For

Not to be taken from the room.

reference

D0208205

THE OXFORD COMPANION TO THE

American MUSICAL

Other Books by Thomas Hischak

The American Musical Film Song Encyclopedia
The American Musical Theatre Song Encyclopedia
American Plays and Musicals on Screen
American Theatre: A Chronicle of Comedy and Drama, 1969–2000
Boy Loses Girl: Broadway's Librettists
Enter the Players: New York Actors in the Twentieth Century
Enter the Playmakers: Directors and Choreographers on the New York Stage
Film It with Music: An Encyclopedic Guide to the American Movie Musical
The Rodgers and Hammerstein Encyclopedia
Stage It with Music: An Encyclopedic Guide to the American Musical Theatre
Theatre as Human Action
The Theatregoer's Almanac: A Collection of Lists, People, History, and Commentary on the American Theatre
Through the Screen Door:
What Happened to the Broadway Musical When It Went to Hollywood
The Tin Pan Alley Song Encyclopedia
Word Crazy: Broadway Lyricists from Cohan to Sondheim

With Gerald Bordman

The Oxford Companion to American Theatre (third edition)

THE OXFORD COMPANION TO THE

American
MUSICAL

Theatre, Film, and Television

THOMAS HISCHAK

OXFORD
UNIVERSITY PRESS

Oxford University Press, Inc., publishes works that further
Oxford University's objective of excellence
in research, scholarship, and education.

Oxford New York
Auckland Cape Town Dar es Salaam Hong Kong Karachi
Kuala Lumpur Madrid Melbourne Mexico City Nairobi
New Delhi Shanghai Taipei Toronto

With offices in
Argentina Austria Brazil Chile Czech Republic France Greece
Guatemala Hungary Italy Japan Poland Portugal Singapore
South Korea Switzerland Thailand Turkey Ukraine Vietnam

Copyright © 2008 by Oxford University Press

Published by Oxford University Press, Inc.
198 Madison Avenue, New York, NY 10016
www.oup.com

Oxford is a registered trademark of Oxford University Press

Library of Congress Cataloging-in-Publication Data
Hischak, Thomas S.
The Oxford Companion to the American Musical:
Theatre, Film, and Television / Thomas Hischak.
p. cm.
Includes bibliographical references (p.   ), discography (p.   ), and index.
ISBN-13: 978-0-19-533533-0
1. Musicals—United States—Dictionaries. I. Title.
ML102. M88H593 2008
782.1'4097303—dc22   2007052436

1 3 5 7 9 8 6 4 2

Printed in the United States of America
on acid-free paper

For my daughter, Karen Soh Hishak

TABLE OF CONTENTS

FOREWORD

Besides being a performer myself, I am also a voice teacher, a coach, and a mentor to other performers. I consider all of these great and delightful things to do. And while I have a certain background to call upon in each of these occupations, and while getting older does mean getting wiser, let's face it, sometimes it means becoming more forgetful too. So in order to stay relevant in film, television, or on stage—in any profession really—we need continuing circles of knowledge and understanding.

To access the relevancy of my experiences and relate them to my students and mentees, I need more and more information and documentation about what has happened in the past, recent or otherwise, because what I've learned in school, from experience, or from life in general is never enough to keep up with the pace of my profession. From time to time I have to be reminded of things that I may have forgotten (or never even knew in the first place) and therefore *The Oxford Companion to the American Musical* gives me great relief. Between the covers of this attractive reference, Thomas Hischak has compiled an impressive amount of information on a wonderful American art form: the musical. Not only will browsing through its entries enable me to continue to grow, but here, in a single volume, I now have free-wheeling access to the precise details about literally hundreds of composers, choreographers, directors, lyricists, musicians, performers, and productions.

That I can be useful to others in this line stretching back centuries is important to me. The process of passing our theatrical history from one generation to the next is ongoing, and to be a part of the ever-growing amount of collective knowledge is not only what keeps me performing, it is also what keeps me young. The information in this *Companion* will keep me feeling current and secure in what I know for many years to come. This new ability to qualify my answers and help anyone by using the product of Tom's research is a great joy as well as a necessity to me.

I'm sure every performer, writer, aficionado, or composer that picks up this book will also find it joyful and necessary in his or her own time and way. My advice then is to simply enjoy it, soak all of this in, contribute however you can, and, above all, use this book to help you put what you learn about yourself and others while experiencing American musicals firsthand into a broad, historical perspective. This can only promote good new things!

Marni Nixon, New York City, January 2008

PREFACE

What is an American musical?

In 1866, an American musical was a five-hour-long extravaganza produced at Niblo's Garden called *The Black Crook* in which melodrama, ballet dancers, and songs were jumbled together for the first time in a very American form of hodge podge. In 1891 an American musical was the singing *Robin Hood* at the Standard Theatre, the most popular homegrown operetta of the nineteenth century, while a few blocks away at the Madison Square Theatre audiences were tapping their toes to "The Bowery" and other tunes in *A Trip to Chinatown*, one of the earliest and best musical comedies. In 1904, an American musical was the very patriotic *Little Johnny Jones* at the Liberty Theatre, defying European shows and characters and its creator–star George M. Cohan proudly proclaiming that he was "A Yankee Doodle Boy." By 1917 an American musical was a sassy, contemporary musical at the tiny Princess Theatre where young composer Jerome Kern was charming audiences with *Oh, Boy!* while at the Shubert Theatre composer Sigmund Romberg was pleasing playgoers with his lush, romantic operetta *Maytime*. In 1927 Americans had their choice of the epic musical play *Show Boat* at the Ziegfeld Theatre or visiting one of the movie houses across the nation and watching Al Jolson sing "Toot Toot Tootsie" on screen in *The Jazz Singer*. In Depression year 1933, the American musical was satirizing the government at the Music Box Theatre with *Of Thee I Sing* or sympathizing with the "forgotten" men in bread lines in the film *Gold Diggers of 1933*.

In wartime 1943, an American musical was *Oklahoma!* at the St. James Theatre celebrating the nation's heartland or the movie *This Is the Army* proclaiming the nation's quest for victory. By 1957 Americans could choose among Robert Preston leading the cast of *The Music Man* in "Seventy-Six Trombones" at the Majestic Theatre, Fred Astaire and Audrey Hepburn on the screen dancing to George Gershwin melodies in *Funny Face*, or staying at home and seeing Julie Andrews on the small screen singing "In My Own Little Corner" in Rodgers and Hammerstein's *Cinderella*. An American musical in 1966 was *The Story of Rudolph the Red-Nosed Reindeer* on NBC-TV, *Fiddler on the Roof* at the Imperial Theatre on Broadway, and *Mary Poppins* at the movies. By 1978, Hollywood musicals were getting scarce, although with a hit like *Grease* they were far from dead; while on Broadway, the original musical revue was gone but with the rousing *Ain't Misbehavin'* at the Longacre Theatre, the cast and patrons were reliving the songs of Fats Waller. An American musical in 1985 was pop-rock music in *Footloose* on the big screen, disco music in *Copacabana* on the little screen, and country-folk music in *Big River* at the Eugene O'Neill Theatre. In 1990, the American musical was willing to give anything a try: singing police squads on television in *Cop Rock*, calypso music in *Once on This Island* at the Booth Theatre, and a Broadway-style score for the animated movie *The Little Mermaid*. The first four years of the new century found movies, such as *The Producers*, *The Full Monty*, and *Hairspray*, showing up on Broadway with songs, just as stage hits like *Chicago*, *Phantom of the Opera*, and *Rent* were on the screen. By 2007, an American musical was millions of young viewers anxiously awaiting the first TV broadcast of *High School Musical 2*, theatregoers buying tickets for the Broadway season's most promising hits, *Young Frankenstein* and *The Little Mermaid*, and moviegoers wondering what film director Tim Burton would do with *Sweeney Todd*.

What is an American musical? Well, it is the entire aforementioned plus much much more. The musical in America is as diverse as the country itself. What is the typical American musical? That is as impossible to pinpoint as to say who or what is the typical American. The purpose of this book is to look at the diversity of the American musical in all three major venues: theatre, film, and television. Too often the musicals of one venue are written about and studied with no regard to the other two. Yet the performers and creative artists who bring us musicals are rarely limited to one genre. To know and understand Julie Andrews or Cole Porter is to look at their work in the theatre, Hollywood, and on television, for that is the purview of the American musical. To see how *Brigadoon* works or doesn't work, one must consider the Broadway, Hollywood, and television productions of the piece. Covering all three areas in a single volume allows one to see how people and musicals appear in different media, the changes made from one venue to another, and the ways in which the American musical is so far-reaching. The result, I hope, is not only a book that is interesting and different but also revealing. Of course, there are difficulties in covering stage, film, and television musicals and their creators together in one work. Space limitations force one to choose carefully who and what to include. I have tried to cover not only major musicals and people in all three media but to include less important entries that represent the breadth of the American musical. Child actor Bobby Breen of the 1930s and cult musical *Flahooley* (1951) may not be essential to a work such as this, but they give one a taste of what was going on at the time and what audiences did and didn't like. Also, there are dozens of subject entries, such as those on pastiche musicals and opera singers in musicals, that explore phenomena that occurred in all three media. Finally, there are listings of awards and recordings, and a chronology of musicals near the end of the book that allows one to see when all these musicals first appeared and how one venue was affected by another.

I have not limited the entries to Americans and American musicals. Foreign works and international artists are included if they were very popular in the States, as with Maurice Chevalier and *Les Misérables*; very influential, such as Richard Barker and *The Threepenny Opera*; or both, as with Noel Coward and *H. M. S. Pinafore*. I have not included operas unless the work was first presented as a theatrical piece, such as *Porgy and Bess* and *Street Scene*. In the case of certain films, there is sometimes a fine line between a comedy and a musical, such as Billy Wilder's *Some Like It Hot*, and between a musical and a film about music, as with the many screen biographies of classical composers in which no one sings or dances. I have tried to concentrate on musicals in which songs are important, although such semimusicals are listed with a person's credits. In order to lead the reader to entries that might be of interest, all titles and people who have their own entry are cross-referenced with SMALL CAPITAL LETTERS so one knows that more information about a certain name or musical is available under a separate entry. To make sure the reader is always aware of the medium of a work being described, icons have been inserted throughout the book. ⮰ indicates a stage work, ▣ represents a film, and ☐ is used to distinguish a television musical. Because many musicals were made or remade by more than a single venue, the icons will make it clear when the entry starts discussing the film version of a stage work or a Broadway mounting of a movie musical. Finally, there is a guide to recordings near the end of the book, which outlines not only stage recordings and soundtracks, but also indicates if the musical is available on video or DVD.

I thank Benjamin Keene, Grace Labatt, and others at Oxford University Press, Ron Mandelbaum and the staff at Photofest, and my wife Cathy for her invaluable help in preparing the manuscript.

List of Entries

A

AARONS, ALEX[ander] A. AND VINTON FREEDLEY. Stage producing team. A pair of farsighted producers, they presented some outstanding musicals by the Gershwins during their brief but memorable partnership in the 1920s. Aarons (1891–1943) was born in Philadelphia, the son of theatre composer and producer Alfred E. Aarons (1865–1936), and began his career in the garment industry. He made his producing debut with *La La Lucille* (1919), the first Broadway musical scored by GEORGE GERSHWIN, but had more success with the early ADELE AND FRED ASTAIRE vehicle *For Goodness Sake* (1922), which he also presented in London. One of the performers in the musical was Vinton Freedley, who gave up acting and turned to co-producing shows with Aarons. Freedley (1891–1969), also a Philadelphia native, played juvenile roles on the stage. His first producing venture with Aarons was the Gershwin brothers' innovative *LADY, BE GOOD!* (1924) and the partners followed it with such Gershwin entries as *Tell Me More* (1925), *TIP-TOES* (1925), *OH, KAY!* (1926), *FUNNY FACE* (1927), *Treasure Girl* (1928), *GIRL CRAZY* (1930), and *Pardon My English* (1933). Aarons and Freedley were so popular that in 1927 they built a Broadway playhouse and christened it the Alvin Theatre, using the beginning of each of their first names. The team also presented such musicals as *HOLD EVERYTHING!* (1928), *Spring Is Here* (1929), and *HEADS UP!* (1929) before ending their partnership in 1933. Freedley continued to produce in a solo capacity and had such successes as COLE PORTER'S *ANYTHING GOES* (1934), *RED, HOT AND BLUE!* (1936), *LEAVE IT TO ME!* (1938), and *LET'S FACE IT!* (1941), as well as *CABIN IN THE SKY* (1940). Aarons left the theatre in the Depression and went to Hollywood but found little success. He served as a production assistant on *BROADWAY MELODY OF 1936* (1935) and was consultant on the Gershwin biomusical *RHAPSODY IN BLUE* (1945) before his premature death.

ABBOTT, GEORGE [Francis] (1887–1995). Stage and film director, writer, and producer. One of Broadway's most successful and durable directors, his eighty-year career also included acting, producing, and playwriting. Abbott was born in Forestville, New York, and educated at Harvard University, where he was a student of George Pierce Baker and a member of the famed 47 Workshop that gave so many American playwrights their start. As an actor, he appeared in Harvard theatricals and performed professionally in Boston before making his New York acting debut in 1913 in *The Misleading Lady* on Broadway. Abbott turned to playwriting in 1925 when he co-wrote *The Fall Guy*, beginning a long career of writing comedies, melodramas, and musical librettos. He made his Broadway directorial debut in 1926 with *Love 'Em and Leave 'Em*, but it was his staging of his own melodrama *Broadway* later that year that propelled his directing career. He would go on to stage some 100 Broadway productions, including many musicals, starting with *JUMBO* (1935). His other musicals, several of which he co-authored, include *ON YOUR TOES* (1936, 1954, and 1983), *THE BOYS FROM SYRACUSE* (1938), *TOO MANY GIRLS* (1939), *PAL JOEY* (1940), *BEST FOOT FORWARD* (1941), *ON THE TOWN* (1944), *Billion Dollar Baby* (1945), *HIGH BUTTON SHOES* (1947), *Look, Ma, I'm Dancin'* (1948), *WHERE'S CHARLEY?* (1948), *CALL ME MADAM* (1950), *OUT OF THIS WORLD* (1950), *A TREE GROWS IN BROOKLYN* (1951), *WONDERFUL TOWN* (1953), *ME AND JULIET* (1953), *THE PAJAMA GAME* (1954 and 1973), *DAMN YANKEES* (1955), *NEW GIRL IN TOWN* (1957), *ONCE UPON A MATTRESS* (1959), *FIORELLO!* (1959), *TENDERLOIN* (1960), *A FUNNY THING HAPPENED ON THE WAY TO THE FORUM* (1962), *FADE OUT—FADE IN* (1964), *FLORA, THE RED MENACE* (1965), *Anya* (1965), *How Now Dow Jones* (1968), and *Music Is* (1976). Abbot directed the Hollywood musical *Why Bring That Up?* (1929) and produced and directed the screen versions of *Too Many Girls* (1940), *The Pajama Game* (1957), and *Damn Yankees* (1958). His unique approach—taut and firm direction mixed with a talent for moving the story along clearly and rapidly—became known as the "Abbott touch" and he influenced many later directors of musical comedy. Autobiography: *Mister Abbott* (1963).

ABBOTT AND COSTELLO. Film comedy team. A highly successful clowning duo in the 1940s and 1950s, neither sang nor danced yet were featured in eighteen Hollywood musicals.

George Abbott. The famous "Abbott Touch" was not limited to fast-paced musical comedies. Abbott was also adept at staging more serious musicals such as *Pal Joey* (1940), *A Tree Grows in Brooklyn* (1951), and *Fiorello!* (1959), with Tom Bosley (pictured) as the tireless young politician Fiorello LaGuardia. Abbott not only directed the musical but co-wrote the libretto with Jerome Weidman. (Photofest)

The tall, thin straight man Bud [born William Alexander] Abbott (1895–1974) was born in Asbury Park, New York, and went into vaudeville where he met the short, rotund comic Lou Costello [born Louis Francis Cristillo] (1906–1959). The two started working together in 1931 and became headliners in variety and burlesque circuits. They were featured in the Broadway revue *Streets of Paris* (1939) and then made their screen debut as two incompetent insurance agents in the musical ONE NIGHT IN THE TROPICS (1940). The duo did not garner much interest until the film BUCK PRIVATES (1941), which was a blockbuster thanks to their verbal and physical comedy. For the next decade and a half the team was box office gold and their thirty films moved UNIVERSAL STUDIOS from the edge of bankruptcy to their most profitable years. Abbott and Costello's humor has not dated well, although classic routines such as "Who's on First?," performed in *The Naughty Nineties* (1945), remain hilari-ous. Their other musical credits include *In the Navy* (1941), *Hold That Ghost* (1941), *Keep 'Em Flying* (1941), *Ride 'Em Cowboy* (1942), *RIO RITA* (1942), *Pardon My Sarong* (1942), *It Ain't Hay* (1943), *In Society* (1944), *Here Come the Coeds* (1945), *Comin' Round the Mountain* (1951), *Lost in Alaska* (1952), and *Dance With Me, Henry* (1956). Costello usually got into trouble, bawled like a giant baby, and Abbott spent his time either scolding or cheating his partner. Their offstage lives, unfortunately, paralleled this situation. The two also performed on television before splitting up in 1957. Memoir: *Lou's on First: The Tragic Life of Hollywood's Greatest Clown*, Chris Costello [his son], 1982; biographies: *The Abbott and Costello Story*, Stephen Cox, John Lofflin (1997); *Abbott and Costello in Hollywood*, Bob Furmanek, Ron Palumbo (1991).

ABORN, MILTON (1864–1933). Stage director. A presenter of popular musicals on Broadway and on tour, he was a leading producer and director of operetta revivals. Aborn was born in Marysville, California, and began in the theatre as a stage manager and an actor. He later teamed with his brother Sargent and produced popular-priced versions of musical favorites and sent them on tour, sometimes managing a half a dozen different troupes at once. But Aborn's first love was operetta and early in the twentieth century the brothers concentrated on them, forming the Aborn Opera Company in 1902. As the golden age for operetta faded in the late 1920s, Aborn revived old favorites by Gilbert and Sullivan, VICTOR HERBERT, and others, usually directing them himself and bringing the repertoire to New York. The last few years of his life were busy with these quickly staged but popular revivals. Sargent Aborn (1867?–1956) is also notable for merging the Witmark Music Library with A. W. Tams, forming the major play-leasing company Tams-Witmark Music Library still in operation today.

ACADEMY AWARDS. The film industry's most powerful and recognized set of prizes, the "Oscars" have been given for achievement in various categories of moviemaking since 1927 by the American Academy of Motion Picture Arts and Sciences. Although the areas of expertise being honored have changed throughout its history, the Academy's actual award has always been a thirteen-and-a-half-inch-high gold-plated statuette known unofficially as the Oscar. The origin of the name is unknown and is the subject of diverse anecdotes. The Academy strives to recognize excellence but throughout its history it has often been a popularity contest or business ploy in disguise. At various points over the decades, Oscars have been given for score, song, choreography, background scoring, and other areas related to musicals. Only ten musicals over the years have won for Best Picture and many others have been nominated. Of the ten musicals, five of the winners were based on Broadway musicals. Looking at the nominations over the decades, one can see the rise and fall of the Hollywood musical by how often musicals were on the list. See also Awards Appendix.

ACROSS THE UNIVERSE (Columbia 2007). Thirty-three songs written by the BEATLES and some startling visual imagery helped viewers get through the routine hippie love story in this awkward, beautiful movie musical. The screenplay by Dick Clement and Ian La Frenais centered on Jude (Jim Sturgess), a shipyard worker from Liverpool. He comes to America looking for his father and befriends Princeton dropout Max (Joe Anderson), with the two living the life of radicals in Greenwich Village. Jude falls in love with Max's sister Lucy

Musicals Nominated for the Best Picture Academy Award

(winners in bold; years given are for the Oscar ceremonies)

1929	**THE BROADWAY MELODY**
	HOLLYWOOD REVUE OF 1929
1930	THE LOVE PARADE
1931	ONE HOUR WITH YOU
	THE SMILING LIEUTENANT
1933	42ND STREET
	SHE DONE HIM WRONG
1934	Flirtation Walk
	THE GAY DIVORCÉE
1935	BROADWAY MELODY OF 1936
	NAUGHTY MARIETTA
	TOP HAT
1936	**THE GREAT ZIEGFELD**
	SAN FRANCISCO
	Three Smart Girls
1937	IN OLD CHICAGO
	ONE HUNDRED MEN AND A GIRL
1938	ALEXANDER'S RAGTIME BAND
1939	THE WIZARD OF OZ
1942	YANKEE DOODLE DANDY
1944	**GOING MY WAY**
1945	ANCHORS AWEIGH
1948	The Red Shoes
1951	**AN AMERICAN IN PARIS**
1954	SEVEN BRIDES FOR SEVEN BROTHERS
	THE COUNTRY GIRL
1956	THE KING AND I
1958	**GIGI**
1961	**WEST SIDE STORY**
1962	THE MUSIC MAN
1964	**MY FAIR LADY**
	MARY POPPINS
1965	**THE SOUND OF MUSIC**
1967	DOCTOR DOOLITTLE
1968	**OLIVER!**
	FUNNY GIRL
1969	HELLO, DOLLY!
1971	FIDDLER ON THE ROOF
1972	CABARET
1975	NASHVILLE
1976	Bound for Glory
1979	ALL THAT JAZZ
1980	COAL MINER'S DAUGHTER
1991	BEAUTY AND THE BEAST
2001	MOULIN ROUGE!
2002	**CHICAGO**
2004	RAY

(Evan Rachel Wood) but everything from her upper-crust mores to the Viet Nam War comes between them. Set against the background of protests, free love, race riots, drugs, and the turbulent American scene, the story aims for mythic proportions but rarely rises above the routine 1960s melodrama. Yet director JULIE TAYMOR films this sometimes trite tale with great panache, letting the songs carry the dialogue and providing such a treat for the eye that everything does become mythic. Army inductees are stripped, examined, and tossed into the war to the strains of "I Want You (She's So Heavy)," a sexually confused lesbian (T. V. Carpio) pleads with "I Want to Hold Your Hand," a drug-infested hippie leader (Bono) claims "I Am the Walrus," and "Let It Be" becomes a gospel-like elegy for the victims of wars and riots. The young cast were not polished singers (neither were the Beatles) yet they sound impressive and their interpretations of the songs carry the day. Also compelling were Dana Fuchs as the Janis Joplin–like singer Sadie and Martin Luther McCoy as her guitarist lover JoJo. Critical and public reactions to the film were widely mixed yet the headstrong movie seems to want it no other way.

🕊 *ACT, THE* (Majestic Theatre 1977). While LIZA MINNELLI triumphed in this musical vehicle built around her considerable talents, the script by George Furth and the score by JOHN KANDER (music) and FRED EBB (lyrics) were less impressive. Film star Michelle Craig (Minnelli) loses her husband and watches her career falter, all told in the format of a Las Vegas nightclub act. Filmmaker Martin Scorsese was the unlikely director, and GOWER CHAMPION was brought in to fix up the direction and choreography. Barry Nelson and a team of hardworking "gypsies" supported Minnelli who was on stage and dancing so much that some of her singing was prerecorded, which did not go over well with the press. Yet as a vehicle it was satisfying for Minnelli fans, of which there are many, and she kept the show running for 233 performances. The songs may not have been top-drawer Kander and Ebb, yet there was still something pleasing about the wry salute to "City Lights," the sexy comic romp "Arthur in the Afternoon," and the satirical number "Little Do They Know" sung by the disgruntled dancers who have to make their star look good. A few years after the show closed, some of the discarded songs from the messy tryout period were recorded and one could see that the musical originally intended was not what opened on Broadway.

ADAMS, EDITH [born Elizabeth Edith Enke] (1927–). Stage, film, and television performer. A blonde singer–actress who spent much of her career in nightclubs, she made some memorable appearances in Broadway and Hollywood comedies and musicals. "Edie" Adams was born in Kingston, Pennsylvania, and educated at the Juilliard School of Music and Columbia School of Drama. After winning some beauty pageants and talent shows, she found recognition in television, most notably on Ernie Kovacs's show, and later married the star. Adams's two outstanding Broadway roles were the amorous Eileen in *WONDERFUL TOWN* (1953) and the determined Daisy Mae in *LI'L ABNER* (1956), but more Americans saw her as the Fairy Godmother in the live broadcast of Rodgers and Hammerstein's TV musical *CINDERELLA* (1957). She acted in several film comedies and made dozens of television appearances, from soap operas to variety shows to cigar commercials.

ADAMS, LEE, AND CHARLES STROUSE. Stage songwriters. Creators of some of the brightest Broadway scores of the 1960s, the duo possessed a vernacular for the American sound and slang of its era. Lee [Richard] Adams (1924–) was born in Mansfield, Ohio, and studied journalism at Ohio State and Columbia University before working for various New York magazines, all the time writing song lyrics as a hobby. Charles [Louis] Strouse 1928–) was born in New York City and studied classical music at the Eastman School of Music, with Aaron Copland at Tanglewood, and with Nadia Boulanger in Paris. He turned from a concert career to writing popular songs and earned his living as a rehearsal pianist on Broadway. Adams and Strouse first collaborated on songs for the summer resort Green Mansions and had some of their work included in the BEN BAGLEY revues *The Littlest Revue* (1956) and *Shoestring '57* (1957), as well as *Catch a Star* (1955) and *Ziegfeld Follies of 1956*. They made an auspicious Broadway debut with their score for the surprise hit *BYE BYE BIRDIE* (1960) and then had less success with their fine scores for *ALL AMERICAN* (1962), *GOLDEN BOY* (1964), and *IT'S A BIRD, IT'S A PLANE, IT'S SUPERMAN!* (1966). The team had a major hit with *APPLAUSE* (1970) but it was their last success together. After writing the London musical *Albert and I* (1972), the partners temporarily parted ways. Strouse teamed with lyricist MARTIN CHARNIN for *ANNIE* (1977), which was his last long-run show. Adams and Strouse reunited for the short-lived New York flops *A Broadway Musical* (1978) and *Bring Back Birdie* (1981). For television they scored theme songs, most memorably "Those Were the Days" for *All in the Family*, the TV musical *ALICE IN WONDERLAND OR WHAT'S A NICE GIRL LIKE YOU DOING IN A PLACE LIKE THIS?* (1966), and the film *The Night They Raided Minsky's* (1968). Although each often wrote outstanding scores with others, neither man enjoyed much success after the 1970s. Adams stumbled with *Ain't Broadway Grand* (1993), and Strouse has had a long run of failures such as *Charlie and Algernon* (1980), *Dance a Little Closer* (1983), *RAGS* (1986), *Nick and Nora* (1993), and *Annie Warbucks* (1992). Both men are traditionalists yet they have found endless variety and creativity in American themes, characters, and settings. Autobiography (Strouse): *Put on a Happy Face: A Broadway Memoir* (2008).

ADAMSON, HAROLD [Campbell] (1906–1980). Film and stage lyricist. A busy contributor to Broadway and the screen, he is most remembered for his songs written with composer JIMMY McHUGH for nineteen Hollywood musicals. Adamson was born in Greenville, New Jersey, and educated at the University of Kansas and at Harvard where he wrote songs for the "Hasty Pudding" shows. By 1930 his work was heard on Broadway in such musicals as *Smiles* (1930), *EARL CARROLL VANITIES* (1931), *Banjo Eyes* (1941), and *AS THE GIRLS GO* (1948). Adamson went to Hollywood in 1933 and, working with a variety of composers, penned dozens of songs for comedies and musicals, such as *DANCING LADY* (1933), *Bottoms Up* (1934), *Reckless* (1935), *Here Comes the Band* (1935), *THE GREAT ZIEGFELD* (1936), *Hit Parade of 1943*, *Bathing Beauty* (1944), *GENTLEMEN PREFER BLONDES* (1953), *JUPITER'S DARLING* (1955), and *An Affair to Remember* (1957). With McHugh he scored *Banjo on My Knee* (1936), *You're a Sweetheart* (1937), *Top of the Town* (1937), *Mad About Music* (1938), *HIGHER AND HIGHER* (1943), *Four Jills in a Jeep* (1944), *SOMETHING FOR THE BOYS* (1944), *Nob Hill* (1945), *Doll Face* (1945), *If You Knew Susie* (1948), and others. Adamson's lyrics run from the dreamy romantic of "I Couldn't Sleep a Wink Last Night" to the silly "Dig You Later (Hubba Hubba)" to the lush "An Affair to Remember" to the spirited "It's a Most Unusual Day."

ADLER, LARRY [Cecil] (1914–2001). Stage and film performer and musician. The virtuoso harmonica player, a favorite in nightclubs and in concerts, was featured in a few Broadway and Hollywood musicals. Adler was born in Baltimore and studied the harmonica as a serious musician. He was soon a unique attraction booked into clubs and was heard on Broadway in the musical *Smiles* (1930), followed by featured spots in the revues *FLYING COLORS* (1932) and *Keep Off the Grass* (1940). Hollywood also found a spot for him in musicals, most memorably playing "Night Over Shanghai" in *The Singing Marine* (1937). His other screen musicals include *Many Happy Returns* (1934), *BIG BROADCAST OF 1937* (1936), and *Music for Millions* (1944). Adler also played on the soundtrack of nonmusicals, such as *Genevieve* (1953), although he was blacklisted at the time and was not credited. Although he was never convicted for Communist activities, he left America in the late 1950s and resided in London for the rest of his life. Adler was responsible for making the harmonica an accepted musical instrument in the world of music and made many recordings of classical as well as popular songs.

ADLER, RICHARD, AND JERRY ROSS. Stage songwriting team. A short-lived but potent collaboration, they were unusual in that both wrote music and lyrics. Adler (1921–) was born in New York City, the son of concert pianist Clarence Adler, but rejected classical music to write pop songs. After serving in the Navy in World War II, he teamed up with Jerry Ross [born Jerrold Rosenberg] (1926–1955) and they worked together on songs for the radio. Ross was born in the Bronx and had acted as a youth in Yiddish Theatre productions. The two songwriters were discovered by FRANK LOESSER who guided them and got their career started when some of their songs were heard on Broadway in *John Murray Anderson's Almanac* (1953). They had a pop single on the charts with "Rags to Riches" and then found success on Broadway for their rousing score for *THE PAJAMA GAME* (1954), quickly followed by the hit *DAMN YANKEES* (1955). The collaboration came to a sudden end with Ross's death at the age of twenty-nine from a lung ailment. Adler never enjoyed such fame again, although he wrote admirable scores alone for the Broadway musicals *KWAMINA* (1961) and *Music Is* (1976). He had better luck on television where he scored the original TV musicals *THE GIFT OF THE MAGI* (1958), *LITTLE WOMEN* (1958), and *OLYMPUS 7-0000* (1966). Adler has also composed symphonic pieces, produced Broadway shows, and promoted political fundraisers and celebrations. He was married to SALLY ANN

Adler and Ross. Although they scored only two book musicals, *The Pajama Game* (1954) and *Damn Yankees* (1955), Richard Adler and Jerry Ross came up with two of the most tuneful and vivacious shows of the 1950s. Doris Day (pictured) joined the Broadway cast for the 1957 film version of *The Pajama Game* and they (literally) gave her plenty of support. (Photofest)

HOWES for a time. Autobiography: *You Gotta Have Heart*, Adler (1990).

🎵 **ADONIS** (Bijou Theatre 1884). Billed as a "burlesque nightmare," this long-forgotten show was quite a hit in its day, running an astonishing 603 performances in the days when three months made a profitable run. William F. Gill collaborated with EDWARD E. RICE on the libretto about the sculptress Talamea (Lillie Grubb) who creates a statue of Adonis so beautiful she falls in love with it and, with the aid of the goddess Artea (Louise V. Essing), brings it to life. The statue is purchased by the Duchess (Jennie Reiffarth), who also is smitten by the chiseled beauty, but Adonis (HENRY E. DIXEY) would rather play the field, so he runs off to the country. He tries to win the love of the country lass Rosetta (Amelia Summerville) even as all the adoring women in town are chasing him. Unlike George Bernard Shaw's *Pygmalion* (1913) and its musical adaptation *MY FAIR LADY*

(1956), *Adonis* ended with the frustrated statue giving up on humans and asking to return to stone. The score was a collection of songs currently available, everything from DAVID BRAHAM to Beethoven to Arthur Sullivan, and the main attraction was the performance by Dixey whose Adonis was both funny and romantic. He was forever identified with the part and played it on and off for twenty years.

ADRIAN, IRIS [born Iris Adrian Hostetter] (1912–1994). Film, television, and stage performer. A durable blonde character actress, she played dumb chorus girls, floozies, and gangsters' molls in over 100 movies, including several musicals. Adrian was born in Los Angeles and began her career when she won a beauty contest that brought her to the attention of FLORENZ ZIEGFELD who put her in his 1929 edition of *ZIEGFELD FOLLIES*. She made her film debut in 1928 and was soon seen in such musicals as *PARAMOUNT ON PARADE* (1930), *Stolen*

Harmony (1935), *GOLD DIGGERS OF 1937* (1936), *Go West* (1940), *ROAD TO ZANZIBAR* (1941), *Too Many Blondes* (1941), *Swing It Soldier* (1941), *ORCHESTRA WIVES* (1942), *The Stork Club* (1945), *THE PALEFACE* (1948), *The Helen Morgan Story* (1957), and *BLUE HAWAII* (1961). Adrian also appeared in many television programs, from variety shows to sit-coms, into the 1980s.

☐ *ADVENTURES OF MARCO POLO, THE* (NBC-TV 1956). ALFRED DRAKE and DORETTA MORROW, who had played father and daughter on Broadway in *KISMET* (1953), were reunited in another exotic tale using classical music. Clay Warnick and Mel Pahl adapted musical themes from Rimsky-Korsakov, and Edward Eager provided lyrics for the score, which included "Uneasy Lies the Head," "Beyond the Sunset," "You'll Be Seeing Me," "The Tartar Song," "The Garden of Imagining," and "Population." While "Market Day" was no "Baubles, Bangles and Beads" and "Xanadu" was not a hit like "Stranger in Paradise," the score was given full voice by Drake and the cast was well reviewed. The teleplay written by William Friedberg and NEIL SIMON followed Polo (Drake) from his home in Venice to Persia, China, and Tibet, and back to Italy, with some playful interludes at the court of Kublai Khan. The script was also praised for not taking itself too seriously. Morrow played the Princess Kokochin and provided the love interest, and the cast also included Arnold Moss, George Mitchell, Paul Ekena, Jerome Kilty, and Beatrice Kraft. One of the five original musicals in the *Max Liebman Presents* series, the broadcast was popular, thanks to Drake and the reputation of LIEBMAN's shows.

AFRICAN AMERICAN MUSICALS. Musical shows utilizing black performers go back to the earliest stage entertainments in America. Minstrel shows were originally composed and performed by African American singers and musicians and were extremely popular with all kinds of audiences, but during the nineteenth century, white artists started performing their version of the minstrel show and derogatory exaggerations that we associate with the term were developed. African American musicals on Broadway can be divided into several different categories. Most musicals and revues with black characters and settings were written by white songwriters, resulting in such shows as *BLACKBIRDS OF 1929* (1929), *PORGY AND BESS* (1935), *CABIN IN THE SKY* (1940), *LOST IN THE STARS* (1949), *HALLELUJAH, BABY!* (1967), and

PURLIE (1970). There were the exceptions when African American creators got to write, direct, and produce their own Broadway shows, as with the early legendary shows *IN DAHOMEY* (1903) and *SHUFFLE ALONG* 1921), but for the most part black artists of the past were accepted as performers only. Another category of African American musical was the exotic Caribbean shows, which placed black performers in quaint, sometimes tribal, surroundings that were palatable to white audiences. *HOUSE OF FLOWERS* (1954), *JAMAICA* (1957), and *ONCE ON THIS ISLAND* (1990) were among the best of this type. *SHOW BOAT* (1927) utilized both white and black characters and choruses, and *FINIAN'S RAINBOW* (1947) was the first Broadway musical to integrate both races in the chorus and supporting roles. Interracial romances were seen in *KWAMINA* (1961) and *NO STRINGS* (1962), showing that fully developed African American characters could exist outside the "all-Negro" musicals of the past. Another category put black characters and idiom into white vehicles, such as *CARMEN JONES* (1944), *THE WIZ* (1975), *TIMBUKTU* (1978), and the all-black versions of *HELLO, DOLLY!* in 1967, *GUYS AND DOLLS* in 1976, and *OH, KAY!* in 1990. Perhaps the most popular form of African American musical remains the revue that celebrates black artists of the past. *BUBBLING BROWN SUGAR* (1976), *AIN'T MISBEHAVIN* (1978), *Eubie* (1978), *One Mo' Time* (1980), *SOPHISTICATED LADIES* (1981), *BLACK AND BLUE* (1989), and *FIVE GUYS NAMED MOE* (1992) were among the best of the many shows of this type. Finally there is the true African American musical, a revue or book show that seeks to explore the black experience through new songs and not through nostalgia. *GOLDEN BOY* (1964), *AIN'T SUPPOSED TO DIE A NATURAL DEATH* (1971), *DON'T BOTHER ME, I CAN'T COPE* (1972), *RAISIN* (1973), *DREAMGIRLS* (1981), *THE TAP DANCE KID* (1983), *JELLY'S LAST JAM* (1992), *BRING IN 'DA NOISE BRING IN 'DA FUNK* (1996), *CAROLINE, OR CHANGE* (2004), and *THE COLOR PURPLE* (2005) were not all written by African American artists but they were laudable shows that sought to reveal the complexity of black life in musical terms.

African American films of any kind were rare in Hollywood until the Civil Rights movement in the 1960s, and even then musical films about black culture were less prevalent than they were on Broadway. Two early musicals that featured African American casts were *Hearts of Dixie* (1929) and *HALLELUJAH* (1929), both containing black stereotypes but generally quite effective. "Race" musicals, both shorts and features, were made throughout the 1930s and 1940s to be shown in black neighborhood movie houses. These low-budget efforts sometimes had African American writers and directors as well as performers, but they were rarely given a wide release. Performers such as the NICHOLAS BROTHERS, BILL ROBINSON, LOUIS ARMSTRONG, CAB CALLOWAY, and LENA HORNE were often featured in mainstream Hollywood musicals, but usually in specialty spots that could easily be edited out for showings in the South. Some pre-1960s musicals that had black artists in major roles were *STORMY WEATHER* (1943), *NEW ORLEANS* (1947), *St. Louis Blues* (1958), and the film versions of the Broadway musicals *Cabin in the Sky* (1943), *Carmen Jones* (1954), and *Porgy and Bess* (1959). Although many more films with African Americans in nonsterotypic roles were made in the late 1960s and thereafter, black musicals were still uncommon, although ethnic-minority performers were now cast in most musicals. *LADY SINGS THE BLUES* (1972), *Leadbelly* (1976), *Scott Joplin* (1977), the film versions of *Lost in the Stars* (1974) and *The Wiz* (1978), to a degree, *THE COTTON CLUB* (1984), and *BIRD* (1988) were among the few African American musicals Hollywood put out at the time. More recently there has been *THE PREACHER'S WIFE* (1996), *RAY* (2004), and *Dreamgirls* (2006), still a small percentage of the limited musical film genre.

Television offered some African American sit-coms and variety shows as early as 1951. *Beulah* and *Amos and Andy* were the most notable of the former, and NAT KING COLE's show of the latter. An original musical titled *A Drum Is a Woman* (1957) about jazz, with Duke Ellington providing the music, was probably the first television musical predominantly about black Americans. Unfortunately, not many followed. The most notable entries were *MINSTREL MAN* (1977), *CINDY* (1978), *POLLY* (1989), and *POLLY—COMIN HOME!* (1990). One of the reasons may be that by the 1970s African Americans were regularly featured in sit-coms, dramas, miniseries, and variety shows, and they were naturally included in mainstream TV musicals, such as the 1997 remake of *CINDERELLA*.

AGER, MILTON (1893–1979). Stage and film composer. A Tin Pan Alley songwriter, he wrote some memorable songs during his brief forays into Broadway and Hollywood musicals. Ager was born in Chicago and began his career playing piano for silent movies and in vaudeville houses. After serving in World War I, he co-founded a music publishing firm and composed such 1920s hits as "I'm Nobody's

Baby," "Hard-Hearted Hannah," and "Ain't She Sweet." Alger's songs were heard in the Broadway shows *Cheer Up* (1917), *What's In a Name?* (1920), *Rain or Shine* (1928), and *John Murray Anderson's Almanac* (1929). With lyricist JACK YELLEN, he provided songs for four Hollywood musicals, most memorably *Chasing Rainbows* (1930), which introduced "Happy Days Are Here Again." His other film credits were *Honky Tonk* (1929), *KING OF JAZZ* (1930), and *They Learned About Women* (1930). Ager's music is lively, catchy, and in the brash Tin Pan Alley style. His daughter was writer Shana Alexander (1925–2005).

AHRENS, LYNN. See FLAHERTY, Stephen, and Lynn Ahrens

AIDA (Palace Theatre 2000). Only the basic story and character names from Verdi's celebrated opera were retained in this soft-rock version of the tragic romance between the Nubian slave-princess Aida (Heather Headley) and the Egyptian prince Radames (Adam Pascal). His betrothed, the princess Amneris (Sherie René Scott), was a spoiled clothes horse and provided comic relief in the grim tale that ended with Aida and Radames buried alive together. Linda Woolverton, DAVID HENRY HWANG, and director Robert Falls wrote the script and the DISNEY company produced it, hiring Bob Crowley to do the creative, anachronistic sets and costumes, which were indeed stunning. The score by ELTON JOHN (music) and TIM RICE (lyrics) included the passionate "Elaborate Lives," the satiric fashion show number "My Strongest Suite," and the evocative "Every Story Is a Love Story," which opened and closed the show in a museum displaying Egyptian artifacts. Critical reaction was guarded, except for enthusiastic praise for Headley's dynamic performance in the title role, but audiences immediately embraced the musical and it ran 1,852 performances.

AIN'T MISBEHAVIN' (Longacre Theatre 1978). Arguably the finest musical revue seen on Broadway since the last holdouts of the genre in the 1950s, the sprightly entertainment celebrated the singer–pianist–songwriter THOMAS "FATS" WALLER by performing thirty songs he either wrote or recorded. RICHARD MALTBY, JR., conceived the idea for the show with Murray Horowitz and they provided new lyrics for some Waller instrumental pieces as well. The five performers—Nell Carter, ANDRE DE SHIELDS, Armelia McQueen,

Ain't Misbehavin'. The five cast members from the acclaimed Broadway revue were as nimble as the five fingers on a hand playing the jaunty music of Thomas "Fats" Waller. There were, left to right, Nell Carter, Armelia McQueen, Ken Page, Charlaine Woodard, and Andre De Shields. (Photofest)

Charlaine Woodard, and KEN PAGE—were dynamic individually and in unison, and the sleek Harlem nightclub-like production was directed by Maltby as a musical joy ride without benefit of narration or commentary. The Off Off Broadway surprise hit moved to Broadway where it stayed for 1,604 performances. In 1982 the quintet of singers made an NBC-TV videotape of the revue, and in 1988 the piece returned to Broadway where it played another 176 times.

AIN'T SUPPOSED TO DIE A NATURAL DEATH (Ambassador Theatre 1971). An explosive musical revue with songs and monologues by Melvin Van Peebles, it looked at the African American experience with anger and sardonic laughter. In an inner-city neighborhood populated by impoverished African Americans, various characters express their bitterness and despair in a series of plotless vignettes, ending with a curse on the white race. The vibrant cast included Arthur French, Minnie Gentry, Sati Jamal, Albert Hall, Marilyn B. Coleman, and Jimmy Hayeson, under the direction of Gilbert Moses. Among the potent songs were

"Just Don't Make No Sense," "Put a Curse on You," "Funky Girl on Motherless Broadway," "Come on Feet Do Your Thing," and "I Got the Blood." Most of the numbers were recited rather than sung so that the accusing lyrics would hit the audience directly. Playgoers both black and white were fascinated and responded for 325 performances. Van Peebles, the father of filmmaker Mario Van Peebles, would put together other inflammatory revues, such as *Don't Play Us Cheap!* (1972) and *Waltz of the Stork* (1982), but none were as successful as this one.

AKST, HARRY (1894–1963). Film and stage composer. A vaudeville pianist and songwriter who later turned to films, he created some unforgettable songs for Tin Pan Alley and Hollywood. Akst was born in New York and began his career playing piano in variety and leading a band. He turned to songwriting when vaudeville acts needed material and soon had such chart hits as "Dinah" and "Baby Face." Akst also contributed songs to the Broadway shows *Ladies First* (1918), *ARTISTS AND MODELS* (1927), and *Calling All Stars* (1934).

His Hollywood career began in 1929 when he wrote, with lyricist GRANT CLARKE, the song "Am I Blue?" for ETHEL WATERS to sing in *ON WITH THE SHOW* (1929), the first hit song introduced by an African American on film. Also with Clarke he scored the movie musicals *Is Everybody Happy?* (1929), *So Long, Letty* (1930), and *Song of the Flame* (1930). With others Akst provided songs for *LEATHERNECKING* (1930), *Song of the West* (1930), *Palmy Days* (1931), *Stand Up and Cheer* (1934), *Paddy O'Day* (1935), *Can This Be Dixie?* (1936), *The Music Goes Round* (1936), *Sing and Be Happy* (1937), *Harvest Melody* (1943), and others. He never gave up playing piano and leading a band and in this capacity Akst appeared in some films as himself, such as *THE SHOW OF SHOWS* (1929), *June Moon* (1931), *42ND STREET* (1933), and *Knee Deep in Music* (1933).

☐ *ALADDIN* (CBS-TV 1958). Prolific songwriter COLE PORTER'S last score was his first for television and, while it offered no beloved standards, it is a lively collection of songs that have the unmistakable Porter flavor. "I Adore You" is the featured love song but there is more spirit in the comic numbers "Come to the Supermarket (in Old Peking)," "Opportunity Knocks But Once," and "No Wonder Taxes Are High," all sung by CYRIL RITCHARD as the Magician–Narrator of the piece. Humorist S. J. PERELMAN wrote the teleplay, setting the tale in its original locale of China, and filled the piece with wry anachronisms that mirrored Porter's playful lyrics. Rising movie star Sal Mineo was Aladdin, Una Merkel was his mother, Basil Rathbone the Emperor, and ANNA MARIA ALBERGHETTI his daughter the Princess Ming Chu whom Aladdin loves. The plot was a series of traps by the Magician to get the magic lamp from Aladdin, and there were plenty of obstacles to keep the commoner and the princess apart. Despite an opulent production by producer RICHARD LEWINE and the *DUPONT SHOW OF THE MONTH* that reportedly cost $500,000, the musical was deemed dull in spots and lacking in charm. Much of the blame was put on Mineo who had proven to be a convincing juvenile delinquent in films but not a musical comedy hero. Also, major talents were not used effectively. The veteran musical star DENNIS KING was cast in the thankless role of the Astrologer, although he got to sing the anthem-like "Trust Your Destiny to Your Star." Also underused were AKIM TAMIROFF and George Hall, whose only song was cut before the broadcast. That number was titled "Wouldn't It Be Fun?" and

was the lament of a famous man who wishes he were not so well known. It was the last song Porter ever wrote and may reflect his own state of mind as his career came to an end. Yet when Ritchard is center stage commenting on life in China and plotting devilish deeds just like a Chinese Captain Hook, it is difficult not to find something to admire in this last hurrah by one of America's greatest songwriters.

☜ A stage version by the Prince Street Players, a Manhattan children's theatre troupe, was adapted into the 60-minute TV musical *Aladdin* (CBS-TV 1967) and used traditional Chinese theatre techniques to tell the familiar story. Aladdin (Fred Grades) has two genies (both played by Will B. Able) to help him win the Princess Mei Ling (Victoria Mallory). The tuneful score was by Jim Eiler and Jeanne Bargy, and the teleplay was written by Paul Zindel, author of teen novels and a few Broadway plays. Unlike the 1958 version with its sly jokes about society, this *Aladdin* is strictly for kids with little in it for adults. The young Mallory, who would later be featured on Broadway in *FOLLIES* (1971) and *A LITTLE NIGHT MUSIC* (1973), is the highlight of the production.

▰ *ALADDIN* (Disney 1992). One of the funniest entries in the DISNEY animated catalog, the adventure musical was a fast-paced *Arabian Nights* farce that only occasionally slowed down for romance, as in the Oscar-winning song "A Whole New World." Aladdin (voice of Scott Weinger, singing by Brad Kane) is a lone "street rat" in this version scripted by Roger Allers and Ron Clements, and the Princess Jasmine (Linda Larkin with LEA SALONGA's singing) is a spunky heroine who flees the palace to see what the real world is like. The two make a sassy pair but the broad comedy comes from the supporting characters, such as the villainous vizier Jafar (JONATHAN FREEMAN), his wisecracking parrot Iago (Gilbert Gottfried), and especially Robin Williams's Genie who was a visual and vocal explosion of lines and sounds, much of his text improvised in the recording session. Also heard on the soundtrack are Douglas Seale, Bruce Adler, Jim Cummings, and Frank Welker. ALAN MENKEN provided the pseudo-exotic music, and HOWARD ASHMAN completed half the lyrics before his premature death. British lyricist TIM RICE finished the score, which included the satirical parade "Prince Ali," the jazzy "One Jump Ahead," the chant-like "Arabian Nights," and the vaudeville showstopper "Friend Like Me." Clements directed with John Musker, and the musical was the top-grossing film of that year. A made-for-video sequel titled *The Return of Jafar* was released in 1994.

ALBERGHETTI, ANNA MARIE (1936–). Stage, film, and television performer. A petite, dark-haired beauty with an opera-quality soprano voice, she played engaging ingénues in the 1950s and 1960s. Alberghetti was born in Pesaro, Italy, the daughter of a concert master and a pianist, and was singing with symphony orchestras by the time she was six years old. After an auspicious debut at Carnegie Hall when she was fourteen, her family settled in America where she sang in concerts and on television variety programs. Alberghetti's first film was the Italian opera movie of *The Medium* (1951) and then she was featured in such Hollywood musicals as HERE COMES THE GROOM (1951), *The Stars Are Singing* (1953), *Ten Thousand Bedrooms* (1957), and *Cinderfella* (1960), as well as the TV musicals ALADDIN (1958), THE JAZZ SINGER (1959), and A BELL FOR ADANO (1959). She made her Broadway debut as the waif Lili in CARNIVAL (1961), followed by many other musicals on tour, particularly WEST SIDE STORY, FANNY, THE FANTASTICKS, and KISMET, which she filmed for television in 1967. Alberghetti has also acted in many movie and television nonmusicals into the new century.

ALBERT, EDDIE [born Edward Albert Heimberger] (1906–2005). Stage, film, and television performer. A genial, lightweight leading man and sometime comic sidekick, he found success in all three media. Born in Rock Island, Illinois, the son of a real estate agent, Albert studied drama at the University of Minnesota before working as a trapeze artist and a radio announcer. He made his Broadway debut in 1936 and gained attention in his second show, *Brother Rat* (1936), in which he played the secretly married cadet Bing Edwards. Making his film debut reprising the role in the 1938 screen version, he went on to play mostly sidekicks and comic supporting roles in many movies over the next forty years, including hoofer Phil Dolen in ON YOUR TOES (1939), the sidekick Eliott Atterbury in *The Girl Rush* (1955), and the peddler Ali Hakim in OKLAHOMA! (1955). Albert returned to the stage on a few occasions, usually with success, and played such musical roles as Antipholus of Syracuse in THE BOYS FROM SYRACUSE (1938), journalist Horace Miller in MISS LIBERTY (1949), playwright Jack Jordan in *Say, Darling* (1958), and a Harold Hill replacement in THE

MUSIC MAN in 1959. Albert was one of the first actors to appear on television, performing in some early experimental broadcasts in 1936. He appeared on many television specials, including the musicals A CONNECTICUT YANKEE (1955), THE CHOCOLATE SOLDIER (1955), and *The Borrowers* (1973). He also was featured on several TV series, most memorably the very popular *Green Acres* in the 1960s. Albert was an influential environmental activist, and Earth Day is set on April 22 (his birthday) in his honor. He was married to actress Margo (1917–1985) and their son was film actor Edward Albert (1951–2006)

ALDA, ROBERT [born Alphonso Giovanni Roberto D'Abruzzo] (1914–1986). Stage and film performer. A solid, handsome singer–actor, he had his two best roles with his Broadway and Hollywood debuts. A native New Yorker and son of a barber, Alda studied architecture at New York University before he started singing in vaudeville and burlesque. Performing on the radio led to a WARNER BROTHERS contract and he made his screen debut as GEORGE GERSHWIN in the biopic *RHAPSODY IN BLUE* (1945). Alda's subsequent musicals, *Cinderella Jones* (1946), *The Man I Love* (1947), and *April Showers* (1948), were not successful and he was soon cast as heavies in nonmusical films. Turning to Broadway, he had better luck with his New York legit debut GUYS AND DOLLS (1950), originating the role of gambler Sky Masterson. Again his subsequent stage efforts were disappointing, although he did shine in the musical *What Makes Sammy Run?* (1964). In 1970 Alda moved to Italy and made European movies until he suffered a stroke in 1984. His son is actor–director **Alan Alda** (1936–), who became famous with the TV series M*A*S*H and appeared in two musicals, THE APPLE TREE (1966) on Broadway and EVERYONE SAYS I LOVE YOU (1996) on screen.

ALEXANDER, JASON [born Jay Scott Greenspan] (1959–). Stage, film, and television performer. The short, stocky comic actor has found success in character roles in all major media. Alexander was born in Newark, New Jersey, and educated at Boston University before making his Broadway debut as producer Joe Josephson in the musical MERRILY WE ROLL ALONG (1981). He began his film career the same year and his television career three years later but often returned to the New York stage, appearing in the musicals *America Kicks Up Its Heels* (1982), FORBIDDEN BROADWAY (1983),

THE RINK (1984), *Personals* (1985), and *JEROME ROBBINS' BROADWAY* (1989). On screen he has played mostly sidekicks and was heard in the animated musical *THE HUNCHBACK OF NOTRE DAME* (1996). Alexander has been most successful on television where he was featured on the series *Seinfeld* in the 1990s and appeared on many different kinds of shows, including the TV musicals *BYE BYE BIRDIE* (1995), *CINDERELLA* (1997), and *A CHRISTMAS CAROL* (2004).

◼ ALEXANDER'S RAGTIME BAND (Fox 1938). The first of a handful of nostalgic films utilizing the vast IRVING BERLIN song catalog, this musical squeezed in twenty-one old favorites and two new numbers, "Now It Can Be Told" and "My Walking Stick." The screenplay by Kathryn Scola, Lamar Trotti, and Richard Sherman followed the on-and-off romantic triangle among bandleader Alexander (TYRONE POWER), band singer Stella Kirby (ALICE FAYE), and composer–pianist Charlie Dwyer (DON AMECHE), spread out from 1911 to 1938 as careers rise and fall and self-sacrificing Charlie steps aside whenever Alexander and Stella are on good terms. Although the three stars never aged, the film captured the changing musical styles over the decades with some accuracy. Faye is particularly effective singing the title number, "Everybody's Doin' It," "All Alone," "Remember," and "What'll I Do?" ETHEL MERMAN, as cabaret singer Jerry Allen

Alexander's Ragtime Band. Irving Berlin refused to let Hollywood make a musical biography of his life but at least we have this song-packed film that came close. Tyrone Power (pictured with Alice Faye) played a composer–pianist who writes the pseudo-rag hit "Alexander's Ragtime Band" and becomes famous. (Photofest)

who is hired to replace Stella after one of her many spats with Alexander, belted out "Pack Up Your Sins and Go to the Devil," "Say It With Music," and "Heat Wave." Also in the cast were HELEN WESTLEY, Jean Hersholt, John Carradine, and JACK HALEY who sang "Oh, How I Hate to Get Up in the Morning." Other Berlin favorites in the score include "When the Midnight Choo-Choo Leaves for Alabam'," "Blue Skies," "A Pretty Girl Is Like a Melody," and "Everybody Step." HENRY KING directed and SEYMOUR FELIX choreographed the DARRYL F. ZANUCK production. It cost a staggering $2 million but the box office was so healthy that other Berlin anthology movies followed.

◼ ALICE IN WONDERLAND (Disney/RKO 1951). Lewis Carroll's sense of satire and the original, highly Victorian look of John Tenniel's illustrations may have been lost in this animated version of the story, but the musical had a distinctive look of its own and the animators' artistry was deliciously surreal at times and often overshone many of the film's characters and songs. A dozen writers were credited with the screenplay, and distinguished novelist Aldous Huxley also contributed to the script, which took *Alice's Adventures in Wonderland* (1865) and sections of Carroll's *Through the Looking Glass* (1872) and created an episodic romp that bounced along without sweetness or pathos, climaxing in a madcap montage that tied the whole extravaganza together. It is perhaps the least sentimental animated musical in the Disney catalog. For the first time, WALT DISNEY employed recognized voices, such as ED WYNN (Mad Hatter), JERRY COLONNA (March Hare), STERLING HOLLOWAY (Cheshire Cat), and J. Pat O'Malley (Walrus, Carpenter, Teedeledee, Tweedledum), and his artists suggested the actors in their drawn characterizations. Kathryn Beaumont voiced Alice with a clear, adult tone that allowed no sweetness, and Verna Felton, who had been so warm as the Fairy Godmother in the previous year's *CINDERELLA*, gave the Queen of Hearts a full-throttle interpretation. SAMMY FAIN (music) and Bob Hilliard (lyrics) wrote the score, which consisted mostly of short songs ("All in a Golden Afternoon," "I'm Late," and the dreamy title number) that rarely stopped the action, or with "The Walrus and the Carpenter" and "The Caucus Race," musicalized the original Carroll text. Clyde Geronimi, Wilfred Jackson, and Hamilton Luske directed the musical, which took five years to make and initially did not do well at the box office. In 1954 it was the first Disney film to be shown on television, although it was edited from seventy-five minutes to one hour to fit into the weekly *Disneyland* spot. It wasn't until the theatrical rereleases in the 1960s that the movie became a beloved classic.

☐ ALICE IN WONDERLAND, OR WHAT'S A NICE KID LIKE YOU DOING IN A PLACE LIKE THIS?

(ABC-TV 1966). More a spoof of the Lewis Carroll story than a sincere attempt at musicalization, this animated version updated the setting and characters and offered a kind of fun far different from the original's Victorian satire. The hip-booted, mini-skirted teen Alice (voice of Janet Waldo) bangs her head as she is reading the Carroll book and imagines her own wonderland with a jiving Cheshire Cat (SAMMY DAVIS, JR.) who wonders "What's a Nice Kid Like You Doing in a Place Like This?," a very Hungarian-sounding Queen of Hearts (ZSA ZSA GABOR), a standup comic Mad Hatter (Harvey Korman) and his wife named Hedda Hatter (Hedda Hopper), and even Fred Flintstone (Alan Reed) and Barney Rubble (Mel Blanc) as a two-headed caterpillar singing "They'll Never Split Us Apart." Comedian Bill Dana wrote the script and, using his José Jiminez voice, played the White Knight, and CHARLES STROUSE (music) and LEE ADAMS (lyrics) provided a lively score that also included "Today's a Wonderful Day," "Life's a Game," and "I'm Home." While the musical cartoon presented by William Hanna and Joseph Barbera is too silly and inconsequential for some tastes, there is much to enjoy all the same.

☐ ALICE IN WONDERLAND, PARTS 1 AND 2

(CBS-TV 1985). At a combined running time of four hours, this star-studded musical version of both *Alice's Adventures in Wonderland* (1865) and *Through the Looking Glass* (1872) is the most complete adaptation of Lewis Carroll's two fantasy works. Producer Irwin Allen, who was noted for his disaster adventure films, filled the production with big names, lots of scenery, and even an action sequence in which the Jabberwock is slain. Some found it riveting, others found it tedious and drawn out. Natalie Gregory is a personable Alice and among the celebrities she runs into are Red Buttons (White Rabbit), SAMMY DAVIS, JR. (Caterpillar and Fr. William), MARTHA RAYE (Duchess), DONALD O'CONNOR (The Lory Bird), ANTHONY NEWLEY (Mad Hatter), Roddy McDowell (March Hare), Arte Johnson (Dormouse), Jayne Meadows

(Queen of Hearts), Telly Savalas (Cheshire Cat), Sherman Hemsley (Mouse), CAROL CHANNING (White Queen), Ringo Starr (Mick Turtle), Lloyd Bridges (White Knight), Steve Lawrence and Eydie Gormé (Tweedledum and Tweedledee), Karl Malden (Walrus), and Jonathan Winters (Humpty Dumpty). Steve Allen wrote the score, which was uneven but sometimes engaging, as with "To the Looking-Glass World," "Hush-a-Bye Lady," "We Are Dancing," and "Alice." Playwright/novelist Paul Zindel wrote the teleplay, which stuck to the original books very closely, making the musical a faithful if not exhilarating experience.

☐ ALICE THROUGH THE LOOKING GLASS (NBC-

TV 1966). While most adaptations of the Lewis Carroll novels concentrate on the more familiar *Alice's Adventures in Wonderland* (1865), this musical focuses on *Through the Looking Glass* (1872) and the more nonsensical and satirical aspects of the fantasy. Albert Simmons' teleplay included most of the famous characters but took liberties with how they were presented. The songs, by Mark Charlap (music) and Elsie Simmons (lyrics), are sprightly and enjoyable, although as far from Victorian Britain as you can get. Judi Rolin was the wide-eyed Alice and among the characters she encountered were the White Queen (NANETTE FABRAY), the Red Queen (AGNES MOOREHEAD), The White King (RICARDO MONTALBAN), the Red King (Robert Coote), Humpty Dumpty (JIMMY DURANTE), the Japperwock (Jack Palance), Tweedledum and Tweedledee (Tom and Dick Smothers), and Lester the Jester (Roy Castle). "I Wasn't Meant to be Queen," "The Backwards Alphabet," "There Are Two Sides to Everything," "Some Summer Day," and "Through the Looking Glass" were the notable numbers. Alan Handley co-produced and directed the ninety-minute musical.

✥ ALL AMERICAN (Winter Garden Theatre

1962). A late entry in the long line of musicals that used a college setting with the big football game, this amiable show did not join the ranks of the campus long runs but was enjoyable for its bright cast and pleasant songs. MEL BROOKS's libretto had a promising start: Hungarian refugee Professor Fodorski (RAY BOLGER) arrives at Southern Baptist Institute of Technology to teach and ends up coaching football. The rest of the plot was routine with an expected romance between students Susan (ANITA GILLETTE) and Edwin (RON HUSMANN) and an unlikely one between the professor and Dean Hawkes-Bullock (Eileen Herlie). Also cast were Fritz Weaver, Will B. Able, and Betty Oakes. The score by CHARLES STROUSE (music) and LEE ADAMS (lyrics) produced the hit ballad "Once Upon a Time," and also commendable were "I've Just Seen Her," "What a Country!," "We Speak the Same Language," and "If I Were You." JOSHUA LOGAN directed and DANNY DANIELS choreographed the musical, which met with mixed notices except for high praise for Bolger. The show lingered for eighty performances, and the disappointed writer Brooks would not return to Broadway for thirty-eight years.

■ **ALL THAT JAZZ** (Fox/Columbia 1979). Despite its title, this backstage musical was more interested in the hard work and the neurotic creators than the razzle dazzle of putting together a Broadway musical. Producer Robert Alan Aurthur assisted director–choreographer BOB FOSSE in writing the screenplay, an obviously autobiographical tale with all the warts showing. Director–choreographer Joe Gideon (Roy Scheider) juggles both a stage musical and a film, popping pills, striving for perfection, cheating on his wife Audrey (LELAND PALMER) with his mistress Kate (ANN REINKING), trying to hang onto his daughter Michelle (Erzsebet Foldi), and eventually suffering a heart attack and dying. This chronicle was interrupted by wry commentary by O'Connor Flood (Ben Vereen) who led the cast in a surreal finale as the Angel of Death (Jessica Lange) took Joe away. This was autobiography at its most abrasive but the musical numbers released some of the tension. Using old and recent song favorites ("Some of These Days," "Bye Bye Love," "After You've Gone," and "Who's Sorry Now?"), Fosse found some new and exciting ways to film dance. Particularly effective was the opening, a montage of the audition process set to "On Broadway." But Joe's open-heart surgery, graphically depicted with a production number swirling around it, was a bit too indulgent even for some Fosse fans. All the same, the movie was moderately successful and remains a unique curiosity piece.

🕭 **ALLEGRO** (Majestic Theatre 1947). Rodgers and Hammerstein's most experimental musical, it was, like all bold experiments that don't completely succeed, either praised as a work of insightful genius or derided as a pretentious bore. OSCAR HAMMERSTEIN's original libretto followed the life of Joe Taylor, Jr. (John Battles), who grows up in a small American town where he falls in love with a local girl, Jennie Brinke (Roberta Jonay). After earning his medical degree, Joe marries Jennie and, against his better wishes, they move to Chicago where he becomes a successful doctor, making lots of money treating neurotic, wealthy patients. Jennie is bored in her marriage, always pushing Joe to rise higher in hospital administration, even as she has love affairs with other men. Everyone but Joe knows the truth, but it particularly hurts his nurse, Emily West (LISA KIRK) who is quietly in love with her boss. Just as Joe is about to accept an even higher position at the hospital, he learns of Jennie's unfaithfulness and becomes aware of his own hypocrisy. He leaves Chicago to become a general practitioner in his hometown, with Emily happily going with him. It may sound like a routine story but Rodgers and Hammerstein wrote the musical without the traditional chorus and plot sequences in mind. Instead they conceived the story of their everyman Joe as taking place in an open space defined by projections, voices, and moving figures. In many ways it was close to the ancient Greek theatre with its speaking chorus (in addition to the usual singing and dancing choruses) commenting on the action and talking to both actors and audience. However, there was also something modern and cinematic in the way that time was compressed, locations were paraded by, and one scene overlapped into the next. AGNES DE MILLE directed and choreographed the unusual show without conventional scenery, and the songs were often extended musical scenes with commentary from the chorus. The sardonic "The Gentleman Is a Dope" was the only hit to come from the score, yet the team also came up with the wistful ballad "I Know It Can Happen Again," the warm "A Fellow Needs a Girl," the sarcastic "Money Isn't Everything," the tender "So Far," and the frantic title song. The mixed notices hurt business and the THEATRE GUILD production ran 315 performances only because of its large advance. Feelings about *Allegro* remain equally divided sixty years later. It remains a brilliant innovative piece but it is also preachy and dull in spots; in other words, a true experiment.

ALLEN, DEBBIE (1950–). Stage, film, and television performer, choreographer, and director. The vivacious African American dancer-turned-choreographer-turned-director, she found fame for her work on television. Allen was born in Houston, Texas, and educated at Howard University. Her mother was the doctor and poet Vivian Ayers. Allen made her Broadway debut as a replacement dancer in *PURLIE* (1970) and then was featured as the restless daughter Beneatha in the musical *RAISIN* (1973) and as a replacement in *AIN'T MISBEHAVIN'* in 1978. Her performance as the tough but dedicated dance teacher Lydia in the movie *FAME* (1980) brought her national attention and she repeated the role in the successful television series (1982–1987). She returned to Broadway and shone as Anita in the 1980 revival of *WEST SIDE STORY* and as Charity in the 1986 mounting of *SWEET CHARITY*. As a choreographer, Allen staged the dances for the TV *Fame*, five ACADEMY AWARDS shows, and the short-lived Broadway musical *Carrie* (1988). Allen is a recognized director who helmed the TV musicals *POLLY* (1989) and *POLLY: COMIN' HOME!* (1990) and many television shows, including dozens of episodes of the series *A Different World* (1988–1993). She is the founder of the Debbie Allen Dance Institute in California and a published author of children's books. Her sister is actress Phylicia Rashad (1948–).

ALLEN, FRED [born John Florence Sullivan] (1894–1956). Stage, film, and television performer. The deadpan comedian with a nasal drawl who was a favorite voice on the radio, he gave droll performances in Broadway and Hollywood musicals as well. Allen was born in Cambridge, Massachusetts, educated at Boston University, and began his career as a vaudeville comic. By 1922 he was doing his witty, funny, low-key monologues on Broadway in such revues as *THE PASSING SHOW* (1922), *Greenwich Village Follies* (1923), *Vogues of 1924, Polly* (1929), *THE LITTLE SHOW* (1929), *THREE'S A CROWD* (1930), and *ZIEGFELD FOLLIES* (1934). Allen was also successful on the screen, making appearances in such film musicals as *THANKS A MILLION* (1935), *Sally, Irene and Mary* (1938), and *LOVE THY NEIGHBOR* (1940). His greatest fame came from his radio show, which he wrote, produced, and performed from 1939 to 1949, which featured a fictitious feud between himself and comic JACK BENNY. Allen also had a show on television in 1953. Autobiographies: *Treadmill to Oblivion* (1954); *Much Ado About Me* (1956); biography: *Fred Allen: His Life and Wit*, Robert Taylor (1991).

ALLEN, GRACIE. See BURNS, George, and Gracie ALLEN

ALLYSON, JUNE [born Ella Geisman] (1917–2006). Film and stage performer. One of Hollywood's favorite "girl next door" stars, the husky-voiced actress–singer seemed to exude optimism and cheerfulness even in her dramatic roles. Allyson was born in the Bronx, the daughter of a builder, and began her career as perky ingénues on Broadway in the musicals *Sing Out the News* (1938), *VERY WARM FOR MAY* (1939), *HIGHER AND HIGHER* (1940), and *PANAMA HATTIE* (1940). Her performance as the coed Minerva in *BEST FOOT FORWARD* (1941) was noticed enough that she made her screen debut reprising the role in the 1943 film version. Allyson was featured as smiling leads in 1940s Hollywood musicals and then in the 1950s turned to dramatic roles. Her most notable musical roles include canteen worker Patsy in *TWO GIRLS AND A SAILOR* (1944), socialite Martha in *Two Sisters From Boston* (1946), college student Connie in *GOOD NEWS!* (1947), bandleader's wife Helen in *The Benny Goodman Story* (1954), and the Park Avenue wife Kay in *The Opposite Sex* (1956), as well as memorable specialty spots in *GIRL CRAZY* (1943), *Thousands Cheer* (1943), *TILL THE CLOUDS ROLL BY* (1946), and *WORDS AND MUSIC* (1948). Her other screen musicals include *Meet the People* (1944), *Music for Millions* (1945), and *You Can't Run Away From It* (1956). Allyson made many nonmusicals in the 1950s but after the death of her husband DICK POWELL in 1963, she struggled with alcoholism and went into semiretirement, only appearing in television programs and occasional plays and nightclubs up to the year of her death. Autobiography: *June Allyson*, with Frances Spatz Leighton (1993).

ALTER, LOUIS (1902–1980). Stage and film composer. Working with a variety of lyricists, the songwriter turned out several hits in his handful of Broadway and Hollywood musicals. Alter was born in Haverill, Massachusetts, and began his career as a vaudeville pianist and singer, even as he started writing songs for himself and other variety artists. He appeared in the Broadway musicals *The Show Of Wonders* (1916) and *Come Along* (1919) and then had his songs heard in the revues *A La Carte* (1927), *EARL CARROLL'S VANITIES* (1928), *Sweet and Low* (1930), and *Ballyhoo of 1930*, as well as the book musical *Hold Your Horses* (1933). Alter provided songs for the movie musicals *Going Highbrow* (1935), *Trail of the Lonesome Pine* (1936), *Sing Baby Sing* (1936), *Rainbow on the River* (1936), *Make a Wish* (1937), *Vogues of 1938*, and *NEW ORLEANS* (1947), the last with lyricist Eddie DeLange and introducing the jazz favorite "Do You Know What It Means to Miss New

Orleans?" With FRANK LOESSER, Alter wrote "Dolores," which introduced FRANK SINATRA to filmgoers in *Las Vegas Nights* (1941).

ALTMAN, ROBERT [Bernard] (1925–2006). Film and stage director. An anti-establishment *auteur* with a distinctive style, he directed three musicals during his long and impressive career. Altman was born in Kansas City, Missouri, served as a bomber in World War II, and then studied engineering at the University of Missouri before turning to writing film scripts. He directed independent films and several television series before finding fame in Hollywood with *M*A*S*H* (1970). Like his subsequent efforts, it was quirky, satiric, and multilayered with overlapping dialogue. These characteristics can be found in his musicals *NASHVILLE* (1975), *Popeye* (1980), and *A Prairie Home Companion* (2006). Altman, who usually contributed to the scripts for his films, never fit into the Hollywood system and throughout his career he was at odds with the studios, which had a love–hate relationship with the brilliant, individualistic director.

ALTON, ROBERT [born Robert Alton Hart] (1897–1957). Stage and film choreographer. For three decades he was one of Broadway and Hollywood's busiest and most successful choreographers. Alton was born in Bennington, Vermont, and studied dance at the Mordkin Ballet and Dramatic School in New York. He was on the stage as a dancer by 1919, moving up from the chorus to assistant choreographer. He made his choreography debut with the Broadway musical *Hold Your Horses* in 1933, followed by dozens of shows into the 1950s, including *ANYTHING GOES* (1934), *HOORAY FOR WHAT!* (1937), *BETWEEN THE DEVIL* (1937), *You Never Know* (1938), *LEAVE IT TO ME!* (1938), *TOO MANY GIRLS* (1939), *DUBARRY WAS A LADY* (1939), *HIGHER AND HIGHER* (1940), *PANAMA HATTIE* (1940), *PAL JOEY* (1940 and 1952), *BY JUPITER* (1942), and *ME AND JULIET* (1953), as well as several popular revues. Alton also enjoyed a very successful Hollywood career, choreographing his first film in 1936 and doing the dance numbers for such movies as *YOU'LL NEVER GET RICH* (1941), *BROADWAY RHYTHM* (1944), *THE HARVEY GIRLS* (1946), *TILL THE CLOUDS ROLL BY* (1946), *GOOD NEWS!* (1947), *THE PIRATE* (1948), *EASTER PARADE* (1948), *WORDS AND MUSIC* (1948), *THE BARKLEYS OF BROADWAY* (1949), *ANNIE GET YOUR GUN* (1950), *SHOW BOAT* (1951), *THE BELLE OF NEW YORK* (1952), *CALL ME MADAM* (1953), *WHITE CHRISTMAS* (1954), and *THERE'S NO BUSINESS LIKE SHOW BUSINESS* (1954). In his choreography, Alton broke away from the traditional chorus line and grouped his dancers in more interesting patterns, also letting featured members of the chorus do specialties in order to individualize the numbers.

AMECHE, DON [born Dominic Felix Amici] (1908–1993). Stage, film, and television performer. The dapper, mustachioed leading man gave some fine performances on the New York stage but always had better luck in Hollywood. Ameche was born in Kenosha, Wisconsin, the son of a tavern owner, and studied for a law degree at Marquette and Georgetown universities and the University of Wisconsin. He began doing campus theatricals at this last school and soon found some success on the radio. Ameche went to New York where he failed to get acting jobs so he headed to California and made his screen debut with 20TH CENTURY-FOX in 1935. He soon became popular for playing lightweight *bon vivant* roles in comedies and musicals, such as *Ramona* (1936), *One in a Million* (1937), *You Can't Have Everything* (1937), *ALEXANDER'S RAGTIME BAND* (1938), *Swanee River* (1939), *The Three Musketeers* (1939), *DOWN ARGENTINE WAY* (1940), *LILLIAN RUSSELL* (1940), *THAT NIGHT IN RIO* (1941), *MOON OVER MIAMI* (1941), *Kiss the Boys Goodbye* (1941), *Something to Shout About* (1943), *Greenwich Follies* (1944), and *Slightly French* (1949). As he matured, Ameche occasionally got more substantial roles, such as the title character in *The Story of Alexander Graham Bell* (1939), but Hollywood preferred him in comedies. With his screen recognition, he returned to Broadway in 1955 to play the middle-aged Steve Canfield in the musical *SILK STOCKINGS* and found success, but his subsequent stage musicals failed to run: *GOLDILOCKS* (1958), *Thirteen Daughters* (1961), and *Henry Sweet Henry* (1967). Ameche made many appearances on television, including the TV musicals *HIGH BUTTON SHOES* (1956) and *JUNIOR MISS* (1957), and in his later years was a highly prized character actor, playing the stage manager in *Our Town* (1989) on Broadway and on screen the senior citizen Arthur in *Cocoon* (1985) and *Cocoon: The Return* (1988).

▆ AMERICAN IN PARIS, AN (MGM 1951). Perhaps the most arty of all MGM musicals, and not just because it is about artists, the film is also a lot of fun, and few movies are more beautiful to look at.

An American in Paris. George Gershwin's concert piece "An American in Paris" provided the music for the extended ballet sequence at the end of the classic musical and the genius of the composer was matched by the genius of the choreographer–dancer Gene Kelly. Just as Gershwin's music is playful, so too was Kelly's visualization of it. Here he strikes an attitude with Leslie Caron. (Photofest)

Plot: Ex-GI Jerry Mulligan remains in Paris after World War II to pursue his dream of becoming an artist. He falls in love with the perfume counter salesgirl Lise Bourvier but she is engaged to the older, dashing Henri Baurel, a music hall entertainer who had saved her life while they were fighting in the Resistance. Jerry, in turn, is pursued by the art patroness Milo Roberts who wants to set him up in his own studio and promote his work. Through a mutual friend, the sardonic pianist Adam Cook, Jerry and Henri become friends without knowing they love the same girl. Once Jerry thinks he has lost Lise forever, he imagines himself in a ballet with all of Paris swirling around him and as he returns to reality he finds that Henri has graciously stepped out of the way so Jerry and Lise can be together.

Producer ARTHUR FREED only gave writer ALAN JAY LERNER the premise of an American artist in Paris and told him to devise a screen-

Cast for *An American in Paris*

Character	Performer
Jerry Mulligan	GENE KELLY
Lise Bourvier	LESLIE CARON
Adam Cook	OSCAR LEVANT
Henri Baurel	Georges Guetary
Milo Roberts	Nina Foch

play using the music of GEORGE GERSHWIN as the score, particularly the symphonic suite "An American in Paris" (1928). The result is a simple but effective story that allows for a variety of Gershwin songs as well as two of his concert pieces. Director VINCENTE MINNELLI, who had started his career as an artist and stage designer, created an artist's view of Paris by filming the musical entirely in a studio and presenting each scene as a painting. This is particularly noticeable in the film's seventeen-minute "An American in Paris" ballet in which

---

An American in Paris Musical Numbers

"Nice Work If You Can Get It"
"Embraceable You"
"Fascinating Rhythm"
"By Strauss"
"I Got Rhythm"
"Tra-La-La"
"Love Is Here to Stay"
"I'll Build a Stairway to Paradise"
"I Don't Think I'll Fall in Love Today"
"Concerto in F" (third movement)
"'S Wonderful"
"Liza"
"An American in Paris"

---

the look of each section is inspired by a different French artist, from Renoir and Utrillo to Dufy and Toulouse-Lautrec. Paris is seen only as Jerry Mulligan sees it, and as a result the musical looks like no other.

When IRA GERSHWIN was approached by Freed about using the music from "An American in Paris" in a musical, the lyricist agreed on the condition that only music by his brother George serve as the score. A variety of songs were used, many with lyrics by Ira, and the movie ended up being a salute to the versatility of George Gershwin. Kelly's singing "I Got Rhythm" with a bunch of French kids or his romancing Caron along the banks of the Seine with "Love Is Here to Stay" are a delightful contrast, just as Guetary, Kelly, and Levant clowning with "By Strauss" is balanced by Levant's earnest playing of the "Concerto in F." *An American in Paris* ended up being a feast for the ear as well as the eye. As for the dancing, many feel that Kelly's choreography and dancing in the film are the finest of his career. The numbers are inventive, stylized, and enchanting. The choreography has less humor than, say, *SINGIN' IN THE RAIN* (1952), but there is a trancelike beauty to the dancing in this movie that is unforgettable.

AMERICAN PLAYHOUSE. An ongoing television series on PBS, this anthology program rarely puts together its own productions but takes drama and musical mountings produced by others and arranges to have them taped for broadcast. The program started in 1982 and, ironically, the first programs came from British stage productions. Over the years, outstanding American classics and new works, both from Broadway and from regional theatre, have been preserved for future generations by

American Playhouse. In the case of musicals, the shows are usually filmed in a theatre with an audience so that laughter and applause can be heard and the theatregoing experience can be somewhat simulated. Among the musicals broadcast on the program were the Broadway productions of the STEPHEN SONDHEIM shows *SUNDAY IN THE PARK WITH GEORGE* (1986), *INTO THE WOODS* (1991), and *PASSION* (1996).

AMERICAN SOCIETY OF COMPOSERS, AUTHORS, AND PUBLISHERS (ASCAP). Music organization. Although copyright laws at the beginning of the twentieth century protected composers, lyricists, and music publishers from illegal reprinting of their sheet music, American artists and their publishers received no payment when orchestras performed their work in restaurants, ballrooms, and other public places. This was completely at odds with the situation in Europe and led to the establishment of ASCAP. Composer Raymond Hubbell, lawyer Nathan Burke, and publisher George Maxwell approached the celebrated composer–conductor VICTOR HERBERT about the idea and Herbert used his influence and popularity to get the project rolling in 1914. The new organization announced that fees would have to be paid to the organization any time the works of one of their artists were performed. Orchestras ignored the ruling until a test case in 1915. ASCAP sued Shanley's Restaurant for playing selections from Herbert's operetta *SWEETHEARTS* (1913) and the case went all the way to the Supreme Court before ASCAP won. With the growing popularity of radio and the invention of other forms by which music could be disseminated, these "performance royalties" became even more important, particularly as they were a more reliable source of income than the "mechanical royalties" paid by record companies to their artists, which were susceptible to creative accounting. A rival group, Broadcast Music, Inc. (BMI), was founded in 1940. Virtually all major composers and lyricists of the American musical have been members of these music associations.

ANASTASIA (Fox 1997). An attempt by 20TH CENTURY-FOX to create a classy animated musical with the quality (and hopefully the box office popularity) of the DISNEY products of the 1990s, this period piece with an unlikely subject matter was quite accomplished in many ways. It was hoped that the screenplay by Susan Gauthier, Bruce Graham, Bob Tzudiker, and Noni White would make audiences forget the film drama *Anastasia* (1956) and accept their story of the teenage Anya (voice of Meg Ryan, singing by Liz Callaway) who cannot remember her past but we know is the surviving Russian princess Anastasia Romanov who miraculously survived when her family was murdered in the revolution. Anya is discovered by the enterprising Dimitri (John Cusack, sung by Jonathan Dokuchitz) and his sidekick Vladimir (Kelsey Grammer) who bring her from St. Petersburg to Paris to present her to the Dowager Empress (ANGELA LANSBURY) as her long lost granddaughter. Dimitri's aims are mercenary but when he falls in love with Anya he changes his tune and helps her battle the back-from-the-grave Rasputin (Christopher Lloyd, sung by Jim Cummings) who has vowed to kill all the Romanovs. Much of the tale was hardly children's fare, such as a sequence showing the Russian revolution and the capture of the Romanovs. But the studio put in some lovable Disney-like characters, such as Rasputin's wacky henchman Bartok the Bat (Hank Azaria) and the life-affirming Parisian Sophie (BERNADETTE PETERS). STEPHEN FLAHERTY (music) and LYNN AHRENS (lyrics) wrote the superior score that included the evocative lullaby "Once Upon a December," the warm character song "Journey to the Past," the creepy conjuring number "In the Dark of the Night," and the rousing "Paris Holds the Key (To Your Heart)." DON BLUTH and Gary Goldman co-produced and co-directed the movie, which was the first feature animated musical in the long history of 20th Century-Fox.

ANCHORS AWEIGH (MGM 1945). Not the first "sailors on leave" musical and far from the last, this agreeable film afforded GENE KELLY and FRANK SINATRA one of their best vehicles to date. ISOBEL LENNART's screenplay, based on the short story "You Can't Fool a Marine" by Natalie Marcin, offered Sinatra, in his first starring role, as the shy sailor Clarence Doolittle, whereas Kelly was the girl-chasing cad Joe Brady. While on leave in Hollywood they meet and are taken with the singer Susan Abbott (KATHYRYN GRAYSON) and help her get an audition with the maestro JOSÉ ITURBI at METRO-GOLDWYN-MAYER. Susan gets a contract, Joe settles down and wins her hand, and Clarence is more than happy with a girl (Pamela Britton) who hails from Brooklyn just like himself. Also cast were Dean Stockwell, Carlos Ramirez, HENRY O'NEILL, Leon Ames, Rags Ragland, and Edgar Kennedy. Sinatra got to sing the enticing ballad "I Fall in Love Too Easily" by JULE STYNE (music) and SAMMY CAHN (lyrics), and pianist–conductor Iturbi presented a few classical selections, but it was the dance sections, choreographed by Kelly and STANLEY DONEN, that were the most memorable: a bombastic sequence in which Kelly wooed Grayson as he scaled the battlements and parapets, a lively "Mexican Hat Dance" routine with Sharon McManus, and a brilliant *pas de deux* "The King Who Couldn't Dance" with the cartoon character Jerry the Mouse, the first combination of live-action dancing with an animated figure. The score also included the Styne–Cahn numbers "I Begged Her," "What Makes the Sunset?," and "The Charm of You." JOE PASTERNAK produced and GEORGE SIDNEY directed.

ANDERSON, EDDIE "ROCHESTER" (1905–1977). Film, television, and stage performer. One of the most familiar African American actors in America in the 1940s and 1950s because of his role as JACK BENNY's sidekick, the gravel-voiced comic was also an accomplished song and dance man. Anderson was born in Oakland, California, the son of a minstrel performer and a tight rope walker, and began singing and doing jokes in vaudeville with his brother Cornelius. He toured in revues and nightclub acts before making his film debut in bit parts in 1932. Although he was in *Green Pastures* (1936) and *SHOW BOAT* (1936), no recognition came until Benny hired him for a comic sketch on his radio program in 1936. The audience response to the chemistry between the two comics was so overwhelming that Anderson and Benny were teamed for decades on radio, in films, and on television. He reprised his character of Rochester, the wise but smart-aleck manservant, in such film musicals as *Man About Town* (1939), *Buck Benny Rides Again* (1940), *LOVE THY NEIGHBOR* (1940), and *What's Buzzin' Cousin?* (1943). Of his many other roles, he is best remembered for hapless Little Joe Jackson in *CABIN IN THE SKY* (1943). Anderson's other screen musicals include *The Music Goes Round* (1936), *Melody for Two* (1937), *GOLD DIGGERS IN PARIS* (1938), *Thanks for the Memory* (1938), *Going Places* (1938), *Honolulu* (1939), *BIRTH OF THE BLUES* (1941), *Kiss the Boys Goodbye* (1941), *STAR-SPANGLED RHYTHM* (1943), *BROADWAY RHYTHM* (1943), and *I Love a Bandleader* (1945). He continued to perform in films and on television through the 1960s and did voiceovers for cartoons in the 1970s.

ANDERSON, JOHN MURRAY (1886–1954). Stage director, producer, and lyricist. A prodigious "jack of all trades," he brought European stagecraft to the Broadway revue. Anderson was born in Newfoundland, Canada, and went to New York City to become a ballroom dancer. Soon he was staging elaborate nightclub revues and designing them as well. In 1919 he used some of British designer Gordon Craig's ideas of suggested scenery and three-dimensional space to design and direct the *Greenwich Village Follies*, a surprise hit that was able to compete with FLORENZ ZIEGFELD's more lavish revues by using simple but effective scenery and costumes. Anderson also introduced "ballet ballads" to the revue, a form of narrative dance that was unique in its day. He produced and staged the six subsequent editions of the *Greenwich Village* series, as well as other revue series, including the celebrated *MUSIC BOX REVUE*, later editions of the *ZIEGFELD FOLLIES*, and two shows titled *John Murray Anderson's Almanac* (1929 and 1953). Anderson directed book musicals, as with *DEAREST ENEMY* (1925), *JUMBO* (1935), *Sunny River* (1941), and *The Firebrand of Florence* (1945), and wrote sketches and lyrics for such Broadway revues as *LIFE BEGINS AT 8:40* (1934), *One for the Money* (1939), *Two for The Show* (1940), *Three to Make Ready* (1946), *NEW FACES OF 1952*, and *Two's Company* (1952). He also directed the early innovative movie musical *KING OF JAZZ* (1930). Anderson's imaginative approach to the revue format greatly influenced the legendary revues of the 1930s. During his long and active career he also staged pageants, civic masques, cabaret floor shows, and circuses, including the circus sequences in the film *The Greatest Show on Earth* (1952). Autobiography: *Out Without My Rubbers* (1954).

ANDERSON, [James] **MAXWELL** (1888–1959). Stage, film, and television writer and lyricist. A distinguished Broadway playwright who wrote many of his dramas in verse, he also was involved with some memorable musicals and proved to be a superb lyricist. Anderson was born in Atlantic, Pennsylvania, and educated at the University of South Dakota and at Stanford. He worked as a journalist and a schoolteacher before turning to the theatre in 1923 and had his first hit the next year with the war play *What Price Glory?*, co-written with Laurence Stallings. Over the next three decades he wrote incisive historical plays, contemporary problem plays, and psychological dramas. Anderson's first Broadway musical was the controversial *KNICKERBOCKER HOLIDAY* (1938), writing the libretto and lyrics, and with composer KURT WEILL presenting the indelible "September Song." He also worked with Weill on the powerful South African musical *LOST IN THE STARS* (1974). Both musicals were later filmed, and Anderson collaborated with composer ALLIE WRUBEL on the screen musical *Never Steal Anything Small* (1959) and with composer ARTHUR SCHWARTZ on the TV musical *HIGH TOR* (1956), which was based on his 1937 play. His musical librettos are incisive and potent and his lyrics can be intoxicating and moving. Biography: *The Life of Maxwell Anderson*, Alfred S. Shivers (1983).

⚉ *ANDRE CHARLOT'S REVUE* (Times Square Theatre 1924). A British import by London impresario–director Andre Chalot, the musical revue was delightful in its own right but is most remembered for introducing GERTRUDE LAWRENCE, BEATRICE LILLIE, and JACK BUCHANAN to American audiences. The sophisticated show was small scale and intimate so the London performers were front and center and easily endeared themselves to Broadway patrons, beginning a love affair with the three stars that would last for four decades. Various songwriters (both British and American) provided the songs; musical highlights included Lawrence's sleek renditions of NOEL COWARD's "Parisian Pierrot" and "Poor Little Rich Girl," the exotic Philip Braham–Douglass Furber number "Limehouse Blues," Lillie dressed as Britannia and clowning through "March With Me!" by Furber and Ivor Novello, and Buchanan joining Lawrence for "I Was Meant for You" by EUBIE BLAKE and NOBLE SISSLE. Also in the cast were JESSIE MATTHEWS, Constance Carpenter, and Herbert Mudin. The Arch Selwyn production was a hit, running 289 performances, and Charlot brought back members of the cast in subsequent editions in 1926 and 1927.

ANDREWS, JULIE [born Julia Elizabeth Wells] (1935–). Stage, film, and television performer. One of America's favorite leading ladies, she appeared in landmark musicals on Broadway, in Hollywood, and on television. Andrews was born in Walton-on-Thames, England, the daughter of entertainers, and sang on the stage as a young girl. Her surprisingly adult soprano voice made her an unusual attraction, and by the age of twelve Andrews

Julie Andrews. Caught between takes of filming *The Sound of Music* (1965) in Salzburg, Austria, some of the von Trapp children seem more weary than sweet, yet there is no question that Julie Andrews and Maria are one and the same in the kids' eyes. (Photofest)

was performing professionally in London concerts and pantomimes. She first came to America in 1954 to recreate her role as Polly in the London musical spoof THE BOY FRIEND and was immediately singled out. After playing the sea captain's wife Lise in the TV musical HIGH TOR (1956), she scored a major triumph as Eliza Doolittle in MY FAIR LADY (1956), first on Broadway and then in London. While appearing in the show in New York, Andrews played the title role in Rodgers and Hammerstein's original television musical CINDERELLA (1957), a live broadcast that was seen by more people than any other up to that time. In 1960 she shone again on Broadway as Queen Guenevere in CAMELOT (1960). Andrews was not chosen to recreate her Eliza in the 1964 film version of *My Fair Lady*, but WALT DISNEY provided her screen debut as MARY POPPINS (1964), beginning her remarkable Hollywood career. She had her greatest screen success as Maria in THE SOUND OF MUSIC (1964), the role she has been most identified with ever since. Other film musical roles followed, including the flapper THOROUGHLY MODERN MILLIE (1967), legendary GERTRUDE LAWRENCE in STAR! (1968), the World War I spy DARLING LILI (1969), and the cross-dressing VICTOR/VICTORIA (1982). She returned to the New York theatre in the Off Broadway STEPHEN SONDHEIM revue *Putting It Together*

(1993) and in the Broadway version of *Victor/Victoria* (1995). Many of Andrews's movies over the past thirty years have been nonmusicals of varying quality, but she remains a bankable Hollywood star, bringing her touch of class and refinement to films as diverse as *The Americanization of Emily* (1964), *Torn Curtain* (1966), *10* (1979), and *The Princess Diaries* (2001). She has also appeared in many television specials and a handful of dramas. Andrews was married to scenic designer Tony Walton before wedding film producer/director BLAKE EDWARDS who directed her in seven films. Under the pen name Julie Edwards, she has written several children's books. With her crystal-clear singing voice, precise diction, and ladylike demeanor, Andrews remains one of the most unique and beloved performers of stage and screen. Biographies: *Julie Andrews*, John Cottrell (1968), *Julie Andrews*, Robert Windeler (1997).

ANDREWS SISTERS. Film performers. A trio of sibling harmony singers and arguably the most famous sister act of all time, they possessed little acting talent but lit up over a dozen Hollywood musicals. Patti (1918–), LaVerne (1911–1967), and Maxene (1916–1995) were born in Minneapolis to Norwegian Greek parents and were put on the stage as youngsters, winning talent contests with their precision singing. The threesome grew up touring in vaudeville and then as adults were featured with bands, finding great success recording hit records such as "Bei Mir Bist Du Schoen" and "The Beer Barrel Polka" in the late 1930s. The Andrews Sisters made their screen debut in the RITZ BROTHERS vehicle *Argentine Nights* (1940) and became stars in BUCK PRIVATES (1941) when they sang "Boogie Woogie Bugle Boy." Playing themselves, the sisters were never the top-billed stars in their films but they never failed to stop the show with their singing. Their other musicals include *Hold That Ghost* (1941), *What's Cookin'?* (1942), *Private Buckaroos* (1942), *Give Out, Sisters* (1942), *Always a Bridesmaid* (1943), *Follow the Boys* (1944), *Moonlight and Cactus* (1944), HOLLYWOOD CANTEEN (1944), and ROAD TO RIO (1947), as well as singing on the soundtracks for the animated musicals MAKE MINE MUSIC (1946) and MELODY TIME (1948). The trio was very popular on radio, where they had their own show, and later on television. After LaVerne's death in 1967, the surviving sisters performed together on occasion, most memorably in the Broadway musical OVER HERE! (1973). On her own, Maxene appeared on tour as old Berthe in *PIPPIN* and in the Off Broadway revue *Swingtime Canteen* (1995).

☐ **ANDROCLES AND THE LION** (NBC-TV 1967). This musical adaptation of George Bernard Shaw's version of the classic fable retained bits of the playwright's philosophical point of view, and RICHARD RODGERS wrote some very British (in fact, some very Noel Coward–like) lyrics for his own music. Since COWARD himself played Caesar, it was appropriate and sometimes delightfully droll.

PETER STONE's teleplay presents the Christian Androcles (Norman Wisdom) as a weakling of a Greek tailor who finds the courage to remove a thorn from the paw of a lion (GEOFFREY HOLDER). His act of kindness is rewarded later when Androcles in thrown into the Roman amphitheatre with other Christians to be eaten by, ironically, the same lion and, in taming him, convinces the emperor Caesar that there is something to Christianity after all. Wisdom got to sing the character songs while the ballads were delivered by JOHN CULLUM as a Roman Captain in love with his Christian captive INGA SWENSON. The talented cast also featured Brian Bedford, PATRICIA ROUTLEDGE, Ed Ames, KURT KASZNAR, and William Redfield. While the Rodgers score can hardly be counted as one of his finest, there is much to admire in the love song "Strangers" and in the lighter numbers "Velvet Paws," "Don't Be Afraid of an Animal," and "The Emperor's Thumb" in which Caesar laments that no matter how much he fusses over his clothes and grooming the crowd only looks at his thumb. In addition to the songs, Rodgers composed some thrilling instrumental pieces for the ninety-minute musical, such as "The Gladiators' Ballet" and "The Arena Pantomime." Marc Merson produced, JOE LAYTON directed, and David Baker choreographed. Critical reaction was very mixed and the broadcast was not widely popular so

Androcles and the Lion remains one of Rodgers' least known works.

☺ **ANIMAL CRACKERS** (44th Street Theatre 1928). A wacky musical vehicle for the MARX BROTHERS, it was their last Broadway appearance before heading to Hollywood. GEORGE S. KAUFMAN and MORRIE RYSKIND wrote the slight but efficient libretto about a valuable painting belonging to Mrs. Rittenhouse that is stolen from her Long Island home during a party. Audiences weren't as interested in the painting and who stole it as they were with the great African explorer Captain Spaulding as portrayed by Groucho and the clowning of his brothers. BERT KALMAR and HARRY RUBY wrote the score that included the daffy "Hooray for Captain Spaulding," which was forever after associated with Groucho. Among the other songs were the coy "Who's Been Listening to My Heart?," the dreamy "Watching the Clouds Go By," and the spoof number "Musketeers," which the brothers performed in outrageous cavalier costumes. SAM H. HARRIS produced the musical, which ran a healthy 191 performances. Although it has never been revived on Broadway, the durable old show has enjoyed productions regionally over the past twenty years, with actors impersonating the Marx Brothers and trying to capture what the silly show was like on Broadway.

🎬 *Animal Crackers* (Paramount 1930) was filmed using the same script and most of the Broadway cast, but the songs were cut (except for "Hooray for Captain Spaulding") and three new ones were added, including the standard "Some of These Days." The film is rather primitive, with the sets looking like stage scenery and the camera pretty much recording the action from a theatre audience's point of view. Yet the Marx Brothers are in top form and the confines of the studio don't seem to inhibit them at all. Kalmar and Ruby wrote "Why Am I So Romantic?" for the film and "Collegiate"

Casts for *Animal Crackers*

Character	1928 Broadway	1930 film
Captain Spaulding	GROUCHO MARX	Groucho Marx
Emanuel Ravelli	CHICO MARX	Chico Marx
The Professor	HARPO MARX	Harpo Marx
Horatio Jamison	ZEPPO MARX	Zeppo Marx
Mrs. Rittenhouse	MARGARET DUMONT	Margaret Dumont
Roscoe Chandler	Louis Sorin	Louis Sorin
Arabella Rittenhouse	Alice Wood	LILLIAN ROTH
John Parker	Milton Watson	Hal Thompson

by Mo Jaffe and Nat Bonx was thrown in, but rarely did the movie feel like a musical. Victor Heerman was the uninspired director but the Marx Brothers, in their second feature, carried the day and the picture was a hit.

ANIMATED MUSICALS. WALT DISNEY and others had been using music and even songs in cartoons and shorts long before the first feature-length animated musical came along with *SNOW WHITE AND THE SEVEN DWARFS* (1937). Disney was America's most recognized innovator with music and animation, presenting his Mickey Mouse shorts and his *Silly Symphony* cartoons. WARNER BROTHERS offered *Looney Tunes* shorts with Bugs Bunny and his friends animated with songs, UNIVERSAL had Oswald the Rabbit, PARAMOUNT had its *Puppetoon* flicks, Columbia offered *Color Rhapsodies*, and independent animators such as Max Fleischer created Popeye and Betty Boop, all of them utilizing music to some degree. When Disney broke new ground by giving the public full-length animated musicals, the other studios were hesitant to follow in his footsteps. Fleischer produced *GULLIVER'S TRAVELS* (1939), but most studios were content to stick to shorts. Disney, however, further developed the new genre of animated musicals with such features as *PINOCCHIO* (1940), *FANTASIA* (1940), *DUMBO* (1941), *THE THREE CABALLEROS* (1945), *SONG OF THE SOUTH* (1946), *CINDERELLA* (1950), *LADY AND THE TRAMP* (1955), and *SLEEPING BEAUTY* (1959). Music was integral to all these features, with some films having extensive scores and providing songs hits. In the 1960s and 1970s, the Disney studio continued, although on much smaller scale, to make such musicals and other studios occasionally joined them with such features as *GAY-PURR-EE* (1962), *YELLOW SUBMARINE* (1968), *A Boy Named Charlie Brown* (1969), *Shinbone Alley* (1971), and *CHARLOTTE'S WEB* (1973). The animation division at Disney declined in the late 1960s, and after Walt Disney's death many animators left the studio to work elsewhere. Feature-length cartoons by various studios started appearing regularly in the 1970s, but few were musicals, most being content to have one theme song and to rely on action and spectacle to tell the story. Only in the 1990s, when the Disney studio was back in full force with *BEAUTY AND THE BEAST* (1991) and *THE LION KING* (1994), did other studios enter the musical market. The quality varied but many of the features found success and helped open up the field of musical animation. Among these non-

Disney entries were *Rock-a-Doodle* (1992), *The Swan Princess* (1994), *Thumbelina* (1994), *A Troll in Central Park* (1994), *The Pebble and the Penguin* (1995), *Cats Don't Dance* (1996), *ANASTASIA* (1997), *Quest for Camelot* (1998), *THE PRINCE OF EGYPT* (1998), and *The Road to El Dorado* (2000). The recent interest in stop-action animation has yielded the Disney-produced musicals *THE NIGHTMARE BEFORE CHRISTMAS* (1993) and *James and the Giant Peach* (1996), and computer animation quickly found an audience with *Toy Story* (1995), *A Bug's Life* (1998), *Antz* (1998), and *Toy Story 2* (1999), all utilizing songs but not traditional musicals. When Disney moved away from musical animation to action animation with such pictures as *Dinosaur* (2000) and *The Incredibles* (2004), other studios followed suit and during the first decade of the twentieth century more animated features were being made than at any other previous time, but rarely were they musicals.

ANN-MARGARET [born Ann-Margaret Olsson] (1941–). Film and television performer. A glittering, leggy star of nightclubs and television, the sexy red-headed singer–actress shone in a handful of movie musicals. Ann-Margaret was born in Valsjobyn, Sweden, and at the age of five came to America where she grew up in Illinois. By the time she was sixteen she was a winner on Ted Mack's television show and sang in nightclubs before making her screen debut in the comedy *Pocketful of Miracles* (1961). Although she played a sweet and wholesome teen in *BYE BYE BIRDIE* (1963), she quickly became known as a sex symbol whose singing and dancing were very sensual. Ann-Margaret's other film musicals were *STATE FAIR* (1962), *The Pleasure Seekers* (1964), *VIVA LAS VEGAS* (1964), *The Swinger* (1966), *TOMMY* (1975), and *Newsies* (1992). She was eventually accepted as a serious actress in the 1970s and played many roles in nonmusical films and television programs. Autobiography: *Ann-Margaret: My Story*, with Todd Gold (1994).

ANNIE (Alvin Theatre 1977). The most successful musical ever made from a comic strip, the sunny, optimistic show became the first family musical hit in many a year and has remained one ever since.

Plot: In the midst of the Great Depression, little Annie is stuck in a Manhattan orphanage run by the harridan spinster Miss Hannigan who makes life miserable for her and the other unfortunate girls living there. Grace Farrell, the secretary to the billionaire Oliver Warbucks,

Casts for *Annie*

Character	1977 Broadway	1982 film	1999 television
Annie	Andrea McArdle	Aileen Quinn	Alicia Morton
Miss Hannigan	DOROTHY LOUDON	CAROL BURNETT	Kathy Bates
Daddy Warbucks	REID SHELTON	Albert Finney	VICTOR GARBER
Grace Farrell	Sandy Faison	ANN REINKING	AUDRA MCDONALD
Rooster	Robert Fitch	TIM CURRY	Alan Cumming
Lily	Barbara Erwin	BERNADETTE PETERS	KRISTIN CHENOWETH

comes looking for a waif to spend Christmas at the Warbucks mansion and, much to Miss Hannigan's dislike, Annie is chosen. Warbucks takes an instant liking to the spirited young-ster and invites Annie to live in the mansion permanently. She is more interested in finding her real parents so Warbucks uses the radio to advertise a search for Annie's folks, only to bring on the fraudulent claimants Rooster, Miss Hannigan's con man brother, and his girl Lily, and the three plan to cash in on Annie's good fortune by claiming to be her real parents. But the trio is found out, the FBI learns that Annie's true parents are dead, and Warbucks adopts Annie and her stray dog named Sandy.

Thomas Meehan's libretto was efficient, funny, and effective, even if it threw out all the politi-cal satire found in Harold Gray's comic strip. The score by CHARLES STROUSE (music) and MARTIN CHARNIN (lyrics) was also effective, providing catchy tunes that were as simplistic as a cartoon. The anthem "Tomorrow" was the kind of Depression chaser that SHIRLEY TEMPLE might have sung in one of her 1930s films, and there was a playful pastiche number called "You're Never Fully Dressed Without a Smile" that also sounded genuine to the era.

Annie (stage) Musical Numbers

"Maybe"
"It's a Hard-Knock Life"
"Tomorrow"
"We'd Like to Thank You (Herbert Hoover)"
"Little Girls"
"I Think I'm Gonna Like It Here"
"N.Y.C."
"Easy Street"
"You Won't Be an Orphan for Long"
"You're Never Fully Dressed Without a Smile"
"Something Was Missing"
"I Don't Need Anything But You"
"Annie"
"New Deal for Christmas"

The Mike Nichols production was first rate, with fluid direction by Charnin, pleasing cho-reography by PETER GENNARO, and a strong cast headed by DOROTHY LOUDON, a veteran character actress who finally got a major role in a Broadway musical and made it a stage triumph. The show ran 2,377 performances, followed by road companies and hundreds of productions in summer stock and schools. The sequel *Annie II: Miss Hannigan's Revenge* (1990) closed out of town in 1990. It was rewritten as *Annie Warbucks* and played Off Broadway in 1993. A revival of the original *Annie* opened on Broadway in 1997 with Nell Carter as Miss Hannigan and ran 239 performances.

🎬 *Annie* (Columbia 1982) went on record as one of the most expensive flops in the his-tory of COLUMBIA PICTURES and helped seal the lid on the big-budget musical coffin. Many changes and mistakes were made in transferring the Broadway hit to the screen: six songs were dropped, the plot was altered, esteemed veteran John Huston was hired to direct even though he had never helmed a musical or anything close to a family picture, and some of the casting was suspect. The studio spent $52 million on the movie but that solved none of its many prob-lems. Aileen Quinn as Annie found little favor and Albert Finney's cartoonish Warbucks was more odd than entertaining. However, CAROL BURNETT was a funny, brawling Miss Hannigan, ANN REINKING was a graceful dancing Grace, and TIM CURRY and BERNADETTE PETERS were fun as Rooster and Lily. The Strouse–Charnin songs seemed less enjoyable on the screen than on the stage, even the hit ballad "Tomorrow" fell flat, and the new production number "Let's Go to the Movies" was a lavish bore. Carol Sobieski wrote the deadly screenplay, Arlene Philips provided the frantic but lifeless chore-ography, and Ray Stark was the misguided pro-ducer. Although the movie was a critical and popular dud on its initial release, it has found an audience over the years on video and DVD.

📺 *Annie* (Disney Channel 1999) was an abridged version of the Broadway show that ran a tight but enjoyable ninety minutes and it was true to the spirit to the original. It was also well cast and playfully performed, with Alicia Morton making a tougher but likable Annie, Kathy Bates as a frowsy and funny Miss Hannigan, and VICTOR GARBER making Warbucks pleasingly pompous. Another plus was up-and-coming Broadway favorites Alan Cumming and KRISTIN CHENOWETH as Rooster and Lily. The best of the stage score was retained, and the production, while not a spectacle, evoked the Depression era well. ROB MARSHALL directed and choreographed the Irene Mecchi teleplay and it was all a delightful reminder of what had made the show so popular in the first place.

🎵 ***ANNIE GET YOUR GUN*** (Imperial Theatre 1946). The most durable and most revived of IRVING BERLIN's musicals, this biographical show about sharpshooter Annie Oakley contained his greatest stage score and afforded ETHEL MERMAN one of her greatest triumphs.

Plot: When hillbilly Annie Oakley comes into town to sell some game that she's shot, she meets up with members of Buffalo Bill's Wild West Show, in particular the dashing Frank Butler who is the show's prize sharpshooter and a bit of a ladies' man. When Buffalo Bill sees how well Annie can shoot, he hires her and soon she starts to eclipse Frank in the show even as she's falling in love with him. His masculine pride hurt, Frank leaves the show and works for another showman while Annie takes Europe by storm when her show goes on tour and she gets plenty of medals from counts and kings. Frank and Annie meet up again when she arrives back in the States and it looks like they are going to get together until Annie dazzles him with all her prizes and still claims to be the better shot. A shooting match is arranged and, taking the advice of the wise old Sitting Bull, Annie lets Frank win the match and thereby wins him.

Lyricist–librettist DOROTHY FIELDS had the idea of a musical with Merman as Annie Oakley and wanted Rodgers and Hammerstein to write the score but they opted to produce the

Annie Get Your Gun. Sharpshooters Frank Butler (Ray Middleton) and Annie Oakley (Ethel Merman) appear to be at another standoff in the Broadway version of Irving Berlin's greatest success, but their fighting is what made the musical so much fun. Other musicals offered sweetness and romance; this one was a romantic brawl. (Photofest)

show instead and contracted JEROME KERN to write the songs with Fields. However, Kern's untimely death altered the plans and Irving Berlin was persuaded to score the libretto written by Dorothy and HERBERT FIELDS. JOSHUA LOGAN directed, HELEN TAMIRIS did the choreography, and the musical was a smash hit from the start. Merman was both raucous and tender as Annie, and RAY MIDDLETON was the perfect foil as Frank Butler.

After composing songs for book musicals for over thirty years, Berlin finally got a surefire libretto to work with in *Annie Get Your Gun* and it prompted him to write a score that was filled

Casts for *Annie Get Your Gun*

Characters	Annie Oakley	Frank Butler	Col. Buffalo Bill Cody
1946 Broadway	ETHEL MERMAN	RAY MIDDLETON	William O'Neal
1950 film	BETTY HUTTON	HOWARD KEEL	Louis Calhern
1957 television	MARY MARTIN	JOHN RAITT	William O'Neal
1966 Broadway	Ethel Merman	Bruce Yarnell	Rufus Smith
2000 Broadway	BERNADETTE PETERS	Tom Wopat	RON HOLGATE

Annie Get Your Gun (stage) Musical Numbers

"Buffalo Bill"
"I'm a Bad, Bad Man"
"Doin' What Comes Natur'lly"
"The Girl That I Marry"
"You Can't Get a Man With a Gun"
"There's No Business Like Show Business"
"They Say It's Wonderful"
"Moonshine Lullaby"
"I'll Share It All With You"
"Ballyhoo"
"My Defenses Are Down"
"Wild Horse Ceremonial Dance"
"I'm an Indian Too"
"Adoption Dance"
"I Got Lost in His Arms"
"Who Do You Love, I Hope"
"I Got the Sun in the Morning"
"Anything You Can Do"

---

not only with hit songs but knowing character numbers and songs about a variety of subjects. Even his love songs, such as "They Say It's Wonderful" and "I Got Lost in His Arms," took the perspective of a specific character, something rarely seen in his work before. The music is pure Broadway, yet it is flavored with a rural tone, and the lyrics are countrified without being corn fed, as in such songs as "Doin' What Comes Natur'lly" and "You Can't Get a Man With a Gun." He even took the image of a backwoods still and turned it into the dreamy "Moonshine Lullaby." More song standards came out of *Annie Get Your Gun* than any other Berlin show, but, just as impressive, he proved that this late in his career he could write a score in the Rodgers and Hammerstein mold. The original production ran 1,147 performances and MARY MARTIN led the first road tour in 1947. The show ran even longer in London than it did in New York, and DOLORES GRAY became a West End star in the role. Merman returned to the part in the 1966 Broadway revival with Bruce Yarnell as Frank and a strong supporting cast that included Rufus Smith, JERRY ORBACH, and Harry Bellaver again playing Sitting Bull. For the new production, Berlin wrote the wry duet "An Old Fashioned Wedding," the last song he ever wrote for Broadway. BERNADETTE PETERS essayed Annie in the 2001 revival with Tom Wopat as Frank and it ran a surprising 1,045 performances. The show remains a favorite in summer stock and in schools; in fact, it is revived more than any other Berlin musical.

■ *Annie Get Your Gun* (MGM 1950) was, by the standards of its day, a faithful screen version of a Broadway hit. Most of the Berlin score was retained and the script was close to the original libretto, with only some secondary characters being cut. Producer ARTHUR FREED contracted JUDY GARLAND to play Annie and she completed the vocal recording and a few scenes before illness forced her to withdraw. BETTY HUTTON, who had always played comic supporting roles in film musicals, was given the plum role and she was not shy about grabbing it and giving it her all. One's appreciation of the movie depends on your reaction to Hutton's broad, funny, full-voiced performance. HOWARD KEEL was a solid Frank Butler, and the supporting cast included Louis Calhern, J. CARROLL NAISH, Edward Arnold, KEENAN WYNN, Benay Venuta, and CLINTON SUNDBERG. GEORGE SIDNEY directed the Sidney Sheldon screenplay, and MGM spent a bundle on the production, all of which it made back when the film was the top-grossing movie of the year.

▢ *Annie Get Your Gun* has been made for television twice, both times with stars who had played the part on stage. In 1957, an NBC broadcast starred Mary Martin and JOHN RAITT as Annie and Frank, with William O'Neal reprising his Buffalo Bill from the original production. Also in the cast were Reta Shaw, Donald Burr, Norman Edwards, Zachary Charles, and Susan Luckey, under the direction of Vincent J. Donahue. The ninety-minute show abridged the script and the score but it was still a joyous production and offered one of Martin's funniest performances. In 1967 Merman and much of the same cast from the 1966 revival went into an NBC studio and taped the production for television. The sixty-year-old star might have got away with playing the young Annie in a large Broadway theatre but on the small screen the effect was disconcerting and she was not able to tone down her broad stage performance so some of the broadcast looked like a parody of Merman as Annie. All the same, it is the only record of a great stage performance and is worth preserving.

ANTI-WAR MUSICALS. Despite Broadway's inclination toward escapism, a number of musicals over the years have expressed strong anti-war sentiments. *JOHNNY JOHNSON* (1936) was as strong as any nonmusical dealing with the crushed idealism of World War I. The wacky *HOORAY FOR WHAT!* (1937) was a broad satire but there was no mistaking its creators' targets; the show featured a poison gas that made the enemy laugh and a prophetic atom bomb-like device. Even in the midst of World War II, *BLOOMER GIRL* (1944) managed to remain palatable by applying its anti-war views to the Civil War. Although such pacifist ideas were anathema in the 1950s and early 1960s, anti-war musicals flourished with the arrival of rock musicals, guerrilla theatre, happenings, and all the other experiments of the late 1960s and early 1970s. Most of these musicals were stronger in content and conviction than in craftsmanship and were usually presented Off Broadway or Off Off Broadway. Yet there were notable exceptions in all three venues. *HAIR* (1968) unabashedly attacked the Vietnam War and the military along with its other establishment targets Off Broadway and then on Broadway. GRETCHEN CRYER and NANCY FORD's *Now Is the Time for All Good Men* (1967) and *THE LAST SWEET DAYS OF ISAAC* (1970) were more subtle but just as potent. The musical *TWO GENTLEMEN OF VERONA* (1971) found anti-war philosophy in Shakespeare, and even the patriotic *1776* (1969) found room for an anti-war song. By the mid-1970s, when America was no longer engaged in a war, the subject had become safe enough that no one was bothered that the old-fashioned, conventional *SHENANDOAH* (1975) was actually a very pacifist musical, although setting it during the Civil War made it easier. During the last few decades, anti-war musicals have become more of a financial risk because the cost of productions has forced them to have a very wide appeal in order to survive.

If Broadway was shy on the subject of pacifism, Hollywood and television were deathly afraid of it. Being mass media entertainments on a grander scale than theatre, both venues were careful not to criticize a war until the general popular opinion agreed with the work doing the criticism. A vivid exception was the nonmusical *Johnny Got His Gun* (1971) about World War I but coming out in the dark days of the Vietnam War. Only when the public turned against that war did such powerful dramas, such as *Coming Home* (1978) and *Born on the Fourth of July* (1989), get made. Rarely were musicals considered the appropriate vehicle for anti-war films. Two outstanding screen musicals about Vietnam, *Hair* (1978) and *ACROSS THE UNIVERSE* (2007), were made long after that war was over and were approached as period pieces.

😎 *ANYONE CAN WHISTLE* (Majestic Theatre 1964). An adventurous if short-lived (nine performances) musical curiosity, it featured a dynamic score by STEPHEN SONDHEIM, a bold and audacious libretto by ARTHUR LAURENTS,

and a grand performance by ANGELA LANSBURY in her first Broadway musical. Because it was so offbeat, so ambitious, and so unsuccessful, the show has risen to a cult status few flop musicals can aspire to. The plot was about an impoverished industrial town that fakes a miracle to draw in the tourists. Added to the mix are the corrupt mayoress Cora Hoover Hooper (Lansbury), the fraudulent psychiatrist J. Bowden Hapgood (Harry Guardino), the daffy nurse Fay Apple (Lee Remick) who is sometimes French, and a chorus of escaped inmates from the local mental institution. Laurents directed the show with a determined effrontery, ending one act with the actors viciously laughing at the audience, and HERBERT ROSS choreographed the dances that ranged from sleazy nightclub numbers to a ballet for lunatics. Just as varied was Sondheim's score, which ranged from the complicated chaos of "Simple" to the quiet title ballad. Other notable songs include "Me and My Town," "There Won't Be Trumpets," "A Parade in Town," and "With So Little to Be Sure Of." Although Laurents' quirky, dated libretto makes *Anyone Can Whistle* difficult to revive, it is still produced on occasion and remains a unique and commendable work.

😎 *ANYTHING GOES* (Alvin Theatre 1934). The most popular and oft-revived Broadway musical of the 1930s, the show captures all the wit, romance, and high spirits of the decade and the COLE PORTER score is one of the finest in American musical comedy.

Plot: The infatuated Billy Crocker is afraid that his beloved Hope Harcourt will throw him over for the English peer Lord Evelyn Oakleigh, whom her mother wants her to marry, so he stows away on the ocean liner that Hope is taking to Europe. Also aboard is the evangelist–nightclub singer Reno Sweeney, who is also interested in Billy, and the convict Moonface Martin, who is disguised as the Rev. Dr. Moon. Billy assumes different disguises as well to get close to Hope, while Moonface gets embroiled in the love triangle, eventually helping Billy win Hope with Reno taking the not-so-stuffy Evelyn for herself.

It is a silly and contrived libretto but one that works, which is remarkable because it was concocted by HOWARD LINDSAY and RUSSEL CROUSE on short notice. The original script by P. G. WODEHOUSE and GUY BOLTON involved a shipwreck that stranded all the characters on a desert island, but when fire destroyed an actual liner off the coast of New

Anything Goes. This modest but energized 1962 revival of the Cole Porter musical ran thirty weeks Off Broadway and, more importantly, it revived interest in the 1934 show and hundreds of amateur productions over the next twenty-five years used this version of the musical. Since there was no complete cast album for the original *Anything Goes*, the Off Broadway recording became the one musical lovers cherished. Lawrence Kasha directed and Ron Field provided the zestful choreography. (Photofest)

Casts for *Anything Goes*

Characters	Reno Sweeney	Billy Crocker	Moonface	Hope Harcourt
1934 Broadway	ETHEL MERMAN	WILLIAM GAXTON	VICTOR MOORE	BETTINA HALL
1936 film	Ethel Merman	BING CROSBY	CHARLES RUGGLES	IDA LUPINO
1962 Off-Broadway	Eileen Rodgers	HAL LINDEN	Mickey Deems	Barbara Lang
1987 Broadway	PATTI LuPONE	HOWARD McGILLIN	Bill McCutcheon	Kathleen Mahoney-Bennett

Jersey, producer VINTON FREEDLEY ordered a new libretto to fit the cast, sets, costumes, and score already prepared. Lindsay directed, Robert Alton choreographed, and the show looked far from a patch-up job, running 420 performances and still entertaining audiences today.

Porter's score is varied and filled with hits, yet it all seems part of a whole. Over the years, various revivals have interpolated other Porter songs into the show and one forgets that the original lineup of songs was pretty

impressive and didn't need outside hits to beef up the score. Merman led the cast in the two most vibrant numbers, the revival-like "Blow, Gabriel, Blow" and the high-flying title number. She also sang the intoxicating "I Get a Kick Out of You" and joined WILLIAM GAXTON for the comic duet "You're the Top," and Gaxton and BETTINA HALL introduced the romantic "All Through the Night." VICTOR MOORE had limited singing polish but he turned the comic "Be Like the Bluebird" into another musical delight. Even the chorus numbers are unusually frothy in this score that seems

Anything Goes (stage) Musical Numbers

"I Get a Kick Out of You"
"Bon Voyage (There's No Cure Like Travel)"
"All Through the Night"
"Sailor's Chantey (There'll Always Be a Lady Fair)"
"Where Are the Men?"
"You're the Top"
"Anything Goes"
"Public Enemy No. 1"
"Blow, Gabriel, Blow"
"Be Like the Bluebird"
"Buddy, Beware"
"The Gypsy in Me"

to bubble like champagne. It is hard to believe that after its long run, *Anything Goes* was not revived regularly until a 1962 Off Broadway production brought it back into circulation. HAL LINDEN led the cast that also featured Eileen Rogers, Barbara Lang, Mickey Deems, Margery Gray, and Kenneth Mars. Guy Bolton revised the script, and the Porter favorites "Let's Misbehave," "Friendship," "Take Me Back to Manhattan," and "De-Lovely" were added to the score. The revival ran 239 performances and became the version that got produced by groups across the country over the next two decades. For the 1987 Broadway revival, Timothy Crouse and JOHN WEIDMAN rewrote the libretto slightly and some of the 1962 interpolations were removed. Added was the tender ballad "Easy to Love," which was originally written for the stage version but was cut when Gaxton couldn't hit the high notes. Ironically, the song was later given to JAMES STEWART to sing in the film *BORN TO DANCE* (1936) and he couldn't hit *any* of the notes. PATTI LUPONE was a vibrant Reno and she was joined by such able players as HOWARD MCGILLIN, Bill McCutcheon, Kathleen Mahoney-Bennett, Anthony Heald, and Linda Hart. JERRY ZAKS directed, MICHAEL SMUIN choreographed, and the Lincoln Center production ran 784 performances.

🎬 Although there were two films titled *Anything Goes*, only one was remotely similar to the stage success. **Anything Goes** (Paramount 1936) should have been as much fun as the Broadway show, for the film let Ethel Merman reprise her vivacious Reno Sweeney. However, only four of Cole Porter's songs made it to the screen and much of the cast was routine. Easygoing BING CROSBY was miscast as Billy and his wooing of

Hope (IDA LUPINO) was so casual that you couldn't believe he'd cross the street to sing to her, much less stow away on board a ship. CHARLES RUGGLES was a low-key but funny Moonface, and ARTHUR TREACHER was the appropriately stuffy Evelyn. Also cast were GRACE BRADLEY, MARGARET DUMONT, and Robert McWade. Merman still got to sing "I Get a Kick Out of You" and the title number, but her "You're the Top" with Crosby was laundered for the screen. HOAGY CARMICHAEL (music) and Edward Heyman (lyric) wrote the smooth ballad "Moonburn" for Crosby to croon, and three other new songs by various tunesmiths were added while Porter's lovely "All Through the Night' was reduced to background music. Lewis Milestone directed the film that is more useful for archival purposes (one of the two times Merman got to recreate a stage role on screen) than for satisfying entertainment. A 1956 *Anything Goes* also made by Paramount featured Crosby again, but the only thing the film had in common with the stage was a shipboard setting. Sidney Sheldon's screenplay concerned two showmen, Bill Benson (Crosby) and Ted Adams (DONALD O'CONNOR), on a world cruise looking for a star for their new show. They found Gaby Duval (Jeanmaire) and Patsy Blair (MITZI GAYNOR), as well as five Porter songs. Crosby got to sing "All Through the Night" this time around, and Gaynor belted out the title song before joining O'Connor for "De-Lovely." JAMES VAN HEUSEN (music) and SAMMY CAHN (lyrics) wrote a handful of new numbers for the film, including the sprightly "You Can Bounce Right Back," which O'Connor sang and danced to in his rubber-boned manner. Also on board were PHIL HARRIS, KURT KASZNAR, Argentina Brunetti, and Richard Erdman, directed by ROBERT LEWIS and choreographed by Ernie Flatt and Roland Petit. It is all pleasant enough but not *Anything Goes*. 📺 An abridged version of *Anything Goes* with MARTHA RAYE as Reno Sweeney was broadcast on NBC-TV's series *Musical Comedy Time* in 1950. Merman reprised her Reno in a 1954 broadcast on NBC's *The Colgate Comedy Hour* in which the musical was reduced to one hour. Still, that was enough time for Merman, BERT LAHR (Moonface), and FRANK SINATRA (Billy) to clown around and do a few of the songs.

🎬 ***APPLAUSE*** (Paramount 1929). An early and uncompromising musical melodrama about show business, the film boasts an unforgettable performance by HELEN MORGAN that has rarely been equaled for raw emotion and simple empathy. Garrett Ford adapted Beth Brown's novel about Kitty Darling, an aging burlesque queen who lives with the two-timing drunk Hitch (Fuller Melish, Jr.). Kitty saves all of her money to support her daughter April (Joan Peters) who is away at a convent school. When April comes to stay, Kitty marries Hitch to make a respectable home for the girl. But Hitch treats Kitty worse as a husband than he did as a lover and has lecherous intentions on April who has fallen in love with the sailor Joe King (Jack Cameron). When April rejects Joe so that she can stay and protect her mother from Hitch, Kitty realizes the only way to free her daughter is to take poison and die. This grim drama was raised to high art by ROUBEN MAMOULIAN's fluid direction (his first film) and Morgan's heartbreaking performances, including her renditions of such torchy classics as "I've Got a Feelin' I'm Fallin'," "What Wouldn't I Do for That Man," and the pathetically cheerful "Give Your Baby Lots of Lovin'," which was used throughout the film as an ironic leitmotif. Although primitive and dated, *Applause* remains a potent work and a landmark in the development of the serious musical film.

🕭 APPLAUSE (Palace Theatre 1970). The musical version of the popular film *All About Eve* (1950), the show was lauded as a valentine to the theatre and a durable vehicle for film star Lauren Bacall in her singing–dancing debut. BETTY COMDEN and ADOLPH GREEN wrote the libretto about musical comedy star Margo Channing (Bacall) who takes on the young widowed fan Eve Harrington (Penny Fuller) as her assistant and soon Eve becomes her understudy and rival in the affections of Eve's lover Bill Sampson (LEN CARIOU). By the end of the show, Eve has clawed her way to the top and is a star but Margo gets Bill and finds a different kind of satisfaction in life. Also featured in the cast were LEE ROY REAMS, Brandon Maggart, Ann Williams, and Bonnie Franklin who led the Broadway "gypsies" in the celebratory title number. The lively score by CHARLES STROUSE (music) and LEE ADAMS (lyrics) also included the affirmation song "But Alive," the 1940s pastiche "Who's That Girl?," the soft-shoe number "One of a Kind," the jarring "Fasten Your Seatbelts," and the bitter "Welcome to the Theatre." Bacall's singing and dancing talents were limited but she carried the show with aplomb all the same. RON FIELD directed and choreographed, and the jaunty musical ran 896 performances. ▢ Bacall and Fuller reprised their stage performances for a 1973 television version in which Larry Hagman played Bill and the supporting cast included Sarah Marshall, Harvey Evans, Robert Mandan, Rod McLennan, and Debbie Bowen. Both the script and the score were abridged and the production lacked the excitement of the original but it does preserve the two female leads' stage performances.

🕭 APPLE TREE, THE (Shubert Theatre 1966). Three one-act musical comedies scored by JERRY BOCK (music) and SHELDON HARNICK (lyrics) made for an enjoyable evening and a first-rate vehicle for BARBARA HARRIS. The songwriters and Jerome Coopersmith collaborated on the libretto, and the three minimusicals were held together by the same cast. In *The Diary of Adam and Eve* (adapted from Mark Twain's story), Adam (ALAN ALDA) is not sure that he likes the new creature in the garden named Eve (Harris), but he eventually grows to love her, even though she listens to the Snake (LARRY BLYDEN) and breaks God's law. Frank R. Stockton's story *The Lady or the Tiger?* took place in a barbaric kingdom where the innocence of Captain Sanjar (Alda), the beloved of Princess Barbára (Harris), is determined by choosing one of two doors, one hiding a maiden and the other a tiger. Jules Feiffer's satirical *Passionella* concerns the dirty chimney sweep Ella (Harris) who becomes a glamorous movie star and gets her Prince Charming (Alda), only to learn that underneath he is as unglamorous as herself. The score produced no hits since the numbers were so plot and character driven, yet it was a delectable set of songs all the same, such as "Feelings," "What Makes Me Love Him?," "I've Got What You Want," "Oh, to Be a Movie Star," and "You Are Not Real." While reviewers had mixed opinions about the three playlets, they cheered in unison for Harris. Stuart Ostrow produced, Mike Nichols directed, and the triple-play entertainment ran 463 performances. The Roundabout Theatre revived the musical in 2006 and again the musical received a mixed press, but there were mostly cheers for the cast, in particular KRISTIN CHENOWETH, who played the three different heroines with panache. Brian D'Arcy James was a solid Adam, Captain Sanjar, and Prince Charming, and MARC KUDISCH stole his scenes as the Snake and other commentating characters. The revival was directed by Gary Griffin and the limited-run production played ninety-nine times.

ARDEN, EVE [born Eunice Quedens] (1912–1990). Stage, film, and television performer. One of Hollywood and television's most recognized character actresses, she usually played the caustic second lead or the acerbic friend of the heroine in comedies and musicals. Arden was born in Mill Valley, California, and began her theatre career in stock companies in San Francisco and Pasadena. She appeared in the Broadway revues *ZIEGFELD FOLLIES* (1934 and 1936) and *Parade* (1935) before getting attention as the smart alec Winnie Spofford in *VERY WARM FOR MAY* (1939). After being featured in *Two for the Show* (1940) and *LET'S FACE IT* (1941), she left Broadway for good and returned to California where she had already played bit parts in the movie musicals *Song of Love* (1929), *DANCING LADY* (1933), *Cocoanut Grove* (1938), *AT THE CIRCUS* (1939), and *No, No, Nanette* (1940). In the next decade Arden appeared in a score of movies in which she refined her sarcastic humor, including such musicals as *ZIEGFELD GIRL* (1941), *Sing for Your Supper* (1941), *Let's Face It!* (1943), *COVER GIRL* (1944), *The Kid From Brooklyn* (1946), *ONE TOUCH OF VENUS* (1948), *My Dream Is Yours* (1949), and *Tea for Two* (1950). Finding wide popularity for her TV series *Our Miss Brooks* in the 1950s, Arden remained in television for four decades doing other series and specials, including the musical spoof *The Royal Follies of 1933* (1967). She occasionally returned to film, as with the screen musicals *GREASE* (1978) and *Grease 2* (1982).

◼ *ARISTOCATS, THE* (Disney 1970). A stylish animated tale about a family of pampered Parisian cats, the musical was the first animated film put out by the studio after the death of WALT DISNEY, but because he had been involved in its preparation it has his mark of quality and integrity. The feline Duchess (voice of EVA GABOR) and her three kittens Toulouse (Gary Dubin), Marie (Liz English), and Berlioz (Dean Clark) are the pride and joy of the elderly Madame Adelaide Bonfammille (Hermione Baddeley) and when the old woman writes her will she leaves her considerable fortune to the cats. The jealous butler Edgar (Roddy Maude-Roxby) kidnaps the felines and drives them out to the French countryside, hoping to inherit the money if the pets are gone. With the help of the mouse Roquefort (STERLING HOLLOWAY), the hound dogs Lafayette (George Lindsey) and Napoleon (Pat Buttram), and the fun-loving alley cat Thomas O'Malley (PHIL HARRIS), the four cats manage to get back to Paris and, after a wild night being entertained by Scat Cat (Scatman Crothers), return home to Madame. Director Wolfgang Reitherman kept the story moving along in a breezy manner, the animation was polished, the background art was atmospheric, and the characterizations were vivid and fun. The songs, mostly by RICHARD M. AND ROBERT B. SHERMAN, ranged from the classically flavored "Scales and Arpeggios" to the swinging "Everybody Wants to Be a Cat." MAURICE CHEVALIER was persuaded to come out of retirement and sing the title song over the credits, the last time he was heard in a movie musical.

ARLEN, HAROLD [born Hyman Arluck] (1905–1986). Stage and film composer. The masterful creator of blues and jazz songs with a feel for African American music, he was renowned on Broadway and in Hollywood for his superb scores with E. Y. HARBURG, IRA GERSHWIN, JOHNNY MERCER, and other top lyricists. Arlen was born in Buffalo, New York, the son of a cantor, and sang in the synagogue as a teenager. He began his career playing piano in New York clubs and doing arrangements for stars and Broadway shows. When his song "Get Happy" was interpolated into *9:15 Revue* (1928) and became a hit, his songwriting career was launched. Working with various lyricists, Arlen wrote scores for *EARL CARROLL VANITIES* (1930), *You Said It* (1931), *LIFE BEGINS AT 8:40* (1934), *ST. LOUIS WOMAN* (1946), *HOUSE OF FLOWERS* (1954), and *SARATOGA* (1959), but his most successful collaborations were with Harburg, the two of them scoring *HOORAY FOR WHAT!* (1937), *BLOOMER GIRL* (1944), and *JAMAICA* (1957). The twosome also wrote the songs for six Hollywood musicals: *The Singing Kid* (1936), *GOLD DIGGERS OF 1937* (1936), *THE WIZARD OF OZ* (1939), *AT THE CIRCUS* (1939), *CABIN IN THE SKY* (1943), and the animated *GAY PURR-EE* (1962). With others Arlen scored *Let's Fall in Love* (1934), *Strike Me Pink* (1936), *BLUES IN THE NIGHT* (1941), *STAR-SPANGLED RHYTHM* (1942), *THE SKY'S THE LIMIT* (1943), *UP IN ARMS* (1944), *HERE COME THE WAVES* (1944), *CASBAH* (1948), *MY BLUE HEAVEN* (1950), *The Petty Girl* (1950), *Mr. Imperium* (1951), *Down Among the Sheltering Palms* (1953), *THE FARMER TAKES A WIFE* (1953), *A STAR IS BORN* (1954), and *THE COUNTRY GIRL* (1954). Although his songs range from "Over the Rainbow" to "Lydia, the Tattooed Lady," from "Ac-cent-chu-ate the Positive" to "The Man That Got Away," there is a distinctive fervor in all Arlen's music that makes it riveting and emotional. Biography: *Harold Arlen: Happy With the Blues*, Edward Jablonski (1986).

ARMSTRONG, [Daniel] LOUIS (1901–1971). Stage, film, and television performer, musician, and songwriter. A giant in the world of jazz music, the raspy-voiced African American played his trumpet and sang in two dozen Hollywood films, usually playing himself and always stopping the show. Armstrong was born in New Orleans and learned to play the bugle and clarinet as a boy, getting jobs playing for funerals, socials, and other gatherings. By the time he was eighteen years old he was a professional playing with the Kid Ory Band and four years later he was in Chicago playing with the Creole Jazz Band. (He was nicknamed "Satchmo," short for Satchelmouth, which was slang for a brass musician.) Armstrong made his first of many recordings in 1923 and was popular enough in clubs that he was featured in the Broadway revue *Hot Chocolates* (1929). He made his feature film debut with *Pennies From Heaven* (1936) and did specialty spots in such musicals as *ARTISTS AND MODELS* (1937), *Doctor Rhythm* (1938), *Jam Session* (1944), *Atlantic City* (1944), *HOLLYWOOD CANTEEN* (1944), *NEW ORLEANS* (1947), *Carnegie Hall* (1947), *A Song Is Born* (1948), *HERE COMES THE GROOM* (1951), *The Strip* (1951), *THE GLENN MILLER STORY* (1954), and *When the Boys Meet the Girls* (1965). He also played characters in *Going Places* (1939), *CABIN IN THE SKY* (1943), *Glory Alley* (1952), *Paris Blues* (1961), and *A Man Called Adam* (1966). But Armstrong is most remembered on screen for playing himself and joining singers in rousing duets, as with BING CROSBY in *HIGH SOCIETY* (1956), DANNY KAYE in *THE FIVE PENNIES* (1959), and BARBRA STREISAND in *HELLO, DOLLY!* (1969). He returned to Broadway to sing and play his trumpet in *Swingin' the Dream* (1939) and made many television appearances over the decades. Armstrong was also famous for his international tours, starting with his renowned European tour in 1932, and for composing several jazz favorites. BEN VEREEN played Armstrong in the TV film *Louis Armstrong: Chicago Style* (1976). Autobiography: *Satchmo: My Life in New Orleans*, 1986; biography: *Satchmo: The Genius of Louis Armstrong*, Gary Giddins (2001).

ARNAZ, DESI [born Desiderio Alberto Arnaz y De Acha III] (1917–1986). Television, film, and stage performer, musician, and producer. Known to most Americans as the crazy Cuban co-star and husband of LUCILLE BALL on television, the accomplished musician and singer was impressive in his handful of musical ventures. Arnaz was born to an aristocratic family in Santiago, Cuba, but fled to Miami after the 1933 revolution led by Baptista. He formed a conga band just as the craze for Latin music was sweeping America, and Arnaz was hired to sing and play the drums in the collegiate musical *TOO MANY GIRLS* (1939) on Broadway. When he made the film version in 1940, the leading lady was Ball and the two wed, but neither of their careers would take off until their television show in the 1950s. Arnaz played himself in the movie musical *Cuban Pete* (1946) and was featured in the films *Four Jacks and a Jill* (1941) and *Holiday in Havana* (1949). He was also a shrewd producer who not only ran the *I Love Lucy* series but was behind other popular television programs, such as *The Untouchables* (1959). His children are performers Desi Arnaz, Jr. (1953–) and Lucie Arnaz (1951–). Autobiography: *A Book* (1977); biography: *Desilu: The Story of Lucille Ball and Desi Arnaz*, Coyne S. Sanders, Tom Gilbert (1994).

AROUND THE WORLD IN EIGHTY DAYS (Grand Opera House/Academy of Music 1875). Jules Verne's novel was musicalized in two different productions that opened in New York within a few weeks of each other. Both emphasized spectacle, songs, and specialty acts and only used the Verne story as an excuse to travel to different locations. The production at the Grand ran only fourteen performances but the shrewd Kiralfy brothers produced the extravaganza at the Academy and it was a hit, running forty-three times and enjoying frequent revivals for the rest of the century. Owen Marlowe played Phileas Fogg and his journey took him through a series of songs and ballets, such as the Grand Funeral Pageant, the Fête of the Snake Charmers, the Revels of the Eccentrics, and the Startling Reptile dances. In 1946, Orson Welles' Mercury Theatre presented its own version titled *Around the World*, which boasted a score by Cole Porter. Welles wrote the adaptation, directed the mammoth production, and played Dick Fix, the copper who chases Fogg (Arthur Margeson) around the globe. It was all very impressive to look at but theatrically unsatisfying, with even most of the songs falling flat. The ballad "Should I Tell You I Love You?" was the best of the lot but was lost in all the sets and costumes. The production ran only seventy-five performances and when it closed, so did the Mercury Theatre.

ARTHUR, BEATRICE [born Bernice Frankel] (1926–). Stage and television performer. The tall, throaty-voiced actress was a long-time popular comedienne on television but she also had an extensive career in the New York theatre in the 1940s, 1950s, and 1960s. A native New Yorker educated at Blackstone College and the Franklin Institute of Science and Art, Arthur studied acting with Edwin Piscator at the New School for Social Research and made her professional acting debut Off Broadway in 1947. She would appear in classics there before getting cast as the competitive Lucy Brown in the record-breaking revival of THE THREEPENNY OPERA (1954). Arthur appeared in other musicals on and Off Broadway, including *Shoestring Revue* (1955) and *Seventh Heaven* (1955), before originating the role of the matchmaker Yente in FIDDLER ON THE ROOF (1964), followed by her hilarious egotistical actress Vera Charles in MAME (1966). She reprised the last in the 1974 film version but Arthur rarely made movies; instead she appeared on television for much of her fifty-year career. As a regular on *Caesar's Hour* in the early 1950s to guest appearances in the late 1990s, Arthur was seen in hundreds of programs, from specials to two of her own series. She returned to the New York stage for her one-person show *Bea Arthur on Broadway: Just Between Friends* (2002). Arthur is married to director–actor GENE SAKS.

ARTISTS AND MODELS. Stage series. A disjointed series of musical revues by various producers, the shows used the premise of artists and their models in order to feature partial nudity and provocative production numbers. In 1923 the SHUBERTS wanted to compete with EARL CARROLL and his fleshy *Vanities* revues so they came up with the title *Artists and Models* and presented plenty of leg and spectacle. Frank Fay was the host who introduced the acts, and Henry Wagstaff Gribble directed the show as one extended sexual fantasy. Critics carped but audiences came for 312 performances. *Artists and Models of 1924* had a thread of a story, about a rural girl who comes to New York and explores Greenwich Village, but it was another revue in which the producers were able to show nude women as long as they were in classical poses. SIGMUND ROMBERG, JAY GORNEY, CON CONRAD, and others contributed to the score but songs were secondary in these shows in which the producers did not waste their money on stars and sunk the money into the scanty costumes and lavish sets. Their thinking was correct, for the second edition ran even longer (519 performances) than the first. The 1927 edition featured such bizarre sights as girls posing in a living tableau of Reims Cathedral and comedy sketches that bordered on the lewd.

The novelty may have been wearing off for the show only ran 151 times. The Depression made its mark on the series when *Artists and Models of 1930* ran only a third as long, despite a much-talked-about parade of girls in Cleopatra's palace. The Shuberts were sharp enough to face the facts and the series ended. Yet the provocative title held on. Different producers presented *Artists and Models of 1943*, which not only offered girls dressed as various perfume bottles but also featured rising comic JACKIE GLEASON and singer Jane Froman. The revue only lasted twenty-seven performances.

Hollywood knew a good title when it heard one, and PARAMOUNT made three musical versions of its own, although they were plotted films and not revues. *Artists and Models* (1937) had as thin a story as any in the era: ad agency president Marc Brewster (JACK BENNY) must see that the top model is crowned at the Artists and Models Ball and he runs into obvious and manufactured complications on the way. Yet the dialogue was snappy, the cast was charming, there were tuneful songs by various songwriters, and even the specialty acts were entertaining. IDA LUPINO and Richard Arlen co-starred with Benny but the real fun came from guest spots by MARTHA RAYE, LOUIS ARMSTRONG, CONNEE BOSWELL, the Yacht Club Boys, and the puppeteering Personettes. Songs included the jazzy "Public Enemy No. 1," the alluring ballads "I Have Eyes" and "Whispers in the Dark," and the swinging duet "Stop, You're Breaking My Heart," to which Ben Blue and JUDY CANOVA sang and danced. RAOUL WALSH directed the Lewis E. Gensler production and it did well enough at the box office that Benny was rehired for *Artists and Models Abroad* (1938). This time he played Buck Boswell who guided a stranded acting troupe around Paris and romancing the Texas heiress Patricia Harper (JOAN BENNETT). It was much less satisfying than the original film, although the score included the lively torch song "What Have You Got That Gets Me?" and the catchy "You're Broke, You Dope," both sung by the Yacht Club Boys. Also cast were MARY BOLAND, Charley Grapewin, Joyce Compton, MONTY WOOLLEY, and Adrienne D'Ambricourt, under the direction of MITCHELL LEISEN. Because the picture was not very popular, Paramount retired the title until it was used for the JERRY LEWIS and DEAN MARTIN vehicle *Artists and Models* (1955). One of the team's better films, it concerned struggling Greenwich Village artist Rick Todd (Martin) who wants to break into the comic book industry by illustrating the fantastical dreams that his roommate Eugene Fullstack (Lewis) has each night. When Eugene dreams of a secret rocket fuel formula and Rick puts it in the comics, federal agents descend on the boys because it is the exact formula that the government is working on. Romance was provided by their neighbors Bessie Sparrowbrush (SHIRLEY MacLAINE) and Abby Parker (Dorothy Malone), and the supporting cast included Eddie Mayehoff, EVA GABOR, Anita Ekberg, and George Winslow. HARRY WARREN (music) and JACK BROOKS (lyrics) wrote an amiable score that included the Italian ballad "Inamorata" and the title song, which was used for a colorful production number displaying artists' models who wore much more than Broadway had seen in earlier revues of the title.

🎭 **AS THE GIRLS GO** (Winter Garden Theatre 1948). An old-style musical comedy built around the talents of its star, the leering comic Bobby Clark, the show also offered an expert score by JIMMY McHUGH (music) and HAROLD ADAMSON (lyrics). William Roos's libretto was set in the future (1952), when Lucille Thompson Wellington (Irene Rich) is elected the first woman president of the United States, making her husband Waldo (Clark) the First Gentleman. Since he's not much of a host, Waldo spends his days chasing after scantily dressed girls and getting in the way of the marriage plans between his son Kenny (Bill Callahan) and Kathy Robinson (Betty Jane Watson). It was all rather slight but Clark's ribald performance made it seem like inspired nonsense. "You Say the Nicest Things, Baby," "I Got Lucky in the Rain," and "It Takes a Woman to Take a Man" were standouts in the sparkling score that also included "There's No Getting Away From You" and the spirited title number. Because of an ASCAP strike at the time, the show's score was never recorded and it has never got the attention it deserved. Reviewers thought the musical thoroughly enjoyable thanks to the clowning of Clark, and the MIKE TODD production ran 420 performances, not quite long enough to turn a profit. Howard Bay directed and designed, and HERMES PAN did the jocular choreography.

🎭 **AS THOUSANDS CHEER** (Music Box Theatre 1933). Arguably IRVING BERLIN's finest musical revue, the show was an outstanding example of the genre during its golden age. MOSS HART wrote all the sketches, which were tied together by a series of newspaper headlines that led into each song or scene. Many celebrities, from JOAN CRAWFORD to Mahatma Gandhi, were satirized, as was high society, the theatre season, the opera world, and even the weather. The superb cast included CLIFTON WEBB, ETHEL WATERS, HELEN BRODERICK, and (in her last Broadway appearance) MARILYN MILLER. HASSARD SHORT staged the many scenes in a graceful and effective manner and the production was beautifully designed. But it was the scintillating Berlin score that made the revue so memorable. The breezy "How's Chances?," the painful lament "Supper Time," the sensuous "Heat Wave," the ballad "Lonely Heart," the bluesy "I've Got Harlem on My Mind," and the perennial favorite "Easter Parade" were among the show's many highlights. The SAM H. HARRIS production ran 400 performances. In 1998, a small-scale revival Off Broadway eschewed the spectacle and concentrated on the songs and sketches. Much of the comedy had dated but the songs proved to be as splendid as ever.

ASHFORD, ROB[ert] (1959–). Stage choreographer. The former dancer has staged the musical numbers for a number of Broadway musicals known for their vibrant choreography. Ashford was born in Orlando, Florida, raised in West Virginia, and educated at Washington and Lee University and Point Park College in Pittsburgh. He danced in the chorus and served as dance captain for such Broadway musicals as ANYTHING GOES (1987), THE MOST HAPPY FELLA (1992), CRAZY FOR YOU (1992), My Favorite Year (1992), and VICTOR/VICTORIA (1995) before becoming associate choreographer for PARADE (1998), KISS ME, KATE (1999), and SEUSSICAL (2000). Ashford made a sensational Broadway debut as a full-fledged choreographer with THOROUGHLY MODERN MILLIE (2002), followed by THE BOYS FROM SYRACUSE (2002), The Wedding Singer (2006), CURTAINS (2007), and GUYS AND DOLLS in London in 2007 and on Broadway in 2008, and Parade in London in 2007. He has choreographed a number of the ENCORES! shows, as well as the film Love Walked In (1997) and the BOBBY DARIN movie musical bio Beyond the Sea (2004).

ASHLEY, CHRISTOPHER (1964–). Stage director. A much-in-demand director of new plays and musicals, much of his work has an unconventional flavor. Ashley was born in Chicago, the son of a college philosophy professor, and educated at Yale University before beginning his career as an assistant director for Driving Miss Daisy (1987). He made his New York directorial debut in 1989 but was most noticed four years later for his staging of the gay life-style comedy *Jeffrey* by Paul Rudnick; Ashley would later direct the 1995 film version and the premiere stage productions of a handful of other Rudnick works. While much of Ashley's directing credits have been Off and Off Off Broadway, he staged three Broadway musicals, the 2000 revival of *THE ROCKY HORROR SHOW*, *All Shook Up* (2005), and *XANADU* (2007), as well as productions of STEPHEN SONDHEIM's *MERRILY WE ROLL ALONG* and *SWEENEY TODD* at the Kennedy Center in Washington and the revised national tour of *SUESSICAL*. He has also directed for such regional theatres as the Center Stage in Baltimore, the Philadelphia Theatre Company, the Williamstown Theatre Festival, the Goodspeed Opera House, and Shakespeare & Company. In 2007 Ashley was named artistic director of La Jolla Playhouse in California.

ASHMAN, HOWARD [born Howard Elliott Gershman] (1950–1991). Stage and film lyricist, director, and writer. An outstanding talent who helped bring about a renaissance in animated film musicals, whose untimely death from AIDS cut short a dazzling theatre and film career. Ashman was born in Baltimore, the son of an ice cream cone manufacturer, and educated at Goddard College and Indiana University. He wrote sketches and lyrics for some Off Off Broadway revues before teaming up with composer ALAN MENKEN for *God Bless You, Mr. Rosewater* (1979), an offbeat musical for which he wrote lyrics and libretto and also directed. The team found fame with the long-running Off Broadway hit *LITTLE SHOP OF HORRORS* (1982), with Ashman again writing and directing. When he staged his first Broadway musical, the underappreciated, short-lived *Smile* (1986), Ashman was discouraged with New York theatre and agreed to write for Disney films. The Ashman–Menken scores for *THE LITTLE MERMAID* (1989) and *BEAUTY AND THE BEAST* (1991) revitalized the animated film musical in Hollywood. He finished half of the score for *ALADDIN* (1992) before his early death, but had a posthumous hit on Broadway when *Beauty and the Beast* was turned into a very popular stage musical in 1994, followed by the stage version of *The Little Mermaid* in 2008.

🖉 **ASPECTS OF LOVE** (Broadhurst Theatre 1990). An atypically small-scale ANDREW LLOYD WEBBER show, the romantic musical emphasized characters rather than spectacle. Based on the novel by David Garnett, the libretto was set in post-World War II

Europe where the handsome Englishman Alex Dillingham (Michael Ball), the French actress Rose Vibert (Ann Crumb), the aging British playboy George Dillingham (Kevin Colson), the bisexual Italian artist Giulietta Trapani (Kathleen Rowe McAllen), and later Rose's daughter Jenny (Danielle Du Clos) fall in and out of love with each other over a period of twenty years. Don Black and Charles Hart wrote the lyrics for Webber's sung-through score, which included "Love Changes Everything," "The First Man You Remember," "Seeing Is Believing," "She'd Be Far Better Off With You," "There Is More to Love," and "Anything But Lonely." The Trevor Nunn–directed musical received mixed notices, although the performers and the lovely production were widely approved. The show had been a major hit in London but only managed to run a year on Broadway, which was because of its large advance sale of tickets.

🖉 **ASSASSINS** (Playwrights Horizons 1991). A daring and darkly comic Off Broadway piece of music–theatre, the STEPHEN SONDHEIM musical looked at the various men and women who have killed or attempted to kill U.S. presidents over the years. In a series of scenes and songs, the historical characters come forward and express themselves; all their distorted dreams and twisted minds are revealed with pathos, humor, and anger. Leading the group is John Wilkes Booth who sees Lincoln as the curse of humanity. He is joined by the angry immigrant Leon Czolgosz, the publicity-hungry Charles Guiteau, the fumbling Sara Jane Moore, the love-smitten John Hinckley, the cultist Lynne "Squeaky" Fromme, and others. The musical climaxes in a Dallas warehouse with Booth encouraging Lee Harvey Oswald to find fame and glory by shooting Kennedy.

John Weidman wrote the disturbing and yet oddly entertaining libretto, and Sondheim wrote a score pastiching American music from past eras: the cakewalking "Ballad of Guitau," the 1960s pop ballad "Unworthy of Your Love," the nineteenth-century narrative "Ballad of Booth," and the disarming march "Another National Anthem." Other songs were timeless commentaries, such as the bouncy "Everybody's Got the Right" and the seething "Gun Song." The PLAYWRIGHTS HORIZONS production, directed by JERRY ZAKS, featured a sterling cast and the limited run sold out quickly. However, the reviews were mixed, with some critics misinterpreting

Casts for *Assassins*

Character	1991 Off Broadway	2004 Broadway
John Wilkes Booth	VICTOR GARBER	MICHAEL CERVERIS
Lee Harvey Oswald	Jace Alexander	Neil Patrick Harris
Charles Guiteau	JONATHAN HADARY	Denis O'Hare
Sara Jane Moore	DEBRA MONK	Becky Ann Baker
Leon Czolgosz	TERRENCE MANN	James Barbour
Squeaky Fromme	Annie Golden	Mary Catherine Garrison
John Hinckley	Greg Germann	Alexander Gemignani
Balladeer	Patrick Cassidy	Neil Patrick Harris

the show as a commendation of assassins and, with patriotism running high because of the Gulf War, it was deemed unwise to transfer the musical to Broadway. After dozens of productions regionally and in London, the disturbing and revealing musical was finally seen on Broadway in 2004 in a ROUNDABOUT THEATRE mounting directed with verve and style by JOE MANTELLO. The reviews were propitious and the limited run was extended for 101 performances.

ASTAIRE, ADELE [born Adele Austerlitz] (1898–1981). Stage performer. Because she did not have a film career, the petite singer–dancer is not as well known as her brother FRED ASTAIRE, but she was as big a star as he on Broadway. Astaire was born in Omaha, Nebraska, and as a teenager appeared with her younger brother in vaudeville before the two settled in New York and were on Broadway together by 1917 in *Over the Top*. The dancing–singing duo were featured in *THE PASSING SHOW* (1918), *Apple Blossoms* (1919), *The Love Letter* (1921), and *For Goodness Sake* (1922) before becoming stars with the GERSHWINS' *LADY, BE GOOD* (1924). The team shone in *FUNNY FACE* (1927), *Smiles* (1930), and *THE BAND WAGON* (1931), as well as in some musicals in London. Adele retired to marry the British Lord Cavendish and never performed again. She was as accomplished a dancer as Fred, possessed a pleasant soprano voice, and had an acute sense of comedy in both her acting and her singing.

ASTAIRE, FRED [born Frederick Austerlitz] (1899–1987). Stage, film, and television performer. Arguably the most graceful, original, and sophisticated song-and-dance man in Hollywood musicals, he enjoyed a successful Broadway career prior to his remarkable film career. Astaire was born in Omaha, Nebraska, and was on the vaudeville stage with his elder sister ADELE ASTAIRE for some years before

Fred Astaire. By usual Hollywood standards, Astaire should not have been a movie star. Yet when he was dancing, singing, joking, and charming his way on the screen, all the rules fell apart. In *Funny Face* (1957) he tries to convince Audrey Hepburn that she has the makings of a model, as if we had any doubts about that. (Photofest)

the team was on Broadway by 1917. After appearing in *THE PASSING SHOW* (1918), *Apple Blossoms* (1919), *The Love Letter* (1921), and *For Goodness Sake* (1922), the team found fame in *LADY, BE GOOD* (1924), followed by the stage hits *FUNNY FACE* (1927), *Smiles* (1930), and *THE BAND WAGON* (1931), and some London successes as well. Although the duo was at the peak of their popularity, Adele gave up show business to marry an Englishman and Fred's career was threatened. He was often seen as the less impressive of the twosome, playing earnest romantic roles while his sister got to play funny heroines. But Astaire proved just as appealing in *Gay Divorce* (1932), his only Broadway musical without Adele, and was whisked off to Hollywood, never to return to the legitimate stage again. He had a featured spot in his debut movie, *Dancing Lady* (1933), and then caught the attention of moviegoers when he and Ginger Rogers were teamed as the secondary couple in *Flying Down to Rio* (1933), dancing "The Carioca" together and giving birth to Hollywood's most famous dancing couple. The twosome were reunited for nine more musicals, most of them major hits: *The Gay Divorcee* (1934), *Roberta* (1935), *Top Hat* (1935), *Follow the Fleet* (1936), *Swing Time* (1936), *Shall We Dance* (1937), *Carefree* (1938), *The Story of Vernon and Irene Castle* (1939), and *The Barkleys of Broadway* (1949). Although moviegoers and studio heads preferred Astaire with Rogers, he did find other dancing partners in *A Damsel in Distress* (1937), *Broadway Melody of 1940*, *You'll Never Get Rich* (1941), *You Were Never Lovelier* (1942), *The Sky's the Limit* (1943), *Yolanda and the Thief* (1945), *Ziegfeld Follies* (1946), *Blue Skies* (1946), and *Easter Parade* (1948). In the 1950s, many of Astaire's musicals did not do as well at the box office, but he still managed to shine in *Three Little Words* (1950), *Let's Dance* (1950), *Royal Wedding* (1951), *The Belle of New York* (1952), *The Band Wagon* (1953), *Daddy Long Legs* (1955), *Funny Face* (1957), and *Silk Stockings* (1957). He turned to dramatic roles with *On the Beach* (1959) and did many television specials in the 1960s and 1970s, returning to Hollywood only for his last screen musical *Finian's Rainbow* (1968) and to narrate the documentaries *That's Entertainment* (1974) and *That's Entertainment Part 2* (1976). Astaire excelled in all manner of dance (tap, soft shoe, ballet, jazz, modern) while maintaining a distinctive persona of wit and romance that has never been equaled. He possessed a thin but appealing singing voice and was an expert interpreter of lyrics by Ira Gershwin, Irving Berlin, Cole Porter, Dorothy Fields, and other top lyricists, allowing him to introduce more song standards than perhaps anyone else in Hollywood after Bing Crosby. Astaire was also actively involved with the dancing he performed, often helping to devise the choreography and finding inventive ways to use locations and inanimate objects in his limitless dancing imagination. Autobiography: *Steps in Time* (1959); biographies: *Fred Astaire*, Sarah Giles (1988); *Fred Astaire: A Wonderful Life*, Bill Adler (1987); *Starring Fred Astaire*, Stanley Green (1977); *The Fred Astaire–Ginger Rogers Book*, Arlene Croce (1972).

At Home Abroad (Winter Garden Theatre 1935). A delightful musical revue that used the gimmick of a world cruise to loosely tie its songs and sketches together, the show featured another fine revue score by Arthur Schwartz (music) and Howard Dietz (lyrics). An American couple traveled the world, from a London department store to the jungles of Africa to a Japanese garden, and kept running into stars such as Beatrice Lillie, Eddie Foy, Jr., Ethel Waters, Eleanor Powell, and Reginald Gardiner wherever they went. The songs included the restless "Thief in the Night," the rhythmic "The Hottentot Potentate," the slaphappy "Got a Bran' New Suit," the tuneful "Love Is a Dancing Thing," the flowing ballad "Farewell, My Lovely," and the risible "Get Yourself a Geisha." Critics cheered the delectable cast, the pleasing score, and the ravishing decor designed by Vincente Minnelli (who also directed), and the Shubert production ran 198 performances.

At the Circus (MGM 1939). Not a top-drawer Marx Brothers vehicle, all the same it has some memorable moments, both musical and comical. In the Irving Brecher screenplay, circus owner Jeff Wilson (Kenny Baker) needs $10,000 to save his operation because his crooked partner John Carter (James Burke) has arranged for the box office money to be stolen so that he can take over the show. Jeff is in love with the performer Julie Randall (Florence Rice) and wants to save the circus for her sake. He enlists the help of the lawyer J. Cheever Loophole (Groucho Marx) who, with the strongman Goliath (Nat Pendleton), his bumbling assistant Punchy (Harpo Marx), and the corrupt Antonio Pirelli (Chico Marx), find the thieves and save the day. Also on hand were Margaret Dumont, Eve Arden, and Fritz Feld. The comedy has three exceptional musical numbers: Harpo plucking out Rodgers and Hart's "Blue Moon" on the harp, Baker and Rice singing "Two Blind Loves" at a lunch counter, and Groucho singing and prancing to "Lydia, the Tattooed Lady" on a train. The last two numbers were by Harold Arlen (music) and E. Y. Harburg (lyrics) who also wrote "Step Up and Take a Bow" and "Swingali" for the film. Mervyn LeRoy produced, Eddie Buzzell directed, and Bobby Connolly choreographed the daffy dancing.

AUBERJONOIS, RENE (1940–) Stage, film, and television performer. A small, lithe character actor who has often stolen the show in supporting roles, he has appeared in everything from Shakespeare to campy musicals. Auberjonois was born in New York City to French Canadian parents and studied at Carnegie Mellon University before getting professional experience in regional theatre. He made an impressive New York debut playing the Fool in *King Lear* (1968), followed by other classical roles for the NEW YORK SHAKESPEARE FESTIVAL. Auberjonois shone in some Broadway musicals as well, most notably the gay fashion designer Sebastian Baye in *Coco* (1969), the Mississippi con man Duke in *BIG RIVER* (1985), the Samuel Goldwyn–like film producer Buddy Fidler in *CITY OF ANGELS* (1989), and the kookie Prof. Abronsius in *Dance of the Vampires* (2002). He has appeared in many nonmusical films, including several directed by ROBERT ALTMAN, and has been in hundreds of television programs, both series and specials. Auberjonois has provided voices for cartoon characters on television and the movies since the early 1960s, such as the French chef Louis in *THE LITTLE MERMAID* (1989).

AUER, MISCHA [born Mischa Ounskowsky] (1905–1967). Film and stage performer. A sad-looking, heavily accented character actor, he played comic eccentrics in many Hollywood comedies and musicals. Auer was born in St. Petersburg, Russia, the grandson of violinist Leopold Auer (whose name he later adopted as an actor in America), and fled his homeland during the 1917 revolution. In New York he studied several musical instruments preparing for a concert career but turned to acting in the 1920s, making his Broadway debut in a 1925 production of *The Wild Duck*. After other jobs on Broadway and on tour, Auer made his first film in 1929 and was then cast as sinister foreigners. Not until the Depression did he become Hollywood's favorite "mad Russian" in lighter fare, including such musicals as *PARAMOUNT ON PARADE* (1930), *DELICIOUS* (1931), *I DREAM TOO MUCH* (1935), *Sons o' Guns* (1936), *Three Smart Girls* (1936), *Top of the Town* (1937), *ONE HUNDRED MEN AND A GIRL* (1937), *Vogues of 1938* (1937), *Merry Go Round of 1938* (1937), *THE JOY OF LIVING* (1938), *SWEETHEARTS* (1938), *HELLZAPOPPIN'* (1941), and *LADY IN THE DARK* (1944). In the 1950s, Auer moved to Europe where he continued to act in films and on stage, returning to Broadway in 1964 to play Popoff in the LINCOLN CENTER revival of *THE MERRY WIDOW*.

AUTRY, GENE [born Orvon Grover Autry] (1907–1998). Film performer, composer, and lyricist. Perhaps America's favorite cowboy singer on radio and film, he was also a prolific songwriter who penned hundreds of Western ballads. Autry was born in rural Texas near Tioga and worked for the railroad and as a telegrapher before he started singing his own songs on the radio. Soon he became famous for his personable singing voice and such hit songs as "That Silver Haired Daddy of Mine" and "Back in the Saddle Again." Autry virtually invented the singing cowboy movie, features that were adventure or action pictures but always had time for a song or two. He appeared in dozens of them in the 1930s and 1940s, some of which could be categorized as musicals: *Tumbling Tumbleweeds* (1935), *Manhattan Merry-Go-Round* (1937), *Melody Ranch* (1940), and others. Autry's popularity spawned a series of comic books, his concerts in huge venues were sellouts, and he had his own television show in the 1950s. He made many hit recordings but, ironically, Autry's top sellers were songs written by others, such as "Here Comes Santa Claus," "Tears on My Pillow," and "Rudolph the Red-Nosed Reindeer." Biographies: *Public Cowboy No. 1: The Life and Times of Gene Autry*, Holly George-Warren (2007); *Gene Autry: His Life and Career*, Don Cusic (2007).

AVALON, FRANKIE [born Francis Thomas Alvallone] (1940–). Film and television performer. The teenage singing heartthrob of the 1960s, he made a series of beach musicals, mostly with fellow teen idol ANNETTE FUNICELLO. Avalon was born in Philadelphia and was a prodigy on the trumpet at the age of nine but as a teen turned to singing and was soon appearing on national television and making hit records. He did a specialty spot in the film *Jamboree* (1957) and came across so well on screen that he was given supporting parts in a handful of films before the studios teamed him with Funicello as the leads in *Beach Party* (1963). Avalon returned to the beach for such musicals as *Muscle Beach* (1964), *Bikini Beach* (1964), *Beach Blanket Bingo* (1965), and *How to Stuff a Wild Bikini* (1967). His less sandy musicals were *Ski Party* (1965), *Jet Set* (1965), *I'll Take Sweden* (1965), and *Fireball 500* (1966), as well as the TV musicals *Who's Afraid of Mother Goose?* (1967) and *The Saga of Sonora* (1973).

Avalon parodied his youthful days when he played Teen Idol in *GREASE* (1978), and he and Funicello got nostalgic with the film *Back to the Beach* (1987), which he produced.

☙ *AVENUE Q* (John Golden Theatre 2003). A sassy, impudent little musical from Off Broadway, it took a little while to catch on in a Broadway house but, helped by encouraging reviews, some awards, and strong word of mouth, the show became a hit that was still running by the beginning of 2008. The characters, both human and puppet, that live in a New York tenement called Avenue Q are thirty-somethings dealing with sexual hang-ups, job loss, friendship difficulties, and other urban and adult problems. The fact that their plight is presented in the style of a children's instructional television program, such as *Sesame Street* and *The Electric Company*, gives the show its gimmick and its irreverent form of comedy. Jeff Whitty wrote the book and Robert Lopez and Jeff Marx collaborated on the score, which included "It Sucks to Be Me," "Everyone's a Little Bit Racist," "There's a Fine, Fine Line," "Schadenfreude," and

"There Is Life Outside Your Apartment." The diversified and talented cast included John Tartaglia, Stephanie D'Abruzzo, Jordan Gelber, Ann Harada, Jennifer Barnhart, Natalie Ventia Belcon, and Rick Lyon. Jason Moore directed, putting a smirk and a smile on everyone's face.

AZENBERG, EMANUEL (1934–). Stage producer. One of the last of the solo producers on Broadway, he has presented most of NEIL SIMON's plays and a variety of offerings over the past four decades, including musicals. The native New Yorker was educated at New York University before embarking on a producing career in 1961. He often works with the Shubert Organization on large expensive projects, but remains one of the few presenters to go solo on a show when he can. Among his musical offerings are *THE ROTHSCHILDS* (1970), *AIN'T SUPPOSED TO DIE A NATURAL DEATH* (1971), *AIN'T MISBEHAVIN'* (1978), *THEY'RE PLAYING OUR SONG* (1979), *SUNDAY IN THE PARK WITH GEORGE* (1984), *JEROME ROBBINS' BROADWAY* (1989), *Side Show* (1997), and *MOVIN' OUT* (2003).

B

🎭 **BABES IN ARMS** (Shubert Theatre 1937). The quintessential "let's put on a show" musical that has often been imitated and parodied, this youthful show was refreshingly original in its day and a surprise hit on Broadway. It also boasted more hit songs than any other RICHARD RODGERS (music) and LORENZ HART (lyrics) musical.

Plot: Some out-of-work vaudevillians take to the road during the Depression, leaving their teenage kids to fend for themselves and avoid the work farm. Led by the young songwriter Val "Valentine" La Mar, his adoring sweetheart Billie Smith, and the would-be socialist Peter, the pack of "babes in arms" puts on a show to raise money and save their parents and themselves. But the revue they stage loses money and the kids are sent to a work farm where a French aviator crossing the Atlantic makes an emergency landing and brings enough publicity to the teens' show to make it a hit.

Producer DWIGHT DEERE WIMAN employed a large cast of youthful unknowns (except for teen film actress MITZI GREEN), kept the sets and costumes to a minimum, and priced the musical with rock-bottom prices. Critics and audiences didn't seem to worry about the weak plot (perhaps the lamest of any Rodgers and

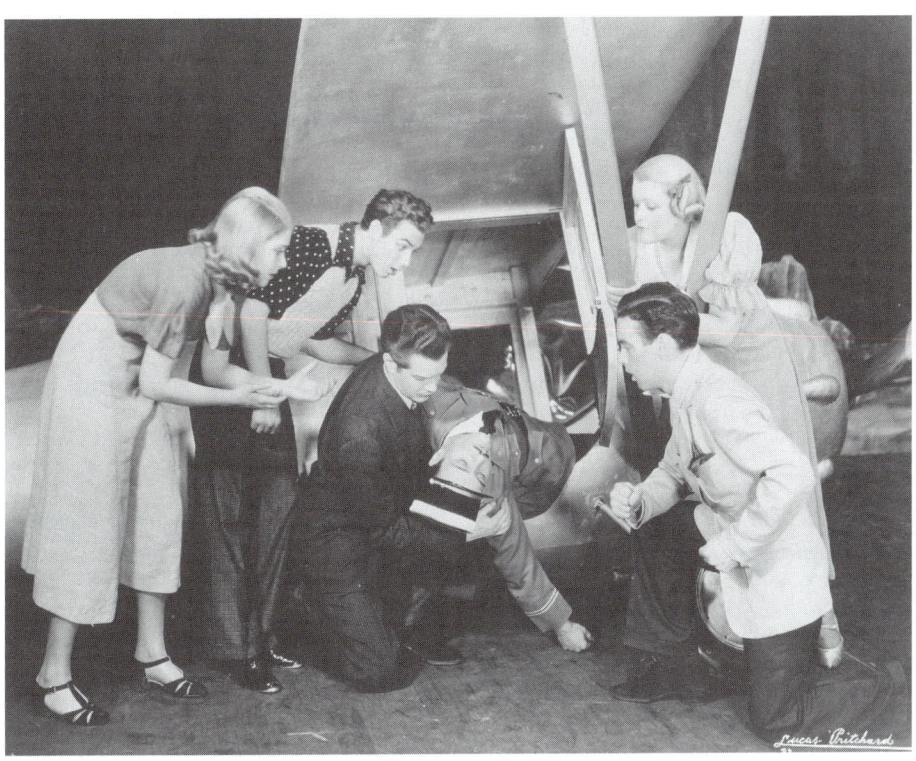

Babes in Arms. The Rodgers and Hart Broadway musical was so thin on plot that a French aviator (Aljan de Loville) had to crash land in the second act to give the story its turning point. Among the "babes" who came to his rescue were (left to right) Mitzi Green, Alex Courtney, Alfred Drake, Ray Heatherton, and Wynn Murray. Because it was a musical comedy, the flyer survived and the publicity turned the teenager's musical revue into a popular attraction. (Photofest)

Casts for *Babes in Arms*

Character	1937 Broadway	1939 film
Val LaMar/Mickey Moran	RAY HEATHERTON	MICKEY ROONEY
Dolores/Patsy Barton	Grace McDonald	JUDY GARLAND
Billie Smith/Rosalie Essex	MITZI GREEN	JUNE PREISSER
Marshall/Don Brice	ALFRED DRAKE	Douglas MacPhail
Baby Rose	Wynn Murray	
DeQuincy Brothers	NICHOLAS BROTHERS	
Joe Moran		CHARLES WINNINGER
Judge		GUY KIBBEE
Martha Steele		MARGARET HAMILTON

Hart success) when there was such a treasure trove of great songs sung and danced by an energetic cast. From the show came such future talents as Ray Heatherton, ALFRED DRAKE, the NICHOLAS BROTHERS, Wynn Murray, DAN DAILEY, ROBERT ROUNSEVILLE, and Grace MacDonald. Robert Sinclair directed and GEORGE BALANCHINE did the choreography, which included the extended dance sequence, "Peter's Journey," a number that foreshadowed the great stage ballets that AGNES DE MILLE would choreograph in the 1940s. Even the costumes by Helene Pons were bargain basement clever, with the kids using dish towels and kitchen utensils to create their Egyptian garb for a production number in their show. As popular as *Babes in Arms* was (289 performances), there were no London or other foreign productions and it has never been revived on Broadway. However, the musical has become a familiar staple in schools and summer stock, using a rewritten libretto that sets the show in a summer theatre with the vaudeville kids now as stage interns. It is not much of an improvement over the ridiculous original, but once again the hit songs keep coming.

Babes in Arms (stage) Musical Numbers

"Where or When"
"Babes in Arms"
"I Wish I Were in Love Again'
"All Dark People"
"Way Out West"
"My Funny Valentine"
"Johnny One-Note"
"Imagine"
"All at Once"
"Peter's Journey"
"The Lady Is a Tramp"
"You Are So Fair"

The musical variety that Rodgers and Hart offered in their score was remarkable by the standards of the day or any time. The haunting "Where or When" may seem too sophisticated for teenagers to sing, just as "The Lady Is a Tramp" is a bit more worldly than these characters appear to be, but like all the songs in the score they make quite an impact even on first hearing. The indelible ballad "My Funny Valentine" is the only number that ties in directly to the play (Billie sings it about Val), yet it certainly has found favor outside of the context of the show. "West End Avenue" is a playful cowboy pastiche with a very urban point of view, "I Wish I Were in Love Again" is a joyous duet that celebrates the heartaches of love, "Johnny One-Note" is a jazzy *tour de force*, and the marching title number is musically stirring even as the lyric is sarcastic. With such a set of songs, it in no wonder audiences willingly overlook the plot.

■ *Babes in Arms* (MGM 1939) was filmed with typical Hollywood backward thinking, the studio retaining much of the flimsy plot of the stage *Babes in Arms* and throwing out most of the score. Only "Where or When" and the title song were used; the score was augmented by a few new numbers ("Good Morning," "Broadway Rhythm," "Daddy Was a Minstrel Man," and "God's Country") and some old favorites such as "You Are My Lucky Star," "Moonlight Bay," "Oh, Susannah," "I'm Just Wild About Harry," and even "Stars and Stripes Forever." On the plus side, the film was able to show off the many talents of MICKEY ROONEY and JUDY GARLAND in the leading roles, now called Mickey Moran and Patsy Barton. Gone was the French aviator, and a new character, Hollywood child star Rosalie Essex (JUNE PREISSER) patterned after SHIRLEY TEMPLE or maybe Mitzi Green herself, was added to come between the two teen lovers. The plot culminated in a big musical revue put on by the kids and the "let's put a show on!" film musical was born. *Babes in Arms* was a Hollywood first on other fronts: it was the first musical produced by ARTHUR FREED and the beginning of the historic Freed Unit, the first picture at MGM directed by BUSBY BERKELEY, and the first teaming of Rooney and Garland, who would go through similar shenanigans in other MGM youth musicals. *Babes in Arms* on screen is all harmless fun but it can hardly be called a Rodgers and Hart musical anymore.

BABES IN TOYLAND (Majestic Theatre 1903). Perhaps the most widely known work by composer VICTOR HERBERT, the family musical was a holiday-time favorite for many decades and some of the songs are still familiar. Lyricist–librettist GLEN MACDONOUGH fashioned a fantastical tale about two children, Jane and Alan, who are set adrift by their wicked Uncle Barnaby and are shipwrecked in Toyland, which is filled with Mother Goose characters. Barnaby follows and enlists the help of the wicked Toymaker to capture the kids, but Jack and Jill, Bo Peep, Mary Quite Contrary, Widow Piper, and her son Tom Tom all help the children escape and Barnaby is brought to justice in the Toyland Palace. At a time when most musicals had a few sets, the Fred Hamlin–JULIAN MITCHELL production was a spectacular parade of scenery, costumes, and special effects. Mitchell also directed and choreographed with such flourishes as a shipwreck, a flower-filled palace for the Moth Queen, and a toy shop bursting with oversized toys. The two standout songs from the score are the lullaby-like "Toyland" and the invigorating "March of the Toys." Also heard were "I Can't Do the Sum," "Never Mind, Bo-Peep," "Song of the Poet," and "Our Castle in Spain." The musical ran a very profitable 192 performances, toured extensively for years, and was revived in New York in 1905, 1929, 1930, and 1979. It also became a staple in the repertoire of operetta companies across the country and still pops up on occasion at Christmastime.

The three film versions of *Babes in Toyland* each have their charms, although the 1934 movie musical by MGM is the superior entry. Although it is only seventy-nine minutes long, the film captured the mystery and joy of the original. In the screenplay by Frank Butler, Hal Roach, and others, Toyland is being invaded by Bogeymen but is saved by the bumbling efforts of the two toymakers Stannie Dum (STAN LAUREL) and Ollie Dee (OLIVER HARDY). The score was greatly abridged but the best stage songs were still there and the recent cartoon ditty "Who's Afraid of the Big Bad Wolf?" was added. WALT DISNEY's 1961 version of *Babes in Toyland* was the company's first live-action musical and no expense was spared. Henry Calin and Gene Sheldon were the comic toymakers but more emphasis was put on their daffy boss played by ED WYNN. The two lost waifs were now the teenage sweethearts Tom Piper (TOMMY SANDS) and Mary Contrary (ANNETTE FUNICELLO), and RAY BOLGER was the villainous Barnaby. They were all either miscast or ineffective and the movie only came to life during the production numbers staged by Tommy Maloney, in particular the dancing fountains during the "Castle in Spain" number. The film may have been overproduced and overdirected by JACK DONOHUE, but at least it was colorful and audiences responded to it. More pleasing is MGM's 1997 animated version of *Babes in Toyland*. The plot was slightly altered, with the young Jack and Jill now sent to Toyland to live with their Uncle Barnaby who hates toys. The seventy-four-minute film retains some of the Herbert songs and has superior animation and voices, including Christopher Plummer, CHARLES NELSON REILLY, Bronson Pinchot, and James Belushi. Like the 1934 film, it is greatly abridged but the spirit of the piece is still there.

Casts for *Babes in Toyland*

Characters	Alan/Tom/Jack	Jane/Mary/Jill	Silas Barnaby	Toymaker
1903 Broadway	William Norris	Mabel Barrison	George W. Denham	Dore Davidson
1934 film	Felix Knight	Marie Wilson	Harry Brandon	William Burress
1961 film	TOMMY SANDS	ANNETTE FUNICELLO	RAY BOLGER	ED WYNN
1986 television	Keneau Reeves	Drew Barrymore	Richard Mulligan	Pat Morita
1997 television	Joey Ashton	Lacey Chabert	Christopher	
(voices)			Plummer	

⬚ The two television versions of the Herbert classic varied greatly. NBC-TV broadcast a live studio production in 1954 with Wally Cox, Jack E. Leonard, Dave Garroway, and the Bil Baird puppets featured in the cast. There seems to be no kinescope of the holiday broadcast so details about the showing are scarce. Plenty is known about NBC's 1986 small-screen, big-budget adaptation, which was written by Paul Zindel. Eleven-year-old Lisa Piper is blown by a blizzard on Christmas eve to Toyland where Mary Contrary is being forced to marry decrepit old Barnaby Barnacle when she really loves Jack Be Nimble. Lisa recruits various Mother Goose characters and the Toymaker and they not only stop the wedding but keep Barnaby from taking over Toyland. Clive Donner directed with such a heavy hand that the actors looked foolish and the fantasy was leaden. Worse, all the Herbert songs but two were cut and new ones by LESLIE BRICUSSE were added so the production is barely *Babes in Toyland* at all.

🎬 **BABES ON BROADWAY** (MGM 1942). A follow-up to the Mickey Rooney–JUDY GARLAND "let's put on a show" film hits *BABES IN ARMS* (1939) and *STRIKE UP THE BAND* (1940), this musical also featured a youthful cast of characters, this time singing and dancing to raise money to send settlement-house kids to the country. The formula was already running thin but the screenplay by Fred Finklehoffe and Elaine Ryan wasted no time getting to the musical numbers, which were exceptional. BURTON LANE, ROGER EDENS (music), Ralph Freed, and E. Y. HARBURG (lyrics) wrote the new songs, including the cozy standard "I Like New York in June (How About You?)," the wry "Anything Can Happen in New York," the raucous "Hoe Down," the patriotic "Chin Up, Cherrio," which encouraged the British to stand up to Hitler, and the zesty title number. Rooney, at the peak of his popularity, got to pull out all the stops, leading both a minstrel show and a barn dance, impersonating Harry Lauder, Walter Hampton, and GEORGE M. COHAN in a dream sequence, and spoofing CARMEN MIRANDA in a hilarious drag routine. ARTHUR FREED produced and BUSBY BERKELEY directed as well as choreographed the frolic, which was filled with more-than-usual musical numbers, including Americana favorites such as "Yankee Doodle Boy," "By the Light of the Silvery Moon," "Swanee River," and "Waiting for the Robert E. Lee."

📖 *BABY* (Ethel Barrymore Theatre 1983). An intimate, knowing little musical by DAVID SHIRE (music) and RICHARD MALTBY, JR. (lyrics),

it was perhaps too small scale for Broadway and probably belonged Off Broadway where the team had more success. Sybille Pearson's libretto was set in a college town where two undergraduate students (Liz Callaway, Todd Graff) living together learn she is pregnant, a married couple (Catherine Cox, Martin Vidnovic) keeps trying unsuccessfully to conceive a child, and a middle-aged couple (BETH FOWLER, James Congdon) with grown kids finds out that she is expecting again. In a series of vignettes, the three couples deal with their particular situations and learn to accept what life has offered them. The songs were perceptive and enjoyable, particularly "The Story Goes On," "I Want It All," "Fatherhood Blues," "Easier to Love," "And What If We Had Loved Like That," and "The Ladies Singin' Their Song." The insightful musical received some favorable notices and managed to run 241 performances, followed by many regional productions.

BACALL, LAUREN [born Betty Joan Perske] (1924–). Film, stage, and television performer. The iconoclastic glamour movie star from the golden age of Hollywood, she has appeared on Broadway on occasion, twice in musical hits. A native New Yorker, Bacall trained at the American Academy of Dramatic Arts but had little luck on the New York stage so she took up modeling and attracted Hollywood, making a sensational screen debut in *TO HAVE AND HAVE NOT* (1944) with Humphrey Bogart (1899–1957) whom she married soon after. The sexy, husky-voiced Bacall played alluring characters in melodramas on the screen but favored comedy when she returned to Broadway in *Goodbye, Charlie* (1959), *Cactus Flower* (1965), and *Waiting in the Wings* (1999). Although her singing and dancing talents were negligible, she triumphed as the temperamental stage star Margo Channing in the musical *APPLAUSE* (1970) and again as the television celebrity Tess Harding in *WOMAN OF THE YEAR* (1981). Bacall has also appeared in many television dramas and specials. After Bogart's death, she was married to actor Jason Robards (1922–2000). Autobiographies: *By Myself and Then Some* (2006); *Now* (1996).

BACHARACH, BURT, AND HAL DAVID. Stage and film songwriting team. The pop song creators whose distinctive sound was a cross between Big Band and light rock, they took time from writing hit songs for the charts to score a few musicals. Bacharach (1928–) was born in Kansas City, Missouri, the son of a syndicated columnist, and studied music at McGill University, Tanglewood, Mannes School of Music, and the Music Academy of the West. He began his career playing piano for USO tours in Korea and arranging and accompanying popular singers such as VIC DAMONE and Marlene Dietrich. Lyricist Hal David (1921–) is a native New Yorker who was educated at New York University before he started collaborating with various composers to come up with many hit singles. He and Bacharach wrote many hit songs for Dionne Warwick and other stars before embarking on their only Broadway musical, *PROMISES PROMISES* (1968). In addition to writing the theme songs for several nonmusical films, the duo scored the film musical *Lost Horizon* (1972) and the TV musical *On the Flip Side* (1966). David is the brother of lyricist MACK DAVID and Bacharach was married to lyricist Carole Bayer Sager (1947–) and actress Angie Dickinson (1937–).

◻ **BACHELOR, THE** (NBC-TV 1956). A charming contemporary musical with a solid score, good plotting, and enjoyable performances, the ninety-minute broadcast was one of the better offerings of the decade and has regrettably been forgotten. Ad exec Larry Blaine (Hal March) keeps three girl friends (Jayne Mansfield, Julie Wilson, and Georgeann Johnson) in anxious anticipation of marrying him while his secretary Marion (CAROL HANEY) is forced to juggle his schedule so the three women don't catch on. Out of frustration and to teach her boss a lesson, Marion arranges a date with all three on the same evening and Larry is found out. The three women demand to know which one he will marry, so Larry forsakes them all and chooses the independent Marion. While quiz show host March was the star, Haney stole the show with her sparkling performance, singing and dancing the numbers that she also choreographed. Steve Allen and Ervin Drake collaborated on the score, which produced two hits, "This Could Be the Start of Something Big" and "Impossible." Also in the well-reviewed score were "My Little Black Book," "The Natives Are Restless Tonight," "The Girl in the Gray Flannel Suite," and "Three Cheers and a Tiger." Joseph Cates produced and directed the *Sunday Spectacular* broadcast, which was written by Arnie Rosen and Coleman Jacoby.

BACON, IRVING (1893–1965). Film performer. A prolific character actor who specialized in rural simpletons, he gave comic performances in over 200 films from the early 1920s until the late 1950s. Bacon was born in St. Joseph, Missouri, the son of popular stage actor Frank Bacon (1864–1922), and began his career in silent comedy shorts directed by Mack Sennett. He started getting interesting supporting roles when sound came in and went on to play pleasant if befuddled clerks, mailmen, ranch hands, bartenders, and other servile characters. Among his musical credits are *GEORGE WHITE'S SCANDALS* (1934), *BIG BROADCAST OF 1937* (1936), *SAN FRANCISCO* (1936), *The Singing Kid* (1936), *Sing You Sinners* (1938), *Every Day's a Holiday* (1937), *Hollywood Merry Go Round of 1938*, *BIG BROADCAST OF 1938*, *College Swing* (1938), *Hollywood Cavalcade* (1939), *SECOND FIDDLE* (1939), *AT THE CIRCUS* (1939), *HOLIDAY INN* (1942), *Footlight Serenade* (1942), *STAR-SPANGLED RHYTHM* (1942), *KNICKERBOCKER HOLIDAY* (1944), *Pin Up Girl* (1944), *WORDS AND MUSIC* (1948), *WABASH AVENUE* (1950), *THE GLENN MILLER STORY* (1954), and *A STAR IS BORN* (1954). In the 1950s Bacon added television to his credits and acted in dozens of westerns and sit-coms. His brother was film director LLOYD BACON.

BACON, LLOYD (1890–1955). Film director and actor. A prolific Hollywood artist with over eighty features to his credit, he was an important figure in early movie musicals. A native of San Jose, California, Bacon had a successful early career as an actor, playing the heavy in many comedy shorts with Charles Chaplin before he started directing two-reelers for Mack Sennett in 1921. His first important feature was the musical *THE SINGING FOOL* (1928). Working with choreographer BUSBY BERKELEY, Bacon created the Depression-era musical at WARNER BROTHERS with such films as *42ND STREET* (1933), *FOOTLIGHT PARADE* (1933), *WONDER BAR* (1934), and *GOLD DIGGERS OF 1937* (1936). Also among his two dozen screen musicals were *Honky Tonk* (1929), *She Couldn't Say No* (1930), *In Caliente* (1935), *Broadway Gondolier* (1935), *Cowboy From Brooklyn* (1938), *Wake Up and Dream* (1946), *I Wonder Who's Kissing Her Now* (1947), *CALL ME MISTER* (1951), *Walking My Baby Back Home* (1953), and *The French Line* (1954). His father was the beloved comic stage actor Frank Bacon (1864–1922) and his brother was the busy film character actor IRVING BACON.

BAGLEY, BEN[jamin James] (1933–1998). Stage producer. One of the most colorful musical producers on the Off Broadway scene in the 1950s and 1960s, he excelled in small and witty revues. Bagley left his hometown in Vermont as a teenager to go to New York where he worked at various jobs before turning to producing. His *The Shoestring Revue* (1955), *The Littlest Revue* (1956), *Shoestring '57* (1957), and *The Decline and Fall of the Entire World as Seen Through the Eyes of Cole Porter* (1965) were smart, funny shows that introduced new songwriters and performers such as CHITA RIVERA, JOEL GREY, and BEATRICE ARTHUR. A compendium of his various revues was presented Off Broadway under the title of *Ben Bagley's Shoestring Revues* (1970). In the 1960s Bagley turned to record producing and put out a series of "Revisited" albums with lesser-known songs by renowned American songwriters.

BAILEY, PEARL (1918–1990). Stage, film, and television performer. The smooth-voiced African American nightclub singer and recording star made only a handful of stage and film appearances but each one was memorable. Bailey was born in Newport News, Virginia, the daughter of a preacher, and started singing in vaudeville and cabarets as a teenager. By the 1940s she was singing in Manhattan's finest supper clubs and in 1946 she made her Broadway debut as the funny barmaid Butterfly in *ST. LOUIS WOMAN*. Bailey also appeared in musicals as the sassy maid Connecticut in *Arms and the Girls* (1950), in the revue *Bless You All* (1950), and as the worldly wise brothel proprietress Madame Fleur in *HOUSE OF FLOWERS* (1954), but her greatest Broadway triumph was as wisecracking Dolly Levi in *HELLO, DOLLY* (1967 and 1975). Although she had appeared on screen in specialty bits in *Variety Girl* (1947) and *Isn't It Romantic?* (1948), she got to play more memorable supporting roles in *CARMEN JONES* (1954), *St. Louis Blues* (1958), and *PORGY AND BESS* (1959). Bailey appeared on many television specials during her long career. Autobiography: *The Raw Pearl* (1968).

BAKER, KENNY [Laurence] (1912–1985). Stage and film performer. A youthful-looking tenor with a naive and innocent persona, he appeared in some dozen Hollywood musicals in the 1930s and 1940s. Baker was born in Monrovia, California, and began his career singing in nightclubs and found recognition on the radio as a singer and sidekick on JACK BENNY's program in the 1930s. His high tenor voice and clean-cut looks made him ideal for films and after doing specialty bits in *KING OF BURLESQUE* (1935), *The King and the Chorus Girl* (1937), *Turn Off the Moon* (1937), and *Mr. Dodd Takes the Air* (1937), he was featured as juvenile leads in *THE GOLDWYN FOLLIES* (1938), *Radio City Revels* (1938), *AT THE CIRCUS* (1939), *THE MIKADO* (1939), *The Hit Parade of 1941* (1940), and *Silver Skates* (1943). Baker's acting abilities were limited so he was demoted to featured supporting roles in such musicals as *STAGE DOOR CANTEEN* (1943), *Doughboys in Ireland* (1944), *THE HARVEY GIRLS* (1945), and *Calendar Girl* (1947). His one Broadway credit was playing the hapless barber Rodney Hatch opposite MARY MARTIN in *ONE TOUCH OF VENUS* (1943), and his only television role was the journalist Horace Miller in the TV version of *MISS LIBERTY* (1951). Baker retired from performing in the early 1950s to become a motivational speaker.

BAKER, WORD [born Charles William Baker] (1923–1995). Stage director. A director and sometime choreographer of works in regional theatre and Off Broadway, he staged America's longest-running musical. Baker was born in Honey Grove, Texas, the son of a druggist and a music teacher, and educated at North Texas State University and the University of Texas. After serving in the anti-air craft artillery during World War II, Baker pursued a career as a theatre designer, making his New York debut in 1956. Two years later he directed a revival of *The Crucible* Off Broadway and then staged some musical revues before he was hired to direct a small musical fable by fellow-Texans TOM JONES and HARVEY SCHMIDT—*THE FANTASTICKS* (1960), which ran a record-breaking forty-three years. Baker's simple but evocative staging of the piece had no dances as such, but the entire musical flowed together like a folk ballet. Later he brought a similar flavor to the musicals by GRETCHEN CRYER and NANCY FORD—*Now Is the Time for All Good Men* (1967), *THE LAST SWEET DAYS OF ISAAC* (1970), and *I'M GETTING MY ACT TOGETHER AND TAKING IT ON THE ROAD* (1978).

BAKER'S WIFE, THE (1976). Probably the most famous and beloved Broadway-bound musical that never made it to Broadway, the show has received many regional productions as well as two London runs and still demands to be heard because of its brilliant STEPHEN SCHWARTZ score. The problematic libretto by JOSEPH STEIN was based on the 1938 French film by Marcel Pagnol about a provincial baker whose young wife runs off with a local lad, causing the older husband such grief that he stops baking. The town is distraught and they try to locate the wife but she has tired of the affair and returns on her own. This rather thin and predictable story did not adapt well to the musical stage and the pre-Broadway touring show went through a series of directors, choreographers, and actors before producer DAVID MERRICK called it quits. Yet Schwartz's score, arguably his finest, was recorded with Paul Sorvino and PATTI LuPONE as the baker and his wife and interest in the musical grew. It was produced Off Broadway in 1985 and in London in 1989 and again in 1995, but none of the productions solved the book problems and both failed to run. All the same, the musical continues to be produced by regional and college theatres. Writing in a much more conventionally romantic style than was typical of him, Schwartz came up with the wistful character number "Gifts of Love," the questioning ballad "Where Is the Warmth?," the evocative French cafe song "Chanson," the narrative "Meadowlark," and other outstanding songs, which have found life outside of the musical.

BALALAIKA (MGM 1939). Based on a 1936 London operetta that never made it to Broadway, this costume drama set to music was set in Russia in revolutionary times but often resembled the old European romances with royalty in disguise as gypsies. All that was kept from the stage work was "At the Balalaika," and the basic story was reworked by Leon Gordon, Charles Bennett, and Jacques Deval as a vehicle for NELSON EDDY. He played Prince Peter Karagin who assumes the guise of a lowly music student in order to woo the revolutionary peasant Lydia Pavlovna (ILONA MASSEY). He helps her become an opera singer and she saves his life by warning him of an assassination at the opera house. Their troubled romance was complicated by the presence of such beloved character actors as CHARLES RUGGLES, FRANK MORGAN, Lionel Atwill, C. Aubrey Smith, Dalies Frantz, and Joyce Compton. GEORGE FORREST and ROBERT WRIGHT penned lyrics for some new music by HERBERT STOTHART and a potpourri of classical pieces taken from Chopin, Bizet, Lehar, Glinka, and Rimsky-Korsakov. Eddy's popularity and the renewed interest in all things Russian (as war escalated in Europe, it looked like Russia would be America's new ally) helped the film do well at the box office. Reinhold Schunzel directed the mostly male cast who often broke out into stirring choral singing.

BALANCHINE, GEORGE [born Gyorgi Melitonovitch Balanchivadzel] (1904–1983). Stage and film choreographer. Arguably the most renowned ballet master of the twentieth century, he also contributed outstanding choreography for over a dozen Broadway musicals. Born in St. Petersburg, Russia, Balanchine danced for impresarios Diaghilev and Colonel de Basil in his native city before moving to London where he choreographed West End revues. He relocated to New York City in 1934 and founded the American Ballet School and the New York Ballet Company. While continuing in classical ballet, he made his Broadway choreography debut with the ZIEGFELD FOLLIES (1936) and, later that year, caused a sensation with his extended dance sequences in RODGERS and HART's ON YOUR TOES, most memorably the jazzy "Slaughter on Tenth Avenue" ballet. Balanchine choreographed the subsequent Rodgers and Hart musicals BABES IN ARMS (1937), I MARRIED AN ANGEL (1938), and THE BOYS FROM SYRACUSE (1938) and then served as co-director as well as choreographer for the landmark folk musical CABIN IN THE SKY (1940). His stage work was so impressive that he was the first artist to be billed as a "choreographer" on Broadway; previous credits usually said "dances by" or "musical numbers staged by." Work with his own ballet school and company decreased his Broadway activities in the 1940s and 1950s, yet he still found time to choreograph LOUISIANA PURCHASE (1940), SONG OF NORWAY (1944), WHERE'S CHARLEY? (1948), and others. For Hollywood, Balanchine did the ballet sections of the films THE GOLDWYN FOLLIES (1938), On Your Toes (1939), STAR-SPANGLED RHYTHM (1942), Follow the Boys (1944), and The Turning Point (1977). He spent the last decades of his life exclusively in classical ballet. Although he came from a European background and a strictly classical form of dance, Balanchine's work on Broadway was often witty and playful in a very American way. Biographies: Balanchine, Bernard Taper (revised 1984); Portrait of Mr. Balanchine, L. Kirstein (1984).

BALL, LUCILLE [Désirée] (1911–1989). Television, film, and stage performer and producer. The undisputed queen of early television, she appeared in over seventy movies before I Love Lucy in 1951, playing everything from glamour girls to innocent ingénues to smart-aleck sidekicks. Ball was born in Jamestown, New York, the daughter of a telephone lineman and a pianist, and went to New York as a teenager to study drama and try to get into the chorus of Broadway musicals but the closest she got to show business was modeling fur coats. Having no luck, she went to California and was selected as one of the Goldwyn Girls, appearing in small roles in musicals such as *Broadway Through a Keyhole* (1933), *ROMAN SCANDALS* (1933), *Moulin Rouge* (1934), *Murder at the Vanities* (1934), *KID MILLIONS* (1934), *ROBERTA* (1935), *TOP HAT* (1935), *I DREAM TOO MUCH* (1935), *FOLLOW THE FLEET* (1936), *JOY OF LIVING* (1938), *Having Wonderful Time* (1938), and *Dance, Girl, Dance* (1940). Ball was finally the leading lady in *TOO MANY GIRLS* (1940), in which she played rich coed Connie Casey but her singing was dubbed. Also in the film was DESI ARNAZ who would become her husband and co-star on television. Her other notable musical roles in Hollywood were nightclub entertainer May Daly who becomes Lady DuBarry in *DUBARRY WAS A LADY* (1943), the movie star "Lucille Ball" who attends a prom at a military academy in *BEST FOOT FORWARD* (1943), and the nouveau riche Agatha in *Fancy Pants* (1950). Her other musicals include *Seven Day's Leave* (1942), *Thousands Cheer* (1943), and *ZIEGFELD FOLLIES* (1946). Ball never became a true star until television where she was not only an inspired clown but a savvy producer and the first woman to own her own studio, Desilu. She later appeared in a handful of film comedies but her two forays into musicals were not successful: as the energetic Wildcat Jackson in the Broadway show *WILDCAT* (1960) and as Mame Dennis in the 1974 film version of *MAME*. Her children are performers Desi Arnaz, Jr. (1953–) and Lucie Arnaz (1951–). Autobiography: *Love, Lucy* (1964/1989); biographies: *Lucille: The Life of Lucille Ball*, Kathleen Brady (2001); *Desilu: The Story of Lucille Ball and Desi Arnaz*, Coyne S. Sanders, Tom Gilbert (1994).

BALLARD, KAYE [born Catherine Gloria Balotta] (1926–). Stage and television performer. A short, squat comic actress and singer with a loud Broadway belt, she has appeared in many Broadway shows over a period of fifty years, yet has been more recognized for her television appearances. A native of Cleveland, Ohio, where she first started performing, Ballard later went into vaudeville on the RKO circuit. She made her Manhattan legit debut Off Broadway in 1946 but didn't get recognition until her sultry, funny Helen in the musical *THE GOLDEN APPLE* (1954). She also shone as the magician's assistant Rosalie in *CARNIVAL* (1961), in the revivals of *WONDERFUL TOWN* (1963) and *THE PIRATES OF PENZANCE* (1981), as Gertrude Berg in the biographical musical

Molly (1973), and in a series of one-person shows in the 1980s and 1990s. Ballad played the stepsister Portia in the original television broadcast of *CINDERELLA* (1957) and many other television appearances followed, including comedy series and specials, and a featured role in the original TV musical *Li'l Abner in Dogpatch Today* (1978). She has also appeared in a handful of films, including the musical *The Girl Most Likely* (1957). Ballard was still acting on the New York stage in 2000.

BALLROOM. See *QUEEN OF THE STARDUST BALLROOM*

BAND WAGON, THE (New Amsterdam Theatre 1931). The best of the ARTHUR SCHWARTZ (music) and HOWARD DIETZ (lyrics) shows and, in the opinion of many, the greatest of all Broadway revues, this beloved musical was as innovative as it was enjoyable. The outstanding cast included FRED and ADELE ASTAIRE, FRANK MORGAN, HELEN BRODERICK, Philip Loeb, John Barker, and Tillie Losch and they all shone in GEORGE S. KAUFMAN's sketches, which were timely and hilarious. The revue also boasted creative direction by HASSARD SHORT who used sliding platforms, moving mirrors, and twin turntables to move the action and highlight ALBERTINA RASCH's stunning choreography. The marvelous Dietz and Schwartz score was filled with future standards: the entrancing waltz "Dancing in the Dark," the oom-pah-pah favorite "I Love Louisa," and the jaunty "New Sun in the Sky." Other numbers included "High and Low," "Sweet Music," "Hoops," and "White Heat." MAX GORDON produced the large-scale production, yet it still had the intimate, elegant quality that distinguished 1930s reviews. Even in the depths of the Depression, the show ran 260 performances. The musical also marked the last Broadway show for Adele Astaire; soon after closing she married a British lord and retired even though she was at the peak of her popularity.

The Band Wagon (MGM 1953) shared nothing but Astaire and a few of the Dietz–Schwartz songs from Broadway, but the film is its own kind of masterwork, poking fun at pretentious musical theatre, backstage movie musicals, detective thrillers, and "let's put on a show" formula films.

Plot: The song-and-dance man Tony Hunter is washed up in show business, getting older with the new style of shows passing him by. Needing a hit comeback vehicle on Broadway,

Cast for *The Band Wagon* (1953 film)	
Character	*Performer*
Tony Hunter	FRED ASTAIRE
Gabrielle Gerard	CYD CHARISSE
Lester Marton	OSCAR LEVANT
Lily Marton	NANETTE FABRAY
Jeffrey Cordova	JACK BUCHANAN
Paul Byrd	JAMES MITCHELL
Colonel Tide	Thurston Hall

he enlists his songwriter friends Lily and Lester Marton to write a tuneful score that will highlight his talents, convinces the popular ballerina Gabrielle Gerard to be his leading lady, and hires the temperamental but brilliant in-vogue director Jeffrey Cordova to stage the show. But Cordova turns the piece into a ponderous musical based on the Faust legend and the musical flops out of town. Once everyone realizes the importance of "entertainment," they rework the show into a light musical comedy revue and it's a smash.

BETTY COMDEN and ADOLPH GREEN wrote the satiric screenplay (the Martons were thinly disguised versions of themselves, just as Jeffrey was based in parts on Orson Welles, JOSÉ FERRER, and VINCENTE MINNELLI who directed the film), and producer ARTHUR FREED hired Dietz and Schwartz to write "That's Entertainment," the movie's only new song. All the other numbers came from the team's various Broadway revues, and the film became a tribute to the talent and versatility of the underappreciated songwriting duo. Musical highlights include

The Band Wagon (film) Musical Numbers
"By Myself"
"A Shine on Your Shoes"
"The Beggar Waltz"
"You and the Night and the Music"
"High and Low"
"Something to Remember You By"
"Dancing in the Dark"
"I Love Louisa"
"That's Entertainment"
"New Sun in the Sky"
"I Guess I'll Have to Change My Plan"
"Louisiana Hayride"
"Triplets"
"The Girl Hunt"

Astaire and Charisse gliding through a moonlit Central Park to the strains of "Dancing in the Dark," Buchanan and Astaire doing a debonair soft shoe to "I Guess I'll Have to Change My Plan," Astaire and LeRoy Daniels tapping through a Times Square penny arcade to "A Shine on Your Shoes," and the hilarious "Triplets" with Astaire, Fabray, and Buchanan howling as three obnoxious infants.

The musical climaxes with a modern mock ballet "The Girl Hunt" in which Astaire, speaking the sly first-person narration written by ALAN JAY LERNER, plays a hard-boiled private eye caught up in a case of bad women and intrigue in a crime-ridden dive. The extended number not only spoofed the then-popular Mickey Spillane novels, but was a wry commentary on the arty ballets Hollywood had recently given the public. "The Girl Hunt" can be seen as the climax and summation of both Astaire's remarkable career and the series of Freed musicals at MGM. Michael Kidd was the film's expert choreographer, and the performances throughout were resplendent. It certainly gave Fabray and Buchanan the best roles of their screen careers. The movie was also Charisse's first starring role and, although what little singing she did was dubbed by India Adams, she is dazzling. Before *The Band Wagon*, Astaire had been considering retirement, feeling he was no longer able to keep up with GENE KELLY and the younger generation. The success of the film revitalized his career.

BARBIER, GEORGE (1865–1945). Film performer. A busy character actor in all genres of film, he excelled at older authority figures who blustered and fretted with a harmless air. Barbier was born in Philadelphia and was educated for the ministry before going on the stage. He made his Broadway debut in 1900 and was featured in several dramas and comedies before going to Hollywood in 1930. Barbier appeared in hundreds of feature films over the next two decades, rarely getting a major role but usually getting a juicy one. His many musicals include *THE SMILING LIEUTENANT* (1931), *ONE HOUR WITH YOU* (1932), *THE BIG BROADCAST* (1932), *THE PHANTOM PRESIDENT* (1932), *Hello, Everybody!* (1933), *THE MERRY WIDOW* (1934), *COLLEGE RHYTHM* (1934), *Broadway Gondolier* (1935), *ON THE AVENUE* (1937), *Little Miss Broadway* (1938), *SWEETHEARTS* (1938), *WEEK-END IN HAVANA* (1941), *Song of the Islands* (1942), *YANKEE DOODLE DANDY* (1942), and *HELLO, FRISCO, HELLO* (1943).

BARI, LYNN [born Marjorie Schuyler Fisher] (1913–1989). Film and television performer. Billed as the "Girl with the Million-Dollar Figure," the dark-haired, apple-cheeked actress played the "other woman" in many Hollywood musicals. Bari was born in Roanoke, Virginia, and grew up in Boston and Los Angeles where she got bit parts in such musicals as *DANCING LADY* (1933), *Stand Up and Cheer* (1934), *GEORGE WHITE'S SCANDALS* (1935), *Music is Magic* (1935), *THANKS A MILLION* (1935), *ON THE AVENUE* (1937), and *REBECCA OF SUNNYBROOK FARM* (1938). The curvaceous beauty graduated to supporting roles with *Walking Down Broadway* (1938), *Battle of Broadway* (1938), *Pack Up Your Troubles* (1939) and other B pictures. When she made quality features, Bari often played the type that women dislike and men crave. By the mid-1940s she was the most idolized pin-up gal for GIs after BETTY GRABLE. Bari's musicals in this era include *LILLIAN RUSSELL* (1940), *SUN VALLEY SERENADE* (1941), *ORCHESTRA WIVES* (1942), *HELLO, FRISCO, HELLO* (1943), *Sweet and Low Down* (1944), and *Margie* (1946). She made many nonmusicals after the war, as well as the musicals *On the Sunny Side of the Street* (1951), *Has Anybody Seen My Gal?* (1952), and *I Dream of Jeanie* (1952), as well as in television where she acted through the 1960s.

BARKER, RICHARD [born Henry de Grey Warter] (1834–1903). Stage director. A pioneering British director of musicals and operettas, he spent a portion of his career in America. It is believed that Barker was born in Bath, England, the son of landed gentry, and was on the stage as a low comedian by 1860. At the same time he pursued a career as a stage director for stock companies and, eventually, London productions. Barker excelled at musical burlesques, operettas, and opera comiques and was one of the first highly paid directors in London, his services considered worth the price. He was long associated with producer Richard D'Oyly Carte and staged many productions at the Savoy Theatre, including works by Gilbert and Sullivan. Barker came to New York in the 1880s and restaged some of his London successes, as well as new pieces, and then returned to England in 1900 to resume his association at the Savoy. Among his thiry-eight New York credits were *The Lion Tamer* (1891), *The Little Trooper* (1894), *The Chieftain* (1895), *The Little Corporal* (1898), and the first Broadway productions of Gilbert and Sullivan's *THE MIKADO* (1885), *Ruddigore* (1887), and *The Yeoman of the Guard* (1888). In a day when directors of musical were little more than traffic managers on stage, Barker had very definite ideas about the movement of actors and the importance of creating an overall visual effect. His work in New York influenced the next generation of American directors and led to a more cohesive staging of musicals.

BARKLEYS OF BROADWAY, THE (MGM 1949). After nine years of partnering with other stars, FRED ASTAIRE and GINGER ROGERS were reteamed for the last time in this tenth musical starring America's favorite dancing couple. When Astaire crooned "You'd Be Hard to Replace" to Rogers, moviegoers wholeheartedly agreed. The screenplay, by BETTY COMDEN and ADOLPH GREEN, involved a pair of dancing stars, Josh and Dinah Barkley, whose career and marriage are threatened by her wish to abandon hoofing and pursue serious acting roles. There were few surprises in the story and the audience came to the decision that Dinah belonged in musical comedy long before she did. BILLIE BURKE, Gale Robbins, GEORGE ZUCCO, CLINTON SUNDBERG, and OSCAR LEVANT were also cast, the last joining Astaire and Rogers for the wry comic number "A Weekend in the Country" and playing Tchaikowsky's "Concerto in B-flat Minor." The new songs, by HARRY WARREN (music) and IRA GERSHWIN (lyrics) in their only collaboration, were all winners, including the Barkleys' "Bouncin' the Blues" at rehearsal, spoofing Scottish dourness in "My One and Only Highland Fling," and Astaire's "Shoes With Wings On" in which he got to dance with dozens of disembodied white shoes. Astaire and Rogers reprised the Gershwins' "They Can't Take That Away From Me," which they had sung on screen twelve years earlier; it was a touching finale to a magical collaboration. ARTHUR FREED produced, CHARLES WALTERS directed, and ROBERT ALTON and HERMES PAN joined Astaire in devising the choreography.

BARNABEE, HENRY CLAY (1833–1917). Stage performer. A horse-faced baritone who was a favorite in operettas, the durable actor–singer played the great comic roles in the musicals of the nineteenth century. Barnabee was born in Jamaica Plains, Massachusetts, and left school to pursue an acting career. He made his professional stage debut in 1865 at the Music Hall in Boston and was soon a member of the distinguished Boston Ideal Opera Company for over two decades, serving as their principal comedian. Barnabee shone as Sir Joseph Porter in *H.M.S. PINAFORE* and other Gilbert and Sullivan comic roles, but he was best remembered for his blustering Sheriff of Nottingham in the operetta *ROBIN HOOD*, a role he played over 2000 times in New York and across the country. Autobiography: *My Wanderings* (1913).

BARNUM (St. James Theatre 1980). Although it may have come nowhere close to capturing the audacious showman P. T. Barnum on stage, the musical was still highly entertaining and JIM DALE in the title role was as much fun as a three-ring circus so few seemed to mind another fictionalized musical biography. Mark Bramble's libretto used the framework of a circus to tell Barnum's story, and the various events and characters in his life were introduced like big-top attractions. Impresario P. T. Barnum searches for oddities, woos and wins the practical Chairy (GLENN CLOSE), has a fling with Swedish singer Jenny Lind (Marianne Tatum), and ends up running the circus with the Ringling Brothers. Also featured in the agile cast were Terri White and Leonard John Crofoot. CY COLEMAN (music) and MICHAEL STEWART (lyrics) wrote the lively score that included the wistful ballad "The Colors of My Life," the jubilant "Join the Circus" and "Come Follow the Band," the jaunty "I Like Your Style," the peppy "Bigger Isn't Better," the clever patter number "Museum Song," and the graceful "Love Makes Such Fools of Us

Barnum. If the real P. T. Barnum was as agile, funny, and delightful as Jim Dale, he could have quit the circus and been a Broadway star. Which is what Dale became after his tour de force performance that involved everything from juggling to singing a rapid patter song to tightrope walking. (Photofest)

All." JOE LAYTON directed and choreographed with inventive and colorful theatrics, and Dale endeared himself to audiences by singing, dancing, walking a tightrope, clowning, and riding a unicycle, most of which had nothing to do with anything. Critics carped but playgoers knew a fun show when they saw one so the musical ran 854 performances

BART, LIONEL [born Lionel Begleiter] (1930–1999). Stage, film, and television composer and lyricist. Of the few British songwriters to find success in America, Bart only had one hit on Broadway but it was a significant one. He was born in the East End of London, the son of a tailor, and as a teenager won a scholarship to study at St. Martin's School of Art. Bart's first job was as a scene painter in the theatre but he soon switched to songwriting. After writing hit songs for British pop singers TOMMY STEELE and Cliff Richard, he found success in the West End with *Fings Ain't Wot They Used to Be* (1959) and *Lock Up Your Daughters* (1959). It was Bart's score for *OLIVER!* (1960) that secured his reputation and when it opened on Broadway in 1963 it was one of very few London musicals to be a hit in the States. Bart's subsequent London musicals *Blitz!* (1962), *Maggie May* (1964), and *Twang!* (1965) never came to New York and his Broadway effort *La Strada* (1969) was short-lived. His TV musical *DR. JEKYLL AND MR. HYDE* (1975) was filmed in London and shown on American television. Bart also composed theme songs for films, such as the James Bond movie *From Russia With Love* (1963). Bad business decisions (he sold off all his rights to *Oliver!* to finance a flop show) and alcoholism contributed to his premature death. Bart had no musical training, yet his songs were spontaneous and contagious and his lyrics delightful in a music hall flavor. Biography: *Bart!*, D. Roper (1994).

BART, ROGER (1962–). Stage, film, and television performer. A small, lively character actor with a continual smirk, he has shone in several musicals and promises to become one of Broadway's best clowns. Bart was born in Norwalk, Connecticut, and educated at the Mason Gross School of Arts at Rutgers University. He made his Broadway debut in 1987 as a replacement for the role of Tom Sawyer in *BIG RIVER* and then appeared on television before returning to the stage as Harlequin in *Triumph of Love* (1997). Bart was widely applauded for his Snoopy in the

1999 Broadway revival of *YOU'RE A GOOD MAN, CHARLIE BROWN* and then received rave notices when he originated the role of the stylish, affected Carmen Ghia in *THE PRODUCERS* (2001). He reprised his performance in the 2005 film version and during the long Broadway run played Leo Bloom for hundreds of performances. Bart was featured as NATHAN LANE's sidekick Xanthias in the musical *The Frogs* (2004) and finally moved from supporting to leading player as Dr. Frederick Frankenstein in *YOUNG FRANKENSTEIN* (2007). He has provided the voices for animated films and television, such as the singing voice of Young Hercules in *HERCULES* (1997), and continues to perform in films and television programs.

BARTON, JAMES (1890–1962). Stage and film performer. A singing–dancing comic in burlesque and vaudeville, he later developed into an accomplished character actor with musical credits on Broadway and in Hollywood. Born in Gloucester, New Jersey, to parents in a minstrel show, Barton was on the stage by the age of two and his years in vaudeville allowed him to polish his comic dancing and popular drunk routine. He was doing his bits on Broadway by 1919, appearing in such revues as *THE PASSING SHOW* (1919 and 1924), *ARTISTS AND MODELS* (1925), and *Sweet and Low* (1930), as well as character parts in the book musicals *The Last Waltz* (1921), *The Rose of Stamboul* (1922), and *Dew Drop Inn* (1923). As he matured into a growly voiced, weathered-faced performer, Barton played serious roles in such plays as *Tobacco Road* (1934 and 1943) and *The Iceman Cometh* (1946). His best musical role was the wistful prospector Ben Rumson in *PAINT YOUR WAGON* (1951). Barton worked in Hollywood on occasion, playing crusty, bigger-than-life types in nonmusical films, such as Kit Carson in *The Time of Your Life* (1948), and in 1950s musicals, such as *The Daughter of Rosie O'Grady* (1950), *WABASH AVENUE* (1950), *HERE COMES THE GROOM* (1951), and *Golden Girl* (1951).

BARTY, BILLY (1924–2000). Film and television performer. Hollywood's most famous and recognized "midget" actor, he played mischievous imps who livened up some screen musicals. Barty was born in Millsboro, Pennsylvania, and was performing by the age of three. He played MICKEY ROONEY's kid brother in a series of comedy shorts in the late 1920s and early 1930s and then appeared in features when sound came in. Among his musical credits are *GOLD DIGGERS OF 1933*, *FOOTLIGHT PARADE* (1933),

ROMAN SCANDALS (1933), *Gift of Gab* (1934), *The Wonderful World of the Brothers Grimm* (1962), *JUMBO* (1962), *Roustabout* (1964), and *Harum Scarum* (1965). Barty appeared in dozens of television programs, had his own kids show, and was acting up to the year of his death. Educated at Los Angeles City College and State University, the three-foot, nine-inch Barty championed the cause of short performers, founding the Little People of America in 1957 and the Billy Barty Foundation in 1975.

BASIE, COUNT [born William Allen Basie] (1904–1984). Film and television musician, conductor, and composer. A popular African American pianist and conductor, he brought his jazz band and its intoxicating music to the screen in eight musicals. Basie was born in Red Bank, New Jersey, and began his career as a piano accompanist for vaudeville. He played with Bernie Moten's orchestra in Kansas City before forming his own jazz band in 1936. Basie's band, as well as his songs, such as "One O'Clock Jump," "Good Morning Blues," and "Jumpin' at the Woodside," was very popular by the 1940s when he appeared as himself in such screen musicals as *Hit Parade of 1943*, *Top Man* (1943), *Crazy House* (1943), and *STAGE DOOR CANTEEN* (1943). Basie remained a top attraction for decades, performing in concerts, nightclubs, many television shows, and later movies such as *Jamboree* (1957), *Cinderfella* (1960), *Made in Paris* (1966), and *Blazing Saddles* (1974). Autobiography: *Good Morning Blues*, with Albert Murray and Dan Morgenstern (2002); biography: *The World of Count Basie*, Stanley Dance (1985).

BASS, JULES. See RANKIN, Arthur.

🎭 ***BAT BOY*** (Union Square Theatre 2001). An Off Broadway musical inspired by the sensational headlines found in tabloid newspapers, the show was odd but endearing in an inexplicable way. When a creature, half-bat, half-boy, is discovered in the hills of West Virginia, the sheriff (Richard Pruitt) brings him to the house of Dr. Thomas Parker (Sean McCourt), the local veterinarian, where he is befriended by the vet's wife Meredith (Kaitlin Hopkins) and their teenage daughter Shelley (Kerry Butler). They educate the creature, whom they name Edgar (Deven May), and he turns out to be quite a scholar, getting a diploma through a correspondence school. But Dr. Parker is insanely jealous of the affection his wife and daughter are showing to Edgar and spreads the word that the creature is the reason the local cattle are dying and he even injects a local girl with poison and says that Bat Boy killed her. The townspeople rise up in anger and search for Edgar but he runs off with Shelley and the two make love, only to be discovered by Meredith and told that Edgar is Shelley's half-brother. The crowd and Dr. Parker surround the creature, Edgar goads the vet to kill him, which he does (as well as himself and Meredith), and Shelley is left to mourn the death of Bat Boy. The script by Keythe Farley and Brian Flemming moved from satire to romance, and the songs by Laurence O'Keefe were similarly silly and touching, such as "Comfort and Joy," "Christian Charity," "Inside Your Heart," "Show You a Thing or Two," and "A Joyful Noise." Scott Schwartz directed the offbeat musical, which had originated in Los Angeles, and it found an audience for 260 performances.

BATTLE, HINTON (1956–). Stage, television, and film performer. The charismatic African American dancer–actor has been singled out and often awarded for each of his Broadway appearances. Battle was born in Neubraecke, Germany, to American parents in the military and he grew up on different army bases across America. He attended the University of California at Los Angeles and trained at the School of American Ballet and the Jones-Hayward School of Ballet before making a sensational Broadway debut as the seemingly spineless Scarecrow in THE WIZ (1975). He was featured in the revues DANCIN' (1980) and SOPHISTICATED LADIES (1981), took over the role of Billy Thunder in DREAMGIRLS (1983), and triumphed as the tap-dancing Uncle Dipsey in THE TAP DANCE KID (1983). Battle originated the role of the Vietnam vet John in the Broadway version of MISS SAIGON (1991) and was one of the many performers to play the slippery lawyer Billy Flynn in the long-running revival of CHICAGO (1998). He has performed in television specials and series and in a few films, such as the tap-dancing demon on *Buffy the Vampire Slayer* (2001) and the mobster Wayne in *Dreamgirls* (2006).

BAXTER, WARNER [Leroy] (1889–1951). Film and stage performer. The dapper leading man in silent films, he played dashing men about town in many talkies, including some memorable musicals. Baxter was born in Columbus, Ohio, and was on the vaudeville stage and worked in stock before making it to Broadway

in 1917. He started appearing in silent movies in 1914 and soon became a matinee idol of sorts. In his first sound film, *In Old Arizona* (1929), he proved to be a serious actor as well. Baxter was featured in the musicals *Stand Up and Cheer* (1934), KING OF BURLESQUE (1935), *Vogues of 1938* (1937), and LADY IN THE DARK (1944), but he is most remembered as the moody theatrical producer Julian Marsh putting on a show in 42ND STREET (1933). Baxter's career fell apart in the 1940s, suffered a nervous breakdown, and underwent a lobotomy before dying of pneumonia.

BAYES, NORA [born Dora Goldberg] (1880– 1928). Stage performer and songwriter. A tiny, deep-voiced belter who shone in vaudeville and Broadway revues, she introduced several song standards in the early years of the twentieth century. It is believed that Bayes was born in Joliet, Illinois, although during her life she gave other locations as her birthplace. She made her vaudeville debut in Chicago in 1899 and was on Broadway by 1901, starring in three editions of the ZIEGFELD FOLLIES, most memorably the 1908 production in which she introduced "Shine On, Harvest Moon," a song she co-wrote. Bayes also appeared the revues *Maid in America* (1915), *The Cohan Revue of 1918* (1917), *Her Family Tree* (1920), and *Snapshots of 1921*. She was featured in such book musicals as *The Jolly Bachelors* (1910), *Little Miss Fix-It* (1911), *Roly Poly* (1912), *Ladies First* (1918), and *Queen o' Hearts* (1922), but she always played herself and most pleased audiences by stepping out of the plot and delivering hit songs such as "Take Me Out to the Ball Game," "Has Anybody Here Seen Kelly?," "Over There," and "The Japanese Sandman." Bayes was married to dancer–songwriter JACK NORWORTH.

BEACH, GARY (1947–). Stage, television, and film performer. A full-voiced, singer–actor on Broadway, he has found most success as an inanimate object and in gay characters. Beach was born in Alexandria, Virginia, and educated at the North Carolina School of the Arts before working in summer stock and in national tours. He made his Broadway debut as a replacement in *1776* in 1970, followed by roles in the musicals *Something's Afoot* (1976) and *The Moony Shapiro Songbook* (1981). He played Duke in the short-lived *Doonesbury* (1983) but got to originate the stage version of the candlestick Lumiere in the long-running BEAUTY AND THE BEAST (1994). Beach finally found wide acclaim as the flamboyant director Roger De Bris in *THE PRODUCERS* (2001), a performance he got to reprise in the 2005 film version. Most recently he was starred in two revivals: as the drag star Albin in *LA CAGE AUX FOLLES* (2004) and Thenardier in *LES MISÉRABLES* (2006). Beach has acted in some films and many television series and specials, including the 1983 TV version of *Doonesbury*.

BEAN, ORSON [born Dallas Frederick Burroughs] (1928–). Stage, television, and film performer. The lightweight, genial actor rarely played leading roles but was always noticed as sidekicks and comic foils to the hero. Bean was born in Burlington, Vermont, and performed as a magician as a boy. In the early 1950s he started doing magic, comedy, and commentary in Manhattan nightclubs and was on Broadway by 1953, usually in comedies and musicals. Bean appeared in the revue *John Murray Anderson's Almanac* (1953) and was featured in the book musicals *Say, Darling* (1959), *SUBWAYS ARE FOR SLEEPING* (1961), *Illya Darling* (1967), and a replacement in *THE ROAR OF THE GREASEPAINT—THE SMELL OF THE CROWD* (1965) and *I'M GETTING MY ACT TOGETHER AND TAKING IT ON THE ROAD* (1981). Always outspoken on matters of politics, Bean was blacklisted by the film studios in the 1950s but afterward gave some impressive dramatic performances, as in *Anatomy of a Murder* (1959) and *Being John Malkovich* (1999). He is most known from his hundreds of appearances on television series, quiz programs, and talk shows.

BEATLES, THE. Film performers, musicians, and songwriters. The most influential rock group of the twentieth century, the British foursome and their songs made some significant film appearances. The quartet consisted of John Lennon (1940–1980), Ringo Starr (1940–), Paul McCartney (1942–), and George Harrison (1943–2001); although Lennon and McCartney were the primary songwriters, all four contributed to the scores of their live-action films, *A HARD DAY'S NIGHT* (1964) and *HELP!* (1965), and the animated *YELLOW SUBMARINE* (1968). The Beatles disbanded in 1970 but their songs were used in such films as *All This and World War II* (1976), *Sgt. Pepper's Lonely Hearts Club Band* (1978), *I Wanna Hold Your Hand* (1978), and *ACROSS THE UNIVERSE* (2007). The foursome can be seen together in the documentary *Let It Be* (1970) and individually in other ROCUMENTARIES and nonmusicals.

BEAUMONT, HARRY (1888–1966). Film director. A prolific director of silents and talkies, he helmed MGM's first musical, *THE BROADWAY MELODY* (1929). Beaumont was born in Abilene, Kansas, and dropped out of school to act in stock companies and vaudeville before making his first films in 1911. Over the next seven years he appeared in over seventy films, collaborated on the scripts, and started directing in 1914. Working for various studios, Beaumont became one of the most trusted and polished directors of the 1920s, handling such stars as John Barrymore and the up-and-coming JOAN CRAWFORD. With the advent of sound, MGM assigned Beaumont to helm the first all-talking, all-singing musical, and *The Broadway Melody* launched the studio's illustrious history with musicals. His subsequent musicals, which were not as impressive, include *Lord Byron of Broadway* (1930), *Children of Pleasure* (1930), *The Florodora Girl* (1930), and *Dance, Fools, Dance* (1931). Beaumont continued to direct through the 1940s but his glory days were far behind him.

BEAUTY AND THE BEAST (Disney 1991). The only animated film ever nominated for the Best Picture Oscar, the musical remains one of the studio's finest accomplishments, a magical mixture of fantasy, romance, and comedy.

Plot: In a French provincial village, the young Belle is considered odd because she likes to read books and does not fawn over the muscular huntsman Gaston like all the other unmarried girls. Also an outcast of sorts is her father Maurice, a crackpot inventor who, on his way to a country fair to show off his latest contraption, gets lost in the forest and stumbles onto a gloomy castle inhabited by enchanted objects who serve a bitter and fearsome Beast. Maurice is made prisoner in the castle and when Belle comes looking for him, she makes a bargain with the Beast: if he will let her father go, she will remain and be his prisoner. The Beast agrees and he tries to act civil toward Belle but his excitable anger gets in the way. With the help of the enchanted candlestick Lumiere, the clock Cogsworth, the teapot Mrs. Potts, and others in the castle, Belle starts to have feelings for the Beast. He lets her go to tend to her sick father only to have Gaston and the villagers, who have heard about the Beast from Maurice, attack the castle. The enchanted objects drive the horde away but the Beast is mortally wounded. Before he dies Belle tells him that she loves him, which removes the curse placed on the Beast and he is transformed back into a prince and lives to marry Belle.

Beauty and the Beast. With its Broadway-like score, engaging characters, solid plotting, and enchanting use of fantasy, this animated film accomplished what Rodgers and Hammerstein had introduced to the musical theatre five decades earlier: a truly integrated musical play. Perhaps that is why it remains the only animated movie ever nominated for the best picture Oscar. And perhaps that's why it seemed such a natural for the Broadway stage. (Photofest)

Casts for *Beauty and the Beast*

Character	1991 film (voices)	1994 Broadway
Belle	Paige O'Hara	Susan Egan
Beast	Robby Benson	TERRENCE MANN
Gaston	Richard White	Burke Moses
Mrs. Potts	ANGELA LANSBURY	BETH FOWLER
Lumiere	JERRY ORBACH	GARY BEACH
Cogsworth	David Ogden Stiers	Heath Lamberts
Maurice	Rex Everhart	TOM BOSLEY
Lefou	Jesse Corti	Kenny Raskin

Linda Woolverton adapted the famous French fairy tale into a moving drama that still allowed for farcical business and comic characters to fill out the story. Directors Gary Tousdale and Kirk Wise gave the film a soft and romantic rendering, and the superior animation and background art evoked a fantastical existence that could be both soothing and frightening. The climactic scene when the Beast is transformed back into a human because of Belle's love may be one of the most affecting in all the Disney canon.

The score by ALAN MENKEN (music) and HOWARD ASHMAN (lyrics) has a French flavor throughout, yet is clearly in the Broadway mold. The opening musical sequence, "Belle," in which characters are introduced and the situation is revealed, is worthy of the Rodgers and Hammerstein kind of musical storytelling. "Be Our Guest" has a delightful *Follies Bergere* feel to it, "Gaston" is a slaphappy drinking song, "Something There" is a poignant character number, and the Oscar-winning title song is

---

Beauty and the Beast (stage)
Musical Numbers

"Belle"
"Gaston"
"Be Our Guest"
"Something There"
"Beauty and the Beast"
"The Mob Song"
"The Battle"

---

a simple narrative raised to a warm and emotional level. The film was very popular and represented a highpoint for the new Disney era of animation in the 1990s.

🐾 **Beauty and the Beast** (Palace Theatre 1994). Disney's first venture into the Broadway arena, the musical was seen as a glorified theme park show by many wary theatre lovers when in fact it was an old-fashioned musical fantasy, the kind that had been entertaining families since the days of BABES IN TOYLAND (1903). Woolverton adapted her own screenplay into an efficient libretto, fleshing out the characters further and allowing room for additional songs written by Menken and TIM RICE who provided the lyrics because Ashman had died since the movie was released. The new numbers focused on character, as with "If I Can't Love Her," "Home," "Me," and "No Matter What," and the rousing "Human Again," which Ashman had written but was cut from the film, was restored in the Broadway version. Disney spent a bundle on the production and got a bang for every buck. "Be Our Guest" turned into a *Ziegfeld Follies* spectacle, and the depiction of the castle and other locations was stunning. The critical response was mostly negative but audiences paid no attention and the musical ran 5,461 performances. Even while it was still running, national tours crisscrossed the country and there were hundreds of productions in summer theatres and schools.

BEAVERS, LOUISE (1902–1962). Film and television performer. The frequently seen African American character actress who only rarely got to play roles beyond cooks or maids in her many films, she enlivened some musicals along the way. Beavers was born in Cincinnati and grew up in Los Angeles, beginning her career as a singer in a touring minstrel troupe. By 1924 she was doing bit parts in films and soon graduated to memorable supporting roles, some of them demanding some potent acting, as in the

dramas *Bombshell* (1933) and *Imitation of Life* (1934). Among her musical credits are GOLD DIGGERS OF BROADWAY (1929), 42ND STREET (1933), SHE DONE HIM WRONG (1933), *Rainbow on the River* (1936), HOLIDAY INN (1942), *DuBarry Was a Lady* (1943), *My Blue Heaven* (1950), *I Dream of Jeanie* (1952), and *You Can't Run Away From It* (1956). Beavers was one of the first African American performers to star in a television series, the popular *Beulah* in the early 1950s.

🎬 **BEDKNOBS AND BROOMSTICKS** (Disney 1971). One of the studio's efforts to recapture the magic (and success) of MARY POPPINS (1964), the musical fantasy with live action and animation has some marvelous sequences but has long sections that are a chore to sit through. Based on a book by Mary Norton, the screenplay by producer Bill Walsh and Don DaGardi concerns three London children (Cindy O'Callaghan, Roy Snart, and Ian Weighill) who are evacuated to the countryside to escape the Blitz and are taken in by the eccentric Eglantine Price (ANGELA LANSBURY) who is studying to become a witch through a correspondence course offered by Emelius Browne (David Tomlinson). The foursome's misadventures include traveling through the air in a magical bed and routing some German invaders with the help of a museum full of medieval armor come to life. The score by RICHARD M. and ROBERT B. SHERMAN is not their best, although there is the lovely ballad–lullaby "The Age of Not Believing" and the catchy "The Beautiful Briny" in which the humans join a selection of fish for an underwater dance contest, with the animated/live action sequence being the highlight of the film. The supporting cast of colorful character actors included Tessie O'Shea, Roddy McDowell, Sam Jaffe, Bruce Forsythe, and REGINALD OWEN. Robert Stevenson directed the musical, which did not do well at the box office initially but later became a favorite on video and DVD.

🐾 **BEGGAR'S OPERA, THE** (1728). One of the first musicals in the English language, the ballad opera by John Gay served as the model for dozens of later works, was the inspiration for THE THREEPENNY OPERA, and is still performed today. Set in the criminal world of London, the story followed the adventures of the dashing thief Macheath who falls in love with Polly, the daughter of Mr. Peachum, a ringleader and powerful fence among the beggars and pickpockets. Macheath elopes with Polly so

Peachum and his wife plan to turn their new son-in-law in to the police for the reward. Before they can, Macheath is betrayed by the prostitute Jenny who loves him and is jealous of Polly. So too is Lucy Lockit, the daughter of the jailer, and she helps Macheath escape, hoping to win his love. Recaptured and sent to the gallows, Macheath is reprieved at the last moment and returns to the arms of Polly. The action of the play is interrupted for romantic duets and rousing chorus numbers so it does not feel like a modern musical at all, but in its theatrical use of music it is the forerunner of our musical theatre. *The Beggar's Opera* was first produced in New York City in 1750 and there were major revivals in 1854, 1855, 1859, 1928, 1957, and 1973. It served as the basis not only for Kurt Weill's *The Threepenny Opera* (1933), but also for *Beggar's Holiday* (1946), an updated version of the tale by DUKE ELLINGTON (music) and JOHN LATOUCHE (lyrics).

There have been film and television versions of *The Beggar's Opera* in different languages and two British productions that are very well done. Laurence Oliver played Macheath (and did his own singing) in a 1953 film directed by Peter Brook. The movie had a dark and atmospheric look to it and the score, although abridged, was performed well by the cast, which also included Dorothy Tutin (Polly), Yvonne Furneaux (Jenny), George Devine (Peachum), Mary Clare (Mrs. Peachum), STANLEY HOLLOWAY (Mr. Lockit), and Daphne Anderson (Lucy).

A 1983 BBC-TV production directed by Jonathan Miller took plenty of liberties with the old musical but much of it was very effective. Roger Daltry made an odd and not-so-menacing Macheath and was supported by Isla Blair (Jenny), Carol Hall (Polly), Straford Johns (Peachum), PATRICIA ROUTLEDGE (Mrs. Peachum), Peter Bayliss (Lockit), and Rosemary Ashe (Lucy).

BELL FOR ADANO, A (CBS-TV 1956). John Hersey's 1944 Pulitzer Prize-winning novel had already been turned into a 1944 play with Fredric March and a 1945 film with John Hodiak as the Italian American Major Joppolo who is in charge of the occupied Italian town of Adano during World War II. The ninety-minute musical version offered Barry Sullivan as the frustrated major who tries to help the villagers but is hindered by government red tape and is eventually replaced by his superiors. But before he goes, Joppolo manages to replace the church bell that the Nazis had taken to melt down for scrap. ANNA MARIA ALBERGHETTI was the local girl who brought some romance into the major's life and some softness into the story. Also cast in the *Ford Star Jubilee* production were Edwin Steffe, Frank Yaconelli, James Howell, Marie Siletti, and Jay Novello. There were not many songs but the score by ARTHUR SCHWARTZ (music) and HOWARD DIETZ (lyrics) was lovely, including the ballad "I'm a Part of You" and the comic "Okay, Mister Major." Schwartz also produced and had some of the exteriors shot in Italy, giving the show a lush, festive atmosphere that did not match the war-torn village setting of the story. Robert Buckner wrote the teleplay and Paul Nickell directed.

BELLE OF NEW YORK, THE (Casino Theatre 1897). An American operetta that found more favor in Europe than in its home country, the musical would resurface a half a century later in Hollywood. Hugh Morton wrote the libretto about the Manhattan playboy Harry Brown (Harry Davenport) who is renounced by his reformer father Ichabod (Dan Daly) so he takes to the streets where he is "saved" by the Salvation Army lass Violet Gray (Edna May). When Ichabod hears, he is so overjoyed he promises to restore Harry's allowance if he will marry Violet. The trouble is, Harry has married Cora Angelique (Ada Dare), so Ichabod plans to annul the marriage. Violet, seeing that Harry loves Cora, purposely offends Ichabod by singing a risqué French song and the annulment is off. Gustav Kerker wrote the pleasant music for Morton's lyrics and the score had two memorable numbers, the sardonic march "The Purity Brigade" and the teasingly sexy "At Ze Naughty Folies Bergere." The musical, produced and directed by GEORGE LEDERER, was well received and ran a very profitable sixty-four performances. However, when it played in London it ran an astonishing 674 performances, making it the first American musical to run over a year in the West End. Productions in Paris and Berlin were also surprisingly successful, partially because Kerker was better known in Europe. Although *The Belle of New York* was revived on Broadway in 1900 and 1921, it was pretty much forgotten by World War II and only diehard operetta companies produce it today.

The Belle of New York (MGM 1952). How and why Hollywood dug up the old operetta is uncertain but the studio must have liked the story, which somewhat resembled the recent Broadway hit *GUYS AND DOLLS* (1950), because producer ARTHUR FREED tossed out the score and retained the turn-of-the-century setting and some of the plot. Robert O'Brien and Irving Elinson wrote the screenplay about the carefree Charlie Hill (FRED ASTAIRE) who has left five brides standing at the altar as he goes about Manhattan living the high life. But he meets his match in the Daughters of the Right worker Angela Bonfils (VERA-ELLEN) who is saving souls in the Bowery. Charlie does everything he can, including giving up his former ways, to win her and succeeds by the final reel. Also in the cast were MARJORIE MAIN, KEENAN WYNN, Alice Pearce, Gale Robbins, and CLINTON SUNDBERG. The film seems more interested in the period details than the story and it does present a picture-perfect view of old New York, particularly during the production number "Thank You, Mr. Currier, Thank You, Mr. Ives," in which Vera-Ellen (singing dubbed by Anita Ellis) appears in various Currier and Ives lithographs as she imagines season after season. The new score by HARRY WARREN (music) and JOHNNY MERCER (lyrics) included the hit song "Baby Doll," as well as "I Wanna Be a Dancin' Man," "When I'm Out With the Belle of New York," and "Seeing's Believing" in which Astaire danced up into the clouds, once again defying gravity. ROBERT ALTON was the imaginative choreographer and CHARLES WALTERS directed.

🕭 **BELLS ARE RINGING** (Shubert Theatre 1956). A conventional musical comedy, it was made special by a radiant star performance of JUDY HOLLIDAY. The talkative New Yorker Ella Peterson (Holliday) likes to chat with her clients who use the answering service Susanswerphone run by Sue (Jean Stapleton). When Ella falls in love with one of her customers, the troubled playwright Jeff Moss (SIDNEY CHAPLIN) who only knows her as the voice of an old lady, she endures a series of misadventures before the two end up in each other's arms. Also featured in the cast were Eddie Lawrence, PETER GENNARO, GEORGE S. IRVING, Bernie West, and Dort Clark. BETTY COMDEN and ADOLPH GREEN wrote the amusing libretto

and the lyrics for JULE STYNE's music and the score produced two standards, "Just in Time" and "The Party's Over." Also in the pleasing score were the determined character song "I'm Goin' Back," the flowing ballad "Long Before I Knew You," the clever list song "Drop That Name," and the comic "It's a Simple Little System." While the press hailed the tuneful score, fresh story line, and the direction and choreography by JEROME ROBBINS and BOB FOSSE, the show was mostly appreciated as a showcase for Holliday in the musical role of her too-short career. The Theatre Guild production ran 924 performances.

Bells Are Ringing was revived on Broadway in 2001 with FAITH PRINCE in the star role. As charming as she was as Ella, too many critics compared her unfavorably to Judy Holliday's stage and screen performance and the musical folded inside of nine weeks. MARC KUDISCH was a personable Jeff, and the supporting cast included BETH FOWLER (Sue) and David Garrison. Tina Landau's direction was faulted as well but there were compliments for JEFF CALHOUN's choreography.

🎬 **Bells Are Ringing** (MGM 1960) came to the screen with its Broadway star recreating her vibrant performance and giving Holliday one of her best movie roles; unfortunately, it was also her last. Comden and Green adapted their stage libretto for the screen and the film is very close to the original, only four songs were cut and two new ones ("Better Than a Dream" and "Do It Yourself") by Styne, Comden, and Green were added. DEAN MARTIN was the playwright Jeff, and Jean Stapleton, Bernie West, and Dort Clark reprised their stage performances. Charles O'Curran choreographed what little dancing was left, and VINCENTE MINNELLI directed, using actual Manhattan locations for certain scenes. The ARTHUR FREED production is nothing above the ordinary but it does preserve Holiday's performance and in doing so makes it worth watching.

BELLS OF ST. MARY'S, THE. See *GOING MY WAY*

Casts for *Bells Are Ringing*

Character	1956 Broadway	1960 film	2001 Broadway
Ella Peterson	JUDY HOLLIDAY	Judy Holliday	FAITH PRINCE
Jeffrey Moss	SYDNEY CHAPLIN	DEAN MARTIN	MARC KUDISCH
Sue	JEAN STAPLETON	Jean Stapleton	BETH FOWLER
Sandor	Eddie Lawrence	EDDIE FOY, JR.	David Garrison

BENCHLEY, ROBERT [Charles] (1889–1945). Stage and film performer and writer. A noted American humorist and theatre critic, the owlish-looking comic appeared on Broadway and in movies, always interjecting a wry and witty note. Benchley was born in Worcester, Massachusetts, and educated at Harvard where he began writing humor pieces and performing comic monologues. After graduation he worked as a journalist and later became a much-read theatre critic, yet he often returned to entertaining private gatherings with his hilarious monologues and even did some for the public in the Broadway show *MUSIC BOX REVUE* (1923). Benchley was involved with film from the early talkies, writing scripts and appearing in a series of comic shorts. He later played supporting roles in several nonmusicals and musicals, such as *DANCING LADY* (1933), *BROADWAY MELODY OF 1938* (1937), *Nice Girl* (1941), *YOU'LL NEVER GET RICH* (1941), *THE SKY'S THE LIMIT* (1943), *Pan-American* (1945), *The Stork Club* (1945), *Duffy's Tavern* (1945), and *THE ROAD TO UTOPIA* (1945) where he can be heard delivering the droll narration. His son was writer Nathaniel Benchley (1915–1981) and his grandson was writer Peter Benchley (1940–2006). Biographies: *Robert Benchley: His Life and Times,* Babette Rosmond (1989); *Robert Benchley,* Nathaniel Benchley (1956).

BENNETT, JOAN [Geraldine] (1910–1990). Film, stage, and television performer. The delicate leading lady in films for over thirty years, the nonsinging beauty was starred in several musicals opposite crooners such as JOHN BOLES and BING CROSBY. Bennett was born in Palisades, New Jersey, the daughter of acclaimed stage actor Richard Bennett (1873–1944), and educated at boarding schools in Connecticut and France. She made her Broadway debut in one of her father's plays in 1928 but that same year went to Hollywood and began her long career in which she moved from gentle ingénues to adult women to mothers to aged *grande dames.* Bennett's musical credits include *PUTTIN' ON THE RITZ* (1930), *Maybe It's Love* (1930), *Careless Lady* (1932), *MISSISSIPPI* (1935), *Two for Tonight* (1935), *Vogues of 1938* (1937), *ARTISTS AND MODELS ABROAD* (1938), and *Nob Hill* (1945). She returned to Broadway in the 1950s and 1960s and made many appearances on television, including the TV musical *JUNIOR MISS* (1957). Her sisters were actresses Constance Bennett (1904–1965) and Barbara Bennett (1906–1958).

BENNETT, MICHAEL [born Michael Di Figlia] (1943–1987). Stage choreographer, director, and performer. An outstanding director–choreographer, he had a short but spectacular career on Broadway. Bennett was born in Buffalo, the son of a machinist, and took dance lessons as a child. By the time he was a teenager he was a celebrity for his dancing on local television, so he dropped out of high school and was cast in a touring production of *WEST SIDE STORY*. This led to jobs in the chorus of Broadway musicals, such as *SUBWAYS ARE FOR SLEEPING* (1961), *Here's Love* (1963), and *Bajour* (1964), and as a featured dancer on the national television show *Hullabaloo.* Bennett started choreographing in stock in 1962 and four years later was staging musical numbers on Broadway with *A Joyful Noise* (1966) and *Henry, Sweet Henry* (1967). His choreography was first widely noticed in *PROMISES, PROMISES* (1968), followed by *Coco* (1969), *COMPANY* (1970), and *FOLLIES* (1971) in which he was also co-director with HAROLD PRINCE. *SEESAW* (1973) was Bennett's first production in which he controlled all the directorial and choreographic aspects, but resounding fame did not come until two years later with *A CHORUS LINE,* which he created in workshops and finessed all the way to Broadway for a record-breaking run. His final director–choreographer credits on Broadway were *BALLROOM* (1978) and *DREAMGIRLS* (1981). Bennett also directed a few nonmusical plays and was the uncredited play doctor on various musicals by others. A manipulative, emotional, and high-powered personality, he was both worshiped and despised by those with whom he worked. Bennett's death from AIDS at the age of forty-three cut short one of the most meteoric directing careers of the century. He was married to dancer–singer Donna McKechnie. Biographies: *"A Chorus Line" and the Musicals of Michael Bennett,* Ken Mandelbaum (1989); *One Singular Sensation: The Michael Bennett Story,* Kevin Kelly (1990).

BENNETT, ROBERT RUSSELL (1894–1981). Stage orchestrator. The leading Broadway orchestrator of the twentieth century, he did the musical arrangements for over 300 stage musicals and helped create the sound of American musicals. Bennett was born in Kansas City, Missouri, to a musical family; his father was a trumpet player and violinist, his mother a pianist. Bennett knew how to play a variety of instruments by the time he was in his teens and then studied composition and began working as a copyist for a music publisher. His first Broadway assignment was orchestrating the score for *Daffy Dill* (1922). By the time he orchestrated ROSE-MARIE two years later, Bennett was the most sought-after talent in his field. He was also the most influential orchestrator in the American theatre, helping to create the Broadway orchestra sound that is so familiar to generations of theatregoers. A list of Bennett's Broadway credits is practically a record of the musical theatre in the 1920s through the 1960s, including such classics as SHOW BOAT (1927), OF THEE I SING (1931), ANYTHING GOES (1934), ANNIE GET YOUR GUN (1946), KISS ME, KATE (1948), MY FAIR LADY (1956), and most of the Rodgers and Hammerstein musicals. Bennett arranged music for plays, films, and television programs, most memorably his orchestrations of RICHARD RODGERS' music for the television documentary series *Victory at Sea* (1954). He also composed many musical works on his own, including operas, choral pieces, tone poems, and band selections. All in all, it is estimated that Bennett orchestrated more music than any other American.

BENNY, JACK [born Benjamin Kubelsky] (1894–1974). Television and film performer. A quiet but commanding comic genius, he is most remembered for his radio and television programs, but the casual, innocent-looking actor also starred in many films, including over a dozen musicals. Benny was born in Chicago, the son of a saloonkeeper, and studied violin as a child. He never mastered the instrument but used it as part of his comic routines throughout his long career. He became popular on the vaudeville circuit before making his film debut in 1929 playing himself in HOLLYWOOD REVUE OF 1929. Benny's roles in the musicals *Chasing Rainbows* (1930), *Lord Byron of Broadway* (1930), and *Transatlantic Merry-Go-Round* (1934) led to better parts in BROADWAY MELODY OF 1936 (1935), THE BIG BROADCAST OF 1937 (1936), *College Holiday* (1936), ARTISTS AND MODELS (1937), ARTISTS AND MODELS ABROAD (1938), and *Man About Town* (1939). By the mid-1930s Benny became even more famous because of radio and was clearly the star of such film musicals as *Buck Benny Rides Again* (1940) and LOVE THY NEIGHBOR (1940). He also did guest bits in HOLLYWOOD CANTEEN (1944), *Somebody Loves Me* (1952), *Beau James* (1957), and GYPSY (1962). Benny's radio show was one of the first to successfully transfer to television and even after his own program ended in 1965 he was still a familiar face on the tube for another ten years. Autobiography: *Sunday Nights at Seven: The Jack Benny Story*, with Joan Benny (1990); biography: *Jack Benny: An Intimate Portrait*, Irving Fein (1976).

BERGEN, EDGAR [born Edgar John Bergren] (1903–1978). Film and television performer. America's premiere ventriloquist, he and his partner, the wooden dummy Charlie McCarthy, were favorites in several media, including a handful of movie musicals. Bergen was born in Chicago and created his co-star McCarthy while attending Northwestern University, with the twosome giving performances to help pay for tuition. After graduation, Bergen went on the vaudeville circuit and then found national fame when he and Charlie were on RUDY VALLEE's radio show. The concept of a ventriloquist impressing audiences on the radio was unique and even bizarre, yet the material was so strong and the characters so well defined that Bergen was a hit. The pair was featured in such film musicals as THE GOLDWYN FOLLIES (1938), *Here We Go Again* (1942), *Around the World* (1943), STAGE DOOR CANTEEN (1943), *Song of the Open Road* (1944), and *Fun and Fancy Free* (1946). Bergen created other puppet characters and featured them as well in his many concert, nightclub, and television appearances, but wisecracking, even lewd McCarthy remained the audience's favorite. The pair was last seen on film in a cameo in THE MUPPET MOVIE (1979), which creator Jim Henson dedicated to Bergen. He is the father of actress Candice Bergen (1946–).

BERGMAN, ALAN AND MARILYN. Film, television, and stage lyricists. The husband and wife team responsible for several pop hits in the 1970s, they have also scored musicals in different media. A native New Yorker, Marilyn Bergman [born Katz] (1929–) was educated at New York University and started writing theme songs for films and television in the 1960s. Alan Bergman (1925–) was born in Brooklyn and educated at UCLA and the University of North Carolina before working in Special Services during World War II. He directed shows for CBS-TV in Philadelphia after the war and married his collaborator Marilyn in 1958. The two provided lyrics for music by SAMMY FAIN, Paul Weston, MICHEL LEGRAND, MARVIN HAMLISCH, and other composers; their songs have been heard in nightclubs, on television, and in films. They also wrote special material for many stars, from Jo Stafford and FRED ASTAIRE to SAMMY

DAVIS, JR. and BARBRA STREISAND. Among their many hit singles are "The Windmills of Your Mind," "What Are You Doing for the Rest of Your Life?," and "The Way We Were." On occasion they would provide lyrics for films, as with the musicals *A STAR IS BORN* (1976) and *YENTL* (1983), and for the TV musical *QUEEN OF THE STARDUST BALLROOM* (1975), which later became the Broadway musical *BALLROOM* (1978). The team also provided the lyrics for the Broadway musicals *Something More!* (1964), *Harlem Nocturne* (1984), and *Street Corner Symphony* (1997).

BERKELEY, BUSBY [born William Berkeley Enos] (1895–1976). Stage and film choreographer and director. The nimble choreographer–director first found success on Broadway and then went to Hollywood where he revolutionized the way movie musicals were filmed. Berkeley was born in Los Angeles, the son of a stage director and a film actress, and moved with his family to New York City when he was three years old. He was on the stage as a youth and then after attending military academy and serving in World War I, he returned to the stage as an adult. Berkeley performed in stock and in small roles on Broadway before turning to choreography in the 1920s, making his New York debut in 1925. He was roundly praised for his dances in *A CONNECTICUT YANKEE* two years later, followed by *The Wild Rose* (1926), *PRESENT ARMS* (1928), *Good Boy* (1928), *Rainbow* (1928), *The Street Singer* (1929), *Sweet and Low* (1930), *Nina Rosa* (1930), and others. Berkeley's choreography differed from most Broadway dancing. Applying the military maneuvers he had learned at school, he used the human figure in an abstract, almost depersonalized way. When Hollywood beckoned, he continued to experiment with his unusual sense of dance on film, as seen in *WHOOPEE* (1930), *FLYING HIGH* (1931), *The Kid From Spain* (1932), *42ND STREET* (1933), *GOLD DIGGERS OF 1933*, *FOOTLIGHT PARADE* (1933), *ROMAN SCANDALS* (1933), *WONDER BAR* (1934), *Twenty Million Sweethearts* (1934), and *DAMES* (1934). Starting with *GOLD DIGGERS OF 1935*, Berkeley sometimes also directed, doing double duty for such musicals as *Hollywood Hotel* (1937), *BABES IN ARMS* (1939), *STRIKE UP THE BAND* (1940), *BABES ON BROADWAY* (1941), *THE GANG'S ALL HERE* (1943), and *Cinderella Jones* (1946). Among his other choreography credits were *GO INTO YOUR DANCE* (1935), *In Caliente* (1935), *The Singing Marine* (1937), *GOLD DIGGERS IN PARIS* (1938), *ZIEGFELD GIRL* (1941), *LADY, BE GOOD* (1941), *CABIN IN THE SKY* (1943), *GIRL CRAZY* (1943), *ROMANCE ON THE HIGH SEAS* (1948), *CALL ME MISTER* (1951), *Two Tickets to Broadway* (1951), *Million Dollar Mermaid* (1952), *Small Town Girl* (1953), *ROSE MARIE* (1954), and *JUMBO* (1962). Berkeley directed and others choreographed *FOR ME AND MY GAL* (1942) and *TAKE ME OUT TO THE BALL GAME* (1949). Although he never returned to Broadway to choreograph after 1930, he did "supervise" the successful 1970 revival of *NO, NO, NANETTE*. Biography: *Showstoppers: Busby Berkeley and the Tradition of Spectacle*, Martin Rubin (1993).

BERLE, MILTON [born Mendel Berlinger] (1908–2002). Television, film, and stage performer. Television's first superstar, he spent many years on the stage and in the movies before he became the beloved "Uncle Miltie" on the tube. Berle was born in New York City and was on stage at the age of five, winning talent contests by impersonating Charles Chaplin. He made a few silent films as a boy and then went into vaudeville with his sister, eventually in 1920 ending up on Broadway in the chorus of a revival of *FLORODORA*. Although Berle was featured in the musicals *EARL CARROLL VANITIES* (1932), *Saluta* (1934), *LIFE BEGINS AT 8:40* (1935), and *ZIEGFELD FOLLIES* (1943), his stage career never took off, so he concentrated on films where he never became a star but was a familiar face, as in such musicals as *NEW FACES OF 1937*, *SUN VALLEY SERENADE* (1941), *Tall, Dark and Handsome* (1941), *Rise and Shine* (1941), and *Always Leave Them Laughing* (1949). The new medium of television was a perfect outlet for his broad clowning talents and his programs in the early 1950s sold more television sets than any other factor. After the golden age of television, Berle returned to Broadway in two unsuccessful plays and had a scattered movie career, but he was always at his best in TV specials and as a guest on other peoples' programs where his vaudeville-like brand of entertainment was most appreciated. Autobiographies: *Out of My Trunk* (1945); *Milton Berle: An Autobiography*, with Haskel Frankel Berle (1974).

BERLIN, IRVING [born Israel Baline] (1888–1989). Stage and film composer and lyricist. America's favorite songwriter, he wrote hundreds of songs for Broadway, Hollywood, and Tin Pan Alley, coming up with more standards than any other figure in popular music. Berlin was born in Temun, Russia, the son of a cantor, and came to America as a child of five,

Irving Berlin. An often shy, self-deprecating man in public, as observed here in 1927 at a rehearsal with some of the chorines from the *Ziegfeld Follies*, Berlin was also a shrewd businessman and nobody's fool. Yet no other American songwriter was able to express so simply and accurately what so many people were feeling, decade after decade. (Photofest)

growing up on New York's Lower East Side. As a teenager he worked as a singing waiter while he wrote songs, although he had no musical education whatsoever. Soon his songs were being published but not until the overwhelming success of "Alexander's Ragtime Band" in 1911 did he move to the forefront of American songwriters, a position he held for five decades. Berlin's first of twenty Broadway scores was *WATCH YOUR STEP* (1914), followed by such notable book musicals as *Stop! Look! Listen!* (1915), *The Century Girl* (1916), *THE COCOANUTS* (1925), *FACE THE MUSIC* (1932), *LOUISIANA PURCHASE* (1940), *ANNIE GET YOUR GUN* (1946), *MISS LIBERTY* (1949), *CALL ME MADAM* (1950), and *MR. PRESIDENT* (1962). He was equally successful at writing songs for Broadway revues, such as *The Cohan Revue* (1917), *YIP, YIP, YAPHANK* (1918), *ZIEGFELD FOLLIES* (1919, 1920, 1927), *MUSIC BOX REVUE* (1922, 1923, 1924), *AS THOUSANDS CHEER* (1933), and *THIS IS THE ARMY* (1942). Only a few of his stage works were filmed but the songs were often used in Hollywood musicals and he wrote original scores for several movies as well. Among his film musicals are *HALLELUJAH* (1929), *Puttin' on the Ritz* (1930), *Mammy* (1930), *TOP HAT* (1935), *FOLLOW THE FLEET* (1936), *ON THE AVENUE* (1937), *ALEXANDER'S RAGTIME BAND* (1938), *CAREFREE*

(1938), *SECOND FIDDLE* (1939), *HOLIDAY INN* (1942), *BLUE SKIES* (1946), *EASTER PARADE* (1948), *WHITE CHRISTMAS* (1954), and *THERE'S NO BUSINESS LIKE SHOW BUSINESS* (1954). Berlin was a genius at capturing the feeling and concerns of America through different eras, echoing the public sentiment even as musical styles changed. His music was once considered unsophisticated and uncomplicated but over the years Berlin's work has been reevaluated and the complexity of his music and the agility of his lyrics are more appreciated than ever. Memoir: *Irving Berlin: A Daughter's Memoir*, Mary Ellen Barrett (2004); biographies: *Irving Berlin*, Jeffrey Magee (2008); *Say It With Music: The Story of Irving Berlin*, Nancy Furstinger (2003); *As Thousands Cheer: The Life of Irving Berlin*, Laurence Bergreen (1996).

BERLIND, ROGER (1931–) Stage, television, and film producer. A busy presenter of plays and musicals, his offerings are eclectic and often challenging. Berlind was born in New York and educated at Princeton before going into business where he did very well. He began his Broadway career as an associate producer for *Rex* (1976) and producer for the short-lived *Music Is* (1976), followed by some forty productions in New York ranging from American revivals to new foreign dramas. Among the musicals he has produced or co-produced are *The 1940's Radio Hour* (1979), SOPHISTICATED LADIES (1981), NINE (1982), THE RINK (1984), *Big Deal* (1986), CITY OF ANGELS (1989), GUYS AND DOLLS (1992), PASSION (1994), *Steel Pier* (1997), THE LIFE (1998), KISS ME, KATE (1999), THE WILD PARTY (2000), WONDERFUL TOWN (2003), CAROLINE, OR CHANGE (2004), CURTAINS (2007), and *LoveMusik* (2007). Berlind has also presented some television dramas and films, mostly screen versions of plays. In 2003, a new theatre at Princeton was named for him.

BERMAN, PANDRO S[amuel]. (1905–1996). Film producer. A proficient producer of musicals and comedies, he presented most of the FRED ASTAIRE–GINGER ROGERS films. Berman was born in Pittsburgh, the son of a film distributor, and began his career as an assistant director in the 1920s. By the arrival of sound he was producing features on his own, including the RKO musicals *Melody Cruise* (1933), *Hips Hips Hooray* (1934), THE GAY DIVORCEE (1934), ROBERTA (1935), TOP HAT (1935), *In Person* (1935), *I DREAM TOO MUCH* (1935), FOLLOW THE FLEET (1936), SWING TIME (1926), *That Girl From Paris* (1936), SHALL WE DANCE (1937), *A DAMSEL IN DISTRESS* (1937), *Having Wonderful Time* (1938), and CAREFREE (1938). Berman moved to MGM in 1940 and produced many pictures over the next twenty-five years, including the musicals ZIEGFELD GIRL (1941), RIO RITA (1942), *Living in a Big Way* (1947), LOVELY TO LOOK AT (1952), and JAILHOUSE ROCK (1957). He was an efficient and creative producer and knew how to cultivate up-and-coming stars, such as Katherine Hepburn, LANA TURNER, ELIZABETH TAYLOR, and ELVIS PRESLEY, in their early films.

BERNARD, SAM [born Samuel Barnett] (1863–1927). Stage performer. A plump, balding comic actor on the musical stage for over forty years, he specialized in dialect parts, particularly German Jewish immigrants. Bernard was born in Birmingham, England, and came to the States as a child. He began his career in American vaudeville and English music halls before finding fame in the 1890s in WEBER AND FIELDS Broadway burlesques, such as *The Geezer* (1896), *The Glad Hand* (1897), *Pousse Cafe* (1897), and *Hoity Toity* (1901). At the turn of the century he left Weber and Fields and starred in his own musicals, such as *The Marquis of Michigan* (1898), *A Dangerous Maid* (1898), *The Man in the Moon* (1899), *The Casino*

Girl (1900), and *The Belle of Bohemia* (1900). Bernard's most famous role was the hapless Yankee "Piggy" Hoggenheimer, a comic type from Britain, which he introduced to New York in the musical *The Girl From Kay's* (1903) and returned to in *The Rich Mr. Hoggenheimer* (1906), *The Belle of Bond Street* (1914), and *Piggy* (1927). His other musical credits include *Nearly a Hero* (1906), *The Girl and the Wizard* (1909), THE MIKADO (1910), *The Century Girl* (1916), *As You Were* (1920), MUSIC BOX REVUE (1921), and *Nifties of 1923*. Bernard occasionally returned to his native country to perform.

BERNIE, BEN [born Benjamin Anzelovitz] (1891–1943). Film and stage performer, conductor, composer, and musician. A popular bandleader with a nasal, talkative personality, he was featured in four Hollywood musicals. Bernie was born in Bayonne, New Jersey, and studied the violin at New York College of Music and the Columbia School of Music. He formed his own orchestra and played in vaudeville before graduating to high-class supper clubs and radio programs. Bernie appeared in the Broadway musical *Here's Howe* (1928) and produced *Cafe de Danse* (1929) even as he composed songs for his band and others, most memorably the standard "Sweet Georgia Brown." He and his band were featured in some film shorts and in the musical features *Shoot the Works* (1934) and *Stolen Harmony* (1935). Bernie starred in WAKE UP AND LIVE (1937) and *Love and Hisses* (1937) in which he played himself and was involved in a feud with columnist Walter Winchell, a fictitious rivalry that had been so popular in his radio broadcasts.

BERNSTEIN, LEONARD (1918–1990). Stage and film composer, lyricist, and conductor. The celebrated composer of all kinds of music and an internationally acclaimed symphony conductor, he found time in his busy career to score some outstanding Broadway musicals. Bernstein was born in Lawrence, Massachusetts, and educated at Harvard and the Curtis Institute of Music before becoming assistant conductor at the Berkshire Music Center and eventually the conductor of the New York Philharmonic. His first piece for the theatre was the ballet *Fancy Free*, which was expanded into the musical comedy ON THE TOWN (1944), written with lyricists BETTY COMDEN and ADOLPH GREEN. Bernstein wrote music and lyrics for the songs in the 1950 Broadway version of PETER PAN starring Jean Arthur before reteaming with Comden and Green for WONDERFUL TOWN (1953). His

Leonard Bernstein. Six Broadway musicals is not an impressive number for an entire career until one realizes that Bernstein was one of the most in-demand conductor–composers in the world of classical music. Here he is at the piano preparing *On the Town* with (left to right) choreographer Jerome Robbins and lyricist–librettists Betty Comden and Adolph Green. (Photofest)

score for *CANDIDE* (1956), written with various lyricists, revealed his ability to spoof the classical music forms he often conducted, and with lyricist STEPHEN SONDHEIM he created a new classic with *WEST SIDE STORY* (1957). Bernstein returned to the theatre decades later for the ill-fated musical *1600 PENNSYLVANIA AVENUE* (1976). He wrote music and lyrics for operatic pieces, such as *Trouble in Tahiti* (1952), and scored theatre–music programs that were unique, such as *Mass* (1971). His many recordings and broadcasts, series of concerts for young audiences, concert hall compositions, and years as a teacher and a conductor made Bernstein one of the most influential and well-known figures of his day. His theatre music uses

a variety of forms, from jazz to Latin to classical, and can be explosive and thrilling as well as tender and reflective. Autobiography: *Findings,* 1982; biographies: *Leonard Bernstein,* Meryle Secrest (1996); *Leonard Bernstein,* Humphrey Burton (1995).

✑ **BEST FOOT FORWARD** (Ethel Barrymore Theatre 1941). A campus musical comedy that is unique in that it is not about the big football game, this surprise hit by unknowns John Cecil Holm (book), HUGH MARTIN, and RALPH BLANE (music and lyrics) ran 326 performances. Bud Hooper, a student at Winsocki Prep School, invites movie star Gale Joy to his high school prom and to his surprise she accepts, angering his girl friend Helen Schlessinger and making the whole campus Hollywood crazy. The carefree show struck the press and the public as ideal wartime escapism and the young talent on stage was impressive, such as ROSEMARY LANE, JUNE ALLYSON, Tommy Dix, and especially NANCY WALKER as the perennial blind date. The standout hit was the contagious fight song "Buckle Down, Winsocki," and the score also included "Just a Little Joint with a Juke Box," "The Three B's," and "I Know You By Heart." GEORGE ABBOTT produced and directed the popular attraction, and GENE KELLY, who had not yet gone to Hollywood, choreographed.

The musical was revived Off Broadway in 1963 and featured another cast of unknowns with a promising future, including LIZA MINNELLI, Paula Wayne, and Christopher Walken (who was going by the name Ronald Walken). Holm made some book revisions and Martin and Blane added some songs they had written for the film *MEET ME IN ST. LOUIS* (1944) that had been cut. DANNY DANIELS directed and choreographed, and the Off Broadway entry ran 224 performances.

🎬 **Best Foot Forward** (MGM 1943) retained much of the zest of the Broadway show and even featured members of the young stage cast. Scriptwriters Irving Brecher and Fred Finklehoffe changed Winsocki to a mili-

Casts for *Best Foot Forward*

Character	1941 Broadway	1943 film	1963 Off Broadway
Bud Hooper	Gil Stratton, Jr.	Tommy Dix	Glenn Walken
Gale Joy	ROSEMARY LANE	LUCILLE BALL	Paula Wayne
Helen Schlesinger	Maureen Cannon	VIRGINIA WEIDLER	Karin Wolfe
Blind Date/Ethel	NANCY WALKER	Nancy Walker	LIZA MINNELLI
Dutch Miller	Jack Jordan, Jr.	Kenny Bowers	Ronald Walken

tary school to give the piece a more patriotic flavor, and Martin and Blane wrote three new songs for the film. Tommy Dix, who had a supporting role on Broadway, graduated to the leading character of Bud, and LUCILLE BALL, her singing dubbed by Martha Mears, played herself as the movie star who comes to campus. Among those from the Broadway production making their screen debuts were June Allyson and Nancy Walker, who reprised her hilarious Blind Date. Also cast were GLORIA DeHAVEN, WILLIAM GAXTON, Virginia Weidler, Kenny Bowers, Chill Wills, and HARRY JAMES and his Music Makers. ARTHUR FREED produced, EDWARD BUZZELL directed, and CHARLES WALTERS did the energetic choreography.

📖 **BEST LITTLE WHOREHOUSE IN TEXAS, THE** (46th Street Theatre 1978). One of a handful of 1970s musicals that was developed and showcased Off Off Broadway and then moved to Broadway for a long run, this satirical show ended up running longer than its colleagues: 1,703 performances. Larry L. King and Peter Masterson wrote the politically incorrect libretto about the infamous brothel known as the Chicken Ranch, which had been a Texas landmark since the 1840s. Its days are numbered when television evangelist Melvin P. Thorpe uses it as a platform for his patriotic, right-wing self-promotion. The local sheriff Ed Earl Dodd tries to protect the Ranch's proprietress Mona Stangley and her girls, but once Thorpe's crusade gets underway not even the governor can stop it. It was all harmless fun, played off of Southern stereotypes and, despite its title, not very provocative. Carol Hall wrote the commendable songs, which were country-flavored yet had a Broadway feel to them as well. Among the most memorable numbers were the rhythmic "20 Fans" that introduced the characters and the situation, the incisive character song "Bus From Amarillo," the plaintive "Hard Candy Christmas," the foot-stomping "The Aggie Song," the mock-gospel number "Twenty-four Hours of Lovin'," and

the wry soft-shoe "The Sidestep." Reviewers particularly lauded co-director/choreographer TOMMY TUNE's inventive dances and the estimable cast headed by Carlin Glynn and Henderson Forsythe, two veteran supporting plays who finally got to shine in leading roles on Broadway.

Most of the creative staff reassembled for the unnecessary sequel *The Best Little Whorehouse Goes Public* (1994) in which the retired Mona (Dee Hoty) is put in charge of a Las Vegas casino where her business sense helps save the bankrupt concern while the knuckle-headed Senator A. Harry Hardast (Ronn Carroll) devises a plan to put the old whorehouse on the stock exchange so everyone can share in the profits. Again some of the songs were expert but little else was condoned by the critics and the show closed after fifteen performances.

🎬 **The Best Little Whorehouse in Texas** (Universal/RKO 1982) utilized few of the talents from the Broadway hit, and the show was rewritten and scrubbed up into a moral fable in which the closing of the Chicken Ranch was viewed as a good thing. King and Peterson's screenplay adjusted the characters of Mona and the sheriff to fit movie stars Dolly Parton and Burt Reynolds, and the story was narrated by wholesome Deputy Fred played by Jim Nabors. Also in the cast were DOM DeLUISE, Lois Nettleton, THERESA MERRITT, Robert Mandan, and Charles Durning who stole the show as the shifty, two-faced governor. Some new songs were added and Parton's hit ballad "I Will Always Love You" was thrown in for good measure, but the movie rarely rose above a bland television special. Colin Higgins co-produced and directed, and Tony Stevens did the exhaustive choreography.

🎬 **BEST THINGS IN LIFE ARE FREE, THE** (Fox 1956). The celebrated songwriting team of De Sylva, Brown, and Henderson, who flourished on Broadway in the 1920s and in Hollywood in the 1930s, was the subject of this routine biomusical that was intermittently

Casts for *The Best Little Whorehouse in Texas*

Character	1978 Broadway	1982 film
Ed Earl Dodd	Henderson Forsythe	Burt Reynolds
Mona Stangley	Carlin Glynn	Dolly Parton
Melvin P. Thorpe	Clint Allmon	DOM DeLUISE
Governor	Jay Garner	Charles Durning
Jewel	Delores Hall	THERESA MERRITT
Deputy Fred		Jim Nabors

saved by the great songs in the trio's song catalog. Lyricist–librettist B. G. DE SYLVA (GORDON MACRAE), lyricist LEW BROWN (Ernest Borgnine), and composer RAY HENDERSON (DAN DAILEY) meet in Atlantic City and soon are writing "Sonny Boy" for AL JOLSON (Norman Brooks) to sing. The trio goes to Broadway and has a string of hits, the only conflicts arising being De Sylva's neglecting his partners to work on projects with others and his efforts to win the love of dancer Kitty Kane (Sheree North, singing dubbed by Eileen Wilson). At least the William Bowers–Phoebe Ephron screenplay left room for plenty of musical numbers, most memorably North and Jacques D'Amboise performing the "Black Bottom" and MacRae singing "The Birth of the Blues" as North danced. Other songs included "Button Up Your Overcoat," "Sunny Side Up," "It All Depends on You," A Talking Picture of You," "Good News," and the title number. Henry Ephron produced, MICHAEL CURTIZ directed, and Rod Alexander did the bubbly choreography.

🎵 **BETWEEN THE DEVIL** (Imperial Theatre 1937). One of the few book musicals scored by ARTHUR SCHWARTZ (music) and HOWARD DIETZ (lyrics), this farcical show was more in the style of the 1910s than the 1930s. Dietz wrote the libretto, which used a timeworn premise. Believing his wife Claudette Gilbert (Adele Dixon) has died in a shipwreck, Peter Anthony (JACK BUCHANAN) weds the pretty Natalie Rives (Evelyn Laye) only to have Claudette show up in good health soon after the wedding. The expected compilations follow but are not resolved, leaving it to the audience to determine which wife Peter sticks with. It was all fairly forgettable except for the score, which offered three hits, the haunting ballad "I See Your Face Before Me," the hilarious "Triplets," and the freewheeling "By Myself." Also heard in the show were "You Have Everything," "I'm Against Rhythm," and "Bye Bye Butterfly Lover." The press thought the tired plot irritating but highly recommended the superb songs and affable players. Patrons only took their advice for ninety-three performances. HASSARD SHORT and John Hayden co-directed the SHUBERT production, and ROBERT ALTON did the choreography.

BIBLICAL MUSICALS. From time to time musicals have shown up on and Off Broadway that use stories from the Bible as their inspiration. For some reason, there was an outpouring of such shows in the 1970s. The gospels were musicalized with *JESUS CHRIST SUPERSTAR* (1971), *GODSPELL* (1971), and *YOUR ARMS TOO SHORT TO BOX WITH GOD* (1976). The Old Testament was also represented when Noah was featured in *TWO BY TWO* (1970), and biblical Joseph was brought to life in *JOSEPH AND THE AMAZING TECHNICOLOR DREAMCOAT* (Off Broadway in 1976 and on Broadway in 1981). The only notable biblical musical not part of this onrush was *THE APPLE TREE* (1966) in which Mark Twain's *The Diary of Adam and Eve* was musicalized. The London musical *Children of Eden* (1991), which told several stories from Genesis, made its American debut in 1998 in regional theatre and has received many productions across the States without ever having landed on Broadway. Hollywood made screen versions of *Godspell* (1973) and *Jesus Christ Superstar* (1973), but rarely offered original biblical musicals, which is curious when one considers how many times the movies have turned to the Bible for film spectaculars. The animated *THE PRINCE OF EGYPT* (1998) is perhaps the only notable example, unless one counts the irreverent spoof *Life of Brian* (1979). Television musicals have touched on the Old Testament with *Noah and the Flood* (1962) and the animated musical *It's a Brand New World* (1977), which told about Noah and Samson. Along with all the Christmas musicals about Santa Claus were some religious treatments of the holiday, such as *The Little Drummer Boy* (1968), *THE LITTLEST ANGEL* (1969), and *The Night the Animals Talked* (1970). Television presented several original operas in the 1950s and some had biblical subjects, most famously *Amahl and the Night Visitors* (1951).

🎵 **BIG BOY** (Winter Garden Theatre 1925). A good example of a disjointed but entertaining AL JOLSON vehicle, this show introduced some standards that would ever after be identified with the star. Jolson played his familiar (and favorite) blackface character Gus who is a stable boy at the Bedford family's stable. Some villains contrive to get Gus fired so that they can fix the race, but Gus outwits them and rides the race horse Big Boy to victory at the Derby. It was a thin plot (written by Harold Atteridge) and was frequently interrupted by special acts and Jolson's stopping the story to deliver whatever songs he was in the mood to sing. At some performances he asked the audience halfway through the show if he could dismiss the rest of the cast and he'd perform solo for the rest of the evening; they always said yes. One could hardly blame them when the songs he delivered included "California, Here I Come," "Keep

Smiling at Trouble," and "If You Knew Susie." J. C. HUFFMAN and ALEXANDER LEFTWICH co-directed the large-scale musical, complete with a moving treadmill for the climatic horse race, and the choreography was by SEYMOUR FELIX and Larry Ceballos. The SHUBERT production looked to be a smash hit, but Jolson fell ill after 56 performances and the show closed down temporarily, hoping to reopen again but it never did.

▪ **BIG BROADCAST, THE** (Paramount 1932). Capitalizing on the popularity of radio during the Depression, the film allowed fans to see what some of their favorite radio stars looked like and it was successful enough to launch a series of PARAMOUNT musicals and copies by other studios. The thin plot by George Marion, Jr., centered on the rivalry between airwaves singer BING CROSBY (playing himself) and Texas millionaire Leslie McWhinney (STUART ERWIN) over the affections of Anita Rogers (Leila Hyams), but the story was happily interrupted by a dozen radio stars. Kate Smith sang "It Was So Beautiful" and her theme song "When the Moon Comes Over the Mountain," CAB CALLOWAY delivered "Minnie the Moocher" and "Kickin' the Gong Around" with his orchestra, the MILLS BROTHERS harmonized through "Tiger Rag" and "Goodbye Blue," Vincent Lopez and his orchestra played their trademark "Nola," and Crosby got to sing his theme song "Where the Blue of the Night Meets the Gold of the Day," as well as "Please," "Dinah," and "Here Lies Love." Also on hand were GEORGE BURNS and GRACIE ALLEN, GEORGE BARBIER, Sharon Lynn, Ralph Robertson, and Alex Melesh, all under the direction of FRANK TUTTLE. **The Big Broadcast of 1936** (Paramount 1935) dealt with both radio and the newfangled invention of the "radio eye" (an early form of television). Broadcast singer Spud Miller (JACK OAKIE) goes by the moniker "Lochinvar" on the airwaves, but his singing is actually dubbed by Smiley (Henry Wadsworth, whose actual singing was provided by KENNY BAKER). When the rich Countess Ysobel de Naigila (LYDA ROBERTI) comes to woo Lochinvar, complications involve Burns and Allen (playing themselves). Crosby was on hand again to sing "I Wished on the Moon" and also featured were the NICHOLAS BROTHERS, BILL ROBINSON, ETHEL MERMAN, Amos and Andy, CHARLES RUGGLES, MARY BOLAND, Benny Baker, Wendy Barrie, band leader Ray Noble, and even the Vienna Boys Choir. NORMAN TAUROG directed and LEROY PRINZ choreographed.

Songs from the *Big Broadcast* films

The Big Broadcast (1932)
"When the Moon Comes Over the Mountain"
"Minnie the Moocher"
"Where the Blue of the Night Meets the Gold of the Day"
"Please"
"Tiger Rag"
"Here Lies Love"
"Shout Sister Shout"
"Hot Toddy"
"Dinah"
"Crazy People"
"Trees"
"The Boswell Weeps"

The Big Broadcast of 1936 (1935)
"I Wished on the Moon"
"Double Trouble"
"Why Dream?"
"It's the Animal in Me"
"Miss Brown to You"
"Why the Stars Come Out at Night"
"Goodnight Sweetheart"
"Through the Doorway of Dreams I Saw You"
"Cheating Machita (Armagura)"

The Big Broadcast of 1937 (1936)
"I'm Talking Through My Heart"
"Vote for Mr. Rhythm"
"Here's Love in Your Eye"
"Hi-Ho the Radio"
"You Came to My Rescue"
"La Bomba"
"Here Comes the Bride"

The Big Broadcast of 1938
"Thanks for the Memory"
"You Took the Words Right Out of My Mouth"
"Brunnhilde's Battle Cry"
"This Little Ripple Had Rhythm"
"Mama, That Moon Is Out Again"
"Don't Tell a Secret to a Rose"
"The Waltz Lives On"
"Truckin'"

The Big Broadcast of 1937 (Paramount 1936) continued the series, this time pitting small-town radio announcer Gwen Holmes (SHIRLEY ROSS) against tenor star Frank Rossman (Frank Forest) while radio network owner Jack Carson (JACK BENNY) had to deal with Mr. and Mrs. Platt (Burns and Allen), sponsors of the station's *Platt Golf Ball Hour*. BENNY GOODMAN provided the swing music, LEOPOLD STOKOWSKI represented the classics, and RALPH RAINGER (music) and LEO ROBIN (lyrics) supplied such delightful songs as "Vote for Mr. Rhythm" (wailed by MARTHA RAYE), "I'm Talking Through My Heart" and "You Came to My Rescue." Raye also sang a swing version of "Here Comes the Bride" at a wedding. One of the nuttier entries, it was directed by MITCHELL LEISEN and choreographed by Prinz. The final entry in the series, **The Big Broadcast of 1938** (Paramount 1938), was perhaps the best one. A transatlantic race between two ocean liners provided the plot and W. C. FIELDS provided the laughs as both the shipping tycoon J. Frothingale Bellows and his twin brother S. B. Bellows. A series of broadcasts from the ships allowed for the musical numbers and most were introduced by radio emcee Buzz Fielding (BOB HOPE in his screen debut). DOROTHY LAMOUR sang "You Took the Words Right Out of My Mouth," opera diva Kirsten Flagstad bellowed Brunnhilde's "Battle Cry" from *Die Walkuere*, and Raye clowned around with "Mama, That Moon Is Here Again." The undisputed high point of the film (and the whole series) was when Buzz ran across his ex-wife Cleo (Shirley Ross) in the bar and the two sang the Oscar-winning duet "Thanks for the Memory" by Rainger and Robin, one of the decade's most touching musical scenes. Also cast were Lynne Overman, Leif Erickson, BEN BLUE, GRACE BRADLEY, Rufe Davis, TOTO GUIZER, and Patricia Wilder. Again Leisen and Prinze directed and choreographed, bringing the series to a very satisfying close.

🔔 **BIG RIVER: THE ADVENTURES OF HUCKLEBERRY FINN** (Eugene O'Neill Theatre 1985). This faithful musical adaptation of Mark

Big River. Composer Kurt Weill was working on a musicalization of Mark Twain's novel when he died in 1950; it took another thirty-five years before Broadway finally saw a musical Huck Finn. The musical came about because producers Rocco and Heidi Landesman were looking for a project to utilize the talents of country songwriter Roger Miller. Twain and Miller were an ideal team, as were Daniel Jenkins (right) and Ron Richardson as Huck and the runaway slave Jim. (Photofest)

Twin's masterwork featured an efficient libretto by William Hauptman and a tuneful country-flavored score by Roger Miller. Most of the major events in the novel were recreated, from Huck (DANIEL JENKINS) running away from his drunken father (John Goodman), his escape on a raft down the Mississippi River with the fugitive slave Jim (Ron Richardson), their meeting with the bogus King (BOB GUNTON) and Duke (RENE AUBERJONOIS), and the mishaps with Tom Sawyer (John Short) that lead to a happy ending. Also in the cast were PATTI CONENOUR, Susan Browning, Peggy Harmon, and Carol Dennis. In his only Broadway effort, country star Miller came up with a true musical score with character songs and choral numbers instead of just disjointed individual songs. "Muddy Water," "Waiting for the Light to Shine," "River in the Rain," "Worlds Apart," "Leaving's Not the Only Way to Go," and "Free at Last" stood out in the exceptional score. DES MCANUFF directed the musical, previously seen at the American Repertory Theatre in Massachusetts and the La Jolla Playhouse in California, and the show overrode mixed notices to run 1,005 performances. In 2003, the Deaf West Theatre Company's production of *Big River*, featuring speaking and deaf actors and singers, arrived on Broadway as part of its national tour and stayed for sixty-seven performances. The revival received more favorable reviews than the original, with critics finding the double cast brought new insights into the familiar tale and the expert staging by director–choreographer JEFF CALHOUN to be exhilarating.

BING, HERMAN (1889–1947). Film performer. A thickly accented, easily excitable German character actor, his comic hysterics were useful in over 100 films, including several musicals. Bing was born in Frankfurt, Germany, and was a circus clown and performer in vaudeville before beginning his film career in his native land. He arrived in Hollywood just as sound was coming in and was quickly picked up for dialect roles, overemphasizing his German accent for comic effect. Among his musical credits are *FOOTLIGHT PARADE* (1933), *THE CAT AND THE FIDDLE* (1934), *THE MERRY WIDOW* (1934), *In Caliente* (1935), *The Night Is Young* (1935), *Every Night at Eight* (1935), *ROSE MARIE* (1936), *THE GREAT ZIEGFELD* (1936), *MAYTIME* (1937), *THE GREAT WALTZ* (1938), *SWEETHEARTS* (1938), *BITTER SWEET* (1940), *BROADWAY MELODY OF 1940*, *Where Do We Go From Here?* (1945), and *NIGHT AND DAY* (1946), as well as the voice of the Ringleader in the animated *DUMBO* (1941). When Bing's career started to collapse in the mid-1940s he committed suicide.

BIOGRAPHICAL MUSICALS. Generally inaccurate and romanticized versions of the truth, musicals based on famous people have always had an appeal in Broadway musicals. Historical personages singing and dancing may not have done much for their status in history books but it makes them more accessible to playgoers. Political figures have been of particular interest. *FIORELLO!* (1959) and *Jimmy* (1969) were about New York mayors Fiorello La Guardia and Jimmy Walker, FDR appeared in *I'D*

Show Business Biographical Musicals on Broadway

Musical	Subject	Impersonator
ANNIE GET YOUR GUN (1946)	Annie Oakley	ETHEL MERMAN
BARNUM (1980)	P. T. Barnum	JIM DALE
BOY FROM OZ, THE (2003)	Peter Allen	Hugh Jackman
BUDDY (1990)	Buddy Holly	Paul Hipp
FUNNY GIRL (1964)	FANNY BRICE	BARBRA STREISAND
GEORGE M! (1968)	GEORGE M. COHAN	JOEL GREY
GYPSY (1959)	GYPSY ROSE LEE	Sandra Church
Harrigan 'n Hart (1985)	EDWARD HARRIGAN	HARRY GROENER
	TONY HART	Mark Hamill
JELLY'S LAST JAM (1992)	Jelly Roll Morton	GREGORY HINES
JERSEY BOYS (2005)	Frankie Valli	John Lloyd Young
MACK AND MABEL (1974)	Mack Sennett	ROBERT PRESTON
	Mabel Normand	BENARDETTE PETERS
Minnie's Boys (1970)	Groucho, Chico	LEWIS J. STADLEN, Irwin Pearl
	HARPO, ZEPPO MARX	Daniel Fortus, Alvin Kupperman
Molly (1973)	Molly Goldberg	Kaye Ballard
Sophie (1963)	SOPHIE TUCKER	Libi Staiger
WILL ROGERS FOLLIES, THE (1991)	WILL ROGERS	Keith Carradine

RATHER BE RIGHT (19337) and *ANNIE* (1977), Teddy Roosevelt was the subject of *Teddy and Alice* (1987), and *Ben Franklin in Paris* (1964) concentrated on the diplomat Franklin and he showed up with a bunch of Founding Fathers in *1776* (1969) just as several presidents and first ladies were featured in *1600 PENNSYLVANIA AVENUE* (1976). Other Americans that inspired stage musicals include baseballer Jack Robinson in *The First* (1981), gangster *Legs Diamond* (1988), and Henry Ford, Houdini, and other celebrities early in the twentieth century in *RAGTIME* (1998). Looking beyond American borders, Broadway has musicalized Joan of Arc and King Charles IV of France in *Goodtime Charley* (1975), Argentina's Eva Peron in *EVITA* (1979), England's King Henry VIII in *Rex* (1976), the French fashion designer Chanel in *Coco* (1969), and the European banking family in *THE ROTHSCHILDS* (1970). Finally, there were several infamous figures portrayed in *ASSASSINS* (1990). Curiously, very few of the musicals just listed were hits, yet Broadway continues to turn to historical figures for ideas.

Broadway producers usually had better luck when the musical biography was about some-

one in show business, particularly musicals. The lives of songwriters and performers obviously lent themselves to the musical form much easier. Artists from vaudeville, Broadway, movies, or the world of popular music brought song standards with them and the scores for such musical biographies were guaranteed to have at least a couple of hit songs. Even when the subject of the musical is well known to playgoers from film footage or television, seeing them impersonated on stage holds some kind of fascination. One can see FANNY BRICE in films or listen to the Four Seasons on CD, yet people will pay to see a copy of them on the stage.

Hollywood far surpassed Broadway when it came to the number of biographical musicals it has turned out over the past seventy years. Often these were also wildly inaccurate but, unlike the many stage flops about famous people, the movie biographical musicals were usually box office hits. The film studios were also smart enough not to attempt musicals about nonshow business figures. They filmed the Broadway historical biographies if they were hits, such as *1776* (1972) and *Evita* (1996), but usually avoided history musicals. You might come up with a

Biographical Film Musicals about Songwriters

Musical	Songwriter(s)	Impersonator(s)
BEST THINGS IN LIFE ARE FREE, THE (1956)	B. G. DeSylva	GORDON MacRae
	Lew Brown	Ernest Borgnine
	Ray Henderson	Dan Dailey
Bound for Glory (1976)	Woody Guthrie	David Carradine
DEEP IN MY HEART (1954)	SIGMUND ROMBERG	JOSÉ FERRER
De-Lovely (2004)	COLE PORTER	KEVIN KLINE
Great Victor Herbert, The (1939)	VICTOR HERBERT	Walter Connolly
Harmony Lane (1935)	Stephen Foster	Douglass Montgomery
I Dream of Jeanie (1952)	Stephen Foster	Bill Shirley
I Wonder Who's Kissing Her Now (1947)	Joe Howard	Mark Stevens
I'll See You in My Dreams (1951)	GUS KAHN	DANNY THOMAS
Irish Eyes Are Smiling (1944)	Ernest R. Ball	DICK HAYMES
My Gal Sal (1942)	Paul Dresser	Victor Mature
My Wild Irish Rose (1947)	Chauncey Olcott	DENNIS MORGAN
NIGHT AND DAY (1946)	COLE PORTER	Cary Grant
RHAPSODY IN BLUE (1945)	GEORGE GERSHWIN	ROBERT ALDA
Scott Joplin (1977)	Scott Joplin	Billy Dee Williams
ST. LOUIS BLUES (1958)	W. C. Handy	NAT KING COLE
Stars and Stripes Forever (1952)	JOHN PHILIP SOUSA	CLIFTON WEBB
Swanee River (1939)	Stephen Foster	DON AMECHE
THREE LITTLE WORDS (1950)	BERT KALMAR	FRED ASTAIRE
	HARRY RUBY	RED SKELTON
TILL THE CLOUDS ROLL BY (1946)	JEROME KERN	Robert Walker
WORDS AND MUSIC (1948)	RICHARD RODGERS	Tom Drake
	LORENZ HART	MICKEY ROONEY
YANKEE DOODLE DANDY (1942)	GEORGE M. COHAN	JAMES CAGNEY

POCAHONTAS (1995) but more than likely you'll end up with oddball features such as *Where Do We Go From Here?* (1945) about Christopher Columbus. When it came to show business, no songwriter, producer, or performer was not worth considering as the subject of a biographical musical. Even if the names were not household ones, such as BERT KALMAR and HARRY RUBY, their songs were familiar and that was enough. A long-forgotten star, such as MARILYN MILLER, may not catch the moviegoer's attention but if she introduced enough song standards, she was ripe for biography. Even a producer, if he was associated with so many stars and songs as FLORENZ ZIEGFELD, got his own musical biography, such as *The Great Ziegfeld* (1936).

Biographical Film Musicals about Performers

Musical	Performer(s)	Impersonator(s)
BENNY GOODMAN STORY, THE (1955)	BENNY GOODMAN	Steve Allen
BIRD (1988)	Charlie Parker	Forest Whitaker
BUDDY HOLLY STORY, THE (1978)	Buddy Holly	Gary Busey
COAL MINER'S DAUGHTER (1980)	Loretta Lynn	Sissy Spacek
DOLLY SISTERS, THE (1945)	JENNY DOLLY	BETTY GRABLE
	ROSIE DOLLY	JUNE HAVER
Doors, The (1991)	Jim Morrison	Val Kilmer
Eddy Cantor Story, The (1953)	EDDIE CANTOR	Keefe Brasselle
Eddy Duchin Story, The (1956)	Eddy Duchin	TYRONE POWER
Fabulous Dorseys, The (1947)	JIMMY DORSEY	Jimmy Dorsey
	TOMMY DORSEY	Tommy Dorsey
FIVE PENNIES, THE (1959)	Red Nichols	DANNY KAYE
FUNNY GIRL (1968)	FANNY BRICE	BARBRA STREISAND
FUNNY LADY (1975)	Fanny Brice	Barbra Streisand
Gene Krupa Story, The (1959)	GENE KRUPA	Sal Mineo
GLENN MILLER STORY, THE (1954)	GLENN MILLER	JAMES STEWART
GREAT CARUSO, THE (1951)	Enrico Caruso	MARIO LANZA
GYPSY (1962)	GYPSY ROSE LEE	NATALIE WOOD
Helen Morgan Story, The (1957)	HELEN MORGAN	ANN BLYTH
I Don't Care Girl, The (1952)	EVA TANGUAY	MITZI GAYNOR
I'LL CRY TOMORROW (1955)	LILLIAN ROTH	SUSAN HAYWARD
Incendiary Blonde (1945)	Texas Guinan	BETTY HUTTON
Interrupted Melody (1955)	Marjorie Lawrence	Eleanor Parker
JOKER IS WILD, THE (1957)	Joe E. Lewis	FRANK SINATRA
JOLSON SINGS AGAIN (1949)	AL JOLSON	LARRY PARKS
JOLSON STORY, THE (1946)	Al Jolson	Larry Parks
La Bamba (1987)	Richie Valens	Lou Diamond Phillips
LADY SINGS THE BLUES (1972)	Billie Holiday	DIANA ROSS
LILLIAN RUSSELL (1940)	LILLIAN RUSSELL	ALICE FAYE
Look for the Silver Lining (1949)	MARILYN MILLER	June Haver
LOVE ME OR LEAVE ME (1955)	RUTH ETTING	DORIS DAY
Perils of Pauline (1947)	Pearl White	Betty Hutton
RAY (2004)	Ray Charles	Jamie Foxx
Seven Little Foys, The (1955)	EDDIE FOY	BOB HOPE
Shine on Harvest Moon (1944)	NORA BAYES	ANN SHERIDAN
So This Is Love (1953)	GRACE MOORE	KATHRYN GRAYSON
Somebody Loves Me (1952)	Blossom Seeley	Betty Hutton
SOUND OF MUSIC, THE (1965)	Maria Von Trapp	JULIE ANDREWS
STAR! (1968)	GERTRUDE LAWRENCE	JULIE ANDREWS
STORY OF VERNON AND IRENE CASTLE, THE (1939)	VERNON CASTLE	FRED ASTAIRE
	IRENE CASTLE	GINGER ROGERS
WALK THE LINE (2005)	Johnny Cash	Joaquin Phoenix
	June Carter	Reese Witherspoon
WITH A SONG IN MY HEART (1952)	Jane Froman	Susan Hayward
Your Cheatin' Heart (1965)	Hank Williams	George Hamilton

Television has not ignored biographies but once again the musical entries are about show business folk, particularly ones with heartbreaking tales, such as *The Ann Jillian Story* (1988) and *Life With Judy Garland: Me and My Shadows* (2001), or closeted lives, such as *Liberace: Behind the Music* (1988). See also CLASSICAL MUSIC IN MUSICALS for stage and film biographies about classical composers.

Birch, Patricia (1934–). Stage, film, and choreographer and director. While not as well known as other choreographer–directors of her generation, the prolific artist was involved in many successful musicals. A native of Scarsdale, New York, Birch was educated at Bennington College before studying dance with Merce Cunningham, Martha Graham, and at the School of the American Ballet. She began her career as a dancer in Graham's company and then appeared in the chorus of some Broadway musicals before taking up theatre choreography in 1956. Birch first found recognition Off Broadway for *You're a Good Man, Charlie Brown* (1967) and had another major hit five years later with *Grease.* Of her many New York credits, arguably her finest work was done with director Harold Prince, staging the musical numbers for *A Little Night Music* (1973), *Candide* (1973 and 1997), *Pacific Overtures* (1976), *Roza* (1987), *Parade* (1998), and *LoveMusik* (2007). Her other New York credits include *The Me Nobody Knows* (1970), *Over Here!* (1974), *Music Is* (1976), *They're Playing Our Song* (1979), and *Welcome to the Club* (1989). Birch turned to directing in 1977 and would perform both duties for musicals in the 1980s and 1990s, including *Happy End* (1977), *Really Rosie* (1984), *What About Luv?* (1991), and *Band in Berlin* (1999). She has choreographed many television specials and the movie musicals *A Little Night Music* (1978), *Grease* (1978), and *Grease 2* (1982), which she also directed. Birch also staged the dances in several nonmusical films, such as *Big* (1988) and *The Stepford Wives* (2004).

Bird (Warner 1988). Charlie "Bird" Parker, the brilliant alto saxophonist who died at the age of thirty-four after an influential but self-destructive career in jazz, was given an appropriately somber biomusical treatment in this film produced and directed by Clint Eastwood. Forest Whitaker portrayed the celebrated musician, and the sounds that came from his sax were authentic recordings that "Yardbird" Parker had made in the early 1950s. Charles McPherson and other jazz musicians contributed to the stunning soundtrack, which included Parker standards "All of Me," "Laura," "This Time the Dream's on Me," "Cool Blues," and "April in Paris." Also in the cast were Diana Venora, Keith David, Michael Zelniker, and Samuel E. Wright as Parker's friend Dizzy Gillespie. Because only instrumental pieces were used, the movie does not feel like a traditional musical, yet the powerful drama comes alive when the music takes over.

Birth of the Blues (Paramount 1941). The first Hollywood musical to deal with the history of jazz and the blues, the film is a Bing Crosby vehicle and feels familiar even as it chronicles a bold musical movement. Harry Tugend and Walter DeLeon wrote the screenplay, which often resembles a traditional backstage musical. Clarinetist Jeff Lambert (Crosby) goes to New Orleans and puts together a Dixieland jazz band incorporating a trumpeter named Memphis (Brian Donlevy), the trombonist Pepper (Jack Teagarden, who did his own playing), and band singer Betty Lou Cobb (Mary Martin). The group fights for recognition in a town that is content with the waltz but eventually the musicians head up north to Chicago where they spread the new sound across America. Inspired by the Original Dixieland Jazz Band, a quintet of players who introduced jazz to mainstream audiences, the film is routine in its plotting but catches fire in the musical numbers. Martin gives what is arguably her finest movie performance, singing "Cuddle Up a Little Closer," joining Crosby on "Wait Till the Sun Shines, Nellie," and letting loose with Teagarden and Crosby on the sly number "The Waiter and the Porter and the Upstairs Maid," written for the film by Johnny Mercer. Most of the numbers were standards and were given exciting interpretations by the cast, such as Ruby Elzy's impassioned rendition of "St. Louis Blues" and Crosby's mournful crooning on "My Melancholy Baby" and the title song. Also cast in the film were Eddie Anderson, J. Carroll Naish, Carolyn Lee, and Harry Barris. Monta Bell and B. G. De Sylva produced the musical and it was directed by Victor Schertzinger right before his premature death.

Bitter Sweet (Ziegfeld Theatre 1929). Noel Coward's most often revived musical, the period operetta is decidedly old fashioned and eschews the Coward wit for romance and lush music. Coward's libretto starts in posh Grovesnor Square where the Marchioness of

Shayne (Evelyn Laye) helps her young niece, who cannot decide whether to marry for love or social position, by telling her own story in flashback. Back in 1875 when she was Sarah Millick, she was engaged to the Marquis of Shayne (John Evelyn) but was in love with her music teacher Carl Linden (Gerald Nodin). The two elope to Vienna and are happy until Carl is killed in a duel five years later. Sarah goes on the stage to support herself, becomes a famous prima donna, and then weds the patient Marquis. Coward's score included the hits "If Love Were All" and "I'll See You Again," as well as "Dear Little Café," "The Call of Life," and "Ziguener." The London success was also popular in New York where the Arch Selwyn–FLORENZ ZIEGFELD production, directed by Coward, ran 159 performances. It was revived on Broadway in 1934 and remains a favorite with operetta companies.

Bitter Sweet was filmed both in England and in Hollywood. British producer–director Herbert Wilcox starred his wife ANNA NEAGLE in a 1933 film version that was a visual and musical treat. Fernand Gravey was Carl, and the supporting cast included Esme Percy, Clifford Haetherley, Ivy St. Helier, and Miles

Mander. Much of the score was retained and the songs were as beautifully presented as the period sets and costumes. MGM's 1940 version was tailored to the singing stars JEANETTE MacDONALD and NELSON EDDY, yet it remained fairly faithful to the original. W. S. VAN DYKE directed a cast that also included George Sanders, Ian Hunter, FELIX BRESSART, Edward Ashley, SIG RUMANN, and Lynne Carver. The VICTOR SAVILLE production was also very attractive and the 1870s were recreated in the glowing manner that only the MGM facilities could provide.

BLACK AND BLUE (Minskoff Theatre 1989). This celebration of blues and jazz from the 1920s and 1930s, performed by an expert African American cast, originated in Paris and was such a hit that the European producers risked putting it on Broadway. The cast included such major talents as Ruth Brown, Linda Hopkins, Bunny Briggs, Ralph Brown, SAVION GLOVER, Dianne Walker, Tanya Gibson, and Carrie Smith, and the song selection, covering everything from "St Louis Blues" to "Body and Soul," was top-notch. Also acclaimed by the press was the choreography by Cholly Atkins,

Black and Blue. It may have taken four choreographers to handle all the dancing in the explosive Broadway revue, but the result was thrilling. One of them was the celebrated dancer Fayard Nicholas who knew a thing or two about hoofing from his many years in Hollywood, Broadway, and television. Three of the African American dancers are captured above in the 1993 documentary-like television film made by Robert Altman and shown on public television. (Photofest)

Henry LeTang, Frankie Manning, and FAYARD NICHOLAS. Claudio Segovia and Hector Orezzoli compiled and directed the vivacious revue and it was a hit, running 829 performances. ❑ Film director ROBERT ALTMAN made a television version of the Broadway production of *Black and Blue* (1993), taping not only the acts on stage but occasionally going backstage between and during numbers, giving the program a documentary feel.

❧ **Black Crook, The** (Niblo's Garden 1866). An extravagant music–dance–drama with everything from ballets to melodrama, the show signified the birth of the American musical theatre. The production was not an innovative stroke of genius as much as a lucky accident, but there was no question of its impact: the Broadway musical began here. The circumstances of the show's origin give *The Black Crook* legendary status and, while much of the story may be apocryphal, some basic facts remain. Impresarios Henry C. Jarrett and Harry Palmer had imported a French ballet troupe to perform at the Academy of Music but the building burnt down in the spring of 1866. William Wheatley, the manager of a large playhouse called Niblo's Garden, had contracted to present a problematic piece of German romanticism called *The Black Crook* by the American dramatist Charles M. Barras, but he saw little chance for success when he read the completed script. Someone suggested to someone that the homeless ballet dancers be added to the melodrama to spice up the tale and provide a bit of leg. Songs from local music shops were added, the ballerinas became spirits, Amazons, and water sprites, and the whole five-and-a-half-hour spectacle opened to a bewildered but enthralled audience. The plot of *The Black Crook* was a clumsy reworking of the Faust legend as the crook-backed magician Hertzog makes a pact with the Arch Fiend (or devil) to gain a year of life with every soul he delivers to him. Hertzog attempts to entrap the virtuous painter Rudolphe, but a fairy queen warns the young artist and takes him off to a magical land where he weds her beautiful daughter. Hertzog, unable to fulfill his promise to the devil, is cast into hell. Added to this melodrama were marches, ballet pieces, solo arias, and comic songs, all presented with lavish scenery and glittering costumes. The combination of dance, spectacle, story, and song was irresistible and the show ran 475 performances in a day when thirty performances were considered a hit. Nothing in the score was very

memorable and the songs changed throughout the long run, as did the performers and some of the scenes. The most talked-about feature of *The Black Crook* was the scantily clad chorines who showed more leg than previously seen outside of ballet. Clergymen and civic leaders who castigated the production from pulpits and newspaper editorials only heightened the public's interest. The show toured extensively and was revived in New York fifteen times between 1870 and 1895. The 1954 musical *The Girl in Pink Tights* was a less-than-accurate version of the circumstances surrounding the original *The Black Crook*.

❧ **Blackbirds of 1928** (Liberty Theatre 1928). The longest-running musical revue of the 1920s, the "all-black" show was legendary for the talent it produced, from tap-master BILL "BOJANGLES" ROBINSON to songwriters JIMMY McHUGH (music) and DOROTHY FIELDS (lyrics). Producer–director Lew Leslie compiled the revue, hiring such African American talents as ADELAIDE HALL, ELIZABETH WELCH, Aida Ward, Tim Moore, Mantan Moreland, Cecil Mack, and the Hall Johnson Choir and giving Cotton Club tunesmiths McHugh and Fields their Broadway break. The combination of the vibrant performers and such future song classics, such as "I Can't Give You Anything But Love" and "Doing the New Low-Down," turned the show into a must-see hit. Also in the score were "Diga, Diga Doo," "I Must Have That Man," and a short musicalized version of the play *Porgy*, six years before the Gershwins' folk opera *Porgy and Bess* appeared. Leslie presented subsequent editions of his *Blackbirds* revue in 1930, 1933, and 1939, but none matched the original's quality or popularity.

BLACKTON, JAY [born Jacob Schwartzdorf] (1909–1994). Stage, television, and film musical conductor and arranger. A first-class conductor of Broadway musicals and recordings, he was much in demand in the 1940s through the 1960s. A native of Brooklyn, Blackton was a child prodigy on the piano, performing at the Brooklyn Academy of Music when he was only twelve years old. He conducted the orchestra for a variety of companies during the 1930s, such as the New York Opera Comique, the Federal Grand Opera Project, and the ST. LOUIS MUNICIPAL OPERA, and then made his Broadway debut as musical director and vocal arranger for *Sunny River* (1941). Two years later he worked with orchestrator ROBERT RUSSELL BENNETT and arranged and conducted the music for OKLAHOMA! (1943), repeating the task for the 1955 movie version and the 1979 Broadway revival. Blackton served as musical director on a number of New York productions, including ANNIE GET YOUR GUN (1946), CALL ME MADAM (1950), A TREE GROWS IN BROOKLYN (1951), WISH YOU WERE HERE (1952), REDHEAD (1959), and GEORGE M! (1968). He conducted the orchestra for a handful of films besides Oklahoma!, most memorably GUYS AND DOLLS (1955), for some television specials, such as the TV musical ANDROCLES AND THE LION (1967), and was musical director on many recordings over the years.

BLAINE, VIVIAN [born Vivian Stapleton] (1921–1995). Stage, film, and television performer. A perky blonde singer from nightclubs who is remembered primarily as the funny Miss Adelaide in the stage and screen versions of GUYS AND DOLLS, she was featured in several movie musicals before her Broadway career, most memorably as the provocative band singer Emily Edwards in STATE FAIR (1945). Blaine was born in Newark, New Jersey, the daughter of a theatrical agent, and was performing as a child and touring with bands in the 1930s before studying at the American Academy of Dramatic Arts. After appearing in cabarets and touring musicals, Blaine was featured in some 1940s movies, such as Jitterbugs (1943), Greenwich Village (1944), SOMETHING FOR THE BOYS (1944), Nob Hill (1945), Doll Face (1945), and THREE LITTLE GIRLS IN BLUE (1946), but the highlights of her career were introducing "That's for Me" and "It's a Grand Night for Singing" in State Fair and her 1950 Broadway debut in Guys and Dolls. Blaine returned to Broadway in Say, Darling (1958) and as replacements for Joanne in COMPANY (1971) and Madame Hortense in ZORBÁ (1984), but for much of her career concentrated on television series and musical specials, such as the TV musicals LET'S FACE IT! (1954) and It's Sunny Again (1956).

BLAIR, JANET [born Martha Jean Lafferty] (1921–2007). Stage and film performer. A wholesome-looking singer–actress with a perky persona, she was cast as the girl next door in several 1940s movies, including five musicals. Blair was born in Altoona, Pennsylvania, and began her career as a band singer, eventually becoming the featured vocalist for Hal Kemp's Orchestra. She made her screen debut in Three Girls About Town (1941) but gained recognition as ROSALIND RUSSELL's younger sister Eileen in the nonmusical film My Sister Eileen (1942). Blair finally got to use her singing talents in the musical Broadway (1942) and was featured as spirited ingénues in Something to Shout About (1943), Tonight and Every Night (1944), Tars and Spars (1946), and The Fabulous Dorseys (1947). Outgrowing such roles in the 1950s, she left Hollywood and returned to band singing as well as the stage, playing Nellie Forbush in the national tour of SOUTH PACIFIC for over 1,000 performances. Blair acted on television in series and specials, such as the TV musicals A CONNECTICUT YANKEE (1955), Strawberry Blonde (1959), and Around the World With Nellie Bly (1960), and returned to films on occasion, such as the musical The One and Only Genuine Original Family Band (1968).

BLAKE, EUBIE [born James Herbert Blake] (1883–1983). Stage composer and musician. A groundbreaking African American songwriter who often collaborated with lyricist NOBLE SISSLE, he gave Broadway its first truly black musical. Blake was born in Baltimore and began his career as a honky tonk and vaudeville pianist, teaming up with Sissle in 1915. The two of them played for the African American conductor James Reese Europe as they toured the States and Europe. The twosome then went into vaudeville together and turned their act into the musical comedy SHUFFLE ALONG (1921), the first Broadway show written, produced, and performed by African Americans. With its merry plot, agile performances, and bright score, which included the future standard "I'm Just Wild About Harry," the musical was a hit. The twosome followed it with the Broadway musicals Elsie (1923), Chocolate Dandies (1924), Shuffle Along of 1933 (1932), Shuffle Along of 1952, and the West End musical London Calling (1923), which introduced "You Were Meant for Me." With lyricist Andy Razaf, Blake also scored Blackbirds (1930). None of these enjoyed the success of his first hit, although some noteworthy songs came from them. Blake's work was celebrated in the Broadway revue Eubie (1978). Memoir: Reminiscing With Sissle and Blake, William Bolcom, Robert Kimball (1973); biographies: Eubie Blake, Al Rose (1983); Eubie Blake: Keys of Memory, Lawrence T. Carter (1979).

BLANE, RALPH [born Ralph Uriah Hunsecker] (1914–1995). Theatre, film, and television composer, lyricist, and arranger. Usually collaborating with HUGH MARTIN, the multitalented songwriter was involved in some major

Broadway and Hollywood musical hits. Blane was born in Broken Arrow, Oklahoma, and began his career as a singer, eventually appearing on Broadway in *New Faces of 1936*, *Hooray for What!* (1937), and *Louisiana Purchase* (1940). He also worked as a vocal arranger for some Broadway shows before he teamed up with Martin in 1944 and the two scored the campus musical *Best Foot Forward* (1941), both contributing to the music and the lyrics. The duo went to Hollywood for the 1943 screen version of the show and stayed, writing their most famous score the first time out with *Meet Me in St. Louis* (1944). Blane collaborated with various composers on the film musicals *Summer Holiday* (1948), *My Dream Is Yours* (1949), *My Blue Heaven* (1950), *Skirts Ahoy* (1952), *Down Among the Sheltering Palms* (1953), and *The French Line* (1954), as well as writing both music and lyrics for *One Sunday Afternoon* (1948). He reteamed with Martin for *Athena* (1954), *The Girl Rush* (1955), and *The Girl Most Likely* (1957). Blane wrote the score alone for the Broadway musical *Three Wishes for Jamie* (1952) and the lyrics for the TV musical *Quillow and the Giant* (1963). Although little remembered today, his songs "Have Yourself a Merry Little Christmas" and "The Trolley Song" are still familiar standards.

BLITZSTEIN, MARC[us Samuel] (1905–1964). Stage composer, lyricist, and writer. Although known primarily as the adaptor of the BRECHT-WEILL classic musical *The Threepenny Opera* (1954), the inventive songwriter wrote challenging and distinguished scores of his own. Blitzstein was born in Philadelphia and educated at the University of Pennsylvania, the Curtis Institute of Music, and the Academy der Kuenste in Berlin. He contributed songs to the Broadway revues *Garrick Gaieties* (1930) and *Parade* (1935) before gaining recognition for his leftist musical *The Cradle Will Rock* (1938). Blitzstein wrote provocative scores for the operatic pieces *Regina* (1949) and *Juno* (1959), although both failed to run and were only appreciated years later. His superb adaptation of the German musical *The Threepenny Opera* afforded the piece to run years Off Broadway. Blitzstein's music is powerful but difficult for many theatregoers and his lyrics are terse and sarcastic. Hank Azaria played Blitzstein in the film *The Cradle Will Rock* (1999). Biography: *Mark the Music: The Life and Work of Marc Blitzstein*, Eric A. Gordon (1990).

BLONDELL, [Rose] **JOAN** (1909–1979). Film, stage, and television performer. The wide-eyed, blonde character actress of over eighty films, she was the perennial wisecracking dame in several memorable movie musicals. Blondell was born in New York, the daughter of a stage comic, and grew up traveling on the vaudeville circuit. She sang and danced in stock and then made her Broadway debut in 1927, appearing in a few plays and the musicals *Ziegfeld Follies* (1929) and *Penny Arcade* (1929). Blondell was brought to Hollywood in 1930 and was given featured roles from the start, playing both leading ladies and supporting characters, usually tough and worldly wise women. Among the many movies she appeared in during the 1930s were the musicals *Gold Diggers of 1933*, *Footlight Parade* (1933), *Dames* (1934), *Broadway Gondolier* (1935), *Colleen* (1936), *Stage Struck* (1936), *Gold Diggers of 1937* (1936), *The King and the Chorus Girl* (1937), and *East Side of Heaven* (1939). By the 1940s Blondell concentrated on nonmusicals and in the 1950s acted in plays in New York and regionally as well as television, including the TV musical *Burlesque* (1955), but returned to the screen for such musicals as *Two Girls on Broadway* (1940), *The Opposite Sex* (1956), *This Could Be the Night* (1957), and *Grease* (1978). She continued acting until the year of her death. Blondell was married to producer MIKE TODD and actor DICK POWELL. Autobiography: *Center Door Fancy* (1972);

Joan Blondell. Between 1930 and 1981, the sassy Blondell appeared in over 130 films and she delivered a smart aleck retort in each one of them. Here she is in *Gold Diggers of 1933* giving that look to William Warren as she dances with Dick Powell. She gave the same look to John Travolta in *Grease* forty-five years later. (Photofest)

biography: *Joan Blondell: A Life Between Takes,* Matthew Kennedy (2007).

🕭 **BLOOD BROTHERS** (Music Box Theatre 1993). A major London hit, the musical melodrama was also popular enough on Broadway to run 840 performances. Willy Russell wrote the score and the libretto that resembled a 1940s "women's picture" but was very effective all the same. When the Liverpool divorced mother Mrs. Johnstone (Stephanie Lawrence) learns she is pregnant with twin boys, she arranges for one of the infants to be raised by the affluent Mrs. Lyons (Barbara Walsh) and keeps the other with her in the slums. Growing up, the two brothers (Con O'Neill and Mark Michael Hutchinson) are acquainted and cross paths several times without knowing they are related, but eventually the truth is revealed and it brings tragedy to both of them. Also in the cast were Warwick Evans, James Clow, Jan Graveson, Ivar Brogger, and Sam Samuelson. Russell's songs were in the light-rock and pop temperament, often reflecting the music of the 1960s and 1970s when the story took place. The numbers included "Marilyn Monroe," "Tell Me It's Not True," "Shoes Upon the Table," "Bright New Day," and "I'm Not Saying a Word." The musical was disfavored by the New York critics but the show held on, slowly gaining an audience thanks to word of mouth and the recasting of pop singer brothers David and Shaun Cassidy as the twins. Bill Kenright produced and co-directed, as he had in London where the musical has been running over twenty years.

🕭 **BLOOMER GIRL** (Shubert Theatre 1944). A popular wartime piece of Americana, the musical took on some heavy issues (slavery, war, and feminism), yet was still an entertaining crowd pleaser for 654 performances. In 1861 upstate New York, feminist and abolitionist Evelina Applegate (CELESTE HOLM) takes after her aunt, Dolly Bloomer (Margaret Douglass), who invented bloomers so women were not restricted by dresses. Evelina refuses to marry the Southern gentleman Jeff Calhoun (David Brooks) picked out by her father, hoop skirt manufacturer Horatio Applegate (Matt Briggs), until she actually meets him and after Jeff comes over to the Union side. FRED SAIDY and Sig Herzig collaborated on the libretto, and the delectable score was by HAROLD ARLEN (music) and E. Y. HARBURG (lyrics). The numbers included the expansive freedom song "The Eagle and Me," the romantic "Right as the Rain," the sarcastic "Sunday in Cicero Falls," the protest march "It Was Good Enough for Grandma (But Not Good Enough for Me)," the flowing ballad "Evelina," and the song cycle "I Got a Song" sung by the runaway slaves. The outstanding supporting cast included DOOLEY WILSON, Mabel Taliaferro, JOAN McCRACKEN, Richard Huey, and Blaine Cordner, under the direction of Harburg and William Schorr, while AGNES DE MILLE choreographed the notable ballets, in particular one illustrating the Civil War. A 1947 Broadway revival of *Bloomer Girl* starring NANETTE FABRAY as Evelina played at the City Center for forty-eight performances. ☐ BARBARA COOK made a delightful Evalina in a 1956 television version on NBC's *Producer's Showcase* series. The impressive cast included Keith Andes, PAUL FORD, Carmen Matthews, JAMES MITCHELL, and Paul McGrath, and the broadcast, produced and directed by Alex Segal, included the original de Mille choreography, including the Civil War ballet.

BLORE, ERIC (1887–1959). Film and stage performer. A round, owlish character actor from England, he was a master at stuffy and fussy British butlers, hotel managers, clerks, waiters, and valets. Blore was born in London and began his career as an insurance agent before going on the stage in comic roles in plays and musicals. He made his Broadway debut in 1923 and was seen in such musicals as *ANDRE CHARLOT'S REVUE* (1924), *Charlot Revue* (1925), *Just Fancy* (1927), *Here's Howe* (1928), *Here Goes the Bride* (1931), *GAY DIVORCE* (1932), and *ZIEGFELD FOLLIES* (1943). Blore had made some films in England before making his Hollywood debut in 1926 and with the coming of sound he was ideal as comic foils in talkies, making over eighty features during the next twenty-five years. His musical credits, which include five FRED ASTAIRE–GINGER ROGERS movies, include *FLYING DOWN TO RIO* (1933), *THE GAY DIVORCE* (1934), *FOLIES BERGERE DE PARIS* (1935), *I DREAM TOO MUCH* (1935), *SWING TIME* (1936), *SHALL WE DANCE* (1937), *JOY OF LIVING* (1938), *Swiss Miss* (1938), *Music in My Heart* (1940), *THE BOYS FROM SYRACUSE* (1940), *ROAD TO ZANZIBAR* (1941), *THE SKY'S THE LIMIT* (1943), *HAPPY GO LUCKY* (1943), *Easy to Look At* (1945), *ROMANCE ON THE HIGH SEAS* (1948), *Love Happy* (1949), and *Fancy Pants* (1950), as well as the voice of Mr. Toad in the animated film *The Adventures of Ichabod and Mr. Toad* (1949) and the TV cartoon *The Wind in the Willows* (1949).

BLOSSOM, HENRY [Martyn, Jr.] (1866–1919). Stage lyricist and writer. An early, literate author of Broadway librettos and lyrics, he collaborated frequently with composer VICTOR HERBERT on some of his greatest successes. Blossom was born in St. Louis and worked for his father's insurance company before turning to writing magazine stories and novels. When he adapted one of his books into a play, it was a hit so Blossom concentrated on writing for the stage thereafter. His lyrics were first heard on the London stage and then were interpolated into Broadway shows before he wrote his first complete libretto and score, *The Yankee Counsel* (1904), with composer Alfred G. Robyn. Blossom first partnered with Herbert for the popular musical comedy *MLLE. MODISTE* (1905), the two of them reteaming for *THE RED MILL* (1906), *The Prima Donna* (1908), *The Only Girl* (1914), *The Princess Pat* (1915), *The Century Girl* (1916), *Eileen* (1917), and *The Velvet Lady* (1919). Blossom's other musicals credits include *The Hoyden* (1907), *The Slim Princess* (1911), *The Man From Cook's* (1912), *All the Ladies* (1912), *A Glimpse of the Great White Way* (1913), and *Follow the Girl* (1919). His librettos were well constructed and more sophisticated than most in his era and his lyrics were often better than average—literate without being stuffy.

BLOSSOM TIME (Ambassador Theatre 1921). The first of several Broadway musicals over the years to use classical music for its score, this popular entry featured themes by Franz Schubert set into songs. DOROTHY DONNELLY wrote the libretto that presented a Schubert who suffered from unrequited love for Mitzi Kranz. His rival, the Baron Franz Schober, sang Schubert's "Song of Love" to Mitzi, thereby winning her heart. In despair, Schubert dies, leaving an unfinished symphony. Donnelly also wrote the lyrics and SIGMUND ROMBERG adapted the Schubert music to create two

hits, "Serenade" and "Song of Love." Also in the score were "Three Little Maids," "Love Is a Riddle," "Tell Me Daisy," and "Lonely Hearts." The SHUBERTS production was an immediate hit, and the producing brothers sent out four road companies at the same time to fill the demand. Over the years, many second-rate tours of the musical crisscrossed the country, and the expression "a road company of *Blossom Time*" was applied to any shabby road show. The musical was revived in New York in 1924, 1926, 1931, 1938, and 1943 and it is still presented by operetta companies. Classical music made accessible to audiences by turning it into songs was an innovation that caught on and many classical composers would be "musicalized" on Broadway over the decades, from Offenbach in *The Love Song* (1925) to Rachmaninoff with *Anya* (1965).

Blossom Time (British International Pictures 1934) created its own musical using Schubert's music and life, which were copyright free because the London film studio did not want to pay the high cost of obtaining the rights to Romberg's version. John Drinkwater and other scriptwriters came up with their own fictional version of the facts—Schubert loving the Viennese beauty Vicki but helping her win the hand of the dashing military officer Rudi who she loves so passionately. The two marry and Schubert pours all his frustration and grief into his music. Opera star Richard Tauber sang the Shubert pieces as art songs and no attempt was made to let them fit into the plot or characters. Musically, the film is very enjoyable but as history and drama it is highly suspect.

BLUE, BEN [Benjamin Bernstein] (1901–1975). Film, stage, and television performer. A sad-faced, agile-dancing comic with a deadpan delivery, he brought his comedy, mime, and hoofing talents from vaudeville to the screen in twenty features, usually in specialty spots. Blue was born in Montreal, Canada, and was

Casts for *Blossom Time*

Character	1921 Broadway	1934 film
Franz Schubert	Bertram Peacock	Richard Tauber
Mitzi/Vicki	Olga Cook	Jane Baxter
Franz Schobel/Rudi	HOWARD MARSH	Carl Esmond
Vogel	Roy Cropper	Cecil Ramage
Archduchess		Athene Seyler
Sharntoff/Wimpassinger	Yvan Servais	Paul Graetz
Von Schwind	Eugene Martinet	

performing in variety as a teenager. After gaining experience touring the vaudeville circuits, he made some silent shorts in Hollywood in the 1920s and got better parts once sound came in. Among his musicals were COLLEGE RHYTHM (1934), *Follow Your Heart* (1936), *Turn Off the Moon* (1937), HIGH, WIDE AND HANDSOME (1937), ARTISTS AND MODELS (1937), *Thrill of a Lifetime* (1937), BIG BROADCAST OF 1938, College Swing (1938), *Cocoanut Grove* (1938), *Paris Honeymoon* (1939), ME AND MY GAL (1942), PANAMA HATTIE (1942), *Thousands Cheer* (1943), BROADWAY RHYTHM (1943), TWO GIRLS AND A SAILOR (1944), *Two Sisters From Boston* (1946), *Easy to Wed* (1946), *My Wild Irish Rose* (1947), and *One Sunday Afternoon* (1948). Blue returned to the stage with the Broadway revue GEORGE WHITE'S SCANDALS (1939) and was very active on television where he had his own show in the 1950s and was a regular on FRANK SINATRA's program. He was still performing on the large and small screen until a few months before his death.

BLUE HAWAII (Paramount 1961). ELVIS PRESLEY and the beautiful scenery in the new state of Hawaii costarred in this musical that often resembled a travelogue with songs. The Hal Kanter screenplay featured the returning GI Chad Gates (Presley) who tells his mother (ANGELA LANSBURY) that he doesn't want anything to do with the family pineapple business and becomes a tour guide showing the islands to a group of comely ladies. Complications arise when he falls for the tourist Ellie Corbett (Jenny Maxwell) even though he has a steady girl named Maile Duval (Joan Blackman). This uninspired story was interrupted by fifteen songs, including the old standards "Aloha Oe," "Hawaiian Wedding Song," and the title song. Among the new numbers by various songwriters were "Rock-a-Hula Baby," "Moonlight Swim," "Beach Boy Blues," "Almost Always True," and the flowing waltz "Can't Help Falling in Love." NORMAN TAUROG directed the HAL B. WALLIS production, which was one of the better Presley films.

Blue Hawaii. Elvis Presley always seemed most comfortable on screen when he sang while accompanying himself on a guitar. In *Blue Hawaii* he had to settle for a ukulele when he serenaded Joan Blackman on the beach. Hollywood placed the King in various locales, from Las Vegas to the Ozark Mountains to New Orleans, in their efforts to hide the fact that all the films were basically the same. (Photofest)

BLUE PARADISE, THE (Casino Theatre 1915). A long-forgotten operetta even though it ran an impressive 356 performances, the musical gave composer SIGMUND ROMBERG his first hit and introduced leading lady VIVIENNE SEGAL to Broadway audiences. Edgar Smith's libretto, based on a Viennese operetta by composer Edmund Eysler, concerned the Vienna lass Mizzi (Segal), a flower seller at the fashionable garden restaurant called the Blue Paradise. She and Rudolph Stoeger (Cecil Lean) are deeply in love but he must leave her and go to America to make his fortune. Rudolph promises to return to her someday and it takes years for him to fulfill that promise, only to find the older Mizzi a scolding harridan who no longer cares for him. Much of Eysler's music was retained, set to lyrics by Herbert Reynolds, but it was the new songs by Romberg that got all the attention, in particular the farewell song "Auf Wiedersehn," which the lovers sang in their dramatic parting scene. Also in the score were Romberg's "One Step Into Love" and "A Toast to Woman's Eyes." Although he had contributed to five earlier Broadway musicals, Romberg was not noticed until this show. Segal was not originally cast as Mizzi but took over the role during the Washington tryout and became the toast of Broadway when the SHUBERT musical opened in New York.

BLUE SKIES (Paramount 1946). One of the most successful Hollywood musicals of the decade, it reunited FRED ASTAIRE and BING CROSBY as a couple of song-and-dance men fighting over the same girl as they sang new and old IRVING BERLIN songs. It was rather too similar to their earlier *HOLIDAY INN* (1942) but no one seemed to mind, especially with twenty musical numbers to while away the time. In Arthur Sheekman's screenplay, based on an idea by Berlin, Jed Potter (Astaire) looks back over the years between 1919 and the present, recalling the romantic triangle consisting of himself, the band singer Mary O'Hara (Joan Caulfield), and his partner Johnny Adams (Crosby) who cannot commit to anything, even his marriage to Mary ending in divorce. The musical numbers ranged from the early Berlin hit "A Pretty Girl Is Like a Melody" to the new "You Keep Coming Back Like a Song," one of the four numbers he wrote for the movie. The most ingenious musical number was Astaire dancing to "Puttin' on the Ritz" while eight miniature Astaires danced behind him on a split screen, all choreographed with rapid-fire precision by HERMES PAN. Since Berlin had written hits for all the different periods covered in the plot, there was a sense of historical accuracy in the film. For the vaudeville section, Berlin wrote "A Couple of Song and Dance Men" and the two stars were at their comic best performing it. Other songs used include "How Deep Is the Ocean," "Heat Wave," "All By Myself," "Always," and the title number. Also featured in the cast were OLGA SAN JUAN, Mikhail Rasummy, Karolyn Grimes, Frank Faylen, and BILLY DE WOLFE who did some of his signature comedy monologues. SOL C. SIEGEL produced and Stuart Heisler directed.

BLUES IN THE NIGHT (Warner 1941). An unsentimental look at itinerant jazz musicians, the musical drama was surprisingly terse and had a wailing anxiety that was best expressed in the title song. The screenplay by Robert Rossen followed jazz pianist and band leader Jigger Pine (Richard Whorf), his clarinetist Nickie Haroyen (Elia Kazan), and his trumpeter Leo Powell (JACK CARSON) who are torn between playing the music they love for little recognition or remuneration or only playing commercial pieces that pay well. Jigger is also torn between his demanding girl friend Kay Grant (Betty Field) who wants him to go mainstream and the new band singer Ginger (PRISCILLA LANE) who encourages him to follow his heart and play what he loves. Except for Kay's convenient death in a car crash, the movie is uncompromising, showing the drudgery of one-night stands, both professional and romantic. HAROLD ARLEN (music) and JOHNNY MERCER (lyrics) wrote the superb bluesy score, including two numbers that would become standards: the flowing ballad "This Time the Dream's On Me" and the haunting title song. The strong supporting cast included Lloyd Nolan, Wallace Ford, HOWARD DA SILVA, and Peter Whitney, who were directed with a sharp eye by Anatole Litvak. The HAL B. WALLIS production was unusually serious and challenging for its time and it still packs a punch.

BLUTH, DON (1938–). Film animator, director, and producer. One of the top figures in animated movie musicals, he is perhaps the most successful such artist outside of the DISNEY COMPANY. Bluth was born in El Paso, Texas, and grew up in rural Utah before his family moved to southern California where he got his first job working in the animation studio for WALT DISNEY. He left the industry to be a Mormon missionary in Argentina for over two years. On returning to the States, Bluth went to

Brigham Young University and then went back to Disney where he was a major contributor to such animated musicals as *Robin Hood* (1973), *The Rescuers* (1977), and PETE'S DRAGON (1977). In 1979 he left Disney and formed his own animation company, producing a string of noteworthy films, such as *The Secret of Nimh* (1982), *The Land Before Time* (1988) and its many sequels, and *All Dogs Go to Heaven* (1989). Bluth-animated musicals include *An American Tail* (1986), *Rock-a-Doodle* (1991), *Thumbelina* (1994), *A Troll in Central Park* (1994), *The Pebble and the Penguin* (1995), and ANASTASIA (1997).

BLYDEN, LARRY [born Ivan Lawrence Blieden] (1925–1975). Stage, television, and film performer. The wiry actor with a strident voice specialized in playing comic sidekicks and secondary leads. Born in Houston, Texas, the son of a lawyer, he was educated at Southern Louisiana Institute and the University of Houston before he went to London to study at the Royal Academy of Dramatic Art and to New York where he studied acting with Stella Adler. Blyden made his Broadway debut in 1949 as a replacement in *Mister Roberts*, followed by such comedies as *Oh, Men! Oh, Women!* (1953), *The Italian Straw Hat* (1957), *Luv* (1966), and *Absurd Person Singular* (1974). He is best remembered for his musical appearances, starting with WISH YOU WERE HERE (1952) and including the sly nightclub owner Sammy Fong in FLOWER DRUM SONG (1958), the sidekick Doc in *Foxy* (1964), the Snake and other roles in THE APPLE TREE (1966), and the slave Hysterium in the 1972 revival of *A FUNNY THING HAPPENED ON THE WAY TO THE FORUM*. Blyden appeared in many television programs, including the TV musicals *He's for Me* (1957) and OLYMPUS 7-0000 (1966). He also had a few film roles, most memorably as the stuffy fiancé Warren in the screen musical ON A CLEAR DAY YOU CAN SEE FOREVER (1970), before his premature death in an automobile accident in Morocco at the age of forty-nine. Blyden was married to actress–choreographer CAROL HANEY.

BLYTH, ANN [Marie] (1928–). Film, stage, and television performer. A dark-haired beauty who was a CHILD STAR on stage before going into movies, she has been impressive in both dramatic and operatic roles. Blyth was born in Mount Kisco, New York, and grew up in Manhattan where she attended the Professional Children's School. As a child she acted in radio soap operas and Broadway plays, as well as sang in the Children's Opera Company. While touring as a teenager she was given a film contract and made her debut as a singing, swinging teen in the musical *Chip Off the Old Block* (1944). Blyth played similar roles in *The Merry Monahans* (1944), *Babes on Swing Street* (1944), *Bowery to Broadway* (1944), and *Top o' the Morning* (1948), even as she shone in dramatic roles in the nonmusicals *Mildred Pierce* (1945) and *Another Part of the Forest* (1948). She had her best musical roles in the 1950s: the understanding Dorothy Caruso in THE GREAT CARUSO (1951), the tavern girl Kathie in THE STUDENT PRINCE (1954), the Canadian opera singer ROSE MARIE (1954), the poet's daughter Marsinah in KISMET (1955), and the tragic torch singer of *The Helen Morgan Story* (1957). In the 1960s and 1970s, Blyth concentrated on television programs, as well as tours, concerts, and summer stock productions of musical classics such as SHOW BOAT, THE KING AND I, THE SOUND OF MUSIC, CARNIVAL, BITTER SWEET, and *A LITTLE NIGHT MUSIC*.

BOBBIE, WALTER (1945–). Stage director and performer. A successful character actor, he turned to directing musicals with rapid success. Bobbie was born in Scranton, Pennsylvania, and educated at the University of Scranton and the Catholic University of America in Washington, DC. He started his acting career in regional theatre and then made his New York debut Off Broadway in 1970. Over the next twenty years he performed in several plays and musicals, most memorably as Nicely Nicely in the 1992 Broadway revival of GUYS AND DOLLS. He also frequently returned to regional theatre, particularly as a member of the company at the Arena Stage in Washington in the late 1970s, and acted in several movies and television shows. Bobbie made his directing debut in New York when the nightclub revue that he staged called *A Grand Night for Singing* transferred to Broadway in 1993. That same year he directed his first of several staged concert versions of musicals for ENCORES!, a series with which he would be long associated. It was his *Encores!* staging of CHICAGO and its record-breaking run on Broadway beginning in 1996 that made Bobbie's reputation as a director. Bobbie's other Broadway musicals include FOOTLOOSE (1998), SWEET CHARITY (2005), and *High Fidelity* (2006). In addition to his New York credits, he has staged musicals regionally and on tour, such as the various road companies of WHITE CHRISTMAS.

BOCK, JERRY, AND SHELDON HARNICK. Stage songwriting team. An outstanding composer–lyricist team, they created some unforgettable Broadway musicals during their twelve-year partnership. Jerry [Jerrold Lewis] Bock (1928–) was born in New Haven, Connecticut, and started composing songs as a high schooler and later at the University of Wisconsin. He wrote songs for summer camp revues and for early television before teaming up with lyricist Larry Holofcener on the score for the Broadway revue *Catch a Star* (1955) and book musical *Mr. Wonderful* (1956). He met lyricist Sheldon [Mayer] Harnick (1924–), a Chicago native, who had written songs (both music and lyrics) while studying at Northwestern University. Harnick saw some of his numbers performed in such New York revues as *New Faces of 1952*, *Two's Company* (1952), *John Murray Anderson's Almanac* (1953), and *Shoestring Revue* (1955). Encouraged by lyricist E. Y. HARBURG to abandon composing and concentrate on lyric writing, Harnick teamed up with Bock and scored the Broadway musicals *The Body Beautiful* (1958), *Fiorello!* (1959), *Tenderloin* (1960), *She Loves Me* (1963), *Fiddler on the Roof* (1964), *The Apple Tree* (1966), and *The Rothschilds* (1970), as well as the TV musical *The Canterville Ghost* (1966). Of the team's musicals, only *Fiddler on the Roof* was filmed, although there was a television version of *She Loves Me* in 1978. When Bock and Harnick broke up their partnership in 1970, Harnick worked on various projects with other composers but found little success. His finest lyrics after Bock were the ones he wrote for RICHARD RODGERS' music for the short-lived *Rex* (1976). Bock's music is versatile and rich, using both a European and an American flavor. Harnick has a talent for honest, unadorned lyrics out of the school of OSCAR HAMMERSTEIN.

BOGARDUS, STEPHEN (1954–). Stage and television performer. A handsome leading man on and Off Broadway, he has managed to play appealing straight and gay characters on stage. Bogardus was born in Norfolk, Virginia, and was educated at Princeton before getting stage experience in stock and in touring productions. He made his New York debut in the musical *The Umbrellas of Cherbourg* (1979) and the next year was cast in the Broadway revival of *West Side Story*. Bogardus first played the gay "other man" Whizzer in the musical *March of the Falsettos* in 1981, returned to the character in *Falsettoland* (1990), and reprised both performances in *Falsettos* (1992). His other musical credits include *No Way to Treat a Lady* (1987), *High Society* (1998), and *Man of La Mancha* (2002), as well as a replacement in *Les Miserables* in 1987 and *James Joyce's The Dead* in 2000. Bogardus has been successful in nonmusicals as well, as with *Love! Valour! Compassion!* (1994), which he filmed in 1997, and on television where he has appeared in soap operas and dramatic series.

BOLAND, MARY [born Marie Anne Boland] (1880–1965). Stage, film, and television performer. A pretty stage ingénue, she later developed into an expert comedienne on Broadway and in Hollywood. Boland was born in Philadelphia into a family of actors and, after a convent education in Detroit, learned her craft in regional stock companies, touring productions, and a handful of silent films. By the time Boland made her Broadway debut in 1905, she was a seasoned actress and became John Drew's leading lady in New York and on the road. It was not until she played the befuddled stepmother in the comedy *Clarence* (1919) that her comic talents were allowed to surface. From then on she concentrated on madcap matrons and zany grande dames in many comedies and two hit musicals, *Face the Music* (1932) and *Jubilee* (1935). In the 1930s Boland went to Hollywood where she made over forty movies, often paired with CHARLES RUGGLES as her put-upon husband. Her screen musicals include *Melody in Spring* (1934), *Two for Tonight* (1935), *Big Broadcast of 1936* (1935), *College Holiday* (1936), *Artists and Models Abroad* (1938), *New Moon* (1940), *Hit Parade of 1941* (1940), and *One Night in the Tropics* (1940). Boland also appeared in some television plays in the 1950s.

BOLES, JOHN (1895–1969). Film performer. A handsome, if somewhat stiff, leading man who starred in silents, he saw his career soar when sound came in and he was a favorite in early film operettas. Boles was born in Greenville, Texas, the son of a banker, and studied at the University of Texas for a medical career. During World War I, he worked in espionage activities in Europe and then studied voice in New York and Paris before making his Broadway debut as a replacement in the musical *Little Jesse James* (1923). After featured roles in *Mercenary Mary* (1925) and *Kitty's Kisses* (1926), Boles went to Hollywood where his dashing, aristocratic looks made him a popular romantic figure in silents. He got to use his voice training when talkies arrived, and he sang the leading role of the Red Shadow in *THE DESERT SONG* (1929), the first film made from a Broadway show. Boles' other musical credits include *RIO RITA* (1929), *Song of the West* (1930), *Careless Lady* (1932), *My Lips Betray* (1933), *Bottoms Up* (1934), *MUSIC IN THE AIR* (1934), *Redheads on Parade* (1935), *CURLY TOP* (1935), *The Littlest Rebel* (1935), *Rose of the Rancho* (1936), *Romance in the Dark* (1938), and *Thousands Cheer* (1943), as well as specialty spots in *KING OF JAZZ* (1930) and *Stand Up and Cheer* (1934). He returned to Broadway to play the art museum curator Whitelaw Savory in *ONE TOUCH OF VENUS* (1943) but by the 1950s he retired from show business.

BOLGER, RAY [born Raymond Wallace Bulcao] (1904–1987). Stage, film, and television performer. The rubber-jointed comic dancer and character actor, immortalized as the Scarecrow in the film *THE WIZARD OF OZ*, was featured on Broadway and in television musicals as well. Born in Dorchester, Massachusetts, he worked as a bank clerk and vacuum cleaner salesman while taking dance lessons and doing summer stock. Bolger was later part of a dance act in

Ray Bolger. The great Broadway and Hollywood dancer was often described as "rubber-limbed," not only because he seemed to bend in unexpected ways but also for his ability to bounce like a rubber ball. Here he is flying high in the Broadway hit *By Jupiter* (1942). (Photofest)

vaudeville before making his Broadway debut in 1926. He was featured in Rodgers and Hart's *HEADS UP!* (1929) and in some revues and then found acclaim with *ON YOUR TOES* (1936) where he played the teacher–hoofer Phil Dolan and got to perform "The Slaughter on Tenth Avenue" ballet. That same year he made his film debut in *THE GREAT ZIEGFELD*, followed by many movies over the next forty years, including *ROSALIE* (1937), *SWEETHEARTS* (1938), *The Wizard of Oz* (1939), *SUNNY* (1940), *Four Jacks and a Jill* (1941), *STAGE DOOR CANTEEN* (1943), *THE HARVEY GIRLS* (1945), *Look for the Silver Lining* (1949), *April in Paris* (1952), and *BABES IN TOYLAND* (1961). Bolger returned to Broadway on several occasions and starred as the mythological assistant Sapiens in Rodgers and Hart's *BY JUPITER* (1942), the Oxford student Charley Wickham in *Where's Charley?* (1948), which he reprised in the 1952 movie, and the foreign professor Fodorski in *All American* (1962). He also danced in six Broadway revues, including *LIFE BEGINS AT 8:40* (1934), *Keep Off the Grass* (1940), and *Three to Make Ready* (1946). Bolger also performed in many television musical specials, series, and dramas.

BOLTON, GUY [Reginald] (1884–1979). Stage and film writer. A prolific author of over fifty stage musicals in New York and London, he was instrumental in developing the new musical comedy model in the 1910s. Bolton was born in Broxbourne, England, to American parents and studied in New York and Paris to be an architect before turning to the theatre in 1912 when his first play opened in London. Although he would occasionally write dramas and comedies for Broadway and the West End, much of his career was occupied with musical librettos. His first on Broadway was *90 in the Shade* (1915) and that same year he teamed up with composer JEROME KERN to write the PRINCESS THEATRE MUSICALS, witty, small-scale, contemporary musicals that foreshadowed the American musical comedies of the 1920s and 1930s. Their first efforts together were *Nobody Home* (1915) and the hit *VERY GOOD EDDIE* (1915) and then British lyricist P. G. WODEHOUSE joined the team and the famous trio penned such groundbreaking shows as *OH, BOY!* (1917), *LEAVE IT TO JANE* (1917), and *OH, LADY! LADY!* (1918). Working with a variety of collaborators, Bolton wrote the books for such musicals as *The Riviera Girl* (1917), *Miss 1917* (1917), *The Rose of China* (1919), *SALLY* (1920), *Tangerine* (1920), *Sitting Pretty* (1924), *LADY, BE GOOD!* (1924), *TIP-TOES* (1925), *The Ramblers* (1926),

OH, KAY! (1926), *RIO RITA* (1927), *The Five O'Clock Girl* (1927), *ROSALIE* (1928), *SIMPLE SIMON* (1930), and *ANYTHING GOES* (1934). He spent much of the 1930s in London where he wrote a dozen West End musicals (most with Wodehouse) and then returned to Broadway for *WALK WITH MUSIC* (1940), *Hold on to Your Hats* (1940), *Jackpot* (1944), *FOLLOW THE GIRLS* (1944), *Ankles Aweigh* (1955), and *Anya* (1965). Many of Bolton's stage works were filmed and he also contributed to the movie musicals *THE LOVE PARADE* (1929), *DELICIOUS* (1931), *Careless Lady* (1932), *ZIEGFELD FOLLIES* (1946), *TILL THE CLOUDS ROLL BY* (1946), *EASTER PARADE* (1948), and *WORDS AND MUSIC* (1948). Although most of Bolton's work was light-hearted musical comedy with few pretensions to musical drama, he was an expert crafts-man and an important innovator for musical comedy structure. Autobiography: *Bring on the Girls! The Improbable Story of Our Life in Musical Comedy*, with Wodehouse (1953).

🕭 *BOMBO* (Jolson's 59th Street Theatre 1921). An extravagant vehicle for AL JOLSON, the show featured a farcical performance by the renowned entertainer and introduced three songs that became standards. The inconse-quential libretto by Harold Atteridge allowed Jolson to play the blackface servant Bombo who accompanies Christopher Columbus (Forrest Huff) on his voyage to discover America. SIGMUND ROMBERG (music) and Atteridge (lyrics) wrote the score but all the hits songs ("California, Here I Come," "Toot, Toot, Tootsie," and "April Showers") were by other tunesmiths and had been added by Jolson before or after opening, one of them interpo-lated in the post-Broadway tour. The produc-ing SHUBERTS provided a lavish production directed by J. C. HUFFMAN, but all the audience cared about for 218 performances was Jolson who triumphed in the new playhouse the Shuberts built and named for him.

BOONE, PAT [born Charles Eugene Boone] (1934–). Film and television performer. The squeaky-clean pop singer who rose to fame in the late 1950s, he brought his agree-able singing voice and ingratiating smile to a handful of movie musicals. Boone was born in Jacksonville, Florida, and was raised in Nashville where he sang on the radio as a teen-ager. After graduating from North Texas State College and Columbia University, he became nationally famous from his appearances on television and sold millions of easy-listening music when rock was starting to take over. In fact, some of his biggest hits were softened ver-sions of rock songs. Boone made his film debut in the musical *Bernadine* (1957), followed by *April Love* (1957), *Mardi Gras* (1958), *All Hands on Deck* (1961), *STATE FAIR* (1962), and *The Main Attraction* (1963), as well as some non-musicals. His acting may have been a bit stiff, but Boone's charisma usually helped and he was very popular on screen. He only returned to films sporadically after the mid-1960s, but he was a frequent and familiar face on televi-sion for decades after. His daughter is singer Debbie Boone (1956–). Autobiography: *Pat Boone's America: 50 Years* (2006); biography: *Pat Boone*, Paul Davis, Cliff Richard, George Hamilton (2002).

BOOTH, SHIRLEY [born Thelma Booth Ford] (1907–1992). Stage, film, and television per-former. An unlikely star with a raspy voice and frumpy figure, she won applause in both tragic and comic roles in all media. The native New Yorker was performing in amateur theatre productions as a preteen and started acting professionally in 1923. Two years later she made her Broadway debut but not until after ten years of playing supporting roles in plays did she gain recognition for her gang-ster's moll Mabel in the comedy *Three Men on a Horse* (1935). For the next thirty-five years Booth played a variety of roles in plays as different as *The Philadelphia Story* (1939) and *Come Back, Little Sheba* (1950). Her first Broadway musical role was columnist Louhedda Hopsons in the spoof *Hollywood Pinafore* (1945), followed by the life-affirm-ing Aunt Cissy in *A TREE GROWS IN BROOKLYN* (1951), the ex-vaudevillian Lottie Gibson in *BY THE BEAUTIFUL SEA* (1954), the tragic Irish mother Juno Boyle in *JUNO* (1959), and the German nun Mother Maria in *Look to the Lilies* (1970). Booth had a limited film career, although she triumphed in the 1952 film of *Come Back, Little Sheba* and appeared in one musical, *Main Street to Broadway* (1953), but she was very successful on television with the popular series *Hazel* in the 1960s. She also did radio broadcasts of famous plays in the 1940s and 1950s. Although Booth's baby voice and broad heart-on-her-sleeve style are open to caricature, she had a surprisingly honest sense of character and could be chillingly moving.

BORDONI, IRENE (1895–1953). Stage performer. The coquettish singer–actress was known for playing naughty Parisian femme fatales on the stages of Europe and America and introducing such provocative songs as "Do It Again" and

"Let's Do It." Bordoni was born on the island of Corsica and was performing in Paris cabarets and revues by the time she was a teenager. She made her Broadway debut in 1912 and was featured in the musical revues *Broadway to Paris* (1912) and *Hitchy-Koo* (1917 and 1918) and then played funny and sexy seductresses in plays and book musicals, most memorably as the temptress Vivienne Rolland in *Paris* (1928) and the vampy Madame Bordelaise in *LOUISIANA PURCHASE* (1940). Bordoni's other Broadway musicals include *As You Were* (1920), *The French Doll* (1922), and *Great Lady* (1938). She appeared in the early film revue *THE SHOW OF SHOWS* (1929) and reprised her Vivienne in the 1929 film version of *Paris*. She got to repeat her Madame Bordelaisew in a 1951 television version of *Louisiana Purchase* and that same year made her last American appearance as the crafty Bloody Mary in a tour of *SOUTH PACIFIC*. Bordoni was married to Broadway producer and songwriter E. Ray Goetz (1886–1954).

BORN TO DANCE (MGM 1936). Although some of his songs had appeared in earlier film musicals, this was songwriter COLE PORTER's first screen assignment and he did not disappoint, writing his first Hollywood standard, "I've Got You Under My Skin." The rich and varied score also included "Rap Tap on Wood," "Easy to Love," "Love Me, Love My Pekinese," and "Swingin' the Jinx Away." They were just part of the many riches in the JACK CUMMINGS production directed by ROY DEL RUTH and choreographed by DAVE GOULD. The Jack McGowan and SID SILVERS screenplay was one of the earlier sailors-on-leave musicals but the plot was more concerned with the newcomer Nora Paige (ELEANOR POWELL) who understudies the temperamental Broadway star Lucy James (VIRGINIA BRUCE) and, to no one's surprise, becomes a star when she steps in for Lucy on opening night. The sailors were Silvers, JAMES STEWART, and BUDDY EBSEN. Also featured

Born to Dance. Eleanor Powell (pictured) was so confident and accomplished in her tap dancing that she always came off looking like a million bucks, even when put into the most ridiculous production numbers. Here she is in the finale of *Born to Dance* as she taps on deck a battleship only Hollywood could devise. (Photofest)

were FRANCES LANGFORD, UNA MERKEL, Raymond Walburn, REGINALD GARDINER, Alan Dinehart, and Georges and Jalna who danced while Bruce sang the intoxicating "I've Got You Under my Skin." The most famous (and later most parodied) number in the film was the nautical finale "Swingin' the Jinx Away" set on a white battleship with Powell swinging down from the crow's nest to tap her way across the shiny deck. The scene would be playfully copied on a small scale in the Off Broadway musical *DAMES AT SEA* (1968).

BORZAGE, FRANK (1893–1962). Film director. Known mostly for his soft-focus romantic weepers, the prodigious director also helmed eight musicals. A native of Salt Lake City, Borzage worked in the silver mines when he was only thirteen and escaped by becoming an actor with a touring theatre company and then in silent films. He appeared in dozens of Westerns and comedies before turning director in 1916 and helming the same kinds of flicks for UNIVERSAL. Borzage's success with *Seventh Heaven* (1927) and similarly sentimental features labeled him a director of "women's pictures" but in truth he excelled at many genres and his eighty-plus credits are filled with top-notch products. Among his musicals were *Flirtation Walk* (1934), *Shipmates Forever* (1935), *Smilin' Through* (1941), and *STAGE DOOR CANTEEN* (1943).

BOSLEY, TOM [Edward] (1927–). Stage and television performer. A short, rotund, smiling character actor best known from television, he also enjoyed some success on Broadway. Bosley was born in Chicago, educated at De Paul University and the Radio Institute of Chicago, and then began acting in stock. He made his Off Broadway debut in 1955 and appeared there in some revivals before finding acclaim with his Broadway debut as Mayor Fiorello La Guardia in the musical *FIORELLO!* (1959). His subsequent musicals, *Nowhere to Go But Up* (1962) and *The Education of H*Y*M*A*N K*A*P*L*A*N* (1968), failed to run so Bosley concentrated on television where he won fame for the series *Happy Days* and hundreds of appearances on other sit-coms, dramatic series, and specials. Bosley returned to Broadway as the French father Maurice in *BEAUTY AND THE BEAST* (1994) and as a replacement for the Jewish grocer Schultz in the revival of *CABARET* in 1998.

BOSTWICK, BARRY (1945–). Stage, television, and film performer. The genial, all-purpose leading man is mostly known for his television appearances but is also an accomplished song-and-dance man with stage credits. Bostwick was born in San Mateo, California, and educated at California-Western and New York University before making his Manhattan stage debut in 1966. After getting supporting roles in classic and new plays and appearing in the musical flop *Soon* (1971), he found recognition as the original Danny Zuko in *GREASE* (1972). Bostwick also shone as the outlaw Jamie Lockhart in *THE ROBBER BRIDEGROOM* (1976) and the amateur sleuth Nick Charles in the short-lived *Nick & Nora* (1991). He then went to television where he acted in dramatic and comedic series, specials, and miniseries. Bostwick only made a few films but became part of a cult phenomenon when he played the nerdy Brad in *THE ROCKY HORROR PICTURE SHOW* (1975). He was also the songwriter-juvenile lead in the film spoof *MOVIE MOVIE* (1978).

BOSWELL, CONNEE (1907–1976). Film performer. A popular band, radio, and recording singer, she made appearances in eight Hollywood musicals. Boswell was born in Kansas City, Missouri, and began in show business as a sibling trio on the radio with her sisters Martha and Vet (Helvetia). The Boswell Sisters were nationally known by the 1930s for their recordings, radio performances, and concerts, including an international tour that made them very popular in Europe. The threesome were featured in the movie musicals *THE BIG BROADCAST* (1932), *Moulin Rouge* (1934), and *Transatlantic Merry-Go-Round* (1934) before the act broke up and Connee went solo. She sang in the films *ARTISTS AND MODELS* (1937), *Kiss the Boys Goodbye* (1941), *Syncopation* (1942), *Swing Parade of 1946*, and *Senior Prom* (1959). She continued to perform until 1975, with the public never knowing that she suffered from crippling polio as a child and always used an upright wheelchair, which was disguised by her long dresses when she appeared in public. She changed her name from Connie to Connee halfway through her career because her polio-stricken hands made it too difficult to sign autographs with the dotted "i."

BOY FRIEND, THE (Royale Theatre 1954). A pastiche show that spoofed the addle-brained musical comedies of the 1920s, the British import also managed to be highly entertaining in its own right. Sandy Wilson wrote the score and libretto, both of which were filled with clichés: rich girl Polly (JULIE ANDREWS) at a

Casts for *The Boy Friend*			
Character	1954 Broadway	1970 Broadway	1971 film
Polly Browne	JULIE ANDREWS	Judy Carne	Twiggy
Tony	John Hewer	Ronald Young	Christopher Gable
Maisie	Ann Wakefield	SANDY DENNIS	Antonia Ellis
Bobby/Tommy	Bob Scheerer	Harvey Evans	TOMMY TUNE
Mme. Dubonnet	Ruth Altman	Jeanne Beauvais	Moyra Fraser
Percy Browne	Eric Berry	Leon Shaw	Bryan Pringle
Dulcie	Dilys Lay	Simon McQueen	Caryl Little
De Thrill			Vladek Sheybal

boarding school for girls on the French Riviera falls in love with delivery boy Tony (John Hewer) who is really an heir in disguise and so and so on. It was as predictable as it was delicious, particularly when the cast was so engaging and the songs were so tuneful. Wilson remained true to the period in his music, and the lyrics were only a bit sillier than the originals had been. "Won't You Charleston With Me?" was not that far removed from the Jimmy Johnson–Cecil Mack original "Charleston," "I Could Be Happy With You" more than echoed Youmans-Caesar's "I Want to Be Happy," and "A Room in Bloomsbury" captured the naive joy of all those "lets get away together" numbers from the era. Also expert were "It's Never Too Late to Fall in Love," "Safety in Numbers," "Fancy Forgetting," and the sprightly title song. Directed by CY FEUER, the small-scale production managed to run 485 performances without benefit of names in the cast, although Andrews (in her first Broadway appearance) certainly became a name thanks to her engaging performance. The musical soon found itself a favorite in schools where it entertained audiences who were too young to be familiar with the kind of theatre being spoofed. A Broadway revival in 1970 featured television star Judy Carne as Polly and both she and the production met with disappointing notices, although critics applauded SANDY DUNCAN as the second lead Maisie. Gus Schirmer directed, Buddy Schwab choreographed, and the revival ran 111 performances.

■ *The Boy Friend* (MGM/EMI 1971) was producer–director KEN RUSSELL'S satire of the stage musical, showing a second-rate theatre company putting on the play and, being a spoof of a spoof, it worked on so many levels that it all started to resemble a psychedelic trip. Yet despite the exaggerated characterizations both on and backstage and the expressionistic sets and costumes, the movie was as enjoyable at times as the stage version. The Hollywood director De Thrill catches a poorly attended matinee of the show in which the company's gofer must go on and play Polly because the star has broken her foot. As De Thrill watches the show, he imagines the piece on screen with a BUSBY BERKELEY-like spectacle and the movie added Hollywood to its satirical targets. Whether one enjoyed or was annoyed with Russell's embellishments, there was still some wonderful singing and dancing to content one. The cast was first-rate, with model Twiggy coming across as the happiest surprise, and one couldn't miss lanky TOMMY TUNE in his film debut showing off his dancing talents as the anxious-to-please hoofer Tommy. Some of Wilson's songs were cut and the familiar standards "You Are My Lucky Star" and "All I Do Is Dream of You" were added to the backstage tale in which Polly really has a crush on the actor playing Tony. Also of interest were Tony Walton's stylized sets for both the stage and the fantasy sequences, helping to give this unique film a look like no other.

🎬 *BOY FROM OZ, THE* (Imperial Theatre 2003). A biographical musical with an unusual twist, the musical succeeded because the star playing the lead was more interesting and more talented than the star being impersonated. The libretto by Martin Sherman and Nick Enright was purportedly about the Australian entertainer Peter Allen, but as performed by a fellow Aussie, the show ended up being a triumph for Hugh Jackman. The plot showed how the gay singer–songwriter Allen found fame in his native country and then headed to England and America where he became a celebrity for his association with JUDY GARLAND (Isabel Keating) and for marrying her daughter LIZA MINNELLI (Stephanie J. Block). After a colorful romp through nightclubs and headlines, he dies of AIDS. Using Allen's pop tunes from the 1970s ("Everything Old Is New Again, "Love Doesn't Need a Reason," "I Honestly Love You," and "I Go to Rio") as its score, the musical biography was a disjointed affair that pleased none of the reviewers but there was nothing but raves for film and television actor Jackman whose popularity allowed the show to run 364 performances.

🖸 *BOYS FROM BOISE, THE* (DuMont 1944). Running two hours, employing a large cast almost entirely of females, and featuring a score of fourteen songs, this musical broadcast was far from simple so it is amazing to learn that it was also the first musical made for television. There had been some musical specials seen previously, but it took a great deal of courage and insanity on the part of producer Sam Medoff and his sponsors to mount such a show on the DuMont network when there were so few televisions out there to receive it. The critics saw it and declared it a bold experiment and a lot of fun as well. A troupe of show girls gets stranded in Boise, Idaho, and takes jobs on a ranch to earn enough money to get them back home. The chorines encounter a crooked ranger owner, a band of rustlers, and an FBI agent out to get his man (who turns out to be a girl). Medoff also wrote the score and, with director Ray Nelson and Constance Smith, the teleplay. The songs ranged from the lively chorus numbers "Rodeo," "Girls of the Eight-to-the-Bar X Ranch," and "Chiki Chiquita" to the more rustic ballads, such as "Sunset Trail," "Broken-Hearted Blues," and "It's a Mystery to Me." The cast was made up of unknowns, although Dolores Wilson would later be featured in Broadway musicals. As one critic put it: "An important and expensive first."

BOYS FROM SYRACUSE, THE (Alvin Theatre 1938). With its tight, solid libretto based on Shakespeare's *A Comedy of Errors* and its scintillating score by RICHARD RODGERS (music) and LORENZ HART (lyrics), the musi-

The Boys From Syracuse. Eddie Albert (left) got the best musical role of his uneven Broadway career as Antipholus of Syracuse who finds love and adventure in Ephesus. Pint-sized Jimmy Savo played his slave Dromio with more vaudeville than ancient Greece in his delightful performance. (Photofest)

cal is one of the most easily revived of all 1930s musicals.

Plot: In the ancient city of Ephesus, the master Antipholus and his slave Dromio arrive from Syracuse and are immediately confused with their twins, the local Antipholus and his slave Dromio who are married to Adriana and Luce, respectively. Complications ensue, especially when the Syracusan Antipholus falls in love with Adriana's sister Luciana. Only after the two Antipholuses' aged father Aegeon, who earlier explained how the two sets of twins were separated in a shipwreck, discovers them both in town does everything end happily.

Casts for *The Boys From Syracuse*

Character	1938 Broadway	1940 film	1963 Off Broadway
Antipholus of Syracuse	EDDIE ALBERT	ALLAN JONES	Stuart Damon
Antipholus of Ephesus	Ronald Graham	Allan Jones	Clifford David
Dromio of Syracuse	JIMMY SAVO	JOE PENNER	Danny Carroll
Dromio of Ephesus	Teddy Hart	Joe Penner	Rudy Tronto
Adriana	Muriel Angelus	Irene Harvey	Ellen Hanley
Luciana/Phyllis	Marcy Wescott	ROSEMARY LANE	Julienne Marie
Luce	Wynn Murray	MARTHA RAYE	Karen Morrow

The inspiration for the show came from Hart's brother Teddy who was always being mistaken for the comic JIMMY SAVO, both of them being short and rather dumpy. GEORGE ABBOTT wrote the efficient libretto and both produced and directed the musical, performing all tasks with masterly control and cleverness. None of Shakespeare's dialogue was used except one line, and the musical was filled anachronisms and slang, making it feel very 1930s, even though it is set in ancient times. Because of its surefire plot and delightful score, the show remains the most produced of the Rodgers and Hart musicals.

Although Hart's alcoholism was slowing down his output at the time, he and Rodgers quickly came up with one of their brightest scores. "Falling in Love With Love" and "This Can't Be Love" were instant hits, but the song that brought the house down each night was the swinging trio "Sing for Your Supper." Also outstanding are the mock revival number "Oh, Diogenes," the soft-shoe "Dear Old Syracuse," the comic duet "What Can You Do with a Man?," and the expository opening "I Had Twins." George Balanchine choreographed the show; his ballet for "Big Brother" was one of the highlights of the second act. The musical also afforded EDDIE ALBERT, Savo, and Teddy Hart with the best roles of their stage careers. *The Boys From Syracuse* ran a profitable ten months on Broadway but did not join the revival repertory until a charming 1963 production Off Broadway directed by Christopher Hewitt and choreographed by Bob Herget. This faithful version (no outside Rodgers and Hart songs were added) ran nearly twice as

long as the original (502 performances) and allowed *The Boys From Syracuse* to become a revival favorite. It also created enough interest for the first British mounting of the musical in 1963 at London's Drury Lane Theatre, leading to productions in Australia and Germany in the 1960s, followed by others wherever American musicals are enjoyed. *The Boys From Syracuse* received its first Broadway revival in 2002, although the show had been seen in a concert version in 1997 as part of the ENCORES! series. SCOTT ELLIS directed the ROUNDABOUT THEATRE production, and ROB ASHFORD choreographed. Despite a strong cast that included Tom Hewitt and Jonathan Dokuchitz (the Antipholuses), Lee Wilkof and CHIP ZIEN (the Dromios), Lauren Mitchell (Adriana), Erin Dilly (Luciana), and Toni diBupno (Luce), the revival received lukewarm notices and was not extended beyond its seventy-three-performance engagement.

The Boys From Syracuse (Universal 1940) was one of the most disappointing film versions of a Rodgers and Hart musical. The screenplay by Leonard Spiegelgass and Charles Grayson reduced the piece to a seventy-three-minute sketch. The garish production, complete with cigar-smoking citizens of antiquity and chariots checkered like modern taxicabs, was neither humorous nor popular. The fault was not with the talented cast but with the lack of wit (both highbrow and lowbrow) on the part of the writing and the direction by EDWARD SUTHERLAND. The Rodgers and Hart score was decimated; some songs were cut, some numbers were reduced to background music, and others were edited to the point of becoming teasers. The two new songs ("Who Are You?" and "The Greeks Have No Word for It"), although by Rodgers and Hart, were forgettable at best. The whole enterprise was so dreary that the film buried the original show in the minds of many and it lay dormant for over twenty years before it was rediscovered by theatre groups thanks to the 1963 Off Broadway revival.

BRACKEN, EDDIE [Vincent] (1915–2002). Film, television, and stage performer. A boyish-looking bumbling comic who befuddled his way through comedies on Broadway and on screen, he shone in a dozen Hollywood musicals, usually as shy and put-upon juveniles. Bracken was born in Queens, New York, and attended Manhattan's Professional Children's School before performing in vaudeville. As

---

The Boys From Syracuse (stage) Musical Numbers

"I Had Twins"
"Dear Old Syracuse"
"What Can You Do With a Man?"
"Falling in Love With Love"
"The Shortest Day of the Year"
"This Can't Be Love"
"Let Antipholus In"
"Ladies of the Evening"
"He and She"
"You Have Cast Your Shadow on the Sea"
"Come With Me"
"Big Brother"
"Sing for Your Supper"
"Oh, Diogenes"

a youth he appeared in several comedy film shorts and then returned to the stage, making his Broadway debut in 1933 and acting in a handful of comedies. His performance as the footballer Jojo Jordan in the musical *TOO MANY GIRLS* (1939) brought him back to Hollywood for the 1940 film version and he stayed to play featured roles in the musicals *THE FLEET'S IN* (1942), *Sweater Girl* (1942), *STAR-SPANGLED RHYTHM* (1942), *HAPPY GO LUCKY* (1943), *Rainbow Island* (1944), *Bring on the Girls* (1945), *Out of This World* (1945), *Duffy's Tavern* (1945), *Ladies' Man* (1947), *SUMMER STOCK* (1950), *Two Tickets to Broadway* (1951), and *About Face* (1952). Bracken was always well known from his farcical performance in some Preston Sturges comedies. He returned to Broadway for the musicals *Shinbone Alley* (1957), *Beg, Borrow or Steal* (1960), as Horace Vandergelder in the 1978 revival of *HELLO, DOLLY!*, and as a replacement for MICKEY ROONEY in *SUGAR BABIES* in 1982. Bracken made many television appearances up to the end of the century, including the original TV musical *STRAWBERRY BLONDE* (1959).

BRADLEY, GRACE (1913–). Film performer. An impish redhead who played second leads, usually in femme fatale roles, the singer–dancer was featured in several 1930s musicals. Bradley was born in Brooklyn and made her feature film debut in 1932. The next year she sang in her first musical, *Too Much Harmony*, and went on to play featured dames in such B pictures as *The Way to Love* (1933), *Girl Without a Room* (1933), *Stolen Harmony* (1935), and *Old Man Rhythm* (1935) before getting attention in better films, such as *Rose of the Rancho* (1936), *ANYTHING GOES* (1936), *WAKE UP AND LIVE* (1937), and *BIG BROADCAST OF 1938*. Bradley's other musical credits include *Three Cheers for Love* (1936), *Sitting on the Moon* (1936), and *There's Magic in Music* (1941). When her appeal waned in the 1940s, she retired.

BRADY, ALICE (1892–1939). Stage and film performer. The versatile actress–singer moved from playing light-headed ingénues to tragic figures on Broadway and then had a movie career where she excelled in daffy matrons in comedies and musicals. The native New Yorker was the daughter of theatrical producer William A. Brady and was educated at the Boston Conservatory of Music for an opera career. Brady appeared in several Gilbert and Sullivan operettas on Broadway (1910–1915) and in musical comedies such as *The Balkan*

Prince (1911), *The Love Letter* (1921), *The Blushing Bride* (1922), *The Yankee Princess* (1922), *Dew Drop Inn* (1923), and *Madame Pompadour* (1924). She had played serious parts in several silent films in the 1910s and by the 1920s she turned to dramatic roles on stage and found a new career climaxing with her performance in *Mourning Becomes Electra* (1931). The next year Brady left Broadway for good and returned to Hollywood, this time getting cast in character parts, such as the screwball mother in *My Man Godfrey* (1936). She played other comic matrons in such musicals as *Broadway to Hollywood* (1933), *THE GAY DIVORCEE* (1934), *GOLD DIGGERS OF 1935*, *Three Smart Girls* (1936), *ONE HUNDRED MEN AND A GIRL* (1937), *Merry Go Round of 1938* (1937), and *JOY OF LIVING* (1938).

BRAHAM, DAVID (1838?–1905). Stage composer. An early and important theatre composer, he wrote the music for several of the *MULLIGAN GUARD* musicals featuring Harrigan and Hart. Braham was born in London and as a teenager came to America where he played violin for a minstrel company. After composing songs for military bands, music halls, and orchestras, he was made musical director at Tony Pastor's Music Hall, the birthplace of American vaudeville. In 1873 Braham joined with performers–producers EDWARD HARRIGAN and TONY HART in scoring their musical spoofs and later their series of pioneering musical farces about the Mulligan Guards, beginning with *The Mulligan Guards' Picnic* (1978). For a decade these popular shows gave the public such songs as "Maggie Murphy's Home," "The Babies on Our Block," "Little Widow Dunn," "The Mulligan Guard," and "Paddy Duffy's Cart." Other Braham musicals with Harrigan and Hart include *CORDELIA'S ASPIRATIONS* (1883), *Dan's Tribulations* (1884), *McKenna's Flirtation* (1889), *Reilly and the Four Hundred* (1890), and *Marty Malone* (1896). Braham and most of his songs are long forgotten but he helped lay the groundwork for a truly American musical comedy sound in the theatre. Biography: *David Braham: The American Offenbach*, Jo Franchecina (2002).

BREAUX, MARC, AND DEEDEE WOOD. Film, television, and stage choreographers. Dancers-turned-choreographers, the married couple is most remembered for the spirited dances they devised for some 1960s film musicals. DeeDee Wood [born Audrey Donella] (1927–) was born in Boston and appeared on Broadway in the chorus of CAN-CAN (1953) and other shows. Marc [Charles] Breaux (1925?–) was born in Carenco, Louisiana, and danced on Broadway in KISS ME, KATE (1948), Catch a Star (1955), LI'L ABNER (1956), and DESTRY RIDES AGAIN (1959); he and Wood served as assistants to choreographer MICHAEL KIDD for the last two. Both co-choreographed DO RE ME (1960) and then he did the dances for Minnie's Boys (1970) and Lovely Ladies, Kind Gentlemen (1970), as well as Breaux directing the TV musical Goldilocks (1970). Wood recreated Kidd's choreography for the 1959 film version of Li'l Abner and then the two found their greatest success doing the imaginative dances for MARY POPPINS (1964). They also co-choreographed THE SOUND OF MUSIC (1965), The Happiest Millionaire (1967), CHITTY CHITTY BANG BANG (1968), and Huckleberry Finn (1974). The two also choreographed many television specials, including the TV version of OF THEE I SING (1972). Breaux alone choreographed the films The Slipper and the Rose (1976) and Sextette (1978).

BRECHER, IRVING S. (1914–). Film writer. A comedy writer for radio stars, he also penned several beloved Hollywood musicals. A native New Yorker, Brecher began his career as a newspaper reporter but soon turned to writing comedy material for MILTON BERLE, AL JOLSON, and other radio celebrities. He turned his talents to Hollywood writing sketches for NEW FACES OF 1937 and stayed to contribute many screenplays for comedies and musicals. Among his film musical credits are THE WIZARD OF OZ (1939), AT THE CIRCUS (1939), Go West (1940), BEST FOOT FORWARD (1943), DUBARRY WAS A LADY (1943), MEET ME IN ST. LOUIS (1944), Yolanda and the Thief (1945), ZIEGFELD FOLLIES (1946), SUMMER HOLIDAY (1948), Somebody Loves Me (1952), and BYE BYE BIRDIE (1963), as well as the 1959 TV version of Meet Me in St. Louis.

BREEN, BOBBY (1927–). Film performer. The singing moppet who was the male equivalent to SHIRLEY TEMPLE in the 1930s, the boy soprano was known for his unabashed sentimentality in acting and high-pitched trilling in singing. Breen was born in Toronto, Canada, and his bird-like singing voice brought him to the attention of Hollywood looking for a CHILD STAR to compete with the reigning queen Temple. He starred in his first feature, LET'S SING AGAIN (1936), and RKO built seven more musical vehicles to showcase him: Rainbow

on the River (1936), Make a Wish (1937), Hawaii Calls (1938), Breaking the Ice (1938), Fisherman's Wharf (1939), and Way Down South (1939). As a fifteen-year-old, Breen did a specialty spot in Johnny Doughboy (1942) and then left Hollywood to sing in nightclubs for the rest of his career.

BREMER, LUCILLE (1917–1996). Film performer. An elegant, statuesque dancer–actress, she was groomed to be a star but after four years in Hollywood retired. Bremer was born in Amsterdam, New York, and grew up in Philadelphia where she took dance lessons as a child and later was in the ballet corps of the Philadelphia Opera Company. While still a teenager she was a Rockette in New York and danced on Broadway in the chorus of PANAMA HATTIE (1940) and other shows. While performing in a nightclub, producer ARTHUR FREED spotted her and gave her a dance specialty in the film This Love of Mine (1944). Bremer played the eldest sister Rose in MEET ME IN ST. LOUIS (1944) and then danced opposite FRED ASTAIRE in Yolanda and the Thief (1945) and ZIEGFELD FOLLIES (1946). After she was featured in TILL THE CLOUDS ROLL BY (1946) and a few nonmusicals, Bremer married and retired from show business.

BRENDEL, EL [born Elmer Goodfellow Brendle] (1890–1964). Film and television performer. A Scandinavian-accented character actor, he specialized in gentle, innocent types who befriended the hero or heroine. Brendel was born in Philadelphia and began his career in vaudeville as a comedian. He made his film debut in 1926 and went on to appear in over sixty films, including a dozen musicals where he usually played someone named Swenson. Brendel's musical credits include The Cock-Eyed World (1929), SUNNY SIDE UP (1929), Happy Days (1930), Just Imagine (1930), DELICIOUS (1931), The Holy Terror (1937), Little Miss Broadway (1938), If I Had My Way (1940), and The Beautiful Bride From Bashful Bend (1949). In the 1950s he concentrated on television and was acting up to a few weeks before his death.

BRENNAN, WALTER [Andrew] (1894–1974). Film and television performer. A veteran character actor of over 100 films, he was a favorite on the big and small screens playing everything from crusty rural types to slick villains. Brennan was born in Swampscott, Massachusetts, and trained for an engineering career before turning to acting in vaudeville and stock. After serving in World War I, he went to Hollywood, made his film debut in 1923, and was kept very busy until the late 1950s when he concentrated on television and had two hit series. Neither a singer nor a dancer, Brennan appeared in several musicals over the decades, including *KING OF JAZZ* (1930), *Sing, Sinners, Sing* (1933), *GEORGE WHITE'S SCANDALS* (1934), *Metropolitan* (1935), *THE STORY OF VERNON AND IRENE CASTLE* (1939), *Rise and Shine* (1941), *CENTENNIAL SUMMER* (1946), and *The One and Only Genuine Original Family Band* (1968).

BRESSART, FELIX (1890–1949). Film performer. An amiable German character actor, he played sweetly comforting types in many Hollywood films, including a handful of musicals during his last ten years. Bressart was born in Eydtkuhnen in East Prussia and went on the German stage as a comic in 1914. He also appeared in European films beginning in 1928 but came to American when the Nazis took over. Bressart made his Hollywood debut in *Three Smart Girls Grow Up* (1939) and went on to play likable foreigners in thirty films before his death. His musicals include *Swanee River* (1939), *BITTER SWEET* (1940), *ZIEGFELD GIRL* (1941), *ICELAND* (1942), *Greenwich Village* (1944), *The Thrill of Brazil* (1946), and *A Song Is Born* (1948).

BRIAN, DONALD (1877–1948). Stage performer. With his dimpled good looks, wavy hair, and light but lyrical singing voice, he became a favorite matinee idol on Broadway in the early decades of the twentieth century. Brian was born in St. John's, Newfoundland, where he sang in a chorus as a child. After an education in Boston, he got roles in stock operetta companies and reached New York in 1899. Brian had featured roles in *The Supper Club* (1901), *The Belle of Broadway* (1902), *LITTLE JOHNNY JONES* (1904), and *FORTY-FIVE MINUTES FROM BROADWAY* (1906), but did not achieve fame until he played Prince Danilo in the first American production of *THE MERRY WIDOW* (1907). His other important musical credit was introducing JEROME KERN's first major song, "They Didn't Believe Me," in *THE GIRL FROM UTAH* (1914). Brian's other Broadway musicals include *The Dollar Princess* (1909), *The Siren* (1911), *The Marriage Market* (1913), *Her Regiment* (1917), *Buddies* (1919), *THE CHOCOLATE SOLDIER* (1921), and replacement roles in *Castles in the Air* (1927), *Yes, Yes, Yvette* (1927), and *MUSIC IN THE AIR* (1933). His

final Broadway appearance was as the fatherly William Graham in *VERY WARM FOR MAY* (1939).

BRICE, FANNY [Fanny Borach] (1891–1951). Stage and film performer. A unique comic singer known for her performances in revues and her voice on the radio, she could move from broad comedy to heart-wrenching torch songs with ease. Brice was a native New Yorker who as a child sang for customers in her family's saloon. Later in burlesque and vaudeville she developed a range of comic characters that she utilized throughout her long career, such as Yiddish-accented spinsters, mocking silent screen vamps, and whining, bratty children. Producer FLORENZ ZIEGFELD cast her as the comedienne in his *Follies of 1910* and was such a hit that she appeared in nine later editions of the *ZIEGFELD FOLLIES*. Brice also shone in other revues, such as *MUSIC BOX REVUE* (1924), *Sweet and Low* (1930), and *Crazy Quilt* (1931), and the book musicals *The Honeymoon Express* (1913) and *Fioretta* (1929). She made a handful of films and was most effective on the screen when she

Fanny Brice. The original "funny girl," Brice was a broad, ingenious comic yet there was always a touch of pathos about her as she lamented about her secondhand clothes and lack of masculine attention. Here she is clowning in the Broadway revue *Ziegfeld Follies* (1936). (Photofest)

played a version of herself and did one of her routines, as in the musicals *Night Club* (1928), *My Man* (1928), *Be Yourself* (1930), *THE GREAT ZIEGFELD* (1936), *Everybody Sing* (1938), and *ZIEGFELD FOLLIES* (1946). Brice was even more successful on the radio, playing Baby Snooks and other caricatures on the airwaves for decades. She was married to showman BILLY ROSE. BARBRA STREISAND played Brice in the Broadway musical *FUNNY GIRL* (1964), the 1968 film version, and the movie sequel *FUNNY LADY* (1975). Also, ALICE FAYE played a thinly disguised version of Brice's life in *Rose of Washington Square* (1939). Biographies: *Fanny Brice: The Original Funny Girl*, Herbert G. Goldman (rev 2002); *Funny Woman: The Life and Times of Fanny Brice*, Barbara Wallace Grossman (1992).

BRICUSSE, LESLIE (1931–). Stage, film, and television composer and lyricist. A successful songwriter of the British and American stages, he also penned some popular film musicals. Bricusse was born in London and educated at Cambridge where he wrote student theatricals. His first West End hit was *STOP THE WORLD—I WANT TO GET OFF* (1961) written with ANTHONY NEWLEY, which transferred successfully to Broadway in 1962. The duo presented their next show, *THE ROAR OF THE GREASEPAINT—THE SMELL OF THE CROWD*, in New York in 1965. Bricusse's other Broadway credits are the book and lyrics for *Pickwick* (1965), *VICTOR/VICTORIA* (1995), and *JEKYLL AND HYDE* (1997). He has also written several other London musicals. Bricusse has enjoyed a busy film career, writing the scores alone for *DOCTOR DOOLITTLE* (1967), *GOODBYE, MR. CHIPS* (1969), and *SCROOGE* (1970), as well as the lyrics for *Victor/Victoria* (1982), and collaborating with Newley again on *WILLY WONKA AND THE CHOCOLATE FACTORY* (1971), as well as the TV musicals *PETER PAN* (1976) and *BABES IN TOYLAND* (1986).

BRIGADOON (Ziegfeld Theatre 1947). One of the American theatre's most romantic musical fantasies, the Scottish-flavored show was the first hit for ALAN JAY LERNER (book and lyrics) and FREDERICK LOEWE (music).

Plot: American tourists Tommy Albright and Jeff Douglas stumble on the remote Scottish village of Brigadoon where Tommy falls for the lovely Fiona MacLaren and Jeff is pursued by the man-hungry Meg Brockie. It doesn't take long for the two foreigners to detect something odd going on and they eventually learn that a miracle allows the town to sleep 100 years each night, keeping it safe from the evils of the ever-changing world. In the subplot, the wedding of Charlie Dalrymple and Fiona's sister Jean is disrupted by the jealous Harry Beaton who attempts to destroy the town by running away but is stopped and accidentally dies. Tommy and Jeff must leave Brigadoon before the next day comes but, once back in New York, Tommy gives up his suffocating fiancée and rushes back to Brigadoon where his sincere love for Fiona allows him to stay.

Lerner's original libretto is a fanciful affair, more akin to a fantastical European operetta, yet it has the solid structure of a Rodgers and Hammerstein Broadway musical. It is a complicated and contrived tale at times, but the blend of romance and fantasy was readily accepted by critics and playgoers and the musical ran 581 performances. CHERYL CRAWFORD produced, ROBERT LEWIS directed, and AGNES DE MILLE did the riveting choreography. *Brigadoon* remains a favorite with all kinds of producing groups.

Lerner and Loewe wrote their first great score for *Brigadoon*, creating atmospheric pieces with a Scottish flavor for the residents of the town and retaining a Broadway sound for Tommy and the modern world. The standout hits were "The Heather on the Hill" and "Almost Like Being in Love," yet

Casts for *Brigadoon*

Character	1947 Broadway	1954 film	1966 television
Tommy Albright	David Brooks	GENE KELLY	ROBERT GOULET
Fiona MacLaren	Marion Bell	CYD CHARISSE	SALLY ANN HOWES
Jean MacLaren	Virginia Bosler	Virginia Bosler	Linda Howe
Jeff Douglas	George Keane	VAN JOHNSON	Peter Falk
Meg Brockie	Pamela Britton	Dodie Heath	Marlyn Mason
Charlie Dalrymple	Lee Sullivan	Jimmy Thompson	Thomas Carlisle
Harry Beaton	James Mitchell	Hugh Laing	Edward Villella

Brigadoon (stage) Musical Numbers

"Once in the Highlands"
"Brigadoon"
"Down on MacConnachy Square"
"Waitin' for My Dearie"
"I'll Go Home With Bonnie Jean"
"The Heather on the Hill"
"The Love of My Life"
"Jeannie's Packing Up"
"Come to Me, Bend to Me"
"Almost Like Being in Love"
"The Wedding Dance"
"The Sword Dance"
"The Chase"
"There But for You Go I"
"My Mother's Weddin' Day"
"Funeral Dance"
"From This Day On"

every song is compelling. The merry "I'll Go Home With Bonnie Jean" and the comic "My Mother's Weddin' Day" sound like authentic Scottish tunes, "Come to Me, Bend to Me" is an entrancing ballad–lullaby, and "Waitin' for My Dearie" and "There But for You Go I" are knowing character songs. Much of the success of *Brigadoon* was dependent on this rich score, for the music casts a spell on the audience and makes the fantasy possible. New York saw major revivals of *Brigadoon* in 1950 with Phil Hanna and Virginia Oswald as Tommy and Fiona, in 1957 with David Atkinson and Oswald, in 1962 with PETER PALMER and SALLY ANN HOWES, in 1964 with Palmer and Linda Bennett, in 1967 with Bill Hayes and Margot Moser, and in 1980 with Martin Vidnovic and Meg Bussert.

■ ***Brigadoon*** (MGM 1954) came to the screen as a ponderous dance show plagued by bad judgment, the biggest being producer ARTHUR FREED's decision to save money and film the pastoral tale in a Hollywood studio with artificial flora and fauna. Half of the glorious score was dropped and replaced with distinctively un-Scottish dance, particularly for GENE KELLY and CYD CHARISSE as Tommy and Fiona. VAN JOHNSON was amusing as Jeff but most of the characters failed to come to life. VINCENT MINNELLI directed, Kelly did the choreography, and Cedric Gibbons designed the phony settings. Even devoid of its stage magic, the film was relatively popular and the songs that survived, such as "Almost Like Being in Love" and "The

Heather on the Hill," became even more popular. ❏ Much more satisfying was ABC-TV's 1966 version of *Brigadoon*, which in ninety minutes captured much of the spirit of the original Broadway musical. ROBERT GOULET and SALLY ANN HOWES shone as Tommy and Fiona, Peter Falk stole all his scenes as Jeff, and Marlyn Mason was a delightful Meg. An added treat was ballet star Edward Villella as Harry Beaton and his performance in the wedding and chase dances choreographed by PETER GENNARO. Ernest Kinoy wrote the efficient teleplay and it was directed by producer Fielder Cook.

🎬 **BRING ON 'DA NOISE, BRING ON 'DA FUNK** (Ambassador Theatre 1996). This vibrant musical revue followed the evolution of American dance, in particular tap, as illustrated through the history of African Americans, from slaves using primitive drums to the hip-hop street dancers of the day. Reg E. Gaines (book and lyrics), Daryl Waters, Zane Mark, and Ann Duquesnay (music) were the authors, but it was the dancing that counted. Choreographer–dancer SAVION GLOVER developed the revue at the PUBLIC THEATRE Off Broadway and the response was so overwhelming that the program transferred to Broadway where it stayed for 1,523 performances. Featured with Glover in the cast were Ann Duquesnay, Jeffrey Wright, Vincent Bingham, Jared Crawford, Jimmy Tate, Dule Hill, Baakari Wilder, and Raymond King. The songs included "The Lynching Blues," "Now That's Tap," "Hittin'," "Chicago Bound," "I Got the Beat," "The Lost Beat Swing," and the title number. George C. Wolfe conceived the idea for the show and produced and directed it.

BRISSON [Pederson], **CARL** (1895–1958). Film performer. With his dapper smile and Continental air, the British song and dance man was featured in a few Hollywood films but never managed to become a screen star. Brisson was born in Copenhagen and began a career as a professional boxer before finding success in the British musical hall and in West End musicals. He starred in the English musical films *Song of Soho* (1930) *Prince of Arcadia* (1933), and *Two Hearts in Waltz Time* (1934) before being brought to Hollywood and groomed as a musical idol with *Murder at the Vanities* (1934). When he failed to appeal to audiences in the musicals *All the King's Horses* (1935) and *Ship Cafe* (1935),

Brisson returned to the British stage. His son was Broadway and film producer Frederick Brisson (1912–1984).

BRITISH MUSICALS. While British films and television shows of any genre were uncommon events in the States until the 1960s, stage musicals from Great Britain playing on Broadway and on tour were a familiar sight. From the pre–Revolutionary War days, plays and ballad–operas from London were a substantial part of the theatre fare in America. The Gilbert and Sullivan comic operettas were the most famous, but far from the only, British imports that were the rage with American playgoers in the late nineteenth century. In the year 1900, the most talked about musical on Broadway was *FLORODORA*, a London transfer, and New Yorkers got their first taste of West End favorites BEATRICE LILLIE, GERTRUDE LAWRENCE, JESSIE MATTHEWS, and JACK BUCHANAN in the imported *ANDRE CHARLOT'S REVUE of 1924.* NOEL COWARD's plays transferred well, as did his operetta hit *BITTER SWEET* (1929). The number of shows from London dwindled during the Depression and did not return in full force for another forty years. There were the occasional British successes after World War II, such as *THE BOY FRIEND* (1954), *STOP THE WORLD — I WANT TO GET OFF* (1962), and *OLIVER!* (1963), but for the most part it was Broadway sending the hits to London. All that started to change in the early 1970s when the ANDREW LLOYD WEBBER–TIM RICE musicals arrived and attracted a wider (and younger) audience than had been seen on Broadway in years. *JESUS CHRIST SUPERSTAR* (1971) began the assault but it was most felt in the team's *EVITA* (1979) and Webber's *CATS* (1982) and *PHANTOM OF THE OPERA* (1988). Even *ME AND MY GIRL*, a 1937 London hit that did not even try to cross the Atlantic back then, came to Broadway in 1986 and charmed everyone. Not only were native British products succeeding but foreign musicals developed and produced in London came over with a vengeance, as in the case of *LES MISÉRABLES* (1987) and *MISS SAIGON* (1991). The British invasion quieted down in the 1990s but since then we have seen such entries as *BLOOD BROTHERS* (1993), *SUNSET BOULEVARD* (1994), *CHITTY CHITTY BANG BANG* (2005), and *MARY POPPINS* (2006). Just as the West End has been saturated with American musicals over the last two decades, there will always be London shows playing on Broadway.

Hollywood turned out so many musicals during the golden age that Americans forget that there was a thriving film industry in Great Britain producing English musicals, very few of which came to the States. *EVERGREEN* (1934) was one of the very few exceptions and it was based on a West End show with a score by Rodgers and Hart. In the 1960s, British and American studios started to co-produce movie musicals with plans for wide distribution in both countries. Many of these were big-budget musicals filmed in England with American–British casts and were often set in Britain and based on English sources. Some of them were purely British products that were financed and promoted in America. *A HARD DAY'S NIGHT* (1964), *HELP!* (1965), *DOCTOR DOOLITTLE* (1967), *HALF A SIXPENCE* (1967), *Chitty Chitty Bang Bang* (1968), *GOODBYE, MR. CHIPS* (1969), *SCROOGE* (1970), *The Boy Friend* (1971), *TOMMY* (1975), and *THE ROCKY HORROR PICTURE SHOW* (1975) were among the British or British American musicals to find a wide audience on American screens. With conglomerates and merging companies, most movies today have many studios or companies behind them and nothing is quite purely American or otherwise. The market is international and the handful of movie musicals that are made today are made and distributed with the whole world in mind.

⬛ BROADWAY MELODY, THE (MGM 1929). This legendary movie boasts a series of firsts in film history: the first all-talking musical film (*THE JAZZ SINGER* had only a few lines of dialogue heard), the first use of Technicolor (for the vibrant "The Wedding of the Painted Doll" sequence), the first score (by NACIO HERB BROWN and ARTHUR FREED) written specifically for a film, the first original screenplay (by Jack McGowan and SID SILVERS) written for a musical, the first production that was shot with some of the music prerecorded, and the first musical to win the Best Picture ACADEMY AWARD. In addition, it had a cunning backstage story, intriguing characters, and flashy production numbers that still hold up. Vaudeville performing sisters Queenie (Anita Page) and Harriet "Hank" Mahoney (Bessie Love) find that their act (and their hearts) is broken up when song-and-dance man Eddie Kerns (CHARLES KING), who is engaged to Hank, falls in love with Queenie. All three were involved in a Broadway production, so there was plenty of opportunity for musical numbers. However, it is the few songs sung outside of the context of a show that were groundbreaking, such as "You Were Meant for Me" becoming a musical

The Broadway Melody. The film that introduced moviegoers to the backstage musical, *The Broadway Melody* was tough, unsentimental, and fascinating. Bessie Love (right) played the no-nonsense "Hank" Mahoney who was not going to let anyone get the better of her on stage, even the conniving Flo (Mary Doran) who knew how to lean on a piano provocatively. (Photofest)

Songs from the *Broadway Melody* films

The Broadway Melody (1929)
"The Broadway Melody"
"You Were Meant for Me"
"The Wedding of the Painted Doll"
"Harmony Babies"
"Youthful Parson Brown"
"The Boy Friend"

Broadway Melody of 1938 (1937)
"You Made Me Love You"
"Everybody Sing"
"Your Broadway and My Broadway"
"Some of These Days"
"Follow in My Footsteps"
"Yours and Mine"
"I'm Feelin' Like a Million"

Broadway Melody of 1936 (1935)
"Broadway Rhythm"
"I Got a Feeling You're Fooling"
"You Are My Lucky Star"
"Sing Before Breakfast"
"All I Do Is Dream of You"
"On a Sunday Afternoon"
"Broadway Rhythm"

Broadway Melody of 1940
"Begin the Beguine"
"Don't Monkey With Broadway"
"I've Got My Eyes on You"
"I Concentrate on You"
"All Ashore"
"Between You and Me"
"Jukebox Dance"

scene. The backstage scenes are not glamorized and there is a sassiness in the dialogue that foreshadows the tough GOLD DIGGERS movies and other Depression films. HARRY BEAUMONT directed the IRVING THALBERG production, which was the first talkie that most Americans at the time saw because it was given such a wide release. Although the title would be reused for other backstagers, the only movie that is an actual remake of *The Broadway Melody* is **Two Girls on Broadway** (MGM 1940). Jerome Chodorov and JOSEPH FIELDS wrote the screenplay, which renamed the sisters Pat (LANA TURNER) and Molly (JOAN BLONDELL) Mahoney, and the Eddie Kerns who comes between them was played by GEORGE MURPHY. Nine of the original songs were used but Freed, Brown, and ROGER EDENS provided "My Wonderful One, Let's Dance," which Turner and Murphy delivered with zest. Other numbers, by various songwriters, included "Broadway's Still Broadway," "Maybe It's the Moon," and "Rancho Santa Fe." S. Sylvan directed the JACK CUMMINGS production, which was choreographed by Eddie Larkin and BOBBY CONNOLLY.

■ BROADWAY MELODY OF 1936 (MGM 1935) had little in common with *The Broadway Melody* except for another marvelous score by Brown and Freed and another backstage story. McGowan and Silvers from the first picture teamed up with Harry Conn and wrote the screenplay about Broadway producer Bob Gordon (Robert Taylor) who is being bribed by a vicious gossip columnist Bert Keeler (JACK BENNY) but is saved by newcomer Irene Foster (ELEANOR POWELL) who goes on in the leading lady's part at the last minute. Just as the show within the movie made Foster a stage star, the film made Powell a screen star. Also cast in the John Considine, Jr., production were UNA MERKEL, FRANCES LANGFORD, Sid Silvers, VILMA and BUDDY EBSEN, JUNE KNIGHT, Harry Stockwell, Nick Long, Jr., and Paul Harvey. The highlights of the score were "I've Got a Feeling You're Fooling," "All I Do Is Dream of You," and "You Are My Lucky Star." ROY DEL RUTH directed, DAVE GOULD and ALBERTINA RAUSCH choreographed, and the picture was such a hit that a sequel was inevitable. **Broadway Melody of 1938** (MGM 1937) again featured Powell and Taylor, this time as performer Sally Lee and producer Steve Raleigh who is having trouble finding money to put on a show. Only when Sally's

race horse wins the grand prize can she save the show, play the leading lady, and win the heart of Steve. SOPHIE TUCKER played Alice Clayton who runs a boarding house for actors and tries to get her daughter Betty (JUDY GARLAND) into show business. Betty is infatuated with Clark Gable, and Garland ran away with the movie when she sang "You Made Me Love You" to his photograph. Betty and her mom end up in the big show as well and what a show it was. Tucker led the cast in singing "Your Broadway and My Broadway" and sang her signature song "Some of These Days." George Murphy joined Powell and Ebsen for "Follow in My Footsteps," and Garland was joined by the ensemble for "Everybody Sing." Del Ruth again directed and the cast also featured Binnie Barnes, Charles Igor Gorin, BILLY GILBERT, WILLIE HOWARD, Raymond Walburn, and Charley Grapewin. The final film in the series, **Broadway Melody of 1940** (MGM 1940), paired FRED ASTAIRE with Powell (surprisingly, their only movie together) and the two created magic together dancing to "Begin the Beguine" on a shiny black floor and surrounded by stars. The song was by COLE PORTER who also provided "I Concentrate on You," "I've Got My Eyes on You," and "Please Don't Monkey With Broadway." This last was sung by dance partners Johnny Brett (Astaire) and King Shaw (Murphy) who are at odds when Broadway star Clare Bennett (Powell) mistakenly chooses King as her new dancing partner. In a way, the silly plot was a reversal of that for the original *The Broadway Melody* so the series had come full circle. This time NORMAN TAUROG directed, and the supporting cast included FRANK MORGAN, Ian Hunter, Florence Rice, Lynne Carver, and HERMAN BING. Astaire and BOBBY CONNOLLY did the choreography, which was sensational.

BROADWAY RHYTHM. See *VERY WARM FOR MAY*

BRODERICK, HELEN (1891–1959). Stage and film performer. A distinctive comedienne who underplayed her characters and used a quiet, wry sense of humor, she was a favorite on Broadway and then in the movies. Broderick was born in Philadelphia, the daughter of an actor, and made her Broadway debut in the chorus of the 1907 edition of the ZIEGFELD FOLLIES. With her deadpan, wisecracking characters she soon was popular in both revues, such as *Nifties of 1923*, *Puzzles of 1925*, and

EARL CARROLL VANITIES (1932), and in book musicals, such as *Jumping Jupiter* (1911), *The Honeymoon Express* (1913), and *Oh, Please!* (1926). Broderick's most memorable Broadway appearances were as the American tourist Violet Hildegarde in *FIFTY MILLION FRENCHMEN* (1929) and a variety of wacky characterizations in the acclaimed revues *THE BAND WAGON* (1931) and *AS THOUSANDS CHEER* (1933). She went to Hollywood in 1933 and was a hit with her first screen musical, *TOP HAT* (1935), followed by *To Beat the Band* (1935), *SWING TIME* (1936), *Life of the Party* (1937), *Naughty But Nice* (1939), *NO, NO, NANETTE* (1940), *STAGE DOOR CANTEEN* (1943), and others. She was the mother of actor Broderick Crawford (1911–1986).

BRODERICK, MATTHEW (1962–). Stage and film performer. The forever-boyish-looking leading man first became a star playing teenagers in film and on Broadway, occasionally doing musicals in the latter venue. The native New Yorker is the son of stage and television actor James Broderick (1928–1982) and studied acting with Uta Hagen. Broderick made his first film when he was twenty-one and soon won attention as the teenage whiz in *War Games* (1983). He made his Broadway debut the same year as the wisecracking youth Eugene in *Brighton Beach Memoirs*, a role he continued in *Biloxi Blues* (1985). Moving back and forth from the stage to the screen, Broderick added musicals to his credits as the ambitious J. Pierrepont Finch in the popular 1995 Broadway revival of *HOW TO SUCCEED IN BUSINESS WITHOUT REALLY TRYING*, and he scored an even bigger triumph as the nerdy Leo Bloom in *THE PRODUCERS* (2001), which he filmed in 2005. His only other film musical credit is providing the voice for the adult Simba in the animated movie *THE LION KING* (1994), although he played Prof. Harold Hill in a 2003 TV version of *THE MUSIC MAN*. Broderick is married to actress Sarah Jessica Parker (1965–).

BRODSZKY, NICHOLAS (1905–1958). Film composer. An opera-flavored composer from Russia, he scored some tuneful Hollywood musicals in the 1950s. Brodszky was born in Odessa and raised in Hungary, studying music in Budapest and Rome before writing his first operetta at the age of twenty-four. He had successful musicals produced on the Hungarian and Austrian stages before scoring Hungarian movie musicals in the 1930s. Brodszky made his Hollywood debut in 1940 providing orchestral music for nonmusicals and then teamed up with lyricist SAMMY CAHN and others to write scores for the musicals *THE TOAST OF NEW ORLEANS* (1950), *Rich, Young and Pretty* (1951), *Small Town Girl* (1953), *Latin Lovers* (1953), additional songs for *THE STUDENT PRINCE* (1954), *Meet Me in Las Vegas* (1956), *The Opposite Sex* (1956), *Ten Thousand Bedrooms* (1957), and the British musical film *Let's Be Happy* (1957). Few of his movies were top drawer, but his songs, such as "Be My Love," "Because You're Mine," and "I'll Never Stop Loving You," were very popular, even though they were far from the pop sound of the decade.

BROOK, THE; OR, A JOLLY DAY AT THE PICNIC (San Francisco's Minstrel Hall 1879). A long-forgotten but important musical program that was a cross between a revue and a musical comedy, it sowed the seeds for both genres. Nate Salsbury of the touring Salsbury Troubadors wrote the entertainment in which a handful of variety performers go on a picnic together and then entertain each other with songs, dances, and vaudeville turns. It ran in the Manhattan venue called San Francisco Minstrel Hall for forty-two performances and was such a sensation that similar concoctions of acts held together by a premise became popular. The songs in *The Brook* came from various sources and included "Pretty as a Picture," "Dorkin's Night," "The Kiss," and "Love, Love, Beautiful Love." The musical toured extensively and was revived in New York in 1881. After that it fell into obscurity but its impact had been made.

BROOKS, JACK (1912–1971). Film lyricist. A British-born songwriter who wrote songs in America with a variety of composers, he even put words to Rimsky-Korsakoff's music for Hollywood. Brooks was born in Liverpool and emigrated to the States in 1916 to write songs for vaudeville and later radio. Having provided hit songs for BING CROSBY, PHIL HARRIS, and others, he was brought to Hollywood in 1939 to score films. With various composers he wrote theme songs for nonmusicals and scores for *Melody Lane* (1941), *Don't Get Personal* (1942), *Here Come the Co-eds* (1945), *The Countess of Monte Cristo* (1948), *Yes, Sir, That's My Baby* (1949), and other B pictures. Brooks received more recognition for his songs for *SON OF PALEFACE* (1952), *The Caddy* (1953), *ARTISTS AND MODELS* (1956), and *Cinderfella* (1960). He turned Rimsky-Korsakoff's classic melodies into songs for *Song of Scheherezade* (1947) and scored the TV musicals *SO HELP ME, APHRODITE* (1960) and *Around the World*

With Nellie Bly (1960). Brook's most famous song is "That's Amore," which he wrote with composer HARRY WARREN for DEAN MARTIN to sing in *The Caddy*.

BROOKS, MEL [born Melvin Kaminsky] (1926–). Film, stage, and television writer, performer, composer, and lyricist. A compulsive, high-energy funnyman who has struck gold in all media, he celebrates traditional comedy schtick with an irreverent flavor. The Brooklyn native began writing comedy sketches for television when he was still in his teens, providing jokes and scripts for SID CAESAR and his *Your Show of Shows*. He made his first film, the animated short *The Critic*, in 1963 and then returned to television to write the spy spoof series *Get Smart*. Brooks' first feature film was *The Producers* (1968), which he co-wrote and directed as he would all his movie projects. Every film had at least a song or two, usually written by Brooks, and some of the comedies border on musicals with their use of song and dance, such as *Blazing Saddles* (1974). He has appeared in many of his films, sometimes in leading roles, sometimes in cameos. Brooks' work in the theatre began when he wrote the libretto for the Broadway musical *Shinbone Alley* (1957). He also scripted the musical ALL AMERICAN (1962) but did not return to the theatre until his successful Broadway version of THE PRODUCERS (2001), which he adapted for the stage with THOMAS MEEHAN and provided a complete musical score. His most recent project is the Broadway version of YOUNG FRANKENSTEIN (2007). His wife was actress Anne Bancroft (1931–2005). Biographies: *It's Good to Be the King: The Seriously Funny Life of Mel Brooks*, James Robert Parish (2007); *Seesaw: A Dual Biography of Anne Bancroft and Mel Brooks*, William Holtzman (1979).

BROWN, GEORGIA [born Lillian Claire Laizer Getel Klot] (1933–1992). Stage, film, and television performer. The dark-haired, full-voiced British singer–actress appeared on Broadway sporadically over a period of thirty years but only had a hit once. Brown was born in London and as a child was sent to Wales to escape the German Blitzkrieg of Britain. She began her career as a cabaret singer, was first noticed on stage in 1956 as the competitive Lucy in a London revival of THE THREEPENNY OPERA, and she joined the New York company Off Broadway in 1957. Brown originated the role of the street tough Nancy in the London

musical OLIVER! and in 1963 reprised her performance in the first Broadway production, winning wide acclaim for her performance. She was similarly praised for her work in three less successful Broadway musicals: the pretend widow *Carmelina* (1979), the Parisian prostitute *Roza* (1987), and the crafty Mrs. Peachum in the 1989 revival titled *3 Penny Opera*. Brown was also a replacement for the Broadway revue *Side By Side By Sondheim* in 1977 and starred in her own revue *Georgia Brown and Friends* (1982). She appeared in a handful of British and American films and television shows.

BROWN, JASON ROBERT (1970–). Stage composer and lyricist. One of the most promising theatre songwriters from the end of the twentieth century, he has written sparkling scores for on and Off Broadway. Brown was born in Ossining, New York, the son of a salesman and a schoolteacher, and wrote songs from an early age. He attended the Eastman School of Music in Rochester for a time but quit to return to Manhattan and write for the theatre. Brown worked as a rehearsal pianist, conductor, music arranger, and music teacher while trying to get his songs heard. His first produced musical, the revue *Songs for a New World* (1995), had a short run but the recording got him noticed. Brown was widely praised for his complex score for the Broadway musical *PARADE* (1998) and the Off-Broadway two-character musical *The Last Five Years* (2001). His other scores include *Urban Cowboy* (2003), *Chanukah Suite* (2005), and *13* (2007). Brown's music is eclectic but mostly contemporary, and his lyrics are known for their incisive character revelation.

BROWN, JOE E[vans]. (1892–1973). Film, stage, and television performer. The wide-mouth, physical comedian who looks like a cartoon character, he was popular in all media even though his vehicles were usually second class. Brown was born in Holgate, Ohio, and left home at the age of nine to be a circus acrobat. After playing semi-pro baseball he went into vaudeville and burlesque before making his Broadway debut in 1918. Brown was cast in farcical supporting roles in comedies and such musicals as *Jim Jam Jems* (1920), *Greenwich Village Follies* (1921), *Betty Lee* (1924), *Captain Jinks* (1925), and *Twinkle Twinkle* (1926). By 1928 he was in silent movies and with the advent of sound was starred in some low-budget comedies that relied on his physical agility for laughs. Brown was also featured in the film musicals ON WITH THE SHOW (1929),

Song of the West (1930), HOLD EVERYTHING (1930), Top Speed (1930), The Lottery Bride (1930), Maybe It's Love (1930), Bright Lights (1935), Sons o' Guns (1936), Joan of the Ozarks (1942), Chatterbox (1943), Pin-Up Girl (1944), and HOLLYWOOD CANTEEN (1944). He returned to the stage, appearing on Broadway in the musical Courtin' Time (1951), and did radio and nightclubs before returning to Hollywood for his two best roles: Cap'n Andy in the 1951 version of SHOW BOAT and millionaire Osgood Fielding III in Some Like It Hot (1959). Brown was busy on television in the 1950s and 1960s. Autobiography: Laughter Is a Wonderful Thing (1959); biography: Joe E. Brown: Film Comedian and Baseball Buffoon, Wes D. Gehring, Conrad Lane (2006).

BROWN, LEW [born Louis Brounstein] (1893–1958). Stage and film lyricist and writer. As part of the team of DeSylva, Brown, and Henderson, the songwriter had a series of Broadway hits in the 1920s and 1930s and scored some notable film musicals as well. Brown was born in Odessa, Russia, and came as a child to America where as a teenager he started writing songs for Tin Pan Alley, finding success with such hits as "Put Your Arms Around Me, Honey" and "Take Me Out to the Ball Game." In 1925 he teamed up with composer RAY HENDERSON and lyricist–writer B. G. DeSYLVA and had their songs heard in the Broadway musicals GEORGE WHITE'S SCANDALS (1925 and 1926) and Piggy (1927). The trio's GOOD NEWS! (1927) was a major hit, followed by Manhattan Mary (1927), HOLD EVERYTHING! (1928), FLYING HIGH (1930), Hot-Cha! (1932), Yokel Boy (1939), and the revues George White's Scandals (1928 and 1931), Strike Me Pink (1933), and Calling All Stars (1934). Most of the trio's stage works were filmed and Brown also contributed lyrics to the original film musicals THE SINGING FOOL (1928), SUNNY SIDE UP (1929), Just Imagine (1930), Stand Up and Cheer (1934), The Music Goes Round (1936), NEW FACES OF 1937, and Swing Fever (1943). Brown's lyrics are colloquial, sassy, and playful and can be described as quintessential Roaring Twenties in their flavor. Among his most famous songs are "Black Bottom," "The Best Things in Life Are Free," "Don't Sit Under the Apple Tree (With Anyone Else But Me)," "The Varsity Drag," and "Birth of the Blues." Ernest Borgnine portrayed Brown in the musical film bio The Best Things in Life Are Free (1956). Biography: The Best Things in Life Are Free: The De Sylva, Brown & Henderson Story, John O'Hara (1955).

BROWN, [Ig]NACIO HERB (1896–1964). Film composer. One of the first American composers to concentrate on film musicals, he wrote some of the most beloved movie songs of the 1930s. Brown was born in Deming, New Mexico, and studied at the Musical Arts High School in Los Angeles before working as a tailor and a real estate agent. He wrote popular songs but instead of going to Broadway as most songwriters did he elected to stay in Hollywood and was ready when sound came in. Brown composed the industry's first full film score for A BROADWAY MELODY (1929) with ARTHUR FREED providing the lyrics. The two also collaborated on HOLLYWOOD REVUE OF 1929, Lord Byron of Broadway (1930), GOING HOLLYWOOD (1930), Sadie McKee (1934), Student Tour (1934), BROADWAY MELODY OF 1936 (1935), and BROADWAY MELODY OF 1938 (1937), as well as new songs for the 1930 film version of GOOD NEWS!. When Freed turned to producing, Brown worked with various lyricists to score Wintertime (1943), Greenwich Village (1944), On an Island With You (1948), and The Kissing Bandit (1948). Several Brown–Freed songs from the 1930s became popular again when they were used in SINGIN' IN THE RAIN (1952). Brown's music is diverse, ranging from jazz and swing to operatic and romantic. Among his many popular songs are "Singin' in the Rain," "Broadway Melody," "You Were Meant for Me," "I've Got a Feelin' You're Foolin'," and "All I Do Is Dream of You."

BRUCE, CAROL [born Shirley Levy] (1919–2007). Stage, television, and film performer. A distinctive throaty-voiced singer–actress, she usually played supporting but memorable roles. Bruce was born in Great Neck, Long Island, and worked as a band singer before making her Broadway debut as a featured singer in GEORGE WHITE'S SCANDALS (1939). The next year she gained attention as the funny seductress Beatrice in LOUISIANA PURCHASE, followed by specialty numbers in the revues New Priorities of 1943 (1942) and Along Fifth Avenue (1949). Bruce was outstanding as the tragic Julie in SHOW BOAT, playing the role in London, on tour, and in the 1946 and 1948 Broadway revivals. She also shone as the jaded Vera Simpson in the 1961 revival of PAL JOEY and as the worldly wise pensione proprietress Signora Fioria in DO I HEAR A WALTZ? (1965). Bruce's other Broadway credits include a replacement in the musical A Family Affair (1962) and in Henry Sweet Henry (1967). She appeared in three screen musicals in the 1940s,

Keep 'Em Flying (1941), *This Woman Is Mine* (1941), and *Behind the Eight Ball* (1942), but made few movies later. Bruce was frequently on television, appearing on variety shows, soap operas, dramatic and comedy series, and specials, such as the musical *MISS LIBERTY* (1951).

BRUCE, VIRGINIA [born Helen Virginia Briggs] (1910–1982). Film and television performer. A classic blonde beauty who was featured in several 1930s movie musicals, the singer–actress was usually cast as the "other woman" who was desirable but not often liked. Bruce was born in Minneapolis and raised in Fargo, North Dakota. She went to California to study at UCLA but was sidetracked when cast in bit parts in early talkies such as the musicals *Why Bring That Up?* (1929), *THE LOVE PARADE* (1929), and *Lilies of the Field* (1930). When Bruce was selected as one of the Goldwyn Girls, she started to appear in better parts in dramas, comedies, and musicals, including *PARAMOUNT ON PARADE* (1930), *Safety in Numbers* (1930), *Let's Go Native* (1930), *WHOOPEE* (1930), *Here Comes the Band* (1935), *Metropolitan* (1935), *THE GREAT ZIEGFELD* (1936), where she appeared at the top of the spiral staircase in the "A Pretty Girl Is Like a Melody" number, and *BORN TO DANCE* (1936) in which she introduced "I've Got You Under My Skin." Her other musical credits include *When Love Is Young* (1937), *Let Freedom Ring* (1939), *Pardon My Sarong* (1942), and *Brazil* (1944). Although her roles got smaller, Bruce continued to act on screen and on television until 1960. She was married for a time to film star John Gilbert (1897–1936).

BRYNNER, YUL [born Taidje Khano] (1911–1985). Stage and film performer. A bald, muscular, severe-looking actor with various credits, he is most remembered for his towering performance as the Siamese monarch in *THE KING AND I* (1951), a role he created on Broadway, repeated on film, revived on Broadway in 1977 and 1985, and played on tour across the country for several years, chalking up more than 4,000 performances. His year and country of birth were shrouded in mystery, one perpetrated by Brynner in his lifetime and by his son after his death. It is now believed that he was born in 1911 on Sakhalin, an island off the coast of Siberia. Brynner performed with gypsies across Europe, worked as a circus trapeze artist, was an announcer on wartime radio broadcasts for the U.S. Office of War Information, and acted in Shakespearean pro-

Yul Brynner. Because he played the King of Siam in *The King and I* (1951) on Broadway, on tour, on the screen, and in New York revivals, Brynner and the role are forever identified with each other. Here is the young Brynner in the original stage production striking a pose he would return to over the next thirty-five years. (Photofest)

ductions before gaining attention on Broadway as the dutiful Chinese husband in the musical *Lute Song* (1946). That show led to his getting cast as the complex monarch in *The King and I*. Brynner returned to Broadway in only one other musical, the ill-fated *Home Sweet Homer* (1976), but he had an active screen career, appearing in such nonmusicals as *The Ten Commandments* (1956), *Anastasia* (1956), *The Brothers Karamazov* (1958), *The Magnificent Seven* (1960), and *Westworld* (1973). Because he got to reprise his stage performance in the 1956 movie of *The King and I*, one of the American theatre's greatest portrayals is captured on film for future generations. Memoir: *Yul: The Man Who Would Be King, A Memoir of Father and Son*, Rock Brynner (1989); biography: *Yul Brynner: A Biography*, Michaelangelo Capua (2006).

BUBBLING BROWN SUGAR (ANTA Playhouse 1976). The glory days of Harlem and venues such as the Cotton Club and the Apollo and Savoy Theatres were recreated and celebrated in this "all-black" revue that was packed with old songs and talented performers. Avon Long, Vernon Washington, Vivian Reed, Josephine Premice, Lonnie McNeil, and Chip Garnett were the featured performers, and the score was composed of favorites written between 1920 and 1940. ROSETTA LENOIRE came up with the concept, co-producer Robert M. Cooper directed, and Billy Wilson choreographed the vivacious dances. The bouncing revue, which had originated Off Broadway at the AMAS Repertory Theatre, ran 766 performances on Broadway.

BUCHANAN, JACK (1891–1957). Stage and film performer, director, and producer. One of England's favorite song and dance men, he appeared only occasionally in Broadway and Hollywood musicals but always made an impression. Buchanan was born near Glasgow, Scotland, and first appeared on the London stage in 1912. The dapper hoofer–singer first came to America with *ANDRE CHARLOT'S REVUE* (1924) and quickly established himself as the very image of the debonair British music hall entertainer. Buchanan appeared in many London musicals, often producing and/or directing them as well, but he only returned to New York for the revues *The Charlot Revue* (1925) and *Wake Up and Dream* (1929) and the book musicals *BETWEEN THE DEVIL* (1937) and *Don't Listen, Ladies* (1948). Similarly in films, he was featured in many British screen musicals but is most remembered in American for his Hollywood appearances in *Paris* (1929), *MONTE CARLO* (1930), and *THE BAND WAGON* (1953).

BUCK PRIVATES (Universal 1941). A war effort musical oozing with patriotic sentiments, the film made *bona fide* movie stars of BUD ABBOTT and LOU COSTELLO and helped propel the career of the ANDREWS SISTERS as well. Necktie salesmen Sliker Smith (Abbott) and Herbie Brown (Costello) are running away from the police and accidentally enter an Army induction center (they think it's a movie house) and soon find themselves bungling through boot camp and military life. Also new to the army are the rich socialite Randolph Parker III (Lee Bowman) and his bodyguard Bob Martin (Alan Curtis) and their adjustments to the army took up much of the screenplay by Arthur T. Horman. But it was Abbott and Costello in the comic supporting roles that stole the show. The Andrews Sisters played themselves and delivered their trademark number "Boogie

Woogie Bugle Boy From Company B" and a swinging "Bounce Me Brother With a Solid Four" (both songs by DON RAYE and Hughie Prince), as well as the old favorite "I'll Be With You in Apple Blossom Time," which got a new lease on life because of the movie. Other Raye-Prince songs included "When Private Brown Meets a Sergeant," "Wish You Were Here," and "You're a Lucky Fellow, Mr. Smith." Alex Gottlieb produced and Arthur Lubin directed the low-budget movie that became the studio's top-grossing film of the year, and Abbott and Costello became box office gold for the rest of the war years.

BUCKLEY, BETTY [Lynn] (1947–). Stage, film, and television performer. A Broadway diva who for several years replaced stars, she originated a few roles before she found stardom. Buckley was born in Big Spring, Texas, and educated at Texas Christian College before going to New York and studying acting with Stella Adler. She made an impressive Broadway debut as Martha Jefferson in the musical *1776* (1969), followed by the revue *What's a Nice Country Like You Doing in a State Like This?* (1973). Buckley replaced the original stars in musical hits such as *PIPPIN* (1973), *I'M GETTING MY ACT TOGETHER AND TAKING IT ON THE ROAD* (1980), *Song and Dance* (1986), and *SUNSET BOULEVARD* (1995), but originated the aged feline Grizabella in the Broadway production of *CATS* (1982), the trouser role of Ned Drood in *THE MYSTERY OF EDWIN DROOD* (1985), the demented mother Margaret in *Carrie* (1988), and the philosopher Hesione in *Triumph of Love* (1997). Buckley has appeared in a number of films and television programs but is only occasionally given the chance to sing. Instead she is very active in nightclubs and in concerts.

BUDDY HOLLY STORY, THE (Columbia 1978). Although it followed the formula rags-to-riches plot of most biographical musicals, Gary Busey's performance as the early rock and roll star was more authentic than most such efforts. The gangly, bucktoothed Busey captured the singer's stage persona (Busey did his own vocals) as well as his shy, awkward personality. The screenplay by Robert Gittler followed the young Texan as he struggled for recognition and eventually became the first white performer to sing at Harlem's Apollo Theatre. His tragic death in a plane crash at the age of twenty-two was, oddly, not included in the film. The supporting cast included Don Stroud, Charles Martin Smith, Conrad Janis,

Maria Richwine, William Jordan, and Amy Johnston, under the direction of Steve Rash. Among the Holly favorites performed in the movie were "That'll Be the Day," "Chantilly Lace," "Peggy Sue," "Rock Around With Ollie Vee," and "You Send Me."

🎵 Not directly based on the film but sharing the same subject was the Broadway musical *Buddy* (Shubert Theatre 1990) in which Paul Hipp played Holly and sang two dozen of his songs. The libretto by Alan Janes covered some of the same biographical material but a good portion of the musical was Holly in concert and Hipp was such an adept impersonator that it was enough for Holly fans. Also in the cast were Jill Hennessy, Russ Jolly, Bobby Prochaska, Kurt Ziskie, and Philip Anthony. Reviews were mixed but the show still managed to run 225 performances, far less than in London where it ran over twenty years.

🎬 **BUGSY MALONE** (Rank/Paramount 1976). A novelty musical in which preteen actors played 1930s gangsters and molls, the movie has an odd charm, an accurate ear and eye for pastiche, and an exceptional score by Paul Williams. Small-time hood Bugsy Malone (Scott Baio) befriends the aspiring chorine Blouse Brown (Florrie Drugger) and gets her a job at the speakeasy run by Fat Sam (John Cassisi). Although Bugsy is falling in love with Blousey, he is easily distracted by the saucy vamp Tallulah (Jodi Foster) and everyone finds themselves tangled in the mob warfare between Sam and Dandy Dan (Martin Lev). The miniature sets and half-pint vintage autos of the period were cleverly done, and the playful tone of the piece was maintained by having whipped cream come out of the tommy guns that the gangsters sported. The performances were polished in the 1930s style, and the singing (much of it dubbed by adults) and dancing were first class. The score included the wistful ballad "Tomorrow," the rousing sing-along "You Give a Little Love," the tender torch song "Ordinary Fool," and the zesty title song that Williams himself sang over the credits. ALAN PARKER wrote and directed the unusual movie and Alan Marshal produced it. It was not a box office hit in the States but became a favorite in England and in the 1990s was turned into a successful stage production in London also using kids. The musical has slowly caught on with amateur groups in Great Britain and America.

BULLOCK, WALTER (1907–1953). Stage and film lyricist and writer. A journeyman songwriter,

who collaborated with RICHARD A. WHITING, VICTOR SCHERTZINGER, JULE STYNE, and others, he scored three SHIRLEY TEMPLE movies and contributed to the scripts of musical and non-musical films. Bullock was born in Shelburn, Indiana, and educated at DePauw University before writing songs for Tin Pan Alley. He went to Hollywood when sound came in but didn't hear his songs used on screen until the mid-1930s. Bullock's musical credits include *Follow Your Heart* (1936), *Nobody's Baby* (1937), *52nd Street* (1937), *Sally, Irene and Mary* (1938), *Little Miss Broadway* (1938), *Just Around the Corner* (1938), *The Three Musketeers* (1939), *The Blue Bird* (1940), and *Hit Parade of 1941*. He also wrote or co-wrote the screenplays for such musicals as SPRINGTIME IN THE ROCKIES (1942), THE GANG'S ALL HERE (1943), *Greenwich Village* (1944), *The I Don't Care Girl* (1953), and THE FARMER TAKES A WIFE (1953). Bullock wrote the book and lyrics for the Broadway musical *Great to Be Alive!* (1950)

BURKE, BILLIE [born Mary William Ethelbert Appleton Burke] (1885–1970). Stage and film performer. Mostly remembered today as the good witch Glinda in the film classic THE WIZARD OF OZ (1939), the red-haired, high-voiced comic singer had a long and fascinating career of sixty years. Burke was born in Washington, DC, the daughter of Barnum and Bailey clown Billy Burke, and was raised and educated in England. She appeared in London plays as early as 1903 and four years later was on Broadway in a series of lightweight comedies and was the toast of the town, courted by millionaires and marrying producer FLORENZ ZIEGFELD who presented her on the stage and in some silent films. After his death in 1932, she worked full time in Hollywood to pay off his debts. Burke was soon a favorite in daffy, quivering character roles in comedies and in a dozen musicals, such as *Everybody Sing* (1938), IRENE (1940), *What's Cookin'?* (1942), *Swing Out, Sister* (1945), *Breakfast in Hollywood* (1946), THE BARKLEYS OF BROADWAY (1949), *Small Town Girl* (1953), and *Pepe* (1960). She served as consultant on the film THE GREAT ZIEGFELD (1936) in which she was portrayed by MYRNA LOY. Burke continued working in stock and in movies into the 1960s. Autobiographies: *With a Feather on My Nose*, with Cameron Shipp (1949); *With Powder on My Nose* (1959).

BURKE, JOE (1884–1950). Stage and film composer and actor. An actor-turned-songwriter, he wrote many memorable songs during his brief stay in Hollywood. Burke was born in Philadelphia and educated at the University of Pennsylvania before working for a publishing firm. He turned to acting and by 1912 was in Hollywood where he appeared in over sixty silent films. When sound came in, he turned to songwriting and his music was heard in the early musical GOLD DIGGERS OF BROADWAY (1929). Burke's lyricist partner was AL DUBIN and together they scored the movies SALLY (1929), LITTLE JOHNNY JONES (1929), She Couldn't Say No (1930), HOLD EVERYTHING (1930), Top Speed (1930), Life of the Party (1930), Sweethearts on Parade (1930), and Oh, Sailor Behave! (1930). When Dubin teamed up with composer HARRY WARREN, Burke left Hollywood and wrote for Tin Pan Alley. He also wrote songs for the Broadway revues EARL CARROLL VANITIES (1928) and ZIEGFELD FOLLIES (1936). Although he is little remembered today, many of his songs remain standards, such as "Carolina Moon," "Moon Over Miami," "Rambling Rose," "Painting the Clouds With Sunshine," and "Tip Toe Through the Tulips."

BURKE, JOHNNY (1908–1964). Film and stage lyricist. One of Hollywood's most reliable and successful songwriters, he collaborated with ARTHUR JOHNSTON, JAMES V. MONACO, and JAMES VAN HEUSEN on many hit songs over a three-decade film career. Burke was born in Antioch, California, and educated at the University of Wisconsin and Crane College before going into vaudeville as a song-and-dance man. He appeared in some Broadway revues and made several film shorts when talkies came in and then concentrated on writing lyrics for Hollywood. With composer Johnston, he scored Go West, Young Man (1936), Pennies From Heaven (1936), and Double or Nothing (1937) and then teamed with Monaco for Doctor Rhythm (1938), Sing You Sinners (1938), East Side of Heaven (1939), The Star Maker (1939), ROAD TO SINGAPORE (1940), If I Had My Way (1940), and RHYTHM ON THE RIVER (1940), all starring BING CROSBY. Burke's most frequent and famous collaborator was Van Heusen, with the two of them scoring twenty musicals together as well as dozens of songs for nonmusicals. Among their musical credits together are LOVE THY NEIGHBOR (1940), Playmates (1941), Dixie (1943), GOING MY WAY (1944), And the Angels Sing (1944), Belle of the Yukon (1944), Cross My Heart (1946), Welcome Stranger (1947), The Emperor Waltz (1948), A CONNECTICUT YANKEE IN KING ARTHUR'S COURT (1949), Top of the Morning (1949), Riding High (1950),

and Mister Music (1950); and four of the ROAD pictures with Crosby and BOB HOPE. (No one wrote more song hits for Crosby than Burke.) He also wrote new lyrics for RUDOLF FRIML'S music for the film remake of THE VAGABOND KING (1956) and for the Broadway musicals Swingin' the Dream (1939), Nellie Bly (1946), Carnival in Flanders (1953), and Donnybrook! (1961), all of which had bright scores but disappointing runs. Burke was an agile writer who could turn an everyday phrase into an intoxicating lyric, and his work is very diverse, from the peppy "Swinging on a Star" and "Pennies From Heaven" to the romantic "But Beautiful" and "Moonlight Becomes You." The Burke–Van Heusen song catalogue was celebrated in the 1995 Broadway musical revue Swinging on a Star.

BURNETT, CAROL (1933–). Stage, television, and film performer. The beloved red-headed, loudmouthed comedienne was a star on Broadway before finding wider fame on television. Burnett was born in San Antonio, Texas,

Carol Burnett. When the Off Broadway musical Once Upon a Mattress transferred to Broadway in 1959, Burnett became a stage star. Later she brought Broadway to television; not in sit-coms, but in variety shows where she sang, danced, and clowned before a live audience, the last of the great stars to do so. (Photofest)

and raised in Hollywood where she trained for an acting career at the local university. After singing and doing comedy in New York nightclubs and small revues, she found recognition as the gawky, funny Princess Winifred in ONCE UPON A MATTRESS (1959). At the same time Burnett was finding fame on television programs so when her Broadway musical *Fade Out—Fade In* (1964) was not a major hit, she left the stage and concentrated on the tube where she became one of its most popular stars because of her TV specials and her variety show. Burnett recreated her Winifred for the 1964 television version of *Once Upon a Mattress* and played the evil Queen in the 2005 TV remake. She returned to Broadway in the comedy *Moon Over Buffalo* (1995) and shone in the musical revue *Putting It Together* (1999). Burnett's movie career has been scattered and uneven, although she has given some funny and moving performances in both comedies and dramas. Her villainous Miss Hannigan was one of the few highlights of the 1982 movie version of *ANNIE*. Burnett and her daughter Carrie Hamilton co-wrote the autobiographical play *Hollywood Arms*, which played on Broadway in 2002. Autobiography: *One More Time* (1986).

BURNS, BOB (1890–1956). Film performer. A comic actor who played philosophical hillbillies, he was featured in a handful of 1930s film musicals, usually opposite MARTHA RAYE as a farcical second couple. Burns was born in Van Buren, Arkansas, and went into vaudeville where he developed his unsophisticated clown with common sense, earning him the title the "Arkansas Philosopher." He was also nicknamed "Bazooka" after the bizarre valve-wind musical instrument he concocted. Burns was so popular in nightclubs and on radio that he was given a specialty spot in the Hollywood musical *The Singing Vagabond* (1935) and played character parts in *Rhythm on the Range* (1936), *Big Broadcast of 1937* (1936), *Waikiki* (1937), *Mountain Music* (1937), *Radio City Revels* (1938), *Tropic Holiday* (1938), and *Belle of the Yukon* (1944). He retired from films in 1944 but remained very popular on the radio where he had his own show from 1941 to 1947. He was married to comic JUDY CANOVA for a time.

BURNS, DAVID (1902–1971). Stage performer. The rotund, scowling-faced, gruff-voiced actor delighted audiences in plays, revues, and book musicals for five decades. Born and educated in New York, Burns spent several seasons in stock and on the road before making his

Broadway debut in 1923 and soon established himself as an excellent comic character actor. His versatility was demonstrated in the caricatures he played in revues such as *MAKE MINE MANHATTAN* (1948), *Alive and Kicking* (1950), *Two's Company* (1952), and *Catch a Star!* (1955), but he is most remembered for introducing delightful supporting characters in book musicals, such as the blustering Mayor Shinn in *THE MUSIC MAN* (1957), the crooked music business executive Brains Berman in *DO RE MI* (1960), the frustrated Roman father Sennex in *A FUNNY THING HAPPENED ON THE WAY TO THE FORUM* (1962), and the miserly Horace Vandergelder in *HELLO, DOLLY!* (1964). Burns' other Broadway musical credits include *FACE THE MUSIC* (1932), *Billion Dollar Baby* (1945), *OUT OF THIS WORLD* (1950), and *Lovely Ladies, Kind Gentlemen* (1970), as well as replacing others in *PAL JOEY* (1941), *OKLAHOMA!* (1946), and *SOUTH PACIFIC* (1952). He was also a favorite in England where he was featured in British films and London musicals in the 1930s. Burns only made a few films, including the musicals *DEEP IN MY HEART* (1954), *IT'S ALWAYS FAIR WEATHER* (1955), and *Let's Make Love* (1960).

BURNS, GEORGE, AND GRACIE ALLEN. Film and television performers. One of the most durable of all comedy teams, the husband and wife comics remained popular in different media for over thirty years. Gracie [Ethel Cecile Rosalie] Allen (1895–1964) was born in San Francisco, the daughter of vaudevillians, and was on the stage as a child. In 1922 she met George Burns [born Nathan Birnbaum] (1896–1996), a New Yorker who had appeared in kiddie acts and as a roller skater in variety as well. The twosome developed an act in which he played the cigar-smoking straight man to her scatterbrained, illogical, yet cheerful character who bordered on the surreal. The team was so successful in nightclubs that they were featured in their first film, *THE BIG BROADCAST* (1932) in which they played themselves as they usually did in their twenty subsequent films. Allen usually sang and they both danced in most of their musicals, which include *INTERNATIONAL HOUSE* (1933), *College Humor* (1933), *WE'RE NOT DRESSING* (1934), *Many Happy Returns* (1934), *Here Comes Cookie* (1935), *BIG BROADCAST OF 1936* (1935), *Love in Bloom* (1935), *BIG BROADCAST OF 1937* (1936), *College Holiday* (1936), *A DAMSEL IN DISTRESS* (1937), *College Swing* (1938), *Honolulu* (1939), and *TWO GIRLS AND A SAILOR* (1944). During the 1930s and 1940s their radio show was one of the most popular programs on the air and it was turned into an equally successful television show in the 1950s. After Allen's premature death, Burns continued to appear in nightclubs and television specials and, after a many years' absence, appeared in films again in the 1970s and 1980s, including the musicals *Sgt. Pepper's Lonely Hearts Club Band* (1978) and *MOVIE MOVIE* (1978) for which he served as the narrator. Biography: *Gracie: A Love Story*, Burns (1996); biography: *George Burns and the Hundred Year Dash*, Martin Gottfried (1996).

BURNS, RALPH (1922–2001). Stage and film orchestrator, composer, and conductor. A much respected Broadway and Hollywood orchestrator, he arranged the music for many classics in both media. Burns was born in Newton, Massachusetts, and educated at the New England Conservatory before working as a pianist for name bands. He started doing the musical arrangements for Broadway musicals in 1955 and contributed to such musicals as *Copper and Brass* (1957), *NO STRINGS* (1962), *LITTLE ME* (1962), *GOLDEN BOY* (1964), *DO I HEAR A WALTZ?* (1965), *SWEET CHARITY* (1966), *NO, NO, NANETTE* (1971), *PIPPIN* (1972), *IRENE* (1973), *CHICAGO* (1975), *THEY'RE PLAYING OUR SONG* (1979), *Big Deal* (1986), *FOSSE* (1999), and *THOROUGHLY MODERN MILLIE* (2002). In Hollywood he was musical director for such musicals as *Sweet Charity* (1969), *CABARET* (1972), *MAME* (1974), *NEW YORK, NEW YORK* (1977), *ALL THAT JAZZ* (1979), *ANNIE* (1982), and *A CHORUS LINE* (1985). Burns conducted the orchestra on many recordings and composed a number of songs as well as film soundtrack music for over twenty nonmusical films

BURNSIDE, R[obert] H[ubberthorne]. (1870–1952). Stage director, lyricist, and writer. A prolific British director and writer, he found success in New York staging musical comedies, including several large extravaganzas and spectacles. Burnside was born in Scotland, the son of an actress and the manager of Glasgow's Gaiety Theatre, and appeared on the stage from a very young age. The family moved to London when Burnside was twelve years old and he entered the legit theatre as a call boy for Edward Terry and then at the Savoy Theatre where the operettas of Gilbert and Sullivan were playing. He emigrated to New York in 1894 and the following year staged his first of sixty musicals before retiring in 1944. Among his New York musical credits are *Thrilby* (1895), *The Earl and the Girl* (1905), *CHIN-CHIN*

(1914), *WATCH YOUR STEP* (1914), *Stop! Look! Listen!* (1915), *When Johnny Comes Marching Home* (1917), *Stepping Stones* (1923), *China Rose* (1925), *Criss Cross* (1926), *Great Day* (1929), and *Hold Your Horses* (1933). Burnside managed and directed the extravaganzas at the mammoth Hippodrome Theatre between 1909 and 1921, sometimes providing librettos and lyrics for them and other musicals as well. In the 1940s he returned to his Gilbert and Sullivan roots and staged a repertory of their operettas in Boston, New York, and on tour.

BURROWS, ABE [born Abram Solman Borowitz] (1910–1985). Stage director and writer. One of Broadway's best musical comedy librettists, he was also a very accomplished director. A native New Yorker, Burrows worked as an accountant and then as a commercial broker before taking up writing for radio, television, and films. He became well known as a chat show host on CBS radio in the 1940s and his written and spoken wit was soon in demand. Burrows entered the theatre when the producers of *GUYS AND DOLLS* (1950) hired him to rewrite the libretto during its troublesome preparation. The musical was an immediate hit and Burrows was much sought after to write his own librettos and to doctor others. Among his Broadway musical scripts were *Make a Wish* (1951), *Three Wishes for Jamie* (1953) *CAN-CAN* (1953), *SILK STOCKINGS* (1955), *Say, Darling* (1958), *First Impressions* (1959), and *HOW TO SUCCEED IN BUSINESS WITHOUT REALLY TRYING* (1961). Burrows's directing career was launched when he staged the musical revue *TWO ON THE AISLE* in 1951. He went on to direct several of his own musicals, as well as his English adaptations of the French comedy *Cactus Flower* (1965) and other plays. Among the musicals he staged but did not write were *Happy Hunting* (1956) and *What Makes Sammy Run?* (1964). Autobiography: *Honest Abe* (1980).

BUSINESS AND LABOR IN MUSICALS. These two recurring subjects in Broadway musicals have been treated satirically, as is often the case of business, or fervently, as sometimes in the matter of labor. From the Fordyce Drop Forge and Tool Factory in *FINE AND DANDY* (1930) to the Louisiana Purchase Company in *LOUISIANA PURCHASE* (1940) to the toymakers B. G. Bigelow, Inc. in *Flahooley* (1951) to the World Wide Wickets Company in *HOW TO SUCCEED IN BUSINESS WITHOUT REALLY TRYING* (1961), big business has proved to be an ideal milieu for lighthearted musical comedy. A less frolicsome approach was taken in *I CAN GET IT FOR YOU WHOLESALE* (1962), which explored greed and ambition in the garment industry, *What Makes Sammy Run?* (1964), which dealt with the ruthless politics of the movie business, and *URINETOWN* (2001) in which the Urine Good Company has the monopoly on pay toilets in a nightmarish future. But they were the exceptions. Most stage musicals set in the world of big business were lighter fare, such as *DO RE MI* (1960), *How Now Dow Jones* (1967), *PROMISES, PROMISES* (1968), and *Big* (1996). Plays dealing with labor and labor relations became prevalent in the 1930s and musicals sometimes tackled the touchy subject. *PINS AND NEEDLES* (1937), produced by a labor union, was often good humored about the topic and the musical revue humanized sociopolitical ideas in a clever way. *THE CRADLE WILL ROCK* (1938), however, was a rather grim and strident musical that pitted the common laborer against the powerful boss Mr. Mister, and the immigrant laborers in *RAGTIME* (1998) were also depicted with compassion. The most successful musical dealing with labor relations was *THE PAJAMA GAME* (1954), but the labor conflicts at the Sleep-Tite Pajama factory often took a back seat to the romantic conflicts. One of the most revealing and nonpreachy musicals about the laborer was *WORKING* (1978), which musicalized the actual words and feelings of those in different occupations. Few of the aforementioned musicals were filmed by Hollywood, and original movie musicals on the subjects of business and labor are rare. The only business that seemed to interest Tinsel Town was show business and there were plenty of musicals about that. In the Depression, films sometime looked at laborers but they were usually out of work, as in *Hallelujah, I'm a Bum!* (1933) and the tribute to the "forgotten Man" on the bread lines in *GOLD DIGGERS OF 1933*. JAMES CAGNEY was a racketeer trying to take over the stevedores' labor union in the musical melodrama *Never Steal Anything Small* (1959), and the film was unusual because it was one of the very few on the labor subject. Perhaps there is something intrinsic in the topic of work that it defies musicalization on screen.

BUTLER, DAVID (1894–1979). Film director. A reliable director of comedies and musicals, he helmed over thirty of the latter between 1929 and 1961. Butler was born in San Francisco, the son of a stage director, and was on stage at the age of three. While getting his education at Stanford University, he continued to act on stage and appeared in silent films until sound came in and he started directing for 20TH CENTURY-FOX. Butler was admired by the studios for his efficient, practical, and on-budget pictures that often did well at the box office. Among his musicals were *SUNNY SIDE UP* (1929), *DELICIOUS* (1931), *The Littlest Rebel* (1935), *CAPTAIN JANUARY* (1936), *Pigskin Parade* (1936), *East Side of Heaven* (1939), *ROAD TO MOROCCO* (1942), *Shine on Harvest Moon* (1944), *My Wild Irish Rose* (1947), *Look for the Silver Lining* (1949), *Tea for Two* (1950), *Lullaby of Broadway* (1951), *WHERE'S CHARLEY?* (1952), *April in Paris* (1952), *By the Light of the Silvery Moon* (1952), *CALAMITY JANE* (1953), and *The Right Approach* (1961). Butler sometimes produced his pictures and occasionally contributed to the scripts.

BUTLER, FRANK (1890–1967). Film performer and writer. An actor-turned writer, he had a busy career in both jobs. Butler was born in Oxford, England, and went on the stage as a comic character actor. He came to America in 1920 and appeared in over forty silent films, usually in supporting roles in comedies. When movies started to speak, Butler gave up acting and took up writing, contributing to over sixty features between 1927 and 1959. Among his musical screenplays are *NEW MOON* (1930), *College Humor* (1933), *BABES IN TOYLAND* (1934), *Coronado* (1935), *Strike Me Pink* (1936), *Waikiki Wedding* (1937), *Tropic Holiday* (1938), *The Star Maker* (1939), *ROAD TO SINGAPORE* (1940), *ROAD TO ZANZIBAR* (1941), *ROAD TO MOROCCO* (1942), *GOING MY WAY* (1944), *The Kid From Brooklyn* (1946), and *ROAD TO BALI* (1952).

BUTTERWORTH, CHARLES [Edward] (1896–1946). Stage and film performer. A comic character actor, he polished his shy, awkward stage persona into a series of routines that delighted audiences on Broadway and then in Hollywood. Butterworth was born in South Bend, Indiana, and received a law degree from Notre Dame, but went into journalism before pursuing an acting career. After many years touring in vaudeville and perfecting his act, he was featured in Broadway revues, such as *Americana* (1926), *Allez-oop* (1927), *FLYING COLORS* (1932), and *Count Me In* (1942), where he delivered comic monologues. Butterworth also played comic supporting roles in *Good Boy* (1928) and *SWEET ADELINE* (1929) before going to Hollywood where he played meek and indecisive characters in over thirty movies, including the musicals *LOVE ME TONIGHT* (1932), *THE*

CAT AND THE FIDDLE (1934), *Hollywood Party* (1934), *The Night Is Young* (1935), *Swing High, Swing Low* (1937), *THE BOYS FROM SYRACUSE* (1940), and *THIS IS THE ARMY* (1943). He was still in great demand when he died prematurely in a car crash at the age of forty-eight.

BUTZ, NORBERT LEO (1967–). Stage performer. A recent and quickly rising musical theatre singer–actor, he has demonstrated an impressive versatility in his handful of New York musicals. Butz was born in St. Louis and educated at the University of Missouri at Columbia and Webster College in his hometown. He got stage experience during his four years at the Alabama Shakespeare Festival before making his Broadway debut as a replacement for Roger and then Mark in *RENT* (1997). He toured as the Emcee in *CABARET* and then played the confused writer Jamie in the Off Broadway musical *The Last Five Years* (2001). His other New York musical credits are the tragic Camille Raquin in *THOU SHALT NOT* (2001), the party-guy Fiero in *WICKED* (2003), and the crude con man Freddy in *DIRTY ROTTEN SCOUNDRELS* (2005). He has made a few film and television appearances.

BUZZELL, [Edward] EDDIE (1895?–1985). Stage and film performer and director. A Broadway comic who moved to Hollywood when sound came in, he ended up directing some thirty movies, including eight musicals. Brooklyn-born Buzzell went on the stage as a boy and was on Broadway by 1920, usually playing the comic sidekick. Among his musicals were *Broadway Brevities of 1920*, *The Gingham Girl* (1922), *No Other Girl* (1924), *THE DESERT SONG* (1926), *Good Boy* (1928), and *Lady Fingers* (1929). In Hollywood he was starred as *LITTLE JOHNNY JONES* (1929) but three years later he gave up performing and started directing comedy shorts for COLUMBIA. Over the next twenty-five years Buzzell worked for several

studios, turning out such musicals as *The Girl Friend* (1935), *Honolulu* (1939), *AT THE CIRCUS* (1939), *Go West* (1940), *Ship Ahoy* (1942), *BEST FOOT FORWARD* (1943), and *NEPTUNE'S DAUGHTER* (1949).

BY JUPITER (Shubert Theatre 1942). The last new musical by RICHARD RODGERS (book and music) and LORENZ HART (book and lyrics), it is little known today but was very popular, the longest-running Rodgers and Hart show on record until the 1983 Broadway revival of *On Your Toes* passed it. Queen Hippolyta and her Amazons rule the ancient land of Pontus while their husbands lie about useless, all because the queen possesses unnatural strength as the wearer of Diana's magic girdle. One of the twelve labors of Hercules is to steal the girdle, so he arrives in Pontus with Theseus and the Greek army. They are no match for Hippolyta's superhuman strength, but when Theseus falls in love with the queen's sister Antiope and the other Amazons are taken with the comely Greeks, the women submit. Hippolyta's weakling husband Sapiens becomes king and Pontus becomes like every place else on earth where the women rule subliminally.

The libretto was adapted by Rodgers and Hart from Julian Thompson's play *The Warrior's Husband* (1932), the vehicle that launched Katharine Hepburn to fame playing Hippolyta. Both the script and the lyrics were filled with sexual innuendo and the gender-battling themes were handled with aplomb. Sapiens was turned into the star role and RAY BOLGER (in his first Broadway lead) took it and ran with it. Particularly charming was the merry duet "Life With Father," which he sang with his mother Pomposa, played by Bertha Belmore who had done the role in the play version a decade earlier. Also in the zesty score were the two hits "Nobody's Heart (Belongs to Me)" and "Ev'rything I Got (Belongs to You)," as well as other estimable songs such

Stage Casts for *By Jupiter*

Character	1942 Broadway	1967 Off Broadway
Sapiens	RAY BOLGER	Bob Dishy
Queen Hippolta	Benay Venuta	Jackie Alloway
Antiope	CONSTANCE MOORE	Sheila Sullivan
Hercules	Ralph Dumke	Charles Rydell
Theseus	Ronald Graham	Robert R. Kaye
Buria	Jane Manners	Rosemarie Heyer
Pomposia	Bertha Belmore	Irene Byatt

as "Wait Till You See Her," "Jupiter Forbid," and "Now That I've Got My Strength." The whole venture was so carefree and intelligently fun that audiences had no idea of the trauma going on behind the scenes. Hart's alcoholism and bouts of depression were so frequent by this time that he had to write much of *By Jupiter* while recuperating in a clinic. The partnership was so strained that Rodgers was starting to consider projects with other lyricists. Although neither songwriter was aware of it at the time, *By Jupiter* turned out to be their last new show together: a year later Hart was dead. The musical was produced by DWIGHT DEERE WIMAN and Rodgers, directed by JOSHUA LOGAN, choreographed by ROBERT ALTON, and ran 427 performances. It might have run longer if its star Bolger had not left to entertain troops in the Far East. A 1967 Off Broadway revival directed by Christopher Hewett with Bob Dishy as Sapiens and Jackie Alloway as Hippolyta was commended by the press and ran 118 performances, but *By Jupiter* has never joined the ranks of the oft-revived Rodgers and Hart shows.

🕮 *BY THE BEAUTIFUL SEA* (Majestic Theatre 1954). A routine story and a pleasant score didn't add up to much of a show, but the multitalented SHIRLEY BOOTH kept the musical comedy afloat for 270 performances. Dorothy and HERBERT FIELDS wrote the libretto about ex-vaudevillian Lottie Gibson (Booth) who runs a boarding house at Coney Island that caters to theatre folk. When she loses her heart to the middle-aged boarder Dennis Emery (Wilbur Evans), she has to gain the affections of his daughter by a previous marriage in order to win Dennis. The commendable supporting cast included Mae Burns, Cameron Prud'Homme, Carol Leigh, Richard France, and Anne Francine, and the company was given some accomplished songs to sing, such as the reflective ballad "Alone Too Long," the raucous revival-like number

"Hang Up," the wry "I'd Rather Wake Up By Myself," and the merry "The Sea Song," which was sung in counterpoint with the standard title tune. Marshall Jamison directed and HELEN TAMIRIS choreographed the Lawrence Carr–Robert Fryer production, but it was Booth's funny, tender performance that made the show work.

🕮 *BYE BYE BIRDIE* (Martin Beck Theatre 1960). A lighthearted spoof of teenagers and their idolization of ELVIS PRESLEY, the musical comedy offered much more and became the surprise hit of the season.

Plot: Before rock and roll singer Conrad Birdie is drafted into the U.S. Army, his manager Albert Peterson and long-time fiancée Rose Grant concoct a publicity gimmick in which the rocker will sing farewell to a randomly selected teenager on television's *The Ed Sullivan Show*. The winner, teen Kim MacAfee (Susan Watson), is thrilled but it wrecks havoc with her boyfriend Hugo, her parents, and the whole town of Sweet Apple, Ohio. After a series of misadventures, Conrad goes off to Uncle Sam, Hugo and Kim are back together, and Rose convinces Albert to give up show business, marry her, and become an English teacher like he always dreamed.

Michael Stewart (book), CHARLES STROUSE (music), and LEE ADAMS (lyric) wrote the show as a musical for high schools and titled it *Going Steady*, but producer Edward Padula thought it worthy of Broadway and hired GOWER CHAMPION to direct and choreograph. It was the first major Broadway assignment for all four men and it launched their careers. The cast, both older and younger generations, was highly proficient with standout performances by DICK VAN DYKE as Albert, CHITA RIVERA in her first leading role as Rose, and Paul Lynde as the frustrated father Mr. McAfee. The score actually has little rock and roll in it, and what's there is closer to pop. "Put on a Happy Face" is a vaudeville soft-shoe number, "Kids" has

Casts for *Bye Bye Birdie*

Character	1960 Broadway	1963 film	1995 television
Albert Peterson	DICK VAN DYKE	Dick Van Dyke	JASON ALEXANDER
Rose Grant/Alverez	CHITA RIVERA	Janet Leigh	Vanessa Williams
Conrad Birdie	Dick Gautier	Jesse Pearson	MARC KUDISCH
Kim MacAfee	SUSAN WATSON	ANN-MARGARET	Chynna Phillips
Hugo Peabody	Michael J. Pollard	Bobby Rydell	Jason Gaffney
Mr. MacAfee	Paul Lynde	Paul Lynde	George Wendt
Mae Peterson	Kay Medford	Maureen Stapleton	Tyne Daly

Bye Bye Birdie. Although it is mostly remembered as a show about teenagers, much of the playing time in *Bye Bye Birdie* is concerned with the adults. Here the usually practical Rose Grant (Chita Rivera) cuts loose with a group of Shriners in one of director–choreographer Gower Champion's lively production numbers. (Photofest)

a Charleston beat, "A Lot of Livin' to Do" is jazzy, "One Boy" is a typical girl-group ballad, and "Hymn for a Sunday Evening" is a mock anthem. The silly but endearing musical was cheered by the critics and ran 607 performances. The show quickly became a perennial favorite with high school theatre groups and has remained so for over four decades

Bye Bye Birdie (Columbia 1963) retained Van Dyke (his screen debut), Lynde and half of the score, but the film was less about the generation gap than a showcase for new talent ANN-MARGARET, who played the teenager Kim but came across more like a Las Vegas headliner. Strouse and Adams wrote a peppy title song for the movie and Ann-Margaret gave it a sultry rendition over the opening credits so the musical was off balance from the very start. Much of the gentle satire of the stage work became farce in the libretto by IRVING BRECHER and the clumsy direction by GEORGE SIDNEY. Some of the supporting cast is enjoy-

able and ONNA WHITE's choreography has its playful moments, but so much of the humor is strained that it's not clear who is making fun of whom. The Fred Kolmar production was a hit at the box office and many have enjoyed the film on video over the years but it is still less satisfying than your local high school production of the show.

More faithful to the original but frightfully lifeless was the 1995 ABC-TV version, which was miscast and mismanaged. Comic sidekick JASON ALEXANDER was as unconvincing as Albert as glamorous Vanessa Williams was wrong for the down-to-earth Rose. GENE SAKS directed at a snail's pace, and ANN REINKING's choreography seemed energetic and pointless. Strouse and Lee wrote a new song, "A Giant Step," for the show when it was touring with TOMMY TUNE as Albert and his height was laughable; having pint-sized Alexander perform the number was the closest the television production came to an original joke.

BYINGTON, SPRING (1886–1971). Film, stage, and television performer. A beloved character actress recognized from all media, the warm and plump comedienne excelled at matronly types, sometimes ditzy in character but usually gentle, wise, and understanding. Byington was born in Colorado Springs, Colorado, and was acting in stock in Denver when she was fourteen years old. After touring for years, she made her Broadway debut in 1924 and acted in twenty plays over the next decade. Although Byington made her first film in 1930, it was her performance as mother "Marmee" in *Little Women* (1933) that brought her recognition and typecast her. Over the next twenty years she appeared in over ninety films, including the musicals *Broadway Hostess* (1935), *The Blue Bird* (1940), *Presenting Lily Mars* (1943), *Thrill of a Romance* (1945), *Meet Me on Broadway* (1946), *In the Good Old Summertime* (1949), and *Because You're Mine* (1952). Byington acted in many television series in the 1950s and 1960, including her own show *December Bride*.

C

CABARET (Broadhurst Theatre 1966). Arguably the most innovative, hard-hitting, and uncompromising musical of the 1960s, the powerful music–drama made few concessions to escapist entertainment, yet it was and remains very popular.

Plot: American writer Clifford Bradshaw goes to Berlin on the eve of the Nazi takeover and is fascinated by the city, the decadent Kit Kat Club, and British singer Sally Bowles. The two drift into a casual affair while the Jewish fruit merchant Herr Schultz romances his landlady Fraulein Schneider and she submits until worries about anti-Semitism force her to break off the engagement. Sally finds that she's pregnant and Cliff offers to marry her and bring her back with him to America. Sally agrees but soon realizes she would make a terrible wife and mother and prefers to continue living the carefree, decadent life in Berlin. The political situation worsens, Cliff leaves Berlin, and Sally goes back to the cabaret where everyone can continue to ignore what is happening around them. Both stories were framed by acts at the cabaret, supervised by the sleazy Master of Ceremonies, and the numbers often commented on the characters and their situation.

Joe Masteroff's libretto was based on John Van Druten's play *I Am a Camera* (1951) and Christopher Isherwood's original stories about Berlin, yet as a musical it goes far beyond both sources, using Brechtian techniques such as the cabaret numbers to explore its dark themes. Producer HAROLD PRINCE directed and RON FIELD choreographed, both with an eye for the unromantic and unsentimental. The role of the Emcee is secondary, but with JOEL GREY's sleazy, knowing performance the character became a guide into man's deepest prejudices and fears. The marvel of the musical is that as cynical and abrasive as it is, the show still entertains and is satisfying on so many levels. JOHN KANDER (music) and FRED EBB (lyrics) wrote two separate scores for *Cabaret*: character songs for the plot scenes and cabaret songs for the nightclub acts. Because of their chilly, distanced tone, all the numbers are of a whole. The love songs and the happy numbers hint at self-deception, the sexy ditties are tainted with self-disgust, and the title song itself is a lie, with no one (including Sally who sings it) believing a word of it. For this reason few of the songs in *Cabaret* "travel" well and have rarely been recorded because they are tied so tightly with the dark tone of the show. Kander and Ebb found plenty of variety even while working within this somber subtext. "Don't Tell Mama" has a British music hall flavor, Fraulein Schneider's solos have a Kurt Weill-like temperament, "Meeskite" has an Eastern European Jewish quality, and "Tomorrow Belongs to Me" is a frightening Nazi anthem because it is so stirring and seemingly positive. The score remains Kander and Ebb's finest achievement.

Cabaret ran a surprising 1,165 performances and has returned to Broadway twice. Joel Grey reprised his electric performance in a 1987 revival again directed by Prince and choreographed by Field. A few revisions were made to the score and the book (such as a hint of homosexuality in Cliff as suggested in the original stories) and the production ran 261 performances. The cast also featured Alyson Reed (Sally), GREGG EDELMAN (Clifford), Regina Resnik (Schneider), and Werner Klemperer (Schultz). In a 1997 revival,

Casts for *Cabaret*			
Character	*1966 Broadway*	*1972 film*	*1998 Broadway*
Sally Bowles	Jill Haworth	LIZA MINNELLI	Natasha Richardson
Clifford Bradshaw/Brian	BERT CONVY	Michael York	John Benjamin Hickey
Master of Ceremonies	JOEL GREY	Joel Grey	Alan Cumming
Fraulein Schneider	LOTTE LENYA		MARY LOUISE WILSON
Herr Schultz	JACK GILFORD		Ron Rifkin
Natalia Landauer		Marisa Berenson	
Fritz Wepper		Fritz Wendel	
Max von Heune		Helmut Griem	

Cabaret. It is not unusual for the Hollywood version of a Broadway musical to undergo all kinds of changes in the transition to the silver screen. What is unusual about *Cabaret* is that as different as the stage and movie versions are, they both are powerful musical dramas with a similarly haunting theme. Pictured is Joel Grey in the 1972 film version with his "two ladies." (Photofest)

Cabaret (stage) Musical Numbers

"Wilkommen"
"So What?"
"Don't Tell Mama"
"Telephone Song"
"Perfectly Marvelous"
"Two Ladies"
"It Couldn't Please Me More"
"Tomorrow Belongs to Me"
"Why Should I Wake Up?"
"The Money Song"
"Married"
"Meeskite"
"If You Could See Her"
"What Would You Do?"
"Cabaret"

ter Sally, and a decadent cast of characters who all ended up in a train going to a concentration camp at the final curtain. The old Henry Miller Theatre was transformed into a sleazy nightclub and the audience sat at tables with the action often occurring right in their midst. Most critics found the ROUNDABOUT THEATRE COMPANY revival exhilarating, although subtlety was not among its merits. Songs from both the original and the movie version were used. Audience response to the potent production was so strong that it ended up running 2,377 performances, one of the longest-running Broadway revivals on record.

■ *Cabaret* (ABC/Allied Artists 1972) was a dynamic reworking of the Broadway musical, rethinking the piece in cinema terms and utilizing material from the Isherwood short stories. Jay Presson Allen and HUGH WHEELER wrote the screenplay, dropping characters and plot lines and adding new ones, and director–choreographer BOB FOSSE put all the musical numbers (save one) in the small,

British director Sam Mendes teamed up with American choreographer ROB MARSHALL and the two turned the musical into a nightmarish journey into Nazi Germany with an androgynously wicked Emcee, a trampy, bit-

smokey, tawdry Kit Kat Klub. LIZA MINNELLI, in her first screen musical (unless you count her brief appearance as a toddler in *IN THE GOOD OLD SUMMERTIME*), lit up the screen as the eager, desperate-to-be-decadent nightclub singer Sally Bowles (changed from a Brit to an American), and she was balanced by a calm amused performance by Michael York as her bisexual lover (changed from the American Cliff to the British Brian). Joel Grey reprised his unforgettable performance as the Emcee, and Helmut Griem and Marisa Berenson were cast in the new subplot about a young Jewish couple whose dreams are thwarted by the growing Nazi party. Only six songs from the Kander–Ebb score made it to the movie but the team wrote two new ones ("Money Money" and "Mein Herr") and interpolated from the trunk "Maybe This Time." Although confined to a small space, the musical numbers were brilliantly staged and very effective using cheap lighting effects and interesting points of view from the audience. The chilling "Tomorrow Belongs to Me" was set in an outdoor beer garden and the song built to a haunting climax as a young Nazi (Oliver Collignon, singing dubbed by Mark Lambert) sang the seemingly innocent anthem. Rarely has the film version of a Broadway musical taken so many liberties with the script and score and ended up being as powerful as the original.

CABIN IN THE SKY (Martin Beck Theatre 1940). A musical fantasy in the style of a "Negro" folk tale, the show is most remembered for its compelling musical score by VERNON DUKE (music) and JOHN LATOUCHE (lyrics) and a penetrating performance by ETHEL WATERS. On the deathbed of luckless Little Joe Jackson, his faithful wife Petunia prays to God to give her misled husband another chance. Joe is given six months to prove himself a good soul, helped in the venture by the Lawd's General and hindered by Lucifer Jr., who tempts Joe with the sultry Georgia Brown. Lynn Root wrote the libretto and it was staged by Albert Lewis with GEORGE BALANCHINE providing the choreog-

raphy (with an assist by Katherine Dunham) and J. Rosamond Johnson supervising the rousing choral singing. In addition to the warm, domestic title song, the score also included the gently swinging ballad "Taking a Chance on Love," the sultry "Honey in the Honeycomb," and the fervent "Love Turned the Light Out." With enthusiastic reviews and a powerhouse cast of some of the finest African Americans in the business, it was surprising the musical did not run longer than 156 performances.

CABIN IN THE SKY (MGM 1943) was one of the few films in the 1940s made by a major studio that utilized a cast of African Americans; in fact, it was the first all-black Hollywood musical since *HALLELUJAH* (1929). John Schrank wrote the screenplay, which was close to the stage libretto except for the ending when the whole plot turned out to be a dream. Ethel Waters got to reprise her Petunia from the stage and it is her greatest musical performance. Also in top form were EDDIE ANDERSON and LENA HORNE, as well as supporting performances by REX INGRAM, Kenneth Spencer, LOUIS ARMSTRONG, John W. "Bubbles" Sublett, Willie Best, Butterfly McQueen, DUKE ELLINGTON and his orchestra, and the Hall Johnson choir. They were all directed with skill by VINCENTE MINNELLI in his first Hollywood assignment. The movie has a rustic yet dreamlike quality about it that is ideal for the fable it tells and music seems to flow throughout the rural community. The three best songs from the stage score were retained for the film, and HAROLD ARLEN (music) and E. Y. HARBURG (lyrics) wrote three new ones, "Li'l Black Sheep," "Life Is Full of Consequence," and the beloved ballad "Happiness Is a Thing Called Joe." *Cabin in the Sky* is an archival treasure, preserving the performances of so many gifted players for future generations.

CAESAR, IRVING [born Isidor Caesar] (1895–1996). Stage and film lyricist. A Tin Pan Alley songwriter who had better luck with revues than book musicals, he wrote the lyrics for

---

Casts for *Cabin in the Sky*

Character	1940 Broadway	1943 film
Petunia Jackson	ETHEL WATERS	Ethel Waters
Little Joe Jackson	DOOLEY WILSON	EDDIE ANDERSON
Lawd's General	TODD DUNCAN	Kenneth Spencer
Lucifer, Jr.	REX INGRAM	Rex Ingram
Georgia Brown	Katherine Dunham	LENA HORNE

some of the biggest hit songs of the 1920s. The native New Yorker was educated at Chautauqua Mountain Institute and City College of New York and worked as a clerk and a press agent before going into vaudeville as a singer. Soon he was writing songs and had a massive hit with composer GEORGE GERSHWIN with "Swanee." Caesar wrote lyrics for the Broadway shows *Greenwich Village Follies* (1922 and 1923) and *Betty Lee* (1924) and then wrote two songs for *NO, NO, NANETTE* (1925) with composer VINCENT YOUMANS: "I Want to Be Happy" and "Tea for Two." It was his only book musical to run but Caesar contributed exceptional songs in his other twelve Broadway shows, including *Sweetheart Time* (1926), *No Foolin'* (1926), *Yes, Yes, Yvette* (1927), *Here's Howe* (1928), *Americana* (1928), *Polly* (1929), *Nina Rosa* (1930), *The Wonder Bar* (1931), *Melody* (1933), *White Horse Inn* (1936), and *My Dear Public* (1943). Caesar saw some of his shows filmed and wrote songs for such original screen musicals as *Crooner* (1932), *GEORGE WHITE'S SCANDALS* (1934), *CURLY TOP* (1935), *Stowaway* (1936), *REBECCA OF SUNNYBROOK FARM* (1938), and *Tea for Two* (1950). His lyrics are simple, direct, and sometimes contagious, as exemplified in the ditties "Tea for Two" and "Animal Crackers in My Soup."

CAESAR, SID [born Isaac Sidney Caesar] (1922–). Television, stage, and film performer. One of television's greatest clowns, with his wacky, satirical bent and ability to imitate any language in gibberish, he only had modest success on Broadway and in Hollywood. Caesar was born in Yonkers, New York, the son of a restaurant owner, studied music at Juilliard, and went into show business as a saxophone player, working with several name bands in the late 1930s. After serving in the Coast Guard in World War II, he started doing standup comedy in clubs and was featured in the New York revues *Tars and Spars* (1944), *MAKE MINE MANHATTAN* (1948), and *Admiral Broadway Revue* (1948). Fame came with his television program *Your Show of Shows* in the 1950s that allowed him to create vivid caricatures and spoof movies in short but potent sketches. Caesar returned to Broadway in 1962 for his only stage success, *LITTLE ME*, which allowed him to play a variety of characters as he had on the tube. His subsequent Broadway shows, the comedy *Four on a Garden* (1988) and the revue *Sid Caesar & Company* (1989), failed to run. His film career was sporadic, appearing in a handful of comedies and in bit parts in the musicals

Tars and Spars (1946), *GREASE* (1978), and *GREASE 2* (1982), but never shining as he had on the small screen. Autobiography: *Where Have I Been?* (1982).

CAGNEY, JAMES [Francis] (1899–1986). Film and stage performer. The fast-talking, scrappy master of both heavies and song-and-dance men, his handful of musicals are unforgettable. Born in New York to an Irish bartender and a Norwegian immigrant, Cagney worked in restaurants and pool halls to put himself through school at Columbia University. But his heart was in musical comedy so after a short hitch in the chorus of the Broadway musical *Pitter-Patter* (1920), he went out on the vaudeville circuit to gain more experience. Hs first job when he returned to New York was as the belligerent Irish hobo Little Red in the melodrama *Outside Looking In* (1925). Cagney spent the rest of the decade on Broadway appearing in other plays and in the revue *Grand Street Follies* (1928 and 1929). When the film studios beckoned, they wanted the toughie and not the hoofer so he was cast in melodramas, finding fame with *The Public Enemy* (1931) and appearing in dozens of gritty gangster films over the next three decades. Cagney's first screen musical was *FOOTLIGHT PARADE* (1933) and he approached the character of producer Chester Kent with all the pugnacious vitality of his nonmusical roles. But the public preferred the actor as a heavy and he only got to appear in one musical, *Something to Sing About* (1937), before he got to play GEORGE M. COHAN in the biopic musical *YANKEE DOODLE DANDY* (1942). It was a smashing portrayal and perhaps the one most identified with the actor, yet his subsequent musicals were scattered and in some he didn't even get to sing or dance: *West Point Story* (1950), *Starlift* (1951), *LOVE ME OR LEAVE ME* (1955), *The Seven Little Foys* (1955), and *Never Steal Anything Small* (1959). Cagney never returned to the stage and never sang or danced for the public during the last twenty-five years of his career. His sister was actress Jeanne Cagney (1919–1984). Autobiography: *Cagney on Cagney* (1975); biographies: *Cagney*, John McCabe (1999); *Cagney: The Actor as Auteur*, Patrick McGilligan (1980).

CAHILL, MARIE (1870–1933). Stage performer. The small, round powerhouse of an entertainer sang comic songs in vaudeville, on Broadway, and on London and Paris stages. The Brooklyn-born comedienne refined her unique way of delivering a song in variety houses in America and England and made her legitimate stage debut in the London musical *Morocco Bound* (1894). The next year she was on Broadway in *Excelsior Jr.*, followed by featured roles in the musicals *The Gold Bug* (1896), *A Runaway Girl* (1897), *Monte Carlo* (1898), *Three Little Lambs* (1899), *Star and Garter* (1900), and *The Wild Rose* (1902). Cahill became a star when she sang "Under the Bamboo Tree" in *Sally in Our Alley* (1902) and continued to star in musicals, which were sometimes built around her talents, such as *Nancy Brown* (1903), *It Happened in Nordland* (1904), *Moonshine* (1905), *Marrying Mary* (1906), *The Boys and Betty* (1908), *Judy Forgot* (1910), *The Opera Ball* (1912), and *90 in the Shade* (1915). Her popularity waned in the 1920s so she went back to vaudeville and music halls in France and England. Cahill returned to Broadway for the revue *Merry-Go-Round* (1927) and had one last hurrah as the Park Avenue matron Mrs. Wentworth looking for a gigolo in *THE NEW YORKERS* (1930).

CAHN, SAMMY [born Samuel Cohen (1913–1993). Stage, film, and television lyricist. The prolific multi-Oscar-winning songwriter had many hits on Tin Pan Alley, on Broadway, and in Hollywood working with a variety of composers. The native New Yorker began his career as a violinist in vaudeville and then turned to writing songs for acts, then for his own band with composer SAUL CHAPLIN, and eventually for stars such as FRANK SINATRA who recorded over eighty Cahn songs. Chaplin collaborated with Cahn on the film scores for the B musicals *Rookies on Parade* (1941), *Time Our for Rhythm* (1941), and *Go West Young Lady* (1941) and then Cahn was paired with composer JULE STYNE, with the two writing dozens of songs together for all media. For Hollywood they scored such musicals as *Youth on Parade* (1942), *Johnny Doughboy* (1942), *Thumbs Up* (1943), *Step Lively* (1944), *Carolina Blues* (1944), *Tonight and Every Night* (1945), *ANCHORS AWEIGH* (1945), *Tars and Spars* (1946), *Cinderella Jones* (1946), *The Kid From Brooklyn* (1946), *Ladies' Man* (1947), *IT HAPPENED IN BROOKLYN* (1947), *ROMANCE ON THE HIGH SEAS* (1948), *Two Guys From Texas* (1948), *It's a Great Feeling* (1949), *West Point Story* (1950), and *Double Dynamite*. Cahn's other frequent film collaborator was composer JIMMY VAN HEUSEN. Together they scored *ANYTHING GOES* (1956), *Pardners* (1956), *Say One for Me* (1959), *Let's Make Love* (1960), *High Time* (1960), *THE ROAD TO HONG KONG* (1962), *ROBIN AND THE SEVEN HOODS* (1964), *The Pleasure Seekers*

(1964), *THOROUGHLY MODERN MILLIE* (1967), and *JOURNEY BACK TO OZ* (1972). With composers NICHOLAS BRODSZKY, VERNON DUKE, and others, Cahn wrote the scores for the films *Always Leave Them Laughing* (1949), *THE TOAST OF NEW ORLEANS* (1950), *Rich, Young and Pretty* (1951), *She's Working Her Way Through College* (1952), *April in Paris* (1952), *PETER PAN* (1953), *Three Sailors and a Girl* (1953), *You're Never Too Young* (1955), *THE COURT JESTER* (1956), *Meet Me in Las Vegas* (1956), *The Opposite Sex* (1956), *Ten Thousand Bedrooms* (1957), and *Rock-a-Bye Baby* (1958). In addition to musical scores, he wrote best-selling theme songs for nonmusical films, such as "Three Coins in the Fountain," "The Tender Trap," "Call Me Irresponsible," and "High Hopes." Cahn's Broadway career was not as extensive and not as successful. With Styne he scored the hit *HIGH BUTTON SHOES* (1947) and the flop *Look to the Lilies* (1970). With Van Heusen he wrote the songs for the short-lived musicals *Skyscraper* (1965) and *Walking Happy* (1966). Cahn performed in the Broadway revue celebrating his work called *Words and Music* (1974) and posthumously had a hit with the stage version of *Thoroughly Modern Millie* (2002). He was also very active in television, writing lyrics for the original TV musicals *OUR TOWN* (1955), *JACK AND THE BEANSTALK* (1967), *The Legend of Robin Hood* (1968), *The Night the Animals Talked* (1970), and *ONCE UPON A BROTHERS GRIMM* (1977). Few lyricists were busier and more diversified than Cahn, yet he was more adept at writing for celebrities than characters, one of the reasons he had so many hit songs. Autobiography: *I Should Care* (1974).

CALAMITY JANE (Warner 1953). It may have been an attempt by WARNER BROTHERS to cash in on the popularity of *ANNIE GET YOUR GUN* (1946 on Broadway and 1950 on film), but this frontier musical about another gun-slinging spitfire had plenty of its own to be proud of. DORIS DAY got to cut loose as she rarely was allowed to and played the title character who protected the Dakota stagecoach line, fetched the Chicago singing star Katie Brown (Allyn McLerie) for the Deadwood saloon, and chased after Wild Bill Hickok (HOWARD KEEL). It was beautifully filmed on location, offered some spirited dances by JACK DONOHUE, and contained a tuneful score by SAMMY FAIN (music) and PAUL FRANCIS WEBSTER (lyrics). "Secret Love' was the standout hit but there was much to enjoy in "The Black Hills of Dakota," "Just

Blew In From the Windy City," "Higher Than a Hawk," "A Woman's Touch," and an extended opening sequence called "The Deadwood Stage," which was a marvel in musical exposition. Dick Wesson, Philip Carey, Gale Robbins, and Paul Harvey were also in the cast, all under the firm direction of DAVID BUTLER.

CALDWELL, ANNE [Payson] (1867–1936). Stage lyricist and writer. A performer-turned-writer in the developing American musical theatre, she was one of the earliest women pioneers in the field. Caldwell was born in Boston and began her career as a singer in operetta, vaudeville, and burlesque, appearing on Broadway in musicals in the 1890s. At the turn of the century she gave up performing and turned to writing lyrics and librettos for musicals, beginning her New York career with the scripts for *Top o' the World* (1907) and *The Lady and the Slipper* (1912). Caldwell collaborated with composer JEAN SCHWARTZ on *When Claudia Smiles* (1914) and then had a major hit with *CHIN-CHIN* (1914) in which she partnered with composer IVAN CARYLL. WITH JEROME KERN she scored *She's a Good Fellow* (1919), *The Night Boat* (1920), *Hitchy-Koo* (1920), *Good Morning, Dearie* (1921), *The Bunch and Judy* (1922), *Stepping Stones* (1923), *The City Chap* (1925), and *Criss-Cross* (1926). With others she wrote scores for *Pom-Pom* (1916), *Jack o' Lantern* (1917), *The Canary* (1918), *The Lady in Red* (1919), *The Sweetheart Shop* (1920), *Tip Top* (1920), *Peg o' My Dreams* (1924), *The Magnolia Lady* (1924), *Oh, Please!* (1926), *Yours Truly* (1927), *Take the Air* (1927), and *Three Cheers* (1928). Caldwell was a practical craftsman and gifted lyricist who was much respected in the rough-and-tumble days when the American musical was still being defined. Her shows are not revived but some of her songs live on, such as "I Know That You Know," "Left All Alone Blues," "Ka-lu-a," and "Wait Till the Cows Come Home."

CALHERN, LOUIS [born Carl Henry Vogt] (1895–1956). Stage and film performer. The tall, distinguished-looking matinee idol of 1920s Broadway graduated to become a favorite character actor in Hollywood. Calhern was a native New Yorker who performed in stock as a child and, after serving in the artillery in World War I, made his Broadway debut in 1922. Two years later he caught the attention of audiences and critics alike in the drama *Cobra* (1924) and went on to play leading men in classics and modern melodramas, often classy and dashing aristo-

crats. Calhern's movie career began in 1921 and stretched to 1956, although he returned to Broadway many times during those decades. Although he was neither a singer nor a dancer, he was featured in several Hollywood musicals, sometimes as the hero's foil, other times as a friendly cohort of the heroine, always a suave fellow. Calhern's musical credits include *DUCK SOUP* (1933), *SWEET ADELINE* (1934), *UP IN ARMS* (1944), *ANNIE GET YOUR GUN* (1950), *Nancy Goes to Rio* (1950), *Two Weeks With Love* (1950), *Main Street to Broadway* (1953), *Rhapsody* (1954), *THE STUDENT PRINCE* (1954), *Athena* (1954), and *HIGH SOCIETY* (1956). The oft-married Calhern numbered actresses Ilka Chase (1905–1978) and Natalie Schafer (1900–1991) among his wives.

CALHOUN, JEFF (1960–). Stage choreographer and director. A former protégé of TOMMY TUNE, he has made a name for himself as a director and choreographer regionally and on Broadway. Calhoun was born in Buffalo and raised in a suburb of Pittsburgh, performing in summer stock and getting his Equity card at the age of sixteen. He attended Northwestern University but left when Tune spotted him in stock and hired him for the tour of *THE BEST LITTLE WHOREHOUSE IN TEXAS*. He assisted Tune on *THE WILL ROGERS FOLLIES* (1991) before making his director–choreographer debut in 1992 with the revue *Tommy Tune Tonite!* Calhoun performed both tasks for the very successful revival of *Grease* in 1994, which Tune supervised, but the two had a falling out in 1995 when Calhoun was replaced by Tune during the problematic tryout tour of *Busker Alley*, which never made it to Broadway. Of his subsequent credits, Calhoun's direction and choreography for the Deaf West Theatre Company's production of *BIG RIVER* were the most acclaimed, with his delicate use of speaking and deaf performers in a seamless musical collage being praised on tour and during its Broadway run. Calhoun has staged a similarly potent production of *OLIVER!* for Deaf West at the Mark Taper Forum in Los Angeles. His other Broadway credits include *The Best Little Whorehouse Goes Public* (1994), *ANNIE GET YOUR GUN* (1999), *BELLS ARE RINGING* (2001), *Taboo* (2003), *Brooklyn* (2004), which he also directed, and *GREY GARDENS* (2006). Calhoun has also choreographed for the prized *ENCORES!* series in New York.

CALL ME MADAM (Imperial Theatre 1950). One of Ethel Merman's best vehicles, the musi-

Casts for *Call Me Madam*		
Character	1950 Broadway	1953 film
Sally Adams	ETHEL MERMAN	Ethel Merman
Cosmo Constantine	Paul Lukas	George Sanders
Kenneth Gibson	RUSSELL NYPE	DONALD O'CONNOR
Princess Maria	Galina Talva	VERA-ELLEN

cal comedy gave her a juicy role and a handful of top-notch IRVING BERLIN songs to sing. The Texas oil widow Sally Adams throws such grand parties in Washington that President Truman appoints her ambassador to the little European country of Lichtenburg. Willing to shower the needy nation with U.S. dollars, she offends the dashing prime minister, Cosmo Constantin, just as she is starting to fall in love with him. Sally's assistant Kenneth Gibson is also enamored of a Lichtenburg native, the Princess Maria, and with Sally's help he wins her heart just as Cosmo and Sally are reconciled. The libretto by HOWARD LINDSAY and RUSSEL CROUSE was tailor-made for Merman, and the jaunty musical was as timely as it was enjoyable, with its references to current politics and Washington gossip. (The Washington hostess Perle Mesta had recently been made ambassador to Luxembourg by Truman.) Berlin wrote one of his brightest and most tuneful scores, including the contrapuntal duet "You're Just in Love," the chipper "The Hostess With The Mostes' on the Ball," the gentle ballad "Marrying for Love," the jaunty "It's a Lovely Day Today," and the political ditty "They Like Ike." The musical was expertly directed by GEORGE ABBOTT and choreographed by JEROME ROBBINS, and with the rave notices and Merman's popularity the show ran 644 performances.

Call Me Madam (Fox 1953) was one of the rare opportunities Ethel Merman got to recreate her stage role on screen and the result was a blockbuster for the star and the studio. Never considered thin and pretty enough for the camera, Merman saw her Annie Oakley and other Broadway roles made by others in Hollywood. But Sally is a middle-aged character and 20TH CENTURY-FOX took a chance and cast her; it is arguably her best film performance. Arthur Sheekman's screenplay followed the stage plot fairly closely and most of the Berlin score survived the transition. His comic lament "What Chance Have I With Love?" from *LOUISIANA PURCHASE* (1940) was given to DONALD O'CONNOR to sing as the aide Kenneth, just as more dancing

was added for him as well. As the Princess Maria, VERA-ELLEN had her singing dubbed by Carole Richards and that role also was given plenty of dance. WALTER LANG directed the SOL C. SIEGEL production, and ROBERT ALTON did the choreography. The result is one of the more faithful stage-to-screen musicals and a thorough delight on every level.

CALL ME MISTER (National Theatre 1946). Servicemen returning to civilian life after World War II was the theme of this very timely hit revue that boasted a talented cast and an outstanding score. Arnold Auerbach and Arnold B. Horwitt wrote the sketches, and HAROLD ROME penned the songs that ranged from the silly to the disturbing. BETTY GARRETT, as a canteen hostess weary of singing Latin numbers for the troops, belted out "South America, Take It Away," soldiers imagined Paul Revere filling out all the paperwork to requisition a horse for his midnight ride, and GIs dreamt about the "Goin' Home Train." There were two very sobering songs in the show as well. Citizens reflected on the recent death of FDR with "The Face on the Dime," and African American-enlisted men, who had served faithfully during the war, pondered the discrimination facing them in civilian life with "The Red Ball Express." The cast, mostly made up of ex-GIs and former USO entertainers, also included JULES MUNSHIN, Lawrence Winters, MARIA KARNILOVA, GEORGE S. IRVING, Bill Callahan, and Paula Bane. Melvyn Douglas and HERMAN LEVIN co-produced, Robert H. Gordon directed, and the revue was a popular favorite, running 734 performances. **Call Me Mister** (Fox 1951) only kept three of Rome's songs and dismissed the premise of enlisted men returning home from the war. Albert Lewin and Burt Styler's screenplay was a romantic comedy set in Japan during the then-current Korean War with USO singer Kay Hudson (BETTY GRABLE) having marital difficulties with her GI husband Sgt. Shep Dooley (DAN DAILEY). It was a tiresome plot about Shep putting on a camp show in order to bring Kate back to him, but many of the musical numbers (staged by BUSBY BERKELEY) were enjoyable. Of the new songs added to the film, the best was "Lament to the Pots and Pans," a comic ditty sung by DANNY THOMAS doing KP duty. Dailey danced to the title number, Grable sang the "Japanese Girl Like American Boy," and the oversized finale called "Love Is Back in Business" crowded enough GIs on screen to launch another D-Day attack. LLOYD BACON directed the FRED KOHLMAR production with panache if not subtlety.

CALLOWAY, CAB[ell] (1907–1994). Stage, film, and television musician, composer, and performer. The energetic African American scat-singing bandleader who flourished for decades in nightclubs and on television, he also made some appearances on Broadway and in films scattered over a fifty-year period. Calloway was born in Rochester, New York, and while studying law at Crane College he started his own band and played in hotels and clubs, eventually quitting school, going professional, and finding fame at Harlem's Cotton Club. With his trademark white suit and zesty jumping about the stage as he conducted, he shouted out "Hi-De-Yo" as he scat-sang jazz pieces, some of which he composed himself. Calloway and his band made many popular recordings (his single "Minnie the Moocher," which he co-wrote, was the first jazz record to sell over one million copies) and were famous enough by 1932 that Calloway and his band were featured in the film musicals THE BIG BROADCAST (1932), INTERNATIONAL HOUSE (1933), *The Singing Kid* (1936), *Manhattan Merry-Go-Round* (1937), STORMY WEATHER (1943), *Sensations of 1945* (1944), and *Hi-De-Ho* (1947). In the 1950s Calloway appeared on television and performed on Broadway, playing Sportin' Life in the 1953 revival of PORGY AND BESS. He also shone on stage as Horace Vandergelder opposite PEARL BAILEY in HELLO, DOLLY! (1967) and as the efficiency expert Hines in THE PAJAMA GAME (1973). He can also be seen in the films *St. Louis Blues* (1958) and *The Blues Brothers* (1980). In the movie THE COTTON CLUB (1984), Calloway was played by LARRY MARSHALL. Autobiography: *Of Minnie the Moocher & Me* (1976); biography: *Hi-Di-Ho Man: The Life of Cab Calloway*, Alyn Shipton (2007); *Cab Calloway*, Dempsey J. Travis (1997).

CAMELOT (Majestic Theatre 1960). A musical play that has become such a favorite of musical theatre patrons, it is often forgotten

Camelot. Just as she played opposite the nonsinging British actor Rex Harrison in *My Fair Lady* (1956), Julie Andrews returned to Broadway with the nonsinging British actor Richard Burton (right) in *Camelot* and once again it was a class act. She may have been the inexperienced one in 1956, but Andrews was the pro in 1960. (Photofest)

how difficult a time its creators had in presenting it and how disappointed both audiences and critics were when it first opened.

Plot: The prearranged marriage between King Arthur and Guenevere does not look so frightening once the two of them accidentally meet and fall in love. Arthur's plan to create the Knights of the Round Table to maintain peace starts successfully, but when his closest friend Lancelot and Guenevere begin a clandestine affair the high ideals of Camelot are threatened. Arthur's bastard son Mordred stirs up further discontent and warfare returns, but not until Arthur knights the youth Thomas and commissions him to carry on the noble goals of Camelot.

The libretto by ALAN JAY LERNER attempted to condense T. H. White's epic history–fantasy novel *The Once and Future King* into a musical theatre format and it was a daunting task, with the show running over four hours in tryouts and songs by FREDERICK LOEWE (music) and Lerner (lyrics) being added and dropped on a

Casts for *Camelot*

Character	1960 Broadway	1967 film
Arthur	Richard Burton	Richard Harris
Guenevere	JULIE ANDREWS	Vanessa Redgrave
Lancelot	ROBERT GOULET	Franco Nero
Mordred	Roddy McDowell	David Hemmings
King Pellinore	Robert Coote	Lionel Jeffries

daily basis. The preparations were also marred by the illness by Lerner, Loewe, and director MOSS HART, who died soon after the musical opened. Casting nonsinger Richard Burton as Arthur was problematic but his acting performance was inspired and JULIE ANDREWS was a luminous Guenevere. Because so many of the creative team from *My Fair Lady* (1956) were reassembled for the show, the highly anticipated musical could not help but disappoint, particularly with its long and disjointed libretto. But the glorious score, superb performances, and dazzling decor helped audiences ignore the mixed notices and make the show a hit. The musical was a particular favorite of President Kennedy and his administration was sometimes likened to Camelot; after his assassination, the musical had an even greater emotional impact on audiences. The original production ran 873 performances, much longer than the opening night reviews could have foreshadowed.

Lerner and Loewe wrote one of their best scores for *Camelot*, perhaps only bettered by *My Fair Lady*. The early character songs, such as Arthur's "I Wonder What the King Is Doing Tonight" and Guenevere's "The Simple Joys of Maidenhood," are lighthearted and knowing, just as their later songs, such as "What Do the Simple Folks Do?" and "I Loved You Once in Silence," have a shadow of doom over them. Lerner's lyrics are masterful throughout, whether in the sarcasm of "The Seven Deadly Virtues" and "C'est Moi" or in the simple emotions of "If Ever I Would Leave You" or "Before I Gaze at You Again." Loewe's music is particularly versatile, from the bouncy "The Lusty Month of May" to the somber "How to Handle a Woman." Whatever script problems still persist in producing *Camelot*, the score remains a sparkling example of two master songwriters at their peak. *Camelot* has grown in popularity over time and is frequently produced in summer stock and by schools. New York has seen three major revivals of the musical, none of them successful. Burton reprised his Arthur at

Camelot (stage) Musical Numbers

"I Wonder What the King Is Doing Tonight"
"The Simple Joys of Maidenhood"
"Camelot"
"C'est Moi"
"The Lusty Month of May"
"You May Take Me to the Fair"
"How to Handle a Woman"
"The Jousts"
"Before I Gaze at You Again"
"If Ever I Would Leave You"
"The Seven Deadly Virtues"
"What Do the Simple Folk Do?"
"The Persuasion"
"Fie on Goodness!"
"I Loved You Once in Silence"
"Guenevere"

the New York State Theatre at Lincoln Center in 1980, although he was deemed far too old and feeble for the role. Richard Harris, who had played Arthur in the 1967 film version, reprised the role on tour and on Broadway in 1981. Meg Bussert was Guenevere, and Richard Muenz was Lancelot. Frank Dunlop directed the production, which struggled for six weeks before returning to the road. (It was also videotaped by *Showtime* cable television and broadcast in 1982.) ROBERT GOULET, the original Lancelot, essayed Arthur in a threadbare-looking production in 1993 that critics dismissed as tacky and artificial. However, there were enough fans of the musical (or Goulet) to keep the production running seven weeks.

Camelot (Warner 1967) took a while to come to the screen because Lerner wanted to solve some of the book problems before a film was made. Because the libretto was a musical comedy in the first act and a musical drama in the second, he somewhat solved the problem in his screenplay by starting the film just as Arthur and Lancelot must go to war and then telling the story as an extended flashback. It was not the most original of ideas but it did tell the audience that this musical was not all comedy. Richard Harris was an earnest Arthur and Vanessa Redgrave a stunning Guenevere. Neither were full-voiced singers, yet they handled the songs with grace and style. Franco Nero (singing dubbed by Gene Merlino) was a humorless Lancelot, just as there wasn't much fun in David Hemmings's deadly Mordred. Most of the Broadway score was used but much of the fantasy was discarded. JOSHUA LOGAN directed with a heavy hand, and the $15 million production rarely looked real or fantastical; usually it resembled an expensive Las Vegas spectacular. The Jack L. Warner production did only marginal business at the box office and the studio lost a bundle. Yet the story and ideals that the story holds are still appealing and many moviegoers still have a soft spot in their heart for *Camelot*.

CAMP (IFC Productions 2003). At a summer theatre camp, teenagers who are viewed as odd show freaks at their high schools can relax and be themselves, singing and dancing in Broadway musical production numbers and acting in dramas that are far beyond their capabilities. The low-budget film, written and directed by Todd Graff, follows the problems of various adolescents, such as the cross-dressing Michael (Robin de Jesus) who wants parental acceptance, the handsome Vlad Baumann (Daniel Letterle) who learns the advantages of being one of the few heterosexuals in theatre, and the glamour girl Jill (Alanna Allen) who is used to getting every part (and boy) she goes after. On the adult side is the washed-up songwriter Bert Hanley (Don Dixon) who bitterly looks at the youthful optimism all around him but sees a glimmer of hope when the kids perform one of his songs. The musical numbers, taken from various Broadway shows, are surprisingly effective. An uneven movie to say the least, it has its own awkward charm.

CAN-CAN (Shubert Theatre 1953). One of COLE PORTER's many Paris-set musicals, this late entry in his career made a stage star of GWEN VERDON. The provocative "can-can" is outlawed in 1893 Paris so when cabaret owner La Mome Pistache features the sinful dance on her stage, the young judge Aristide Forestier goes to investigate and ends up falling in love with the proprietress. One of her dancers, Claudine, is being wooed by the artist Boris and the art critic Hillarie and only a farcical duel on a rooftop will satisfy the rivals. The libretto by ABE BURROWS may have been a patchwork affair, but the entertainment values were high enough to make the show the musical hit of the season, running 829 performances. Most critics felt the Porter score was lacking, yet some standards came from the show: "I Love Paris," "It's All Right With Me," and the high-kicking title song. Also heard in the musical were "Allez-Vous En (Go Away)," "C'est Magnifique," and "Never Give Anything Away." Lilo was the top-billed star but it was the funny, sexy Verdon who walked off with the most cheers and began her reign as Broadway's favorite dancing star. Author Burrows directed the CY FEUER–Ernest Martin production and MICHAEL KIDD choreographed the vivacious dances. In 1962 a New York City Light Opera production featured Genevieve (Pistache), George Gaynes (Forestier), Mara Lynn (Claudine) Gabriel Dell (Boris), and Ferdinand Hilt (Hillarie). The 1981 Broadway revival, for which Burrows revised his libretto and directed, failed to please the critics or excite playgoers and closed after five performances even though it had much to recommend it. Zizi Jeanmaire (Pistache), RON HUSMANN (Aristide), Pamela Sousa (Claudine), Avery Schreiber (Boris), and Swen Swenson (Hillarie) led the cast and Roland Petit did the choreography.

Can-Can (Fox 1960) featured such talents as SHIRLEY MACLAINE, FRANK SINATRA, and MAURICE CHEVALIER so the result should have been more delectable than this lackluster film. DOROTHY KINGSLEY and Charles Lederer wrote the screenplay, which turned

Casts for *Can-Can*		
Character	*1953 Broadway*	*1960 film*
Simone Pistache	Lilo	SHIRLEY MACLAINE
Claudine	GWEN VERDON	Juliet Prowse
Francois Durnais		FRANK SINATRA
Paul Barrierre		MAURICE CHEVALIER
Forrestier	Peter Cookson	Louis Jourdan
Boris	HANS CONREID	
Hillarie	ERIK RHODES	

Mme. Pistache's love interest into the lawyer Durnais who defends her in court, and the script built up the role of the judge Barrierre so that Chevalier could be cast opposite Louis Jourdain as they had in *Gigi* (1958). Half of the Porter stage score was cut, three of his hits from other shows ("Just One of Those Things," "Let's Do It," and "You Do Something to Me") were added, and most of the songs were misused, such as having the luscious "I Love Paris" only sung over the credits. WALTER LANG directed the JACK CUMMINGS production, while HERMES PAN did the choreography, best appreciated when Juliet Prowse was featured. The movie did well at the box office and helped boost MacLaine's screen career.

CANDIDE (Martin Beck Theatre 1956). Although it contains one of the musical theatre's greatest scores, this beloved comic operetta had major book problems that for twenty years kept it from becoming a hit. In Lillian Hellman's original libretto, the lowly born youth Candide loves the highborn Cunegonde and only after adventures that take him across continents searching for the meaning of life and trying to live by the cockeyed philosophy taught to him by his tutor Pangloss does he finally win her and settle for the simple life of a farmer. Voltaire's satiric novella played uncomfortably on the stage, and the dazzling sets by Oliver Smith and picturesque direction by Tyrone Guthrie seemed to weigh down the cartoonish story and characters. Aisle sitters advocated the ravishing score sung by a bright, talented cast but, in the end, could not recommend the ambitious musical and it closed after seventy-three performances. However, *Candide* refused to fade away. The cast recording remained a big seller for years, and the show's overture became a staple with orchestras around the world. Listening to the celebrated score one can see why music lovers would not let *Candide* die. Composer LEONARD BERNSTEIN playfully pastiched a handful of operas and operettas in the music but one did not have to recognize the in-jokes to appreciate the lush, sprightly score. Richard Wilbur, JOHN LATOUCHE, Dorothy Parker, and Bernstein himself contributed to

the witty lyrics that often satirized the emotions that the music was expressing. Among the many highlights were the mock aria lament "Glitter and Be Gay," the philosophical "The Best of All Possible Worlds," the idiotically cheerful "Oh, Happy We," the Latin-flavored "I Am Easily Assimilated," the nonsensical "You Were Dead, You Know," the daffy choral number "Bon Voyage," the wistful ballad "It Must Be So," the swirling "What's the Use?," and the fervent "Make Our Garden Grow."

Candide found new life in 1974 when a revised revival from the Chelsea Theatre Center of Brooklyn transferred to Broadway and ran 740 performances. HUGH WHEELER wrote a completely new libretto, STEPHEN SONDHEIM provided some new lyrics for Bernstein's music, and HAROLD PRINCE directed the operetta as a joyous, circus-like cartoon. A young and physical Candide jumped from one continent to another just as he leapt from one platform to another in Eugene Lee's ingenious setting that was constructed throughout the large playhouse, putting audience members on the stage and some of the action in the balcony. The delightful romp was a hit and the new version placed the musical in the repertory of theatre and opera companies around the world. In 1997, director Prince returned to the musical for producer Garth H. Drabinsky and, using the Wheeler script, created a carnival atmosphere in a conventional theatre setting. JIM DALE shone as Voltaire, Pangloss, and other characters but reviews were mixed so the musical struggled to run 103 performances.

CANOVA, JUDY [born Juliet Canova] (1913–1983). Film and stage performer. A singing hillbilly comic who was very popular on screen and on the radio, her yodeling and broad clowning were unique in her day, especially for a female entertainer. Canova was born in Starke, Florida, and began her career singing, playing the guitar, and yodeling in a nightclub act with her two siblings. She was soon dubbed the "Jenny Lind of the Ozarks" and the "Queen of Corn" and was featured in twenty movie musicals, mostly B pictures at Republic Studios and usually with members of her

---

Casts for *Candide*

Character	1956 Broadway	1974 Broadway	1997 Broadway
Candide	ROBERT ROUNSEVILLE	Mark Baker	Jason Danieley
Cunegonde	BARBARA COOK	Maureen Brennan	Harolyn Blackwell
Pangloss, etc.	Max Adrian	LEWIS J. STADLEN	JIM DALE
Old Lady	IRRA PETINA	June Gable	ANDREA MARTIN

family in the cast. Among her credits are *Going Highbrow* (1935), *In Caliente* (1935), *Thrill of a Lifetime* (1937), *ARTISTS AND MODELS* (1937), *Sis Hopkins* (1941), *Puddinhead* (1941), *Sleepytime Gal* (1942), *True to the Army* (1942), *Joan of Ozark* (1942), *Sleepy Lagoon* (1943), *Louisiana Hayride* (1944), *Hit the Hay* (1945), *Singin' in the Corn* (1946), *Oklahoma Annie* (1952), *The Wac From Walla Walla* (1952), *Untamed Heiress* (1954), *Carolina Cannonball* (1955), and *Lay That Rifle Down* (1955). Canova made a few stage appearances, being featured in the Broadway musicals *Calling All Stars* (1934), *ZIEGFELD FOLLIES* (1936), and *Yokel Boy* (1939), and for twelve years had a very popular radio show of her own. After a long absence from the screen she played the sheriff's wife in the musical *The Adventures of Huckleberry Finn* (1960) and in 1971 she starred in the national road tour of *NO, NO, NANETTE*. Canova was married to actor BOB BURNS for a time.

◼ **CAN'T HELP SINGING** (Universal 1944). With more than a passing nod to *OKLAHOMA!*, which opened on Broadway the year before, this frontier musical captured the enthusiasm for land (there was even a rousing song celebrating "Californ-i-ay") and the pioneer spirit of the Rodgers and Hammerstein musical, yet the movie has a charm of its own. Lewis R. Foster and director Frank Ryan penned the screenplay set in 1847 in which Caroline (DEANNA DURBIN), the daughter of East Coast senator Frost (Ray Collins), ignores her father's threats and sets off across country to wed an army officer, but on the wagon train heading to California falls in love with the outdoorsman Johnny Lawlor (ROBERT PAIGE). AKIM TAMIROFF and LEONID KINSKEY supplied the humor as the pair of European fortune hunters Prince Gregory and Koppa who are bumbling across the prairie. Also cast were David Bruce, Andrew Tombes, Thomas Gomez, June Vincent, Clara Blandick, and Olin Howland. JEROME KERN (music) and E. Y. HARBURG (lyrics) provided the best original score of Durbin's career, mixing operetta and Broadway sounds in such songs as "Any Moment Now," "Swing Your Partner," "More and More," and the lilting title number. Felix Jackson produced the film, which boasted magnificent Technicolor photography and stunning outdoor locations.

◻ **CANTERVILLE GHOST, THE** (ABC-TV 1966). Oscar Wilde's 1887 short story about a 300-year-old ghost (Michael Redgrave) who haunts an old English mansion was musicalized with a fine, low-key score by Jerry Bock (music) and SHELDON HARNICK (lyrics). In BURT SHEVELOVE's teleplay, an American family buys the mansion and, when they are not frightened away by the ghost, he befriends them and they help the spirit resolve the issues that keep him from resting in peace. Shevelove also directed the *ABC Stage 67* production, which was taped on location in Kent. The cast, most of whom had limited singing abilities, also included Douglas Fairbanks, Jr., Natalie Schafer, and pop singer Peter Noone of Herman's Hermits. The critics stomped on the musical, finding little life in the players or the score, yet "Canterville Hall," "Vengeance," "Undertow," and "Overhead" are commendable songs in the melodic, sincere Bock–Harnick style.

CANTOR, EDDIE [born Isidore Itkowitz] (1892–1964). Stage, film, and television performer. One of America's favorite clowns, the durable comedy star rarely strayed far from his skipping, leering persona who rolled his "banjo" eyes as he sang suggestive lyrics and then waved his handkerchief about as he exited. Cantor was born in Manhattan's Lower East Side, the son of Russian immigrants who died when he was a child. He was on the stage professionally by the age of fifteen and soon he was on vaudeville stages in England as well as in America. Producer FLORENZ ZIEGFELD gave Cantor his Broadway debut in *The Midnight Frolic* (1917) and the animated little comic went over so well he was featured in five editions of the *ZIEGFELD FOLLIES* and introduced several song standards. Cantor was also a success in book musicals, playing wimpy and anti-romantic characters such as the hypochondriac Henry in *WHOOPEE* (1928). His other Broadway credits include *Broadway Brevities of 1920*, *Make It Snappy* (1922), *Kid Boots* (1923), and *Banjo Eyes* (1941). When Cantor reprised his Henry in the 1930 film version of *Whoopee*, his screen career was launched and he played silly heroes in such musicals as *Palmy Days* (1931), *The Kid From Spain* (1932), *ROMAN SCANDALS* (1933), *KID MILLIONS* (1934), *Strike Me Pink* (1936), *Ali Baba Goes to Town* (1937), and *Forty Little Mothers* (1940). He played himself or Cantor-like roles in *THANK YOUR LUCKY STARS* (1943), *HOLLYWOOD CANTEEN* (1944), *Show Business* (1944), *If You Knew Susie* (1948), and *The Story of Will Rogers* (1952), as well as providing the singing vocals for Keefe Brasselle in *The Eddie Cantor Story* (1953). He also had a very successful career on the radio in the 1930s and his own television show in the 1950s. Autobiographies:

My Life in Your Hands (1928); *Take My Life* (1957); *The Way I See It* (1959); *I Remember Them* (1962); biography: *Banjo Eyes: Eddie Cantor and the Birth of Modern Stardom*, Herbert G. Goldman (1997).

■ **CAPTAIN JANUARY** (Fox 1936). The first of four SHIRLEY TEMPLE films released that year, this picture is a good example of how the busy moppet kept the studio afloat during the Depression years. The movie is also a testament to her surprising vocal range (she even sang a section of Donizetti's *Lucia di Lammermoor*) and heart-tugging theatrics. In the screenplay by Sam Hellman, Gladys Lehman, and Harry Tugend, the shipwrecked Helen Mason (Temple) is rescued by kindly old Captain January (GUY KIBBEE) but the purveyors of the law want to separate the two and put the child in an institution. Among all the melodramatics were some lively songs by LEW POLLOCK (music), SIDNEY MITCHELL, and JACK YELLEN (lyrics), including the optimistic "Early Bird," the affectionate "The Right Somebody to Love," and the merry "At the Codfish Ball." BUDDY EBSEN joined Temple for a memorable dance routine, and Slim Summerville provided some rustic humor as the captain's cribbage-playing friend Captain Nazro. Jane Darwell, June Lang, Jerry Tucker, Sasa Haden, and Nella Walker were also in the cast directed by DAVID BUTLER. The DARRYL F. ZANUCK–B. G. DE Sylva production, like all the Temple vehicles of the period, was a box office hit.

■ **CAREFREE** (RKO 1938). FRED ASTAIRE finally got to play someone besides a song and dance man in his eighth musical with GINGER ROGERS. He was cast as psychiatrist Tony Flagg who is treating Amanda Cooper (Rogers) because she cannot decide whether or not to marry Stephen Arden (Ralph Bellamy). This and other elements in the script by Ernest Pagano and Allan Scott took a lot of imagination on the audience's part but it was easier to buy when Dr. Flagg was also a terrific hoofer, in one scene even tap dancing on the golf course. In another switch for Astaire, he was not pursuing Rogers this time. Amanda realizes she like her psychiatrist more than stuffy Arden and chases the hoofer until she gets him. IRVING BERLIN wrote three news songs for the film and they were radiant: "Change Partners," "I Used to Be Colorblind," and the latest Berlin dance song "The Yam." JACK CARSON, LUELLA GEAR, FRANKLIN PANGBORN, and HATTIE MCDANIEL filled out the cast, who

were directed by MARK SANDRICH. PANDRO S. BERMAN produced, and HERMES PAN choreographed with Astaire's assistance.

CARIOU, LEN (1939–). Stage, television, and film performer. A respected classical actor in Canada, England, and regional theatre, he later became a favorite leading man in Broadway musicals. Cariou was born in St. Boniface, Manitoba, Canada, and educated at St. Paul's College in Winnipeg. After selling farm equipment and men's clothing, he studied acting at the Stratford Festival School and later was a member of its company, playing dozens of classical roles. Cariou also acted in distinguished theatres in England and America before making his Broadway debut in 1968. Two years later he was LAUREN BACALL's leading man in the musical *APPLAUSE* (1970), followed by such musical roles as the lawyer Frederik Egerman in *A LITTLE NIGHT MUSIC* (1973), the murderous *SWEENEY TODD, THE DEMON BARBER OF FLEET STREET* (1979), veteran hoofer Harry Aikens in *Dance a Little Closer* (1983), and Theodore Roosevelt in *Teddy and Alice* (1987). Cariou frequently returns to classical and other nonmusical plays. He has only made a handful of films, including the 1978 screen version of *A Little Night Music*, but has been very active on television since 1990.

CARLISLE, KITTY [born Catherine Holzman] (1917–2007). Stage, film, and television performer. A classy, poised soprano with high fashion tastes in clothes and demeanor, she was equally proficient with comedies and musicals as she was with opera and television quiz shows. Born in New Orleans and educated at first-class private schools in Switzerland, London, Paris, and Rome, Carlisle trained for an opera career and studied acting at the Royal Academy of Dramatic Art. She made her Broadway debut as the title heroine in the 1932 revival of *RIO RITA* and then found higher recognition in the trouser role of Prince Orlofsky in *Champagne, Sec* (1933). Carlisle starred in such operettas as *White Horse Inn* (1936) and *Three Waltzes* (1937), even as she was featured in such Hollywood musicals as *Murder at the Vanities* (1934), *She Loves Me Not* (1934), *Here in My Heart* (1934), *A NIGHT AT THE OPERA* (1935), *Larceny With Music* (1943), and *HOLLYWOOD CANTEEN* (1945). In the 1950s she found success in some comedies on Broadway, played Lilli Vanessi/Katharine in the 1956 revival of *KISS ME, KATE*, and started appearing on television, as with the TV musicals *A Waltz Dream* (1951) and *Holiday* (1956). Carlisle would become a familiar face to most Americans for her years on the quiz programs *I've Got a Secret* and *To Tell the Truth*. During her long and productive life, she sang in opera houses, returned to Broadway in 1983 to play the patroness of the arts Peggy Porterfield in ON YOUR TOES, and ran the New York State Council on the Arts for over twenty years. Carlisle put together a one-person nightclub act in 2005 and was still performing it a few months before her death at ninety-three. She was married to playwright–director MOSS HART. Autobiography: *Kitty* (1984).

CARLISLE, MARY (1912–2007). Film performer. A striking blonde actress who usually played wholesome coeds, she made over fifty films in the 1930s and early 1940s without becoming a star. Carlisle was born in Boston and grew up in southern California. After high school she started getting bit parts in films and then graduated to featured roles and leading parts, although mostly in B pictures. She played opposite BING CROSBY in three musicals: *College Humor* (1933), *DOUBLE OR NOTHING* (1937), and *Doctor Rhythm* (1938). Carlisle's other musical credits are *Sweetheart of Sigma Chi* (1933), *Palooka* (1934), *Million Dollar Ransom* (1934), *The Old Homestead* (1935), *Hawaiian Nights* (1939), and *Rovin' Tumbleweed* (1939). She retired from films in 1943 and ran an Elizabeth Arden studio in Beverly Hills in the 1950s. Autobiography: *Wide-Eyed in Babylon* (1974).

🕭 **CARMEN JONES** (Broadway Theatre 1943). OSCAR HAMMERSTEIN's adaptation of Bizet's opera *Carmen* (1875) reset in America with African American characters was much more than a gimmick and even music critics hailed it as an effective, thought-provoking venture. In a southern American town during World War II, the most provocative (and trouble-making) employee at the parachute factory is Carmen Jones who is arrested by the military for causing a ruckus once again. She uses her

Carmen Jones. The bewitching Dorothy Dandridge was an accomplished singer but did not have the vocal ability necessary for the opera score so she was dubbed in the 1954 film. It did not diminish her resplendent performance as the reckless, enticing Carmen who seduces and destroys army officer Harry Belafonte. (Photofest)

seductive ways on Joe, the corporal assigned to guard her, and soon Joe has forgotten his local sweetheart Cindy Lou and runs off to Chicago with Carmen. The boastful Husky Miller, a champion boxer on the military base, also goes to Chicago for a major bout in the ring. The unfaithful Carmen is drawn to the boxer and Joe, in a jealous rage, stabs her to death as the sounds of cheering from the offstage boxing match fill the stage. Hammerstein wrote the new libretto and fashioned African American slangy lyrics to Bizet's famous music. From this new score came such memorable musical numbers as "Dat's Love," "Dere's a Café on

Casts for *Carmen Jones*

Character	1943 Broadway	1954 film
Carmen Jones	Muriel Smith/Muriel Rahn	DOROTHY DANDRIDGE
Joe	Luther Saxon/Napoleon Reed	Harry Belafonte
Husky Miller	Glenn Bryant	Joe Adams
Cindy Lou	Carlotta Franzell/Elton J. Warren	Olga James
Frankie	Jessica Russell	PEARL BAILEY

de Corner," "Stan' Up and Fight," "Beat Out Dat Rhythm on a Drum," "My Joe," and "Dis Flower." Critical reaction to the new version of the opera was enthusiastic. Hammerstein's handling of the characters and his new lyrics helped audiences enjoy *Carmen* with a new perspective. Also praised were the new orchestrations by ROBERT RUSSELL BENNETT, the atmospheric settings by Howard Bay, and the way director–lighting designer HASSARD SHORT bathed each scene with a different color palette. *Carmen Jones* was a surprise hit, running 502 performances on Broadway and coming back twice for return engagements while it toured the country.

■ *Carmen Jones* (Fox 1954) lost something in the transition to the screen, as most operas do. The screenplay by Harry Kleiner condensed the plot, character development was gone, and too often the glorious music was cut for banal dialogue scenes. Hollywood's finest African American actors were assembled for the screen version but, because they were actors and not wide-ranged singers, most of the major characters were dubbed. DOROTHY DANDRIDGE is a spellbinding Carmen and, with Marilyn Horne's singing voice, her numbers work. Harry Belafonte as Joe (dubbed by LeVern Hutcherson) is less effective; his performance was perhaps too naive, little more than putty in Carmen's hands. Olga James did her own vocals as Cindy Lou, and Joe Adams was a robust Husky Miller (dubbed by Marvin Hayes). The cast was filled out by such notable talents as PEARL BAILEY, DIAHANN CARROLL, and BROCK PETERS. Producer OTTO PREMINGER's direction was too literal and too flat, and the high theatrics of opera sometimes became annoyingly melodramatic on screen. All the same, the picture is worth seeing for Dandridge.

CARMICHAEL, HOAGY [born Hoagland Howard Carmichael] (1899–1981). Film and television composer, musician, and performer. The distinctive songwriter, pianist, and actor who appeared in films as a supporting character with a cigarette dangling out of his mouth, he was one of the most successful of all popular music composers. Carmichael was born in Bloomington, Indiana, and studied law at Indiana University before becoming a bandleader, music arranger, and eventually a songwriter. He recorded some of his own works singing in his lazy drawl and his unique quality caught on. Carmichael became famous for his 1931 song "Star Dust," a musical composition that didn't catch on

until Mitchell Parrish added a lyric; it went on to become one of the most recorded songs of all time. Some of Carmichael's songs were placed in movies as early as 1936 and he himself appeared in *To Have and Have Not* (1944), *The Best Years of Our Lives* (1946), *Canyon Passage* (1946), *Night Song* (1947), *YOUNG MAN WITH A HORN* (1950), *The Las Vegas Story* (1952), *Timberjack* (1955), and others, often singing a song or two even in nonmusicals. Among the film musicals he scored were *Road Show* (1941), *Mr. Bug Goes to Town* (1941), *True To Life* (1943), and *GENTLEMEN PREFER BLONDES* (1953). Carmichael acted and sang in several television shows from the early 1950s to the early 1970s. Among his many best-selling songs are "Ole Buttermilk Sky," "Georgia on My Mind," "Rockin' Chair," "Heart and Soul," and "In the Cool, Cool, Cool of the Evening." Autobiographies: *The Stardust Road* (1946), *Sometimes I Wonder* (1965); biography: *Stardust Melody: The Life and Music of Hoagy Carmichael*, Richard M. Sudhalter (2003).

CARMINATI, TULLIO [born Count Tullio Carminati de Brambilla) (1894–1971). Stage and film performer. An elegant leading man on the European and Broadway stage, the suave actor–singer appeared in a handful of musicals in New York and in Hollywood. Carminati was born in Zara, Italy (present-day Croatia), and began acting on the stage as a teenager. By 1910 he was in European films but continued to perform in the theatre opposite major stars such as Eleanore Duse. Carminati came to America in 1925 and made an auspicious Broadway debut in the comedy *Strictly Dishonorable* (1929). He quickly became a matinee idol and was featured in two musicals, *MUSIC IN THE AIR* (1932) and *Great Lady* (1938). Although he made a few silent films in America in the 1920s, he didn't get noticed until sound came in and his distinguished, continental voice could be heard. Carminati's screen musicals are *Moulin Rouge* (1934), *ONE NIGHT OF LOVE* (1934), *Let's Live Tonight* (1935), and *Paris in Spring* (1935), as well as the British films *London Melody* (1937) and *Sunset in Vienna* (1937). He aged gracefully and played character parts in American and European films into the 1960s.

CARNELIA, CRAIG (1949–). Stage composer, lyricist, and performer. A highly talented songwriter, he has written compelling scores for thirty years without ever having a major hit or receiving wide recognition. Carnelia was born in Floral Park, New York, and began his career as an actor–singer, eventually getting cast as one of the many replacements for Matt during the original run of *THE FANTASTICKS*. He started singing his own songs in cabarets and then scored the Off Broadway revues *Notes: Songs* (1978), *Diamonds* (1984), and *No Frills Revue* (1987) before some of his songs were heard on Broadway in *WORKING* (1978). His first full score for Broadway was the commended but short-lived *Is There Life After High School?* (1982) and his songs in the Off Broadway musical *Three Postcards* (1987) were also praised. Carnelia collaborated with composer Marvin Hamlisch on the score for the dark musical *Sweet Smell of Success* (2002) and the two also provided songs for the play *Imaginary Friends* (2002). He continues to perform his works in cabarets and has made several recordings. His music is contemporary and highly accessible, while his lyrics have a superior sense of character, pathos, and drama.

CARNIVAL. *See LILI*

🕭 **CAROLINE, OR CHANGE** (Eugene O'Neill Theatre 2004). A poetic, atmospheric sung-through musical by Tony Kushner (book and lyrics) and JEANINE TESORI (music), it may have been lean on plot but was rich in characterization and the bluesy score was sometimes intoxicating. The African American servant Caroline Thibodeaux (TONYA PINKINS) does the laundry in the basement of the Jewish Gellman family home in Louisiana, finding companionship with her singing washing machine, dryer, and the young Noah Gellman (Harrison Chad) who idolizes her. The divorced Caroline has her own children to worry about, one in Viet Nam, the teenage Emmie (Anika Noni Rose) running around with radical ideas, and the younger ones always needing something she cannot afford. On the day President Kennedy is assassinated, the Gellman family is in shock but the Thibodeaux kids feel it has nothing to do with them. Noah's stepmother Rose (Veanne Cox), in her efforts to help the moody boy gain responsibility, tells Caroline she can keep any loose change he forgets to take out of his pockets and soon Noah is helping the Thibodeaux family by purposely leave money in clothes sent down in the laundry. The relationship between Caroline and Noah is forever changed when he accidentally leaves a $20 bill, given to him by his grandfather (Larry Keith), in his pocket and she insists it is hers to keep. At the same time the friction between Caroline and Emmie explodes and Caroline's

frustration with her life pushes her to turn a corner and learn to live with sorrow. The musical numbers were more extended musical scenes than songs, yet there were many memorable moments, as in "Moon Change," "Lot's Wife," "Roosevelt Pertrucius Coleslaw," "No One Waitin'," "Gonna Pass Me a Law," and "Underwater." Critics carped about the details but unanimously extolled Pinkins unsentimental, compelling performance. The GEORGE C. WOLFE-directed production, which had originated Off Broadway at the PUBLIC THEATRE and then moved to Broadway, had difficulty finding an audience and closed after 136 performances. The musical was better appreciated in Los Angeles and London with Pinkins reprising her fascinating Caroline.

CARON, LESLIE [Claire Margaret] (1931–). Film and television performer. The slight, dark-haired beauty from France, she has given delectable screen performances in dramas and musicals. Caron was born in Boulogne-Billancourt, France, the daughter of a French father and an American mother, and began ballet lessons when she was ten years old. While still a teenager she danced with Roland Petit's Ballets des Champs and when GENE KELLY saw her perform he cast her as Lise Bouvier in *AN AMERICAN IN PARIS* (1951). Caron remained in Hollywood to act in nonmusicals but was most known for her musical roles: the orphaned waif *LILI* (1953), the Cinderella-like Ella in *The Glass Slipper* (1955), the refugee Julie in *DADDY LONG LEGS* (1955), and the tomboy *GIGI* (1958). With her enticing French accent, delicate dancing, and wide-eyed charm, Caron was a distinctive ingénue and unique in Hollywood. Although she gave up musicals after *Gigi*, she has continued to act sporadically in American and European films and television.

🕭 **CAROUSEL** (Majestic Theatre 1945). The second Broadway collaboration of RICHARD RODGERS (music) and OSCAR HAMMERSTEIN (book and lyrics), the complex, dark musical is considered by many to be their finest achievement.

Plot: Julie Jordan and Carrie Pipperidge, young mill workers in a New England town, visit a local carnival where the dashing but tough carousel barker Billy Bigelow is immediately attracted to Julie, much to the displeasure of the jealous carousel owner Mrs. Mullin. She kicks the girls out and fires Billy and then pleads for him to return. But Billy is drawn to Julie and, after arguing that they do not love

Carousel. Whereas most musicals in the 1940s started with an overture and then an opening chorus number, this innovative show began with a pantomime in which the major characters were introduced without words. The scene was set to Richard Rodgers' intoxicating "Carousel Waltz" and the music climaxed just as the confrontation between some of the characters reached a peak. From the start it was a musical like no other. (Photofest)

each other, the two succumb to the inevitable and get married. It is not a happy marriage with Billy out of work, the couple living off the charity of Julie's Aunt Nettie, and Billy unable to conform to respectable conventions. When he learns that Julie is pregnant, Billy is determined to make some money quickly so he falls into a scheme with the dishonest Jigger Craigin to rob a payroll courier. The robbery goes wrong and, facing capture, Billy falls on his own knife and dies. Arriving in heaven, Billy is told by the Starkeeper that he may return to earth briefly to help his daughter Louise, now a troubled teenager as restless as Billy was. The encounter with Louise goes badly, with Billy offering her a star and her refusing to accept it. At Louise's high school graduation, Billy is able to impart some confidence to his daughter and to let Julie know that he still loves her. The subplot concerns Carrie and her beau, the fisherman Mr. Snow. The two court and wed and have a brood of children, becoming the

bastion of respectability that so annoys Louise and Billy.

The THEATRE GUILD had produced Ferenc Molnar's fantasy–drama *Liliom* in 1921 and it was a notable success, running 300 performances. Rodgers and Hammerstein were interested in adapting it into a musical, but they feared the Budapest setting and the Hungarian characters were too foreign for Broadway audiences so Hammerstein reset the story in a New England mill town in the late 1800s, changed all of the names, created a comic subplot out of some minor characters, and gave the musical a more hopeful ending. As plotted out by Rodgers and Hammerstein, the score was even more integrated into the plot than *OKLAHOMA!* (1943) with dialogue sections and sometimes whole scenes set to music. The lengthy so-called "Bench Scene," in which Billy and Julie get to know each other, argue, and finally submit to each other to the strains

Casts for *Carousel*

Characters	Billy Bigelow	Julie	Carrie	Mr. Snow
1945 Broadway	JOHN RAITT	JAN CLAYTON	Jean Darling	Eric Mattson
1956 film	GORDON MACRAE	SHIRLEY JONES	Barbara Ruick	ROBERT ROUNSEVILLE
1957 Broadway	HOWARD KEEL	BARBARA COOK	Pat Stanley	RUSSELL NYPE
1967 television	ROBERT GOULET	Mary Glover	Marlyn Mason	Jack DeLon
1994 Broadway	Michael Hayden	Sally Murphy	AUDRA McDONALD	Duane Boutte

Characters	Nettie	Jigger	Mrs. Mullin	Louise
1945 Broadway	Christine Johnson	Murvyn Vye	Jean Casto	Bambi Linn
1956 film	Claramae Turner	Cameron Mitchell	Audrey Christie	Susan Luckey
1957 Broadway	Maria Powers	James Mitchell	Kay Medford	Bambi Linn
1967 television	Patricia Neway	Pernell Roberts	Marge Redmond	Linda Howe
1994 Broadway	Shirley Verrett	Fisher Stevens	Kate Buddeke	Sandra Brown

of "If I Loved You," is considered the most perfectly integrated piece of music–drama in the American theatre. So too is Billy's seven-minute "Soliloquy," a masterwork of musical stream of consciousness. Broadway had seen a few anti-heroes before (most memorably the heel Joey Evans in Rodgers and Hart's *PAL JOEY* in 1940), but never before had such a flawed, belligerent central character been portrayed from within so effectively. Julie was a much more complex version of a Broadway ingénue and her growth from a determined yet impressionable girl to a knowing woman is one of the most subtly engaging of all Rodgers and Hammerstein heroines. The use of humor and the comic subplot of Carrie and Mr. Snow are handled very carefully in the musical. Carrie is no addle-brained Ado Annie, but is a gleeful and confident foil to the dreamy, reticent Julie. Mr. Snow may come across as a bit of a buffoon at first but the humor changes as he becomes self-righteous and a symbol of the respectability that so disgusts Billy. Only the villainous Jigger comes close to a stock character, yet Hammerstein gives him a sardonic sense of humor and an outrageous cockiness that makes you realize how Billy's good qualities make him worth saving. As with *Oklahoma!*, dance again grew out of the characters, and the second act ballet explores the psychological state of not one, but two characters: Billy and his troubled teenager daughter Louise. The end result of all of Rodgers and Hammerstein's planning and writing is a musical play even richer and more integrated than *Oklahoma!* It is little wonder that *Carousel* remained Rodgers' personal favorite all his life.

Much of the same team from *Oklahoma!* were reassembled, including director ROUBEN

Carousel (stage) Musical Numbers

"Carousel Waltz"
"You're a Queer One, Julie Jordan"
"When I Marry Mr. Snow"
"If I Loved You"
"June Is Bustin' Out All Over"
"When the Children Are Asleep"
"Blow High, Blow Low"
"Soliloquy"
"This Was a Real Nice Clambake"
"Geraniums in the Winder"
"Stonecutters Cut It on Stone"
"What's the Use of Wondrin'"
"You'll Never Walk Alone"
"Ballet"

MAMOULIAN and choreographer AGNES DE MILLE. Both were able to match the proficiency of the earlier show, with the book scenes having an even darker edge to their presentation and the dances alternating between buoyant celebration, as in "June Is Bustin' Out All Over" and "Blow High, Blow Low," and painful restlessness, as in Louise's solo sections in the second act ballet. The direction and dancing came together in seamless harmony in the musical's opening "Carousel Waltz" pantomime. Instead of a traditional overture, Rodgers and Hammerstein opted for a lengthy musical prologue introducing the major characters and conflicts without spoken or sung words. It was a unique way to start a musical and immediately told audiences that *Carousel* was going to be different. Several songs from the show became standards, such as "If I Loved You," "You'll Never Walk Alone," "June Is Bustin' Out All Over," and "What's the Use of Wond'rin'," and the "Carousel Waltz" became one of Rodgers' most recognized and beloved waltzes. Yet even the character songs such as "Soliloquy" and "When I Marry Mr. Snow" found recognition even though it was awkward to perform them outside the context of the show. There is more music in *Carousel* than any other Rodgers and Hammerstein musical, prompting many to term it an operetta. Critics may not have agreed on what to call it but the reviews were highly favorable and the musical ran 890 performances, far less than *Oklahoma!* but quite impressive for such a demanding musical drama. *Carousel* would never become as popular as the other Rodgers and Hammerstein masterworks; for many it is a musical more respected than loved. However, it is the show that has inspired generations of later librettists and songwriters to tackle themes and subject matter previously deemed too serious for the musical stage.

The first national tour of *Carousel* ran two years, remaining for five months just in Chicago. The New York City Center revived the musical in 1949 with STEPHEN DOUGLASS (Billy), Iva Withers (Julie), Margot Moser (Carrie), and Christine Johnson and Eric Mattson reprising their Nettie and Mr. Snow. The New York Light Opera Company reprised *Carousel* for seventy-nine performances in 1954 with a cast that featured Chris Robinson (Billy), Jo Sullivan (Julie), Jean Handzlik (Nettie), BARBARA COOK (Carrie), and Don Blackey (Mr. Snow) under the direction of William Hammerstein, Oscar's son. The same company offered a 1957 revival, this time with Barbara Cook as Julie. The next year the New York City Light Opera Company sent a production of *Carousel* to the Brussels Exposition. JAN CLAYTON reprised her Julie for the prestigious production, which also featured David Atkinson (Billy), Ruth Kobart (Nettie), Joan Hovis (Carrie), and RUSSELL NYPE as Enoch Snow. Richard Rodgers and the Music Theatre of Lincoln Center presented the 1965 revival with JOHN RAITT reprising his Billy. The production, which ran forty-seven performances, also featured Eileen Christy (Julie), Katherine Hilgenberg (Nettie), SUSAN WATSON (Carrie), REID SHELTON (Mr. Snow), and JERRY ORBACH (Jigger). The next year the New York City Light Opera Company brought *Carousel* back to the City Center for twenty-two performances with a cast that included Bruce Yarnell (Billie), CONSTANCE TOWERS (Julie), Patricia Neway (Nettie), NANCY DUSSAULT (Carrie), and Jack DeLon (Mr. Snow). Although there had been some revivals of *Carousel* in Great Britain, none attracted so much attention as a 1992 Royal National Theatre production directed by NICHOLAS HYTNER and choreographed by Sir Kenneth MacMillan in which the script and score were radically rethought. Hytner opened the musical not with the carousel but in the textile factory where Julie and Carrie work, with the waltzing opening music slowed down to a grinding pattern of toil. The staging then followed the girls after work to the shipyards and then to the carnival where other major characters were introduced. The American actor Michael Hayden played Billy not as a large gruff man but a smaller, pent-up, frustrated time bomb and the familiar scenes and songs took on a new energy. The acclaimed production transferred to Broadway in 1994, winning several awards and running 322 performances.

Carousel (Fox, 1956) is perhaps the most disappointing film version of a Rodgers and Hammerstein musical. The screenplay by Henry and Phoebe Ephron cuts lengthy song–dialogue sections to get the script down to size; other songs were cut after they had been filmed because the movie was still running too long. When FRANK SINATRA walked off the set the first day of shooting, GORDON MACRAE was called in to play Billy and, reunited with SHIRLEY JONES as Julie, the romantic couple from *Oklahoma!* filled the same shoes in *Carousel*. Jones gives a valiant performance, but MacRae, whose singing is fine, seems lost as Billy, huffing, puffing, and pulling up his pants every few seconds to show that he is tough. The rest of the cast is competent but the direction and choreography are not. Director HENRY KING shot miles of postcard-like footage in Boothbay Harbor, Maine, and then left a lot of it on the cutting room floor. The intimate duet "When the Children Are Asleep" was filmed in the middle of a crowded flotilla and there always seemed to be a sailboat passing by behind all of the dialogue scenes, as if to prove that everyone really went to Maine. The scenes filmed in the California studios look artificial and the action is often wooden. Even the long engrossing "Bench Scene" comes across only as long on screen. One interesting directorial touch was having Billy sing "Soliloquy" as he walked along the shore with crashing waves; it often distracted from what MacRae was singing but it added a tension that was sorely needed. Rod Alexander staged the dances in the film and they are energetic, fervent, and hollow. He used much of de Mille's original choreography in the extended ballet without crediting her; she had to go to court to get recognition and compensation. The film critics were surprisingly supportive and *Carousel* was very successful at the box office, with the soundtrack recording becoming a bestseller. ☐ *Carousel* (ABC-TV 1967) had to cut the stage work down to an hour and forty minutes and it was no easy feat for scriptwriter Sidney Michaels, but this abridged *Carousel* was surprisingly effective. Whereas the movie was too wide in its scope, television was ideal for concentrating on the characters. ROBERT GOULET sings the role of Billy beautifully and manages to capture quite a bit of the character, even showing the more fragile side of this confused bully. The rest of the cast is commendable, with Patricia Neway outstanding in her rendition of "You'll Never Walk Alone." (She had introduced the similar anthem "Climb Ev'ry Mountain" in the stage version of *THE SOUND OF MUSIC* eight years earlier.) Paul Bogart directed, Edward Villela choreographed, the studio production values were simple but pleasing, and the tone of the production seemed right. This modest television production was able to do what the overproduced film version could not.

CARPENTER, CARLETON (1926–). Film, stage, and television performer and composer. A slim, boyish dancer–singer of only a few musicals, he nevertheless always stood out and shone in supporting roles. Carpenter was born in Bennington, Vermont, and began his career dancing in nightclub shows. He made his Broadway debut in a play in 1944 and then was featured in the revue *Three to Make Ready* (1946). Carpenter was brought to Hollywood and made three musicals that came out in 1950: *THREE LITTLE WORDS*, *SUMMER STOCK*, and *Two Weeks With Love*, in which he sang "Aba Daba Honeymoon" with DEBBIE REYNOLDS; their recording of the song was a best seller. He returned to Broadway to appear in *John Murray Anderson's Almanac* (1953) and then concentrated on nonmusical films and on television where he was in the TV musicals *Paris in the Springtime* (1956) and *Mother Goose* (1958). Carleton returned to Broadway again in 1993 as a replacement in *CRAZY FOR YOU*. He has also composed popular songs, such as "Christmas Eve," "I Wouldn't Mind," and "Cabin in the Woods."

CARR, ALLEN [born Allan Solomon] (1937–1999). Film, television, and stage producer. A Hollywood producer who had a brief, flashy, and notable career that included some hit musicals. The Chicago native grew up in Atlanta, Georgia, and began his career as an artists' manager, guiding the careers of ANN-MARGARET, Peter Sellers, Paul Anka, PEGGY LEE, and others. After working as a promoter for *Playboy* executive Hugh Hefner, he turned to producing, presenting his first film in 1969 and his first television show in 1973. Carr handled the promotion campaign for the sleeper hit *SATURDAY NIGHT FEVER* (1977) and then was producer for the megahit *GREASE* (1978), co-writing the screenplay as well. He found less success with the screen musicals *Can't Stop the Music* (1980) and *GREASE 2* (1982) but on Broadway presented some profitable plays and the long-running *LA CAGE AUX FOLLES* (1983).

CARILLO, LEO (1881–1961). Film and television performer. A familiar Hollywood character actor of many movies in the 1930s and 1940s, he specialized in stereotypic Hispanic types. Carillo was born in Los Angeles to an aristocratic Latin family and educated at St. Vincent of Loyola College before working as a newspaper writer and a cartoonist. He went into vaudeville as a dialect comedian and by 1915 was playing character parts in Broadway comedies and dramas. Carrillo made his screen debut in 1927 and went on to play bandits, doctors, ranch hands, servants, and other types in over eighty movies. His musical credits include *Moonlight and Pretzels* (1933), *In Caliente* (1935), *Love Me Forever* (1935), *Manhattan Merry-Go-Round* (1937), *52nd Street* (1937), *LILLIAN RUSSELL* (1940), *ONE NIGHT IN THE TROPICS* (1940), *What's Cookin'?* (1942), *Bowery to Broadway* (1944), *Ghost Catchers* (1944), *Moonlight and Cactus* (1944), and *Mexicana* (1945). In 1950 Carrillo turned to television and became widely known as the agreeable sidekick Pancho on the long-running series *The Cisco Kid*.

CARROLL, DAVID (1950–1992). Stage and television performer. A handsome actor–singer on Broadway, he was proving to be one of the most impressive leading men in stage musicals when he died of AIDS. Carroll was born in Rockville Centre, New York, and educated at Dartmouth College where he co-founded a repertory theatre company. He made his Broadway debut in the chorus of *WHERE'S CHARLEY?* (1974) and then played the title role in the popular 1976 Off Broadway revival of *JOSEPH AND THE AMAZING TECHNICOLOR DREAMCOAT*. Carroll was featured in the Broadway musicals *Rodgers and Hart* (1975) and *Oh, Brother!* (1981) before playing the leading role of Adam in the short-lived stage version of *SEVEN BRIDES FOR SEVEN BROTHERS* (1982). He was noticed and commended more for his Rodolfo opposite Linda Ronstadt in the Off Broadway *La Boheme* (1984), Rat in *Wind in the Willows* (1985), Russian contestant Anatoly in *CHESS* (1988), and Waiter in *Cafe Crown* (1989) before getting rave notices for his tragic Baron in *GRAND HOTEL* (1989). Carroll also made some appearances in television series before dying while recording the cast album of *Grand Hotel*.

CARROLL, DIAHANN [born Carol Diahann Johnson] (1935–). Stage, film, and television performer. The sleek, classy, African American beauty of concerts, nightclubs, and television made two memorable Broadway musical appearances: as the young prostitute Ottilie in the *HOUSE OF FLOWERS* (1954) and as chic fashion model Barbara Woodruff in *No Strings* (1962). Carroll was born in the Bronx and attended New York University before beginning her successful singing and acting career. She made her film debut as Myrt in the 1954 screen version of *CARMEN JONES* and was also featured as Clara in the movie of *PORGY AND BESS* (1959). Much of Carroll's career was on television where she appeared in dozens of musical specials, original dramas, and weekly series, including the breakthrough sit-com *Julia* in the early 1970s, which was the first to star a young black actress. She was married to singer VIC DAMONE for a time. Autobiography: *Diahann: An Autobiography* (1986).

CARROLL, EARL (1892–1948). Stage producer, director, and lyricist. A colorful showman on Broadway, often in the news as a producer, lyricist, theatre builder, and director, he is best remembered for the series of revues that bore his name. A native of Pittsburgh, Carroll sold playbill programs in local theatres as a boy. After spending some years as a seaman, he went to New York and broke into show business as a lyricist, with some of his songs being used in Broadway musicals. He turned to producing plays in 1919 but had no success until 1923 when he presented his first of many revues that he directed and named after himself. The *EARL CARROLL VANITIES* featured scantily clad girls and off-color humor, made no pretense to art, and were popular enough to warrant a dozen subsequent editions between 1924 and 1940. Carroll also produced and directed a handful

of book musicals, most memorably *Murder at the Vanities* (1933), which was filmed in 1934, and presented plays staged by others. He produced three movie musicals for Hollywood: *Stowaway* (1936), *Love Is News* (1937), and *A Night at Earl Carroll's* (1940). Carroll made and lost fortunes during his lifetime, building and losing two New York theatres named after himself. He befriended millionaires and racketeers and died in a plane crash at the age of fifty-six. Biography: *The Body Merchant*, Ken Murray (1976).

CARROLL, JOHN [born Julian LaFaye] (1906–1979). Film and television performer. A dashing, mustached leading man who excelled at Continental types, the actor–singer played romantic lovers in 1930s films and character parts in his later years. Carroll was born in New Orleans and at the age of twelve ran away from home to work in various jobs before going to sea and ending up in Europe where he studied voice. Having experience also as a race car driver, Carroll broke into films as a stunt man and then started getting cast in acting roles when sound came in. After bit parts in such musicals as *Marianne* (1929), *The Rogue Song* (1930), *Monte Carlo* (1930), *NEW MOON* (1930), and *GO INTO YOUR DANCE* (1935), he started playing romantic Latins in nonmusicals and the musicals *Hi, Gaucho* (1936), *Rose of the Rancho* (1938), *Go West* (1940), *SUNNY* (1941), *LADY, BE GOOD* (1941), *RIO RITA* (1942), *Hit Parade of 1943*, and *Fiesta* (1947). Carroll was also effective as more mature types, as in the musicals *Hit Parade of 1951* (1950) and *THE FARMER TAKES A WIFE* (1953). He appeared on television before retiring in the late 1960s.

CARROLL, NANCY [born Ann Veronica La Hiff] (1903–1965). Film and stage performer. A charming wide-eyed, red-haired leading lady of the 1930s, she was one of the first stars of the talkies and bewitched audiences, particularly when paired with CHARLES "BUDDY" ROGERS. The native New Yorker was singing and dancing on the musical stage as a teenager and was in the chorus of some 1920s Broadway musicals. While performing in a play in California, she was spotted by a PARAMOUNT agent and appeared in a few silents, becoming a star with the arrival of sound. Carroll shone in many dramas and comedies but her special flair in musicals was unique. Among her musical credits are *The Shopworn Angel* (1929), *Close Harmony* (1929), *Dance of Life* (1929), *Sweetie* (1929), *Honey* (1930), *PARAMOUNT*

ON PARADE (1930), *FOLLOW THRU* (1930), *Transatlantic Merry-Go-Round* (1934), *After the Dance* (1935), and *That Certain Age* (1938). Carroll stopped making films in 1938 but came back in the public eye in the 1950s in television dramas and series.

CARROLL, PAT[ricia Angel Ann Bridget] (1927–). Stage and television performer. A plump, comic actress who excelled at playing the villain or the best friend in comedies and musicals, she turned to more serious roles later in her career. Carroll was born in Shreveport, Louisiana, and educated at Sacred Heart College and Catholic University of America before starting her career as a cabaret singer. By the early 1950s she had appeared in dozens of stock productions across the country and started appearing regularly on television in variety shows. Carroll was featured on Broadway in the revues *Come What May* (1955) and *Catch a Star!* (1955) and as the cab driver Hildy in the 1959 revival of *ON THE TOWN*, but most of her career was on the tube, which best suited her performance style. Possibly her most memorable appearance was as the stepsister Prunella in the 1965 TV remake of *CINDERELLA*. By the 1980s Carroll returned to the New York theatre in serious roles and performed everything from Shakespeare to new plays in regional theatre. She also is in much demand for doing voices for animated television shows and films, particularly the sea witch Ursula in *THE LITTLE MERMAID* (1989) and its video sequels.

CARROLL, VINNETTE (1922?–2002). Stage director and producer. An ambitious presenter of new African American musicals, she was a leading figure in New York theatre in the 1970s and 1980s. Carroll was a native New Yorker, educated at Long Island, Columbia, and New York universities, as well as at the New School for Social Research. She studied with Stella Adler, Edwin Piscator, and Lee Strasberg for an acting career and performed in both New York and London before turning to directing in 1960. Throughout the decade Carroll directed revivals and new African American musicals before founding the Urban Arts Corps Theatre in 1969 and dedicating her energies to new works. From the Off Broadway company came such popular musicals as *But Never Jam Today* (1969), *DON'T BOTHER ME, I CAN'T COPE* (1971), and *YOUR ARMS TOO SHORT TO BOX WITH GOD* (1976), all of which moved to Broadway. Carroll also staged vibrant productions, which often took the form of a revival meeting or a gospel service. She and her company served as an inspiration for many fledgling African American writers, performers, and directors.

CARSON, JACK [Elmer] (1910–1963). Film performer. A stocky character actor in many films, he usually played second leads ranging from heavies in westerns to buffoonish sidekicks in musicals. Carson was born in Carman, Manitoba, Canada, and educated at Carlton College before going into vaudeville as a comic. He started in Hollywood as an extra in the mid-1930s but was not noticed until the early 1940s when his agile, facial expressions and broad double take were appreciated. Among Carson's twenty-three musicals are *Having Wonderful Time* (1938), *CAREFREE* (1938), *LOVE THY NEIGHBOR* (1940), *BLUES IN THE NIGHT* (1941), *The Hard Way* (1942), *Shine on Harvest Moon* (1944), *Two Guys From Milwaukee* (1946), *The Time, the Place and the Girl* (1946), *April Showers* (1948), *ROMANCE ON THE HIGH SEAS* (1948), *Two Guys From Texas* (1948), *It's a Great Feeling* (1949), *My Dream Is Yours* (1949), *Dangerous When Wet* (1953), *Red Garters* (1954), and *A STAR IS BORN* (1954). In addition to some ninety films, Carson played candidate Wintergreen in the popular 1952 Broadway revival of *OF THEE I SING* and was also active on television, appearing in the TV musicals *The Adventures of Huckleberry Finn* (1957) and *The Happiest Day* (1961) before his premature death.

CARVER, BRENT (1951–). Stage and television performer. A versatile and busy leading man who has only been seen sporadically in New York, the actor–singer made an impression each time. Carver was born in Cranbrook, British Columbia, Canada, and studied at the University of British Columbia until he left to pursue a professional acting career. He played classical and contemporary roles in regional theatres across Canada and the United States and by the mid-1980s was a favorite at the Stratford Festival in his native country, playing everything from Hamlet to Tevye. Carver's two Broadway musical credits are the gay window dresser Molina in *KISS OF THE SPIDER WOMAN* (1993) and the wrongly accused Leo Frank in *PARADE* (1998), both performances highly praised by the press. He has appeared in films and in many television dramas in Canada and the States and played Gandalf in the premiere production of the stage musical *The Lord of the Rings* (2006) in Toronto.

🎬 *CASBAH* (Marston/Universal 1948). The romantic Charles Boyer–Hedy Lamar film *Algiers* (1938) was turned into a musical by scriptwriters Leslie Bush-Fekete and Arnold Manoff, and the rich, flowing score by HAROLD ARLEN (music) and LEO ROBIN (lyrics) helped the romance if not the intrigue. The French jewel thief Pepe Le Moko (TONY MARTIN) has fled his native country for Algiers and takes up with the tobacco shop owner Inez (YVONNE DE CARLO). When he falls in love with the French visitor Gaby (Marta Toren), Inez's jealousy is aroused and she helps Inspector Slimare (Peter Lorre) corner Pepe who dies with Gaby's name on his lips. Hugo Hass, Thomas Gomez, Douglas Dick, Gene Walker, and Katherine Dunham and her dancers were also cast in the torrid romance. The songs included "It Was Written in the Stars," "Hooray for Love," "What's Good About Goodbye," "and "For Every Man There's a Woman." John Berry directed the Nat G. Goldstone production, and Bernard Pearce choreographed the pseudo-exotic dance numbers.

CASSIDY, JACK [born John Joseph Edward Cassidy] (1927–1976). Stage and television performer. The dimpled, smiling actor–singer played both cads and heroes, always bringing a satirical leer to his comedy. Cassidy was born in Richmond Hill, New York, and was only fifteen years old when he started appearing in the chorus of Broadway shows, such as *SOMETHING FOR THE BOYS* (1943), *Sadie Thompson* (1944), *Marinka* (1945), *The Firebrand of Florence* (1945), and *THE RED MILL* (1945). After being featured in bits in the revues *INSIDE U. S. A.* (1948), *Small Wonder* (1948), and *Alive and Kicking* (1950), Cassidy got recognition for his summer camp dancing instructor Chick Miller in *WISH YOU WERE HERE* (1952). Many of his subsequent musicals failed to have long runs, but he was always noticed, as with the cutthroat Macheath in *THE BEGGAR'S OPERA* (1957), ladies' man Kodaly in *SHE LOVES ME* (1963), Hollywood idol Byron Prong in *FADE OUT–FADE IN* (1964), and the corrupt Max Mencken in *IT'S A BIRD, IT'S A PLANE, IT'S SUPERMAN!* (1966). Cassidy's other musical credits include *Sandhog* (1954), *Shangri-La* (1956), and *Maggie Flynn* (1968). He appeared in a few films and in many television shows before his premature death in a fire. Cassidy was married to SHIRLEY JONES and is the father of performers David, Shaun, Ryan, and Patrick Cassidy.

CAST RECORDINGS AND SOUNDTRACKS. An original cast recording of a Broadway show, made by members of the company and featuring most or all of the score as performed on stage, is a relatively recent innovation. The invention of the phonograph in 1877 coincides with the developing American musical theatre, for it was at that time that musicals started to boast original scores with possible hit songs. Yet the earliest recordings of songs from Broadway on cylinders and 78-rpm discs rarely used the stage performers. It was felt that recording artists were better suited for these records, and often the house band for the recording company played their own orchestrated version of the song. When a performer of renown did get to record his or her hit song, rarely did it resemble the manner in which it was done in the theatre. In Great Britain, however, recording companies felt differently, and in 1900 the complete score for the musical *FLORODORA* was recorded on 78s. On several occasions the British would record the West End versions of American musicals,

Cast Recordings and Soundtracks. Many stage musicals live on because of the cast recording. This is still true today, despite video and other forms of technology. Pictured is Max Crumm as Danny Zuko making the cast recording of the 2007 Broadway revival of *Grease*. (Wire Image)

and the earliest and most accurate recordings of ROSE-MARIE (1924), LADY, BE GOOD (1924), NO, NO, NANETTE (1925), and other shows were made this way. The first American to try and preserve stage scores accurately on records was Jack Kapp who took selections from BLACKBIRDS OF 1928 and the 1932 revival of SHOW BOAT and recorded them with the original artists on the Brunswick label in 1932. Kapp was also responsible for putting all of the songs and some narration from THE CRADLE WILL ROCK (1938) on six 78s, using the original cast as well as composer MARC BLITZSTEIN as narrator. The first complete cast recording of a full-scale Broadway musical was Kapp's 78s of OKLAHOMA! (1943) on the Decca label. When the long-playing (LP) record, capable of having twenty-five minutes of music on each side, was introduced in 1948, the concept of the original cast recordings became even more practical. The first major hit in the LP format was SOUTH PACIFIC (1949) on the Columbia label. LP recordings did have one drawback: musicals originally issued on several 78s were now forced to edit the score to fit within fifty minutes. The Broadway show album as we know it today was developed by Goodard Lieberson, a record producer and president of Columbia Records from 1956 to 1966. It was Lieberson who tried to recapture the stage experience on the recording by adding lead-in dialogue for songs and editing longer musical passages in order to include their essence on the LP. Using these techniques, almost every Broadway musical in the late 1950s and 1960s, successful or not, was recorded for posterity. But the rise of rock music and the new directions the music industry was taking in the late 1960s made original cast albums less and less profitable and too many shows in the 1970s and 1980s went unrecorded. The introduction of the compact disc (CD) in the 1980s meant that the scores for Broadway musicals could be recorded with fewer omissions, but CDs did not manage to make show recordings popular enough to compete with mainstream popular music. CDs do allow for previously recorded musicals to be reissued with additional tracks, and CDs are ideal for recording complete scores for classic musicals from the past with contemporary performers. But the original cast recording is still not big business in the eyes of record companies.

Recordings of movie and television musicals, or soundtrack recordings, have a different history. Because the score for a film musical is done before the movie is shot, there is no need to go back into the recording studio and make a record. A recording company could just pick and choose which musical selections to release as a single or an album without the overhead expense of recording anything. This did not mean that complete soundtrack recording were readily available. Too often only the highlights were put on record and released when the movie came out as a way of promoting the film. Other times a single song from a movie musical might be released as a single and find success. As movie musicals included more songs, particularly in the 1940s, it was not possible to fit all the musical numbers from a film on one LP and a truly "complete score" was a rare things. Decades later, even when the original studio recordings were lost, record companies where able to extract a recording from the film itself, fading into the dialogue right before a song began and fading out after the musical number ended. These are not as polished as the studio-made Broadway recording but they are complete and accurate. Also see the *Guide to Recordings* at the back of the book.

CASTLE, [Nicholas] **NICK** (1910–1968). Film choreographer. A busy screen choreographer with nearly fifty musicals to his credit, he worked at a variety of studios and choreographed all the major musical stars. Castle was born in Brooklyn and danced in vaudeville before going to Hollywood in the mid-1930s. He made his debut with *Love and Hisses* (1937) and received recognition for the SHIRLEY TEMPLE musicals REBECCA OF SUNNYBROOK FARM (1938), *Little Miss Broadway* (1938), and *The Little Princess* (1939). Castle's other choreography credits include DOWN ARGENTINE WAY (1940), BUCK PRIVATES (1941), HELLZAPOPPIN (1941), ORCHESTRA WIVES (1942), STORMY WEATHER (1943), THIS IS THE ARMY (1943), SOMETHING FOR THE BOYS (1944), *Nob Hill* (1945), *You're My Everything* (1949), SUMMER STOCK (1950), ROYAL WEDDING (1951), *Stars and Stripes Forever* (1952), *Red Garters* (1954), *Seven Little Foys* (1955), ANYTHING GOES (1956), *Rock-a-Bye Baby* (1958), and STATE FAIR (1962). He was the father of movie writer and director Nick Castle (1947–).

CASTLE, VERNON AND IRENE. Stage performers. America's premiere dance team at the turn of the twentieth century, the husband and wife duo popularized ballroom dancing and instigated a dance craze in Europe and North America, introducing the Castle Walk, Turkey Trot, Maxie, and new forms of polka and tango.

Born Vernon Blythe (1887–1918) in Norfolk, England, he appeared in the dancing chorus of some British and American musicals before he met Irene Foote (1893–1969), a dancer from New Rochelle, New York, who had been on Broadway in the chorus. The couple wed and first appeared together on Broadway in *About Town* (1906), *The Mimic World* (1908), *The Summer Widowers* (1910), and *The Hen-Pecks* (1911), while he was featured solo in *The Girl Behind the Counter* (1907), *Old Dutch* (1909), *The Midnight Sons* (1909), and *The Lady of the Slipper* (1912). It was when the two danced together in a new act in Paris in 1912 and introduced the sprightly but elegant "Castle Walk" that they found fame, performing in ballrooms across Europe and America and starring in the Broadway musicals *The Sunshine Girl* (1913), WATCH YOUR STEP (1914), and *Miss 1917* (1917) and in the silent film *The Whirl of Life* (1915), which Vernon also wrote. The couple was at the peak of their popularity when he died in a plane crash while training for duty in World War I. Irene Castle appeared in several silent films after his death, had three unsuccessful marriages, and then spent her later years as an animal rights activist. FRED ASTAIRE and GINGER ROGERS played the couple in the screen musical THE STORY OF VERNON AND IRENE CASTLE (1939), for which Irene served as consultant. Autobiography: *Castles in the Air* (1958).

CAT AND THE FIDDLE, THE (Globe Theatre 1931). A contemporary operetta by JEROME KERN (music) and OTTO HARBACH (book and lyrics), the melodic piece was a refreshingly effective blend of the old and the new. At the Music Conservatoire in Brussells, the Rumanian composer Victor Florescu (Georges Metaxa) writes serious music while his sweetheart, the American composer Shirley Sheridan (BETTINA HALL), writes jazz. A producer plans to present Victor's opera *The Passionate Pilgrim* but insists on interpolating some of Shirley's tunes to liven it up. Victor is furious until he

learns that he and Shirley can harmonize nicely onstage and off. Also in the splendid cast were ODETTE MYRTIL, EDDIE FOY, JR., José Ruben, Doris Carson, Lawrence Grossmith, and George Meader. The entrancing score included the hits "Try to Forget" and "The Night Was Made for Love," and there were also such delightful numbers as "She Didn't Say Yes (She Didn't Say No)," "I Watch the Love Parade," "One Moment Alone," "Poor Pierrot," and "A New Love Is Old." MAX GORDON produced and José Ruben directed the unusual but thoroughly enjoyable musical, which ran 395 performances.

The Cat and the Fiddle (MGM 1934) came to the screen with all of its Broadway score intact, a rare feat even for the best of stage musicals. Screenwriters Bella and Samuel Spewak made changes in the plot, particularly at the end when the prima donna Odette walks out of the show and Shirley has to go on in her place. That opening night performance was shot in the new three-color Technicolor and enthralled audiences. It was JEANETTE MacDONALD's first MGM movie and her popularity grew because of the film. William K. Howard directed, ALBERTINA RASCH choreographed, and the producer was Bernard Hyman.

CATLETT, WALTER (1889–1960). Stage and film performer. A favorite character actor who specialized in blustering, scatterbrained types, he was featured in a dozen Broadway musicals and in many movies, including some musicals. Catlett was born in San Francisco, educated at St. Ignatius College, started acting in 1906, and gained plenty of vaudeville and touring experience before he made his Broadway debut in the musical *The Prince of Pilsen* (1910). Catlett was soon featured in New York and London musicals, most memorably as the unscrupulous theatrical agent Otis Hooper in SALLY (1920) and the cigar-chomping lawyer J. Watterson Watkins introducing the title song in LADY, BE GOOD (1924). His other Broadway musicals

Casts for *The Cat and the Fiddle*

Character	1931 Broadway	1934 film
Victor Florescu	George Metaxa	Ramon Novarro
Shirley Sheridan	BETTINA HALL	JEANETTE MACDONALD
Odette	ODETTE MYRTIL	VIVIENNE SEGAL
Pompineau	George Meader	
Clement/Jules Daudet	José Ruben	FRANK MORGAN
Prof. Bertier		Jean Hersholt

include *So Long, Letty* (1916), *ZIEGFELD FOLLIES* (1917), *Follow the Girl* (1918), *Little Simplicity* (1918), *Dear Sir* (1924), *Lucky* (1927), *Here's Howe* (1928), and *Treasure Girl* (1928). Catlett made his screen debut in 1924 and, over the next thirty years, played dozens of colorful character roles, including those in the musicals *EVERY NIGHT AT EIGHT* (1935), *ON THE AVENUE* (1937), *Every Day's a Holiday* (1938), *Going Places* (1939), *My Gal Sal* (1942), *YANKEE DOODLE DANDY* (1942), *UP IN ARMS* (1944), *Look for the Silver Lining* (1949), *The Inspector General* (1949), *Dancing in the Dark* (1950), and *HERE COMES THE GROOM* (1951). Perhaps his most recognized role was never seen: the voice of the conning fox J. Worthington Foulfellow in the animated classic *PINOCCHIO* (1940).

CATS (Winter Garden Theatre 1982). The international sensation from London, the musical had many characters but only the thinnest of plots and was performed more like a revue than a book musical. A variety of singing–dancing feline characters are introduced, they celebrate at a midnight ball, and then the aged cat Grizabella dies and is guided to the beyond by the wise Old Deuteronomy. ANDREW LLOYD WEBBER set T. S. Elliot's poems to music, and TREVOR NUNN co-directed (and provided the lyric for "Memory") with choreographer GILLIAN LYNNE. Among the other songs were "The Moments of Happiness," "The Journey to the Heaviside Layer," "Jellicle Songs for Jellicle Cats," "Old Deuteronomy," "Macavity," "The Old Gumbie Cat," "Grizabella, the Glamour Cat," and "Bustopher Jones." The unexpected British hit was given an American cast and the phenomenon was as popular on Broadway as it had been in England where Eliot's *Old Possum's Book of Practical Cats*, the source material, was better known. Initial reviews were welcoming without being enthusiastic;

Cats. It may not have had much in the way of story and character development, but the British musical was certainly theatrical, using dance and ritual in a way that was universally understood. No wonder so many foreign tourists made a performance of *Cats* a required attraction while visiting New York City. The felines pictured are from the original Broadway company. (Photofest)

Casts for *Cats*

Character	1982 Broadway	1998 television
Grizabella	BETTY BUCKLEY	Elaine Paige
Old Deuteronomy	KEN PAGE	Ken Page
Rum Tum Tugger	TERRENCE MANN	John Partridge
Mistoffolees	Timothy Scott	Jacob Brent
Rumpleteazer	Christine Langner	Jo Gibb
Mungojerrie	Rene Clemente	Drew Varley
Bustopher Jones	Stephen Hanan	James Barron
Gus the Theatre Cat		John Mills

during the 7,485 performances that the musical ran, the show was often decried in the press and mocked by some playgoers but it didn't stop it from becoming the longest-running musical for awhile. CAMERON MACKINTOSH and David Geffen co-produced with Webber's Really Useful Theatre Company, Inc.

☐ Plans for a film version (live-action or animated) of *Cats* were tossed about for years with such figures as Steven Spielberg and Tom Stoppard attached to the projects, but in the end Webber settled for a video production using both American and British players. Although the 120-minute production was taped in a studio, it resembled the original stage production, both designed by John Napier. David Mallet directed and Gillian Lynne recreated her original choreography so there were few surprises for the millions who had seen *Cats* on stage. Some critics thought the busy camera work distracted from the piece, whereas others thought it helped. The cast was first rate, with many of them having done the show in London or New York, and a special treat was veteran actor John Mills as Gus the Theatre Cat, a character sung about but not seen in the stage version.

CAWTHORN, JOSEPH (1867–1949). Stage and film performer. A short, round, prematurely balding "Dutch" comic, he fractured the English language with his thick German dialect in several musicals on Broadway and in Hollywood. A native of New York, Cawthorn began his career as a child performer in vaudeville and minstrel shows and then as an adult found work in British music halls and touring productions across America. He made his Broadway debut in 1897 and got his first recognition the next year as the gypsy father Boris in the operetta *THE FORTUNE TELLER*. Over the next twenty-five years Cawthorn appeared as character types in such musicals as *The Rounders* (1899), *Mother Goose* (1903), *Fritz in Tammany Hall* (1905), *The Hoyden* (1907), *The Sunshine*

Girl (1913), *THE GIRL FROM UTAH* (1914), *The Canary* (1918), *The Half Moon* (1920), *The Blue Kitten* (1922), and *SUNNY* (1925). While playing the cockeyed inventor Dr. Pill in the fantasy musical *Little Nemo* (1908), he improvised a description of an imaginary beast he called a "whiffenpoof." Some Yale students who were in the audience took the name for their new glee club. Cawthorn made many films between 1924 and 1942, including featured spots in the musicals *LOVE ME TONIGHT* (1932), *SWEET ADELINE* (1934), *Twenty Million Sweethearts* (1934), *THE CAT AND THE FIDDLE* (1934), *MUSIC IN THE AIR* (1934), *NAUGHTY MARIETTA* (1935), *GOLD DIGGERS OF 1935*, *THE GREAT ZIEGFELD* (1936), and *LILLIAN RUSSELL* (1940).

☙ **CELEBRATION** (Ambassador Theatre 1969). An intriguing experiment in which TOM JONES (book and lyrics) and HARVEY SCHMIDT (music) attempted to create a musical that was primitive, bare bones theatre. The innocent but determined Orphan (Michael Glenn-Smith) wishes to plant a garden but is deterred by the coming of winter, his infatuation with the ambitious singer Angel (SUSAN WATSON), and the interference by the jealous millionaire Rich (Ted Thurston). Potemkin (Keith Charles), the narrator and con man, sets up a battle between youth–summer and maturity–winter and Orphan wins the battle and Angel. The allegorical piece was performed as an ancient ritual, often using masks on a mostly bare stage. The score was eerie yet accessible, with songs such as "It's You Who Makes Me Young," "I'm Glad to See You've Got What You Want," "Survive," and the compelling title number. The critics were somewhat fascinated and complimentary but audiences only came for 109 performances. Many felt *Celebration* belonged Off Broadway and Jones and Schmidt must have agreed for all their subsequent musicals played there. CHERYL CRAWFORD and Richard Chandler produced, Jones directed, and Vernon Lusby choreographed. The musical was briefly revived Off Broadway in 2007.

◼ **CENTENNIAL SUMMER** (Fox 1946). Without question an attempt by 20TH CENTURY-FOX to come up with their own *MEET ME IN ST. LOUIS* (1944), the period musical rarely measured up to the early film but it boasted JEROME KERN'S last score and the songs were as resplendent as the story and characters were mediocre. Instead of the St. Louis World's Fair of 1904, scriptwriter Michael Kanin, adapting Albert E. Idell's novel, set the story during the Philadelphia Exposition of 1876. The Rogers family, parented by Dorothy Gish and WALTER BRENNAN, is caught up in the excitement, especially daughters Edith (Linda Darnell) and Julia (JEANNE CRAIN, singing dubbed by Louann Hogan), who both fall for the Frenchman Philippe Lascalles (Cornel Wilde) when he comes to visit the fair. Also caught in the mild complications were characters played by William Eythe, Constance Bennett, Barbara Whiting, Avon Long, Larry Stevens, and Kathleen Howard. OSCAR HAMMERSTEIN, LEO ROBIN, and E. Y. HARBURG contributed lyrics for Kern's lovely music, resulting in the soulful ballad "All Through the Day," the rustic "Cinderella Sue," the cheerful "Up With the Lark," and the torchy "In Love in Vain." Despite such accomplished songs, very little in the movie, produced and directed by OTTO PREMINGER, was very involving.

CERVERIS, MICHAEL (1960–). Stage, television, and film performer. A dynamic, bald-headed leading man who has played a variety of musical roles, there is always something a bit magnetic if not sinister about his persona. Cerveris was born in Bethesda, Maryland, grew up in West Virginia, and was educated at Yale. He acted in regional theatre and television, playing a regular on the television series *FAME* in 1986–1987, before getting cast in the title role of *TOMMY* in the original California production. Cerveris made an impressive Broadway debut reprising his performance in 1993. He also shone on Broadway as the ship architect Thomas Andrews in *TITANIC* (1997), John Wilkes Booth in *ASSASSINS* (2004), murderer *SWEENEY TODD* (2005), and composer KURT WEILL in *LoveMusik* (2007). Cerveris also played Hedwig in the musical *HEDWIG AND THE ANGRY INCH* both Off Broadway and in London's West End. He has acted in several films and television productions.

CHAKIRIS, GEORGE (1934–). Film, television, and stage performer. A dark, dashing leading man of Greek origin, the former dancer shone as brooding, sexy characters. Chakiris was born in Norwood, Ohio, and sang in choirs as a boy, affording him a film debut at the age of twelve singing in the chorus of *Song of Love* (1947). As an adult he went back to Hollywood where he danced in the chorus of such movie musicals as *GENTLEMEN PREFER BLONDES* (1953), *BRIGADOON* (1954), *WHITE CHRISTMAS* (1954), *The Girl Rush* (1955), and *Meet Me in Las Vegas* (1956). The next year he started getting speaking parts in films but left Hollywood to originate the role of the gang leader Riff in the London stage production of *WEST SIDE STORY* in 1958. Three years later he found fame playing the Puerto Rican gang leader Bernardo in the 1963 film version. Chakiris only appeared in one other film musical, *The Young Girls of Rochefort* (1967), and played the Caliph in the TV version of *KISMET* (1967), but he sang and danced in his popular nightclub appearances and returned to stage musicals regionally in the 1990s. In addition to nonmusical films in America and Europe, he has been a regular in different television series, specials, and dramas.

CHAMPION, GOWER [Carlyle] (1920–1980). Stage and film choreographer, performer, and director. The oft-awarded dancer-turned-director–choreographer was known for his staging that was as bright and stylish as it was witty. Champion was born in Geneva, Illinois, the son of an ad executive, and when his parents divorced he was raised in Los Angeles by his mother, a successful dressmaker in Hollywood. He quit high school to form a dance act and then, after serving in the Coast Guard, he teamed up with Marjorie Belcher and they became famous as Marge and Gower Champion, one of the country's favorite dance duos in nightclubs, on television, and in movies. Champion danced in a few Broadway musicals, such as *The Streets of Paris* (1939), *The Lady Comes Across* (1942), and *Count Me In* (1942) and then went to Hollywood were he was featured solo in *TILL THE CLOUDS ROLL BY* (1946) and with Marge in *Mr. Music* (1950), *SHOW BOAT* (1951), *Everything I Have Is Yours* (1952), *LOVELY TO LOOK AT* (1952), *GIVE A GIRL A BREAK* (1953), *Jupiter's Darling* (1955), and *Three for the Show* (1955). The couple also starred in the TV musicals *A Bouquet for Millie* (1953) and *What Day Is It?* (1956). He returned to the

New York stage in 1948 to direct and choreograph the revue *Small Wonder,* followed by the popular Broadway revue LEND AN EAR (1948), as well as the TV musical *Cindy's Fella* (1959). The quintessential Champion style was first witnessed in his staging of the surprise hit BYE BYE BIRDIE (1960), finding clever and amusing ways to illustrate the effects of rock and roll on America. Yet he also shone with his delicate and atmospheric production of the French tale CARNIVAL the next year. Giant hits such as HELLO, DOLLY! (1964), I DO! I DO! (1966), and 42ND STREET (1980) made Champion the most sought-after director–choreographer on Broadway for two decades, yet his genius for creating imaginative and vibrant musicals was also noticeable in less successful ventures, such as THE HAPPY TIME (1968) and MACK AND MABEL (1974). His other Broadway musicals include *Make a Wish* (1951), SUGAR (1972), IRENE (1973), *Rockabye Hamlet* (1976), and *A Broadway Musical* (1978), as well as a handful of nonmusicals. Champion's premature death was announced to a shocked cast and audience at the end of the opening-night performance of *42nd Street.* He was perhaps the last in the line of BUSBY BERKELEY-like artists who instinctively knew how to provide dazzling entertainment values in all that he touched. Biographies: *Before The Parade Passes By*, John Anthony Gilvey (2005); *Gower Champion: Dance and American Musical Theatre*, David Payne-Carter (1999).

CHAMPION, MARGE [born Marjorie Celeste Belcher] (1921–). Film and television performer and choreographer. A beaming dancer–singer in Hollywood musicals, she is most remembered for her performances with her then-husband GOWER CHAMPION. A native of Los Angeles, her father was Ernest Belcher, a dance coach for the movies, and he saw that his daughter took dance lessons as a child. As an adult she worked as a model and was used to create the initial drawings and movements for the heroine of WALT DISNEY'S SNOW WHITE AND THE SEVEN DWARFS (1937) and the Blue Fairy in PINOCCHIO (1940). Champion did dance specialties in three movie musicals under the name Marjorie Bell: THE STORY OF VERNON AND IRENE CASTLE (1939), TILL THE CLOUDS ROLL BY (1944), and *Mr. Music* (1950). She married hoofer Gower Champion in 1947 and the two worked together in nightclubs and on screen in such musicals as SHOW BOAT (1951), *Everything I Have Is Yours* (1952), LOVELY TO LOOK AT (1952), GIVE A GIRL A BREAK (1953), *Jupiter's Darling* (1955), and *Three for the Show* (1955), as well as the television musicals *A Bouquet for Millie* (1953) and *What Day Is It?* (1956). Gower Champion had started choreographing in the late 1940s and she assisted her husband in staging the dances for the Broadway musicals LEND AN EAR (1948), *Make a Wish* (1951), and HELLO, DOLLY! (1964). In the 1960s she acted in nonmusical films and television shows, and also choreographed some television specials, including the TV musical QUEEN OF THE STARDUST BALLROOM (1975). Champion was a dance teacher for many years and choreographed some nonmusical films and the Broadway play-with-music *Stepping Out* (1987). She made a belated Broadway singing–dancing debut as the veteran hoofer Emily Whitman in the 2001 revival of FOLLIES.

CHANNING, CAROL [Elaine] (1921–). Stage and television performer. The popular wide-mouthed, big-eyed blonde comedienne is one of the most distinctive talents in the American theatre. Channing was born in Seattle, raised in San Francisco, and educated at Bennington College before going to New York in 1941 to appear in nightclubs where she developed her stage persona: a naive yet knowing bleached blonde with an open mouth and a giving heart. After appearing on Broadway in LET'S FACE IT! (1941), she first won over audiences in the revue LEND AN EAR (1948) in which she played a flapper in a musical spoof of the Roaring Twenties. Channing became a full-fledged star as the gold digger Lorelei Lee in GENTLEMEN PREFER BLONDES (1949) and later had an even bigger hit as matchmaker Dolly Levi in HELLO, DOLLY! (1964), a role she returned to on tour and in New York over the next thirty years. Her other musical credits include a replacement for Ruth Sherwood in WONDERFUL TOWN (1954), *The Vamp* (1955), *Show Girl* (1961), and LORELEI (1974), an updated version of her earlier success. Channing possesses a growling voice that ranges from a deep baritone to a high-pitched squeak and a glowing stage presence that did not always translate to other media. All the same, she appeared in many television specials, including the TV musicals *Svengali and the Blonde* (1955) and ALICE IN WONDERLAND (1985), and in a handful of films, most memorably THOROUGHLY MODERN MILLIE (1967) and voices for the animated musicals *Shinebone Alley* (1971) and *Tumbelina* (1994). Autobiography: *Just Lucky I Guess* (2002).

Carol Channing. The sparkling, cartoonish performer was too mannered, too theatrical for most television shows and films and was at her best on stage where she knew how to engage an audience with her wide expressions and unusual voice. Here she is in the Hollywood musical *Thoroughly Modern Millie* (1967) as the daffy millionairess Muzzy, one of her few cinema roles and one that was pure Channing. (Photofest)

CHAPLIN, SAUL [born Saul Kaplan] (1912–1997). Film composer, orchestrator, and producer. A notable Tin Pan Alley songwriter, he was successful in films first for his music abilities and then for his producing skills. Chaplin was born in Brooklyn and educated at the New York City School of Commerce. He began his career as a pianist for bands and then turned to songwriting, composing the music for such song hits as "Bei Mir Bist Du Schon" and "Until the Real Thing Comes Along." Chaplin collaborated with lyricists SAMMY CAHN, JOHNNY MERCER, and others to write the scores for the movie musicals *Go West, Young Lady* (1941), *Rookies on Parade* (1941), *Time Out for Rhythm* (1941), *Redhead From Manhattan* (1943), *Cowboy Canteen* (1944), *Meet Me on Broadway* (1946), *Countess of Monte Cristo* (1948), and *Merry Andrew* (1959), serving as co-producer on the last. But Chaplin was even more respected as an arranger of musical scores, working on such movie musicals as *ON THE TOWN* (1949), *SUMMER STOCK* (1950), *AN AMERICAN IN PARIS* (1951), *LOVELY TO LOOK AT* (1952), *KISS ME, KATE* (1953), *SEVEN BRIDES FOR SEVEN BROTHERS* (1954), *HIGH SOCIETY* (1956), and *WEST SIDE STORY* (1961). When he turned to producing films in the late 1950s, he presented *LES GIRLS* (1957), *CAN-CAN* (1960), *THE SOUND OF MUSIC* (1965), *STAR!* (1968), and *MAN OF LA MANCHA* (1972). Although Chaplin was never a household name, he was a giant of Hollywood musicals and the author of songs widely beloved, none sung more often than "The Anniversary Song."

CHAPLIN, SYDNEY [Earle] (1926–). Stage and film performer. A genial, lightweight leading man with an unpretentious, deep singing voice, he found himself in two Broadway hits. Chaplin was born in Los Angeles, son of the celebrated filmmaker Charles Chaplin, and educated at Lawrenceville Academy before joining the army. Fearing comparisons with his father, he avoided films and acted on the stage with the Circle Theatre in Los Angeles before going to Broadway where he made an impressive debut as the playwright Jeff Moss in *BELLS ARE SINGING* (1956). Chaplin was also praised for his society dropout Tom Bailey in *SUBWAYS ARE FOR SLEEPING* (1961) and as gambler Nick Arnstein in *FUNNY GIRL* (1964). He made his screen debut in his father's film *Limelight* (1952) but appeared in few other movies, preferring to sing in nightclubs and in concerts and performing in musicals in Europe, such as *SWEET CHARITY* in Paris. Chaplin appeared on American television on occasion, as with the TV version of *WONDERFUL TOWN* (1958) and the original musical *Keep in Step* (1959). He found a different kind of success owning and managing the very popular restaurant Chaplin's in Palm Springs, California. Chaplin is the half-brother of actress Geraldine Chaplin (1944–).

CHARISSE, CYD [born Tulia Ellice Finklea] (1921–). Film, stage, and television performer. The leggy, dark-haired beauty who had to be dubbed in musicals, she was one of Hollywood's finest dancing stars. Charisse was born in Amarillo, Texas, and took ballet lessons as a child. By the time she was sixteen years old, she was dancing with the Ballet Russe and grabbed the attention of Hollywood where she was given supporting roles in the musicals *Something to Shout About* (1944), *THE HARVEY GIRLS* (1946), and specialty bits in *ZIEGFELD FOLLIES* (1946), *TILL THE CLOUDS ROLL BY* (1946), *The Kissing Bandit* (1948), *SINGIN' IN THE RAIN* (1952), *Easy to Love* (1953), and *DEEP IN MY HEART* (1954). Charisse played leading roles in such beloved musicals as *THE BAND WAGON* (1953), *BRIGADOON* (1955), *IT'S ALWAYS FAIR WEATHER* (1955), *Meet Me in Las Vegas* (1956), and *SILK STOCKINGS* (1956). Her other musical films include *Fiesta* (1947), *The Unfinished Dance* (1947), *On an Island With You* (1948), *Sombrero* (1952), and *Black Tights* (1962). With the demise of movies musicals, she attempted dramatic roles in films and on television but was more successful dancing in nightclubs with her husband TONY MARTIN. Late in her career, Charisse turned to the stage, appearing in a 1972 Australian production of *No, No, NANETTE* and taking over the role of the aging ballerina Grushinskaya in *GRAND HOTEL* on Broadway in 1990. Autobiography: *The Two of Us*, with Martin (1976).

CHARLOTTE'S WEB (Paramount 1973). E. B. White's beloved children's book was musicalized and animated without vulgarizing it, and the result was a charming and entertaining film for kids and adults. Earl Hammer, Jr. adapted White's story faithfully, retelling the adventures of the pig Wilbur (voice of Henry Gibson) who is saved from the slaughter by the love of the farm girl Fern (Pamelyn Ferdin) and the ingenuity of the spider Charlotte (DEBBIE REYNOLDS). Of the supporting characters voiced by AGNES MOOREHEAD, CHARLES NELSON REILLY, Dave Madden, Danny Bonaduce, Martha Scott, and Don Messick, the most fun was the rat Templeton, which Paul Lynde played with relish. RICHARD M. and ROBERT B. SHERMAN supplied the tuneful songs, including the gentle ballad "Mother Earth and Father Time," the comic "A Veritable Smorgasbord," and the haunting title song. Rex Allen narrated the tale, and Joseph Barbera and William Hanna produced the unpretentious but effective film.

CHARNIN, MARTIN [Jay] (1934–). Stage director and lyricist. A reputable Broadway lyricist, he directed several of his own and other's musicals. A native New Yorker and the son of an opera singer, Charnin was educated at Cooper Union for the Advancement of Science and Art. He began his career as an actor–dancer and appeared in several New York productions, most memorably as the gang member Big Deal in the original cast of *WEST SIDE STORY* (1957). That same year he made his directing debut in Boston and started writing articles and stories for magazines; two years later he gave up performing to concentrate on writing and directing. Charnin's Manhattan directorial debut was the 1968 Off Broadway musical *Ballad for a Firing Squad*, for which he also provided the lyrics. He often directed and wrote lyrics for his productions, as in his most successful effort, *ANNIE* (1977). Charnin wrote lyrics for several Off Broadway revues as well as the Broadway musicals *Hot Spot* (1963), *La Strada* (1969), *TWO BY TWO* (1970), *I Remember Mama* (1979), *The Madwoman of Central Park West* (1979), *The First* (1981), and *Sid Caesar & Company* (1989). He staged the musicals *Bar Mitzvah Boy* in London, *Jeanne La Pucelle* in Canada, and has also written and directed for television, such as the TV musical *FEATHERTOP* (1961).

CHENOWETH, KRISTIN [Dawn] (1968–). Stage and television performer. A perky, tiny blonde bombshell of an entertainer with an opera-quality voice, she has excelled as bright and funny musical comedy characters. Chenoweth was born with part-Cherokee ancestry in Broken Arrow, Oklahoma, and educated at

Oklahoma City University where she studied voice. With her wide-range coloratura soprano voice, she planned on an opera career but was sidetracked when cast in musicals Off Broadway, later playing Luisa in THE FANTASTICKS. Chenoweth was featured in her first Broadway musical, the short-lived Steel Pier (1997), played several supporting roles in the Off Broadway musical A NEW BRAIN (1998), and then received recognition for her daffy Sally in the 1999 Broadway revival of YOU'RE A GOOD MAN, CHARLIE BROWN. She was a star by the time she originated the role of the good witch Glinda in WICKED (2003) and was also praised for her three characterizations in the revival of THE APPLE TREE (2006). Chenoweth played the floozie Lily in the TV version of ANNIE (1999) and Marian Paroo in television's The Music Man (2003) She has acted in several television shows and had her own series in 2001.

CHESS (Imperial Theatre 1988). A London success that floundered on Broadway, the musical play by former ABBA members Benny Andersson and Bjorn Ulvaeus (music), with lyrics by TIM RICE, offered a rich score if an undernourished story. The temperamental American Freddie (Philip Casnoff) and the moody Russian Anatoly (DAVID CARROLL) are rivals in an international chess tournament, as well as competing suitors for the love of the Hungarian refugee Florence (JUDY KUHN) who ends up leaving Freddie for the Soviet player. Also in the cast were Harry Goz, Marcia Mitzman, Richard Muenz, Neal Ben-Ari, and Paul Harman. The hit song from the show was the pulsating "One Night in Bangkok," and there were also such commendable numbers as "I Know Him So Well," "Heaven Help My Heart," "Someone Else's Story," "Terrace Duet," and "You and I." The West End hit was deemed too anti-American for Broadway so the script was rewritten by Richard Nelson and an already problematic show was made weaker. Critics appreciated the exciting score and the featured players but dismissed the rest of the show as a noisy and flashy bore so it ran only sixty-eight performances. TREVOR NUNN directed and Lynn Taylor Corbett choreographed. A revised version of the musical later toured and has been produced by various theatre groups in Great Britain and the States.

CHEVALIER, MAURICE [Auguste] (1888–1972). Film and television performer. Perhaps the greatest of all French entertainers, the rogu-

ish bon vivant song and dance man captivated audiences on both sides of the Atlantic, never straying far from his bow tie, straw hat boulevardier persona. Chevalier was born in poverty in Paris and worked in a factory as a child, later becoming an acrobat in variety. He served in the French army during World War I and learned his broken English from British soldiers while in a German prisoner-of-war camp. Chevalier first became popular in Paris cafes and then was the star of the famous Folies Bergere. He made some films in France but it was his Hollywood debut in INNOCENTS OF PARIS (1929) that made him an international star. His other musical films of the period were THE LOVE PARADE (1929), PARAMOUNT ON PARADE (1930), The Big Pond (1930), Playboy of Paris (1930), THE SMILING LIEUTENANT (1931), ONE HOUR WITH YOU (1932), LOVE ME TONIGHT (1932), A Bedtime Story (1933), The Way to Love (1933), THE MERRY WIDOW (1934), FOLIES BERGERE (1935), and the British films The Beloved Vagabond (1936) and Break the News (1938). Chevalier left films in the 1940s and concentrated on concerts, nightclubs, and later television specials. He made a triumphal return to the musical screen as the charming Honore in GIGI (1958) and was featured in the musicals CAN-CAN (1960), Pepe (1960), Jessica (1962), and I'd Rather Be Rich (1964), as well as lending his voice to the animated THE ARISTOCATS (1970). Chevalier was a unique talent in that he always played himself in every role he undertook and the audience would have it no other way. Autobiographies: The Man in the Straw Hat (1949), With Love (1960), I Remember It Well (1970); biographies: Maurice Chevalier, David Bret (2003); The Good Frenchman: The True Story of the Life and Times of Maurice Chevalier, Edward Behr (1993).

CHICAGO (46th Street Theatre 1975). A vibrant, satirical concept musical by JOHN KANDER (music), FRED EBB (book and lyrics), and BOB FOSSE (book), the jazzy piece used the techniques of vaudeville to tell a wildly improbable tale of sin and insincerity in 1920s Chicago. Roxie Hart shoots her lover when he tries to walk out on her and then gets big-time lawyer Billy Flynn to defend her and, more important, keep her name on the front page. Her fellow murderess Velma Kelly is worried about her own publicity and is Roxie's rival until both are pushed out of the limelight and end up doing a double act together in vaudeville. The musicalization of Maurine Dallas Watkins' satire Chicago (1926) took the form

Chicago. Director–choreographer Bob Fosse cast the Broadway production with veteran hoofers (Gwen Verdon and Chita Rivera) who were probably far too old for the roles and came across as weathered but determined broads, enforcing the tawdry nature of the piece. For the film version, director–choreographer Rob Marshall used the youthful and sexy Renee Zellweger (left) and Catherine Zeta-Jones as the "merry murderesses" who were just as determined but in their prime. (Photofest)

of a vaudeville show with each musical number announced by an M.C. and echoing a particular 1920s song or song type. "All That Jazz," "Nowadays," "Cell Block Tango," "All I Care About (Is Love)," "Class," "When You're Good to Mama," "Mister Cellophane," and "Razzle Dazzle" were among the many musical treats. Although it featured Broadway's two top dancing stars GWEN VERDON and CHITA RIVERA, the musical was considered a "Fosse show" because of his stylized direction and distinctive choreography. Reviews were approving with reservations but audiences had little trouble enjoying the dark, satirical musical for 898 performances. A well-received *ENCORES!* concert led to the 1996 Broadway revival directed by WALTER BOBBIE. ANN REINKING played Roxie and recreated Fosse's

Casts for *Chicago*

Character	1976 Broadway	1996 Broadway revival	2002 film
Roxie Hart	GWEN VERDON	ANN REINKING	Renée Zellweger
Velma Kelly	CHITA RIVERA	BEBE NEUWIRTH	Catherine Zeta-Jones
Billy Flynn	JERRY ORBACH	JAMES NAUGHTON	Richard Gere
Mama Morton	MARY McCARTY	Marcia Lewis	Queen Lafitah
Amos Hart	Barney Martin	JOEL GREY	John C. Reilly
Mary Sunshine	M. O'Haughey	D. Sabella	Christine Baranski

choreography in this slimmed-down revival with no scenery and simple costumes. Both critics and playgoers thought the satiric musical more timely than ever and embraced its dark humor. The production was produced by Barry and Fran Weissler who have wisely kept the economical and popular attraction going with a series of guest stars over the years, making it the longest-running revival in Broadway history.

■ *Chicago* (Miramax 2002) was made because of the popularity of the 1996 stage revival and it ended up being the sleeper of the year, winning the Best Picture Oscar and opening doors for subsequent film musicals based on Broadway shows. Bill Condon's screenplay changed the "vaudeville" musical into a period piece in which the heroine Roxie imagines everyone and everything around her as a vaudeville act. The concept opened up all kinds of possibilities for director–choreographer Rob Marshall and the movie ended up being both a visual and a musical treat. None of the cast members were known for their singing abilities except for the pop star Queen Latifah and most had no extensive dance experience, yet the movie has a polish and professional confidence that reminds one of the golden days of studio musicals. Most of the Kander and Ebb score was retained and the partners wrote a new number, "I Move On," which was heard over the final credits. The film's only drawback is the dizzying camera work and MTV-like editing that some felt distracted rather than added to the musical.

Child Stars. Playgoers in the nineteenth century had a fascination with children on stage, applauding all-children theatre companies (the miniature versions of *H.M.S. Pinafore* were particularly popular) and turning some tots into stars. Some productions of *Uncle Tom's Cabin* were built around young actresses who played Little Eva, and children characters such as *Peck's Bad Boy* and *Little Lord Fauntleroy* were audience favorites. The most famous child star of the nineteenth century was Charlotte Crabtree (1847–1924), affectionally called Lotta by her thousands of fans. She was the Shirley Temple of her day, winning the hearts of theatregoers wherever she went. While her vehicles were heart-tugging melodramas, such as *Little Nell and the Marchioness* (1867) and *Musette, or Little Bright Eyes* (1867), Lotta always sang and danced a number or two. She retained her youthful looks and played children's roles until she retired

at the age of forty-four years old, leaving an estate of $4 million when she died. There were no child stars on Broadway or on tour in the twentieth century that came close to that kind of popularity. In fact, there were very few kid stars in plays or musicals. One of the reasons was the movies.

From the earliest silent shorts, moviemakers realized the potency of children on screen for both pathos and comedy. Mary Pickford, Jackie Coogan, and the *Our Gang* kids were probably the most popular child stars of the silent era. Little Davey Lee brought audiences to tears when he died in the early screen musical *The Singing Fool* (1928), and talkies were more than anxious to have tots who could sing and dance as well as break hearts. They found it all in Shirley Temple, the most famous of all child stars, who made her first feature in 1933 at the age of five and was the most beloved movie figure (adult or child) for the rest of the decade. Jane Withers was a different type than Temple, and Bobby Breen was a male counterpart of the curly blonde moppet; both made several musicals in the 1930s as well. Mickey Rooney had been performing on the screen since he was a toddler but became a box office headliner as a teenager. Like Donald O'Connor, who also started in musicals as a child, Rooney would be able to brave a career as an adult performer, a rarity for kid performers then and now. Other teenage favorites who appeared in movie musicals were Judy Garland, Deanna Durbin, Virginia Weidler, Ann Blyth, Bobby Driscoll, Tommy Rettig, Natalie Wood, Tommy Kirk, Annette Funicello, and Frankie Avalon.

🎵 *Chin-Chin* (Globe Theatre 1914). A vehicle for the popular Broadway comics Fred Stone and Dave Montgomery, this raucous version of the Aladdin tale was the musical hit of its season. Anne Caldwell and R. H. Burnside collaborated on the libretto in which the evil Abanazar (Charles T. Aldrich) tries to steal the magic lamp from Aladdin (Douglas Stevenson) and sell it to the American millionaire Cornelius Bond (R. E. Graham) who wants to stop Aladdin from marrying his daughter Violet (Helen Falconer). The two knuckleheaded but clever genies inside the lamp, Chin Hop Hi (Stone) and Chin Hop Lo (Montgomery), don various disguises and whisk Aladdin off to exotic lands in their efforts to win him the lamp and the girl. Caldwell and James O'Dea wrote the lyrics for Ivan Caryll's music, the most notable songs being "Goodbye, Girls,

I'm Through" and "Ragtime Temple Bells." Montgomery and Stone triumphed in the CHARLES DILLINGHAM production but it was to be their last Broadway show; Montgomery died unexpectedly two years later.

CHISHOLM, ROBERT (1898–1960). Stage performer. The full-voiced leading man was heard in operettas on Broadway and then, when that genre waned, in musical comedies. Chisholm was born in Melbourne, Australia, and trained in his hometown and at London's Royal Academy of Music before he was singing professionally in the British provinces and in Australia. He made his London debut in 1925 and two years later was on Broadway as the unlikely black overseer Shep Keyes on an African plantation in *Golden Dawn* (1927). Chisholm fared better as HELEN MORGAN'S leading man in *SWEET ADELINE* (1929) and played Macheath in the first American production of *THE THREEPENNY OPERA* (1933). His other operetta credits include *Luana* (1930), *The Two Bouquets* (1938), *Knights of Song* (1938), *Susanna, Don't You Cry* (1939), *Night of Love* (1941), and *BLOSSOM TIME* (1943). By the 1940s, Chisholm was playing supporting roles in musicals very different from the operettas he had once starred in, such as *HIGHER AND HIGHER* (1940), *A CONNECTICUT YANKEE* (1943), *ON THE TOWN* (1944), *Billion Dollar Baby* (1945), *Park Avenue* (1946), and *Bless You All* (1950). During summers he often went to the ST. LOUIS MUNICIPAL OPERA and other regional theatres where he starred in *ROSE-MARIE*, *THE FIREFLY*, and other old operetta favorites.

CHITTY CHITTY BANG BANG (Warfield/ United Artists 1968). A big budget musical fantasy, the British American production got a bang for its buck even if it never became another *MARY POPPINS* (1964). Producer Albert Broccoli was anxious to capture the magic of the earlier film and even hired leading man DICK VAN DYKE and songwriters RICHARD M. and ROBERT B. SHERMAN to do the score. But the screenplay by Roald Dahl and director Ken Hughes, based on an Ian Fleming children's book, was rather convoluted, with fantasy, flashbacks, and reality so jumbled that it was best not to think about it and enjoy the ride. Crackpot British inventor Caractacus Potts finally comes up with something that works, a floating–flying car that his two young children Jemina and Jeremy call Chitty Chitty Bang Bang, but the Baron Bomburst of Vulgaria and his henchmen steal the car and capture the children. Potts and his sweetheart Truly Scrumptious rescue the kids as well as other unwanted children in Vulgaria and fly away on their magical car. Despite a personable cast and excellent production values, there were long stretches in the film that did not work but the songs were mostly delightful, particularly "Me Ol' Bamboo," "Toot Sweet," "Hushabye Mountain," "Truly Scrumptious," and the catchy title tune. MARC BREAUX and DEEDEE WOOD provided the spirited choreography and most of the big production numbers played nicely. The movie was modestly successful at the box office, doing better business in Great Britain where the Fleming book was better known.

Chitty Chitty Bang Bang (Hilton Theatre 2005) was also an expensive undertaking, trying to put all of the film's special effects on stage and mostly succeeding. Jeremy Sams wrote the libretto, which clarified the story and had more humor than the screen version. The Sherman brothers wrote three new numbers, none of which were as good as the original ones, Adrian Noble directed with a light touch, and GILLIAN LYNNE choreographed. The comic book-like fable was

---

Casts for *Chitty Chitty Bang Bang*

Character	1968 film	2005 Broadway
Caractacus Potts	DICK VAN DYKE	RAUL ESPARZA
Truly Scrumptious	SALLY ANN HOWES	Erin Dilly
Grandpa Potts	Lionel Jeffries	Philip Bosco
Jemima	Heather Ripley	Ellen Marlow
Jeremy	Adrian Hall	Henry Hodges
Baron	Gert Frobe	MARC KUDISCH
Baroness	Anna Quayle	Jan Maxwell
Child Catcher	Robert Helpmann	Kevin Cahoon
Toymaker	Benny Hill	Frank Raiter

applauded by the press more for its special effects than for its heart, although the performers were roundly praised as well. The London hit did not fare as well in New York where the expensive production forced it to close after 285 performances.

۞ **CHOCOLATE SOLDIER, THE** [*Der Tapfere Soldat*] (Lyric Theatre 1909). A German operetta based on George Bernard Shaw's comedy *Arms and the Man* (1894), the lyrical musical comedy would become a favorite on two continents. The Bulgarian aristocrat Nadina (Ida Brooks Hunt) is engaged to the dashing, if silly, Alexius Spiridoff (George Tallman) so when she allows the Swiss soldier of fortune Bumerli (Jack E. Gardner) to hide in her bedroom during a retreat, her ideas of valor are shaken. When confronted with both men after the war, Nadina finds herself favoring the practical Bumerli over the pompous Spiridoff who has been romancing her cousin Mascha (Edith Bradford) behind her back. Oscar Straus wrote the entrancing music, and Stanislau Stange translated the German libretto and lyrics by Rudolph Bernauer and Leopold Jacks. Among the most memorable musical numbers were the waltzing "My Hero," the gushing duet "That Would Be Lovely," the anxious trio "Romanze," and the comic sextet "The Tale of a Coat." The comic operetta premiered in Vienna in 1908 and was soon being produced everywhere, with the first American production running 296 performances. Major New York revivals were seen in 1910, 1921, 1930, 1931, 1934, 1942, and 1947, as well as dozens of productions by operetta companies across the country. ▪ In addition to several foreign language screen versions, a Hollywood film was made by MGM in 1941, which foolishly dropped the Shaw plot and instead adapted the play *The Guardsman* by Ferenc Molnar using the Straus songs. Karl Lang (NELSON EDDY) and his wife Maria (RISË STEVENS) are married opera singers in Vienna performing *The Chocolate Soldier* and he is so jealous of her that he disguises himself as the flamboyant Cossack Vassily Vassilivetch and tries to test her fidelity. The screenplay by Leonard Lee and Keith Winter gave Eddy one of his few opportunities to cut loose and play the fool and, as directed by ROY DEL RUTH, he is surprisingly animated. Also in the cast were Nigel Bruce, Florence Bates, Dorothy Gilmore, Nydia Westman, and Max Barwyn. ❑ Risë Stevens got to play the original heroine Nadina in a 1955 NBC-TV version of *The Chocolate Soldier* with EDDIE ALBERT as her Bumerli. Will Glickman, NEIL

SIMON, and Billy Friedberg adapted the operetta for television and Jeffrey Hayden directed the MAX LIEBMAN production.

۞ **CHORUS LINE, A** (Shubert Theatre 1975). A musical theatre phenomenon that few could foresee as a Broadway blockbuster, the show had such wide appeal and struck a nerve with audiences that it remains an emotional favorite for many.

Plot: As eighteen dancers audition for a chorus of eight in a new Broadway musical, the director Zach interviews them and asks each to reveal something about themselves. This leads to reminiscences, confessions, and expressions of both joy and despair, particularly for Cassie who used to be Zach's lover. By the end of the audition, eight fortunate dancers are chosen but everyone returns in a musical salute to chorus dancers everywhere.

A Chorus Line. How a show that paid tribute to "gypsies," those unknown chorus dancers, ever found success outside the world of theatre folk is one of the mysteries and charms of the long-running musical. Creator Michael Bennett dedicated the show to anyone who had ever danced in a group, and that included enough patrons to let the musical run fifteen years. (Photofest)

Casts for *A Chorus Line*

Character	1975 Broadway	1985 film	2006 Broadway
Zach	Robert LuPone	Michael Douglas	Michael Berresse
Cassie	DONNA McKECHNIE	Alyson Reed	Charlotte d'Ambroise
Diana	PRISCILLA LOPEZ	Yamil Borges	Natalie Cortez
Sheila	Carole Bishop	Vicki Frederick	Deidre Goodwin
Paul	Sammy Williams	Cameron English	Jason Tam
Val	Pamela Blair	Audrey Landers	Jessica Lee Goldyn
Connie	Baayork Lee	Jan Gan Boyd	Yuka Takara
Mike	Wayne Cilento	Charles McGowan	Jeffrey Schecter

Developed in workshops with director–choreographer MICHAEL BENNETT and using taped interviews with actual Broadway dancers, the concept musical focused on characters and their shared emotions rather than plot. James Kirkwood and Nicholas Dante shaped the material into a libretto using the framework of an audition, and MARVIN HAMLISCH (music) and Edward Kleban (lyrics) wrote songs that built on the ideas expressed in the interviews. The show opened Off Broadway at the PUBLIC THEATRE and was rapturously received by audiences and critics. After 101 performances it transferred to Broadway where it broke the record for the longest-running musical, running 6,137 performances. Although book, score, and dancers were all praised, *A Chorus Line* was mostly a triumph for Bennett who rose to the top ranks of director–choreographers because of the musical. Since much of the show is dancing, *A Chorus Line* has fewer songs than most stage musicals. In many ways the songs are extensions to or alternatives to the confessional monologues that the dancers deliver. "Nothing," "I Can Do That," "Sing!," and "Dance: Ten; Looks: Three" are very specific, exploring one's person's dilemma, while other numbers, such as "Hello Twelve, Hello Thirteen, Hello Love" and "At the Ballet," echo the thoughts and feelings of many of the auditionees. Kleban's lyrics are incisive and personal, and Hamlisch's music never strays far from the Broadway idiom, as if these dancers can only express themselves with theatre music. "What I Did for Love" and "One" were the only songs to find wide popularity because they can work outside of the context of the musical. When *A Chorus Line* closed after fourteen years, an emptiness was felt on Broadway. Not only because the show had been running so long, but because its presence on Broadway symbolized something permanent to its many fans. Sixteen years later, the musical was revived and a new generation got to experience what so many older theatregoers fondly remembered. Bob Avian, who had served as assistant director on the original, restaged the musical in 2006 exactly as Bennett had first presented it so there were few surprises in this production, which also used the original set and costume designs. Critics welcomed the show back to Broadway and audiences responded as if it were a new hit.

A Chorus Line (stage) Musical Numbers

"I Hope I Get It"
"And …"
"At the Ballet"
"Sing!"
"Hello Twelve, Hello Thirteen, Hello Love"
"Nothing"
"Dance: Ten; Looks: Three"
"One"
"Tap Combination"
"What I Did for Love"

■ *A Chorus Line* (Universal 1984) was an attempt to film an unfilmable stage work and it did not please the show's millions of fans. Of course, no screen version could have done that but surely everyone deserved better than the lackluster treatment that screenwriter Arnold Schulman and director Richard Attenborough came up with. The relationship between director Zach and his former lover Cassie (who is now auditioning for him) was a minor but intriguing subplot in the stage musical. The film used it as the main story line, diminishing the importance of the auditionees, thereby ignoring what made the musical work on stage. The choreography by Jeff Hornaday was routine and generic, the dancers capable but uninteresting, and the filming claustrophobic. Most of the Hamlisch–Kleban score was retained and the songwriters wrote some new numbers that failed to register with the audience. The movie that couldn't be made became the movie that shouldn't have been made.

☐ **CHRISTMAS CAROL, A** (CBS-TV 1954). Fredric March played Scrooge in this musical, sometimes operatic, version scored by Hollywood composer Bernard Herrmann and playwright–lyricist MAXWELL ANDERSON. The sixty-minute broadcast abridged the Charles Dickens novella to make room for the songs but critics agreed that Anderson's teleplay was economical and straightforward. Basil Rathbone was Marley's Ghost, RAY MIDDLETON was the Ghost of Christmas Present, and also featured were Bob Sweeney, Craig Hill, Bonnie Franklin, Queenie Leonard, Peter Miles, Christopher Cook, and the Robert Wagner Chorale. The rich, evocative score included the songs "On This Darkest Day of Winter," "Dear God of Christmas and the New Year," "Marley's Ghost," "What Shall I Give My Lad/Girl for Christmas?," and "A Very Merry Christmas," as well as instrumental themes that Herrmann also composed. The broadcast was popular enough that it was shown again the following Christmas season. Ralph Levy produced and directed and DONALD SADDLER choreographed. See also THE STINGIEST MAN IN TOWN (1956 and 1978).

🕭 **CHRISTMAS CAROL, A** (Paramount Madison Square Garden Theatre 1995). A large-scale musical reminiscent of the theatrical spectacles of the 1920s and 1930s, this version of Dickens' perennial favorite was not in a Broadway venue but was the work of top theatre talents. MIKE OCKRENT and LYNN AHRENS adapted the famous ghost story into a family entertainment, and ALAN MENKEN (music) and Ahrens (lyrics) wrote a top-notch score that director Ockrent and choreographer SUSAN STROMAN used to provide lavish and exciting production numbers. Marley and fellow ghosts flew through the air dragging their chains, Fezziwig's dance became a glittering Christmas Eve ball, Scrooge confronted debtors in a bustling Royal Exchange, and the Ghost of Christmas Present joined a chorus line of girls in a Victorian music hall show. Tony Walton's sets not only filled the huge Paramount Theatre stage, but the scenery continued along the side of the house so that the audience was surrounded by Victorian London. Like the buckets of snow that fell on the actors and the patrons during the finale, the show was an obvious, joyous romp.

Although the show ran less than ninety minutes, *A Christmas Carol* boasted a full musical score and an excellent one at that. Highlights included the warm ballad "A Place Called Home," the evocative "The Lights of Long Ago," the foot-stomping "Mr. Fezziwig's Annual Christmas Ball," the rhythmic "Link By Link," the toe-tapping "Abundance and Charity," and the fervent yet cliché-free "God Bless Us, Everyone." The annual holiday presentation ran about seventy performances each season and continued for six years. ☐ The script and the score were later used in a 2004 television special on NBC directed by Arthur Allan Seidelman. The broadcast featured an all-star cast led by Kelsey Grammer as Scrooge and Dan Siretta did the choreography. The spectacle and feeling of communal cheer were lost on the small screen and it seemed little different or better than any other holiday special.

CHURCHILL, FRANK (1901–1942). Film composer. Working with various lyricists, the songwriter wrote several enduring Disney song classics during his brief career. Churchill was born in Rumford, Maine, and educated at the University of California before starting his career as a pianist for theatre productions in California. He was signed by WALT DISNEY to write songs for his cartoon shorts

Casts for *A Christmas Carol*				
	Scrooge	Ghost of Jacob Marley	Ghost Of Christmas Past	Ghost of Christmas Present
1994	Walter Charles	Jeff Keller	Ken Jennings	Michael Mandell
1995	TERRENCE MANN	Paul Kandel	Ken Jennings	BEN VEREEN
1996	Tony Randall	Paul Kandel	Ken Jennings	Ben Vereen
1997	HAL LINDEN or Roddy McDowell	Paul Kandel	Joel Blum	KEN PAGE
1998	Roger Daltry	Paul Kandel	Ken Jennings	Roz Ryan
1999	TONY ROBERTS	Paul Kandel	Didi Conn	Reginald VelJohnson
2004 (TV)	Kelsey Grammer	JASON ALEXANDER	Jane Krakowski	Jesse L. Martin

and, with lyricist Ann Ronell, wrote "Who's Afraid of the Big Bad Wolf?" for *The Three Little Pigs* (1933). Churchill collaborated with lyricist LARRY MOREY to write the score for the studio's first animated feature, *SNOW WHITE AND THE SEVEN DWARFS* (1937), which included "Whistle While You Work," "Heigh-Ho," "Some Day My Prince Will Come," and other favorites. His other film musicals were *Breaking the Ice* (1938), *DUMBO* (1941), *The Reluctant Dragon* (1941), and *BAMBI* (1942), as well as dozens of cartoon songs. Churchill committed suicide at the age of forty.

CINDERELLA (Disney 1950). The familiar Charles Perrault fairy tale was given added touches of humor and romance in this animated version that has become one of the most fondly remembered of DISNEY musicals. As with the earlier *SNOW WHITE AND THE SEVEN DWARFS* (1937), the heroine (voice of Ilene Woods, singing dubbed by Helene Stanley) was much more memorable than her prince

(William Phipps, singing dubbed by Mike Douglas), and over the years young girls have identified with Cinderella perhaps more than any other Disney character. In addition to the expected characters, such as the cold-hearted stepmother Lady Tremaine (Eleanor Audley), the vain stepsisters Drizella (Rhoda Williams) and Anastasia (Lucille Bliss), and the warm Fairy Godmother (Verna Felton), the screenplay by Ken Anderson and others added such delightful supporting characters as the villainous cat Lucifer (June Foray) and a gang of friendly mice led by Jacques and Gus (both voiced by James McDonald). MACK DAVID, JERRY LIVINGSTON, and Al Hoffman collaborated on the magical score that ranged from the heartfelt "A Dream Is a Wish Your Heart Makes," "Sing, Sweet Nightingale," and "So This Is Love" to the merry "Work Song" to the nonsense delight "Bibbidi Bobbidi Boo." The musical fantasy is timeless and unforgettable, from the mice making Cinderella's ball gown to the gleaming castle that inspired the

Cinderella. The team of Rodgers and Hammerstein turned to television only once but the result was a lyrical and enchanting musical that is still impressive. The live broadcast was one of the most complicated productions the young medium of television had yet seen and the musical was perfectly scaled to the small screen. Pictured are Julie Andrews and Jon Cypher as Cinderella and her Prince being filmed during the legendary broadcast. (Photofest)

centerpiece of the Walt Disney World theme park in Florida. There have been four other musical film versions of the Cinderella tale, all live-action features: *First Love* (1939) with DEANNA DURBIN, *The Glass Slipper* (1955) with LESLIE CARON, *Cinderfella* (1960) with JERRY LEWIS, and *THE SLIPPER AND THE ROSE* (1976) with Gemma Craven.

▢ **CINDERELLA** (CBS-TV 1957). Rodgers and Hammerstein's only musical for the small screen was as ambitious and innovative as any of their complex stage works and has endured as a beloved favorite through two television remakes and hundreds of stage productions.

Plot: The King and Queen announce a ball at the palace hoping that their son, the Prince, will meet a prospective wife. All the ladies in the kingdom are excited by the news, in particular two unlikely candidates: the quarreling sisters Portia and Joy. Their stepsister Cinderella also dreams of meeting the Prince but her stepmother will not allow Cinderella to attend. After the women leave for the ball, Cinderella's Fairy Godmother appears and supplies her with a gown and a coach. Arriving at the ball, Cinderella meets the Prince who is immediately enchanted with her and the two fall in love. Soon the clock strikes midnight and Cinderella flees, leaving one of her glass slippers behind. A search of the kingdom for the owner of the slipper brings Cinderella and the Prince together for a happy ending.

OSCAR HAMMERSTEIN penned the teleplay and the lyrics for the music by RICHARD RODGERS, both of them knowing the limitations of a live broadcast. JULIE ANDREWS, currently appearing on Broadway in *MY FAIR LADY*, was cast as the heroine, even though she was unknown except by theatre audiences. Because the rest of the cast was drawn mostly from Broadway, the broadcast did not have much star power behind it except for the famous songwriters. Hammerstein disliked magic and fantasy so this version of the beloved Charles Perrault tale is rather down to earth, the Cinderella is very human with a poetic imagination instead of magical friends, and the Godmother is more like a reassuring relative than a fairy. The score, however, was filled with magic, and several songs joined the repertory of familiar Rodgers and Hammerstein favorites, particularly the ballads "A Lovely Night," "Ten Minutes Ago (I Saw You)," and "In My Own Little Corner" and the comic delight "Stepsisters' Lament." RICHARD LEWINE produced and Ralph Nelson directed the live color broadcast, which ran ninety minutes with only three commercial breaks that were used for costume changes. All the sets for the musical were crowded into one studio so the action was pretty much continuous. The show was seen by 107 million viewers (a record at the time) in its one and only showing on March 31. Because the original was on kinescope, a DVD version was not available until 2004. ✑ A stage version of Rodgers and Hammerstein's *Cinderella* was produced at the London Coliseum in December of 1958, using the television score but redoing the script into a holiday pantomime. TOMMY STEELE was the star, appearing as the servant Buttons, a role not in the American broadcast. Stage versions of the musical started to be produced regionally in the States in the 1960s, and the musical was presented by the New York City Opera in 1993 and 1995 and at Madison Square Garden Theatre in 2001. Today the Rodgers and Hammerstein Organization licenses stage rights for the musical and it is produced by many amateur and professional theatre groups each year.

Cinderella Television Casts

Character	1957 version	1965 version	1997 version
Cinderella	JULIE ANDREWS	Lesley Ann Warren	Brandy Norwood
Prince	Jon Cypher	Stuart Damon	Paolo Montalban
Stepmother	Ilka Chase	Jo Van Fleet	BERNADETTE PETERS
Stepsister Portia	KAYE BALLARD		
[Prunella]		PAT CARROLL	
[Minerva]			Natalie Desselle
Stepsister Joy	Alice Ghostley		
[Esmerelda]		Barbara Ruick	
[Calliope]			Veanne Cox
Fairy Godmother	EDIE ADAMS	CELESTE HOLM	Whitney Houston
King	HOWARD LINDSAY	WALTER PIDGEON	VICTOR GARBER
Queen	Dorothy Stickney	GINGER RODGERS	Whoopi Goldberg

> ## Cinderella (1957) Musical Numbers
>
> "The Prince Is Giving a Ball"
> "In My Own Little Corner"
> "Your Majesties"
> "Impossible/It's Possible"
> "Ten Minutes Ago (I Saw You)"
> "Stepsisters' Lament"
> "Waltz for a Ball"
> "Do I Love You Because You're Beautiful?"
> "When You're Driving Through the Moonlight"
> "A Lovely Night"

CBS-TV remade *Cinderella* in 1965 with Lesley Ann Warren as the heroine, supported by a strong cast from Hollywood and Broadway. The broadcast, produced and directed by Charles S. Dubin, was filmed in color on videotape so it was available for subsequent showings. Except for the addition of one song, "Loneliness of Evening" sung by the Prince, the score is identical. Warren may not be another Julie Andrews but she is charming in the musical. Although it is considered inferior to the original, this is the version that more viewers saw over the years so it is fondly remembered by many. In 1997, the DISNEY Channel broadcast its own version of Rodgers and Hammerstein's *Cinderella* with an ethnically diverse cast featuring African American pop singer Brandy Norwood as Cinderella. Some new songs were added ("There's Music in You" and "The Deepest Love in All the World"), as well as the Rodgers and LORENZ HART number "Falling in Love With Love" and Rodgers' "The Sweetest Sounds" from other sources, and the score was reorchestrated to give the musical a more contemporary sound. The Robert L. Freedman teleplay added its own contemporary touches as well, yet the spirit of the original was still there. The lush, literally sparkling production was directed by Robert Iscove and choreographed by ROB MARSHALL and was very successful. There were three other *Cinderella* musicals on television that were not scored by Rodgers and Hammerstein. CBS's *Studio One* broadcast a live sixty-minute version in 1953 titled *Cinderella, '53*, which featured songs by COLE PORTER. No copy of the musical exists and it is believed that the songs were Porter standards, although which ones is unknown. Arnold Schulman wrote the teleplay about a poor but beautiful girl (Ann Crowley) from Tenth Avenue who falls for a princely society gent (David Atkinson) even though she has never spoken to him. NBC's *Lincoln-*

Mercury Startime set the classic story in the Wild West and called it *Cindy's Fella* (1959). Cindy is the stepdaughter of Widow Parke and gets to go to a barn dance with the help of the guitar-strumming drifter who acts as a Fairy Godmother and turns a peddler's wagon into a coach. The interesting twist is that Cindy decides she doesn't love the rich ranchman's son but settles for the peddler, Azel Dorsey, instead. The up-and-coming director–choreographer GOWER CHAMPION staged the sixty-minute musical, which had songs by Conrad Salinger. The impressive cast featured Kathie Brown, Lois Smith, JAMES STEWART, George Gobel, and James Best. The *Cinderella* tale was also given a refreshing new look with the TV musical *CINDY* (1978).

CINDY (ABC-TV 1978). Setting the Cinderella fairy tale in Harlem of 1943 allowed the musical to use period standards such as "Stompin' at the Savoy," "Take the A Train," "Mood Indigo," and "I'm Getting Sentimental Over You" alongside some new numbers by Stan Daniels and Howard Roberts to evoke the era. Cindy (Charlaine Woodard) comes from the South to live in New York with her weak-willed father and vicious stepmother. There is little magic involved in getting her to the Sugar Hill Ball where she dances with a dashing Marine on leave. Cindy loses a sneaker rather than a glass slipper and when the Marine finds her, she forsakes him for the local youth that she's fallen in love with. The African American cast was top notch and included Cleavant Derricks, Mae Mercer, Scoey Mitchell, Clifton Davis, Alaina Reed, and Nell-Ruth Carter. William A. Graham directed the stylish two-hour production, and DONALD MCKAYLE choreographed the vivacious dance numbers.

CITY OF ANGELS (Virginia Theatre 1989). A musical spoof on a grand scale, this ingenious, tuneful musical written by LARRY GELBART (book), CY COLEMAN (music), and David Zippel (lyrics) was as much like a 1940s hit even as it mocked the 1940s. Detective novelist Stine (GREGG EDELMAN) goes to Hollywood where producer Buddy Fidler (RENE AUBERJONOIS) is making a film of one of his books featuring the private eye Stone (JAMES NAUGHTON). Stine's business and romantic complications echo those in his novel until both have a happy ending. The expert cast also included RANDY GRAFF, Dee Hoty, Kay McClelland, RACHEL YORK, Scott Waara, and Shawn Elliott. The clever pastiche of 1940s private eye films and Big Band songs pleased both critics and playgoers, and the production, directed by Michael Blakemore, had many playful touches, such as all the sets and costumes in black and white for the film scenes and in color for reality. The score included such delicious numbers as the swinging duet "You're Nothing Without Me," the wry character song "You Can Always Count on Me," the frustrated lament "What You Don't Know About Women," the seductive ballads "Lost and Found" and "With Every Breath I Take," and the be-boop "Ev'rybody's Gotta Be Somewhere." The musical ran 878 performances and then toured successfully.

CLARE, SIDNEY (1892–1972). Film lyricist. A little-known but widely sung songwriter, he flourished in Hollywood in the 1930s. Clare was born in New York and went into vaudeville as a singer–dancer, writing material for himself and eventually turning to songwriting. Songs by Clare were used on Broadway in THE PASSING SHOW (1921), The Midnight Rounders (1921), The Mimic World (1921), and EARL CARROLL'S VANITIES (1932). He arrived in Hollywood in 1933 and wrote the lyrics for RKO's first musical, Street Girl (1029). Working with composers OSCAR LEVANT, JAY GORNEY, SAM STEPT, HARRY AKST, and others, Clare contributed scores to the movie musicals Tanned Legs (1929), Love Comes Along (1930), Jimmy and Sally (1933), Wild Gold (1934), Transatlantic Merry-Go-Round (1934), This Is the Life (1935), Music Is Magic (1935), Paddy O'Day (1935), Song and Dance Man (1936), Can This Be Dixie? (1936), Star for a Night (1937), The Holy Terror (1937), Sing and Be Happy (1937), and Rascals (1938). Ironically, Clare's two most famous songs—"Keeping Myself for You" and "On the Good Ship Lollipop"—did not come from the aforementioned movies but were written and interpolated in others' films. Clare and his movies are long forgotten but some of his songs endure, such as "Please Don't Talk About Me When I'm Gone," "You're My Thrill," "Polly Wolly Doodle," and "Ma, He's Making Eyes at Me."

CLARK, BOBBY [Edwin] (1888–1960). Stage, screen, and television performer. A very popular vaudeville and Broadway clown, he kept audiences in stitches for over fifty years. Clark was born in Springfield, Ohio, and when he was twelve years old teamed up with another local, Paul McCullough (1883–1936), and went on the vaudeville stage in 1905 as a comedy duo. The short, stubby Clark wore painted-on eyeglasses and sported a too-short cane and

a cigar as he leered his way across the stage and growled about his latest scheme. The tall, beefy McCullough wore a mustache and usually played Clark's spineless stooge. The two were a hit in variety and burlesque, and even on the circus circuit, which brought them to New York for the first time in 1919. The team was featured in Broadway revues and book musicals, such as Peek-a-Boo (1919), Carnival (1919), MUSIC BOX REVUE (1922 and 1924), The Ramblers (1926), STRIKE UP THE BAND (1930), Here Goes the Bride (1931), Walk a Little Faster (1932), and Thumbs Ups! (1934). McCullough committed suicide in 1936 and Clark continued on in musical comedies, playing characters that allowed him to retain some of his broad comic bits, most memorably the scoundrel Joe Bascom on the lam in MEXICAN HAYRIDE (1944) and as the skirt-chasing Waldo Wellington who is married to the first female president of the United States in AS THE GIRLS GO (1948). His other Broadway musicals include ZIEGFELD FOLLIES (1936), Streets of Paris (1939), Star and Garter (1942), and SWEETHEARTS (1944). Clark wrote and appeared with McCullough in a series of comedy film shorts in the 1920s and appeared solo in THE GOLDWYN FOLLIES (1938), as well as on some early television specials, such as the TV musical Once Upon an Eastertime (1954). His final stage appearance was as the devilish Applegate in the national tour of DAMN YANKEES (1956).

CLARK, PETULA [Sally Owen] (1932–). Film, television, and stage performer. A British pop singer of the 1960s, the chipper, wholesome singer starred in both stage and movie musicals. Clark was born in Ewell, England, and was singing professionally in music halls and on radio when she was only eleven years old. In the 1940s she was a child star in British films and by the 1950s was in France making recordings and singing in nightclubs. Clark burst onto the music scene in England and America with pop hits such as "Downtown" and "Don't Sleep in the Subway." Over the years she would make over 100 recordings that sold seventy million records, the best-selling female vocalist in the United Kingdom. Clark made two Hollywood musicals: as the Irish lass Sharon in FINIAN'S RAINBOW (1968) and as the music hall singer Katherine in GOODBYE, MR. CHIPS (1969). She has appeared in many nonmusical films and dozens of television programs on both sides of the Atlantic. Clark has also returned to musicals on the London stage, playing Maria in THE SOUND OF MUSIC in 1981, Grizabella in CATS in 1990, Mrs. Johnstone in Blood Brothers in 1993 (a performance she reprised on Broadway in 1994), and movie queen Norma Desmond in *SUNSET BOULEVARD* in 1995. Biography: *This Is My Song: A Biography of Petula Clark*, Andrea Kon (1983).

CLARK, VICTORIA (1959–). Stage performer. A superb singer–actress who has always been given supporting roles in musicals, she dazzled Broadway with her performance in *THE LIGHT IN THE PIAZZA* (2005) and opened a new phase in her career. Clark was born in Dallas, Texas, and studied music at Yale and New York University, singing soprano roles in operetta while still a student. She made her Broadway debut in the 1992 revival of *GUYS AND DOLLS* and was featured in *A Grand Night for Singing* (1993), *HOW TO SUCCEED IN BUSINESS WITHOUT REALLY TRYING* (1995), *TITANIC* (1997), and replacements in *CABARET* in 1999 and *URINETOWN* in 2003. She finally got a leading role as the troubled tourist Margaret Johnson in *The Light in the Piazza*. Clark has sung on the soundtracks of the animated films *THE HUNCHBACK OF NOTRE DAME* (1996) and *ANASTASIA* (1997) and has acted in a few television programs and films, including *THE CRADLE WILL ROCK* (1999).

CLARKE, GRANT (1891–1931). Stage and film lyricist. A Broadway and Tin Pan Alley songwriter, he contributed to the first Hollywood musical and some early talkies in his brief career. Clarke was born in Akron, Ohio, and went into the theatre as an actor, performing in stock companies and even appearing in Broadway plays before turning to songwriting. He contributed songs to the Broadway musicals *The Wall Street Girl* (1912), *The Pleasure Seekers* (1913), *Hands Up* (1915), and *ZIEGFELD FOLLIES* (1921), as well as songs for vaudeville stars AL JOLSON, FANNY BRICE, EVA TANGUAY, and others. Clarke went to Hollywood and wrote lyrics for the landmark film *THE JAZZ SINGER* (1927); his "Mother of Mine, I Still Have You" with Louis Silvers was the first song ever written for a talkie. Collaborating with composer HARRY AKST, he wrote scores for the movie musicals *ON WITH THE SHOW* (1929), *Is Everybody Happy?* (1929), *So Long, Letty* (1930), and *Song of the Flame* (1930) before his premature death from alcoholism. Among Clarke's song standards are "Am I Blue?," "Ragtime Cowboy Joe," and "Second Hand Rose."

CLASSICAL MUSIC IN MUSICALS. For many years Broadway had used classical music for ballets or specialty spots and sometimes a particular song was "inspired" from a classical piece, but it was the success of *BLOSSOM TIME* (1921) that began the practice of whole scores coming from the world of classical music. SIGMUND ROMBERG adapted themes by Franz Schubert to create the songs for the biographical musical about the composer's

---

Biographical Film Musicals about Classical Composers

Musical	Composer(s)	Impersonator(s)
Amadeus (1984)	Wolfgang Amadeus Mozart	Tom Hulce
BLOSSOM TIME (1934)	Franz Schubert	Richard Tauber
GREAT WALTZ, THE (1938)	Johann Strauss, Jr.	Fernand Gravet
GREAT WALTZ, THE (1972)	Johann Strauss, Jr.	Horst Buchholtz
Immortal Beloved (1994)	Ludwig van Beethoven	Gary Oldman
Lisztomania (1975)	Franz Liszt	Roger Daltry
Magnificent Rebel, The (1962)	Ludwig van Beethoven	Karl Boehm
Music Lovers, The (1970)	Peter I. Tchaikovsky	Richard Chamberlain
Song of Love (1947)	Johannes Brahms	Robert Walker
	Robert Schumann	Paul Henreid
Song of My Heart (1948)	Peter I. Tchaikovsky	Frank Sundstrom
SONG OF NORWAY (1970)	Edvard Grieg	Toralv Maurstad
Song of Scheherezade (1947)	Nikolai Rimsky-Korsakov	Jean-Pierre Aumont
Song to Remember, A (1944)	Frederic Chopin	Cornel Wilde
Song Without End (1960)	Franz Liszt	Dirk Bogart
Story of Gilbert and Sullivan (1953)	W. S. Gilbert	Robert Morley
	Arthur Sullivan	Maurice Evans
Topsy-Turvy	W. S. Gilbert	Jim Broadbent
	Arthur Sullivan	Allan Corduner
Waltz King, The (1963)	Johann Strauss, Jr.	Kerwin Matthews

life. It was a sensation and both audiences and producers wanted more. While some of the musicals that followed, such as Grieg's SONG OF NORWAY (1944), were also biographies, most were shows that used classical music that evoked the tone or time period of the musical. The most successful such adaptations were OSCAR HAMMERSTEIN'S CARMEN JONES (1944) using music by Bizet and GEORGE FORREST and ROBERT WRIGHT'S KISMET (1953) using themes from Borodin. Lesser known efforts include Chopin for *White Lilacs* (1928) and *Polanaise* (1945), Kreisler for *Rhapsody* (1944), Villa-Lobos for *Magdalena* (1948), Offenbach for *The Love Song* (1925) and *The Happiest Girl in the World* (1961), various Strausses for THE GREAT WALTZ (1934), THREE WALTZES (1937), and *Mr. Strauss Goes to Boston* (1945), Tchaikovsky for *Nadja* (1925) and *Music in My Heart* (1947), Rachmaninoff for *Anya* (1965), and John Philip Sousa for *Teddy and Alice* (1987). On television, the music of Rimsky-Korsakov was used for the score for the original musical THE ADVENTURES OF MARCO POLO (1956).

Hollywood filmed the most successful of these stage works and made several of their own classically scored musicals. These were almost always biographies of composers and, although there was usually little or no singing, there was plenty of famous music in the films. Like most biographical films, accuracy was not highly valued and many of these movies can be categorized as fiction, but the music was the real thing and that is what counted.

CLAYTON, JAN [born Jane Byral] (1917–1983). Stage, television, and film performer. A slender blonde singer–actress who was frequently seen on television, she is most remembered for creating the role of Julie Jordan in CAROUSEL (1945). Clayton was born in Tularosa, New Mexico, and was featured in films by the time she was eighteen years old and made several pictures over the next ten years, none of which utilized her clear, expressive soprano singing voice. She made a sensational Broadway debut in *Carousel*, introducing "If I Loved You" and "What's the Use of Wond'rin'?," and then she took over the role of Magnolia in the 1946 revival of SHOW BOAT. Clayton made her first of many television appearances in 1949 and over the next three decades would appear in hundreds of episodes of westerns, dramas, and sit-coms, mostly memorably as the mother in the popular series *Lassie* from 1954 to 1957. She made a brief return to Broadway in 1972 as a replacement in the musical FOLLIES. Because of her bouts with alcoholism and run-ins with movie executives, Clayton never became the star that her talents deserved. She was married to actor Russell Hayden for a time and, with Samuel Marx, wrote *Rodgers and Hart: Bewitched, Bothered and Bewildered* (1976).

CLOONEY, ROSEMARY (1928–2002). Film and television performer. A renowned Big Band singer and jazz stylist, the attractive blonde and her smooth and mellow vocal talents were utilized in only a few but notable films. Clooney was born in Maysville, Kentucky, and as a teenager sang with her sister Betty on a Cincinnati radio station. The two sang in clubs together until Rosemary went solo and sang with name bands, leading to a record contract that made her one of the most popular singers of the 1950s. Her most remembered movie role is the band singer Betty Haynes in WHITE CHRISTMAS (1954), but she was also featured in *The Stars Are Singing* (1953), *Here Come the Girls* (1953), *Red Garters* (1954), and DEEP IN MY HEART (1954). Clooney was very popular on radio and then on television and she continued singing and recording into the 1980s. She was married to actor JOSÉ FERRER (1909–1992), is the sister of television host Nick Clooney (1934–), and aunt to film actor–director George Clooney (1961–). Autobiographies: *This For Remembrance* (1982); *Girl Singer: An Autobiography* (2001).

CLORINDY; OR, THE ORIGIN OF THE CAKE WALK (Casino Theatre 1898). A musical theatre footnote but a noteworthy one, this short musical "afterpiece" was the first show written and performed by African Americans to play in a major Broadway house. Producer–director EDWARD E. RICE presented a vaudeville entertainment entitled *Rice's Summer Nights* for fifty-five performances on the rooftop of the Casino Theatre. Added during the run was *Clorindy* by Will Marion (music) and Paul Lawrence Dunbar (book and lyrics). The "African singing and dancing novelty" featured such songs as "Every Coon Had a Lady Friend But Me," "Who Dat Say Chicken in Dis Crowd?," and "Darktown Is Out Tonight." The last song enjoyed some popularity at the time, and the show itself was well received as a delightful warm-weather diversion. Dunbar would later become better known as a poet and civil rights advocate.

Close, Glenn (1947–). Stage, film, and television performer. The regal star of Broadway and Hollywood, she can play crazed femme fatales as easily as classy ladies of quality. Close was born in Greenwich, Connecticut, the daughter of a surgeon who took her with him on his missionary work in Africa. After graduating from the College of William and Mary, she toured as a folk singer before going to New York and making her legit debut in 1974. Close was featured in plays and musicals on and Off Broadway throughout the 1970s, such as the Princess Mary in *Rex* (1976) and then played the level-headed wife Charity in *Barnum* (1980). She has been awarded for her performances in plays in New York and in London, and her most notable musical role on Broadway was the looney silent screen star Norma Desmond in *Sunset Boulevard* (1994). Close made an impressive screen debut as the liberated mother Jenny Fields in *The World According to Garp* (1982), followed by a variety of popular films but none of them musicals except the animated *Tarzan* (1999) for which she provided the voice of the mother Kala. She played nurse Nellie Forbush in the 2001 TV version of *South Pacific* and has appeared on many other television shows.

Closer Than Ever. See *STARTING HERE, STARTING NOW*

■ **Coal Miner's Daughter** (Universal 1980). What might have been a routine "rags-to-riches" biographical musical about a celebrity, this unsentimental film about country singer Loretta Lynn was raised to a higher level by the dynamic performance of Sissy Spacek. Thomas Rickman adapted Lynn's autobiography, beginning with the marriage of thirteen-year-old Loretta Webb (Spacek) from the hills of Kentucky to the war veteran "Doo" Lynn (Tommy Lee Jones). A disappointment as a wife, she shows a talent for writing and singing songs about her life in the hills so Doo promotes her at the local radio station. Lynn's rise to fame in Nashville was handled with unromantic realism, as were her bouts with depression and a nervous breakdown right on stage. Beverly D'Angelo shone as her friend Patsy Cline who died in a plane crash, the news of which contributed to Lynn's downfall. Also in the cast were William Sanderson, Levon Helm, Phyllis Boyens, and Robert Elkins, under the direction of Michael Apted. Songs by Lynn and others were heard in the film, including "Honky-Tonk Girl," "You're Lookin' at

Country," "Sweet Dreams of You," and the title number. Spacek did her own singing and held the movie together with her tough, determined, yet vulnerable portrayal of the Nashville recording star.

Coca, Imogene [born Imogene Fernandez de Coca] (1908–2001). Television and stage performer. The tiny comedienne with wide eyes and a large mouth appeared in farcical sketches and sang comic songs in musical revues on Broadway but became more famous for her hilarious antics on television. Coca was born in Philadelphia, the daughter of a violinist–bandleader and a dancer, and went into vaudeville as a dancer at the age of nine. She made her Broadway debut in the chorus of *When You Smile* (1925) and soon was featured in such revues as *Bunk of 1926*, *The Garrick Gaieties* (1930), *Shoot the Works!* (1931), and *Flying Colors* (1932), but found wide recognition for her daffy characters in *New Faces of 1934*. Coca was so popular that, inexplicably, she was featured as a "new face" again in *New Faces of 1936*. Her other Broadway musicals include *Bubbling Over* (1926), *Queen High* (1928), *Fools Rush In* (1934), *Who's Who* (1938), *The Straw Hat Revue* (1939), *All in Fun* (1940), and *Concert Varieties* (1945). Coca got involved with early television and it was as Sid Caesar's partner in comedy on *Your Show of Shows* that she became a nationwide favorite. She appeared in many other television programs, including two series of her own in the 1960s, and returned to Broadway for two plays in the 1950s and as wacky senior citizens in the musicals *On the Twentieth Century* (1978) and *My Old Friends* (1985). She was married to actor King Donovan (1918–1987).

🎵 **Coco** (Mark Hellinger Theatre 1969). The only Broadway musical starring film legend Katharine Hepburn, the biographical show about French designer Gabrielle "Coco" Chanel was tailored to the star's very limited singing ability, yet she triumphed in the role all the same. Alan Jay Lerner's libretto presented highlights from the life of the famous fashion designer with emphasis on her attempting to make a comeback after World War II and failing miserably in Paris, only to have her designs picked up by American department stores. It was not the most gripping of stories but Hepburn's characterization demanded attention and she carried the show, even as she could barely croak out her few songs. She was supported by a first-rate cast that included GEORGE ROSE, RENE AUBERJONOIS, David Holliday, Gale Dixon, Jon Cypher, and Jeanne Arnold. Lerner also provided the lyrics for ANDRÉ PREVIN's music and some of the songs were laudable, such as the sarcastic "The World Belongs to the Young," the cheery "When Your Lover Says Goodbye," the tender "Always Mademoiselle," and the slaphappy "The Money Rings Out Like Freedom." The press unfairly dismissed the musical and just concentrated on the valiant Hepburn who sold enough tickets to let the show run 332 performances and then go on a successful tour. Frederick Brisson produced, Michael Benthall directed, and MICHAEL BENNETT choreographed.

COCOANUTS, THE (Lyric Theatre 1925). The plot, the score, and the supporting players all took a back seat in this hilarious MARX BROTHERS vehicle, their biggest Broadway hit. GEORGE S. KAUFMAN and MORRIE RYSKIND wrote the libretto about the recent land development boom in Florida and the wealthy dowager Mrs. Potter who stays at a hotel run by Henry Schlemmer and has her valuable necklace stolen. Even the scriptwriters admitted little of their dialogue survived by opening night because the zany brothers usually ad libbed their way through the show. IRVING BERLIN wrote the score, which included "A Little Bungalow," "Florida By the Seas," "Why Am I a Hit With the Ladies?," and "Monkey Doodle Doo," but the best song, "Always," was cut before opening. SAM H. HARRIS produced, Oscar Eagle directed, and SAMMY LEE choreographed, but none had any control over the Marx Brothers who turned chaos into inspired fun. Audiences were delighted and the show ran 377 performances in two engagements. The musical has been revived regionally by repertory and college theatres with the actors impersonating the Marx Brothers and the show still plays well on stage.

The Cocoanuts (Paramount 1929) was the brothers' first feature film, a stagy studio version of their Broadway hit and very primitive in regards to sound and camerawork. However, it is a facetious romp and still holds up today. While the brothers were performing ANIMAL CRACKERS (1928) on Broadway at night, they filmed The Cocoanuts in a Long Island studio with the early sound cameras enclosed in giant glass boxes to cut down on their noise. Consequently, the camera rarely moves and much of the film is like a staged play. It was enough to capture their antics, and this first movie gives one a better idea of their stage presence than the later more polished Hollywood vehicles. Only half of the Broadway score was retained for the film, and Berlin wrote the catchy "When My Dreams Come True" for the screen lovers. Most of the highlights in the movie are not musical, such as the prankish auction led by Groucho and the famous "viaduct" conversation with Chico. Sammy Lee again did the choreography, and the directors were JOSEPH SANTLEY and Robert Florey.

COHAN, GEORGE M[ichael]. (1878–1942). Stage and film performer, director, songwriter, and producer. Broadway's greatest showman in the early decades of the twentieth century, he was a one-man dynamo who created and performed in plays and musicals with confidence and usually with success. Cohan was born in Providence, Rhode Island, into a family of vaudeville performers. As a child he appeared on stage with his parents and sister; the family was billed as the Four Cohans. While still a teenager, he began to write, direct, compose songs, and manage the foursome and they soon became one of the most popular acts on the variety circuit. But Cohan wanted to conquer Broadway. After a few false starts, he had a hit in 1904 writing the book and songs, directing, co-producing, and starring in the newfangled

Casts for *The Cocoanuts*

Character	1925 Broadway	1929 film
Henry Schlemmer	GROUCHO MARX	Groucho Marx
Willie the Wop	CHICO MARX	Chico Marx
Silent Sam	HARPO MARX	Harpo Marx
Jamison	ZEPPO MARX	Zeppo Marx
Mrs. Potter	MARGARET DUMONT	Margaret Dumont
Polly Potter	Mabel Withee	Mary Eaton
Bob Adams	Jack Barker	OSCAR SHAW
Penelope Martin	Janet Velie	Kay Francis

ally producing and directing them himself, as with FORTY-FIVE MINUTES FROM BROADWAY (1906), *George Washington, Jr.* (1906), *The Talk of New York* (1907), *Fifty Miles From Boston* (1908), *The Man Who Owns Broadway* (1909), *The Little Millionaire* (1911), *Hello, Broadway!* (1914), *The Royal Vagabond* (1919), LITTLE NELLIE KELLY (1922), *The Rise of Rosie O'Reilly* (1923), *The Merry Malones* (1927), and *Billie* (1928). His direction was as rapid fire as his onstage delivery of lines and songs, yet he understood the power of sentiment as well and paced his musicals accordingly. Cohan also wrote, produced, and directed nonmusical plays, most memorably *Seven Keys to Baldpate* (1913) and *The Tavern* (1920). As times changed, his scripts and style of musical were considered old fashioned by many, but his appeal as a performer never waned, finding hits late in life in the Eugene O'Neill play *Ah, Wilderness!* (1933) and the Rodgers and Hart musical I'D RATHER BE RIGHT (1937). Cohan only appeared in one Hollywood musical, the commendable THE PHANTOM PRESIDENT (1932), but he was vividly portrayed by JAMES CAGNEY in the musical bio-pic YANKEE DOODLE DANDY (1942), as he was years later by JOEL GREY in the Broadway musical GEORGE M! (1968). Cohan was not a subtle artist in any of his talents, but he created a new all-American sound for the Broadway musical and wrote songs that departed drastically from European operetta. Autobiography: *Twenty Years of Broadway* (1925); biographies: *George M. Cohan: Prince of the American Theatre*, Ward Morehouse (rev. 1972); *George M. Cohan: The Man Who Owned Broadway*, John McCabe (1973).

COHEN, ALEXANDER H[enry]. (1920–2000). Stage producer. The presenter of classy plays on Broadway, including new works, star revivals, and British imports, also produced musicals but often with less success than his other projects. The native New Yorker began his producing career in 1941 with a quick flop and then later the same year struck gold with the long-running thriller *Angel Street*. He would become one of the most active solo producers over the next fifty years, finding commercial success on occasion and often bringing exceptional fare to Broadway. Cohen's musicals credits include *Of V We Sing* (1942), *Bright Lights of 1944*, *Make a Wish* (1951), *At the Drop of a Hat* (1959), *Rugantino* (1964), *Baker Street* (1965), *A Time for Singing* (1966), *At the Drop of Another Hat* (1966), DEAR WORLD (1969), *Words and Music* (1974), *I Remember*

George M. Cohan. The multitalented showman was at heart a performer, proud to be called cocky and brash. Cohan loved playing "Cohan" on and off the stage. This photo of him exudes cockiness, from the tilt of his hat to the tip of his cane. (Photofest)

musical LITTLE JOHNNY JONES. Like many of his subsequent shows, it was a fast-paced, slangy, tuneful romp that the critics dismissed but the audiences loved. Cohan continued to present similar shows for three decades, usu-

Mama (1979), and *A DAY IN HOLLYWOOD—A NIGHT IN THE UKRAINE* (1980). For many years he produced the television coverage of the TONY AWARDS and two years before he died Cohen performed a successful one-man show, *Star Billing* (1998), in which he talked about his decades in the theatre. His wife is actress–producer Hildy Parks.

COHENOUR, PATTI (1952–). Stage and television performer. An operatic-voiced ingénue on Broadway, the petite blonde later became a solid character actress. Cohenour was born in Albuquerque, New Mexico, and educated at the University of New Mexico. She made her Broadway debut in the ensemble of the short-lived musical *A Doll's Life* (1982) and then played the featured role of Mary Jane Wilkes in *BIG RIVER* (1985). Cohenour graduated to major roles in *THE MYSTERY OF EDWIN DROOD* (1985), where she played the scared soprano Rosa Bud, and *THE PHANTOM OF THE OPERA* (1988) in which she played Christine for matinees and later took over the part full time. She also sang leading roles in the Off Broadway musical productions of *THE PIRATES OF PENZANCE* (1981) and *La Boheme* (1984), both for the NEW YORK SHAKESPEARE FESTIVAL. Cohenour has been very active in regional theatre, performing in musicals and plays. She returned to Broadway as the Mother Abbess in *THE SOUND OF MUSIC* (1998) and as the Italian matriarch Signora Naccarelli in *THE LIGHT IN THE PIAZZA* (2005), eventually playing the leading role of Margaret. She has appeared in a handful of television programs, including the musical *GEPETTO* (2000).

COLE, JACK (1914–1974). Stage and film choreographer. An outstanding choreographer, his dances for Broadway and Hollywood were varied yet distinctive in style. Cole was born in New Brunswick, New Jersey, and began his career as a dancer with the Denishawn Dance Company, later forming his own troupe that specialized in Asian forms. He was in the chorus of such Broadway musicals as *Thumbs Up!* (1934) and *May Wine* (1935) before making his choreography debut in 1942 with the ETHEL MERMAN vehicle *SOMETHING FOR THE BOYS*. Cole appeared in and choreographed the 1943 edition of the *ZIEGFELD FOLLIES* and the revue *Alive and Kicking* (1950), but his first hit was *KISMET* (1953) in which he was able to utilize his training in exotic dance from Asia. His other Broadway credits include *Magdalena* (1948), *JAMAICA* (1957), *A FUNNY*

THING HAPPENED ON THE WAY TO THE FORUM (1962), *Foxy* (1964), and *MAN OF LA MANCHA* (1965), as well as both directing and choreographing *Donnybrook* (1961) and *Kean* (1961). Cole also enjoyed a notable film career staging the dance numbers for several movie musicals in the 1940s and 1950s, including *COVER GIRL* (1944), *THE JOLSON STORY* (1946), *The Thrill of Brazil* (1946), *ON THE RIVIERA* (1951), *THE MERRY WIDOW* (1952), *THE FARMER TAKES A WIFE* (1953), *GENTLEMEN PREFER BLONDES* (1953), *THERE'S NO BUSINESS LIKE SHOW BUSINESS* (1954), *Kismet* (1955), *LES GIRLS* (1957), and *Let's Make Love* (1960), as well as the TV musical *Keep in Step* (1959). His choreography was marked with a unique blend of the foreign with American jazz. Cole was also an influential teacher, training such dancers as GWEN VERDON (who was his assistant for seven years) and CAROL HANEY. Biography: *Unsung Genius: The Passion of Dancer-Choreographer Jack Cole*, Glenn Loney (1984).

COLE, NAT "KING" [born Nathaniel Adams Cole] (1919–1965). Film and television performer and musician. A velvet-voiced singer and pianist who conquered radio, records, and television, the handsome African American artist made some twenty films before his untimely death. Cole was born in Montgomery, Alabama, and grew up in Chicago where he played the organ at church and then started his own band as a teenager. In 1939 he formed the instrumental jazz group the King Cole Trio and only later did he start singing as part of the act. After hit recordings, popular nightclub appearances, and international tours, Cole was brought to Hollywood where he appeared in the movie musicals *Here Comes Elmer* (1943), *Pistol Packin' Mamma* (1943), *Pin-Up Girl* (1944), *Stars on Parade* (1944), *Swing in the Saddle* (1944), *See My Lawyer* (1945), *Breakfast in Hollywood* (1946), *Make Believe Ballroom* (1949), and *Small Town Girl* (1953). Most of these were B movies and Cole usually played himself in a specialty spot. He did get to play a major character role as W. C. Handy in *St. Louis Blues* (1958). Cole was one of the first African Americans to have his own television variety show and he made many appearances on others' programs as well. His last screen appearance was one of the balladeers in *Cat Ballou* (1965). His daughter is singer Natalie Cole (1950–). Biographies: *Nat King Cole*, Daniel Mark Epstein (2000); *Nat King Cole*, James Haskins (1991); *Nat King Cole: An Intimate Biography*, Maria Cole [his wife] (1971).

COLEMAN, CY [born Seymour Kaufman] (1929–2004). Stage composer. One of the most tuneful of Broadway songwriters, his scores bounce with vitality and a full jazzy, brassy sound. A native New Yorker, Coleman was a child prodigy on the piano and was performing at Carnegie Hall and other prestigious venues when he was only six years old. But his heart was in jazz and the Big Band sound so as a teenager he formed his own band and played in nightclubs, eventually writing original material to play. Coleman and lyricist CAROLYN LEIGH had some hit singles, such as "Witchcraft" and "The Best Is Yet to Come," before they scored the Broadway musical *WILDCAT* (1960) for star LUCILLE BALL. Their score for *LITTLE ME* (1962) was tailored to fit the talents of another television star, comic SID CAESAR. Coleman teamed with veteran lyricist DOROTHY FIELDS for *SWEET CHARITY* (1966) and *SEESAW* (1973), with MICHAEL STEWART for *I LOVE MY WIFE* (1977) and *BARNUM* (1980), and with BETTY COMDEN and ADOLPH GREEN for *ON THE TWENTIETH CENTURY* (1978) and *THE WILL ROGERS FOLLIES* (1991). With others he scored *Welcome to the Club* (1989), *CITY OF ANGELS* (1989), and *THE LIFE* (1997). Coleman's music is optimistic and full throttle, much as in the spirit of GEORGE M. COHAN, but with a distinctive jazz influence.

■ **COLLEGE RHYTHM** (Paramount 1934). Although it had an impossible premise for a musical (two department stores go collegiate and complete via a football game), the film offered a breezy pace, splendid cast, and a vivacious score by HARRY REVEL (music) and MACK GORDON (lyrics). All-American halfback Francis J. Finnigan (JACK CARSON) and the team depend on Joe (JOE PENNER) and his pet duck as the team mascot and are too superstitious to go into the football field without them there. Frank's roommate is Larry Stacey (LANNY ROSS) who plays the piccolo in the pep band and sings in the glee club. The two love the same girl, coed Gloria Van Dayham (Mary Brian), so Frank refuses Larry's offer to work in his father's department store. The Depression hits and Frank is on the streets until he swallows his pride, joins Stacey's Department Store, and leads them to victory over the rival Whipple's Emporium. The screenplay was laughable, but the songs, such as "Stay As Sweet As You Are," "Take a Number From One to Ten," "Let's Give Three Cheers for Love," and the pulsating title number, were delightful compensation. So too were the supporting play-ers, including LYDA ROBERTI, Helen Mack, FRANKLIN PANGBORN, GEORGE BARBIER, Dean Jagger, and Robert McWade. NORMAN TAUROG directed the Adolph Zukor production.

COLONNA, JERRY [born Gerardo Luigi Colonna] (1904–1986). Film and television performer. A broad comic who rolled his eyes, bristled his bushy mustache, and bellowed through clenched teeth, he was an audience favorite in nightclubs, on radio, on television, and in twenty movies. Colonna was born in Boston and started as a trombone player in the Columbia Orchestra in the 1930s but soon found he could make audiences laugh with his wild facial expressions. He was a hit in nightclubs and on the radio with BOB HOPE who traded barbs with him for decades. Colonna went to Hollywood in 1937 and was featured in such musicals as *ROSALIE* (1937), *Little Miss Broadway* (1938), *Garden of the Moon* (1938), *College Swing* (1938), *Naughty But Nice* (1939), *ROAD TO SINGAPORE* (1940), *Sis Hopkins* (1941), *You're the One* (1941), *True to the Army* (1942), *STAR-SPANGLED RHYTHM* (1942), *Atlantic City* (1944), *ROAD TO RIO* (1947), *Meet Me in Las Vegas* (1956), and *THE ROAD TO HONG KONG* (1962). He also provided voices for the animated musicals *MAKE MINE MUSIC* (1946) and *ALICE IN WONDERLAND* (1951). Colonna made many television appearances, including the small screen version of *REVENGE WITH MUSIC* (1954) and the original TV musical *PINOCCHIO* (1957). Biography: *The Story of Professor Colonna*, Bob Colonna, John Williams (2007).

☙ **COLOR PURPLE, THE** (Broadway Theatre 2005). A much anticipated musical based on Alice Walker's popular novel, the stage version disappointed some fans of the book but found its own advocates. In Marsha Norman's libretto, the African American Celie (LaChanze) moves from put-upon teenager to self-empowered woman in the American South as she battles tough black men and is given strength by determined black women. The entire cast was exceptional, including Felicia P. Fields, Elisabeth Withers-Mendes, Brandon Victor Dixon, Kingsley Leggs, Renee Elise Goldsberry, and Krisha Marcano. The songs by Brenda Russell, Allee Willis, and Stephen Bray may have lacked variety but were lively extensions of the characters' emotions. "Hell, No!," "Too Beautiful for Words," "Mysterious Ways," "Push da Button," "I'm Here," "What About Love?," "Somebody Gonna Love You," and the title song were the most memorable. The musical was often celebratory and jubilant, turning the book's most grim scenes into theatrical moments of discovery. Critics differed in their opinions on the script and score but applauded the fine cast, particularly LaChanze. Gary Griffin directed and Donald Byrd choreographed. The show took a while to catch on with audiences but under the shrewd promotion of co-producer Oprah Winfrey it eventually was embraced by the public for 910 performances.

COLUMBIA PICTURES. Founded in 1924 as a minor operation on Hollywood's "poverty row," the studio emerged in the 1930s as one of the major league players and has remained so ever since. Its success has been attributed to the astute leadership of ruthless Harry Cohn, a former salesman who was one of the company's founders, the artistry of directors such as Frank Capra, and the popularity of stars such as RITA HAYWORTH. The studio found its first footing producing economic second features (or B movies) and occasionally had a box office hit, although rarely in the musical genre. In the 1940s, Hayworth kept the musical end of the company afloat with such vehicles as *YOU'LL NEVER GET RICH* (1941), *YOU WERE NEVER LOVELIER* (1942), and *COVER GIRL* (1944), and the popular musical biographies such as *THE JOLSON STORY* (1946) and *JOLSON SINGS AGAIN* (1949) certainly helped. By the 1950s, Columbia dealt with the threat of television by investing in the new medium and establishing the subsidiary Screen Gems. Studio musicals during the decade were scarce but evident, ranging from the star-driven *PAL JOEY* (1957) to the prestige opera *PORGY AND BESS* (1959). Musicals at Columbia fared better in the 1960s, finding box office success with *BYE BYE BIRDIE* (1963), *FUNNY GIRL* (1968), and *OLIVER!* (1969). Along with other studios, Columbia had the burden of large expensive fiascos such as *ANNIE* (1982), which helped seal the fate on Hollywood musicals. The company was taken over by conglomerates in the 1980s, first by Coca-Cola and then by the SONY Corporation. Its most recent musical entries have been *RENT* (2005), *THE PRODUCERS* (2005), and *ACROSS THE UNIVERSE* (2007).

COLUMBO, RUSS [born Ruggerio Eugenio de Rudolpho Columbo] (1908–1934). Film performer and composer. A mellow Big Band singer whose crooning style was intimate and caressing, he was on his way to becoming the new BING CROSBY when he died at the age of twenty-six. Columbo was born in Philadelphia and began as a band singer with Gus Arnheim's orchestra. He later started his own band with himself as vocalist and became very popular on radio and records. Columbo played himself in the early film musicals *Street Girl* (1929) and *Dynamite* (1929) and then graduated to character parts in *Broadway Through a Keyhole* (1933), *Moulin Rouge* (1934), and *Wake Up and Dream* (1934), which he also composed the score. Columbo wrote the song hits "Prisoner of Love," "Coffee in the Morning," and "You Call It Madness (But I Call It Love)." He can best be described as a forerunner of FRANK SINATRA with a similar intimate style of song delivery. Columbo died of an accidental and freakish gunshot wound.

COMDEN, BETTY, AND ADOLPH GREEN. Stage, film, and television lyricists and writers. The longest songwriting partnership in the history of the Broadway musical, the twosome contributed to classic shows on stage and in Hollywood. Comden [born Basyal Cohen] (1915–2006) was born in Brooklyn and educated at New York University before entering show business as a singer in small clubs and cabaret. Green (1915–2002) was also a native New Yorker who started as a performer. The two met and, with JUDY HOLLIDAY, formed a group called the Revuers that presented musical spoofs and songs that commented on current events. Comden and Green wrote their own material and some of it was used when they teamed up with Green's college roommate LEONARD BERNSTEIN for *ON THE TOWN* (1944) in which Comden and Green also performed. That same year they played bit parts in the movie musical *Greenwich Village* (1944), but it was clear that their future lay in writing and not performing. Comden and Green collaborated with composer Morton Gould on the short-lived Broadway musical *Million Dollar Baby* (1945) and then went to Hollywood where they wrote the screenplay and/or the songs for *GOOD NEWS!* (1947), *TAKE ME OUT TO THE BALL GAME* (1949), *THE BARKLEYS OF BROADWAY* (1949), *On the Town* (1949), *SINGIN' IN THE RAIN* (1952), *THE BAND WAGON* (1953), and *IT'S ALWAYS FAIR WEATHER* (1955). They returned to Broadway and wrote the songs for the revue *TWO ON THE AISLE* (1951), their first collaboration with composer JULE STYNE. The twosome reteamed with Bernstein for the hit *WONDERFUL TOWN* (1953) and then did a series of shows with Styne: *PETER PAN* (1954), *BELLS ARE RINGING* (1956), *Say, Darling* (1958), *DO RE*

Mi (1960), *SUBWAYS ARE FOR SLEEPING* (1961), *FADE OUT–FADE IN* (1964), and *HALLELUJAH, BABY!* (1967). With composer CY COLEMAN they scored *ON THE TWENTIETH CENTURY* (1978) and *THE WILL ROGERS FOLLIES* (1991). Their other Broadway musical credits are the book for *APPLAUSE* (1970) and the score for *A Doll's Life* (1982). Many of their stage works were filmed, and they wrote new scores for *What a Way to Go* (1964) and the television musical *I'm Getting Married* (1967). Comden and Green never gave up singing and got to perform their own works in the successful Broadway revue *A Party With Comden and Green* (1958); Comden also appeared in some nonmusical plays and films. Their lyrics, librettos, and screenplays are usually in the conventional musical comedy tradition but they have an energy and playfulness that keeps them from being dated. Many mistakenly thought that Comden and Green were married; she was wed to Stephen Kyle and Green's wife is actress–singer PHYLLIS NEWMAN. Autobiography: *Off Stage*, Comden (1995).

COMIC STRIP MUSICALS. Before the advent of cartoons on film and television, newspaper comic strips and pulp comics were even more popular than they are today so it is not surprising to find that musicals based on comics go way back. Broadway saw a lot of musicals around the turn of the twentieth century that were inspired by comic strips. The cartoons and their musical versions are long gone but some of the names still are familiar: *Hogan's Alley* (1896), *The Katzenjammer Kids* (1900), *Foxy Grandpa* (1902), *Happy Hooligan* (1902), *Mickey Finn* (1903), *Buster Brown* (1905), *Panhandle Pete* (1906), and *Little Nemo* (1908), the last by no less a composer than VICTOR HERBERT. In the 1920s there were a series of musicals based on the comic strip *Bringing Up Father* featuring the battling married couple Maggie and Jiggs. Broadway saw only *Bringing Up Father* (1925) but on the road there were the musicals *Bringing Up Father in Florida*, *Bringing Up Father in Ireland*, *Bringing Up Father on Broadway*, and *Bringing Up Father on the Seashore*. The most famous comic strip stage musicals arrived after World War II. *LI'L ABNER* (1956) brought Al Capp's satirical characters from Dogpatch, U.S.A. to life on Broadway, and the musical comedy was filmed in 1959 and an abridged television version was broadcast in 1971. Similarly satirical was *IT'S A BIRD, IT'S A PLANE, IT'S SUPERMAN!* (1966), which took a lighthearted look at the ever-popular Man of Steel. A tele-

vision version of the musical was broadcast in 1975. Charles Schultz's beloved strip *Peanuts* became the long-running Off Broadway musical *YOU'RE A GOOD MAN, CHARLIE BROWN* (1967), which was remade for television twice: a live action version in 1973 and an animated one in 1985. The most successful comic strip musical of all was *ANNIE* (1977) based on Harold Gray's *Little Orphan Annie* series of comics. The musical was filmed by Hollywood in 1982 and for television in 1999. Its Off-Broadway sequel *Annie Warbucks* (1993) failed to catch on. The Off-Broadway musical *Snoopy* (1982) was not nearly as successful as the earlier Schultz show, but it was put on television in 1988. Similarly, *Doonesbury* (1983), based on Garry Trudeau's politically potent comic strip, was not a hit on Broadway but was filmed that same year. Hollywood has long depended on comic strips and pulp heroes for adventure and science fiction movies, from *Blondie* to *Batman*, yet rarely were these action pictures musicals. *Popeye the Sailor Man* had been a comic strip long before it was turned into a series of cartoon shorts, and the film musical *Popeye* (1980) played up the cartoonish aspects of the tales with live actors. Also highly stylized was the screen musical *Dick Tracy* (1990), which made efforts to turn famous actors into cartoon-looking villains. Finally, two Broadway musicals concerned cartoonists in their plots: *Rumple* (1957) dealt with a comic strip with a cartoon character named Rumple (RAY BOLGER) and the Trudeau-like cartoonist Sam in *WOMAN OF THE YEAR* (1981) was known for his Tessie Cat character in the newspapers.

■ COMMITMENTS, THE (United Artists 1991), A low-budget film with a casual, knockabout quality to it, the musical has become a cult favorite and a unique look at small-time hopes and dreams. Based on a novel by Roddy Doyle, the story concerns out-of-work Dubliner Jimmy Rabbitte (Robert Arkins) who forms a band called the Commitments and hires some back-up singers to bring the sound of rock and roll to staid old Dublin. The formation of the group, their struggles to get bookings, the modest success they find, and the break up because of infighting are all handled with humor, honesty, and lack of sentiment. Michael Aherne, Angeline Ball, Maria Doyle Kennedy, Dave Finnegan, Bronagh Gallagher, Felim Gormley, Johnny Murphy, and others are right on target as the restless, confused, but endearing young musicians and singers. Among the songs they performed were "Try a Little

Tenderness," "Bye Bye Baby," "Take Me to the River," "Chain of Fools," and "Treat Me Right." ALAN PARKER directed with a precise eye for the everyday ridiculous behavior of such people.

COMO, PERRY [born Pierto Ronald Como] (1912–2001). Film and television performer. The durable singing star known for his relaxed performance style and cozy, unexciting persona, he was featured in four Hollywood musicals without catching fire but went on to enthrall millions on television. Como was born in Cannonsburg, Pennsylvania, and worked as a barber while he sang in amateur groups. When he went professional, he sang with Ted Weems' band and became popular enough that he was featured in the movie musicals *SOMETHING FOR THE BOYS* (1944), *Doll Face* (1945), *If I'm Lucky* (1946), and *WORDS AND MUSIC* (1948). Moviegoers were only modestly impressed so Como returned to singing in nightclubs and making records. His popular television show premiered in 1948 and for the next three decades he would be a familiar face in his and others' musical programs. Biography: *Dream Along With Me and Perry Como*, Art Vallee (2006).

COMPANY (Alvin Theatre 1970). One of the most innovative and influential musicals of its decade, this concept show by George Furth (book) and STEPHEN SONDHEIM (music and lyrics) paved the way for less-linear, more psychological musicals.

Plot: On his thirty-fifth birthday, Manhattan bachelor Robert is bombarded with memories and images of his married friends and three past girl friends. Looking at the various kinds of marriages and trying to learn from his failed relationships, Robert finally learns that he will have to give into commitment in order to be truly alive.

There was no traditional plotline but instead a series of episodes, scattered in time, and forming a mosaic in which the audience learned about Bobby even as he was putting the pieces together for himself. Scenes overlapped in an expressionistic manner, and characters who had never met each other appeared on the stage at the same time, with past memories and regrets combining into a whole. Producer–director HAROLD PRINCE staged the musical unconventionally as well. The action took place on different levels and at various locales, sometimes merged on scenic designer's Boris Aronson's collage-like setting that used steel, Plexiglas, and projections. MICHAEL BENNETT choreographed and, although there were few conventional dances as such, the whole show moved like a frantic urban ballet. The astonishingly perceptive score was Sondheim's best to date and it had a contemporary sound that forced the show to be timely and relevant. Although the tone of the whole score was one of high-energy tension, there was amazing variety from song to song. The opening title number was a complex collision of voices, whereas the reflective "Sorry–Grateful" was nearly monosyllabic in its simplicity. The ANDREWS SISTERS-like trio "You Can Drive a Person Crazy" had a 1940s sound with a 1970s sensibility, whereas "Side By Side By Side" was an old-fashioned soft-shoe number with a wry subtext. The rapid "Getting Married Today" contrasted nicely with the cautious ballad "Someone Is Waiting." "Barcelona" was an awkward postcoital scene put to music, "The Ladies Who Lunch" had a subtle Latin beat that exploded as it progressed, and the heart-wrenching "Being Alive" was a cry for help that served as an emotional release for Bobby and the audience. The critics recognized *Company* as something new and provocative, and audiences had no trouble enjoying the unusual but satisfying experience for 690 performances. However, neither the press nor the

Broadway Casts for *Company*			
Character	*1970 cast*	*1995 cast*	*2006 cast*
Bobby	Dean Jones	BOYD GAINES	RAÚL ESPARZA
Joanne	ELAINE STRITCH	DEBRA MONK	Barbara Walsh
Sarah	Barbara Barrie	Kate Burton	Kristin Huffman
Harry	Charles Kimbrough	ROBERT WESTENBERG	Keith Buterbaugh
Amy	Beth Howland	Veanne Cox	Heather Laws
Marta	Pamela Myers	La Chanze	Angel Desai
Kathy	DONNA McKECHNIE	Charlotte d'Ambroise	Kelly Jeanne Grant
April	Susan Browning	Jane Krakowski	Elizabeth Stanley
Larry	Charles Braswell	Timothy Lanfield	Bruce Sabath

Company. What little story there was in this compelling musical took place in the hero's head: his memories, regrets, and fears. Dean Jones (foreground) played Bobby, a bachelor with lots of friends but few real connections. Not until he is willing to get entangled with someone does he have a chance of finding happiness. This is not the plot of a traditional musical on Broadway. (Photofest)

Company Musical Numbers

"Company"
"The Little Things You Do Together"
"Sorry–Grateful"
"You Could Drive a Person Crazy"
"Have I Got a Girl for You"
"Someone Is Waiting"
"Another Hundred People"
"Getting Married Today"
"Side By Side By Side"
"What Would We Do Without You?"
"Poor Baby"
"Tick Tock"
"Barcelona"
"The Ladies Who Lunch"
"Being Alive"

a Broadway hit. Inventive nonlinear musicals such as *A CHORUS LINE* (1975) and *JELLY'S LAST JAM* (1992), not to mention Sondheim's own *SUNDAY IN THE PARK WITH GEORGE* (1984) and *ASSASSINS* (1991), would be possible because of what *Company* introduced.

Difficult to revive because the sound and tone of *Company* are so specifically 1970s, the musical has nonetheless received hundreds of productions by professional and amateur groups. Later playgoers (and directors) have found Bobby difficult as well, suggesting that he is gay or that his fear of commitment is hidden in some mysterious subtext. Yet commendable revivals are not that uncommon. *Company* has been revived on Broadway twice. The 1995 ROUNDABOUT THEATRE production, directed by SCOTT ELLIS, received mixed notices for the musical, the production, and even the cast, although BOYD GAINES was a personable Robert. A 2006 mounting, which originated at the Cincinnati Playhouse in the Park, was

public was aware that the show was opening up new possibilities for musical theatre. There had been concept musicals before this one but they had felt experimental; *Company* felt like

more rewarding. Director John Doyle dispensed with scenery and costume changes and played the musical as a group of musicians telling the story, with each cast member playing at least one musical instrument. The concept met with mixed opinions by the press but all agreed that the cast was first rate and that RAUL ESPARZA's Bobby was a revelation, making the character both cynical and vulnerable, charming, and desperate. The Roundabout revival lasted sixty-eight performances, and the Doyle production was extended for 247 performances. The musical was broadcast on PBS-TV in 2008.

CONCEPT MUSICALS. Difficult to define and, consequently, even harder to trace historically, this form of stage musical has sometimes been attributed to any show that is bold and original in some aspect. A better definition might be any musical that puts as much importance on the unique manner of its presentation as on its content. Concept musicals tend to be less linear and more thematic than the usual fare, which suggests that the plays and musicals by Bertolt Brecht might be the source of the genre. Looking specifically at Broadway, many point to *LADY IN THE DARK* (1940) as the granddad of the concept musical. The show was highly expressionistic and took a psychological approach to characters, with the plot being secondary in importance. *ALLEGRO* (1947) was a less successful musical but one that also used a bold method of telling a rather conventional story. *LOVE LIFE* (1948), another box office disappointment, may be the best candidate for the first concept musical; it disregarded the traditional use of time, interrupted its action with jolting vaudeville numbers that commented on the story, and even tried to illustrate sociological ideas by paralleling them to a long-term personal relationship. *WEST SIDE STORY* (1957) has been called a concept musical because of its unique use of dance, but few musicals are more traditional when it comes to plotting and characters. *ANYONE CAN WHISTLE* (1964) was so disarming in its presentation and *HALLELUJAH, BABY!* (1967) was so all-encompassing in its scope that they have also been pointed out as fledging concept shows. The allegorical *CELEBRATION* (1969) was similarly offbeat and unconventional; the fact that all three shows failed at the box office was also indicative of something conceptual.

Wherever it may have come from, the concept musical truly arrived with *COMPANY* (1970), a musical that managed to be palatable to audiences even as it broke just about every rule of musical comedy. *Company* was expressionistic and psychological, it played around with time and place, and it was unabashedly contemporary. The show was successful in its own right but, more importantly, it opened doors for similarly adventurous musicals: *GODSPELL* (1971), *FOLLIES* (1971), *A CHORUS LINE* (1975), *CHICAGO* (1975), *PACIFIC OVERTURES* (1976), *EVITA* (1979), *NINE* (1982), *GRAND HOTEL* (1989), *ASSASSINS* (1990), *JELLY'S LAST JAM* (1992), *TOMMY* (1993), *RENT* (1996), *FLOYD COLLINS* (1996), *BRING IN 'DA NOISE BRING IN 'DA FUNK* (1996), *HEDWIG AND THE ANGRY INCH* (1998), *THE WILD PARTY* (2000), *SEUSSICAL* (2000), *URINETOWN* (2001), *MOVIN' OUT* (2002), *CAROLINE, OR CHANGE* (2004), *SPRING AWAKENING* (2006), and others. Some of the techniques of the concept musical would work their way into even traditional, escapist Broadway musicals, such as *BARNUM* (1980), *THE WILL ROGERS FOLLIES* (1991), *JERSEY BOYS* (2005), and *TARZAN* (2006). One only has to look at the titles just listed and see that very few of them have been made into movies to understand Hollywood's resistance to concept musicals. Film tends to be a realistic medium and these shows do not want to look and sound like real life. All the same, some movie concept musicals have been made. How else to describe such films as *TOMMY* (1975), *THE ROCKY HORROR PICTURE SHOW* (1975), *ALL THAT JAZZ* (1980), *PENNIES FROM HEAVEN* (1981), *THE NIGHTMARE BEFORE CHRISTMAS* (1993), *MOULIN ROUGE* (2001), and *ACROSS THE UNIVERSE* (2007)? Where the concept musical is heading and what form it will take next is anybody's guess; its unpredictability and tendency to surprise are among its strongest elements.

CONEY ISLAND (Fox 1943). BETTY GRABLE, at the peak of her popularity with movie audiences stateside and with GIs overseas, was showcased in this period musical filled with pleasant songs and performances. George Seaton's screenplay centers on saloon singer Kate Farley (Grable) at the turn-of-the-century amusement park of the title. Two business rivals, con man Eddie Johnson (George Montgomery) and slick promoter Joe Rocco (CESAR ROMERO), each want to manage Kate, but she has set her sights on someday playing the big time at Hammerstein's Broadway theatre. Complications are doubled when both men fall in love with her as well and try to sabotage the other's chances for winning her. The sprightly supporting cast included

CHARLES WINNINGER, PHIL SILVERS, Matt Briggs, Paul Hurst, and Leo Diamond. Several old standards from the period were dusted off for the score, such as "Cuddle Up a Little Closer," "The Darktown Strutters' Ball," "Pretty Baby," and "Put Your Arms Around Me, Honey," and RALPH RAINGER (music) and LEO ROBIN (lyrics) supplied such new pastiche numbers such as "Take It From There," "Lulu From Louisville," and the elaborate finale "There's Danger in Dance," which HERMES PAN choreographed with dozens of chorus couples illustrating the perils of passionate dancing through the ages. WALTER LANG directed the WILLIAM PERLBERG production and, with no small thanks to Grable, it was a big hit. Seven years later both 20TH CENTURY-FOX and Grable returned to the property and called it **Wabash Avenue** (Fox 1950). The new screenplay by Charles Lederer and Harry Tugend was set in Chicago during the 1892 World's Fair. Grable was a shimmy dancer named Ruby Summers in a Windy City dive, and the men fighting over her this time were Andy Clark (VICTOR MATURE) and Mike Stanley (PHIL HARRIS). The supporting cast was as impressive as in the earlier feature: REGINALD GARDINER, MARGARET HAMILTON, JAMES BARTON, Barry Kelley, and Jacqueline Dalya. The old ditty "I Wish I Could Shimmy Like My Sister Kate" was revived, and Josef Myrow (music) and MACK GORDON (lyrics) wrote several new songs, such as "Baby, Won't You Say You Love Me?," "Walking Along With Billy," "Wilhellmina," and "Down on Wabash Avenue." Perlberg again produced, HENRY KOSTER directed, and Billy Daniels choreographed. Although Grable's popularity was not as strong as in the war years, the remake did good business.

CONNECTICUT YANKEE, A (Vanderbilt Theatre 1927). The only RICHARD RODGERS (music) and LORENZ HART (lyrics) show from the 1920s that is still revived on occasion, the musical had a solid libretto by HERBERT FIELDS based on Mark Twain's fable *A Connecticut Yankee in King Arthur's Court*. On the eve of his wedding in Hartford, Connecticut, Martin is clobbered on the head with a champagne bottle by his fiancée Fay Morgan for flirting with Alice, sending him into an unconscious stupor where he dreams he is back in Camelot in 528 AD. King Arthur, the magician Merlin, and others in the court are suspicious of the oddly dressed stranger and plan to burn him at the stake until Martin recalls a bit of astronomy and correctly predicts an eclipse of the sun. Greatly impressed, the citizens of Camelot dub Martin "Sir Boss" and watch amazed as he introduces a radio, telephone, and other twentieth-century wonders to the Middle Ages. Most impressed is the Lady Alisandre who is falling in love with Martin; least impressed is the sorceress Morgan le Fay who plots to destroy the alien. She almost succeeds in doing so, but Martin awakes from his dream, realizes he doesn't love Fay, and pursues Alice for a happy ending.

The script's premise was ripe for opportunities to make fun of modern idioms and ideas in a medieval setting. Fields' libretto was joked filled but never strayed far from the central story. The Rodgers and Hart score was a sparkling mixture of medieval touches, 1920s jazz, archaic phrases, and modern slang, as indicated in the title "Thou Swell." The biggest hit from the show was "My Heart Stood Still" (which had been introduced earlier that year in London) and also enjoyable were "On a Desert Island With Thee," "I Feel at Home With You," and "Evelyn, What Do You Say?" Produced by LEW FIELDS and Lyle D. Andrews, directed by ALEXANDER LEFTWICH, and choreographed by BUSBY BERKELEY, the musical ran 418 performances on Broadway, becoming one of the team's biggest hits, and then it toured extensively. A dozen years later, during the last days of his collaboration with Hart, Rodgers was looking for a project that his

Broadway Casts for *A Connecticut Yankee*

Character	1927 cast	1943 cast
Martin	WILLIAM GAXTON	DICK FORAN
Alisandre	Constance Carpenter	Julie Warren
Morgan Le Fay	Nana Bryant	VIVIENNE SEGAL
King Arthur	Paul Everton	ROBERT CHISHOLM
Sir Galahad	Jack Thompson	Chester Stratton
Evelyn	June Cochrane	VERA-ELLEN
Merlin	William Norris	Kohn Cherry

unreliable partner could handle and suggested reviving *A Connecticut Yankee*. Hart agreed and together they wrote five new songs for the 1943 revival, which Rodgers produced himself. The book was updated to wartime America with Martin and his friends in the military and the jokes and idioms were brought up to date as well. VIVIENNE SEGAL was Fay/Morgan de Fay and got to sing the best of the new songs, the diabolical comedy number "To Keep My Love Alive." The merry song about how Morgan le Fay had bumped off all of her husbands was the last lyric Hart ever wrote, yet is was as fresh and sassy as any in his prodigious but short career. The reviews were very laudatory so it was disappointing that the revival ran only 135 performances. It was the last Broadway entry by the team; Hart died a few days after it opened. ❑ A condensed adaptation of the Rodgers and Hart's *A Connecticut Yankee* was seen on NBC-TV in 1955 as an entry in the program *Max Liebman Presents*. EDDIE ALBERT was Martin, JANET BLAIR played Alisandre, Gale Sherwood was Morgan le Fay, and Boris Karloff portrayed King Arthur.

🎬 **Connecticut Yankee in King Arthur's Court** (Paramount 1949) was also based on Twain's tale but offered a different script and a new score by JAMES VAN HEUSEN (music) and JOHNNY BURKE (lyrics). Edmund Beloin's screenplay was set in 1912 Connecticut where the singing blacksmith Hank Martin (BING CROSBY) is bumped on the head and dreams he is in Camelot. He befriends a bumbling Sir Sagimore (William Bendix), helps King Arthur (Cedric Hardwicke), and falls for redheaded Lady Alisande (Rhonda Fleming). Although Martin had to outwit the villains Merlin (Murvyn Vye) and Morgan Le Faye (Virginia Field), the complications were rather low key, as was the soothing crooning by Crosby who sang the optimistic "If You Stub Your Toe on the Moon," the genial "Busy Doing Nothing," and the love duet "Once and for Always." The film is one of Crosby's few period pieces and he looks more comfortable in medieval garb than he did in some of his other costume musicals. Tay Garnett directed the lavish yet tasteful production and it is still very enjoyable.

CONNELL, JANE [born Jane Sperry Bennett] (1926–). Stage, television, and film performer. The tiny character actress with a giant, squeaking voice became a Broadway favorite late in her career. Connell was born in Berkeley, California, and attended the local university before getting years of experience in stock and in nightclubs. She was thirty years old when she made her Broadway debut in *Shoestring Revue* (1955) and later that year gained recognition as the crafty Mrs. Peachum in the long-running Off Broadway production of THE THREEPENNY OPERA (1955). Connell was Princess Winifred in the original London production of ONCE UPON A MATTRESS (1960) and appeared in a series of musicals on and Off Broadway, including NEW FACES OF '56, THE GOLDEN APPLE (1962), *No Shoestrings* (1962), and *Drat! The Cat!* (1965) and then won praise for her introverted governess Miss Gooch in MAME (1966), a role she repeated on tour, in stock, in revival, and in the 1974 film. Her other musical roles were the delightfully insane Gabrielle in DEAR WORLD (1969), the aghast Duchess in ME AND MY GIRL (1986), the overbearing mother in CRAZY FOR YOU (1992), and the Widow Douglas in *The Adventures of Tom Sawyer* (2001), as well as a replacement for piano player Jeanette Burmeiter in THE FULL MONTY (2002). Connell has stolen the show in a few Broadway comedies as well and has appeared in a handful of films and television shows.

CONNOLLY, [Robert] **BOBBY** (1895–1944). Stage and film choreographer. A very busy Broadway and Hollywood choreographer, he was known for his appealing, toe-tapping dances. Connolly was born in Encino, California, and was dancing on Broadway by 1920. He made his choreography debut in 1926, had his first hit later that year with THE DESERT SONG, and the next year had all of New York tapping to "The Varsity Drag" and other peppy numbers from GOOD NEWS! His other stage credits include FUNNY FACE (1927), THE NEW MOON (1928), *Treasure Girl* (1928), FOLLOW THRU (1929), *Spring Is Here* (1929), FLYING HIGH (1930), *America's Sweetheart* (1931), *Free for All* (1931), *Hot-Cha!* (1932), and TAKE A CHANCE (1932), as well as two editions of the ZIEGFELD FOLLIES. With the waning of Broadway musicals during the Depression, Connolly went to Hollywood where he choreographed over thirty movie musicals in the 1930s and 1940s, including *Moonlight and Pretzels* (1933), *Flirtation Walk* (1934), SWEET ADELINE (1935), GO INTO YOUR DANCE (1935), *The Singing Kid* (1936), *Ready, Willing and Able* (1937), *Fools for Scandal* (1938), *Honolulu* (1939), THE WIZARD OF OZ (1939), AT THE CIRCUS (1939), BROADWAY MELODY OF 1940, TWO GIRLS ON BROADWAY (1940), *Ship Ahoy* (1942), FOR ME AND MY GIRL (1942), and *I Dood It* (1943). He was not an innovative choreographer but an endlessly resourceful one who kept his dances lively and contagious.

CONRAD, CON [born Conrad K. Dober] (1891–1938). Film and stage composer. A Tin Pan Alley and Broadway composer who was one of the first to go to Hollywood and write for the talkies, he wrote "The Continental," the first song to win an Academy Award. Conrad was born in New York and educated at a military academy before working as a pianist in vaudeville and silent film houses. He turned to performing briefly but found more success writing songs that became hits, such as "Barney Google," "Ma, He's Making Eyes at Me," and "Prisoner of Love." His songs were heard in the Broadway musicals *Greenwich Village Follies* (1923), *Moonlight* (1924), *ARTISTS AND MODELS* (1924), *Mercenary Mary* (1925), *Kitty's Kisses* (1926), *Americana* (1926), and *Take the Air* (1927) before he went to Hollywood at the beginning of the sound era. With various lyricists he scored the early musicals *Fox Movietone Follies* (1929), *Broadway* (1929), *The Cockeyed World* (1929), *Happy Days* (1929), *Let's Go Places* (1930), *Movietone Follies of 1930*, *The Gift of Gab* (1934), *THE GAY DIVORCEE* (1934), and *Reckless* (1935). Among his many song hits are "Margie," "You've Got to See Mama Every Night," and "Singin' the Blues Till My Daddy Comes Home."

CONREID, HANS (1917–1982). Stage, film, and television performer. A versatile character actor who played a variety of foreign types, from snarling Nazis to finicky Brits, the thin and beady-eyed comic added a dash of spice to several musicals. Conreid was born in Baltimore and educated at Columbia University and then began his acting career on the radio with Orson Welles' Mercury Theatre Company. He made his film debut in 1938 and was quickly typecast as eccentric supporting characters, although he was also exceptional in the leading role of the diabolical piano teacher Terwilliger in the musical *THE 5,000 FINGERS OF DR. T* (1953). Among his other musical credits are *BITTER SWEET* (1940), *Crazy House* (1943) *ON THE TOWN* (1949), *THE BARKLEYS OF BROADWAY* (1949), *Nancy Goes to Rio* (1950), *SUMMER STOCK* (1950), *I'll See You in My Dreams* (1951), *Texas Carnival* (1951), *Rich, Young and Pretty* (1951), *Rock-a-Bye Baby* (1958), and *ROBIN AND THE SEVEN HOODS* (1964). He also shone on many radio shows and on Broadway as the artist Boris in *CAN-CAN* (1953). Conreid was very active on television, appearing in dozens of programs, most memorably as a regular on *The Danny Thomas Show*, and in the TV musicals *Manhattan Tower* (1956), *HIGH TOR* (1956), *HANSEL AND GRETEL* (1958), *FEATHERTOP* (1961), and *The Royal Follies of 1933* (1967) and in the small screen version of *KISMET* (1967). He has lent his voice to many cartoons and animated films, most memorably as the voice of Captain Hook in *PETER PAN* (1953) and that of the villain Snidley Whiplash on *The Bullwinkle Show*. Conreid was still performing on television within a few weeks of his death.

CONTACT (Vivian Beaumont Theatre 2000). A dance musical triptych that was not typical Broadway fare, it ended up being a giant hit at 1,010 performances. Choreographer SUSAN STROMAN conceived and staged the unusual entertainment written by JOHN WEIDMAN (although there was hardly any dialogue) that consisted of three tales told mostly in dance and using recordings of classical and pop standards as the score. An aristocrat (Séan Martin Huingston) disguises himself as his own servant (Scott Taylor) in order to frolic with a lady (Stephanie Michels) on a swing; the abused wife (KAREN ZIEMBA) of a mobster escapes into a fantasy world while dining at an Italian restaurant; and a suicidal man (BOYD GAINES) chases an elusive girl (Deborah Yates) about town only to discover that she lives in the apartment above his. Although there was no singing and the characters were sketches at best, most critics recommended the entertainment for its dancing and playgoers took their advice for two and a half years. The LINCOLN CENTER THEATRE production premiered in their Off Broadway downstairs space and then moved upstairs to their larger Broadway venue after the show caught on. ❑ A performance of *Contact* was broadcast live on the PBS-TV program *Live From Lincoln Center* in 2002, and the tape is a vivid record of the production.

CONVY, BERT [born Bernard Whalen Convy] (1934–1991). Stage and television performer. The busy television celebrity who appeared in sit-coms, quiz shows, and original dramas began as the juvenile lead in Broadway musicals. A native of St. Louis who grew up in southern California, Convy was a professional baseball player for the Philadelphia Phillies's farm team until 1957 when he started acting in stock companies. Two years later he made his Broadway debut in *Billy Barnes Revue* (1959), followed by the musicals *Vintage '60* (1960), *No Where to Go But Up* (1962), *The Beast in Me*

(1963), and a replacement for El Gallo in *THE FANTASTICKS* (1963). Convy then got to originate two of the musical theatre's finest juvenile roles, the radical Russian Perchik in *FIDDLER ON THE ROOF* (1964) and the American writer Cliff Bradshaw in *CABARET* (1966). By the end of the decade he left the stage to concentrate on television where he was a familiar favorite for the next twenty years. Convy returned to Broadway as a replacement for film director Guido Contini in *NINE* (1983). He died of a brain tumor at the age of fifty-seven.

COOK, BARBARA (1927–). Stage and television performer. One of the finest voices ever to grace the Broadway stage, she had only one major Broadway success but has remained a star over the years through her appearances in revivals, concerts, and recordings. A native of Atlanta, Georgia, Cook had no professional experience when she went to New York and got her first job on Broadway as the ingénue Sandy in the offbeat musical *FLAHOOLEY* (1951). Her only Broadway hit was *The Music Man* (1957),

Barbara Cook. It's one thing to be caught in a string of Broadway flops; it's quite another to light up the stage each time. In addition to an astounding singing voice, Cook has a stage presence that is unmistakable. Here she is in her shortest run, the musical *Something More!* (1964). (Photofest)

in which she originated the role of the librarian Marian Paroo. The rest of Cook's stage credits were in admired musicals that failed to have long runs, such as *PLAIN AND FANCY* (1955), *CANDIDE* (1956), *The Gay Life* (1960), *SHE LOVES ME* (1963), *Something More!* (1964), and *THE GRASS HARP* (1971). She had more success with Broadway revivals, playing Carrie in the 1954 and Julie in the 1957 revivals of *CAROUSEL*, Anna in the 1960 Broadway production of *THE KING AND I*, and Magnolia in the 1966 revival of *SHOW BOAT*. By the mid-1970s, her weight and her string of short runs led Cook to a second and equally celebrated career in concerts, cabarets, and nightclubs. Cook acted in a few nonmusicals in New York and was featured in the musical *Carrie* in London in 1987. She also was featured in two original TV musicals, *HANSEL AND GRETEL* (1958) and *O'Halloran's Luck* (1961). Cook returned to Broadway in a series of one-woman concert shows that were sellouts. She has recorded extensively and is considered one of the greatest interpreters of theatre songs and standards. Because of her superlative voice, engaging stage persona, and history with ambitious musicals, Cook has grown into a theatre legend with a popularity matched only by the Broadway greats.

COOK, JOE [born Joseph Lopez] (1890–1959). Stage and film performer. A much-loved comic on vaudeville, Broadway, and London stages, he was a unique clown with his wide-mouthed innocent look as he juggled or explained his oddball inventions. Cook was born in Evansville, Indiana, where he quit school to join a traveling show when he was twelve. Later he and his brother had a juggling act on the vaudeville circuit, which brought them to New York in 1907. But it was as a solo act that Cook became famous, performing his comic monologues in such Broadway revues as *Hitchy-Koo* (1919), *EARL CARROLL VANITIES* (1923, 1924, 1925), and *It Happens on Ice* (1940). He also shone in some book musicals, most memorably as Joe Squibb, the incompetent factory manager in *FINE AND DANDY* (1930). Cook's other musical credits include *Rain or Shine* (1928) and *Hold Your Horses* (19333), as well as *Fanfare* (1932) and other shows in London. He wrote and performed a few comedy film shorts in the 1930s and reprised his stage performance in the movie *Rain or Shine* (1930).

COOPER, MARILYN (1936–). Stage and television performer. The dowdy character actress, who has appeared in Broadway musicals for over forty years, has stolen the show on many occasions. A native New Yorker who was educated at New York University, Cooper made her Broadway debut in MR. WONDERFUL (1956) and soon had featured roles in such popular shows as WEST SIDE STORY (1957), GYPSY (1959), MAME (1969), ON THE TOWN (1971), and GREASE (1997), but she is perhaps best remembered as the bedraggled housewife Jan Donovan in WOMAN OF THE YEAR (1981). Her other musical credits include I CAN GET IT FOR YOU WHOLESALE (1962), HALLELUJAH, BABY! (1967), Golden Rainbow (1968), TWO BY TWO (1970), BALLROOM (1978), Cafe Crown (1989), and The Petrified Prince (1994). She has also acted in comedies on Broadway, on television, and in a handful of films.

COP ROCK. See THAT'S LIFE

☐ **COPACABANA** (CBS-TV 1985). Singer–songwriter Barry Manilow's 1978 song "Copacabana" was atypical for a pop hit in that it used a Latin–disco beat and was a narrative ballad telling the story of pianist Tony who loves but loses the Copa singer Lola. The musical tale was expanded into a two-hour musical pastiche by James Lipton with a score by Bruce Sussman and Jack Feldman that captured the 1940s in a silly but affectionate way. Manilow himself played Tony, Annette O'Toole was Lola, and Joseph Bologna was the Havana club owner Rico Castelli who comes between the two. Also cast were Estelle Getty, Ernie Sabella, James T. Callahjan, Cliff Osmond, Silvana Gallardo, and Dwier Brown. Among the new songs written for the broadcast were "Let's Go Steppin'," "Call Me Mr. Lucky," "Big City Blues," "Who Needs to Dream," and "Aye Caramba." Manilow made one of the very few acting appearances of his long career and one doesn't need to be a fan to enjoy his goofy, likable Tony. While the Dick Clark-produced musical spoofed the 1940s film musicals that were heavy on South American characters and color, there was an affection for the old genre as well. Waris Hussein directed and Grover Dale choreographed.

📖 **CORDELIA'S ASPIRATIONS** (Theatre Comique 1883). Generally acknowledged to be the best of the Harrigan and Hart musical farces, this slapstick show featured the recurring Mulligan family, Irish immigrants who have settled in the brawling neighborhoods of Manhattan at the end of the nineteenth century. In EDWARD HARRIGAN's script, the young wife Cordelia

Mulligan (Annie Yeamans) has illusions of grandeur and forces her happy husband Dan (Harrigan) to leave their ghetto home and move uptown where she puts on pretensions of class. When she is tricked by her unscrupulous brother Planxty (H. A. Fisher) into signing away all her money to him, Cordelia despairs and takes poison, only to learn that the bottle belongs to the maid Rebecca Allup (TONY HART) and is filled with booze. Cordelia gives up her aspirations and she and Dan move back downtown. Harrigan wrote the lyrics for DAVID BRAHAM's music, and the score included the risible songs "Dad's Dinner Pail" and "Mulligan Guard's March." The rough and tumble musical ran 176 performances.

COSLOW, SAM[son] (1902–1982). Film and stage lyricist and composer. Usually working with composer ARTHUR JOHNSTON, the Tin Pan Alley songwriter scored two dozen film musicals and wrote plenty of song standards. The native New Yorker wrote lyrics (and sometimes music as well) for a publishing company he co-founded. Coslow's songs were used on Broadway in ARTISTS AND MODELS (1924) and in the early movie musicals Dance of Life (1929), THE VAGABOND KING (1930), Honey (1930), This Is the Night (1932), and Blonde Venus (1932). He teamed up with composer Johnston for the first time for Hello, Everybody (1933), and the two went on to score College Humor (1933), Too Much Harmony (1933), Murder at the Vanities (1934), Many Happy Returns (1934), and Belle of the Nineties (1934). Coslow wrote music and lyrics for the movies All the King's Men (1935), Turn Off the Moon (1937), Mountain Music (1937), Out of This World (1945), and Copacabana (1947) and provided lyrics for various composers for Coronado (1935), Goin' to Town (1935), Thrill of a Lifetime (1937), This Way Please (1937), Every Day's a Holiday (1937), Love on Toast (1938), and You and Me (1938). Among his many popular songs are "Cocktails for Two," "My Old Flame," "Just One More Chance," and "Sing You Sinners." Autobiography: Cocktails for Two (1977).

COSTELLO, LOU. See ABBOTT and COSTELLO

■ **COTTON CLUB, THE** (Orion 1984). Because it was one of the most talked about movies that year (mainly about how its cost escalated to $47 million), the finished picture was a disappointment and a financial dud. However, the musical melodrama had some thrilling moments and there were some first-rate performances amidst all the clutter. The screenplay by William Kennedy, Mario Puzo, and director Francis Ford Coppola centered on the rivalry between gangsters Dutch Schultz (James Remar) and Owney Madden (Bob Hoskins) and was set in Harlem's Cotton Club between 1928 and 1931 when the celebrated nightclub featured African American talent on stage but the patrons were strictly white. Into this fact-based gangland war are the white cornet player Dixie Dwyer (Richard Gere) trying to break into the all-black entertainment and African American hoofer Sandman Williams (GREGORY HINES) trying to break into Broadway. The love interests for the two men were Vera Cicero (Diane Lane) and Lila Rose Oliver (Lonette McKee), and the supporting cast of characters was one of the most impressive of the decade, with appearances by Nicholas Cage, Fred Gwynne, GWEN VERDON, MAURICE HINES, Julian Beck, Diana Venora, Woody Strode, Larry Fishburne, Jennifer Grey, Giancarlo Eposito, LARRY MARSHALL, and Charles "Honi" Coles. The songs were all period standards and presented as Cotton Club numbers, although none was shown in its entirety. Gregory Hines, Henry LeTang, and MICHAEL SHUIN choreographed them with panache and added to the feverish tone of the film. "Crazy Rhythm," "Am I Blue?," "Doin' the New Low-Down," "Copper-Colored Gal," and "Minnie the Moocher" were among the songs that sprung to life in a setting where most were first heard. Coppolo captured the Roaring Twenties and the Harlem milieu beautifully, even if the plotting was sometimes a mess and the relationships throughout were rather disjoined. Robert Evans produced the problematic but intriguing musical.

COUNTESS MARITZA (Shubert Theatre 1926). A European operetta by the popular composer EMMERICH KALMAN, this was one of the few such imports that retained the original score when it was produced on Broadway. HARRY B. SMITH adapted the Hungarian script about the wealthy Countess Maritza (Yvonne D'Arle) who is surrounded by fortune hunters but truly loved by the impoverished Count Tassilo (Walter Woolf). He disguises himself as an overseer on the countess' estate and sings rustic folk songs with the peasant workers, thereby getting her attention. The countess discovers the count's true identity and dismisses him but, once she realizes his love is sincere, apologizes by letter and the two are united.

Smith also wrote the lyrics for Kalman's music, and the hit of the operetta was "Play, Gypsies—Dance, Gypsies." Also in the score were "I'll Keep on Dreaming," "The Call of Love," and "The One I'm Looking For." J. C. HUFFMAN directed the SHUBERT production and it ran a very profitable 321 performances, followed by a revival in 1928 and many regional productions by light opera companies.

COUNTRY GIRL, THE (Paramount 1954). A melodrama masquerading as a musical (or vice versa), this movie, based on the powerful 1950 Clifford Odets play, had only four songs but they were intrinsic to the action. Director-screenwriter George Seaton changed the play from a story of an alcoholic, unemployable actor trying for a comeback to one about has-been singer Frank Elgin (BING CROSBY) who is cast in a Broadway musical, but many of the dynamics stayed the same. His put-upon wife Georgie (Grace Kelly) builds him up even as she keeps reminding him of his failed past and, when she starts to fall in love with the show's director Bernie Dodd (William Holden), the situation becomes so tense that Frank starts drinking again, only to pull himself together and make a new start. Crosby was given the most challenging role of his career and came through beautifully, not depending on his singing to carry the picture. He did croon the quartet of songs that HAROLD ARLEN (music) and IRA GERSHWIN (lyrics) wrote for the film—"It's Mine, It's Yours," "The Search Is Through," "Dissertation on the State of Bliss" (aka "Love and Learn"), and "The Land Around Us"—so his fans were appeased.

COURT JESTER, THE (Paramount 1965). One of DANNY KAYE's best vehicles, the period musical allowed him to clown around in song and dialogue, both of which were sparkling. MELVIN FRANK and Norman Panama produced, directed, and wrote the silly screenplay about the medieval potboy Hubert Hawkins (Kaye) who disguises himself as a jester to break into the court ruled by Sir Ravenhurst (Basil Rathbone) and help the mysterious Black Fox (Edward Ashley) regain the throne. While inside, he dallies with the Princess Gwendolyn (ANGELA LANSBURY) and the maid Jean (Glynis Johns) and finds time to engage in a hysterical verbal exchange with Lady Griselda (Mildred Natwick) as she explains to him that "the pellet with the poison is in the vessel with the pestle." Also joining the raucous fun were Cecil Parker, John Carradine, Robert Middleton, Michael

Pate, Herbert Rudley, and Noel Drayton. The songs by Sylvia Fine (music) and SAMMY CAHN (music) were designed to show off Kaye's considerable talents, from the cockeyed "Maladjusted Jester" to the lovely ballad "I'll Take You Dreaming." The other songs were "Outfox the Fox," "Life Could Not Better Be," and "My Heart Knows a Love Song."

■ COVER GIRL (Columbia 1944). Intended as another showcase for RITA HAYWORTH, the musical was dominated by the up-and-coming GENE KELLY, proving to be a better actor and more versatile dancer than previously seen. Paul Gangelin and Marion Parsonnet wrote the screenplay about dancer Rusty Parker (Hayworth, singing dubbed by Martha Mears) who works in a Brooklyn nightclub run by Danny McGuire (Kelly) but she dreams of moving into the big time. Danny is in love with her and, with his sidekick Genius (PHIL SILVERS), do what they can to promote Rusty's career. When she wins a contest to be the cover girl for a popular magazine, Rusty becomes famous, forgets her old friends, and nearly marries the Broadway producer Noel Wheaton (Lee Bowman) before coming to her senses and returning to her Brooklyn buddies. In one section of the movie, the magazine publisher John Coudair (Otto Kruger) recalls Rusty's grandmother Maribelle Hicks whom he idolized and Hayworth got to play her in a flashback, singing "Sure Thing." JEROME KERN (music) and IRA GERSHWIN (lyrics) wrote the score, which also included "Put Me to the Test," "Make Way for Tomorrow" (lyric by E. Y. HARBURG), and the hit ballad "Long Ago and Far Away." The film boasts two memorable production numbers. While the chorus sang the title number, Hayworth ran down a seemingly endless ramp, her hair and dress blowing seductively, a scene ripe for parody over the years. More impressive was Kelly's *pas de deux* with his alter ego as he scampered down a lonely Brooklyn street. CHARLES VIDOR directed, ARTHUR SCHWARTZ produced, and SEYMOUR FELIX and Val Rasset were the credited choreographers; Kelly and Stanley Donen devised the "alter ego" number themselves.

COWARD, NOEL [Pierce] (1899–1973). Stage, film, and television performer, playwright, songwriter, and director. The multitalented artist, whose very name conjures up images of sophisticated and witty theatre, was one of the most popular Brits in America. Coward was born in Teddington, England, the son of a piano

salesman, and raised in Surrey where he went on the variety stage as a boy. He first received acclaim as a songwriter and playwright and then became a familiar and much-loved figure performing on the stage. Most of Coward's plays transferred successfully to America but only a handful of his London musicals reached Broadway, such as *This Year of Grace* (1928), *BITTER SWEET* (1929), *Conversation Piece* (1934), *Tonight at 8:30* (1936), and *Set to Music* (1939). His musicals *Sail Away* (1961) and *The Girl Who Came to Supper* (1963) premiered in New York and he directed *High Spirits* (1964), the musical version of his popular play *Blithe Spirit*. Coward appeared in several of his plays and musicals on Broadway, and he was seen in a number of nonmusical films from both Hollywood and Great Britain. He also appeared in nightclubs and on American television specials, such as the TV musical *ANDROCLES AND THE LION* (1967). Autobiographies: *Present Indicative* (1937); *Future Indefinite* (1954); *Past Conditional* (1986); biographies: *A Talent to Amuse*, Sheridan Morley (1969); *Remembered Laughter: The Life of Noel Coward*, Cole Lesley (1976); *Noel Coward: A Biography*, Philip Hoare (1998).

🖎 CRADLE WILL ROCK, THE (Windsor Theatre 1938). A legendary play-with-songs production that is as famous for its opening night as it is for itself. MARC BLITZSTEIN wrote the score and the libretto that was set in Steeletown, U.S.A., a city run by Mr. Mister (Will Geer) for the benefit of himself and his spoiled family. He controls the press, overrides the church, and rules everything through his own Liberty Committee. The upstanding labor organizer Larry Foreman (HOWARD DA SILVA) leads the steelworkers in a revolt and topples Mister and his gang. Also in the original cast were Olive Stanton, HIRAM SHERMAN, Blanche Collins, Peggy Coudray, and John Adair. One of the most controversial works of the decade, the leftist musical parable was produced by the Federal Theatre Project, but just before it was to open on Broadway at the Maxine Elliott Theatre, pressure from the government forced its cancellation and an injunction was put on its actors. Director Orson Welles booked the small Venice Theatre Off Broadway and marched the opening night audience to it where the musical was performed without scenery or costumes with the cast performing from their seats in the audience and Blitzstein accompanying them on a piano. The excitement of the unique, passionate opening night prompted Welles to move the show to the Mercury Theatre for a series of Sunday evenings and then regular performances began, the actors now on stage but the bare-bones production still on an empty stage. Blitzstein's songs were powerful commentaries on the situation rather than traditional musical theatre numbers. "Nickle Under the Foot," "The Freedom of the Press," "The Rich," "Joe Worker," "Art for Art's Sake," and the title song were among the most memorable musical moments. Critics and several audience members thought the piece a simpleminded rant with clumsy writing and tuneless songs, but the vibrant cast and the electricity the whole experience conjured up each night was strong enough to attract playgoers for 108 performances. ALFRED DRAKE starred as Larry Foreman, and Will Geer reprised his Mr. Mister in a 1947 Broadway revival directed by Howard Da Silva, the original Foreman. Also in the cast were VIVIAN VANCE, Muriel Smith, David Thomas, Jesse White, and Jack Albertson. The production ran thirty-four performances. *The Cradle Will Rock* is revived by colleges and regional theatres on occasion but usually proves more interesting historically than theatrically. ▨ The 1999 film *The Cradle Will Rock* by Touchstone Pictures was more about the circumstances leading up to the opening night of the 1938 production. The screenplay by director Tim Robbins mixes fact and fiction, yet the movie is an interesting depiction of the times. Scenes from the musical were shown near the end of the film.

CRAIN, JEANNE (1925–2003). Film and television performer. An attractive girl-next-door movie star, she appeared in several musicals, although she could not sing and was always dubbed. Crain was born in Barstow, California, the daughter of a high school English teacher, and studied acting at the University of California at Los Angeles. After winning a beauty contest at the age of sixteen, she turned to modeling with great success. Hollywood signed her in 1943 and she made her film debut in a bit part in the musical THE GANG'S ALL HERE. Two years later she enchanted moviegoers with her fresh, engaging performance as farm girl Margy Frake in the musical STATE FAIR (1945) where she introduced "It Might as Well Be Spring" using Louanne Hogan's singing voice. Crain's subsequent musicals included CENTENNIAL SUMMER (1946), *Margie* (1946), *You Were Meant for Me* (1948), *Gentlemen Marry Brunettes* (1955), *The Second Greatest Sex* (1955), and THE JOKER IS

WILD (1957). She was equally popular in light comedies and melodramas, such as *Apartment for Peggy* (1948), *A Letter to Three Wives* (1949), *Pinky* (1949), and *O. Henry's Full House* (1952). Crain appeared on television in a handful of series, dramas, and specials, such as the 1959 TV version of the musical MEET ME IN ST. LOUIS. Her popularity waned in the 1960s, although she made occasional screen appearances into the 1970s.

CRAWFORD, CHERYL (1902–1986). Stage producer and director. An ambitious independent producer and proponent of repertory theatre, she presented a variety of noteworthy musicals on Broadway. Crawford was born in Albany, New York, and was educated at Smith College where she directed plays. She began her career working for the prestigious THEATRE GUILD and was one of the founders of the radical Group Theatre for whom she directed plays. Crawford struck out on her own as a producer in the early 1940s and gained recognition for the well-received 1942 revival of PORGY AND BESS. Among her musical offerings were ONE TOUCH OF VENUS (1943), BRIGADOON (1947), LOVE LIFE (1948), REGINA (1949), FLAHOOLEY (1951), PAINT YOUR WAGON (1951), *Jennie* (1963), and CELEBRATION (1969). She was a founder of the short-lived American Repertory Theatre, a founder of the Actors' Studio, and the director of the American National Theatre and Academy play series. Because many of Crawford's productions were uncommercial and challenging, she had only a few hits. But she was all the more respected for her good taste and high expectations. Autobiography: *One Naked Individual: My Fifty Years in the Theatre* (1977).

CRAWFORD, JOAN [born Lucille Fay LeSueur] (1904–1977). Film performer. The glamorous, often mannered, frequently imitated movie star, her long and varied career included seven movie musicals. Crawford was born in San Antonio, Texas, and began her career as a Charleston dancer, winning contests and getting bookings in nightclubs. While appearing in the chorus of the Broadway musicals *Innocent Eyes* (1924) and THE PASSING SHOW (1924), she was spotted by a Hollywood agent who put her on screen as a flapper in silent films. The bright-eyed, wide-lipped beauty caught on and was a star even before sound came in and audiences got to hear her alluring speaking voice. Crawford was featured in the movie musicals HOLLYWOOD REVUE OF 1929, DANCING

LADY (1933), *Sadie McKee* (1934), *Ice Follies of 1939*, HOLLYWOOD CANTEEN (1944), *It's a Great Feeling* (1949), and *Torch Song* (1953). Since she was most loved for her melodramatic roles, often playing ambitious gals who get what they want, Crawford did not fit into escapist musicals so they formed a minor part in her durable five-decade career. She was married to actors Douglas Fairbanks, Jr. (1909–2000) and FRANCHOT TONE. Autobiography: *A Portrait of Joan* (1962); biographies: *Joan Crawford: Hollywood Martyr*, David Bret (2006); *Joan Crawford*, Lawrence J. Quirk, William Schoell (2002); *Joan Crawford*, Bob Thomas (1979).

CRAWFORD, MICHAEL [born Michael Patrick Dumble-Smith] (1942–). Stage, television, and film performer. A popular British actor–singer on the Broadway and West End stage, his unusual career went from playing goofy, awkward juveniles to romantic matinee idols to campy character parts. Crawford was born in Salisbury, England, and as a youth was in the St. Paul's Cathedral boys' choir. He quit school to take up acting, working first on BBC radio and then on television. Crawford was soon a familiar face in Great Britain from his West End comedies and comedy series on television. He made his film debut in 1958 and played characters younger than himself for many years.

Crawford's notable musical roles on screen were the hapless Hero in *A FUNNY THING HAPPENED ON THE WAY TO THE FORUM* (1966) and the gawky clerk Cornelius Hackl in *HELLO, DOLLY!* (1969). Crawford returned to the London stage in the 1970s and became a favorite leading man in the musicals *Billy* (1974), *Flowers for Algernon* (1979), *BARNUM* (1981), and *THE PHANTOM OF THE OPERA* (1985), reprising his performance on Broadway in 1988. With his new-found celebrity, he appeared in concerts, in Las Vegas spectaculars, and on television specials with great success. When Crawford returned to the stage it was as a comic character actor in two short-lived musicals, playing the affected Count von Krolock in *Dance of the Vampires* (2002) on Broadway and the greasy Count Fosco in *Woman in White* (2004) in London. Autobiography: *Parcel Arrived Safely: Tied With String* (2000); biography: *Phantom: Michael Crawford Unmasked*, Anthony Hayward (1993).

CRAZY FOR YOU. See *GIRL CRAZY*

CROSBY, BING [born Harry Lillis Crosby] (1903–1977). Film and television performer.

Arguably America's favorite singer, who recorded more songs and had more hits than any other entertainer, he played an easy-going, affable, and unconventional romantic figure in over sixty Hollywood musicals. Crosby was born in Tacoma, Washington, and educated at Gonzaga University where he started singing with a campus band. He was not singing professionally very long before conductor PAUL WHITEMAN teamed him with two other singers, billed them as the Rhythm Boys, and featured them in his concerts and in the film *KING OF JAZZ* (1930). Crosby soon went solo, got his own radio show, started his phenomenal recording career, and was given specialty bits in such movie musicals as *Reaching for the Moon* (1931), *THE BIG BROADCAST* (1932), and *Confessions of a Co-Ed* (1932). He moved into character parts with *College Humor* (1933) and was seen in leading roles in several 1930s musicals, including *GOING HOLLYWOOD* (1933), *WE'RE NOT DRESSING* (1934), *She Loves Me Not* (1934), *MISSISSIPPI* (1935), *Two for Tonight* (1935), *ANYTHING GOES* (1936), *Rhythm on the Range* (1936), *PENNIES FROM HEAVEN* (1936), *Waikiki Wedding* (1937), *DOUBLE OR NOTHING* (1937), *Doctor Rhythm* (1938), *Sing You Sinners* (1938), *East Side of Heaven* (1939), and *The Star Maker* (1939). Crosby first teamed up with BOB HOPE in *ROAD TO SINGAPORE* (1940) and the chemistry was dynamite; the two went on to make six more *Road* pictures together. Crosby's other 1940s musicals include *BIRTH OF THE BLUES* (1941), *HOLIDAY INN* (1942), *Dixie* (1943), *GOING MY WAY* (1944), *HERE COME THE WAVES* (1944), *THE BELLS OF ST. MARY'S* (1945), *BLUE SKIES* (1946), *The Emperor Waltz* (1948), and *A CONNECTICUT YANKEE IN KING ARTHUR'S COURT* (1949). As he aged gracefully, Crosby played more mature roles where he was less a romantic figure than a comfortable old friend. However, he remained a box office favorite and still his records sold in the millions. The 1950s saw an even more laid back Crosby in such musicals as *HERE COMES THE GROOM* (1951), *WHITE CHRISTMAS* (1954), *THE COUNTRY GIRL* (1954), *ANYTHING GOES* (1956), and *HIGH SOCIETY* (1956). By the 1960s he was appearing more and more on television and gently eased his way out of movies, making his last screen appearances in the musicals *High Time* (1960), *Pepe* (1960), *THE ROAD TO HONG KONG* (1962), and *ROBIN AND THE SEVEN HOODS* (1964). He also acted in two TV musicals, *HIGH TOR* (1956) and *The Road to Lebanon* (1966). Crosby appeared in several nonmusicals during his long career but rarely did his public accept him unless he was singing. The original crooner, Crosby was one of the first singers to use the radio microphone to seduce his listeners and represented a style of singing that contrasted greatly with the belters and operatic singers that were typical. His acting talents were modest but his comic timing and interpretation of a lyric were outstanding, making everything look easy. Crosby was married to actress Dixie Lee (1911–1952) and singer Kathryn (Grant) Crosby; his brother was BOB CROSBY and his son was actor Gary Crosby (1933–1995). Autobiography: *Call Me Lucky*, with Gary Giddins, Pete Martin (1953); memoirs: *Bing and Other Things*, Kathryn Crosby (1967); *Going My Own Way*, Gary Crosby (1983); biographies: *Going My Way: Bing Crosby and American Culture*, Ruth Prigozy, Walter Raubicheck (2007); *Bing Crosby: The Hollow Man*, Donald Shepherd, Robert F. Slatzer (1981); *Bing*, Charles Thompson (1975).

CROSBY, BOB [born George Robert Crosby] (1913–1993). Film and television musician and performer. While never as famous as his brother BING CROSBY, the Dixieland bandleader had a successful career on the big and little screens. Crosby was born in Spokane, Washington, the son of a bookkeeper, and educated at Gonzaga University before following in his elder brother's footsteps and singing with various bands. He sang with Ted Weems and then the DORSEY BROTHERS before forming his own band, the Bob Crosby Orchestra. As opposed to the growing swing fad, Crosby's band emphasized old-time Dixieland and jazz and audiences responded, making them popular enough to be featured in the Hollywood musicals *Rhythm on the Roof* (1934), *Let's Make Music* (1940), *Rookies on Parade* (1941), *Reveille With Beverly* (1943), *Thousands Cheer* (1943), *Meet Miss Bobby Sox* (1944), *Pardon My Rhythm* (1944), and others. Crosby played character parts in such musicals as *Sis Hopkins* (1941), *Kansas City Kitty* (1944), *My Gal Loves Music* (1944), and *The Singing Sheriff* (1944). After the group disbanded during World War II, Crosby formed a new band, Crosby and the Bobcats, and they found success on radio and television. Crosby had his own television show in the 1950s and was more popular than ever. He continued to sing and conduct into the 1980s.

CROSLAND, ALAN (1894–1936). Film director. A historically noteworthy movie director because of his use of sound in films, he helmed seven musicals. A native New Yorker, Crosland worked as an actor and stage manager in the theatre before joining the Edison Company and directing silents starting in 1914. After many movies, Crosland made history in the 1920s by directing *Don Juan* (1926), the first film with synchronized sound effects, and *THE JAZZ SINGER* (1927), the first talkie and first screen musical. His other movie musicals are *ON WITH THE SHOW* (1929), *Song of the Flame* (1930), *Big Boy* (1930), *Viennese Nights* (1930), *Children of Dreams* (1931), and *King Solomon of Broadway* (1935). Crosland also directed several nonmusicals before his premature death in an automobile accident.

CROUSE, RUSSEL. See LINDSAY, Howard, and Russel CROUSE

CRYER, GRETCHEN, AND NANCY FORD. Stage songwriting team. The first successful female songwriting partnership in the American theatre, the actress–lyricist Cryer and composer Ford wrote some delightful pop-rock scores in the 1970s. Cryer (1935–) was born in Dunreith, Indiana, and educated at De Pauw University where she met fellow student Ford (1935–), a musician born in Kalamazoo, Michigan. The two started collaborating while doing graduate work at Yale University, with Cryer writing the libretto and lyrics and Ford the music. While Ford played pit piano for Manhattan shows, Ford performed in such musicals as *LITTLE ME* (1962), *110 IN THE SHADE* (1963), and *1776* (1969). The songwriters' first New York production was the Off Broadway anti-war musical *Now Is the Time for All Good Men* (1967), followed by the rock musical comedy *THE LAST SWEET DAYS OF ISAAC* (1970), which brought them wide recognition. The team's musical *Shelter* (1973) was produced on Broadway but did not survive long. However, the feminist musical *I'M GETTING MY ACT TOGETHER AND TAKING IT ON THE ROAD* (1978) ran over 1,000 performances Off Broadway. Cryer played the leading role herself. Cryer and Ford have taught classes, run workshops, and performed their work in cabarets and theatre conventions. The team's most recent work is the musical version of *Anne of Green Gables* (2007), which was produced Off Broadway and then toured. The scores by Cryer and Ford are contemporary, very knowing, filled with fertile ideas, and have the flavor of pop music even as they function as theatre pieces. Cryer's son is television actor Jon Cryer (1965–).

CUGAT, XAVIER [born Francisco de Asis Javier Cugat Mingall de Bru y Deulofeu] (1900–1990). Film and television musician, conductor, and performer. The Cuban "Rhumba King" who helped popularize Latin music in the States, the rotund bandleader appeared with his band in fifteen Hollywood musicals. Cugat was born near Barcelona, Spain, and moved to Havana, Cuba, with his family when he was three years old. When he was older the family emigrated to Los Angeles where he got a job as a cartoonist for the *Los Angeles Times*. In 1928 Cugat formed his own band and became popular in southern California for their performances at the Cocoanut Grove nightclub. In the 1930s, Cugat brought attention to Latin dance music and was responsible for the rhumba becoming a national fad. Cugat and his band were featured in such movie musicals as *Go West, Young Man* (1936), *YOU WERE NEVER LOVELIER* (1942), *The Heat's On* (1943), *STAGE DOOR CANTEEN* (1943), *Bathing Beauty* (1944), *TWO GIRLS AND A SAILOR* (1944), *Weekend at the Waldorf* (1945), *Holiday in Mexico* (1946), *No Leave, No Love* (1946), *On an Island With You* (1948), *A DATE WITH JUDY* (1948), *Luxury Liner* (1948), and *NEPTUNE'S DAUGHTER* (1949). He usually played himself but was capable enough an actor to be part of the plot, not just in a specialty spot. In the 1950s and 1960s he made many television appearances and performed in movies in Europe. Autobiography: *Rhumba Is My Life* (1948).

CUKOR, GEORGE (1899–1983). Film and stage director. One of Hollywood's finest directors of movie stars (particularly women), he started in the theatre working with stage stars. Cukor was a native New Yorker who as a teenager decided to make the theatre his career. At the age of eighteen he was a professional stage manager and in 1920 be began directing for stock companies. Cukor was working on Broadway by 1925 and for the rest of the decade got sterling performances from Ethel Barrymore, Jeanne Eagels, Laurette Taylor, and other female theatre stars in New York and on tour. With the arrival of talking pictures, he relocated to California where his illustrious film career began. Although Cukor worked with a variety of genres, he was eventually known in Hollywood as a "woman's director" for the many award-winning performances actresses gave in his films. He only directed five musicals—*A STAR IS BORN* (1954), *LES GIRLS* (1957), *Let's Make Love* (1960), *MY FAIR LADY* (1964), and *The Bluebird* (1976)—and contrib-uted to parts of two others—*ONE HOUR WITH YOU* (1932) and *Song Without End* (1960)—yet again he provided opportunities for actresses such as JUDY GARLAND and AUDREY HEPBURN to shine. Biographies: *George Cukor: Master of Elegance*, Emanuel Levy (1994); *George Cukor: A Double Life*, Patrick McGilligan (1991).

CULLUM, JOHN (1930–) Stage and television performer. A charismatic, full-voiced baritone with tawny hair and dramatic facial features, he has been impressive in both classical plays and Broadway musicals. Cullum was born in Knoxville, Tennessee, and educated at the University of Tennessee before making his Broadway debut in a revival of *Saint Joan* (1956). At first he was seen mostly in Shakespeare revivals and then got to sing on Broadway as Sir Dinahan in *CAMELOT* (1960). Cullum's first leading musical role was psychiatrist Mark Bruckner in *ON A CLEAR DAY YOU CAN SEE FOREVER* (1965) followed by replacing others in *MAN OF LA MANCHA* in 1967 and *1776* in 1970. He was highly praised for his pacifist Charlie Anderson in *SHENANDOAH* (1975 and 1989), his manic theatrical producer Oscar Jaffee in *ON THE TWENTIETH CENTURY* (1978), the corrupt Caldwell B. Caldwell in *URINETOWN* (2001), and Max the dog in *DR. SEUSS' HOW THE GRINCH STOLE CHRISTMAS* (2006), as well as such revival performances as the king in *THE KING AND I* (1972), Billy Bigelow in *CAROUSEL* (1973), Cap'n Andy in *SHOW BOAT* (1996 and 1997), and the father H. C. Curry in *110 IN THE SHADE* (2007). Cullum has appeared in several nonmusical plays on and Off Broadway, in a few films, such as the musical *1776* (1972), and in several television dramas, series, and specials, such as the TV musical *ANDROCLES AND THE LION* (1967). His son is actor John David Cullum (1966–).

CUMMINGS, IRVING (1888–1959). Film director and performer. The former silent screen actor directed over seventy features, including fifteen musicals mostly at 20TH CENTURY-FOX with the studio's biggest stars, from SHIRLEY TEMPLE to BETTY GRABLE. Cummings was born in New York City and acted in LILLIAN RUSSELL's company before entering films in 1909, quickly becoming a leading man in dozens of silents. By 1922 he was directing features and over the next two decades helmed all kinds of movies, although he is most remembered for his Fox musicals. Cummings' screen musicals include *Cameo Kirby* (1930), *CURLY TOP* (1935), *Poor Little Rich Girl* (1936), *Little*

Miss Broadway (1938), LILLIAN RUSSELL (1940), DOWN ARGENTINE WAY (1940), THAT NIGHT IN RIO (1941), LOUISIANA PURCHASE (1941), SPRINGTIME IN THE ROCKIES (1942), *Sweet Rosie O'Grady* (1943), and THE DOLLY SISTERS (1945).

CUMMINGS, JACK [born Jacob Kominsky] (1905–1989). Film producer. A very successful producer at MGM, he presented over two dozen musicals, including several beloved classics. Cummings was born in New Brunswick, Canada, the nephew of movie executive Louis B. Mayer. He began his career at MGM at the age of seventeen as an office boy and worked his way through various departments until he was producing features in 1935. Among his notable musicals are BORN TO DANCE (1936), BROADWAY MELODY OF 1938 (1937), BROADWAY MELODY OF 1940, TWO GIRLS ON BROADWAY (1940), *Go West* (1940), *Ship Ahoy* (1942), *I Dood It* (1943), BROADWAY RHYTHM (1944), *Bathing Beauty* (1944), IT HAPPENED IN BROOKLYN (1947), NEPTUNE'S DAUGHTER (1949), THREE LITTLE WORDS (1950), LOVELY TO LOOK AT (1952), KISS ME, KATE (1953), SEVEN BRIDES FOR SEVEN BROTHERS (1954), *Interrupted Melody* (1955), and VIVA LAS VEGAS (1964).

CUMMINGS, [Charles Clarence] **ROBERT** [Orville] (1918–1990) Film, stage, and television performer. A handsome, youthful-looking leading man who excelled at light comedy, he enjoyed a long and impressive career in different media. Cummings was born in Joplin, Missouri, and educated at Carnegie Tech and the American Academy of Dramatic Arts. The enterprising young actor went to Broadway posing as a British thespian named Blade Stanhope Conway and was quickly cast in plays. When he decided to try Hollywood in 1935, Cummings called himself Bruce Hutchins and told studio agents he was a rich Texan. Again he was immediately cast as appealing if bumbling juveniles. Among his sixty films are fifteen musicals in which he usually played Ivy League types. His musical credits include *Millions in the Air* (1935), *Three Cheers for Love* (1936), *College Swing* (1938), *Three Smart Girls Grow Up* (1939), *Spring Parade* (1940), ONE NIGHT IN THE TROPICS (1940), MOON OVER MIAMI (1941), *The Petty Girl* (1950), *Lucky Me* (1954), and *Beach Party* (1963). Cummings found greater fame on television where he had his own sit-com in the 1950s and another in the 1960s, still playing hapless young men. He continued doing films through the 1960s and

appeared on dozens of other television programs through the 1970s.

CUNNINGHAM, JOHN (1932–) Stage, film, and television performer. A reliable, all-purpose actor in all media, he was usually cast in supporting roles but has been a solid asset in both plays and musicals. Cunningham was born in Auburn, New York, and educated at Dartmouth and Yale, serving in the army in between schools. He made his New York debut in the chorus of MY FAIR LADY in 1960 and played El Gallo in THE FANTASTICKS in 1962, but spent most of the decade at the American Shakespeare Festival in Connecticut. Cunningham either originated roles or replaced actors in the musicals *Hot Spot!* (1963), CABARET (1967), ZORBÁ (1968), *1776* (1969), COMPANY (1970), *Birds of Paradise* (1987), *Anna Karenina* (1992), TITANIC (1997), and *Amour* (2002). He has acted in plays both on and Off Broadway and in regional theatre, particularly at the Williamstown Theatre Festival, and has appeared in many films and television programs, although none of them were musicals.

■ **CURLY TOP** (Fox 1935). SHIRLEY TEMPLE got to introduce one of her most popular ditties, "Animal Crackers in My Soup," in this sentimental musical in which the optimistic moppet got to tug on the heart strings of Depression America. Millionaire Edward Morgan (JOHN BOLES) is enchanted with the little orphan Elizabeth Blair (Temple) and so he adopts her and her older sister Mary (Rochelle Hudson) under the guise of the unseen "Mr. Jones." Elizabeth decides to play matchmaker and Mary ends up in Edward's arms just as they learn the true identity of Mr. Jones. Jane Darwell, Esther Dale, Etienne Giradot, ARTHUR TREACHER, and Rafaela Ottiano filled out the cast directed by IRVING CUMMINGS and RAY HENDERSON. IRVING CAESAR and Edward Heyman contributed to the score, which also included "The Simple Things in Life," "When I Grow Up," and the title number in which Boles sang while Temple tap danced atop a white piano. The picture was very popular, and the story was reused by 20TH CENTURY-FOX later in the movie musical DADDY LONG LEGS (1955) with LESLIE CARON and FRED ASTAIRE playing the roles as older characters.

CURRY, TIM[othy James] (1946–). Stage, television, and film performer. A gaunt, mesmerizing character actor of British and American films and television, he was a recognized stage actor in England before finding fame in America and has appeared on Broadway on occasion. Curry was born in Grappenhall, Cheshire, England, the son of a Methodist navy chaplain, and attended Cambridge and the University of Birmingham. By 1968 he was on the London stage and he first came to Broadway to reprise his outlandish performances as the oversexed scientist Dr. Frank-N-Furter in *THE ROCKY HORROR SHOW* on Broadway in 1975. Although the musical was short lived in New York, Curry became widely known on both sides of the Atlantic when he repeated his performance in the film version titled *THE ROCKY HORROR PICTURE SHOW* (1975). Curry returned to the New York stage sporadically, originating the role of Mozart in the Broadway production of *Amadeus* (1980) and playing such musical roles as the Hollywood star Alan Swann in *My Favorite Year* (1989), Scrooge in *A CHRISTMAS CAROL* (2000), and King Arthur in *SPAMALOT* (2005). He has many film credits, including the con man Rooster in *ANNIE* (1982) and Long John Silver in *Muppets' Treasure Island* (1996), and has appeared in several television shows, as well as providing the voices for dozens of characters in animated films and TV programs.

🖎 **CURTAINS** (Hirschfeld Theatre 2007), A rarity on Broadway in the first decade of the twenty-first century, this musical comedy featured an original libretto and was not based on a movie, play, or book. RUPERT HOLMES and PETER STONE were the co-authors of the musical whodunit in which the players were more interesting than who done it. After the curtain call for the musical *Robbin' Hood of the Old West*, which is trying out at the Colonial Theatre in Boston in 1959 before heading to Broadway, the temperamental, untalented star Jessica Cranshaw (Patty Goble) is somehow poisoned on stage and the investigating police Lieutenant Frank Cioffe (David Hyde Pierce) soon realizes that everyone involved with the show is a possible suspect. Quarantining the whole cast and crew in the theatre, he questions the brassy producer Carmen Bernstein (DEBRA MONK), her rich husband Sidney (Ernie Sabella), their sexy, ambitious daughter Bambi (Megan Sikora), the songwriting couple Georgia Hendricks (KAREN ZIEMBA) and Aaron Fox (Jason Danieley), and the under-

study Niki Harris (Jill Paice) with whom Cioffe falls in love. After a lot of nasty revelations and two more murders, the culprit turns out to be a theatre critic. Also in the cast were Edward Hibbert, John Bolton, Michael McCormick, Michael X. Martin, and Noah Racey. The score was by JOHN KANDER (music) and FRED EBB (lyrics) and had such fun songs as the joyous anthem "Show People," the gentle "I Miss the Music," the practical "It's a Business," the flowing ballad "Thinking of Him," and the *OKLAHOMA!* spoof "Wide Open Spaces." So many years in preparation that librettist Stone and lyricist Ebb had died before it arrived on Broadway, the musical was cobbled together and given a polish by director SCOTT ELLIS and choreographer ROB ASHFORD. Critics were halfhearted about the show but not about the bright performances, Pierce in particular. Audiences were less fussy and the musical entertained crowds on Broadway for 511 performances.

CURTIZ, MICHAEL [born Mikhaly Kertesz] (1888–1962). Film director. The prolific Hollywood director who filmed everything and anything, he found time to helm fifteen musicals with everyone from AL JOLSON to ELVIS PRESLEY. Curtiz was born in Budapest, the son of an architect and an opera singer, and educated at Markoszy University and Hungary's Royal Academy of Theatre and Art. He worked in a circus before entering films as an actor and by 1912 was directing Hungarian movies. After serving in World War I, Curtiz was a political refugee who directed films in Austria and then Germany, getting the attention of Hollywood studios who were impressed by his epic silent features. WARNER BROTHERS brought him to California in 1926 and he stayed to direct well over 100 movies during the next thirty years. Curtiz's variety was as impressive as his quantity of output, helming film classics as different as *The Adventures of Robin Hood* (1938) and *Casablanca* (1943). His musicals are similarly varied and include *Mammy* (1930), *YANKEE DOODLE DANDY* (1942), *THIS IS THE ARMY* (1943), *NIGHT AND DAY* (1946), *ROMANCE ON THE HIGH SEAS* (1948), *YOUNG MAN WITH A HORN* (1950), *THE JAZZ SINGER* (1953), *WHITE CHRISTMAS* (1954), *THE VAGABOND KING* (1956), *THE BEST THINGS IN LIFE ARE FREE* (1956), *The Helen Morgan Story* (1957), and *King Creole* (1958).

D

DA COSTA, MORTON [born Tecosky] (1914–1989). Stage and film director. A first-class Broadway director, he was equally proficient with musicals and plays. Da Costa was born in Philadelphia, educated at Temple University, and later taught at Temple's School of Theatre. He began acting in stock and then co-founded a theatre company of his own in Dayton, Ohio, in 1937, producing and often directing some sixty plays there. He made his New York acting debut in *The Skin of Our Teeth* (1942) and appeared in several Broadway productions in the 1940s before turning to directing in 1947. Da Costa's staging of revivals at the City Center brought him to the attention of producers and in the 1950s he directed a handful of Broadway nonmusical hits, including *Mister Roberts* (1955) and *Auntie Mame* (1956). His biggest musical hit was *THE MUSIC MAN* (1957) but he also staged *PLAIN AND FANCY* (1955), *SARATOGA* (1959), *Maggie Flynn* (1968), and *A Musical Jubilee* (1975). Da Costa directed a handful of films as well, including the screen versions of *Auntie Mame* (1958) and *The Music Man* (1962), which he also produced.

DA SILVA, HOWARD [born Herbert Silverblatt] (1909–1986). Stage, film, and television performer and director. A deep-voiced, bulky character actor of all media, he could play the heavy as effectively as the cuddly teddy bear. Da Silva was born in Cleveland, the son of a tailor and a suffragette, and grew up in the Bronx. He moved with his family to Pittsburgh where he worked in the steel mills in order to finance his education at Carnegie Tech. Da Silva made his New York acting debut in 1929 with Eve Le Gallienne's Civic Repertory Theatre and over the next forty years appeared on stage in a variety of works, including the musical roles of Larry Foreman in *THE CRADLE WILL ROCK* (1937), the original Jud Fry in *OKLAHOMA!* (1943), the political boss Ben in *FIORELLO!* (1959), and Benjamin Franklin in *1776* (1969).

He made his screen debut in 1936 and played supporting roles in several films until he was blacklisted as a Communist during the 1950s so he concentrated on the theatre, directing as well as acting. Da Silva returned to movies in the 1960s and made a half dozen features, including the screen version of *1776* (1972). He also appeared in many television dramas and series before and after his blacklisting period.

DADDY LONG LEGS (Fox 1955). The maturing FRED ASTAIRE got to romance a much younger woman, LESLIE CARON, in this musical version of the Jean Webster novel, which had been filmed as a nonmusical in 1919 and 1931 and as the musical *CURLY TOP* (1935). Phoebe and Henry Ephron tailored the story to fit the stars. The millionaire Jervis Pendleton III (Astaire) adopts the French orphan Julie Andre (Caron) without revealing he is her guardian; she has been told it is Mr. Smith but, having seen his long shadow once, calls him Daddy Long Legs. Julie comes to America to go to school, she and Jervis fall in love, and the guardian becomes the husband. Terry Moore, Thelma Ritter, Fred Clark, Larry Keating, Ralph Dumke, and Charlotte Austin played the supporting characters, and JOHNNY MERCER wrote both music and lyrics for the score, the standout hit being "Something's Gotta Give." Ray Anthony's Orchestra was on hand for the college dance number "Sluefoot," and the intoxicating "Dream" was used for a dance sequence in which Julie dreams about what her guardian might be like. Jean Negulesco directed the Samuel G. Engel production, which was choreographed by David Robel, Roland Petit, and Astaire.

DAILEY, DAN[iel James] (1914–1978). Film, stage, and television performer. A pleasant, light-haired song-and-dance man with a confident, friendly demeanor, he worked in all media but is most remembered for his eighteen Hollywood musicals. The native New Yorker was on the stage as a child and worked in vaudeville and burlesque before being cast as one of the teenagers in the Broadway musical *BABES IN ARMS* (1937). He was featured in *Stars in Your Eyes* (1939) and then headed west where he made his film debut in 1940. Dailey was cast in some dramatic roles but it didn't take the studios long to see that he was ideal musical comedy material. After small roles in *Hullabaloo* (1940) and *ZIEGFELD GIRL* (1941), he graduated to better parts in *LADY, BE GOOD* (1941), *PANAMA HATTIE* (1942), *Give Out Sisters*

(1942), *Mother Wore Tights* (1947), *You Were Meant for Me* (1948), *Give My Regards to Broadway* (1948), *When My Baby Smiles at Me* (1948), *You're My Everything* (1949), *My Blue Heaven* (1950), *Call Me Mister* (1951), *Meet Me at the Fair* (1952), and *The Girl Next Door* (1953). As he aged with grace, Dailey played fathers and more mature types, yet retained his popularity in such musicals as *There's No Business Like Show Business* (1954), *It's Always Fair Weather* (1955), *Meet Me in Las Vegas* (1956), and *The Best Things in Life Are Free* (1956). He also did specialty bits in *I'll Get By* (1950) and *Pepe* (1960) and was featured in the TV musicals *Burlesque* (1955) and *Paris in Springtime* (1956). In the 1960s Dailey returned to Broadway in a few comedies and appeared in nightclubs and on many television shows.

DALE, JIM [born James Smith] (1935–). Stage, television, and film performer. The multitalented actor–singer–dancer has found success in a number of fields, but is best known in America for his athletic, charismatic performances in musicals. Dale was born in Rothwell, England, and trained for a career in ballet, but by 1952 he was doing standup comedy, worked as a disc jockey, and even found some notoriety as a pop singer in Great Britain. Dale became a familiar face in England for his television appearances and roles in the *Carry On* series of film comedies. His career then took a new turn and he pursued acting in classical theatre, playing comic roles in productions by the Young Vic. When that company visited New York in 1974, Dale wowed audiences and critics with his agile, hilarious performance as the sly servant *Scapino*. He has since returned to the New York stage in a variety of roles, including the singing–dancing entrepreneur Phinias T. Barnum in *Barnum* (1980), a replacement for the cocky cockney Bill Snibson in *For Me and My Gal* (1987), a selection of daffy characters in *Candide* (1997), and the corrupt Mr. Peachum in *The Threepenny Opera* (2006). Dale has appeared in a number of films, including the musical *Pete's Dragon* (1977), and has written songs for television and movies, most memorably the lyrics for "Georgy Girl." He has also recorded many audio books, in particular the *Harry Potter* works.

DALEY, CASS (1915–1975). Film and television performer. A gangly, bucktoothed comedienne who excelled in physical humor, outlandish singing, and contortion-like dancing, she was featured in movie musicals during the World War II years and into the 1950s. Daley was born in Philadelphia and began her show business career as a band singer. She soon discovered that she had a talent for broad comedy and found favor as a unique performer in concerts, on the radio, in nightclubs, and on Broadway in *Ziegfeld Follies* (1936). Daley was featured in ten Hollywood musicals, sometimes playing herself, as in *Crazy House* (1943), *Duffy's Tavern* (1945), *Variety Girl* (1947), and *Here Comes the Groom* (1952), other times playing comic characters, as with *The Fleet's In* (1942), *Star-Spangled Rhythm* (1942), *Riding High* (1943), *Out of This World* (1945), *Ladies' Man* (1947), and *Red Garters* (1954). She appeared on some early television shows and then retired from public life.

DALRYMPLE, JEAN [Van Kirk] (1910–1998). Stage producer. A busy and far-reaching presenter of New York theatre, she was general director of the City Center Light Opera, which presented thirty musical revivals during her tenure. Dalrymple was born in Morristown, New Jersey, and began in the theatre writing sketches for vaudeville and then became a press agent on Broadway. By the late 1940s she was producing plays and oversaw many popular play revivals at the City Center. Between 1957 and 1968 she ran the Light Opera Center and presented such musical revivals as *Brigadoon* (1957 and 1963), *Carousel* (1957), *The Most Happy Fella* (1959), *Finian's Rainbow* (1960), *Pal Joey* (1963), *West Side Story* (1965), and *Guys and Dolls* (1965). These productions often featured outstanding casts and, in many cases, were the first major revivals of these memorable musicals. Autobiographies: *September Child* (1963); *From the Last Row* (1975).

DAMES (Warner-Vitaphone 1934). The plot may have been weaker than most of the older **Warner Brothers** golden age musicals but the songs by **Harry Warren** (music) and Al Dubin (lyrics) were superior so the movie was very enjoyable. Delmar Daves' screenplay is a routine backstage affair in which chorine Mabel Anderson (**Joan Blondell**) has to go on for the leading lady Barbara Hemingway (**Ruby Keeler**), just as Keeler had done a year earlier in *42nd Street*. Thrown into the plot are the eager young producer Jimmy Higgens (**Dick Powell**), millionaire Ezra Ounce (**Hugh Herbert**), who's looking for deserving individuals to give money to, and Barbara's monied Uncle Horace (**Guy Kibbee**) who

Mabel blackmails into backing the show. BUSBY BERKELEY choreographed three outstanding production numbers for the film. Powell sang the title song to a group of producers, explaining what audiences want in a Broadway show, and the scene dissolved to a spectacular series of geometric patterns formed by chorus girls. "I Only Have Eyes for You" became a salute to Keeler as her face appears everywhere in Powell's imagination, from subway ads to a chorus of chorines wearing Keeler masks. Most ingenious of all was "The Girl at the Ironing Board" in which Blondell is pressing men's garments and they spring to life and start dancing around her. Zasu Pitts, Arthur Vinton, PHIL REGAN, and Arthur Aylesworth filled out the cast of the DARRYL F. ZANUCK production directed by RAY ENRIGHT.

📖 *DAMES AT SEA* (Bouwerie Lane Theatre 1968). An Off Broadway spoof of early Hollywood musicals, the small-scale production mocked the large-scale films by WARNER BROTHERS in the 1930s even as it held an affection for the old tuners. George Haimsohn and Robin Miller wrote the silly libretto in which naive Ruby (BERNADETTE PETERS) from Centerville, Utah, arrives in Manhattan with dreams of becoming a Broadway star. After she befriends the songwriting sailor Dick (David Christmas) and gets cast in the chorus of a show, the producer loses his backing and the musical has to be performed on the deck of a ship. This causes the star Mona (Tamara Long) to get seasick so Ruby has to go on in her place and tap dances her way to fame. The musical, performed by only six actors, was filled with clichés from the RUBY KEELER– DICK POWELL films, and the score by Jim Wise (music), Haimsohn, and Miller (lyrics) was composed of clever pastiche numbers, such as "Raining in My Heart," "Good Times Are Here to Stay," "Choo-Choo Honeymoon," "That Mister Man of Mine," "Singapore Sue," and the toe-tapping title number. Neal Kenyon

directed and choreographed, and the modest little show developed a following, running 575 performances. The musical also brought the first recognition for Peters who would go from there to Broadway and stay for over forty years. *Dames at Sea* continues to be produced in summer stock and other regional theatre groups. ☐ ANN-MARGARET played Ruby in a 1971 NBC-TV version of *Dames At Sea* and, with ANN MILLER playing Mona, the taping was the real thing. Also in the cast were Fred Gwynne, Anna Meara, and Harvey Evans.

📖 *DAMN YANKEES* (46th Street Theatre 1955). A sly, modern take on the Faust legend, the baseball musical comedy was a breezy fantasy loaded with talent on stage and behind the scenes.

Plot: Joe Boyd, a middle-aged fan of the Washington Senators baseball team, is so distressed at their losing record that he sells his soul to the devil, Mr. Applegate, for a winning season. Joe is transformed into the young slugger Joe Hardy, the Senators start winning, and, to protect his investment, Applegate conjures up the temptress Lola to see that Joe doesn't return home to his wife Meg. But Joe sneaks out of Applegate's contract, still manages to win the big game, and happily becomes the older Joe Boyd again and rejoins his wife.

GEORGE ABBOTT and Douglass Wallop cowrote the libretto, based on Wallop's novel *The Year the Yankees Lost the Pennant*, and it was filled with holes plotwise but never was dull, and the songs by RICHARD ADLER and JERRY ROSS filled in the gaps nicely. It also helped that the cast was first rate, with GWEN VERDON making sex funny as the vamp Lola and RAY WALSTON getting the best role of his career as the devilish Applegate. There are many similarities between Adler and Ross's earlier score for THE PAJAMA GAME (1953) and the songs for *Damn Yankees*, with both shows utilizing a variety of music styles, such

Casts for *Damn Yankees*

Character	1955 Broadway	1958 film	1967 television	1994 Broadway
Joe Hardy	STEPHEN DOUGLASS	Tab Hunter	Jerry Lanning	Jarrod Emick
Applegate	RAY WALSTON	Ray Walston	PHIL SILVERS	VICTOR GARBER
Lola	GWEN VERDON	Gwen Verdon	Lee Remick	BEBE NEUWIRTH
Meg Boyd	Shannon Bolin	Shannon Bolin	Fran Allison	Linda Stephens
Joe Boyd	Robert Shafer	Robert Shafer	RAY MIDDLETON	Dennis Kelly
Van Buren	Russ Brown	Russ Brown	Jim Backus	Dick Latessa
Gloria Thorpe	Rae Allen	Rae Allen	Linda Lavin	Vicki Lewis

as a tango, a hoe-down number, a mambo-like song, a vaudeville turn, and so on. But that doesn't diminish one's enjoyment of the spirited *Damn Yankees* songs. There was no stand-out hit like "Hey There" but the score was filled with memorable tunes and clever lyrics. The more raucous numbers such as "Shoeless Joe From Hannibal, Mo" and "Who's Got the Pain" are nicely balanced by the slower, heartfelt "A Man Doesn't Know" and "Near to You." The Latin-flavored "Whatever Lola Wants" and the soft-shoe "Those Were the Good Old Days" are playful pastiches, and the harmonizing "Heart" also echoes the sound of barbershop quartets of the past. Yet *Damn Yankees* sounds contemporary and even when revived today it is kept in the 1950s because that is the predominant tone of the score as well as the book. Abbott directed with his usual razor-sharp timing, and BOB FOSSE did the resplendent choreography. Except for campus-set shows with the big football game, sports musicals had usually failed in the past; *Damn Yankees* broke the curse and ran 1,019 performances. Even though the musical has been a favorite with all kinds of producing groups over the years, a Broadway revival wasn't produced until 1994. Director JACK O'BRIEN tinkered with the book, attempting to make some of the incomprehensible loose ends of the plot tie together, but it still was a cockeyed fantasy and it was the musical numbers that scored. The cast was splendid, as was the choreography by KATHLEEN MARSHALL, and the show was a hit all over again, running 718 performances. Late in the run JERRY LEWIS took over the role of Applegate (his belated Broadway debut) and he toured with the show before reprising his performance in a London production.

🎬 ***Damn Yankees*** (Warner 1958) was one of the most faithful stage-to-screen transitions of the decade, with the director, choreographer, and most of the cast repeating their stage work for the film. Veteran filmmaker STANLEY DONEN assisted Abbott in the direction and current heartthrob Tab Hunter played Joe Hardy, but much is exactly as it was on Broadway. Some scenes look stagy, such as Verdon's delivery of "A Little Brains, A Little Talent" and the team players' "Heart," but other numbers, such as "Six Months Out of Every Year" and "Shoeless Joe From Hannibal, Mo," opened up nicely. More importantly, Walston and Verdon's performances were preserved, even if the camera reveals that she is a bit too old to play Lola. Just about all of the score survived the transition as well, and Adler wrote two new and forgettable numbers alone because Ross had died soon after the Broadway production opened. One can complain that Abbott's rapid theatre staging is lost on screen

Damn Yankees. Aside from college football, sports and musicals rarely mixed well on Broadway. Maybe it was funny, sexy Gwen Verdon, or maybe it was the sprightly production, but *Damn Yankees* was a hit. Here is Verdon as the seductive Lola in the 1958 screen version, working her charms on Tab Hunter. (Photofest)

Damn Yankees (stage) Musical Numbers

"Six Months Out of Every Year"
"Goodbye, Old Girl"
"(You've Gotta Have) Heart"
"Shoeless Joe from Hannibal, Mo"
"A Man Doesn't Know"
"A Little Brains, a Little Talent"
"Whatever Lola Wants (Lola Gets)"
"Not Meg"
"Who's Got the Pain?"
"The American League"
"The Game"
"Near to You"
"Those Were the Good Old Days"
"Two Lost Souls"

and parts of the picture drag, but it's a wonderful record of a Broadway favorite. ❏ *Damn Yankees* (NBC-TV 1967) had a terrific cast, from the principals PHIL SILVERS, Lee Remick, and Jerry Lanning, to the team members, such as Lee Goodman, Eugene Troobrick, Bob Dishy, and Jim Backus. It was a shame the production values were bargain basement and the 100-minute broadcast was so unpolished. Kirk Browning directed and Ernie Flatt choreographed and it looks like everyone could have use used a few more days of rehearsal. All the same, Silvers is an ideal Applegate and Remick surprises one throughout the broadcast.

DAMONE, VIC [born Vito Rocco Farinola] (1928–). Film and television performer. A slight, dark, and handsome singer who was very popular in nightclubs, on television, and on records, he was featured in a handful of 1950s movie musicals. Damone was born in Brooklyn and left school early to work as a movie theatre usher, even as he was singing in choirs and amateur groups. His career was launched when he won Arthur Godfrey's talent contest in 1945 and was soon making a name for himself in clubs. Damone played himself or did specialty spots in the film musicals *The Strip* (1951), *DEEP IN MY HEART* (1954), and *Meet Me in Las Vegas* (1956) and then got to play singing juveniles in *Rich, Young and Pretty* (1951), *Athena* (1954), *HIT THE DECK* (1955), and *KISMET* (1955). He acted in nonmusical films and has done many television shows, including the TV musicals *THE STINGIEST MAN IN TOWN* (1956) and *THE DANGEROUS CHRISTMAS OF RED RIDING HOOD* (1965). Damone was married to actresses Pier Angeli (1932–1971) and DIAHANN CARROLL.

DAMSEL IN DISTRESS (RKO 1937). FRED ASTAIRE's first film without GINGER ROGERS after partnering with her seven times was a disappointment at the box office, yet it is a wondrous musical in many ways. American dancer Jerry Halliday (Astaire) is in London doing a show and is smitten by the aristocratic Lady Alyce (Joan Fontaine) so he pursues her to the countryside and eventually rescues her from her stuffy life at Totleigh Castle. Ernest Pagano, S. K. Lauren, and P. G. WODEHOUSE wrote the screenplay based on one of Wodehouse's many comic novels and in addition to the expected British characters, played by REGINALD GARDINER, Constance Collier, Montagu Love, Harry Watson, and band leader Ray Noble, the writers threw in the American press agents

GEORGE BURNS and GRACIE ALLEN. Because Fontaine did not dance or sing in the script, the studio hoped that comparisons with Rogers would not be made. Instead Astaire's dance numbers were solos and there was a delightful number titled "Stiff Upper Lip" with Burns and Allen in which the threesome danced through an amusement park fun house complete with turning barrels and distorted mirrors. The exceptional score was by the GERSHWIN brothers and also included the hypnotic "A Foggy Day (In London Town)," the jazzy "I Can't Be Bothered Now," the harmonizing madrigal "Nice Work If You Can Get It," and the breezy "Things Are Looking Up." HERMES PAN and Astaire came up with the ingenious choreography, and the PANDRO S. BERMAN production was directed by GEORGE STEVENS with a felicitous touch.

DANCE IN MUSICALS. One of the unique aspects of the first musical, *THE BLACK CROOK* (1866), was its troupe of ballet dancers worked into the show to provide something in addition to melodrama and song, so one might say that dancing has been part of the American musical from the very start. In the early musicals, the existence of a chorus line defined the Broadway show. Dance was such a vital element that a musical without dances and pseudo-ballet sequences was unheard of. By the turn of the twentieth century, ballet was replaced by more up-to-date dances, such as the cake walk, tango, ballroom dancing, and even ragtime hoofing. *WATCH YOUR STEP* (1914) was the first "syncopated" musical with performers VERNON and IRENE CASTLE and composer IRVING BERLIN redefining theatre dance rhythms. However, the idea of dance truly incorporated into the action did not yet exist. GEORGE BALANCHINE and other choreographers provided stunning dance and ballet sequences in the 1930s musicals (most memorably the "Slaughter on Tenth Avenue from 1936's *ON YOUR TOES*), but dances were set pieces that existed on their own. It was AGNES DE MILLE who took dance and ballet and used it not only to tell a story but to explore characterization. In *OKLAHOMA!* (1943), *BRIGADOON* (1947), and other shows, de Mille presented a form of theatre dance that shaped the way we still view Broadway dancing. JEROME ROBBINS developed the form further by applying modern dance in musicals such as *ON THE TOWN* (1944), and in *WEST SIDE STORY* (1957) he used dance to illustrate tension as well as story, character, and mood. The emergence of the director–choreographer in the 1960s revealed the new role dance played in the creation of musicals; now the whole show was choreographed, and formal, separate dance numbers were somewhat passé. Musicals such as *FIDDLER ON THE ROOF* (1964), *MAN OF LA MANCHA* (1966), *COMPANY* (1970), and other seemingly nondance shows were, in fact, one uninterrupted set piece. More recently this has been seen in such musicals as *DREAMGIRLS* (1981), *NINE* (1982), *CATS* (1982), *ONCE ON THIS ISLAND* (1990), *JELLY'S LAST JAM* (1992), *KISS OF THE SPIDER WOMAN* (1993), *THE LION KING* (1997), *SEUSSICAL* (2000), *THOROUGHLY MODERN MILLIE* (2002), and *TARZAN* (2006). Finally, there are the unique shows that are all dance or all about dance, a fairly recent phenomenon and a popular one: *A CHORUS LINE* (1975), *DANCIN'* (1978), *THE TAP DANCE KID* (1983), *Song and Dance* (1985), *JEROME ROBBINS' BROADWAY* (1989), *BRING IN 'DA NOISE BRING IN 'DA FUNK* (1996), *FOOTLOOSE* (1998), *FOSSE* (1999), *CONTACT* (1999), and *MOVIN' OUT* (2002).

The use of dance in film follows a slightly different path. The early movie musicals simply copied the chorus line from Broadway and shot the number from a theatre audience's point of view. How else does one watch a line of girls? Stage choreographer BUSBY BERKELEY first came to Hollywood to redo his stage dances for the screen version of *WHOOPEE!* (1930) and, in his first time out, thought there were other ways to film the girls. Instead of setting a dance number and then filming it from different angles to be edited later, Berkeley used one camera and chose what the audience would see of the dance at any one point in time. He utilized close-ups of the girls, views looking through their legs, and their bodies forming designs that could only be appreciated from an overhead shot. Soon the Berkeley dances were not only different from Broadway dancing, but they were seen in production numbers that could not possibly take place in a Broadway theatre. Not all film choreographers were as extravagant and cockeyed as Berkeley but they were all influenced by him. After *42ND STREET* (1933) and the other Berkeley-choreographed movies of the 1930s, the chorus line on film was dead. Just as Broadway had shows that featured ballets or extended dance sequences, so did Hollywood allow some of its musicals to leave the narrative and move into pure dance. Dream ballets were the easiest way to get into these dances but other methods worked as well, such as a big number in the big show or the hero/heroine just imagining something in terms of dance. Among the many films to

feature such extended dance numbers were *GOLD DIGGERS OF 1935*, *On Your Toes* (1939), *ZIEGFELD FOLLIES* (1946), *WORDS AND MUSIC* (1948), *ON THE TOWN* (1949), *AN AMERICAN IN PARIS* (1951), *HANS CHRISTIAN ANDERSEN* (1952), *SINGIN' IN THE RAIN* (1952), *THE BAND WAGON* (1953), *LILI* (1953), *A STAR IS BORN* (1954), *OKLAHOMA!* (1955), and *CAROUSEL* (1956). One will not find dream ballets in today's movie musicals, and the dancing in *SATURDAY NIGHT FEVER* (1977) and *DIRTY DANCING* (1987) could never be mistaken for the choreography in the *GOLD DIGGERS* or FRED ASTAIRE–GINGER ROGERS films. Yet Berkeley's influence is still with us. How else can you describe the way dance was presented in *MOULIN ROUGE* (2001) and *CHICAGO* (2002)?

DANCIN' (Broadhurst Theatre 1978). Choreographer–director BOB FOSSE finally solved his problems with librettists, songwriters, characters, plot, and untried songs: he got rid of them all and devised this evening of dance pieces set to music by such diverse songwriters as GEORGE M. COHAN, Cat Stevens, JOHN PHILIP SOUSA, Neil Diamond, and the team of LEIBER and STOLLER. The revue's twenty-three numbers were performed by sixteen dancers, many of whom had worked with Fosse in the past, such as ANN REINKING, Wayne Cilento, Jill Cook, Rene Ceballos, Gail Benedict, John Mineo, Sandahl Bergman, Christopher Chadman, Vicki Frederick, and Charles Ward. Fosse's choreography was varied enough to avoid repetition and the revue quickly caught on, running an astonishing 1,744 performances. After the celebrated choreographer's death, Ann Reinking and Chet Walker restaged musical numbers from *Dancin'* and his other shows and put them together in a revue entitled **Fosse** (Broadhurst Theatre 1999). The talented dancers included Valarie Pettiford, Scott Wise, Jane Lanier, Eugene Fleming, Dana Moore, Sergio Trujillo, Desmond Richardson, and Elizabeth Parkinson, and the revue was directed by RICHARD MALTBY, JR. Critics were divided about the show, some seeing it as a celebration of a unique artist, others a tired retread of numbers not as well executed as in the originals. Audiences tended to agree with the former and the show ran 1,100 performances.

DANCING LADY (MGM 1933). METRO-GOLDWYN-MAYER'S answer to WARNER BROTHERS' *42ND STREET* (1933), this backstage musical is more memorable for the people in it than what happens in the story. Alan Rivkin and P. J. Wolson adapted James Warner

Bellah's novel for the screen, but they may as well have taken the script from the Warner classic. Chorus girl Janie "Duchess" Barlow (JOAN CRAWFORD) hopes to make it big on Broadway but her rich boyfriend Tod Newton (Franchot Tone) secretly bribes the backers to pull out and keep the musical *Dancing Lady* from opening. Tough-as-nails director Patch Gallagher (Clark Gable) puts his own money into the show and puts Janie in the leading role when the star cannot go on, all ending happily if not surprisingly. In addition to seeing nonmusical stars Crawford and Gable giving strong performances in a musical, the film is noteworthy for introducing FRED ASTAIRE who played the Broadway hoofer named "Fred Astaire." Also cast were NELSON EDDY, May Robson, WINNIE LIGHTNER, ROBERT BENCHLEY, Ted Healy, Grant Mitchell, STERLING HOLLOWAY, and Art Jarret who delivered the hit song "Everything I Have Is Yours." The score was composed of new songs written by three different teams: RODGERS and HART, JIMMY MCHUGH and DOROTHY FIELDS, and BURTON LANE and HAROLD ADAMSON. Astaire partnered with Crawford for "Heigh-Ho, the Gang's All Here" and "Let's Go Bavarian," and Eddy sang the lavish finale "The Rhythm of the Day" about the throbbing pulse of big city life. As directed by ROBERT Z. LEONARD and choreographed by SAMMY LEE and Eddie Prinz, the David O. Selznick production was a mishmash of styles but an agreeable experience all the same.

DANDRIDGE, DOROTHY [Jean] (1923–1965). Film, stage, and television performer. One of the first African American actress to become a movie star and the first black woman to grace the cover of *Life Magazine*, she gave some outstanding performances in her brief film career. Dandridge was born in Cleveland, Ohio, the daughter of a minister and a film actress, and began performing at the age of four with her sister in a vaudeville act billed "The Wonder Children." The sisters sang in the Hollywood musicals *THE BIG BROADCAST OF 1936* (1935) and *Easy to Take* (1936) and then Dorothy was featured as a child singer in the MARX BROTHERS movie *A DAY AT THE RACES* (1937) before gaining further attention as a teenager introducing "Chattanooga Choo-Choo" in *SUN VALLEY SERENADE* (1941). Soon she was a regular on the radio, was featured as a specialty in the movie musicals *Hit Parade of 1943* and *Atlantic City* (1944), became a popular singer in nightclubs, and acted in the early television series *Beulah*. Dandridge's singing voice

was not capable of handling opera so she was dubbed for her two most famous movie musicals, *CARMEN JONES* (1954) and *PORGY AND BESS* (1959). In the early 1960s, the glamorous beauty was swindled out of her fortune, went bankrupt, and committed suicide with a drug overdose at the age of thirty-eight. She was married to dancer Harold Nicholas of the famed NICHOLAS BROTHERS and Halle Berry played her in the TV movie *Introducing Dorothy Dandridge* (1999). Autobiography: *Everything and Nothing* (1970).

◻ **DANGEROUS CHRISTMAS OF RED RIDING HOOD, THE, or OH WOLF, POOR WOLF.** (ABC-TV 1965). Songwriters JULE STYNE (music) and BOB MERRILL (lyrics) went from their Broadway hit *FUNNY GIRL* (1964) to television where they again found themselves writing for a rising star, in this case LIZA MINNELLI, who plays Red with tenderness and awe. The main character in Robert Emmett's teleplay is the Wolf (CYRIL RITCHARD) who tells the story from his point of view, claiming he was a victim of circumstances. VIC DAMONE was the prince disguised as a Woodsman, and

The Dangerous Christmas of Red Riding Hood.
A few months after starring in *Flora, the Red Menace* (1965) on Broadway, seventeen-year-old Liza Minnelli (pictured) was starred in this television musical opposite veteran Cyril Ritchard; she dazzled audiences in both productions. (Photofest)

the British rock group, the Animals, played the pack of wolves. The sixty-minute musical was slight but entertaining, particularly when the principals engaged in such songs as "You'll Need a Song," "My Riding Hood," and "Ding-a-Ling, Ding-a-Ling." Also enjoyable were the raucous "We're Gonna Howl Tonight," the merry "Along the Way," and the "Woodsman's Serenade." The story was set at Christmastime (Red is bringing Christmas presents to Granny) so there was even a holiday song, "We Wish the World a Happy Yule," for the finale. RICHARD LEWINE produced the engaging musical, which was directed by Sid Smith and choreographed by LEE THEODORE.

DANIELE, GRACIELA (1939–). Stage and film choreographer and director. A distinctive dancer-turned-choreographer-turned-director, she is equally at home with brassy Broadway dance as with ethnic-flavored choreography. Daniele was born in Buenos Aires, Argentina, and educated there at the Theatre Colon. She was a ballet dancer for the Opera Ballet of Nice, France, in the early 1960s and then came to New York and studied dance with Matt Mattox before appearing in the chorus of Broadway musicals such as *What Makes Sammy Run?* (1964), *PROMISES, PROMISES* (1968), and *FOLLIES* (1971). She assisted such choreographers as BOB FOSSE and MICHAEL BENNETT and then made her Manhattan choreography debut Off Broadway in 1971. Her choreography was first noticed on Broadway in the 1979 revival of *THE MOST HAPPY FELLA*, followed by a number of musicals that showed off her versatility, including *THE PIRATES OF PENZANCE* (1980), *ZORBÁ* (1983), *THE RINK* (1984), *THE MYSTERY OF EDWIN DROOD* (1985), *The Goodbye Girl* (1993), *RAGTIME* (1998), and *The Pirate Queen* (2007). Daniele first directed as well as choreographed with the Latin American dance musical *Tango Apasionado* (1987), followed by *Dangerous Games* (1989), *ONCE ON THIS ISLAND* (1990), *HELLO AGAIN* (1994), *Chronicle of a Death Foretold* (1995), *A NEW BRAIN* (1998), *ANNIE GET YOUR GUN* (1999), *Marie Christine* (1999), *Dessa Rose* (2005), *Chita Rivera: A Dancer's Life* (2005), *Bernarda Alba* (2006), and *The Glorious Ones* (2007). She has also done choreography for films, most memorably a series of Woody Allen movies, including the musical *EVERYONE SAYS I LOVE YOU* (1996). Daniele is married to lighting designer Jules Fisher (1937–).

DANIELS, BEBE [Virginia] (1901–1971). Film performer. A dark-haired beauty with lots of spirit, she was a veteran of hundreds of silent shorts before she made movie musicals in the 1930s. Daniels was born in Dallas, Texas, and was on the stage at the age of four. After touring the country in kid parts, she went to Hollywood when she was nine and was cast as a child in many two-reelers, mostly westerns. With the arrival of sound, Daniels moved easily into musicals, playing the title role in *RIO RITA* (1929). Her other musical credits are *Love Comes Across* (1930), *Dixiana* (1930), *Reaching for the Moon* (1931), and *Music Is Magic* (1935), but she is best remembered as the temperamental star Dorothy Brock in *42ND STREET* (1933). Daniels married the British actor Ben Lyon (1901–1979) and the two went to England where he was featured in the musicals *The Song You Gave Me* (1933), *A Southern Maid* (1933), and *Hi, Gang!* (1941). The couple remained in England where she appeared in West End musicals and later they had a very popular radio show together. Autobiography: *Life With the Lyons* [both] (1953); Biography: *Bebe and Ben*, Jill Allgood (1973).

DANIELS, DANNY (1924–). Stage and television choreographer. A resourceful choreographer and sometime director, he has staged both intimate Off Broadway revues and large brassy Broadway musicals. Daniels was born in Albany, New York, the son of a salesman, and studied at various dance studios before beginning a busy dancing career. In addition to appearing in many tours of musicals and with dance companies, Daniels was in the dancing chorus of such Broadway hits as *BEST FOOT FORWARD* (1941), *MAKE MINE MANHATTAN* (1948), and *KISS ME KATE* (1948). In 1953 he founded the Danny Daniels Dance America Company and toured the country. By 1956 he was staging numbers Off Broadway for such fondly remembered intimate revues as *The Littlest Revue* (1956) and *Shoestring '57 (1956)*. He made his Broadway choreography debut in 1962 with *ALL AMERICAN*, followed by other shows of varying success, including *High Spirits* (1964), *ANNIE GET YOUR GUN* (1966), *Walking Happy* (1966), *I Remember Mama* (1979), and *THE TAP DANCE KID* (1983). Daniels resurrected his dance company in 1974 and choreographed works for it in California. He also devised the dances for many television specials and in a number of films, most memorably *The Night They Raided Minsky's* (1968) and *PENNIES FROM HEAVEN* (1981). Daniels' choreography might have been in the traditional mode but it was notable for its vitality and wit, such as his chorus doing a tap number wearing sneakers in *The Tap Dance Kid*.

DANIELS, WILLIAM (1927–). Stage, television, and film performer. The loud, strident character actor became a familiar face late in his career because of his television appearances but he has diversified theatre experience as well. Born in Brooklyn to a performing family, Daniels was on the stage from the age of four and first appeared on Broadway as one of the children in the long-running comedy *Life With Father* (1943). After attending Northwestern University, he trained with Lee Strasberg at the Actors Studio and appeared in some notable plays on and Off Broadway, such as the original production of Edward Albee's *The Zoo Story* (1960) and as the narrow-minded social worker in *A Thousand Clowns* (1962), a role he repeated on screen in 1965. Daniel's first Broadway musical appearance was as the stuffy fiancé Warren in *ON A CLEAR DAY YOU CAN SEE FOREVER* (1965), followed by his most memorable stage role, the quarrelsome John Adams in *1776* (1969), which he reprised on film in 1972. He replaced LEN CARIOU as the lawyer Frederik Egerman in *A LITTLE NIGHT MUSIC* in 1974 and then concentrated on television where he was successful in comedy and drama series, as well as in a number of movies. He is married to actress Bonnie Bartlett (1929–) with whom he has often acted.

DARE, [Daniel] **DANNY** (1905–1996). Stage and film choreographer and producer. A successful Broadway and Hollywood choreographer, he turned to producing films late in his career. Little is confirmed about Dare's early life but by 1923 he was dancing on Broadway and in 1929 he choreographed the landmark revue *THE LITTLE SHOW* (1929). His other Broadway musical credits include *SWEET ADELINE* (1929), *Sweet and Low* (1930), *You Said It* (1931), *Tattle Tales* (1933), and *Meet the People* (1940), which he also wrote, directed, and produced. Dare was working in Hollywood by 1935 and choreographed such musicals as *Three Cheers for Love* (1936), *HOLIDAY INN* (1942), *STAR-SPANGLED RHYTHM* (1942), *HERE COME THE WAVES* (1944), *And the Angels Sing* (1944), *Incendiary Blonde* (1945), and *ROAD TO UTOPIA* (1945). He turned to producing for PARAMOUNT in 1945 and presented such musicals as *Duffy's Tavern* (1945), *Variety Girl* (1947), *ROAD TO RIO* (1947), and *Isn't It Romantic?* (1948).

DARLING LILI (Paramount 1970). While it may have been a bit of a mess as it tried to decide whether it was a farce, an adventure, or a romance, the musical was held together by star JULIE ANDREWS who conquered the material and got to sing the haunting "Whistling Away the Dark," lyricist JOHNNY MERCER's last great song. HENRY MANCINI composed the music and, while the other numbers could not match it, the musical end of the movie held its own. The screenplay by producer–director BLAKE EDWARDS and William Peter Blatty, however, was problematic. During World War I, the British singing star Lili Smith (Andrews) is really a German spy Lili Schmidt who is passing information on to the enemy. American flying ace Major William Larrabee (Rock Hudson) is on to her game but is charmed all the same, with the two of them engaging in some romantic banter reminiscent of Hudson's tangles with DORIS DAY in their many 1960s comedies. The contrived ending insisted Lili see the error of her ways and switch sides. Some wartime standards, such as "It's a Long Long Way to Tipperary" and "Pack Up Your Troubles in Your Old Kit Bag," were added for period flavor, but the film never felt like a period piece. Although Andrews got to do a mock striptease (choreographed by HERMES PAN in the final days of his career) and play a bad girl, it was her familiar crisp and wholesome persona that carried the movie. The musical was a box office failure but over the years has acquired a kind of cult status.

DATE WITH JUDY, A (MGM 1948). Teenagers prevailed in this bright musical comedy that was very popular with postwar audiences looking to the domestic side of life. Based on a 1941 radio program, the screenplay by DOROTHY KINGSLEY and Dorothy Cooper centered on the Foster household in which papa (Wallace Beery) is privately taking rhumba lessons from Rosita Cochellas (CARMEN MIRANDA) to surprise his wife (Selena Royle) on their anniversary. His teenage daughter Judy (JANE POWELL) misconstrues their meetings as an affair, which adds to her anxiety over choosing between the youthful Oogie Pringle (Scotty Beckett) and the older Stephen Andrews (Robert Stack) as her date to the dance. Because Oogie's beautiful, calculating sister Carol (ELIZABETH TAYLOR) is after Stephen herself, there are plenty of complications. Also cast were Leon Ames, CLINTON SUNDBERG, George Cleveland, Jerry Hunter, Lloyd Corigan, and XAVIER CUGAT as himself getting mixed up in the plot and leading the band at the dance. The score was by a variety of songwriters, but the standout hit "It's a Most Unusual Day" was by JIMMY MCHUGH (music) and HAROLD ADAMSON (lyrics). Other numbers included "Cuanto La Gusta," "I've Got a

Date With Judy," "Judaline," and "Strictly on the Corny Side." RICHARD THORPE directed the JOE PASTERNAK production with just enough schmaltz, and STANLEY DONEN choreographed the lively dance numbers.

DAVID, HAL. See BACHARACH, Burt

DAVID, MACK (1912–1993). Film and television lyricist. A prolific Tin Pan Alley songwriter who wrote theme songs for dozens of Hollywood nonmusicals and television programs, he scored a few musicals as well. David was born in New York and educated at Cornell University and St. John's University Law School. He turned to songwriting in the late 1920s and, usually collaborating with composer JERRY LIVINGSTON, wrote the scores for the movie musicals *Main Street Follies* (1935), *The Love Department* (1935), *Dublin in Brass* (1935), WALT DISNEY'S *CINDERELLA* (1949), and three JERRY LEWIS–DEAN MARTIN service musical comedies—*At War With the Army* (1950), *Sailor Beware* (1951), and *Jumping Jacks* (1952). David also scored the TV musicals *The Land of Green Ginger* (1958) and *Mother Goose* (1958). Among his popular songs are "A Dream Is a Wish Your Heart Makes," "I Don't Care If the Sun Don't Shine," "Falling Leaves," "Baby, It's You," and "Bibbidi Bobbidi Boo." His brother is lyricist HAL DAVID.

DAVIES, BRIAN (1939–). Stage and television performer. A favorite juvenile actor on Broadway in the 1960s, the round-cheeked singer–actor originated some notable roles in musicals. Davies was born in the Rhondda Valley in Wales but came to America when he was ten and grew up in Indianapolis. After attending Indiana University, he went on the stage and originated two familiar roles on Broadway: the young Nazi Rolf in *THE SOUND OF MUSIC* (1959) and the hapless lover Hero in *A FUNNY THING HAPPENED ON THE WAY TO THE FORUM* (1962). He did not return to Broadway until he played the Dubliner Mr. Browne in the musical *JAMES JOYCE'S THE DEAD* (2000). Davies has acted in a few films and has appeared on many television programs playing regulars in soap operas and courtroom dramas.

DAVIES, MARION [born Marion Cecilia Douras] (1897–1961). Film and stage performer. The wide-eyed blonde beauty mostly remembered as the mistress of newspaper tycoon William Randolph Hearst, the singer–actress was featured in nine movie musicals in which she demonstrated that she was more than a pretty face. Davies was born in New York and was a show girl on the Manhattan stage, appearing in the chorus of the Broadway musicals *CHIN CHIN* (1914), *Nobody Home* (1915), and *Miss Information* (1915). She got featured roles in the musicals *Stop! Look! Listen!* (1915), *ZIEGFELD FOLLIES* (1916), *Betty* (1916), *OH, BOY!* (1917), *Miss 1917* (1917), *Words and Music* (1917), and *Ed Wynn's Carnival* (1920). Davies entered silent films in 1917 and Hearst founded Cosmopolitan Pictures in 1919 to showcase her in romantic period costume pieces. For the next four years she starred in melodramas that were highly publicized by Hearst but audiences didn't embrace the manufactured star and the studio collapsed. Ironically, audiences loved Davies when she was in light comedies and, when sound came in, musicals. Her movie musicals include *HOLLYWOOD REVUE OF 1929*, *Marianne* (1929), *The Florodora Girl* (1930), *Blondie of the Follies* (1932), *GOING HOLLYWOOD* (1933), *Hearts Divided* (1936), *Cain and Mabel* (1936), and *Ever Since Eve* (1937). Davies retired from films in the late 1930s and became a successful businesswoman and company executive. Autobiography: *The Times We Had* (1985); biography: *Marion Davis*, Fred Lawrence Guiles (1972).

DAVIS, JOAN [born Madonna Josephine Davis] (1907–1961). Film and television performer. An awkward comedienne with a continual forlorn look on her face, she lit up the screen in two dozen Hollywood musicals. Davis was born in St. Paul, Minnesota, the daughter of a train dispatcher, and was on the stage as a child, later doing a comedy act in vaudeville. She started making comedy shorts in Hollywood in 1934 and then later was featured in such musical features as *Millions in the Air* (1935), *ON THE AVENUE* (1937), *WAKE UP AND LIVE* (1937), *Sing and Be Happy* (1937), *Thin Ice* (1937), *Love and Hisses* (1937), *Sally, Irene and Mary* (1938), *My Lucky Star* (1938), *Just Around the Corner* (1938), *SUN VALLEY SERENADE* (1941), *Two Latins From Manhattan* (1941), *Yokel Boy* (1942), *Show Business* (1944), *Kansas City Kitty* (1944), *GEORGE WHITE'S SCANDALS* (1945), and *If You Knew Susie* (1948). Although she became a familiar face on screen, real fame came from her many radio broadcasts in the 1940s and her popular television series *I Married Joan* in the 1950s. Biography: *Hold That Joan: The Life, Laughs and Films of Joan Davis*, Ben Ohmart (2006).

DAVIS, JOHNNY SCAT [born John Gustave Davis] (1910–1983). Film performer and musician. The Big Band favorite who scat-sang on the radio and on records, he was featured in character parts in six Hollywood musicals. Davis was born in Brazil, Indiana, and played trumpet as a youngster. When he started playing in bands he discovered a talent for scat-singing like a musical instrument. Soon he was the featured vocalist with Fred Waring's Orchestra and was featured in the movie musicals *Varsity Show* (1937), *Cowboy From Brooklyn* (1938), *Garden of the Moon* (1938), *You Can't Ration Love* (1944), and *KNICKERBOCKER HOLIDAY* (1944), but he is most remembered for introducing "Hooray for Hollywood" in *HOLLYWOOD HOTEL* (1937). Davis also acted in several nonmusical films and then left the movies in the 1940s to concentrate on recordings and nightclubs.

DAVIS, SAMMY, JR. (1925–1990). Stage, film, and television performer. The electric African American entertainer found success in every medium, from vaudeville to television. The New Yorker was born into a family of hoofers and at a young age Davis was dancing in vaudeville and in some movie shorts. Touring the country as one of the Will Mastin Trio, he developed his jazzy singing style, expert hoofing, and wry sense of comedy. In 1956 Davis made his adult film debut in *The Benny*

Sammy Davis, Jr. On the stage as a child, Davis was a polished veteran by the time he starred in his first Broadway show in 1956. He returned as boxer Joe Wellington in *Golden Boy* (1964), giving a performance that was applauded for it vocal and physical punch. Here Davis (left) demonstrates his prowess for Kenneth Tobey. (Photofest)

Goodman Story and his Broadway debut as the star of *MR. WONDERFUL*, followed by many more films, and returned to Broadway as the boxer Joe Wellington in *GOLDEN BOY* (1964) and the everyman Littlechap in *STOP THE WORLD—I WANT TO GET OFF* (1978). At the same time Davis was very active in nightclubs, in concerts, and on television specials, such as the TV musical *ALICE IN WONDERLAND* (1985). He got to sing and dance in many of his films even when they were not musicals, such as the "rat pack" films with FRANK SINATRA and his last movie *Tap* (1989). Davis' screen musicals include *Sweet and Low* (1947), *PORGY AND BESS* (1959), *Pepe* (1960), the German film *THE THREEPENNY OPERA* (1962), *ROBIN AND THE SEVEN HOODS* (1964), *SWEET CHARITY* (1969), and *Stop the World—I Want to Get Off* (1978). Autobiographies: *Yes, I Can* (1965); *Why Me?* (1989); *Sammy*, with Burt and James Boyar (2000); biographies: *Gonna Do Great Things: The Life of Sammy Davis Jr.*, Gary Fishgall (2003); *Sammy Davis, Jr., My Father*, Tracey Davis with Delores Barclay (1996).

DAWN, HAZEL [born Hazel Dawn La Tout] (1891–1988). Stage performer. A wide-eyed blonde who charmed audiences in New York and London, her vehicles were rarely first class but she was never less than stellar. Dawn was born in Ogden City, Utah, and trained in Europe as a violinist and singer. She made her London debut in 1909 in *Dear Little Denmark*, followed by featured roles in *The Balkan Princess* (1910) and *The Dollar Princess* (1910). Dawn made a sensational Broadway debut in *THE PINK LADY* (1911) in which she accompanied herself on the violin as she sang "My Beautiful Lady." After reprising her performance in London, she starred in some Broadway farces and the musicals *The Little Café* (1913), *The Debutante* (1914), *The Century Girl* (1916), *Nifties of 1923*, *Keep Kool* (1924), and *Great Temptations* (1926). Dawn also starred in several silent films in the 1910s. She was at the peak of her popularity when she retired to get married in 1931.

■ **DAY AT THE RACES, A** (MGM 1937). Even though this MARX BROTHERS vehicle had more musical numbers than usual, the highlights were mostly comic sequences rather than songs. George Seaton, Robert Pirosh, and George Oppenheimer collaborated on the screenplay in which the wealthy philanthropist Emily Upjohn (MARGARET DUMONT) brings in the horse doctor Hugo Hackenbush (Groucho Marx) to save her sanitarium, but he only manages to bring Judy Standish (Maureen O'Sullivan) and Gil Stewart (ALLAN JONES) together while ice cream vendor Tony (Chico Marx) causes trouble and jockey Stuffy (Harpo Marx) saves the day by winning a horse race in the farcical climax. Douglass Dumbrille, SIG RUMANN, Esther Muir, Robert Middlemass, and Ivie Anderson were on hand to be insulted by Groucho. "Tomorrow Is Another Day," "Blue Venetian Waters," and "A Message From the Man in the Moon" were written by various songwriters, but the standout musical number was "All God's Chillun Got Rhythm" by Bronislaw Kaper, GUS KAHN, and Walter Jurmann in which pied piper Harpo led a gang of African American kids (including a young DOROTHY DANDRIDGE) in a jubilant celebration of gospel, jazz, and swing choreographed by DAVE GOULD. Co-producer SAM WOOD directed the fast-paced frolic.

DAY, DENNIS [born Eugene Dennis McNulty] (1916–1988). Film and television performer. A boyish high tenor who usually played lame-brained sidekicks, he was featured in eight Hollywood musicals. Born in the Bronx, Day was a boy singer in the choir of St. Patrick's Cathedral before going to Manhattan College. He was discovered by JACK BENNY, who first featured the young singer on his radio show in 1939; the two would become comic foils for each other on film and in Benny's successful television show in the 1950s. Day sang in such movie musicals as *Buck Benny Rides Again* (1940), *The Powers Girl* (1942), *Sleepy Lagoon* (1943), *Music in Manhattan* (1944), *I'll Get By* (1950), *The Golden Girl* (1951), and *The Girl Next Door* (1953), as well as singing on the soundtrack for the animated film *MELODY TIME* (1948). He appeared on many different television shows but continued to perform with Benny until the comic's death in 1974.

DAY, DORIS [born Doris Mary Anne von Kappelhoff] (1924–). Film and television performer. For many years America's favorite wholesome, girl-next-door movie star, playing virginal heroines into middle age, she was also a superb song stylist and a very accomplished actress with several memorable films to her credit. Day was born in Cincinnati and dreamt of a dance career until a car accident ended her hopes of becoming a ballerina. As a teen she started singing and was eventually the featured vocalist with Les Brown's Band. Day made an auspicious screen debut in the leading role in the musical *ROMANCE ON THE HIGH SEAS* (1948),

launching her movie career and putting her records high on the charts. She was cast in a series of musicals in which she was optimistic, chipper, and engaging, such as *It's a Great Feeling* (1949), *My Dream Is Yours* (1949), *Tea for Two* (1950), *West Point Story* (1950), *Lullaby of Broadway* (1951), *On Moonlight Bay* (1951), *I'll See You in My Dreams* (1951), *April in Paris* (1952), *By the Light of the Silvery Moon* (1953), *Lucky Me* (1954), THE PAJAMA GAME (1957), and *JUMBO* (1962). She got meatier parts in nonmusicals but on occasion one of her musical roles gave her a chance to stretch her acting muscles, such as *YOUNG MAN WITH A HORN* (1950), CALAMITY JANE (1953), *Young at Heart* (1954), and *LOVE ME OR LEAVE ME* (1955). Day found a new career in the 1960s as the bubble-headed heroine in a series of coy sex comedies with ROCK HUDSON and then found success with her own television show from 1968 to 1971 and a cable show in the 1980s. She has retired from performing and has been active in animal rights organizations. Autobiography: *Doris Day: Her Own Story* (1975); biographies: *Doris Day*, Eric Braun (2004); *Considering Doris Day*, Tom Santopietro (2007).

DAY, EDITH [Marie] (1896–1971). Stage performer. An American leading lady who, after a handful of musical hits on Broadway, went to London for the rest of her celebrated career. Day was born and educated in Minneapolis and made her Broadway stage debut in 1915 in *Pom-Pom*. Two years later she gained recognition as the heroine Grace in the aviation musical *Going Up!* and then had even greater success as the Irish Cinderella Irene O'Dare in *IRENE* (1917). Her last Broadway appearances were as Kitty in *Orange Blossoms* (1922) and as the heroine Nina Benedetto in *WILDFLOWER* (1923) in which she introduced the song "Bambalina." Day then went to London where she was later dubbed the "Queen of Drury Lane" for her series of musical hits at the Drury Lane Theatre. There she played the leading roles in *ROSE-MARIE* (1925), *THE DESERT SONG* (1927), *SHOW BOAT* (1928), and *RIO RITA* (1930), as well as other musicals and operettas. Day continued performing on the London stage into the 1960s, playing the wry tourist Mrs. Sweeney in *Sail Away* (1962). She was a baby-faced, dark-haired pixie whose bright and slightly pop eyes lit up the stage.

DAY IN HOLLYWOOD, A—A NIGHT IN THE UKRAINE (John Golden Theatre 1980). An unusual evening that consisted of a revue and a one-act musical farce, this loving movie salute and parody may have been thin Broadway fare but was so well executed that audiences came for 588 performances. Dick Vosburgh (book and lyrics) and Frank Lazarus (music) wrote the musical double bill, the first half a tribute to movie musicals with a chorus line of ushers performing old songs from Hollywood and new numbers about Tinsel Town. The second half was a slap-happy MARX BROTHERS version of Chekhov's one-act comedy *The Bear* with lots of Russian jokes and tuneful pastiche songs. The skill-ful cast included PRISCILLA LOPEZ, David Garrison, Frank Lazarus, Peggy Hewett, Stephen James, and Kate Draper, and some of the new songs they delivered were "Just Go to the Movies," "I Love a Film Cliché," "Samovar the Lawyer," "The Best in the World," and "Natasha." While some critics found the evening an extended sketch planted within a revue, others enjoyed the piece for the unpretentious fun that it was, particu-larly the young cast and TOMMY TUNE's end-lessly creative direction and (with THOMMIE WALSH) choreography.

DE KOVEN, [Henry Louis] **REGINALD** (1861–1920). Stage composer. Little remembered and rarely produced today, the prolific composer was the most respected theatre artist of his day and wrote the most-produced American operetta of the nineteeth century, *ROBIN HOOD* (1891). De Koven was born in Middleton, Connecticut, and educated at Oxford University in England, as well as at music schools in Germany and Italy. He went into business and made his fortune and then retired and wrote twenty-four oper-ettas for Broadway, starting with *The Begum* (1887) and concluding with *Her Little Highness* (1913). In addition to *Robin Hood*, the first endur-ing American operetta, De Koven scored such pieces as *Don Quixote* (1889), *The Knickerbockers* (1892), *The Algerian* (1893), *The Fencing Master* (1893), *Rob Roy* (1894), *The Mandarin* (1896), *The Highwayman* (1897), *Papa's Wife* (1899), *The Little Duchess* (1901), *Maid Marian* (1892), *The Jersey Lily* (1903), *Happyland* (1905), *The Student King* (1906), *The Golden Butterfly* (1908), and *The Wedding Trip* (1911). Seventeen of his oper-ettas were written with librettist–lyricist HARRY B. SMITH and, although they were foreign in set-ting, the two men strived to create an American sound in their scores. Memoir: *A Musician and His Wife*, Anna De Koven (1926).

DE-LOVELY. See *NIGHT AND DAY*

DE MILLE, AGNES [George] (1905–1993). Stage choreographer and director. Arguably Broadway's most influential choreographer, she created a long list of unforgettable musi-cal numbers in legendary shows. She was born in New York City, the daughter of playwright William C. de Mille, the granddaughter of playwright Henry C. de Mille, and the niece of film director Cecil B. De Mille (the only family member to capitalize the "De"). After gradu-ating from the University of California at Los Angeles, de Mille studied dance in London with Theodore Koslov, Marie Rambert, and Anthony Tudor. Returning to America, she performed with various companies, started a troupe of her own, and appeared on Broadway in the *Grand Street Follies* (1928). In the 1930s she started to make a name for herself as a choreographer with New York City's Ballet Theatre (later known as the American Ballet Theatre) where she developed such memora-ble dance pieces as *Three Virgins and a Devil* and *Rodeo*. de Mille choreographed some regional theatre productions and then two popular London attractions before making her Broadway debut with her dances for *HOORAY FOR WHAT!* in 1937. It was de Mille's choreog-raphy for *OKLAHOMA!* (1943) that revolution-ized theatre dance, using ballet not just to tell a story but to illustrate the psychological state of the characters, as in the famous ballet titled "Laurey Makes Up Her Mind." Not only was de Mille in great demand after *Oklahoma!*, but many other choreographers copied her ideas and producers added similar ballet sequences to their shows. Not content with repeating her-self, de Mille experimented with dance in many of her subsequent projects, some of which she also directed. Among her Broadway chore-ography credits were *ONE TOUCH OF VENUS* (1943), *BLOOMER GIRL* (1944), *CAROUSEL* (1945), *BRIGADOON* (1947), *GENTLEMEN PREFER BLONDES* (1949), *PAINT YOUR WAGON* (1951), *The Girl in Pink Tights* (1954), *Goldilocks* (1958), *JUNO* (1959), *KWAMINA* (1961), and *110 IN THE SHADE* (1963). de Mille directed *OUT OF THIS WORLD* (1950) and both directed and choreographed *ALLEGRO* (1947) and *Come Summer* (1969). As a young dancer she appeared in a few of her uncle's silent films but had very little to do with Hollywood throughout her long career except to restage her dances for the screen version of *Oklahoma!* (1955) and her ballets were recre-ated for the movie of *Carousel* (1956). Because her fame as a choreographer coincided with the advent of the fully integrated play, her con-tribution to the development of theatre dance is sometimes underestimated. After de Mille, it would no longer be so easy for a musical to just break into hoofing because it was time for a dance. She was also the first to insist that the music for ballets and extended dance numbers be composed in collaboration with the choreographer. A very vocal advocate for government support of the arts, de Mille wrote a dozen books on her life and her art, including *Dance to the Piper* (1952), *And Promenade Home* (1957), *Speak to Me, Dance With Me* (1973), and *Reprieve: A Memoir* (1981). Biography: *No Intermissions: The Life of Agnes de Mille*, Carol Easton (2000).

DE PAUL, GENE (1919–1988). Stage and film composer. A lesser-known but very successful songwriter in Hollywood, his scores with lyricists JOHNNY MERCER and DON RAYE are filled with musical favorites. The native New Yorker studied music privately and played piano for dance orchestras, sometimes singing with bands as well. He started writing songs for Tin Pan Alley and found enough success that he was hired by the studios in 1941 to score movie musicals with Raye. Among the team's film credits are the musicals *In the Navy* (1941), *Moonlight in Hawaii* (1941), *Keep 'Em Flying* (1941), *Behind the Eight Ball* (1941), *Hellzapoppin'* (1941), *Ride 'Em Cowboy* (1942), *Pardon My Sarong* (1942), *Hi Ya Chum* (1943), *Larceny With Music* (1943), *Broadway Rhythm* (1944), *A Song Is Born* (1948), and the animated *Ichabod and Mr. Toad* (1949). De Paul's first collaboration with Mercer brought forth the Hollywood classic *SEVEN BRIDES FOR SEVEN BROTHERS* (1954), and the two also worked together on the Broadway musical *Li'l Abner* (1956) and the film *You Can't Run Away From It* (1956). Among de Paul's song hits are "Teach Me Tonight," "Cow-Cow Boogie," "I'll Remember April," and "You Don't Know What Love Is."

DE SHIELDS, ANDRE (1946–). Stage performer, director, and choreographer. The agile African American singer–dancer–actor usually stood out even in a talented ensemble, bringing a vibrant excitement to his stage roles. De Shields was born in Baltimore and educated at the University of Wisconsin and New York University before getting work as a backup singer for BETTE MIDLER. After appearing in the Chicago company of *HAIR*, he made his New York debut Off Broadway in 1973 and two years later was on Broadway, stopping the show as the title role in *THE WIZ* (1975 and

1993). De Shields' other major hit was *AIN'T MISBEHAVIN'* (1978), which he reprised in 1988. The rest of his on and Off Broadway musicals failed to run, such as *Harlem Nocturne* (1984), *Just So* (1985), *Stardust* (1987), and *Play On!* (1997), but he made an impressive comeback as the elderly would-be stripper Horse Simmons in *THE FULL MONTY* (2000). De Shields has made some television appearances and is a respected stage director and choreographer regionally.

DE SYLVA, B. G. [born George Gard De Sylva] (1895–1950). Stage and film lyricist, writer, and producer. A multitask, multitalented songwriter who worked with a wide variety of artists, he contributed to twenty-three Broadway and twenty-one movie musicals. The native New Yorker, familiarly known as "Buddy" De Sylva, grew up in California and started writing lyrics as a student at the University of Southern California. Some of his songs were interpolated into Broadway shows before he and composer GEORGE GERSHWIN had their first full score heard in *La La Lucille* (1919). The two also collaborated on songs for three editions of *GEORGE WHITE'S SCANDALS* (1922, 1923, 1924), as well as the book musical *Sweet Little Devil* (1924). De Sylva teamed with other composers for *Orange Blossoms* (1922), *The Yankee Princess* (1922), *BIG BOY* (1925), *Captain Jinks* (1925), and *Queen High* (1926), also writing the libretto for the last. But his most famous collaborators were composer RAY HENDERSON and lyricist LEW BROWN. The trio first worked together on *George White's Scandals* (1925) and came up with such a scintillating score that they reteamed for a series of hit musicals: *GOOD NEWS!* (1927), *Manhattan Mary* (1927), *George White's Scandals* (1928), *HOLD EVERYTHING!* (1928), *FOLLOW THRU* (1929), and *FLYING HIGH* (1930). Again De Sylva wrote the books for most of these and by the 1930s turned to producing as well. He presented and wrote the librettos for *TAKE A CHANCE* (1932), *DUBARRY WAS A LADY* (1939), *LOUISIANA PURCHASE* (1940), and *PANAMA HATTIE* (1940). De Sylva also contributed single songs to musicals by others; some of his biggest hits were such interpolations as "Look for the Silver Lining" and "California Here I Come." De Sylva was equally busy and successful in Hollywood where he, Brown, and Henderson scored the early musicals *THE SINGING FOOL* (1928), *Say It With Songs* (1929), *SUNNY SIDE UP* (1929), *Just Imagine* (1930), and *Indiscreet* (1931), as well as the screen versions of their stage hits. After scoring *My Weakness* (1933) with composer RICHARD A. WHITING, De Sylva took up movie producing and presented such musicals as *Under the Pampas Moon* (1935), *The Littlest Rebel* (1935), *CAPTAIN JANUARY* (1935), *Sing, Baby, Sing* (1936), *POOR LITTLE RICH GIRL* (1936), *Merry-Go-Round of 1938* (1937), *You're a Sweetheart* (1937), *BIRTH OF THE BLUES* (1941), *LADY IN THE DARK* (1943), and *The Stork Club* (1946). De Sylva was very active in musical publishing and was a co-founder of Capitol Records. The story of De Sylva, Brown, and Henderson was told in the film bio *THE BEST THINGS IN LIFE ARE FREE* (1956) in which GORDON MACRAE played De Sylva. Among his many song standards are "Sonny Boy," "I'll Build a Stairway to Paradise," "If You knew Suzie," and "It All Depends on You." De Sylva's talent was for carefree, exuberant lyrics and breezy librettos that reflected the spirit of the Jazz Age. Biography: *The Best Things in Life Are Free: The De Sylva, Brown & Henderson Story*, John O'Hara (1955).

DEAR WORLD (Mark Hellinger Theatre 1969). Perhaps songwriter Jerry Herman's most ambitious effort, this musical version of Jean Giraudoux's French fantasy–comedy *The Madwoman of Chaillot* (1948) was sometimes exhilarating and other times deadly dull. The Paris madwoman Countess Aurelia (ANGELA LANSBURY) discovers one day that there are some greedy, unpleasant people in the world so with her cohort the Sewerman (Milo O'Shea) and the approval of her looney friends Gabrielle (JANE CONNELL) and Constance (Carmen Mathews), Aurelia passes judgment on the villains of the world and sends them to their death in her cellar. JEROME LAWRENCE and ROBERT E. LEE wrote the charmless libretto that seemed to ignore the wistful nature of the play, but some of Herman's songs captured it beautifully, such as " I Don't Want to Know;" "And I Was Beautiful," "Each Tomorrow Morning," and "Kiss Her Now." Other numbers, such as the noisy title song, were inappropriately razzle dazzle. Even the most negative

notices admitted that Lansbury's performance was luminous but not even she could keep the musical on the boards for more than 132 performances. ALEXANDER H. COHAN produced and the show was staged by JOE LAYTON.

DEAREST ENEMY (Knickerbocker Theatre 1925). This first collaboration between librettist HERBERT FIELDS and songwriters RICHARD RODGERS (music) and LORENZ HART (lyrics) resulted in a charming musical comedy set during the Revolutionary War. The British army, under the leadership of General Howe, has taken New York City in 1776 so the wily Mrs. Murray and other women on "Murray Hill" plan to wine and dine the General and his officers, giving time for George Washington in Harlem Heights to amass his troops and get reinforcements. Mrs. Murray is aided in her plan by her feisty niece, Betsy Burke, who proceeds with the distraction even after she falls in love with the British Captain John Copeland. The ladies' delaying tactics, which include everything from food and wine to sexual teasing, are a success. In the ensuing battle of Washington Heights, Washington and the colonists are victorious and John is taken prisoner. In an epilogue after the war, Betsy and John are reunited.

No established producers would present the witty historical musical so HELEN FORD's husband George Ford produced it on a slim budget. The critics raved about both the clever libretto and the melodic, tangy score, comparing the enterprise to a Gilbert and Sullivan piece. "Here in My Arms" was the standout hit song, although "Bye and Bye" and "Here's a Kiss" were also popular. Also in the score were "Old Enough to Love," "I Beg Your Pardon," "Sweet Peter," and "Where the Hudson River Flows." The show was Rodgers and Hart's first hit book musical, running 286 performances, and they would continue to work with Fields on other inventive musicals over the next decade. *Dearest Enemy* was successful on the road and then somewhat disappeared, rarely revived even though it has

Casts for *Dearest Enemy*		
Character	*1925 Broadway*	*1955 television*
Betsy Burke	HELEN FORD	Anne Jeffreys
Capt. John Copeland	CHARLES PURCELL	Robert Sterling
General Howe	Harold Crane	CYRIL RITCHARD
Mrs. Murray	Flavia Arcaro	Cornelia Otis Skinner

a strong story, fun characters, and a lovely score. A stylish revival by the Goodspeed Opera House in 1976 revealed that the wit and charm were still very much in evidence.

☐ **Dearest Enemy** (NBC-TV 1955) was an abridged but relatively faithful adaptation of the stage work, presented on the series *Max Liebman Presents*. Only one song from the Broadway score was dropped, although some numbers were reassigned to different characters. The television version focused on Cyril Ritchard as General Howe, which was not a singing role in the original play. Ritchard was given several numbers and his foppish delivery of them brought Gilbert and Sullivan to mind once again. The teleplay was by William Friedberg and Neil Simon, the broadcast was produced and directed by Max Liebman, and James Starbuck did the period choreography.

DeCamp, Rosemary (1910–2001). Film and television performer. One of Hollywood's favorite choices for understanding mothers, helpful friends, and consoling sisters, the warm character actress was seen in several movie musicals. DeCamp was born in Prescott, Arizona, and began her career singing on the radio. She made her film debut in 1941 and was quickly typecast as friendly supporting characters in nonmusicals and musicals such as *Yankee Doodle Dandy* (1942), *This Is the Army* (1943), *Bowery to Broadway* (1944), *The Merry Monahans* (1944), *Rhapsody in Blue* (1945), *Two Guys From Milwaukee* (1946), *Look for the Silver Lining* (1949), *On Moonlight Bay* (1951), *By the Light of the Silvery Moon* (1953), *Main Street to Broadway* (1953), and *So This Is Love* (1953). In the 1950s, DeCamp concentrated on television, appearing in dozens of series, including a stint as a regular on *The Bob Cummings Show*. She continued acting on both the large and the small screen throughout the 1980s.

DeCarlo, Yvonne [born Margaret Yvonne Middleton] (1922–2007). Film, television, and stage performer. With her dark and exotic looks, the black-haired beauty often played sexy femme fatales or seductive slave girls in her many movies, including some notable musicals. DeCarlo was born in Vancouver, British Columbia, Canada, and took dancing and acting lessons as a child preparing to become a child star in films. But she did not find bit parts on screen until her late teen years after experience on stage and in nightclubs. DeCarlo was finally noticed when cast in the title role

of *Salome Where She Danced* (1945) and went on to play similarly sultry characters in many films. Her musical credits include *Road to Morocco* (1942), *Youth on Parade* (1942), *Rhythm Parade* (1943), *Let's Face It!* (1943), *Here Come the Waves* (1944), and *Casbah* (1948). She found greater fame on television as the campy Lily Munster in the TV series *The Munsters*. DeCarlo made a belated but triumphal Broadway debut as the faded actress Carlotta Campion who sang "I'm Still Here" in the musical *Follies* (1971). She continued acting on television and in films into the 1990s. Autobiography: *Yvonne: An Autobiography*, with Doug Warren (1987).

🎬 **Deep in My Heart** (MGM 1954). This biographical musical about composer Sigmund Romberg boasted a superb performance by José Ferrer as the operetta master and there were enough stars and songs to distract from the trite rags-to-riches plot. Because operetta was a risky item in the 1950s, many of Romberg's musical comedy numbers were featured and provided the most fun: Gene Kelly and his brother Fred (in their only film appearance together) showing off their pectorals with "I Like to Go Swimmin' With Wimmen," Ferrer and opera star Helen Traubel cutting loose in "The Leg of Mutton Rag," Ann Miller turning "It" into a seductive showcase for herself, and Ferrer and Rosemary Clooney singing the sly "Mr. and Mrs." Some of the operetta selections included Jane Powell and Vic Damone in the duet "Will You Remember?," Tony Martin and Joan Weldon in "Lover, Come Back to Me," William Ovis crooning "Serenade," and Howard Keel giving full force to "Your Land and My Land." Yet the most memorable musical number in the film is José Ferrer's one-man *tour de force* "Jazzadoo" in which he describes, acts out, and sings his latest musical comedy creation. David Burns, Walter Pidgeon, Merle Oberon, Paul Henreid, Doe Avedon, and Jim Backus filled out the cast of singing and nonsinging, fictional and factual characters. Leonard Spigelgass wrote the predictable screenplay, Eugene Loring did the choreography, and Stanley Donen directed the Roger Edens production.

DeHaven, Gloria [Mildred] (1925–). Film and television performer. A glamorous leading lady or second lead in several MGM musicals, the singer–actress shone in innocent and sympathetic roles. DeHaven was born in Los Angeles, the daughter of actor–director Carter

DeHaven (1886–1977) and actress Flora Parker DeHaven (1883–1950), and was in vaudeville and on screen as a child actress. After playing bit parts in films as a teenager, she became a band singer with BOB CROSBY's and Jan Savitt's orchestras, returning to Hollywood and playing one of the coeds in the musical *BEST FOOT FORWARD* (1943). Her other musical credits include *Thousands Cheer* (1943), BROADWAY RHYTHM (1944), *TWO GIRLS AND A SAILOR* (1944), *Step Lively* (1944), *SUMMER HOLIDAY* (1946), *Yes, Sir, That's My Baby* (1949), *SUMMER STOCK* (1950), *Two Tickets to Broadway* (1951), *Down Among the Sheltering Palms* (1952), *So This Is Paris* (1954), and *The Girl Rush* (1955). In the period musical *THREE LITTLE WORDS* (1950), DeHaven played her own mother. She also performed in the short-lived Broadway musical *Seventh Heaven* (1955). DeHaven acted in nonmusical films until the end of the century and appeared in many television programs. She was married to actor JOHN PAYNE.

DEL RIO, DOLORES [born Dolores Martinez Asunsolo y Lopez Negrete] (1905–1983). Film performer. The first Mexican actress to become a Hollywood star, the dark-eyed beauty made only a few but memorable musicals. Del Rio was born in Durango, Mexico, to an aristocratic family and, after marrying into high society, moved to Hollywood with her husband Jaime Martinez Del Rio with the hopes of her becoming an actress and he a screenwriter. She made her screen debut in 1925 and immediately enthralled moviegoers as a female version of the exotic Rudolph Valentino. The arrival of sound boosted her career even further and she was put in four musicals: *FLYING DOWN TO RIO* (1933), *Wonder Bar* (1934), *I Live for Love* (1935), and *In Caliente* (1935). When her popularity waned in the 1940s, Del Rio returned to Mexico and became a film star in her native land. In the 1960s she returned to Hollywood for occasional bit parts in movies. Biographies: *Dolores Del Rio*, Cinta Franco Dunn (2003); *The Invention of Dolores Del Rio*, Joanne Hershfield (2000).

DEL RUTH, ROY (1895–1961). Film director. A polished professional in silents and talkies, he is most remembered for his lavish MGM musicals. Del Ruth was born in Philadelphia and began his career as a journalist but switched to writing scripts for two-reel comedies in 1914, eventually directing shorts and then features by the mid-1920s. For nearly forty years he turned out a variety of pictures for different studios, including twenty-three musicals. De Ruth directed *THE DESERT SONG* (1929), the first sound film version of a Broadway musical, followed by such screen musicals as *GOLD DIGGERS OF BROADWAY* (1929), *HOLD EVERYTHING* (1930), *KID MILLIONS* (1934), *FOLIES BERGERE* (1935), *BROADWAY MELODY OF 1936* (1935), *THANKS A MILLION* (1935), *BORN TO DANCE* (1936), *ON THE AVENUE* (1937), *BROADWAY MELODY OF 1938* (1937), *The Star Maker* (1939), *THE CHOCOLATE SOLDIER* (1941), *DuBARRY WAS A LADY* (1943), *BROADWAY RHYTHM* (1944), *On Moonlight Bay* (1951), *Starlift* (1951), and *Three Sailors and a Girl* (1953).

◼ DELICIOUS (Fox 1931). The romantic team of JANET GAYNOR and CHARLES FARRELL, who captured the hearts of America in silent and then early talking features, were starred together in this intimate, sentimental musical. In SONYA LEVIEN's screenplay, Swedish immigrant Heather Gordon (Gaynor), having escaped the clutches of the lecherous Ellis Island official O'Flynn (Lawrence O'Sullivan), soon finds herself having to choose between the affections of Russian composer Sascha (Raul Roulien) and American playboy Larry Beaumont (Farrell). There was no question where the audience's sympathies lay but there were some wonderful GERSHWIN brothers songs to make the contest interesting: the delicate lullaby "Somebody From Somewhere," a satirical number about lyric writing called "Blah, Blah, Blah," and the very Gershwinesque "Delicious." The comedy was provided by MISCHA AUER and the Swedish comic EL BRENDEL who massacred the English language every time he opened his mouth. DAVID BUTLER directed the gentle film with a delicate touch.

DELL'ISOLA, SALVATORE (1901–1989). Stage and film musical director. One of Broadway's top conductors in the 1940 and 1950s, he was frequently associated with RODGERS and HAMMERSTEIN productions. Dell'Isola was born in Italy and came to America when he was in his teens. He began his career as a musician in vaudeville pit orchestras and then was hired as a violinist for the Metropolitan Opera orchestra where he played for ten years. He conducted the RKO orchestra in the 1920s and 1930s. Dell'Isola first worked with Rodgers' music when he conducted the tour of *OKLAHOMA!* in the mid-1940s and then served as the musical director for the team's Broadway productions of *ALLEGRO* (1947), *SOUTH PACIFIC* (1949), *ME AND JULIET* (1953), *PIPE DREAM* (1955), and

Flower Drum Song (1958). Among his other New York stage credits were the 1954 revival of *On Your Toes* and *Ankles Aweigh* (1955). Dell'Isola was a frequent conductor at the Westbury Music Fair for many years.

DeLuise, Dom (1933–). Film, stage, and television performer. A rotund, smiling comic actor who usually played the hero's hapless sidekick in films, he appeared in a few musicals and lent his voice to many others. DeLuise was born in Brooklyn and educated at Tufts University before acting in stock companies and appearing in nightclubs. He gained recognition for his appearances on television variety shows and eventually had his own show. DeLuise returned to the stage in the Off Broadway musical *All in Love* (1961) and was featured on Broadway in *The Student Gypsy* (1963) and as a replacement in *Here's Love* (1964). He also was active in summer stock for many years. DeLuise began acting in film comedies in the 1960s and later appeared in the musicals *Blazing Saddles* (1974), *The Muppet Movie* (1979), and *The Best Little Whorehouse in Texas* (1982), but most of his musical credits are vocals for animated films, including *An American Tail* (1986), *Oliver and Company* (1988), *All Dogs Go to Heaven* (1989), *An American Tail: Fievel Goes West* (1991), *A Troll in Central Park* (1994), *All Dogs Go to Heaven 2* (1996), and *An All Dogs Christmas Carol* (1998), as well as many television cartoons and made-for-video features.

Demarest, William (1892–1983). Film and television performer. One of Hollywood's most distinctive character actors, the paunch-faced comic and his crude wisecracking manner lit up over 140 movies between 1926 and 1976. Demarest was born in St. Paul, Minnesota, and worked in vaudeville, carnivals, stock theatres, and even professional boxing before making his film debut in the silents era. Among his many memorable films was a series of Preston Sturges farces in the 1940s in which he stole the show each time with his sarcastic barking.

Among Demarest's musical credits are *The Jazz Singer* (1927), *The Broadway Melody* (1929), *The Great Ziegfeld* (1936), *Rosalie* (1937), *Wake Up and Live* (1937), *Rebecca of Sunnybrook Farm* (1938), *True to the Army* (1942), *Pardon My Sarong* (1942), *Behind the Eight Ball* (1942), *Johnny Doughboy* (1942), *The Jolson Story* (1946), *Red, Hot and Blue* (1949), *Jolson Sings Again* (1949), *The Strip* (1951), *Dangerous When Wet* (1953), *Jupiter's Darling* (1955), *Pepe* (1960), and *Viva Las Vegas* (1964). He found a whole new audience on television, particularly as a regular on the series *My Three Sons* in the 1960s.

Desert Song, The (Casino Theatre 1926). One of the most popular of all American operettas, this exotic, romantic musical by Frank Mandel (book), Sigmund Romberg (music), Otto Harbach, and Oscar Hammerstein (book and lyrics) holds up better than most 1920s works of the genre.

Plot: The French military stationed in the mountains of Morocco are fighting the rebellious Riffs, who are led by a mysterious captain known as the Red Shadow. Pierre Birabeau, the shy and seemingly awkward son of the French commander, loves the beautiful Margot Bonvalet but she has little time for him. When the masked Red Shadow steals away with Margot into the desert, he leaves her with only a red cloak as evidence of his identity. She pines for her mysterious lover and, after the Riffs and the French reach a peace settlement, is pleasantly surprised to learn that he is Pierre in disguise.

Suggested by the real life Abd-el-Krim, a Berber chieftain who was in the news with a recent Riff uprising, the romantic tale was also timely because of America's fascination with cinema hero Rudolph Valentino as the Sheik. There was also a song, "It," that was an homage to the silver screen's "it girl" Clara Bow. Since most operettas were set in the past, one that was contemporary was a novelty. Yet it

Casts for *The Desert Song*

Characters	Pierre/Paul	Margot	General	Fontaine
1926 Broadway	Robert Halliday	Vivienne Segal	Edmund Elton	Glen Dale
1929 film	John Boles	Carlotta King	Edward Martindel	John Miljan
1943 film	Dennis Morgan	Irene Manning	Gene Lockhart	Bruce Cabot
1953 film	Gordon MacRae	Kathryn Grayson	Ray Collins	Steve Cochran
1955 television	Nelson Eddy	Gale Sherwood	Otto Kruger	John Conte

The Desert Song (stage) Musical Numbers

"High on a Hill"
"The Riff Song"
"Margot"
"I'll Be a Buoyant Girl"
"Why Did We Marry Soldiers"
"French Military Marching Song"
"Romance"
"Then You Will Know"
"It"
"The Desert Song"
"My Little Castagnette"
"Song of the Brass Key"
"One Good Boy Gone Wrong"
"Eastern and Western Love"
"Let Love Go"
"One Flower in Your Garden"
"One Alone"
"The Sabre Song"
"Farewell"
"All Hail to the General"
"Let's Have a Love Affair"

still had the appeal of a faraway exotic land and romantic characters who could express themselves with soaring music. The standout hits from the show were the ballads "One Alone" and "Romance," the rousing chorale "The Riff Song," and the dreamy title number. Romberg wrote some of his most romantic melodies for the score, but the lyrics by Harbach and Hammerstein were sometimes pedestrian as the young Hammerstein was still learning his craft. Produced by LAURENCE SCHWAB and Mandel, directed by Arthur Hurley, choreographed by BOBBY CONNOLLY, The Desert Song ran 471 performances on Broadway and for over three years on the road. The operetta also proved a hit in England, France, and Australia. Major New York revivals were seen in 1946, 1973, 1987, and 1989, and for decades it was a staple with summer stock and operetta companies.
    The Desert Song (Warner Brothers–Vitaphone 1929) was the first Broadway musical to be filmed with sound. The early talkie starred JOHN BOLES and Carlotta King as the Red Shadow and Margot. Much of the Broadway score survived the transition and the movie also followed the highly romantic stage plot, which, like the early sound film techniques, came across as rather primitive. The screenplay was by Harvey Gates, ROY DEL RUTH directed, and a new song, "Then You Will Know," was added to the favorites

that were retained from the Broadway score. In 1932 Warner Brothers released a two-reel version of the operetta, running about twenty-minutes and featuring Alexander Gray and Bernice Claire, both of whom had played the Red Shadow and Margot on stage together. **The Desert Song** (Warner Brothers 1943) was set in 1937 with French Morocco battling the Nazis and the Red Shadow (DENNIS MORGAN) was an American freedom fighter from the Spanish Civil War who leads the Riffs against the German occupiers. Irene Manning was Margot and again the best songs from the Broadway score were used, supplemented by others ("Long Live the Night," "Fifi's Song," and "Gay Parisienne"), not by Romberg. The screenplay was by producer Robert Buckner, the film was directed by Robert Florey, and LEROY PRINZ did the choreography. **The Desert Song** (Warner Brothers 1953) dropped the term "Red Shadow" because of the jitters over the Cold War and made the hero (GORDON MACRAE) a Riff rebel named Paul Bonnard with KATHRYN GRAYSON as a general's daughter who loves him. The score was somewhat shortchanged in this version. Roland Kibbee wrote the screenplay, BRUCE HUMBERSTONE directed, and Prinz was again the choreographer. ▢ NBC-TV broadcast a live, abridged adaptation of The Desert Song in 1955 with NELSON EDDY and Gale Sherwood. It was produced and directed by MAX LIEBMAN and choreographed by Rod Alexander, with a teleplay by William Friedberg, NEIL SIMON, and Will Glickman.

DESTRY RIDES AGAIN (Imperial Theatre 1959). A musicalization of the popular 1939 film of the same title, this DAVID MERRICK production was a modest hit at 473 performances but has pretty much disappeared from memory and revivals. Thomas Jefferson Destry, Jr. (Andy Griffith), the new sheriff of the western town of Bottleneck, is a peace-loving man but he holds his own up against the bully Kent (Scott Brady) and the sultry saloon gal Frenchy (DOLORES GRAY) who tries to seduce him. Also in the top-notch cast were MARC BEAUX, Swen Swenson, George Reeder, Elizabeth Watts, and Jack Prince. The libretto by Leonard Gershe had a happy ending with Frenchy, who was shot and killed in the film, alive and getting hitched to Destry. The surprisingly forgettable score was by the reliable songwriter HAROLD ROME. "I Know Your Kind," "Once Knew a Fella," "Respectability," and "That Ring on the Finger" served their purpose, which in this case meant highlighting the spirited performers and giving director–choreographer MICHAEL KIDD the opportunity to provide some vivacious dances.

DEUTSCH, ADOLPH (1897–1980). Film and stage orchestrator and composer. The oft-awarded conductor and musical arranger composed the soundtracks for many nonmusical films and did the musical direction for many classic musicals. Deutsch was born in London and educated at the London Polytechnic and the Royal Academy of Music. He came to America in 1910 and arranged music for dance bands and later celebrated orchestras such as that of PAUL WHITEMAN. Deutsch was musical director for the Broadway musicals *Here Goes the Bride* (1931), *Pardon My English* (1933), and *As Thousands Cheer* (1933), even as he arranged music and / or conducted such movie musicals as *The Smiling Lieutenant* (1931), *Fools for Scandal* (1938), *Cowboy From Brooklyn* (1938), *Take Me Out to the Ball Game* (1949), *The Barkleys of Broadway* (1949), *Annie Get Your Gun* (1950), *Show Boat* (1951), *The Belle of New York* (1952), *The Band Wagon* (1953), *Seven Brides for Seven Brothers* (1954), *Deep in My Heart* (1954), *Oklahoma!* (1955), *Funny Face* (1957), and *Les Girls* (1957). He also composed original soundtrack scores for over fifty nonmusicals.

DEWOLFE, BILLY [born William Andrew Jones] (1907–1974). Film, television, and stage performer. A delightful gap-toothed, lisping comic with a pencil-thin mustache and a very proper persona, his quiet but hilarious clowning was seen in nine Hollywood musicals. DeWolfe was born in Wollaston, Massachusetts, and sang and danced in vaudeville as a teenager. He later got bookings in nightclubs where he did his comic monologues to great acclaim and then taking his antics to London where he was a hit in music halls and even played the London Palladium. After serving in the Navy in World War II, DeWolfe headed to Hollywood where he made his debut in the musical *Dixie* (1943). He usually played minor character roles but was often given a chance to reprise one of his nightclub routines. His other musical credits are *Duffy's Tavern* (1945), *Blue Skies* (1946), *The Perils of Pauline* (1947), *Variety Girl* (1947), *Isn't It Romantic?* (1948), *Tea for Two* (1950), *Lullaby of Broadway* (1951), and *Call Me Madam* (1953). DeWolfe was featured in the Broadway revues *John Murray Anderson's Almanac* (1953) and *Ziegfeld Follies* (1957),

appeared in several musical revivals in stock and summer theatre, and made many television appearances.

DICK TRACY (Touchstone/Disney 1990). This cartoonish adventure was such a dazzling display of stylized settings, use of color, cartoonish makeup, and high-flying performances that it was difficult to detect a superb score by STEPHEN SONDHEIM hidden or edited out of recognition. Producer–director Warren Beatty played the stolid title detective with an earnest gleam in his eye, Glenne Headley was his patient sweetheart Tess Trueheart, and Charlie Korsmo was the street kid they befriended. But it was the villains, cops, and other supporting roles that provided all the fun: Charles Durning, Dustin Hoffman, James Caan, Michael J. Pollard, DICK VAN DYKE, Cathy Bates, Catherine O'Hara, Estelle Parsons, Paul Sorvino, James Tolkan, and, best of all, Al Pacino in an over-the-top performance as the hood Big Boy Caprice. The musical numbers were limited to Big Boy's nightclub where sexy songstress Bubbles Mahoney (Madonna) and the piano player 88 Keys (MANDY PATINKIN) delivered four dynamite songs, none enjoyed in its entirety as the camera usually cut away to the action elsewhere. "Sooner or Later (I Always Get My Man)" stuck with enough viewers that it won an Oscar, but just as proficient were the rowdy "Back in Business," the plaintive "What Can You Lose," and the jazzy "More," with which Big Boy tried to teach the chorus girls to sing at a comical rehearsal. The script by Jim Cash and Jack Epps, Jr., Beatty's fluid direction, and the dynamic use of matte paintings and stylized scenery helped make this film look like no other.

DIENER, JOAN (1930–2006). Stage performer. The striking blonde singer–actress was very effective in operetta and more serious musical plays. Diener was born in Columbus, Ohio, and educated at Sarah Lawrence College before embarking on a musical career. She had several successes in the opera world and in revivals of operetta, but most of her Broadway musicals were short runs. In the two exceptions she was indeed exceptional: the sultry Lalume in *Kismet* (1953) and the whore Aldonza in *Man of La Mancha* (1965, 1972, and 1992). Diener's other musical stage credits include *Small Wonder* (1948), *Cry for Us All* (1970), and *Home Sweet Homer* (1976). Despite her photogenic beauty, she did not get to reprise any of her stage roles on screen; in fact, she never made a movie at all. Diener was married to director ALBERT MARRE.

DIETZ, HOWARD (1896–1983). Stage and film lyricist and writer. The incisive lyricist had two very different careers: as a leading songwriter, usually paired with composer ARTHUR SCHWARTZ, and as an executive at MGM where he was in charge of publicity for over thirty years. Dietz was born in New York and studied journalism at Columbia University where he got involved with campus theatricals. While he wrote advertising slogans for companies, he penned lyrics as well and had a few songs interpolated into Broadway shows. Dietz collaborated with composer JEROME KERN on *Dear Sir* (1924) and with JAY GORNEY on *Merry-Go-Round* (1927) and then found success when he teamed up with Schwartz to score the innovative revue THE LITTLE SHOW (1929). The twosome also provided songs for the inventive revues *The Second Little Show* (1930), THE BAND WAGON (1931), FLYING COLORS (1932), AT HOME ABROAD (1935), and INSIDE U. S. A. (1948). They had less success with their book musicals REVENGE WITH MUSIC (1934), BETWEEN THE DEVIL (1937), THE GAY LIFE (1961), and *Jennie* (1963), although some exceptional songs came from the scores. With composer VERNON DUKE, Dietz provided the scores for the short-run musicals *Jackpot* (1944) and *Sadie Thompson* (1944). For many of these musicals Dietz also wrote the libretto or sketches. His advertising career at MGM ran parallel to his Broadway writing and on occasion wrote for the movies, such as the screenplay for the musical *Hollywood Party* (1934) and the score for *Under Your Spell* (1936) with Schwartz. Songs from the Dietz–Schwartz stage revues were used in the Hollywood musicals *Dancing in the Dark* (1949) and *The Band Wagon* (1953), with the team writing the new song "That's Entertainment" for the latter. The twosome also collaborated on the score for the TV musical *A BELL FOR ADANO* (1956). Dietz's lyrics are known for their wit, intoxicating sense of mystery and romance, and ability to lead to dancing. He was married to costume designer Lucinda Ballard (1906–1993). Autobiography: *Dancing in the Dark* (1974).

DILLINGHAM, CHARLES [Bancroft] (1868–1934). Stage producer. The prolific and tasteful presenter of some 200 Broadway productions from the turn of the twentieth century into the 1930s, he produced over sixty musical shows, both revues and book musicals. Dillingham was born in Hartford, Connecticut, the son of a minister, and worked as a journalist on various newspapers before turning to writing theatre reviews for the *New York Evening Sun*. After working as a press agent for CHARLES FROHMAN and a manager for actress Julia Marlowe, he took up producing on his own and presented new comedies and dramas, British imports, adaptations of foreign works, and all kinds of musicals. Among his many notable musical offerings are *Babette* (1903), MLLE. MODISTE (1905), THE RED MILL (1906), *The Tattooed Man* (1907), *The Lady of the Slipper* (1912), CHIN-CHIN (1914), WATCH YOUR STEP (1914), *Stop! Look! Listen!* (1915), *The Century Girl* (1916), *Jack O' Lantern* (1917), *Apple Blossoms* (1919), *Tip Top* (1920), *The Night Boat* (1920), *Good Morning, Dearie* (1920), *Stepping Stones* (1923), SUNNY (1925), *China Rose* (1925), *Criss Cross* (1926), *Oh, Please!* (1926), *Sidewalks of New York* (1927), *She's My Baby* (1928), *Ripples* (1930), and *NEW FACES* (1934). Dillingham also produced musical extravaganzas at the mammoth Hippodrome Theatre. He was wiped out in the stock market crash and died a few years later.

DIRTY DANCING (Vestron 1987). There was so much dancing and such unrelenting soundtrack music that this movie seemed like a full-fledged musical even though the characters hardly sang a note. Eleanor Bergstein's screenplay is set in a 1960s Catskills resort where the reclusive teen Frances "Baby" Houseman (Jennifer Grey) is vacationing with her family. There is a lot of "uninhibited" dancing going on and Baby soon discovers the joy of dancing and sex, both with the resort's star dancer Johnny Castle (Patrick Swayze). The film ended with the requisite Big Show, in this case a full-throttle dance piece featuring Baby that endears her to her family (and to audiences). The solid supporting cast featured JERRY ORBACH, Jack Weston, LONNIE PRICE, Kelly Bishop, Cynthia Rhodes, and Charles "Honi" Coles, and the songs heard on the soundtrack included new numbers by various writers, most memorably "(I've Had) The Time of My Life," and older favorites such as "You Don't Own Me" and "Be My Baby." Emile Ardolino directed the Linda Gottlieb production, and Kenneth Ortega choreographed the vigorous dancing. Both the movie and the soundtrack recording were very popular and redefined what was meant by a musical film in the 1980s.

Dirty Dancing. Sex and dancing got a bit intertwined in this pop musical where there was little singing but a lot of hoofing. Patrick Swayze and Jennifer Grey (pictured) didn't need to sing to express themselves when they had the dance floor on which to engage in their two favorite pastimes. (Alamy)

DIRTY ROTTEN SCOUNDRELS (Imperial Theatre 2005). Another musical comedy based on a popular film, this show was so polished and well acted that few realized or cared that it was paper thin and sophomoric to boot. On the French Riviera, two American con men, the debonair ladies' man Lawrence Jameson (John Lithgow) and the crass shyster Freddy Benson (NORBERT LEO BUTZ), make a bet over who can fleece the all-American "soap queen" Christine Colgate (Sherie Rene Scott), with each scoundrel playing dirty tricks on the other to impede his success. The rivals become buddies despite themselves and at least have each other when it turns out that Christine was conning them all the time. Also featured in the cast were JOANNA GLEASON, Gregory Jbara, and Sara Gettelfinger. Jeffrey Lane wrote the libretto, taken from the 1988 film, which was based on the 1964 movie *Bedtime Story*, and David Yazbek provided the songs, including "Give Them What They Want," "The More We Dance," "Great Big Stuff," "Like Zis/Like Zat," "What Was a Woman to Do?," and "Love Sneaks In." Many critics found the humor broad and the performances over-sized yet recommended it; audiences took their advice for 627 performances. JACK O'BRIEN was the clever director, and JERRY MITCHELL did the choreography.

DISNEY COMPANY. See WALT DISNEY COMPANY

DISNEY, WALT[er Elias] (1901–1966). Film producer. The one-man dynamo behind cartoon shorts, animated features, live-action adventure film, television programs, nature documentaries, big-budget screen musicals, and theme parts, he also pioneered the use of music on film just as he revolutionized animation. Disney was born in Chicago and, after serving in World War I, studied at the Kansas City Art Institute. In the early 1920s he set up his own animation studio to provide cartoons for a chain of movie theatres and, after several failures, found success with the creation of Mickey Mouse and other beloved cartoon characters. With the arrival of sound, Disney experimented with ways to coordinate not only sound but music to the moving images, and his cartoon shorts soon became minimusicals using classical music as well as original songs such as "Who's Afraid of the Big Bad Wolf?" His decision to produce a feature-length animated musical was laughed at by the industry, but SNOW WHITE AND THE SEVEN DWARFS (1937) proved to be a sleeper hit and Disney proceeded to offer a series of animated classics, most of which had full musical scores. In addition to book musicals such as PINOCCHIO (1940), DUMBO (1941), CINDERELLA (1950), ALICE IN WONDERLAND (1951), PETER PAN (1954), THE LADY AND THE TRAMP (1955), SLEEPING BEAUTY (1959), and THE JUNGLE BOOK (1967), Disney produced anthology musicals, such as FANTASIA (1940), THE THREE CABALLEROS (1945), MAKE MINE MUSIC (1946), Fun and Fancy Free (1947), and MELODY TIME (1948), as well as films that mixed animation and live action, as with SONG OF THE SOUTH (1946) and MARY POPPINS (1964). He also offered live-action comedies and drama that included music and sometime introduced song favorites. The creative and executive power of Disney was so great that the WALT DISNEY COMPANY took years to recover from his death. Memoir: The Disney Story, Diane Disney Miller [his daughter] (1957); biographies: Walt Disney: The Triumph of the American Imagination, Neal Gabler (2006); Walt Disney: An American Original, Bob Thomas (1994); Walt Disney: Hollywood's Dark Prince, Marc Eliot (1993).

DIXEY, HENRY E. (1859–1943). Stage performer and writer. An unusual comic actor–singer in that he was extremely handsome and often wore tight-fitting costumes to show off his physique, he became a widely popular matinee idol in the 1880s. Dixey was born in Boston and by the age of ten was acting professionally at the Boston Athenaeum. He made an inauspicious Broadway debut in 1874 as the back end of a cow in the musical EVANGELINE and then appeared in the musicals Babes in the Woods (1879), Fantinitza (1880), Billee Taylor (1880), New Evangeline (1880), Hiawatha (1880), The Mascot (1883), and The Merry Duchess (1883), some of which he co-authored. Dixey teamed up with composer EDWARD RICE and wrote and starred in ADONIS (1886), triumphing in the title role for 600 performances in New York in two engagements and taking it on tour and to London with such acclaim that he became known as Adonis Dixey. Although much of Dixey's subsequent career was anticlimactic in comparison, he did star in several Broadway classic revivals, new plays, and musicals, such as Gayest Manhattan (1897), Erminie (1898),

The Burgomaster (1900), Chu Chin Chow (1917), and The Merry Malones (1928). As dashing as he looked on stage, Dixey was still a comic actor, often engaging in clownish buffooning and even appearing in drag on occasion.

DIXON, LEE (1914–1953). Stage and film performer. The gangly, agile singer–dancer was busy on the vaudeville and Broadway stage, as well as in films, but his only notable role came near the end of his short career. A native of Brooklyn, New York, Dixon danced from childhood, appearing in the chorus of Broadway musicals as a teenager. He was a hoofer in vaudeville before making his film debut as a dancer in the musical A Modern Cinderella (1932). Dixon made eight other movies, including the musicals GOLD DIGGERS OF 1937 (1936), Ready, Willing and Able (1937), The Singing Marine (1937), Varsity Show (1937), DOUBLE OR NOTHING (1940), and Double Rhythm (1946). He returned to Broadway to play a featured role in HIGHER AND HIGHER (1940) but it was his overeager cowboy Will Parker in the original OKLAHOMA! (1943) that was his greatest performance. Dixon died of alcoholism at the age of forty-two.

DO I HEAR A WALTZ? (46th Street Theatre 1965). The only collaboration between RICHARD RODGERS (music) and STEPHEN SONDHEIM (lyrics), the small-scale musical suffered from a problematic book and production but resulted in a superior score. ARTHUR LAURENTS adapted his own play The Time of the Cuckoo (1952), which had been made into the popular film Summertime (1955), and Elizabeth Allen was featured as the spinster Leona Samish who discovers a romantic interlude with the Italian shop owner Renato Di Rossi (Sergio Franchi) during her vacation in Venice. The cast also included CAROL BRUCE, Stuart Damon, Julienne Marie, Madeleine Sherwood, and Jack Manning. SHIRLEY BOOTH and Katharine Hepburn had been so memorable as Leona in the play and film versions that Allen was up against some stiff competition and did not survive the comparisons. The critics also found the leading man leaden and the script weak. The score would only be appreciated in hindsight: the lyrical "Moon in My Window," the ballads "Someone Like You" and "Take the Moment," the caustic "We're Gonna Be All Right," and the entrancing title song. Rodgers was still such a popular composer that his name on a marquee was appealing enough to audiences to let the show run 220 performances.

📖 **Do Re Mi** (St. James Theatre 1960). Glowing notices for stars PHIL SILVERS and NANCY WALKER and the quick popularity of the song "Make Someone Happy" helped this flawed but interesting musical run 400 performances. Small-time operator Hubert Cram (Silvers) is always coming up with get-rich-quick schemes, much to the distress of his faithful wife Kay (Walker). Hubie gets mixed up with a jukebox racket that is not strictly legal and is left by his partners to face jail. The subplot concerned the up-and-coming singer Tilda Mullen (NANCY DUSSAULT) and her romance with record producer John Henry Wheeler (John Reardon). Garson Kanin wrote the quirky libretto and directed the cast, which also included DAVID BURNS, George Givot, and George Mathews. JULE STYNE (music), BETTY COMDEN, and ADOLPH GREEN (lyrics) penned the score, which also had such memorable numbers as the flowing ballad "I Know About Love," the spry character song "Adventure," the pop "What's New at the Zoo?," the soft-shoe "It's Legitimate," and the moaning "Cry Like the Wind." DAVID MERRICK produced the offbeat show that had imaginative cartoonish sets designed by Boris Aronson.

🎬 **Doctor Dolittle** (APJAC/Fox 1967). It may have been overlong and overproduced (it just about bankrupted 20TH CENTURY-FOX) but there was a cockeyed kind of charm in the musical fantasy as it lumbered from sequence to sequence revealing new and unusual creatures and special effects along the way. The Hugh Lofting stories were adapted for the screen by LESLIE BRICUSSE who also wrote the songs, and REX HARRISON was cast as the magical doctor who is taught hundreds of languages by his pet parrot Polynesia (voice of Ginny Tyler). The doctor sets off with his comrades Albert Blossom (Richard Attenborough), Emma Fairfax (Samantha Eggar), and Matthew Mugg (ANTHONY NEWLEY) to use his linguistic knowledge and encounters the Giant Lunar Moth, a double llama called Pushmi–Pullyu, the Great Pink Sea Snail, and a homesick seal named Sophie to whom the doctor sang the mellifluous "When I Look Into Your Eyes." Other songs included "Beautiful Things," "Something in Your Smile," and the Oscar-winning "Talk to the Animals." Richard Fleischer directed without ever quite pinning down what style the movie was supposed to be, and HERBERT ROSS devised the choreography.

DOLAN, ROBERT EMMETT (1906–1972). Stage and film composer, musical arranger, and pro-ducer. A respected musical director both on Broadway and in Hollywood, he was involved with dozens of musicals in both venues and also composed soundtrack scores for many nonmusical films. Dolan was born in Hartford, Connecticut, and educated at Loyola College and studied piano with various teachers before getting a job as a rehearsal and orchestra pianist for Broadway musicals. He was the musical director for many shows from the 1920s through the 1960s and composed the music for two Broadway musicals, *Texas, Li'l Darlin'* (1949) and *Foxy* (1964). However, much of Dolan's career was in Hollywood where he arranged and/or conducted the music for such musicals as *BIRTH OF THE BLUES* (1941), *HOLIDAY INN* (1942), *STAR-SPANGLED RHYTHM* (1943), *Dixie* (1943), *LADY IN THE DARK* (1944), *THE BELLES OF ST. MARY'S* (1945), *BLUE SKIES* (1946), *ROAD TO UTOPIA* (1946), and many others. Dolan turned to movie producing in the 1950s and presented such musicals as *WHITE CHRISTMAS* (1954), *The Girl Rush* (1955), and *ANYTHING GOES* (1956).

DOLLY SISTERS. Stage performers. Two dark almond-eyed beauties with a bewitching stage persona, they were the most famous sister act in the early decades of the twentieth century. Jenny [born Janszieka Deutsch] (1892–1941) and Rosie Dolly [born Roszika Deutsch] (1892–1970) were born in Budapest, Hungary, but were raised in New York's Lower East Side. The siblings began singing together in vaudeville and quickly rose to the top of their profession, with their four-week run at the Palace Theatre breaking all records for a sister act. They made their Broadway debut in character parts in the musical *The Echo* (1910) and then FLORENZ ZIEGFELD featured them in his *ZIEGFELD FOLLIES* (1911). The sisters performed together in the Broadway shows *A Winsome Widow* (1912), *The Merry Countess* (1912), *Her Bridal Night* (1916), and *Greenwich Village Follies* (1924), as well as the London musicals *Jig-Saw* (1920), *League of Notions* (1921), and *The Fun of the Fayre* (1921). Jennie appeared without Rosie in *The Honeymoon Express* (1913), and Rosie went solo in *Lieber Augustin* (1913), *The Whirl of the World* (1914), and *Hello, Broadway!* (1914). BETTY GRABLE and JUNE HAVER played the siblings in the Hollywood musical *THE DOLLY SISTERS* (1945).

🎬 **Dolly Sisters, The** (Fox 1945). Little attempt at historical accuracy was made when telling the story of the Hungarian-born beauties Jennie and Rosie Dolly who started in vaudeville and on Broadway. The two dark-haired Europeans were played by blonde all-Americans BETTY GRABLE and JUNE HAVER, and the settings, costumes, makeup, and even the new songs seemed more 1940s than turn of the century. The screenplay by John Larkin and Marian Spitzer was similarly fictional, offering Harry Fox (JOHN PAYNE) and Irving Netcher (Frank Lattimore) as the sisters' love interests, with the matchmaking being done by impresario OSCAR HAMMERSTEIN I (Frank Middlemass). S. K. SAKALL was on hand as their cuddly Uncle Latsie and also cast in supporting roles were REGINALD GARDINER, Gene Sheldon, SIG RUMANN, Colette Lyons, and Trudy Marshall. "I Can't Begin to Tell You" by JAMES V. MONACO (music) and MACK GORDON (lyrics) was the best of the original numbers, which were augmented by period favorites such as "I'm Always Chasing Rainbows," "Smiles," and "The Sidewalks of New York." GEORGE JESSEL, who knew about the period firsthand, produced and IRVING CUMMINGS directed with SEYMOUR FELIX doing the choreography. The whole production seems garish by modern sentiments but, mainly because of Grable's popularity, the movie was a box office hit.

DONAHUE, JACK (1892–1930). Stage performer and writer. A rubber-limbed dancer who lit up a number of musicals, he was on the brink of major stardom when he died at the age of thirty-eight. Donahue was born in Charlestown, Massachusetts, and was only eleven years old when he joined a medicine show. He danced in vaudeville and burlesque before making his Broadway debut in the chorus of *The Woman Haters* (1912), followed by the musicals *Angel Face* (1919), *ZIEGFELD FOLLIES* (1920), *Molly Darling* (1922), and *Be Yourself* (1924). Donahue was the romantic partner for MARILYN MILLER in *SUNNY* (1925) and *ROSALIE* (1928) and then starred in *Sons o' Guns* (1929). He wrote the libretto for the last show, as well as for *Princess Charming* (1930) that opened after his death. Autobiography: *Letters of a Hoofer to His Ma* (1911). [He is not to be confused with dancer–choreographer JACK DONOHUE.]

DONALDSON, WALTER (1893–1947). Film and stage composer. A successful Tin Pan Alley songwriter who often collaborated with lyricist GUS KAHN, he only made a few forays into the Broadway and Hollywood musical but came up with some impressive hits all the same. The Brooklyn native worked in a brokerage firm on Wall Street before getting a job as pianist for a music publishing company, later co-founding his own firm. Donaldson already had a few single song hits to his credit before he scored the Broadway musicals *Sweetheart Time* (1926) and *WHOOPEE* (1928), the latter with Kahn. When *Whoopee* was filmed in 1930, Donaldson and Kahn went to Hollywood where they scored the screen musicals *KID MILLIONS* (1934) and *Operator 13* (1934). With lyricist HAROLD ADAMSON, he wrote some songs for *THE GREAT ZIEGFELD* (1936) and then returned to the Alley and music publishing. Among Donaldson's many song hits are "Carolina in the Morning," "Love Me or Leave Me," "My Mammy," "My Blue Heaven," "My Buddy," and "Yes, Sir, That's My Baby." In the film bio of Kahn titled *I'll See You in My Dream* (1951), Donaldson was played by Frank Lovejoy.

DONEN, STANLEY (1924–). Film director, choreographer, and producer. A leading figure in postwar Hollywood musicals, he devised some of the most memorable innovations in how to film a musical. Donen was born in Columbia, South Carolina, and educated at the University of South Carolina before appearing as a dancer on Broadway in *PAL JOEY* (1940). He became the protégé of the show's star GENE KELLY and helped Kelly choreograph *BEST FOOT FORWARD* (1941) before both headed to Hollywood and worked on *COVER GIRL* (1944) together. Donen was solo choreographer for *Jam Session* (1944), *Kansas City Kitty* (1944), *ANCHORS AWEIGH* (1945), *Holiday in Mexico* (1946), *A DATE WITH JUDY* (1948), *The Kissing Bandit* (1948), and *TAKE ME OUT TO THE BALL GAME* (1949) before choreographing and co-directing *ON THE TOWN* (1943) with Kelly. It was the first musical shot on location in New York and was innovative in its quick-cutting montages and travelogue-like approach to location filming. The two men co-directed and choreographed *SINGIN' IN THE RAIN* (1952) and *IT'S ALWAYS FAIR WEATHER* (1955) and Donen directed *ROYAL WEDDING* (1951), *GIVE A GIRL A BREAK* (1953), *SEVEN BRIDES FOR SEVEN BROTHERS* (1954), *DEEP IN MY HEART* (1954), and *FUNNY FACE* (1957). He turned to producing as well as directing with *THE PAJAMA GAME* (1957) and repeated both chores for *DAMN YANKEES* (1958), *The Little Prince* (1973), and *MOVIE MOVIE* (1978). Donen also directed and produced nonmusicals, most memorably *Charade* (1963) and *Two for the Road* (1967), and he returned to Broadway in 1993 to direct the ill-fated musical *The Red Shoes*. He was responsible for some of the era's most unique

Stanley Donen. Some felt that the director–choreographer was at his best when co-directing and co-choreographing with Gene Kelly (center). A ripe example of their ingenuity was this number from *It's Always Fair Weather* (1955) in which three drunk GIs dance down Manhattan's Third Avenue with trash can lids on their feet. Joining Kelly in the risible dance were Michael Kidd (left) and Dan Dailey (right). (Photofest)

musical sequences, such as FRED ASTAIRE dancing on the ceiling in *Royal Wedding*, Kelly's dance with the cartoon Jerry the Mouse in *Anchors Aweigh*, and the wet title number in *Singin' in the Rain*. Biographies: *Dancing on the Ceiling: Stanley Donen and His Movies*, Stephen M. Silverman (1996); *Stanley Donen*, Joseph Andrew Casper (1995).

DONNELLY, DOROTHY [Agnes] (1880–1928). Stage lyricist and writer. A respected songwriter and playwright in the early decades of the twentieth century, she helped improve the writing quality of American operettas. Donnelly was born in New York, the daughter of a theatre manager, and began her career as a successful actress on the New York stage, playing a variety of roles, including George Bernard Shaw's *Candida* in its first American production. While still performing, Donnelly started adapting European operettas for Broadway and then went on to write original librettos and lyrics for *BLOSSOM TIME* (1921), *THE STUDENT PRINCE* (1924), *My Maryland* (1927), and *My Princess* (1927), all with composer SIGMUND ROMBERG. Her other musical credits were the librettos for *Flora Bella* (1916) and *Fancy Free* (1918) and both book and lyrics for *Poppy* (1923) and *Hello, Lola* (1926). Her writing career was cut short by her premature death but during her ten years in writing operettas she offered intelligent and passionate lyrics, logical librettos, and a sense of sincerity not often found in the operetta form. Biography: *Dorothy Donnelly: A Life in the Theatre*, Lorraine Arnal McLean (1999).

DONOHUE, [John Francis] **JACK** (1908–1984). Stage and film choreographer and director. A prodigious dancer–choreographer, he was busy in Hollywood between 1934 and 1966 but returned to Broadway regularly. The native New Yorker attended military school and worked as a broker and a riveter before taking up a dance career. Donohue started hoofing in vaudeville and by 1927 was on Broadway in the dancing chorus of ZIEGFELD FOLLIES, followed by appearances in *GOOD NEWS!* (1927), *FOLLOW THRU* (1929), *America's Sweetheart* (1931), and other musicals. He made his choreography debut in 1932 and staged the musical numbers for some Broadway musicals in the 1930s, most memorably *MUSIC IN THE AIR* (1932), even as he started a productive film career choreographing *GEORGE WHITE'S SCANDALS* (1934), *Music in the Air* (1934), *The Little Colonel* (1935), *CURLY TOP* (1935), *THANKS A MILLION* (1935), *The Littlest Rebel* (1935), and *CAPTAIN JANUARY* (1936). Donohue relocated to England in the late 1930s where he performed and choreographed in London and then returned to America to resume his Broadway career in 1944 with *Seven Lively Arts*, followed by *Top Banana* (1951), *OF*

THEE I SING (1952), *MR. WONDERFUL* (1956), and *Rumple* (1957), which he also directed. Although he was a well-known choreographer in New York, Donohue was more famous for the films he choreographed, including five SHIRLEY TEMPLE movies in the 1930s, *LOUISIANA PURCHASE* (1941), *THE FLEET'S IN* (1942), *BEST FOOT FORWARD* (1943), *GIRL CRAZY* (1943), *BROADWAY RHYTHM* (1944), *IT HAPPENED IN BROOKLYN* (1947), *CALAMITY JANE* (1953), *Top Banana* (1954), *Lucky Me* (1954), and *BABES IN TOYLAND* (1961), the last two which he also directed. Donohue also directed and choreographed television specials for such stars as FRANK SINATRA, RED SKELTON, and DEAN MARTIN.

DON'T BOTHER ME, I CAN'T COPE (Playhouse Theatre 1972). Racial strife and the angst of modern living were handled with a sometimes light, self-mocking touch in this vibrant revue that celebrated African American song and dance without resorting to nostalgia. MICKI GRANT wrote the splendid songs, most memorably the angry "Fighting for Pharaoh," the crooning "Thank Heaven for You," the rousing "Good Vibrations," and the sly title number, and the animated cast included Grant, Alex Bradford, Bobby Hill, Hope Clarke, and Arnold Wilkerson. Conceived and directed by VINNETTE CARROLL for her Off Off Broadway Urban Arts Corps, the revue caught on with white and black playgoers and ran 1,065 performances before touring successfully.

DOOLEY, RAY [born Rachel Rice Dooley] (1896–1984). Stage performer. A raucous singer–comedienne who had a variety of funny caricatures always on hand, she was a favorite in vaudeville and in Broadway revues. Dooley was born in Glasgow, Scotland, the daughter of an American circus clown, and was raised and educated in Philadelphia. She was coached by her father in comic techniques and as a member of the family's act did impersonations of bratty children. The act was popular enough to eventually play the Palace Theatre in New York and by 1917 Dooley was on Broadway in the revue *Words and Music*. Often performing with her husband EDDIE DOWLING, she was featured in such revues as *Hitchy-Koo of 1918*, *ZIEGFELD FOLLIES* (1919, 1920, 1921, and 1925), *Nifties of 1923*, *No Foolin'* (1926), *EARL CARROLL VANITIES* (1928), and *Thumbs Up!* (1934), as well as the book musicals *The Bunch and Judy* (1922) and *Sidewalks of New York* (1927). Dooley made only one film, the comedy *Honeymoon Lane*

(1931) written and co-starring Dowling, but it is a lively illustration of her animated comic talents.

DOORS, THE (Tri-Star 1991). Despite its title, the biographical musical was not about the celebrated 1960s band as much as it was about the unstable rock star Jim Morrison (Val Kilmer). J. Randal Johnson and director Oliver Stone penned the screenplay, which followed Morrison from his childhood, told in sepia-toned vignettes, to college days in Los Angeles, through his formation of the band with himself as composer and lead singer, his descent into drugs, alcohol, and sex, to his premature death in Paris at the age of twenty-seven. Parts of the film have a documentary feel, whereas other sections are pure melodrama. Kilmer not only looked alarmingly like Morrison but he did his own singing and sounded like him as well. Meg Ryan, Kathleen Quinlan, Frank Whaley, Kevin Dillon, Kyle MacLachlan, Billy Idol, Dennis Burkler, and Josh Evans were among the supporting players, although the picture belonged to Kilmer who seems to explode on screen right before your eyes. Songs by the Doors and other 1960s groups were used for the soundtrack, such as "Five to One," "Light My Fire," "When the Music Is Over," "Touch Me," and "Soft Parade."

DORSEY, JIMMY AND TOMMY. Film musicians and conductors. Two of the giants of the Big Band era, together and then separately they provided wonderful music, introduced major vocalists, and appeared in several movies. Jimmy (1904–1957) and Tommy Dorsey (1905–1956) were both born in Shenandoah, Pennsylvania, the sons of a cornet player in local bands who encouraged music lessons for both boys. Jimmy learned the saxophone and clarinet and started his career in the orchestras of PAUL WHITEMAN, Red Nichols, and the California Ramblers. Tommy studied the trombone and also played for various orchestras before the brothers teamed up in 1933 and found recognition with the Dorsey Brothers' Band. Two years later they parted ways and had separate careers that included concerts, nightclubs, recordings, and movies. Jimmy Dorsey and his band were featured in the Hollywood musicals *LADY, BE GOOD!* (1941), *THE FLEET'S IN* (1942), *I Dood It* (1943), *Four Jills and a Jeep* (1944), *Lost in Harlem* (1944), *HOLLYWOOD CANTEEN* (1944), *Music Man* (1948), and *Make Believe Ballroom* (1949). Tommy Dorsey and his band performed in such musicals as

Las Vegas Nights (1941), *Ships Ahoy* (1942), *Presenting Lili Mars* (1943), *DuBARRY WAS A LADY* (1943), *GIRL CRAZY* (1943), *Swing Fever* (1943), *BROADWAY RHYTHM* (1944), *The Thrill of a Romance* (1945), *A Song Is Born* (1948), and *Disc Jockey* (1951). The brothers were reunited for the film bio *The Fabulous Dorseys* (1947) in which they played themselves. Biographies: *Tommy and Jimmy: The Dorsey Years*, Herb Sanford (1980); *Jimmy Dorsey*, Robert L. Stockdale (1998); *Tommy Dorsey: Livin' in a Big Way*, Peter J. Levinson (2006).

◼ DOUBLE OR NOTHING (Paramount 1937). An odd and unique little musical film vehicle for BING CROSBY, it was filled with surprises along the way, many of them in the unusual way the musical numbers were handled. A millionaire, believing that people are basically honest, states in his will that wallets containing $500 each be left in various spots in Manhattan to see who is honest enough to return them to the lawyer's address placed inside. New Yorkers Lefty Boylan (Crosby), Liza Lou Lane (MARTHA RAYE), John Pederson (WILLIAM FRAWLEY), and Half Pint (Andy Devine) return the money and are given the chance to make $5000 each if they can double their $500 in a month's time. Only Lefty is successful, having invested in a nightclub where he crooned nightly for the patrons. The supporting cast included MARY CARLISLE, Benny Baker, Fay Holden, Harry Barris, and Samuel S. Hines. The songs, by various tunesmiths, were memorable in themselves but benefited by their distinctive staging by director Theodore Reed. Crosby makes shadow puppets on the wall while singing "It's the Natural Thing to Do," the music for the sidewalk dance number "All You Want to Do Is Dance" comes from a car radio, Raye satirizes stripteasers with "It's On, It's Off," and a nightspot orchestra creates their sounds vocally while accompanying "The Moon Got in My Eyes." Benjamin Glazer produced the offbeat musical, which remains intriguing.

DOUGLASS, STEPHEN (1921–). Stage performer. An affable leading man in 1950s musicals, he only had one hit but shone in several revivals. Douglass was born in Mt. Vernon, Ohio, and trained at the American Theatre Wing School under the tutelage of actor Walter Hampton. With his boyish good looks and rich voice, he was ideal for operetta heroes, and his first professional job was in stock in *NAUGHTY MARIETTA*. After appearing in two editions

of BILLY ROSE's nightclub revue *Diamond Horseshoe*, Douglass was hired as a replacement for Billy Bigelow in *CAROUSEL* (1947) and he repeated his performance in London. He got to originate featured characters in the musicals *Make a Wish* (1951) and *THE GOLDEN APPLE* (1954) and replaced JOHN RAITT in *THE PAJAMA GAME* (1954) before finding himself in a hit as the young baseballer Joe Hardy in *DAMN YANKEES* (1955). He also played the cartoonist Nelson Crandal in *Rumple* (1957), the Sheriff File in *110 IN THE SHADE* (1963), and was featured in the TV musical *The Mercer Girls* (1953). But Douglass was more in demand for revival roles, such as Edward Grieg in *SONG OF NORWAY* (1958), Tommy Albright in *BRIGADOON* (1961), Gaylord Ravenal in *SHOW BOAT* (1966), and as replacement for ROBERT PRESTON in *I DO! I DO!* (1968). Douglass retired from show business in 1969 but his lyrical, full voice is preserved on several cast recordings.

DOWLING, EDDIE [born Joseph Nelson Goucher] (1895–1976). Stage and film performer, writer, director, and producer. A respected stage artist who had many careers, including a substantial one in musical comedy, Dowling was born in Woonsocket, Rhode Island, and as a youth worked as a cabin boy on an ocean liner. He began his acting career in Providence and then went to England where he toured in a song-and-dance troupe. Returning to America, Dooley went on the vaudeville circuit with his wife, comedienne RAY DOOLEY, and the two appeared in such Broadway musicals as *ZIEGFELD FOLLIES* (1919 and 1920), *The Sidewalks of New York* (1927), and *Thumbs Up!* (1934). He also appeared solo in *The Velvet Lady* (1919), *Sally, Irene and Mary* (1922 and 1925), *Tell Me More* (1925), and *Honeymoon Lane* (1926), some of which he also wrote. In the late 1930s, Dowling left musical comedy and concentrated on serious drama as an actor, director, and producer, finding wide success with such classic plays as the original *The Time of Your Life* (1939) and *The Glass Menagerie* (1945). In an about face, his last Broadway acting credit was as replacement for the old miner Ben Rumson in *PAINT YOUR WAGON* (1952). Dowling wrote, directed, and/or appeared in a handful of films in the 1920s and 1930s.

◼ DOWN ARGENTINE WAY (Fox 1940). Two movie stars were created with this delightful Latin-flavored musical: BETTY GRABLE, who got the leading role when illness forced ALICE FAYE out, and CARMEN MIRANDA, who reached a wide audience for the first time and knocked them off their feet. The nearly invisible plot by Karl Tunberg and Darrel Ware concerned the American heiress Glenda Crawford (Grable) who travels to Argentina to buy a horse from wealthy Ricardo Quintana (DON AMECHE) and falls into a romance with him despite the disapproval of his rich father Don Diego (Henry Stephenson). Miranda was not put into the storyline at all; in fact, her specialty numbers were filmed in New York where she was appearing on Broadway. Nevertheless the Brazilian bombshell stopped the show with "South American Way" and "Mama Yo Quiero." Grable got to sing the ballad "Two Dreams Met" and show off her gams dancing to "Down Argentina Way." Leggy CHARLOTTE GREENWOOD, who managed to dance and get laughs at the same time, and the NICHOLAS BROTHERS were also showcased. The songs, mostly by HARRY WARREN (music) and MACK GORDON (lyrics), also included "Sing to Your Senorita" and some dance instrumentals. The movie, directed by IRVING CUMMINGS and choreographed by NICK CASTLE, was so successful that a series of Latin American musicals, often featuring Miranda, Ameche, and Grable or Faye, were launched by 20TH CENTURY-FOX.

DOWNS, JOHNNY [Morey] (1913–1994). Film and stage performer. An agile singer–dancer who usually played clean-cut college types in Hollywood musicals of the 1930s, he enjoyed a long career on stage and screen. The Brooklyn native was in films as a child, appearing in many silent shorts and playing one of the *Our Gang* kids for a time. As an adult he sang and danced in the Broadway musical *Strike Me Pink* (1933) and then returned to Hollywood where he had a bit part in *BABES IN TOYLAND* (1934). He was then cast in juvenile roles in such B musicals as *Coronado* (1935), *Pigskin Parade* (1936), *College Holiday* (1936), *Turn Off the Moon* (1937), *Thrill of a Lifetime* (1937), *Blonde Trouble* (1937), *Hold That Coed* (1938), *Swing, Sister, Swing* (1938), *Hawaiian Nights* (1939), *I Can't Give You Anything But Love* (1940), *Melody and Moonlight* (1940), *Moonlight in Hawaii* (1941), *All American Coed* (1941), *Behind the Eight Ball* (1941), *Campus Rhythm* (1943), and *Trocadero* (1944). Downs returned to Broadway in the musicals *Are You With It?* (1945) and *Hold It!* (1948) and then in Hollywood got cast in better musicals but in smaller parts, such as with *RHAPSODY IN BLUE* (1945), *The Kid From Brooklyn* (1946), *CALL ME MADAM* (1953), *Cruisin' Down the River* (1953), and *Here Come the Girls* (1953).

He left films in the 1950s and did a local television show in Los Angles for kids in which he showed old *Our Gang* shorts.

☐ **DR. JEKYLL AND MR. HYDE** (NBC-TV 1973). Hollywood star Kirk Douglas got to play the two-sided hero in this musical adaptation of Robert Louis Stevenson's 1886 novel, and opinions about the broadcast came down to whether one liked his energetic, ardent performance or not. Susan Hampshire was the doctor's sweetheart, Donald Pleasance his lab assistant Smudge, and Susan George the singer Annie who falls prey to the evil Mr. Hyde side of his personality. The musical was taped in England, and several distinguished stage actors were cast, including Michael Redgrave and STANLEY HOLLOWAY. None of them were experienced singers so the songs by LIONEL BART (with some assist by Mel Mandel and Norman Sachs) were not given full voice. "Our Time Together," "Right Before My Eyes," "The Way the World Was Meant to Be," "Poor Annie," and "Experiment (Whatever It Is)" were agreeable numbers if not very memorable. Sherman Yellen wrote the teleplay, which was reasonably faithful to the novel, and the 90-minute broadcast was produced by Burt Rosen and directed by David Winters. See also: *JEKYLL AND HYDE* (1997).

☐ **DR. SEUSS' HOW THE GRINCH STOLE CHRISTMAS** (CBS-TV 1966). A beloved animated musical and a perennial holiday favorite, the Chuck Jones production is probably second only to Charles Dickens' *A Christmas Carol* for popularity, repeated viewing, and nostalgic memories.

Plot: Every December the Grinch has to endure the cheerful singing and the gleeful anticipation of Christmas by the citizens of Whoville. Then on Christmas Day their joyous camaraderie and the noise of their celebrations are further irritations. Unable to endure another such holiday, the Grinch dresses up like Santa Claus, disguises his dog Max as a reindeer, and on Christmas eve sneaks into Whoville late at night and steals all the decorations, gifts, and banquet food from the houses of the Whos. When Christmas morning comes, he expects anguish and sorrow but the Whos happily welcome the holiday just the same. The realization that Christmas is more than just trappings and presents makes the Grinch have a change of heart. He returns all the gifts and is guest of honor at the Christmas feast.

Casts for *Dr. Seuss' How the Grinch Stole Christmas*

Character	1966 television (voices)	2006 Broadway
Narrator	Boris Karloff	JOHN CULLUM
Grinch	Boris Karloff	Patrick Page
Old Max		John Cullum
Young Max		Rusty Ross
Cindy Lou Who	June Foray	Nicole Bocchi or Caroline London
Singer	Thurl Ravenscroft	

Dr. Seuss' How the Grinch Stole Christmas. An Ebeneezer Scrooge for the twentieth century, the Grinch is similarly reborn by the end of the tale. As voiced by Boris Karloff, the Grinch is one of the most memorable of all animated characters. (Photofest)

Author–artist Theodore Geisel, who used the pen name Dr. Seuss, had never let any of his illustrated books be made into an animated show, but producer–director Jones convinced him that the thirty-minute musical would remain faithful to the celebrated book. Geisel wrote the teleplay and the lyrics, which were set to music by composer Mark Charlap with background music by Eugene Poddany. There were only three distinct songs—"Welcome Christmas," "Trim Up the Tree," and "You're a Mean One, Mr. Grinch!"—but because the narration and dialogue were all in rhymed verse, the program was highly lyrical. Geisel initially did not want horror movie veteran Boris Karloff to voice the Grinch, fearing he might frighten children, but once the recording was made it was clear it was a classic performance.

Jones recreated the look of the original book and brought the characters to life with delightful visuals. Max, for example, never utters a sound yet the character is brilliantly developed in the production. Critical raves and immediate public adulation turned the animated musical into a holiday favorite and has been broadcast every December since 1966.

A nonmusical stage adaptation of *How the Grinch Stole Christmas* was first presented by the Milwaukee's Children's Theatre Company in the 1990s, and a musical version was created by JACK O'BRIEN in the late 1990s when he was artistic director at the Old Globe Theatre in San Diego. An expanded version of that production arrived on Broadway in 2006 and ran 107 performances during the holiday season. The stage libretto and additional lyrics were by Timothy Mason, and Mel Marvin composed the new music. The TV songs were retained but to turn the short cartoon into a full-length musical some of the Who characters were further developed and seven new songs were added: "Whatchama Who," "I Hate Christmas," "One of a Kind," "Now's the Time," "Once in a Year," "Who Likes Christmas?," and "Santa for a Day." Karloff's narration was taken by Old Max looking back on the events of the story and again the look of the book was recreated in the sets and costumes. Reviews were mixed but audiences were not so reticent and the engagement was so successful it returned for the 2007 Christmas season.

DRAKE, ALFRED [born Alfredo Capurro] (1914–1992). Stage and television performer. One of the American Theatre's most esteemed leading men, he created some classic roles in Broadway musicals and was a highly regarded Shakespearean actor as well. A native New Yorker who was educated at Brooklyn College, Drake started in the chorus of Gilbert and Sullivan stock companies before making his Broadway debut in 1935 in a production of *THE MIKADO.* Two years later he was featured in Rodgers and Hart's *BABES IN ARMS.* After appearing on Broadway in the musicals *The*

Alfred Drake. No one epitomized the virile, Broadway baritone of the 1940s and 1950 as Drake did, playing macho roles but not afraid to look foolish on occasion. Here he is as the wily beggar and poet Hajj in the Broadway production of *Kismet* (1953). (Photofest)

Two Bouquets (1938) and *Out of the Frying Pan* (1941), the revues *One for the Money* (1939) and *The Straw Hat Revue* (1939), and playing Orlando in *As You Like It* (1941), Drake found fame in OKLAHOMA! (1943) where he originated the role of Curly. The full-voiced baritone also originated two other beloved musical roles: Fred Graham/Petruchio in KISS ME, KATE (1948) and the poet Hajj in KISMET (1953). He was offered the role of the king in THE KING AND I (1951) but turned it down because it didn't have enough singing; but in 1952 Drake played the King when YUL BRYNNER was on vacation. His other Broadway musicals include

Sing Out Sweet Land (1944), *The Beggar's Holiday* (1946), THE CRADLE WILL ROCK (1947), *Kean* (1961), and GIGI (1975). Drake never got to reprise his famous stage roles on screen but he appeared in a few films, starred in the TV musicals NAUGHTY MARIETTA (1955), THE ADVENTURES OF MARCO POLO (1956), *Yeoman of the Guard* (1957), and *Kiss Me, Kate* (1958), as well as in many television specials where he got to sing some of the songs that he had introduced on Broadway.

✧ **DREAMGIRLS** (Imperial Theatre 1981). One of the most dazzling musicals of the 1980s, the show was another triumph for director–choreographer MICHAEL BENNETT. Tom Eyen's libretto, loosely based on the real-life trio The Supremes, followed three African American singers, Deena Jones, Effie White, and Lorrell Robinson, as they climb the show biz ladder with the help of their ruthless manager Curtis Taylor, Jr., who is not above discarding one of the trio (and his former lover) and replacing her when he thinks it's good for business. With success comes heartaches and damaged relationships with friends, family, and spouses. Yet the women girls triumph in the end by being true to themselves and their personal dreams. The songs by Henry Krieger (music) and Eyen (lyrics) captured the Motown sound in the character numbers, such as "Family," "And I'm Telling You I Am Not Going," "I Am Changing," and "When I First Saw You," as well as the onstage pop songs such as "One Night Only," "Steppin' to the Bad Side," and the title number. The gritty yet sparkling musical was given a stunning production by Bennett, which showed off the talented cast and pop score. Critical approval and strong word of mouth kept the show on the boards for 1,522 performances. Bennett recreated the original production in 1987 with a new cast (Alisa Gyse, Arnetia Walker, LILLIAS WHITE, Weyman Thompson, and Herbert Rawlings, Jr.) and it was embraced again by playgoers for 168 performances.

Casts for *Dreamgirls*

Character	1981 Broadway	2006 film
Effie Melody White	Jennifer Holliday	Jennifer Hudson
Deena Jones	Sheryl Lee Ralph	Beyoncé Knowles
Lorrell Robinson	Loretta Devine	Anika Noni Rose
Curtis Taylor, Jr.	Ben Harney	Jamie Foxx
James Thunder Early	Cleavant Derricks	Eddie Murphy
C. C. White	Obba Babatundé	Keith Robinson
Michelle Morris	Deborah Burrell	Sharon Leal
Marty	Vondie Curtis-Hall	Danny Glover

Dreamgirls (Dreamworks/Paramount 2006) was on the planning boards for years but not until the success of the film version of *CHICAGO* (2002), which Bill Condon wrote, was the project green lit with Condon as writer and director. Because Bennett's stage production moved in and out of different places and switched from the audience's point of view to that of the actors', the show seemed cinematic already. Condon built on Bennett's ideas and jumped from location to location even during one song, giving the film a vibrant if sometimes dizzying feeling. The cast was not only excellent but also full of surprises. Newcomer Jennifer Hudson triumphed as Effie, the amiable Jamie Foxx gave a vicious performance as Curtis, and Eddie Murphy revealed a whole new side to his many talents. Everyone did their own singing and it was riveting to hear them. The Kreiger–Eyen score was well served by the movie, with most of the songs retained, and some new numbers ("I Love You I Do," "Patience," and "Listen") were added. The integration of music and scenes was particularly effective and the movie was well paced. The Broadway show that fans feared would never come to the screen finally arrived and it was worth the wait.

DRESSLER, MARIE [born Leila Marie Koeber] (1869–1934). Stage and film performer. The popular comedienne with a bulldog face, large imposing body, and commanding voice first found fame on Broadway and then made an unforgettable impression in some movies before she died. Dressler was born in Coburg, Canada, the daughter of a music teacher, and by the time she was fourteen she was a professional actress working in stock. She made her New York debut in the musical *The Robber of the Rhine* (1892) and soon established herself as a superb comic in plays and musicals, including *Princess Nicotine* (1893), *Giroflé-Girrrflá* (1894), *The Lady Slavey* (1896), *Hotel Topsy-Turvy* (1898), *The King's Carnival* (1901), *The Lady of Fame* (1902), *Higgledy Piggledy* (1904), *Twiddle Twaddle* (1906), *Roly Poly* (1912), *Marie Dressler's All Star Gambols* (1913), *The Century Girl* (1916), *THE PASSING SHOW* (1920), *The Dancing Girl* (1923), and many others. Dressler's most famous role was the boarding house drudge Tillie Blobbs who fantasizes herself in romantic settings in the musical *Tillie's Nightmare* (1910). She was so popular in the role that she reprised the part in the silent films *Tillie's Punctured Romance* (1914), *Tillie's Tomato Surprise* (1915), and

Tillie Wakes Up (1917). But Dressler didn't become a movie star until sound came in and audiences could hear her overbearing voice, as in the nonmusical classics *Anna Christie* (1930), *Min and Bill* (1930), and *Dinner at Eight* (1933). She appeared in the screen musicals *THE HOLLYWOOD REVUE OF 1929*, *The Vagabond Lover* (1929), and *Chasing Rainbows* (1930), and she was also a favorite on the vaudeville circuit. Autobiographies: *The Story of an Ugly Duckling* (1924); *My Own Story* (1934); biography: *Marie Dressler*, Matthew Kennedy (2006).

DRISCOLL, BOBBY [Cletus] (1937–1968). Film and television performer. The tragic child star of DISNEY movies, he shone in musicals and adventure films during his brief career. Driscoll was born in Cedar Rapids, Iowa, and made his feature film debut when he was six years old. His musical credits include *SONG OF THE SOUTH* (1946), *If You Knew Susie* (1948), *So Dear to My Heart* (1948), and vocals for the animated *MELODY TIME* (1949), but he is most remembered as Jim Hawkins in the nonmusical *Treasure Island* (1950) and for providing the voice of *PETER PAN* in the 1953 animated musical. Driscoll made several television appearances in the 1950s but when he stopped getting cast in the 1960s he took to drink and became a drug addict, dying of an overdose at the age of thirty-one.

DROWSY CHAPERONE, THE (Marquis Theatre 2006). An unlikely and surprising Broadway hit, the lighthearted musical pastiche recalled *THE BOY FRIEND* (1954) in its ability to parody with accuracy and affection. Sitting in his apartment with his record collection of old musicals, the Man in the Chair (Bob Martin) shares with the audience one of his favorite vintage albums, *The Drowsey Chaperone*, and as he describes it the 1920s musical comedy comes to life about him. The silly plot is about the stage star Janet Van De Graaff (SUTTON FOSTER) who wants to give up show biz to marry the handsome Robert Martin (Troy Britton Johnson). Theatre producer Fedlzieg (Lenny Wolpe) tries to break them up using two gangsters disguised as pastry chefs. Also causing complications is Janet's chaperone (Beth Leavel), who is always soused, or "drowsy" in Roaring Twenties slang. The delightful cast also included Georgia Engel, Eddie Korbich, Edward Hibbart, Jennifer Smith, Jason and Garth Kravits, Danny Burstein, and Kecia Lewis-Evans. Bob Martin and Don McKellar wrote the zany libretto, and Lisa Lambert and Greg Morrison penned the

Twenties-like song, such as "Show Off," "As We Stumble Along," "Love Is Always Lovely in the End," "Accident Waiting to Happen," and "Cold Feets." The playful musical spoof echoed the period with oddball precision but it was the ongoing commentary by the Man in the Chair that allowed the show-within-a-show to sparkle in an original way. Critical response was positive and after a slow start audiences discovered the pleasant little diversion and kept it running for 674 performances. The musical, which had originated in Canada and been successfully produced in southern California, was directed and choreographed by Casey Nicholaw, who raised silliness to a high art.

DuBarry Was a Lady (46th Street Theatre 1939). A sparkling COLE PORTER score and superior clowning by stars BERT LAHR and ETHEL MERMAN turned the musical into first-class entertainment. Louis Blore (Lahr), the washroom attendant at the ritzy Manhattan Club Petite, has long loved the chorine May Daly (Merman) but she seems too interested in the handsome Alex Barton (Ronald Graham). Louis plots to put knockout drops in Alex's cocktail but mistakenly drinks the concoction himself and falls into a deep slumber during which he dreams he is King Louis XIV of France and May is his mistress Du Barry. Yet even in his dream Louis cannot win May and he awakes just as the king is about to be assassinated. Also involved in the fun were BETTY GRABLE, Benny Baker, CHARLES WALTERS, and Kay Sutton. B. G. DE SYLVA and HERBERT FIELDS collaborated on the contrived but nimble libretto, and Porter provided such song delights as "Friendship," "Well, Did You Evah?," "But in the Morning, No!," "Do I Love You?," "Katie Went to Haiti," and "It Was Written in the Stars." DeSylva produced, EDGAR MACGREGOR directed, ROBERT ALTON did the choreography, and the audience roared for 408 performances.

DuBarry Was a Lady (MGM 1943) dropped Lahr, Merman, and all but three of the Porter songs so it is not surprising that the result is a lackluster and even annoying movie musical. RED SKELTON and LUCILLE BALL would later become two of television's greatest clowns so it is disconcerting to see them trying so hard and not being funny on screen. Even the reliable GENE KELLY looks uncomfortable as he plays a leading man who hasn't much to do. The IRVING BRECHER screenplay retained the premise of the stage work, but the scenes in the French court were tedious and the supporting roles, such as the conjurer Taliostra played by a young and fascinating ZERO MOSTEL, are underused. Porter's "Friendship," "Do I Love You?," and "Katie Went to Haiti" were supplemented by new numbers by ROGER EDENS, Ralph Freed, BURTON LANE, and others. "DuBarry Was a Lady," "I Love an Esquire Girl," "Madame, I Love Your Crepes Suzettes," and "Ladies of the Bath" were mildly enjoyable, and VIRGINIA O'BRIEN'S deadpan delivery of Edens' "No Matter How You Slice It, It's Still Salome" was much more than that. ROY DEL RUTH was the uninspired director, and CHARLES WALTERS, who had been featured in the Broadway production, choreographed the film.

DUBIN, AL (1891–1945). Film and stage lyricist. One of Hollywood's earliest and best songwriters, he scored over thirty musicals and had dozens of hits in his twenty-year career. Dubin was born in Zurich, Switzerland, and emigrated to America with his family two years later. He worked for different music publishers in New York and then, after serving in World War I, contributed songs to the Broadway musicals *Charlot Revue* (1925) and *White Lights* (1927) before heading to Hollywood in 1929. Dubin's first collaborator was composer JOE BURKE and the two scored the early screen musicals *GOLD DIGGERS OF BROADWAY* (1929),

Casts for *Du Barry Was a Lady*

Character	1939 Broadway	1943 film
Louis Blore	BERT LAHR	RED SKELTON
May Daly	ETHEL MERMAN	LUCILLE BALL
Alex/Alec	Ronald Graham	GENE KELLY
Alice/Ginny	BETTY GRABLE	VIRGINIA O'BRIEN
Charley/Dauphin	Benny Baker	Rags Ragland
Harry Norton	CHARLES WALTERS	
Taliostra		ZERO MOSTEL

SALLY (1929), *She Couldn't Say No* (1930), *HOLD EVERYTHING!* (1930), *Top Speed* (1930), *Life of the Party* (1930), and *Oh, Sailor Behave* (1930). After writing the songs for *Her Majesty Love* (1931) with composer Walter Jurmann, he was teamed up with composer HARRY WARREN and the duo enjoyed one of the most successful collaborations in the history of Hollywood musicals. Among their two dozen musicals together were *42ND STREET* (1933), *GOLD DIGGERS OF 1933*, *FOOTLIGHT PARADE* (1933), *ROMAN SCANDALS* (1933), *Moulin Rouge* (1934), *WONDER BAR* (1934), *Twenty Million Sweethearts* (1934), *DAMES* (1934), *GOLD DIGGERS OF 1935*, *GO INTO YOUR DANCE* (1935), *Broadway Gondolier* (1935), *Shipmates Forever* (1935), *Stars Over Broadway* (1935), *Colleen* (1936), *GOLD DIGGERS OF 1937* (1936), *Cain and Mabel* (1936), *Mr. Dodd Takes the Air* (1937), *The Singing Marine* (1937), *GOLD DIGGERS IN PARIS* (1938), and *Garden of the Moon* (1938). Dubin returned to Broadway to provide songs

for the musical revues *Streets of Paris* (1939), *Keep Off the Grass* (1940), and *Star and Garter* (1942) and then teamed with JAMES V. MONACO for some songs in the film musical *STAGE DOOR CANTEEN* (1943) before his premature death from alcoholism. Nearly four decades later he had a hit on Broadway with the stage version of *42nd Street* (1980). Dubin was the first lyricist to create a catalog of hit songs written for the screen, leaving behind such standards as "Lullaby of Broadway," "Shuffle Off to Buffalo," "I Only Have Eyes for You," "We're in the Money," "Tip Toe Through the Tulips," and "I'll String Along With You." Biography: *Lullaby of Broadway: The Life of Al Dubin*, Patricia Dubin McGuire [his daughter] (1983).

DUCK SOUP (Paramount 1933). Arguably the MARX BROTHERS' funniest film, it has no love songs to slow down the action and the musical numbers are all comic. HARRY RUBY and BERT KALMAR wrote the songs and the

Duck Soup. There are not many songs in this Marx Brothers film but the ones that are there are incorporated into the action, much like a comic operetta. The spoof on war and patriotism was one of the few Hollywood products to take the satirical approach seen on Broadway in such musical satires as *Strike Up the Band* (1930), *Of Thee I Sing* (1931), and *Let 'Em Eat Cake* (1933). Pictured (left to right) in *Duck Soup* are Chico, Zeppo, Groucho, and Harpo Marx. (Photofest)

screenplay, which was set in the tiny kingdom of Freedonia where Rufus T. Firefly (Groucho Marx) is the zany dictator and the wealthy Mrs. Teasdale (MARGARET DUMONT) keeps the country funded. After the Ambassador Trentino of Sylvania (Louis Calhern) is insulted by Firefly, the two nations go to war and Chicolini (Chico Marx), Pinky (Harpo Marx), and Lt. Bob Rolard (Zeppo Marx) are the military brains of the Freedonian army. Just as the script celebrated comic anarchy and mocked nationalism, the songs satirized everything from GEORGE M. COHAN to Gilbert and Sullivan: the empty anthem "Freedonia," the foot-stomping spiritual "The Country's Going to War," and the patter song "The Laws of My Administration." LEO MCCAREY directed with wild abandon, allowing the plot to stop for such classic bits as Harpo and Groucho dressed identically in nightshirts and simulating a mirror between them. Today the Herman J. Mankiewicz-produced movie is considered a classic but it was not very popular on its initial release and did so poorly at the box office that PARAMOUNT dropped the brothers and they went to MGM.

DUKE, VERNON [born Vladimir Dukeksky] (1903–1969). Stage and film composer. The creator of both concert and popular music, the Russian songwriter gave Broadway and Hollywood some superior scores. Duke was born in Parafianovo, Russia, and trained in classical music at the Kiev Conservatory and composed music for the Ballet Russe before emigrating west and writing several London musical comedies between 1926 and 1930. He continued on to New York and made his Broadway debut with *Walk a Little Faster* (1932), followed by songs in *ZIEGFELD FOLLIES* (1934 and 1936), *CABIN IN THE SKY* (1940), *Banjo Eyes* (1941), *The Lady Comes Across* (1942), *Jackpot* (1944), *Sadie Thompson* (1944), *Two's Company* (1952), and *The Littlest Revue* (1956). His lyricist collaborators include JOHN LATOUCHE, HOWARD DIETZ, and IRA GERSHWIN, with whom he helped complete the score for the movie musical *THE GOLDWYN FOLLIES* (1938) after GEORGE GERSHWIN died. Duke also scored the Hollywood musicals *She's Working Her Way Through College* (1952) and *April in Paris* (1952) with lyricist SAMMY CAHN, and his songs were used in the TV musical *Autumn in New York* (1952). Duke's music could be quite complex and sophisticated, yet he managed to be accessible as well, as proven by such hit songs as "I Can't Get Started (With You)," "I Like the Looks of You," "April in

Paris," "Autumn in New York," and "Taking a Chance on Love." His concert music was written under his Russian birth name. Biography: *Passport to Paris* (1955).

DUMBO (Disney/RKO 1941). Although it is the shortest of all Disney animated features (only sixty-four minutes long), every moment counts in this tenderhearted tale of a misfit elephant who never speaks throughout the whole film. Mr. Stork (voice of STERLING HOLLOWAY) delivers the baby elephant Dumbo to his mother at the circus where his oversized ears are the subject of much scorn by the other animals. Only Timothy Q. Mouse (Edward Brophy) befriends Dumbo and, once it is discovered that Dumbo can fly by flapping his large ears, the mouse champions the elephant into becoming the star of the circus. The animation was expert throughout, but the dream sequence "Pink Elephants on Parade" contained the most innovative use of color and line yet seen on film. Oliver Wallace, NED WASHINGTON, and FRANK CHURCHILL collaborated on the songs, which also included the catchy "When I See an Elephant Fly," the rhythmic "Casey Junior," and the lilting "Baby Mine." Among the many vibrant voices heard on the soundtrack were CLIFF EDWARDS, Verna Felton, HERMAN BING, Billy Bletcher, Jim Carmichael, and Eddie Holden. The Ben Sharpsteen-directed musical was one of the top-grossing movies of the year and has remained a favorite ever since.

DUMONT, MARGARET (1889–1965). Film, stage, and television performer. A stately, very proper character actress forever remembered as the foil in seven MARX BROTHERS films, the buxom but elegant singer–actress was also featured in other movie musicals and on Broadway. Dumont was born in Brooklyn and went on the stage as a child, even appearing in a silent movie in 1917. She made her Broadway debut in 1921 and was seen in a handful of plays before playing the wealthy matron Mrs. Potter in the musical *THE COCOANUTS* (1925) starring the Marx Brothers. Dumont joined them again for *ANIMAL CRACKERS* (1928) and then reprised both performances in the 1929 and 1930 film versions. She went to Hollywood with the brothers and appeared in five more of their films, *DUCK SOUP* (1933), *A NIGHT AT THE OPERA* (1935), *A DAY AT THE RACES* (1937), *AT THE CIRCUS* (1939), and *The Big Store* (1941), as well as over fifty other movies over the next three decades. Among her screen musical credits are *ANYTHING GOES* (1936), *Song and Dance*

Man (1936), *The Life of the Party* (1937), *Born to Sing* (1942), *Sing Your Worries Away* (1942), *Rhythm Parade* (1942), *Up in Arms* (1944), *Bathing Beauty* (1944), and *What a Way to Go!* (1964), as well as some television shows in the 1950s. Dumont aspired to be a serious actress but was rarely given the opportunity and claimed not to understand the Marx Brothers' humor at all.

DUNBAR, DIXIE [born Christina Elizabeth Dunbar] (1919–1991). Film and stage performer. A perky, tap-dancing treat who was in both Broadway and Hollywood musicals as a youngster, she shone in a dozen screen musicals and then retired from films at the age of nineteen. Dunbar was born in Montgomery, Alabama, and grew up in Atlanta, Georgia, where she took dance lessons at an early age. Renamed "Dixie" because of her Southern drawl, she was soon singing and dancing in nightclubs and with name bands, making her Broadway debut in *GEORGE WHITE'S SCANDALS* (1934) and shining in *LIFE BEGINS AT 8:40* (1934). That same year Dunbar made her film debut in a character part in *George White's Scandals* (1934), followed by featured roles in such musicals as *KING OF BURLESQUE* (1935), *The First Baby* (1935), *Sing, Baby, Sing* (1935), *Pigskin Parade* (1935), *ONE IN A MILLION* (1935), *Sing and Be Happy* (1937), and *Life Begins in College* (1937). When she was relegated to smaller roles in *REBECCA OF SUNNYBROOK FARM* (1938), *ALEXANDER'S RAGTIME BAND* (1938), *Walking Down Broadway* (1938), and *The Freshmen Year* (1938), Dunbar returned to Broadway and appeared in *Yokel Boy* (1939) and then performed in nightclubs for a time before retiring.

DUNCAN, SANDY (1946–). Stage and television performer. A tiny, perky singer–actress with bright eyes and a wide smile, she possesses a squeaky but pleasant little voice that has limited her to lightweight roles, often as ditzy and naive characters, yet hasn't stopped her from some buoyant performances. Duncan was born in Henderson, Texas, and educated at Lon Morris College and soon was performing in musicals in her home state. She made her Broadway debut as the mayor's daughter Zaneeta Shinn in *THE MUSIC MAN* (1965), followed by featured roles in the revivals *CAROUSEL* (1966), *FINIAN'S RAINBOW* (1967), and *THE SOUND OF MUSIC* (1967). After replacing the female lead in the Off Broadway musical *YOUR OWN THING* (1968), Duncan was noticed as the spunky heroines in *Canterbury*

Tales (1969) and the flighty Maisie in *THE BOY FRIEND* (1970) and then had her biggest hit as *PETER PAN* (1979) in the longest-running production of that musical on record. She was also praised as a replacement in *MY ONE AND ONLY* (1985) and *CHICAGO* (2002). Duncan has toured extensively in musicals such as *Peter Pan*, *THE KING AND I*, and *ANYTHING GOES*. She made only a few films but many televisions appearances, from commercials to her own series, playing a boy again in the TV musical *PINOCCHIO* (1976). Duncan has also provided the voices for characters in animated movies, such as *The Fox and the Hound* (1981), *Rock-a-Doodle* (1991), and *The Swan Princess* (1994). She was married to actor Bruce Scott and is currently wed to singer–dancer Don Correia with whom she has often performed.

DUNCAN, [Robert] **TODD** (1903–1998). Stage performer. The full-voiced African American opera singer made only a few appearances on Broadway, but all of them were memorable. Duncan was born in Danville, Kentucky, and was educated at Butler University and Columbia University, after which he taught elocution at Howard University. It was while he was teaching music at Municipal College for Negroes in Louisville, Kentucky, that Duncan turned to a performing career. He made an auspicious Broadway debut as Porgy in the original *PORGY AND BESS* (1935), returning to the role in various venues and back in New York in 1942 and 1943. Duncan also shone as the Lawd's General in *CABIN IN THE SKY* (1940) before pursuing opera roles at the New York City Opera and other companies. He returned to Broadway to give a powerful performance as the South African minister Stephen Kumalo in *LOST IN THE STARS* (1949). Duncan retired from performing on stage in 1951 and spent the rest of his life teaching and making recordings, over 2,000 of them. He can be seen and heard in the film musical *Syncopation* (1942).

DUNN, JAMES [Howard] (1905–1967). Film, stage, and television performer. An affable song-and-dance man with a smiling, good-guy persona, he was featured in eight Hollywood musicals, mostly B pictures. The native New Yorker went on the vaudeville stage and appeared in some silent films before making his Broadway debut in 1930 in a play. Discouraged by his stalled career, Dunn went to Hollywood in 1931 and was picked up by the studios for juvenile leads in such musicals as *Dance Team* (1932), *Jimmy and Sally* (1933), *TAKE A CHANCE*

(1933), *Stand Up and Cheer* (1934), *Baby, Take a Bow* (1934), *365 Nights in Hollywood* (1934), *Bright Eyes* (1934), and GEORGE WHITE'S SCANDALS (1935). He returned to Broadway and was featured in the musical *PANAMA HATTIE* (1940) and then tried Hollywood again, getting some challenging roles in nonmusicals. By the 1950s his drinking problem hindered his career but he acted in television up until a few weeks of his death.

DUNNE, IRENE [Marie] (1898–1990). Stage and screen performer. An aristocratic beauty with a flowing soprano voice, she was popular in musicals, comedies, and dramas. Dunne was born in Louisville, Kentucky, the daughter of a steamship inspector and a musician, and was raised and educated in rural Indiana. After studying at the Indianapolis Conservatory, she went to the Chicago Musical College to train as an opera singer. When she failed to get accepted by the Metropolitan Opera in New York in 1920, she turned to musical theatre and got a job as the title heroine in the national touring company of *IRENE*. Dunne made her Broadway debut in 1922 and was featured in a half dozen forgettable musicals before getting cast as Magnolia in the 1929 tour of *SHOW BOAT*. She was so effective in the role that she got to reprise her performance in the 1936 screen version of the musical. Dunne never returned to Broadway but was seen in over forty movies, including the musical roles of the high-society Daphne in *LEATHERNECKING* (1930), the pathetic saloon singer Addie in *SWEET ADELINE* (1935), the princess-in-disguise Stephanie in *ROBERTA* (1935), the frontier performer Sally in *HIGH, WIDE AND HANDSOME* (1937), the Broadway star Maggie in *JOY OF LIVING* (1938), and the tragic Terry in *Love Affair* (1939). Dunne was also a bankable movie star in nonmusicals, praised for her fine performances in *Cimarron* (1931), *The Age of Innocence* (1934), *The Awful Truth* (1937), *Anna and the King of Siam* (1946), *Life With Father* (1947), *I Remember Mama* (1948), *The Mudlark* (1950), and other films. Dunne retired in 1952 and concentrated on political causes, diplomacy (she was a UN delegate), charities, and business. Biography: *Irene Dunne: First Lady of Hollywood*, Wes D. Gehring (2003).

DUPONT SHOW OF THE MONTH/WEEK, THE. An anthology series on television that offered dramatizations and musicals with name casts, the ambitious show was carried by all three major networks at different times because of its classy reputation. It was first called *DuPont Theatre* (1956–1957) on ABC and each week presented a thirty-minute drama or comedy. As *The DuPont Show of the Month* (1957–1961) on CBS, each show ran ninety minutes and condensed versions of classic novels, plays, and musicals were offered. When the show moved to NBC, it was called *The DuPont Show of the Week* (1961–1964), and the sixty-minute program switched to dramatizations of actual events and documentary. In its heyday, DuPont provided quality programs and featured stars from Broadway and Hollywood. Among the musicals produced by the show were *JUNIOR MISS* (1957), *ALADDIN* (1958), and *THE RED MILL* (1958).

DURANTE, JIMMY [Francis] (1893–1980). Stage, film, radio, and television performer. The beloved comic, with his prominent "schnozzola" of a nose, raspy voice, funny walk, and "New Yorkese" speech, was a much-loved favorite in all media. The native New Yorker worked as a photographic engraver and honky-tonk pianist before he started doing comedy in vaudeville as part of the comedy team with Lou Clayton (1890–1950) and Eddie Jackson (1896–1980). The act was a hit and the trio even played Manhattan's Palace Theatre before the threesome found themselves on Broadway in *Show Girl* (1929) and *THE NEW YORKERS* (1930). In 1930, Durante began his solo career on stage and in films. He was featured on Broadway in comic roles in *Strike Me Pink* (1930), *JUMBO* (1935), *RED, HOT AND BLUE!* (1936), and *Stars in Your Eyes* (1939) and in the revue *Keep Off the Grass* (1940). Durante made over two dozen screen musicals, but he is most remembered as the piano-playing pal Nick Lombardi to FRANK SINATRA in *IT HAPPENED IN BROOKLYN* (1947) and the circus owner Pop Wonder in *Jumbo* (1962). His other screen credits include *Roadhouse Nights* (1930) with Jackson and Clayton, *THE PHANTOM PRESIDENT* (1932), *Broadway to Hollywood* (1933), *GEORGE WHITE'S SCANDALS* (1934), *Sally, Irene and Mary* (1938), *Little Miss Broadway* (1938), *TWO GIRLS AND A SAILOR* (1944), *Music for Millions* (1944), *Two Sisters From Boston* (1945), *On an Island With You* (1948), and *Beau James* (1957). Durante was very popular on radio and in nightclubs and then when television was introduced found a whole new audience through guest appearances and TV specials, such as the musical *Alice Through the Looking Glass* (1966). He also wrote songs for some of his vehicles, such as one of his signature numbers "Inka Dinka Doo." Biographies: *Jimmy Durante*,

David Bakish (1995); *Goodnight, Mrs. Calabash*, William Cahn (1963); *Schnozzola*, Gene Fowler (1951).

DURBIN, DEANNA [born Edna Mae Durbin) (1921–). Film performer. A classically trained singer who excelled at playing wholesome youths with a bubbly personality, she was one of the top box office attractions for a time and a leader in record sales. Durbin was born in Winnipeg, Canada, and raised in California where she showed a talent for singing at a young age. By the age of fourteen she was starring in such screen musicals as *Three Smart Girls* (1935), ONE HUNDRED MEN AND A GIRL (1937), *Mad About Music* (1938), *That Certain Age* (1938), *Three Smart Girls Grow Up* (1939), *First Love* (1939), *It's a Date* (1940), *Spring Parade* (1940), *Nice Girl!* (1941), and *It Started With Eve* (1941). As Durbin matured and her roles approached adulthood, she remained popular and starred in the musicals *The Amazing Mrs. Holliday* (1943), *Hers to Hold* (1943), *His Butler's Sister* (1943), CAN'T HELP SINGING (1944), *Lady on a Train* (1945), *Because of Him* (1946), *I'll Be Yours* (1947), *Something in the Wind* (1947), UP IN CENTRAL PARK (1948), and *For the Love of Mary* (1948). At the age of twenty-seven, Durbin left films and retired to France where for decades she has refused film offers and requests for interviews. Biography: *Deanna Durbin: Fairy Tale*, W. E. Mills (1996).

DUSSAULT, NANCY (1936–). Stage and television performer. A petite, blonde singer–dancer with an opera-ranged voice, she has had a busy Broadway career between originating and reviving musical roles. Dussault was born in Pensacola, Florida, educated at Northwestern, and received an extensive musical training before she started appearing in summer stock musicals. He made her New York debut in the Off Broadway revue *Diversions* (1958) and then was featured in revivals of STREET SCENE (1959), THE MIKADO (1959), and THE CRADLE WILL ROCK (1960) before getting noticed as the fledging pop singer Tilda in DO RE MI (1960). Dussault's other original role of note was the anthropologist Emily Kirsten in *Bajour* (1964), but she also shone as a replacement for Maria in THE SOUND OF MUSIC (1962) and in leading roles in Broadway revivals of CAROUSEL (1966), FINIAN'S RAINBOW (1967), and SOUTH PACIFIC (1969). After doing tours and regional productions, she returned to Broadway as a replacement in *Side By Side By Sondheim* (1977) and INTO THE WOODS (1988). Dussault has appeared on television in many series and musical specials and late in her career took up teaching at UCLA.

DVORAK, ANN [born Anna McKim] (1912–1979). Film performer. A child performer who grew up to become an acclaimed actress in dramatic pieces, the dark-haired beauty was a dancer–singer in some early screen musicals. Dvorak was born in New York, the daughter of a film manager and a silent film actress, and appeared in silents as a child. Dvorak studied dance and when sound came in became a dance instructor for MGM musicals. She appeared in the chorus of HOLLYWOOD REVUE OF 1929 and *Lord Byron of Broadway* (1930) and then was featured in such musicals as *The Crooner* (1932), *College Coach* (1933), *The Way to Love* (1933), *Sweet Music* (1935), *Bright Lights* (1935), THANKS A MILLION (1935), *Manhattan Merry-Go-Round* (1937), *Masquerade in Mexico* (1945), *Abeline Town* (1946), and *The Bachelor's Daughters* (1946). During the 1930s and 1940s, Dvorak gave some compelling performances in melodramas such as *Scarface* (1932) and *G Men* (1934). After entertaining the troops during World War II and acting in a few early television dramas she retired from the screen.

DWAN, [Joseph Aloysius] **ALLAN** (1885–1981). Film director and producer. A prolific and versatile director from the early silents into the 1950s, he often produced his own pictures. Dwan was born in Toronto, the son of a garment manufacturer, and studied electrical engineering at Notre Dame. He got interested in film after graduation when the lighting company he worked for got a contract for a movie studio. At first he sold scripts to the studio and by 1911 he was directing shorts and serving as technical advisor for such directors as D. W. Griffith, helping develop crane and dolly camera movement for *Intolerance* (1916) and other movies. Dwan was directing features by the 1920s and helmed many popular Douglas Fairbanks–Mary Pickford films as well as some of Gloria Swanson's best vehicles. When sound came in, he continued to work steadily and ended up directing some 400 movies by the time he retired in 1958. Dwan's thirteen musicals, half of which he also produced, include *Hollywood Party* (1934), REBECCA OF SUNNYBROOK FARM (1938), *Young People* (1940), *Rise and Shine* (1941), *Here We Go Again* (1942), *Calendar Girl* (1947), *Northwest Outpost* (1947), *I Dream of Jeanie* (1952), and *Sweethearts on Parade* (1953).

EARL CARROLL VANITIES. Stage musical series. Between 1923 and 1940, EARL CARROLL presented eleven editions of his revue in his efforts to rival the *ZIEGFELD FOLLIES* and *GEORGE WHITE'S SCANDALS*. These shows were considered the most risqué and comedy oriented of the various Broadway revue series and they had the reputation of being smutty and nothing more than tarted-up burlesques, yet some outstanding talent (mostly comics) first found recognition in the shows and the comedy was often first class. JIMMY SAVO, PATSY KELLY, W. C. FIELDS, JOE COOK, HELEN BRODERICK, SOPHIE TUCKER, LILLIAN ROTH, JACK BENNY, and MILTON BERLE were among the comics and singers who graced the *Vanities* stage. But what audiences most came to see were the girls. Carroll's beauties were presented in sexy and sometimes lewd exhibitions, which kept the producer at odds with the law and secured the series' popularity. Carroll himself directed the shows and contributed to the sketches, music, and lyrics, although few memorable songs came from the series. Two films were made using the Carroll name and the reputation of the *Vanities*, although Hollywood made sure that there was nothing objectionable to be seen. Of course, both movies had plots added so the revue format of the stage shows was only to be found in the show within the show. In *Earl Carroll Vanities* (Republic 1945), the Princess Drinia of Turania (CONSTANCE MOORE) comes to New York City with her mother, Queen Elena (Mary Forbes), and ends up appearing in a *Vanities* show on Broadway. Dennis O'Keefe provided the love interest and also in the cast were EVE ARDEN, Otto Kruger, Alan Mowbray, Stephanie Bachelor, and Pinky Lee. The Frank Gill, Jr., screenplay was nonsense but agreeably so, and the *Vanities* production numbers, staged by SAMMY LEE, were more lavish than Carroll could afford on Broadway. The JOSEPH SANTLEY-directed film featured some pleasant if not memorable songs by Kim Gannon and Walter Kent, including "Endlessly" and "Who Dat Up Dere?" *Earl Carroll Sketchbook* (Republic 1946) was also a backstager penned by Gill with Parke Levy. Constance Moore was back as Pamela Thayer, a singing star who has romantic and professional complications with her songwriter Tyler Brice (William Marshall). In addition to such fine supporting players such as EDWARD EVERETT HORTON, Barbara Jo Allen, Bill Goodwin, and Hilary Brooke, the film boasted some commendable songs by JULE STYNE (music) and SAMMY CAHN (lyrics), including "I've Never Forgotten," "What Makes You So Beautiful, Beautiful?," and "Oh Henry." Interpolated into the movie was "I Got a Right to Sing the Blues," a song HAROLD ARLEN (music) and TED KOEHLER (lyrics) wrote for one of Carroll's *Vanities* and arguably the best song to come out of the whole series.

EARNEST IN LOVE. See *WHO'S EARNEST?*

EASTER PARADE (MGM 1948). FRED ASTAIRE, who had gone into a brief retirement, launched a new phase in his remarkable career with this musical favorite. The forty-eight-year-old hoofer was paired with JUDY GARLAND, who was practically half his age and not known for her dancing abilities, but the team set off sparks all the same and the movie was a giant hit.

Plot: The dancing team of Don Hewes and Nadine Hale is broken off in 1911 when Nadine dumps Don to accept a role in the *Ziegfeld Follies*. Determined to continue on without her, Don takes the rookie dancer Hannah Brown as his new partner and vows to make her as popular as Nadine. Even though Hannah is not physically nor vocally like Nadine, Don tries to turn her into a copy of his former partner. Once he allows Hannah to be herself, the new team becomes popular and jealous Nadine tries to break it up by dancing with Don at a nightclub and suggesting to Hannah that he is still in love with her. The wealthy New Yorker Johnny Harrow has fallen in love with Hannah but she

Cast for *Easter Parade*	
Character	*Performer*
Hannah Brown	JUDY GARLAND
Don Hewes	FRED ASTAIRE
Jonathan Harrow III	PETER LAWFORD
Nadine Hale	ANN MILLER
Francois	JULES MUNSHIN

Easter Parade. The prominent billing of songwriter Irving Berlin in this original one-sheet poster shows that the tunesmith was as important a name as any star. The fact that the movie offered seventeen Berlin songs was as much a selling point as Fred Astaire or Judy Garland. (Photofest)

loves Don. By Easter Sunday, Hannah and Don are romantic as well as dancing partners and stroll down Fifth Avenue in the Easter parade.

Both old and new IRVING BERLIN songs were used for the score, all of them top drawer. "A Fella With an Umbrella," "Better Luck Next Time," and "It Only Happens When I Dance With You" were the quieter numbers, while ANN MILLER did some furious tapping in "Shaking the Blues Away" and Astaire danced in distorted time with images of himself in "Stepping Out With My Baby." The comic highlight of the score was Garland and Astaire cutting loose as a duo of happy hobos in "A Couple of Swells." The title number, introduced on Broadway fifteen years before in the revue AS THOUSANDS CHEER (1933), became more popular than ever.

While *Easter Parade* is a perennial favorite now and seems so familiar, the film originally planned was quite different. The screenplay by Sidney Sheldon, FRANCES GOODRICH, and ALBERT HACKETT was written for GENE KELLY and Garland as a follow-up to their work together on THE PIRATE (1948). When Kelly broke his ankle, Astaire was asked to come out of semiretirement to take his place. Producer ARTHUR FREED cast CYD CHARISSE as Nadine but she also suffered an accident and had to be replaced by Miller who was too tall for Astaire and had to dance in flat shoes. Director VINCENTE MINNELLI was having marital problems with Garland so he left once filming began and was replaced by CHARLES WALTERS. Rarely has a film so unlucky in preparation turned out so well.

EBERSOLE, CHRISTINE (1953–). Stage and television performer. The stately blonde actress–singer can play everything from sexpots to royalty in both plays and musicals. Ebersole was born in Winnetka, Illinois, and educated at MacMurray College before studying at the American Academy of Dramatic Arts. She made her Broadway debut as a replacement in the play *Angel Street* (1976) and then appeared in a minor role in ON THE TWENTIETH CENTURY (1978), but recognition first came with her funny, sexy Ado Annie in the 1979 revival of OKLAHOMA! The next year Ebersole played Guenevere in the Broadway revival of CAMELOT and then was busy with plays on and Off Broadway and on television where she became a familiar face from series and specials, such as the TV version of GYPSY (1993).

In addition to some acclaimed performances in nonmusicals on Broadway, she was widely praised for her temperamental Dorothy Brock in *42ND STREET* (2001) and her double roles as Edith Bouvier Beale and her daughter Edie in *GREY GARDENS* (2006).

EBSEN, BUDDY [born Christian Rudolph Ebsen, Jr.] (1908–2003). Film, television, and stage performer. A tall and lanky dancer who became a favorite in Hollywood and on television, he usually played sidekicks and country bumpkins with very lucrative success. Ebsen was born in Belleville, Illinois, the son of a dance instructor, and went into vaudeville as a hoofer with his sister Vilma (1911–2007) and then danced in the chorus of the Broadway musicals *WHOOPEE!* (1928), *FLYING COLORS* (1932), and *ZIEGFELD FOLLIES* (1934). He studied at Rollins College and then made his film debut with Vilma in *BROADWAY MELODY OF 1936* (1935). When he went solo he was noticed for his agile and eccentric dancing in the musicals *CAPTAIN JANUARY* (1936), *BORN TO DANCE* (1936), *Banjo on My Knee* (1936), *BROADWAY MELODY OF 1938* (1937), *Girl of the Golden West* (1938), *My Lucky Star* (1938), *They Met in Argentina* (1941), *Sing Your Worries Away* (1942), and *Red Garters* (1954). Ebsen was originally cast as the Tin Man in *THE WIZARD OF OZ* (1939) but after nine days of shooting developed skin poisoning from the silver makeup and was replaced by JACK HALEY. He appeared in many nonmusical films and returned to Broadway in the musical *Yokel Boy* (1939) and in the 1946 revival of *SHOW BOAT*. Ebsen found his greatest popularity on television where he acted in many series and specials and had two very successful series of his own, *The Beverly Hillbillies* in the 1960s and *Barnaby Jones* in the 1970s. He returned to the big screen on occasion, as with the musical *The One and Only Genuine Original Family Band* (1968). Autobiography: *The Other Side of Oz*, with Stephen Cox (1994).

EDDY, NELSON (1901–1967). Film and television performer. The king of Hollywood operettas, he is most remembered for his films with JEANETTE MACDONALD. Eddy was born in Providence, Rhode Island, and was a boy soprano in church choirs until he was old enough to get jobs as a telephone operator and a news reporter. He grew up in Philadelphia where he joined the local Civic Opera and then toured in operettas until he was signed to a Hollywood contract in 1933, the year he made his screen debut. After the movie musicals

Broadway to Hollywood (1933), *DANCING LADY* (1933), and *Student Tour* (1924), Eddy was teamed with MacDonald in *NAUGHTY MARIETTA* (1935); the duo was an immediate hit and the two were paired in seven more musicals: *ROSE MARIE* (1936), *MAYTIME* (1937), *SWEETHEARTS* (1938), *The Girl of the Golden West* (1938), *NEW MOON* (1940), *I MARRIED AN ANGEL* (1942), and *BITTER SWEET* (1940). He also starred with different leading ladies in *ROSALIE* (1937), *Let Freedom Ring* (1939), *BALALAIKA* (1939), *THE CHOCOLATE SOLDIER* (1941), *The Phantom of the Opera* (1943), *KNICKERBOCKER HOLIDAY* (1944) and *Northwest Outpost* (1947). Eddy also provided singing vocals for the Disney-animated musical *MAKE MINE MUSIC* (1946). In the 1950s he concentrated on concerts, nightclubs, recordings, and television where he had his own show. The stiff, baby-faced, wavy-haired baritone may seem the stuff of parody today, but he was considered a dashing romantic figure in his day and he and MacDonald were the most famous singing team in Hollywood history.

EDELMAN, GREGG (1958–). Stage and television performer. The all-purpose leading man possesses a strong and expressive singing voice that has allowed him to shine in several musicals. Edelman was born in Chicago and educated at Northwestern before making his Broadway debut in the chorus of *EVITA* (1979). After playing Cliff Bradshaw in the 1987 revival of *CABARET*, he was applauded for his ambivalent pulp writer Stine in *CITY OF ANGELS* (1989). Edelman also shone as the Russian aristocrat Levin in the musical version of *Anna Karenina* (1992), the suspicious Colonel Ricci in *PASSION* (1994), the commanding delegate Edward Rutledge in *1776* (1997), the Wolf and Prince in *INTO THE WOODS* (2002), and frustrated editor Robert Baker in *WONDERFUL TOWN* (2003). His other Broadway musical credits, many of them as replacements for leading characters, include *CATS* (1982), *OLIVER!* (1984), *ANYTHING GOES* (1987), *FALSETTOS* (1992), *LES MISERABLES* (1999), and *Reefer Madness* (2002). Edelman has acted in a number of nonmusical films and television programs. He is married to singer–actress Carolee Carmello (1962–).

EDENS, ROGER (1905–1970). Film producer, songwriter, music arranger, and director. One of Hollywood's unsung talents, he was involved with dozens of popular musicals in a variety of jobs. Born in Hillsboro, Texas, Edens started his career as a piano accompanist for ballroom dancers. He went to Hollywood in 1933 to arrange music but was soon writing extra songs for movie musicals, supervising the music, and eventually producing films. Either with ARTHUR FREED or on his own he produced such notable musicals as *BABES IN ARMS* (1939), *LITTLE NELLIE KELLY* (1940), *LADY, BE GOOD* (1941), *BABES ON BROADWAY* (1941), *Yolanda and the Thief* (1945), *THE HARVEY GIRLS* (1946), *THE PIRATE* (1948), *EASTER PARADE* (1948), *WORDS AND MUSIC* (1948), *THE BARKLEYS OF BROADWAY* (1949), *ANNIE GET YOUR GUN* (1950), *ROYAL WEDDING* (1951), *SHOW BOAT* (1951), *AN AMERICAN IN PARIS* (1951), *THE BELLE OF NEW YORK* (1952), *THE BAND WAGON* (1953), *BRIGADOON* (1954), *DEEP IN MY HEART* (1954), *JUMBO* (1962), *THE UNSINKABLE MOLLY BROWN* (1964), and *HELLO, DOLLY!* (1969). Edens provided songs and arrangements for other musicals, which he co-produced, such as *STRIKE UP THE BAND* (1940), *ZIEGFELD GIRL* (1941), *ZIEGFELD FOLLIES* (1946), *GOOD NEWS!* (1947), *TAKE ME OUT TO THE BALL GAME* (1949), *ON THE TOWN* (1949), *SINGIN' IN THE RAIN* (1952), and *FUNNY FACE* (1957). Although his name was little known to the general public, Edens was one of the most important artists behind the golden age of Hollywood musicals.

EDWARDS, BLAKE [born William Blake McEdwards] (1922–). Film and television director, producer, and screenwriter. A colorful showman with an up-and-down career, he helmed five musicals amidst his many hits and flops. Edwards was born in Tulsa, Oklahoma, into a family of stage and movie people, and he began his career as an actor in a handful of movies in the 1940s. He contributed to several film scripts, including the musicals *All Ashore* (1953) and *MY SISTER EILEEN* (1955), and also produced some films before he directed his first feature in 1955. Parallel to his work in Hollywood, Edwards was also active in television, producing the hit series *Peter Gunn* and *Mr. Lucky*. After a few stumbles in the late 1960s, Edwards gave up on Hollywood and went to England where he found success with the *Pink Panther* movie sequels. Returning to the States he had a series of comedy hits, some featuring his wife JULIE ANDREWS, whom he directed in the musical *DARLING LILI* (1969). His other musicals were *Bring Your Smile Along* (1955), *He Laughed Last* (1956), *High Time* (1960), and *VICTOR/VICTORIA* (1982), also starring Andrews, which the couple brought to Broadway in 1995.

EDWARDS, CLIFF[ton A.] (1895–1971). Stage, film, and television performer. The high-pitched singer, known as Ukulele Ike for his strumming on the ukulele as he accompanied himself, was one of the most popular singers of his day but is mostly remembered today as the voice of Jiminy Cricket. Edwards was born in Hannibal, Missouri, and left school at the age of fourteen to go to St. Louis and sing in saloons. His recording of "Ja Da" was a hit and he became a headliner in vaudeville and was featured in the Broadway musicals *The Mimic World* (1921), *LADY, BE GOOD!* (1924), and *ZIEGFELD FOLLIES* (1927). Edwards introduced "Singin' in the Rain" in his first film, *HOLLYWOOD REVUE OF 1929*, and was also featured in *Marianne* (1929), *So This Is College* (1929), *Lord Byron of Broadway* (1930), *Montana Moon* (1930), *GOOD NEWS!* (1930), *The Prodigal* (1931), *TAKE A CHANCE* (1933), and *GEORGE WHITE'S SCANDALS* (1934 and 1935). He returned to Broadway for the revue *George White's Scandals* (1935) and then was back in Hollywood for *The Girl of the Golden West* (1938), *Prairie Stranger* (1941), and *Salute for Three* (1943). Perhaps Edwards' most memorable film performances were unseen: he did the voice for Jim Crow in the animated feature *DUMBO* (1941) and the voice of Jiminy Cricket in *PINOCCHIO* (1940) and again in *Fun and Fancy Free* (1946). He had his own television show in 1949, appeared on many other programs, and continued to voice Jiminy in dozens of Disney programs.

EL CAPITAN (Broadway Theatre 1896). The best of the handful of operettas JOHN PHILIP SOUSA wrote for Broadway, this musical comedy set in South America was outrageous fun, thanks to the skillful clowning of DE WOLF HOPPER. Charles Klein wrote the action-packed libretto about a band of rebels who seeks to overthrow Don Medigua (Hopper), the viceroy of Peru. Medigua captures and executes the rebels' leader El Capitan and disguises himself as the outlaw to infiltrate the enemy ranks. He also takes the opportunity to flirt with the lovely Estrelda (Edna Wallace Hopper) before leading the rebels in circles, tiring them out by the time the Spanish army arrives. Tom Frost and Sousa wrote the lyrics for the stirring music, some of it from previous Sousa instrumental pieces. The standout hit was the rousing march "El Capitan's Song," which later became a concert favorite under the title "El Capitan March." Other songs include "Sweetheart," "I'm Waiting," and "A

Typical Tune of Zanzibar." As much as the press and the public enjoyed the story and the score, it was Hopper's farcical performances that allowed the show to run 112 performances. The operetta was revived in New York in 1897 and 1898 and is still performed on occasion by light opera companies.

ELLINGTON, DUKE [born Edward Kennedy Ellington] (1899–1974). Stage and film musician, conductor, and composer. A world-renowned jazz composer and interpreter, the African American pianist composed three Broadway musicals and he and his orchestra performed in specialty spots in six Hollywood musicals. Ellington was born in Washington, DC, formed his own band at the age of nineteen, and in 1923 went to New York and was a hit at the Cotton Club in Harlem. By the 1930s he was nationally known for his unique jazz sound and his song compositions, such as "Sophisticated Lady," Mood Indigo," and "It Don't Mean a Thing (If It Ain't Got that Swing)." Ellington and his band were featured in the films *Check and Double Check* (1930), *Murder at the Vanities* (1934), *Belle of the Nineties* (1934), *Hit Parade of 1937*, CABIN IN THE SKY (1942), and *Reveille With Beverly* (1943), and he composed the songs for the movie *Paris Blues* (1961). On Broadway he scored the musicals *Blue Holiday* (1945), *Beggar's Holiday* (1946), and *Pousse-Café* (1966), and his songs were featured in the Broadway revue SOPHISTICATED LADIES (1981). Ellington was popular in concerts, nightclubs, on records, and he made several international tours spreading the sound of jazz around the world. Autobiography: *Music Is My Mistress* (1975); biographies: *Duke Ellington: The Piano Prince and His Orchestra*, Andrea and Brian Pinkney (2007); *Beyond Category: The Life and Genius of Duke Ellington*, John Edward Hasse, Wynton Marsalis (1995).

ELLIS, MARY [born Mary Belle Elsas] (1898–2003). Stage performer. The lyrical musical star of Broadway and the West End was also adept at opera and nonmusical comedies. A native New Yorker, Ellis studied art and took singing lessons and by the age of eighteen was performing featured roles at the Metropolitan Opera alongside Caruso, Chapliapine, and other greats. But after three years she gave up her opera career and pursued acting, making her Broadway debut as Nerissa in *The Merchant of Venice* (1922). Ellis's first musical role was her best: the French Canadian songstress ROSE-MARIE (1924). Although she appeared in more plays on Broadway and in some London musicals, she never did another musical in New York. Ellis made some films in the 1930s, including the musical *All the King's Horses* (1934) and then when she was in her nineties she made a few more movies and some television dramas. She was married to actor Basil Sydney (1894–1968).

ELLIS, SCOTT (1957–). Stage director. An estimable director of plays and musical revivals, he has gathered a considerable number of credits in a rather short time. Ellis was born in Washington, DC, and studied at the Goodman School of Drama in Chicago before making his Manhattan directing debut Off Broadway in 1987 with a revival of the musical FLORA, THE RED MENACE. He was first singled out for his staging of the KANDER and EBB revue *And the World Goes 'Round* (1991) and then began his successful association with the ROUNDABOUT THEATRE, staging several popular revivals, including the musicals SHE LOVES ME (1993), COMPANY (1995), *1776* (1997), and THE BOYS FROM SYRACUSE (2002). Ellis also staged *Steel Pier* (1997), *The Adventures of Tom Sawyer* (2001), the revue *The Look of Love* (2003), and CURTAINS (2007).

ENCORES! Concert series. An ambitious series of staged concert versions of Broadway musicals, the much cherished program frequently revives lesser-known shows that might never see a traditional Broadway revival. Each spring since 1994, three musicals have been presented at the City Center Theatre, usually for three performances, using name performers and recognized creative staff. *Encores!* shows are not just concerts or readings but a staged production with choreography and costumes. The complete musical (libretto and score) is presented and sometimes the result is an accurate recreation of the original. The books for older shows are often revised or edited. All of the offerings have been book musicals except ZIEGFELD FOLLIES OF 1936 and the compilation program *Stairway to Paradise*, which took numbers from several classic Broadway revues. The *Encores!* productions of CHICAGO, WONDERFUL TOWN, THE APPLE TREE, and GYPSY were later restaged and opened as full Broadway productions, mostly with the same principal performers from the concert versions. Also, many of the programs were recorded and released on CD, affording the first full recordings of such shows as *Pardon My English* and FACE THE MUSIC.

Encores! Productions

1994: *FIORELLO!, ALLEGRO, LADY IN THE DARK*
1995: *CALL ME MADAM, OUT OF THIS WORLD, PAL JOEY*
1996: *ONE TOUCH OF VENUS, DU BARRY WAS A LADY, CHICAGO*
1997: *SWEET ADELINE, PROMISES PROMISES, THE BOYS FROM SYRACUSE*
1998: *STRIKE UP THE BAND, LI'L ABNER, ST. LOUIS WOMAN*
1999: *BABES IN ARMS, ZIEGFELD FOLLIES OF 1936, DO RE MI*
2000: *ON A CLEAR DAY YOU CAN SEE FOREVER, TENDERLOIN, WONDERFUL TOWN*
2001: *A CONNECTICUT YANKEE, BLOOMER GIRL, HAIR*
2002: *CARNIVAL, GOLDEN BOY, THE PAJAMA GAME*
2003: *HOUSE OF FLOWERS, THE NEW MOON, NO STRINGS*
2004: *CAN-CAN, Pardon My English, BYE BYE BIRDIE*
2005: *A TREE GROWS IN BROOKLYN, PURLIE, THE APPLE TREE*
2006: *KISMET, 70, GIRLS, 70, OF THEE I SING*
2007: *FACE THE MUSIC, FOLLIES, Stairway to Paradise, GYPSY*
2008: *APPLAUSE, JUNO, NO NO NANETTE*

A similar program in New York City is Off Broadway's *Musicals in Mufti* series sponsored by the York Theatre Company. This series offers more obscure works from the past and may not attract the big-name performers and directors as *Encores!* but has a faithful following of its own. Another Manhattan series is *Musicals Tonight! Inc.*, which has been offering staged readings of past musicals since 1998.

ENGEL, LEHMAN (1910–1982). Stage conductor and composer. A renowned Broadway musical director and conductor, he was also one of the first to write books about the structure and workings of the American musical. Engel was born in Jackson, Mississippi, and educated at the University of Cincinnati, Juilliard School of Music, and with Rogers Sessions before beginning his career composing incidental music for Broadway plays. He turned to conducting with the legendary musical *THE CRADLE WILL ROCK* (1937) and went on to supervise the music for twenty Broadway shows over the next forty years, including *CALL ME MISTER* (1946), *WONDERFUL TOWN* (1953), *FANNY* (1954), *LI'L ABNER* (1956),

JAMAICA (1956), *DESTRY RIDES AGAIN* (1959), *TAKE ME ALONG* (1959), *I CAN GET IT FOR YOU WHOLESALE* (1962), and *Bajour* (1964). Lehman was also a scholar and mentor, teaching at both the American Musical and Dramatic Academy and at New York University, as well as founding and running the BMI–Lehman Engel Theatre Workshop, the first program to study the art of lyric and libretto writing. Among his books are *Musical Shows: Planning and Producing* (1957), *The American Musical Theatre* (1967), *Words and Music* (1972), and an autobiography, *This Bright Day* (1974).

ENRIGHT, RAY[mond E.] (1896–1965). Film director. A durable director from the silent film days, he helmed a series of light musicals for WARNER BROTHERS and First National in the 1930s. Enright was born in Anderson, Indiana, and began his film career editing and writing for Charles Chaplin and Mack Sennett. By 1927 he was directing and over the next twenty-five years worked with just about every major studio turning out westerns, comedies, romances, and musicals. Enright's thirteen musicals include *Song of the West* (1930), *Golden Dawn* (1930), *Twenty Million Sweethearts* (1934), *DAMES* (1934), *Ready, Willing and Able* (1937), *The Singing Marine* (1937), *GOLD DIGGERS IN PARIS* (1938), *Going Places* (1938), and *Naughty But Nice* (1939).

ERLANGER, A[braham]. **L**[incoln]. (1860–1930). Stage producer and manager. One of the American theatre's most powerful (and ruthless) presenters of plays and musicals, the stage mogul controlled the workings of the theatre for decades and was responsible for over fifty musical productions just in New York City. Erlanger was born in Cleveland, Ohio, and entered show business booking tours of melodramas across the country. He teamed with producer Marc Klaw and formed an agency that grew and became the Theatrical Syndicate, which controlled over 650 theatres from coast to coast and managed the careers of stars, playwrights, and actors in vaudeville and legit theatre. The monopoly was not broken until the SHUBERT BROTHERS gradually bought up enough theatres to start their own syndicate of sorts in the twentieth century. Erlanger himself personally produced such musicals as *The Brownies* (1894), *THE ROGERS BROTHERS in Central Park* (1900) and its many sequels, *Sleeping Beauty* (1901), *HUMPTY DUMPTY* (1904), *The Ham Tree* (1905), *FORTY-FIVE MINUTES FROM BROADWAY* (1906), *Little Nemo* (1908), *THE PINK LADY* (1911), *The Count* of *Luxembourg* (1912), *Miss Springtime* (1916), *The Riviera Girl* (1917), *The Velvet Lady* (1919), *Two Little Girls in Blue* (1921), *The Perfect Fool* (1921), *The Yankee Princess* (1922), *Honeymoon Lane* (1926), and *ZIEGFELD FOLLIES* (1927).

ERROL, LEON [born Leonce Errol Simms] (1881–1951). Stage and film performer. An agile, sour-faced, and balding comic, he was featured in Broadway musicals and revues and then enjoyed a successful film career. A native of Sydney, Australia, Errol was pursuing a medical degree at the local university when he went onto the vaudeville stage to earn money for tuition. He was such a hit that he gave up medicine and soon was performing in circuses, Shakespeare plays, and comic operas. While touring in the States, he was hired by producer FLORENZ ZIEGFELD to appear in the 1910 edition of the *ZIEGFELD FOLLIES*. Errol's rubber-legged drunk routine and other comic bits were so well received that he was featured in six later editions, as well as in the revues *Hitchy-Koo* (1917 and 1918) and *Ziegfeld Midnight Frolic* (1921). Errol also shone in book musicals, most memorably as "Connie," the exiled Grand Duke in *SALLY* (1920). His other musicals include *A Winsome Widow* (1912), *The Century Girl* (1916), *Louie the 14th* (1925), *Yours Truly* (1927), and *Fioretta* (1929), some of which he also co-wrote. Errol was a respected director as well and staged sections of the *Follies* revues as well as the musicals *Words and Music* (1917) and *The Blue Kitten* (1922). He made his film debut as a specialty act in *PARAMOUNT ON PARADE* (1930), followed by many comedy shorts, and then two dozen musicals in which he usually played harassed and henpecked husbands, including *WE'RE NOT DRESSING* (1934), *Coronado* (1935), *Melody Lane* (1941), *Strictly in the Groove* (1943), *HIGHER AND HIGHER* (1943), *Babes on Swing Street* (1944), *Riverboat Rhythm* (1946), and *Footlight Varieties* (1951).

ERWIN, STUART (1903–1967). Film and television performer. A beefy character actor who played bumbling but likable guys in over 100 films, he was seen in a handful of screen musicals. Erwin was born in Squaw Valley, California, and educated at the University of California before going on the stage in stock companies. He made his film debut in 1928 and over the next twenty years was a familiar face in light comedies and musicals such as *Sweetie* (1929), *PARAMOUNT ON PARADE* (1930), *THE BIG BROADCAST* (1932), *INTERNATIONAL HOUSE* (1933), *GOING HOLLYWOOD* (1933), *Pigskin*

Parade (1936), *Dance, Charlie, Dance* (1937), and *I'll Take Romance* (1937). Erwin also performed in the Broadway musical *Great to Be Alive!* (1950). He made fewer films in the 1950s because of his own television show, which ran four years, and his many appearances on other programs.

ESPARZA, RAÚL (1970–). Stage performer. A mesmerizing Cuban American actor–singer with impressive versatility, he has quickly become one of the most praised and admired performers on the musical theatre scene. Esparza was born in Wilmington, Delaware, and raised in Miami, Florida, and then educated at New York University. After performing at various regional theatres, he was cast as Che in a 1999 tour of *EVITA*. Esparza made his Broadway debut in 2001 as a replacement for the Emcee in *CABARET* and then was featured as Riff Raff in *THE ROCKY HORROR SHOW* (2000). Off Broadway he received plaudits for his performances as the young songwriter Johnny in *Tick, Tick ... Boom!* (2001) and then returned to Broadway as the outrageous Phillip Sallon in *Taboo* (2003), the crackpot inventor Caractaus Potts in *CHITTY CHITTY BANG BANG* (2005), and confused bachelor Bobby in the 2006 revival of *COMPANY*. Few performers have garnered so much attention and adulation in so short a time.

ETTING, RUTH (1907–1978). Stage and film performer. One of America's greatest torch singers, she spent most of her career performing in nightclubs but her handful of Broadway appearances were unforgettable. Etting was born in David City, Nebraska, and studied to become a fashion designer but at the age of eighteen she appeared in a Chicago revue and her distinctive way with a song brought her recognition. She was featured in the Broadway revues *ZIEGFELD FOLLIES* (1927 and 1931) and *9:15 Revue* (1930) and in the book musicals *WHOOPEE* (1928), introducing "Love Me or Leave Me," and *Simple Simon* (1930), singing "Ten Cents a Dance." She also appeared in the film musicals *ROMAN SCANDALS* (1933), *Hips Hips Hooray* (1934), and *Gift of Gab* (1934). Etting was a slim, fragile blonde whose sad life often mirrored her torchy numbers. DORIS DAY played her in the biopic *LOVE ME OR LEAVE ME* (1955).

🎭 **EVANGELINE, OR THE BELLE OF ACADIA** (Niblo's Garden Theatre 1874). Billed as an "American Opera-Bouffe Extravaganza," the musical was actually a burlesque of the Longfellow poem of the title. In the libretto by J. CHEEVER GOODWIN, Evangeline (Ione Burke) and her neighbors are expelled from their Acadian village by the British and she is separated from her sweetheart Gabriel (Carrie Thompson in a trouser role). The two lovers endure a series of adventures as they travel separately from New England to Africa to the Wild West before being reunited. The heroine's hardships were more comic than arduous, and a sequence with a dancing cow became an audience favorite. *Evangeline* was one of the earliest musicals in which all the songs in the score were written by the same team, in this case EDWARD E. RICE (music) and Goodwin (lyrics), although none found fame outside of the show. The musical originated in Boston and only played sixteen performances during its initial New York engagement but it soon became one of the most popular shows in the last third of the nineteenth century. Manhattan saw revivals in 1877, 1878, 1885, 1887, 1888, 1889, 1892, and 1896; the 1885 engagement ran 251 performances. Also, many acclaimed performers first found recognition in productions of the musical, including HENEY E. DIXEY, Francis Wilson, and William H. Crane.

📺 *EVENING PRIMROSE* (ABC-TV 1966). Broadway songwriter STEPHEN SONDHEIM's only television musical is as unusual and challenging as many of his stage works. It boasts a superb score that confirms his remarkable talent years before he became a Broadway institution. Based on a short story by John Collier, the James Goldman teleplay tells its offbeat but engaging tale with simplicity and charm. The poet Charles Snell (Anthony Perkins) is weary of the modern world and spends his evenings in a Manhattan department store where he only needs to avoid the night watchman in order to be free of people. But Charles soon learns that the store in inhabited by other refugees from the world, ghostly figures who want to keep their existence secret. Only the young Ella Harkins (Charmian Carr), who was brought to the store when she was six years old, longs to see the outside world. She and Charles fall in love but when he makes plans to help her escape, the Dark Men (whose job is to dispose of anyone who might jeopardize the arrangement) take her away and Charles is left contemplating his own fate. The *ABC Stage 67* broadcast was not aimed at the mainstream public but for viewers looking for something out of the ordinary, which the musical was. It was also haunting

Evening Primrose. An unusual love story even for the nontraditional songwriter Stephen Sondheim, this television musical was about a haunted place and the show itself haunts anyone who has ever seen it (which is not all that many). (Photofest)

and memorable. Unpolished singer Perkins and dancer Carr (who was familiar to audiences from the recent film version of *THE SOUND OF MUSIC* where she played Liesl) gave sincere, affecting performances, and the supporting cast included Dorothy Stickney, Larry Gates, and Dorothy Sands. Paul Bogart directed the atmospheric piece, which was filmed in Stern Brothers' store in Manhattan. Because the musical ran under sixty minutes, there are only four songs but each one is outstanding: "I Remember," "Take Me to the World," "If You Can Find Me, I'm Here," and "When?" Although there is no soundtrack recording, some of the songs have been recorded many times and show up in Sondheim revues and concerts.

🎵 *EVER GREEN* (Adelphi Theatre–London 1930). A splendid musical comedy by RICHARD RODGERS (music) and LORENZ HART (lyrics), it premiered in London but didn't come to America until the screen version four years later. The libretto by Benn W. Levy was about

Harriet Green (JESSIE MATTHEWS) who, hoping to break into show business, pretends to be her sixty-year-old grandmother, a London actress of some repute before she moved to Australia many years before. Harriet tells her public that her secrets of cosmetology have kept her so young looking and, becoming a sort of freak attraction, she is starred in a musical show. Although she is falling in love with the young Tommy Thompson (Sonnie Hale), Harriet does not tell him the truth until her deception is revealed. By that time Tommy loves her and the public adores her on stage so all ends happily. *Ever Green* was a first-class vehicle for stage favorite Matthews and had a superior score, with the best number being the entrancing "Dancing on the Ceiling," which FLORENZ ZIEGFELD had rejected for a Broadway production of his earlier in the year. Also heard in the London hit were "Dear, Dear," "In the Cool of the Evening," "No Place But Home," and "If I Give in to You." Producer Charles B. Cochran spared no expense, and scenic designer Ernst Stern, using the first revolving stage in London, recreated everything from a Spanish festival to a Paris Casino to the Albert Hall on the large stage. The production ran 254 performances, one of the healthiest runs for Americans writing an original show for the West End, and was fondly remembered for years in England.

■ *Evergreen* (Gaumont 1934) condensed the plot (and the title) and highlighted Matthews, Britain's only bankable movie musical star of the decade. Instead of impersonating her grandmother, Harriet pretends to be her mother in the screen version. Her sweetheart Tommy (Barry Mackay) now is a press agent who aids her in her deception. Also in on the hoax is the flamboyant director Leslie Benn (Sonnie Hale). Much of the Rodgers and Hart score was jettisoned for the film and, since the team were in Hollywood when *Evergreen* was shot in England, the new numbers were written by Harry Woods, very much in the music hall manner: "When You've Got a Little Springtime in Your Heart," "Over My Shoulder," "Daddy Wouldn't Buy Me a Bow Wow," and "Just By Your Example." The movie is as silly as the play but, again, Matthews is the attraction and American took to her, making *Evergreen* one of the very few British film musicals to find success in the States.

■ *EVERY NIGHT AT EIGHT* (Paramount 1935). A routine backstage musical with a not-quite-famous-yet ALICE FAYE in the leading role, the film has a superior score by JIMMY McHUGH, DOROTHY FIELDS, and others, and Faye sings them on her way to stardom. Struggling singers Dixie Foley (Faye), Susan Moore (FRANCES LANGFORD), and Daphne O'Connor (PATSY KELLY) are fired from their job at a mint-julep factory, so bandleader Tops Cardona (GEORGE RAFT) takes over their management and they become singing stars. Because Faye was not as established as Langford, the Graham C. Baker and Gene Towne screenplay had Tops end up in the arms of Susan rather than Dixie. Yet all three women are superb in the movie, singing such musical gems as the mellow "I'm in the Mood for Love," the sprightly "I Feel a Song Comin' On," the swinging "Take It Easy," and the breezy ballad "Speaking Confidentially." The supporting cast included WALTER CATLETT, HERMAN BING, Harry Barris, and bandleader Ted Fio Rito as himself. Action film director RAOUL WALSH helmed the musical, which was produced by Walter Wanger.

■ *EVERYONE SAYS I LOVE YOU* (Miramax 1997). A pleasing mixture of contemporary comedy and nostalgic romance, this unusual movie celebrated the musicals of old while it also satirized them. Woody Allen wrote and directed the comedy of manners about rich New Yorkers looking for love in Manhattan, Venice, and Paris, and he had the characters, very few of them experienced singers, express themselves by breaking into old song standards. Goldie Hawn, ALAN ALDA, Edward Norton, and some others sounded fine, whereas Allen, Julia Roberts, Tim Roth, and others struggled vocally. However, the effect was deliciously unpretentious if one accepted the premise (and most did not). GRACIELA DANIELE'S choreography was contagiously fun: Hawn floated through the air as she and Allen sang "I'm Through With Love" on the banks of the Seine, doctors and patients in a hospital romped up and down the corridors singing "Makin' Whoopee," various New Yorkers (including store mannequins) joined Norton in singing "Just You, Just Me," and a party of Parisians dressed liked GROUCHO MARX pranced in the Ritz Hotel singing "Hooray for Captain Spaulding" in French. A one-of-a-kind movie, it either charmed or annoyed audiences and critics, yet was another unique contribution to the musical form by America's most successful auteur film director.

☙ *EVITA* (Broadway Theatre 1979). A well-established London hit by the time it arrived

Evita. Barbra Streisand, Meryl Streep, and Patti LuPone were among the many performers who over the years were rumored to play Eva Peron on the screen. By the time the film was finally made, seventeen years after the musical opened on Broadway, the only box office name that the studios were willing to gamble on was Madonna, a singer often as notorious as Evita herself. The Argentines were not pleased until Madonna herself went to Buenos Aires and campaigned for acceptance. She won the right people over and the movie was allowed to be partially filmed in Argentina. (Photofest)

on Broadway, this sung-through musical by ANDREW LLOYD WEBBER (music) and TIM RICE (lyrics) boasted what was arguably the best score either ever wrote and it was a dynamic production directed by HAROLD PRINCE. The libretto chronicled the life of the famous/infamous Eva Peron (PATTI LuPONE) from an ambitious girl of fifteen to a popular actress on the radio to the first lady of the nation to international celebrity to her death at thirty-three from cancer. Commenting on the saga throughout was the young radical Che Guevera (MANDY PATINKIN) who gave a sociopolitical point of view to the proceedings. The show's standout hit was "Don't Cry for Me, Argentina," but the score was filled with thrilling numbers, such as the sly duet "I'd Be Surprisingly Good for You," the crooning love song "On This Night of a Thousand Stars," the plaintive "Another Suitcase in Another Hall," the soaring ballad "High Flying Adored," the sarcastic "And the Money Kept Rolling In," the pulsating "Buenos Aires," and the rousing "A New Argentina." The Broadway production made LuPone a star and launched Patinkin's career as well, but the most ingenious talent

Casts for *Evita*

Character	*1979 Broadway*	*1997 film*
Eva Peron	PATTI LuPONE	MADONNA
Che/various	MANDY PATINKIN	Antonio Banderas
Juan Peron	BOB GUNTON	Jonathan Pryce
Magaldi	Mary Syers	Jimmy Nail
Peron's Mistress	Jane Ohringer	Andrea Corr

involved was Prince, who utilized multimedia, Bechtian techniques, and even Russian biomechanics to raise the gossipy subject matter to high art. The authors seemed to be ambivalent about their feeling toward Eva Peron, for she is depicted as both saint and whore, and Prince's chilly, detached presentation gave the show a documentary feel that let the audience draw their own conclusions. The ROBERT STIGWOOD production ran 1,567 performances and toured for several years.

Evita (Hollywood Pictures 1997) was the only big-budget film musical made in the 1990s and every penny showed up on the screen. However, there was much more than spectacle involved and the screen version was as emotionally enthralling as it was visually stunning. Director ALAN PARKER co-wrote the screenplay with Oliver Stone, keeping the show completely sung and filming the tale in Argentina and eastern Europe with thousands of extras and a whirlwind of lavish scenes depicting the life of Eva Peron on the scale that it affected her nation. Madonna was surprisingly effective as Evita, not only handling the giant singing role but managing to balance the vulnerable and vicious sides of the character. The stage character of Che was turned into a series of Argentines who appeared in each scene, all played by Antonio Banderas with a smooth but seething presence. The score was somewhat abridged, and Webber and Rice wrote a new number, "You Must Love," which won the Oscar. *Evita* proved that the big movie musical was not dead and gone forever, but the picture only had marginal box office success and the studios once again shied away from screen versions of Broadway hits for several years.

FABRAY, NANETTE [born Ruby Bernadette Nanette Fabares] (1920–). Stage, film, and television performer. The vivacious, red-headed singer–actress worked in all media for over sixty years without ever becoming a major star but was always applauded by critics and audiences alike. Fabray was born in San Diego, California, and was on the vaudeville stage at the age of three, billed as Baby Nanette. She made several films as a child, working as one of the kids in the *Our Gang* comedy shorts for a while. She took time off from performing to study dance in southern California, singing at Juilliard, and acting at the Max Reinhardt School of Theatre. She made her Broadway debut in the revue *Meet the People* (1940), followed by supporting roles and replacements in the musicals *LET'S FACE IT!* (1941), *BY JUPITER* (1943), *My Dear Public* (1943), *Jackpot* (1944), and *BLOOMER GIRL* (1945). Farbray's first substantial role was New Jersey housewife Sara Longstreet in *HIGH BUTTON SHOES* (1947) and she was also praised for her work in the short-lived musicals *LOVE LIFE* (1948), *Arms and the Girl* (1950), and *Make a Wish* (1951). She left the theatre in the 1950s and concentrated on movies, giving a sensational performance in the musical *THE BAND WAGON* (1953), and on television where she replaced IMOGENE COCA as SID CAESAR's comic partner on *Your Shows of Shows*. Fabray appeared on hundreds of programs, from quiz shows to musical specials, including the TV musicals *High Button Shoes* (1956), *A Man's Game* (1957), *SO HELP ME, APHRODITE* (1960), *ALICE THROUGH THE LOOKING GLASS* (1966), and *GEORGE M* (1970). She returned to the New York stage on occasion, as in the musical *MR. PRESIDENT* (1962), and was still performing in plays and on television in the 1990s. Fabray is the aunt of television-film actress Shelley Fabares (1942–).

FACE THE MUSIC (New Amsterdam Theatre 1932). A high-spirited musical satire about the Depression that opened in the depths of the Depression, it boasted a lively score by IRVING BERLIN and a witty libretto by MOSS HART. Broadway producer Hal Reisman (Andrew Tombes) needs money to put on a show so he goes to the Automat where all the wealthy have taken to dining since the Crash and he secures the financial help of Mrs. Martin Van Buren Meshbesher (MARY BOLAND). What Hal doesn't know is that her husband is a cop and their wealth comes from police corruption so Hall is soon embroiled in a scandal and only by the show being a hit does he get everyone off the hook. Also in the cast were J. HAROLD MURRAY, Katherine Carrington, DAVID BURNS, and Hugh O'Connell. The merry score included the convivial "Let's Have Another Cup of Coffee," the romantic "On a Roof in Manhattan," the sassy "I Say It's Spinach (And to Hell With It)," and the caressing "Soft Lights and Sweet Music." GEORGE S. KAUFMAN and HASSARD SHORT co-directed the SAM H. HARRIS production and ALBERTINA RASCH did the choreography. It was delicious fun top to bottom but the musical suffered from comparisons with the recent musical satire *OF THEE I SING* (1931) so it only managed to run 165 performances.

FADE OUT–FADE IN (Mark Hellinger Theatre 1964). A vehicle for the comic star CAROL BURNETT after her success in *ONCE UPON A MATTRESS* (1959) and on television, the show had a difficult time of it and bad feelings between the star and the production's management kept her away from Broadway for thirty years. BETTY COMDEN and ADOLPH GREEN wrote the libretto spoofing Hollywood in the 1930s and allowing Burnett to use her many comic and singing talents. When an unknown chorus girl Hope Springfield (Burnett) is accidentally given a major role in a Hollywood musical, the mistake is not discovered until filming is complete. Studio head Lionel Z. Governor (Lou Jacobi) orders the film hidden away in a vault but his nephew Rudolf (Dick Patterson) believes in Hope, gets the movie seen by a preview audience, and Hope becomes a star. Also in the top-notch cast were JACK CASSIDY, TIGER HAYNES, Tina Louise, and Mitchell Jason. The score by JULE STYNE (music) and Comden and Green (lyrics) was disappointing, with the best numbers being the dreamy "The Usher From the Mezzanine" and the SHIRLEY TEMPLE pastiche "You Mustn't Be Discouraged." The press felt that featured star Burnett deserved a better libretto and score but her farcical performance was something to cheer about. The production soon had to close due to Burnett's back injuries. During the three-month hiatus the script and score were revised somewhat, the producers sued Burnett, and the lawyers argued the legal implications. When the court ordered Burnett to return to the show, business was weak and it closed for good after 271 performances. GEORGE ABBOTT directed the Lester Osterman–Jule Styne production and Ernest Flatt did the choreography.

FAIN, SAMMY [born Samuel Feinberg] (1902–1989). Stage, film, and television composer. A busy and much respected songwriter little known outside of show business circles, he worked with many different lyricists on many flops and hits, usually turning out exceptional music in both. The native New Yorker began in vaudeville as a singer and then was heard on the radio before turning to playing piano in nightclubs, often featuring his own compositions. He made his Hollywood debut in 1930 and his Broadway bow the next year, and for three decades wrote many musicals for both media. Fain collaborated with lyricists Irving Kahal, SAM COSLOW, SAMMY CAHN, PAUL FRANCIS WEBSTER, and others on such Hollywood musicals as *Young Man of Manhattan* (1930), FOOTLIGHT PARADE (1933), *College Coach* (1933), *DAMES* (1934), *Sweet Music* (1935), NEW FACES OF 1937, *Meet the People* (1944), GEORGE WHITE'S SCANDALS (1945), *Two Sisters From Boston* (1946), *No Leave, No Love* (1946), CALL ME MISTER (1951), THE JAZZ SINGER (1953), *Three Sailors and a Girl* (1953), CALAMITY JANE (1953), *Lucky Me* (1954), *April Love* (1957), *Mardi Gras* (1958), *The Big Circus* (1959), and the animated musicals ALICE IN WONDERLAND (1953) and PETER PAN (1953). He also wrote theme songs for many nonmusical films, such as "I'll Be Seeing You" and "Love Is a Many Splendored Thing." Parallel to his Hollywood career, Fain scored the Broadway musicals *Everybody's Welcome* (1931), HELLZAPOPPIN' (1938), *George White's Scandals* (1939), *Boys and Girls Together* (1940), *Sons o' Fun* (1941), *Toplitzsky of Notre Dame* (1946), *Alive and Kicking* (1950), FLAHOOLEY (1951), *Ankles Aweigh* (1955), *Catch a Star* (1955), ZIEGFELD FOLLIES (1957), *Christine* (1960), and *Something More* (1964), as well as the TV musical *A Diamond for Carla* (1959). Fain's music is remarkably eclectic and difficult to categorize except to say that it is strong on melody and frequently is very contagious.

FALSETTOS (John Golden Theatre 1992). It took this sly contemporary musical thirteen years and three Off Broadway productions to finally arrive on Broadway and when it did it was heartily welcomed for 487 performances. The neurotic New Yorker Marvin (MICHAEL RUPERT) leaves his wife Trina (Barbara Walsh) and teenage son Jason (Jonathan Kaplan) to be with his male lover Whizzer (STEPHEN BOGARDUS). This drives Trina to her ex-husband's psychiatrist Mendel (CHIP ZIEN) and the two fall in love and marry. When Whizzer finds Marvin as impossible to live with as Trina did, he leaves Marvin. Some years later, when Whizzer is diagnosed with AIDS, he and Marvin are reunited. Jason refuses to be bar mitzahed until Whizzer can attend so everyone, including the two lesbians (Carolee Carmello and Heather MacRae) from next door, gather in Whizzer's hospital room for the ceremony. Before Whizzer dies, Marvin is able to make peace with him and realize the love they had was real. Songwriter WILLIAM FINN had told the story over the course of three plays previously seen Off Broadway: *In Trousers* (1979), *March of the Falsettos* (1981), and *Falsettoland* (1990). A song ("I'm Breaking Down") from the first was combined with the later two sung-through musicals to create the full evening program *Falsettos*, which was first produced regionally and then became an unlikely but solid hit on Broadway. Other highlights in the score include "The Thrill of First Love," "The Games I Play," "Trina's Song," "The Baseball Game," "Unlikely Lovers," "The Chess Game," "Holding to the Ground," and "What Would I Do?" JOHN LAPINE co-wrote the libretto with Finn and directed the Barry and Fran Weissler production.

FAME (MGM 1980). Set in Manhattan's High School of the Performing Arts over a four-year period, this popular movie wavered between a gritty, realistic look at show business and a romanticized "let's put on a show" musical. In Christopher Gore's screenplay, the young hopefuls struggle through auditions, classes, rehearsals, setbacks, family troubles, and sexual anxiety, every once in a while bursting into song and dance everywhere from the street to the cafeteria. The film was highly charged, joyfully noisy, and very engaging to younger moviegoers. ALAN PARKER directed Irene Cara, Lee Curreri, Barry Miller, Antonia Francschi, Gene Anthony Ray, and other young performs, with Anne Meara, ALBERT HAGUE, and DEBBIE ALLEN on hand to play faculty members. Most of the songs were by Michael Gore (music) and Dean Pitchford (lyrics), with the most memorable being

"I Sing the Body Electric," "Red Light," and the explosive title number. *Fame* was one of the first films to employ digital audio on the soundtrack and it was recorded onto a compact disc, two years before CDs were introduced. ☐ Allen, Ray, Curreri, and Hague reprised their roles in the popular television series that began in 1982. Allen appeared in forty-eight episodes, later directing and choreographing several shows. ☙ A stage version of the musical *Fame* was very successful in London in the 1990s and has been revived in the West End in the new century. The show has been produced regionally in the States, including many school productions, and played Off Broadway under the title *Fame on 42nd Street* (2004)

☙ **FANNY** (Majestic Theatre 1954). A highly romantic and sentimental musical, it proved to be the first Broadway venture for producer DAVID MERRICK and his first hit as well. In the French port of Marsailles, Marius (WILLIAM TABBERT), the son of waterfront café owner César (EZIO PINZA), loves the young Fanny (FLORENCE HENDERSON) but he longs to see the world so he sails away not knowing that she is pregnant by him. The elderly sail maker Panisse (WALTER SLEZAK) agrees to marry Fanny and raise the child as his own. Years later Marius returns home and realizes he still loves Fanny. On his deathbed, Panisse tells Marius to marry Fanny and raise their son. Director JOSHUA LOGAN and S. N. Behrman condensed Marcel Pagnol's film trilogy *Marius*, *Fanny*, and *César* into one musical play, and HAROLD ROME wrote a warm, low-key score that included such songs as "Love Is a Very Light Thing," "Welcome Home," "Be Kind to Your Parents," "Restless Heart," "Why Be Afraid to Dance?," and the title number. Audiences took to the French-flavored musical and kept it on the boards for 888 performances. ▦ Logan also directed the 1961 screen version, which cut all the musical numbers and just told the melodramatic story. LESLIE CARON (Fanny), Horst Buchholtz (Marius), MAURICE CHEVALIER (Panisse), and Charles Boyer (Cesar) led the cast.

▦ **FANTASIA** (Disney/RKO 1940). Even by the standards of WALT DISNEY and his artists, this animated musical anthology was a surprisingly unique musical experience and remains one of the wonders of moviemaking. Eight classic concert pieces were illustrated and animated in various ways to bring the music to life rather than just serve as background. Bach's "Toccata and Fugue in D Minor" became an abstract expression of lines and music; Dukas'

Fantasia. Walt Disney gambled on *Fantasia* and he lost; the picture failed at the box office. It would take decades to reach the classic status it enjoys today. Pictured is Mickey Mouse in the most famous of the musical segments, "The Sorcerer's Apprentice." (Photofest)

"The Sorcerer's Apprentice" told a story with Mickey Mouse as an overeager wizard in training who loses control of his magic; Tchaikovsky's "The Nutcracker Suite" came to life as a nature ballet with fairies, flowers, fish, and even dancing mushrooms; Beethoven's "Pastoral Symphony" served for mythological characters; Ponchielli's "La Gioconda" was turned into a comic ballet featuring ostriches, crocodiles, and hippos; Stravinsky's "Rite of Spring" showed the creation of the planet and primeval life; Mussorgsky's "Night on Bald Mountain" illustrated the battle between good and evil with devils, ghosts, and skeletons; and Schubert's "Ave Maria" presented a dawn of tranquility and hope. Each section had a distinct visual style and its own director, all under the supervision of Ben Sharpsteen and the specific vision of Disney himself. The music was performed by the Philadelphia Orchestra conducted by LEOPOLD STOKOWSKI who appeared on screen between segments and Deems Taylor was the host/narrator. *Fantasia* was not a success when released even though critical reaction was enthusiastic. Considered by many at the time as Disney's most expensive folly, the film did not find favor until the 1960s when art houses started to show it. In 1982 the old print was refurbished and a new soundtrack conducted by Irwin Kostal replaced the original.

Sixty years later, a sequel *Fantasia 2000* (Disney 2000) was released that retained the Dukas sequence and presented seven new concert pieces. Beethoven's Fifth Symphony was interpreted abstractly; Respighi's "Pines of Rome" became a water ballet for whales; GEORGE GERSHWIN's "Rhapsody in Blue" captured busy Depression-era New Yorkers in busy Al Hirschfeld-like line drawings; Shostakovich's Piano Concerto No. 2 served to illustrate a Hans Christian Andersen tale, "The Steadfast Soldier"; a movement from Saint-Saens' "Carnival of the Animals" was used for a playful sequence with bouncing flamingos and a yo-yo; Elgar's "Pomp and Circumstance" provided the music for all the animals marching onto Noah's Ark with Donald Duck as Noah's frustrated helper; and Stravinsky's "Firebird Suite" dramatized a mythic parable about a sprite and an elk restoring life to a ravaged forest. James Levine conducted the Chicago Symphony, and various guest stars, such as ANGELA LANSBURY, Quincy Jones, BETTE MIDLER, and Steve Martin, introduced each section. Again critical response was favorable but the musical collage did not do well at the box office, although it was a brisk seller on DVD.

🕮 *FANTASTICKS, THE* (Sullivan Street Playhouse 1960). The finest of all Off Broadway musicals and an ageless wonder, the simple musical ran forty-two years, the longest running theatre production in the history of New York theatre.

Plot: The young lovers Matt and Luisa are neighbors, separated by a wall that their fathers, Hucklebee and Bellomy, have put up because they want their children to think they are enemies. In fact, they are using reverse psychology hoping that the two will fall in love. When they have to call off the pretend feud, the fathers hire the bandit El Gallo to try and abduct Luisa, knowing that Matt will save her and the two families can then become friends. All goes according to plan but once the happy ending comes the lovers find that they are disenchanted with each other in the harsh sunlight and they part. Matt goes off to see the world and is treated cruelly, while Luisa makes plans for a romantic future with El Gallo, only to be abandoned by him. With the two lovers hurt and more mature, they realize that they have a more genuine love for each other and there is a second, more honest, happy ending.

Originally presented as a one-act musical for a summer season at Barnard College, the show caught the attention of producer Loto Nore and he urged the authors to write a full-length version for Off Broadway. TOM JONES wrote the libretto, based on Edmond Rostand's play *Les Romanesques*, and the delicate lyrics to go with the sparkling music by HARVEY SCHMIDT, and the intimate piece was like a magical musical fable. It was staged with imaginative simplicity by WORD BAKER using only a wooden platform and a trunkful of props, and the cast of mostly newcomers was earnest and charming. JERRY ORBACH was particularly effective as El Gallo and the musical's narrator, commenting on the action and characters with a mixture of wry humor and somber reflection. Lore struggled to raise the $16,500 to open in the 144-seat Sullivan Street Theatre and the few reviewers who came were modest in their praise. After the show won the Vernon Rice Award, business picked up and soon word of mouth did the rest, helped by the popularity of the song "Try to Remember." The cast recording also helped and, without ever being a hot ticket, *The Fantasticks* slowly and surely became a hit.

Casts for *The Fantasticks*

Character	1960 Off Broadway	1964 television	1995 film	2006 Off Broadway
El Gallo	JERRY ORBACH	RICARDO MONTALBAN	Jonathan Morris	Burke Moses
Matt	KENNETH NELSON	John Davidson	Joseph McIntyre	Santino Fontana
Luisa	Rita Gardner	SUSAN WATSON	Jean Louisa Kelly	Sara Jean Ford
Hucklebee	William Larsen	BERT LAHR	Brad Sullivan	Leo Burmester
Bellomy	Hugh Thomas	STANLEY HOLLOWAY	JOEL GREY	Martin Vidnovic

The Fantasticks Musical Numbers

"Try to Remember"
"Much More"
"Metaphor"
"Never Say No"
"It Depends on What You Pay"
"Soon It's Going to Rain"
"The Abduction Ballet"
"Happy Ending"
"This Plum Is Too Ripe"
"I Can See It"
"Plant a Radish"
"Round and Round"
"They Were You"

Although the score is eclectic, using jazz, Latin, folk, and waltzes effectively, there is a quality to all the songs that suggests an unadorned way of looking at the world. The bouncy overture, unique in that it uses no songs from the show, created a carnival feeling but on an intimate scale. The character songs are direct and funny because they are unembellished. The mock operetta duet "Metaphor" overflows with youthful energy, in contrast to the quiet, knowing duet "They Were You" that seems to be aching with wisdom. "Try to Remember" has the structure of a folk song and has the power to hypnotize the listener, preparing one for the fairy tale-like story that is to follow. Jones and Schmidt were not afraid of an old-fashioned soft-shoe song like "Plant a Radish" or a simple waltz such as "Round and Round." Most remarkably, the score doesn't sound like 1960 or 1970 or any other year. Part of the show's universal appeal is that both the story and the songs are simply timeless. Few American musicals have traveled as well as The Fantasticks. Within a decade of its opening in New York, productions were done in places all around the world (an estimated seventy different countries), many where they had never heard an American musical before. The piece also remained a favorite with all kinds of theatre groups in the States, chalking up hundreds of revivals each year. All the time the show continued on in its original Off Broadway home. New Yorkers accepted it as a local landmark, something that would always be there. But it was not to be. In 2002, the building was sold, the income from the small theatre was deemed inefficient in a real estate boom, and the show was forced to close after 17,162 performances. It was greatly missed and few were surprised when The Fantasticks was revived in 2004 in another intimate space, this time uptown in the theatre district, and ran 628 performances.

☐ In 1964, HALLMARK HALL OF FAME broadcast an abridged version of The Fantasticks with an impressive cast that included BERT LAHR, RICARDO MONTALBAN, STANLEY HOLLOWAY, John Davidson, and SUSAN WATSON. It was the first time a television version had been shown of a musical still running in New York. George Schaefer directed the studio production, which resembled the Off Broadway version in its simplicity. For decades there had been talk of a film version of the musical but no one really expected it to happened since it seemed to be such an obviously bad idea. A television studio could capture the intimacy of the piece but what possibly could film have to offer? In 1995, UNITED ARTISTS thought otherwise, Jones wrote the screenplay, and Michael Ritchie directed. The result is probably the worst film version of a musical ever made. Conceptually, acting-wise, cinematically, and visually it was beyond anyone's most fearsome nightmare of what could be done to this charming little musical. The studio must have had such a feeling since they kept the film on the shelf for five years and then gave it a very limited release in 2000 before putting it out on video.

FARMER TAKES A WIFE, THE (Fox 1953). A musical version of the 1935 Henry Fonda–JANET GAYNOR film of the same name, the frontier musical had trouble capturing the locale and tone of life on the Erie Canal in 1850 but had no difficulty offering lively performances and commendable songs. JOSEPH FIELDS, WALTER BULLOCK, and Sally Benson adapted the novel Rome Haul by Walter D. Edmonds into a screenplay about canal boat driver Daniel Harrow (Dale Robertson) and his rivalry with boat owner Jothum Klore (JOHN CARROLL) over the boat's cook Molly Larkin (BETTY GRABLE). Waiting to see who got her was a tiresome exercise relieved by spirited dances choreographed by JACK COLE (with a young GWEN VERDON seen kicking up her heels) and some pleasing songs by HAROLD ARLEN (music) and DOROTHY FIELDS (lyrics). The exuberant "Today I Love Everybody," the lazy ballad "With the Sun Warm Upon Me," and the chipper "We're in Business" were the standout numbers. The comedy was supplied by Thelma Ritter and EDDIE FOY, JR., although they seemed as out of place in the period musical as the rest of the cast. Henry Levin directed the Frank P. Rosenberg production.

FARRELL, CHARLES (1901–1990). Film and television performer. A handsome if stiff leading man, he was paired with JANET GAYNOR in twelve movies (including four musicals) and they were the era's favorite romantic screen couple. Farrell was born in Onset Bay, Massachusetts, and educated at Boston University before going on the stage and acting in stock companies. He made his silent screen debut in 1923 and soon became a romantic idol, also praised for his acting in such pictures as the melodrama *Seventh Heaven* (1927). His popularity was sustained when sound came in and he acted in many dramas and sang in such musicals as *SUNNY SIDE UP* (1929), *Happy Days* (1930), *High Society Blues* (1930), *DELICIOUS* (1931), *Girl Without a Room* (1933), and *Just Around the Corner* (1938), as well as the British film *Moonlight Sonata* (1937). Farrell made one Broadway appearance, in the revue *ZIEGFELD FOLLIES* (1931). When his screen career started to fade in the 1940s, he went into business and made a fortune founding the Palm Springs Racquet Club. Farrell then enjoyed a new career on television as a regular on the series *My Little Margie* (1952–1955).

FAYE, ALICE [born Alice Jeanne Leppert] (1915–1998). Film and stage performer. The queen of 20TH CENTURY-FOX musicals in the late 1930s and 1940s, the shapely blonde's husky speaking voice and deep contralto singing voice were a welcome change from chirping sopranos. Faye was born in New York, the daughter of a policeman, and was singing and dancing professionally as a teenager. When Faye was cast in the Broadway chorus of *GEORGE WHITE'S SCANDALS* (1931), she was spotted by RUDY VALLEE who hired her to sing with his band. She made her film debut in a small role in *George White's Scandals* (1934) and quickly was given better parts in such musicals as *She Learned About Sailors* (1934), *365 Nights in Hollywood* (1924), *EVERY NIGHT AT EIGHT* (1935), *KING OF BURLESQUE* (1936), *Poor Little Rich Girl* (1936), *Sing, Baby, Sing* (1936), and *Stowaway* (1936). She was a full-fledged star by the time she made *ON THE AVENUE* (1937) and shone in the musicals *WAKE UP AND LIVE* (1937), *You Can't Have Everything* (1937), *You're a Sweetheart* (1937), *Sally, Irene and Mary* (1938), *IN OLD CHICAGO* (1938), *ALEXANDER'S RAGTIME BAND* (1938), *ROSE OF WASHINGTON SQUARE* (1939), *LILLIAN RUSSELL* (1940), *TIN PAN ALLEY* (1940), *THAT NIGHT IN RIO* (1941), *The Great American Broadcast* (1941), *WEEKEND IN HAVANA* (1941), *HELLO, FRISCO, HELLO* (1943), *THE GANG'S ALL HERE* (1943), and *Four Jills in a Jeep* (1944). Disagreements with the Fox studio head DARRYL F. ZANUCK and the emergence of BETTY GRABLE as the war years' favorite blonde prompted Faye to retire in 1945, but she returned two decades later to play maternal roles in the film musicals *STATE FAIR* (1962) and *The Magic of Lassie* (1978). Faye returned to the stage with a national tour of *GOOD NEWS!* that played on Broadway in 1974. She was married to TONY MARTIN for a time and then she wed PHIL HARRIS and the two had a popular radio show between 1948 and 1954. Biography: *Alice Faye: A Life Beyond the Silver Screen*, Jane Lenz Elder (2002).

☐ **FEATHERTOP** (ABC-TV 1961). Taken from one of Nathaniel Hawthorne's more fantastical short stories, the sixty-minute musical was an odd concoction of revenge and romance. John Marsh's teleplay moved the story from New England to early nineteenth-century Louisiana where the sorceress Madame Eau Charme (Cathleen Nesbitt) is rudely turned away from a ball by the governor (HANS CONRIED) so she uses her magic powers to get even. She constructs a creature named Feathertop (Hugh O'Brien) who appears as a scarecrow to everyone but the governor's beautiful daughter Julie (JANE POWELL) who only sees a handsome gentleman. Madame Charme instructs Feathertop to make Julie fall in love him him, thereby rendering the girl ridiculous in the eyes of society. But Feathertop falls in love with Julie, denounces the sorceress, and becomes mortal so that he can remain with Julie. The performances were praised by the press, as was the charming score by MARY RODGERS (music) and MARTIN CHARNIN (lyrics), which included "Easy Come, Easy Go," "Perfect Strangers," "Gentleman of Breeding," "The Day I Say I Do," and "Intimate Friends." Tony Charmoli produced and choreographed, and Dean Whitmore directed the unusual musical.

FELIX, SEYMOUR (1892–1961). Stage and film choreographer and director. A top Hollywood choreographer and sometime director, he also had his fair share of hits on Broadway in the 1920s. Felix was born in New York City and was dancing on stage as a child. By the time he was fifteen, he toured the country on the vaudeville circuit and then returned to Manhattan to choreograph some of AL JOLSON's nightclub shows. Felix made his Broadway choreography debut in 1923 but his big hits did not come until later in the decade: *PEGGY-ANN* (1926), *HIT THE DECK!* (1927), *ROSALIE* (1928), and *WHOOPEE* (1938). His other Broadway credits include *ARTISTS AND MODELS OF 1924*, *Gay Paree* (1926), *SIMPLE SIMON* (1930), and *Strike Me Pink* (1933). When the Depression hit Broadway hard, Felix went west and staged the dances for thirty film musicals, directing a few of them as well. Among his screen credits are *SUNNY SIDE UP* (1929), *THE CAT AND THE FIDDLE* (1934), *KID MILLIONS* (1934), *THE GREAT ZIEGFELD* (1936), *ON THE AVENUE* (1937), *ALEXANDER'S RAGTIME BAND* (1938), *TIN PAN ALLEY* (1940), *YANKEE DOODLE DANDY* (1942), *LET'S FACE IT!* (1943), *COVER GIRL* (1944), *THE DOLLY SISTERS* (1945), *MOTHER WORE TIGHTS* (1947), *Give My Regards to Broadway* (1948), *Oh, You Beautiful Doll* (1949), *Down Among the Sheltering Palms* (1952), and *The 'I Don't Care' Girl* (1953).

FERRER, JOSÉ [born José Vicente Ferrer de Otero y Cintron] (1912–1992). Stage and film performer and director. A compelling and versatile actor of stage and screen, he was also an exceptional director on Broadway. Ferrer was born in Santurce, Puerto Rico, grew up in New York City, and studied at Princeton University to become an architect. He made his acting debut in 1934 on a show boat cruising Long Island Sound, and the next year he was on Broadway where over the next four decades he played everything from classical tragedy and contemporary farce to dark melodramas. Ferrer began directing in the 1940s, making his Broadway debut in 1942 but finding more success in the 1950s with such hits as *Stalag 17* (1951), *My 3 Angels* (1953), the 1953 revival of *Charley's Aunt*, and *The Andersonville Trial* (1959). His musicals included *Oh, Captain!* (1958), *Juno* (1959), and *Carmelina* (1979). Ferrer made his film debut in 1948 and went on to make dozens of movies in Hollywood, Great Britain, Canada, Germany, France, Italy, and Spain. Perhaps the role he was most identified with was *Cyrano de Bergerac*, which he played on stage and screen, directing himself in the 1953 Broadway revival. Ferrer's sole screen musical role was that of SIGMUND ROMBERG in *DEEP IN MY HEART* (1954) and his only Broadway musical appearance was *MAN OF LA MANCHA* in 1966. He also directed the film remake of *STATE FAIR* (1962). Ferrer was married to stage actress Uta Hagen (1919–2004) and singer ROSEMARY CLOONEY (1928–2002).

FEUER, CY, AND ERNEST MARTIN. Stage producing partners. One of the most successful teams to produce musicals on Broadway in the 1950s and 1960, Feuer was also an accomplished director. Cy Feuer [born Seymour Arnold Feuer] (1911–2006) was born in New York and studied at Juilliard School of Music before playing trumpet in orchestras and dance bands. He was hired as a film composer by Republic Studios in 1938 and eventually ran the music department there between 1945 and 1947, supervising over 100 B movies. Ernest Martin [born Markowitz] (1919–1993) was born in Pittsburgh and teamed with Feuer to produce FRANK LOESSER's first Broadway musical *WHERE'S CHARLEY?* (1948). Feuer and Martin went on to present Loesser's *GUYS AND DOLLS* (1950) and *HOW TO SUCCEED IN BUSINESS WITHOUT REALLY TRYING* (1962), as well as the musicals *CAN-CAN* (1953) and *THE BOY FRIEND* (1954). Feuer directed as well as co-produced with Martin the Broadway shows *SILK STOCKINGS* (1955), *Whoop-Up!* (1958), *LITTLE ME* (1962), *Skyscraper* (1965), and *Walking Happy* (1966). In 1975 the partners became co-managers of the Los Angeles and San Francisco Light Opera Association and oversaw many musicals in those cities. Feuer and Martin also produced the film versions of *Where's Charley?* (1952), *CABARET* (1972), and *A CHORUS LINE* (1985). Autobiography: *I Got the Show Right Here*, Feuer with Jed Feuer (2003).

FIDDLER ON THE ROOF (Imperial Theatre 1964). A Jewish musical whose universal themes made it a favorite around the world, the show was filled with riches, from a heartfelt score by JERRY BOCK (music) and SHELDON HARNICK (lyrics) to a towering performance by ZERO MOSTEL.

Plot: Dairyman Tevye and his wife Golde are like all the other Jewish citizens of the Russian village of Anatevka, holding on to traditions of how to do everything. His daughters start to break from the old ways, falling in love and finding spouses without the aid of a matchmaker. Even more upsetting, one daughter marries outside of the Hebrew faith. After some demonstrations of their distaste for the Jews living in their community, the Cossacks order the Jews to leave the village and it seems that the world is coming to an end. By the final curtain the villagers set off for new lives in the New World, bringing their traditions with them.

Fiddler on the Roof. In a small Russian village, the arrangement of marriage between the butcher Lazar Wolf, played by Michael Granger (left), and the daughter of the dairyman Tevye, the irrepressible Zero Mostel (right), is enough reason to celebrate with song and dance. Here the two men toast each other with "To Life," the most raucous number in the Broadway production. (Photofest)

Casts for *Fiddler on the Roof*

Character	1964 Broadway	1971 film	2004 Broadway
Tevye	ZERO MOSTEL	Topol	Alfred Molina
Golde	MARIA KARNILOVA	Norma Crane	RANDY GRAFF
Yente	BEATRICE ARTHUR	Molly Picon	Nancy Opel
Tzeitel	Joanna Merlin	Rosalind Harris	Sally Murphy
Hodel	Julia Migenes	Michele Marsh	Laura Michelle Kelly
Chava	Tanya Everett	Neva Small	Tricia Paoluccio
Motel	AUSTIN PENDLETON	Leonard Frey	John Cariani
Perchik	BERT CONVY	Paul Michael Glaser	Robert Petkoff
Lazar Wolf	Michael Granger	Paul Mann	David Wohl

JOSEPH STEIN wrote the tender, funny, and efficient libretto, based on Sholom Aleichem's stories, and let the simple charm of the characters carry the plot. By emphasizing the Jewish community from the beginning, the story took on a folk tale-like quality and the village types were as familiar as they were endearing. JEROME ROBBINS directed and choreographed with a delicate touch, avoiding spectacle and cleverness and relying on traditional images, such as a family at prayer or the celebrants at a wedding. Even the choreography grew from the rustic lives of the people and the bottle dance at the wedding took on a mythic feeling of ancient ritual. The excellent cast was led by Zero Mostel as Tevye, revealing levels of pathos and vulnerability that he had rarely been given a chance to display before. So many of the songs from *Fiddler on the Roof* have become so familiar over the years that one forgets how daring it was to write a score that avoided slick jokes, overt emotion, and other forms of theatrics. Harnick's lyrics are marvels of simplicity and sincerity, the humor growing gently out of the characters and the emotions quietly expressed. Bock's music is ethnic sounding without being clichéd and there is a richness in even the most uncomplicated melodies. "Sunrise Sunset" has become the most recognized song, helped no doubt by its use in weddings over the decades, "Matchmaker, Matchmaker" is the catchiest tune, and "If I Were a Rich Man," with its cantor-like chanting, is the most revealing of the many character numbers. Although it is mostly a quiet score, it has its moment of joy, as in the riotous "To Life" and the celebratory "Miracles of Miracles." The charm song "Do You Love Me?" may just be the most charming of that genre ever written. Producer HAROLD PRINCE and the creative staff thought that their touching Jewish show would have limited appeal but were proud of it. They were all surprised when it became universally embraced and moved people of all religions and races. The original production ran 3,242 performances, a new record at the time, and was followed my many tours and mountings by regional theatre, summer stock, community groups, schools, synagogues, and even churches. Mostel reprised his Tevye in a 1976 Broadway revival, which duplicated the original production. Israeli actor Topol, who had played Tevye in the film version, returned to the role in a popular New York revival in

1990. British director David Leveaux staged a Broadway production in 2004 that met with diverse critical reactions. Some thought the somber, more realistic approach and Alfred Molina's gentle, subtler Tevye to be refreshing interpretations; other critics found both player and production bland and lifeless.

■ *Fiddler on the Roof* (Mirisch/United Artists) was a faithful screen version of the stage work, with all but two of the Bock–Harnick songs retained and Robbins' famous choreography recreated by Tom Abbott. Director Norman Jewison treated the material with respect and integrity, but the pace was slow and the overlong (180 minutes) movie rarely captured the spirit and exuberance of the Broadway production. Topol was more than adequate as Tevye, Norma Crane underplayed his wife Golde, and even scene stealer Molly Picon seemed subdued as the matchmaker Yente. However, the location filming was poetic and evocative, the surreal "Tevye's Dream" was a cinematic treat, and there was a rustic tone to the picture that was engaging. Not only were the songs well sung but a bonus treat was Isaac Stern's brilliant violin playing during the opening credits. In 1979 the film was rereleased in Dolby stereo with thirty-two minutes cut out, resulting in what many felt was an improved movie.

FIELD, RON[ald] (1934–1989). Stage and television choreographer, director, and dancer. A first-rate choreographer–director, he had a checkered career on Broadway. Field was born in Queens, New York, and was on the stage dancing as a child. After attending the High School of the Performing Arts, he graduated to the Broadway chorus in the 1950s, appearing in *Seventeen* (1951), *KISMET* (1953), and *THE BOY FRIEND* (1954). During that decade he also danced in over 300 television shows. He first came to the attention of theatre audiences in 1962 with his energetic choreography for the long-running Off Broadway revival of *ANYTHING GOES*. Later that same year he staged dances for Broadway, receiving major acclaim for his choreography for *CABARET* (1966). His ethnic dances for *ZORBA* (1968) and his direction and contemporary choreography for *APPLAUSE* (1970) were also lauded, but Field had little success with *Nowhere to Go But Up* (1962), *Cafe Crown* (1964), *King of Hearts* (1978), and *RAGS* (1986). He also choreographed the revivals of *SHOW BOAT* (1966), *PETER PAN* (1979), and *Cabaret* (1987), many television specials and variety shows in the 1960s and 1970s, including

---

Fiddler on the Roof Musical Numbers

"Tradition"
"Matchmaker, Matchmaker"
"If I Were a Rich Man"
"Sabbath Prayer"
"To Life"
"Miracle of Miracles"
"The Tailor, Motel Kamziol (Tevye's Dream)"
"Sunrise, Sunset"
"Bottle Dance"
"Wedding Dance"
"Now I Have Everything"
"Do You Love Me?"
"I Just Heard"
"Far From the Home I Love"
"Anatevka"

the TV musical *Pinocchio* (1976), and night-club acts for LIZA MINNELLI, ANN-MARGARET, CHITA RIVERA, GWEN VERDON, and other stars. Field was also active in regional theatres and in London before his premature death.

FIELDS, DOROTHY (1904–1974). Stage and film lyricist and writer. An astute, highly gifted songwriter who worked with the finest composers of her day, she had one of the longest Broadway careers in the history of the American musical, from 1928 to 1973. Fields was born in Allenhurst, New Jersey, the daughter of the celebrated stage comic and producer LEW FIELDS, and as a boarding school student wrote light verse. In the late 1920s she teamed up with composer JIMMY McHUGH and some of their songs were introduced at the Cotton Club in Harlem in 1927. The next year they scored the popular Broadway revue *BLACKBIRDS OF 1928*, which introduced "I Can't Give You Anything But Love" and other memorable songs. The team provided the score for *Hello, Daddy* (1928) and *International Revue* (1930) and then went to Hollywood where they scored the musicals *Love in the Rough* (1930), *Cuban Love Song* (1931), *Hooray for Love* (1935), and *EVERY NIGHT AT EIGHT* (1935). Fields worked with composer JEROME KERN for the first time when they wrote some additional songs for the 1935 screen version of *ROBERTA* and would reteam for *I DREAM TOO MUCH* (1935), *SWING TIME* (1936), *JOY OF LIVING* (1938), and *ONE NIGHT IN THE TROPICS* (1940). She returned to Broadway to co-author with her brother HERBERT FIELDS the librettos for the musical hits *LET'S FACE IT!* (1941), *SOMETHING FOR THE BOYS* (1943), *MEXICAN HAYRIDE* (1944), and *ANNIE GET YOUR GUN* (1946). Fields collaborated with composer ARTHUR SCHWARTZ on the Broadway musicals *Stars in Your Eyes* (1939), *A TREE GROWS IN BROOKLYN* (1951), and *BY THE BEAUTIFUL SEA* (1954), with SIGMUND ROMBERG on *UP IN CENTRAL PARK* (1945), with Morton Gould on *Arms and the Girl* (1950), and with ALBERT HAGUE on *REDHEAD* (1959). In Hollywood she worked with various composers on the scores for *In Person* (1935), *The King Steps Out* (1936), *Mr. Imperium* (1951), *Excuse My Dust* (1951), *Texas Carnival* (1951), and *THE FARMER TAKES A WIFE* (1953), as well as the TV musical *JUNIOR MISS* (1953). Just when most thought Fields was going to retire, she teamed up with the much-younger CY COLEMAN and wrote vivacious scores for the Broadway musicals *SWEET CHARITY* (1966) and *SEESAW* (1973). Among her many song standards are "On the Sunny Side of the Street," "Exactly Like You," "Hey Big Spender," "Never Gonna Dance," "A Fine Romance," and "The Way You Look Tonight," the first song by a female songwriter to win the Oscar for Best Song. Fields was a practical craftsman when writing stage librettos and a prodigious talent with lyric writing, equally at home with character songs, romantic ballads, and jazz-flavored dance numbers. Few have made the crossover from one medium to another and from one decade to another so effortlessly. Her other brother was writer JOSEPH FIELDS. Biography: *On the Sunny Side of the Street*, Deborah Grace Winer (1997).

FIELDS, HERBERT (1897–1958). Stage and film writer. One of Broadway's most significant librettists, he worked closely with Rodgers and Hart on several of their early musicals and then later collaborated with other top artists on Broadway and Hollywood. A member of a famous theatrical family, his father was comic–producer LEW FIELDS (of the legendary team of Weber and Fields), his brother JOSEPH FIELDS was a respected playwright, and his sister DOROTHY FIELDS was one of America's finest lyricists. Herbert Fields was born in New York City and educated at Columbia University before beginning his career as an actor and appearing in some plays and silent films. By 1925 he was writing plays and librettos, as well as directing and choreographing musicals. He first worked professionally with RICHARD RODGERS and LORENZ HART doing the dances for their revue *THE GARRICK GAIETIES* (1925) and then wrote the librettos for their musicals *DEAREST ENEMY* (1925), *The Girl Friend* (1926), *PEGGY-ANN* (1926), *A CONNECTICUT YANKEE* (1927), *PRESENT ARMS* (1928), *Chee-Chee* (1928), and *America's Sweetheart* (1931). Many of these early musicals were highly experimental and refreshingly different, and the trio of Rodgers–Hart–Fields was widely acclaimed. He also wrote librettos for the Broadway musicals *HIT THE DECK* (1927), *FIFTY MILLION FRENCHMEN* (1929), *THE NEW YORKERS* (1930), *DuBARRY WAS A LADY* (1939), *PANAMA HATTIE* (1940), and, with his sister Dorothy, *LET'S FACE IT!* (1941), *SOMETHING FOR THE BOYS* (1943), *MEXICAN HAYRIDE* (1944), *UP IN CENTRAL PARK* (1945), *ANNIE GET YOUR GUN* (1946), *Arms and the Girl* (1950), *BY THE BEAUTIFUL SEA* (1954), and *REDHEAD* (1959). Fields saw many of his stage works filmed and he contributed to the scripts for other musicals as well, such as *MISSISSIPPI* (1935), *Fools for Scandal* (1938), *JOY OF LIVING* (1938), and *Honolulu* (1939).

FIELDS, JOSEPH (1895–1966). Stage and film writer. The author of many Broadway hit plays and successful Hollywood films, his few musicals were very popular. The eldest of the three famous children of comedian–producer LEW FIELDS, Joseph Fields was a native New Yorker who was educated at New York University for a law career before serving in World War I. He remained in Paris after the war and began writing fiction and nonfiction for magazines. Returning to America in 1923, Fields wrote sketches for the ZIEGFELD FOLLIES before heading to California in 1931 and scripting his first of several films, including the musicals *Fools for Scandal* (1938), *TWO GIRLS ON BROADWAY* (1940), *LOUISIANA PURCHASE* (1942), and *THE FARMER TAKES A WIFE* (1953). He often returned to Broadway and wrote plays, usually in collaboration with others. Among his nonmusical hits were *My Sister Eileen* (1940), *Junior Miss* (1941), *The Doughgirls* (1942), *Anniversary Waltz* (1954), and *The Tunnel of Love* (1957). Fields also collaborated on the librettos for four stage musicals: *GENTLEMEN PREFER BLONDES* (1949), *WONDERFUL TOWN* (1953), *The Girl in Pink Tights* (1954), and *FLOWER DRUM SONG*, co-written with OSCAR HAMMERSTEIN. Most of Fields' stage efforts were filmed and usually he worked on the screenplay, as he did for the 1961 screen version of *Flower Drum Song*.

FIELDS, LEW [born Lewis Maurice Shanfield] (1867–1941). Stage performer, and producer. A beloved figure on the vaudeville and Broadway stage, he was also a proficient producer and presented several early musicals by RODGERS and HART. Born into an immigrant family of the Lower East Side of Manhattan, Fields began his career in vaudeville, teaming up with comic JOE WEBER and performing a "Dutch" comedy act across the country. The tall, bearded Fields and the short, plump Weber were so popular that by 1896 they were able to purchase their own Broadway theatre where they presented a series of musical comedy "burlesques" that parodied the shows and stars currently on Broadway. Among the most popular of these musical spoofs were *The Art of Maryland* (1896), *Hurly Burly* (1898), *Cyranose de Bricabrac* (1898), *FIDDLE-DEE-DEE* (1900), *Hoity Toity* (1901), *Twirly Whirly* (1902), *Whoop-Dee-Doo* (1903), and *An English Daisy* (1904). The team split up in 1903 and Fields turned to producing and occasionally starring in his productions. Between 1904 and his retirement in 1930, Fields produced over forty musicals and plays, including the early Rodgers

and Hart shows scripted by his son HERBERT FIELDS: *The Girl Friend* (1926), *PEGGY-ANN* (1926), *A CONNECTICUT YANKEE* (1927), *PRESENT ARMS* (1928), and *Chee-Chee* (1928). Other Fields-produced musicals include *It Happened in Nordland* (1904), *The Midnight Sons* (1909), *Old Dutch* (1909), *The Jolly Bachelors* (1910), *Tillie's Nightmare* (1910), *Roly Poly* (1912), *Step This Way* (1916), *HIT THE DECK* (1927), *Hello Daddy* (1929), and *Vanderbilt Revue* (1930). Fields also appeared in approximately half of these productions. He was also the father of playwright JOSEPH FIELDS and lyricist–librettist DOROTHY FIELDS. Biography: *From the Bowery to Broadway: Lew Fields and the Roots of American Popular Theatre*, Armon Fields and L. Marc (1993).

FIELDS, W. C. [born William Claude Dukenfield] (1879–1946). Stage and film performer. The unique, round-nosed, muttering comic usually played a variation on the misanthropic, juggling tramp–con man that he developed in vaudeville. Fields was born in Philadelphia and ran away from home as a youth, teaching himself to juggle and performing on the variety circuit. He refined his act on the road and in British music halls, even making a brief appearance on Broadway in *The Ham Tree* (1905). By the time he returned to New York in a specialty spot in *WATCH YOUR STEP* (1914), he was a recognized attraction and the next year was starred in the 1915 version of the *ZIEGFELD FOLLIES*, followed by eight more editions and the revues *GEORGE WHITE'S SCANDALS* (1922) and *EARL CARROLL'S VANITIES* (1925). Fields also appeared in book musicals, most memorably as Prof. Eustace McGargle in *Poppy* (1923). He made his feature film debut in 1924 and was featured in dozens of comedies over the next two decades, including the musicals *Her Majesty Love* (1931), *INTERNATIONAL HOUSE* (1933), *MISSISSIPPI* (1935), *Poppy* (1936), *BIG BROADCAST OF 1938*, *Follow the Boys* (1944), *Song of the Open Road* (1944), and *Sensations of 1945* (1944). Fields wrote several of his movie vehicles as well as his many radio broadcasts in the 1930s and 1940s. Rod Steiger played him in the film *W. C. Fields and Me* (1976). Autobiography: *W. C. Fields By Himself*, edited by Ronald Fields [his grandson] (1972); biography: *The Man on the Flying Trapeze: The Life and Times of W. C. Fields*, Simon Louvish (1997).

FIERSTEIN, HARVEY (1954–). Stage, film, and television performer and writer. The sometimes outrageous and always fascinating character actor with a raspy voice also scripted estimable Broadway plays and musicals. A native of Brooklyn, he worked as a female impersonator at the age of fifteen and then attended Pratt Institute before making his professional acting debut Off Off Broadway in 1971. Fierstein saw his first plays produced Off Off Broadway, and in 1982 three of his one acts were combined to make the Off Broadway and then Broadway hit *Torch Song Trilogy* (1982). He has written other plays but has concentrated mostly on musicals since the 1980s. Fierstein wrote the librettos for the hit *La Cage aux Folles* (1983) and the flop *Legs Diamond* (1988) and then was busy in the 1990s acting on television and in films. He returned to his drag queen roots when he played the Baltimore housewife Edna Turnblad in the original Broadway cast of *Hairspray* (2002) and then shone in one of his few nongay stage performances when he was a replacement for Tevye in *Fiddler on the Roof* in 2004. Fierstein's distinctive voice can be heard in the animated musical *Mulan* (1998) and its video sequel. His most recent project is the Broadway musical *A Catered Affair* (2008), which he co-wrote and appeared in.

🎵 **Fifty Million Frenchmen** (Lyric Theatre 1929). COLE PORTER's first Broadway hit, this lighthearted "musical comedy tour of Paris" ran 254 performances and established the songwriter as a talent to be reckoned with. HERBERT FIELDS' efficient libretto was a comic–romantic tale about the American millionaire Peter Forbes (WILLIAM GAXTON) in Paris who makes a wager that he can win the hand of tourist Looloo Carroll (Genevieve Tobin) within a month without using his money. He disguises himself as a tour guide and, in the process of showing Looloo the sights, falls in love with her and relinquishes the wager. Also in the first-rate cast were HELEN BRODERICK, Betty Compton, Jack Thompson, Thurston Hall, and Evelyn Hoey, who introduced the comic "Find Me a Primitive Man." The standout hit of the score was "You Do Something to Me," and other delights included "You Don't Know Paree," "You've Got That Thing," and "Paree, What Did You Do to Me?" Gaxton established himself as one of Broadway's favorite leading men with this show, and also noteworthy in the Ray E. Goetz production were Norman Bel Geddes' sets that recreated many of the Paris landmarks on stage. MONTE WOOLLEY directed with a playful touch, and Larry Ceballos did the choreography.

🎵 **Fine and Dandy** (Erlanger's Theatre 1930). The only full Broadway score by the underappreciated composer Kay Swift, the musical comedy is worth remembering for its expert score. Swift, one of Broadway's very few female composers until the 1970s, collaborated with Paul James (lyrics) and came up with a jazzy, spirited set of songs that were reminiscent of GEORGE GERSHWIN, her mentor, assistant, and friend. When Mrs. Fordyce (Dora Maugham) inherits the Fordyce Drop Forge and Tool Company from her late husband, she causes labor-management problems as well as romantic complications for various lovers who work in the factory. Matters get worse when she names the incompetent buffoon Joe Squibb (JOE COOK) as manager, but the minority stockholders stage a hostile takeover, offer Joe $100,000 to quit and never try to manage anything ever again, and he happily weds along with two other couples. The silly libretto by Donald Ogden Stewart and Cook was mostly a vehicle for the latter, a popular comic on Broadway. He was surrounded by such players as Nell O'Day, Dave Chasen, Alice Boulden, and ELEANOR POWELL, who was featured for her energetic tapping. The score included the rhythmic "Can This Be Love?," the sprightly "I'll Hit a New High," the oddly engaging "Let's Go Eat Worms in the Garden," the bouncy "The Jig Hop," and the raucous title number. Despite opening at the onset of the Depression, the Morris Green–Lewis Gensler production was a major hit, running 255 performances. Swift later contributed songs to various revues but never again had the opportunity to score a complete stage musical.

🎵 **Finian's Rainbow** (46th Street Theatre 1947). One of Broadway's most beguiling masterworks, the satiric musical fantasy by BURTON LANE (music), E. Y. HARBURG (book and lyrics), and FRED SAIDY (book) deals with racial prejudice and other weighty topics, yet seems as light as air.

Plot: After he steals a crock of gold from the leprechaun Og in Ireland, Finian McLonergan and his daughter Sharon come to America where Finian hopes to plant it near Fort Knox and see it multiply. Og is in hot pursuit and, having lost his crock, is turning more human every day. Sharon falls in love with the radical Woody Mahoney. He is organizing the black and white sharecroppers against the bigoted Senator Billboard Rawkins who only learns to reform after having been temporarily turned into an African American to see what it is like to be at the other end of his segregation laws.

Casts for *Finian's Rainbow*

Character	1947 Broadway	1960 Broadway	1968 film
Finian	Albert Sharpe	Bobby Howes	FRED ASTAIRE
Sharon	Ella Logan	Jeannie Carson	PETULA CLARK
Og	DAVID WAYNE	Howard Morris	TOMMY STEELE
Woody	Donald Richards	Biff Maguire	Don Francks
Susan	Anita Alverez	Anita Alvarez	Barbara Hancock
Sen. Rawkins	Robert Pitkin	Sorrell Booke	KEENAN WYNN

Finian's Rainbow. Few musical fantasies work on film. *The Wizard of Oz* (1939) is the most notable exception; *Finian's Rainbow* is more typical; it struggled and only occasionally succeeded. Petula Clark, pictured with Don Francks, usually found herself in uneven screen musicals so she turned to the London theatre and did much better. (Photofest)

to the Rainbow." There was also the jubilant revival-like "The Great Come-and-Get-It Day," the mock gospel number "The Begat," and the playful "Something Sort of Grandish." Much of the rest of the score was composed of pointed comic numbers, such as "When the Idle Poor Become the Idle Rich," "Necessity," and "When I'm Not Near the Girl I Love (I Love the Girl I'm Near)." Bretaigne Windust directed, MICHAEL KIDD did the clever choreography, and the critics advocated the show enthusiastically. Audiences took their advice and *Finian's Rainbow* ran 725 performances. Because the musical is about sensitive issues, revivals have been infrequent and many theatre groups are wary of producing it. New York saw a 1955 production at the City Center featuring HELEN GALLAGHER (Sharon) and Merv Griffin (Woody) with dances by ONNA WHITE based on Kidd's original choreography. At the same venue in 1960, a bright and tuneful production was presented by the New York City Light Opera Company with HERBERT ROSS directing and choreographing and Jeannie Carson as Sharon. Less impressive was the same company's 1967 revival with FRANK McHUGH as Finian and NANCY DUSSAULT as Sharon, supported by Stanley Grover, SANDY DUNCAN, Len Gochman, Carol Brice, and Howard I. Smith.

A bold and joyous experiment that worked beautifully on stage, the fantasy was highly enjoyable and got its message across without preaching. The musical boasted the first fully integrated chorus (white and blacks singers and dancers in the same ensemble) in Broadway history and its ideas were as uncompromising as they were entertaining. Not only was the wicked libretto highly satirical, the brilliant score also was incisively potent even as it was disarmingly escapist. "How Are Things in Glocca Morra" was the Irish-flavored hit ballad but also popular were the up-tempo love song "Old Devil Moon" and the dreamy "Look

Finian's Rainbow (stage) Musical Numbers

"This Time of the Year"
"How Are Things in Glocca Morra?"
"Look to the Rainbow"
"Old Devil Moon"
"Something Sort of Grandish"
"If This Isn't Love"
"Necessity"
"That Great Come-and-Get-It Day"
"When the Idle Poor Become the Idle Rich"
"Fiddle Faddle"
"The Begat"
"When I'm Not Near the Girl I Love"

■ *Finian's Rainbow* (Warner/Seven Arts 1968) took twenty-one years to jump from stage to screen and it is easy to see why when one considers the subject matter. However, by the late 1960s the studios were feeling more daring so a big-budget production was planned and major stars were signed. Satire and whimsical fantasy are both difficult to capture on screen and *Finian's Rainbow* was no exception. The screenplay by Saidy and director Francis Ford Coppola retained some of the potent aspects of the stage work, such as the senator (KEENAN WYNN) turning black, but made many other changes in the storyline, none of them for the better. Shot partially in a studio and partially on location, the difference is obvious and jarring. The film is heavy and realistic and the whimsy is gone, as is the romance since there is no chemistry between PETULA CLARK (Sharon) and Don Francks (Woody), and TOMMY STEELE's leprechaun is so narcissistic that one cannot believe he could love any girl, near or not. A good portion of the score survived the transition, and some of the musical numbers are well filmed and performed. "The Great Come-and-Get-it Day" is a joyous romp in a field, and the wry "The Begat" is a delightful ride through the countryside in a broken down convertible. As uneven as the film is, it is well worth seeing for the quiet, genial farewell performance by FRED ASTAIRE as Finian. In his last screen musical, he lightly dances an Irish jig and the low-energy, aged hoofer still has grace and style as he executes HERMES PAN's choreography. A totally satisfying film of such an elusive stage musical as *Finian's Rainbow* was probably not possible so we must be content with the memory of Astaire trippingly going down the road in the film's final moments.

FINN, WILLIAM (1952–). Stage composer and lyricist. An offbeat yet highly accessible songwriter, his musicals are bursting with neuroses and energy. Finn was born in Boston and studied music at Williams College where he started writing intimate and unusual musicals. His one-act musicals *In Trousers* (1979), *March of the Falsettos* (1981), and *Falsettoland* (1990) were produced Off Broadway and then combined under the title *FALSETTOS* and produced successfully on Broadway in 1992. Finn's other musical credits include *Dangerous Games* (1989), *Romance in Hard Times* (1989), *A NEW BRAIN* (1998), *Elegies: A Song Cycle* (2003), and the long-running *THE 25TH ANNUAL PUTNAM COUNTY SPELLING BEE* (2004). A revue of his songs, entitled *Make Me a Song*, ran Off

Broadway in 2007. Most of Finn's works are sung-through (with help on the "book" by JAMES LAPINE), deal with harassed and volatile Jewish urbanites, and have a strong sense of family, even if the families are usually dysfunctional.

✿ **FIORELLO!** (Broadhurst Theatre 1959). A musical biography of the beloved New York City mayor Fiorello LaGuardia, the show also took a satirical look at American politics. In the efficient libretto by JEROME WEIDMAN and GEORGE ABBOTT, the young Italian American lawyer LaGuardia (TOM BOSLEY) begins in the ethnic neighborhoods of New York and works his way up to mayor by being honest, stubborn, and always one of the people. HOWARD DA SILVA was outstanding as LaGuardia's political nemesis Ben Marino, Ellen Hanley and Patricia Wilson were the two women in Fiorello's life, and the supporting cast included Nathaniel Frey, Pat Stanley, Mark Dawson, and Eileen Rodgers. JERRY BOCK (music) and SHELDON HARNICK (lyrics) wrote the superior score that included the dandy comic songs "Politics and Poker" and "Little Tin Box," the plaintive ballad "When Did I Fall in Love?," the determined character song "The Very Next Man," the silly rhapsodic "I Love a Cop," and the waltzing "Til Tomorrow." The musical may have been an idealized portrait of the beloved LaGuadia, but the strong book, vibrant score, and gifted cast kept the show from getting sentimental. The popular attraction made a star of Bosley and launched the career of songwriters Bock and Harnick. Abbott directed, PETER GENNARO choreographed, and it was produced by HAROLD PRINCE and Robert E. Griffith, running 795 performances and winning the PULITZER PRIZE. Yet for all its acclaim when it opened, *Fiorello* was never filmed and is rarely revived. A two-week production by the New York City Light Opera in 1962 with Sorrell Booke as LaGuardia has been the musical's only major Manhattan revival.

✿ **FIREFLY, THE** (Lyric Theatre 1912). Composer RUDOLF FRIML's first Broadway assignment, it afforded him a sensational debut and its star EMMA TRENTINI one of her greatest triumphs. OTTO HARBACH wrote the lyrics and libretto, a Cinderella tale about Italian street singer Nina Corelli (Trentini) who disguises herself as a cabin boy on a yacht to be near the man she loves, Jack Travers (Craig Campbell), when he and some friends sail off to Bermuda. Also aboard is the music teacher

Herr Franz (Henry Vogel) who hears Nina singing and wants the "boy" for his choir. He takes Nina as a pupil and three years later she is a famous opera prima donna and in a better position to win the hand of Jack. The contrived story was overshadowed by Trentini's thrilling performance and the luscious Friml–Harbach score that included the hits "Giannina Mia," "Sympathy," and "Love Is Like a Firefly." VICTOR HERBERT was originally contracted to write the score but he feuded with the temperamental Trentini and pulled out of the production. Producer ARTHUR HAMMERSTEIN hired the young Czech immigrant Friml who wanted to write serious music but needed the job. *The Firefly* put him in the ranks of the top American composers of operettas for the next twenty years. As for Trentini, this was her last American success. No one would work with the difficult diva and she returned to Europe. *The Firefly* ran 120 performances and has remained in the repertoire of light opera companies ever since.

■ ***The Firefly*** (MGM 1937) bore little resemblance to the stage work, with only five of the songs being retained and the libretto thrown out for a completely new one by FRANCES GOODRICH and ALBERT HACKETT. The Spanish singer Nina Maria Azara (JEANETTE MACDONALD) works as spy to save King Ferdinand VII (Tom Rutherford) from the Napoleonic invasion while the counterspy Don Diego (ALLAN JONES) is working for the French. He catches on to her but by then they have fallen in love and, after the smoke clears from battle, the two are reunited. It wasn't much of an improvement over the old 1912 plot, but MacDonald and Jones had a special rapport on screen and kept the picture moving. The most famous musical scene in the film is when the two go for a ride through the Pyrenees in a donkey cart and Jones sings "Donkey Serenade," the hit song by Friml, HERBERT STOTHART (music), ROBERT WRIGHT, and GEORGE FORREST (lyrics) that became Jones' signature number throughout his long career. ROBERT Z. LEONARD directed the cast, which also included Warren William, BILLY GILBERT, Douglass Dumbrille, Henry Daniell, Leonard Penn, and Belle Mitchell.

🕮 ***Five Guys Named Moe*** (Eugene O'Neill Theatre 1992). A hit London revue that had to settle for a not-shabby 445 performances on Broadway, the CAMERON MACKINTOSH production celebrated the music of songwriter–saxophonist Louis Jordan. In the Clarke Peters "book," the African American young man Nomax (Jerry Dixon) suffers from an unsatisfactory love life but he is consoled and cheered up by five singers (Doug Eskew, Milton Craig Nealy, Glenn Turner, Jeffrey D. Sams, and Kevin Ramsey) who leap out of Nomax's radio and perform songs that were written and/or popularized by Jordan, such as "Ain't Nobody Here But Us Chickens," "Push Ka Pi Shi Pie," "Early in the Morning," "Choo Choo Ch-Boogie," and "Is You or Is You Not My Baby?" The pop numbers were staged by director–choreographer Charles Augins, performed with zest by the small company, and a good deal of audience participation was encouraged so word of mouth kept the revue on the boards for over a year. ☐ The long-running London production of *Five Guys Named Moe* was videotaped in 1995 and broadcast on British television. An Australian film version of the musical was in production in 2007.

■ ***Five Pennies, The*** (Dena/Paramount 1959). A musical biography that relied more on sentiment than historical accuracy, it told the story of cornet player Red Nichols and at least the music was true to its period (the 1920s and 1930s). Danny Kaye played Nichols and, for the most part, forsook his clowning for pathos. Barbara Bel Geddes (singing dubbed by Eileen Wilson) was his noble and suffering wife Bobbie, and Susan Gordon was their polio-stricken young daughter Dorothy who survived to grow up to be Tuesday Weld. Also on hand were BOB CROSBY, Ray Anthony (as JIMMY DORSEY), Harry Guardino, Nichols himself to provide the cornet playing on the soundtrack, and, most memorably, LOUIS ARMSTRONG whose duet of "When the Saints Come Marching In" with Kaye was the highlight of the movie. Jack Rose and director Melville Shavelson wrote the maudlin screenplay, and Sylvia Fine provided the new songs, including "Lullaby in Ragtime," "Good Night, Sleep Tight," and the touching title number. Among the old favorites heard were "After You've Gone," "Out of Nowhere," and "Runnin Wild."

■ ***5,000 Fingers of Dr. T, The*** (Columbia 1953). A musical fantasy that looks and feels like no other film, this Dr. Seuss adventure, once viewed, cannot be forgotten. Allan Scott and Theodore Geisel, better known as Dr. Seuss, wrote the screenplay about young Bartholomew Collins (Tommy Rettig) who is forced to practice the piano when he would rather be outside playing baseball. When the youth doses off, he dreams that his piano teacher Mr. Terwilliker (HANS CONREID) becomes the diabolical Dr. T who has imprisoned 500 boys in his dungeon and forces them to play on long curling pianos that only Dr. Seuss could dream up. Also in the prison are nonpiano musicians who have grown green and moldy and finally break out in song and dance. Bartholomew, with the help of his widowed mother Heloise (Mary Healy) and the kindly plumber August Zabladowski (Peter Lind Hayes), outwits Dr. T, and the boy awakes to find the plumber and his mother in love. Much of the film doesn't quite work, but Rudolph Sternad's optical illusion sets (inspired from the illustrated Seuss book), Conreid's zany performance, and the tuneful songs by Frederick Hollander (music) and Geisel (lyrics) help one get through the weak spots. "The Kid's Song," "Get Together Weather," "The Dressing Song (My Do-Me-Do Duds)," "Dream Stuff," and "Ten Happy Fingers" are catchy in the distinct Seuss style. Roy Rowland directed the Stanley Kramer production, and EUGENE LORING provided the cockeyed choreography.

FLAHERTY, STEPHEN, AND LYNN AHRENS. Stage and film songwriting team. The only durable, consistently captivating Broadway team to come out of the 1980s or 1990s, they are highly versatile and very productive. Lyricist and librettist Ahrens (1948–) was born in New York and educated at Syracuse University for a journalism career. After writing television commercials and children's shows, such as *Schoolhouse Rock* (1973), she met composer Flaherty at a BMI Musical Theatre Workshop in 1983. Flaherty (1960–) was born in Pittsburgh and studied music at the Cincinnati Conservatory of Music. The team's first effort, *Lucky Stiff* (1988), was little noticed Off Broadway (although later became popular with all kinds of theatre groups) but their Caribbean-flavored ONCE ON THIS ISLAND (1990) transferred to Broadway for a modest run. *My Favorite Year* (1992), their first Broadway project, failed to run but RAGTIME (1998) was a critical and popular hit. The team's subsequent musicals are SEUSSICAL (2000), *A Man of No Importance* (2002), *Dessa Rose* (2005), and *The Glorious Ones* (2007). The two also scored the animated musical film ANASTASIA (1997), and Ahrens collaborated with composer ALAN MENKEN on the Madison Square Garden musical *A CHRISTMAS CAROL* (1994). Ahrens and Flaherty are known for their acute sense of pastiche, strong melodic lines, powerful characterization, and polished integrated scores.

FLAHOOLEY (Broadhurst Theatre 1951). An offbeat musical satire that had an unsuccessful run of only forty performances on Broadway, the show lives on as a cult favorite because of its quirky plot and exhilarating score by SAMMY FAIN (music) and E. Y. HARBURG (lyrics). The wacky libretto by Harbach and FRED SAIDY makes fun of big business, the McCarthy witch hunts, the atom bomb, and modern consumerism; it's a script that either delights or infuriates theatregoers. Toy manufacturer B. G. Bigelow (ERNEST TRUEX) takes the advice of his ideas man Sylvester (Jerome Courtland) and puts out a laughing doll named Flahooley to compete with all the crying dolls on the market. Soon Arab spies, a vigilante group, puppets, and a magic lamp are thrown into the mix and chaos ensues. The talented cast also included BARBARA COOK, Yma Sumac, Irwin Corey, Fay DeWitt, Edith Atwater, Louis Nye, and Lulu Bates, and the cunning score featured such songs as "Here's to Your Illusions," "He's Only Wonderful," "The Springtime Cometh," "You Too Can Be a Puppet," and "The World Is Your Balloon." Harburg and Saidy co-directed, HELEN TAMIRIS choreographed, and CHERYL CRAWFORD was the brave producer. The oddball musical had been a smash hit in Philadelphia during the tryout tour but the Manhattan critics would have none of it and the cockeyed musical never found an audience. It would later become one of the most cultist of cult musicals, although revivals are very rare.

FLASHDANCE (Paramount 1983). A Cinderella story for the 1980s, this contemporary romance relied on a lot of dance and an insistent series of songs on the soundtrack to become what was known as a musical in that decade. The screenplay by Thomas Hedley, Jr., and Joe Eszterhas followed the adventures of Pittsburgher Alex Owens (Jennifer Beals) who works as a steel welder during the day and dances at a go-go club at night, all the time dreaming of becoming a prima ballerina with the Pittsburgh Ballet. Her fairy godmother of sorts is her boss Nick Hurley (Michael Nouri) who gets her an audition and by the end becomes her Prince Charming as well. The ridiculous premise was given a rock video staging with dances that elicited more laughs than intended, but young audiences somehow bought into it and the film was a major hit. The pounding score by

Giorgio Moroder, Irene Cara, and Keith Forsey made for a popular soundtrack, with the song "Flashdance ... What a Feeling" even winning the Oscar. Adrian Lyne directed the movie, and Jeffrey Hornaday did the cockamamie choreography, which at one point included buckets of water falling on the dancing Alex.

FLEET'S IN, THE (Paramount 1942). A wartime frolic with an old-hat story, the musical nevertheless was an enjoyable nautical romp. The premise for the Walter DeLeon–Sid Silvers screenplay had served as the plot for two previous nonmusicals. The shy sailor Casey Kirby (William Holden) is mistakenly believed by everyone to be a notorious ladies' man. His fellow gobs make a bet with each other that Casey can kiss in public the beautiful but aloof nightclub singer known as the Countess (Dorothy Lamour). Of course the very unwolf-like sailor wins the kiss and his misguided reputation prevails. As the Countess's brazen roommate Bessie Day, Betty Hutton made a sensational screen debut singing "Build a Better Mousetrap" and, with her love interest Barney Waters (Eddie Bracken), performed "Arthur Murray Taught Me Dancing in a Hurry." Victor Schertzinger (music) and Johnny Mercer (lyrics) wrote the bouncy score that also included the hits "I Remember You" and "Tangerine," both performed by Tommy Dorsey and his orchestra (vocals by Bob Eberle and Helen O'Connell) and were identified forever after with the bandleader. Also in the cast were Cass Daley, Gil Lamb, Leif Erickson, and Betty Jane Rhodes. Schertzinger directed the Paul Jones production, and Jack Donohue did the swing choreography. The musical was remade in 1951 as the Jerry Lewis–Dean Martin vehicle *Sailor Beware*.

FLORA, THE RED MENACE (Alvin Theatre 1965). Memorable if for no other reason than it introduced the songwriting team John Kander (music) and Fred Ebb (lyrics) to Broadway and gave Liza Minnelli her first major role, the musical comedy by George Abbott and Robert Russell had much to enjoy. Producer Harold Prince had planned the production for the new stage star Barbra Streisand, but when he couldn't get her he cast nineteen-year-old Minnelli who had impressed him in an Off Broadway revival of *Best Foot Forward* (1963). It was a daring choice given the size of the role but the show afforded Minnelli an auspicious Broadway debut. Recent art school graduate Flora Meszaros (Minnelli) has trouble finding a job during the Depression and gets involved with the Communist Party through her idealistic boy friend Harry Toukarian (Bob Dishy). Both her career and her romance go bust but Flora takes the advice of the philosophical Mr. Weiss (Joe E. Marks) and continues on finding strength within herself. The young but impressive cast also included Mary Louise Wilson, Cathyrn Damon, James Cresson, Danny Carroll, and Gordon Dillworth. Loosely based on Lester Atwill's novel *Love Is Just Around the Corner*, the musical was far from being as political or thought-provoking as its subject matter and critics were unimpressed by everything except the young, energetic Minnelli. What they failed to notice was such sparkling songs as "A Quiet Thing," "Dear Love," "You Are You," "Sing Happy," and "All I Need Is One Good Break." Abbott directed, Lee Theodore choreographed, and audiences came for only eighty-seven performances. *Flora, the Red Menace* has been infrequently revived Off Broadway and in regional theatres.

FLORODORA (Casino Theatre 1900). An import from London where it ran 455 performances, this provocative musical comedy was a sensation in New York, running 553 performances and creating the mystique of the "Florodora Girl." On the Philippine Island of Florodora, the elderly perfume manufacturer Cyrus Gilfain (R. E. Graham) wants to marry the pretty Dolores (Fannie Johnston), the daughter of the man he has swindled. But she loves the company manager Frank Abercoed (Sydney Deane), the man whom Gilfain wants his daughter Angela (May Edouin) to wed, and Angela loves Captain Arthur Donegal (Cyril Scott). To serve as the matchmaker in all these affairs is the put-upon phrenologist Anthony Tweedlepunch (Willie Edoin) who goes to Wales just as all the others do because Gilfain has bought a castle there. The castle is somewhat haunted, which helps frighten the villainous Gilfain into letting true love have its course. Owen Hall wrote the daffy libretto, which was convenient for fitting in the charming songs by Leslie Stuart (music and Lyrics), Paul Rubens, and Frank Clement (lyrics), including "The Shade of the Palm," "When I Leave Town," "I Want to Be a Military Man," "The Silver Star of Love," and "When You're a Millionaire." But the musical highlight of the show was "Tell Me, Pretty Maiden" in which six lovely ladies with parasols flirted coquettishly with six male admirers. New Yorkers were fascinated by the sextet of beauties, termed the "Florodora Girls," and they became famous, most of them eventually giving up show business and marrying millionaires. *Florodora* was a favorite on the road and was revived in New York in 1902, 1905, and 1920, with the last production running an impressive 150 performances.

🐦 **FLOWER DRUM SONG** (St. James Theatre 1958). An atypical show by the team of RICHARD RODGERS (music) and OSCAR HAMMERSTEIN (lyrics), it was a lighthearted musical comedy with sassy nightclub numbers, broad cartoonish characters, and a plot ending with old operetta-like trickery. Sammy Fong, a nightclub owner in San Francisco's Chinatown, is in love with the sexy, all-American chorine Linda Low but is betrothed to the "picture bride" Mei Li who has just arrived from China with her father, Dr. Li. In order to get out of the contract, Sammy pairs the innocent Mei Li with the young Chinese American Wang Ta who is unofficially engaged to Linda. Sammy breaks up that engagement by bringing Wang Ta's father, Wang Chi, and aunt, Madam Liang, to the nightclub where Linda's striptease-like act shocks the relatives. Mei Li and Wang Ta fall in love, much to the disappointment of the melancholy seamstress Helen Chao, and Sammy only gets to wed Linda by disguising her at the wedding ceremony as the veiled Mei Li. Based on the novel *The Flower Drum Song* by C. Y. Lee, the musical took a lighthearted look at the clash between East and West, parents and children, and new ways versus tradition. JOSEPH FIELDS adapted Lee's book and brought it to Rodgers and Hammerstein, later sharing libretto credit with Hammerstein. The novel was unique and appealed to the team, but it was also more serious in spots than the authors wanted. For example, in the novel the lonely Helen commits suicide over her unrequited love for Wang Ta. Fields and Hammerstein created the char-

acter of the sly Sammy Fong and switched the emphasis from the father Wang Chi to the younger couples. Except for LARRY BLYDEN (replacing Larry Storch during the Boston tryouts) in Chinese makeup, the cast was Asian, a Broadway first; however, some complained that the characters sometimes were mere Oriental stereotypes. Regardless, the production, staged by GENE KELLY (his only Broadway directing credit) and choreographed by CAROL HANEY, was superbly mounted and highly entertaining and ran for 600 performances. The score, although often in a lighter vein than the team's other work, is still one of their finest. The most famous number, "I Being a Girl," was later a staple in beauty pageants, even though there is a sarcastic subtext in the lyric. The haunting ballads "You Are Beautiful" and "Love, Look Away" are superb, the comic "Don't Marry Me" is one of the funniest in the Rodgers and Hammerstein canon, and the Asian-flavored "A Hundred Million Miracles" serves as the theme song for the piece, uniting the score with its optimistic philosophy. Although critical reaction was mixed, audiences enjoyed the musical for a year and a half.

Because of the demand for an all-Asian cast, *Flower Drum Song* did not receive many regional productions but an inspired revival opened on Broadway in 2002 that took a very different approach to the show. Asian American playwright HENRY DAVID HWANG rewrote the original libretto, turning the musical comedy into a musical play with a darker subtext to the story and the characters. Mei Li (LEA SALONGA) escapes from Communist China in 1961 and arrives in San Francisco where she finds work at the Golden Pear Theatre, a traditional but failing Chinese theatre venue run by Wang Chi-Yang (Randall Duk Kim). She falls in love with his outspoken son Ta (José Llana) who thinks he's in love with nightclub singer Linda

---

Casts for *Flower Drum Song*

Character	1958 Broadway	1961 film	2003 Broadway
Mei-Li	Miyoshi Umeki	Miyoshi Umeki	LEA SALONGA
Sammy Fong	LARRY BLYDEN	Jack Soo	José Llana
Wang Ta	Ed Kenny	James Shigita	José Llana
Linda Low	Pat Suzuki	Nancy Kwan	Sandra Allen
Helen Chao	Arabella Hong	Reiko Sato	
Madame Laing	JUANITA HALL	Juanita Hall	Jodi Long
Wang Chi-Yang	Keye Luke	Benson Fong	Randall Duk Kim
Chao			Hoon Lee

(Sandra Allen). Just as Ta starts to appreciate his Chinese heritage, his father, with the help of the wily agent Madam Liang (Jodi Long), turns the theatre into a nightclub that satirizes Chinese clichés. The heartbroken Mei Li plans to emigrate to Hong Kong but at the last minute Ta realizes he loves her and together they plan to reconcile their Asian roots with their new home. The elaborate production, directed and choreographed by Robert Longbottom, received mixed notices but there was little disagreement about the outstanding performers and the lavish production values. The new version premiered at the Mark Taper Forum in Los Angeles where it was very successful but only lasted on Broadway for 169 performances.

Flower Drum Song (Universal-International 1961) was a very faithful screen adaptation of the Broadway musical; all the stage songs were retained except one and four stage cast members appeared on screen: Miyoshi Umeki, JUANITA HALL, and Patrick Adiarte (as Wang Ta's younger brother Wang San) reprised their stage roles and Jack Soo graduated from a minor character to play the leading comic part of Sammy. Because Fields adapted his own libretto, the screenplay followed the play closely, although some of the dance numbers were expanded, such as a lengthy ballet that follows "Love, Look Away." Director HENRY KOSTER went for a less realistic telling of the story, such as having Mei Li and her father enter the country illegally by popping out of a crate in San Francisco. Nancy Kwan was dazzling as Linda Low (even though her singing was dubbed by B. J. Baker), Soo was very funny as Sammy, and Umeki was as endearing on screen as she was in the theatre. An added bonus is hearing the young Marilyn Horne sing the vocals for Reiko Sato for "Love, Look Away." The film version was very colorful, had lavish sets, and some vibrant choreography by HERMES PAN. The movie was popular, but again some Asian Americans complained of stereotyping. However, it remains the only Asian American musical film and has much to recommend it.

Floyd Collins (Playwrights Horizons 1996). An engrossing little musical with an unusual subject, the Off Broadway piece introduced songwriter ADAM GUETTEL to the theatregoing public and they would not forget the impact he made with his stunning score. In the winter of 1925, the Kentucky farmer Floyd Collins (Christopher Innvar) is exploring a cave on the family property when he gets trapped 150 feet below the surface. The efforts

to rescue him make national news and the site soon turns into a media circus as journalists and thousands of curious onlookers arrive. By the time the rescuers reach Collins, he has died of exposure and the circus disbands. Tina Landau's libretto, based on a true event, eschewed conventional storytelling and used dreams, flashbacks, and other theatrical devices to explore the mindset of Floyd and his family. The score was an eclectic mix of country, ragtime, and avant garde music, resulting in such fascinating numbers as "The Call," "The Riddle Song," "Is That Remarkable?," and "The Ballad of Floyd Collins." Landau directed the ingenious production, and the piece was greeted enthusiastically by the press and the PLAYWRIGHTS HORIZONS subscribers during its limited run of twenty-five performances. Since then *Floyd Collins* had received many productions in colleges and regional theatres.

Flying Colors (Imperial Theatre 1932). A sparkling musical revue starring CLIFTON WEBB and TAMARA GEVA, it boasted a delightful score by ARTHUR SCHWARTZ (music) and HOWARD DIETZ (lyrics). Cheers for its funny sketches (by Dietz, GEORGE S. KAUFMAN, and others), strong score, distinguished dancing, and bevy of talented performers ought to have made the show a long-run hit but it had to settle for 188 performances on Depression-weary Broadway. The talented cast also included CHARLES BUTTERWORTH, PATSY KELLY, BUDDY and VILMA EBSEN, PHILIP LOEB, IMOGENE COCA, and LARRY ADLER, and among the songs were "Alone Together," "Louisiana Shoeshine," "Shine on Your Shoes," "Smokin' Reefers," "Fatal Fascination," "Mother Told Me So," and "A Rainy Day." MAX GORDON produced, Dietz directed, both ALBERTINA RASCH and a young AGNES DE MILLE did the choreography, and Norman Bel Geddes' designed the innovative scenery, which utilized a moving dance floor.

Flying Down to Rio (RKO 1933). A landmark musical not only for introducing the dance team of FRED ASTAIRE and GINGER ROGERS, but the South American-set film initiated a nationwide interest in Latin-flavored music.

Plot: The American playboy Roger Bond, a bandleader who is also an aviator, meets the Brazilian beauty Belinha De Rezande in Miami and realizes it is true love. But Belinha is engaged to dashing countryman Julio Riberio and can't decide which of the two men she loves. Roger's band, the Yankee Clippers, is engaged to open a new hotel in Rio de Janeiro so he pursues Belinha

Flying Down to Rio. Has there ever been a wackier and more ridiculously wonderful sequence than the title number in this film musical? Only in Hollywood would someone try to entertain hotel guests by flying biplanes overhead with chorus girls strapped to the wings. The scene thrilled moviegoers because finally on the screen was a musical number that didn't look like a stage show. (Photofest)

in her native country. His idea man, hoofer Fred Ayres, has an idea for a sensational number to open the hotel. While he sings "Flying Down to Rio" in the hotel plaza, a fleet of airplanes fly overhead, each one with scantily clad chorus girls dancing on the wings. The show is a success and Roger wins Belinha's hand.

While the high-flying finale, choreographed by DAVE GOULD, is the most remembered scene because of it audacious craziness, the musical highlight of the movie came when Astaire and Rogers danced to "The Carioca" atop seven white pianos in a nightclub. The sleek, attractive new couple and the romantic strains of the Latin music changed the history of movie dancing. The two only had secondary roles but it was clear that this was where the magic was.

Edward Eliscu, GUS KAHN, and VINCENT YOUMANS collaborated on the film's four

Cast for *Flying Down to Rio*

Character	Performer
Belinha De Rezende	DOLORES DEL RIO
Roger Bond	GENE RAYMOND
Julio Riberio	Raul Roulien
Honey Hale	GINGER ROGERS
Fred Ayres	FRED ASTAIRE
Señor Carlos De Rezende	Walter Walker
Doña Elena De Rezende	Blanche Friderici
Carioca Singer	Etta Moten
Mr. Butterbass	ERIC BORE

Flying Down to Rio Musical Numbers

"Music Makes Me"
"The Carioca"
"Orchids in the Moonlight"
"Flying Down to Rio"

songs and they too were revolutionary. The rhythm number "Music Makes Me" and the warm ballad "Orchids in the Moonlight" did not have the brash, Broadway sound of *42ND STREET* (1933), that year's other landmark film. Youmans' music was not only Latin but it introduced a more serene, fox-trot pattern that would dictate much of the dance music in the 1930s. Also, "The Carioca" started a rage for the samba and other south-of-the-border dances and music. THORNTON FREELAND directed and HERMES PAN and Astaire assisted Gould in the choreography. Much of *Flying Down to Rio* is preposterous and silly, particularly to contemporary viewers, yet the strangely affecting musical was one of the most important of the decade.

FLYING HIGH (Apollo Theatre 1930). The last Broadway musical by the illustrious team of DeSylva, Brown, and Henderson, it did not boast their finest score but the show had BERT LAHR in top form and that was plenty. The libretto by John McGowan, LEW BROWN, and B. G. DESYLVA cashed in on the 1920s flying craze prompted by Charles Lindbergh's famous transatlantic flight. From the day the dashing aviator Tod Addison accidentally parachuted onto the apartment balcony of Eileen Cassidy, he has been in love with her but the usual musical comedy complications keep them apart until the finale. Tod's mechanic Rusty Krause has the opposite problem: he is being chased by the hefty, determined Pansy Sparks. To escape from her latest pursuit, Rusty steals Tod's plane and flies off, only remembering that he doesn't know how to fly when he is aloft. In his panic, he breaks a record for the longest flight and becomes a hero. "Thank Your Father" was the only song by DeSylva, Brown (lyrics), and RAY HENDERSON (music) to become popular; the rest of the score included "Red Hot Chicago," "I'll Know Him," "Good for You–Bad for Me," and the title number. GEORGE WHITE

produced and co-directed, BOBBY CONNOLLY did the choreography, and the silly but enjoyable show ran 357 performances despite the onset of the Depression.

Flying High (MGM 1931) brought Bert Lahr to Hollywood for the first time and he was hilarious reprising his Rusty Krause on screen. The screenplay by A. P. Younger doesn't stray too far from the stage work but all of the Broadway songs were cut except the title number, which was a bit severe when George White also produced the film. JIMMY MCHUGH (music) and DOROTHY FIELDS (lyrics) provided the new songs, most memorably "Happy Landing" and "We'll Dance Till Dawn," and BUSBY BERKELEY choreographed them with his still-emerging style of focusing on individual chorines with his camera. CHARLOTTE GREENWOOD was funny as Pansy but it is Lahr's frantic, oversized performance that keeps the movie alive. ❑ Bert Lahr got to reprise his Rusty yet again on the small screen when the NBC television series *Musical Comedy Tonight* broadcast an abridged version of *Flying High* in 1951.

FOLIES BERGERE DE PARIS (Fox/United Artists 1935). A vehicle for America's favorite Frenchman, MAURICE CHEVALIER, the film had such a reliable bedroom farce plot that it served for three popular movie musicals. Bess Meredyth and Hal Long adapted the play "The Red Cat" into a breezy screenplay about the wealthy French businessman Baron Fernand Cassini (Chevalier) who is married to Genevieve (Merle Oberon) but has Mimi (ANN SOTHERN) as his mistress. When the baron has to be at a business meeting and a grand ball at the same time, he hires *Folies Bergere* entertainer Eugene Charlier (Chevalier), who looks like him and impersonates the rich man in his act, to take his place. Genevieve has not been informed of the switch and she and Eugene spend a lovely night together. She later

Casts for *Flying High*		
Character	*1930 Broadway*	*1931 film*
Rusty Krause	BERT LAHR	Bert Lahr
Tod Addison/Sport Wardell	OSCAR SHAW	Pat O'Brien
Eileen Cassidy/Smith	Grace Brinkley	Kathryn Crawford
Pansy Sparks/Potts	Kate Smith	CHARLOTTE GREENWOOD
Dr. Brown		CHARLES WINNINGER
Mrs. Smith		Hedda Hopper
Fred Smith		GUY KIBBEE

acknowledges that he is an impostor but neither the baron nor Eugene ever quite knows when she realized the true identity of her bedtime partner. The score, by various songwriters, featured "I'm Lucky," "You Took the Words Right Out of My Mouth," and "Rhythm of the Rain." The last served for a lavish *Folies* production number choreographed by DAVE GOULD with Chevalier, SOTHERN, and the chorus singing and dancing away with twirling umbrellas in a studio-manufactured downpour. ROY DEL RUTH directed the DARRYL F. ZANUCK production with a light touch and Chevalier got one of the juiciest roles of his career.

Without too many plot changes, the studio moved the locale to Brazil and remade the film as **That Night in Rio** (Fox 1941) with DON AMECHE in the double leading role. This time it was song-and-dance man Larry Martin who becomes Baron Manuel Duarte and his worldly wise wife Cecilia (ALICE FAYE) may or may not know who it was she slept with. The baron's mistress is Carmen (CARMEN MIRANDA) and she too gets the two look-alikes confused. S. Z. SAKALL, J. CARROLL NAISH, LEONID KINSKEY, Lillian Porter, and Curt Bois were cast to add to the confusion. HARRY WARREN (music) and MACK GORDON (lyrics) penned the Latin-flavored score and gave Miranda two of her biggest hits, "Chica Chica Boom Chic" and "I Yi Yi Yi Yi (I Like You Very Much)." Also heard were "Cae Cae," "They Met in Rio," and the lullaby "Boa Noite (Good Night)." IRVING CUMMINGS directed the FRED KOHLMAR production, and HERMES PAN provided the Latin dances. Ten years later the same tale resurfaced with a French setting again as **On the Riviera** (Fox 1951) with DANNY KAYE as both American entertainer Jack Martin and businessman Henri Duran. Gene Tierney was his wife Lili and Corinne Calvet was his mistress Colette. The most far-cical of the three versions, the film allows Kaye to run wild with his verbal pyrotechnics and physical sense of humor. Sylvia Fine wrote some songs particularly suited to his style, such as "Poppo the Puppet," "Rhythm of a New Romance," and the Gallic title number, which Kaye sang in a broad Chevalier impersonation as an inside joke. Yet the most memorable song in the film, the one Kaye would return to throughout his long career, was "Ballin' the Jack" by Jim Burris and Chris Smith. WALTER LANG was the astute director, SOL C. SIEGEL produced, and JACK COLE did the choreography. Interestingly, cameraman Leon Shamroy worked on all three movies.

🎭 **FOLLIES** (Winter Garden Theatre 1971). Not the lavish, escapist revue that its title suggested and what some of its audience expected, this dark musical play is about the follies people have committed in the past and how their present is still haunted by them.

Plot: At a reunion of performers from the *Weismann Follies* held in a soon-to-be-razed old theatre, two married couples return to the place where they first met and reminisce even as they are haunted by the ghosts of the past, including the younger versions of themselves. Diplomat Ben Stone and his acid-toned wife Phyllis are drifting apart and traveling salesman Buddy Plummer knows his wife Sally is still carrying a torch for Ben. The reunion turns into an expressionistic *Follies* show in which the foursome's past mistakes are musicalized and by dawn the two couples are reunited with painful resolve.

James Goldman wrote the incisive libretto in which the dialogue and characters were both charged with wit, brains, and remorse. STEPHEN SONDHEIM wrote two scores: a knowing and sometimes devastating set of character songs

Stage casts for *Follies*		
Character	*1971 Broadway*	*2001 Broadway*
Phyllis Stone	ALEXIS SMITH	Blythe Danner
Ben Stone	JOHN McMARTIN	Gregory Harrison
Sally Plummer	Dorothy Collins	Judith Ivey
Buddy Plummer	GENE NELSON	TREAT WILLIAMS
Carlotta Campion	Yvonne De Carlo	Polly Bergen
Stella Deems	MARY McCARTY	Carol Woods
Hattie Walker	Ethel Shutta	BETTY GARRETT
Heidi Schiller	Justine Johnson	Joan Roberts
Solange LaFitte	Fifi D'Orsay	Jane White

Follies. The final musical number in the show, "Live, Laugh, Love," was performed by the self-loathing Ben (John McMartin) as a debonair hat-and-cane routine, complete with a smiling chorus line. What would have served as a joyful finale in any other Broadway musical instead became a nightmare. Ben kept forgetting the lyric, which was full of lies, and he tried to stop the number only be be overruled by the dances. What followed was a noisy, frightening collage of people and snatches of song, then all the ghosts departed and there was silence. That was *Follies*. (Photofest)

for the present and a tuneful, seemingly frolicsome set of pastiche songs for the old *Follies* numbers. Book and score collided passionately just as past and present did throughout the show, so even the most lighthearted and silly ditties had a sobering subtext. Just as the score had many songs, the story had many characters who moved in and out of the action, just as ghosts of the past paraded through the present with chilling effect. Co-directors HAROLD PRINCE and MICHAEL BENNETT staged the complex piece in a dreamlike trance, yet intrusive flashes of reality broke through at times, making the dream more like a nightmare.

Even critics and audience members who found *Follies* too abrasive or dreary for their tastes admitted that the score was a remarkable achievement. Songs for the present-day story may have been too harsh for some but

one could not deny the brilliant craftsmanship of numbers such as "Could I Leave You?," "The Right Girl," "In Buddy's Eyes," and "Too Many Mornings." "I'm Still Here" became quite well known for its wry commentary on time and change, and the octet "The Girls Upstairs" in which the past and present couples intersect was an amazing bit of musical storytelling. The pastiche songs are easier to love, especially if one takes them out of the context of the show and sees them as delightful set pieces. Various songwriters from the past were echoed in "Beautiful Girls,' "One Last Kiss," "Who's That Woman?," "Broadway Baby," "Losing My Mind," and others. Unlike the pastiche songs in *THE BOY FRIEND* (1954) or *DAMES AT SEA* (1968) in which one laughs at the past even as you enjoy the familiar tone, the pastiche numbers in *Follies* are so accurate and sincere in their frivolity that one cannot mock

Follies Musical Numbers

"Beautiful Girls"
"Don't Look at Me"
"Waiting for the Girls Upstairs"
"Rain on the Roof"
"Ah, Paris!"
"Broadway Baby"
"The Road You Didn't Take"
"Bolero d'Amour"
"In Buddy's Eyes"
"Who's That Woman?"
"I'm Still Here"
"Too Many Mornings"
"The Right Girl"
"One More Kiss"
"Could I Leave You?"
"Loveland"
"You're Gonna Love Tomorrow"
"Love Will See Us Through"
"The God-Why-Don't-You-Love-Me Blues"
"Losing My Mind"
"The Story of Lucy and Jessie"
"Live, Laugh, Love"

them. To the characters in the plot these escapist songs are telling their story and it is a frightening thing to behold. Sondheim goes beyond spoof and reaches a level of self-awareness in these numbers that make them richer than the originals that inspired them

The most expensive Broadway musical to date, *Follies* was overflowing with memorable performances, dazzling choreography (by Bennett), and stunning sets and costumes. However, most critics complained about the cynical tone and fatalistic theme of the piece and recommended it with severe reservations. The Harold Prince production ran 552 performances but never came close to paying off its high-cost investment. Over time the musical has become one of the most celebrated of all American stage works and even with its flaws the show remains some kind of classic. All the same, revivals are difficult and the show is beyond the resources of most theatre groups. Yet productions are done on a regular basis and in the most unlikely places. In New York the only Broadway revival to date was presented by the ROUNDABOUT THEATRE in 2001. While it could not hope to match the lavishness and the star power of the original, the production, directed by Matthew Warchus, received mostly favorable notices and critics thought the script and score even stronger than commentators did in 1971. The cast was roundly commended,

as was KATHLEEN MARSHALL's choreography, and the limited run of 116 performances was well attended.

FOLLIES OF 1907, THE. See *ZIEGFELD FOLLIES*

FOLLOW THAT BIRD (Warner 1985). A feature film musical presented by the Children's Television Workshop and the creators of *Sesame Street*, the movie (like the TV show) was aimed at young children, yet there was plenty for adults to enjoy as well. The Judy Freudberg and Tony Geiss screenplay related what happens when Big Bird (voice of Carroll Spinney) is sent to a foster family of birds and he misses his friends back on Sesame Street. One day he steals away and journeys to be reunited with the urban gang but they have gone off in search of Big Bird so there follows a series of missing each other before everyone is together again. The cast included such familiar muppets as Kermit the Frog (Jim Henson), Cookie Monster (Frank Oz), the Count (Jerry Nelson), and Sully Monster (Richard Hunt), as well as the human actors Linda Bove, Emilio Delgado, Sonia Manzano, Roscoe Orman, and Alaina Reed Hall. There were also cameos by Chevy Chase, John Candy, Sandra Bernhard, Joe Flaherty, and Sally Kellerman. Oscar the Grouch (also Spinney) opened the film with a satire on *Patton* (1970) by addressing the viewers in front of a huge American flag and urging everyone to sing "The Grouch Anthem." Other musical treats (by various songwriters) included Waylon Jennings and Big Bird singing the country tune "Ain't No Road Too Long" as they rode along in a truck full of turkeys, and the whole cast, human and cloth, joining in singing the tender lullaby "One Little Star." Tony Garnett produced, Ken Kwapis directed, and Jim Henson was in charge of the puppeteering. Some of the same team reunited fifteen years later for *The Adventures of Elmo in Grouchland* (1999), which had fun paralleling *THE WIZARD OF OZ* (1939).

FOLLOW THE FLEET (RKO 1936). With FRED ASTAIRE and GINGER RODGERS and seven new IRVING BERLIN songs, no one minded that the plot had been used previously on Broadway and in Hollywood. Dwight Taylor and Allan Scott's screenplay was based on the play *Shore Leave* (1922), which had become the Broadway musical *HIT THE DECK* (1927), which had been filmed in 1930 (and would be again in 1955). Ex-hoofer Bake

Baker (Astaire) is in the navy leading a band and with his buddy Bilge Smith (RANDOLPH SCOTT) goes on leave in San Francisco where they come across Sherry Martin (Rogers) and her sister Connie (HARRIET HILLIARD) at the Paradise Ballroom. Connie falls for Bilge and makes plans to refurbish an old schooner for him, necessitating a benefit performance highlighted by Baker and Sherry performing "Let's Face the Music and Dance," perhaps Berlin's most seductive and magical song. Other musical numbers included Astaire and the sailors chanting "We Saw the Sea" and then breaking into "I'd Rather Lead a Band" on deck, Hilliard's solo renditions of the ballads "But Where Are You?" and "Get Thee Behind Me, Satan," and Rogers and Astaire cutting loose on the dance floor with "Let Yourself Go" and rehearsing "I'm Putting All My Eggs in One Basket" as a competitive dance on board the schooner. MARK SANDRICH directed for producer PANDRO S. BERMAN, and HERMES PAN and Astaire did the choreography.

📖 **FOLLOW THE GIRLS** (Century Theatre 1944). A rather juvenile piece of escapism during wartime, the silly musical comedy was a particular favorite with enlisted men going through New York to overseas assignments. Burlesque queen Bubbles LaMarr (GERTRUDE NIESEN) does her bit for the war effort by taking over a canteen where there are plenty of girls and only service personnel are allowed. This means Bubbles' rotund 4-F boy friend Goofy Gale (JACKIE GLEASON) has to dress up like a WAVE to get in to see his own sweetheart. GUY BOLTON, Eddie Davis, and Fred Thompson wrote the libretto and Phil Charig (music), Dan Shapiro, and Milton Pascal (lyrics) the songs and none were much to speak of; "I Wanna Get Married," "You Don't Dance," and "You're Perf" were the better efforts. The thin storyline left room for plenty of specialty acts so the musical often resembled a glorified burlesque show. The press recommended it as escapist entertainment and war-weary playgo-ers kept the musical running for 882 performances.

📖 **FOLLOW THRU** (46th Street Theatre 1929). As the title suggests, this musical comedy was about golf, although romance and laughs were featured more than the sport. The libretto by B. G. DeSYLVA and LAURENCE SCHWAB was set at the Bound Brook Country Club and concerned the rivalry between Lora Moore and Ruth Van Horn for the club's golf championship and for the handsome golf pro Jerry Downs. Also on the chase is the brash Angie Howard who is after the hapless but endearing department store heir Jack Martin. It takes a lot of plotting and some delightful DeSylva, LEW BROWN, and RAY HENDERSON songs before the two men are snapped up for good. From the score came the popular "Button Up Your Overcoat," as well as such fun numbers as "You Wouldn't Fool Me, Would You?," "I Want to Be Bad," "My Lucky Star," and the title song. While the whole cast was applauded, it was newcomer JACK HALEY who got the most praise for his shy, funny portrayal of a weakling. EDGAR MacGREGOR directed the Schwab–FRANK MANDEL production, BOBBY CONNOLLY was the choreographer, and the "musical slice of country club life" ran a very profitable 403 performances.

🎬 **Follow Thru** (Paramount 1930) afforded Jack Haley his screen debut and it was an auspicious one, with his performance leading to other reticent, comic roles in twenty films over the next sixteen years. His partner ZELMA O'NEAL was retained from the stage production but of the Broadway score only "Button Up Your Overcoat" and "I Want to Be Bad" were kept. DeSylva, Brown, and Henderson, and various other songwriters, provided new numbers for the film, including "A Peach of a Pair," "It Must Be You," and "Then I'll Have Time for You." The favorite screen couple NANCY CARROLL and CHARLES "BUDDY" ROGERS played the leading couple but again it was Haley and O'Neal who were more fun. Schwab adapted his libretto for the screen with

Casts for *Follow Thru*		
Character	*1929 Broadway*	*1930 film*
Jerry Downs	John Barker	CHARLES "BUDDY" ROGERS
Lora Moore	Irene Delroy	NANCY CARROLL
Ruth Van Horne	Madeline Cameron	Thelma Todd
Angie Howard	ZELMA O'NEAL	Zelma O'Neal
Jack Martin	JACK HALEY	Jack Haley
J. C. Effingham		EUGENE PALLETTE

Lloyd Corrigan and it was not too different from the original; the two also directed the movie, which was shot in early Technicolor so the golf course was actually green.

▄ **FOOTLIGHT PARADE** (Warner 1933). Even though it has a dynamite score by HARRY WARREN (music) and AL DUBIN (lyrics) and others and vintage performances by JAMES CAGNEY and company, the musical is most remembered for the fantastical BUSBY BERKELEY production numbers that seem to top themselves in the film's last reel. Instead of being about putting on a Broadway show, the Manuel Seff and James Seymour screenplay was about the production of "prologues," minimusicals presented in movie theatres as preshow entertainment. The hyperactive producer Chester Kent (Cagney in his first screen musical) produces prologues for a chain of Manhattan movie houses but all his ideas are being stolen by the competition. His secretary Nan Prescott (JOAN BLONDELL) loves her boss so she discovers who the culprit is and, putting the romantic couple Scotty Blair (DICK POWELL) and Bea Thorn (RUBY KEELER) in featured spots, Chester rehearses three prologues at the same time and premieres them in three different theatres on the same night. That fact that these minimusicals were so huge and lavish that no one theatre could accommodate them just adds to the ridiculousness of the backstager. When the three prologues are finally unveiled, reality has quite disappeared. For the "By a Waterfall" number, dozens of girls dive and swim for nearly fifteen minutes while Powell and Rudy dream away in each other's arms. "Honeymoon Hotel" showed groups of newlyweds checking in to a Jersey City hotel and preparing for bed, with a lot of singing and smirking about the activities to follow. The final prologue is "Shanghai Lil" in which the melancholy sailor Cagney searches through a Chinese saloon and an opium den looking for (and eventually finding) his long-lost Lil (Keeler) before they both set out for sea. Irving Kahal and SAMMY FAIN contributed to the score, which also included "Ah, the Moon Is Here" and "Sittin' on a Backyard Fence," and the colorful supporting cast included GUY KIBBEE, Ruth Donnelly, Claire Dodd, FRANK MCHUGH, HERMAN BING, and HUGH HERBERT. In many ways the movie really belongs to Cagney who propels the action, sings with no-nonsense bite, and dances with the determination of an athlete. LLOYD BACON directed the DARRYL F. ZANUCK production with just enough crazy abandonment to make it all work.

▄ **FOOTLOOSE** (Indie Prod./Paramount 1984). Although it had a plot that would make the corniest 1930s musical blush, the film was a hit because so many moviegoers bought the prereleased soundtrack album that they went *into* the theatres singing the songs. Dean Pitchford's screenplay asked us to believe that dancing has been outlawed in the small midwestern town of Beaumont. Newcomer Ren McCormack (Kevin Bacon) arrives from the big city and routs the restless teens to battle the local minister Rev. Moore (John Lithgow) to allow everyone to cut the rug and they win, just as Ren wins the heart of the minister's daughter Ariel (Lori Singer). Former choreographer HERBERT ROSS directed, letting Lynne Taylor-Corbett handle the dances, and the movie kept moving even though it had nowhere to go. Except for the title song by Kenny Loggins, the rest of the score was written and tacked onto the soundtrack after filming was complete. The result was another 1980s musical in which no one in the cast sang, but some of the songs (by Pitchford and various composers) became hits: "Let's Hear It for the Boy," "Almost Paradise," and "Holding Out for a Hero."

🎵 **Footloose** (Richard Rodgers Theatre 2000) emphasized dance and the choreography by A. C. Ciulla was the only aspect of the production the critics didn't veto. Pitchford

Casts for *Footloose*		
Character	*1984 film*	*2000 Broadway*
Ren McCormack	Kevin Bacon	Jeremy Kushnier
Ariel Moore	Lori Singer	Jennifer Laura Thompson
Rev. Moore	John Lithgow	Stephen Lee Anderson
Vi Moore	Dianna Wiest	Dee Hoty
Willard Hewitt	Chris Penn	Tom Plotkin
Rusty	Sarah Jessica Parker	Stacy Francis
Woody	John Laughlin	

Footloose. By the 1980s, a Hollywood musical could survive very well without a score as long as there was plenty of dancing and a pounding soundtrack to dance to. In *Footloose*, Kevin Bacon (center) played a trouble-making teen who defies the local law and teaches the kids to dance. (Photofest)

and director WALTER BOBBIE wrote the stage libretto, and new musical numbers were added to the soundtrack songs from the film and given to different characters to sing but the show never felt like a book musical. Audiences who loved the film and enjoyed the dancing had no trouble keeping the show on the boards for 709 performances, and the musical enjoyed subsequent productions regionally and in London.

FOR ME AND MY GAL (MGM 1942). A period musical that used World War I-era standards for its score, the film introduced GENE KELLY to movie audiences and gave JUDY GARLAND her first formidable screen partner other than MICKEY ROONEY. The cocky Kelly and the hesitant Garland made an electric duo, especially when they delivered the title song together. The screenplay by Richard Sherman, Fred Finklehoffe, and SID SILVERS was heavier than the usual musical fare. The vaudeville trio of Harry Palmer (Kelly), Jo

Hayden (Garland), and Jimmy Metcalf (GEORGE MURPHY) work their way from a hick berg in Iowa to New York City but there are complications. Jimmy loves Jo, Jo loves Harry, and Harry only loves success. Just as it looks like the trio is to play the Palace Theatre, Harry gets his draft notice. He purposely smashes his hand in a trunk and is rejected by the army (and by Jo). Only after seeing the error of his ways and entertaining the troops in Europe does Harry reunite with Jo for a triumph at the Palace. "Oh, You Beautiful Doll," "After You've Gone," "When You Wore a Tulip," "Till We Meet Again," and "Where Do We Go From Here?" were among the old favorites sung with gusto by the cast. BUSBY BERKELEY directed and left the choreography to BOBBY CONNOLLY, although Kelly devised some of his own dances. The ARTHUR FREED production was a box office success, Kelly's movie career was launched, and Garland's went in a new, more adult direction.

FOR THE BOYS (Fox 1991). A musical vehicle for BETTE MIDLER, the fifty-year melodramatic saga was buoyed by some terrific renditions of popular songs through the ages. The screenplay by Marshall Brickman, Nel Jemenez, and Lindy Laub followed the tempestuous love–hate relationship between USO entertainers Dixie Leonard (Midler) and Eddie Sparks (James Caan) from when they first work together during World War II until they come to some kind of understanding in the 1990s. During those years they perform for American troops in the Korean and Vietnam wars even as they separate and reconcile like clockwork. What never got tiresome were the songs from those periods and Midler hit the right notes in every time period. Caan also held his own and some of their duets were very potent. Among the old and not-so-old favorites performed were "Stuff Like That There," "P. S. I Love You," "Dreamland," "Come Rain or Come Shine," "In My Life," "Baby, It's Cold Outside," "For All We Know,' "Every Road Leads Back to You," "Billy-a-Dick," and "I Remember You" used as a kind of leitmotif throughout the movie. Mark Rydell directed the musical, which was not well reviewed but found an audience because of Midler's popularity (and performance).

FORAN, DICK [born John Nicholas Foran] (1910–1979). Film and television performer. A rugged-looking, red-haired leading man who made over 200 feature films, many of them

B westerns, he started as a song-and-dance man and occasionally returned to musicals. Foran was born in Flemington, New Jersey, and educated at Princeton before starting his career singing on the radio and with bands. He made his screen debut with a specialty spot in the musical *Stand Up and Cheer* (1934) and then went on to play singing heroes in westerns and tough but nice types in many other genres as well. Among his musical credits are *Lottery Lover* (1935), *Shipmates Forever* (1935), *Song of the Saddle* (1935), *Cowboy From Brooklyn* (1938), *In the Navy* (1941), *Keep 'Em Flying* (1941), *Behind the Eight Ball* (1941), *Private Buckaroo* (1942), and *Hi, Buddy* (1943). Foran also starred in the 1943 Broadway revival of *A CONNECTICUT YANKEE*. He appeared in dozens of television programs in the 1950s and 1960s, including the TV musical *Burlesque* (1955).

FORBIDDEN BROADWAY (1982). A very small-scale revue that spoofed Broadway shows and stars, it was first presented at Palsson's supper club and for over twenty-five years has continued as it moved from one Off Broadway location to another. The revue has gone through many editions over the years, each time slightly retitled and updated to lampoon the most recent shows. Gerard Alessandrini writes and directs each new edition, which usually uses the original music from stage musicals but is reset with satirical lyrics. The shows mock all of the Broadway entries democratically and most songwriters are pleased to allow their music to be used in the revues. The cast members are usually unknowns but with a talent for impersonation or mimicry and sometimes when the material is weak the performances make the show still worthwhile. A parallel program called *Forbidden Hollywood* was attempted in the early 1990s but it failed to catch on.

FORD, HELEN [born Helen Isabel Barnett] (1897–1982). Stage performer. A tiny, perky soprano, she lit up the stage in several 1920s musicals. Ford was born in Troy, New York, and was on the stage as a child. She made her New York debut in 1919 and the next year was featured as Toinette in OSCAR HAMMERSTEIN'S first musical, *Always You*. Ford became a star as the enterprising Mary Thompson in *The Gingham Girl* (1922), followed by *Helen of Troy, New York* (1923), and *No Other Girl* (1924). She began a fruitful relationship with the young songwriters RICHARD RODGERS and LORENZ HART and librettist HERBERT FIELDS when she

starred as the rebellious colonial Betsy Burke in *DEAREST ENEMY* (1925), followed by playing the title roles in the trio's *PEGGY-ANN* (1926) and *Chee-Chee* (1928). Ford's last two Broadway musicals were *Champagne Sec* (1933) and *Great Lady* (1938). Much of the rest of her career was spent performing on tour and in England, but she returned to Broadway in 1942 as Lucy in a revival of *The Rivals*.

FOREVER PLAID (Steve McGraw's 1990). A tiny entertainment that became a long-run hit Off Broadway, the revue was a pleasing blend of mockery and affection for the all-guy quartets of the 1950s and early 1960s. Stuart Ross wrote, directed, and choreographed the show about an amateur group called the Plaids, consisting of Sparky (Jason Graae), Jinx (Stan Chandler), Smudge (David Engel), and Frankie (Guy Stroman), who died in a car crash on the way to their first professional gig and are now in heaven doing their act. Patterned after the Four Aces, The Four Lads, the Four Freshmen, and other four-part harmony groups, the Plaids sing the popular nonrock songs of the 1950s, including such easy-listening favorites as "Three Coins in the Fountain," "Heart and Soul," "Shangri-La," and "Love Is a Many-Splendored Thing." There is some amusing chitchat between the numbers but most of the revue is the songs, sung with skill and sincerity. Audiences of all ages enjoyed the show for 1,811 performances, most with a nostalgic fondness, some laughing at the naiveté of the foursome and their repertoire, and many just discovering the songs for the first time and liking them. The economic little revue remains popular in summer stock, community theatres, and schools.

FORREST, GEORGE. See WRIGHT, Robert, and George FORREST

FORTUNE TELLER, THE (Wallack's Theatre 1898). VICTOR HERBERT'S sixth Broadway entry, this exotic and romantic operetta is the musical that firmly placed him as the premiere operetta composer in America. HARRY B. SMITH wrote the lyrics and the libretto about the heiress Irma (Alice Nielson) who is studying ballet in Budapest and falls in love with the handsome hussar Ladislas (Frank Rushworth) even though she is being coerced to marry Count Berezowski (Joseph Herbert). Irma hires the gypsy girl Musette (also Nielson), who looks like her, to take her place and entertain the count while Irma goes to Ladislas. Musette's gypsy lover Sandor (Eugene Cowles) learns that she is seeing a count and the complications mount. The piece was written as a vehicle for Neilson but Cowles got to join her on the operetta's two most famous numbers, "Gypsy Love Song" and "Romany Life." Also in the score were "Always Do as People Say You Should," "Gypsy Jan," and "The Lily and the Nightingale." The original production of *The Fortune Teller* was a touring one so it only stayed in New York for forty performances but the operetta would be regularly revived across the country for the next thirty years.

FORTY-FIVE MINUTES FROM BROADWAY (New Amsterdam Theatre 1906). Arguably GEORGE M. COHAN's best musical, it is a tightly constructed melodrama that has only five songs but each one is first rate and they fit neatly into the plot. Cohan's libretto is set in New Rochelle, New York, a community only forty-five minutes from Times Square by train, and concerns Tom Bennett (DONALD BRIAN) who inherits his uncle's estate and plans to use the money to wed the celebrated actress Flora Dora Dean (Lois Ewell). The people of New Rochelle were hoping that the deceased millionaire left his fortune to his dedicated maid and nurse Mary Jane Jenkins (FAY TEMPLETON), which is why the devious Dan Cronin (James H. Manning) had been courting Mary, hoping to get his hands on the money. Tom's secretary Kid Burns (VICTOR MOORE) goes to New Rochelle to go through the papers and falls in love with Mary. When he discovers the real will, one that leaves everything to Mary, he is afraid Mary will think he is a fortune hunter if he proposes marriage to her. Mary destroys the will to see if Kid really loves her and, when she finds out he does, is happy to lose the money to Tom in order to find true happiness. The waltzing "Mary's a Grand Old Name," the robust "I Want to Be a Popular Millionaire," the catchy "So Long, Mary," the wry "Gentlemen of the Press," and the satiric title number were all tuneful treats and the cast delivered them with panache. Templeton was an established star and Moore became a Broadway favorite as Kid Burns. In fact, Cohan immediately wrote *The Talk of New York* (1907) with Burns as the central character and Moore played the role again. *Forty-Five Minutes From Broadway* was staged by Cohan with razor-sharp precision and the Klaw–Erlanger production ran ninety performances.

42ND STREET (Warner-Vitaphone 1933). A pivotal movie in the history of the musical film, it revitalized the genre after two years of declining interest. It is the quintessential backstager and almost every aspect of it later became a cliché from overuse.

Plot: Hopeful Peggy Sawyer from Sioux City, Iowa, comes to New York to be on Broadway and is cast in the chorus of the new musical *Pretty Lady*, which is being produced by the moody, cold producer Julian Marsh who has lost all his money in the stock market crash. The money comes from wealthy Abner Dillon, and the Broadway star Dorothy Brock is the box office guarantee. Peggy befriends dancer–singer Billy Lawler, who teaches her the ropes, and "Anytime" Annie, who realizes that Peggy has what it takes. When Dorothy gets drunk and breaks her ankle, the backer Dillon insists that his girl friend Annie take over the lead but Annie convinces Julian that Peggy is the girl to save the show. After Julian admonishes to Peggy, "Sawyer, you're going out a youngster, but you've got to come back a star," she plays the lead in *Pretty Lady* and indeed becomes a star. As everyone celebrates, the loner Julian sits in the alley and quietly smokes his cigarette.

Casts for *42nd Street*

Character	1933 film	1980 Broadway	2001 Broadway
Julian Marsh	WARNER BAXTER	JERRY ORBACH	Michael Cumpsty
Peggy Sawyer	RUBY KEELER	Wanda Richert	Kate Levering
Billy Lawler	DICK POWELL	LEE ROY REAMS	David Elder
Dorothy Brock	BEBE DANIELS	TAMMY GRIMES	CHRISTINE EBERSOLE
Abner Dillon	GUY KIBBEE	Don Crabtree	Michael McCarty
Lorraine/Maggie	UNA MERKEL	Carole Cooke	MARY TESTA
Bert Barry	NED SPARKS	Joseph Bova	JONATHAN FREEMAN
Pat Denning	George Brent	James Congdon	Richard Muenz
Annie	GINGER ROGERS	Karen Prunczik	Mylinda Hull

42nd Street. Broadway musicals had chorus lines; Hollywood musicals had Busby Berkeley. It may have been all about a Broadway show, but *42nd Street* always looked like a film because choreographer Berkeley thought in terms of the camera, not the proscenium. This still from the movie's title number may seem like just a series of chorus lines but once Berkeley and his single camera got down into the crowd the look was completely different. (Photofest)

James Seymour and Rian James based their screenplay on Bradford Ropes's novel, which was much darker and risqué. Some of what survives is the somber, bitter character of Julian Marsh but mostly the musical is escapist fun. Also, *42nd Street* didn't look like the many Hollywood musicals that glutted the market in the preceding few years. BUSBY BERKELEY'S choreography did not recall a Broadway staging at all; his use of the camera to follow individuals in a production number or to view performers from angles not possible in a theatre made the film a true Hollywood musical rather than a film of a stage-like show. LLOYD BACON directed (with uncredited help from MERVYN LEROY) and there is a fast-paced urgency in the film that comes across in the rapid, wisecracking dialogue as well as in the production numbers. It was Keeler's first character part on screen and the movie made her a bigger star than "Peggy Sawyer." The movie was the first of twenty-three films scored by HARRY WARREN (music) and AL DUBIN (lyrics), the songwriters most associated with WARNER BROTHERS musicals. Although they only wrote five songs for the movie, it can be considered their masterwork for it captures both the anxiety and the carefree abandon of the Depression. The spirited "Young and Healthy" is full of optimism, there is a plaintive matter-of-fact quality in "You're Getting to Be a Habit With Me," a slyness creeps into "Shuffle Off to Buffalo," and there is something downright sinister about the joyful decadence of the title number. Depression audiences loved the gritty texture of the film as well as its escapism, and the score reflects this. The success of the movie prompted Warner Brothers to produce a series of similar backstagers with Berkeley creating more elaborate showpieces with each film. Few in the series would match the overall impact of *42nd Street* but it would be a golden age for the ridiculously joyous backstage movie musical.

42nd Street Musical Numbers

1933 film
"It Must Be June"
"You're Getting to Be a Habit With Me"
"Shuffle Off to Buffalo"
"Young and Healthy"
"Forty-Second Street"

Added for 1980 Broadway
"Shadow Waltz"
"Go Into Your Dance"
"Getting Out of Town"
"Dames"
"I Know Now"
"We're in the Money"
"Sunny Side to Every Situation"
"Lullaby of Broadway"
"About a Quarter to Nine"

🕮 ***42nd Street*** (Winter Garden Theatre 1980) used the basic plot of the movie and interpolated hit songs from several Warner Brothers films scored by Warren so the show sometimes resembled a revue about Hollywood musicals rather than a book musical. However, the whole package was so slickly done and the production values so spectacular that it was hard not to enjoy the piece. MICHAEL STEWART and Mark Bramble wrote the stage libretto in which the book scenes were reduced to short exchanges of dialogue in order to incorporate the nine added songs. A possible romantic interest was suggested between Peggy and Marsh and at one point in the musical he fires her from the show during the tryout tour. That allows Marsh and all the cast to go to the Philadelphia train station and convince Peggy to come and play the lead, using "Lullaby of Broadway" as their persuasion song. DAVID MERRICK was the shrewd producer of *42nd Street* and he spared no expense, making it the most lavish show Broadway had seen in years. The ingenious director–choreographer GOWER CHAMPION pulled it all together, in many ways becoming the show's true star. When Champion died on opening night, Merrick milked the sentiment from the occasion and promoted the musical as good old-fashioned entertainment, keeping it alive on Broadway for 3,486 performances, the biggest hit of his hit-filled career. A 2001 Broadway revival was directed by co-author Bramble with RANDY SKINNER providing the vivacious choreography. While sets and costumes could not compete with the original, there was much to enjoy in the bright production and the talented cast. The durable musical

was well reviewed and audiences kept it on the boards for 1,524 performances.

FOSSE. See *DANCIN'*

FOSSE, [Robert Louis] **BOB** (1927–1987). Stage, film, and television choreographer, director, and dancer. A celebrated artist who found success in all forms of entertainment, he had a style as distinctive and quirky as his personality. Fosse was born in Chicago, Illinois, the son of a salesman, and started dance lessons at the age of nine, performing professionally as a teen in local nightclubs, burlesque houses, and waning vaudeville theatres. He moved to New York City in 1946 and appeared in the chorus of a handful of forgotten Broadway musicals before going to Hollywood and getting better roles in movie musicals such as *KISS ME KATE* (1953), *GIVE A GIRL A BREAK* (1953), and *MY SISTER EILEEN* (1955). Fosse made his choreographer debut on Broadway with *THE PAJAMA GAME* in 1954 and his jazz-influenced style was immediately recognized as unique. His dances were rarely lyrical or ballet-like; instead the human body was contorted and used in new and unusual ways, everything from the tilt of the head to the outstretched fingertips working together to create a highly theatrical look. Fosse staged the dances for *DAMN YANKEES* (1955), *BELLS ARE RINGING* (1956), *Copper and Brass* (1957), *NEW GIRL IN TOWN* (1957), and *HOW TO SUCCEED IN BUSINESS WITHOUT REALLY TRYING* (1961), and both directed and choreographed *REDHEAD* (1959), *LITTLE ME* (1962), *SWEET CHARITY* (1966 and 1986), *PIPPIN* (1972), *CHICAGO* (1975), and *Big Deal* (1986). He recreated his stage choreography for the film versions of *The Pajama Game* (1957), *Damn Yankees* (1958), and *Sweet Charity* (1968), also directing the last. Fosse directed four other movies, including the musicals *CABARET* (1972) and *ALL THAT JAZZ* (1979). For television, he staged the popular special *Liza With a Z* (1972). He put together an evening of original dance pieces called *DANCIN'* (1978), and after his death a collection of his numbers was compiled as *FOSSE* (1999); both were Broadway hits. Fosse was a temperamental and demanding director–choreographer with an obsessive drive, yet he was highly respected and dancers always returned to work with him again. He was married to dancing star GWEN VERDON who was featured in five of his Broadway musicals. Biographies: *Bob Fosse*, Jenai Cutcher (2005); *All His Jazz: The Life and Death of Bob Fosse*, Martin Gottfried (1990/2003); *Razzle Dazzle: The Life and Work* *of Bob Fosse*, Kevin Boyd Grubb (1989); *Bob Fosse's Broadway*, Margery Beddow (1996).

FOSTER, SUSANNA [born Susanna DeLee Flanders Larson] (1924–). Film performer. A sprightly actress with a surprisingly high vocal range, the operatic teen singer was PARAMOUNT'S answer to DEANNA DURBIN. Foster was born in Chicago and was on screen by the age of twelve and then going to MGM where she was groomed for a screen career alongside JUDY GARLAND and MICKEY ROONEY. Her high soprano was used in her film debut, *The Great Victor Herbert* (1939), and then she played singing teens in such B musicals as *There's Magic in Music* (1941) and *Glamour Boy* (1941). She is most remembered as the frightened opera singer Christine in *Phantom of the Opera* (1943). Few of her subsequent musicals were noteworthy: *Top Man* (1943), *Follow the Boys* (1944), *This Is the Life* (1944), *Bowery to Broadway* (1944), *The Climax* (1944), *Frisco Sal* (1945), and *That Night With You* (1945). She left Hollywood in 1945 and appeared with her husband Wilbur Evans in operetta revivals in regional theatres and on tour before falling into obscurity. One of the finest voices of the era was neglected and misused by Hollywood.

FOSTER, SUTTON [Lenore] (1975–). Stage and television performer. A recently recognized singer–dancer with a traditional musical comedy persona, she has excelled in period musicals that allow her to flaunt her comic and musical talents. Foster was born in Statesboro, Georgia, and raised in Troy, Michigan, beginning her professional career in the national tour of *THE WILL ROGERS FOLLIES*. After studying for a while at Carnegie-Mellon University she performed in regional theatre, winning the title role in *THOROUGHLY MODERN MILLIE* at the La Jolla Playhouse in California. Foster's performance was so accomplished that she got to originate the role on Broadway in 2002, winning great acclaim. After playing the tomboy Jo in the Broadway musical version of *Little Women* (2005), she was again applauded for her vivacious performance as the starlet Janet in *THE DROWSY CHAPERONE* (2006). Her most recent Broadway credit is the yodeling fräulein Inga in *YOUNG FRANKENSTEIN* (2007). Foster has also acted on television. Her husband is stage actor Christian Borle (1973–) and her brother is stage actor Hunter Foster (1969–).

FOWLER, BETH (1940–). Stage and film performer. The matronly but classy singer–actress has given several memorable performances in supporting and leading roles in musicals. Fowler was born in Jersey City, New Jersey, educated at Caldwell College, and made her Broadway debut in the short-lived musical *Gantry* (1970). She shone as one of the lieder singers in *A LITTLE NIGHT MUSIC* (1973), the tragic Julie in the 1976 revival of *SHOW BOAT*, the doubtful mother-to-be Arlene in *BABY* (1983), the Victorian pie maker Mrs. Lovett in the 1989 revival of *SWEENEY TODD*, the teapot Mrs. Potts in *BEAUTY AND THE BEAST* (1994), the answering service owner Sue in *BELLS ARE RINGING* (2001), and the celebrity-crazy Marion Woolnough in *The Boy From Oz* (2003). Fowler's other musical credits include *1600 PENNSYLVANIA AVENUE* (1976), *FINIAN'S RAINBOW* (1977), *PETER PAN* (1979), *Preppies* (1983), *TAKE ME ALONG* (1985), and *Teddy and Alice* (1987). She has appeared in a handful of films, such as one of the singing nuns in *Sister Act* (1992) and *Sister Act 2: Back in the Habit* (1993).

FOY, EDDIE [born Edwin Fitzgerald] (1854–1928). Stage performer. A popular vaudeville star with a pointed nose and mumbling delivery, he played clownish sidekicks in a dozen Broadway musicals. The native New Yorker made his variety debut in Chicago and toured for years before reaching New York, making his legit debut in the comedy *Jack-in-the-Box* (1886). Soon his acrobatic dancing and puckish persona made him a favorite on Broadway and he was featured in such musicals as *Off the Earth* (1895), *Hotel Topsy-Turvy* (1898), *An Arabian Girl* (1899), *The Strollers* (1901), *The Wild Rose* (1902), *Mr. Bluebeard* (1903), *The Earl and the Girl* (1905), *Mr. Hamlet of Broadway* (1908), *Up and Down Broadway* (1910), and *Over the River* (1912). Foy left the legit stage in 1912 and toured with his children in a celebrated act, Eddie and the Seven Little Foys, even appearing together in a few silent films. By the late 1920s, the kids outgrew the act and Foy continued on alone. Only one of his offspring, EDDIE FOY, JR., continued on as a performer. BOB HOPE played the senior Foy in the biopic *The Seven Little Foys* (1955). Autobiography: *Clowning Through Life* (1928); biography: *Eddie Foy*, Armond Fields (1999).

FOY, EDDIE, JR. [born Edwin Fitzgerald, Jr.] (1905–1983). Stage, film, and television performer. The spry, physical comic played scene-stealing supporting roles in several Broadway and Hollywood musicals. He was born in New Rochelle, New York, the son of successful vaudeville comic EDDIE FOY, and was put on the stage as a boy in the variety act Eddie and the Seven Little Foys. Foy Jr., made his

Broadway debut in *Show Girl* (1929) and over the next thirty years frequently returned to the stage, most memorably as the zany American tourist Kid Conner in *THE RED MILL* (1945), a replacement for the con man Harrison Floy in *HIGH BUTTON SHOES* (1948), and efficiency expert Hines in *THE PAJAMA GAME* (1954). His other stage musicals include *Ripples* (1930), *Smiles* (1930), *THE CAT AND THE FIDDLE* (1931), *AT HOME ABROAD* (1935), *Rumple* (1957), and *Donnybrook* (1961). Foy made his screen debut in *Queen of the Night Clubs* (1929), followed by dozens of movie, including the musicals *LEATHERNECKING* (1930), *Broadway Through a Keyhole* (1933), *Four Jacks and a Jill* (1941), *Yokel Boy* (1942), *Dixie* (1943), *And the Angels Sing* (1944), *THE FARMER TAKES A WIFE* (1953), *Lucky Me* (1954), and *BELLS ARE RINGING* (1960). He played his father in two films, *LILLIAN RUSSELL* (1940) and *YANKEE DOODLE DANDY* (1942), and reprised his Hines in the screen version of *The Pajama Game* (1957). Foy appeared in many televisions shows, including the TV musicals *No Man Can Tame Me* (1959), *The Seven Little Foys* (1964), and *OLYMPUS 7-0000* (1966). He was the brother of film director producer Bryan Foy (1896–1977).

FRANK, MELVIN (1913–1988). Film director, scriptwriter, and producer. Usually working with his collaborator Norman Panama, he wrote several memorable screenplays and often directed and produced as well. Frank was born in Chicago and met Panama at the University of Chicago, the two of them going to Hollywood after graduation and writing comedies and musicals, including *HAPPY GO LUCKY* (1943), *THANK YOUR LUCKY STARS* (1943), *And the Angels Sing* (1944), *Duffy's Tavern* (1945), *ROAD TO UTOPIA* (1946), and *WHITE CHRISTMAS* (1954). He added director and sometimes producer to his credits for several more movies, including the musicals *THE COURT JESTER* (1956), *THE ROAD TO HONG KONG* (1962), and *A FUNNY THING HAPPENED ON THE WAY TO THE FORUM* (1966), which he co-wrote and produced. Frank's one Broadway effort was the popular *LI'L ABNER* (1956), which he co-wrote and directed and redid for the screen in 1959.

FRASER, ALISON (1955–). Stage and television performer. The vibrant, full-voiced actress–singer has been lauded for her vivid performances in plays and musicals but has not yet come across the role or vehicle to make her a stage star. Fraser was born in Natick, Massachusetts, and educated at Carnegie Mellon and the Boston Conservatory of Music. She made her Off Broadway debut in 1975 and then was cast in two of the *FALSETTOS* musicals: *In Trousers* (1979) and *March of the Falsettos* (1981), originating the character of the frustrated wife Trina in the second. Fraser's two most memorable Broadway appearances were as the twin heroines Josefine and Monica in *Romance, Romance* (1988) and the Yorkshire maid Martha in *THE SECRET GARDEN* (1991). Her other musical credits include *Beehive* (1986), a replacement in *THE MYSTERY OF EDWIN DROOD* (1986), *Swingtime Canteen* (1995) and *GYPSY*. She has performed on television in both children's shows and dramatic series, has done many voices for animated programs, and has recorded two solo albums.

FRAWLEY, WILLIAM [Clement] (1887–1966). Television, film, and stage performer. A beloved character actor of over 150 films and a notable television career, the paunchy comic usually played gruff but warmhearted types. Frawley was born in Burlington, Iowa, and began his career in vaudeville as a song-and-dance man. He eventually made it to Broadway where he performed in the musicals *Merry, Merry* (1925), *Bye, Bye, Bonnie* (1927), *She's My Baby* (1928), *Here's Howe* (1928), *Sons o' Guns* (1929), *Tell Her the Truth* (1932), and in comedies as well. Frawley went to Hollywood in 1932 where he was featured in supporting but notable roles in all genres of film, including such musicals as *Moonlight and Pretzels* (1933), *Harmony Lane* (1935), *Strike Me Pink* (1936), *HIGH, WIDE AND HANDSOME* (1937), *Mad About Music* (1938), *ROSE OF WASHINGTON SQUARE* (1939), *St. Louis Blues* (1949), *ONE NIGHT IN THE TROPICS* (1940), *RHYTHM ON THE RIVER* (1940), *Moonlight in Havana* (1942), *Sing Out, Sisters* (1942), *GOING MY WAY* (1944), *Lake Placid Serenade* (1944), *ZIEGFELD FOLLIES* (1946), *I Wonder Who's Kissing Her Now* (1947), *MOTHER WORE TIGHTS* (1947), *My Wild Irish Rose* (1947), and *The Lemon Drop Kid* (1951). He found greater fame as Fred Mertz on the long-running television series *I Love Lucy* and in the 1960s was a regular on *My Three Sons*. Biography: *Meet the Mertzes: The Life Stories of I Love Lucy's Other Couple*, Rob Edelman, Audrey Kupferberg (1999).

FRAZEE, JANE [born Mary Jane Freshe] (1918–1985). Film and television performer. A leading lady in many B musicals in Hollywood, the attractive singer–actress was well known to audiences without ever becoming a major star. Frazee was born in Duluth, Minnesota, and was in vaudeville as a child, touring in a kiddie act with her sister Ruth. The two performed together for years, appearing in nightclubs and on the radio, but split when the studios wanted only Jane. After some musical shorts, Frazee made her feature debut in *Melody and Moonlight* (1940) and was featured or starred in twenty-six other musicals, including *BUCK PRIVATES* (1941), *San Antonio Rose* (1941), *HELLZAPOPPIN'* (1941), *What's Cookin'?* (1942), *Get Hep to Love* (1942), *Moonlight in Havana* (1942), *When Johnny Comes Marching Home* (1942), *Hi' Ya Chum* (1943), *Rhythm of the Islands* (1943), *Rosie the Riveter* (1944), *Kansas City Kitty* (1944), *Swing in the Saddle* (1944), *Calendar Girl* (1947), *SPRINGTIME IN THE ROCKIES* (1947), *The Gay Ranchero* (1948), and *Grand Canyon Trail* (1948). Frazee retired from films in the late 1940s and turned to television where she appeared in many programs and was a regular on the series *Beulah* before giving up show business and going into real estate.

FREED, ARTHUR [born Arthur Grossman] (1894–1973). Film producer and songwriter. Arguably the most influential producer of Hollywood musicals, he was also an expert lyricist with many hit songs to his credit. A native of Charleston, South Carolina, Freed began his career as a song plugger for a music publisher and then performed in vaudeville before enlisting in the service during World War I. After the armistice, Freed returned to vaudeville where he started writing song lyrics for his act and for others. His first hit song, "I Cried for You," came out in 1923, but Freed changed careers again and went to Hollywood where he directed silent films. With the coming of sound, MGM hired him to write lyrics for original songs to be featured in the talkies. With composer NACIO HERB BROWN, he wrote the scores for such early film musicals as *THE BROADWAY MELODY* (1929), *HOLLYWOOD REVUE OF 1929* (1929), *GOOD NEWS!* (1930), *GOING HOLLYWOOD* (1933), *BROADWAY MELODY OF 1936* (1935), and *BROADWAY MELODY OF 1938* (1937). After serving as co-producer for the classic *THE WIZARD OF OZ* (1939), Freed abandoned lyric writing for producing. He established the celebrated "Freed Unit" at MGM and for the next twenty years presented some of the greatest of all Hollywood musicals, including *BABES IN ARMS* (1939), *STRIKE UP THE BAND* (1940), *LITTLE NELLY KELLY* (1940), *LADY, BE GOOD* (1941), *BABES ON BROADWAY* (1941), *FOR ME AND MY GAL* (1942), *CABIN IN THE SKY* (1943), *DUBARRY WAS A LADY* (1943) *BEST FOOT FORWARD* (1943), *GIRL CRAZY* (1943), *MEET ME*

IN ST. LOUIS (1945), *THE HARVEY GIRLS* (1946), *TILL THE CLOUDS ROLL BY* (1947), *Good News!* (1947), *SUMMER HOLIDAY* (1948), *EASTER PARADE* (1948), *WORDS AND MUSIC* (1948), *TAKE ME OUT TO THE BALL GAME* (1949), *THE BARKLEYS OF BROADWAY* (1949), *ON THE TOWN* (1949), *ANNIE GET YOUR GUN* (1950), *ROYAL WEDDING* (1951), *SHOW BOAT* (1951), *AN AMERICAN IN PARIS* (1951), *THE BELLE OF NEW YORK* (1952), *SINGIN' IN THE RAIN* (1952), *THE BAND WAGON* (1953), *BRIGADOON* (1954), *IT'S ALWAYS FAIR WEATHER* (1955), *SILK STOCKINGS* (1957), *GIGI* (1958), and *BELLS ARE RINGING* (1960). For what is arguably his greatest achievement, *Singin' in the Rain*, the catalogue of Freed's old songs with Brown was used. His brother was movie lyricist Ralph Freed (1907–1973).

FREELAND, THORNTON (1898–1987). Film director. Working both in America and in Great Britain, he helmed a number of light comedies and escapist musicals. Freeland was born in Hope, North Dakota, and was on the stage as a youth before joining Vitagraph at the age of eighteen as a cutter, cameraman, and then director just as sound came in. He helmed a series of musicals in the early 1930s, including *Be Yourself* (1930), *WHOOPEE* (1930), *FLYING DOWN TO RIO* (1933), and *GEORGE WHITE'S SCANDALS* (1934). Freeland relocated to England in 1935 and directed several films there, including the musicals *Brewster's Millions* (1935), *Paradise for Two* (1937), and *Gaiety Girls* (1938) and then returned to Hollywood during the war and turned out more light fare, including the musical *Too Many Blondes* (1941), before retiring in 1949.

FREEMAN, JONATHAN (1950–). Stage and television performer. A tall, deep-voiced character actor, he has often been singled out for his comic performances in supporting roles in musicals. Freeman was born in Bay Village, Ohio, and educated at Ohio University. He made his New York debut in *Sherlock Holmes* (1974) and then was featured in the musicals *Platinum* (1978), *SHE LOVES ME* (1993), *BEAUTY AND THE BEAST* (1994), *HOW TO SUCCEED IN BUSINESS WITHOUT REALLY TRYING* (1995), *PETER PAN* (1998), *ON THE TOWN* (1998), *A Class Act* (2001), *42ND STREET* (2001), *THE PRODUCERS* (2001), and *THE LITTLE MERMAID* (2008). Freeman's distinctive and versatile voice has been used for the Bil Baird Marionette Theatre productions and many Disney television shows and movies, most memorably as the voice of the villain Jafar in *ALADDIN* (1992) and its video sequels. He has appeared in several television programs and a few films.

FREES, PAUL [born Solomon Hersh Frees] (1920–1986). Television and film actor. Dubbed the "Man of a Thousand Voices" for his vast collection of dialects and impersonations, he provided the voices for dozens of animated characters in hundreds of films and television programs. Frees was born in Chicago and worked in radio before he served in World War II, afterward studying at the Chouinard Art Institute before returning to the radio microphone. By 1942 he was in Hollywood where he recorded over mispronunciations by foreign actors, dubbed voices for foreign films, and lent his voice to animated characters in shorts at WALT DISNEY PICTURES and other studios. With the arrival of television, Frees was busier than ever and voiced such series characters as Boris Badenov and Inspector Fenwick in *The Bullwinkle Show*, Professor Ludwig Von Drake in *The Wonderful World of Disney*, The Thing in *The Fantastic Four*, George Harrison in *The Beatles*, and the Pillsbury Doughboy. In addition to animated feature film musicals, such as

One Hundred and One Dalmatians (1961) and *GAY PURR-EE* (1962), Frees provided voices for fifteen original animated musicals on television, including *MR. MAGOO'S CHRISTMAS* (1962), *Cricket on the Hearth* (1967), *Frosty the Snowman* (1969), *SANTA CLAUS IS COMIN' TO TOWN* (1970), *Here Comes Peter Cotton Tail* (1971), *Rudolph's Shiny New Year* (1976), *The Hobbit* (1977), *THE STINGIEST MAN IN TOWN* (1978), *RUDOLPH AND FROSTY'S CHRISTMAS IN JULY* (1979), and *THE WIND IN THE WILLOWS* (1987). His recorded voice can heard throughout the Disneyland and Disney World theme parks, from The Pirates of the Caribbean to the Haunted Mansion.

FRIML, RUDOLF [Charles] (1879–1972). Stage and film composer. One of the American theatre's premiere composers of operettas, he enjoyed a sensational career until operettas went out of fashion. Friml was born in Bohemia into a poor but musical family and at an early age displayed remarkable musical

Rudolf Friml. The acclaimed composer was left high and dry when the Depression hit and Broadway was no longer interested in operetta. Luckily Hollywood put out a series of movie operettas in the 1930s and Friml saw some of his stage works filmed. MGM totally rewrote *The Firefly* (1937) but much of Friml's music survived, including this number which was sung and danced by Jeanette MacDonald. (Photofest)

abilities. Friends of the family raised money so that the youth could study at the Prague Conservatory where he received a scholarship and studied with Antonin Dvorák. Friml first came to America as the accompanist for famed violinist Jan Kubelik, remaining in the States where he wrote and performed without much success. When composer VICTOR HERBERT refused to work with temperamental soprano EMMA TRENTINI, the job of composer for *THE FIREFLY* (1912) fell to Friml who found sudden fame for such compositions as "Giannina Mia" and "Love Is Like a Firefly." Subsequent operettas, such as *High Jinks* (1913), *Katinka* (1915), *Kitty Darlin'* (1917), *The Little Whopper* (1919), and *Cinders* (1923), were not as successful, but he found success again when he teamed up with lyricists OTTO HARBACH and OSCAR HAMMERSTEIN on the phenomenally popular *ROSE-MARIE* (1924). The trio also scored *The Wild Rose* (1926) before parting ways. While the heyday of operetta flourished, Friml also had hits with his scores for *THE VAGABOND KING* (1925) and *THE THREE MUSKETEERS* (1928) but failed with *The White Eagle* (1927), *Luana* (1930), and *Music Hath Charms* (1924). Hollywood filmed *The Vagabond King* in 1930 and 1956, *The Firefly* in 1937, and *Rose Marie* in 1936 and 1954 and he contributed some songs for them. Friml also wrote music for the screen musicals *The Lottery Bride* (1930), *Music for Madame* (1937), and *Northwest Outpost* (1947), none of which were popular. As Broadway's fascination with operetta declined, Friml tried to compose in the more prevalent musical comedy mode but he had no success, but in his heyday few composed such lilting melodies and vigorous marches.

FROHMAN, CHARLES (1860–1915). Stage producer and manager. A much-admired and respected presenter of theatre on both sides of the Atlantic, the enterprising producer offered Broadway thirty musicals during his career, as well as another thirteen in London. Frohman was born in Sandusky, Ohio, the son of a traveling peddler, and went to New York at the age of twelve to work for various newspapers. By 1877 he was helping to book touring theatre productions and, with his brothers Daniel and Gustave, eventually managed the prestigious Madison Square Theatre in Manhattan. Frohman began producing in 1888 and over the next three decades presented new American plays, vehicles for stars, foreign language works adapted for Broadway, British hits, and musicals, including

His Excellency (1895), *The Girl From Up There* (1901), *Three Little Maids* (1903), *The Rich Mr. Hoggenheimer* (1906), *The Hoyden* (1907), *The Dollar Princess* (1909), *The Arcadians* (1910), *The Girl From Montmartre* (1912), *The Marriage Market* (19213), *The Laughing Husband* (1914), and *THE GIRL FROM UTAH* (1914). Frohman managed theatres in New York and London, was famous for creating and nurturing stars, such as Ethel Barrymore, Maude Adams, and John Drew, and for the high quality and good taste of his productions. He was at the height of his career when he drowned during the sinking of the *Lusitania*. Biography: *Charles Frohman: Manager and Man*, Isaac F. Marcosson, Daniel Frohman (1916).

FRONTIER MUSICALS. Since professional theatre in the twentieth century was mainly an urban activity and most composers, lyricists, and librettists were born and raised in cities, the musical theatre has always concentrated on city locations, primarily New York followed by Paris as the most frequent settings. A musical set in the wilderness or even a small town was always in the minority, as many Broadway shows were about Broadway. However, as musical comedies focused on cities, nightclubs, penthouses, and such, operettas (particularly the ones from Europe) tended to be rural and even pastoral. American operettas followed that pattern with *NAUGHTY MARIETTA* (1910), *ROSE-MARIE* (1924), *RIO RITA* (1927), *SHOW BOAT* (1937), *NEW MOON* (1928), and other works that mostly took place in the American countryside. One of the surprising aspects of *OKLAHOMA!* (1943) was its frontier setting for a nonoperetta musical. Usually when musical comedies were set outdoors, as with *WHOOPEE!* (1928) and *GIRL CRAZY* (1930), it was to make fun of the rural hicks. *Oklahoma!* took a more affectionate view of the characters and was not only set in the country, it was *about* the land as well. Other musicals over the years that had such a frontier aspect include *ANNIE GET YOUR GUN* (1946), *PAINT YOUR WAGON* (1951), *DESTRY RIDES AGAIN* (1959), *THE UNSINKABLE MOLLY BROWN* (1960), *SHENANDOAH* (1975), and *BIG RIVER* (1985). It was in Hollywood that the frontier musical was far from a minority. From the earliest silents, movies were about the outdoors and westerns and other rural films held a fascination for moviegoers. The first film musicals copied Broadway, setting their tales in New York and being about the big show. It wasn't long before the studios realized that their musicals could go places where even the most lavish Broadway shows could not. When *Naughty Marietta* (1935), *Rose-Marie* (1936), *Show Boat* (1936), and other rural stage works were filmed, the crew went on location and showed the audience the Mississippi River or the Canadian Rockies. Soon Hollywood started writing its own frontier musicals, created with the outdoors in mind, and were opened up to take advantage of location shooting. Among the many such films were *Hallelujah* (1929), *Mississippi* (1935), *High, Wide and Handsome* (1936), *Riding High* (1943), *Can't Help Singing* (1945), *Belle of the Yukon* (1945), *The Harvey Girls* (1946), *The Kissing Bandit* (1948), *The Paleface* (1948), *The Beautiful Blonde From Bashful Bend* (1949), *Son of Paleface* (1952), *Calamity Jane* (1953), *The Farmer Takes a Wife* (1953), *Seven Brides for Seven Brothers* (1954), and *Pocahontas* (1995). Early television, confined to a small studio and often broadcast live, had even more limitations than the stage and frontier musicals looked rather artificial so they were avoided. However, even when the TV camera left the studio and went on location, few rural musicals were made. Perhaps it was too difficult to compete with Hollywood's wide screen exteriors or maybe television studios thought much like Broadway and were more interested in urban settings. In either case, most TV musicals with a frontier setting were those based on stage works.

FRYER, ROBERT (1920–2000). Stage and film producer. A presenter of Broadway plays and musicals from the 1950s through the 1980s, he often co-produced with Lawrence Carr. Fryer was born in Washington, DC, and educated at Western Reserve University before working as a casting director and assistant producer. His first Broadway musical was *A Tree Grows in Brooklyn* (1951) co-produced with GEORGE ABBOTT, followed by *Wonderful Town* (1953), *By the Beautiful Sea* (1954), *Shangri-La* (1956), *Redhead* (1959), *Saratoga* (1959), *Hot Spot* (1963), *Sweet Charity* (1966), *Mame* (1966), *Chicago* (1975), *On the Twentieth Century* (1978), *They're Playing Our Song* (1979), *Sweeney Todd* (1979), *Merrily We Roll Along* (1981), and *A Doll's Life* (1982). Fryer also produced several plays, which were, like his musical, eclectic in style, subject, and flavor. He presented the TV version of *Wonderful Town* (1958) and produced a dozen films, including the screen *Mame* (1974). Near the end of his career he served as artistic director of the Ahmanson Theatre in Los Angeles.

FULL MONTY, THE (Eugene O'Neill Theatre 2000). A musical version of the popular 1997 British film, the show was Americanized with the location moved from industrial England to Buffalo, New York, although the title (an English expression meaning complete nudity) stayed the same. A group of out-of-work factory laborers in Buffalo find that money is to be made during ladies' night at strip joints so they put together a striptease act and advertise that full frontal nudity will be the climax of the show. The plan wrecks havoc on their personal lives until the big night comes and they are a hit. TERRENCE MCNALLY wrote the efficient libretto, and David Yazbek wrote the pop songs, which included "You Rule My World," "Breeze Off the River," "You Walk With Me," "Big Black Man," " Big-Ass Rock," and "Let It Go." Some critics may have had their doubts about the musical but everyone thought the cast exceptional: PATRICK WILSON, Jason Danieley, ANDRE DE SHIELDS, John Ellison Conlee, Todd Weeks, Romain Frugé, Kathleen Freeman, Emily Skinner, and Annie Golden. JACK O'BRIEN was the inventive director, the playful dances were choreographed by JERRY MITCHELL, and favorable word of mouth helped keep the show on the boards for 770 performances.

FUNICELLO, ANNETTE (1942–). Television and film performer. The most famous member of the *Mickey Mouse Club* gang, the dark-haired smiling actress went from playing a wholesome preteen wearing Mickey ears on television to a wholesome teen wearing a bathing suit in films. Funicello was born in Utica, New York, and started her television career in 1956, appearing in WALT DISNEY shows and other programs on occasion. She made her big screen debut in the Disney adventure film *Johnny Tremain* (1957) followed by a few other nonmusicals and the musical *Babes in Toyland* (1961). She outgrew her TV spot but continued to appear in Disney films even as she did a string of beach musical movies in the 1960s, usually paired with FRANKIE AVALON. *Beach Party* (1963), *Muscle Beach Party* (1964), *Bikini Beach* (1964), *Beach Blanket Bingo* (1965), *Fireball 500* (1966), *How to Stuff a Wild Bikini* (1967), and *Pajama Party* (1967) were naive, tuneful, and harmless musicals that were very popular. Funicello made television appearances sporadically in the 1970s and 1980s. The TV movie *Frankie and Annette: The Second Time Around* (1978) and the "reunion" film musical *Return to the Beach* (1987) with Avalon were welcomed by nostalgic moviegoers. Her autobiography, *A Dream Is a Wish Your Heart Makes: My Story* (1995), recounted her battle with multiple sclerosis and Eva La Rue played Funicello in the TV movie version of the book.

☙ FUNNY FACE (Alvin Theatre 1927). The combination of the Gershwins and the Astaires made this musical comedy a special treat and it inspired another hit fifty-six years later. The libretto by Fred Thompson and Paul Gerard Smith centered on the strict guardian Jimmy Reeves (FRED ASTAIRE) who refuses to let his ward Frankie (ADELE ASTAIRE) have her jewels, so she schemes with her sweetheart, the aviator Peter Thurston (ALLEN KEARNS), to attempt to steal them. Also after the jewels are two comic crooks, Herbert (VICTOR MOORE) and Dugsie (William Kent), who fail in their efforts because they cannot get along with each other. By the final curtain, Jimmy comes round and Frankie has her jewels and her flyer. It wasn't the most original of plots but it left plenty of room for song and dance, both of which were superior. GEORGE GERSHWIN (music) and his brother IRA GERSHWIN (lyrics) came up with such musical gems as the smooth "He Loves and She Loves," the slaphappy "'S Wonderful," the toe-tapping "High Hat," the tongue-in-cheek "The Babbitt and the Bromide," and the entrancing title song. BOBBY CONNOLLY was the choreographer and provided the Astaires with some sensational dance routines, and the AARONS–FREEDLEY production, directed by EDGAR MACGREGOR, ran 250 performances. **My One and Only** (St. James Theatre 1983) started out as a revival of *Funny Face* but by the time it opened, the production had gone through four directors, cast changes, a new book, scenery alterations, and a new title. Barnstorming American pilot Captain Billy Buck Chandler (TOMMY TUNE) plans to fly solo from New York to Paris but is distracted by a romance with an English champion swimmer Edith Herbert (Twiggy) and run-ins with bootlegging minister J. D. Montgomery (Roscoe Lee Browne), Russian spy Prince Nicolai (Bruce McGill), and philosophical Mr. Magix (Charles "Honi" Coles) of Harlem. Six songs from *Funny Face* were retained and supplemented with other Gershwin numbers, such as "I Can't Be Bothered Now," "Nice Work If You Can Get It," "Kickin' the Clouds Away," and "Sweet and Low Down." Critics stated that it was all an anachronistic mess but topflight entertainment thanks to the luscious old tunes, the congenial performers, and the contagious dancing. Tune and THOMMIE

WALSH were the final director–choreographers, PETER STONE and Timothy S. Mayer the credited librettists, and the show was a surprise hit, running 767 performances.

🎬 **Funny Face** (Paramount 1957) kept Fred Astaire, the title, and the title song from the Broadway musical and went off in its own direction, resulting in one of the most stunning-looking musicals of the 1950s. It was about fashion photography and the celebrated photographer Richard Avedon served as consultant so the look of the film was unique. The on-site locations in New York City and Paris certainly helped as director STANLEY DONEN turned each sequence into a dazzling magazine spread. Leonard Gershe's screenplay was about fashion photographer Dick Avery (Astaire) who discovers the brainy Jo Stockton (AUDREY HEPBURN, doing her own singing) working in a Greenwich Village bookstore and is determined to make a star model out of her. With the help of fashion magazine editor Maggie Prescott (KAY THOMPSON), who wants the women of the world to "think pink," he whisks Jo off to Paris for a shoot and, succumbing to the charms of the man and the city, she falls in love with Dick while becoming a famous cover girl. EUGENE LORING and Astaire did the choreography, with the most memorable moments being Astaire's solo "Let's Kiss and Make Up," in which a raincoat and umbrella become his partner, and a lyrical *pas de deux* with Hepburn and Astaire dancing to "He Loves and She Loves" through a morning mist rising from a pond. The other Gershwin songs used included "Clap Yo' Hands," "How Long Has This Been Going On?," and "'S Wonderful," while ROGER EDENS (music) and Gershe (lyrics) added "Bonjour, Paris!," "On How to Be Lovely," and "Think Pink!"

☙ FUNNY GIRL (Winter Garden Theatre 1964). Purportedly a musical biography about the great comedienne–singer FANNY BRICE, the show ended up being a vehicle for the sensational newcomer BARBRA STREISAND. Isobel Lennart's libretto followed the awkward, stage-struck Fanny from her futile auditions to get on stage to her discovery by FLORENZ ZIEGFELD to her becoming a comic singing star of the *Ziegfeld Follies*. But Fanny has less luck in keeping her husband, the gambling addict Nicky Arnstein (Sydney Chaplin), and when he is convicted for a phony bond scheme, he goes to jail and Fanny is left only with her career. JULE STYNE (music) and BOB MERRILL (lyrics) wrote the pleasing score that included

Casts for *Funny Girl*		
Characters	*1964 Broadway*	*1968 film*
Fanny Brice	BARBRA STREISAND	Barbra Streisand
Nick Arnstein	SYDNEY CHAPLIN	Omar Sharif
Mrs. Brice	KAY MEDFORD	Kay Medford
Eddie Ryan	Danny Meehan	Lee Allan
Florenz Ziegfeld	Roger De Koven	WALTER PIDGEON

the runaway hit "People" and other accomplished songs such as "The Music That Makes Me Dance," "His Love Makes Me Beautiful," "I'm the Greatest Star," "You Are Woman," "Don't Rain on My Parade," and "Who Are You Now?" Streisand's performance made her a star but it was her last Broadway appearance. Garson Kanin directed, CAROL HANEY choreographed, and Ray Stark produced. Helped by strong reviews and the popularity of the song "People," the musical ran 1,348 performances, remaining popular even after Streisand left the show.

🎬 *Funny Girl* (Rastar/Columbia) was a first-class film version of the Broadway hit and, just as the stage work had made Streisand a Broadway star, the screen version made her a movie star. Only half of the Styne–Merrill songs were used in the film and a few new ones were added, including a title number and the standard "My Man." Lennart adapted her libretto into a commendable screenplay, opening up the action effectively, such as putting the determined song "Don't Rain on My Parade" on a series of transports ending on a tugboat in the New York harbor. Most of the supporting characters from the stage were abridged or deleted, but Omar Sharif managed to be a strong presence as the gambler Nick. WILLIAM WYLER directed with skill, and HERBERT ROSS staged the *Follies* numbers with wit and style. Yet all it really came down to was Streisand who was in every scene and sang every song. With the confidence of a veteran trouper, she turned her screen debut into a polished tour de force.

🎬 *Funny Lady* (Rastar/Columbia 1973). A musical sequel to the popular *Funny Girl* (1968), it utilized the some of the same creative team and offered another high-powered performance by BARBRA STREISAND as FANNY BRICE, but it was a rather disjointed affair and was not as popular at the box office. All the same, there are many enjoyable aspects to the films, such as a lively performance by James Caan and some delightful production numbers. The screenplay by Jay Presson Allen and

Arnold Schulman begins with Fanny's gambler husband Nick Arnstein (Omar Sharif) getting out of jail and asking for a divorce. Fanny marries songwriter–producer BILLY ROSE (Caan) on the rebound but his infidelities destroy the marriage and Brice is alone once again. The plot was mercifully broken up by eighteen songs, some standards from the period, such as "Am I Blue?," "I Found a Million Dollar Baby in a Five-and-Ten Cent Store," "It's Only a Paper Moon," and "Great Day," and new ones by JOHN KANDER (music) and FRED EBB (lyrics), including the breezy "How Lucky Can You Get," the plaintive "Isn't This Better?," and the affirming "Let's Hear It For Me." HERBERT ROSS directed and also choreographed the production numbers.

🎬 *FUNNY THING HAPPENED ON THE WAY TO THE FORUM, A* (Alvin Theatre 1962). One of the most amusing musical comedies of the post-war era, it also marked the first full score, music and lyrics, by STEPHEN SONDHEIM. The raucous libretto by BURT SHEVELOVE and LARRY GELBART was based on some Roman plays by Plautus, and the ancient Roman setting and characters were retained but the musical was also a vaudeville-like romp filled with merry anachronisms. The conniving slave Pseudolus promises his young master Hero that he will get him the beautiful virgin Philia as his wife in exchange for granting Pseudolus his freedom. Since Philia has been purchased by the puffed-up soldier Miles Gloriosus and Hero's hen-pecked father Senex lusts after the girl himself, there are plenty of comic complications. To convince Miles that his intended has died of plague, Pseudolus stages a mock funeral with fellow slave Hysterium acting as the dead virgin. It all goes awry and, after a farcical chase involving all the characters, Hero gets Philia and Pseudolus wins his freedom. Sondheim's songs were often clever pastiches of vaudeville, burlesque, and old-time musical farces and each one was as tuneful as it was funny. Highlights from the score include the marching theme song "Comedy Tonight," the soft-shoe number "Everybody Ought to

A Funny Thing Happened on the Way to the Forum. The anachronistic musical set in ancient Rome relied on vaudeville and burlesque humor and required resourceful comics rather than actors. With Zero Mostel, pictured back to back with Roberta Keith, it had both. (Photofest)

GEORGE ABBOTT directed with his customary talent for fact-paced musical comedy but it was JEROME ROBBINS, who was called in during the out-of-town tryouts, who gave the show its winning touch. JACK COLE choreographed the dances, and HAROLD PRINCE produced the show, which was well received by the press and the public and ran 964 performances. The musical has long been a favorite with all kinds of theatre groups. There have also been two Broadway revivals. Shevelove directed a 1972 production that was highly praised but could only find an audience for five months. PHIL SILVERS led the strong cast as Pseudolus, and LARRY BLYDEN was particularly applauded as Hysterium. NATHAN LANE starred as Pseudolus in a sprightly 1996 revival directed by JERRY ZAKS. Some critics quibbled about the young cast's ability to do the old-time schtick but admitted the musical was still a joyous romp. Audiences agreed for 715 performances.

🎬 **A Funny Thing Happened on the Way to the Forum** (United Artists 1966) kept Zero Mostel and JACK GILFORD from the Broadway cast but tossed out all but five of the songs, and three of them were heard in a very abridged form. Scriptwriters MELVIN FRANK and Michael Pertwee kept all the best jokes, condensed the silly plot somewhat, and came up with a comedy with songs. RICHARD LESTER directed with an eye for the offbeat, making ancient Rome something of a freak show and cross-cutting from place to place as he did in the BEATLES movies *A HARD DAY'S NIGHT* (1964) and *HELP!* (1965). Lester does stage the opening "Comedy Tonight!" with flair but "Everybody Ought to Have a Maid" was given a busy, jokey treatment so that one laughed at what the director was doing rather than what the characters were singing. The cast is strong throughout and the movie certainly moves at a good clip. The result is a pleasing comedy but an unsatisfying musical.

Have a Maid," the vapid love song "Lovely," the bouncy "Pretty Little Picture," the nervous character ditty "I'm Calm," and the sly duet "Impossible." The cast included some seasoned comics, in particular ZERO MOSTEL who served as narrator and tied all the shenanigans together with his oversized performance.

Casts for *A Funny Thing Happened on the Way to the Forum*

Characters	1962 Broadway	1966 film	1972 Broadway	1996 Broadway
Pseudolus	ZERO MOSTEL	Zero Mostel	PHIL SILVERS	NATHAN LANE
Hero	BRIAN DAVIES	MICHAEL CRAWFORD	John Hansen	Jim Stanek
Hysterium	JACK GILFORD	Jack Gilford	LARRY BLYDEN	Mark Linn-Baker
Senex	DAVID BURNS	Michael Hordern	Lew Parker	LEWIS J. STADLEN
Domina	Ruth Kobart	Patricia Jessel	Lizbeth Pritchett	MARY TESTA
Lycus	John Carradine	PHIL SILVERS	Carl Ballantine	Ernie Sabella
Philia	Preshy Marker	Annette Andre	Pamela Hall	Jessica Boevers
Miles	RON HOLGATE	Leon Greene	Carl Lindstrom	Cris Groenendaal
Erronius	Raymond Walburn	Buster Keaton	REGINALD OWEN	William Duell

G

GABOR, EVA AND ZSA ZSA. Stage, film, and television performers. Two glamorous, heavily accented sisters from Hungary who were as known for their many marriages and celebrity as their performances, both were featured in musicals. The Gabors were born in Budapest and were well-known beauties before they came to America. Zsa Zsa Gabor [born Sari Gabor] (1917–) was on the Vienna stage at the age of fifteen and was crowned Miss Hungary in 1936. She arrived in America in 1941 and became famous for her marriages to and divorces from actor George Sanders, hotelier Conrad Hilton, and five others, collecting jewels and notoriety along the way. Appearances on television led to roles in movies, including the musicals *LOVELY TO LOOK AT* (1952), *LILI* (1952), and *Pepe* (1960). Zsa Zsa Gabor also acted in comedies on tour and on Broadway. Her flair for being celebrated for being a celebrity has been carried by her step-great-granddaughter Paris Hilton. Eva Gabor (1910–1995) was the more accomplished actress of the sisters, beginning her career as a cafe singer and ice-skating performer in her native country. She came to America in the late 1930s and made many Hollywood films, including the musicals *ARTISTS AND MODELS* (1955) and *GIGI* (1958), and did voices for the animated features *THE ARISTOCATS* (1970), *THE RESCUERS* (1977), and *The Rescuers Down Under* (1990). Eva Gabor acted in a few Broadway comedies and was a replacement in the musical *Tovarich* (1963). She appeared on dozens of television programs but is most remembered as the ditzy New Yorker Lisa living on the farm in the comedy series *Green Acres* (1965–1971). Although Eva Gabor was considered the more stable of the two sisters, she was married five times. A third sister, Magda Gabor (1914–1997), was also well known for her six marriages (including one to George Sanders as well) and her scattered television appearances. Autobiographies: *Orchids and Salamis* [Eva] (1951); *One Lifetime Is Not Enough* [Zsa Zsa] (1991). Biographies: *Such Devoted Sister: Those Fabulous Gabors*, Peter Harry Brown (1985); *Eva Gabor: An Amazing Woman*, Camyl Sosa Belanger (2005).

GAINES, BOYD [Payne] (1953–). Stage and television performer. The boyish-looking, very physical leading man has usually attracted attention in even small roles in both plays and musicals. Gaines was born in Atlanta and trained at Juilliard before making his New York stage debut in 1978. He appeared in classic and modern revivals Off Broadway and then found recognition in the play *The Heidi Chronicles* (1989). Gaines entered musicals late, garnering attention for his lovesick Georg in *SHE LOVES ME* (1993), followed by lauded performances as bachelor Robert in *COMPANY* (1995), writer Cliff Bradshaw in *CABARET* (1999), the suicidal Michael in *CONTACT* (1999) and Herbie in *GYPSY* (2008). Gaines has acted in many plays and on television in dramatic series as well as sit-coms. He has made a few films, including *FAME* (1980).

GALLAGER AND SHEAN. Stage performers. One of the most famous of all vaudeville comedy duos, the "Dutch comics" appeared together on Broadway and in a few films during their brief but unforgettable career. The American Ed Gallagher (1873?–1949) was a skinny, bespectacled straight man who began his career doing comic military sketches with his partner Joe Barnett for several years. In 1919 he teamed up with Al Shean [born Albert Schonberg] (1868–1949) who was born in Dornum, Germany, but grew up in New York City where he went into vaudeville as a member of the Manhattan Comedy Four. Shean was short and stocky with a thick German accent and the two men were hilarious foils for each other. Their most famous routine was singing "Mr. Gallagher and Mr. Shean" in which they asked each other a series of silly questions. Gallagher and Shean stopped the show when they performed it in the *ZIEGFELD FOLLIES* (1922) and later recorded it. The team's other Broadway musicals were *Rose Maid* (1912), *Greenwich Village Follies* (1923), and the 1924 edition of *Ziegfeld Follies*. The partners quarreled and split up on occasion, finally parting for good in 1925. Gallagher suffered a nervous breakdown and retired but Shean continued on and had success as a character actor in plays and musicals, most memorably the elderly music teacher D. Lessing in *MUSIC IN THE AIR* (1932). He reprised the role in the 1934 film version and appeared in many other films, including ZIEGFELD GIRL (1941) in which he sang "Mr. Gallagher and Mr. Shean" with CHARLES WINNINGER as Gallagher. Shean's other screen musicals include *Sweet Music* (1935), SAN FRANCISCO (1936), ROSALIE (1937), THE GREAT WALTZ (1938), *Broadway Serenade* (1939), and *The Daughter of Rosie O'Grady* (1942). Shean was the uncle of the MARX BROTHERS.

GALLAGHER, HELEN (1926–). Stage and television performer. An energetic singer–actress who never quite achieved stardom on Broadway, she replaced stars and headed revivals in New York and across the country and finally became famous on television. A native of Brooklyn, Gallagher studied dance at the American Ballet School and then appeared in the chorus of the Broadway musicals *Seven Lively Arts* (19440, *Mr. Strauss Goes to Boston* (1945), *Billion Dollar Baby* (1945), and BRIGADOON (1947) before getting featured in HIGH BUTTON SHOES (1947), *Touch and Go* (1949), and *Make a Wish* (1951). She received wide recognition for her funny Gladys in the 1951 revival of PAL JOEY and then played leading roles in the revivals of GUYS AND DOLLS (1955), FINIAN'S RAINBOW (1955), *Brigadoon* (1957), and OKLAHOMA! (1958). Gallagher was roundly commended for her sarcastic Nicky in SWEET CHARITY (1966) and later took over the title role and then was again praised for her light-footed Lucille in the 1971 revival of NO, NO, NANETTE. Her other New York musicals include *Hazel Flagg* (1953), *Portofino* (1958), MAME (1968), *Cry for Us All* (1970), *A Broadway Musical* (1978), and SUGAR BABIES (1979 and 1981). Gallagher was in the TV musical *Paris in the Springtime* (1956) and returned to television in the 1970s where she appeared on hundreds of programs, from music specials to soap operas.

GALLAGHER, RICHARD "SKEETS" (1891–1955). Stage and film performer. A blonde-haired, easy-going song-and-dance man with a breezy demeanor, he was featured in Broadway and Hollywood musicals in the 1920s and 1930s. Gallagher was born in Terre Haute, Indiana, and studied for a law career for a time but succumbed to the stage and did an act in vaudeville before making his Broadway debut in the musical *Above the Clouds* (1922). After playing lightweight roles in the musicals *Up She Goes* (1922), *Marjorie* (1924), *The Magnolia Lady* (1924), *The City Chap* (1925), and *Lucky* (1927), he went to California where he was cast in second leads or supporting parts in over fifty

movies, including the musicals *Close Harmony* (1929), *Pointed Heels* (1929), *Honey* (1930), PARAMOUNT ON PARADE (1930), *Let's Go Native* (1930), *Love Among the Millionaires* (1930), *Too Much Harmony* (1933), *Hats Off* (1936), *Zis Boom Bah* (1942), and *Jam Session* (1944).

GANG'S ALL HERE, THE (Fox 1943). This colorful extravaganza was 20TH CENTURY-FOX's most expensive musical of the war years and one only has to look at director–choreographer BUSBY BERKELEY's production numbers to see where the money went. "The Lady in the Tutti-Fruitti Hat" number featured CARMEN MIRANDA, wagon loads of colorfully dressed peasants on a plantation, and thousands of bananas (including some large phallic ones making risqué patterns) all combined to form geometric patterns. For the finale, "The Polka Dot Polka," ALICE FAYE, a gang of children from different time periods, and a nightclub chorus all performed in front of revolving mirrors that made dizzying kaleidoscopic images. It was Berkeley's first film in Technicolor and the effect was practically psychedelic. The screenplay by WALTER BULLOCK centered on the showgirl Edie Allen (Faye) at a Manhattan nightclub who is romanced by the playboy soldier Andy Mason (James Ellison). He tells her his name is Casey and then is shipped off to the Pacific. Not until he returns a war hero and Edie is hired with other chorines to entertain at Andy's family mansion do they meet again and she makes him forget the fiancée Vivian Potter (Sheila Ryan) his family has chosen for him. CHARLOTTE GREENWOOD, EDWARD EVERETT HORTON, Phil Baker, and EUGENE PALLETTE wandered in and out of the plot to grab laughs when Miranda was occupied elsewhere, and BENNY GOODMAN provided the requisite band needed to fill out the production numbers. HARRY WARREN (music) and LEO ROBIN (lyrics) wrote most of the score, which also included the hit ballads "No Love, No Nothin'" and "A Journey to a Star," both sung by Faye in her last film for nineteen years. WILLIAM LEBARON produced and stopped worrying about the expense once the movie opened and was a hit.

GARBER, VICTOR [Joseph] (1949–). Stage, television, and film performer. The tall, baby-faced leading man of plays and musicals has played everything from Jesus Christ to the devil. Garber was born in London, Ontario, Canada, and worked in regional and stock companies before playing Jesus in a Toronto production of GODSPELL in 1972. The next year he reprised the role in the film version and then headed to New York where he made his debut in the classic drama *Ghosts* (1973). Garber established himself in some plays, such as the hit thriller *Deathtrap* (1978), before appearing as the sailor Anthony Hope in *SWEENEY TODD* (1979) and frequently returned to comedies and dramas on stage and later in films and on television. His other New York musical credits include a replacement for songwriter Vernon in *THEY'RE PLAYING OUR SONG* (1981), various wacky characters in *LITTLE ME* (1982), John Wilkes Booth in *ASSASSINS* (1991), and the devil Mr. Applegate in *DAMN YANKEES* (1994). Garber rarely got to sing in his films but he shone in TV musicals, playing the King in *CINDERELLA* (1997), Daddy Warbucks in *ANNIE* (1999), and Mayor Shinn in *THE MUSIC MAN* (2003). He was also featured in the original TV rock opera *Jack: A Flash Fantasy* (1977).

GARDINER, [William] **REGINALD** (1903–1980). Stage, film, and television performer. The dapper English character actor of the London and New York stage appeared in fourteen Hollywood musicals, usually playing butlers or aristocrats with the same snob persona. Gardiner was born in Wimbleton, England, and educated at the Royal Academy of Dramatic Art. He delivered wry comic monologues and impersonated trains and wallpaper in British variety, the legit stage, and in a few English films before coming to America and appearing in the Broadway revue *AT HOME ABROAD* (1935) with **BEATRICE LILLIE**. He returned for *THE SHOW IS ON* (1936) and *An Evening With Beatrice Lillie* (1952) and as Alfred Doolittle in *MY FAIR LADY* (1964), but much of his time was spent in California where he made his Hollywood debut in *BORN TO DANCE* (1936). Gardiner, with his clipped speech and clipped mustache, played supporting roles in such musicals as *DAMSEL IN DISTRESS* (1937), *SWEETHEARTS* (1938), *Everybody Sing* (1938), *Sweet Rose O'Grady* (1943), *THE DOLLY SISTERS* (1945), *I Wonder Who's Kissing Her Now* (1947), *WABASH AVENUE* (1950), *Ain't Misbehavin'* (1955), and *Rock-a-Bye Baby* (1958). He also appeared on television in sit-coms, quiz shows, and specials.

GARLAND, JUDY [born Frances Ethel Gumm] (1922–1969). Film and television performer. Bonding with her audience with a greater emotional grip than perhaps any other movie musical star, the actress–singer–dancer won moviegoers over with her innocence in her

Judy Garland. Throughout her film career, Garland introduced many song standards, from "Over the Rainbow" to "The Man That Got Away." Yet she was also an expert interpreter of old favorites in such period musicals such as *In the Good Old Summertime* (1949) where she sang "Play That Barber Shop Chord" with a barber shop quartet. (Photofest)

early films, her sense of eager romance in her adult movies, and her struggle for survival in her later concerts and television appearances. Garland was born in Grand Rapids, Minnesota, the daughter of vaudevillians, and was on stage at the age of three. By the time she was five she was touring in a polished vaudeville act with her sisters called the Gumm Sisters Kiddie Act, getting a reputation as the "little girl with the great big voice." When the act broke up, Garland's ambitious stage mother brought her to Hollywood and as a young teen she made some musical shorts before getting featured in the musicals *Pigskin Parade* (1936), *BROADWAY MELODY OF 1938* (1937), *Everybody Sing* (1938), *Listen, Darling* (1938), and *Love Finds Andy Hardy* (1938), her first teaming with **MICKEY ROONEY**. Full-fledged stardom came with her luminous performance in *THE WIZARD OF OZ* (1939), followed by a series of successful "let's put on a show" musicals with Rooney: *BABES IN ARMS* (1939), *Andy Hardy Meets Debutante* (1940), and *STRIKE UP THE BAND* (1940). With

LITTLE NELLIE KELLY (1940) and *ZIEGFELD GIRL* (1941), Garland edged into adulthood and remained popular in musicals such as *BABES ON BROADWAY* (1941), *FOR ME AND MY GAL* (1942), *Presenting Lily Mars* (1943), and *GIRL CRAZY* (1943). She was perhaps at the peak of her powers in the films *MEET ME IN ST. LOUIS* (1944), *THE HARVEY GIRLS* (1946), *THE PIRATE* (1948), *EASTER PARADE* (1948), and *IN THE GOOD OLD SUMMERTIME* (1949), also shining in specialty spots in *Thousands Cheer* (1943), *ZIEGFELD FOLLIES* (1946), *TILL THE CLOUDS ROLL BY* (1946), and *WORDS AND MUSIC* (1948). The strain of her difficult life, her battle with pills and alcohol, and her failed marriages started to show in *SUMMER STOCK* (1950) but when she returned to the screen in *A STAR IS BORN* (1954), she gave what many feel is her greatest performance. Garland's final musical credits were doing voices for *Pepe* (1960) and the animated *GAY-PURR-EE* (1962) and the disappointing *I Could Go On Singing* (1962). She made several nonmusicals and appeared on many television programs, having her own variety show in the 1960s. Although Garland was primarily a singer with the ability to interpret a song in a personal and sometimes even desperate way, her acting and dancing talents were considerable and her persona on the screen was never less than magnetic. Judy Davis played the legendary singer in the TV biomusical *Life With Judy Garland: Me and My Shadows* (2001). Her five husbands include composer David Rose (1910–1990), director VINCENTE MINNELLI, and producer Sidney Luft (1915–2005), and her daughters are LIZA MINNELLI and Lorna Luft (1952–). Memoir: *Me and My Shadows: A Family Memoir*, Lorna Luft (1999); biographies: *Heartbreaker*, John Meyer (2006); *Get Happy: The Life of Judy Garland*, Gerald Clarke (2001); *Judy*, Gerold Frank (1999).

GARRETT, BETTY (1919–). Stage, film, and television performer. A veteran of many forms of show business, the wisecracking singer–comedienne never because a major star in any venue but was a recognized face and applauded performer in many musicals. Garrett was born in St. Joseph, Missouri, the daughter of a traveling salesman, and grew up in Tacoma, Washington, winning a scholarship to the Neighborhood Playhouse School in Manhattan where she studied acting, singing, and dancing. She made her professional acting debut in the Mercury Theatre production of *Danton's Death* (1938) and then appeared in the revues *You Can't Sleep Here* (1940), *A Piece of Our Mind* (1940), *All in Fun* (1941), *Let*

Freedom Ring (1942), and *Of V We Sing* (1942) before getting featured in *SOMETHING FOR THE BOYS* (1943). Garrett appeared in *Jackpot* (1944) and *Laffing Room Only* (1944) before bringing down the house singing "South America, Take It Away" in *CALL ME MISTER* (1946). She made her movie debut in the musical *Big City* (1948), followed by major roles in *WORDS AND MUSIC* (1948), *TAKE ME OUT TO THE BALL GAME* (1949), *NEPTUNE'S DAUGHTER* (1949), and *ON THE TOWN* (1949). She and her husband LARRY PARKS appeared together in nightclub acts but when he was blacklisted in the 1950s her career also suffered. Garrett got to shine again on screen in *MY SISTER EILEEN* (1955) and on Broadway as a replacement for JUDY HOLLIDAY in *BELLS ARE RINGING* (1958). By the 1960s she concentrated on television where she appeared in specials, dramas, and sit-coms. Garrett returned to Broadway on occasion, playing the housemaid Katie in *MEET ME IN ST. LOUIS* (1980) and the old hoofer Hattie in *FOLLIES* (2001). Autobiography: *Betty Garrett and Other Songs: A Life on Stage and Screen* (2000).

GARRICK GAIETIES, THE (Garrick Theatre 1925). A small-scale musical revue that helped push the genre toward a more satirical, literate level, the show is also noteworthy for establishing the careers of songwriters RICHARD RODGERS (music) and LORENZ HART (lyrics). The New York subway system, President Calvin Coolidge, the Scopes "Monkey Trial" (performed by apes), the Three Musketeers, and the THEATRE GUILD (who produced the show) and its arty productions were all spoofed in sketches by Benjamin M. Kaye, Sam Jaffe, Edith Meiser, MORRIE RYSKIND, and others. Planned as a fundraiser for the Guild, the revue was written, staged, and performed by young members of the company, including Philip Loeb, Edith Meiser, STERLING HOLLOWAY, June Cochrane, Betty Starbuck, LIBBY HOLMAN, Sanford Meisner, Romney Brent, and Lee Strasberg. The show, scheduled for a single matinee and one evening performance, so charmed the critics and audiences that the Guild extended it and had a money-maker for 211 performances. Seven songs by the young Rodgers and Hart were featured, most famously the ballad "Manhattan," which quickly became a standard, and "Sentimental Me," which was also popular. Also in the show were "April Fool," Mr. and Mrs.," "The Three Musketeers," "Do You Love Me (I Wonder)?," and "Black and White." Much of the creative staff and cast members from the first edition were reunited for *The Garrick Gaieties of 1926*, which ran a healthy 174 performances. Again most of the score was by Rodgers and Hart and again they had a standout hit with "Mountain Greenery." Spoofed this time around were Nijinsky and the ballet world, sports, operetta, and recent Guild productions. Also in the score were "Keys to Heaven," "What's the Use of Talking?," and "Sleepyhead." There was also an extended operetta spoof "Rose of Arizona," which is considered the forerunner for later musical pastiches such as *LITTLE MARY SUNSHINE* (1959) and *THE DROWSY CHAPERONE* (2006). A version containing material from both editions toured in the fall of 1926. Four years later the series returned a final time. *The Garrick Gaieties of 1930*, which was presented in the Guild's larger home theatre, still managed a healthy run. Rodgers and Hart did not contribute any songs this time around, but the score included the early work of IRA GERSHWIN, JOHNNY MERCER, E. Y. HARBURG, MARC BLITZSTEIN, and VERNON DUKE. None of the songs became hits and the third edition of *The Garrick Gaieties* was more remembered for introducing performers IMOGENE COCA, RAY HEATHERTON, and, in a return engagement of the show, ROSALIND RUSSELL.

GAXTON, WILLIAM [born Arturo Antonio Gaxiola] (1893–1963). Stage and film performer. The good-looking leading man of Broadway musicals and a few films had a distinguished appearance that was in contrast to the brash, pushy schemers that he usually played. Gaxton was born in San Francisco where he attended military school and the University of California before going into vaudeville. His comedy act got enough notice that he was added to the cast of the 1922 edition of *MUSIC BOX REVUE*, after which he became a favorite in musical comedies. Among his many notable roles were the New Englander Martin stuck in Camelot in *A CONNECTICUT YANKEE* (1927), the millionaire Peter posing as a tour guide in Paris in *FIFTY MILLION FRENCHMEN* (1929), the presidential John P. Wintergreen in *OF THEE I SING*

(1931) and *LET 'EM EAT CAKE* (1933), the enterprising stowaway Billy Crocker in *ANYTHING GOES* (1934), foreign correspondent Buckley Joyce Thomas in *LEAVE IT TO ME!* (1938), and the shady lawyer Jim Taylor in *LOUISIANA PURCHASE* (1940). His other Broadway musicals include *White Horse Inn* (1936), *Keep 'Em Laughing* (1942), *Hollywood Pinafore* (1945), and *Nellie Bly* (1946). Gaxton was often paired with comic VICTOR MOORE, with the former's fast-talking bombast providing a delightful contrast with Moore's slow, wimpy delivery. Gaxton did not get to reprise any of his great Broadway roles on film but he was featured in the movie musicals *STAGE DOOR CANTEEN* (1943), *BEST FOOT FORWARD* (1943), *Something to Shout About* (1943), *The Heat's On* (1943), and *Diamond Horseshoe* (1945), as well as the TV musical *The Box Supper* (1950).

GAY DIVORCE (Ethel Barrymore Theatre 1932). A notable COLE PORTER musical that introduced the song "Night and Day," it concluded FRED ASTAIRE's Broadway career. Wishing to get a divorce from her scientist husband, Mimi Bratt (Claire Luce) arranges with her lawyers to be caught in a seaside hotel room with the professional correspondent Tonetti (ERIK RHODES). Guy Holden (Astaire), who is in love with Mimi, follows her to the hotel where he is mistaken for correspondent and complications ensue. By the finale Mimi gets her divorce and Guy. Dwight Taylor wrote the lighthearted musical comedy, which also featured ERIC BLORE, LUELLA GEAR, G. P. Huntley, Jr., Betty Starbuck, and Roland Bottomley. Other songs in the Porter score included "After You, Who?," "I Still Love the Red, White and Blue," "I've Got You on My Mind," "Mr. and Mrs. Fitch," and "You're in Love." Used to seeing Astaire with his sister Adele, the critics were not so supportive of the dancing star in his first show without her. But the success of the song "Night and Day" turned the musical into a hit, running 248 performances. HOWARD LINDSAY directed, and Carl Randall and Barbara Newberry did

Casts for *Gay Divorce* and *The Gay Divorcee*

Character	1932 Broadway *Gay Divorce*	1934 film *The Gay Divorcee*
Guy Holden	FRED ASTAIRE	Fred Astaire
Mimi Pratt/Glossop	Claire Luce	GINGER ROGERS
Rodolfo Tonetti	ERIK RHODES	Erik Rhodes
Aunt Hortense	LUELLA GEAR	ALICE BRADY
Pinky Fitzgerald		EDWARD EVERETT HORTON

the choreography. Soon after the show closed, Astaire went to Hollywood, never to return to the stage.

▓ The Gay Divorcee (RKO 1934) reached the screen with little of Broadway's *Gay Divorce* intact, including the title. The Hollywood censors thought that something as unseemly as a divorce could not be happy, but they reasoned that a divorced person might be, so the title was altered. Producer PANDRO S. BERMAN tossed out the entire Porter score except the popular "Night and Day" and new songs by various tunesmiths were added, most memorably "The Continental" by CON CONRAD and HERB MAGIDSON, which was the first number to win the Best Song Oscar. Other numbers included "Don't Let It Bother You," "A Needle in a Haystack," and "Let's Knock K-nees," which BETTY GRABLE and EDWARD EVERETT HORTON sang as they strummed ukuleles. For the first time Astaire and Ginger Rogers were playing the leading roles together in a screen musical and the chemistry hinted at in their previous supporting roles blossomed when they danced to "Night and Day" and "The Continental." The choreography was by HERMES PAN and DAVE GOULD, and MARK SANDRICH directed.

☙ GAY LIFE, THE (Shubert Theatre 1961). ARTHUR SCHWARTZ (music) and HOWARD DIETZ (lyrics), the masters of revue score, once again attempted a book musical and once again wrote a fine score for an unsuccessful show. Fay and Michael Kanin wrote the libretto, based on Arthur Schnitzler's Austrian play *Anatol*. The Viennese playboy Anatol von Huber (Walter Chiari) vows never to marry but he is no match for the determined Liesl Brandel (BARBARA COOK) who outwits his many lovers and gets him to the altar. The musical was filled with period charm and delightful songs but critics were divided on the libretto and the leading man, although Cook was praised and there were fine supporting performances by JULES MUNSHIN, Elizabeth Allen, Jeanne Bal, Loring Smith, and Lu Leonard. The Schwartz–Dietz score contained such expert songs as the joyful ballad "Magic Moment," the characters numbers "Who Can? You Can" and "Why Go Anywhere at All?," the revelatory "Something You Never Had Before," and the raucous "Come A-Wandering With Me." Gerald Freedman directed and HERBERT ROSS choreographed the uneven show, which ran 113 performances.

▓ GAY PURR-EE (UPA/Warner 1962). A rare case at the time of an animated musical not by WALT DISNEY, this fanciful diversion was not gripping enough for kids but a treat for adults who enjoyed splendid songs sung by top performers. Chuck and Dorothy Jones wrote the serviceable screenplay about a French house cat named Mewsette (voice of JUDY GARLAND) who longs to see the lights of Paris so she leaves her beau, the field cat Jaune-Tom (ROBERT GOULET), and sets off on her own and ends up in the clutches of the city slicker Meowice (PAUL FREES). Luckily Juane-Tom and his friend Robespierre (Red Buttons) arrive in Paris and rescue her. Also heard on the soundtrack were HERMIONE GINGOLD, MOREY AMSTERDAM, Mel Blanc, June Foray, Thurl Ravenscroft, and Julie Bennett. While the animation could not compete with Disney, the backgrounds in the style of Matisse, Modigliani, Cezanne, Toulouse-Lautrec, and Van Gogh were radiant. HAROLD ARLEN (music) and E. Y. HARBURG (lyrics) wrote the commendable songs, including "Paris Is a Lonely Town," "Little Drops of Rain," "Roses Red, Violets Blue," "Take My Hand, Paree," and "Mewsette."

GAYNOR, JANET [born Laura Augusta Gaunor] (1906–1984). Film and television performer. A small, dimpled All-American sweetheart who rose to fame and maintained her stardom through the 1930s, the actress–singer shone in five early musicals. A native of Philadelphia who was raised in San Francisco, she went to Hollywood as a teenager and got bit parts in silents shorts. By the time she was twenty she was a screen star specializing in delicate and adorable heroines in melodramas and comedies. Gaynor retained the same persona when sound came in and she played lovable waifs or immigrants in talkies. She did a bit part in the musical *Happy Days* (1930) but was starred in four others: as the Yorkville "Cinderella" Molly Carr in *SUNNY SIDE UP* (1929), the nouveau riche "Juliet" Eleanor Divine in *High Society Blues* (1930), Scottish immigrant Heather Gordon in *DELICIOUS* (1931), and Princess Marie Christine disguised as a manicurist in *Adorable* (1933). When her popularity started to wane in the late 1930s, Gaynor retired from films but decades later returned for a supporting role in *Bernadine* (1957) and made sporadic television appearances up to 1981. She was married to costume designer Gilbert Adrian (1903–1959) and producer Paul Gregory (1920–).

GAYNOR, MITZI [born Francesca Mitzi de Czanyi von Gerber] (1931–). Film and television performer. The leggy, buoyant singer–dancer lit up some TWENTIETH-FOX musicals in the 1950s, most memorably the 1958 screen version of *SOUTH PACIFIC*. Gaynor was born (supposedly of Hungarian aristocratic blood) in Chicago, the daughter of a ballerina, and was dancing on stage from an early age. By the time she was a teenager, Gaynor was in the ballet troupe of the Los Angeles Civic Light Opera. She made her film debut in 1949 and was featured in such movie musicals as *My Blue Heaven* (1950), *Golden Girl* (1951), *Bloodhounds of Broadway* (1952), *The "I Don't Care" Girl* (1953), *THERE'S NO BUSINESS LIKE SHOW BUSINESS* (1954), *ANYTHING GOES* (1956), *THE JOKER IS WILD* (1957), and *LES GIRLS* (1958), but her best musical role was her last, as the "cockeyed optimist" Nellie Forbush in *South Pacific*. Gaynor retired from films in 1963 and concentrated on nightclub appearances and on television where she shone in a series of musical specials in the 1960s.

GEAR, LUELLA [born Gardner Van Nort] (1807–1980). Stage, film, and television performer. The acerbic character actress rarely played leading roles but was always noticed for her sharp sense of comedy in plays and musicals. A native of New York City, Gear was educated in her home city and in Brussels and then made her Broadway debut in the musical *Love o' Mike* (1917). Two years later she was noticed as one of the chorines on the hunt in the comedy *The Gold Diggers*, followed by many other worldly wise dames. Gear's most memorable role was the patroness of the arts Peggy Porterfield in *ON YOUR TOES* (1936). Her other musical credits include *Elsie* (1923), *Poppy* (1923), *Queen High* (1926), *The Optimists* (1928), *GAY DIVORCE* (1933), *LIFE BEGINS AT 8:40* (1934), *The Streets of Paris* (1939), *Crazy With the Heat* (1941), *Count Me In* (1942), and *My Romance* (1948). Gear appeared in a few films, including the musical *CAREFREE* (1938), and in early television, including the TV version of *LADY IN THE DARK* (1954).

GELBART, LARRY (1928–). Stage, television, and film writer. A successful author of comedies in every media, he wrote two memorable Broadway librettos. Gelbart was born in Chicago and while still in high school was writing comedy sketches for radio and television shows, later contributing to the comedy shows of Red Buttons, BOB HOPE, SID CAESAR, Jack

Parr, and others. Gelbart wrote the libretto for the short-lived musical *The Conquering Hero* (1961) and the next year had a hit as the co-author of *A FUNNY THING HAPPENED ON THE WAY TO THE FORUM* (1962). His other notable Broadway musical credit was the clever script for *CITY ANGELS* (1989). Gelbart wrote comedies for Broadway and scripted many films, such as *Oh God* (1977) and *Tootsie* (1982), as well as the musical *MOVIE MOVIE* (1978). For television he developed and wrote many of the episodes of *M*A*S*H*. Autobiography: *Laughing Matters* (1998).

GELD, GARY (1935–). Stage composer. A little known but exceptional theatre songwriter, he collaborated with lyricist PETER UDELL on some memorable Broadway musicals. Geld was born in Patterson, New Jersey, and educated at New York University and Juilliard. In 1959 he formed his own music publishing company, which handled hit singles he wrote with Udell, such as "Sealed With a Kiss" and "Ginny Come Lately." Geld and Udell's first Broadway score was the rousing *PURLIE* (1970), followed by an even bigger hit, the pastoral *SHENANDOAH* (1975). Their score for *Angel* (1978) was also splendid but the musical did not run. He has also written songs for films. Geld's music mixes pop, rhythm and blues, and folk in a way that is still very much Broadway.

GEMIGNANI, PAUL. Stage and film musical director and conductor. A respected musical director mostly identified with STEPHEN SONDHEIM musicals, the much-awarded conductor has been associated with over thirty Broadway musical since 1971. In addition to most Sondheim musicals since *FOLLIES* (1971), Gemignani has conducted *ON THE TWENTIETH CENTURY* (1978), *EVITA* (1979), *DREAMGIRLS* (1981), *THE RINK* (1984), *JEROME ROBBINS' BROADWAY* (1989), *Big* (1996), *KISS ME, KATE* (1999), *110 IN THE SHADE* (2007), and many others. He has also directed the music for films and recordings.

GENNARO, PETER (1919–2000). Stage, television, film choreographer, and dancer. A dancer-turned-choreographer who had an up-and-down Broadway career, he was very successful in other media. Gennaro was born in Metairie, Louisiana, and made his dancing debut with the San Carlo Opera Company and then appeared on Broadway in the chorus of such musicals as *MAKE MINE MANHATTAN* (1948), *GUYS AND DOLLS* (1950), *Arms and the*

Girl (1950), THE PAJAMA GAME (1954), and BELLS ARE RINGING (1956). His New York choreography debut was *Seventh Heaven* in 1955, followed by his co-choreography with JEROME ROBBINS for WEST SIDE STORY two years later. Many of Gennaro's musicals, such as MR. PRESIDENT (1962), *Bajour* (1964), *Jimmy* (1969), and *Carmelina* (1979), failed to run, but he had hits with FIORELLO! (1959), THE UNSINKABLE MOLLY BROWN (1960), the 1973 revival of IRENE, and ANNIE (1977). He was also very busy (and very successful) choreographing television variety programs and specials with BING CROSBY, JUDY GARLAND, PERRY COMO, MITZIE GAYNOR, and others. Gennaro choreographed the TV version of BRIGADOON (1966) and directed and choreographed the TV musical *Who's Afraid of Mother Goose?* (1967). He assisted on the choreography for the film version of *West Side Story* (1961) and recreated his stage dances for the movie *The Unsinkable Molly Brown* (1964).

🎭 GENTLEMEN PREFER BLONDES (Ziegfeld Theatre 1949). A musical comedy that boasted a spirited libretto, a tune-filled score, and splashy production values, the show is most remembered for CAROL CHANNING who rose to stardom playing the flapper Lorelei Lee. The libretto was by JOSEPH FIELDS and Anita Loos, based on her best-selling comic novel. Gold digger Lee and her pal Dorothy Shaw set off for Europe, all expenses paid by Lorelei's "daddy," the wealthy button manufacturer Gus Esmond. On the ocean liner crossing the Atlantic, Lorelei is attracted to the stuffy Brit Henry Spofford because of a diamond tiara of Mrs. Spofford's that she has her eye on. In Paris the two girls get caught up in intrigues with lawyers and diamonds, but all ends happily when they perform together in a nightclub show and Gus forgives all of Lorelei's indiscretions. JULE STYNE (music) and LEO ROBIN (lyrics) wrote

Gentlemen Prefer Blondes. While the stage version retained the Roaring Twenties time period, the 1953 movie ignored it and dressed its stars in slick and sexy 1950s clothes. Marilyn Monroe (left) and Jane Russell both looked terrific but you could hardly call them flappers. (Photofest)

the splendid songs, the most memorable being the marching credo "Diamonds Are a Girl's Best Friend," the lullaby-like "Bye, Bye, Baby," and the risible character number "A Little Girl From Little Rock." Except for the sets and costumes, the show had little of the wit and feel for the Roaring Twenties but it did have Channing whose wide-eyed, ditzy Lorelei was not the novel's sly heroine but a musical comedy cari-

Casts for *Gentlemen Prefer Blondes* and *Lorelei*

Character	1949 Broadway	1953 film	Lorelei (1974)
Lorelei Lee	CAROL CHANNING	MARILYN MONROE	Carol Channing
Guy Holden	Yvonne Adair	JANE RUSSELL	Tamara Long
Dorothy Shaw	Jack McCauley	Tommy Noonan	PETER PALMER
Gus Esmond	Eric Brotherson	George Winslow	LEE ROY REAMS
Henry Spofford	ALICE PEARCE		Dody Goodman
Mrs. Spofford	Rex Evans		
Sir Francis Beekman	Reta Shaw	Charles Coburn	Jack Fletcher
Lady Beekman		Norma Varden	Jean Bruno
Ernie Malone		Elliot Reid	
Henry Spofford III		George Winslow	

cature that was thoroughly delicious. Channing would play variations of the bubble-headed Lorelei for the rest of her long and prodigious career. JOHN C. WILSON directed the Oliver Smith–HERMAN LEVIN production, AGNES DE MILLE choreographed, and the musical ran 740 performances. Regional revivals have been infrequent, probably because the show depends on a strong personality to play Lorelei, and its only Broadway revival was a short-lived 1995 production by the GOODSPEED OPERA HOUSE in Connecticut, which transferred to Broadway and closed in two weeks. Critics complained that the mounting looked like a frugal summer stock offering and lamented the lackluster staging. The cast was headed by K. T. Sullivan (Lorelei), Karen Prunzik (Dorothy), Allen Fitzgerald (Gus), and George Dvorsky (Spofford).

Channing returned to the role, not in a revival but in **Lorelei** (Palace Theatre 1974), a slightly rewritten version of *Gentlemen Prefer Blondes*. The libretto by Kenny Solms and Gail Parent kept the best scenes and songs from the original and added a prologue and epilogue showing the elderly, wealthy Lorelei to frame the "new" musical. BETTY COMDEN and ADOLPH GREEN provided lyrics for some new Styne tunes ("I Won't Let You Get Away," "Men," "Lorelei," and "Looking Back") but the show's saving grace once again was Channing. ROBERT MOORE directed the Lee Gruber–Shelly Gross production, which had toured extensively before arriving on Broadway, Ernest Flatt did the choreography, and despite weak reviews (except for Channing) the show ran 321 performances.

Gentlemen Prefer Blondes (Fox 1953) dropped much of the stage plot and all but three of the songs, reworking the piece into a showcase for MARILYN MONROE whose Lorelei was less daffy and sexier than Channing's interpretation. Monroe sparkled in the role and was supported by JANE RUSSELL, the two of them having some ter-

rific numbers together. Charles Lederer's screenplay took the story out of the 1920s and made it a contemporary tale in which the wealthy Sir Beekman hires the detective Ernie Malone to keep Lorelei away from his son. Emphasis was still placed on Lorelei's fascination with diamonds and she had plenty of them by the final double wedding. Numbers from the Styne–Robin score were delivered with style, and two new songs by HOAGY CARMICHAEL (music) and HAROLD ADAMSON, "Ain't There Anybody Here for Love?" and "When Love Goes Wrong (Nothing Goes Right)," were splendid as well. JACK COLE was the clever choreographer, and Howard Hawks directed the SOL C. SIEGEL production. 20TH CENTURY-FOX spent a fortune on the lavish film but it turned out to be a box office diamond mine all its own.

GEORGE M! (Palace Theatre 1968). A musical biography about the great Broadway showman GEORGE M. COHAN, the colorful, fast-paced show didn't reveal much about the famous man but it provided an opportunity to hear his songs and to see JOEL GREY's tour de force performance. MICHAEL STEWART and John and Fran Fran Pascal wrote the by-the-numbers libretto that took Cohan from his days in vaudeville with his family to his Broadway triumphs to his declining days and eventual retirement from the stage. Because over thirty Cohan songs were sung, many in large production numbers, dialogue was kept to the minimum and dancing was often featured. The press didn't think very highly about the storytelling but praised Grey and applauded the way director–choreographer JOE LAYTON brought the old songs to life. Also, many fondly remembered JAMES CAGNEY and the film bio *YANKEE DOODLE DANDY* (1942) and comparisons were not favorable. Although it was not a comfortable time for flag waving because of the national discontent with the Viet Nam War, the musical still found an audience for 427 performances.

Casts for *George M!*

Character	1968 Broadway	1970 television
George M. Cohan	JOEL GREY	Joel Grey
Jerry Cohan	Jerry Dodge	JACK CASSIDY
Josie Cohan	BERNADETTE PETERS	Bernadette Peters
Agnes Nolan	Jill O'Hara	Blythe Danner
Nellie Cohan	Betty Ann Grove	NANETTE FABRAY
Ethel Levy	Jamie Donnelly	ANITA GILLETTE
Sam H. Harris	Harvey Evans	Red Buttons

▢ Joel Grey and BERNADETTE PETERS got to reprise their stage performances in a 1970 NBC-TV version and were joined by a top-notch cast. Just as the Broadway production had been presented on a bare stage with pieces of scenery added for the big numbers, the television version took place in a studio and had the same rehearsal-like quality. Once again Grey was magnetic (even if not very close to the real Cohan in style) and the dancing was laudable.

🖗 *GEORGE WHITE'S SCANDALS.* Stage series. The closest rival to the *ZIEGFELD FOLLIES*, this series of musical revues by producer GEORGE WHITE had many unique attributes of its own. White conceived the idea for the series when he was a dancer in the *Follies*. He wanted to create a kind of revue in which contemporary music and modern dance could be featured so he wrote sketches and lyrics, secured various composers, and made sure there was plenty of dance in *George White Scandals* (1919) as well as appearing in the show himself. The revue was a success and over the next twenty years White would present twelve more editions. Unlike FLORENZ ZIEGFELD who put more emphasis on stars and spectacle than songs, White sought out the newest and best song-writers for his shows. GEORGE GERSHWIN, RAY HENDERSON, LEW BROWN, RICHARD A. WHITING, and others got their first recognition writing songs for the *Scandals*. Three editions stand out as the best. The 1922 revue was scored by Gershwin (music) and B. G. DeSYLVA (lyrics) and featured the hit song "I'll Build a Stairway to Paradise" and an ambitious mini-opera called "Blue Monday" using an African American cast and a score filled with jazz and blues. Although it did not go over well with audiences and was cut after opening, the piece was a notable forerunner for Gershwin's later *PORGY AND BESS* (1935). Joining White on stage were W. C. FIELDS, WINNIE LIGHTNER, Jack McGowan, Dolores Costello, and PAUL WHITEMAN and his orchestra and the show ran eighty-eight performances. The 1926 edition of *George White's Scandals* is generally considered his best, mostly because of the score. DeSylva, Brown, and Henderson wrote most of the songs, including the standards "Black Bottom," "Lucky Day,' and "Birth of the Blues." Gershwin's "Rhapsody in Blue' was performed and W. C. Handy's "St. Louis Blues" was interpolated. The splendid cast included WILLIE and EUGENE HOWARD, ANN PENNINGTON, HARRY RICHMAN, Frances Williams, and the Fairbanks Twins. The pro-

duction was a box office sensation, running 424 performances. The Howards returned for the 1931 *Scandals* and were joined by such talents as ETHEL MERMAN, RUDY VALLEE, RAY BOLGER, Everett Marshall, and an unknown ALICE FAYE. Lew Brown and Ray Henderson did the songs, with the best being "Life Is Just a Bowl of Cherries" but also featuring "The Thrill Is Gone," "My Song," "This Is the Missus," and the first-act finale "That's Why Darkies Were Born," which presented the plight of African Americans without stereotype or cliché. The 1931 edition was also known for its elaborate production values, designed by Ziegfeld's house artist Joseph Urban. As usual, White produced, directed, and choreographed and the revue ran 202 performances. Although no one could rival Ziegfeld's opulence and sense of spectacular showmanship, the *Scandals* made a valuable contribution to the American musical theatre that, in many ways, was more long lasting than the *Follies*.

🎬 Three Hollywood films bore the title *George White's Scandals* but they were back-stagers rather than revues. White was often producer and director and the production numbers often resembled his stage shows. The 1934 20TH CENTURY-FOX film called *George White's Scandals* is noteworthy for introducing Alice Faye to moviegoers. She was a last-minute replacement for Lillian Harvey who quit right before filming began. It is a tired backstage tale about whether or not crooner Jimmy Ryan (Rudy Vallee) will win the heart of chorine Kitty Donnelly (Faye), but the songs by Henderson, IRVING CAESAR, and JACK YELLEN were commendable. "You Nasty Man," "Your Dog Loves My Dog," "Every Day Is Father's Day," and "Hold My Hand" were well sung, and BUSBY BERKELEY's staging of the big production numbers (one had chorus girls diving into a giant glass of champagne) were fun. Also in the cast were JIMMY DURANTE, CLIFF EDWARDS, DIXIE DUNBAR, Gregory Ratoff, and Adrienne Ames, but it was Faye the audiences cared about most and her film career was launched. In the 1935 film *George White's Scandals*, White played himself in the story about a producer who books singers Honey Walters (Faye) and Eddy Taylor (James Dunn) for his *Scandals* in New York. The big break for the couple also brings romantic complications but everything is patched up by opening night. The score by Yellen, HERB MAGIDSON, Cliff Friend, and others featured the songs "Oh, I Didn't Know," "You Belong to Me," "It's an Old Southern Comfort," and "I Got Shoes,

You Got Shosies." Although Faye was starred, the hit of the film was tap-dancing ELEANOR POWELL who made her screen debut in a featured part. *George Whites Scandals of 1945* was an RKO release that revived the song "Life Is Just a Bowl of Cherries," which JACK HALEY and JOAN DAVIS sang together. He played the stage comic Jack Evans who is romancing the comic singer Joan Mason (Davis) in an uninteresting backstage story, which also featured Philip Terry, Martha Holliday, MARGARET HAMILTON, and Ethel Smith who played swing numbers on the organ. The songs, by various tunesmiths, included "I Wake Up in the Morning," "Who Killed Vaudeville?," and "I Want to Be a Drummer" performed by GENE KRUPA and his orchestra. It was the least accomplished of the three *Scandals* films and not a box office hit so the series was retired.

GERSHWIN, GEORGE [born Jacob Gershwin] (1898–1937). Stage and film composer. One of the greatest and most original of Broadway and Hollywood songwriters, he did masterful work in both light musical comedy and tragic opera. Born in Brooklyn, New York, to a poor immigrant family, he showed musical abilities at an early age. Gershwin studied piano and composition with some respected teachers and worked as a song plugger before his song "Swanee" became a hit when AL JOLSON sang it in *SINBAD* (1919). He wrote his first complete Broadway score that same year, was represented in five editions of *GEORGE WHITE'S SCANDALS* and other revues, and then teamed up with his lyricist-brother IRA GERSHWIN for a series of bright and jazz-flavored musicals such as *LADY, BE GOOD!* (1924), *Tell Me More!* (1925), *TIP-TOES* (1925), *OH, KAY!* (1926), *FUNNY FACE* (1927), *ROSALIE* (1928), *Treasure Girl* (1928), *Show Girl* (1929), *STRIKE UP THE BAND* (1930), *GIRL CRAZY* (1930), *OF THEE I SING* (1931), *Pardon My English* (1933), and *LET 'EM EAT CAKE* (1933). His only operetta was *Song of the Flame* (1925) and, working with Ira and Dubose Heyward, Gershwin scored the unique American opera *PORGY AND BESS* (1935) before going to Hollywood and writing three film scores—*SHALL WE DANCE* (1937), *DAMSEL IN DISTRESS* (1937), and *THE GOLDWYN FOLLIES* (1938)—before his early death from a brain tumor. Several of the Gershwin stage musicals were filmed and their songs were used in the early screen musical *Delicious* (1931). After George's death, other songs provided the score for such movie musicals as *RHAPSODY IN BLUE* (1945), *THE SHOCKING MISS PILGRIM* (1947), *AN*

AMERICAN IN PARIS (1951), *FUNNY FACE* (1957), *Kiss Me, Stupid* (1964), and *When the Boys Meet the Girls* (1965). He also enjoyed two posthumous Broadway hits, *MY ONE AND ONLY* (1983) and *CRAZY FOR YOU* (1992). Gershwin enjoyed a remarkable concert career in his short life, introducing such beloved orchestral pieces as "American in Paris" and "Rhapsody in Blue," which were featured in films titled after them and in *KING OF JAZZ* (1930). In a span of less than twenty years, Gershwin explored several areas of American music, opened up new musical forms, and created an extensive repertoire of concert music and popular songs. Biographies: *Gershwin, a Biography*, Edward Jablonsky (1987); *George Gershwin: A New Biography*, William G. Hyland (2003); *George Gershwin: His Life and Work*, Howard Pollack (2006).

GERSHWIN, IRA [born Israel Gershwin] (1896–1983). Stage and film lyricist. Too often overshadowed by his composer brother GEORGE GERSHWIN, the meticulous, gifted songwriter was one of the finest American lyricists and contributed to many innovative or landmark musicals. Gershwin was born in Brooklyn and

George and Ira Gershwin. George (left) wrote the music while Ira (right) penned the lyrics and each complemented each other beautifully, even if George got most of the attention. Ira preferred it that way for he deferred to his brother's genius. (Photofest)

started writing light verse and lyrics while a student at Columbia University. Since his brother was gaining notoriety as a popular composer, Ira wrote under the penman Arthur Francis so as not to ride on his fame. His first Broadway score was for *Two Little Girls in Blue* (1921) with composer VINCENT YOUMANS and then he teamed up with his brother for *LADY, BE GOOD!* (1924), the first of a series of jazz-influenced scores they wrote for Broadway. The brothers subsequent shows together were *Tell Me More!* (1925), *TIP-TOES* (1925), *OH, KAY!* (1926), *FUNNY FACE* (1927), *ROSALIE* (1928), *Treasure Girl* (1928), *Show Girl* (1929), *STRIKE UP THE BAND* (1930), *GIRL CRAZY* (1930), *OF THEE I SING* (1931), *Pardon My English* (1933), and *LET 'EM EAT CAKE* (1933). Ira Gershwin collaborated with other composers on the London musical *That's a Good Girl* (1928) and the Broadway revue *LIFE BEGINS AT 8:40* (1934) and then the brothers teamed with lyricist DuBose Heyward to write the folk American opera *PORGY AND BESS* (1935). The brothers went to Hollywood during the Depression to score films together but Ira returned to Broadway to write songs for *ZIEGFELD FOLLIES* (1936) with composer VERNON DUKE. The Gershwins wrote the scores for the Hollywood musicals *SHALL WE DANCE* (1937), *DAMSEL IN DISTRESS* (1937), and *THE GOLDWIN FOLLIES* (1938) before George's untimely death. It took time for Ira Gershwin to recover from the loss of his brother and primary collaborator but by 1941 he was back on Broadway with the innovative *LADY IN THE DARK* (1941) with music by KURT WEILL. The two reteamed for the short-lived *The Firebrand of Florence* (1945) and then Gershwin suffered a second flop with *Park Avenue* (1946) with composer ARTHUR SCHWARTZ. The two failures ended his stage career but Gershwin remained active in Hollywood for another decade. With JEROME KERN he scored *COVER GIRL* (1944) and with Weill *Where Do We Go From Here?* (1945). He wrote lyrics from some of his brother's "trunk" music for *THE SHOCKING MISS PILGRIM* (1947) and then collaborated with composer HARRY WARREN on *THE BARKLEYS OF BROADWAY* (1949), with BURTON LANE on *GIVE A GIRL A BREAK* (1943), and with HAROLD ARLEN on *A STAR IS BORN* (194) and *THE COUNTRY GIRL* (1954). Gershwin then retired, although musicals using his old songs surfaced on the screen, as with *FUNNY FACE* (1957), *Kiss Me, Stupid* (1964), and *When the Boys Meet the Girls* (1965), and on Broadway with *MY ONE AND ONLY* (1983) and *CRAZY FOR YOU* (1992). Among Ira Gershwin's many talents were his unique use of slang in lyric writing, an ingenious turn of phrase in his romantic songs, and a satirical wit that was accurate and delightful. Although he did not write an autobiography, his ideas about songwriting and his past shows are revealed in his book *Lyrics on Several Occasions* (1959). Biographies: *Fascinating Rhythm: The Collaboration of George and Ira Gershwin*, Deena Ruth Rosenberg (1998); *The Gershwin Years*, Edward Jablonski, Lawrence Stewart (1973).

GEVA, TAMARA [born Sheversheieva Gevergeva] (1907–1997). Stage and film performer. An alluring Russian dancer, she lit up some 1930s Broadway musicals. Geva was born in St. Petersburg, Russia, and was a renowned ballet dancer with Diaghilev's Monte Carlo Ballet before she came to New York as part of the Russian revue *Chauve-Souris* (1922). She had a small role in the musical *WHOOPEE!* (1928) and choreographed parts of the production. Geva's enticing dancing was featured in the Broadway revues *THREE'S A CROWD* (1930) and *FLYING COLORS* (1932) and then she wowed audiences as the Russian ballerina Vera Barnova in *ON YOUR TOES* (1936), dancing the modern ballet "Slaughter on Tenth Avenue" with RAY BOLGER. The show was choreographed by her ex-husband GEORGE BALANCHINE. Geva made some European films in the 1920s and appeared in Hollywood shorts and comedies as well as in the screen musicals *Manhattan Merry-Go-Round* (1937) and *ORCHESTRA WIVES* (1942). Autobiography: *Split Seconds: A Remembrance* (1986).

◻ GIFT OF THE MAGI (CBS-TV 1958). O. Henry's famous short story was turned into a lovely, intimate musical scripted by Wilson Lehr and scored by RICHARD ADLER. Eli Wallach acted as the narrator to tell the story of a young, penniless married couple in early twentieth-century Manhattan who give each other a perfect Christmas gift. Jim Young (GORDON MacRAE) sells his prized gold watch in order to buy some dazzling tortoise shell combs for his wife's beautiful long hair. Della Young (SALLY ANN HOWES) sells her hair to wigmaker Madame Sofroni (Bibi Osterwald) in order to buy Jim a gold chain for his pocket watch. On Christmas morning they realize that their sacrifices have led to an ironic testament of their love. The two stars were in fine voice for such pleasing songs as "A Better Word Than Love," "What to Do?," "My Sugar Is the Salt of the Earth," and "Christmas in Your Heart." George Schaefer co-produced and directed the sixty-minute broadcast. An NBC television musical *The Gift of the Magi* in 1978 retained the title, plot, and period, but was opened up by scriptwriter Sidney Michaels to show the immigrant experience during the ninety-minute show. Debby Boone and John Rubenstein were the young couple, and Peter Graves, as O. Henry, served as narrator. Fred Tobias (music) and Stanley Lebowsky (lyrics) provided the score. ✄ Off Broadway saw a 1984 musical version called *The Gifts of the Magi*, which added scenes from other O. Henry stories to fill out an full evening's entertainment. Mark St. Germain (book and lyrics) and Randy Courts (book and music) wrote the musical, which featured Leslie Hicks and Jeff McCarthy as the young couple.

Gigi. Groomed to become a high-class Parisian courtesan, the tomboy Gigi (Leslie Caron) must learn how to tell real jewels from fake ones. The task bores her, as do most things about Parisian high life. *Gigi* has got to have the most unpromising premise for a musical yet it works beautifully. (Photofest)

■ **GIGI** (MGM 1958). The last great movie musical of the 1950s, the unlikely hit was, in many ways, the last of the classic musicals that Hollywood had done so efficiently for decades.

Plot: During *la belle epoque* in Paris, the bored nobleman Gaston Lachailles scoffs at the carefree life of his *bon vivant* uncle Honoré and the other Parisians and prefers spending his time with the tomboy Gigi, the granddaughter of the retired courtesan Madame Alvarez. Gigi is being groomed by her Aunt Alicia to become a high-class courtesan someday and as she matures Gaston considers making her his mistress. But realizing he truly loves Gigi, he proposes marriage instead.

ALAN JAY LERNER's screenplay was based on the French writer Colette's novella, which had been produced as a nonmusical French film in 1950 with Danielle Delorme and a play on Broadway in 1954 with AUDREY HEPBURN. LESLIE CARON played the role in the London stage version and got to reprise her performance on screen, this time with songs. The subject of grooming a courtesan was not typical musical fare in Hollywood but Lerner insisted

on staying true to Colette's book and producer ARTHUR FREED backed him up before worried studio executives. The film was shot mostly in Paris by director VINCENTE MINNELLI, using such famous landmarks as Maxim's restaurant, the Bois de Boulogue, and the Tuileries, but some scenes had to be reshot in a California studio when the first cut of the movie was not falling into place. MAURICE CHEVALIER served as the musical's narrator and helped give the picture a Gallic flavor that was much needed. Songwriters FREDERICK LOEWE (music) and Lerner (lyrics) were riding high on their success with *MY FAIR LADY* (1956) on Broadway when they embarked on writing *Gigi* and there was the inevitable fear that comparisons would be made. There are several similarities between the two shows and some songs serve the same purpose in each musical. However, there is a European flavor to the *Gigi* score that is very distinct from the British tone of *My Fair Lady*. The celebratory trio "The Night They Invented

Casts for *Gigi*

Character	1958 film	1973 Broadway
Gigi	LESLIE CARON	Karin Wolfe
Gaston Lachaille	Louis Jourdan	Daniel Massey
Honore Lachaille	MAURICE CHEVALIER	ALFRED DRAKE
Madame Alvarez	HERMIONE GINGOLD	MARIA KARNILOVA
Aunt Alicia	Isabel Jeans	AGNES MOOREHEAD
Liane d'Exelmans	EVA GABOR	Sandahl Bergman

Champagne" holds the same plot position as "The Rain in Spain" does in the earlier musical, yet there is something explicitly Continental about the *Gigi* number. The title song was the standout hit but also embraced were such character-based songs as "I Remember It Well" and "I'm Glad I'm Not Young Anymore," as well as the sly "Thank Heaven For Little Girls" and tender "Say a Prayer for Me Tonight." *My Fair Lady* might be considered the finest Broadway score of the decade and *Gigi* the best of the movie scores. At one point during the editing, MGM wanted to stop spending any more money on the overbudget film and release it as it was. Not until Lerner offered to buy the picture outright and release it though another studio did the executives relent and the musical took the form it has today. Critical and public response was enthusiastic and the film won an armful of Oscars. If *Gigi* signaled the end of an era never to be seen again, at least the era went out in a blaze of glory.

🕮 *Gigi* (Uris Theatre 1973) was reworked and adapted for the stage by Lerner, he and Loewe wrote six new songs, and a top-notch cast was assembled so it was dismaying to critics that the result was so lifeless and without charm. "In This Wide, Wide World," "I Never Want to Go Home Again," "Paris Is Paris Again," "The Contract," and "The Earth and Other Minor Things" were commendable songs but they lacked theatricality, probably because of the way they were staged because even the superb songs from the movie failed to work effectively on stage. Edwin Lester produced, Joseph Hardy directed, and ONNA WHITE choreographed the misguided production, which lasted only 103 performances. This same stage version of *Gigi* has been produced by regional theatres and schools and is often popular so one tends to blame the Broadway production rather than the material.

Gigi (film) Musical Numbers

"Thank Heaven for Little Girls"
"It's a Bore"
"(I Don't Understand) The Parisians"
"Gossip"
"She Is Not Thinking of Me"
"The Night They Invented Champagne"
"I Remember It Well"
"Gigi"
"I'm Glad I'm Not Young Anymore"
"Say a Prayer for Me Tonight"

GILBERT, BILLY [born William Gilbert Barron] (1893–1971). Film, television, and stage performer. A huge character actor who specialized in small but very noticeable roles in over 200 feature films from silents to the 1960s, the rotund giant was seen in many musicals. Gilbert was born in Louisville, Kentucky, the son of Metropolitan Opera singers, and at the age of twelve was doing comedy on the vaudeville circuits. He made his film debut in 1916 and clowned opposite Charlie Chaplin and Laurel and Hardy in the silent days. When sound came in, Gilbert often played heavily accented comic characters. Among his musical credits are CURLY TOP (1935), A NIGHT AT THE OPERA (1935), *Millions in the Air* (1935), ON THE AVENUE (1937), THE FIREFLY (1937), BROADWAY MELODY OF 1938 (1937), ONE HUNDRED MEN AND A GIRL (1937), ROSALIE (1937), JOY OF LIVING (1938), *My Lucky Star* (1938), TIN PAN ALLEY (1940), NO, NO, NANETTE (1940), WEEKEND IN HAVANA (1941), Song of the Islands (1942), ANCHORS AWEIGH (1945), and *Down Among the Sheltering Pines* (1953), as well as the TV musicals THE CHOCOLATE SOLDIER (1950), REVENGE WITH MUSIC (1951), JACK AND THE BEANSTALK (1956), and *Mother Goose* (1958). In vaudeville, Gilbert was famous for his sneezing routine, which was utilized in several of his screen appearances; he also provided the voice and the sneezing for Sneezy in SNOW WHITE AND THE SEVEN DWARFS (1938). On Broadway, he was in the revivals of THE RED MILL (1945), *The Chocolate Soldier* (1947), and SALLY (1948). Gilbert also wrote and appeared in the musical *Buttrio Square* (1952) and was a replacement in the FANNY in 1955.

GILBERT, RAY (1912–1976). Film composer. A successful Tin Pan Alley songwriter, he managed to write several familiar favorites in his limited Hollywood career. Gilbert was born in Hartford, Connecticut, and began in show business writing songs for such vaudeville stars as SOPHIE TUCKER, HARRY RICHMAN, and CHARLES "BUDDY" ROGERS. He went to Hollywood in 1939 and wrote songs for shorts and features by the WALT DISNEY COMPANY, most memorably "Zip-a-Dee-Doo-Dah" for SONG OF THE SOUTH (1946). His other film musicals include THE THREE CABALLEROS (1944), MAKE MINE MUSIC (1946), and *The Adventures of Ichabod and Mr. Toad* (1949). Among Gilbert's song hits are "You Belong to My Heart," "Blame It on the Samba," and "Cuanto le Gusta." He was married to actress JANIS PAIGE.

GILFORD, JACK [born Jacob Aaron Gellman] (1907–1990). Stage, film, and television performer. The small, withered-looking comedian rarely played a leading role but was always a delight as supporting characters in plays and musicals. Gilford was born in New York, the son of a divorced mother who supported her family as a bootlegger. He began his show business career as a standup comic in nightclubs and then went on to vaudeville and eventually appeared on Broadway in revues such as *Meet the People* (1940), *Count Me In* (1942), *Alive and Kicking* (1950), and *Once Over Lightly* (1955). Gilford also played characters parts, most memorably the mute King Septimus in *ONCE UPON A MATTRESS* (1959), which he reprised in the 1964 and 1972 television versions, the nervous slave Hysterium in *A FUNNY THING HAPPENED ON THE WAY TO THE FORUM* (1962), which he also played in the 1966 film, the Jewish fruit merchant Herr Schultz in *CABARET* (1966), and the Bible salesman Jimmy Smith in the 1971 revival of *NO, NO, NANETTE*. He was a favorite in comedies, such as *Three Men on a Horse* (1969) and *Sly Fox* (1976), and in dramas, as in *The Diary of Anne Frank* (1955) and *The Tenth Man* (1959). Gilford appeared in several films and was active in 1950s television, performing in variety shows and specials, such as the musical *HIT THE DECK* (1950). But he was blacklisted for a time and concentrated on Broadway until the 1960s when he returned to television and made hundreds of appearances on sit-coms, commercials, dramas, and specials, such as the TV musical version of *OF THEE I SING!* (1972).

GILLETTE, ANITA [born Anita Luebben] (1936–). Stage and television performer. The bright-eyes singer–actress with a solid Broadway belt originated ingénues in some 1960s musicals but had better vehicles when she replaced others. Gillette was born in Baltimore and worked as a secretary before studying acting at the Peabody Conservatory with Lee Strasberg and ROBERT LEWIS. After appearing in stock, she made her Broadway debut as a replacement in *GYPSY* (1960) and then played ingénue leads in the short-lived musicals *ALL AMERICAN* (1962), *MR. PRESIDENT* (1962), *Kelly* (1965), and *Jimmy* (1969). Gillette shone as the replacement for Lili in *CARNIVAL* (1961), Sarah Brown in *GUYS AND DOLLS* (1965), Sally Bowles in *CABARET* (1968), a role she played on tour and in summer theatres for years, and Sonia Wolsk in *THEY'RE PLAYING OUR SONG* (1980). She was applauded for her performances in comedies, in particu-

lar *Chapter Two* (1977), and was a favorite on television where she appeared in dramatic and comedy series, as well as the TV musicals *PINOCCHIO* (1968) and *GEORGE M!* (1970).

GINGOLD, HERMIONE [Ferdinanda] (1897–1987). Stage and film performer. A haughty, raffish British comedienne with a piercing throaty voice, her unique comic talents were enjoyed on both sides of the Atlantic. Gingold was born and educated in London and was on the stage by the age of eleven. After years of experience in music halls and in London musicals, she came to America and made a sensational debut in *John Murray Anderson's Almanac* (1953) doing wacky monologues and playing various characters of diverse classes. Gingold only made a few subsequent Broadway musical appearances but they were memorable: the conniving Mrs. Bennet in *First Impressions* (1959), the revue *From A to Z* (1960), and the aging courtesan Madame Armfeldt in *A LITTLE NIGHT MUSIC* (1973), which she reprised in London and in the 1977 film. She also replaced others on Broadway in *MILK AND HONEY* (1962) and *Side By Side By Sondheim* (1977). Gingold was a frequent guest on television shows and specials, such as the TV musical *A Special London Bridge Special* (1972), and made several movies, most memorably as the Parisian Madame Alvarez in *GIGI* (1958) and the Mayor's wife Eulalie Shinn in *THE MUSIC MAN* (1962), as well as providing a voice for the animated film musical *GAY PURR-EE* (1962). Autobiographies: *The World Is Square* (1958); *How to Grow Old Disgracefully* (1988).

GIRL CRAZY (Alvin Theatre 1930). With more song hits than any other Gershwin show, this sparkling piece of fluff is arguably the brothers' best musical comedy.

Plot: Manhattan playboy Danny Churchill is sent by his father to Custerville, Arizona, because there are no nightclubs, no gambling casinos, and hardly a woman in sight. Arriving by cab, driven all the way from New York by taxi driver Gieber Goldfarb, Danny turns the town into a swinging dude ranch and falls in love with postmistress Molly Gray. Goldfarb runs for sheriff and converses with the Indians in Yiddish while Kate Fothergill, the saloon keeper's daughter, leads the town in singing and celebrating.

GUY BOLTON and John McGowan wrote the funny libretto that made fun of both prairie folk and city slickers, and the script was

Girl Crazy. Ginger Rogers had a brief but memorable stage career before she went to Hollywood. As Molly, the postmistress of Custerville, Arizona, in the Broadway version of *Girl Crazy*, she was wooed by the city slicker Allen Kearns (right) and introduced the standards "Embraceable You" and "But Not for Me." (Photofest)

Girl Crazy (stage) Musical Numbers
"Bidin' My Time"
"The Lonesome Cowboy"
"Could You Use Me?"
"Bronco Busters"
"Barbary Coast"
"Embraceable You"
"Goldfarb, That's I'm!"
"Sam and Delilah"
"I Got Rhythm"
"Land of the Gay Caballero"
"But Not for Me"
"Treat Me Rough"
"Boy! What Love Has Done to Me"
"(When It's) Cactus Time in Arizona"

tailored to the superior cast: WILLIE HOWARD provided the Jewish schtick, ALLEN KEARNS the romantic flavor, GINGER ROGERS the pert female point of view, and ETHEL MERMAN the big voice to turn her songs into a clarion call for fun. Although it was only a supporting role, her Kate was a show stopper and Merman's career was off and running. Three beloved standards came from the score by GEORGE GERSHWIN (music) and IRA GERSHWIN (lyrics): "I Got Rhythm," "But Not for Me," and "Embraceable You." However, numbers such as "Bidin' My Time," "Could You Use Me?," "Sam and Delilah," and "Boy! What Love Has Done to Me" were also popular and are still recognized. The use of jazz in the score is exhilarating, giving the show a rhythm

that propels it in a way found in few musical comedies. Even the ballads move forward, helped by Ira Gershwin's driving lyrics. ALEX A. AARONS and VINTON FREEDLEY produced the slaphappy musical, ALEXANDER LEFTWICH directed, GEORGE HALE choreographed, and the show ran 272 performances despite the Depression. It seems that with such a funny script and grand collection of songs that *Girl Crazy* would be revived regularly but such was not the case. Regional productions popped up once in a while but Broadway ignored the show until it came back as a retitled, reworked musical in 1992.

🎵 *Crazy for You* (Shubert Theatre 1992) made so many script and song changes that it could hardly be called a revival. The new libretto by Ken Ludwig was still set in a sleepy Western town but playboy Bobby Child (HARRY GROENER) now sets out to save an old theatre with the help of postmistress Polly Baker (Jodi Benson), the hindrance of Bobby's mother (JANE CONNELL), and the complications by the impresario Bela Zangler (Bruce Adler). The best songs from *Girl*

Casts for *Girl Crazy*

Character	1930 Broadway	1932 film	1943 film
Danny Churchill	ALLEN KEARNS	Eddie Quillin	MICKEY ROONEY
Molly/Ginger Grey	GINGER ROGERS	Arline Judge	JUDY GARLAND
Kate Fothergill/Foster	ETHEL MERMAN	Kitty Kelly	
Gieber Goldfarb/cabbie	WILLIE HOWARD	BERT WHEELER	
Slick Fothergill/Foster	William Kent	ROBERT WOOLSEY	
Patsy		Dorothy Lee	
Tessie		MITZI GREEN	
Polly Williams			NANCY WALKER
Bud Livermore			Gil Stratton

Crazy were retained and others were replaced with familiar Gershwin favorites from other shows and the movies, such as "I Can't Be Bothered Now," "Someone to Watch Over Me," "Slap That Bass," and "They Can't Take That Away From Me." The result was a hit parade of standards, some of which fit uncomfortably into the new show, but they were stunningly choreographed by SUSAN STROMAN. MICHAEL OCKRENT directed. Both critics and playgoers were thrilled to encounter a unpretentious, lively musical comedy so it ran over 1,622 performances, by far the longest run for a Gershwin show. After a successful tour, the new–old musical became a staple in summer, school, and community theatres, something that had never happened to *Girl Crazy*.

If Broadway ignored *Girl Crazy* for decades, Hollywood certainly didn't, making three film versions over the years. RKO's 1932 film was the most faithful if not the most enjoyable. The comedy team of BERT WHEELING and ROBERT WOOLSEY were featured, turning supporting comic characters into the leads. Five of the Gershwin songs from Broadway were used and the brothers wrote a new one, "You've Got What Gets Me," which was also quite good. Merman, of course, is missed, as is the sprightly tone of the stage work. WILLIAM A. SEITER directed the WILLIAM LeBARON production with competence but without flair, and BUSBY BERKELEY did the surprisingly uninteresting choreography. MGM made a more successful version of *Girl Crazy* in 1943 as a vehicle for MICKEY ROONEY and JUDY GARLAND and it was one of their best films together. Fred Finklehoffe's screenplay kept the original premise but changed the details, making the heroine Ginger the daughter of the dean of the local college and there was a rodeo to raise money for the school. Six songs from the stage score were used, the Gershwins' "Fascinating Rhythm" was interpolated into the film, and a new number, "Happy Birthday Ginger" by ROGER EDENS, was added. All of the songs were cleverly staged by choreographer CHARLES WALTERS (although the "I Got Rhythm' finale was done by Busby Berkeley) and performed with gusto by the skillful cast. NORMAN TAUROG directed the ARTHUR FREED production and it was a box office hit. MGM's *When the Boys Meet the Girls* (1966) kept a ranch setting and five Gershwin songs but it only resembles *Girl Crazy* in the slightest way. The Robert E. Kent screenplay concerned the married couple Ginger (Connie Francis) and Danny (HARVE PRESNELL) who

run a dude ranch for divorcées and how their marriage is threatened with the predatory Tess Rawley (Sue Ann Langdon) sets her eye on Danny. The supporting cast was an odd gathering, including Peter Noone with his Herman's Hermits, LOUIS ARMSTRONG, LIBERACE, Fred Clark, Frank Faylen, Joby Baker, and Sam the Sham (Domingo Samudio) and the Pharaohs. The Gershwin numbers were not well presented, and the pop songs by various songwriters were also unimpressive.

GIRL FROM UTAH, THE (Knickerbocker Theatre 1914). A British import of minor importance, the musical contained some songs by a young JEROME KERN, his first Broadway score. The libretto by James T. Tanner was about the American girl Una Trance (JULIA SANDERSON) who runs away from her Mormon husband in Salt Lake City and goes to England where she falls in love with Sandy Blair (DONALD BRIAN), the dashing leading man at the Gaiety Theatre. The British score by Paul A. Rubens, Sidney Jones (music), Percy Greenbank, and Adrian Ross (lyrics) was considered weak by the American producer CHARLES FROMAN so he hired the unknown Kern to write a handful of new songs for the Broadway production. One of them was "They Didn't Believe Me," one of the most influential songs in the history of the American theatre. The ballad introduced a modern 4/4 time that broke away from the waltz tempo and created the pattern for the musical comedy songs for the next fifty years.

GIVE A GIRL A BREAK (MGM 1953). Intended as a B picture with a small budget and a lot of newcomers in the cast and on the artistic staff, the unpretentious backstage musical turned out to be a pleasing combination of bright talents and sparkling songs. FRANCES GOODRICH and ALBERT HACKETT wrote the screenplay in which Janet Hallson (Dona Martell), the star of a Broadway show in rehearsal, has a fight with the director, Ted Sturgis (GOWER CHAMPION), and walks out on the production. Auditions are held and her replacement comes down to three girls: Ted's former dancing partner Madelyn Corlane (MARGE CHAMPION); Joanna Moss (Helen Wood), the choice of the composer Leo Belney (KURT KASZNAR); and Suzie Doolittle (DEBBIE REYNOLDS), the protégé of the assistant director, Bob Dowdy (BOB FOSSE). The competition keeps the plot crackling until Joanna finds out she's pregnant, Madelyn falls in love with Ted and doesn't care about her career, and Suzie gets the plum part. STANLEY DONEN directed and choreographed, with Gower Champion assisting in the dances and starting his remarkable career as a choreographer. The score by BURTON LANE (music) and IRA GERSHWIN (lyrics) had no hits but offered a handful of delicious songs, including the patriotic love song "In Our United State," the upbeat "It Happens Every Time," and the tongue-in-cheek rouser "Applause, Applause."

GLASER, LULU [born Lilian Glaser] (1874–1958). Stage performer. A fetching, frizzy-haired singer–actress, she played appealing gamines in plays and musicals and was a favorite in vaudeville. Glaser was born in Allegheny City, Pennsylvania, and got her first Broadway job in the chorus of the musical *The Lion Tamer* (1891). In true legendary Broadway style, Glaser took over the leading role of Angeline when the star was taken ill and she wowed audiences and critics. She was featured in *The Merry Monarch* (1892), *Erminie* (1893), *The Little Corporal* (1898), and other musicals before playing the strolling player Anne in *Sweet Anne Page* (1900), which allowed her to show off her boisterous stage persona. Glaser also shone as the spunky country lass *Dolly Varden* (1902), *The Madcap Princess* (1904), *Miss Dolly Dollars* (1905), *Mlle. Mischief* (1908), *Miss Dudelsack* (1911), and other starring vehicles. When her popularity on Broadway waned in the 1910s, she turned to vaudeville where she was very welcome for years. Glaser was married to comic actor DE WOLF HOPPER.

GLEASON, JACKIE [born Herbert John Gleason] (1916–1987). Stage, film, and television performer. The rotund comic with a booming voice and expressive face found some success in every area of show business but was at his best on television. Gleason was born in Brooklyn and dropped out of school to work as a carnival barker, in vaudeville, and on the radio. He made his Broadway debut as a replacement in *HELLZAPOPPIN'* (1938) and then was featured in the revues *Keep Off the Grass* (1940) and *ARTISTS AND MODELS* (1943) before getting recognition as the rejected draftee Goofy Gale in *FOLLOW THE GIRLS* (1944). Gleason was starred in *Along Fifth Avenue* (1949) and made an impressive return to Broadway a decade later as the tipsy Uncle Sid in *TAKE ME ALONG* (1959). He appeared in three movie musicals, *Navy Blues* (1941), *ORCHESTRA WIVES* (1942), and *SPRINGTIME IN THE ROCKIES* (1942), but they did not suit his clowning style as television did. On his own variety show, in *The Honeymooners*

series, and as a guest on others' programs, Gleason became one of the tube's biggest stars. He appeared in many specials, including the TV version of *No, No, Nanette* (1950). Gleason returned to movies on occasion, sometimes winning more praise for his serious roles than his comic ones. He also composed, conducted, and produced several albums of mood music. Biographies: *The Great One: The Life and Legend of Jackie Gleason*, William A. Henry (1992); *Jackie Gleason: An Intimate Portrait of the Great One*, W. J. Weatherby (1992).

GLEASON, JOANNA [born Johanna Hall] (1950–). Stage, film, and television performer. The classy leading lady of musicals and plays, she specializes in intelligent if slightly affected women. Gleason was born in Winnipeg, Canada, the daughter of television producer (and later game show host) Monty Hall and an actress, and grew up in New York City and southern California. She was educated at Occidental College and the University of California at Los Angeles before doing theatre in California. Gleason made an auspicious Broadway debut as the New Jersey housewife Monica in the musical *I LOVE MY WIFE* (1977) and then appeared in a series of dramas and comedies. She also shone as the childless Baker's Wife in *INTO THE WOODS* (1987), the upper-class sleuth Nora Charles in the short-lived *Nick & Nora* (1991), and the wealthy Muriel Eubanks in *DIRTY ROTTEN SCOUNDRELS* (2005). Gleason has appeared in several movies and many television series and specials, although rarely has she gotten to sing in either medium. She is married to actor Chris Sarandon (1942–).

GLENN MILLER STORY, THE (Universal 1954). The best of the many biographical musicals about Big Band conductors, the sentimental but well-directed, well-acted film is also one of the better biomusicals to come out of Hollywood. Valentine Davies and Oscar Brodney's screenplay followed the usual rags-to-riches format, and because Miller had died in a plane crash going to entertain troops in World War II, it could not help but be sentimental. JAMES STEWART played Miller as a dedicated, very human artist searching for the distinctive sound that would make his band special, JUNE ALLYSON was his overly understanding wife Helen, and LOUIS ARMSTRONG, GENE KRUPA, Ben Pollock, FRANCES LANGFORD, and others from the 1940s played themselves. Joe Yukl, who had been in the Miller band, did Stewart's trombone playing on the soundtrack and the most dedicated fans knew that the sound was authentic. All of the Miller song favorites were heard, from "Basin Street Blues" and "In the Mood" to "Pennsylvania 6–5000" and "Chattanooga Choo-Choo," and audiences nostalgic for the previous decade were in bliss. Anthony Mann directed the Aaron Rosenberg production, which also featured Harry Morgan, GEORGE TOBIAS, Charles Drake, SIG RUMANN, and Barton MacLane.

GLOVER, SAVION (1973–). Stage performer and choreographer. An electric African American dancer and creator of unique dance programs, he has lit up the Broadway stage several times in his young career. Glover was born in Newark, New Jersey, and attended the local arts high school. He also trained at the Broadway Dance Center and studied tap with Michael Blevins before making his Broadway debut at the age of ten as a replacement in *THE TAP DANCE KID* in 1983. He was featured in the revue *BLACK AND BLUE* (1989) and that same year was in the film *Tap* (1989) dancing with tap masters SAMMY DAVIS, JR. and GREGORY HINES. In 1990 Glover joined the cast of the children's television show *Sesame Street*, taking time out to return to Broadway as the young Jelly Roll Morton in *JELLY'S LAST JAM* (1992), dancing again with Hines. With director GEORGE C. WOLFE, Glover created, choreographed, and danced in the innovative musical *BRING IN 'DA NOISE, BRING IN 'DA FUNK* (1996). He has choreographed television specials, tours, and films, such as *Bamboozled* (2000) and *Happy Feet* (2006). In 2005 he toured with his own dance show, *Improvography II*. Glover's work is a thrilling mixture of traditional dance and modern movement, put together in a fascinating manner that has wide audience appeal.

Go INTO YOUR DANCE (Warner 1935). Another chiché-filled backstager with a superior score by HARRY WARREN (music) and AL DUBIN (lyrics), this one was unique in that it was the only feature film to co-star AL JOLSON and RUBY KEELER (who was Mrs. Jolson at the time). Earl Baldwin's screenplay was based on a novel by Bradford Robes, whose earlier book was the source for *42ND STREET* (1933). Egotistical entertainer Al Howard (Jolson) is on the outs because no one will work with him, but humble dancer Dorothy Wayne (Keeler) believes in Al and manages to open a nightclub in New York in which he can be featured. Some gangsters and a bum murder rap slow down her plans but the night spot

eventually opens with a splash and the two end up dancing atop a globe to "A Latin From Manhattan." Other songs in the score included the rhythmic "About a Quarter to Nine" and the snappy title number. A touching but sad moment in the musical was HELEN MORGAN, in the supporting role of Luana Wells, the gangster's mistress, sitting on a piano and delivering the morose torch song "The Little Things You Used to Do." Alcoholism had pretty much destroyed Morgan's career by this time, but Jolson insisted that she be given the cameo part and she was incredibly poignant. Also in the cast were AKIM TAMIROFF, Glenda Farrell, Barton MacLane, PATSY KELLY, PHIL REGAN, and Benny Rubin. ARCHIE MAYO directed the gritty musical, and BOBBY CONNOLLY did the choreography.

GODSPELL (Cherry Lane Theatre 1971). An intimate, exhilarating musical version of St. Matthew's Gospel, the surprise Off Broadway hit introduced songwriter STEPHEN SCHWARTZ to theatregoers. John-Michael Tebelak's libretto chronicled the life of Jesus from his baptism to his death, enacted by an ensemble of circus-like performers using jokes, mime, vaudeville bits, and songs. "Day By Day" was the most popular number in the show but also becoming favorites were "All for the Best," "Bless the Lord," "Turn Back, O Man," "We Beseech Thee," "Save the People," "Light of the World," and "All Good Gifts." The free-spirited, tuneful musical was directed by author Tebelak with energy and affection and the show ran 2,118 performances. A 1976 Broadway production, also directed by Tebelak, retained the staging and spirit of the original and ran 527 performances, and a revival is set for Broadway in 2008. The show continues to be one of the most frequently produced musicals in schools, community, regional, and summer stock theatres as well as in churches.

Godspell (Columbia 1973) was certainly opened up from its small Off Broadway roots, with the biblical musical now taking place all over New York City and celebrating its many locations like no other movie since *ON THE TOWN* (1949). VICTOR GARBER was the androgynous flower child Jesus, and David Haskell was the hobo hoofer who played John the Baptist and then later Judas. Tebelak wrote the screenplay with director David Greene, and the cast dashed all over the cityscape, from tap dancing on top of the World Trade Center towers to high kicking in front of a twinkling sign in Times Square. Most of the stage songs

Godspell. The tiny Off Broadway musical was opened up for the 1973 film, using various Manhattan locations to frolic, sing, dance, and act out parables. Here Victor Garber (center with the Superman shirt) and his disciples bring their props along with them as they hit Central Park. (Photofest)

Casts for *Godspell*

Character	1971 Off Broadway	1973 film	1976 Broadway
Jesus	Stephen Nathan	VICTOR GARBER	Don Scardino
John/Judas	David Haskell	David Haskell	Tom Rolfing
	Peggy Gordon	Katie Hanley	Laurie Falso
	Herb Braha	Merrell Jackson	Bobby Lee
	Joanne Jonas	Joanne Jonas	Valerie Williams
	Robin Lamont	Robin Lamont	Robin Lamont
	Gilmer McCormick	Gilmer McCormick	Lamar Alford
	Jeffrey Mylett	Jeffrey Mylett	Marley Sims
	Lamar Alford	Jerry Sroka	Elizabeth Lathram
	Sonia Manzano	Lynne Thigpen	Lois Foraker

were used and Schwartz wrote a new number, "Beautiful City," that capsulated the musical celebration of Manhattan as a city of love.

■ **GOING HOLLYWOOD** (Cosmopolitan/MGM 1933). A musical vehicle for MARIAN DAVIES presented by her benefactor William Randolph

Hearst, the film used Tinsel Town as *42ND STREET* (1933) used Broadway, both conveniently disabling the star so that a newcomer could go on and save the show. Donald Ogden Stewart's screenplay made Davies that newcomer as French teacher Sylvia Bruce who follows her sweetheart Billy Williams (BING

CROSBY) to Hollywood where he hopes to become a star. Sylvia rescues Billy from drink and the arms of the hussy Lili Yvonne (Fifi D'Orsay) and then goes to the sound stage and makes a stellar debut in a feature film musical. Davies gave one of her most radiant performances of her mismanaged career, and newcomer Crosby saw his screen career take off when he sang the fervent "Temptation" in a Tijuana saloon as he hallucinated and saw the unfaithful D'Orsay's face in his liquor glass. The other songs by NACIO HERB BROWN (music) and ARTHUR FREED (lyrics) included "We'll Make Hay While the Sun Shines," "After Sundown," "Our Big Love Scene," and the jaunty title song. The supporting cast included STUART ERWIN, NED SPARKS, PATSY KELLY, and Bobby Watson, all under the no-nonsense direction of RAOUL WALSH. The Walter Wanger production was the first screen musical to use Hollywood and the movie business as its setting, but it would be far from the last.

🎬 **GOING MY WAY** (Paramount 1944). One of the studio's biggest hits of the decade, the sentimental musical drama helped keep BING CROSBY the top box office attraction for several years running. In many ways it was a break-out film for the crooner, playing the gentle priest Fr. Chuck O'Malley in FRANK BUTLER and Frank Cavette's screenplay based on a story by director LEO MCCAREY. Sent to a rundown urban parish where aging, conservative Fr. Fitzgibbon (Barry Fitzgerald) is pastor, Fr. O'Malley organizes a boys' choir out of the riffraff on the street, brings a young couple together, raises money for the poor parish, and even brings Fr. Fitzgibbon's ninety-year-old mother from Ireland for Christmas. It was sentiment stuff all around but it was handled with taste by the director and the cast. The supporting cast included Gene Lockhart, FRANK MCHUGH, Jean Heather, and opera singer RISË STEVENS as opera singer Genevieve Linden who helps Fr. O'Malley get the choir heard by record producer Max Dolan (WILLIAM FRAWLEY). What he heard was the gentle title ballad and the hit novelty number "Swinging on a Star," both by JAMES VAN HEUSEN (music) and JOHNNY BURKE (lyrics). The film collected a choir loft full of Oscars and was soon followed by the sequel **The Bells of St. Mary's** (Rainbow/RKO 1945). Crosby reprised his role of Fr. O'Malley, and Van Heusen and Burke again provided him with a hit song, "Aren't You Glad You're You?" The understanding Fr. O'Malley sang it to the dejected Patsy Gallagher (Joan Carroll), one of the students in a poor parish school run by the not-so-understanding Sister Mary Benedict (Ingrid Bergman). Fr. O'Malley has recently been transferred to the school and he and the Sister Superior clash before sentimentality conquers all. The Dudley Nichols screenplay was tamer and more tired than the earlier work and there were only four songs in the movie, one of them a hymn, so the sequel didn't feel much like a musical. Also featured in the cast were Henry Travers, William Gargan, Ruth Donnelly, Martha Sleeper, Rhy Williams, Una O'Connor, and Richard Tyler. McCarey again directed with that heart-tugging way of his and the sequel was nearly as popular as *Going My Way*.

GOLD DIGGERS IN PARIS. See *GOLD DIGGERS OF BROADWAY*

🎬 **GOLD DIGGERS OF BROADWAY** (Warner 1929). An agreeable backstager in the distinct WARMER BROTHERS style, the movie inspired a series of five Gold Digger sequels, some of them much better than this original. Robert Lord's screenplay had a plot seen earlier in a 1919 play on Broadway and in a 1923 silent film. Three chorus girls (WINNIE LIGHTNER, Nancy Welford, and ANN PENNINGTON) are after wealthy husbands and help fool a Boston snob (Conway Tearle), who comes to New York, into paying off the gold digger who is after his nephew. After a night on the town, during which the stuffy uncle is put in a compromising position, all ends happily as each girl gets the chump of her choice. Songs by JOE BURKE (music) and AL DUBIN (lyrics) were used in the plot and in the show that the chorines are appearing in, giving the film a lift, especially when they were as catchy as "Tip Toe Through the Tulips" and "Painting the Clouds With Sunshine." The cast also included Lilyan Tashman, William Blakewell, and Nick Lucas, all under the direction of ROY DEL RUTH with a folksy kind of familiarity with backstage life. Some sections of the film were in the new Technicolor process, which certainly impressed audiences. The next installment, **Gold Diggers of 1933** (Warner 1933) was the best of the series, dealing with a backstage milieu again but now it was Broadway in the depths of the Depression. The musical is one of the few to deal with the economic condition that had so affected audiences watching the film. Some of the 1929 plot remained with GINGER ROGERS, JOAN BLONDELL, RUBY KEELER, and Aline McMahon as chorus girls whose show is closed down in rehearsal because the producer ran out of money. The nephew this time was a songwriter (DICK POWELL) who loved the Keeler character but whose family sets out to break up the relationship. More emphasis was put on the production numbers, and choreographer BUSBY BERKELEY turned each one of the HARRY WARREN (music) and Al Dubin (lyrics) songs into a visual as well as a musical feast. Rogers and the chorines were dressed in outfits made of coins for the optimistic "We're in the Money;" lovers cuddled and kissed in "Pettin' in the Park" until a sudden thunder shower sent the girls scurrying for cover and they were shown changing out of their wet clothes in silhouette; and violin-playing chorus girls formed patterns and even glowed in the dark for "The Shadow Waltz." The finale was a tribute to war veterans out of a job during the Depression, with Etta Moten and Blondell singing "Remember My Forgotten Man" as flashbacks of soldiers marching off to war dissolved into the same men now in bread lines. It was musical comedy at its most socially conscious and yet was still enormously entertaining. The DARRYL F. ZANUZK production, which also featured Warren William, NED SPARKS, GUY KIBBEE, Clarence Nordstrom, and BILLY BARTY, was directed by MERVYN LEROY.

The Broadway backstage locale was abandoned for **Gold Diggers of 1935** (Warner 1935), which was directed and choreographed by Berkeley. The Manuel Seff and Peter Milne screenplay was set in a New Hampshire summer resort where the gold digging is done by

a Russian con man (ADOLPH MENJOU) who is trying to fleece a society matron (ALICE BRADY) even as a secretary (Glenda Farrell) is blackmailing a wealthy snuff box collector (Hugh Herbert) and a struggling medical student (Dick Powell) is falling in love with an heiress (GLORIA STUART). The songs were again by Warren and Dubin and it was the large production numbers that counted, such as having fifty-six pianos played by fifty-six girls for "The Words Are in My Heart," with the pianos moving about to create designs and patterns. The "Lullaby of Broadway" sequence was the most ambitious, a narrative ballet that showed twenty-four hours in the hedonistic life of a New York chorus girl. A long shot of Winifred Shaw's face grew from a distant speck of light into a facial close-up that dissolved into the Manhattan skyline. What followed was a montage of the city's nightlife that climaxed with the chorine being pushed out a window to her death. It was Berkeley's most dramatic film sequence and relied on precision dancing and dynamic camera work rather than gimmicks.

Joan Blondell finally got to play the leading lady in **Gold Diggers Of 1937** (Warner 1936). In Warren Duff's screenplay, an insurance salesman (Powell) tries to sell a theatrical producer (VICTOR MOORE) a huge policy so that his cronies could have enough money to produce a Broadway show after he dies. The old man continues to live but the show goes on anyway, featuring a military finale, "All's Fair in Love and War" by Warren and

---

Songs from the *Gold Diggers* films

The Gold Diggers of Broadway (1929)
"Tiptoe Through the Tulips"
"Painting the Clouds With Sunshine"
"And They Still Fall in Love"
"What Will I Do Without You?"

Gold Diggers of 1935
"Lullaby of Broadway"
"The Words Are Written in My Heart"
"Going Shopping With You"

Gold Diggers in Paris (1938)
"Day Dreaming (All Night Long)"
"The Latin Quarter"
"I Wanna Go Back to Bali"
"A Stranger in Paree"
"Put That Down in Writing"
"Waltz of the Flowers"
"My Adventure"

Gold Diggers of 1933
"We're in the Money"
"Remember My Forgotten Man"
"Pettin' in the Park"
"The Shadow Waltz"
"I've Got to Sing a Torch Song"

Gold Diggers of 1937 (1936)
"With Plenty of Money and You"
"All's Fair in Love and War"
"Let's Put Our Heads Together"
"Speaking of the Weather"

Dubin, in which Blondell led dozens of goose-stepping chorus girls in a battle of the sexes. The same songwriters also came up with the catchy "With Plenty of Money and You," whereas HAROLD ARLEN (music) and E. Y. HARBURG (lyrics) penned "Let's Put Our Heads Together," which fifty couples sang as they rocked to the rhythm of the music in giant rocking chairs. Berkeley choreographed and LLOYD BACON directed. The series ended with *Gold Diggers in Paris* (Warner 1938), a frail musical in which RUDDY VALLEE and his nightclub dancing girls are invited to a Paris festival with the misunderstanding that they are a ballet troupe. Berkeley again staged the musical numbers, although on a much less lavish scale than earlier in the series. Warren and Dubin's "The Latin Quarter" was a breezy song about the Left Bank that Berkeley choreographed with grace, and Warren and JOHNNY MERCER penned the ballad "Day Dreaming (All Night Long)," which Vallee and ROSEMARY LANE sang together. RAY ENRIGHT directed the film that did so poorly at the box office that *Gold Diggers* sequels were discontinued. Years later the series returned somewhat with *Painting the Clouds With Sunshine* (1951), a remake of the original *Gold Diggers of Broadway* with VIRGINIA MAYO, Lucille Norman, and Virginia Gibson as the three showgirls and some old standards (including two from the 1929 film) were dusted off and used again.

GOLD DIGGERS OF 1933/1935/1937. See *GOLD DIGGERS OF BROADWAY*

GOLDEN APPLE, THE (Phoenix Theatre 1954). One of the American musical theatre's most beloved failures, the brilliant and charming show failed to run but has gained plenty of fans over the years. Soon after Ulysses (STEPHEN DOUGLASS) and his men return from the Spanish American War to their little town of Angel's Roost, Washington, the traveling salesman Paris (Jonathan Lucas) runs off with Helen (KAYE BALLARD), the wife of Sheriff Menelaus, so Ulysses, Hector (JACK WHITING), and the other war heroes follow in pursuit. After several adventures, Ulysses beats Paris in a boxing match and then returns home to his faithful wife Penelope (Priscilla Gillette). Also in the excellent cast were Bibi Osterwald, Portia Nelson, Jerry Stiller, and David Hooks. This retelling of *The Iliad* and *The Odyssey* tales was sung through with no dialogue, with the score by Jerome Moross (music) and JOHN LATOUCHE (lyrics) echo-

ing different kinds of American music and employing clever, tongue-in-cheek lyrics. Among the memorable songs were the languid seduction song "Lazy Afternoon," the domestic number "It's the Going Home Together," the warm ballad "Windflowers," and the Hawaiian-flavored "By Goona-Goona Lagoon." The smart little musical was so lauded when it opened Off Broadway that after six weeks it moved to Broadway where surprisingly it only lasted 125 performances. A favorite cult show, it was far ahead of its time and its score is still treasured as one of the most unique of the decade.

GOLDEN BOY (Majestic Theatre 1964). A musicalization of Clifford Odets' 1937 boxing drama of the same title, the musical play was primarily a showcase for the talents of SAMMY DAVIS, JR. The African American boxer Joe Wellington (Davis) from Harlem is on the brink of breaking into the big time but when he finds that his white girl friend Lorna Moon (Paula Wayne) is sleeping with his manager Tom Moody (Kenneth Tobey), Joe gets drunk and dies in a car crash. Also in the fine cast were Billy Daniels, Terrin Miles, Louis Gossett, and Lola Falana. William Gibson and Odets collaborated on the libretto and the adaptation was sometimes awkward but there were enough potent scenes and songs that parts of the show were thrilling, such as Davis' dazzling performance and DONALD McKAYLE's choreography and fight sequences. CHARLES STROUSE (music) and LEE ADAMS (lyrics) wrote their most atypical score and it was filled with adept songs, such as "I Want to Be With You," "Night Song," "While the City Sleeps," "Don't Forget 127th Street," "This Is the Life," "Gimme Some," and "No More." The musical overcame mixed notices and ran 568 performances on the popularity of Davis.

GOLDILOCKS (Lunt-Fontane Theatre 1958). A musical satire of Hollywood by Walter and Jean Kerr (book and lyrics), Leroy Anderson (music), and Joan Ford (lyrics), the show featured the unique ELAINE STRITCH in one of her few Broadway leads. In the days of the early silent film business in New Jersey, the rising movie mogul Max Grady (DON AMECHE) and his star, Broadway performer Maggie Harris (Stritch), are always at odds, but Maggie ends up throwing over the socialite George Randolph Brown (RUSSELL NYPE) to marry Max. Pat Stanley, Nathaniel Frey, and MARGARET HAMILTON were also in the cast directed by Walter Kerr. The score was first rate, with such songs as "I Never Know When," "Who's Been Sitting in My Chair?," "I Can't Be in Love," "The Beast in You," "The Pussy Foot," and "If I Can't Take It With Me." Some wonderful performances, a tuneful score, and witty choreography by AGNES DE MILLE were all weighed down by a mediocre book, but there was enough to entertain audiences for 161 performances.

■ GOLDWYN FOLLIES, THE (Goldwyn/ United Artists 1938). The movie is not a true *Follies*, being a plotted musical rather than a revue, but there are a succession of specialty spots that pad out the thin storyline contrived by screenwriter Ben Hecht. Short-order cook Danny Beecher (KENNY BAKER) is trying to make it in Hollywood as a singer with the help of his girl friend Hazel Dawes (Andrea Leeds, singing dubbed by Virginia Verrill). Movie producer Oliver Merlin (ADOLPHE MENJOU) has selected Hazel to be his "Miss Humanity," the average moviegoer who will evaluate his products from the point of view of the public. There are some misunderstandings about the relationship between Hazel and Oliver that are cleared up before Danny gets his girl and a studio contract. The story was mercifully interrupted by unrelated acts such as the RITZ BROTHERS, opera diva Helen Jepson, BOBBY CLARK, EDGAR BERGEN and his dummy Charlie McCarthy, and singer Ella Logan. VERA ZORINA appeared in a ballet segment choreographed by GEORGE BALANCHINE that featured music by VERNON DUKE. Originally the dance piece was to be done to new music by GEORGE GERSHWIN who, with his brother Ira, supplied the songs for the film, but George died during production and Duke had to complete the score. Four outstanding songs were introduced in the film, although they were not shown to their best advantage and had to wait to become famous later when they had been recorded. "I Love to Rhyme," "Love Walked In," "I Was Doing All Right," and "(Our) Love Is Here to Stay" each deserved a better film. It was a sad anticlimax for George Gershwin's too-brief movie career. Producer SAMUEL GOLDWYN spent so much money on the picture (it was done in the new three-color Technicolor) that, despite its healthy box office, he abandoned plans to do other *Follies* as FLORENZ ZIEGFELD had done on Broadway.

GOLDWYN, SAMUEL [born Shmuel Gelgfisz] (1879–1974). Film producer. One of Hollywood's most colorful and tireless executives, the prolific producer presented seventeen screen musicals and made Broadway musical players such as EDDIE CANTOR and DANNY KAYE into movie stars. Goldwyn was born in Warsaw, Poland, and at the age of eleven emigrated to England where he worked for a blacksmith. Arriving in American in 1892 as Samuel Goldfish, he settled in Gloversville, New York, where he learned to sew gloves and later became a traveling salesman and learned about business. With his brother-in-law Jesse L. Lasky, he formed a film production company and hired the young Cecil B. De Mille to direct, having a hit early on with *The Squaw Man* (1914). Going into business with theatre producer Edgar Selwyn, he put their names together and founded Goldwyn Pictures, legally changing his name to Goldwyn as well. A later merger created METRO-GOLDWYN-MAYER but Goldwyn wanted to be his own boss and for most of his career he was an independent producer. He made every kind of picture and had a good number of hits in each genre. His musical credits are *WHOOPEE!* (1930), *One Heavenly Night* (1930), *Palmy Days* (1931), *The Kid From Spain* (1932), *ROMAN SCANDALS* (1933), *KID MILLIONS* (1934), *Strike Me Pink* (1936), *THE GOLDWYN FOLLIES* (1938), *They Shall Have Music* (1939), *UP IN ARMS* (1934), *Wonder Man* (1945), *The Kid From Brooklyn* (1946), *The Secret Life of Walter Mitty* (1947), *A Song Is Born* (1948), *HANS CHRISTIAN ANDERSEN* (1952), *GUYS AND DOLLS* (1955), and *PORGY AND BESS* (1959). His son is producer Samuel Goldwyn, Jr. (1926–). Biography: *Goldwyn: A Biography*, A. Scott Berg (1998).

🎵 GOOD NEWS! (46th Street Theatre 1927). The best book musical by the team of DeSylva, Brown, and Henderson, this toe-tapping campus show was one of the most popular musicals of the 1920s and is still revived on occasion. LAURENCE SCHWAB and B. G. DeSYLVA's libretto was set at Tait College and, as in most collegiate musicals, the plot revolved around football. The team's star player Tom Marlowe may not be able to play in the big game if he fails his astronomy exam. The brainy Connie Lane, who is in love with Tom but fears his affections lie elsewhere, agrees to tutor Tom and in the process he falls in love with Connie, passes the test, and wins the game.

The plot was packed with zany characters, and the songs by RAY HENDERSON (music), LEW BROWN, and DeSylva (lyrics) were exuberant,

Good News! The brainy Connie Lane (June Allyson) tries to coach the footballer Tom Marlowe (Peter Lawford) for his French exam in the second film version, but he has his mind on romance. Everyone in the cast looked a bit old for college undergrads but that didn't distract from all the musical fun. (Photofest)

making college life look like one big party. Five standards came from the score: the dreamy "Just Imagine," the swinging "Lucky in Love," the optimistic "The Best Things in Life Are Free," the foot-stomping "Varsity Drag," and the spirited title number. EDGAR MACGREGOR directed the Schwab–FRANK MANDEL production and BOBBY CONNOLLY devised the vivacious dances. The critics cheered and so did playgoers for 557 performances. For decades the musical was a staple in schools and summer stock, and the occasional revival today proves that *Good News!* is as durable as it is fun. Broadway saw no revivals until 1974. With a changed score, a new setting in the 1930s, and film stars ALICE FAYE and JOHN PAYNE in supporting roles that were built up to please audiences, the production toured the country for months and played many New York previews, during which time Payne was replaced by GENE NELSON. When the botched production finally opened, the damning reviews closed the

show in two weeks. ABE BURROWS directed and DONALD SADDLER choreographed, all for naught.

🎬 *Good News!* (MGM 1930) did not begin to capture the vitality and playfulness of the Broadway hit, and the studio, nervous about the public's growing disenchantment with movie musicals, cut two of the best songs ("The Best Things in Life Are Free" and "Lucky in Love") in order to shorten the picture. The screenplay by Francis Marion did not stray too far from the stage libretto but campus frivolity did not look as appealing in the early days of the Depression as it had in the prosperous Roaring Twenties. However, there are moments to enjoy in the film, particularly the "Varsity Drag" and the title song choreographed with splash by SAMMY LEE. There were a few new numbers ("Students Are We," "If You're Not Kissing Me," and "But I'd Like to Make You Happy") but the best things in the film were from the stage. MacGregor directed the movie with Nicke Grinde and, as MGM feared, it was not a box office success. The same studio had much better luck seventeen years later. *GOOD NEWS!* (MGM 1947) boasted a slightly updated screenplay by BETTY COMDEN and ADOLPH GREEN (in their first screen assignment) that tightened up the plot and the movie was cast with screen favorites JUNE ALLYSON

Casts for *Good News!*

Character	1927 Broadway	1930 film	1947 film
Tom Marlowe	John Price Jones	Stanley Smith	PETER LAWFORD
Constance Lane	Mary Lawlor	Mary Lawlor	JUNE ALLYSON
Bobby Randall	Gus Shy	Gus Shy	RAY MCDONALD
Babe/Dixie O'Day	Inez Courtney	Bessie Love	JOAN MCCRACKEN
Patricia Bingham	Shirley Vernon	Lola Lane	Pat McClellan
Flo	ZELMA O'NEAL	Penny Singleton	Georgia Lee

and PETER LAWFORD surrounded by some of the brightest young players on the lot. Much of the stage score was used and there were two new numbers that measured up to them: the conversational duet "The French Lesson" by ROGER EDENS (music), Comden, and Green (lyric) sung by Lawford and Allyson, and the contagious romp "Pass That Peace Pipe" by Edens, HUGH MARTIN, and RALPH BLANE that JOAN MCCRACKEN and RAY MCDONALD led in a campus ice cream parlor. The choreography was by ROBERT ALTON and CHARLES WALTERS (who also directed) and this time MGM had a hit.

GOODBYE, MR. CHIPS (APJAC/MGM 1969). The intimate, sentimental tale of a British schoolteacher was turned into a big budget Hollywood musical and, despite its many problems, ended up being an intimate sentimental film all the same. Terence Rattigan adapted James Hilton's beloved novella, which had been a hit nonmusical film in 1939, and LESLIE BRICUSSE wrote the songs, which added a tenderness to the story or sugar-coated the tale even further, depending on your outlook. Peter O'Toole was quietly enthralling as Arthur Chipping, affectionately called "Mr. Chips" by the boys at the boarding school where he teaches. PETULA CLARK was the London musical hall singer Katherine Bridges who falls in love with the reticent fellow and causes a ruckus at the school when she marries him and turns out not to be the demur kind of faculty wife that is the norm. Katherine dies entertaining the troops in World War I and Chips continues on, teaching generations of boys. Michael Redgrave, Sian Phillips, Michael Bryant, and George Baker were among the very British supporting cast and the film was shot on location in English so it certainly had the right look and feel. There was an authentic ring about the school anthem "Fill the World With Love," and the love song "Walk Through the World" was the kind of low-key ballad a schoolteacher like Chips would sing. HERBERT Ross directed with restraint, avoiding production numbers and musical comedy staging. Sometimes the characters sang their thoughts on the soundtrack rather than expressing them openly. It was all too quiet for the public who stayed away in droves, making the film a major financial disaster.

GOODMAN, BENNY [David] (1909–1986). Film musician, composer, and conductor. The famed clarinetist and bandleader dubbed the King of Swing, he had the most famous orchestra in America in the late 1930s and 1940s and was featured in eight Hollywood musicals. A native of Chicago, Goodman was educated at the Lewis Institute in his home town and then was a clarinet player for various bands before forming his own in 1934. Radio performances led to the sale of millions of records, and Goodman and his band were in great demand in concerts across the country, in Europe, South America, and even the Far East. He composed some of his band's most popular songs, such as "Stompin at the Savoy" and "Two O'Clock Jump." Goodman mostly played himself on screen and his band was usually on hand for his appearances in THE BIG BROADCAST OF 1937 (1936), HOLLYWOOD HOTEL (1937), The Powers Girl (1942), Syncopation (1942), THE GANG'S ALL HERE (1943), STAGE DOOR CANTEEN (1943), Sweet and Lowdown (1944), and A Song Is Born (1948). Goodman's clarinet playing was heard in the animated feature MAKE MINE MUSIC (1946) and he provided the playing for the film bio The Benny Goodman Story (1955) in which Steve Allen impersonated the celebrated musician. Biography: Swing, Swing, Swing: The Life and Times of Benny Goodman, Ross Firestone (1998).

GOODRICH, FRANCES, AND ALBERT HACKETT. Stage and film writing team. The successful Broadway and Hollywood writers adapted many stage musicals for the screen and wrote some excellent original ones as well. Frances Goodrich (1890–1984) was born in Belleville, New Jersey, and educated at Vassar College before beginning her career as an actress, making her Broadway debut in 1918 and getting small roles in plays over the next ten years. She turned to writing in the late 1920s and had her first play on Broadway in 1930, a comedy co-written with Hackett, and the next year they married. Albert [Maurice] Hackett (1900–1995) was born in New York into an acting family and was on the stage as a youth. He made his Broadway debut in 1909 and appeared in a handful of comedies, including Up Pops the Devil (1930), his first collaboration with Goodrich. The couple wrote other plays for Broadway, most notably The Diary of Anne Frank (1955). Goodrich and Hackett went to Hollywood in 1931 for the film version of Up Pops the Devil and soon found themselves adapting plays and musicals for the studios and writing original scripts. Their musical credits include NAUGHTY MARIETTA (1935), ROSE MARIE (1936), THE FIREFLY (1937), LADY IN THE DARK

(1944), *The Pirate* (1948), *Summer Holiday* (1948), *Easter Parade* (1948), *In the Good Old Summertime* (1949), *Give a Girl a Break* (1954), and *Seven Brides for Seven Brothers* (1954).

Goodspeed Opera House. Theatre company. Built in 1876 by William H. Goodspeed to contain a 400-seat playhouse and offices for his mercantile business in East Haddam, Connecticut, the Victorian Gothic structure served as an operating theatre until it closed in 1920. The building was scheduled to be demolished in the 1950s until concerned citizens rallied to save the structure and organized the Goodspeed Opera House Foundation to restore the building to a working theatre again. The Goodspeed reopened in 1963 and since that time has offered a wide variety of musical productions, from rarely produced works to popular favorites to new musicals. The company opened a second space in the 1980s called the Norma Terris Theatre, a more intimate space named after the 1920s Broadway star who lived nearby for so many years. Among the new musicals the Goodspeed has sent to Broadway are *Man of La Mancha*, *Shenandoah*, *Something's Afoot*, *Harrigan 'n Hart*, and *Annie*. The company has also seen some of their revivals transfer to New York, such as *Whoopee!*, *Gentlemen Prefer Blondes*, *Very Good Eddie*, *The Five O'Clock Girl*, and *Oh, Kay!*

Gordon, Mack [born Morris Gittler] (1904–1959). Film and stage lyricist. One of Hollywood's busiest songwriters, he collaborated with Harry Revel, Harry Warren, and others on hundreds of songs for over fifty screen musicals. Gordon was born in Warsaw, Poland, and emigrated to America with his family in 1908. He began in show business as an actor–singer in vaudeville and then started writing lyrics with composer Revel; their songs were featured in the Broadway musicals *Ziegfeld Follies* (1931), *Fast and Furious* (1931), *Everybody's Welcome* (1931), *Smiling Faces* (1932), and *Strike Me Pink* (1933). Although some songs by Gordon had been used in the Hollywood musicals *Song of Love* (1929), *Pointed Heels* (1929), and *Swing High* (1930), he and Revel didn't become resident songwriters for films until *Broadway Through a Keyhole* (1933). Over the next five years they scored over two dozen screen musicals, including *Sitting Pretty* (1933), *We're Not Dressing* (1934), *Shoot the Works* (1934), *She Loves Me Not* (1934), *College Rhythm* (1934), *Love in Bloom*

(1935), *Stolen Harmony* (1935), *Two for Tonight* (1935), *Collegiate* (1935), *Poor Little Rich Girl* (1936), *Stowaway* (1936), *Wake Up and Live* (1937), *You Can't Have Everything* (1937), *Love and Hisses* (1937), *Love Finds Andy Hardy* (1938), *My Lucky Star* (1938), and *Thanks for Everything* (1938). After writing both music and lyrics for *Star Dust* (1940), Gordon teamed with composer Warren for such 1940s musicals as *Young People* (1940), *Down Argentine Way* (1940), *That Night in Rio* (1941), *The Great American Broadcast* (1941), *Sun Valley Serenade* (1941), *Weekend in Havana* (1941), *Orchestra Wives* (1942), *Iceland* (1942), *Springtime in the Rockies* (1942), *Sweet Rosie O'Grady* (1943), *Diamond Horseshoe* (1945), and *Summer Stock* (1950). With other composers he wrote the songs for *Song of the Islands* (1942), *Pin-Up Girl* (1944), *Sweet and Lowdown* (1944), *Irish Eyes Are Smiling* (1944), *The Dolly Sisters* (1945), *Three Little Girls in Blue* (1946), *Mother Wore Tights* (1947), *Wabash Avenue* (1950), *Call Me Mister* (1951), *I Love Melvin* (1953), *The Girl Next Door* (1953), and *Bundle of Joy* (1956). Gordon's many hit songs include "Chattanooga Choo Choo," "You Make Me Feel So Young," "You'll Never Know," and "Did You Ever See a Dream Walking?"

Gordon, Max [born Mechel Salpeter] (1892–1978). Stage producer. The flamboyant Broadway producer who had the temperament of an actor, he produced some of the most distinctive musicals of the 1930s. The native New Yorker started in show business as a press agent and then became a talent agent in vaudeville before joining up with Sam H. Harris to produce plays and musicals. Later he would go solo and become one of the most successful producers of his era. Most of Gordon's musical credits were in the 1930s when revues flourished and his offerings in that genre were among the best: *Three's a Crowd* (1930), *The Band Wagon* (1931), *Flying Colors* (1932), and *Sing Out the News* (1938). His book musicals were *The Cat and the Fiddle* (1931), *Roberta* (1933), *The Great Waltz* (1934), *Jubilee* (1935), *Very Warm for May* (1939), *The Firebrand of Florence* (1945), *Hollywood Pinafore* (1945), and *Park Avenue* (1946). In the 1940s he concentrated on comedies, such as *My Sister Eileen* (1940) and *Born Yesterday* (1945). Autobiography: *Max Gordon Presents* (1963).

Gorney, Jay (1896–1990). Stage and film composer. A little known songwriter today, the Russian-born composer wrote for Broadway and Hollywood and gave America its unofficial theme song for the Depression, "Brother, Can You Spare a Dime?" Gorney was born in Bialystok, Russia, and in 1906 emigrated to America where he studied at the University of Michigan. During World War I he was a bandmaster for the navy and then turned to composing popular songs. He contributed to the Broadway musicals THE PASSING SHOW (1923), *Top-Hole* (1924), *Vogues of 1924*, ARTISTS AND MODELS (1925), *Merry-Go-Round* (1927), *Earl Carroll's Sketchbook* (1929), EARL CARROLL'S VANITIES (1930), ZIEGFELD FOLLIES (1931), *Shoot the Works* (1931), and *Americana* (1932), the last in which he and lyricist E. Y. HARBURG introduced the cry of the common man, "Brother, Can You Spare a Dime?" Gorney went to Hollywood in 1933 and wrote commendable songs with Harburg and others for second-rate movies musicals: *Jimmy and Sally* (1933), *Moonlight and Pretzels* (1933), *Wild Gold* (1934), *Lottery Lover* (1935), *Redheads on Parade* (1935), *The Heat's On* (1943), and *Hey, Rookie* (1944). One of his best Hollywood songs was "Baby, Take a Bow," which was interpolated into the SHIRLEY TEMPLE vehicle *Stand Up and Cheer* (1934). Gorney returned to Broadway in the 1940s and wrote songs for the revues *Meet the People* (1940), *Heaven on Earth* (1948), and *Touch and Go* (1949). He was also chairman of the music division of the Dramatic Workshop at the New School in Manhattan and later also taught for the American Theatre Wing. His daughter is actress–dancer Karen Lynn Gorney (1945–). Biography: *Brother, Can You Spare a Dime? The Life of Composer Jay Gorney*, Sondra K. Gorney [his wife] (2005).

GOULD, DAVE (1899–1969). Stage and film choreographer and director. A Broadway choreographer who found greater success in Hollywood, he gave audiences some of the most spectacular musical sequences of the 1930s. Gould was born in Budapest, Hungary, and danced in musicals before becoming a choreographer in the late 1920s. His Broadway credits include *Hello Yourself!* (1928), *Grand Street Follies* (1929), *The Second Little Show* (1930), FINE AND DANDY (1930), *The Gang's All Here* (1931), and *Hey Nonny Nonny!* (1932). Gould went to Hollywood and quickly learned to expand his thinking regarding dance. After choreographing *Melody Cruise* with little notice, he gained wide recognition with his dances for FLYING DOWN TO RIO (1933), particularly the airborne finale with chorines strapped to airplanes. One of his other unforgettable

production numbers is the stylish finale of BORN TO DANCE (1936) set on a gleaming white battleship. Gould's other screen musicals include *Hollywood Party* (1934), THE GAY DIVORCEE (1934), FOLIES BERGERE (1935), BROADWAY MELODY OF 1936 (1935), *A DAY AT THE RACES* (1937), BROADWAY MELODY OF 1938 (1937), THE BOYS FROM SYRACUSE (1940), *Rhythm Parade* (1942), *My Best Gal* (1944), and *Rosie the Riveter* (1944), as well as the dances in several nonmusical films. He returned to Broadway to choreograph the revue *Sing Out the News* (1938). In the 1940s, Gould also directed eighteen musical film shorts.

GOULET, ROBERT [Gerald] (1933–2007). Stage, film, and television performer. The rich-voiced baritone appeared in only a few Broadway musicals but performed in many on tour, in stock and summer theatre, and on television. Goulet was born in Lawrence, Massachusetts, grew up in Edmonton, Canada, and later studied voice at the Royal Conservatory of Music in Toronto. After playing in musical revivals across Canada, he made a sensational Broadway debut as Lancelot in CAMELOT (1960). He returned to Broadway as the French Canadian photographer Jacques Bonnard in THE HAPPY TIME (1968), King Arthur in *Camelot* in 1993, and a replacement for the Gay nightclub owner Georges in LA CAGE AUX FOLLES (2004). Goulet made many films, although he rarely got to sing in them. He starred on dozens of television programs, from dramatic series to musical specials, such as the TV versions of BRIGADOON (1966), CAROUSEL (1967), and KISS ME, KATE (1968). Goulet recorded many records and provided singing and speaking voices for several animated TV shows and films, including GAY PURR-EE (1962) and *Toy Story 2* (1999). He was married to singer–actress CAROL LAWRENCE for a time.

GRABLE, BETTY [born Elizabeth Ruth Grable] (1916–1973). Film, stage, and television performer. The queen of Technicolor musicals in the 1940s and the American GI's favorite pin-up girl during the war, the shapely blonde with the million-dollar legs appeared in bit roles in thirty-one films before becoming a star. Grable was born in St. Louis and began dance lessons at the age of three. Her ambitious stage mother brought her thirteen-year old daughter to Hollywood in 1930 and, lying about the girl's age, got her cast in the chorus or in minor roles in such musicals as *Let's Go Places* (1930), WHOOPEE! (1930), *Palmy Days*

(1931), *Sweetheart of Sigma Chi* (1933), *THE GAY DIVORCEE* (1934), *Old Man Rhythm* (1935), *Collegiate* (1936), *FOLLOW THE FLEET* (1936), *Pigskin Parade* (1936), *Thrill of a Lifetime* (1937), *College Swing* (1938), and *Give Me a Sailor* (1938). Frustrated with the way her career was stalled, Grable went to Broadway where she got a featured role in *DUBARRY WAS A LADY* (1939). Back in Hollywood she finally got her big break when the leading role planned for ALICE FAYE in *DOWN ARGENTINE WAY* (1940) was open and the studio needed another blonde. Grable shone in the part and quickly became the decade's favorite new discovery. She starred in twenty-three more film musicals, including *TIN PAN ALLEY* (1940), *MOON OVER MIAMI* (1941), *SPRINGTIME IN THE ROCKIES* (1942), *CONEY ISLAND* (1943), *Sweet Rosie O'Grady* (1943), *Four Jills in a Jeep* (1944), *Pin-Up Girl* (1944), *THE DOLLY SISTERS* (1945), *THE SHOCKING MISS PILGRIM* (1947), *MOTHER WORE TIGHTS* (1947), *That Lady in Ermine* (1948), and *When My Baby Smiles at Me* (1948). Grable managed to remain popular after the war years and into the 1950s with such musicals as *WABASH AVENUE* (1950), *My Blue Heaven* (1950), *CALL ME MISTER* (1951), and *THE FARMER TAKES A WIFE* (1953). She also made many nonmusical films, most memorably *How to Marry a Millionaire* (1953). After making the musical *Three for the Show* (1955), she left Hollywood, never to return. She made many nightclub and television appearances and took over the role of Dolly Levi in *HELLO, DOLLY!* on Broadway in 1967 before her premature death from lung cancer. Grable was known for her feisty screen persona, chipper singing voice, and gorgeous legs, which 20TH CENTURY-FOX insured for $1 million in a crafty publicity stunt. She was married to actor Jackie Coogan (1914–1984) and bandleader HARRY JAMES. Biographies: *Betty Grable: The Girl With the Million Dollar Legs*, Tom McGee (1995); *Betty Grable: The Reluctant Movie Queen*, Doug Warren (1981).

GRAFF, RANDY (1955–). Stage and television performer. A flexible actress–singer with a solid, belt voice, she has been effective in comic and serious musicals, as well as in dramas and comedies. Graff was born in Brooklyn and educated at Wagner College before making her New York debut as a replacement in *GREASE* (1972). After appearing in an Off Broadway revival of *PINS AND NEEDLES* (1978), *Savará* (1979), and *A ... My Name Is Alice* (1984), Graff received plaudits as Fantine in the original Broadway cast of *LES MISÉRABLES* (1987).

She followed that with the double roles of Girl Fridays Donna and Oolie in *CITY OF ANGELS* (1989). Her other musical credits include *A ... My Name Is Still Alice* (1991), *FALSETTOS* (1993), *HIGH SOCIETY* (1998), *Class Act* (2000), and as Golde in the 2004 revival of *FIDDLER ON THE ROOF*. Graff had a small role in the film version of *RENT* (2005) and has acted in some television series.

GRAND HOTEL (Martin Beck Theatre 1989). Much more than a musicalization of the soap opera-like play by Vicki Baum, the musical eschewed traditional narrative for a bold, expressionistic approach to recreating the various levels of society in 1928 Berlin. Luther Davis wrote the ambitious libretto, and the score by ROBERT WRIGHT and GEORGE FORREST was augmented by songs by MAURY YESTON. TOMMY TUNE directed and choreographed, setting the tale in a surreal hotel with no walls but plenty of chairs to denote different locations. Liliane Montevecchi was the fading ballerina Grushinskaya, DAVID CARROLL the dishonest Count Felix von Gaigan who loves her, Jane Krakowski the eager stenographer Flaemmchen, Timothy Jerome the failed businessman Preysing, Michael Jeter the dying accountant Otto Kringelein, and Karen Akers the ballerina's overly devoted companion Raffaela. Among the many estimable songs were "Love Can't Happen," "We'll Take a Glass Together," "I Want to Go to Hollywood," "Fire and Ice," "Who Couldn't Dance With You?," "Maybe My Baby Loves Me," and "I Waltz Alone." The production was fraught with difficulties before opening, and songwriter Yeston was called in to rewrite half of the score but by opening the stylish, beautifully performed musical came together enough to get appreciative notices. Tune tinkered with the production even after opening and, with audience approval, settled in for a run of 1,077 performances.

GRAND TOUR, THE (Palace Theatre 1979). One of songwriter JERRY HERMAN's more ambitious shows, it was not one of his many hits, although it was highly commendable. In Mark Bramble and MICHAEL STEWART's libretto, the Jewish refugee S. L. Jacobowsky (JOEL GREY) travels across war-torn Europe with the Polish Col. Stjerbinsky (RON HOLGATE), the two slowly becoming friends despite their very different backgrounds and beliefs. This musical version of the popular play *Jacobowsky and the Colonel* (1944) retained much of the whimsy and charm of the original, and several of the songs were first rate, such as "I'll Be Here Tomorrow," "Marianne," "You I Like," "One Extraordinary Thing," and "For Poland." Gerald Freedman directed the excellent cast, which also included Florence Lacey, Stephen Vinovich, Grace Keagy, and Mark Waldrop, and DONALD SADDLER choreographed. Critical reaction was mixed and the musical had trouble finding an audience, closing after sixty-one performances.

GRANT, MICKI (1941?–). Stage lyricist, composer, writer, and performer. The Chicago native was educated at the University of Illinois, Roosevelt University, and De Paul University and began her career as a member of the theatrical group Center Aisle Players. In New York she appeared in several Off Broadway and Broadway plays and the musical *Tambourines to Glory* (1963). In 1970 Grant formed a partnership with producer–director VINNETTE CARROLL and they presented a series of nine musical revues at the Urban Arts Corps, some of which went on to Broadway. Grant wrote the music, lyrics, book, and performed in *DON'T BOTHER ME, I CAN'T COPE* (1972), contributed lyrics to *YOUR ARMS TOO SHORT TO BOX WITH GOD* (1976) and *WORKING* (1978), and wrote the book and score for *It's So Nice to Be Civilized* (1980). She has made many television appearances over the years, including the musical version of *THE CRADLE WILL ROCK* (1964). Grant was also one of the first African Americans to become a regular on a television soap opera.

🕮 **GRASS HARP, THE** (Martin Beck Theatre 1971). An offbeat little musical that lasted on Broadway for only seven performances, the show has reached cult status because of its delectable score. In order to avoid the commercial plans of her sister Verena (Ruth Ford) to manufacture a dropsy cure she has developed, the unconventional Dolly Talbo (BARBARA COOK) retreats to a tree house with her young relative Collin (RUSS THACKER) and the African American–Native American servant Catherine Creek (Carol Brice) until she realizes you cannot totally escape the world so she returns and accepts life as it is. Kenward Elmslie adapted Truman Capote's novella and play and wrote the lyrics for Claibe Richardson's music. The score was a charming mix of gospel, operetta, blues, and musical comedy, with such delightful numbers as "Yellow Drum," "I'll Always Be in Love," "Marry With Me," "Reach Out,"

and "The Babylove Miracle Show," a cycle of songs delivered with panache by Karen Morrow as a cockeyed evangelist.

GRAY, DOLORES (1924–2002). Stage, film, and television performer. A statuesque musical comedy performer with a Broadway belt and a brassy persona, she seldom found herself originating roles but often triumphed as a replacement. Born in Chicago, Gray was given singing and dancing lessons by her mother who was then singing in San Francisco nightclubs and performing on the radio. Gray was only a teenager when she started singing in clubs where she was later discovered by RUDY VALLEE who made her a regular on his radio show. Her Broadway debut was in the revue *Seven Lively Arts* (1944), followed by character parts in the short-lived book musicals *Are You With It?* (1945) and *Sweet Bye and Bye* (1946), which never made it to New York. Gray became a London star when she played Annie Oakley in *ANNIE GET YOUR GUN* (1946) for three years. Returning to Broadway, she enthralled audiences in the revue *TWO ON THE AISLE* (1951) and then shone as the sexy "widow" Cornelia in the flop *Carnival in Flanders* (1953), saloon singer Frenchy in *DESTRY RIDES AGAIN* (1959), and vain actress Lorraine Sheldon in the unsuccessful *Sherry!* (1967). Once again Gray became a favorite in London when she played Mama Rose in *Gypsy* in 1973 and finally was in a Broadway hit again when she was a replacement for Dorothy Brock in *42ND STREET* in 1986. She made her last hurrah on the London stage in *Follies* in 1987. She made only three movie musicals but each role was choice: the TV star Madeline Bradbille in *IT'S ALWAYS FAIR WEATHER* (1955), the sultry Lalume in *KISMET* (1955), and the Park Avenue gossip Sylvia in *The Opposite Sex* (1956). Gray frequently returned to supper clubs and appeared on many musical programs on television.

GRAYSON, KATHRYN [Zelma Kathryn Elizabeth Hedrick] (1922–). Film performer. A pretty and perky coloratura, she was featured in 1940s and 1950s movie musicals. Born in Winston-Salem, North Carolina, Grayson began her career singing on the radio. Hollywood signed her in 1941 and the next year she was playing the title heroine in *RIO RITA*. Grayson was featured in *Seven Sweethearts* (1942), *Thousands Cheer* (1943), *ANCHORS AWEIGH* (1945), *ZIEGFELD FOLLIES* (1946), *Two Sisters From Boston* (1946), *TILL THE CLOUDS ROLL BY* (1946), *IT HAPPENED IN BROOKLYN* (1947), *The Kissing Bandit* (1948),

THE TOAST OF NEW ORLEANS (1950), SHOW BOAT (1951), LOVELY TO LOOK AT (1952), THE DESERT SONG (1953), KISS ME, KATE (1953), THE VAGABOND KING (1956), and others. Grayson left films in the late 1950s and concentrated on stage, concert, and nightclub appearances, although she played some television roles through the 1980s. She was married to singer–actor JOHNNY JOHNSTON.

GREASE (Broadhurst Theatre 1972). One of the most popular and durable of all American musicals, the 1950s pastiche may have a weak book and routine songs, but it seems to please audiences every time it surfaces, which is frequently. Jim Jacobs and Warren Casey wrote the songs and the script about the "greasers" at Rydell High School in Chicago in the 1950s. Danny Zuko has fallen in love with the virtuous Sandy Dumbrowski instead of one of the streetwise Pink Ladies led by Betty Rizzo and peer pressure seems to be against the couple. But Sandy learns to conform to more sluttish ways and thereby ends up in Danny's arms. Many of the songs

have become popular favorites, such as "We Go Together," "Summer Nights," "Freddy, My Love," "Greased Lightnin'," "Look at Me, I'm Sandra Dee," "It's Raining on Prom Night," "Beauty School Dropout," and "Born to Hand-Jive." What started in Chicago as an amateur production in a trolley barn opened Off Broadway and after 128 performances transferred to Broadway where it stayed for 3,388 performances, breaking the record for the longest-running musical. Tom Moore directed and PATRICIA BIRCH choreographed. National tours and hundreds of school productions followed, and Grease remains one of the most produced musicals today. Broadway has seen two revivals of Grease. A garish, broadly played and fast-moving production in 1994, directed and choreographed by JEFF CALHOUN, was viewed with disfavor by most critics but audiences already familiar with the show and its movie version were not so fussy and it ran 1,503 performances, one of the longest-running revivals on record. The 2007 revival, directed and choreographed by KATHLEEN MARSHALL, received a lot of hype when its Danny and Sandy were chosen on a network television show in which amateurs auditioned for a panel of judges but the public voted on the winners. Again the reviews were dismissive but by then the show had such a huge advance that it didn't matter.

Grease (Paramount 1978) was so popular at the box office ($100 million by its tenth anniversary and a hit all over again when it was rereleased in theatres in 1998) that Hollywood was convinced a musical could make money only if it was a youth product. Several imitations followed, but few were as much fun as Grease. Bronte Woodard's screenplay changed Sandy into an Australian exchange student so that the Aussie pop singer Olivia Newton John could play her. She was partnered with JOHN TRAVOLTA as Danny who, like most of the cast, was far too old for high school but had screen charisma. Plot changes were minor and several cameo roles were written in for veteran performers EVE ARDEN, SID CAESAR, Dody Goodman, JOAN BLONDELL, Alice Ghostley, and FRANKIE AVALON. Most of the stage score was used, and some new songs, by various tunesmiths, proved to be just as popular: "Hopelessly Devoted to You," "You're the One That I Want," and a title song sung by Frankie Valli over the opening credits. Patricia Birch recreated her Broadway dances, and Randal Kleiser directed without a feeling for the period or much else. The

Grease. The original "high school musical," the show ran so long on Broadway that it went through a lot of leather jackets and poodle skirts. It also went through many cast replacements, such as the pictured Adrian Zmed as greaser Danny Zuko and Andrea Walters as the virginal Sandy Dumbrowski. (Photofest)

Casts for *Grease*

Character	1972 Broadway	1978 film	1994 Broadway	2007 Broadway
Danny	BARRY BOSTWICK	JOHN TRAVOLTA	Ricky Paul Goldin	Max Crumm
Sandy	Carole Demas	Olivia Newton-John	Susan Wood	Laura Osnes
Rizzo	Adrienne Barbeau	Stockard Channing	Rosie O'Donnell	Jenny Powers
Frenchy	Marya Small	Didi Conn	Jessica Stone	Kirsten Wyatt
Doody	James Canning	Barry Pearl	Sam Harris	Ryan Patrick Binder
Kenickie	Timothy Meyers	Jeff Conaway	Jason Opsahl	Matthew Saldivar
Marty	Katie Hanley	Dinah Manoff	Megan Mullally	Robyn Hurder
Jan	Garn Stephens	Jamie Donnelly	Heather Stokes	Lindsay Mendez
Miss Lynch	Dorothy Leon		Marcia Lewis	Susan Blommaert

inevitable sequel, *Grease 2* (Paramount 1982) was virtually ignored by the public since neither Travolta nor Newton-John were in it, yet it had its own merits. Birch directed as well as choreographed and there was some creative camera work and sense of style. In the screenplay by Ken Finkleman, high schooler Stephanie Zinone (Michelle Pfeiffer) was the cool one and British exchange student Michael Carrington (Maxwell Caulfield) had to become a biker to win her in time for the finale, a rock and roll luau with hoola hoops. It was all harmless nonsense and no better or worse than the earlier film, but it didn't click with young audiences so it died.

GREAT CARUSO, THE (MGM 1951). The best and most successful of MARIO LANZA's seven films, the musical biography of the celebrated Italian tenor was so popular that many Americans became interested in opera and Hollywood jumped in with a half a dozen other opera singer bios during the decade. The screenplay by SONYA LEVIEN and William Ludwig was trite and inaccurate, but watching Enrico Caruso struggle from the cafés in Naples to singing at the Met was another variation of the Cinderella tale and Lanza played it beautifully. ANN BLYTH was Caruso's high society wife Dorothy who got to sing the film's biggest hit, "The Loveliest Night of the Year," which Irving Aaronson and PAUL FRANCIS WEBSTER adapted from an old Mexican waltz tune. Lanza sang opera selections from Verdi, Puccini, and Leocavallo, and he was joined by opera singers Dorothy Kirsten, Blanche Thebom, Teresa Celli, Nicola Moscona, and Giuseppe Vandengo. The forty-eight-year-old Caruso's collapsing and dying on stage while singing *Martha* was the film's tearful climax. Sadly, Lanza himself would die of a heart attack at the age of thirty-eight after bouts with obesity, drugs, and alcohol, so watching the movie today adds an additional level of empathy. RICHARD THORPE directed the JOE PASTERNAK production, and Peter Herman Adler staged the opera sequences.

GREAT PERFORMANCES. Television series. Music concerts, opera, ballet, classic and modern plays, and musicals have been broadcast on the PBS-TV series since it began in 1974. Perhaps the most famous presentation in the history of the series was the multipart *Brideshead Revisited* (1982). While some of the musical showings are documentary programs exploring the work of a certain artist, such as *Judy Garland: The Concert Years* or *Irving Berlin's America*, many have been complete performances of stage musicals produced by others but captured on video for the series. Among the musicals (some in concert format) seen on the program were *PORGY AND BESS, BLACK AND BLUE, SOUTH PACIFIC, JOSEPH AND THE AMAZING TECHNICOLOR DREAMCOAT, PASSION, THE MIKADO, SHOW BOAT, CANDIDE, OKLAHOMA!, JESUS CHRIST SUPERSTAR, CATS, KISS ME KATE,* and *COMPANY.*

GREAT WALTZ, THE (Center Theatre 1934). A biographical musical about composer Johann Strauss, Jr., the production was one of the biggest and most extravagant of the decade, performed in a 3,822-seat venue rather than a traditional Broadway house. The actors, singers, dancers, and musicians totaled over 175 people, and the scenery and costumes were as opulent as they were plentiful. MOSS HART's libretto, based on an English operetta on the same subject, concerned the jealousy composer Strauss Sr. has for his up-and-coming composer son, with the father finally conceding to his successor in a climatic scene at the Dommeyer's Gardens in Vienna. Desmond Carter put lyrics to Strauss's familiar waltzes and came

The Great Ziegfeld. The Hollywood musical biography that launched a series of such movies, the film is still impressive for its grandeur and sense of elegant excess. Pictured is the "You Never Looked So Beautiful" production number with the requisite glittering costumes and spiral staircase. (Photofest)

Casts for *The Great Waltz*

Character	1934 Broadway	1938 film	1955 television	1972 film
Johann Strauss	GUY ROBERTSON	Fernand Gravet	Keith Andes	Horst Buchholz
Johann Strauss, Sr.	H. Reeves-Smith		Henry Sharp	Nigel Patrick
Olga/Poldi/Carla	Marie Burke	Luise Rainer		Mary Costa
Carla Donner		Miliza Korjus		
Resi Ebesteder			Patrice Munsel	
Hans Ebesteder			BERT LAHR	

up with such songs as "Love Will Find You," "You Are My Song," "With All My Heart," and "Danube So Blue." MAX GORDON produced the mammoth project, HASSARD SHORT directed, and ALBERTINA RASCH choreographed the large ballet troupe. The show ran 298 performances in two separate engagements and was one of the most talked about spectacles of its era.

🎵 *The Great Waltz* (MGM 1938) is not a film version of the stage spectacular but a very different piece altogether, although it is still about Strauss and his music is used to create songs. The screenplay by Samuel Hoffenstein and Walter Reisch picks up where the stage version ends. After Strauss II becomes famous in Vienna, his faithful, selfless wife Poldi shares in his glory. When he has an affair with the beautiful diva Carla Donner, his wife patiently waits for him to come to his senses and return to her. Because the acting was solid, the dialogue lively, and the decor ravishing, the melodramatic movie held together very well. OSCAR HAMMERSTEIN put music to the familiar melodies and came up with such delectable songs as "I'm in Love With Vienna," "There'll Come a Time," "One Day When We Were Young," "Only You," and "Voices of Spring." However, the musical highlight of the film required no lyrics at all. Strauss rode through a forest in his carriage and all the sounds of nature and the music from shepherds' flutes give him the idea for "Tales from the Vienna Woods." The Bernard Hyman production was directed by Julien Duvivier (with uncredited help from Josef Von Sternberg and Victor Fleming) and Rasch again choreographed the waltzes. The same studio returned to the Viennese composer thirty-four years later with *The Great Waltz* (MGM 1972), a less inspired biography, which was sometimes more laughable than entrancing. The screenplay by producer–director Andrew L. Stone covered much of Strauss' life and it all seemed rather clichéd given the wooden dialogue and the stiff performances. ROBERT WRIGHT and GEORGE FORREST wrote the lyrics for Strauss' music and came up with songs such as "Pitter Patter Polka," "Louder and Faster," and "Love Is Music." The movie's only saving grace is the singing, which is expert, particularly that of Mary Costa. This time around ONNA WHITE devised the choreography. ☐ Producer MAX LEIBMAN presented a television version of Strauss's life also called *The Great Waltz* (NBC-TV 1955). Billy Friedberg and NEIL SIMON wrote the teleplay, and the cast featured Keith Andes as Strauss. Leibman and Bill Hobin co-directed the live broadcast, which is not believed to exist on kinescope so it is lost.

🎬 **GREAT ZIEGFELD, THE** (MGM 1936). An early and opulent biographical musical about Broadway producer FLORENZ ZIEGFELD, the film has rarely been topped for pure showmanship and glamour.

Plot: At the midway of the 1893 Chicago World's Fair, sideshow barker Florenz Ziegfeld promotes his attraction, strong man The Great Sandow, and hones his showmanship skills. Soon he is producing revues on Broadway and is known for his celebrated *Follies*. He brings the provocative French singer ANNA HELD to New York on a wave of publicity and then marries her. But the marriage is a difficult one and Ziegfeld divorces her when he meets and falls in love with actress BILLIE BURKE. The high point in his Broadway career is the night in 1927 when his production of *Show Boat* opens but soon the Depression wipes him out

Cast for *The Great Ziegfeld*	
Character	*Performer*
Florenz Ziegfeld	WILLIAM POWELL
ANNA HELD	LUISE RAINER
BILLIE BURKE	MYRNA LOY
Audrey Lane	VIRGINIA BRUCE
Jack Billings	FRANK MORGAN
Fanny Brice	FANNY BRICE
The Great Sandow	Nat Pendleton
Ray Bolger	RAY BOLGER
Sam Sampson	REGINALD OWEN
Dr. Ziegfeld	Joseph Cawthorn
Mary Lou	Jean Chatburn
WILL ROGERS	A. A. Trimble
Schultz	HERMAN BING
Sidney	Ernest Cossart
Gene Buck	WILLIAM DEMAREST

financially and he dies in 1932 thinking back on all his past triumphs.

WILLIAM ANTHONY MCGUIRE's screenplay was a mixture of fact and fiction with plenty of celebrities from the past portrayed by themselves or by others. It was a long chronicle (176 minutes) with a lot of dialogue and plenty of production numbers but audiences had seen few show business biographies in 1936 so the picture was also a novelty. SEYMOUR FELIX choreographed the musical numbers, the most famous being IRVING BERLIN's "A Pretty Girl Is Like a Melody" staged on a giant spiral staircase with dozens of singers, dancers, and musicians posed on the 175 steps. So many memorable songs came from Ziegfeld productions that the score was a treasure trove of standards and they were performed with taste

The Great Ziegfeld Musical Numbers

"Won't You Come and Play With Me?"
"It's Delightful to Be Married"
"If You Knew Susie"
"Shine on Harvest Moon"
"A Pretty Girl Is Like a Melody"
"You Gotta Pull Strings"
"She's a (Ziegfeld) Follies Girl"
"You"
"You Never Looked So Beautiful (Before)"
"Yiddle on Your Fiddle"
"Queen of the Jungle"
"My Man"
"A Circus Must Be Different in a Ziegfeld Show"

and panache by the large cast. Surprisingly, many of the book scenes were also excellent, and the performances by WILLIAM POWELL, MYRNA LOY, and particularly LUISE RAINER were outstanding. The musical direction, the decor and costumes, and the direction by ROBERT Z. LEONARD were also superior. The HUNT STROMBERG production spawned a string of show biz musical biographies for decades, which are still being made on occasion. *The Great Ziegfeld* is the granddaddy of them all and still one of the best.

GREEN, ALFRED E. (1889–1960). Film director. A reliable if not distinctive movie director, he turned out dozens of silent and sound films over a fifty-year career. Green was born in Ferris, California, and began his film career as an actor before directing two-reelers and then features in 1917. He tackled any genre and usually came in on time and under budget, with most of his products being a B movie grade. Of his fourteen musicals, *THE JOLSON STORY* (1946) was his most notable effort. Green's other musicals include *Sweet Kitty Bellairs* (1930), *Here's to Romance* (1935), *Mr. Dodd Takes the Air* (1937), *Shooting High* (1940), *Tars and Spars* (1946), *The Fabulous Dorseys* (1947), *Copacabana* (1947), *The Eddie Cantor Story* (1953), and *Top Banana* (1954).

GREEN, ADOLPH. See COMDEN, Betty, and Adolph GREEN

GREEN, JOHNNY (1908–1989). Film and stage composer, orchestrator, musician, and conductor. A vastly talented songwriter from Tin Pan Alley, he arranged the music for many beloved Hollywood musicals, from *AN AMERICAN IN PARIS* (1951) to *WEST SIDE STORY* (1961). Green was born in Far Rockaway, New York, the son of two musicians, and educated at Harvard where he formed the Harvard Gold Coast Orchestra. Bandleader Guy Lombardo was so impressed with Green's musical arrangements that he hired him to orchestrate numbers for his own band. At the same time Green was composing popular songs and had several hits, such as "I Cover the Waterfront," "Easy Come, Easy Go," "Out of Nowhere," and "Body and Soul." He scored the Broadway musicals *Here Goes the Bride* (1931), *Murder at the Vanities* (1933), and *Beat the Band* (1942), and was a musical arranger for others, such as *BY JUPITER* (1942). In Hollywood, Green was known more as a music director than a composer, although he scored the musicals *The Sap From Syracuse*

(1930), *Start Cheering* (1938), *Bathing Beauty* (1944), *Easy to Wed* (1946), and *Something in the Wind* (1947) with various lyricists and wrote the soundtrack score for many nonmusicals. Yet it was his expert musical arrangements for over forty screen musicals that made Green one of the most respected artists in Hollywood. His band made many recordings, including several with FRED ASTAIRE, and he had a popular radio show called *World of Music* (1933 to 1940). Green was married to actress–consumer affairs expert Betty Furness (1916–1994).

GREEN, MITZI [born Elizabeth Keno] (1920–1969). Film and stage performer. A precocious child star in films, the animated moppet managed to keep singing as a teenage and young adult as well. Green was born in the Bronx, the daughter of vaudevillians, and was on the stage at the age of three. Five years later she was billed as "Little Mitzi" and was featured in the *Our Gang* series of early short talkies. She also played supporting roles in feature films at Paramount, including the musicals *Honey* (1930), *PARAMOUNT ON PARADE* (1930), *Love Among the Millionaires* (1930), *GIRL CRAZY* (1932), and *Transatlantic Merry-Go-Round* (1934). Just as she was outgrowing child roles, she starred on Broadway as the teenager Susie Ward in *BABES IN ARMS* (1937), followed by featured roles in the Broadway musicals *Walk With Music* (1940), *Let Freedom Ring* (1942), and *Billion Dollar Baby* (1945). Green returned to Hollywood in the 1950s for the screen musicals *Lost in Alaska* (1952) and *Bloodhounds of Broadway* (1952) but found no success. After a few television appearances she retired.

GREENWILLOW (Alvin Theatre 1960). FRANK LOESSER's only unsuccessful Broadway musical, the charming and underrated work has a quirky, problematic book but a superior score. The libretto by Loesser and Lesser Samuels, based on B. J. Chute's novel, was about the young Gideon Briggs (Anthony Perkins) who lives in the rural town of Greenwillow and loves Dorrie Whitbred (Ellen McCown). The Briggs family is cursed with a wanderlust that drives the men in each generation to abandon their family and journey through the world. With Dorrie's love and help, Gideon overcomes the family curse and remains in Greenwillow. Also in the strong cast were PERT KELTON, Cecil Kellaway, William Chapman, Lee Cass, and Bruce MacKay. Loesser's songs are rich with rustic color and very different from the slick numbers seen in some of his other works.

The ardent "Never Will I Marry" enjoyed some popularity, but just as fine were the fervent "The Music of Home," the declamatory "Summertime Love," the wistful "Walking Away Whistling" and "Faraway Boy," the wry "What a Blessing," and the farcical "Could've Been a Ring." The story was deemed too slight to be theatrical so the fine score and gifted cast could do little to bring the show to life. Only the healthy advance for the musical allowed it to run ninety-seven performances. Revivals are rare but efforts to rewrite the libretto have met with some success and someday *Greenwillow* may become producible.

GREENWOOD, [Frances] CHARLOTTE (1893–1978). Stage and film performer. A tall, lanky blonde dancer famous for her flat-footed steps and high kicks, she played many comic sidekicks on screen during the latter part of her career. Born in Philadelphia in the theatrical rooming house her mother ran, Greenwood was educated in Boston and Norfolk, Virginia, before going into vaudeville as a dancer. She made her Broadway debut in 1905 but wasn't noticed until she played the supporting role of Letitia Proudfoot in *Pretty Mrs. Smith* (1914). Greenwood so enamored audiences with her funny, gawky Letitia that producer Oliver Morosco featured her in a series of "Letty" musicals that played on Broadway and on tour for eight years. She also was featured in several London musicals in the 1930s. Greenwood began her film career in 1915 and appeared in many silent movies and later talkies, such as *So Long, Letty* (1930), *Palmy Days* (1931), and *FLYING HIGH* (1931), returning to Broadway on occasion for such successes as the *MUSIC BOX REVUE* (1922) and *OUT OF THIS WORLD* (1950). By the 1940s, she was a favorite comedienne in Hollywood, playing supporting comic roles in movie musicals, such as *DOWN ARGENTINE WAY* (1940), *MOON OVER MIAMI* (1941), *Tall, Dark and Handsome* (1941), *SPRINGTIME IN THE ROCKIES* (1942), *THE GANG'S ALL HERE* (1943), *Wake Up and Dream* (1946), *Oh, You Beautiful Doll* (1949), *Dangerous When Wet* (1953), and *The Opposite Sex* (1956). OSCAR HAMMERSTEIN wanted Greenwood to play Aunt Eller in the original Broadway production of *OKLAHOMA!* (1943) but she had movie commitments; she got to play the crusty but worldly wise Eller Murphy on screen in 1955, which was perhaps her most fully realized movie role. Autobiography: *Never Too Tall* (1947); biography: *Charlotte Greenwood*, Grant Hayter-Menzies (2007).

GREY, CLIFFORD [born Percival Davis] (1887–1941). Stage and film lyricist and writer. An English-born songwriter and libretto author who found success on both the London and the New York stage, the prolific writer also was busy in Hollywood as well. Grey was born in Birmingham, England, and educated at King Edward VI School before he started contributing lyrics to London revues and musicals. By the World War I years, he had several long-running shows in the West End, most of which he had also written the librettos. In 1920, Grey took a two-week holiday in New York and ended up staying most of the decade, writing lyrics and/or librettos for Broadway musicals *SALLY* (1920), *The Hotel Mouse* (1922), *Lady Butterfly* (1923), *Vogues of 1924*, *Marjorie* (1924), *ARTISTS AND MODELS* (1924 and 1925), *Annie Dear* (1924), *June Days* (1925), *Gay Paree* (1925), *Mayflowers* (1925), *A Night in Paris* (1926), *The Great Temptations* (1926), *The Merry World* (1926), *HIT THE DECK* (1927), *The Optimists* (1928), *The Madcap* (1928), *Sunny Days* (1928), *THE THREE MUSKETEERS* (1928), and *Ups-a-Daisy* (1928). By 1929 he was in Hollywood writing scores with JEROME KERN, LEO ROBIN, and others, even as he continued to contribute to Broadway and West End shows. Grey's screen musicals are *THE LOVE PARADE* (1929), *Devil May Care* (1929), *Sally* (1929), *Hit the Deck* (1930), *The Rogue Song* (1930), and *THE SMILING LIEUTENANT* (1931). He also organized shows for the British and American troops before his untimely death.

GREY GARDENS (Walter Kerr Theatre 2006). A poignant musical inspired by a documentary film, the show met with mixed reactions but everyone agreed that CHRISTINE EBERSOLE was giving the performance of her career. At the Long Island mansion Grey Gardens, Edith Bouvier Beale (Ebersole) is preparing a garden party in 1941 to announce the engagement of her daughter Edie (Erin Davis) to the dashing heir Joe Kennedy (Matt Cavenaugh). With the assistance of her pianist-in-residence George Gould Strong (Bob Stillman), Edith plans to sing some of her song favorites for the gathering, much against the wishes of Edie who is also worried about her relationship with Joe and his celebrated family. When Edith's husband telegrams to say he is going off to Mexico to get a divorce, the scandal breaks up the engagement and Edie runs away. Thirty years later, Grey Gardens is a dilapidated shambles, overrun with cats and reported to the local health officials. The aging Edith (Mary Louise Wilson) still lives there and has grown as eccentric as the middle-aged Edie (Ebersole), the two arguing about the past, reliving golden moments, and Edie still trying to escape but emotionally unable to move. Also featured in the excellent cast were JOHN McMARTIN and Michael Potts. Doug Wright wrote the libretto, the second act of the musical based on the 1975 documentary film of the same title, while the first act was an assembly of fact and fiction about the two famous Bouvier women. Scott Frankel (music) and Michael Korie (lyrics) wrote the compelling score that pastiched 1940s songs in the first act and had a chilling, contemporary sound in the second. "Another Winter in a Summer Town," "The Revolutionary Costume for Today," "Will You?," "Daddy's Girl," "Jerry Likes My Corn," "Around the World," "The Girl Who Has Everything," and "The Cake I Had" were among the highlights. First presented Off Broadway by PLAYWRIGHTS HORIZONS, the offbeat but engrossing musical was rewritten and recast and arrived on Broadway to rave notices for Ebersole's twin performances but still disagreement about the show itself. Michael Greif directed with delicacy and the musical ran 307 performances.

GREY, JOEL [born Joel David Katz] (1932–). Stage and film performer. The pint-sized, energetic song-and-dance man lit up a number of hit and flop musicals during his long career. Grey was born in Cleveland, the son of comedian Mickey Katz (1909–1985), and was on the vaudeville stage as a youth. After studying acting at the Neighborhood Playhouse and appearing in nightclubs, he made his legit debut Off Broadway in *The Littlest Revue* (1956). Grey replaced stars in STOP THE WORLD—I WANT TO GET OFF (1963) and HALF A SIXPENCE (1965) before landing the role of the sleazy Master of Ceremonies in CABARET (1966), a performance he repeated on film in 1972 and on Broadway in 1987. His other major hits were as GEORGE M. COHAN in GEORGE M! (1968), the overlooked Amos in the 1996 revival of CHICAGO, and the Wizard in WICKED (2003). Grey also gave admirable performances in two short-lived musicals: as King Charles of France in *Goodtime Charley* (1975) and as the Jewish refugee Jacobowsky in *The Grand Tour* (1977). He made several films, including the musicals THE FANTASTICKS (1995) and *Dancer in the Dark* (2000), and many television appearances, including the musical specials JACK AND THE BEANSTALK (1956), LITTLE WOMEN (1958), *George M!* (1970), and *Yeoman*

of the Guard (1982). He is the father of actress Jennifer Grey (1960–).

GRIMES, TAMMY (1934–). Stage, film, and television performer. A small, fiery actress with a buzz-saw voice, she has excelled in classics, modern dramas, and comedies and in musicals. Grimes was born in Lynn, Massachusetts, and educated at Stephens College and the Neighborhood Playhouse School before making her Broadway debut replacing Kim Stanley as Cherie in *Bus Stop* in 1955. She was featured in *The Littlest Revue* (1956) and a few plays before finding fame as the raucous backwoods gal Molly in THE UNSINKABLE MOLLY BROWN (1960). Grimes' other memorable musical roles were the elusive ghost Elvira in *High Spirits* (1964) and the temperamental star Dorothy Brock in 42ND STREET (1980). Her other musical credits include *A Musical Jubilee* (1975), *Sunset* (1983), and *Tammy Grimes: A Concert in Words and Music* (1988). Grimes has made some films, including the camp classic musical *Can't Stop the Music* (1980), and has appeared on many television programs, including her own show in the 1960s and the TV musicals *Holiday* (1956), *Sextuplets* (1957), GIFT OF THE MAGI (1958), *Archy and Mehitabel* (1960), and *The Borrowers* (1973). She was married to actor Christopher Plummer (1927–) for a time and their daughter is actress Amanda Plummer (1957–).

GROENER, HARRY (1951–). Stage, film, and television performer. The bright-eyed singer–dancer–actor has played broad supporting characters as well as leading men. Groener was born in Augsburg, Germany, the son of a concert pianist and an opera singer, and was educated at the University of Washington and the Pacific Conservatory of Performing Arts. He also studied dance at the San Francisco Conservatory of Ballet and performed for that city's ballet troupe before taking acting roles in regional theatre. Groener made an exciting Broadway debut as Will Parker in the 1979 revival of OKLAHOMA! and was singled out for his performances in the short-lived musicals *Oh, Brother!* (1981), *Is There Life After High School?* (1982), and *Harrigan 'n Hart* (1985). He found himself in major hits as Munkustrap in CATS (1982) and playboy Bobby Child in CRAZY FOR YOU (1992), played NOEL COWARD in *If Love Were All* (1999), and shone as a replacement for George in SUNDAY IN THE PARK WITH GEORGE (1985) and King Arthur in SPAMALOT (2006). Groener has acted in many television shows and films, although rarely have his singing–dancing talents been used.

GROODY, LOUISE (1897–1961). Stage performer. A spirited singer–dancer in musicals in the 1920s, she was known for her dimpled good looks and exuberant dancing. Groody was born in Waco, Texas, and educated in San Antonio before heading to New York where she became a cabaret dancer. Her act became so popular that producers featured her in *Around the Map* (1915), *Toot-Toot!* (1918), *Fiddlers Three* (1918), *The Night Boat* (1920), *Good Morning Dearie* (1921), *Frank Fay's Fables* (1922), and *One Kiss* (1923) before she got her two best roles: the unconventional Nanette in *NO, NO, NANETTE* (1925) and the determined saloon gal Loulou in *HIT THE DECK!* (1927). After appearing in few nonmusicals on Broadway, Groody turned to vaudeville for the rest of her career.

GUETTEL, ADAM (1964). Stage composer and lyricist. One of the most promising and accomplished songwriters at the turn of the twentieth century, he has garnered plenty of attention in his recent career. Guettel was born in New York, the son of composer MARY RODGERS and the grandson of RICHARD RODGERS. As a boy, he sang in the children's chorus at the Metropolitan Opera and then was educated at Yale University where he began writing experimental musicals in a new, innovative form quite unlike the traditional form of his grandfather. Guettel uses atonal music, folk and blues, and a bit of opera, all put together in a thrilling manner. Guettel first gained recognition with the Off Broadway musical *FLOYD COLLINS* (1996), followed by praise for his song cycle *Saturn Returns* (1998) and lyrical Italianate musical *THE LIGHT IN THE PIAZZA* (2005).

GUIZAR, TITO [born Federico Arturo Guizar Tolentino] (1909–1999). Stage and film performer and musician. A popular singing star in Mexico, the guitar-strumming troubadour graced eight Hollywood musicals. Guizar was born in Guadalajara, Mexico, and was noticed for his singing and guitar playing so he was sent to New York to record songs. While there he went on the radio and was so popular that he got his own radio program, was heard in nightclubs, and did concerts at various venues, including Carnegie Hall. Guizar was given specialty spots in the Hollywood musicals *Under the Pampas Moon* (1935) and *BIG BROADCAST OF 1938* and was embraced by moviegoers so he was featured in *Tropic Holiday*

(1938), *St. Louis Blues* (1939), *Blondie Goes Latin* (1941), and *Brazil* (1944). He remained a major star in Mexico for decades, making movies and appearing on television into the 1990s.

■ **GULLIVER'S TRAVELS** (Paramount 1939). One of the very few feature-length animated musicals not from the DISNEY studio, this entertaining adventure cannot compete with the craftsmanship of the Disney artists but it still has much to offer. Based on the Lilliput section of Jonathan Swift's satire, the plot concerned two rival kingdoms who are about to make peace because Princess Glory (singing voice of Jessica Dragonette) of Lilliput and Prince David (LANNY ROSS) of Lupescu have fallen in love and wish to wed. But before the wedding can take place the two governments disagree on which country's official song should be played at the wedding. It is at this impasse that giant Gulliver (Sam Parker) is washed up on the beach and is discovered by the excitable town crier Gabby (Pinto Colvig). The Lilliputians tie up the giant and transport him to the town but he awakes and breaks loose as the Lupescuians attack and Gulliver forces a peace, pointing out that the official songs "Faithful" and "Forever" can be sung together in perfect harmony. Other songs written by RALPH RAINGER (music) and LEO ROBIN (lyrics) for the film include "It's a Hap-Hap-Happy Day" and "Bluebirds in the Moonlight." Producer–director–animator Max Fleischer kept the comic characters broad and the lovers dull and the tone of the musical is often lighthearted fun.

GUNTON, BOB [born Robert Patrick Gunton, Jr.] (1945–). Stage, television, and film performer. A solid, flexible actor–singer who has given outstanding performances in all media, he has often been highly praised although he's never hit star status. Gunton was born in Santa Monica, California, and educated at St. Peter's College and the University of California before serving as a sergeant in Viet Nam where he was decorated. He made his New York acting debut Off Broadway in 1971 and often returned to that venue in hard-hitting plays. Gunton was cast in the musical *Happy End* (1976), eventually taking over the leading role of Billy Cracker, and was featured in the short-run musicals *WORKING* (1978) and *King of Hearts* (1978). He found wide recognition as the dictator Juan Peron in *EVITA* (1979), followed by a zesty performances as King in *BIG RIVER* (1985) and many plaudits for his *SWEENEY TODD* (1989). Gunton's other musical credits include *Roza* (1987) and *THE MUSIC MAN* (1988). He has acted in several films and very many television programs, although rarely was his strong singing voice heard.

🕮 **GUYS AND DOLLS** (46th Street Theatre 1950). Perhaps the most durable of all American musical comedies, it is so tightly written, has such vibrant characters, and the score is so splendid that the show is practically indestructible.

Plot: Gambler Nathan Detroit has enough on his mind trying to find a new location for his famous floating crap game, when his longtime sweetie, the nightclub singer Adelaide, wants to know when they are finally going to get married. To raise the cash to secure a place for the big game, Nathan bets the slick lady-killer Sky Masterson that he can't get the prim Save-a-Soul Mission worker Sarah Brown to go to Havana with him. Sky wins the bet but, because he has fallen in love with Sarah, he reforms. Sarah helps Adelaide take Nathan in tow and the musical ends with a double wedding.

Guy and Dolls. The story of showgirl Miss Adelaide (Vivian Blaine) and gambler Nathan Detroit (Sam Levene) could hardly be called a comic subplot. Both featured couples in the musical are major to the plot and score. With comic pros Blaine and Levene, the Adelaide–Nathan scenes and songs were unforgettable. (Photofest)

Producers CY FEUER and ERNEST MARTIN hired Jo Swerling to fashion a musical out of a series of stories and characters by Damon Runyon, but the show was a hopeless mess until ABE BURROWS was brought in and created the clever libretto. *Guys and Dolls* is unique in that the two romantic couples are equally interesting rather than one being major and the other secondary. It also has several supporting characters that are delightful and colorful, helping to create a Runyonesque landscape where whimsy and farce coexist. FRANK LOESSER wrote his most famous score for *Guys and Dolls*. Not only did the ballads become popular but the character songs are also familiar favorites. "Adelaide's Lament" is one of the funniest, cleverest, and most revealing character numbers ever written, the duets "Sue Me" and "Marry the Man Today" are ingeniously straightforward, the solos "If I Were a Bell" and "My Time of Day" are masterful examples of a character letting down his/her guard, and the revival-like "Sit Down, You're Rockin' the Boat" remains one of Broadway's best eleven o'clock numbers. Every song in the show is effective, even the quiet Irish-flavored "More I Cannot Wish You," providing a quaint touch of sincerity amidst all of the plotting and deceiving. A score this good could have hidden a weaker libretto but luckily it didn't have to. The original production was pure gold, with GEORGE S. KAUFMAN directing and MICHAEL KIDD providing the nimble choreography. The Broadway production ran 1,200 performances, followed by tours and then mountings by every kind of theatre group imaginable.

The musical has returned to New York on five occasions. A 1955 City Center revival featured Walter Matthau (Nathan), HELEN GALLAGHER (Adelaide), Ray Shaw (Sky), and Leila Martin (Sarah). A New York City Light Opera production in 1965 featured Alan King (Nathan), Sheila MacRae (Adelaide), JERRY ORBACH (Sky), and ANITA GILLETTE (Sarah). VIVIAN BLAINE reprised the most celebrated role of her career when she played Miss Adelaide in a 1966 New York City Light Opera revival. Jan Murray was Nathan and the other featured players included Barbara Meister (Sarah) and Hugh O'Brien (Sky). All of these were limited engagements but the 1976 revival was a commercial venture that lasted 239 performances. An African American cast, directed and choreographed with panache by Billy Wilson, gave the old musical a refreshing new interpretation without subtracting any of the

Casts for *Guys and Dolls*

Characters	Sky Masterson	Sarah Brown	Nathan Detroit	Adelaide
1950 Broadway	ROBERT ALDA	Isabel Bigley	SAM LEVENE	VIVIAN BLAINE
1955 film	Marlon Brando	Jean Simmons	FRANK SINATRA	Vivian Blaine
1976 Broadway	James Randolph	Ernestine Jackson	Robert Guillaume	Norma Donaldson
1992 Broadway	Peter Gallagher	Josie de Guzman	NATHAN LANE	FAITH PRINCE

Guys and Dolls (stage) Musical Numbers

"Runyonland"
"Fuge for Tinhorns"
"Follow the Fold"
"The Oldest Established"
"I'll Know"
"A Bushel and a Peck"
"Adelaide's Lament"
"Guys and Dolls"
"If I Were a Bell"
"My Time of Day"
"I've Never Been in Love Before"
"Take Back Your Mink"
"More I Cannot Wish You"
"Crapshooters' Dance"
"Luck Be a Lady"
"Sue Me"
"Sit Down, You're Rockin' the Boat"
"Marry the Man Today"

Woman in Love," the last two to beef up Sinatra's portion of the songs; all three numbers, written by Loesser, were forgettable and have been forgotten. However, Goldwyn did some things right. He let VIVIAN BLAINE reprise her hilarious Adelaide on screen, hired MICHAEL KIDD to restage his Broadway dances, and got stage designer Oliver Smith to create a cartoonish Runyonland in the studio. The result was a movie far better than most expected. Brando did his own singing and found a sincere charm in the con man Sky. Jean Simmons, also doing her own singing, was surprisingly effective as Sarah. The supporting cast was excellent, including the three bookies, STUBBY KAYE, Johnny Silver, and B. S. Pully, who had sung "Fugue for Tinhorns" on Broadway. The movie has a stylized look that complements the material, and Kidd's production numbers were energetic and fun. Goldwyn's gamble paid off; the film was one of the top-grossing pictures of the year.

🐊 **GYPSY** (Broadway Theatre 1959). One of the American musical theatre's masterworks, the show has a story, characters, songs, and a theatricality that have rarely been equaled.

Plot: The aggressive divorcée Rose is determined that her daughter June become a child star in vaudeville so she takes her and her younger sister Louise on the road with a kiddie act. With the help of Rose's boy friend–manager Herbie, they manage to get some bookings in the waning days of variety. When the grown-up June elopes with Tulsa, one of the boys in the act, Rose turns her energies to making the untalented Louise a star and she does, but it is in burlesque. No longer needed, Rose explodes with frustration and only reconciliation with her daughter helps her go on.

comic and lyrical fun. Running almost as long as the original was the 1992 production. JERRY ZAKS directed the slick, fast-paced mounting that emphasized the comedy but still had its softer moments. The popular attraction ran 1,143 performances, breaking the record for the longest-running revival in a full-size Broadway house.

■ *Guys and Dolls* (Goldwyn/MGM 1955) was a gamble on the part of producer SAM GOLDWYN who purchased the film rights for a record $1 million and then proceeded to cast the movie with an eye toward disaster. Nonsinger Marlon Brando was cast as the singing Sky Masterson, while singer FRANK SINATRA was contracted for the nonsinging role of Nathan Detroit. Joseph L. Mankiewicz, who had never directed a musical before, was hired to write and helm the $5 million production. Two of the Broadway show's biggest hits, "A Bushel and a Peck" and "I've Never Been in Love Before," were cut and added were "Pet Me, Poppa," "Adelaide," and "A

Loosely based on stripper GYPSY ROSE LEE's autobiography, the telling libretto by ARTHUR LAURENTS focuses on Rose, the stage mother of all stage mothers, and Merman gave the

Casts for *Gypsy*

Characters	Mama Rose	Louise	Herbie	June
1959 Broadway	ETHEL MERMAN	Sandra Church	Jack Klugman	Lane Bradbury
1962 film	ROSALIND RUSSELL	NATALIE WOOD	Karl Malden	Ann Jillian
1974 Broadway	ANGELA LANSBURY	Zan Charisse	Rex Robbins	Maureen Moore
1993 television	BETTE MIDLER	Cynthia Gibb	Peter Reigert	Jennifer Rae Beck
1991 Broadway	Tyne Daly	Crista Moore	Jonathan Hadary	Tracy Venner
2003 Broadway	BERNADETTE PETERS	Tammy Blanchard	John Dossett	Kate Reinders
2008 Broadway	PATTI LUPONE	Laura Benantí	BOYD GANES	Leigh Ann Lanki

Gypsy Musical Numbers

"May We Entertain You"
"Some People"
"Small World"
"Baby June and Her Newsboys"
"Mr. Goldstone (I Love You)"
"Little Lamb"
"You'll Never Get Away From Me"
"Dainty June and Her Farmboys"
"If Momma Was Married"
"All I Need Is the Girl"
"Everything's Coming Up Roses"
"Madame Rose's Toreadorables"
"Together, Wherever We Go"
"You Gotta Get a Gimmick"
"Let Me Entertain You"
"Rose's Turn"

most complex performance of her long career as the funny, infuriating character. However, all the characters were vivid, from the slowly emerging Louise to the three strippers (MARIA KARNILOVA, Chotzi Foley, and Faith Dane) who instruct Louise on how little talent is needed to do their job. The script is a chronicle in the form of a fable and it moves swiftly and efficiently as few librettos do. Composer JULE STYNE, working with young lyricist STEPHEN SONDHEIM, wrote his greatest score with *Gypsy*. The show has the brassy, Broadway sound of his other work, but the complexity of the characters and the shrewd lyrics must have inspired him for there are moments where the music aches with emotion, such as the desperate "Everything's Coming Up Roses" and the explosive "Rose's Turn." Sondheim's lyrics can be incisive, as in the character numbers "If Momma Was Married" and "Small World," or carefree and slaphappy as in "Together, Wherever We Go" and the vaudeville numbers. All of the songs are so tied to character that it is surprising that any of them became

popular outside of the context of the show. Yet it is a well-known and beloved score that seems to retain its power just as the musical itself only gets better with age. LELAND HAYWARD and DAVID MERRICK produced the original production, JEROME ROBBINS was the astute director–choreographer, and the well-reviewed show ran 702 performances.

While it is not the easiest musical to cast or produce, revivals have been plentiful with various kinds of theatre groups. Broadway has seen four successful revivals with four very different Roses. ANGELA LANSBURY had triumphed in the role in London so the production, directed by author Laurents, was brought to Broadway in 1974 where critics cheered her very human, very different interpretation of Rose. Television favorite Tyne Daly was applauded by the press for her fiery, funny Rose and the 1989 revival, which ran 582 performances, took a few months off and then returned for another 105 performances. The soft-featured, mellow-voiced, baby-faced BERNADETTE PETERS may not have been the ideal choice to play the abrasive Rose but most critics felt the power-house performer pulled it off with aplomb and turned the routine 2003 production into something special, running 451 performances. PATTI LUPONE, who played Rose to great acclaim in a 2007 *ENCORES!* concert, reprised her performance in a 2008 Broadway revival.

■ *Gypsy* (Warner 1962) came to the screen with its libretto and score (minus only one song) intact, was given a handsome production directed by MELVIN FRANK that captured the vaudeville era and the sleazy burlesque milieu, and was well acted and sung. But the heart and soul of the musical were missing when the studio decided not to let Ethel Merman recreate her dynamic performance on screen. ROSALIND RUSSELL was adequate in the role and certainly captured the humor, if not the terror, in the complicated character. But who wants to see an adequate Rose? NATALIE WOOD (singing dubbed by MARNI NIXON) made the transition from wall flower to stripper believable and touching and the rest of the cast was commendable. All in all, the movie is one of the more faithful stage-to-screen projects, but the ghost of Merman haunts the picture and one keeps wondering what it would have been like if her legendary performance had been captured on screen forever.

❑ BETTE MIDLER was a highly effective Rose in a CBS-TV production that was very faithful to the orginal stage libretto. Peter Riegert was Herbie and the strong supporting cast included Cynthia Gibb, CHRISTINE EBERSOLE, Jennifer Rae Beck Michael Jeter, ANDREA MARTIN, and Edward Asner.

H

☙ **H. M. S. PINAFORE** (Standard Theatre 1879). One of the most influential of all musical works, the British comic operetta by W. S. Gilbert (book and lyrics) and Arthur Sullivan (music) has probably been produced more often than any other musical in the English language. Captain Corcoran (Eugene Clarke) has engaged his lovely daughter Josephine (Eva Mills) to marry the elderly Sir Joseph Porter (Thomas Whiffen), the First Lord of the Admiralty, but she loves the common seaman Ralph Rackstraw (Henri Laurent). When the lovers try to elope, they are foiled by the ugly sailor Dick Deadeye (William Davidge) and a happy ending is only achieved when the bumboat woman Little Buttercup (Blanche Galton) reveals that Ralph is of highborn blood and the Captain of common ancestry. The public reaction to the operetta was overwhelming and within months the whole country was *Pinafore* crazy singing the songs and buying products that capitalized on the show. No previous American or British musical ever had such an attraction, and revivals, many of them pirated, were in abundance for several years. The silly, satirical libretto remains stage worthy but the test of any operetta is its score and the songs in *H.M.S. Pinafore* are brilliance itself. "We Sail the Ocean Blue," "When I Was a Lad (I Served a Term)," "Sorry Her Lot (Who Loves Too Well)," "I Am the Monarch of the Sea," "Never Mind the Why or Wherefore," "I Am the Captain of the Pinafore," "A British Tar Is a Soaring Soul," and "Things Are Seldom What They Seem" are just some of the delicious numbers in this timeless piece. The original New York ran 175 performances but the musical returned soon and often. Not counting Off Broadway productions, it is recorded that seventy major revivals have been produced in New York, more than any other musical work.

HACKETT, BUDDY [born Leonard Hacker) (1924–2003). Stage, film, and television performer. A short, round comic with a twisted smile and a spitting voice, he was noticed in all media for his energetic and farcical performances. Hackett was born in Brooklyn and left his father's upholstery business to do comedy in the Borscht Belt resorts and nightclubs. His routines, which always bordered on the obscene, made him a favorite in Las Vegas for decades and television audiences enjoyed his many (and much milder) appearances over the years. Hackett occasionally left standup comedy to appear on Broadway, as with a few comedies in the 1950s and as the fortune teller Garside in the musical *I Had a Ball* (1964), and to act in movies, including the musicals *Walking My Baby Back Home* (1953), *The Wonderful World of the Brothers Grimm* (1962), *THE MUSIC MAN* (1962), and *Muscle Beach Party* (1964). His distinctive voice was used in some animated programs and films, most memorably as the sea gull Scuttle in *THE LITTLE MERMAID* (1989).

HADARY, JONATHAN (1948–). Stage and television performer. A solid, all-purpose leading man in plays and musicals, he can play eccentrics as well as low-key roles. Hadary was born in Chicago and educated at Tufts University before acting in regional theatres and stock. He made his New York debut Off Broadway in 1974 and was noticed two years later as the fat teenager Herschel in the longrunning comedy *Gemini*. Hadary appeared in many Off Broadway productions, including the musicals *God Bless You, Mr. Rosewater* (1979), *Scrambled Feet* (1979), and *Tomfoolery* (1981), and then was on Broadway as Herbie in *GYPSY* (1989 and 1991). He also shone as the self-deluded Charles Guiteau in *ASSASSINS* (1991) and as replacements for Nathan Detroit in *GUYS AND DOLLS* (1993) and King Arthur in *SPAMALOT* (2006). Hadary's other New York musicals include *Weird Romance* (1992) and *All Shook Up* (2005). He has acted in a few films and many television programs, although not in a singing role.

HAGUE, ALBERT [born Albert Marcuse] (1920–2001). Stage and television composer and performer. Hague was born in Berlin, Germany, but escaped from the Nazis and fled to Rome where he studied at the Royal Conservatory of St. Cecilia. When Italy allied with Germany he emigrated to America where he continued his studies at the University of Cincinnati and then worked as a singer–actor while he wrote music. Hague provided original music for the ballet piece *Dance Me a Song* (1950) and then composed the scores for the Broadway musicals *PLAIN AND FANCY* (1955), *REDHEAD* (1959), *The Girls Against the Boys* (1959), *Cafe Crown* (1964), and *The Fig Leaves Are Falling* (1969). He composed the songs for the TV musical *The Mercer Girls* (1953) and is best known for his music for the TV animated musical *DR. SEUSS' HOW THE GRINCH STOLE CHRISTMAS* (1966), which was adapted for Broadway in 2006 and 2007. Hague returned to performing in the 1980s, appearing as Benjamin Shorofsky in the film musical *FAME* (1980) and in the subsequent televisions series, as well as on other series and programs.

🎵 *HAIR* (Biltmore Theatre 1968). An important musical landmark because it brought rock music and a counterculture sensibility to Broadway, the show also opened up, for a time at least, new possibilities for the American musical. The anti-war hippie Claude (James Rado) is to be drafted into the army and his pal Berger (Gerome Ragni) and other members of the "tribe" encourage him to burn his draft card and continue his life of free love, drugs, and peace. But in the end Claude is drafted and dies in Viet Nam and the tribe mourns his lost. The thin plot was an excuse for vibrant musical numbers and satirical skits celebrating the anti-establishment sentiments that were growing in America. Ragni and Rado wrote the script and the nimble lyrics for GALT MACDERMOT's compelling music. Some of the songs, such as "Aquarius," "Good Morning Starshine," "Let the Sun Shine In," and "Easy to Be Hard," became pop hits in a way few theatre songs at the time could, and equally accomplished were such numbers as "Where Do I Go?," "Frank Mills," "Ain't Got No," and "I Got Life." The musical was presented Off Broadway for ninety-four performances before it was revised, redirected by TOM O'HORGAN, and opened on Broadway to mostly favorable notices. The show's anti-patriotic stance, advocation of drugs, and brief nudity made the musical shocking to many and the musical was highly controversial. The curious and the converted came for 1,750 performances. It was the first rock musical seen on Broadway and was very influential in changing the sound of the Broadway score. Not that many subsequent shows would be rock musicals, but *Hair* had the first amplified musicians, which meant all the performers were obviously miked and there was no pretense that they weren't. Before long, musical theatre amplification became the norm. Michael Butler was *Hair*'s canny producer and he supervised touring and international productions, turning one show into an ongoing enterprise. Although there would eventually be many regional and amateur productions, *Hair* was revived on Broadway only once. The 1977 production was again directed by O'Horgan but reviewers felt the new production lacked the spark of the original. It certainly lacked the shock value and audience appeal, closing after five weeks. The cast included Randall Easterbrook (Claude), Michael Hoit (Berger), Cleavant Derricks, Ellen Foley, Scott Thornton, and Alaina Reed.

🎬 *Hair* (United Artists 1979) came to the screen a decade after the peak of the anti-war protests and the Age of Aquarius movement so there was a touch of nostalgia in director Milos Forman's movie version. Scriptwriter Michael Weller took the plotless "tribal love rock musical" and fashioned a thin story about the Oklahoma youth Claude who travels to New York City before being inducted into the Army and falls in with a group of hippies in Central Park. He adopts the tribe's lifestyle of drugs, sex, and nonconformity and then is inducted into the military. When some members of the tribe come to visit him at his army base, Berger takes Claude's place so that he can enjoy a day with his old friends. On that day, the troops are suddenly mustered into planes and flown to Viet Nam where Berger is killed and Claude and the tribe are left standing amidst the thousands of grave markers in Arlington Cemetery.

Casts for *Hair*

Character	1968 Broadway	1978 film
Claude	James Rado	John Savage
Berger	Gerome Ragni	TREAT WILLIAMS
Sheila	Lynn Kellogg	Beverly D'Angelo
Woof	Steve Curry	Don Dacus
Hud	Lamont Washington	Dorsey Wright
Jeanie	Sally Eaton	Annie Golden
Dionne	MELBA MOORE	Cheryl Barnes

Most of the stage songs were used in the film, although they were often assigned to different characters or presented in different situations. Twyla Tharp did the sprightly choreography and, with Forman, recreated the era effectively. The controversy and sense of discovery that theatregoers first experienced in the theatre were gone but the movie was stirring all the same.

HAIRSPRAY (Neil Simon Theatre 2002). Similar to *GREASE* (1972) in its depiction and celebration of high schoolers of the past, the tuneful, funny musical was an immediate hit and continues to be on Broadway, on tour, and on the screen. Hefty teenager Tracy Turnblad lives in Baltimore in 1962 and dreams of appearing on the Corny Collins dance show on local television. When the program sponsors an open contest for Miss Teenage Hairspray,

Tracy enters and, with the reluctant help of her mother, the overabundant Edna, protests the exclusion of "Negroes" from the competition. Despite the efforts of the conniving Velma Von Tussle and her ambitious daughter Amber, Tracy ends up winning the crown and the handsome teen Link Larkin and striking a blow for desegregation. "You Can't Stop the Beat," "Good Morning, Baltimore," "Big, Blond and Beautiful," "It Takes Two," "Timeless to Me," "Mama, I'm a Big Girl Now," and "Without Love" were among the tuneful numbers. Based on the 1988 cult film by John Waters, the cartoonish fable by Mark O'Donnell, THOMAS MEEHAN (book), Marc Shaiman (music and lyrics), and Scott Wittman (lyrics) captured the attitudes and musical sound of the era, and a strong cast (particularly newcomer Marissa Jaret Winokur and HARVEY FIERSTEIN's outrageous drag Edna), under the astute direction

Hairspray. Female impersonators have been popular on Broadway since the 1880s with such popular performers as Tony Hart and Julian Eltinge specializing in distaff roles in musicals. By the last decades of the twentieth century "drag" meant gay instead of the lost art of female impersonation. So it was interesting to see Harvey Fierstein (left) play a woman in *Hairspray*, rather than a campy drag queen. In the original Broadway cast the daughter Tracy was played by Marissa Jaret Winokur (right). (Photofest)

Casts for *Hairspray*

Character	2002 Broadway	2007 film
Tracy Turnblad	Marissa Jaret Winokur	Nikki Blonsky
Edna Turnblad	HARVEY FIERSTEIN	JOHN TRAVOLTA
Link Larkin	Matthew Morrison	Zac Efron
Motormouth Mabelle	Mary Bond Davis	Queen Latifah
Wilbur Turnblad	Dick Latessa	Christopher Walken
Amber Von Tussle	Laura Bell Bundy	Brittany Snow
Velma Von Tussle	Linda Hart	Michelle Pfeiffer
Penny Pingleton	Kerry Butler	Amanda Bynes
Seaweed J. Stubbs	Corey Reynolds	Elijah Kelley

of JACK O'BRIEN and animated choreography by JERRY MITCHELL, turned the cliché-ridden tale into a joyous romp.

🎬 *Hairspray* (New Line-Warner 2007) was greatly anticipated because of the ongoing popularity of the stage musical and the appearance of former greaser JOHN TRAVOLTA in drag playing Edna, and most moviegoers were not disappointed. Leslie Dixon altered the plot somewhat, particularly at the end when it was not Tracy who wins the contest but the African American preteen Little Inez (Taylor Parks), but much was familiar and the spirit of the Broadway hit could be felt. Where Fierstein's Edna was a funny steamroller of a woman, Travolta's interpretation was reticent, shy, and cute. Michelle Pfeiffer dominated much of the movie for the role of Velma had been built up some, yet newcomer Nikki Blondsky made a commendable screen debut as Tracy. Adam Shankman directed and choreographed the Craig Zadan–Neil Meron production, which had a strong box office on its initial release and looks to enjoy a long-lasting appeal.

HALE, ALAN (1892–1950). Film and stage performer and director. One of Hollywood's most recognized character actors, the large yet gentle player was Errol Flynn's sidekick in several movies and played a variety of types in over 100 other films. Hale was born in Washington, DC, and prepared for a career as an opera singer but was quickly discouraged so in 1911 he started acting in silent films. He made his Broadway debut in 1913 and appeared in a handful of plays, as well as the musicals *Rock-a-Bye Baby* (1918) and *A Lonely Romeo* (1919), before returning to movies and directing features for Cecil B. De Mille in the 1920s. Hale was much more in demand as an actor so he concentrated on character parts for the next twenty years, playing heavies, lovable teddy bears, sinister authority figures, and jolly buffoons. Among his musical credits are *REBECCA*

OF SUNNYBROOK FARM (1932), *HIGH, WIDE AND HANDSOME* (1937), *Music for Madame* (1937), *Listen, Darling* (1938), *ON YOUR TOES* (1939), *THIS IS THE ARMY* (1943), *THANK YOUR LUCKY STARS* (1943), *NIGHT AND DAY* (1946), *The Time, the Place and the Girl* (1946), and *My Wild Irish Rose* (1947). His look-alike son was actor Alan Hale, Jr. (1921–1990), remembered as the Skipper on the television series *Gilligan's Island*.

HALEY, JACK (1899–1979). Stage, film, and television performer. A lightweight leading man most remembered as the Tin Man in the film classic *THE WIZARD OF OZ* (1939), he usually played comic wide-eyed hicks or lovable losers. Haley was born in Boston and went into vaudeville right after school and found some success as part of the comedy act Crafts and Haley. By 1924 he was well known enough to be featured in the Broadway revues *Round the Town* (1924) and *Gay Paree* (1925) and then was noticed as the wimpy chain store heir Jack Martin in *FOLLOW THRU* (1929), which he reprised in the 1930 film, his screen debut. Haley played leading roles in the Broadway musicals *Free for All* (1931), *TAKE A CHANCE* (1932), *HIGHER AND HIGHER* (1940), and *INSIDE U.S.A.* (1948), but most of his time in the 1930s and 1940s was spent in Hollywood where he appeared in such musicals as *Sitting Pretty* (1933), *Coronado* (1935), *Pigskin Parade* (1936), *POOR LITTLE RICH GIRL* (1936), *WAKE UP AND LIVE* (1937), *REBECCA OF SUNNYBROOK FARM* (1938), *ALEXANDER'S RAGTIME BAND* (1938), *Navy Blues* (1941), *MOON OVER MIAMI* (1941), *Higher and Higher* (1943), *GEORGE WHITE'S SCANDALS* (1945), and *People Are Funny* (1946). He was cast in his most famous role, the Tin Man in *The Wizard of Oz*, when he replaced BUDDY EBSEN who had an allergic reaction to the silver powder used in the makeup. Haley made several television appearances in the 1950s, including an abridged TV version of *The Wizard of Oz*

(1956). His son was film producer Jack Haley, Jr. (1933–2001).

🎬 **HALF A SIXPENCE** (Broadhurst Theatre 1965). A British import with a very English story and a music hall-like score, the happy musical comedy was one of the few West End products that decade to find success on Broadway. When the struggling draper's apprentice Arthur Kipps inherits a fortune, he neglects his lower-class sweetheart Ann Pornick and takes up with the aristocratic Helen Walsingham. After Helen's brother Young Walsingham loses Arthur's fortune in bad investments, Arthur happily returns to Ann and opens a book shop. Based on H. G. Wells' novel *Kipps*, the musical by Beverley Cross (book) and David Heneker (music and lyrics) boasted a tuneful score and a star turn by the animated TOMMY STEELE who had originated it in England. Among the zesty songs were "Money to Burn," "If the Rain's Got to Fall," "She's Too Far Above Me," "Flash Bang Wallop," and the jaunty title number. Although not as popular as in London, the show still ran a very profitable 512 performances. GENE SAKS was the efficient director, and ONNA WHITE provided the vigorous choreography.

🎞 *Half a Sixpence* (Paramount 1967) may have been overlong and overproduced for such a simple, affecting tale but much of the production was first-class fun so one learned to overlook its faults. Cross adapted his stage libretto into a by-the-numbers screenplay, GEORGE SIDNEY directed it efficiently, and GILLIAN LYNNE staged the spirited (if rather lengthy) dances. Tommy Steele reprises his West End–Broadway performance and he is funny and energetic, filling the wide screen with singing and dancing that never could be called subtle. Julia Foster gives a more down-to-earth performance as Ann, yet she has her ostentatious moments as well. Underused but delightful all the same is CYRIL RITCHARD as Chitterlow, the fellow who brings Kipps the word of his inheritance and sticks around for the fun. Because some production numbers go on and on, some songs from the stage score had to be cut, but what's left is the best of the lot.

HALL, ADELAIDE (1901–1993). Stage performer. The short, round African American cabaret singer with a powerful and sizzling way with a song lit up musical revues in New York and London. A native of Brooklyn, Hall made her first public appearance in the legendary "all-Negro" musical *SHUFFLE ALONG* (1921). She then became popular in vaudeville and in nightclubs but returned to Broadway for the revues *Runnin' Wild* (1923) and *BLACKBIRDS OF 1928*, in which she partnered with BILL ROBINSON. Hall toured Europe in the show and became one of the first and most popular African American performers on two continents. She also gave memorable performances in the Broadway book musicals *Brown Buddies* (1930) and *JAMAICA* (1957). Hall was featured in a few London musicals, most memorably as Hattie in *KISS ME, KATE* (1951), and made a final Broadway appearance in *Black Broadway* (1980). She was still performing in concerts on her ninetieth birthday. Biography: *Sophisticated Lady: A Celebration of Adelaide Hall*, Stephen Bourne (2001).

HALL, ALEXANDER (1894–1968). Film director. A routine Hollywood director who specialized in comedies, he helmed seven musicals of secondary note. Hall was born in Boston and was on the stage as a boy and in films by 1914. After serving in World War I, he returned to movies as an editor and then started directing when sound came in. Hall's most acclaimed movie was the comedy–fantasy *Here Comes Mr. Jordan* (1941) but he directed several genres, including such musicals as *Torch Singer* (1933), *Little Miss Marker* (1934), *Give Us This Night* (1936), *Because You're Mine* (1952), and *Let's Do It Again* (1953).

HALL, BETTINA (1906–1997). Stage performer. A pretty, clear-voiced musical comedy singer–actress, she also had credits in operetta and opera. Hall was born in North Easton, Massachusetts, and by the age of twenty was

---

Casts for *Half a Sixpence*

Character	1965 Broadway	1967 film
Arthur Kipps	TOMMY STEELE	Tommy Steele
Ann Pornick	Polly James	Julia Foster
Harry Chitterlow	James Grout	CYRIL RITCHARD
Helen Walsingham	Carrie Nye	Penelope Horner
Young Walsingham	John Cleese	James Villiers

singing professionally in Gilbert and Sullivan operettas, appearing on Broadway in *Iolanthe* (1927), *THE MIKADO* (1927), and *THE PIRATES OF PENZANCE* (1927). She sang major opera roles for the American Opera Company and then returned to Broadway for a series of musicals, including *THE LITTLE SHOW* (1929), *Three Little Girls* (1930), and *Meet My Sister* (1930). Hall was most remembered for playing the American composer Shirley Sheridan in *THE CAT AND THE FIDDLE* (1931) and the at-sea heroine Hope Harcourt in *ANYTHING GOES* (1934). Her other musicals include *The Only Girl* (1934) and *Susanna, Don't You Cry* (1939). She retired from show business in the 1940s when she married. Her sister was singer–actress Natalie Hall (1904–1994), the female lead in *Through the Years* (1932) and *MUSIC IN THE AIR* (1932), who also retired young.

HALL, JUANITA [born Juanita Long] (1901–1968). Stage and screen performer. A beloved African American character actress, she also passed for Asian in less discriminating times and originated two Oriental roles in Rodgers and Hammerstein musicals. Hall was born in Keysport, New Jersey, and trained at Juilliard before singing with the renowned Johnson Hall Choir. She made her Broadway acting debut in the drama *Stevedore* (1934) and was soon a featured singer in such musicals as *Sweet River* (1936), *Sing Out, Sweet Land!* (1944), *ST. LOUIS WOMAN* (1946), and *STREET SCENE* (1947). Fame did not come to the short, rotund actress until 1949 with her performance as the Polynesian racketeer Bloody Mary in *SOUTH PACIFIC* (1949), a role she recreated in the 1958 film version. After costarring with PEARL BAILEY in the musical *HOUSE OF FLOWERS* (1954), Hall had another Broadway hit in 1958 with *FLOWER DRUM SONG* in which she played the caustic Madame Liang. She repeated the role in the 1961 movie version. Sadly, Hall's singing voice deteriorated when she was in her fifties. She did her own vocals for the film of *Flower Drum Song* but her singing was dubbed by MURIEL SMITH for the screen's *South Pacific*.

HALL NATALIE. See HALL, Bettina

HALLELUJAH (MGM 1929). The first all-black talking feature film, this semimusical is an impressive achievement by any standards as a result of producer–director KING VIDOR's demand for authenticity and avoidance of stereotyping. Southern cotton farm worker Zeke Johnson (Daniel L. Haynes) loves the honest, sincere Missy Rose (Victoria Spivy) but the temptress Chick (Nina Mae McKinney) lures him into a crooked crap game where he is cheated out of $100, all the money he received for selling his family's cotton crop. In his anger and frustration, Zeke accidentally shoots his younger brother Spunk (Everett McHarrity) and then runs away in agony. When he returns to his home county, he has been saved and is now the preacher Brother Zekiel, moving the crowds with his spiritual strength. He asks Missy Rose to marry him but when Chick comes to Zekiel to be saved, he is again ensnared by her seductive power. It was highly melodramatic, and the many Negro spirituals used throughout the movie practically turn the piece into an opera, six years before GEORGE GERSHWIN did just that with *Porgy and Bess*. Two new IRVING BERLIN songs were added to the traditional numbers and both were effective: "Waiting at the End of the Road," sung by Zeke and the other plantation workers (dubbed by the Dixie Jubilee Singers) as they waited in line to sell their bales of cotton, comparing it to waiting to get into heaven, and "Swanee Shuffle," the sultry number Chick sang to tempt Zeke. The film was shot on location (dialogue and music were added later in the studio) so it has a documentary look to it that is still potent. Although rarely seen today, the early musical is a landmark of sorts and explores African American culture more effectively than movies would for another three decades.

HALLELUJAH, BABY! (Martin Beck Theatre 1967). An ambitious if uneven musical about African Americans over the decades, it boasted a dynamic performance by young LESLIE UGGAMS. In an expressionistic use of time, the determined, hopeful African American Georgina (Uggams) lives through the twentieth century aging very little, working as a maid in the 1910s, a cabaret singer in the 1920s, a WPA actress in the Depression, entertaining the troops during World War II, a nightclub star in the 1950s, and involved in the Civil Rights movement in the 1960s. Uggams was supported by a first-class cast that included Robert Hooks, Lillian Hayman, Allen Chase, Barbara Sharma, Alan Weeks, Winston DeWitt Hemsley, and MARILYN COOPER. ARTHUR LAURENTS penned the intriguing libretto, and JULE STYNE (music), BETTY COMDEN, and ADOLPH GREEN (lyrics) wrote the eclectic score that ranged from Broadway to blues to boogie. Among the notable songs were "Now's the Time," "My Own Morning," "Being Good Isn't Good Enough," "Feet Do Yo' Stuff," and "Talking to Yourself." BURT SHEVELOVE directed and Kevin Carlisle choreographed the musical experiment, which the press applauded for Uggams's performance and the show ran an unprofitable 293 performances.

▀ HALLELUJAH, I'M A BUM (United Artists 1933). An unusual movie musical that gave AL JOLSON his most demanding screen role, the film offers a low-key but heartbreaking performance with none of the gushing he used when crying "Mammy!" on stage. The film, scripted by Broadway playwrights Ben Hecht and S. N. Behrman, is the antithesis of the GOLD DIGGERS movies of the same decade; the bittersweet tale was about the many homeless in the Depression who lived in Central Park as opposed to the chorines who were struggling on Broadway. When Mayor John Hastings (FRANK MORGAN) has a quarrel with his fiancée June Marcher (Madge Evans), she tries to commit suicide but is rescued by Bumper (Jolson), a tramp in the park who rules as mayor of the homeless. June suffers from amnesia and cannot recall her past but she and Bumper fall in love, only for her to leave him for the real mayor when she regains her memory. It was a far cry from escapism, yet the songs by RICHARD RODGERS (music) and LORENZ HART (lyrics) had extended sections of rhythmic dialogue so the movie often sounded like a cockeyed romantic operetta. Jolson got to sing "You Are Too Beautiful" to Evans, a restrained ballad that he delivered to perfection. Other numbers included the sly "What Do You Want With Money?," "I've Got to Get Back to New York," and the philosophical title song that had to be recorded twice, with the word 'tramp' substituted for the England release because "bum" refers to buttocks in British slang. (The musical was retitled *Hallelujah, I'm a Tramp* in Great Britain.) The sterling supporting cast included Harry Langdon, Chester Conklin, and Edgar Connor, and LEWIS MILESTONE directed with a semidocumentary look and feel. The Joseph M. Schenck production was a box office failure but a triumph in inventive musical filmmaking.

HALLIDAY, ROBERT (1891–1975). Stage performer. A handsome, full-voiced baritone, he starred in a handful of Broadway musicals in the 1920s and 1930s, originating two famous roles in operetta. Halliday was born in Loch Lomond, Scotland, and studied at Glasgow University for an engineering career. When he started singing with a choral group that traveled across Scotland, he decided to pursue a musical career and in 1913 emigrated to America, where he performed in vaudeville and toured with operetta companies. Halliday made his Broadway debut in 1921 and in a few years he was a leading man in musicals such as *Dew Drop Inn* (1923), *Topsy and Eva* (1924), *Holka Polka* (1925), and *TIP-TOES* (1925). His best roles came in two OSCAR HAMMERSTEIN–SIGMUND ROMBERG operettas: the dashing "Red Shadow" Pierre Birabeau in THE DESERT SONG (1926) and the freedom fighter Robert Misson in THE NEW MOON (1928). Halliday's other stage credits include *Princess Charming* (1930), *Music Hath Charms* (1934), and *White Horse Inn* (1936). After a sixteen-year absence, he returned to Broadway in the short-lived *Three Wishes for Jamie* (1936). Halliday was married to singer EVELYN HERBERT, his co-star in *The New Moon*.

HALLMARK HALL OF FAME. Television series. Arguably the most famous, most comprehensive, and most accomplished anthology program in the history of broadcasting, this celebrated series has offered everything from historical dramas to musical comedies since it was begun in 1952. During its long history, the show has been seen on ABC, NBC, CBS, and PBS-TV. For its first three years it was a weekly program but after 1956 the shows were treated as specials and were broadcast irregularly, although in its heyday there would be five or six programs each season. Sponsored by Hallmark Cards, the program had a host in the early years but later presented dramas, comedies, and musicals without commentary and let the high-quality programs speak for themselves. Some of the memorable musical programs over the years (most of them original musicals) have included *The Mercer Girls* (1953), *HANS BRINKER OR THE SILVER SKATES* (1958), *THE FANTASTICKS* (1964), *PINOCCHIO* (1968), *THE LITTLEST ANGEL* (1969), *YOU'RE A GOOD MAN, CHARLIE BROWN* (1973), *The Borrowers* (1973), *PETER PAN* (1976), and some operas, most notably the premiere of *Amahl and the Night Visitors* (1951).

HAMILTON, MARGARET (1902–1985). Film, television, and stage performer. Although she will always be remembered as the Wicked Witch of the West in the film classic THE WIZARD OF OZ (1939), the lean, pinched-faced character actress played spinsters, housekeepers, and even kindly ladies in many other films. Hamilton was born in Cleveland and worked as a kindergarten teacher (future actors William Windom and Jim Backus were among her pupils) before going on the stage, making her Broadway debut in 1932. The next year she made her first of over fifty films, including the musicals *I'll Take Romance* (1937), BABES IN ARMS (1939), GEORGE WHITE'S SCANDALS (1945), WABASH AVENUE (1950), *Comin' Round the Mountain* (1951), and supplying the voice of Aunt Em in the animated JOURNEY BACK TO OZ (1974). Hamilton returned to the New York stage in the musicals *Goldilocks* (1958), *Come Summer* (1969), and OKLAHOMA! (1969). She also acted in many television programs from the early 1950s to the early 1980s. Autobiography: *Countryside Musings* (1977).

HAMLISCH, MARVIN (1944–). Stage, film, and television composer and music arranger. The oft-awarded musical jack of all trades, he has written and arranged music for every medium, often with great success. The native New Yorker was born into a musical family and showed outstanding musical talent as a child. He was the youngest student ever accepted into the Juilliard School of Music and did further study at Queens College while he worked as a rehearsal pianist for Broadway shows. Hamlisch did vocal or dance music arrangements for such shows as FUNNY GIRL (1964), *Henry, Sweet, Henry* (1967), *Golden Rainbow* (1968), *Minnie's Boys* (1970), and SEESAW (1973) and then made his mark as the composer for the long-running *A CHORUS LINE* (1975). This was followed by the hit THEY'RE PLAYING OUR SONG (1979), but his subsequent musicals—*Smile* (1986), *The Goodbye Girl* (1993), *Sweet Smell of Success* (2002), and *Imaginary Friends* (2002)—did not run despite some excellent scores. Hamlisch has also enjoyed a productive career in films, composing his first of dozens of soundtrack scores in 1968 and writing memorable movie theme songs, such as "Sunshine, Lollipops and Roses," "Nobody Does It Better," and "The Way We Were." His masterful musical arrangements for the film *The Sting* (1973) brought about a renewed interest in composer Scott Joplin and ragtime music, and he arranged the music for old favorites in the movie musical PENNIES FROM HEAVEN (1981). Hamlisch also wrote the songs for the TV drama–musical *The Entertainer* (1976), which he also produced. Autobiography: *The Way I Was* (1992).

HAMMERSTEIN, ARTHUR (1872–1955). Stage producer. A prodigious presenter of operetta on the Broadway stage, he produced works by VINCENT YOUMANS, RUDOLF FRIML, GEORGE GERSHWIN, JEROME KERN, OTTO HARBACH, and his nephew OSCAR HAMMERSTEIN. Born in New York City, the son of the colorful impresario OSCAR HAMMERSTEIN I, he worked

as his father's assistant in running the elder's theatres and productions. Soon after Oscar I presented NAUGHTY MARIETTA (1910) on Broadway, he shifted his attention to creating an opera company so he put his son Arthur in charge of running the Hammerstein enterprises. The younger Hammerstein had a hit with his first solo effort, THE FIREFLY (1912), which introduced composer Rudolf Friml to Broadway. Hammerstein would produce nine more Friml operettas, including the legendary ROSE-MARIE (1924) which Oscar II co-wrote. Although he was hesitant to encourage Oscar II in a theatrical career, wanting to follow the family's wishes and have the youth become a lawyer, Arthur Hammerstein relented to his nephew's requests and hired him as an assistant and stage manager. Soon he relented further and produced Oscar's first Broadway musical, *Always You* (1920), followed by the younger Hammerstein's *Tickle Me* (1920), *Jimmie* (1920), *Daffy Dill* (1922), WILDFLOWER (1923), *Song of the Flame* (1925), *The Wild Rose* (1926), *Golden Dawn* (1927), *Good Boy* (1928), and SWEET ADELINE (1929). When the Depression changed the Broadway musical, Arthur could not adapt and he declared bankruptcy, losing the famed Hammerstein Theatre and his clout as a producer. He produced one film, the musical *The Lottery Bride* (1930).

HAMMERSTEIN, OSCAR, I (1847–1919). Stage producer, manager, and writer. One of the most colorful showmen of his day, the dapper impresario presented operettas and musicals, built theatres, and ran an entertainment empire. Born in Berlin, Germany, in 1863, the son of a stock exchange trader, Hammerstein started training at the local music conservatory as a violinist at the age of three. He soon learned that he was not a musician but at the conservatory he developed a love for opera that became his passion throughout his life. He ran away from home at the age of sixteen and worked his way to New York where he labored making cigars, soon inventing a patent on a machine that improved the rolling of tobacco products. With the money earned from this, he began investing in playhouses, theatre companies, and real estate. Hammerstein built his first of many theatres in 1889, the Harlem Opera House, but soon lost it due to poor management. This would be the sad pattern for the rest of his life, building (and losing) such famous playhouses as the Columbus, Manhattan, Republic, and Olympia Theatres. His most successful venture was the Victoria Theatre, which became for a time the most profitable vaudeville house in

Oscar Hammerstein. Because his grandfather, impresario Oscar Hammerstein, was so famous, the younger Hammerstein added the "II" after his name so that he would not be confused with his more celebrated namesake. The great lyricist–librettist is pictured (right) with his celebrated partner Richard Rodgers as they prepare *South Pacific* (1949). (Photofest)

New York. Much of this success was attributed to his son William Hammerstein, the father of Oscar Hammerstein II. He booked the acts and made several artists into stars. Oscar I was more interested in musicals, producing and writing a handful of them in the 1890s. His most notable contribution to the musical form was producing VICTOR HERBERT's operetta classic *NAUGHTY MARIETTA* (1910), but opera remained Hammerstein's first love and he spent most of his theatre profits on building the Manhattan Opera House and producing opera productions between 1906 and 1910 in competition with the Metropolitan Opera. He eventually lost both the opera house and the company but he never lost his zest for life, his-bigger-than-life persona, and the respect of his colleagues. Oddly, the younger Oscar barely knew his grandfather. They only met on a few occasions and barely exchanged any words. Because of the resounding fame of his grandfather, Oscar Hammerstein added the "II" to his name when he started in show business even though he was not technically a "second." Biography: *Oscar Hammerstein I*, Vincent Sheean (1956).

HAMMERSTEIN, OSCAR [Greeley Clendenning], **II** (1895–1960). Stage, film, and television lyricist and playwright. Arguably the American musical theatre's premiere lyricist and librettist, he was sometimes a producer and director as well. Hammerstein was born in

New York City into a famous theatrical family; his grandfather was the colorful theatre and opera impresario OSCAR HAMMERSTEIN I and his uncle ARTHUR HAMMERSTEIN was a prosperous Broadway producer. He was educated at Columbia University to become a lawyer but his involvement in the campus theatre productions convinced him to follow in the family profession. Hammerstein began as a stage manager for his uncle's productions and then took up writing nonmusical plays but with no success. He wrote his first lyrics and libretto for the short-lived *Always You* (1920) and followed it with a forty-year career writing all forms of musicals, from operettas to musical comedy to the musical play, which he pretty much invented with *SHOW BOAT*. Hammerstein usually wrote both the book and the lyrics for his shows, sometimes collaborating with more experienced writers such as OTTO HARBACH during the first half of his career. He also collaborated with many of the major composers of the American theatre. With HERBERT STOTHART he wrote *Tickle Me* (1920), *Jimmie* (1920), and *Daffy Dill* (1922). He collaborated with RUDOLF FRIML on *ROSE-MARIE* (1924) and *The Wild Rose* (1926), with GEORGE GERSHWIN on *Song of the Flame* (1925), with VINCENT YOUMANS on *WILDFLOWER* (1923), *Mary Jane McKane* (1923), and *Rainbow* (1928), and with SIGMUND ROMBERG on *THE DESERT SONG* (1926), *THE NEW MOON* (1928), *East Wind* (1931), *May Wine* (1935), and *Sunny River* (1941). One of the most fruitful of Hammerstein's collaborations was with composer JEROME KERN, resulting in *SUNNY* (1925), *Show Boat* (1927), *SWEET ADELINE* (1929), *MUSIC IN THE AIR* (1932), and *VERY WARM FOR MAY* (1939). Hammerstein's most famous partnership was with composer RICHARD RODGERS, the two first working together on Broadway with the landmark *OKLAHOMA!* (1943), followed by *CAROUSEL* (1945), *ALLEGRO* (1947), *SOUTH PACIFIC* (1949), *THE KING AND I* (1951), *ME AND JULIET* (1953), *PIPE DREAM* (1955), *FLOWER DRUM SONG* (1958), and *THE SOUND OF MUSIC* (1959). The duo also scored the film musical *STATE FAIR* (1945), the television musical *CINDERELLA* (1957), produced plays and musicals on Broadway, most memorably *ANNIE GET YOUR GUN* (1946), and supervised the film version of their stage hits. Hammerstein even had a surprise hit with *CARMEN JONES* (1943), an American version of the opera *Carmen*. He saw most of his early works filmed by Hollywood but his original movie musicals were rarely successes at the box office. With Romberg he wrote original scores for *Viennese*

Nights (1930), *Children of Dreams* (1931), and *The Night Is Young* (1935), and with Kern he scored *HIGH, WIDE AND HANDSOME* (1937). Hammerstein also contributed to other screen musicals, including *Give Us This Night* (1936), *Swing High, Swing Low* (1937), *THE GREAT WALTZ* (1938), *The Lady Objects* (1938), and *THE STORY OF VERNON AND IRENE CASTLE* (1939). Hammerstein directed his stage musicals on occasion, although often he was uncredited, as in the case of *Show Boat* and *The King and I*. The contribution Hammerstein made to the American musical cannot be overestimated. He brought an integrity to the stage libretto, raised the level of truthfulness in operetta books, created the serious musical play, introduced the integrated musical, and left a model for musical play construction that has served artists ever since. Biography: *Getting to Know Him: A Biography of Oscar Hammerstein II*, Hugh Fordin (1977).

HANEY, CAROL (1924–1964). Stage and screen choreographer and performer. A multitalented dancer and comic actress, her career as a Broadway choreographer was gaining momentum when she died at the age of forty. Haney was born in New Bedford, Massachusetts, took dance lessons as a child, and while still in her teens opened her own dance studio. She went to California after graduation and studied dance with Ernest Belcher (the father of MARGE CHAMPION) and Eduardo Cansino (the father of RITA HAYWORTH). Her first jobs were dancing in nightclubs where she met choreographer JACK COLE who cast her in his shows, as well as making her his assistant on some movie musicals. Haney also danced in films, getting featured spots in *ON THE TOWN* (1949), *Tea For Two* (1950), *INVITATION TO THE DANCE* (1956), *SUMMER STOCK* (1959), and others. GENE KELLY then hired her to be his assistant for *AN AMERICAN IN PARIS* (1951) and *SINGIN' IN THE RAIN* (1952). While dancing in the movie version of *KISS ME, KATE* (1953), she met BOB FOSSE who cast her as the comic secretary Gladys in the Broadway production of *THE PAJAMA GAME* (1954) and she stopped the show singing and dancing "Hernando's Hideaway." Haney made her Broadway choreography debut with the dances for *FLOWER DRUM SONG* (1958), followed by *Bravo Giovanni* (1962), *SHE LOVES ME* (1963), *Jennie* (1963), and *FUNNY GIRL* (1964) before succumbing to diabetes. She choreographed a handful of television specials and the TV musical *The Bachelor* (1956). She was married to actor LARRY BLYDEN.

🖵 **HANS BRINKER, OR THE SILVER SKATES** (NBC-TV 1958). Mary Mapes Dodge's children's story, first published in 1865, was musicalized by *HALLMARK HALL OF FAME* with plenty of emphasis on the skating, even boasting Olympic champion Dick Button in the action sequences. Even the stars, Tab Hunter and Peggy King, took to the ice without doubles, but such supporting players as Basil Rathbone, Carmen Matthews, and Sheila Smith got to stay on the artificial snow. Sally Benson's teleplay depicted the poor Dutchman Hans Brinker (Hunter) and his sister Trinka (King) who cannot afford silver skates like their friends but must use wooden skates. When the siblings' father gets seriously ill, Hans and Trinka travel to Amsterdam to enlist the help of a famous doctor. Hans falls in love with the doctor's daughter, the father is cured, and Hans wins the skating contest with his new silver skates. HUGH MARTIN wrote the pleasant score that included "The More the Merrier," "Clop, Clop, Clop," "I Happen to Love You," "Ice," and "Hello, Springtime." However, the score and even the characters took a back seat to the skating, which was done on a huge rink built inside NBC's studio in Brooklyn. Mildred Freed Alberg and Paul Feigay co-produced the ninety-minute broadcast, which was directed by Sidney Lumet. Because of Button and America's new fascination with championship skating, the musical was very popular. NBC returned to the old story in 1969 for a different musical version, also titled *Hans Brinker or The Silver Skates*, that was filmed in Holland and ran two hours, filling in many of the details omitted from the earlier broadcast. Bill Manoff wrote the teleplay, and Mark Charlap provided the score, which had lively numbers such as "Proper Manners" and tender moments like "Golden Tomorrows." Robin Askwith was the title character but much more fun were CYRIL RITCHARD, Eleanor Parker, and Richard Basehart in supporting roles. The decor was impressive, as was the skating, but critics felt much of the musical dragged and tended toward the maudlin on more than one occasion.

🎬 **HANS CHRISTIAN ANDERSEN** (Goldwyn/RKO 1952). This biographical musical contains FRANK LOESSER's best film score, a lovely mixture of ballads, rousing chorus numbers, and playful children's ditties. MOSS HART's screenplay about the life of the Danish storyteller was so inaccurate that the government of Denmark insisted on a disclaimer at the beginning of the film saying that this was a fairy tale version of the fairy tale author's life. Cobbler Andersen (DANNY KAYE in a surprisingly restrained performance) leaves his little village

Hans Christian Andersen. After clowning, actor Danny Kaye most liked pulling heartstrings. He did both in this pseudo-biography about the Danish writer of children's tales. Here he embraces a Danish tot played by Noreen Corcoran. (Photofest)

with his apprentice Peter (Joey Walsh) and travels to Copenhagen where he makes shoes for the famous ballerina Doro (Jeanmaire) and is smitten with her. His affection is not returned and, after providing the plot for her "Little Mermaid" ballet, Andersen returns home and becomes an author. The plot was far from gripping, but the musical interruptions were resplendent and included some colorful ballets choreographed by Roland Petit who also performed in them. The songs included the vigorous waltz "Wonderful Copenhagen," the dreamy "Anywhere I Wander," the tuneful duet "No Two People," and the children's numbers based on Andersen stories: "The Ugly Duckling," "Inch Worm," "Thumbelina,' and "The King's Clothes." CHARLES VIDOR directed with a light touch and the colorful decor was very storybook-like. Producer SAMUEL GOLDWYN gambled $4 million on the elaborate production (he boasted that $14,000 was spent just on shoes) and the audiences loved it so the musical grossed $6 million within a year. A 1974 London stage version of the movie was titled *Hans Andersen* and starred TOMMY STEELE.

HANSEL AND GRETEL (NBC-TV 1958). The familiar fairy tale classic was given a very musical treatment with star performers and lots of dancing, opening up the tale to include the whole village in the story. The Town Crier

(STUBBY KAYE) served as narrator for the musical that gave the Witch (HANS CONRIED) four apprentices named Eenie, Meenie, Mynie, and Moe, built up the parts of the siblings' parents (RISË STEVENS and RUDY VALLEE), and made Hansel (Red Buttons) and Gretel (BARBARA COOK) less the victims as the instigators of all the merriment. Yasha Frank's teleplay (written in verse) was not as concerned with the original tale as with providing opportunity for delightful production numbers. Alec Wilder (music) and William Engvick (lyrics) wrote the tuneful score, which included "What Are Little Boys/ Girls Made Of?," "Much Too Happy Dancing," "Market Today," "Eenie Meenie Mynie and Moe," and "Men Rule the World." Paul Bogart directed the sixty-minute romp, and ONNA WHITE did the zesty choreography.

HAPPY GO LUCKY (Republic 1943). A good example of a small-scale, unpretentious 1940s musical, this one had all the elements delightfully in place. In the screenplay by MELVIN FRANK, Norman Panama, and others, the nightclub cigarette girl Marjory Stuart (MARY MARTIN) disguises herself as an heiress and goes down to the Caribbean Islands to land a rich husband, finicky Alfred Monroe (RUDY VALLEE) in particular. She is aided by the American beachcomber Pete Hamilton (DICK POWELL), whom she falls in love with just as his pal Wally Case (EDDIE BRACKEN) is ensnared by the robust Bubbles Hennessy (BETTY HUTTON). JIMMY MCHUGH (music) and FRANK LOESSER (lyrics) provided a tuneful score that included the pseudo-calypso "Sing a Tropical Song," the seductive "Let's Get Lost," the breezy title number, and two comic specialty songs for Hutton's siren voice, "The Fuddy Duddy Watchmaker" and "Murder, He Says." Mabel Paige, ERIC BLORE, Clem Bevans, and Harry Barris made up the supporting cast, and the modest Harold Wilson production was directed by Curtis Bernhardt.

HAPPY TIME, THE (Broadway Theatre 1968). An intimate musical play with an atypically quiet score by JOHN KANDER (music) and FRED EBB (lyrics), it just missed being a hit. The itinerant photographer Jacques Bonnard (ROBERT GOULET), the black sheep of the family, returns to the French Canadian town of his birth where he is worshipped by his adolescent nephew Bibi (MICHAEL RUPERT), welcomed by his ex-girl friend Laurie Mannon (Julie Gregg), gently scolded by his libertine of a father (DAVID WAYNE), and scorned by the rest of the relatives until he picks up and leaves. Although it was based on Samuel Taylor's 1950 comedy of the same name, the plot was mostly original and only the setting and some of the characters were the same. The libretto by N. Richard Nash was deemed thin by the critics but the score was first rate. The self-deceptive "I Don't Remember You," the joyous "The Life of the Party," the wistful "(Walking) Among My Yesterdays," the merry "A Certain Girl," and the evocative title number were among the score's highlights. GOWER CHAMPION directed, choreographed, and filled the stage with myriad slide projections, which helped and hindered the gentle little musical, and the DAVID MERRICK production held on for an unprofitable 285 performances.

HARBACH, OTTO [born Otto Abels Hauerbach] (1873–1963). Stage lyricist and playwright. One of the first musical theatre craftsman to aim for better books and lyrics on Broadway, he had a good number of hits among his dozens of musicals. Harbach was born in Salt Lake City, Utah, to Danish immigrant parents and worked his way through Knox College, teaching English and public speaking after graduation at Whitman College in the state of Washington. In 1901 he moved to New York City to take graduate courses at Columbia University, but soon his money ran out and he took a series of jobs, mostly writing for small newspapers. When Harbach discovered Broadway and musical comedy, he shifted his attention to writing lyrics and librettos and had some success with his first collaborator, composer Karl Hoschna. Their most memorable musical was *MADAME SHERRY* (1910), which produced the song standard "Every Little Movement (Has a Meaning All Its Own)." Hoschna died young so Harbach turned to other composers and co-writers for the rest of his career. Between 1908 and 1936, he wrote over forty musicals (in 1925 he had five shows running on Broadway) with RUDOLF FRIML, JEROME KERN, LOUIS HIRSCH, HERBERT STOTHART, VINCENT YOUMANS, GEORGE GERSHWIN, SIGMUND ROMBERG, and others. Harbach first worked with the young OSCAR HAMMERSTEIN in 1920, teaching him the craft of lyric writing, urging him toward librettos that were more integrated with the songs, and approaching musical theatre writing as a serious art form. Among the musicals Harbach and Hammerstein worked on together were *Tickle Me* (1920), *Jimmie* (1920), *WILDFLOWER* (1923), *ROSE-MARIE* (1924), *SUNNY* (1925), *Song of the Flame* (1925), *The Wild Rose* (1926), *THE DESERT SONG* (1926), *Golden Dawn* (1927), and *Good Boy* (1928). Harbach's most

notable musicals without Hammerstein include *THE FIREFLY* (1912), *Going Up!* (1917), *MARY* (1920), *NO, NO, NANETTE* (1925), *THE CAT AND THE FIDDLE* (1931) and *ROBERTA* (1932), the last two with Kern. Ironically, Harbach never achieved his goal of a fully integrated musical play, but his pupil Hammerstein did with *SHOW BOAT* (1927), *OKLAHOMA!* (1943), and other musical classics.

HARBURG, E. Y. [born Isidore Hochberg] (1896–1981). Stage, film, and television lyricist and writer. The sly Broadway songwriter and librettist who used fantasy and satire to write about weighty issues, he was better known for his tamer and more accessible Hollywood efforts. Harburg (called Yip by his family and friends) was born in New York and educated at City College of New York, where he wrote light verse and submitted it to local newspapers, and then worked for his father's electronics business. When the stock market crash wiped out the family business, Harburg was free to pursue his dreams of writing lyrics and soon some of his songs written with composer JAY GORNEY and others were sung in the Broadway revues *Earl Carroll Sketchbook* (1929), *EARL CARROLL VANITIES* (1930), *Ballyhoo of 1932*, *Americana* (1932), *Walk a Little Faster* (1932), *ZIEGFELD FOLLIES* (1934), and *LIFE BEGINS AT 8:40* (1934). His song "Brother, Can You Spare a Dime?," written with Gorney, was one of the famous songs to come from these shows, and none had more impact on Americans during the Depression than the musical cry of desperation heard in his lyrics. Harburg's first Broadway book musical was the satiric *HOORAY FOR WHAT!* (1937) written with HAROLD ARLEN, the composer he had collaborated with on the movie musicals *The Singing Kid* (1936) and *GOLD DIGGERS OF 1937* (1936). When the two men scored the film classic *THE WIZARD OF OZ* (1939) they entered the top ranks of American songwriters. Harburg and Arlen went on to score the Hollywood musicals *AT THE CIRCUS* (1939), new songs for *CABIN IN THE SKY* (1943), *Meet the People* (1944), and the animated *GAY-PURR-EE* (1962). On Broadway the team wrote the Civil War-era musical *BLOOMER GIRL* (1944) and the sardonic *JAMAICA* (1957). Harbach collaborated with composer JEROME KERN on the film musical *CAN'T HELP SINGING* (1944), with BURTON LANE on the movie *Ship Ahoy* (1942) and the Broadway musicals *Hold on to Your Hats* (1940) and *FINIAN'S RAINBOW* (1947), and with SAMMY FAIN the oddball stage musical *FLAHOOLEY* (1951). His other musical credits are the Hollywood films *The Sap From Syracuse* (1930), *Moonlight and Pretzels* (1933), *Cairo*

(1942), and *California* (1946), the Broadway musicals *The Happiest Girl in the World* (1961) and *Darling of the Day* (1968), and the TV musical *The Great Man's Whiskers* (1973). Harburg contributed to the scripts of several of his stage works, covering such topics as feminism, slavery, big business, prejudice, the atom bomb, and war. However, all of his musicals can be categorized as comedies for he thought it was through humor that the theatre could tackle the most fearsome topics. His lyrics are considered among the wittiest in the American musical and yet he wrote such simple, heartfelt classic songs such as "Look to the Rainbow," "April in Paris," "What a Wonderful World," and "Over the Rainbow." Biography: *Who Put the Rainbow in The Wizard of Oz? Yip Harburg, Lyricist*, Harold Myerson, Ernest Harburg [his son] (1993).

HARD DAY'S NIGHT, A (United Artists 1964). A low-budget feature made to cash in on the international popularity of the BEATLES, the film's purpose was more to gain the rights to the soundtrack album than to present anything of quality. Yet director RICHARD LESTER and scriptwriter Alun Owen took the opportunity to make a frenetic mock documentary about a typical day in the life of the "Fab Four," and the result was an original, freewheeling celebration of rock that was a forerunner to the later MTV videos. The movie, filmed in black and white to save money, had a *cinema vérité* quality that was very tongue in cheek as the foursome ran from hordes of females, took Paul McCartney's grandfather (Wilfred Brambell) on a train ride to a rehearsal, and ended the day performing in a theatre full of screaming fans. The songs were by the group, some written for the film ("And I Love Her," "Can't Buy Me Love," "I Should Have Known Better," and the title number), others already famous ("All My Loving," "If I Fell," and "She Loves You"). The musical was a critical as well as a financial hit and remains an unpretentious, nostalgic look back at the period.

HARNICK, SHELDON. See BOCK, Jerry, and Sheldon HARNICK

A Hard Day's Night. Before there was Monty Python and MTV there was Richard Lester's two freewheeling Beatles movies, *A Hard Day's Night* (1964) and *Help!* (1965). The first was a psuedo-documentary filmed on the streets of London as the Fab Four ran from fans and sometimes others, as pictured here. It was loosely plotted, carefree, and a big hit. Of course, the Beatles were so popular that any film with them would have been box office gold. But this was actually quite good. (Photofest)

HARRIGAN, NED, AND TONY HART. Stage performers and producers. A popular and influential comedy team on Broadway, the two clowns played an important role in the development of musical comedy in America. Edward [Green] Harrigan (1844–1911) was born in New York and began in show business in touring minstrel shows and variety. He made a few Broadway appearances in comic parts in 1870 and then the next year teamed up with Tony Hart [born Anthony J. Cannon] (1855–1891), a fellow comic born in Worcester, Massachusetts. The short, round Hart ran away from an abusive home and sang in New York saloons, performed in circuses, and clowned in minstrel shows before doing a comedy act with Harrigan, playing the hyperactive buffoon to Harrigan's fatherly, more mature foil. Soon the two were headlining in vaudeville, with Harrigan writing the sketches and collaborating with various composers on songs in the act. These rough-and-tumble performances were extended and became the first American musical comedies on Broadway. Between 1878 and 1893, Harrigan wrote and produced some two dozen of these farcical musicals, the most famous being the *MULLIGAN GUARD* musicals in which he played a battling Irishman and Hart took on outrageous male and female parts. The Harrigan and Hart shows celebrated the cultural diversity of American with one group of immigrants fighting and outwitting another group, all in wild and carefree pandemonium. The two comics were so successful that they owned their own Broadway theatre and laid the groundwork for other notable comedy teams to follow, such as WEBER and FIELDS, GALLAGHER and SHEAN, the MARX BROTHERS, HOPE and CROSBY, and MARTIN and LEWIS. HARRY GROENER (Harrigan) and Mark Hamill (Hart) played the duo in the short-lived Broadway musical *Harrigan 'n' Hart* (1985). Biographies: *Ned Harrigan: From Corlear's Hook to Harold Square*, Richard Moody (1980); *The Merry Partners:* E. J. Kahn (1955).

HARRIS, BARBARA (1935–). Stage, film, and television performer. The baby-faced, grainy-voiced actress has scattered credits in all media and is never less than fascinating each time. Harris was born in Evanston, Illinois, and studied at the Goodman Theatre School and the University of Chicago before joining the improvisational group Second City, touring with them and making her New York City debut in 1961 when the troupe played Broadway. She was cited for her versatility in such revues as *Alarums and Excursions* (1962), *When the Owl Screams* (1963), and *Open Season at Second City* (1964) and then shone in the plays *Oh Dad, Poor Dad ...* (1962) and *Mother Courage and Her Children* (1963). Harris was at her best in musicals, winning applause as the kooky psychic Daisy Gamble in *ON A CLEAR DAY YOU CAN SEE FOREVER* (1965) and as three very different heroines in *THE APPLE TREE* (1966). After serving as a replacement in *Mahagonny* (1970), she left the New York theatre and concentrated on television, where she appeared in several series and films, including the musicals *NASHVILLE* (1975) and *MOVIE MOVIE* (1978). Harris is considered one of the best female improvisationalists of her era but that talent was rarely illustrated in her big and small screen performances. She currently is teaching and directing.

HARRIS, PHIL[ip] (1904–1995). Film and television performer. The gravel-voiced character actor with a Southern flavor, he was expert at playing con men, shady businessmen, and overconfident Romeos in many films, television shows, and on the radio. Harris was born in Linton, Indiana, the son of a musician, and grew up in Nashville, Tennessee, where he played drums at an early age. He started his own band in 1931, playing the drums and singing, and became popular enough to interest Hollywood. Harris was featured in the movie musicals *Melody Cruise* (1933), *Turn Off the Moon* (1937), *Man About Town* (1939), *Dreaming Out Loud* (1940), *Buck Benny Rides Again* (1940), *I Love a Band Leader* (1946), *WABASH AVENUE* (1950), *Starlift* (1951), *HERE COMES THE GROOM* (1951), and *ANYTHING GOES* (1956), but his finest musical roles were probably as the voices for Baloo the Bear in *THE JUNGLE BOOK* (1967), the cool cat J. Thomas O'Malley in *THE ARISTOCATS* (1970), Little John in *ROBIN HOOD* (1973), and the fowl Patou in *Rock-a-Doodle* (1991). Harris was very popular on the radio, first as the music director and sidekick on JACK BENNY's show and then later on his own show with his wife ALICE FAYE. He also appeared in dozens of television programs, including the TV musical *Manhattan Tower* (1956), and made many recordings over the years.

HARRIS, SAM[uel] H[enry]. (1872–1941). Stage producer and manager. One of the most respected and beloved theatrical producers of his day, he presented shows by the greatest songwriters of the first half of the twentieth century, from GEORGE M. COHAN and IRVING

BERLIN to COLE PORTER and KURT WEILL. The native New Yorker worked various jobs until he became the promoter of prizefighter Terry McGovern, later managing the athlete's vaudeville appearances. He produced some touring theatricals before teaming with Cohan to produce his legendary hit LITTLE JOHNNY JONES (1904) on Broadway, followed by other Cohan musicals such as *George Washington Jr.* (1906), *The Talk of New York* (1907), *Fifty Miles From Boston* (1908), *The Yankee Prince* (1908), *The American Idea* (1908), *The Man Who Owns Broadway* (1909), *The Little Millionaire* (1911), the 1912 revival of FORTY-FIVE MINUTES FROM BROADWAY, *Hello, Broadway* (1914), *The Cohan Revue* (1916), *Going Up* (1917), and *The Royal Vagabond* (1919). Harris and Cohan broke off the partnership over disagreements about Actors Equity and Harris went solo, presenting such popular musicals as the four editions of the MUSIC BOX REVUES (1921–1924), the MARX BROTHERS musicals THE COCOANUTS (1925) and ANIMAL CRACKERS (1928), the landmark GERSHWIN musical OF THEE I SING (1931) and its short-lived sequel LET 'EM EAT CAKE (1933), Berlin's FACE THE MUSIC (1931) and AS THOUSANDS CHEER (1933), Porter's JUBILEE (1935), RODGERS and HART's I'D RATHER BE RIGHT (1937), and Weill's LADY IN THE DARK (1941). Harris presented many nonmusical plays as well and owned and managed theatres in New York.

HARRISON,   REX [born Reginald Carey Harrison] (1908–1990). Stage and film performer. The actor who represented to Americans the very model of the urbane Englishman in witty comedies, he was also an expert in playing darker roles. Harrison was born in Huyton, England, the son of a cotton broker, and studied acting in Liverpool, later performing with the Liverpool Repertory Theatre when he was only sixteen. He made his London debut in 1930 and was a familiar face in the West End and in some British films by the time he came to America in 1936, but it was not until he returned to Broadway in *Anne of a Thousand Days* (1948) that he was a star. Considered one of the greatest Shavian actors, he also played romantic leads in many films and returned to Broadway in plays over the years, acting in *The Circle* (1989) just weeks before his death. Yet of all his roles, Harrison is most remembered as Henry Higgins in MY FAIR LADY (1956), which he reprised in London in 1958, on screen in 1964, on tour, and back on Broadway in 1981. His only other screen

musicals were *Main Street to Broadway* (1953) and *DOCTOR DOLITTLE* (1967). Among his many wives were actresses Rachel Roberts (1927–1980), Kay Kendall (1926–1959), and Lilli Palmer (1914–1986). His son is actor Noel Harrison (1934–). Autobiographies: *Rex* (1974); *A Damned Serious Business: My Life in Comedy* (1991); biography: *Fatal Charm: The Life of Rex Harrison*, Alexander walker (2002).

HART,   LORENZ [Milton] (1895–1943). Stage and film songwriter. One of the American theatre's most nimble and penetrating lyricists, his partnership with composer RICHARD RODGERS resulted in some of Broadway's brightest scores and a few innovative Hollywood musicals as well. The New York-born Hart was educated at Columbia University where he wrote and performed in original college musicals. He left school to earn money as a translator for the SHUBERT BROTHERS who frequently imported foreign musicals for their many theatres. Hart teamed up with Rodgers in 1919 and one of their songs was interpolated into the Broadway musical *A Lonely Romeo* (1919), followed by *Poor Little Ritz Girl* (1920), their first score heard on Broadway. The young songwriters were first noticed for their songs in the revue THE GARRICK GAIETIES (1925). For the next eighteen years the team scored over two dozen musicals for Broadway, the West End, and Hollywood. Their early stage hits included DEAREST ENEMY (1925), PRESENT ARMS (1928), *The Girl Friend* (1926), PEGGY-ANN (1926), *Betsy* (1926), A CONNECTICUT YANKEE (1927), *Chee-Chee* (1928), *Spring Is Here* (1929), HEADS UP! (1929), SIMPLE SIMON (1930), and *America's Sweetheart* (1931), as well as the London shows *Lido Lady* (1926), *One Dam Thing After Another* (1927), and *EVER GREEN* (1930). The team was lured to Hollywood during the Depression where they scored eight original musicals, most memorably the experimental LOVE ME TONIGHT (1932), THE PHANTOM PRESIDENT (1932), and HALLELUJAH, I'M A BUM (1933). Returning to New York, Rodgers and Hart had a string of successes with JUMBO (1935), ON YOUR TOES (1936), BABES IN ARMS (1937), I'D RATHER BE RIGHT (1937), I MARRIED AN ANGEL (1938), THE BOYS FROM SYRACUSE (1938), TOO MANY GIRLS (1939), HIGHER AND HIGHER (1940), and BY JUPITER (1941). By the 1940s Hart's alcoholism was affecting their productivity, yet PAL JOEY (1940) is considered by many to be their richest work. The last effort by the team was the 1943 revival of *A Connecticut Yankee*; he died a few days after the revival opened. Most of the Rodgers and Hart musicals were filmed by Hollywood with varying success. The British filmed *Evergreen* in 1934, and the story of the partners was the subject of the musical-bio *WORDS AND MUSIC* (1948). Hart had a remarkable talent for polysyllabic and internal rhymes, yet he could also write a direct, heartbreaking lyric as well. Biographies: *Lorenz Hart: A Poet on Broadway*, Frederick Nolan (1994); *Thou Swell: The Life and Lyrics of Lorenz Hart*, Dorothy Hart (1976).

HART, MOSS (1904–1961). Stage and film writer and director. A masterful playwright and librettist, late in his career he also became a highly regarded theatre director. Hart was born in New York City and struggled as an actor and a writer until he collaborated with veteran playwright GEORGE S. KAUFMAN on the comedy *Once in a Lifetime* in 1930. The Kaufman–Hart team went on to write several plays, most memorably *You Can't Take It With You* (1936), *The Man Who Came to Dinner* (1939), and the musical *I'D RATHER BE RIGHT* (1937). On his own or with other collaborators, Hart found success with the musicals *FACE THE MUSIC* (1932), *AS THOUSANDS CHEER* (1933), *THE GREAT WALTZ* (1934), *JUBILEE* (1935), *Sing Out the News* (1938), *LADY IN THE DARK* (1941), and *MISS LIBERTY* (1949), which he also directed. Hart staged several plays on Broadway, as well as the musicals *MY FAIR LADY* (1956) and *CAMELOT* (1960). Many of his plays were made into movies and he scripted some original stories for Hollywood, including the musicals *BROADWAY MELODY OF 1936* (1935), *HANS CHRISTIAN ANDERSEN* (1952), and *A STAR IS BORN* (1954). He was married to singer–actress KITTY CARLISLE. Autobiography: *Act One* (1959); Biography: *Dazzler: The Life and Times of Moss Hart*, Steven Bach (2001).

■ *HARVEY GIRLS, THE* (MGM 1946). Perhaps the best of the frontier musicals inspired by the success of *OKLAHOMA!* (1943) on stage, this western adventure boasted a splendid score and sparkling performances throughout. Easterner Susan Bradley (JUDY GARLAND) travels to Sandrock, New Mexico, in 1880 to work as a waitress in Frank Harvey's restaurant chain that promises good food and a genteel eating atmosphere in the rugged West. Susan and the other Harvey girls are pitted against the less wholesome gals in town, particularly at the Alhambra Saloon run by Ned Trent (John Hodiak) and presided over by the worldly wise Em (ANGELA LANSBURY). The rivalry gets

nasty but Susan ends up in the arms of Ned, thanks to a quick change of heart by Em. The HARRY WARREN (music) and JOHNNY MERCER (lyrics) score was filled with gems. Garland sang the yearning ballad "In the Valley (Where The Evening Sun Goes Down)" and joined the crowd in the Oscar-winning "On the Atchison, Topeka and the Santa Fe," choreographed by ROBERT ALTON and arguably the best train number in movie musicals. Lansbury (dubbed by Virginia Reese) led her girls in the sly "Oh, You Kid," and Garland, MARJORIE MAIN, and RAY BOLGER joined the Harvey girls in the contagious waltz "Swing Your Partner Round and Round." Garland and fellow waitresses VIRGINIA O'BRIEN and CYD CHARISSE (dubbed by Marion Doengers) lamented that "It's a Great Big World," and O'Brien sarcastically sang about "The Wild Wild West." Also in the cast were KENNY BAKER, singing the ballad "Wait and See," Chill Wills, Stephen McNally, and Selena Royle. ARTHUR FREED was the producer, and GEORGE SIDNEY directed with the right amount of suspense and playfulness.

HASTINGS, HAROLD (1916–1973). Stage and television orchestrator and conductor. One of Broadway's most talented music directors, he arranged and orchestrated twenty-two musicals, including many by producer HAROLD PRINCE. Hastings was born in New York and educated at New York University. He began his career as a conductor of radio and early television orchestras and then composed background music for commercials. Hastings made his Broadway debut as the composer of incidental music for the revue *Tickets Please!* (1950) and then went on to arrange and/or orchestrate such musicals as *Top Banana* (1951), *THE PAJAMA GAME* (1954), *DAMN YANKEES* (1955), *NEW GIRL IN TOWN* (1957), *ONCE UPON A MATTRESS* (1959), *FIORELLO!* (1959), *KWAMINA* (1961), *A FUNNY THING HAPPENED ON THE WAY TO THE FORUM* (1962), *SHE LOVES ME* (1963), *FLORA, THE RED MENACE* (1965), *Baker Street* (1965), *CABARET* (1966), *ZORBÁ* (1968), *COMPANY* (1970), *FOLLIES* (1971), *The Selling of the President* (1972), and *A LITTLE NIGHT MUSIC* (1973). Hastings also conducted or arranged the music for the TV musicals *GIFT OF THE MAGI* (1958), *Keep in Step* (1959), and *Damn Yankees* (1967).

HAVER, JUNE [born June Stovenour] (1926–2005). Film performer. A blonde singer–dancer whom 20TH CENTURY-FOX groomed to be another BETTY GRABLE, she gave buoyant, spirited performances in a dozen Hollywood musicals. Haver was born in Rock Island, Illinois, and was on the stage at an early age, later singing on the radio and with different bands. After a few musical shorts, she made her feature film debut in a minor role in *THE GANG'S ALL HERE* (1943) but soon graduated to better roles in *Irish Eyes Are Smiling* (1944) and *Where Do We Go From Here?* (1945). Haver costarred with Grable in *THE DOLLY SISTERS* (1945) and usually had leading roles from then on. Her other musical credits are *THREE LITTLE GIRLS IN BLUE* (1946), *Wake Up and Dream* (1946), *I Wonder Who's Kissing Her Now* (1947), *Oh, You Beautiful Doll* (1949), *Look for the Silver Lining* (1949), *The Daughter of Rosie O'Grady* (1950), *I'll Get By* (1950), and *The Girl Next Door* (1953). She left films in 1953 to enter a convent but after a few months gave up the religious life and married FRED MACMURRAY, making only a few television appearances during the rest of her life.

HAVOC, JUNE [born Ellen Evangeline Hovick] (1916–). Stage, film, and television performer. During her eighty-year career, the slim blonde with the sharp tongue has acted in vaudeville, legit, nightclubs, movies, radio, and television, and even wrote and directed on occasion, yet she is most remembered as the source for the character of Baby June in *GYPSY* (1959). Havoc was born in Vancouver, British Columbia, Canada, and was put into silent shorts and in vaudeville by her pushy stage mother. With her sister GYPSY ROSE LEE, she was a headliner on variety's Orpheum Circuit, but with the waning of vaudeville in the Depression she performed in marathon dances, nightclubs, and Catskills resorts. Havoc made her Broadway debut in the musical *Forbidden Melody* (1936) and was featured in *PAL JOEY* (1940) and *MEXICAN HAYRIDE* (1944) and starred in the short-lived *Sadie Thompson* (1944). She made her screen musical bow in *Four Jacks and a Jill* (1941) and was featured in such musicals as *HELLO, FRISCO, HELLO* (1943), *When My Baby Smiles at Me* (1948), and *RED, HOT AND BLUE* (1949), but stardom again eluded her so she went into television where she did everything from variety shows to soap operas to her own series in the 1960s. Havoc also did dramatic as well as musical radio programs. She was on television and in movies into the 1990s, including the campy musical *Can't Stop the Music* (1980), and often returned to the New York stage, playing Miss Hannigan in *ANNIE* in 1982. Havoc wrote about her dance marathon days in the Broadway play *Marathon '33* (1964) and wrote two memoirs: *Early Havoc* (1960) and *More Havoc* (1980).

HAYMES, [Richard Benjamin] **DICK** (1916–1980). Film and television performer. One of America's favorite crooners in the 1950s and 1960s, the handsome singer appeared in leading roles even though his acting talents were limited. Born in Buenos Aires, Argentina, to an English father and an Irish mother who was a singer, Haymes was educated in Switzerland, France, and England before arriving in the States in 1936. His first jobs were as a radio announcer and singer and then he was a vocalist for name bands, such as those of HARRY JAMES and TOMMY DORSEY. Although he was a low-key performer, his popularity on records and radio led to a Hollywood contract where he appeared in over a dozen movie musicals between 1943 and 1953. Perhaps Haymes' most satisfying performances were as the farm boy Wayne Frake in *STATE FAIR* (1945), the stuffy businessman John Pritchard in *THE SHOCKING MISS PILGRIM* (1947), and the journalist John Matthews in *UP IN CENTRAL PARK* (1948). His other screen musicals include *DUBARRY WAS A LADY* (1943), *Four Jills in a Jeep* (1944), *Irish Eyes Are Smiling* (1944), *Carnival in Costa Rica* (1947), *ONE TOUCH OF VENUS* (1948), *All Ashore* (1953), and *Cruisin' Down the River* (1953), as well as the TV musical *The Lord Don't Play Favorites* (1956). Haymes's career (and life) suffered from five failed marriages (including Joanne Dru and RITA HAYWORTH), immigration problems, and bankruptcy, yet he appeared in nightclubs and on television shows into the 1970s.

HAYNES, TIGER [born George Haynes] (1914–1994). Stage, film, and television performer. The seemingly ageless African American dancer–singer was still playing agile hoofers in his seventies. Haynes was born in St. Croix, Virgin Islands, and made his Broadway debut playing George Washington and other sketch characters in *NEW FACES OF 1956*. He was applauded as the smiling, tapping BOJANGLES ROBINSON in *FADE OUT–FADE IN* (1964), the softhearted Tin Man in *THE WIZ* (1975), the ghost of Marley in *Comin' Uptown* (1979), and a replacement for the toe-tapping minister J. D. Montgomery in *MY ONE AND ONLY* (1984). Haynes's other Broadway musicals include *FINIAN'S RAINBOW* (1960), *KISS ME, KATE* (1965), *TWO GENTLEMEN OF VERONA* (1972), *THE PAJAMA GAME* (1973), *A Broadway Musical* (1978), and *Taking My Turn* (1983). He appeared in a number of films, including the musical *ALL THAT JAZZ* (1979), and television programs, acting up until a few months before his death.

HAYWARD, LELAND (1902–1971). Stage producer. A colorful, aggressive showman, he produced many plays and musicals on Broadway, including two of RODGERS and HAMMERSTEIN'S biggest hits. A native of Nebraska City, Nebraska, Hayward was educated at Princeton University and began his career in films, working in the publicity department at UNITED ARTISTS, as a script supervisor at First National, and then as a talent agent. His first Broadway production was the successful drama *A Bell for Adano* (1944) and over the next twenty years he produced (alone or with others) such plays as *State of the Union* (1945) and *Mister Roberts* (1948) and the musicals *SOUTH PACIFIC* (1949), *CALL ME MADAM* (1950), *WISH YOU WERE HERE* (1952), *GYPSY* (1959), *THE SOUND OF MUSIC* (1959), and *MR. PRESIDENT* (1962). Hayward produced a few films as well, including the screen version of *Mister Roberts* in 1955. He was married to actress Margaret Sullavan (1911–1960).

HAYWARD, SUSAN [born Edythe Marrener] (1918–1975). Film performer. A red-haired, husky-voiced passionate actress of over sixty films, she made six musicals, two of which were popular biographies. Hayward was born in Brooklyn and after high school worked as a model before going to Hollywood in 1937 to be tested for Scarlett O'Hara in *Gone With the Wind* (1939). Her screen test led to minor roles in feature films but stardom would not come until the early 1940s for melodramas that displayed her intense characterizations on screen. While Hayward was not suited to light musical comedy, she was cast in such musicals as *HOLLYWOOD HOTEL* (1937), *Sis Hopkins* (1941), *STAR-SPANGLED RHYTHM* (1942), and *Hit Parade of 1943*. Her best musical roles were portraying tragic figures in show business: Jane Froman in *WITH A SONG IN MY HEART* (1952) and LILLIAN ROTH in *I'LL CRY TOMORROW* (1955). Hayward continued making films into the 1970s. Biographies: *Susan Hayward: Her Life and Films*, Kim R. Holston (2002); *A Star Is a Star Is a Star: The Lives and Loves of Susan Hayward*, Christopher P. Andersen (1980).

HAYWORTH, RITA [born Margarita Carmen Cansino] (1918–1987). Film performer. COLUMBIA PICTURES'S reigning star of the 1940s, the redheaded beauty exuded a sensual quality in all her roles, yet still managed to play the all-American girl. Hayworth was born in Brooklyn, the daughter of professional dancers from Spain who had danced in the *ZIEGFELD FOLLIES*, and was taught to dance at an early age, making her professional debut when she was twelve years old. While performing in night-clubs, Hayworth was signed by Hollywood and made her screen debut in 1935 but did not get much recognition until her performance in the melodrama *Only Angels Have Wings* (1939). She was soon one of the screen's hottest stars appearing in dramas, comedies, and musicals. Her best musical roles were the Broadway actress Sheila Winthrop in *YOU'LL NEVER GET RICH* (1941), the aspiring model Rusty Parker in *COVER GIRL* (1944), the femme fatale *Gilda* (1946), and the society dame Vera Simpson in *PAL JOEY* (1957). Hayworth's other musical credits include *Under the Pampas Moon* (1935), *Paddy O'Day* (1935), *Music in My Heart* (1940), *My Gal Sal* (1942), *YOU WERE NEVER LOVELIER* (1942), *Tonight and Every Night* (1945), *Down to Earth* (1947), *Affair in Trinidad* (1952), and *Miss Sadie Thompson* (1953). Her singing was frequently dubbed, but Hayworth's dancing was the important thing, especially when paired with FRED ASTAIRE or GENE KELLY. She continued to make films into the 1970s. Hayworth's five husbands included Orson Welles (1915–1985), Prince Aly Khan (1911–1960), and DICK HAYMES. Biographies: *Being Rita Hayworth: Labor, Identity, and Hollywood Stardom*, Adrienne L. McLean (2004); *If This Is Happiness: A Biography of Rita Hayworth*, Barbara Leming (1991).

🎵 **HEADS UP!** (Alvin Theatre 1929). A lesser known musical comedy scored by RICHARD RODGERS (music) and LORENZ HART (lyrics), it offered two noteworthy songs and some fine comic performances. The wealthy socialite Mrs. Trumbell enjoys little jaunts on her yacht *Silver Lady* without knowing that her captain Denny and her cook Skippy Dugan are using the boat for rum running. Coast Guard Lieutenant Jack Mason suspects that the *Silver Lady* is trafficking in illegal booze, but before Mason can board her the captain sets the yacht aflame to destroy the evidence. Jack doesn't get his contraband but he does catch Denny and wins the hand of Mrs. Trumball's daughter Mary. Titled *Me for You*, the musical was in such trouble in Detroit that producers ALEX A. AARONS and VINTON FREEDLEY threw out the libretto written by Owen Davis and hired John McGowan and Paul Gerald Smith to create a totally new one using the songs, sets, and cast already assembled. The result was an uneven but enjoyable enough show, directed and choreographed by GEORGE HALE, that managed to survive 144 performances in the early days of the Depression. The performers, including a young RAY BOLGER squeezed into the plot after Detroit, were splendid, in par-

Casts for *Heads Up!*		
Character	*1929 Broadway*	*1930 film*
Jack Mason	JACK WHITING	CHARLES "BUDDY" ROGERS
Mary Trumbell	Barbara Newberry	Margaret Breen
Skippy Dugan	VICTOR MOORE	Victor Moore
Mrs. Trumbul	Janet Velie	Helen Carrington
Capt. Denny	Robert Gleckner	Harry Shannon
Betty Trumbul		HELEN KANE

ticular VICTOR MOORE whose lovable Skippy kept tinkering with oddball inventions until one actually worked. Two popular Rodgers and Hart songs, "A Ship Without a Sail" and "Why Do You Suppose?," came from the otherwise mediocre score.

■ *Heads Up!* (Paramount 1930) retained Victor Moore for the film but all but two of the Rodgers and Hart songs were gone and a new number ("If I Knew You Better") by director VICTOR SCHERTZINGER was added. The screenplay by Jack Kirkland and McGowan was similar to McGowan's libretto but more emphasis was placed on the rivalry between Jack and the captain over Mary. Added to the mix was a new featured character, Mary's funny kid sister Betty, which HELEN KANE played with relish. Too much of the film takes itself too seriously and the comedy is often strained. Musically it is unimpressive, with even "A Ship Without a Sail" failing to register.

HEARN GEORGE (1934–). Stage, film, and television performer. A powerful baritone with a strong stage presence, the versatile singer–actor has been extolled for his performances in the classics, musicals, and everything between. Hearn was born in St. Louis and educated at Southwestern University before acting in regional theatres. His early Manhattan credits were in classical revivals by the NEW YORK SHAKESPEARE FESTIVAL and then he made his Broadway debut in the short-lived musical *A Time for Singing* (1966). Hearn impressed audiences when he took over the roles of John Dickinson in *1776* in 1971 and *SWEENEY TODD* in 1980 and when he originated the character of cabaret performer Albin in *LA CAGE AUX FOLLES* (1983) and ex-director Max in *SUNSET BOULEVARD* (1994).

His other musicals include *I Remember Mama* (1979), *A Doll's Life* (1982), *KISMET* (1985), *MEET ME IN ST. LOUIS* (1989), *Putting It Together* (1999), and a replacement for the Wizard in *WICKED* in 2004 and 2006. Hearn has appeared in some films and many television programs, from dramas to sit-coms to musicals specials. His *Sweeney Todd* was videotaped for TV in 1982 and again in 2001. Hearn has been married to actresses Betsy Joslyn (1954–) and Dixie Carter (1939–).

HEDWIG AND THE ANGRY INCH (Jane Street Theatre 1998). An Off Broadway cult hit, the offbeat musical took the form of a concert with Hedwig narrating his/her tale between songs. Young Hansel was born in East Berlin the year the wall went up and grows into a confused transsexual. He marries an American G.I. to get to the States but has to have a sex change operation to qualify. The operation is botched and Hedwig is left with an inch of undetermined sexual embarrassment. Once in America, she is dumped by the G.I. and has an affair with a military brat named Tommy Gnosis who becomes a rock star using Hedwig's songs, who then too abandons her. Left singing rock-and-roll dirges in third-class dives, Hedwig continues on, searching for a personal and sexual identity. The bewigged, heavily made up JOHN CAMERON MITCHELL, who also wrote the script, was mesmerizing, singing the rock score by Stephen Trask, telling his/her story with a phony German accent, and exuding a strange sensuality that was sexy without knowing which sex it was. Among the songs sung were "Origin of Love," "Angry Inch," "Wicked Little Town" and "Tear Me Down." The little musical, directed by Peter Askin, quickly caught on and ran 857 performances.

Casts for *Hedwig and the Angry Inch*		
Character	*1998 Off Broadway*	*2001 film*
Hedwig	JOHN CAMERON MITCHELL	John Cameron Mitchell
Tommy Gnosis	John Cameron Mitchell	Michael Pitt
Yitzhak	Miriam Shore	Miriam Shore

HEDWIG AND THE ANGRY INCH (New Line 2001) not only starred Mitchell in his own screenplay but he directed the movie himself, opening up the story and showing much of what was only described in the stage version. The film often got bogged down in the cinematic tricks and the bizarre storyline was not always clear; consequently, the characters rarely seemed as interesting as they had in the theatre. But the things that made *Hedwig and the Angry Inch* rock on stage were still there: the propulsive score, the weird concept, and Mitchell's astonishing performance.

HEINDORF, RAY (1908–1980). Film orchestrator, arranger, and composer. A much admired musical director in Hollywood, he supervised the music at WARNER BROTHERS for forty years. Heindorf was born in Haverstraw, New York, and educated at the Troy Conservatory before arriving in Hollywood just as sound came in. He supervised the music for *HOLLYWOOD REVUE OF 1929* and went on to arrange, orchestrate, and/or conduct the music for 150 films. His many musicals include *SWEET ADELINE* (1934), *Broadway Gondolier* (1935), *GOLD DIGGERS OF 1937* (1936), *The Singing Marine* (1937), *GOLD DIGGERS IN PARIS* (1938), *ON YOUR TOES* (1939), *YANKEE DOODLE DANDY* (1942), *THIS IS THE ARMY* (1943), *THE DESERT SONG* (1943), *UP IN ARMS* (1944), *Wonder Man* (1945), *RHAPSODY IN BLUE* (1945), *NIGHT AND DAY* (1946), *ROMANCE ON THE HIGH SEAS* (1948), *YOUNG MAN WITH A HORN* (1950), *Tea for Two* (1950), *THE JAZZ SINGER* (1953), *A STAR IS BORN* (1954), *THE PAJAMA GAME* (1957), *DAMN YANKEES* (1958), *THE MUSIC MAN* (1962), *FINIAN'S RAINBOW* (1968), and *1776* (1972). Heindorf also wrote original soundtrack scores for over thirty nonmusical films and individual songs, such as "Some Sunday Morning," "Pete Kelly's Blues," and "Sugarfoot."

HELD, ANNA (1873–1918). Stage performer. With her round, soft face, reddish hair, appealing figure, and—most intoxicating of all—her wide twinkling eyes, she was America's favorite Parisienne performer at the turn of the twentieth century. It is believed that Held was born in either Warsaw or Paris, the daughter of working class folk whose plight was worsened when her father died young. Held's mother took the child to London where she was put on stage in music halls and in the chorus of British musicals. By the time she was in her teens, Held went back to Paris where she appeared in revues. At the age of twenty-three she was hired by the

Anna Held. What was sex appeal to Americans at the turn of the twentieth century? Someone who was curvy, soft, seemingly innocent but hopefully not, and French. Anna Held was all of these plus more. Her singing of slightly risqué songs in Broadway musicals made her the most desirable woman in New York. (NYPL)

Folies-Bergere but broke her contract when producer FLORENZ ZIEGFELD saw her and offered to bring her to New York. With typical Ziegfeld ballyhoo, Held was championed as the world's greatest beauty (much ado was made of her supposed milk baths that she took every day to keep her skin soft), and with her Broadway debut in *A Parlor Match* (1896) she captured the hearts of theatregoers by singing suggestive songs with a coquettish innocence and a thick French accent. Her other musicals were *La Poupée* (1897), *Papa's Wife* (1899), *The Little Duchess* (1901), *Mam'selle Napoleon* (1903), *Higgledy Piggledy* (1904), *The Parisian Model* (1906), and *Miss Innocence* (1908). Her vehicles were never noteworthy (sometimes her character was simply called Anna) and her singing voice was not exceptional, but Held's disarming performances never failed to please. Ziegfeld himself was captivated and married her in 1901, but the marriage lasted less than a decade and Held's career suffered without his backing. All the same, she remained popular in vaudeville and in 1916 she returned to Broadway with success in the musical *Follow Me*. In the 1936 film *THE GREAT ZIEGFELD*, Held was portrayed by LUISE RAINER. A 1954 book claimed to be Held's long-lost autobiography, but it was soon discovered that it was written by her daughter, former vaudeville performer Liane Carrera. Biography: *Anna Held and the Birth of Ziegfeld's Broadway* by Eve Golden (2000).

HELLO AGAIN (Mitzi E. Newhouse Theatre 1994). An arresting little musical that captures the musical sounds and sexual mores of different decades in the twentieth century, the Off Broadway show featured a cast of up-and-coming talents and brought wider recognition to songwriter MICHAEL JOHN LaCHIUSA. Loosely based on Arthur Schnitzler's 1903 comedy of amoral manners *La Ronde*, LaChiusa's libretto follows ten sexual encounters in which one partner in each coupling appears in the next episode, with each segment taking place in a different era. The Whore (DONNA MURPHY) beds the circa 1900 Soldier (David A. White) who then seduces the Nurse (Judy Blazer) before he ships out for World War II; the Nurse then sleeps with the 1960s College Boy (Michael Park) who then seduces the Young Wife during the Depression, and on and on. In the last scene the 1990s Senator (John Dossett) has a confrontation with the Whore and the plotting has come full circle. GRACIELA DANIELE directed and choreographed the outstanding cast, which also featured JOHN CAMERON MITCHELL, Carolee Carmello, Malcolm Gets, Dennis Parlato, and Michele Pawk. LaChiusa's songs pastiched each period accurately and effectively and among the most memorable numbers were "The One I Love,' "Mistress of the Senator," "The Bed Was Not My Own," "Listen to the Music," "We Kiss," "I Gotta Little Time," and the title song. The engagement at LINCOLN CENTER was limited to sixty-five performances but the musical was well received and much attention was placed on the young LaChiusa.

HELLO, DOLLY! (St. James Theatre 1964). The most popular musical comedy of its decade, the sparkling, happy show represented Broadway escapism at its best and afforded a triumph for producer DAVID MERRICK, star CAROL CHANNING, director–choreographer GOWER CHAMPION, and songwriter JERRY HERMAN.

Plot: When the Yonkers businessman Horace Vandergelder hires matchmaker Dolly Levi to find him a wife, little does he suspect that Dolly has herself in mind. She also matches up the clerk Cornelius Hackl with the milliner widow Irene Molloy, the woman Horace is thinking of marrying, and works things so that Horace's niece Ermengarde gets to wed her sweetheart, the artist Ambrose Kemper. Despite a fiasco at the Harmonia Gardens Restaurant, where Horace loses his wallet and gets into a free-for-all on the dance floor, Dolly calms his anger and accepts his marriage proposal.

The libretto by MICHAEL STEWART was closely adapted from Thornton Wilder's comedy *The Matchmaker* (1955), with the story somewhat condensed but the major characters and sense of comic adventure still evident. Many of the songs flow right out of Wilder's dialogue, and the production numbers are spaced effectively so that the show is a well-balanced musical romp. The title song became a major recording hit for LOUIS ARMSTRONG and others, one of the few theatre songs of the decade to travel so far, but all of Herman's score is superior. The propulsive "Put on Your Sunday Clothes" is a musical scene that builds like an accelerating train, the merry march "It Takes a Woman" is foolishly self-deceptive, the gentle "Ribbons Down My Back" provides the show's quietest moment, the mock aria "So Long, Dearie" is a clever contrast from the welcoming title song that preceded it, and the first act finale "Before the Parade Passes By" is a joyous affirmation of life.

Casts for *Hello, Dolly!*

Character	1964 Broadway	1975 Broadway	1969 film
Dolly Levi	CAROL CHANNING	PEARL BAILEY	BARBRA STREISAND
Horace Vandergelder	DAVID BURNS	Billy Daniels	Walter Matthau
Cornelius Hackl	CHARLES NELSON REILLY	Terrence Emanuel	MICHAEL CRAWFORD
Irene Molloy	Eileen Brennan	Mary Louise	Marianne McAndrew
Barnaby Tucker	Jerry Dodge	Grenoldo Frazier	Danny Lockin
Minnie Fay	Sondra Lee	Chip Fields	E. J. Peaker

Hello, Dolly! The Jerry Herman musical is all about "adventure" and all of the characters set off for New York City hoping to find just that. Dolly Levi is the impetus but she also has the best adventure of them all. Here she is welcomed by the staff of the Harmonia Gardens Restaurant. No, that is not the original production. That is seventy-four-year-old Carol Channing in the 1995 Broadway revival. (Photofest)

Hello, Dolly! (stage) Musical Numbers

"I Put My Hand In"
"It Takes a Woman"
"Put on Your Sunday Clothes"
"Ribbons Down My Back"
"Motherhood"
"Dancing"
"Before the Parade Passes By"
"Elegance"
"The Waiters' Gallop"
"Hello, Dolly!"
"The Polka Contest"
"It Only Takes a Moment"
"So Long, Dearie"

Cheered by the press and embraced by the public, *Hello, Dolly!* ran 2,844 performances, thanks to Merrick's shrewd policy of replacing Channing with such stars as GINGER ROGERS, BETTY GRABLE, MARTHA RAYE, and ETHEL MERMAN. When business started to wane in 1968, Merrick recast the entire show with African American performers and starred PEARL BAILEY as Dolly. It was a gimmick but a unique move to apply color-blind casting on Broadway for the first time. By the time *Hello, Dolly!* finally closed in 1970, it was the record holder for the longest-running musical to date. There have been three Broadway revivals of the musical. Bailey returned in 1974 for six weeks as part of her national tour, and Channing reprised her Dolly Levi in 1978, welcomed back by both the press and the public and staying for 145 performances. EDDIE BRACKEN was her Horace, and the cast also included LEE ROY REAMS, Florence Lacey, Robert Lydiard, and Alexandra Korey. When it was announced that Channing was to play Dolly again in 1995, there was some concern that a geriatric performance might diminish the memory of the star's greatest Broadway triumph. But both critics and playgoers were pleased to see that the ageless Channing was still funny and spirited and the revival did brisk business for 118 performances. Reams directed and the cast included Jay Garner, Michael DeVries, Florence Lacy, Cory English, and Lori Ann Mahl.

■ *Hello, Dolly!* (Fox 1969) reunited, for the last time, several artists from the famous "Freed Unit" of the glory days of MGM: ROGER EDENS as associate producer, GENE KELLY as director, MICHAEL KIDD as choreographer, costumer Irene Sharaff, and even cinematographer Harry Stradling and set designer Jack Martin Smith. The musical did resemble the old days in its colorful period spectacle and celebratory dancing, but the movie almost seemed out of place in the 1960s and was poorly received by the press. Much fuss was made over Channing being passed over for twenty-seven-year-old BARBRA STREISAND playing the middle-aged matchmaker. Ironically, she was the overproduced, over budget film's saving grace and proved that the superstar could hold her own in a mammoth production. Streisand made no attempt to age herself, tackled the humor with a Jewish flavor (Dolly Levi is Jewish, after all), and sang the songs with polish and style. The movie had some other joys as well. Much of the Broadway score was retained, two new songs—"Just Leave Everything to Me" and "Love Is Only Love"—by Herman were added, and the numbers were often given top-notch staging, as in a bucolic rendering of "Dancing" in a park, the contagious "Put on Your Sunday Clothes" climaxing with a train setting off from Yonkers for Manhattan, Streisand cutting loose and mocking her own exuberance with "So Long, Dearie," and the rousing title number in which Louis Armstrong joined Streisand and the two created sparks that could rival the best moments from Hollywood's golden age. Although *Hello, Dolly!* did very well at the box office, it still lost money because of its record $24 million cost.

HELLO FRISCO, HELLO. See *KING OF BURLESQUE*

☺ *HELLZAPOPPIN'* (46th Street Theatre 1938). A recording-breaking revue, it owed its long run (1,404 performances) to the clowning of OLE OLSON and CHIC JOHNSON and the unabashed plugging it got from Walter Winchell's newspaper column rather than from any artistic merit. Olsen, Johnson, and Tom McKnight wrote the slaphappy, antic show, which offered forgettable songs (by SAMMY FAIN, Charles Tobias, and others) and juvenile sketches satirizing Hitler, Mussolini, and FDR, but mostly it had the zany comedy team of Olson and Johnson who would do anything for a laugh and often did. There was a wild tone to the loud, abrasive, but contagious revue and audiences turned it into a hit even though it had no other stars, no spectacle, and a terrible set of critical notices. Producers Olson and Johnson changed some of the songs and sketches during the long run, calling the show *The New Hellzapoppin* after June of 1941.

■ *Hellzapoppin'* (Universal 1941) sported a thin plot by Warren Wilson and Nat Perrin because Hollywood distrusted revues but with all its disjointed acts and scattershot humor, the film was pretty much a revue. Jeff Hunter (ROBERT PAIGE) loves Kitty Rand (JANE FRAZEE) but the wealthy Woody Taylor (Lewis Howard) is after her so Jeff puts on a big show with Olsen and Johnson (playing themselves) and gets Kitty a starring part in the revue, thereby winning her heart. Although the satirical targets were tamer on screen than they had been on Broadway, the movie was still a frenzied, anything-for-a-laugh circus with MISCHA AUER, MARTHA RAYE, Shemp Howard, HUGH HERBERT, and others thrown in for farcical bits or songs. The stage score was pretty much discarded and replaced by slightly better but still unimpressive numbers by GENE DE PAUL and DON RAYE. H. C. POTTER directed, Edward Prinz and NICK CASTLE choreographed, and the silly picture actually did well at the box office.

■ *HELP!* (United Artists 1965). With the success of the BEATLES' first film *A HARD DAY'S NIGHT* (1964), which was made on the cheap, the studio upped the budget, commissioned Marc Behm and Charles Wood to come up with a screenplay that had a real story this time around, and rehired RICHARD LESTER to direct, this time in color. The resulting film was just as popular as the earlier effort but less accomplished. Spoofing the current James Bond films, the farce had the foursome caught up in a plot to blow up the world and a religious cult with a high priest (Leo McKern) chasing them about for a missing sacrificial ring that Ringo was wearing. The frolicking took place on ski slopes, a beach in the Bahamas, and on Salisbury Plain with tanks coming to the rescue. It all looked a bit forced but the music was still classic rock and roll: "Ticket to Ride," "You're Gonna Lose That Girl," "You've Got to Hide Your Love Away," and the exclamatory title song. There was much to enjoy, particularly for Beatles fans, but everything was manufactured and artificial and it seemed to show up on the Liverpool lads' faces at times. It is not surprising that they turned down future offers to star in movies, happy to provide the voices for *YELLOW SUBMARINE* (1968) and appear in a few ROCKUMENTARIES.

HENDERSON, FLORENCE [Agnes] (1934–). Stage, television, and film performer. A perky, bright-eyed singer–actress, she found recognition in the theatre before finding greater success on television. Born in Dale, Indiana, the youngest of ten children of a sharecropper family, Henderson was educated in Kentucky before studying at the American Academy of Dramatic Arts. She made her Broadway debut as a minor character in the musical *WISH YOU WERE HERE* (1952) and then took over the role of Laurey in the national tour of *OKLAHOMA!*, playing it again in the New York City Center revival in 1953. Henderson also led the first national tour of *THE SOUND OF MUSIC* in 1961, playing Maria for over two years. In 1967 she played Nellie Forbush in a popular New York revival of *SOUTH PACIFIC*, repeating her performance in many stock and summer theatres. Henderson also originated two musical roles on Broadway: the title French heroine in *FANNY* (1954) and the sly American actress Mary Morgan in *The Girl Who Came to Supper* (1963). She was featured in the TV musicals *The Adventures of Huck Finn* (1957) and *LITTLE WOMEN* (1958). After appearing in many tours and stock productions, Henderson found fame on television with the family sitcom *The Brady Bunch* in the 1970s, followed by many sequels into the 1990s. She appeared on many other televisions shows and in a few films, including the musical *SONG OF NORWAY* (1970) in which she played composer Edvard Grieg's wife Nina.

HENDERSON, LUTHER [Lincoln] (1919–2003). Stage and television orchestrator and musician. A creative supervisor and arranger of music for the theatre, the oft-awarded African American musician took the music of THOMAS "FATS" WALLER and Jelly Roll Morton and brought them to new appreciation with the musicals *AIN'T MISBEHAVIN'* (1978) and *JELLY'S LAST JAM* (1992). Henderson was born in Kansas City, Missouri, and was educated at the Juilliard School of Music before serving as staff orchestrator for the Navy School of Music. He arranged music for other orchestras, such as DUKE ELLINGTON's band and the Canadian Brass, before making his Broadway debut doing the dance arrangements for *FLOWER DRUM SONG* (1958), followed by vocal, dance, and/or music arrangements for such shows

as *DO RE MI* (1960), *Bravo Giovanni* (1962), *Hot Spot* (1963), *FUNNY GIRL* (1964), *I Had a Ball* (1964), *HALLELUJAH, BABY!* (1967), *Golden Rainbow* (1968), *PURLIE* (1970), *NO, NO, NANETTE* (1971), *GOOD NEWS!* (1974), *Doctor Jazz* (1975), *So Long, 174th Street* (1976), *Lena Horne: The Lady and Her Music* (1981), *BLACK AND BLUE* (1989), and *Play On!* (1997). He also arranged the music on many recordings and for some television specials.

HENDERSON, RAY [born Raymond Brost] (1896–1970). Stage and film composer. As the composer member of the trio of De Sylva, Brown, and Henderson, he was responsible for some of Broadway's brightest and most tuneful musicals of the 1920s. Henderson was born in Buffalo, New York, the son of a musician, and studied music at the Chicago Conservatory before starting his career as pianist in a dance band. Soon he was in New York arranging music for song publishers and writing such hit songs as "That Old Gang of Mine," "Bye Bye Blackbird," "Five Foot Two, Eyes of Blue," and "I'm Sitting on Top of the World," some of which were interpolated into Broadway revues. In 1925 Henderson teamed with lyricist LEW BROWN and lyricist–librettist B. G. DE SYLVA to score *GEORGE WHITE'S SCANDALS* (1925). With such hits as "Lucky Day" and "The Birth of the Blues," the trio was in much demand and scored three more *Scandals* over the years. The threesome had an even bigger hit with their first book musical, *GOOD NEWS!* (1927), followed by *Manhattan Mary* (1927), *HOLD EVERYTHING!* (1928), *FOLLOW THRU* (1929), *FLYING HIGH* (1930), *Hot-Cha!* (1932), and *Strike Me Pink* (1933). When the trio parted ways, Henderson scored another *Scandals* (1935) and *ZIEGFELD FOLLIES* (1943) with lyricist JACK YELLEN, *Say When* (1934) with TED KOEHLER, and the London musical *Transatlantic Rhythm* (1936) with IRVING CAESAR. Many of Henderson's book musicals were filmed by Hollywood and he wrote original scores for the movie musicals *THE SINGING FOOL* (1928), *Say It With Songs* (1929), *SUNNY SIDE UP* (1929), *Just Imagine* (1930), and *Indiscreet* (1931) with De Sylva and Brown. With Koehler and Caesar he also wrote the songs for *CURLY TOP* (1935). Henderson's music is melody-driven, very carefree, and often with a flavor of blues and jazz. Among his many beloved songs are "Button Up Your Overcoat," "Life Is Just a Bowl of Cherries," "It All Depends on You," "You're the Cream in My Coffee," and "The Thrill Is Gone." In the movie musical bio *THE BEST THINGS IN LIFE*

Are Free (1956), Henderson was portrayed by DAN DAILEY. Biography: *The Best Things in Life Are Free: The De Sylva, Brown & Henderson Story*, John O'Hara (1955).

HENIE, SONJA (1910–1969). Film performer. An Olympic gold medal figure-skating star from Norway, the bubbly blonde was turned into a leading lady in movie musicals for her skating talents more than for her singing or dancing. Henie was born in Oslo, Norway, the daughter of a fur wholesaler, and was on skates at the age of six. By the time she was fourteen she was the figure-skating champion of Norway and she won medals at the Olympics in 1928, 1932, and 1936. Henie turned professional and was starred in ice shows around the world, stopping off in Hollywood from time to time to make ten movie musicals. While her English and acting abilities were limited, she managed to sparkle in the light comedy plots and dazzle in the skating sequences that were worked into the films. Her musical credits are *One in a Million* (1936), *Thin Ice* (1937), *Happy Landing* (1938), *My Lucky Star* (1938), *SECOND FIDDLE* (1939), *SUN VALLEY SERENADE* (1941), *ICELAND* (1942), *Wintertime* (1953), *It's a Pleasure* (1945), and *The Countess of Monte Cristo* (1948). When her screen career waned in the late 1940s, she concentrated on ice extravaganzas and remained very popular until she retired in 1960. Biography: *Queen of Ice, Queen of Shadows: The Unsuspected Life of Sonja Henie*, Raymond Strait (1990).

HEPBURN, AUDREY [born Edda van Heemstra Hepburn-Ruston] (1929–1993). Stage and film performer. The Belgium-born international film actress, whose slender, gamin looks and classic beauty made her a fashion icon as well as a movie star, ventured into musicals on a few occasions. Hepburn was born near Brussels, the daughter of an English banker and a Dutch baroness, and was educated in England and Belgium, studying ballet and later working as a model. She had bit parts in a few British films in the 1950s and then made an auspicious Broadway debut as *Gigi* (1951) in the nonmusical version of the Colette tale. Hepburn returned to Broadway only once, as the sprightly *Ondine* (1954), but by then she was a major movie celebrity thanks to her performance in *Roman Holiday* (1953). Among her many film roles, her two musical performances are among the most fondly remembered: the bookstore clerk-turned-model Jo Stockton in *FUNNY FACE* (1957), in which she did her own singing, and the Cockney Eliza Doolittle in *MY FAIR LADY* (1964), in which her singing was dubbed by MARNI NIXON. Hepburn can also be heard singing "Moon Rover" in her own voice in the nonmusical movie *Breakfast at Tiffany's* (1961). She was in semiretirement for the later part of her life, dedicating her time to charitable causes, in particular UNICEF. Biography: *Enchantment: The Life of Audrey Hepburn*, Donald Spoto (2007); memoir: *Audrey Hepburn, An Elegant Spirit: A Son Remembers*, Sean Hepburn Ferrer (2005).

HERBERT, EVELYN [born Evelyn Hostetter] (1898–1975). Stage performer. The full-throttle soprano, considered one of the finest voices heard in 1920s operettas, had a brief but impressive Broadway career. A native of Philadelphia, Herbert studied voice in Chicago and New York, singing major opera roles in both cities, but the strain of such parts damaged her voice so she turned to musical theatre. She made her Broadway debut in *Stepping Stones* (1923) and for the next ten years gave such memorable performances as the Civil War lass Barbara Frietchie in *My Maryland* (1927) and the French aristocrat Marianne Beaunoir in *THE NEW MOON* (1928). Herbert's other Broadway musicals were the *Love Song* (1925), *Princess Flavia* (1925), *The Merry World* (1926), *Princess Charming* (1930), and *Melody* (1933). With the waning of operetta during the Depression, she retired after making one final Broadway appearance in the revival of *BITTER SWEET* (1934). Herbert was married to singer–actor ROBERT HALLIDAY, with whom she performed on occasion.

HERBERT, HUGH (1887–1952). Film performer. A fidgety, stammering comic who would rub his hands together and let out a "woo-woo," he played supporting and some leading roles in over 100 movies. Herbert was born in Binghamton, New York, and began his career writing and performing in sketches in vaudeville. He was featured in the Broadway musical *Polly of Hollywood* (1927) and then went west when sound came in, writing scripts and acting in features. Herbert often played eccentric millionaires, mama's boys, befuddled professors, and other silly types in the movies, including over two dozen musicals such as *FOOTLIGHT PARADE* (1933), *College Coach* (1933), *WONDER BAR* (1934), *DAMES* (1934), *SWEET ADELINE* (1935), *GOLD DIGGERS OF 1935* (1936), *Colleen* (1936), *Sing Me a Love Song* (1936), *The Singing Marine* (1937), *HOLLYWOOD HOTEL*

(1937), GOLD DIGGERS IN PARIS (1938), THE GREAT WALTZ (1938), La Conga Nights (1940), Hit Parade of 1941 (1940), HELLZAPOPPIN' (1941), STAGE DOOR CANTEEN (1943), Ever Since Venus (1944), Music for Millions (1944), ONE TOUCH OF VENUS (1948), A Song Is Born (1948), and The Beautiful Blonde From Bashful Bend (1949). Herbert continued acting in films until a few weeks before his death.

HERBERT, VICTOR [August] (1859–1924). Stage composer, conductor, and musician. The first major composer for the American musical theatre, the multitalented songwriter laid the foundation for the Broadway operetta. Herbert was born in Dublin, Ireland, and was raised and educated in Germany where he studied the cello and later played in the Court Orchestra at Stuttgart. He emigrated to America when his wife, opera singer Therese Forster, was hired to sing at the Metropolitan Opera and Herbert played cello in the orchestra. His first musical compositions were in the classical mode and were performed by various symphonies, which he conducted. Herbert gained renown in his new homeland as an exceptional conductor, heading the Pittsburgh Symphony for some years and returning to conducting throughout his long life. He eventually turned his composing skills to operetta and made his Broadway debut with *Prince Ananias* (1894), followed by over forty other musicals written with such lyricist–librettists as HARRY B. SMITH, HENRY BLOSSOM, GLEN MACDONOUGH, and RIDA JOHNSON YOUNG. Among the most famous of his operettas are *The Wizard of the Nile* (1895), *The Serenade* (1897), *The Idol's Eye* (1897), THE FORTUNE TELLER (1898), *Cyrano de Bergerac* (1899), *The Viceroy* (1900), BABES IN TOYLAND (1903), *It Happened in Nordland* (1904), MLLE. MODISTE (1905), THE RED MILL (1906), *Algeria* (1908), *Little Nemo* (1908), NAUGHTY MARIETTA (1910), *The Enchantress* (1911), SWEETHEARTS (1913), *The Only Girl* (1914), *The Princess Pat* (1915), *The Century Girl* (1916), *Eileen* (1917), *The Velvet Lady* (1919), *Orange Blossoms* (1922), and *The Dream Girl* (1924). Hollywood filmed the Herbert operettas *Mlle. Modiste*, retitled *KISS ME AGAIN* (1931), *Babes in Toyland* (1934 and 1961), *Naughty Marietta* (1935), and *Sweethearts* (1938), usually with major script changes but with the best of the scores preserved. Walter Connolly played the composer in the musical film *The Great Victor Herbert* (1939). Although the influences of European operetta can be found in most of his works, the operettas are distinctly American as well.

Herbert used the Viennese waltz, the German march, and French and English ballads in his musicals, yet filtered them through an American idiom. Herbert was also instrumental in the founding of the AMERICAN SOCIETY OF COMPOSERS, AUTHORS AND PUBLISHERS (ASCAP), which looks after the interests of songwriters. Biographies: *Victor Herbert: A Life in Music*, Edward Waters (1955); *Victor Herbert: A Theatrical Life*, Neil Gould (2007).

HERCULES (Disney 1997). Although many liberties were taken with Greek mythology, this animated musical comedy ended up being one of the funniest in the Disney catalogue thanks to a witty script and some hilarious voices. A set of gospel-singing Muses (voices of Cheryl Freeman, La Chanze, Vanéese Y. Thomas, Roz Ryan, and LILLIAS WHITE) narrates the tale of how Hercules, the infant son of Zeus (Rip Torn), was kidnapped by the god Hades (James Woods) who orders his henchmen Pain (Bob Goldthwait) and Panic (Matt Frewer) to destroy him. But Hercules survives and is raised by mortals, growing up to become a superhero trained by the satyr Philoctetes (Danny DeVito). When Hades releases the Titans from their bondage and has them attack Mt. Olympus, Hercules (Tate Donovan) saves the day and even outwits Hades by winning the love of his spy Megara (Susan Egan). Despite all the derring-do, the film never took itself at all seriously and was filled with sly anachronisms in the dialogue and in the songs by ALAN MENKEN (music) and David Zippel (lyrics). Teenage Hercules (ROGER BART) sang the stirring "Go the Distance," but the rest of the score was more sassy, from the rousing "Gospel Truth" and "Zero to Hero," both sung by the Muses, to the self-aware ballad "I Won't Say (I'm in Love)," sung by Egan. The film reached its comic high points in the characterizations of Hades and Philoctetes, with both Woods and DeVito bringing a modern slyness to the classical material. John Musker and Ron Clements co-produced and co-directed the fast-paced joy ride of a film.

HERE COME THE WAVES (Paramount 1944). A World War II-era military musical, it stands out from the others because of its superior score by HAROLD ARLEN (music) and JOHNNY MERCER (lyrics) and for the way BING CROSBY made fun of the current fad of bobby-soxers swooning over singers like himself and FRANK SINATRA. (Crosby even satirizes Sinatra by crooning "That Old Black Magic" in the newcomer's style.) The screenplay by Ken Englund, Zion Myers, and Allan Scott focused on singing idol Johnny Cabot (Crosby) who, with his pal Windy (SONNY TUFTS), meets a twin sister act, Susan and Rosemary Allison (both played by BETTY HUTTON), falling for one sister and being mocked by the other. When Johnny joins the Navy, he is assigned to putting on a benefit entertainment with the W.A.V.E.S. (including the sisters), and the resulting show is a humdinger. Crosby and Tufts (in black face) introduced the movie's hit song, "Ac-cent-tchu-ate the Positive," Crosby and Hutton sang the romantic duets "I Promise You" and "Let's Take the Long Way Home," and Hutton was at her comic best bragging "There's a Fellow Waiting in Poughkeepsie." MARK SANDRICH produced and directed the nautical frolic with a careful yet carefree touch.

🎬 **HERE COMES THE GROOM** (Paramount 1951). It may have had a convoluted plot but this BING CROSBY vehicle had enough stars and felicitous musical numbers to brighten up the dreariest story. International correspondent Pete Garvey (Crosby) runs an adoption agency in Paris for war orphans, two of which he brings back to the States to adopt with his fiancée, Bostonian Emmadel Jones (JANE WYMAN). But Emmadel is now engaged to the dashing Wilbur Stanley (FRANCHOT TONE) and Pete must get a wife within five days or the kids will be deported back to Europe. Luckily the French orphans melt Emmadel's heart and she switches sweethearts. Crosby and Wyman sang the Oscar-winning "In the Cool Cool Cool Cool of the Evening" by HOAGY CARMICHAEL (music) and JOHNNY MERCER (lyrics), Crosby and CASS DALEY jumped and jived to "Misto Cristo Colombo" by RAY EVANS and JAY LIVINGSTON, and Crosby put the two orphans to bed singing the English and French lullaby "Bonne Nuit–Good Night" by the same team. Also on hand for musical and comic fun were LOUIS ARMSTRONG, DOROTHY LAMOUR, ALEXIS SMITH, JAMES BARTON, PHIL HARRIS, WALTER CATLETT, and ANNA MARIA ALBERGHETTI who sang an aria from *Rigoletto*. Frank Capra produced and directed the tuneful romp.

HERMAN, JERRY (1931–). Stage and television composer and lyricist. A master of singable musical comedy songs, the versatile songwriter has had mega hits and major flops on Broadway, with excellent songs in both. Herman was born in New York, the son of a piano teacher, and was raised in New Jersey

where he began playing at a young age. He was educated at the Parsons School of Design and Miami University in Ohio where he scored the musical revue *I Feel Wonderful*, which was produced Off Broadway in 1954. Herman's Broadway debut was the Israeli-set musical *MILK AND HONEY* (1961) followed by the mammoth hits *HELLO, DOLLY!* (1964) and *MAME* (1966). He experimented with nontraditional musical forms in the short-lived *DEAR WORLD* (1969) and wrote rich and engrossing scores for *MACK AND MABEL* (1974) and *THE GRAND TOUR* (1979) but neither show ran. Herman bounced back with the popular *LA CAGE AUX FOLLES* (1983). In addition to revivals, Herman's songs have returned to Broadway in the retrospective revues *Jerry's Girls* (1985) and *Jerry Herman on Broadway* (2001). *Hello, Dolly!* (1969) and *Mame* (1974) were filmed by Hollywood and he provided an original score for the TV musical *MRS. SANTA CLAUS* (1996). Herman's scores have been criticized as uninventive and too traditional, but his sprightly, hummable melodies and playful, engaging lyrics are too often underestimated. Autobiography: *Showtune: A Memoir*, with Marilyn Stasio (1996).

📖 **HIGH BUTTON SHOES** (Century Theatre 1947), A carefree period musical comedy that evoked Americana with a nostalgic smile, the show was notable as composer JULE STYNE's first Broadway effort and for launching PHIL SILVERS's career as a top banana in legit theatre. In 1913, con man Harrison Floy (Silvers) sells the people of New Brunswick, New Jersey, useless swamp land and then, with his partner Pontdue (Joey Faye), takes off for Atlantic City with the money. Henry (JACK McCAULEY) and Sara Longstreet (NANETTE FABRAY), one of the families swindled by Floy, follow him to the shore where a merry chase ensues, ending in the college town of Rutgers where Floy foolishly bets on the big football game and loses it all. The talented cast also included Mark Dawson, Nathaniel Frey, HELEN GALLAGHER, Johnny Stewart, and Lois Lee. Stephen Longstreet wrote the efficient libretto based on his semiautobiographical novel *The Sisters Liked Them Handsome*, although the script was mostly by the uncredited GEORGE ABBOTT who also directed. SAMMY CAHN provided the lyrics for Styne's music and they came up with the hit songs "Papa, Won't You Dance With Me?," and "I Still Get Jealous." Just as delightful were "There's Nothing Like a Model T," "On a Sunday By the Sea," and "Nobody Ever Died for Dear Old Rutgers." In addition to Silvers's risible performance as the fast-talking swindler Floy, the show's other star was JEROME ROBBINS whose choreography, in particular a madcap "Mack Sennett Ballet," was the talk of the town. The well-received musical ran 727 performances but, curiously, was never filmed or revived on Broadway. ❏ There was a condensed television version on NBC-TV in 1956 with an estimable cast headed by Hal March (Floy), Joey Faye (Pontdue), DON AMECHE (Henry Longstreet), and Nanette Fabray reprising her Sara Longstreet.

❏ **HIGH SCHOOL MUSICAL** (Disney Channel 2006). An unpretentious teen musical with no stars and little promotion, the show was a surprise hit that became one of the most-watched programs in the history of cable television. The teleplay by Peter Barsocchini was merely the latest incarnation of the MICKEY ROONEY-JUDY GARLAND "let's put on a show" musical. Two teens, the jock Troy Bolton (Zac Efron) and the "brainiac" Gabriella Montez (Vanessa Anne Hudgens), meet in a karaoke session on vacation at a ski

resort and the next fall find themselves classmates in his Albuquerque, New Mexico, high school. Troy is the basketball star but because of Gabrielle he considers trying out for the high school musical. This does not sit well with Troy's father (Bart Johnson), who is the basketball coach, and with his teammates. Troy and Gabrielle also have to contend with the diva Charpay Evans (Ashley Tisdale) and her affected brother Ryan (Lucas Grabeel) who are always cast in the leading roles. By the end, Troy and Gabrielle teach everyone that you have to be yourself and not be categorized as a jock, a brain, or anything else. What might have been just another routine high school romance was turned into a joyous celebration of youthful energy by director and co-choreographer Kenny Ortega who turned a basketball practice into a high-flying dance and lunch in the cafeteria into an explosion of teen angst. The pulsating score, written by a variety of tunesmiths, included "Start of Something New," "What I've Been Looking For," "Breaking Free," "When There Was Me and You," "Get'cha Head in the Game,"

High School Musical. The musical hits *Grease* and *Hairspray* were set in high schools of the past, drawing on nostalgia and a fascination with the outdated lifestyle of yesteryear. The Disney made-for-cable *High School Musical* was contemporary and teen audiences connected with the plot and characters without having to put them in a time frame. Here Zac Efron leads the cast in the musical's finale. (Photofest)

and "We're All in This Together." The musical broadcast was so popular and demand was such that Disney added extra air dates, the DVD was an instant bestseller, and the show was quickly turned into a stage work that has been produced by both professional and amateur theatre groups. The inevitable sequel, **High School Musical 2** (Disney Channel 2007), was heavily promoted and broke viewership records with its first broadcast. Most of the same cast and crew returned but the freshness of the original was gone and the contrived plot was no longer set in the high school but at the swanky country club where Troy, Gabrielle, and their friends get summer jobs while Sharpay and other members sip cool drinks by the pool. The complications, such as Sharpay chasing Troy to perform with her in the talent show and the lure of a basketball scholarship coming between Troy and his friends, were forced and unconvincing. Even the musical numbers lacked the energy and free abandon of the earlier program. The score, again by several different songwriters, included "You Are the Music in Me,' "All for One," "What Time Is It?," "Gotta Go My Own Way," and "Work This Out."

HIGH SOCIETY (Siegel/MGM 1956). One of those rare cases in which a musical is so enjoyable that one is able to (temporarily) forget the matchless source material, this musicalization of Philip Barry's comedy of manners *The Philadelphia Story* (1939) is its own masterwork thanks to songwriter COLE PORTER and some delightful star turns.

Plot: On the eve of her wedding to the stuffy millionaire George Kittridge, the spoiled heiress Tracy Lord is visited in her Newport summer mansion by two men who give her second thoughts. One is her ex-husband, songwriter C. Dexter Haven, who is in town for the jazz festival and is still liked by Tracy's family, par-

ticularly her younger sister Caroline. The other man is the radical journalist Mike Connor who has come with the wisecracking photographer Liz Imbrie to cover the wedding. To avoid a scandal, the family pretends that Uncle Willie is really Tracy's father because her real father is off philandering with a chorus girl in New York. Although Tracy and her riches represent everything he is against, Mike is drawn to her and the two go off for a midnight swim. George is shocked, breaks off the engagement, and Dexter rescues the day by offering to marry her once again since they obviously still love each other.

Katharine Hepburn had played Tracy on Broadway and in the popular 1940 film so it was difficult for moviegoers to replace her in their minds. However, Grace Kelly was so different in her sex appeal and classiness that she made her own Tracy work. The singing chores fell to BING CROSBY and FRANK SINATRA as Dexter and Mike and again comparisons were hard to make. Some of the Barry wit was sacrificed when screenwriter John Patrick abridged the original, but Porter's lyrics were pretty witty in themselves. The score is arguably the finest set of songs Porter ever wrote for one movie, from the lyrical ballads "True Love' and "You're Sensational" to the tongue-in-cheek character songs "Who Wants to Be a Millionaire?" and "Well, Did You Evah?" (the last was from a Porter stage score). Perhaps the highlight of this musical feast was Crosby and LOUIS ARMSTRONG bringing down the house with "Now You Has Jazz." Singing and joking and making love, the cast is in superb form and the chemistry between Kelly and both Crosby and Sinatra makes the triangle all the more intriguing. (This was Kelly's last film; she retired after filming was complete to become the Princess of Monaco.) CHARLES WALTERS directed the SOL C. SIEGEL production with a touch of class of his own.

Casts for *High Society*

Character	1956 film	1998 Broadway
Tracy Samantha Lord	Grace Kelly	Melissa Errico
C. K. Dexter Haven	BING CROSBY	Daniel McDonald
Mike Connor	FRANK SINATRA	STEPHEN BOGARDUS
Liz Imbrie	CELESTE HOLM	RANDY GRAFF
Uncle Willie	LOUIS CALHERN	JOHN McMARTIN
George Kittredge	John Kund	MARC KUDISCH
Caroline/Dinah Lord	Lydia Reed	Anna Kendrick

High Society (film) Musical Numbers

"High Society Calypso"
"Little One"
"Who Wants to Be a Millionaire?"
"True Love"
You're Sensational"
"I Love You, Samantha"
"Now You Has Jazz"
"Well, Did You Evah?"
"Mind If I Make Love to You?"

🎵 A stage version of *High Society* was first produced in London in 1987 with Natasha Richardson, Stephen Rea, and Trevor Eve as the romantic triangle. In the States, a version opened on Broadway in 1998 with a libretto by Arthur Kopit. Several Porter songs from other shows were added to the film score and, in a few cases, Susan Birkenhead wrote new or revised lyrics to try to make the numbers fit into the plot. Despite a young but very talented cast, the show was knocked by the press as lifeless and uninvolving. Christopher Renshaw directed and Lar Lubovitch choreographed the musical that had originated at the American Conservatory Theatre in San Francisco where it had been well received. On Broadway it only lasted 144 performances but has since found success in regional theatre.

▢ **HIGH TOR** (CBS-TV 1956). Maxwell Anderson's 1937 verse play was a ghostly fantasy with somber undertones about man's restlessness with the present. The musical version, with teleplay and lyrics by Anderson, was lighter but still wistful. Van Van Dorn (BING CROSBY) owns a mountain in New York State called High Tor and refuses to sell it to real estate agents because he likes to go there to fish and escape the modern world. After a quarrel with his fiancée Judith (Nancy Olsen), Van climbs the mountain and spends the night, running into the real estate agents, some bank robbers, and the ghosts of long-dead Dutch sailors who climbed the mountain after they were shipwrecked. Van meets the lovely ghost Lise (JULIE ANDREWS), the wife of a ship captain thought lost at sea. The two fall in love but as dawn comes they realize that death separates them so Van returns to Judith and sells the mountain. The appearance of long-time favorite Crosby and newcomer Andrews helped make the unusual but enjoyable broadcast very popular. ARTHUR SCHWARTZ produced and composed the music for the songs, which were exceptional: "Living One Day at a Time," "A Little Love, A Little While," "Once Upon a Long Ago," "Sad Is the Life of a Sailor's Wife," "When You're in Love," and "John Barleycorn." The notable supporting cast included Everett Sloane, HANS CONRIED, Lloyd Corrigan, and John Pickard. The *Ford Star Jubilee* broadcast was CBS's first original musical and they spent a hefty $300,000 on the elaborate production, the most expensive TV musical up to that time. Although the venture received mixed notices, it was an impressive achievement.

🎬 **HIGH, WIDE AND HANDSOME** (Paramount 1937). A transitional piece that lyricist–librettist OSCAR HAMMERSTEIN wrote between the Broadway classics *SHOW BOAT* (1927) and *OKLAHOMA!* (1943), this marvelous frontier musical with music by JEROME KERN has a little bit of each show in it.

Plot: In the western hills of Pennsylvania in 1859, the farmer Peter Cortlandt takes in the itinerant medicine man Doc Watterson, his daughter Sally, and their sidekick Maurice. When Peter discovers oil on his land, he attempts to build a pipeline to bring the oil out of the hills, but the railroad robber baron Walter Bremman opposes him every step of the way. A romance between Peter and Sally blossoms and then is disrupted. In the film's climatic scene, Sally brings along the personnel from a traveling circus, dwarfs and elephants included, to drive away the railroad goons and allow Peter to complete his pipeline.

The screenplay by Hammerstein and ROUBEN MAMOULIAN painted a broad panorama of frontier life, including medicine shows, backwoods saloons, a circus, riverboat entertainment, and country square dances, and employed a rich set of supporting characters, particularly DOROTHY

Cast for *High, Wide and Handsome*

Character	Performer
Sally Waterson	IRENE DUNNE
Peter Cortlandt	RANDOLPH SCOTT
Molly	DOROTHY LAMOUR
Joe Varesi	AKIM TAMIROFF
Red Scanlan	Charles Bickford
Doc Waterson	Raymond Walburn
Samuel	BEN BLUE
Maurice	WILLIAM FRAWLEY
Grandma Cortlandt	Elizabeth Patterson
Walter Bremman	ALAN HALE

High, Wide and Handsome Musical Numbers

"High, Wide and Handsome"
"Can I Forget You?"
"Will You Marry Me Tomorrow, Maria?"
"The Folks Who Live on the Hill"
"The Things I Want"
"Allegheny Al"
"He Wore a Star"
"Grandma's Song"

LAMOUR as the knowing saloon singer Molly. The movie was shot on location near Chino, California, and the look of the picture is rustic and poetic.

The original score by Kern–Hammerstein was the best the two of them ever wrote for Hollywood and the songs were more integrated into the story than in most previous movie musicals, helped by Hammerstein's plotting and Mamoulian's expert direction. The gentle domestic ballad "The Folks Who Live on the Hill" was the standout number but also laudable were the farewell song "Can I Forget You?," the frolicking "Allegheny Al," the bluesy "The Things I Want," and the rollicking title number. One can see in the script and score some of the rustic Americana of *Oklahoma!* and the heartfelt melodrama of *Show Boat*. Producer ARTHUR HORNBLOW, JR., the creators of the film, and the studio were all very proud of the expensive but classy movie and reviews were laudatory, yet *High, Wide and Handsome* did modest box office and never paid off its high price tag.

HIGHER AND HIGHER (Shubert Theatre 1940). A lesser RICHARD RODGERS (music) and LORENZ HART (lyrics) effort, the musical comedy came

and went and only later did a song standard emerge from it. The libretto by Gladys Hurlbut and JOSHUA LOGAN takes place at the Drake Mansion in New York City where word has gotten to the servants that the Drakes are bankrupt and all the staff will be out of work. When the family leaves town, the butler Zachary Ash, the maid Sandy Moore, and the other servants hatch a plan to disguise the parlor maid Minnie Sorenson as a Drake debutante and get her married to the wealthy Patrick O'Toole. In the midst of their charade, the Drakes return, causing enough complications to give time for Zachary and Minnie to realize they love each other. An interesting premise for a musical comedy turned into a nightmare during the show's preparation. Logan wrote the piece with dancer VERA ZORINA in mind but she was unavailable so producer DWIGHT DEERE WIMAN replaced her with nondancing singer Marta Eggert. The book was such a shambles out of town that Hurlbut was brought in to doctor the script; her biggest contribution was to add a performing seal, which, unfortunately, became the high point of the musical. Little of the score was appreciated at the time, although years later "It Never Entered My Mind" became a standard, and there was much to admire in "From Another World," "Ev'ry Sunday Afternoon," "Mornings at Seven," "How's Your Health?," and "Disgustingly Rich." The musical, directed by Logan and choreographed by ROBERT ALTON, struggled on for 108 performances without showing a profit.

Higher and Higher (RKO 1943) was made as a showcase for rising sensation FRANK SINATRA who played himself, a popular singer who lives next door to the servants, again headed by Haley who, in the screenplay by Jay Dratle and Ralph Spence, was now called Mike O'Brien. Michele Morgan was the parlor maid and, odd at it may seem, she threw over

Casts for *Higher and Higher*

Character	1940 Broadway	1943 film
Zachary Ash/Mike O'Brien	JACK HALEY	Jack Haley
Minnie/Millie	Marta Eggerth	Michele Morgan
Sandy	SHIRLEY ROSS	MARY WICKES
Patrick O'Toole/Frank Sinatra	Leif Erickson	FRANK SINATRA
Byng	ROBERT CHISHOLM	Paul Hartman
Victor Fitzroy Victor		Victor Borge
Cyrus Drake		LEON ERROL
Mickey		Marcy McGuire

Sinatra for Haley in the end. All but one of the Rodgers and Hart songs ("Disgustingly Rich") were tossed out and a new score was provided by JIMMY McHUGH (music) and HAROLD ADAMSON (lyrics), including "I Couldn't Sleep a Wink Last Night," "A Lovely Way to Spend an Evening," "The Music Stopped," and "It's a Most Important Affair." Most of the numbers were sung by Sinatra, which was fine for his hordes of bobby-soxer fans but not good for anyone connected with the stage musical.

HILLIARD, HARRIET. See NELSON, Ozzie, and Harriet HILLIARD

HINES, GREGORY [Oliver] (1946–2003). Stage, film, and television performer and choreographer. The African American singer–actor was one of the most acclaimed tap dancers of the post–World War II era. Hines was born in New York, the son of entertainer Maurice Hines, and was on stage as a boy, appearing with his brother Maurice on Broadway in the chorus in *The Girl in Pink Tights* (1954). They formed the Hines Kids act in the 1950s, and then in the 1960s the two brothers danced with their father as Hines, Hines and Dad in nightclubs, on television specials, and on tour. Both Hines brothers were familiar faces from television and some films when they were featured in the Broadway revues *Eubie* (1978) and *SOPHISTICATED LADIES* (1981). Gregory Hines also shone as Scrooge in *Comin' Uptown* (1979) and as Jelly Roll Morton in *JELLY'S LAST JAM* (1992). Of the movies he made, his expert dancing was witnessed in *The Cotton Club* (1984), *White Nights* (1985), and *Tap* (1989), and he was in the musical film *THE PREACHER'S WIFE* (1996). Hines appeared frequently on television, in series, his own show in the 1990s, and in many specials, including the TV biography *Bojangles* (2001). He was also a teacher and a choreographer on occasion, contributing to the dances in *Jelly's Last Jam* and other shows. His brother **Maurice Hines** (1943–) is also a choreographer and has turned to directing musicals as well. He conceived, staged, and starred in the Broadway revue *Uptown … It's Hot!* (1986) and directed and choreographed the dance revue *Hot Feet* (2006). Hines was in the short-lived musical *Bring Back Birdie* (1981) but much of his performing has been in regional theatre and on tour, such as playing Nathan Detroit in the national company of *GUYS AND DOLLS* and dancing in the revues *Harlem Suite, Havana Night,* and *Broadway Soul Jam,* directing and choreographing the last two. He is also the first African American to direct at Radio City Music Hall.

Hines has appeared in a few films, including *The Cotton Club* (1984), and made many television appearances as well.

HINES, MAURICE. See HINES, Gregory

HIRSCH, LOUIS A[chille]. (1887–1924). Stage composer. A vibrant songwriter with significant musicals on Broadway and the West End, his impressive career was cut short by his premature death. The native New Yorker was educated at City College of New York and the Stern Academy in Berlin before beginning his career writing songs for Lew Dockstader's Minstrels and for Tin Pan Alley. Hirsch was hired by the SHUBERTS to be their staff composer and he made his Broadway debut writing their musical *He Came From Milwaukee* (1910), followed by *The Revue of Revues* (1911), *Vera Violetta* (1911), *The Whirl of Society* (1912), and *THE PASSING SHOW* (1912), as well as thirteen shows for other producers. His most memorable book musicals were *Going Up!* (1917) and *MARY* (1920), both written with lyricist OTTO HARBACH. Hirsch's other book musicals are *The Grass Widow* (1917), *The Rainbow Girl* (1918), *Oh, My Dear* (1918), *See-Saw* (1919), *The O'Brien Girl* (1921), and *Betty Lee* (1924). His revues include *ZIEGFELD FOLLIES* (1915, 1916, and 1918) and *Greenwich Village Follies* (1922 and 1923). Hirsch also scored four London musicals in the 1910s. His songs, such as "The Love Nest," "The Tickle Toe," and "Neath the Southern Moon," were very popular in their day and one cannot help but speculate about the musical gems that would have been written had Hirsch lived longer.

HIT THE DECK! (Belasco Theatre 1927). A merry musical comedy with a daffy 1920s sensibility, the show boasted a superior score by VINCENT YOUMANS (music), LEO ROBIN, CLIFFORD GREY, and IRVING CAESAR (lyrics). The saucy, carefree Loulou Martin runs a dockside coffee house in Newport, Rhode Island, and loves the rough-and-ready gob Bilge Smith. When he goes off to sea, Loulou follows him, going all the way to China where she presents him with his own ship. Bilge is suspicious of a girl rich enough to take care of him, so Loulou agrees to sign all her money over to their first child and the twosome head for the altar. HERBERT FIELDS wrote the libretto, which was based on the 1922 play *Shore Leave*, making the characters tougher and more liable to break into song. Two of the numbers they sang were giant hits, "Sometimes I'm Happy" and "Hallelujah." Also in the score were "Why, Oh,

Casts for *Hit the Deck*

Character	1927 Broadway	1930 film
Bilge	CHARLES KING	JACK OAKIE
Loulou	LOUISE GROODY	Polly Walker
Lavinia	Stella Mayhew	Marguerita Padula
Charlotte Payne	Madeline Cameron	Ethel Clayton
Donkey/Dinty	Brian Donlevy	Andy Clark
Lt. Alan Clark	JACK MCCAULEY	Wallace MacDonald

Why?," "Lucky Bird," "Harbor of My Heart," and "Join the Navy." Co-producer LEW FIELDS directed with ALEXANDER LEFTWICH, the choreography was by SEYMOUR FELIX, and the happy show ran 352 performances.

■ The Broadway hit inspired three Hollywood musicals, the most faithful version being **Hit the Deck!** (RKO 1930) starring JACK OAKIE and Polly Walker. Director Luther Reed's screenplay followed the Fields script pretty closely but only three songs from the stage score were used. Other Youmans tunes were interpolated, most memorably "Keeping Myself for You" (lyric by SIDNEY CLARE) and "More Than You Know" (lyric by Edward Eliscu and BILLY ROSE). The two leads were personable but much of the film fell flat and it was not a box office hit. That didn't discourage RKO from remaking the musical in 1936 but calling it *FOLLOW THE FLEET*. (See separate entry.) Two decades later the musical resurfaced again as **Hit the Deck!** (MGM 1955) but the title and some of the songs were all that remained from the Broadway show. Screenwriters SONYA LEVIEN and William Ludwig jettisoned most of the Fields characters and plot and just kept the navy uniforms. William Clark (TONY MARTIN), Danny Smith (RUSS TAMBLYN), and Rico Ferrari (VIC DAMONE) are three sailors on leave in San Francisco but spend more time making trouble than romancing. Rico is smitten with Danny's sister Susan (JANE POWELL), who is so anxious to get a part in the stage show *Hit the Deck!* that she agrees to meet a womanizing producer in his hotel room. The three gobs try to save her virtue

by destroying the hotel suite but only get in trouble with Admiral Daniel Xavier Smith (WALTER PIDGEON) who just happens to be Danny and Susan's father. All that mattered were the musical numbers, staged beautifully by HERMES PAN, and the fine cast, which also included DEBBIE REYNOLDS, ANN MILLER, J. CARROL NAISH, and Kay Armen. Eleven Youmans songs were used, including the best from the stage and 1930 version, so the movie was a feast of riches from this too-often underrated composer.

HOLD EVERYTHING! (Broadhurst Theatre 1928). A frolicsome musical about professional boxing, it is mostly remembered for its score and for making a star out of comic BERT LAHR. The libretto by B. G. DeSYLVA and John McGowan centered on the welterweight boxer Sonny Jim Brooks who loves Sue Burke and has ambitions for the title. But his affections and professional plans are threatened by the high society Norine Lloyd until Jim's challenger insults Sue and he regains the fighting spirit and wins the girl and the match. More interesting than the romantic triangle was the punch-drunk pug Gink Schiner played by BERT LAHR with hilarious ignorance. The score by RAY HENDERSON (music), DeSylva, and LEW BROWN (lyrics) was full of splendid songs, with the most famous being "You're the Cream in My Coffee," but also including "Too Good to Be True," "Don't Hold Everything," and "To Know You Is to Love You." The ALEX A. AARONS–VINTON FREEDLEY production was a runaway hit, entertaining audiences for 409 performances.

Casts for *Hold Everything!*

Character	1928 Broadway	1930 film
Jim Brooks/George La Verne	JACK WHITING	Georges Carpentier
Gink Schiner	BERT LAHR	JOE E. BROWN
Sue Burke	Ona Munson	Sally O'Neill
Norine Lloyd	Betty Compton	Dorothy Revier
Nosey Bartlett	VICTOR MOORE	Bert Roach
Pop O'Keefe	Edmund Elton	Edmund Breese
Toots Breen	Nina Olivette	WINNIE LIGHTNER

▦ *Hold Everything* (Warner 1930) foolishly dropped Lahr and "You're the Cream in My Coffee," as well as the rest of the score, and turned the musical into a vehicle for comic JOE E. BROWN as Gink Schiner. The slight and nervous character Brown came up with was funny but no match for the inspired clowning of Lahr. The screenplay by Robert Lord followed the stage plot fairly closely, and real-life boxing champ Georges Carpentier was the eager boxer, renamed Georges La Verne. The new score by JOE BURKE (music) and AL DUBIN (lyrics) was pleasant if not exceptional; the songs included "All Alone Together," "Take It on the Chin," When Little Red Roses Get the Blues for You," and "Girls We Remember." ROY DEL RUTH directed, Larry Ceballos choreographed, and the movie was popular with Brown's many fans.

HOLDER, GEOFFREY (1930–). Stage, film, and television performer and choreographer. The tall, athletic, deep-voiced African American dancer–actor usually plays supporting roles but he's hard to miss and easy to enjoy. Holder was born in Port-of-Spain, Trinidad, and trained in dance at an early age by his brother Boscoe Holder who had his own dance company. Holder took over the running of the company as an adult and then in 1954 he and the company came to America where, as Geoffrey Holder and Company, they performed into the 1960s. Holder danced in (and help choreograph) the Broadway musical *HOUSE OF FLOWERS* (1954) and then danced for several years at the Metropolitan Opera. He returned to Broadway in the late 1950s to act in plays, and in 1957 he started appearing in films and on television, moving from dance to dramas to musicals, sometimes designing costumes as well. Holder's most significant Broadway credit is *THE WIZ* (1975), which he directed and designed the costumes, turning an out-of-town flop into a musical triumph. He repeated both jobs for *Timbuktu* (1978), a stylish retelling of *KISMET* in Africa. Holder was in the movie musicals *DOCTOR DOOLITTLE* (1967) and *ANNIE* (1982), was the narrator for *CHARLIE AND THE CHOCOLATE FACTORY* (2005), and acted in the TV musicals *ALADDIN* (1958) and *ANDROCLES AND THE LION* (1967). His distinctive voice and screen charisma have been utilized for many television commercials.

HOLGATE, RON[ald] (1937–). Stage performer. The rich-voiced baritone was a reliable leading man in both new musicals and revivals for many years and then became a seasoned character actor. Holgate was born in Aberdeen, South Dakota, and educated at Northwestern before studying for an opera career at the New England Conservatory and the Music Academy of the West. He made his opera debut in Boston in 1958, but soon switched to musical theatre, making his Broadway bow in 1961. After appearing in the ensemble of *MILK AND HONEY* (1962), Holgate gained recognition for his pompous Miles Gloriosus in *A FUNNY THING HAPPENED ON THE WAY TO THE FORUM* (1962). He was also praised for his vivacious Richard Henry Lee in *1776* (1969), grumpy Col. Stjerbinsky in *THE GRAND TOUR* (1979), and American tourist Phil Arkin in the Off Broadway revival of *Milk and Honey* in 1994. Holgate's other New York musical credits include a replacement for Vittorio Vidal in *SWEET CHARITY* (1969), *Musical Chairs* (1980), gangster Big Jule in *GUYS AND DOLLS* (1992), Buffalo Bill in *ANNIE GET YOUR GUN* (1999), and millionaire Harrison Howell in *KISS ME, KATE* (1999). He has acted in some nonmusicals, most memorably as Italian opera star Tito Merelli in *Lend Me a Tenor* (1989), and played the ruthless Caldwell B. Cladwell in the 2003 tour of *URINETOWN*. Holgate reprised his Richard Henry Lee in *1776* (1972), his only screen musical.

▦ *HOLIDAY INN* (Paramount 1942). Although it will always be remembered as the film in which BING CROSBY introduced IRVING BERLIN's "White Christmas," the musical is chock full of other musical and romantic treats as well.

Plot: Nightclub partners Ted Hanover and Jim Hardy break up over a girl, Lila Dixon, so Jim moves to the country and turns an old Connecticut homestead into an inn that's only open on holidays. When he falls for aspiring singer Linda Mason, Jim tries to keep her identity from Ted so as not to lose her too. Each holiday brings a new show to the inn and another opportunity to keep the wolf-like Ted at bay. Ted eventually discovers Linda and whisks her off to Hollywood to make a movie about the inn. Jim goes to the studio and in the setting of the artificial inn wins her back.

Cast for *Holiday Inn*	
Character	*Performer*
Jim Hardy	BING CROSBY
Ted Hanover	FRED ASTAIRE
Linda Mason	MARJORIE REYNOLDS
Lila Dixon	Virginia Dale
Danny Reed	Walter Abel
Mamie	LOUISE BEAVERS

Claude Binyon's screenplay was inspired from a story by Elmer Rice and an idea that Berlin and playwright Moss Hart had for a Broadway revue based on all the major American holidays. It is a fanciful conceit to believe that a business that's only open for the holidays could survive, but part of the charm of the film is the carefree way it goes about its way to entertain. What is unusual in the story is the fact that Astaire, for the first time in his movie career, does not get the girl, but then his is not a very likable character. Only Astaire's charm allows him to carry it off. The setting for the musical is also unique. The homey Connecticut inn seemed idyllic to wartime audiences, and the mood and setting for "White Christmas" make for one of the most cozy and romantic scenes in the history of movie musicals.

Berlin's "Easter Parade" was the only song in the score not written for the film. The new holiday songs have been overshadowed by the tremendous popularity of the Oscar-winning "White Christmas," but others are also quite good and are given effective introductions. Crosby sang "Be Careful, It's My Heart," a warm ballad for Valentine's Day, "Let's Start the New Year Right," is a chipper New Year's ditty, and the Fourth of July is celebrated with Astaire tapping to "Let's Say It With Firecrackers" as dozens of tiny explosions erupted at his feet. The most problematic number in the film for modern audiences is the revival-like "Abraham" for Lincoln's birthday, which Crosby and Marjorie Reynolds (dubbed by Martha Mears) performed as two black-faced minstrels. The nonholiday songs were also given memorable treatments, such as Crosby attempting to dance like Astaire while Astaire tries to croon like Crosby in "I'll

---

Holiday Inn **Musical Numbers**

"I'll Capture Your Heart Singing"
"Lazy"
"You're Easy to Dance With"
"White Christmas"
"Happy Holiday"
"Holiday Inn"
"Let's Start the New Year Right"
"Abraham"
"Be Careful, It's My Heart"
"I Can' Tell a Lie"
"Easter Parade"
"Let's Say It With Firecrackers"
"Song of Freedom"
"Plenty to Be Thankful For"

Capture Your Heart Singing," and Virginia Dale and Astaire gliding across the dance floor with "You're Easy to Dance With." DANNY DARE and Astaire did the inventive choreography, MARK SANDRICH produced and directed the film with a breezy style, and the movie was a giant hit. It remains a familiar favorite because of its reappearance every December on television, video, and DVD.

HOLLIDAY, JUDY [born Judith Tuvim] (1922–1965). Stage and film performer. The vibrant, not-so-dumb-blonde comedienne made a limited number of Broadway and Hollywood appearances in her short life but most of them were special. Holliday was born in New York City where she began her theatre career as a telephone operator for Orson Welles' Mercury Theatre. By the late 1930s she teamed up with ADOLPH GREEN and BETTY COMDEN, with the three calling themselves the Revuers and playing in nightclubs and Off Broadway theatres. While Comden and Green found success as writers and performers, Holliday's career seemed stalled so she went to California and made a few films, including the musicals *Greenwich Village* (1944) and *SOMETHING FOR THE BOYS* (1944), without getting noticed. It was her performance as Billie Dawn, the feisty mistress of a junk dealer in the play *Born Yesterday* (1946), that launched her Broadway career and she became a movie star when she reprised the performance on film in 1950. After playing the overimaginative Georgina in the 1951 revival of the fantasy comedy *Dream Girl*, Holliday had a major hit with the musical *BELLS ARE RINGING* (1956), written for her by Comden and Green. She triumphed in the 1960 film version as well. Holliday's only other Broadway musical was the short-lived *Hot Spot* (1963), and she made a handful on nonmusical movies before her untimely death by cancer at the age of forty-three. With her baby voice and precise comic instincts, Holliday gave her characters a delicious blend of naiveté and slyness.

HOLLOWAY, STANLEY [Augustus] (1890–1982). Stage, film, and television performer. A raucous character actor from Great Britain, he made only a few but very memorable appearances in musicals in the States. The native Londoner began his career in music halls and by 1919 was singing and dancing in West End musicals. Holloway became a London favorite for his clowning in a series of the revues called *The Co-Optimists* between 1921 and 1930, and his British film debut was in a 1929 screen version of the show. He made his Broadway musical debut as Alfred Doolittle in *My Fair Lady* (1956) and his Hollywood bow in the 1964 film version. Holloway also performed in two American television musicals, as Pooh-Bah in *The Mikado* (1950) and the father Bellamy in *The Fantasticks* (1964). His son is actor Julian Holloway (1944–) who played Doolittle in the 1993 Broadway revival of *My Fair Lady*. Autobiography: *Wiv' a Little Bit of Luck* (1969).

HOLLOWAY, STERLING [Price] (1905–1992). Stage, film, and television performer. An easily recognizable character actor with his lanky frame and raspy voice, the unusual song-and-dance man played country bumpkins, telegram boys, clerks, and soda jerks in over 100 films but is mostly known as the voice of Winnie the Pooh. Holloway was born in Cedartown, Georgia, and was a juvenile actor on the regional stage. He made his Broadway debut in 1923 in a drama but two years later got to introduce the first RODGERS and HART song hit "Manhattan" in the revue *The Garrick Gaieties* (1925). Holloway was featured in the 1926 and 1930 editions of the *Gaieties* but rarely returned to Broadway because of his busy film and television schedule. He appeared in a few silent films but with the coming of sound his high-pitched drawl was an asset and he was frequently cast in comedies, dramas, and musicals, such as *Gold Diggers of 1933*, *Dancing Lady* (1933), *The Merry Widow* (1935), *Varsity Show* (1937), *Doctor Rhythm* (1938), *Iceland* (1942), *Hit Parade of 1941* (1940), and *The Beautiful Blonde From Bashful Bend* (1949). Holloway's best musical performances were in animated films where he provided the voices of Mr. Stork in *Dumbo* (1940), the Cheshire Cat in *Alice in Wonderland* (1951), Kaa the Snake in *The Jungle Book* (1967), Roquefort the Mouse in *The Aristocats* (1970), and various parts in *The Three Caballeros* (1945) and *Make Mine Music* (1946). He appeared in dozens of television shows, including many Disney programs, and had his own series in the mid-1950s. He first voiced Winnie the Pooh in 1966 and provided the bear's voice in many cartoons and features up until Holloway's death.

HOLLYWOOD CANTEEN. See *STAGEDOOR CANTEEN*

HOLLYWOOD HOTEL (Warner 1937). A songfest of a musical about the crazy world of Tinsel Town, the film starts out with a bang and rarely lets up. Taking its title from a popular radio program, the movie begins with Georgia (JOHNNY "SCAT" DAVIS), Alice (FRANCES LANGFORD), and other friends accompanied by BENNY GOODMAN's orchestra riding to the St. Louis airport to bid farewell to Ronnie Bowers (DICK POWELL) by singing "Hooray for Hollywood," a tongue-in-cheek salute that became the unofficial theme song of the place. Once in California, Ronnie is reduced to providing the singing voice for ham actor Alexandre Dupre (Alan Mowbray), but he gets to meet aspiring actress Virginia Stanton (ROSEMARY LANE) who is playing a double for the temperamental star Mona Marshall (LOLA LANE). Of course Ronnie and Virginia fall in love, and after a series of musical numbers at the famed Hollywood Hotel, get to go on and show the world their stuff. RICHARD A. WHITING (music) and JOHNNY MERCER (lyrics) wrote the scintillating score that also included the romantic ballad "Silhouetted in the Moonlight," the frolicsome "I'm Like a Fish Out of Water" (which Ronnie and Virginia sang as they splashed in a fountain), the dreamy "I've Hitched My Wagon to a Star," and "Let That Be a Lesson to You," which director–choreographer BUSBY BERKELEY staged at a drive-in diner with carhops whizzing by and dancers prancing on the tops of parked cars. HUGH HERBERT, Ted Healy, Glenda Farrell, Edgar Kennedy, Allyn Joslyn, Mabel Todd, RONALD REAGAN, and Jerry Cooper filled out a cast that ribbed the cinema capital (even gossip columnist Louella Parsons was on hand to play herself) and provided vivacious entertainment at the expense of the studios.

HOLLYWOOD REVUE OF 1929 (MGM 1929). The first of the all-star revues that the studios put out in the early days of the talkies to show off their roster of talent, this one was a lavish, if mixed-bag, affair with everything from ballet to comedy turns to Shakespeare to song-and-dance numbers. JACK BENNY and Conrad Nagel emceed the revue, which was directed by Charles F. Reisner and choreographed by SAMMY LEE, ALBERTINA RASCH, and Natasha Natova. John Gilbert and Norma Shearer did the balcony scene from *Romeo and Juliet*, Buster Keaton and LAUREL and HARDY provided the comedy, JOAN CRAWFORD danced as a flapper to "Got a Feelin' for You," Nagel (dubbed by CHARLES KING) sang "You Were Meant for Me," MARION DAVIES cut loose with "Tommy Atkins on Parade," Charles King sang "Orange Blossom Time" while the Albertina Rasch Ballet fluttered around him, and much of the cast joined CLIFF EDWARDS in "While Strolling Through the Park One Day." The film's most memorable number was the introduction of the NACIO HERB BROWN–ARTHUR FREED song "Singin' in the Rain" with Edwards strumming his ukulele while a cast in slickers danced through the pounding rain.

HOLM, CELESTE (1919–). Stage, film, and television performer. A sparkling blonde actress–singer, she appeared on Broadway consistently for more than fifty years and in films for over forty years. Holm was born in New York City to Norwegian immigrants and then educated in Holland and France before returning to America to go to high school in Chicago. She took drama classes at the University of Chicago, as well as singing and dancing lessons. Holm got her experience in stock and in tours before making her Broadway debut in 1938. Although Holm appeared in nine plays over the next five years, it was not until her funny, rustic Ado Annie in OKLAHOMA! (1943) that she was noticed. She made her Hollywood debut in the musical THREE LITTLE GIRLS IN BLUE (1946) but was more successful in nonmusicals such as Gentleman's Agreement (1947) and All About Eve (1950). Her movie musicals Carnival in Costa Rica (1947) and Road House (1948) did little for her career but she shone as the wisecracking photographer Liz Imbrey in High Society (1956) and Aunt Polly in Tom Sawyer (1973). She also acted and sang in many television programs over the decades, including the TV musicals JACK AND THE BEANSTALK (1956), CINDERELLA (1965), POLLY (1989), and POLLY—COMIN' HOME! (1990). Yet Holm always returned to the New York theatre, playing everything from Ibsen and Shaw to bedroom farces and one-woman shows, still performing on stage in 2000. Her Broadway musical credits include the rebellious Evalina in BLOOMER GIRL (1944), a replacement for Anna in THE KING AND I when GERTRUDE LAWRENCE died in 1952, one of the many Auntie Mames in the musical MAME in 1968, and the frazzled school teacher Julia Faysle in the short-lived The Utter Glory of Morrissey Hall (1979). For her charitable work, Holm has received honors from the King of Norway and the president of the United States.

HOLM, HANYA [born Johanna Eckert] (1893–1992). Stage choreographer. The eclectic German-born choreographer created a variety of dance styles in her dozen Broadway productions, including the popular classics KISS ME, KATE and MY FAIR LADY. Holm was born in Worms, Germany, and danced in Max Reinhardt productions before immigrating to America in 1931 to found the Mary Wigman School of the Dance (later changed to the Hanya Holm School). She worked as a dancer until her choreography debut, staging "The Eccentricities of Davy Crockett" for the revue Broadway Ballads in 1948. Her subsequent Broadway credits include Kiss Me, Kate (1948), OUT OF THIS WORLD (1950), My Darlin' Aida (1952), THE GOLDEN APPLE (1954), My Fair Lady (1956), CAMELOT (1960), and Anya (1965). Holm choreographed the television version of THE VAGABOND KING (1956) and directed and choreographed the TV musical PINOCCHIO (1957). She employed a variety of styles and techniques in her many very different projects. Holm was the first Broadway choreographer to copyright her dances. Biographies: Hanya Holm: A Pioneer in American Dance, Marilyn Cristofori (1992); Hanya Holm: The Biography of an Artist, W. Sorrell (1969).

HOLMAN, LIBBY [born Elizabeth Holtzman] (1906–1971). Stage performer. A dark-haired, deep-voiced torch singer who spent of her career singing in nightclubs, she made some memorable appearances in Broadway musicals. Holman was born in Cincinnati where she attended the local university before entering show business as an actress in stock. She made her Broadway debut in the legendary revue GARRICK GAIETIES (1925) and then appeared in the subsequent revues Greenwich Village Follies (1926), Merry-Go-Round (1927), and Ned Wayburn's Gambols (1929) before gaining wide recognition singing "Moanin' Low" in THE LITTLE SHOW (1929). Holman's other hit revue was THREE'S A CROWD (1930) in which she introduced "Body and Soul." She also fared well in book musicals, playing the seductive Lola in Rainbow (1928), the desirable newlywed Maria in REVENGE WITH MUSIC (1934), and the French society lady Mme. Baltin in You Never Know (1938). Holman left the theatre to concentrate on records and nightclub appearances, although she returned to Broadway in Libby Holman's Blues, Ballads, and Sin-Songs (1954). Her life was a series of bad marriages, torrid affairs with wealthy men and women, scandals, and suicides, including her own at the age of sixty-five. Biographies: Dreams That Money Can Buy: The Tragic Life of Libby Holman, Jon Bradshaw (1985); Libby Holman: Body and Soul, Hamilton Darby Perry (1983).

HOLTZ, LOU (1893–1980). Stage performer. An ethnic comic who shuttled between vaudeville and the legit theatre for thirty years, he was famous for his slightly risqué stories told in a thick Yiddish dialect and ending his act with a kooky rendition of "O Solo Mio."

Holtz was born and educated in San Francisco and started in variety in 1914. The next year he was on Broadway doing his specialty act in the revues *A World of Pleasure* (1915), followed by GEORGE WHITE'S SCANDALS (1919, 1920, and 1921), and *The Dancing Girl* (1923). Holtz then moved into character roles in book musicals, most memorably as the clownish Monty Sipkin wooing a rich gal in *Tell Me More* (1925) and the crook Pinkie Pincus who enrolls in college to set up a rackets system in *You Said It* (1931). His other musical credits include *Manhattan Mary* (1927), *Calling All Stars* (1934), *Priorities of '42* (1942), and *Star Time* (1944).

HOORAY FOR WHAT! (Winter Garden Theatre 1937). A musical satire that poked fun at the international tension building in Europe, the show was primarily an ED WYNN vehicle and, therefore, more silly than pointed. The horticulturist Chuckles Wynn (Wynn) accidentally discovers a gas that not only kills fruit-eating insects but humans as well. Soon every nation has spies trying to steal the formula for warfare purposes. One spy gets a look at the formula reflected in a mirror so it is written down backwards and only produces a laughing gas. E. Y. HARBURG, HOWARD LINDSAY, and RUSSEL CROUSE wrote the libretto as a biting dark comedy but star Wynn had much of the bitter satire cut by the time the show opened on Broadway. HAROLD ARLEN (music) and Harburg (lyrics) wrote the splendid score, which included the mocking flag-waver "God's Country," the anti-romantic "Down With Love," the wry ballad "Moanin' in the Morning," the swinging "In the Shade of the New Apple Tree," and the marching title song. Lindsay directed the cast, which also included Paul Haakon, June Clyde, VIVIAN VANCE, JACK WHITING, Robert Shafer, and Detmar Poppen. VINCENTE MINNELLI did the colorful décor, and the dances were by ROBERT ALTON and beginner AGNES DE MILLE. Wynn's popularity helped the show run 200 performances.

HOPE, BOB [born Leslie Townes Hope] (1903–2003). Stage, film, and television performer.

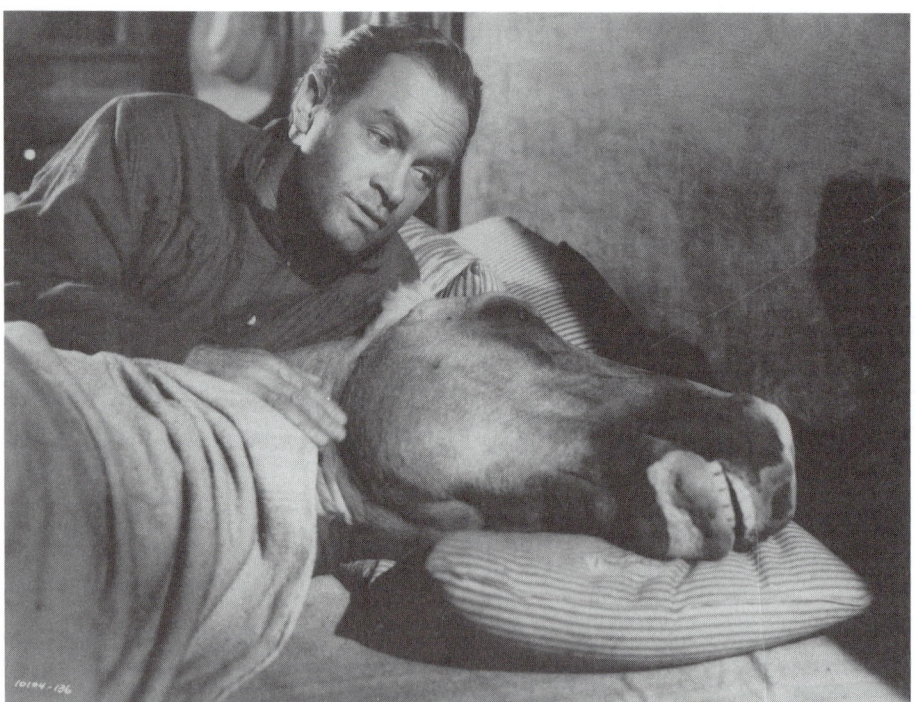

Bob Hope. The durable entertainer was at his best when he played put-upon, deceived, conned, and framed innocents who never got the girl and ended up the dupe. In the movie musical *Son of Paleface* (1952) he had to share a bed with a horse when he was really hoping for Jane Russell. But Hope, as always, took it in his stride. (Photofest)

One of the English-speaking world's favorite entertainers, Broadway and Hollywood musicals were part of his long and illustrious career. Hope was born in Eltham, England, and came to America at the age of four and grew up in Cleveland. He worked as a clerk, newsboy, soda jerk, and even a boxer before going into show business as a song-and-dance man on the variety circuit. Hope's wisecracking, self-deprecating style of comedy caught on and by the late 1920s he was featured in the Broadway revues *The Ramblers* (1926), *Ups-a-Daisy* (1928), and *Ballyhoo of 1932*, and the book musicals *Sidewalks of New York* (1927) and *Smiles* (1930). He was finally noticed as the American bandleader Huckleberry Haines in *ROBERTA* (1933) and starred in *Say When* (1934), *ZIEGFELD FOLLIES* (1936), and *RED, HOT AND BLUE* (1936). Hope made his screen debut in *BIG BROADCAST OF 1938* and never returned to Broadway, concentrating on films, his own radio program, television specials, and personal appearances over the next fifty years. On screen he was featured in the musicals *College Swing* (1938), *Give Me a Sailor* (1938), and *Thanks for the Memory* (1938) before teaming up with BING CROSBY for *ROAD TO SINGAPORE* (1940), followed by six more *Road* pictures over the next twenty-two years. Hope's other memorable musicals include *LOUISIANA PURCHASE* (1941), *LET'S FACE IT!* (1943), *THE PALEFACE* (1948), *Fancy Pants* (1950), *The Lemon Drop Kid* (1951), *SON OF PALEFACE* (1952), *The Seven Little Foys* (1955), *Beau James* (1957), *I'll Take Sweden* (1967), and specialty bits in *STAR SPANGLED RHYTHM* (1942), *Duffy's Tavern* (1945), *Scared Stiff* (1953), *THE FIVE PENNIES* (1959), and *THE MUPPET MOVIE* (1979). Hope made many other films but by the 1970s he concentrated on television specials and concerts, playing at hundreds of venues across the country and in Great Britain. He was also known for and decorated for entertaining American and British troops during every conflict from World War II to the Persian Gulf War in the 1990s. Although Hope became an institution of sorts and was highly awarded and revered as the ultimate patriotic American during his later years, he always kept his sarcastic persona, spoofing political figures and world problems, and retaining his vaudeville-like delivery. He wrote several comic memoirs, including *They Got Me Covered* (1941), *Have Tux, Will Travel* (1954), *I Owe Russia $1,200* (1963), *The Last Christmas Show* (1974), *The Road to Hollywood: My 40-Year Love Affair With the Movies* (1977), and *Don't Shoot, It's Only Me* (1990). Biographies: *Bob Hope: A Life in Comedy*, William Robert Faith (2003); *Bob Hope: The Road Well-Traveled*, Lawrence J. Quirk (2000).

HOPKINS, LINDA [born Melinda Helen Matthews] (1925–). Stage, film, and television performer. A brassy, sassy African American singer who has recorded jazz, the blues, and gospel, she has stopped the show in her few Broadway appearances. Hopkins was born in New Orleans and sang as a child so when Mahalia Jackson discovered the eleven-year-old girl with the giant voice she arranged for lessons and promoted her career. Hopkins was a recognized recording star before she turned to performing in musicals. On screen she has sung in the films *Rockin' the Blues* (1956), *Honkytonk Man* (1982), and *Wild Women Blues* (1997). On Broadway she was a featured vocalist in *PURLIE* (1970), was acclaimed for her performance in *Inner City* (1971), impersonated her idol Bessie Smith in *Me and Bessie* (1975), and starred in the revue *BLACK AND BLUE* (1989). Her TV musicals are *Mitzi … Roarin' in the 1920s* (1976), in which she played Bessie Smith again, *Purlie* (1981), and *Black and Blue* (1993). Hopkins was still touring and singing as the new century began.

HOPPER, DE WOLF [born William DeWolf Hopper] (1858–1935). Stage performer. A tall, animated clown with a deep basso voice, he was one of America's greatest musical comedy stars, entertaining audiences in New York, London, and on the road for fifty years. A native New Yorker, Hopper was educated to become a lawyer like his father but soon after he entered the bar he left to become a serious actor. When he was hired for a series of comic operettas, he realized that his forte was comedy and he became an outstanding singing character actor. Hopper made his Broadway debut in 1879 and impressed audiences in minor and then major roles, becoming a full-fledged star as the dandified judge Filacoudre in *Castles in the Air* (1890). He appeared in thirty musicals in New York and London, most memorably as the sly regent of a bankrupt Siam in *WANG* (1891), the viceroy of Peru who disguises himself as his enemy to stop a revolution in *EL CAPITAN* (1896), and various comic roles in Gilbert and Sullivan revivals. Among his other notable musicals were *The Begum* (1887), *FIDDLE-DEE-DEE* (1900), *Hoity Toity* (1901), *Hop o' My Thumb* (1913), *THE PASSING SHOW* (1917), *Erminie* (1921), and *White Lilacs* (1928). Hopper played himself in some early talkies and starred in some silent films in the 1910s, including *Casey at the Bat* (1916) in which he played baseballer Casey. The poem "Casey at the Bat" was long associated with Hopper who recited it for over forty years in musical revues, on records, on the radio, and in films. Among his six wives were musical comedy star LULU GLASER and actress–columnist Hedda Hopper (1885–1966), and his son was television actor William Hopper (1915–1970). Autobiography: *Once a Clown, Always a Clown*, with Wesley Winans Stout (1927).

HORNBLOW, ARTHUR, JR. (1893–1976). Stage and film producer. A notable presenter on both Broadway and in Hollywood, he produced ten movie musicals over a period of twenty years. A native New Yorker, Hornblow was educated at Dartmouth College and the New York Law School but his law career was interrupted by service in World War I, after which he switched his career to writing and producing theatre productions. Eight of his plays appeared on Broadway, including the popular melodrama *The Captive* (1926). He relocated to Hollywood when talkies came in and served as a producer for SAMUEL GOLDWYN, then PARAMOUNT, and then as an independent. Among his many movies were the musicals *MISSISSIPPI* (1935), *Swing High, Swing Low* (1937), *HIGH, WIDE AND HANDSOME* (1937), *Waikiki Wedding* (1937), *ARTISTS AND MODELS ABROAD* (1938), *Man About Town* (1939), *Million Dollar Mermaid* (1952), and *OKLAHOMA!* (1955). He was married to screen actress MYRNA LOY.

HORNE, LENA [Calhoun] (1917–). Stage, television, and film performer. The sleek, slim, and sexy African American song stylist appeared only a limited number of times on Broadway and in films but was never less than sensational. A native of Brooklyn, Horne was singing in public at an early age and quit school as a teenager to tour the cabaret circuit. She worked her way from the chorus at the Cotton Club in Harlem to being one of its star attractions and was featured in two Broadway shows, *Dance With Your Gods* (1934) and *BLACKBIRDS OF 1939*. Horne made her screen debut in *The Duke Is Tops* (1938) and did a specialty number in *PANAMA HATTIE* (1942) before dazzling moviegoers as the seductive Georgia Brown in *CABIN IN THE SKY* (1943). Her only other screen musical roles were in *STORMY WEATHER* (1943), *BROADWAY RHYTHM* (1944), and *THE WIZ* (1978), but she did specialty numbers in such musicals as *I Dood It* (1943), *Swing Fever* (1943), *Thousands Cheer* (1943), *TWO GIRLS AND A SAILOR* (1944), *ZIEGFELD FOLLIES* (1946), *TILL THE CLOUDS ROLL BY* (1946), *WORDS AND MUSIC*

(1948), *The Duchess of Idaho* (1950), and *Meet Me in Las Vegas* (1956). After 1956, Horne concentrated on nightclubs and records, although she returned to Broadway triumphantly on two occasions: as the elusive Savannah in *JAMAICA* (1957) and in her one-woman show *Lena Horne: The Lady and Her Music* (1981). She also appeared on many television variety shows and specials. Autobiographies: *In Person—Lena Horne* (1950); *Lena* (1965); biography: *Lena: A Personal and Professional Biography of Lena Horne*, James Haskins, Kathleen Benson (1986).

HORTON, EDWARD EVERETT (1886–1970). Film, stage, and television performer. The quintessential nervous, bubbling, frustrated sidekick in 120 movies, the finicky character actor fussed his way through thirty-four film musicals. Horton was born in Brooklyn, the son of a newspaper proofreader, and was educated at Oberlin College and Columbia University where he started acting. He made his Broadway debut in a play in 1912 and then toured with stock companies getting experience and refining his double takes and his fluttering "Oh, dear!" Horton entered films in 1922 and was soon playing comic leads. When the talkies arrived, he found his nasal voice a detriment until he was cast in persnickety character parts. Among Horton's musicals are *Reaching for the Moon* (1931), *THE GAY DIVORCEE* (1934), *THE MERRY WIDOW* (1934), *The Night Is Young* (1935), *In Caliente* (1935), *TOP HAT* (1935), *The Singing Kid* (1936), *SHALL WE DANCE* (1937), *College Swing* (1938), *Paris Honeymoon* (1939), *ZIEGFELD GIRL* (1941), *SUNNY* (1941), *I Married an Angel* (1942), *SPRINGTIME IN THE ROCKIES* (1942), *THANK YOUR LUCKY STARS* (1943), *THE GANG'S ALL HERE* (1943), *Brazil* (1944), *Cinderella Jones* (1946), and *Down to Earth* (1947). Horton had his own radio show in the 1930s and frequently returned to the stage, usually in summer stock where he played the silly playboy Henry Dewlip in the comedy *Springtime for Henry* over 1,700 times over the years, including a run on Broadway in 1951. He also enjoyed a busy television career, acting in dozens of programs, such as the TV musical *Manhattan Tower* (1956), and providing the voices for animated shows, notably *The Bullwinkle Show*.

HOUSE OF FLOWERS (Alvin Theatre 1954). An atmospheric musical set on a Caribbean island, the unusual show boasted an intriguing plot and an excellent score. On a West Indies island there is plenty of rivalry between two competing brothels and their proprietors,

Madame Fleur (PEARL BAILEY) and Madame Tango (JUANITA HALL). When one of Fleur's prettiest girls, Ottilie (DIAHANN CARROLL), refuses to be "sold" to a wealthy businessman because she loves the local youth Royal (Rawn Spearman), Fleur has Royal kidnapped. But all ends well, with the two houses even surviving an epidemic of mumps. The expert cast also included Enid Mosier, Ada Moore, RAY WALSTON, GEOFFREY HOLDER, Alvin Ailey, and Frederick O'Neal. Truman Capote adapted his own story and also proved to be an estimable lyricist for HAROLD ARLEN's music. The score was both poignant and amusing, with such songs as "A Sleepin' Bee," "Two Ladies in de Shade of de Banana Tree," "I Never Has Seen Snow," "Don't Like Goodbyes," and the title number. Most critics praised the score, the superior cast, and the stunning sets and costumes by Oliver Messel. All the same, the unusual musical had a tone that was too foreign for many playgoers and the show only lasted 165 performances. The renowned play director Peter Brook, in one of his rare musical ventures, staged the show and HERBERT ROSS did the rhythmic choreography. A revised 1968 revival Off Broadway also failed to run.

HOW THE GRINCH STOLE CHRISTMAS. See *DR. SEUSS' HOW THE GRINCH STOLE CHRISTMAS*

HOW TO SUCCEED IN BUSINESS WITHOUT REALLY TRYING (46th Street Theatre 1961). An entertaining satire about big business in America, the FRANK LOESSER show was also one of the least romantic musicals ever to become a hit.

Plot: Window washer J. Pierrepont Finch uses a guide book to climb the corporate ladder of the World Wide Wickets Company. He gets hired by casually mentioning the name of the president of the company, J. B. Biggley, as if they were friends. Finch begins in the mail room but soon he does get friendly with Biggley, pretending they have the same alma mater, and soon he is in an executive position. Finch almost tumbles when Biggley's sexy mistress Hedy Le

Rue is thrown his way but he avoids disaster and ends up as head of advertising. Even when his ad campaign (a treasure hunt) fails and the corporate offices are ransacked, Finch comes out smelling like a rose and is heading toward chairmanship of the board with his supportive girl Rosemary at his side.

Shepherd Mead's tongue-in-cheek book of the same title, the source for the musical, had no plot or characters but offered wry commentary on corporate ladder climbing. Willie Gilbert and Jack Weinstock wrote a libretto that had so many problems that ABE BURROWS was called in to rewrite it, turning the work into a brash, cynical, and strangely delightful musical comedy. Loesser's score produced few hits and it's not difficult to see why. The songs for the show are mostly unsentimental, cynical, and antiromantic. Even the big love song, "I Believe in You," was sung by the hero to himself in the mirror as he was shaving. There is a snide subtext to the numbers: the philosophical "The Company Way" is Machiavellian in its thinking, "Coffee Break" is about obsession without passion, "A Secretary Is Not a Toy" is cautionary yet leering, and even the mock revival number "Brotherhood of Man" is cheerful but dishonest, with the whole number celebrating Finch's Teflon-like ability to come out on top. It took courage to write a score with no take-home tunes but they sharpened the show considerably and the songs are essential to maintaining the temper of the script. ROBERT MORSE became a star as the lovably conniving Finch and old-time crooner RUDY VALLEE was a sensation as Biggley. Burrows directed, BOB FOSSE did the quirky choreography, and the CY FEUER and ERNEST MARTIN production ran 1,417 performances, helped no doubt by winning the PULITZER PRIZE. *How to Succeed in Business Without Really Trying* has not received as many revivals as Loesser's other hits and New York has only seen two. The New York City Light Opera production in 1966 had fewer stars but was quite effective. Leo Gochman played Finch and was supported by BILLY DEWOLFE

Casts for *How to Succeed in Business Without Really Trying*

Character	1961 Broadway	1966 film	1995 Broadway
J. Pierrepont Finch	ROBERT MORSE	Robert Morse	MATTHEW BRODERICK
J. B. Biggley	RUDY VALLEE	Rudy Vallee	Ronn Carroll
Rosemary Pilkington	Bonnie Scott	MICHELE LEE	Megan Mullally
Hedy La Rue	Virginia Martin	Maureen Arthur	Luba Mason
Bud Frump	CHARLES NELSON REILLY	Anthony Teague	Jeff Blumenkrantz

How to Succeed in Business without Really Trying. Rudy Vallee (right) started his career singing college songs through a megaphone. Here he is decades later singing the college fight song "Grand Old Ivy" with Robert Morse, and it looks like Vallee misses his megaphone. (Photofest)

(Biggley), Sheila Sullivan (Rosemary), Betty Linton (Hedy), and Lee Goodman (Frump). MATTHEW BRODERICK had the charm to make Finch endearing as well as devilish in a popular 1995 production directed by DES McANUFF and choreographed by WAYNE CILENTO. Favorable notices and Broderick's popularity helped the revival run 548 performances.

How to Succeed in Business Without Really Trying Musical Numbers

"How To (Succeed)"
"Happy to Keep His Dinner Warm"
"Coffee Break"
"The Company Way"
"A Secretary Is Not a Toy"
"Been a Long Day"
"Grand Old Ivy"
"Paris Original"
"Rosemary"
"Cinderella Darling"
"Love From a Heart of Gold"
"I Believe in You"
"The Yo Ho Ho" (Pirate Dance)
"Brotherhood of Man"

How to Succeed in Business Without Really Trying (Mirsch/United Artists 1966) may have cut five songs from the Broadway show but just about everything and everyone else made the transfer from stage to screen. Morse and Vallee reprised their Finch and Biggley, and MICHELE LEE, who had taken over the role of Rosemary in New York, was cast in the film. Director David Swift wrote the faithful screenplay, and Dale Moreda recreated Fosse's choreography. The only real difference was one of tone; the movie was less abrasive. "I Believe in You" was a straightforward love song for Finch and Rosemary, and the cartoonish look of the film gave the piece a fairy tale quality so its targets were less real. Yet the movie remains one of the most faithful film versions of a Broadway musical and although the 1960s clothes and hair styles have dated, the show has not.

HOWARD, KEN [born Kenneth Joseph Howard, Jr.] (1944–). Stage, television, and film performer. A tall, blond, athletic leading man who became a very familiar face on television in the 1970s and 1980s, he has given some memorable musical performances as well. Howard was born in El Centro, California, and was educated at Amhurst College and Yale before working in stock. His first Broadway credit was in a supporting role in PROMISES, PROMISES (1968) and then gained recognition for his Thomas Jefferson in *1776* (1969), which he reprised on the screen in 1972. Howard acted in both dramas and comedies on Broadway and shone in two musicals: as the lawyer Jerry Ryan in SEESAW (1973) and as several presidents in *1600 PENNSYLVANIA AVENUE* (1976). He has acted in some films and in hundreds of episodes in television series, although his singing voice was rarely heard in either medium.

HOWARD, WILLIE AND EUGENE. Stage performers. The brother comedians were popular in vaudeville and brought their antics to some two dozen Broadway musicals, mostly revues. Eugene Howard [born Isidore Levkowwitz] (1881–1965) was born in Neustadt, Germany, and immigrated to America where as a boy he was in the chorus of the Broadway musicals THE BELLE OF NEW YORK (1897) and *A Million Dollars* (1899). His younger brother Willie Howard [born Wilhelm Levkowitz] (1886–1949) was born in Paramus, New Jersey, and as a boy soprano sang in the musical *The Little Duchess* (1901). The two siblings later formed a comedy act and performed on the vaudeville circuit, with the diminutive, mimicking Willie playing against his taller, dapper brother. The twosome were featured on Broadway in *The Whirl of the World* (1914), *The Show of Wonders* (1916), *Ballyhoo of 1932*, ZIEGFELD FOLLIES (1934), THE SHOW IS ON (1937), six editions of THE PASSING SHOW, and seven versions of GEORGE WHITE'S SCANDALS. Willie was the more flexible of the two comics and appeared in a series of comedy film shorts in the 1930s. He was sometimes cast as characters in book musicals, most memorably as the Jewish cab driver Gieber Goldfarb who becomes sheriff out West in GIRL CRAZY (1930). Eugene retired in 1940 but Willie continued to perform for another eight years, featured on Broadway in *Crazy With the Heat* (1941), *Priorities of 1942*, *My Dear Public* (1943), and the revival of SALLY (1948).

HOWES, SALLY ANN (1930–). Stage, film, and television performer. The bright-eyed, lovely blonde singer–actress has starred in several London musicals and a few on Broadway, although in America she is better known from her movies. Howes was born in London, the daughter of popular West End comic Bobby Howes (1895–1972), and was on stage and in films as a child. After schooling at Queenswood College, she found adult roles in such West End musicals as *Fancy Free* (1951), *Bet Your Life* (1952), PAINT YOUR WAGON (1953), *Romance in Candlelight* (1955), and *Summer Song* (1956). Howes was so polished a performer that she was selected to replace JULIE ANDREWS in MY FAIR LADY in 1958. Her other Broadway roles were the British doctor Eve in Africa in KWAMINA (1961), Fiona in the 1963 revival of BRIGADOON, the Hollywood secretary Kit Sargent in *What Makes Sammy Run?* (1964), and the Irish aunt Julia Morkan in JAMES JOYCE'S THE DEAD (1999). Howes returned to the movies as an adult and made several pictures, most memorably the musical fantasy CHITTY CHITTY BANG BANG (1968) in which she played the candy heiress Truly Scrumptious. She has appeared on many American and British television programs, from game shows to musical specials, such as the original TV musical THE GIFT OF THE MAGI (1958). Howe played in many of the great musicals, from THE KING AND I to *A LITTLE NIGHT MUSIC*, on tour in America and Great Britain. She was married for a time to songwriter RICHARD ADLER.

HOYT, CHARLES H[ale]. (1860–1900). Stage lyricist, writer, and producer. An early pioneer of American musical comedy, he wrote the landmark Broadway musical *A TRIP TO CHINATOWN* (1891) and prepared the way for shows that deviated from operetta. Hoyt was born in Concord, Massachusetts, and studied law at Boston Latin School until he tried ranching and then writing for a Boston newspaper where he created comic characters in his column. When theatrical producer William Harris, Sr., had an open spot and needed a play, Hoyt wrote the hit farce *Gifford's Luck* (1881). Turning to the theatre full time, Hoyt wrote a series of comic farces, adding songs to them until they started to resemble modern musical comedy. His musical credits, for which he usually wrote both libretto and lyrics, are *The Maid and the Moonshiners* (1886), *A Black Sheep* (1891), *A Parlor Match* (1896), and *A Day and Night in New York* (1898), but it was his blending of songs, characters, and plot in *A Trip to Chinatown* that was his masterwork and can be viewed as the great grandfather of today's musical comedy. Hoyt suffered from mental instability and after a few failures he had a breakdown and was confined to an insane asylum before his untimely death at the age of forty. Biography: *The Life and Work of Charles H. Hoyt*, Douglas L. Hunt (1945).

HUFFMAN, J[esse]. **C.** (1869–1935). Stage director. A very prolific Broadway director, he specialized in light musical comedies and operettas. Huffman was born in Bowling Green, Ohio, the son of a Civil War general, and began his professional acting career as a teenager. When he started to stage plays for a stock company in Pittsburgh, he gave up acting and concentrated on directing. Popular actor Richard Mansfield saw his work in stock and brought him to New York to stage some of his productions. Huffman soon showed a talent for directing loosely plotted book musicals and musical revues and in 1911 the SHUBERT BROTHERS made him general director for their growing empire of productions in New York and on the road. Records are inaccurate but it has been estimated that Huffman staged over two hundred shows that either originated or played in New York. While some of these were very popular musical comedies, such as the series of THE PASSING SHOW revues and the AL JOLSON vehicles SINBAD (1918), BOMBO (1921), and BIG BOY (1925), Huffman only got quality material in the genre of operetta, staging the original productions of BLOSSOM TIME (1921), THE STUDENT PRINCE OF HEIDELBERG (1924), *Princess Flavia* (1925), *Countess Maritza* (1926), *My Maryland* (1927), and *Nina Rosa* (1932).

HUGHES, [James Mercer] LANGSTON (1902–1967). Stage lyricist and writer. One of the very few American theatre lyricists who is also considered a significant poet, the African American author brought an authentic sense of black life to his musicals. Hughes was born in Joplin, Missouri, and as a teenager moved with his family to Cleveland where many of his plays were tried out. He attended Columbia University to study engineering but left when he turned to a writing career and in the 1920s his poetry was first published in magazines. After traveling to Africa, Europe, and Asia and writing about his experiences, Hughes settled in New York during the "Harlem Renaissance" and, discovering blues and jazz, was prompted to write for the musical theatre but was delayed while he studied at Lincoln University and devoted much of his time to poetry and essays. He made a bold and impressive Broadway debut with his drama *Mulatto* (1935), which was a surprise hit, but he wouldn't be heard on Broadway again until his sterling lyrics for the KURT WEILL musical *STREET SCENE* (1947). Concentrating on musicals, he wrote both the music and the lyrics for *The Barrier* (1950)—a musical version of *Mulatto*—and the book and lyrics for the folk musicals *Simply Heavenly* (1957) and *Tambourines to Glory* (1963) and the gospel musicals *Black Nativity* (1961) and *Jericho-Jim Crow* (1964). Hughes also wrote a few scripts for films, such as *Way Down South* (1939), and television dramas, and his *Simply Heavenly* was produced on television in 1959. He also wrote many plays that were not published or produced until after his death, such as *Mule Bone* (1991). Hughes' lyrics are often as penetrating as his poetry, using simple but incisive imagery and filled with the character's frustration or joy. Autobiography: *The Big Sea*, with Arnold Rampersad (1993); biography: *The Life of Langston Hughes*, A. Rampersad (1988).

☙ **HUMAN COMEDY, THE** (Royale Theatre 1984). An ambitious and often enthralling musical play, it was very atmospheric but too low key for Broadway. In a small California town during World War II, the residents go through their everyday lives with dread and hope. For the widowed Kate Maccauley (Bonnie Koloc), all her concerns are for her children who are either in the war or at home dealing with the pains of growing up. The death of her son Marcus (Don Kehr) brings momentary tragedy, but then life struggles on, particularly when Marcus's Army friend Spangler (Rex Smith) comes to town looking for the family he's heard so much about. The

large cast of characters also included featured performances by Mary Elizabeth Mastrantonio, Stephen Geoffreys, Josh Blake, Gordon Connell, Caroline Peyton, and Debra Byrd. Based on William Saroyan's novel, the sung-though musical by GALT MACDERMOT (music) and William Dumaresq (book and lyrics) employed a variety of musical styles, and the songs were revealing expressions of everyday emotions, as with "Beautiful Music," "Long Past Sunset," "Somewhere, Someone," "The Birds in the Sky," and "What Am I Supposed to Do?" The Wilford Leach-directed musical was so well received Off Broadway at the PUBLIC THEATRE that producer JOSEPH PAPP moved it to Broadway where playgoers seemed to ignore it and it was forced to close after thirteen performances. Because of its unusual casting and music demands, the lovely musical is rarely revived.

HUMBERSTONE, H. BRUCE (1903–1984). Film and television director. Adept at helming thrillers and musicals, he worked with the most popular blonde stars of his day, from BETTY GRABLE to ALICE FAYE to SONJA HENIE. A native of Buffalo, Humberstone was educated at military school and then when into films as a teenager, working first as a script clerk and then as an actor. He began directing in 1932 and found success with the Charlie Chan series and crime melodramas. He also revealed a lighter touch in his eleven Hollywood musicals, such as *SUN VALLEY SERENADE* (1941), *ICELAND* (1942), *HELLO, FRISCO, HELLO* (1943), *Pin-Up Girl* (1944), *Wonder Man* (1945), *THREE LITTLE GIRLS IN BLUE* (1946), *She's Working Her Way Through College* (1952), and *THE DESERT SONG* (1953).

☙ **HUMPTY DUMPTY** (Olympic Theatre 1868). This "spectacular ballet pantomime" was one of the biggest hits of its day and was responsible for creating a long-standing Broadway tradition. A. Reiff, Jr. (music) and G. L. Fox (book and lyrics) wrote the extravaganza that consisted of a series of adventures that befall a group of children (played by adults) who travel from New York City to various fantasy locations. The longest-running Broadway production to date (483 performances), *Humpty Dumpty* was so popular with children that Wednesday matinees were offered for the first time and soon all Broadway entries followed suit. Fox produced and played the title character, a role he repeated 1,128 times in New York and on the road. The musical was revived in

New York in 1871, 1873, and 1876, followed by sequels and variations such as *Humpty Dumpty Abroad!* (1873), *Humpty Dumpty at Home* (1874), *Humpty Dumpty at School* (1874), *Humpty Dumpty in Every Clime* (1875), and *Humpty Dumpty's Dream* (1878).

HUNCHBACK OF NOTRE DAME, THE (Disney 1996). Sometimes a rather dark and sensual animated musical, other times a playful family entertainment, this visually and musically thrilling version of the Victor Hugo classic tale is a feast of contrasts. Irene Mecchi's screenplay gave the novel a bit of a tweaking, adding comic gargoyles and a satirical hero who mocks his macho image, yet the hypnotic pull of the story and the characters were still there, and the vivid look of the movie, the concise storytelling, and the vibrant score made it one of the studio's finer achievements. ALAN MENKEN (music) and STEPHEN SCHWARTZ (lyrics) wrote the songs, some of which, such as the opening "The Bells of Notre Dame," combined narrative and character beautifully. The hunchback Quasimodo (voice of Tom Hulce) yearned for life "Out There," the gypsy Esmeralda (Demi Moore, singing voice of Heidi Mollenbauer) prayed "God Help the Outcasts," the three gargoyles (JASON ALEXANDER, Charles Kimbrough, and MARY WICKES, whose singing was dubbed by Mary Stout) hammed it up with "A Guy Like You," and the crowd celebrated a festival where everything turned dangerously "Topsy Turvy." The most potent number was the contrasting songs "Heaven's Light," sung by Quasimodo as he basks in the warmth of Esmeralda's smile, and "Hellfire," in which the villainous priest Frollo (Tony Jay) sung both of his hatred and lust for the gypsy girl as the flames in his fireplace conjure up erotic images of passion and punishment. KEVIN KLINE voiced the stalwart hero Phoebus and also heard were Jim Cummings, David Ogden Stiers, Paul Kandel, JANE WITHERS, and Mary Kay Bergman. Gary Trousdale and Kirk Wise directed with bold strokes, and the animation and backgrounds were both stunning. American moviegoers did not flock to the

The Hunchback of Notre Dame. While the Feast of Fools is going on in the streets of Paris, the hunchback Quasimodo (pictured) celebrates far above them in the towers of Notre Dame, wishing he could be part of it all. When his wish comes true, he is humiliated by the crowd. Such potent drama was not diminished because it was an animated film; in many ways animation was ideal for such a misunderstood character. (Photofest)

musical as they had with most Disney entries in the 1990s, yet the movie was extremely popular in Europe, so the company's stage version was produced in Germany.

HUNTER, ROSS [born Martin Fuss] (1920–1996). Film and television producer and performer. A Hollywood presenter of big-name melodramas, he also performed in and produced musicals during his unusual career. Hunter was born in Cleveland and educated at Western Reserve University before working as a schoolteacher and serving in Army intelligence during World War II. He entered movies as an actor and appeared in some 1940s films, including the musicals *Louisiana Hayride* (1944), *She's a Sweetheart* (1944), *Ever Since Venus* (1944), *Hit the Hay* (1945), and *Sweetheart of Sigma Chi* (1946). With his acting career going nowhere, Hunter went back to teaching, only to return to Hollywood in 1951 as a producer. Over the next thirty years he presented over sixty movies, including the musicals *FLOWER DRUM SONG* (1964), *I'd Rather Be Rich* (1964), *THOROUGHLY MODERN MILLIE* (1967), and *Lost Horizon* (1973). Hunter also produced some TV movies in the 1970s. His films were meant to be audience pleasers by featuring big stars and providing laughs or tears.

HUSMANN, RON (1937–). Stage and television performer. A handsome, full-voiced leading man, the actor–singer was applauded in 1960s musicals on Broadway. Husmann was born in Rockford, Illinois, and educated at Northwestern University. Right after graduation he was seen in bit parts in the Broadway musical *FIORELLO!* (1959) and then quickly moved into leading roles as journalist Tommy in *TENDERLOIN* (1960), college athlete Edwin Bricker in *ALL AMERICAN* (1962), beleaguered Captain Fisby in *Lovely Ladies, Kind Gentlemen* (1970), sailor Gabey in *ON THE TOWN* (1971), a replacement in *IRENE* in 1973, and the Parisian judge Forestier in the 1981 revival of *CAN-CAN*. Husmann has appeared on many variety shows, series, soap operas, and specials on television, including the TV version of *ONCE UPON A MATTRESS* (1972), and acted in a few films.

HUTTON, BETTY [born Elizabeth June Thornton] (1921–2007). Film, stage, and television performer. Billed as the "Blonde Bombshell" because of her high-powered singing and comic bombast, the animated singer–

actress lit up the screen in eighteen movie musicals. Hutton was born in Battle Creek, Michigan, and was raised in Detroit where she started singing in school and by the time she was a teenager was a vocalist for local bands. Hutton later sang with name bands, such as the Vincent Lopez Orchestra, and was featured on Broadway in *Two for the Show* (1940) and *PANAMA HATTIE* (1940) before making her film debut in a bit part in the musical *THE FLEET'S IN* (1942). She was frequently cast in supporting roles in musicals, comedies, and dramas, but the nature of her exuberant personality always made her noticeable, as in such musicals as *STAR-SPANGLED RHYTHM* (1942), *HAPPY GO LUCKY* (1943), *LET'S FACE IT!* (1943), *And the Angels Sing* (1944), *HERE COME THE WAVES* (1944), *Duffy's Tavern* (1945), *The Stork Club* (1945), and *Cross My Heart* (1946). Hutton eventually played leading roles, impersonating notable celebrities such as nightclubber Texas Guinan in *Incendiary Blonde* (1945), screen actress Pearl White in *The Perils of Pauline* (1947), sharpshooter Annie Oakley in *ANNIE GET YOUR GUN* (1950), and singer Blossom Seeley in *Somebody Loves Me* (1952). Her other musical credits include *Dream Girl* (1948), *RED, HOT AND BLUE* (1949), *Let's Dance* (1950), and *Sailor Beware* (1951). Despite her unforgettable presence in musicals and comedies, such as the farcical *Miracle at Morgan's Creek* (1944), and her own television show in the 1950s, the oft-married Hutton soon fell out of favor and years later was discovered living on charity and battling mental illness. She made a comeback of sorts, replacing CAROL BURNETT on Broadway in *FADE OUT–FADE IN* in 1965 and DOROTHY LOUDON in *ANNIE* in 1980, and making some television appearances in the 1970s. No one put a song over as Hutton, blasting out the words with her full-throttle voice and explosive expressions and turning her comic numbers, such as "Poppa Preach to Me" and "Murder, He Says," into animated delights. Her sister was singer MARION HUTTON.

HUTTON, MARION [born Marion Thornton] (1919–1987). Film performer. The noted Big Band singer with a singing style much subtler than that of her sister BETTY HUTTON, she was featured in six Hollywood musicals. Hutton was born in Battle Creek, Michigan, and raised in Detroit. She started singing with bands after her high school years and eventually became a featured vocalist with GLENN MILLER and his orchestra. Hutton sang with Miller's band in the films *SUN VALLEY SERENADE* (1941) and

ORCHESTRA WIVES (1942) and then did specialty spots in Crazy House (1943) and Babes on Swing Street (1944). She got to play characters roles in In Society (1944) and Love Happy (1949) but moviegoers did not take to her so she returned to band singing.

HWANG, DAVID HENRY (1957–). Stage and film writer. America's preeminent Asian American playwright, he has also contributed to musicals on Broadway. Hwang was born in Los Angeles to Chinese immigrants and was educated at Stanford and Yale Universities. By 1980s his plays about Asians and Asian Americans were produced Off Broadway and he made an auspicious Broadway debut with the hit play M. Butterfly (1988). Hwang co-authored the script for the long-running musical AIDA (2000), wrote the new libretto for the 2002 revival of FLOWER DRUM SONG, and contributed to the script for the stage version of TARZAN (2006). He has also written film scripts and librettos for opera. In his works, Hwang views the Asian American experience with humor, pathos, and a sense of awe at ancient ritual.

HYTNER, NICHOLAS (1956–). Stage and film director and producer. A remarkably versatile British director–manager whose handful of Broadway productions illustrate his talent for diversified theatre experiences, he has staged a few memorable musicals on both sides of the Atlantic. Hytner was born in Manchester, England, the son of a barrister, and educated at Cambridge University. He made his professional directing debut regionally in 1983 and was soon working for the finest theatre companies in the United Kingdom. He has served as associate or artistic director for the Royal Exchange Theatre in Manchester, Leeds Playhouse, LINCOLN CENTER in New York, and in 2003 he was named artistic director of the Royal National Theatre. Hytner's productions often emphasize bold visual design and marked tableaus, as seen in the musical MISS SAIGON, which he directed first in London and then on Broadway in 1991 for his New York debut. Perhaps his most memorable Broadway offering was the poetic, reenvisioned revival of CAROUSEL (1994) that gave the old musical a new look and a fresh approach. Hytner staged Sweet Smell of Success (2000) on Broadway and has also directed for many opera companies across the States and in Europe, as well as a handful of films, most notably The Madness of King George (1994) and The History Boys (2006).

I

popular song from the musical but also admirable were the pensive "What Is a Woman?," the angry "The Honeymoon Is Over," the jubilant "I Love My Wife," the boastful "A Well Known Fact," the defiant "Flaming Agnes," and the bouncy title number. GOWER CHAMPION directed, and bravos for the two stars and the tuneful score made the DAVID MERRICK production an instant hit, running 560 performances. The economical little musical has long been a favorite in summer stock and has been revived Off Broadway.

I CAN GET IT FOR YOU WHOLESALE (Shubert Theatre 1962). An unsentimental musical about the garment industry, the show avoided the Jewish stereotypes usually associated with the subject and offered an incisive score by HAROLD ROME. Ambitious and callous Harry Bogen (Elliott Gould) claws his way through the fashion business, disposing of friends and ideals as he aims for the mighty dollar. When his plans collapse and he is wiped out, only his understanding mother (LILLIAN ROTH) and faithful sweetheart Ruthie (MARILYN COOPER) are left to sympathize with him. Based on his novel, JEROME WEIDMAN'S libretto was uncompromising and sometimes ruthless in its depiction of Depression-era Jews in the garment district. ARTHUR LAURENTS directed the strong cast, which also included Sheree North, HAROLD LANG, Bambi Linn, BARBRA STREISAND, Ken LeRoy, and Jack Kruschen. Rome's excellent score included "The Sound of Money," "Have I Told You Lately?," "Miss Marmelstein," "A Gift Today," and "Momma, Momma." Some critics found the DAVID MERRICK production bold and intriguing, whereas others found it too brash and charmless. Audiences came to see for themselves for 300 performances. Today the musical is most remembered for the debut of Streisand as the scene-stealing secretary Miss Marmelstein.

I Do! I Do! (46th Street Theatre 1966). One of the very few two-character Broadway musicals, the show starred MARY MARTIN and ROBERT PRESTON as the two characters so no one felt cheated. TOM JONES (book and lyrics) and HARVEY SCHMIDT (music) wrote the musical version of Jan de Hartog's comedy *The Fourposter* (1951). Agnes and Michael go through decades of married life, from their wedding day to the time when their kids are grown and move away and the couple sells the house and bids farewell to their old four-poster bed. "My Cup Runneth Over" was the most

I DREAM TOO MUCH (RKO 1935). A musical melodrama about the opera world, the film was Metropolitan Opera diva LILY PONS' first and best film, proving that the diminutive star could act as well as sing. The screenplay by James Gow and others presented Pons as Annette Monard, a simple girl from the French provinces who is discovered by impresario Paul Darcy (Osgood Perkins) and taken to Paris. Once there her voice is trained and her heart is stolen by the idealistic Johnny Street (Henry Fonda), a young composer struggling to break into the opera business. They marry but Annette becomes famous and he doesn't, so she foregoes her career to devote her energies to promoting his. Hollywood came up with what it thought was a happy ending: Johnny's opera is turned into a musical comedy, which becomes a hit with Annette as the leading lady. The supporting cast included ERIC BLORE, Lucien Littlefield, MISCHA AUER, LUCILLE BALL, and Paul Porcasi. In addition to the expected opera arias, the score included some marvelous new numbers by JEROME KERN (music) and DOROTHY FIELDS (lyrics): the swinging "I Got Love," the lullaby "The Jockey on the Carousel," and the entrancing title song. John Cromwell directed the PANDRO S. BERMAN production and the movie was a hit, but Pons's three subsequent efforts were not so popular so she gave up on Hollywood.

I LOVE MY WIFE (Ethel Barrymore Theatre 1977). A small, contemporary musical comedy by CY COLEMAN (music) and MICHAEL STEWART (book and lyrics), it had a provocative enough premise to sell tickets but was satisfying in an old-fashioned conventional way. Two married couples in Trenton, New Jersey—Alvin (Lenny Baker) and Cleo (Ilene Graff) and Wally (JAMES NAUGHTON) and Monica (JOANNA GLEASON)—think they are missing out on the sexual revolution so they decide to swap partners, only to find that they only love their spouses. The only other characters were four musicians who played various walk-on roles and commented on the action with their songs, the most memorable being "Hey There, Good Times." Other numbers included "Lovers on Christmas Eve," "Someone Wonderful I Missed," "Everybody Today Is Turning On," and the title song. The press questioned the logic of the libretto but enjoyed the tuneful score and bright performances by the four young and promising players. Audiences were more enthusiastic and kept the GENE SAKS-directed show running 872 performances.

🎭 I LOVE YOU, YOU'RE PERFECT, NOW CHANGE (Westside Theatre 1996). The durable little musical revue that continues to run Off Broadway, the show was (and still is) unique in that it's all about heterosexual relationships, something frequently ignored over the past few decades. Joe DiPietro wrote the sketches and lyrics for Jimmy Roberts' music, and both the scenes and the songs were routine at best but struck a nerve with audiences who recognized the clichés about dating and marriage. "Cantata for a First Date," "Single Man Drought," "He Called Me," "Marriage Tango," "On the Highway of Love," and the title number were typical of the score, which offered few surprises. The economical, four-character show has also been very popular with summer theatres, community groups, and dinner theatres.

🎭 I MARRIED AN ANGEL (Shubert Theatre 1938). A sly musical fantasy by RICHARD RODGERS (book and music) and LORENZ HART (book and lyrics), it was adult, sophisticated fun and charmed audiences for 338 performances. The Budapest banker Willie Palaffi is not very faithful to his shrewish fiancée Anna and he soon breaks off the engagement, vowing the only woman he will ever wed will be an angel. From heaven arrives an actual Angel with wings and Willie is smitten with her, marries her, and in making love to her she loses her

I Married an Angel. The team of Rodgers and Hart was such a potent force on Depression-weary Broadway that they enjoyed hit after hit while other songwriters only found success in the 1930s in Hollywood. The duo not only scored the hit fantasy *I Married an Angel* but wrote the libretto, based on an Hungarian play. (Photofest)

wings. However, Angel is still angelic, honest to a fault, and not versed in the deceptive and hypocritical ways of humans until Willie's sister, the Countess Peggy Palaffi, teaches her. Peggy also helps save Willie's bank from creditors who descend on him; she makes a deal with the wealthy backer Harry Szigetti and saves the day. The idea for the musical, based on a Hungarian play by János Vaszary, began as a movie musical some years before when Rodgers and Hart were in Hollywood. The team wrote a few of the numbers before the studio canceled the production. The project was revived as a Broadway musical with Rodgers and Hart

Casts for *I Married an Angel*

Character	1938 Broadway	1942 film
Willie Palaffi	DENNIS KING	NELSON EDDY
Angel	VERA ZORINA	JEANETTE MACDONALD
Countess Peggy	VIVIENNE SEGAL	Binnie Barnes
Harry Szigetti	WALTER SLEZAK	Douglas Dumbrille
Peter		EDWARD EVERETT HORTON
Anna	Audrey Christie	

writing the adaptation themselves, although director JOSUHA LOGAN also contributed to the libretto. The DWIGHT DEERE WIMAN production turned out to be the most popular musical fantasy of the decade with a superb score, an outstanding cast, and some memorable dance numbers choreographed by GEORGE BALANCHINE, most notably the satiric "At the Roxy Music Hall" in which the giant film palace and its extravagant shows were spoofed. The title song and "Spring Is Here" were the standout hits, and also enjoyable were "Did You Ever Get Stung?," "A Twinkle in Your Eye," and "I'll Tell the Man in the Street." There have been no Broadway revivals but the musical fared very well in Budapest where its 1938 production used Vaszary's original Hungarian title, *Angyalt vettem feleségul.*

I Married an Angel (MGM 1942) was a tired JEANETTE MACDONALD-NELSON EDDY vehicle and only a shadow of the Broadway show. Hollywood was afraid of all the risqué jokes in the libretto about the angel losing her wings (read "virginity"), so Anita Loos' script sanitized and drained the satire, music, and dance out of the piece. What was left was a routine tale about a banker Palaffi who falls asleep at his own birthday party, dreams he marries an Angel, and then awakes to find a secretary who looks just like her. ROBERT WRIGHT and GEORGE FORREST wrote a few new, forgettable songs ("Now You've Met the Angel," "There Comes a Time," and "But What of Truth") and even ruined the torchy "Spring Is Here" by rewriting the lyric as a meaningless duet for MacDonald and Eddy. One of Rodgers and Hart's most exhilarating musical experiments became dreary on the screen. The movie, produced by HUNT STROMBERG, directed W. S. VAN DYKE, and choreographed by Ernest Matray, was not popular and MacDonald and Eddy never worked together again.

Iceland (Fox 1942). A showcase for Hollywood's one and only ice skating star, SONJA HENIE, the musical only came to life when the Norwegian skater was on the ice or when the HARRY WARREN (music) and MACK GORDON (lyrics) songs were being performed. The screenplay by Helen Logan and Robert Ellis revolved around the uninteresting love triangle involving Reykjavik girl Katin Jonsdottir (Henie), her local boy friend Sverdrup Svenssen (STERLING HOLLOWAY), and the American Marine officer Capt. James Murfin (JOHN PAYNE). While the threesome

straightened out their differences, Joan Merrill got to sing the hit song "There Will Never Be Another You" with Sammy Kaye's orchestra. She also performed the sly "You Can't Say No to a Soldier," and JACK OAKIE joined Henie and Payne in the chummy "It's a Lovers' Knot." Also cast were FELIX BRESSART, Osa Massen, and Fritz Feld. James Gonzles staged Henie's skating numbers, which were engaging, even if her two patriotic songs, "I Like a Military Tune" and "Let's Bring New Glory to Old Glory," were a bit tiresome even for loyal wartime Americans. H. BRUCE HUMBERSTONE directed the WILLIAM LeBARON production, and HERMES PAN choreographed the non-ice numbers.

I'D RATHER BE RIGHT (Alvin Theatre 1937). A satirical musical comedy scored by RICHARD RODGERS (music) and LORENZ HART (lyrics), its main attraction was the return of GEORGE M. COHAN to the Broadway stage after a decade's absence. On the Fourth of July, sweethearts Phil Barker (Austin Marshall) and Peggy Jones (Joy Hodges) are in Central Park lamenting the fact that they cannot get married until President Roosevelt balances the budget and Phil's boss can give him a raise. When Phil falls asleep in the park, FDR (Cohan) appears in his dream and tries to help the young couple out. What follows is a vaudeville-like parade of songs and sketches in which Roosevelt tries everything to cure the nation's financial woes, from $100 postage stamps to using pickpockets to collect taxes. In the dream, many figures in the news appear, from FDR's rival Alf Langdon to newsman Walter Lippman to the entire Supreme Court. Unable to succeed in his task, Roosevelt urges the young couple to marry anyway and have hope in the future.

Rodgers and Hart's only collaboration with the great satirist GEORGE KAUFMAN, who wrote the libretto, the musical was more topical than any of the team's other works. It was a funny, if contrived plot and Hart's lyrics met Kaufman's wit every inch of the way. Unfortunately, *I'd Rather Be Right* did not inspire Rodgers to his better efforts. Only the flowing ballad "Have You Met Miss Jones?" found popularity, and it was the only nonsatirical number in the show. Other songs included "Off the Record," "We're Going to Balance the Budget," "Sweet Sixty-Five," and the breezy title number. There was great anticipation over the musical because of Cohan's appearance and the first (and only) time he performed in a musical he had not written. While this led to many problems in rehearsals (Cohan hated Rodgers and Hart as much as he despised FDR), on stage Cohan held the musical together and was largely responsible for its run of 290 performances. The show was produced by SAM H. HARRIS and directed by Kaufman. Because of its topicality, *I'd Rather Be Right* is very rarely revived.

🎬 I'LL CRY TOMORROW (MGM 1955). A

hard-hitting biographical musical about the hard-hitting life of singer–actress LILLIAN ROTH, the movie gave SUSAN HAYWARD one of the best roles of her career. Roth's shocking, best-selling autobiography was adapted for the screen by Helen Deutsch and Jay Richard Kennedy, none of whom pulled any punches when it came to revealing the seamier side of show business and marriage. The oft-wed Roth (Hayward), who was a star of stage and screen in the 1930s, battles alcoholism, wife-beating, and loss of fame even as she continues to sing torch songs in crummy dives. Hayward did her own singing and recreated such Roth favorites as "Happiness Is (Just) a Thing Called Joe," "Sing You Sinners," and "When the Red Red Robin Comes Bob Bob Bobbin Along." Jo Van Fleet turned in a powerful performance as Roth's pushy mother, EDDIE ALBERT, Don Taylor, and Richard Conte played Roth's husbands, and Daniel Mann directed them all with a gritty kind of honesty.

👥 I'M GETTING MY ACT TOGETHER AND TAKING IT ON THE ROAD (Public Theatre

1978). The finest of the handful of contemporary musicals by NANCY FORD (music) and GRETCHEN CRYER (book and lyrics), this long-running Off Broadway show was one of the few works of the decade that dealt effectively with women's issues, yet it was far more than a feminist musical. The thirty-nine-year-old singer–actress Heather (Cryer) auditions her new nightclub act for her manager Joe (Joel Fabiani), hoping to convince him that she should present a more honest portrayal of herself rather than the glossy, fanciful persona that she has faked in the past. Joe believes the false image is more lucrative but, in a series of songs, which she wrote, Heather expresses her frustration of trying to please men throughout her life: her father, her ex-husband, and now Joe. By the end of her rehearsal, Heather has liberated herself from her past doubts and faces the future with a more confident and self-fulfilled attitude. The intimate musical was alternately funny and sobering, and Cryer's autobiographical tale and powerful performance were both exhilarating. The pop score included such commendable

songs as "Dear Tom," "Natural High," "Strong Woman Number," "Miss America," and "In a Simple Way I Love You." The WORD BAKER-directed show ran six months at the PUBLIC THEATRE and then producer JOSEPH PAPP moved it to the Circle in the Square downtown where it stayed for 1,165 performances.

🎵 IN DAHOMEY (New York Theatre 1903).

The first musical comedy written and performed by African Americans to play before white audiences in a Broadway house, the landmark show was a farcical piece with top-notch performers. When Rareback Pinkerton (George Walker) goes to Florida to con an old millionaire out of his money, he brings along his bumbling assistant Shylock Homestead (BERT WILLIAMS). Soon Rareback finds out that Shylock has a considerable fortune of his own so he bamboozles him, using the money to live the life of leisure in Florida and then in Africa until Shylock finally catches on. Will Marion Cook wrote the libretto and music, and celebrated poet Paul Laurence Dunbar provided the lyrics but the songs took second place to the hilarious byplay of comics Walker and Williams who had first found success in vaudeville. White audiences were hesitant to attend yet the musical ran a still-surprising fifty-nine performances. When Walker and Williams took the show to London where there was less prejudice, the musical ran seven months in 1904.

🎬 IN OLD CHICAGO (Fox 1938). One of

Hollywood's rare musical disaster movies, the film had the Great Chicago Fire of 1871 providing the disaster and ALICE FAYE providing the singing. Saloon singer Belle Fawcett (Faye) can't decide between the goodhearted Jack O'Leary (DON AMECHE) or his dark-hearted brother Dion (TYRONE POWER) so in the meantime she and the cast sing old favorites such as "How Many Miles Back to London Town?" and new songs such as the waltzing "I've Taken a Fancy to You" by LEW POLLOCK (music) and SIDNEY CLARE (lyric) and the vivacious title number by HARRY REVEL (music) and MACK GORDON (lyric). The romantic triangle was sorted out just about the time the brothers' family cow knocks over a lantern in the barn and the fire breaks out. From that point the music stopped and the film became a catastrophic spectacle. ALICE BRADY, as Mrs. O'Leary, was a standout in the supporting cast, which also featured Andy Devine, Brian Donlevy, Phyllis Brooks, Sidney Blackmer, and Burton Churchill. Producer DARRYL F. ZANUCK spent $1.8 million on the picture, one of the most expensive of the decade, and director HENRY KING made sure it all showed up on the screen.

IN THE GOOD OLD SUMMERTIME (MGM 1949).

Although this period musical couldn't hold a candle to the classic film comedy *The Shop around the Corner* (1940) on which it was based, it was a cheerful, colorful diversion all the same and gave both JUDY GARLAND and VAN JOHNSON a chance to show off their comic skills. ALBERT HACKETT, FRANCES GOODRICH, and Ivan Tors reset the Hungarian play *Parfumerie* in Chicago at the turn of the twentieth century and used period songs for the score. The Budapest perfume shop became a music store run by Otto Oberkugen (S. K. SAKALL) and his adoring assistant Nellie Burke (SPRING BYINGTON). Two employees at the store, Andrew Larkin (Johnson) and Veronica Fisher (Garland), are always quarreling, neither knowing that the secret pen pal each has been writing to is the other. The complications were pleasant enough and the fine supporting cast included Buster Keaton, Lillian Bronson, CLINTON SUNDBERG, Marcia Van Dyke, and LIZA MINNELLI as the toddler that Andrew and Veronica produce in the film's finale. The old standards used included "I Don't Care," "Meet Me Tonight in Dreamland," "Play That Barbershop Chord," "Put Your Arms Around Me, Honey," and the bucolic title song. As performed by Garland and company, they seemed fresh as new. ROBERT Z. LEONARD directed the JOE PASTERNAK production and ROBERT ALTON handled the choreography.

IN THE HEIGHTS (Richard Rodgers Theatre 2008).

The first musical written, scored, and performed by Hispanic artists to reach Broadway, the joyous celebration of life and love in a Washington Heights neighborhood managed to be cutting edge and pleasantly accessible at the same time. Lin-Manuel Miranda wrote the score and played the central character Usnavi, named by his father on Ellis Island when he saw a U. S. Navy ship go by.

Although his dream is to own a bar on a beach in the Dominican Republic, Usnavi is smitten with the freewheeling Vanessa (Karen Olivo) who is very much a New York City girl. Quiara Alegria Hudes' libretto was more episodic than linear, but many of the vignettes were engaging, and the score, which included hip-hop, salsa, rap, merengue, and traditional Broadway forms, was thrilling. Various neighbors and family members were played by Mandy Gonzales, Christopher Jackson, Robin de Jesus, PRISCILLA LOPEZ, Carlos Gomez, Olga Merediz, and Seth Stewart. The musical began as a student project when Miranda was attending Wesleyan University and then developed over time until it opened Off Broadway in 2007 to enthusiastic reviews. It was revised and slightly recast before transferring to Broadway twelve months later.

INGRAM, REX (1895–1969). Stage, film, and television performer. An imposing, deep-voiced actor–singer, the tall, muscular African American played in everything from musical revues to absurdist plays. Ingram was born in Cairo, Illinois, the son of riverboat stoker, and educated at Northwestern University for a medical career but instead opted for acting. He made his film debut in *Tarzan of the Apes* (1918), followed by other silent films. Ingram got experience on the stage in California and then made his Broadway debut in the comedy *Theodora, the Queen* (1934). Over the next thirty years he was seen in contemporary dramas, such as *Stevedore* (1934), to classics, as with *Lysistrata* (1946), to theatre of the absurd, such as *Waiting for Godot* (1957). His musical credits include the Broadway revue *Sing Out the News* (1938), the wry villain Lucifer Jr. in CABIN IN THE SKY (1940), the saloon owner Bigelow Brown in ST. LOUIS WOMAN (1946), and the African villager Nana Mwalla in KWAMINA (1961). Ingram's film career took off when he played De Lawd in the screen version of *The Green Pastures* (1936) and is most remembered as Jim opposite MICKEY ROONEY in *The Adventures of Huckleberry Finn* (1939). He reprised his Lucifer Jr. in the 1943 screen version of *Cabin in the Sky*, his only screen musical. Ingram made many television appearances in the 1960s and, after shooting a Christmas episode on *The Bill Cosby Show*, died of a heart attack.

INNOCENTS OF PARIS (Paramount 1929).

An early Hollywood talkie that made MAURICE CHEVALIER a star in America, the primitive musical still has its charms. In his first feature-length film in English, the young Frenchman stumbled through the melodramatic plot battling weak dialogue and a new language but when the musical numbers came along he soared with confidence and audiences were enamored with the funny, sexy Gallic entertainer. The screenplay by Ethel Doherty and Ernest Vajda concerns the Parisian junk dealer Maurice Marney (Chevalier) who wants to be an entertainer, rescues a child from drowning in the Seine, and then falls in love with the tot's aunt, Louise Leval (Sylvia Beecher).

Should he marry Louise and become a family man or follow his dream to go into show business? Maurice chose true love but fortunately he sang and danced a few numbers before he did. RICHARD A. WHITING (music) and LEO ROBIN (lyrics) wrote the new songs, including the Chevalier signature song "Louise," the suggestive "Wait 'Til You See Ma Cherie," and the torchy "On Top of the World Alone." Chevalier also included two favorites from his Paris nightclub act, "Valentine" and "Dites-Moi Ma Mere," sporting his straw hat and cane and displaying the polish of a veteran hoofer. Jesse L. Lasky produced, Richard Wallace directed, and LEROY PRINZ choreographed.

INSIDE U.S.A. (Century Theatre 1948). A sparkling musical revue that used a tour of the nation as the springboard for its songs and sketches, the show featured an expert score by ARTHUR SCHWARTZ (music) and HOWARD DIETZ (lyrics). Inspired by a popular nonfiction book by John Gunther, the musical explores different facets of American life, often in sarcastic sketches by Arnold Auerbach, MOSS HART, and Arnold B. Horwitt. BEATRICE LILLIE and JACK HALEY were the stars, and also featured were dancer Valerie Bettis, singer John Tyler, and comic monologist Herb Shriner, as well as newcomers Carl Reiner, Lewis Nye, Rod Alexander, and Thelma Carpenter. The most memorable songs included "Haunted Heart," "Rhode Island Is Famous for You," "We Won't Take It Back," "At the Mardi Gras," and "My Gal Is Mine Once More." While reviewers didn't think the show measured up to the Dietz–Schwartz revues of the 1930s, there was still plenty to enjoy and audiences had fun for 339 performances.

INTERNATIONAL HOUSE (Paramount 1933). This grab bag of a movie had a more cockeyed and contrived plot than most 1930s musicals, but once W. C. FIELDS arrived in his "auto giro," moviegoers stopped worrying about it and enjoyed the fireworks. Francis Martin and Walter DeLeon concocted the screenplay about a Chinese scientist Doctor Wong (Edmund Breese) who has invented a new communications device called a radioscope, an early form of television set, and invites delegates from around the world to come to the International House Hotel in China and bid on it. Tommy Nash (STUART ERWIN) arrives from America but comes down with the measles and has to be quarantined. Luckily for the audience, GEORGE BURNS and GRACIE ALLEN were the hotel doctor and nurse who tended to him. Then Fields arrives on the roof and

proceeds to take over the film with his one-liners and sight gags, causing havoc by driving throughout the hotel in a miniature car. The musical numbers came from the specialty acts that were demonstrated on the radioscope. RALPH RAINGER (music) and LEO ROBIN (lyrics) provided the songs, with the best being the mock kiddie number "My Bluebird's Singing the Blues" delivered tongue-in-cheek by Baby Rose Marie, "Thank Heaven for You" crooned by RUDY VALLEE while Fields made wisecracks at every musical rest, and the daffy "She Was a China Teacup and He Was Just a Mug," which STERLING HOLLOWAY sang as chorus girls dressed as cups danced around him. Also on hand were Bela Lugosi (as a sinister Russian delegate Petronovich), Peggy Hopkins Joyce, FRANKLIN PANGBORN, Lumsden Hare, and CAB CALLOWAY, whose rendition of "Reefer Man" is not easily forgotten. The agreeable mess of a film was directed by A. EDWARD SUTHERLAND.

INTO THE WOODS (Martin Beck Theatre 1987). A merry yet disturbing musical fantasy, the STEPHEN SONDHEIM show became one of his most frequently produced works across the country. In a fairy tale forest, characters from old and new children's tales meet and help each other achieve their happy ending. But in the second act the same characters are called to account for their actions, such as killing a giant and marrying a prince one hardly knows, and they strive to reach a more mature recognition of their wishes. JAMES LAPINE wrote the complex, if sometimes convoluted, libretto and directed the unusual musical, which boasted a superior cast and a remarkable score. Among the many outstanding songs were "Children Will Listen," "Giants in the Sky," "No One Is Alone," "Agony," "Moments in the Woods," "On the Steps of the Palace," "No More," "Hello, Little Girl," "It Takes Two," and the title number. The press may have been undecided about the uncomfortable mixture of children's theatre and dark adult themes but audiences quickly embraced the musical and it ran 765 performances. The show had originated at the Old Globe Theatre in San Diego and after its New York success the musical was produced by schools, summer theatre, community groups, and regional theatres.

Into the Woods returned to Broadway in 2002 and although it was again directed by Lapine, the new production had a very different look and feel to it. Critical reaction was more positive this time and the revival ran 279 performances.

Broadway casts for *Into the Woods*

Character	1987 Broadway	2002 Broadway
Witch	BERNADETTE PETERS	Vanessa Williams
Baker	CHIP ZIEN	Stephen DeRosa
Baker's Wife	JOHANNA GLEASON	Kerry O'Malley
Cinderella	Kim Crosby	Laura Benanti
Red Riding Hood	Danielle Ferland	Molly Ephraim
Jack	Ben Wright	Adam Wylie
Jack's Mother	Barbara Bryne	Marylouise Burke
Mysterious Man/Narrator	Tom Aldredge	JOHN MCMARTIN
Wolf/Prince	ROBERT WESTENBERG	GREGG EDELMAN

The original New York production and cast of *Into the Woods* were videotaped in the theatre with a live audience and the beautifully filmed show was broadcast on PBS-TV in 1991. It is an excellent record of musical and invaluable for archival and entertainment purposes.

INVITATION TO THE DANCE (MGM 1956). Clearly a labor of love on the part of GENE KELLY who conceived, directed, choreographed, and danced in it, this musical celebration of dance has moments of brilliance and pretentiousness but it is rarely dull. The studio was less in love with the arty film than Kelly and delayed releasing it for four years. The movie has no dialogue or songs but premiered three ballets meant to expose the public to classical and modern dance. In "Circus," with music by Jacques Ibert, Kelly played a tight-rope-walking Pierrot who falls to his death when his beloved (Claire Sombert) forsakes him for another. "Ring Around the Rosie" was the most satisfying ballet, with ANDRE PREVIN providing the music for a tale of a bracelet that a husband gives to his wife, who passes it to an artist, and it travels from person to person until a whore completes the circle by giving it to the husband. The final sequence, "Sinbad the Sailor," was set to Rimsky–Korsakov's *Scheherazade* and utilized both live action and animation in telling a story about a sailor (Kelly), his genie (David Kasday), and the storyteller Scheherazade (CAROL HANEY). The movie is a one-of-a-kind experience, although few could argue the experience should be repeated.

IRENE (Vanderbilt Theatre 1919). One of Broadway's favorite (and most successful) Cinderella musicals, it has been copied many times over the decades but rarely improved upon. The libretto by James Montgomery is straightforward and simple, yet still engaging. Irene O'Dare (EDITH DAY) is an Irish lass who works as an upholsterer's assistant and is sent to a Long Island mansion to reupholster cushions. While there she falls in love with Donald Marshall (Walter Regan), the wealthy son of the estate's owner. Through the help of the male couturier known as Madame Lucy (Bobbie Watson), Irene poses as a socialite to show off Lucy's gowns, wins the heart of high society, and marries Donald. "Alice Blue Gown" was the hit song from the HARRY TIERNEY (music) and JOSEPH MCCARTHY (lyrics) score, which also featured the Chopin-inspired "Castle of Dreams," "The Last Part of Ev'ry Party," "Skyrocket," and the adoring title number. EDWARD ROYCE directed the lighthearted musical and it ran 675 performances, the longest run to date of any musical and a record that would not be beaten for eighteen years. National tours of *Irene* crisscrossed the country for years, and the show was revived on Broadway in 1923 with Dale Winter as the heroine and in 1973 with DEBBIE REYNOLDS as Irene. Much of the book and several of the songs were changed for this popular revival directed by GOWER CHAMPION and choreographed by PETER GENNARO. Some critics thought the old show hopelessly dated but audiences disagreed and it ran for 604 performances.

Casts for *Irene*

Character	1919 Broadway	1940 film	1973 Broadway
Irene O'Dare	EDITH DAY	ANNA NEAGLE	DEBBIE REYNOLDS
Donald Marshall	Walter Regan	Ray Milland	Monte Markham
Mrs. O'Dare	Dorothy Walters	May Robson	PATSY KELLY
Madame Lucy	Bobbie Watson	Roland Young	GEORGE S. IRVING

■ *Irene* (RKO 1940) may not look like much now but it was very popular in its day, perhaps because moviegoers entering a world war found escapism in the simple romantic tale. The screenplay by Alice Duer Miller stayed close to the original but half of the songs were dropped. ANNA NEAGLE's singing and dancing talents don't seem very impressive but her performance is bubbling with charm and her grand entrance at a fashionable high society gathering still works. Henry Wilcox directed and Aida Broadbent choreographed, both competently if not excitingly. RKO wanted the picture to star FRED ASTAIRE and GINGER ROGERS but they declined, saying the musical was too old-fashioned. They were right, of course, but it is the old-fashioned quality that makes *Irene* so endearing.

◎ *IRMA LA DOUCE* (Plymouth Theatre 1960). A musical comedy from France, a rarity on Broadway in any era, the sexy, funny show was a charming, slightly naughty delight. The struggling law student Nestor-Le-Fripe (Keith Michell) loves the Parisian prostitute Irma-La-Douce (Elizabeth Seal) and is jealous of her many clients. He disguises himself as a rich old man named Oscar and gets Irma to give up her many customers in order to become Oscar's exclusive companion. Before he realizes it, Nestor is soon equally jealous of Oscar. He "kills" Oscar, is convicted for the crime and sent to Devil's Island, and then escapes and returns to France where he proves his innocence and wins Irma's heart. The Paris hit by Alexandre Breffort (book and lyrics) and Marguerite Monnot (music) was translated and adapted by the British writers Julian More, David Heneker, and Monty Norman and was a major success in London, running over 1,000 performances. The Broadway production retained director Peter Brook and leading man Michell, and the cast also included CLIVE REVILL, Zack Matalon, GEORGE S. IRVING, and Elliott Gould. The hit song from the show was "Our Language of Love," and also enjoyable were "Dis-Donc," "That's a Crime," "The Bridge of Caulaincourt," and "There Is Only One Paris for That." Although not a giant hit on Broadway as it was in the West End, the DAVID MERRICK production still ran a profitable 524 performances. ■ The 1963 Mirsch/United Artist film version of *Irma la Douce*, with SHIRLEY MACLAINE as the title heroine, rewrote the script considerably and cut all the songs. THE BILLY WILDER film was very popular, and audiences remember *Irma la Douce*

only as a comedy, which may explain why there are so few revivals of the musical.

IRVING, GEORGE S. [born George Irving Shelasky] (1922–). Stage and television performer. The busy character actor who specializes in foreigner types on Broadway and in opera houses, he performed for twenty-five years before becoming a familiar favorite in supporting roles. Irving was born in Springfield, Massachusetts, and trained for an opera career. After appearing in operettas in stock, he made his Broadway debut in the original cast of *OKLAHOMA!* (1943) and thereafter was usually seen in musicals. Irving had minor or supporting roles in two dozen Broadway musicals, including *CALL ME MISTER* (1946), *GENTLEMEN PREFER BLONDES* (1949), *Two's Company* (1952), *ME AND JULIET* (1953), *BELLS ARE RINGING* (1956), *Shinbone Alley* (1957), *IRMA LA DOUCE* (1960), *Bravo Giovanni* (1962), *Anya* (1965), and *THE HAPPY TIME* (1968), and then found recognition as Madame Lucy in the 1973 revival of *IRENE*. He subsequently was given noteworthy supporting roles in such musicals as *So Long, 174th Street* (1976), *I Remember Mama* (1979), *Copperfield* (1981), *THE PIRATES OF PENZANCE* (1981), *ON YOUR TOES* (1983), and *ME AND MY GIRL* (1986). Irving frequently returns to the opera, such as in *CINDERELLA* and *THE MERRY WIDOW* at the New York City Opera in the 1990s, and has been featured in many plays, most memorably as the title character in the satire *An Evening With Richard Nixon and ...* (1972). He has appeared in a few films and television programs, such as the TV musicals *Holiday* (1956) and *RUGGLES OF RED GAP* (1957). Irving was married to actress MARIA KARNILOVA.

■ *IT HAPPENED IN BROOKLYN* (MGM 1947). Although the film was a low-budget attempt to cash in on the popularity of singer FRANK SINATRA, the modest musical had some bountiful pleasures. In Isobel Lennart's screenplay, G.I. Danny Miller (Sinatra) returns to his home in Brooklyn after the war to fall hopelessly in love with the music teacher Anne Fielding (KATHRYN GRAYSON) but loses her to composer Jamie Shellgrove (PETER LAWFORD). It didn't seem fair but Lawford was the bigger movie star and at least Sinatra got to sing the beguiling JULE STYNE-SAMMY CAHN ballad "Time After Time," which became one of his biggest hits of the 1940s. Sinatra also got to join school janitor Nick Lombardi (JIMMY DURANTE) in "The Song's Gotta Come From the Heart" and "I Believe," paid tribute to his home with

"Brooklyn Bridge," and pleased customers in a music store by swinging to "It's the Same Old Dream." Perhaps Sinatra went on one song too many when he and Grayson performed a duet from Mozart's *Don Giovanni*, but his many fans were forgiving and the Richard Whorf-directed picture was a hit.

☞ *It's a Bird, It's a Plane, It's Superman!*

(Alvin Theatre 1966). An agreeable musical comedy suggested by the popular comic strip, the show failed to run despite its playful production values and splendid score by CHARLES STROUSE (music) and LEE ADAMS (lyrics). Posing as newspaper reporter Clark Kent, Superman (Bob Holiday) fights crime in the city of Metropolis, even as he is being romantically pursued by his co-worker Lois Lane (Patricia Marand). The conniving Max Mencken (JACK CASSIDY) and the mad scientist Dr. Abner Sedgwick (Michael O'Sullivan) team up and try to blow up City Hall and then send an atomic missile toward Metropolis, but Superman saves the day as usual. David Newman and Robert Benton wrote the tongue-in-cheek libretto, which never took itself seriously, and producer HAROLD PRINCE directed the piece like a colorful cartoon. The score produced one major hit song, "You've Got Possibilities," and such delightful numbers as "It's Superman," "You've Got What I Need," "Ooh, Do You Love You!," "Doing Good," "So Long, Big Guy," and "The Woman for the Man." Most of the critics pronounced the show unpretentious fun, but the public didn't respond and it closed after 129 performances. ☐ ABC-TV made a small screen version of *It's a Bird, It's a Plane, It's Superman!* in 1975 but director Jack Regas did not capture the playful, satiric tone of the musical. ROMEO MULLER wrote the teleplay and only a handful of the stage songs were used, plus a new one by Strouse and Lee titled "It's a Free Country." The talented but misguided cast included David Wilson (Superman), Lesley Ann Warren (Lois Lane), Kenneth Mars (Mencken), DAVID WAYNE (Sedgwick), Loretta Swit, and Allen Ludden.

▦ *It's Always Fair Weather* (MGM

1955). It may have resembled a sequel to *On the Town* (1949) with its reunion of three sailors in New York City, one of them played by GENE KELLY from the earlier film, but this cynical and even bitter musical had nothing to do with the wartime optimism of the 1940s. Fellow gobs Ted Riley (Kelly), Doug Hallerton (DAN DAILEY), and Angie

Valentine (MICHAEL KIDD) agree at the end of the war to meet in ten year's time and see how they are getting on. Their reunion reveals that they no longer feel any comradeship and are even annoyed with each other. Their animosity is heightened when the television coordinator Jackie Leighton (CYD CHARISSE) puts the three men on a local interview program hosted by the phony Madeline Bradville (DOLORES GRAY). When Ted is hunted down by a crooked boxing promoter, the old friends gang together once more and help each other out. BETTY COMDEN and ADOLPH GREEN wrote the unusual screenplay and the lyrics for ANDRÉ PREVIN's music, with the songs having little to do with the story but wonderful all the same. The male trio danced down the street with trash can lids on their feet and were seen in split screen singing "Once Upon a Time," Charisse (dubbed by Carole Richards) sang "Baby, You Knock Me Out" to a gym full of pugilists, Gray stopped the show with the satiric "Thanks a Lot But No Thanks" and noted "Music Is Better Than Words," and Kelly roller-skated down Broadway proclaiming "I Like Myself." STANLEY DONAN and Kelly co-directed and co-choreographed, their last teaming before going separate ways.

ITURBI, JOSÉ (1895–1980). Film and televi-

sion musician, conductor, and performer. An internationally renowned classical conductor and concert pianist, he added a touch of class to seven Hollywood musicals. Iturbi was born in Valencia, Spain, of Basque ancestry and was so gifted on the piano that at the age of twelve he was playing professionally as an accompanist for silent films. He studied at the Conservatoire de Musique in Paris and then taught piano at the Conservatory of Geneva even as he played in nightclubs. Iturbi came to America in 1929 and was soon a recognized virtuoso, playing with various name orchestras and for a time serving as the conductor of the Rochester Philharmonic. He always played himself in his 1940s movie musicals even when he was a character in the plot. His keyboarding and conducting could be seen in the films *Thousands Cheer* (1943), *Two Girls and a Sailor* (1944), *Music for Millions* (1944), *Anchors Aweigh* (1945), *Holiday in Mexico* (1946), *Three Darling Daughters* (1948), and *That Midnight Kiss* (1949), as well as providing the piano playing for Cornel Wilde as Chopin in *A Song to Remember* (1945). Iturbi also made television appearances up through the 1960s.

J

□ **JACK AND THE BEANSTALK** (NBC-TV 1956). An unknown JOEL GREY played the teenage Jack in this very popular musical broadcast as part of the *PRODUCER'S SHOWCASE* series. Using the format of a dream, Jack climbs the beanstalk and all the characters he meets up in the clouds resemble the people he knows back on the ground, giving the tale a psychological twist. DENNIS KING narrated and the supporting cast was loaded with talent: CELESTE HOLM, CYRIL RITCHARD, BILLY GILBERT, Peggy King, Arnold Stang, Leora Dana, and the Ray Charles Chorus to fill out the musical numbers written by Jerry Livingston (music) and Helen Deutsch (lyrics), who also wrote the teleplay. The spirited songs included "The Ballad of Jack and the Beanstalk," "He Never Looks My Way," "Sweet World," "Where Are the White Birds Flying?," "The March of the Ill-Assorted Guards," "Song of the Harp," and "I'll Go Along With You." The critics were not impressed but the broadcast broke records for a ninety-minute show. Alvin Cooperman produced and Clark Jones directed. A decade later CBS came up with their own musical *Jack and the Beanstalk* when Jim Eiler adapted and directed a Prince Street Players production for the small screen, writing the songs with Jeanne Bargy. Set in medieval England, this witty, irreverent version has Jack (Hal Holden) climb the beanstalk to discover a friendly singing and dancing Giant (Will B. Able) but an evil Baron (Robert Dagny) who serves as the villain. Most of the cast were unknowns but Joan Roberts from Broadway's *OKLAHOMA!* (1943) played Jack's mother. The catchy songs included "It's a Magical, Musical Day," "Take a Giant Step," "Oh, Them Golden Eggs," "Fee, Fi, Fo, Fum," and "I'm Gonna Climb Up." The next year NBC returned to the story for a 1967 musical that mixed live action and animation. GENE KELLY produced, directed, and played Jeremy Keen, an adult companion to Jack (Bobby Riha) who climbs up the stalk with him. They discover a bumbling Giant (voice of Ted Cassidy), the beautiful Princess Serena (voiced by Janet Waldo and sung by MARNI NIXON), and a pair of animated birds who do a terrific trio with Kelly called "The Woggle Bird Song." The other delightful songs, written by JAMES VAN HEUSEN (music) and SAMMY CAHN (lyrics), include "Half Past April and a Quarter," "One Starry Moment," "I Sure Hate Love," "A Tiny Bit of Faith," and "It's Been Nice." The William Hanna–Joseph Barbera production was innovative, clever, and highly appealing to kids and adults.

🎵 **JACQUES BREL IS ALIVE AND WELL AND LIVING IN PARIS** (Village Gate 1968). An unlikely hit, this intimate musical revue celebrating the songs of Belgian pop composer–singer Jacques Brel became one of the longest-running shows in the history of Off Broadway. Eric Blau and Mort Shuman translated and adapted Brel's lyrics, and without benefit of narration or commentary, Brel's musical world was brought to life by four performers (Shuman, Elly Stone, Shawn Elliott, and Alice Whitfield) who presented the numbers cabaret style. Because the songs were often character driven, the evening was surprisingly theatrical. Among the many songs performed were "If We Only Had Love," "Old Folks," "Marathon," "Brussels," "Alone," "Madeleine," "Timid Frieda," "Carousel," and "You're Not Alone." The little revue, directed by Moni Yakim, built slowly and became a surprise hit, running 1,847 performances, followed by hundreds of productions in cabarets, summer stock, and regional theatres. A 1972 Broadway production, also directed by Yakim and featuring Stone, played a limited engagement of fifty-one performances in the Royale Theatre, and critics complained that the revue lost its intimacy in the larger house. The show has since been revived on Off Broadway where it probably belongs. ▨ Some of the original cast members appeared in a 1975 film version of the revue directed by Denis Héroux as a collage of scenes set all over Paris. The fancy cutting and contrived dramatic settings for the songs were more annoying than revealing and the fine singers rarely could compete with all the visuals. All the same, there were poignant moments, including Brel himself who sings a number in his native language.

▨ **JAILHOUSE ROCK** (MGM 1957). ELVIS PRESLEY's third Hollywood musical, it was one of his best efforts and revealed that the King could act when needed. Vince Everett (Presley) is sent to jail for manslaughter. There he befriends fellow inmate Hunk Horton (Mickey Shaughnessy), a former country music singer who teaches him about the record business. After Vince is released, he pursues his dream, rises to the top of the rock and roll industry, and callously forgets his friends until one of them, Peggy Ann Alden (Judy Tyler), sets Vince straight with her love for him. The Guy Trosper screenplay presented an unsentimental view of the music business and gave Presley a more complex, perplexed character to play than he was usually handed. MIKE STOLLER and JERRY LEIBER wrote the songs for the film, with the best three being the confessional love song "(You're So Square,) Baby, I Don't Care," the pleading "Treat Me Nice," and the propulsive title number that went to the top of the charts. RICHARD THORPE directed the movie in black and white, giving it a documentary feel at times, and PANDRO S. BERMAN produced. One of the highlights of the movie was newcomer Tyler, recently seen on Broadway in Rodgers and Hammerstein's PIPE DREAM (1955) and deemed to be the most promising new face in Hollywood; however, two days after filming was complete, the twenty-three-year-old actress died in a car crash.

🐚 **JAMAICA** (Imperial Theatre 1957). A tropical musical with a less than inspired libretto but a sparkling score, the show was a vehicle for LENA HORNE and in that respect did not disappoint. The poor Caribbean fisherman Koli (RICARDO MONTALBAN) loves the beautiful, worldly Savannah (Horne) but she is more interested in leaving her little island home for the bright life on the island of Manhattan. She almost gets there when she latches on to the hustling Joe Nashua (Joe Adams), but when Koli saves Savannah's young brother in a hurricane, she decides to stay and wed Koli. The superior cast also included Josephine Premice, ADELAIDE HALL, ERIK RHODES, and Ossie Davis. E. Y. HARBURG and FRED SAIDY originally wrote the script for popular singer Harry Belafonte who was not available so the libretto was rewritten for Horne when the casting changed and the strain sometimes showed. Yet the songs, by HAROLD ARLEN (music) and Harburg (lyrics), written with Horne in mind, were sensational and her delivery of "Cocoanut Sweet," "Ain't It the Truth," "Napoleon," "Push the Button," and "Take It Slow, Joe" were magical. Also in the score were "Monkey in the Mango Tree," "Savannah," and "Leave the Atom Alone." DAVID MERRICK produced,

ROBERT LEWIS directed, and JACK COLE was the choreographer, but all that mattered was Horne who kept the show on the boards for 555 performances.

JAMES, BRIAN D'ARCY (1968–). Stage, television, and film performer. A recent, quickly rising leading man with traditional but striking good looks, he has gained a lot of attention on Broadway in a short time. James was born in Saginaw, Michigan, the son of a lawyer and a children's books publisher, and studied theatre at Northwestern University before acting in regional theatre and in the national tour of LES MISÉRABLES. He made his Broadway debut as a replacement in BLOOD BROTHERS in 1994 and then played various roles in the 1994 revival of CAROUSEL before getting recognition as the stoker Barrett in TITANIC (1997). James was highly praised for his ambitious Sidney in SWEET SMELL OF SUCCESS (2002) and for his leading male roles in the musical trilogy THE APPLE TREE (2006). His other musical credits include the Off Broadway productions of FLOYD COLLINS (1996) and THE WILD PARTY (2000), replacing NORBERT LEO BUTZ as Freddy in DIRTY ROTTEN SCOUNDRELS in 2006, and regionally as nightclubber Bob Wallace in the stage version of WHITE CHRISTMAS (2006 and 2007). James had made a handful of films and television appearances.

JAMES, HARRY [Haag] (1916–1983). Film and television musician and conductor. Perhaps the finest trumpeter of the Big Band era, the thin, mustached conductor–musician was featured in sixteen Hollywood musicals, usually playing himself and with his band. James was born in Albany, Georgia, the son of circus performers, and began in show business at the age of four as a contortionist. As an adult he played trumpet in the circus band and then was elevated to a featured trumpeter in BENNY GOODMAN's orchestra, appearing with them in the movie musical HOLLYWOOD HOTEL (1937). He formed his own band in 1939, called Harry James and his Music Makers, and quickly became popular in nightclubs, on the radio, and on records. In addition to his expert trumpet playing and the band itself, James was noted for introducing new singers, such as DICK HAYMES, Kitty Kallen, Connie Haines, Helen Forrest, and FRANK SINATRA. James's film musicals include *Private Buckaroo* (1942), SPRINGTIME IN THE ROCKIES (1942), *Syncopation* (1942), TWO GIRLS AND A SAILOR (1944), BEST FOOT FORWARD (1943), *Bathing Beauty* (1944), *I'll Get By* (1950), *Carnegie Hall* (1950), *The*

Benny Goodman Story (1955), *The Opposite Sex* (1956), *The Big Beat* (1957), and *Ladies Man* (1961). He was the musical director and did the trumpet playing for Kirk Douglas in the film *Young Man With a Horn* (1950). He also made several television appearances in the 1950s and 1960s. James continued to do concerts up until a few days before his death from cancer. He was married for a time to Betty Grable. Biography: *Trumpet Blues: The Life of Harry James*, Peter J. Levinson (2001).

James Joyce's The Dead (Belasco Theatre 2000). A quiet, atmospheric, but engrossing musical play, it had been so well received Off Broadway at Playwrights Horizons that it transferred to Broadway, only to struggle for 112 performances. The Dublin spinster sisters Julia (Sally Ann Howes) and Kate Morkan (Marni Nixon) throw a Christmas gathering with their niece Mary Jane (Emily Skinner) and the guests are a varied lot, some living in the past and others trying not to remember the past. Gabriel Conroy (Christopher Walken) narrates the story, and a confession by his wife Gretta (Blair Brown), that the only love of her life was a boy who died years ago, served as the main crisis of the piece. Also in the ensemble cast were Stephen Spinella, Broan Davies, Alice Ripley, John Kelly, and Daisy Eagan. Richard Nelson wrote the libretto, based on one of Joyce's short stories in *The Dubliners*, and provided the lyrics for Shaun Davey's music, resulting in such songs as "The Living and the Dead," "Three Jolly Pigeons," "Goldenhair," "Wake the Dead," "Naughty Girls," and "When Lovely Lady." Nelson directed the musical and Sean Curran choreographed the Irish dancing, which was highly commended.

Janis, Elsie [born Elsie Bierbower] (1889–1956). Stage performer and producer. A slim, spirited comic singer and renowned mimic, she was the unofficial queen of vaudeville in America and Great Britain and made a dozen appearances on Broadway. Janis was born in Columbus, Ohio, and was pushed on the stage at a young age by her overbearing stage mother. Billed as Little Elsie, she toured the country and made her Broadway debut in *When We're Forty-One* (1905), followed over the years by such shows as *The Hoyden* (1907), *The Fair Coed* (1909), *The Lady of the Slipper* (1912), *Miss Information* (1915), *The Century Girl* (1916), *Miss 1917* (1917), *Elsie Janis and Her Gang* (1919 and 1922), and *Puzzles of 1925*. In London she shone in two editions of *The Passing Show* (1914 and 1915) and other musicals. Even in her character roles, Janis did her specialties: singing snappy comic songs and doing outrageous impersonations of the celebrities of the day. She also wrote sketches and songs for some of her vehicles, and in the later part of her career produced and directed them on occasion. Yet she always returned to vaudeville and, because of her extended tours among the American and British troops during World War I, she was equally beloved in both countries and earned the nickname "Sweetheart of the A.E.F." (American Expeditionary Force). When her domineering mother died in 1932, Janis retired from show business even though she was still extremely popular. Autobiography: *So Far So Good* (1932).

Jazz Singer, The (Warner-Vitaphone 1927). Commonly known as the first talking feature film, the picture is actually a silent movie with sound added for the songs only. Yet however one categorizes it, the movie is a major landmark and is still surprisingly effective.

Plot: Young Jakie Rabinowitz lives on Manhattan's Lower East Side and is a concern to his parents, especially when the youth is caught singing jazz and ragtime in a local saloon. Jakie refuses to study to be a cantor like his father and four generations of Rabinowitzs before him, so he runs away from home and, under the name Jack Robin, goes into show business. The years pass and, with the love and encouragement of dancer May, Jakie finds success, singing in nightclubs and returning to New York to be in a Broadway show. He hears he father is dying so he goes to the local synagogue and sings the Yom Kippur service in the old man's place. Jakie then opens on Broadway and, with his mother sitting in the front row, sings "My Mammy" to her.

Film casts for *The Jazz Singer*

Character	1927 version	1952 version	1980 version
Jakie/Jerry/Yussel	Al Jolson	Danny Thomas	Neil Diamond
His father, a cantor	Warner Oakland	Eduard Franz	Laurence Olivier
His mother	Eugenie Besserer	Mildred Dunnock	Caitlin Adams
May/Judy/Molly	May McAvoy	Peggy Lee	Lucie Arnaz
Young Jakie	Bobby Gordon		

Alfred A. Cohn's screenplay is based on Samson Raphaelson's 1925 play, which had starred GEORGE JESSEL on Broadway. Unlike the stage work, the action in the film glides through the immigrant neighborhoods and opens up the story to present the neighbors and other characters who influence Jakie's life. Although much of the movie is dated, there are still marvelous things to enjoy. Director ALAN CROSLAND shot the exteriors on location in New York, and the depiction of the neighborhood, the smoky saloons and nightclubs, and the backstage of the theatre has a tawdry realism to it. The plotting is solid, character development is not complex but clear, and of course there is the riveting presence of AL JOLSON. Jessel was contracted to reprise his stage performance on film but when he learned that there were to be sound sections, he demanded more money so WARNER BROTHERS went with Jolson. In both the silent and the sound sections of the movie, the stage entertainer managed to grab one's attention and hold it with confident gusto. In the more serious scenes he avoids melodramatics and lets a simple frown or the turn of the head say it all. It was Jolson's first feature film and he embraced the camera like a silent film veteran. The script called for sound to be used only when the actors started singing, either the songs or the Hebrew chants. However, Jolson was used to inserting phrases and brief comments in his stage performances so when he did the same on film the audience actually heard his speaking voice as well as his singing. Jakie tells the applauding patrons in a San Francisco night spot "Wait a minute! Wait a minute! You ain't heard nothing yet!" before he breaks into "Toot, Toot, Tootsie," and there is a lovely section when Jolson ad-libs some words of affection to actress Eugenie Besserer, who plays his mother, while he sits at the piano and sings "Blue Skies." That is about all the dialogue that is heard in the movie but it was enough to start a revolution. All the songs used in *The Jazz Singer* but one were numbers already familiar to audiences. GRANT CLARKE, Louis Silvers, and Jolson wrote "Mother of Mine, I Still Have You" for the film and he sang it in blackface at a rehearsal while his mother watched tearfully from the wings. It has the distinction of being the first true movie song. Although it did not become a major hit, the number was very effective on screen and it opened up a whole new avenue for promoting songs. The birth of the movie musical also meant the beginning of selling popular songs by way of Hollywood. But Warner Brothers was not concerned with

> ### *The Jazz Singer* (1927) Musical Numbers
> "My Gal Sal"
> "Waiting for the Robert E. Lee"
> "Kol Nidre"
> "Dirty Hands, Dirty Faces"
> "Toot, Toot, Tootsie"
> "Kaddish"
> "Blue Skies"
> "Mother of Mine, I Still Have You"
> "My Mammy"

Jolson talking or the selling of songs when they gambled everything on the newfangled process of Vitaphone. Nearly bankrupt before the picture opened, *The Jazz Singer* saved the studio and changed the course of film history.

The same studio remade *The Jazz Singer* in 1953 with DANNY THOMAS as Jerry Golding, the son of Cantor and Mrs. Golding (Eduard Franz and Mildred Dunnock), who returns from serving in the Korean war and decides to go into show business. This time it was Judy Lane (PEGGY LEE) who provided the love and support, and again Jerry went to the synagogue at the last moment. As with the original film, the songs were mostly recognized standards ("Birth of the Blues," "Just One of Those Things," "Lover," and "I'll String Along With You"), which choreographer LEROY PRINZ staged in a very contemporary way. MICHAEL CURTIZ directed competently but there is no flavor in the locale or the characters. The screenplay by Frank Davis, Leonard Stern, and Lewis Metzler was very sentimental and seemed less palatable in the 1950s so the film did only marginal business. A third version of *The Jazz Singer* (EMI 1980) updated the story, and Herbert Baker's screenplay was about Yussell Rabinovitch (Neil Diamond) who becomes rock singer Jess Rabinovitch. Molly Bell (Lucie Arnaz) was his girl friend and in this version the cantor father (Laurence Oliver) doesn't die but lives to accept his son's calling and is seen at a rock concert cheering the boy on. Much of it was embarrassing (Olivier's hammy performance was the laugh of the industry) and director Richard Fleischer did little to make the script or the characters work. Yet Diamond had natural charisma and some of the songs, by Diamond and associates, were enjoyed by younger audiences. ("Love on the Rocks" and "America" were both on the charts.) As a tribute to the film's legacy, Diamond donned blackface in one number. Most moviegoers drawn to the film could hardly understand the connection and just thought it a matter of bad taste. ☐ In 1959, JERRY LEWIS played the central character as Joey Rabinowitz in a NBC-TV version of *The Jazz Singer* on the *Ford Startime* anthology series. Joey was more a standup comic than a singer but much of the plot was the same. Molly Picon and Eduard Franze were his parents, and also in the cast were ANNA MARIA ALBERGHETTI, Barry Gordon, Alan Reed, and Del Moore.

JEAN, GLORIA [born Gloria Jean Schoonover] (1928–). Film and television performer. A cheery, wholesome singer actress, she was groomed by UNIVERSAL STUDIOS to play the teenage roles that DEANNA DURBIN was outgrowing. Jean was born in Buffalo, New York, and grew up in Scranton, Pennsylvania, where she was singing in vaudeville and on the radio as a child. At the age of twelve she was signed by Hollywood and made her first film musical, *The Underpup* (1939), followed by chipper adolescent roles in such musicals as *If I Had My Way* (1940), *A Little Bit of Heaven* (1940), *What's Cookin'?* (1942), *Get Hep to Love* (1942), *When Johnny Comes Marching Home* (1942), *Cinderella Swings It* (1943), *Moonlight in Vermont* (1943), *Follow the Boys* (1944), *Pardon My Rhythm* (1944), *The Ghost Catchers* (1944), *The Reckless Age* (1944), *I'll Remember April* (1945), and *Easy to Look At* (1945). Jean never was as popular as Durbin and by the late 1940s her roles got smaller, as in *Copacabana* (1947), *I Surrender, Dear* (1947), *Manhattan Angel* (1949), *There's a Girl in My Heart* (1949), and *An Old-Fashioned Girl* (1949). She was in a few nonmusicals in the 1950s and early sixties and made several appearances on television before retiring in 1963.

JEKYLL & HYDE (Plymouth Theatre 1997). A pop opera treatment of Robert Louis Stevenson's classic tale *The Strange Case of Dr. Jekyll and Mr. Hyde*, the musical was generally dismissed by the press but quickly developed a cult status and ran 1,543 performances. Composer FRANK WILDHORN had released a recording of the score long before the production was put together and it sold over 250,000 copies so for many the show was a hit before the first rehearsal. Robert Cuccioli played the dual main character, and Linda Eder was the prostitute Lucy that he loved and murdered. Also in the cast were George Merritt, Christiane Noll, Brad Oscar, and Barrie Ingham. LESLIE BRICUSSE, provided the lyrics for Wildhorn's music, and the score included the hit ballad "This Is the Moment," as well as "A New Life," "Someone Like You," "Once Upon a Dream," and "Lost in the Darkness."

JELLY'S LAST JAM (Virginia Theatre 1992). A musical biography of Jelly Roll Morton, the stylized show took a nontraditional and more conceptual approach to its subject matter and afforded GREGORY HINES his best stage role. In the limbo-like Jungle Inn, the deceased composer Morton (Hines) arrives and is forced by the Chimney Man (Keith David) to reenact his life. From his days as a dancing youth (SAVION GLOVER) to his rise to fame to his later years when he is neglected by the public, Morton is seen as a selfish, volatile, and even racist character who abuses friends, such as Jack the Bear (Stanley Wayne Mathis), and lovers, such as Anita (TONYA PINKINS). GEORGE C. WOLFE wrote the uncompromising libretto, and Susan Birkenhead wrote lyrics for music by Morton and LUTHER HENDERSON who adapted the blues and jazz material into a musical play format. Among the electrifying numbers were "Lovin' Is a Lowdown Blues," "The Whole World's Waitin' to Sing Your Song," "That's How You Jazz," and "The Last Chance Blues." Author Wolfe directed and Hope Clarke devised the choreography, one of the highlights of which was Hines and Glover tapping up a storm together as Morton young and old. While aisle sitters felt the premise was thin and the main character not very likable, they admitted that Hines and his fellow performers made everything shine and the dark, brooding musical managed to be enjoyable all the same. Audiences agreed and the musical ran 569 performances.

JENKINS, DANIEL (1963–). Stage, television, and film performer. An affable yet not typical leading man, he has been roundly praised for his handful of Broadway appearances. The native New Yorker, the son of actor Ken Jenkins, appeared in tours and Off Broadway before making an auspicious Broadway debut as Huck Finn in the musical *BIG RIVER* (1985). After acting as a replacement in the drama *Angels in America* (1993), he returned to musicals in the leading role of Josh Baskin in *Big* (1996). For the 2003 revival of *Big River* using speaking and deaf performers, Jenkins played Mark Twain and provided the voice of Huck. He also shone as the repressed banker George Banks in the Broadway cast of *MARY POPPINS* (2006). In addition to Off Broadway, *ENCORES!*

musicals, and regional theatre, Jenkins has acted on television and in some films, including *THE CRADLE WILL ROCK* (1999).

JEROME ROBBINS' BROADWAY (Imperial Theatre 1989). In this spectacular musical revue, memorable production numbers from Robbins' musicals, complete with original sets and costumes, were staged by the legendary director–choreographer himself with a young cast who brought his celebrated dances back to life. The cast included JASON ALEXANDER, Charlotte D'Amboise, FAITH PRINCE, Scott Wise, Robert La Fosse, Debbie Shapiro, Michael Kubala, Jane Lanier, JOEY McKNEELY, Susan Fletcher, and Luis Perez. The numbers came from such varied shows as *THE KING AND I*, *PETER PAN*, *HIGH BUTTON SHOES*, *GYPSY*, *WEST SIDE STORY*, *ON THE TOWN*, *FIDDLER ON THE ROOF*, and *MISS LIBERTY*. Enthusiastic reviews and wide audience appeal allowed the revue to run 634 performances but it was not a financial success because of the large cast and expensive production.

JERSEY BOYS (August Wilson Theatre 2005). A combination juke box musical and musical biography, the show (which originated at the La Jolla Playhouse in California) was an immediate hit on Broadway and continues to pack them in. In Marshall Brickman and Rick Elice's libretto, Frankie Valli (John Lloyd Young) and fellow New Jerseyites Tommy DeVito (Christian Hoff), Nick Massi (J. Robert Spencer), and Bob Gaudio (Daniel Reichard) leave their lives of petty crimes on the streets and form a singing quartet called the Four Seasons. The foursome introduces a new sound to pop singing in the 1950s and 1960, complete with a squealing tenor and a seething sexuality. Among the pop hits heard were "Can't Take My Eyes Off of You," "Working My Way Back to You," "Sherry," "Rag Doll," and "Oh, What a Night." Critics bemoaned the clunky book, lack of characterizations, and the nonintegrated lineup of hit singles, but admitted that the four players captured the Seasons's sound with accuracy and fervor. Audiences were not so particular, and old and new fans

Jersey Boys. Nostalgia on Broadway used to mean a fondness for old musicals. By the 1990s it also meant a love for old songs and singing groups which had nothing to do with Broadway. Among the biggest "jukebox" musical hits were *Smokey Joe's Cafe* (1995), *Mamma Mia!* (2001), and, pictured above, *Jersey Boys* (2005), in which the Four Seasons and their unique sound were recreated on stage. (Wire Image)

embraced the rags-to-riches show that was directed by DES MCANUFF and choreographed by Sergio Trujillo.

JESSEL, GEORGE [Albert] (1898–1981). Stage, film, and television performer, songwriter, and producer. One of vaudeville's favorite comics with his telephone monologues to his mother becoming classics in the field, he was featured in Broadway plays and musicals before finding greater success in other media. Jessel was born in the Bronx and began performing as a child to earn money to support his family. After working as a kid in variety, he joined Gus Edwards' popular schoolchildren act and played the best vaudeville circuits. As an adult Jessel continued to perform and took on producing as well. He made his Broadway debut in the cast of the revue *Shubert Gaieties* (1919) and then shone in *THE PASSING SHOW* (1923) before getting the best role of his career: the cantor's son Jackie Rabinowitz who goes into show business in *The Jazz Singer* (1925). Jessel played the character more than a thousand times in New York, on the road, and back on Broadway in 1929, but he unwisely turned down the opportunity to make the movie version of the play because he wanted more money. He made a few more Broadway appearances, as in *Sweet and Low* (1930), *High Kickers* (1941), and *Show Time* (1942), but concentrated on radio, where his monologues went over very well, and then in television where he appeared on hundreds of programs including his own show, later serving as toastmaster saluting stars. Jessel acted in only a few films but produced fourteen pictures in the 1940s and 1950s, including the musical biographies *THE DOLLY SISTERS* (1945) and *The I Don't Care Girl* (1953) and a series of tuners inspired from old songs, such as *I Wonder Who's Kissing Her Now* (1947), *When My Baby Smiles at Me* (1948), and *Oh You Beautiful Doll* (1949). Perhaps his greatest legacy is the sentimental songs he co-wrote with others, such as "My Yiddishe Mama," "Sonny Boy," and his theme song "My Mother's Eyes." Jessel's three

wives included film star Norma Talmadge (1893–1957). Autobiographies: *So Help Me* (1943); *This Way, Miss* (1955).

JESUS CHRIST SUPERSTAR (Mark Hellinger Theatre 1971). The first musical by ANDREW LLOYD WEBBER (music) and TIM RICE (lyric) to play on Broadway, the biblical rock musical was the first shot in the British invasion and a popular favorite ever since. During the last seven days in the life of Jesus (Jeff Fenholt), he struggles with his decision to be betrayed by Judas Iscariot (BEN VEREEN) and be crucified in order to save his disciples, including Mary Magdalene (Yvonne Elliman) who is in love with him. Already familiar to theatregoers because of its best-selling album and touring concert productions, the Broadway version was a colorful, flashy demonstration of surreal theatrics directed by TOM O'HORGAN. The score featured the hit numbers "I Don't Know How to Love Him" and "Superstar," as well as such memorable songs as "Heaven on Their Minds," "Everything's Alright," "What's the Buzz?," "Hosanna," and "King Herod's Song." Some critics balked at the gaudy elements of the ROBERT STIGWOOD production but audiences embraced the musical for 720 performances and it became a favorite in theatres across the country. In 1977, *Jesus Christ Superstar* was presented on Broadway concert style with minimal sets and costumes, much as the rock opera had been done before it was turned into a Broadway production. All the same, fans of the piece were able to keep it running for 96 performances. The cast included William Daniel Grey (Jesus), Patrick Jude (Judas), and Barbara Niles (Mary Magdalene). A 2000 Broadway revival fared less well. With a lot of T-shirts on stage, the production struck commentators as cheap and lacking in imagination. Glenn Carter (Jesus), Tony Vincent (Judas), and Maya Days (Mary Magdalene) led the company directed by Gale Edwards. Tepid notices and lack of interest by the public forced the show to close after six weeks.

Casts for *Jesus Christ Superstar*

Character	1971 Broadway	1973 film
Jesus	Jeff Fenholt	Ted Neeley
Judas	BEN VEREEN	Carl Anderson
Mary Magdalene	Yvonne Elliman	Yvonne Elliman
Herod	Paul Ainsley	Joshua Mostel
Pontius Pilate	Barry Dennen	Barry Denham

Jesus Christ Superstar. The Andrew Lloyd Webber and Tim Rice rock musical may have seemed a bit irreverent when first presented on Broadway, particularly in director Tom O'Horgan's outlandish production, but over the years the piece has become so well accepted that churches are among the many theatre groups who regularly revive it. Pictured is Jeff Fenholt as Jesus in the original Broadway mounting. (Photofest)

Jesus Christ Superstar (Universal 1973) approached the movie with a play-within-a-play premise, with the actors disembarking from a bus in the desert and the story told as a kind of outdoor pageant. Filming on location in Israel, director Norman Jewison and choreographer Robert Iscove found clever ways to keep the visuals lively. Ted Neeley and Carl Anderson led the cast as Jesus and Judas and they later reprised their roles in stage versions and concerts. The Webber–Rice score was kept pretty much intact, knowing that the fans of the rock musical would notice any monkeying with the score. The movie was a modest success on its first release but has remained a favorite of fans over the years. ❑ An Australian television version of *Jesus Christ Superstar* in 2000 was based on a modern dress 1996 London production and was similar in look to the 2000 Broadway revival. It featured Glenn Carter (Jesus), Jerome Pradon (Judas), Renee Castle (Mary Magdalene), Rik Mayall (Herod), and Fred Johnson (Pilate).

JOHN, ELTON [born Reginald Kenneth Dwight] (1947–). Stage and film composer, musician, and performer. Perhaps the most durable British rock star of all time with a career spanning four decades without losing momentum, the singer–pianist turned to the musical late in his career and came up with major hits. John was born in Pinner, England, and educated at London's Royal Academy of Music. Since 1970 he has been an internationally famous rock singer and composer with record-breaking albums and sold-out concerts around the world. His usual lyricist for his albums is Bernie Taupin (1950–), but he teamed with TIM RICE to write the scores for the animated movie musicals *THE LION KING* (1994) and *The Road to El Dorado* (2000). On Broadway he wrote new songs with Rice for the 1997 stage version of *The Lion King* and the two teamed up for an original score for *AIDA* (2000). Taupin and John reteamed for the short-lived stage musical *Lestat* (2006) on Broadway but in London John had a giant hit with *Billy Elliott* (2005) with lyrics by Lee

Hall, arriving on Broadway in 2008. John is as popular a performer as a composer and has appeared on television specials and in a handful of films, including the musical *TOMMY* (1989) in which he played the Pinball Wizard. He has sung on the soundtrack of several films, including the musicals *The Lion King* and *The Road to El Dorado*. Biographies: *Elton*, David Buckley (2007); *Sir Elton*, Philip Norman (2001).

JOHNNY JOHNSON (44th Street Theatre 1936). KURT WEILL's first Broadway assignment after emigrating to America, the powerful anti-war musical contained the bite and fervor of his European works. The pacifist sculptor Johnny Johnson (Russell Collins) is sent to Europe when World War I breaks out, is wounded and sent to a hospital, recovers, and is deemed insane when he doesn't want to return to the trenches so is put in an insane asylum. Returning home after the war, he sells toys on street corners, but not toy guns or soldiers, and encounters Minny Belle (Phoebe Brand), the girl he once loved but lost because of his pacifist ideas. Also in the impressive cast were Grover Burgess, Sanford Meisner, Art Smith, Lee J. Cobb, Will Lee, Susanna Senior, Paul Mann, Luther Adler, Roman Bohnen, Morris Carnovsky, Eunice Stoddard, Elia Kazan, and Ruth Nelson. Paul Green wrote the funny, frightening libretto as well as the lyrics for Weill's music, resulting in such unforgettable numbers as "Johnny's Song (Listen to My Song)," "Mon Ami, My Friend," "Aggie's Sewing Machine Song," "Cowboy Song (Oh, the Rio Grande)," and "Captain Valentine's Tango." The leftist Group Theatre produced and Lee Strasberg directed the anti-war drama with songs that often moved into fantasy and allegory. Some critics appreciated the strange, haunting score but audiences only came for sixty-eight performances. The musical has been produced at colleges and by adventurous theatre groups over the years, and in 1971 there was a Broadway revival with Ralph Williams as the title hero. Critics admired the anti-war piece in the Viet Nam era but audiences were not interested in a period piece about a past war so it closed on opening night. José Quintero directed a cast that included Alice Cannon, Gordon Minard, Norman Chase, Paul Michael, and James Billings.

JOHNSON, BILL (1916–1957). Stage performer. A talented, stalwart singer–actor, his short career consisted of strong performances in short-run musicals. Johnson was born in Baltimore and educated at the University of Maryland for an engineering degree, which he pursued for a while before getting major roles in summer stock musicals. He also had many singing engagements with orchestras and in nightclubs before making his Broadway debut in the revue *Two for the Show* (1940). After appearing in *All in Fun* (1940) and *Banjo Eyes* (1941), Johnson was featured opposite ETHEL MERMAN in *SOMETHING FOR THE BOYS* (1943) and played the leading role in the early Lerner and Loewe musical *The Day Before Spring* (1945). He fared better in London, where he played Frank Butler in *ANNIE GET YOUR GUN* in 1947 and Fred Graham / Petruchio in *KISS ME, KATE* in 1951. It looked like his big break finally came when he was cast as the philosophical marine biologist Doc in Rodgers and Hammerstein's *PIPE DREAM* (1955), but the musical had a short run and Johnson died two years later in an automobile accident.

JOHNSON, CHIC. See OLSEN and JOHNSON

JOHNSON, [Charles] **VAN** (1916–). Film, stage, and television performer. The handsome heartthrob of bobby-soxers in the 1940s for his boyish good looks and appearances in so many musicals, he was dubbed the voiceless FRANK SINATRA. Johnson was born in Newport, Rhode Island, the son of a plumber, and sang and danced in the chorus in summer stock before making his Broadway debut in *NEW FACES OF 1936*. He was one of the college students in *TOO MANY GIRLS* (1939) and then was hired as the understudy to GENE KELLY in *PAL JOEY* (1940). That same year Johnson made his film debut in the screen version of *Too Many Girls*. Although it was not a very large part, moviegoers demanded to see more of the sandy-haired boy-next-door type. He got the leading role in *TWO GIRLS AND A SAILOR* (1944) and remained a star for decades. Although he was given some demanding acting roles in nonmusicals, Johnson usually played the affable nice guy in light comedies and musicals, such as *Thrill of a Romance* (1945), *Easy to Wed* (1946), *No Leave, No Love* (1946), *TILL THE CLOUDS ROLL BY* (1946), *IN THE GOOD OLD SUMMERTIME* (1949), *The Duchess of Idaho* (1950), *Grounds for Marriage* (1950), *Easy to Love* (1953), *BRIGADOON* (1955), and *Kelly and Me* (1957). Johnson has made many television appearances, including the TV musical *THE PIED PIPER OF HAMELIN* (1957), and returned to Broadway in some comedies and as replacements in the musicals *ON A CLEAR DAY YOU CAN*

SEE FOREVER in 1966 and LA CAGE AUX FOLLES in 1987. Autobiography: *The Luckiest Guy in the World* (1947); biography: *Van Johnson: MGM's Golden Boy*, Ronald L. Davis (2001).

JOHNSTON, ARTHUR [James] (1898–1954). Film and theatre composer. A prominent Tin Pan Alley songwriter, he scored a dozen Hollywood musicals, mostly with lyricist SAM COSLOW. The native New Yorker played piano and plugged tunes by others before he saw his songs published. He made his Broadway debut with his score for *Dixie to Broadway* (1924) and then did vocal arrangements for *ROSALIE* (1928) and *Hello, Daddy* (1928) before going to Hollywood. Johnston composed soundtrack music for some early nonmusical talkies and then teamed with Coslow to write the songs for the screen musicals *Hello, Everybody* (1933), *College Humor* (1933), *Too Much Harmony* (1933), *Murder at the Vanities* (1934), *Many Happy Returns* (1934), and *Belle of the Nineties* (1934). With lyricist GUS KAHN he scored *The Girl Friend* (1935) and *THANKS A MILLION* (1935), and with JOHNNY BURKE he wrote the songs for *Go West Young Man* (1936), *Pennies From Heaven* (1936), and *DOUBLE OR NOTHING* (1937). Among Johnston's hit songs are "Cocktails for Two," "Pennies From Heaven," "My Old Flame," and "Just One More Chance."

JOHNSTON, JOHNNY (1915–1996). Stage and film performer. A popular radio, band, and nightclub crooner, he sang in some 1940s Hollywood musicals and a few Broadway shows. Johnston was born in St. Louis and began his career playing the guitar and singing in saloons and cabarets. He later found recognition on the radio and became a favorite in swanky nightclubs, also appearing on Broadway in the musical *Roll, Sweet Chariot* (1934). Johnston made his film debut in the musical *Sweater Girl* (1942) and was featured in *Priorities on Parade* (1942) but found more notoriety when he introduced "That Old Black Magic" in *STAR-SPANGLED RHYTHM* (1942). He was also featured in the musicals *You Can't Ration Love* (1944) and *This Time for Keeps* (1946) before going back to clubs and recordings. He returned to Broadway to play the ne'er-do-well Johnny Nolan in *A TREE GROWS IN BROOKLYN* (1951) and made a final film appearance in *Rock Around the Clock* (1956) before moving on to television where he had his own series *Make That Spare* (1960–1964). Johnston was one of the first artists signed by the new Capitol Records and had many best-sellers, including his version of "Laura" that sold over a million copies. He was married to singer–actress KATHRYN GRAYSON for a time.

■ **JOKER IS WILD, THE** (AMBL/Paramount 1957). A downbeat biographical musical about singer-turned-comic Joe E. Lewis, the melodrama with songs afforded FRANK SINATRA one of the best roles of his career. During Prohibition, crooner Lewis (Sinatra) decides to leave one mobster's nightclub to work for a rival hood. In retribution, he is attacked one night by some thugs and his vocal cords are so damaged that he cannot sing again so Lewis becomes a stand-up comic, making jokes about his alcohol and gambling addictions. The Oscar Saul screenplay was terse and matter of fact, and Sinatra, who knew Lewis personally, found a harsh and gritty reality in the character that, although unlikable, was fascinating. EDDIE ALBERT was Austin Mack, Lewis' longtime friend and accompanist, JEANNE CRAIN played the Chicago socialite Letty Page, and MITZI GAYNOR the showgirl Martha Stewart, both of whom Lewis weds and divorces, never willing to give either his love. Ironically, the hit song from the film, JAMES VAN HEUSEN and SAMMY CAHN's "All the Way," was about the kind of affection Lewis was not capable of. Also heard in the movie were "I Cried for You," "At Sundown," and "If I Could Be With You One Hour Tonight." CHARLES VIDOR directed perhaps too well, for the uncomfortable film was not a success at the box office. However, Sinatra got a best-selling record from the experience, and the movie was later reissued as *All the Way* to capitalize on it.

JOLSON, AL [born Asa Yoelson] (1886–1950). Stage and film performer. Arguably the leading entertainer in America during the first half of the twentieth century, the charismatic singer–actor introduced hit songs and memorable moments in different media. Born in present-day Lithuania, the son of a cantor, Jolson was brought to America as a youngster and lived in Washington, DC. He was on stage from childhood, singing in vaudeville and minstrel shows, before making his Broadway bow in 1911 in *La Belle Paree*. Usually appearing in black face and talk-singing his sentimental ballads, Jolson soon became an audience favorite and was featured in a series of popular shows on Broadway, including *The Honeymoon Express* (1913), *Robinson Crusoe, Jr.* (1916), *SINBAD* (1918), *BOMBO* (1921), and *BIG BOY* (1925). He made cinema history when he starred in

THE JAZZ SINGER (1927), the first talkie and
the first screen musical. Other movie musicals
followed, such as THE SINGING FOOL (1928),
Mammy (1930), *Big Boy* (1930), WONDER
BAR (1934), GO INTO YOUR DANCE (1935), *The
Singing Kid* (1936), *Rose of Washington Square*
(1939), and *Swanee River* (1939). Jolson usually
played broad, sentimental characters on the
screen that were just an extension of his stage
persona, yet his performance as the down-and-
out but hopeful Bumper in HALLELUJAH, I'M A
BUM (1933) showed a talent for more subtle
characterization. His other Broadway credits
include *Wonder Bar* (1931) and *Hold Onto Your
Hats* (1940), and he enjoyed renewed popularity with the biopics THE JOLSON STORY (1946)
and *JOLSON SINGS AGAIN* (1949) in which he
provided his singing voice for actor LARRY
PARKS. Jolson remained a potent recording star up to his death. He was married to
singer–dancer RUBY KEELER. Autobiography:
Mistah Jolson (1951); biographies: *Jolson: The
Legend Comes to Life*, Herbert G. Goldman
(1988); *Jolson: The Story of Al Jolson*, Michael
Freedland (1995).

JOLSON SINGS AGAIN.   See JOLSON STORY,
THE

🎬 JOLSON STORY, THE (Columbia 1946). It
may have been filled with clichés and untruths,
but this film was one of the most popular musical biographies ever made and remains a solid
piece of entertainment. LARRY PARKS played
the great entertainer (the sixty-six-year-old
Jolson supplied his singing on the soundtrack),
WILLIAM DEMAREST was Steven Martin, the
man who discovered him, and Evelyn Keyes
was his showgirl wife RUBY KEELER (although
she was called Julie Benson in the movie to keep
ex-wife Keeler from suing). The screenplay by
Stephen Longstreet and Sidney Buchman was
closer to THE JAZZ SINGER (1927) than Jolson's
real story, but that's the way audiences wanted
it. Young Asa Yoelson (Scotty Beckett) runs
away from his home and his cantor father
(Ludwig Donath), changes his name to Jolson,
and becomes a star when he dons blackface and
learns to go down on one knee. He weds Julie
but she yearns for a home life and convinces
him to retire. But the urge to perform is too
great within him and his audience comes first.
The marriage breaks up and Jolson becomes
a bigger star than ever. The real Jolson's ego-
tism came across as enthusiasm and love for
his public in the screen version, and the fading
entertainer found a whole new audience to love

The Jolson Story. The very popular movie
biography not only revived interest in Al Jolson
(his records went to the top of the charts) but it
made a movie star out of Larry Parks, pictured as
Jolson in a production number from the film.
Jolson provided Park's singing voice but it did not
diminish Park's mesmerizing performance.
(Photofest)

him back. Jolson's catalogue of song favorites
was used unsparingly, including "Toot, Toot,
Tootsie," "You Made Me Love You," "Rock-
a-Bye Your Baby With a Dixie Melody," "I'm
Sitting on Top of the World," and "Swanee."
There was only one original number in the
score, "Anniversary Song" by Jolson and
SAUL CHAPLIN based on an old waltz tune,
which Jolson/Parks sang to his parents; the
Jolson recording sold over a million discs.
ALFRED E. GREEN directed, JACK COLE choreographed, and Sidney Skolsky produced
the biography that Buchman had been trying
to get Hollywood to film for several years.
Initial reaction was negative because Jolson
was considered old news. But Harry Cohn at
COLUMBIA held a fondness for Jolson and eventually greenlit the project. *The Jolson Story* was
a surprise hit, bringing in $8 million at the box
office. A sequel was inevitable.
🎬 Jolson Sings Again (Columbia 1949)
was not as accomplished a film as the earlier
biography but was still extremely popular.
Parks again played Jolson (with Jolson again

providing the singing) who, in the screenplay by Buchman again, goes off to entertain troops in World War II. He suffers a physical collapse, is cared for and brought back to health by the nurse Ellen Clark (Barbara Hale) whom he later marries, and makes a big comeback at a Hollywood benefit show. It was no more truthful than the first film, but neither was it as engaging. The musical numbers remained the highlights, repeating some favorites from the first movie and adding plenty more, including "For Me and My Gal," "I'm Looking Over a Four Leaf Clover," "Sonny Boy," "Carolina in the Morning," and "Is It True What They Say About Dixie?" Demarest and Ludwig returned in their old roles, and the cast also featured Myron McCormick, Bill Goodwin, and Tamara Shayne. The most bizarre scene in the movie is when Jolson hears of the film they are making of his life and he goes to meet the actor who will portray him, with Parks playing both roles thanks to double exposure. Buchman produced and HENRY LEVIN directed.

JONES, ALLAN (1907–1992). Stage, film, and television performer. A personable tenor, he made an impressive leading man in several film musicals between 1935 and 1945. Jones was born in Old Forge, Pennsylvania, the son of a coal miner, and worked in the mines himself as a young man. He later studied music at Syracuse University and in Paris and then returned to America where he toured in musicals and made a few appearances in Broadway shows, such as the 1934 revival of BITTER SWEET. Jones made his film debut in *Reckless* (1935) and was noticed for his crooning in the MARX BROTHERS'S *A NIGHT AT THE OPERA* (1935) and *A DAY AT THE RACES* (1937). His most notable musical roles were gambler Gaylord Ravenel in *SHOW BOAT* (1936), the spy Don Diego in *THE FIREFLY* (1937), in which he first sang his signature song, "The Donkey Serenade," and the twin Antipholuses in *THE BOYS FROM SYRACUSE* (1940). Jones' other screen musicals include *Everybody Sing* (1938), *The Great Victor Herbert* (1939), *Honeymoon in Bali* (1939), *ONE NIGHT IN THE TROPICS* (1940), *There's Magic in Music* (1941), *True to the Army* (1942), *Moonlight in Havana* (1942), *When Johnny Comes Marching Home* (1942), *Rhythm of the Islands* (1943), *Sing a Jingle* (1944), and *Honeymoon Ahead* (1945). He returned to Broadway in *Jackpot* (1944) and made a few films in the 1960s, including the musical *A Swingin' Summer* (1965). The rest of his career was spent in concerts and nightclubs, making recordings, and appearing on television specials. He is the father of popular singer Jack Jones (1938–).

JONES, SHIRLEY [Mae] (1934–). Film, stage, and television performer. A popular singer–actress with impressive credits in all media, the attractive blonde embodies the demure musical heroine. Born in Smithton, Pennsylvania, the daughter of a brewer, Jones was named after SHIRLEY TEMPLE. As a girl she started taking singing lessons and won a beauty contest before going to New York to pursue a career on Broadway. Jones appeared as one of the nurses in *SOUTH PACIFIC* (1949), and Rodgers and Hammerstein were so struck with her talent that they signed her to play Laurey in the 1955 screen version of their *Oklahoma!* She was so accomplished in her film debut that Jones went on to play an even more complex heroine, Julie Jordan, in the 1956 screen version of *CAROUSEL*. Her subsequent screen musicals were *April Love* (1957), *Never Steal Anything Small* (1959), and *Pepe* (1960), but only the librarian Marian Paroo in *THE MUSIC MAN* (1962) would offer her much of a challenge. Jones was just as impressive in nonmusical films, particularly in *Elmer Gantry* (1960). She finally made it back to Broadway in *Maggie Flynn* (1968) but it failed to run; she had more luck as a replacement in *42ND STREET* in 2004. Jones was also very successful on television, appearing on many specials, including the TV musical spoof *The Royal Follies of 1933* (1967), and starring in the long-running series *The Partridge Family* in the 1970s. She continues to perform on television, in occasional films, and was on stage as recently as 2007. Jones was married to actor–singer JACK CASSIDY before wedding comedian Marty Engles (1936–), and she is the mother of singer–actors Patrick, David, and Shaun Cassidy. Autobiography (with Engles): *Shirley and Marty: An Unlikely Romance* (2006).

JONES, TOM, AND HARVEY SCHMIDT. Stage songwriting team. Often departing from the norm in their stage projects, the partners created some unique musicals, none more unique and successful than *THE FANTASTICKS* (1960). Lyricist and librettist Tom Jones (1928–) was born in Littlefield, Texas, the son of a turkey farmer, and attended the University of Texas where he studied theatre directing. There he met Harvey Schmidt (1929–), an art major from Dallas who played piano by ear, and they collaborated on some student shows before heading to New York where they contributed songs to Julius Monk's Off Broadway revues. The young partners wrote a one-act version of THE FANTASTICKS for a summer program and when they expanded it and presented the musical Off Broadway in 1960, the intimate, small-scale show slowly caught on and became an American institution, running forty-three years. Jones and Schmidt were wooed by Broadway and provided expert but traditional scores for *110 IN THE SHADE* (1963) and *I DO! I DO!* (1966) and a more innovative score for the ritualistic *CELEBRATION* (1969). The twosome then returned to Off Broadway, founded the Portofino Theatre Workshop, and experimented on small, innovative pieces, most memorably *Philemon* (1975). Other works have premiered regionally and have not come to New York except the Off Broadway entry *Roadside* (2002). In 1997 the two songwriters appeared in a popular retrospective revue called *The Show Goes On*. The scores by Jones and Schmidt are highly lyrical, often very simple in melody, and usually poetic and sincere in the lyrics.

JOSEPH AND THE AMAZING TECHNICOLOR DREAMCOAT (Royale Theatre 1982).

Fourteen years elapsed from its initial presentation in a London school to its appearance on Broadway, but by that time many Americans knew the musical well from the many amateur productions across the country. Biblical Joseph, the favorite son of Jacob, is sold by his jealous brothers into slavery and is taken to Egypt. Imprisoned for being falsely accused of trying to seduce the wife of the pyramid builder Potiphar, Joseph reveals a talent for interpreting dreams and when he explains a puzzling dream that the Pharaoh has been having, Joseph rises in stature and becomes Pharaoh's right-hand man. A famine torments the land and Joseph's brothers come to Egypt where he tests them and then forgives them. The original 1968 cantata that ANDREW LLOYD WEBBER (music) and TIM RICE (lyric) wrote was only twenty minutes long and over the years songs have been added to fill out the story and make it a full

(if still short) evening's entertainment. The tuneful score consists of serious ballads and clever pastiche numbers. "Any Dream Will Do," "Close Every Door," "Those Canaan Days," "Jacob and Sons," and "One More Angel in Heaven" were among the notable songs. The colorful, joyous 1982 production, directed and choreographed by Tony Tanner, originated Off Broadway and was so successful that it transferred to Broadway where it stayed for 747 performances. Michael Damian was featured as Joseph in a slick 1993 revival directed by Steven Pimlot. Notices were unenthusiastic but audience response was healthy enough to run 231 performances. Also in the cast were Kelli Rabke (Narrator), Robert Torti (Pharaoh), and Clifford David (Potiphar). The musical remains a favorite in schools and summer stock.

❏ While Hollywood never attempted to film *Joseph and the Amazing Technicolor Dreamcoat*, television was not so shy. Webber himself produced and directed a 1991 British TV version starring pop star Jason Donovan as Joseph. Also British was a very colorful and lavish 1999 production with an impressive cast led by pop favorite Donny Osmond. Even the minor roles, such as Jacob, the butler, and Potiphar's wife, were played by stars Richard Attenborough, Alex Jennings, and Joan Collins, respectively. A 2000 television version from New Zealand featured Jerome Winterburn and included a large children's chorus in the production.

JOURNEY BACK TO OZ (Warner 1974).

Lacking the original's imagination, wit, and sense of magic, this animated sequel to *THE WIZARD OF OZ* (1939) was chock full of top talent for the voices, all of whom deserved better material. Fred Ladd and Norm Prescott wrote the screenplay in which another twister knocks Dorothy (voice of LIZA MINNELLI) unconscious and she wakes up in Oz where Witch Mombi (ETHEL MERMAN) is trying to conquer the Emerald City with the help of giant green elephants that she conjures up out of a brew.

Casts for *Joseph and the Amazing Technicolor Dreamcoat*

Character	1982 Broadway	1991 television	1999 television	2000 television
Joseph	Bill Hutton	Jason Donovan	Donny Osmond	Jerome Winterburn
Narrator	Laurie Beechman	Linzi Harely	Maria Friedman	Keri Harper
Pharaoh	Tom Cader	David Easter	Robert Torti	Shane Cortese
Potiphar	David Ardeo	Aubrey Woods	Ian McNeice	David Dougherty

The witch's slave Pumpkinhead (Paul Lynde) helps Dorothy warn the Scarecrow (MICKEY ROONEY), who is now king of Oz , and the Lion (MILTON BERLE) and Tin Man (DANNY THOMAS) try to help but it is Dorothy, Pumpkinhead, and the carousel horse Woodenhead (Herschel Bernardi) who save the land. Other voices heard included RISË STEVENS, Paul Ford, Jack E. Leonard, Mel Blanc, Larry Storch, and MARGARET HAMILTON who was Aunt Em this time around. The animation was flat and uninspired, and the direction by Hal Sutherland was pedestrian at best. The score by JIMMY VAN HEUSEN (music) and SAMMY CAHN (lyrics) included the lovely ballads "There's a Far Away Land" and "That Feeling of Home" for Minnelli, the encouraging "You Have Only You" for Stevens as Glinda, and the riotous "Be a Witch" for Merman. The film was made in 1962 by the Filmation Company but was not released until a dozen years later by WARNER BROTHERS without much hoopla. With such talent in the cast, the musical is a major disappointment and one can only imagine what a wonderful movie it could have been.

JOY OF LIVING (RKO 1938). A screwball comedy with music, the film suffered from a weak plot but was saved by a strong score and fine performances. Broadway star Maggie Garret (IRENE DUNNE) is too uptight to enjoy life, although her wacky relatives and other parasites are sure having a great time. It takes the Boston banking heir Dan Brewster (Douglas Fairbanks, Jr.) to teach Maggie to live by doing Donald Duck impersonations, taking her to a beer hall and a skating rink, and whisking her off to a South Seas island. JEROME KERN (music) and DOROTHY FIELDS (lyrics) wrote the songs, the best three being the swinging lullaby "You Couldn't Be Cuter," the farewell ballad "What's Good About Goodnight?," and the flowing "Just Let Me Look at You," which was used throughout the film as a leitmotif. The supporting cast reads like a who's who of favorite Hollywood character actors: GUY KIBBEE, LUCILLE BALL, ALICE BRADY, ERIC BLORE, BILLY GILBERT, FRANKLIN PANGBORN, MISCHA AUER, FUZZY KNIGHT, Jean Dixon, and Warren Hymer. They all deserved a better script than the one producer–director Tay Garnett offered them.

JUBILEE (Imperial Theatre 1935). While it may have been one of COLE PORTER's less successful Broadway entries, it boasted a superior cast and some unforgettable songs. The royal family of a fictional European nation is restless and bored with court life. The threat of a rebellion allows the King (Melville Cooper), Queen (MARY BOLAND), Prince James (CHARLES WALTERS), and Princess Diana (Margaret Adams) to sneak out of the palace and have some incognito fun, such as the King indulging in parlor games, the Queen palling around with the ape man Mowgli (Mark Plant) from the movies, and their children indulging in romance. The revolt doesn't happen, the royals are recognized, and everyone returns to their old ways. Also cast were JUNE KNIGHT, Derek Williams, Olive Reeves-Smith, Montgomery Clift, Jackie Kelk, and May Boley. MOSS HART wrote the risible libretto and the players all shone in it, just as they did performing such Porter gems as "Begine the Beguine," "Just One of Those Things," "Why Shouldn't I?," "A Picture of Me Without You," "The Kling-Kling Bird on the Divi-Divi Tree," and "When Love Comes Your Way." Notices were favorable but the musical was too sophisticated and filled with too many in-jokes to appeal to the public so it ran only 169 performances. MAX GORDON produced, HASSARD SHORT and MONTY WOOLLEY co-directed, and ALBERTINA RASCH choreographed, all of them in top form.

JULIA, RAUL [born Raul Rafael Carlos Julia y Arcelay] (1940–1994). Stage, film, and television performer. The robust, masculine leading man in musicals and plays, he exuded a sensuous, dangerous quality even in his comic roles. Julia was born in San Juan, Puerto Rico, and educated at the University of Puerto Rico before studying acting in New York. He made his Manhattan debut in a Spanish-language production Off Broadway in 1964 and then toured the boroughs with the NEW YORK SHAKESPEARE FESTIVAL's mobile unit. Julia was long associated with that organization, playing Shakespeare roles in Central Park where he first got recognition as Proteus in the musical *TWO GENTLEMEN OF VERONA* (1971). His other musical success for producer JOE PAPP and the Festival was Macheath in the revival of *THE THREEPENNY OPERA* (1977), which he reprised in the film *Mack the Knife* (1989). Julia's New York musical credits also include leading roles in *YOUR OWN THING* (1968), *THE ROBBER BRIDEGROOM* (1974), *WHERE'S CHARLEY?* (1974), *NINE* (1982), and *MAN OF LA MANCHA* (1992). He made a number of diverse films, ranging from the tragic *The Kiss of the Spider Woman* (1985) to the satirical *The Addams Family* (1991), and appeared in many television programs before his premature death from a stroke at the age of fifty-three.

🎭 **JUMBO** (Hippodrome Theatre 1935). A "musical extravaganza" that filled the large venue with circus acts and RICHARD RODGERS (music) and LORENZ HART (lyrics) songs, the show was one of the most fondly remembered in the history of the 45,000-seat Hippodrome. Rival circus owners Matthew Mulligan and John A. Considine have always been suspicious of each other so neither is especially happy when Considine's daughter Mickey and Mulligan's son Matt fall in love. Considine already has enough problems, such as his drinking and the bankruptcy his circus is facing. His ambitious but inept press agent, Claudius B. Bowers, tries to fix things by burning down Considine's house to collect the insurance. The two lovers solve everything by merging the two circuses into one and securing peace and prosperity. Ben Hecht and Charles MacArthur wrote the libretto, leaving room for circus acts, and producer BILLY ROSE had designer Albert Johnson turn the space into a gigantic circus tent where acrobats, jugglers, trapeze artists, and animal acts were featured. The extravaganza was declared a circus rather than a musical by Actors' Equity and audiences were inclined to agree. However, the human performances were lauded (JIMMY DURANTE's was the star turn) and the Rodgers and Hart score produced three standards, "My Romance," "Little Girl Blue," and "The Most Beautiful Girl in the World," as well as "The Circus Is on Parade," "Laugh," and "Over and Over Again." PAUL WHITEMAN and his orchestra provided the music, parading into the "tent" circus style, and the complicated production was held together by the ingenious direction of JOHN MURRAY ANDERSON and, in his first staging of a book musical, GEORGE ABBOTT. Reviews were complimentary and business was brisk for over seven months, but the expensive production could never recoup its costs and closed in the red after 233 performances.

🎬 ***Billy Rose's Jumbo*** (MGM 1962) was made twenty-seven years after the stage production. Why it took Hollywood so long is curious, since the scale of the story cried out for the big screen. In the screenplay by Sidney Sheldon, Durante was Pop Wonder, one of the two rival circus proprietors, and it was the fight over the elephant Jumbo that propelled the plot. DORIS DAY and Stephen Boyd (dubbed by James Joyce) played the lovers with Dean Jagger as Durante's rival and MARTHA RAYE as Pop's love interest, Lulu. Some of the Rodgers and Hart score was dropped, two familiar songs by the team ("This Can't Be Love" and "Why Can't I?") were interpolated, and ROGER EDENS wrote a new finale number, "Sawdust, Spangles and Dreams." Although the golden age of movie musicals was over by 1962, there was much in *Jumbo* that was old-fashioned fun, such as BUSBY BERKELEY's choreography in his forty-second and last film. Billy Rose had nothing to do with the movie, but MGM titled it *Billy Rose's Jumbo* for those old enough to recall the Hippodrome spectacular. CHARLES WALTERS directed the Martin Melcher–JOE PASTERNAK production, which did impressive business, probably due to the popularity of Doris Day at the time.

🎬 **JUNGLE BOOK, THE** (Disney 1967). The last animated film that WALT DISNEY produced, it is one of the most musical of all his features, with the songs by Terry Gilkyson and RICHARD M. and ROBERT B. SHERMAN becoming the movie's highlights instead of pleasant diversions along the way. Larry Clemmons, Ralph Wright, Ken Anderson, and Vance Gerry adapted Rudyard Kipling's Mowgli stories into a simple tale of the "man-cub" Mowgli (voice of Bruce Reitherman) who is orphaned

---

Casts for *Jumbo*

Character	1935 Broadway	1962 film
Mickey/Kitty	Gloria Grafton	DORIS DAY
Matt Jr./Sam	Donald Novis	Stephan Boyd
Claudius B. Bowers	JIMMY DURANTE	
Matt Mulligan	W. J. McCarthy	
John A. Considine	Arthur Sinclair	
Pop Wonder		Jimmy Durante
Lulu		MARTHA RAYE
John Noble		Dean Jagger

in the jungles of India and raised by the panther Bagheera (Sebastian Cabot). When the deadly tiger Shere Kahn (George Sanders) returns to the area, Bagheera convinces Baloo the Bear (PHIL HARRIS) to escort the boy to the "man-village." The journey is merrily interrupted by wonderful vaudeville turns, such as Baloo cutting loose with "The Bear Necessities" and King Louis of the Apes (Louis Prima) going wild with "I Wanna Be Like You." J. Pat O'Malley, STERLING HOLLOWAY, Verna Felton, Chad Stuart, Lord Tim Abbott, Clint Howard, and Ben Wright also loaned their voices for such numbers as the brusque "Colonel Hati's March," the slithering "Trust in Me," and the harmonizing "That's What Friends Are For." Directed by Wolfgang Reitherman, it was also one of the most artistic of Disney's later efforts, richly illustrated and beautifully animated.

○ JUNIOR MISS (CBS-TV 1957). Having been a best-selling book by Sally Benson, a Broadway comedy hit in 1941, and a film in 1945, this musical version on the DU PONT SHOW OF THE MONTH held few surprises but the tried-and-true plot still entertained and there were some commendable songs by BURTON LANE (music) and DOROTHY FIELDS (lyrics) to add some flavor. JOSEPH STEIN and Will Glickman wrote the teleplay in which teenager Judy Graves (Carol Lynley) and her friend Fluffy Adams (Diana Lynn) come to the ill-formed conclusion that Judy's father (DON AMECHE) is having an affair and they try to correct matters, only making things worse. The top-notch supporting cast included Joan Bennett, Jill St. John, DAVID WAYNE, Paul Ford, and Suzanne Sidney. The songs "A Man Is an Animal," "Have Feet–Will Dance," "I'll Buy It," "Let's Make It Christmas All Year Round," "Happy Heart," and the title number reflected the slaphappy nature of the piece. RICHARD LEWINE produced and Ralph Nelson directed.

🎵 JUNO (Winter Garden Theatre 1959). An ambitious, beautifully scored musical drama, it could not survive its negative reviews and closed after only sixteen performances. JOSEPH STEIN wrote the libretto and MARC BLITZSTEIN the score for this musicalization of Sean O'Casey's classic drama *Juno and the Paycock* (1926) and it was done with taste and talent and was performed by a superlative cast. SHIRLEY BOOTH did not get to display her comic gifts as the troubled Juno but she proved to be an adroit actress. Melvyn Douglas was her shiftless husband Jack Boyle, Jack MacGowran was his drinking comrade Joxer, Monte Amundsen was the pregnant daughter Mary, and TOMMY RALL was the tragic son Johnny. Also in the strong ensemble cast were Nancy Andrews, JEAN STAPLETON, Sada Thompson, and Earl Hammond, all under the direction of JOSÉ FERRER. The expert songs included "Bird Upon the Tree," "One Kind Word," "I Wish It So," "We're Alive," and "My True Heart." One of the most impressive aspects of the ambitious musical was AGNES DE MILLE's emotional choreography. Some aisle sitters found the musical more grim than the original play, which had been laced with Irish humor at times, but the piece and its estimable score would later be better appreciated in opera houses.

K

KAHN, GUS [born Gustave Gerson Kahn] (1886–1941). Film and stage lyricist. One of Tin Pan Alley's greatest songwriters, he also contributed scores to over a dozen Hollywood musicals even as he continued to turn out hit songs on the Alley. Kahn was born in Koblenz, Germany, and his family emigrated to American when he was four, settling in Chicago. He began writing specialty numbers for vaudeville acts and then turned to Tin Pan Alley where his single songs started selling. Some of his lyrics were heard in the Broadway musicals *Jumping Jupiter* (1911), *THE PASSING SHOW* (1916), and *SINBAD* (1918) and then he got to score *Holka Polka* (1925) and *Kitty's Kisses* (1926). Kahn's only Broadway hit was *WHOOPEE!* (1928) with composer WALTER DONALDSON, although his very popular song "Liza" came from *Show Girl* (1929) written with the GERSHWIN brothers. The 1930 film version of *Whoopee!* brought Kahn to Hollywood for the first time and he returned to score such musicals as *FLYING DOWN TO RIO* (1933), *Caravan* (1934), *KID MILLIONS* (1934), *Operator 13* (1934), *The Girl Friend* (1935), *THANKS A MILLION* (1935), *Three Smart Girls* (1937), *A DAY AT THE RACES* (1937), *Everybody Sing* (1938), *Honolulu* (1939), *Broadway Serenade* (1939), *Spring Parade* (1940), and *Go West* (1940). Among his composer collaborators were VINCENT YOUMANS, ARTHUR JOHNSTON, Bronislaw Kaper, and Walter Jurmann, and his many song hits include "Ain't We Got Fun?," "Toot Toot Tootsie," "Carolina in the Morning," "Yes, Sir, That's My Baby," "Love Me or Leave Me," and "It Had to Be You." It is estimated that a Kahn song has been used in over 250 movies over the years. DANNY THOMAS portrayed Kahn in the Hollywood biomusical *I'll See You in My Dreams* (1951).

KAHN, MADELINE [born Madeline Gail Wolfson] (1942–1999). Stage, television, and film performer. The bold, offbeat comedienne had a multi-range singing voice; she also had dozens of funny character voices. A native of Boston, Kahn was educated at Hofstra University as a speech therapist but she also trained for an opera career. After singing in nightclubs and appearing in the chorus of *KISS ME, KATE* (1965), she honed her skills in the Off Broadway musical revues *Just for Openers* (1965), *Mixed Doubles* (1966), and *Below the Belt* (1966) before getting attention on Broadway in *NEW FACES OF 1968*. She also shone in the musicals *Promenade* (1969) and *TWO BY TWO* (1970) but did not achieve stardom until such 1970s movies as *Paper Moon* (1973) and *Young Frankenstein* (1974). Kahn returned to Broadway a star in 1978 and gave a stellar performance as film idol Lily Garland in the musical *ON THE TWENTIETH CENTURY*. She had her own television series in the 1980s and appeared on many other programs and then made two triumphal returns to the nonmusical Broadway stage with *Born Yesterday* (1989) and *The Sisters Rosensweig* (1992) before her premature death from cancer at the age of fifty-seven. Although Kahn made no movie musicals except the filmed revue *Scrambled Feet* (1983), she got to sing a song or two in a number of her movie comedies.

KALMAR, BERT, AND HARRY RUBY. Stage and film songwriting team. With Kalmar providing the lyrics, Ruby composing the music, and both often writing the libretto, the two offered some delightful, lighthearted musicals on Broadway and in Hollywood. [Al]Bert Kalmar (1884–1947) was born in New York and began in show business as a child musician and then as a comedian in vaudeville. He graduated to the legitimate stage early in the new century and even appeared on Broadway in *Li'l Mose* (1908) before turning to songwriting. Harry Ruby [born Harry Rubinstein] (1895–1974) was also a native New Yorker who played piano in vaudeville and then took up songwriting. The two men teamed up for the Broadway musical *Helen of Troy* (1923) and then went on to score *No Other Girl* (1924), *The Ramblers* (1926), *The Five O'Clock Girl* (1927), *ANIMAL CRACKERS* (1928), *Top Speed* (1929), and *High Kickers* (1941), sometimes writing the scripts as well. The two also penned the librettos for others' musicals, such as *Holka Polka* (1925) and *She's My Baby* (1928), and Kalmar collaborated with JEROME KERN on *Lucky* (1927) and with HERBERT STOTHART on *Good Boy* (1928). In addition to the screen versions of some of their Broadway hits, Kalmar and Ruby also wrote original scores for the film musicals *Check and Double Check* (1930), *HORSE FEATHERS* (1932), *The Kid From Spain* (1932), *DUCK SOUP* (1933), *Hips Hips Hooray* (1934), *Walking on Air* (1936), and *Everybody Sing* (1938). The twosome's many hit songs include "Who's Sorry Now?," "Three Little Words," "I Wanna Be Loved By You," and "A Kiss to Build a Dream On." FRED ASTAIRE (Kalmar) and RED SKELTON (Ruby) portrayed the songwriters in the Hollywood biomusical *THREE LITTLE WORDS* (1950).

KANDER, JOHN, AND FRED EBB. Stage and film songwriting team. One of the longest, closest, and most dazzling of Broadway duos, the two songwriters offered everything from escapist musical comedy to dark and haunting musical drama. John [Harold] Kander (1927–) was born in Kansas City, Missouri, and studied at Oberlin College and Columbia University before working as a music director in summer theatres and orchestrating scores on Broadway. He got to hear his own songs on Broadway with *A Family Affair* (1962) with lyricist–librettists William and James Goldman. Fred Ebb (1928–2004) was a native New Yorker who was educated at Columbia and contributed lyrics to some Broadway revues, such as *From A to Z* (1960). Kander and Ebb met in 1962 and collaborated on some songs for recording stars, most memorably Barbra Streisand and "My Coloring Book." The star they would be most associated with over the decades was LIZA MINNELLI who made her Broadway debut in the team's first musical together, *FLORA, THE RED MENACE* (1965). The twosome's subsequent Broadway shows varied in subject matter, tone, and success, yet there was always something distinctive and high quality about their scores for *CABARET* (1966), *THE HAPPY TIME* (1968), *ZORBA* (1968), *70, GIRLS, 70* (1971), *CHICAGO* (1975), *THE ACT* (1977), *WOMAN OF THE YEAR* (1981), *THE RINK* (1984), *KISS OF THE SPIDER WOMAN* (1993), *Steel Pier* (1997), and *CURTAINS* (2007), which opened three years after Ebb had died. Other stage musicals by the team, such as *The Visit* and *Over and Over*, have been produced regionally and may yet arrive on Broadway. Kander and Ebb also had an impressive Hollywood career. Their only stage works to be filmed were *Cabaret* (1972) and *Chicago* (2002), for which they wrote some new songs, and the team created originals songs for *FUNNY LADY* (1975), *A Matter of Time* (1976), and *NEW YORK, NEW YORK* (1977). They also scored the TV musicals *Three for the Girls* (1973) and *Sam Found Out* (1988). Kander has written theme music for films and television dramas. Autobiography: *Colored Lights* [by both] (2004).

KANE, HELEN [born Helen Schroeder] (1904–1966). Stage, film, and television performer. A popular singer–dancer across the country because of her many vaudeville appearances in the 1920s, she possessed a squeaky baby voice and a round, dimpled face that lit up a few Broadway and Hollywood musicals. Kane was born in the Bronx and as a teenager went into variety, working with the MARX BROTHERS for a while. She made a rousing Broadway debut on Broadway in *A Night in Spain* (1927) and had a bigger hit the next year in *Good Boy* in which she sang "I Wanna Be Loved By You," the number that became her theme song. Because of the squealing phrase she inserted into the song, Kane became known as the "Boop-Boop-a-Doop" girl. Her voice and look inspired the Max Fleishman cartoon character Betty Boop, and at the height of her popularity there were Betty Boop dolls and look-alike contests. Kane was featured in five early screen musicals, *Sweetie* (1929), *Pointed Heels* (1929), *PARAMOUNT ON PARADE* (1939), *HEADS UP!* (1930), and *Dangerous Dan McGrew* (1930), and then made a final Broadway appearance in *Shady Lady* (1933). When her popularity waned in the late 1930s she retired, although she made a few television appearances in the 1950s. DEBBIE REYNOLDS played Kane in the screen bio *THREE LITTLE WORDS* (1950), although Kane herself provided the singing vocals.

KARNILOVA, MARIA [born Maria Karnilovich Dovgolenka] (1920–2001). Stage and film performer. The sharp-voiced, lively character actress slowly worked her way to top billing over a period of twenty-five years. Karnilova was born in Hartford, Connecticut, and trained for a career in ballet at the Metropolitan Opera School where he had performed as a child. She was later a soloist for the Ballet Theatre and toured internationally before making her Broadway debut in the chorus of *Stars in Your Eyes* (1938). Karnilova was a featured dancer in such musicals as *Hollywood Pinafore* (1945), *CALL ME MISTER* (1946), *MISS LIBERTY* (1949), *OUT OF THIS WORLD* (1950), *Two's Company* (1952), and *THE BEGGAR'S OPERA* (1957) before getting noticed as the stripper Tessie Tura in the original *GYPSY* (1959). Thereafter she played character parts, most memorably the Russian mother Golde in *FIDDLER ON THE ROOF* (1964 and 1981) and the aging courtesan Hortense in *ZORBA* (1968). Her other musical credits include *Bravo Giovanni* (1962), *GIGI* (1973), *Bring Back Birdie* (1981), and *CINDERELLA* (1993) at the New York City Opera in which she played the Queen opposite the King of her husband

GEORGE S. IRVING. Karnilova made only a few appearances on television and in films, although she was featured in THE UNSINKABLE MOLLY BROWN (1964).

KASZNAR, KURT [born Kurt Serwischer] (1913–1979). Stage and film performer. A colorful character actor with a deep, growly voice that never lost its Austrian flavor, he played supporting roles in a few Broadway musicals and in several screen musicals. Born in Vienna, Austria, Kasznar was educated at Minerva University in Zurich before training for the stage with Max Reinhardt. He later performed for Reinhardt, and he first came to America in 1937 as part of the international tour of Reinhardt's company. Kasznar stayed in New York City where he wrote, produced, and acted in plays in the 1940s and then became a favorite supporting player on stage and screen in the 1950s and 1960s. On Broadway he was the Austrian impresario Max in THE SOUND OF MUSIC (1959) and was seen also in the musicals *The Eternal Road* (1937), *Crazy With the Heat* (1941), and *Seventh Heaven* (1955). On screen Kasznar appeared in the musicals LOVELY TO LOOK AT (1952), LILI (1953), KISS ME, KATE (1953), GIVE A GIRL A BREAK (1953), MY SISTER EILEEN (1955), and ANYTHING GOES (1956), as well as in the TV musicals ANDROCLES AND THE LION (1967) and *The Royal Follies of 1933* (1967).

KAUFMAN, GEORGE S[imon]. (1889–1961). Stage and film writer and director. The celebrated comic playwright and social curmudgeon wrote and directed several important musicals. Kaufman was born in Pittsburgh, the son of an unsuccessful businessman, and attended Western University of Pennsylvania (today the University of Pittsburgh) for a time before going into journalism. After working for a newspaper in Washington, DC, he went to New York where he took theatre classes at Columbia University and wrote theatre reviews, later becoming the drama critic for the *New York Times*. He gave up this position in 1930 because his playwriting career was blossoming, writing hit comedies with Marc Connelly, Edna Ferber, and others. Although he had unofficially taken on the direction of some of his own plays, it was Kaufman's inventive and razor-sharp staging of *The Front Page* in 1928 that proved him to be a commendable director of others' works as well. In 1930 he collaborated with playwright MOSS HART for the first time, and their hit farce *Once in a Lifetime* was the first of several popular plays

together. In 1931 Kaufman co-wrote and staged the landmark musical satire OF THEE I SING. He also wrote and directed LET 'EM EAT CAKE (1933), I'D RATHER BE RIGHT (1937), *Hollywood Pinafore* (1945), and *Park Avenue* (1946). Other musicals for which Kaufman contributed to the script include *Helen of Troy, New York* (1923), *Be Yourself!* (1924), THE COCOANUTS (1925), ANIMAL CRACKERS (1928), STRIKE UP THE BAND (1930), *Sing Out the News* (1938), and SILK STOCKINGS (1955). He also directed musicals by others, such as FACE THE MUSIC (1932) and GUYS AND DOLLS (1950). Biographies: *George S. Kaufman*, Rhoda-Gale Pollack (1988); *George S. Kaufman: His Life, His Theatre*, Malcolm Goldstein (1979); *George S. Kaufman and His Friends*, Scott Meredith (1974); *George S. Kaufman: An Intimate Portrait*, Howard Teichmann (1973).

KAY, HERSHY (1919–1981). Stage orchestrator. A prominent arranger and orchestrator of musicals, he was much sought after in the 1940s through the 1970s for his superb musical artistry. Kay was born in Philadelphia and educated at the Curtis Institute of Music where he was a classmate of LEONARD BERNSTEIN. He made his Broadway debut working with Bernstein on the orchestrations for the composer's first show ON THE TOWN (1944). Kay would also arrange Bernstein's PETER PAN (1950), CANDIDE (1956), and *1600 PENNSYLVANIA AVENUE* (1976), as well as such diverse musicals as THE GOLDEN APPLE (1954), JUNO (1959), ONCE UPON A MATTRESS (1959), 110 IN THE SHADE (1963), *Drat! The Cat!* (1965), A CHORUS LINE (1975), ON THE TWENTIETH CENTURY (1978), EVITA (1979), and BARNUM (1980). Kay also orchestrated classical and popular music into concert pieces, such as his celebrated Sousa medley for the Boston Pops.

KAYE, DANNY [born David Daniel Kominsky] (1913–1987). Film, stage, and television performer. A popular comic actor–singer–dancer who was as limber with his tongue as with the rest of his body, he triumphed in all media and entertained several generations of audiences. A native of Brooklyn and the son of a tailor, Kaye left school as a teenager to perform as a comic in "Borscht Belt" nightclubs and then in vaudeville. After appearing in some film shorts, he made his Broadway debut in *The Straw Hat Revue* (1939) and then found fame as the fast-talking art director Russell Paxton in LADY IN THE DARK (1941) where he rattled off the names of dozens of Russian composers in the show-stopping number "Tchaikovsky."

He starred in *LET'S FACE IT!* (1941) and then was off to Hollywood where he shone in some twenty films, most of them catering to his special talents for clowning, comic dancing, and vocal pyrotechnics. Among his noteworthy movies were *UP IN ARMS* (1944), *Wonder Man* (1945), *The Kid From Brooklyn* (1946), *The Secret Life of Walter Mitty* (1947), *A Song Is Born* (1948), *The Inspector General* (1949), *ON THE RIVIERA* (1951), *HANS CHRISTIAN ANDERSEN* (1952), *WHITE CHRISTMAS* (1954), *THE COURT JESTER* (1956), *Merry Andrew* (1958), and *THE FIVE PENNIES* (1959). In the 1960s, Kaye was occupied mostly with concert tours and then he returned to Broadway after a thirty-year absence to play Noah in the Biblical musical comedy *TWO BY TWO* (1970). A frequent performer on television, he played Captain Hook in the TV musical *PETER PAN* (1976) and Gepetto in the musical version of *PINOCCHIO* (1976), as well as the voices for animated musicals. His final years were busy with charitable causes and benefit performances. Kaye was married to songwriter Sylvia Fine (1913–1991) who often wrote special material for him. Biography: *Nobody's Fool: The Lives of Danny Kaye*, Martin Gottfried (1994).

KAYE, JUDY (1948–). Stage performer. The short, dark-haired, powerful-voiced singer–actress of Broadway musicals has also performed opera and in concert with renowned symphonies. Born in Phoenix, Arizona, and educated at the University of California at Los Angeles and Arizona State, Kaye worked in stock in California before making her Broadway debut in 1977 as a replacement for Rizzo in *GREASE*. She became famous the next year when she moved from a minor role in *ON THE TWENTIETH CENTURY* to the leading lady Lily Garland when star MADELINE KAHN suddenly left the musical. Kahn's other notable musical roles include the temperamental opera singer Carlotta in *THE PHANTOM OF THE OPERA* (1987), labor organizer Babe in the 1989 revival of *THE PAJAMA GAME*, the anarchist Emma Goldman in *RAGTIME* (1998), the former pop singer Rosie in *MAMMA MIA* (2002), and the untalented opera diva Florence Foster Jenkins in *Souvenir* (2005). Her other musical credits include *Oh, Brother!* (1981), *The Moony Shapiro Songbook* (1981), *Love* (1984), and its revised version *What About Luv?* (1991). In 2007 Kaye played Mrs. Lovett in a national tour of *SWEENEY TODD*.

KAYE, STUBBY [born Bernard Kotzin] (1918–1997). Stage, film, and television performer.

The short, rotund character actor–singer was a favorite on Broadway for lighting up the stage in supporting roles. A native New Yorker, Kaye launched his career in 1939 when he won a talent contest on the radio show *Major Bowes Amateur Hour*. He made his London debut in 1942 as a member of a USO show and an auspicious Broadway debut as Nicely-Nicely Johnson in *GUYS AND DOLLS* (1950), stopping the show with his rousing rendition of "Sit Down, You're Rockin' the Boat." Kaye was also a hit as Marryin' Sam in *L'IL ABNER* (1966) and he got to reprise both roles on screen. He returned to Broadway to play the coach Pooch in *GOOD NEWS!* (1974) and as the seedy burlesque comic Gus in *Grind* (1985). Kaye was very active in touring shows and concerts but also made some films, getting to sing in *Cat Ballou* (1965) and *SWEET CHARITY* (1969). He appeared on many television shows, had his own children's show on the tube in the 1960s, and was in the original TV musicals *PINOCCHIO* (1957), *HANSEL AND GRETEL* (1958), and *SO HELP ME, APHRODITE* (1960).

KEARNS, ALLEN (1893–1956). Stage performer. A reliable leading man in Broadway and London musicals, he played juvenile roles for nearly thirty years. Born in Brockville, Ontario, Canada, Kearns was on stage as a boy, appearing in Gus Edwards's kiddie act in vaudeville, and when he was still a teenager made his Broadway debut in the chorus of *Tillie's Nightmare* (1910). He graduated to small but noticeable roles in such musicals as *The Red Petticoat* (1912), *Miss Daisy* (1914), *Good Morning, Judge* (1919), *Tickle Me* (1920), *Tangerine* (1921), *Little Jessie James* (1923), and *Mercenary Mary* (1925) and then was cast in the leading role of the glue millionaire Steve Barton in the GERSHWINS'S *TIP-TOES* (1925), a part he reprised in London the next year. Kearns's other major musical roles were also in Gershwin musicals: the aviator Peter Thurston in *FUNNY FACE* (1927) and the playboy Danny Churchill in *GIRL CRAZY* (1930). His youthful looks allowed him to play the young beau into his late forties, starring in such musicals as *Here's Howe* (1928) and *Hello, Daddy* (1928), and the London shows *Castles in the Air* (1927), *Up With the Lark* (1927), and *Love Laughs* (1935). Kearns acted in a few early talkies and did plays on Broadway and stock until the late 1940s.

KEEL, HOWARD [born Harold Clifford Leek] (1919–2004). Film, stage, and television performer. A stalwart, full-voiced baritone, he played the virile leading man in many Hollywood musicals. Keel was born in Gillespie, Illinois, and grew up in California where he later worked as an aircraft salesman. He started singing in clubs and at aircraft sales conventions, and eventually went professional and performed in California stock theatres. Keel made his Broadway debut as a replacement for Billy Bigelow in *Carousel* in 1945 and reprised the role in a 1957 Broadway revival. In 1946 he took over the role of Curly in *Oklahoma!* on Broadway, played it in the original 1947 London production, and repeated his performance on tour. Keel got to originate only two roles on Broadway—in the short-run musicals *Saratoga* (1959) and *Ambassador* (1972)—but he was very busy in Hollywood where he made an impressive screen debut playing Frank Butler in *Annie Get Your Gun* (1950). His other memorable movie roles include the gambler Gaylord Ravenal in *Show Boat* (1951), the frontiersman Bill Hickock in *Calamity Jane* (1953), the egotistical Fred/Petruchio in *Kiss Me Kate* (1953), the backwoodsman Adam Pontipee in *Seven Brides for Seven Brothers* (1954), and the wily poet Hajj in *Kismet* (1955). Keel also appeared in the musicals *Pagan Love Song* (1950), *Texas Carnival* (1951), *Lovely to Look At* (1952), *I Love Melvin* (1952), *Kiss Me, Kate* (1953), *Rose Marie* (1954), *Seven Brides for Seven Brothers* (1954), *Deep in My Heart* (1954), and *Jupiter's Darling* (1955). In 1963 he replaced Richard Kiley in *No Strings* on Broadway and continued to sing on television, in clubs and concerts, and in stock revivals into the 1990s.

KEELER, RUDY [born Ethel Hilda Keeler] (1909–1993). Stage and film performer. One of the first musical stars to find fame in the movies rather than the stage, she possessed a round, almost expressionless face and her buck-and-wing dancing was far from graceful but she symbolized a youthful, carefree optimism that was very appealing in the Depression. Keeler was born in Halifax, Nova Scotia, Canada, but her family moved to New York City when she was young and provided dance lessons when she was nine years old. By her teen years she was performing in cabarets and in minor roles on Broadway in *The Rise of Rosie O'Reilly* (1923), *Bye Bye Bonnie* (1927), *Lucky* (1927), and *Sidewalks of New York* (1927). Keeler finally got star billing for *Show Girl* (1929) in which she introduced the standard "Liza," and producer Florenz Ziegfeld wanted her for the leading lady in *Whoopee* (1928) but she opted to go to Hollywood with her husband AL JOLSON. After a guest bit in *Show Girl in Hollywood* (1930), she found fame as the chorine Peggy Sawyer who saves the show in *42nd Street* (1933), followed by a series of Warner Brothers musicals in which she was usually teamed with DICK POWELL: *Gold Diggers of 1933* (1933), *Footlight Parade* (1933), *Dames* (1934), *Flirtation Walk* (1934), *Go Into Your Dance* (1935), *Shipmates Forever* (1935), *Colleen* (1936), and *Ready, Willing and Able* (1937). After divorcing Jolson and making *Sweetheart of the Campus* (1941), Keeler remarried and retired, only making a few television appearances in the 1950s and early 1960s. She temporarily came out of retirement and returned to Broadway after forty-one years as the matron Sue Smith in the 1971 revival of *No, No, Nanette*. In the musical biopic *The Jolson Story* (1946), Keeler was played by Evelyn Keyes, but because Keeler refused permission to use her name, Jolson's wife was called Julie Benson.

KELLY, GENE [born Eugene Curran Kelly] (1912–1996). Stage, film, and television performer, director, and choreographer. The cinema's preeminent dancer–choreographer, he made a big splash on Broadway before going to Hollywood where his athletic style of dance made him unique. A native of Pittsburgh, Pennsylvania, the son of a sales executive and a former actress, Kelly was educated at Penn State and the University of Pittsburgh in economics. He had taken dance lessons as a child and as a young adult worked as a dance instructor to support himself while he tried to get acting jobs in New York. He made his Broadway debut in the chorus of *Leave It to Me!* (1938) and the next year was featured in the revue *One for the Money* while he choreographed nightclub acts and revues in Manhattan. Kelly was first noticed in the nonmusical *The Time of Your Life* (1939) in which he played the desperate Harry the Hoofer. That part got him the leading role of the unscrupulous Joey Evans in Rodgers and Hart's *Pal Joey* (1940), which made him famous. After choreographing the Broadway musical *Best Foot Forward* (1941), Kelly went to Hollywood where he made his screen debut in the musical *For Me and My Gal* (1942), followed by one of the most spectacular careers in movie history. He performed in *DuBarry Was a Lady* (1943), *Ziegfeld Follies* (1946), *Les Girls* (1957), *Xanadu* (1980), and other musicals but he is better remembered for the movies he both choreographed and danced in, such as *Cover Girl* (1944), *Anchors Aweigh* (1945), *The*

PIRATE (1948), *WORDS AND MUSIC* (1948), *TAKE ME OUT TO THE BALL GAME* (1949), *SUMMER STOCK* (1950), *AN AMERICAN IN PARIS* (1951), *BRIGADOON* (1954), and *What a Way to Go* (1964). Kelly directed as well as choreographed and performed in *ON THE TOWN* (1949), *SINGIN' IN THE RAIN* (1952), *IT'S ALWAYS FAIR WEATHER* (1955), and *INVITATION TO THE DANCE* (1956), as well as directing *HELLO, DOLLY!* (1969). He also acted in nonmusical movies and returned to New York to direct *FLOWER DRUM SONG* in 1958. Kelly's gymnastic-like dancing, imaginative choreography, innovative use of cinema effects in movie musicals, and astute direction made him a giant in the American film musical. He was married to actress Betsy Blair for a time. Biographies: *Gene Kelly: A Life of Dance and Dreams*, Alvin Yudoff (1999); *Gene Kelly: A Biography*, Clive Hirschhorn (1985).

KELLY, PATSY [born Sarah Veronica Rose Kelly] (1910–1981). Stage, film, and television performer. The dumpy, wisecracking character actress had two Broadway careers separated by forty years. Kelly was born in Brooklyn and was dancing on the stage as a child, later going into vaudeville with her neighborhood friend RUBY KEELER. She made her Broadway debut in 1927, and her comic sass lit up such revues as *Harry Delmar's Revels* (1927), *Earl Carroll Sketch Book* (1929), *EARL CARROLL VANITIES* (1930), and *FLYING COLORS* (1932), as well as the book musicals *Three Cheers* (1928) and *WONDER BAR* (1930). Kelly went to Hollywood and made her screen debut in *GOING HOLLYWOOD* (1933), followed by a dozen other musicals in which she usually played smart-aleck maids or secretaries. Among her film credits are *GO INTO YOUR DANCE* (1935), *THANKS A MILLION* (1935), *Pigskin Parade* (1936), *WAKE UP AND LIVE* (1937), *Hit Parade of 1941* (1940), *Road Show* (1941), and *Sing Your Worries Away* (1942). Kelly continued to make nonmusical movies into the late 1970s and enjoyed a triumphant return to Broadway in two revivals: as the sarcastic maid Pauline in *NO, NO, NANETTE* (1971) and the Irish mother Mrs. O'Dare in *IRENE* (1973). She was very active on television from the mid-1950s until a few months before her death.

KELTON, PERT (1907–1968). Stage, film, and television performer. A delicious comedienne and character actress, the small, plump singer–actress managed to steal the scene in every media. Kelton was born on a cattle ranch in Great Falls, Montana, the daughter of

vaudevillians, and was on stage at the age of three. She worked her way into legitimate theatre and made her Broadway debut as MARILYN MILLER's chum in *SUNNY* (1925), followed by featured roles in plays and the musicals *The Five O'Clock Girl* (1927), *The DuBarry* (1932), and *All in Fun* (1940). Kelton made her screen debut as the sidekick Rosie in *SALLY* (1929), but most of her film roles were in comedies. She returned to Broadway as the sly Mrs. Paroo in *THE MUSIC MAN* (1957) and reprised her performance in the 1962 film version. Kelton also shone in some Broadway comedies in the 1960s and gave a delightful performance as Gramma Briggs in *GREENWILLOW* (1960). She made many television appearances, including the original Alice Kramden in *The Honeymooners*.

KERN, JEROME [David] (1885–1945). Stage and film composer. An innovative, vastly talented artist who reshaped the sound of the American musical, he created several outstanding scores for Broadway and Hollywood. Kern was born in New York City, the son of a German-born merchandiser and an American-born mother of Bohemian descent who taught the boy piano. At the age of ten, he moved with his family to Newark, New Jersey, and while in high school began composing for school and community shows. He studied at the New York College of Music before his songs were interpolated into other songwriters' shows. Kern gained some recognition when his "How'd You

Jerome Kern. The versatile and endlessly creative composer worked so well with so many different lyricists that it seemed like he brought out the best in each collaborator. Here he is pictured with lyricist Dorothy Fields when they were working together on the film *Swing Time* (1936). (Photofest)

Like to Spoon With Me?" was inserted into *The Earl and the Girl* (1905) and for the next decade he saw more of his songs interpolated into Broadway and London musicals. The London hit *THE GIRL FROM UTAH* (1914) was brought to New York and a handful of Kern songs were added, including "They Didn't Believe Me," a very innovative number that helped define the new form of ballad that would later dominate theatre music. With librettist GUY BOLTON and lyricist P. G. WODEHOUSE, Kern wrote a series of intimate, intelligent musical comedies dubbed the *PRINCESS MUSICALS* because most of them were staged in the small Princess Theatre. *VERY GOOD EDDIE* (1915), *OH, BOY!* (1917), *LEAVE IT TO JANE* (1917), and others were not only popular but inspired a new generation of songwriters to aim for more integrated, literate musicals. After scoring the hit musical *SALLY* (1920), Kern worked with OTTO HARBACH and OSCAR HAMMERSTEIN for the first time on *SUNNY* (1925). With Harbach he would write such popular shows as *THE CAT AND THE FIDDLE* (1931) and *ROBERTA* (1933), but it was with Hammerstein that Kern had his greatest triumphs, including the legendary *SHOW BOAT* (1927), *SWEET ADELINE* (1929), and *MUSIC IN THE AIR* (1932). Among Kern's many other Broadway musicals were *Nobody Home* (1915), *Have a Heart* (1917), *The Night Boat* (1920), *Sitting Pretty* (1924), *Criss-Cross* (1926), and *VERY WARM FOR MAY* (1939), as well as the short-lived London musical *Three Sisters* (1934) that is much admired today. Kern saw many of his stage works filmed and when productivity on Broadway waned during the Depression, he spent most of his time in Hollywood where, with various collaborators, he scored such screen musicals as *I DREAM TOO MUCH* (1935), *SWING TIME* (1936), *HIGH, WIDE AND HANDSOME* (1937), *JOY OF LIVING* (1938), *ONE NIGHT IN THE TROPICS* (1940), *YOU WERE NEVER LOVELIER* (1942), *COVER GIRL* (1944), *CAN'T HELP SINGING* (1944), and *CENTENNIAL SUMMER* (1946). He returned to New York to score *ANNIE GET YOUR GUN* (1946) but died of a heart attack before he could begin. Kern's remarkable melodic gifts and his pioneering with the ballad and the musical play cannot be overestimated and his music is still potent today. Biographies: *The World of Jerome Kern*, David Ewen (1960); *Jerome Kern: His Life and Music*, Gerald Bordman (1980); *Jerome Kern*, Stephen Banfield (2006).

KERT, LARRY [born Frederick Lawrence] (1930–1991). Stage performer. The dark-featured,

boyish actor–singer spent most of his career replacing others in Broadway musicals but he got to originate one important character. Kert was born in Los Angeles and studied acting with Sanford Meisner at the Neighborhood Playhouse in New York. He began his career singing in nightclubs and then appeared in the musicals *Tickets, Please!* (1950), *John Murray Anderson's Almanac* (1953), and as a replacement in *MR. WONDERFUL* (1956) before getting cast as Tony in the original cast of *WEST SIDE STORY* (1957 and 1960). Kert played Tony in London, on tour, and in regional theatres for several years because most of his other New York shows were short-lived, including the musicals *A Family Affair* (1962), *La Strada* (1969), *Music! Music!* (1974), *A Musical Jubilee* (1975), *Changes* (1980), *RAGS* (1986), and *The Rise of David Levinsky* (1987). He had better luck replacing others in leading roles in *I CAN GET IT FOR YOU WHOLESALE* (1962), *CABARET* (1968), *Side By Side By Sondheim* (1977), and most memorably as the confused bachelor Bobby in *COMPANY* (1970), which he took over soon after opening night and reprised in London. Kert often returned to concerts and nightclub and he only rarely appeared on television or film, with his performance in *New York, New York* (1977) mostly left on the cutting room floor.

KIBBEE, GUY [Bridges] (1882–1956). Film and stage performer. A paunchy character actor who specialized in cheerful millionaires and crafty civic leaders, he was a familiar face on screen after a long career in the theatre. Kibbee was born in El Paso, Texas, and started as a teenager in show business by acting on a riverboat and then in legitimate theatres across the country, even playing on Broadway in 1930. The next year he went to Hollywood where he was immediately cast in character parts in comedies, action pictures, and musicals, such as *FLYING HIGH* (1931), *42ND STREET* (1933), *GOLD DIGGERS OF 1933*, *FOOTLIGHT PARADE* (1933), *WONDER BAR* (1934), *DAMES* (1934), *CAPTAIN JANUARY* (1936), *JOY OF LIVING* (1938), *BABES IN ARMS* (1939), *GIRL CRAZY* (1943), and *Dixie Jamboree* (1944). Kibbee also made a few television appearances before his death from Parkinson's disease.

KID MILLIONS (Goldwyn/United Artists 1934). The simplistic plot may have resembled a two-reeler comedy but no expense was spared on this EDDIE CANTOR vehicle and it turned out to be one of his best. The screenplay by Nunnally

Johnson, Nat Perrin, and Arthur Sheekman was a frolic about the archeologist's son Eddie Wilson, Jr. (Cantor) in Brooklyn who inherits $77 million but to claim it must go to Egypt where he is chased over the sands by con men out to fleece him of his dough. Director ROY DEL RUTH and choreographer SEYMOUR FELIX provided lavish and playful production numbers. Cantor sang IRVING BERLIN's "Mandy" in blackface as part of a minstrel show on board ship, and the NICHOLAS BROTHERS cut loose with "I Want to be a Minstrel Man" by BURTON LANE (music) and HAROLD ADAMSON (lyrics), who also wrote the hit ballad "Your Head on My Shoulder" sung by the young lovers ANN SOTHERN and GEORGE MURPHY (in his screen debut). ETHEL MERMAN played Cantor's mother (even though she was seventeen years his junior) and belted out Berlin's "An Earful of Music." She was also featured in the Technicolor finale, "Ice Cream Fantasy," by WALTER DONALDSON (music) and GUS KAHN (lyric), set in a Brooklyn ice cream factory.

KIDD, MICHAEL [born Milton Greenwald] (1919–2007). Stage and screen choreographer, performer, and director. An exceptionally talented Broadway and Hollywood choreographer, his work is famous for its energy and vitality. Kidd was born in Brooklyn and began studying at New York City College for an engineering degree when he began to take ballet lessons and decided to pursue a dance career instead. By 1942 he was a featured dancer with the American Ballet Theatre and appeared in "Billy the Kid" and other notable pieces. Kidd made a spectacular choreography debut on Broadway in 1947 with FINIAN'S RAINBOW, followed by such hits as GUYS AND DOLLS (1950), CAN-CAN (1953), LI'L ABNER (1956), and DESTRY RIDES AGAIN (1959), all considered outstanding dance musicals. He also directed the last two productions and would do double duty on some subsequent shows, such as WILDCAT (1960), SUBWAYS ARE FOR SLEEPING (1961), Ben Franklin in Paris (1964), THE ROTHSCHILDS (1970), GOOD NEWS! (1974), and THE MUSIC MAN (1980). Among his other choreographer credits on Broadway are LOVE LIFE (1948), Arms and the Girl (1950), Here's Love (1963), Skyscraper (1965), and The Goodbye Girl (1993). Kidd choreographed his first movie musical, WHERE'S CHARLEY?, in 1952 and went on to do the memorable dances in The Girl Next Door (1953), THE BAND WAGON (1953), SEVEN BRIDES FOR SEVEN BROTHERS (1954), GUYS AND DOLLS (1955), STAR! (1968), HELLO, DOLLY! (1969),

and others. Kidd has also performed in films on occasion, as in IT'S ALWAYS FAIR WEATHER (1954), Smile (1975), and MOVIE MOVIE (1978). He both directed and choreographed the movie musical Merry Andrew (1958) and the TV version of PETER PAN (1976). His choreography could be raucous and athletic, as in the "Sadie Hawkins Day" ballet in Li'l Abner and the barn-raising sequence in Seven Brides for Seven Brothers, witty and continental as in the "Garden of Eden" ballet in Can-Can, or contemporary and jazzy, as in "Station Rush" in Subways Are for Sleeping, but there was always a robust, explosive quality to his work that was particularly exciting.

KILEY, RICHARD (1922–1999). Stage, film, and television performer. A tall, imposing leading man with a flowing baritone voice, he starred in many memorable Broadway musicals and was very effective in nonmusical dramas as well. Kiley was born in Chicago and educated at Loyola University, started his acting career in his home town, and then worked in radio before making his Broadway debut in a revival of The Trojan Women in 1947. After a handful of other plays, Kiley was first noticed as the Caliph singing "Stranger in Paradise" in KISMET (1953). He would go on to star in such musicals as REDHEAD (1959), NO STRINGS (1962), I Had a Ball (1964), and Her First Roman (1968), but is most remembered as Cervantes/Don Quixote in MAN OF LA MANCHA (1965), which he reprised on Broadway in 1972 and 1977. Kiley also shone in several plays in New York, particularly Advise and Consent (1960), Absurd Person Singular (1974), and All My Sons (1987). He appeared in a handful of films, the only musical being The Little Prince (1974), and many television dramas and miniseries.

KING AND I, THE (St. James Theatre 1951). RICHARD RODGERS and OSCAR HAMMERSTEIN's first venture into a property that was not American in either setting or character, the beloved musical favorite was written with honesty and integrity and resulted in a Broadway version of the Orient that was tasteful, exotic, and very moving.

Plot: The Welsh widow Anna Leonowens and her young son Louis arrive in Siam where she has been hired as a teacher for the King's son, Prince Chulalongkorn, and the many children the King has sired with his various wives. Right away Anna and the King are at odds, he insisting on her living in the palace when her contract calls for a separate house for her and

The King and I. "The Small House of Uncle Thomas" number, in which the abolitionist novel *Uncle Tom's Cabin* was reimagined through an Asian slave's point of view, was one on the many wonders in the Rodgers and Hammerstein musical. Pictured is the number in the original Broadway production, ingeniously choreographed by Jerome Robbins. (Photofest)

Louis. Anna would leave immediately but she is charmed by the anxious and loving faces of the children and decides to stay. Also new to the court is the Burmese slave Tuptim who is a "gift" for the King, but she and her emissary Lun Tha are in love and hope to escape together. While the tension between the King and Anna remains, they soon develop a healthy respect for each other and she helps the King and his wives prepare for a visit by foreign dignitaries to show that the Siamese monarch is not the barbarian that rumors say he is. At the state occasion, Tuptim and members of the court perform a version of *Uncle Tom's Cabin* that Tuptim has written, condemning slavery and ruthless monarchs. After the performance Tuptim and Lun Tha flee the palace but are captured by the King's guards. The King tries to punish Tuptim by flogging her himself but he cannot, plagued by Anna's accusations

and his doubts about his barbarism. Anna and Louis make preparations to leave Siam but she is called to the deathbed of the King who encourages the Prince to rule as he sees fit. The King dies and Anna remains to guide the young King.

GERTRUDE LAWRENCE brought the idea of musicalizing Margaret Landon's 1944 novel *Anna and the King of Siam* to Rodgers and Hammerstein, having bought the stage rights and knowing that the role of Anna Leonowens was perfect for her. There had been a popular film version in 1946 with IRENE DUNNE and REX HARRISON but OSCAR HAMMERSTEIN's libretto fleshed out each character and created a rivalry that was complicated by respect and perhaps a little love. He also developed the secondary plot concerning Tuptim and Lun Tha, turning the latter from a priest to a lover and the former

Casts for *The King and I*

Characters	Anna Leonowens	King	Tuptim	Lady Thaing
1951 Broadway	GERTRUDE LAWRENCE	YUL BRYNNER	DORETTA MORROW	Dorothy Sarnoff
1956 film	Deborah Kerr	Yul Brynner	RITA MORENO	Terry Saunders
1977 Broadway	CONSTANCE TOWERS	Yul Brynner	June Angela	Hye-Young Choi
1985 Broadway	Mary Beth Peil	Yul Brynner	Patricia Welch	Irma-Estel LaGuerre
1996 Broadway	DONNA MURPHY	Lou Diamond Phillips	Joohee Choi	Taewon Kim
1999 film (voices)	Miranda Richardson	Martin Vidnovic	Ami Arabe	
(singing voices)	Christiane Noll	Martin Vidnovic	Tracy Venner Warren	

from a feisty slave to a voice of conscience for the King. There is more dialogue in *The King and I* than in any other of the team's musicals, and the writing is terse, funny, and involving. The King was considered a supporting role (Lawrence was obviously the star) so he was given only one solo song and YUL BRYNNER was billed on the playbill after the designers and conductor. It was only years later that *The King and I* was considered a two-star vehicle and, by the end of his career, Brynner had turned it into a one-star show, his own.

Rodgers knew he could not rely on the traditional Broadway sound for the score. Nor could the music be accurately Asian, for theatregoers would find the high-pitched, nonmelodic sounds strange and even irritating. So Rodgers composed a score that was richly flavored with Oriental touches. The result is music that is

exotically majestic when it needs to be and quiet and delicate when necessary. Songs for the Englishwoman Anna contain European music and lyrics, such as the lively polka "Shall We Dance?" or the operetta ballad "Hello, Young Lovers." Songs for the Asian characters were more fragile, for the lyrics must denote their unfamiliarity with English and yet not reduce the characters to pigeon-English clichés. Tuptim's songs are simple and heartfelt, and Lady Thiang's "Something Wonderful" has a direct and unfussy lyric while Rodgers' music soars with emotion. Perhaps the most wondrous of these Asian numbers is the King's "A Puzzlement." With his broken English phrases, forceful arguments, and painful self-doubts, it is a masterpiece of a character song. Just as the score could not be a standard set of Broadway songs, the choreography in the show could not rely on all-American chorus lines or tap routines. Choreographer JEROME ROBBINS brilliantly devised very Asian movements for the formal "March of the Royal Siamese Children" and the theatrical "The Small House of Uncle Thomas" ballet, which contrasted with the formal minuet of the Europeans and the free-wheeling polka for "Shall We Dance?" John Van Druten was the nominal director for the musical but it is believed that Hammerstein himself restaged many of the scenes. With the ingenious scenic design by Jo Mielziner and the stunning costumes by Irene Sharaff, *The King and I* was perhaps the most resplendent looking of all the Rodgers and Hammerstein musicals. The songwriters produced the show themselves and it ran 1,246 performances.

The King and I has seen more Broadway revivals than any of the works by the celebrated team. A 1956 production by the New

The King and I (stage) Musical Numbers

"I Whistle a Happy Tune"
"My Lord and Master"
"Hello, Young Lovers"
"March of the Royal Siamese Children"
"A Puzzlement"
"The Royal Bangkok Academy"
"Getting to Know You"
"We Kiss in a Shadow"
"Shall I Tell You What I Think of You?"
"Something Wonderful"
"Western People Funny"
"I Have Dreamed"
"The Small House of Uncle Thomas" Ballet
"Shall We Dance?"

York City Center Light Opera Company starred JAN CLAYTON as Anna and Zachary Scott as the King. The same company presented the musical in 1960 with BARBARA COOK and Farley Granger, and again in 1963 with Eileen Brennan and Manolo Fabregas. Rodgers was the producer behind the Music Theatre of Lincoln Center production in 1964 with Darren McGavin and RISE STEVENS; Michael Kermoyan played the King in 1968 opposite CONSTANCE TOWERS. She reprised her Anna in a 1977 revival that brought Yul Brynner back to Broadway as the King, remaining for a remarkable 696 performances. Brynner toured with the musical extensively in the 1980s and played the role one last time on Broadway in 1985 with Mary Beth Peil as his Anna for 191 performances. Christopher Renshaw directed an Australian production that portrayed a darker and more sinister Siam, a less elegant but more forceful Anna (Haley Mills), and a younger, more physical King (Tony Marinyo). The acclaimed production came to Broadway in 1996 with Lou Diamond Phillips and DONNA MURPHY as the King and Anna and remained for 781 performances before transferring to London in 2000. *The King and I* remains a staple with summer theatres, school, stock companies, and community theatre groups.

■ *The King and I* (Fox 1956) is arguably the finest film adaptation of any Rodgers and Hammerstein musical, even better than the more popular movie THE SOUND OF MUSIC (1965). Some will go so far as to say that it is the only musical by the team that is actually better on the screen than the stage, since ERNEST LEHMAN's screenplay trims the stage libretto, cuts three songs, and makes for a more compact and powerful show. Comparisons aside, it is safe to say that it is a beautifully directed, designed, acted, and sung movie and true to the Broadway show without seeming stage bound. WALTER LANG directed with a delicate but firm touch and nothing in the movie seems dated or overwrought five decades later. It certainly helped having Yul Brynner back as the king, as well as Sharaff's costumes and Robbins' choreography from the Broadway production. The studio scenic designers and ALFRED NEWMAN's masterful direction of the music were also major pluses. DEBORAH KERR was not a singer so MARNI NIXON provided her singing voice. Kerr gives an outstanding performance, balancing Anna's icy British reserve with her temperamental Welsh wit. Brynner's recreation of his stage performance is towering and the rivalry between his King and this

Anna hits all of the exciting levels of their relationship. The Charles Brackett production was a box office hit and remains popular on DVD. However, the animated film version of *The King and I* (Morgan Creek/Warner 1999) is easily the worst screen treatment of any Rodgers and Hammerstein property. Geared toward children, the story is reduced to a carefree sing-along with annoyingly superficial characters, cuddly animals (including a dragon), a forced love story, and a wasteland of scenes without wit or intelligence. At least some of the songs survive nicely and the singing vocals throughout are very proficient. (A nice compensation is hearing BARBRA STREISAND sing "I Have Dreamed," "We Kiss in a Shadow" and "Something Wonderful" on the soundtrack.) Perhaps someone thought that this travesty would be a swell introduction to Rodgers and Hammerstein for kids. Yet children have enjoyed *The King and I* for over five decades without relying on dancing dragons. The movie was condemned by the press and ignored by the public, although the DVD is available and doing damage somewhere.

KING, CHARLES (1889–1944). Stage and film performer. A light-footed, lightweight song-and-dance man, he introduced several song standards on Broadway and on the screen. A native New Yorker, King worked in minstrel shows and vaudeville before making his Broadway debut in the chorus of *The Yankee Prince* (1908). After minor roles in *The Mimic World* (1908), *The Slim Princess* (1911), *The Winsome Widow* (1912), *The Geisha* (1913), and THE PASSING SHOW OF 1913, he was featured in WATCH YOUR STEP (1914) and introduced "Play a Simple Melody." King's other memorable musical roles were Irish lad Jerry Conroy who sang the title song in LITTLE NELLIE KELLY (1922), the dense but enamored sailor Bilge Smith in HIT THE DECK (1927) singing "Sometimes I'm Happy," and the bootlegger Al Spanish in THE NEW YORKERS (1938). His other stage musicals include *Miss 1917* (1917), GEORGE WHITE'S SCANDALS (1921), *No Foolin'* (1926), and PRESENT ARMS (1928). King had a short but noteworthy tenure in films, introducing the songs "You Were Meant for Me' in THE BROADWAY MELODY (1929) and "Happy Days Are Here Again" in *Chasing Rainbows* (1930). His other two screen musicals were HOLLYWOOD REVUE OF 1929 and *Oh, Sailor Behave* (1930).

■ **KING CREOLE** (Paramount 1958). An ELVIS PRESLEY vehicle that didn't look or sound like the glossy features that the star was usually stuck with, the film afforded him one of his best performances. Based on the Harold Robbins novel *A Stone for Danny Fisher*, the screenplay by Herbert Baker and Michael V. Gazzo centered on New Orleans bus boy Danny (Presley) who, despite the meddling of some local thugs and his suffocating family members, gets to be a singer in a Bourbon Street nightclub. MICHAEL CURTIZ's direction captured the gritty, tawdry milieu (the movie was filmed in black and white) of the French Quarter at dawn and behind the scenes of the party hot spots. It probably helped that Presley was surrounded by solid nonmusical actors such as Walter Matthau, Vic Morrow, Dean Jagger, Dolores Hart, and Jan Shepard, who all gave tough and honest performances. Carolyn Jones, in one of her best roles, was memorable as the mobster's girl friend Ronnie who falls for the younger Danny even as she belittles him. Even the score was a cut above the usual Presley film. A pushcart peddler (Kitty White) moaned out the bluesy "Crawfish" (by Fred Wise and Ben Wiseman) at the top of the film, and audiences knew this was not a Las Vegas concert movie. The same team wrote the torchy rock ballad "Don't Ask Me Why," and JERRY LEIBER and MIKE STOLLER penned the title song, both numbers sung by Presley and both best-selling records. The most satisfying song was Claude De Metrius' "Hard Headed Woman" (also a hit), which was heard only briefly off camera.

KING, DENNIS (1897–1971). Stage, television, and film performer. A versatile singer–actor who played everything from Shakespeare to operetta, he originated some dashing musical theatre roles on Broadway. King was born in Coventry, England, and educated in Birmingham where he joined the repertory as an apprentice and worked his way up to manager and actor. He made his London debut in 1919 and his Broadway bow two years later in the play *Clair de Lune*. Settling in America and becoming a U. S. citizen, King became a stage star in 1924 when he played the fur trapper Jim Kenyon in *ROSE-MARIE*, introducing "Indian Love Call" with MARY ELLIS. For the next forty years he performed in New York and London in a variety of roles, most memorably the outlaw poet Francois Villon in *THE VAGABOND KING* (1925), the swashbuckling D'Artagnan in *THE THREE MUSKETEERS* (1928), gambler Gaylord Ravenal in the 1932 revival of *SHOW BOAT*, the aristocrat Willie Palaffi in Rodgers and Hart's *I MARRIED AN ANGEL* (1938), Bruno

Mahler in the 1951 revival of *MUSIC IN THE AIR*, and a number of classic works by Shakespeare, Ibsen, and Shaw. His last Broadway appearance was in 1969 as the transvestite Baron von Epp in the play *A Patriot for Me*. King made only a handful of films, including the early talkie *The Vagabond King* (1930), but was featured in many television programs, mostly specials such as the TV musicals *KNICKERBOCKER HOLIDAY* (1950), *BABES IN TOYLAND* (1950), *JACK AND THE BEANSTALK* (1956), *ALADDIN* (1958), and *THE MIKADO* (1960). He is the father of actors Dennis King, Jr., and John Michael King (1926–) who introduced "On the Street Where You Live" in *MY FAIR LADY* (1956).

KING, HENRY (1892–1982). Film director. A much-demanded Hollywood director with over fifty films to his credit, he helmed all genres and made eight musicals. King was born in Christiansburg, Virginia, where he was raised on his family's plantation before becoming an actor in vaudeville, burlesque, legitimate theatre, and silent films. He started directing in 1915 and soon showed a talent for using wide open spaces on film to create a sense of Americana. Although his adventure movies were the most popular, King also handled character pieces equally well. His early musicals *I Love You Wednesday* (1933), *Marie Galante* (1934), and *Ramona* (1936) were not successful but he was more in his element with *IN OLD CHICAGO* (1938), *ALEXANDER'S RAGTIME BAND* (1938), *Margie* (1946), *Wait Till the Sun Shines, Nellie* (1952), and *CAROUSEL* (1956).

KING OF BURLESQUE (Fox 1935). A low-budget backstager that concentrated on characters rather than spectacle, the musical worked nicely thanks to a strong cast and a superior score. Harry Tugend and Gene Markey's screenplay is about burlesque entrepreneur Kerry Bolton (WARNER BAXTER) who wants to go high class so he persuades his sweetheart Pat Doran (ALICE FAYE) and cohort Joe Cooney (JACK OAKIE) to move uptown and try Broadway. In the process he falls for and marries the society dame Rosalind Cleve (Mona Barrie), so Pat flees to London where she becomes a star in the West End. When Bolton's big Broadway revue flops, Rosalind ditches him and the dejected producer turns to drink. But Pat returns, bankrolls his new nightclub, and all ends happily with a swell show that includes turns by KENNY BAKER, THOMAS "FATS" WALLER, DIXIE DUNBAR, and others. JIMMY MCHUGH (music) and TED KOEHLER (lyrics) wrote most of the score, which included the vibrant "Spreading Rhythm Around," the optimistic "I'm Shooting High," the waltzing "Lovely Lady," and the rhythmic "I've Got My Fingers Crossed." Sidney Lanfield directed the DARRYL F. ZANUCK production. Faye, Oakie, and the same plot all returned in **Hello, Frisco, Hello** (Fox 1943). The screenplay by Robert Ellis, Helen Logan, and Michael Macaulay reset the story at the turn of the twentieth century in San Francisco's Barbary Coast district where Johnny Carroll (JOHN PAYNE), Trudy Evans (Faye), Dan Daley (Oakie), and Beulah Clancy (JUNE HAVER) are entertainers. Although Johnny loves Trudy, he weds the Nob Hill socialite Bernice Croft (LYNN BARI) to get money to open his nightclub, but the marriage is a fiasco and he loses everything. Trudy goes to Broadway and the West End, becomes a star, and then returns to bail out the divorced Johnny. Also in the cast are Laird Cregar, Ward Bond, GEORGE BARBIER, and Aubrey Mather. The many period songs, such as "Has Anybody Here Seen Kelly?," "By the Light of the Silvery Moon," and "Hello, Frisco," and a memorable new one, "You'll Never Know" by HARRY WARREN (music) and MACK GORDON (lyric), were presented beautifully by director H. BRUCE HUMBERSTONE and choreographer Val Raset.

KING OF JAZZ (Universal 1930). An early film revue put together by the Broadway revue expert JOHN MURRAY ANDERSON, the movie was spectacular by any standards and many of the visuals were copied in subsequent Hollywood musicals. The focal point of the jam-packed show (there were seventy numbers performed in 101 minutes) was PAUL WHITEMAN and his orchestra, the most popular band in America at the time and the custodians of jazz in nightclubs and on records. In one of Anderson's many inventive staging ideas, Whiteman and his boys performed GEORGE GERSHWIN's "Rhapsody in Blue" atop a mammoth piano. For "The Melting Pot of Music" sequence, music and performers from eight different countries gathered, with all of the music coming out of one giant cauldron in the form of jazz. BING CROSBY made his screen debut as one of the Rhythm Boys singing "So the Bluebirds and the Blackirds Got Together" and joined the Brox Sisters and others for "A Bench in the Park" with couples snuggling on various layers of turf. Other songs by various tunesmiths included "Happy Feet," "It Happened in Monterey," "Mississippi Mud,"

and "Ragamuffin Romeo." Carl Laemmle, Jr. produced the inspired, overabundant musical show.

KINGSLEY, DOROTHY (1909–1997). Film and television writer. A former radio writer for such stars as BOB HOPE and EDGAR BERGEN, she turned to movies in the 1940s and scripted several noteworthy musicals. Kingsley was born in New York, the daughter of silent screen star Alma Hanlon and Broadway press agent Walter Kingsley, and broke into show business writing comedy sketches for radio stars. She arrived in Hollywood in 1940 to write jokes for Bergen's specialty spots in the films *Look Who's Laughing* (1941) and *Here We Go Again* (1942) and stayed, scripting such musicals as *BEST FOOT FORWARD* (1943), *GIRL CRAZY* (1943), *BROADWAY RHYTHM* (1944), *Bathing Beauty* (1944), *Easy to Wed* (1946), *On an Island With You* (1948), *A Date With Judy* (1948), *Neptune's Daughter* (1949), *Two Weeks With Love* (1950), *Texas Carnival* (1951), *Small Town Girl* (1953), *Dangerous When Wet* (1953), *Kiss Me, Kate* (1953), *Seven Brides for Seven Brothers* (1954), *Jupiter's Darling* (1955), *Pal Joey* (1957), *Can-Can* (1960), *Pepe* (1960), and *Half a Sixpence* (1967). Kingsley also wrote television scripts in the 1960s before retiring to run a winery in Carmel Valley in California.

KINSKEY, LEONID (1903–1998). Film and television performer. A thickly accented character actor on the stages of Europe, he became a favorite in Hollywood for his eccentric foreigners. Kinskey was born in St. Petersburg, Russia, and traveled about Europe acting in different companies. He even performed on a tour to South America before arriving in the States in 1931 and made his screen debut in *THE BIG BROADCAST* (1932). He was noticed in the comedy *Trouble in Paradise* (1932) and quickly was in demand for eastern European types over the next two decades, most memorably as the bartender Sascha in *Casablanca* (1942). Among his many musical credits are *DUCK SOUP* (1933), *THE CAT AND THE FIDDLE* (1934), *Strictly Dynamite* (1934), *HOLLYWOOD PARTY* (1934), *THE MERRY WIDOW* (1934), *Rhythm on the Range* (1936), *THE BIG BROADCAST OF 1937* (1936), *MAYTIME* (1937), *ONE HUNDRED MEN AND A GIRL* (1937), *THE BIG BROADCAST OF 1938*, *THE GREAT WALTZ* (1938), *ON YOUR TOES* (1939), *DOWN ARGENTINE WAY* (1940), *THAT NIGHT IN RIO* (1941), *WEEKEND IN HAVANA* (1941), *I MARRIED AN ANGEL* (1942), *Presenting Lily Mars* (1943), *CAN'T HELP*

SINGING (1944), *Nancy Goes to Rio* (1950), and *The Helen Morgan Story* (1957). Kinskey also acted in many television programs in the 1950s and 1960s.

KIRK, LISA (1925–1990). Stage, film, and television performer. A stately, attractive singer–actress who could play highbrow or lowbrow, she was a favorite in nightclubs, on Broadway, and on television. Kirk was born in Brownsville, Pennsylvania, and trained at the Pittsburgh Playhouse before making her Broadway bow in the play *Good Night, Ladies* (1945). Two years later, she stopped the show each night singing "The Gentleman Is a Dope" in *ALLEGRO* (1947). Her other Broadway triumph was as Lois Lane/Bianca in the original production of *KISS ME, KATE* (1948). Kirk made many television appearances and a few films, providing some of the singing vocals for ROSALIND RUSSELL in the film version of *GYPSY* (1962). She returned to the stage as the veteran hoofer Lottie in the musical play *MACK AND MABEL* (1974) and made her last Broadway appearance in a revival of the play *Design for Living* (1984).

☙ *KISMET* (Ziegfeld Theatre 1953). The most successful and accomplished of the series of musicals ROBERT WRIGHT and GEORGE FORREST adapted from classical music, this bewitching Arabian Nights show was a light-hearted fantasy with radiant singing and gorgeous production values. Edward Knoblock's romantic adventure play *Kismet* (1911) was set to the stirring music of Alexander Borodin and, with expert lyrics by Wright and Forrest, the musical boasted a marvelous score. "Stranger in Paradise" and "Baubles, Bangles and Beads" were the runaway hits, but also intoxicating were "And This Is My Beloved," "Night of My Nights," "Fate," "Rahadlakum," "Gesticulate," and "Rhymes Have I." In the libretto by Charles Lederer and Luther Davis, ALFRED DRAKE was the beggar poet Hajj who becomes the emir of Baghdad for a day, marries his daughter Marsinah (DORETTA MORROW) to

the Caliph (RICHARD KILEY), and woos Lalume (JOAN DIENER), the wife of the Wazir (Henry Calvin). ALBERT MARRE directed, JACK COLE did the exotic choreography, and the lavish sets and costumes were by Lemuel Ayers. A hit on the West Coast, the Edwin Lester–Lederer production was embraced by the New York press and ran 583 performances. The operetta-like musical was popular with light opera groups and in summer stock and returned to Broadway twice. Drake reprised his wily Hajj and Calvin his Wazir in a 1965 Lincoln Center production that recreated the original staging, choreography, and design. Also in the cast were Lee Venora (Marsinah), Richard Banke (Caliph), and Anne Jeffreys (Lalume). Retitled *Timbuktu!* (Mark Hellinger Theatre 1978) and reset in the ancient empire of Mali, the new version was performed by an African American cast and found a new audience for 221 performances. Some character names and sections of dialogue changed but the glorious score was left pretty much intact. Davis adapted his own libretto, and the colorful, exotic production was directed, choreographed, and costumed by GEOFFREY HOLDER.

🎬 *Kismet* (MGM 1955). was filmed by director VINCENT MINNELLI with a luscious decor that matched its luscious music, but the resulting musical lacked the excitement of the stage. HOWARD KEEL is a lively Hajj, DOLORES GRAY a classy Lalume, and Sebastian Cabot a funny Wazir, but much of the rest of the cast is dull and the movie drags when it should sparkle. The score was abridged and the Borodin music seemed less impressive on the screen even though the singing was accomplished. Davis and Lederer wrote the screenplay from their libretto but the story seemed more silly than magical. The ARTHUR FREED production had modest box office success and the film is mostly forgotten, one of the reasons the musical is not revived as much as it used to be. ▢ A condensed version of *Kismet* was broadcast by ABC-TV in 1967 with JOSÉ FERRER as Hajj. His singing was not as impressive as earlier performers who had played the part

---

Casts for *Kismet*

Character	1953 Broadway	1955 film	1978 Broadway (Timbuktu!)
Hajj	ALFRED DRAKE	HOWARD KEEL	Ira Hawkins
Marsinah	DORETTA MORROW	ANN BLYTH	MELBA MOORE
Caliph/Mansa of Mali	RICHARD KILEY	VIC DAMONE	GILBERT PRICE
Lalume/Sahleem	JOAN DIENER	DOLORES GRAY	EARTHA KITT
Wazir	Henry Calvin	Sebastian Cabot	George Bell

but his beautiful speaking voice and sense of comedy got him through. His fellow players were ANNA MARIA ALBERGHETTI (Marsinah), Barbara Eden (Lalume), GEORGE CHAKIRIS (Caliph), and HANS CONRIED (Wazir).

KISS ME AGAIN. See MLLE. MODISTE

KISS ME, KATE (New Century Theatre 1948). COLE PORTER's best (and most successful) musical, the show boasts one of the best librettos ever written for Broadway and Porter wrote his most dazzling collection of songs to go with it.

Plot: While a musical version of Shakespeare's *The Taming of the Shrew* is performing in a Baltimore theatre, the stars Fred Graham and Lilli Vanessi, who used to be married to each other, play Petruchio and Kate and battle both on- and offstage. Also in the cast are sweethearts Lois Lane and Bill Calhoun who are plagued by Bill's gambling addition. When Bill signs Fred's name to an IOU for some gangsters, two henchmen come to the theatre to collect the money from Fred and end up helping him keep Lilli from walking out on the show. Just as Shakespeare's story comes to a happy ending, Fred and Lilli are reconciled by the finale of both shows.

Bella and Sam Spewack wrote the brilliant libretto in which the modern story comments on the Shakespearean one, and the other way around as well. Even more accomplished, one gets the sense of having seen the whole Shakespeare tale when in effect only a few scenes/songs were shown. The writers also created backstage characters that are just as much fun as the Shakespearean characters. The Spewacks' two comic henchmen, with no direct parallels to the Elizabeth tale, are among the funniest supporting characters of the era, speaking in a genteel slang that foreshadows the Runyonesque types of *GUYS AND DOLLS* (1950).

Kiss Me, Kate. The Broadway production of the musicalized *The Taming of the Shrew* was so well written and scored that for the first time in Cole Porter's career Hollywood didn't rework the whole thing and toss out half his songs. Pictured in the film version are (left to right) the eligible bachelorettes played by Jeanne Coyne, Carol Haney, and Ann Miller. Those three flashes of flying movement are Bobby Van, Bob Fosse, and Tommy Rall. (Photofest)

Casts for *Kiss Me, Kate*

Characters	Fred/Petruchio	Lili/Kate	Lois/Bianca	Bill/Lucentio
1948 Broadway	ALFRED DRAKE	Patricia Morison	LISA KIRK	HAROLD LANG
1953 film	HOWARD KEEL	KATHRYN GRAYSON	ANN MILLER	TOMMY RALL
1958 television	Alfred Drake	Patricia Morison	Julie Wilson	Bill Hayes
1964 television	Howard Keel	Patricia Morison	Millicent Martin	Reginald Beckwith
1968 television	ROBERT GOULET	CAROL LAWRENCE	Jessica Walter	Michael Callan
1999 Broadway	BRIAN STOKES MITCHELL	MARIN MAZZIE	Amy Spanger	Michael Berresse

Kiss Me, Kate (stage) Musical Numbers

"Another Op'nin', Another Show"
"Why Can't You Behave?"
"Wunderbar"
"So in Love"
"We Open in Venice"
"Tom, Dick or Harry"
"I've Come to Wive It Wealthily in Padua"
"I Hate Men"
"Were Thine That Special Face"
"Cantiamo D'Amore"
"Kiss Me, Kate"
"Too Darn Hot"
"Where Is the Life That Late I Led?"
"Always True to You (In My Fashion)"
"Bianca"
"Brush Up Your Shakespeare"
"I Am Ashamed That Women Are So Simple"

Porter wrote two scores for *Kiss Me, Kate*: a psuedo-Elizabethan set of songs for the musical of *The Taming of the Shrew* that is taking place on stage of a Baltimore theatre and a contemporary score for the backstage story. They are very distinct, yet all part of a whole because *The Taming of the Shrew* songs are filled with anachronisms, as if Porter was making fun of what the musical theatre does to the classics. However, both scores have their serious and comic songs, their choral numbers, and their love songs. The way the two scores balance each other is one of the many remarkable aspects of *Kiss Me, Kate*. While numbers such as "So in Love," "Too Darn Hot," and "Wunderbar" have found success outside of the context of the show, the score is amazingly integrated with the script. This is particularly impressive when one considers that for twenty-five years Porter had been writing scores for musical comedies in which such integration was not necessary. After the change in musical structure brought on by *OKLAHOMA!* (1943), Porter confessed that the theatre had passed him by and he stuck to writing for the movies. But given an excellent script, he proved he could write a score in the Rodgers and Hammerstein model and still have it sparkle like his old songs did. Critics immediately recognized the development in his work and cheered it, as they did about JOHN C. WILSON's direction, HANYA HOLM's choreography, and everything else in the Saint Subber–Lemuel Ayers production. The show ran a happy 1,070 performances, by far the biggest hit of Porter's stage career.

While *Kiss Me, Kate* was a popular favorite in the repertory of summer stock, regional theatres, and schools, it was not a success again in New York City for fifty years. A touring production was brought back to Broadway at popular prices in 1952 and, surprisingly, audiences were not interested so it only stayed a week. The cast was headed by Robert Wright (Fred/Petruchio), Holly Harris (Lilli/Kate), Marilyn Day (Lois/Bianca), and Frank Derbas (Bill/Lucentio). BERT SHEVELOVE staged the New York Light Opera Company production in 1956 that featured David Atkinson (Fred/Petruchio), KITTY CARLISLE (Lilli/Kate), Barbara Ruick (Lois/Bianca), and Richard France (Bill/Lucentio). The same company produced a revival in 1965 that featured Patricia Morison reprising her Lilli Vanessi/Katherine from the original production. She was supported by Robert Wright (Fred/Petruchio), Nancy Ames (Lois/Bianca), and Kelly Brown (Bill/Lucentio); neither production ran beyond its limited engagement. Finally, in 1999, *Kiss Me, Kate* was a Broadway hit again, running 881 performances. Although there were minor script changes and the insertion of "From This Moment On" from the film, this joyous revival directed by Michael Blakemore and choreographed by KATHLEEN MARSHALL was faithful to the original and pleased both the press and the public with its timeless entertainment value. BRIAN STOKES MITCHELL and MARIN MAZZIE were the battling Fred/Petruchio and Lilli/Kate with Amy Spanger and Michael Berresse as the secondary pair.

■▮ **Kiss Me, Kate** (MGM 1953) was the most faithful screen version of any Cole Porter stage work. Most of the stage score was retained and the screenplay by DOROTHY KINSLEY stayed close to the original after an awkward opening scene that took place away from the theatre. HOWARD KEEL and KATHRYN GRAYSON were in full voice and full bluster as the battling couple on and offstage, ANN MILLER and TOMMY RALL shone as the secondary couple, and the supporting cast was first rate, particularly KEENAN WYNN and James Whitmore as the two gangsters. HERMES PAN was the choreographer but dancer BOB FOSSE got to stage one number, "From This Moment On," which was added to the score. The movie was filmed in 3-D so director GEORGE SIDNEY sometimes had characters tossing objects at the camera to get the three-dimensional effect; but the 3-D fad faded quickly and most moviegoers have seen the non-3-D version. ▯ There have been three television versions of *Kiss Me, Kate*. Drake and Morison reprised their stage performances in a ninety-minute broadcast in 1958 directed by George Schaefer. Also in the cast were Julie Wilson (Lois/Bianca), Bill Hayes (Bill/Lucentio), and Jack Klugman and Harvey Lembeck as the gangsters. In England, the BBC made a version in 1964 with Keel recreating his film Fred/Petruchio and Morison her stage Lilli/Kate. David Askey directed the condensed, ninety-five-minute broadcast. ABC-TV offered a pleasing (if condensed) version in 1968 with ROBERT GOULET and his then-wife CAROL LAWRENCE as the battling couple. Paul Bogart directed, LEE THEODORE choreographed, and Marty Ingels and JULES MUNSHIN stole their scenes as the henchmen. Also, the 1999 London revival, with American performers Brent Barrett (Fred) and RACHEL YORK (Lilli) in the leads, was filmed during a performance and broadcast on television in the States in 2003. Because it was a duplicate of the popular 1999 Broadway revival, the video is valuable for archival reasons.

◈ **KISS OF THE SPIDER WOMAN** (Broadhurst Theatre 1993). A dark musical play by TERRENCE MCNALLY (book), JOHN KANDER (music), and FRED EBB (lyrics), it was an unlikely candidate for a long run but was so powerful that favorable notices and strong word of mouth helped it run 906 performances. The gay window dresser Molina (BRENT CARVER) and the dedicated revolutionary Valentin (Anthony Crivello) are cell mates in a South American country ruled by a dictatorship. While Valentin broods and pines to rejoin his comrades, Molina escapes from reality by fantasizing movie musicals in his head that feature the alluring Aurora (CHITA RIVERA). The two very different men become friends and even lovers before Molina is gunned down in an effort to make Valentin reveal his cohorts on the outside. The Latin-flavored score, which consisted of poignant character songs and flashy production numbers that took place inside Molina's imagination, included "Where You Are," "Dear One," "Gimme Love," "Anything for Him," "She's a Woman," "You Could Never Shame Me," "Dressing Them Up," and "The Day After That." Based on Manuel Puig's novel, which had been made into a popular film, the musical managed to find plenty of life and color despite its grim story and setting. Critics saluted veteran Rivera and the strong principals as well as HAROLD PRINCE's inventive direction.

KITT, EARTHA [May] (1928–). Stage, television, and film performer. The durable African American singer–actress with a feline demeanor and a unique, resonating voice, she has been a longtime favorite in cabarets and swank supper clubs and performed intermittently on the New York stage over a period of sixty years. Kitt was born in North, South Carolina, grew up in Harlem, and attended the High School of the Performing Arts. She joined Katherine Dunham's dance company and toured Europe before making her Broadway bow in two of Dunham's dance concerts, *Blue Holiday* (1945) and *Bal Negre* (1946). It was in *NEW FACES OF 1952* that she gained wide attention for her smoldering singing style as she delivered the song "Monotonous." Kitt returned to the New York stage for such musical roles as the cat Mehitabel in *Shinebone Alley* (1957), the seductive *La-Lume in TIMBUKTU!* (1978), the conniving actress Dolores in *THE WILD PARTY* (2000), a replacement for Liliane La Fleur in *NINE* (2003), and the bohemian Parisian in *Mimi le Duck* (2006). On screen she danced in *CASBAH* (1948), reprised her performance in the film version of *New Faces of 1952* called *New Faces of 1954*, and was featured in *St. Louis Blues* (1958). Kitt appeared in hundreds of television shows, from drama and comedy series to quiz programs and musical specials. She also lent her voice to many animated movies and TV shows. Kitt has long been an outspoken activist for civil rights and against war, causing her to be blacklisted at times, and she often returned to Europe to perform, especially Paris where she has been a particular favorite. Autobiographies: *Thursday's Child* (1956); *A Tart Is Not a Sweet* (1976); *I'm Still Here: Confessions of a Sex Kitten* (1992).

KLINE, KEVIN [Delaney] (1942–). Stage, film, and television performer and director. A high-energy leading man with a dynamic presence on stage and screen, he has excelled at playing everything from farce to King Lear. Kline was born in St. Louis, the son of a record store owner, and educated at Indiana University and Juilliard and then toured the country as a member of John Houseman's Acting Company. His first acting jobs in Manhattan were in 1970 with the NEW YORK SHAKESPEARE FESTIVAL, an organization he would long be associated with, playing (and sometimes directing) many classical roles, including Hamlet twice. It was through the Acting Company that Kline appeared in musicals in New York, memorably Macheath in *THE BEGGAR'S OPERA* (1973) and outlaw Jaime Lockhart in *THE ROBBER BRIDEGROOM* (19775), and then he received many plaudits for his pompous fiancé Bruce Granit in *ON THE TWENTIETH CENTURY* (1978). Two years later he triumphed as the Pirate King in a very popular New York Shakespeare Festival revival of *THE PIRATES OF PENZANCE*. Most of Kline's subsequent stage credits have been in classical works but he has returned to a few musicals on the screen, such as the 1983 film of *The Pirates of Penzance*, the Cole Porter musical bio *DE-LOVELY* (2004), and *A Prairie Home Companion* (2006). He has shone in many nonmusicals films and occasionally on television in everything from soap operas to historical dramas, and his quicksilver voice has been used in such animated films as *THE*

HUNCHBACK OF NOTRE DAME (1996) and *The Road to El Dorado* (2000). Klein is married to actress Phoebe Cates (1963–).

KNICKERBOCKER HOLIDAY (Ethel Barrymore Theatre 1938). An uncomfortably satiric musical by the distinguished verse playwright MAXWELL ANDERSON (book and lyrics) and KURT WEILL (music), the show drew parallels between the current president FDR and the Dutch dictator Pieter Stuyvesant, which did not sit well with many critics and theatregoers. Stuyvesant (Walter Huston) arrives in New Amsterdam in 1647 to be the new governor of the colony and imposes laws that take away many of the freedoms the locals have long enjoyed. He also wishes to marry the much-younger Tina Tienhoven (Jeanne Madden), the daughter of a councilor and a girl in love with the town's outspoken radical, Brom Broeck (Richard Kollmar). When Brom protests the proposed marriage and Stuyvesant's dictatorship, he is sentenced to be hanged until the old governor considers how history will remember him and, wanting to cut a finer figure, blesses the union of the happy couple. The musical is remembered for Huston's charming performance (although he was too charming for the role as written) and for the indelible ballad "September Song." The rest of the score was also expert, including "It Never Was You," "How Can You Tell an American?," "There's Nowhere to Go But Up," and "Will You Remember Me?" The Playwrights' Company production, directed by JOSHUA LOGAN, managed to run 168 performances on the strength of Huston's appeal and the popularity of "September Song."

Knickerbocker Holiday (United Artists 1944) came to the screen so watered down and toothless that, with its period sets and pretty costumes, it resembled an old-fashioned operetta. Only three songs (including the popular "September Song") were retained from the stage score, and new numbers ("Love Has Made This Such a Lovely Day,"

Casts for *Knickerbocker Holiday*

Character	1938 Broadway	1944 film	1950 television
Pieter Stuyvesant	Walter Huston	Charles Coburn	DENNIS KING
Brom Broeck	Richard Kollmer	NELSON EDDY	JOHN RAITT
Tina Tienhoven	Jeanne Madden	Constance Dowling	DORETTA MORROW
Washington Irving	RAY MIDDLETON		
Tienhoven	Mark Smith	Ernest Cossart	
Ulda Tienhoven		Shelley Winters	

"Holiday," and "One More Smile") were provided by JULE STYNE (music), SAMMY CAHN (lyrics), and others. Surprisingly, movie favorite Huston did not get to reprise his beloved stage performance and Charles Coburn took his place, playing Stuyvesant as the grumpy, tired businessman that he usually played in the movies. Roosevelt was at the peak of his popularity when the film was released and neither he nor anyone else would have found the movie offensive since the parallels between the two were extricated from the plot and the character. ❑ A condensed version of *Knickerbocker Holiday* was broadcast on television's *Pulitzer Prize Playhouse* in 1950. The veteran operetta performer DENNIS KING played Stuyvesant on the sixty-minute broadcast.

KNIGHT, FUZZY [born John Forrest Knight] (1901–1976). Film and stage performer. A crusty character actor who played comic sidekicks in over 200 westerns, he also was in Broadway and Hollywood musicals. Knight was born in Fairmont, West Virginia, and educated at the University of West Virginia for a law career but instead went into vaudeville as a comic, singer, and bandleader. He later graduated to nightclubs and then to Broadway where he was featured in the musicals *Here's Howe* (1928) and *Ned Wayburn's Gambols* (1929). Although he made his screen debut in 1929, Knight didn't get noticed until MAE WEST caught his nightclub act and cast him in *SHE DONE HIM WRONG* (1933) and from then on he was in great demand. When he wasn't in the saddle, Knight appeared in such screen musicals as *Sitting Pretty* (1933), *MUSIC IN THE AIR* (1934), *Belle of the Nineties* (1934), *GEORGE WHITE'S SCANDALS* (1935), *Mountain Music* (1937), *JOY OF LIVING* (1938), *Hi, Good Lookin'* (1944), *Swing Out, Sister* (1945), and *SHOW BOAT* (1951).

KNIGHT, JUNE [born Margaret Rose Valliquietto] (1913–1987). Stage and film performer. A pretty blonde flapper with pencil-thin eyebrows, she sang and danced her way through a number of Broadway and movie musicals in ingénue roles. Knight was born in Hollywood, took dancing lessons as a child, and was put in silent films as a dancing youth. After appearing on Broadway in the chorus of *Topsy and Eva* (1925) and *FIFTY MILLION FRENCHMEN* (1929), she got further experience acting in theatre stock in California and singing in cabarets. Returning to Broadway, Knight was singled out in the musical *Hot-Cha!* (1932) and then got her two best roles: showbiz hoofer Toni

Ray in *TAKE A CHANCE* (1932) and the sassy Karen O'Kane in *JUBILEE* (1935) where she sang "Just One of Those Things" and danced to "Begin the Beguine." Knight appeared in a few nonmusicals, was featured in the musical revival of *SWEETHEARTS* (1947), and appeared in a handful of movies in the 1930s, including the musicals *Madam Satan* (1930), *Take a Chance* (1933), *Gift of Gab* (1934), *Wake Up and Dream* (1934), *Redheads on Parade* (1935), and *BROADWAY MELODY OF 1936* (1935), in which she sang "I've Got a Feelin' You're Foolin'."

KOEHLER, TED (1894–1973). Stage and film lyricist. From the Cotton Club to Hollywood, the masterful songwriter often collaborated with composer HAROLD ARLEN and came up with unforgettable songs, most famously "Stormy Weather." Koehler was born in Washington, DC, and worked as an engraver and pianist in silent film houses before writing songs for vaudeville acts. With Arlen he scored songs for several of Harlem's Cotton Club revues and his songs were heard on Broadway in such shows as *9:15 Revue* (1930), *Americana* (1932), *EARL CARROLL'S VANITIES* (1932), *George White's Music Hall Varieties* (1932), and *Say When* (1934). Koehler went to Hollywood in 1934 and, working with Arlen, JIMMY McHUGH, BURTON LANE, and other composers, wrote songs for the musicals *Let's Fall in Love* (1934), *CURLY TOP* (1935), *KING OF BURLESQUE* (1935), *Dimples* (1936), *ARTISTS AND MODELS* (1937), *STORMY WEATHER* (1943), *UP IN ARMS* (1944), *Rainbow Island* (1944), and *My Wild Irish Rose* (1947). Among his many other hit songs are "Animal Crackers in My Soup," "Get Happy," "I Gotta Right to Sing the Blues," "Let's Fall in Love," and "I've Got the World on a String."

KOHLMAR, FRED (1905–1969). Film producer. An eclectic Hollywood producer who presented everything from westerns to screwball comedies, he also supervised some notable screen musicals in the 1940s and 1950s. Kohlmar was born in New York and began his career as a talent agent and then moved into producing as an assistant to SAM GOLDWYN. By the late 1930s he was presenting feature films at various studios and finding success in many different genres. Kohlmar's musicals are *THAT NIGHT IN RIO* (1941), *LET'S FACE IT!* (1943), *Riding High* (1943), *Bring on the Girls* (1945), *You Were Meant for Me* (1948), *CALL ME MISTER* (1951), *Down Among the Sheltering Pines* (1953), *MY SISTER EILEEN* (1955), *PAL JOEY* (1957), and *BYE BYE BIRDIE* (1963).

KOSTA, TESSA (1893–1981). Stage performer. A dark-haired soprano beauty, she was considered one of the finest singer–actresses of the 1920s. Kosta was born in Chicago and learned her craft on the road, eventually playing the leading lady in *THE PINK LADY* (1911). She made her Broadway bow in *The Beauty Shop* (1919) and three years later was starring as the slave girl Marjanah in *Chu Chin Chow*. Kosta was also a success as the Bulgarian aristocrat Nadina in *THE CHOCOLATE SOLDIER* (1921), the Russian revolutionary Aniuta in *Song of the Flame* (1925), and a series of royals: *Princess Virtue* (1921), *Princess April* (1924), and *Princess Ida* (1925). Her other musical credits include *Stop! Look! Listen!* (1916), *The Royal Vagabond* (1919), *Lassie* (1920), *The Rose of Stamboul* (1922), *Caroline* (1923), and a revival of *THE FORTUNE TELLER* (1929). By the end of the decade, Kosta disappeared and fell into obscurity until her death was recorded.

KOSTER, HENRY [born Herman Kosterlitz] (1905–1988). Film director. The German-born director helmed many comedies and musicals, mostly for producer JOE PASTERNAK who discovered him. Koster was born in Berlin and educated at the local Academy of Fine Arts before pursing careers as a painter, cartoonist, journalist, film critic, and scriptwriter for the German film industry. Pasternak promoted him to director in 1932 but the following year Koster fled the Nazis and went to Paris and finally Hollywood where he started directing in 1936 with the DEANNA DURBIN musical *Three Smart Girls* (1937). He would helm five more musicals for the teenage star and became one of UNIVERSAL's most reliable directors. Koster's other screen musicals include *ONE HUNDRED MEN AND A GIRL* (1937), *First Love* (1939), *Music for Millions* (1944), *Two Sisters From Boston* (1946), *The Inspector General* (1949), *WABASH AVENUE* (1950), *My Blue Heaven* (1950), *Stars and Stripes Forever* (1952), *FLOWER DRUM SONG* (1961), and *The Singing Nun* (1966).

KRAFT TELEVISION THEATRE. Television series. A showcase for new dramas, comedies, and musicals, this esteemed program that flourished during the golden days of early television introduced more promising playwrights, actors, and directors than perhaps any other single series. The show ran from 1947 to 1958 and was shown first on NBC and then ABC before returning to NBC in 1955. Of the 650 episodes broadcast, only a few were musicals, including the original musicals *Come to Me* (1957) with Farley Granger, Julie Wilson, and MARGARET O'BRIEN, *Drummer Man* (1957) with Sal Mineo, *Sextuplets* (1957) with TAMMY GRIMES and Fred Gwynne, and *Singin' Idol* (1957) with TOMMY SANDS. A later program, *The Kraft Music Hall* (1967–1971), was a musical variety show.

KRUPA, GENE [born Eugene Bertram Krupa] (1909–1973). Film and television musician and conductor. The flashy gum-chewing drummer who headed his own band, he made specialty appearances in eleven Hollywood musicals. Krupa was born in Chicago and by the age of twenty was touring in professional bands, eventually becoming the featured drummer for BENNY GOODMAN's orchestra. He made many jazz recordings with different musicians and was soon known for his flamboyant style of performing as well as his music. Krupa formed his own band in 1938 and experimented with new drumming techniques and instruments, making him an innovator in jazz percussion. He always played himself in his movie musicals, which include *BIG BROADCAST OF 1937* (1936), *HOLLYWOOD HOTEL* (1937), *Ball of Fire* (1941), *Syncopation* (1942), *GEORGE WHITE'S SCANDALS* (1945), *Beat the Band* (1946), *Make Believe Ballroom* (1949), *THE GLENN MILLER STORY* (1954), and *The Benny Goodman Story* (1960). Krupa also made many television appearances from 1949 to 1972. Sal Mineo impersonated the celebrated musician in *The Gene Krupa Story* (1960) with Krupa himself providing the drumming on the soundtrack. Biographers: *The World of Gene Krupa: That Legendary Drummin' Man*, Bruce H. Klauber (1991); *Gene Krupa: His Life and Times*, Bruce Crowther (1988).

KUDISCH, MARC (1966–). Stage performer. A powerful, masculine leading man with a playful streak to his performances, he has recently become much in demand for Broadway musicals. Kudisch was born in Hackensack, New Jersey, and grew up in Ft. Lauderdale, Florida, studying theatre at Florida Atlantic University. He played Conrad Birdie in the 1992 tour of *BYE BYE BIRDIE*, reprising his performance in the 1995 television version. Kudisch made his Broadway debut as Reuben in the 1993 revival of *JOSEPH AND THE AMAZING TECHNICOLOR DREAMCOAT*, followed by replacing others in *BEAUTY AND THE BEAST* in 1995 and *THE SCARLET PIMPERNEL* in 1999. He shone on Broadway as the stuffy George Kittredge in *HIGH SOCIETY* (1998), the hedonistic Jackie in *THE WILD*

PARTY (2000), the playwright Jeff Moss in *BELLS ARE RINGING* (2001), the dashing executive Mr. Graydon in *THOROUGHLY MODERN MILLIE* (2002), the proprietor in *ASSASSINS* (2004), the diabolical Baron Bomburst in *CHITTY CHITTY BANG BANG* (2005), and the snake and other roles in *THE APPLE TREE* (2006). Off Broadway he was seen in the musicals *See What You Wanna See* (2002), *The Thing About Men* (2003), and *The Glorious Ones* (2007). He has done several musicals in regional theatre and has appeared on television in series, commercials, and soap operas.

KUHN, JUDY (1958–). Stage and television performer. The slim, dark-haired leading lady of Broadway musical hits and flops who has a sparkling clear soprano voice, she has also made many notable recordings. The native New Yorker was educated at Oberlin College's Conservatory of Music before making her Broadway debut in the short-lived *Oh, Brother!* (1981) and then appeared in *THE MYSTERY OF EDWIN DROOD* (1985) before giving a powerful performance as the tragic immigrant Bella in *RAGS* (1986). That musical quickly closed but Kuhn's next musical ran for years: *LES MISÉRABLES* (1987) in which she originated the role of grown-up Cosette in New York. Her other memorable performances include the Hungarian refugee Florence in *CHESS* (1988), the Budapest salesgirl Amalia Balash in the popular revival of *SHE LOVES ME* (1993), and various roles in the Off Broadway revue revival *As THOUSANDS CHEER* (1999). Kuhn played Betty Schaefer in the Los Angeles production of *SUNSET BOULEVARD* (1993) and was featured in the London musical *Metropolis*. In 2007, twenty years after playing the orphaned Cosette, she returned to play her mother Fantine during the Broadway revival of *Les Misérables*. She has appeared in several nonmusicals, on some television dramas and musical specials, and in a few films, also doing the singing vocals for the heroine of the animated *POCAHONTAS* (1995) and its video sequel.

🕮 **KWAMINA** (54th Street Theatre 1961). An unconventional musical with a challenging subject, the piece was perhaps too challenging for audiences in the early 1960s for it closed after thirty-two performances, despite some encouraging reviews. The European-educated African doctor Kwamina (Terry Carter) returns to his native village in a newly freed West African nation where he confronts and then falls in love with the white Englishwoman Eve (SALLY ANN HOWES), their romance threatened by old traditions and radical new movements in the country. Robert Alan Aurthur wrote the uncomfortable libretto and RICHARD ADLER the exhilarating score, which included African-flavored numbers, such as "The Cocoa Bean Song," "Nothing More to Look Forward To," and "One Wife," and European-based numbers, such as "Another Time, Another Place" and "Ordinary People." ROBERT LEWIS directed the superior cast, which also included Robert Guillaume, Ethel Ayler, and BROCK PETERS, and AGNES DE MILLE devised the ritual dances. Some critics faulted the book but found much to admire in the ALFRED DE LIAGRE, JR. production even if most playgoers were wary of such a show.

KYSER, KAY [born James King Kern Kyser] (1897–1985). Film musician, conductor, and performer. A radio favorite with his show *Kay Kyser's Kollage of Musical Knowledge*, the hawk-nosed bandleader with glasses and academic regalia was featured in nine movie musicals. Kyser was born in Rocky Mount, North Carolina, the son of two pharmacists, and studied at the University of North Carolina at Chapel Hill where he played clarinet and led his own campus band. By 1938 he was on the radio as the "Ol' Professor" with his musical quiz show, which ran until 1949. Kyser usually played himself in his Hollywood musicals, which include *That's Right, You're Wrong* (1939), *You'll Find Out* (1940), *Playmates* (1941), *My Favorite Spy* (1942), *STAGE DOOR CANTEEN* (1943), *Thousand Cheer* (1943), *Swing Fever* (1943), *Around the World* (1943), and *Carolina Blues* (1944). Kyser and his band were also very popular in concerts and on records, and several singers got their start with the orchestra, including Harry Babbitt, Ginny Simms, and Mike Douglas. Biography: *Kay Kyser and His Orchestra*, Charles Garrod (1999).

L

LA BAMBA (Columbia 1987). A youthful, vivacious musical biography, it was one of the few Hollywood films ever shot in both English and Spanish so as to reach a wide Hispanic audience as well as traditional moviegoers. It was an appropriate decision because the subject of the movie was young Chicano singer Richie Valens, portrayed by Lou Diamond Phillips with David Hidalgo dubbing the singing for him. Luis Valdez wrote and directed the film and, as bio pics go, it was one of Hollywood's better efforts. California teenager Valens is discovered while still a student in high school, and he soars to stardom via three hit songs. The conflicts revolved around Valens's difficult relationship with his volatile brother Bob (Esai Morales), and all ends tragically when Valens dies at the age of seventeen in the same plane crash that killed Buddy Holly (Marshall Crenshaw). Also in the cast were Rosanna DeSoto, Elizabeth Penã, Joe Pantoliano, Danielle von Zerneck, and Rick Dees. The group Los Lobos provided the musical accompaniment for the Valens's favorites, such as "All My Love, All My Kisses," "Baby, Baby," "Come On, Let's Go," "Little Darlin'," "Saturday Night," and the title number.

LA CAGE AUX FOLLES (Palace Theatre 1983). The first Broadway musical to have homosexual characters in the major roles, the musical otherwise was a very conventional crowd pleaser with plenty of glitter and hummable songs. St. Tropez nightclub owner Georges and his longtime lover and main attraction, female impersonator Albin, find their lives turned upside down when Georges's son Jean-Michel wants to bring his fiancée Anne and her conservative parents, Edouard and Marie Dindon, to meet his family. The two gay men attempt to come across as straight as possible but Albin ends up getting into drag to play Jean-Michel's "mother." Closely patterned after the popular 1978 French film, the libretto by HARVEY FIERSTEIN was traditional in most ways and even the central gay couple seemed old-fashioned and familiar. JERRY HERMAN wrote the tuneful score, which included such numbers as "The Best of Times," "I Am What I Am," "Song on the Sand," "A Little More Mascara," and the title number. Appreciative reviews and strong word of mouth made it the first gay musical to become a mainstream hit. ARTHUR LAURENTS directed, Scott Salmon choreographed with panache, and the musical comedy ran 1,761 performances.

Productions of *La Cage aux Folles* waned in the later 1980s when the AIDS epidemic made the lighthearted show seem in questionable taste, but by 2004 it was back on Broadway with GARY BEACH (Albin) and Daniel Davis (Georges) heading a capable cast directed by JERRY ZAKS and choreographed by JERRY MITCHELL. Although it lacked the quality and impact of the original and was cited as dated by some reviewers, the well-acted revival was deemed to be still very enjoyable and audiences agreed for 229 performances.

LA PLUME DE MA TANTE (Royale Theatre 1958). French cuisine, airlines, romance, entertainers, and phrases were all satirized in this unique and much-lauded revue that had been a hit in Paris and London before DAVID MERRICK brought it to Broadway for a profitable run of 835 performances. Many of the sketches were silent and no understanding of French was necessary to enjoy the songs and dialogue.

Broadway casts for *La Cage aux Folles*		
Character	*1983 Broadway*	*2004 Broadway*
Albin	GEORGE HEARN	GARY BEACH
Georges	Gene Barry	Daniel Davis
Jean-Michel	John Weiner	Gavin Creel
Anne	Leslie Stevens	Angela Gaylor
Jacqueline	Elizabeth Parrish	Ruth Williamson
Edouard Dindon	Jay Garner	Michael Mulheren
Marie Dindon	Merle Louise	Linda Balgord

Robert Dhery wrote the skits and lyrics and Gerald Calvi composed the music, and the delightful cast included author Dhery, Pierre Olaf, Colette Brosset, Ross Parker, and Jean Lefevre. Most remembered from the revue was a hilarious number in which four monks sedately pulled bell ropes to the tune of "Frere Jacques," but as the music got faster and faster the foursome got wilder and wilder, ending up tied in knots and dangling in the air.

LaChiusa, Michael John (1962–). Stage composer, lyricist, and writer. One of the most original, engrossing, and challenging songwriters at the end of the twentieth century, he has written musicals that are uncompromising in their goals and, consequently, rarely have found wide acceptance. LaChiusa was born in Chautauqua, New York, and briefly attended a junior college in Boston before going to New York to write musicals that demand more from audiences than escapism. Working with writers and lyricist such as Jeffrey Essmann and Doug Wright, he wrote music for some Off Off Broadway musicals in 1989 to 1993 but was first noticed for his *First Lady Suite* (1993) for which he wrote book, music, and lyrics, his pattern for most of his subsequent works. LaChiusa received high praise for his Off Broadway musical *Hello Again* (1993) but his Broadway efforts *Marie Christine* (1999) and *The Wild Party* (2000) were more admired than embraced by the public. His other New York works include *The Petrified Prince* (1994), *Chronicle of a Death Foretold* (1995), *Little Fish* (2003), *See What I Wanna See* (2005), and *Bernarda Alba* (2006). LaChiusa's music is eclectic, echoing different time periods and styles, his lyrics are terse and piercing, and his books inventive and offbeat.

▉ Lady and the Tramp (Disney 1955). Although it was not based on a classic fairy tale or a familiar children's book, the animated musical immediately became a Disney favorite with audiences and has remained so over the decades. The sharp, truthful characterizations of the canine characters and the very human feelings of rejection and love that they possess keep the movie potent and enjoyable for each new generation that experiences it. The pampered but affectionate cocker spaniel Lady (voice of Barbara Luddy) feels on the outs when a new human baby in the household usurps her position as the family's only pet. After being pushed aside and then blamed for mischief she didn't do, Lady runs off. But the outside world is even less accepting and

only through the wily machinations of the street mutt Tramp (Larry Roberts) does Lady regain her place in the home and find a mate as well. The supporting characters were a colorful crew: the aging bloodhound Trusty (Bill Baucon), the wiry Scottish terrier Jock (Bill Thompson), the sassy, sexy canine Peg, and two stuck-up Siamese cats (all three voiced by Peggy Lee). Lee wrote the songs with Sonny Burke, including the sly parody "Siamese Cat Song," the torchy "He's a Tramp," and the romantic ballad "Bella Notte" sung by Italian restaurateur Tony (George Givot) while Lady and the Tramp engage in the most famous spaghetti dinner in filmdom. The first Disney-animated film in Cinemascope, it required over 150 artists and animators and the result is stunning. Set in a New England town in 1910, the movie is a wonderful piece of Americana as well as first-class entertainment.

✎ Lady, Be Good! (Liberty Theatre 1924). The first collaboration of George (music) and Ira Gershwin (lyrics) to reach Broadway, the musical also turned Adele and Fred Astaire into bona fide Broadway stars. Angry because Dick Trevor (Fred Astaire) has not returned her affections, property owner Josephine Vanderwater (Jayne Auburn) evicts Dick and his sister Susie (Adele Astaire) from her apartment building and they take residence on the sidewalk until the crafty lawyer "Watty" Watkins (Walter Catlett) comes up with a plan. He has Susie disguise herself as a Mexican wife so that Watty can collect his fee from a divorce case. The ruse causes complications when the man Susie loves, Jack Robinson (Alan Edwards), finds out she is "married" and it takes some doing to repair the damage and allow Dick to win his own sweetheart, Shirley Vernon (Kathlene Martyn). Guy Bolton and Fred Thompson wrote the efficient libretto, which was tailored to the singing–dancing talents of the Astaire siblings and the two took the town by storm. However, the more far-reaching effect of *Lady, Be Good!* was its score. The show was the first to use the new jazz sound effectively in a musical comedy format, and the new sound would influence musical comedy songs for decades, relying on a rhythm totally divorced from operetta. "Oh, Lady Be Good!" and "Fascinating Rhythm" were the two most popular numbers, but also expert were "So Am I," "Hang on to Me," "Little Jazz Bird," and "The Half of It Dearie Blues." The Alex A. Aaron and Vinton Freedley production ran 330 performances and launched the Broadway careers of the Gershwins and the Astaires.

■ *Lady, Be Good!* (MGM 1941) kept the title song and "Fascinating Rhythm," tossed out the rest of the stage score and plot, and substituted it with a dull story about songwriters Dixie Donegan (ANN SOTHERN) and Eddie Crane (ROBERT YOUNG) who are romantic as well as professional partners. When success goes to their heads, the couple breaks up, followed by a series of reconciliations and further partings that try the patience of even the most forgiving movie musical fan. ELEANOR POWELL, as a character who hardly entered the plot, gave the film its only winning moments, such as a lavish production number that featured her, eight grand pianos, and a hundred men in white tie and tails tapping to "Fascinating Rhythm." Also effective was Sothern's rendition of "The Last Time I Saw Paris," a poignant ballad by JEROME KERN (music) and OSCAR HAMMERSTEIN (lyrics) that was interpolated into the film and won the Oscar for Best Song. Also in the score were "Your Words and My Music" and "You'll Never Know" by ROGER EDENS and ARTHUR FREED. NORMAN Z. LEONARD directed without much energy, and the supporting cast included Lionel Barrymore, RED SKELTON, JOHN CARROLL, VIRGINIA O'BRIEN, DAN DAILEY, REGINALD OWEN, and PHIL SILVERS, all of whom had been better and would be again in other films.

🕮 *LADY IN THE DARK* (Alvin Theatre 1941). One of the most experimental Broadway shows of its era, the inventive musical play by MOSS HART (book), KURT WEILL (music), and IRA GERSHWIN (lyrics) utilized expressionism and other theatrical techniques and still ended up being an enjoyable hit. Magazine editor Liza Elliott is having so much difficulty of late making decisions about business and personal affairs that she goes into therapy with Dr. Brooks. Under analysis, surreal musical dream sequences illustrate her fears, wishes, and disappointments. By the end of her analysis, Liza knows she loves her business and sparing partner Charley Johnson who can complete a song she once knew in childhood. The innovative musical confined most of the musical numbers to the dream sequences and, co-directed by HASSARD SHORT and Hart, the show flowed in and out of reality in a unique way. GERTRUDE LAWRENCE was the star attraction, although

Lady in the Dark. In the old days all it took sometimes was one song in a Broadway hit and a star was born. It happened with Mary Martin singing "My Heart Belongs to Daddy" in *Leave It to Me* (1938) and three years later it happened to Danny Kaye (pictured) singing the tongue-twisting "Tschaikowsky" in *Lady in the Dark.* (Photofest)

Casts for *Lady in the Dark*

Character	1940 Broadway	1944 film	1954 television
Liza Elliott	GERTRUDE LAWRENCE	GINGER ROGERS	ANN SOTHERN
Charley Johnson	MacDonald Carey	Ray Milland	James Daly
Russell Paxton	DANNY KAYE	MISCHA AUER	CARLETON CARPENTER
Kendall Nesbitt	Bert Lytell	WARNER BAXTER	Paul McGrath
Randy Curtis	VICTOR MATURE	Jon Hall	
Dr. Brooks	Donald Randolph	Barry Sullivan	Sheppard Strudwick

DANNY KAYE stopped the show each night with his fast-talking solo "Tschaikowsky" and he too became a star. Other songs to become popular were the dreamy lullaby "My Ship" and the sly narrative number "Jenny," as well as "Girl of the Moment," "This Is New," and "One Life to Live." The SAM H. HARRIS production received rave notices and ran 162 performances in its first engagement, returning in 1941 for another 305 performances, and yet again in 1943 for another eighty-three performances. Revivals have been rare, although a London production in 1997 with Maria Friedman as Liza was a major hit.

■ *Lady in the Dark* (Paramount 1944) starred GINGER ROGERS as Liza Elliott and she did not disappoint her many fans, although anyone who knew the stage work and Lawrence's performance was not impressed. The screenplay by FRANCES GOODRICH and ALBERT HACKETT sticks with the Broadway musical's premise but what was intriguing on stage came across as confused in the disjointed movie. Much of the Weill–Gershwin score was cut or abridged and the song "My Ship" was reduced to a few bars of background music, thereby removing the key to Liza's character. Billy Daniels choreographed the production numbers, with the best one being the circus dream in which Rogers performs "Jenny," but both Danny Kaye and his song "Tchaikovsky" were gone, although MISCHA AUER played the role without a song. New songs, written by various tunesmiths, were added, including "Suddenly It's Spring," "Artists' Waltz," and "Dream Lover." MITCHELL LEISEN directed the B. G. DeSYLVA production and it did very well at the box office, although it has pretty much been forgotten since then. ▢ MAX LEIBMAN produced an eighty-five-minute version *of Lady in the Dark* for NBC-TV in 1954 with ANN SOTHERN as Liza and critics applauded her performance as one of her best. A good number of the stage songs were included in the condensed version, and Rod Alexander staged the production numbers.

■ *LADY SINGS THE BLUES* (Paramount 1972). While it distorted more facts than it used and loyal fans of the legendary jazz singer Billie Holiday might be discontented with DIANA ROSS when they could listen to the real Holiday on records, the biographical musical was nevertheless intriguing as well as entertaining. Following the usual rags-to-riches format that had been working since the 1930s, the film followed young Billie from the streets of Harlem to her triumph at Carnegie Hall, all the time showing her drug addiction, battles with racism while touring the country, and the tempestuous relationship with her husband Louis McKay (Billy Dee Williams). Holiday's death by a heroin overdose was alluded to in a film montage, another old device that still worked. Richard Pryor was outstanding as Billie's co-addict and friend Piano Man, and the expert supporting cast included Sid Melton, James Callahan, Virginia Capers, Paul Hampton, and Scatman Crothers. Ross delivered the Holiday song hits in a smooth, velvety style that sounded more contemporary than the raw, aching voice of Holiday herself, but the old standards were interpreted well, including "Strange Fruit," "Good Morning, Heartache," "The Man I Love," "'Tain't Nobody's Bizness If I Do," "Lover Man," "God Bless the Child," and the title number. Sidney J. Furie directed Ross in her first character role on screen and it made her a movie star.

LAHR, BERT [born Irving Lahrheim] (1895–1967). Stage, film, and television performer. One of America's most inspired clowns, he is mostly remembered as the Cowardly Lion in the movie musical favorite THE WIZARD OF OZ (1939) but the rubber-faced, razor-sharp comic had a long and varied career. The native New Yorker dropped out of school and worked in burlesque and vaudeville for years, refining his quirky persona and odd but hilarious noises he produced in his throat. He made his Broadway debut in *Delmar's Revels* (1927) and then first attracted wide attention as the punch-drunk boxer Gink Schiner in *HOLD*

EVERYTHING! (1928). Lahr kept Broadway audiences in stitches in a series of musical hits: as the buffoonish airplane mechanic Rusty Krause in *FLYING HIGH* (1930), the speakeasy waiter Alky Schmidt in *Hot-Cha!* (1932), the doped-up washroom attendant Louis Blore who dreams he is King Louis XV of France in *DUBARRY WAS A LADY* (1939), and a variety of comic characters in the revues *George White's Music Hall Varieties* (1932), *LIFE BEGINS AT 8:40* (1934), *GEORGE WHITE'S SCANDALS* (1935), *THE SHOW IS ON* (1936), *Seven Lively Arts* (1944), *TWO ON THE AISLE* (1951), and *The Boys Against the Girls* (159). He began his movie career when he reprised his Rusty in *Flying High* (1931) but except for *The Wizard of Oz* and a few other films, Lahr's manic comedy talents never showed as well on screen as on stage. His other movie musicals include *Merry-Go-Round* (1937), *Love and Hisses* (1937), *Just Around the Corner* (1938), *Zaza* (1939), *Sing Your Worries Away* (1942), *Ship Ahoy* (1942), *Meet the People* (1944), *Always Leave Them Laughing* (1949), *ROSE MARIE* (1954), *The Second Greatest Sex* (1955), and *The Night They Raided Minsky's* (1968). Lahr was popular on the radio (he had his own show for a time) and made a number of television appearances, including the TV musicals *ANYTHING GOES* (1954), *LET'S FACE IT!* (1954), *THE GREAT WALTZ* (1955), and *THE FANTASTICKS* (1964). He returned to Broadway for such diverse productions as the first New York production of the absurdist classic *Waiting for Godot* (1956), the French farce *Hotel Paradiso* (1957), the satire *The Beauty Part* (1962), and the Klondike musical *Foxy* (1964). His son, critic John Lahr (1941–), wrote his biography: *Notes on a Cowardly Lion* (1969).

LAINE, FRANKIE [born Francesco Paul LoVecchio] (1913–2007). Film performer. One of America's favorite singers on records and in nightclubs in the late 1940s and 1950s, he made a half-dozen Hollywood musicals without creating much of a stir. Laine was born in Chicago, the son of immigrants from Sicily, and sang in the church choir as a boy. After working in offices and in sales, he became a champion marathon dancer during the Depression but his singing career didn't take off until he was discovered by HOAGY CARMICHAEL who helped him get nightclub bookings and a recording contract. Laine was at the peak of his popularity when he sang in the movies *Make Believe Ballroom* (1949), *When You're Smiling* (1950), *On the Sunny Side of the Street* (1951), *Rainbow 'Round My Shoulder* (1952), *Bring Your Smile Along* (1955),

Meet Me in Las Vegas (1956), and *He Laughed Last* (1956), yet the public preferred Laine on records and in personal appearances so he stuck to those and television for the rest of his career. Autobiography: *That Lucky Old Son*, with Joseph F. Laredo (1993); biography: *Reaching for a Star: Frankie Laine*, Craig Cronbaugh (2005).

LAMAS, FERNANDO [Alvaro] (1915–1982). Film, stage, and television performer and director. One of Hollywood's favorite Latin lovers, the handsome actor possessed an agreeable baritone singing voice that made his musical roles very romantic. Lamas was born in Buenos Aires, Argentina, and became an established movie star in his native country before he was brought to Hollywood in 1950 where he was cast as muscular, sporting types in such musicals as *Rich, Young and Pretty* (1951), *THE MERRY WIDOW* (1952), *Dangerous When Wet* (1953), *ROSE MARIE* (1954), and *The Girl Rush* (1955). He also made a noteworthy Broadway appearance as the Duke of Granada opposite ETHEL MERMAN in the musical *Happy Hunting* (1956). Lamas started directing in the 1960s, helming a few films and many television programs. He was married to actress Arlene Dahl (1928–) and ESTHER WILLIAMS, and his son is actor Lorenzo Lamas (1958–).

LAMB, GIL[bert L.] (1904–1995). Film, stage, and television performer. With his long sad face and eccentric dancing style, the odd character actor was noticeable in some forty films. Lamb was born in Minneapolis and was in vaudeville, stock, and some musical film shorts before making his Broadway bow in *Hold on to Your Hats* (1940). He went to Hollywood the next year and was cast in supporting roles of an offbeat nature, including characters in the musicals *THE FLEET'S IN* (1942), *STAR-SPANGLED RHYTHM* (1943), *Riding High* (1943), *Rainbow Island* (1944), and *Hit Parade of 1947* (1946). He returned to Broadway to play Ichabod Crane in the musical *Sleepy Hollow* (1948) but it failed to run so he made more films and many television appearances, such as the TV version of *BABES IN TOYLAND* (1950). Lamb played small roles in the film musicals *BELLS ARE RINGING* (1960) and *BYE BYE BIRDIE* (1963) and made a final Broadway appearances as the senior citizen Walter in *70, GIRLS, 70* (1971).

LAMOUR, DOROTHY [born Mary Leta Dorothy Slaton] (1914–1996). Film and stage performer. Typecast as an exotic, primitive jungle princess when she donned a sarong in nonmusical films, the dark-haired, sultry beauty appeared in over thirty movie musicals, most fondly remembered as the beautiful distraction in the seven BOB HOPE–BING CROSBY *ROAD* pictures. Lamour was born in New Orleans and won beauty contests and sang in bands before making her Hollywood debut as a chorus girl in the musical *FOOTLIGHT PARADE* (1933). When she appeared in a sarong in the nonmusical *Jungle Princess* (1936), she was widely noticed and was similarly clothed in such films as *The Hurricane* (1937), *Typhoon* (1940), *Aloma of the South Seas* (1941) and many others. Lamour's early musicals were *College Holiday* (1936), *Swing High, Swing Low* (1937), *HIGH, WIDE AND HANDSOME* (1937), *Thrill of a Lifetime* (1937), *BIG BROADCAST OF 1938*, *Her Jungle Love* (1938), *Tropic Holiday* (1938), *St. Louis Blues* (1939), and *Man About Town* (1939), but it was in *ROAD TO SINGAPORE* (1940) that her exotic persona was used in a satirical, musical way and she revealed a playful side rarely seen before. She costarred with Hope and Crosby in six of the Road musical comedies and made a cameo in the final entry, *THE ROAD TO HONG KONG* (1962). Among her other musical credits are *Johnny Apollo* (1940), *Moon Over Burma* (1940), *THE FLEET'S IN* (1942), *Beyond the Blue Horizon* (1942), *STAR-SPANGLED RHYTHM* (1942), *Dixie* (1943), *Riding High* (1943), *And the Angels Sing* (1944), *Rainbow Island* (1944), *Duffy's Tavern* (1945), *Variety Girl* (1947), *Slightly French* (1949), and *HERE COMES THE GROOM* (1951). In the 1950s Lamour acted on television and occasionally turned to the stage, performing on Broadway as a replacement in *Oh, Captain!* in 1958 and playing Dolly Levi in *HELLO, DOLLY!* on tour in the 1960s. She continued to perform into the late 1980s. Autobiography: *My Side of the Road* (1980).

LANDIS, CAROLE [born Frances Lillian Mary Ridste] (1919–1948). Film performer. The shapely, leggy blonde who was a favorite of G.I.s during World War II for her many USO shows overseas, she shone in some 1940s Hollywood musicals even though she was rarely in a leading role. Landis was born in Fairchild, Wisconsin, and won beauty contests as a teenager. After working at various jobs in her hometown, she went to San Francisco where she sang and danced in nightclubs. Hollywood discovered her in 1937, and after bit parts in the musicals *A DAY AT THE RACES* (1937), *BROADWAY MELODY OF 1938* (1937), *Varsity Show* (1937), *HOLLYWOOD HOTEL* (1937), and *GOLD DIGGERS IN PARIS* (1938), she got secondary roles in such musicals as *Road Show* (1941), *MOON OVER MIAMI* (1941), *Cadet Girl* (1941), *My Gal Sal* (1942), *ORCHESTRA WIVES* (1942), *The Powers Girl* (1942), and *Wintertime* (1943). Perhaps her best performance was playing herself in *Four Jills in a Jeep* (1944), which was based on her true adventures entertaining the troops. She also was featured in the Broadway musical *A Lady Says Yes* (1945). The oft-married, unstable Landis died of an overdose of sleeping pills at the age of twenty-nine. Biography: *Carole Landis: A Tragic Life in Hollywood*, E. J. Fleming (2005).

LANE, BURTON [born Burton Levy] (1912–1997). Stage and film composer. Although not as well known as he ought to be, the gifted songwriter worked with the finest lyricists of his era and turned out exceptional scores on Broadway and in Hollywood. The native New Yorker composed songs as a child and got his first job as a teenager playing piano in a music publisher's office. Some songs he wrote with lyricist HAROLD ADAMSON were heard in the Broadway revue *EARL CARROLL VANITIES* (1931) and then Lane and Adamson went to Hollywood where they scored the musicals *DANCING LADY* (1933) and *Bottoms Up* (1934). Lane collaborated with FRANK LOESSER (who was only writing lyrics at the time) on *College Swing* (1938), *Cocoanut Grove* (1938), and *St. Louis Blues* (1939) and then returned to Broadway where he teamed with lyricist E. Y. HARBURG for the first time, with the two scoring the revue *Hold on to Your Hats* (1940) and later on the classic musical fantasy *FINIAN'S RAINBOW* (1947). Lane crisscrossed back and forth between New York and California for years, working with his past collaborators and finding success with new ones, most notably ALAN JAY LERNER with whom he wrote the film score for *ROYAL WEDDING* (1951) and the Broadway scores for *ON A CLEAR DAY YOU CAN SEE FOREVER* (1965) and *Carmelina* (1979). Lane's other movie musicals are *Strictly Dynamite* (1934), *She Married a Cop* (1939), *Dancing on a Dime* (1941), *BABES ON BROADWAY* (1941), *Ship Ahoy* (1942), *Rainbow Island* (1944), *GIVE A GIRL A BREAK* (1953), *Jupiter's Darling* (1955), and *The Adventures of Huckleberry Finn* (1960), as well as the TV musical *JUNIOR MISS* (1957). He even provided his own lyrics for the Broadway musical *Laffing Room Only* (1947). Lane's musical talents were considerable, filled with versatility, inventiveness, and strong melodic lines. His sense of variety can be seen in his catalogue of song hits, with such diverse entries as "Old Devil Moon," "Heigh Ho, the Gang's All Here," "Too Late Now," "Feudin' and Fightin'," "Look to the Rainbow," "How Could You Believe Me When I Said I Loved You … ?," and "If This Isn't Love."

LANE, LOLA, PRISCILLA, AND ROSEMARY. Film and stage performers. Three attractive siblings with wholesome good looks and pleasing singing voices, they were featured in several Hollywood musicals but rarely together. The dark-haired Lola Lane [born Dorothy Mullican] (1909–1981) was born in Macy, Indiana, the daughter of a dentist, but raised in the Iowa corn belt with her four sisters. She learned to play piano as a child and earned money as an accompanist in the local silent film theatre before studying music at a nearby conservatory. She and her elder sister Leta went to New York together in 1926 to perform in vaudeville and were promoted by showman Gus Edwards in variety. The two siblings appeared Off Broadway in the revue *Greenwich Village Follies* (1927) and when Lola was cast in a play the next year, she was signed by a Hollywood agent. The doll-faced Rosemary Lane [born Rosemary Mullican] (1914–1974) and the blonde Priscilla Lane [born Priscilla Mullican] were both born in Indianola, Iowa, and attended Simpson College before going into show business as vocalists for Fred

Waring's Pennsylvanians. The sisters made their film debuts with that chorale in the musical *Varsity Show* (1937), and the next year the three siblings were cast in the melodrama *Four Daughters* (1938), followed by some other sentimental dramas that were very popular. Each of the Lane sisters made musicals. Lola was featured in *Fox Movietone's Follies* (1929), *Let's Go Places* (1930), GOOD NEWS! (1930), and HOLLYWOOD HOTEL (1937). Rosemary played character parts in *Hollywood Hotel* (1937), GOLD DIGGERS IN PARIS (1938), THE BOYS FROM SYRACUSE (1940), *Time Out for Rhythm* (1941), *Chatterbox* (1943), *Harvest Melody* (1943), and *Trocadero* (1944). She also returned to Broadway in the musical *Best Foot Forward* (1941). Priscilla had the most successful career, appearing in major roles in many nonmusicals and two other musicals: *Cowboy From Brooklyn* (1938) and *BLUES IN THE NIGHT* (1941).

LANE, NATHAN [born Joseph Lane] (1956–). Stage, film, and television performer. The pudgy comic actor–singer has the qualities and talents of the great Broadway clowns, yet

Nathan Lane. Because they rarely write great comic roles in new musicals, the inspired funnyman Nathan Lane (far left) needs to appear in revivals of older shows to get the kind of parts in which he excels. Even when he originated the role of Max Bialystock in *The Producers* (2001), he was in the shadow of Zero Mostel who had created the nonsinging role on screen. Here Lane appears in another Mostel role, the clever slave Pseudolus in the 1996 revival of *A Funny Thing Happened on the Way to the Forum*. He is followed by Mark Linn-Baker, Ernie Sabella, and William Duell. (Photofest)

he has successfully appeared in serious and classic plays as well. Lane was born in Jersey City, New Jersey, the son of a policeman, and worked as a telemarketer, pollster, singing telegram delivery boy, and stand-up comic before he began acting in dinner theatres and stock. He was on the New York stage by 1978 and was first noticed for his comic shenanigans as the overeager playwright Roland Maule in a Broadway revival of the comedy *Present Laughter* (1982). Lane appeared in a variety of productions on and Off Broadway, including the musicals *Merlin* (1983), *Love* (1984), and *Wind in the Willows* (1985), before he became a full-fledged star as Nathan Detroit in the popular 1992 revival of GUYS AND DOLLS. He also shone as Pseudolus in *A FUNNY THING HAPPENED ON THE WAY TO THE FORUM* (1996) before getting his best musical role to date, Shyster producer Max Bialystock in THE PRODUCERS (2001), which he repeated in London and on the screen. Lane played Dionysus in the stage musical *The Frogs* (2004) and acted in several nonmusicals on Broadway. He has appeared in a number of films and television programs, although rarely did they give him the chance to sing or dance. Lane's versatile voice has been used effectively in animated television shows and movies, mostly memorably as the voice of the meerkat Timon in THE LION KING (1994) and its video sequels and as the mouse *Stuart Little* (1999) and its sequel.

LANFIELD, SIDNEY (1898–1972). Film and television director. During his two decades in Hollywood, he helmed many comedies, melodramas, and musicals. Lanfield was born in Chicago and worked as a jazz musician and in vaudeville before entering the movie business as a writer in 1926. Four years later he was directing for 20TH CENTURY-FOX and was known for his light touch, as seen in the musicals *Moulin Rouge* (1934), *KING OF BURLESQUE* (1935), *Sing, Baby, Sing* (1936), *WAKE UP AND LIVE* (1937), *SECOND FIDDLE* (1939), and *Swanee* (1939). After directing *YOU'LL NEVER GET RICH* (1941) for COLUMBIA, Lanfield worked for PARAMOUNT and turned out such musicals as *LET'S FACE IT* (1943), *The Lemon Drop Kid* (1951), and *Shirts Ahoy* (1952). He left Hollywood for early television where he helmed over 200 shows, including original dramas and long-running series.

LANG, HAROLD (1920–1971). Stage, television, and film performer. The athletic dancer–singer, with a strong background in ballet, was usually seen in supporting roles in Broadway musi-

cals. Lang was born in Day City, California, and pursued a dance career, getting hired by the Ballets Russe de Monte-Carlo and the American Ballet Theatre and touring with them before making his Broadway musical debut in the chorus of *Mr. Strauss Goes to Boston* (1945). After supporting roles in *Three to Make Ready* (1946) and *Look, Ma, I'm Dancin'* (1948), he got the plum role of careless, breezy hoofer Bill Calhoun in KISS ME, KATE (1948). Lang was featured in the short-lived *Make a Wish* (1951) and then was acclaimed for his amoral Joey Evans in the popular 1951 revival of PAL JOEY, which he reprised in London in 1954. His other musicals were *Shangri-La* (1956), ZIEGFELD FOLLIES (1957), ON THE TOWN (1959), *I CAN GET IT FOR YOU WHOLESALE* (1962), and *The Decline and Fall of the World as Seen Through the Eyes of Cole Porter Revisited* (1965). Lang frequently returned to ballet and danced with various companies on tour. He also appeared in several television shows and some movies, including the musicals *The Story of Gilbert and Sullivan* (1953), *Dance Little Lady* (1955), and *It's a Wonderful World* (1956).

LANG, PHILIP J. (1911–1986). Stage and television orchestrator. One of the busiest and most respected musical arrangers on Broadway, he also orchestrated for television, films, ballet companies, the Boston Pops, Radio City Music Hall, and the Metropolitan Opera. The native New Yorker was educated at Ithaca College, Columbia University, and Juilliard. He orchestrated music for bands and music ensembles before making his Broadway debut with the orchestrations for *Billion Dollar Baby* (1945). Over the next forty years he orchestrated over fifty Broadway shows of diverse styles and temperament. His credits include *HIGH BUTTON SHOES* (1947), *WHERE'S CHARLEY?* (1948), *CAN-CAN* (1953), *FANNY* (1954), *MY FAIR LADY* (1956), *JAMAICA* (1957), *REDHEAD* (1959), *DESTRY RIDES AGAIN* (1959), *CAMELOT* (1960), *SUBWAYS ARE FOR SLEEPING* (1961), *HELLO, DOLLY!* (1964), *THE ROAR OF THE GREASEPAINT–THE SMELL OF THE CROWD* (1965), *MAME* (1966), *GEORGE M!* (1968), *APPLAUSE* (1970), *SUGAR* (1972), *MACK AND MABEL* (1974), *ANNIE* (1977), *42ND STREET* (1980), and *Peg* (1983). He also orchestrated the movie musicals *LI'L ABNER* (1959), *The Night They Raided Minsky's* (1968), and *HELLO, DOLLY!* (1969) and many television specials, including the TV musical *Stover at Yale* (1957). Lang taught instrumental music at the University of Michigan in Ann Arbor and the University of Colorado at Boulder and wrote a textbook on scoring music for bands.

LANG, WALTER (1896–1972). Film director. A master at glossy, entertaining comedies and musicals, he helmed some of the best screen versions of Broadway hits. Lang was born in Memphis, Tennessee, and worked as a fashion illustrator and as an actor on the stage before entering films in the early 1920s as a clerk at a Manhattan production company. By 1926 he was directing silents for COLUMBIA but by the mid-1930s was at 20TH CENTURY-FOX where he stayed for thirty years. Lang was one of the first directors to effectively use the lush look of Technicolor, and his movies often have a bright, even garish look to them. Among his twenty musicals were *Hooray for Love* (1935), *The Blue Bird* (1940), *Tin Pan Alley* (1940), *Moon Over Miami* (1941), *Weekend in Havana* (1941), *Coney Island* (1943), *State Fair* (1945), *Mother Wore Tights* (1947), *You're My Everything* (1949), *On the Riviera* (1951), *With a Song in My Heart* (1952), *Call Me Madam* (1953), *There's No Business Like Show Business* (1954), *The King and I* (1956), and *Can-Can* (1960).

LANGFORD, FRANCES [born Frances Newbern] (1913–2005). Film, stage, and television performer. A radio singer with a smooth and creamy voice, the small, round-faced actress appeared in twenty-seven movie musicals, usually in supporting roles in grade A films and leads in inferior products. Langford was born in Lakeland, Florida, and began singing in public at an early age. Her caressing voice made her a radio favorite, particularly when she teamed up with BOB HOPE on a series of broadcasts. Langford was featured in the Broadway musical *Here Goes the Bride* (1931) and then made her screen debut in the musical *Every Night at Eight* (1935). She gained moviegoers' attention when she sang "Broadway Rhythm" in *Broadway Melody of 1936* (1935). Among her subsequent musicals are *Born to Dance* (1936), *Too Many Girls* (1940), *Swing It, Soldier* (1941), *Yankee Doodle Dandy* (1942), *Follow the Band* (1943), *This Is the Army* (1943), *Never a Dull Moment* (1943), *The Girl Rush* (1944), *People Are Funny* (1946), *Bamboo Blonde* (1946), *Beat the Band* (1947), and *The Glenn Miller Story* (1954), as well as singing on the soundtrack for the animated *Melody Time* (1948). Langford was also a very successful recording star and made several appearances on television variety shows.

LANSBURY, ANGELA (1925–). Stage, film, and television performer. The many-sided actress who has conquered every medium, she did not become a musical star until late in her career. The native Londoner, the daughter of a Labour Party leader and an actress, took singing and dancing lessons as a child and then continued her studies in New York City when she was evacuated during the Blitz. Lansbury was still a teenager when she made a noticeable film debut in *Gaslight* (1944), followed by many films over the next three decades. Some of them were musicals, such as *The Harvey Girls* (1946), *Till the Clouds Roll By* (1946), *The Court Jester* (1956), and *Blue Hawaii* (1961), although often her singing was dubbed. It was not until Lansbury appeared on Broadway in the musical *Anyone Can Whistle* (1964) and was a smash in *Mame* (1966 and 1983) that she was considered a singer and she got to do her own vocals in the movie musicals *Bedknobs and Broomsticks* (1971) and *The Pirates of Penzance* (1983), as well as provide voices for the animated musicals *Beauty and the Beast* (1991) and *Anastasia* (1997). Her other stage musical credits were the loony Countess Aurelia in *Dear World* (1969), Mama Rose in the London and Broadway revival of *Gypsy* (1974), a replacement for Anna Leonowens in *The King and I* (1978), and Mrs. Lovett in *Sweeney Todd* (1979). Lansbury appeared in nonmusical plays in London and New York and then found a whole new audience on television in the long-running series *Murder She Wrote* in the 1980s and 1990s, also appearing on many specials, including the TV musical *Mrs. Santa Claus* (1996). She returned to Broadway in 2007 in the play *Deuce*. From the start of her film career, Lansbury often played characters much older than herself so she has always been more a character actress than a leading lady, bringing a sparkling stage presence to her work and mixing humor and subtle nuance as she shifts from lovable to chilling in the blink of an eye. Biography: *Balancing Act: The Authorized Biography of Angela Lansbury*, Martin Gottfried (1999).

LANZA, MARIO [born Alfredo Arnold Cocozza] (1921–1959). Film performer. One of the greatest tenor voices of the twentieth century, the robust, handsome singer chose Hollywood over the opera world and the tragic consequences have at least left behind some sterling singing on film. Lanza was born in Philadelphia, the son of a disabled vet and a seamstress, and took singing lessons as a child. He dropped out of high school to work in his grandfather's grocery business and then in 1942 auditioned for conductor Serge Koussevitzky who featured the young singer at Tanglewood.

Lanza started recording in the late 1930s and, after serving in World War II, became popular in concerts as well. He also sang opera but when Hollywood beckoned he went west and was starred in the musical *That Midnight Kiss* (1949). Moviegoers were as entranced as classical music lovers were and Lanza's subsequent musicals THE TOAST OF NEW ORLEANS (1950) and THE GREAT CARUSO (1951) were international hits. But the temperamental singer was difficult to work with, suffering from alcoholism and emotional insecurity, and when he put on too much weight, he was dropped from THE STUDENT PRINCE (1954) after recording the soundtrack; actor Edmund Purdom played the title role using Lanza's singing voice. The great tenor's next three films—*Serenade* (1956), THE SEVEN HILLS OF ROME (1958), and *For the First Time* (1959)—were not as popular so Lanza moved to Europe, made some foreign films, and sang in concerts until his premature death by a heart attack. With his hit recordings of both classical and popular music, Lanza did much to promote opera and classical music in mainstream America. Biographies: *Mario Lanza: Singing to the Gods*, Derek Mannering (2005); *Mario Lanza: Tenor in Exile*, Roland L. Bessette (2003).

LAPINE, JAMES (1949–). Stage director and playwright. A prodigious writer–director with a varied and impressive list of credits over the past three decades, his musical efforts have been associated with songwriters STEPHEN SONDHEIM and WILLIAM FINN. Lapine was born in Mansfield, Ohio, educated at Franklin and Marshall College, and studied design at the California Institute of the Arts and at Yale University. When he taught design at the last institution, Lapine was drawn to writing and directing for the theatre and made his New York debut in both fields in 1977 with the Off Broadway work *Photograph*. He staged his own social comedies *Twelve Dreams* and *Table Manners* before writing and directing his first musical, Sondheim's SUNDAY IN THE PARK WITH GEORGE (1984). Lapine also worked with Sondheim on INTO THE WOODS (1987 and 2002) and *PASSION* (1994), both of which he co-wrote and directed. He has collaborated with Finn in a similar capacity, directing *March of the Falsettos* (1981), *Falsettoland* (1990), *FALSETTOS* (1992), and THE 25TH ANNUAL PUTNAM COUNTY SPELLING BEE (2005). Lapine also staged the musical *Amour* (2002) and several plays, including Shakespeare productions in Central Park.

LARSON, JONATHAN (1960–1996). Stage composer, lyricist, and writer. The author of the rock musical sensation *RENT* (1996), his death before the show opened not only cut short a very promising career but leaves many questions about the direction such a career would have gone. Larson was born in White Plains, New York, and educated at Adelphi University before moving to New York where he wrote musicals seen Off Off Broadway and in workshops. The New York Theatre workshop picked up his musical *Rent* for a limited run in 1996 and the day before it was to start previewing, Larson died of an aneurysm so he never saw the great success the show has become. One of his earlier works was revised by David Auburn and was produced Off Broadway as *Tick, Tick ... Boom!* (2001). The three-person autobiographical show, about a struggling composer–lyricist, named Johnnie (RAÚL ESPARZA), demonstrated that Larson was much more than a one-play talent.

☙ LAST SWEET DAYS OF ISAAC (East Side Playhouse 1970). The first rock musical to suggest that strong characterization, adept narrative, and even wit could be found in the new sound, the Off Broadway work brought recognition to the songwriting team of NANCY FORD (music) and GRETCHEN CRYER (book and lyrics). The musical consisted of two playlets about the loss of opportunity and the lack of communication in the modern world. In the first act, Isaac (AUSTIN PENDLETON) and Ingrid (Fredricka Weber) are trapped in an elevator and slowly learn to shed their inhibitions. In the second, Isaac is in jail and tries to communicate with the blonde inmate Alice (Weber) by way of a television screen, only to learn on the news that he has died in a protest demonstration. Highlights from the rock–folk score included "A Transparent Crystal Moment," "Love You Came to Me," "Somebody Died Today," "I Want to Walk to San Francisco," and the title number. The offbeat but likable musical, directed by WORD BAKER, quickly found an audience and ran 485 performances. Hopelessly dated today and rarely revived, the show was potent and timely in its day.

LATOUCHE, JOHN [born John Patrick Digges Treville La Touche] (1917–1956). Stage lyricist and writer. An exceptional talent and a renegade against tradition, the gifted lyricist only began to achieve his considerable potential during his short career. Latouche was born in Baltimore, Maryland, and grew up in

Richmond, Virginia. He won a literary contest in 1932 and moved to New York where he attended Columbia University for a time, leaving to concentrate on writing for the theatre. Latouche wrote and appeared in the revue *The Pepper Mill* (1937) and contributed sketches and lyrics for the ever-changing revue *PINS AND NEEDLES* (1937). He found recognition when his tone poem "Ballad for Americans," written with composer Earl Robinson, was sung on the radio by PAUL ROBESON and interpolated into the Broadway revue *Sing for Your Supper* (1939), for which he wrote lyrics and sketches. After contributing to the revue *From Vienna* (1939), Latouche wrote his first book musical, *CABIN IN THE SKY* (1940), providing the lyrics for VERNON DUKE's music; the two also collaborated on *Banjo Eyes* (1941) and *The Lady Comes Across* (1941). With DUKE ELLINGTON, he scored the jazz-flavored *Beggar's Holiday* (1946) and with composer Jerome Moross he wrote *Ballet Ballads* (1948) and the sung-through *THE GOLDEN APPLE* (1954). Latouche's other Broadway credits were *Rhapsody* (1944), *Polonaise* (1945), and *The Vamp* (1955). He also wrote the libretto for the opera *The Ballad of Baby Doe* (1956) and contributed a few lyrics to *CANDIDE* (1956) before his premature death from a heart attack. Latouche was a gregarious, sometimes outrageous and difficult talent, yet was beloved by all who worked with him. His lyrics are enticing, filled with easy-going poetic images and a haunting turn of phrase. His work was celebrated in the Off Broadway revue *Taking a Chance on Love* (2000).

LAUREL, STAN, AND OLIVER HARDY. Film comedy team. The most successful comedy team in the history of the movies, popular in both silents and talkies, the oddly matched duo rarely sang or danced, yet were featured in eight Hollywood musicals. The thin, weepy Stan Laurel [born Arthur Stanley Jefferson] (1890–1965) was born in Ulverston, England, the son of theatre people, and was on stage as a teenager, later appearing in comedies, dramas, and music halls. He was Charlie Chaplin's understudy in Fred Karno's touring company and when the troupe toured the States in 1912, Laurel stayed and went into American vaudeville before making his film debut in 1917. The large, bullying Oliver [Norvell] Hardy (1892–1957) was born in Harlem, Georgia, the son of a lawyer, and was singing in a touring minstrel show at the age of eight. When he was older he enrolled at

the University of Georgia with the intention of following in his father's footsteps, but left school in 1910 and started doing bit parts in silent films. In 1926 the director Leo McCarey suggested that the two very different comics work together and they were teamed in some shorts at the Hal Roach studios. By 1927 they were working exclusively with each other, staying together for thirty years and making over 100 films, a fourth of them features. Their musical credits are *HOLLYWOOD REVUE OF 1929*, *The Rogue Song* (1930), *The Devil's Brother* (1933), *Hollywood Party* (1934), *BABES IN TOYLAND* (1934), *The Bohemian Girl* (1936), *Swiss Miss* (1938), and *Jitterbugs* (1943), as well as *Riding High* (1950) in which Hardy performed without Laurel. The duo left Hollywood in 1945, toured together in British music halls for a time, and then parted ways. Biographies: *Stan and Ollie, The Roots of Comedy: The Double Life of Laurel and Hardy*, Simon Louvish (2005); *Laurel and Hardy: The Magic Behind the Movies*, Randy Skretvedt, Jordan R. Young (1994); *Stan: The Life of Stan Laurel*, Fred Lawrence Guiles (1991).

LAURENTS, ARTHUR (1918–). Stage and film writer and director. The author of two of the finest American musical librettos, he is also an accomplished director of his own and others' works. Laurents was born in Brooklyn, New York, and educated at Cornell University before making his Broadway playwriting debut in 1954 with the commended but short-lived drama *Home of the Brave*. Of his subsequent plays, only *The Time of the Cuckoo* (1952) managed a long run, but Laurents had much more success writing librettos for musicals. His first two efforts, *WEST SIDE STORY* (1957) and *GYPSY* (1959), were his greatest achievements and he followed them with noteworthy librettos for *ANYONE CAN WHISTLE* (1964), *DO I HEAR A WALTZ?* (1965), and *HALLELUJAH, BABY!* (1967). Laurents also scripted some Off Broadway musicals, the Broadway misfire *Nick & Nora* (1991), and several screenplays, most memorably *Rope* (1948), *Anastasia* (1956), *The Way We Were* (1973), and *The Turning Point* (1977). He first turned to directing when he staged his own play *An Invitation to a March* in 1960, followed two years later with his direction of the musical *I CAN GET IT FOR YOU WHOLESALE*. In 1964 he staged his own *Anyone Can Whistle* but had more success directing the 1984 hit *La Cage aux Folles* and various revivals of *Gypsy* in New York, London, and on tour. Autobiography: *Original Story By* (2000).

LAWFORD, PETER [born Peter Sydney Ernest Aylen] (1923–984). Film and television performer. A British-born leading man who played debonair men of wealth in many non-musicals, the handsome, nasal-voiced, low-key actor was also a favorite in musicals despite his thin singing voice and limited dancing talents. Lawford was born in London, the son of a knighted World War I hero, and grew up in Paris where he was educated and appeared in some British films as a boy actor. Although he made a film in Hollywood in 1938 when he was visiting America, his movie career really started in the 1940s when he was cast as affable Brits in *Mrs. Miniver* (1942), *A Yank at Eton* (1942), and other nonmusicals. Most of his career was spent playing laid-back gentlemen in dramas and comedies but audiences also enjoyed him in such musicals as *GIRL CRAZY* (1930), *Two Sisters From Boston* (1945), *IT HAPPENED IN BROOKLYN* (1946), *GOOD NEWS!* (1947), *On an Island With You* (1948), *EASTER PARADE* (1948), *ROYAL WEDDING* (1951), *Pepe* (1960), and *A Man Called Adam* (1966). Lawford was one of the popular "Rat Pack" stars who made a series of films together in the 1960s, and he appeared on many television programs, from quiz shows to dramas to variety shows to specials, such as the TV musical *RUGGLES OF RED GAP* (1957). Biography: *Peter Lawford*, James Spada (1992).

LAWRENCE, CAROL [born Carol Maria Laraia] (1932–). Stage and television performer. The striking actress–singer has given memorable performances in both Broadway musical hits and flops. Lawrence was born in Melrose Park, Illinois, and was on Broadway at the age of eighteen in *NEW FACES OF 1952*. After appearances in *SOUTH PACIFIC* (1952), *PLAIN AND FANCY* (1955), *Shangri-La* (1956), and *ZIEGFELD FOLLIES* (1957), she finally won recognition as Maria in the original cast of *WEST SIDE STORY* (1957 and 1960). Her performance as the ambitious Creole heroine Clio Dulaine in *SARATOGA* (1959) was also praised, although the musical did not run. Lawrence also shone as the roving reporter Angela McKay in *SUBWAYS ARE FOR SLEEPING* (1961) and as a replacement for Agnes in *I Do! I Do!* (1967). Thereafter she concentrated on television, appearing on variety shows, soap operas, sit-coms, game shows, cooking programs, and her own talk show, as well as the TV musical versions of *HIGH BUTTON SHOES* (1966) and *KISS ME, KATE* (1968). Lawrence often returned to the stage, touring in productions of *THE SOUND OF MUSIC*, *FUNNY GIRL*, *THE UNSINKABLE MOLLY BROWN*, *SWEET CHARITY*, *WOMAN OF THE YEAR*, and *SUGAR BABIES*, as well as Los Angeles revivals of *MAME*, *DO I HEAR A WALTZ?*, and *FOLLIES*, and she was back on Broadway in 1993 as a replacement for Aurora in *KISS OF THE SPIDER WOMAN*. She has been a favorite in nightclubs and in concerts. Lawrence was married to singer–actor ROBERT GOULET for a time. Autobiography: *Carol Lawrence: The Backstage Story*, with Phyllis Hobe (1990).

LAWRENCE, GERTRUDE [born Gertrude Alexandra Dagmar Lawrence Klasen] (1989–1952). Stage and film performer. One of the most beloved stars of the London and New York stages, her singing voice was thin, but her angular beauty, sparkling sense of comedy, and warm, playful stage presence made her a one-of-a-kind performer. A native Londoner, Lawrence was the daughter of an actress who brought her on tour when she was a child. By the age of twelve, she was a professional dancer in pantomimes, revues, and musicals and was a West End favorite by the time she first came to

Gertrude Lawrence. For someone with an unsteady and uncertain singing voice, the beloved British star introduced many song standards on Broadway. Here she is in *Oh, Kay!* (1926) singing the heart-tugging "Someone to Watch Over Me" to her rag doll. (Photofest)

America in 1924 to appear in *ANDRE CHARLOT'S REVUE*. Broadway immediately welcomed her, and she returned often over the next twenty-eight years. Lawrence excelled at both musical comedy roles, such as the British aristocrat Kay disguised as a servant in *OH, KAY!* (1926), and comic parts, as in her tempestuous Amanda Prynne in *Private Lives* (1931) and a variety of roles in *Tonight at 8:30* (1936), both written for her by her co-star and lifelong friend NOEL COWARD. Her two greatest roles were the indecisive magazine editor Liza Elliott in *LADY IN THE DARK* (1941) and English schoolteacher Anna Leonowens in *THE KING AND I* (1951). Other musicals she appeared in on Broadway were *Charlot Revue* (1925), *Treasure Girl* (1928), and *International Revue* (1930). Lawrence starred in several London musicals, made a few films, including the early musical *Battle of Paris* (1929) and a guest spot in the musical *STAGE DOOR CANTEEN* (1943), and was a favorite of American and British G.I.s during World War II because of her many tours to military bases. She died of cancer during the run of *The King and I*. JULIE ANDREWS played Lawrence in the biopic *STAR!* (1968). Autobiography: *A Star Danced* (1945); biographies: *Gertrude Lawrence as Mrs. A.*, Richard Aldrich [her husband] (1954); *Gertrude Lawrence*, Sheridan Morley (1981).

LAWS, MAURY (1922?–). Television composer, conductor, and music arranger. A prolific composer of scores for original television musicals, he mostly created songs for animated specials that were offered as holiday fare. Laws was born in rural North Carolina and played guitar as a child, working professionally with bands by the time he was sixteen years old. After serving in World War II, he settled in New York where he played in clubs and studied music privately. Laws worked as a music arranger for top recording artists of the 1950s, which led to doing their television specials and his own career on the tube. His first important television job was as music director for the animated *THE STORY OF RUDOLPH, THE RED-NOSED REINDEER* (1964). Laws would go on to compose, arrange, and/or conduct over twenty TV musicals, including *The Cricket on the Hearth* (1967), *The Little Drummer Boy* (1968), *The Mouse on the Mayflower* (1968), *Frosty the Snowman* (1969), *SANTA CLAUS IS COMIN' TO TOWN* (1970), *Here Comes Peter Cotton Tail* (1971), *The Emperor's New Clothes* (1972), *THE YEAR WITHOUT A SANTA CLAUS* (1974), *'Twas the Night Before Christmas* (1974), *Rudolph's Shiny New Year* (1976), *The Hobbit* (1977), *The*

Easter Bunny Is Comin' to Town (1977), *Jack Frost* (1979), *RUDOLPH AND FROSTY'S CHRISTMAS IN JULY* (1979), *Pinocchio's Christmas* (1980), *Return of the King* (1980), and *THE WIND IN THE WILLOWS* (1987).

LAYTON, JOE [born Joseph Lichtman] (1931–1994). Stage, film, and television choreographer and director. A resourceful choreographer–director, he was often saddled with weak vehicles but still was able to shine on occasion. Layton was born in Brooklyn, studied at the School of Music and Art and at various ballet studios, and was on the Broadway stage by the age of sixteen, cast as a replacement in the dancing chorus of *OKLAHOMA!* in 1947. He also appeared in such Broadway hits as *HIGH BUTTON SHOES* (1947), *GENTLEMEN PREFER BLONDES* (1949), and *WONDERFUL TOWN* (1953) and on television; he was one of the featured dancers in the celebrated live broadcast of *CINDERELLA* in 1956. He made his New York choreography debut with an Off Broadway revival of *ON THE TOWN* in 1959, creating such a strong impression that he was hired to do the dances for *ONCE UPON A MATTRESS* and *THE SOUND OF MUSIC* that same year. *GREENWILLOW* the next year was the first in a long line of admirable failures that Layton choreographed over the decades, such as *TENDERLOIN* (1960), *Sail Away* (1961), *Drat! The Cat!* (1965), *DEAR WORLD* (1969), *Bring Back Birdie* (1981), and *Harrigan 'n' Hart* (1985). His two outright hits were *GEORGE M!* (1968) and *BARNUM* (1980). Layton began to direct as well as choreograph with *NO STRINGS* in 1962, followed by double duty for such musicals as *The Girl Who Came to Supper* (1963), *TWO BY TWO* (1970), and *Platinum* (1978). He staged special programs for BARBRA STREISAND, BETTE MIDLER, DIANA ROSS, Harry Connick, Jr., and other stars on Broadway, television, and in nightclubs. He also directed productions abroad, most memorably *Gone With the Wind* in London in 1972. Layton choreographed a few films, most notably *THOROUGHLY MODERN MILLIE* (1967), and produced the screen version of *ANNIE* (1982). For the small screen, Layton directed the TV musicals *Once Upon a Mattress* (1964), *The Belle of 14th Street* (1967), *ANDROCLES AND THE LION* (1967), and *THE LITTLEST ANGEL* (1969).

LEATHERNECKING. See *PRESENT ARMS*

LEAVE IT TO JANE (Longacre Theatre 1917). Although not technically a PRINCESS THEATRE musical because it did not play at the

Princess Theatre, the bouncy collegiate show had the same creators as the famous musical series and fulfilled all its goals to present literate musical comedies with contemporary characters. GUY BOLTON and P. G. WODEHOUSE wrote the libretto, based on the 1904 comedy *The College Widow*, about Jane Witherspoon (Edith Hallor), the daughter of the president of Atwater College, who secures a victory for Atwater's football team over that of the rival Bingham College. She does this by flirting and coercing the All-American halfback Billy Bolton (Robert G. Pitkin) not to enroll at Bingham but to come to Atwater. He does, Atwater wins the big game, and Billy wins Jane. This slight but useful storyline allowed for ample song-and-dance opportunities, and the score by JEROME KERN (music) and Wodehouse (lyrics) used those opportunities to present such delightful numbers as the bouncy "Just You Watch My Step," the comic "Cleopaterer," the sultry "The Siren's Song," and the celebratory title song. EDWARD ROYCE directed, David Bennett choreographed, and the happy show ran 167 performances. A 1958 Off Broadway revival of *Leave It to Jane* ran a surprising two years.

LEAVE IT TO ME! (Imperial Theatre 1938). A COLE PORTER musical with a better-than-average book, the satirical musical comedy is most remembered for introducing MARY MARTIN to Broadway audiences. Alonzo P. Goodhue (VICTOR MOORE), the unwilling American ambassador to Russia, only got the job because his wife (SOPHIE TUCKER) contributed so much money to FDR's reelection campaign. He sets off for Moscow with brash newsman Buckley Joyce Thomas (WILLIAM GAXTON), and Goodhue tries everything he can to get recalled to the States, including shooting a politico in Red Square, but his efforts only make him a hero. Only after trying to create world peace is Goodhue deemed incompetent by Washington and brought home. The cast also featured TAMARA, GEORGE TOBIAS, Walter Armin, and Mary Martin as the coy secretary Dolly Winslow who did a funny striptease in a Siberian train station to the song "My Heart Belongs to Daddy." Also in the delectable Porter score were "Most Gentlemen Don't Like Love," "Get Out of Town," "From Now On," and "Tomorrow." The farcical libretto was by Bella and Sam Spewack who adapted their satirical comedy *Clear All Wires* (1932) and updated the political jokes. Sam Spewack directed the VINTON FREEDLEY production

and ROBERT ALTON was the choreographer. After running 291 performances on Broadway, the show toured the country but lost some of its humor when Stalin and Hitler signed their pact. The script had to be rewritten and when the production returned to Broadway in 1939 it ran only two more weeks.

LeBaron, William (1883–1958). Film producer. The presenter of thirty-two Hollywood musicals, he supervised many films of all genres for different studios during his career. LeBaron was born in Elgin, Illinois, and educated at Chicago University and New York University. He took up playwriting for a time and then was a managing editor at *Collier's* magazine before starting in films in 1919 as a writer. LeBaron showed a talent for business and became general manager of Cosmopolitan Productions and then an executive at RKO, PARAMOUNT, and other studios. He began producing films in 1924 and was known for his handling of stars such as W. C. FIELDS, MAE WEST, ALICE FAYE, and BETTY GRABLE. LeBaron's musical credits include *RIO RITA* (1929), *SHE DONE HIM WRONG* (1933), *College Humor* (1933), *I'm No Angel* (1933), *All the King's Horses* (1935), *Here Comes Cookie* (1935), *Rose of the Rancho* (1936), *Give Us This Night* (1936), *Poppy* (1936), *RHYTHM ON THE RIVER* (1940), *Kiss the Boys Goodbye* (1941), *WEEKEND IN HAVANA* (1941), *Song of the Islands* (1942), *ORCHESTRA WIVES* (1942), *SPRINGTIME IN THE ROCKIES* (1942), *ICELAND* (1942), *STORMY WEATHER* (1943), *THE GANG'S ALL HERE* (1943), *Pin-Up Girl* (1944), *Sweet and Low Down* (1944), *THREE LITTLE GIRLS IN BLUE* (1946), and *Carnegie Hall* (1947).

Lederer, George W. (1861–1938). Stage director and producer. An early and important presenter of musicals, he had a long and varied theatre career. Lederer was born in Wilkes Barre, Pennsylvania, and worked as a journalist, vaudeville writer, drama critic, and actor before entering into management by co-producing a tour of the musical *Florizel* in 1878. With Thomas Canary he took over the Casino Theatre and from 1893 to 1903 presented and directed many musicals there, including *THE PASSING SHOW* (1894), the first important American revue, and *THE BELLE OF NEW YORK* (1897), the first American musical to achieve international success. Among his other Broadway musicals were *The Whirl of the Town* (1897), *The Belle of Bohemia* (1900), *The Casino Girl* (1900), *Sally in Our Alley* (1902), *The Charity Girl* (1912), and *Peaches* (1923). After running the New York and Bijou Theatres, Lederer produced and directed some of his hits in London. In his later years he co-produced (and often directed) popular musicals with H. H. Frazee, most notably the long-running *MADAME SHERRY* (1910), and then spent many years as the general manager for producer SAM H. HARRIS. Lederer was still producing the occasional show in the 1930s.

LEE, GYPSY ROSE [born Rose Louise Hovick] (1914–1970). Stage, film, and television performer and writer. America's most famous striptease artist, she was neither a voluptuous beauty nor a particularly talented performer but her sophisticated parody of sex and use of suggestion rather than vulgarity made her unique in burlesque and a delightful diversion in plays and musicals. Lee was born in Seattle and was in vaudeville as a child, pushed by her stage mother across the country, but with little success. Yet later she was an immediate hit in burlesque houses and she eventually worked her way up to Minskey's in New York City, the premiere striptease palace. Lee was shrewd enough to expand her career and wrote novels, screenplays, and plays, most of which she appeared in. Her Broadway musical credits include *Hot-Cha!* (1932), *Melody* (1933), *ZIEGFELD FOLLIES* (1936), a replacement for ETHEL MERMAN in *DuBarry Was a Lady* (1940), and *Star and Garter* (1942). Lee's novels and plays were filmed by Hollywood, and she appeared in a number of movies (usually using the name Louise Hovick), including the musicals *Sally, Irene and Mary* (1937), *Ali Baba Goes to Town* (1937), *You Can't Have Everything* (1937), *My Lucky Star* (1938), *STAGE DOOR CANTEEN* (1943), and *Belle of the Yukon* (1944). Lee even appeared on television in game shows and various series. Her memoir *Gypsy* (1957) served as the basis for the 1959 Broadway musical. Her sister is singer–actress JUNE HAVOC. Memoir: *Gypsy and Me*, Erik Lee Preminger [her son] (1984).

LEE, MICHELE [born Michelle Lee Dusick] (1942–). Stage, television, and film performer. A statuesque leading lady, she has been equally proficient in musicals and nonmusicals. Lee was born in Los Angeles, the daughter of film makeup artist Jack Dusick, and was a singer and dancer in school musicals before heading to Broadway where she was cast in the revue *Vintage '60* (1960). A small role in the musical *Bravo Giovanni* (1962) led to her getting hired as a replacement for Rosemary in *How to*

SUCCEED IN BUSINESS WITHOUT REALLY TRYING in 1962, a performance she got to reprise in the 1967 film version. Lee's other notable musical role was the Manhattan dancer Gittel Mosca in *SEESAW* (1973). She has acted in many nonmusical plays, films, and television shows, including over 300 appearances on *Knott's Landing*, directing many episodes as well. Lee got to sing and dance on the small screen in the TV versions of *ROBERTA* (1969) and *OF THEE I SING* (1972). She was married to actor James Farentino (1938–).

LEE, PEGGY [born Norma Delores Egstrom] (1920–2002). Film and television performer and lyricist. The unique recording star known for her smoky and precise way with a song, the classy blonde also acted in films and wrote songs. Lee was born in Jamestown, North Dakota, the daughter of a railway station agent, and sang on the local radio. Her big break came when BENNY GOODMAN heard her and hired Lee as a vocalist for his band. Soon she was known nationally for her recordings and was a favorite for decades in nightclubs and in concerts. Lee did specialty spots in the movie musicals *The Powers Girl* (1942), *STAGE DOOR CANTEEN* (1942), and *Mr. Music* (1950) and then got to play a leading character role in the 1953 remake of *THE JAZZ SINGER*. Her finest screen performance was as the saloon singer Rose Hopkins in *PETE KELLY'S BLUES* (1955). Collaborating with composer Sonny Burke, Lee wrote the lyrics for songs in the animated musical *LADY AND THE TRAMP* (1953) and provided the voices for the Siamese cats, the wife Darling, and the sexy canine Peg. She performed on dozens of television variety shows over the years and made her Broadway debut at the age of sixty-two in the autobiographical musical *Peg* (1983) for which she sang old favorites and new songs that she wrote for the short-lived show. Autobiography: *Miss Peggy Lee* (2002); biography: *Fever: The Life and Music of Miss Peggy Lee*, Peter Richmond (2007).

LEE, [Samuel] SAMMY [born Levy] (1890–1968). Stage and film choreographer. A first-class Broadway choreographer, he staged the dances for a number of hits in a rather short period of time. Lee was born in New York City and started as a dancer in vaudeville and then in Broadway musicals. When cast in a featured dancing role in the operetta *THE FIREFLY* (1912), Lee took over some of the choreography chores, but he was not a recognized choreographer himself until the 1920s when he staged twenty-six musicals during the decade, including such works as *The Gingham Girl* (1922), *Mary Jane McKane* (1923), *LADY, BE GOOD!* (1924), *Tell Me More* (1925), *NO, NO, NANETTE* (1925), *THE COCOANUTS* (1925), *TIP-TOES* (1925), *The Ramblers* (1926), *OH, KAY!* (1926), *RIO RITA* (1927), and the original *SHOW BOAT* (1927), as well as editions of the *ZIEGFELD FOLLIES*, *MUSIC BOX REVUE*, and *EARL CARROLL VANITIES*. He started choreographing film musicals in 1929 and rarely returned to Broadway after that. Among his twenty screen musicals were *It's a Great Life* (1929), *HOLLYWOOD REVUE OF 1929*, *Adorable* (1933), *DANCING LADY* (1933), *KING OF BURLESQUE* (1935), *NEW FACES OF 1937*, *Life of the Party* (1937), *Honolulu* (1940), *TWO GIRLS AND A SAILOR* (1944), and *Earl Carroll Vanities* (1945).

LEFTWICH, ALEXANDER [Thornton] (1884–1947). Stage director. An actor-turned-director, he staged some of the brightest Broadway musical hits of the 1920s. Leftwich was born in Philadelphia and began his theatre career in his teens as an actor in Baltimore. After performing for many years in stock, Leftwich relocated to New York City where he was an assistant to producers Jesse Lasky and Cecil B. De Mille before they went to Hollywood. He started directing acts on the B. F. Keith vaudeville circuit and then staged plays for producer Daniel Frohman in the 1910s and for the SHUBERTS in the 1920s. But Leftwich is most known for directing a string of memorable musicals after he left the Shuberts: *HIT THE DECK* (1927), *A CONNECTICUT YANKEE* (1927), *FUNNY FACE* (1927), *Rain or Shine* (1928), *PRESENT ARMS* (1928), *Spring Is Here* (1929), *STRIKE UP THE BAND* (1930), *GIRL CRAZY* (1930), *Sweet and Low* (1930), and others. During the Depression he ran the Federal Theatre Project in California and later was a successful film producer.

📖 *LEGALLY BLONDE* (Palace Theatre 2007). One of the many popular movies turned into musicals during the first decade of the new century, this featherweight show held few surprises for the fans of the original product but satisfied them all the same. When her law student boyfriend Warner (Richard H. Blake) dumps her because she's just another dumb blonde, the bubbly Elle Woods (Laura Bell Bundy) gets into Harvard Law School to convince him that she has brains and to win him back. Once there she falls for teaching assistant Emmett Forrest (Christian Borle) who loves her for herself and, in the happy end-

ing, wins Emmett and a big court case. Also in the cast were Orfeh, MICHAEL RUPERT, Kate Shingle, and Nikki Snelson. Heather Hach penned the by-the-numbers libretto based on the 2001 film, and Laurence O'Keefe and Nell Benjamin collaborated on the songs, which included "Chip on My Shoulder," "Find My Way," "What You Want," "Omigod You Guys," "Bend and Snap," "Ireland," and the title number. The unpretentious musical never took itself too seriously and spoofed itself with cheerful energy. Reviews were mildly approving but audience reaction was less restrained and the show, directed and choreographed by JERRY MITCHELL, continues to find an audience despite the fact that MTV broadcast a taping of the musical six months after the production opened, the first time such a broadcast had been done of a show still running on Broadway.

LeGRAND, MICHEL [Jean] (1932–). Film and stage composer. One of the busiest and most successful composers in Hollywood and European films, he is most known for his theme songs but he has scored musicals as well. He was born in Paris, the son of an actor and composer, and studied piano at the Paris Conservatoire. LeGrand began his career writing songs for French singing stars and for jazz musician Dizzy Gillespie. He then recorded some albums, which eventually caught on and made him famous in Europe. LeGrand started scoring French nonmusical films in the 1960s and then became internationally famous for his film opera *Les Parapluies de Cherbourg/ The Umbrellas of Cherbourg* (1964). He wrote the soundtrack music for many Hollywood films, with several of the theme songs becoming hits, such as "The Windmills of Your Mind," "What Are You Doing the Rest of Your Life?," and "The Summer Knows." His other movie musical credits include the score for the French film *The Young Girls of Rochefort* (1967), instrumental music for *LADY SINGS THE BLUES* (1972), and the songs (with lyricists ALAN and MARILYN BERGMAN) for *YENTL* (1983). LeGrand contributed music to the Broadway revue *Zizi* (1964) and decades later his French stage musical *Amour* was presented on Broadway in 2002.

LEHMAN, ERNEST (1920–2005). Film writer and producer. A multitalented Hollywood screenwriter, he wrote some skillful movie adaptations of Broadway musicals. A native of New York City, Lehman was educated at City College of New York for a business career. He became a financial editor even as he started writing short stories, novels, and radio scripts. His first produced screenplay was *The Inside Story* (1948), followed by such notable movies as *Executive Suite* (1954), *Sabrina* (1954), *Sweet Smell of Success* (1957), *North By Northwest* (1959), and *Who's Afraid of Virginia Woolf?* (1966). Lehman was adept at adapting plays and books for the screen, opening up the action without diminishing the original. His craftsmanship can be seen in such screen musicals as *THE KING AND I* (1956), *WEST SIDE STORY* (1961), *THE SOUND OF MUSIC* (1965), and *HELLO, DOLLY!* (1969). Lehman produced some of his films in the 1960s and directed on a few occasions. Among his novels and nonfiction are *The Sweet Smell of Success* and *Screening Sickness*.

LEIBER, JERRY, AND MIKE STOLLER. Film songwriters. The pop lyricist and composer of many 1950s and 1960s hits, the two songwriters also provided original scores for seven *ELVIS PRESLEY* movie musicals. Jerry Leiber (1933–) was born in Baltimore and grew up in Los Angeles where he met Mike Stoller (1933–), a native of Belle Harbor, New York, who was studying at Los Angeles City College. The two shared an interest in rhythm and blues music and started collaborating, getting their first song recorded in 1950. Writing for such singers as Jimmy Witherspoon, Charles Brown, Wilbert Harrison, Little Willie Littlefield, and Big Mama Thornton, and for groups such as the Coasters and the Drifters, the twosome had many hits on the charts. When their 1955 Freddie Bell and the Bellboys song "Hound Dog" was recorded the next year by Presley and was a mammoth hit, Leiber and Stoller were hired to write songs for the rock and roll singer's films *JAILHOUSE ROCK* (1957), *Loving You* (1957), *KING CREOLE* (1958), *Girls! Girls! Girls!* (1962), *Fun in Alcapulco* (1964), *Roustabout* (1964), and *Tickle Me* (1965). The collaborators' songs were celebrated in the long-running Broadway revue *SMOKEY JOE'S CAFE* (1995). Leiber and Stoller were influential in bringing rhythm and blues to mainstream America. Among their many hit songs are "On Broadway," "Jailhouse Rock," "Charlie Brown," "Kansas City," "Love Potion No. 9," and "Yakety Yak."

LEIGH, CAROLYN (1926–1983). Stage and television lyricist. A vivacious songwriter with a buoyant sense of wordplay, she contributed lyrics to a handful of tuneful Broadway shows. Leigh was born in the Bronx and attended Queens College and New York University before writing for radio programs and advertising companies. She moved to television in the early 1950s and wrote scripts and lyrics for revamped operettas as well as for the TV musical *Heidi* (1955). Collaborating with composer CY COLEMAN, she wrote a series of hit singles, including "It Amazes Me," "Firefly," "Witchcraft," and "The Best Is Yet to Come." Leigh also had major success writing "Young at Heart" with composer Johnny Richards. She made her Broadway debut writing half of the songs for *PETER PAN* (1954) with composer Mark Charlap and then, after contributing some lyrics to *ZIEGFELD FOLLIES* (1957), she and Coleman collaborated on the scores for the LUCILLE BALL vehicle musical *WILDCAT* (1960) and the SID CAESAR vehicle *LITTLE ME* (1962). With composer Elmer Bernstein, she scored the musical *How Now Dow Jones* (1967). At its best, Leigh's work is inspired fun and her lyrics have a brassy, confident tone and sit happily on the music that was provided for her.

LEIGH, JANET [born Jeanette Helen Morrison] (1927–2004). Film and television performer. A top dramatic movie star in the 1950s and 1960s, the fresh-faced, attractive actress also had a charming presence in comedies and musicals. Leigh was born in Merced, California, and studied music at the College of the Pacific until she was discovered by film star Norma Shearer and given a screen test. She made her film debut in 1947 and quickly became a popular ingénue on screen, later maturing to dramatic roles in nonmusicals such as *Touch of Evil* (1958) and *Psycho* (1960). Leigh's musical credits include *WORDS AND MUSIC* (1948), *Two Tickets to Broadway* (1951), *Walking My Baby Back Home* (1953), *Living It Up* (1954), *PETE KELLY'S BLUES* (1955), *MY SISTER EILEEN* (1955), *Pepe* (1960), and *BYE BYE BIRDIE* (1963). She made very few films after the 1960s but was seen on many television shows into the new century. Leigh was married to actor Tony Curtis (1925–) and her daughter is actress Jamie Lee Curtis (1958–). Autobiography: *There Really Was a Hollywood* (1984).

LEIGH, MITCH [born Irwin Michnik] (1928–). Stage and television composer, director, and producer. A Broadway and television songwriter, he only had one major hit but it was a significant one. Leigh was born in New York and educated at the Yale University School of Music and began his career as a jazz musician. He wrote incidental music for some Broadway plays in the early 1960s and then made an auspicious debut as a score composer with MAN OF LA MANCHA (1965). His subsequent Broadway musicals—Cry for Us All (1970), Home Sweet Homer (1976), Savara (1979), Chu Chem (1989), and Ain't Broadway Grand (1993)—were short-lived. Leigh turned to directing and producing in the 1980s, staging touring and Broadway productions of THE KING AND I with YUL BRYNNER and producing Broadway revivals of MAME (1983), The King and I (1985), and Man of La Mancha (1992 and 2002), as well as the revue The Gershwins' Fascinating Rhythm (1999). He also wrote music for television, scoring the TV musical ONCE UPON A BROTHERS GRIMM (1977) and composing music for television commercials, such as the "Cracker Jack Theme Song" and "Nobody Doesn't Like Sara Lee."

LEISEN, MITCHELL [born James Leisen] (1898–1972). Film and television director. Moving from career to career, he found success everywhere he went in show business. Leisen was born in Menominee, Michigan, the son of a brewery owner, and trained as an architect at Washington University in St. Louis before working in the art department of the Chicago Tribune. He went to Hollywood in 1919 and designed costumes for Cecil B. DeMille and later set decoration for other directors as well. Leisen started directing in 1933, and the look of his pictures was always outstanding even if many were weepy romantic movies with little substance. His dozen screen musicals include Murder at the Vanities (1934), BIG BROADCAST OF 1937 (1936), Swing High, Swing Low (1937), BIG BROADCAST OF 1938, ARTISTS AND MODELS ABROAD (1938), LADY IN THE DARK (1944), Tonight We Sing (1953), and The Girl Most Likely (1957). By the late 1950s, Leisen left Hollywood and became a busy director in television, helming several series and specials, including the TV musical Mother Goose (1958). He also returned to design, doing interior design and running a fashionable tailor shop in Beverly Hills.

LEMMON, JACK [born John Uhler Lemmon III] (1925–2001). Film, television, and stage performer. One of Hollywood's most cherished actors who gave many memorable comic and serious performances, he appeared in musicals on occasion. Lemmon was born in Newton, Massachusetts, and was educated at prep school and at Harvard before joining the navy. He worked in a variety of jobs before turning to acting, studying with Uta Hagen.

After appearing in some early television soap operas and working on radio, he made his Broadway debut in a revival of the comedy Room Service (1953). The next year Lemmon made his first film, the comedy It Should Happen to You (1954), and only returned to Broadway a few times later in his career. Although he was cast in comic supporting roles at first, his versatility was eventually discovered and for four decades he played a wide range of characters, from the daffy Jerry in drag in the semimusical Some Like it Hot (1959) to the recovering alcoholic Joe Clay in the gritty drama Days of Wine and Roses (1962). Lemon's other musicals were Three for the Show (1955), MY SISTER EILEEN (1955), You Can't Run Away From It (1956), and Pepe (1960), and he got to sing in the television play The Entertainer (1976). His son is actor **Chris Lemmon** (1954–). Biographies: A Twist of Lemmon: A Tribute to My Father, Chris Lemmon with Kevin Spacey (2006); Some Like It Cool: The Charmed Life of Jack Lemmon, Michael Freedland (2003).

☙ LEND AN EAR (National Theatre 1948). A clever musical revue by Charles Gaynor (sketches, music, and lyrics), it is most remembered today for bringing recognition to two major talents: comedienne CAROL CHANNING and director–choreographer GOWER CHAMPION. They both were integral to the highlight of the revue, a hilarious musical pastiche called "The Gladiola Girl," which captured the joy and zaniness of 1920s musical comedies. The show, which spoofed a variety of subjects, also featured GENE NELSON, Yvonne Adair, George Hall, Bob Scheerer, and Arthur Maxwell. Among the other playful songs were "I'm Not in Love," "Three Little Queens of the Silver Screen," "Molly O'Reilly," and "Give Your Heart a Chance to Sing." The show, which originated in Pittsburgh, was a surprise hit on Broadway, running 460 performances.

LENNART, ISOBEL (1915–1971). Stage and film writer. A reliable Hollywood screenwriter who penned light comedies, adventures, dramas, and musicals, Lennart was born in Brooklyn and started writing for the movies in the early 1940s. Her musical credits include ANCHORS AWEIGH (1945), Holiday in Mexico (1946), IT HAPPENED IN BROOKLYN (1947), The Kissing Bandit (1948), Skirts Ahoy! (1952), LOVE ME OR LEAVE ME (1955), Meet Me in Las Vegas (1956), and Merry Andrew (1958). Lennart also wrote the libretto for the Broadway musical FUNNY GIRL (1964) and did the screen version in 1968.

LeNoire, Rosetta [born Rosetta Olive Burton] (1911–2002). Stage, television, and film performer and producer. An untiring African American character actress, she appeared in dozens of New York stage productions between 1936 and 1983, a number of them musicals. A native New Yorker, LeNoire was educated at Hunter College and worked as a secretary while she trained at the American Theatre Wing School. She made her professional stage debut as one of the witches in Orson Welles' legendary all-black production of *Macbeth* (1936), followed by noteworthy roles in plays and musicals both on and Off Broadway. LeNoire's musical credits include *The Hot Mikado* (1939), *Finian's Rainbow* (1955), *Lost in the Stars* (1958 and 1972), *Destry Rides Again* (1959), *South Pacific* (1961), *Sophie* (1963), *Tambourines to Glory* (1963), *Cabin in the Sky* (1964), *I Had a Ball* (1964), and *Show Boat* (1966). She acted in a number of films and many television programs, from soap operas and sit-coms to dramas and miniseries. LeNoire founded and was artistic director of the AMAS Musical Theatre, Inc., which presented original African American works, two of which transferred to Broadway: *Bubbling Brown Sugar* (1976) and *It's So Nice to Be Civilized* (1980).

LENYA, LOTTE [born Karoline Wilhelmine Charlotte Blamauer] (1898–1981). Stage and film performer. The internationally known singer–actress with an abrasive, haunting voice, she sang the songs of her husband KURT WEILL on stage, in nightclubs and concerts, and on recordings. Lenya was born in Penzing near Vienna and was in show business as a child, performing as a tightrope walker, ballet dancer, and singer. She began her acting career in Germany where she met Weill and originated roles in four of his Berlin music dramas, including the streetwalker Jenny Diver in *The Threepenny Opera* (1928), reprising her performance in a German film in 1931. When the Nazis took over, Lenya and Weill fled to Paris and then to New York where she made her Broadway debut in the drama *The Eternal Road* (1937), followed by seven other productions spread over the next thirty years. Her three musical roles were the wry Duchess in Weill's *The Firebrand of Florence* (1945), Jenny in the long-running Off Broadway revival of *The Threepenny Opera* (1954), and the Berlin landlady Fraulein Schneider in *Cabaret* (1966). Lenya spent much of her career performing in clubs and concerts and making recordings of

her husband's works. She appeared in some films, most memorably *The Roman Spring of Mrs. Stone* (1961) and *From Russia With Love* (1963). DONNA MURPHY played Lenya in the Broadway musical biography *LoveMusik* (2007). Biography: *Lenya: A Life*, Donald Spoto (1989).

LEONARD, ROBERT Z[igler]. (1889–1968). Film director and producer. Known more for his craftsmanship than his creativity, the prolific director specialized in lush melodramas and lavish musicals. Leonard was born in Chicago, was on the stage as a child, and then was educated at the University of Colorado. He starred in some silent films before turning to directing in 1914. Over the next forty years he helmed more than eighty pictures for various studios, his best work being at MGM. Among his fifteen musicals are *Marianne* (1929), *Dancing Lady* (1933), *The Great Ziegfeld* (1936), *Maytime* (1937), *The Firefly* (1937), *Broadway Serenade* (1939), *New Moon* (1940), *Ziegfeld Girl* (1941), *In the Good Old Summertime* (1949), *Duchess of Idaho* (1950), *Everything I Have Is Yours* (1952), and *Kelly and Me* (1957). For a handful of these and for some nonmusicals, Leonard also served as producer.

LERNER, ALAN JAY, AND FREDERICK LOEWE. Stage and film songwriters and writers. After Rodgers and Hammerstein, the duo was the most successful and beloved Broadway musical team of the post–World War II decades. Alan Jay Lerner (1918–1986) was born into a wealthy New York family, the owners of the chain of retail clothing stores called the Lerner Shops, and educated at Harvard, Juilliard, and Oxford Universities, writing librettos and lyrics for campus shows and then working in radio as a scriptwriter. Frederick Loewe (1901–1988) was born in Berlin, Germany, to a musical family and was a child prodigy on the piano, playing with the Berlin Symphony at the age of thirteen and two years later writing the hit song "Katrina." He studied with celebrated music teachers in Europe before emigrating in 1924 to America where he could not make a living with music and for ten years worked as a boxer, a busboy, a cow puncher, and even a gold prospector. Loewe finally had some of his songs interpolated into the Broadway revues *Petticoat Fever* (1935) and *The Illustrators' Show* (1936) and then his full score was heard in the short-lived operetta *Great Lady* (1938). Lerner and Loewe met in 1942 and collaborated on the admirable but unsuccessful Broadway musicals *What's Up* (1943) and *The Day Before*

Lerner and Loewe. The first Broadway hit for lyricist–librettist Lerner was *Brigadoon* in 1947, which placed he and composer Frederick Loewe in the top ranks of theatre songwriters. The 1954 screen version of *Brigadoon* was only a shadow of the stage work and both Lerner and Loewe were very disappointed in it. Pictured from the film are Jimmy Thompson and Virginia Bosler during the wedding dance. (Photofest)

Spring (1945) before having their first hit with *Brigadoon* (1947). Lerner worked with composer Kurt Weill on the experimental musical *Love Life* (1948) and then reteamed with Loewe for the modest success *Paint Your Wagon* (1951) and the giant success *My Fair Lady* (1956). During this time Lerner was also active in Hollywood, scoring the movie musical *Royal Wedding* (1951) with composer Burton Lane and writing the screenplay for the classic *An American in Paris* (1951). Both Lerner and Loewe had a mammoth Hollywood hit together with *Gigi* (1958) and then returned to Broadway to score *Camelot* (1960). Loewe retired in the1960s, only returning to the stage to write some new songs for the 1973 Broadway version of *Gigi* and to score the ill-fated movie musical *The Little Prince* (1974). Lerner continued on with other collaborators but rarely found success on Broadway again. His late stage credits are *On a Clear Day You Can See Forever* (1965), *Coco* (1969), *Carmelina*

(1979), *1600 Pennsylvania Avenue* (1976), and *Dance a Little Closer* (1983). Loewe's music is rich in variety, has strong melodic lines, and blends the operetta and Broadway sound with very pleasing results. Lerner always wrote or co-wrote the librettos for his musicals, which vary in quality, although the script for *My Fair Lady* remains one of the finest musical adaptations in the American theatre. His lyrics are consistently literate, witty, and elegantly memorable. Autobiography: *The Street Where I Live* [Lerner] (1978); biographies: *Alan Jay Lerner*, Edward Jablonski (1996); *Inventing Champagne: The Worlds of Lerner and Loewe*, Gene Lees (1990).

LeRoy, Hal [born John LeRoy Schotte] (1913–1985). Stage, film and television performer. The tall, slim boyish-looking hoofer featured in both Broadway and Hollywood musicals, he was known for his rapid tap dancing routines. LeRoy was born in Cincinnati and danced in vaudeville and nightclubs before making his Broadway bow in the musical *The Gang's All Here* (1931). He and Mitzi Mayfair were not top billed in *ZIEGFELD FOLLIES* (1931) but they stole the show with their machine gun-like tapping. The next year LeRoy made his film debut and danced in some musical shorts before returning to Broadway to appear in *Strike Me Pink* (1933), *Thumbs Up!* (1934), and *Count Me In* (1942). His most notable stage and screen performance in a book musical was as college footballer Al Terwilliger in *TOO MANY GIRLS* (1939), which he reprised on film in 1940. In the 1940s LeRoy returned to nightclubs and made many appearances on television, including the small screen version of *RIO RITA* (1950).

LEROY, MERVYN (1900–1987). Film director and producer. A versatile Hollywood show-man, he excelled in directing many kinds of films and was a shrewd producer as well. LeRoy was born in San Francisco and as a boy saw his family business destroyed by the famous earthquake of 1906. He sold newspapers on the street and then went into show business, first as a singer in vaudeville and then in the movies where he worked his way up from the wardrobe department to cameraman to director in 1927. LeRoy made his name directing some hard-hitting melodramas for WARNER BROTHERS, such as *Little Caesar* (1931) and *I Am a Fugitive From a Chain Gang* (1932). At the same time he was turning out musicals such as *LITTLE JOHNNY JONES* (1930), *Show Girl in Hollywood* (1930), *GOLD DIGGERS OF 1933*, and *SWEET ADELINE* (1935). By 1937 LeRoy was also producing for MGM and presented such musicals as *The King and the Show Girl* (1937), *Mr. Dodd Takes the Air* (1937), *Fools for Scandal* (1938), *THE WIZARD OF OZ* (1939), and *AT THE CIRCUS* (1939). After World War II, he concentrated on nonmusicals but still directed *LOVELY TO LOOK AT* (1952), *Million Dollar Mermaid* (1952), *Latin Lovers* (1953), and both produced and directed *ROSE MARIE* (1954) and *GYPSY* (1962). Autobiography: *Mervyn LeRoy: Take One* (1974).

LES GIRLS (MGM 1957). Despite the many modest pleasures this film offers, what lingers most in the memory is Kay Kendall's inspired performance that hints at what the beloved English comedienne could have done had she made more American movie musicals. John Patrick's screenplay was clever, allowing three different women (Kendall, Taina Elg, and MITZI GAYNOR) to each tell her version of what happened a decade earlier when they were billed as Les Girls and worked with song-and-dance man Barry Nichols (GENE KELLY) in a Paris nightclub. Of course each version of the truth varies widely from the others, giving Kelly a chance to give three slightly different performances. COLE PORTER was so ill at the time that he barely managed to complete the score (it was his last film assignment), but it had its moments: Kelly and Kendall (dubbed by Betty Wand) breaking into "You're Just Too Too," Kelly singing "Why Am I So Gone?" and then going into a ballet with Gaynor that spoofed Marlon Brando and the leather-jacketed motorcycle gangs currently in the movies, and the lovely ballad "Ca C'est L'Amour." However, the musical highlight of the movie wasn't a Porter number at all but Kendall trying to sing Bizet's "Habañera" from Carmen when she was pleasantly drunk. GEORGE CUKOR directed the SOL C. SIEGEL production, which was choreographed by Kelly and JACK COLE.

LES MISÉRABLES (Broadway Theatre 1987). A musical pageant of sorts, the big, emotional, spectacular musical has played around the world, finding success everywhere it goes. The determined Jean Valjean is sentenced to jail for stealing a loaf of bread in nineteenth-century France, escapes, and over the next seventeen years is hounded by the obsessed police officer Javert. The epic pop opera retains many of the characters from Victor Hugo's classic novel, including the tragic Fantine, her daughter Cosette whom Jean adopts, the student Marius who loves Cosette, the despicable couple the Thenardiers, and their love-torn daughter Eponine. Alain Boublil wrote the French libretto and lyrics, and Claude-Michel Schonberg composed the music for the piece that premiered as a pageant in France and then was translated and adapted by lyricist Herbert Kretzmer and co-directors TREVOR NUNN and John Caird for a London production that was a giant hit. Word of the show reached New York quickly, and there was an advance of $11 million for the Broadway production, making it a hit before the press had their say. Most critics approved of the long, sung-though "pop-era," and American audiences had no trouble embracing it as well, making it one of the most successful of all musicals, running 6,680 performances in New York. Among the many musical numbers were such favorites as "I Dreamed a Dream," "Bring Him Home," "Who Am I?,"

Les Misérables. Operetta on a grand opera scale, the French musical was decidedly old fashioned and yet still very appealing to audiences everywhere from London to China. Pictured is the original Broadway cast in the Act One finale "One Day More." (Photofest)

Casts for *Les Misérables*

Character	1987 Broadway	2006 Broadway
Jean Valjean	Colm Wilkinson	Alexander Gemignani
Javert	TERRENCE MANN	Norm Lewis
Fantine	RANDY GRAFF	Daphne Rubin-Vega
Marius	David Bryant	Adam Jacobs
Cosette	JUDY KUHN	Ali Ewoldt
Thenadier	Leo Burmeister	GARY BEACH
Madame Thenadier	Jennifer Butt	Jenny Galloway
Enjolras	Michael McGuire	Aaron Lazar
Eponine	Frances Ruffelle	Celia Keenan-Bolger

"One Day More," "Empty Chairs at Empty Tables," "Master of the House," "In My Life," and "Castle on a Cloud." In addition to the fine voices, the CAMERON MACKINTOSH production boasted stunning scenery by John Napier and dramatic lighting by John Hersey. Road companies toured the world for decades and then an abridged version became a popular choice for high schools and summer theatres.

Billed as a revival, the 2006 Broadway production was a copy of the original with the same creative staff providing the direction, choreography, and technical aspects. Reviewers were more matter of fact than enthusiastic about the new production and cast but audiences accepted the show as if it was a new hit. The six-month limited engagement was so popular that it was extended for a total of 479 performances.

LESLIE, JOAN [born Joan Agnes Theresa Sadir Brodel] (1925–). Film and television performer. A petite, wholesome-looking actress who exuded sweetness and trust, she was featured in eleven Hollywood musicals even though her singing had to be dubbed. Leslie was born in Detroit and was a child actress, making her film debut in kids' roles in 1936 under the name Joan Brodel. When she graduated to adult roles, she changed her name and found wide recognition for her performance in the melodrama *High Sierra* (1941). Leslie's musical credits are *Star Dust* (1940), *YANKEE DOODLE DANDY* (1942), *The Hard Way* (1942), *THE SKY'S THE LIMIT* (1943), *THIS IS THE ARMY* (1943), *THANK YOUR LUCKY STARS* (1943), *HOLLYWOOD CANTEEN* (1944), *Where Do We Go From Here?* (1945), *RHAPSODY IN BLUE* (1945), *Cinderella Jones* (1946), and *Two Guys From Milwaukee* (1946). When her popularity waned in the 1950s she retired from films, although she continued to act on television into the 1990s.

LESLIE, LEW [born Lewis Lessinsky] (1886–1963). Stage producer and director. The predominant presenter of African American entertainment on Broadway in the 1920s and 1930s, he introduced FLORENCE MILLS, ETHEL WATERS, BILL ROBINSON, and other black artists to white audiences. Leslie was born in Orangeburg, New York, and performed in vaudeville before becoming manager of the famous New York nightclub Café de Paris. It was while running the club that he discovered the appeal of African American singers and dancers so he produced the all-black *Plantation Revue* (1922). It was popular enough that Leslie followed it up with *Dixie to Broadway* (1924) and *BLACKBIRDS OF 1928*. The latter was so successful that he went on to present other *Blackbird* revues in 1930, 1933, and 1939. He also did four London versions of his Broadway shows. Leslie's only nonethnic show was *International Revue* (1930). He was married to vaudeville star Belle Baker (1895–1957).

LESTER, RICHARD (1932–). Film and television director. Using a manic, frenzied way of shooting and editing his work, he created a distinctive style of filming that was ahead of its time. Lester was born in Philadelphia and was educated at the University of Pennsylvania for a career in clinical psychology but instead went into television and by 1952 was directing commercials and programs for CBS-TV. Two years later he relocated to England and entered British television where he presented a series of comedy programs for Peter Sellers. Soon Lester was directing films and found recognition for his haphazard but entertaining musical films with the BEATLES: *A HARD DAY'S NIGHT* (1964) and *HELP!* (1965). He used a similarly jaunty style for the screen version of *A FUNNY THING HAPPENED ON THE WAY TO THE FORUM* (1966). His subsequent films have ranged from adventures to farces.

LET'S FACE IT! (Imperial Theatre 1941). An escapist wartime musical comedy scored by COLE PORTER, the show featured the recently discovered talent DANNY KAYE. HERBERT and DOROTHY FIELDS penned the libretto, an updated musicalization of the comedy *The Cradle Snatchers* (1925) about three Long Island wives who are suspicious of their husbands' so-called hunting trips so they invite three G.I.s from the local army base to be entertained in one of their homes. Before you know it, the husbands, the husbands' girlfriends, and the G.I.s' girlfriends show up. The Porter score offered no runaway hits but there was much to enjoy in "Let's Not Talk About Love," "Ev'rything I Love," "Ace in the Hole," "I Hate You, Darling," "Farming," and the title number, as well as the specialty number "Melody in Four F" written for Kaye by Sylvia Fine and MAX LEIBMAN. The show

---

Casts for *Let's Face It!*

Character	1941 Broadway	1943 film	1954 television
Jerry Walker	DANNY KAYE	BOB HOPE	GENE NELSON
Winnie Potter	Mary Jaye Walsh	BETTY HUTTON	VIVIAN BLAINE
Cornelia Pigeon/Figeson	Edith Meiser	Zasu Pitts	Ann Staunton
Henry Clay Pigeon	Fred Irving Lewis	Andrew Tombes	Larry J. Blake
Nancy Collister	VIVIAN VANCE	Phyllis Povah	GLORIA JEAN
Eddie/Barney Hilliard	Jack Williams	Dave Willock	Robert Strasuss
Maggie Watson	EVE ARDEN	Eve Arden	Betty Furness
Julian Watson	Joseph Macauley	Raymond Walburn	Barry Kelley
Jean Blanchard	NANETTE FABRAY	Marjorie Weaver	Pat Horn
Frankie Burns	Benny Baker	Cully Richards	BERT LAHR

did not boast the best libretto or score but it was deemed first-rate entertainment thanks to the cast directed by EDGAR MACGREGOR and choreographed by CHARLES WALTERS. The VINTON FREEDLEY production ran 547 performances. *Let's Face It!* was Kaye's first starring role on Broadway and his last legit stage appearance for thirty years.

■🎬 **Let's Face it!** (Paramount 1943) was even more complicated than the stage plot; Harry Tugend's screenplay kept all the stage characters and added some farce by having the G.I. Jerry Walker (Bob Hope) cleverly run an enemy submarine to ground by holding a mirror up to its periscope. With so much plot, the studio cut all but two of the Porter songs ("Let's Not Talk About Love" and the title number) and added a few new ones by JULE STYNE (music) and SAMMY CAHN (lyrics), such as "Who Did? I Did." SIDNEY LANFIELD directed the piece as a farce, which it was, since there was little to remind one that it was a musical. 🖵 A 1954 *The Colgate Comedy Hour* broadcast of *Let's Face It!* featured a starry cast led by Gene Nelson as Jerry, although Bert Lahr pretty much stole the show. MICHAEL TODD co-produced the show and Fred Kelly (brother to Gene) choreographed it.

🎬 **LET'S SING AGAIN** (RKO 1936). The film that introduced youngster BOBBY BREEN to Depression audiences, the movie did not provide another SHIRLEY TEMPLE but the boy endeared himself enough to make seven more tearful melodramas in which he sang his heart out in that high, bird-like chirp he possessed. EDDIE CANTOR discovered Breen on his radio show, and producer Sol Lesser was impressed enough to build a movie around him. In the screenplay by Don Swift and Daniel Jarrett, the youth Billy Gordon (Breen) is abandoned by his Neapolitan mother, put in an orphanage, escapes to join a touring circus, is adopted by the kindly Joe Pasquale (Henry Armetta), and then comes across his real father while hitchhiking to New York to sing in an opera. Also cast were George Houston, Vivienne Osborne, Grant Withers, Inez Courtney, Lucien Littlefield, and Richard Carle. Breen got to sing a handful of songs, with the best being the Depression-chasing title number by JIMMY MCHUGH (music) and GUS KAHN (lyric), which became a hit when the boy recorded it. To really show off their singing moppet, the studio had Breen sing "La Dona e Mobile" from Verdi's *Rigoletto* as some kind of freak show attraction. Kurt Newmann directed with the wherewithal to keep the focus on Breen.

LET 'EM EAT CAKE. See *OF THEE I SING*

LEVANT, OSCAR (1906–1972). Film and television musician, composer, and performer. The cynical, piano-playing hypochondriac who played sardonic best friends of the hero in several movie musicals, he was also a first-rate songwriter and concert pianist. Levant was born in Pittsburgh, the son of a watch repairman, and as a teenager studied piano in New York, grooming himself for a concert career while he earned money playing in nightclub bands and in pit orchestras for Broadway musicals. He got a small part in the play *Burlesque* (1927) and wrote some of the music for the musical *Ripples* (1930) but the rest of his career was in Hollywood where he made his debut in *The Dance of Life* (1929). Usually sitting at a piano and smoking while he made witty insults, Levant helped enliven eight more movie musicals: *RHYTHM ON THE RIVER* (1940), *Kiss the Boys Goodbye* (1941), *RHAPSODY IN BLUE* (1945), *You Were Meant for Me* (1948), *THE BARKLEYS OF BROADWAY* (1949), *AN AMERICAN IN PARIS* (1951), *The I Don't Care Girl* (1953), and *THE BAND WAGON* (1953). Throughout his life he returned to the concert stage, made recordings, and wrote both symphonic and popular music. With lyricists Sidney Clare, DOROTHY FIELDS, and others, Levant wrote the score for the Hollywood musicals *Street Girl* (1929), *Tanned Legs* (1929), *Love Comes Along* (1930), *Music Is Magic* (1935), and *In Person* (1936), as well as soundtrack music for nonmusicals. He was a favorite on television, playing classical and popular music and showing off his deadly wit on quiz shows, variety programs, and talk shows. Levant was a close friend of GEORGE GERSHWIN, and his piano interpretations of the composer's work are considered among the finest on record. Autobiographies: *A Smattering of Ignorance* (1942), *Memoirs of an Amnesiac* (1965), *The Unimportance of Being Oscar* (1968); biography: *A Talent for Genius: The Life and Times of Oscar Levant*, Sam Kashner, Nancy Schoenberger (1998).

LEVENE, SAM [born Samuel Levine] (1905–1980). Stage and film performer. One of Broadway's favorite character actors, for fifty years he played cops, con men, theatrical types, gamblers, and hassled husbands, all with his thick New Yorkese accent and sour-looking expressions. He only appeared in a few musicals but shone on each occasion. The native New Yorker was pursuing a law career when he took up acting, getting his training at the American Academy of Dramatic Arts. By 1927

Levene was on Broadway and, although he was rarely cast in the leading role, he usually stole the show as supporting characters. His most famous nonmusical credits include *Dinner at Eight* (1932), *Three Men on a Horse* (1935), *Room Service* (1939), *Light Up the Sky* (1948), *The Devil's Advocate* (1961), *The Sunshine Boys* (1972), and the acclaimed revival of *The Royal Family* (1975). Although he was a weak singer, Levene was cast as the gambler Nathan Detroit in the original cast of *GUYS AND DOLLS* (1950) and reprised the role in London. His two other musical credits were the race-track fanatic Patsy in *Let It Ride!* (1961), a role he created in the comedy *Three Men on a Horse*, and the wisecracking waiter Hymie in *Cafe Crown* (1964); both shows failed to run. Levene played the same character types in his thirty movies, including the musicals *Sing Your Worries Away* (1942), *I Dood It* (1943), *Three Sailors and a Girl* (1953), and *The Opposite Sex* (1956).

LEVEY, ETHEL [born Ethelia Fowler] (1881–1955). Stage performer. A bubbly, high-kicking dancer–singer with a surprisingly deep voice, she played major roles in both Broadway and West End musicals. Born in San Francisco where she first started dancing on the stage, Levey came to New York in 1897 and was regularly featured in the music halls of Weber and Fields, Koster and Bial, and Hyde and Berman. She met and married GEORGE M. COHAN and made her Broadway debut in his *The Govenor's Son* (1901), followed by his *Running for Office* (1903), *LITTLE JOHNNY JONES* (1904), and *George Washington, Jr.* (1906). By the end of the decade, Levey and Cohan divorced and, after she starred in *Nearly a Hero* (1908), she began a new career in London, where she appeared in musicals for the next fifteen years. Among her London revues were *Hello, Ragtime!* (1912), *Hullo, Tango!* (1913), *Follow the Crowd* (1916), *Look Who's Here* (1916), *Three Cheers* (1916), *Here and There* (1917), and *Yes!* (1923), and she shone in the book musicals *WATCH YOUR STEP* (1914), *Oh, Julie!* (1920), and *The Blue Kitten* (1925). Levey returned to Broadway in featured parts in *Sunny River* (1941) and *Marinka* (1945) but neither show ran so she retired.

LEVIEN, SONYA (1895–1960). Film writer. The prolific Hollywood screenwriter, she penned several notable musicals, both originals and adaptations of stage works. Leven was born in Russia and educated in America at New York University where she studied law, later entering the legal profession for a time. She was a magazine editor before taking up writing and when some of her stories were adapted into films she got interested in screenwriting. Leven scripted her first film in 1921 and remained active into the 1960s. Among her musical credits are *Song o' My Heart* (1930), *DELICIOUS* (1931), *REBECCA OF SUNNYBROOK FARM* (1932), *IN OLD CHICAGO* (1938), *ZIEGFELD GIRL* (1941), *RHAPSODY IN BLUE* (1945), *STATE FAIR* (1945), *THE GREAT CARUSO* (1951), *THE MERRY WIDOW* (1952), *THE STUDENT PRINCE* (1954), *HIT THE DECK* (1955), *Interrupted Melody* (1955), *OKLAHOMA!* (1955), and *Pepe* (1960).

LEVIN, HENRY (1909–1980). Film, and television director. Working in a variety of genres for several different studios, the movie director specialized in lighter fare, including seven musicals. Levin was born in Trenton, New Jersey, and educated at the University of Pennsylvania before beginning his career as an actor in New York, appearing in a handful of plays presented by the THEATRE GUILD in the late 1930s and early 1940s. After serving as a dialogue director in Hollywood, he helmed his first feature in 1944, followed by fifty more films before he moved to television in the 1960s and directed many made-for-TV movies. His screen musicals include *JOLSON SINGS AGAIN* (1949), *THE FARMER TAKES A WIFE* (1953), *Bernardine* (1957), *April Love* (1957), *Where the Boys Are* (1960), and *Wonderful World of the Brothers Grimm* (1962).

LEVIN, HERMAN (1907–1990). Stage producer. A much-respected presenter of plays and musicals who had his fair share of hits and flops, he is remembered as the producer who struggled for years to bring *MY FAIR LADY* (1956) to the Broadway stage. Levin was born in Philadelphia and was a practicing lawyer before turning to producing with the Broadway revival of *The Gondoliers* in 1940. In addition to the original *My Fair Lady* and its 1976 revival, his musical hits were *CALL ME MISTER* (1946) and *GENTLEMEN PREFER BLONDES* (1949). Less successful were *Bless You All* (1950), *The Girl Who Came to Supper* (1963), *Tricks* (1973), and *Lovely Ladies, Kind Gentlemen* (1979). His nonmusical productions ranged from *No Exit* (1946) to *The Great White Hope* (1968).

LEWINE, RICHARD (1910–2005). Television producer and stage composer. One of America's most important TV producers, in regard to musicals, he also was a gifted songwriter. The native New Yorker studied music at Columbia University while he wrote songs for Broadway musicals such as *Fools Rush In* (1934), *Naughty*

Naught (1937), *The Fireman's Flame* (1937), and *The Girl From Wyoming* (1938); he would return to the stage later in life to score MAKE MINE MANHATTAN (1948) and *The Girls Against the Boys* (1959). After serving in World War II, Lewine got involved with television in its earliest days and worked his way into production and management, eventually becoming vice president of CBS-TV from 1952 to 1961. It was Lewine who conceived the idea of Rodgers and Hammerstein scoring a new musical version of CINDERELLA (1956) and broadcasting it live with the new Broadway star Julie Andrews as the heroine. He also produced the original TV musicals JUNIOR MISS (1957), ALADDIN (1958), THE DANGEROUS CHRISTMAS OF RED RIDING HOOD (1965), *On the Flip Side* (1966), and PINOCCHIO (1968). In the 1950s and 1960s, he and Robert Englander created the famous Young People's Concerts featuring LEONARD BERNSTEIN, and Lewine produced such memorable specials as *Together With Music* (1955) with NOEL COWARD and MARY MARTIN, and *My Name is Barbra* (1965) with BARBRA STREISAND. Lewine was also a recognized author of books on musical theatre songs.

LEWIS, JERRY [born Joseph Levitch] (1926–). Film, television, and stage performer, writer, and director. A durable and enduring comic, the agile, squawking clown had two film careers: one with his partner DEAN MARTIN in seventeen movie musicals and then as a solo artist often writing, producing, and directing his own screen vehicles. Lewis was born in Newark, New Jersey, to a family of show people and as a child often joined their act in Catskills resorts. He quit school to do stand-up comedy and was a seasoned professional when he and Martin were cast in secondary roles in the film musical *My Friend Irma* (1949) and were an immediate hit with moviegoers. They starred in *My Friend Irma Goes West* (1950) and fifteen other films, with the forever-juvenile Lewis as the erratic clown and Martin as the straight man who providing the singing and

Jerry Lewis. The irrepressible comic wrote, directed, and starred in so many film comedies in the 1960s and 1970s that one forgets his career began in movie musicals with partner Dean Martin. Here Lewis (right) does a hat and cane routine with Martin in *The Caddy* (1953). (Photofest)

the romance. Between 1950 and 1956, the duo was the top box office attraction in America. The most notable of their musical collaborations are *At War With the Army* (1950), *Sailor Beware* (1951), *The Stooge* (1952), *Scared Stiff* (1953), *The Caddy* (1953), *Living It Up* (1954), *You're Never Too Young* (1955), ARTISTS AND MODELS (1955), and *Pardners* (1956), as well as a cameo in ROAD TO BALI (1952). After the team split up, Lewis made several solo features in which he matured somewhat but still played the naive clown. His musicals without Martin include *Rock-a-Bye Baby* (1958), *Cinderfella* (1960), *The Ladies' Man* (1961), and *The Nutty Professor* (1963). Lewis remained a favorite for decades in nightclubs and on television where he had his own show and hosts his annual Muscular Dystrophy Telethon. Lewis made his late Broadway debut as the devil Applegate in DAMN YANKEES in 1995 and then toured with the show. Autobiographies: *Jerry Lewis in Person* (1982), *Dean and Me (A Love Story)*, with James Kaplan; biography: *King of Comedy: the Life and Art of Jerry Lewis*, Shawn Levy (1997).

LEWIS, ROBERT (1909–1994). Stage director. A versatile director with a long career in New York theatre, he was also one of America's most influential acting teachers. Lewis was born in Brooklyn, the son of a jeweler and a musician, and studied the cello at the Institute of Musical Art at City College. He soon turned to acting, studying at Juilliard and appearing on stage and sometimes directing for Eva Le Gallienne's Civic Repertory Theatre. By 1939, Lewis gave up acting to concentrate on directing, staging plays regionally and on tour, and then making a noticeable New York debut directing William Saroyan's *My Heart's in the Highlands* (1939). Over the next forty years, he directed classics, thrillers, comedies, melodramas, and musicals, such as BRIGADOON (1947), REGINA (1949), JAMAICA (1957), KWAMINA (1961), *Foxy* (1964), and ON A CLEAR DAY YOU CAN SEE FOREVER (1965). Lewis had become interested in Stanislavsky's acting theories when he was a member of the Group Theatre in the 1930s. In 1947 he co-founded the Actors Studio and remained with the organization as a director and teacher for many years. Lewis also taught at various universities and directed regionally throughout his life. Autobiography: *Slings and Arrows: Theatre in My Life* (1984).

LIEBMAN, MAX (1902–1981). Television and stage producer, writer, and director. A clever writer of sketches on Broadway, he later became an enterprising presenter of television specials, including both old and new musicals in his programming. Liebman was born in Vienna and got started on Broadway writing comedy sketches for the revues *The Illustrators' Show* (1936), *The Straw Hat Revue* (1939), *Crazy With the Heat* (1941), MAKE MINE MANHATTAN (1948), and *Alive and Kicking* (1950), as well as producing *Wine, Women and Song* (1942) and *From the Second City* (1961). He entered television as the producer of *The Admiral Broadway Revue* (1949) and became famous when he created SID CAESAR's *Show of Shows* in 1950. In his 1954–1955 series titled *Max Liebman Presents*, he offered major stars in condensed versions of such celebrated Broadway musicals as BABES IN TOYLAND, LADY IN THE DARK, NAUGHTY MARIETTA, A CONNECTICUT YANKEE, THE CHOCOLATE SOLDIER, THE DESERT SONG, THE GREAT WALTZ, and DEAREST ENEMY. Liebman also produced original TV musicals, such as SATINS AND SPURS (1954), *Heidi* (1955), THE ADVENTURES OF MARCO POLO (1956), *Holiday* (1956), and *Paris in the Springtime* (1956), directing several of the shows himself. He also produced musical specials featuring MAURICE CHEVALIER, JACKIE GLEASON, and others.

LIFE, THE (Ethel Barrymore Theatre 1997). An unsentimental musical play that showed the seamier side of life on the streets of New York City, the show was composer CY COLEMAN's last Broadway effort. The pimps, prostitutes, drug dealers, and their clients prowl sleazy 42nd Street (before it was cleaned up) where long-term relationships are next to impossible. David Newman, Ira Gasman, and Coleman collaborated on the hard-as-nails libretto, and the various characters were played by Sam Harris, LILLIAS WHITE, Pamela Isaacs, Chuck Cooper, Kevin Ramsey, Bellamy Young, Vernel Bagneris, and Sharon Wilkins. Gasman also wrote the lyrics for Coleman's music, resulting in such terse numbers as "Check It Out!," "The Oldest Profession," "My Way or the Highway," "Use What You Got," "We Had a Dream," "Easy Money," and "My Body." The musical had been workshopped in 1990 and songs had been recorded long before the Broadway version materialized so there was considerable anticipation for the show directed by Michael Blakemore and choreographed by JOEY MCKNEELY. Critics were more impressed by the talented cast than the musical itself but word of mouth was favorable enough to let the show run an (unprofitable) 465 performances.

◻ **LIFE AND ADVENTURES OF SANTA CLAUS, THE** (CBS-TV 1985). A stop-motion animated musical with an intriguing story and wonderful voices, the sixty-minute production was one of the best TV musicals of its decade. Based on a novel by L. Frank Baum, Julian P. Gardner's teleplay lets the Great Ak (voice of ALFRED DRAKE) tell the story of how Santa Claus came to be. The abandoned infant named Claus is raised by a lioness and a fairy in the Forest of Bursee and when he is an adult he learns about the evil and hardships in the world. Claus (Earl Hammond) is determined to relieve the suffering by working with the residents of the Laughing Valley of Ho-Ha-Ho to make presents and deliver them to children in the orphanages. The evil King Awgwa (Earle Hyman) tries to stop Claus but he enlists the help of the reindeer to fly out of the valley and deliver the gifts on Christmas Eve. For his efforts the Council of Immortals bestows the title Santa (saint) on Claus and makes him immortal. Gardner wrote the lyrics for Bernard Hoffer's music, and the score ranged from the solemn "Ora E Sempre" to the silly "Ho-Ha-Ho" with such tuneful numbers as "Babe in the Woods" "A Child," and "Big Surprise." ARTHUR RANKIN, JR., and JULES BASS produced and directed and, as with their earlier stop-motion works, the visuals were splendid.

◔ **LIFE BEGINS AT 8:40** (Winter Garden Theatre 1934). A fondly remembered musical revue from the Depression years, the show boasted top-flight songs and beloved stars. Its title was taken from Walter Pitkin's best-selling book *Life Begins at Forty* and the sketches by David Freedman and others were tailored to the comic talents of BERT LAHR, LUELLA GEAR, and Brian Donlevy, while the songs by HAROLD ARLEN (music), IRA GERSHWIN, and E. Y. HARBURG (lyrics) were ideal for RAY BOLGER, Frances Williams, Earl Oxford, and DIXIE DUNBAR. "You're a Builder-Upper," "What Can You Say in a Love Song?," "Fun to Be Fooled," "Shoein' the Mare," "I Couldn't Hold My Man," and "My Paramount-Publix-Roxy-Rose" were among the skillful numbers. The SHUBERTS produced, Philip Loeb and JOHN MURRAY ANDERSON co-directed, ROBERT ALTON and Charles Weidman did the choreography, and the revue ran 237 performances despite the hard times on Broadway.

◔ **LIGHT IN THE PIAZZA, THE** (Vivian Beaumont Theatre 2005). A beguiling operatic piece that was scheduled for a limited run at Lincoln Center, the show was so well reviewed and the musical caught on with audiences that it was held over for 504 performances. The North Carolina tourist Margaret Johnson (VICTORIA CLARK) takes an extended vacation in Florence, Italy, with her beautiful daughter Clara (KELLI O'HARA) who is grown up but is brain damaged and has the emotional development of a child. When the local youth Fabrizio Naccarelli (Matthew Morrison) is smitten with Clara, Margaret assumes he is just another Italian on the make and tries to keep the two apart. But Fabrizio and Clara are soon deeply in love and, sensing that her daughter is accepted for who she is and has a chance for the married happiness she lacks, Margaret agrees to the wedding. Also in the superior cast were Mark Harelik, Sarah Uriarte Berry, PATTI CONENOUR, Michael Berresse, and Beau Gravitte. Based on Elizabeth Spencer's novella, the libretto by Craig Lucas was both amusing and moving, and the compelling score by ADAM GUETTEL was operatic without being artificial. Among the lovely numbers in the show were "Love to Me," "Dividing Day," "The Beauty Is," "Let's Walk," "The Joy You Feel," "Say It Somehow," "Fable," and the title number. Bartlett Sher directed the atmospheric production, which had been previously seen in regional theatre, and Clark gave one of the most poignant performances of the decade. ◻ The final performance of *The Light in the Piazza* was broadcast live on the PBS-TV program *Live From Lincoln Center* in 2006 and the tape is a vivid record of the production.

LIGHT OPERA OF MANHATTAN (LOOM). Theatre company. A Manhattan institution that began in 1968 with a season of Gilbert and Sullivan offerings, over the years they expanded the repertory to include many American and foreign operettas not often seen in New York or elsewhere. The company moved its home from location to location over the decades, hitting such financial problems that it temporarily closed in 1986. But fervent patrons and supporters of the company resurrected the troupe and it managed to hang on until 1989 when it closed for good. Some foreign works were presented with new translations, and the productions often revised the librettos of the older musicals but were usually faithful to the music as written. VICTOR HERBERT, SIGMUND ROMBERG, and RUDOLF FRIML's popular and sometimes lesser known works were the backbone of LOOM's American repertory.

LIGHTNER, WINNIE [born Winnifred Josephine Reeves] (1901–1971). Stage and film performer. A blonde firecracker of a performer, she sang and danced in vaudeville, on Broadway, and in some early talkies. Lightner was born in Greenport, New York, and went into variety as a comedienne in 1919. She made her Broadway bow in GEORGE WHITE'S SCANDALS (1922), followed by two more editions of Scandals and other revues such as Gay Paree (1925 and 1926) and Harry Delmar's Revels (1927), introducing such songs as "I'll Build a Stairway to Paradise" and "Somebody Loves Me." Lightner left the stage when sound came in and made her screen debut in HOLLYWOOD REVUE OF 1929, quickly establishing herself as a top star in the new field of movie musicals. She was featured in the SHOW OF SHOWS (1929), HOLD EVERYTHING (1930), Life of the Party (1930), She Couldn't Say No (1930), and DANCING LADY (1933) and then, at the peak of her popularity, she retired when she married director ROY DEL RUTH.

Li'l Abner. Unknown actor–singer Peter Palmer (pictured with Edith Adams as Daisy Mae) had the beefy good looks to play the dense country bumpkin Abner Yokum so the producers cast him rather than a bankable star in the Broadway and film productions. (Photofest)

🎭 **LI'L ABNER** (St. James Theatre 1956). A musicalization of Al Capp's popular comic strip, the show was indeed cartoonish in its look and performances. When the ramshackle community of Dogpatch is selected as an atomic bomb testing site because it is deemed by the government as the most useless place in the nation, the hillbilly residents are up in arms and their rag-tag lifestyle is only saved by a historical mistake. The familiar Capp characters included lazy Abner, his amorous sweetheart Daisy Mae, his spunky Mammy Yokum, the congenial Marryin' Sam, the put-upon Pappy Yokum, the loud-mouth General Bullmoose, and the sultry Appassionata Von Climax. Co-producers Norman Panama and MELVIN FRANK penned the libretto in which much of Capp's wicked satire became merely farcical on stage. The tuneful score by GENE DE PAUL (music) and JOHNNY MERCER (lyrics) featured such countrified numbers as "Namely You," "Jubilation T. Cornpone," "(Don't That Take the) Rag Off'n the Bush," "The Country's in the Very Best of Hands," and "I'm Past My Prime." Reviewers recommended the animated performances and the raucous production, including the riotous direction and choreography by MICHAEL KIDD, and the show ran 693 performances.

🎬 **Li'l Abner** (Paramount 1959) was about as faithful a movie could be to its original Broadway source, for most of the cast, score,

Casts for *Li'l Abner*		
Character	*1956 Broadway*	*1959 film*
Li'l Abner	PETER PALMER	Peter Palmer
Daisy Mae	EDITH ADAMS	Leslie Parrish
Marryin' Sam	STUBBY KAYE	Stubby Kaye
Mammy Yokum	Charlotte Rae	Billie Hayes
Pappy Yokum	Joe E. Marks	Joe E. Marks
General Bullmoose	Howard St. John	Howard St. John
Stupefyin' Jones	Julie Newmar	Julie Newmar
Earthquake McGoon	Bern Hoffman	Bern Hoffman
Appassionata Von Climax	Tina Louise	Stella Stevens

libretto, and choreography were repeated on the screen. In fact, with its stylized settings and cartoonish costumes, the movie seemed more theatrical than cinematic. However, the production is so lively and the performances so vibrant that one is not bothered by the staginess of Melvin and Panama's direction. Kidd's choreography (recreated by DEEDEE WOOD) for the "Sadie Hawkins Day" ballet is even more fun on screen, even if the chase is all set on a sound stage. *Li'l Abner* is that rare case when Hollywood did not tamper with something that worked, and this musical farce worked very well on stage and screen. ❑ ABC-TV presented a greatly abridged version of the show in 1971, cramming what they could in the half-hour broadcast. Ray Young (Abner) and Nancee Parkinson (Daisy Mae) led the cast, which included Billie Hayes and Billy Belcher as Mammy and Pappy Yokum.

LILI (MGM 1953). With only one song, a lot of background music, and a lengthy dream ballet, the movie barely qualifies as a musical yet there is something so lyrical about its charm that it feels like a full-scale musical. Based on a story by Paul Gallico, the simple plot centered on the French orphan Lili Daurier who gets hired by a traveling carnival show and falls girlishly in love with the dashing magician Marco the Magnificent while she is loved by the bitter cripple Paul Berthalet who speaks to (and eventually woos) Lili through his puppets. The lone song, "Hi-Lili, Hi-Lo," was by Bronislaw Kaper (music) and Helen Deutsch (lyric) who also wrote the screenplay. As sung by LESLIE CARON and the puppets, the simple carousel-like ditty was endearing and became a hit. CHARLES WALTERS directed the film and, with Dorothy Jarnasc, choreographed the ballet in which Lili dreams of the two men in her life. The whole venture was so fragile and bittersweet it might have been a French art house film, yet it was popular at the box office.

🕊 *Carnival* (Imperial Theatre 1961) was the first time a Hollywood musical inspired a Broadway musical, a reversal of the usual order of things. *Lili* was turned into the stage musical *Carnival* with a libretto by MICHAEL STEWART and a whole new score by BOB MERRILL that featured its own carousel-like hit song, "Theme From Carnival" but better known as "Love Makes the World Go Round." Also in the splendid score were the plaintive "Mira," the ballads "Her Face" and "Always Always You," the comic number "Humming," and the joyous "Grand Imperial Cirque de Paris." Like its film source, the stage production had a quaint, European flavor to it, yet as directed and choreographed by GOWER CHAMPION with colorful theatricality it was also a satisfying Broadway show. Critical cheers from the press helped the DAVID MERRICK production run 719 performances. Revivals in summer stock and with other groups were consistent for a time and the musical returned to Broadway in 1968 in a month-long engagement by the City Center Light Opera Company featuring Victoria Mallory (Lili), Leon Bibb (Paul), Richard France (Marco), KAREN MORROW (Rosalie), and Pierre Olaf reprising his Jacquot from the original.

LILLIAN RUSSELL (Fox 1940). The costumes and the interior settings of the 1890s were so well done in this biographical film that audiences were led to believe that the story was close to the truth. Not only was the screenplay by WILLIAM ANTHONY McGUIRE inaccurate, it was dull, which in Hollywood terms was the greater sin. However, the life of the hourglass-figured Russell, who starred in vaudeville, on Broadway, and most memorably in a series of JOE WEBER and LEW FIELDS revues, was a lively subject for a musical. Instead young Lillian (ALICE FAYE) is just another show girl yearning for fame and when she gets it she comes across as just another leading lady. Russell's four notorious marriages were reduced to two bland ones: with songwriter Edward Solomon (DON AMECHE) and newspaper reporter Alexander Moore (Henry Fonda). Her flamboyant association with Diamond Jim Brady (Edward Arnold) was turned into a tired

---

Casts for the *Lili* musicals

Character	1953 film Lili	1961 Broadway Carnival
Lili	LESLIE CARON	ANNA MARIA ALBERGHETTI
Paul Berthalet	Mel Ferrer	JERRY ORBACH
Marco	Jean-Pierre Aumont	JAMES MITCHELL
Rosalie	ZSA ZSA GABOR	KAYE BALLARD
Jacquot	KURT KASZNAR	Pierre Olaf

friendship that could not create much interest or many sparks. Faye is solid and reliable as always, although nothing close to a character emerges. Her renditions of the period songs, which were usually accurate for the time, were pleasing if never exciting: "Come Down, Ma Evenin' Star," "Ma Blushin' Rosie," "After the Ball," "The Band Played On," and others. There was another touch of authenticity: Weber and Fields came out of retirement and performed one of their comic routines in the film, although not with Russell/Faye. IRVING CUMMINGS was the dutiful director, SEYMOUR FELIX did the graceful choreography, and the picture was produced by Gene Markey and DARRYL F. ZANUCK.

LILLIE, BEATRICE [born Constance Sylvia Gladys Munston] (1894–1989). Stage, television, and film performer. The uniquely inspired clown, who retained her regal and lady-like demeanor while doing outrageous things such as roller skating while wearing an evening gown, she lit up musical revues in New York and London. Born in Toronto, Lillie performed as a child in Canada and then in England when her family moved there when she was a teenager. By 1914 she was making a name for herself in musical halls and London revues such as *Not Likely!* (1914), *Now's the Time* (1915), *Cheep* (1917), *Tabs* (1918), *Pot Luck* (1921), and *The Nine O'Clock Revue* (1922). Lillie first came to Broadway in *ANDRÉ CHARLOT'S REVUE* (1924) with JACK BUCHANAN and GERTRUDE LAWRENCE and was immediately embraced by New York audiences. Over the next thirty years she would return in such revues as *Charlot Revue* (1925), *This Year of Grace* (1928), *THE THIRD LITTLE SHOW* (1931), *Walk a Little Faster* (1932), *AT HOME ABROAD* (1935), *THE SHOW IS ON* (1936), *Set to Music* (1939), *Seven Lively Arts* (1944), *INSIDE U.S.A.* (1948), *An Evening With Beatrice Lillie* (1952), and *ZIEGFELD FOLLIES* (1957). Lillie occasionally appeared in book musicals, such as *Oh, Please* (1926) and *She's My Baby* (1928), and late in her career triumphed as the daffy medium Madame Arcati in *High Spirits* (1964). Her kind of humor went over well on the radio but not in films, with her appearances in the musicals *THE SHOW OF SHOWS* (1929), *Are You There?* (1930), *Doctor Rhythm* (1938), and *THOROUGHLY MODERN MILLIE* (1967) only serving as a faint record of her stage persona, as were her handful of television appearances in the 1950s. Autobiography: *Every Other Inch a Lady* (1972); biography: *Beatrice Lillie: The Funniest Woman in the World*, Bruce Laffey (1990).

LINCOLN CENTER THEATRE. Theatre organization. This performing arts center in Manhattan has a long and roller coaster-like history but for the past two decades has emerged as a potent theatre operation that has offered many notable musical productions. Built in the 1960s and covering blocks of cityscape on Amsterdam Avenue and Broadway, Lincoln Center was the largest and most ambitious arts project in the city's history. The complex includes the Metropolitan Opera House, the New York State Theatre, the Avery Fisher Hall, the Alice Tully Hall, and two legitimate theatres spaces: the Broadway-contracted Vivian Beaumont Theatre and the Off Broadway space the Mitzi Newhouse Theatre. The Repertory Theatre of Lincoln Center was established in 1960 before the complex was built, and by 1964 the company was performing classics and new works in the Vivian Beaumont, but rarely musicals. The repertory company offered some outstanding productions, but was the victim of financial and managerial problems and floundered for years. While JOSEPH PAPP ran the theatre for a few seasons in the 1970s, he offered some musicals, most memorably the 1976 revival of *THE THREEPENNY OPERA*, but soon he gave up on the problematic institution and returned to his activities Off Broadway. The New York City Opera, however, has flourished at the New York State Theatre and occasionally revives musicals and operettas as part of its repertory. Also, in the 1960s RICHARD RODGERS was the producer of the Music Theatre of Lincoln Center, which offered classic musical revivals in the larger venues. The theatre sector of Lincoln Center closed down for a few years in the 1980s and then returned as Lincoln Center Theatre in 1986, abandoning the repertory system and booking works in both the large upstairs space and the intimate downstairs venue. Under Gregory Mosher, Bernard Gersten, and later Andre Bishop, Lincoln Center Theatre has become a highly respected and artistically vibrant organization. In addition to new American and British plays and classic revivals, Lincoln Center has been a major force in offering new musicals and outstanding revivals. Among the latter have been productions of *ANYTHING GOES* (1987), *CAROUSEL* (1994), and *SOUTH PACIFIC* (2008). The new musicals to premiere at Lincoln Center Theatre include *My Favorite Year* (1992), *HELLO AGAIN* (1994), *PARADE* (1998), *A NEW BRAIN* (1998), *Marie Christine* (1999), *It Ain't Nothing But the Blues* (1999), *CONTACT* (2000), *A Man of No Importance* (2002), *The Frogs* (2004), *THE LIGHT IN THE PIAZZA* (2005), *Bernarda Alba* (2006), and *The*

Glorious Ones (2007). Often Lincoln Center Theatre finds that one of its productions is so popular that it must move to another Broadway house in order to continue its season. In some cases, the company has opened plays and musicals in another Broadway playhouse because their home venues are booked. Such has been the case with the musicals *Sarafina* (1988), *THE MOST HAPPY FELLA* (1992), and *Thou Shalt Not* (2001).

LINDEN, HAL [born Harold Lipshitz] (1931–). Stage and television performer. The genial leading man with a perennial smile and pleasant singing voice, he acted on Broadway for years but only found stardom right before he left the theatre to become famous on television. The Bronx native was educated at the High School of the Performing Arts, Queens College, and City College before playing clarinet for some touring bands and in the Army during World War II. After studying acting with Paul Mann and others and appearing in summer stock, Linden made his Broadway bow in 1958 as a replacement for the leading man in *BELLS ARE RINGING* (1958). Originating roles or replacing others in the musicals *WILDCAT* (1961), Off Broadway in *ANYTHING GOES* (1962), *Something More!* (1964), *Illya Darling* (1967), *THE APPLE TREE* (1967), and *The Education of H̃´Y´M´A´N K´A´P´L´A´N* (1968) brought him little attention, but his masterful performance as Mayer Rothschild in *THE ROTHSCHILDS* (1970) finally gave him recognition. Linden concentrated on television in the 1970s and became a familiar favorite because of the series *Barney Miller* but he returned to Broadway occasionally in plays and musicals, such as *THE PAJAMA GAME* (1972) and *CABARET* (2002). He has appeared in only a few films but in many television series and specials.

LINDSAY AND CROUSE. Playwriting team. One of the most successful writing duos in the American theatre, they scripted seven Broadway musicals together. Howard Lindsay [born Herman Nelke] (1889–1968) was born in Waterford, New York, and educated at Harvard University before he began his career as an actor and stage manager in New York City. Lindsay first found success as a director when he staged the popular comedy *Dulcy* in 1921. While continuing to direct, Lindsay also took up writing and his first play, *Tommy*, appeared on Broadway in 1927. He wrote his first musical libretto in 1934 when, as director of *ANYTHING GOES*, he and press agent Russel Crouse had to rewrite the original libretto. Crouse (1893–

1966) was born in Findlay, Ohio, and worked as a journalist in Cincinnati and then in New York before he became a press agent for the THEATRE GUILD. He had contributed to the script for two musicals before teaming up with Lindsay and writing *Anything Goes*. The new team went on to a twenty-five-year collaboration that included such hit plays as *Life With Father* (1939), *Strip for Action* (1942), *State of the Union* (1945), and *Remains to Be Seen* (1951), as well as the musicals *RED, HOT AND BLUE!* (1936), *HOORAY FOR WHAT!* (1937), *CALL ME MADAM* (1950), *Happy Hunting* (1956), *THE SOUND OF MUSIC* (1959), and *MR. PRESIDENT* (1962). Lindsay continued to act and direct throughout his productive career, as well as co-producing such successes as *Arsenic and Old Lace* (1941) and *Detective Story* (1949). Lindsay was married to actress Dorothy Stickney whom he directed and acted with on several occasions. Biography: *Life with Lindsay and Crouse*, Cornelia Otis Skinner (1976).

LION KING, THE (Disney 1994). Eschewing the DISNEY tradition of starting with a classic fairy tale or well-known story, the studio commissioned an original screenplay by Irene Mecchi, Jonathan Reynolds, and Linda Woolverton. It may have borrowed generously from *Hamlet* and the studio's own *Bambi* (1942), but the story and characters were solid, engaging, and lent themselves to an often serious musical film.

Plot: The lion patriarch King Mufasa rules over all the animals on the African savanna from Pride Rock and the birth of his son Simba is celebrated by all the creatures. Young Simba grows to be a playful but impatient cub that eagerly looks forward to being the lion king someday. During a stampede of wildebeests, Mufasa is pushed into the path of the herd and is trampled to death. Simba is convinced by his evil uncle Scar that the cub was responsible for the death of his father, when it was Scar himself who murdered his brother in order to take over the pride. Simba runs away and grows up under the "no worries" philosophy of the meerkat Timon and the warthog Pumbaa. Scar proves to be a neurotic, ineffective king and his allies the hyenas are starting to turn against him. Simba is encouraged by the wise-old baboon Rafiki to return home and avenge his father's death and in the battle that follows the truth of who really murdered Mufasa is revealed. Scar is destroyed, Simba mates with his childhood sweetheart, and the animals once again come to pay homage when the couple present their newborn cub to the pride.

The Lion King. Film is supposed to be cinematic and theatre is supposed to be theatrical; *The Lion King* was both. Looking at the movie, one cannot imagine it on a stage. Watching the Broadway version, one cannot picture such a thing on the screen. That is how well the two versions of the musical did their job. Pictured is Tsidii Le Loka as Rafiki singing "The Circle of Life" in the original Broadway production. (Photofest)

Casts for *The Lion King*

Character	1994 film (voices)	1997 Broadway
Mufasa	James Earl Jones	SAMUEL E. WRIGHT
Adult Simba	MATTHEW BRODERICK	Jason Raize
Young Simba	Jonathan Taylor Thomas	Scott Irby-Ranniar
Scar	Jeremy Irons	John Vickery
Timon	NATHAN LANE	Max Casella
Pumbaa	Ernie Sabella	Tom Alan Robbins
Rafiki	Robert Guillaume	Tsidii Le Loka
Zazu	Rowman Atkinson	Geoff Hoyle
Nala	Moira Kelly	HEATHER HEADLEY

No animated film had taken on so many heavy issues, met them head on, and succeeded like *The Lion King*. The stampede in which Mufasa died was as powerful as any live-action adventure, yet the comedy of Timon and Pumbaa had the heart and soul of vaudeville. Directors Roger Allers and Rob Minkoff captured not only the look and feel of the African savannah, but also the kinship of community, which drives the plot. The depiction of the many different kinds of animals that are connected to the pride is both lyrical and stunning, like a ballet of nature enfolding before our eyes. The background art and animation are equally as evocative. The film may be the visual masterpiece of the modest renaissance in Disney animation that began with *THE LITTLE MERMAID* (1989). ELTON JOHN (music) and TIM RICE (lyrics) wrote the pop score, which sometimes bordered on the fervent, especially in the opening number "The Circle of Life," which combined music, animation, and ritual in a way rarely seen on the screen before. Other songs include Timon and Pumbaa's freewheeling "Hakuna Matata," Scar's Fascist creed "Be Prepared," and the Oscar-winning ballad "Can You Feel

The Lion King (film) Musical Numbers

"The Circle of Life"
"I Just Can't Wait to Be King"
"Be Prepared"
"Hakuna Matata"
"Can You Feel the Love Tonight?"

the Love Tonight?" used behind the romantic scenes between adult Simba and Nala. The superb musical background score by Hans Zimmer gave the movie an authentic-sounding African rhythm not found in the songs. The soundtrack recording was very popular. As for the film itself, it was the biggest sleeper hit in the history of the Disney studios. From a totally unknown entity came the top-grossing animated movie of all time.

🖐 **The Lion King** (New Amsterdam Theatre 1997) was not so much dramatized for the stage as rethought in ritual and theatrical terms by director–designer JULIE TAYMOR and the result was a dazzling display of musical celebration that pleased even the most adamant anti-Disney critics. Mecchi adapted her screenplay with Roger Allers, fleshing out the characters by adding new songs for Scar, adult Simba and Nala, and others. Also, some rousing choral singing based on African rhythms gave the show an almost spiritual aura at times. Tim Rice, Lebo M, and Taymor set new lyrics to music by John, Zimmer, and Mark Mancina, and they came up with such expert new numbers as "Shadowland," "The Morning Report," "They Live in You," "Chow Down," and "Endless Night." The show was a hit with audiences from the start and still manages to sell out a decade after it opened. *The Lion King* was the first open-run attraction in the newly restored New Amsterdam Theatre and the beginning of the revitalization of 42nd Street.

🖐 **LITTLE JOHNNY JONES** (Liberty Theatre 1904). The multitalented George M. Cohan's third Broadway effort and his first hit, the tuneful musical not only made him a major showman but solidified the brash Cohan sound that would influence so many subsequent shows. The American jockey Johnny Jones (Cohan) is in England to ride his horse Yankee Doodle in the Derby and is falsely accused of throwing the race by the villainous Brit Anthony Antsey (Jerry Cohan). The cocky little hero must remain in England to clear his name and sends a detective friend to search for evidence aboard a ship sailing out of Southampton harbor. The detective signals Johnny on the pier by setting off some skyrockets and Johnny celebrates by singing and dancing on the pier in the musical's most famous scene. But the jockey's problems continue in America where Antsey kidnaps Johnny's fiancée Goldie (ETHEL LEVEY), brings her to a Chinatown haunt, and sets up Johnny for two crimes. Johnny and the detective rescue Goldie, clear Johnny's name, and finally get Antsey behind bars. The three-act "musical play," as Cohan billed it, was an action packed melodrama with songs, and Cohan directed the piece in a brisk, broad manner. Critics complained that the story was crude and the lyrics too slangy but audiences immediately liked the Cohan sound, and "Give My Regards to Broadway" and "Yankee Doodle Boy" became instant hits. Also in the score were "Life's a Funny Proposition After All," "They're All My Friends," and "A Girl I Know." SAM H. HARRIS produced the musical and it ran fifty-two performances in its first engagements and then returned twice in 1905 and again in 1907. Broadway didn't see *Little Johnny Jones* again until a 1982 production directed by Gerald Gutierrez and choreographed by DAN SIRETTA. The largely rewritten revival starred television star Donny Osmond, and both the performer and the production were panned by the press, forcing the show to close on opening night.

Casts for Little Johnny Jones

Character	1904 Broadway	1929 film
Johnny Jones	GEORGE M. COHAN	EDDIE BUZZELL
Goldie/Mary	ETHEL LEVEY	Alice Day
Anthony Anstey	Jerry Cohan	
Henry Hapgood	DONALD BRIAN	
Timothy D. McGee	Sam J. Ryan	
Wyman		Wheeler Oakman
Carbon		Ray Turner
Ed Baker		Robert Edeson

■ **Little Johnny Jones** (Warner/First National 1929) kept the two famous Cohan songs but not Cohan, casting instead the wiry little comic EDDIE BUZZELL as Johnny and he was the movie's only saving grace. Adelaide Heilbron's screenplay not only condensed the events of the stage show, but sucked the life out of them as well and the dull melodrama only came to life when Buzzell sang "Yankee Doodle Boy" and "Give My Regards to Broadway." MERVIN LEROY directed the film, which has primitive sound and clumsy camera work. Much more enjoyable is the lengthy segment in *YANKEE DOODLE DANDY* (1942), the biographical movie musical about Cohan, in which JAMES CAGNEY plays Cohan/Johnny in three musical scenes from *Little Johnny Jones*.

❧ **LITTLE MARY SUNSHINE** (Orpheum Theatre 1959). A delightful musical spoof satirizing 1920s operettas, the Off Broadway show found a steady audience for 1,143 performances. Little Mary Sunshine (Eileen Brennan) is the proprietress of the Colorado Inn in the Rocky Mountains where she sings chipper, optimistic songs to the guests and the locals. When she is threatened with eviction, Captain Jim Warington, (William Graham), the forest ranger Billy Jester (JOHN MCMARTIN), and the Colorado Rangers come to her rescue and not only is the inn saved but Jim wins the heart of Mary. Rick Besoyan wrote the risible libretto and the pastiche numbers, which ribbed *ROSE-MARIE* (1924), *RIO RITA* (1927), and other operettas, yet there was still a kind of affection in the spoof and the songs were enjoyable in themselves. "Look for a Sky of Blue," "Colorado Love Call," "Mata Hari," "Once in a Blue Moon," "In Izzenschnooken on the Lovely Essenzook Zee," and the title number were among the songs that echoed past operetta hits. The musical was very popular with summer stock and amateur theatre groups for years, enjoyed by audiences often too young to be familiar with the show's musical targets.

❧ **LITTLE ME** (Lunt-Fontanne Theatre 1962). A broad musical farce that was more a series of funny sketches than a cohesive book musical, the show was a showcase for the inspired comic SID CAESAR and as such was very satisfying. The infamous Belle Poitrine decides to write her scandalous memoirs recalling how as a young woman she found wealth and fame through her connection with different men, many of them played by Caesar. The merry libretto, taken from Patrick Dennis' comic novel, was by NEIL SIMON who wrote it with Caesar (his old television boss) in mind, while CY COLEMAN (music) and CAROLYN LEIGH (lyrics) provided the cunning score, which produced two hits, "Real Live Girl" and "I've Got Your Number." Also highly enjoyable were "Be a Performer!," "Here's to Us," "The Other Side of the Tracks," "Boom-Boom," and the title song. Caesar was outstanding but also commendable were the supporting cast and the witty choreography by BOB FOSSE. CY FEUER directed and, with Ernest Martin, produced the musical, which ran 257 performances.

Because the musical was a star vehicle, it lost something in the 1982 Broadway revival when Caesar's roles were divided between veteran character actor James Coco and young leading man VICTOR GARBER. Also, the critics noted that without Caesar the script seemed less accomplished, although they felt the songs held up. The revival, directed by Robert Drivas and choreographed by PETER GENNARO, ran only thirty-six performances. *Little Me* did much better in 1998 when another television star, MARTIN SHORT, starred in the ROUNDABOUT THEATRE revival. Short played all the characters Caesar had and then a few more in the slightly revised libretto by Simon, and FAITH PRINCE played Belle in the past and the present, although even combined there wasn't much of a character there. Again the press faulted the libretto but praised the performers and the production, directed and choreographed by ROB

Broadway casts for *Little Me*

Character	1962 Broadway	1982 Broadway	1998 Broadway
Noble Eggleston		VICTOR GARBER	
Amos Pinchley		James Coco	
Prince Cherney		James Coco	
Val Du Val, etc.	SID CAESAR	Victor Garber	MARTIN SHORT
Belle Then	Virginia Martin	Mary Gordon Murray	FAITH PRINCE
Belle Now	Nancy Andrews	Jessica James	Faith Prince
Bernie, etc.	Joey Faye		Michael McGrath

MARSHALL, and the limited engagement of 101 performances was well attended.

📽 **LITTLE MERMAID, THE** (Disney 1989). The movie that began the DISNEY renaissance in animated musicals in the 1990s, the film offered a classic story, superb animation, vibrant characters, and a Broadway-like score full of hit songs.

Plot: The mermaid Ariel is not happy in her underwater world, even though she is the daughter of King Triton. She has often swum to the surface and observed humans, even collecting the objects from their world that have sunk into the sea. Despite the arguments of the crab Sebastian that life under the sea is the best of all existences, Ariel yearns to be human, especially when she sees and falls in love with Prince Eric. After a fight with her father, Ariel makes a pact with the sea witch Ursula to exchange her beautiful voice for human legs. The deal involves Ariel getting Eric to kiss her or else she becomes the slave of the witch. Ursula tricks Ariel by appearing as a beautiful woman with Ariel's voice but the plot is uncovered just in time and Eric slays the sea witch and Ariel becomes a mermaid again. Triton, seeing how much she loves Eric, uses his powers to make Ariel human once again and she is reunited with Eric.

Loosely adapted from the Hans Christian Andersen tale, the screenplay by Roger Allers and directors Ron Clements and John Musker gave the tragic story a happy ending and added an array of colorful secondary characters to bring intrigue and humor to the story. In the Disney tradition, Ariel was surrounded by lively companions, in this case the fearful Flounder and the cockeyed seagull Scuttle. Also a tradition, the villainess had her henchmen, two slithering, silent eels named Flotsom and Jetsom. The background art was colorful and

---

The Little Mermaid (film) Musical Numbers

"Daughters of Triton"
"Part of Your World"
"Under the Sea"
"Poor Unfortunate Souls"
"Les Poissons"
"Kiss the Girl"

---

fairy tale-like and the animation was buoyant and playful. Composer ALAN MENKEN began his string of award-winning movie scores with *The Little Mermaid* and the songs, written with lyricist HOWARD ASHMAN, reminded audiences of what a top-notch Broadway score used to sound like. Not only were the musical numbers tuneful and imaginative, they also were marvelous character pieces that moved the story along effectively. Ariel's wistful "Part of Your World," the Oscar-winning calypso number "Under the Sea," the bombastic aria "Poor Unfortunate Souls," and the romantic, Caribbean-flavored "Kiss the Girl" were more than musical diversions, they were the heart of the movie. *The Little Mermaid* was a box office hit and opened the door for an exciting decade of musical animation from the Disney studio. The movie was popular enough to inspire a cartoon series on television and some made-for-video sequels.

📖 **The Little Mermaid** (Lunt-Fontanne Theatre 2007) sought to capture the magic of the beloved screen musical on stage and, despite an expensive and clever production and a personable cast, the show struggled to live up to its predecessor. Doug Wright's libretto made changes in the plot that did not please some fans of the movie, and new songs ("I Want the Good Times Back," "The World Above," "Sweet Child," "Beyond My Wildest Dreams,"

Casts for The Little Mermaid

Character	1989 film (voices)	2007 Broadway
Ariel	Jodi Benson	Sierra Boggess
Ursula	PAT CARROLL	Sherie René Scott
Prince Eric	Christopher Daniel Barnes	Sean Palmer
Sebastian	SAMUEL E. WRIGHT	Tituss Burgess
Scuttle	BUDDY HACKETT	Eddie Korbich
Flounder	Jason Marin	Cody Hanford
		J. J. Singleton
Louis	RENE AUBERJONAIS	John Treacy Egan
King Triton	Kenneth Mars	Norm Lewis
Grimsby	Ben Wright	JONATHAN FREEMAN

"Positoovity," and others) by Menken (music) and Glenn Slater (lyrics) were added to fill out the story and the characters. Reviewers and audiences had mixed reactions to everything about the show, from the sets, costumes, and rollerblading underwater creatures to the direction by Francesca Zambello and choreography by Stephen Mear, although most reviewers applauded Sheri Rene Scott's hilarious sea witch Ursula. A huge advance and high audience satisfaction point to another hit for Disney.

LITTLE NELLIE KELLY (Liberty Theatre 1922). Described by the press as an old-fashioned musical comedy a bit out of place in the Roaring Twenties, the show was an audience favorite and ran 276 performances, longer than any other GEORGE M. COHAN musical. Nellie (Elizabeth Hines), the daughter of Irish police officer Kelly (Arthur Deagon), works in DeVere's Department Store where she is seen by the wealthy swell Jack Lloyd (Barratt Greenwood). In order to get closer to her, Jack invites all the employees at DeVere's to a party at his aunt's Fifth Avenue mansion. The Irish laborer Jerry Conroy (CHARLES KING), who has long loved Nellie, crashes the party and when the aunt's string of pearls is stolen he is suspected. In time Jerry is cleared and Nellie turns down the high life with Jack to be with her own kind. As in the past, Cohan wrote the libretto and score and served as producer and director; also, as in the past, he came up with a hit song in "Nellie Kelly, I Love You." Other songs in the tuneful score were "You Remind Me of My Mother," "They're All My Boys," "Dancing My Worries Away," "All in the Wearing," and "Till My Luck Comes Rolling Along."

Little Nellie Kelly (MGM 1940) only kept the title song and the Irish flavor of the Broadway hit and told a different story all together. John McGowan's screenplay starts in Ireland where Nellie Noonan (JUDY GARLAND) wants to marry the local lad Jack Kelly (GEORGE MURPHY) but her father (CHARLES WINNINGER) is against it. They wed anyway and move to New York City where Jack becomes a policeman. Papa follows them to America and sponges off the young couple, never warming up to the husband. In a bold move on the screenwriter's part, Nellie dies in childbirth but the infant lives, growing up to be Nellie Kelly (also Garland) who falls for Dennis Fogarty (Douglas MacPhail). Again the grandfather Noonan tries to stop it, so the girl's father and sweetheart have to scheme and arrange for the happy ending. The movie gave Garland her first adult roles and she was very effective, performing "Singin' in the Rain" and some Irish ditties and handling the dramatic scenes well. Also in the score were Cohan's title song, the old favorite "Danny Boy," and "A Pretty Girl Milking Her Cow," adapted by ROGER EDENS who also wrote "It's a Great Day for the Irish" for the film. NORMAN TAUROG's direction was steady and the melodramatic musical is still engaging.

LITTLE NIGHT MUSIC, A (Shubert Theatre 1973). A beguiling musical fairy tale for adults, the STEPHEN SONDHEIM musical remains one of the few post–World War II shows that can rightly be described as sophisticated.

Plot: Swedish lawyer Frederik Egerman has married the young, virginal Anne and she remains a virgin so he is drawn to his past mistress, the actress Desiree Armfeldt, whose current lover is the egotistical soldier Count Carl-Magnus Malcolm. Romantic and sexual complications converge when the count's wife Charlotte informs Anne of the affair, even as Anne finds herself drawn to her brooding stepson Henrik who is her own age. Desiree

---

Casts for *A Little Night Music*

Character	1973 Broadway	1978 film
Fredrik Egerman	LEN CARIOU	Len Cariou
Desiree Armfeldt	Glynis Johns	ELIZABETH TAYLOR
Madame Armfeldt	HERMIONE GINGOLD	Hermione Gingold
Anne Egerman	Victoria Mallory	Lesley-Anne Down
Henrik/Erich Egerman	Mark Lambert	Christopher Guard
Count Carl-Magnus	LAURENCE GUITTARD	Laurence Guittard
Countess Charlotte	Patricia Elliott	Diana Rigg
Petra	D. Jamin-Bartlett	Lesley Dunlop
Frederika	JUDY KUHN	Chloe Franks

arranges for her mother, the aging courtesan Madame Armfeldt, to invite the Egermans to her country estate for the weekend, but the Count and Charlotte crash the party and the romantic intrigues get quite complicated. The relationships are resolved during one brief midsummer moonlit night: Anne elopes with Henrik, the Count returns to his wife, Frederik and Desiree are united, and old Madame Armfeldt quietly dies.

HUGH WHEELER freely adapted Ingmar Bergman's film *Smiles of a Summer Night* (1955) and came up with a comedy of manners that was as witty as it was romantic. Producer HAROLD PRINCE directed the superb cast, keeping the action as lyrical and flowing as the score, the gently gliding scenery by Boris Aronson, and the elegant costumes by Florence Klotz. Although the show was basically a drawing room comedy set to music and had no chorus or splashy production numbers, the musical was popular, running 601 performances. Sondheim's score included the hit ballad "Send in the Clowns," the most popular song from all of his shows, and it is a masterwork, but the entire score was brilliant. Although all the songs use a waltz tempo or a variation of a waltz, the operetta-like score is filled with variety. Among the many highlights were the ambitious "The Miller's Son," the duet lament "Every Day a Little Death," the bustling "The Glamourous Life," the dreamy "Liaisons," the delectable triptych "Now/Later/Soon," the droll comic duet "You Must Meet My Wife," the sprightly "Remember?," and the captivating concerted number "A Weekend in the Country." The score is so appealing that opera and light opera companies often revive *A Little Night Music*

but the show really belongs in a theatre since it demands a refined acting ensemble as well as accomplished singers and the musical must be directed with a light but confident touch. All the same, the show is produced by all kinds of groups in America and in Europe.

■ *A Little Night Music* (Sascha-Wein-New World 1978) retained the director, screenwriter, and several cast members from Broadway so it came as something of a shock when the movie was not only disappointing but a deadly disaster. Some critics blamed ELIZABETH TAYLOR who did not have the looks, voice, or demeanor of Desiree, but that cannot account for the lifeless performances by most of the other players and the lack of wit, romance, and sophistication that made the original so special. To avoid comparisons with Bergman's film, screenwriter Wheeler reset the tale in Austria, which not only cut out songs about the sun never setting but also took away the Scandinavian milieu that was so magical. No major changes were made in the plotting, yet the scenes fell flat and the humor was strained. However, there were a few compensations. Diana Rigg was a sly, knowing Charlotte, Lesley-Ann Down an engaging Ann (even if she was far too old for the role), and Sondheim wrote a wonderful new number called "The Letter Song." The foreign-financed movie was given a very limited release and then pretty much disappeared, not doing much harm to the reputation of the stage work. ❑ Much more satisfying is a 1990 television broadcast of the New York City Opera production of *A Little Night Music* directed by SCOTT ELLIS and featuring SALLY ANN HOWES (Desiree), George Lee Andrews (Frederick), Regina Resnik (Madame Armfeldt), Maureen Moore (Charlotte), Michael McGuire (Count), Beverly Lambert (Anne), and Kevin Anderson (Henrik). It is no match for the original Broadway production but compared to the movie it is very satisfying.

A Little Night Music (stage) Musical Numbers

"Night Waltz"
"Now/Later/Soon"
"The Glamourous Life"
"Remember?"
"You Must Meet My Wife"
"Liaisons"
"In Praise of Women"
"Every Day a Little Death"
"A Weekend in the Country"
"The Sun Won't Set"
"It Would Have Been Wonderful"
"Perpetual Anticipation"
"Send in the Clowns"
"The Miller's Son"

🎬 *LITTLE SHOP OF HORRORS* (Orpheum Theatre 1982). The long-running Off Broadway camp musical, the science fiction spoof was offbeat enough to be different and yet engaging enough to be appealing to a wide audience. The nerdy botanist Seymour Krelbourn, who works in the floundering flower shop of Mr. Mushnik and silently loves the sensual salesgirl Audrey, comes upon a mysterious plant that brings him fame and fortune as long as he feeds it human blood. As the plant continues to grow, so do its demands until Seymour is feeding it body parts from

Casts for *Little Shop of Horrors*

Character	1982 Off Broadway	1986 film	2003 Broadway
Seymour	Lee Wilkof	Rick Moranis	Hunter Foster
Audrey	Ellen Greene	Ellen Greene	Kerry Butler
Mr. Mushnik	Hy Anzell	Vincent Gardenia	Rob Bartlett
Orin, etc.	Franc Luz	Steve Martin	Douglas Sills

Mushnik and Audrey's sadistic boyfriend dentist Orin. Eventually the plant devours Seymour, Audrey, and everyone on planet earth, even threatening the audience. HOWARD ASHMAN wrote the incongruous libretto, based on the low-budget 1960 film, and he also penned the clever lyrics for ALAN MENKEN's 1960s pastiche music. The pop score included "Suddenly Seymour," "Somewhere That's Green," "Feed Me," "Skid Row," "Dentist," "Grow for Me," and the title song. Ashman directed the small but ingenious production, which caught on in due time and ran 2,209 performances. Hundreds of productions in regional theatre, summer stock, and schools followed, and the musical continues to be a favorite across the country. A 2003 Broadway revival directed by JERRY ZAKS may not have been as vivid as the original but it boasted a fine cast and a high-tech plant that was more spectacular than the Off Broadway version. Despite lackluster notices, the production was popular enough to run 372 performances.

■ ***Little Shop of Horrors*** (Geffen/Warner 1986) followed the Off Broadway musical fairly closely until the end when screenwriter Ashman had Seymour kill the plant and he and Audrey survive to live happily ever after. However, there was a cautionary epilogue of sorts that was typical of 1960s sci fi films: new sprouts popped up in the garden and winked at the audience. Frank Oz directed the movie, giving it the colorful, garish look of the period, and the special effects have some of the cheesiness of the cheap thrillers that the musical spoofs. Ellen Greene reprised her Audrey from the stage and her fellow players were all excellent, particularly Rick Moranis as Seymour, exuding a goofiness and sincerity that worked beautifully. Most of the stage score was used, and Menken and Ashman wrote a new number for the plant, "Mean Green Mother From Outer Space," which was as silly and accurate as the rest of the score.

✎ ***Little Show, The*** (Music Box Theatre 1929). Not little by today's standards, this intimate revue was a refreshing surprise because it was more cerebral and satiric than the revues FLORENZ ZIEGFELD and GEORGE WHITE were presenting at the time. The musical is also notable for bringing recognition to songwriters ARTHUR SCHWARTZ (music) and HOWARD DIETZ (lyrics), the finest team to score revues during its golden age in the 1930s. Their "I Guess I Have to Change My Plan" and "Hammacher-Schlemmer, I Love You" were their main contributions to the show, and the score also featured "Moanin' Low," "A Little Hut in Hoboken," and "Can't We Be Friends" by other tunesmiths. Dietz, GEORGE S. KAUFMAN, and others wrote the sketches, which were heads above the usual revue fare, and the sparkling cast included CLIFTON WEBB, LIBBY HOLMAN, BETTINA HALL, FRED ALLEN, JACK McCAULEY, Peggy Conklin, Constance Cummings, and Romney Brent. DWIGHT DEERE WIMAN and ALEXANDER LEFTWICH co-directed the Wiman–William A. Brady, Jr., production, which ran 321 performances. Because the revue was such a hit, two subsequent editions were presented, although neither was a success. *The Second Little Show* (1930) offered some Dietz–Schwartz songs and had a less than stellar cast, while *The Third Little Show* (1931) featured BEATRICE LILLIE, ERNEST TRUEX, Constance Carpenter, and Edward Arnold and introduced NOEL COWARD's "Mad Dogs and Englishman."

📺 ***Little Women*** (CBS-TV 1958). Louisa May Alcott's 1868 beloved novel had been brought to the big screen at least seven times and to the small screen five times before this first musical version was broadcast so even audiences who had not read the famous novel were more than passing familiar with the story. Wilson Lehr had the unenviable task of condensing the novel into one hour and still leave room for eight songs so maybe it was just as well the story of the four March sisters was not unknown. Jo (Jeannie Carson) and her sisters (FLORENCE HENDERSON, Zina Bethune, and MARGARET O'BRIEN) wait with their mother Marmee (RISË STEVENS) for their father to return from the Civil War but have time for amateur dramatics, romance with the neighbor Theodore "Laurie" Lawrence (JOEL GREY), and endure hardships before the end of the plot. Also featured in the cast were Bill Hayes, Roland Winters, and Jane Rose. Critics carped about the abridged script but commended the pleasing score by RICHARD ADLER, which included "The Four of Us," "How do You Write a Book?," "Dance, Why Not?," "Man of the Family," "Love I Mean" and "Party Shoes." William Corrigan directed the Davis Suskind–Albert Selden production. 📖 Musical versions of *Little Women* for the stage have appeared in regional theatre and Off Broadway over the decades, but the only one to reach Broadway was a 2004 production starring SUTTON FOSTER as Jo and Maureen McGovern as Marmee. Allan Knee (book), Jason Howard (music), and Mindi Dickstein (lyrics) devised the musical for touring to schools and community centers. After negative notices on Broadway and an unprofitable run, the musical found favor on tour and in high school productions.

📁 **LITTLEST ANGEL, THE** (NBC-1969). One of the most popular of all *Hallmark Hall of Fame* broadcasts, the holiday program boasted a strong cast, a fine score, and a story that was sentimental without being cloying. Lan O'Kun wrote the score and, with Patricia Gray, co-wrote the teleplay, based on Charles Tazewell's 1946 story. The eight-year-old shepherd boy Michael (Johnnie Whitaker) dies and goes to heaven where he is made the littlest angel and put under the guidance of the angel Patience (Fred Gwynne). Michael has trouble flying and getting used to robes and a halo and longs to return to earth to get his box of children's treasures. When God (E. G. Marshall) announces that his son Jesus is to be born, all the angels prepare gifts for the infant. Michael can only offer his box of treasures and the humble offering pleases God so much he places the box in the sky and it becomes the Star of Bethlehem. The estimable supporting cast included CAB CALLOWAY, Tony Randall, John McGiver, GEORGE ROSE, Connie Stevens, James Coco, Cris Alexander, and Evelyn Russell. The songs included "Once Upon Another Time," "The Heavenly Ever After," "I Bring You Good Tidings," "The Master of All I Survey," "Where Is the Blue?," and "May It Bring Him Pleasure." JOE LAYTON directed and choreographed the very popular broadcast, which was later turned into a stage piece for schools.

LIVINGSTON, JAY, AND RAY EVANS. Film songwriters. While few of their Hollywood musicals were high-quality products, the scores usually were delightful and several hit songs came from their twenty musical films. Jay Livingston [born Jacob Harold Levinson] (1915–2001) was born in McDonald, Pennsylvania, and studied piano as a boy, working in local clubs as a high schooler. He attended the University of Pennsylvania where he met Ray[mond Bernard] Evans (1915–2007), a fellow student born in Salamanca, New York. The two played in the campus dance orchestra before working professionally in nightclubs and on cruise ships as they wrote songs together. Some of Evans' music was heard in the Broadway revue *Sons o' Fun* (1941) and then the two wrote songs for the comedy team OLSEN and JOHNSON. By 1943 the pair were in Hollywood scoring such musicals as *Footlight Glamour* (1943), *Isn't It Romantic?* (1948), *THE PALEFACE* (1948), *My Friend Irma* (1949), *My Friend Irma Goes West* (1950), *Fancy Pants* (1950), *The Lemon Drop Kid* (1951), *HERE COMES THE GROOM* (1951), *SON OF PALEFACE* (1952), *Those Redheads From Seattle* (1953), *Red Garters* (1953), *The Big Beat* (1958), *A Private's Affair* (1959), and *All Hands on Deck* (1961). Ironically, many of their most famous songs, such as "Mona Lisa," "Que Sera Sera," "To Each His Own," and "Tammy," were written as theme songs for nonmusical films. Livingston and Evans also scored the TV musicals *SATINS AND SPURS* (1954) and *No Man Can Tame Me* (1955), wrote television theme songs such as "Bonanza" and "Mr. Ed," and scored the Broadway musicals *Oh Captain!* (1958) and *Let It Ride* (1961).

LOESSER, FRANK [Henry] (1910–1969). Stage and film composer and lyricist. A songwriter who reversed the usual pattern by having a successful Hollywood career before he struck gold on Broadway, the versatile, sparkling talent spent years as a lyricist before writing both words and music. The native New Yorker grew up in a musical family, his father a piano teacher and his brother Arthur later became a respected concert pianist. He wrote popular songs as a child, later attended the City College of New York for a time, and then worked as a newspaper reporter before writing sketches and lyrics for vaudeville acts, radio shows, and summer resorts. In 1931 he had his first song published, "In Love With a Memory of You," written with the later celebrated composer William Schuman. Some of Loesser's lyrics were heard in the Broadway revue *The Illustrators's Show* (1936) and then he headed to Hollywood where, working with BURTON LANE, JULE STYNE, and other composers, he provided the lyrics for such musicals as *College Swing* (1938), *St. Louis Blues* (1939), *Man About Town* (1939), *DESTRY RIDES AGAIN* (1939), *Buck Benny Rides Again* (1940), *Dancing* *on a Dime* (1941), *Las Vegas Nights* (1941), *Sis Hopkins* (1941), *Kiss the Boys Goodbye* (1941), *True to the Army* (1942), *Sweater Girl* (1942), *Seven Days' Leave* (1942), *HAPPY GO LUCKY* (1943), and *THANK YOUR LUCKY STARS* (1943). When Loesser's solo effort "Praise the Lord and Pass the Ammunition" became one of the most popular songs of the war years, he decided to write his own music all the time and did so for the rest of his career. After scoring the films *The Perils of Pauline* (1947) and *Variety Girl* (1947), he returned to Broadway and had a hit with his first score, *WHERE'S CHARLEY?* (1948). This was followed by the musical comedy classic *GUYS AND DOLLS* (1950), the operatic *THE MOST HAPPY FELLA* (1956), the charming but unsuccessful *GREENWILLOW* (1960), and the satirical *HOW TO SUCCEED IN BUSINESS WITHOUT REALLY TRYING* (1961). Loesser continued his ties with Hollywood, writing songs for the musicals *NEPTUNE'S DAUGHTER* (1949), *RED, HOT AND BLUE* (1949), *Let's Dance* (1950), and *HANS CHRISTIAN ANDERSEN* (1955). He founded his own music publishing company and used it not only for his own works but to bring attention to new songwriters whom he nurtured, such as RICHARD ADLER, JERRY ROSS, and MEREDITH WILLSON. Loesser was an eclectic songwriter who seemed as inspired in slick Broadway musical comedy as in Italian opera and rustic folk music. His second wife is singer–actress Jo Sullivan and his younger daughter is singer Emily Loesser. Memoir: *A Most Remarkable Fella: Frank Loesser and the Guys and Dolls in His Life: A Portrait by His Daughter*, Susan Loesser (2000).

LOEWE, FREDERICK. See LERNER, Alan Jay, and Frederick LOEWE

LOGAN, JOSHUA [Lockwood] (1908–1988). Stage and film director, playwright, and producer. A prodigious theatre and movie showman, he had a winning touch with everything from new dramas to fanciful musical comedies. Logan was born in Texarkana, Texas, the son of a successful lumber man. His father died when Logan was three, so he was raised in South Mansfield, Louisiana, by his mother and stepfather, an officer at the Culver Military Academy. Logan was educated at Princeton University where he participated in campus theatricals. After graduation he hired some of his classmates and in 1928 founded the University Players on Cape Cod. By 1931 the troupe was located in Baltimore where Logan directed revivals and new works, including *Carrie Nation*, which transferred to Broadway and provided him with his first New York directing credit in 1932. Winning a scholarship from the Moscow Art Theatre, he spent six months in Russia studying with Stanislavsky before returning to work in films, serving as a dialogue coach and directing his first feature in 1938. It was the success of Logan's staging of *On Borrowed Time* on Broadway that same year that secured his stage career and he would move back and forth between New York and Hollywood for the next forty years. Logan had many hits in all categories but many felt it was his staging of musicals that was the most noteworthy. For Broadway he directed *I MARRIED AN ANGEL* (1938), *KNICKERBOCKER HOLIDAY* (1938), *Stars in Your Eyes* (1939), *Two for the Show* (1940), *HIGHER AND HIGHER* (1940), *BY JUPITER* (1942), *THIS IS THE ARMY* (1942), *ANNIE GET YOUR GUN* (1946), *SOUTH PACIFIC* (1949), *WISH YOU WERE HERE* (1952), *FANNY* (1954), *ALL AMERICAN* (1962), and *MR. PRESIDENT* (1962). Logan co-authored the libretto for *South Pacific* and wrote other scripts and screenplays as well. He was not as accomplished directing his three screen musicals: *South Pacific* (1958), *CAMELOT* (1967), and *PAINT YOUR WAGON* (1969). In his prime, Logan was considered one of the best directors in America and he had a list of hits to prove it. Autobiographies: *Josh: My Up and Down, In and Out Life* (1976); *Movie Stars, Real People and Me* (1978).

LONG RUNS ON AND OFF BROADWAY. The concept of a Broadway musical running for years is a relatively new one. In the early years of the twentieth century, a musical that ran 100 performances was considered a hit. In fact, financially it was possible to be a success by running less than that. But as costs escalated it became necessary for a show to have a long run in order to turn a profit. What is considered a long run varied from decade to decade. In the 1920s one could play for 100 performances on Broadway and tour for a full season and make a handsome profit. By the 1940s, a hundred performances were profitable for a play but not a musical. *OKLAHOMA!* (1943) was the first Broadway musical to count its run in years rather than months. No one thought one show could run so long (although in London there were already several musicals that had passed the 1,000 mark) but it was only the beginning. As musicals needed to run longer to turn a profit, long runs became the norm for a hit show. Over the decades musicals such as *MY FAIR LADY* (1956), *HELLO, DOLLY!* (1964), *GREASE* (1972), and *CATS* (1982) held the record for the longest-running Broadway show. Today we expect to see such records broken on a regular basis.

Longest-Running Broadway Musicals

Musical	Opening season	Number of performances
PHANTOM OF THE OPERA	1987–1988	8,000+
CATS	1982–1983	7,485
LES MISÉRABLES	1986–1987	6,680
A CHORUS LINE	1975–1976	6,137
OH, CALCUTTA! (revival)	1976–1977	5,959
BEAUTY AND THE BEAST	1993–1994	5,461
RENT	1995–1996	5,012
CHICAGO (revival)	1996–1997	4,500+
MISS SAIGON	1990–1991	4,097
THE LION KING	1997–1998	4,000+
42ND STREET	1980–1981	3,486
GREASE	1972–1973	3,388
FIDDLER ON THE ROOF	1964–1965	3,242
HELLO, DOLLY!	1963–1964	2,844
MY FAIR LADY	1955–1956	2,717
THE PRODUCERS	2000–2001	2,502
CABARET (revival)	1997–1098	2,378
ANNIE	1976–1977	2,377
MAMMA MIA!	2001–2002	2,500+
MAN OF LA MANCHA	1965–1966	2,328
OKLAHOMA!	1942–1943	2,212
SMOKEY JOE'S CAFE	1994–1995	2,036
HAIRSPRAY	2002–2003	2,500+
PIPPIN	1972–1973	1,944
SOUTH PACIFIC	1948–1949	1,925
THE MAGIC SHOW	1973–1974	1,920
AIDA	1999–2000	1,852
DANCIN'	1977–1978	1,774
LA CAGE AUX FOLLES	1983–1984	1,761
HAIR	1967–1968	1,750

Longest-Running Off Broadway Musicals

Musical	Year opened	Number of performances
THE FANTASTICKS	1960	17,162
Stomp	1994	5,000+
NUNSENSE	1985	3,672
I LOVE YOU, YOU'RE PERFECT, NOW CHANGE	1996	4,000+
THE THREEPENNY OPERA	1954	2,611
FORBIDDEN BROADWAY 1982–1987	1982	2,332
Naked Boys Singing!	1999	2,500+
LITTLE SHOP OF HORRORS	1982	2,209
GODSPELL	1971	2,124
JACQUES BREL ...	1968	1,847
FOREVER PLAID	1990	1,811
YOU'RE A GOOD MAN, CHARLIE BROWN	1967	1,597
One Mo' Time	1980	1,372

In an age when a musical can run 800 performances and still lose money, the long run has become a necessity rather than a triumph.

LOPEZ, PRISCILLA (1948–). Stage and television performer. The animated Hispanic actress–singer–dancer has shone brightly in both plays and musicals. Lopez was born in the Bronx and educated at the High School of the Performing Arts before appearing in the Broadway chorus of *Henry, Sweet Henry* (1967) and *Her First Roman* (1968). She replaced others in *YOUR OWN THING* (1969), *COMPANY* (1971), and *PIPPIN* (1974) and was in the cast of the revue *What's a Nice Country Like You Doing in a State Like This?* (1973) before finding fame in *A CHORUS LINE* (1975) in which she originated the role of the Puerto Rican dancer Diana. Lopez made a delightful Harpo Marx in *A DAY IN HOLLYWOOD/A NIGHT IN THE UKRAINE* (1980) and then concentrated on plays (many of them Off Broadway), although she was a replacement for Liliane La Fleur in *NINE* (1982) and was featured in *IN THE HEIGHTS* (2008). Since the mid-1980s she has appeared in some films and many television programs, although very rarely have her singing–dancing talents been used.

LORELEI. See *GENTLEMEN PREFER BLONDES*

LORING, EUGENE [born Leroy Kerpestein] (1914–1982). Film, stage, and television choreographer. A classically trained dancer-turned-choreographer, he staged significant dances in all three media. Loring was born in Milwaukee, Wisconsin, and trained for classical ballet as a youth. He danced and later choreographed many pieces for the Ballet Theatre, the most celebrated being *Billy the Kid*. Loring appeared in the dancing chorus of *Alma Mater* (1935) on Broadway and then danced and choreographed *Filling Station* (1939), *The Ballet Caravan* (1939), *CARMEN JONES* (1943), *Three Wishes for Jamie* (1952), *Buttrio Square* (1952), and *SILK STOCKINGS* (1955). He is better known for his fourteen screen musicals, choreographing FRED ASTAIRE in *Yolanda and the Thief* (1945), *ZIEGFELD FOLLIES* (1946), *FUNNY FACE* (1957) and *Silk Stockings* (1957). His other Hollywood musical credits include *Fiesta* (1946), *MEXICAN HAYRIDE* (1948), *The Inspector General* (1949), *THE TOAST OF NEW ORLEANS* (1950), *THE 5000 FINGERS OF DR. T* (1953), *Torch Song* (1953), *DEEP IN MY HEART*

(1954), *Meet Me in Las Vegas* (1956), and *Pepe* (1960). Loring also choreographed some television specials, most memorably Rodgers and Hammerstein's *CINDERELLA* (1956).

LORRAINE, LILLIAN [born Eulallean de Jacques] (1892–1955). Stage performer. A statuesque singer who was a favorite of producer FLORENZ ZIEGFELD, her classic features and pleasing singing allowed her to shine in Broadway revues. Lorraine was born in San Francisco and began performing professionally as a young child. She made her Broadway debut in the chorus of *The Tourists* (1906) and then was featured in *The Gay White Way* (1907) and *Miss Innocence* (1908). Supposedly the mistress of Ziegfeld, she was given a prominent place in five editions of his *Follies* between 1909 and 1918. Her other Broadway musicals are *Over the River* (1912), *The Whirl of the World* (1914), *Odds and Ends* (1917), *The Little Blue Devil* (1919), and *The Blue Kitten* (1922). Lorraine is most remembered for introducing "By the Light of the Silvery Moon" in the 1909 *Follies* and "Row Row Row" in the 1912 *Follies*. She also made some silent films in the 1910s and 1920s.

LOST IN THE STARS (Music Box Theatre 1949). KURT WEILL's last and arguably most powerful effort, it is a moving musical drama set in South Africa. The black minister Stephen Kumalo leaves his village and travels to Johannesburg to find his son Absalom whom he has not heard from in many months. Absalom needs money for his pregnant girl friend Irina so he takes part in a robbery in which the white liberal Arthur Jarvis is killed. His father is James Jarvis, the prosperous white man in Kumalo's village. Absalom is executed and both Stephen and James are drawn together, each having lost a son. MAXWELL ANDERSON adapted Alan Paton's novel *Cry, the Beloved Country* and wrote the lyrics; both were gripping and uncompromising. Weill's music was an entrancing blend of American, European, and African sounds, resulting in such numbers as the aching torch song "Trouble Man," the mournful "Cry, the Beloved Country,"

Casts for *Lost in the Stars*		
Character	1949 Broadway	1974 film
Stephen Kumalo	TODD DUNCAN	Brock Peters
James Jarvis	Leslie Banks	Paul Rogers
Absalom Kumalo	Julian Mayfield	Clifton Davis
Irina	Inez Matthews	MELBA MOORE

the lullaby ballad "Stay Well," and the poignant title song. ROUBEN MAMOULIAN directed with grace, and the cast, black and white, was exceptional, but the bleak tale was difficult to sell on Broadway where it was greeted with mixed notices and struggled to run 273 performances. Revivals have been rare and they are usually produced by opera companies. Gene Frankel directed the 1972 Broadway revival, which had originated at the Kennedy Center in Washington and was commended for its fine singing even if most reviewers thought the musical not worth reviving. BROCK PETERS led the cast as Kumalo and was supported by Jack Gwillim (Jarvis), GILBERT PRICE (Absalom), Margaret Cowie (Irina), and Don Fenwick (Arthur). The production only lasted thirty-nine performances.

Lost in the Stars (American Film Theatre 1974) was well sung, with much of the score as well as the script surviving the transition, but it is a poorly made film with uneven acting and an uncomfortable mixture of realistic location footage and artificial studio scenes. Alfred Hayes wrote the screenplay, Daniel Mann directed, and Paula Kelly did the choreography. On its initial release only subscribers to the experimental American Film Theatre could see the movie. It was later released on video but never reached a wide audience.

LOUDON, DOROTHY (1933–2003). Stage and television performer. The big-voiced comic actress–singer excelled at bigger-than-life characters in which her Broadway belt could best be utilized. The Boston native was educated at Syracuse University, Emerson College, and the American Academy of Dramatic Arts before embarking on a career singing and doing hilarious impersonations in nightclubs. Loudon made her Broadway debut in the short-lived musical *Nowhere to Go But Up* (1962), followed by the musical failures *Noel Coward's Sweet Potato* (1968) and *The Fig Leaves Are Falling* (1969). She finally received wide recognition as the cartoonish Miss Hannigan in *ANNIE* (1977)

and revealed a more subtle characterization as widow Bea Asher in *BALLROOM* (1978). Loudon replaced ANGELA LANSBURY in *SWEENEY TODD* in 1980 and returned five years later for the revue *Jerry's Girls* (1985). She was also successful in nonmusicals, such as *Noises Off* (1983) and *The Matchmaker* (1991). Loudon enjoyed a long and fruitful career on television as a regular on Gary Moore's 1960s variety show and appearing on hundreds of programs ranging from game shows to drama series.

LOUISIANA PURCHASE (Imperial Theatre 1940). A timely musical comedy about political corruption, the show boasted one of IRVING BERLIN's best stage scores. Naive and unworldly Senator Oliver P. Loganberry is sent to New Orleans to investigate the questionable tactics of the Louisiana Purchasing Company. The company's president, Jim Taylor, throws temptation in the senator's way by sending the Viennese refugee Marina Van Linden to seduce him and then has the restaurateur Madame Yvonne Bordelaise work her wiles on the politician. Instead of a scandal, Oliver weds Yvonne and the company is spared because a picket line keeps the senator from testifying. Inspired by the tales of graft in Huey Long's administration in the South, MORRIE RYSKIND and B. G. DE SYLVA wrote the satirical libretto, which may have been forced but offered plum roles for the comedy team of WILLIAM GAXTON and VICTOR MOORE and offered excellent song opportunities for Berlin who obliged with such delectable numbers as the mock lament "You're Lonely and I'm Lonely," the philosophical "Fools Fall in Love," the revival-like "The Lord Done Fixed Up My Soul," the flowing ballad "Tomorrow Is a Lovely Day," the comic gems "What Chance Have I (With Love)?" and "Outside of That I Love You," the hot-blooded "Latins Know How," and the contagious title song. De Sylva produced, EDGAR MACGREGOR directed, GEORGE BALANCHINE did the choreography, and the show was the hit of the season, running 444 performances.

Casts for *Louisiana Purchase*

Character	1940 Broadway	1941 film
Jim Taylor	WILLIAM GAXTON	BOB HOPE
Sen. Oliver P. Loganberry	VICTOR MOORE	Victor Moore
Marina Van Linden	VERA ZORINA	Vera Zorina
Madame Bordellaise	IRENE BORDONI	Irene Bordoni

■ **_Louisiana Purchase_** (Paramount 1942) allowed Moore, Bordoni, and Zorina to reprise their stage roles, but all but four of Berlin's fifteen songs were cut and no new numbers were added so the film doesn't feel much like a musical. BOB HOPE played Taylor and provided the movie with its best scenes, none of them musical. Jerome Chodorov and JOSEPH FIELDS wrote the screenplay, which tended to showcase Hope and, except for the funny opening when the lawyers at the studio worry about getting sued for the parallels to real people, there is not much wit left in the story. IRVING CUMMINGS directed without much flavor, with the movie never feeling like any place but a California studio. Largely forgotten today, the screen _Louisiana Purchase_ probably discouraged revivals of the stage version at the time; today, productions are hardly ever heard of. ❑ Victor Moore and Irene Bordoni got to play Senator Loganberry and Madame Bordelaise again in 1951 in the abridged version of _Louisiana Purchase_ on the NBC-TV series _MUSICAL COMEDY TIME_.

🕊 **LOVE LIFE** (46th Street Theatre 1948). A fascinating if problematic musical experiment, the show foreshadowed the more creative musicals of the 1960s and 1970s, particularly _CABARET_ (1966) and _CHICAGO_ (1975). ALAN JAY LERNER wrote the adventurous libretto, the story of the ageless married couple Sam (RAY MIDDLETON) and Susan Cooper (NANETTE FABRAY) from 1791 to 1948. The chronicle of their marriage was framed by a series of vaudeville acts that commented on their up-and-down relationship, which happened to parallel the ups and downs of the nation. Lerner also wrote the lyrics for KURT WEILL's music, and the score was a rich pastiche of different kinds of American music: "Green-Up Time," "Love Song," "Here I'll Stay," "Progress," "This Is the Life," and "Economics." Elia Kazan directed the CHERYL CRAWFORD production, and the press thought the musical highly original but uneven, although there were plenty of compliments for the score and the two principals. There was enough interest on the part of playgoers for the show to run 252 performances. Revivals have been rare, yet the musical has developed a cult following as one of the earliest concept musicals.

■ **LOVE ME OR LEAVE ME** (MGM 1953). Portraying torch singer RUTH ETTING gave DORIS DAY her first acting challenge and she rose to it effectively in this unsentimental biographical musical that also boasted another strong performance by JAMES CAGNEY. Daniel Fuchs and ISOBEL LENNART wrote the tough-as-nails screenplay in which dance hall hostess Etting is discovered by small-time mobster "Gimp" Snyder (Cagney) who is not above using unethical means to further her career. Snyder's jealousy, even after he marries Etting, is notorious and when she falls in love with pianist Johnny Alderman (Cameron Mitchell), Snyder shoots him. Alderman survives, Snyder goes to jail, and in the film's only Hollywood concession, all three are reunited years later as Snyder, now out of jail, opens his new club. Cagney was as charismatic as ever but Day held her own in both the book scenes and in her interpretation of such Etting songs as "Ten Cents a Dance," "Shaking the Blues Away," "You Made Me Love You," and the title number. There were also two new torch songs for Day to sing, "Never Look Back" by Chilton Price and "I'll Never Stop Loving You" by NICHOLAS BRODSZKY (music) and SAMMY CAHN (lyrics), which became a best-selling record for Day. CHARLES VIDOR directed the taut melodrama, which was produced by JOE PASTERNAK.

■ **LOVE ME TENDER** (Fox 1956). ELVIS PRESLEY made his screen debut in this period melodrama, which was a musical only by virtue of the popular recording star picking up his guitar on four occasions and singing. Robert Buckner's screenplay was set during the Civil War when the Texas farm boy Clint Reno (Presley) works the farm while his brother Vance (Richard Egan) goes off to fight for the South. Clint has long loved Vance's girl friend Cathy (Debra Paget) so when word comes that Vance has died in battle, Clint proposes to Cathy and they wed. But Vance is alive and returns home, causing a family uproar and legal ones since Vance stole money from the Federal government during a train robbery. All the dramatics were temporarily stopped for Presley to sing "Poor Boy," "We're Gonna Move," "Let Me," and the title song, which was a new version of the folk standard "Aura Lee." Presley was surrounded by a skillful cast, which also included Robert Middleton, Mildred Dunnock, William Campbell, Neville Brand, James Drury, and Bruce Bennett, yet he held his own acting wise and gave an understated performances. Robert D. Webb directed the David Weisbart production, which did well enough at the box office that Presley's film career was off and running.

■ *LOVE ME TONIGHT* (Paramount 1932). A sophisticated musical fairy tale for adults, the innovative film blended song, background music, character, plot, camera work, and editing in a miraculous manner never seen before and only rarely accomplished since.

Plot: The Parisian tailor Maurice Courtelin follows the Vicomte de Vareze to his provincial chateau to collect an unpaid debt. When he arrives, Maurice is mistaken for a baron and, after rescuing the haughty Princess Jeanette from a runaway carriage, falls in love with her. The princess's man-hungry friend Countess Valentine suspects Maurice is not a baron but is too busy chasing after him to do anything about it. When everyone at the chateau finds out the truth about Maurice's lowly social position, he boards the first train back to Paris. Jeannette chases after him on horseback, bravely stands in front of the oncoming train, and claims her lover regardless of rank.

Love Me Tonight. Before Jeanette MacDonald (pictured) was paired with Nelson Eddy in a series of movie operettas, she enjoyed a very different partnership with the French performer Maurice Chevalier in four films. Here they are in *Love Me Tonight* as the princess in love with the tailor. (Photofest)

The delightful score by RICHARD RODGERS (music) and LORENZ HART (lyrics), which includes the hit songs "Lover," "Isn't It Romantic?," and the title number, is so tightly woven into the witty screenplay by Samuel Hoffenstein, Waldemar Young, and George Marion, Jr. that the movie sometimes resembles a cockeyed operetta. Yet there is nothing stuffy or slow moving about the musical as it bounces along in a slaphappy manner. Much of the credit must go to producer–director ROUBEN MAMOULIAN (replacing GEORGE CUKOR at the last minute) who broke new ground in finding cinematic ways to present a musical tale. Just as Rodgers and Hart's rhythmic dialogue led into and out of songs, Mamoulian moved the camera in clever ways to comment on the action. MacDonald sang the operatic "Lover" as she bounced along in a carriage, with the music rising and falling with her movements. Chevalier delivered the seductive "Mimi" to MacDonald but as filmed he delivered most of it to her horse. A deer hunt in the woods became a slow-motion ballet of people, horses,

and stags. Perhaps the most memorable of the many thrilling sequences was near the opening of the film in which the song "Isn't It Romantic?" began on a Paris street and was carried in a taxi to a train to a marching regiment to a gypsy singer to the Vicomte's chateau. *Love Me Tonight* is arguably the best of the four Chevalier–MacDonald vehicles. It boasts Rodgers and Hart's finest screen score, with both the comic and the romantic numbers

Love Me Tonight Musical Numbers

"That's the Song of Paree"
"Isn't It Romantic?"
"Lover"
"Mimi"
"A Woman Needs Something Like That"
"The Poor Apache"
"Love Me Tonight"
"The Son of a Gun Is Nothing But a Tailor"

Love Me Tonight Cast

Character	Performer
Maurice Courtelin	MAURICE CHEVALIER
Princess Jeanette	JEANETTE MACDONALD
Count Gilbert de Vareze	CHARLES RUGGLES
Count de Savignac	CHARLES BUTTERWORTH
Countess Valentine	MYRA LOY
Duke	C. Aubrey Smith
Aunts	Elizabeth Patterson, Ethel Griffies, Blanche Friderici

striking gold. Just as impressive, it showed the team experimenting with the musical form on screen just as they had found new ways to present music on stage. The duo would experiment further with the movie musicals *THE PHANTOM PRESIDENT* (1932) and *HALLELUJAH, I'M A BUM* (1933) until the Hollywood system would defeat them and send them back to Broadway.

🎬 **LOVE PARADE, THE** (Paramount 1929). Too little known today, this early movie musical was filled with important firsts. It was director–producer ERNEST LUBITSCH'S first talkie, JEANETTE MACDONALD's first film (and the first of four MacDonald–MAURICE CHEVALIER musicals), and the first attempt to integrate songs and music into the whole picture rather than settling for tacked-on numbers. In fact, Chevalier's talk–singing of "Nobody's Using It Now" is the screen's first musical soliloquy. The screenplay by GUY BOLTON and Ernest Vajda told a fanciful tale about Queen Louise (MacDonald) of Sylvania who has heard so much about the amorous goings-on of Count Alfred Renard (Chevalier), her emissary in Paris, that she summons him home out of anger and curiosity. The two are immediately infatuated with each other and wed but Alfred soon tires of the idle life in court and wishes to return to the high life of Paris. The marriage is saved only by Louise naming Alfred the king. It was a tale befitting an antique European operetta, but the famous "Lubitsch touch" made all the difference, resulting in a breezy, witty movie in which each song became an opportunity for fluid camera work and an intimate peek into character. VICTOR SCHERTZINGER (music) and CLIFFORD GREY (lyrics) penned the scintillating score, which included the wistful "Paris, Stay the Same," the trilling "Dream Lover" (the song that introduced MacDonald to film audiences), the pounding "March of the Grenadiers," the sly "Let's Be Common," and the airy serenade "My Love Parade." The delightful supporting cast included Lupino Lane, LILLIAN ROTH, Edgar Norton, and EUGENE PALLETTE.

🎬 **LOVE THY NEIGHBOR** (Paramount 1940). A famous (and fictitious) feud between JACK BENNY and FRED ALLEN had been entertaining radio listeners in the 1930s so producer–director MARK SANDRICH used the humorous rivalry as the plot for a musical, hiring Ernest Pagano, William Morrow, Zion Myers, and Edmund Beloin to come up with a screenplay that featured the two quarreling stars. Benny and Allen played themselves and MARY MARTIN

was Allen's niece Mary Allen who returns to New York from South America. Benny's valet EDDIE "ROCHESTER" ANDERSON has a sweetheart arriving on the same boat so the battling starts when Allen and Benny meet on the dock, their cars collide, insults are exchanged, and the fun begins. Mary gets cast in a Broadway show Benny is producing and takes it on herself to bring a truce between the two men. She finally succeeds only to have Allen hire Rochester away from Benny and the feud is on again. The supporting cast included Verree Teasdale, Virginia Dale, Theresa Harris, Richard Denning, and JACK CARSON. The JAMES VAN HEUSEN–JOHNNY BURKE score offered Anderson the comic love song "Dearest, Dare I?," and Martin got three choice numbers: "Do You Know Why?," "Isn't That Just Like Love?," and COLE PORTER'S "My Heart Belongs to Daddy," which she had sung in *LEAVE IT TO ME!* (1938) on Broadway where it launched her career.

LOVELY TO LOOK AT. See *ROBERTA*

LOY, MYRNA [born Myrna Adele Williams] (1905–1993). Film and television performer. A Hollywood leading lady who played lusty vamps in the silents, smart comic heroines in the 1930s, and sophisticated ladies and mothers thereafter, the sloe-eyed beauty appeared in seven musicals during the first decade of the talkies. Loy was born in Raidersburg, near Helena, Montana, the daughter of a cattleman who had served in the state legislature, and was dancing at the age of twelve. When her father died, the family moved to Los Angeles where she started doing bit parts in films. Soon she was cast as sultry mistresses and women of easy virtue but never became too well known. Loy can be spotted as a chorine in the first talkie *THE JAZZ SINGER* (1927) and then played supporting roles in the early musicals *THE DESERT SONG* (1929), *THE SHOW OF SHOWS* (1929), *Cameo Kirby* (1930), and *Bride of the Regiment* (1930). Her comic talents were first fully realized in the musical *LOVE ME TONIGHT* (1922) in which she played the madcap Countess Valentine. Loy also shone as BILLIE BURKE in *THE GREAT ZIEGFELD* (1936). The rest of her career was in nonmusicals where she became one of Hollywood's favorite stars, adding class to comedy and sincerity to melodrama. Loy continued acting on screen into the 1980s and also appeared in many television shows beginning in the 1950s. She was married to director ARTHUR HORNBLOW, JR. for a time. Autobiography: *Myrna Loy: Being and Becoming*, with James Kotsillibas (1988).

LUBITSCH, ERNST (1892–1947). Film director and producer. An internationally famous director, he is most remembered for his sly comedies of manners and musicals that have the frothy "Lubitsch touch." He was born in Berlin and was a comic on the stage before he started acting in early German films. By 1914 Lubitsch was directing silents, some of which found renown throughout Europe and in America. After visiting the States a few times, he settled in Hollywood in the mid-1920s and over the next twenty-five years turned out delightful social satires about love, sex, and money. The Lubitsch touch can be seen in his seven musicals as well, such as *THE LOVE PARADE* (1929), *MONTE CARLO* (1930), *THE SMILING LIEUTENANT* (1931), *ONE HOUR WITH YOU* (1932), and *THE MERRY WIDOW* (1934). He also served as producer for many of his movies. Biography: *Ernst Lubitsch: Laughter in Paradise*, Scott Eyman (2000).

LUKER, REBECCA (1961–). Stage and television performer. A stately blonde-leading lady on Broadway, her finest performances have been in revivals of musical classics. Luker was born in Helena, Alabama, and studied music at the University of Montevello before working with an opera company in Michigan. She made her Broadway bow in the ensemble of *THE PHANTOM OF THE OPERA* (1988) and a year later assumed the leading role of Christine Daáe. Luker played the ghostly Lily in *THE SECRET GARDEN* (1991) followed by a series of plum revival roles: Magnolia in *SHOW BOAT* (1995), Fiona in *BRIGADOON* (1996), Maria in *THE SOUND OF MUSIC* (1998), and Marian in *THE MUSIC MAN* (2000). She was a replacement for Claudia in *NINE* (2003) and most recently was Mrs. Banks in *MARY POPPINS* (2006). Luker has performed in concert with various symphonies across the country and has appeared on several television musical specials.

LUPINO, IDA (1914–1995). Film and television performer and director. An English-born leading lady who typified strong-willed American women in her many dramatic films, the actress made eight musicals during her career even though her singing had to be dubbed. Lupino was born in London to a show business family who had been in the theatre since the seventeenth century and trained at the Royal Academy of Dramatic Art. She made her British film debut at the age of fifteen and then was brought to Hollywood in 1934 where she played minor roles in secondary pictures, including the musical *Paris in Spring* (1935).

Lupino was featured in *ANYTHING GOES* (1936) and *ARTISTS AND MODELS* (1937) but didn't get major recognition until her performance in the melodrama *The Light That Failed* (1940). Her career included many similarly dramatic non-musicals, yet she was also cast in the musicals *The Hard Way* (1942), *THANK YOUR LUCKY STARS* (1943), *HOLLYWOOD CANTEEN* (1944), *The Man I Love* (1946), and *Road House* (1948). In the 1950s Lupino also wrote screenplays, produced films, and was one of the few women directors in Hollywood. She also acted in dozens of television shows. Lupino was married to actor Howard Duff (1913–1990) and played opposite him in films and on television for many years. Biographies: *Ida Lupino*, William Donati (2000); *Queen of the Bs: Ida Lupino Behind the Camera*, Annette Kuhn (1995).

LuPONE, PATTI [Ann] (1949–). Stage, television, and film performer. With her dark and piercing looks, staunch voice, and sometimes chilly persona, she seems an unlikely leading lady for musical theatre, but this remarkably versatile performer has conquered every kind of theatre role. LuPone was born on Long Island at Northport, New York, the daughter of a school administrator and a librarian, and was educated at Juilliard where she played a variety of roles because her teachers there did not know how to classify her. When she became a founding member of John Houseman's Acting Company, she continued to hone her versatility on tour by playing different kinds of roles in very different pieces, some of which played on Broadway briefly in 1972. When the Acting Company brought the musical *THE ROBBER BRIDEGROOM* to Broadway in 1975, LuPone was praised for her funny backwoods heroine Rosamund. Her performance as the quietly unhappy wife Genevieve in the musical *THE BAKER'S WIFE* (1976) was her first starring role but the troubled production closed on the road. Stardom on Broadway would not come until her penetrating performance as the ambitious Eva Peron in *EVITA* (1979), perhaps the role with which she is still most identified. After a series of plays and the short-lived musical *Working* (1978), LuPone scored another hit as the raucous Reno Sweeney in the 1987 revival of *ANYTHING GOES*. In 1993 she was given one of the juiciest musical roles of the decade: the fading but still feisty silent movie queen Norma Desmond in *SUNSET BOULEVARD*, written for her by composer *ANDREW LLOYD WEBBER* who had scored Evita. LuPone premiered the musical in London and was contracted to recreate her performance on Broadway, but in a mis-

Patti Lupone. The role of Eva Peron was not the most sympathetic of musical characters yet LuPone triumphed as the ambitious Evita. She then made a career of playing similarly tough, fascinating women, such as Reno Sweeney in *Anything Goes*, Mrs. Lovett in *Sweeney Todd*, and Mama Rose in *Gypsy*. (Photofest)

guided attempt to sweeten the box office appeal by putting a movie star in the role, Webber and the producers gave the Broadway Norma to GLENN CLOSE who had played the part successfully in California. Also in London, LuPone originated the role of Fantine in *LES MISERABLES* (1985). In more recent years, her musical projects have consisted mostly of one-woman shows and staged concert versions of such demanding musicals as *SUNDAY IN THE PARK WITH GEORGE*, *SWEENEY TODD*, *CANDIDE*, *PASSION*, *GYPSY*, and *REGINA*. In 2005, eighteen years after her last appearance on Broadway in a musical, she returned to play the practical, ghoulish Mrs. Lovett in a revival of *Sweeney Todd*. She reprised her *ENCORES!* performance as Rose in *Gypsy* on Broadway in 2008. LuPone has appeared in a few films and in many television series and specials. Her brother is actor Robert LuPone (1946–).

LYNN, DIANA [born Delores Loehr] (1926–1971). Film and television performer. A child prodigy at the piano, the lively, round-faced actress was the piano-playing kid sister in several 1940s movies but failed to catch on in adult roles. Lynn was born in Los Angeles, the daughter of an oil executive and a piano teacher, and was a concert pianist at the age of ten. She did specialties in the movies *There's Magic in Music* (1941) and *STAR-SPANGLED RHYTHM* (1942) and then got supporting roles in the musicals *And the Angels Sing* (1944), *Out of This World* (1945), *Duffy's Tavern* (1945), *Variety Girl* (1947), *My Friend Irma* (1949), *My Friend Irma Goes West* (1950), *Meet Me at the Fair* (1952), and *You're Never Too Young* (1955). However, she is best remembered as the outspoken teen in nonmusical comedies such as *The Miracle at Morgan's Creek* (1944) and *Our Hearts Were Young and Gay* (1944). Although Hollywood was not interested in her after the mid-1950s, Lynn appeared in many television series, dramas, and specials, such as the TV musical *JUNIOR MISS* (1957).

LYNNE, GILLIAN [born Jillian Barbara Pyrke] (1926–). Stage and film choreographer. One of Great Britain's most applauded choreographers, her work has been visible on Broadway and film for decades. Lynne was born in Bromley, England, the daughter of a businessman and a dancer, and educated at the Arts Educational School before studying at the Royal Ballet School. She first performed with the Sadler's Wells Ballet Company in 1944 and then with various other troupes until she turned to choreographing in 1963, presenting a program at the Edinburgh Festival. Three years later she made her Broadway debut staging the musical numbers for *THE ROAR OF THE GREASEPAINT—THE SMELL OF THE CROWD*, followed by the musical *Pickwick* (1965), which she first choreographed in London. Lynne's only American musical was *How Now, Dow Jones* (1967), but she was well represented on Broadway with such British imports as *CATS* (1982), *THE PHANTOM OF THE OPERA* (1988), *ASPECTS OF LOVE* (1990), and *CHITTY CHITTY BANG BANG* (2005). Among the many films she has choreographed are *Wonderful Life* (1964), *Every Day's a Holiday* (1965), *200 Motels* (1971), *HALF A SIXPENCE* (1967), *MAN OF LA MANCHA* (1972), *The Old Curiosity Shop* (1975), and *YENTL* (1983). In England she not only choreographed musicals, but also the dances in many Royal Shakespeare Company productions and for various ballet companies around the world. Lynne's choreography is based on ballet, yet she has also employed everything from jazz to music hall in her work.

M

two finest were the Princess Bozena who poses as a maid in *The Spring Maid* (1910) and the laundress Sylvia who turns out to be royalty in *Sweethearts* (1913). Among her other Broadway musical credits are *The Chieftain* (1895), *In Gay Paree* (1899), *The Cadet Girl* (1900), *An English Daisy* (1904), *The Belle of Mayfair* (1906), *The Prince of Bohemia* (1910), and the revival of *Florodora* (1920). Although her superb voice was still thrilling audiences, McDonald retired when she reached the age of forty and could no longer play ingénues.

MacDermot, Galt (1928–). Stage composer. An eclectic Broadway composer mostly known for his music for *Hair* (1968), he also wrote some accomplished scores for lesser-known works. MacDermot was born in Montreal, the son of a diplomat, and was educated at Upper Canada College and Bishop's University before studying music in Capetown, South Africa, where he started writing operas. He settled in New York in the late 1960s and met Gerome Ragni and James Rado, his collaborators on *Hair*. MacDermot worked with playwright John Guare on the score for *Two Gentlemen of Verona* (1971) before reuniting with Rado and Ragni for two notorious Broadway flops, *Dude* (1972) and *Via Galactica* (1972). His superb score for *The Human Comedy* (1983) was heard Off Broadway but the musical failed to run when it transferred to Broadway. MacDermot's other musical credits include *My Fur Lady* (1957), *Isabel's a Jezebel* (1970), *The Karl Marx Play* (1973), *Time and the Wind* (1995), and a series of musicals in Trinidad with playwright Derek Walcott, including *The Joker of Saville* (1974) and *Steel* (1991). He has also written songs for recording artists and for films, including *Cotton Comes to Harlem* (1970) and some nonmusicals. MacDermot is a versatile composer who uses everything from African rhythms to pop to opera in his work.

MacDonald, Christie (1875–1962). Stage performer. A dainty and demure soprano with an exceptional voice, she starred in several operettas at the turn of the twentieth century. McDonald was born in Pictou, Nova Scotia, Canada, and educated in Boston before she started singing professionally on the road. By 1984 she was on Broadway and by 1900 became a star as the Normandy princess who disguises herself as a peasant in *The Princess Chic*. Of her many operetta roles, McDonald's

MacDonald, Jeanette [Anna] (1901–1965). Stage and film performer. One of filmdom's favorite sopranos, her teaming with singer Nelson Eddy resulted in the most popular singing duo in the history of Hollywood. Born and educated in Philadelphia, MacDonald studied voice in New York before landing her first jobs in the chorus in Broadway musicals. Soon the delicate, blonde beauty was playing ingénue roles in operettas and musical comedies, including *Tip-Toes* (1925), *Yes, Yes, Yvette* (1927), *Sunny Days* (1928), *Angela* (1928), and *Boom Boom* (1929). Few of these shows were hits and MacDonald never became a stage star; in 1929 she signed a film contract and never returned to the theatre. From her first film, *The Love Parade* (1929) with Maurice Chevalier, MacDonald was a sensation, going on to star in over two dozen musicals before retiring twenty years later to concentrate on concerts and recordings. She also costarred with Chevalier in *One Hour With You* (1932), *Love Me Tonight* (1932), and *The Merry Widow* (1934), but she is most remembered for her eight movies with Eddy: *Naughty Marietta* (1935), *Rose Marie* (1936), *Maytime* (1937), *The Girl of the Golden West* (1938), *Sweethearts* (1938), *New Moon* (1940), *Bitter Sweet* (1940), and *I Married an Angel* (1942). With other leading men she starred in the musicals *The Vagabond King* (1930), *Monte Carlo* (1930), *The Cat and the Fiddle* (1934), *San Francisco* (1936), *The Firefly* (1937), *Smilin' Through* (1941), *Cairo* (1942), *Three Darling Daughters* (1948), *The Sun Comes Up* (1949), and others. While she was sometimes dubbed the "Iron Butterfly" for her cold beauty and superhuman voice, MacDonald was beloved by audiences, and her partnership with Eddy was uniquely grandiose. She was married to screen actor Gene Raymond (1908–1998). Biography: *The Jeanette MacDonald Story*, Robert Parish (1976).

MacDonough, Glen (1870–1924). Stage lyricist and writer. The author of some two dozen Broadway musicals early in the twentieth century, the librettist–lyricist worked with the finest American and European composers of his day. MacDonough was born in Brooklyn and began his career as an actor and then wrote farces before turning to musicals with *The Gold Bug* (1896) with composer Victor Herbert. The two would also collaborate on the classic fantasy *Babes in Toyland* (1903) as well as *It Happened in Nordland* (1904), *Wonderland* (1905), *Algeria* (1908), and *The Rose of Algeria* (1909). With composer John Philip Sousa, he wrote book and lyrics for *Chris and the Wonderful Lamp* (1900). MacDonough was also known for his adaptations of European operettas and musicals, such as Johann Strauss' *Vienna Life* (1901) and Franz Lehár's *The Count of Luxembourg* (1912) and *Eva* (1912). His other Broadway credits include *The Belle of Bridgeport* (1900), *The Midnight Sons* (1909), *The Jolly Bachelors* (1910), *The Summer Widowers* (1910), *The Queen of the Movies* (1914), *Fads and Fancies* (1915), *The Kiss Burglar* (1918), and *Hitchy-Koo* (1918 and 1920). MacDonough was a competent and versatile writer whose work sometimes was enchanting and superior fun.

MacGregor, Edgar J. (1879–1957). Stage director. One of Broadway's busiest directors for over thirty years, he specialized in musicals. MacGregor was born in Rochester, New York, and began his career as an assistant to actor William Gillette and actress Jane Crowl. He was directing on Broadway by 1910 and staged several plays before hitting his stride with the musical *The Kiss Burglar* in 1918. Thereafter he would concentrate on musicals, directing nearly thirty of them, such as *The Gingham Girl* (1922), *Captain Jinks* (1925), *Queen High* (1926), *The Desert Song* (1926), *Honeymoon Lane* (1926), *Good News!* (1927), *Funny Face* (1927), *The New Moon* (1928), *Follow Thru* (1929), *Through the Years* (1932), and *Take a Chance* (1932). In 1932 MacGregor went to Hollywood to direct but did not fare as well so he returned to Broadway in 1939 to stage a handful of other hits, such as *DuBarry Was a Lady* (1939), *Louisiana Purchase* (1940), *Panama Hattie* (1940), and *Let's Face It!* (1941). He excelled at fast-paced, bright musical comedy and was as adept at working with early musical forms such as with Roaring Twenties jazz and Big Band musicals.

Mack and Mabel (Majestic Theatre 1974). It may not have been another hit for composer–lyricist Jerry Herman, but this musical did boast what many consider his strongest score. Early film pioneer Mack Sennett (Robert Preston) discovers Mabel Normand (Bernadette Peters) working in a deli and turns her into a silent screen star by featuring her in comic one-reelers. The two also embark on a shaky romance and when Mabel leaves Mack to manage her own career she falls into the clutches of the sinister William Desmond Taylor (James Mitchell) and dies of a drug overdose. Michael Stewart wrote the libretto and it was a downbeat (and true) story that did not please the critics or the public. Even with first-rate performances by the two stars and the sterling songs, the show struggled to run sixty-five performances. Over the years the score has become even more admired, and revivals in London and regionally have been prompted by the desire to have these songs performed. The sardonic ballad "I Won't Send Roses," the merry frolic "Hundreds of Girls," the revealing "Look What Happened to Mabel," the feisty "Wherever He Ain't," the ironic "Tap Your Troubles Away," and the indelible torch song "Time Heals Everything" were among the finest songs of the decade. Gower Champion directed and choreographed the David Merrick production and it was superior in all departments, but *Mack and Mabel* was not the escapist musical Jerry Herman fans expected.

Mackintosh, Cameron [Anthony] (1946–). Stage producer. One of the world's most successful theatrical producers with megahits playing on several continents, he has presented everything from spectacular pop-operas to intimate musical revues. Mackintosh was born in Enfield, England, and studied acting before taking work as a stagehand at the Drury Lane Theatre and as an assistant stage manager of a tour of *Oliver!* in order to get acquainted with all aspects of theatre production. He began producing shows regionally in Great Britain and then presented revivals and new works in London, including *Tomfoolery* (1981) and *Little Shop of Horrors* (1982), before having his first West End success with *Cats* (1981), which he brought to Broadway the next year. Teaming with composer–producer Andrew Lloyd-Webber, he presented *Song and Dance* (1985) and *The Phantom of the Opera* (1988) in New York after their successful openings in London. Mackintosh's other

Broadway hits are *Les Misérables* (1987) and *Miss Saigon* (1990), both of which he previously produced in England. His other New York musical credits are the 1984 revival of *Oliver!*, *Five Guys Named Moe* (1992), the 1995 revival of *Carousel*, *Putting It Together* (1999), the 2002 revival of *Oklahoma!*, and *Mary Poppins* (2006), which he co-produced with Disney Productions. Among his many London musicals that did not come to New York are *Trelawney* (1972), *Blondel* (1983), *Martin Guerre* (1996), and *The Witches of Eastwick* (2000). Mackintosh is a shrewd, dedicated, obstinate, and powerful producer who understands publicity, showmanship, and public tastes. Biography: *Hey, Mr. Producer: The Musical World of Cameron Mackintosh*, Sheridan Morley, Ruth Leon (1998).

MacLaine, Shirley [born Shirley MacLean Beaty] (1934–). Film and stage performer. A durable leading lady in Hollywood, the redheaded actress–singer–dancer has shone in everything from melodramas to comedies to musicals, still finding juicy roles after fifty years of movie acting. MacLaine was born in Richmond, Virginia, where she took dance lessons as a child. After graduating from high school she headed to New York and was cast in the chorus of *Me and Juliet* (1953). The next year she was hired for the chorus of *The Pajama Game* and as understudy for featured player Carol Haney. When Haney was injured during the run, MacLaine went on in her place and dazzled the audience, which included Hollywood producer Hal B. Wallis. MacLaine made a noticeable film debut in a leading role in the comedy *The Trouble With Harry* (1955), followed by some fifty movies in all genres. Her film musical roles include the Greenwich Village resident Bessie Sparrowbush in *Artists and Models* (1955), Parisian dance hall proprietor Simone Pistache in *Can-Can* (1960), lucky widow Louisa May Benson in *What a Way to Go!* (1964), and taxi-dancer Charity Hope Valentine in *Sweet Charity* (1968). MacLaine has returned to Broadway in special showcases and has acted on many television series and specials. She has written many autobiographies, memoirs, and reflections on her beliefs, most notably *Don't Fall Off the Mountain* (1985) and *My Lucky Stars: A Hollywood Memoir* (1996). Her brother is film actor Warren Beatty (1937–).

MacMurray, Fred[rick Martin] (1908–1991). Film, television, and stage performer. One of the most personable leading men on the large and small screens, the solid, unfussy actor appeared in all genres, including thirteen movie musicals. MacMurray was born in Kankakee, Illinois, the son of a concert violinist, and played saxophone in local bands to earn tuition money for Carroll College. After graduation he continued playing in touring orchestras and made a few film appearances in the late 1920s before going to Broadway where he was in the ensemble of the musicals *Three's a Crowd* (1930) and *Roberta* (1933). After working in vaudeville, he returned to Hollywood in 1935 and was cast as nice leading man types in nonmusicals such as *Alice Adams* (1935). That same year he played one of the musicians in the musical *Beat the Band*, and many of his subsequent musicals would have him as a nonsinging musician in the plot. MacMurray's other musicals are *The Princess Comes Across* (1936), *Champagne Waltz* (1937), *Swing High, Swing Low* (1937), *Cocoanut Grove* (1938), *Sing You Sinners* (1938), *Café Society* (1939), *Star-Spangled Rhythm* (1942), *And the Angels Sing* (1944), *Never a Dull Moment* (1950), and *The Happiest Millionaire* (1967). While he excelled at playing less-than-good characters in dramas such as *Double Indemnity* (1944) and *The Apartment* (1960), MacMurray is mainly remembered for his affable roles in a series of Disney comedies and his long-running television series *My Three Sons*. He was married to actress–singer June Haver. Biography: *Fred MacMurray*, Charles Tranberg (2007).

MacRae, Gordon (1921–1986). Film, television, and stage performer. A masculine, full-voiced baritone with a genial persona, he starred in a dozen movie musicals in the 1950s. MacRae was born in East Orange, New Jersey, the son of a toolmaker–singer and a concert pianist, and went to schools in Buffalo and Syracuse before becoming a band vocalist. After serving as a navigator in World War II, MacRae returned to singing, first on the radio and then on Broadway in the revue *Three to Make Ready* (1946). This appearance led to a movie contract, and he made his screen debut in 1948 in *The Big Punch*. MacRae starred in such musicals as *Tea for Two* (1950), *West Point Story* (1950), *On Moonlight Bay* (1951), *By the Light of the Silvery Moon* (1953), *The Desert Song* (1953), and *Three Sailors and a Girl* (1953) before getting his best film roles: the cowboy hero Curly in *Oklahoma!* (1955) and the troubled carousel barker Billy Bigelow in *Carousel* (1956). He also played songwriter B. G. DeSylva

Gordon Macrae. While most leading men in movie musicals came from Broadway, MacRae pretty much started his career on screen and managed to play several musical roles before the golden age of the Hollywood musical faded away. Here he is in what is arguably his best performance, as Curly in *Oklahoma!* (1955) with his bride Laurey, played by Shirley Jones. (Photofest)

in the biopic *THE BEST THINGS IN LIFE ARE FREE* (1956), but with the waning of movie musicals in the 1960s, MacRae concentrated on concerts, summer stock, touring companies, and television where he had a show of his own and appeared in many specials, including the TV musicals *THE GIFT OF THE MAGI* (1958) and *The Young Man From Boston* (1965). He was married to actress Sheila MacRae (1924–) and is the father of actresses Meredith (1944–2000) and Heather MacRae (1946–).

MADAME SHERRY (New Amsterdam Theatre 1910). The finest of the six collaborations between Karl Hoschna (music) and OTTO HARBACH (book and lyrics), this smart and clever musical comedy managed to be ahead of its time and still popular with audiences. Edward Sherry (Jack Gardner) heads a dance school of the Isadora Duncan style that loses money but is funded by his millionaire– archeologist Uncle Theophilus (Ralph Herz) to whom Edward has told a couple of lies to, such as his being married and having two children. When the uncle unexpectedly arrives, Edward must convince his housekeeper and her kids to act as his wife and family. Theophilus is only fooled for a time and just as he is about to cut off funding to his nephew, Edward is able to announce that he is love with Theophilus' niece Yvonne (Lina Abarbanell) and they are to be wed. Although the plot had shown up in earlier musicals in Europe, Harbach's treatment was very contemporary and American. It was also farsighted in how music was used. The hit song "Every Little Movement (Has a Meaning All Its Own)" was sung as part of a dance lesson and then was reprised throughout the show in different tempos and taking on different meanings, serving to unify the score and bring the lovers together. The other numbers included "The Smile She Means for You," "I Want to Play House With You," "The Birth of Passion," and the interpolated "Put Your Arms Around Me, Honey." GEORGE LEDERER directed and co-produced the "modern" musical, which was the hit of the season, running 231 performances.

MAGIC SHOW, THE (Cort Theatre 1974). A magic act disguised as a little musical, the show was dismissed by the press who only recommended its conjuring tricks but that was enough for audiences who kept the show on the boards for 1,920 performances. Rob Randall penned the libretto about the Passaic Top Hat, a floundering nightclub in New Jersey, which tries to avoid bankruptcy by hiring a magic act featuring the young magician Doug (Doug Henning). The rest of the evening consisted of dazzling feats of illusion interrupted by pop songs by STEPHEN SCHWARTZ, some of them quite entertaining, such as "Style," "Lion Tamer," "West End Avenue," and "Two's Company." Also in the cast were David Ogden Stiers, Anita Morris, Robert LuPone, Dale Soules, Cheryl Barnes, and Annie McGreevey, but the only one who counted was Henning who was well known from his many television appearances. One of the longest-running shows on record, it has pretty much disappeared and revivals are next to nonexistent, although some of the songs have long been favorites in cabarets and nightclub acts.

MAGIDSON, HERB (1906–1986). Film and stage lyricist. A reliable Hollywood songwriter, he collaborated with many composers but mainly with ALLIE WRUBEL. Magidson was born in Braddock, Pennsylvania, and first heard his lyrics on Broadway in the play with music *The Song Writer* (1928). The next year he was in Hollywood writing songs for the musicals *The Forward Pass* (19239), *LITTLE JOHNNY JONES* (1929), *Bright Lights* (1931), and *The Gift of Gab* (1934). Magidson gained wide recognition for his lyrics for the song "The Continental," which he wrote with composer CON CONRAD and was used in *THE GAY DIVORCEE* (1934), winning the first Oscar for best song. After scoring *GEORGE WHITE'S SCANDALS* (1935) and *Hats Off* (1936), he teamed with Wrubel for such musicals as *Life of the Party* (1937), *Radio City Revels* (1938), and *Sing Your Way Home* (1945). His other Hollywood musicals are *Priorities on Parade* (1942), *Sleepy-Time Gal* (1942), and *Music in Manhattan* (1944), as well as songs for nonmusicals. Magidson also returned to Broadway to write songs for *George White's Music Hall Varieties* (1932) and *George White's Scandals* (1939). While few of his films were first-class affairs, he managed to come up with such hit songs as "Midnight in Paris," "Singin' in the Bathtub," "Gone With the Wind," and "Enjoy Yourself (It's Later Than You Think)."

MAIN, MARJORIE [born Mary Tomlinson] (1890–1975). Film and stage performer. One of Hollywood's favorite character actresses,

the wizened-looking matron played crusty, no-nonsense women in dozens of films, including some beloved musicals. Main was born in Acton, Indiana, the daughter of a minister, and after attending Franklin College went on the stage, playing in vaudeville and on Broadway in the 1920s in comedies and dramas. She made her film debut in 1931 and then went back to Broadway to play a featured role in the musical *MUSIC IN THE AIR* (1932) and in more plays. Main was widely noticed when she played Humphrey Bogart's tragic mother in the play *Dead End* (1935) and reprised her performance in the 1937 film. For a while she was cast in such serious roles but most remember her for her comedies, in particular the *Ma and Pa Kettle* movies in the 1940s and 1950s. Main added a touch of zest in such musicals as *Music in the Air* (1934), *NAUGHTY MARIETTA* (1935), *MEET ME IN ST. LOUIS* (1944), *THE HARVEY GIRLS* (1946), *SUMMER STOCK* (1950), *THE BELLE OF NEW YORK* (1952), and *ROSE MARIE* (1954). Biography: *Marjorie Main: The Life and Films of Hollywood's Ma Kettle*, Michelle Vogel (2006).

MAKE MINE MANHATTAN (Broadhurst Theatre 1948). One of the last in the era of original Broadway revues, this delightful show about living in New York was refreshingly witty and tuneful. Arnold B. Horwitt wrote the sketches and lyrics for RICHARD LEWINE'S music, and the revue featured a talented cast of comics, some prankish sketches, and a sprightly score that included the swinging "Saturday Night in Central Park," the bouncy "My Brudder and Me," the comic lament "Subway Song," the wry "Gentleman Friend," and the silly tribute to "Schraffts." The exceptional cast included DAVID BURNS, SID CAESAR, Sheila Bond, Eleanor Bagley, DANNY DANIELS, Biff McGuire, Joshua Shelley, Max Showalter, and Jack Kilty. The revue veteran HASSARD SHORT directed with MAX LIEBMAN, and Lee Sherman choreographed the surprise hit, which ran 429 performances.

MAKE MINE MUSIC (Disney 1946). A swinging animated musical anthology by the DISNEY studio, its superb art was matched by the superior music. The film consisted of ten segments with music ranging from classical to bebop. The most familiar item was Prokofiev's "Peter and the Wolf" with narration by STERLING HOLLOWAY, while the most ambitious was the grand finale "Opera Pathetique," featuring the opera-loving whale Willie who longs to sing at the Met. Celebrated passages from Rossini, Wagner, Donizetti, and other operas were heard in playful contrast with the old spiritual "Shortnin' Bread," and all the voices (tenor, alto, soprano, bass, and even the chorus) were sung by NELSON EDDY. Other memorable sections include the ANDREWS SISTERS singing the musical tale of "Johnny Fedora and Alice Blue Bonnet" (by RAY GILBERT and ALLIE WRUBEL) about two hats in a department store window who fall in love; a surreal visualization of the old standard "After You've Gone" performed by the BENNY GOODMAN Quartet; a poetic piece involving a flamingo and the moon called "Blue Bayou" (by Gilbert and Bobby Worth); a tale about feuding hillbillies illustrated while the King's Men sang "The Martins and the Coys" (by Ted Weems and Al Cameron); and the swinging "All the Cats Join In" (by Alec Wilder, Gilbert, and Eddie Sauter) in which hyperactive bobby-soxers jitterbug in a malt shop to the music of Goodman and his orchestra. Each segment had its own director and animation staff, all under the supervision of Joe Grant. The inventive film was not popular at the box office but individual sections become favorites when shown separately as shorts in the theatres and on WALT DISNEY's television show in the 1950s.

MALTBY, RICHARD, JR., AND DAVID SHIRE. Stage songwriters and director. An Off Broadway lyricist–composer team who write engaging revues and book musicals, although they have seen little success on Broadway. Richard Maltby, Jr. (1937–) was born in Ripon, Wisconsin, the son of band leader and music arranger Richard Maltby, and was educated at Yale University where he met fellow student David Shire (1937–), a music student from Buffalo. Their Off Broadway musical *The Sap of Life* (1961) was short-lived but their subsequent revues STARTING HERE, STARTING NOW (1977) and CLOSER THAN EVER (1989) were well received by the press and the public. Maltby and Shire's two Broadway efforts, *BABY* (1983) and *Big* (1996), boasted superior scores but neither managed to run. The team's most recent effort is the London musical *Take Flight* (2007). Maltby has had Broadway success with AIN'T MISBEHAVIN' (1978), which he conceived, directed, and wrote some lyrics, and MISS SAIGON (1991), for which he adapted the French lyrics. He had less success with the Broadway musicals *Nick and Nora* (1991), *Ring of Fire* (2006), and *The Pirate Queen* (2007). Maltby is also a respected director who staged some of his own works, as well as the musicals

Song and Dance (1985) and *FOSSE* (1999). Shire has composed music soundtracks for over 100 Hollywood and television nonmusicals, as well as the musical SATURDAY NIGHT FEVER (1977). He was wed to actress Talia Shire (1946–) and is married to actress Didi Conn (1951–).

🎭 **MAME** (Winter Garden Theatre 1966). The antic adventures of the unconventional Mame Dennis may have been familiar to audiences from the best-selling book *Auntie Mame*, the hit play version (1956), and the 1958 film version, but the musical seemed as fresh as a new work, with the songs and dancing making the bigger-than-life story even more fun.

Plot: The orphaned Patrick Dennis arrives with his governess Agnes Gooch at the Manhattan apartment of his aunt Mame who has been given custody of the boy in his late father's will. Although the will insists on a conventional upbringing, the unconventional Mame shows Patrick the world of 1920s New York, complete with speakeasies, theatres, and other adventures. When the crash comes, Mame is forced to work for a living and takes the advice of her actress friend Vera Charles and tries the stage, but Mame's debut is a disaster. Luckily she meets up

Mame. There may not have been too many surprises in the characters and plot of the oft-told tale of Auntie Mame, but the Broadway musical had one giant surprise in Angela Lansbury (left) who became a musical star late in her career. Pictured with Lansbury is Beatrice Arthur as her caustic pal Vera. (Photofest)

Casts for *Mame*

Character	1966 Broadway	1974 film
Mame Dennis	ANGELA LANSBURY	LUCILLE BALL
Vera Charles	BEATRICE ARTHUR	Beatrice Arthur
Young Patrick	Frankie Michaels	Kirby Furlong
Adult Patrick	Jerry Lanning	Bruce Davison
Beauregard Burnside	Charles Braswell	ROBERT PRESTON
Agnes Gooch	JANE CONNELL	Jane Connell

with the dashing Southern gent Beauregard Jackson Pickett Burnside who brings Mame and Patrick down South to meet his narrow-minded relatives. Mame turns a cockeyed fox hunt into a personal triumph and she marries Beau. But Beau falls off a mountain on their honeymoon and the widowed Mame continues on, trying to steer Patrick away from conventionality. When he gets engaged to a stuck-up girl with a wretchedly right-wing family, Mame rescues him. Patrick eventually marries a more open-minded woman and has a son whom Mame is ready to take charge in raising as well.

Jerome Lawrence and Robert E. Lee wrote the efficient libretto, retaining the highlights of the earlier versions and making room for the sparkling JERRY HERMAN songs. "If He Walked Into My Life" and the title song were the instant hits but as time has passed it is the seasonal "We Need a Little Christmas" that is the most famous, one of the very few theatre songs to join the repertory of holiday favorites. Also delightful were the comic numbers, such as "Bosom Buddies" and "Gooch's Song," the celebratory numbers, such as "It's Today," "Open a New Window," and "That's How Young I Feel," and the tender ballad "My Best Girl." ANGELA LANSBURY became a Broadway musical star with her funny, classy, endearing Mame, and she was supported by a strong cast under the direction of GENE SAKS. ONNA WHITE was the choreographer, and the production numbers were showstoppers. The show ran 1,508 performances, during which time Mame was also played by CELESTE HOLM, JANIS PAIGE, Jane Morgan, and ANN MILLER. *Mame* was popular on the road and has remained a favorite with stock, summer, and community theatres. Original cast members Lansbury and Connell were reunited with the original sets, direction, and choreography for a 1983 Broadway revival but critics were brutally dismissive of the 1960s musical form so the revival struggled to run five weeks.

Mame (stage) Musical Numbers

"St. Bridget"
"It's Today"
"Open a New Window"
"The Man in the Moon"
"My Best Girl"
"We Need a Little Christmas"
"The Fox Hunt"
"Mame"
"Bosom Buddies"
"Gooch's Song"
"That's How Young I Feel"
"If He Walked Into My Life (Today)"

■ *Mame* (Warner 1974) sounded like a hit on paper with television's queen of comedy as Mame and the director, choreographer, Beatrice Arthur, and Jane Connell from the Broadway production returning for the film. Paul Zindel's screenplay was faithful to the original and much of the Herman score was retained. However, the result was, to put it mildly, disappointing. Much blame has been put on LUCILLE BALL who was too old, too feeble, and unable to sing the songs. Yet even scenes without her fail to come to life, and there seems to be a pallor over the whole movie, not unlike the gauze used on all of Ball's close-ups. The film made it quite clear that the heart of the musical is Mame and when she lacks energy, charm, and zest, nothing else works. WARNER BROTHERS spent a bundle on the movie, and the sets, costumes, and other production elements were first class. Despite all the promotion given the musical, word of mouth traveled faster than the bad reviews and the film was a box office failure.

MAMMA MIA! (Winter Garden Theatre 2001). A weak libretto, lack of stars, and damning notices couldn't keep this musical from becoming a hit because audiences walked into the theatre singing the songs and decided they liked it before the curtain went up. Catherine

Mamma Mia! The advance word on the Australian musical was so strong that millions of dollars worth of tickets were sold without patrons wondering what it was, who was in it, or who put it together. All they knew was ABBA and that was enough. Pictured is the curtain call at a 2006 performance when *Mamma Mia!* celebrated its fifth anniversary on Broadway. (Wire Image)

Casts for *Mamma Mia!*

Character	2001 Broadway	2008 film
Donna Sheridan	Louise Pitre	Meryl Streep
Sophie Sheridan	Tina Maddigan	Amanda Seyfield
Rosie	JUDY KAYE	Julie Walters
Tanya	Karen Mason	Christine Baranski
Sky	Joe Machota	Dominic Cooper
Sam Carmichael	David W. Keeley	Pierce Brosnan
Harry Bright	Dean Nolen	Colin Firth
Bill Austin	Ken Marks	Stellan Skarsgard

Johnson wrote the contrived libretto about Sophie Sheridan who is getting married on a Greek Island and wants her father to be there. The trouble is, her mother, the ex-rock singer Donna, says her father could be any one of three men from her wild past so Sophie invites all three to the wedding. Also on hand are Donna's ex-singing mates Rosie and Tanya so the trio relives their youth by singing their old hits. Those song favorites were by Benny Andersson, Björn Ulvaeus, and Stig Anderson, better known as ABBA, the popular Swedish rock group from the 1970s. Such familiar songs as "Dancing Queen," "Lay All Your Love on Me," "Super Trouper,' and the title number were sandwiched into the contrived plot but no one seemed to worry because the audience was invited to dance in the aisles to the old favorites. The international hit from Australia was a sellout from the start and continues to draw audiences of all ages.

UNIVERSAL PICTURES filmed a screen version of *Mamma Mia!* with a star-studded cast, something the many stage productions around the world did not bother with. Johnson adapted her own libretto for the screen, and Phyllida Lloyd, who directed the Broadway version, also directed the movie, which was released in 2008.

MAMOULIAN, ROUBEN (1898–1987). Stage and film director. An extraordinary helmer of landmark Broadway and Hollywood musicals, he was one of the most visual of all directors. Mamoulian was born in Tiflis, in the Georgian state of Russia, to an Armenian family. His father was a bank president so Mamoulian was educated in Paris as well as at the University of Moscow for a law career, but instead enrolled at Evgeny Vakhtangov's Third Studio, a school connected with the Moscow Art Theatre. A theatre company he organized in his hometown in Georgia traveled to England in 1920 and Mamoulian stayed to study theatre at the University of London. First coming to America in 1923, he directed opera at the Eastman School of Music in Rochester, New York, before making his Manhattan directorial debut with the Theatre Guild's production of *Porgy* (1927). As his reputation grew, Mamoulian was invited to direct films in Hollywood, but he continued to return to the stage and directed some landmark musicals of his era, such as *PORGY AND BESS* (1935), *OKLAHOMA!* (1943), *ST. LOUIS WOMAN* (1946), *CAROUSEL* (1945), and *LOST IN THE STARS* (1949). He also directed the first American production of Turgenev's *A Month in the Country*, as well as other non-musicals. Mamoulian's film career was just as impressive, directing musical classics such as *APPLAUSE* (1929), *LOVE ME TONIGHT* (1932), and *HIGH, WIDE AND HANDSOME* (1937). His other film musicals include *The Gay Desperado* (1936), *SUMMER HOLIDAY* (1947), and *SILK STOCKINGS* (1957). Mamoulian was particularly talented at handling a large number of actors on stage, turning crowd scenes into focused and theatrical paintings. In film, he used unique cinematic devices to introduce characters or a story, as in the stunning opening of *Love Me Tonight*. Mamoulian's background in art and music also served him well and few productions were as visually vibrant as his, bringing a European sense of decor to American works. Biographies: *Rouben Mamoulian*, Tom Miln

(1969); *Reinventing Reality: The Art and Life of Rouben Mamoulian*, Mark Spergel (1993).

🕭 **MAN OF LA MANCHA** (ANTA Theatre 1965). An unlikely musical hit that originated at the GOODSPEED OPERA HOUSE in Connecticut, this musicalization of the Spanish epic novel *Don Quixote* by Cervantes not only dramatized the novel but depicted the plight of its author as well.

Plot: When the Spanish author Miguel de Cervantes and his servant are thrown into jail by the Spanish Inquisition and await trial, their fellow inmates hold their own tribunal. In his defense, Cervantes acts out the story of the madcap knight errant Don Quixote and his faithful squire Sancho Panza and their misadventures with imaginary dragons, evil knights, and the beautiful Lady Dulcinea who is really the bitter whore Aldonza. Quixote helps defend the honor of Dulcinea by fighting off the muleteers who taunt her and then asks the innkeeper to dub him a knight, which he does mockingly. The muleteers take their revenge by raping and beating Aldonza and she tries to make Quixote see her as the whore she is but he cannot. The madman's relatives send Dr. Carrasco to try and cure Quixote and, dressed as the mysterious Knight of Mirrors, the doctor shocks the old man back into reality. Quixote takes to his deathbed but before he dies Aldonza appears and reminds him of the glorious knight he once was. The story told, the fellow prisoners declare Cervantes to be like his fictional hero and he agrees as he and his servant are led to face the Inquisition.

Dale Wasserman condensed the long novel efficiently by dramatizing the key events as part of Cervantes' defense, and director ALBERT MARRE kept all the action in Howard Bay's atmospheric prison setting, letting one imagine the different locales as Cervantes conjured them up. Also, JACK COLE's inventive choreography grew out

Casts for *Man of La Mancha*

Character	1966 Broadway	1972 film	2002 Broadway
Cervantes/Don Quixote	RICHARD KILEY	Peter O'Toole	BRIAN STOKES MITCHELL
Aldonza/Dulcinea	JOAN DIENER	Sophia Loren	Mary Elizabeth Mastrantonio
Sancho Panza	Irving Jacobson	James Coco	Ernie Sabella
Innkeeper	RAY MIDDLETON	Harry Andrews	Don Mayo
Padre	ROBERT ROUNSEVILLE	Ian Richardson	Mark Jacoby
Dr. Carrasco	Jon Cypher	John Castle	STEPHEN BOGARDUS

Man of La Mancha. Cervantes loved the theatre and wrote over twenty plays so dramatizing *Don Quixote* as its author Cervantes might have done was not so far-fetched a premise. Pictured from the original Broadway production is Richard Kiley (center) as Quixote with Joan Diener as Aldonza and Irving Jacobson as Sancho. (Photofest)

Man of La Mancha (stage) Musical Numbers

"Man of La Mancha (I, Don Quixote)"
"It's All the Same"
"Dulcinea"
"I'm Only Thinking of Him"
"I Really Like Him"
"What Does He Want of Me?"
"Little Bird, Little Bird"
"Barber's Song"
"Golden Helmet of Mambrino"
"To Each His Dulcinea"
"The Impossible Dream (The Quest)"
"The Combat"
"The Dubbing"
"Knight of the Woeful Countenance"
"The Abduction"
"Moorish Dance"
"Aldonza"
"The Knight of Mirrors"
"A Little Gossip"
"The Psalm"

of the improvised play within a play. It was all as theatrical as it was emotional thanks to the outstanding performances, particularly RICHARD KILEY who got the role of a lifetime. The score by MITCH LEIGH (music) and Joe Darion (lyrics) was operatic with a strong Spanish flavor, yet pure Broadway in its characterization and sense of narrative. The runaway hit was "The Impossible Dream," one of the most popular theatre songs of the decade, and there was a heightened sense of lyricism also in the ballads "To Each His Dulcinea," "What Does He Want With Me?," and "Dulcinea," the comic numbers "I Really Like Him" and "Barber's Song," and the dramatic character songs such as "It's All the Same" and "Aldonza." Rave notices and the popularity of "The Impossible Dream" helped the dark but affirming musical run 2,328 performances. In 1972, Kiley reprised his splendid performance and was reunited with original cast members JOAN DIENER, Irving Jacobson, and ROBERT ROUNSEVILLE in an accurate duplication of the original production for a limited seventeen-week engagement. A 1977 Broadway revival also featured Kiley with Emily Yancy (Aldonza), Tony Martinez (Sancho), Bob Wright (Innkeeper), and Taylor Reed (Padre). Albert Marre again directed and the production ran 124 performances. RAUL JULIA essayed the double role of Cervantes–Don Quixote on Broadway in 1992 and the press was divided on his performance, as they were about Sheena Easton (Aldonza), but the revival found an audience for three months. BRIAN STOKES MITCHELL was a masterful Quixote/Cervantes in a very different-looking revival in 2002 directed by Jonathan Kent. Again the press was mixed but the public came for 304 performances.

Man of La Mancha (United Artists 1972) was oddly cast, considering the operatic nature of the musical, for few of the players were singers and only Peter O'Toole was dubbed. Also strange was the fact that the cast was mostly British, giving the film a *Masterpiece Theatre* kind of sound that was no more Spanish than an American production. O'Toole (partially dubbed by Simon Gilbert) acted the role of Quixote to perfection, James Coco got his laughs as Sancho, and even the Italian-accented Sophia Loren had moments of fiery passion, but when any of them began to sing the picture fell apart. One expected the movie to open up the story and leave the prison but in Wasserman's screenplay it was not handled smoothly and with the uninspired, clumsy direction by Arthur Hiller, one couldn't tell the difference between reality and the story of Cervantes's imagination. Much of the stage score survived but when it was sung so poorly that was not necessarily a selling point. The picture was not well reviewed and was not a box office hit.

⚜ **MAN WITH A LOAD OF MISCHIEF** (Jan Hus Playhouse 1966). An enchanting Off Broadway musical with a European air to it, the intimate, small-cast show managed to run 240 performances and later became a cult favorite, although revivals are not frequent. Based on a forgotten play of the same name by Ashley Dukes, the libretto by Ben Tarver is about six characters at a nineteenth-century English inn. A lady (VIRGINIA VESTOFF) of high society, running away from a lord (Raymond Thorpe) who wishes to marry her, comes to the inn run by the innkeeper (Tom Noel) and his wife (Leslie Nicol). The lord arrives at the inn with his manservant (REID SHELTON) with the intention of winning the lady's hand but instead is attracted to the maid (Alice Cannon) and has a one-night frolic with her while the lady befriends the manservant who turns out to be more noble that his master. The exceptional score by John Clifton (music and lyrics) and Tarver (lyrics) was true to the period and very theatrical, as with the flippant "Goodbye, My Sweet," the wistful "Little Rag Doll," the expansive "Hulla-Baloo-Balay," the enticing "Come to the Masquerade," the saucy "Once You've Had a Little Taste," and the lyrical "Make Way for My Lady!" The musical was a rare entry for Off Broadway in the 1960s, being a chamber piece that embraced the romanticism of past styles.

MANCINI, HENRY (1924–1994). Film and television composer and arranger. The prolific and oft-awarded composer of movie soundtrack scores and theme songs, he also wrote a few musicals as well. Mancini was born in Cleveland, raised in Pennsylvania, and educated at Carnegie Tech Music School and Juilliard before working as a pianist in dance bands. He was hired as a staff arranger and composer by UNIVERSAL PICTURES in 1951 and was noticed for his handling of the music in THE GLENN MILLER STORY (1954). From that point on Mancini was one of the busiest composers in Hollywood, scoring over 175 movies and creating such song hits as "The Days of Wine and Roses," "Moon River," "Dear Heart," and "Charade," as well as such familiar instrumentals as "Baby Elephant Walk" and "The Pink Panther Theme." He also wrote themes for television shows, such as *Peter Gunn* and *Mr. Lucky*. Mancini collaborated with lyricist JOHNNY MERCER on the superb score for the movie musical *DARLING LILI* (1969) and with LESLIE BRICUSSE on the songs for *VICTOR/VICTORIA* (1982), which arrived on Broadway in 1995.

MANDEL, FRANK (1884–1958). Stage writer and producer. The author of both plays and librettos, he was also a successful producer on Broadway. Born in San Francisco and educated at the University of California and the Hastings Law School, Mandel went to New York where he worked as a journalist and later a playwright. Although he wrote, collaborated, and/or translated several plays in his career, he is mostly remembered for the musical librettos he wrote with others. Mandel first collaborated with OSCAR HAMMERSTEIN on the book for *Tickle Me* (1920), and the two also worked together on *Jimmie* (1920), *Queen o' Hearts* (1922), THE DESERT SONG (1926), THE NEW MOON (1928), *Free for All* (1931), *East Wind* (1931), and *May Wine* (1945). With other collaborators he wrote the librettos for such musical hits as *MARY* (1920) and *NO, NO, NANETTE* (1925). Mandel teamed with LAURENCE SCHWAB to produce a series of musicals, including *Captain Jinks* (1925), *The Desert Song*, GOOD NEWS! (1927), *The New Moon*, FOLLOW THRU (1929), *America's Sweetheart*, *Free for All*, and *East Wind* (1931).

MANN, TERENCE [Vaughn] (1951–). Stage, film, and television performer. The rugged, weathered-looking leading man, usually cast as villains or anti-heroes, has given outstanding performances in musical hits and flops. Mann was born in Clearwater, Florida, and educated at the North Carolina School of the Arts and Jacksonville University before making his Broadway debut in the ensemble of *BARNUM* (1981). The next year he originated the role of the rambunctious feline Rum Tum Tugger in *CATS*, followed by a potent portrayal of the dastardly police officer Javert in LES MISÉRABLES (1987). Mann was a replacement for various roles in *JEROME ROBBINS' BROADWAY* (1989) and then shone as the labor organizer Saul in *RAGS* (1986), the embittered immigrant Leon Czolgosz in *ASSASSINS* (1991), the prince-turned-beast in *BEAUTY AND THE BEAST* (1994), a delightful Scrooge in *A CHRISTMAS CAROL* (1995) at Madison Square Garden Theatre, the villain Chauvelin in THE SCARLET PIMPERNEL (1997), a replacement for Frank-N-Furter in *THE ROCKY HORROR SHOW* (2001), and one of the eight actors portraying John Lennon in *Lennon* (2005). He has appeared in many television programs, including soap operas and drama series, and a handful of films, although his musical talents were only used in the movie of *A CHORUS LINE* (1985) and the TV musical *MRS. SANTA CLAUS* (1997). He is married to dancer–singer Charlotte d'Amboise (1964–).

MANTELLO, JOE (1962–). Stage director and performer. A dynamic actor-turned-director with a strong visual sense, he seems to triumph with everything from solo shows to huge Broadway musicals. Mantello was born in Rockford, Illinois, and educated at the North Carolina School of Arts and at the Circle Rep Company. He made his New York acting debut Off Broadway in 1986 and in 1993 was acclaimed for his portrayal of the Jewish radical Louis Ironson in *Angels in America* on Broadway. But he was more interested in directing, co-founding the Edge Theatre in Manhattan in 1984 and starting to stage works Off Off Broadway. His directing abilities were first noticed in the triple-monologue drama *Three Hotels* (1993), and he entered the ranks of top directors when his Off Broadway production of *Love! Valour! Compassion!* (1995) transferred to Broadway. Since then Mantello has offered everything from surreal tragicomedies to thought-provoking dramas to musicals as diverse as the spectacular *WICKED* (2003) and the revival of *ASSASSINS* (2004).

MARRE, ALBERT [born Moshinski] (1925–). Stage director. A prominent Broadway director for forty years, he is known mostly for his musical productions. Marre was born in New York City and educated at Oberlin College and Harvard University before serving in the Army during World War II. After the war he ran the Allied Repertory Theatre in Berlin, Germany, and then returned to the States where he was managing director of the Brattle Theatre Company in Cambridge, Massachusetts, directing dozens of productions between 1948 and 1952. Marre made his Manhattan debut in 1951 and the next year was named artistic director of the New York City Center Drama Company where he staged classic revivals. He became a recognized Broadway director with the hit musical *KISMET* in 1953, followed by musical and nonmusical successes over the next thirty-five years. Marre is most remembered for staging *MAN OF LA MANCHA* (1965) first on Broadway and then in revivals. His other New York musicals include *Shangri-La* (1956), *The Conquering Hero* (1961), *MILK AND HONEY* (1961), *Cry for Us All* (1970), *Home Sweet Homer* (1976), and *Chu Chem* (1989). His wife was actress–singer JOAN DIENER who appeared in many of his musical productions.

MARSH, HOWARD (?–1969). Stage performer. A handsome tenor with a lyrical voice, he got to originate two of the greatest roles in American operetta. Marsh managed to keep details of his youth, including his birth year, a secret but it has been confirmed that he was born in Bluffton, Indiana, and was on the New York stage by 1917 in *The Grass Widow*. The next year he was a replacement for Rudolfo in *MAYTIME* and appeared in the revue *Greenwich Village Follies* (1920) before getting attention as Baron Franz Schober in *BLOSSOM TIME* (1921). Marsh's true claim to fame was as the original Prince Karl Franz in *THE STUDENT PRINCE* (1924) and the original Gaylord Ravenal in *SHOW BOAT* (1927). His other musical credits include *Cherry Blossoms* (1927), *The Well of Romance* (1930), a revival of *ROBIN HOOD* (1932), and several Gilbert and Sullivan operettas. In 1932 Marsh retired from the stage and became a banker in New Jersey.

MARSHALL, GEORGE (1891–1975). Film director. With one of the longest directing careers in Hollywood history, from 1916 to 1969, he helmed a wide variety of genres, including twenty-two musicals. Marshall was born in Chicago, was educated at military school, and worked is various jobs before entering the movies as an extra. After acting and writing chores he started directing westerns for Universal. He served in World War I and then went to 20TH CENTURY-FOX where he directed both shorts and features and eventually developed a talent for light comedies and musicals, working with the screen's greatest comics from W. C. FIELDS to BOB HOPE to JERRY LEWIS. Marshall's musicals include *She Learned About Sailors* (1934), *365 Nights in Hollywood* (1934), *THE GOLDWYN FOLLIES* (1938), *Destry Rides Again* (1939), *STAR-SPANGLED RHYTHM* (1942), *Riding High* (1943), *And the Angels Sing* (1944), *Incendiary Blonde* (1945), *The Perils of Pauline* (1947), *Variety Girl* (1947), *My Friend Irma* (1949), *Fancy Pants* (1950), *Never a Dull Moment* (1950), *Scared Stiff* (1953), and *Red Garters* (1954).

MARSHALL, KATHLEEN (1962–). Stage and television director and choreographer. A recent but a much-in-demand artist, she has found wide commendation working with diverse musical styles. Marshall was born in Madison, Wisconsin, and raised in Pittsburgh, Pennsylvania. She appeared as a child in professional musicals at the local Civic Light Opera and then attended Smith College, where she majored in English, and the University of Massachusetts, where she studied theatre. When her brother ROB MARSHALL was made choreographer for a tour of *THE MYSTERY OF EDWIN DROOD*, he hired her as his assistant. She choreographed regionally, particularly at the Old Globe Theatre in San Diego, and made her New York choreography debut in 1995 staging the dances for the City Center's *Encores!* concert production of *Call Me Madam*. Marshall's first Broadway assignment was choreography for the short-lived revue *Swinging on a Star* (1995), followed by new works such as *Violet* (1997) and *Suessical* (2000), and revivals, such as *1776* (1997), *Kiss Me, Kate* (1999), *Follies* (2001), and *Little Shop of Horrors* (2003). She moved into directing and choreographing with the 2000 Off Broadway production of *Saturday Night*, followed by the 2003 popular revival of *Wonderful Town*, which grew out of her *Encores!* concert version, and revivals of *Two Gentlemen of Verona* (2005) in Central Park, *The Pajama Game* (2007), and *Grease* (2007). For television, Marshall choreographed the small screen version of *The Music Man* (2003) and the TV remake of *Once Upon a Mattress* (2005). Her work is marked by freshness and exuberance even as it stays within a conventional musical comedy framework.

MARSHALL, LARRY (1944–). Stage, film, and television performer. An energetic African American singer–dancer–actor, he was featured in several Broadway musicals and plays but few ran very long and stardom eluded him. Marshall was born in Spartanburg, South Carolina, and was educated at Fordham University and the New England Conservatory. He made his Broadway bow in 1970 as a replacement for Berger in *Hair*, followed by various roles in *Inner City* (1971) and Hamlet in the rock musical *Rockabye Hamlet* (1976). Marshall first played Sportin' Life in the 1976 revival of *Porgy and Bess* and reprised the part throughout his career on tour, in opera houses, and back on Broadway in 1983. His other New York musicals include *A Broadway Musical* (1978), *Comin' Uptown* (1979), *Oh, Brother!* (1981), *Big Deal* (1986), *3 Penny Opera* (1989), *Play On!* (1997), and replacements for Horse Simmons in *The Full Monty* (2002) and Mister in *The Color Purple* (2006). Marshall played classical roles for the New York Shakespeare Festival and made some television and film appearances, including the movie musicals *Jesus Christ Superstar* (1973) and *The Cotton Club* (1984) in which he impersonated Cab Calloway.

MARSHALL, ROB (1960–). Stage, film, and television director and choreographer. A dancer-turned-choreographer-turned-director, he has an impressive track record during

a relatively short period of time. Marshall was born in Madison, Wisconsin, and at the age of four moved with his family to Pittsburgh, Pennsylvania, when his father was hired for the English faculty at the University of Pittsburgh. He was educated at Carnegie-Mellon University before being cast in a touring production of *A Chorus Line*, followed by some jobs in Broadway musicals (he was dance captain for *The Rink*). Marshall started to choreograph regionally, doing the dances for *Bells Are Ringing* at the Goodspeed Opera House in 1990. His New York debut was choreographing an Off Broadway revival of *She Loves Me* in 1993, which transferred to Broadway. After choreographing *Kiss of the Spider Woman* (1993), *Damn Yankees* (1994), *The Petrified Prince* (1994), *Company* (1995), *Victor/Victoria* (1995), and *A Funny Thing Happened on the Way to the Forum* (1996), he made his directorial debut co-staging with Sam Mendes the highly praised 1998 revival of *Cabaret*. Marshall directed and choreographed the revival of *Little Me* in 1998 and then turned to other media, staging the television version of *Annie* in 1999, the dances for the film *The Cradle Will Rock* (1999), and triumphing as director and choreographer for the award-winning movie version of *Chicago* (2003). His dances are in the traditional Broadway mode but often his direction is unique and resourceful. His sister is stage choreographer–director Kathleen Marshall.

MARTIN, ANDREA (1947–). Stage, television, and film performer and writer. The short, frizzy-haired comedienne and mimic known to millions of Americans and Canadians because of her television appearances on *SCTV*, she turned to the theatre in the 1990s. Martin was born in Portland, Maine, and educated at Stephens College, Emerson College, and the Sorbonne in Paris. She appeared in the Toronto production of *Godspell* (1972) with fellow unknowns Martin Short and Victor Garber and then began working in comedy clubs and doing improvisation, becoming a regular player in the Second City improv group where she wrote and played dozens of hilarious caricatures. In the late 1970s the group turned to television and presented the long-running Canadian TV program and appeared on Broadway twice in the 1980s. Martin quickly established herself as an expert supporting player with her performance as the television comedy writer Alice Miller in the short-lived Broadway musical *My Favorite Year* (1992), followed by acclaimed appearances as the complaining Old Lady in *Candide*

(1997), crusty Aunt Eller in *OKLAHOMA!* (2002), a replacement for the wife Golde in *FIDDLER ON THE ROOF* (2005), and the secretive Frau Brucher in *YOUNG FRANKENSTEIN* (2007). She has also appeared in nonmusicals, including Shakespeare productions, and had her own Off Broadway show, the satirical *Nude Nude Totally Nude* (1996), which she wrote. Martin has appeared in hundreds of televisions programs, from *Star Trek* to *Sesame Street*, as well as the TV version of *GYPSY* (1993). She has acted in several movies, notably the musicals *Stepping Out* (19910) and *Hedwig and the Angry Inch* (2001), and has provided lively voices for many animated television shows and films, such as the movie musical *ANASTASIA* (1997).

MARTIN, DEAN [born Dino Paul Crocetti] (1917–1996). Film and television performer. The handsome Italian American crooner who was straight man for JERRY LEWIS in sixteen films and in nightclubs, he later found his niche playing laid-back playboys in nonmusicals. Martin was born in Steubenville, Ohio, and was a prizefighter, steel mill worker, and a professional gambler before he started singing in nightclubs across the country. While singing at an Atlantic City club, he met Lewis and the two did an act together before appearing in the film *My Friend Irma* (1949), which launched their screen partnership. Among the other Martin–Lewis musicals are *At War With the Army* (1950), *Sailor Beware* (1951), *The Stooge* (1952), *Scared Stiff* (1953), *The Caddy* (1953), *Living It Up* (1954), *ARTISTS AND MODELS* (1955), and *Pardners* (1956). After the duo went their separate ways, Martin did solo work in the movie musicals *Ten Thousand Bedrooms* (1957), *BELLS ARE RINGING* (1960), *ROBIN AND THE SEVEN HOODS* (1964), and *Kiss Me Stupid* (1965), as well as in many nonmusicals, such as the "Rat Pack" films in the 1960s. Martin was very popular on records, in nightclubs, and later on television where his relaxed persona on his own variety show was legendary. His son was Dean Paul Martin, better known as Dino (1951–1987). Memoirs: *Memories Are Made of This: Dean Martin Through His Daughter's Eyes*, Deana Martin, Wendy Holden (2005); *That's Amore: A Son Remembers Dean Martin*, Ricci Martin (2004); biographies: *Dean Martin: King of the Road*, Michael Freedland (2006); *Dino: Living High in the Dirty Business of Dreams*, Nick Tosches (1999).

MARTIN, HUGH (1914–). Film and stage composer, arranger, and lyricist. Mostly remem-

bered for his accomplished scores written with RALPH BLANE, he was a respected musical arranger and songwriter on Broadway before going on to Hollywood success. Martin was born in Birmingham, Alabama, and educated at the Birmingham Conservatory of Music. He started in show business as a singer and was cast in the ensembles of the Broadway musicals *HOORAY FOR WHAT!* (1937) and *LOUISIANA PURCHASE* (1940) where he met Blane and they started to collaborate on songs. Martin did vocal arrangements for such musicals as *THE BOYS FROM SYRACUSE* (1938), *One for the Money* (1939), *Streets of Paris* (1939), *TOO MANY GIRLS* (1939), *DUBARRY WAS A LADY* (1939), and *CABIN IN THE SKY* (1940) before he and Blane had their own score heard in the campus musical *BEST FOOT FORWARD* (1941), with both contributing to the music and the lyrics. The duo went to Hollywood for the 1943 screen version of the show and stayed, writing their most famous score the first time out: *MEET ME IN ST. LOUIS* (1944). Their other screen musicals are *Abbott and Costello in Hollywood* (1945), *Athena* (1954), *The Girl Rush* (1955), and *The Girl Most Likely* (1957), as well as the TV musical *HANS BRINKER OR THE SILVER SKATES* (1958). Returning to Broadway where he sang in *The Lady Comes Across* (1942), Martin did both music and lyrics for *Look, Ma, I'm Dancin'* (1948) and *Make a Wish* (1951) and collaborated with Timothy Gray on *High Spirits* (1964). He also returned to arranging choral music on Broadway, working on such shows as *Heaven on Earth* (1948), *AS THE GIRLS GO* (1948), *GENTLEMEN PREFER BLONDES* (1949), *Top Banana* (1951), *Hazel Flagg* (1953), and *LORELEI* (1974). Martin and Blane reteamed to write some new songs for the Broadway version of *MEET ME IN ST. LOUIS* (1989). Their most popular songs remain "Have Yourself a Merry Little Christmas."

MARTIN, MARY [Virginia] (1913–1990). Stage, film, and television performer. One of the giants of the American musical theatre, the effervescent singer–actress had several Broadway hits and some noteworthy musical films as well. Martin was born in Weatherford, Texas, and educated in Nashville and at the University of Texas before working as a dance instructor and performing in nightclubs. She made a famous Broadway debut in 1938 singing "My Heart Belongs to Daddy" as she did a funny striptease at a Siberian railroad station in *LEAVE IT TO ME!* Martin was starred as the statue Venus coming to life in *ONE TOUCH OF VENUS* (1943) and then demonstrated a

Mary Martin. Without belting or mugging, Martin managed to charm her audiences with a warm rapport that made one feel she was performing just for you. In *One Touch of Venus* (1943) she pulled a chair down to the footlights and sat and explained in the song "That's Him" how she felt about the barber Rodney Hatch. (Photofest)

totally different persona as the faithful Chinese wife Tchao-ou Niang in *Lute Song* (1946). The role of optimistic nurse Nellie Forbush in *SOUTH PACIFIC* (1949) was written with Martin in mind and in many ways it was her greatest performance, allowing her to be both funny and charming in her uniquely high-spirited way. She worked with Rodgers and Hammerstein again a decade later when she played the novice Maria in *THE SOUND OF MUSIC* (1959). Martin's other Broadway musicals include *PETER PAN* (1954), *Jennie* (1963), and *I Do! I Do!* (1966), and in London and on tour she played the title roles in *ANNIE GET YOUR GUN* and *HELLO, DOLLY!* Her film career began in 1938 doing vocals for Margaret Sullavan in *Shopworn Angel*, followed by ten movie musicals, including *The Great Victor Herbert* (1938), *RHYTHM ON THE RIVER* (1940), *LOVE THY NEIGHBOR* (1940), *Kiss the Boys Goodbye* (1941), *BIRTH OF THE BLUES* (1941), *HAPPY GO LUCKY* (1943), *NIGHT AND DAY* (1946), and *Main Street to Broadway* (1953). Few of her screen performances captured her stage magic and she never became a

bankable Hollywood star. However, she shone on the new medium of television, reprising her *Peter Pan* in 1960 and appearing in many musical specials over the years. Martin possessed a pleasing mezzo-soprano belt and she delivered her lines in a staccato form that made her stand out from most other musical ingénues. Her son is television star Larry Hagman (1931–). Autobiography: *My Heart Belongs* (1976).

MARTIN, TONY [born Alvin Morris] (1912–). Film and television performer. The handsome crooner whose romantic way with a song made him a favorite on records and in nightclubs, he played leading men in some twenty movie musicals over three decades. Martin was born in San Francisco and as a teenager played in and led his own band, going professional after graduation. He later played saxophone in Tom Gerun's orchestra and then left in 1935 to try Hollywood. Martin played bit parts in the musicals *FOLLOW THE FLEET* (1936) and *POOR LITTLE RICH GIRL* (1936) before getting character parts in *Sing, Baby, Sing* (1936), *Pigskin Parade* (1936), *Banjo on My Knee* (1936), *Sing and Be Happy* (1937), *You Can't Have Everything* (1937), *Sally, Irene and Mary* (1938), *Music in My Heart* (1940), and *ZIEGFELD GIRL* (1941). It was his romantic performance as the dashing Pepe LeMoko in the musical *CASBAH* (1948) that made him a favorite leading man, and he shone in *Two Tickets to Broadway* (1951), *Easy to Love* (1953), and *HIT THE DECK* (1955). Martin also did specialty spots in *TILL THE CLOUDS ROLL BY* (1946), *DEEP IN MY HEART* (1954), and *Meet Me in Las Vegas* (1956). He made few films after 1956 but was a frequent guest on television, singing on variety shows and specials, such as the TV musical *High Pitch* (1955). Martin was married to *ALICE FAYE* for a time and then wed *CYD CHARISSE*, with whom he has performed in nightclubs.

MARX BROTHERS. Stage, film, and television performers. Perhaps the most inspired and anarchic of all American comedy teams, their timeless comedy remains popular in memory and on celluloid. The brothers were Leonard "Chico" Marx (1886–1961) who spoke with a fractured Italian accent; Milton "Gummo" Marx (1893–1977) who gave up performing early on to become a manager; Adolph "Harpo" Marx (1888–1964) who wore a blond curly wig, played the harp, and never spoke; Julius "Groucho" Marx (1890–1977) who wore a painted mustache, sported a cigar, and made lewd wisecracks; and Herbert "Zeppo" Marx (1901–1979) who was the straight man for the others. The brothers were all born in New York and began in vaudeville together in 1917, coached by their stage mother Minnie and encouraged by their uncle AL SHEAN. One of their acts was expanded into the Broadway show *I'll Say She Is* (1924), followed by the musicals *THE COCOANUTS* (1925) and *ANIMAL CRACKERS* (1928), both of which were filmed more or less as they appeared on stage. The brothers concentrated on movies during the 1930s, turning out the musical comedies *HORSE FEATHERS* (1932), *DUCK SOUP* (1933), *A NIGHT AT THE OPERA* (1935), *A DAY AT THE RACES* (1937), and *AT THE CIRCUS* (1939), as well as such nonmusicals as *Monkey Business* (1931) and *Room Service* (1938). Their popularity waned in the 1940s, hastened by the unsuccessful *Go West* (1940), *The Big Store* (1941), *A Night in Casablanca* (1946), and *Love Happy* (1949). Groucho made brief solo appearances in the musicals *Copacabana* (1947), *Mr. Music* (1950), and *Double Dynamite* (1951), and Harpo did a guest bit in *STAGE DOOR CANTEEN* (1943). By 1949 the brothers separated and only Groucho enjoyed a continued career on radio and then television, even making a cameo appearance in a few films. Chico returned to Broadway in the revue *Take a Bow* (1944) and did some radio before retiring in the 1950s. Harpo made television appearances on occasion until his death, the first of the brothers to die. By the 1960s there was a revival of interest in the brothers and their movies became cult favorites. Only Groucho was still performing and found himself in demand for concerts and personal appearances. With their zany, physical humor, outrageous puns and verbal jokes, and touches of inspired chaos, the Marx Brothers were unique even as they represented the best of old-time vaudeville comedy. Autobiographies: *Harpo Speaks*, Harpo with Rowland Barber (1961); *Groucho and Me*, Groucho (1959); *Memoirs of a Mangy Lover*, Groucho (1964); *The Secret Word Is Groucho*, Groucho with Hector Arce (1976).

MARY (Knickerbocker Theatre 1920). A popular Cinderella musical that led the way for other similar shows in the 1920s, this romantic frolic introduced the song "The Love Nest," which swept the nation. The secretary Mary Howells (Janet Velie) is in love with Jack Keene (Jack McGowan), the son of her boss, Mrs. Keene (Georgia Caine), but Jack only seems interested in his dream of manufacturing low-priced, portable homes, which he calls "love nests," which will be affordable for young married couples just starting out. He goes out West to set up a factory to make the prebuilt homes but while digging the foundation he strikes oil. Now independently wealthy and not dependent on his mother, Jack returns East and realizes that he loves Mary. The silly libretto by OTTO HARBACH and FRANK MANDEL was prophetic about prefab homes but more importantly it lent itself to some catchy songs by LOUIS HIRSCH (music) and Harbach (lyrics), including "We'll Have a Wonderful Party," "That May Have Satisfied Grandma," "Down on That Old Kansas Farm," "Waiting," and the adoring title number. Producer GEORGE M. COHAN had touring companies of the musical out months before the New York opening so "The Love Nest" was already a hit when *Mary* premiered in Manhattan. The show ran 220 performances and started a vogue for musicals with simple female titles: *SALLY* (1920), *Suzette* (1921), *Liza* (1922), *Caroline* (1923), *Adrienne* (1923), *Marjorie* (1924), *ROSE-MARIE* (1924), *SUNNY* (1925), *PEGGY-ANN* (1926), *Betsy* (1926), *Judy* (1927), *ROSALIE* (1928), and so on.

MARY POPPINS (Disney 1964). Producer WALT DISNEY's finest musical film and the best musical fantasy since *THE WIZARD OF OZ* (1939), the movie is a splendid combination of top talent, unforgettable songs, and an intriguing tale that appeals to different ages for different reasons.

Plot: In 1910 London, the stuffy banker Mr. Banks lives on Cherry Tree Lane where his household is anything but calm. Mrs. Banks is active in the women's suffrage movement and his two young children Jane and Michael go through nannies as fast as they are hired. The arrival of Mary Poppins, an unconventional nanny who flies off a cloud and into the Banks house in answer to an advertisement in the paper, changes everything. With her magical ways, she makes everything, even cleaning a room or taking medicine, an adventure. With her pal Bert, the chimney sweep–sidewalk chalk artist, Mary and the children enter one of his pictures and have a merry day with carousel horses who go off on their own, dancing penguins, and nonsense songs with raucous street buskers. Mr. Banks, in his efforts to show his children the practical and serious side of life, takes them to his dour place of employment but the kids accidentally start a run on the bank and it looks like Mr. Banks will be fired and the family destitute. However, the experience forces him to become a more understanding and even playful father. He gets his job back, the family is closer than ever, and Mary Poppins, her job done, flies off to new adventures.

Mary Poppins. The golden age of the Hollywood musical had passed by 1964 but some scenes from the Disney musical convinced one that they were not forgotten. Pictured is Julie Andrews as the title character cutting loose with the chimney sweeps in the raucous "Step in Time" choreographed by Marc Breaux and DeeDee Wood. (Photofest)

Casts for *Mary Poppins*

Character	1964 film	2006 Broadway
Mary Poppins	JULIE ANDREWS	Ashley Brown
Bert	DICK VAN DYKE	Gavin Lee
Mr. Banks	David Tomlinson	DANIEL JENKINS
Mrs. Banks	Glynis Johns	REBECCA LUKER
Jane Banks	Karen Dotrice	Katherine Doherty
		Katheryn Faughnan
Michael Banks	Matthew Garber	Matthew Gumley
		Henry Hodges
Uncle Albert	ED WYNN	
Ellen	Hermione Baddeley	
Mrs. Brill	Reta Shaw	Jane Carr
Bird Woman	Jane Darwell	Cass Morgan
Mr. Dawes	Dick Van Dyke	
Miss Andrew		Ruth Gottschall

Bill Walsh and Donald Da Gradi wrote the top-notch screenplay that was based on P. L. Travers' children's books, yet took plenty of liberties with various aspects of the popular series. JULIE ANDREWS made a "practically perfect" screen debut as Mary, finding charm in efficiency and playfulness even while maintaining a stiff upper lip. Karen Dotrice and Matthew

Garber gave uninspired performances as the children but the rest of the cast was lively and animated even when they were in live action. DICK VAN DYKE got to play the Cockney Bert, as well as the caricatured old bank president Mr. Dawes, and the veteran comic Ed Wynn, in his last screen appearance, was a cartoon come alive as Bert's jolly Uncle Albert who can't help floating up in the air every time he laughs. The use of animation and live action was the most sophisticated and inventive yet seen, and the decor for both real and fantastical worlds was colorful and evocative. RICHARD M. and ROBERT B. SHERMAN wrote their best film score for *Mary Poppins*. The variety is considerable, yet all the songs seem to be part of one musical point of view. The Oscar-winning "Chim-Chim-Cheree" is easy-going yet mysterious, and many of the songs linger in memory not only because they are tuneful but they often have similarly twofold emotion to them. The other hits from the score were the vigorous march "A Spoonful of Sugar," the slaphappy nonsense song "Supercalifragilisticexpialidocius," the rousing polka "Step in Time," and the expansive "Let's Go Fly a Kite." Yet equally as accomplished were the lullaby "Stay Awake," the contagious romp "Jolly Holiday," and the indelible ballad "Feed the Birds." Rarely has the music for a children's movie gone so many wonderful places. Robert Stevenson directed the huge production with just the right tone that allowed reality and fantasy to coexist, MARC BREAUX and DEEDEE WOOD choreographed (the rooftop "Step in Time" number was particularly exciting), and Peter Ellenshaw did the special effects, which were as wondrous as they were fun. *Mary Poppins* was such a hit at the box office that Disney and other studios tried desperately for years to copy the formula and repeat its success, yet never succeeding.

Mary Poppins (film) Musical Numbers

"The Perfect Nanny"
"Sister Suffragette"
"The Life I Lead"
"A Spoonful of Sugar"
"Jolly Holiday"
"Supercalifragilisticexpialidocius"
"Stay Awake"
"I Love to Laugh"
"Feed the Birds"
"Fidelity, Fiduciary Bank"
"Chim-Chim-Cheree"
"Step in Time"
"Let's Go Fly a Kite"

Mary Poppins (New Amsterdam Theatre 2006) had been such a hit in London that the advance sale, thanks to the Disney promotion machine, was considerable so the mixed notices seemed to make little difference. Julian Fellows wrote the libretto, omitting several scenes from the film, changing some of the characters considerably (Mrs. Banks is no longer a suffragette but a Victorian lady feeling inadequate), and using material from the original Travers stories, such as bringing in Mr. Banks' gorgon of a governess Miss Andrew when Mary Poppins abandons the family for a while. At times it was a darker tale, frightening even, yet most of the production numbers were bright, lavish, and often only slightly connected to the plot. "Step in Time" resembled the movie's setting and situation, but "Supercalifragilisticexpialdocius," "A Spoonful of Sugar," and "Jolly Holiday" seemed more like numbers in a music hall revue, dazzling but without purpose. Five of the Sherman brothers songs were cut and seven new ones by Anthony Drewe and George Stiles were added, including "Brimstone and Treacle," "Anything Can Happen," "Being Mrs. Banks," "and "Practically Perfect." CAMERON MACKINTOSH co-produced with Disney Theatrical Productions, Richard Eyre directed, and Matthew Bourne choreographed and none of them were shy about spending money; the production values were sensational, particularly Bob Crowley's sets and costumes. Although *Mary Poppins* was not as difficult a ticket to get as when Disney's *THE LION KING* (1997) first opened, business was brisk and a long run is expected.

MASSEY, ILONA [born Ilona Hajmassy] (1912–1974). Film and stage performer. A Hungarian opera singer with an international reputation in films and opera houses, the stunning blonde sang in five Hollywood musicals. Massey was born in poverty in Budapest and worked as a seamstress to pay for music lessons. She sang in the chorus at the Staats Opera before graduating to leading stage roles and featured parts in Viennese films. Massey was brought to Hollywood in 1937 to sing opposite EDDY NELSON in *ROSALIE* (1937) and the two were also teamed in *BALALAIKA* (1939) and *Northwest Outpost* (1947). Her other Hollywood musicals are *New Wine* (1942) and *Holiday in Mexico* (1945). She was starred on Broadway in *ZIEGFELD FOLLIES* (1943) and then made many nonmusicals where she was usually cast as a sultry spy. Massey also acted on television and had her own variety show in the 1950s. The avid anti-Communist became an American citizen in 1947 and was active in movements to boycott Russian trade.

MATTHEWS, JESSIE [Margaret] (1907–1981). Stage and film performer. A popular singing–dancing star of the London stage and British screen, she is one of the very few Brits to find notoriety in America even though she rarely worked on Broadway or in Hollywood. A native Londoner, one of eleven children in an impoverished family, Matthews was dancing on the stage professionally by the age of ten. As a teenager, she appeared in the chorus of London musicals and acted in some silent films. After understudying GERTRUDE LAWRENCE, she was featured in three revues in New York: *ANDRE CHARLOT'S REVUE* (1924), *EARL CARROLL VANITIES* (1927), and *Wake Up and Dream!* (1929). Of her London book musicals, Matthews gave her best performance in Rodgers and Hart's *EVER GREEN* (1930), which she filmed (as *Evergreen*) in 1934. Her other British stage musicals include *One Dam Thing After Another* (1927), *This Year of Grace* (1928), *Hold My Hand* (1931), *Come Out to Play* (1940), and *Maid to Measure* (1948). Matthews was the most famous musical personality in 1930s British movies, starring in the musicals *Out of the Blue* (1931), *The Good Companions* (1933), *It's Love Again* (1936), *Sailing Along* (1937) and others, and her popularity spread to America where she starred in a few Hollywood films, including the musical *TOM THUMB* (1958). A graceful dancer with a winning personality, Matthews was dubbed the "Dancing Divinity" and continued to perform into the 1980s. She was married to actor–singer–director Sonny Hale (1902–1959). Autobiography: *Over My Shoulder* (1974); biography: *Jessie Matthews*, Michael Thornton (1974).

MATURE, VICTOR [John] (1913–1999). Film and stage performer. The muscular American actor with European good looks, he was mostly known for his rugged action pictures in the 1940s and 1950s but revealed a lighter side in his musicals. Mature was born in Louisville, Kentucky, was educated at a military academy, and acted in stock companies and at the Pasadena Playhouse before making his screen debut in 1939. He played only minor roles so he went to Broadway where he was noticed as the hunky movie star Randy Curtis in *LADY IN THE DARK* (1941). After serving in World War II,

he returned to Hollywood and got better parts, usually cast as beefy athletes, tough cowboys, noble slaves, and biblical characters. Mature possessed a self-mocking grin that he showed to advantage in the screen musicals *Song of the Islands* (1942), *MY GAL SAL* (1942), *Footlight Serenade* (1942), *Seven Days' Leave* (1942), *RED, HOT AND BLUE* (1949), *Las Vegas Story* (1952), and *Million Dollar Mermaid* (1952). Never a subtle or nuanced actor, Mature got to spoof his own image and shortcomings as an untalented movie star in the film *After the Fox* (1966) and then he retired.

MAXWELL, [Marvel] **MARILYN** (1921–1972). Film, television, and stage performer. A curvy blonde with bright eyes and a smooth singing voice, she shone in a handful of Hollywood musicals and is most remembered introducing the seasonal favorite "Silver Bells" with BOB HOPE in *The Lemon Drop Kid* (1951). Maxwell was born in Clarinda, Iowa, and grew up on the road as her mother was a piano accompanist for the touring dancer Ruth St. Denis. She was on stage as a young child and then later sang with bands and acted at the Pasadena Playhouse. Maxwell made her screen debut in 1942 and was seen in small roles in the musicals *Presenting Lily Mars* (1943), *DuBarry WAS A LADY* (1943), *Thousands Cheer* (1943), and *Swing Fever* (1943). Fame came when she was featured on Hope's radio show and when she toured with him during World War II to entertain the troops. Her touching supporting performance as the saloon gal Belle in *SUMMER HOLIDAY* (1948) led to leading roles in the musicals *The Lemon Drop Kid, Rock-a-Bye-Baby* (1958), and *The Lively Set* (1964). In the 1950s Maxwell also performed on television where she had her own show, played many roles in stock, and even toured with a nostalgic burlesque show.

MAYO, [Archibald L.] **ARCHIE** (1891–1968). Film director. A busy director at WARNER BROTHERS and 20TH CENTURY-FOX, he helmed every kind of movie, including eight musicals. Mayo was born in New York City and was on the stage briefly before working as an extra in 1916. Soon he was directing comedy shorts and by 1926 was helming features as diverse as *The Sap* (1929) and *The Petrified Forest* (1936). Mayo's musicals include *My Man* (1928), *Is Everybody Happy?* (1929), *GO INTO YOUR DANCE* (1935), *The Great American Broadcast* (1941), *ORCHESTRA WIVES* (1942), and *Sweet and Low Down* (1944).

MAYO, VIRGINIA [born Virginia Clara Jones] (1920–2005). Film, television, and stage performer. The voluptuous leading lady of the 1940s who was partnered with DANNY KAYE in musicals, the glamorous blonde was an accomplished actress with many dramatic roles to her credit, but audiences liked her best in light comedies and musicals. Mayo was born in St. Louis, the daughter of a newspaper reporter, and took dancing lessons as a child. She performed in vaudeville, at the local MUNICIPAL OPERA, and had a featured role on Broadway in the musical *Banjo Eyes* (1941) before a talent scout from Hollywood spotted her and she was cast in a small role in the bio-drama *Jack London* (1943). Mayo was in the chorus of Kaye's first musical, *UP IN ARMS* (1944), and was noticed by audiences and producers so she got better parts in such musicals as *Seven Days' Leave* (1944), *Wonder Man* (1945), *The Kid From Brooklyn* (1946), *The Secret Life of Walter Mitty* (1947), and *A Song Is Born* (1948), the last four also with Kaye. Her other screen musicals are *Always Leave Them Laughing* (1949), *The West Point Story* (1950), *Painting the Clouds With Sunshine* (1951), *Starlift* (1951), *She's Working Her Way Through College* (1952), and *She's Back on Broadway* (1953). Mayo made few films after 1957 but was frequently seen on television. While her singing in movie musicals usually had to be dubbed, Mayo's screen presence was impressive in both dramas and lighter fare. Autobiography: *Virginia Mayo: The Best Years of My Life*, with L. Van Savage (2002).

MAYTIME (Shubert Theatre 1917). Although it was inspired by a German operetta, this musical hit was a favorite with wartime audiences and American troops stopping in New York on their way to Europe.

Plot: The New York heiress Otillie Van Zandt loves the poor working-class Richard Wayne but the romance is broken up by Otillie's class-conscious father Colonel Van Zandt and Ottilie is persuaded to marry her weak-willed cousin Claude. Fifteen years later, Richard and Otillie meet at Mme. Delphine's nightclub. He has been very successful in business and is now one of New York's most monied and respected men. The two lament what might have been and then part. Twenty-five years later, Claude has died and left so many debts that Ottilie has been forced to sell her home. Richard buys it at auction, presenting it as a gift to Ottilie. Three decades later, both Richard and Ottilie are dead but their grandchildren Dicky and Otillie have fallen in love and plan their future together as they sit in the same garden where Richard and Otillie had fallen in love.

RIDA JOHNSON YOUNG adapted the European operetta *Wie einst im Mai*, Americanized the setting and the characters, and the producing SHUBERTS billed the show as a "musical play" with no mention of its German roots. Young also wrote the graceful lyrics for SIGMUND ROMBERG's entrancing music, and the score was one of the finest of its era. "Will You Remember?" was the most popular number because it was used so effectively throughout the musical as a leitmotif for the two different generations of lovers. However, there was a lovely bittersweet flavor to all the score, keeping the show very romantic without being tragic. *Maytime* was a sensation from the start. The demand for tickets was so great that the Shuberts opened a second company of the show in a theatre across the street to handle the demand for tickets. Road companies proliferated for years, and the operetta has remained in the frequently performed repertory of light opera companies ever since.

Cast for *Maytime*	
Ottille Van Zandt	PEGGY WOOD
Richard Wayne	CHARLES PURCELL
Col. Van Zandt	Carl Stall
Matthew Van Zandt	William Norris
Claude	Douglas J. Wood
John Rutherford	Ralph Herbert
Ermintrude D'Albert	Gertrude Vanderbilt
Rudolpho	Arthur Albro
Dicky Wayne	Charles Purcell

Maytime (stage) Musical Numbers

"In Our Little Home, Sweet Home"
"It's a Windy Day at the Battery"
"Gypsy Song"
"Will You Remember (Sweetheart)?"
"Jump Jim Crow"
"The Road to Paradise"
"Spanish Dance"
"Odd Lots, Job Lots"
"Reminiscence"
"Selling Gowns"
"Dancing Will Keep You Young"
"Only One Girl for Me"

■ *Maytime* (MGM 1937) only used one song from the Romberg–Young score, the lovely "Will You Remember?," and it was used throughout the movie as the romantic theme song. The rest of the score was a hodge-podge of opera selections, old standards, and new numbers by HERBERT STOTHART, ROBERT WRIGHT, and GEORGE FORREST, including selections from a fictitious opera called *Czaritza*. Gone with the stage score was the story, replaced by a melodramatic screenplay by Noel Langley in which the heroine, an aging opera star named Marcia Mornay (JEANETTE MACDONALD), advises a young man in love to follow his heart and then, in a long flashback, recalls her own youth. As a budding opera diva, she fell in love with the handsome singer Paul Allison (NELSON EDDY) but her shrewd manager Nicolai Nazaroff (John Barrymore) convinced her to think of her career first, so she broke off the romance and wed Nazaroff. When Paul came back into her life later, the jealous Nazaroff shot and killed him. The story ends back in the present with Marcia singing a duet version of "Will You Remember?" with Paul's ghost. While the stage work was quietly affecting, the movie is rather blatant and obvious. However, it is a beautifully produced film with impressive production values, and the singing by MacDonald and Eddy is first rate even if the acting is a bit strident. ROBERT Z. LEONARD directed the movie, which also featured HERMAN BING, Lynne Carver, Tom Brown, Paul Porcasi, and SIG RUMANN, and it was another box office hit for MacDonald and Eddy.

MAZZIE, MARIN (1960–). Stage and television performer. The classy, beautiful singer–actress has established herself as a major Broadway musical artist after only a few but impressive performances. Mazzie was born in Rockford, Illinois, and educated at Western Michigan University before appearing in musicals in regional theatre. She made her New York debut as Kitty in an Off Broadway revival of *WHERE'S CHARLEY?* (1983) and then was a replacement for leading roles in *BIG RIVER* (1985) and *INTO THE WOODS* (1989). Mazzie originated the role of the Italian mistress Clara in *PASSION* (1994) and then played the complex, maturing Mother in *RAGTIME* (1998), receiving plaudits for both performances. She also shone as the fiery Lilli Vanessi/Katherine in the popular 1999 revival of *KISS ME, KATE*, which she reprised in London in 2002. Most recently Mazzie has been a replacement for Aldonza/Dulcinea in *MAN*

OF LA MANCHA (2003) and for the Lady of the Lake in *SPAMALOT* (2007). She has appeared on television in series and musical specials.

MCANUFF, DES (1952–). Stage director and producer. A versatile director who has staged everything from avant-garde pieces to splashy Broadway musical revivals, he is also a recognized producer in regional theatre. McAnuff was born in Toronto, Canada, and studied briefly at the Ryerson Polytechnical Institute before quitting school to write for television. He wrote, produced, and directed stage productions in Toronto before coming to the States when he was twenty-four years old. McAnuff made his New York debut in 1977 with his surreal staging of the fantasy *The Crazy Locomotive* Off Broadway. The next year he co-founded the Dodger Theatre Company and continued to direct in Manhattan and regionally. McAnuff served as artistic director of the La Jolla Playhouse in California from 1983 to 1994 where he introduced new works, such as *BIG RIVER* (1985), *THE WHO'S TOMMY* (1993), and *JERSEY BOYS* (2005), and revived traditional ones, such as *HOW TO SUCCEED IN BUSINESS WITHOUT REALLY TRYING* (1995), and sending them on to Broadway. His productions tend to be very visual and to use bold images, such as the wooden plank version of the Mississippi River in *Big River* and the use of television screens in *Tommy*. As a producer, he and his Dodger Theatricals have produced his Broadway directing credits as well as *FOOTLOOSE* (1998), *URINETOWN* (2001), *THOROUGHLY MODERN MILLIE* (2002), *Dracula, the Musical* (2004), *Good Vibrations* (2005), and others. McAnuff has taught on the faculty of Juilliard and the University of California at San Diego, and he has written plays and composed music for film and television. In 2007 he was named producing director of the Stratford Festival in Canada.

MCCAREY, [Thomas] **LEO** (1898–1969). Film director, producer, and writer. One of Hollywood's most successful directors and screenwriters, he helmed ten musicals and produced the most popular of them. McCarey was born in Los Angeles, where he worked as a boxer and a miner before going to law school but gave up his practice in 1918 to become an assistant director and a writer for comedy shorts for Hal Roach and Charles Chaplin. He supervised and wrote many of the LAUREL and HARDY silents before moving on to features where he specialized in comedies such as

Ruggles of Red Gap (1935) and *The Awful Truth* (1937), often serving as writer and producer as well. McCarey's musicals range from the zany *Duck Soup* (1933) to the sentimental *Going My Way* (1944). His other musicals include *Red Hot Rhythm* (1929), *The Kid From Spain* (1932), *Belle of the Nineties* (1934), *Love Affair* (1939), *The Bells of St. Mary's* (1945), and *An Affair to Remember* (1957).

McCarthy, Joseph. See TIERNEY, Harry

McCarty, Mary (1923–1980). Stage, television, and film performer. A tough-looking character actress with a fine singing belt, she gave top-notch performances in every media and every genre. McCarty was born in Winfield, Kansas, and was on screen as a juvenile, usually playing one of the secondary kids in vehicles for Shirley Temple or Jane Withers. As an adult she sang with bands and in nightclubs, acted in a few 1940s films, and appeared in the Broadway musicals *Sleepy Hollow* (1948), *Small Wonder* (1948), *Miss Liberty* (1949), and *Bless You All* (1950). McCarty's screen musicals as an adult include *Ice-Capades Revue* (1942), *Hit Parade of 1947*, *The French Line* (1954), *Babes in Toyland* (1961), and *All That Jazz* (1979). She enjoyed a comeback on Broadway with her show-stopping performances as the old hoofer Stella Deems in *Follies* (1971) and then as a replacement for Mrs. O'Dare in *Irene* in 1973 and as the prison matron Mama Morton in the original cast of *Chicago* (1975). McCarty was a regular on the early TV variety series *The Admiral Broadway Revue* (1949) and appeared on many shows in the 1950s. She returned to television at the end of her career, completing a season as a regular on *Trapper John, M.D.* before she died.

McCauley, Jack [Bernard] (1900–1980). Stage performer. A genial leading man in musicals, his gentle singing voice and light-footed soft-shoe technique made him a laid-back favorite. A native New Yorker, McCauley made his Broadway bow in *Earl Carroll Vanities* (1923) and was featured in other revues, such as *The Little Show* (1929), *Hey Nonny Nonny!* (1932), *Life Begins at 8:40* (1935), *At Home Abroad* (1935), *The Show Is On* (1936), *The Streets of Paris* (1939), *Count Me In* (1942), *Ziegfeld Follies* (1943), and *Sing Out, Sweet Land* (1944). He played character parts in the book musicals *Hit the Deck* (1927) and *The Gang's All Here* (1931), but his two best roles were his last two: the breezy father Henry

Longstreet in *High Button Shoes* (1947) and the "button king" Gus Esmond in *Gentlemen Prefer Blondes* (1949).

McCracken, Joan (1917–1961). Stage and film performer. A superb ballet dancer on Broadway, she was also adept at comic character roles. A native of Philadelphia, McCracken studied dance as a child, and was an early student of George Balanchine before becoming a professional dancer for the American Ballet Company, Eugene Loring's Dance Players, Radio City Music Hall, and tours across the States and in London. She made her Broadway debut as the farm girl Sylvie in *Oklahoma!* (1949) in which she was also featured in the "Laurey Makes Up Her Mind" dream ballet. McCracken was very funny as the impatient Daisy in *Bloomer Girl* (1944), the moll Maribelle Jones in *Billion Dollar Baby* (1945), and the exuberant dancer Betty Lorraine in *Me and Juliet* (1953). She also shone in a handful of dramas, particularly in *The Big Knife* (1949). McCracken appeared on screen in *Hollywood Canteen* (1944) and played the vivacious co-ed Babe Doolittle in the second movie version of *Good News!* (1946). Before her premature death from heart disease and diabetes, she toured with various dance companies and was featured in some television musical specials. McCracken was married to dancer–choreographer–director Bob Fosse for a time.

McDaniel, Hattie (1895–1952). Film and television performer. Although she will be forever remembered as Mammy in *Gone With the Wind* (1939), the round African American character actress acted in different media and broke social barriers in each one. McDaniel was born in Wichita, Kansas, the daughter of a Baptist preacher and his church-singing wife, and sang as a child. She was a band vocalist before making her screen debut in 1932 and was quickly noticed for her large size, expressive eyes, and firm voice. McDaniel rarely got to play anything but maids and other servile types but she usually shone with dignity and humor. Her finest musical role was the riverboat cook Queenie in *Show Boat* (1936) but she also lit up such musicals as *I'm No Angel* (1933), *Harmony Lane* (1935), *The Little Colonel* (1935), *Music Is Magic* (1935), *Carefree* (1938), *Merry-Go-Round of 1938*, *Thank Your Lucky Stars* (1946), and *Song of the South* (1946). McDaniel was the first African American to sing on network radio, the first to win an Academy Award (for *Gone*

With the Wind), the first to star in her own television series (*Beulah*), and the first to be buried in Los Angeles's exclusive Rosedale Cemetery. Biographies: *Hattie McDaniel: Black Ambition, White Hollywood*, Jill Watt (2007); *Hattie: The Life of Hattie McDaniel*, Carlton Jackson (1993).

McDᴏɴᴀʟᴅ, Aᴜᴅʀᴀ [Ann] (1970–). Stage, television, and film performer. With her opera-quality voice—a crystal clear soprano that seems to rise out of deep, earthy tones— and her classic kind of beauty that mixes the softness of Western tradition with striking African features, she is one of the most unique actress–singers working today. McDonald was born in 1970 in Berlin, Germany, the daughter of American parents who were stationed there in the military, and grew up in Fresno, California. She was educated at Juilliard in New York and the American Conservatory Theatre School in San Francisco before making her Broadway debut as a replacement in *Tʜᴇ Sᴇᴄʀᴇᴛ Gᴀʀᴅᴇɴ* in 1991. McDonald quickly gained recognition as the perky textile worker Carrie in the 1994 revival of *Cᴀʀᴏᴜsᴇʟ*, and the next season she shone as the indignant opera student Sharon in *Master Class* (1995), followed by her tragic servant girl Sarah in *Rᴀɢᴛɪᴍᴇ* (1998), the murderous Creole in *Marie Christine* (1999), and the spinster Lizzie in *110 ɪɴ ᴛʜᴇ Sʜᴀᴅᴇ* (2007). McDonald also shine in the nonmusicals *Henry IV* (2003) and *A Raisin in the Sun* (2004). In addition to her CDs in which she tackles both new works and song standards, McDonald is very popular on the concert stage and has sung with several of the nation's finest symphonies. She has also given notable performances in staged concert versions of *Pᴀssɪᴏɴ, Sᴜɴᴅᴀʏ ɪɴ ᴛʜᴇ Pᴀʀᴋ ᴡɪᴛʜ Gᴇᴏʀɢᴇ, Dʀᴇᴀᴍɢɪʀʟs*, and other challenging works, some of which have been televised. McDonald has appeared in many other musical specials on television, including the TV version of *Aɴɴɪᴇ* (1999). She has also acted in a few films, including the musical *Tʜᴇ Cʀᴀᴅʟᴇ Wɪʟʟ Rᴏᴄᴋ* (1999).

McDᴏɴᴀʟᴅ, Gʀᴀᴄᴇ ᴀɴᴅ Rᴀʏ. Stage and film performers. Dancing and singing siblings on Broadway and in films, both exuded a perky, wholesome, spirited persona in their musicals. Grace (1918–1999) and Ray McDonald (1920–1959) were born in Boston and went into vaudeville at a young age, honing their tapping skills and becoming polished performers by the time they made their Broadway bow as two of the teens in *Bᴀʙᴇs ɪɴ Aʀᴍs* (1937), stopping the show each night with their sprightly rendition of "I Wish I Were in Love Again." Grace was featured in the revue *One for the Money* (1939) and the book musical *Vᴇʀʏ Wᴀʀᴍ ꜰᴏʀ Mᴀʏ* (1939) while Ray was in the revue *Crazy With the Heat* (1941) before they were brought to Hollywood together. Ironically, the two never appeared in the same film musical together. The boyish-looking Ray played well-scrubbed juveniles who shone, singing the title song in *Tɪʟʟ ᴛʜᴇ Cʟᴏᴜᴅs Rᴏʟʟ Bʏ* (1946) with Jᴜɴᴇ Aʟʟʏsᴏɴ and introducing "Pass That Peace Pipe" with Jᴏᴀɴ McCʀᴀᴄᴋᴇɴ in *Gᴏᴏᴅ Nᴇᴡs!* (1947). His other screen musicals were *Bᴀʙᴇs ᴏɴ Bʀᴏᴀᴅᴡᴀʏ* (1941), *Born to Sing* (1942), *Presenting Lily Mars* (1943), *There's a Girl in My Heart* (1949), and *All Ashore* (1952). He returned to Broadway for the short-lived musical *Park Avenue* (1946) and appeared on some television variety shows before his premature death. Grace McDonald had a more successful career, making seventeen Hollywood musicals in the 1940s and playing more substantial roles, although many of them were B pictures. She made her screen debut in *Dancing on a Dime* (1941) and gained recognition the next year introducing "Mr. Five By Five" in *Behind the Eight Ball* (1942). Her other musicals include *What's Cookin'?* (1942), *Give Out Sisters* (1942), *Strictly in the Groove* (1943), *It Ain't Hay* (1943), *Gals, Inc.* (1943), *Crazy House* (1943), *Follow the Boys* (1944), *My Gal Loves Music* (1944), *Honeymoon Ahead* (1945), and *See My Lawyer* (1945). Grace married a Marine and retired from films. Ray McDonald was married to actress Peggy Ryan (1924–2004).

McGɪʟʟɪɴ, Hᴏᴡᴀʀᴅ (1953–). Stage and television performer. A dark and dashing leading man with a rich, operatic voice, he is usually cast in sinister roles. A native of Los Angeles, McGillin was educated at the University of California at Santa Barbara before beginning his television career in the 1970s, appearing in soap operas, miniseries, sit-coms, and drama series. He was a soloist in concerts with major symphony orchestras before making his New York debut at the Pᴜʙʟɪᴄ Tʜᴇᴀᴛʀᴇ as Marcel in *La Boheme* (1984). After serving as a replacement for various roles in *Sᴜɴᴅᴀʏ ɪɴ ᴛʜᴇ Pᴀʀᴋ Wɪᴛʜ Gᴇᴏʀɢᴇ* (1984), McGillin was noticed as the delightfully suspicious John Jasper in *Tʜᴇ Mʏsᴛᴇʀʏ ᴏꜰ Eᴅᴡɪɴ Dʀᴏᴏᴅ* (1985), followed by *Aɴʏᴛʜɪɴɢ Gᴏᴇs* (1987) in which he played stowaway Billie Crocker opposite Pᴀᴛᴛɪ LᴜPᴏɴᴇ. In 1988 he took over as the Phantom in *Tʜᴇ Pʜᴀɴᴛᴏᴍ ᴏꜰ ᴛʜᴇ Oᴘᴇʀᴀ*, returning to it again in 1999 and singing the role over 1,600 times, more than any other performer. McGillin's other New York musical credits include SHE LOVES ME (1993) and AS THOUSANDS CHEER (1998), as well as replacing others in major roles in THE SECRET GARDEN (1991) and KISS OF THE SPIDER WOMAN (1999). His powerful singing–acting voice has been used in the animated films THE SWAN PRINCESS (1994), THE HUNCHBACK OF NOTRE DAME (1996), and South Park: Bigger, Longer and Uncut (1999).

McGUIRE, WILLIAM ANTHONY (1885–1940). Stage and film director and writer. A multitalent who wrote and directed plays and musicals in the 1920s, he could not sustain his career. McGuire was born in Chicago and worked as a journalist for the South Bend (Indiana) News while he started to write plays. He first found success with his plays Six Cylinder Love (1921) and Twelve Miles Out (1925) but soon concentrated on musicals, writing sketches for various revues, including the ZIEGFELD FOLLIES, and book shows, such as Kid Boots (1923), ROSALIE (1928), THE THREE MUSKETEERS (1928), WHOOPEE! (1928), and other hits. He also directed the last three, as he did with a handful of other plays and musicals, such as Betsy (1926), Show Girl (1929), Ripples (1930), and Smiles (1930). McGuire was a smart showman and a practical writer and director, understanding the value of entertainment rather than art, but his career suffered from his alcoholism and by the 1930s no one would work with him anymore. He then went to Hollywood and wrote scripts for such musicals as The Kid From Spain (1932), ROMAN SCANDALS (1933), THE GREAT ZIEGFELD (1936), Rosalie (1937), LILLIAN RUSSELL (1940), and ZIEGFELD GIRL (1941) before his premature death.

McHUGH, FRANK [born Francis Curray McHugh] (1898–1981). Film, television, and stage performer. A busy character actor with a silly, high-pitched giggle and a forlorn look, he played best friends and other congenial types in over 125 films, including twenty-one musicals. McHugh was born in Homestead, Pennsylvania, where his parents ran a stock theatre company and he gained acting experience from a young age. He made his Broadway bow in 1927 and was in some comedies, dramas, and the musical Show Girl (1929) before heading to Hollywood for a busy career of thirty years. Among his musical credits are Top Speed (1930), KISS ME AGAIN (1931), FOOTLIGHT PARADE (1933), Happiness Ahead (1934), GOLD DIGGERS OF 1935, Stars Over Broadway (1935),

Stage Struck (1936), Mr. Dodd Takes the Air (1937), GOING MY WAY (1944), Bowery to Broadway (1944), STATE FAIR (1945), Carnegie Hall (1947), THERE'S NO BUSINESS LIKE SHOW BUSINESS (1954), Say One for Me (1959), and Easy Come, Easy Go (1967). McHugh concentrated on television in the 1960s and returned to Broadway as a replacement for Senex in A FUNNY THING HAPPENED ON THE WAY TO THE FORUM in 1963.

McHUGH, JIMMY (1892–1969). Stage and film composer. A very successful songwriter who struck gold in nightclubs, on Tin Pan Alley, on Broadway, and in Hollywood, he mostly collaborated with lyricists DOROTHY FIELDS and HAROLD ADAMSON. McHugh was born in Boston and worked as an office boy at the Boston Opera House, later plugging, writing, and publishing songs. He first gained attention for the songs he wrote with Fields for the Cotton Club revues in Harlem, some of which were heard in the team's Broadway revue BLACKBIRDS OF 1928. After scoring Hello, Daddy (1928) and International Revue (1930), McHugh and Fields went to Hollywood where they provided the songs for the early musical Love in the Rough (1930), followed by Hooray for Love (1935) and EVERY NIGHT AT EIGHT (1935). McHugh was teamed with lyricist TED KOEHLER for KING OF BURLESQUE (1935) and Dimples (1936) and then began his fruitful collaboration with Adamson, with the two writing scores for nineteen movie musicals, including Banjo on My Knee (1936), Hitting a New High (1937), Top of the Town (1937), Mad About Music (1938), That Certain Age (1938), HIGHER AND HIGHER (1943), Four Jills in a Jeep (1944), SOMETHING FOR THE BOYS (1944), Nob Hill (1945), Doll Face (1945), Calendar Girl (1947), and If You Knew Susie (1948). With FRANK LOESSER he wrote songs for Buck Benny Rides Again (1940), Seven Days' Leave (1942), and HAPPY GO LUCKY (1943), and with JOHNNY MERCER You'll Find Out (1940) and You're the One (1941). He returned to Broadway to score The Streets of Paris (1939) with AL DUBIN and AS THE GIRLS GO (1948) with Adamson. McHugh wrote dozens of hit songs, including "I Can't Give You Anything But Love," "I'm in the Mood for Love," "On the Sunny Side of the Street," "I Feel a Song Comin' On," "Cuban Love Song," and "I Couldn't Sleep a Wink Last Night." Several of his songs were used in the movie musical The Helen Morgan Story (1957), in which he made a brief screen appearance, and in the Broadway revue SUGAR BABIES (1979).

McKayle, Donald (1930–). Stage, film, and television choreographer and director. An expert choreographer and sometime director, he made a splash more than once on Broadway even though his work there was limited. McKayle was born in New York City and educated at City College of New York before founding the Donald McKayle Dance Company in 1951, choreographing new and familiar pieces for the next seventeen years. He staged his first dances for the theatre in 1961 when he did the choreography for the Off Broadway revue *Free and Easy*. After doing the period dances in classic revivals by the New York Shakespeare Festival, he made an auspicious Broadway debut with his choreography for the boxing musical *Golden Boy* in 1964. McKayle's dances also sparkled in two vibrant Broadway revues, *Sophisticated Ladies* (1981) and *It Ain't Nothin' But the Blues* (1999). He directed and choreographed the award-winning *Raisin* (1973). McKayle also worked in regional theatre and in London, choreographed some films, such as *Bedknobs and Broomsticks* (1971) and *The Jazz Singer* (1980), and television musicals, such as *Minstrel Man* (1977) and *Cindy* (1978). He taught at several schools—from Juilliard to the University of Oregon to the Neighborhood Playhouse—and choreographed for such dance companies as the Harkness Ballet and the Alvin Ailey City Center Dance Theatre. His work could be very traditional, as in the smooth, gliding numbers in *Sophisticated Ladies*, or inventively original, such as the explosive boxing sequences set to music in *Golden Boy*.

McKechnie, Donna (1940–). Stage, television, and film performer. The tall, leggy dancer–actress has rarely played leads on Broadway but has always lit up the stage in supporting roles in musicals. McKechnie was born in Detroit and took ballet lessons as a child. At the age of fifteen she ran away from home and went to New York to become a dancer. McKecknie was on Broadway in the chorus of *How to Succeed in Business Without Really Trying* (1961) before getting featured in *The Education of H'Y'M'A'N K'A'P'L'A'N* (1968). She worked with choreographer Michael Bennett for the first time as one of the dancing office workers in *Promises, Promises* (1968). The two later married and she did his choreography as Kathy in *Company* (1970) and as Cassie in *A Chorus Line* (1975). Her other musical credits include *On the Town* (1971), *Music! Music!* (1974), *Annie Warbucks* (1993), and *State Fair* (1996). McKechnie has played leading roles in touring productions, such as *Sweet Charity*, and has appeared in a few films, including a dancer in *Billie* (1965) and as the singing Rose in *The Little Prince* (1974). She began her long television career as a dancer in *Hullabaloo* in the 1960s and in the 1980s was featured on the TV series *Fame*. McKechnie has also appeared in television series and specials. Autobiography: *Time Steps: My Musical Comedy Life* (2006).

McKneely, Joey (1965–). Stage choreographer. A recent yet impressive choreographer, he has widely varied credits. McKneely was born in New Orleans, Louisiana, and went to New York City right after high school graduation to be a dancer on Broadway. For seven years he appeared in such productions as *Roza* (1987), *Starlight Express* (1987), *Carrie* (1988), and *Jerome Robbins' Broadway* (1989). He turned to choreographing in the mid-1990s, working regionally and choreographing tours of *Crazy for You* and *Annie Get Your Gun*. McKneely made an auspicious Broadway debut in 1995 staging the musical numbers in the long-running revue *Smokey Joe's Cafe*, followed by the dances in darker musicals such as *The Life* (1997) and *The Wild Party* (2000), and his musical staging of the lounge-like numbers in *The Boy From Oz* (2003) was also applauded. McKneely did uncredited work on *The Capeman* (1998) and *On the Town* (1999). McKneely is an eclectic choreographer, assimilating various kinds of dance, from Roaring Twenties to Motown pop to Las Vegas-type show biz. He has also choreographed for the popular *Encores!* series in New York.

McLeod, Norman Z[enos]. (1898–1964). Film director. A Hollywood director with fifteen musicals to his credit, he worked with the greatest comics of his day, from the Marx Brothers to Danny Kaye. McLeod was born in Grayling, Michigan, the son of a clergyman, educated at the University of Washington, and served as a pilot in World War I before entering films in 1919 as an animator and titles writer for silents. His experience flying got him the job as assistant director on Howard Hawks' *Wings* (1927) and the next year he started directing features on his own. McLeod helmed all genres but was most accomplished with comedies and musicals. Among his credits in the latter category were *Horse Feathers* (1932), *Many Happy Returns* (1934), *Coronado* (1935), *Pennies From Heaven* (1936), *Lady, Be Good* (1941), *Panama Hattie* (1942), *The Kid From Brooklyn* (1946), *The Secret Life of Walter Mitty* (1947), *Road to Rio* (1947), and *The Paleface* (1948).

McMartin, John (1932–). Stage, television, and film performer. A dapper, sandy-haired leading man who later eased into another career as crusty and colorful senior citizens, he has enjoyed a varied career over nearly fifty years. McMartin was born in Warsaw, Indiana, raised in Minnesota, and educated at Columbia University. He made an auspicious New York debut as Billy Jester in the Off Broadway spoof LITTLE MARY SUNSHINE (1959) and in 1966 was widely applauded for his neurotic Oscar in SWEET CHARITY, which he got to reprise in the 1969 screen version. His other memorable musical roles include the disillusioned Benjamin Stone in FOLLIES (1971), Cap'n Andy in the popular 1995 revival of SHOW BOAT (1995), the wistful, drunken uncle Willie in HIGH SOCIETY (1998), the Mysterious Man in INTO THE WOODS (2002), and the blueblood Major Bouvier in GREY GARDENS (2006). McMartin's other stage musicals include The Conquering Hero (1961) and Happy New Year (1980). He has also appeared in a variety of plays in New York and in regional theatre and been featured on television for many years in everything from soap operas to sit-coms. McMartin has made a number of movies but very rarely was he given a chance to sing on screen.

McNally, Terrence (1939–). Stage writer. The prolific author of comedies and dramas on and Off Broadway, he turned to writing musicals late in his career and sometimes found remarkable success. McNally was born in St. Petersburg, Florida, raised in Corpus Christie, Texas, and studied at Columbia University. By the late 1960s his plays were being produced Off Broadway and, although several would eventually transfer to Broadway, the ideal venue for his edgy and knowing works was in the smaller Off Broadway houses. Among his many admired plays are The Ritz (1973), Frankie and Johnny in the Clair de Lune (1987), Love! Valour! Compassion! (1994), and Master Class (1995). McNally first got involved with musicals when he did unaccredited work on Here's Where I Belong (1968) and then decades later was asked to rewrite the libretto for THE RINK (1984). His subsequent New York musical scripts include KISS OF THE SPIDER WOMAN (1993), RAGTIME (1998), THE FULL MONTY (2000), and A Man of No Importance (2002), all adapted from previous source material. While his plays are usually loosely plotted and take a Chekhov-like approach to playwriting, McNally's musical librettos are tightly structured, economically plotted, and true to their source material.

Me and Juliet (Majestic Theatre 1953). An atypical Rodgers and Hammerstein work in that it is more musical comedy than musical play, the show may be the team's least effective work yet it still has some superb songs. Backstage during the run of a Broadway musical called Me and Juliet, assistant stage manager Larry (Bill Hayes) falls in love with the chorine Jeanie (Isabel Bigley) and, despite the interference of Jeanie's ex-boy friend, electrician Bob (Mark Dawson), the two are united by the time the onstage show comes to its happy conclusion. Also in the large cast were RAY WALSTON, JOAN MCCRACKEN, Arthur Maxwell, and GEORGE S. IRVING. OSCAR HAMMERSTEIN's original libretto avoided all of the clichés of backstage musicals but didn't replace them with much that was very interesting, resulting in a rather dull show. However, the performers were proficient enough, Jo Mielziner's complicated sets showing different view points of the stage were impressive, and director GEORGE ABBOTT and choreographer ROBERT ALTON kept the piece moving. The score may not rank with the team's best but it included the tango-like ballad "No Other Love," the bubbly "It's Me," the flowing "Marriage Type Love," the wry "Intermission Talk," and the bizarre tribute to audiences called "The Big Black Giant." Reviews registered disappointment and the musical ran 358 performances, only on the strength of its huge advance sale. Revivals are very rare indeed.

Me and My Girl (Marquis Theatre 1986). It took nearly half a century for this London hit to come to Broadway but the production was so joyous it was worth the wait. The carefree Cockney Bill Snibson (Robert Lindsay) is discovered to be the long-lost heir to an earldom but when he tries to bring his Lambeth girlfriend Sally Smith (Maryann Plunkett) with him into high society, the bluebloods turn their noses up until she becomes lady-like enough for their tastes. The exceptional cast also included JANE CONNELL, GEORGE S. IRVING, Jane Summerhays, Timothy Jerome, Nick Ullett, and Thomas Toner. The 1937 British musical comedy by Noel Gay (music), L. Arthur Rose, and Douglas Furber (book and lyrics) was given a bit of revision by Stephen Fry for a 1985 London revival and was so popular the producers risked bringing it to Broadway. The reviews were enthusiastic (especially for the clowning of Lindsay), the public was thrilled, and the new–old show ran 1,420 performances. The charming score included the contagious hit "(Doin') The Lambeth Walk" and such tuneful numbers as "Once You Lose Your Heart," "Leaning on a Lamppost," "You Would If You Could," and the jolly title song. MIKE OCKRENT directed and Gillian Gregory choreographed the musical, which was the premiere attraction at the new Marquis Theatre.

ME NOBODY KNOWS, THE (Helen Hayes Theatre 1970). An uncommonly poignant musical, the revue voiced the concerns and dreams of children and young adults in contemporary inner city society. Stephen M. Joseph, Herb Shapiro (book), Gary William Friedman (music), and Will Holt (lyrics) wrote the piece, which was based on Robert H. Livingston's book, a collection of writings from kids, and the show was an engrossing collage of voices and songs that expressed their feeling about a variety of subjects and revealed an undaunted optimism despite their environment. The young cast included Irene Cara, Northern J. Calloway, José Fernandez, Hattie Winston, Melanie Henderson, and Kevin Lindsay, and among the memorable songs were "Dream Babies," "Sounds," "If I Had a Million Dollars," "Light Sings," and "Let Me Come In." The musical had a successful run Off Broadway and was welcomed on Broadway by both the press and the public. Livingston directed and PATRICIA BIRCH choreographed the revue that ran 378 performances.

MEDFORD, KAY [born Maggie O'Regin] (1914–1980). Stage, film, and television performer. A delightful character actress with a continual look of disapproval, she specialized in playing mothers of different ethnic backgrounds. The native New Yorker worked as a waitress in nightclubs while waiting for her big break and then put together her own act and eventually found success in cabarets in New York and London. She made her Broadway bow in *PAINT YOUR WAGON* (1951) and thereafter was employed steadily in all three media. Medford is most remembered for playing Fanny Brice's mother in *FUNNY GIRL* (1964), both on Broadway and in the 1968 film version, and DICK VAN DYKE's stage mother Mae Peterson in *BYE BYE BIRDIE* (1960). Her other stage musicals include *John Murray Anderson's Almanac* (1953), *Almost Crazy* (1955), *MR. WONDERFUL* (1956), *CAROUSEL* (1957), and *PAL JOEY* (1963). Medford made several films and was featured on many television series and variety shows.

MEEHAN, THOMAS (1929–). Stage and film writer. One of the least known and yet most prosperous Broadway librettists, he has written or co-written some of the biggest hits of the past three decades. The native New Yorker was educated at Hamilton College and then tried writing plays but found no encouragement so he wrote for television and for *The New Yorker* magazine. Meehan turned to screenwriting in 1970, co-writing the MEL BROOKS films *To Be or Not to Be* (1983) and *Spaceballs* (1987), and then struck gold with his first Broadway musical, *ANNIE* (1977). Although his scripts for *I Remember Mama* (1979) and *Ain't Broadway Grand* (1993) did not succeed, his librettos (co-written with Brooks) for *THE PRODUCERS* (2001) and for *HAIRSPRAY* (2002) were well-crafted and inspired, as well as very popular. He revised the London musical *Bombay Dreams* (2004) for Broadway to little avail but was in much better form for *YOUNG FRANKENSTEIN* (2007), also co-written with Brooks. Meehan also co-authored the screenplays for *Annie* (1982) and *The Producers* (2005).

MEEK, DONALD (1878–1946). Stage and film performer. A small, balding character actor who often played worried men whose personality tended to reflect the actor's name, he appeared in hundreds of theatre productions in New York and on the road before finding a second, lucrative career in Hollywood. Born and educated in Glasgow, Scotland, Meek was a child performer who acted with Henry Irving and then toured to Australia, Boston, and New York before he ever appeared on a London stage. He served in the Spanish-American War where he contracted yellow fever and lost most of his hair, prompting him to play character parts. Meek made his Broadway bow in the musical *Going Up!* (1917) and was a familiar face on stage up through 1932, featured in comedies and the musicals *Nothing But Love* (1919) and *My Princess* (1927). He made a few silent films in the 1920s but in the 1930s he returned to Hollywood and was used in dozens of comedies, melodramas, and musicals, such as *Murder at the Vanities* (1934), *THE MERRY WIDOW* (1934), *TOP HAT* (1935), *PENNIES FROM HEAVEN* (1936), *ARTISTS AND MODELS* (1937), *Little Miss Broadway* (1938), *Hullabaloo* (1940), *BABES ON BROADWAY* (1942), *DuBARRY WAS A LADY* (1943), *TWO GIRLS AND A SAILOR* (1944), and *STATE FAIR* (1945).

MEET ME IN ST. LOUIS (MGM 1944). A musical favorite with audiences over the

Casts for *Meet Me in St. Louis*

Character	1944 film	1959 television	1989 Broadway
Esther Smith	JUDY GARLAND	JANE POWELL	Donna Kane
John Truitt	Tom Drake	Tab Hunter	Jason Workman
Mr. Smith	Leon Ames	WALTER PIDGEON	GEORGE HEARN
Mrs. Smith	Mary Astor	MYRNA LOY	Charlotte Moore
Tootie Smith	MARGARET O'BRIEN	Patty Duke	Courtney Peldon
Rose Smith	LUCILLE BREMER	JEANNE CRAIN	Juliet Lambert
Grandpa	Harry Davenport	ED WYNN	Milo O'Shea
Katie	MARJORIE MAIN	Reta Shaw	BETTY GARRETT

decades because of its warm nostalgia, the film succeeds because it is sentimental without being maudlin. The nearly plotless movie celebrates domestic life, which was more precious than ever during World War II when the musical was first released.

Plot: In the summer of 1903, all of St. Louis is excited because in one year the World's Fair will be held there. The Smith family of Kensington Avenue goes through the four seasons with anticipation, heartbreak, and finally joy. The eldest daughter Rose gets engaged, her sister Esther falls in love with the boy next door, and little Tootie Smith has a Halloween adventure she'll never forget. When banker Mr. Smith is offered a higher position if he will move to the New York City office, the family is in turmoil. Once father realizes how much their old house and old friends mean to them, he turns down the offer and the Smiths go off to the opening of the Louisiana Purchase Exposition of 1904.

Fred Finklehoffe and IRVING BRECHER wrote the uneventful yet totally satisfying screenplay, based on a series of stories by Sally Benson. Director VINCENTE MINNELLI turned each section into a visual and emotional postcard, and choreographer CHARLES WALTERS staged the songs with a simple but thrilling joy, as in the famous "The Trolley Song." However, many of the movie's memorable moments come from book scenes, such as the mischievous Tootie's bold confrontation with a "witch" on Halloween. The cast was splendid from the stars to the minor bit parts, each a vivid characterization that seemed to glow through the haze of nostalgia for an America long gone. Producer ARTHUR FREED later stated that *Meet Me in St. Louis* was his favorite of all the musicals he presented at MGM and it is not difficult to understand why. Some period songs were mixed with new numbers by HUGH MARTIN and RALPH BLANE and it is a credit to their score

Meet Me in St. Louis (film) Musical Numbers

"Meet Me in St. Louis (Louis)"
"The Boy Next Door"
"Skip to My Lou"
"Under the Bamboo Tree"
"Over the Bannister"
"The Trolley Song"
"You and I"
"Have Yourself a Merry Little Christmas"

that all the musical numbers blend into a whole. Old favorites included "Skip to My Lou" and "Under the Bamboo Tree," with the second done as a charming parlor entertainment by JUDY GARLAND and MARGARET O'BRIEN. "The Trolly Song" sounded like an old standard, the wistful "The Boy Next Door" had the simplicity of an early Tin Pan Alley ballad, and "Have Yourself a Merry Little Christmas" has proven its timelessness by remaining a holiday favorite for over five decades. Of all the scores Martin and Blane wrote together and with others for Broadway and Hollywood, none approaches the warm and emotional pull that this one has.

☐ *Meet Me in St. Louis* (CBS-TV 1959) could not capture the period charm in a studio but it did have an all-star cast who were successful in making the characters come alive without recalling the famous movie performers. The two-hour broadcast, also written by Finklehoffe and Belcher, was able to keep much of the story and score from the screen, and the David Susskind production was tenderly directed by George Schaefer. ☉ *Meet Me in St. Louis* (Gershwin Theatre 1989) was not so fortunate. The libretto by HUGH WHEELER built up some of the secondary roles, such as the maid Katie, played with zest by BETTY GARRETT, weakened the story by concentrating on the minor plot points, and failed to shed any light on the characters. New songs by Blane and Martin, including "Wasn't It Fun?," "Be Anything But a Girl," "Paging Mr. Sousa," and "You Are for Loving," added little and even the familiar, beloved numbers were not presented effectively. The leading roles were played competently by unknowns and the supporting cast was composed of veterans who were more interesting than the material they had to work with. The critics thought the production poorly directed and choreographed and could find little to recommend. Audiences came for an unprofitable run of 252 performances. The musical was later revised to resemble the movie more and has been produced successfully by amateur groups across the country.

MELODY TIME (Disney 1948). The last of a series of animated musical anthology films that WALT DISNEY made in the 1940s, this one is perhaps the best because of its wide variety, encompassing American folklore, boogie woogie, and Latin-flavored pieces. The film is made up of seven different segments, with the most familiar two based on mythic folk heroes: "The Story of Johnny Appleseed," with the voice of DENNIS DAY as Johnny, and "Pecos Bill," featuring ROY ROGERS and the Sons of the Pioneers, BOBBY DRISCOLL, and Luana Patten. A jazzy version of Rimsky–Korsakov's "The Flight of the Bumble Bee" called "Bumble Boogie" was performed by Freddie Martin and his orchestra (Jack Fina at the piano), and the ANDREWS SISTERS sang about "Little Toot" (by ALLIE WRUBEL), a small tugboat who saves an ocean liner. More solemn was a rendition of Joyce Kilmer's poem "Trees" (music by Oscar Rasbach) sung by Fred Waring and his Pennsylvanians, contrasted by the lively "Blame It on the Samba" (by RAY GILBERT and Ernesto Nazareth) in which Donald Duck and José Carioca cut loose in a Latin cafe. The remaining segment was "Once Upon a Wintertime," in which a young couple is rescued from an icy river by helpful animals and featured the singing voice of FRANCES LANGFORD. Each section had its own director, and the whole film was under the supervision of Ben Sharpsteen. Much admired today, none of the Disney anthologies were box office hits when first released.

MENJOU, ADOLPHE [Jean] (1890–1963). Film performer. With his precise mustache, suave demeanor, and well-tailored clothes, the debonair character actor had one of Hollywood's longest screen careers (1914 to 1960), which included two dozen musicals. Menjou was born in Pittsburgh, the son of a hotel manager, and was educated at military school and then at Cornell University for an engineering career. Instead he worked at various odd jobs and performed in vaudeville before appearing in some silent films, interrupting his career to serve in World War I. Returning to the movies after the war, Menjou soon found himself a matinee idol on the silent screen and the heartthrob lover or urbane playboy in such films as *Through the Back Door* (1921), *The Three Musketeers* (1921), and *A Woman of Paris* (1923). With the arrival of sound, he continued to play dapper types, even if they were older in years, in over eighty talkies, including such musicals as *Fashions in Love* (1929), *Morocco* (1930), *NEW MOON* (1930), *Little Miss Marker* (1934), *GOLD DIGGERS OF 1935*, *Broadway Gondolier* (1935), *One in a Million* (1936), *ONE HUNDRED MEN AND A GIRL* (1937), *THE GOLDWYN FOLLIES* (1938), *Syncopation* (1942), *YOU WERE NEVER LOVELIER* (1942), *Sweet Rosie O'Grady* (1943), *Step Lively* (944), *My Dream Is Yours* (1949), *Dancing in the Dark* (1949), and *Bundle of Joy* (1956).

MENKEN, ALAN (1950–). Stage and film composer. One of the most successful, awarded, and versatile of Hollywood composers since the golden age of movie musicals passed, he has created an impressive body of work in a relatively short time. Menken was born in New Rochelle, New York, the son of a dentist, and studied at New York University before writing music for television's *Sesame Street* in the late 1960s. While attending the LEHRMAN ENGEL Musical Theatre Workshops at BMI, he met lyricist–librettist HOWARD ASHMAN and the two collaborated on the short-lived Off Broadway musical *God Bless You, Mr. Rosewater* (1979) before writing the long-running musical pastiche *LITTLE SHOP OF HORRORS* (1982). The WALT DISNEY COMPANY hired the team to score animated musicals, and their first effort, the very successful *THE LITTLE MERMAID* (1989), ushered in a modest renaissance in animated musicals. The team's *BEAUTY AND THE BEAST* (1991) and *ALADDIN* (1992) were also hits, although Ashman died during the preparation of the latter and lyricist TIM RICE provided the unfinished lyrics. Menken's other animated musicals, with various collaborators, are *POCAHONTAS* (1995), *THE HUNCHBACK OF NOTRE DAME* (1996), and *HERCULES* (1997). He has scored the live-action movie musical *Newsies* (1992), the Off Broadway sci-fi musical *Weird Science* (1992), and the Madison Square Garden Theatre stage version of *A CHRISTMAS*

CAROL (1994). Menken also wrote new songs for the Broadway versions of *Beauty and the Beast* (1994) and *The Little Mermaid* (2008), as well as for the film version of *Little Shop of Horrors* (1986). His music is very tuneful, rich in harmonies, and captures the flavor of the period and locations, which vary widely from one musical to another.

MENZEL, IDINA [born Idina Kim Mentzel] (1971–). Stage and film performer. A big-voiced, nontraditional leading lady in musicals, she has quickly become a Broadway favorite who seems headed for a major career. Menzel was born in New York and raised in Syosset, New York, and studied theatre at New York University before appearing in some Off Broadway musicals. She was an unknown entity when cast as the performance artist Maureen in the Off Broadway production of *RENT* (1996) but by the time the show reached Broadway she and some of her fellow cast members were considered stars. Menzel played the hardened Kate in the Off Broadway musical *THE WILD PARTY* (2000), was a replacement for Amneris in *AIDA* in 2001, and then confirmed her power to thrill an audience as the misunderstood Elphaba in *WICKED* (2003), which she reprised in London. She then returned to Off Broadway to give taut performances as two different women in the musical *See What I Wanna See* (2005). In addition to the film version of *Rent* (2005), Menzel has appeared in handful of nonmusical movies as well. She is married to actor Taye Diggs (1971–).

MERCER, JOHNNY [born John Herndon Mercer] (1909–1976). Stage and film lyricist and composer. A favorite songwriter in Hollywood and on Broadway, he possessed an estimable talent for writing idiomatic lyrics filled with regional slang and folksy familiarity. Mercer was born in Savannah, Georgia, and as a youngster had ambitions to be a singer. He went to New York and got some singing jobs, was a vocalist with bands touring across the country, and started writing lyrics. Some of his songs were heard in the Broadway revues *GARRICK GAIETIES* (1930) and *Blackbirds of 1939*, but he had better luck in Hollywood writing scores for such musicals as *Old Man Rhythm* (1935), *To Beat the Band* (1935), *Ready, Willing and Able* (1937), *Varsity Show* (1937), *HOLLYWOOD HOTEL* (1937), *Cowboy From Brooklyn* (1938), *Garden of the Moon* (1938), *Going Places* (1938), and *Naughty But Nice* (1939) with such composers as RICHARD A. WHITING and HARRY WARREN.

Mercer collaborated with HOAGY CARMICHAEL on the score for the Broadway musical *Walk With Music* (1940) and for the next thirty years would work on both coasts with various composers, writing hit songs for both successful and unsuccessful shows. With HAROLD ARLEN, he scored the Broadway musicals *ST. LOUIS WOMAN* (1946), *SARATOGA* (1959), and the films *BLUES IN THE NIGHT* (1941), *STAR-SPANGLED RHYTHM* (1942), *THE SKY'S THE LIMIT* (1943), and *HERE COME THE WAVES* (1944). With GENE DE PAUL, he wrote the songs for the Broadway musical satire *LI'L ABNER* (1956) and the movies *SEVEN BRIDES FOR SEVEN BROTHERS* (1954) and *You Can't Run Away From It* (1956). Mercer sometimes wrote both music and lyrics, as with the Broadway show *Top Banana* (1951) and the movie musical *DADDY LONG LEGS* (1955). His other Broadway credits are *Texas, Li'l Darling* (1949) and *Foxy* (1964) and his other Hollywood musicals include *You'll Find Out* (1940), *Second Chorus* (1940), *You're the One* (1941), *THE FLEET'S IN* (1942), *YOU WERE NEVER LOVELIER* (1942), *True to Life* (1943), *THE HARVEY GIRLS* (1946), *Dangerous When Wet* (1953), *Merry Andrew* (1958), and *DARLING LILI* (1969). He also wrote many memorable theme songs for nonmusical films, such as "Moon River" and "The Days of Wine and Roses." Mercer never gave up on his singing, making many recordings over the years of his own and others' songs, and he was a cofounder of Capitol Records in 1942. His work was celebrated in the Broadway revue *Dream* (1997). Autobiography: *Portrait of Johnny: The Life of John Herndon Mercer*, with Gene Lees (2006); biography: *Skylark: The Life and Times of Johnny Mercer*, Philip Furia (2004).

MERKEL, UNA (1903–1986). Film, stage, and television performer. Specializing in wisecracking dames and no-nonsense friends of the heroine, the pinched-face character actress added a bit of zest to twenty-one Hollywood musicals. Merkel was born in Covington, Kentucky, and began her career as a stand-in for silent screen star Lillian Gish whom she resembled. She made her Broadway debut in 1927 and appeared in several comedies and dramas before returning to Hollywood and getting leading roles in melodramas in the 1920s and she remained a busy actress after sound came in. Merkel is best remembered for her supporting roles in dozens of films from the 1930s into the 1960s. Among her musical credits are *42ND STREET* (1933), *THE MERRY WIDOW* (1934 and 1952), *BROADWAY MELODY OF 1936* (1935), *BORN TO DANCE* (1936),

DESTRY RIDES AGAIN (1935), *ROAD TO ZANZIBAR* (1941), *THIS IS THE ARMY* (1943), *My Blue Heaven* (1950), *Rich, Young and Pretty* (1951), *WITH A SONG IN MY HEART* (1952), *I Love Melvin* (1953), *Bundle of Joy* (1956), *The Girl Most Likely* (1957), *Summer Magic* (1963), and *Spinout* (1966). Merkel returned to Broadway to play the mother Essie Miller in the musical *TAKE ME ALONG* (1959). She appeared in some television shows in the 1950s and 1960s, including the TV musical *ALADDIN* (1958).

MERMAN, ETHEL [born Ethel Zimmerman] (1908–1984). Stage, film, and television performer. The bold, brassy singer–actress had a famous Broadway belt, sparkling clear diction, and brazen comic timing that made her a one-of-a-kind star who could carry any musical with her Herculean stage power. Merman was born in Astoria, New York, educated on Long Island, and worked as a typist before she started singing in cabarets. She appeared in vaudeville with the comedy team of Clayton, Jackson, and [Jimmy] DURANTE and even played the Palace Theatre in Manhattan before making a sensational Broadway debut singing "I Got Rhythm" in *GIRL CRAZY* (1930). After impressive supporting performances in *GEORGE WHITE'S SCANDALS* (1931) and *TAKE A CHANCE* (1932), Merman triumphed in her first leading role, the evangelist–nightclub singer Reno

Ethel Merman. For decades the star had been acclaimed as everything from the finest belter to the funniest broad but no one called her an actress until *Gypsy* (1959). Her pushy, desperate, outrageous, yet vulnerable Mama Rose was a surprise, to say the least. Here she is with her young daughters played by Karen Moore (left) and Jacqueline Mayro. (Photofest)

Sweeney in *ANYTHING GOES* (1934). From that point on Broadway shows were built around her and she got to play such memorable characters as the manicurist-turned-society dame Nails O'Reilly Dusquesne in *RED, HOT AND BLUE!* (1936), Hollywood star Jeanette Adair in *Stars in Your Eyes* (1939), cabaret singer May Daly-turned-aristocrat-Madame DuBarry in *DUBARRY WAS A LADY* (1939), Latin American saloon owner Hattie Maloney in *PANAMA HATTIE* (1940), defense worker Blossom Hart in *SOMETHING FOR THE BOYS* (1943), sharpshooter Annie Oakley in *ANNIE GET YOUR GUN* (1946 and 1966), ambassador Sally Adams in *CALL ME MADAM* (1950), Philadelphia matron Liz Livingstone in *Happy Hunting* (1956), stage mother Rose in *GYPSY* (1959), and a replacement for matchmaker Dolly Levi in *HELLO, DOLLY!* (1970). Some of these shows were little more than vehicles and would have quickly closed had not Merman been in them. However, in musicals such as *Annie Get Your Gun* and *Gypsy*, they offered her more demanding roles and Merman rose to the occasion and proved herself much more than a savvy comic. Her movie career was scattered and Hollywood never quite knew how to use Merman on screen. She only got to recreate two of her stage portrayal on film: Reno Sweeney in *Anything Goes* (1936) and Sally Adams in *Call Me Madam* (1953). She usually played supporting characters, as in *WE'RE NOT DRESSING* (1934), *KID MILLIONS* (1934), *Strike Me Pink* (1935), *Happy Landing* (1938), *ALEXANDER'S RAGTIME BAND* (1938), and *Straight, Place and Show* (1938), or just specialty bits, as with *Follow the Leader* (1930), *BIG BROADCAST OF 1936* (1935), and *STAGE DOOR CANTEEN* (1943). Only in *THERE'S NO BUSINESS LIKE SHOW BUSINESS* (1954) was she the leading lady but as a mother figure with younger stars in the romantic spots. Her many television appearances on variety shows, ranging from *The Colgate Comedy Hour* to *The Muppet Show*, give a better picture of the stage Merman who knew how to hold an audience as few others ever did. Autobiographies: *Who Can Ask for Anything More?* (1955); *Merman*, with George Eells (1978); biographies: *Brass Diva: The Life and Legends of Ethel Merman*, Caryl Flinn (2007); *Ethel Merman: The Biggest Star on Broadway*, Geoffrey Mark (2005).

MERRICK, DAVID [born David Lee Margulois] (1911–2000). Stage and film producer. The most flamboyant and celebrated Broadway producer of the post-World War II American theatre, he presented over thirty musicals of varying quality but he always made sure everyone heard about them. Merrick was born in St. Louis and received his law degree from St. Louis University before serving as an assistant producer to Herman Shumlin. His first solo effort, the musical *FANNY* (1954), was a hit and over the decades it was followed by such popular musicals as *JAMAICA* (1957), *DESTRY RIDES AGAIN* (1959), *GYPSY* (1959), *IRMA LA DOUCE* (1960), *CARNIVAL* (1951), *OLIVER!* (1962), *HELLO, DOLLY!* (1964), *I DO! I DO!* (1966), *PROMISES, PROMISES* (1968), and *42ND STREET* (1980). Merrick also had his fair share of short-run flops, such as *Foxy* (1964), *Pickwick* (1965), and *OH, KAY!* (1990), but even his less accomplished musical productions were kept alive for a while by his shrewd showmanship and audacious publicity gimmicks, as with *SUBWAYS ARE FOR SLEEPING* (1962), *How Now, Dow Jones* (1967), and *SUGAR* (1972). His other musical credits are *TAKE ME ALONG* (1959), *DO RE MI* (1960), *I CAN GET IT FOR YOU WHOLESALE* (1962), *STOP THE WORLD—I WANT TO GET OFF* (1962), *110 IN THE SHADE* (1963), *Oh, What a Lovely War!* (1964), *THE ROAR OF THE GREASEPAINT—THE SMELL OF THE CROWD* (1965), *THE HAPPY TIME* (1968), *MACK AND MABEL* (1974), *VERY GOOD EDDIE* (1975), and *STATE FAIR* (1996). He also produced dozens of nonmusicals, from prestigious British imports to contemporary American comedies, and he produced a few nonmusical films in the 1970s. Merrick is considered the last of Broadway's great showmen. He made producing theatre a passion rather than a business venture. Biography: *David Merrick: The Abominable Showman*, Howard Kissell (1993).

MERRILL, BOB [born Henry Robert Merrill Lavan] (1921–1998). Stage, film, and television composer and lyricist. The busy and successful songwriter who could write songs as diverse as "People" and "How Much Is That Doggie in the Window?," he scored a number of hits alone and with collaborators. Merrill was born in Atlantic City, New Jersey, and raised in Philadelphia where he began his career as an actor. While serving in World War II, he started writing novelty songs and after the war wrote scripts for television and jingles for commercials. He also tried acting in movies and working on a ranch in Arizona before turning to serious songwriting, even though he had no musical training. Merrill had several songs on the charts before scoring the Broadway musical *NEW GIRL IN TOWN* (1957), which was a modest hit. More successful were *TAKE ME*

ALONG (1959) and *CARNIVAL* (1961) and then he collaborated with composer JULE STYNE and wrote lyrics only for *FUNNY GIRL* (1964) and *SUGAR* (1972), as well as the TV musicals *MR. MAGOO'S CHRISTMAS CAROL* (1962) and *THE DANGEROUS CHRISTMAS OF RED RIDING HOOD* (1965). On his own, Merrill scored the movie musical *Wonderful World of the Brothers Grimm* (1962) and the Broadway musical *Henry, Sweet Henry* (1967). His final musical credits are the Off Broadway musical *Hannah ... 1939* (1990) and the short-lived Broadway musical *The Red Shoes* (1993), which he wrote under the pen name Paul Stryker. After years without any new successes, he committed suicide. Merrill's lyrics can be both brash and silly as they are sometimes tender and inspired, and his music often has a grace and style not usually found in big Broadway musical comedies.

MERRILY WE ROLL ALONG (Alvin 1981). A short-lived STEPHEN SONDHEIM musical that was beset with libretto and production problems, the show nevertheless has a superior score and has found life after Broadway. In 1980, the famous composer and film producer Franklin Shepard (Geoffrey Horne) addresses the graduating class of Lake Forest Academy and preaches about fighting for your ideals, but in the subsequent scenes, which go backward to 1955, we see that the younger Frank (Jim Walton) lost his idealism, as well as friends and wives, by selling out. The cast also featured LONNY PRICE, Ann Morrison, JASON ALEXANDER, Sally Klein, and Terry Finn. George Furth adapted the 1934 GEORGE S. KAUFMAN–MOSS HART play of the same title, updating the tale and changing the characters from artists and writers to theatre folk. Director HAROLD PRINCE cast the show with young performers to make an ironic comment on youthful idealism, but many of the scenes about jaded adults did not play and the story line was often more confusing than intriguing. However, the Sondheim score was rich with variety: poignant character songs, lovely ballads, and incisive character numbers. Two of the songs, "Not a Day Goes By" and "Good Thing Going," enjoyed some popularity, and also excellent were the pathetically cheerful "Old Friend," the unsentimental "Now You Know," the wistful "Like It Was," the narrative number "Opening Doors," the psychotic "Franklin Shepard, Inc.," the satirical "Bobbie and Jackie and Jack," and the propulsive title song. There were a few compliments for the score but generally critics denounced the experimental piece as a failure and it closed after sixteen performances. Subsequent productions regionally (with slightly revised books) found more success, and the musical has developed into a cult favorite with many productions each year.

MERRITT, THERESA (1922–1998). Stage, television, and film performer. The hefty African American actress–singer moved back and forth from plays to musicals and found fame later in her career. Merritt was born in Emporia, Virginia, and began her career singing backup for Buddy Holly, Harry Belafonte, and other stars. She made her Broadway debut in the musical *Trumpets of the Lord* (1963) but was thereafter frequently cast in dramas as well. Among her musical credits are *Tambourines to Glory* (1963), *GOLDEN BOY* (1964), *Don't Play Us Cheap* (1972), *THE WIZ* (1976), and *God's Trombones* (1989 and 1997). Merritt's two outstanding performances were as the mother earth figure Bernice in the Off Broadway musical version of *The Member of the Wedding* called *F. Jasmine Addams* (1971) and the temperamental blues singer Ma Rainey in the play-with-songs *Ma Rainey's Black Bottom* (1984). Merritt appeared on many television programs, including her own series *That's My Mama* in the 1970s, and in several movies, most memorably as Aunt Em in *THE WIZ* (1979) and the red-hot housekeeper Jewel in *THE BEST LITTLE WHOREHOUSE IN TEXAS* (1982).

☙ MERRY WIDOW, THE (New Amsterdam Theatre 1907). The international hit musical that ushered in a new age of comic operetta, the Viennese piece remains one of the most produced musicals around the world. The light and lyrical show by Franz Lehar (music), Viktor Leon, and Leo Stein (book and lyrics) premiered in Vienna in 1905 and quickly swept Europe, revitalizing the waning waltz operetta form of the nineteenth century and introducing one of the most beloved of all musical scores. Based on a French play by Henri Meilhac, the plot concerns the impoverished European country of Marsovia and its efforts to get its richest citizen, the widow Sonia, to marry a Marsovian and keep her wealth in the country. The ambassador Popoff goes to Paris where Sonia lives and convinces the Marsovian Prince Danilo, who idles away his time in Paris cafes and nightspots, to propose to the widow. The fact that Sonia and Danilo were once lovers complicates rather than helps the situation and not until some court intrigues do the two get together again. The contagious "The Merry Widow Waltz" was the runaway hit from the operetta but also beloved by audiences were "Maxim's (Girls, Girls, Girls)" "Vilja," "Oh, Say No More," "Butterflies," "The Cavalier," "Love in My Heart," and "A Dutiful Wife." The first American production of *The Merry Widow* used a translation by Basil Hood and, featuring Ethel Jackson and DONALD BRIAN as Sonia and Danilo, was a giant success, running 416 performances. The show was so popular it started a craze for Merry Widow hats, dresses, cigarettes, and even corsets. Since then there have been twenty-eight major revivals in New York City, as well as hundreds in opera and operetta theatres across the country. One of the most successful of the Broadway revivals was the 1942 production starring Marta Eggerth and Jan Kiepura using a translation by Adrian Ross, Robert Gilbert, Sidney Sheldon, and Ben Roberts that ran 322 performances.

🎬 There have been two Hollywood versions of the operetta since sound came in. *The Merry Widow* (MGM 1934) starred JEANETTE MacDONALD and MAURICE CHEVALIER as Sonia and Danilo and featured lyrics by LORENZ HART and a screenplay by Ernest Vajda and Samson Rapaelson. The action was set back in the 1880s and the nation was called Marshovonia but most of the story was the same. ERNEST LUBITSCH directed with a graceful air, ALBERTINA RASCH did the swirling waltzes, and the Irving Thalberg production was a feast for the eye and the ear. The chemistry between MacDonald and Chevalier was elegant and witty, and the supporting cast, which included EDWARD EVERETT HORTON, HERMAN BING, UNA MERKEL, Minna Gombell, GEORGE BARBIER, STERLING HOLLOWAY, and DONALD

Casts for *The Merry Widow*

Characters	Sonia	Prince Danilo	Popoff/Baron Zelta
1907 Broadway	Ethel Jackson	DONALD BRIAN	R. E. Graham
1934 film	JEANETTE MacDONALD	MAURICE CHEVALIER	EDWARD EVERETT HORTON
1952 film	LANA TURNER	FERNANDO LAMAS	Richard Hayden
1955 television	Ann Jeffreys	Brian Sullivan	Edward Everett Horton

MEEK, was top-notch. Also lovely to look at was *The Merry Widow* (MGM 1952) but the performances and the music were less impressive. LANA TURNER (singing dubbed by Trudy Erwin) and FERNANDO LAMAS were starred, and in SONYA LEVIAN and William Ludwig's screenplay the widow was an American who had been married to a Marshovian and Danilo was a count she falls in love with while visiting the little nation. The story was as bland as the singing and even choreographer JACK COLE seemed to run out of ideas when it came to the waltzes. Curtis Bernhart directed the JOE PASTERNAK production, which also featured Una Merkel, Richard Hayden, Thomas Gomez, and John Abbott. ❑ Producer MAX LEIBMAN made a ninety-minute television version in 1955 with Anne Jeffreys and Brian Sullivan as the widow and Danilo and, abridged as it was, the production still had its charm. Dancers Bambi Linn and Rod Alexander were featured in the studio broadcast that had little in the way of spectacle but the music was still glowing.

METRO-GOLDWYN-MAYER (MGM). The biggest and most prestigious studio in Hollywood for much of the 1930s and 1940s, it was formed in 1924 by the merger of the Metro Picture Corporation, SAMUEL GOLDWYN's company, and Loew's subsidiary run by Louis B. Mayer. The three-way combination, plus Loew's vast chain of movie theatres, made MGM a powerful company from the start, and under Mayer's leadership and the expert management of Irving Thalberg as head of production it quickly became the king of Hollywood studios. By the time sound came in, MGM had the staff, facilities, and stars to grow rapidly and turn out more and better pictures than its competitors. It quickly established its reputation for movie musicals with such early hits as *THE BROADWAY MELODY* (1929), *THE HOLLYWOOD REVUE OF 1929*, and *RIO RITA* (1929). In the 1930s, the studio found great success with the *BROADWAY MELODY* series, the JEANETTE MACDONALD–NELSON EDDY operettas, the first biographical musical *THE GREAT ZIEGFELD* (1936), and the landmark fantasy musical *THE WIZARD OF OZ* (1939). MGM remained strong in the 1940s with the MICKEY ROONEY–JUDY GARLAND backstagers, unusual entries such as *CABIN IN THE SKY* (1943) and *ZIEGFELD FOLLIES* (1946), period musicals such as *MEET ME IN ST. LOUIS* (1944) and *THE HARVEY GIRLS* (1946), GENE KELLY and FRANK SINATRA vehicles such as *ANCHORS AWEIGH* (1945) and *ON THE TOWN* (1949), and FRED ASTAIRE showcases such as *EASTER PARADE* (1948) and *THE BARKLEYS OF BROADWAY* (1949). Many of these musicals were products of the Freed Unit consisting of producer ARTHUR FREED with directors VINCENTE MINNELLI, CHARLES WALTERS, and STANLEY DONEN. The studio also made many film versions of Broadway hits, such as *NAUGHTY MARIETTA* (1935), *ROSE MARIE* (1936), *BABES IN ARMS* (1939), *GIRL CRAZY* (1943), *BEST FOOT FORWARD* (1943), *ANNIE GET YOUR GUN* (1950), *SHOW BOAT* (1951), *KISS ME, KATE* (1953), *BRIGADOON* (1954), *THE STUDENT PRINCE* (1954), *GUYS AND DOLLS* (1955), *JUMBO* (1962), *GYPSY* (1962), and *THE UNSINKABLE MOLLY BROWN* (1964). MGM was hit with corporate problems, as well as a decline in movie attendance in the 1950s, but several popular musicals were still made, including *AN AMERICAN IN PARIS* (1951), *SINGIN' IN THE RAIN* (1952), *THE BAND WAGON* (1953), *SEVEN BRIDES FOR SEVEN BROTHERS* (1954), *HIGH SOCIETY* (1956), *SILK STOCKINGS* (1957), and *GIGI* (1958). By the 1960s the giant was severely wounded and the studio even auctioned off memorabilia in its property and costume warehouses to raise the much-needed cash, and in the 1970s the studio stopped releasing its own films. A merger with UNITED ARTISTS in 1981 formed the short-lived MGM/UA Entertainment, and by 1986 the studio was bought by Turner Broadcasting, which virtually turned the company into a library of classics from the past. What made the MGM musicals so special was the high level of artistry in every department, from the star talent to the art directors to the orchestras. The resulting products were lavish but rarely gaudy, boldly presented with attention paid to details, sometimes innovative but always entertaining.

MEXICAN HAYRIDE (Winter Garden Theatre 1944). A popular wartime diversion with a Latin-flavored COLE PORTER score, the musical comedy was a showcase for comedian BOBBY CLARK who did not disappoint his many fans. Down in Mexico where he is on the lam from the FBI, Joe Bascom (Clark) teams up with Lombo Campos (George Givot) in a numbers scheme and soon must don a variety of disguises to keep from being identified. The subplot involved the lady bullfighter Montana (JUNE HAVOC) and the American agent David Winthrop (Wilbur Evans) who suspects she might be in the racket with Joe. HERBERT and DOROTHY FIELDS wrote the slight but funny libretto tailored to Clark's comic talents, and Porter provided such pleasing songs as "Count Your Blessings," "I Love You" "There Must Be

Someone for Me," "Carlotta," "Abracadabra," and "Sing to Me Guitar." The MICHAEL TODD production ran 481 performances, probably on the strength of Clark in one of his most hilarious performances, but the critics were also pleased with the serviceable plot, the charming score, and the shining supporting players. ▣ UNIVERSAL PICTURES made a screen version of *Mexican Hayride* in 1948 as a vehicle for BUD ABBOTT and LOU COSTELLO, but they cut all the songs and just used some of Porter's tunes for background music.

MIDDLETON, RAY[mond Earl] (1907–1984). Stage, television, and film performer. The robust, strapping leading man with an exceptional baritone voice, he appeared intermittently on Broadway for thirty years. Middleton was born in Chicago and studied music at the University of Illinois and Juilliard for an opera career, but by 1933 he was on Broadway, playing leading roles in the musicals *ROBERTA* (1933) and *KNICKERBOCKER HOLIDAY* (1938). After appearing in *GEORGE WHITE'S SCANDALS* (1939) and serving in the Air Force during World War II, he found wider recognition as sharpshooter Frank Butler in the original cast of *ANNIE GET YOUR GUN* (1946). Middleton also shone as the symbolic husband Sam Cooper in the short-lived musical allegory *LOVE LIFE* (1948) and as a replacement for Emile de Becque in *SOUTH PACIFIC* (1950 and 1965). He frequently returned to opera but was back on Broadway to play the baffled Innkeeper in *MAN OF LA MANCHA* (1965). Middleton made some films, such as *1776* (1972), and appeared on many television series and specials, including the TV versions of *PANAMA HATTIE* (1954) and *DAMN YANKEES* (1967).

MIDLER, BETTE (1945–). Film, television, and stage performer. The sometimes outrageous, often bawdy, and always fascinating singer–actress with a big voice and even bigger emotions, she has occasionally left the world of pop music to pursue musicals. Midler was born in Honolulu and educated at the University of Hawaii at Manoa before going to New York where she was cast as a replacement on Broadway in *FIDDLER ON THE ROOF* in 1967. She jump started her career by singing in a gay bathhouse and a record contract followed, making her a nationally known pop singer by 1972. On her albums and in her concerts, Midler often sang standards and 1940s Big Band favorites. She made an auspicious film debut in the musical *THE ROSE* (1979) but her subsequent films

were nonmusicals, with the exception of *FOR THE BOYS* (1991). Midler provided the vocals for the pampered cat Georgette in the animated musical *OLIVER AND COMPANY* (1988) and was a sensational Mama Rose in the TV version of *GYPSY* (1993). In addition to many television appearances, she has given concerts across the country and on Broadway on three occasions. Autobiography: *Bette Midler: A View From a Broad* (1981); biographies: *Bette Midler: Still Divine*, Mark Bego (2002); *Bette: An Intimate Biography of Bette Midler*, George Mair (1996).

MIKADO, THE (Fifth Avenue Theatre 1885). One of the most popular of Gilbert and Sullivan's comic operettas, the musical was a hit from the start and rivals *H.M.S. PINAFORE* (1879) as the most produced of the team's works. Nanki-Poo (Courtice Pounds), the son of the Japanese Emperor, the Mikado (F. Federici), disguises himself as a minstrel singer and falls in love with the beautiful Yum-Yum (Geraldine Ulmar) who is engaged to her guardian Ko-Ko (George Thorne), the lord high executioner. Since an edict decrees that someone in the town must be executed before a month has passed, Nanki-Poo agrees to be the victim if he can be married to Yum-Yum for the month. The arrival of the Mikado with Nanki-Poo's betrothed, the fearsome spinster Katisha (Elsie Cameron), complicates matters and only by having Ko-Ko wed Katisha can the young lovers be united. W. S. Gilbert wrote the satirical libretto and the lyrics for Arthur Sullivan's music, and the score included such operetta favorites as "A Wandering Minstrel, I," "Three Little Maids (From School Are We)," "The Sun Whose Rays," "As Some Day It May Happen That a Victim Must Be Found (I've Got a Little List)," "The Flowers That Bloom in the Spring," "On a Tree By a River a Little Tom-Tit (Tit-Willow)," "Here's a How-de-Do," "A More Humane Mikado Never (Let the Punishment Fit the Crime)," and "Behold the Lord High Executioner." The first authorized production in New York (a pirated version opened a few months earlier) was produced by Richard D'Oyly Carte, directed by RICHARD BARKER, and ran 250 performances. Since then New York has seen over sixty major revivals, making it the most-produced musical in the English language in Manhattan, if not the world. In 1939 there were two updated versions of *The Mikado* on Broadway. *The Swing Mikado*, a Federal Theatre Project revival from Chicago, rearranged Sullivan's music into a Big Band swing version with an African American cast. A few months later producer MICHAEL TODD put together his own all-black version and called it *The Hot Mikado*. Charles L. Cook reorchestrated the score, and BILL ROBINSON starred as the title character.

🎬 **The Mikado** (Universal 1939) is Hollywood's only version of the comic operetta, although there have been many British and foreign language screen adaptations. The D'Oyly Carte favorite Martyn Green, who had played Ko-Ko hundreds of times on stage, reprised his risible performance in this VICTOR SCHERTZINGER-directed film that had lush and exotic production values. KENNY BAKER was top billed as Nanki-Poo and also featured were Jean Colin (Yum-Yum), John Barclay (Mikado), Sydney Granville (Pooh-Bah), and Constance Willis (Katisha), all members of the D'Oyly Carte company at the time. ☐ There have been over fifteen television broadcasts of *The Mikado* in English, some videos of stage productions and others made for television. Perhaps the most interesting one was a NBC-TV 1960 version on *The Bell Telephone Hour* starring GROUCHO MARX as Ko-Ko. Martyn Green wrote the sixty-minute adaptation and directed the all-star cast that included DENNIS KING (Mikado), ROBERT ROUNSEVILLE (Nanki-Poo), Barbara Meister (Yum-Yum), STANLEY HOLLOWAY (Pooh-Bah), and Helen Traubel (Katisha).

MILESTONE, LEWIS [born Milstein] (1895–1980). Film director and screenwriter. Known mostly for his dramatic features, he made four musicals, one an early classic. Milestone was born near Odessa, Russia, to a prosperous Jewish family who objected to his desire to become an actor so he studied engineering for a time before emigrating to America. While serving in the U. S. Army in World War I, he learned about moviemaking when he was assigned to a Signal Corps crew filming combat footage. After the war Milestone went to Hollywood where he worked first as an editor and writer before directing features in 1925. His most famous film, *All Quiet on the Western Front* (1930), grew from his experiences during the war. His first musical was *HALLELUJAH, I'M A BUM* (1933), an experimental movie that looked and sounded like no other. Milestone's other musicals were more routine: *Paris in Spring* (1935), *ANYTHING GOES* (1936), and *Melba* (1953).

🎬 **MILK AND HONEY** (Martin Beck Theatre 1961). A musical that used the modern state of Israel for its setting and subject, the show was the first Broadway effort by songwriter JERRY HERMAN. Don Appell wrote the libretto about the middle-aged American Phil (Robert Weede) who, separated from his wife, goes to Israel to visit his daughter Barbara (Lanna Saunders) who is living on a kibbutz with her Israeli husband David (TOMMY RALL). There he meets the American tourist Ruth (Mimi Benzell) and they fall into an autumnal romance, although it is complicated by Phil's marriage and Barbara's homesickness for America. For comic relief, there was a subplot about a widowed New York City yenta (Molly Picon) who is also visiting Israel looking for a suitable husband. Herman's score was a lovely mixture of ethnic and traditional Broadway sounds. The only song to enjoy any popularity was "Shalom," but also accomplished were "Independence Day Hora," "Let's Not Waste a Moment," "There's No Reason in the World," "Hymn to Hymie," and the rousing title number. Critics applauded the score, opera singers Weede and Benzell, and the scene-stealing comedienne Picon. ALBERT MARRE directed, DONALD SADDLER did the robust choreography, and the musical ran 543 performances.

MILLER, ANN [born Lucille Ann Collier] (1923–2004). Film and stage performer. One of Hollywood's most accomplished tap dancers, the dark-haired, apple-cheeked singer–actress rarely played leading roles on screen but was so memorable as second leads or the "other woman" that she became a star. Miller was born in Chireno, Texas, and grew up in southern California where she took dance lessons as a child and later got jobs dancing in nightclubs. She was only a teenager when she was cast in such movie musicals as *NEW FACES OF 1937*, *Life of the Party* (1937), *Radio City Revels* (1938), *Having Wonderful Time* (1938), *TOO MANY GIRLS* (1940), *Hit Parade of 1941* (1940), *Melody Ranch* (1940), *Time Out for Rhythm* (1941), and *Go West Young Lady* (1941). Although Miller got better roles in *True to the Army* (1942), *Priorities on Parade* (1942), *Reveille With Beverly* (1943), *What's Buzzin', Cousin?* (1943), *Carolina Blues* (1944), *Eadie Was a Lady* (1945), and *The Thrill of Brazil* (1946), she didn't get wide recognition until she danced with FRED ASTAIRE in *EASTER PARADE* (1948). She was better billed and more recognized in *The Kissing Bandit* (1948), *ON THE TOWN* (1949), *Texas Carnival* (1951), *Two Tickets to Broadway* (1951), *LOVELY TO LOOK AT* (1952), *Small Town Girl* (1953), *KISS ME,*

Ann Miller. Although she already had featured spots in eighteen movie musicals, the tap-dancing favorite did not get noticed by the public until she danced with Fred Astaire in *Easter Parade* (1948). Here she is doing a solo turn in the same movie, exuding a confidence in her dancing that was legendary. (Photofest)

KATE (1953), *DEEP IN MY HEART* (1954), *HIT THE DECK* (1955), and *The Opposite Sex* (1956). Throughout her career Miller has performed in musicals on the stage. She made her Broadway debut in the revue *GEORGE WHITE'S SCANDALS* (1939) and then decades later was a replacement for *MAME* in 1967. Miller costarred with MICKEY ROONEY in the popular Broadway salute to burlesque, *SUGAR BABIES* (1979), and later toured in the show. She also acted on stage in *ANYTHING GOES*, *HELLO, DOLLY!*, *FOLLIES*, and other musicals regionally and on tour. Miller was still performing into the 1990s.

MILLER, [Alton] **GLENN** (1904–1944). Film musician, conductor, and composer. The beloved trombone-playing orchestra leader and a giant of the Big Band era, he appeared in only two Hollywood musicals and inspired a third, yet introduced a handful of hit songs on screen. Miller was born in Clarinda, Iowa, and played trombone in the campus band while a student at the University of Colorado. He left school to play professionally with Ben Pollack's band and then studied music in New

York and composed the instrumental favorite "Moonlight Serenade." After playing in the DORSEY Brother's band he formed his own in 1935 and the new orchestra's recordings quickly climbed the charts. Hollywood cast Miller as himself in the musicals *SUN VALLEY SERENADE* (1941) and *ORCHESTRA WIVES* (1942) and he got to introduce "The Kiss Polka," "I Know Why (And So Do You)," "Chattanooga Choo Choo," "Serenade in Blue," " and "I've Got a Gal in Kalamazoo." Miller was at the peak of his popularity when he died in a plane crash while en route to Europe to entertain the troops. His life and music were the subject of the biomusical film *THE GLENN MILLER STORY* (1954) in which Jimmy Stewart played the bandleader and Joe Yukl did the trombone playing on the soundtrack. Biographies: *Chattanooga Choo Choo: The Life and Times of the World Famous Glenn Miller Orchestra*, Richard Grudens (2004); *Glenn Miller and His Orchestra*, George T. Simon (1988).

MILLER, MARILYN [born Mary Ellen Reynolds] (1898–1936). Stage and film performer. One of the brightest stars of Broadway musicals in the 1920s, the petite blonde's effervescent dancing and singing made her a beloved favorite in both revues and book musicals. Miller was born in Evansville, Indiana, and at the age of five started performing in the family's vaudeville act, touring the world for a decade before being discovered in London by producer LEE SHUBERT. He cast her in three editions of *THE PASSING SHOW* (1914, 1915, and 1917) and then she went on to star in the *ZIEGFELD FOLLIES* (1918 and 1919). Miller was applauded for her character roles as well, particularly the optimistic dishwasher *SALLY* (1920) who becomes a Ziegfeld star, the circus bareback rider *SUNNY* (1925), and the Princess Romanza in *ROSALIE* (1928). Her other musical credits include *The Show of Wonders* (1916), *Fancy Free* (1918), and *Smiles* (1930), and she got to reprise her *Sally* on screen in 1929 and her *Sunny* in 1930. After filming *Her Majesty Love* (1931), Miller returned to Broadway in the legendary revue *AS THOUSANDS CHEER* (1933) before her premature death at the age of thirty-seven. Although she played optimistic heroines who found a Cinderella-like happiness at the end of her musicals, Miller's short life was far from fairy tale-like, with three unhappy marriages and a destructive alcohol addiction. A sanitized version of her life was portrayed in the movie biomusical *Look for the Silver Lining* (1947) in which JUNE HAVER played Miller, and Judy

Garland portrayed her briefly in *TILL THE CLOUDS ROLL BY* (1946). Biography: *The Other Marilyn*, Warren G. Harris (1985).

MILLS BROTHERS. Film performers. A harmonizing trio (later a quartet) made up of siblings, they were known for their low-key, smooth sound on records, radio, and in eleven Hollywood musicals. Herbert (1912–1989), Harry (1913–1982), and Donald (1925–1999) Mills were born in Piqua, Ohio, and started doing close harmony singing in nightclubs. They were joined by their brother John (1911–1936) and the quartet found fame on the radio and on records. The four brothers played themselves and were featured in the movie musicals *THE BIG BROADCAST* (1932), *Twenty Million Sweethearts* (1934), *Operator 13* (1934), *Strictly Dynamite* (1934), and *Broadway Gondolier* (1935), introducing "Lulu's Back in Town" in the last. When John died of tuberculosis, the brother's father John Mills, Sr. (1889–1967) joined his sons and they were a quartet again, seen in the films *Rhythm Parade* (1942), *He's My Guy* (1943), *Chatterbox* (1943), *Reveille With Beverly* (1943), *When You're Smiling* (1950), and *The Big Beat* (1957). The Mills Brothers remained popular for decades and when the father died in 1967 the group was again a trio and continued to perform into the 1980s. Biography: *The Mills Brothers*, Charles Garrod (1994).

MINNELLI, LIZA [May] (1946–). Stage, film, and television performer. The hypercharged yet vulnerable actress–singer–dancer has conquered all forms of entertainment, including some memorable musicals in all media. The daughter of JUDY GARLAND and VINCENTE MINNELLI, the Los Angeles native was put on screen as a toddler in the finale moments of *In the Good Old Summertime* (1949) and was later educated at the Sorbonne in Paris before studying acting with Uta Hagen and Herbert Berghof. She appeared in summer stock as a teenager and then made her New York debut in an Off Broadway revival of *BEST FOOT FORWARD* (1963). Minnelli made an auspicious Broadway bow as the spunky artist Flora in *FLORA, THE RED MENACE* (1965) and then concentrated on concerts, recordings, and television, appearing on variety shows and specials, such as the TV original musicals *THE DANGEROUS CHRISTMAS OF RED RIDING HOOD* (1965) and voice of Dorothy in the animated film *JOURNEY BACK TO OZ* (1974) She made her adult screen debut in 1967 but became a full-fledged movie star with

Liza Minnelli. Audiences love the multitalented Minnelli but want her with sparkles, glitter, and razzle dazzle. When she donned a sweatshirt and played the unglamorous, confused Angel who returns home to her estranged mother, played by Chita Rivera, in the somber Broadway musical *The Rink* (1984), the show struggled to run. (Photofest)

her first film musical, *CABARET* (1972). Minnelli brought her popular 1972 television special *Liza With a Z* to Broadway in 1974, took over temporarily for GWEN VERDON in *CHICAGO* in 1975, and then starred in her own Broadway vehicle as Las Vegas singer Michelle Craig in *THE ACT* (1977). Her screen musical *A Matter of Time* (1976) was a failure but there was much to applaud in *NEW YORK, NEW YORK* (1977), just as there was in her performance as the disillusioned waif Angel in the Broadway musical *THE RINK* (1984). Thereafter Minnelli spent her time in concerts and on television, including the original TV musical *Sam Found Out* (1988). She has returned to Broadway as a replacement for JULIE ANDREWS in *VICTOR/VICTORIA* in 1997 and in such concert shows as *Minnelli on Minnelli* (1999). While Minnelli has suffered from physical and mental ailments and has been tabloid fodder for decades, she remains a major star in the old-fashioned manner with fans who are as devoted to her as those for her mother. Among her husbands were producer Jack Haley, Jr. (1933–2001) and entertainer Peter Allen (1944–1992). Biographies: *Under the Rainbow: The Real Liza Minnelli*, George

Mair (1996); *Liza Minnelli: Born a Star*, Wendy Leigh (1994).

MINNELLI, VINCENTE [born Lester Anthony Minnelli] (1903–1986). Stage and film director and designer. A major director of Hollywood musicals, he started with some impressive designs and staging on Broadway. Minnelli was born in Chicago, Illinois, to a family of vaudeville entertainers and was on stage at the age of three. Showing an aptitude for drawing, he quit school as a teenager and worked painting billboards and as an apprentice at a photographer's studio. Minnelli entered show business as a stage manager and costume designer for live shows produced by a Chicago motion picture theatre chain, but ended up in New York designing sets and costumes for large spectaculars at Radio City Music Hall and for musical revues on Broadway, including the *ZIEGFELD FOLLIES*. In 1935 he both designed and co-directed the popular revue *AT HOME ABROAD* (1935), followed by the colorful revue *THE SHOW IS ON* (1936) and the book musicals *HOORAY FOR WHAT!* (1937) and *VERY WARM FOR MAY* (1939). Equally impressed with Minnelli's designs as well as his staging, Hollywood hired him in 1940 and his illustrious cinema career began, never returning to Broadway again. His first feature was *CABIN IN THE SKY* (1943), followed by such notable musicals as *MEET ME IN ST. LOUIS* (1944), *Yolanda and the Thief* (1945), *ZIEGFELD FOLLIES* (1946), *THE PIRATE* (1948), *AN AMERICAN IN PARIS* (1951), *THE BAND WAGON* (1953), *BRIGADOON* (1954), *KISMET* (1955), *GIGI* (1958), *BELLS ARE RINGING* (1960), and *ON A CLEAR DAY YOU CAN SEE FOREVER* (1970). He was married to film star JUDY GARLAND and the father of singer–actress LIZA MINNELLI. Autobiography: *I Remember It Well* (1974); biography: *Vincente Minnelli: Hollywood's Dark Dreamer*, Emanuel Levy, 2007.

◻ **MINSTREL MAN** (CBS-TV 1977). A hard-hitting, uncompromising look at racial prejudice in the decades after the Civil War, the two-hour musical was remarkable in many ways, not the least of which is that it was highly entertaining. African American song-and-dance man Harry Brown, Jr. (Glynn Turman) hopes to run his own minstrel troupe, reclaiming a style of entertainment that has been taken over by whites in blackface. His quiet brother Rennie (Stanley Bennett Clay), a pianist and composer, wants to forget the old Negro traditions and create ragtime and new music for a new age. Harry's efforts turn tragic when a redneck audience turns on the all-black minstrels and lynches Harry. Rennie and the rest of the company remove their blackface makeup and lament the narrow confines of their creative abilities. The score consisted of period standards, such as "Hot Time in the Old Town Tonight," "The Band Played On," "Turkey in the Straw," and "Wait Till the Sun Shines, Nellie," and new numbers by Fred and Meg Karlin that echoed the era, such as "Ragtime Special" and "Early in the Morning." The teleplay by Richard A. and Esther Shapiro was rich in characterization and allowed for the joyous as well as the tragic elements of the story to surface. William A. Graham directed the production, which was taped on location in Mississippi, and DONALD MCKAYLE devised the expert choreography.

MIRANDA, CARMEN [born Maria do Carmo Miranda Da Cunha] (1909–1955). Film and stage performer. Billed as the "Brazilian Bombshell" because of her flamboyant personality, colorful costumes, and tongue-twisting English, the highly animated singer lit up the screen in supporting roles in fourteen Hollywood musicals. Miranda was born in Marco de Canavezes, Portugal, and when she was very young her family moved to Brazil where they ran a produce business in Rio de Janeiro. She started singing on local radio and then became a popular recording and movie star in Brazil. The SHUBERT BROTHERS brought Miranda to New York where they featured her in the Broadway revue *Streets of Paris* (1939) in which she sang "South American Way." She made her Hollywood debut as a specialty number in *DOWN ARGENTINE WAY* (1940) and then was given character parts in such musicals as *THAT NIGHT IN RIO* (1941), *WEEKEND IN HAVANA* (1941), *SPRINGTIME IN THE ROCKIES* (1942), *THE GANG'S ALL HERE* (1943), *Four Jills in a Jeep* (1944), *Greenwich Village* (1944), *SOMETHING FOR THE BOYS* (1944), *Doll Face* (1945), *Copacabana* (1947), *A DATE WITH JUDY* (1948), *Nancy Goes to Rio* (1950), and *Scared Stiff* (1953). Miranda often appeared in American nightclubs and on early television before her premature death from a heart attack.

✍ **MISS LIBERTY** (Imperial Theatre 1949). One of IRVING BERLIN's gentler, more evocative scores was heard in this musical that was not one of his long-run hits because of libretto problems. Hapless Manhattan news photographer Horace Miller (EDDIE ALBERT) tries to further his career by going to France and finding the original model for the Statue of Liberty. He mistakes the Parisian model Monique (Allyn McLerie) as the inspiration for Bartholdi's statue and brings her to New York with great hoopla. On arrival, both are denounced as frauds but they end up in each other's arms. Robert Sherwood's uneven book also had featured roles for MARY MCCARTY, Ethel Griffies, TOMMY RALL, and Herbert Berghof, and the entire cast, under the direction of MOSS HART, was commendable. So too was the score, which produced no runaway hits but included such enticing numbers as "Let's Take an Old-Fashioned Walk," "Paris Wakes Up and Smiles," "Just One Way to Say I Love You," "Only for Americans," and "Give Me Your Tired, Your Poor" with music set to the poem inscribed at the Statue of Liberty. Also of note was JEROME ROBBINS' inventive choreography. The large advance for the new Berlin musical allowed the show to run 308 performances despite a disappointing response from the press and public. ☐ An NBC-TV version of *Miss Liberty* was broadcast on *Musical Comedy Time* in 1951 with KENNY BAKER as Horace and with DORETTA MORROW and CAROL BRUCE.

☙ *MISS SAIGON* (Broadway Theatre 1991). An eagerly awaited hit from London that arrived on Broadway with a record advance, this modern retelling of the *Madame Butterfly* story was another success for the creators of *LES MISÉRABLES* (1987). American G.I. Chris (Willy Falk) falls in love with the young prostitute Kim (LEA SALONGA) during the last days of the Vietnam War and the two are separated in the rush of activity as the Americans leave Saigon to the approaching Communists. Years later Kim and her young son try to reach America with the help of the conniving Eurasian known as the Engineer (Jonathan Pryce) but they only get to Bangkok where she is reunited with Chris, now married to the American Ellen (Liz Callaway). In order to ensure that her son gets to America, Kim leaves the boy with Chris and commits suicide. Claude-Michel Schönberg wrote the music and American RICHARD MALTBY, JR. adapted the French libretto and lyrics by Alain Boublil. The show was virtually sung through and included such powerful numbers as "The Last Night of the World," "The Movie in My Mind," "Sun and Moon," "The American Dream," "Bui-Doi," "I Still Believe," "Why God Why?," and "Now That I've Seen Her." Critics carped, dismissing the CAMERON MACKINTOSH produc-

tion and only applauding the performers and the spectacular scenic effects (most memorably the helicopter scene) and the inventive direction by NICHOLAS HYTNER. Audiences disagreed, keeping the musical on the boards for 4,097 performances, followed by successful tours and then many regional productions.

◧ *MISSISSIPPI* (Paramount 1935). One of BING CROSBY's few period musicals, the film began production with LANNY ROSS in the leading role but he was so dull in the rushes that the studio replaced him with their more reliable star. Based on Booth Tarkington's novel and play *Magnolia*, the screenplay concerned the nineteenth-century pacifist Tom Grayson (Crosby) who will not fight a duel even to defend the honor of his fiancée Elvira Rumford (Gail Patrick). Not only do the Rumfords break off the engagement but Tom's family disowns him, so he gets a job singing on a riverboat piloted by the eccentric Commodore Jackson (W. C. FIELDS). During a saloon brawl, Tom must defend himself with a pistol and proves to be a crack shot. He fends off the instigator of the fight, who accidentally shoots himself with his own gun, so the Commodore bills Tom as "the singing killer." Tom eventually falls in love with Elvira's sister Lucy (Joan Bennett) and it takes all his courage and fortitude to prove to the Rumford family that he is worthy of her. Also in the cast were QUEENIE SMITH, Fred Kohler, John Miljan, and Edward Pawley. Songwriters RICHARD RODGERS (music) and LORENZ HART (lyrics) had left Hollywood and returned to New York before production even began. When Crosby asked for a ballad suitable for his persona, the twosome quickly came up with "It's Easy to Remember," which became a hit record for him after the film was released. Other songs in the score included "Down By the River" and "Soon," which also was on the charts with a recording by Crosby. As suitable as the songs were for the popular crooner, the character of Tom was not ideal for Crosby and the droll performance by Fields became the focal point of the movie. Also, the story was showing its age. *Magnolia* had been filmed as *Cameo Kirby* in 1914, 1923, and 1930 (the last being a musical version as well). A. EDWARD SUTHERLAND directed the ARTHUR HORNBLOW, JR., production.

MITCHELL, BRIAN STOKES (1957–). Stage and television performer. The dashing, ethnically mixed baritone has quickly developed into a musical leading man in the old tradition, usually playing classic roles in revivals. Mitchell was born in Seattle and grew up on army bases in Guam and the Philippines where his father was a civil engineer for the military. He began acting professionally in regional theatres in California before beginning a successful career in television in 1979, appearing in several series. He returned to the stage in the 1980s, making his New York debut in 1986 and the next performing in his first Broadway musical, *Mail* (1987). Mitchell was featured in the short-lived revival of *Oh, Kay!* (1990) and was a replacement for leading roles in *Jelly's Last Jam* (1993) and *Kiss of the Spider Woman* (1994). He finally found wide recognition as the pianist-turned-radical Coalhouse Walker in *Ragtime* (1998). His other notable musical roles on Broadway are Fred Graham/Petruchio in *Kiss Me Kate* (1999) and Cervantes/Don Quixote in *Man of La Mancha* (2002). Mitchell is active in regional theatre, concerts, and recordings and has shone in nonmusicals as well. His racial makeup is a mixture of African and Native American, German, and Scottish and he has played Hispanic and other races as well. Yet Mitchell is an old-fashioned kind of stage star whose performances are character driven and his rich, full voice is used richly but without excess.

MITCHELL, JERRY (1961–). Stage choreographer and director. A much-in-demand choreographer, he has had several hits in a short period of time. Mitchell was born in Paw Paw, Michigan, and began his career as a dancer, appearing in a handful of New York productions, most memorably as a featured dancer in *The Will Rogers Follies* (1991). He soon became more interested in choreographing so after serving as JEROME ROBBINS' assistant for the retrospective musical *Jerome Robbins' Broadway* (1989), he moved to film and television, making his professional debut as the choreographer on the movie *Scent of a Woman* (1992). Mitchell was associate choreographer for the 1994 Broadway revival of *Grease* and was first noticed for his staging of the musical numbers for *Hedwig and the Angry Itch* four years later. He found success with his dances for *The Full Monty* (2000), *The Rocky Horror Show* (2000), *Hairspray* (2002), *La Cage aux Folles* (2004), *Dirty Rotten Scoundrels* (2005), and other Broadway musicals, yet arguably his finest work to date was the extended dance sequences for the short-lived stage version of the movie musical *Swing Time* (1936), which was called *Never Gonna Dance* (2003) on Broadway. Mitchell served as director and

choreographer for *Legally Blonde* (2007). He has staged dances for national tours and for films and was resident choreographer for such television shows as *The Rosie O'Donnell Show* and *The Drew Carey Show*.

MITCHELL, JOHN CAMERON (1963–). Stage, film, and television performer and writer. The boyish-looking actor–singer has given a number of remarkable performances in his young career. Mitchell was born in El Paso, Texas, the son of actor Cameron Mitchell (1918–1994) and educated at Northwestern University. After making his Broadway debut as a replacement in the chorus of *Big River* (1985), he was noticed as the Yorkshire conjurer Dickon in *The Secret Garden* (1991) and then the toy boy Young Thing in *Hello Again* (1994). Mitchell also impressed critics with his performances in nonmusical plays, films, and television dramas. He co-wrote and played the title character in *Hedwig and the Angry Inch* (1998), reprising his performance on film in 2001 and directing it as well. Mitchell has recently concentrated in directing music videos and films.

MITCHELL, JULIAN (1852–1926). Stage director and choreographer. Arguably the most prolific stager of musicals in Broadway history, he directed and choreographed all types of musical entertainment. Mitchell was probably born in New York City, the nephew of popular stage star Maggie Mitchell, and was a dancer in a revival of *The Black Crook* in 1873 before setting out on tour with his aunt's production of *Mignon*. Mitchell worked as an actor and later as a director and choreographer for producer CHARLES HOYT, and it was his staging of the pioneering musical comedy *A Trip to Chinatown* in 1891 that made Mitchell the most in-demand director and choreographer in New York. By 1900 he abandoned acting to concentrate on his busy directing career, which lasted into the 1920s, even though he was virtually deaf in his final years. Among the legendary musicals Mitchell staged were *The Fortune Teller* (1898), *Cyranose de Bric-a-Brac* (1898), *Fiddle-Dee-Dee* (1900), *Twirly Whirly* (1902), *The Wizard of Oz* (1903), *Babes in Toyland* (1905), *It Happened in Nordland* (1904), *The Red Mill* (1906), *The Pink Lady* (1911), *Mary* (1920), *Little Nellie Kelly* (1922), *Sunny* (1925), and several editions of the *Ziegfeld Follies*. He was equally adept at musical burlesques, farce comedies, spectaculars, operettas, lavish revues, and up-to-date musical comedies. Records vary but it is estimated that he staged over eighty musicals. Mitchell was not a subtle director and liked oversized scenery, energetic dancing, and a tight tempo. His shows were often large but they moved effortlessly and demanded more from his chorus than the static tradition of just filling the stage with extras. Mitchell did not concentrate on the text as much as the musical numbers, although few of his projects had laudable scripts. No one else helped design and shape the look of the Broadway musical in the early years of the century more than Mitchell.

MITCHELL, SIDNEY (1888–1942). Film and stage lyricist. Working with a wide variety of composers, the former Broadway songwriter scored eighteen Hollywood musicals in the 1930s. Mitchell was born in Baltimore and first had his lyrics sung on Broadway in the ZIEGFELD FOLLIES (1918). He never got to write a complete score or a book musical on Broadway but his songs were featured in the revues THE PASSING SHOW OF 1921 (1920), *The Whirl of New York* (1921), and GEORGE WHITE'S SCANDALS (1923). Mitchell was in Hollywood when sound came in and wrote songs for three 20TH CENTURY-FOX musicals in 1929: *Fox Movietone Follies*, *Broadway*, and *The Cockeyed World*. Collaborating with CON CONRAD, LEW POLLOCK, SAM STEPT, and others, he scored such screen musicals as *Let's Go Places* (1930), *I Like It That Way* (1934), *Dancing Feet* (1936), *Trail of the Lonesome Pine* (1936), CAPTAIN JANUARY (1936), *Pigskin Parade* (1936), *One in a Million* (1936), *Thin Ice* (1937), IN OLD CHICAGO (1938), REBECCA OF SUNNYBROOK FARM (1938), and *Kentucky Moonshine* (1938). "All My Life," "Sugar," "You Turned the Tables on Me," and "At the Codfish Ball" are among his most known songs.

🕭 **MLLE. MODISTE** (Knickerbocker Theatre 1905). With its solid libretto, enticing songs that tied into the plot, and sharp characterizations, it is easy to see why critics considered this VICTOR HERBERT operetta the best American musical yet written.

Plot: Captain Etienne de Bouvray is in love with Fifi, a sales girl in a Paris hat shop on the Rue de la Paix, but the romance is frowned upon by Fifi's employer, Mme. Cecile, and by Etienne's rich uncle, the Compte de St. Mar. The wealthy American tourist Hiram Bent comes into the shop one day and takes a liking to Fifi, asking her what her dreams are. Fifi obliges with a song cycle explaining what she would be like on the stage. Hiram is impressed enough that he pays for singing lessons for the girl. A year later the Compte de St. Mar is throwing a party and the entertainment is the singer Mme. Bellini, the toast of all Paris. The star turns out to be Fifi and she so charms the partygoers and the Compte that he consents to a match with his nephew Etienne.

HENRY BLOSSOM wrote the well-constructed libretto in which often the action did not stop for the songs but the musical numbers continued the story and character development in a unique way. All of the characters were given distinct personality traits that raised them above the usual musical types, and much of the dialogue was vivid and amusing. Blossom also penned the lyrics for Herbert's wonderful music, and "Kiss Me Again," which was only one section of Fifi's extended "If I Were on the Stage" song medley, became the show's biggest hit. Also memorable were "The Time, the Place and the Girl," "I Want What I Want When I Want It," and "The Mascot of the Troop." The CHARLES DILLINGHAM production was cheered by the press and the public and ran 202 performances. The musical also made Fritzi Scheff a star and she played Fifi on and off for over twenty years and was asked to sing "Kiss Me Again" in all her public appearances.

Casts for *Mlle. Modiste* and *Kiss Me Again*

Character	Mlle. Modiste (1905)	Kiss Me Again (1931)
Mlle. Fifi	FRITZI SCHEFF	Bernice Claire
Etienne de Bouvray/Paul	Walter Percival	WALTER PIDGEON
Compt de St. Mar/St. Cyr	William Pruette	Claude Gillingwater
Hiram Bent/Francois	Claude Gillingwater	FRANK McHUGH
Mme. Cecile	Josephine Bartlett	Judith Vosselli
Marie Louise	Louise Le Baron	June Collyer
Rene La Motte	Howard Chambers	EDWARD EVERETT HORTON

Mlle. Modiste Musical Numbers

"Furs and Feathers, Buckles and Bows"
"When the Cat's Away the Mice Will Play"
"The Time, the Place and the Girl"
"If I Were On the Stage (Kiss Me Again)"
"Love Me, Love My Dog"
"Hats Make the Woman"
"I Want What I Want When I Want It"
"Ze English Language"
"The Mascot of the Troop"
"The Dear Little Girl Who Is Good"
"The Keokuk Culture Club"
"The Nightingale and the Star"

🕮 **Kiss Me Again** (First National 1931) was Hollywood's version of *Mlle. Modiste* and it was surprisingly faithful, retaining seven of the Herbert–Blossom songs (and no outside interpolations) and the basic story, although some of the characters' names changed. Bernice Claire and WALTER PIDGEON were the young lovers, and Claude Gillingwater, who had played the young American Hiram in the original stage production, now played the disapproving uncle. Julian Josephson and Paul Perez wrote the screenplay, and WILLIAM A. SEITER directed the film with an eye for the romantic.

MONACO, JAMES V. (1885–1945). Film composer. Usually working with lyricist JOHNNY BURKE, the Tin Pan Alley songwriter scored eleven Hollywood musicals, seven of them featuring BING CROSBY. Monaco was born in Fornia, Italy, and when he came to America found work as a pianist in nightclubs in New York. After writing some hit singles for Tin Pan Alley, he contributed music to the Broadway shows ZIEGFELD FOLLIES (1912 and 1931), *The Night Boat* (1920), and *Harry Delmar's Revels* (1927). One of his songs, "Dirty Hands, Dirty Faces," was sung by AL JOLSON in *THE JAZZ SINGER* (1927). When the Depression hit, Monaco stayed in New York writing songs for stars rather than fleeing to Hollywood. By the time he wrote his first film songs for *Doctor Rhythm* (1938) with Burke, he was an established composer in the business. With Burke he also wrote scores for the screen musicals *Sing You Sinners* (1938), *East Side of Heaven* (1939), *The Star Maker* (1939), *ROAD TO SINGAPORE* (1940), *If I Had My Way* (1940), *RHYTHM ON THE RIVER* (1940), *STAGE DOOR CANTEEN* (1943), *Pin-Up Girl* (1944), *Sweet and Low Down* (1944), and *Irish Eyes Are Smiling* (1944). Among his many hit songs are

"You Made Me Love You (I Didn't Want to Do It)," "Row, Row, Row," "I Can't Begin to Tell You," and "I've Got a Pocketful of Dreams."

MONK, DEBRA (1949–). Stage, film, and television performer and songwriter. An arresting character actress usually cast in supporting roles, she never fails to be noticed for her broad characterizations and belt singing. Monk was born in Middleton, Ohio, and educated at Frostburg State College in Maryland and Southern Methodist University in Texas. She had extensive experience in regional theatre before making her New York debut Off Broadway in 1978 and was first noticed as a performer and co-author of the songs in the quasi-revues *Pump Boys and Dinettes* (1982) and *Oil City Symphony* (1987). Monk played the funny and disturbing would-be assassin Sara Jane Moore in *ASSASSINS* (1991), the caustic New Yorker Joanne in *COMPANY* (1995), and as a replacement for Mama Morton in *CHICAGO* (2005). She has even shone in the short-lived musicals *Nick and Nora* (1991), *Steel Pier* (1997), and *Thou Shalt Not* (2001). Monk also played Mrs. Paroo in the television version of *THE MUSIC MAN* (2003). She was finally billed as a star in the Broadway musical *CURTAINS* (2007) in which she played the suspicious producer Carmen Bernstein. Monk has also been praised and awarded for some of her sterling performances in nonmusical plays, television dramas, and films.

MONROE,   MARILYN [born Norma Jean Mortensen] (1926–1962). Film performer. A Hollywood legend and icon of sexuality, the voluptuous blonde often played damaged females but in her musicals she was usually confident and fun. Monroe was born in Los Angeles into a broken home, grew up in an orphanage and in foster homes, and worked in an aircraft factory before going into films. She had a bit part in a few movies, including the musical *THE SHOCKING MISS PILGRIM* (1947), and sang two songs in the B musical *Ladies of the Chorus* (1949) before getting noticed in short but memorable scenes in the nonmusicals *The Asphalt Jungle* (1950) and *All About Eve* (1950). By the time she played Lorelei Lee in *GENTLEMEN PREFER BLONDES* (1953), Monroe was a bona fide star and, although her short career was filled with ups and downs, she remained a shining emblem of Hollywood glamour, even long after her premature death. Her other musical credits are *River of No Return* (1954), *THERE'S NO BUSINESS LIKE SHOW*

Marilyn Monroe. The Hollywood legend often played insecure and even pathetic types on screen but when she was singing and dancing in one of her movie musicals she displayed a polish and wherewithal that radiated confidence, as seen in this publicity photo taken when Monroe was filming *Gentlemen Prefer Blondes* (1953). (Photofest)

BUSINESS (1954), *Some Like It Hot* (1959), and *Let's Make Love* (1960). Monroe's husbands included baseballer Joe DiMaggio (1914–1999) and playwright Arthur Miller (1915–2005). Biographies: *Marilyn Monroe: The Biography*, Donald Spoto (2001); *Marilyn Monroe*, Barbara Leaming (2000); *Legend: The Life and Death of Marilyn Monroe*, Fred Lawrence Guiles (1992).

MONTALBAN, RICARDO [born Ricardo Gonzalo Pedro Montalban y Merino) (1920–). Film, television, and stage performer. The dashing leading man in musicals and dramas who could be either congenial or menacing, he was usually cast as Latin lovers in his nine Hollywood musicals. Montalban was born near Mexico City and educated partially in the States before returning to his native country to make films. He made his Hollywood debut in the musical *Fiesta* (1947) and then went back and forth between dramas and musicals over the next two decades. Montalban's musical credits are *On an Island With You* (1948), *The Kissing Bandit* (1948), *NEPTUNE'S DAUGHTER* (1949), *Two Weeks With Love* (1950), *Sombrero* (1953), *Latin Lovers*

(1953), *The Singing Nun* (1966), and *SWEET CHARITY* (1968), as well as the TV musical *ALICE THROUGH THE LOOKING GLASS* (1966). He has also appeared on Broadway in plays and in the musicals *Seventh Heaven* (1955) and *JAMAICA* (1957). Montalban acted in many television programs and continues to perform on the large and the small screens. Autobiography: *Reflections: A Life in Two Worlds* (1980); biography: *Ricardo Montalban: The Unauthorized Biography*, Matt O'Grady (1992).

MONTE CARLO (Paramount 1930). A featherweight musical comedy by producer–director ERNEST LUBITSCH, it was one of the superb musicals he made in the 1930s that seemed to float magically rather than unspool on the screen. The screenplay by Ernest Vajda and Vincent Lawrence, based on a German play, focused on the impoverished Countess Helene Mara (JEANETTE MACDONALD) who leaves her wealthy fiancé Count Otto Von Seibenheim (Claud Allister) at the altar and flees to Monte Carlo where she meets the aristocratic Count Rudolph Falliere (JACK BUCHANAN) who is disguised as the barber Rudy. She falls in love with him but their social differences are an obstacle to her pride. Not until she runs into Rudolph at the opera and learns of his exalted position in the world does she accept him. Also in the cast were Zasu Pitts, Tyler Brooke, John Roach, Albert Conti, and Lionel Belmore. Lubitsch told the story with charm, a wry satirical subtext, and delicate cinematographic skill. Helene and Rudolph sang the duet "Give Me a Moment, Please" on the phone and attended the fictional opera *Monsieur Beaucaire* where the plot paralleled their own situation. The most famous scene in the movie is Helene's train ride on the *Blue Express* to Monte Carlo with MacDonald singing "Beyond the Blue Horizon," waving to peasants working in the field, and the peasants joining her in song, all perfectly set to the rhythm of the train and the clinking on the rails. RICHARD A. WHITING, LEO ROBIN, and W. Franke Harling wrote the superior score, which also included the uptempo ballad "Always in All Ways." Buchanan and MacDonald made a charming couple but he left Hollywood after this film and didn't return for twenty-three years.

MONTGOMERY, DAVE (1870–1917). Stage performer. With his partner FRED STONE, he was part of the funniest and most popular musical comedy team during the first decade of the twentieth century. Montgomery was born in

St. Joseph, Missouri, and as a teenager toured with Haverley's Minstrels before teaming up with Stone in 1894 and going into vaudeville together. Their comedy was broad, based on pratfalls and exaggerated makeup, but the act developed and later added a more verbal kind of humor in which their rapid and polished repartee shone. The team's first Broadway show was *The Girl From Up There* (1901), which they repeated in London, but greater fame came with the musical comedy THE WIZARD OF OZ (1903) in which Montgomery played the Tin Woodman to Stone's Scarecrow. The pair were just as enjoyable as American tourists bumbling their way through Holland in THE RED MILL (1906) and as two Chinese sidekicks in CHIN-CHIN (1914). The team's other musical credits were *The Old Town* (1909) and *The Lady of the Slipper* (1912). Montgomery's untimely death in 1917 while they were preparing a new show quickly ended Broadway's favorite duo, although Stone continued performing solo with on-and-off success for many years.

MOON OVER MIAMI (Fox 1941). A tuneful and colorful musical diversion with a Latin flavor, the film found enough south-of-the-border romance without going any further than Florida. The screenplay by Vincent Lawrence and Brown Tolmes, based on the 1938 London play *Three Blind Mice*, concerned the waitress Kay Latimer (BETTY GRABLE) who pulls together her money and heads to Miami to snag a millionaire. Her sister Barbara (CAROLE LANDIS) poses as her secretary and her Aunt Susan (CHARLOTTE GREENWOOD) pretends to be her maid. Kay almost gets the wealthy playboy Jeffrey Bolton III (ROBERT CUMMINGS) but falls in love with not-so-wealthy playboy Phil McNeil (DON AMECHE). The opportunity for musical numbers was easy to come by, and the dances staged by HERMES PAN and JACK COLE sparkled, as did much of the score by RALPH RAINGER (music) and LEO ROBIN (lyrics), with the best songs being the freewheeling "Kindergarten Conga," the spirited ballad "You Started Something," and the daffy character song "Is That Good?," which Greenwood sang with hotel waiter JACK HALEY. WALTER LANG directed the lighthearted musical, some of it filmed on location in Florida, and it was very popular at the box office. The movie was recycled as **Three Little Girls in Blue** (Fox 1946), and the screenwriter Valentine Davies pushed the setting back to 1902. Farm girl Pam Charters (JUNE HAVER) of Red Bank, New Jersey, sets out for Atlantic City with her

sisters Liz (VIVIAN BLAINE) and Myra (VERA-ELLEN, singing dubbed by Carol Stewart) posing as her secretary and maid. The sisters end up with fortune hunter Van Damn Smith (George Montgomery, dubbed by Ben Gage), waiter Mike Bailey (Charles Smith, dubbed by Del Porter), and titled aristocrat Steve Harrington (Frank Latimore). CELESTE HOLM took Greenwood's place and supplied the comedy. Joseph Myrow (music) and MACK GORDON (lyrics) wrote the songs and some of them ("Somewhere in the Night," "This Is Always," and "On the Boardwalk in Atlantic City") captured the period nicely. However, the big hit song was the swinging, very-1940s "You Make Me Feel So Young," which was used for a dream ballet featuring Smith and Vera-Ellen. Lyricist Mack Gordon produced, H. BRUCE HUMBERSTONE directed, and SEYMOUR FELIX provided the choreography.

MOORE, CONSTANCE (1919–2005). Film, stage, and television performer. A blonde singer with glowing stage presence, she was featured in eighteen movie musicals, many of them B pictures, yet she failed to become a recognized star. Moore was born in Sioux City, Iowa, and raised in Dallas, Texas, and began as a vocalist for various bands. After singing on the radio she was brought to Hollywood where she made her screen debut in 1937 with a bit part in *You're a Sweetheart*. Moore played leads and supporting characters in all genres but was most effective in musicals, such as *Swing That Cheer* (1938), *Hawaiian Nights* (1939), *Laugh It Off* (1939), *Argentine Nights* (1940), *I'm Nobody's Sweetheart Now* (1940), *La Conga Nights* (1940), *Las Vegas Nights* (1941), *Show Business* (1944), *Atlantic City* (1944), EARL CARROLL VANITIES (1945), *Mexicana* (1945), *Earl Carroll Sketchbook* (1946), *In Old Sacramento* (1946), and *Hit Parade of 1947*. Moore also shone as the Amazon Antiope in the Broadway musical *BY JUPITER* (1942).

MOORE, GRACE [born Mary Willie Grace Moore] (1901–1947). Stage and film performer. The blonde, icy beauty was a dazzling opera soprano who gave memorable performances in some Broadway and Hollywood musicals. Moore was born in Slabtown, Tennessee, the daughter of an army colonel, and was educated in Nashville. Although she trained for an opera career, her first professional engagements were in the theatre, featured in the Broadway revues *Hitchy-Koo* (1920) and MUSIC BOX REVUE (1923 and 1924) where she introduced IRVING

BERLIN's "What'll I Do?" and "All Alone." Moore also appeared in the book musicals *Up in the Clouds* (1922) and *The DuBarry* (1932). She eventually got to her opera career, making her Metropolitan Opera debut in 1928 and later performing in Paris, Monte Carlo, and London. When sound came in, Moore tried Hollywood and her seven musical films helped popularize opera on the screen. Dubbed the Tennessee Nightingale, she was most applauded for her Italian opera diva Mary Barrett in ONE NIGHT OF LOVE (1934), but all of her musical films found favor with the public: *A Lady's Morals* (1930), NEW MOON (1930), *Love Me Forever* (1935), *The King Steps Out* (1936), *When You're in Love* (1937), and *I'll Take Romance* (1937). Moore returned to the opera house in the late 1930s and died in a plane crash over Denmark while on a European tour. KATHRYN GRAYSON played her in the musical biopic *So This Is Love* (1953). Autobiography: *You're Only Human* (1944).

MOORE, MELBA [born Melba Hill] (1945–). Stage, film, and television performer. A petite African American with a powerful vocal belt, the actress–dancer–singer gave some vivacious performances on Broadway in the 1960s and 1970s. The native New Yorker came from a musical family, her father a saxophone player who ran a club in Harlem, and she studied voice and dance at the New York High School of the Performing Arts before attending Montclair State College. She taught school for a while and then worked as a backup singer on recordings throughout the 1960s, making her Broadway debut as a member of the original cast of *HAIR* (1968), eventually moving into the role of Sheila. Moore lit up Broadway with her scintillating performance as the Southern orphan Lutiebelle in *PURLIE* (1970), a performance she reprised on the 1981 TV version. She shone as the poet's daughter Marsinah in the African reworking of *KISMET* called *TIMBUKTU!* (1978) and then returned to the New York stage decades later as a replacement for Fantine in *LES MISÉRABLES* in 1995. Moore has performed in a number of films, including the musicals *LOST IN THE STARS* (1974) and *Hair* (1979), and has appeared on television in variety shows, series, and specials. Her amazing four-octave range singing voice can be heard on many recordings.

MOORE, ROBERT (1927–1984). Stage, television, and film director and performer. A proficient director of plays and musicals, he had a large proportion of stage triumphs in his too-short life. Moore was born in Detroit, Michigan, and educated at the Catholic University of America in Washington, DC, before beginning his acting career in the 1940s. He was performing in New York by 1948, finding work on stage, on television, and in films. Moore never abandoned his acting career but started directing in the late 1950s, making his Off Broadway bow in 1961 with a revival of *The Ticket-of-Leave Man*. He became a much-in-demand director after his penetrating staging of *The Boys in the Band* in 1968, the first mainstream play about the homosexual lifestyle. This was followed by such Broadway hits as the comedy *The Last of the Red Hot Lovers* (1969), the thriller *Deathtrap* (1978), and the musicals *PROMISES, PROMISES* (1968), *LORELEI* (1974), *THEY'RE PLAYING OUR SONG* (1979), and *WOMAN OF THE YEAR* (1981). Before his untimely death, Moore also directed television dramas, sit-coms, and films, including three NEIL SIMON movies.

MOORE, VICTOR [Frederick] (1876–1962). Stage, film, and television performer. With his short dumpling frame, chicken-like walk, and whining voice, he was an easily recognized and much beloved character actor of musicals on Broadway and in Hollywood. Moore was born in Hammonton, New Jersey, and educated in Boston where he got his first acting job in 1893. After gaining experience in summer stock and touring with John Drew, he went into vaudeville with his wife Emma Littlefield and their comedy act caught on. Moore made an impressive Broadway bow as the resourceful secretary Kid Burns in GEORGE M. COHAN's *FORTY-FIVE MINUTES FROM BROADWAY* (1906); he was so liked by the audience that Cohan wrote the musical sequel *The Talk of New York* (1907) so that Moore could play Burns again. Throughout the 1920s and 1930s, he was a familiar presence on Broadway, often playing the helpless man who is easily persuaded to do things that make him miserable. He was first paired with the brash, self-assured WILLIAM GAXTON in 1931, and the contrasting duo lit up six musicals together. Moore originated such delightful characters as the Long Island butler Shorty McGee in *OH, KAY!* (1926), the hapless burglar Herbert in *FUNNY FACE* (1927), the befuddled Vice President Alexander Throttlebottom in *OF THEE I SING* (1931) and *LET 'EM EAT CAKE* (1933), gangster Moonface Martin disguised as a preacher in *ANYTHING GOES* (1934), the reluctant ambassador Alonzo P. Goodhue in *LEAVE IT TO ME!* (1938), and the squeaky-clean Senator Loganberry in *LOUISIANA*

PURCHASE (1940). His other musical credits include *The Happiest Night of His Life* (1911), *Allez-Oop!* (1927), *HOLD EVERYTHING* (1928), *HEADS UP!* (1929), *Princess Charming* (1930), *Hollywood Pinafore* (1945), and *Nellie Bly* (1946). Moore made many silent film shorts in the 1910s and later got to repeat his stage roles in the film musicals *Heads Up!* (1930) and *Louisiana Purchase* (1941). He was also featured in fourteen Hollywood musicals, including *Dangerous Dan McGrew* (1930), *The Gift of Gab* (1934), *SWING TIME* (1936), *GOLD DIGGERS OF 1937* (1936), *Life of the Party* (1937), *STAR-SPANGLED RHYTHM* (1942), *Riding High* (1943), *Carolina Blues* (1944), *Duffy's Tavern* (1945), and *ZIEGFELD FOLLIES* (1946). He appeared in some early television broadcasts, continued making nonmusical films up to 1955, and returned to Broadway one last time in 1957 to play the Starkeeper in *CAROUSEL*.

MOOREHEAD, AGNES [Robertson] (1906–1974). Stage, television, and film performer. The sharp-featured character actress usually played haughty or neurotic women on stage and in films but comic ladies on television and in musicals. Moorehead was born in Clinton, Massachusetts, the daughter of a minister, and educated at Muskingum College in Ohio, the University of Wisconsin, and Bradley University before becoming a high school English teacher and directing the school plays. She had performed in ballet as a child and was a professional dancer in her teens and each summer when she wasn't teaching Moorehead returned to the stage in summer theatres and in vaudeville. Eventually she gave up teaching, studied acting at the American Academy of Dramatic Arts, and made her Broadway debut in a play in 1929. She was also performing on national radio with ORSON WELLES who made Moorehead a member of his Mercury Theatre troupe in 1940. When Welles went to Hollywood, he brought his players with him and Moorehead made her screen debut as his mother in *Citizen Kane* (1941). After giving a superb performance in *The Magnificent Ambersons* (1942), she was established in Hollywood and over the next thirty years appeared in dozens of films, almost always in supporting roles. Although she was not a singer, Moorehead was featured in such musicals as *SUMMER HOLIDAY* (1948), *SHOW BOAT* (1951), *Main Street to Broadway* (1953), *Those Redheads From Seattle* (1953), *The Opposite Sex* (1956), *Meet Me in Las Vegas* (1956), and *The Singing Nun* (1966). She became a familiar face

on television because of the series *Bewitched* (1964–1972) and appeared on many other programs as well, such as the TV musicals *ROBERTA* (1955) and *ALICE THROUGH THE LOOKING GLASS* (1966). Moorehead returned to Broadway on occasion, as in the musical *GIGI* (1973), and frequently toured in readers theatre programs, one-woman shows, and poetry readings.

MORENO, RITA [born Rosita Dolores Alveri] (1931–). Stage, film, and television performer. This spirited, Hispanic actress–singer–dancer is one of the few performers to win an Academy, Tony, Emmy, and Grammy Award. Moreno was born in Humacao, Puerto Rico, and grew up in New York City where she was a professional dancer as a child and first appeared on Broadway at the age of thirteen in the play *Skydrift* (1945). Moreno made her film debut in 1945 and was featured in such musicals as *THE TOAST OF NEW ORLEANS* (1950), *Pagan Love Song* (1950), *SINGIN' IN THE RAIN* (1952), *Latin Lovers* (1953), and *THE VAGABOND KING* (1956), but her two best screen roles were the concubine Tuptim in *THE KING AND I* (1956) and the fiery Anita in *WEST SIDE STORY* (1961). She also appeared in dramas and comedies on screen and on Broadway and was frequently seen on television on everything from miniseries and children's programs to sit-coms and dramas.

MORGAN, DENNIS [born Stanley Morner] (1910–1994). Film and television performer. An operatic tenor with a chiseled handsome face, he was a favorite leading man in 1940s Hollywood musicals. Morgan was born in Prentice, Wisconsin, and began his career as a radio announcer and then sang opera in small-time companies before going to Hollywood in 1936. In his first musical, *THE GREAT ZIEGFELD* (1936), he was cast as the tuxedoed man who sings "A Pretty Girl Is Like a Melody" during the movie's most spectacular production number, yet his voice was dubbed by ALLAN JONES. Morgan got better parts and did his own singing in such musicals as *The Hard Way* (1942), *THE DESERT SONG* (1943), *THANK YOUR LUCKY STARS* (1943), *Shine On, Harvest Moon* (1944), *HOLLYWOOD CANTEEN* (1944), *Two Guys From Milwaukee* (1946), *The Time, the Place and the Girl* (1946), *My Wild Irish Rose* (1947), *Two Guys From Texas* (1948), *One Sunday Afternoon* (1948), *It's a Great Feeling* (1949), and *Painting the Clouds With Sunshine* (1951). Morgan portrayed heroic types in comedies and action features as well, often with JACK CARSON as his sidekick. In the 1950s he made fewer films and did a lot of television, from variety shows to Westerns to his own show in 1959. He retired from performing in 1980.

MORGAN, FRANK [born Francis Phillip Wupperman] (1890–1949). Stage and film performer. The colorful and much recognized character actor could play jovial types, menacing ones, or a combination of both, as in his Professor Marvel/Wizard in THE WIZARD OF OZ (1939). The native New Yorker was the son of a wealthy manufacturer and tried a handful of different jobs before he decided to follow in his elder brother Ralph's footsteps and become an actor. After training at the American Academy of Dramatic Arts, Morgan made his Broadway debut in a minor role in a 1914 revival of *A Woman Killed With Kindness*. He also started making films at the same time, managing both stage and movie careers until the 1930s when he devoted all his time to Hollywood. Of Morgan's two dozen Broadway credits, only a handful were musicals but he shone as King Cyril in ROSALIE (1928) and as various characters in the famous revue THE BAND WAGON (1931). His other stage musicals included *Rock-a-Bye Baby* (1918), *Her Family Tree* (1920), and *Hey Nonny Nonny!* (1932). In Hollywood Morgan quickly became a familiar face and was known for his nervous chuckle and wide-eyed double takes. He appeared in over seventy films, mostly at MGM, including twenty-one musicals, although usually he did not sing. In addition to the Wizard, his memorable roles include the Mayor in HALLELUJAH, I'M A BUM (1933), the frustrated Governor in NAUGHTY MARIETTA (1935), the promoter Billings in THE GREAT ZIEGFELD (1936), the king in *Rosalie* (1937), and the boozy Uncle Sid in SUMMER HOLIDAY (1948). Morgan's other screen musicals include *Queen High* (1930), *Broadway to Hollywood* (1933), THE CAT AND THE FIDDLE (1934), *Dimples* (1936), SWEETHEARTS (1936), BROADWAY MELODY OF 1940, *Hullabaloo* (1940), and *Yolanda and the Thief* (1945). His brother Ralph Morgan (1883–1956) was a popular stage and screen actor, usually playing villains, and his niece was the busy stage–film–televison actress Claudia Morgan (1912–1974).

MORGAN, HELEN [born Helen Riggins] (1900–1941). Stage and film performer. One of America's great torch singers, she gave some piercing performances on Broadway and on screen during her short but vibrant career. Born in Danville, Ohio, Morgan worked in a biscuit

Helen Morgan. The delicate singer–actress gave her greatest performance on stage and screen as Julie in *Show Boat* who must hide the fact that she is a mulatto married to a white man. Here she is (right) in the 1936 film version caught off guard when the cook Queenie (Hattie McDaniel) recognizes the song Julie sings as an African American favorite. (Photofest)

factory and as a manicurist before she started to sing in Chicago nightclubs and in vaudeville. She made her Broadway debut in GEORGE WHITE'S SCANDALS (1925) and also appeared in *Americana* (1926) before finding the role of her career, the tragic mulatto Julie in the original production of SHOW BOAT (1927). Her renditions of "Can't Help Lovin' Dat Man" and "Bill" made her famous and she reprised them in the 1929 part-talkie version of *Show Boat* before appearing as Julie in the celebrated 1936 film version. *Show Boat*'s songwriters OSCAR HAMMERSTEIN and JEROME KERN wrote the Broadway musical SWEET ADELINE (1929) with her in mind, and as the pathetic saloon singer Addie she introduced the torchy standard "Why Was I Born?" That same year Morgan triumphed as the tragic burlesque performer Kitty Darling in the film musical APPLAUSE, and then in 1932 she played Julie once again in the Broadway revival of *Show Boat*. Her other credits include the Broadway revue GEORGE WHITE'S SCANDALS (1936) and the film musicals *Glorifying the American Girl* (1929), *Roadhouse Nights* (1930), *You Belong to Me* (1934), GO INTO YOUR DANCE (1935), and *Frankie and Johnnie* (1935). Bouts with alcohol and depression harmed her career and after a few more appearances in clubs, she died of cirrhosis of the liver at the age of forty-one. Although Morgan might be described as a saloon singer, she was atypical of the type, being small and frail with a high but delicate soprano voice. Few performers have been able to convey such heartbreak and vulnerability in her singing as she did. In the biopic *The Helen Morgan Story* (1957), ANN BLYTH played Morgan and Googie Grant provided her singing vocals. Biography: *Helen Morgan: Her Life and Legend*, Gilbert Maxwell (1975).

MORROW, DORETTA [born Doretta Marano] (1928– 1968). Stage performer. A small, dark-haired soprano, she originated three of the musical theatre's best ingénue roles. A native of New York City, by the age of eighteen Morrow was on Broadway as the heroine Gretchen in the 1946 revival of *THE RED MILL*. Two years later she created the part of the perky English lass Kitty Verdun in *WHERE'S CHARLEY?* and then played the tragic concubine Tuptim in *THE KING AND I* (1951). Morrow's other important ingénue role was the poet's daughter Marsinah in *KISMET* (1953). Before death from cancer at the age of forty, she performed on the London stage, on tour, in one film, the musical *Because You're Mine* (1952). She also sang on television specials, such as the small screen versions of *KNICKERBOCKER HOLIDAY* (1950), *MISS LIBERTY* (1951), and *THE BEGGAR'S OPERA* (1952), and the original TV musicals *Once Upon an Eastertime* (1954), *Holiday* (1956), and *THE ADVENTURES OF MARCO POLO* (1956). Morrow possessed a lovely lyric soprano voice that did justice to "I Have Dreamed," "Stranger in Paradise," "We Kiss in a Shadow," "Baubles, Bangles and Beads," and other standards she introduced.

MORSE, ROBERT (1931–). Stage, television, and film performer. The eternally boyish leading man with a mischievous gap-toothed smile has given some memorable performances in musical hits and flops. Morse was born in Newton, Massachusetts, and after serving in the Navy in the early 1950s trained at the American Theatre Wing School and in stock companies. He made an impressive Broadway debut as the naive clerk Barnaby Tucker in the original cast of the farce *The Matchmaker* (1955), a role he got to recreate on film in 1958, followed by other youthful roles in Broadway musicals: the brash young producer Ted Snow in *Say, Darling* (1958) and the poetic New England teenager Richard Miller in *TAKE ME ALONG* (1959). Morse's most famous performance was as the sly, ambitious corporate climber J. Pierpont Finch in *HOW TO SUCCEED IN BUSINESS WITHOUT REALLY TRYING* (1961), which he reprised in the 1967 screen version. He also shone as the cross-dressing musician Jerry in

SUGAR (1972) and the would-be actor David in the short-lived *So Long, 174th Street* (1976). Morse made his screen debut in the ensemble of *ON THE TOWN* (1949) but very few of his films would be musicals. He has been very busy on television, appearing in everything from soap operas and quiz shows to drama series and providing voices for animated shows. He also starred in *THAT'S LIFE* (1969), one of the few weekly musical series ever attempted on the small screen. Morse made a triumphal return to Broadway as the writer–society czar Truman Capote in the one-person play *Tru* (1989).

MORTON, JOE (1947–). Stage, film, and television performer. A proficient African American actor who is equally adept at comedy and drama, he gave some electric performances in Broadway musicals. The native New Yorker was educated at Hofstra University and made his Manhattan acting debut in 1968 and was a replacement in *HAIR* (1970). After appearing in minor roles in the musicals *Salvation* (1969) and *Tricks* (1973) and replacing a lead in *TWO GENTLEMEN OF VERONA* (1973), he was applauded for his frustrated chauffeur Walter Younger in *RAISIN* (1973). Morton acted in several classic plays and new dramas on and Off Broadway and returned to musicals as one of the Habim twins in *Oh, Brother!* (1981) and in *Honky Tonk Nights* (1986). He has appeared in many films and television shows, although his singing talents have rarely been utilized in those media.

MOST HAPPY FELLA, THE (Imperial Theatre 1956). FRANK LOESSER'S adventurous and uneven attempt at Italianate opera, the show was a mixture of musical comedy and operetta with superb songs in both styles. The aging vineyard owner Tony (Robert Weede) proposes to the San Francisco waitress Rosabella (Jo Sullivan) in a letter and she accepts, arriving in the Napa Valley and expecting the handsome Joe (Art Lund) whose photo Tony sent her. It takes a while for Rosabella to get over her disappointment and learn to love the child-like Tony but eventually she does. Also involved in the action were Tony's jealous sister Marie (Mona Paulee), Rosabella's pal Cleo (Susan Johnson), and the comic Herman (Shorty Long). Loesser himself adapted Sidney Howard's drama *They Knew What They Wanted* (1924) and filled the show with songs, twice the usual number of a Broadway musical. "Joey, Joey, Joey," "My Heart Is So Full of You," "Somebody, Somewhere," and "Warm

All Over" were among the memorable opera-like songs, while "Standing on the Corner" and "Big D" were the best of the musical comedy numbers. The talented cast did justice to both kinds of songs, and Joseph Anthony directed the piece like a drama. Reviews were mixed but audiences responded favorably enough to let the show run 676 performances. The musical is usually revived by opera and operetta companies, and New York has seen four commendable productions over the years. Norman Atkins was the vineyard owner Tony, Paula Stewart was his bride Rosabella, and Art Lund (reprising his original performance of Joe) was the man who comes between them in a 1959 New York City Light Opera production. The same organization produced a 1966 revival with Lund as Joey and Norman Atkins (Tony), Barbara Meister (Rosabella), Karen Morrow (Cleo), and Jack De Lon (Herman). There were plenty of compliments for opera singer Giorgio Tozzi's Tony and the 1979 production directed by JACK O'BRIEN, but audiences were not interested in the operatic show and it closed after six weeks. Also in the cast were Sharon Daniels (Rosabella), Richard Muenz (Joe), Louisa Flanigan (Cleo), and Adrienne Leonetti (Marie). A scaled-down production, which reduced the orchestrations to a two-piano arrangement, had originated at the GOODSPEED OPERA HOUSE in Connecticut and some commentators felt the intimacy of it worked better for the musical so it transferred to the small Booth Theatre on Broadway in 1992 where it pleased audiences for 244 performances. The revival, directed by Gerald Gutierrez, featured Spiro Malas (Tony), Sophie Hayden (Rosabella), Charles Pistone (Joe), Liz Larsen (Cleo), and Scott Waara (Herman).

MOSTEL, ZERO [born Samuel Joel Mostel] (1915–1977). Stage, film, and television performer. The oversized, over-the-top comic actor has given unforgettable performances in all media but the stage was the genre where his bigger-than-life persona flourished. A native of Brooklyn, Mostel studied at City College and New York University to be a painter but worked as a longshoreman, a factory laborer, and in other jobs during the Depression. He performed stand-up comedy in clubs, on the radio, and in the Off Broadway revues *Keep 'Em Laughing* (1942) and *Top Notchers* (1942) before making his screen debut in a featured comic part in the musical *DuBARRY WAS A LADY* (1943). After serving during World War II, Mostel's movie and stage careers started

to take off. He rarely did screen musicals but on Broadway he was noticed as Peachum in *Beggar's Holiday* (1946) and in the revues *Concert Varieties* (1945) and *Once Over Lightly* (1955). Mostel found his two best roles late in his career: the conniving slave Pseudolus in *A FUNNY THING HAPPENED ON THE WAY TO THE FORUM* (1962) and the philosophical Russian Jew Tevye in *FIDDLER ON THE ROOF* (1964 and 1976). Because he was blacklisted in the 1950s for refusing to name Communists he knew, he got no film or television work but was active in theatre, acting in such demanding dramas as *Ulysses in Nighttown* (1958 and 1974). In the 1960s he appeared again on the large and small screens but, except for vehicles such as the movie comedy *The Producers* (1968) and the TV musical spoof of Westerns called *The Saga of Sonora* (1973), Mostel was not as potent as he was on stage. His son is character actor Josh Mostel (1946–).

▶ MOTHER WORE TIGHTS (Fox 1947). One of BETTY GRABLE's many period musicals, this one was her most successful, grossing over $4 million and spurning three more films with her co-star DAN DAILEY. Producer–writer Lamar Trotti's screenplay, based on a book by Miriam Young, began in 1900 with the vaudeville couple Myrtle (Grable) and Frank Burt (Dailey) on the road and trying to raise a family. As their daughters Iris (Mona Freeman) and Mickie (Connie Marshall) grow up, they rebel against their parents' barnstorming lifestyle, especially when Iris gets out of finishing school and is embarrassed by her family. But time passes and everything is cured by a tear, a song, and a dance. Old vaudeville song favorites were used in the score, and Josef Myrow (music) and MACK GORDON (lyrics) wrote new numbers, including the pastiche soft-shoe "Kokomo, Indiana," the jaunty "On a Little Two-Seat Tandem," and the ballad "You Do" that was used effectively as a leitmotif throughout the film. The supporting cast of characters was as lively as the stars: Robert Arthur, Sara Allgood, WILLIAM FRAWLEY, Vanessa Brown, SIG RUMANN, Chick Chandler, Ruth Nelson, Señor Wences, Lee Patrick, and the voice of Ann Baxter who narrated the story as the grown-up Mickie. WALTER LANG directed, and the dances were choreographed by SEYMOUR FELIX and Kenny Williams.

▶ MOULIN ROUGE! (Bazmark/Fox 2001). A frenetic musical extravaganza in which music, broad performances, and hyperactive camera-

Moulin Rouge! Nothing in this feverish movie musical was done simply, making it a visual roller coaster ride that thrilled many filmgoers. While Ewan McGregor kisses Nicole Kidman, John Leguizano looks on. Is he upside down or is that just his reflection in a mirror? In *Moulin Rouge!* it was always a trick of the eye. (Photofest)

work bombarded the audience, most of them young and loving every second of it. Director Baz Luhrmann and Craig Pearce wrote the screenplay, which sent the young Englishman Christian (Ewan McGregor) to Paris to become a poet and ends up being a drinking pal of Toulouse-Lautrec (John Leguizano) and other bohemian artists. They write a show for producer Harold Zidler (Jim Broadbent) who runs the famous Moulin Rouge nightspot. Christian falls in love with the sultry star of the club, Satine (Nicole Kidman), but their romance is thwarted by the wealthy Duke (Richard Roxburgh) who will support the financially strapped Moulin Rouge if Satine can be his. The colorful circus of a movie was fast paced, with the camera zooming in and out of locales with breakneck speed, and the editing so fervent that it made most MTV videos look static. The songs, from various sources and time periods and sung by cast members, as well as other artists on the soundtrack, were given a high pressure treatment, as was the vigorous choreography by John O'Connell. Musical numbers as diverse

as "Nature Boy," "Your Song," "Come What May," "Lady Marmalade," and "El Tango de Roxanne" all seemed to explode on the screen, causing some viewers to declare *Moulin Rouge* the most innovative, exciting musical in decades and others to run out of the theatre in panic.

MOVIE MOVIE (Warner 1978). A tongue-in-cheek double bill that pastiched movies of the 1930s, one of the two minifeatures was an accurate yet loving parody of the kind of BUSBY BERKELEY musical that WARNER BROTHERS produced during the Depression. The opening half of the bill was a clever spoof of boxing films and much of the same cast appeared in *Baxter's Beauties*, a musical about Broadway producer Spats Baxter (George C. Scott) who only has a few more months to live but insists on putting on one last big show. The Ruby Keeler-like Kitty (RACHEL YORK) comes to New York to be on Broadway and befriends unknown songwriter Dick Cummings (BARRY BOSTWICK) and gets in the chorus of Baxter's show. When the leading lady Isobel Stuart

(Trish Van Devere) gets drunk, Kitty has to go on in her place and becomes a star. The affectionate spoof was written by LARRY GELBART, directed with precise style by STANLEY DONEN, and choreographed with Berkeley-like nonsense by MICHAEL KIDD. Gelbart and Ralph Burns penned a few pastiche songs, one of which, "Just Shows to Go Ya," was as infectiously silly as the real thing.

☼ **MOVIN' OUT** (Richard Rodgers Theatre 2002). An exciting dance show set to contemporary music, the musical also managed to have vivid characters and stories. Director–choreographer Twyla Tharp fashioned two dozen Billy Joel pop songs and a few classical pieces into a danced chronicle about the generation that grew up during the turbulent 1960s. Since the Joel songs often told a story, the program was theatrically satisfying as well as choreographically thrilling. Michael Cavanaugh did most of the vocals in the Joel style and the stories were enacted by such vibrant dancers as John Selya, Scott Wise, Elizabeth Parkinson, Benjamin G. Bowman, Ashley Tuttle, and Keith Roberts. Rave reviews and a lot of Joel fans helped turn the piece into a long-run (1,303 performances) hit.

⛶ **MR. MAGOO'S CHRISTMAS CAROL** (NBC-TV 1962). One of the shortest of the many versions of Charles Dickens's holiday favorite, the thirty-minute animated musical squeezes in the basic plot, six songs, and even some backstage fumbling by the nearsighted Mr. Magoo (voice of Jim Backus). The teleplay by Barbara Chain takes the premise that Magoo is appearing as Scrooge in a Broadway musical production of *A Christmas Carol*. While he stumbled into wrong doors and through scenery backstage, his performance in the piece was straightforward Dickens. JACK CASSIDY, Morey Amsterdam, PAUL FREES, Jane Kean, Royal Dano, Joan Gardner, and Les Tremayne were among those providing the other voices. JULE STYNE (music) and BOB MERRILL (lyrics) wrote a very Broadway-sounding set of songs that included "It's Great to Be Back on Broadway," "Ringle, Ringle," "All Alone in the World," "We're Despicable," and "Winter Was Warm." While the musical might be a little too slick for Dickens's purists, there is something contagious and memorable about the show. The Henry Saperstein–Lee Orgel production was the first made-for-television animated musical and it set a standard for the many to follow.

☼ **MR. PRESIDENT** (St. James Theatre 1962). IRVING BERLIN's last Broadway show, it was a major disappointment regarding plot, characters, and even the songs. When President Stephen Decatur Henderson (Robert Ryan) loses his reelection bid, his wife Nell (NANETTE FABRAY) is pleased to leave the White House. But Henderson feels he still has something to offer the country. When he realizes a senate opening comes with too many compromises, he decides to run again for the presidency. Also in the cast were ANITA GILLETTE, Jack Haskell, Jack Washburn, and Stanley Grover, under the direction of JOSHUA LOGAN. HOWARD LINDSAY and RUSSEL CROUSE wrote the unexciting libretto, and Berlin's songs, many echoing earlier and better ones by him, included "This Is a Great Country," "Meat and Potatoes," "Pigtails and Freckles," "Let's Go Back to the Waltz," "Don't Be Afraid of Romance," and "In Our Hide-Away." High expectations for a new show by the team that created *Call Me Madam* (1950) led to a record-breaking advance but disappointment in the musical forced the LELAND HAYWARD production to close after 265 performances. None of Berlin's songs became popular so he retired from show business and from public life.

☼ **MR. WONDERFUL** (Broadway Theatre 1956). A vehicle used to introduce popular singer SAMMY DAVIS, JR. to Broadway, the thin musical served its purpose and Davis shone for 383 performances. Struggling African American singer Charlie Welch (Davis) is strictly small time until his fiancée Ethel Pearson (Olga James) and his pal Fred Campbell (Jack Carter) persuade him to take a booking at Miami Beach's swanky Palm Club and it opens the door to the big time. Also in the cast were Will Maston, Sammy Davis, Sr., CHITA RIVERA, Pat Marshall, and Hal Loman. JOSEPH STEIN and Will Glickman wrote the libretto, and JERRY BOCK, Larry Holofcener, and George Weiss collaborated on the score, which produced two hits, "Too Close for Comfort" and the title number. Also in the contemporary-sounding score were "Without You, I'm Nothing" and "Talk to Him." Much of the second act was Davis's act with his father and Will Maston singing songs from their days as the Will Maston Trio.

⛶ **MRS. SANTA CLAUS** (CBS-TV 1996). Songwriter JERRY HERMAN and television favorite ANGELA LANSBURY, who had worked together on Broadway in *MAME* (1966) and *DEAR WORLD* (1969), were reunited for this lavish two-hour musical set in 1910. Anna Claus (Lansbury) is an active participant in the

Christmas preparation in the Mark Saltzman teleplay. She heads the manufacture of toys in the North Pole and charts a new route for Santa (Charles Durning) but the old man is distracted, seems to be ignoring his wife, and losing his enthusiasm for Christmas. A week before Christmas eve, Anna tries out the new route but a blizzard waylays her in New York City's Lower East Side where she befriends some of the immigrants, organizes the child laborers who work in a sweat shop run by the evil Augustus P. Tavish (TERRENCE MANN), and even acts as matchmaker for a young couple. When Anna returns to the North Pole, Santa is so glad to see her that he asks her to accompany him on his rounds this year. Also in the cast were Michael Jeter, David Norona, Debra Wiseman, Rosalind Garris, Lynsey Bartilson, and Bryan Murray. The catchy songs included "Seven Days Til Christmas," "Avenue A," "Whistle," " He Needs Me," "Almost Young," "The Best Christmas of All," and "Mrs. Santa Claus." Aside from a first-class performance by Lansbury, the musical boasted impressive production values and bubbly dance numbers choreographed by ROB MARSHALL. David Shaw produced the two-hour show and Terry Hughes directed it.

MULAN (Disney 1998). A unique and exotic animated musical that attempted to take an Eastern point of view, the Chinese adventure was filled with many marvelous things even if that attempt was not always successful. The screenplay was based on a Chinese legend about the girl Mulan (voice of Ming-Na, singing by LEA SALONGA), the daughter of an ailing, aging warrior. Attempts by Mulan's relatives and the local matchmaker to train the headstrong girl into becoming a submissive female and prospective bride fail. When the Huns attack China and the Emperor (Pat Morita) demands that every family provide a fighter, Mulan disguises herself as a boy and joins the army where she proves her ability to fight, falls in love with her superior officer Shang (B. D. Wong, singing by Donny Osmond), and then saves China by outwitting the enemy. The tale may have been Chinese but some aspects of the movie were pure Disney, such as Mulan's comic sidekick Mushu the Dragon (Eddie Murphy). Some of Mulan's fellow comrades in arms were also closer to Hollywood than the Great Wall, although the characterizations and voices of HARVEY FIERSTEIN, James Hong, Jerry Tondo, and Gedde Watanabe were first class. Among the other talents to lend speaking and/or singing voices were June Foray, MARNI

NIXON, James Shigeta, Miriam Margolyes, BETH FOWLER, and Freeda Foh Shen. With so much action there was not room for many songs, but the ones written by Matthew Wilder (music) and David Zippel (lyrics) were delightful, from Mulan's pensive ballad "Reflection" to the slaphappy "A Girl Worth Fighting For." There was also a sweeping musical soundtrack score by Jerry Goldsmith and stunning background art that added greatly to the setting and tone of the film. Tony Bancroft and Barry Cook directed the unusual musical, which was not one of the studio's major hits when it opened but has grown in popularity over the years.

MULLER, ROMEO (1928–1992). Television writer. The busy author of many television musical specials and original TV musicals, he penned several holiday programs for family viewing. Muller was born in the Bronx and raised on Long Island where as a child he wrote and performed puppet shows. He started his career as an actor but often found himself writing scripts and one of his plays was produced Off Broadway. It was while writing comedy material for JACK BENNY that Muller first worked in television, the medium he would devote his life to. In 1964 he first worked with producers ARTHUR RANKIN, JR. and JULES BASS on the animated musical special *Return to Oz* and then together they created the animated classic *THE STORY OF RUDOLPH THE RED-NOSED REINDEER* (1964). Muller also scripted the original animated musicals *The Cricket on the Hearth* (1967), *The Little Drummer Boy* (1968), *The Mouse on the Mayflower* (1968), *Frosty the Snowman* (1969), *SANTA CLAUS IS COMIN' TO TOWN* (1970), *Here Comes Peter Cottontail* (1971), *It's a Brand New World* (1977), *The Easter Bunny Is Comin' to Town* (1977), *THE STINGIEST MAN IN TOWN* (1978), *Jack Frost* (1979), *RUDOLPH AND FROSTY'S CHRISTMAS IN JULY* (1979), *Pinocchio's Christmas* (1980), *Return of the King* (1980), and *THE WIND IN THE WILLOWS* (1987). He also wrote many nonmusical TV specials and live-action programs. In the 1980s Muller wrote, produced, and did the narration for the *Strawberry Shortcake* series for children.

MULLIGAN GUARDS MUSICALS, THE. Stage series. Seven antic musical comedies at the end of the nineteenth century, these popular shows written, produced, and performed by EDWARD HARRIGAN and TONY HART were the forerunners for the fast-paced musicals by GEORGE M. COHAN and others. The shows were outrageous farces that related the misadventures of the Irish Mulligan Guards, a boisterous, hard-drinking social and military club in the slums of New York. The characters in the musicals were Irish, German, Italian, African American, and Jewish immigrants, and the way Harrigan and Hart utilized ethnic idioms and street vernacular would influence later shows with slang and current expressions in the librettos and lyrics. DAVID BRAHAM composed the music for the series and among the popular songs to come from the shows were "Maggie Murphy's Home," "The Mulligan Guard," "Babies on Our Block," and "Paddy Duffy's Cart." The series began as a vaudeville sketch in 1873 and by 1878 the first full-length show, *The Mulligan Guards' Picnic*, was on Broadway and ran a month. *The Mulligan Guards' Ball* (1879) is considered the best of the series, a riotous tale about the rivalry between the Irish group and the African American Skidmore Guards who have both booked the same ballroom for their annual ball. The series ended with *The Mulligan's Silver Wedding* (1880), although some of the characters reappeared in later musicals.

MUNSHIN, JULES (1915–1970). Film, stage, and performer. A tall, forlorn-looking comic actor, he usually played supporting roles in comedies and musicals and frequently managed to steal the limelight from the principals. The native New Yorker began his career clowning in vaudeville and in Catskills resorts and then entertained fellow soldiers during World War II. Munshin made an auspicious Broadway debut playing different daffy characters in the musical revue CALL ME MISTER (1946), which led to a Hollywood contract. He was noticed in secondary roles in *EASTER PARADE* (1948), *TAKE ME OUT TO THE BALL GAME* (1949), and *That Midnight Kiss* (1949) and then got his best film role as Ozzie on leave with sailors GENE KELLY and FRANK SINATRA in *ON THE TOWN* (1949). Munshin was also featured in *SILK STOCKINGS* (1957) and *Ten Thousand Bedrooms* (1957). He returned to Broadway for plays and the musical revues *Bless You All* (1950) and *Show Girl* (1961) and then played the Viennese confidant Max in the book musical *THE GAY LIFE* (1961). Munshin performed in many television shows, including the musicals *It's Sunny Again* (1956), *The Emperor's New Clothes* (1960), *Archie and Mehitabel* (1960), and *KISS ME, KATE* (1968), before his premature death from a heart attack.

MUPPET MOVIE, THE (ITC 1979). The famous cloth characters from television came to the big screen and had quite a success even though the film was rarely as inspired as the Muppets were on the small screen. The serviceable screenplay by Jerry Juhl and Jack Burns followed Kermit the frog (operated and voiced by Jim Henson) as he leaves the swamp and heads to Hollywood with his friends Miss Piggy, Fozzie Bear, Rowlf the dog, and others, voiced by such talents as Frank Oz, Jerry Nelson, Richard Hunt, and Dave Goelz. Although he doesn't know it, Kermit is being hunted down by entrepreneur Doc Hopper (Charles Durning) who wants the singing–dancing green fellow to be spokesman for his fast-food chain of fried frogs' legs. Along the way the Muppets meet up with guest stars in cameo roles, from veterans BOB HOPE, MILTON BERLE, and EDGAR BERGEN, to more recent celebrities such as Steve Martin, Richard Pryor, and MADELINE KAHN. PAUL WILLIAMS and Kenny Ascher wrote an agreeable set of songs, most memorably "The Rainbow Connection," which became a hit, and Kermit's signature song, but the musical numbers often lacked the panache that characterized the television show's numbers. Still, there was something pleasant about "Movin' Right Along" and "I'm Going to Go Back There Some Day." Over the years there were other Muppet features, most of them musicals, and with stronger storylines and better production numbers they were sometimes more satisfying than this original. Among the films utilizing the cloth characters were *The Great Muppet Caper* (1981), *The Muppets Take Manhattan* (1984), *The Muppet Christmas Carol* (1992), *Muppets Treasure Island* (1996), and *Muppets From Space* (1999).

MURPHY, DONNA (1958–). Stage, television, and film performer. A dark, exotic singer–actress, she possesses a smokey singing voice and a sensual yet distant presence. Born in Corno, New York, and raised on Long Island and in Topsfield, Massachusetts, Murphy was educated at New York University and studied acting with Stella Adler before making her Broadway debut as a replacement for Sonia in *THEY'RE PLAYING OUR SONG* in 1979. She appeared in the ensemble of *THE MYSTERY OF EDWIN DROOD* (1985) and eventually graduated to playing the title character. Murphy was featured in the Off Broadway musicals *Birds of Paradise* (1987), *Showing Off* (1989), *Privates on Parade* (1989), and *Song of Singapore* (1991) before getting attention as the Whore in *HELLO AGAIN* (1994). She was roundly commended for her ugly spinster Fosca in *PASSION* (1994), as well as for her performances as Anna in the

1996 revival of *The King and I*, sarcastic Ruth Sherwood in the 2003 revival of *Wonderful Town*, and LOTTE LENYA in *LoveMusik* (2007). Murphy has acted in a variety of films and television programs, but rarely has gotten to sing in any of them.

MURPHY, GEORGE [Lloyd] (1902–1992). Film performer. A congenial song-and-dance man, he cavorted in twenty Hollywood musicals and then played in dramatic roles before going into politics. Murphy was born in New Haven, Connecticut, the son of an Olympic training coach, and attended Yale University for a few years before quitting to work at various jobs. He was dancing in nightclub shows when he teamed up with Julie Johnson, later his wife, and they went into vaudeville together. Murphy eventually got to Broadway where he played secondary roles in the musicals *Shoot the Works* (1931), *Of Thee I Sing* (1931), and *Roberta* (1933). The next year he was in Hollywood playing carefree types in such musicals as *Kid Millions* (1934), *After the Dance* (1935), *Top of the Town* (1937), *Broadway Melody of 1938* (1937), *You're a Sweetheart* (1937), *Little Miss Broadway* (1938), *Broadway Melody of 1940*, *Two Girls on Broadway* (1940), *Little Nellie Kelly* (1940), *Rise and Shine* (1941), *For Me and My Gal* (1942), *The Powers Girl* (1942), *This Is the Army* (1943), *Broadway Rhythm* (1944), *Step Lively* (1944), and *Big City* (1948). Murphy left musicals for dramatic parts but when his popularity dropped he retired from show business and took up politics, first in the entertainment unions and then as a Republican senator for California. Autobiography: *Say, Didn't You Used to Be George Murphy?* (1970).

MURRAY, J. HAROLD [born Harry Rulten] (1891–1940). Stage and film performer. A rugged-looking, sandy-haired baritone, he appeared in a number of Broadway musicals in the 1920s and 1930s. Murray was born in South Berwick, Maine, and was a professional boy singer in choral groups and later in vaudeville. After being educated in Boston, he made his Broadway bow in *The Passing Show* (1920) followed by thirteen musicals in which he gradually worked his way to leading man. Murray is best remembered as Texas Ranger Capt. Jim Stewart in *Rio Rita* (1927), the theatrical Pat Mason in *Face the Music* (1932), and introducing "Autumn in New York" in the revue *Thumbs Up!* (1934). His other musical credits include *The Whirl of the World* (1921), *Make It Snappy* (1922), *Caroline* (1923), *Vogues of 1924*, *Captain Jinks* (1925), *China Rose* (1925), *Castles*

in the Air (1926), and *East Wind* (1931). Before his untimely death at the age of forty-nine, Murray appeared in several musical movie shorts in the 1930s as well as a handful of feature films, including the musicals *Happy Days* (1929), *Married in Hollywood* (1929), *Cameo Kirby* (1930), and *Women Everywhere* (1930).

MUSIC BOX REVUES. Stage series. A beloved series of four musical revues between 1921 and 1924, they were named after the new Music Box Theatre on West 45th Street. Producer SAM H. HARRIS and songwriter IRVING BERLIN built the midsized playhouse with an eye to presenting intimate, small-scale shows that would contrast with the lavish revues put on by FLORENZ ZIEGFELD and GEORGE WHITE. The shows boasted scores by Berlin, and some famous songs came from the series, including "What'll I Do?," "All Alone," "Pack Up Your Sins and Go to the Devil," "Everybody Step," and "Say It With Music," the theme song for the series. The revues were also famous for their literate sketches by GEORGE S. KAUFMAN and other wits. Perhaps the most fondly remembered sketch was ROBERT BENCHLEY'S "The Treasurer's Report," which he performed himself in the 1922 edition. Although the *Music Box Revues* did not last as long as other musical series, it was one of the best and later revues strived to copy it in quality.

MUSIC IN THE AIR (Alvin Theatre 1932). An attempt to create a modern operetta after the golden age of the genre had passed, the musical succeeded nicely and the JEROME KERN (music) and OSCAR HAMMERSTEIN (lyrics) score was filled with charming numbers. The elderly Bavarian music teacher, Dr. Walther Lessing (AL SHEAN), his pupil–composer Karl Reder (WALTER SLEZAK), and Karl's sweetheart Sieglinde (Katherine Carrington), who is Lessing's daughter, set out for Munich to get a song of theirs published, but the big city nearly devours them. The predatory prima donna Frieda Hatzfeld (Natalie Hall) goes after Karl and the lusty composer Bruno Mahler (TULIO CARMINATI) pursues Sieglinde. When the diva cannot perform on opening night of Karl's opera, Sieglinde takes her place and, contrary to cliché, fails to impress the audience. Fed up with the big time in Munich, Lessing, Sieglinde, and Karl return home to make music the way they like. Hammerstein wrote the libretto, which lent itself to such lovely songs as "I've Told Ev'ry Little Star," "There's a Hill Beyond a Hill," "The Song Is You," "When Spring Is in the Air," "In Egern on the Tegern

Sea," "We Belong Together," "And Love Was Born," and "One More Dance." Critical reaction to the old-style operetta was positive, as was audience appeal, and the musical ran 342 performances. Because anti-German sentiments were still prevalent in the 1950s, Hammerstein changed the location of his story from Bavaria to Switzerland for the 1951 Broadway revival, which captured the warm romantic glow of the original. The star-filled cast included CHARLES WINNINGER, DENNIS KING, and Jane Pickens, directed by Hammerstein himself. Although the reviews were propitious, audiences were no longer much interested in operetta, modern or not, and the revival ran only seven weeks.

🎬 **Music in the Air** (Fox 1934) cut four of the stage songs but opened up the musical, filming on location in the Alps and building up the role of opera singer Freida for Gloria Swanson in her only musical. The screenplay by Howard Young and BILLY WILDER concentrated on Frieda's attempt to seduce Karl (Douglass Montgomery) in order to make her lover Bruno (JOHN BOLES) jealous. The script stuck with Hammerstein's ending and did not turn Sieglinde (June Lang) into a German RUBY KEELER and become a star. The dialogue sparkled, Swanson and the rest of the cast were in top form, and the movie was a delight, one of Kern and Hammerstein's more successful transitions from stage to screen.

👁 **MUSIC MAN, THE** (Majestic Theatre 1957). One of Broadway's most beloved musicals, the crowd-pleasing show is also very innovative and unique in many ways.

Plot: When the con man Professor Harold Hill comes to the small Iowa town of River City, he points out the dangers of the new pool parlor in town and gets the citizens all excited about forming a boys' marching band to protect the youth from the evils of the world. With the help of his old pal Marcellus Washburn, Hill collects money for instruments and uniforms even as he keeps the suspicious Mayor Shinn and the other authorities off balance. The unmarried piano teacher Marian Paroo sees right through the phony "professor" and is about to expose his fraud to the mayor when the Wells Fargo Wagon comes to town with the instruments and she sees the look of delight on the face of her shy little brother Winthrop when he receives his coronet. While Hill stalls, waiting for the uniforms to arrive, Marian falls in love with him. When he is found out, she even defends him reminding her fellow citizens of all the joy he has brought to the town. When the boys enter and proceed to produce squawks and screeches from their instruments, the townspeople are thrilled and all is forgiven.

Meredith Willson wrote the funny, engaging libretto with Franklin Lacey, basing the story and characters on his own experiences growing up in a small Iowa town early in the twentieth century. Unlike most musicals that focus on two couples and a few bit parts, *The Music Man* is filled with unforgettable characters that are drawn with affection and humor. From the pompous mayor and his affected wife to Marian's Irish mother and the coarse sales-

Casts for *Music in the Air*

Character	1932 Broadway	1934 film	1951 Broadway
Karl Reder	WALTER SLEZAK	Douglass Montgomery	Mitchell Gregg
Sieglinde	Katherine Carrington	June Lang	Lillian Murphy
Dr. Walther Lessing	AL SHEAN	Al Shean	CHARLES WINNINGER
Frieda Hatzfeld	Natalie Hall	Gloria Swanson	Jane Pickens
Bruno Mahler	TULIO CARMINATI	JOHN BOLES	DENNIS KING

Casts for *The Music Man*

Character	1957 Broadway	1962 film	2000 Broadway	2003 television
Harold Hill	ROBERT PRESTON	Robert Preston	Craig Bierko	MATTHEW BRODERICK
Marian Paroo	BARBARA COOK	SHIRLEY JONES	REBECCA LUKER	KRISTIN CHENOWETH
Marcellus	Iggie Wolfington	BUDDY HACKETT	Max Casella	David Aaron Baker
Mayor Shinn	DAVID BURNS	Paul Ford	Paul Benedict	VICTOR GARBER
Mrs. Shinn	Helen Raymond	HERMIONE GINGOLD	Ruth Williamson	Molly Shannon
Mrs. Paroo	PERT KELTON	Pert Kelton	Katherine McGrath	DEBRA MONK

man Charley Cowell who turns in Hill, the characters are vibrant and alive. Harold Hill is a unique leading role, a con man with few admirable qualities, yet he manages to charm audiences just as Hill charms the citizens of River City. Willson's talent for characterization is matched by his musical numbers, which are also unusual. The score is so famous and so many of the songs well known that one forgets how unique they are. Rarely has a musical used such different kinds of American music in a Broadway score. The opening "Rock Island" is an auctioneer-like patter that rises and falls with the speed of the train the salesman are riding. "Piano Lesson" uses traditional piano scales to form the pattern and melody for an argument between mother and daughter. Elsewhere in the score barbershop quartets, square dance music, soft-shoe, and rhythm songs can be found. Even the march "Seventy Six Trombones," the most famous song in the score, is slowed down and used as the wistful ballad "Goodnight, My Someone," with the characters of Harold Hill and Marian linked by the same song played at a different tempo, just as their characters have a different viewpoint. *The Music Man* is considered a nostalgic, old-fashioned show by many but its score is actually daring and bold. Critical raves for the script, score, and the cast (particularly ROBERT PRESTON in his musical debut) made the Kermit Bloomgarden production the biggest hit of the season, running 1,375 performances. MORTON DA COSTA directed with a flair for the rustic, and ONNA WHITE did the inventive choreography, which included a marvelous dance in the library that started with stiff, restricted moves and built into a frenzy of bodies and books. The musical toured with great success and then became a perennial favorite with all kinds of theatre groups. New York has seen three revivals of *The Music Man*. Bert Parks starred as Harold Hill in a 1965 revival by the New York City Light Opera. In 1980, MICHAEL KIDD directed and choreographed a production at the City Center that never seemed to come to life, mostly because of the miscast DICK VAN DYKE as Harold Hill. Meg Bussert was Marian, and Iggie Wolfington, who originated the role of Marcellus, played Mayor Shinn. More successful was a 2000 Broadway revival with the little-known performer Craig Bierko playing Harold Hill in a lavish mounting directed and choreographed by SUSAN STROMAN. REBECCA LUKER was deemed a luminous Marian, and the bright and bouncy show was a popular attraction for 699 performances.

The Music Man (stage) Musical Numbers
"Rock Island"
"Iowa Stubborn"
"(Ya Got) Trouble"
"Piano Lesson"
"Goodnight, My Someone"
"Seventy-Six Trombones"
"Sincere"
"The Sadder-But-Wiser Girl"
"Pickalittle (Talkalittle)"
"Goodnight, Ladies"
"Marian the Librarian"
"My White Knight"
"The Wells Fargo Wagon"
"It's You"
"Shipoopi"
"Lida Rose"
"Will I Ever Tell You?"
"Gary, Indiana"
"Till There Was You"

The Music Man (Warner 1962) lost none of its luster when it transferred to the screen with Robert Preston reprising his magnetic performance. SHIRLEY JONES was a splendid Marion and the rest of the cast was equally skillful. The screenplay by Marian Hargrove opened up the action without weakening it and the fantasy-like ending, in which Hill's imaginary band comes to life, was right in keeping with the theme of the musical. Onna White recreated her choreography and the production values were expert, making River City idealized without looking phony. The movie, produced and directed by Morton Da Costa, was a box office hit and remains a favorite. It also preserves one of the American musical theatre's legendary performances by capturing Preston's Harold Hill on film. ❏ Because *The Music Man* is so popular with amateur groups it seems indestructible, yet the 2003 ABC-TV production was more disappointing than any high school effort. MATTHEW BRODERICK was a smiling, charming Harold Hill without any persuasive powers, KRISTIN CHENOWETH was miscast and every line she uttered rang false, and most of the townspeople came across as petty and annoying rather than funny and eccentric. Sally Robinson's teleplay was faithful to the original libretto and KATHLEEN MARSHALL's choreography was enjoyable, but the direction by Jeff Bleckner was heavy-handed and clumsy. It was clear that no musical is indestructible.

MUSICAL COMEDY TIME. Television series. This was a short-lived but impressive anthology program on NBC in 1950–1951 in which abridged versions of Broadway musicals were produced, sometimes with members of the original cast. Among the offerings were BERT LAHR in *FLYING HIGH*, JACKIE GLEASON in *NO, NO, NANETTE*, VICTOR MOORE and IRENE BORDONI in *LOUISIANA PURCHASE*, NANCY WALKER in *WHOOPEE!*, and DENNIS KING in *BABES IN TOYLAND*.

MY FAIR LADY (Mark Hellinger Theatre 1956). ALAN JAY LERNER (book and lyrics) and FREDERICK LOEWE's (music) greatest triumph as well as one of the glories of the American theatre, the unlikely hit may be the best post-World War II Broadway show.

Plot: London phonetics professor Henry Higgins observes the Cockney flower girl Eliza Doolittle selling her wares outside St. Paul's Church after the opera lets out and boasts that with proper training in speech he could pass her off as a duchess. Liza comes to Higgins' home asking for speech lessons and he bets his fellow bachelor friend Colonel Pickering that he will turn the squawking, ignorant girl into a lady in six months. The training is rigorous and ruthless and after showing her off at the Ascot races, Higgins and Pickering bring her to an embassy ball where she not only comes across as a lady but charms the royal members present. The bet having been won, Eliza turns on Higgins, demanding to be treated like the lady he has made her and threatening to wed the youth Freddie Hill who has been courting her. Higgins denounces Liza as an ungrateful upstart but after she walks out on him he realizes that he is rather fond of her and is more than pleased when she eventually returns to continue their relationship on more equal terms. The comic subplot concerns Eliza's father Alfred, a common dustman, who inherits a bundle of money and is forced to become respectable, much against his nature and sense of happiness.

George Bernard Shaw's drawing room comedy *Pygmalion* (1914) opened up elegantly for the musical stage and the Cinderella tale may have resembled the romantic musicals of the 1920s, yet it was highly literate and witty with the romance muted almost to invisibility. Lerner's libretto is one of the masterpieces of adaptation, with the new scenes capturing the old play's style so accurately that it is hard to tell where Shaw leaves off and Lerner starts. Even the ending, more romanticized than the play, is in character. *My Fair Lady* is such an established and familiar classic that one forgets how unlikely it was for Broadway success. There is no overt love story, the action is that of a drawing room comedy, there is more talk than music, the story requires very little dancing, the major characters are more comic than romantic, and there is absolutely nothing American about it. Several other songwriters, including RODGERS and HAMMERSTEIN, had attempted to musicalize *Pygmalion* and gave up in frustration. The musical Lerner and Loewe created is not only unusual but also rather daring. The score is a master blending of operetta, British music hall, and musical comedy with unforgettable songs in each genre. The standout hits were the ballads "I Could Have Danced All Night" and "On the Street Where You Live," but few theatre songs are as easily recognized as "The Rain in Spain." In fact, the whole score was so memorable that American (and later British) music lovers opted to own the original cast album rather than just recordings of the top songs by various artists. Numbers such as "Wouldn't It Be Loverly," "Get Me to the Church on Time," "With a Little Bit of Luck," "Just You Wait," and "Show Me" seem unlikely to work outside of the context of the show, yet they also are well known. Another astonishing feat is the way Higgins is musicalized. He is not a romantic person and cannot

My Fair Lady. Some critics found Audrey Hepburn's cockney flower girl Eliza unconvincing but everyone admitted she made quite a lady. In this still from the 1964 film, Hepburn is dressed for the races at Ascot and even Rex Harrison's Henry Higgins seems impressed. (Photofest)

Casts for *My Fair Lady*

Characters	Henry Higgins	Eliza Doolittle	Alfred Doolittle
1956 Broadway	REX HARRISON	JULIE ANDREWS	STANLEY HOLLOWAY
1964 film	Rex Harrison	AUDREY HEPBURN	Stanley Holloway
1976 Broadway	Ian Richardson	Christine Andreas	GEORGE ROSE
1981 Broadway	Rex Harrison	Nancy Ringham	Milo O'Shea
1993 Broadway	Richard Chamberlain	Melissa Errico	Julian Holloway

express himself in musical terms. Also, the role was cast with the nonsinging REX HARRISON. Yet Higgins' character songs "I've Grown Accustomed to Her Face," "I'm an Ordinary Man," and "A Hymn to Him" are triumphs in musical characterization. Equally impressive is the way the songs for Eliza develop from the simple-phrased "Wouldn't It Be Loverly" to witty "Just You wait" to the complex "Without You." Few Broadway scores are so effective in tracing the change in the character's psyches. Rave reviews for Harrison, JULIE ANDREWS, and all the cast, the sharp yet poignant direction of MOSS HART, and the Edwardian sets and costumes by Oliver Smith and Cecil Beaton helped make the HERMAN LEVIN production the hit of the decade, running 2,717 performances and breaking the current record.

Five New York revivals over the years have kept the musical fresh in the memory of Manhattan theatregoers. The New York City Light Opera Company recreated the original staging and design in 1964 and featured Myles Eason as Henry Higgins and MARNI NIXON as Eliza. The supporting cast included REGINALD GARDNER (Doolittle), RUSSELL NYPE (Freddy), Byron Webster (Pickering), and Margery Maude (Mrs. Higgins). The same organization featured Fritz Weaver (Higgins) and Inga Swenson (Eliza) in 1968 with GEORGE ROSE (Doolitle), Evan Thomas (Freddy), Byron Webster (Pickering), and Margery Maude (Mrs. Higgins). For the twentieth anniversary of the musical, the original sets, costumes, and staging were recreated for a well-received 1976 production with Ian Richardson (Higgins), Christine Andreas (Eliza), and Robert Coote, the original Pickering. Produced again by Herman Levin, the revival ran 377 performances. The seventy-three-year-old Harrison returned to his most famous role, and the ninety-two-year-old Cathleen Nesbitt again played his mother in a 1981 revival that faithfully recreated the original look if not spirit of the musical. Both Harrison and the production looked tired but audiences wanted to see both so the limited engagement in the large Uris

My Fair Lady (stage) Musical Numbers

"Street Entertainers"
"Why Can't the English?"
"Wouldn't It Be Loverly?"
"With a Little Bit of Luck"
"I'm an Ordinary Man"
"Just You Wait"
"The Rain in Spain"
"I Could Have Danced All Night"
"Ascot Gavotte"
"On the Street Where You Live"
"The Embassy Waltz"
"You Did It"
"Show Me"
"Get Me to the Church on Time"
"Hymn to Him"
"Without You"
"I've Grown Accustomed to Her Face"

Theatre was extended to fifteen weeks. Mixed notices greeted the 1993 Howard Davies-directed revival in which the scenery was more abstract than romantic and the performances uneven. Richard Chamberlain was a somber Higgins but Melissa Errico was complimented for her sparkling Eliza. Julian Holloway, the son of STANLEY HOLLOWAY, who had originated the role of Alfred Doolittle, took on this father's part. The production ran 165 performances and then took off on an extended (and successful) national tour. *My Fair Lady* remains a favorite with all kinds of theatre groups in America and Europe.

🎬 *My Fair Lady* (Warner 1964) had to try and live up to the reputation of the Broadway production so some disappointment was inevitable. When producer Jack Warner opted not to use Julie Andrews and wanted Cary Grant to play Higgins, omens were not good. But Grant refused to play it, AUDREY HEPBURN (singing dubbed by MARNI NIXON) was a very effective Eliza, and much of the movie was very enjoyable. Lerner wrote the efficient screenplay, the score was not tampered with in any noticeable way, and the production values, idealized and with a studio look to them, were in the style of the golden age movie musicals. GEORGE CUKOR directed and the film moved too slowly at times, just as Harrison's performance sometimes seemed a bit more weary than was comfortable. However, when the movie worked, it worked beautifully. Warner paid over $5 million for the screen rights and spent a bundle on the production but the film was a major box office hit and turned a healthy profit.

MY GAL SAL (Fox 1942). A biographical musical about songwriter Paul Dresser, the movie did not let the facts stand in the way of making a vehicle for RITA HAYWORTH. Seyon I. Miller, Karl Tunberg, and Darrel Ware concocted the screenplay in which the fictitious musical comedy star Sally Elliott (Hayworth) is the love of Dresser's life. The unlikely VICTOR MATURE played Dresser from his humble beginnings as a medicine show performer to a Broadway composer, although the real Dresser never quite made it to the Great White Way and died in poverty. Ironically, only six Dresser songs were used (including "On the Banks of the Wabash" and the title tune) and new ones were added by RALPH RAINGER (music) and LEO ROBIN (lyrics), with the best one being "Here You Are," which actually sounded like a Dresser song. Hayworth's singing was dubbed by Nan Wynn and lacked her sultry, deep register, but the star did not disappoint in other ways, giving a vibrant performance and looking sensational in Gay Nineties attire. Also in the cast were John Sutton, PHIL SILVERS, James Gleason, CAROLE LANDIS, WALTER CATLETT, Curt Bois, Andrew Tombes, and HERMES PAN, who also choreographed the numbers with Val Raset. IRVING CUMMINGS was the efficient director.

MY MAN (Warner-Vitaphone 1928). The studio's first feature after *THE JAZZ SINGER* (1927), it also was only partially a talkie that featured a major Broadway star, this time FANNY BRICE. Producer DARRYL F. ZANUCK contributed to the melodramatic screenplay about the struggling singer Fannie Brand (Brice) who falls for Joe Halsey (Guinn Williams), a muscular guy who models exercise equipment in a store window. They are about to get married but Fannie's jealous sister Edna (Edna Murphy) steals Joe away from her. The distraught Fannie is rescued by theatrical producer Landau (Andre De Segurola) who

puts her on the stage. The movie only came to life (and into sound) when Brice sang her recognized favorites such as "I'd Rather Be Blue," "Second Hand Rose," "If You Want a Rainbow (You Must Have the Rain)," "I'm an Indian, Too," and the title song. ARCHIE MAYO directed the primitive movie, which remains one of the best film records of a great star.

MY ONE AND ONLY. See *FUNNY FACE*

MY SISTER EILEEN (Columbia 1955). By the time this modest but enjoyable musical was released, audiences had had many chances to experience the story of Ohio sisters Ruth and Eileen Sherwood and their adventures in Greenwich Village. The series of New Yorker stories by Ruth McKenney had been turned into a hit comedy on Broadway in 1940 and on screen in 1942. A musical version titled *WONDERFUL TOWN*, with music by LEONARD BERNSTEIN and book and lyrics by BETTY COMDEN and ADOLPH GREEN, opened on Broadway in 1953 and was a hit. However, Hollywood wasn't finished with the property and this version, with a screenplay by director Richard Quine and BLAKE EDWARDS, featured a young, spirited cast and a new score by JULE STYNE (music) and LEO ROBIN (lyrics). The sarcastic Ruth (BETTY GARRETT) and the pretty Eileen (JANET LEIGH) encountered pretty much the same misadventures as in the past, JACK LEMMON, BOB FOSSE (who also choreographed), and TOMMY RALL were the men interested in them, and the supporting cast was filled out by KURT KASZNAR, Dick York, Lucy Marlow, Barbara Brown, and Horace McMahon. While the songs were mostly serviceable rather than memorable, they were given a sparkle by young Fosse just turning from acting to choreographing. However, "Give Me a Band and My Baby" and "It's Bigger Than You and Me" were a lot of fun and showed off the lively cast effectively. The movie is a testament to the versatility and showmanship of Garrett who rarely got a leading role, a shameful realization when one sees her set the screen on fire as the funny, knowing, exuberant Ruth.

MYRTIL, ODETTE [born Odette Quignard] (1898–1978). Stage and film performer. An international singer applauded on stages in New York, London, and Paris, she also made a number of Hollywood musicals. The Paris native made her professional debut at the age of thirteen singing and playing the violin in variety halls and was still a teenager when she was featured on Broadway in the *ZIEGFELD FOLLIES* (1914 and 1915). After appearing in London musicals, Myrtil returned to New York as an adult and sang in the musicals *Vogues of 1924*, *The Love Song* (1925), *Countess Maritza* (1926 and 1928), *White Lilacs* (1928), and *Broadway Nights* (1929). Her most remembered Broadway role was the temperamental opera singer Odette in *THE CAT AND THE FIDDLE* (1931) and she shone replacing leading players in *ROBERTA* (1934) and *SOUTH PACIFIC* (1952). Myrtil's other musical credits include *THE RED MILL* (1945), *Maggie* (1953) and *SARATOGA* (1959). She was cast as supporting characters (usually French) in many movies, including the musicals *YANKEE DOODLE DANDY* (1942), *I MARRIED AN ANGEL* (1942), *Thousands Cheer* (1943), *RHAPSODY IN BLUE* (1945), and *HERE COMES THE GROOM* (1951), and played herself in the film drama *The Last Time I Saw Paris* (1954). Myrtil was also a fashion designer, designing the costumes for several 1940s Hollywood films, and ran a famous restaurant called Chez Odette in Bucks County, Pennsylvania.

📖 ***MYSTERY OF EDWIN DROOD, THE*** (Imperial Theatre 1985). A musical whodunit in which the audience decided on who the murderer was, the show was certainly different and, presented in the format of a British music hall performance, was also very foreign for a Broadway product. However, the lively piece was so enjoyable that audiences got over its strangeness and kept it on the boards for 608 performances. In the Victorian England cathedral town of Cloisterham, the arrogant young Edwin Drood (BETTY BUCKLEY in a trouser role) quarrels with a variety of characters and then mysteriously disappears, throwing suspicion on a handful of people. Since the story was based on Charles Dickens's unfinished novel, the solution of who murdered Drood is posed to the audience who vote on the likely culprits and then the tale is completed accordingly. The music hall Chairman (GEORGE ROSE) acted as host and narrated the story, and the Victorian actors often broke character to comment on the action or sing a song out of context. The cast of characters (and suspects) were played by HOWARD McGILLIN, Patti Cohenour, Cleo Laine, George N. Martin, Jana Schneider, John Herrera, and Joe Grifasi. Rupert Holmes wrote the clever libretto and the score, which was filled with parlor songs, music hall turns, and merry production numbers. "Moonfall," "Don't Quit While You're Ahead," "The Wages of Sin," "Perfect Strangers," "Off to the Races," "The Writing on the Wall," and "Both Sides of the Coin" were among the most memorable numbers. Wilfred Leach directed with ingenious touches, and GRACIELA DANIELE devised the raucous choreography. After a rousing reception during the summer in Central Park, the NEW YORK SHAKESPEARE FESTIVAL production was presented on Broadway by producer JOSEPH PAPP and proved to be a durable hit. The musical was later produced by many regional theatres, summer stock, and college groups.

N

NAISH, J[oseph Patrick] **CARROLL** (1897–1973). Film, stage, and television performer. An Irish American character actor who specialized in foreign dialects and played Italians, Latins, Asians, Native Americans, eastern European Jews, and even Arabs, he was rarely cast as Irishmen because of his dark complexion. The native New Yorker dropped out of school to join the Navy during World War I and then traveled across Europe picking up different languages. When a tramp steamer dropped him off in southern California he started working as an extra and then as a stunt man in the movies. Taking up acting he went back to New York and appeared in some plays on Broadway but by 1930 was back in Hollywood where he stayed for forty years playing character types in over 150 films of all genres. Naish's musical credits include *Cheer Up and Smile* (1930), *The Kid From Spain* (1932), *DOWN ARGENTINE WAY* (1940), *THAT NIGHT IN RIO* (1941), *BIRTH OF THE BLUES* (1941), *Carnival in Costa Rica* (1947), *The Kissing Bandit* (1948), *ANNIE GET YOUR GUN* (1950), *THE TOAST OF NEW ORLEANS* (1950), and *HIT THE DECK* (1955). He also appeared in many television series and specials.

■ *NASHVILLE* (Paramount/ABC 1975). An intriguing, one-of-a-kind film by auteur director ROBERT ALTMAN, it is not often thought of as a musical, yet it has more songs (twenty-three) than just about every other Hollywood tuner. Twenty-four distinct characters in the Tennessee music capital were followed during a couple of weeks while a presidential campaign is going on. Part documentary and part satire., the intricate movie was a collage of characters and themes taking place on stage, backstage, and everywhere else in the city. Joan Tewkesbury wrote the complicated screenplay with help from the cast (sections of dialogue and some scenes are clearly improvised), who also penned some of the many songs in the piece. Keith Carradine, Ronee Blakely,

Lily Tomlin, Gwen Welles, Henry Gibson, BARBARA HARRIS, Shelley Duvall, Karen Black, Ned Beatty, Michael Murphy, KEENAN WYNN, and Geraldine Chaplin were standouts in a large cast that was never less than riveting to watch. Altman produced and directed the sprawling giant of a movie with cockeyed affection for the country music business and the American character itself. The songs, ranging from hillbilly parodies to bluegrass to folk to light rock and roll, gave the film its tempo and verve. Carradine wrote and sang the Oscar-winning "I'm Easy" and the lazy "It Don't Worry Me," but just as accomplished were the heartbreaking "Dues," the naive patriotic "200 Years," the wistful "My Idaho Home," the rhythmic "Tapedeck in His Tractor," the moaning "Memphis," and others.

NAUGHTON, JAMES (1945–). Stage, film, and television performer. The solid, handsome leading man of musicals and nonmusicals always brings a casual, lightweight quality to his roles. Naughton was born in Middleton, Connecticut, and educated at Brown and Yale Universities before making a noteworthy Manhattan debut as Edmund in a 1971 revival of *Long Day's Journey Into Night*. While he would play a variety of roles on the stage, he is most remembered for his musical performances: the wife-swapping Wally in *I LOVE MY WIFE* (1977), the hard-boiled detective Stone in *CITY OF ANGELS* (1989), and the first of many Billy Flynns in the long-running 1996 revival of *CHICAGO*. Naughton has appeared in some films and many television series over the years, but his musical talents were seldom used.

✪ *NAUGHTY MARIETTA* (New York Theatre 1910). It may not have been VICTOR HERBERT'S biggest hit, but the operetta was musically his finest work and is still a remarkable theatre piece.

Plot: French New Orleans in the 1780s is being terrorized by the pirate Bras Pique whose true identity is unknown, and Captain Dick Warrington and his rangers are sent by the King of France to find the culprit. The peasant girl Marietta, who is really the Countess d'Altena who has fled France and come to New Orleans, is attracted to Etienne, the son of the lieutenant governor, but it is Dick who loves her even when he discovers her true identity and is ordered to bring her back to France. By this time Marietta has learned that Etienne is Bras Pique and she is his prisoner, only to be rescued by Dick. Etienne escapes with his

Casts for *Naughty Marietta*

Character	1910 Broadway	1935 film	1955 television
Marietta d'Altena	EMMA TRENTINI	JEANETTE MACDONALD	Patrice Munsel
Capt. Dick Warrington	Orville Harrold	NELSON EDDY	ALFRED DRAKE
Etienne Grandet	Edward Martindel		
Adah	Marie Duchene		
Governor		FRANK MORGAN	John Conte
Madame d'Annard		Elsa Lancaster	
Prince de Namours		Douglass Dumbrille	
Schuman		Joseph Cawthorn	
Yvonne			Gale Sherwood
Louis D'Arc			Don Driver

pirates and Marietta realizes she loves Dick, especially when he can complete the song fragment that has haunted her.

RIDA JOHNSON YOUNG wrote the forced but effective libretto, and impresario OSCAR HAMMERSTEIN I cast the operetta with singers from his financially troubled Manhattan Opera Company. Knowing that he was writing for highly trained singers, Herbert composed his most difficult and rhapsodic music, and Young supplied the gushing lyrics. The recurring "Ah, Sweet Mystery of Life" was used effectively throughout the score and became the operetta's biggest hit, but also popular were the marching "Tramp! Tramp! Tramp!," the vivacious "Italian Street Song," the dreamy ballad "'Neath the Southern Moon," and the waltzing "I'm Falling in Love With Someone." The musical was a triumph for Herbert and for opera singer EMMA TRENTINI (Marietta) and the original production ran 136 performances. *Naughty Marietta* returned to New York for short engagements in 1929 and 1931 and for decades was a favorite with operetta and light opera companies, still being produced today on occasion.

■ *Naughty Marietta* (MGM 1935) introduced the singing team of JEANETTE MACDONALD and NELSON EDDY to movie audiences and it was love at first sight. The movie not only inspired seven more movie musicals with the pair but also paved the way for the popularity of film operettas through the rest of the decade. The script by FRANCES GOODRICH and ALBERT HACKETT took many liberties with the stage libretto, having Marietta attacked by pirates while sailing from France to New Orleans and being rescued by Dick Warrington. There were a lot of contrived complications once they

Naughty Marietta (stage) Musical Numbers

"Tramp! Tramp! Tramp!"
"Taisez-Vous"
"Naughty Marietta"
"It Never, Never Can Be Love"
"If I Were Anybody Else But Me"
"'Neath the Southern Moon (For Thee)"
"Italian Street Song"
"The Marionette Song"
"(You) Marry a Marionette"
"New Orleans Jeunesse Doree"
"Opening of the Ball (Loves of New Orleans)"
"(The Sweet) Bye and Bye"
"Live for Today"
"I'm Falling in Love With Someone"
"It's Pretty Soft for Simon"
"Dream Melody (Ah, Sweet Mystery of Life)"

arrived in America as she continued to hide her true identity but all was resolved in an illogical but romantic fashion. The highlights from the Herbert–Young score were retained and, as sung by the two stars, the songs were so thrilling that audiences embraced the old favorites all over again. W. S. VAN DYKE directed with efficiency, the movie looked as beautiful as it sounded, and *Naughty Marietta* was a hit once again. ☐ MAX LEIBMAN produced a seventy-five-minute version of the operetta for NBC-TV and it was well sung by Patrice Munsel and ALFRED DRAKE in the leading roles. The broadcast was part of an ambitious series titled *Max Leibman Presents*, which offered abridged versions of musicals and operettas with name talents.

NEAGLE, ANNA [born Florence Marjorie Robertson] (1904–1986). Film and stage performer. A musical star of the London stage and films, she was mostly known for her historical films in Hollywood but also starred in some musicals. Neagle was born in London and by the age of fourteen was dancing in the chorus of West End musicals. She was discovered by producer Herbert Wilcox (who later married her) and he promoted her first as a stage star and then as a musical star in a dozen British films starting in 1932. Neagle came to Hollywood during the 1940s and made a series of melodramas that had her playing Florence Nightingale, Queen Victoria, and other inspirational women in history. She also played the title roles in three American musicals, *IRENE* (1940), *NO, NO, NANETTE* (1941), and *SUNNY* (1941), all produced by Wilcox. She left films in the 1960s and returned to the London stage and appeared in musicals into the 1980s. Autobiographies: *It's Been Fun* (1941); *There's Always Tomorrow* (1974).

NEDERLANDER, JAMES AND DAVID. Stage managers, owners, and producers. The father and then the son built up an organization of Broadway theatres that is second only to the Shuberts and helped fill them with plays and musicals. David T. Nederlander (1886–1965) was born in Detroit and in 1912 founded the Nederlander organization when he bought a ninety-nine-year lease on the Detroit Opera House. The company expanded under the leadership of his son James [Morton] Nederlander (1922–) who bought up theatres across the country, as well as outdoor ampitheatres in Los Angeles, Minneapolis, and Santa Barbara where name attractions were booked. Today the Nederlanders own nine Broadway playhouses, another nine regionally in the States, and three in London. In addition to presenting international dance, opera, and ethnic companies on Broadway, James Nederlander has produced such musicals as *ON A CLEAR DAY YOU CAN SEE FOREVER* (1965), *APPLAUSE* (1970), *PETER PAN* (1979 and 1990), *JOSEPH AND THE TECHNICOLOR DREAMCOAT* (1982), *ME AND MY GIRL* (1986), and *THE WILL ROGERS FOLLIES* (1991).

NELSON, GENE [born Leander Eugene Berg] (1920–1996). Film, stage, and television performer and director. An athletic dancer in the GENE KELLY style, he usually played supporting roles in 1950s movie musicals and often stole the show. Nelson was born in Seattle, Washington, and began taking dance lessons as a boy, studying with NICK CASTLE and appearing in revues at Los Angeles's Paramount movie theatre.

He toured with SONJA HENIE's ice show for three years before making his screen debut as a dancer in *THIS IS THE ARMY* (1943). Nelson was featured in such musicals as *I Wonder Who's Kissing Her Now* (1947), *The Daughter of Rosie O'Grady* (1950), *Tea for Two* (1950), *The West Point Story* (1950), *Lullaby of Broadway* (1951), *Painting the Clouds With Sunshine* (1951), *She's Working Her Way Through College* (1953), *She's Back on Broadway* (1953), *Three Sailors and a Girl* (1953), and *So This Is Paris* (1954) before getting the plum role of the eager cowboy Will Parker in *OKLAHOMA!* (1955), dazzling audiences with his vivacious singing and dancing of "Kansas City." Nelson appeared in some dramatic roles on screen before concentrating on directing in the 1960s and 1970s, helming two ELVIS PRESLEY films, *Kissin' Cousins* (1964) and *Harum Scarum* (1965), and directing many episodes of television series and appearing in specials, such as the TV musicals *LET'S FACE IT!* (1954), *A Man's Game* (1957), and *Shangri-La* (1960). He made a triumphant comeback as a performer as the frustrated Buddy in the Broadway musical *FOLLIES* (1971).

NELSON, KENNETH (1930–1993). Stage performer. A youthful-looking actor–singer, he played teenagers when he was far beyond his teen years and then found difficulty getting cast in adult roles. Nelson was born in Rocky Mount, North Carolina, and grew up in San Antonio, Texas, and later attended Baylor University before studying acting with Uta Hagen in New York. At the age of twenty-one he made his Broadway bow as seventeen-year-old Willie Baxter in the musical *Seventeen* (1951). Nine years later he was still playing a teenager, but in the best role of his career: naive lover Matt in the original cast of *THE FANTASTICKS* (1960). Nelson appeared in the musicals *Night-Cap* (1958), *The Sap of Life* (1961), as replacements for Littlechap in *STOP THE WORLD—I WANT TO GET OFF* (1963) and Kipps in *HALF A SIXPENCE* (1965), and as the sly narrator Sakini in the short-lived *Lovely Ladies, Kind Gentlemen* (1970). He also acted in nonmusicals, most memorably as the gay host Michael in *The Boys in the Band* (1968), a role he reprised in London and on film. Nelson relocated to London in 1971 and concentrated on British television for the rest of his career.

NELSON, OZZIE, AND HARRIET HILLIARD. Film and television performers and bandleader. A collegiate-looking conductor and his wife with the tiny but expressive voice, the couple were featured in Hollywood musicals but found greater fame on television without doing any conducting or singing. Ozzie Nelson [born Oswald George Nelson] (1906–1975) was born in Jersey City, New Jersey, and was educated at Rutgers University where he was a top athlete and formed his own band. After graduation he went professional and his orchestra was gaining in popularity when he met Harriet Hilliard [born Peggy Lou Snyder] (1909–1994). She was born in Des Moines, Iowa, into a show business family and performed as a child. After high school she went into vaudeville as a singer and attracted the attention of bandleader Nelson who made her his featured vocalist and later his wife. Her singing with Nelson on the radio led to Hilliard's being cast in supporting roles in the movie musicals *Follow the Fleet* (1936), *New Faces of 1937*, *Life of the Party* (1937), *Cocoanut Grove* (1938), *Jukebox Jennie* (1942), *Hi, Buddy* (1943), *Gals, Incorporated* (1943), and *Swingtime Johnny* (1944). Nelson and his band were heard in *Strictly in the Groove* (1942) and *People Are Funny* (1946). Nelson and Hilliard performed together in the films *Sweetheart on Campus* (1941), *Honeymoon Lodge* (1943), *Hi, Good Lookin'* (1944), and *Take It Big* (1944). The two began their famous radio show in 1944 and it moved to television in 1952, remaining on the air for fourteen years. The musical aspects of the show were phased out in the 1940s so for most of its run *The Adventures of Ozzie and Harriet* was a situation comedy. Their sons, actor–director David Nelson (1936–) and singer Ricky Nelson (1940–1985), played themselves on the show, growing up on television and giving the bland but cozy show a sincerity found in few sitcoms. Autobiography: *Ozzie* (1973)

NEPTUNE'S DAUGHTER (MGM 1949). The most profitable of the many ESTHER WILLIAMS vehicles, this breezy and melodic romp offered a better score than was usually found in the swimming star's movies. DOROTHY KINGSLEY wrote the screenplay about ex-swimming champion Eve Barrett (Williams) who runs a swimsuit manufacturing company and is throwing a big fashion show when Latin American polo star José O'Rourke (RICARDO MONTALBAN) comes to town. Eve's oversexed sister Betty (BETTY GARRETT) mistakes the clubhouse masseur Jack Spratt (RED SKELTON) for the famous sportsman and harmless merriment results. KEENAN WYNN, Ted De Corsia, Mel Blanc, and XAVIER CUGAT and his orchestra were thrown into the mix while JACK DONOHUE staged some spectacular water ballets for Williams. However, it is the delightful score by FRANK LOESSER that sticks in the memory, particularly the Oscar-winning duet "Baby, It's Cold Outside," which made no sense since the story took place in summer. The number had been written years earlier for Loesser and his first wife to sing at parties. Also in the score were "I Love Those Men" and "My Heart Beats Faster." EDWARD BUZZELL directed the colorful JACK CUMMINGS production.

NEUWIRTH, BEBE [Beatrice] (1958–). Stage, television, and film performer. The lithe, mannered dancer–singer is also a fine comedienne in films and television sit-coms. Neuwirth was born in Princeton, New Jersey, the daughter of a mathematician and an artist, studied dance at Juilliard, and danced with the Princeton ballet Company. By 1980 she was on Broadway as a replacement for Sheila in *A Chorus Line*, followed by a replacement position in *Dancin'* (1978) and appearances in the musicals *Little Me* (1982), *Upstairs at O'Neals* (1982), and *Kicks* (1984) before getting noticed as the taxi dancer Nicki in *Sweet Charity* (1986). Neuwirth was finally starring on Broadway as the seductress Lola in the 1994 revival of *Damn Yankees*, was applauded as the murderess Velma in the 1996 revival of *Chicago*, and was featured in the dance revue *Fosse* (2001). She has acted in a handful of films and in many television programs, including recurring characters on the series *Cheers* and *Law and Order*.

NEVER GONNA DANCE. See *SWING TIME*

NEW BRAIN, A (Mitzi Newhouse Theatre 1998). An inventive, deeply moving Off Broadway musical by WILLIAM FINN, the sung-through piece was autobiographical yet there was no self pity or moroseness about it. Gordon Schwinn (Malcolm Gets) writes songs for a children's television show character, the frog Mr. Bungee (CHIP ZIEN), but dreams of creating a body of songs that say something worthwhile. When he collapses in a restaurant one day and is hospitalized, his friends gather around him, including his ex-lover Roger (Christopher Innvar) and Gordon's fretful mother Mimi (Penny Fuller). A brain tumor is discovered and treatments in the hospital bring on hallucinations of the present, such as a tormenting Mr. Bungee, and the past, as with memories of a gambling-addict father and Gordon's former happiness with Roger. The tumor is operated on successfully and by the time Gordon comes back to life his perspective had changed, deciding he will now live for "Time and Music." Other numbers in the superb score include "And They're Off," "Sailing," "Family History," "Gordo's Law of Genetics," and "The Music Still Plays On." GRACIELA DANIELE directed and choreographed the small-scale musical, and the LINCOLN CENTER production ran a limited engagement of 78 performances.

🕭 *NEW FACES* MUSICALS. Stage series. Seven musical revues presented by LEONARD SILLMAN between 1934 and 1968 in which the focus was on new performers, the series also introduced songs and scripts by budding talents as well. The number of famous actors, singers, and dancers who came from the shows is impressive, ranging from Henry Fonda to MADELEINE KAHN, and the new writers to get early work in the revues include MEL BROOKS, Ronny Graham, SHELDON HARNICK, E. Y. HARBURG, Luther Davis, NEIL SIMON, Dean Fuller, and Marshall Barer,

🎬 Twice Hollywood took some of the talent and material from the best revues and put them on screen, giving the newcomers even more exposure, although neither film version was a box office smash. *New Faces of 1937* (RKO 1936) was a misnomer, as the only cast member making anything close to a screen debut was ANN MILLER. The film was not a revue but a tired backstage story that was enlivened by not-so-new MILTON BERLE, HARRIET HILLIARD, JOE PENNER, Tommy Mack, Bert Gordon, and Patricia Wilder. What was new were the SAMMY FAIN (music) and LEW BROWN songs, the best being "Our Penthouse on Third Avenue" and "Love Is Never Out of Season." Much more

satisfying was *New Faces* (Fox 1954), a fairly faithful recreation of the *New Faces of 1952* stage revue, the most successful in the stage series (365 performances). EARTHA KITT sang "Monotonous" as she had on Broadway and was given the interpolated hit songs "C'est Si Bon" and "Santa Baby" to purr as well. The other highlight of the film was Paul Lynde's comedy monologues and sketches, most of which he wrote himself. Also from Broadway were Robert Clary, June Carroll, Alice Ghostly, and CAROL LAWRENCE, with new "new faces" added for the movie. The production values look cheap and there is no effort made to open up the show, yet it is an entertaining archival record of these promising performers.

🕭 *NEW GIRL IN TOWN* (46th Street 1957). An entertaining vehicle for the Broadway dancing star GWEN VERDON, the show also had a substantial plot, characters, and score. GEORGE ABBOTT adapted Eugene O'Neill's drama *Anna Christie* (1921) into a musical play about the ex-prostitute Anna (Verdon) who falls for the sailor Mat (George Wallace) and keeps his love even after he finds out about her past. Cameron Prud'homme was her crusty father and Thelma Ritter stole all her scenes as the caustic Marthy. BOB MERRILL wrote the commendable songs, including "It's Good to Be Alive," "Flings," "Sunshine Girl," "There Ain't No Flies on Me," "At the Check Apron Ball," and "On the Farm." The gritty realistic drama became primarily a dance show but with Verdon center stage few minded. Abbott directed, BOB FOSSE did the boisterous choreography, and the unlikely show (produced by HAROLD PRINCE, Frederick Brisson, and Robert Griffith) ran 461 performances

Casts from the *New Faces* (stage) revues

New Faces of 1934	*New Faces of 1936*	*New Faces of 1943*	*New Faces of 1952*
IMOGENE COCA	Jack Smart	Irwin Corey	Alice Ghostley
Henry Fonda	Helen Craig	Diane Davis	June Carroll
Dolores Hart	VAN JOHNSON	John Lund	EARTHA KITT
Gus Schirmer	Billie Haywood	ALICE PEARCE	Paul Lynde
Nancy Hamilton	Karl Swenson	Dorothy Dennis	Robert Clary
Teddy Lynch	RALPH BLANE	Tony Farrar	CAROL LAWRENCE
New Faces of 1956	*New Faces of 1962*	*New Faces of 1968*	
JANE CONNELL	Marian Mercer	Robert Klein	
Virginia Martin	Tom Arthur	MADELEINE KAHN	
Bill McCutheon	Joey Carter	Gloria Bleezarde	
INGA SWENSON	Patti Karr	Brandon Maggart	
Maggie Smith	Mickey Wayland	Trudy Carson	
TIGER HAYNES	Juan Carlos Copes	Dorothy Frank	

NEW MOON, THE (Imperial Theatre 1929). Considered the last of the great American operettas, this lyrical musical romance scored by SIGMUND ROMBERG ended the era dominated by VICTOR HERBERT, RUDOLF FRIML, and Romberg.

Plot: The French nobleman Robert Misson has revolutionary sympathies so he flees his native country and goes to New Orleans in the 1790s disguised as a servant and falls in love with the aristocratic Marianne, the daughter of his employer. Robert, his cohort Phillippe, and their fellow revolutionaries plan to overthrow the royalists in the New World but Robert's disguise is betrayed, he believes by Marianne. When he is put aboard the ship *The New Moon* to return to France and stand trial, Marianne stows away to be with him. The ship is attacked by pirates but they turn out to be Phillippe and his friends come to rescue Robert. The revolutionaries settle on the Isle of Pines and begin to lead a democratic lifestyle but Marianne and Robert are not reunited until he learns of her innocence and word arrives from France that the Revolution has begun and they are all free.

OSCAR HAMMERSTEIN, FRANK MANDEL, and LAURENCE SCHWAB collaborated on the intricate but pleasing libretto, and Hammerstein wrote the lyrics for Romberg's music, resulting in a superlative set of songs. The waltzing ballads "One Kiss," "Lover, Come Back to Me," and "Wanting You" all became famous, as did the rousing "Stouthearted Men," the gushing tribute "Marianne," and the melancholy lament "Softly, As in a Morning Sunrise." The operetta had a disastrous out-of-town tryout tour and the New York opening was delayed for eight months while the creators reworked the piece. When *The New Moon* finally opened it was cheered by the press and the public and ran 509 performances, a final celebratory hurrah before the stock market crash and the end of the old-style American operetta. New York saw major revivals of the operetta in 1942,

1944, 1986, and 1988. *The New Moon* continues to be produced by light opera companies.

Hollywood made two versions of the operetta, both dropping the "The" and retitled *New Moon*. The 1930 MGM film was reset in Russia with a heroine called Princess Tanya (GRACE MOORE) in love with the dashing Lieutenant Petroff (LAWRENCE TIBBETT) even though she is engaged to the government agent Boris Brusiloff (ADOLPHE MENJOU). The dynamics in the Sylvia Thalberg and Frank Butler screenplay were completely different but the songs still made sense and were effective, especially as sung by the two celebrated opera stars. MGM remade *New Moon* in 1940 as a vehicle for JEANETTE MACDONALD and NELSON EDDY, and the Robert Arthur and Jacques Deval screenplay was closer to the stage libretto, although some of the names were different. Once again it was the songs that counted, and the popular singing couple did justice to those numbers that survived the transition. ROBERT

The New Moon (stage) Musical Numbers

"Dainty Wisp of a Thistledown"
"Marianne"
"The Girl on the Prow"
"Gorgeous Alexander"
"An Interrupted Love Song"
"Tavern Song (Red Wine)"
"Softly, As in a Morning Sunrise"
"Stouthearted Men (Liberty Song)"
"Fair Rosita"
"One Kiss"
"Ladies of the Jury"
"Wanting You"
"A Chanty"
"Funny Little Sailor Man"
"Lover, Come Back to Me"
"Love Is Quite a Simple Thing"
"Try Her Out at Dancing"
"Never (For You)"

Casts for *(The) New Moon*

Character	1928 Broadway	1930 film	1940 film
Marianne/Tanya	EVELYN HERBERT	GRACE MOORE	JEANETTE MACDONALD
Robert/Michael/Charles	ROBERT HALLIDAY	LAWRENCE TIBBETT	NELSON EDDY
Vicomte Ribuad	Max Figman		GEORGE ZUCCO
Alexander	Gus Shy		
Phillippe	William O'Neal		
Governor		ADOLPHE MENJOU	
Valerie de Rossac			MARY BOLAND

Z. LEONARD directed with a romantic touch, yet the movie has a rustic, more rugged quality than a dreamy, operetta one. Both films did well at the box office because of the popularity of the singing stars.

NEW ORLEANS (United Artists 1947). With one of the greatest collections of jazz talents in one movie, this film could have been a classic but instead it was a tiresome melodrama with wonderful musical interruptions. Young Miralee Smith (Dorothy Patrick) upsets her high society mother (Irene Rich) and forsakes the world of classical music for jazz even as she rejects her well-connected beaux and falls for Nick Duquesne (Arturo de Cordova). Shelly Winters, Marjorie Lord, John Alexander, and Richard Hageman were also cast in the forgettable tale that was strung out over forty years. The movie attempted to show the rise and development of jazz during those forty years and as a history lesson it was suspect. However, the appearance of Billie Holiday singing "Do You Know What It Means to Miss New Orleans" (by LOUIS ALTER and Edgar De Lange) with LOUIS ARMSTRONG and his New Orleans Ragtime Band with Woody Herman joining in will tell you an awful lot about the power of jazz. Other renowned jazz musicians who showed up on screen included Kid Ory, Zutty Singleton, Barney Bigard, Bud Scott, Charlie Beal, Red Callender, and Meade Lux Lewis. Director Arthur Lubin didn't know how to film such talents in performance but they were there to be heard, as were such jazz favorites as "Basin Street Blues," "New Orleans Stomp," "The Blues Are Brewin'," "Honky Tonk Train Blues," "Ahim-Me-Sha-Wabble," "Mahogany Hall Stomp," and "Where the Blues Were Born in New Orleans."

NEW YORK CITY CENTER LIGHT OPERA COMPANY. Theatre company. The large Manhattan venue called the City Center may not be ideal for musical theatre but it has been the home for various organizations that have presented revivals there since the 1949 production of CAROUSEL. Between 1955 and 1968, the New York City Center Light Opera Company produced a series of musicals and operettas, first under the supervision of William Hammerstein and then under JEAN DALRYMPLE. Because the venue has 2,683 seats, these revivals could not run very long and hope to fill the theatre so the number of performances given is not impressive until one considers the number of patrons who saw the shows. During Dalrymple's tenure (1957 to 1968), over thirty revivals were presented, in many cases the first New York productions after the original runs. Sometimes the demand for tickets was great enough that a show had to leave the tightly booked City Center and continue its run in a traditional house. This happened on eight occasions with revivals such as BRIGADOON (1957), THE MOST HAPPY FELLA (1959), PAL JOEY (1963), and GUYS AND DOLLS (1965). Today the only musical theatre event in the City Center is the popular ENCORES! series and they usually perform in the large house for only three performances.

NEW YORK DRAMA CRITICS CIRCLE AWARD. Theatre awards. In 1935 a group of New York theatre critics, unhappy with some recent decisions made for the PULITZER PRIZE for drama, founded the New York Theatre Critics Circle with an eye to awarding their own honors to plays and musicals on Broadway. The group has also held regular meetings over the years to discuss the state of the American theatre and form a united front on certain issues. However, it is the awards that the public and the theatre community are most interested in. The categories are sometimes tricky, with awards on some occasions going to the best American play, best musical, and best foreign play, other times going to the best play and musical regardless of nationality and once in a while special citations are given to musicals and foreign works. While winning the New York Drama Critics Circle Award may not have the same box office effect as the Pulitzer and the TONY AWARD, it is considered a prestigious honor of sorts since it tends not to be a popularity contest and aims to be about the quality of theatre. The history of the awards points out some embarrassing errors but for the most part the works that won deserved some kind of attention.

NEW YORK, NEW YORK (United Artists 1977). Director Martin Scorsese's attempt to capture the stylized look and feel of a 1940s studio musical, the film was very 1970s in its sensibility and often musically very satisfying. Earl MacRauch and Mardik Martin scripted the loose chronicle of freewheeling saxophone player Jimmy Doyle (Robert De Niro) who meets the struggling band singer Francine Evans (LIZA MINNELLI) during the frenzied VJ Day celebration in New York's Rainbow Room. The two embark on a bumpy courtship and marriage only to split after their child is born. The story was a downer in the expected Scorsese vein but the music made it worth sitting through. The sounds of the Big Band era

New York Drama Critics Circle Award-Winning Musicals	
1946	CAROUSEL
1947	BRIGADOON
1949	SOUTH PACIFIC
1950	The Consul
1951	GUYS AND DOLLS
1952	PAL JOEY (revival)
1953	WONDERFUL TOWN
1954	THE GOLDEN APPLE
1955	The Saint of Bleecker Street
1956	MY FAIR LADY
1957	THE MOST HAPPY FELLA
1958	THE MUSIC MAN
1959	LA PLUME DE MA TANTE
1960	FIORELLO!
1961	CARNIVAL
1962	HOW TO SUCCEED IN BUSINESS WITHOUT REALLY TRYING
1964	HELLO, DOLLY!
1965	FIDDLER ON THE ROOF
1966	MAN OF LA MANCHA
1967	CABARET
1968	YOUR OWN THING
1969	1776
1970	COMPANY
1971	FOLLIES
1972	TWO GENTLEMEN OF VERONA
1973	A LITTLE NIGHT MUSIC
1974	CANDIDE (revival)
1975	A CHORUS LINE
1976	PACIFIC OVERTURES
1977	ANNIE
1978	AIN'T MISBEHAVIN'
1979	SWEENEY TODD
1980	EVITA
1983	LITTLE SHOP OF HORRORS
1984	SUNDAY IN THE PARK WITH GEORGE
1987	LES MISÉRABLES
1988	INTO THE WOODS
1990	CITY OF ANGELS
1991	THE WILL ROGERS FOLLIES
1993	KISS OF THE SPIDER WOMAN
1996	RENT
1997	VIOLET
1998	THE LION KING
1999	PARADE
2000	JAMES JOYCE'S THE DEAD
2001	THE PRODUCERS
2003	HAIRSPRAY
2006	THE DROWSY CHAPERONE
2007	SPRING AWAKENING

"Honeysuckle Rose," "The Man I Love," "Blue Moon," and others, and JOHN KANDER (music) and FRED EBB (lyrics) provided a handful of new songs that were expert, including "There Goes the Ball Game," "But the World Goes Round," and the runaway hit "Theme From New York, New York," which joined the list of song standards about Manhattan. The movie initially ran over four hours, so the studio cut ninety minutes before releasing it. Lost was a lengthy musical montage called "Happy Endings" featuring Minnelli and LARRY KERT, which recalled the extended "Born in a Trunk" section that Minnelli's mother JUDY GARLAND had performed in A STAR IS BORN (1954). When New York, New York was reissued in 1981, the number was reinstated.

NEW YORK SHAKESPEARE FESTIVAL. Stage organization. With its humble roots in low-budget productions of Shakespeare presented in the various boroughs of New York City for free, the organization has grown into one of the city's largest and most respected producing groups. JOSEPH PAPP founded the New York Shakespeare Festival in 1954 with a charter from the State of New York Education Department to "encourage and cultivate interest in poetic drama with emphasis on William Shakespeare and his Elizabethan contemporaries," but over the years the festival has included new works, including musicals. The company acquired a permanent home at the outdoor Delacorte Theatre in Central Park in 1962 where summer productions were offered free of charge and the practice continues to this day. That venue has seen the premiere of such new musicals as TWO GENTLEMEN OF VERONA (1971) and THE MYSTERY OF EDWIN DROOD (1985) and revivals such as THE PIRATES OF PENZANCE (1980) and ON THE TOWN (1998), all of which transferred to Broadway. In 1967 the festival purchased the old Astor Library near Washington Square and the Off Broadway organization known as the **Public Theatre** was born. This multispace complex with several theatres of different sizes was conceived as a winter home for the company's productions, but it expanded into a year-round operation that emphasized new works. Again, several notable musicals were born here, such as A CHORUS LINE (1975), I'M GETTING MY ACT TOGETHER AND TAKING IT ON THE ROAD (1978), Runaways (1978), THE HUMAN COMEDY (1984), BRING ON 'DA NOISE BRING ON 'DA FUNK (1996), and CAROLINE, OR CHANGE (2004). After the death of Papp in 1991 the organization suffered some administrative problems but over the past decade or so has

flowed throughout with Georgie Auld dubbing De Niro's sax playing. Minnelli sang some old favorites ("You Are My Lucky Star,"

strengthened and continues to be a vital force in New York theatre.

🔑 *NEW YORKERS, THE* (Broadway Theatre 1930). A cynical, bitter even, view of upper-class Manhattan, the musical was still palatable to audiences because of its delightful COLE PORTER score and the fact that the HERBERT FIELDS's libretto was presented as nothing but a dream. Socialite Alice Wentworth (Hope Williams) of Park Avenue takes up with gang-ster–bootlegger Al Spanish (CHARLES KING) and they are joined by fumbling mobster Jimmie Deegan (JIMMY DURANTE), Alice's father (Richard Carle), and his mistress Lola McGee (ANN PENNINGTON). Also scheming away are Alice's mother (MARIE CAHILL) and her gigolo Alfredo (Maurice Lapue) as they all go down to Miami to party. The law catches up with Al and he is arrested, not for his many murders or booze operations, but for parking too close to a fire hydrant. Just as Alice loses her lover she awakes from her dream brought on by an injection from her family doctor. Also in the cast were Rags Ragland, Kathryn Crawford, Frances Williams, Lou Clayton, and Eddie Jackson. The Porter songs included the sultry "Love for Sale," the breezy "Take Me Back to Manhattan," the dreamy rhythm number "Let's Fly Away," and the matter-of-fact salute "I Happen to Like New York." Reviewers hailed the irreverent, slaphappy musical satire and the show would have run longer than 168 performances had not the Bank of America folded three days after the musical opened and America was thrown into the dark-est days of the Depression. The musical was directed with wit by MONTY WOOLLEY and the choreography was by GEORGE HALE.

NEWLEY, ANTHONY (1931–1999). Stage, film, and television performer, composer, lyricist, and writer. The hyperactive, multitalented star of two continents, he managed a busy perform-ing and writing career side by side for decades. Newley was born in London's East End and attended the Italia Conti Stage School as a teenager. By the time he was sixteen he was featured in several British films, most memora-bly as the young Artful Dodger in *Oliver Twist* (1948). After serving in World War II, he con-centrated on his singing career and made some hit records. He also performed in musicals in the West End and played major roles in such British film musicals as *The Good Companions* (1957), *The Lady Is a Square* (1959), and *Jazz Boat* (1960). Newley made his Broadway bow when he performed in the British revue *Cranks*

(1956) in New York. In London he co-wrote the book, music, and lyrics (with Leslie Bricusse), directed, and played the hero Littlechap in *STOP THE WORLD—I WANT TO GET OFF* (1961) and the next year brought it to Broadway for a long run. Newley had the same jobs for *THE ROAR OF THE GREASEPAINT–THE SMELL OF THE CROWD* (1965), which originated in New York. His performing in the States after that was lim-ited to nightclubs, concerts, and television and he continued to write musicals for the stage and screen. With Bricusse he scored the movie musical *WILLY WONKA AND THE CHOCOLATE FACTORY* (1971) and the TV musical *PETER PAN* (1976). Newley wrote music and lyrics on his own and performed in the film musi-cals *DOCTOR DOLITTLE* (1967), *Can Hieronymus Merkin Ever Forget Mercy Humppe and Find True Happiness?* (1969), and *Mr. Quilp* (1975), which was later rereleased as *The Old Curiosity Shop*. He also acted in the TV musicals *ALICE IN WONDERLAND* (1985) and *POLLY—COMIN' HOME!* (1990). Newley was a bombastic per-former with a reedy voice that was unique and he wrote equally bombastic but thrilling songs such as "What Kind of Fool Am I?," "Who Can I Turn To?," "Gonna Build a Mountain," "Talk to the Animals," and "Candy Man." He was married to actress Joan Collins (1933–) for a time.

NEWMAN, ALFRED (1901–1970). Film con-ductor, composer, and music director. An oft-awarded and highly respected maestro, he was in charge of the music for over 200 Hollywood movies. Born in New Haven, Connecticut, Newman was a child prodigy on the piano, giving concerts by the time he was seven and conducting both symphony orchestras and Broadway musicals in his twenties. He went to Hollywood at the age of thirty and directed the music for the musical *WHOOPEE!* (1930), followed by many musicals over the next forty years. He won Academy Awards for nine movies, including the musicals *ALEXANDER'S RAGTIME BAND* (1938), *TIN PAN ALLEY* (1940), *MOTHER WORE TIGHTS* (1947), *WITH A SONG IN MY HEART* (1952), *CALL ME MADAM* (1953), and *THE KING AND I* (1956). Newman's other notable musicals include *ROMAN SCANDALS* (1933), *BROADWAY MELODY OF 1936* (1935), *LILLIAN RUSSELL* (1940), *STATE FAIR* (1945 and 1962), *CAROUSEL* (1956), *SOUTH PACIFIC* (1958), and *CAMELOT* (1967). He composed music for concerts as well as films, but his only screen musical with Newman songs was *The Blue Bird* (1940) with lyrics by WALTER BULLOCK. He is the father of screen composer David Newman

(1954–), the brother of film music director LIONEL NEWMAN, and the uncle of singer–composer Randy Newman (1943–).

NEWMAN, LIONEL (1916–1989). Film and television musician, music director, and conductor. As the musical director at 20TH CENTURY-FOX for many years, the versatile musician and composer made his mark on the Hollywood musical. Newman was born in New Haven, Connecticut, and began his career as piano accompanist for MAE WEST. He started in movies in 1943 as a rehearsal pianist and eventually became a much-respected music arranger, supervising the music in 250 musicals and nonmusicals. Newman's musical credits include *You Were Meant for Me* (1948), *Give My Regards to Broadway* (1948), *WABASH AVENUE* (1950), *ON THE RIVIERA* (1951), *GENTLEMEN PREFER BLONDES* (1953), *The I Don't Care Girl* (1953), *THE FARMER TAKES A WIFE* (1953), *THERE'S NO BUSINESS LIKE SHOW BUSINESS* (1954), *DOCTOR DOLITTLE* (1967), *HELLO, DOLLY!* (1969), and *At Long Last Love* (1975). He also composed music for some forty movies and television shows, including the musicals *Bloodhounds of Broadway* (1952), *LOVE ME TENDER* (1956), *THE BEST THINGS IN LIFE ARE FREE* (1956), and *Let's Make Love* (1960). He is the younger brother of ALFRED NEWMAN.

NEWMAN, PHYLLIS (1933–). Stage and television performer. The attractive, dark-haired, energetic actress–singer has appeared on Broadway for over a period of fifty years, often playing lively, ditzy supporting roles. Newman was born in Jersey City, New Jersey, and was educated at Case Western Reserve University and Columbia and had actor training with Wynn Handman. She made her Broadway debut in the ensemble of the musical *WISH YOU WERE HERE* (1952), followed by the revue *I Feel Wonderful* (1954) and the role of Jane Bennet in the musical version of *Pride and Prejudice* titled *First Impressions* (1959). Newman garnered plaudits as the funny ex-beauty queen Martha Vail in *SUBWAYS ARE FOR SLEEPING* (1961) and then began her career on television and in nightclubs. She returned to Broadway in plays and musicals past the year 2000, featured in such musicals as *THE APPLE TREE* (1967), *ON THE TOWN* (1971), *The Madwoman of Central Park West* (1979), *I'M GETTING MY ACT TOGETHER AND TAKING IT ON THE ROAD* (1980), and *I MARRIED AN ANGEL* (1986). Newman has appeared in several films and on hundreds of television programs, from talk shows and series to game shows and musical specials, including the TV musicals *THE*

VAGABOND KING (1956) and *OLYMPUS 7-0000* (1966). She was married to lyricist–librettist ADOLPH GREEN.

NEWMAR, JULIE [born Julia Chalene Newmeyer] (1933–). Film, stage, and television performer. A leggy, voluptuous actress–singer best remembered for her sexy Stupefyin' Jones in the Broadway and Hollywood musicals *LI'L ABNER*, she was a popular television performer in the 1960s. Newmar was born in Los Angeles, the daughter of a former football player and a former *Follies* girl, and studied ballet before attending the University of California at Los Angeles. She danced in Los Angeles Opera productions before getting minor roles in the movie musicals *THE BAND WAGON* (1953), *The Eddie Cantor Story* (1953), and *SEVEN BRIDES FOR SEVEN BROTHERS* (1954). Newmar then went to New York where she made her Broadway debut as a featured ballerina in *SILK STOCKINGS* (1955). The next year she was noticed in *Li'l Abner* and she reprised her Jones in the 1959 screen version. She concentrated on television after that and was featured in variety shows, specials, and as a regular in three series. Newmar returned to the stage on occasion, heading tours of *DAMN YANKEES* and *DAMES AT SEA*.

NICHOLAS BROTHERS. Stage and film performers and choreographers. Two of the greatest tap dancers and athletic hoofers in the history of show business, the African American brothers appeared on Broadway and were featured in nine movie musicals where they never failed to amaze. Fayard [Antonio] Nicholas (1914–2006) was born in Mobile, Alabama, and Harold [Lloyd] Nicholas (1921–2000) was born in Winston-Salem, North Carolina, coming from a show business family. The brothers danced in vaudeville and found fame at the Cotton Club in Harlem when they were young and then were featured in the movie musicals *KID MILLIONS* (1934) and *BIG BROADCAST OF 1936* (1935). The brothers were also highlights in the Broadway musicals *ZIEGFELD FOLLIES* (1936) and *BABES IN ARMS* (1937). While they were rarely given character roles to play in Hollywood, the Nicholas Brothers were given special spots in such musicals as *DOWN ARGENTINE WAY* (1940), *TIN PAN ALLEY* (1940), *The Great American Broadcast* (1941), *SUN VALLEY SERENADE* (1941), *ORCHESTRA WIVES* (1942), *STORMY WEATHER* (1943), and *THE PIRATE* (1948). Also, Harold danced without Fayard in *The Reckless Age* (1944) and *Carolina Blues* (1944). Although they were less attractive to the studios once they matured into adult performers, the two remained popular in nightclubs and concerts in the States and in England. Returning to Broadway, Harold played the leading role of Li'l Augie in *St. Louis Woman* (1946) while Fayard was the supporting character Barney. Fayard also worked on Broadway four decades later when he co-choreographed the popular revue *Black and Blue* (1989). The Nicholas Brothers had a unique talent for being gymnastically athletic in their dancing while they maintained an elegance and sense of humor that was thrilling. Harold Nicholas was married to Dorothy Dandridge. Biography: *Brotherhood in Rhythm: The Jazz Tap Dancing of the Nicholas Brothers*, Constance V. Hill (2002).

Niesen, Gertrude (1911–1975). Film, stage, and television performer. A small but sensual blonde singer with an alluring foggy voice, she was a star in nightclubs and on Broadway but was buried in B musicals in Hollywood. The native New Yorker started singing and dancing in vaudeville and then found recognition on the radio, in supper clubs, and on Broadway in the musical revues *Calling All Stars* (1934) and *Ziegfeld Follies* (1936). Niesen was contracted by Hollywood in 1937 and was given featured roles in the forgettable screen musicals *Top of the Town* (1937), *Start Cheering* (1938), *A Night at Earl Carroll's* (1940), *Rookies on Parade* (1941), and *He's My Guy* (1943). She played herself and did specialty spots in the A-grade musicals *Thumbs Up!* (1943) and *This Is the Army* (1943). The next year she was the talk of Broadway as the sexy, funny Bubbles LaMarr in the raucous musical comedy *Follow the Girls* (1944). After playing a band singer in the film *The Babe Ruth Story* (1948), Neisen left the movies and concentrated on nightclubs and television.

■ **Night and Day** (Warner 1946). This autobiographical musical about songwriter Cole Porter may get the award for being the most inaccurate of the many fictionalized screen bios that Hollywood has presented over the years. Even though it dealt with events and shows of recent memory and many of the people involved were still alive and working (including Porter himself), the movie was a travesty all around. Porter's homosexuality and snobbery were understandably omitted, but his zest for life and ability to charm and entertain were lost in Cary Grant's proper and detached performance. Songs and stars were attributed to the wrong shows, and the context of the celebrated numbers was changed to satisfy the production numbers by director Michael Curtiz and choreographer LeRoy Prinz, neither of whom were at their best here. On the plus side, Alexis Smith was elegant as Porter's stately wife Linda Lee, Mary Martin recreated her stage triumph "My Heart Belongs to Daddy," and Porter's close friend Monty Woolley was played by Woolley himself, although he didn't have much to do. Ginny Simms sang several of the songs that had been originated by Ethel Merman, while Jane Wyman, Eve Arden, Alan Hale, Dorothy Malone, Victor Francen, Selena Royle, Herman Bing, Carlos Ramirez, Donald Woods, Mel Tormé, and others wandered in and out of the unexciting story. Despite all its shortcomings, the film was very popular and Porter himself professed to have loved it, his real life not at all touched on by the movie. Nearly six decades later Hollywood again put Porter's life on screen. *De-Lovely* (MGM 2004) was not afraid to deal with Porter's sexuality but it was not brave enough to present the songwriter's songs without a glaze of fantasy and modern presentations that would help audiences get through a bunch of old songs. Contemporary cabaret singers such as John Barrowman, Sheryl Crow, Diana Krall, Vivian Green, and Elvis Costello sang the Porter standards with a hip, even funky interpretation that appealed to younger moviegoers but just about suffocated the numbers. It was the conceit of Jay Cocks' screenplay that the story was told through the recently dead Porter's point of view so it made even less sense that the songwriter would conjure up visions of later generations destroying his songs. Kevin Kline's performance as Porter was charming, sly, and ambiguous enough to play all the sexual angles. Ashley Judd was the knowing Linda, and in supporting roles were Jonathan Pryce, Kevin McNally, Sandra Nelson, Allan Cordner, Peter Polycarpou, Keith Allen, and James Wilby. Because the whole film was a fantasy of sorts, they were directed by Irwin Winkler to shift from realism to expressionism as freely as they wished. Judd kept both feet on the ground the entire film and came off best. As in *Night and Day*, most of the musical numbers were sung out of their original context, mixing shows and performers willy nilly. Caroline O'Connor at least got to wear a sailor outfit when she performed "Anything Goes" but one wonders if Fred Astaire's "Night and Day" was given to Jack (Barrowman) because he was one of Porter's one-night stands. A truthful movie musical about Cole Porter has yet to be made.

NIGHT AT THE OPERA, A (MGM 1935). The favorite MARX BROTHERS movie for many fans, this joyous musical farce featured the brothers at their creative peak and it included several beloved sequences. GEORGE S. KAUFMAN and MORRIE RYSKIND, who had written for the comic siblings on Broadway, concocted the wacky screenplay in which the four brothers stow away on an ocean liner to New York, disguise themselves as Russian aviators to get ashore, and wreck havoc on a performance of *Il Trovatore*. The story also concerned the struggling tenor Ricardo Baroni (ALLAN JONES) and his sweetheart Rosa Castaldi (KITTY CARLISLE) and their efforts to sing opera, but except for a few duets they didn't get in the way too much and there was enough screen time for the famous stateroom scene, for Otis B. Driftwood (Groucho Marx) to woo and insult Mrs. Claypool (MARGARET DUMONT), for Fiorello (Chico Marx) to play "All I Do Is Dream of You" on the piano, and for Tomasso (Harpo Marx) to pluck out "Alone" on the harp. This last was written for the film by NACIO HERB BROWN (music) and ARTHUR FREED (lyric) and was sung beautifully by Jones and Carlisle. Another laudable number was the sing-along ditty "Cosi Cosa" by Bronislaw Kaper, Walter Jurmann, and NED WASHINGTON. Irving Thalberg produced, giving the Marx Brothers the most lavish production of their Hollywood career, and SAM WOOD directed with unaccredited help from Edmund Golding.

NIGHTMARE BEFORE CHRISTMAS, THE (Touchstone/Disney 1993). A highly stylized and highly imaginative animated musical, the movie was a visual treat and musically was intriguing as well. Screenwriters Caroline Thompson and Michael McDowell adapted Tim Burton's illustrated story and it was given a macabre stop-action treatment by director Henry Selick. Jack Skellington (voice of Chris Sarandon, singing by Danny Elfman) is the "Pumpkin King" of Halloweentown but is getting bored with the same scary goings on year after year. Then he discovers Christmastown and the holiday of Christmas and gets excited once again, creating his own frightening version of the merry holiday. His enthusiasm runs away with him as he kidnaps Santa Claus and tries to take over his job, only to be feared by the rest of the world and shot down from the sky. He returns to Halloweentown, rescues his sweetheart Sally (Catherine O'Hara) from the clutches of Oogie Boogie (KEN PAGE), and returns to being a

Halloween hero. The story was populated with bizarre and fascinating supporting characters, such as the evil Dr. Finkelstein (William Hickey), the frustrated Mayor (Glenn Shadix), and the three mischievous sidekicks Lock (Paul Reubens), Shock (O'Hara), and Barrel (Elfman). The decor for the film was as stunning as the creatures that inhabited it, and Danny Elfman wrote a score that was both disarming and exciting. "This Is Halloween," "Making Christmas," "Jack's Lament," "Sally's Song," "What's This?," and "Oogie Boogie's Song" were among the musical numbers, each one staged with mesmerizing style. Burton produced the atypical holiday film and, as dark as it was, children seemed to enjoy it as much as adults. Burton and Elfman joined forces again for *The Corpse Bride* (2005), another stop-action horror tale that was also visually compelling but the characters were less fascinating, despite such voices as Johnny Depp and Helen Bonham Carter, and the story was only mildly interesting. One watched the fanciful movie in a detached way and it did not share the earlier film's success.

NINE (46th Street Theatre 1982). The musicalization of Federico Fellini's 1963 surreal film classic $8\frac{1}{2}$ (1963) may not have been what devotees of the original wanted but it was a spectacular concept musical that was continually fascinating. The burnt-out Italian film director Guido Contini arrives in Venice without a clue as to what his next movie will be and, in his confusion, all the women in his life, from his mother and wife to his mistress and agent, appear to him in a steam bath and taunt him for his misguided life. Arthur Kopit penned the intriguing libretto (based on a treatment by Mario Fratti) and MAURY YESTON wrote the outstanding score that was Italian flavored yet filled with variety. "My Husband Makes Movies," "Ti Voglio Bene (Be Italian)," "Simple," "A Call From the Vatican," "Only With You," "Be On Your Own," "Unusual Way," and the title song were among the many entrancing musical numbers. RAUL JULIA was adept as the confused Guido, and the supporting cast of women was sensational. The show was criticized for trivializing the film masterwork but most critics agreed that TOMMY TUNE's direction and choreography were splendid enough to make the musical a solid hit in its own right. After a slow start at the box office, *Nine* gained momentum and ran 732 performances.

Nine was revived on Broadway in 2003 with film star Antonio Banderas, who shone as

Broadway casts for *Nine*		
Character	*1982 Broadway*	*2003 Broadway*
Guido Contini	RAUL JULIA	Antonio Banderas
Luisa	Karen Akers	Mary Stuart Masterson
Carla	Anita Morris	Jane Krakowski
Liliane le Fleur	Liliane Montevecchi	CHITA RIVERA
Claudia	Shelly Burch	Laura Benanti
Seraghina	Kathi Moss	Myra Lucretia Taylor
Mother	Taina Elg	Mary Beth Peil

the womanizing Guido Contini in a stylish ROUNDABOUT THEATRE mounting directed by David Leveaux. Also applauded were the various actresses who surrounded him and the startling production values. The production ran 285 performances. ▉ A screen version of *Nine* is planned by Lucamar Productions with Javier Bardem as Guido and directed and choreographed by ROB MARSHALL for a 2008 release.

NIXON, MARNI [born Marni McEathron] (1929–). Film and stage performer. One of the most famous singing voices in Hollywood, although only seen by movie audiences once, she sang the vocals for nonsinging stars in some famous film musicals. A native of Altadena, California, Nixon studied violin and singing as a child and then she and her sister formed a kiddie act for vaudeville. When she was a bit older she trained as an opera singer and became a soloist with the Roger Wagner Chorale. Nixon's clear, soprano voice allowed her to sing everything from opera to pop in nightclubs, in concerts, and on recordings, and by 1948 she was in Hollywood dubbing the vocals for MARGARET O'BRIEN in *Big City*. Her most famous "unseen appearances" were singing for Deborah Kerr in *THE KING AND I* (1955), for NATALIE WOOD in *WEST SIDE STORY* (1961), and for AUDREY HEPBURN in *MY FAIR LADY* (1964), and she also dubbed for JEANNE CRAIN, JANET LEIGH, MARILYN MONROE, and even some animated geese in *MARY POPPINS* (1964). Nixon dubbed Kerr a second time when she provided her singing for the songs in *An Affair to Remember* (1957). Movie audiences finally got to see Nixon's face when she played Sister Sophia in the 1965 screen version of *THE SOUND OF MUSIC* where she joined in singing "(How Do You Solve a Problem Like) Maria?" She has also performed on the New York stage in the musicals *The Girl in Pink Tights* (1954), *Taking My Turn* (1984), *JAMES JOYCE'S THE DEAD* (2000), *FOLLIES* (2001), and *NINE* (2003). She continues to sing in concerts and on soundtracks, such as the voice of the grand-

mother in the animated film *MULAN* (1998), and in 2007 played Mrs. Higgins in the national tour of *MY FAIR LADY*. Autobiography: *I Could Have Sung All Night*, with Stephen Cole (2006).

No, No, NANETTE (Globe Theatre 1925). With its silly plot, oversized characters, and slaphappy songs, it is little wonder why this is considered the quintessential 1920s musical comedy.

Plot: Bible publisher Jimmy Smith seems to be the model of respectability, living with his wife Sue, their sarcastic maid Pauline, and his orphaned niece Nanette. Yet Jimmy has been giving financial support to three different women in three different cities because he met them on his business travels and just wanted to make them happy. When Nanette has a quarrel with her boyfriend Tom, she goes off to Atlantic City followed by everyone else and Jimmy's three women also show up on the boardwalk, adding to the complications. A subplot concerns the married couple Lucille and Billy who are having a misunderstanding as well. Everything is resolved satisfactorily at Jimmy's cottage on the Jersey shore. Sue forgives him and, to keep him from being tempted to help other needy women, she goes out and spends all his money.

OTTO HARBACH and FRANK MANDEL wrote the screwball libretto (based on the play *My Lady Friend*) and it is pure 1920s escapism. VINCENT YOUMANS composed the sprightly music, and Harbach provided most of the lyrics; the show's two biggest hits, "I Want to Be Happy" and "Tea for Two," had lyrics by IRVING CAESAR. Also memorable were the flowing ballad "I've Confessed to the Breeze," the bouncy "Too Many Rings Around Rosie," the jazzy "You Can Dance With Any Girl at All," the mock blues number "Where Has My Hubby Gone? Blues," and the vivacious title song. The original company spent so much time on the road during the tryout tour that some of the songs were already nationwide hits by the time *No,*

Casts for *No, No, Nanette*

Character	1925 Broadway	1930 film	1940 film	1971 Broadway
Nanette	LOUISE GROODY	Bernice Claire	ANNA NEAGLE	SUSAN WATSON
Jimmy Smith	CHARLES WINNINGER	Lucien Littlefield	Roland Young	JACK GILFORD
Sue Smith	Eleanor Dawn	Louise Fazenda	HELEN BRODERICK	RUBY KEELER
Lucille	Josephine Whittell	Lilyan Tashman		HELEN GALLAGHER
Billy Early	Wellington Cross	Bert Roach		BOBBY VAN
Pauline	Georgia O'Ramey	Zasu Pitts	Zasu Pitts	PATSY KELLY

No, No, Nanette (stage) Musical Numbers

"Flappers Are We"
"The Call of the Sea"
"Too Many Rings Around Rosie"
"I'm Waiting for You"
"I Want to Be Happy"
"No, No, Nanette"
"The Deep Blue Sea"
"My Doctor"
"Fight Over Me"
"Tea for Two"
"You Can Dance With Any Girl at All"
"Hello, Hello, Telephone Girlie"
"Who's the Who? (Where Has My Hubby Gone? Blues)"
"Pay Day Pauline"

No, Nanette opened in New York. In fact, the London company opened before the Broadway production. H. H. Frazee produced and directed the New York show, SAMMY LEE did the agile choreography, and the musical ran 321 performances. (The West End production was even more popular, running 665 performances.) *No, No, Nanette* was also a major hit on its post-Broadway tour, staying in Chicago for over a year. By the Depression the show was considered too frivolous and it pretty much faded from view until a 1971 revival directed by BERT SHEVELOVE with effervescent choreography by DONALD SADDLER. The vibrant, colorful production became the surprise hit of the season, running 861 performances, touring successfully, and putting the old musical back into the repertory of summer stock and schools.

🎬 ***No, No, Nanette*** (First National 1930) jettisoned most of the songs (only the two Youmans–Caesar hits are retained, as well as the title song) and a few forgettable numbers by other tunesmiths were added. The Howard Emmet Rogers screenplay is somewhat faithful to the original, and Bernice Claire is an appealing Nanette. The rest of the cast is uneven but the production numbers, staged by Larry Ceballos, are enjoyable and one gets an idea of what the Broadway show might have been like. ***No, No, Nanette*** (RKO 1940) was very disappointing. Ken Englund's screenplay was so plot heavy that the five songs retained from the stage were mostly used as background scoring. The movie is more a vehicle for ANNA NEAGLE as a not-young-enough but very flighty Nanette and her dancing is highlighted; however, when a song comes along, the characters only get a few bars out and then they are off and running. It is a curiously unfunny comedy and an unsatisfying musical, yet Naegle was popular and the movie was not the box office dud one might suspect. ❏ The NBC-TV anthology series *Musical Comedy Tonight* broadcast a very abridged version of *No, No, Nanette* in 1951 with JACKIE GLEASON as Jimmy and Ann Crowley as Nanette.

🎵 ***NO STRINGS*** (54th Street Theatre 1962). A small-scale, contemporary musical scored by RICHARD RODGERS, it was an unusual Broadway entry but a very accomplished one. When the prize-winning author David Jordan (RICHARD KILEY) from Maine has writer's block, he bums around Europe where he has an affair with an attractive American model, Barbara Woodruff (DIAHANN CARROLL), who is African American but works with success in Europe where there are fewer racial prejudices. The two consider returning to the States and marrying but the reality of it is too risky so they part. The talented supporting cast included Alvin Epstein, Don Chastain, Polly Rowles, and Noelle Adam. Samuel Taylor penned the intriguing, unsentimental libretto, and Rodgers, in his first Broadway musical after the death of OSCAR HAMMERSTEIN, wrote both lyrics and music and came up with some estimable songs, such as the enticing hit "The Sweetest Sounds," the revealing ballads "Nobody Told Me" and "Look No Further," the zesty "Loads of Love," and the bittersweet title number. As the double-meaning title stated, there were no string instruments in the orchestra so the score had a sound that seemed modern and unique. Critics were mixed on the book and score but praise for the two stars was not so divided and the show, directed and choreographed with ingenuity by JOE LAYTON, ran 580 performances on their popularity.

NORWORTH, JACK [born John Knauff] (1879–1959). Stage and film performer and songwriter. The popular song-and-dance man of vaudeville and Broadway is mostly remembered as the performing and writing partner of NORA BAYES, yet his career extended beyond their marriage. Norworth was born in Philadelphia and ran away from home as a youth to work in a minstrel show. He did a blackface comedy act in vaudeville and then refined his act as a singer of tongue-twisting comic songs. By 1906 he was on Broadway and two years later he appeared in Ziegfeld's *Follies of 1908* with his second wife Bayes and the two were a sensation together introducing "Shine On, Harvest Moon," which they wrote. The couple was featured in *The Jolly Bachelors* (1910), *Little Miss Fix-It* (1911), and *Roly-Poly* (1912) before they divorced and Norworth continued to act in plays on Broadway. He sang and danced in such London musicals as *Hullo, Tango* (1914), *Rosy Rapture* (1915), *Looking Around* (1915), and *Oh! La-La!* (1915), often writing songs for them as well. He returned to the States to appear in *Odds and Ends of 1917*, *EARL CARROLL VANITIES* (1925), and some nonmusicals. Norworth made a few films, including the musical *Queen of the Night Clubs* (1929), and appeared on a few television shows in the 1950s. His greatest legacy is not as a performer but as a songwriter: he penned the lyric for "Take Me Out to the Ball Game," one of the most frequently sung songs in America. Norworth's first wife was actress Louise Dresser (1882–1965).

NUGENT, ELLIOTT (1896–1980). Stage and film director, writer, producer, and performer. The all-around show business personality handled many jobs and found success in all of them, including the direction of a half-dozen movie musicals. Nugent was born in Dover, Ohio, the son of vaudeville and Broadway actor J. C. Nugent (1868–1947), and was on stage from the age of four. He attended Ohio State University, where he befriended the young writer James Thurber, and then returned to the stage acting and writing sketches and then later plays, making a splash as co-author (with his father) and star of the comedy *Kempy* (1922). Nugent had a series of hits on Broadway, most memorably *The Male Animal* (1940), which Nugent co-wrote with Thurber and played the leading role. At the same time he acted in many films and in the 1930s started directing and producing them as well. Although he had not dealt with musicals on the stage, he was successful in directing them on the screen, as with *She Loves Me Not* (1934), *Strictly Dynamite* (1934), *Love in Bloom* (1935), *Give Me a Sailor* (1938), *UP IN ARMS* (1944), and *Just for You* (1952), as well as many nonmusical movies. Nugent's film career collapsed in the early 1950s because of his alcoholism and depression but he returned to Broadway and managed to direct and produce plays until he retired in 1957. Few artists had so varied and all-encompassing a career. Autobiography: *Events Leading Up to Comedy* (1965).

NUNN, TREVOR (1940–). Stage and film director and producer. An outstanding British director, he is equally proficient at staging classics, challenging new works, and giant musicals. Nunn was born in Ipswich, England, the son of a cabinetmaker, and by the age of sixteen had founded his own theatre company, the Ipswich Youth Drama Group. After attending Cambridge University, where he directed dozens of student productions, Nunn made his professional directing debut in Coventry in 1962 and his London bow three years later. By the time he was twenty-eight, he was named artistic director of the Royal Shakespeare Company (RSC) where he did some of his finest work. It was his highly popular RSC production of *The Life and Adventures of Nicholas Nickleby* (1981) that afforded Nunn his Broadway debut, followed by the two musical megahits *CATS* (1982) and *LES MISÉRABLES* (1987). His other Broadway musicals include *STARLIGHT EXPRESS* (1987), *CHESS* (1988), *ASPECTS OF LOVE* (1990), *SUNSET BOULEVARD* (1994), *OKLAHOMA!* (2002), and *The Woman in White* (2005). Nunn has also directed plays on film and musicals for television, such as *PORGY AND BESS* (1993) and *Oklahoma!* (1999). Many of his productions, especially the musicals, offer striking visual images, yet his attention is usually on the text and finding the truth of the characters. A good example is the approach he took with the revival of *Oklahoma!* in which the musical comedy characters were handled with an almost Stanislavsky-like realism.

☙ **NUNSENSE** (Cherry Lane Theatre 1985). An Off Broadway long-run hit with a thin libretto and an even thinner score, the small-cast, economical show has proved to be a godsend to theatre groups across the country looking for an inexpensive, guaranteed moneymaker. Five nuns, the only survivors among their order of an epidemic of food poisoning, put on an amateur show to raise money for their sisters' burials. Dan Groggin wrote the book and the songs, and the amateurish production that the nuns presented was not much different from *Nunsense* itself. The critics barely paid attention to the one-joke musical but word of mouth kept the show on the boards for 3,672 performances. There were several less successful sequels, such as *Nunsense II*, a country-western *Nunsense*, and even a Jewish version and an all-male drag variation called *Nunsense Ah-Men!*

NYPE, RUSSELL (1924–). Stage and television performer. The lanky, bespectacled character actor–singer was rarely cast in leading roles but often stole the show in plays and musicals in the 1950s and 1960s. Nype was born in Zion, Illinois, and educated at Lake Forest College before making his Broadway debut as the spineless Leo Hubbard in the musical *REGINA* (1949). The next year he received wide recognition as the diplomatic aide Kenneth Gibson singing "You're Just in Love" with ETHEL MERMAN in *CALL ME MADAM* (1950). Nype's other memorable Broadway roles include the high-society bachelor George Randolph Brown in *GOLDILOCKS* (1958), the sarcastic American tourist Jeff in revivals of *BRIGADOON* (1963 and 1967), and clerk Cornelius Hackl in *HELLO, DOLLY!* (1970) in which he was reunited with Merman. His other musical credits include *Great to Be Alive* (1950), *CAROUSEL* (1957), *MY FAIR LADY* (1964), and *Lady Audley's Secret* (1972). Nype acted in many national tours of Broadway hits and has appeared on several television programs, including the musical specials *THE THIRTEEN CLOCKS* (1953), *ONE TOUCH OF VENUS* (1955), and *KISS ME, KATE* (1968).

OAKIE, JACK [born Lewis Delaney Offield] (1903–1978). Film, stage, and television performer. A portly and often jolly character actor, he specialized in doing double (and even triple) takes as he played good-natured buffoons and sidekicks of the hero. Oakie was born in Sedalia, Missouri, raised in Oklahoma (hence his stage name), and then moved to New York where he worked for a brokerage firm. After performing in the company's amateur theatricals, he went into vaudeville as a comic and developed his farcical facial ticks and bombastic double takes. Oakie reached Broadway in the chorus of *LITTLE NELLIE KELLY* (1922) and then was featured in the Broadway revues *Innocent Eyes* (1924) and *ARTISTS AND MODELS* (1925). By 1928 Oakie was in Hollywood where he acted in eighty films over the next twenty years, half of them musicals. His early musicals include *Close Harmony* (1929), *Street Girl* (1929), *Sweetie* (1929), *PARAMOUNT ON PARADE* (1930), *HIT THE DECK* (1930), *Let's Go Native* (1930), and *Dancers in the Dark* (1932). Although he was well over thirty years old, the studio kept casting him as a college student in such musicals as *College Humor* (1933), *COLLEGE RHYTHM* (1934), *Collegiate* (1936), and *Rise and Shine* (1941), earning him the sardonic title "The World's Oldest Freshman." Among Oakie's many other musicals are *Too Much Harmony* (1933), *Murder at the Vanities* (1934), *BIG BROADCAST OF 1936* (1935), *KING OF BURLESQUE* (1935), *That Girl From Paris* (1936), *Thanks for Everything* (1938), *TIN PAN ALLEY* (1940), *The Great American Broadcast* (1941), *ICELAND* (1942), *Song of the Islands* (1942), *HELLO, FRISCO, HELLO* (1943), *Sweet and Low Down* (1944), *Bowery to Broadway* (1944), *The Merry Monahans* (1944), *On Stage Everybody* (1945), and *When My Baby Smiles at Me* (1948). Of his many nonmusicals, his most famous role is the Mussolini-like Benzini in Charlie Chaplin's *The Great Dictator* (1940). From the mid-1950 to the early 1970s, Oakie

concentrated on television work, appearing in many programs, including the TV musical *Burlesque* (1955).

O'BRIEN, JACK (1939–). Stage and television director and producer. A popular and versatile director with major New York and regional credits in all forms of theatre, he staged a handful of musical comedies for Broadway. O'Brien was born in Saginaw, Michigan, and educated at the University of Michigan before relocating to New York in the early 1960s and teaching theatre at Hunter College. He studied with director–producers Ellis Rabb and John Houseman and in 1969 was Rabb's assistant at the Association of Producing Artists. That same year he made his directorial debut in Manhattan and directed for the first time at the Old Globe Playhouse in San Diego. O'Brien was later artistic director at the Old Globe between 1981 and 1991, staging everything from classic revivals to new musicals. He is also a much-sought-after director of opera. O'Brien's chameleon-like directing talents have allowed him to shine in delicate character comedies, epic historical pieces, and dense intellectual plays, but his biggest hits have been musicals on Broadway, such as *PORGY AND BESS* (1976), *THE MOST HAPPY FELLA* (1979), *DAMN YANKEES* (1994), *THE FULL MONTY* (2002), *HAIRSPRAY* (2002), and *DIRTY ROTTEN SCOUNDRELS* (2005). He has also directed dramas for television.

O'BRIEN, MARGARET [born Angela Maxine O'Brien] (1937–). Film and television performer. One of Hollywood's most polished child actors, she will always be remembered as JUDY GARLAND's little sister Tootie in *MEET ME IN ST. LOUIS* (1944). O'Brien was born in San Diego and at the age of four had a bit part in the film musical *BABES ON BROADWAY* (1941). The next year she had a more noticeable role in the nonmusical *Journey for Margaret* and for the next ten years was much in demand. O'Brien did a specialty in *Thousands Cheer* (1943) and then found fame in *Meet Me in St. Louis*, followed by the musicals *Music for Millions* (1944), *The Unfinished Dance* (1947), and *Big City* (1948). She also gave shining performances in nonmusicals but when O'Brien reached adolescence her popularity waned. She retired from films in 1951 but years later came back to do dinner theatre, a few movies, and lots of television, including the TV musicals *Come to Me* (1957) and *LITTLE WOMEN* (1958). Biography: *Margaret O'Brien: A Career*

Chronicle and Biography, Allan R. Ellenberger, Robert Young, Margaret O'Brien (2004).

O'BRIEN, [William Joseph] **PAT**[rick] (1899–1983). Film performer. Filmdom's favorite Irish cop, priest, detective, or coach, the stout but handsome actor was featured in leading man roles in light movie musicals in the 1930s. O'Brien was born in Milwaukee and went to military school with JAMES CAGNEY, the two joining the Navy together during World War I. (He and Cagney would later make nine films together.) After the war the two friends attended drama school in New York and then O'Brien went into vaudeville and by 1926 was on Broadway in plays and in one musical, *THE GREAT WALTZ* (1934). He made his screen debut in 1929 and acted in nearly 100 films over the next three decades. O'Brien's musical credits are *FLYING HIGH* (1930), *College Coach* (1933), *Twenty Million Sweethearts* (1934), *Flirtation Walk* (1934), *In Caliente* (1935), *Stars Over Broadway* (1935), *Cowboy From Brooklyn* (1938), *Garden of the Moon* (1938), *Broadway* (1942), *His Butler's Sister* (1943), and *Some Like It Hot* (1959). He acted in early television and was in many series, specials, and dramas up into the 1980s. Autobiography: *The Wind at My Back* (1963).

O'BRIEN, VIRGINIA [Lee] (1921–2001). Film performer. The delightfully deadpan singing comedienne of Hollywood musicals, her flat but funny delivery of songs earned her the nickname "Miss Red Hot Frozen Face." O'Brien was born in Los Angeles, the daughter of a police detective, and took singing and dancing lessons. She received stage experience in local theatres and then got her break in the professional musical *Meet the People* in 1939; she was so frightened that she froze on stage and sang her number wide-eyed and paralyzed. The audience roared and O'Brien had her trademark. She began making movies the following year and shone in the musicals *Hullabaloo* (1940), *The Big Store* (1941), *LADY, BE GOOD* (1941), *Ship Ahoy* (1942), *PANAMA HATTIE* (1942), *DuBARRY WAS A LADY* (1943), *Thousands Cheer* (1943), *Meet the People* (1944), *TWO GIRLS AND A SAILOR* (1944), *THE HARVEY GIRLS* (1945), *TILL THE CLOUDS ROLL BY* (1946), and *ZIEGFELD FOLLIES* (1946). O'Brien also made comedies, several of them with RED SKELTON. She retired in 1947 when the studio did not renew her contract but she made nonmusical films in 1955 and 1976 as well as performing on stage occasionally, most mem-orably as Parthy in *SHOW BOAT* in 1984 at the Long Beach Civic Light Opera.

OCKRENT, MIKE (1946–1999). Stage director. An esteemed British director, he was chalking up a list of hits on Broadway when he died at the peak of his career. Ockrent was born in London, educated at Edinburgh University for a career in physics, and then trained at the Perth Theatre in Scotland. He started directing regionally and then was named artistic director of the Traverse Theatre in Edinburgh from 1973 to 1976. After directing such West End successes as *FOLLIES*, *Watch on the Rhine*, and *Educating Rita*, he became a founding member of the Play Group in New York and remained to direct his first Broadway production in 1979. Ockrent returned to Manhattan to restage his West End musical hit *ME AND MY GIRL* in 1986, followed by a handful of other plays and musicals, such as *CRAZY FOR YOU* (1992) and *Big* (1996). He also staged the large-scale musical version of *A CHRISTMAS CAROL* at the Paramount Theatre at Madison Square Garden and was preparing to direct *THE PRODUCERS* before his untimely death from leukemia. That production was later staged by his wife, choreographer SUSAN STROMAN. Ockrent was known for his spirited and clever staging of musicals, often finding playful ways to present rather routine situations.

O'CONNOR, DONALD [David Dixon Ronald] (1925–2003). Film, stage, and television performer. A nimble, energetic song-and-dance man who seemed to defy gravity in his sprightly dancing, he lit up many movie musicals for a period of twenty years. O'Connor was born in Chicago into a show business family and performed in vaudeville as a child. At the age of twelve he made his movie musical debut doing a specialty act with his brothers in *Melody for Two* (1937) and then was signed by PARAMOUNT where he played juvenile roles in such nonmusicals as *Tom Sawyer Detective* (1938) and *Beau Jeste* (1939). While still a teenager, O'Connor was featured in such musicals as *SING YOU SINNERS* (1937), *ON YOUR TOES* (1939), *Private Buckaroo* (1942), *Give Out Sisters* (1942), *Get Hep to Love* (1942), *When Johnny Comes Marching Home* (1942), *Top Man* (1943), *Follow the Boys* (1944), *The Merry Monahans* (1944), and *Bowery to Broadway* (1944). With his ever-youthful looks, O'Connor was able to play young men for many years and, while he was cast in major roles in nonmusicals, such as the *Francis the Talking Mule* series of comedies,

Donald O'Connor. Although he was not the leading character, O'Connor (left) gave his greatest performance as Cosmo Brown in *Singin' in the Rain* (1952). He was not only able to keep up with Gene Kelly (right) in such numbers as "Fit as a Fiddle," but he triumphed on his own in the hilarious "Make 'Em Laugh" solo. (Photofest)

he usually was in secondary roles in musicals. His most beloved and remembered performance was as funnyman Cosmo Brown in *SINGIN' IN THE RAIN* (1952), but he was also outstanding as the photographer's assistant Melvin Hoover in *I Love Melvin* (1952), ambassador's aide Kenneth Gibson in *CALL ME MADAM* (1953), ex-G.I. Jigger Millard in *Walking My Baby Back Home* (1953), troubled performer Tim Donohue in *THERE'S NO BUSINESS LIKE SHOW BUSINESS* (1954), and the Broadway star Ted Adams in *ANYTHING GOES* (1956). His other musical credits include *Patrick the Great* (1945), *Are You With It?* (1948), *Feudin', Fussin' and a-Fightin'* (1948), and *The Milkman* (1950). O'Connor made many television appearances, including his own series and the TV musicals *THE RED MILL* (1958), *OLYMPUS 7-000* (1966), and *ALICE IN WONDERLAND* (1985), and was on Broadway as the disgruntled Albert in *Bring Back Birdie* (1981) and as Cap'n Andy in the 1983 revival of *SHOW BOAT*.

OF THEE I SING (Music Box Theatre 1932). One of the boldest and most brilliant of all satirical American musicals, the show was more comic operetta than standard musical comedy, yet it was very up to date.

Plot: Presidential candidate John P. Wintergreen and his cronies come up with an election gimmick, stating that their platform is love and whichever girl wins their nationwide beauty contest will marry Wintergreen and go to the White House with him as First Lady. The Southern belle Diana Devereaux wins but by that time Wintergreen has fallen in love and married his secretary Mary Turner because she bakes the most delectable corn muffins. As soon as Wintergreen is elected, Diana brings him up on charges of breech of promise and the French ambassador gets involved because it turns out Diana is very distantly related to Napoleon. To avoid an international incident, the Senate brings on an impeachment trial only to have

Casts for *Of Thee I Sing*

Character	1931 Broadway	1952 Broadway	1972 television
John P. Wintergreen	WILLIAM GAXTON	JACK CARSON	Carroll O'Connor
Alexander Throttlebottom	VICTOR MOORE	Paul Hartman	JACK GILFORD
Mary Turner	Lois Moran	Betty Oakes	Cloris Leachman
Diana Devereaux	Grace Brinkley	Lenore Lonergan	MICHELE LEE

Of Thee I Sing Musical Numbers

"Wintergreen for President"
"Who Is the Lucky Girl to Be?"
"The Dimple on My Knee"
"Because, Because"
"As Chairman of the Committee"
"How Beautiful"
"Never Was a Girl So Fair"
"Some Girls Can Bake a Pie"
"Love Is Sweeping the Country"
"Of Thee I Sing"
"(Here's a) Kiss for Cinderella"
"I Was the Most Beautiful Blossom"
"Hello, Good Morning"
"Who Cares?"
"Garson, S'il Vous Plait"
"The Illegitimate Daughter"
"We'll Impeach Him"
"The Senatorial Roll Call"
"Jilted"
"I'm About to Be a Mother"
"Posterity (Is Just Around the Corner)"
"Trumpeter, Blow Your (Golden) Horn"
"On That Matter No One Budges"

Of Thee I Sing. As the sheet music cover proudly states, the musical won the prestigious Pulitzer Prize, the first musical to do so. But the prize went to librettists George S. Kaufman and Morrie Ryskind and lyricist Ira Gershwin and not to composer George Gershwin because the prize is a literary award and the judges felt music was not literature. (Photofest)

the case thrown out when it is learned that Mary is expecting a baby and the Senate won't condemn an expectant father. Diana settles for marriage with the Vice President, the nonentity Alexander Throttlebottom, and all are happy.

GEORGE S. KAUFMAN and MORRIE RYSKIND wrote the satiric libretto that was worthy of W. S. Gilbert in its combination of nonsense and deadly serious jabs at the superficial ways of government. The script is so strong that it might have stood as a comedy all on its own but the score by GEORGE GERSHWIN (music) and IRA GERSHWIN (lyrics) raised the humor

to a sublime level. The lyrics also echo Gilbert, and the flag-waving music gives the satire an extra kick. There are twice as many songs in *Of Thee I Sing* than the usual musical comedy and the extended musical sequences propel the action along with glee. Considering how plot and character driven the songs are, it is surprising that some became popular on their own, such as "Love Is Sweeping the Country," "Who Cares?," and the title number. The unique musical was praised by the critics for everything from the witty script to the radiant performances to the melodious score. It was the first musical to win the PULITZER PRIZE and the first to be published in book form, another testament to the strong libretto and lyrics. SAM H. HARRIS produced, co-author Kaufman directed, and Chester Hale choreographed. After running 441 performances, the production toured and then returned to New York for another thirty-two performances.

For the 1952 Broadway revival, some of the topical references in the script were updated but too many aislesitters thought the legendary show had dated poorly. There were mostly cheers for the cast but audiences seemed less interested in satire in the 1950s so the production, directed again by Kaufman, ran only seventy-two performances. Revivals in regional theatre are common during election years and there is something timeless about the musical, probably because its targets are still there. ❑ An abridged version of *Of Thee I Sing* was made by CBS-TV in 1972 and the script was faithful to the original, even if it seemed watered down for the tube. The popular television star Carroll O'Connor starred as Wintergreen and he was more gruff than sly but the supporting cast was strong. The production was routine and what was once abrasive seemed only mildly amusing in this version directed by Roger Beatty, Dick Hall, and Dave Powers and choreographed by Marc Beaux.

🎭 **Let 'Em Eat Cake** (Imperial Theatre 1933) was a sequel to *Of Thee I Sing* and reunited much of the backstage and onstage personnel from the earlier show. President John P. Wintergreen (William Gaxton) loses his reelection bid so he starts a fascist party in America called the Blue Shirts and leads a revolution that takes over the government. Vice President Alexander Throttlebottom (Victor Moore) acts as umpire in a baseball game between the Supreme Court and the League of Nations and, because of his unpopular call of a play, is sentenced to the guillotine, only to be rescued by the forced happy ending brought on by Mary (Lois Moran) and the women of the country. Kaufman and Ryskind again penned the libretto, and the Gershwins wrote the new score, which included such risible numbers as "Blue, Blue, Blue," "Union Square," "Down With Everyone Who's Up," "On and On and On," and the warm duet "Mine," which became a hit and was interpolated into later revivals of *Of Thee I Sing*. Although *Let 'Em Eat Cake* shared much the same satirical wit of the earlier work and the cast was still expert, the musical was not well received. The political climate had changed in America and a satire about fascism in the land did not sit well with audiences when such dark news was coming from Europe. Kaufman directed the Sam H. Harris production but it ran only ninety performances. Over the years the Gershwin's score has grown in appreciation but the musical itself is still an unsatisfying oddity.

🎭 **Oh Boy!** (Princess Theatre 1917). Arguably the finest of the Princess Theatre musicals, this high-spirited musical comedy by Jerome Kern (music), P. G. Wodehouse (book and lyrics), and Guy Bolton (book) bubbled with silly goings-on and scintillating songs. Without telling his wealthy, domineering guardian-aunt Penelope (Edna May Oliver), George Budd (Tom Powers) has married Lou Ellen (Marie Cahill) and doesn't know how to break the news. His pal Jim Marvin (Hal Forde) and his girl Jackie (Anna Wheaton) invade George's apartment when the Budds are away and are surprised by a visit by the aunt. The Budds return to find Jackie pretending to be Lou Ellen and then, when other country club friends come by, Jackie masquerades as the aunt herself. It was all lovable nonsense punctuated by such delicious songs as "Till the Clouds Roll By," "Nesting Time in Flatbush," "An Old-Fashioned Wife," "The Land Where the Good Songs Go," and "You Never Knew About Me." Edward Royce co-directed and choreographed the William Elliott–F. Ray Comstock production, which ran 463 performances in the intimate little theatre.

🎭 **Oh, Calcutta!** (Belasco Theatre 1971). A notorious revue that explored humankind's sexual hang-ups through the ages, the musical did so with the cast nude for long sections of the show. British critic Kenneth Tynan put together the adult program of sketches by Jules Feiffer, John Lennon, Jacques Levy, Leonard Melfi, Sam Shepard, and others, and the group The Open Window wrote the songs, which included "Coming Together, Going Together," "Much Too Soon," "I Want It," and "I Don't Have a Song to Sing." The revue premiered Off Broadway in 1969 where it received mostly negative reviews but was controversial and sensational enough to run 704 performances. When it transferred to Broadway it ran 610 performances. A replica of the original *Oh, Calcutta!* opened in the tiny Edison Theatre in 1976 and ran an astounding 5,959 performances. Many of the patrons were foreign tourists who were drawn by the promotion campaign in different languages. ❑ A video/film version of the revue was made in 1972, taped during a performance and showing the audience arriving at the theatre and the actors backstage applying makeup to their nude bodies before the show begins. Broadcast on cable and in a limited run in theatres, *Oh, Calcutta!* on the screen is not what audiences wanted and the film was not popular.

⚭ *OH KAY!* (Imperial Theatre 1926). A vehicle for the British star GERTRUDE LAWRENCE, the Gershwin musical also boasted one of the brothers' best scores. Kay (Lawrence) knows that millionaire Jimmy Winter (OSCAR SHAW) is rarely at his Long Island estate so she suggests to her rum-running brother Shorty McGee (VICTOR MOORE) and his cohort Larry Potter (Harland Dixon) that they use the waterside location for business. When Jimmy comes home unexpectedly, Shorty disguises himself as the new butler and Kay as the new maid. Jimmy and Kay fall in love even though he is engaged to be married to the high society dame Constance Appleton (Sascha Beaumont). The authorities raid the house, find the rum, and are about to deport Kay as an illegal alien until it is revealed that Jimmy has married her. GUY BOLTON and P. G. WODEHOUSE wrote the contrived but funny libretto and the top-notch cast played it for all it was worth. They also did justice to such popular Gershwin numbers as the wistful "Someone to Watch Over Me," the dreamy "Maybe," the sassy "Do, Do, Do," the vivacious "Fidgety Feet," and the jubilant "Clap Yo' Hands." John Harwood directed the ALEX A. AARONS–VINTON FREEDLEY production, SAMMY LEE devised the animated choreography, and the musical ran 256 performances. Producer DAVID MERRICK revived *Oh, Kay!* in 1990 and cast the musical with African Americans, changing the setting to contemporary Harlem. It was an uncomfortable fit but the cast was vibrant enough and the direction and choreography by DAN SIRETTA were quite spirited. Audiences came for seventy-seven performances before Merrick closed the show, went back into rehearsal, recast the leading roles, and started previewing the new version, but it never reopened. The commendable cast included Angela Teek (Kay), BRIAN [Stokes] MITCHELL (Jimmy), Stanley Wayne Mathis, Gregg Burge, Tamara Tunie Bouquett, and Alexander Barton.

⚭ *OH, LADY! LADY!* (Princess Theatre 1918). The last of the GUY BOLTON (book), P. G. WODEHOUSE (book and lyrics), and JEROME KERN (music) collaborations for the PRINCESS THEATRE MUSICAL series, this intimate, contemporary show reflected the spirit of the innovative series. Willoughby Finch (Carl Randall) is about to be wed to Mollie Farrington (VIVIENNE SEGAL) when the Farrington jewels are stolen and suspicion falls on Willoughby's valet Spike (Edward Abeles), a former jewel thief. Also complicating the situation is the arrival of May Barber (Carroll McComas) from Ohio to deliver some lingerie for Molly. It seems May was once engaged to Willoughby and her presence so upsets Molly that she calls off the wedding. It takes Spike to find the jewel thieves and to get Molly and Willoughby back together again. The nimble score featured "Moon Song," "Before I Met You," "When the Ships Come Home," "Not Yet," and "Greenwich Village." The best song written for the show was "Bill" but it did not fit in the production and was discarded before opening; Kern used it nine years later in *SHOW BOAT* (1927). Edward Royce co-directed and choreographed *Oh, Lady! Lady!* and the merry little musical ran 219 performances.

O'HARA, KELLI (1977–). Stage and television performer. A very recent and very promising talent who has already given a number of outstanding performances in New York musicals, the blonde singer–actress is Broadway's latest discovery. O'Hara was born in rural Oklahoma and studied voice at Oklahoma City University and privately in New York. She made her Broadway debut as a replacement for Kate in *JEKYLL & HYDE* in 2000 and then was seen as Young Hattie (then Young Phyllis) in the revival of *FOLLIES* (2001). O'Hara's first major role was the determined sister Susan in *Sweet Smell of Success* (2002) and, although she was highly praised, the show was short-lived. Off Broadway she shone as the elusive Parisian Albertine in *My Life with Albertine* (2003) and then played Lucy in the ill-fated *Dracula, the Musical* (2004) on Broadway. Acclaim and a long run finally came with her piercing performance as the befuddled Clara Johnson in *THE LIGHT IN THE PIAZZA* (2006). O'Hara won another round of raves for her Babe Williams in the 2006 revival of *THE PAJAMA GAME* and she played Nellie Forbush in the LINCOLN CENTER THEATRE production of *SOUTH PACIFIC* in 2008. She has also acted on television in series and soap operas.

OHIO LIGHT OPERA, THE. Theatre organization. One of the handful of operetta companies going strong in the twenty-first century, the summer theatre company was founded in 1979 and is located on the campus of the College of Wooster. They specialize in Gilbert and Sullivan productions but have also presented many European operettas and American works going back to the nineteenth century, including such rarely seen operettas as REGINALD DE KOVEN'S *ROBIN HOOD* (1890), VICTOR

HERBERT'S *Eileen* (1917), and KURT WEILL–IRA GERSHWIN'S *The Firebrand of Florence* (1945).

O'HORGAN, TOM (1926–). Stage director. An ever-controversial director, his outlandish experiments in staging have been seen in musical hits and flops. O'Horgan was born in Chicago and educated at DePaul University before coming to New York and getting involved with the avant-garde theatre company Cafe LaMama. He quickly became known because of his staging of six short plays for that company in 1966, and two years later he was directing the Broadway production of the rock musical *HAIR*. While many of his subsequent projects were small pieces Off and Off Off Broadway, his bombastic theatrics sometimes were seen on Broadway, such as the musicals *JESUS CHRIST SUPERSTAR* (1971), *Inner City* (1971), *Dude* (1972), and *Sgt. Pepper's Lonely Hearts Club Band on the Road* (1974).

OKLAHOMA! (St. James Theatre 1943). Not only the most important of the RICHARD RODGERS (music) and OSCAR HAMMERSTEIN (book and lyrics) musicals, it is also the single most influential work in the American musical theatre.

Plot: The Oklahoma territory is experiencing a land rush, which creates friction between the farmers and the cowmen. There is also friction between the cowboy Curly McLain and the farm hand Jud Fry over Laurey Williams, who lives with her Aunt Eller on the farm where Jud works. Although Laurey much prefers Curly, she agrees to go to the box social with Jud in order to punish Curly for taking her for granted. She immediately regrets her decision and has a nightmare in which she sees the sinister Jud intrude on her wedding to Curly and carry her away. At the box social Curly outbids Jud for the picnic hamper that Laurey has prepared, even though he has to sell everything he owns to do it. Jud threatens Curly and Laurey so she fires him and Curly and Laurey confess they love each other. At their wedding celebration, a drunk Jud shows up with a knife and challenges Curly; in the scuffle, Jud falls on his own knife and dies. So that the newlyweds can leave on their honeymoon, Aunt Eller convinces the local judge to hold the trial immediately. Curly is acquitted and the couple leads the neighbors in a celebration of their new statehood as they leave on their honeymoon. The comic subplot also concerns a romantic triangle: the flirtatious Ado Annie

Oklahoma! For a landmark musical filled with historical significance, the show has always been a lot of fun as well. Agnes de Mille's choreography for the second act opener "The Farmer and the Cowman" (pictured in the original production) showed that the "new" musical model was not without the simple joys of song and dance. (Photofest)

Casts for *Oklahoma!*

Characters	Curly	Laurey	Ado Annie	Will Parker
1943 Broadway	ALFRED DRAKE	Joan Roberts	CELESTE HOLM	LEE DIXON
1955 film	GORDON MACRAE	SHIRLEY JONES	Gloria Grahame	GENE NELSON
1969 Broadway	Bruce Yarnell	Leigh Berry	April Shawhan	LEE ROY REAMS
1979 Broadway	LAURENCE GUITTARD	Christine Andreas	CHRISTINE EBERSOLE	HARRY GROENER
2002 Broadway	PATRICK WILSON	Josephina Gabrielle	Jessica Boevers	Justin Bohon

Characters	Aunt Eller	Jud Fry	Ali Hakim	
1943 Broadway	Betty Garde	HOWARD DA SILVA	Joseph Buloff	
1955 film	CHARLOTTE GREENWOOD	Rod Steiger	EDDIE ALBERT	
1969 Broadway	MARGARET HAMILTON	Spiro Malas	Ted Beniades	
1979 Broadway	MARY WICKES	Martin Vidnovic	Bruce Adler	
2002 Broadway	ANDREA MARTIN	Shuler Hensley	Aasif Mandvi	

Carnes is promised to Will Parker but is also drawn to the wily peddler Ali Hakim. Caught in a compromising position with Annie, Hakim is going to be forced into a shotgun wedding with her, but he arranges to buy Will's wedding presents at such inflated prices that Will has enough money to marry Annie himself.

Theresa Helburn, the co-producer of the THEATRE GUILD, is credited with coming up with the idea of musicalizing Lynn Riggs' pastoral play *Green Grow the Lilacs* (1931) and Rodgers was enthusiastic but when he presented the idea to partner LORENZ HART, the lyricist immediately dismissed it. When Rodgers approached Hammerstein, he immediately agreed. It seems like such a perfect match today but at the time it was far from promising. Hammerstein was viewed on Broadway as a has-been, an old-fashioned operetta writer whose time was long gone. The Theatre Guild was also seen as washed up, the renowned organization deeply in debt and their track record with musicals unimpressive. (Although they had produced Gershwin's masterpiece *Porgy and Bess* in 1935, none of their musical efforts had made a profit since *The Garrick Gaieties* series in the 1920s.) When word hit the street that for the first time Rodgers was writing a musical with someone other than Hart, predictions were dire for the whole enterprise. As Rodgers, Hammerstein, and the creative staff worked on *Away We Go!*, as it was then titled, none of them thought

about breaking new ground and building a landmark. However, they knew what they were doing was different. A cowboy musical would traditionally start with a barn dance or square dance (as suggested by the title), but Rodgers and Hammerstein liked the quiet beginning of Riggs' play and opened their musical with Aunt Eller churning butter and Curly entering singing "Oh, What a Beautiful Mornin'." Hammerstein remained true to the characters when mapping out the story and the songs, but there is much in the musical that is not in the play, such as Will Parker and his comic wooing of Ado Annie. They cast unknown (although hardly inexperienced) performers for the production, and director ROUBEN MAMOULIAN approached the musical piece as a dramatic play. Choreographer AGNES DE MILLE, whose track record on Broadway was dismal, took the same approach to the dances and, although there were some major battles between her and Mamoulian, the two ended up creating a seamless piece of musical drama. The innovative ballet that ended the first act was mostly de Mille's idea, as was her suggestion to illustrate Jud's naughty French postcards in Laurey's dream. The out-of-town tryouts in New Haven and Boston allowed the team to polish the show, making several changes, including retitling the musical *Oklahoma!* when that song stopped the show each night. Word of mouth was mixed and conflicting reports were sent back to New York. The famous telegram

> ### Oklahoma! (stage) Musical Numbers
>
> "Oh, What a Beautiful Mornin'"
> "The Surrey With the Fringe on Top"
> "Kansas City"
> "I Cain't Say No"
> "Many a New Day"
> "It's a Scandal! It's an Outrage!"
> "People Will Say We're in Love"
> "Pore Jud Is Daid"
> "Lonely Room"
> "Out of My Dreams"
> "Laurey Makes Up Her Mind" Ballet
> "The Farmer and the Cowman"
> "All er Nothin'"
> "Oklahoma"

by producer MIKE TODD announcing "No gags, no gals, no chance" was not a lone voice; some backers seeing the show for the first time were convinced that this odd new musical was doomed. Other observers were ecstatic over the show, although most of them probably wondered how such a piece would appeal to New York critics and audiences. Because there were such low expectations for the new musical, the impact *Oklahoma!* made was all the more dynamic. The rave reviews touched upon all aspects of the show, from the book and score to the cast and the dancing. The demand for tickets was unprecedented as the show became more popular in the months that followed, eventually running 2,212 performances, a new record by far. Also, *Oklahoma!* was the first Broadway musical to prompt an original cast recording as we know it today.

The history of the Broadway musical can accurately be divided into what came before *Oklahoma!* and what came after it. It was the first fully integrated musical play and its blending of song, character, plot, and even dance would serve as the model for Broadway shows for decades to follow. No song from the score could be reassigned to another actor, no less another show, because each was drawn from the character so fully that it became an integral piece of the character's development within the plot. The songs in *Oklahoma!* continued the plot and characterization, rather than interrupting them. By the time Curly has finished singing the seemingly casual "The Surrey With the Fringe on Top," the dramatic situation has altered. Every musical number became a little one-act play of sorts. The musical was also unique in other ways. Without waving a flag as GEORGE M. COHAN had done in his

patriotic shows, *Oklahoma!* celebrated the American spirit, which was particularly potent in 1943 with the country deep in World War II. *Oklahoma!* also celebrated the rural life, whereas most musicals were decidedly urban. The characters in the story were not placed in the tragic circumstances of, say, *SHOW BOAT* (1927), but they were fully developed all the same and the sincerity of their everyday emotions was refreshing after the slick, Broadway types that populated most Broadway shows. Even the so-called villain Jud is a complex creation, arousing conflicting emotions in the audience just as he confuses Laurey's feelings about him. Finally, *Oklahoma!* used dance as never seen before, the hoofing growing out of the characters and their emotions rather than from disjointed dance cues. Will Parker's lively retelling of life in "Kansas City" grew into a dance demonstrating what he'd seen in the big city and soon the stage was exploding with competitive cowboys doing the two-step. Laurey's indecision about her feelings for Curly and Jud led into the famous "Laurey Makes Up Her Mind" Ballet, the American theatre's first fully realized psychological dance piece. Even the rousing chorus number "The Farmer and the Cowman" is a challenge dance that echoes the conflicts between the two rival groups. The impact *Oklahoma!* had on the American musical theatre cannot be overestimated. Even the silliest, least consequential musical comedies after 1943 were directly affected by the Rodgers and Hammerstein landmark show. No longer could the plot turn on a dime to reach its expected conclusion. No longer could a performer break out of character to sing a specialty number that had no relation to the rest of the show. And no longer could a musical be thrown together with the traditional elements of entertainment without the audience expecting some sort of cohesive logic to it all. Few Broadway products would accomplish what *Oklahoma!* did on stage, but all of them would be judged by the example set by the Rodgers and Hammerstein masterwork.

A year and a half into the Broadway run, the first of several touring productions was launched and productions of *Oklahoma!* would remain on the road across the States and Canada through 1954. There have been eight major New York revivals of the musical. The national tour featuring Ridge Bond and Patricia Northrop as Curly and Laurey played on Broadway for seventy-two performances in 1951 and then at the New York City Center for forty performances in 1953. The

New York Light Opera Company brought back Betty Garde, the original Aunt Eller, for its 1958 revival, which also featured GENE NELSON recreating his film performance as Will Parker and HELEN GALLAGHER as a highly commended Ado Annie. The same organization revived *Oklahoma!* in 1963 with PETER PALMER and Louise O'Brien as Curly and Laurey (and Garde back again as Eller), and in 1965 with John Davidson and SUSAN WATSON as the lovers and risible performances by Karen Morrow and JULES MUNSHIN as Annie and Ali. Rodgers himself produced the 1969 revival at LINCOLN CENTER for eighty-eight performances. Oscar's son William Hammerstein staged the lauded 1979 Broadway revival, which featured a power-house cast led by LAURENCE GUITTARD and Christine Andreas. An acclaimed 1999 British revival directed by TREVOR NUNN was unique in that it did not use the original Agnes de Mille choreography but offered a new dance inter-pretation by American choreographer SUSAN STROMAN. Also unusual, the actress Josefina Gabrielle who played Laurey also danced the role of dream Laurey in the "Laurey Makes Up Her Mind" ballet. Hugh Jackman was a charismatic Curly, as was American actor Shuler Hensley a riveting Jud. The Royal National Theatre production transferred to Broadway in 2002 with Gabrielle and Hensley reprising their performances with an American cast. *Oklahoma!* has never lost its popularity; it remains to this day the most-produced Rodgers and Hammerstein musical, averaging about 600 productions a year.

Oklahoma! (Magna 1955) was a faith-ful screen adaptation of the stage work, opening a dozen years after the musical had premiered on Broadway. Rodgers and Hammerstein shrewdly did not make arrangements for a film version of *Oklahoma!* until the Broadway production and the last national tour had closed, keeping the movie studios hungry and anxious for ten years. They chose the small, independent Magna company and supervised every aspect of the production, from the casting to the locations. The only cast members from the Broadway production to appear on screen were dancers Bambi Linn and Marc Platt. SHIRLEY JONES was the only principal in the movie who had never made a film before, but she was a veteran of Rodgers and Hammerstein stage productions. The rest were experienced in film musicals, although most had never had such important roles before. CHARLOTTE GREENWOOD finally got to play Aunt Eller, the part she had been offered in 1943 but was unable to play due to film commitments. All of the players did their own singing. Such would have not been the case had James Dean or Paul Newman played Curly, Joanne Woodward was Laurey, and Eli Wallach as Jud; they had all tested for the film and were seriously considered. Jud's "Lonely Room" and Ali Hakim's only song, "It's a Scandal! It's an Outrage!," were cut from the film but the rest of score was intact, beautifully conducted by JAY BLACKTON who had worked on the stage version. Interior scenes were shot in California but for the exteriors a location was selected in Arizona where period farm houses were built and acres of corn were planted. The respected director Fred Zinnemann had never helmed a musical before but was selected with the hope of making *Oklahoma!* not look like a Hollywood musical. In many ways the risk paid off, for the movie doesn't have the glossy look and feel of a back lot musical. Zinnemann got sincere and nicely nuanced performances from his cast, although the pace of the film lacks the immediacy of Mamoulian's stage direction and the lengthy screen musical is sluggish at times. Agnes de Mille recreated her dances for the screen and they serve as a colorful record of her stage work, but even they seem less impressive in the movie. Filmed in a new wide-screen pro-cess called Todd-AO, the movie often seemed bigger than it had to be. The open prairie is well served by such an expansive look but *Oklahoma!* has always been about characters, not scenery. Most of the reviews were compli-mentary and the picture was a box office hit. In 1956 20TH CENTURY-FOX rereleased the film in CinemaScope, which is the format most have seen it in over the years.

OLIVER! (Imperial Theatre 1963). A tune-ful London hit, the show held the record for the most successful West End musical on Broadway (774 performances) until the British invasion of the 1970s. LIONEL BART wrote the score and the libretto for the musicalization of Charles Dickens' classic novel *Oliver Twist.* The adventures of the orphan boy Oliver Twist take him from the workhouse to London, where he is befriended by a band of pickpock-ets run by Fagin, to finding his long-lost rela-tives only after robbery, betrayal, and murder have been committed. Considering how dark the story was at times, most of the songs were cheerful music hall-like numbers, such as "I'd Do Anything," "You've Got to Pick a Pocket or Two," "Food, Glorious Food," "It's a Fine Life," and "Consider Yourself." Also

Casts for *Oliver!*

Character	1963 Broadway	1968 film	1984 Broadway
Oliver Twist	Bruce Prochnick	Mark Lester	Braden Danner
Fagin	CLIVE REVILL	Ron Moody	Ron Moody
Nancy	GEORGIA BROWN	Shani Wallis	PATTI LuPONE
Artful Dodger	David Jones	Jack Wild	David Garlick
Bill Sikes	Danny Sewell	Oliver Reed	Graeme Campbell

in the score was the tender ballad "Where Is Love?.," the plaintive torch song "As Long As He Needs Me," and the stream-of-conscience character number "Reviewing the Situation." Critics felt the novel was expertly condensed and musicalized, and the London smash was a hit on Broadway as well. DAVID MERRICK co-produced with London producer Donald Albery, and Peter Coe directed the atmospheric production. Only Danny Sewell as the murderous Bill Sikes remained from the original Broadway cast when producer David Merrick brought the show back to New York in 1965 after its long tour, staying for sixty-four performances. The principals were Robin Ramsay (Fagin), Donnie Smiley (Nancy), Victor Stiles (Oliver), and Joey Baio (Artful Dodger). Ron Moody, who had scored a triumph as Fagin in the movie version of the musical, reprised the role on Broadway in 1984 but audiences weren't interested in a revival of the British show and it folded after two weeks. *Oliver!* has long been a favorite of all kinds of producing groups, from professional regional theatres to schools.

▪ *Oliver!* (Columbia 1968) was given prestige treatment by Hollywood, hiring the distinguished British director Carol Reed to helm this, his only musical, spending big bucks on recreating Victorian London, and securing ONNA WHITE to choreograph the huge production numbers. It certainly was big, and the lively movie translated into a big box office hit. Curiously, Columbia did not cast any stars, using the stage actor Ron Moody who had played Fagin in London and giving the plum role of Nancy to singer Shani Wallis who was little known in the States. Mark Lester was a bland Oliver but the rest of the cast shone, from the creepy performance by Oliver Reed as Bill Sikes to the animated shenanigans by little Jack Wild as the Artful Dodger. The movie may have been overproduced but it seemed everyone liked it that way. A clever animated version of the story titled OLIVER AND COMPANY was made by the DISNEY studio in 1988.

▪ OLIVER AND COMPANY (Disney 1988). Although this musical was made right before the studio's animation renaissance began with THE LITTLE MERMAID (1989), it has the artistry, confidence, and entertainment value of the later hits. Roger Allers and his fellow screenwriters adapted Dickens' *Oliver Twist* into an animal tale set in contemporary New York City. The orphaned kitten Oliver (voice of Joey Lawrence) falls into a gang of street-smart dogs led by Dodger (Billy Joel) and overseen by the human Fagin (DOM DeLUISE). When Oliver is rescued by the wealthy little girl Jenny (Natalie Gregory), the pampered French poodle Georgette (BETTE MIDLER) sees the stray as a threat and works with the gang to get rid of him. All of the characters were vivid and funny, with skillful voice work from Cheech Marin, Richard Mulligan, Sheryl Lee Ralph, Roscoe Lee Browne, and Robert Loggia. The score, by a variety of pop songwriters, was equally vibrant, especially the rhythmic "Why Should I Worry?," the satirical "Perfect Isn't Easy," the pulsating "Streets of Gold," and the bluesy "Once Upon a Time in New York City." The animation was superb, with Manhattan presented in a sharp, stylized manner that was neither too gritty nor glorified. George Scribner directed and Barry Manilow composed the very urban soundtrack music. The success of the movie, helped by the popularity of the stars heard on the soundtrack, encouraged the Disney studio to invest more money and talent in its neglected animation department.

OLSEN AND JOHNSON. Stage and film performers, writers, and producers. A raucous comedy team who entertained audiences with broad clowning, high-pitched laughter, and unrelentless slapstick, they found more success on Broadway than any other vaudeville comic duo. Ole Olsen [born John Siguard Olsen] (1892–1963) was born in Peru, Indiana, and attended Northwestern University before going into vaudeville in 1914. The next year he teamed up with Chic Johnson [born Harold

Ogden Johnson] (1891–1962), a Chicago native who attended the same college. The two immediately got bookings on the variety circuit and even performed in Great Britain and Australia. The duo was quite famous when they appeared in the film musical *Oh, Sailor Behave!* (1931) and were added to the Broadway musical *TAKE A CHANCE* (1933) in which they played character parts. But the team's zany antics were better displayed in sketches, so they produced and starred in the revue *HELLZAPOPPIN'* (1938), a giant hit that broke box office records. Olsen and Johnson repeated the silly show in London and then on screen in 1941. Their subsequent Broadway revues, and shows they produced without appearing in, were less successful, as with *Streets of Paris* (1939), *Sons o' Fun* (1941), *Count Me In* (1942), *Laffing Room Only* (1944), and *Pardon Our French* (1950). The team often wrote the sketches and lyrics for their shows and for revues presented by others, and they played themselves in some movies, including the musicals *Crazy House* (1943), *The Ghost Catchers* (1944), and *See My Lawyer* (1945). Unlike most comedy duos, in which one member plays straight man to the other's clowning, both Olsen and Johnson were extroverted, broad performers and their jokes and bits came fast and furiously.

☐ **OLYMPUS 7-0000** (ABC-TV 1966). RICHARD ADLER, who had co-written Broadway's baseball hit *DAMN YANKEES* (1955), turned to football for this musical fantasy and was only intermittently successful. Adler and Jerome Chodorov wrote the teleplay in which the architecture student Todd (LARRY BLYDEN) at a small New England college is coach for the school's losing football team, played by real footballer Joe Namath and the New York Jets. Mary (PHYLLIS NEWMAN) is in love with Todd and wants to help so she dials Olympus 7-000 on the phone and asks Hermes (DONALD O'CONNOR), the messenger god, for help. With Hermes' magical powers the team starts winning and Todd is wooed by big time colleges to be their coach. But Mary loves Todd as he is and keeps Hermes from the crucial game. The team loses, the offers dry up, and Todd

returns to Mary and architecture. Lou Jacobi and EDDIE FOY, JR. were among the supporting players. Adler's score was pleasant enough but suffered in comparison to the *Damn Yankees* set of hits. All the same, there was something pleasing about "I've Got Feelings," "The Three of Us," "I Get Around," "Better Things to Do," and the title song. Adler and Willard Levitas co-produced the sixty-minute musical for *ABC Stage 67*.

☯ **ON A CLEAR DAY YOU CAN SEE FOREVER** (Mark Hellinger Theatre 1965). An interesting if problematic musical about ESP, the musical comedy by ALAN JAY LERNER (book and lyrics) and BURTON LANE (music) may have had script difficulties but there was nothing the matter with the score and the glowing performance by BARBARA HARRIS. Chain-smoking, overtalkative Daisy Gamble goes to Dr. Mark Bruckner to hypnotize her into giving up cigarettes to please her straight-laced fiancé Warren Smith. When Daisy is under hypnosis, the psychiatrist discovers that in an earlier life Daisy was the eighteenth-century lady Melinda Wells. Just as Daisy falls in love with Mark, he is infatuated with Melinda and the romantic triangle is only solved when Daisy's ESP saves Mark's life and the two twentieth-century characters are united. An interesting premise seemed to go haywire by the second act but Harris was as engaging as her songs, which included the enticing "Hurry! It's Lovely Up Here," the jubilant "On the S. S. Bernard Cohn," and the torchy "What Did I Have That I Don't Have?" Also in the expert score were "Come Back to Me," "She Wasn't You," "Wait Till We're Sixty-Five," and the haunting title song. Lerner produced and ROBERT LEWIS directed the musical, which overrode mixed notices to run 272 performances.

🎬 **On a Clear Day You Can See Forever** (Paramount 1970) was a tuneful, decorative vehicle for BARBRA STREISAND who was ideally suited to play the loquacious Daisy from Brooklyn. The movie was built around her, with Lerner's screenplay eliminating characters and songs so as to give her more

Casts for *On a Clear Day You Can See Forever*		
Character	*Broadway 1965*	*1970 film*
Daisy Gamble	BARBARA HARRIS	BARBRA STREISAND
Marc Bruckner / Charbot	JOHN CULLUM	Yves Montand
Warren Smith	WILLIAM DANIELS	LARRY BLYDEN

screen time and it was the film's saving grace. Yves Montand gave a tired, dull performance as the psychiatrist, who was Frenchified into Marc Chabot, and the other characters were so minor as to be forgettable. Lerner rewrote his story, spending more time on the flash-backs to Regency England, and came up with a new ending that was no more satisfying than the stage one. He also collaborated with Lane on some new songs, most memorably "Love With All the Trimmings" and "Go to Sleep," which Daisy sang as a duet with her alter ego. VINCENTE MINNELLI directed without much energy, for any time Streisand is not on the screen, the picture seems to come to a dead halt. The production values are quite impres-sive, both the modern and period clothes hav-ing fun with excess and the location shooting in England for the flashbacks very atmospheric.

ON THE AVENUE (Fox 1937). What might have been a routine backstager rose above the others because of its effervescent IRVING BERLIN score and the appealing cast. Producer Gene Markey and William Conselman wrote the tired screenplay about Gary Blake (DICK POWELL), the star, author, and producer of a Broadway revue called *On the Avenue*. When

Blake satirizes the wealthy Caraway family in one of the show's sketches, the socialite Mimi Caraway (Madeleine Carroll) objects and the two lock horns and then lips, much to the dis-appointment of the revue's leading lady Mona Merrick (ALICE FAYE). Most of the songs in the film were presented as part of the revue and never tied in with the plot but they were wonderful all the same. "This Year's Kisses," "Slumming on Park Avenue," "He Ain't Got Rhythm," "The Girl on the Police Gazette," "You're Laughing at Me," and "I've Got my Love to Keep Me Warm" were performed (mostly by Faye) and staged with zest. Also in the film were the RITZ BROTHERS, Alan Mowbray, GEORGE BARBIER, JOAN DAVIS, WALTER CATLETT, Stepin Fetchit, SIG RUMANN, Cora Witherspoon, BILLY GILBERT, and LYNN BARI. ROY DEL RUTH directed, and the inven-tive production numbers were choreographed by SEYMOUR FELIX.

ON THE RIVIERA. See *FOLIES BERGERE DE PARIS*

ON THE TOWN (Adelphi Theatre 1944). A fanciful musical comedy filled with dance, the show marked the Broadway debut of four major

On the Town. While not the first movie musical to shoot on location, there was something exciting about the way New York City was more than just a backdrop for the action. Pictured are the three sailors, played by (left to right) Frank Sinatra, Jules Munshin, and Gene Kelly, at Rockefeller Center. (Photofest)

creative talents: composer LEONARD BERNSTEIN, lyricist–librettists BETTY COMDEN and ADOLPH GREEN, and choreographer JEROME ROBBINS. Sailors Ozzie, Chip, and Gabey, whose ship is docked at the Brooklyn Navy Yard, get a twenty-four hour leave and explore New York City looking for adventure and romance. They find it in the form of cab driver Hildy, anthropology student Claire de Loon, and ballerina–cooch dancer Ivy. By the end of the leave the three couples part with bittersweet satisfaction. The libretto was an extended version of the Bernstein–Robbins ballet piece "Fancy Free," and the plotting was still sketchy but the show featured some lengthy dance numbers that continued the stories so few Broadway musicals felt so "musical." The vibrant "New York, New York" became the most popular song, but the score was filled with wonderful numbers, such as the manic "I Get Carried Away," the torchy "Lonely Town," the quietly celebratory "Lucky to Be Me," the farcical "Come Up to My Place," the vivacious "You Got Me," the swinging "I Can Cook Too," and the poignant parting song "Some Other Time." Robbins' choreography was jazzy, clever, and funny, as seen in such ballet pieces as "Miss Turnstiles" and "Coney Island." Critics cheered the new talents as well as veteran GEORGE ABBOTT who directed and the show was a surprise hit, running 463 performances. RON FIELD directed and choreographed a cast of young and promising talents in a 1971 Broadway revival, but the lavish production played to small audiences and had to shutter in nine weeks. Even less successful was a 1998 revival, which lasted only sixty-five performances. GEORGE C. WOLFE directed the lively production in Central Park and the audience response was encouraging enough that he moved the show into one of Broadway's biggest venues only to see it fold in two months. Critical complaints centered on the dancing, which was deemed uninspired, and the uneven cast.

■ **On the Town** (MGM 1949) was a lively, spirited film co-directed and co-choreographed by STANLEY DONEN and GENE KELLY that decimated the stage score but retained the lengthy ballets and the music Bernstein wrote for them. Producer ARTHUR FREED bought the screen rights to *On the Town* but admitted he didn't like the songs so he hired ROGER EDENS to compose new ones, and Comden and Green wrote new lyrics, with the best addition being "Prehistoric Man." Kelly was joined by Frank Sinatra and JULES MUNSHIN to play the three sailors and VERA-ELLEN, ANN MILLER, and BETTY GARRETT were their love interests. In addition to the extended dance sequences, the movie was also unique in the way it used on-location filming in New York City, using the celebrated tourist sights as the background for the action. Comden and Green wrote the screenplay that did not stray too far from the original stage story, and the action moved briskly even if the plot was as thin as before.

▧ **ON THE TWENTIETH CENTURY** (St. James Theatre 1978). A riotous musical farce with outstanding production values and an animated mock-operetta score, the musical was superior in all areas, yet could not find an audience beyond 453 performances. BETTY COMDEN and ADOLPH GREEN adapted the popular comedy *Twentieth Century* (1933) about the egotistical Broadway producer Oscar Jaffe (JOHN CULLUM) who needs the movie star Lily Garland (MADELINE KAHN) to be in his next show or he won't get the backing. Oscar discovered Lily and was once her lover as well but times have changed and she is now famous and Oscar is struggling. When the religious fanatic Mrs. Primrose (IMOGENE COCA) agrees to back Oscar's play because it is about Mary Magdalene, he nearly wins Lily over to his side. But Mrs. Primrose turns out to be a penniless nut case so only when he fakes his own deathbed scene does he get Lily to sign

Casts for *On the Town*

Character	1944 Broadway	1949 film	1971 Broadway	1998 Broadway
Gabey	John Battles	GENE KELLY	RON HUSMANN	Perry Laylon Ojeda
Ozzie	ADOLPH GREEN	JULES MUNSHIN	Remak Ramsay	Robert Montano
Chip	Cris Alexander	FRANK SINATRA	Jess Richards	Jesse Tyler Ferguson
Ivy Smith	Sono Osato	VERA-ELLEN	DONNA MCKECHNIE	Tai Jimenez
Claire	BETTY COMDEN	ANN MILLER	PHYLLIS NEWMAN	Sarah Knowlton
Hildy Esterhazy	NANCY WALKER	BETTY GARRETT	BERNADETTE PETERS	Lea Delaria
Lucy Schmeeler	ALICE PEARCE	Alice Pearce	MARILYN COOPER	Annie Golden

a contract. Also in the cast were George Coe, Dean Dittman, George Lee Andrews, JUDY KAYE, and newcomer KEVIN KLINE who stole his scenes as Lily's hyperactive fiancé Bruce Granit. All the action took place on the train *Twentieth Century* as it went from Chicago to New York, and the endlessly inventive set designs by Robin Wagner were one of the show's highlights. HAROLD PRINCE directed, encouraging the performers to give over-the-top performances that matched the vigorous score by CY COLEMAN (music), Comden, and Green (lyrics). "Repent," "Veronique," "Our Private World," "Never," "Life Is Like a Train," and the title song were among the most memorable numbers.

ON WITH THE SHOW (Warner 1929). An early and primitive backstager, the pleasant musical revealed the goings-on behind the scenes of a Broadway show in out-of-town tryouts. Robert Lord wrote the screenplay in which scenes from the musical on stage were shown in such a way that the audience could follow both the on- and offstage plots. The temperamental star Nita French (Betty Compson) quarrels with the producers and walks out during the performance, so newcomer Kitty (Sally O'Neil) has to go on in her place. It was one of the first times this ruse had been used in a talkie and seemed unique enough at the time. Also unique was the way time was used. The movie started with the audience assembling in the house, all the action occurred during the performance, and it ended with the company's curtain call. The concept remains interesting, yet much of the film falls flat. The studio decided to shoot the entire movie in color and the technical problems, both visual and aural, make it a difficult picture to watch. Also, Compson and O'Neil do poorly, both of them having their singing dubbed by Josephine Houston, and Compson's dancing is so inad-

equate that she needed a double for some of the numbers. The highlight of the musical is the presence of young ETHEL WATERS as a plantation worker in the show within the show. GRANT CLARKE and HARRY AKST wrote her two songs, "Birmingham Bertha" and "Am I Blue?," the latter the first hit song introduced by an African American on screen. ALAN CROSLAND directed the DARRYL F. ZANUCK production, and Larry Ceballos was the choreographer.

ON YOUR TOES (Imperial Theatre 1936). A landmark musical for its use of dance, this sparkling show by GEORGE ABBOTT (book), RICHARD RODGERS (book and music), and LORENZ HART (book and lyrics) was both arty and a satire on the arts.

Plot: Hoofer Phil Dolan Jr. grew up in vaudeville but now teaches music at Knickerbocker University where his sweetheart Frankie Frayne writes songs, such as "It's Got to Be Love," and his student Sidney Cohn composes modern ballets, such as "Slaughter on Tenth Avenue." Junior convinces the wealthy patroness of the arts Peggy Porterfield to get Sergei Alexandrvitch to have his Russian ballet company present the new jazz ballet. During rehearsals the prima ballerina Vera Barnova gets a little too interested in Junior, causing distress for Frankie and arousing enough anger in Vera's jealous boyfriend–dancing partner Konstantine Morrosine that he hires two hit men to shoot Junior when the ballet ends. While Phil is dancing in the "Slaughter on Tenth Avenue," he is slipped a note about the murder plot and is instructed to keep dancing no matter what. So Junior keeps dancing until the police arrive and both the ballet and the musical can end.

The idea for the musical originated in Hollywood as a possible vehicle for FRED ASTAIRE but nothing came of it so Rodgers and

Broadway casts for *On Your Toes*

Character	1936 Broadway	1939 film	1954 Broadway	1983 Broadway
Phil Dolan	RAY BOLGER	EDDIE ALBERT	BOBBY VAN	Lara Teeter
Vera	TAMARA GEVA	VERA ZORINA	Vera Zorina	Natalia Makarova
Frankie	Doris Carson		Kay Coulter	Christine Andreas
Serge	MONTY WOOLLEY	ALAN HALE	Ben Astar	GEORGE S. IRVING
Peggy	LUELLA GEAR	Gloria Dickson	ELAINE STRITCH	Dina Merrill
Konstantine	Demetrios Vilan	ERIK RHODES	Nicolas Orloff	George de la Pena
Sidney Cohn	David Morris		Joshua Shelley	Peter Slutsker

On Your Toes (stage) Musical Numbers

"Two a Day for Keith"
"The Three B's"
"It's Got to Be Love"
"Too Good for the Average Man"
"There's a Small Hotel"
"The Heart Is Quicker Than the Eye"
"La Princess Zenobia" Ballet
"Quiet Night"
"Glad to Be Unhappy"
"On Your Toes"
"Slaughter on Tenth Avenue" Ballet

Hart teamed up with Abbott and put together one of the better librettos of the decade. GEORGE BALANCHINE, choreographing his first book musical, was able to use dance, both classical ballet and modern, in a way that continued the story rather than just interrupting it. The two extended dance numbers, the "Princess Zenobia" ballet and the famous "Slaughter on Tenth Avenue," were not highbrow interpolations but witty and even satiric pieces that were, nonetheless, performed by classically trained dancers. Because there was so much dance in the show there were fewer songs, yet all were outstanding and "There's a Small Hotel" and "Glad to Be Unhappy" became standards. Also, Rodgers' music for the dance sections revealed new facets of his composing talents. The show made a Broadway star out of RAY BOLGER, and the DWIGHT DEERE WINMAN production ran 315 performances. BOBBY VAN played Junior in the 1954 Broadway revival and, as accomplished as he was, the show seemed to need a star. However, the 1983 revival featured the unknown Lara Teeter as Junior and it ran 505 performances and then toured and transferred successfully to London. Abbott directed both revivals, the second being his last Broadway triumph.

On Your Toes (Warner–First National 1939) came to the screen without Ray Bolger, which was odd since he had already been featured in three movie musicals and had just completed *The Wizard of Oz* (1939). But even Bolger would not have been able to save the hatchet job that WARNER BROTHERS did to *On Your Toes*. None of the songs were sung, some were heard as background music only, and only the (much abridged) ballet music was used. The screenplay by Jerry Wald and Richard Macaulay was dreary, particularly as directed by Ray Enright, EDDIE ALBERT was a tiresome Junior, and only Balanchine's choreography

featuring VERA ZORINA had a spark of life to it. What could have been one of the great movie musicals was botched beyond recognition.

ONCE ON THIS ISLAND (Booth Theatre 1990). A simple but intoxicating musical set in the Caribbean, the show brought the first Broadway recognition to creators LYNN AHRENS (book and lyrics) and STEPHEN FLAHERTY (music). A group of storytellers on an island in the French Antilles act out the fable of Ti Moune (La Chanze), an orphan girl who saves the life of the rich heir Daniel (Jerry Dixon) after an automobile accident by promising her soul to the gods. The two fall in love but when Daniel is forced to wed the rich girl his family has chosen for him, Ti Moune dies and becomes a tree that overlooks and protects Daniel's children. Also in the vibrant African American cast were Kecia Lewis-Evans, Sheila Gibbs, Milton Craig Nealy, Nikki Rene, Eric Riley, and Gerry McIntyre. Based on Rosa Guy's novel *My Love, My Love*, the musical was so well received Off Broadway at PLAYWRIGHTS HORIZONS that it moved to Broadway where it found an audience for 469 performances. GRACIELA DANIELLE directed and choreographed the Caribbean-flavored show, and the score featured such evocative numbers as "Forever Yours," "Mama Will Provide," "Waiting for Life," "The Human Heart," "We Dance," and "A Part of Us."

ONCE UPON A BROTHERS GRIMM (CBS-TV 1977). Even at two hours, this complicated, large-scale musical about the famous storytelling brothers was overcrowded with characters and tales. Yet amid the confusion were delicious moments and some superb dance numbers. The teleplay by Jean Campbell showed Jakob (Dean Jones) and Wilhelm Grimm (Paul Sand) traveling through a forest in their carriage to deliver a copy of their stories to the king when they get lost in the woods and run across their character creations reenacting such tales as *Little Red Riding Hood*, *Tom Thumb*, *Sleeping Beauty*, *Hansel and Gretel*, *Cinderella*, and *Rumpelstilskin*. Cleavon Little, CHITA RIVERA, Teri Garr, CLIVE REVILL, Sorrell Booke, Don Correia, Arte Johnson, MADELINE KAHN, and Ruth Buzzi were among the many actors needed to tell the stories, and the Los Angeles Ballet Company was employed to handle the many dance sequences. MITCH LEIGH (music) and SAMMY CAHN (lyrics) wrote over a dozen songs for the show, including "Happily Married Wolf," "The Only Way to Go Is Up," "Life Is Not a Fairy Tale," "Don't Tell Me I'm Flying," "Schlaf Mein Kind," "Day of Days," and "Life Can Be a Fairy Tale." The danced recreations of the tales, choreographed by RON FIELD, received the highest praise and the critics admitted that many of the players gave expert performances, but generally the ambitious musical disappointed.

🐦 **ONCE UPON A MATTRESS** (Alvin Theatre 1959). The anachronistic musical version of the old *Princess and the Pea* fairy tale was such a hit at the Off Broadway Phoenix Theatre that the show moved to Broadway for 460 performances and made CAROL BURNETT a stage star. In the libretto by Jay Thompson, Dean Fuller, and Marshall Barer, no one in the kingdom can marry until the hapless Prince Dauntless is wed, and his mother the Queen has seen to it that no girl is good enough for her boy. But the unconventional, spunky Princess Winifred outwits the Queen, passes her test of sensitivity even as she sleeps on a pile of mattresses, and there is a happy ending for everyone, including the once-mute King who silences his bossy wife. MARY RODGERS (music) and Barer (lyrics) wrote the merry score that included "Happily Ever After," "In a Little While," "Shy," "Yesterday I Loved You," "Very Soft Shoes," "Normandy," and "Sensitivity." The tuneful score and funny libretto took a back seat to newcomer Burnett who was applauded by the press and the public for her comic Princess "Fred." GEORGE ABBOTT directed and JOE LAYTON choreographed the musical, which also featured Harry Snow, Matt Mattox, Anne Jones, and Allen Case. *Once Upon a Mattress* has remained a favorite in summer stock and schools, and it was revived on Broadway in 1996. Sarah Jessica Parker was considered a bright and personable performer but most critics felt her Princess Winifred was not raucous enough to hold together the musical revival directed by Gerald Gutierrez. Yet Parker had her fans and the colorful, clever production, which included tap-dancing knights in armor, was enjoyable enough that audiences came for 187 performances.

☐ Carol Burnett appeared in all three television productions of *Once Upon a Mattress*. She reprised her stage performance as "Fred" in a 1964 version on CBS-TV in which most of the Broadway cast appeared. It was directed by Joe Layton and Dave Geisel and, although numbers were cut to fit the show into the ninety-minute broadcast, the spirit of the stage musical was still there. A 1972 remake on CBS-TV reunited Burnett with other cast members in a ninety-minute new version with a slightly revised script and directed by Dave Powers and RON FIELD. A 2005 ABC-TV production starred Burnett again but this time she played the Queen and some scenes and songs were reassigned to build up the supporting role. Tracey Ullman was a delightful Winifred and the supporting cast was very talented. KATHLEEN MARSHALL directed and choreographed the broadcast, which had colorful, fairy tale-like production values.

🎬 **ONE HOUR WITH YOU** (Paramount 1932). Although it may not compare favorably with the best MAURICE CHEVALIER–JEANETTE MACDONALD vehicles, the musical still sparkles with wit, playful performances, and a fine score by OSCAR STRAUS, LEO ROBIN, and RICHARD A. WHITING. In SAMSON RAPHAELSON's screenplay, Dr. André Bertier (Chevalier) is happily married to Colette (MacDonald) but is tempted by his wife's flirtatious friend Mitzi Olivier (Genevieve Tobin). Colette pushes the two together to test her husband and merry complications follow. Also in the cast were Roland Young, CHARLES RUGGLES, GEORGE BARBIER, Josephine Dunn, Richard Carle, Charles Judels, and Donald Novis. Parts of the movie were directed by ERNST LUBITSCH and the rest by GEORGE CUKOR (there were fights about final billing), but a frothy and suggestive tone runs throughout the musical. Although only the title song became a hit, all the numbers are first rate and are smoothly integrated into the story. The doctor praises the charms of "Oh, That Mitzi!" and recommends that she take a tonic "Three Times a Day" while she seductively suggests she come and see him thrice daily. The married couple slyly notes

Casts for *Once Upon a Mattress*

Characters	Winifred	Dauntless	Queen	King
1959 Broadway	CAROL BURNETT	Joseph Bova	Jane White	JACK GILFORD
1964 television	Carol Burnett	Joseph Bova	Jane White	Jack Gilford
1996 Broadway	Sarah Jessica Parker	David Aaron Baker	Mary Lou Rosato	Heath Lamberts
2005 television	Tracey Ullman	Denis O'Hare	Carol Burnett	Tom Smothers

"What a Little Thing Like a Wedding Ring Can Do" and affectionately confirms that "We Will Always Be Sweethearts." Most nimble of all, Chevalier sings to the camera, asking the men in the audience "What Would You Do?" in his situation; he concludes the song with a wink and explains, "That's what I did too!"

🎵 **110** in the **Shade** (Broadhurst Theatre 1963). A gentle and affecting musical that couldn't survive any longer than 330 performances on Broadway in a season that offered big spectacles and glamorous stars, this musicalization of N. Richard Nash's play *The Rainmaker* (1954) boasted a lovely score and commendable performances. The DAVID MERRICK production featured Robert Horton as the con man Bill Starbuck who promises to bring rain for a fee and Inga Swenson was the feisty spinster Lizzie Curry who sees through him but is attracted to him all the same. Nash penned the character-driven libretto, and HARVEY SCHMIDT (music) and TOM JONES (lyrics) wrote the heartfelt score, which included the plaintive ballads "Love, Don't Turn Away" and "Simple Little Things," the grandiose numbers "Melisande" and "Raunchy," the atmospheric songs "Another Hot Day" and "Everything Beautiful Happens at Night," and the giddy "Little Red Hat." Joseph Anthony directed and AGNES DE MILLE did the rustic dances.

Revivals have been infrequent but New York saw a production by the City Opera in 1992 that featured KAREN ZIEMBA as Lizzie and she was supported by Brian Sutherland (Starbuck), Richard Muenz (File), and Henderson Forsythe (H. C. Curry). SCOTT ELLIS directed and SUSAN STROMAN choreographed. The ROUNDABOUT THEATRE COMPANY offered a Broadway production in 2007 directed by LONNY PRICE, which did well during its limited run of ninety-four performances. AUDRA MCDONALD was deemed a luminous Lizzie by the press and the public and the musical itself was praised, many

commentators stating that the tender show held up very well.

🎬 **ONE HUNDRED MEN AND A GIRL** (Universal 1937). A modern yet charming fairy tale, the musical featured teenager DEANNA DURBIN who, with her energetic smile and heavenly soprano voice, seemed to have come out of a storybook herself. As the daughter of the unemployed trombonist John Cardwell (ADOLPHE MENJOU), Patricia (Durbin) struggles to form an orchestra for her father and his out-of-work fellow musicians. Patricia not only gets a patron and a hall but even convinces world-famous maestro LEOPOLD STOKOWSKI (playing himself) to come and conduct them. At the opening night concert, the ambitious teen is called to the stage for acknowledgment and, when asked to sing, launches into an air from *La Traviata*. Durbin got to sing some other numbers as well, and movements by Tchaikovsky, Liszt, Mozart, and Berlioz were performed by the orchestra. The strong supporting cast included ALICE BRADY, EUGENE PALLETTE, MISCHA AUER, BILLY GILBERT, Alma Kruger, and Jack Smart. HENRY KOSTER directed the film, which was Durbin's second picture, and it secured her career.

🎬 **ONE IN A MILLION** (Fox 1936). Although the Norwegian skating champion SONJA HENIE had been in many newsreels, this Hollywood musical was her feature debut and she established herself as a screen favorite the first time out. Producer DARRYL F. ZANUCK signed the blonde athlete to a nine-picture contract without ever auditioning her for singing or acting abilities. Yet the gamble paid off the moment Henie hit the ice and audiences were enthralled. In the screenplay by Leonard Praskins and Mark Kelly, Greta (Henie), the daughter of Swiss innkeeper Heirich Muller (Jean Hersholt), prepares for the Olympics while she is urged by Tad Spencer (ADOLPHE MENJOU) to join him and skate to the music of his all-

---

Broadway casts for *110 in the Shade*

Character	1963 Broadway	2007 Broadway
Lizzie	Inga Swenson	AUDRA MCDONALD
Starbuck	Robert Horton	Steve Kazee
H. C. Curry	Will Geer	JOHN CULLUM
File	STEPHEN DOUGLASS	Christopher Innvar
Jimmy	Scooter Teague	Bobby Steggert
Snookie	Lesley Warren	Carla Duren
Noah	Steve Roland	Chris Butler

girl orchestra. Greta is also being wooed by the brash American reporter Bob Harris (DON AMECHE). By the final reel, Greta gives in to Bob, skates for Tad, and ends up performing in a lavish ice show at Madison Square Garden. Along the way the RITZ BROTHERS, Leah Ray, DIXIE DUNBAR, Arline Judge, NED SPARKS, and Borah Minnevitch and his Harmonica Rascals were on hand to provide comedy and/or music. The songs by LEW POLLACK (music) and SIDNEY MITCHELL (lyrics) were not particularly memorable, although the title number (used several times throughout the movie) started to sound catchy. SIDNEY LANFIELD directed, NICK CASTLE did the choreography, and Jack Haskell staged the skating sequences.

ONE NIGHT IN THE TROPICS (Universal 1940). It may have had a silly and improbable excuse for a plot but the West Indies musical offered some masterful songs by JEROME KERN (music), OSCAR HAMMERSTEIN, DOROTHY FIELDS, and OTTO HARBACH, all of which were written four years earlier for an unproduced musical called *Riviera*. The screenplay by Gertrude Purcell and Charles Grayson was set on the fictional Caribbean island of San Marcos where insurance salesman Jim Moore (ALLAN JONES) makes his playboy friend Steve Harper (ROBERT CUMMINGS) buy a policy promising to settle down and marry his fiancée Cynthia Merrick (Nancy Kelly). However, Jim ends up paying heavily because he himself falls in love with Cynthia and on the day she is to wed Steve the two run off together. MARY BOLAND, Peggy Moran, WILLIAM FRAWLEY, and LEO CARILLO were somehow involved in the plot but seemed to get lost in it, just as the fine songs were. The scintillating rhumba "Remind Me," the heartfelt "Your Dream (Is the Same as My Dream)," and the lovely "You and Your Kiss" were topflight numbers by three brilliant songwriters at their peak, but the film bombed at the box office and it took a while for the songs to catch on. UNIVERSAL lost a bundle on the lavish film directed by A. EDWARD SUTHERLAND but eventually had the last laugh: producer Leonard Spigelgass hired two radio comics, BUD ABBOTT and LOU COSTELLO, to play undercover men in the movie and the team immediately clicked. They would go on to make twenty-eight more movies for the studio and save the company from bankruptcy.

ONE NIGHT OF LOVE (Columbia 1934). The first Hollywood musical to feature a bona fide opera singer, GRACE MOORE, in a leading role, the film was such a hit that studios started wooing famous divas to come to California. Moore played the American soprano Mary Barett who is studying in Italy with her devoted teacher Monteverdi (TULLIO CARMINATI). Her dream of becoming an opera star is somewhat sidetracked by her romance with the visiting American Bill Houston (Lyle Talbot), but eventually Mary realizes that music is her true love and ends up starring at the Metropolitan Opera in New York. Moore sang selections from *Lucia di Lammermoor*, *Madama Butterfly*, *Carmen*, and other standard repertoire pieces, and audiences found that they liked the highbrow music in limited dosages. With lyricist GUS KAHN, director VICTOR SCHERTZINGER composed a flowing title song, which also became a hit, although Schertzinger was the first to point out that the main melody came from Puccini.

ONE TOUCH OF VENUS (Imperial 1943). Much lighter and carefree than other musicals by composer KURT WEILL, this fantasy afforded MARY MARTIN her first starring role on Broadway. The barber Rodney Hatch has bought an engagement ring for his bossy fiancée Gloria and tries it out on a statue of Venus in a museum. The statue comes to life and falls for Rodney, giving him a better self-image. But once Venus sees how humdrum the life of a housewife is in the twentieth century, she turns back to stone and Rodney has the strength to break up with Gloria. Humorist S. J. PERELMAN and comic poet Ogden Nash collaborated on the libretto that was alternately witty and romantic, and Nash wrote some delicious lyrics for Weill's flowing music, with the big hit being "Speak Low (When You Speak Love)." Also in the scintillating score were the matter-of-fact tribute "That's Him," the enticing "I'm a Stranger Here Myself," the sly "The Trouble With Women," and the haunting "Foolish Heart." The reviews extolled the script, score, and cast, especially Martin, and the CHERYL CRAWFORD production ran 567 performances. Elia Kazan directed and AGNES DE MILLE choreographed the dances, including two outstanding modern ballets, "Forty Minutes for Lunch" and "Venus in Ozone Heights."

One Touch of Venus (Universal 1948) not only dropped Mary Martin but also all of the songs except the popular "Speak Low" and the comic "The Trouble With Women." With so few new ones added, the film hardly felt like a musical at all. The Harry Kurnitz and Frank Tashlin screenplay removed all

Casts for *One Touch of Venus*

Character	1943 Broadway	1948 film	1955 television
Venus	MARY MARTIN	AVA GARDNER	JANET BLAIR
Rodney/Eddie Hatch	KENNY BAKER	Robert Walker	RUSSELL NYPE
Whitelaw Savory	JOHN BOLES	Tom Conway	George Gaines
Gloria Kramer	Ruth Bond	OLGA SAN JUAN	
Molly Grant	Paula Lawrence	EVE ARDEN	Laurel Shelby
Joe Grant		DICK HAYMES	

vestiges of wit and what was left was a dreary, charmless fantasy with AVA GARDNER (singing dubbed by Eileen Wilson) giving one of her worst performances as Venus. The rest of the cast showed more life but not enough to save it from WILLIAM A. SEITER's clumpy direction. ◻ Much more pleasing was the 1955 abridged NBC-TV version with JANET BLAIR as Venus and RUSSELL NYPE as Rodney. The ninety-minute program was broadcast live from Dallas, Texas, and was directed by George Schaefer.

OPERA SINGERS IN MUSICALS. In the days when operettas flourished on Broadway, there was sometimes little difference between a bona fide opera singer and a Broadway operetta star. Many were trained the same way, and the ones who could not find renown as an opera house star often turned to stage operettas. During the first few decades of the twentieth century, celebrated singers such as EMMA TRENTINI, EVELYN HERBERT, DONALD BRIAN, CHRISTIE MACDONALD, and HOWARD MARSH sang in Broadway operettas with their opera-quality voices and seemed no different from what patrons were hearing in the opera house. But Broadway operettas faded during the Depression and such voices were not needed; a musical comedy voice was sufficient. When an opera singer appeared in a Broadway musical later in the century, it was not an everyday event. Metropolitan basso EZIO PINZA was so effective in *SOUTH PACIFIC* (1949) that Broadway producers sometimes sought opera stars for their shows if appropriate. Among the notable appearances by opera stars on Broadway were Pinza again in *FANNY* (1954), Helen Traubel in *PIPE DREAM* (1955), Robert Weede in *THE MOST HAPPY FELLA* (1956), and Weede and Mimi Benzell in *MILK AND HONEY* (1961). Today when opera stars attempt a Broadway musical such as *CANDIDE* (1956) or *SWEENEY TODD* (1979), they usually do it in an opera house where such shows are produced on occasion.

The use of opera singers in the movies is a very different story. Opera singers had appeared on film in silent shorts and features even though their singing talents could hardly be enjoyed under the circumstances. Opera diva Mary Garden actually had a considerable following from her performances in silent films. Met soprano GRACE MOORE was the first opera singer to find success in the talkies. After appearing in two film musicals in 1930, she found acclaim for her performance as a struggling American opera singer in *ONE NIGHT OF LOVE* (1934). Aside from radio broadcasts, it was the first mainstream exposure Americans had to opera and the movie was such a hit that all the studios starting courting singers from the Metropolitan Opera and European troupes. Moore made four more films and was soon joined by LILY PONS, the French coloratura who starred in such vehicles as *I DREAM TOO MUCH* (1935) and *That Girl From Paris* (1936). Mezzo-soprano GLADYS SWARTHOUT was the opera diva at PARAMOUNT, where she was featured in *Rose of the Rancho* (1935) and *Give Us This Night* (1936), mezzo RISE STEVENS was heard in a handful of the same studio's films, and ILONA MASSEY appeared in five musicals in the 1930s and 1940s. Male opera singers were not forgotten. Richard Tauber performed in a handful of British musical movies in the 1930s, Nino Matini sang in four films in the same decade, as well as Pinza in *Carnegie Hall* (1947) and a few 1950s films. Danish-born heldertenor Lauritz Melchior, one of the world's greatest interpreters of Wagner operas, found himself in such Hollywood musicals as *Thrill of a Romance* (1945), *Two Sisters From Boston* (1946), and *Luxury Liner* (1948). In a reversal of the usual pattern, James Melton made such an impression in his 1930s musicals that he later moved on to the Met. The most beloved of all screen opera singers was the dashing tenor MARIO LANZA who probably prompted more interest in opera than any other singer. Lanza made seven musicals and provided the vocals for *THE STUDENT PRINCE* (1954). He was the most promising of all the classical singers but his temperamental lifestyle and addiction to drugs and alcohol ended his career prematurely. More recently, tenor Luciano Pavorotti made his bid for movie stardom with *Yes, Giorgio* (1982) but failed miserably. Few of these opera singers enjoyed lengthy movie careers because their novelty quickly wore out or they maintained such a busy stage and concert schedule that it was difficult to continue on in Hollywood. Since films of opera have become more common, many of the great opera singers today are now preserved on film, but their ability to cross over to musicals remains a rare feat.

OPERETTAS. While they are no longer with us in name, the effects of this seemingly antique form of musical theatre are still present on Broadway. By definition, operetta refers to a light form of opera that utilizes dialogue and tends toward the amusing rather than the thought provoking. Such a general definition would include most musical comedies and even a good portion of musical plays. The true American operetta is a fanciful form of musical that put its emphasis on singing and romance. Such shows flourished from the 1890s until the Depression and patterned themselves on the lyrical works coming from Europe in the nineteenth century. American operetta grew out of opéra bouffe and opéra comique from France, ballad opera and comic opera from England, and the waltzing opera from Vienna. These forms had been coming across the Atlantic from early in the century and by the 1860s were a stronghold in legitimate theatres as well as opera houses. The popularity of Gilbert and Sullivan's comic operettas during the Victorian period secured operetta a place on Broadway, and by the second half of the 1800s American composers were attempting a homegrown version of the genre. REGINALD DEKOVEN was one of the most prolific composers inspired by the European models, and his *ROBIN HOOD* (1891) was a major success, although it is more European than American in subject and music. JOHN PHILIP SOUSA would present a more American sound in his operettas even though they were usually set in exotic locales far from North America. The American theatre's three outstanding masters of operetta, composers VICTOR HERBERT, SIGMUND ROMBERG, and RUDOLF FRIML, also tended toward non-American settings at first but later favored French Louisiana, the Canadian Rockies, and other North American locales. These three, and their many imitators, wrote enough operettas that the genre comprised a sizable portion of the musicals on Broadway up through

the 1920s. The Depression made the old-style operettas seem frivolous and out of date and the genre seemed to die out. In fact, it just adapted itself into a slightly more "modern" form and continued on under the name of musical play. *THE CAT AND THE FIDDLE* (1931), *OF THEE I SING* (1931), and *MUSIC IN THE AIR* (1932) dare not bill themselves as operettas but that was what they were, disguised by being more savvy and telling stories that did not resemble those about quaint princesses, gypsies, and romantic outlaws. A decade later the musicals by Rodgers and Hammerstein, particularly *CAROUSEL* (1945) and *THE KING AND I* (1951), were certainly operettas but were so much better written that they could never be mistaken for *THE FORTUNE TELLER* (1898) or *ROSE-MARIE* (1924). Musicals patterned after Rodgers and Hammerstein, such as *BRIGADOON* (1947) and *THE MOST HAPPY FELLA* (1956), were also pure operetta but again they didn't feel like the old genre and were palatable to audiences. By the 1960s audiences had pretty much forgotten the old-style operettas and producers didn't worry about it either. Although no one would bill a new work as an operetta, there was no pretending that there wasn't a lot of operetta characteristics in such shows as *SHE LOVES ME* (1963), *MAN OF LA MANCHA* (1965), *A LITTLE NIGHT MUSIC* (1973), *ON THE TWENTIETH CENTURY* (1978), *SWEENEY TODD* (1979), *THE PHANTOM OF THE OPERA* (1988), *THE SECRET GARDEN* (1991), *BEAUTY AND THE BEAST* (1994), *TITANIC* (1997), and *THE LIGHT IN THE PIAZZA* (2005). Operetta never left Broadway, it just changed its tune slightly.

Hollywood may not seem to be a location where operettas would thrive because they involve so much music, yet even before sound came in there were popular movie versions of stage operettas. The silent *The Student Prince* (1923), for example, was a major hit. The reason was plot. Operettas always told a good story, usually an implausible and ridiculous story, but they were strong on plot and the movies have always leaned toward pieces that told a clear and involving story. The first Broadway musical to be filmed was an operetta, *THE DESERT SONG* (1929), and soon every major operetta going back to *BABES IN TOYLAND* (1903) was filmed and many of them were hits. One of the weird ironies about the American musical is the way the Depression affected operetta. The stock market crash ended the stage operetta but it gave birth to the movie operetta. What audiences would not abide in a theatre in the 1930s was perfectly thrilling to moviegoers during the same decade. So in addition to filming *THE MERRY WIDOW* (1934), *NAUGHTY MARIETTA* (1935), *ROSE MARIE* (1936), *MAYTIME* (1937), *SWEETHEARTS* (1938), and all the other Broadway operetta hits, Hollywood created their own operettas. *THE LOVE PARADE* (1929), *THE SMILING LIEUTENANT* (1931), *LOVE ME TONIGHT* (1932), *ONE NIGHT OF LOVE* (1934), *I DREAM TOO MUCH* (1935), *HIGH, WIDE AND HANDSOME* (1937), *THE GREAT WALTZ* (1938), and *BALALAIKA* (1939) were among the original operettas that the studios made to meet the demand. It was not a demand that continued into the 1940s. Operettas quickly went out of favor during the war years and even after the war they were never as popular again. Out of the handful of screen versions of stage operettas made in the 1950s, a very small percentage made any money at the box office, and the only original Hollywood operettas were those built around a popular operatic star, such as MARIO LANZA. When the "new" operettas from Broadway, such as the Rodgers and Hammerstein shows, were filmed in the 1950s and 1960, they were given the prestige treatment. In fact, these newer operatic musicals were filmed with more fidelity than Hollywood ever gave the old-time operettas. The studios used to toss out the ridiculous operetta plots and replace them with equally silly new ones. But when *OKLAHOMA!* (1955) or *MY FAIR LADY* (1964) came to the screen, everyone was careful. The old operetta genre was gone and no longer could JEANETTE MACDONALD and NELSON EDDY gloss over a weak story with their glorious singing.

ORBACH, JERRY [born Jerome Bernard Orbach] (1935–2004). Stage, television, and film performer. The likable, durable leading man of musicals and comedies, he became known to most Americans late in his career for his dramatic roles on television. Orbach was born in the Bronx, the son of a vaudevillian and a radio singer, was educated at the University of Illinois and Northwestern, and trained with Herbert Berghof and Lee Strasberg. After dozens of productions in stock, he was cast as an understudy in the legendary Off Broadway revival of *THE THREEPENNY OPERA* and in 1957 took over the role of MacHeath. Orbach originated the role of El Gallo in the record-breaking musical *THE FANTASTICKS* (1960) and then made his Broadway debut as the bitter cripple Paul in *CARNIVAL* (1961). He originated the musical roles of young executive Chuck Baxter in *PROMISES PROMISES* (1968), slippery lawyer Billy Flynn in *CHICAGO* (1975), and Broadway producer Julian Marsh in *42ND STREET* (1980),

as well as memorable performances in revivals of *THE CRADLE WILL ROCK* (1964), *GUYS AND DOLLS* (1965), *CAROUSEL* (1965), and *ANNIE GET YOUR GUN* (1966), which was filmed for television in 1967. Orbach left Broadway in the 1980s and concentrated on television, appearing in dozens of programs before finding fame on *Law and Order*. He made several non-musical films and provided the vocals for the candlestick Lumiere in the animated musical *BEAUTY AND THE BEAST* (1991). In 2007 an Off Broadway theatre was named after Orbach, a fitting tribute for the man who led the cast of Off Broadway's biggest hit.

■ **ORCHESTRA WIVES** (Fox 1942). Perhaps the quintessential Big Band musical, it was about a touring band and featured GLENN MILLER, his orchestra, and his mainstay vocalists in a film that is surprisingly dark and far from cheerful. The screenplay by Karl Tunberg and Darrell Ware concerned the bitchy and vindictive behavior of the musicians' wives toward Connie Ward (Ann Rutherford) when she marries a member of the orchestra. The movie pulled no punches about the sometime dreary life of touring from city to city in a band bus, and even after the happy ending (Connie gets the band together again after their petty differences have led them to separate), it is clear that a musician's life was far from glamorous. It was not the downbeat story but the music that counted and the movie was filled with the best: "People Like You and Me," "Serenade in Blue," "At Last," and "I've Got a Gal on Kalamazoo," all written by HARRY WARREN (music) and MACK GORDON (lyrics). The vocalists were Tex Beneke, Billy May, Ray Eberle, Hal McIntyre, Marion Hutton, and the Modernaires, with the dancing NICHOLAS BROTHERS setting the stage on fire. George Montgomery, JACKIE GLEASON, Harry Morgan, and CESAR ROMERO were among the musicians (all dubbed by the real Miller boys), and CAROLE LANDIS, LYNN BARI, Mary Beth Hughes, TAMARA GEVA, and Virginia Gilmore were among the wives. ARCHIE MAYO directed the WILLIAM LEBARON production.

▢ **OUR TOWN** (NBC-TV 1955). An outstanding cast and a superior score made this musical version of Thornton Wilder's 1938 play one of the best television specials of the 1950s.

Plot: The stage manager narrates the musical, introducing the town of Grover's Corners, New Hampshire, and some of its residents. During a typical day early in the twentieth century, local editor Mr. Webb and his family

Cast of *Our Town*

Character	Performer
Stage manager	FRANK SINATRA
George Gibbs	Paul Newman
Emily Webb	Eva Marie Saint
Dr. Gibbs	ERNEST TRUEX
Mrs. Gibbs	Sylvia Field
Mr. Webb	Paul Hartman
Mrs. Webb	Peg Hillias
Rebecca Gibbs	Shelley Fabares

Our Town Musical Numbers

"Our Town"
"Love and Marriage"
"The Impatient Years"
"A Perfect Married Life"
"Look to Your Heart"
"Wasn't It a Wonderful Wedding?"

Our Town. Photo stills from a live television broadcast are hard to come by but this shot of (left to right) Paul Newman, Eva Marie Saint, and Frank Sinatra rehearsing the musical version of *Our Town* is somewhat revealing, if for no other reason than to see what one wore to rehearsal in the summer of 1955. (Photofest)

and Dr. Gibbs and his family go about their lives, dealing with simple everyday joys and disappointments. In the second act the courtship and wedding of George Gibbs and Emily Webb are dramatized. The final act mostly takes place in the local cemetery where Emily, who has died in childbirth, has joined the other deceased members of the town. The stage manager grants her wish to return to life for one day but the experience only convinces her that the living are too busy to fully appreciate the gift of life.

David Shaw adapted Wilder's play into a concise teleplay that retained the simplicity and charm of the original. The songs by JAMES VAN HEUSEN (music) and SAMMY CAHN (lyrics) were also in keeping with the tone of the play, and FRANK SINATRA, serving as narrator and commentator, did most of the singing. Delbert Mann directed the *PRODUCER'S SHOWCASE* presentation with just the right delicate touch and the whole production came together as few live performances can. The broadcast was unusual in that the cast of thirty took up so much studio

space that the forty-member orchestra was put in another room and watched the monitor for cues. Because the original play was performed on a bare stage, the use of a television studio for the musical was in keeping with Wilder's vision. However, the playwright was not happy with the broadcast, thought it too sentimental, and asked that it not be shown again. He was also concerned that the musical version might eclipse the original plays, much as *HELLO, DOLLY!* (1964) overshadowed his *The Matchmaker* (1955) for many years and *MY FAIR LADY* (1956) outshone *Pygmalion* (1914) in the public eye. However, the nonmusical *Our Town* remains one of the most produced of all American plays and hardly seems in danger of fading away because of a musical version.

The true legacy of the television musical is its score. Cahn thought it the finest set of lyrics he ever wrote, admitting that Wilder's dialogue inspired his words. Van Heusen's music is contagious and some songs are not forgotten after only one hearing. The standout hit was "Love and Marriage," the most successful song to come from a TV musical. Sinatra's recording climbed the charts and stayed there for months. Later generations would know the number as the theme song for the TV series *Married With Children.* Also memorable were "The Impatient Years," "Look to Your Heart," and the evocative title song. Sinatra's favorite musical director, Nelson Riddle, handled the music for the broadcast and, while the arrangements may not conjure up New England, they are expert all the same. Fred Coe and Henry Jaffe produced the musical, which was well reviewed, highly awarded, and widely watched. 🕮 Songwriters TOM JONES and HARVEY SCHMIDT have a stage musical of the play *Our Town* titled *Grover's Corners* that has been produced regionally but has not yet played in New York.

🕮 **OUT OF THIS WORLD** (New Century Theatre 1950). A lesser known COLE PORTER musical with a marvelous score, it did not produce any standards and so is unjustly forgotten. Jupiter (George Jongeyans) leaves Mt. Olympus and goes to modern Greece where he has a fling with the recently married Helen (Priscilla Gillette). Jupiter's wife Juno (CHARLOTTE GREENWOOD) is a force to be reckoned with and, when her anger is aroused, Jupiter returns to the heavens and Helen goes back to her dull life. Also in the cast were William Redfield, William Eythe, and DAVID BURNS. The ancient tale of *Amphitryon* was updated by Dwight Taylor and Reginald Lawrence with a lot of slang in the script and in Porter's witty lyrics, but the show seemed more contrived than inspired. The songs, however, were the real thing, with such delights as the dreamy "Use Your Imagination," the caustic lament "Nobody's Chasing Me," the expansive "I Am Loved," and the sly "I Sleep Easier Now" among the most memorable numbers. Greenwood's return to Broadway after twenty-three years in the movies was quite an occasion and she did not disappoint, particularly in her comic songs. AGNES DE MILLE, HELEN TAMIRIS, and GEORGE ABBOTT shared directing–choreographing chores and it was a polished, playful production, but with mixed notices it could run only 157 performances.

🕮 **OVER HERE!** (Shubert Theatre 1974). A modest bit of musical comedy escapism, the show was unusual for the 1970s in that it was set on the home front during World War II and echoed the Big Band sound of the era. The singing de Paul sisters (Maxene and Patty Andrews) are entertaining the troops stateside but need a third songbird for their act. They hire Mitzi (Jane Snell) for their cross-country tour but discover she's a German spy so they turn her in and continue on as a duo. Also cast were such promising talents as ANN REINKING, TREAT WILLIAMS, SAMUEL E. WRIGHT, JOHN TRAVOLTA, April Shawhan, Marilu Henner, MacIntyre Dixon, and Bette Henritz. Will Holt wrote the silly but practical libretto, and RICHARD M. and ROBERT B. SHERMAN provided the pastiche songs, including "Buy a Victory Bond," "Wait for Me, Marlena," "My Dream for Tomorrow," "We Got It!," and the title number. The two surviving ANDREWS SISTERS from the actual wartime era were the main attraction but the press also applauded the young performers and the boogie-woogie-flavored score and audiences came for 348 performances. Tom Moore directed and PATRICIA BIRCH did the jitterbug-inspired choreography.

OWEN, [John] **REGINALD** (1887–1972). Stage and film performer. The adaptable British actor was a familiar figure on Broadway and the West End and then became more famous as one of Hollywood's busiest character actors. Owen was born in Wheathampstead, England, and attended acting school in London before making his professional debut in 1905. After playing everything from kings and butlers to villains and lovable sidekicks on the London stage, he came to America in 1924, returning several times during the next decade and appeared in new and classic plays as well as the musicals *THE THREE MUSKETEERS* (1928) and *Through the Years* (1932). When sound came in, Owen went to Hollywood where he acted in dozens of films, usually in supporting roles but on occasion in leads, as with his Scrooge in *A Christmas Carol* (1938). Among his screen musicals were *MUSIC IN THE AIR* (1934), *ROSE MARIE* (1936), *THE GREAT ZIEGFELD* (1936), *ROSALIE* (1937), *Hullabaloo* (1940), *LADY, BE GOOD* (1941), *I MARRIED AN ANGEL* (1942), *Cairo* (1942), *THE PIRATE* (1948), *Red Garters* (1954), *MARY POPPINS* (1964), and *BEDKNOBS AND BROOMSTICKS* (1971). Owen returned to Broadway in the comedy *Affairs of State* (1950) and then at the age of eighty-five played the wandering Erronius in the 1972 revival of *A FUNNY THING HAPPENED ON THE WAY TO THE FORUM*.

P

Kanagawa," the sly "Chrysanthemum Tea," the philosophic "A Bowler Hat," and the multicultural spoof "Please Hello." The show had trouble finding an audience and closed after 193 performances.

When *Pacific Overtures* was revived in a small-scale Off Broadway mounting in 1984, it was better received, not so much because the production directed by Fran Soeder was better but because reviewers and audiences were more open to the experiment and it ran 109 performances. Japanese director–choreographer Amon Miyamoto had staged the musical in his native country and that renowned production had toured to some major American cities, performed in Japanese with English supertitles. The ROUNDABOUT THEATRE invited Miyamoto to restage the musical in 2004 with Asian American actors and the result was a captivating production that differed greatly from the original Broadway one, using traditional Noh Theatre techniques rather than Kabuki ones. Notices were mostly salutatory, and the limited run of sixty-nine performances was well attended.

🌱 **PACIFIC OVERTURES** (Winter Garden Theatre 1976). An uncompromising experiment by songwriter STEPHEN SONDHEIM, librettist JOHN WEIDMAN, and producer–director HAROLD PRINCE to musicalize the Westernization of Japan from the arrival of Commodore Perry in 1859 to the present day, the show met with very mixed reactions by critics and playgoers but over time has been accepted as a uniquely accomplished work. Taking the Japanese point of view, the musical was narrated by the Reciter (Mako), and the history personified by two men, the samurai Kayama (Isao Sato) who succumbs to Westernization, and his friend Manjiro (Sab Shimono), who becomes an anti-Western rebel. The clash between the two men echoed the internal conflict in the island nation, which eventually succumbs to progress and then quickly becomes a major player in the modern age. Sondheim's songs used elements of Asian music and Japanese haiku but were still in the Broadway mold, just as Prince used Kabuki theatre techniques in staging the episodic musical. Some found these Oriental touches innovative and rewarding, others distant and uninvolving. The press was in agreement about the strong all-Asian cast and the stunning production designed by Boris Aronson. The ingenious score included such fascinating numbers as the multiviewpoint song "Someone in a Tree," the lyrical " Pretty Lady," the evocative "Poems," the ribald "Welcome to

PAGE, KEN (1954–). Stage, television, and film performer. A rotund, full-voiced African American actor–singer, he has lit up several musicals in character roles. A native of St. Louis, Page studied theatre at the local Fontbonne College before performing in stock. He made a lively Broadway debut as Nicely-Nicely in the all-black revival of *GUYS AND DOLLS* (1976), stopping the show with his gospel number "Sit Down, You're Rockin' the Boat." Page found further acclaim as one of the agile quintet in the popular revue *AIN'T MISBEHAVIN'* (1978 and 1988), recreating his performance in the 1982 television version, and then was a replacement for the Cowardly Lion in *THE WIZ* (1979). He later played the Lion in the Madison Square Garden Theatre version of the movie *THE WIZARD OF OZ* (1997 and 1998),

Stage casts for *Pacific Overtures*			
Character	*1976 Broadway*	*1984 Off Broadway*	*2004 Broadway*
Reciter, etc.	Mako	Ernest Abuda	B. D. Wong
Manjiro	Sab Shimono	John Caleb	Paolo Montalban
Kayama	Isao Sato	Kevin Gray	Michael K. Lee
Shogan's mother, etc.	Alvin Ing	Chuck Brown	Alvin Y. Ing
Madam, etc.	Ernest Harada	Thomas Ikeda	Francis Jue
Lord Abe	Alvin Y. Ing	Tony Marino	Sab Shimono
Tamate	Soon-Teck Oh	Timm Fujii	Yoko Fumoto

as well as the Ghost of Christmas Present in the same venue's musical *A Christmas Carol* (1997). Page's other notable Broadway credit is the role of the wise old feline Deuteronomy in the original New York cast of *CATS* (1982), a performance he reprised in London and in the 1998 television version. He also starred as God in the London musical *Children of Eden* (1991) and has performed in many regional theatres, such as his hometown's ST. LOUIS MUNICIPAL OPERA. Page has appeared in a handful of movies, including *DREAMGIRLS* (2006), and on television, as in the TV musicals *POLLY* (1989) and *Polly—Comin' Home!* (1990). His voice has been used for many animated films, most memorably as the deep-voiced Oogie Boogie in *THE NIGHTMARE BEFORE CHRISTMAS* (1993).

PAIGE, JANIS [born Donna Mae Tjaden] (1922–). Stage, film, and television performer. The redheaded leading lady made her name in Hollywood and then turned to Broadway musicals before settling into television. Paige was born in Tacoma, Washington, and studied for an opera career but while volunteering as a waitress and singer at the Hollywood Canteen was discovered by a talent scout and put on the screen in 1944. She usually played the lively friend of the heroine in several 1940s and 1950s movies, including the musicals *Bathing Beauty* (1944), *HOLLYWOOD CANTEEN* (1944), *The Time, the Place and the Girl* (1946), *Love and Learn* (1947), *ROMANCE ON THE HIGH SEAS* (1948), *One Sunday Afternoon* (1948), *Two Gals and a Guy* (1951), and *SILK STOCKINGS* (1956). Paige appeared on Broadway a few times, most memorably in musicals as the labor organizer Babe Williams in *THE PAJAMA GAME* (1954), the Macy's executive Doris Walker in *Here's Love* (1963), and as the replacement for ANGELA LANSBURY in *MAME* (1968). She played many classic musical roles in summer stock and was popular on the nightclub circuit, sometimes with JACK CARSON who was paired with her in films. Paige has been active in television since

the 1950s, acting in hundreds of comedy and drama series and musical specials, such as the TV musicals *The Happiest Day* (1961) and *ROBERTA* (1969). She was married to songwriter RAY GILBERT.

PAIGE, ROBERT [born John Arthur Page] (1910–1987). Film and television performer. Often paired with singer–actress JANE FRAZEE, the handsome leading man of Hollywood musicals was usually stuck in B movies but still had some shining moments. Paige was born in Indianapolis, Indiana, to British parents and attended West Point Academy until he left to pursue an acting career. He began as a radio singer and then announcer. After appearing in a few film shorts, Paige made his feature debut in 1935 and gradually graduated to romantic leads. In his twenty-two screen musicals, he was partnered with Frazee seven times, yet his most memorable performance was in the DEANNA DURBIN vehicle *CAN'T HELP SINGING* (1944) in which he joined her in introducing "Californ-i-ay" and the title song. Paige's other musical credits include *Cain and Mabel* (1936), *The Lady Objects* (1938), *Dancing on a Dime* (1941), *San Antonio Rose* (1941), *HELLZAPOPPIN'* (1941), *What's Cookin'?* (1942), *Pardon My Sarong* (1942), *Get Hep to Love* (1942), *Hi Buddy* (1943), *Cowboy in Manhattan* (1943), *Crazy House* (1943), *Follow the Boys* (1944), *Shady Lady* (1945), and *BYE BYE BIRDIE* (1963). In addition to many nonmusicals, Paige was a familiar face on television both as an actor and as a quiz show host.

📚 *PAINT YOUR WAGON* (Shubert Theatre 1951). A robust and engaging musical set during the California gold rush, it brought further recognition to the team of ALAN JAY LERNER (book and lyrics) and FREDERICK LOEWE (music). In 1853, Ben Rumsen discovers gold on his land and soon a mining camp springs up around him. His daughter Jennifer, being the only female in the camp, attracts a

Casts for *Paint Your Wagon*

Character	1951 Broadway	1969 film
Ben Rumsen	JAMES BARTON	Lee Marvin
Jennifer Rumsen	OLGA SAN JUAN	
Julio Valveras	Tony Bavaar	
Pardner		Clint Eastwood
Elizabeth		Jean Seberg
Rotten Luck Willie		HARVE PRESNELL
Mad Jack Dugan		RAY WALSTON

lot of attention but her heart goes out to the Mexican prospector Julio Valveras. The lode runs out, Ben dies, and Jennifer and Julio begin life together as farmers. It was an efficient, well-written libretto but the spirit of the gold rush was more to be found in the stimulating score. The two runaway hits were the pensive ballads "I Talk to the Trees" and "They Call the Wind Maria," but also highly skillful were "I'm On My Way," "I Still See Elisa," "What's Goin' On Here?," "Another Autumn," and "Wand'rin' Star." The rousing musical also boasted a strong cast and lively dances choreographed by AGNES DE MILLE. Daniel Mann directed the CHERYL CRAWFORD production, which, despite its run of 289 performances, lost money.

■ **Paint Your Wagon** (Paramount 1969) was one of the era's overproduced and overspent ($17 million) behemoths that helped make the big-budget Hollywood musical extinct. Shot on location in Oregon, where director JOSHUA LOGAN built a complete mining town (and then destroyed it in the movie's climax) and starring the highly paid nonsingers Lee Marvin and Clint Eastwood, the musical seemed doomed to financial failure from the start. Lerner wrote the screenplay that tossed out much of the plot, characters, and charm of the original and substituted a new story (with writer Paddy Chayevsky) about a ménage à trois with old-timer Ben (Marvin) and greenhorn Pardner (Eastwood) both in love with the Mormon castaway Elizabeth (Jean Seberg, singing dubbed by Anita Gordon). Having been one of two wives before, she willingly shares both men until respectability forces her to choose Pardner. The boom town goes bust (literally) and Ben sets out looking for new and unspoiled wilderness. Half of the Broadway score was dropped and Lerner collaborated with composer ANDRÉ PREVIN on a handful of new songs. In one of the film's few pleasing moments, HARVE PRESNELL gave full voice to "They Call the Wind Maria" and it was lovely to hear even if he had no distinct character to give the song a point of view. Lerner produced the movie, which was a critical and box office fiasco.

🎵 **PAJAMA GAME, THE** (St. James Theatre 1954). An unpretentious musical comedy that offered a rousing good time, it also introduced a handful of talents in their first major Broadway effort: producers Frederick Brisson, HAROLD PRINCE, and Robert Griffith, choreographer BOB FOSSE, and songwriters JERRY ROSS and RICHARD ADLER.

Plot: Labor-management relations at the Sleep-Tite Pajama Factory in Cedar Rapids, Iowa, are not improved when the new manager, Sid Sorokin, and the union spokesperson, Babe Williams, fall in love. Romantic and professional differences just about close the factory but matters are resolved when the wily secretary Gladys pulls a few strings with her jealous boyfriend, time-study expert Hines, and the workers get a raise.

Director GEORGE ABBOTT wrote the efficient libretto with Richard Bissell, based on Bissell's novel *7 1/2 Cents*, and the cast was engaging, playing the broad comic types with relish. The Adler–Ross score was chock full of memorable ditties, with the biggest hits being the dreamy ballad "Hey There," the tango "Hernando's Hideaway," and the jazzy "Steam Heat." Also delightful were the waltzing "I'm Not at All in Love," the comic duet "I'll Never Be Jealous Again," the rhymic "Think of the Time I Save," and the country-western spoof "There Once Was a Man." The tuneful, funny show was the best reviewed musical of the season and ran longer than any other, 1,063 performances. In addition to becoming a favorite in summer stock and schools, *The Pajama Game* has seen four major New York revivals. The 1957 City Center production featured Larry Douglas (Sid), Jane Kean (Babe), Pat Stanley (Gladys), and Paul Hartman (Hines). An interracial cast was the distinctive feature of the 1973 revival in which CAB CALLOWAY's comic Hines and HAL LINDEN's full-voiced Sid were most appreciated by the press. Original director GEORGE ABBOTT staged the production, which ran sixty-five performances. The New York City Opera offered theatre performers Richard Munez (Sid), JUDY

Casts for *The Pajama Game*				
Character	*1954 Broadway*	*1957 film*	*1974 Broadway*	*2006 Broadway*
Sis Sorokin	JOHN RAITT	John Raitt	HAL LINDEN	Harry Connick, Jr.
Babe Williams	JANIS PAIGE	DORIS DAY	Barbara McNair	KELLI O'HARA
Hines	EDDY FOY, JR.	Eddie Foy, Jr.	CAB CALLOWAY	Michael McKean
Gladys	CAROL HANEY	Carol Haney	Sharon Miller	Megan Lawrence
Mabel	Reta Shaw	Reta Shaw	Mary Jo Catlett	Roz Ryan

KAYE (Babe), Lenora Nemetz (Gladys), and Avery Saltzman (Hines) in a 1989 production at Lincoln Center. In 2006, KATHLEEN MARSHALL directed and choreographed a ROUNDABOUT THEATRE revival and she was applauded on both counts, as was the personable cast. Pop singer–songwriter Harry Connick, Jr. was a sexy, engaging Sid, KELLI O'HARA a smart and vibrant Babe, Megan Lawrence a dizzy, funny Gladys, and Michael McKean a merry Hines. The limited run quickly sold out and then was extended for 129 performances before Connick had to move on to other commitments.

■ *The Pajama Game* (Warner 1957) came to the screen with just about the entire cast and creative staff of the Broadway show and although the film looked stage bound on occasion, it was a delightful copy of the original. DORIS DAY played Babe and Abbott shared directing chores with STANLEY DONEN, but the rest was pretty much the same. Only four of the fifteen Adler–Ross songs were dropped and there were no outside interpolations so musically the movie was just as faithful. Some of Fosse's choreography opened up nicely for the screen, particularly in the frolicking "Once a Year Day," and the final number "7 1/2 Cents"

The Pajama Game Musical Numbers

"The Pajama Game"
"Racing With the Clock"
"A New Town Is a Blue Town"
"I'm Not at All in Love"
"I'll Never Be Jealous Again"
"Hey There"
"Her Is"
"Sleep-Tite"
"Once a Year Day"
"Small Talk"
"There Once Was a Man"
"Steam Heat"
"Think of the Time I Save"
"Hernando's Hideaway"
"Jealousy Ballet"
"7 1/2 Cents"

---

was turned into a pajama fashion show. All the performances were bright and funny and the musical remains unpretentious fun.

🎞 ***PAL JOEY*** (Ethel Barrymore Theatre 1940). Possibly the first adult musical because of its uncompromising look at its seedy and cynical characters, the show is arguably the finest work by RICHARD RODGERS (music) and LORENZ HART (lyrics).

Plot: Joey Evans is a third-rate night-club hoofer in Chicago who borrows money and beds chorus girls with no idea of taking responsibility for either action. He woos and wins the naive stenographer Linda English and then quickly dumps her when a bigger fish comes along in the form of the wealthy, bored society dame Vera Simpson, a gal who barely keeps up a respectable front for her husband's sake. Vera and Joey are on the same wavelength and their torrid affair is without pretense on each of their parts. She rents a trysting place for them to meet and builds him a glitzy nightclub to star in. But when Vera tires of Joey and some blackmailers make the situation sticky, she dismisses both problems with simple, professional ease. Vera, it turns out, is a smarter version of Joey. She offers the heel back to Linda who, having wised up to him, refuses, and Joey moves off into new territory and new, unsatisfying conquests.

Based on a series of O'Hara stories in *The New Yorker* magazine, *Pal Joey* was Rodgers and Hart's final and perhaps most provocative experiment. The tone throughout was tough and anti-romantic and the musical made no effort to charm or appease the audience. The amoral Joey was not presented as a villain, but neither did he make any apologies to the world and he had no intention of changing. Joey was the American musical theatre's first anti-hero and, as portrayed by GENE KELLY, he could fascinate even as he irritated. Hart created a hard-as-nails attitude in his lyrics, with even the love songs coming across as a con, and Rodgers' music is cool, distant, and uncomfortably

---

Casts for *Pal Joey*

Character	1940 Broadway	1952 Broadway	1957 film
Joey Evans	GENE KELLY	HAROLD LANG	FRANK SINATRA
Vera Simpson	VIVIENNE SEGAL	Vivienne Segal	RITA HAWORTH
Linda English	Leila Ernst	Pat Northrop	Kim Novak
Gladys	JUNE HAVOC	HELEN GALLAGHER	Barbara Nichols
Melba Snyder	Jean Casto	ELAINE STRITCH	

Pal Joey. Gene Kelly (center) left Broadway after playing the lead in only one Broadway musical. But what was Broadway's loss was Hollywood's gain. All the same, one wonders what Kelly might have done on Broadway in the 1940s and 1950s. Pictured is a moment from Robert Alton's "Joey Looks to the Future" ballet in the Broadway production of *Pal Joey*. Kelly's future was just as elegant. (Photofest)

insincere. The score may not have produced as many hit songs as some of their previous shows but it was their most ambitious set of songs. The show was produced and directed by GEORGE ABBOTT and choreographed by ROBERT ALTON who found sarcasm even in the dances. Although some critics were not happy with the unsavory aspects of *Pal Joey*, the musical ran 374 performances on Broadway and did very well on the road. "Bewitched" soon became a standard but the show itself was pretty much forgotten by the end of the decade. In 1950 VIVIENNE SEGAL and HAROLD LANG made a studio recording of the score that was so popular they were cast in a 1952 Broadway revival that ran 540 performances. There were less successful New York revivals in 1961 with BOB FOSSE (Joey) and CAROL BRUCE (Vera), in 1963 with Fosse and Viveca Lindfors (Vera), and in 1976 with Christopher Chadman (Joey) and Joan Copeland (Vera). While it would never enjoy the number of stock and amateur

productions as the less disturbing Rodgers and Hart musicals, *Pal Joey* was far ahead of its time and competent revivals prove it is for all time.

🎬 ***Pal Joey*** (Columbia 1957) was slow in coming to the screen because Hollywood was not interested in trying to film the problematic musical until the popular 1952 revival sparked interest with the studios. It took five more years to decide how to cast it and what to do with the cynical, unconventional nature of the characters and story. The result was a sanitized, watered down, and reconfigured movie that might have been made in the days of Hollywood's heaviest censorship. With FRANK SINATRA as Joey, the character was changed from a Chicago dancer to a San Francisco crooner in the screenplay by DOROTHY KINGSLEY. Vera (RITA HAYWORTH, dubbed by Jo Ann Greer) was still high society but a former stripper (so that she could sing the risible song "Zip") and Linda (Kim Novak, dubbed by Trudi Erwin) was now a dumb chorine. Nearly half of the

Pal Joey (stage) Musical Numbers

"You Mustn't Kick It Around"
"I Could Write a Book"
"Chicago"
"That Terrific Rainbow"
"Love Is My Friend"
"Happy Hunting Horn"
"Betwitched (Bothered and Bewildered)"
"Joey Looks Into the Future" Ballet
"The Flower Garden of My Heart"
"Zip"
"Plant You Now, Dig You Later"
"In Our Little Den (of Iniquity)"
"Do It the Hard Way"
"Take Him"

stage score was dropped, and famous, cheerier Rodgers and Hart numbers from other shows, such as "There's a Small Hotel," "My Funny Valentine," and "The Lady Is a Tramp," were inserted even though they did not fit the characters or the plot. There was even a happy ending with Joey reformed and going off into the sunset with Linda. How sad that Rodgers, who had been treated so shabbily by Hollywood in the 1930s and saw his scores with Hart mangled beyond recognition, should have to see the same thing happen to *Pal Joey* two decades later. GEORGE SIDNEY directed the FRED KOLMAR production and HERMES PAN did the routine choreography.

📽 **PALEFACE, THE** (Paramount 1948) With only three songs, the film barely qualifies as a musical but all three numbers were gems and one cannot help but remember the trio of tunes when recalling the comedy. Frank Tashlin's slaphappy screenplay gave BOB HOPE one of the best roles of his long career. "Painless" Peter Potter is a quack dentist from the East who travels the Wild West looking for a quick buck but finding sexy, gun-slinging Calamity Jane (JANE RUSSELL) instead. She talks the timid Painless into marrying her so that she has a front for her activities as a government agent. The resulting complications gave Hope a chance to play his fumbling, wisecracking persona to the hilt. Saloon gal Pepper (Iris Adrian) sang Joseph J. Lilley's "Get a Man" with a sardonic grin and tried to seduce the hapless Painless with "Meetcha 'Round the Corner (At Half Past Eight)," and Painless sang the Oscar-winning "Buttons and Bows" to Jane as he longed for the creature comforts back East. Both songs were by JAY LIVINGSTON and RAY EVANS and blended

into the silly plot with ease. NORMAN Z. MCLEOD directed the comedy and it was so popular that a sequel followed. **Son of Paleface** (Paramount 1952) takes place some years later when Painless Potter is dead and memorialized by a statue in the town square and his son, Painless Potter, Jr. (Hope), recently graduated from Harvard, returns to the West to claim his inheritance. The son is as cowardly as his dad and no match for the bandit Mike "the Torch" Delroy (Russell) disguised as a saloon singer. The government agent Roy Barton (ROY ROGERS) is on to "Mike" but is starting to fall for her. He eventually captures her (and her heart) and Hope got a hilarious scene trying to sleep in a bed with a horse so everyone was happy. Robert L. Welch and Joseph Quillan collaborated with Tashlin on the screenplay, and Evans and Livingston wrote the congenial ballad "California Rose" for Rogers to sing and he and Russell reprised "Buttons and Bows" from the earlier film. Also in the score was JACK BROOKS' "Am I in Love?" for Hope and Russell, sung while she gave him a shave. Tashlin directed the movie and it was a rare case when a sequel was as enjoyable (if not more so) as the original.

PALLETTE, EUGENE (1889–1954). Film performer. One of Hollywood's most easily identified character actors with his round girth and frog voice, he made hundreds of features and was a frequent visitor to musicals. Pallette was born in Winfield, Kansas, and went on the stage where he played leading roles in stock before making his first film in 1910 as a thin, handsome juvenile. He appeared in over 150 silent shorts and features before sound arrived and, with his added weight and odd voice, was cast in character parts. Among Pallette's musical credits are *THE LOVE PARADE* (1929), *Pointed Heels* (1929), *PARAMOUNT ON PARADE* (1930), *Let's Go Native* (1930), *Playboy of Paris* (1930), *All the King's Horses* (1935), *Stowaway* (1936), *ONE HUNDRED MEN AND A GIRL* (1937), *A Little Bit of Heaven* (1940), *THE GANG'S ALL HERE* (1943), *Lake Placid Serenade* (1944), *Pin-Up Girl* (1944), and *Step Lively* (1944). He also was a familiar voice on the radio and in some animated shorts.

PALMER, LELAND (1945–). Stage, television, and film performer. A vivacious singer–dancer who was very active in New York musicals in the 1960s and 1970s, the wide-eyed, very physical performer was seen by some as the next GWEN VERDON but her career was not sustained. Palmer was born in Port Washington,

New York, and made her Broadway debut as a dancer in the musical *Bajour* (1964) and then was noticed for her performance as the dancing Miss Jimmie in *A Joyful Noise* (1966). She was a replacement for Minnie Fay in *Hello, Dolly!* in 1967 and the next year received wide recognition as the cross-dressing Viola in the Off Broadway rock musical *Your Own Thing* (1968). After dancing in *Applause* (1970) and taking over the role of the gypsy Bonnie, she dazzled audiences with her gymnastic dancing as the sly queen Fastrada in *Pippin* (1972). The show's director–choreographer BOB FOSSE then cast Palmer in his film musical *All That Jazz* (1979) as the singing–dancing Audrey Paris, a role clearly based on Fosse's ex-wife Verdon. In the 1980s she turned to television and appeared regularly on three sit-coms.

PALMER, PETER (1931–). Stage and film performer. A tall, muscular leading man with chiseled good looks, he gave some significant performances in musicals before going into television. Palmer was born in Milwaukee, raised in St. Louis, and educated at the University of Illinois at Champaign-Urbana where he received a football scholarship and took the team all the way to the Rose Bowl. While in the Army he won a talent contest that put him on Ed Sullivan's television show and the producers preparing the musical version of *Li'l Abner* (1956) spotted him. Palmer made an impressive Broadway debut as the hillbilly yokel Abner Yokum and then went on to play Tommy Albright in *Brigadoon* and Curly in *Oklahoma!* at the City Center in 1963. Although his television career began in the mid-1960s, he returned to Broadway to play the wealthy Gus Esmond in the CAROL CHANNING musical *Lorelei* (1974).

PAN, HERMES [born Hermes Panagiotopulos] (1905?–1990). Film and television choreographer. Perhaps the most sought-after choreographer during Hollywood's golden age of musicals, his career is closely tied to that of FRED ASTAIRE. Little is known about Pan's early years except that he was born in either Nashville or Memphis, Tennessee, and was an experienced dancer by the time he arrived in Hollywood when sound came in. He served as assistant dance director on *Flying Down to Rio* (1933), *The Gay Divorcee* (1934), and *Roberta* (1935) before doing the choreography solo for *Old Man Rhythm* (1935). Later that same year Pan found fame for his choreography for *Top Hat*, followed by

fifty more musicals, among them *Follow the Fleet* (1936), *Swing Time* (1936), *Shall We Dance* (1937), *A Damsel in Distress* (1937), *Carefree* (1938), *The Story of Vernon and Irene Castle* (1939), *That Night in Rio* (1940), *Sun Valley Serenade* (1941), *Weekend in Havana* (1941), *Springtime in the Rockies* (1942), *Blue Skies* (1946), *The Barkleys of Broadway* (1949), *Three Little Words* (1950), *Lovely to Look At* (1952), *The Student Prince* (1954), *Hit the Deck* (1955), *Silk Stockings* (1956), *Porgy and Bess* (1959), *Can-Can* (1960), *Flower Drum Song* (1961), *My Fair Lady* (1964), *Finian's Rainbow* (1968), and *Darlin' Lili* (1969). He was a featured dancer in several films he choreographed, such as *Moon Over Miami* (1941), *My Gal Sal* (1942), *Coney Island* (1943), *Sweet Rosie O'Grady* (1943), *Pin-Up Girl* (1944), *Kiss Me, Kate* (1953), and *Pal Joey* (1957). Pan physically resembled Astaire and was called the star's alter ego, with the two working together on seventeen films and several television specials. He was also long associated with BETTY GRABLE, choreographing ten of her screen musicals.

PANAMA HATTIE (46th Street Theatre 1940). Not a top-drawer COLE PORTER show but, thanks to ETHEL MERMAN and a few catchy tunes, the musical comedy was entertaining enough to run 501 performances on a Broadway still recovering from the Depression. The brazen Hattie Maloney (Merman), a bar girl in the Panama Canal Zone, and the Philadelphia scion Nick Bullett (James Dunn) fall in love but marriage is out of the question until the snooty Geraldine (Joan Carroll), Nick's eight-year-old daughter by his first marriage, approves of Hattie. HERBERT FIELDS and B.G. DE SYLVA penned the inconsequential libretto that seemed better with the sparkling cast and such cunning Porter songs as "Make It Another Old-Fashioned, Please," "Let's Be Buddies," "I've Still Got My Health," and "I'm Throwing a Ball Tonight." EDGAR MACGREGOR directed and ROBERT ALTON choreographed the DeSylva-produced star vehicle; as long as Merman stuck with the show it was a hit.

Panama Hattie (MGM 1942) offered the slight, tiny-voiced ANN SOTHERN in the belting role of Hattie and she was unable to carry the film, leaving the vibrant supporting cast to carry the day, not that here was much of a film worth carrying. The screenplay retained the same premise and built up some of the secondary characters but the score was a mixed bag of some

Casts for *Panama Hattie*			
Characters	1940 Broadway	1942 film	1954 television
Hattie	ETHEL MERMAN	ANN SOTHERN	Ethel Merman
Nick/Dick	James Dunn	DAN DAILEY	RAY MIDDLETON
Geraldine	Jean Carroll	Jackie Horner	
Red		RED SKELTON	
Florrie/Flo	BETTY HUTTON	VIRGINIA O'BRIEN	
Woozy/Rags	Rags Ragland	Rags Ragland	Art Carney
Scat Briggs	Pat Harrington		
Windy/Rowdy	Frank Hyers	BEN BLUE	Jack E. Leonard
Vivian/Jay	ARTHUR TREACHER	Alan Mowbray	

Porters songs (only a few from the stage version) and others by various tunesmiths, with the best being "Fresh as a Daisy" sung by VIRGINIA O'BRIEN. Another highlight was LENA HORNE's specialty spot singing Porter's "Just One of Those Things." The rest of the movie relied on the comedy of RED SKELTON, Rags Ragland, Ben Blue, and others. The film was not a box office hit and the movie hurt Sothern's career. Hollywood would only cast her in secondary roles after it was clear she could not handle the lead in a major musical. ☐ Merman got to play Hattie again in a 1954 television version on CBS. Details about the live (and thought lost) broadcast are scarce but RAY MIDDLETON, Art Carney, and Jack E. Leonard were also in the cast.

PANGBORN, FRANKLIN (1893–1958). Film, stage, and television performer. A thin, nervous character actor who made dozens of films in the 1930s and 1940s, he fussed and fumed as a harassed maitre d', hotel manager, or store clerk in comedies and musicals. Pangborn was born in Newark, New Jersey, and acted in stock before making his Broadway debut in 1911, appearing in dramas and playing leading roles such as Messala in a revival of *Ben-Hur*. After serving in the Army during World War I, he went into movies and made several silents as a villain or romantic lead. But with his thinning face and simpering voice he was cast in character parts once sound arrived. Pangborn's musical credits include *FLYING DOWN TO RIO* (1933), *INTERNATIONAL HOUSE* (1933), *COLLEGE RHYTHM* (1934), *REBECCA OF SUNNYBROOK FARM* (1938), *JOY OF LIVING* (1938), *CAREFREE* (1938), *Hit Parade of 1941* (1940), *Strictly in the Groove* (1942), *Crazy House* (1943), *Reveille With Beverly* (1943), *Two Guys From Milwaukee* (1946), and *ROMANCE ON THE HIGH SEAS* (1948). He made a few television appearances before his death, including the TV musical *Svengali and the Blonde* (1955).

PAPP, JOSEPH [born Yosi Papirofsky] (1921–1991). Stage producer and director. An extraordinary producer–director who was a towering figure in New York theatre for nearly forty years, he was responsible for several outstanding musicals Off and on Broadway. Papp was born in Brooklyn and studied at Hollywood's Actors Laboratory, serving as managing director in the late 1940s. After understudying the two sons and stage managing a tour of *Death of a Salesman*, he returned to New York where in 1954 he founded the Shakespeare Theatre Workshop, a troupe dedicated to presenting classic revivals free to the public. This evolved into the NEW YORK SHAKESPEARE FESTIVAL, offering free plays in Central Park in the summer, and later the PUBLIC THEATRE, a year-round operation that produced new and old works in a multitheatre building Off Broadway. Papp ran these operations for the rest of his life, presenting hundreds of productions that included unconventional Shakespeare revivals with ethnic casts, controversial or experimental dramas, and new and revived musicals, such as in *HAIR* (1967), *TWO GENTLEMEN OF VERONA* (1971), *A CHORUS LINE* (1975), *THE THREEPENNY OPERA* (1976), *Runaways* (1978), *I'M GETTING MY ACT TOGETHER AND TAKING IT ON THE ROAD* (1978), *THE PIRATES OF PENZANCE* (1980), *THE HUMAN COMEDY* (1983), and *THE MYSTERY OF EDWIN DROOD* (1985). Papp directed plays on occasion, usually Shakespeare productions. He was a volatile, passionate producer and one of the most important theatre personages of the postwar years. Biography: *Joe Papp: An American Life*, Helen Epstein (1994).

🎭 *PARADE* (Vivian Beaumont Theatre 1998). A dark and disturbing musical drama, it was a powerful piece that introduced songwriter JASON ROBERT BROWN to Broadway. In 1913 Atlanta, the Northern Jew Leo Frank (BRENT

CARVER) is accused of raping and murdering a fourteen-year old girl who worked in the factory that he managed. Found guilty in a patently biased courtroom, Leo's wife Lucille (Carolee Carmello) pushes for an appeal and just when it seems justice will prevail, a mob takes Leo from his jail cell and lynches him. Also in the talented cast were Evan Pappas, Herndon Lackey, Don Chastain, Kirk McDonald, Jessica Molaskey, Rufus Bonds, Jr., John Hickok, and Christy Carlson Romano. Alfred Uhry wrote the terse libretto based on a true incident, and Brown added to the tension with his incisive character songs, arresting choral numbers, and period pastiches. "All the Wasted Time," "The Old Red Hills of Home," "You Don't Know This Man," "This Is Not Over Yet," "How Can I Call This Home?," "Big News!," and "That's What He Said" were among the many memorable numbers. HAROLD PRINCE directed the grim musical that was admired by much of the press but was a hard sell to the public, so the LINCOLN CENTER production folded after eighty-five performances.

◢ PARAMOUNT ON PARADE (Paramount 1929). Unlike MGM's *HOLLYWOOD REVUE OF 1929* (1929) and WARNER BROTHERS' *THE SHOW OF SHOWS* (1929), this studio revue depended less on spectacle and more on star turns by everybody from MISCHA AUER to Fay Wray. JACK OAKIE, RICHARD "SKEETS" GALLAGHER, LEON ERROL, VIRGINIA BRUCE, Mitzie Mayfair, and the Paramount Publix Ushers acted as hosts and emcees introducing so many songs, comedy sketches, and dramatic scenes that eleven directors were used in the filming. Musical highlights included MAURICE CHEVALIER as a gendarme strolling through a Paris park filled with loving couples and crooning RICHARD A. WHITING and LEO ROBIN's "All I Want Is Just One Girl"; Clara Bow, Oakie, and a chorus of Marines singing and dancing to the self-mocking ELSIE JANIS–Jack King ditty "I'm True to the Navy Now"; LILLIAN ROTH and CHARLES "BUDDY" ROGERS claiming "Any Time's the Time to Fall in Love" by the same songwriters; Ruth Chatterton as a Montmarte prostitute lamenting "My Marie" by Whiting and Ray Egan; HELEN KANE as a flapper–teacher asking the Janis–King musical question "What Did Cleopatra Say?"; and a marvelous finale with chimney sweep Chevalier and a chorus of comely sweepettes singing SAM COSLOW's "Sweeping the Clouds Away" as they formed kaleidoscopic patterns while Chevalier climbed a ladder up into the clouds.

PARAMOUNT PICTURES. The celebrated movie studio was formed in 1916 when Adolph Zukor's Famous Players Film Company merged with H. H. Hodkinson's Paramount Pictures Corporation to become one of the "big five" studios in Hollywood. Actress Mary Pickford, producer SAMUEL GOLDWYN, and director Cecil B. De Mille helped ensure both the quality and the box office popularity of the new company, which specialized in family entertainment. The studio released some very innovative and unique musicals in the 1930s, although few of them made money: *MONTE CARLO* (1930), *THE SMILING LIEUTENANT* (1931), *LOVE ME TONIGHT* (1932), *ONE HOUR WITH YOU* (1932), *THE PHANTOM PRESIDENT* (1932), *WE'RE NOT DRESSING* (1934), and *HIGH WIDE AND HANDSOME* (1937). Paramount barely avoided bankruptcy in 1933 and didn't reach financial security until the 1940s, thanks to the *BIG BROADCAST* series, the "ROAD" pictures with BOB HOPE and BING CROSBY, and other musicals featuring Crosby such as *HOLIDAY INN* (1942), *GOING MY WAY* (1944), and *BLUE SKIES* (1946). The comedy team of DEAN MARTIN and JERRY LEWIS helped the studio ride through the 1950s, as did such musical hits as *WHITE CHRISTMAS* (1954) and *FUNNY FACE* (1957). The 1960s included some costly flops, such as *PAINT YOUR WAGON* (1969), but the 1970s brought some marginal hits, such as *LADY SINGS THE BLUES* (1972), and blockbusters, such as *SATURDAY NIGHT FEVER* (1977) and *GREASE* (1978). Aside from the occasional success such as *FLASHDANCE* (1983) and *DREAMGIRLS* (2006), musicals at Paramount dwindled into obscurity by the 1980s. The conglomerate Gulf & Western bought the studio in 1983, and in 1989 the company adopted the current title Paramount Communications. Today the studio is owned by Viacom, which also controls Nickelodeon, MTV, and Showtime television.

PARKER, ALAN (1944–). Film director. The British director who works on both sides of the Atlantic, he has helmed everything from documentaries to socially relevant dramas to musicals. Parker was born in London and was an advertising executive before he entered films as a writer. He directed documentaries and television commercials before making his first feature, the British gangster musical *BUGSY MALONE* (1976), which featured a cast of preteens and teenagers. Among his subsequent screen musicals were *FAME* (1980), *Pink Floyd–The Wall* (1982), *THE COMMITMENTS*

(1991), and *Evita* (1996). Parker often writes or co-authors the screenplays for his films.

PARKS, LARRY [born Sam Klusman Lawrence Parks] (1914–1975). Film and stage performer. A routine contract player at Columbia, the full-voiced singer–actor suddenly became a star when he impersonated AL JOLSON in two movies. Parks was born in Olathe, Kansas, grew up in Joliet, Illinois, and was educated at the University of Illinois with plans to become a doctor. Once he got involved with campus theatre productions he gave up on medicine and got acting experience in touring productions and summer stock. Going to New York in 1937, he was cast in dramas put on by the Group Theatre; four years later he was in Hollywood playing small or supporting roles in melodramas and featured parts in mostly B musicals such as *Sing for Your Supper* (1941), *You Were Never Lovelier* (1942), *Is Everybody Happy?* (1943), *Reveille With Beverly* (1943), *She's a Sweetheart* (1944), *Stars on Parade* (1944), and *Hey, Rookie* (1944). When Parks was cast as the title entertainer in *THE JOLSON STORY* (1946), his singing was dubbed by Jolson himself, but that did not detract from Park's powerful performance. After appearing in the musical *Down to Earth* (1947), he secured his newfound stardom with his performance in *JOLSON SINGS AGAIN* (1949). But just as suddenly his career crashed when he was accused of being a Communist by the House Un-American Activities Committee. Although he was not officially blacklisted, Columbia canceled his contract and Parks had to turn to nightclubs and the stage to find work. On Broadway he was the replacement for the leading man in *BELLS ARE RINGING* in 1957 and was featured in the musical *Beg, Borrow or Steal* (1960). In stock he acted in plays, often with his wife BETTY GARRETT who stood by him and also performed with him in clubs and later on television. But Parks career never recovered and he retired in 1962.

PASSING SHOW SERIES, THE. Stage series. More a catch-phrase title than a planned set of musical revues, the shows were scattered over a period of thirty years and had little in common. The series was spawned by a landmark production called *The Passing Show* in 1894, generally considered the first American musical revue. Its producer GEORGE LEDERER called it a "review" because the show reviewed the events of the day and spoofed the arts, such as operas in a number called "Round the Opera in Twenty Minutes." There were also satires on recent plays, acrobatics, ballet pieces, and songs from various sources. The production was not strictly a revue in the modern sense because there was a slight plot to try and tie the numbers together, but it was clear that audiences came for the sketches and musical numbers, not the story. The cast had over 100 people so the first *The Passing Show* was indeed a spectacle and it ran a very profitable 110 performances. The SHUBERTS revived the title in 1912 and used it for their series of elaborate revues that attempted to rival FLORENZ ZIEGFELD and his *ZIEGFELD FOLLIES*. There was a new edition annually (except 1920) until 1924 and the shows were popular. They may not have given Ziegfeld a run for his money, but the Shuberts's *Passing Shows* featured name talents, such as MARILYN MILLER, CHARLOTTE GREENWOOD, WILLIE and EUGENE HOWARD, ED WYNN, DE WOLF HOPPER, ADELE and FRED ASTAIRE, FRED ALLEN, MARIE DRESSLER, and others. Even comic Jefferson DeAngelis, who had been in the 1894 original, appeared in the Shuberts's versions. *The Passing Show* series also featured funny sketches, many written by Harold R. Atteridge, and introduced some song hits, such as "Smiles," "Goodbye Broadway, Hello France," "I'm Forever Blowing Bubbles," and "Carolina in the Morning."

PASSION (Plymouth Theatre 1994). An unusual chamber musical by JAMES LAPINE (book) and STEPHEN SONDHEIM (music and lyrics), it was a difficult piece for many and remains the songwriter's most elusive work. In 1863 Italy, the dashing officer Giorgio (Jere Shea) must leave his married mistress Clara (MARIN MAZZIE) in Milan when he is sent to a remote outpost commanded by Colonel Ricci (GREGG EDELMAN). The colonel's homely, sickly sister Fosca (DONNA MURPHY) falls obsessively in love with Giorgio even though he does not return her feelings. Over time he loses Clara, who is afraid to divorce her husband and lose her son, and Georgio starts to understand the power of a love like Fosca's but it is too late. He suffers a nervous breakdown and recovers to learn that Fosca has died. Also in the cast were Tom Aldredge, Francis Ruiviar, Cris Groendaal, and George Dvorsky. Much of the score was so integrated with the plot and characters that few individual songs stood out, but there was something haunting about "Happiness," "Loving You," "I Read," "I Wish I Could Forget You," and "No One Has Ever Loved Me." Based on I. U. Tarchetti's novel *Fosca* and the Italian film

Passione D'Amore (1981), the musical boasted graceful performances and beautiful decor but most critics found the characters dreary and the score too unmelodic to enjoy. The musical was definitely an acquired taste, even for Sondheim fans, but revivals later surfaced that helped some appreciate the strange piece. Author Lapine directed the elegant production, which ran 280 performances.

PASTERNAK JOSEPH (1901–1991). Film producer. A Hungarian-born Hollywood producer who worked with various studios during his long career, he presented some sixty movie musicals between 1937 and 1966. Pasternak was born in Szilagy-Somylo in present-day Hungary and came to America as a teenager, working as a bus boy and a waiter at the PARAMOUNT commissary before getting a job as a director's assistant in 1932. As he progressed into management, he was assigned by UNIVERSAL to oversee musical films made in Berlin. Just as the studio was facing bankruptcy, Pasternak returned to Hollywood, discovered DEANNA DURBIN, and featured her in the musicals *Three Smart Girls* (1937), *ONE HUNDRED MEN AND A GIRL* (1937), *Mad About Music* (1938), *That Certain Age* (1938), *Three Smart Girls Grow Up* (1939), and other tailor-made vehicles, thereby saving the studio. He also promoted such stars as JANE POWELL, KATHRYN GRAYSON, MARIO LANZA, ESTHER WILLIAMS, and JUNE ALLYSON during his career. Many of Pasternak's products were wholesome, family fare, such as *A DATE WITH JUDY* (1948), *IN THE GOOD OLD SUMMERTIME* (1949), *SUMMER STOCK* (1950), and *HIT THE DECK* (1955), yet he also presented more provocative musicals such as *DESTRY RIDES AGAIN* (1939) and *LOVE ME OR LEAVE ME* (1955). He revived interest in operetta with his productions of *THE MERRY WIDOW* (1952) and *THE STUDENT PRINCE* (1954). Among Pasternak's many other musical credits are *A Little Bit of Heaven* (1940), *Presenting Lily Mars* (1943), *TWO GIRLS AND A SAILOR* (1944), *ANCHORS AWEIGH* (1945), *Two Sisters From Boston* (1946), *Luxury Liner* (1948), *The Kissing Bandit* (1948), *THE TOAST OF NEW ORLEANS* (1950), *THE GREAT CARUSO* (1951), *Rich, Young and Pretty* (1951), *Because You're Mine* (1952), *Small Town Girl* (1953), *Athena* (1954), *Meet Me in Las Vegas* (1956), *The Opposite Sex* (1956), *This Could Be the Night* (1957), *Where the Boys Are* (1960), *JUMBO* (1962), *Girl Happy* (1965), and *Spinout* (1966). Autobiography: *Easy the Hard Way* (1956).

PASTICHE MUSICALS. When a show imitates the musical styles of earlier eras, it might be termed a pastiche musical. Many a modern musical has included a pastiche nightclub act or a show-within-a-show number for atmospheric effect or variety, as in *GYPSY* (1959), *FUNNY GIRL* (1964), *CABARET* (1966), *ANNIE* (1977), *THE WILL ROGERS FOLLIES* (1991), and *CURTAINS* (2007). But a true pastiche musical consistently echoes a previous style throughout. Most pastiche musicals have come in the form of a spoof of the past. An early example was "The Gladiola Girl" lampoon in the revue *LEND AN EAR* (1948), making fun of 1920s musical comedy. It has been followed by other gently mocking pastiche shows such as *THE BOY FRIEND* (1954), *DAMES AT SEA* (1968), *GREASE* (1972), *OVER HERE!* (1974), *Charlotte Sweet* (1982), *LITTLE SHOP OF HORRORS* (1982), *HAIRSPRAY* (2002), and *THE DROWSY CHAPERONE* (2006). Sometimes the spoofing is aimed at a very specific target, such as SHIRLEY TEMPLE in *Curly McDimple* (1967), *Sesame Street* in *AVENUE Q* (2003), and specific songwriters in the Off Broadway musical *The Musical of Musicals* (2003). A recent phenomenon is to spoof past musicals in certain numbers in the show without the musical itself being a pastiche. This happens with the mocking of *NAUGHTY MARIETTA* songs in *THOROUGHLY MODERN MILLIE* (2002), Judy Garland's "Born in a Trunk" number in *THE PRODUCERS* (2001), and ANDREW LLOYD WEBBER songs in *SPAMALOT* (2005). Much more difficult to do is to pastiche past styles without spoofing them. All of the numbers in *CHICAGO* (1975), for example, are pastiche numbers patterned on 1910s and 1920s songs and several are comic but the echoing of the past is a conscientious effort to recapture the sound and tone of those old favorites. "Serious" pastiche can also be found in such musicals as *FOLLIES* (1971), *JELLY'S LAST JAM* (1992), *RAGTIME* (1998), *THE WILD PARTY* (2000), *CAROLINE, OR CHANGE* (2004), and *GREY GARDENS* (2006).

Hollywood has been wary of pastiching because movies are supposed to have a contemporary appeal and even a historical or period musical must be palatable to the modern moviegoers. When the studios did musicals set in a past era, they simply lifted song standards from that era, which is not pastiching but the real thing. Period biographical musicals such as *THE GREAT ZIEGFELD* (1936), *THE STORY OF VERNON AND IRENE CASTLE* (1939), *LILLIAN RUSSELL* (1940), and *YANKEE DOODLE DANDY* (1942) used songs popularized by the actual person. Yet old songs were also used in period musicals that were totally fiction, such as *ALEXANDER'S RAGTIME BAND* (1938), *TIN PAN ALLEY* (1940), *FOR ME AND MY GAL* (1942), *HELLO, FRISCO, HELLO* (1943), *MOTHER WORE TIGHTS* (1947), *IN THE GOOD OLD SUMMERTIME* (1949), and *THERE'S NO BUSINESS LIKE SHOW BUSINESS* (1954). Even the deconstructed period musical *PENNIES FROM HEAVEN* (1981) used old recordings of old songs. Sometimes in 1950s movies one ran across a delightful pastiche number within a film, such as the music hall numbers in *ROYAL WEDDING* (1951), the Mickey Spillane spoof "The Girl Hunt" ballet in *THE BAND WAGON* (1953), and the French cabaret numbers in *LES GIRLS* (1957). But for the most part the pastiche musicals on screen are those based on Broadway pastiches shows, such as *The Boy Friend* (1971) or *Chicago* (2002). The few original films that include pastiche numbers include *Thoroughly Modern Millie* (1967), *NASHVILLE* (1975), *BUGSY MALONE* (1976), and *MOVIE MOVIE* (1979). The situation is not much different with television musicals. The medium is supposed to be the most up to date of the three, and nostalgia for the past usually means reruns of old TV shows. But a few original musicals can be classified as pastiche pieces, such as *Royal Follies of 1933* (1967), *MINSTREL MAN* (1977), *Hi-Hat* (1978), and *COPACABANA* (1985).

PATINKIN, MANDY [born Mandel Bruce Patinkin] (1952–). Stage, television, and film performer. A magnetic performer who specializes in intense or flamboyant characters, he is a nontraditional leading man who can play everything from Shakespeare to avant garde roles. Patinkin was born in Chicago, the son of a cookbook author, and was singing in temple by the age of nine. He studied for a time at the University of Kansas, the North Carolina School of the Arts, and Juilliard before working several years in regional theatre. Patinkin made his Off Broadway bow in 1974 and acted in several NEW YORK SHAKESPEARE FESTIVAL classics before he was first noticed on Broadway as the despondent lover Mark in the drama *The Shadow Box* (1977). He found wider recognition as the wry commentator Che in the original American cast of *EVITA* (1979) and would become known in New York for other riveting musicals roles: the two artists named George in *SUNDAY IN THE PARK WITH GEORGE* (1984), the sex changed Peter in *The Knife* (1987), the moody Archibald Craven in *THE SECRET GARDEN* (1991), a replacement for the neurotic

Marvin in *FALSETTOS* (1993), and the crazed vaudevillian Burrs in *THE WILD PARTY* (2000). Patinkin has enjoyed a very different career in film, where his only musicals were *YENTL* (1983) and *DICK TRACY* (1990), and on television where he is known for his performances in drama series such as *Chicago Hope*. He has recorded several albums and frequently does solo concerts, bringing his shows to Broadway on five occasions.

PATRIOTIC MUSICALS. When patriotism runs high, it shows up in the American musical. Going back to the Spanish-American War, patriotic songs on Tin Pan Alley appeared when the country's temperament was fervent with nationalism. Theatre audiences didn't necessarily want to see war plays and musicals during wartime but they did like to see patriotic musical numbers. The *ZIEGFELD FOLLIES* and other revues made sure there was a flag-waving number in each edition when nationalism ran high. GEORGE M. COHAN's musicals, such as *LITTLE JOHNNY JONES* (1904) and *George Washington, Jr.* (1906), also included songs celebrating America, whether there was a war on or not. The theme of many of his musicals was the superiority of the American spirit over the foreigner's philosophy and Cohan was not shy about it. During World War I, Broadway often rode on the wave of patriotism. Some shows, such as *YIP YIP YAPHANK* (1918), were outright advertisements for patriotism and contributed directly to the cause by raising money for the Army Relief Fund. Patriotism was ailing during the Depression and Broadway had more musicals satirizing the government and American ideals than in patriotic sentiments, as seen with *OF THEE I SING* (1931) and *I'D RATHER BE RIGHT* (1937). Of course that reversed during World War II. *OKLAHOMA!* (1943) was not about any war but its reaffirmation of the American character made it a highly patriotic show in the 1940s. However, even lighthearted musical comedies during wartime had plots that dealt with servicemen just to remain timely and keep the boys in uniform in the spotlight, as with *LET'S FACE IT!* (1941), *SOMETHING FOR THE BOYS* (1943), and *FOLLOW THE GIRLS* (1944). In the 1950s one found more musicals making fun of American policy, as with *CALL ME MADAM* (1950) and *SILK STOCKINGS* (1955), than those that might be termed patriotic. By the 1960s and 1970s it was best to put a musical in the distant past if one wanted to celebrate America, as with *GEORGE M!* (1968) and *Shenandoah* (1975). Recent years have brought musicals that tried to look at both sides of the American dream, as with *Assassins* (1991) and *Ragtime* (1998), and the result was far from the blind patriotism of Cohan's shows.

Movie musicals during World War II were more than entertainment, they were morale boosters. Even the most ridiculous musical comedy was very sincere about the war effort and was not afraid to show it. Films such as *Star-Spangled Rhythm* (1942), *This Is the Army* (1943), *Stagedoor Canteen* (1943), *Hollywood Canteen* (1944), *Thank Your Lucky Stars* (1943), and *Two Girls and a Sailor* (1944) did not so much create a patriotic fervor as much as it promoted and fed such a spirit. These kinds of movie musicals dropped off quickly in the late 1940s when many Americans wanted to forget the war and move on with lives. From that point on, a Broadway or Hollywood musical that had a patriotic theme tended to be more subtle, such as the gentle affection for Americana in *The Music Man* (1957) and *Big River* (1985) or the more realistic depictions of wartime as in *The Human Comedy* (1984) and *For the Boys* (1991). Perhaps the only musical of the last decades of the twentieth century that was overtly patriotic was *Annie* (1977), which was patterned after a Cohan kind of show.

PAYNE, JOHN (1912–1989). Film, television, and stage performer. A personable leading man who was more reliable than exciting, he played opposite the favorite blondes of the 1940s, including ALICE FAYE, BETTY GRABLE, JUNE HAVER, and SONJA HENIE. Payne was born in Roanoke, Virginia, the son of an opera soprano, and was educated at Roanoke College, Columbia University, and Juilliard before getting experience in stock. He sang in the Broadway revue *At Home Abroad* (1935) before heading to Hollywood where he was soon cast as wholesome leading men in such musicals as *Hats Off* (1936), *Love on Toast* (1938), *College Swing* (1938), *Garden of the Moon* (1938), and *Star Dust* (1940). By the 1940s he was partnered with 20th Century-Fox's top females stars in the musical hits *Tin Pan Alley* (1940), *Weekend in Havana* (1941), *Sun Valley Serenade* (1941), *Iceland* (1942), *Springtime in the Rockies* (1942), *Hello, Frisco, Hello* (1943), and *The Dolly Sisters* (1945). His other musical credits include *The Great American Broadcast* (1941), *Footlight Serenade* (1942), and *Wake Up and Dream* (1946). As Payne aged and his boyish looks grew more severe, he switched to westerns and action pictures. By the 1950s

he concentrated on television where he had his own show and appeared on many others. In 1973 Payne reunited with Alice Faye for a touring production of *Good News!* that was a nostalgic favorite with audiences. He was married to actresses Anne Shirley (1918–1993) and GLORIA DeHAVEN.

PEARCE, ALICE (1913–1966). Television, film, and stage performer. A farcical character actress with a homely but expressive face and a squawky voice, she was a bright addition to several musicals. Pearce was born in New York, the daughter of a bank vice president, and educated in European schools and at Sarah Lawrence College before working in summer stock. Her comedy routines in nightclubs led to her Broadway debut playing various daffy characters in the revue *New Faces of 1943* (1942). Pearce's career was launched with her merry performance as the sneezing roommate Lucy Schmeeler in *On the Town* (1944). She was featured in the musicals *Look, Ma, I'm Dancin'* (1948), *Small Wonder* (1948), and *Gentlemen Prefer Blondes* (1949) before going to Hollywood to reprise her Lucy in the 1949 screen version of *On the Town*. Pearson had small but noticeable parts in the film musicals *The Belle of New York* (1952), *The Opposite Sex* (1956), and *Kiss Me, Stupid* (1964). She returned to Broadway for the revue *John Murray Anderson's Almanac* (1953), as a replacement for proprietor Sue in *Bells Are Ringing* in 1957, and in featured roles in *Copper and Brass* (1957) and *Sail Away* (1961). Pearce was most known for her many television appearances, including her own show in 1949 and her nosey Gladys Kravitz on the series *Betwitched* right before her premature death from cancer.

PEGGY-ANN (Vanderbilt Theatre 1926). An inventive musical fantasy by HERBERT FIELDS (book), RICHARD RODGERS (music), and LORENZ HART (lyrics), the clever show used expressionism in a lighthearted way. Peggy-Ann (HELEN FORD) has a dreary existence slaving away in a boarding house in Glen Falls, New York, but when she dreams her world is full of excitement. Soon Peggy-Ann is out of Glen Falls and on Manhattan's Fifth Avenue, then on a yacht raided by pirates, and then at the races in Cuba. During her dream she encounters policemen with pink hair and mustaches, talking animals, oversized objects, and even finds herself at her own wedding wearing only her underwear. Once Peggy-

Ann awakes, she makes up with her boy friend Guy Pendleton (Lester Cole) and agrees to live in the real world. Adapted from the popular musical *Tillie's Nightmare* (1910) that had starred MARIE DRESSLER, *Peggy-Ann* had fun experimenting with Freudian clichés and expressionistic theatrics. The dream in the earlier musical was an excuse for vaudeville-like entertainment; Fields's libretto was more interested in the heroine's neuroses. There were also a few unusual touches, such as starting the show with dialogue rather than a musical number, changing the scenery in view of the audience, and ending the show quietly with Peggy-Ann and Guy dancing together in the dark. It was not so much innovative as different and, because *Peggy-Ann* never took itself very seriously, it was great fun. The musical offered no take-home hits, although later "Where's That Rainbow?" enjoyed some popularity, but such numbers as "Maybe It's Me," "A Tree in the Park," "A Little Birdie Told Me So," "Havana," and "Give This Little Girl a Hand" worked nicely in the show. Robert Milton directed and SEYMOUR FELIX choreographed the Lyle D. Andrews–LEW FIELDS production, which ran 333 performances.

PENDLETON, AUSTIN (1940–). Stage, film, and television performer, director, and playwright. The lean, bespectacled, nasal character actor turned to stage directing in the 1970s but is still a familiar face performing in different media. Pendleton was born in Warren, Ohio, and educated at Yale before making a noticeable Broadway debut as the stuttering mama's boy Jonathan in the comedy *Oh Dad, Poor Dad ...* (1962). His first musical in New York was *FIDDLER ON THE ROOF* (1964) in which he originated the role of the tailor Motel, followed by such musical performances as the anti-establishment poet Isaac in *THE LAST SWEET DAYS OF ISAAC* (1970), the suicidal Harry Berlin in *What About Luv?* (1991), and a replacement for the dying clerk Otto in *GRAND HOTEL* (1991). Even as Pendleton acted in many nonmusicals on and Off Broadway, he started directing in regional theatre and then New York, helming such notable plays as the ELIZABETH TAYLOR revival of *The Little Foxes* (1981) and the dramas *The Runner Stumbles* (1976) and *Spoils of War* (1988), as well as the Broadway musical *Shelter* (1973). He also turned to writing in the 1990s and scripted such Off Broadway plays as *Booth* (1994) and *Orson's Shadow* (2005). Pendleton has appeared in many films, the only musical being *THE MUPPET SHOW* (1979), and

dozens of television programs, including the TV musical version of *GEORGE M!* (1970).

PENNER, JOE [born Josef Pinter] (1905–1941). Stage and film performer. Using baby talk and such phrases as "You wanna buy a duck?" and "Oh, you nasty man!," the broad comic was a hit on Depression-era radio and popped up in a handful of Hollywood musicals. Penner was born in Nagechkereck, Hungary, and came to America as a child, going into vaudeville as a teenager and burlesque as an adult. His act got him cast in the Broadway musicals *The Vanderbilt Revue* (1930) and *East Wind* (1931), but it was when RUDY VALLEE discovered him and put Penner on his popular radio show that the silly comedian became an immediate sensation and soon had his own show on the airwaves. He usually played himself or someone named Joe in his six movie musicals, although he got to be the clownish twin Dromios in *THE BOYS FROM SYRACUSE* (1940). His other musical credits are *COLLEGE RHYTHM* (1934), *Collegiate* (1936), *NEW FACES OF 1937*, *Life of the Party* (1937), and *Go Chase Yourself* (1938). Penner was still very popular when he died of a heart attack at the age of thirty-six.

🎞 *PENNIES FROM HEAVEN* (Columbia 1936). A good example of a mediocre film made memorable by BING CROSBY playing a likable fellow who sings his way into the audience's (and other characters') favor. The Jo Swerling screenplay was about Depression drifter and street singer Larry Poole (Crosby) who is caught smuggling and lands in jail where a convicted murderer gives him the address of his victim's family. When Larry is released, he goes to the Smith home and befriends the family, especially the ten-year-old Patsy (Edith Fellows) and Gramp Smith (DONALD MEEK). It was pretty treacly stuff but ARTHUR JOHNSTON and JOHNNY BURKE wrote a handful of choice songs and Crosby made the most of them: the heartfelt ballads "Let's Call a Heart a Heart" and "So Do I," the simple, prayer-like "One, Two, Button Your Shoe," the rousing "Skeleton in the Closet," which he sang with LOUIS ARMSTRONG, and the wistful, optimistic title tune. NORMAN Z. MCLEOD directed the melodrama, which also featured Madge Evans, John Gallaudet, William Stack, Nana Bryant, and Tommy Dugan. ***Pennies from Heaven*** (MGM 1981) was not a remake but an inventive, dark, and uneven musical that used old standards in its fantasy sequences. Based on Dennis Potter's television series in

Great Britain, the screenplay (also by Potter) depicted Chicago sheet-music salesman Arthur Parker (Steve Martin) who trudges through the Depression and escapes from his dreary wife Joan (Jessica Harper) and pathetic mistress Eileen (BERNADETTE PETERS) by imagining his life situations turned into glamorous BUSBY BERKELEY-like musical production numbers. Martin and the other cast members lip-synced to celebrated old recordings of the songs, so the effect was almost Brechtian rather than entertaining. HERBERT ROSS directed the film on stylized Edward Hopperesque settings by Ken Adams, and DANNY DANIELS choreographed the musical numbers ingeniously. Arthur and Eileen were in a movie theatre watching FRED ASTAIRE and GINGER ROGERS dance to "Let's Face the Music and Dance" and suddenly the real-life couple appeared in the movie couple's place on the screen. "Love Is Good for Anything That Ails You" was "sung" by Peters as she conducted an orchestra of children. Perhaps the best number was the title song using the old recording by Arthur Tracy as a tramp (Vernel Bagneris) pranced on the street in a shower of golden pennies. The unusual film was not a box office success, yet is a vivid memory for those who saw it.

PENNINGTON, ANN (1893–1971). Stage and film performer. A flashy, dimpled-kneed dancer who stood just under five feet tall, she lit up many a Broadway revue with her energetic kicking and hoofing. Pennington was born in Wilmington, Delaware, grew up in Camden, New Jersey, and started dancing in nearby Philadelphia before going into vaudeville. She made her Broadway bow in ZIEGFELD FOLLIES (1913) and was featured in six subsequent editions between 1914 and 1924. Pennington was even better known for her five appearances in GEORGE WHITE'S SCANDALS between 1919 and 1928, in particular the 1926 edition in which she introduced the song and dance "Black Bottom." Her other Broadway credits include the revue *Miss 1917* (1917) and the book musicals *Jack and Jill* (1923), *THE NEW YORKERS* (1930), and *Everybody's Welcome* (1931). She made several silent films, some early musical shorts, and was featured in bit parts in the musical features *Happy Days* (1929), *Tanned Legs* (1929), *Is Everybody Happy?* (1929), *GOLD DIGGERS OF BROADWAY* (1929), and played herself in the Western *Texas Terrors* (1940). Pennington's popularity waned after the Roaring Twenties but she continued to dance in operettas on the road into the 1940s, one of which, *THE STUDENT PRINCE* (1943), briefly came to Broadway.

PERELMAN, S[imeon] **J**[oseph]. (1904–1979). Stage, film, and television writer. The celebrated American humorist took time from his comic essays and stories to contribute to a handful of musicals. Perelman was born in Brooklyn and grew up in Providence, Rhode Island, where he attended Brown University and wrote comic pieces for the school's humor magazine. He never finished college but was soon employed writing for *The New Yorker* magazine and other literary periodicals. Perelman was brought to Hollywood to write gags for the MARX BROTHERS comedy *Monkey Business* (1931) and also wrote material for their musical *HORSE FEATHERS* (1932), as well as the scripts for the musicals *Sitting Pretty* (1933) and *THE BIG BROADCAST OF 1936* (1935). He also penned some nonmusical screenplays, such as *Around the World in Eighty Days* (1956). On Broadway, Perelman contributed sketches for the musical revue *Walk a Little Faster* (1932) and the book for the musical fantasy *ONE TOUCH OF VENUS* (1943), which was filmed in 1948. Perelman also wrote the script for COLE PORTER's TV musical *ALADDIN* (1958). He published several collections of his comic pieces during his lifetime and others have been compiled since his death. Biography: *S. J. Perelman: A Life*, Dorothy Herrmann (1988).

PERLBERG, WILLIAM (1896–1968). Film producer. A Hollywood presenter who often worked with director GEORGE SEATON, he produced fourteen movie musicals spread across his long career. The native New Yorker began his career as a talent agent and then as an assistant to producer Harry Cohn before writing scripts and directing a few films in the early 1930s. He produced sixty films between 1936 and 1965, including the musicals *The King Steps Out* (1936), *The Lady Objects* (1938), *Hello, Frisco, Hello* (1943), *CONEY ISLAND* (1943), *SWEET ROSIE O'GRADY* (1943), *Diamond Horseshoe* (1945), *Where Do We Go From Here?* (1945), *THE SHOCKING MISS PILGRIM* (1947), *WABASH AVENUE* (1950), *Somebody Loves Me* (1952), and *THE COUNTRY GIRL* (1954).

PETE KELLY'S BLUES (Mark VII/Warner 1955). A gritty gangster melodrama that was also trying to be a backstage musical, the film was often fascinating, sometimes tedious. Richard L. Breen's screenplay was about the conflict between trumpet player Pete Kelly (Jack Webb), who plays in a Kansas City speakeasy in 1927, and the bootlegger–owner Frank McCarg (Edmond O'Brien), who is trying to edge into the talent agency business. Also at the club are singer Rose Hopkins (PEGGY LEE) who has taken to drink as her career declines, and various lowlifes and patrons played by Andy Devine, Lee Marvin, Martin Melnar, Mort Marshall, Jayne Mansfield, Matty Matlock, and Ella Fitzgerald. Webb's trumpet playing was dubbed by Dick Cathcart and Lee sang most of the movie's twelve songs, all old standards ("Bye Bye Blackbird," "Somebody Loves Me," "Sugar," "Hard-Hearted Hannah," and others) except for the new title song by Ray Heindorf (music) and SAMMY CAHN (lyric). Lee's acting and singing were outstanding, the highpoint of her movie career, and producer–director Webb created an effective *film noir* atmosphere for the haunting little film.

PETER PAN (Imperial Theatre 1950). The first musical version of the beloved 1905 James M. Barrie classic, it was more a play with songs but those songs were by LEONARD BERNSTEIN (music and lyrics) and were quite accomplished. Jean Arthur played the boy Peter and Boris Karloff was Captain Hook in this lively and popular production that ran 321 performances. The show used the original Barrie script but added the merry numbers "Who Am I?," "The Pirate Song," "Never Land," "My House," "Peter, Peter," and "The Plank." John Burrell directed the production, Ralph Alswang designed the playful sets, and Motley designed the clever costumes. One critic described Arthur's performance as looking and sounding like MARY MARTIN, four years before Martin played Peter in another musical version.

Peter Pan (Disney/RKO 1953) used stunning animation to go places that stage versions of Barrie's story could only suggest, and the movie was a visual treat from start to finish. The screenplay was more interested in action than talk so much of Barrie's dialogue was cut or simplified, yet there was room for such delightful SAMMY FAIN (music) and SAMMY CAHN (lyrics) songs as "You Can Fly," "The Elegant Captain Hook," "What Makes the Red Man Red?," and "Your Mother and Mine." Other numbers included "Tee-Dum Tee-Dee," "A Pirate's Life," and "Never Smile at a Crocodile." Since most stage Peter Pans had always been played by women, it was refreshing to see the boyish character voiced by BOBBY DRISCOLL, and HANS CONREID made the most of the plum role of Captain Hook. Perhaps the only radical departure from the traditional version was the sensual, very temperamental characterization of the fairy Tinker Bell, which the Disney artists modeled after MARILYN MONROE. The film is a timeless treat and remains popular with each new generation that experiences it.

Peter Pan (Winter Garden Theatre 1954) featured Mary Martin as the high-flying

---

Casts for *Peter Pan*

Character	1950 Broadway	1953 film (voices)	1954 Broadway	1960 television
Peter Pan	Jean Arthur	BOBBY DRISCOLL	MARY MARTIN	Mary Martin
Capt. Hook	Boris Karloff	HANS CONREID	CYRIL RITCHARD	Cyril Ritchard
Wendy	Marcia Henderson	Kathryn Beaumont	Kathy Nolan	Maureen Bailey
Michael	Charles Taylor	Tommy Luske	Joseph Stafford	Kent Fletcher
John	Jack Diamond	Paul Collins	Robert Harrington	Joey Trent
Mrs. Darling	Peg Hillias	Heather Angel	Margalo Gillmore	Margalo Gillmore
Smee	Joe E. Marks	Bill Thompson	Joe E. Marks	Joe E. Marks
Tiger Lily	Gloria Patrice		Sondra Lee	Sondra Lee

Character	1976 television	1979 Broadway	1990 Broadway	
Peter Pan	Mia Farrow	SANDY DUNCAN	Cathy Rigby	
Capt. Hook	DANNY KAYE	GEORGE ROSE	Steven Hanan	
Wendy	Briony McRoberts	Marsha Kramer	Cindy Robinson	
Michael	Ian Sharrock	Jonathan Ward	Chad Hutchinson	
John	Adam Stafford	Alexander Winter	Britt West	
Mrs. Darling	Virginia McKenna	BETH FOWLER	Lauren Thompson	
Smee	Tony Sympson	Arnold Soboloff	Don Potter	
Tiger Lily	Paula Kelly	Maria Pogee	Holly Irwin	

Peter Pan. In rehearsals Jule Styne argued that the two stars, Mary Martin and Cyril Ritchard (pictured), must have one song together. So the songwriters devised the funny but unnecessary specialty number "Mysterious Lady," which gave the stars their duet. The number is usually cut in revivals. (Photofest)

hero, and the musical is the most beloved and fondly remembered stage version of the story, mainly because so many have seen her performance on video and DVD. The production started out as another play version starring Martin and CYRIL RITCHARD with a few songs by Mark Charlap (music) and CAROLYN LEIGH (lyrics) added. Producers Edwin Lester and Richard Halliday were not pleased with the way the production was

shaping up in rehearsals and decided to make it a full-scale musical and brought in more experienced hands, composer JULE STYNE and lyricists BETTY COMDEN and ADOLPH GREEN, to write the rest of the score. Both teams contributed expert numbers, with Charlap–Leigh writing the more boisterous numbers, such as "I'm Flying," "I Won't Grow Up," and "I've Got to Crow," while the Styne–Comden–Green team wrote the more fanciful or lyrical songs, such as "Mysterious Lady," "Captain Hook's Waltz," and "Neverland." JEROME ROBBINS directed and choreographed the musical fantasy with grace and playfulness, and Martin and Ritchard gave sterling performances. Although the press was enthusiastic about the show, the original run of only 152 performances was disappointing. Only after the televised version in 1960 did the musical become a stage favorite. This musical version of *Peter Pan* has been revived on Broadway four times. In 1979, SANDY DUNCAN found her own distinctive way to play Peter, and advanced technology allowed for some complex flying stunts and a sprightly laser Tinker Bell. GEORGE ROSE also shone as Captain Hook and Mr. Darling in the lively production directed and choreographed by Rob Iscove. The popular attraction ended up running 551 performances, the longest running of any version of *Peter Pan*. Olympic-winning gymnast Cathy Rigby played Peter in a 1990 revival and was applauded for her buoyant performance as well as her expert flying. The limited engagement of forty-five performances in New York was part of a long national tour and business was so good that Rigby and the production returned in 1991 for forty-nine more performances. Having toured as Peter on and off over the past seven years, Cathy Rigby returned to Broadway once again in 1998 and was welcomed by playgoers for twenty-seven weeks. Paul Schoeffler was her Captain Hook.

❑ ***Peter Pan*** (NBC-TV 1960) is one of the most famous of all television broadcasts, very popular in its day and ever since thanks to rebroadcasts, video, and DVD. The program was a slightly condensed version of the 1954 Broadway musical and it reunited Mary Martin and Cyril Ritchard to recreate their Peter Pan and Captain Hook for posterity. The show had originally been broadcast live in 1955 with the stage cast and was so popular that NBC did another live broadcast in 1956. The program was finally taped in 1960, which is the version that was shown many times over the years. The production was also very stage bound and the scenery is far from impressive. Martin was perhaps far too old to pass as a preteen boy, particularly in front of the unflattering camera, yet she believed in her characterization so much and it showed in her performance that one could not help but go along with it. The show is still magical, with even the primitive flying techniques coming across as special. The program was directed by Vincent J. Donehue and choreographed by Robbins. **Peter Pan** (NBC-TV 1976) was a HALLMARK HALL OF FAME production starring Mia Farrow (Peter), DANNY KAYE (Captain Hook), and a new score by ANTHONY NEWLEY and LESLIE BRICCUSE. Andrew Birkin and Jack Burns wrote the teleplay, which did not deviate much from the conventional version, making room for sixteen songs, and giving Kaye a little leeway for his kind of clowning. Farrow played up the boyishness of the character and managed to carry her songs with her thin singing voice. The production, directed by Dwight Hemion, seemed more geared to young children and adult viewers may have gotten impatient with it at times. Among the songs were "By Hook or By Crook," "Never Never Land," "Love Is a House," "If I Could Build a World of My Own," "They Don't Make 'Em Like Me Anymore," "I'll Teach You How to Fly," and "Once Upon a Bedtime," which JULIE ANDREWS sang over the credits.

PETE'S DRAGON (Disney 1977). A large, lumbering musical with plenty of stars, songs, and scenery, the movie was overproduced and not as much fun as it should have been, yet there were moments that were very entertaining. Malcolm Marmorstein's screenplay followed the adventures of orphan Pete (Sean Marshall) who escapes from his hillbilly foster family the Gogans and arrives in the Maine town of Passamaquoddy with his dragon Elliott, a large, friendly, clumsy creature who mumbles incoherently and disappears whenever others are around. Pete is befriended and taken in by Nora (Helen Reddy), the daughter of the inebriated lighthouse keeper Lampie (MICKEY ROONEY), but soon the Gogans, led by the villainous Lena (Shelley Winters), come looking for Pete and the evil Dr. Terminus (JIM DALE) comes looking for Elliott to use for medical experiments. Also in the large cast were Red Buttons, Jane Kean, Jim Backus, Jeff Conaway, Gary Morgan, and Charles Tyner. Elliott was the only animated character in the live-action feature and his performance was more endearing than some of the overblown ones by the humans. The songs by Al Kasha and Joel

Hirschhorn ranged from tuneful to annoying but there was a nice balled for Reddy to sing called "Candle on the Water." ONNA WHITE did the vigorous, hyperactive choreography and the unimaginative direction was by Don Chaffey. It is a movie best enjoyed by children or adults who remember seeing it as children.

PETERS,   BERNADETTE [born   Bernadette Lazzara] (1948–). Stage and film performer. The baby-faced, baby-voiced singer–actress–dancer has remained one of Broadway's favorite leading ladies for thirty years, playing a variety of comic and tragic characters with distinct individuality and versatility. Peters was born in Ozone Park, New York, and trained at Manhattan's Quintano School for Young Professionals even as she was singing and dancing professionally as a child. She was on Broadway as one of the kids in THE MOST HAPPY FELLA (1959), toured as one of the child performers in GYPSY, and was featured in the Off Broadway musicals Riverwind (1966) and Curly McDimple (1967) before getting noticed as GEORGE M. COHAN's sister Josie in GEORGE M! (1968). In her subsequent hit and flop musicals, Peters gave unforgettable performances as the tap-dancing Ruby in the musical spoof DAMES AT SEA (1968), the Italian waif Gelsomina in La Strada (1969), the sassy cab driver Hilda in ON THE TOWN (1971), the silent screen star Mabel Normand in MACK AND MABEL (1974), the Parisian model Dot and her daughter Marie in SUNDAY IN THE PARK WITH GEORGE (1984), the British Emma at sea in America in Song And Dance (1985), the funny-sad Witch in INTO THE WOODS (1987), the struggling dancer Paula in The Goodbye Girl (1993), the sharpshooter Annie Oakley in ANNIE GET YOUR GUN (1999), and the ambitious stage mother Rose in GYPSY (2003). Although she has appeared in several films and television programs, rarely has Peters shone as she has on stage. She was featured in the movie musicals PENNIES FROM HEAVEN (1981) and ANNIE (1982) and in the TV musicals George M! (1970), ONCE UPON A MATTRESS (1973), and CINDERELLA (1997). Peters is also popular in concerts, in nightclubs, and on recordings.

PETERS,   BROCK [born George   Fisher] (1927–2005). Stage, television, and film performer. A muscular, rugged-looking African American actor–singer, his powerful presence was ideal for dramas and virile action movies but he was also effective in a handful of musicals. Peters was born in New York's Harlem district, the son of African and West

Indian parents, and studied at the Music and Arts High School and City College of New York. His first professional job was in a 1949 tour of *Porgy and Bess* and then he made his screen debut as Sergeant Brown in the film version of *Carmen Jones* (1954). Peters made his Broadway bow in the drama *Mister Johnson* (1956) and then was a singer in the musical *The Body Beautiful* (1958) before playing the tribesman Obitsebi in *Kwamina* (1961). He was praised for his performance as South African minister Stephen Kumalo in the 1972 Broadway revival of *Lost in the Stars*, a role he reprised on screen in 1974. Peters' most notable screen musical part was the vicious Crown in the 1959 film version of *Porgy and Bess*. He acted in dozens of films, perhaps most memorably in *To Kill a Mockingbird* (1962), and many television series, specials, and miniseries.

Petina, Irra (1908–2000). Stage and film performer. The Russian-born contralto with an opera-quality voice, she often turned to musicals during her long career but rarely found herself in a hit. Petina was born in Petrograd (now St. Petersburg), Russia, to an aristocratic family with close connections to Czar Nicholas II. Her family fled to China during the revolution and she was educated there in music. Her opera career led her to America and the Metropolitan Opera where she made her debut in 1933 and sang there regularly for twenty years. Petina first turned to the musical stage when she played the opera singer Louisa Giovanni in *The Song of Norway* (1944), her only Broadway show to enjoy a long run. She was featured in *Magdalena* (1948) and *Hit the Trail* (1954) but both were short-lived. Petina's finest performance on Broadway was the wily Old Lady in *Candide* (1956) but even that extraordinary musical failed to run. Her final Broadway attempt was *Anya* (1965) in which he got to play a Russian aristocrat. Petina made an uncredited appearance in the Hollywood musical *Balalaika* (1939) and played herself in *There's Magic in Music* (1941).

📖 **Phantom of the Opera, The** (Majestic Theatre 1987). The long-running champ on Broadway, playing longer than any previous musical, the show is a phenomenon like no other, finding success wherever it is presented and bringing fans back for repeat viewings like no other theatre attraction. As in the Gaston Leroux novel and the many film and television versions of it, the disfigured Phantom haunts the Paris Opera House and kidnaps the young opera singer Christine Daaé whom he loves and wants to use to introduce his music to the world. The nobleman Raoul also loves Christine and tries to protect her from the Phantom, particularly after the deformed fiend cuts loose a chandelier during a performance and it crashes down onto the stage. The Phantom hypnotizes Christine and brings her to his underground lair, but he is followed and surrounded, only to escape seemingly into thin air. Andrew Lloyd Webber composed his most romantic score for the sung-through show, and Richard Stilgoe and Charles Hart provided the purple lyrics. Among the highlights in the very popular score were "The Music of the Night," "All I Ask of You," "Masquerade," "The Point of No Return," "Prima Donna," "Think of Me," "Angel of Music," "Wishing You Were Somehow Here Again," and the title number. Harold Prince staged the piece like grand opera and the visuals often provided the dramatics missing in the somewhat muddled story line. A gigantic hit in London before it opened on Broadway, the musical boasted a $16.5 million advance but no one, including its creators, foresaw that it would remain a hot ticket for years and become the longest-running musical in the American theatre. Cameron Mackintosh co-produced the expensive, elaborate show with Webber's Really Useful Theatre Company, Inc., and with its many tours it has turned out to be a highly profitable industry as well as a hit musical

🎬 **The Phantom of the Opera** (Warner 2004) was long in coming and garnered a lot of anticipation by fans of the stage musical. What they found was not a disaster by any means but

Casts for *The Phantom of the Opera*

Character	1988 Broadway	2004 film
Phantom	Michael Crawford	Gerard Butler
Christine Daaé	Sarah Brightman	Emmy Rossum
Raoul	Steve Barton	Patrick Wilson
Carlotta Guidcelli	Judy Kaye	Minnie Driver
Madame Giry	Leila Martin	Miranda Richardson

The Phantom of the Opera. Florenz Ziegfeld is probably turning over in his grave, furious that he didn't think of a lavish musical version of the Gaston Leroux novel. It was his kind of show and, as staged by Harold Prince, he would have loved the "Masquerade" number (pictured) most of all: gorgeous costumes and a staircase. Both were designed by the superb Maria Bjornson who must get credit for helping to make *The Phantom of the Opera* such a crowd pleaser. (Photofest)

neither was it what most theatregoers wanted from a screen version. Since the story had already been filmed several times, there were going to be few surprises even for those unfamiliar with the stage version. The screenplay made every effort to open up the action, even placing some scenes in a cemetery when one of the main points of the story is that the Phantom haunts the opera house because his deformity keeps him a prisoner there. What the movie was able to do well was show the opera productions, both onstage and backstage, and the opening sequence in which the decaying theatre returns to life in a flashback was unquestionably stunning. Vocally, the film was faithful to the score, even if Gerard Butler made a bland Phantom and Patrick Wilson looked uncomfortably stiff in the one-dimensional role of Raoul. Newcomer Emmy Rossum had the youth and glow that made it believable she could drive these two men to fight over her. Also, in the musical's rare comic moments, Minnie Driver was a lively, funny Carlotta. Joel Schumacher directed with care if not inspiration and the result was a very polished if not vibrant film. Considering the popularity of the stage version, the movie was a box office disappointment. It already seems to have disappeared even as the Broadway, London, and road companies of *The Phantom of the Opera* live on and on.

PHANTOM OF THE PARADISE (Fox 1974). A disco-rock version of Leroux's classic tale *The Phantom of the Opera*, the clever movie develops its wacky premise with style and holds together much better than one would expect. Director Brian De Palma wrote the screenplay about crazed pop composer Winslow Leach (William Finley) whose face was deformed by an accident with a record press. When the music publisher Swan (PAUL WILLIAMS) steals one of Leach's song, the composer becomes the Phantom and haunts the popular Paradise Discotheque run by Swan. Both the Phantom and Swan crave the love of singer Phoenix (Jessica Harper). They make a deal that if the Phantom will compose a rock opera version of the *Faust* legend, Swan will produce it. The opera is written but Swan angers the Phantom by hiring the eccentric rock singer Beef (Gerrit Graham) to sing the title role, leading to a climax in which both Swan and the Phantom are destroyed. Williams wrote the songs, the most satisfying being the rock ballad "Old Souls," the Beach Boys spoof "Upholstery," and the moody "Phantom Theme." The movie did marginal business but later developed a cult following.

■ PHANTOM PRESIDENT, THE (Paramount 1932). An imaginative musical with an inventive score by RICHARD RODGERS (music) and LORENZ HART (lyrics), it afforded GEORGE M. COHAN his feature film debut. The screenplay by Walter DeLeon and Harlan Thompson revealed a political campaign committee trying to get the banker Theodore K. Blair (Cohan) elected president but they don't know what to do about their candidate's stuffy and unappealing personality. Then they catch the act by the singing and dancing medicine man Peter "Doc" Varney (also Cohan) and his sidekick Curly Cooney (JIMMY DURANTE). Doc is a dead ringer for Blair so they hire the charismatic con man to impersonate the candidate during the campaign and drum up votes. Doc agrees and immediately he's a hit with the voters, not to mention Blair's fiancée Felicia Hammond (Claudette Colbert). Come election day the party is victorious, the real Blair is exiled off to the North Pole, and Doc and Felicity head for the White House. The great Broadway showman (and egomaniac) Cohan caused numerous problems on the set but on screen his performance in this, his only film musical, was electric. Cohan's oversized persona (and Durante's comic contribution) allowed the outlandish fable to work, and Rodgers and Hart's score was neatly tied into the story and the characters. For example, the speeches and delegates' reactions at the presidential convention sequence are all set to music. Other notable numbers included "The Country Needs a Man," "Somebody Ought to Wave a Flag," and the warm ballad "Give Her a Kiss," which was only heard on the car radio. Depression-era moviegoers didn't respond to the stylistic movie, it was a dud at the box office, and Cohan never attempted another musical on screen. Only years later did the film get recognition and develop a following.

PIDGEON, WALTER [Davis] (1897–1984). Film, stage, and television performer. The soft-spoken, gentlemanly leading man of many films, he began in musicals and occasionally returned to them. Pidgeon was born in East St. John, New Brunswick, Canada, and was educated at the University of New Brunswick and the New England Conservatory of Music. After serving as a pilot in World War I, he began his acting career in Boston and in 1925 appeared on Broadway in the revue *Puzzles of 1925*. The next year Pidgeon was in Hollywood acting in silents and when sound came in he was cast as the baritone leading man in the screen musicals *Melody of Love* (1928), *Show Girl in Hollywood* (1930), *Bride of the Regiment* (1930), *Viennese Nights* (1930), *Sweet Kitty Bellairs* (1930), *KISS ME AGAIN* (1931), and *The Hot Heiress* (1931). He soon developed into a favorite in nonmusicals, particularly in the 1940s in movies such as *How Green Was My Valley* (1941) and *Mrs. Miniver* (1942). When he was cast in later musicals he rarely got to sing, as with *The Girl of the Golden West* (1938), *Listen, Darling* (1938), *It's a Date* (1940), *Holiday in Mexico* (1946), *Million Dollar Mermaid* (1952), *DEEP IN MY HEART* (1954), *HIT THE DECK* (1955), and *FUNNY GIRL* (1968). Pidgeon returned to Broadway on a few occasions and he got to sing as the patriarch Nat Miller in the musical *TAKE ME ALONG* (1959). He acted in many television programs, including the TV musicals *MEET ME IN ST. LOUIS* (1959) and *CINDERELLA* (1965).

□ PIED PIPER OF HAMELIN, THE (NBC-TV 1957). An ambitious attempt to combine a classic tale with classical music and poetic dialogue, the musical inspired from Robert Browning's narrative poem was an uneven affair. Producer Hal Stanley wrote the script in rhymed verse, drawing on Browning at times, and with Irving Taylor penned the lyrics, which were set to celebrated musical themes by Edward Grieg. The plot depicted the town of Hamelin run by a corrupt Mayor (Claude Rains) who has the children of the village working in a sweatshop rather than out playing. When a flood drives all the river rats into the town, a Pied Piper (VAN JOHNSON) appears and offers to rid the village of the rats for a huge fee, 50,000 guilders, which is how much there is in the treasury. The Mayor agrees but once the Piper uses his magic flute to lead the rats away, the greedy Mayor refuses to pay so the Piper uses the same flute to lure away all the children, bringing them to a cave that opens into a mystical land. The citizens revolt, oust the Mayor, pay the Piper, and the children return. The large cast also included Kay Starr, Lori Nelson, Jim Backus, and Stanley Adams. The production values were first class (the broadcast was in color), and the performances were broad but playful. Critics differed on the effectiveness of the Grieg music set to lyrics, although the same thing had been done with success on Broadway with *SONG OF NORWAY* (1944). Songs such as "Flim Flam Floo," "Welcome Song," "Feats of Piper," "Fools Gold," and "Mother's Lament" could be taken as high-flying numbers riding on Grieg's wonderful music or an awkward blend of words and melody. The ninety-minute broadcast was directed by Broadway veteran Bretaigne Windust with some nice touches, such as never showing the rats but indicating their presence by menacing shadows.

PINOCCHIO (Disney/RKO 1940). The second animated feature from WALT DISNEY and for many the greatest of all the studio's work, the film combined a gripping story, memorable characters, tuneful songs, and remarkable animation that has rarely been equaled.

Plot: The tale is narrated by Jiminy Cricket who is also in the plot as Pinocchio's conscience. The good-hearted Gepetto carves the marionette Pinocchio and prays on the wishing star that he might become a real boy. The Blue Fairy arrives that night and magically brings the puppet to life but says he must prove himself before becoming human. Pinocchio and Jiminy head off to school the next day but are sidetracked by the conniving J. Worthington Foxwell, thereby setting up a series of misadventures that include the greedy puppeteer Stromboli, the horrors of Pleasure Island, and

rescuing Gepetto from inside Monstro the whale. The trials prove Pinocchio to be worthy and he becomes a real boy.

Based on the 1880 story by Carlo Collodi, the screenplay is a marvelous blending of comedy, suspense, and warmth with both villainous and lovable characters vividly coming to life. Certain scenes, once viewed, can never be forgotten, such as the stringless Pinocchio dancing with marionettes in Stromboli's theatre, the frantic chase escaping from the whale, and the horrifying transition of the boy Lampwick into a donkey at Pleasure Island. The animation is even more skillful than that for the studio's previous effort, *SNOW WHITE AND THE SEVEN DWARFS* (1937), and the masterly background art captures the cozy, continental European village as effectively as the garish, almost surreal Pleasure Island.

Pinocchio (film) Musical Numbers

"When You Wish Upon a Star"
"Little Woodenhead"
"Give a Little Whistle"
"Turn on the Old Music Box"
"Hi Diddle Dee Dee (An Actor's Life for Me)"
"I've Got No Strings"

Casts for Pinocchio

Character	1940 film (voices)	1957 television	1965 television
Pinocchio	Dickie Jones	MICKEY ROONEY	John Joy
Gepetto	Christian Rub	WALTER SLEZAK	David Life
Jiminy Cricket	CLIFF EDWARDS		
Honest John/Fox	WALTER CATLETT	Martyn Green	
Blue Fairy	Evelyn Venable	Fran Alison	Jodi Williams
Cat		Matt Mattox	
Stromboli	Charles Judels		
Ringmaster		JERRY COLONNA	
Lampwick	Frankie Darro		
Coachman			Jim Eiler

Character	1968 television	1976 television	2000 television (Geppetto)
Pinocchio	Peter Noone	SANDY DUNCAN	Seth Atkins
Gepetto	Burl Ives	DANNY KAYE	Drew Carey
Jiminy Cricket			
Honest John/Fox		Flip Wilson	RENE AUBERJONOIS
Blue Fairy			Julia Louis-Dreyfus
Cat		Liz Torres	
Stromboli			Brent Spiner
Ringmaster			
Lampwick			
Coachman		CLIVE REVILL	

Pinocchio. Who else but Walt Disney and his writers would think to personify a character's conscience in an animated movie? But Jiminy Cricket (right) was one of the many brilliant touches in the 1940 film and audiences liked him so much he returned on the large and small screen for decades after. (Photofest)

The songs by Leigh Harline (music) and NED WASHINGTON (lyrics) are not only enjoyable in themselves but also fit nicely into the narrative. The Oscar-winning "When You Wish Upon a Star" sets the mood and theme and foreshadows Gepetto's wish, which sets the action in motion. "Honest" John's "Hi Diddle Dee Dee" is a merry persuasion song that is so tuneful that there's no question of its working on Pinocchio. Jiminy's "Give a Little Whistle" is a contagious ditty that cements the friendship between the "conscience" and his young charge. Paul J. Smith composed the accomplished background score, and Ben Sharpsteen headed the staff of directors and animators. The character of Jiminy Cricket (a Disney creation not in the original tale) was immediately embraced by moviegoers and the studio used him for decades in other features and on television, with the spry little fellow becoming an unofficial host for the world of Disney. Also a signature of sorts was the song "When You Wish Upon a Star," which has become the unofficial theme song for everything Disney, from films and television to theme parks and cruise liners. *Pinocchio* has dated perhaps less than any other animated film; what was frightening then still is, and what was once joyous still soars.

☐ At least five television musicals based on Collodi's story have been made. *Pinocchio* (NBC-TV 1957) squeezed many of the same adventures into a sixty-minute broadcast written by Yasha Frank in verse. MICKEY ROONEY'S Pinocchio struck some as endearing, others as embarrassing. The cast included some popular character actors and the score by Alec Wilder (music) and William Engvick (lyrics) had its charm, such as the songs "Listen to Your Heart," "The Fox's Pitch," "Pinocchio's Song," and "The Jolly Coachman." David Susskind produced and Paul Bogart directed. Eight years later, *Pinocchio* (1965 CBS-TV) featured the Prince Street Players, a Manhattan children's theatre group, in a TV adaptation with songs by Jim Eiler and Jeanne Bargy. Numbers such as "You Can Sing" and "I Don't Want to Go to School" didn't help propel the sixty-minute musical but the songs were pleasant enough, especially "A Real Little Boy," "How Will I Ever Get Along?," and "The Coach Is Coming." The broadcast was well received by the press and was shown again in 1967. Peter Noone, a popular singer because of his rock group Herman's Hermits, played the title character in *Pinocchio* (NBC-TV 1968), a HALLMARK HALL OF FAME production presented by RICHARD LEWINE and directed by Sid Smith. The songs by Walter Marks were commendable, such as "Chip Off the Old Block," "Beautiful People," "Walk With Him," and "Wonderful World, Hello," as were such supporting players as Burl Ives, Charlotte Rae, Mort Marshall, and Pierre Epstein. This ninety-minute version also featured marionette work by Bil Baird. Also ninety minutes and directed by Sid Smith was *Pinocchio* (CBS-TV 1976) featuring DANNY KAYE as Gepetto and SANDY DUNCAN as the wooden boy. The songs this time were by Billy Barnes and included such numbers as " This Little Boy of Mine," "I'm Talkin' to Myself," "I Like It!," and "I'm Not Worried—Yes I Am!" RON FIELD co-directed and choreographed and this adaptation had a more Broadway feel than the others. There was a touch of Broadway also in the score by STEPHEN SCHWARTZ for **Geppetto** (ABC-TV 2000). Ballads such as "My Empty Heart" and "Since You Took My Heart Away" balanced nicely with character songs "Satisfaction Guaranteed," "Toys," and "Pleasure Island." Television comic Drew Carey produced the Disney offering and starred himself as Geppetto (spelled differently from all the other adaptations). The David I. Stern teleplay focused on the puppet maker quite a bit so one's reaction to the musical was based on one's appreciation of the star. The supporting cast was first rate and Tom Moore directed. There was also an animated musical version titled *Pinocchio's Christmas* (NBC-TV 1980), a sequel that featured Pinocchio and Gepetto preparing a puppet show for the holidays.

PINK LADY, THE (New Amsterdam Theatre 1911). Although the musical and its score are long forgotten, the show was the biggest hit of its season, running a very impressive 312 performances. Even though he is engaged to be wed to Angele (Alice Dovey) in the near future, the Parisian Lucien Gabriel (William Elliott) wants to have one last fling with his favorite girl from his wild youth, the enticing Claudine (HAZEL DAWN) who has the nickname the Pink Lady because of the color of her wardrobe. He takes Claudine to a restaurant in the woods of Compiegne where they accidentally come across Angele and Lucien tries to pass Claudine off as the wife of a friend. Also complicating things is a satyr who is running through the forest stealing kisses from young ladies. C. M. S. McLellan's libretto was silly and his lyrics for IVAN CARYLL's music light as air, resulting in such frothy numbers as "Donny Didn't, Donny Did," "On the Saskatchewan," "Hide and Seek," and the hit song "My Beautiful Lady," which Dawn sang as she accompanied herself on the violin. The Klaw–Erlanger production made her a star and gave composer Caryll the biggest hit of his fourteen Broadway musicals.

PINKINS, TONYA (1962–). Stage and television performer. The sleek, sensuous African American actress–singer left her busy television career to appear in Broadway musicals, each time giving a riveting performance. Pinkins was born in Chicago and educated at Carnegie-Mellon University before making her debut in the young cast of the short-lived musical MERRILY WE ROLL ALONG (1981). A decade later she wowed audiences with her sexy Anita in JELLY'S LAST JAM (1991), followed by the Argentine Clotilde in *Chronicle of a Death Foretold* (1995), the classy Lady Liv in *Play On!* (1997), and the controlling Kate in THE WILD PARTY (2000). Arguably her finest performance was as the Louisiana maid Caroline in CAROLINE OR CHANGE (2004), a role she reprised in California and then in London. Pinkins has also acted in nonmusical plays, such as *The Merry Wives of Windsor* (1994) and *Radio Golf* (2007). She appeared in a few films and many television programs, including a long stint on the soap opera *All My Children*, but her musical talents were rarely used in those media.

PINS AND NEEDLES (Labor Stage 1937). One of the longest-running revues in Broadway history, the show started out as an amateur theatrical but eventually turned into a landmark of sorts. Although it was produced by the International Ladies Garment Workers' Union, the revue was far from ponderous or sermonizing. Instead the sketches (by Arthur Arent, MARC BLITZSTEIN, and others) and songs (by HAROLD ROME) took a lighthearted look at labor relations, world affairs, and even love. The cast consisted of union workers, most with little or no stage experience, yet the production was far from an embarrassing amateur affair, particularly with its first-class score. Scheduled for a few weekends when the cast was not working at their real trade, the little but potent revue quickly caught on and offered more performances per week, even as the program changed slightly to reflect the latest headlines. By the time it had changed theatres a few times and offered revised editions, it had run 1,108 performances. The cast included Millie Weitz, Ruth Rubinstein, Al Levy, Lynne Jaffee, Hy Goldstein, Nettie Harary, and Paul Seymour, and among the first-rate songs were "Sing Me a Song With Social Significance," "Sunday in the Park," "Four Little Angels of Peace," "Nobody Makes a Pass at Me," "Chain Store Daisy," "One Big Union for Two," and "Doin' the Reactionary."

PINZA, EZIO [born Fortunato Pinza] (1892–1957). Stage, film, and television performer. A leading basso at the Metropolitan Opera, he appeared in two Broadway musicals and in a handful of films. Pinza was born to an impoverished family in Rome, Italy, and began singing at a young age, never learning how to read music but performing some of the most challenging of opera roles. After a celebrated career in the great opera houses of the world, Pinza turned to the theatre late in life, making a sensational Broadway debut as the French planter Emile de Becque in SOUTH PACIFIC (1949), a role written by OSCAR HAMMERSTEIN with Pinza in mind. His other stage role was the French cafe owner César in FANNY (1954). Pinza also sang in a handful of films, including *Carnegie Hall* (1947), *Mr. Imperium* (1950), *Strictly Dishonorable* (1951), and *Tonight We Sing* (1953), and on several television specials. Autobiography: *Ezio Pinza: An Autobiography*, with Robert Magidoff (1959).

PIPE DREAM (Shubert Theatre 1955). The least known (and least successful) musical by RICHARD RODGERS (music) and OSCAR HAMMERSTEIN (book and lyrics), it is also their most offbeat and atypical show. In Cannery Row, a seaside town in California, the local folks all like Doc (BILL JOHNSON), a penniless marine biologist who lives an unconventional, easy-going life and can't even afford to buy a microscope so his pals Mac (G. D. Wallace) and Hazel (Mike Kellin), with the help of Fauna (Helen Traubel), the madame at the local whorehouse, hold a raffle to buy Doc a microscope. When the lonely drifter Suzy (Judy Tyler) comes to town, they decide that she would make a good companion for Doc and act as matchmaker for the two. Doc and Suzy fall in love but she questions how he can love a prostitute so she plans to leave town. Hazel breaks Doc's arm, knowing Suzy will stay with Doc to nurse him, and the plan works. Hammerstein adapted John Steinbeck's novella *Sweet Thursday*, an unusual choice since none of the characters had much integrity, idealism, or strength of purpose, the elements that usually attracted the librettist to a project. The result was a musical that was loose, freewheeling, and more than a little naughty. The score produced no major hits but there is a lovely poignancy in many of the songs, such

as "Ev'rybody's Got a Home But Me" and "All at Once You Love Her." Also notable were "All Kinds of People," "A Lopsided Bus," "The Man I Used to Be," "Suzy Is a Good Thing," "The Happiest House on the Block," and "The Party That We're Gonna Have Tomorrow Night." Opera star Traubel did not come across as well as everyone hoped but the rest of the cast, under Harold Clurman's direction, was quite engaging. The reviews were mostly dismissive but the show had chalked up the largest advance yet seen on Broadway (just over $1 million) so it managed to run 246 performances, even if many of those performances were far from full. *Pipe Dream* was intriguing, cockeyed, and sometimes even touching. It was the kind of flop worthy of such highly talented men.

PIPPIN (Imperial Theatre 1972). A grand hocus-pocus act of a musical, it became dazzling entertainment because director–choreographer

Pippin. Ben Vereen (center) had already given an impressive performance on Broadway as Judas in the original production of *Jesus Christ Superstar* (1971) but the next year he was roundly cheered as the cat-like Leading Player in *Pippin*, tying the haphazard story together by serving as narrator, host, commentator, and even young Pippin's antagonist in the finale. (Photofest)

BOB FOSSE seemed to pull magic out of thin air. Young Pippin (John Rubinstein), the son of Charlemagne (Eric Berry), searches for self-fulfillment in the world by experimenting with war, sex, and politics, only to realize that, despite what the Leading Player (BEN VEREEN) suggests, satisfaction only comes from domestic happiness. The multitalented company also included Jill Clayburgh, LELAND PALMER, Irene Ryan, and Christopher Chadman. Roger O. Hirson wrote the loose libretto, and STEPHEN SCHWARTZ provided a splendid set of songs, including "Magic to Do," "Morning Glow," "With You," "No Time at All," "Corner of the Sky," and "On the Right Track." The plotting was thin and forced but the reviewers rejoiced in Fosse's inventive staging and in the mesmerizing theatrics of performer Vereen. Stuart Ostrow produced the show, which ran 1,944 performances, and the musical soon became a favorite with schools, summer stock, and community theatres across the country.

PIPPIN, DONALD (1931–). Stage and television orchestrator, musical director, and composer. A much respected arranger and director of music for Broadway shows, he has guided several notable musicals to successful opening nights. Pippin was born in Macon, Georgia, and in the 1950s wrote songs, such as "Hold Me in Your Arms," and was a staff musician for ABC television. He composed dance music for *Ankles Aweigh* (1955) on Broadway and then made his debut as musical director for the British import *Oliver!* (1962). For the next three decades he would be the first choice for musical director by JERRY HERMAN, CY COLEMAN, and other composers. Among his many Broadway credits are *110 IN THE SHADE* (1963), *Ben Franklin in Paris* (1964), *MAME* (1966), *APPLAUSE* (1970), *SEESAW* (1973), *MACK AND MABEL* (1974), *A CHORUS LINE* (1975), *WOMAN OF THE YEAR* (1981), *LA CAGE AUX FOLLES* (1983), *Teddy and Alice* (1987), *The Red Shoes* (1993), and *Dream* (1997). Pippin has also returned to television on occasion such as doing the musical direction for the TV musical *MRS. SANTA CLAUS* (1996).

PIRATE, THE (MGM 1948). Perhaps the most cartoonish live-action musical from Hollywood's golden age, the artificial sets, garishly colored costumes, and larger-than-life characters performing with wild abandon strike some as inspired, others as wearing. FRANCES GOODRICH and ALBERT HACKETT adapted S. N. Behrman's 1942 Broadway play set on a fictional Caribbean Island. The dreamy senorita Manuela (JUDY GARLAND), who is bored with her fiancé Don Pedro (WALTER SLEZAK), fantasizes about being carried off by the dashing pirate Macoco, also known as Mack the Black. When the strolling actor Serafin (GENE KELLY) and his troupe come to town, he woos her by suggesting to her that he is the pirate but suffers her anger when she learns the truth. It turns out that Don Pedro is the real Macoco, and Manuela, her illusions dashed, joins Seraphin and his players. It was an adult fairy tale played with grand passions, silly athletics, and not a touch of subtlety. COLE PORTER penned the score and tried to match all the derring-do on the set: the sly "Niña," the overly romantic "Love of My Life," the rousing "Mack the Black," the wistful "You Can Do No Wrong," and the celebratory "Be a Clown," which the anti-gravity NICHOLAS BROTHERS performed with Kelly. Also in the cast were Gladys Cooper, REGINALD OWEN, GEORGE ZUCCO, and Lola Albright, all under VINCENTE MINNELLI's colorful direction and choreographed by Kelly and ROBERT ALTON. The movie did poorly at the box office but has found its advocates over the years.

PIRATES OF PENZANCE, THE (Fifth Avenue Theatre 1879). One of the most produced and most fun comic operettas by W. S. Gilbert (book and lyrics) and Arthur Sullivan (music), its ridiculous plot is balanced with one of their finest scores. The pirate apprentice Frederic (Hugh Talbot) wishes to give up his disreputable profession and marry Mabel (Blanche Roosevelt), one of the many lovely daughters of Major General Stanley (J. H. Ryley), but the Pirate King (Signor Brocolini) finds a loophole in Frederic's apprenticeship contract and will not release him. Only after the pirate maid Ruth (Alice Barnett) reveals that Frederic and the pirate horde are all aristocrats by birth are Mabel and Frederic united. The marvelous score included such memorable numbers as "Poor Wandering One," "I Am the Very Model of a Modern Major General," "When Frederic Was a Little Lad," "When a Felon's Not Engaged in His Employment," and "With Cat-like Tread." The authors and producer Richard D'Oyly Carte wished to stop pirated productions of their new work so the musical opened in New York before London, the only Gilbert and Sullivan operetta to have its world premiere on Broadway. It ran ninety-one performances in its initial engagement and New York has seen over forty major revivals since then. The most notable production of recent decades was the 1981 mounting by the NEW YORK SHAKESPEARE FESTIVAL in Central

Park. The lively, rough-and-tumble mounting, directed by Wilford Leach and choreographed by GRACIELA DANIELE, featured pop singers Linda Ronstadt (Mabel) and Rex Smith (Frederic), as well as KEVIN KLINE (Pirate King), GEORGE ROSE (Maj. Gen. Stanley), and Estelle Parsons (Ruth). The production was such a hit that producer JOSEPH PAPP moved it to Broadway where it ran 772 performances, the most successful Gilbert and Sullivan revival on record. *The Pirates of Penzance* remains a favorite with light opera, summer stock, community, and school theate groups.

☙ **PLAIN AND FANCY** (Mark Hellinger Theatre 1955). A pleasing musical comedy set in an Amish community, it managed to be a hit without being a sensational blockbuster. New Yorkers Ruth Winters (Shirl Conway) and Dan King (Richard Derr) arrive in Pennsylvania Dutch country to sell a barn Dan has inherited and they get involved with the local Amish citizens, including the fun-loving Hilda Miller (BARBARA COOK) and the stubborn farmer Papa Yoder (Stefan Schnabel) who is forcing his daughter Katie (Gloria Marlowe) to marry the dense Ezra Reber (Douglas Fletcher Rodgers) when she loves his brother, the outcast Peter Reber (David Daniels). After a barn raising and a ruckus in which Peter clears his name, all ends happily for the rural folk and the two city dwellers return home engaged to each other. JOSEPH STEIN and Will Glickman penned the proficient libretto, and ALBERT HAGUE (music) and Arnold B. Horwitt (lyrics) wrote some accomplished songs, particularly the runaway hit "Young and Foolish." Also heard were "Plenty of Pennsylvania," "It Wonders Me," "Follow Your Heart," "I'll Show Him!," and "City Mouse, Country Mouse." Its unique setting, genial characters, and pleasant score didn't add up to a must-see attraction but it was an entertaining show that ran a profitable 461 performances. MORTON DA COSTA was the efficient director, and HELEN TAMIRIS provided the lively choreography.

PLAYWRIGHTS HORIZONS. Stage company. Perhaps no other Off Broadway theatre organization has been more successful in introducing notable new plays and playwrights than this small but potent company. Their track record with new musicals is also impressive, premiering challenging works and even sending some on to Broadway. Founded in 1971 by Robert Moss as a writers' showcase, the group was the first to feature such songwriters and librettists as WILLIAM FINN, JAMES LAPINE, ADAM GUETTEL, and JEANINE TESORI. Among the musicals to premiere at Playwrights Horizons were *March of the Falsettos* (1981), *SUNDAY IN THE PARK WITH GEORGE* (1984), *ONCE ON THIS ISLAND* (1990), *Falsettoland* (1990), *ASSASSINS* (1990), *FLOYD COLLINS* (1996), *VIOLET* (1997), *JAMES JOYCE'S THE DEAD* (2000), and *GREY GARDENS* (2006).

🎬 **POCAHONTAS** (Disney 1995). Walt Disney loved American history and produced several live-action feature films on the subject during his lifetime but this is the only animated musical dealing with history that the studio has ever presented. It was far from accurate in historical details, but as a love story it was beautifully told and rather low key for a children's movie. In fact, many children were bored. None of the animals talked, there was no fantasy or magic save a little conjuring by Grandmother Willow (voice of Linda Hunt), the issues were mature ones (ecological awareness, racial intolerance, the evils of imperialism), and at the end the lovers are separated. No wonder adults found more to savor than kids. Pocahontas (Irene Bedard, singing by JUDY KUHN) was portrayed as a full-grown woman rather than the young girl she really was, and Captain John Smith (Mel Gibson) looked more like a movie star than an explorer, but their scenes together were honest, funny, and very moving. The Englishmen were portrayed as simply greedy but the Native Americans were handled sympathetically without being patronizing. The melodic songs by ALAN MENKEN (music) and STEPHEN SCHWARTZ (lyrics) sometimes took an inspirational tone, especially with the Oscar-winning "Colors of the Wind," yet equally impressive was the reflective "Just Around the Riverbend." Mike Gabriel and Eric Goldberg directed with care and the art backgrounds were rich, verdant, and even primeval.

POLITICS IN MUSICALS. America's fascination with politics, the alternate form of mass entertainment, has encouraged Broadway and Hollywood to occasionally present works about the dramatics of elections, administrations, and political games. While plays and nonmusical films have often taken a serious view of these matters, musicals usually took a satiric or even farcical one. On Broadway the government and its political machinery have been the targets of such musicals as *STRIKE UP THE BAND* (1930), *OF THEE I SING* (1931), *LET 'EM EAT CAKE* (1933), *RED, HOT AND BLUE!* (1936), *I'D RATHER BE RIGHT* (1937), *KNICKERBOCKER HOLIDAY* (1938), *LEAVE IT TO ME!* (1938), *LOUISIANA PURCHASE*

(1940), *ANYONE CAN WHISTLE* (1964), and *URINETOWN* (2001). Less satirical but still within the range of musical comedy were *George Washington, Jr.* (1907), *FIORELLO!* (1959), *MR. PRESIDENT* (1962), *Ben Franklin in Paris* (1964), *1776* (1969), *Jimmy* (1969), and *Teddy and Alice* (1987). On a much more serious level were *THE CRADLE WILL ROCK* (1938), *Cry for Us All* (1970), *1600 PENNSYLVANIA AVENUE* (1976), *PACIFIC OVERTURES* (1976), *EVITA* (1979), and *ASSASSINS* (1990). Hollywood has offered few musicals involved with politics. Perhaps it is too touchy a subject when appealing to the masses. In addition to the aforementioned stage works that were filmed, movie musicals dealing with politics include *THE LOVE PARADE* (1929), *THE PHANTOM PRESIDENT* (1932), *HALLELUJAH, I'M A BUM* (1933), *DUCK SOUP* (1933), *ROMAN SCANDALS* (1933), *THANKS A MILLION* (1935), and *HIGH, WIDE AND HANDSOME* (1937).

POLLACK, LEW (1895–1946). Film composer. Usually working at 20TH CENTURY-FOX, the songwriter collaborated with SIDNEY MITCHELL and a variety of other lyricists on seventeen movie musicals. The native New Yorker wrote songs for vaudeville and had an early hit with "My Yiddishe Momme." Some of his music was heard on Broadway in *THE PASSING SHOW OF 1921* (1920) and then he went to Hollywood when sound came in, writing theme songs for *Seventh Heaven* (1927) and other nonmusical melodramas. By 1936 his first full score was heard in *Song and Dance Man*, written with lyricist SIDNEY CLARE. Most of Pollack's musicals were with Mitchell, such as *CAPTAIN JANUARY* (1936), *Pigskin Parade* (1936), *ONE IN A MILLION* (1936), *Thin Ice* (1937), *Life Begins in College* (1937), *IN OLD CHICAGO* (1938), *REBECCA OF SUNNYBROOK FARM* (1938), and *Kentucky Moonshine* (1938). With HERB MAGIDSON, Mort Greene, Charles Newman, and others, he scored *The Yanks Are Coming* (1942), *Tahiti Honey* (1943), *Jitterbugs* (1943), *Sweethearts of the USA* (1944), *Seven Days Ashore* (1944), *Music in Manhattan* (1944), *The Girl Rush* (1944), and *Bamboo Blonde* (1946). Pollack's most famous songs include "Sing, Baby, Sing," "It's Love I'm After," "Charmaine," and "You Do the Darndest Things, Baby."

◻ *POLLY* (NBC-TV 1989). WALT DISNEY had featured his young protégé Hayley Mills in the nonmusical film *Pollyanna* (1960) and the company returned to Eleanor H. Porter's 1911 story three decades later for this musical version on *The Magical World of Disney* that was set among African Americans. In 1955, the orphaned Polly (Keshia Knight Pulliam) goes to live with her rich, humorless Aunt Polly (Phylicia Rashad) in Harrington, Alabama, and with her cheerful demeanor Polly brings joy to a sour household and even a sweetheart for her revitalized aunt. The supporting cast included Brandon Quintin Adams, BROCK PETERS, CELESTE HOLM, Barbara Montgomery, KEN PAGE, Dorian Harewood, and Butterfly McQueen. The sentimental but winning tale was enlivened by some charming musical numbers by Joel McNeely, such as "Shine a Light," "By Your Side," "Honey Ain't Got Nothin' on You," and "Something More." William Blinn wrote the two-hour teleplay, and director DEBBIE ALLEN did the lively choreography. Ratings were so strong that most of the creative staff and cast returned for **Polly—Comin' Home!** (NBC-TV 1990). In the sequel set in 1956, Polly gets involved in more matchmaking, a political race in which Miss Snow (Celeste Holm) runs for mayor, and even some sticky moments having to do with segregation. Considered more contrived and syrupy than the original, the two-hour musical still offered some commendable songs, such as "I Can't Hear My Heart" and "What a Gentlemen Does," a nimble performance by ANTHONY NEWLEY, and some sprightly dancing.

PONS, LILY [born Alice Josephine Pons] (1904–1976) Film performer. One of the Metropolitan Opera's favorite coloraturas, the petite, dark-haired singer was courted by Hollywood after the success of opera singer GRACE MOORE on the screen. Pons was born in Draguingnan, France, of Italian and French ancestry, and entered the Paris Conservatoire at the age of thirteen. After World War I her career took off, singing in the leading opera houses in Europe and making her Met debut in 1931. Over the next thirty years Pons would give 280 performances at the celebrated Manhattan opera house. She played character parts in the movie musicals *I DREAM TOO MUCH* (1936), *That Girl From Paris* (1936), and *Hitting a New High* (1937) and then performed as herself in *Carnegie Hall* (1947). While Pons' movie career did not take off as hoped, she was very popular on the radio and was beloved for her many concerts entertaining the troops during World War II. She was married to Andre Kostelanetz (1901–1980) who conducted many of her performances.

▬ **POOR LITTLE RICH GIRL** (Fox 1936). A typical SHIRLEY TEMPLE vehicle, the musical was a pleasing mix of contemporary, toe-tapping razzle-dazzle and good old-fashioned sentimentality. The story had already been seen on screen as a Mary Pickford silent and it still held together efficiently. The neglected, motherless Barbara (Temple), the daughter of soap manufacturer Richard Barry (Michael Whalen), runs away from home and is befriended by the married vaudevillians Jerry (ALICE FAYE) and Jimmy Dolan (JACK HALEY) who, spotting talent, put her in the act. Soon the singing–dancing moppet has the three of them in the big time, but when they sing together on a radio show sponsored by a rival soap company, dad comes back and promises to change his ways. HARRY REVEL (music) and MACK GORDON (lyrics) wrote some tailor-made tunes for Temple, including "You Gotta Eat Your Spinach, Baby," "When I'm With You," "Oh, My Goodness," "But Definitely," and the tapping production number "Military Man." IRVING CUMMINGS directed the DARRYL F. ZANUCK–B. G. DE SYLVA production, which also featured GLORIA STUART, Sara Haden, Jane Darwell, and (briefly) TONY MARTIN.

PORGY AND BESS (Alvin Theatre 1935). America's greatest folk opera, it is also considered musical theatre because its creators, GEORGE GERSHWIN (music), IRA GERSHWIN (lyrics), and DuBose Heyward (book and lyrics), considered it a theatre piece and premiered the work in a Broadway playhouse rather than an opera house. Among the African American residents of Catfish Row in Charleston is the cripple Porgy who has fallen in love with the loose vixen Bess even though she is the mistress of the belligerent Crown. When Crown kills a neighbor in a crap game and takes off, Porgy and Bess find temporary happiness together. When Crown returns, Porgy kills him and is arrested. Bess is lured away to New York by the drug dealer Sportin' Life and the released Porgy sets off in his wagon to find her. Based on the play *Porgy* (1927), the opera featured such classic musical numbers as "I Loves You, Porgy," "Summertime," "Bess, You Is My Woman Now," "It Ain't Necessarily So," "I Got Plenty o' Nuttin'," "My Man's Gone Now," "There's a Boat Dat's Leavin' Soon for New York," and "A Woman Is a Sometime Thing." The production was reviewed by both music and theatre critics, with the latter writing more enthusiastically about the piece. There was also praise for the vibrant cast, the outstanding production values, and the evocative direction by ROUBEN MAMOULIAN. But Depression audiences were not interested and the THEATRE GUILD production ran only 124 performances, a major financial loss. Sadly, it was the last new work by George Gershwin to be heard on Broadway. The first major New York revival of *Porgy and Bess* was in 1942. Producer CHERYL CRAWFORD cut some of the recitatives, TODD DUNCAN and Anne Brown reprised their Porgy and Bess, and the supporting cast included Avon Long (Sportin' Life), Warren Coleman (Crown), Ruby Elzy (Serena), and Harriet Jackson (Clara). The revival ran 286 performances and returned to New York twice while it was touring the country. An international tour of the opera that had played Russia came to New York in 1953 where it was received so warmly that it stayed for nine months, twice as long as the original run. LeVern Hutcherson, Leslie Scott, and Irving Barnes alternated as Porgy, Leontyne Price and Urylee Leonardos sang Bess, and CAB CALLOWAY stopped the show every

Casts for *Porgy and Bess*

Character	1935 Broadway	1959 film	1976 Broadway
Porgy	TODD DUNCAN	Sidney Poitier (Robert McFerrin)	Donnie Ray Albert, Abraham Lind-Oquendo, Robert Mosley
Bess	Anne Brown	DOROTHY DANDRIDGE (Adele Addison)	Clamma Dale, Esther Hinds, Irene Oliver
Crown	Warren Coleman	BROCK PETERS	Andrew Smith, George Robert Merritt
Sportin' Life	John W. Bubbles	SAMMY DAVIS, JR.	LARRY MARSHALL
Clara	Abbie Mitchell	DIAHANN CARROLL	Betty D. Lane
Serena	Ruby Elzy	Ruth Attaway	Wilma Shakesnider, Delores Ivory-Davis
Maria	Georgette Harvey	PEARL BAILEY	Carol Bric

Porgy and Bess. Among the many attributes of the original Broadway production of the folk opera was the sterling direction by Rouben Mamoulian. The Russian-born director was particularly adept at handling crowd scenes, as evidenced in this production shot showing the residents of Catfish Row reacting to the bully Crown (center with arms raised) as he turns a crap game into a fight. The atmospheric setting was designed by another Russian, Sergei Soudeikine. (Photofest)

performance as Sportin' Life. In 1961, William Warfield and Irving Barnes alternated as Porgy, while Leesa Foster and Martha Flowers took turns as Bess in the New York Light Opera production directed by William Ball. The same company produced a 1964 revival with Warfield and Veronica Tyler as the title couple with support from Robert Guillaume (Sportin' Life), Marie Young (Clara), William Dilliard (Crown), Gwendolyn Walters (Serena), and Carol Brice (Maria). The 1976 Houston Grand Opera production, directed by JACK O'BRIEN, was the first time the opera was seen in New York in its entirety, including musical passages and recitatives cut from the original before opening. Critical and popular cheers greeted the powerful production and the alternating cast of singers, and the revival ran 122 performances. The same production, with cast changes, returned to New York in 1982 and performed at the mammoth Radio City

Music Hall for forty-five performances. Most recently, the New York City Opera offered a production directed by Tazwell Thompson as part of its 2000 season's repertory. Alvy Powell and Richard Hobson alternated as Porgy, and Bess was played by Marquita Lister and Kishna Davis. Other opera companies have included the piece in their repertory but a nonopera revival is rare.

Porgy and Bess (Columbia 1959) was a disappointment to opera lovers because much of the score had to be cut to fit into a standard length movie, yet the singing is glorious because the two principals were dubbed by opera singers Robert McFerrin and Adele Addison. That left Sidney Poitier and DOROTHY DANDRIDGE to do the acting and they did not disappoint. OTTO PREMINGER directed with a heavy hand but much of the film is very effective, from the recreation of Catfish Row to the acting of the minor characters. N. Richard Nash wrote the screenplay, which was an efficient condensation of the original, and HERMES PAN did the little choreography needed. The SAMUEL GOLDWYN production (it was his last film) was disfavored by the critics and did not do the business it might have. Over the years the Gershwin estate has kept viewings to a minimum, dissatisfied with the way the opera was edited for the screen. However, the movie is an always competent, sometimes thrilling, screen version of an opera, one of the most difficult of all musical films to make.

PORTER, COLE (1891–1964). Stage, film, and television composer and lyricist. The celebrated American songwriter whose songs and lifestyle represented the sophisticated high life for over forty years, he was equally successful in Hollywood as on Broadway and scored classic musicals in both media. Porter was born into a wealthy family in Peru, Indiana, and was educated at Yale where his football fight songs and campus productions were legendary. He studied law at Harvard but he had known since he was a child that music would be his life. He wrote both music and lyrics throughout his career and there was always something distinctive about a Cole Porter song. His lyrics have a breezy elegance, a farcical wit, and sometimes a romantic yearning that is almost painful. Porter's music tended toward the exotic and the Latin sound, often similar in tempo but variable in mood and melody. Some of his songs were interpolated into Broadway musicals in the 1910s and his first full score for *See America First* (1916) did not get much attention. It was the song "Let's Do It (Let's Fall in Love)" in *Paris* (1928) that was first noticed by the public and with *FIFTY MILLION FRENCHMEN* (1929) Porter was established on Broadway. Most of his musicals were hits and most introduced at least one song standard. During the Depression years he offered *THE NEW YORKERS* (1930), *GAY DIVORCE* (1932), *ANYTHING GOES* (1934), *JUBILEE* (1935), *RED, HOT AND BLUE!* (1936), *You Never Know* (1938), *LEAVE IT TO ME!* (1938), and *DuBARRY WAS A LADY* (1939). Porter's Broadway shows during the war years were less accomplished but were usually saved by bright stars and some memorable songs, as with *PANAMA HATTIE* (1940), *LET'S FACE IT!* (1941), *SOMETHING FOR THE BOYS* (1943), *MEXICAN HAYRIDE* (1944), *Seven Lively Arts* (1944), and *Around the World in 80 Days* (1946). He got his best libretto with *KISS ME, KATE* (1948) and turned out what is

considered his greatest score. He managed to keep writing remarkable songs in the 1950s with the shows *OUT OF THIS WORLD* (1950), *CAN-CAN* (1953), and *SILK STOCKINGS* (1955). Porter also scored the London musicals *Wake Up and Dream* (1929) and *Nymph Errant* (1933). Most of Porter's stage musicals were filmed, although often the scores were abridged and songs by others were sometimes added. However, he wrote some sparkling original scores for Hollywood as well and again many of his song standards were introduced on screen. Porter's movie scores are *The Battle of Paris* (1929), *BORN TO DANCE* (1936), *ROSALIE* (1937), *BROADWAY MELODY OF 1940*, *YOU'LL NEVER GET RICH* (1941), *THE PIRATE* (1948), *HIGH SOCIETY* (1956), and *LES GIRLS* (1957). His songs were used in the musical biographies *NIGHT AND DAY* (1946) and *DE-LOVELY* (2004), as well as the TV musical *Cinderella '53* (1953) and the misconceived screen musical *At Long Last Love* (1975). At the end of his career Porter scored the TV musical *ALADDIN* (1958). Autobiography: *The Cole Porter Story, As Told to Richard G. Hubler* (1965); biographies: *Cole Porter*, William McBrien (2000); *Cole Porter: A Biography*, Charles Schwartz (1988); *Cole Porter: The Life That Late He Led*, George Eells (1967).

POTTER, H[enry] **C**[odman] (1904–1977). Stage and film director. A versatile Broadway and Hollywood director who found success with everything from screwball musical comedy to historical dramas, he helmed five movie musicals. Potter was born in New York City and educated at Yale University and then attended the famous 47 Workshop at Harvard University. He began his career in stage management in stock companies in 1928 and one year later was directing on Broadway. Among his hit plays were *Kind Lady* (1935) *A Bell for Adano* (1944), *Anne of the Thousand Days* (1948), and *Sabrina Fair* (1953). Potter's film career started in 1935 and he would direct a variety of movies over the next twenty years. His screen musicals were *Romance in the Dark* (1938), *THE STORY OF VERNON AND IRENE CASTLE* (1939), *Second Chorus* (1940), *HELLZAPOPPIN'* (1941), and *Three for the Show* (1955).

POWELL, DICK [born Richard Ewing Powell] (1904–1963). Film and television performer, director, and producer. The boyish leading man of 1930s musicals and a dramatic actor in 1940s melodramas, he had a long and varied career in show business but he is best remembered in a series of WARNER BROTHERS musicals, usually paired with RUBY KEELER. Powell was born in Mountain View, Arkansas, and began his career as a band vocalist. He made his screen debut in the musical *Blessed Event* (1932) and the next year rose to stardom as the singing–dancing Billy Lawlor in *42ND STREET* (1933). Powell crooned through many backstage musicals, often playing an eager songwriter-turned-singer and several times named Dick. His 1930s musical credits include *GOLD DIGGERS OF 1933*, *FOOTLIGHT PARADE* (1933), *DAMES* (1934), *WONDER BAR* (1934), *Twenty Million Sweethearts* (1934), *Happiness Ahead* (1934), *Flirtation Walk* (1934), *GOLD DIGGERS OF 1935*, *Broadway Gondolier* (1935), *Shipmates Forever* (1935), *THANKS A MILLION* (1935), *Colleen* (1936), *Stage Struck* (1936), *GOLD DIGGERS OF 1937* (1936), *ON THE AVENUE* (1937), *THE SINGING MARINE* (1937), *Varsity Show* (1937), *HOLLYWOOD HOTEL* (1937), *Cowboy From Brooklyn* (1938), *Going Places* (1938), and *Naughty But Nice* (1939). Although he wearied of playing the same part over and over, audiences wanted more so even as he turned to dramatic roles in the 1940s, he still was seen in such musicals as *In the Navy* (1941), *STAR-SPANGLED RHYTHM* (1942), *HAPPY GO LUCKY* (1943), *True to Life* (1943), *Riding High* (1943), and *Meet the People* (1944). By the end of the decade Powell was accepted in detective roles and by the 1950s he eased out of acting altogether and produced and directed television series, making an appearance on occasion up into the 1960s, as with his own television show in 1961–1962. He also produced and directed some feature films, including the musical *You Can't Run Away From It* (1956). Powell was married to JOAN BLONDELL and then JUNE ALLYSON. Biography: *The Dick Powell Story*, Tony Thomas (1992).

POWELL, ELEANOR [Torrey] (1912–1982) Film and stage performer. The undisputed Hollywood queen of tap dancing, the tall, leggy dancer displayed her machine-like tapping on Broadway but didn't become famous until she strutted her stuff on the screen. Born and educated in Springfield, Massachusetts, Powell started dancing professionally at the age of eleven and by the time she was seventeen she was tapping away in the Broadway revue *The Optimists* (1928). Her talent for making tapping look easy and sexy allowed her to shine in revues, such as *Hot-Cha!* (1932), *George White's Music Hall Varieties* (1932), and *AT HOME ABROAD* (1935), and in book musicals such as *FOLLOW THRU* (1929), and *FINE*

AND DANDY (1930). Yet she never quite became a Broadway star so Powell went to Hollywood in 1935 where she found fame from her performances in a series of musicals, most memorably *BROADWAY MELODY OF 1936* (1935), *BORN TO DANCE* (1936), *BROADWAY MELODY OF 1938* (1937), *ROSALIE* (1937), and *BROADWAY MELODY OF 1940* and *LADY, BE GOOD* (1941). She continued to dance on screen until 1944, featured in *GEORGE WHITE'S SCANDALS* (1935), *Honolulu* (1939), *Ship Ahoy* (1942), *I Dood It* (1943), *Thousands Cheer* (1943), and *Sensations* (1944), and then retired only to make a guest appearance in *Duchess of Idaho* (1950). Powell continued to dance in nightclubs and for charity benefits long after her film career ended. She was married for a time to movie actor Glenn Ford (1916–2006).

POWELL, JANE [born Suzanne Lorraine Burce] (1929–). Film, television, and stage performer. The chipper, wholesome blonde with an operatic soprano singing voice, she became a favorite in Hollywood musicals when she was only a teenager. Powell was born in Portland, Oregon, and sang on the radio as a child. She was fifteen years old when she made her screen debut in 1944, playing herself in *Song of the Open Road*. Powell was soon given better roles, usually as a vivacious, optimistic teen who fixes up everybody's problems in musicals such as *Delightfully Dangerous* (1945), *Holiday in Mexico* (1946), *Three Darling Daughters* (1948), *Luxury Liner* (1948), *A DATE WITH JUDY* (1948), and *Nancy Goes to Rio* (1950). She got to mature into a leading lady with *Two Weeks With Love* (1950), *ROYAL WEDDING* (1951), *Rich, Young and Pretty* (1951), *Small Town Girl* (1953), *Three Sailors and a Girl* (1953), *Athena* (1954), *SEVEN BRIDES FOR SEVEN BROTHERS* (1954), *HIT THE DECK* (1955), and *The Girl Most Likely* (1957). Powell did a specialty spot in *DEEP IN MY HEART* (1954) and starred in the TV musicals *RUGGLES OF RED GAP* (1957), *MEET ME IN ST. LOUIS* (1959), *Hooray for Love* (1960), and *FEATHERTOP* (1961). Powell made few films after 1958, concentrating on television and the stage. She did tours and summer stock productions of *MY FAIR LADY*, *OKLAHOMA!*, *THE SOUND OF MUSIC*, *CAROUSEL*, *I DO! I DO!*, and *SOUTH PACIFIC* in the 1960s and 1970s and replaced DEBBIE REYNOLDS on Broadway in *IRENE* in 1974. Powell is married to former child star Dickie Moore (1925–). Autobiography: *The Girl Next Door and How She Grew* (1988).

POWELL, WILLIAM [Horatio] (1892–1984). Film performer. One of Hollywood's most debonair, gentlemanly, and pliable stars, the nonsinging actor was cast in seven musicals, playing FLORENZ ZIEGFELD in two of them. Powell was born in Pittsburgh, the son of an accountant, and attended the University of Kansas for a time before going to New York to study at the American Academy of Dramatic Arts. He was on the Broadway stage by 1912 and acted in a handful of plays without getting much recognition so he went to Hollywood in 1922 where he was cast as suave villains in melodramas. With the advent of sound he started playing sophisticated, well-dressed millionaires and detectives and got to combine both in the popular *Thin Man* series with MYRNA LOY. Powell gracefully aged into a character actor and late in his career returned to Broadway in comedies. His musical credits are *Pointed Heels* (1929), *PARAMOUNT ON PARADE* (1930), *Fashions of 1934*, *Reckless* (1935), *THE GREAT ZIEGFELD* (1936), *ZIEGFELD FOLLIES* (1946), and *Dancing in the Dark* (1949). Powell was married briefly to actress Carole Lombard (1908–1942). Biographies: *William Powell: The Life and Films*, Roger Bryant (2006); *Gentleman: The William Powell Story*, Charles Francisco (1985).

POWER, TYRONE [Edmund, Jr.] (1913–1958). Film and stage performer. A popular matinee idol in various genres of film, the handsome nonsinging actor shone in leading roles in a handful of movie musicals. Power was born in Cincinnati to a famous acting family who had been on the American stage since the 1820s and began on the stage in bit parts in his father's productions of the classics. He got experience in stock and then acted on Broadway in modern and classical plays in the 1930s. Power went to Hollywood in 1937 and was quickly established as a dashing leading man in modern melodramas, costume dramas, mysteries, and such musicals as *Thin Ice* (1937), *IN OLD CHICAGO* (1938), *ALEXANDER'S RAGTIME BAND* (1938), *ROSE OF WASHINGTON SQUARE* (1939), *SECOND FIDDLE* (1939), and *The Eddy Duchin Story* (1956). Power's popularity waned in the 1950s so he returned to the stage, playing on Broadway in a few dramas, and made fewer films. He died of a heart attack while in Spain filming *Solomon and Sheba* (1959). Biographies: *Tyrone Power: The Last Idol*, Fred Lawrence Guiles (1990); *The Secret Life of Tyrone Power*, Hector Arce (1979).

◼ PREACHER'S WIFE, THE (Touchstone/Goldwyn 1996). A holiday musical without Santa or many Christmas carols but a lot of gospel singing, this warmhearted melodrama–

fantasy evoked the holiday spirit all the same. The story was a familiar one, having been a novel by Robert Nathan called *The Bishop's Wife* and filmed as a nonmusical in 1947. In the Nat Maudlin and Allan Scott screenplay, the African American preacher Rev. Henry Biggs (Courtney B. Vance) is so busy keeping his inner city church and parishioners going that he neglects his wife Julia (Whitney Houston) and their young son Jeremiah (Justin Pierre Edmund). The angel Dudley (Denzel Washington) comes down from heaven to help and finds that he is attracted to Julia, a former nightclub singer who now is a soloist in the church choir. Dudley overcomes his rekindled interest in worldly things and helps the reverend to appreciate his family in time for Christmas. The expert supporting cast included GREGORY HINES, Jennifer Lewis, Loretta Devine, and Lionel Richie, and the picture was directed with tenderness by Penny Marshall. The songs, by various artists, were mostly gospel numbers sung in the church but the standout hit was "I Believe in You and Me" (by David Wolfert and Sandy Linzer), sung by Julia when she and her husband visit a nightclub.

PREISSER, JUNE (1921–1984). Film and stage performer. A twinkling blonde with a slightly naughty air about her, she tried to coax MICKEY ROONEY away from JUDY GARLAND in two "let's put on a show" musicals. Preisser was born in New Orleans and demonstrated a bizarre talent for agile dancing and body contortion at an early age. She went into vaudeville with her sister Cherry, the two kids entertaining audiences in America and in Europe with their gymnastic skills. FLORENZ ZIEGFELD caught the sisters' act and put them in the 1934 and 1935 editions of his *ZIEGFELD FOLLIES*. Hollywood wasn't interested in Cherry but the button-nosed June was signed to play the "other woman" in *BABES IN ARMS* (1939) and *STRIKE UP THE BAND* (1940). Preisser was also featured with Rooney in some of the *Andy Hardy* nonmusical films. Her other screen musical credits include *Dancing Co-ed* (1939), *Sweater Girl* (1942), *Babes on Swing Street* (1944), *Let's Go Steady* (1945), *Junior Prom* (1946), *Freddie Steps Out* (1946), *Sarge Goes to College* (1947), *Two Blondes and a Redhead* (1947), and *Campus Sleuth* (1948). She was also featured in the Broadway revue *Count Me In* (1942). When Preisser grew out of adolescence, the public lost interest. After starring in *ANNIE GET YOUR GUN* on stage in Los Angeles, she retired.

PREMINGER, OTTO (1905–1986). Stage and film actor, director, and producer. A severe

German character actor, he later became one of Hollywood's most successful directors and helmed five musicals. Born in Vienna, Austria, the son of a high-level politician, Preminger studied law at the University of Vienna before turning to the theatre and working as an actor and assistant for Max Reinhardt. He directed his first film in Germany in 1931 and then came to America in 1935 to restage the drama *Libel* on Broadway and stayed, directing plays and then learning more about movies in California. Hollywood cast him as Teutonic heavies in several films, and then he became just as famous as a director for *Laura* (1944), which he also produced. Preminger's other screen hits include *The Moon Is Blue* (1953), *The Man With the Golden Arm* (1955), *Saint Joan* (1957), *Anatomy of a Murder* (1959), and *Advise and Consent* (1962). Perhaps his two most challenging movies were the ethnic musicals *CARMEN JONES* (1954) and *PORGY AND BESS* (1959). Preminger's other screen musicals were *Under Your Spell* (1936), *CENTENNIAL SUMMER* (1946), and *That Lady in Ermine* (1948). He continued to act, direct, and produce into the 1980s. Autobiography: *Preminger* (1978).

🎬 **PRESENT ARMS** (Mansfield Theatre 1928). A nautical musical comedy scored by RICHARD RODGERS (music) and LORENZ HART (lyrics), the show shared its setting, characters, writer, and even an actor from the recent success *HIT THE DECK!* (1927) but audiences didn't mind and let it run a profitable 155 performances. The uncouth marine Chick Evans, who is stationed at the naval base at Pearl Harbor, loves the aristocratic British Lady Delphine but doesn't know how to go about wooing her, especially since she is being courted by the wealthy German, Ludwig Von Richter. So Chick impersonates a Captain and tries to hide his gruff manners. His deception is soon discovered and all seems lost until he valiantly rescues the passengers from a yachting accident. Chick is promoted to a real Captain and he wins the

hand of Delphine. HERBERT FIELDS, who had written the libretto for *Hit the Deck!*, penned this script as well, and CHARLES KING, who had played the rough and tough sailor in that show, played a similarly unsophisticated gob again. The plot was serviceable, the performers were engaging, and the songs enjoyable. The only number to enjoy wide popularity was "You Took Advantage of Me," sung not by the principals but by the saucy English tourist Edna and Sergeant Atwell, played by BUSBY BERKELEY, who also choreographed the musical. Also in the score were "A Kiss for Cinderella," "Blue Ocean Blues," "Do I Hear You (Saying "I Love")?," "Hawaii," and "Tell It to the Marines." ALEXANDER LEFTWICH directed the LEW FIELDS production; both had served in the same capacities for *Hit the Deck!*

🎬 **Leathernecking** (RKO 1930) was the new title given to the film version of *Present Arms* and, despite its title change, the movie adhered to the original libretto rather closely. Yet all but two of the Rodgers and Hart songs were dropped and others ("All My Life," "Shake It Off With a Smile," and "Careless Kisses") by HARRY AKST, Benny Davis, SIDNEY CLARE, and OSCAR LEVANT were substituted. Edward Cline directed the Louis Sarecky production and Pearl Eaton did the choreography. It is a charming, if not very memorable, film but no longer a Rodgers and Hart musical. (In Great Britain the movie was released as *Present Arms* since few Brits knew that a "leatherneck" was slang for a Marine.)

PRESLEY, ELVIS [Aron] (1935–1977). Film and television performer. A legendary rock and roll icon who remains as popular today, if not more so, than when he was alive, the throaty singer with the gyrating hips made thirty-three movie musicals tailored to his image and his audience. Presley was born in Tupelo, Mississippi, and spent his teen years in Memphis, Tennessee, where he started singing and signed with a local record company. In 1955 RCA Records discovered him and soon he was changing the

---

Casts for *Present Arms* and *Leathernecking*

Character	Present Arms (1927)	Leathernecking (1930)
Chick Evans/Frank	CHARLES KING	Ken Murray
Lady Delphine	Flora Le Breton	IRENE DUNNE
Ludwig Von Richter	Anthony Knilling	Wilhelm von Brincken
Edna Stevens	Joyce Barbour	Lilyan Tashman
Sergeant Atwell/Evans	BUSBY BERKELEY	EDDIE FOY, JR.
Hortense	Gaile Beverley	Louise Fazenda

face of American pop music. Hollywood did not hesitate to put Presley on screen where he made his film debut in *LOVE ME TENDER* (1956). What followed was a series of vehicles that rarely gave the singer a chance to act or his fans a chance to see their idol as anything more than a star. However, in his more challenging films, such as *JAILHOUSE ROCK* (1957) and *KING CREOLE* (1958), it is clear that Presley was capable of more than the manufactured plots and stereotypic parts he was given. Among his musical credits are *Loving You* (1957), *GI Blues* (1960), *BLUE HAWAII* (1961), *Kid Galahad* (1962), *Fun in Alcapulco* (1963), *VIVA LAS VEGAS* (1964), *Roustabout* (1964), *Girl Happy* (1965), *Frankie and Johnny* (1966), *Spinout* (1966), *Easy Come Easy Go* (1967), *Clambake* (1968), *Live a Little Love a Little* (1968), *The Trouble With Girls* (1970), and *Change of Habit* (1970). Presley left films and concentrated on concerts, recordings, television specials, and nightclubs until his premature death at the age of forty-two. Among the many film and television biomusicals about the popular singer are *Elvis* (1979), *This Is Elvis* (1981), *Elvis* (1990), and *Elvis* (2005). Biographies: *Elvis Presley: The Man, the Life, the Legend*, Pamela Clarke Keogh (2004); *Inner Elvis: A Psychological Biography of Elvis Presley*, Peter O. Whitmer (1997).

PRESNELL, [George] **HARVE**[y] (1933–). Film, television, and stage performer. A muscular, virile baritone who found humor and warmth in his macho heroes, he arrived in Hollywood too late to find the kinds of musical parts (and movie musicals) that were ideal for him. Presnell was born in Modesto, California, and trained for an opera career while doing concerts in southern California. Songwriter MEREDITH WILLSON heard him sing at the Hollywood Bowl and signed him to play Johnny "Leadville" Brown in his Broadway musical *THE UNSINKABLE MOLLY BROWN* (1960), winning applause and the chance to reprise his performance in the 1964 screen version. Presnell played the dude ranch owner Danny Churchill in the movie musical *When the Boys Meet the Girls* (1965) and the gold prospector Rotten Luck Willie in *PAINT YOUR WAGON* (1969), singing "They Call the Wind Maria." With so few movie musical being made by the 1970s, Presnell turned to television where he appeared in dozens of series, soap operas, and specials, such as the TV musical *The Great Man's Whiskers* (1973). He also returned to the stage, touring in productions of *ANNIE GET YOUR GUN, ON A CLEAR DAY YOU CAN SEE FOREVER*, and other

musicals. He played Rhett Butler in the musical stage version of *Gone With the Wind* (1972) in London. Presnell was back on Broadway as a replacement for Daddy Warbucks in *ANNIE* in 1978 and also toured in the part. Off Broadway he played the same character in the sequel *Annie Warbucks* (1993). He continues to act in nonmusical films and on television.

PRESTON,   ROBERT [born Robert Preston Meservey] (1918–1987). Stage and film performer. A solid leading man with rough masculine features and a commanding voice, he appeared in plays and movies for twenty-five years before he became one of Broadway's top song and dance stars. Preston was born in Newton Highlands, Massachusetts, and was raised in California where he trained at the Pasadena Playhouse school. He began making films in 1938 but was usually featured in B movies or in supporting roles in first-class pictures. After a dozen years of this, Preston's frustration prompted him to try Broadway where he gave some notable performances in

Robert Preston. The forty-year-old veteran of stage and screen, whose career seemed to be going nowhere, found a new career in musical comedy with Professor Harold Hill in *The Music Man*, a role he originated on Broadway in 1957 and on screen in 1962. Here he is with Shirley Jones in the finale of the movie version. (Photofest)

comedies in the 1950s. Although he had never appeared in a musical before, Preston was cast as con man Harold Hill in THE MUSIC MAN (1957) after many other stars turned it down and it launched his new career on Broadway. The screen version in 1962 finally made him a bona fide movie star as well. Preston's other stage musical roles were the wily diplomat Benjamin Franklin in *Ben Franklin in Paris* (1964), the perennial husband Michael in *I Do! I Do!* (1966), and the silent movie pioneer Mack Sennett in MACK & MABEL (1974). He also shone in nonmusicals as diverse as *The Lion in Winter* (1966) and *Sly Fox* (1977). Early in his Hollywood career, Preston had appeared in nonsinging roles in screen musicals such as *Moon Over Burma* (1940), *Variety Girl* (1947), and *Big City* (1962). He returned to the musical screen as plantation owner Beauregard Burnside in MAME (1974) and as the gay entrepreneur Toddy in VICTOR/VICTORIA (1982).

PREVIN, ANDRÉ [born Andreas Ludwig Priwin] (1929–). Film and stage composer, conductor, and musical director. One of the few American composers to find recognition in both classical and popular music, the world-renowned conductor of classical music has contributed to musicals on and off over the decades. Previn was born in Berlin, Germany, of Russian Jewish ancestry and quickly proved to be a prodigy at the piano, entering Berlin's High School of Music when he was six years old. His family fled Germany and settled in France where Previn attended the Paris Conservatoire until the fall of France and the family went to California where a relative worked in the music department at UNIVERSAL STUDIOS. Previn was still in high school when he started doing musical arrangements for MGM musicals. He later conducted the orchestras for such musicals as THREE LITTLE WORDS (1950), *Small Town Girl* (1953), KISS ME, KATE (1953), GIVE A GIRL A BREAK (1953), IT'S ALWAYS FAIR WEATHER (1955), SILK STOCKINGS (1957), GIGI (1958), PORGY AND BESS (1959), BELLS ARE RINGING (1960), MY FAIR LADY (1964), and JESUS CHRIST SUPERSTAR (1973). Previn composed the musical soundtracks for forty nonmusicals and wrote songs for the musicals *It's Always Fair Weather* (1955), *Pepe* (1960), and *PAINT YOUR WAGON* (1969), as well as music for one of the ballets in INVITATION TO THE DANCE (1956). On Broadway he collaborated with lyricist ALAN JAY LERNER on the Katharine Hepburn musical *Coco* (1969). Among his many wives are writer Dory Langdon Previn (1925–) and

actress Mia Farrow (1945–). Biography: *André Previn: A Biography*, Martin Bookspan, Ross Yockey (1981).

PRICE, GILBERT (1942–1991). Stage performer. A handsome, full-voiced African American singer–actor on Broadway, he was never in a long-run hit, yet always shone in supporting roles. The native New Yorker trained at the American Theatre Wing School and made his off Broadway debut in 1962. Three years later he was on Broadway stopping the show with his heartfelt rendition of "Feeling Good" in THE ROAR OF THE GREASEPAINT–THE SMELL OF THE CROWD (1965). Gilbert also shone as the wayward son Absalom in LOST IN THE STARS (1972), the never-aging servant Lud in *1600 PENNSYLVANIA AVENUE* (1976), and the dashing Mansa of Mali in TIMBUKTU! (1978). His other musical credits in New York include *Promenade* (1969), *Six* (1971), and *The Night That Made America Famous* (1975). Price appeared in concerts and on a few television programs before his premature death at the age of forty-nine.

PRICE, LONNY (1959–). Stage director and performer. An energetic actor-turned-director, he brings to the staging of musicals the same vitality he has shown in performing. Price was born in New York City and performed as a child in regional theatre. He was educated at the High School of the Performing Arts and at Juilliard before beginning his adult acting career Off Broadway in 1979. A few years later he was roundly praised for his electric performance as Charley in the musical MERRILY WE ROLL ALONG (1981), followed by appearances in RAGS (1986), *A Class Act* (2000), and others. Although he would return to acting during the subsequent decades, Price concentrated on directing, beginning in 1990 with an Off Broadway revival of THE ROTHSCHILDS. Most of his New York credits have been musicals, such as *JUNO* (1992), *A Class Act*, *Urban Cowboy* (2003), and *110 IN THE SHADE* (2007). As accomplished as his full-scale productions have been, Price is probably at his best in directing staged concerts of musicals, presenting such difficult pieces as SWEENEY TODD, CANDIDE, SUNDAY IN THE PARK WITH GEORGE, and PASSION with theatricality and spirit, using some production elements such as costumes and props, and turning the orchestra and chorus into the scenery for the piece.

PRINCE, FAITH (1957?–). Stage and television performer. The wide-eyed, demonstrative actress–singer with a powerful Broadway belt, she excels at playing not-so-dumb blondes (even though her hair is red). Prince was born in Augusta, Georgia, raised in Lynchburg, Virginia, and educated at the University of Cincinnati where she studied voice before performing in musicals in regional theatre. She made her New York debut in the Off Broadway revue *Scrambled Feet* (1980) and then was a replacement for Audrey in *LITTLE SHOP OF HORRORS* (1983). After performing in the revues *Living Color* (1986), *Groucho: A Life in Revue* (1986), and *Urban Blight* (1988), Prince was featured in various showy roles in *JEROME ROBBINS' BROADWAY* (1989) and then played the frustrated wife Trina in *Falsettoland* (1990) and the murder victim Lorraine in *Nick and Nora* (1991). Wide recognition finally came with her funny, touching performance as Miss Adelaide in the 1992 revival of *GUYS AND DOLLS*. Her subsequent musicals were as a replacement for Anna in *THE KING AND I* (1997), the notorious femme fatale Belle in *LITTLE ME* (1998), a replacement for the Dubliner Gretta Conroy in *JAMES JOYCE'S THE DEAD* (2000), the optimistic Ella Peterson in *BELLS ARE RINGING* (2001), and the repressed spinster Lily Byrne in *A Man of No Importance* (2002). Prince has appeared in a few films and many televisions series, including a regular stint on *Huff*.

PRINCE OF EGYPT, THE (DreamWorks 1998). Based on the Bible and Cecil B. De Mille, this animated musical was very serious minded and used animation the way the older De Mille movies used spectacle. The screenplay by Philip LaZebnik and Nicholas Myer follows the plot of De Mille's live-action epic *The Ten Commandments* (1956) almost scene by scene. The Jewish baby Moses is set adrift in a basket on the Nile, is rescued by the pharaoh's family, and is raised as the adopted brother of Rameses (voice of Ralph Fiennes). The adult Moses (Val Kilmer) learns of his Jewish heritage, falls in love and weds the shepherd girl Tzipporah (Michele Pfeiffer), and then leads his people out of Egypt after the plagues have crippled Rameses's kingdom and destroyed his son. The crossing of the Red Sea, the destruction of the Egyptian army, and Moses receiving the Ten Commandments on tablets all followed in the expected way. This retelling was distinguished by the animation, which, while not on a par with the DISNEY studios, was still impressive, particularly the background art. The supporting cast was also noteworthy, with voices provided by Sandra Bullock, Jeff

Goldblum, Danny Glover, Patrick Stewart, Helen Mirren, and, for the much-needed comic relief, Steve Martin and MARTIN SHORT. STEPHEN SCHWARTZ wrote the songs, with the most popular one being "When You Believe," which had a hit recording by Whitney Houston and Mariah Carey. Other songs included "All I Ever Wanted," "Playing With the Big Boys," and "Through Heaven's Eyes," and there was a stirring musical background score by Hans Zimmer.

PRINCE, HAROLD [born Harold Smith Price] (1928–). Stage director, producer. The most awarded and, arguably, the most consistently adventurous of all director–producers, he has presented more landmark and recording-breaking musicals than any other individual in the American theatre. Prince was born in New York City, the stepson of a stockbroker, and educated at the University of Pennsylvania where he was active in campus dramatics. Prince began his career as a stage manager for GEORGE ABBOTT and was influenced greatly by the veteran director–producer. After serving in the army, Prince teamed up with Frederick Brisson and Robert E. Griffith in 1954 and produced *THE PAJAMA GAME*, the first of a long line of musical hits over the next decade: *DAMN YANKEES* (1955), *NEW GIRL IN TOWN* (1957), *WEST SIDE STORY* (1957), *FIORELLO!* (1959), *A FUNNY THING HAPPENED ON THE WAY TO THE FORUM* (1962), *FIDDLER ON THE ROOF* (1964), and others. Prince turned to directing in 1962 when he was brought in as a replacement to stage the musical *A Family Affair*, but his reputation grew with his direction of *SHE LOVES ME* (1963), *CABARET* (1966), *ZORBÁ* (1968), and other shows in the 1960s that he produced as well. It was with the STEPHEN SONDHEIM musical *COMPANY* in 1970 that Prince's full powers were unleashed, and the collaborations between the two artists over the next decade were perhaps the most ambitious and innovative series of musicals since the Rodgers and Hammerstein revolution. Challenging works such as *FOLLIES* (1971), *A LITTLE NIGHT MUSIC* (1973), *PACIFIC OVERTURES* (1976), *SWEENEY TODD* (1979), and *MERRILY WE ROLL ALONG* (1981) were only occasionally box office hits, but they represented the American musical at its most daunting. Prince often found more commercial success directing musicals by others, in particular *EVITA* (1979) and *PHANTOM OF THE OPERA* (1988), yet his talent for provocative staging and exciting directorial ideas can be found in these somewhat "safer" productions as well. Although he was most interested in developing new work, Prince shone with admirable revivals of CANDIDE (1974 and 1997) and SHOW BOAT (1994), and he brought his special gifts to nonmusicals on occasion. By the 1990s, Prince was one of the senior directors working on Broadway, yet his projects, such as THE KISS OF THE SPIDER WOMAN (1993), The Petrified Prince (1994), and PARADE (1998), were still the work of a youthful, experimental artist. Among Prince's other musical directing credits are Baker Street (1965), IT'S A BIRD, IT'S A PLANE, IT'S SUPERMAN (1966), ON THE TWENTIETH CENTURY (1978), A Doll's Life (1982), Grind (1985), Roza (1987), and LoveMusik (2007). The winner of many awards, he chooses only to direct works with subjects that intrigue him intellectually and he has little interest in repeating past projects or pursuing something that does not have something new to say or a fresh way to say it. Few artists have contributed so much to the American theatre over such a long period of time. Autobiography: Contradictions: Notes on 26 Years in the Theatre (1974); biographies: Harold Prince and the American Musical, Foster Hirsch (1989); Harold Prince: From "Pajama Game" to "Phantom of the Opera," Carol Ilson (1989).

PRINCESS THEATRE MUSICALS. Stage series. A short-lived (1915–1919) but extremely influential series of intimate musical comedies, they were very popular in their day and foreshadowed the shape of Broadway shows of the future. The musicals were presented in Manhattan's Princess Theatre, a 299-seat venue that was considered too small for traditional stage shows. Literary agent Elisabeth Marbury and theatre owner F. Ray Comstock had an idea for a series that would feature small, contemporary musicals by new composers, performed by a resident company of actors. It was planned to be the world's first musical repertory theatre, but the shows that followed were not done in repertory and the cast differed from musical to musical. However, the series was successful as an alternative to the large-scale operettas and lavish musical revues that dominated Broadway at the time. Because of the small stage, the shows could not have large chorus lines or opulent scenery, and the size of the orchestra pit limited the number of musicians to eleven players. The first entry in the series was Nobody Home (1915) with music by JEROME KERN, libretto by GUY BOLTON, and lyrics by Schuyler Greene. Aside from its

small scale, the musical comedy about young lovers and mistaken identity was not much different from the standard fare of the day. But the second entry, the same team's VERY GOOD EDDIE (1915), was a major hit and a literate, witty musical comedy of manners that somewhat integrated the songs into the plot. Less successful was Go to It (1916) with a score by John Golden and Anne Caldwell. P. G. WODEHOUSE joined Kern and Bolton for the next Princess musical, OH, BOY! (1917), and the illustrious team of Bolton, Wodehouse, and Kern was born. The series would reach its goal of expert modern musical comedy in the shows by this trio who blended story, character, and song together in a charming and surprisingly intelligent way. Although officially not part of the series because it played at another theatre, the team's LEAVE IT TO JANE (1917) had all the superior qualities of the Bolton–Wodehouse–Kern shows. Their OH, LADY! LADY! (1918) was another hit in the series, but it was the last at the Princess Theatre by the popular triumvirate. LOUIS HIRSCH took over the composing for Oh, My Dear! (1918) and, although it was mildly popular, Kern's music was greatly missed. The final Princess Theatre offering, Toot Sweet (1919), with a score by RICHARD A. WHITING and Ray Egan, was an unsuccessful revue that departed from the series's initial intention. The bold experiment ended after only seven shows in four years but the Princess musicals were fondly remembered and inspired the next generation of songwriters such as RICHARD RODGERS, LORENZ HART, COLE PORTER, and others who later acknowledged the series as the reason they first pursued musical theatre.

PRINZ, LE ROY (1895–1983). Film choreographer. Hollywood's most prolific choreographer, he did the dances for some sixty screen musicals, mostly at PARAMOUNT and WARNER BROTHERS. Prinz was born in St. Joseph, Missouri, and served in the Foreign Legion and as an aviator before choreographing films for Max Reinhardt in Europe and for the Folies Bergere in Paris. He arrived in Hollywood just as sound came in and assisted with the dances in Innocents of Paris (1929). The next year he choreographed on his own, going on to do such musicals as Too Much Harmony (1933), BIG BROADCAST OF 1936 (1935), SHOW BOAT (1936), Waikiki Wedding (1937), HIGH, WIDE AND HANDSOME (1937), ROAD TO SINGAPORE (1940), TOO MANY GIRLS (1940), YANKEE DOODLE DANDY (1942), THIS IS THE ARMY (1943), THANK

YOUR LUCKY STARS (1943), *THE DESERT SONG* (1943), *RHAPSODY IN BLUE* (1945), *NIGHT AND DAY* (1946), *Look for the Silver Lining* (1949), *Tea for Two* (1950), *On Moonlight Bay* (1951), *I'll See You in My Dreams* (1951), *THE JAZZ SINGER* (1953), *Three Girls and a Sailor* (1953), *The Helen Morgan Story* (1957), and *SOUTH PACIFIC* (1958).

PRODUCERS, THE (St. James Theatre 2001). The first giant hit musical of the new century, the irreverent, farcical show was inspired silliness that looked back to the days of unpretentious musical fun.

Plot: Over-the-hill Broadway producer Max Bialystock plots with the nebbish accountant Leo Bloom to raise twice as much money needed to finance a big musical and, after it flops on Broadway, keep half without the investors expecting any profits. The odd twosome secure the rights for the tasteless musical *Springtime for Hitler* from Nazi sympathizer–author Franz Liebkind and then enlist the services of the flamboyantly tacky director Roger De Bris in order to guarantee failure. When the show becomes a politically incorrect smash hit, the two producers are eventually apprehended by the police and sentenced to prison where they continue their entrepreneurial ways behind bars and then, when released, back on Broadway.

MEL BROOKS and THOMAS MEEHAN wrote the hilarious libretto, taken from Brooks's popular 1968 movie, and Brooks also wrote the score, a clever (and sometimes touching) pastiche of old-time Broadway musical styles. While a few of the numbers were one-joke ditties, many others were full-fledged character songs, ballads, and choral pieces. NATHAN LANE and MATTHEW BRODERICK were roundly cheered for their winning performances, yet the entire cast was superior and director–choreographer SUSAN STROMAN handled the farcical material with conviction and panache. The musical was a smash from the start and remained one of the hottest tickets on Broadway for several years, eventually playing 2,502 performances.

The Producers (Universal 2005) came to the screen with most of the cast and creative staff from the Broadway hit, yet the movie was poorly reviewed and did not do well at the box office. Producer Mel Brooks and director–choreographer Susan Stroman consciously made the decision to film the movie in a studio with an artificial look reminiscent of the Hollywood musicals of the 1950s. Critics slammed the picture for its staginess and uncinematic look, wanting the show to be opened up for the camera. Much of what happens on screen is a replica of what happened on the Broadway stage, yet something was missing. The performers were all in top form and the material was the same, yet the excitement and spirit of the stage show did not

---

The Producers (stage) Musical Numbers

"Opening Night"
"The King of Broadway"
"We Can Do It"
"I Wanna Be a Producer"
"In Old Bavaria"
"Der Guten Tag Hop Clop"
"Keep It Gay"
"When You Got It, Flaunt It"
"Along Came Bialy"
"That Face"
"Haben Sie Gehoert Das Deutsche Band?"
"You Never Say 'Good Luck' on Opening Night"
"Springtime for Hitler"
"Where Did We Go Right?"
"Betrayed"
"'Til Him"
"Prisoners of Love"
"Goodbye"

Casts for *The Producers*

Character	2001 Broadway	2005 film
Max Bialystock	NATHAN LANE	Nathan Lane
Leo Bloom	MATTHEW BRODERICK	Matthew Broderick
Ulla	Cady Huffman	Uma Thurman
Roger DeBris	GARY BEACH	Gary Beach
Carmen Ghia	ROGER BART	Roger Bart
Franz Liebkind	Brad Oscar	Will Ferrell

The Producers. The Mel Brooks musical is distinct in that every character that pops up in the libretto is a comic gem and Brooks gave each a farcical song to express themselves. In this still from the 2005 film version, the Nazi playwright Franz Liebkind (center), played by Will Ferrell, sings "In Old Bavaria" to producers Leo Bloom (left) and Max Bialystock, played as they were on Broadway by Matthew Broderick and Nathan Lane. (Photofest)

always transfer to film. For moviegoers who had seen the musical in New York or on tour, the film was a pleasant and enjoyable recollection of the fun experience in the theatre. Those unfamiliar with the piece were left wondering what all the fuss had been about. As time passes the movie version of *The Producers* will probably be seen in a better light, appreciated as it is as a competent record of an outstanding musical comedy.

PRODUCERS' SHOWCASE. Television series. A high-quality anthology program on NBC-TV from 1954 to 1957, it was known for its expensive production values and big name stars, yet the fare was often quite highbrow. Under the supervision of Fred Coe, the program offered a dramatic or musical program once a month, some adapted from stage works or literature, and others that were original. The musical offerings were quite impressive and included such notable shows as the MARY MARTIN *PETER PAN* (1955, rebroadcast in 1956), *The King and Mrs. Candle* (1955) with CYRIL RITCHARD and Irene Manning, *OUR TOWN* (1955) with FRANK

SINATRA, *JACK AND THE BEANSTALK* (1956) with JOEL GREY, *The Lord Don't Play Favorites* (1956) with LOUIS ARMSTRONG, *BLOOMER GIRL* (1956) with BARBARA COOK, and *RUGGLES OF RED GAP* (1957) with Michael Redgrave.

PROMISES PROMISES (Shubert Theatre 1968). The only Broadway musical by the pop songwriting team of BURT BACHARACH (music) and HAL DAVID (lyrics), the contemporary-sounding show was refreshingly buoyant and one wishes that the songwriters had returned to the stage again. The affable young executive Chuck Baxter (JERRY ORBACH) rises in his company by loaning his bachelor apartment out to his married bosses looking for a trysting place. When he gets romantically involved with Fran Kubelik (Jill O'Hara), the ill-treated mistress of J. D. Sheldrake (Edward Winter), Chuck gains the courage to break off the corporate arrangements. Also in the cast were A. Larry Haines, Marian Mercer, Paul Reed, Vince O'Brien, and Norman Shelly. NEIL SIMON wrote the literate and funny libretto, based on the BILLY WILDER film *The Apartment* (1960), and the slick DAVID

MERRICK production was directed by ROBERT MOORE and choreographed by MICHAEL BENNETT. The very 1960s score included two runaway hits, "I'll Never Fall in Love Again" and the pulsating title number. Also expert were "She Likes Basketball," "Whoever You Are," "Knowing When to Leave," "Wanting Things," and "You'll Think of Someone." The press applauded the script, score, and cast, particularly Orbach, who became a Broadway star with this show, and the musical ran 1,968 performances. Unfortunately, *Promises, Promises* was such a product of its time that it is rarely revived today.

PULITZER PRIZE FOR DRAMA. The most prestigious of all drama awards, it has only been given to musicals on seven occasions. The awards were created in 1917 by Joseph Pulitzer to recognize various areas of writing, from history to poetry. The School of Journalism at Columbia University decides on the winners and can withhold an award if they feel no new work justifies recognition. For the award in drama, the prize is given to the playwright for the script, not for a production, and late in its history winners have included plays that had not yet been produced in New York. The first time the award was given to a musical was in 1932 for *OF THEE I SING* (1931). Because it is a literary award, the committee gave the award to librettists GEORGE S. KAUFMAN and MORRIE RYSKIND and lyricist IRA GERSHWIN but not to composer GEORGE GERSHWIN because music was not considered a literary art. This kind of narrow-minded thinking was later corrected. Like all awards, there have been some glaring errors throughout its history, major works have been overlooked, and questionable works honored. Most would agree that the seven musicals chosen were deserving but could name many others that should have been honored.

Pulitzer Prize–Winning Musicals	
1932	*OF THEE I SING*
1950	*SOUTH PACIFIC*
1960	*FIORELLO!*
1962	*HOW TO SUCCEED IN BUSINESS WITHOUT REALLY TRYING*
1976	*A CHORUS LINE*
1985	*SUNDAY IN THE PARK WITH GEORGE*
1996	*RENT*

PURCELL, CHARLES (1883–1962). Stage performer. A favorite leading man in operettas in the 1910s and 1920s, his boyish good looks and smooth baritone voice made him ideal for romantic roles. Purcell was born in Chattanooga, Tennessee, and studied voice in the States but made his professional singing debut in London in 1904. Four years later he was on Broadway where he usually played princes, military officers, and other dashing heroes. One of his early successes was the practical Lt. Bummerli in *THE CHOCOLATE SOLDIER* (1915), a role he would return to often on the road and in New York over the next twenty years. Purcell's two other notable roles were the working-class Richard Wayne in *MAYTIME* (1917) and the British Capt. John Copeland in *DEAREST ENEMY* (1925). His many other musical credits include *Pretty Mrs. Smith* (1914), *ZIEGFELD FOLLIES* (1915), *The Lady's Glove* (1917), *Monte Cristo, Jr.* (1919), *Poor Little Ritz Girl* (1920), *The Rose Girl* (1921), *Oh, Please* (1926), *Judy* (1927), *Shady Lady* (1933), and *Park Avenue* (1946). Purcell appeared in one film: as a singer in *The Yanks Are Coming* (1942).

PURLIE (Broadway Theatre 1970). A joyous musical comedy about racial strife, the rousing and often touching show utilized gospel and folk sounds within a conventional Broadway framework. The preacher Purlie Victorious Judson (Cleavon Little) returns to his southern homeland to revive an old church and help empower the African Americans who are under the thumb of the bigoted Ol' Cap'n Cotchipee (John Heffernan). Purlie tries to pass off the young Lutiebelle (MELBA MOORE) as the ancestor and rightful owner of the land the church sits on and, with the help of the Cap'n's liberal son Charley (C. David Colson), wins the day. Also in the spirited cast were Sherman Hemsley, LINDA HOPKINS, Novella Nelson, and Helen Martin. The funny libretto by Ossie Davis and PHILIP ROSE was based on Davis' comedy *Purlie Victorious* (1961), and the vibrant score was by GARY GELD (music) and PETER UDELL (lyrics). "I Got Love," "First Thing Monday Mornin'," "Walk Him Up the Stairs," "New Fangled Preacher Man," "Down Home," and the adoring title number were among the highlights of the show, which was produced and directed by Rose and choreographed by Louis Johnson. Enthusiastic reviews and strong word of mouth allowed the musical to run 688 performances and then it returned to New York in 1972 as part of a national tour featuring Robert Guillaume (Purlie) and Patti Jo (Lutiebelle).

PUTTIN' ON THE RITZ (United Artists 1930). The musical backstager marked the film debut of Broadway's beloved song and dance man HARRY RICHMAN, but the camera did not capture the performer's talents so he only made one other Hollywood film. The screenplay by James Gleason and William K. Wells told the too-familiar story of vaudevillian Harry Raymond (Richman) who makes it big on Broadway, lets success go to his head, falls from popularity, and then is saved by the love of faithful Dolores Fenton (Joan Bennett). It was worth sitting through to enjoy the songs, especially two new IRVING BERLIN gems, the flowing "With You" and the dapper title number, one of the songwriter's most sophisticated and breezy works. Richman himself contributed to the score, collaborating with various tunesmiths on the fatalistic "There's Danger in Your Eyes, Cherie" and the crooning serenade "Singing a Vagabond Song," which became Richman's theme song on radio and in nightclubs for years. Edward Sloman directed the cast, which also included James Gleason, Aileen Pringle, Lilyan Tashman, Richard Tucker, Eddie Kane, and Purnell Pratt. It is a primitive talkie in many ways, yet has an authenticity about its backstage milieu that cannot be found in later, better movies.

☐ **Queen of the Stardust Ballroom** (CBS-TV 1975). A low-key yet engaging musical about an autumnal romance, the story focused on Bronx widow Bea Asher (Maureen Stapleton) who feels that life has passed her by until she starts going to the local Stardust Ballroom where late-middle-age couples do the dances from the 1930s and 1940s. There she meets and eventually falls in love with the personable mailman Al Rossi (Charles Durning). Bea's conventional upbringing causes her to balk when she finds out that Al is married but she gets over it and the two of them dance in the annual contest and she is crowned queen of the ballroom. Flushed with excitement from her triumph and new outlook on life, Bea goes home and quietly dies in her sleep. Jerome Kass' teleplay was quietly engrossing, letting the characters slowly reveal themselves and the performances by Stapleton and Durning were masterful, even if their singing was realistically unprofessional. Billy Goldenberg (music) and Alan and Marilyn Bergman (lyrics) wrote the songs, which included "Call Me a Fool," "I Love to Dance," "Suddenly There's You," "Pennies and Dreams," and "Who Gave You Permission?" Marge Champion choreographed the ballroom dances, which were delightful without being sensational. Sam O'Steen directed the two-hour broadcast, which had little appeal for young viewers but was praised by the press and fondly embraced by the more mature public. ☙ Director–choreographer Michael Bennett was among the many who applauded the broadcast and his first project after *A Chorus Line* (1975) was to create a Broadway version of the musical. Retitled **Ballroom** (1978), it had an expanded libretto by Kass and more songs by the Bergmans and Goldenberg. Dorothy Loudon (Bea) and Vincent Gardenia (Al) headed the cast, which also included Marilyn Cooper, Danny Carroll, Lynn Roberts, Bernie Knee, Peter Alzado, Barbara Erwin, Dorothy Danner,

John Hallow, and Rudy Tronto. Critics felt the story did not play as well on stage as it had on the small screen (Bea did not die in the Broadway version) but there was applause for Bennett's smooth direction and engaging ballroom dances. The new songs included "Fifty Per Cent," "I Wish You a Waltz," "Somebody Did Alright for Herself," "One By One," "Dreams," and "Goodnight Is Not Goodbye." The show ran only 116 performances, quite a letdown for Bennett after *A Chorus Line*.

☐ **Quillow and the Giant** (NBC-TV 1963). A children's musical that used puppets and live actors together effectively, this sixty-minute *NBC Children's Theatre* broadcast was as charming as it was imaginative. The giant Hunder (Win Stracke) terrorizes the countryside, going from village to village demanding food and gifts as well as someone to tell him a good story. When Hunder comes to the village where the toymaker Quillow (George Latshaw) lives, the townspeople feed the giant as Quillow tells him a tale about a monster that suffers from an incurable disease and is only cured by bathing in the Yellow Sea. Hunder is convinced that he is dying and rushes off, relieving the land of his threatening presence. Later a traveler passing through town tells Quillow and the villagers that a giant was observed walking into the sea and disappearing beneath the water never to be seen again. No writer was credited but the plot came from the James Thurber story *The Great Quillow* and the songs were by Wade Barnes (music) and Ralph Blane (lyrics). "How Many Stars?," "I Hunder," "Nothing Is the Hardest Thing to Do," "Full Moon Street," "I Believe in Something," and "No Such Word as Can't" were simple, child-like numbers but worked well in the fairy tale musical. Strache was an enjoyable giant, towering over the puppet villagers around him, and David Barnhizer directed with just enough touch of whimsy.

Quine, Richard (1920–1989). Film and stage performer and director. A youthful, eager singer–dancer in 1940s screen musicals, he later became a busy Hollywood director. Quine was born in Detroit, the son of an actor, and was a child dancer in vaudeville and then an actor on radio before making his screen debut at the age of twelve. He appeared in juvenile roles in several films, including the musicals *Dames* (1934), *Babes on Broadway* (1941), *For Me and My Gal* (1942), and *Words and Music* (1948), before giving up acting and turning to directing in the late 1940s. Quine's musical credits as director include *On the Sunnyside of the Street* (1951), *Sound Off* (1952), *Rainbow 'Round My Shoulder* (1952), *All Ashore* (1953), *Cruisin' Down the River* (1953), *So This Is Paris* (1954), and *MY SISTER EILEEN* (1955). He also appeared in two Broadway shows, the musical *VERY WARM FOR MAY* (1939), and the comedy *My Sister Eileen* (1940), the basis for his 1955 musical film. Quine frequently contributed to the scripts for his films and continued directing movies and some television through the 1970s. When he was no longer offered quality projects, he committed suicide.

R

RADIO BROADCASTS OF MUSICALS. In addition to playing recordings of songs from Broadway musicals and singers performing a hit tune from a musical on a radio program, there were also shows that recreated, in abridged versions, stage musicals for the airwaves. These programs sometimes allowed stars to sing highlights from the scores they had performed on Broadway or in the movies. *Lux Radio Theatre* was one of the most notable of such programs. CHARLES WINNINGER sang numbers and did some dialogue sections from *SHOW BOAT* (1927), JUDY GARLAND performed highlights from *THE WIZARD OF OZ* (1939), and AL JOLSON recreated musical moments from the legendary talkie *THE JAZZ SINGER* (1927). *The Maxwell House Showboat* was a program that also used Winninger, this time as host Captain Henry who introduced numbers from musicals that were loosely tied together with a story line. *Command Performance* and *The Railroad Hour* were other programs, the latter hosted by GORDON MACRAE who sang short versions of musical and operetta scores with guest sopranos. Once in a while a musical was written especially for radio. ARTHUR SCHWARTZ (music) and HOWARD DIETZ (lyrics) wrote original songs for the weekly NBC-Radio program *The Gibson Family* in 1935 and CBS-Radio countered with their own series with RICHARD RODGERS (music) and LORENZ HART (lyrics) providing the songs, but after *Let's Have Fun* was broadcast in 1935, no other shows followed. A popular radio musical in 1945 entitled *Dick Tracy in B-Flat* did not have original songs but provided comic lyrics to familiar numbers, creating a parody score not unlike those performed in *FORBIDDEN BROADWAY*. BING CROSBY played Tracy in the two-hour broadcast and the star-studded supporting cast included BOB HOPE, DINAH SHORE, JUDY GARLAND, THE ANDREWS SISTERS, FRANK MORGAN, and FRANK SINATRA. It says something about the power of radio in those pretele-vision days that such a gathering of stars could be assembled for a single show.

RADIO MUSICALS. While Broadway only used radio as its subject in a few musicals, Hollywood seemed obsessed with the airwaves and film after film was made in the 1930s and 1940s about radio and radio stars. This is ironic when one considers that radio was Tinsel Town's biggest competition for audiences in those decades. Many popular movie stars began in and found fame on the radio, including RUDY VALLEE, BOB HOPE, FRANCES LANGFORD, JACK BENNY, JANE FRAZEE, BING CROSBY, EDGAR BERGMAN, KATE SMITH, KENNY BAKER, DINAH SHORE, RUSS COLUMBO, and GEORGE BURNS and GRACIE ALLEN. Also, all the popular Big Band directors found fame on the radio before being featured in the movies. When all the aforementioned stars were first put on screen, they usually played themselves or fictional radio stars, the thinking of the studios being that moviegoers would most easily accept them in films if the milieu was a familiar one. Some of these radio personalities became movie stars with no problem, whereas others struggled on the screen and eventually returned to the medium that proved more successful. The plots of PARAMOUNT's *THE BIG BROADCAST* (1932) and the other films in the series all revolved around a radio show, as did many of the SHIRLEY TEMPLE vehicles at 20TH CENTURY-FOX. Over the years other films dealing with broadcast entertainment included *Say It With Songs* (1929), *Hello Everybody* (1933), *Torch Singer* (1933), *Myrt and Marge* (1934), *Twenty Million Sweethearts* (1934), *Strictly Dynamite* (1934), *Gift of Gab* (1934), *Millions in the Air* (1935), *Sing, Baby, Sing* (1936), *With Love and Kisses* (1937), *WAKE UP AND LIVE* (1937), *Mr. Dodd Takes the Air* (1937), *Love and Hisses* (1937), *The Hit Parade* (1937), *Melody and Moonlight* (1940), *A Little Bit of Heaven* (1940), *LOVE THY NEIGHBOR* (1940), *The Great American Broadcast* (1941), *I'll Tell the World* (1945), *Ladies' Man* (1947), and *My Dream Is Yours* (1949). When television came in, radio gradually changed from a wide entertainment medium to a music medium and few movies were about this new venue. Perhaps the fondest and most nostalgic tribute to the old-style medium was Woody Allen's film *Radio Days* (1987).

RAFT, GEORGE [born George Ranft] (1895–1980). Film, stage, and television performer. A brooding, distrustful-looking actor who specialized in gangster roles on the screen, he was also an accomplished dancer and was featured in a dozen musicals. A native New Yorker who grew up in the infamous neighborhood of Hell's Kitchen, he left home at the age of thirteen and worked as a boxer and then a ballroom dancer, winning Charleston contests and getting work in nightclubs. Raft danced on Broadway in the musicals *The City Chap* (1925) and *Padlocks of 1927* and then made his screen debut as a gigolo in the musical *Queen of the Night Clubs* (1929). With his riveting performance in the melodrama *Scarface* (1932), Raft was typecast as heavies but he still got to dance in such musicals as *Palmy Days* (1931), *Bolero* (1934), *Rhumba* (1935), *Stolen Harmony* (1935), *EVERY NIGHT AT EIGHT* (1935), *Broadway* (1942), *Follow the Boys* (1944), *Nob Hill* (1945), *Some Like It Hot* (1959), and *The Ladies Man* (1961). His off-screen life sometimes paralleled his film roles and he ran casinos in London and Havana and was associated with underworld figures, which brought on problems of deportation and tax evasion in the 1950s and 1960s. Raft had his own television show in 1952. His life was romanticized in the film biography *The George Raft Story* (1961) in which he was played by Ray Danton. Biographies: *George Raft*, Lewis Yablonsky (2000); *The George Raft File*, James Parish (1973).

🎭 *RAGS* (Mark Hellinger Theatre 1986). A highly anticipated musical that was a major disappointment, quickly closed, but refuses to fade away because of its superb score. Jewish immigrant Rebecca Herschkowitz (Teresa Stratas) arrives in New York City with her young son David (Josh Blake) to find her husband Nathan (LARRY KERT) who has preceded them to the New World. Also new to America is Avram Cohen (Dick Latessa) and his daughter Bella (JUDY KUHN) who is soon wooed by the enterprising youth Ben (LONNY PRICE). Before Rebecca finds Nathan, she is drawn to the radical Saul (TERRENCE MANN) even though she does not agree with his politics. But when Bella dies in the Triangle Shirt Factory fire and Nathan turns out to be a political stooge, Rebecca's ideas change and she embraces activism and Saul. Also in the large and talented cast were Marcia Lewis, Rex Everhart, and Michael Cone. The libretto by JOSEPH STEIN was chock full of characters, subplots, and ideas, making the show a bit overwhelming for audiences. CHARLES STROUSE (music) and STEPHEN SCHWARTZ (lyrics) wrote the rich and varied score that captured the period and yet

was still accessible and very moving. Among the many memorable songs were "Blame It on the Summer Night," "Children of the Wind," "Greenhorns," "Easy for You," "Three Sunny Rooms," and the explosive title number. Critics approved of the scintillating songs and the outstanding cast, but the complicated and depressing book was cited as insurmountable and the notices were so negative that the musical, directed by GENE SAKS and choreographed by RON FIELD, closed after four performances. (Interestingly, the very similar musical *Ragtime* with an equally complex book and serious subject matter was a hit a dozen years later.) In 1991, the American Jewish Theatre revived the musical Off Broadway and, while criticisms of the script continued, the score was deemed better than ever.

🎭 *RAGTIME* (Ford Center Theatre 1998). A large, engrossing musical epic that boasted a

Ragtime. There were many major characters in this epic musical but they were all proficiently drawn and acted with skill. Pictured are Audra McDonald as Sarah and Brian Stokes Mitchell as Coalhouse Walker; their performances firmly placed them in the top ranks of Broadway players, both in plays and musicals. (Photofest)

compelling libretto, score, cast, and production, the show felt like a hit but even at 861 performances, the expensive undertaking lost money.

Plot: Three groups of Americans are followed during the early years of the twentieth century: a WASP family in New Rochelle in which mother and father follow tradition religiously but find their lives turned upside down by events new to them; the newly arrived immigrant Tateh with his young daughter who struggles through hardship and labor strikes to emerge as an early movie pioneer; and the African American ragtime pianist Coalhouse Walker who goes on a destructive rampage when his fiancée Sarah is killed. The three stories overlap with mother's younger brother joining Coalhouse's gang as they take J. P. Morgan's famous library hostage and plan to blow it up unless wrongs are righted. Father becomes the negotiator and, with Booker T. Washington's help, gets Coalhouse to surrender, only to be gunned down the moment he gives himself up. Mother has found that she cannot return to the old ways and divorces father to marry Tateh, raising their children as well as the orphaned illegitimate son of Coalhouse and Sarah. Woven into these stories are several historical figures of the day, such as the magician Harry Houdini, the scandalous Evelyn Nesbit, the labor organizer Emma Goldman, and the manufacturer Henry Ford.

TERRENCE MCNALLY adapted E. L. Doctorow's popular novel, putting many of its numerous events and characters on stage, and it was enthralling without being overwhelming.

Cast for *Ragtime*	
Character	*Performer*
Coalhouse Walker	BRIAN STOKES MITCHELL
Sarah	AUDRA MCDONALD
Father	Mark Jacoby
Mother	MARIN MAZZIE
Tateh	Peter Friedman
Emma Goldman	JUDY KAYE
Evelyn Nesbit	Lynette Perry
Younger brother	Stephen Sutcliffe
Little boy	Alex Strange
Grandfather	Conrad McLaren
Harry Houdini	Jim Corti
Booker T. Washington	Tommy Hollis
Henry Ford	Larry Daggett
J. P. Morgan	Mike O'Carroll

***Ragtime* Musical Numbers**
"Ragtime"
"Goodbye, My Love"
"Journey On"
"The Crime of the Century"
"What Kind of Woman"
"A Shtetl Iz Amereke"
"Success"
"Gettin' Ready Rag"
"Henry Ford"
"Nothing Like the City"
"Your Daddy's Son"
"New Music"
"Wheels of a Dream"
"The Night That Goldman Spoke at Union Square"
"Lawrence, Massachusetts"
"Gliding"
"Justice"
"President"
"Till We Reach That Day"
"Harry Houdini, Master Escapist"
"Coalhouse's Soliloquy"
"What a Game"
"Atlantic City"
"Buffalo Nickel Photoplay, Inc."
"Our Children"
"Sarah Brown Eyes"
"He Wanted to Say"
"Back to Before"
"Look What You've Done"
"Make Them Hear You"

STEPHEN FLAHERTY (music) and LYNN AHRENS (lyrics) wrote the ingenious score that included ragtime, blues, vaudeville, ethnic, patriotic, and Broadway sounds to create a musical melting pot that echoed not only the period but the different forces at work in society. Some critics carped about the abridged dramatization of the long, complex novel but audiences embraced the epic tale and the large, compelling production directed by Frank Galati and choreographed by GRACIELA DANIELE. The musical was the first attraction in the newly built Ford Center for the Performing Arts.

RAINER, LUISE (1910–). Film, stage, and television performer. After enjoying a brief but spectacular career in Hollywood, including two memorable musicals, the dark-haired, slightly accented actress suddenly disappeared from the public eye. Rainer was born in Dusseldorf, Germany, a member of an aristocratic Jewish family, and was a child performer on stage in Austria and Germany before training with renowned director Max Reinhardt and acting in his company. After making a few European films she was forced to leave Europe because of the Nazis and went to Hollywood in 1934 where she was featured in *Escapade* (1935). She made only eight more films but three of them were outstanding and afforded her exceptional roles: the fragile performer ANNA HELD in *THE GREAT ZIEGFELD* (1936), the Chinese peasant O'Lan in nonmusical *The Good Earth* (1937), and Johann Strauss' wife Poldi Vogelhuber in *THE GREAT WALTZ* (1938). By 1942 Rainer had left films and appeared on Broadway in the play *A Kiss for Cinderella* (1942) before visiting troops overseas. After the war she retired in Europe but on a few occasions returned to acting, appearing on American television in 1965 and 1984, and in the film *The Gambler* (1997). She was once married to playwright Clifford Odets (1906–1963).

RAINGER, RALPH [born Ralph Reichenthal] (1901–1942). Film and stage composer. One of Hollywood's busiest composers in the 1930s and early 1940s, he often collaborated with lyricist LEO ROBIN and turned out such song hits as "Love in Bloom" and "Thanks for the Memory," which became the signature songs for JACK BENNY and BOB HOPE. Rainger was born in New York and pursued a law career until he got a job as a pianist and later composer for Broadway musicals, such as *Queen High* (1926), *Cross My Heart* (1928), and *Tattle Tales* (1933). By 1932 he was in Hollywood collaborating with lyricist SAM COSLOW on the musicals *This Is the Night* (1932) and *Blonde Venus* (1932). Rainger first teamed up with Robin for *THE BIG BROADCAST* (1932) and the team would go on to score thirty more films together. Among their musicals are *INTERNATIONAL HOUSE* (1933), *Little Miss Marker* (1934), *Millions in the Air* (1935), *Palm Springs* (1936), *College Holiday* (1936), *Waikiki Wedding* (1937), *Give Me a Sailor* (1938), *ARTISTS AND MODELS ABROAD* (1938), *Paris Honeymoon* (1939), *GULLIVER'S TRAVELS* (1939), *MOON OVER MIAMI* (1941), *MY GAL SAL* (1942), *Footlight Serenade* (1942), *CONEY ISLAND* (1943), *Riding High* (1943), and the sequel films *Big Broadcast of 1926, 1937,* and *1938*. Rainger also wrote songs for many nonmusicals before his premature death in a plane crash.

RAISIN (46th Street Theatre 1973). A warm and honest musical based on Lorraine Hansberry's landmark African American drama *A Raisin*

in the Sun (1959), the show was faithful to its source and offered some splendid performances. Chauffeur Walter Lee Younger (JOE MORTON) lives in a cramped Chicago tenement with his wife Ruth (Ernestine Jackson), their young son Travis (Ralph Carter), his widowed mother Lena (Virginia Capers), and his college student sister Beneatha (DEBBIE ALLEN). He hopes to use the life insurance check from his late father to invest in a liquor store but Lena wishes to use it for a down payment on a nice detached house that happens to be in a white neighborhood. Walter loses his portion of the insurance check when one of the partners in the liquor store runs off with all the money. The white members of their new neighborhood offer to buy back the house to keep the Youngers away but Walter and Lena learn to keep their dignity and move in anyway. Robert Nemiroff and Charlotte Zaltzberg penned the libretto, and Judd Woldin (music) and Robert Brittan (lyric) wrote the admirable score that included "Measure the Valleys," "Sidewalk Tree," "A Whole Lotta Sunlight," "Man Say," and "Sweet Time." DONALD MACKAYE directed and choreographed the musical that ran 847 performances but has rarely been heard of since.

RAITT, JOHN (1917–2005). Stage, film, and television performer. A muscular, full-voiced baritone who exuded virility on stage, he created two memorable musical theatre roles on Broadway. Raitt was born in Santa Ana, California, where he was educated and received voice training. He sang in operas and operettas with the Los Angeles Civic Light Opera before getting work in the musical theatre. Raitt played Curly in the Chicago company of *OKLAHOMA!* and then made a sensational Broadway debut as the tough Billy Bigelow in *CAROUSEL* (1945), one of the most challenging and complex characters in the American musical theatre. Raitt did not get to reprise his Billy on screen, but his stage performance as the factory supervisor Sid Sorokin in *THE PAJAMA GAME* (1954) was repeated in the 1957 film version. His other films include *LITTLE NELLIE KELLY* (1940), *ZIEGFELD GIRL* (1941), and *Ship Ahoy* (1942). Raitt's other Broadway musicals, such as *Magdalena* (1948), *Three Wishes for Jamie* (1952), *Carnival in Flanders* (1953), and *A Joyful Noise* (1966), did not run even though he was generally praised for his performances. He repeated his Billy in the 1965 Broadway revival of *Carousel* and then spent much of the rest of his career in stock doing popular musicals such as *KISMET*, *CAMELOT*, *SOUTH PACIFIC*, and *KISS ME, KATE*. During his busy sixty-year career, Raitt also performed in concerts and on many television series and specials, such as the TV musicals *KNICKERBOCKER HOLIDAY* (1950), *REVENGE WITH MUSIC* (1951), *THE THIRTEEN CLOCKS* (1953), *ANNIE GET YOUR GUN* (1957), and *No Man Can Tame Me* (1959). His daughter is singer–songwriter Bonnie Raitt and the two recorded some songs together.

RALL, TOMMY (1929–). Stage and film performer. The agile dancer–singer from the world of ballet, he shone in supporting roles on Broadway and in Hollywood musicals. Rall was born in Kansas City, Missouri, and trained for a dance career at an early age. After appearing in stage musicals in Los Angeles and San Francisco he became a member of the American Ballet Theatre. Rall crossed over to musical comedy with featured roles in the Broadway musicals *Look, Ma, I'm Dancin'* (1948), *Small Wonder* (1948), *MISS LIBERTY* (1949), and *CALL ME MADAM* (1950). He made a sensational film debut as the dancing gambler Bill Calhoun opposite ANN MILLER in *KISS ME, KATE* (1953) and was also featured in *INVITATION TO THE DANCE* (1954), *SEVEN BRIDES FOR SEVEN BROTHERS* (1954), *MY SISTER EILEEN* (1955), and *Merry Andrew* (1958). Returning to Broadway he scored a triumph as the restless IRA member Johnny Boyle in the short-lived musical *JUNO* (1959) and as the Israeli activist David in *MILK AND HONEY* (1961). Rall returned to the American Ballet Theatre in the mid-1950s but often made room for musical appearances on Broadway, such as in *Cafe Crown* (1964) and *Cry for Us All* (1970), and in memorable bit parts in the movies *FUNNY GIRL* (1968) and *PENNIES FROM HEAVEN* (1981).

RANKIN, ARTHUR, JR., AND JULES BASS. Television producing and directing team. A tireless and influential pair of presenters whose company Rankin–Bass meant quality programming for families, they wrote, directed, and produced many memorable TV musicals. Arthur Rankin J. (1924–) was born in New York, the son of writer and film actor Arthur Rankin, and entered early television as a graphics designer at ABC in 1948. He soon graduated to art director and then produced live shows, including adaptations of the classics. Jules Bass (1935–) was born in Philadelphia and educated at New York University before working at a Manhattan advertising agency. In 1960 he went into television production and teamed up with Rankin to produce and direct a

series of TV specials over the next thirty years that would revolutionize children's programming using traditional animation with live action, stop-acting techniques, and stylized animation. They were particularly successful in musicalizing new and familiar holiday stories. Among the many original musicals they produced and/or directed are *Return to Oz* (1964), *THE STORY OF RUDOLPH THE RED-NOSED REINDEER* (1964), *The Ballad of Smokey the Bear* (1966), *The Cricket on the Hearth* (1967), *The Little Drummer Boy* (1968), *The Mouse on the Mayflower* (1968), *Frosty the Snowman* (1969), *SANTA CLAUS IS COMIN' TO TOWN* (1970), *Here Comes Peter Cottontail* (1971), *The Emperor's New Clothes* (1972), *'Twas the Night Before Christmas* (1974), *A YEAR WITHOUT A SANTA CLAUS* (1974), *Rudolph's Shiny New Year* (1976), *The Easter Bunny Is Comin' to Town* (1977), *The Hobbit* (1977), *THE STINGIEST MAN IN TOWN* (1978), *Jack Frost* (1979), *RUDOLPH AND FROSTY'S CHRISTMAS IN JULY* (1979), *Pinocchio's Christmas* (1980), *Return of the King* (1980), and *THE LIFE AND ADVENTURES OF SANTA CLAUS* (1985). Rankin and Bass presented some feature animated films, such as *The Daydreamer* (1966) and *The Mad Monster Party* (1969), and some nonmusical programs. Their last collaboration was the TV musical *THE WIND IN THE WILLOWS* (1987), although Rankin continued on and produced the animated feature film version of *THE KING AND I* (1999).

RAPHAELSON, SAMSON (1896–1983). Stage and film writer. A Broadway playwright who wrote many films in the 1930s and 1940s, his play *THE JAZZ SINGER* was the catalyst for the talking movies. A native New Yorker, Raphaelson was educated at the University of Illinois and began his career as an ad man and then a newspaper writer before turning to playwriting. His first Broadway effort was the drama *The Jazz Singer* (1925) starring GEORGE JESSEL. When the piece was rewritten as a film vehicle for AL JOLSON and songs were added, the talkies were born. Raphaelson went to Hollywood in 1926 and scripted several early sound films, including some comedies for director ERNST LUBITSCH. Among the musicals he wrote are *THE SMILING LIEUTENANT* (1931), *ONE HOUR WITH YOU* (1932), *THE MERRY WIDOW* (1934), *THE HARVEY GIRLS* (1946), *ZIEGFELD FOLLIES* (1946), *That Lady in Ermine* (1948), *IN THE GOOD OLD SUMMERTIME* (1949), *Mr. Music* (1950), and *Main Street to Broadway* (1953). Raphaelson returned to Broadway throughout his career to write plays, some of which were very successful, and then for the last decade of his life taught playwriting at Columbia University.

RAPP, ANTHONY [Dean] (1971–). Stage and film performer. An affable, animated singer–actor who found sudden success in *RENT*, he has been on the stage professionally since the age of nine. Rapp was born in Joliet, Illinois, and in 1981 was cast as the young prince in the Broadway-bound musical *The Little Prince and the Aviator* but it shuttered on the road. Five years later he played the youth Freddy in the short-lived Broadway drama *Precious Sons* (1986) and was featured as a child in the television soap opera *All My Children*. Rapp trained at the Interlochen Arts Camp and at New York University and then played supporting roles in some Broadway and Off Broadway plays before originating the role of the video artist Mark in *Rent* (1996 and 2007), a character he reprised in the 2005 film version. He also played the title character in the Broadway revival of *YOU'RE A GOOD MAN, CHARLIE BROWN* (1999) before returning to Off Broadway nonmusical projects. Rapp is active in regional theatre and in touring productions and has made several movies since 1987. His brother is playwright–novelist Adam Rapp (1968–). Autobiography: *Without You: A Memoir of Love, Loss, and the Musical 'Rent'* (2006).

RASCH, ALBERTINA (1891–1967). Stage and film choreographer. An Austrian-born choreographer who brought a distinctive, balletic look to many Broadway book musicals and revues, she also did the dances for a dozen Hollywood musicals. Rasch was born in Vienna and trained and performed in the Opera Ballet in Austria before she was brought to New York in 1911 to be a featured dancer in the SHUBERT brothers' musical spectacles at the Hippodrome Theatre. Rasch danced in a handful of Broadway musicals as well and then toured in vaudeville before returning to Manhattan to make her choreography debut with the 1925 edition of *GEORGE WHITE SCANDALS*. Her first of many Broadway hits was *RIO RITA* (1927), followed by such popular book musicals as *THE CAT AND THE FIDDLE* (1931), *FACE THE MUSIC* (1932), *JUBILEE* (1935), *PAL JOEY* (1940), and *LADY IN THE DARK* (1941). It was her exotic staging of the choreography for Cole Porter's "Begine the Beguine" in *Jubilee* that made such an impact on first-night audiences and secured the song's success. Because her dances were not as character driven as those of AGNES DE MILLE and other younger choreographers' work, Rasch's finest efforts were

often to be found in revues, such as the 1930s classics *THREE'S A CROWD* (1930), *THE BAND WAGON* (1931), and *FLYING COLORS* (1932). Her background in ballet was evident, yet Rasch found ways to incorporate newer styles in her works, as with jazz and modern dance in *The Band Wagon* and expressionistic movement in *Lady in the Dark*. Rasch was married to prolific screen composer Dimitri Tiomkin so she had connections to Hollywood where she choreographed such films as *HOLLYWOOD REVUE OF 1929*, *GOING HOLLYWOOD* (1933), *The Cat and the Fiddle* (1934), *BROADWAY MELODY OF 1936* (1935), *ROSALIE* (1936), *THE FIREFLY* (1937) and *SWEETHEARTS* (1938).

RATOFF, GREGORY [born Eugene Leontovitch] (1897–1960). Film director and performer. The portly character actor of stage and screen often played directors and producers in films in the 1930s and by the end of the decade was behind the camera where he helmed many films, including eight musicals. Ratoff was born in St. Petersberg, Russia, and studied acting at the Moscow Art Theatre before coming to America in 1930. He played a variety of types in Hollywood movies, including roles in the musicals *I'm No Angel* (1933), *GEORGE WHITE'S SCANDALS* (1934), *KING OF BURLESQUE* (1935), *Sing, Baby, Sing* (1936), and *Top of the Town* (1937). Ratoff made his directing debut in 1936 and was later responsible for such hits as *Intermezzo* (1939) and *The Corsican Brothers* (1941). His screen musicals include *ROSE OF WASHINGTON SQUARE* (1939), *Footlight Serenade* (1942), *Irish Eyes Are Smiling* (1944), *Where Do We Go From Here?* (1945), and *Carnival in Costa Rica* (1947).

RAY (Universal 2004). The musical biography of the celebrated blues and jazz singer Ray Charles could have become a teary-eyed testimonial to an African American who overcame tremendous odds and succeeded, but the nuanced performance by Jamie Foxx and the tough, unsentimental screenplay by James L. White made the movie much more honest and, in turn, more moving. Born poor in rural Georgia and going blind at the age of seven, the young Charles is encouraged by his fearless single mother Aretha (Sharon Warren) to pursue a musical career. Despite Jim Crow laws in the South and more subtle racial discrimination in the North, Charles breaks onto the charts with his records, tours Europe many times, and becomes a major force in rhythm and blues, jazz, gospel, and even country music, breaking boundaries by sometimes mixing two of the sounds together. However, his weakness for drugs and women starts to deteriorate his personal life and only after he turns himself around and defeats his own demons does he feel like a winner. Also in the strong cast were Kerry Washington as Charles' long-suffering wife Dela Bea and Regina King as his mistress Margie Hendricks. Charles, who died right after filming was completed, provided the vocals for Foxx who did his own piano playing and gave a riveting, multifaceted performance. Among the many Charles favorites heard in the film were "Georgia on My Mind," "I Can't Stop Loving You," "I Got a Woman," "Unchain My Heart," "Hit the Road Jack," and "Let the Good Times Roll." Director Taylor Hackford secured the rights to Charles' life story in 1987 but couldn't find a studio to finance it so the movie was made as an independent feature by Anvil Films and released through UNIVERSAL.

RAYE, DON [born Donald MacRae Wilhoite, Jr.] (1909–1985). Film and stage lyricist. Usually working with composer GENE DE PAUL, the Hollywood lyricist scored fourteen musicals in the 1940s. Raye was born in Washington, DC, and first had his songs interpolated into a film with *Argentine Nights* (1940). He burst onto the music scene when he collaborated with composer Hughie Prince on the wartime favorite "Boogie Woogie Bugle Boy," which the ANDREWS SISTERS introduced in the film musical *BUCK PRIVATES* (1941). Raye first worked with de Paul on *In the Navy* (1941) and the two went on to score such movies as *Moonlight in Hawaii* (1941), *Keep 'Em Flying* (1941), *Behind the Eightball* (1941), *San Antonio Rose* (1941), *HELLZAPOPPIN* (1941), *Ride 'Em Cowboy* (1942), *Pardon My Sarong* (1942), *Larceny With Music* (1943), *BROADWAY RHYTHM* (1944), *A Song Is Born* (1948), and *Ichabod and Mr. Toad* (1949). He contributed to the Broadway musical *Almost Crazy* (1955) and had individual songs interpolated into many musical and nonmusical films.

RAYE, MARTHA [born Margaret Teresa Yvonne O'Reed] (1908–1994). Stage, film, and television performer. The elastic-mouthed comedienne with a siren voice lit up shows in all media with her animated energy and raucous sense of comedy. Raye was born in Butte, Montana, the daughter of traveling vaudevillians, was on the stage at the age of three, and by the time she was a teenager was an accomplished singer. She appeared on Broadway in *Calling All Stars* (1934) and *Hold On to Your Hats* (1940) and made her screen debut in 1935. Soon Raye

was featured in such musicals as *Rhythm on the Range* (1936), *BIG BROADCAST OF 1937* (1936), *College Holiday* (1936), *Waikiki Wedding* (1937), *Mountain Music* (1937), *ARTISTS AND MODELS* (1937), *DOUBLE OR NOTHING* (1937), *BIG BROADCAST OF 1938, College Swing* (1938), *Give Me a Sailor* (1938), *Tropic Holiday* (1938), *THE BOYS FROM SYRACUSE* (1940), *Navy Blues* (1941), *Keep 'Em Flying* (1941), *HELLZAPOPPIN'* (1941), *Four Jills in a Jeep* (1944), and *Pin-Up Girl* (1944). She was a favorite in nightclubs and with the American G.I.s she entertained during World War II, the Korean War, and in Viet Nam. Raye was also popular on television where she had her own show and appeared on many other programs, including the original musicals *Skinflint* (1979) and *ALICE IN WONDERLAND* (1985), and in the TV versions of *ANYTHING GOES* (1950) and *PIPPIN* (1981). Later in her career she found good roles as the overemotional Lulu in the movie musical *JUMBO* (1962) and as a replacement for Dolly Levi on Broadway in *HELLO, DOLLY!* (1967). Among her husbands were composer David Rose (1910–1990) and dancer Nick Condos (1915–1988). Biography: *Take It From the Big Mouth: The Life of Martha Raye*, Jean Maddern Pitrone (1999).

RAYMOND, GENE [born Raymond Guion] (1908–1998). Film, television, and stage performer. A blond leading man who started as a child actor in films, he played the romantic (if unexciting) leading man in many films in the 1930s. The native New Yorker was on the stage at the age of five and studied at the Professional Children's School in his hometown before making his Broadway debut in 1921. Raymond appeared in ten plays in the 1920s, as well as in the musical *Say When* (1928). By 1931 he was in films and soon was playing leading roles, as in the musicals *FLYING DOWN TO RIO* (1933), *Sadie McKee* (1934), *Transatlantic Merry-Go-Round* (1934), *Hooray for Love* (1935), *The Girl From Paris* (1936), and *The Life of the Party* (1937). Raymond moved on to character parts in *Smilin' Through* (1941), *HIT THE DECK* (1955), and *I'd Rather Be Rich* (1964). He was very active on television, appearing in dozens of shows into the 1970s. Raymond was married to JEANETTE MACDONALD.

REAGAN, RONALD [Wilson] (1911–2004). Film and television performer. The personable leading man in Hollywood, television, and government, he did not sing on the screen yet was featured in seven musicals. Reagan was born in Tampico, Illinois, and educated at

Eureka College before starting his career as a sportscaster on the radio. He made his screen debut in 1937 and was cast as likable if often bland leading characters in comedies, melodramas, and musicals, such as *Going Places* (1938), *Naughty But Nice* (1939), *Juke Girl* (1942), *THIS IS THE ARMY* (1943), *It's a Great Feeling* (1949), and *She's Working Her Way Through College* (1952). Occasionally Reagan got a meaty role in nonmusicals, such as with *Knute Rockne—All American* (1940) and *King's Row* (1942), but his film career was not dazzling so he moved to television in the 1950s and found success in series, variety shows, quiz programs, and as the host of anthology shows. His political career started as president of the Screen Actors Guild and then graduated to Governor of California and President of the United States. Autobiography: *An American Life* (1999).

☐ **REALLY ROSIE** (CBS-TV 1975). Artist–writer Maurice Sendak had created the character of Rosie, a precocious little girl with an adult-like attitude at times, in a children's book that was popular. There was little plot except that Rosie has decided to make a movie of her life and coerces all her neighborhood friends to try out using silly poems and ghastly tales. The book was musicalized in this delightful thirty-minute animated revue in which Carole King's contagious music allowed the lyrics (by Sendak and Lou Adler) to spring to life. "Chicken Soup With Rice," "One Was Johnny," "Alligators All Around," "Avenue P," "Screaming and Yelling," and "Pierre" are among the unforgettable ditties that were performed by the kids, as animated by Sendak. King provided the vocals for Rosie, and other voices were done by Mark Hampton, Alice Playten, Baille Gerstein, and Dale Soules. 🎵 The soundtrack recording was very popular and prompted a stage version of *Really Rosie* that was produced Off Broadway in 1980, followed by many productions in schools, summer camps, and community centers.

REAMS, LEE ROY (1942–). Stage performer and director. A cheery, all-American type singer–dancer, he appeared in musicals on Broadway and on the road and then later turned to directing and choreographing revivals of the shows he once appeared in. Reams was born in Covington, Kentucky, and educated at the University of Cincinnati Conservatory of Music. He began his career as a dancer in Juliet Prowse's nightclub act and then made his Broadway bow in the chorus of *SWEET CHARITY* (1966), also appearing in the 1969 film version.

After playing cowboy Will Parker in the 1969 revival of *OKLAHOMA!*, he was applauded as the gay hairdresser Duane Fox in *APPLAUSE* (1970). Reams was featured on Broadway in *LORELEI* (1974) and *SHOW BOAT* (1976), sang and danced in the Off Broadway revues *Sterling Silver* (1979) and *Potholes* (1979), and then was lauded for his energetic Billy Lawlor in the Broadway version of *42ND STREET* (1980). He played clerk Cornelius Hackl with CAROL CHANNING in the 1978 revival of *HELLO, DOLLY!* and then directed and choreographed the musical on tour, in regional theatres, and for Channing's 1995 return to Broadway. Reams has directed other classic musicals on tour and in regional theatre and both directed and performed on Broadway in *An Evening With Jerry Herman* (1998). He has also shone on Broadway in such replacement jobs as Alban in *LA CAGE AUX FOLLES* (1987), Lumiere in *BEAUTY AND THE BEAST* (1995), and Roger De Bris in *THE PRODUCERS* (2006).

🎬 **REBECCA OF SUNNYBROOK FARM** (Fox 1938). Based on an oft-told story already filmed in 1917 and 1932, this SHIRLEY TEMPLE vehicle strayed far from the Kate Douglas Wiggin story than had its two nonmusical predecessors, but the movie was one of the moppet's best and musically it was outstanding. In the Ken Tunberg and Don Ettlinger screenplay, city girl Rebecca (Temple) joins her Aunt Miranda (HELEN WESTLEY) on Sunnybrook Farm to get away from show business. However, radio producer Tony Kent (RANDOLPH SCOTT) puts her on the air and Rebecca becomes a hit, attracting her greedy stepfather Harry Kipper (WILLIAM DEMAREST). Six different tunesmiths contributed to the score, and the film is filled with wonderful musical numbers, particularly two with farmhand Aloysius (BILL ROBINSON), the freewheeling "An Old Straw Hat" and the march tune "Parade of the Wooden Soldiers." Other new songs included "Come and Get Your Happiness," "Alone With You," and "Au Revoir." At one point in the film, the ten-year-old veteran sat down at the piano and sang a medley of her past hits, such as "Animal Crackers in My Soup," "When I'm With You," and "On the Good Ship Lollipop." ALLAN DWAN directed the DARRYL F. ZANUCK production, which also featured JACK HALEY, GLORIA STUART, Phyllis Brooks, Slim Summerville, Alan Dinehart, and DIXIE DUNBAR.

🎵 **RED, HOT AND BLUE!** (Alvin Theatre 1936). A silly political satire with some memorable COLE PORTER songs, the show featured three of Broadway's favorite comic stars, ETHEL MERMAN, JIMMY DURANTE, and BOB HOPE. Millionairess Nails O'Reilly (Merman) raises money to ease the national debt by holding a contest to see who can locate Bob Hale's (Hope) long-lost sweetheart, a gal who accidentally sat on a waffle iron as a child and still has the markings to prove it. Everyone looks for the mystery girl, including the convict Policy Pinkle (Durante) who'd rather be in jail with the polo team. Contest or no, Bob ends up with Nails. The cast was filled with talent, including Lew Parker, Polly Walters, Forrest Orr, Grace Hartman, VIVIAN VANCE, Dorothy Vernon, Thurston Crane, and Paul Hartman. HOWARD LINDSAY and RUSSEL CROUSE wrote the ridiculous libretto, and Porter provided such delights as "It's De-Lovely," "Down in the Depths (On the 90th Floor)," "Ridin' High," "A Little Skipper From Heaven Above," and the risible title tune. The script may have struck critics as slapshot but the scintillating score and the three sportive stars more than compensated. VINTON FREEDLEY produced, co-author Lindsay directed, GEORGE HALE choreographed, and the show ran 183 performances.

📖 **RED MILL, THE** (Knickerbocker Theatre 1906). Lighter fare than usual for a VICTOR HERBERT operetta, the show was written as a vehicle for two popular comics so it often resembles a musical comedy. The two Americans Con Kidder and Kid Conner are taking the grand tour of Europe and end up penniless in Katwyk-aan-Zee, Holland, where they help the romance between the burgomaster's daughter Gretchen and the sea captain Van Damm, even though her father wants her to marry the Governor of Zeeland. When the burgomaster learns of his daughter's affections for Van Damm, he locks her up in the red mill but Con and Kid take on a series of disguises (such as Sherlock Holmes and Watson) and rescue her. The Governor takes a liking to

Gretchen's Aunt Bertha, the young lovers are united in marriage, and Con and Kid take the next boat back to New York.

HENRY BLOSSOM wrote the efficient, amusing libretto and it served comics FRED STONE and DAVE MONTGOMERY well, their clowning and musical comedy songs balancing nicely with the more operatic numbers for the lovers. Blossom also wrote the lyrics for Herbert's music and they came up with such popular favorites as "The Streets of New York," "Moonbeams," and "The Isle of Our Dreams." Also expert were "Because You're You," "Every Day Is Ladies Day With Me," and "When You're Pretty and the World Is Fair." The CHARLES DILLINGHAM production, directed by Fred Latham, was a solid hit, running 274 performances. Even more successful was a 1945 Broadway revival that starred EDDIE FOY, JR. as Kid Conner. Both script and lyrics were slightly revised for this very popular mounting directed by BILLY GILBERT that ran 531 performances. ❑ An unusual but enjoyable version of *The Red Mill* was broadcast on CBS-TV's *The DuPont Show of the Month* in 1958 with SHIRLEY JONES as Gretchen. The cast also included DONALD O'CONNOR, Edward Andrews, ELAINE STRITCH, comedy duo Mike Nichols and Elaine May, and (oddest of all) HARPO MARX as the narrator.

📖 **REDHEAD** (46th Street Theatre 1959). A merry vehicle for Broadway's favorite dancing star, GWEN VERDON, the musical was unusual in that it was a whodunit. In London of the early 1900s, an actress has been murdered and someone with red hair has been seen leaving the scene of the crime. Musical hall entertainer Tom Baxter (RICHARD KILEY) and Essie Whimple (Verdon), who works in her aunt's Simpson Sisters Waxworks, set out to find the murderer and in the process fall in love. HERBERT and DOROTHY FIELDS, Sidney

Casts for *The Red Mill*

Character	1906 Broadway	1945 Broadway
Con Kidder	FRED STONE	Michael O'Shea
Kid Conner	DAVE MONTGOMERY	EDDIE FOY, JR.
Gretchen	Augusta Greenleaf	Ann Andre
Capt. Van Damm	Joseph M. Ratliff	Robert Hughes
Governor	Neal McCay	Edward Dew
Jan Van Borkem	Edward Begley	Frank Jaquet
Tina	Ethel Johnson	Dorothy Stone
Bertha/Juliana	Allene Crater	Martha Errolle

Sheldon, and David Shaw collaborated on the tricky libretto, and ALBERT HAGUE (music) and Dorothy Fields (lyrics) wrote a delightful score that produced no hits but was commendable all the same. "Merely Marvelous," "Look Who's in Love," "She's Not Enough Woman for Me," "Erbie Fitch's Twitch," and "The Uncle Sam Rag" were among the notable musical numbers choreographed and (for the first time) also directed by BOB FOSSE. The musical mystery was less about solving a crime as it was about Verdon's energetic and funny performance, which audiences came to see for 452 performances.

REED, VIVIEN (1947–). Stage, television, and film performer. A vivacious African American singer and dancer, she has rarely found herself in a hit but always gets rave reviews. Reed was born in Pittsburgh and won a scholarship to Juilliard where she studied both voice and dance. In the 1960s she was a successful rhythm and blues vocalist, with some of her recordings high on the charts. Reed made her Broadway debut in the short-lived revue *That's Entertainment* (1971), followed by featured spots in DON'T BOTHER ME, I CAN'T COPE (1972), BUBBLING BROWN SUGAR (1976), *It's So Nice to Be Civilized* (1980), *The High Rollers Social and Pleasure Club* (1992), and *Marie Christine* (1999). She has been a soloist for various dance companies, briefly appeared on a television series, and acted in the films *Headin' for Broadway* (1980) and the French movie *La Rumba* (1987) in which she played Josephine Baker.

REGAN, PHIL[ip Joseph Aloysius] (1906–1996). Film performer. A handsome Irish tenor in Hollywood, he never became a major star because most of his musicals were either forgettable or B movies. Regan was born in Brooklyn and was a police department detective who liked to sing in nightclubs, billed as "The Singing Cop." He eventually quit the force and concentrated on singing, making his screen debut in the musical *Student Tour* (1934). He was featured in the popular films *Dames* (1934), *Sweet Adeline* (1935), and *Go Into Your Dance* (1935) and then found himself playing Irish leading men in such films as *Laughing Irish Eyes* (1936), *Outside of Paradise* (1938), *She Married a Cop* (1939), *Sunbonnet Sue* (1945), *Swing Parade of 1946*, and *Sweetheart of Sigma Chi* (1946). Regan's other film credits include *In Caliente* (1935), *Broadway Hostess* (1935), *HAPPY-GO-LUCKY* (1936), *Manhattan Merry-Go-Round* (1937), *Las Vegas Nights* (1941), *Sweet Rosie O'Grady* (1943), and a bit part in *THREE LITTLE WORDS* (1950). He retired from movies in 1946 but continued to sing, hosting the *Phil Regan Armed Forces Radio Show* in 1951.

REGINA (46th Street Theatre 1949). With its sweeping arias and extended musical passages, the show was closer to opera than musical play. The scheming characters of Lillian Hellman's drama *The Little Foxes* (1939) were revived in this operatic adaptation by MARC BLITZSTEIN who also wrote the challenging score. The ruthless Southern Regina (Jane Pickens) tries to outwit her husband (William Wilderman) and two brothers (David Thomas and George Lipton) by securing her share of a business venture that the greedy family is planning. Regina's schemes force her to let her husband die of a heart attack but she wins her money and ends up losing her daughter (Priscilla Gillette). Also in the cast was Brenda Lewis who shone as the faded Southern belle Birdie. Blitzstein's complex score included such powerful numbers as "The Best Thing of All," "Birdie's Aria," and "Rain Quartet." The critics found the theatrics a bit too static and the music too difficult so the ambitious musical closed after fifty-six performances. Since then, *Regina* has become more appreciated and is revived on occasion, usually by opera companies.

REILLY, CHARLES NELSON (1931–2007). Stage and television performer and director. A nimble character actor in comedies and musicals, he turned to directing very different kinds of theatre pieces late in his career. A native New Yorker, Reilly was educated at the University of Connecticut, later studying acting with Uta Hagen and Herbert Berghof. He worked in summer stock before making his New York acting debut in 1956. Usually playing supporting roles, he shone in three 1960s musical hits: as Mr. Heckel in *BYE BYE BIRDIE* (1960), Bud Frump in *HOW TO SUCCEED IN BUSINESS WITHOUT REALLY TRYING* (1961), and Cornelius Hackl in *HELLO, DOLLY!* (1964). Reilly's other New York musicals included *BEST FOOT FORWARD* (1956), *LEND AN EAR* (1959), *Billy Barnes Revue* (1959), *Parade* (1960), and *Skyscraper* (1965). A popular favorite on television, he appeared on sit-coms, game shows, and specials and has provided the voices for many animated characters on TV and film. Reilly's theatre directing credits include *The Belle of Amherst* (1976) with Julie Harris, one of the most successful of all one-person shows. He performed his own Off Broadway one-man show, *Save It for the Stage:*

The Life of Reilly (2001), which was filmed as *The Life of Reilly* (2006).

REINKING, ANN (1949–). Stage and film performer and choreographer. The leggy, statuesque dancer most associated with BOB FOSSE musicals, she later helped recreate his choreography for Broadway. Reinking was born in Seattle and trained at the Joffrey school and the Herbert Berghof Studio before dancing as a rockette at Radio City and then making her Broadway bow as a replacement in the chorus of CABARET (1969). After dancing in *Coco* (1969) and *Wild and Wonderful* (1971), she first worked with Fosse as a member of the ensemble of PIPPIN (1972). Reinking was featured in OVER HERE! (1974), played Joan of Arc in the short-lived *Goodtime Charley* (1975), was a replacement for Cassie in *A CHORUS LINE* (1976), and then got wide recognition for her performance in Fosse's DANCIN' (1978). She replaced stars in such Fosse roles as Roxie Hart in CHICAGO (1977) and Charity in SWEET CHARITY (1986) and then performed and staged the revues *One More Song/One More Dance* (1983) and *Ann Reinking: Music Moves Me* (1984). She was also responsible for

recreating Fosse's choreography for the very popular revival of *Chicago* (1996) in which she played Roxie. Reinking conceived, directed, and choreographed the Broadway and London dance revue FOSSE (1999) and during the long run performed in it at times. She also staged and choreographed the revue the *Look of Love* (2003) and choreographed the TV version of BYE BYE BIRDIE (1995). Reinking made her film debut as a dancer in MOVIE MOVIE (1978) and was featured in the musicals ALL THAT JAZZ (1979) and ANNIE (1982).

RENT (Nederlander Theatre 1996). The popular rock musical loosely based on the Puccini opera *La Boheme*, the thrilling show was both the Broadway debut and the swan song for the gifted author–composer–lyricist JONATHAN LARSON.

Plot: Struggling composer Roger Davis and video artist Mark Cohen live in the East Village of Manhattan in the 1990s with other bohemian artists and try to be true to their artistic vision while struggling with sour love affairs, poverty, and AIDS. Roger reluctantly falls in love with the dancer Mimi Marquez; Mark's ex-girl friend, performance artist Maureen

Rent. What does a chorus number look like in a rock musical? A lot like "La Vie Boheme," the finale of the first act of *Rent*. The cast of characters celebrates the bohemian life with joy and defiance, making for a very theatrical number even as it captures the spirit of the whole work. Pictured is the original Broadway cast. (Photofest)

Casts for *Rent*

Character	1996 Broadway	2005 film
Roger Davis	Adam Pascal	Adam Pascal
Mimi Marquez	Daphne Rubin-Vega	Rosario Dawson
Mark Cohen	ANTHONY RAPP	Anthony Rapp
Maureen Johnson	IDINA MENZEL	Idina Menzel
Joanne Jefferson	Fredi Walker	Tracie Thoms
Tom Collins	Jesse L. Martin	Jesse L. Martin
Angel Schunard	Wilson Jermaine Heredia	Wilson Jermaine Heredia
Benjamin Coffin III	Taye Diggs	Taye Diggs

Johnson, takes up with legal aid worker Joanne Jefferson; and ex-professor Tom Collins finds true love with drag queen Angel Schunard. Over the course of a year, these relationships are threatened by jealousy, infidelity, and death. In the end, the survivors find hope with each other and discover from Mimi, who was close to death but returned, that the deceased Angel urges them to love and live on.

The sung-through rock musical uses a variety of musical styles, from the tango to blues to folk, but at heart it is a contemporary sounding score that is not afraid of using rock to do what theatre songs are supposed to do. The show is character driven and the songs often are specific to certain people in the drama. Most of the characters are struggling artists, yet they cannot be lumped together as simple types. Larson's lyrics are poignant but rarely sentimental, romantic but far from gushing. He is not afraid to show his character's weaknesses and builds an empathy with the audience by sometimes showing them at their worst. While most rock musicals of the past concentrated on protest or celebration, *Rent* is more incisive, looking at youth and youthful ideas with humor, sadness, and honesty. The musical was first produced at the New York Theatre Workshop, directed by Michael Greif, but before the first preview performance the young Larson died suddenly. Reviewers were drawn to the Off Off Broadway venue and liked what they saw. The seven-week engagement sold out and then the show transferred to Broadway without losing any of its intimacy and power. The highly praised production launched the careers of its young, unknown cast and ran 5,012 performances. The contemporary musical continues to appeal to audiences young and old in nonprofessional performances.

🎬 *Rent* (Columbia 2005) reunited most of the original cast members but director Chris

Rent Musical Numbers

"Tune Up"
"Voice Mail"
"Rent"
"You Okay Honey?"
"One Song Glory"
"Light My Candle"
"Today for You"
"You'll See"
"Tango: Maureen"
"Life Support"
"Out Tonight"
"Another Day"
"Will I?"
"On the Street"
"Santa Fe"
"We're Okay"
"I'll Cover You"
"Christmas Bells"
"Over the Moon"
"La Vie Boheme"
"I Should Tell You"
"Seasons of Love"
"Happy New Year"
"Take Me or Leave me"
"Without You"
"Contact"
"Halloween"
"Goodbye, Love"
"What You Own"
"Your Eyes"

Columbus took a more realistic and sentimental approach to the material so the movie was often very moving but rarely as gritty and uncompromising as the stage work. All the high points of Larson's score are in the film but it is no longer sung-through. Dialogue scenes interrupt the score and all the recitative and musical transitions are gone. While the story was presented on an expressionistic metal sculpture of a set on Broadway, the movie is very realistic, including visual flash-backs for events only sung about in the original. The stage performers adjusted well to the screen (for many it was their film debut), and the performances by old and new cast members are commendable throughout. The acting and singing have been softened for the movie treatment and what was sometimes "in your face" in the theatre is now safely distanced or even removed. The screenplay by Stephen Chbodsky fills in many details that the stage libretto didn't worry about so the story seems more conventional. Many devotees of the stage *Rent* and most of the critics disparaged the film but it is unlikely that a movie could have been made that captured the dangerous and exciting experience of *Rent* in the theatre.

RESCUERS, THE (Disney 1977). An oft-neglected little gem from the DISNEY studio, this musical adventure took a while to catch on and eventually became a favorite on video and DVD. Based on Margery Sharp's books *The Rescuers* and *Miss Bianca*, the screenplay showed the plight of the orphan Penny (voice of Michelle Stacy) who is kidnapped from the orphanage and kept prisoner in a houseboat deep in the Everglades swamp by Madame Medusa (Geraldine Page) and her bumbling sidekick Snoops (Joe Flynn). The villainess needs the little girl to crawl into a partially flooded pirate's cave and recover the Devil's Eye, the world's largest diamond. Penny writes a note pleading for help and puts it in a bottle, which floats out to sea and is found by the Rescue Aid Society, an organization of mice located in the basement of the United Nations building in New York. The unflappable Miss Bianca (EVA GABOR) and the reluctant Bernard (Bob Newhart) are given the assignment to rescue Penny and, with the help of various creatures in the swamp, they succeed and Penny's future is secured by the valuable diamond. The cast was filled with marvelous supporting characters that were voiced with panache, such as the hapless albatross Orville (Jim Jordan), the out-of-breath dragonfly Evinrude (James MacDonald), and various swamp dwellers played by Jeanette Nolan, Pat Buttram, George Lindsey, Dub Taylor, John McIntire, Bernard Fox, and John Fiedler. Page's performance bounced back and forth from curdling sweet to bombastic outrage, and Medussa joined the ranks of the most notable Disney villains. SAMMY FAIN collaborated with Carol Connors and Ayn Robbins on the songs, most memorably the ballad "Someone Is Waiting for

You." Wolfgang Reitherman produced and co-directed with Art Stevens and John Lounsbery, and the depiction of the swampy Devil's Bayou was evocative and frightening.

REVEL, HARRY (1905–1958). Film and stage composer. A veteran of Broadway and West End musicals, the prolific songwriter scored over thirty movie musicals, many with lyricist MACK GORDON. Revel was born in London and was a prodigy at the piano at a young age. He studied at the Guildhall School of Music and then in Austria and Germany. Revel published his first popular song at the age of fifteen and in his twenties wrote an opera while studying in Germany. Some of his songs were interpolated into West End musicals in 1927 and the next year he emigrated to America. He contributed to the scores of such Broadway musicals as *ZIEGFELD FOLLIES* (1931), *Fast and Furious* (1931), *Everybody's Welcome* (1931), *Marching By* (1932), and *Smiling Faces* (1932). By 1933 he was writing songs for PARAMOUNT with Gordon, including *Broadway Through a Keyhole* (1933), *Sitting Pretty* (1933), *WE'RE NOT DRESSING* (1934), *She Loves Me Not* (1934), *COLLEGE RHYTHM* (1934), *Love in Bloom* (1935), and *Stolen Harmony* (1935). At 20TH CENTURY-FOX the team scored *POOR LITTLE RICH GIRL* (1936), *Stowaway* (1936), *WAKE UP AND LIVE* (1937), and several others. By the 1940s Revel was collaborating with other lyricists and provided songs for *Four Jacks and a Jill* (1941), *Sing Your Worries Away* (1942), *The Mayor of 44th Street* (1942), *It Ain't Hay* (1943), *The Ghost Catchers* (1944), *Minstrel Man* (1944), and others. He returned to Broadway in 1945 to score *Are You With It?* "Did You Ever See a Dream Walking?," "There's a Lull in My Life," and "You Say the Sweetest Things, Baby" are among Revel's many hit songs.

REVENGE WITH MUSIC (New Amsterdam Theatre 1934). The first attempt by revue songwriters ARTHUR SCHWARTZ (music) and HOWARD DIETZ (lyrics) to write a book musical, the operetta failed to work but some lovely songs came from the show. The Spanish governor Don Emilio (CHARLES WINNINGER) tries unsuccessfully to bed the lovely Maria (LIBBY HOLMAN) on her wedding night and her bridegroom Carlos (Georges Metaxa) takes his revenge by wooing the too-willing Dona Isabella (Ilka Chase), the governor's wife. Dietz adapted the familiar Spanish story into a routine libretto that was often saved by the score, including the two hit ballads "You and the Night and the Music" and "If There Is Someone Lovelier Than You." Also heard in the show were "In the Middle of the Night," "When You Love Only One," and "In the Noonday Sun." Reviewers found the old-fashioned operetta plot quaint at best but raved about the melodic score and ravishing production values, particularly the colorful, revolving sets by Albert Johnson, so the show managed to run 158 performances. ☐ An abridged version of *Revenge With Music* was broadcast on NBC-TV's series *Musical Comedy Time* in 1951. The cast included ANNE JEFFREYS (Maria), JOHN RAITT (Carlos), Audrey Christie (Dona Isabella), and BILLY GILBERT (Don Isabella).

REVILL, CLIVE [Selsby] (1930–). Stage, television, and film performer. The deep-voiced, animated character actor of the London and Broadway stages, his musical appearances are few but unforgettable. Revill was born and educated in Wellington, New Zealand, and worked as an accountant before turning to acting. After appearing in stock in his native country, he came to New York and was cast as the wily servant Sam Weller in the comedy *Mr. Pickwick* (1952). Revill continued on to England where he studied at the Old Vic School in London and played many classical roles at the Ipswich Repertory Theatre and the Shakespeare Memorial Theatre in Stratford. He became most known for his bar owner Bob-Le-Hotu in the musical *IRMA LA DOUCE* (1957), a role he reprised on Broadway in 1960. He had an even bigger success originating the role of Fagin in the original New York production of *OLIVER!* (1963). Revill's subsequent new musical on Broadway was as Sheridan Whiteside in the short-lived *Sherry!* (1967) but he was lauded when he replaced the role of the Chairman in *THE MYSTERY OF EDWIN DROOD* (1988). He has appeared in many Gilbert and Sullivan operettas in England and America and was in the television versions of *THE MIKADO* (1982) and *The Sorcerer* (1982). Revill has acted in dozens of films, including the musical *The Little Prince* (1974), and many television programs, such as the TV musicals *PINOCCHIO* (1976), *ONCE UPON A BROTHERS GRIMM* (1977), *The Frog Prince* (1986), and *Rumplestiltskin* (1987).

REVIVALS AND REMAKES. With half of the musical entries on Broadway today being revivals, it is interesting to recall that the concept of reviving an old musical in a new production is a relatively new one. In the nineteenth century, hits such as *THE BLACK CROOK* (1866), *EVANGELINE* (1874), *ADONIS* (1884), and

a handful of European operettas returned to New York a half dozen or more times but usually these were road companies and were not much different than the originals. It was common in the 1910s and 1920s for popular musicals to tour after their initial Broadway run and then to reopen in New York a year or two later for a "return engagement." These were not, strictly speaking, revivals since they were the same production with often the same casts. A true revival is a production in which the musical is rethought, redesigned, and reinterpreted by different artists from those who had originated the work. Early in the twentieth century the only shows regularly revived in New York were Gilbert and Sullivan operettas and many of those were visits by the D'Oyly Carte Opera Company from England. *SHOW BOAT* (1927) was one of the few American musicals that were not disposed of after making money in New York and on tour. The musical was revived on Broadway in 1932 with pretty much the original cast and production, but the 1946 production was a true revival, with a new song and script changes. New York has seen seven major productions of *Show Boat* since then, making it the most revived American musical in the twentieth century. Other notable revivals before the 1960s include the 1943 productions of *THE MERRY WIDOW* and *A CONNECTICUT YANKEE*, the 1945 *THE RED MILL*, the 1947 *SWEETHEARTS*, a 1951 revival of *MUSIC IN THE AIR*, the 1952 *PAL JOEY*, and a 1953 *PORGY AND BESS*. By the 1970s, Broadway revivals proliferated. There were fewer new musicals than ever before and new productions of old shows looked very appealing to producers, looking for a familiar product to sell, and for artists, willing to work with superior material. Among the notable revivals of the decade were *NO, NO, NANETTE* (1971), *IRENE* (1973), *CANDIDE* (1974), *GOOD NEWS!* (1974), *VERY GOOD EDDIE* (1976), *THE KING AND I* (1977), and *OKLAHOMA!* (1979). Because the costs of production had escalated by the 1980s and 1990s, even a revival was a risky business proposition on Broadway but that did not deter producers from offering such noteworthy revivals as *THE PIRATES OF PENZANCE* (1981), *ON YOUR TOES* (1983), *ZORBÁ* (1983), *SWEET CHARITY* (1986), *ANYTHING GOES* (1987), *Gypsy* (1989), *GUYS AND DOLLS* (1992), *THE MOST HAPPY FELLA* (1992), *SHE LOVES ME* (1993), *Show Boat* (1994), *CAROUSEL* (1994), *HOW TO SUCCEED IN BUSINESS WITHOUT REALLY TRYING* (1995), *A FUNNY THING HAPPENED ON THE WAY TO THE FORUM* (1996), *THE SOUND OF MUSIC* (1998), and *KISS ME, KATE* (1999). It seems in recent years that a musical does not

<table>
<tr><td>

Some Notable Movie Musical Remakes

BABES IN TOYLAND (1934 and 1961)

Cameo Kirby (1930 and 1935 as *MISSISSIPPI*)

CONEY ISLAND (1943 and 1950 as *WABASH AVENUE*)

DESERT SONG, THE (1929, 1943, and 1953)

FOLIES BERGERE DE PARIS (1935 and 1941 as *THAT NIGHT IN RIO* and 1951 as *ON THE RIVIERA*)

GIRL CRAZY (1932 and 1943)

GOOD NEWS! (1930 and 1947)

JAZZ SINGER, THE (1927, 1952, 1980)

KING AND I, THE (1956 and 1999: animated)

MOON OVER MIAMI (1941 and 1946 as *THREE LITTLE GIRLS IN BLUE*)

NEW MOON (1930 and 1940)

NO, NO, NANETTE (1930 and 1940)

RIO RITA (1929 and 1942)

ROBERTA (1935 and 1952 as *LOVELY TO LOOK AT*)

ROSE MARIE (1936 and 1954)

SHOW BOAT (1929, 1936, and 1951)

STAR IS BORN, A (1954 and 1976)

STATE FAIR (1945 and 1962)

SUNNY (1930 and 1941)

Sweetheart of Sigma Chi, The (1933 and 1946)

THANKS A MILLION (1935 and 1946 as *If I'm Lucky*)

TIN PAN ALLEY (1940 and 1950 as *I'll Get By*)

VAGABOND KING, THE (1930 and 1956)

VARSITY SHOW (1937 and 1950 as *Fine and Dandy*)

</td></tr>
</table>

have to be forty years old (or more) to warrant a Broadway revival. Some shows are reappearing in New York before a generation has passed. Consider such not-so-old revivals as *GREASE* (1972, 1994, 1996, and 2007), *PACIFIC OVERTURES* (1976 and 2004), *SWEENEY TODD* (1979 and 2005), *NINE* (1982 and 2003), *INTO THE WOODS* (1987 and 2002), and *42ND STREET* (1980 and 2001), not to mention *A CHORUS LINE* (1975 and 2006) and *LES MISÉRABLES* (1987 and 2006), which are exact replicas of the original productions and not true revivals. Some see the large numbers of revivals on Broadway as a sign of a dwindling American musical theatre. Others feel the great shows of the past ought to be revived, not as museum pieces but as part of a living cultural heritage.

Hollywood's version of a revival is a remake. Movie musicals were occasionally remade (often by the same studio because they usually owned the rights) because the property was considered appealing enough to attract a new audience. Before the arrival of videotapes and DVDs, and even more so before television started broadcasting old movies in the late 1950s, a film could easily disappear. Once a few years had passed, one's memory of a particular movie may have been vivid but there was no place for one to actually see it again. As a result, it was financially sound to remake a movie after ten years and capitalize on new box office potential. Musicals were no exception, and musical remakes were not uncommon up through the 1950s. Interestingly, most of the musicals remade were based on Broadway works. Even television was mindful of the short life of a broadcast (particularly a live one) so it made sense to remake TV musicals such as *PETER PAN* and *CINDERELLA*.

REVUE MUSICALS. Frequently confused with vaudeville or a variety show, the Broadway musical revue was a program of songs, dances, and sketches that created a plotless entity. Rather than just a bill of acts, the show was put together by its creators to present a balanced and somewhat unified whole. It was planned, designed, scored, directed, and choreographed with the same kind of integrity used in book musicals. Some revues were held together thematically, whereas others were tied together less obviously. The first distinctively American revue was *THE PASSING SHOW* (1894), although its roots go back further. Many revues were part of a series, with the most famous one being the *ZIEGFELD FOLLIES*, which producer FLORENZ ZIEGFELD presented between 1907 and 1931; others continued the series after his death. Other celebrated revue series include the *GEORGE WHITE SCANDALS*, *EARL CARROLL'S VANITIES*, THE *MUSIC BOX REVUES*, *Greenwich Village Follies*, *GARRICK GAIETIES*, and *ARTISTS AND MODELS*. IRVING BERLIN and the team of ARTHUR SCHWARTZ (music) and HOWARD DIETZ (lyrics) are generally considered the best songwriters of American revues but there were many outstanding shows scored by others as well. The golden age for the Broadway revue began with *The LITTLE SHOW* (1929) and lasted into the early 1940s. Among the superior revues from this period were *THREE'S A CROWD* (1930), *THE BAND WAGON* (1931), *AS THOUSANDS CHEER* (1933), *LIFE BEGINS AT 8:40* (1934), *AT HOME ABROAD* (1935), *THE SHOW IS ON* (1936), *PINS AND NEEDLES* (1938), *HELLZAPOPPIN'* ((1938), and *THIS IS THE ARMY* (1942). The genre started to wane after World War II and by the 1950s and 1960s revues with original scores were usually to be found Off Broadway if anywhere at all, such as the MALTBY and SHIRE musicals *STARTING HERE, STARTING NOW* (1977) and *CLOSER THAN EVER* (1989). In the 1970s, a new breed of musical revue became popular: the nostalgic recollection of the work of former greats. The music of "FATS" WALLER was collected for *Ain't Misbehavin'* (1977), *Eubie* (1978) celebrated composer EUBIE BLAKE, *Sophisticated Ladies* (1981) honored DUKE ELLINGTON, and the pop music songs by the team of LEIBER and STOLLER provided the score for the long-running *Smokey Joe's Cafe* (1995). Other shows, such as *Bubbling Brown Sugar* (1976), *Sugar Babies* (1979), *Tintypes* (1980), *Black and Blue* (1989), *Five Guys Named Moe* (1992), and *Swing!* (1999) concentrated on a particular culture or on a period of music from the past. Also, dance has sometimes been the format for a revue, as with *Dancin'* (1978), *Fosse* (1999), *Contact* (2000), and *Movin' Out* (2002). However, the full-scale Broadway revue with original songs and top-class production numbers is a thing of the past.

Movie revue musicals had a brief but potent life during the early days of sound. Each studio gathered their talent on contract and put together a revue of songs, sketches, dances, dramatic scenes, and ballet and tied the whole program together with one or more master of ceremonies. Because the novelty of talking pictures was still fresh and the spectacle could be impressive (some even had color sections), these revues were popular for a few years. MGM offered *The Hollywood Revue of 1929*, WARNER BROTHERS made *On With the Show* (1929) and *The Show of Shows* (1929), UNIVERSAL had *King of Jazz* (1930), and *Paramount on Parade* (1930) showed off that studio's stars. When the appeal of these musicals declined in the early 1930s, the studios abandoned the revue format and later disguised their variety shows as *The Big Broadcast* (1932), *The Broadway Melody of 1936* (1935), and other films that offered a parade of talents but tied them together with the thinnest of plots. The titles of the famous Broadway revues such as *Ziegfeld Follies, George White's Scandals, Earl Carroll Vanities, Artists and Models,* and *Greenwich Village Follies* were all used by Hollywood for movie musicals that had a plot that was an excuse for a series of production numbers, but a true movie revue would be a rare thing. The few exceptions include *Ziegfeld Follies (1946)*, *New Faces* (1954), and *Jacques Brel Is Alive and Well and Living in Paris* (1975), as well as the animated anthology musicals such as *The Three Caballeros* (1945) and *Make Mine Music* (1946). For many years television took up the musical revue in the form of weekly variety shows that featured stars, songs, sketches, and production numbers. *The Hollywood Palace, The Ed Sullivan Show, The Carol Burnett Show,*

and many others were very popular and offered shows that were a cross between vaudeville and the opulent Broadway revue, but by the 1980s such programs lost their appeal and the revue faded away in another medium.

REYNOLDS, [Mary Frances] **DEBBIE** (1932–). Film, television, and stage performer. The seemingly ever-youthful, perky blonde singer–dancer of 1950s and 1960s movies, she was part of the last generation of stars during the golden age of Hollywood musicals. Reynolds was born in El Paso, Texas, and her wholesome, girl-next-door looks allowed her to win some beauty pageants, which led to a movie contract. She made her screen debut in 1948 and was noticed in her first musical, *The Daughter of Rosie O'Grady* (1950), followed by featured roles in *Three Little Words* (1950), *Two Weeks With Love* (1950), and *Mr. Imperium* (1951). Reynolds found wide popularity as the cheery Kathy Selden who dubs singing vocals during the early talkies in *Singin' in the Rain* (1952) and her other standout role was the feisty

Debbie Reynolds. Often saddled with second-rate movie musicals, the chipper Reynolds usually shone all the same. Here she is in *Two Weeks With Love* (1950), a film most remembered for her duet "The Aba Daba Honeymoon" with Carlton Carpenter. The movie was not a hit but the Reynolds–Carpenter recording of the song sold a million discs. (Photofest)

Molly in *THE UNSINKABLE MOLLY BROWN* (1964). Her other screen musicals include *Skirts Ahoy* (1952), *The Affairs of Dobie Gillis* (1952), *GIVE A GIRL A BREAK* (1952), *I Love Melvin* (1952), *Athena* (1954), *HIT THE DECK* (1955), *Bundle of Joy* (1956), and *The Singing Nun* (1966). Reynolds was also a favorite in film comedies and in nightclubs. She made her belated Broadway debut in *IRENE* (1973) and appeared on many television programs, including her own show in 1970. Reynolds has provided voices for animated television shows and films, such as *CHARLOTTE'S WEB* (1973) and *Rugrats in Paris* (2000). She was still making films in the 2006. Reynolds was married to singer Eddie Fisher (1928–) and their children are actress Carrie Fisher (1956–) and television director Todd Fisher (1958–). Autobiography: *Debbie: My Life*, with David Patrick Columbia (1988).

REYNOLDS, MARJORIE [born Marjorie Goodspeed] (1917–1997). Film and television performer. A former child actress, she grew into an attractive blonde leading lady in 1940s films, including several musicals. Reynolds was born in Buhl, Idaho, and appeared in silent films at a very young age. Under the name Marjorie Moore she played preteens and adolescents in 1930s movies, including bit parts in the musicals *Wine, Women and Song* (1933) and *Collegiate* (1935). Changing her name to Marjorie Reynolds, she was cast in adult roles in dramas and musicals, most memorably as the aspiring singer that both FRED ASTAIRE and BING CROSBY fight over in *HOLIDAY INN* (1942). Her other musical credits include *STAR-SPANGLED RHYTHM* (1942), *Dixie* (1943), *Bring on the Girls* (1945), *Duffy's Tavern* (1945), *That Midnight Kiss* (1949), and *Juke Box Rhythm* (1959). When her film career declined in the 1950s, she moved to television and found new success in *The Life of Riley* and other shows.

▦ *RHAPSODY IN BLUE* (Warner 1945). This biographical musical didn't have very much to say about the life of composer GEORGE GERSHWIN (and what was said wasn't very accurate) but with twenty-four musical numbers and an agreeable cast to present them it was a highly entertaining movie and a box office hit. Howard Koch and Eliot Paul wrote the screenplay that was as dull as it was fictitious, showing young George (Mickey Roth) and his brother Ira (Darryl Hickman) growing up in New York with their folksy parents (Morris Carnovsky and ROSEMARY DeCAMP), eventually becoming Broadway's acclaimed songwriters George (ROBERT ALDA) and Ira Gershwin (Herbert Rudley). The routine rags-to-riches plot was given a touch of authenticity by performers who actually knew Gershwin, such as AL JOLSON, Hazel Scott, Anne Brown, GEORGE WHITE, PAUL WHITEMAN (who conducted the title composition), and OSCAR LEVANT (who played the "Piano Concerto in F"). Also on hand to perform the songs or fill out the cast were ALEXIS SMITH, Charles Coburn, Albert Basserman, Julie Bishop, Andrew Tombes, and JOAN LESLIE who got the most numbers even though she had to be dubbed by Louanne Hogan. Among the beloved songs heard were "Swanee," "I Got Rhythm," "The Man I Love," "Somebody Loves Me," "Fascinating Rhythm," "Clap Yo' Hands," and "Love Walked In." Irving Rapper was the uninspired director, and LeRoy PRINZ did the choreography.

RHODES, ERIK [born Ernest Sharpe] (1906–1990). Film, stage, and television performer. A character actor in 1930s films who specialized in Continental types, he livened up a handful of movie musicals. Rhodes was born in El Reno, Oklahoma, and pursued an acting career on radio and the stage, making his Broadway debut in a play in 1928. The next year he was in the cast of the innovative revue *THE LITTLE SHOW* (1929), followed by *Hey Nonny Nonny!* (1932) and *GAY DIVORCE* (1932) in which he played the effete Italian Tonetti. Rhodes got to reprise his performance in the film version retitled *THE GAY DIVORCEE* (1934) and was thereafter usually cast as eccentric Europeans. His other musical films include *TOP HAT* (1935), *Old Man Rhythm* (1935), *Music for Madame* (1937), and *ON YOUR TOES* (1939). Rhodes returned to the stage in 1947 and was featured in the Broadway musicals *Dance Me a Song* (1950), *CAN-CAN* (1953), *Shinebone Alley* (1957), *JAMAICA* (1957), and as a replacement for Lycus in *A FUNNY THING HAPPENED ON THE WAY TO THE FORUM* in 1963. He infrequently returned to films and was acting on television into the 1960s.

▦ *RHYTHM ON THE RIVER* (Paramount 1940). A low-budget, unpretentious BING CROSBY vehicle, the engaging little musical was one of his best thanks to a sparkling score by JOHNNY BURKE and JAMES V. MONACO and some enjoyable performances by a first-class cast. Dwight Taylor's screenplay let Crosby play the laid-back songwriter Bob Sommers who'd rather live the lazy life on his modest houseboat on the river than deal with the hectic world of

Tin Pan Alley. Bob happily ghostwrites music for the dried-out songwriter Oliver Courtney (Basil Rathbone) until he meets Courtney's ghostwriting lyricist Cherry Lane (MARY MARTIN). The two fall in love and start making music together under their own names. VICTOR SCHERTZINGER directed the film, which also featured OSCAR LEVANT as Courtney's wry assistant Billy Starbuck, Charley Grapewin, OSCAR SHAW, Lillian Cornel, WILLIAM FRAWLEY, and Jeanne Cagney. In addition to the lyrical title song, the score included the romantic ballads "That's for Me" and "Only Forever," the sly narrative number "Ain't It a Shame About Mame?," and the teary torch song "I Don't Want to Cry Anymore," which Schertzinger wrote himself and interpolated into the Burke–Monaco score.

RICE, EDWARD E[verett]. (1848–1924). Stage composer, producer, and director. A pioneering writer and presenter of musicals, he not only produced hits but paved the way for later musical comedies. Rice was born in poverty in Brighton, Massachusetts, and ran away from home to be an actor. As an adult he joined up with lyricist–librettist J. CHEEVER GOODWIN and wrote the very popular musical *Evangeline* (1874), one of the first musical burlesques. Rice would go on to write other musicals, such as *Hiawatha* (1880), *Adonis* (1884), and *Excelsior, Jr.* (1895), but most of his energies would be spent on producing and directing. He created an American brand of musical farce–comedy that was instrumental in developing the Broadway musical in a direction different than European operettas. Rice was also noted for the talent he discovered and promoted, such as LILLIAN RUSSELL, HENRY E. DIXEY, FAY TEMPLETON, and JEROME KERN. Among the many musicals he produced and/or directed are *Billee Taylor* (1881), *Little Christopher Columbus* (1894), *The French Maid* (1897), *The Show Girl* (1902), and *Mr. Wix of Wickham* (1904). One of Rice's most unique contributions was *CLORINDY; OR, THE ORIGIN OF THE CAKE WALK* (1898), the first musical written and performed by African Americans that was presented for white audiences in a Broadway playhouse.

RICE, TIM[othy Miles Bindon] (1944–). Stage and film lyricist. An extremely popular songwriter, the British lyricist seems to find success with whichever composer he teams up with. Rice was born in Amersham, England, and educated at Lansing College before beginning his career in music broadcasting and recording. Collaborating with composer ANDREW LLOYD WEBBER, Rice wrote the lyrics for a trio of successful pop-rock musicals that were hits in both England and America: *JOSEPH AND THE AMAZING TECHNICOLOR DREAMCOAT* (1968), *JESUS CHRIST SUPERSTAR* (1971), and *EVITA* (1979). Of his other London musicals, only *CHESS* (1988) reached Broadway but he was well represented in America with the lyrics he contributed to the stage versions of *BEAUTY AND THE BEAST* (1994) and *THE LION KING* (1997), as well as the original musical *AIDA* (2000) with composer ELTON JOHN. While his shows with Webber were either made into movies or filmed for video, Rice wrote lyrics directly for the screen with the animated musicals *ALADDIN* (1992), *The Lion King* (1994), and *Road to El Dorado* (2000).

RICHMAN, HARRY [born Harry Reichman] (1885–1972). Stage and film performer. A dapper song-and-dance man, he spent most of his career in vaudeville and nightclubs but was enjoyed in a number of Broadway musicals as well. Richman was born in Cincinnati and went into variety as a young man, touring across the country for several years. He was a gifted pianist and sometime composer and some of his early jobs were as accompanist to MAE WEST, NORA BAYES, and the DOLLY SISTERS. Richman impersonated AL JOLSON and other stars in his act and then developed his own style as a top-hatted hoofer who twirled his cane as he sang in a slightly lisped voice. His most significant Broadway appearances were in the 1926 edition of *GEORGE WHITE'S SCANDALS*, in which he introduced "The Birth of the Blues," and *The International Revue* (1930), where he sang "On the Sunny Side of the Street." Richman's other revues include *George White's Scandals* (1928 and 1932), *ZIEGFELD FOLLIES* (1931), and *Priorities of 1943*, and he played character parts in the book musicals *Queen o' Hearts* (1922) and *Say When* (1934). He made a notable film debut in *PUTTIN' ON THE RITZ* (1930) where he introduced the title song and his recording of the number was very popular. Richman also appeared in the Hollywood musical *The Music Goes Round* (1936) and the British film *Kicking the Moon Around* (1938), as well as composing songs that were used in the movies *Near the Rainbow's End* (1930), *Stars of Arizona* (1937), and *Kelly and Me* (1957). Autobiography: *A Hell of a Life* (1966).

RING, BLANCHE (1871?–1961). Stage performer. One of the twentieth century's first and biggest musical comedy stars, she introduced more hit songs than perhaps any other performer between 1900 and 1920. Born in Boston sometime in the early 1870s, Ring's family was in show business and she was on stage as a child performer, later touring the country with such stars as Nat Goodwin and Chauncey Olcott and then becoming a vaudeville star in her own right. She was a tiny blonde with a big belting voice and knew how to engage a crowd, being one of the first singers to get her audiences to sing along with her. Ring made a rousing Broadway debut in *The Defender* (1902) in which she introduced "In the Good Old Summertime." Over the next three decades she would appear in two dozen Broadway musicals, often playing the lively, clever girl who was as brash as her singing, as well as some comedies and shows in London where she was also very popular. Among her musical credits are *The Jersey Lily* (1903), *His Majesty* (1906), *Miss Dolly Dollars* (1906), *The Midnight Sons* (1909), *The Yankee Girl* (1910), *When Claudia Smiles* (1914), THE PASSING SHOW OF 1919, *The Broadway Whirl* (1921), *House Boat on the Styx* (1928), STRIKE UP THE BAND (1930), *De Luxe* (1935), and *Right This Way* (1938). More memorable than most of her vehicles were the songs she introduced, including "I've Got Rings on My Fingers," "Waltz Me Around, Willie," "Yip-I-Addy-I-Ay," "Bedelia," and "Come Josephine in My Flying Machine." Ring appeared in two silent films and two talkies, singing only in *If I Had My Way* (1940). She was married for a time to actor CHARLES WINNINGER.

🕮 **RINK, THE** (Martin Beck Theatre 1984). A gritty yet fascinating musical by JOHN KANDER (music) and FRED EBB (lyrics), the show was much more than the stars vehicle it seemed. After a failed marriage and years of running a roller skating rink on the boardwalk of an East Coast amusement park, Anna (CHITA RIVERA) is ready to sell the place and retire when her estranged daughter Angel (LIZA MINNELLI) unexpectedly shows up and wants to keep the place open for business. Mother and daughter argue, reminisce, and then finally come to some kind of understanding. Also in the cast were JASON ALEXANDER, Ronn Carroll, SCOTT ELLIS, Mel Johnson, Jr., and Scott Holmes. TERRENCE MCNALLY wrote the character-centered libretto (his first one for Broadway) and the two stars gave thrilling, honest performances. The Kander and Ebb score produced no mainstream hits but was filled with superior

songs, such as the questioning solo "Colored Lights," the comic duet "The Apple Doesn't Fall," the plaintive ballad "Marry Me," the vaudeville-like "What Happened to the Old Days?," the painful flashback "All the Children in a Row," and the exhilarating "Blue Crystal." The dark and painful storyline did not provide the glittering kind of show Minnelli was usually associated with so there was disappointment on the part of the reviewers and the public. Everyone agreed that Rivera was giving one of her best performances but it wasn't enough so the musical closed when Minnelli's contract ran out after 204 performances. A. J. Antoon directed the atmospheric piece and GRACIELA DANIELE choreographed.

🕮 **RIO RITA** (Ziegfeld Theatre 1927). A large-scale operetta set on the Texas–Mexico border, the highly romantic musical was one of the most successful shows of the 1920s. Captain Jim Stewart and his Texas Rangers are on the hunt for the notorious bandit known as the Kinkajou but he is not too busy to find time to fall in love with the lovely but hot-tempered Rio Rita Ferguson. The oily General Esteban also has his eye on Rita and persuades her that her brother Roberto is the Kinkajou. He then convinces her that Jim does not love her and he is only interested in her to get to Roberto. It turns out that Esteban is the real Kinkajou and Jim not only captures his man but wins Rita's heart for good. The libretto by GUY BOLTON and Fred Thompson left room for comedy as well as romance, creating the sidekick characters of Chick and Ed who were played with farcical skill by the team of WHEELER and WOOLSEY. The score by HARRY TIERNEY (music) and JOSEPH MCCARTHY (lyrics) was filled with stirring numbers such as "The Ranger's Song," "If You're in Love You'll Waltz," "The Kinkajou," "Following the Sun Around," and the title number. Producer FLORENZ ZIEGFELD hired Joseph Urban to design the spectacular sets, which held a chorus of 100 chorines, and he used the show to open his new playhouse named after himself. John Harwood directed, ALBERTINA RASCH and SAMMY LEE shared the choreography chores, and the musical ran 494 performances.

🎬 **Rio Rita** (RKO 1929) was the first successful screen version of a Broadway musical, receiving both critical and popular approval. Producer WILLIAM LEBARON brought the stage work to the screen with all but two of its songs, its comedians Wheeler and Woolsey making their film debut, and even divided the movie

Casts for *Rio Rita*			
Character	*1927 Broadway*	*1929 film*	*1942 film*
Rita	Ethelind Terry	BEBE DANIELS	KATHRYN GRAYSON
Jim Stewart/Ricardo	J. HAROLD MURRAY	JOHN BOLES	JOHN CARROLL
General	Vincent Serrano	Georges Renavent	
Roberto	Walter Petrie	Don Alvarado	
Dolly/Dottie	Ada May	Dorothy Lee	Joan Valerie
Chick Bean/Doc	BERT WHEELER	Bert Wheeler	BUD ABBOTT
Ed Lovett/Wishy	ROBERT WOOLSEY	Robert Woolsey	LOU COSTELLO
Lucette Brunswick			Patricia Dane
Maurice Crandall			Tom Conway
Harry Gantley			Barry Nelson

into two acts with the second half in color. The screenplay by director Luther Reed and Russell Mack was close to the stage libretto, and the characters of Rita (BEBE DANIELS), Jim (JOHN BOLES), and Esteban (George Renavent) played well on the screen. Tierney and McCarthy wrote a new song for the film, the entrancing "You're Always in My Arms (But Only in My Dreams)," and the musical favorites from the stage were well served. It is an early and somewhat primitive film in many ways, yet the spectacle is impressive and the performances enjoyable in an operetta fashion. MGM made a version of *Rio Rita* in 1942 as a vehicle for comics BUD ABBOTT and LOU COSTELLO in the Wheeler and Woolsey roles. About half of the score was cut to make room for added comedy bits by the popular team. The screenplay by Richard Connell and Gladys Lehman was also a hatchet job, resetting the story during World War II and adding spies and comic intrigues to the story. As directed by S. Sylvan Simon, the movie is a funny vehicle for Abbott and Costello but far from satisfying as a musical. ☐ An abridged version of *Rio Rita* featuring PATRICIA MORISON as Rita was broadcast on NBC-TV's anthology series *Musical Comedy Time* in 1950.

RITCHARD, CYRIL [born Cyril Trimmell-Ritchard] (1897–1977). Stage, film, and television performer and director. With his bleating voice punctuated with a giggling laugh, no one was better at playing fops, dandies, and aesthetes on the British and London stage and there are vivid television records to keep the memory of him alive. Ritchard was born in Sydney, Australia, and started to study medicine at the local university but by 1917 turned to acting. After performing in plays and musicals in his native country and stopping in New York to appear on Broadway in the revue *Puzzles*

of 1925, he continued on to England where he made silent films and sang in music halls. Eventually he became famous in both Australia and Great Britain for his comic performances in classic plays and musicals. Ritchard first found notice on Broadway as the foppish Tattle in John Gielgud's production of *Love for Love* (1947) and returned in some other comedies of manners before finding acclaim for his Captain Hook in the musical *PETER PAN* (1954), a performance he reprised for television in 1960. His other memorable musical roles were the philosophical Pluto in *The Happiest Girl in the World* (1961), the upper-class Sir in *THE ROAR OF THE GREASEPAINT–THE SMELL OF THE CROWD* (1965), and the merry millionaire Osgood Fielding Jr. in *SUGAR* (1975). Ritchard also starred in several comedies on Broadway, most of which he directed himself, and occasionally sang in operas at the Met and other venues. He only made a handful of films, including the musical *HALF A SIXPENCE* (1967), but appeared on many television programs, including the TV musicals *The King and Mrs. Candle* (1955), *DEAREST ENEMY* (1955), *JACK AND THE BEANSTALK* (1956), *ALADDIN* (1958), *THE DANGEROUS CHRISTMAS OF RED RIDING HOOD* (1965), and *HANS BRINKER OR THE SILVER SKATES* (1969). Ritchard was married to actress–singer Madge Elliott (1896–1955) and during the early part of his career the two performed together in many revues and musicals in Australia and England, labeled the "musical Lunts" by their many fans.

RITTMAN, TRUDE (1909–2005). Stage music arranger. One of the unsung talents of the American musical theatre, she arranged the dance and choral music for over fifty Broadway shows.

Rittman was born in Mannheim, Germany, and emigrated to America in 1937 where soon she was working as a piano accompanist for concerts and the GEORGE BALANCHINE dance company. Trained in musical composition, she worked with such composers as Aaron Copland, Virgil Thompson, LEONARD BERNSTEIN, and MARC BLITZSTEIN in creating the dance music for ballets and operas. Rittman was the first person to work with choreographers in deciding how the music for the dances should be constructed and she single-handedly created the title of dance music arranger. She worked closely with AGNES DE MILLE on many dance concerts and Broadway musicals, beginning with ONE TOUCH OF VENUS (1943). Her collaboration with de Mille in developing RICHARD RODGERS's melodies into choreographic music for OKLAHOMA! (1943) was one of the reasons that the musical's ballets and other musical numbers were so well integrated with the story and character. Rittman would do similar arrangements for other Rodgers and Hammerstein musicals and her contribution to their success cannot be overestimated. For example, Rittman composed most of the music for "The Small House of Uncle Thomas" ballet in THE KING AND I (1951). Among her many other Broadway credits were FINIAN'S RAINBOW (1947), BRIGADOON (1947), PETER PAN (1954), MY FAIR LADY (1956), and CAMELOT (1960). Rittman also composed music for ballets and television specials.

RITZ BROTHERS. Stage, film, and television performers. The zany, if not terribly witty, trio of comics were audience favorites in the 1930s and 1940s, invading Broadway and Hollywood musicals for slapstick diversion. Al (1901–1965), Jimmy (1903–1985), and Harry (1906–1986) were born in Newark, New Jersey, sons of a haberdasher named Joachim from Austria. They grew up in Brooklyn and went into vaudeville as each finished high school, with the trio gaining fame for their noisy and physical comedics and eccentric singing. (There was a fourth brother named George who did not perform but acted as the team's manager.) After appearing in nightclubs, they were featured on Broadway in two editions of EARL CARROLL VANITIES and in Florida Girl (1925). The brothers made their screen debut in a 1934 short and then were cast in thirteen musical features over the next decade, including Sing, Baby, Sing (1936), One in a Million (1936), ON THE AVENUE (1937), You Can't Have Everything (1937), THE GOLDWYN FOLLIES (1938), Straight, Place and Show (1938), The Three Musketeers (1939), Argentine Nights (1940), Behind the Eight Ball

(1942), and Never a Dull Moment (1943). The team retired from films in 1944 but continued to perform in clubs and on television until the death of Al in 1965. Never as inspired as the MARX BROTHERS, the threesome was nonetheless a spirited amusement that was much appreciated by Depression-era audiences.

RIVERA, CHITA [born Dolores Conchita Figueroa Del Rivero] (1933–). Stage, film, and television performer. One of Broadway's finest and more durable singing–dancing stars, she has managed to shine in both hit and flop musicals decade after decade. Rivera was born in Washington, DC, the daughter of a Puerto Rican musician, but grew up in New York and trained at the American School of Ballet. She was on Broadway by 1952 as a replacement in the choruses of CALL ME MADAM (1952), GUYS AND DOLLS (1953), and CAN-CAN (1954) and then was featured in Shoestring Revue (1955), Seventh Heaven (1955), and Mr. WONDERFUL (1956). Her fiery performance as Anita in the original cast of WEST SIDE STORY (1957) brought her acclaim and from then on her work was always applauded even if her vehicles were less than successful. Rivera's Broadway credits are the spirited Rose in BYE BYE BIRDIE (1960) and Bring Back Birdie (1981), the sultry gypsy Anyanka in Bajour (1964), the publicity-hungry Velma Kelly in CHICAGO (1975), the conniving Queen in Merlin (1983), the Italian mother Anna in THE RINK (1984), the movie goddess Aurora and the deadly Spider Woman in THE KISS OF THE SPIDER WOMAN (1993), and the ex-Folies de Bergere star Liliane in NINE (2003), as well as the revues Jerry's Girls (1985) and the autobiographical Chita Rivera: The Dancer's Life (2005). She has performed in the touring versions of many musicals and in concert, as well as on several musical specials on television, including ONCE UPON A BROTHERS GRIMM (1954) and PIPPIN (1987). Rivera was featured as Nicki in the film SWEET CHARITY (1969) but she made few other movies, although she can be spotted in cameo roles in Sgt. Pepper's Lonely Hearts Club Band (1978) and CHICAGO (2002). In addition to being an outstanding dancer, Rivera possesses a charismatic stage presence, a wry sense of comedy, and a masterful way with a song.

RKO PICTURES. It may have been one of Hollywood's smaller studios with fewer productions and a limited number of stars in its employ, but it was still a very influential organization, particularly in the area of musicals.

Its roots were in vaudeville at the turn of the twentieth century when the Keith and Orpheum circuits were among the most powerful players in variety entertainment. The film studio was founded in 1928 when the two businesses merged with a Minneapolis nickelodeon chain and titled itself Radio-Keith-Orpheum Pictures. The company hit its peak in the 1930s with a series of very popular films, such as *King Kong* (1933), *Little Women* (1933), *The Informer* (1935), *Becky Sharp* (1935), *Stage Door* (1937), *Bringing Up Baby* (1938), and *The Hunchback of Notre Dame* (1939). RKO was mostly known in the Depression years for its beloved series of FRED ASTAIRE and GINGER ROGERS musicals utilizing the music of VINCENT YOUMANS, IRVING BERLIN, JEROME KERN, and GEORGE GERSHWIN. Among the screen classics of this era were *FLYING DOWN TO RIO* (1933), *ROBERTA* (1935), *TOP HAT* (1935), *FOLLOW THE FLEET* (1936), *SWING TIME* (1936), and *SHALL WE DANCE* (1937). Aside from distributing WALT DISNEY's animated films, the studio generated few musicals after 1940. Enterprising billionaire Howard Hughes bought the company in 1948 but the studio dwindled further under his sporadic leadership. Its financial troubles in the 1950s caused RKO to switch to the blossoming venue of television. The RKO studios were sold to Desilu in 1953, and the library of old films was purchased by entertainment business mogul Ted Turner in the 1980s.

ROAD PICTURES. One of the most popular movie series in the history of Hollywood, these seven BOB HOPE and BING CROSBY musicals by PARAMOUNT were predictable, self-mocking, and highly entertaining. In all the screenplays, many written by FRANK BUTLER and Don Hartman, Crosby was the straight man, sang the

Road Pictures. There was a predictability to the seven *Road* movies, from the cast to the plots, but the jokes were new and there were a few surprises along the way, be it a talking camel or Bob Hope playing his own aunt. One thing you could count on is that Hope (left) and Bing Crosby would somehow meet up with Dorothy Lamour (center). Here they are clowning around in *Road to Zanzibar* (1941). (Photofest)

ballads, and got the girl (DOROTHY LAMOUR) in the end. Hope was the put-upon chump, always got into difficult straits because of Crosby, and invariably fell for Lamour but lost her or any other beautiful woman who came along. The movies were known for their unpretentious gags, ridiculous plots, and breaking of character. The two comics often spoke directly into the camera and made fun of Paramount, Hollywood, and their own careers. In **Road to Singapore** (1940), Joshua Mallon (Crosby), the son of shipping millionaire Joshua Mallon IV (Charles Coburn), doesn't want to marry high-society Gloria Wycott (Judith Barrett) so he runs off with his penniless friend Ace Lannigan (Hope) to the South Seas. There they rescue Mima (Lamour) from the sinister Caesar (Anthony Quinn) who makes his living whipping cigarette ends out of Mima's mouth. The songs were by JOHNNY BURKE, JAMES V. MONACO, and VICTOR SCHERTZINGER (who also directed), the best being the rhythmic ditty "Sweet Potato Piper." The movie was far from the best in the series but the Hope–Crosby–Lamour chemistry was magic and the picture was very popular. The three stars were quickly reassembled for **Road to Zanzibar** (1941), which was a better comedy all around. Con men Chuck Reardon (Crosby) and Hubert "Fearless" Frazier (Hope) have to skip town when they sell a phony diamond mine to an unhappy customer, so they go to Africa where they meet the con women Donna Latour (Lamour) and Julia Quimny (UNA MERKEL) on safari. In addition to spoofing every jungle picture ever made, the film offered two pleasing ballads by BURKE and JAMES VAN HEUSEN (who would score the rest of the *Road* musicals): "You're Dangerous" and "It's Always You." The supporting cast included ERIC BLORE, Douglass Dumbrille, Iris Adrian, and Lionel Royce, under Schertzinger's direction once again.

Road to Morocco (1942) had fun ribbing *Arabian Nights* movies as the carefree bums Jeff Peters (Crosby) and Orville "Turkey" Jackson (Hope) are shipwrecked on the shore of North Africa and set off across the desert only to find themselves rescuing Princess Shalmar (Lamour) from the murderous chieftain Mullay Kasim (Anthony Quinn). One of the funniest of the entries, the film included a sequence when Hope played his own Aunt Lucy. The movie also boasted a superb score headed by "Moonlight Becomes You," the biggest-selling song to come out of the whole series. Screenwriter Frank Butler directed this time around. **Road to Utopia** (1945) is generally considered the classic of the seven movies. The story, told in flashback, concerned turn-of-the-twentieth-century vaudevillians Duke Johnson (Crosby) and Chester Hooton (Hope) who head for the Klondike with a map

---

Songs from the *Road* Pictures

Road to Singapore (1940)	*Road to Zanzibar* (1941)	*Road to Morocco* (1942)
"Too Romantic"	"You're Dangerous"	"Moonlight Becomes You"
"The Moon and the Willow Tree"	"It's Always You"	"Ain't Got a Dime to My Name"
"Sweet Potato Piper"	"You Lucky People, You"	"Constantly"
"Kaigoon"	"On the Road to Zanzibar"	"Road to Morocco"
"Captain Custard"	"Birds of a Feather"	

Road to Utopia (1945)	*Road to Rio* (1947)	*Road to Bali* (1952)
"Put It There, Pal"	"But Beautiful"	"Hoots Mon"
"Personality"	"You Don't Have to Know the Language"	"Chicago Style"
"Good-Time Charley"	"Experience"	"The Merry-Go-Runaround"
"It's Anybody's Spring"	"Apalachicolas Fla"	"To See You"
"Welcome to My Dreams (And How Are You?)"	"Cavaquinho"	"Moonflowers"
"Would You"	"Brazil"	

The Road to Hong Kong (1962)
"Warmer Than a Whisper"
"Let's Not Be Sensible"
"Teamwork"
"The Road to Hong Kong"

showing the location of a lost gold mine. They team up with saloon singer Sal Van Hoyden (Lamour) and, pursued by a set of villains, set off via dog sleds on a merry misadventure. For a change, Hope wins Lamour when Crosby is set adrift on an ice floe and is presumed dead. Jumping to the present, the older Chester and Sal complete the story just as Duke shows up, not too surprised to note that the couple's baby, Junior Hooton, is a spitting image of Crosby. Once again the songs were superior, with the most popular being the sassy and suggestive "Personality," but also enjoyable were the enticing ballad "Welcome to My Dreams" and the optimistic "It's Anybody's Spring." Hal Waker directed the Norman Panama–MELVIN FRANK screenplay with slaphappy abandon. **Road to Rio** (1947) was more conventional, a little less inspired, but just as popular as the others. When musicians Scat Sweeney (Crosby) and Hot Lips Barton (Hope) accidentally burn down the carnival where they work, the two hop aboard a boat for Rio de Janeiro. On the journey they meet Brazilian heiress Lucia Maria de Andrade (Lamour) who is being hypnotized by her evil Aunt Catherine (Gale Sondergaard) into marrying a fortune-hunting Brazilian she does not love. Once in Rio, the two musicians foil the crooks and stop the wedding in time. The ANDREWS SISTERS joined in on the singing this time, and the Burke–Van Heusen score included the hit ballad "But Beautiful" and the sly and peppy "You Don't Have to Know the Language." The popular song "Brazil" by Ary Barroso was interpolated into the score for atmospheric flavor. NORMAN Z. McLEOD was the director and the script this time was by Edmund Beloin and Jack Rose.

Moviegoers had to wait five years for **Road to Bali** (1952) and, although some of the jokes were aging along with the stars, it was still an enjoyable romp. Vaudevillians George Cochran (Crosby) and Harold Gridley (Hope) were once again on the run, the duo heading for the South Seas searching for hidden treasure but finding Princess Lal (Lamour) instead. The movie was enlivened by brief guest appearances by Humphrey Bogart, BOB CROSBY, JANE RUSSELL, and the newest comedy team, DEAN MARTIN and JERRY LEWIS. The songs were not as memorable this time around, although Hope and Crosby got to put on kilts and sing the risible Scottish parody "Hoots Mon." After a decade with no more *Road* pictures, audiences assumed the series was over and so box office for **The Road to Hong Kong** (Melnor/ United Artists 1962) was not overwhelm-

ing. The only film to add "the" to its title, it added nothing else and was an uninspired affair with the spirit of the series missing. Director Norman Panama wrote the screenplay with Melvin Frank and once again the two stars were con men. Harry Turner (Crosby) and Chester Babcock (Hope) try to sell rocket ships in Tibet but are run out of the country, travel to Hong Kong, and get involved with spies looking for a secret rocket fuel formula. Although the twosome briefly meet Lamour when they visit a nightclub where she performs, the woman they fight over this time is the agent Diane (Joan Collins). By the end of the story, the two comics are shot off into space where they come across fellow spacemen FRANK SINATRA and DEAN MARTIN. Van Heusen wrote the songs with SAMMY CAHN this time and three of them were delightful: the buddy trio "Teamwork," the soothing ballad "Warmer Than a Whisper," and the romantic duet "Let's Not Be Sensible." Again there were cameo appearances by David Niven, Peter Sellers, and JERRY COLONNA, but it wasn't enough to disguise the lack of excitement. The *Road* pictures were products of their time, yet are still very enjoyable. Various studios have tried to copy the formula over the years but never successfully, although the animated musical *The Road to El Dorado* (2000) was popular.

ROAR OF THE GREASEPAINT, THE–THE SMELL OF THE CROWD (Shubert Theatre 1965). An allegorical British musical by LESLIE BRICUSSE and ANTHONY NEWLEY (book, music, and lyrics), the show premiered on Broadway rather than in the West End. The "haves" of this world are represented by the self-serving Sir (CYRIL RITCHARD) and the "have nots" by the put-upon Cocky (Newley) and no matter what game they play, be it money, power, or love, Cocky always loses. By the end of the musical, Cocky realizes that the Sirs of the world need the have nots like himself, which gives him the power to reach some sort of agreement with Sir. Also featured in the cast were Sally Smith, GILBERT PRICE, and Joyce Jillson. The estimable score included three song hits, "Who Can I Turn To (When Nobody Needs Me)," "A Wonderful Day Like Today," and "Nothing Can Stop Me Now," and also quite accomplished were "Look at That Face," "The Joker," "My First Love Song," and "Feeling Good." A cross between the theatre of the absurd and old-time music hall, the unusual musical offered star turns by Newley (who also directed) and Ritchard but the reviews were mixed and the DAVID MERRICK production ran an unprofitable 231 performances. For several years after the offbeat piece was very popular with summer stock, colleges, and community theatre groups.

🖉 **ROBBER BRIDEGROOM, THE** (Harkness Theatre 1975). A raucous yet charming backwoods musical comedy by Alfred Uhry (book and lyrics) and Robert Waldman (music), the show boasted a vivacious score and stimulating young performers. Mississippi planter Clemment Musgrove (David Schramm) and his second wife Salome (Mary Lou Rosato) want their daughter Rosamund (PATTI LuPONE) to wed Jamie Lockhart (KEVIN KLINE) but she is more interested in the dashing, romantic bandit who she encountered in the woods. Of course the bandit is Jamie but there is a lot of confusion, plotting, and even a kidnapping before all ends happily. The country-flavored songs included "Steal With Style," "Sleepy Man," "Love Stolen," "The Pricklepear Bloom," "Goodbye Salome," and "Riches." The playful musicalization of Eudora Welty's novella was presented by the Acting Company as part of its touring repertory and ran only fifteen performances in New York as part of the tour. The show was so well received by the press that it returned to Broadway in 1976 with some cast changes but the spirit of the original remained and it pleased audiences for 145 performances. Gerald Freedman directed and DONALD SADDLER choreographed the musical, which toured successfully and then was later popular in colleges and summer theatres.

ROBBINS, JEROME [born Rabinowitz] (1918–1998). Stage and film choreographer and director. A choreography giant in the fields of modern ballet and musical theatre, he became the most powerful director–choreographer on Broadway in the 1950s and 1960s. Robbins was born in New York City and raised in nearby Weehawken, New Jersey, the son of an unsuccessful businessman. When his sister Sonia began to study dance, he learned everything that she did and was soon recognized as a dance prodigy by the innovative dance instructor Senia Gluck-Sandor. Robbins briefly attended New York University, but had to drop out for financial reasons. Instead he studied dance with Anthony Tudor and other ballet masters before getting cast in the chorus of Broadway musicals in the late 1930s. It was Robbins' choreography for the Ballet Theatre's *Fancy Free*, set to music by LEONARD BERNSTEIN, that led

to *ON THE TOWN*, the 1944 Broadway debut for both men. In the 1940s and 1950s, Robbins was busy choreographing on Broadway and in the ballet world, staging such unforgettable numbers as the farcical "Mack Sennett Ballet" in *HIGH BUTTON SHOES* (1947) and the imaginative narrative "Small House of Uncle Thomas" in *THE KING AND I* (1951). His other choreography assignments included *Billion Dollar Baby* (1945), *Look, Ma, I'm Dancin'* (1948), *MISS LIBERTY* (1949), *CALL ME MADAM* (1950), and *Two's Company* (1952). Robbins moved into directing and choreographing musicals with *PETER PAN* (1954) and explored ways in which dance and story were interwoven seamlessly, as in such classics as *BELLS ARE RINGING* (1956), *WEST SIDE STORY* (1957), *GYPSY* (1959), and *FIDDLER ON THE ROOF* (1964). He assisted in recreating some of his stage work for the film versions of *The King and I* (1956) and *West Side Story* (1961), and his Broadway choreography served as the basis for the film version of *Fiddler on the Roof* (1971). By the mid-1960s, Robbins abandoned the theatre and concentrated on ballet, running such distinguished companies as the American Ballet Theatre. He returned to the New York stage one last time in 1989 for the retrospective revue *JEROME ROBBINS' BROADWAY*. He also directed a handful of nonmusicals on Broadway, most memorably the New York premiere of Bertolt Brecht's *Mother Courage and Her Children* (1963). Something of a genius when it came to making dance tell a story and reveal unspoken emotions, he took AGNES DE MILLE'S ideas of theatre dance and went farther than anyone had imagined it could go. Robbins was a tyrannical, difficult person to work with or for and was roundly hated by many in the theatre community, yet no one was more respected for his ideas and talent and many were willing to be antagonized by Robbins because the results were always brilliant. Biographies: *Jerome Robbins: His Life, His Theatre, His Dance*, Deborah Jowitt, 2004; *Dance With Demons: The Life of Jerome Robbins*, Greg Lawrence (2001); *Jerome Robbins: That Broadway Man*, Christine Conrad (2000).

🖉 **ROBERTA** (New Amsterdam Theatre 1933). A lackluster musical comedy with a superior score, the show was saved by a hit song. All-American football player John Kent (RAY MIDDLETON) inherits a Paris dress shop called Roberta from his Aunt Minnie (FAY TEMPLETON) so he goes to France with his pal Huckleberry Haines (BOB HOPE) where he falls in love with his aunt's able assistant

Casts for *Roberta* and *Lovely to Look At*

Character	*Roberta* 1933 Broadway	*Roberta* 1935 film	*Lovely to Look At* 1952 film
Stephanie	TAMARA	IRENE DUNNE	KATHRYN GRAYSON
John Kent/Tony	RAY MIDDLETON	RANDOLPH SCOTT	HOWARD KEEL
Huckleberry Haines/Al Marsh	BOB HOPE	FRED ASTAIRE	RED SKELTON
Comtesse/Bubbles	LYDA ROBERTI	GINGER ROGERS	ANN MILLER
Aunt Minnie	FAY TEMPLETON	HELEN WESTLEY	
Jerry			GOWER CHAMPION
Clarisse			MARGE CHAMPION

Stephanie (TAMARA). John's old flame Sophie (Helen Gray) arrives to complicate matters but he ends up with Stephanie, who turns out to be a Russian princess in disguise. Also in the sparkling cast were GEORGE MURPHY, LYDA ROBERTI, and Sydney Greenstreet. OTTO HARBACH wrote the tired, old-fashioned libretto based on Alice Duer Miller's novel *Gowns By Roberta*, as well as the piquant lyrics for JEROME KERN's lovely music. The musical opened to unfavorable reviews and the box office floundered until the song "Smoke Gets in Your Eyes" became a huge hit on the radio and the shrewd producer MAX GORDON advertised *Roberta* as "the 'Smoke Gets in Your Eyes' show." Business picked up and the musical ran a profitable 295 performances. Also in the score were the flowing ballads "Yesterdays" and "The Touch of Your Hand," the adoring "You're Devastating," the sassy "I'll Be Hard to Handle" (lyric by Bernard Dougall), and the jazzy "Let's Begin." HASSARD SHORT directed the splendid cast and José Limon choreographed the lavish production numbers.

■ *Roberta* (RKO 1935) lost much of its terrific score on screen but the musical gained FRED ASTAIRE and GINGER ROGERS in the secondary roles of bandleader Huckleberry Haines and a phony Russian countess who were much more fun than the leading roles played by IRENE DUNNE and RANDOLPH SCOTT. The screenplay by Jane Murfin and others was somewhat contrived but an improvement over the stage libretto and much of the movie is topflight entertainment. DOROTHY FIELDS collaborated with Kern on two splendid new songs, "Lovely to Look At" and "I Won't Dance" (based on an OSCAR HAMMERSTEIN lyric), and the movie was directed with pizzazz by WILLIAM A. SEITER with choreography by Astaire and HERMES PAN. The film was very popular and decades later was remade as **Lovely to Look At** (MGM 1952). The screenplay by GEORGE WELLS and HARRY RUBY went back to the source material and told of American comic Al Marsh who inherits the

Paris dress shop and goes to France with his buddies Tony and Jerry to find the store, run by sisters Stephanie and Clarisse, facing bankruptcy. The boys help put on a big fashion show, save the shop, and win the hearts of the sisters and the provocative Bubbles Cassidy. It was not as solid as the earlier film but there was still much to enjoy, including Kern–Harbach songs from the original stage score not used in the 1935 film and a daffy new number called "Lafayette." VINCENTE MINNELI directed the lush production, which was filled with talented players and forty-two gowns by Adrian for the fashion show finale. Pan again was the choreographer, and the MELVYN LEROY production was a hit at the box office. ❏ Bob Hope reprised his Huckleberry Haines in a much-abridged and updated 1969 television version of *Roberta* on NBC. MICHELE LEE, John Davidson, and JANIS PAIGE were also featured in the ninety-minute broadcast.

ROBERTI, LYDA (1906–1938). Stage performer. A platinum blonde who excelled at playing man-hungry females, she made some memorable appearances in 1930s musicals before her premature death. Roberti was born in Warsaw, Poland, the daughter of a circus clown, and grew up traveling with him around the world. Arriving in the States, she went into vaudeville where her thick but sexy accent was a novelty and by 1931 she was on Broadway in the musical revue *You Said It*, followed by *Pardon My English* (1933) and *ROBERTA* (1933). Roberti made her screen debut in 1932 and completed only eleven features before her fatal heart attack. Her musicals were *Dancers in the Dark* (1932), *The Kid From Spain* (1932), *Torch Singer* (1933), *COLLEGE RHYTHM* (1934), *GEORGE WHITE'S SCANDALS* (1935), *BIG BROADCAST OF 1936* (1935), and *Nobody's Baby* (1937). Roberti was much imitated by other performers, including GINGER ROGERS who used a Roberti accent when she played the Polish actress's role in the film version of *Roberta* (1935).

ROBERTS, [Anthony David] **TONY** (1939–). Stage, film, and television performer. A lightweight comic actor in musicals and plays, he has shone in major and supporting roles for several decades. Born in New York City, the son of radio and television announcer Ken Roberts, he was educated at the High School of the Performing Arts and Northwestern before making his Broadway debut as a minor character in a play in 1962. He replaced others as the leading man in comedies such as *Never Too Late* (1964) and *Barefoot in the Park* (1965) before getting attention as the Wall Street trader Charley in the musical *How Now, Dow Jones* (1967). Roberts' other notable musical roles are the musician-on-the-run Joe in *Sugar* (1972), the wheeler-dealer Luther Billis in *South Pacific* (1987), the sarcastic tourist Jeff in *Brigadoon* (1991), the gay nightclub entrepreneur Toddy in *Victor/Victoria* (1995), Scrooge in the Madison Square Garden Theatre musical *A Christmas Carol* (1999), and Danny Maguire/ Zeus in *Xanadu* (2007). He has also replaced others in leading roles in the long-running musicals *Promises, Promises* (1971), *They're Playing Our Song* (1979), *Jerome Robbins' Broadway* (1990), and *Cabaret* (2003). In addition to nonmusical plays, Roberts has acted in many movies, including several Woody Allen films, and television programs, although his singing talents have seldom been required.

ROBERTSON, GUY (1892–?) Stage performer. An attractive wavy-haired baritone, he made a dashing hero in several operettas. Robertson was born in Denver and trained for a career in engineering until World War I service interrupted his education. After the armistice he turned to performing and made his Broadway debut in 1919. He was playing juvenile leads in musicals by 1922 and for the next decade was a favorite in musicals and operettas, including *Daffy Dill* (1922), *Wildflower* (1923), *Song of the Flame* (1925), *The Circus Princess* (1927), *White Lilacs* (1928), *Nina Rose* (1930), *Marching By* (1932), *All the King's Horses* (1934), *The Great Waltz* (1934), and *Right This Way* (1938). Robertson performed on the road and in stock companies for several years and then returned to Broadway one last time in 1939 as a replacement in *Very Warm for May*. No record of Robertson's death has been verified.

ROBESON, PAUL [born Paul Leroy Bustill Robeson] (1898–1976). Stage and film performer. One of the greatest of all African American performers, the powerful actor–singer excelled at everything from musicals to Shakespeare. Robeson was born in Princeton, New Jersey, the son of a Presbyterian minister, and was educated for law at Rutgers University (where he was a top athlete) and Columbia University (during which he played professional football for a time). About the time he was admitted to the bar he started performing professionally, appearing in the chorus of the landmark all-black musical *Shuffle Along* (1921) on Broadway. Robeson's first success as a dramatic actor was in *All God's Chillun Got Wings* (1924), followed by his towering performance as Brutus Jones in the expressionistic *The Emperor Jones* (1925), which he reprised in a 1933 film. The role of the dockhand Joe in *Show Boat* (1927) was written for him by Oscar Hammerstein and Jerome Kern, but Robeson was engaged to perform in Europe so he didn't get to play it until the London production in 1928. His performance and stirring rendition of "Ol' Man River" were repeated in the 1936 film version of *Show Boat* and he sang it throughout his career as kind of identity for himself and his race. Another highlight in his stage career was playing *Othello* on Broadway in 1943 and in 1945. Robeson repeated many of his stage roles in London, and much of his career was occupied with concerts in America and Europe. His Communist sympathies put him out of favor in the 1950s, although he still gave concerts on occasion, and in his final years he became a recluse. Robeson was a huge, muscular bass–baritone with a rich speaking voice and eyes that could either twinkle or send chills. Autobiography: *Here I Stand* (1971); biographies: *Paul Robeson*, Virginia Hamiliton (1974); *Paul Robeson*, Martin Duberman (1995).

ROBIN AND THE SEVEN HOODS (PC/ Warner 1964). A modern parody of the Robin Hood legend, the film was a kind of parody of a movie musical as the stars kidded and smirked their way through the movie as if on an unrehearsed television special. All the same, there is a lot to savor here, such as Bing Crosby's pleasing performance and Frank Sinatra's throwaway performance (it was the final movie musical for both of them), and the songs by James Van Heusen (music) and Sammy Cahn (lyrics) were enjoyable, especially the soft-shoe "Style," the revival-like "Mr. Booze," the sing-along "Don't Be a Do-Badder," and the popular anthem "My Kind of Town (Chicago)." The David R. Schwartz screenplay is a cross between a poor man's *Guys and Dolls* and a television sketch, but sometimes a funny one. Chicago gangster Robbo (Sinatra) is pitted against the rival mobster Guy Gisborn (Peter

Falk) over the gang headed by Big Jim Stevens (Edward G. Robinson) before he is gunned down. Big Jim's daughter Marian (Barbara Rush) hopes to get revenge for her dad's murder and insinuates herself into both warring factions, causing business and romantic complications. Robbo's merry men included Little John (DEAN MARTIN), Will (SAMMY DAVIS, JR.), and Allen A. Dale (Crosby), with Victor Buono, Hank Henry, Allen Jenkins, Jack LaRue, HANS CONREID, SIG RUMANN, and Philip Crosby filling out the cast. As a sort of "Rat Pack" vehicle, it was one of the Sinatra–Martin–Davis team's better efforts; as a musical, it made one long for the days when these performers still cared.

📽️ **ROBIN HOOD** (Standard Theatre 1891). The most popular American operetta of the nineteenth century, the show is the most (and only) remembered musical by composer REGINALD DE KOVEN. The libretto by HARRY B. SMITH adheres to the English legend up to a point and all the well-known characters are there, including Robert, the Earl of Huntington (Tom Karl), who is robbed of his lands by the wicked (and comic) Sheriff of Nottingham (HENRY CLAY BARNABEE) so he becomes the outlaw Robin Hood. The sheriff tries to marry Robin's beloved Maid Marion (Caroline Hamilton) to the crooked Guy of Gisbourne (Peter Lang) but Robin and his merry men rescue her before the wedding can take place. One of Robin's comrades, Alan-a-Dale, was played by Jessie Bartlett Davis as a trouser role and she got to sing the score's most famous song, the interpolated "Oh, Promise Me" (lyric by Clement Scott), at the wedding before it was interrupted by the bandits. The gushing ballad swept the country and was used for weddings for many decades after. Also in the score were "Brown October Ale," "Tinkers' Chorus," and "Ah, I Do Love Thee." The original production of *Robin Hood* was a touring production from Boston and only played forty performances in its initial Broadway stop but the musical returned to New York over a dozen times over the years and was long a favorite with operetta and opera companies. DeKoven wrote a sequel to the musical called *Maid Marion* (1902) but it was not nearly as successful.

🎬 Of the many screen versions of the Robin Hood legend, only one musical emerged, the animated **Robin Hood** (Disney 1973). In this clever and lively version, all of the familiar characters are played by different animals, Robin (voice of Brian Bedford) and Marian (Monica Evans) as foxes, Prince John (Peter Ustinov) a lion, the Sheriff (Pat Buttram) a wolf, Little John (PHIL HARRIS) a bear, and so on. Other voices heard included Carole Shelley, Andy Devine, George Lindsey, Terry-Thomas, J. Pat O'Malley, and Roger Miller who played Alan-a-Dale as a rooster troubadour who narrated the story and sang his own song "Oo-de-Lolly." Other songs by Miller and others included "Not in Nottingham," "Whistle Stop," "Love," and "Phony King of England." The clever screenplay was by Larry Clemmons and Ken Anderson, and Wolfgang Reitherman directed with a playful touch, making even the villains fun.

ROBIN, LEO (1900–1984). Film and stage lyricist. One of Hollywood's most prolific songwriters, he scored over fifty screen musicals, many with composer RALPH RAINGER, as well as some Broadway musicals and Tin pan Alley hits. Robin was born in Pittsburgh and pursued careers as an actor and a newspaper reporter before turning to writing lyrics. His songs were first heard on Broadway in 1927 and it was his score for *HIT THE DECK!* (1927) with composer VINCENT YOUMANS that launched his new career. Robin also scored the musicals *Judy* (1927), *Allez-Oop* (1927), *Just Fancy* (1927), and *Hello Yourself!* (1928) before going to Hollywood and collaborating with composer RICHARD A. WHITING on the songs for *Innocents of Paris* (1929). With Whiting and others he scored *Fashions in Love* (1929), *The Dance of Life* (1929), *MONTE CARLO* (1930), *ONE HOUR WITH YOU* (1932), and others before teaming with Rainger on some thirty musicals, including *THE BIG BROADCAST* (1932) and its sequels in 1936, 1937, and 1938, *A Bedtime Story* (1933), *INTERNATIONAL HOUSE* (1933), *Little Miss Marker* (1934), *Millions in the Air* (1935), *Palm Springs* (1936), *College Holiday* (1936), *Waikiki Wedding* (1937), *Give Me a Sailor* (1938), *ARTISTS AND MODELS ABROAD* (1938), *Paris Honeymoon* (1939), *GULLIVER'S TRAVELS* (1939), *MOON OVER MIAMI* (1941), *MY GAL SAL* (1942), *Footlight Serenade* (1942), *CONEY ISLAND* (1943), and *Riding High* (1943). Robin worked with a variety of composers after Rainger died in 1942, most memorably JULE STYNE with whom he scored the Broadway musical *GENTLEMEN PREFER BLONDES* (1949), the films *Meet Me After the Show* (1951), *Two Tickets to Broadway* (1951), *MY SISTER EILEEN* (1955), and the TV musical *RUGGLES OF RED GAP* (1957). Robin's film credits with others include *THE GANG'S ALL HERE* (1943), *CENTENNIAL SUMMER*

(1946), *CASBAH* (1948), *That Lady in Ermine* (1948), *Just for You* (1952), *Small Town Girl* (1953), and *Latin Lovers* (1953). He returned to Broadway one last time to provide lyrics for SIGMUND ROMBERG's music in *The Girl in Pink Tights* (1954). Although Robin never became a household name, he wrote some beloved songs, ranging from "Thanks for the Memory" and "Blue Hawaii" to "Beyond the Blue Horizon" and "Diamonds Are a Girl's Best Friend."

ROBINSON, BILL [born William Luther Robinson] (1878–1949). Stage and film performer and choreographer. The smiling African American hoofer, nicknamed "Bojangles," is generally considered America's greatest tap dancer and there is enough film footage to support that opinion. Robinson was born in Richmond, Virginia, where he performed for pennies on the streets as a child. He went into vaudeville as a teenager, was eventually a headliner in the best variety houses, and then was featured in the Broadway musicals *BLACKBIRDS OF 1928*, *Brown Buddies* (1930), *Blackbirds* (1933), *The Hot Mikado* (1939), *All in Fun* (1940), and *Memphis Bound* (1945). Robinson made his movie debut as a specialty act in *Dixiana* (1930) and then was cast as supporting characters in seven more musicals, four of them—*The Little Colonel* (1935), *The Littlest Rebel* (1935), *REBECCA OF SUNNYBROOK FARM* (1938), and *Just Around the Corner* (1938)—opposite SHIRLEY TEMPLE who paired with him in some unforgettable tap numbers. He choreographed most of his dances on stage and screen and provided the choreography for the Temple vehicle *Dimples* (1936) even though he did not appear in the picture. Robinson's other screen musicals are *Hooray for Love* (1935), *BIG BROADCAST OF 1936* (1935), and *STORMY WEATHER* (1943), as well as some nonmusicals. He frequently returned to vaudeville and nightclubs, such as the Cotton Club in Harlem, and was an activist for black performers, being a founding member of the

Bill Robinson. Like most African American performers, Robinson was limited to what he could do in a Hollywood film and often had to play a servant to explain his presence in a musical. Not so in *Stormy Weather* (1943) in which Robinson and the African American cast played the major characters. Pictured here is Robinson (left) with Dooley Wilson a year after the latter was immortalized as the piano-playing Sam in *Casablanca* (1942). (Photofest)

Negro Actors Guild of America (NEGA). Robinson had a genius for making tap dancing look effortless and was instrumental for changing the form from a heavy, flat-footed kind of dance to a light, on the toes or on the heels kind of style. In a joint 1989 resolution, Congress designated his birthday (May 25) as National Tap Dancing Day. Biography: *Mr. Bojangles: The Biography of Bill Robinson*, James Haskins, N. R. Mitgang (1988).

ROCK MUSICALS. Broadway was slow to pick up on rock and roll. It was over a decade after the new sound was heard on radio, television, and in movies that a rock musical opened on Broadway. In the late 1960s and early 1970s there was an abundance of rock scores heard on and Off Broadway and then the phase passed. However, the impact had been made and the rock musicals left an indelible mark on Broadway, and all musicals today have been influenced by the music, orchestrations, and artificially generated sound that rock introduced. *Hair* opened Off Broadway in 1967 and the next year was on Broadway; it was controversial, abrasive, satirical, and (most importantly) a hit. By its very nature, a rock musical tends to be unconventional and more experimental than traditional shows, not only in subject matter but also in structure and presentation. The music is often more pounding, with more emphasis on the beat and less on the lyrics, and the musical usually is a free-flowing celebration, protest, or both. The rock shows are usually less literary and more anachronistic and rely on a variety of audiovisual effects. Most significantly, the orchestrations for rock musicals require a good deal of electronic instruments so mechanical amplification is a must. Broadway was slow to embrace the rock sentiment but *Hair* opened the floodgates and the rock sound popped up everywhere. Within a short time the theatre saw such successes as *JESUS CHRIST SUPERSTAR* (1971) and *GODSPELL* (1971) and flops such as *Dude* (1972) and *Via Galactica* (1972). By the mid-1970s, rock shows were dwindling but not the rock sound. Some later works, such as The Who's *TOMMY* (1993), *RENT* (1996), *HEDWIG AND THE ANGRY INCH* (1998), and *SPRING AWAKENING* (2006), would be true rock musicals but most shows were content in having a rock and roll flavor at times. Touches of the sound are predominant in *THE WIZ* (1975), *EVITA* (1979), *DREAMGIRLS* (1981), *Starlight Express* (1987), *THE PHANTOM OF THE OPERA* (1988), *MISS SAIGON* (1991), *AIDA* (2000), *HAIRSPRAY* (2002), and even *TARZAN* (2006), although few of those could rightfully be called a rock musical. Even conventional Broadway musicals started using electronic instruments and amplified sound, and the timbre of the traditional musical score was altered. The violin may have been the primary instrument in the operetta days and the woodwinds and brass in the musical comedy days, but the guitar was the key instrument in rock. Today that has been replaced by the electric keyboard, which is often used to artificially create the sounds needed for a Broadway score. Like it or not, Broadway sounds different because of rock musicals.

Rock and roll was heard in the movies almost from the very start of the new form. In fact, the film *ROCK AROUND THE CLOCK* (1956), featuring Bill Haley and the Comets, the Platters, and other rock pioneers heard on the soundtrack, was greatly responsible for spreading the new sound. Early rock films such as *Rock Rock Rock* (1956), *Don't Knock the Rock* (1957), *Carnival Rock* (1957), and *Mr. Rock 'n' Rock* (1957) were cheaply made movies that were addressed directly to the youth market, but the ELVIS PRESLEY musicals were mainstream hits, and Hollywood realized before television and theatre that there was money to be made from the new sound. Many of the rock movie musicals over the years have been screen versions of stage works, from *Jesus Christ Superstar* (1973) and *THE ROCKY HORROR PICTURE SHOW* (1975) to *Hedwig and the Angry Inch* (1998) and *Rent* (2004). To these the studios added their own versions of rock musicals, often in a format that did not resemble a stage piece. *A HARD DAY'S NIGHT* (1964), *HELP!* (1965), *Head* (1968), *YELLOW SUBMARINE* (1968), *PHANTOM OF THE PARADISE* (1974), *A STAR IS BORN* (1976), *I Wanna Hold Your Hand* (1978), *American Hot Wax* (1978), *THE BUDDY HOLLY STORY* (1978), *Thank God It's Friday* (1978), *Rock 'n' Roll High School* (1979), *Quadrophenia* (1979), *THE ROSE* (1979), *FAME* (1980), *THE JAZZ SINGER* (1980), *FLASHDANCE* (1983), *FOOTLOOSE* (1984), *Labyrinth* (1986), *DIRTY DANCING* (1987), *LA BAMBA* (1987), *THE COMMITMENTS* (1991), *THE DOORS* (1991), *THAT THING YOU DO* (1996), *Spice World* (1998), *The Road to El Dorado* (2000), *MOULIN ROUGE* (2001), and *ACROSS THE UNIVERSE* (2007) all rely heavily on rock. Add to those the many nonmusical films that utilize a rock soundtrack and one can see that Hollywood has done very well by rock and roll.

ROCKUMENTARIES. Film documentaries covering a rock concert, festival, tour, or recording session were dubbed "rockumentaries" in the 1970s as the relatively new genre needed a label. These behind-the-scenes movies go back to the 1950s when rock was gaining a foothold. *Rockin' the Blues* (1956) chronicled performances by several African American artists (the Hurricanes, the Miller Sisters, Flournoy Miller, the Harptones) who were just starting to popularize the rock and roll sound. Films focusing on rock groups were common by the late 1950s, but a major documentary about them would not come along until the *T.A.M.I. Show* (1964), which covered the Teenage Awards Music International in California and featured the Rolling Stones, Lesley Gore, Marvin Gaye, the Beach Boys, the Supremes, Gerry and the Pacemakers, and others. Similar films included *The Big T.N.T. Show* (1966), *You Are What You Eat* (1968), and *Monterey Pop* (1969). The rockumentary that would prove the most effective (and influential to subsequent films of the genre) was *WOODSTOCK* (1970), Michael Wadleigh's coverage of the legendary 1969 festival in Bethel, New York. Other notable rockumentaries during the 1970s included *Gimme Shelter* (1970), about a Rolling Stones tour; *Mad Dogs and Englishmen* (1970), with Joe Cocker and entourage touring America; *Let It Be* (1970), covering the BEATLES's last recording session; *The Concert for Bangladesh* (1972), featuring George Harrison and various performers at a Madison Square Garden benefit concert; *Let the Good Times Roll* (1973), with a nostalgic look at rock artists from the 1950s; *The Grateful Dead* (1977); and *The Last Waltz* (1978), Martin Scorsese's vivid coverage of a farewell tour by The Band. By the 1980s, MTV and other television outlets were covering the rock scene pretty thoroughly and patrons were not as willing to pay to see a film about the rock stars they could see for free on TV. All the same there were rockumentaries such as *Black Flag Live* (1984), *The Decline of Western Civilization, Part II: The Metal Years* (1988), *Madonna: Truth or Dare* (1991), *The Punk Rock Movies* (1992), and *1991: The Year Punk Broke* (1992). With the new century, a flood of rockumentaries arrived, including *Festival Express* (2003), *KISS Loves You* (2004), *Metallica: Some Kind of Monster* (2004), *No Direction Home: Bob Dylan* (2006), and *Party at Ground Zero* (2007). There have also been a handful of television and movie spoofs of rockumentaries over the years, most notably *The Rutles: All You Need Is Cash* (1978) and *THIS IS SPINAL TAP* (1984).

ROCKY HORROR SHOW, THE (Belasco Theatre 1975). A musical spoof of science fiction, porno, and rock films, the London hit failed on Broadway but finally found success as a film–theatre experience. Richard O'Brien's libretto concerned the innocent, naive couple Janet (Abigale Haness) and Brad (Bill Miller) who take refuge in a mansion where the transvestite Frank N. Furter (TIM CURRY) lives with his stud creation Rocky (Kim Milford) and various other bizarre folk. Frank has sexual designs on both Janet and Brad but the couple are rescued by Dr. Scott (Meat Loaf) who knows that all of the house's inhabitants come from outer space. O'Brien also wrote the rock score, which included "Sweet Transvestite," "What Ever Happened to Saturday Night," "Time Warp," "Charles Atlas Song," "Once in a While," and "The Sword of Damocles." The show was a campy success in London, where it eventually ran over five years in a dilapidated movie house, but on Broadway it captured little of the same tawdry atmosphere even though the Belasco theatre was turned into a cabaret for the production. The oddball but likable musical only managed to run thirty-two performances and did not become popular in the States until the 1975 film version. *The Rocky Horror Show* returned to Broadway in 2000

Casts for *The Rocky Horror (Picture) Show*

Character	1975 Broadway	1975 film	2000 Broadway
Dr. Frank-N-Furter	TIM CURRY	Tim Curry	Tom Hewitt
Janet Weiss	Abigale Haness	Susan Sarandon	Alice Ripley
Brad Majors	Bill Miller	BARRY BOSTWICK	Jarrod Emick
Riff Raff	Ritz O'Brien	Richard O'Brien	RAÚL ESPARZA
Magenta	Jamie Donnelly	Patricia Quinn	Daphne Rubin-Vega
Eddie	Meatloaf	Meatloaf	Lea DeLaria
Columbia	Bonnie Enten	Nell Campbell	Joan Jett
Dr. Von Scott	Meatloaf	Jonathan Adams	Lea Delaria
Rocky Horror	Kim Milford	Peter Hinwood	Sebastian LaCause
Narrator	William Newman		Dick Cavett

and it was a well-known commodity by then and managed to run 356 performances. Critical reaction to the cult classic was very positive this time around with praise for CHRISTOPHER ASHLEY'S atmospheric staging in the thrust stage space of Circle in the Square and plaudits for the high-style performances as well. JERRY MITCHELL did the choreography, John Rockwell designed the clever setting, and the show recreated the movie experience by selling the props necessary to participate in the event.

■ *The Rocky Horror Picture Show* (Fox 1975) became the ultimate cult film in the decade following its release as patrons dressed up, brought props, and participated in midnight showings of the spoof in cities across the country. O'Brien's screenplay is close to the original but the word "picture" was added to the title to make it clear that this was a film and not a copy of the stage performance. Tim Curry repeated his bizarre, hilarious Dr. Frank-N-Furter and the young couple were played by unknowns BARRY BOSTWICK and Susan Sarandon who became famous because of the movie. The action of the play is opened up by director Jim Sharman, and the production numbers are staged inside the castle with cinematic flair. The popularity of the film prompted some revivals of the stage version (including the 2000 Broadway mounting) but for devotees, the only real *Rocky Horror* experience is in a movie house filled with costumed, singing spectators.

RODGERS, MARY (1931–). Stage composer. One of the very few woman theatre composers in America before the 1960s, she is the daughter of RICHARD RODGERS and an accomplished songwriter in her own right. A native New Yorker, Rodgers studied music at the Mannes School before going to Wellesley College for a time, writing music for campus musicals. Her most known musical is the fairy tale romp *ONCE UPON A MATTRESS*, which was a surprise hit first Off Broadway and then on Broadway in 1959. Rodgers also wrote songs for the musicals *Hot Spot* (1963), *The Mad Show* (1966), and *WORKING* (1978), the television musical *FEATHERTOP* (1961), and also for children's records. She is the author of children's books as well, most memorably *Freaky Friday* (1972), which has been filmed twice by Hollywood and once for television. She is the mother of composer–lyricist ADAM GUETTEL.

RODGERS, RICHARD [Charles] (1902–1979). Stage, film, and television composer, lyricist, and producer. The dean of Broadway compos-

ers with a career of sixty years in the theatre, films, and television, he collaborated with two brilliant (and very different) lyricists, LORENZ HART and OSCAR HAMMERSTEIN. Rodgers was born into a middle-class Jewish family, the son of a physician, and before he even began school he had taught himself to play piano by ear. By the time Rodgers was sixteen years old, his first complete musical score was produced by an amateur theatre group and he wrote several other shows while a student at Columbia University. He met Hart in 1919 and the two immediately hit it off and started collaborating on songs that they submitted to theatrical producers. A Rodgers and Hart song was

Richard Rodgers. Before Rodgers and Hammerstein (top photo) there was Rodgers and Hart (bottom photo). It's no coincidence that two of the greatest songwriting teams shared the same composer. Rodgers is at the piano with Hart in the foreground. If they look like two very different kinds of men that's because they were. (Photofest)

first heard on Broadway in *A Lonely Romeo* (1919) and only a portion of their score was retained for *Poor Little Ritz Girl* (1920), but the team found recognition for their songs for *THE GARRICK GAIETIES* (1925), followed by *DEAREST ENEMY* (1925), the first of a series of delightful collaborations between Rodgers and Hart and librettist HERBERT FIELDS. The subsequent Rodgers–Hart–Fields musicals were *The Girl Friend* (1926), a second edition of *The Garrick Gaieties* (1926), *PEGGY-ANN* (1926), *A CONNECTICUT YANKEE* (1927), *PRESENT ARMS* (1928), *Chee-Chee* (1928), and *America's Sweetheart* (1931). Other Rodgers and Hart musicals of the period include *Spring Is Here* (1929), *HEADS UP!* (1929), and *SIMPLE SIMON* (1930) and the London hit *EVER GREEN* (1930). During the darkest days of the Depression, the team accepted tempting offers from Hollywood to score movie musicals and they headed west, writing *The Hot Heiress* (1931) and three very innovative musicals, *LOVE ME TONIGHT* (1932), *THE PHANTOM PRESIDENT* (1932), and *HALLELUJAH, I'M A BUM* (1933). They had less success with *Hollywood Party* (1934) and *MISSISSIPPI* (1935) and returned to New York where they had a series of stage hits: *JUMBO* (1935), *ON YOUR TOES* (1936), *BABES IN ARMS* (1937), *I'D RATHER BE RIGHT* (1937), *I MARRIED AN ANGEL* (1938), *THE BOYS FROM SYRACUSE* (1938), and *TOO MANY GIRLS* (1939). The final Rodgers and Hart musicals were *HIGHER AND HIGHER* (1940), *PAL JOEY* (1940), *BY JUPITER* (1942), and the 1943 revival of *A Connecticut Yankee*. (The career of Rodgers and Hart was fictionalized in the 1948 movie musical *WORDS AND MUSIC*.) When Hart, who was suffering from severe depression and alcoholism, abruptly turned down Rodgers' idea to musicalize the pastoral play *Green Grow the Lilacs*, Rodgers turned to Hammerstein and the result was *OKLAHOMA!* (1943), the show that revolutionized the musical play. In 1945 they wrote their only original screen score for *STATE FAIR*, which was also popular. The subsequent Rodgers and Hammerstein collaborations were not all hits but each was an attempt to further experiment with the musical form. *CAROUSEL* (1945), which many considered their finest hour, was a success but their expressionistic *ALLEGRO* (1947) was not. *SOUTH PACIFIC* (1949) and *THE KING AND I* (1951) were critical and popular triumphs, whereas *ME AND JULIET* (1953) and *PIPE DREAM* (1955) were major disappointments. The team took the surprising move of scoring an original live television musical, *CINDERELLA* (1957), something that had never before been

attempted on such a scale, and it was a landmark on the small screen. By this time most of the Rodgers and Hammerstein shows were being filmed as well. On Broadway, *FLOWER DRUM SONG* (1958) and *THE SOUND OF MUSIC* (1959) received mixed notices from the press but were roundly applauded by audiences. Hammerstein's death from cancer in 1960 was the end of an era but Rodgers continued on. He provided some new songs (both music and lyrics) for the 1962 remake of *State Fair* and for the film of *The Sound of Music* (1965), wrote the score for the contemporary Broadway musical *NO STRINGS* (1962) and the television musical *ANDROCLES AND THE LION* (1967), and collaborated with others on *DO I HEAR A WALTZ?* (1965), *TWO BY TWO* (1970), *Rex* (1976), and *I Remember Mama* (1979). Despite an operation for throat cancer that nearly robbed him of his speech, Rodgers worked up until the year that he died. The contribution of Richard Rodgers to the American musical cannot be overstated. His enticing use of melody and harmony, his endless variety, his ability to capture a mood or a place or a character in a few notes, and his untiring search for new ways in which music can become theatre—these are among his gifts to the American musical. His daughter is composer MARY RODGERS and his grandson is composer–lyricist ADAM GUETTEL. Autobiography: *Musical Stages* (1975); biographies: *Somewhere for Me: A Biography of Richard Rodgers*, Meryle Secrest (2001); *Richard Rodgers*, William Hyland (1998).

ROGERS BROTHERS. Stage performers. A comedy duo who had musicals tailor made for them, the "Dutch" comics were audience favorites around the turn of the twentieth century. Gus (1869–1908) and Max (1873–1932) Rogers were born in New York with the surname Solomon and began performing comic routines together in 1885. When Tony Pastor featured them at his music hall, the twosome caught on and by 1899 were on Broadway in the musical *A Reign of Error*. To rival the popular team of WEBER and FIELDS, producer A. L. ERLANGER starred the Rogers Brothers in a series of musical farces that were excuses for the clowning: *The Rogers Brothers in Wall Street* (1899), *The Rogers Brothers in Central Park* (1900), *The Rogers Brothers in Washington* (1901), *The Rogers Brothers in Harvard* (1902), *The Rogers Brothers in London* (1903), *The Rogers Brothers in Paris* (1904), *The Rogers Brothers in Ireland* (1905), and *The Rogers Brothers in Panama* (1907). The series ended with the death of Gus

Rogers in 1908 and his brother's career faltered and then faded.

ROGERS, CHARLES [Edward] **"BUDDY"** (1904–1999). Film and stage performer. An affable leading man in silents and talkies, he had a wholesome and endearing quality that made him so charming in his nine movie musicals, several of them costarring NANCY CARROLL. Rogers was born in Olathe, Kansas, and educated at the University of Kansas before taking up acting. He studied at the Paramount Pictures School before making his screen debut in 1926, appearing in several silents, most memorably *Wings* (1927). When sound came in, Rogers was cast in boy-next-door roles in such musicals as *Close Harmony* (1929), *PARAMOUNT ON PARADE* (1930), *Safety in Numbers* (1930), *FOLLOW THRU* (1930), and *HEADS UP!* (1930). He made his Broadway debut in the musical revue *Hot-Cha!* (1932) and then returned to Hollywood to make the musicals *Best of Enemies* (1933), *TAKE A CHANCE* (1933), *Old Man Rhythm* (1935), *This Way Please* (1937), and the British movies *Dance Band* (1925) and *Let's Make a Night of It* (1937). Rogers returned to Broadway for the revues *Laffing Room Only* (1944) and *Hold It* (1948) and then concentrated on nonmusical films until 1957 when he retired. He was married to film star Mary Pickford (1893–1979).

ROGERS, GINGER [born Virginia Katherine McMath] (1911–1995). Film, stage, and television performer. Perhaps the quintessential Hollywood musical star, she was a glamorous, funny blonde whose dancing and singing could be romantic or silly. Rogers was born in Independence, Missouri, and took singing and dancing lessons as a young child, being groomed for show business by her determined, divorced stage mother. After appearing in vaudeville and winning some Charleston contests, Rogers made her Broadway debut in the musical *Top Speed* (1929), followed by the major role of postmistress Molly Gray in *GIRL CRAZY* (1930). Her performance led to a Hollywood contract and she played wisecracking blondes in a series of B pictures before getting noticed as the smart-aleck Anytime Annie in *42ND STREET* (1933). Rogers was featured in *GOLD DIGGERS OF 1933* and *Sitting Pretty* (1933) before she was teamed for the first time with FRED ASTAIRE in secondary roles in *FLYING DOWN TO RIO* (1933). When the two danced "The Carioca" together, the public was enthralled and they soon became the most famous dance team in the history of the movies. Rogers was partnered with Astaire in *THE*

GAY DIVORCEE (1934), *ROBERTA* (1935), *TOP HAT* (1935), *FOLLOW THE FLEET* (1936), *SWING TIME* (1936), *SHALL WE DANCE* (1937), *CAREFREE* (1938), *THE STORY OF VERNON AND IRENE CASTLE* (1939), and *THE BARKLEYS OF BROADWAY* (1949). Rogers's musicals with other leading men were *Twenty Million Sweethearts* (1934), *In Person* (1935), *Having Wonderful Time* (1938), and *LADY IN THE DARK* (1944). She also appeared in many comedies and dramas through the 1950s before retiring from films and doing concerts and nightclubs. She returned to Broadway as a replacement for Dolly Levi in *HELLO, DOLLY!* in 1965, played *MAME* in London in 1969, and appeared on television on occasion, most memorably singing NOEL COWARD songs in *Tonight at 8:30* (1954) and as the queen in the remake of Rodgers and Hammerstein's *CINDERELLA* (1965). Autobiography: *Ginger: My Story* (1991); biography: *Shall We Dance: The Life of Ginger Rogers*, Sheridan Morley (1995).

ROGERS, ROY, AND DALE EVANS. Film and television performers. A singing cowboy couple who were first paired in the movies, they became more popular on television with a series that always included a song or two. Rogers (1911–1998) was born Leonard Franklin Slye in Cincinnati and went to California to pick fruit, remaining to form a singing group called the Sons of the Pioneers. The singers were featured on the radio and in a few films, such as *Tumbling Tumbleweeds* (1935), and then Rogers was cast in B westerns where he sang cowboy ballads. Evans (1912–2001) was born Frances Octavia Smith in Uvalde, Texas, and broke into show business as a nightclub singer and made it to Hollywood where she was featured in *ORCHESTRA WIVES* (1942), *Swing Your Partner* (1943), and other musicals. Rogers and Evans married in 1947 and appeared together in *Apache Rose* (1947) but were not considered a singing team until 1951 when they had their popular television show, which lasted, in one form or another, until 1962. Rogers sometimes returned to films as a solo, as with *SON OF PALEFACE* (1952) and doing the vocals for the animated anthology *MELODY TIME* (1948). He was a shrewd businessman who promoted everything from cowboy wear to restaurants with his name on them. Evans wrote their theme song "Happy Trails to You." Biography: *The Cowboy and the Senorita: A Biography of Roy Rogers and Dale Evans*, Howard Kazanjian (2005).

ROGERS, WILL [born William Penn Adair Rogers] (1879–1935). Stage and film performer. One of America's favorite and most unique humorists, he was popular in all media, including radio and newspapers, and appeared in ten Broadway musicals. Rogers, who was part Cherokee, was born in Oologah Indian Territory in present-day Oklahoma and was educated at Kemper Military School and College in Missouri and then began his career as a performing cowboy in a Wild West show. He played Madison Square Garden in 1905 doing roping and riding tricks, but then turned to verbal comedy, chewing gum and telling yarns as he twirled his lasso. Rogers made his Broadway debut as a specialty act in *The Wall Street Girl* (1912), followed by *Hands Up* (1915), *Town Topics* (1915), *THE PASSING SHOW* (1917), *Three Cheers* (1928), and seven editions of the *ZIEGFELD FOLLIES* between 1916 and 1924. Roger's wry, philosophical comments about the news events of the day were on the radio and in his own newspaper column. He appeared in several silent films but his kind of humor was verbal so he did not become a movie star until sound came in, appearing in some two dozen nonmusical talkies in which he played crusty, easy-going rural characters. Rogers died in a plane crash in Alaska with aviator Wiley Post. His son Will Rogers, Jr. (1911–1993), an actor who later became a celebrated newspaper publisher and congressman, played Rogers in the movie *The Story of Will Rogers* (1952) and in the screen musicals *Look for the Silver Lining* (1949) and *The Eddie Cantor Story* (1953). Buff Brady portrayed Rogers in *W. C. Fields and Me* (1976), and Keith Carradine played him in both the Broadway musical *THE WILL ROGERS FOLLIES* (1991) and the film *Mrs. Parker and the Vicious Circle* (1994). Biographies: *Will Rogers: A Biography*, Ben Yagoda (2000); *Will Rogers: His Life and Times*, Richard Ketchum (1973).

ROMAN SCANDALS (Goldwyn/United Artists 1933). The most lavish, ridiculous, and farcical EDDIE CANTOR vehicle, the movie doesn't sit well with modern audiences but was considered great fun in its time. WILLIAM ANTHONY MCGUIRE headed the team of writers who concocted the plot about delivery boy Eddie (Cantor) in West Rome, Oklahoma, who is upset over the political corruption in the small burg and dreams he is in ancient Rome where corruption is on an even larger scale. He is the food-tasting slave of Emperor Valerius (Edward Arnold) whose wife Agrippa (Verree Teasdale) is always trying to poison him. Eddie helps out the lovers Princess Sylvia (GLORIA STUART) and Josephus (David Manners) and then proves the emperor to be a corrupt cheat,

thereby becoming the hero of Rome before waking up. The film had everything from RUTH ETTING singing the torch song "No More Love" to a chariot race. HARRY WARREN (music) and AL DUBIN (lyrics) wrote the score, and BUSBY BERKELEY staged the musical numbers, two of them outstanding for opulence and questionable taste. While Etting sang her torchy number, the camera drooled over dozens of slave girls chained to the walls, naked except for their long blonde hair, and writhing as a grotesque jailer went about lashing his whip. (It is believed that this scene did more to bring on the censorship-based Production Code in Hollywood than any other.) The other unforgettable scene took place in a Roman bath house with Eddie (in blackface) urging hundreds of black and white beauties to "Keep Young and Beautiful" while they exercised and applied makeup, surrounded by revolving mirrors, to make themselves attractive for men. Also in the score were "Build a Little Home" and "Put a Tax on Love." Frank Tuttle directed the SAMUEL GOLDWYN production.

ROMANCE ON THE HIGH SEAS (Warner 1948). The pleasant musical romance was Doris Day's first film and it made her a star, helped no doubt by the fact that she got to introduce two JULE STYNE–SAMMY CAHN hit songs, "It's Magic" and "Put 'Em in a Box, Tie 'Em with a Ribbon, and Throw 'Em in the Deep Blue Sea." The screenplay by Julius J. and Philip G. Epstein concerned the wealthy New Yorker Mrs. Elvira Kent (JANIS PAIGE) who suspects her husband Michael (Don DeFore) of infidelity so she hires singer Georgia Garrett (Day) to impersonate her and sail to Rio on a luxury liner while she stays behind to spy on him. Michael thinks his wife is meeting another man on board so he hires detective Peter Virgil (JACK CARSON) to keep an eye on her. What happens then was no surprise, but Day made quite an impression with moviegoers, the newcomer to film coming across as an experienced pro. Also on board were OSCAR LEVANT, S. Z. SAKALL, Fortunio Bonanova, ERIC BORE, FRANKLIN PANGBORN, and specialty numbers by the Samba Kings, Avon Long, and the Page Cavanaugh Trio, all efficiently directed by MICHAEL CURTIZ and choreographed by BUSBY BERKELEY in one of his more restrained moods.

ROMBERG, SIGMUND (1887–1951). Stage and film composer. One of Broadway's finest operetta composers in the European tradition, he was versatile enough to write all kinds of music throughout his forty-year career. Romberg was born in Nagy Kaniza, Hungary, studied violin as a child, and then went to Vienna to train for a career in engineering. While there he became involved with the Theater-an-der-Wien and started composing for the musical stage. He emigrated to New York in 1909 and took various jobs while trying to get his songs interpolated into shows. His work caught the attention of producer J. J. Shubert who hired the young Hungarian in 1914 as the house composer for the SHUBERT BROTHERS's theatrical enterprises. Romberg first found fame when his song "Auf Wiedersehn" was interpolated into THE BLUE PARADISE (1915), which was a bestseller. His first of many outstanding operettas was MAYTIME (1917), followed by dozens of others, including BLOSSOM TIME (1921) and THE STUDENT PRINCE (1924), Princess Flavia (1925), THE DESERT SONG (1926), My Maryland (1927), My Princess (1927), THE NEW MOON (1928), Nina Rosa (1930), East Wind (1931), Melody (1933), May Wine (1935), Forbidden Melody (1936), and Sunny River (1941). For the Shuberts he scored many revues, in particular the profitable THE PASSING SHOW series, and musical comedies, including two vehicles for AL JOLSON: SINBAD (1918) and BOMBO (1921). Although the appeal for old-time operetta died out during the Depression, Romberg was able to adjust and use opera elements in musicals, as seen in his later shows UP IN CENTRAL PARK (1945) and The Girl in Pink Tights (1954). His most renowned stage works were filmed by Hollywood and he also scored three movie musicals with OSCAR HAMMERSTEIN: Viennese Nights (1930), Children of Dreams (1931), and The Night Is Young (1935). His life and work were subjects of the biopic DEEP IN MY HEART (1954). More adaptable than his operetta contemporary RUDOLF FRIML, Romberg had a long career on Broadway (over fifty musicals) and on the screen (twelve films), bringing the sound of European operetta to America complete with rich, memorable melodies. Biographies: Deep in My Heart, Elliott Arnold (1949); Sigmund Romberg, William A. Everett, (2006).

ROME, HAROLD [Jacob] (1908–1993). Stage and film composer and lyricist. A songwriter who often used music to present sociopolitical ideas, he was expert in capturing the feelings of the working class in his scores. Rome was born in Hartford, Connecticut, and studied law and architecture at Yale before he found writing songs for adult summer camps more rewarding. He scored the amateur revue PINS

AND NEEDLES (1937) for the garment workers union in a small New York theatre and it was so popular it ran over 1,000 performances. Rome also echoed the voice of the average man in the revues Sing Out the News (1938), Let Freedom Sing (1942), CALL ME MISTER (1946), and Bless You All (1950). His book musicals were WISH YOU WERE HERE (1952), FANNY (1954), and DESTRY RIDES AGAIN (1959). Rome returned to the garment industry for his hard-hitting musical I CAN GET IT FOR YOU WHOLESALE (1962) and scored the ethnic show The Zulu and the Zayda (1965). He also scored the musical Gone With the Wind (1972), which was seen in Toyko and London. Only his musicals Call Me Mister (1951) and Fanny (1961) were filmed; much of the score was dropped in the former and his songs were reduced to background music in the latter. While Rome's work was often left wing, it was always seasoned with humor and sincere insight into everyday emotions.

ROMERO, CESAR [Julio] (1907–1994). Film and television performer. One of Hollywood's favorite Latin lovers, he was a suave leading man who later developed into a playful character actor. A native New Yorker born to Cuban parents, he began his career as a ballroom dancer in nightclubs and performed in the Broadway musicals Lady Do (1927) and Street Singer (1929) before making his screen debut in 1933. Romero made his name as the Cisco Kid in a series of adventure shorts and then played foreign types in comedies and dramas. He found himself dancing again in Metropolitan (1935) and went on to play feature and leading roles in the musicals Happy Landing (1938), My Lucky Star (1938), Tall, Dark and Handsome (1941), The Great American Broadcast (1941), WEEKEND IN HAVANA (1941), ORCHESTRA WIVES (1942), SPRINGTIME IN THE ROCKIES (1942), CONEY ISLAND (1943), Carnival in Costa Rica (1947), That Lady in Ermine (1948), HAPPY GO LUCKY (1951), and others. In all, he appeared in over eighty films. Romero found a new career on television, particularly as the Joker in the Batman series and in the dramatic serial Falcon Crest in the 1980s, but he continued to act on screen until a few years before his death.

ROONEY, MICKEY [born Joe Yule] (1920–). Film, stage, and television performer. The beloved and durable pint-sized actor–singer–dancer with a perennial adolescent glow about him, he has enjoyed one of the longest careers in show business, from playing toddlers to senior citizens on the screen. Rooney was

Mickey Rooney. In the late 1930s and early 1940s, Rooney played unbelievably talented teenagers who wrote the songs, played musical instruments, directed the show, and starred in his own productions, often with Judy Garland at his side. It was all so believable because Rooney himself seemed to be able to do all those things. Well, he didn't write songs but he sure knew how to perform. Pictured are Hollywood's favorite teen couple in a publicity shot for *Babes on Broadway* (1941). (Photofest)

born in Brooklyn, the son of vaudevillian Joe Yule, and was on the stage by the time he was fifteen months old, singing, dancing, and telling jokes as part of the family act. He made his first silent movie short in 1926 and as the comic strip character Mickey Maguire appeared in over fifty films before sound came in. Cast in supporting roles in early talkies, including the musicals *Broadway to Hollywood* (1933), *I Like It That Way* (1934), and *Reckless* (1935), he found further recognition as Puck in Max Reinhardt's movie version of *A Midsummer Night's Dream* (1935) but true stardom did not come until he played adolescent Andy Hardy in the B picture *A Family Affair* (1937); it was so popular Rooney starred in fourteen more Hardy films, including the musicals *Love Finds Andy Hardy* (1938) and *Andy Hardy Meets Debutante* (1940). Even this series of hits would be overshadowed by the "let's put on a show"

musicals with JUDY GARLAND, including *BABES IN ARMS* (1939), *STRIKE UP THE BAND* (1940), *BABES ON BROADWAY* (1941), *GIRL CRAZY* (1943), and *Thousands Cheer* (1943). At the same time, he also appeared in many famous nonmusical films. After World War II, Rooney was forced to graduate to more mature roles and concentrated on nonmusical films, yet still shone in the musicals *SUMMER HOLIDAY* (1948) and *WORDS AND MUSIC* (1948). His later screen musicals were *The Strip* (1951), *Sound Off* (1952), *All Ashore* (1958), *PETE'S DRAGON* (1977), and *The Magic of Lassie* (1978). Rooney was a frequent visitor to television, appearing in his own show in the 1950s and on hundreds of programs and specials, including some powerful dramas and the TV musical *PINOCCHIO* (1957), as well as providing the voices for many animated shows and films. At the age of fifty-nine he made his Broadway debut in the revue *SUGAR BABIES*

(1979) and was a hit, returning to the New York stage as a replacement for Will Roger's father Clem in THE WILL ROGERS FOLLIES (1993) and as Professor Marvel/Wizard in the Madison Square Garden Theatre musical version of THE WIZARD OF OZ (1998). He was still acting in films in 2007. Rooney's unceasing energy and pixie charm seem to render him timeless and he has carried the showmanship from his vaudeville days into everything he has done for eighty years. Among his eight wives were actresses AVA GARDNER and Martha Vickers (1925–1971). Autobiographies: *i.e.* (1965); *Life Is Too Short* (1991); biography: *The Nine Lives of Mickey Rooney*, Arthur Marx (1988).

ROSALIE (New Amsterdam Theatre 1928). A FLORENZ ZIEGFELD musical extravaganza, which required lavish sets by Joseph Urban and a huge cast to sing songs by GEORGE and IRA GERSHWIN, SIGMUND ROMBERG, and P. G. WODEHOUSE, the show starred MARILYN MILLER who had one of her greatest triumphs in this massive, clumsy presentation. GUY BOLTON and WILLIAM ANTHONY McGUIRE concocted the libretto about the Lindbergh-like Richard Faye from West Point who flies across the Atlantic to the Kingdom of Romanza to be near the Princess Rosalie whom he loves. When the royal family visits New York, Richard serves as part of the honor guard and the lovers are united again but Rosalie cannot marry a commoner. After a lot of fretting and spectacular production numbers, the king abdicates so Rosalie is no longer royalty and she can marry Richard. McGuire directed the huge production, SEYMOUR FELIX choreographed the dances, and Michel Fokine did the ballets. The score included the Romberg–Wodehouse numbers "Oh Gee! Oh Joy!," "Kingdom of Dreams," and "West Point Bugle," while the Gershwins provided "Ev'rybody Knows I Love Somebody," "Let Me Be a Friend to You," "Show Me the Town," and "How Long Has This Been Going On?," the last totally overlooked by the press and public and not finding popularity until years later. Critics commented that the musical hodgepodge was a grand entertainment thanks to Miller's sprightly singing and dancing and the show ran 335 performances.

Rosalie (MGM 1937) scrapped all the Broadway songs and Cole Porter provided a new score, with the highlight being the entrancing "In the Still of the Still." Also heard were "Why Should I Care?," "I've a Strange New Rhythm in My Heart," "Who Knows?," and "Spring Love Is in the Air." McGuire produced the film and rewrote his libretto for the screen, turning the flyer Richard into college football player Dick Thorpe (NELSON EDDY) and Rosalie (ELEANOR POWELL) as a European princess in America going to the same school. The two fall in love but she is engaged to Prince Paul back in Romanza. The difficulty was settled when Dick puts down a political coup in Romanza and gives up football to become king and spouse to Rosalie. Like the Broadway show, the movie was a lavish spectacle, with director W. S. VAN DYKE putting hundreds of extras on the set for the big finale. The excesses throughout were as silly as they were impressive and the picture was a big hit.

ROSE, THE (TCF 1979). The rock musical melodrama that marked BETTE MIDLER's screen debut, the film afforded her the opportunity to give a no-holds-barred performance that turned her from a light rock and camp figure into a movie star. The screenplay by Bo Goldman and Bill Kerby is loosely based on the tragic life of the late Janis Joplin, here called Mary Rose Foster (Midler) and known to her adoring fans as "The Rose." The popular rock and roll star is pushed by her manager Rudge Campbell (Alan Bates) to keep up a demand-

---

Casts for *Rosalie*

Character	1928 Broadway	1937 film
Princess Rosalie	MARILYN MILLER	ELEANOR POWELL
Lt. Richard Fay/Dick Thorpe	Oliver McClennan	NELSON EDDY
King Cyril/Fredrick	FRANK MORGAN	Frank Morgan
Queen	Margaret Dale	Edna May Oliver
Bill Delroy	JACK DONAHUE	RAY BOLGER
Prince Paul		Tom Rutherford
Countess Brenda		ILONA MASSEY
Chancellor		REGINALD OWEN

ing concert tour schedule that leads her deeper into alcohol and drugs. She finds some fleeting happiness in the arms of the ex-soldier Huston Dyer (Frederic Forrest) but life is too much for The Rose so, back in her Florida hometown for a concert performance, she overdoses on heroin and dies on stage. It was all pretty melodramatic but Midler was so magnetic that the film never flagged. A variety of pop composers provided the songs, all sung by Midler, including "Midnight in Memphis," "Stay With Me," "Whose Side Are You On?," "Sold My Soul to Rock and Roll," and the tender title number heard only over the final credits but it became the biggest hit of the lot. Mark Rydell directed the cast, which also featured Harry Dean Stanton, Barry Primus, David Keith, Sandra McCabe, and Will Hare. Midler's movie career would be prodigious but uneven, and she only rarely returned to the movie musical genre.

ROSE, BILLY [born William Samuel Rosenberg] (1899–1966). Stage producer and lyricist. A celebrated showman who presented all forms of live entertainment, from Broadway and nightclub shows to expositions and aquacades, he was one of the most colorful and aggressive individuals in show business. The native New Yorker began his career writing lyrics for the Broadway musical *Great Day!* (1929) and the revues *Charlot's Revue of 1926*, *Padlocks of 1927*, *Harry Delmar's Revels* (1927), *Sweet and Low* (1930), and *Crazy Quilt* (1931). He also produced the last two and continued to present such diverse Broadway musicals as *JUMBO* (1935), *CARMEN JONES* (1943), and *Seven Lively Arts* (1944). He bought and sold New York theatres, presented massive entertainments at world's fairs, and owned and operated several nightclubs throughout his career. Although he only scored a few shows, his song catalogue is impressive, with such hits as "More Than You Know," "I Found a Million Dollar Baby (In a Five-and-Ten-Cent Store)," and "It's Only a Paper Moon." He was married to FANNY BRICE for a time and was portrayed by James Caan in the musical film *FUNNY LADY* (1975). Biographies: *Only a Paper Moon: The Theatre of Billy Rose*, Stephen Nelson (1987); *Billy Rose: Manhattan Primitive*, Earl Conrad (1969); *The Nine Lives of Billy Rose*, Polly Rose Gottlieb (1968).

ROSE, GEORGE (1920–1988). Stage, film, and television performer. A round, twinkling character actor who has played everything from Shakespeare to music hall, he often stole the show in supporting roles. Rose was born in Bicester, England, and studied at the Central School of Speech Training and Dramatic Art before becoming a member of the Old Vic Company. He toured America with that troupe in 1946 and 1959 but didn't find recognition on Broadway until he played the common man in the drama *A Man for All Seasons* (1961). Rose settled in Manhattan in the 1960s and for two decades played a variety of characters on Broadway, including the musical roles of the shopkeeper Hobson in *Walking Happy* (1966), Alfred Doolittle in *MY FAIR LADY* (1968 and 1976), various dirty old men in *Canterbury Tales* (1969), French businessman Louis Greff in *COCO* (1969), Captain Hook in *PETER PAN* (1979), Major-General Stanley in *THE PIRATES OF PENZANCE* (1980), which he made for television in 1980 and for film in 1983, the diplomat Dr. Josef Winkler in *Dance a Little Closer* (1983), and the music hall Chairman in *THE MYSTERY OF EDWIN DROOD* (1985). Rose made many British and American films and appeared on some television specials.

ROSE, PHILIP [born Rosenberg] (1921–). Stage producer and director. A groundbreaking producer of unlikely plays, he also directed most of his musical productions. Rose was born in New York City and began his career as a singer, first performing professionally in stock in 1945. After starting a successful record company specializing in rhythm-and-blues artists, Rose became interested in producing and in 1959 struggled against all odds to bring Lorraine Hansberry's drama *A Raisin in the Sun* to New York. It was the first play by an African American woman to be presented on Broadway and a landmark in the history of the American theatre. Rose produced a number of other plays but in the 1970s he became interested in musicals and produced and directed a series of them, most memorably the hits *PURLIE* (1970) and *SHENANDOAH* (1975). His less successful musicals included *Angel* (1978), *My Old Friends* (1978), *Comin' Uptown* (1979), and *The Amen Corner* (1983). Autobiography: *You Can't Do That on Broadway!* (2004)

ROSE-MARIE (Imperial 1924). With its highly romantic score, lush scenic background, and rhapsodic lovers, the show may be the quintessential American operetta.

Plot: Rose-Marie la Flamme, the daughter of a French trapper, works as a singer at Lady Jane's Hotel in the Canadian Rockies. She is in love with the fur trapper Jim Kenyon, even

Casts for *Rose-Marie*

Character	1924 Broadway	1936 film	1954 film
Rose-Marie	MARY ELLIS	JEANETTE MACDONALD	ANN BLYTH
Jim/Bruce/Mike	DENNIS KING	NELSON EDDY	HOWARD KEEL
Edward Hawley	Frank Greene		
Black Eagle	Arthur Ludwig		Chief Yowlachie
Wanda	Pearl Regay		Joan Taylor
Herman/Barney	William Kent		BERT LAHR
John Flower		JAMES STEWART	
Myerson		REGINALD OWEN	
Bella		Gilda Gray	
James Duval			FERNANDO LAMAS

Rose-Marie. While some found Nelson Eddy (pictured) as wooden as the totem pole seen behind him, once he started singing all was forgiven. Here he is with Jeanette MacDonald in the first sound version of the stage operetta *Rose-Marie* (1936). (Photofest)

OTTO HARBACH and OSCAR HAMMERSTEIN wrote the libretto that made some bold advances for the American musical. The plot is much more intricate and the characters more complex than had previously been seen on the Broadway stage. The death of Black Eagle, for example, was a radical innovation for conventional operetta. The songs were so interwoven with the story that the authors did not want them listed individually in the program; the aim was for a "sung-through" operetta, although there were plenty of book scenes. Today we would consider *Rose-Marie* far from a fully integrated musical but in its day it was an exciting and revelatory experience. The glorious score by RUDOLF FRIML, HERBERT STOTHART, (music), Harbach, and Hammerstein (lyrics) was filled with wonderful songs, with the standout hits being "Indian Love Call" and the title number. Also estimable were the rousing march "The Mounties," the rhythmic "Totem Tom-Tom," the lyrical "The Door of My Dreams," the chipper "Pretty Things," and the lively duet "Why Shouldn't We?" The ARTHUR HAMMERSTEIN production was directed by Paul Dickey and choreographed by David Bennett. The Broadway production ran 557 performances and there were several national touring companies and a 1927 revival in New York. The 1925 London version starring EDITH DAY and Derek Oldham ran over two years, and *Rose-Marie* was even more popular in Paris where it ran 1,250 performances. For many years the musical was a staple in summer stock and with light opera companies.

though she is persistently pursued by the devious city slicker Edward Hawley. Jealous of Jim, Hawley frames him as the murderer of the drunken Indian Black Eagle and in grief Rose-Marie agrees to wed Hawley. The real culprit was the half-breed Wanda who accidentally killed Black Eagle in a fight. Jim's friend, Hard-Boiled Herman, gets the truth out of Wanda who stops Rose-Marie's wedding to Hawley just in time. Jim's name is cleared and he and Rose-Marie are reunited.

■ A 1928 silent film version, believed to be lost, featured JOAN CRAWFORD as the heroine and James Murray as Jim. It was not the only American operetta to be made into a silent movie but it says something about the strength of the musical's plot that Hollywood

---

Rose-Marie (stage) Musical Numbers

"Viva la Canadienne"
"Hard-Boiled Herman"
"Rose-Marie"
"The Mounties"
"Lak Jeem"
"Indian Love Call"
"Pretty Things"
"Why Shouldn't We?"
"Totem Tom-Tom"
"Only a Kiss"
"I Love Him"
"The Minuet of the Minute"
"One Man Woman"
"The Door of My Dreams"

---

thought the story worth filming without the benefit of song. (Sheet music with highlights of the stage score was provided for movie theatres who added piano, organ, or full orchestra accompaniment.) *Rose Marie* (MGM 1936) featured JEANETTE MACDONALD as the unhyphenated Rose Marie and NELSON EDDY was the hero, changed from a fur trapper to the Mountie Sergeant Bruce who is looking for a murderer who happens to be Rose Marie's brother (JAMES STEWART). In the screenplay by FRANCES GOODRICH, ALBERT HACKETT, and Alice Duer Miller, the heroine was promoted from a hotel singer to a famous Canadian opera singer who sets off for the Rockies to save her brother, with Jim on her trail and soon in her heart. Only four songs from the stage score were used, with the rest of the music coming from familiar standards ("Dinah" and " Some of These Days"), two new numbers ("Pardon Me, Madame" and "Just for You") by Stothart and GUS KAHN, and established opera arias for MacDonald. Some of the movie was shot by director W. S. VAN DYKE on location, and "Indian Love Call" was even more effective in a realistic, rural setting. As competent as the HUNT STROMBERG movie is, it has none of the bite of the stage version, yet it was extremely popular with moviegoers. The same studio remade *Rose Marie* (MGM 1954) in color CinemaScope and the scenery often outshone the screenplay (by Ronald Millar and George Froeschel), which was a mixture of the stage libretto and the 1936 movie. ANN BLYTH was Rose Marie, a Mountie named Mike Malone (HOWARD KEEL) was the hero, and Rose Marie ends up in the arms of the fur trapper Duval (FERNANDO LAMAS). The low-caste Wanda from the stage became a ravishing

Indian princess (Joan Taylor), the daughter of the chief of the tribe. The one improvement in the movie was a delightful turn by BERT LAHR singing "I'm a Mountie Who Never Got His Man" by GEORGE STOLL and Herbert Baker. Other new numbers by Hammerstein, PAUL FRANCIS WEBSTER, and others included "The Right Place for a Girl," "Free to Be Free," "I Have the Love," and "Love and Kisses." The film, produced and directed by MERVYN LEROY and choreographed by BUSBY BERKELEY, was not a success at the box office and by the 1960s the musical *Rose-Marie* was little more than a corny relic from the past and "Indian Love Call" the stuff of parody.

ROSE OF WASHINGTON SQUARE (Fox 1939). Although it did not advertise itself as a biographical musical about entertainer FANNY BRICE, the film's plot was so similar to her life that the comedienne sued 20TH CENTURY-FOX and got a hefty out-of-court settlement. In co-producer Nunnally Johnson's screenplay, the heroine is Rose Sargent (ALICE FAYE) who climbs to the top of her profession but her love for the disreputable con man Barton DeWitt Clinton (TYRONE POWER) keeps dragging her down. Eventually he goes to prison, she sings Brice's signature number "My Man," and everybody knew this was not fiction. The score consisted of several old standards (such as "I'm Just Wild About Harry" and the title tune), AL JOLSON sang an armful of his old hits (including "California, Here I Come" and "My Mammy"), and HARRY REVEL (music) and MACK GORDON (lyric) provided a new ballad, "I Never Knew That Heaven Could Speak." GREGORY RATOFF directed the DARRYL F. ZANUCK production, which also featured WILLIAM FRAWLEY, Joyce Compton, Hobart Cavanaugh, Louis Prima, and Moroni Olsen. The whole story would be told without disguises in *FUNNY GIRL*.

ROSS, DIANA [Ernestine Earle] (1944–). Film and television performer. The classy African American singer–actress, who first became famous as a pop singer, has dipped into the musical with mixed results. Ross was born in Detroit and started singing with a gospel group at her church before she found fame as the lead singer of the pop group the Supremes. After the trio disbanded, Ross sang solo with success and pursued a film career, making a smashing debut as legendary blues singer Billie Holiday in the musical bio *LADY SINGS THE BLUES* (1972). She was less impressive as a grown-up Dorothy in the ill-fated musical *THE WIZ* (1978). Ross has made some nonmusical films and has appeared on television in TV movies and variety specials. The popular musical *DREAMGIRLS* (1981) is loosely based on Ross and the Supremes. Autobiographies: *Going Back*, with Rosanne Shelnutt (2004); *Upside Down: Wrong Turns, Right Turns and the Road Ahead* (1997); biography: *Diana Ross*, J. Randy Taraborrelli (2007).

ROSS, HERBERT [David] (1927–2001). Stage and screen choreographer, director, and dancer. A prosperous film director of nonmusicals, he started out as a prominent choreographer (and sometime director) on Broadway. Ross was born in Brooklyn, New York, and in the 1940s studied dance with Doris Humphrey, Helena Platova, and Caird Leslie, as well as acting with Herbert Berghof. He made his acting debut in 1942 in a tour of *Macbeth* and was performing in plays on Broadway the next year. While appearing in the dancing chorus of such musicals as *FOLLOW THE GIRLS* (1944), *BLOOMER GIRL* (1944), and *INSIDE U.S.A.* (1948), he also danced with various ballet companies. By 1951 Ross was choreographing on Broadway and, on occasion, directing as well. His shows included *A TREE GROWS IN BROOKLYN* (1951), *Three Wishes for Jamie* (1952), *HOUSE OF FLOWERS* (1954), *THE GAY LIFE* (1961), *I CAN GET IT FOR YOU WHOLESALE* (1962), *DO I HEAR A WALTZ?* (1965), *ON A CLEAR DAY YOU CAN SEE FOREVER* (1965), and *THE APPLE TREE* (1966). Perhaps his finest work of the 1960s was the clever, quirky choreography he devised for the short-lived musical *ANYONE CAN WHISTLE* (1964). In 1954 Ross choreographed his first film, *CARMEN JONES*, followed by *DOCTOR DOLITTLE* (1967) and *FUNNY GIRL* (1968). He staged many television specials in the 1950s and 1960s. By 1969 he left the stage for the movies, directing the musicals *GOODBYE MR. CHIPS* (1969) and *FUNNY LADY* (1975) and several nonmusical hits such as *The Sunshine Boys* (1975), *The Turning Point* (1977), *The Goodbye Girl* (1977), and *Steel Magnolias* (1989). When Ross returned to Broadway a decade later, it was to direct the popular Neil Simon comedies *Chapter Two* (1977) and *I Ought to Be in Pictures* (1980).

ROSS, LANNY [born Lancelot Patrick Ross] (1906–1988). Film performer. A handsome blond tenor with an opera-quality voice, he was a favorite on the radio but was also featured in some films. Ross was born in Seattle and sang in nightclubs and on records before becoming a radio singing star. He made his screen debut in the musical short *Yours Sincerely* (1933) and then went on to make such feature musicals as *Melody in Spring* (1934), *COLLEGE RHYTHM* (1934), *The Lady Objects* (1938), and *STAGE DOOR CANTEEN* (1943). Ross provided the singing voice of Prince David in the animated musical *GULLIVER'S TRAVELS* (1939), as well as in the musical short *Tune Up and Sing* (1934).

ROSS, SHIRLEY [born Bernice Gaunt] (1909–1975). Film and stage performer. A redheaded band singer who never quite became a movie star, she got to introduce some song favorites on screen. Ross was born in Omaha, Nebraska, and grew up in California where she studied for a time at UCLA. She sang with various bands and on the radio before getting a Hollywood contract in 1933. She played bit parts in *Bombshell* (1933), *HOLLYWOOD PARTY* (1934), *THE MERRY WIDOW* (1934), and other PARAMOUNT films and in the nonmusical *Manhattan Melodrama* (1934) she was a nightclub singer who crooned "The Bad in Every Man," which was later revised to become "Blue Moon." Ross was given featured and leading roles in the musicals *SAN FRANCISCO* (1936), *BIG BROADCAST OF 1937* (1936), *Hideaway Girl* (1937), *Waikiki Wedding* (1937), *Blossoms on Broadway* (1937), *BIG BROADCAST OF 1938* (in which she sang "Thanks for the Memory" with BOB HOPE), *Thanks for the Memory* (1938), *Paris Honeymoon* (1939), *Café Society* (1939), and others. Ross was also featured in the Broadway musical *HIGHER AND HIGHER* (1940) where she introduced the song standard "It Never Entered My Mind." She retired from singing in 1943. Among the other hit songs she got to sing on screen were "Two Sleepy People" and "The Lady's in Love With You."

ROTH, LILLIAN [born Lillan Rutstein] (1910–1980). Stage and film performer. The dark-haired, round-faced belter was the quintessential flapper on Broadway and in the movies, yet she never became a major star because of her tragic life. Roth was born in Boston and was on the vaudeville stage as a young child, acting kid roles on Broadway at the age of six, and featured in *Ziegfeld's Midnight Frolics* (1927) when she was still a teenager. She was also featured in the Broadway revues *Padlocks of 1927* and *EARL CARROLL VANITIES* (1928 and 1931). In Hollywood she was given featured roles in the early musicals *Illusion* (1929), *THE LOVE PARADE* (1929), *THE VAGABOND KING* (1930), *Honey* (1930), *PARAMOUNT ON PARADE* (1930),

ANIMAL CRACKERS (1930), *Madam Satan* (1930), and *TAKE A CHANCE* (1933). Roth disappeared from the public eye in the 1930s and not until her appearance on television's *This Is Your Life* in 1954 did America know of her many ruined marriages and bouts of alcoholism. Her best-selling autobiography *I'll Cry Tomorrow* (1954) was turned into a successful movie in 1955 with SUSAN HAYWARD playing Roth. She made a comeback appearing in nightclubs, on television, in a few films, and in the Broadway musicals *I CAN GET IT FOR YOU WHOLESALE* (1962) and *70, GIRLS, 70* (1971).

ROTHSCHILDS, THE (Lunt-Fontanne Theatre 1970). An expertly crafted musical play about the famous banking family, the Jewish show was viewed as the flip side of *FIDDLER ON THE ROOF* (1964). The lives and fortunes of the wealthy Jewish Rothschild family were chronicled starting with its humble beginnings in the Frankfort ghetto, where patriarch Mayer Rothschild (HAL LINDEN) weds Gutele (Leila Martin). With his sons, Mayer begins his business and it grows until the family is a powerful influence at the Congress of Vienna. Also in the cast were Keene Curtis, Timothy Jerome, David Garfield, Chris Sarandon, Paul Hecht, Allan Gruet, Jill Clayburgh, and Robby Benson. Sherman Yellen adapted Frederic Morton's biography of the same title, and JERRY BOCK (music) and SHELDON HARNICK (lyrics) wrote the proficient score that included "In My Own Lifetime," "One Room," "Everything," "Sons," "Rothschild and Sons," and "He Tossed a Coin." The musical, directed and choreographed by MICHAEL KIDD, was compared unfavorably by several critics to the songwriters' earlier *Fiddler on the Roof*, but taken on its own the show was a pleasing mixture of history, sentiment, and warm comedy. Linden became a bona fide Broadway star with his performance and audiences embraced the musical for 507 performances.

ROUNDABOUT THEATRE COMPANY. Theatre organization. After many years of presenting low-budget revivals in a variety of inhospitable venues, this organization became one of New York's most potent producing groups on and Off Broadway in the 1990s. Founded in 1965 by Gene Feist to present nonmusical revivals in a church, the company persevered for decades and gradually grew, found a wider audience base, and expanded its repertoire. By the 1980s it boasted the largest subscription audience of any theatre group in town and started presenting shows on Broadway as well as off. By the 1990s its musical revivals were particularly accomplished, several of them so popular that they had to move to a larger or different house so that the season could continue. Among the Roundabout musicals were *SHE LOVES ME* (1993), *COMPANY* (1995), *1776* (1997), *CABARET* (1998), *LITTLE ME* (1998), *FOLLIES* (2001), *THE BOYS FROM SYRACUSE* (2002), *BIG RIVER* (2003), *PACIFIC OVERTURES* (2004), *ASSASSINS* (2004), *THE PAJAMA GAME* (2006), *THE THREEPENNY OPERA* (2006), *THE APPLE TREE* (2006), *110 IN THE SHADE* (2007), and *SUNDAY IN THE PARK WITH GEORGE* (2008). The only original musicals produced by the company were the revues *A Grand Night for Singing* (1993) and *The Look of Love* (2003).

ROUNSEVILLE, ROBERT [Field] (1914–1974). Stage, television, and film performer. A superior operatic tenor who sang some of Broadway's most challenging roles, he also played several classic characters in European operettas. A native of Attleboro, Massachusetts, Rounseville trained for the opera but began his career pursuing musical theatre jobs. He made his Broadway debut in the chorus of *BABES IN ARMS* (1937) and was seen in bit parts in such Broadway musicals as *KNICKERBOCKER HOLIDAY* (1938) and *HIGHER AND HIGHER* (1940) before being cast in a major role in the 1943 revival of *THE MERRY WIDOW* and a featured part in *UP IN CENTRAL PARK* (1945). Rounseville played major roles in Gilbert and Sullivan operettas on Broadway and was praised for his Gaylord Ravenal in the 1954 and 1961 revivals of *SHOW BOAT*. He also shone on Broadway as the title hero in *CANDIDE* (1956) and as the Padre in *MAN OF LA MANCHA* (1965) where he introduced "To Each His Dulcinea." His other stage credits in New York include revivals of *BRIGADOON* (1957) and *SONG OF NORWAY* (1958). Rounseville made only a few films, most memorably as Mr. Snow in *CAROUSEL* (1956), and a few television appearances, such as *THE MIKADO* (1960), but concentrated on concerts and touring productions of operettas where his pure, rich tenor voice was most appreciated.

ROUTLEDGE, [Katherine] **PATRICIA** (1929–). Stage, film, and television performer. The many-sided British actress–singer, who suffered a series of flops on Broadway, yet was always applauded, finally became famous in America late in her career because of television. Routledge was born in Birkenhead, England, the daughter of a haberdasher, and was educated at the University of Liverpool, the Guildhall School of Music, and Bristol Old Vic Theatre School. By 1954 she was acting in London, easily moving back and forth between plays and musicals, and in 1966 she came to Broadway for the first time in the farce *How's the World Treating You?* Routledge returned for two short-lived musicals, playing the life-affirming widow Alice Challice in *Darling of the Day* (1968) and as various First Ladies in *1600 PENNSYLVANIA AVENUE* (1976), and in two shows that closed before reaching New York: *Love Match* (1968) and *Say Hello to Harvey* (1981). In 1980 she was a replacement for Ruth in the popular revival of *THE PIRATES OF PENZANCE* but never appeared on Broadway again, returning to England to do more theatre, films, and television, including the TV musicals *ANDROCLES AND THE LION* (1967) and *The Pirates of Penzance* (1980). It wasn't until the 1990s that Routledge became well known as Hyacinth Bucket in the BBC series *Keeping Up Appearances*.

ROYAL WEDDING (MGM 1951). The first musical STANLEY DONEN directed alone, it was also the first major leading role for JANE POWELL and the first Hollywood assignment for writer–lyricist ALAN JAY LERNER. They all did themselves proud and came up with an entertaining musical that falls short of being a classic because of some weak performances in the personage of PETER LAWFORD and Sarah Churchill (Winston Churchill's daughter). In Lerner's screenplay, the brother and sister Broadway performers Tom (FRED ASTAIRE) and Ellen Bowen (Powell) bring their musical hit to London as Great Britain prepares for the wedding of Princess Elizabeth to Philip Mountbatten. Ellen falls in love with the English Lord John Brindale (Lawford) while Tom is entranced by the publican's daughter Anne Ashmond (Churchill). Since neither romance was particularly engrossing, it fell to the musical numbers to carry the film and they did more than that. Lerner wrote the lyrics for BURTON LANE's music and every song was a gem, including the entrancing ballads "Open Your Eyes" and "Too Late Now," the sexy comedy number "Every Night at Seven," the raucous music hall turn "How Could You Believe Me When I Said I Loved You When You Know I've Been a Liar All My Life?," the stomping "Sunday Jumps," and the ecstatic "You're All the World to Me," which Astaire sang and, in the movie's most famous scene, danced on the walls and ceiling of his hotel

room. NICK CASTLE and Astaire did the choreography, which also included a clever pas de deux for Astaire and a hat stand. Also in the cast were KEENAN WYNN (playing twin brothers, only one of whom was British), Albert Sharpe, and Viola Roache.

ROYCE, EDWARD [born James William Reddall] (1870–1964). Stage director and choreographer. He staged many American and British musicals in the 1910s and 1920s, including early landmark efforts by JEROME KERN. Royce was born in Bath, England, the son of musical comedy star E. W. Royce, and began his career as a scenic designer, but he soon followed in his father's footsteps and took up dancing. Eventually he became more interested in choreography and started to stage dances in West End musicals at the turn of the century. By 1905 Royce was directing as well as choreographing British musicals. He was brought to America by his friend Jerome Kern, making his Broadway debut in 1913 and going on to direct and choreograph Kern's *Have a Heart* (1917), *OH, BOY!* (1917), *LEAVE IT TO JANE* (1917), *OH, LADY! LADY!* (1918), and *SALLY* (1920). Royce also staged such hits as *Going Up!* (1917), *IRENE* (1919), *Kid Boots* (1923), *Billie* (1928), and a few editions of the *ZIEGFELD FOLLIES*. In 1929 he choreographed a few early movie musicals and then returned to England for the rest of his declining career. As a creative member of the team who put together the PRINCESS MUSICALS in the 1910s, Royce was instrumental in the American musical's development from large, dazzling extravaganzas to smaller, more intimate and intelligent works. His choreography was sprightly and contagious, as in the "Tickle Toe" in *Going Up!*, and his staging of those early literate book musicals was effective enough to be noticed at the time.

RUBY, HARRY. See KALMAR, Bert

RUDOLPH AND FROSTY'S CHRISTMAS IN JULY (ABC-TV 1979). Two favorites from previous Rankin–Bass animated musicals were teamed together for this convoluted but enjoyable ninety-minute musical that boasted fun songs and top-notch voices. ROMEO MULLER's teleplay is a complicated tale about the evil Winterbolt (voice of PAUL FREES) who wants to destroy the beloved inhabitants of the North Pole. Rudolph the red-nosed reindeer (Billie Mae Richards) is tricked into joining the circus and is encouraged by the crooked reindeer Scratcher (Alan Sues) into stealing the box office take, thereby causing his nose to stop glowing. Frosty (Jackie Vernon) and his family want to see the circus but to travel south in July means they will melt so they are given magic amulets by Winterbolt that stop working once it is too late. It takes all the efforts of Rudolph's pal Milton (Red Buttons), Santa Claus (MICKEY ROONEY), the circus manager Lily Loraine (ETHEL MERMAN), and the cold breath of Crystal (Shelley Winters) to get everyone back North. The cockeyed plot was relieved by some holiday favorites, such as "Frosty the Snowman" and "Rudolph the Red-Nosed Reindeer" and new numbers by MAURY LAWS, Johnny Marks, and Michael Colicchio, including "Christmas in July," "I See Rainbows," and "Everything I've Always Wanted." As belted out by Merman and others, the musical numbers were sportive fun. ARTHUR RANKIN, JR. and JULES BASS produced and directed.

RUDOLPH THE RED-NOSED REINDEER. See *STORY OF RUDOLPH THE RED-NOSED REINDEER, THE*

RUGGLES, [Charles Sherman] **CHARLES** (1886–1970). Stage, film, and television performer. One of Broadway and Hollywood's favorite character actors, he specialized in playing well-dressed but nervous types who were usually gullible and/or henpecked. Ruggles was born in Los Angeles and in 1914 he made both his screen and Broadway debuts. While he mostly appeared in comedies in both media, he was a delightful addition to many musicals. On Broadway he was featured in *THE PASSING SHOW OF 1918*, *Tumble In* (1919), *Queen High* (1926), *Rainbow* (1928), and *Spring Is Here* (1929). Of his over 100 movies, Ruggles acted in some two dozen musicals, including The *Battle of Paris* (1929), *Queen High* (1930), *THE SMILING LIEUTENANT* (1931), *ONE HOUR WITH YOU* (1932), *LOVE ME TONIGHT* (1932), *BIG BROADCAST OF 1936* (1935), *ANYTHING GOES* (1936), *Turn Off the Moon* (1937), *BALALAIKA* (1939), *Incendiary Blonde* (1945), *Give My Regards to Broadway* (1948), *Look for the Silver Lining* (1949), and *I'd Rather Be Rich* (1964). He returned to Broadway and acted in some comedies in the late 1950s and 1960s. Ruggles was also a familiar favorite on television, appearing on many shows, including the TV version of *CAROUSEL* (1967), and providing the narration for the Aesop's Fables section of the animated *The Bullwinkle Show* in the 1960s. His brother was actor–director WESLEY RUGGLES.

🖵 *RUGGLES OF RED GAP* (NBC-TV 1957). Harry Leon Wilson's 1915 novel had been filmed in 1918, 1923, 1935, and 1950 (as *Fancy Pants*) with success so this musical version broadcast on *Showcase Productions* held few surprises for many viewers. David Shaw's teleplay sticks close to the original but builds up the love story and love songs rather than the comedy. The uncouth couple Effie (IMOGENE COCA) and Egbert Floud (DAVID WAYNE) from Red Gap, Washington, win the services of the gentlemanly British butler Ruggles (Michael Redgrave) in a poker game in Europe and bring him home to their cattle ranch, passing the sophisticated fellow off as an English colonel to impress the locals. Ruggles is a hit with the townspeople and manages to eventually become his own man, running a restaurant in his new homeland. The estimable cast also included JANE POWELL, PETER LAWFORD, Joan Holloway, Paul Lynde, HAL LINDEN, GEORGE S. IRVING, and Fred Stewart. Critics found the story less effective this time around but commended the score by JULE STYNE (music) and LEO ROBIN (lyrics), which included "It's a Glorious Fourth," "It's Terribly, Horribly, Frightfully Nice," "I Have You to Thank," "Oh, Those Americans," "The Way to a Family's Heart," "A Ride on a Rainbow," and "Kickapoo Kick." Two years later Styne recycled the music from one of the numbers, "I'm in Pursuit of Happiness," to use in *GYPSY* (1959) as "You'll Never Get Away From Me." Redgrave surprised audiences with a pleasing singing voice and the rest of the cast was in high spirits with their songs as well. Charles Friedman produced the ninety-minute musical that was directed by Clark Jones.

RUGGLES, WESLEY (1889–1972). Film director and performer. A comic actor in early two-reelers, he turned to directing and made many silent and sound movies, including seven musicals. Ruggles was born in Los Angeles and by 1914 was one of the Keystone Kops and a supporting player in Charles Chaplin's early comedies. He directed his first silent in 1917 and was busy throughout the 1920s and 1930s, helming a variety of genres, including the early musicals *Street Girl* (1929) and *Honey* (1930). Ruggles career was uneven but he managed to direct such important films as *Cimarron* (1931) and *I'm No Angel* (1933). His other screen musicals included *College Humor* (1933), *Bolero* (1934), *Shoot the Works* (1934), and *SING YOU SINNERS* (1938). He was the brother of actor CHARLES RUGGLES.

RUMANN, SIG [born Siegfried Albon Rumann] (1884–1967). Film and stage performer. A busy character actor who appeared in over 100 movies after a stage career, he was a favorite as blustering Prussian authority figures. Rumann was born in Hamburg and studied electrotechnology in college before pursuing an acting career. He performed on the German stage and screen before serving in the Kaiser's army during World War I. Rumann came to America in 1924 and five years later was on Broadway in a handful of comedies and dramas, most memorably *Grand Hotel* (1930). He made his Hollywood debut in a bit part in the musical *Lucky Boy* (1929) and soon was cast as foreigners in comedies, dramas, and musicals, including *A NIGHT AT THE OPERA* (1935), *ON THE AVENUE* (1937), *MAYTIME* (1937), *A DAY AT THE RACES* (1937), *Thin Ice* (1937), *THE GREAT WALTZ* (1938), *Honolulu* (1939), *BITTER SWEET* (1940), *THE DOLLY SISTERS* (1945), *NIGHT AND DAY* (1946), *MOTHER WORE TIGHTS* (1947), *The Emperor Waltz* (1948), *ON THE RIVIERA* (1951), *THE GLENN MILLER STORY* (1954), *WHITE CHRISTMAS* (1954), and *ROBIN AND THE SEVEN HOODS* (1964). Rumann continued acting on screen and on Broadway into the 1960s.

RUPERT, MICHAEL (1951–). Stage and television performer. The likable leading man in New York musicals, he has an everyman look and demeanor, yet has excelled in playing colorful neurotics. Rupert was born in Denver and trained at the Pasadena Playhouse as a teenager before making an impressive Broadway debut as the French Canadian adolescent Bibi in the musical *THE HAPPY TIME* (1968). As an adult performer, he has been most associated with the character of Marvin, the difficult homosexual in the musicals *March of the Falsettos* (1981), *Falsettoland* (1992), and the compilation of them titled *FALSETTOS* (1992). Rupert also shone as another neurotic, the uncertain Oscar in *SWEET CHARITY* (1986), as law Professor Callahan in *LEGALLY BLONDE* (2007), and replacing leading roles in *PIPPIN* (1974), *CITY OF ANGELS* (1990), and *RAGTIME* (1999). His other musical credits include *Festival* (1979), *Shakespeare's Cabaret* (1981), *Mail* (1988), and *Putting It Together* (1993). Rupert has written scripts and composed songs, most memorably for the Off Broadway musical *3 Guys Naked From the Waist Down* (1985), and has acted in a few films and many television programs.

RUSSELL, JANE [born Ernestine Jane Geraldine Russell] (1921–). Film, television, and stage performer. The buxom brunette who became famous for her measurements, she remained in the public eye because of her playful performances in comedies and musicals. Russell was born in Bemidji, Minnesota, the daughter of an actress, and did some modeling while she studied acting at Max Reinhardt's Theatrical Workshop. Millionaire producer Howard Hughes chose Russell for his controversial western *The Outlaw* (1943) in which she was shamelessly exploited but the notoriety led to better film vehicles, including the musicals *THE PALEFACE* (1948), *Double Dynamite* (1951), *The Las Vegas Story* (1952), *SON OF PALEFACE* (1952), *GENTLEMEN PREFER BLONDES* (1953), *The French Line* (1953), and *Gentlemen Marry Brunettes* (1955). Russell was also popular in nightclubs and on television and made a belated Broadway debut in 1971 when she took over the role of Joanne in *COMPANY*. While in her eighties, she was still performing on occasion. Autobiography: *My Path and Detours* (1985).

RUSSELL, [Henry] **KEN**[neth] (1927–). Film and television director. The controversial British director, known for his bombastic style and overblown images on screen, helmed two noteworthy musicals, which also met with controversy. Russell was born in Southampton, England, served in the British Navy and the RAF force before turning to performing, first as a dancer and then as an actor. He abandoned the stage when he took up photography and later made short films and documentaries for television, including fictionalized biographies on famous composers that caused a stir. Russell directed his first feature film in 1963 and became famous for his second, *Women in Love* (1969). He remade some of his composer pieces as full-length movies, such as *The Music Lovers* (1970), *Mahler* (1974), and *Lisztomania* (1975). His film version of the stage musical *THE BOY FRIEND* (1971) and the rock opera *TOMMY* (1975) were both reviled and praised but his dance film *Valentino* (1977) had few advocates. In the 1990s Russell returned to television and made several drama specials. Autobiography: *Altered States: The Autobiography of Ken Russell* (1991); biography: *Phallic Frenzy: Ken Russell and His Films*, Joseph Lanza (2007).

RUSSELL, LILLIAN [born Helen Louise Leonard] (1861–1922). Stage performer. The blue-eyed, blonde singer–actress whose corseted hourglass figure became the standard by which beauty was measured, she was arguably the first superstar of the American stage. Russell was born in Clinton, Iowa, the daughter of a newspaper editor and a women's rights advocate, and was raised in Chicago before moving to New York where she studied voice. She started appearing in the chorus of Broadway operettas in 1877 but her career didn't blossom until Tony Pastor hired her for his Music Hall, gave her a new name, and marketed her as a singing comedienne in a series of Gilbert and Sullivan spoofs. Soon musicals and operettas were being written for her and the public was crazy about "Airy Fairy Lillian." By the end of the century she had starred in over thirty Broadway shows, including *The Great Mogul* (1891), *Billee Taylor* (1883), *Pepita* (1886), *The Maid and the Moonshiner* (1886), *Nadjy* (1889), *The Grand Duchess* (1889), *Girofle-Girofla* (1891), *Princess Nicotine* (1893), *La Perichole* (1895), *The Little Duke* (1895), *The American Beauty* (1996), *La Belle Helene* (1899), and *Erminie* (1899). When her popularity started to wane around 1900, she rejuvenated it by joining up with WEBER and FIELDS and played the female star in their rough-and-tumble musical burlesques such as *Fiddle-Dee-Dee* (1900), *Hoity Toity* (1901), *Twirly Whirly* (1902), and *Whoop-Dee-Doo* (1903). By 1910 Russell concentrated on vaudeville, but she returned to Broadway in 1912 for the Weber and Fields reunion *Hokey Pokey*. She was a temperamental star, disposing of bills, contracts, friends, and husbands throughout her life, but she personified the era and represented everything glamorous about the theatre. ALICE FAYE played the celebrated songstress in the movie musical *LILLIAN RUSSELL* (1940) and Weber and Fields came out of retirement to appear as themselves in the film. Biography: *Lillian Russell*, Armond Fields (1999).

RUSSELL, ROSALIND (1912–1976). Stage, film, and television performer. The fast-talking, sarcastic comedienne of many movies between 1934 and 1971, she made only a few musical appearances on screen and stage but they were all memorable. Russell was born in Waterbury, Connecticut, the daughter of a lawyer and a fashion editor, and studied acting at the American Academy of Dramatic Arts before working in stock. She made her Broadway bow in the third edition of *THE GARRICK GAIETIES* (1930) and then, after appearing in one play, was off to Hollywood where she specialized in playing smart, efficient career girls in comedies and a few musicals, such as *The Night Is Young* (1934) and *Reckless* (1935). Russell returned to Broadway after two decades and rejuvenated her career as the sly spinster Ruth Sherwood in the musical *WONDERFUL TOWN* (1953), a role

she had played in the film comedy *My Sister Eileen* (1942). After making the screen musical *The Girl Rush* (1955), Russell found her greatest role: the wacky *Auntie Mame* on Broadway in 1956 and on screen in 1958. Although she would make several movies after that, only one was a musical, *GYPSY* (1962) in which she played the driven stage mother Rose. Russell made a number of television appearances, including the small-screen version of *Wonderful Town* (1958). She was married to producer Frederick Brisson (1912–1984). Autobiography: *Life Is a Banquet* (1977); biography: *Forever Mame: The Life of Rosalind Russell*, Bernard F. Dick, (2006).

RYAN, PEGGY [O'Rene] (1924–2004). Film, television, and stage performer. A chipper child and teenage singer–dancer, she enlivened several movie musicals in the 1940s and was often paired with DONALD O'CONNOR, the two of the becoming the JUDY GARLAND and MICKEY ROONEY of B movies. Ryan was born in Long Beach, California, the daughter of vaudeville dancers, and was on stage as a child. She made her screen debut at the age of thirteen and was cast as a spunky adolescent named Peggy in such low-budget musicals as *Top of the Town* (1937), *Private Buckaroo* (1942), and *Give Out Sisters* (1942), the last two with O'Connor. The two also danced together in *Get Hep to Love* (1942), *When Johnny Comes Marching Home* (1942), *Mr. Big* (1943), *Top Man* (1943), *Chip Off the Old Block* (1944), *Follow the Boys* (1944), *This Is the Life* (1944), *The Merry Monahans* (1944), *Bowery to Broadway* (1944), and *Patrick the Great* (1945). Ryan appeared in several nonmusical movies, most memorably *The Grapes of Wrath* (1940), and in two Broadway revues, *Meet the People* (1940) and *Count Me In* (1942). Her other movie musicals are *Babes in Swing Street* (1944), *Here Come the Coeds* (1945), *That's the Spirit* (1945), *On Stage Everybody* (1945), *There's a Girl in My Heart* (1949), and *All Ashore* (1952). In the last film she was paired with RAY MCDONALD, whom she married. Ryan retired from movies in the 1950s and ran a dancing school. When she later moved to Hawaii she appeared on the television series *Hawaii Five-O* for seven years.

RYSKIND, MORRIE (1895–1985). Stage and film writer. A little known but very successful author of Broadway musicals and Hollywood scripts, he contributed to several major works with the GERSHWINS and others. The Brooklyn native was educated at Columbia and began his career writing sketches for the

Broadway revues *The 49ers* (1922), *Merry-Go-Round* (1927), and *Ned Wayburn's Gambols* (1929), also penning some of the lyrics. He turned to book musicals when he co-wrote the libretto for the Marx Brothers vehicle *Animal Crackers* (1928) and then collaborated with the Gershwins and George S. Kaufman on *Strike Up the Band* (1930), *Of Thee I Sing* (1931), and *Let 'Em Eat Cake* (1933). Ryskind also wrote the musicals *The Gang's All Here* (1931) and *Louisiana Purchase* (1940). He made his Hollywood debut when he adapted the Marx Brothers stage works *The Cocoanuts* (1929) and *Animal Crackers* (1930) for the screen. He scripted many non-musical comedies and such musicals as *Palmy Days* (1931), *A Night at the Opera* (1935), *Anything Goes* (1935), *Man About Town* (1939), and *Where Do We Go From Here?* (1945).

S

SADDLER, DONALD (1918–). Stage choreographer. A productive choreographer on Broadway and in regional theatre, he has had full careers in musicals as well as classical and modern dance. Saddler was born in Van Nuys, California, the son of a landscape designer, and educated at Los Angeles City College before studying dance with Carmelita Maracci, Anthony Tudor, and Madame Anderson Ivantzova. He began his career as a dancer in nightclubs in 1939 and then started performing with various dance companies, in particular the Harkness Ballet where he would become the artistic director in the 1960s. Saddler appeared in the dancing chorus of a handful of Broadway musicals in the 1940s and had a featured role in *HIGH BUTTON SHOES* (1947). He turned to choreographing in 1948 with the Markova-Dolin Dance Company and made an auspicious Broadway bow with his dances for *WONDERFUL TOWN* (1953), followed by such musicals as *MILK AND HONEY* (1961), *Rodgers & Hart* (1975), *THE ROBBER BRIDEGROOM* (1975), *THE GRAND TOUR* (1979), *Teddy and Alice* (1987), and the revivals of *NO, NO, NANETTE* (1971), *GOOD NEWS!* (1974), and *ON YOUR TOES* (1983). He also choreographed for different dance companies, regional theatre, and opera organizations such as the City Opera and the Metropolitan Opera, and he both directed and choreographed the Off Broadway revue *From Berlin to Broadway With Kurt Weill* (1972). Although he comes from a ballet background, Saddler's choreography is wide ranged and varied, from Russian ballet in *On Your Toes* to the backwoods folk dances in *The Robber Bridegroom* to the contagious tap dancing in *No, No, Nanette*.

SAIDY, FRED [born Fareed Milhelm Saidy] (1907–1982). Stage, film, and television writer. The author of some bold and provocative musical librettos, he often collaborated with the controversial E. Y. HARBURG. Saidy was born in Los Angeles and began his career as a journalist before writing sketches for Broadway, films, and early television. His first Broadway book musical was the anti-war, feminist *BLOOMER GIRL* (1944) in which he collaborated with writer Sig Herzig, lyricist Harburg, and composer HAROLD ARLEN. Saidy adapted the piece for television in 1956. He worked with Harburg again on *FINIAN'S RAINBOW* (1947), *FLAHOOLEY* (1951), *JAMAICA* (1957), and *The Happiest Girl in the World* (1961), each musical filled with potent leftist ideas. Saidy contributed to the scripts for the Hollywood musicals *STAR-SPANGLED RHYTHM* (1942), *I Dood It* (1943), *Meet the People* (1944), and the screen version of *Finian's Rainbow* (1968), as well as the television musical *SATINS AND SPURS* (1954).

ST. LOUIS MUNICIPAL OPERA. Locally known as the "Muny," the outdoor theatre in Forest Park of urban St. Louis seats 11,000 people and features a stage big enough to accommodate a large chorus, spectacular scenery, and even horses pulling carriages. The venue opened in 1919 with a revival of *ROBIN HOOD* (1891) and for several decades the repertoire consisted of American and European operettas. Later on musical comedies were added and today comprise most of the summer season. The organization also presents touring Broadway shows in their winter home, the mammoth Fox Theatre, an opulent movie palace built in the silent movie era.

ST. LOUIS WOMAN (Martin Beck Theatre 1946). An intriguing musical about African Americans, the show had libretto problems but there was nothing wrong with the superior score and stimulating performances. Della Green (Ruby Hill) of 1898 St. Louis is the mistress of saloon owner Bigelow Brown (REX INGRAM) but her affections shift to the affable jockey Little Augie (HAROLD NICHOLAS) who is on a winning streak. Bigelow sets out to shoot Augie but he's killed first by one of his spurned girlfriends. As Bigelow dies, he puts a curse on Augie and the winning streak ends, as does the romance with Della until she returns to him for the final curtain. Also in the gifted cast were PEARL BAILEY, FAYARD NICHOLAS, June Hawkins, JUANITA HALL, and Lorenzo Fuller. Arna Bontemps and Countee Cullen adapted Bontemps' novel *God Sends Sunday* for the stage and HAROLD ARLEN (music) and JOHNNY MERCER (lyrics) wrote such unforgettable hits as "Come Rain or Come Shine," "I Had Myself a True Love," and "Any Place I Hang My Hat Is Home." Also quite commendable were "Legalize My Name," "Ridin' on the Moon," "Sleep Peaceful, Mr. Used-to-Be," "A Woman's Prerogative," and "Cakewalk With Your Lady." ROUBEN MAMOULIAN directed and CHARLES WALTERS choreographed the musical, which received a mixed press and ran only 113 performances.

SAKALL, S. Z. [born Eugene Gero Szakall] (1884–1955). Film performer. A short, round character actor who was so endeared to audiences that he was nicknamed Cuddles, he specialized in nervous and frustrated managers, uncles, impresarios, and other types as he slapped his cheeks in anxiety and fractured the language with his thick eastern European accent. Sakall was born in Budapest, Hungary, and became a popular figure in German movies until he had to flee the Nazis and make films in Hungary and Austria. He arrived in America in 1940 and that same year was on screen in bit parts in the musicals *It's a Date* (1940) and *Spring Parade* (1940). Sakall got juicier roles in *THAT NIGHT IN RIO* (1941), *Broadway* (1942), *YANKEE DOODLE DANDY* (1942), and other musicals. He also appeared in many nonmusicals, such as *Casablanca* (1943). Sakall's many other musicals include *THANK YOUR LUCKY STARS* (1943), *Shine On Harvest Moon* (1944), *Wonder Man* (1945), *THE DOLLY SISTERS* (1945), *The Time, the Place and the Girl* (1946), *ROMANCE ON THE HIGH SEAS* (1948), *IN THE GOOD OLD SUMMERTIME* (1949), *Look for the Silver Lining* (1949), *The Daughter of Rosie O'Grady* (1950), *Tea for Two* (1950), *Painting the Clouds With Sunshine* (1951), *Small Town Girl* (1953), and *THE STUDENT PRINCE* (1954).

SAKS, GENE [Jean Michael] (1921–). Stage, film, and television director and performer. An animated character actor-turned-director, he is one of the best stagers of comedy of his generation and on occasion he has directed

musicals. Saks was born in New York City and educated at Cornell University and the Dramatic Workshop of the New School for Social Research. He began his acting career Off Broadway in the late 1940s, co-producing and performing in a series of works at the Cherry Lane Theatre. He also trained at the Actors Studio before getting roles on Broadway and in television dramas. Saks turned to directing in the early 1960s, making his Broadway debut staging the comedy *Enter Laughing* in 1963. His acute sense of comic timing as a performer carried over to his directing and soon he was one of the most sought-after directors for contemporary comic works, particularly those by NEIL SIMON. Saks' musical credits include *HALF A SIXPENCE* (1965), *MAME* (1966), *I LOVE MY WIFE* (1977), and *RAGS* (1986). He helmed the movie *Mame* (1974), the television adaptation of *BYE BYE BIRDIE* (1995), and films versions of several Broadway plays, although rarely was his sharp sense of humor as evident on the screen. Throughout his long career he continued to act in movies and on television on occasion

☞ **SALLY** (New Amsterdam Theatre 1920). A Cinderella musical given a splashy production by producer FLORENZ ZIEGFELD, the show made MARILYN MILLER the First Lady of musical comedy on Broadway. The orphaned Sally Rhinelander works as a dishwasher at the Elm Tree Alley Inn in Greenwich Village where her friend is the exiled Duke Constantine of Czechogovinia whom everyone calls "Connie." The monied Blair Farquar comes to the restaurant to hire workers for a party he's throwing and is smitten by Sally. The day of the party he is thrilled when the dancer that theatrical agent Otis Hooper has booked doesn't show and Sally gets to perform. Hooper is so impressed that he gets Sally into the *Ziegfeld Follies* where she becomes a star and wins the hand of Blair. GUY

Casts for *Sally*		
Character	1920 Broadway	1929 film
Sally	MARILYN MILLER	Marilyn Miller
Blair Farquar	Irving Fisher	Alexander Gray
"Connie"	LEON ERROL	JOE E. BROWN
Otis Hooper	WALTER CATLETT	T. Roy Barnes
Mrs. Ten Broek	Dolores	Maude Turner Gordon
Rosie	May Hay	PERT KELTON
Pops	Alfred P. James	Ford Sterling
Jimmy Spelvin	Stanley Ridges	

BOLTON wrote the simple but efficient libretto, and the score was the work of several hands, including JEROME KERN, VICTOR HERBERT (music), CLIFFORD GREY, P. G. WODEHOUSE, and others (lyrics). Kern was responsible for the hit "Look for the Silver Lining," as well as for the memorable "Little Church Around the Corner," "The Wild Rose," "Whip-poor-will," "The Lorelei," "On With the Dance," and the title number, while Herbert's music was used for the "Butterfly Ballet." Ziegfeld spared no expense, hiring Joseph Urban for the lavish scenery and featuring Miller in one of her best vehicles. Notices were like valentines and the musical ran 561 performances. Miller and much of the same cast returned to Broadway with the show in 1923 and the 1948 revival featured BAMBI LINN (Sally), WILLIE HOWARD (Connie), Robert Shackleton (Blair now called Mickey), and Jack Goode (Otis). The William Berbey–HUNT STROMBERG production only lasted thirty-six performances.

Sally (Warner/First National 1929) afforded Marilyn Miller her screen debut as she reprised her Sally in this elaborate, overstuffed film directed by John Francis Dillon. Yet even surrounded by hundreds of extras, Miller's singing and dancing talents hold their own and one gets a glimpse of why she was so beloved on the stage. Most of the Kern songs were dropped and new ones by JOE BURKE (music) and AL DUBIN (lyrics) were added, including ""All I Want to Do, Do, Do Is Dance," "Walking Off Those Balkan Blues," and "What Will I Do Without You?" Larry Ceballos choreographed the giant production numbers, some of which were in color.

SALONGA, LEA [born Maria Lea Carmen Imutan Salonga] (1971–). Stage and television performer. A classic beauty with a clear, enthralling singing voice, she has become one of the most famous Asian actresses in the West. Salonga was born in Manila and by the age of seven was singing in musicals in her native country, recording her first album when she was ten years old, and as a teen had her own Manila television show. She attended Ateneo De Manila University to study dermatology but left college to continue singing and in 1989 made a thrilling London debut as the refugee Kim in the musical MISS SAIGON, reprising her performance to great acclaim on Broadway in 1991. After doing some musicals in the Philippines, Salonga was back on Broadway as a replacement for Eponine in LES MISÉRABLES in 1992 and then returned to *Miss Saigon* in 1999. Her other outstanding performance was as the Chinese picture bride Mei-Lei in the revised Broadway revival of *FLOWER DRUM SONG* (2002). When she returned again to *Les Misérables* as a replacement in 2007, she played the role of Fantine. In addition to many recordings, Salonga has sung at Carnegie Hall and other famous venues around the world. She has appeared on Philippine and American television and in a few films, although she was not seen in her two best film roles: the singing voice for the animated Jasmine in *ALADDIN* (1992) and the female warrior *MULAN* (1998).

SAN FRANCISCO (MGM 1936). A Hollywood product that was a rarity on two fronts, it was a musical disaster film and it was a disaster picture in which the characters and the story were as intriguing as the special effects. Anita Loos and Robert Hopkins penned the screenplay in which opera singer Mary Blake (JEANETTE MacDONALD) goes to San Francisco's notorious Barbary Coast district in 1906 to sing in a saloon run by Blackie Norton (Clark Gable). She begins a romance with the tough but charming proprietor, but soon high society calls and Mary is singing at the Tivoli Opera House to the delight of all the swells on Nob Hill. Blackie refuses to turn genteel to keep Mary and their relationship is at an impasse when the earthquake strikes and the two lovers, surviving the disaster and looking at life differently now, are reunited. Spencer Tracy, in a career-boosting performance as the priest Fr. Mullin who runs a Barbary Coast mission, led the supporting cast that included Jack Holt, Ted Healy, Jessie Ralph, SHIRLEY Ross, Margaret Irving, Edgar Kennedy, and AL SHEAN. W. S. VAN DYKE directed, Val Raset choreographed, and James Basevi did the spectacular earthquake sequence that is still stunning to behold. BRONISLAW KAPER (music) and GUS KAHN (lyric) wrote the title song, which was used as both a rousing anthem and a tender hymn, and NACIO HERB BROWN (music) and ARTHUR FREED (lyric) provided the waltzing "Would You?" The rest of the score was composed of either old standards (such as "At the Georgia Camp Meeting" and "Battle Hymn of the Republic") or selections from classical opera (*La Traviata* and *Faust*).

SAN JUAN, OLGA (1927–). Stage and film performer. Dubbed the "Puerto Rican Pepper Pot" for her vivacious and spicy personality, the attractive singer–dancer lit up a number of 1940s musicals. San Juan was born in

Brooklyn and while she was a still a teenager she was performing at the famous Copacabana Club in Manhattan. The rhumba singer and dancer made her film debut in 1943 and, with the emphasis Hollywood was putting on Latin American culture during World War II, she was soon featured in such musicals as *Rainbow Island* (1944), *Out of This World* (1945), *Duffy's Tavern* (1945), *BLUE SKIES* (1946), *Variety Girl* (1947), *The Countess of Monte Cristo* (1948), *ONE TOUCH OF VENUS* (1948), *Are You With It?* (1948), and *The Beautiful Blonde From Bashful Bend* (1949). San Juan played the feisty prospector's daughter Jennifer Rumson in the Broadway musical *PAINT YOUR WAGON* (1951). She was married to actor Edmund O'Brien (1915–1985) for a time.

SANDERSON, JULIA [born Julia Sackett] (1887–1975). Stage performer. A petite, doll-faced soprano who starred in several Broadway musicals in the 1910s and 1920s, she usually played the secondary female lead, a lively soubrette opposite the show's comics. Sanderson was born in Springfield, Massachusetts, the daughter of an actor, and was on the stage as a child. By the age of fifteen, she had years of experience and made her Broadway bow in the chorus of *A Chinese Honeymoon* (1902). Sanderson moved up from the chorus in her next show, *Winsome Winnie* (1903), to replace the title character, the next year was widely noticed as the exotic Mataya in *WANG* (1904), and was finally a star as the Utopian lass Eileen Cavanaugh in *The Arcadians* (1910). Her two other significant roles were the Mormon wife Una Trance in *THE GIRL FROM UTAH* (1914), in which she introduced JEROME KERN's trend-setting ballad "They Didn't Believe Me," and Shirley Dalton, a visitor to the mythical island called *Tangerine* (1921). Her other musical credits include *Fantana* (1905), *The Tourists* (1906), *Kitty Grey* (1909), *The Sunshine Girl* (1913), *Rambler Rose* (1917), and *Hitchy-Koo of 1920*, as well as the leading lady in tours of such musical hits as *NO, NO, NANETTE* and *OH, KAY!* When she was past the age of playing ingénues, Sanderson went into vaudeville with her husband Frank Crumit (1889–1943); the two of them became very popular together on radio from 1929 to 1943. She was also married to actor Tod Sloan (1874–1933) for a time.

SANDRICH, MARK (1900–1945). Film director and producer. The director of some of the most popular of RKO musicals in the 1930s, in particular five with FRED ASTAIRE and GINGER ROGERS, he later turned to producing and directing at PARAMOUNT. Sandrich was born in New York City and educated at Columbia before entering silent films in 1922 as a properties man. He worked his way up to directing, helming many shorts before his first sound feature in 1929. Sandrich hit his stride during the Depression with such popular musicals as *THE GAY DIVORCEE* (1934), *TOP HAT* (1935), *FOLLOW THE FLEET* (1936), *SHALL WE DANCE* (1937), and *CAREFREE* (1938). In 1940 he joined Paramount and both produced and directed the seasonal classic *HOLIDAY INN* (1942). Sandrich's other musical credits include *Melody Cruise* (1933), *Hips Hips Hooray* (1934), *Man About Town* (1939), *Buck Benny Rides Again* (1940), *LOVE THY NEIGHBOR* (1940), and *HERE COME THE WAVES* (1944), producing the last three as well. He died while filming *BLUE SKIES* (1946).

SANDS, TOMMY [Adrian] (1937–). Film and television performer. A popular rock-and-roll singer and guitarist, the teenage heartthrob was featured in some musicals during his brief career. Sands was born in Chicago, the son of a band singer, and taught himself to play the guitar when he was a child. Soon he was singing on the radio and at the age of fourteen had recordings on the charts. Sands played a young ELVIS PRESLEY-like singer in the television drama *The Singing Idol* (1957), one of the first programs about rock and roll, which made him nationally famous. He made his screen debut in the musical *Sing, Boy, Sing* (1958), followed by *Mardi Gras* (1958), *Love in a Goldfish Bowl* (1961), *BABES IN TOYLAND* (1961), and a few nonmusicals. A mental and physical breakdown cut short his career but after he moved to Hawaii, where he ran a nightclub and a clothing business, he appeared on episodes of the television series *Hawaii Five-O* in the 1970s. Sands has returned to the concert stage on rare occasions, as with a rock festival in England in 1990. He was married to singer Nancy Sinatra (1940–) for a time.

◻ SANTA CLAUS IS COMING TO TOWN (ABC-TV 1970). The oft-broadcast animated musical attempts to explain the origins of Santa Claus, the flying reindeer, the red suit and white beard, and even why he comes down the chimney on Christmas eve. ROMEO MULLER wrote the imaginative teleplay that is narrated by a mailman (voice of FRED ASTAIRE) who explains how the orphaned Kris was left as a baby on the doorstep of the Kringle family of elves who made toys. The grown-up Kris (MICKEY ROONEY) defies the law of the Burgermeister (PAUL FREES) and promises to deliver toys to the children of Sombertown. When the Burgermeister orders everyone to lock their doors, Kris goes down the chimneys. When pursued as an outlaw, Kris changes his name to Claus, uses flying reindeer to escape the Burgermeister, and hides out in the North Pole, returning once a year to deliver toys. In addition to the title song standard from 1934, the score offered new numbers by MAURY LAWS (music) and JULES BASS (lyrics), such as "My World Is Beginning Today," "What Better Way to Tell You," "First Toymaker to the King," and "Put One Foot in Front of the Other." The sixty-minute fantasy was declared unpretentious fun by the press and embraced by the public, prompting the network to show it each December. ARTHUR RANKIN, JR. and Bass produced and directed.

SANTLEY, JOSEPH (1889–1971). Film and television director and stage performer. A leading man in Broadway musicals in the 1910s and 1920s, he turned to directing in Hollywood and helmed over two dozen musicals. Santley was born in Salt Lake City, the stepson of actor Eugene Santley, and was on the stage by the age of three and starring as a juvenile lead on Broadway by 1910. He appeared as a youth and then as an adult in such musicals as *When Dreams Come True* (1913), *Stop! Look! Listen!* (1915), *Betty* (1916), *She's a Good Fellow* (1919), *The Half Moon* (1920), *The Wild Rose* (1926), *Lucky* (1927), and three editions of the *MUSIC BOX REVUE*. Santley first directed in 1925 when he staged and starred in *Mayflowers* (1925). Arriving in Hollywood just as sound came in, he helmed several shorts before co-directing his first feature, the MARX BROTHERS vehicle *THE COCOANUTS* (1929) with Robert Florey. Ironically, it would be the only important work of his many Hollywood musicals, which included *Swing High* (1930), *Laughing Irish Eyes* (1936), *Swing, Sister, Swing* (1938), *Music in My Heart* (1940), *Dancing on a Dime* (1941), *Sis Hopkins* (1941), *Ice-Capades* (1941), *Yokel Boy* (1942), *Thumbs Up!* (1943), *Here Comes Elmer* (1943), *Brazil* (1944), *Make Believe Ballroom* (1949), and *When You're Smiling* (1950). Santley was one of the first Hollywood directors to turn to television, and in 1951 he left films and produced and directed many variety specials. He

was married to British performer Ivy Sawyer with whom he often co-starred during his Broadway years.

SARATOGA (Winter Garden Theatre 1959). More a disappointment than a flop, this epic musical play might have succeeded under different circumstances. The much anticipated musical, based on Edna Ferber's sprawling novel *Saratoga Trunk*, might have been another wide-reaching musical like *Show Boat* (1927) but the clumsy libretto by director MORTON DA COSTA and his overstuffed production weighed down the talented performers and the result was ponderous and unmoving. The illegitimate Clio Dulaine (CAROL LAWRENCE), who has been scorned by society, and the bitter Clint Maroon (HOWARD KEEL), who seeks revenge on the railroad tycoons who stole his family's land, team up to make a fortune together but, after various events ranging from race track shenanigans to a riot, instead end up falling in love. Also in the large and capable cast were ODETTE MYRTIL, Carol Brice, Warde Donovan, and Edith King. The score by HAROLD ARLEN (music) and JOHNNY MERCER (lyrics) was as ambitious and uneven as the plot but had some commendable songs, including "Game of Poker," "Love Held Lightly," "Countin' Our Chickens," and the title song. The reviews were not supportive, with the only compliments going to the cast and Cecil Beaton for his period sets and costumes, and the show ran eighty performances only on the strength of its large advance. Sadly, it was Arlen's last Broadway effort.

SATINS AND SPURS (NBC-TV 1954). BETTY HUTTON had played sharpshooter Annie Oakley in the movie musical *ANNIE GET YOUR GUN* (1950) so she seemed ideally cast as rodeo cowgirl Cindy Smathers in this ninety-minute musical offered as part of the *Max Liebman Presents* series. But Hutton's career was falling apart, her voice was failing, and she was difficult to work with so the live broadcast was fraught with problems. Producer MAX LIEBMAN, William Friedberg, NEIL SIMON, Will Glickman, and FRED SAIDY collaborated on the teleplay in which Sally comes to New York to ride in a Wild West Show in Madison Square Garden. The photographer–journalist Tony (Kevin McCarthy) interviews Sally and then writes a story on her, making her out to be a hick in the big city. She is furious and about to leave town when it becomes clear to both of them that they're in love. Tony builds her up in the press as a talented performer and Sally ends up on Broadway. The thin plot was filled out by some enjoyable songs by JAY LIVINGSTON (music) and RAY EVANS (lyrics), such as "Wildcat Smathers," "Back Home," "You're Right for Me," "Whoop Diddy Ay," and the title number. It was NBC's first color spectacular and the network built up so much anticipation that many were disappointed by the ninety-minute show. (Many viewers with black and white television sets thought that they would receive the show in color as promised.) Hutton insisted that her husband Charles O'Curran direct and choreograph but he disagreed with the other staff members, the preparations were agonizing, and the live broadcast ended up being seven minutes short. A desperate Steve Allen gave the viewers a quick tour of the studio and Hutton came back on the air to thank everybody for all their hard work. ABC was embarrassed by the whole fiasco but still there were many worthwhile aspects to the show, including Hutton who was still a powerhouse even as she had to speak–sing some of her numbers, and the score was not without its merits.

■ **SATURDAY NIGHT FEVER** (Paramount 1977). Showing that the crudest of society's discontents can achieve ecstasy on the dance floor, the movie made a screen star of JOHN TRAVOLTA and gave disco dancing a much-needed lift. Norman Wexler's screenplay, inspired by a magazine article about a Brooklyn disco, centered on the aimless youth Tony Manero (Travolta) who has a dead-end job working in a paint store by day and getting into trouble with gangs and girls at night. However, on Saturday nights he transforms into a dance sensation at the local disco club and finds some fleeting joy and meaning to his life. The story followed Tony's ambiguous relationship with the ambitious Stephanie Mangano (Karen Lynn Gorney) who disparages his lifestyle but serves as his dancing partner so that they can win a

couples contest at the disco. They win, but Tony, having watched his equally dissatisfied pal Bobby (Barry Miller) jump off a bridge in frustration, realizes his Saturday night's glory is not the answer. The plot may have resembled a 1950s urban melodrama but Travolta's magnetic performance and the Bee Gee's pounding disco music on the soundtrack made it all seem new and exciting. Lester Wilson staged the vibrant disco dancing and John Badham's direction went right to the nerve. None of the characters sang, but such hit numbers as "Staying Alive," "More Than a Woman," and "How Deep Is Your Love?" by Barry, Robin, and Maurice Gibb made it one of the most musical films of the 1970s. It was also one of the most popular, although the sequel *Staying Alive* (1983), also with Travolta, was a critical and box office dud.

🎬 **Saturday Night Fever** (Minskoff Theatre 1999) seemed a natural for Broadway because of its dancing but the stage adaptation made some errors in judgment, the most damaging one being to turn the pop songs heard in the film to musical theatre numbers sung by characters. Not only did they not fit but many of the popular songs were less effective when bent to fit situations and characters that were not in mind when the numbers were first written. Several additional songs ("Disco Duck," "Boogie Shoes," "Disco Inferno," and "Open Sesame") by various tunesmiths were added but they seemed just as vague and didn't have the propulsive power of the screen numbers. The dramatics in the screenplay came off as cheap melodramatics in the libretto by Nan Knighton. The young and energetic cast was complimented more for its dancing than acting or singing and it was the many disco numbers that kept audiences happy. Arlene Phillips directed and choreographed the ROBERT STIGWOOD production and, despite damning reviews, the show was an audience pleaser for 501 performances.

Casts for *Saturday Night Fever*

Character	1977 film	1999 Broadway
Tony Manero	JOHN TRAVOLTA	James Carpinello
Stephanie Mangano	Karen Lynn Gorney	Paige Price
Annette	Donna Pescow	Orfeh
Bobby	Barry Miller	Paul Castree
Joey	Joseph Cali	Sean Palmer
Gus	Bruce Ornstein	Richard H. Blake

Saturday Night Fever. Although disco and leisure suits may have passed with the 1970s, this film still has the power to grab viewers. Younger audiences may think the movie is a period piece like the other John Travolta musicals *Grease* (1978) and *Hairspray* (2007), but *Saturday Night Fever* was very contemporary and was considered very hip. Pictured is Travolta on the dance floor with Karen Lynn Gorney. (Photofest)

SAVILLE, VICTOR (1896–1979). Film director and producer. The British showman managed to have a noteworthy career in both England and America, directing a handful of musicals in both countries. Saville was born in Birmingham, England, and entered the movie business first as a salesman and then as a production manager and screenwriter. He directed his first feature in 1927 and during the 1930s was one of the British film industry's top directors, helming a variety of genres and making such musicals as *Sunshine Susie* (1931), *The Good Companions* (1933), *EVERGREEN* (1934), and *It's Love Again* (1936). Saville went to Hollywood in 1940 and had more luck as a producer than a director, presenting such musicals as *BITTER SWEET* (1940), *Smilin' Through* (1941), *THE CHOCOLATE SOLDIER* (1941), and *TONIGHT AND EVERY NIGHT* (1945). Returning to England in 1960, he founded his own production company but only made one feature before retiring.

SAVO, JIMMY (1892?–1960). Stage and film performer. The round-faced, pint-sized comic was very popular in vaudeville and found success in Broadway musicals on occasion. Savo was born in Ferni, Italy, but grew up in New York City, going into variety at a young age. By the 1920s he was a well-known comic in vaudeville and was featured on Broadway in *Vanities of 1923*, followed by other revues such as *Vogues of 1924*, *Ritz Revue* (1924), *John Murray Anderson's Almanac* (1929), *Parade* (1935), and *Wine, Women and Song* (1942). His two book musical credits were notable, playing the twin Dromio of Syracuse in *THE BOYS FROM SYRACUSE* (1938) and the lusty Rawa of Tanglinia in Lerner and Loewe's first musical *What Up* (1943). Savo appeared in a few silent and talking films, including the musicals *Reckless Living* (1938) and *Merry-Go-Round of 1938*. On stage he usually sported a beat-up derby hat, baggy clothes, and a child-like grin as he sang and danced. Autobiography: *I Bow to the Stones* (1963).

SCANDALS. *See GEORGE WHITE'S SCANDALS*

🐚 SCARLET PIMPERNEL, THE (Minskoff Theatre 1997). A costume musical adventure based on Baroness Orcy's 1905 swashbuckling novel, the show underwent three Broadway premieres in its efforts to become a hit. The English aristocrat Percy Blakeney (Douglas Sills) seems a worthless fop to his wife Marguerite (Christine Andreas) and others in 1794 London. In reality it is a put-on show. Percy disguises himself as the legendary Scarlet Pimpernel and rescues people from the guillotine in revolution-torn France, despite the machinations of the diabolical Chauvelin (TERRENCE MANN) who is always on his trail. Nan Knighton wrote the libretto and the lyrics for FRANK WILDHORN's rousing music, resulting in such numbers as "When I Look at You," "Believe," "Into the Fire," "She Was There," "Storybook," and "Falcon in the Dive." The colorful musical, directed by Peter Hunt and choreographed by Adam Pelty, was roundly panned by the press with only Sills getting anything close to a compliment. However, audiences seemed to enjoy the campy adventure and the show managed to run 373 performances. The producers then did an unusual thing: the production closed, the creative staff made changes, some of the company was recast, a new director (Robert Longbottom) was brought on board, and it reopened in 1998 at the same theatre. Critics returned to state that the changes were for the better but still did not recommend the show. Audiences returned for another 239 performances. The producers repeated the revision process again and the musical opened for a third time in 1999 and ran another 132 performances. After all that, the show never got out of the red but the musical has enjoyed some revivals by amateur groups.

SCHEFF, FRITZI [born Anna Friedrike Jaeger] (1879–1954). Stage, television, and film performer. An internationally acclaimed opera singer with a shapely figure and fiery performing style, she turned to Broadway musicals later in her career. Scheff was born in Vienna, the daughter of an opera singer, and studied voice at Hoch's Conservatory in Frankfort. She first rose to prima donna status in Munich and then traveled across Europe and ended up at the Metropolitan Opera in New York in 1901. Producer CHARLES DILLINGHAM persuaded Scheff to try the legit stage and featured her as the feisty freedom fighter *Babette* in 1903, which immediately established her as a prominent Broadway star. Of her dozen musical performances, her most important was as the Parisian would-be singer Fifi in *MLLE. MODESTE* (1905) introducing "Kiss Me Again." It was a role she

toured with and revived several times, still playing it at the age of fifty. Her other musical credits include *The Two Roses* (1904), *The Prima Donna* (1908), *The Duchess* (1911), *Pretty Mrs. Smith* (1914), and some Gilbert and Sullivan operettas. Savo also performed in vaudeville between 1913 and 1930 and appeared in a few films, playing herself in *Follies Girl* (1943). By the 1930s, she was cast mostly in supporting roles in plays, still on the stage as late as 1948 and in a few television programs in the 1950s, including a small-screen version of *Mlle. Modiste* in 1951.

SCHERTZINGER, VICTOR (1890–1941). Film director, songwriter, and conductor. An unusual combination of talents, he was a recognized director of movie musicals and a composer, sometimes fulfilling both duties in the same film. Schertzinger was born in Mahanoy City, Pennsylvania, and educated in music at Brown University and at the University of Brussels before beginning a career as a concert violinist in Europe. When he returned to America he conducted Broadway musical orchestras before going to Hollywood in 1916 and writing orchestra scores to be performed with silent movies. Soon he was directing as well and when sound came in, Schertzinger was providing songs for early musicals such as *THE LOVE PARADE* (1929) and *Fashions in Love* (1929). He co-directed *PARAMOUNT ON PARADE* (1930) and then went on to direct and score (with lyricists GUS KAHN, JOHNNY BURKE, JOHNNY MERCER, and others) such musicals as *HEADS UP!* (1930), *ONE NIGHT OF LOVE* (1934), *Love Me Forever* (1935), *Follow Your Heart* (1936), *Something to Sing About* (1937), *ROAD TO SINGAPORE* (1940), *RHYTHM ON THE RIVER* (1940), *Kiss the Boys Goodbye* (1941), and *THE FLEET'S IN* (1942). Among the film musicals he directed but not scored were *THE MIKADO* (1939), *ROAD TO ZANZIBAR* (1941), and *BIRTH OF THE BLUES* (1941).

SCHULMAN, SUSAN H. (1943?–). Stage director. A skillful director, primarily of musicals, she brings a poetic sensibility to all of her productions. Schulman was born in New York City where she attended the High School of the Performing Arts before going to Yale and Hofstra Universities. She made her New York directing debut Off Off Broadway in 1978 and then spent several years in regional theatre. She first gained attention for a small-scale but powerful revival of *SWEENEY TODD* Off Off Broadway in 1989 that was so well received it transferred to Broadway. Her other notable Manhattan musicals include the elegant and mystical staging of *THE SECRET GARDEN* (1991), the offbeat but moving Off Broadway musical *VIOLET* (1997), and a refreshingly sincere revival of *THE SOUND OF MUSIC* (1998). Schulman's other New York musical credits include *Jack's Holiday* (1995), *Time and Again* (2001), *Little Women* (2005), and Off Broadway revivals of *COMPANY* (1987) and *MERRILY WE ROLL ALONG* (1994). She has directed national tours, concert versions of musicals for the *ENCORES!* series, and at regional theatres such as the Stratford Festival in Canada.

SCHWAB, LAURENCE (1893–1951). Stage writer and producer. A shrewd Broadway producer who, usually working with fellow writer–producer FRANK MANDEL, presented some of the biggest hits of the 1920s. Schwab was born in Boston and educated at Harvard before he took up producing musicals on Broadway. With Mandel he presented such shows as *The Gingham Girl* (1922), *Captain Jinks* (1925), *THE DESERT SONG* (1926), *GOOD NEWS!* (1927), *THE NEW MOON* (1928), *FOLLOW THRU* (1929), *America's Sweetheart* (1931), *Free for All* (1931), and *East Wind* (1931), contributing to the scripts for many of the musicals as well. As an independent producer he presented the musicals *Sweet Little Devil* (1924), *Queen High* (1926), *TAKE A CHANCE* (1932), and *May Wine* (1935). Schwab also presented a handful of nonmusicals on Broadway. While many of his musicals were filmed, he only acted as movie producer on *Follow Thru* (1930) and *Queen High* (1930).

SCHWARTZ, ARTHUR (1900–1984). Stage, film, and television composer and producer. A masterful songwriter who wrote all kinds of musicals with different collaborators, he is most remembered for the scores he wrote for musical revues with lyricist HOWARD DIETZ. Schwartz was born in Brooklyn, the son of a lawyer, and while he studied for a legal career played piano for silent movie theatres. He started writing his own music for college musicals and later had some songs interpolated into Broadway revues but continued his career as a lawyer. Not until he teamed up with Dietz and they had a hit with the innovative *THE LITTLE SHOW* (1929) did Schwartz give up the bar and concentrate on songwriting. With Dietz he scored such beloved revues as *THREE'S A CROWD* (1930), *THE BAND WAGON* (1931), *FLYING COLORS* (1932), *AT HOME ABROAD* (1935), and *INSIDE U.S.A.* (1948). They had less luck with their book musicals *REVENGE WITH MUSIC* (1934), *BETWEEN THE DEVIL* (1937), *THE GAY LIFE* (1961) and *Jennie* (1963), although some superior songs came from the shows. Schwartz scored the book musicals *A TREE GROWS IN BROOKLYN* (1951)

and *BY THE BEAUTIFUL SEA* (1954) with lyricist DOROTHY FIELDS and with others the Broadway shows *The Grand Street Follies* (1929), *Princess Charming* (1930), *Virginia* (1937), *Stars in Your Eyes* (1939), and *Park Avenue* (1946), as well as the London musicals *Here Comes the Bride* (1930), *The Co-Optimists* (1930), *Nice Goings On* (1933), *and Follow the Sun* (1936). Although none of Schwartz's stage works were filmed by Hollywood, many of his songs were put into movie musicals, most memorably in *THE BAND WAGON* (1953), which added a plot and drew on the Dietz–Schwartz catalogue. Working with Dietz, E. Y. HARBURG, JOHNNY MERCER, FRANK LOESSER, and others, Schwartz scored a number of original film musicals, including *Under Your Spell* (1936), *That Girl From Paris* (1936), *Navy Blues* (1941), *Cairo* (1942), *THANK YOUR LUCKY STARS* (1943), *The Time, the Place and the Girl* (1946), *Dancing in the Dark* (1949), *Excuse My Dust* (1951), *Dangerous When Wet* (1953), and *You're Never Too Young* (1955), as well as producing *COVER GIRL* (1944) and *NIGHT AND DAY* (1946). He also scored the original TV musicals *HIGH TOR* (1956) and *A BELL FOR ADANO* (1957), which he produced as well. Schwartz's music ranges from the brooding romantic to the bright and sophisticated, often with a pleasantly haunting flavor to it.

SCHWARTZ, JEAN (1878–1956). Stage composer. A long-forgotten but prolific songwriter from the early years of the twentieth century, he wrote the music for over thirty Broadway musicals, several of them hits. Schwartz was born in Budapest, Hungary, and was brought to America when he was ten years old and was forced to work to support his family. Among his many early jobs were pianist at Coney Island, a song plugger for a music company, and a rehearsal pianist for Broadway shows. Collaborating with lyricist William Jerome (1865–1932), he saw some of his songs interpolated into other songwriters' shows before the twosome scored *Piff! Paff! Pouf!* (1904) together. They would reteam for such musicals as *Lifting the Lid* (1905), *The Ham Tree* (1905), *Fritz in Tamany Hall* (1905), *The White Cat* (1905), *Lola From Berlin* (1905), *In Haiti* (1909), and *Up and Down Broadway* (1910). Schwartz had greater success with lyricist Harold Atteridge, scoring *The Honeymoon Express* (1913), *THE PASSING SHOW* (1913, 1918, 1919, 1920, 1923, and 1924), *Monte Cristo Jr.* (1919), *Make It Snappy* (1922), *Topics of 1923*, *ARTISTS AND MODELS* (1923), and *Innocent Eyes* (1924). Working with Alfred Bryan, ANNE CALDWELL, and other lyricists, Schwartz also wrote *When Claudia Smiles* (1914), *Hello, Alexander* (1919), *Shubert Gaieties* (1919), *The Century Revue* (1920), *A Night in Spain* (1927), and *Sunny Days* (1928). Ironically, most of Schwartz's biggest song hits, such as "Bedalia," "Mr. Dooley," and "Rock-a-Bye Your Baby With a Dixie Melody," were not from his scores but from others' shows in which they were interpolated.

SCHWARTZ, STEPHEN (1948–). Stage and film composer, lyricist, and director. The author of long-run hits and admirable misses, he can create songs ranging from the traditional Broadway style to the contemporary pop sound. Born in New York and raised on Long Island, Schwartz was educated at Juilliard and Carnegie-Mellon University, where he wrote original musicals before embarking on a career as a record company executive and producer. While still in his early twenties, he had three New York musical hits to his credit: *GODSPELL* (1971), *PIPPIN* (1972), and *THE MAGIC SHOW* (1974). His tender score for *THE BAKER'S WIFE* (1976) demonstrated the versatility of the young composer–lyricist but the troublesome show closed before reaching New York. After the unsuccessful Broadway musicals *WORKING* (1978), which he also directed, and *RAGS* (1986), for which he wrote lyrics for CHARLES STROUSE's music, Schwartz turned to Hollywood where he wrote lyrics for the animated musicals *THE HUNCHBACK OF NOTRE DAME* (1996) and *PRINCE OF EGYPT* (1998). He returned to Broadway triumphantly with his score for the popular *WICKED* (2003). His other works include the theatre–music concert piece *Mass* (1971), in which he wrote lyrics for LEONARD BERNSTEIN's music, the Biblical musical *Children of Eden* (1991), which was produced in London and regionally in the States, the TV musical *GEPPETTO* (2000), and the Off Broadway children's musical *Captain Louie* (2005). Schwartz's music and lyrics are imaginative and varied, using rock, vaudeville soft-shoe, gospel, pop, and romantic operetta. His son is director Scott Schwartz who has staged several Broadway and Off Broadway works, including the musical *Jane Eyre* (2000).

SCOTT, [George] **RANDOLPH** [Crane] (1898– 1987). Film performer. One of Hollywood's favorite cowboy stars, the tall, rugged-looking actor also shone in some comedies and in a few major musicals. Scott was born in Orange, Virginia, and educated for an engineering career at Georgia Tech and the University of North Carolina before and after serving in World War I. After graduation he turned to acting and, having gotten experience at the Pasadena Playhouse, went into films in 1927. By the mid-1930s Scott had established himself as a cowboy star and retained the image for twenty years. He usually played physically strong but romantically shy heroes and he was often cast that way in musicals as well. His musical credits include *Hello, Everybody!* (1933), *ROBERTA* (1935), *FOLLOW THE FLEET* (1936), *HIGH, WIDE AND HANDSOME* (1937), *REBECCA OF SUNNYBROOK FARM* (1938), *Follow the Boys* (1944), *Belle of the Yukon* (1944), and *Starlift* (1951). He served as associate producer for many of his films in the 1950s. A shrewd investor, Scott retired from Hollywood in the early 1960s as one of the richest men in California.

SCROOGE (Cinema Center/Waterbury 1970). Hoping for another *Oliver!* with another Dickens tale set in Victorian London, this musical version of *A CHRISTMAS CAROL* was given a big budget, lots of songs, and a name cast. The film was not a major hit on its initial release but has become a perennial favorite over the years. Because there had been many film versions of the story since 1901, there were few surprises in the plot and the songs sometimes seem to slow up the action rather than add much to the famous ghost story. However, there were certainly rewards along the way. Albert Finney was a lively, memorable Scrooge, the decor by Terry Marsh was exquisite, and the titles sequence illustrated by Ronald Searle was very inventive. Ronald Neame directed efficiently, coming up with some unusual casting for the three spirits; the aged Edith Evans was the spirit of Christmas past, Kenneth More was the present, and the future was darkly portrayed by Paddy Stone who also provided the music hall-like choreography. Also in the cast were Alec Guinnes (Marley), Laurence Naismith, Michael Medwin, David Collings, Gordon Jackson, Anton Rodgers, and Suzanne Neve. LESLIE BRICUSSE wrote the screenplay and the songs which were not top drawer, although the catchy "Thank You Very Much" was pleasing enough to stick around a while. Other numbers included "I Like Life," "Father Christmas," "Happiness," and "The Beautiful Day."

SEATON, GEORGE (1911–1979). Film director, producer, and screenwriter. The former actor-turned-writer co-produced a series of movies with WILLIAM PERLBERG, including a number of musicals in the 1950s. Seaton was born in South Bend, Indiana, and began as an actor in radio, finding recognition as the first Lone

Ranger of the airwaves. In 1933 he went to Hollywood and wrote several films, including the musicals *A Day at the Races* (1937), *That Night in Rio* (1941), and *Coney Island* (1943). His first directing assignment was *Diamond Horseshoe* (1945), which he also wrote, and he did both jobs again for *The Shocking Miss Pilgrim* (1947) and *Aaron Slick From Pumkin Creek* (1951). Seaton teamed up with Perlman in 1952 and they co-produced many movies, including the musicals *Somebody Loves Me* (1952), *Little Boy Lost* (1953), and *The Country Girl* (1954).

■ SECOND FIDDLE (Fox 1939). This musical was a timely spoof of a topic very much on the minds of moviegoers in 1939: the casting of Scarlett O'Hara in *Gone With the Wind* (1939). In Harry Tugend's screenplay, Consolidated Pictures brings in candidate number 436 to test for the role of Violet Jansen in the period epic *Girl of the North*, who turns out to be Trudi Hovland (SONJA HENIE), a school teacher and skating instructor from Minnesota. Although he is smitten by her, publicity executive Jimmy Sutton (TYRONE POWER) sets up a phony romance between Trudi and movie star Roger Maxwell (RUDY VALLEE) in order to get her in all the papers and build up anticipation by the public. But the confused and overwhelmed Trudi flees Hollywood and Jimmy follows her all the way back to Minnesota where he stays and finds happiness married to a teacher. Edna May Oliver was quite droll as Trudi's wise Aunt Phoebe and the other supporting players included Lyle Talbot, Mary Healy, Alan Dinehart, Minna Gombell, and the Brian Sisters. IRVING BERLIN wrote the score and although no classics came from the film, there was much to enjoy in the sincere ballads "I Poured Myself Into a Song" and "When Winter Comes," the torchy "I'm Sorry for Myself," the nostalgic "An Old Fashioned Tune Is Always Nice," and the swinging "Back to Back," which poked fun at Berlin's own "Cheek to Cheek." SIDNEY LANFIELD directed the Gene Markey production and Harry Losee did the choreography.

☺ SECRET GARDEN, THE (St. James Theatre 1991). A delicate, atmospheric musical play, it met with divided reactions but survived to run 706 performances and find a second life in

The Secret Garden. Oft filmed for the large and small screen, the classic Frances Hodgson Burnett novel was turned into a bewitching Broadway musical populated with the ghosts of deceased characters who are only spoken about in the original story. Daisy Eagan (pictured) was the young heroine Mary Lennox whose imagination seems to conjure up the ghosts. Here she is with her crippled cousin Colin, played by John Babcock. (Photofest)

theatres across the country. The young orphan Mary Lennox (Daisy Eagan) goes to Yorkshire to live on the country estate of her morose, widowed uncle Archibald Craven (MANDY PATINKIN) and offers new hope to him, his crippled son Colin (John Babcock), and herself when she brings her late aunt's garden back to life. Also in the talented cast were REBECCA LUKER, ALISON FRASER, ROBERT WESTENBERG, JOHN CAMERON MITCHELL, Tom Toner, and Barbara Rosenblat. Marsha Norman adapted the beloved Frances Hodgson Burnett novel for the stage, giving it a lovely Victorian flavor with a touch of mysticism. She also penned the lyrics for Lucy Simon's engaging music, and the score was filled with period songs, rustic folk pieces, and expansive Broadway-style numbers. "Lily's Eyes," "Come to My Garden," "Where in the World," "Race You to the Top of the Morning," "The Girl I Meant to Be," "Hold On," "Winter's on the Wing," "Wick," and "A Fine White Horse" were among the memorable musical numbers. The critics were sharply divided in finding the gentle musical enthralling or boring but there was less indecision about the strong performances, the ravishing decor that reminded one of a children's pop-up book, and SUSAN H. SCHULMAN's poetic direction.

🕸 **SEESAW** (Uris Theatre 1973). A fondly remembered musical that struggled for 296 performances before throwing in the towel, it was the first true "MICHAEL BENNETT musical," his having written the libretto and directed and choreographed the show. The musical version of William Gibson's two-character comedy-drama *Two for the Seesaw* (1958) was opened up and decorated with lots of razzle dazzle but it still told the intimate tale of a failed romance between kookie New York dancer Gittel Mosca (MICHELE LEE) and married Midwest lawyer Jerry Ryan (KEN HOWARD). Also in the cast was TOMMY TUNE as the gay choreographer David, and Bennett let him stage his own show-stopping number, "It's Not Where You Start (It's Where You Finish)." Also in the sprightly score by CY COLEMAN (music) and DOROTHY FIELDS (lyrics) were "Nobody Does It Like Me," "Welcome to Holiday Inn," "We've Got It," "Ride Out the Storm," "My City," "He's Good for Me," "I'm Way Ahead," and the flowing title song. Mixed notices greeted the problematic show but those who loved it were very vocal and efforts were made by fans, the cast, and the producers to keep it running. *Seesaw* was Fields' last Broadway credit, ending her forty-five-year stage career.

SEGAL, VIVIENNE (1897–1992). Stage, film, and television performer. A skillfully adaptable singer–actress, she was a leading lady on Broadway for many years because of her ability to perform both operetta and musical comedy. Born in Philadelphia, the daughter of a renowned physician, Segal trained for an opera career and appeared in some local productions before making an impressive Broadway debut as Mizzy in *THE BLUE PARADISE* (1915). For the next forty years she would appear in all kinds of musicals, moving from perky ingénue to mature character player. Among her most memorable roles were the French heroine Margot Bonvalet in *THE DESERT SONG* (1926), royal court member Constance Bonacieux in *THE THREE MUSKETEERS* (1928), the sassy Countess Peggy in *I MARRIED AN ANGEL* (1938), the devious Morgan le Fay in *A CONNECTICUT YANKEE* (1943), and the worldly wise Vera Simpson in the original 1940 production and the acclaimed 1951 revival of *PAL JOEY*. Among her other Broadway credits were *OH, LADY! LADY!* (1918), *The Little Whopper* (1919), *The Yankee Princess* (1922), *Adrienne* (1923), *ZIEGFELD FOLLIES* (1924), *Castles in the Air* (1926), *THE CHOCOLATE SOLDIER* (1931), *Music in My Heart* (1947), and *Great to Be Alive!* (1950). She made only a few films, such as *Golden Dawn* (1930) and *Viennese Nights* (1930), and only a handful of television appearances. Segal had a round baby face, dark hair, and a wide-ranged singing voice that allowed her to trill high notes as well as deliver comic lyrics.

SEITER, WILLIAM A. (1891–1964). Film director. The former silent screen actor helmed over sixty movies during a forty-year career, including some two dozen musicals. Seiter was born in New York City and worked as a writer and an artist before appearing in silents as one of the Keystone Kops. By 1918 he was directing two-reelers and then graduated to features in 1920. Seiter helmed all genres but was most accomplished with lightweight or romantic pictures. Among his musicals were *Smiling Irish Eyes* (1929), *SUNNY* (1930), *GIRL CRAZY* (1932), *Hello, Everybody* (1933), *ROBERTA* (1935), *Dimples* (1936), *Stowaway* (1936), *Life of the Party* (1937), *Sally, Irene and Mary* (1938), *YOU WERE NEVER LOVELIER* (1942), *Four Jills in a Jeep* (1944), *That Night With You* (1945), *I'll Be Yours* (1947), *UP IN CENTRAL PARK* (1948), and *ONE TOUCH OF VENUS* (1948).

SEQUELS. The popularity of certain musicals has prompted producers and writers to try to repeat the success on occasion, sometimes continuing to strike gold and other times resulting in major disappointment. Broadway has seen more of the latter than the former, particularly in recent history. The stage sequels that worked the best were those revolved around a star and/or a character. Comic actor J. K. Emmet was so popular in the musical *Fritz, Our Cousin German* (1870) that he played the funny immigrant Fritz for the rest of his career, appearing in nine sequels on Broadway and on tour. CHARLOTTE GREENWOOD first found fame as the silly Letitia Proudfoot in the musical *Pretty Mrs. Smith* (1914) and was featured in five different "Letty" musicals on tour, some of which also played in New York. Other comics who found success in musical sequels were EDWARD HARRIGAN and TONY HART in the *Mulligan Guard* shows and the ROGERS BROTHERS. Most later attempts to return to the characters in one hit musical in

another were not satisfying. Hollywood has a better track record with sequels, although even there some substantial flops have occurred. While critics argued that the sequels were rarely as accomplished as the originals, the box office sometimes said different. *THE BELLS OF ST. MARY* (1944), for example, was just as popular as *GOING MY WAY* (1945). Some screen musical sequels hardly qualify for the category, only retaining parts of the title and the general premise or milieu. No one character returned in the *Gold Diggers* or *Broadway Melody* movies, yet the musical sequels continued the character types and plot situations found in the originals. Television loves spin-offs, building a new series on the strength of a character/actor in a popular show, yet there have not been too many television musical sequels. Perhaps the runaway success of *HIGH SCHOOL MUSICAL 2* (2007) might change the networks' thinking on that.

Stage Musical Sequels

ANNIE (1977)	*Annie Warbucks* (1993)
BEST LITTLE WHOREHOUSE IN TEXAS, THE (1978)	*The Best Little Whorehouse Goes Public* (1994)
BYE BYE BIRDIE (1960)	*Bring Back Birdie* (1981)
FORTY-FIVE MINUTES FROM BROADWAY (1906)	*The Talk of New York* (1907)
Fritz, Our Cousin German (1870)	*Fritz in Ireland* (1879), etc.
MULLIGAN GUARD'S PICNIC, THE (1878)	*THE MULLIGAN GUARD'S BALL* (1879), etc.
NUNSENSE (1985)	*Nunsense II: The Second Coming* (1992), etc.
OF THEE I SING (1931)	*LET 'EM EAT CAKE* (1933)
Pretty Mrs. Smith (1914)	*So Long, Letty* (1916), etc.
ROBIN HOOD (1891)	*Maid Marian* (1902)
Rogers Brothers in Wall Street (1899)	*Rogers Brothers in Washington* (1901), etc.
YOU'RE A GOOD MAN, CHARLIE BROWN (1967)	*Snoopy* (1982)

Film Musical Sequels

ARTISTS AND MODELS (1937)	*ARTISTS AND MODELS ABROAD* (1938)
BIG BROADCAST, THE (1932)	*THE BIG BROADCAST OF 1936* (1935), etc.
BROADWAY MELODY, THE (1929)	*THE BROADWAY MELODY OF 1936* (1935), etc.
FANTASIA (1940)	*FANTASIA 2000* (2000)
FUNNY GIRL (1968)	*FUNNY LADY* (1975)
GOING MY WAY (1944)	*THE BELLS OF ST. MARY'S* (1945)
GOLD DIGGERS OF BROADWAY, THE (1929)	*THE GOLD DIGGERS OF 1933*, etc.
GREASE (1978)	*Grease 2* (1982)
HARD DAY'S NIGHT, A (1964)	*HELP!* (1965)
JOLSON STORY, THE (1946)	*JOLSON SINGS AGAIN* (1949)
MUPPET MOVIE, THE (1979)	*The Great Muppet Caper* (1981), etc.
PALEFACE, THE (1948)	*SON OF PALEFACE* (1952)
RESCUERS, THE (1977)	*The Rescuers Down Under* (1990)
ROAD TO SINGAPORE (1940)	*ROAD TO ZANZIBAR* (1941), etc.
SATURDAY NIGHT FEVER (1977)	*Staying Alive* (1983)
Sister Act (1992)	*Sister Act 2: Back in the Habit* (1993)
Three Smart Girls (1936)	*Three Smart Girls Grow Up* (1939)
Toy Story (1995)	*Toy Story 2* (1999)
WIZARD OF OZ, THE (1939)	*JOURNEY BACK TO OZ* (1974); *Return to Oz* (1985)

Television Musical Sequels

Frosty the Snowman (1969)	*Frosty Returns* (1995)
High School Musical (2006)	*High School Musical 2* (2007)
Kingdom Chums: Little David's Adventure (1986)	*Kingdom Chums: The Original Top Ten* (1993)
POLLY (1989)	POLLY—COMIN' HOME! (1990)
SANTA CLAUS IS COMIN' TO TOWN (1970)	*A YEAR WITHOUT A SANTA CLAUS* (1974)
STORY OF RUDOLPH THE RED NOSED	*Rudolph's Shiny New Year* (1976)
REINDEER, THE (1964)	RUDOLDH AND FROSTY'S CHRISTMAS IN JULY (1979)

SERIES OF MUSICALS. Unlike Hollywood, which has found success with a series of musicals about the same characters or character types, Broadway has been limited mostly to series of revues, such as the *THE PASSING SHOW*, *ZIEGFELD FOLLIES*, *GEORGE WHITE'S SCANDALS*, *EARL CARROLL VANITIES*, *ARTISTS AND MODELS*, and the *MUSIC BOX REVUES*. On the few occasions when a book musical continued on in a series, it was because of a star and the character that star played, as with CHARLOTTE GREENWOOD's "Letty" musicals, J. K. Emmett's "Fritz" musicals, and shows by comic teams such as the RODGERS BROTHERS and EDWARD HARRIGAN and TONY HART. These would be the equivalent to Hollywood's Andy Hardy films. However, in the movies there were several series that were not determined by a star or a personality. When films such as *THE GOLD DIGGERS OF BROADWAY* (1929), *THE BROADWAY MELODY* (1929), and *THE BIG BROADCAST* (1932) were big hits, the studios retained part of the title and offered subsequent musicals with different characters in similar settings. Other series were less definite but audiences perceived them as part of a series. The RKO musicals of the 1930s with FRED ASTAIRE and GINGER ROGERS, the MGM "let's put on a show" films starring MICKEY ROONEY and JUDY GARLAND, and the series of operettas that paired JEANETTE MacDONALD and NELSON EDDY might be considered series as well. One of the most popular of all film series, the *ROAD* pictures featuring BOB HOPE and BING CROSBY, varied the titles and plots very little and remained favorites because they were so familiar each time. Television, of course, has long been all about series: drama, comedy, variety show, soap opera, and even anthology shows. In fact, the reason there are few (if any) series today on stage and screen may be attributed to television, which thrives on continuing stories and characters on a weekly basis.

⚙ *SEUSSICAL* (Richard Rodgers Theatre 2000). A much anticipated musical that failed to meet the public and critics' high expectations, the show was based on the beloved children's stories by Theodore Geisel, better known as Dr. Seuss. Kind-hearted Horton the Elephant (Kevin Chamberlain) discovers a population of microscopic beings called Whos and befriends the lonely misfit youth JoJo (Anthony Blair Hall) without being able to see him. When Horton tries to tell others about the Whos, he is labeled crazy and brought to court where the collective voice of JoJo and all the Whos prove Horton is sane. The Cat in the Hat (David Shiner) served as narrator and several different stories were enacted as well, with featured cast members Michele Pawk, Janine LaManna, Erick Devine, Sharon Wilkins, Stuart Zagnit, and Alice Playten. LYNN AHRENS (lyric) and STEPHEN FLAHERTY (music) wrote the libretto and the sparkling score that included "How Lucky You Are," "Sola Sollew," "Notice Me, Horton," "Alone in the Universe," "Oh, the Thinks You Can Think," "It's Possible (McElligot's Pool)," and "Amazing Mayzie." Frank Galati directed the clever, colorful production, and KATHLEEN MARSHALL did the spirited choreography. While the press applauded the tuneful score and the animated performers, the rambling plot made up of different tales was disappointing. With such mixed notices the expensive musical had to struggle to run an unprofitable 197 performances. With some script revisions, the musical did well on tour and eventually became a favorite in schools and summer stock. *Seussical* returned to New York in 2007 in a condensed version and played a limited engagement as part of a family series at the Victory Theatre. This time it was much better received by the press and public.

▮ *SEVEN BRIDES FOR SEVEN BROTHERS* (MGM 1954). Perhaps the most exciting and enjoyable of all the frontier musicals to come out of Hollywood, it has a smart and funny script by FRANCES GOODRICH, ALBERT HACKETT, and DOROTHY KINGSLEY; a soaring score by GENE

DE PAUL (music) and JOHNNY MERCER (lyrics); and exuberant choreography by MICHAEL KIDD, with the whole package managing to be wholesome and sexy at the same time.

Plot: Set in the mountains of Oregon in the 1850s, the story centers on the seven Pontipee brothers who are crude, brawling, ignorant, restless, and lonely for women. When eldest brother Adam goes into town and gets himself a wife by wooing the just-as-restless Milly, the other siblings start hankering for wives too. Milly tries to teach the boys genteel manners but when they go into town to socialize, everyone breaks out in fist fights. Out of frustration (and a little encouragement from Adam), the six brothers steal into town one night, steal six young unmarried women, and bring them back home to the cabin high in the mountains. They soon realize the error of their ways but an avalanche blocks the pass back to civilization until spring and the brothers have time to learn how to woo the ladies successfully.

The unlikely plot for a musical was based on a Stephen Vincent Benet story, which was a folksy version of the ancient episode known as the Rape of the Sabine women. The fact that the film is done in good taste and still is a lot of fun is a tribute to the fine writing. STANLEY DONEN directed with just enough brashness to make the crazy tale work and the characterization grew from cartoon types to engaging people is a cockeyed situation. Although it was filmed on the MGM back lot, the movie had a rugged, outdoors feel to it. The settings evoke rustic charm and the scruffy Pontipee brothers were delightfully ragtag in a musical way. The original plan was to use existing folk songs to give the picture an authentic musical sound, but producer JACK CUMMINGS was persuaded to use De Paul and Mercer who had never collaborated before. Mercer's bucolic lyrics are

especially potent in "Spring, Spring, Spring" and "Wonderful, Wonderful Day," while De Paul's moaning music for "Lonesome Polecat" is bluesy and dreamy. Because so many of the songs were tied directly to the plot and

Seven Brides for Seven Brothers. From the poster you'd think the dancers could fly. After you've seen Michael Kidd's choreography, you know they can. The ad hints at naughtiness, saying it is filmed in "blushing color." Rarely has a Hollywood musical come so close to being off color and still ended up being so wholesome. (Photofest)

Casts for *Seven Brides for Seven Brothers*

Character	1954 film	1982 Broadway
Adam Pontipee	HOWARD KEEL	DAVID-JAMES CARROLL
Milly	JANE POWELL	Debby Boone
Benjamin Pontipee	Jeff Richards	D. Scot Davidge
Frank Pontipee	TOMMY RALL	Michael Ragan
Caleb Pontipee	Matt Mattox	LARA TEETER
Gideon Pontipee	RUSS TAMBLYN	Craig Peralta
Ephraim Pontipee	Jacques d'Amboise	Jeffrey Reynolds
Daniel Pontipee	Marc Platt	JEFF CALHOUN
Dorcas	JULIE NEWMAR	Manette LaChance
Ruth Jebson	Ruta Lee	Sha Newman

Seven Brides for Seven Brothers (film) Musical Numbers

"Bless Your Beautiful Hide"
"Wonderful, Wonderful Day"
"When You're in Love"
"Goin' Co'tin'"
"House-Raising Dance"
"Lonesome Polecat"
"Sobbin' Women"
"June Bride"
"Spring, Spring, Spring"

characters, the film produced no runaway hits, yet the score as a whole became well known. The most remembered musical number in the film was not sung but featured dancing: the high energy "House-Raising Dance," which Kidd choreographed with acrobatics, gymnastics, and vivid challenge dancing as the Pontipee brothers and the boys from town compete and try to impress the girls. Never before had dance been used so effectively in a wilderness setting and both the rivalry dance and the axe-chopping "Lonesome Polecat" numbers look like no other. Kidd and Donen cast dancers for the brothers, yet they all deliver solid acting performances. HOWARD KEEL makes the brusque Adam likable and JANE POWELL is luminous as the knowing Milly. Donen handles the tricky parts of the story well, for this after all is basically a story of musical rape. The whole movie shouldn't work yet it does so beautifully.

🕏 **Seven Brides for Seven Brothers** (Alvin Theatre 1982) was roundly castigated by the press and held up as an example of a film classic destroyed on Broadway. Lawrence Kasha, David Landay, and Joel Hirschhorn collaborated on the libretto and the new songs, which included "Glad That You Were Born," "Love Never Goes Away," and "One Man." Reviews concentrated on the sloppy script, the dull new songs, the mistreatment of the celebrated movie numbers, and the lackluster performers. Kasha directed the tawdry production, which had toured extensively before trying Broadway, but it only lasted there for five performances.

▪ **SEVEN HILLS OF ROME, THE** (MGM 1958). A fine showcase for singer MARIO LANZA, the film musical is a valentine to the singer and the city of Rome, both in top form. The uninspired screenplay by Art Cohn and Giorgio Prosperi centered on the American television star Marc Revere (Lanza) who has a quarrel with his heiress fiancée Carol Ralston (Peggy Castle). When she runs off to Rome, Marc pursues her, meeting the impoverished but delightful Rafaella Marini (Marissa Allasio) on the train into Rome. She has been left without a place to live so Marc finds her lodgings with his pianist cousin Pepe Bonelli (Renato Rascel). It takes a while before Marc eventually realizes he loves Rafaella and not Carol, but the songs were a pleasing diversion while the audience patiently waited for him to come to his senses. The supporting cast featured Italian actors, and the movie, filmed in color in Technirama on location, offered ravishing views of the Eternal City. Lanza gave one of his more playful performances, not only singing opera selections and new numbers by a variety of songwriters, but also clowning about and doing impersonations of DEAN MARTIN, FRANKIE LAINE, PERRY COMO, and LOUIS ARMSTRONG. The 1954 hit "Arrivederci, Roma" was used hauntingly in the film and other songs included "Never Till Now," "There's Gonna Be a Party Tonight," "Come Dance With Me," "Italian Calypso," and the title number. Roy Rowland directed, keeping his focus on the two stars, Lanza and Rome.

🕏 **1776** (46th Street Theatre 1969). An unlikely musical hit and the surprise of its season, the historical piece boasted one of the most literate of all Broadway librettos. John Adams, Ben Franklin, Thomas Jefferson and other delegates at the Continental Congress in Philadelphia struggle to get the rest of the representatives to approve and sign the Declaration of Independence and officially break away from England. At times it looks like an impossible task, but with perseverance and some painful compromises, the group finally ratifies the document. PETER STONE wrote the libretto that was amusing, interesting, and even gripping, and Sherman Edwards provided a set of songs that ranged from the silly to the solemn, including "Sit Down, John," "Molasses to Rum," "He Plays the Violin," "Till Then," "Is Anybody There?," "Cool, Cool Considerate Men," "The Egg," and "Momma, Look Sharp." Peter Hunt directed the Stuart Ostrow production and it was greeted with surprise and rave notices, running 1,217 performances. The musical toured successfully and saw some regional productions, although the nearly all-male cast made *1776* a difficult show for most schools and community theatres. The 1997 ROUNDABOUT THEATRE production in New York, directed by SCOTT ELLIS, was so well

Casts for *1776*

Character	1969 Broadway	1972 film	1997 Broadway
John Adams	WILLIAM DANIELS	William Daniels	Brent Spiner
Benjamin Franklin	HOWARD DA SILVA	Howard Da Silva	Pat Hingle
Thomas Jefferson	KEN HOWARD	Ken Howard	Paul Michael Valley
Abigail Adams	VIRGINIA VESTOFF	Virginia Vestoff	Linda Emond
Martha Jefferson	BETTY BUCKLEY	Blythe Danner	Lauren Ward
Edward Rutledge	Clifford David	JOHN CULLUM	GREGG EDELMAN
Richard Henry Lee	RON HOLGATE	Ron Holgate	Merwin Foard
John Dickinson	Paul Hecht	John Madden	Michael Cumpsty
Courier	Scott Jarvis	Stephen Nathan	Erik J. McCormack

received by the press and the public that after three months Off Broadway it moved to the larger Gershwin Theatre on Broadway and remained for a total of 333 performances.

■ *1776* (Columbia 1972) was so faithful to the Broadway original (the entire creative staff and most of the cast were in the film) that one kept looking for the curtain. Peter Hunt again directed but he couldn't find a cinematic way to handle the material so the movie is very static. However, most of the score and the dialogue were retained and the admirable stage performances are captured on film, even if none of them are as impressive as they were in the theatre. As with the stage version, what sounded like dull history was once again vivid storytelling.

🎔 *70, GIRLS, 70* (Broadhurst Theatre 1971). A farcical musical that never quite worked, nonetheless it boasted a vivacious score by JOHN KANDER (music) and FRED EBB (lyrics). A Manhattan old-folks home is down in funds but high in spirits so, under the leadership of Ida Dodd (Mildred Natwick), the senior citizens take up burglary to bring them the things that make life a little more comfortable. Also in the cast of aged stage veterans were LILLIAN ROTH, HANS CONRIED, Joey Faye, GIL LAMB, Lucie Lancaster, and Lillian Hayman. JOE MASTEROFF and the songwriters collaborated on the awkward libretto, loosely based on Peter Coke's play *A Breath of Spring* and the 1960 British film *Make Mine Mink*, and the joyous if often silly musical celebrated old age by featuring older performers who were still vibrant and entertaining. The songs they had to sing were just as spry and vivacious, such as "Coffee in a Cardboard Cup," "Broadway, My Street," "See the Light," "Home," "Go Visit (Your Grandmother)," "The Elephant Song," and "Yes." Most critics and audiences did not quite know how to take

the odd musical and it floundered for thirty-six performances but the vibrant score is still very much alive.

SHAKESPEARE MUSICALS. Hollywood has shied away from musicals based on Shakespeare plays, but Broadway and Off Broadway have musicalized the Bard on several occasions. Since most stage musicals are based on previous plays and stories it makes sense that producers and writers were attracted to some of the best plays and stories ever written. The fact that most of Shakespeare's comedies and even some tragedies already have songs in them has not deterred writers from further musicalizing the tales. The two most popular musicals based on Shakespeare are *THE BOYS FROM SYRACUSE* (1938), taken from *The Comedy of Errors*, and *KISS ME, KATE* (1948), based on *The Taming of the Shrew*, unless one counts *WEST SIDE STORY* (1957) and its updating of *Romeo and Juliet*. The lovers of Verona also inspired a 1970 Off Broadway musical called *Sensations*. *A Midsummer Night's Dream* got a jazz facelift in *Swingin' the Dream* (1939) and the pastoral comedy appeared Off Broadway as *Babes in the Woods* (1964). Even the melancholy Dane discovered rock in *Rockabye Hamlet* (1976) but Broadway only welcomed him for two weeks. *The Two Gentlemen of Verona* lost the title's "the" and became the musical *TWO GENTLEMEN OF VERONA* (1971) in Central Park and then on Broadway. *Twelfth Night* is Shakespeare's most musical play with more songs than any other so it is understandable that it has been musicalized four times: the delightful *YOUR OWN THING* (1968) spoofed the Bard and rock musicals and had a long run Off Broadway; the musically interesting *Music Is* (1976), which lasted only a week on Broadway; *Love and Let Love* (1968), which did not do much better Off Broadway; and the stylish African American musical *Play On!* (1997), which used music by

DUKE ELLINGTON. For those not content with *The Boys From Syracuse*, there was *Oh, Brother!* (1981), a silly reworking of *The Comedy of Errors* set in oil-rich Iran with the Ayatollah singing and dancing.

■ **SHALL WE DANCE** (RKO 1937). With the finest score the GERSHWINS ever wrote for the movies and FRED ASTAIRE and GINGER ROGERS at their peak, this musical comedy treasure beguiles, amuses, and even brings a tear to the eye.

Plot: The American dancer Pete Peters is in London to do a ballet but, much to the distress of his manger Jeffrey Baird, he prefers jazz and modern dance. When he first sees and is smitten with the American musical comedy star Linda Keene, Pete puts on a phony Russian accent and pretends to be an affected ballet star named Petrov. The disguise doesn't last long and soon the two are aboard a ship returning to New York when rumors circulate that the two are married. Unable to refute the stories in the press, the couple decides to wed and then have a very public divorce. Once married they realize they love each other and drop the idea of the divorce.

Allan Scott and Ernest Pagano wrote the contrived screenplay, which seems to search for improbable complications just to keep the plot going. The dialogue is less strained and Astaire in particular gets to do some silly stuff. Director MARK SANDRICH did his best to help the picture make sense but all he could do was film it with style. The same could be said for the unmotivated production numbers choreographed by Astaire, Harry Losee, and HERMES PAN. The whole musical is a trivial nothing, yet the characters still enchant. When it looks like they must go through the divorce and part, singing the indelible "They Can't Take That Away From Me," there is genuine empathy.

Every number in the George and Ira Gershwin score is pure gold, right down to the instrumental piece "Walking the Dog" that has its own cockeyed charm. Astaire and Rogers sing and dance to the title number in a sleek ballroom high up in a skyscraper, Astaire taps all over the white art deco engine room of the ocean liner with "Slap That Bass," the couple roller skate in Central Park as they playfully admonish "Let's Call the Whole Thing Off," Astaire performs the bouncy "(I've Got) Beginner's Luck" while Rogers has fun with the musical words in "They All Laughed," and their duet version of "They Can't Take That Away From

Cast for *Shall We Dance*	
Character	*Performer*
Pete Peters (aka Petrov)	FRED ASTAIRE
Linda Keene	GINGER ROGERS
Jeffrey Baird	EDWARD EVERETT HORTON
Cecil Flintridge	ERIC BLORE
Arthur Miller	Jerome Cowan
Lady Tarrington	Ketti Gallian
Jim Montgomery	William Brisbane
Specialty dancer	Harriet Hoctor

Shall We Dance Musical Numbers
"Slap That Bass"
"Walking the Dog"
"(I've Got) Beginner's Luck"
"They All Laughed"
"Let's Call the Whole Thing Off"
"They Can't Take That Away From Me"
"Shall We Dance?"

Me" is restrained yet unforgettable. Rarely have so many beloved standards come from one Hollywood musical. PANDRO S. BERMAN was the lucky producer, although it was the audience who were the most fortunate.

SHAW, OSCAR [born Oscar Schwartz] (1889–1967). Stage and film performer. A boyishly handsome leading man in Broadway musicals, his toothy grin, slicked-back dark hair, and jovial style were as consistent as the juvenile roles he played for twenty years. The Philadelphia native was educated at the University of Pennsylvania before going on the Broadway stage as a singer in the chorus of *The Mimic* (1908). After playing second leads in the landmark musicals *VERY GOOD EDDIE* (1915) and *LEAVE IT TO JANE* (1917), he rose to primary roles in such musicals as *Two Little Girls in Blue* (1921), *Good Morning, Dearie* (1921), *Dear Sir* (1924), *OH, KAY!* (1926), *The Five O'Clock Girl* (1927), *FLYING HIGH* (1930), and *Everybody's Welcome* (1931), as well as some London musicals. Shaw was also given featured spots in the revues *THE PASSING SHOW* (1912), *Ziegfeld's Midnight Frolic* (1916), *Ziegfeld's Nine O'Clock Frolic* (1921), and *MUSIC BOX REVUE* (1924). He made a few silent films and was in the screen musicals *THE COCOANUTS* (1929) and *RHYTHM ON THE RIVER* (1940). Shaw was a solid song-and-dance man but not a very flexible actor, so his career faded once he grew too old to play juveniles.

SHAW, WINIFRED [born Winifred Leo Momi] (1910?–1982). Stage and film performer. The dark-haired, serious-looking torch singer was featured in some memorable production numbers in 1930s musicals. Although some said she was born in Hawaii in 1899, it was believed that San Francisco was her birthplace in 1910 and that her parents were traveling vaudeville performers. Shaw also worked in variety and made it to Broadway in a featured role in *SIMPLE SIMON* (1931). She made her screen debut in a 1934 comedy and then later that year was featured in the musical *Million Dollar Ransom*. She usually starred in second-class films but was more noticed in minor roles in much better musicals, such as *GOLD DIGGERS OF 1935* (1935) in which she sang "Lullaby of Broadway." Her other musicals include *Wake Up and Dream* (1934), *SWEET ADELINE* (1935), *In Caliente* (1935), *Broadway Hostess* (1935), *The Singing Kid* (1936), *Ready, Willing and Able* (1937), and *Melody for Two* (1937). Shaw also played a cabaret singer and sang a number or two in several nonmusicals, such as *The Case of the Curious Bride* (1935), *Sons o' Guns* (1936), *Smart Blonde* (1937), and *King of the Islands* (1938). She left Hollywood in 1939 and disappeared from the public eye.

SHE DONE HIM WRONG (Paramount 1933). MAE WEST'S first starring role in Hollywood, the musical was a resounding success in all departments. Harvey F. Thew and John Bright's screenplay was adapted from the 1928 Broadway play *Diamond Lil*, which West wrote and starred in, and they left room for the self-mocking sex goddess to sing a handful of songs. The shady saloon gal Lady Lou (West) sings on the Bowery in the 1890s and deals in white slave trade as she keeps several men on the string. The tough broad's downfall comes about when she falls for Captain Cummings (Cary Grant), a policeman disguised as a Salvation Army officer. Audiences were immediately taken with West's nasal double entendres (this is the film in which she asked Grant, "Why don't you come up and see me sometime?") and moan-like singing voice that made her unlike any other movie star. The songs were just as sultry as the singer, including Shelton Brooks' "I Wonder Where My Easy Ride's Gone," RALPH RAINGER and LEO ROBIN'S "A Guy What Takes His Time," and the old standbys "Pretty Baby" and "Frankie and Johnny." Lowell Sherman directed the WILLIAM LEBARON production, which also featured Owen Moore, Gilbert Roland, Noah Beery, David Landau, FUZZY KNIGHT, Rafaela Ottiano, LOUISE BEAVERS, and Grace La Rue.

SHE LOVES ME (Eugene O'Neill Theatre 1963). A thoroughly enchanting musical based on a familiar but durable premise, the show boasted one of the best JERRY BOCK (music) and SHELDON HARNICK (lyrics) scores, if not *the* best. Two employees, Georg Nowack and Amalia Balash, at a Budapest parfumerie quarrel by day and write love letters to each other by night, only knowing each other's identity as "dear friend." When Georg is fired because his boss Mr. Maraczek (Ludwig Donath) thinks that his wife's lover is Georg rather than the real culprit, fellow worker Kodaly (JACK CASSIDY), matters soften between Amalia and Georg. By Christmas Eve the truth is revealed and both are happy with the outcome. Also in the superior cast were Barbara Baxley, Nathaniel Frey, and Ralph Williams. JOE MASTEROFF wrote the delicate yet funny libretto based on a Hungarian play by Miklos Laszlo (which had already been filmed twice and would be again), and producer–director HAROLD PRINCE staged the valentine of a show with charm and wit. The beloved score included the hyperactive ballad "Tonight at Eight," the stream-of-consciousness piece "Ice Cream," the delicate "Will He Like Me?," the risible narrative "A Trip to the Library," the waltzing "Days Gone By," the dedicated march "I Resolve," the sarcastic "Grand Knowing You," the frantic

---

Casts for *She Loves Me*

Character	1963 Broadway	1978 television	1993 Broadway
Georg Nowack	Daniel Massey	Robin Ellis	BOYD GAINES
Amalia Balash	BARBARA COOK	Gemma Craven	JUDY KUHN
Ilona Ritter	Barbara Baxley	Diane Langton	Sally Mayes
Steven Kodaly	JACK CASSIDY	David Kernan	HOWARD McGILLIN
Mr. Maraczek	Ludwig Donath	Derek Smith	Louis Zorich
Ladislav Sipos	Nathaniel Frey	Peter Sallis	Lee Wilkof
Arpad Laszlo	Ralph Williams	Nigel Rathbone	Brad Kane

She Loves Me. For a highly romantic musical, there is plenty of humor and sass in the libretto and score. Since the two lovers do not get together until the final moments of the show there are no gushing duets and the solo ballads are more touching than torchy. Yet the musical is so charming from top to bottom that it seems like a nonstop romance. Pictured are Amalia (Barbara Cook) and Georg (Daniel Massey) in an awkward moment, being serenaded by a restaurant violinist when neither is in a romantic mood. (Photofest)

"Twelve Days to Christmas," and the jubilant title song. The charming, beautifully performed musical was well reviewed but its run (301 performances) was hampered by an overabundance of big, glossy musicals on Broadway that season. The score quickly became a cult favorite but revivals were not frequent until three decades later.

The ROUNDABOUT THEATRE revived *She Loves Me* in 1993, and the production, directed by SCOTT ELLIS, captured the romantic magic of the lyrical musical. The cast was roundly praised and the production was so popular that the Roundabout moved it out of its home space at the Criterion Center and into a Broadway house so that it could continue its scheduled season. By the time the revival closed, it had played 355 performances and brought a lot of attention to the neglected musical. Productions in regional theatre, summer stock, colleges, and community theatres followed. ◻ A 1978 BBC-TV production directed by Michael Simpson was broadcast on American television via PBS-TV. The cast was excellent, if a bit too British for American viewers' idea of Budapest characters, and a good portion of the score was retained for the 105-minute broadcast.

SHEAN, AL. See GALLAGHER and SHEAN

SHELTON, REID (1924–1997). Stage and television performer. A durable song-and-dance man who appeared in many Broadway musicals, he did not find wide recognition until late in his career as Daddy Warbucks in *ANNIE* (1977). Shelton was born in Salem, Oregon, and educated at the University of Michigan before making his Broadway debut in *WISH YOU WERE HERE* (1952). His other Broadway musicals include *WONDERFUL TOWN* (1953), *BY THE BEAUTIFUL SEA* (1954), *MY FAIR LADY* (1956), *Oh, What a Lovely War!* (1964), *CAROUSEL* (1965), *Canterbury Tales* (1969), *THE ROTHSCHILDS* (1970), and *1600 PENNSYLVANIA AVENUE* (1976). In addition to his funny, tender Daddy Warbucks, Shelton's other outstanding performance was as the brooding manservant Charles in the Off Broadway musical *MAN WITH A LOAD OF MISCHIEF* (1966). He left the theatre in the 1980s and appeared in dozens of television dramas and comedies.

🎵 **SHENANDOAH** (Alvin Theatre 1975). An old-fashioned but effective period musical play, the show boasted a pleasant score and enjoyable performances. The pacifist Virginia farmer Charlie Anderson (JOHN CULLUM) refuses to participate in the Civil War waging around him and he keeps his sons on the farm until the youngest one, Robert (Joseph Shapiro), is kidnapped by Union soldiers and then the brothers join the father in the fight. Also cast were Joel Higgins, Ted Agress, Jordan Suffin, David Russell, Penelope Milford, Chip Ford, and Donna Theodore. James Lee Barrett, PETER UDELL, and PHILIP ROSE wrote the by-the-numbers libretto, based on the 1965 film of the same title, and Gary Geld (music) and Udell (lyrics) provided the agreeable songs, including "Over the Hill," "Next to Lovin' (I Like Fightin')," "Freedom," "The Pickers Are Coming," "Violets and Silverbells," "We Make a Beautiful Pair," and "Meditation." Co-author Rose produced and directed and Robert Tucker did the vigorous choreography. The musical was deemed sentimental and artificial by the press but audiences thought otherwise and enjoyed the wholesome show for 1,050 performances and it was later popular in summer stock. When Cullum and much of the creative staff reassembled on Broadway for a 1989 recreation of the original, critics again disdained the piece and declared the revival lackluster and tired so it only lasted a month.

SHERIDAN, [Clara Lou] **ANN** (1915–1967). Film and television performer. Publicized by the studios as the "Oomph Girl" for her no-nonsense sex appeal and down-to-earth persona, the slim beauty appeared in several musicals before carving a niche as a dramatic actress. Sheridan was born in Denton, Texas, and trained for an education career at the North Texas State Teachers College. When she won a beauty contest, she was brought to Hollywood, making her screen debut in 1933. Sheridan made twenty films in two years without getting much recognition, including the musicals *Bolero* (1934), *Murder at the Vanities* (1934), *COLLEGE RHYTHM* (1934), *Rhumba* (1935), and *MISSISSIPPI* (1935). By the mid-1930s she was noticed in some comedies and musicals and became popular in major roles in the musicals *Sing Me a Love Song* (1936), *Cowboy From Brooklyn* (1938), *Naughty But Nice* (1939), *Navy Blues* (1941), *THANK YOUR LUCKY STARS* (1943), *Shine on Harvest Moon* (1944), and *The Opposite Sex* (1956). Her performance in the drama *King's Row* (1942) established her as a serious actress and she remained a major star until the late 1950s. Sheridan then turned to television for the rest of her career.

SHERMAN BROTHERS. Film and stage composers and lyricists. The most successful songwriting team in the history of DISNEY PICTURES, the two siblings invented new words as well as memorable songs. Richard M. Sherman (1928–) and Robert B. Sherman (1925–) were born in New York and both were educated at Bard College. They had written some pop hits, such as "Tall Paul" and "You're Sixteen," before WALT DISNEY hired them to provide songs for the nonmusicals *The Parent Trap* (1961) and *In Search of the Castaways* (1962). Soon the brothers became the studio's unofficial tunesmiths in residence, penning the scores for *SUMMER MAGIC* (1963), *MARY POPPINS* (1964), *The Happiest Millionaire* (1967), *The One and Only Genuine Original Family Band* (1968), and *BEDKNOBS AND BROOMSTICKS* (1968), as well as the animated features *The Sword in the Stone* (1963), *THE JUNGLE BOOK* (1967), *THE ARISTOCATS* (1970), and, years later, *The Tigger Movie* (2000). For other studios the Shermans scored *CHITTY CHITTY BANG BANG* (1968), the animated films *CHARLOTTE'S WEB* (1972) and *Snoopy Come Home* (1972), and wrote both screenplays and scores for the musicals *Tom Sawyer* (1973), *Huckleberry Finn* (1974), *THE SLIPPER AND THE ROSE* (1976), and *The Magic of Lassie* (1978). The Broadway versions of *Chitty Chitty Bang Bang* (2005) and *Mary Poppins* (2006) retained much of the brothers' film songs and they wrote original songs for the war-time musical comedy *OVER HERE!* (1974) and the TV musical *Goldilocks* (1970). The Shermans' songs can be buoyant, tender, silly, and contagious, as well as popular. It is estimated that "It's a Small World (After All)," which they wrote for Disneyland, has been heard by many millions. Their lyrics are also memorable, even when they used made-up words such as "Higitus Figitus," "Fortuosity," "Gratifaction," and "Supercalifragilisticexpialidocius."

SHERMAN, HIRAM (1908–1989). Stage and television performer. A chubby character actor who often made a strong impression in supporting roles, he appeared in classics, comedies, and musicals. The Boston native, the son of a newspaper cartoonist, was educated at the University of Illinois and studied acting at the Goodman Theatre School in Chicago. After working professionally in stock in that city, he went to New York where he made his Broadway bow in the Federal Theatre Project's farce *Horse Eats Hat* (1936), followed by other productions by the same organization, including the legendary musical *THE CRADLE WILL ROCK* (1937 and 1964). When the group was discontinued, Orson Welles hired Sherman for his Mercury Theatre where he appeared in a variety of works as well as on Broadway where he was featured in the revue *Sing Out the News* (1938) and played the temperamental director Ogden Quiler in *VERY WARM FOR MAY* (1939). Sherman was seen in very early television broadcasts in the late 1940s and was a frequent face on the small screen into the 1960s, although he consistently returned to Broadway in plays and musicals. He was a replacement for the role of Jeff in *BRIGADOON* (1949), shone in the revues *Two's Company* (1952), *Three for Tonight* (1955), and *International Soirée* (1958) and was lauded for his Wall Street tycoon Wingate in *How Now, Dow Jones* (1967). Sherman appeared in a handful of London musicals and in a few films as well.

SHEVELOVE, BURT[on] (1915–1982). Stage and television director and writer. Active on Broadway and in television, he staged both new works and popular revivals. Shevelove was born in Newark, New Jersey, and educated at Brown and Yale Universities. After writing and directing small shows Off Broadway, he made his Broadway debut with the revue *Small Wonder* (1949) for which he staged and provided sketches and lyrics. His greatest Broadway triumph was co-writing the libretto for *A FUNNY THING HAPPENED ON THE WAY TO THE FORUM* (1962) with LARRY GELBART. He also was acclaimed for his direction of the long-running 1971 revival of *No, No, NANETTE* and the 1972 revival of *A Funny Thing Happened on the Way to the Forum*. Shevelove's other direct-

ing credits on Broadway include *HALLELUJAH, BABY!* (1967), *Rodgers & Hart* (1975), *So Long, 147th Street* (1976), and *Happy New Year* (1980). He produced and directed many television specials for different stars, directed the TV musical *Hooray for Love* (1960), and both wrote and directed the TV musical *THE CANTERVILLE GHOST* (1966). Shevelove was represented on Broadway posthumously when *The Frogs*, a musical he wrote with STEPHEN SONDHEIM for Yale University in 1974, arrived on Broadway in 2004.

SHOCKING MISS PILGRIM, THE (Fox 1947). A curiosity of a musical about women's suffrage in the 1870s, it featured BETTY GRABLE and a new GEORGE GERSHWIN score a full decade after his death. The great composer's brother IRA GERSHWIN took some of the many musical compositions left behind after Gershwin's premature death and wrote lyrics to them, coming up with a handful of new songs, only one of which ("For You, For Me, For Evermore") found any popularity. Also of more than passing interest were the satirical "Back Bay Polka," the reflective "Changing My Tune," and the sly "Aren't You Kinda Glad We Did?," which, despite its provocative title, was about an innocent ride in a carriage without a chaperone. The songs would have found more renown if the film had been better. The screenplay by co-director GEORGE SEATON concerned the progressive Bostonian Cynthia Pilgrim (Grable) who gets a job as a "typewriter" in a shipping factory and gets involved in the suffragette movement. Her boss John Pritchard (DICK HAYMES) disagrees with Cynthia's political agenda but finds himself falling in love with her anyway. The supporting cast included oddball artistic characters living at Cynthia's boarding house: Elizabeth Patterson, Anne Revere, Allyn Joslyn, Gene Lockhart, Arthur Shields, Lilian Bronson, and Charles Kemper. WILLIAM PERLBERG produced the musical, which was awkward and unsatisfying. The nineteenth-century costumes and sets seemed overly artificial, Haymes gave one of his most wooden performances, and Grable's character was confusing and not very endearing. Only during some of the musical numbers does one get a glimmer of vitality.

SHORE, DINAH [born Frances Rose Shore] (1917–1994). Film and television performer. The beloved recording artist was featured in several 1940s movie musicals in an effort to make her a film star but it was on television that the smooth-voiced blonde became a national favorite. Shore was born in Winchester, Tennessee, and educated at Vanderbilt University before she started singing on local and then New York radio stations. She became famous after singing on EDDIE CANTOR's radio program and her recordings were bestsellers. Shore made her screen debut in *Thank Your Lucky Stars* (1943), followed by *Belle of the Yukon* (1944), *Up in Arms* (1944), *Follow the Boys* (1944), *Till the Clouds Roll By* (1946), and *Aaron Slick From Pumpkin Crick* (1951), as well as singing on the soundtracks for the animated *Make Mine Music* (1946) and *Fun and Fancy Free* (1946). She turned to television in the 1950s and was the first female to host her own variety show. Shore also appeared on dozens of other television programs throughout the 1980s. She was married to actor George Montgomery (1916–2000). Biography: *Dinah! A Biography*, Bruce Cassiday (1979).

SHORT, [Hubert Edward] HASSARD (1877–1956). One of the most prolific and innovative directors of musicals from the 1920s through the 1940s, he changed the look of the Broadway musical. Short was born in rural Lincolnshire, England, and ran away from home at the age of fifteen to become an actor. He made his London debut in 1895 and six years later emigrated to New York where he appeared in a number of Broadway productions, most memorably *Peg o' My Heart* (1912). His first New York directing assignment was the hit play *The Man From Home* in 1908 but he was not noticed until his staging of sketches for the Lambs' Club annual benefit revues called *Gambols* (1911 to 1913). Directing his first Broadway musical in 1920, Short's mastery of visuals and the use of lighting stood out. He replaced footlights with lighting instruments hung in the auditorium, used elevator and revolving stages, added color to light, used mirrors on stage effectively, and even had whiffs of perfume sent out into the house for certain numbers. Perhaps the high points of this kind of visual magic were seen in his direction of the landmark revues *The Band Wagon* (1931), with its twin turntables and the use of moving platforms to introduce and conclude scenes, and *As Thousands Cheer* (1933), with the scenery ablaze with newspaper headlines that introduced each scene. He staged three editions of the *Music Box Revue*, *Greenwich Village Follies* (1925), *Three's a Crowd* (1930), *Star and Garter* (1942), *Seven Lively Arts* (1944), *Make Mine Manhattan* (1948), and other popular revues, as well as such

beloved book musicals as *Sunny* (1925), *Face the Music* (1932), *Jubilee* (1935), *Between the Devil* (1937), *Very Warm for May* (1939), *Lady in the Dark* (1941), *Something for the Boys* (1943), *Carmen Jones* (1943), *Mexican Hayride* (1944), and the 1946 revival of *Show Boat*.

SHORT, MARTIN [Hayter] (1950–). Film, television, and stage performer and writer. The slightly built, animated comic actor with a hundred faces and voices, he has returned to the musical stage on occasion. Short was born in Hamilton, Ontario, Canada, the son of an executive and a concert violinist, and educated at McMaster University where he started performing in campus shows. Relocating to Toronto, he appeared in the first professional production there of *Godspell* in 1972. Joining the improv group Second City in 1977, Short worked his way up and was a favorite on the Canadian television series *SCTV*, which was shown in the States, and then on *Saturday Night Live* and eventually his own syndicated show, serving as one of the writers on all three. He started making comedy films in 1979 but only rarely has his style of comedy worked on the screen, yet on stage he shines like the great clowns of the past. On Broadway he has played the hyper actor Elliott Garfield in the musical version of *The Goodbye Girl* (1993), a handful of comic caricatures in *Little Me* (1998), and a variety of characters in the mock musical autobiography *Martin Short: Fame Becomes Me* (2006), which he also co-wrote. Short has returned to the stage regionally, such as playing Leo Bloom in the Los Angeles and Toronto companies of *The Producers*.

SHOW BOAT (Ziegfeld Theatre 1927). The American musical theatre's first masterpiece and arguably still the finest musical play, the show had a libretto and score with a larger scope and a more complex temperament than any work before it, bringing to fruition the dream of JEROME KERN (music) and OSCAR HAMMERSTEIN (book and lyrics) to create a piece of serious music–theatre.

Plot: In the 1880s, Cap'n Andy Hawkes pilots the show boat *Cotton Blossom* up and down the Mississippi River, bringing stage melodramas to the riverside towns and cities. His wife Parthy doesn't like raising her daughter Magnolia among show people and river riff raff so she is particularly suspicious of Gaylord Ravenal, a dashing-looking gentleman who she (rightly) suspects is a river gambler. When the local sheriff learns that Julie La Verne, the featured actress on the *Cotton Blossom*, is a mulatto and is married to a white man, Steve, the couple is forced to flee and Gaylord and Magnolia take over the leading roles in the show boat's repertoire. The two fall in love and, with Cap'n Andy's help, elope and move to Chicago. Ravenal's gambling luck deserts him and, unable to face his failure, he abandons Magnolia and their little girl Kim. Magnolia gets a job singing in a Chicago nightclub after the star of the show quits; the star is the alcoholic Julie and, unknown to Magnolia, she hears Magnolia's audition and quits so that her friend can get the job. On New Year's Eve the Cap'n and Parthy are reunited with Magnolia at the nightclub where she is such a success that her singing career is launched. Years pass and Kim has grown up and is now a Roaring Twenties singing and dancing star. Magnolia decides to retire from performing and, joining her parents and Kim back on the *Cotton Blossom*, she

is reunited with the aged Ravenal once again. Throughout the years, the African American riverboat worker Joe and his wife, the cook Queenie, remain on the *Cotton Blossom* and observe the changes that occur in the Hawkes family. As much as life on the Mississippi may change, Joe knows that the river itself is unaware of the plight of humans and continues on regardless of people's fortunes or failures.

Hammerstein's adaptation of Edna Ferber's sprawling novel was a masterwork of storytelling and character development. He not only condensed and clarified the book's many events and characters, but he rethought them in terms of a musical theatre production. The Kern–Hammerstein score was richer and more varied than any other yet heard, filled with operetta numbers, folk and blues music, and bright musical comedy songs. *Show Boat* is also the first musical to hold together so well thematically, with the song "Ol' Man River"

Casts for *Show Boat*

Characters	Magnolia	Ravenal	Julie	Joe
1927 Broadway	NORMA TERRIS	HOWARD MARSH	HELEN MORGAN	Jules Bledsoe
1929 film	Laura La Plante	Joseph Schildkraut	Alma Rubens	Stepin Fetchit
1932 Broadway	Norma Terris	DENNIS KING	Helen Morgan	PAUL ROBESON
1936 film	IRENE DUNNE	ALLAN JONES	Helen Morgan	Paul Robeson
1946 Broadway	JAN CLAYTON	Charles Fredericks	CAROL BRUCE	Paul Robeson
1951 film	KATHRYN GRAYSON	HOWARD KEEL	AVA GARDNER	William Warfield
1966 Broadway	BARBARA COOK	STEPHEN DOUGLASS	CONSTANCE TOWERS	William Warfield
1983 Broadway	Sheryl Woods	Ron Raines	Lonette McKee	Bruce Hubbard
1994 Broadway	REBECCA LUKER	Mark Jacoby	Lonette McKee	Michel Bell

Characters:	Cap'n Andy	Parthy	Queenie	
1927 Broadway	CHARLES WINNINGER	Edna May Oliver	Tess Gardella	
1929 film	Otis Harlan	Emily Fitzroy		
1932 Broadway	Charles Winninger	Edna May Oliver	Tess Gardella	
1936 film	Charles Winninger	HELEN WESTLEY	HATTIE MCDANIEL	
1946 Broadway	Ralph Dumke	Ethel Owen	Helen Dowdy	
1951 film	JOE E. BROWN	AGNES MOOREHEAD	Frances E. Williams	
1966 Broadway	DAVID WAYNE	MARGARET HAMILTON	ROSETTA LENOIRE	
1983 Broadway	DONALD O'CONNOR	Avril Gentles	Karla Burns	
1994 Broadway	JOHN MCMARTIN	ELAINE STRITCH	Gretha Boston	

Show Boat. The role of Joe was written with Paul Robeson (pictured) and his great, deep voice in mind, but the African American singer–actor didn't play Joe until the 1932 revival and the 1936 film and it is a subtle but towering performance. Here he is with his wife Queenie, played by Hattie McDaniel, in the film version. (Photofest)

Show Boat (stage) Musical Numbers

"Cotton Blossom"
"Where's the Mate for Me?"
"Make Believe"
"Ol' Man River"
"Can't Help Lovin' Dat Man"
"Life Upon the Wicked Stage"
"Till Good Luck Comes My Way"
"Mis'ry's Comin' Around"
"I Might Fall Back on You"
"Queenie's Ballyhoo"
"You Are Love"
"At the Fair"
"Dandies on Parade"
"Why Do I Love You?"
"In Dahomey"
"Bill"
"Goodbye, My Lady Love"
"After the Ball"
"Hey, Feller"

---

linking the score just as the Mississippi ties together the plot and characters. Several standards came out of the score, including "Make Believe," "You Are Love," "Can't Help Lovin' Dat Man," "Why Do I Love You?," and "Ol' Man River," but *Show Boat* is much more than a string of hit songs. Each number comments on the action or the characters, even if it is part of the show being presented on the boat or in a nightclub. The score has variety, yet it is all of a piece. Even the interpolated songs—the old standards "After the Ball" and "Goodbye, My Lady Love," and "Bill," which Kern wrote years before with a lyric by P. G. WODEHOUSE—are used effectively and seem created for the musical. Never before had a Broadway score taken its characters (and the audience) to so many places emotionally and thematically.

Producer FLORENZ ZIEGFELD's original production boasted one of the most extraordinary casts of any Broadway musical. HELEN MORGAN's poignant, tragic Julie, NORMA TERRIS and HOWARD MARSH moving from youthful lovers to mature adults, and the vibrant comic performances by CHARLES WINNINGER and Edna May Oliver, as Cap'n Andy and his harridan wife Parthy, and SAMMY WHITE and EVA PUCK, as the show boat's comedy couple, Frank and Ellie, were all unforgettable. The African American performers were startlingly proficient, surprising audiences who had never seen black characters who moved

beyond happy song and dance. Jules Bledsoe and Tess Gardella helped frame the show with their quietly affecting portrayals of Joe and Queenie. Ziegfeld spared no expense on this, his most atypical show. Joseph Urban designed the many sets, that cast numbered over 100, and Hammerstein himself took over much of the direction of the mammoth production. Critical and popular responses were overwhelming and *Show Boat* ran 572 performances.

Over the years the musical has not only been revived but revised so that there is no one definite version of *Show Boat*. The musical successfully toured across America for seven months (with IRENE DUNNE playing Magnolia) and later returned to New York on eight occasions. Terris, Morgan, Winninger, and Oliver were among the returning players in the 1932 return engagement on Broadway that ran 180 performances. New to the production were DENNIS KING as Ravenal and PAUL ROBESON playing Joe, which was originally written for him but was unable to play because of bookings in England. The 1946 revival, produced by Hammerstein and Kern with the former directing with HASSARD SHORT, starred JAN CLAYTON and Charles Fredericks as the central couple and it ran a very profitable 418 performances. For this production, Kern and Hammerstein wrote a new number, "Nobody Else But Me"; it was the last song Kern ever wrote. The New York City Center production in 1948 was far less successful, as was the New York City Light Opera mounting, which played two different engagements in 1954. The same company revived *Show Boat* in 1961, and its commendable cast included Jo Sullivan (Magnolia), ROBERT ROUNSEVILLE (Ravenal), Andrew Frierson (Joe), and Anita Darian (Julie). One of the most fondly remembered revivals was the Music Theatre of Lincoln Center's 1966 production with BARBARA COOK (Magnolia), STEPHEN DOUGLASS (Ravenal), William Warfield (Joe), and CONSTANCE TOWERS (Julie). The Houston Grand Opera, the Kennedy Center, and other organizations presented a *Show Boat* in 1983 that starred DONALD O'CONNOR as Cap'n Andy and had lesser-known performers giving excellent performances as Magnolia (Sheryl Woods), Ravenal (Ron Raines), Joe (Bruce Hubbard), and Julie (Lonette McKee). McKee reprised her Julie in the acclaimed 1994 revival directed by HAROLD PRINCE, which used dance (choreographed by SUSAN STROMAN) to tie together the many events in the second act. The cast featured REBECCA LUKER and Mark Jacoby as Magnolia and Ravenal. The much-awarded production ran 946 performances, nearly twice as long as the original. Although it is an expensive and difficult musical to produce, cast, and perform, *Show Boat* has remained in the popular musical theatre repertoire for over eighty years.

■ There have been three film versions of *Show Boat*, although only two are full-fledged musicals. **Show Boat** (Universal 1929) was a silent film version of Ferber's book that was in production when the musical opened on Broadway. Universal added sound to some scenes, put Negro spirituals in the background, and filmed an eighteen-minute prologue in which members of the Broadway company sang some of the hits from the musical. The result is an odd, disjointed movie but it does have those historic clips of the original players. Laura La Plante and Joseph Schildkraut are Magnolia and Ravenal in the nonmusical story and they are often quite effective, but the supporting characters are mostly stereotypic and melodramatic. The movie was produced by Carl Laemmle and it was his son Carl Leammle, Jr. who produced the first talkie version of **Show Boat** (Universal 1936), which was directed by James Whale with choreography by LEROY PRINZ. Helen Morgan, Charles Winninger, and others from the original cast were reunited for this superb sound version, beautifully filmed, acted, and sung. Irene Dunne and ALLAN JONES shine as Magnolia and Ravenal, Paul Robeson is a towering Joe, and every player down to the smallest role is excellent. Some songs from the stage score had to be cut, and Hammerstein and Kern wrote three new ones, "I Have the Room Above Her," "Ah Still Suits Me," and "Gallivantin' Around," some of which were later incorporated into stage revivals of the show. Hammerstein's screenplay made changes in the later part of the story and the ending is closer to a Hollywood finale rather than the bittersweet conclusion of the play. But all in all this *Show Boat* is a film classic and is still powerful and pleasing. The 1946 Kern biopic *TILL THE CLOUDS ROLL BY* opens with a fifteen-minute sequence in which the opening night of *Show Boat* is illustrated. It is a beautifully edited and sung condensation featuring KATHRYN GRAYSON as Magnolia, TONY MARTIN as Gaylord, LENA HORNE as Julie, Caleb Peterson as Joe, and VIRGINIA O'BRIEN as Ellie. In some ways the sequence was a screen test by MGM in preparation for a full-length, color remake of the entire musical, although only Grayson was used in the subsequent film. **Show Boat** (MGM 1951) was produced by ARTHUR FREED, directed by GEORGE SIDNEY, and choreographed by ROBERT ALTON. The use of color and location shooting distinguished the MGM remake but, some fine performances aside, it is disappointing. Grayson and HOWARD KEEL as Magnolia and Ravenal are in top form vocally but neither performance is totally convincing. Ava Gardner (dubbed by Annette Warren) is effective in the enlarged part of Julie, but too many of the other supporting cast are only superficially entertaining. The screenplay by John Lee Mahin also made many changes in the later half of the plot, some of which work well. Julie, for instance, is instrumental in bringing Magnolia and Ravenal back together at the end of the film. However, after the outstanding 1936 version, this *Show Boat* seems unnecessary. ❏ A superior production of *Show Boat* by the Paper Mill Playhouse in New Jersey was taped before a live audience and broadcast on PBS-TV's *Great Performances* in 1989. The production, directed by Robert Johanson, featured EDDIE BRACKEN (Cap'n Andy), Rebecca Baxter (Magnolia), Richard White (Ravenal), P. L. Brown (Joe), Shelly Burch (Julie), Ellia English (Queenie), Marsha Bagwell (Parthy), LEE ROY REAMS (Frank), and Lenora Nemetz (Ellie).

🕭 **SHOW IS ON, THE** (Winter Garden Theatre 1936). A merry musical revue by topnotch talents, it used the world of show business as its unifying gimmick. David Freedman and MOSS HART wrote the sketches, and the score was by a potpourri of famous songwriters, such as HOAGY CARMICHAEL, GEORGE and IRA GERSHWIN, RICHARD RODGERS, LORENZ HART, and VERNON DUKE. Among the songs they contributed were "By Strauss," "Buy Yourself a Balloon," "(There's) Rhythm (In That Heart of Mine)," "Little Old Lady," "Song of the Woodman," "As Long As You've Got Your Health," and "Now." The adept cast included BERT LAHR, BEATRICE LILLIE, Paul Haakon, Mitzi Mayfair, Robert Shafer, REGINALD GARDINER, JACK MCCAULEY, and Ralph Riggs. With such expert players, topical and hilarious sketches, and laudable songs, the Shuberts' production was considered the last great revue of the decade. VINCENTE MINNELLI directed and designed, Harry Losee choreographed, and *The Show Is On* ran 237 performances and then returned in 1937 for another two weeks.

SHOW OF SHOWS, THE (Warner 1929). Even more a hodgepodge of acts than most early musical showcases in Hollywood, this Broadway-like revue more resembled a vaudeville lineup with just about every performer at WARNER BROTHERS somehow getting into the act. In addition to the expected songs and dances, the revue featured a spoof of melodramas, Rin Tin Tin barking out an introduction, John Barrymore reciting a speech from Shakespeare, a sketch performed by BEATRICE LILLIE, MYRNA LOY as a Chinese princess being serenaded by Nick Lucas, and guest spots for Lupino Lane, Douglas Fairbanks, Jr., Dolores Costello, IDA LUPINO, Richard Barthelmess, IRENE BORDONI, Noah Beery, WINNIE LIGHTNER, ANN SOTHERN, SID SILVERS, Loretta Young, Ben Turpin, and on and on, hosted by Frank Fay who also wrote some of the sketches. Two musical numbers stood out: "Meet My Sister," performed by eight sets of sisters from around the world, and the lengthy finale in which Betty Compson and Alexander Gray sang "Lady Luck" while fifteen acts broke in and reprised parts of the song as well. John G. Adolfi directed the sprawling DARRYL F. ZANUCK production, which remains interesting more for archival reasons than entertainment ones.

SHUBERT BROTHERS. Stage producers and directors. Although not the most high-minded or innovative of Broadway showmen, the siblings always kept the tired businessman in mind and appealed to a wide audience in their many theatres. Lee (1873–1953), Sam S. (1876–1905), and J. J. (1878–1963) were all born in Lithuania

with the surname Szemanski and were sent for by their father who had emigrated first to England and then America, settling in Syracuse, New York. Sam started as an actor but later joined with his brothers in buying theatres across the country, producing road companies, and eventually presenting shows on Broadway. They broke the nationwide theatre monopoly of the Theatrical Syndicate and then created a monopoly of their own. At the peak of their empire, the Shuberts owned thirty-one theatres in New York City and another seventy across the country. Between 1902 and 1948, they produced about 500 Broadway shows, 125 of them musicals. All three brothers (until Sam's early death) were involved in each production but it was J. J. Shubert who was in charge of the musicals, sometimes directing them also. Among the many Shubert musicals were such noteworthy shows as *A Chinese Honeymoon* (1902), *The Earl and the Girl* (1905), *Up and Down Broadway* (1910), *The Honeymoon Express* (1913), THE BLUE PARADISE (1915), MAYTIME (1917), SINBAD (1918), BLOSSOM TIME (1921), BOMBO (1921), THE STUDENT PRINCE (1924), BIG BOY (1925), COUNTESS MARITZA (1926), *My Maryland* (1927), LIFE BEGINS AT 8:40 (1934), AT HOME ABROAD (1935), THE SHOW IS ON (1936), HOORAY FOR WHAT! (1937), *The Streets of Paris* (1939), BETWEEN THE DEVIL (1937), HELLZAPOPPIN' (1938), *My Romance* (1948), and the revue series THE PASSING SHOW (1912 to 1924) and ARTISTS AND MODELS (1912 to 1924), which were the Shuberts' answer to the ZIEGFELD FOLLIES. Presenting a sizable percentage of the musicals seen on Broadway during the first half of the twentieth century, the brothers were a major force in the history of the genre.

SHUBERT ORGANIZATION. Stage organization. After the theatre empire formed by the SHUBERT BROTHERS was broken up in the 1960s, the company moved from a family business to a large and efficient corporation that owns and operates theatres and produces Broadway shows. In 1972 the lawyers Bernard B. Jacobs and Gerald Schoenfeld took over management of the organization, establishing the Shubert Foundation, which sponsors philanthropic projects in the arts and oversees the valuable Shubert archives. Also since the 1970s, the company has actively participated in producing (or usually co-producing) Broadway plays and musicals instead of just owning and managing playhouses. The company owns theatres on and Off Broadway and in major cities across the country, so they remain a very important player in live theatre in America. Among the musicals that the Shubert Organization had a hand in presenting were *AIN'T MISBEHAVIN'* (1978), *DREAMGIRLS* (1981), *LITTLE SHOP OF HORRORS* (1982), *SUNDAY IN THE PARK WITH GEORGE* (1984), *CITY OF ANGELS* (1989), *JEROME ROBBINS' BROADWAY* (1989), *PASSION* (1994), *Amour* (2002), and *SPAMALOT* (2005).

🕮 **SHUFFLE ALONG** (63rd Street Music Hall 1921). Not only the first successful, full-length musical written, directed, and performed by African American artists, it was also one of the most joyous shows of the decade. In the city of Jimtown, grocery store partners Steve Jenkins (Flourney Miller) and Sam Peck (Aubrey Lyles) are each running for mayor, each promising the other that he will be made chief of police. After Steve wins and Sam heads the police department, corruption sets in and the reform candidate Harry Walton (Roger Matthews) gets the people behind him and soon Steve and Sam are back in the grocery store. Flournoy Miller and Aubrey Lyles penned the risible libretto, and EUBIE BLAKE (music) and NOBLE SISSLE (lyrics) wrote the scintillating score. "I'm Just Wild About Harry" was the runaway hit and also delightful were "Love Will Find a Way," "Bandana Days," "Baltimore Buzz," "If You Haven't Been Vamped By a Brownskin," "(I'm) Simply Full of Jazz," "I'm Craving for That Kind of Love," and the title number. The show tried out in various cities before getting a berth in a Broadway house far from the mainstream. Word slowly filtered down and soon the musical was a must-see sensation, eventually running 484 performances. While the plot was familiar from black vaudeville, the score was a refreshing collection of innovative and durable songs that struck reviewers and playgoers as contemporary and gleeful. *Shuffle Along* also opened the door for all-black musicals that could appeal to white and black audiences. Other editions of *Shuffle Along* were presented in 1928 and 1932 but neither was successful. In 1952 a production of *Shuffle Along* opened on Broadway but, with only two of the original score's songs and a whole new libretto, this production hardly qualified as a revival, although as a new musical it was also severely lacking. Flournoy Miller and Gerard Smith's new plot now concerned a group of African American soldiers in Italy at the end of World War II, in particular the WAC Lucy Duke (Dolores Martin) who, thinking her husband was killed in action, begins a new romance

only to have her spouse (Miller) return. Noble and Sissle wrote some new numbers ("Swanee Moon," "Give It Love," "Rhythm of America," and "My Day") and appeared as themselves in the show, which ran only four performances.

SIDNEY, GEORGE (1911–2002). Film director and producer. A prolific director with a thirty-year career in Hollywood, he is most remembered for his MGM musicals in the 1940s and 1950s. Sidney was born on Long Island, New York, and was on the stage as a child. After appearing in a few Tom Mix Westerns, he worked his way up at MGM from sound technician to editor to director of short subjects, two of which won Academy Awards in the early 1940s. Sidney moved on to features in 1941 and helmed such memorable musicals as *ANCHORS AWEIGH* (1945), *THE HARVEY GIRLS* (1946), *ANNIE GET YOUR GUN* (1950), *SHOW BOAT* (1951), *KISS ME KATE* (1953), *Jupiter's Darling* (1955), and *PAL JOEY* (1957). He left MGM and produced and directed independently for such musicals as *Pepe* (1960), *BYE BYE BIRDIE* (1963), *VIVA LAS VEGAS* (1964), and *HALF A SIXPENCE* (1967). Sidney was also president of Hanna-Barbera Productions for a time and supervised many animated shorts.

SIEGEL, SOL C. (1903–1982). Film producer. A versatile presenter of all kinds of films, he worked for several studios before becoming an independent force. The native New Yorker was educated in journalism at Columbia and worked for the *Herald Tribune* before going out to Hollywood in 1934 to organize the creation of Republic Pictures. Siegel stayed and ran the studio until 1940 when he moved on to bigger companies, making his reputation first with westerns and then all genre pictures. By the 1950s he was vice president at MGM, yet continued to oversee individual productions, just as he would when he went independent in the 1960s. Among Siegel's musical credits include *Glamour Boy* (1941), *Priorities on Parade* (1942), *BLUE SKIES* (1946), *Welcome Stranger* (1947), *My Blue Heaven* (1950), *ON THE RIVIERA* (1951), *CALL ME MADAM* (1953), *GENTLEMEN PREFER BLONDES* (1953), *THERE'S NO BUSINESS LIKE SHOW BUSINESS* (1954), *HIGH SOCIETY* (1956), *LES GIRLS* (1957), and *Merry Andrew* (1959).

🕮 **SILK STOCKINGS** (Imperial Theatre 1955). COLE PORTER's last Broadway show, the amusing musical comedy was uneven but enjoyable and some of the songs were splendid. The chilly

Casts for *Silk Stockings*		
Character	*1955 Broadway*	*1957 film*
Steve Canfield	DON AMECHE	FRED ASTAIRE
Ninotchka	Hildegarde Neff	CYD CHARISSE
Peter Ilyitch Boroff	Philip Sterling	Wim Sonneveld
Janice/Peggy Dayton	Gretchen Wyler	JANIS PAIGE
Commissar Markovitch	GEORGE TOBIAS	George Tobias
Ivanov	Henry Lascoe	Joseph Buloff
Bibinski	David Opatoshu	JULES MUNSHIN
Brankov	Leon Belasco	Peter Lorre

Soviet officer Ninotchka (Hildegarde Neff) arrives in Paris to bring home the Russian composer Peter Ilyitch Boroff (Philip Sterling) who is being wooed by Hollywood to score movie soundtracks. The American theatrical agent Steve Canfield (DON AMECHE) plans to fend off Ninotchka by seducing her with the romance of Paris and he succeeds so well the two eventually take off for the West together. GEORGE S. KAUFMAN, Leueen MacGrath, and ABE BURROWS struggled with adaptation of the film classic *Ninotchka* (1939) starring Greta Garbo and it never came close to the brilliant screen version but the songs were often fun, particularly "All of You," "Paris Loves Lovers," "It's a Chemical Reaction, That's All," " Siberia," "Stereophonic Sound," and the title number. In addition to the libretto problems, there were staff changes and plenty of rewriting out of town. The result was a shaky musical that intermittently came to life. CY FEUER directed and co-produced with ERNEST MARTIN, and *Silk Stockings* overcame its disappointing reviews and managed to run 478 performances.

 Silk Stockings (MGM 1957) made a better movie musical than a stage work thanks to the presence of FRED ASTAIRE, CYD CHARISSE, and the rest of the superior cast. The screenplay by Leonard Gershe and Leonard Spigelgass was an improvement on the Broadway libretto, highlighting the three Soviet emissaries Ivanov, Bibinski, and Brankov who were played with comic panache by Joseph Buloff, JULES MUNSHIN, and Peter Lorre. Charisse was no Garbo in the book scenes but when she sang (dubbed by Carole Richards) or danced with Astaire the movie was heavenly. ROUBEN MAMOULIAN directed the film in a studio sound stage, but the ARTHUR FREED production felt like Paris all the same. EUGENE LORING, HERMES PAN, and Astaire all contributed to the choreography and it was able to go places even *Ninotchka* could not go.

SILLMAN, LEONARD (1908–1982). Stage and television producer, director, and performer. A versatile showman who acted, danced, produced, and directed in New York and regionally for over forty years, he launched the careers of dozens of actors and writers through his popular *NEW FACES* revues. Sillman was born in Detroit, Michigan, and at a young age went into vaudeville, singing and dancing in various acts before he was hired by comedian–producer LEW FIELDS to perform in his shows. Sillman later teamed up with comedienne IMOGENE COCA and their vaudeville act played the Palace Theatre in New York in 1926. After appearing in book musicals in New York and on the road, he produced, directed, and performed in his first revue in California in 1930. Four years later Sillman presented his first *New Faces* revue, followed by seven editions over the next three decades. Many of the Sillman revues toured or appeared regionally, but he frequently returned to New York where he staged revues in Broadway houses, such as *Fools Rush In* (1934), *All in Fun* (1940), *If the Shoe Fits* (1946), and *Mask and Gown* (1957). He was also very active in producing and directing on television and in some films. His playful and satiric style of directing revues influenced others, and the Sillman touch was seen in many Off Broadway revues in the 1950s and 1960s. Autobiography: *Here Lies Leonard Sillman, Straightened Out at Last* (1963).

SILVERS, PHIL (1911–1985). Television, stage, and film performer and producer. One of television's greatest clowns, the balding, bespectacled comic had a long and varied career that included vaudeville, burlesque, radio, and nightclubs, as well as Hollywood and Broadway musicals. The Brooklyn native sang in variety as a teenager and made some silent comedy shorts before going into burlesque where he eventually became one of the top comics at Minsky's. Silvers was featured in the Broadway musical *Yokel Boy* (1939) and then the next year started making talking films beginning with the musical *Hit Parade of 1941* (1940). In Hollywood he often played sidekicks or the friend of the leading man, as in the musicals *LADY, BE GOOD* (1941), *Ice-Capades* (1941), *My GAL SAL* (1942), *Footlight Serenade* (1942), *CONEY ISLAND* (1943), *COVER GIRL* (1944), *Four Jills in a Jeep* (1944), *SOMETHING FOR THE BOYS* (1944), *Diamond Horseshoe* (1945), *If I'm Lucky* (1946), *SUMMER STOCK* (1950), and *Lucky Me* (1954). Silvers never became a screen star but he was roundly praised on Broadway as the con man Harrison Floy in the musical *HIGH BUTTON SHOES* (1947) and his low comic Jerry Biffle in *Top Banana* (1951), which he repeated on screen in 1954. True stardom came with his Sergeant Bilko comedy shows on television in the 1950s, making him one of the most familiar performers in America. Throughout the rest of his career, Silvers returned to musicals, as with the TV musicals *Keep in Step* (1959) and *DAMN YANKEES* (1967), in which he played the devilish Applegate, and in the film version of *A FUNNY THING HAPPENED ON THE WAY TO THE FORUM* (1967). On Broadway he shone as the wheeler-dealer Herbie Cram in *DO RE MI* (1960) and as the clever Pseudolus in the 1972 revival of *A Funny Thing Happened on the Way to the Forum*. Silvers sometimes produced plays and television shows, such as the long-running *Gilligan's Island*, in the 1960s, and continued acting in films and on television into the 1980s. Autobiography: *The Laugh Is on Me* (1974).

SILVERS, SID (1901–1976). Stage and film performer and writer. A pint-sized physical comedian on Broadway and in Hollywood, he also had a concurrent career writing scripts for musicals. The Brooklyn native performed routines he scripted himself in vaudeville and eventually appeared in musicals revues, writing his own sketches and later entire librettos, usually in collaboration with others. He made his Broadway debut in *ARTISTS AND MODELS* (1925) and then both acted and contributed to the book and lyrics to *A Night in Spain* (1927) and *TAKE A CHANCE* (1932). His writing credits on Broadway also include *Pleasure Bound* (1929), *You Said It* (1931), and *NEW FACES OF 1956*. Silvers did a specialty spot in the movie *THE SHOW OF SHOWS* (1929), followed by appearances in *Dancing Sweeties* (1930), *My Weakness* (1933), *Transatlantic Merry-Go-Round* (1934), and *52nd Street* (1937). He wrote and appeared in *Bottoms Up* (1934), *BROADWAY MELODY OF 1936* (1935), and *BORN TO DANCE* (1936). His

other writing credits include *Follow the Leader* (1930), *BROADWAY MELODY OF 1938* (1937), *THE FLEET'S IN* (1942), *FOR ME AND MY GAL* (1942), *Two Tickets to Broadway* (1951), and was one of the many authors of the screenplay for *THE WIZARD OF OZ* (1939).

SIMMS, GINNY [Ellen] (1916–1994). Film performer. A beautiful high-cheeked vocalist popular in the Big Band era, she was featured in ten Hollywood musicals. Simms was born in San Antonio, Texas, and raised in California. While studying at Fresno State Teachers College, she sang with a trio and got interested in singing professionally. When she was performing in San Francisco, bandleader KAY KAYSER heard her and selected Simms as his featured vocalist. She played herself and sang with the band in the movie musicals *That's Right, You're Wrong* (1939), *You'll Find Out* (1940), and *Playmates* (1942). Simms then went solo and played character parts in *Here We Go Again* (1942), *Seven Day's Leave* (1942), *Hit the Ice* (1943), *BROADWAY RHYTHM* (1944), *Shady Lady* (1945), *NIGHT AND DAY* (1946), and *Disc Jockey* (1951). She had a popular radio show in the 1940s.

SIMON, [Marvin] **NEIL** (1927–). Stage, film, and television writer. One of America's most popular (and successful) comic writers, he penned the scripts for some long-running Broadway musicals. Simon was born in the Bronx and grew up in Brooklyn, later taking some courses at New York University. He began his writing career in radio and then contributed to sketches on SID CAESAR's popular television show. Simon's first association with musicals was writing scripts for the original TV movies *SATINS AND SPURS* (1954), *Heidi* (1955), *Paris in Springtime* (1956), and *THE ADVENTURES OF MARCO POLO* (1956). Also in 1955 he adapted a series of musicals and operettas for television, including *A CONNECTICUT YANKEE, THE CHOCOLATE SOLDIER, THE DESERT SONG,* and *THE GREAT WALTZ.* Simon helped write sketches for the Broadway musical revues *Catch a Star* (1955) and *NEW FACES OF 1956* and then had a hit of his own with the comedy *Come Blow Your Horn* (1961). This was followed by one the longest runs of hit plays in the Broadway record books, some twenty-five plays with only a few not showing a profit. Simon's Broadway musical scripts are *LITTLE ME* (1962), *SWEET CHARITY* (1966), *PROMISES PROMISES* (1969), *THEY'RE PLAYING OUR SONG* (1979), and *The Goodbye Girl* (1993), all but the last reaching hit status. He has also proven to be a noted play doctor who provided uncredited material for others' plays and musicals, most memorably *A CHORUS LINE* (1975). Like his plays, Simon's musical librettos tend to be slick, urban, and very well crafted. Many of Simon's plays and musicals have been filmed and he has written several original screenplays as well. In 1983 Broadway's Alvin Theatre was renamed the Neil Simon Theatre. Autobiographies: *Rewrites* (1996); *The Play Goes On* (1999).

📖 **SIMPLE SIMON** (Ziegfeld Theatre 1930). A loosely plotted extravaganza was little more than an excuse for showing off the talents of popular comic ED WYNN, the musical boasted a Rodgers and Hart song classic. Coney Island news agent Simon Eyyes (Wynn) doesn't like to read the depressing headlines on the newspaper he sells, preferring to read fairy tales. In his imagination many of these innocent tales come to life and he joins the heroes and heroines who are wearing modern clothes and using contemporary slang. Simon encounters Cinderella, Prince Charming, Jack and Jill, Little Red Riding Hood, Miss Muffett, Bluebeard, King Cole, the cat with the fiddle, and a giant frog who shares Simon's urban picnic lunch. Although Simon eventually awakes from his fantasies, he still refuses to acknowledge the ills of reality and is soon dreaming again. WYNN and GUY BOLTON wrote the slapdash libretto, and RICHARD RODGERS (music) and LORENZ HART (lyrics) provided the songs, the best being the torchy standard "Ten Cents a Dance," which RUTH ETTING sang while riding on top of a piano on a bicycle peddled by Wynn. Also in the score were "I Still Believe in You," "Don't Tell Your Folks," "Send for Me," and "I Can Do Wonders With You." Two superior songs, the wistful "He Was Too Good to Me" and the exuberant "Dancing on the Ceiling," were cut from the score by producer FLORENZ ZIEGFELD because he feared they were slowing down the farcical show. Everything on stage was tailored to Wynn's specifications, such as his demonstration of silly inventions (including a mouse trap with no entrance so the little creatures wouldn't get hurt) and his lisping exclamations ("Oh, how I love the woodth!" became the latest catch phrase). However, Wynn's fans could only keep *Simple Simon* on the boards for 135 performances so Ziegfeld sent his star on tour for six months where he paid off his investment.

SINATRA, FRANK [born Francis Albert Sinatra] (1915–1998). Film and television performer.

A durable vocalist who managed to maintain a faithful following for five decades, the blue-eyed crooner had an extensive career in movie musicals. Sinatra was born in Hoboken, New Jersey, the son of Italian immigrants, and launched his singing career when he won first prize on radio's *Major Bowes Amateur Hour*. Soon he was a featured vocalist with the HARRY JAMES and TOMMY DORSEY bands, appearing on screen with the latter orchestra in *Las Vegas Nights* (1941) and *Ship Ahoy* (1942). Sinatra was the first band vocalist to break away and go solo with success. He soon was the singing idol of young women and his concerts were known for the hysterics of his hysterical fans. After playing himself in the movie musicals *Reveille With Beverly* (1943) and *HIGHER AND HIGHER* (1943), Sinatra graduated to character parts, usually young, callow, and sheepish juveniles who were hesitant with women but won them over with his singing, as seen in *Step Lively* (1944), *ANCHORS AWEIGH* (1945), *IT HAPPENED IN BROOKLYN* (1947), *TAKE ME OUT TO THE BALL GAME* (1949), *ON THE TOWN* (1949), and *Strictly Dynamite* (1951). Sinatra moved into dramatic roles in the 1950s and played more adult roles in the musicals *GUYS AND DOLLS* (1955), *HIGH SOCIETY* (1956), *THE JOKER IS WILD* (1957), *PAL JOEY* (1957), *CAN-CAN* (1960), and *ROBIN AND THE SEVEN HOODS* (1964). He also made guest appearances or did specialty spots in *TILL THE CLOUDS ROLL BY* (1946), *Meet Me in Las Vegas* (1955), *Pepe* (1960), and *THE ROAD TO HONG KONG* (1962) and played the stage manager in the television musical *OUR TOWN* (1955). Sinatra's special way with a song and relaxed singing style made him a longtime favorite, but he also possessed a strong film presence and managed to be intriguing even when his vehicles were second rate. Among his wives were AVA GARDNER and Mia Farrow (1945–), and his children are singers Nancy Sinatra (1940–) and Frank Sinatra, Jr. (1944–). Biographies: *Frank Sinatra: The Man, the Music, the Legend*, Jeanne Fuchs, Ruth Prigozy (2007); *Frank Sinatra: An American Legend*, Nancy Sinatra (1998).

📖 **SINBAD** (Winter Garden Theatre 1918). A large-cast extravaganza produced by the SHUBERTS, the musical was a vehicle for AL JOLSON and all it needed was its star. In the silly libretto by Harold Atteridge, Jolson played the black-faced slave Inbad in ancient Baghdad who poses as Sinbad the sailor, allowing for all kinds of disguises, shenanigans, and songs. Atteridge wrote the lyrics for SIGMUND ROMBERG's music but none of their songs found any fame. The hits, such as "Rock-a-Bye Your Baby With a Dixie Melody," "Avalon," "My Mammy," and "Swanee," were all numbers by various tunesmiths that Jolson interpolated into the show before and during the run and then later on the road. J. C. HUFFMAN directed the scattershot show and it was a crowd pleaser, running 388 performances before setting out on an equally successful tour.

■ SING YOU SINNERS (Paramount 1938). Singing and fighting brothers was the premise of this unusual but likable musical that boasted a topnotch score. Claude Binyon's screenplay is a domestic tale about three squabbling Beebe brothers: the hardworking David (FRED MACMURRAY), horse gambler Joe (BING CROSBY), and their pint-sized kid brother Mike (DONALD O'CONNOR). The usual family infighting is further ignited when Joe is attracted to David's fiancée Martha Randal (Ellen Drew). Joe wins a pile at the race track, buys a junk shop and a race horse, and the siblings are united (temporarily) when Mike rides the horse to victory. It was an offbeat plot line for a musical but one that worked., especially when Crosby sang two JAMES V. MONACO–JOHNNY BURKE song hits, "I've Got a Pocketful of Dreams" and "Don't Let That Moon Get Away." However, the highlight of the film was the three brothers cutting loose with HOAGY CARMICHAEL and FRANK LOESSER's cautionary ditty "Small Fry," which also became a hit. WESLEY RUGGLES produced and directed the film, which also featured Elizabeth Patterson (as the boys' mother Daisy), John Gallaudet, Paul White, Irving Bacon, William Haade, and Herbert Corthell.

■ SINGIN' IN THE RAIN (MGM 1952). It may or may not be the greatest of all Hollywood musicals, but it is probably more fun than any other.

Plot: Silent screen idol Don Lockwood meets the chorus girl Kathy Selden who dreams of being a serious actress and scoffs at Don's dashing but phony film performances. All the same he falls in love with her and when sound comes in and the studio is worried about what to do with the nasal-sounding star Lina Lamont, he gets Kathy a job lip-syncing the voice for Lina on screen. The film is made and at the premiere the audience cheers Lina's beautiful singing voice. When it is revealed that Kathy is the real voice, she gets a contract and stars in the studio's next film musical.

Singin' in the Rain. One of the refreshing aspects of this movie classic is the way it takes nothing too seriously. In the long ballet sequence near the end, Gene Kelly (pictured) dances with the seductive Cyd Charisse and there is a slightly mocking tone in the choreography and in their performances. (Photofest)

Casts for *Singin' in the Rain*

Character	1952 film	1986 Broadway
Don Lockwood	GENE KELLY	Don Correia
Kathy Selden	DEBBIE REYNOLDS	Mary D'Arcy
Cosmo Brown	DONALD O'CONNOR	Peter Slutsker
Lina Lamont	Jean Hagen	Faye Grant
R. F. Simpson	Millard Mitchell	Hansford Rowe
Zelda Zanders	RITA MORENO	Mary Ann Kellogg
Featured dancer	CYD CHARISSE	

BETTY COMDEN and ADOLPH GREEN wrote the satirical screenplay using the HERB NACIO BROWN–ARTHUR FREED catalogue of songs as their inspiration. It is a splendid script that bounces along easily, with each scene punctuated with a song. The difficulties in making early talkies were presented hilariously and accurately, and the result was a good-natured spoof of Hollywood in general. Newcomer DEBBIE REYNOLDS was a sparkling revelation, GENE KELLY was at his best being both silly and romantic, and Jean Hagen gives one of the funniest supporting roles in Hollywood movies as the nasty, irritating Lina. The plot found room for sidekick DONALD O'CONNOR to give his most nimble performance ever and for naughty flapper CYD CHARISSE to make quite an impact wearing a Louise Brooks-like wig in a sultry pas de deux with Kelly. Even without the musical numbers, this film would have been a comic treasure. Except for the nonsense ditty "Moses (Supposes)" written by Comden, Green, and ROGER EDENS for the film and a new Brown–Freed number, "Make 'Em Laugh" for O'Connor to perform in one of the movie's most memorable scenes, the score was composed of old favorites that were so marvelously staged by co-director–choreographers Kelly and STANLEY DONEN that they are usually remembered for this film rather than their initial screen appearances. The title number was the most famous case in point. Kelly joyously splashing down the street as he's "Singin' in the Rain" is movie musical heaven. The big "Broadway Rhythm" ballet at the end was more playful than Kelly's usual long dance pieces and reaffirmed the satirical tone of the whole picture. Although it was only moderately successful in its first release, *Singin' in the Rain* has achieved cult status over the years and represents the finest hour of its stars and the whole Freed unit.

🕭 ***Singin' in the Rain*** (Gershwin Theatre 1985) was a misguided attempt to recreate the film on stage, falling rain and all. The movie musical had been adapted successfully for the stage in London but the New York version, directed and choreographed by Twyla Tharp, was deemed a miserable ordeal to sit through by the press. All the same, audiences wanted to relive the old film again and kept the large show on the boards for 367 performances. The unfortunate performers forced to compete with the movie performances were young and energetic but it was a fruitless endeavor, particularly when the libretto by Comden and Green was a pale version of their witty screenplay. The revised version of *Singin' in the Rain*, which later toured, was considered an improvement over the Broadway production, which is the version theatres produce when the show is revived in summer stock, schools, and community theatres.

🎬 **SINGING FOOL, THE** (Warner 1928). Although it may be little seen (or remembered) today, this part-talkie musical was the top-grossing movie in Hollywood history until *SNOW WHITE AND THE SEVEN DWARFS* (1937) came along nearly a decade later. C. Graham Baker and Joseph Jackson wrote the highly sentimental screenplay about the rise to fame of singing waiter Al Stone (AL JOLSON). When he finally achieves success and it goes to his head, Al's wife Molly (Josephine Dunn) walks out on him, leaving Al to raise their little boy Sonny Boy (Davey Lee). The child gets ill, Al sings "Sonny Boy" to him before the boy dies, and then Al sinks into despair, only to be rescued by the love of cigarette girl Grace (Betty Bronson). Jolson's unabashed, maudlin performance was tempered by his mighty delivery of the songs by various tunesmiths, including "It All Depends on You," "I'm Sittin' on Top of the World," "There's a Rainbow 'Round My Shoulder," and "Keep Smilin' at Trouble." LLOYD BACON directed the melodrama with all the emotional stops pulled out and audiences flocked to the theatres in droves. Like the earlier *THE JAZZ SINGER* (1927), the film was silent except for the musical numbers. The biggest hit of the many hits was "Sonny Boy," which, legend has it, B. G. DESYLVA, LEW BROWN, and RAY HENDERSON wrote with every saccharine cliché they could think of as a joke. The catchy

---

Singin' in the Rain (film) Musical Numbers

"Singin' in the Rain"
"Fit as a Fiddle"
"All I Do Is Dream of You"
"Make 'Em Laugh"
"I've Got a Feelin' You're Foolin'"
"The Wedding of the Painted Doll"
"Should I?"
"Beautiful Girl"
"You Were Meant for Me"
"Moses (Supposes)"
"Good Morning"
"Would You?"
"Broadway Melody"
"You Are My Lucky Star"

ballad sold over three million copies of sheet music and sales of Jolson's recording went over a million discs.

SIRETTA, DAN (1940?–). Stage choreographer. A vivacious dancer-turned-choreographer, he has a knack for staging revivals of old classic musicals. Siretta was educated at Juilliard and made his Broadway debut as a dancer in *FIORELLO!* (1959). He appeared in such musicals as *MR. PRESIDENT* (1962), *The Girl Who Came to Supper* (1963), *Walking Happy* (1966), and *Coco* (1969) before turning to choreographing in regional theatre. Siretta's dances for the GOODSPEED OPERA HOUSE production of the early JEROME KERN musical *VERY GOOD EDDIE* were seen on Broadway when the show transferred to New York in 1976. Manhattan has also seen his choreography for such vintage musical revivals as *Going Up!* (1976), *WHOOPEE!* (1979), *The Five O'Clock Girl* (1981), *LITTLE JOHNNY JONES* (1982), *TAKE ME ALONG* (1985), and *OH, KAY!* (1990), which he also directed. Siretta also choreographed the TV musical *A CHRISTMAS CAROL* (2004).

SISSLE, NOBLE (1889–1975). Stage lyricist and performer. The first African American lyricist to find success on Broadway, he was also an animated performer and interpreter of his songs. Sissle was born in Indianapolis and teamed up with composer EUBIE BLAKE, his only collaborator, in 1915 to sing with the pioneering black conductor James Reese Europe and his band. After Europe was murdered in 1919, the twosome did a vaudeville act together in which they avoided the traditional minstrel show caricatures and put emphasis on love and celebration songs, which they wrote themselves. They turned their act into a full-length show, the landmark musical *SHUFFLE ALONG* (1921), the first major hit on Broadway that was written, produced, and performed by African Americans. The rhythmic score and vivacious dancing set the pattern for black musicals for decades. Sissle performed a major role in the show, as he did with most of the team's subsequent musicals: *Elsie* (1923), *Chocolate Dandies* (1924), *Shuffle Along of 1933* (1932), *Shuffle Along of 1952*, and the West End musical *London Calling* (1923), which introduced "You Were Meant for Me." None of these enjoyed the success of their first hit, although some noteworthy songs came from them. He later conducted his own band, which was popular on tour and was featured in some film shorts. The team's songs were celebrated in the Broadway revue *Eubie* (1978). Sissle's lyric writing must be acknowledged not only for its own high quality but also for the groundwork it laid for later African American songwriters. Memoir: *Reminiscing With Sissle and Blake*, William Bolcom, Robert Kimball (1973).

◊ **1600 PENNSYLVANIA AVENUE** (Mark Hellinger Theatre 1976). A unanimously panned musical that lasted only seven performances on Broadway, it is a show that refuses to disappear because of its intriguing score by LEONARD BERNSTEIN (music) and ALAN JAY LERNER (lyrics). A musical history of the White House and its inhabitants up through the early 1900s, the show offered KEN HOWARD as all the presidents through Teddy Roosevelt and PATRICIA ROUTLEDGE as their first ladies. The African American servants Lud (GILBERT PRICE) and Seena (Emily Yancy) barely aged as the decades and different people flew by and only the house itself remained constant. The ambitious but disjointed libretto was by Lerner and the out-of-control musical became the fiasco of its season, the disaster on stage only surpassed by the fighting and tensions that occurred backstage during its painful preparation. Robert Whitehead and Roger L. Stevens produced, Gilbert Moses directed, and George Faison choreographed, and none were on friendly terms with the songwriters by opening night. The critics' only compliments were for the two leading players and few seemed to even notice the score. There was no original cast recording made so it took years before songs from the musical were performed or recorded and it eventually became clear that a worthwhile score existed underneath all the ashes. A reconstructed version of many of the songs was made in 2000 under the title *White House Cantata* and one can finally hear what kind of musical *1600 Pennsylvania Avenue* was meant to be. "Take Care of This House," "Duet for One," "Lud's Wedding/I Love My Wife," "The President Jefferson Sunday Luncheon Party March," and "If I Was a Dove" were among the many memorable numbers in the very American-sounding score.

SKELTON, [Richard Bernard] **RED** (1910–1997). Television and film performer. The beloved clown with a nervous chuckle, rubber face, and physical comedy appeared in just about every form of entertainment but didn't find fame until the arrival of television. Skelton was born in Vincennes, Indiana, the son of a circus clown who died before his son was born. He quit school at a young age to beg on the streets and later toured with a medicine show even though he was not yet an adolescent. Skelton worked on show boats, in circuses, burlesque, and vaudeville before finding some recognition on radio. His comic monologues led to a movie contract and he was cast as sidekicks or childish buffoons in a number of films, including the musicals *Having a Wonderful Time* (1938), *LADY, BE GOOD* (1941), *PANAMA HATTIE* (1942), *Ship Ahoy* (1942), *DuBARRY WAS A LADY* (1943), *I Dood It* (1943), *Thousands Cheer* (1943), *Bathing Beauty* (1944), *ZIEGFELD FOLLIES* (1946), *NEPTUNE'S DAUGHTER* (1949), *The Duchess of Idaho* (1950), *THREE LITTLE WORDS* (1950), *Excuse My Dust* (1951), *Texas Carnival* (1951), and *LOVELY TO LOOK AT* (1952). Skelton also had a popular radio show in the 1940s. Rarely was he cast in leading roles on screen but he became familiar enough to audiences that he was given his own television show in 1951 and it was a hit for twenty years. Television was the best medium for Skelton to demonstrate his versatility, letting him play a variety of characters that ranged from the farcical to the whimsical. He returned to Hollywood in the 1960s to make some nonmusicals and then spent the rest of his career doing concerts and personal appearances. Biographies: *Seeing Red: The Skelton in Hollywood's Closet*, Wes D. Gehring (2001); *Red Skelton*, Arthur Marx (1979).

SKINNER, RANDY (1952–). Stage, film, and television choreographer and director. This impressive choreographer's work has been seen only occasionally on Broadway, yet with effective results. Skinner was born in Columbus, Ohio, and educated at Ohio State University. He provided the lively dances for the short-lived *Ain't Broadway Grand* (1993) and both directed and choreographed the stage version of the Rodgers and Hammerstein film *STATE FAIR* (1996) before finding more success with the 2001 revival of *42ND STREET*. Skinner directed and choreographed *Lone Star Love* Off Broadway in 2004. He has choreographed regionally at the Kennedy Center, George Street Playhouse, Great Lakes Shakespeare Festival, Goodspeed Opera House, and other theatres and for national tours, such as the various road companies of *WHITE CHRISTMAS*, and for productions that traveled to Moscow and Japan. His work has been seen on television and film and he has choreographed for the *ENCORES!* series at the City Center.

■ **SKY'S THE LIMIT, THE** (RKO 1943). A minor musical effort but one worth noting for an atypical performance by FRED ASTAIRE (not wearing tails for the first time in his movie career) and the score by HAROLD ARLEN (music) and JOHNNY MERCER (lyrics). The Lynn Root and Frank Fenton screenplay centered on Flying Tiger war hero Fred Atwell (Astaire) who is not interested in glory and tends to be a moody loner. When his squadron sets off on a cross-country victory tour, Fred ducks out and, assuming the name Fred Burton, goes incognito and hits several bars. He meets and falls in love with the photographer Joan Marion (JOAN LESLIE) but she thinks he's only as drifter and will have nothing to do with him until the happy ending. Astaire was far from debonair in this picture, frequently drunk and unpleasant, if not morose as when he introduced the Arlen–Mercer standard "One for My Baby (And One More for the Road)." The score also included "A Lot in Common With You" and the standard "My Shining Hour." Leslie's singing had to be dubbed by Sally Sweetland but her dancing was good enough to keep up with Astaire. The supporting cast was a strong one, including ROBERT BENCHLEY, Robert Ryan, Elizabeth Patterson, Marjorie Gateson, ERIC BLORE, and conductor Freddie Slack who played himself and provided his orchestra for some of the music.

SLEZAK, WALTER [Leo] (1902–1983). Stage, film, and television performer. An opera-voiced singer, he played leading men in Broadway musicals and later character parts in Hollywood movies. Born in Vienna, Austria, the son of opera tenor Leo Slezak, he worked as a bank clerk to finance his medical studies and then was discovered by film director MICHAEL CURTIZ. Slezak appeared in several German and Austrian silents even as he started to sing on the Berlin stage. American producer LEE SHUBERT brought Slezak to New York where he made his Broadway debut in 1930 in the musical *Meet My Sister*. He found recognition as the music student Karl in the operetta *MUSIC IN THE AIR* (1932), followed by featured roles in *May Wine* (1935) and *I MARRIED AN ANGEL* (1938). Slezak put on weight in the late 1930s so when he made his first Hollywood film in 1942 he was cast in comic character roles. He appeared in dozens of movies, including the musicals *Step Lively* (1944), *THE PIRATE* (1948), *The Inspector General* (1949), *CALL ME MADAM* (1953), *Ten Thousand Bedrooms* (1957), and *The*

Wonderful World of the Brothers Grimm (1962). Slezak returned to Broadway in 1954 to play the elderly wooer Panisse in the musical *FANNY* and appeared in many television series and specials, including the TV musicals *PINOCCHIO* (1957), *Fenwick* (1968), and *The Legend of Robin Hood* (1968). He retained his operatic singing voice and sang at the Metropolitan Opera and other opera houses in the 1950s. Slezak retired in 1976 and lived in Switzerland for the rest of his life. Autobiography: *What Time's the Next Swan?* (1962).

SLIPPER AND THE ROSE, THE (Paradine/Universal 1976). A charming, beautifully filmed musical version of the Cinderella story, the British film offers few surprises but some first-rate performances and musical numbers. Director Bryan Forbes co-wrote the screenplay with songwriters Robert B. and RICHARD M. SHERMAN and, except for naming the kingdom Euphrania and adding the character of the Dowager Queen (Edith Evans), it sticks to the classic fairy tale. Gemma Craven was the put-upon Cinderella tormented by her stepmother (Margaret Lockwood) and stepsisters (Rosalind Ayres and Sherrie Hewson) and Richard Chamberlain was the prince who must wed to please his royal parents (Michael Hordern and Lally Bowers). A particular delight is Annette Crosbie as a funny, outspoken Fairy Godmother. The Sherman brothers provided the delightful score, which included the heartfelt "Once I Was Loved" for Cinderella, the comic "What Has Love Got to Do With Getting Married? for the Prince and his grandmother, the magical "Suddenly It Happened" for the Fairy Godmother and Cinderella, and the entrancing title song subtitled "He Danced With Me/She Danced With Me" for Cinderella and the Prince. The whole film looks and sounds very British, of course, making it a bit foreign and all the more fantastical.

SLOANE, A[lfred] **BALDWIN** (1872–1925). Stage composer. A prolific Broadway songwriter little remembered today, he scored nearly thirty musicals in a sixteen-year period at the turn of the twentieth century. Sloane was born in Baltimore where he started writing songs for local amateur productions. In New York he saw some of his work interpolated in Broadway shows but didn't get to write a complete score until *Jack and the Beanstalk* (1896). Working with a variety of lyricists, he composed the music for such musicals as *Broadway to Tokyo* (1900), *The Belle of Broadway* (1902), *The Mocking Bird* (1902), *THE WIZARD OF OZ* (1903), *The Summer Widowers* (1910), *Hokey Pokey* (1912), *Greenwich Village Follies* (1919 and 1920), and *China Rose* (1925). Perhaps his only song remembered today is "Heaven Will Protect the Working Girl," which MARIE DRESSLER introduced in *Tillie's Nightmare* (1910).

SMILING LIEUTENANT, THE (Paramount 1931). A scintillating fairy tale for adults, this MAURICE CHEVALIER vehicle boosted his ever-growing popularity and provided some continental sophistication to contrast the more vulgar musicals that were flooding the market at the time. SAMSON RAPHAELSON, Ernest Vajda, and ERNEST LUBITSCH adapted OSCAR STRAUSS's 1907 Viennese operetta for the screen. CLIFFORD GREY wrote English lyrics for the songs, and Lubitsch produced and directed with the lightness of a soufflé. Lieutenant Nikolaus von Preyn (Chevalier) has an eye for the ladies but, for some reason not worth explaining, he weds the rather plain Princess Anna (Miriam Hopkins) even though he is more attracted to the flirtatious Franzi (Claudette Colbert) who leads an all-women orchestra. Realizing she cannot compete with a princess, Franzi gives up "Niki" and even provides Anna with tips on how to make herself more beautiful and how to act more vivacious. CHARLES RUGGLES, GEORGE BARBIER, Hugh O'Connell, and Robert Strange rounded out the cast, and the waltzing score included "Breakfast Table Love," "One More Hour of Love," and "While Hearts Are Singing (Live for Today)."

SMITH, ALEXIS [born Gladys Smith] (1921–1993). Film and stage performer. The statuesque, elegant leading lady of films didn't become a musical star until she was fifty years old. Smith was born in Penticon, Canada, and performed in summer stock in her native country before going to Los Angeles City College where she was discovered by Hollywood talent agents and first put on the screen in 1940. She was usually cast as the cool, charming female or the calculating "other woman," and, although she rarely did any singing or dancing on screen, she appeared in six notable musicals: *THANK YOUR LUCKY STARS* (1943), *HOLLYWOOD CANTEEN* (1944), *RHAPSODY IN BLUE* (1945), *NIGHT AND DAY* (1946), *HERE COMES THE GROOM* (1951), and *Beau James* (1957). Never becoming a major star, she retired from the screen at the end of the 1950s and did a little television acting. Smith made a smashing Broadway debut as the jaded ex-*Follies* chorine Phyllis in the musical *FOLLIES* (1971) and returned to the New York stage three more times, including the short-lived musical *Platinum* (1978) in which she was lauded as the movie-star-turned-rock star Lila Halliday. She appeared in *APPLAUSE* and other musicals on tour and did a few more movies and television programs before her death at the age of seventy-two. Smith was a vibrant, witty musical performer and it is a shame no one knew it until so late in her career. She was long married to actor Craig Stevens (1918–2000).

SMITH, EDGAR [McPhail] (1857–1938). Stage lyricist and writer. An all-purpose author, he wrote plays, librettos, and lyrics for some 150 shows on Broadway. The Brooklyn native attended Pennsylvania Military Academy before beginning his career as an actor and, while working with various companies, he started writing sketches and then plays. His Broadway career started when he was asked to adapt European operettas and musicals for New York audiences, such as *Les Brigands* (1889) and *The Grand Duchess* (1890). He was so successful that he started writing original librettos and lyrics. In 1897 Smith teamed up with comics WEBER and FIELDS and, with composer JOHN STROMBERG, wrote musical burlesques featuring the "Dutch" comedians. *Pousse-Café* (1897), *Hurly Burly* (1898), *Cyranose de Bric-a-Brac* (1898), *Fiddle-Dee-Dee* (1900), *Hoity Toity* (1901), *Twirly Whirly* (1902), and others were very popular and Smith was much in demand. Even as he wrote nonmusicals, he continued to script and score musicals until 1930, collaborating with A. BALDWIN SLOANE, VICTOR HERBERT, and others for such works as *Dream City and the Magic Knight* (1906), *The Girl Behind the Counter* (1907), *Old Dutch* (1909), *Tillie's Nightmare* (1910), *Up and Down Broadway* (1910), *La Belle Paree* (1911), *Roly Poly* (1912), *THE BLUE PARADISE* (1915), *Robinson Crusoe, Jr.* (1916), *My Lady's Glove* (1917), *The Whirl of New York* (1921), *The Street Singer* (1929), and *Hello, Paris* (1930).

SMITH, HARRY B[ache] (1860–1936). Stage lyricist and writer. The American theatre's most prolific writer of lyrics and librettos, the reliable if rarely inspired author is believed to have written over 300 scripts for musicals in New York, Chicago, and elsewhere and to have penned some 6,000 lyrics. Smith was born in Buffalo and was working as a drama and music critic for Chicago's *Evening Journal* when he started writing scripts and lyrics for touring companies coming though town. Soon he was in such demand that he gave up journalism and concentrated on theatre, writing quickly but intelligently to order. Before he retired in 1932 he had penned 123 musicals for Broadway. Smith's first New York entry was *The Begum* (1887) with composer REGINALD DeKOVEN. The two collaborated on many other shows, none more popular than *ROBIN HOOD* (1891), the most produced American operetta of the nineteenth century. Throughout his career, Smith worked with such renowned composers as A. BALDWIN SLOANE, VICTOR HERBERT, John Stromberg, JOHN PHILIP SOUSA, JEROME KERN, Ivan Caryll, SIGMUND ROMBERG, and IRVING BERLIN, and adapted musicals by such Europeans as Gustave Kerker, Emmerich Kalman, Franz Lehar, OSCAR STRAUS, and Jacques Offenbach. A list of his most notable works would include *The Serenade* (1897), *THE FORTUNE TELLER* (1898), *The Singing Girl* (1899), *The Casino Girl* (1900), *The Little Duchess* (1901), *Babette* (1903), *The Rich Mr. Hoggenheimer* (1906), *ZIEGFELD FOLLIES* (1907 through 1910 and 1912), *The Spring Maid* (1910), *Gypsy Love* (1911), *A Winsome Widow* (1912), *SWEETHEARTS* (1913), *THE GIRL FROM UTAH* (1914), *WATCH YOUR STEP* (1914), *Stop! Look! Listen!* (1915), *Angel Face* (1919), *Princess Flavia* (1925), *COUNTESS MARITZA* (1926), *Cherry Blossoms* (1927), *Three Little Girls* (1930), and *Marching By* (1932). While Smith's work may appear clichéd and routine by later standards, he was an intelligent, dedicated writer who was highly respected by his colleagues and the audiences of his day. His brother was librettist and lyricist ROBERT B. SMITH. Autobiography: *First Nights and First Editions* (1931); biography: *Harry B. Smith: Dean of American Librettists*, John Franceschina (2003).

SMITH, QUEENIE (1898–1978). Stage, film, and television performer. A small, round-faced, energetic singer–dancer who usually stopped the show playing supporting roles, she epitomized the Roaring Twenties flapper. The native New Yorker began dance training when she was just a child at the Metropolitan Opera Ballet School where she later performed as an adult. In 1919 she left ballet for the musical stage where she played second leads in *Roly-Boly Eyes* (1919), *Just Because* (1922), *Orange Blossoms* (1922), and *Helen of Troy, New York*

(1923). Smith's two most memorable roles were spunky Dixie trying to reform a crook in *Sitting Pretty* (1924) and the down-and-out vaudevillian Tip-Toes Kaye looking for a rich husband in *TIP-TOES* (1925). Her later musicals include *Be Yourself* (1924), *Judy* (1927), *Street Singer* (1929), and *A Little Racketeer* (1932), as well as replacing the starring part of Loulou in *HIT THE DECK* (1927). During the Depression, Smith turned to Hollywood where she made many films, including the musicals *MISSISSIPPI* (1935), *SHOW BOAT* (1936), *ON YOUR TOES* (1939), and *MY SISTER EILEEN* (1955). For many years she was the drama teacher at Hollywood Professional School, training many future stars, and she acted in dozens of television programs up until the year of her death.

SMITH, ROBERT B[ache] (1875–1951). Stage lyricist and writer. The long-forgotten Broadway author and lyric writer has been overshadowed by his prolific brother HARRY B. SMITH, yet he contributed to some thirty Broadway musicals in the early years of the twentieth century. Smith was born in Chicago and began writing as a reporter for the *Brooklyn Eagle* before he became press agent for the celebrated Casino Theatre in Manhattan. After writing sketches and lyrics for burlesque and vaudeville houses, his work was seen on Broadway with the WEBER and FIELDS musical spoof *Twirly Whirly* (1902) in which he collaborated with composer John Stromberg on the hit song "Come Down, Ma Evenin' Star." Few of Smith's subsequent shows were of that quality. Before retiring in 1920, he wrote the lyrics and/or co-wrote the scripts for such shows as *A China Doll* (1904), *Fantana* (1905), *The Girl and the Wizard* (1909), *The Spring Maid* (1910), *Gypsy Love* (1911), *The Rose Maid* (1913), *SWEETHEARTS* (1913), *The Debutante* (1914), *Follow Me* (1916), *Angel Face* (1919), and *The Girl in the Spotlight* (1920).

SMOKEY JOE'S CAFE (Virginia Theatre 1995). The longest-running Broadway revue on record, the show was a celebration of the pop songs by the team of JERRY LEIBER and MIKE STOLLER. Numbers first sung by artists such as ELVIS PRESLEY in the 1950s and 1960s were turned into a vivacious and unpretentious revue that was smartly directed by JERRY ZAKS and choreographed by JOEY MCKNEELY. The original cast included Brenda Braxton, Ken Ard, Victor Trent Cook, Michael Park, and Pattie Darcy Jones, and among the many songs they performed were "On Broadway," "Stand By Me,' "I'm a Woman," "Treat Me Nice," "Yakety Yak," "Fools Fall in Love," "Keep on Rollin'," "Charlie Brown," and "That Is Rock and Roll." Reviewers thought it a harmless enough entertainment but audiences embraced it and by the time the show closed it had given 2,036 performances.

SNOW WHITE AND THE SEVEN DWARFS (Disney/RKO 1937). A landmark film that was a series of firsts: the first feature-length animated movie, the first cartoon to use life models to simulate human movement, the first animated feature to use a multiplane camera to achieve depth, the first movie musical to produce (in 1944) a best-selling soundtrack, and the first Hollywood film to earn over $6 million on its initial release. However, the movie's greatness lies in the fact that it doesn't look like the primitive first of anything.

Plot: Every time the Queen asks her Magic Mirror who is the fairest in the land, it replies that she is. But when Snow White grows up and the mirror tells the Queen that the young orphan is the fairest, the jealous monarch orders the huntsman to take the girl deep into the forest and kill her. Unable to carry out her wishes, he tells Snow White to flee and never return to the castle. The lost Snow White stumbles upon the cottage of the seven dwarfs whom she befriends. When the Queen learns from the mirror that Snow White lives, she swallows a potion turning her into an aged old crone and goes to the cottage offering Snow White a poisoned apple. One bite and Snow White falls into a comma before the dwarfs return and chase the queen/crone to the edge of a ravine where she falls and dies while trying to destroy the dwarfs with a boulder. The dwarfs do not have the heart to bury the still-lovely Snow White and are kneeling in reverence before her

Cast for *Snow White and the Seven Dwarfs*

Character	Performer
Snow White	Adriana Caselotti
Queen	Lucille La Verne
Prince	Harry Stockwell
Doc	Roy Atwell
Sneezy	BILLY GILBERT
Grumpy/Sleepy	Pinto Colvig
Happy	Otis Harlan
Bashful	Scotty Mattraw
Dopey	Eddie Collins
Magic Mirror	Moroni Olsen
Huntsman	Stuart Buchanan

Snow White and the Seven Dwarfs. The dwarfs have no names or distinct characters in the original Grimm fairy tale but Walt Disney and his writers and animators, with their love of lively supporting characters, were not going to miss out on bringing the seven little men to life. They considered many adjectives before narrowing the list to seven (including Doc who is the only noun) and then proceeded to script and animate the much-loved dwarfs. One has only to look at their faces and you can probably remember their names. (Photofest)

body when a Prince whom Snow White has once glimpsed comes into the forest, kisses the sleeping Snow White, and she awakes to see that her prince has truly come.

Producer WALT DISNEY and hundreds of artists labored for four years on the project, which the film community saw as a grand folly. The very idea of a cartoon lasting eighty-three minutes, of animated characters singing love songs to each other, and of artists creating a complex and detailed art decor for a kid's movie was laughable. However, the film changed the way audiences thought about cartoons, children's movies, and Disney. The script took liberties with the original Grimm Brothers' tale and created names and individual characters for the dwarfs. Although softening some of the original story's more gruesome aspects, the film was still frightening and powerful at times, yet warmhearted and fanciful in other spots. Never had moviegoers got so caught up in an animated tale and the public, both children and adults, liked the experience.

> ### Snow White and the Seven Dwarfs Musical Numbers
> "I'm Wishing"
> "One Song"
> "With a Smile and a Song"
> "Whistle While You Work"
> "Heigh-Ho"
> "Bluddle-Uddle-Um-Dum"
> "Isn't This a Silly Song?" (Dwarfs' Yodeling Song)
> "Some Day My Prince Will Come"

FRANK CHURCHILL (music) and Larry Morey (lyrics) wrote the songs, several of which became hits, and just about all of them are now part of musical folklore. The songwriters turned to operetta for the romantic numbers, such as "One Song," "I'm Wishing," and "Someday My Prince Will Come," and then used musical comedy for the dwarfs, as with "Heigh-Ho" "and "The Dwarfs' Yodeling Song." Also very effective was the music background score by

Leigh Harline and Paul J. Smith, adding suspense and drama throughout. It is interesting that Disney saw his initial animated feature as a musical, but then he had been experimenting with music in cartoons for some time and always saw music and action linked. *Snow White and the Seven Dwarfs* started a tradition of animated features being musicals and very few Disney products over the decades would offer animation without songs. To celebrate the fiftieth anniversary of the film, the studio rereleased it in 1987 with 4,000 prints seen in fifty-eight countries on the same day, the largest opening day in the history of the movies.

📽 Stage versions of Disney's *Snow White and the Seven Dwarfs* have been produced on occasion over the last forty years, usually in large venues such as the ST. LOUIS MUNICIPAL OPERA or Radio City Music Hall in New York. These have tended to emphasize spectacle so the story and characters were usually diminished and only the audience's familiarity with the film allowed the show to connect in their minds. Of all the Disney films that the studio has looked at as possible Broadway entries, *Snow White and the Seven Dwarfs* has not been on the list of possibilities. It seems that Walt Disney's first masterpiece cannot be improved upon.

📺 **So HELP ME, APHRODITE** (NBC-TV 1960). NANETTE FABRAY got a juicy role that demonstrated her many talents in this sixty-minute musical with fantasy elements. Danny Arnold's teleplay concerned Sally, a waitress at a diner frequented by truck drivers, who is always fantasizing about being famous, being Pocahontas, being Marie Antoinette, being anyone but Sally. All this daydreaming makes her a forgetful and inefficient waitress and she would get fired but the owner of the diner is hopelessly in love with her. When Sally's daydreams, which are filled with the truckers in various guises, get

to be too much, she comes back to the real world and accepts the love of her boss. Tony Randall, Jean-Pierre Aumont, STUBBY KAYE, and Robert Strauss were also in the cast, and the songs were by Arnold (lyrics) and JACK BROOKS (music and lyrics). "Save a Place on the Wall," "You've Got to Keep a Woman in the Right-Hand Lane," "Po-Po-Pocahontas," and "Who Needs It" were used to illustrate Sally's fantasies, and Fabray was a marvel as she evolved into different personages in the flash of an eye. Larry Burns produced the *Ford Startime* broadcast and Bob Henry directed.

📽 **SOMETHING FOR THE BOYS** (Alvin Theatre 1943). One of several ETHEL MERMAN–COLE PORTER combinations, this musical did not reveal songwriter Porter at his best but Merman was so the show ran 422 performances. Chorine-turned-defense worker Blossom Hart (Merman) and her cousins, nightclub singer Chiquita Hart (Paula Lawrence) and carnival pitchman Harry Hart (Allen Jenkins), inherit a Texas ranch, which is near an army base. Blossom falls for Sgt. Rocky Fulton (BILL JOHNSON) and invites him and other enlisted men to the ranch but the army mistakes the farm for a brothel and puts it off limits. In the end Blossom is vindicated and declared a hero when the fillings in her teeth pick up the distress signals from a faltering government plane and it is rescued. HERBERT and DOROTHY FIELDS penned the ridiculous libretto and Porter provided the hit song "Hey, Good Lookin'." Also in the score were "Could It Be You?," "By the Mississinewah," "When My Baby Goes to Town," "He's a Right Guy," and the title song. The plot was a shambles and much of the score disappointing but Merman made both seem like gold and the critics declared the musical a delightful diversion. MICHAEL TODD produced, HASSARD SHORT and Herbert Fields co-directed, and JACK COLE choreographed.

Casts for *Something for the Boys*

Character	1943 Broadway	1944 film
Blossom Hart	ETHEL MERMAN	VIVIAN BLAINE
Sgt. Rocky Fulton	BILL JOHNSON	Michael O'Shea
Chiquita Hart	Paula Lawrence	CARMEN MIRANDA
Harry Hart	Allen Jenkins	PHIL SILVERS
Sgt. Laddie Green	Stuart Langley	PERRY COMO
Melanie Walker	Frances Mercer	Sheila Ryan
Lt. Grubbs/Crothers	Jack Hartley	Glenn Langan
Mary-Francis	BETTY GARRETT	

■ **Something for the Boys** (Fox 1944) came to the screen with only the title song, which was a shame, and without Merman, which was worse. Instead, CARMEN MIRANDA was starred and the action was moved from Texas to the backwoods of Kentucky, as if that was a better milieu for the Brazilian bombshell. Miranda was at the peak of her popularity and stole every movie in which she had previously appeared, but her funny, outrageous performance as Chiquita Hart (her sister Blossom was played by VIVIAN BLAINE) was starting to look too familiar. Her career started to wane with *Something for the Boys* and this and very few of her subsequent movies were hits. JIMMY MCHUGH (music) and HAROLD ADAMSON (lyrics) wrote the new songs for the film, which included "I Wish We Didn't Have to Say Goodnight," "Samba Boogie," "Wouldn't It Be Nice?," and "Boom Brachee." The supporting cast included PERRY COMO, making his screen debut and singing "I'm in the Middle of Nowhere."

SON OF PALEFACE. See *PALEFACE, THE*

SONDHEIM, STEPHEN [Joshua] (1930–). Stage, television, and film songwriter. The most daring and often demanding composer–lyricist of his era, he wrote scores for many Broadway musicals that have met with uneven popular success but usually receive high acclaim by critics and dedicated audiences. Sondheim was born in New York City, the son of a prosperous businessman, and was educated at the George School in Newtown, Pennsylvania, where he met James Hammerstein, the youngest son of OSCAR HAMMERSTEIN. Sondheim soon became familiar with the whole Hammerstein family, who lived nearby in Bucks County, and Oscar adopted the precocious young man as his protégé. Sondheim attended Williams College where he studied music with Milton Babbitt and scored collegiate musicals. After graduation he wrote radio scripts and crossword puzzles, finally making his Broadway writing debut as the lyricist for *WEST SIDE STORY* (1957). He also penned the lyrics for *GYPSY* (1959) before Broadway heard its first Sondheim score— music and lyrics—in the popular *A FUNNY THING HAPPENED ON THE WAY TO THE FORUM* (1962). His emerging experimentation was seen in the short-lived musical *ANYONE CAN WHISTLE* (1964) and, after writing lyrics for *DO I HEAR A WALTZ?* (1965), he hit his stride with a series of musicals in the 1970s that were not always commercially successful but never

Stephen Sondheim. Although he has won many awards and honors, few of his musicals have been financial hits. He demands much from himself and from his audiences; that is the Sondheim legacy. This photo of the songwriter was taken in 1963 when he was writing *Anyone Can Whistle* (1964). (Photofest)

less than fascinating: *COMPANY* (1971), *FOLLIES* (1971), *A LITTLE NIGHT MUSIC* (1973), *PACIFIC OVERTURES* (1976), and *SWEENEY TODD, THE DEMON BARBER OF FLEET STREET* (1979). His adventurous *MERRILY WE ROLL ALONG* (1981) had a short run, but *SUNDAY IN THE PARK WITH GEORGE* (1984) and *INTO THE WOODS* (1987) found wider acceptance. Sondheim's other musical credits include *Saturday Night* (1954 and 2000), new lyrics for *CANDIDE* (1974), *ASSASSINS* (1991), *PASSION* (1994), *The Frogs* (2004), and *Bounce* (2003), which never made it to New York. The musical revues *Side By Side By Sondheim* (1977), *Marry Me a Little* (1980), and *Putting It Together* (1993 and 1999) celebrate his songs. The only Sondheim musicals to be filmed have been *West Side Story* (1961), *Gypsy* (1962), *A Funny Thing Happened on the Way to the Forum* (1967), *A Little Night Music* (1978), and *Sweeney Todd* (2007), although others have been preserved on video. He has also scored songs for a few movies, such as *DICK TRACY* (1990) and *The Birdcage* (1996), for the TV musical *EVENING PRIMROSE* (1966), and written instrumental music for films and plays. While Sondheim's tough, ingenious and sometimes abrasive scores might not have wide appeal, there is an uncompromising quality and an acute sense of dedication that ties him with Oscar Hammerstein as the younger songwriter has continued his teacher's quest for high craftsmanship and experimentation in the musical theatre form. In many ways Sondheim can be viewed as the continuation of the bold adventure begun by Hammerstein in the 1920s. Biography: *Stephen Sondheim, A Life*, Meryle Secrest (1998).

☞ **SONG OF NORWAY** (Imperial Theatre 1944). One of the most successful of all the musicals utilizing classical music, this biographical operetta about the life of Edvard Grieg did not have a very gripping story but the music was wonderful. The Norwegian composer Grieg is married to the faithful Nina but the seductive prima donna Louisa Giovanni lures him away from Nina and his homeland and sets him up in Italy until the voices of his wife and Norway call him back home. Milton Lazarus penned the routine libretto, and ROBERT WRIGHT and GEORGE FORREST adapted Grieg's music and wrote romantic lyrics for the classical themes, turning it all into a very pleasing Broadway score. "Strange Music" was the most popular number but also enjoyable were "Hill of Dreams," "Freddie and His Fiddle," "Now!," "Three Loves," and "Midsummer's Eve." The highly romanticized musical was a hit on the West Coast so producer Edwin Lester brought it to New York where it was welcomed by the press and playgoers, running for 860 performances. Charles K. Freeman directed the cast of first-rate singers, and GEORGE BALANCHINE did the choreography. *Song of Norway* was a favorite with light opera and summer stock companies for years.

■ **Song of Norway** (ABC 1970) would never have been filmed except that the phenomenal success of the film THE SOUND OF MUSIC (1965) had the studios scouring the files for similar properties. Someone in California decided that the Scandinavian fiords would do for *Song of Norway* what the Alps did for that outdoors blockbuster. Any Norwegian operetta film was most likely to fail in the 1970s but few suspected it would end up as bad as this. The screenplay by Virginia and Andrew Stone was embarrassingly sentimental and incompetent, and even the great music was bearable only when used as background to the lovely scenery. Toralv Maurstadt and FLORENCE HENDERSON were Mr. and Mrs. Grieg and they had to be the cinema's odd couple of the decade. Andrew Stone was the director and LEE THEODORE the unfortunate choreographer. If the Hollywood operetta wasn't totally dead by 1970, this movie certainly killed it.

■ **SONG OF THE SOUTH** (Disney/RKO 1946) Although it was not Disney's first blending of animation and live action, the process had never been perfected and used as effectively as it was in this folklore musical. Dalton S. Reymond and a team of scriptwriters adapted Joel Chandler Harris' *Tales of Uncle Remus* into an inspired piece of filmmaking that has bothered some modern sensibilities. The live-action portion of the film concerned young Johnny (BOBBY DRISCOLL) whose parents separate and he goes to live in the South where he befriends Uncle Remus (James Baskett) and the local farm girl Ginny (Luana Patten). Johnny's dealings with his overprotective mother (Ruth Warrick), his grandmother (Lucile Watson), and some bullies in the neighborhood are interrupted by the animated stories that Remus tells him about Brer Rabbit (voice of Johnny Lee), Brer Fox (Baskett), and Brer Bear (Nicodemus Stewart). The animated sequences are much more satisfying than the melodrama involving the humans, but the whole movie has a lazy charm about it that was often winning. Various tunesmiths wrote the songs, most of them excellent: "Everybody's Got a Laughing Place," "How Do You Do?," "Sooner or Later," and

Casts for *Song of Norway*		
Character	*1944 Broadway*	*1970 film*
Edvard Grieg	Lawrence Brooks	Toralv Maurstad
Nina Hagerup	Helena Bliss	FLORENCE HENDERSON
Louisa Giovanni	IRRA PETINA	
Rikard Nordraak	Robert Shafer	Frank Poretta
Count Peppi'Berg	Sig Arno	Robert Morley
Bjoernson		Harry Secombe
Krogstad		Edward G. Robinson

the Oscar-winning "Zip-a-Dee-Doo-Dah" by RAY GILBERT and ALLIE WRUBEL. Harve Foster directed the live-action part of the film and Wilfred Jackson oversaw the animated tales. Although the movie was very popular in both the South and across the States in its first release, some African American groups complained about the antiquated view of southern blacks, and rumblings got so loud during the civil rights movement in the 1960s that the studio withdrew the film from circulation. It was not made available again until 1972.

🎭 **SOPHISTICATED LADIES** (Lunt-Fontanne Theatre 1981). One of the better musical revues that followed in the footsteps of *AIN'T MISBEHAVIN'* (1978) and featured the work of an African American composer, this show offered thirty-six numbers by DUKE ELLINGTON and the result was delightful. Choreographer DONALD MCKAYLE conceived of the revue as a nightclub floor show but it was director Michael Smuin who took over and made the musical one of the most glittering productions of the decade.

Sophisticated Ladies. The music of Duke Ellington conjures up images of the Harlem renaissance and this revue brought those images to life. The first-rate cast was led by Gregory Hines and Judith Jamison (pictured) who could evoke attitude in each little facial expression and gesture. (Photofest)

Songs composer Ellington wrote with various lyricists were given a lavish and sleek presentation by a nimble cast in glittering art deco settings. The dynamic cast included GREGORY HINES, Judith Jamison, HINTON BATTLE, Terri Klausner, Gregg Burge, Mercedes Ellington, and Phyllis Hyman. Among the musical highlights were "Satin Doll," "I Let a Song Go Out of My Heart," "It Don't Mean a Thing (If It Ain't Got that Swing)," "I'm Beginning to See the Light," "I'm Just a Lucky So-and-So," "Mood Indigo," "Do Nothing Till You Hear From Me,' and "Sophisticated Lady." Critical cheers translated into a run of 767 performances.

SOTHERN, ANN [born Hariette Lake] (1909–2001). Film, stage, and television performer. A bouncy blonde singer–actress with a pleasantly nasal voice, she enjoyed a long career that covered various media. Sothern was born in Valley City, North Dakota, the daughter of a soprano concert singer, and educated at the University of Washington. She trained for a singing career and using her birth name was cast in a bit part in the movie musical *THE SHOW OF SHOWS* (1929). Sothern then went to New York where she eventually played leading roles in the Broadway musicals *America's Sweetheart* (1931) and *Everybody's Welcome* (1931). She toured as the female principal in *OF THEE I SING* before returning to Hollywood and getting another bit part in *Broadway Through a Keyhole* (1933). In 1934 she changed her name to Ann Sothern and started getting featured roles in comedies and mostly B musicals, such as *Let's Fall in Love* (1934), *Melody in Spring* (1934), *Kid Millions* (1934), *FOLIES BERGERE DE PARIS* (1935), *Hooray for Love* (1935), *The Girl Friend* (1935), and *Walking on Air* (1936). Sothern got to better quality pictures in the 1940s, including a series of "Maisie" farces and the musicals *LADY, BE GOOD* (1941), *PANAMA HATTIE* (1942), *Thousands Cheer* (1943), *April Shows* (1948), *WORDS AND MUSIC* (1938), and *Nancy Goes to Rio* (1950). In the 1950s she appeared in dramatic roles on film and in two of her own television shows. Sothern returned to the theatre in touring productions and was still acting in the late 1980s.

🎭 **SOUND OF MUSIC, THE** (Lunt-Fontanne Theatre 1959). Arguably the most well-known musical by RICHARD RODGERS (music) and OSCAR HAMMERSTEIN (lyrics) because of its famous movie version and many regional revivals, it is also the only work by the team that Hammerstein did not write the libretto.

Casts for *The Sound of Music*

Character	1959 Broadway	1965 film	1998 Broadway
Maria	MARY MARTIN	JULIE ANDREWS	REBECCA LUKER
Capt. Von Trapp	Theodore Bikel	Christopher Plummer	Michael Siberry
Mother Abbess	Patricia Neway	PEGGY WOOD	PATTI COHENOUR
Liesl	Laurie Peters	Charmian Carr	Sara Zelle
Rolf	BRIAN DAVIES	Daniel Truhitte	Dashiell Eaves
Max Detweiler	KURT KASZNAR	Richard Haydn	Fred Applegate
Elsa Schraeder	Marion Marlowe	ELEANOR PARKER	Jan Maxwell

Plot: The Mother Abbess and her advisors at the Austrian Abbey at Nonnberg are not sure the spirited postulant Maria Rainer is a good candidate for the religious order so Maria is sent to serve as governess for the seven children of the widower Captain Georg Von Trapp. The children are reluctant to like the new governess until she teaches them to sing and she even manages to soften the stern exterior of their father. Although he is engaged to wed the sophisticated baroness Elsa Schrader, the Captain finds himself attracted to Maria. When the Nazis take over Austria, the Captain and the Baroness disagree on how to handle the political situation and break off the engagement. The Captain and Maria wed but, on returning from their honeymoon, the Captain is ordered to serve in the German Navy. Rather than bow to the Nazis, he and his family slip away during a musical festival in which they are performing and escape over the mountains to Switzerland and freedom.

HOWARD LINDSAY and RUSSEL CROUSE based their libretto on Maria Von Trapp's 1948 autobiography *The Story of the Van Trapp Family Singers*, which had been filmed as two sequential German movies, *Die Trapp Familie* (1956) and *Die Trapp Familie in Amerika* (1958). The previous Lindsay and Crouse musicals, such as *RED, HOT AND BLUE* (1936), *CALL ME MADAM* (1950), and *Happy Hunting* (1956), were loosely held together star vehicles; however, when they wrote the libretto for *The Sound of Music*, it came out in the pattern of a Rodgers and Hammerstein show, complete with governess, kids, big inspiring ballad, and all the rest. Since neither Hammerstein nor Rodgers had a hand in writing the script, it is curious how those who dislike the show's sweetness blame the songwriters. In some ways *The Sound of Music* is a gentle parody of a Rodgers and Hammerstein musical. Yet the libretto also has some of the team's fine points: a solid story, logical integration of script and score, and

some serious issues to contend with. Those too familiar with the later film version forget that politics and the subjugation of one country by another are important elements in the stage musical. There is also a sarcasm at times that is used to offset all the naiveté of Maria and the squeals of children's laughter. The baroness and her pal Max are cynical, practical people who seem to have wandered into the story from *PAL JOEY*. The two songs by Rodgers and Hammerstein that illustrate their wry sense of sophistication, "How Can Love Survive?" and "No Way to Stop It," were not in the movie but they are very necessary in the play. The score for *The Sound of Music* is a variable one, but one tends to remember the lightweight ditties such as "Do-Re-Mi," "Sixteen Going on Seventeen," "My Favorite Things," "and "The Lonely Goatherd." The title song is much fuller in imagery and exultation than these; it is an anthem as deeply felt as the more somber "Climb Ev'ry Mountain." The humor in "Maria" might be too bland for some tastes but it is the comic lament of a trio of nuns, not musical comedy figures. Like them or not, the songs fit the show. The preparation of *The Sound of Music* was done mostly without Hammerstein who already knew about his terminal cancer. Late in the rehearsal period, Rodgers and the creative staff realized that the Von Trapp family needed a new song to sing at the festival, not another reprise. They asked Hammerstein to oblige and he wrote the folk song "Edelweiss," a simple and unadorned number about the Austrian mountain flower. It was the last lyric he ever wrote. Rodgers and Hammerstein produced the show with LELAND HAYWARD and Richard Halliday, VINCENT J. DONEHUE directed, and JOE LAYTON did the choreography. The reviews were mixed but the popular reaction was not so divided and the musical immediately became an audience favorite, running 1,443 performances and selling over $1 million worth of cast albums. The first national tour featured FLORENCE

The Sound of Music (stage) Musical Numbers

"Preludium"
"The Sound of Music"
"Maria"
"My Favorite Things"
"Do-Re-Mi"
"Sixteen Going on Seventeen"
"The Lonely Goatherd"
"How Can Love Survive?"
"Laendler Dance"
"So Long, Farewell"
"Climb Ev'ry Mountain"
"No Way to Stop It"
"Ordinary Couple"
"Processional"
"Edelweiss"

HENDERSON as Maria and remained on the road for two years. The Broadway production was recreated for London in 1961 with Jean Bayless and Roger Dann in the leads and remained at the Palace Theatre for 2,385 performances, three years longer than the Broadway run. *The Sound of Music* quickly became a favorite with every kind of theatre group in America, from high schools to Broadway revivals. The musical returned to Manhattan in 1967 when the New York City Light Opera Company revived it with CONSTANCE TOWERS as Maria and Robert Wright as the Captain. The 1990 revival by the New York City Opera, featuring Debby Boone and LAURENCE GUITTARD, was not well received but a 1998 production directed by SUSAN SCHULMAN and starring REBECCA LUKER and Michael Siberry was enthusiastically applauded and ran 533 performances. Notable London revivals include a 1981 version with PETULA CLARK, a 1992 production with Liz Robertson, and a 2006 revival in which Maria, Connie Fisher, was chosen by the public voting on candidates on a series of television auditions called *How Do You Solve a Problem Like Maria?*

 The Sound of Music (Fox 1965) has been seen around the world by more people than perhaps any other film musical. In some American cities, the number of citizens who saw it doubled the population figures. Legends about individuals who have seen it over 600 times are staggering because they are more than just legends. It is perhaps the most beloved movie of all time, loved in a way you can't embrace *The Birth of a Nation* or *Gone With the Wind*. It is also a film much derided for its sentimentality, sweetness, and wholesomeness. *The Sound of Music* is the movie people love to hate, just as it is the movie they hate to love. The movie is also one of the least American musicals, sometimes closer to European operetta than Broadway, and extremely proficient, highly polished, and beautifully filmed. All of the right pieces fell into place and, not to belittle the creative people behind it, *The Sound of Music* was a very fortunate fluke. Consider the film that might have been. William Wyler, an expert Hollywood director with no musical experience, was slated to direct; he withdrew and was replaced by producer ROBERT WISE who had done many exciting things with the film version of *WEST SIDE STORY* (1961). Movie stars AUDREY HEPBURN, DORIS DAY, and Romy Schneider were considered for Maria. JULIE ANDREWS had not yet appeared on the screen but when the producers saw some early footage of *MARY POPPINS* (1964), they grabbed her. Although 20TH CENTURY-FOX was on a budget-cutting campaign, the producers insisted that the movie had to have some location shooting in Austria. Someone must have sensed that Salzburg was the other star of the show. ERNEST LEHMAN's screenplay is sometimes an improvement over the stage libretto, even if it cut out much of the political elements of the story and replaced them with romantic ones. Rodgers wrote both music and lyrics for two new songs ("Something Good" and "I Have Confidence") and they were excellent. Choreographers MARC BREAUX and DEEDEE WOOD worked with Lehman and Wise in opening up the musical as few musicals have ever been opened up for the screen. Everything seemed to work. Christopher Plummer might not have been too happy, taking on the role of the Captain only because he wanted to sing and then finding his songs dubbed by Bill Lee. PEGGY WOOD, the great operetta star of old, also had to be dubbed (by Margery McKay) because her glorious soprano voice was gone. But these were minor difficulties. For the most part, *The Sound of Music* was charmed from the start and has remained charmed ever since. The wildly mixed film reviews echoed those of the Broadway critics. Moviegoers didn't care about the reviews and ticket sales passed $79 million in 1965 dollars. As sometimes happens, the popularity of the movie made the stage musical more famous and there were more productions of *The Sound of Music* on the boards than before the film opened. Although it has been available on video for several years, movie houses still present *The Sound of Music* on the big screen. By the end of the century, "sing-along" showings of the movie became a fad in Great Britain and then in the States, with the audience dressing up like the characters and singing the songs either from memory or from the lyrics projected on the screen. This sort of thing only happens to films such as THE ROCKY HORROR PICTURE SHOW, but *The Sound of Music* is, in its own wholesome way, a cult film as well.

SOUSA, JOHN PHILIP (1854–1932). Stage composer, conductor, and musician. America's celebrated "March King" who wrote and conducted some of the nation's most beloved orchestral pieces, he was also a respected composer of comic operettas on Broadway. Sousa was born in Washington, DC, the son a Portuguese father and Bavarian mother, and studied music as a boy. He got further experience as an apprentice to the U.S. Marine Band before getting work conducting pit orchestras for Broadway musicals. Sousa turned to composing for the stage and saw his first work, *The Smugglers* (1879), and three other operettas produced in Philadelphia. The next year he was made bandmaster of the Marine Band and gained fame as a conductor and for the marches he composed for the band, yet Sousa still pursued a stage career. His first Broadway show, EL CAPITAN (1896), was his most successful, and working with various lyricists he also scored *The Bride Elect* (1989), *The Charlatan* (1989), *Chris and the Wonderful Lamp* (1900), *The Free Lance* (1906), and *The American Maid* [aka *The Glass Blowers*] (1913). Sousa sometimes wrote songs added to others' scores and he and his band appeared on the Hippodrome stage in the Broadway revue *Hip Hip Hooray* (1915). Because of his renown as a march composer, Sousa's theatre work was long neglected and only recently has started to be revived by opera companies. CLIFTON WEBB played the conductor–composer in the film bio *Stars and Stripes Forever* (1952), and Sousa's march melodies were turned into songs for the Broadway musi-

cal *Teddy and Alice* (1987). Autobiography: *Marching Along* (1928); biography: *John Philip Sousa: American Phenomenon*, Paul E. Bierley (2001).

SOUTH PACIFIC (Majestic Theatre 1949). Perhaps the most adult of the RICHARD RODGERS (music) and OSCAR HAMMERSTEIN (book and lyrics) musicals, its story is not dictated merely by romance but also by prejudice and fear.

Plot: During the Pacific campaign of World War II, the young nurse Nellie Forbush from Little Rock, Arkansas, falls in love with the older, gentlemanly Emile de Becque who left France years ago to become a planter on an island where the Allies are now stationed. The upper-class Lieutenant Joe Cable from Philadelphia arrives on the island to prepare for a dangerous mission and falls for the beautiful Polynesian girl Liat; the two young lovers are brought together by Liat's crafty mother, the black marketeer Bloody Mary. When Nellie learns that Emile has had a Polynesian wife who died and left him two children, her prejudices force her to turn down Emile's proposal of marriage, just as Joe realizes he has no future with Liat and leaves her. The disillusioned Emile agrees to help Joe with his mission and the two depart for a remote island where they will radio news about the Japanese fleet. Joe is killed in the endeavor but Emile manages to return to the base where Nellie, who has learned to love Emile's two Eurasian children, is willing to conquer her prejudices and marry Emile.

Hammerstein and director JOSHUA LOGAN adapted two stories from James Michener's *Tales of the South Pacific* (1947) and took characters from some of the other tales to create a cohesive libretto that not only intertwined the two plots but linked them thematically. Both love stories are threatened by the inner prejudices of the American characters. The supposedly unintelligent hick Nellie from the

---

Casts for *South Pacific*

Character	1949 Broadway	1958 film	2001 television
Nellie Forbush	MARY MARTIN	MITZI GAYNOR	GLENN CLOSE
Emil de Becque	EZIO PINZA	Rosanno Brazzi	Rade Serbedzija
Bloody Mary	JUANITA HALL	Juanita Hall	Lori Tan Chinn
Lt. Joe Cable	WILLIAM TABBERT	John Kerr	Harry Connick, Jr.
Liat	Betta St. John	France Nuyen	Natalie Mendoza
Luther Billis	Myron McCormick	RAY WALSTON	Robert Pastorelli

South Pacific. Oscar Hammerstein usually wrote his librettos solo but, being too old to serve in World War II, he had no first-hand experience with military personnel. Director Joshua Logan had and he assisted Hammerstein in writing the tough GI dialogue. His contribution was such that by opening night Logan was credited as co-author. Pictured is the male chorus singing "There Is Nothin' Like a Dame" in the original Broadway production. (Photofest)

American South is looking for adventure and romance but when she learns of Emile's first wife and their Polynesian children, she loses her courage. The educated Joe Cable from Mainline Philadelphia is seemingly an enlightened and more broadminded American, but the upper-class prejudices that he grew up with are stronger than his love for Liat. Ironically, the hick learns to overcome her doubts and accepts Emile and his children; Joe cannot and only his death in the mission keeps him from dealing with the problem. Rodgers and Hammerstein, who became co-producers of their own work with *South Pacific*, wrote the musical with stars in mind. MARY MARTIN was the toast of Broadway and EZIO PINZA a favorite in the opera world. However, they were a very unlikely pair for a Broadway musical, just as Nellie and Emile are an unlikely couple: he is an older and distinguished foreigner and she is a youthful all-American gal. Pinza was a deep basso instead of the traditional Broadway leading man who was either a baritone or a tenor. The songwriters worried that a bass singing a duet with Martin's belting alto-soprano voice might strike audiences as odd so the two characters never sing in unison until far into the second act when playgoers were used to the vocal combination. The score for *South Pacific* is one of the team's most varied, with some of their funniest songs alongside some of their most beautiful. "Some Enchanted Evening" was the most popular number but nearly all of the songs became famous. It is also a score full of surprises. The show opens and closes with the child-like French ditty "Dites Moi" rather than a choral number. Nellie and Emile's first duet, "Twin Soliloquies," is one song divided into musical asides, climaxing not with the two voices singing but in the orchestra where the music covers over their interrupted thoughts. The haunting ballad "Bali Ha'i" is sung by

Bloody Mary, a comic supporting character, and a dishonest one at that. Joe's "Younger Than Springtime" is sung to a lover who barely understands what he is saying. Nellie's revelation that she is in love with "A Wonderful Guy" is more silly than rhapsodic and her "I'm Gonna Wash That Man Right Outa My Hair" means the opposite of what she says. Most unusual of all is "You've Got to Be Carefully Taught," Joe's bitter accusation in which he is the accused one. This last song, which summarized the theme of the musical, caused some trouble during rehearsals and there was talk of cutting it so it would not offend certain audience members. But Rodgers and Hammerstein felt it was essential and it remained in the score. Later there were cities in the deep South that would not book the tour of *South Pacific* because of that number. For a star vehicle, here was a musical with a lot to say. Reviews for the Broadway production were highly laudatory and Martin and Pinza were similarly praised, although the musical remained a top attraction even after the stars left. *South Pacific* ran 1,925 performances, and the Broadway cast recording remained a bestseller for years. The first touring company, with JANET BLAIR (Nellie) and Richard Eastham (Emile), ran for five years, and the 1951 London company with Mary Martin and Wilbur Evans (Emile) ran 802 performances. There have been six major New York revivals of *South Pacific*, beginning with a New York City Light Opera production in 1955 with Sandra Deel and Richard Collett as Nellie and Emile and Sylvia Syms as Bloody Mary. JUANITA HALL reprised her Mary in the 1957 Light Opera production starring Mindy Carson as Nellie and Robert Wright as Emile, and the same organization revived the musical in 1961, with Allyn Ann McLerie and William Chapman in the leads, and in 1965, with Betsy Palmer and RAY MIDDLETON. Richard Rodgers and the Music Theatre of Lincoln Center produced *South Pacific* in 1967 with JOE LAYTON directing a cast that included FLORENCE HENDERSON (Nellie), Giorgio Tozzi (Emile), and Irene Byatt (Bloody Mary). The musical was presented by the New York City Opera in 1987 with Susan Bigelow and Marcia Mitzman alternating as Nellie and Justino Diaz and Stanley Wexler taking turns as Emile. A LINCOLN CENTER THEATRE revival with KELLI O'HARA (Nellie) and Paulo Szot (Emile), directed by Bartlett Sher, opened in 2008. *South Pacific* remains a popular favorite in summer stock, amateur theatres, and schools.

South Pacific (stage) Musical Numbers

"Dites-Moi"
"A Cockeyed Optimist"
"Twin Soliloquies"
"Some Enchanted Evening"
"Bloody Mary"
"There Is Nothin' Like a Dame"
"Bali Ha'i"
"I'm Gonna Wash That Man Right Outa My Hair"
"A Wonderful Guy"
"Younger Than Springtime"
"Happy Talk"
"Honey Bun"
"You've Got to Be Carefully Taught"
"This Nearly Was Mine"

South Pacific (Magna/20th Century-Fox 1958) was also directed by Joshua Logan and was filmed on the Hawaiian island of Kauai with its beautiful postcard vistas, which are frequently ruined by Logan's decision to use color filters to denote mood; the multicolored faces singing on screen quickly became an industry joke. Logan moves people as awkwardly as he does his camera and everyone seems to be hanging around on beaches waiting for the drama to start. Paul Osborn's screenplay diminishes Hammerstein script without straying too far from the original. Some dialogue scenes are leaden, whereas others are extraneous. The movie opens with a dull conversation in an airplane and never picks up much steam thereafter. All of the stage songs were retained and "My Girl Back Home," which was cut during the pre-Broadway tryout tour, was reinstated. Musically the movie is strong, even if several of the voices are dubbed. Both DORIS DAY and ELIZABETH TAYLOR were seriously considered for Nellie before pert MITZI GAYNOR got the part. She did not disappoint, although one suspects there's more to the character than Gaynor's easy smile and pretty frowns. The Italian screen star Rossano Brazzi brought plenty of class to the role of Emile, although even the grayed temples could not hide the fact that he was not all that much older than Nellie. Opera singer Giorgio Tozzi provided Brazzi's singing voice and it was a beautiful sound, all the more enjoyable because one believes such a sound could come from the deep-spoken Brazzi. Bill Lee did the singing for the somewhat wooden John Kerr as Joe Cable and Juanita Hall got to reprise her Bloody Mary on screen. Unfortunately she could no longer hit the high notes of "Bali Ha'i" so she was dubbed by Muriel Smith who had played the role on the London stage. RAY WALSTON's Luther Billis is perhaps too low key even for a movie but at least he adds the necessary cynicism to offset all that lovely scenery. Film critics mostly found fault with *South Pacific* but the film was very popular at the box office and remains a favorite on television, on videotape, and on DVD.

☐ *South Pacific* (ABC-TV 2001) was an odd mixture of faithful Rodgers and Hammerstein and some headstrong changes that give one pause. GLENN CLOSE's Nellie was neither young nor a hick, exuding more sophistication than an empress. Rade Serbedzija was a short, scruffy, beach bum of an Emile who sang with a tenor voice. Whether this was foolhardy casting or a refreshing reinterpretation is a matter of opinion. Lori Tan Chinn's Bloody Mary was a creepy, unsentimental Bloody Mary and one not far from what Michener originally had in mind. Only Harry Connick, Jr.'s Joe Cable was traditional, although his acting was sometimes as stiff as Kerr's in the film. The Broadway score was mostly retained

("Happy Talk" was cut for some reason) and well orchestrated, conducted, and sung. The teleplay by Lawrence C. Cohen was hell-bent on showing wartime action scenes, as if that was ever what *South Pacific* was about. The production values were admirable and much of the production, directed by Richard Pearce, moved at a good pace.

🔊 *SPAMALOT* (Shubert Theatre 2005). A musical spoof based on (and mocking) a movie spoof, the show took nothing (including its own merits) very seriously and consequently was one of the funniest and least pretentious entries on Broadway in years. King Arthur (TIM CURRY) sets out to find the Holy Grail and, even with the help of Sir Lancelot (Hank Azaria), Sir Galahad (Christopher Sieber), Sir Robin (David Hyde Pierce), and his squire Patsy (Michael McGrath), he flounders from one misadventure to another until the Lady of the Lake (Sara Ramirez) guides him to the correct spot and wins the king's heart and hand as well. Loosely based on the silly, disjointed film *Monty Python and the Holy Grail* (1975), the musical version retained some of the fans'

Spamalot. Camelot met Las Vegas in this madcap musical farce that never ran out of ideas for inspired silliness. Even the scenery by Tim Hatley was funny, such as ye olde medieval roulette wheel. Standing in the center are (left to right) Sir Robin (David Hyde-Pierce), King Arthur (Tim Curry), and the Lady of the Lake (Sara Ramirez). (Wire Image)

favorite scenes from the movie and augmented the spoof with new songs and daffy plot twists. Eric Idle provided the libretto, lyrics, and some of the music, and John Du Prez wrote the rest of the music. Two songs ("Knights of the Round Table" and "Always Look on the Bright Side of Life") from the Pythons' films were joined by such risible new ditties as "The Song That Goes Like This," "Find Your Grail," "You Won't Succeed on Broadway," "Diva's Lament," "I'm All Alone," "Where Are You?," and "I Am Not Dead Yet." Mike Nichols directed and Casey Nicholaw choreographed with just the right touch of absurdist folly and both the press and the public responded with cheers and laughs. The musical continues to run, enjoyed by many who are not Python fans or even familiar with the film.

SPARKS, NED [born Edward A. Sparkman] (1883– 1957). Stage and film performer. A gravel-voiced character actor with a grumpy face, he enjoyed a notable career on Broadway and then a busy twenty-five years in Hollywood. Sparks was born in Guelph, Ontario, Canada, and educated at the University of Toronto before going on the stage. By 1921 he was on Broadway in comedies and was featured in three musicals: *My Golden Girl* (1920), *Jim Jam Jems* (1920), and *The All-Star Idlers of 1921*. The next year Sparks was in Hollywood where he appeared in many silents but didn't get recognition until sound came in. He played unsmiling, cigar-chewing sarcastic types in over 100 movies, including the musicals *LEATHERNECKING* (1930), *42ND STREET* (1933), *GOLD DIGGERS OF 1933*, *Too Much Harmony* (1933), *GOING HOLLYWOOD* (1933), *SWEET ADELINE* (1935), *GEORGE WHITE'S SCANDALS* (1935), *Sweet Music* (1935), *Collegiate* (1936), *ONE IN A MILLION* (1937), *WAKE UP AND LIVE* (1937), *The Star Maker* (1939), and *STAGE DOOR CANTEEN* (1943).

SPIALEK, HANS (1894–1983). Stage orchestrator and music arranger. One of Broadway's busiest orchestrators in the 1930s and 1940s, he arranged the music for some memorable ballet pieces in musical comedies. Spialek was born in Vienna, Austria, where he received a classical music education and studied composition. He made his Broadway debut orchestrating *Sweetheart Time* (1926) and over the next twenty-two years Spialek arranged the music for over one hundred Broadway shows and dance programs, including the hits *ROSALIE* (1928), *GAY DIVORCE* (1932), *ANYTHING GOES* (1934), *I MARRIED AN ANGEL* (1938), *Du Barry*

WAS A LADY (1939), *PAL JOEY* (1940), and *WHERE'S CHARLEY?* (1948). Perhaps Spialek's greatest contribution was the modern ballet orchestrations he made of RICHARD RODGERS's music for "Slaughter on Tenth Avenue" and the "Princess Zenobia" ballet in *ON YOUR TOES* (1936), the "Big Brother" ballet in *THE BOYS FROM SYRACUSE* (1938), and "Peter's Journey" ballet in *BABES IN ARMS* (1937). Musicologists have long enjoyed Spialek's musical puns in his arrangements, such as bits from Debussy's *Prelude to the Afternoon of a Faun* in "Big Brother" and Rimsky–Korsakov's *Scheherezade* in "Peter's Journey."

SPRING AWAKENING (Eugene O'Neill Theatre 2006). An expressionistic musical about the perils of adolescence, the powerful piece was lauded as new and daring when both the story and the style were over 100 years old. The young teenagers in a nineteenth-century German town are sexually confused, sexually ignorant, or just sexually charged as their strict upbringing adds to the tension. It drives the academically weak student Moritz (John Gallagher, Jr.) to suicide and leads the nonconformist Melchior (Jonathan Groff) and too-innocent Wendla (Lea Michele) into a sexual liaison that leaves her pregnant and has him sent away to a reformatory. She dies during a botched abortion and Melchior is left haunted and comforted by the ghosts of Moritz and Wendla. Also in the compelling cast were Stephen Spinella, Christine Estabrook, Jonathan B. Wright, Lilli Cooper, Skylar Astin, and Lauren Pritchard. Steven Sater's libretto closely followed Frank Wedekind's 1891 expressionistic drama, and the musical retained a period look and feel in the book scenes but burst into rock and hand-held microphones for the musical numbers by Duncan Sheik (music) and Sater (lyrics). "The Bitch of Living," "Mama Who Bore Me," "I Believe," "The Word of Your Body," and "My Junk" were among the notable songs. Michael Mayer staged the tricky piece with the right touch and Bill T. Jones choreographed the few but memorable dances. First presented the previous season Off Broadway by the Atlantic Theatre Company, it was so successful that the production moved to Broadway where it was welcomed with enthusiastic notices. Box office business was sluggish at first but, as word of mouth spread, the musical became very popular, especially with young audiences.

SPRINGTIME IN THE ROCKIES (Fox 1942). A facile BETTY GRABLE vehicle that was all about nothing, its musical numbers are so enjoyable that the picture seemed like solid gold. WALTER BULLOCK and Ken Englund wrote the screenplay about the Broadway performers Vicky Lane (Grable) and Dan Christy (JOHN PAYNE) who love each other but are always fighting (he has a roving eye for the ladies), so when she runs off to Lake Louise in the Canadian Rockies with her former dancing partner Victor Prince (CESAR ROMERO), Payne follows and tries to make Vicky jealous by flirting with the Latin femme fatale Rosita Murphy (CARMEN MIRANDA). It was a plot that ached for interruptions and the interruptions were delicious. Grable and Payne performed the zesty duet "Run Little Raindrop," Miranda sang "Chattanooga Choo-Choo" in Portuguese, vocalist Helen Forrest introduced "I Had the Craziest Dream" with HARRY JAMES and his band, and the whole cast, including high-kicking CHARLOTTE GREENWOOD, fidgety EDWARD EVERETT HORTON, and roly-poly JACKIE GLEASON, cut loose with HERMES PAN'S choreography for the "Pan American Jubilee" finale. HARRY WARREN (music) and MACK GORDON (lyrics) penned the catchy songs, and IRVING CUMMINGS directed with gusto.

STADLEN, LEWIS J. (1947–). Stage, television, and film performer. An energetic comic character actor who has often appeared in scene-stealing supporting roles, he has the polish and panache of old-time vaudeville comedians even though he is several generations removed from them. The Brooklyn native, the son of voice-over artist Allen Swift, trained at the Neighborhood Playhouse and the Stella Adler Studio before getting his first professional work in a 1966 tour of *FIDDLER ON THE ROOF*. He made a rollicking Broadway debut as the young GROUCHO MARX in the musical *Minnie's Boys* (1970); his imitation of the famous comic was so well received that Stadlen later toured as Marx in a one-man show. He has appeared in many New York comedies and a few musicals, such as Dr. Pangloss and a variety of other wacky characters in *CANDIDE* (1974), the nervous messenger Sosia in *Olympus on My Mind* (1986), and the Roman father Senex in *A FUNNY THING HAPPENED ON THE WAY TO THE FORUM* (1996). Stadlen was a replacement for the role of Max Bialystock in *THE PRODUCERS* (2003) on Broadway and played it on tour, as he has with *GUYS AND DOLLS* and other musicals. He has acted in a handful of films and many television programs where his musical talents were not required.

STAGEDOOR CANTEEN (Lesser/United Artists 1943). A musical that saluted the American Theatre Wing and its wartime efforts, the film was also a revue hidden by a very thin plot. The Wing was a New York organization that sponsored the famous New York hot spot Stagedoor Canteen for servicemen during World War II. In Delmer Daves' screenplay, G.I. Dakota Smith (William Terry) meets canteen hostess Eileen Burke (Cheryl Walker) and they have a wartime romance with the usual setbacks and complications. The movie was really just a parade of stars who were making appearances at the canteen. Theatrical grande dames such as Katharine Hepburn, Helen Hayes, Katharine Cornell, Ina Claire, and Judith Anderson showed up to wash dishes and pass out food while music was provided by Big Band favorites BENNY GOODMAN, XAVIER CUGAT, KAY KYSER, Freddie Martin, and Guy Lombardo, with vocals by LANNY ROSS, RAY BOLGER, PEGGY LEE, and many others. A variety of songwriters contributed to the scattershot score, the best numbers being RODGERS and HART's comic "The Girl I Love to Leave Behind" and JAMES V. MONACO and AL DUBIN's teary ballad "We Mustn't Say Goodbye." The unusual revue was popular and, because ninety percent of the box office went to the Theatre Wing, it was a great morale booster. The West Coast jumped on the band wagon and offered *Hollywood Canteen* (Warner 1944), the Los Angeles version of Manhattan's Stagedoor Canteen. There being more stars in the neighborhood, the movie was stuffed with nearly thirty names-above-the-title celebrities, from the swinging ANDREWS SISTERS to the violin virtuoso Efrem Zimbalist. Again there was a slim plot (also penned by director Daves) about sailors Sgt. Nowland (Dane Clark) and Cpl. Slim Green (Robert Hutton) on sick leave from the Pacific campaign and Slim winning a contest that gives him a dream date with JOAN LESLIE. JIMMY DORSEY, Carmel Cavallaro, and their bands provided the music, and several songs by Hollywood songwriters were introduced. Among the many notable moments: ROY ROGERS and the Sons of the Pioneers singing COLE PORTER's "Don't Fence Me In," EDDIE CANTOR and Nora Martin proclaiming "We're Having a Baby (My Baby and Me)," LESLIE and KITTY CARLISLE bidding "Sweet Dreams, Sweetheart," and the ANDREWS SISTERS singing how they got "Corns for My Country" by waiting on all the servicemen.

STAPLETON, JEAN [born Jeanne Murray] (1923–). Television, stage, and film performer. The bony, precise character actress forever remembered as Edith Bunker on the television series *All in the Family*, she has enjoyed a busy career before and after her glory days on the tube. The native New Yorker was educated at Hunter College, after which she worked as a secretary while studying acting at the American Apprentice Theatre, the American Actors Company, and the American Theatre Wing. Stapleton sang with the Robert Shaw Clorale and was in stock before making her New York acting debut in 1948. She first found attention in colorful supporting roles in musicals: baseball fan Sister in *DAMN YANKEES* (1955) and answering service owner Sue in *BELLS ARE RINGING* (1956), reprising both performances in the screen versions. While she played supporting roles on Broadway in the 1960s, she performed major musical roles in summer stock, continuing to do so even after she became famous on television. Her other New York musical theatre credits include *JUNO* (1959), *FUNNY GIRL* (1964), and the stepmother in *CINDERELLA* (1996). Stapleton has acted in many movies and televisions shows, including the TV musical version of *Something's Afoot* (1984).

STAR! (Fox 1968). It may have intended to celebrate the life and career of GERTRUDE LAWRENCE, the British star who had conquered the West End and Broadway in the 1920s and remained popular for decades, but the film shed little light on Lawrence and a lot on a very different British star, JULIE ANDREWS, who impersonated her. At the peak of her popularity, Andrews valiantly held the long (175 minutes), overextended, overproduced biographical musical together, helped by terrific old tunes by NOEL COWARD, COLE PORTER, KURT WEILL, and the GERSHWINS. William Fairchild wrote the rags-to-riches screenplay that followed Lawrence from her humble beginnings in the Clapham section of London to her music hall days and then her celebrity on both sides

of the Atlantic. Her lifetime friend Coward (Daniel Massey) and her supportive second husband Richard Aldrich (Richard Crenna) were the anchors in Lawrence's stormy life, yet audiences got weary of her tale long before the picture concluded. Luckily MICHAEL KIDD choreographed some lively numbers, such as "The Physician" and "Jenny," and director ROBERT WISE made the whole thing look and feel right. Other songs, most of them performed by Andrews, included "Parisian Pierrot," "Burlington Bertie From Bow," "My Ship," "Someday I'll Find You," "Someone to Watch Over Me," "Limehouse Blues," and the new title song by JAMES VAN HEUSEN and SAMMY CAHN. When the picture bombed at the box office, the studio cut nearly an hour out of the original and rereleased it as *Those Were the Happy Days*, but it failed again. Over the years the long version has found its admirers and there is still a lot to be said about Andrews' performance.

STAR IS BORN, A (Transcona/Warner 1954). JUDY GARLAND's last major musical and, in the opinion of many, it featured her finest performance.

Plot: Band singer Esther Blodgett meets alcoholic movie star Norman Maine at a Hollywood benefit where he literally stumbles into her act and, after he hears her sing in a smoky little nightclub, is determined to help her climb to stardom. The two marry but as Vicky Lester (as she is renamed by the studio) climbs to success, Maine descends until in despair he ends up drowning himself.

The story was already familiar to movie audiences, the tale having been told as a nonmusical film in 1937 with JANET GAYNOR and Fredric March as Esther and Norman. MOSS HART wrote the unsentimental screenplay for the musical version, and GEORGE CUKOR directed it with style and a knowing touch. The performances throughout were riveting, Garland going places with a character that she had never been asked to go before. James Mason and the

Film casts for *A Star Is Born*

Character	1954 version	1976 version
Esther Blodgett/Hoffman	JUDY GARLAND	BARBRA STREISAND
Norman Maine/Howard	James Mason	Kris Kristofferson
Matt Libby/Bobbie Ritchie	JACK CARSON	Gary Busey
Oliver Niles/Gary Danziger	Charles Bickford	Oliver Clark
Danny McGuire	Tom Noonan	

A Star Is Born. Although it was a big, expensive musical with some complicated production numbers, often the most memorable moments in the movie were small scale, such as Judy Garland singing "The Man That Got Away" in a smoke-filled, after-hours club. Another was the number "Someone at Last" in which Garland (pictured with James Mason) acts out in her living room the movie she is making, playing all the parts and describing the production numbers. (Photofest)

A Star Is Born (1954 film) Musical Numbers

"Gotta Have Me Go With You"
"The Man That Got Away"
"Born in a Trunk"
"Swanee"
"It's a New World"
"Here's What I'm Here For"
"Someone at Last"
"Lose That Long Face"

supporting cast were also expert, with each scene playing beautifully and the story gaining in its pull as it went along. The picture was perhaps the most sobering of backstagers and it ran over three hours in its first cut so the studio cut two scenes and two numbers to bring the running time to 154 minutes. The cutting did not help the structure of the film and it still seemed long without making any sense at times. Some of the missing footage was restored and added to the 1983 rerelease and most felt the picture was improved by the additions. Always a movie that was demanding of its audience, the full version of *A Star of Born* asks a lot from the viewers but gives back double in return.

The dynamic score by HAROLD ARLEN (music) and IRA GERSHWIN (lyrics) is varied, yet all of a piece, capturing the slick world of show business in both ballads and mocking songs. The standout hit was "The Man That Got Away," which Garland sang in the empty nightclub after hours with some musician friends. As Mason watches her and realizes her talent, the screen seems to glow with awareness. Her recording of the song was one of her biggest hits and after "Over the Rainbow" may be the number that most defines Garland. Another musical masterwork in the film is the extended "Someone at Last" song sequence, sung by Esther/Vicky to her husband, demonstrating the inane musical she is making at the studio. It's a comic tour de force that matches the earlier torch song in power. The two numbers cut by the studio were "Lose That Long Face" and "Here's What I'm Here For," both revealing character numbers as well as catchy songs. Also impressive was the swinging "Gotta Have a Go With You" and the optimistic ballad "It's a New World." The famous "Born in Trunk" montage was written by ROGER EDENS and Leonard Gershe after the Arlen–Gershwin score was complete. Its opening and closing sections are the stuff of parody today (*THE PRODUCERS* particularly had fun with it) but it still is a vibrant way to get into the long montage of old song favorites used to show the struggles of a young singer trying to make it in show biz. Musically, *A Star Is Born* is as rich and complex as the drama it has to tell. The two working together make the film so potent.

The Hollywood remake of **A Star Is Born** (Warner/Barwood-First Artists 1976) featured its era's superstar BARBRA STREISAND with Kris Kristofferson in the world of rock concerts rather than Tinsel Town. Although the milieu and the songs were very different, the plot was surprisingly similar. The screenplay by John Gregory Dunne, Joan Didion, and director Frank Pierson focused on ambitious pop singer Esther Hoffman (Streisand) who rises to the top while her mentor and husband John Norman Howard (Kristofferson) descends into drugs and suicide by crashing his Ferrari. Just as the earlier film sought to expose the hypocrisy of the show business of their day, the remake provided a very unglamorous view of rock singers and their world. PAUL WILLIAMS and Streisand collaborated on the Oscar-winning song "Evergreen" (aka "Love Theme From *A Star Is Born*") and it was the best number in the score, although there was much to like in Rupert Holmes' "Queen Bee," "Woman in the Moon" by Williams and Kenny Ascher, and "I Believe in Love" by Alan and MARILYN BERGMAN and Kenny Loggins. The critics carped but the movie was a resounding hit at the box office.

STARLIGHT EXPRESS (Gershwin Theatre 1987). An allegorical musical in which trains are personified and became characters in a story, the British show lost something in the transfer to Broadway. The underdog steam-train engine Rusty (Greg Mowry) wants to win the big race but his competition, including the show-off diesel locomotive Greaseball (Robert Torti) and the sleek electric engine Electra (Ken Ard), is fierce and only with the help of his Poppa (Steve Flowler) and the love of the carriage car Pearl (Reva Rice) does he win the day. Also featured in the cast were Andrea McArdle, Jane Krakowski, Jamie Beth Chandler, and Barry K. Bernal. ANDREW LLOYD WEBBER (music) and Richard Stilgoe (lyrics) wrote the sung-through musical, and the score was a collection of pop, rock, blues, country-western, and gospel. "Only You," "Lotta Locomotion," "Make Up My Heart," "One Rock & Roll Too Many," "Light at the End of the Tunnel," "U.N.C.O.U.P.L.E.D.," "Poppa's Blues," and the title song were among the notable musical numbers. TREVOR NUNN directed the elaborate production in which the cast performed on roller skates and raced through the huge steel setting made of bridges and ramps, all of which was more interesting than the characters or the plot. The British love for trains had made the musical a London hit but for the Broadway version the tale was reworked into a children's fable imagined by a young boy. Critics were only impressed with the technical side of the extravaganza, at $8 million the most expensive Broadway musical yet seen, but audiences kept the flashy show alive for 761 performances, which wasn't enough to make a profit.

STAR-SPANGLED RHYTHM (Paramount 1942). The first of a handful of wartime musicals that used a slender plot as an excuse to feature plenty of stars, the picture was a patriotic bonanza packed with PARAMOUNT celebrities. Harry Turgend and a flock of writers penned the screenplay about G.I. Johnny Webster (EDDIE BRACKEN) who, wanting to impress his shipmates, schemes with switchboard operator Polly Judson (BETTY HUTTON) to pass off John's father, Bronco Billy Webster (VICTOR MOORE), a gatekeeper at Paramount, as a studio executive. The plan starts off successfully but soon Billy finds himself in charge of a huge stage show for servicemen. HAROLD ARLEN (music) and JOHNNY MERCER (lyrics) wrote the score and struck gold twice: "That Old Black Magic," sung by JOHNNY JOHNSTON and danced by VERA ZORINA, and "Hit the Road to Dreamland," introduced by MARY MARTIN, DICK POWELL, and the Golden Gate Quartet. Also enjoyable were Paulette Goddard, DOROTHY LAMOUR, and Veronica Lake spoofing their image with "A Sweater, a Sarong, and a Peek-a-Boo Bang," CASS DALEY lamenting "He Loved Me Till the All-Clear Came," and Hutton riding in a jeep full of sailors and slyly singing "I'm Doing It for Defense." Other stars stopping by the set were BING CROSBY, BOB HOPE, FRED MacMURRAY, FRANCHOT TONE, SUSAN HAYWARD, EDDIE "ROCHESTER" ANDERSON, Alan Ladd, MacDonald Carey, MARJORIE REYNOLDS, and many others. George Marshall directed the agreeable hodge-podge and it was so successful that it was followed by other wartime pseudo-revues such as STAGE DOOR CANTEEN (1943), THANK YOUR LUCKY STARS (1943), Thousands Cheer (1943), HOLLYWOOD CANTEEN (1944), and Follow the Boys (1944)

🎵 *STARTING HERE, STARTING NOW* (Barbarann Theatre 1977). An exciting three-person Off Broadway musical revue with a smart, knowing score, the show brought the first recognition to songwriters DAVID SHIRE (music) and RICHARD MALTBY, JR. (lyrics). The songs were very contemporary in subject and spirit and covered a variety of topics, usually with wit and intelligence. "Crossword Puzzle," "Flair," "Watching the Parade Go By," "I Don't Remember Christmas," "What About Today," and the title song were among the many gems in the score performed by Magery Cohen, George Lee Andrews, and Loni Ackerman. Maltby directed and the revue ran 120 performances, followed by many productions in little theatres, cabarets, and other intimate spaces. The songwriters offered a similarly perceptive revue eleven years later with **Closer Than Ever** (Cherry Lane Theatre 1989), which took a more mature viewpoint and explored the various decisions and compromises that people make later in life. "You Want to Be My Friend," "One of the Good Guys," "What Am I Doin'?," "If I Sing," "Miss Byrd," "Life Story," and the title number were outstanding numbers in the bright and literate score. Maltby again directed a cast that consisted of Richard Munez, Sally Mayes, Patrick Scott Brady, Brent Barrett, and Lynne Wintersteller and the revue ran 288 performances.

🎬 *STATE FAIR* (Fox 1945). The only movie musical that RICHARD RODGERS (music) and OSCAR HAMMERSTEIN (lyrics) scored together, the folksy tale is a simple and loving look at Americana.

Plot: As the Frake family prepares to leave their farm for the Iowa State Fair, the father Abel makes a bet with a neighbor that his boar Blue Boy will win the top prize and that every family member will have a great time at the fair. His wife Melissa is entering her homemade mincemeat in the competition, son Wayne is hoping to win his prizes on the midway, and daughter Margy is looking forward to getting away from her dull fiancé. At the fair Wayne falls into a too-casual romance with a band singer, Emily Edwards, and Margy is attracted to the newsman Pat Gilbert. Although Blue Boy and the mincemeat both win ribbons, the younger Frakes are less lucky in love. Emily realizes that she has no future with the naive Wayne and Pat rushes off when he learns of a job at a Chicago newspaper. Returning home, Wayne happily goes back to his old girl friend. Abel claims his bet and when Margy hears from Pat that he wants to marry her, she is overjoyed, so the neighbor admits that all had a good time at the fair and pays up.

After the Broadway success of *OKLAHOMA!* (1943), Rodgers and Hammerstein received a flow of offers from Hollywood, but both had had unpleasant experiences with the studio system in the 1930s and were reluctant to go back. Then 20TH CENTURY-FOX asked them to musicalize *State Fair*, a novel by Philip Strong that the studio had filmed successfully in 1933 as a nonmusical. It was similar to *Oklahoma!* in its midwestern setting, rural characters, and rustic humor. Hammerstein collaborated on the screenplay with SONYA LEVIEN and they came up with a pleasantly old-fashioned piece about the American heartland. Fox wanted their in-house ingénue ALICE FAYE to play the daughter Margie but she surprised the studio and the world by abruptly retiring in 1944, so up-and-coming JEANNE CRAIN was cast, even though her singing had to be dubbed by

Casts for *State Fair*			
Character	*1945 film*	*1962 film*	*1996 Broadway*
Abel Frake	CHARLES WINNINGER	Tom Ewell	John Davidson
Melissa Frake	Fay Bainter	ALICE FAYE	Kathryn Crosby
Margy Frake	JEANNE CRAIN	Pamela Tiffin	Andrea McArdle
Wayne Frake	DICK HAYMES	PAT BOONE	Ben Wright
Emily	VIVIAN BLAINE	ANN-MARGARET	DONNA McKECHNIE
Pat/Jerry	Dana Andrews	Bobby Darin	Scott Wise

State Fair. Jeanne Crain (pictured with Dick Haymes) could act but couldn't sing so she was dubbed in the 1945 version of *State Fair*. Haymes could sing but his acting was always a bit on the stiff side and no one has figured out how you can dub acting. You can't have everything, not even in Hollywood. The two played brother and sister in the film, which explains their tentative hand holding here. (Photofest)

Louanne Hogan. The rising singing star DICK HAYMES played her brother and the veteran actors CHARLES WINNINGER and Fay Bainter played their parents. To contrast the folksy Frake family, Dana Andrews and VIVIAN BLAINE brought a tough, urban edge to the characters that the Frake siblings fell in love with. The production values were top notch, with WALTER LANG directing with just the right touch of whimsy and romance. Although there are only six songs and three reprises in the film, each number counted and all of them were superior. The opening "Our State Fair" introduced the family as the song bounced through the household, and the movie ended with the merry "All I Owe Ioway," a sillier version of the boastful "Oklahoma." The numbers for the city characters, such as "That's for Me" and "Isn't It Kinda Fun," had a touch of swing and jazz, and Rodgers wrote one of his most infectious waltz melodies for "It's a Grand Night for Singing." The highlight of the superb score was the Oscar-winning "It

> **State Fair (1945 film) Musical Numbers**
>
> "Our State Fair"
> "It Might as Well Be Spring"
> "That's For Me"
> "It's a Grand Night for Singing"
> "Isn't It Kinda Fun?"
> "All I Owe Ioway"

Might As Well Be Spring," a tender character song that became the most famous of all the numbers. Because of the look and temperament of *State Fair*, the film tends to date and is best enjoyed now as a nostalgic example of a 1940s homespun musical.

Fox remade the musical in 1962 when many studios were remaking their old black and white pictures. Producer Charles Brackett wanted a new, colorful *State Fair* with a young cast that would appeal to the ever-younger moviegoing public. The new screenplay by

Richard L. Breen reset the tale in Texas, to get away from corn-fed Iowa and padded the thin story to nearly two hours. The score was reorchestrated to make some of the numbers sound more contemporary and five new songs were added. Since Hammerstein had died in 1960, Rodgers obliged and wrote both music and lyrics for the new numbers, "More Than Just a Friend," "Never Say No to a Man," "This Isn't Heaven," "Willing and Eager," and "It's the Little Things in Texas." While none came close to the quality of the original score, they served the plot and gave the parents something to sing. Character actor Tom Ewell was well cast as the father and the studio pulled off a real coup in getting Alice Faye to come out of seventeen years of retirement to play the mother. The scenes between the two have a cozy quality that older audiences enjoyed, even though younger viewers got restless. Popular singers (but limited actors) PAT BOONE and Bobby Darin were paired with the vivacious ANN-MARGARET and the vapid Pamela Tiffin (dubbed by Anita Gordon); there wasn't a spark of chemistry in the whole quartet. JOSE FERRER's clumsy direction, the television-special-like dancing by NICK CASTLE, and the garish wide screen photography seemed to be making a mockery of what the first film was all about. It was not accidental; this was a 1960s pop musical and as such it did very well at the box office.

🐖 Although it was seen on the screen twice, *State Fair* did not appear on stage until a 1969 production at the ST. LOUIS MUNICIPAL OPERA. Lucille Kallen adapted the two screenplays into a stage libretto and songs from both movie versions were used. The "Muny" being a huge outdoor theatre, real animals could be used (including the prize hog Blue Boy) and the fair midway was recreated on the mammoth stage. Because of its large scale, few other theatres considered producing the stage *State Fair* until a rewritten, scaled-down version arrived on Broadway twenty-seven years later. The libretto for the Broadway **State Fair** (Music Box Theatre 1996) was by Tom Briggs and Louis Mattioli. Familiar personalities John Davidson and Kathryn Crosby were cast as the parents to appeal to the road's audiences but the younger characters were played by Broadway pros DONNA MCKECHNIE, Andrea McArdle, Scott Wise, and Ben Wright. The THEATRE GUILD liked the tour and wanted it on Broadway, but the funds were not there until veteran producer DAVID MERRICK, who also hadn't been represented on Broadway

for several seasons, came up with the cash and New York saw its last "new" Rodgers and Hammerstein musical. Critics complained about the threadbare road production and declared the libretto dated without being charming. However, the score was not to be dismissed, featuring not only songs from both movie versions but lesser-known Rodgers and Hammerstein songs from *ME AND JULIET* (1953), *ALLEGRO* (1947), *PIPE DREAM* (1955), and even a song cut from *Oklahoma!* entitled "Boys and Girls Like You and Me." RANDY SKINNER provided the energetic choreography and co-directed with Oscar's son James Hammerstein, and the result was far from the yawn that the critics declared. The production held on for fifteen weeks and then closed deep in the red. The stage *State Fair* marked the end of two long and notable careers, those of Merrick and the Theatre Guild. Since then the musical has become popular with summer stock and schools looking for a new–old musical by the famous team.

STEELE, TOMMY [born Thomas Hicks] (1936–). Stage and film performer. A smiling blond song-and-dance man, he was a popular favorite on the London stage but Americans know him from his few Hollywood musicals. The native Londoner began his career as a merchant seaman but in the 1950s became a rock-pop singing idol with best-selling records and concert appearances and playing himself in the film musical *The Tommy Steele Story* (1957). He turned to theatre in 1958 when he played the hoofing servant Buttons in the London stage version of RODGERS and HAMMERSTEIN's *CINDERELLA*. The musical *HALF A SIXPENCE* was written for him and his performance as the lively Cockney Kipps was so successful in the West End in 1963 that he reprised it on Broadway in 1965 and on film in 1967. Hollywood cast Steele as the chipper butler John Lawless in *The Happiest Millionaire* (1967) and the leprechaun Og in *FINIAN'S RAINBOW* (1968). He also starred in the British film musicals *The Duke Wore Jeans* (1958), *Tommy the Toreador* (1959), *It's All Happening* (1963), and *The Dream Maker* (1964), as well as the West End musicals *Hans Andersen* (1974), *SINGIN' IN THE RAIN* (1983), and *Some Like It Hot* (1992).

STEIN, JOSEPH (1912–). Stage, film, and television writer. A respected Broadway librettist, he has had both giant hits and giant flops in his notable career. Stein was born in New York and educated at the City College of New

York and Columbia for a career in social work before turning to writing for radio. In the 1950s he wrote sketches for SID CAESAR and *All Star Revue*, as well as the script for the TV musical *JUNIOR MISS* (1957). While some of his sketches appeared in the Broadway revues *LEND AN EAR* (1948), *Alive and Kicking* (1950), and *ZIEGFELD FOLLIES* (1956), his first book musical was *PLAIN AND FANCY* (1955). This modest success was followed by *MR. WONDERFUL* (1956), *The Body Beautiful* (1958), *TAKE ME ALONG* (1959), *JUNO* (1959), *FIDDLER ON THE ROOF* (1964), *ZORBÁ* (1968), the revised *IRENE* (1973), *So Long, 174th Street* (1976) based on his 1963 play *Enter Laughing*, *King of Hearts* (1978), *Carmelina* (1979), and *RAGS* (1986). Stein also collaborated with songwriters KANDER and EBB on the musical *Over and Over*, based on the play *The Skin of Our Teeth*, which has been seen in different versions (and titles) regionally. Of all his Broadway musicals, the only one to be filmed was *Fiddler on the Roof* (1971) for which he wrote the screenplay. Many of his stage librettos are about strong communities, from the Pennsylvania Dutch people of *Plain and Fancy* to the Russian villagers in *Fiddler on the Roof* to ethnic neighbors of Manhattan's Lower East Side in *Rags*.

STEPT, SAM H. (1897–1964). Stage and film composer. Working with a variety of lyricists, the songwriter scored a dozen Hollywood musicals. Stept was born in Odessa, Russia, and after emigrating to America worked as a bandleader before turning to composing. His songs were heard on Broadway in *George White's Music Hall Varieties* (1932 and 1933), *Shady Lady* (1933), and *Yokel Boy* (1939). Stept had a parallel career in Hollywood. Collaborating with Bud Green, SIDNEY MITCHELL, TED KOEHLER, NED WASHINGTON, LEW BROWN, and others, he scored such musicals as *Syncopation* (1929), *Lucky in Love* (1929), *Playing Around* (1930), *Shady Lady* (1933), *This Is the Life* (1935), *Dancing Feet* (1936), *Laughing Irish Eyes* (1936), *Hit Parade of 1937*, *Having Wonderful Time* (1938), and *Yokel Boy* (1942). Songs of his were also heard in nonmusical films. Stept's most famous song is "Don't Sit Under the Apple Tree (With Anyone Else But Me)."

STEVENS, GEORGE (1904–1975). Film director. A distinguished and versatile Hollywood director, he only helmed three musicals but two of them are classics. Stevens was born in Oakland, California, the son of two actors, and was on the stage as a child. He started in movies as a cameraman in 1921 and then worked his way to directing shorts for Hal Roach and others. By 1933 Stevens was helming features and the next year found recognition with *Alice Adams*, his first of many insightful character dramas. Among his most famous pictures were *Woman of the Year* (1942), *A Place in the Sun* (1951), *Shane* (1953), and *Giant* (1956). Stevens' first musical *Nitwits* (1935) was forgettable but not his subsequent features *SWING TIME* (1936) and *A DAMSEL IN DISTRESS* (1937). His son was film executive George Stevens, Jr. (1932–). Biography: *Giant: George Stevens, a Life on Film*, Marilyn Ann Moss (2004).

STEVENS, RISË [born Risë Steenberg] (1913–). Stage, film, and television performer. An acclaimed opera star, the beautiful singer often turned to musicals in different media during her long career. Stevens was born in New York and studied voice at Juilliard and in Europe. She made her Metropolitan Opera debut in 1939 and over the next twenty years sang all the major mezzo-soprano roles. Concurrent with her opera career, Stevens became nationally known for her appearances in movies, on the radio, and on television. She sang opposite NELSON EDDY in the 1941 film version of *THE CHOCOLATE SOLDIER* and played the opera star Genevieve Linden in *GOING MY WAY* (1941). Stevens did a specialty spot in *Carnegie Hall* (1949) and then in the 1950s used television to promote opera, appearing in one of the Met's first telecasts in 1954. She performed in the original TV musicals *HANSEL AND GRETEL* (1958) and *LITTLE WOMEN* (1958) and sang all kinds of music in her many television appearances. Throughout her career Stevens made many recordings of operettas and musicals, as well as the opera repertory, and played some of the classic Broadway musical roles, such as Anna Leonowens in *THE KING AND I* for Lincoln Center Music Theatre in 1964. Stevens also did the voice of the good witch Glinda in the animated movie musical *JOURNEY BACK TO OZ* (1972). Biography: *Risë Stevens: A Life in Music*, John Pennino (2005).

STEWART, JAMES [Maitland] (1908–1997). Film, stage, and television performer. Arguably the most versatile and consistently accomplished screen actor in Hollywood history, he could do just about everything but sing and dance, yet he appeared in eight movie musicals. Stewart was born in Indiana, Pennsylvania, and educated at Princeton for a career in architecture, but a summer spent in stock persuaded him to become an actor. He began his career in the New York theatre, making his Broadway bow in 1932 and appearing in seven other plays without getting much attention. In 1935 he and his friend Henry Fonda went to Hollywood where each began prodigious careers on screen. At first Stewart usually played the common man whom audiences could identify with and it was in such a role that he was cast in the musicals *Rose Marie* (1935), *Born to Dance* (1936), *Ice Follies of 1939*, *Destry Rides Again* (1939), *Pot o' Gold* (1941), and *Ziegfeld Girl* (1941). By the 1950s he had widened his scope of characters considerably and had his best musical role as the title band leader in *The Glenn Miller Story* (1954). He appeared in one more musical two decades later, *The Magic of Lassie* (1978). Stewart returned to Broadway with success as tipsy Elwood P. Dowd in the comedy *Harvey* (1947 and 1970) and made many television appearances, including a show of is own in the 1970s. Biography: *Pieces of Time: The Life of James Stewart*, Gary Fishgall, Lisa Drew (1998).

Stewart [Rubin], **Michael** (1929–1987). Stage and television writer and lyricist. The author of some of Broadway's brightest musical hits, he was also an adept lyric writer. Stewart was born in New York and educated at Yale but he learned his craft writing sketches and songs for summer camp shows. Some of his material was used in some off Broadway revues, on Broadway in *The Shoestring Revue* (1955), and in Sid Caesar's television show. Stewart's first Broadway book musical was the surprise hit *Bye Bye Birdie* (1960), followed by the successful *Carnival* (1961) and the long-run giant *Hello, Dolly!* (1964). His other hits were *George M!* (1968), *I Love My Wife* (1977), and *Barnum* (1980), both of which he wrote lyrics as well as the scripts, and *42nd Street* (1980). Stewart also had many disappointments during his career, such as the musicals *Mack and Mabel* (1974), *The Grand Tour* (1979), *Bring Back Birdie* (1981), *Harrigan 'n Hart* (1985), and four others that never made it to Broadway. His librettos, half of which were adaptations of plays, were economical, well structured, and playful, and his lyrics were sometimes ingenious and inspired.

Stigwood, **Robert** [Colin] (1934–). Stage and film producer. An international presenter of everything from rock concerts to London musicals, the impresario presented some trans-

atlantic stage hits and a series of movie musicals in the 1970s that ranged from record-breaking successes to renowned flops. Stigwood was born in Adelaide, Australia, and made his fortune in England promoting pop singers and records. He produced *Hair* (1968) in London, followed by *Joseph and the Amazing Technicolor Dreamcoat* (1972) and *Pippin* (1973), and both the West End and Broadway productions of *Jesus Christ Superstar* (1971 and 1972) and *Evita* (1978 and 1979). Stigwood was also active in the movies and produced *Jesus Christ Superstar* (1973), *Tommy* (1975), *Bugsy Malone* (1976), *Saturday Night Fever* (1977), *Grease* (1978), *Sgt. Peppers Lonely Hearts Club Band* (1978), *Times Square* (1980), *Grease 2* (1982), and *Staying Alive* (1983). In the 1990s he returned to the theatre and produced the London musical revival of *Grease* (1993) and the stage version of *Saturday Night Fever* (1998), which he transferred to Broadway in 1999. Stigwood also produced the long-gestating film version of *Evita* (1996).

◻ **Stingiest Man in Town, The** (NBC-TV 1956). Talents from Broadway, ballet, and the opera world merged to perform this ninety-minute musical version of *A Christmas Carol*, which trimmed the Dickens tale to make room for songs, dance, and even a piano concerto concert. Janice Torre wrote the adaptation and penned the lyrics for Fred Spielman's music, and it is an accomplished score featuring such numbers as "It Might Have Been," "An Old Fashioned Christmas," "I Wear a Chain," "Birthday Party of the King," "Golden Dreams," "Mankind Should Be My Business," "Yes, There Is a Santa Claus," and the title song. In addition to the twelve songs, the musical featured a ballet of toys and composer Spielman performed his piano "Concerto Inferno" in the cemetery scene. Critics complained that the show was full of everything except Dickens, yet there were compliments all around for the cast headed by Basil Rathbone as Scrooge. Also cast were such diverse talents as Vic Damone, Patrice Munsel, Johnny Desmond, Martyn Green, The Four Lads, Robert Weede, Olive Dunbar, Robert Wright, John McGiver, Betty Madigan, and John Heawood who also choreographed. Joel Spector produced the ninety-minute *Alcoa Hour* broadcast and Dan Petrie directed. Using the same score, NBC made an animated version of *The Stingiest Man in Town* in 1978 and recast it with voices of celebrities of the day. Walter Matthau was an appropriately grumpy Scrooge and the tale was narrated by a small winged insect named B.A.H. Humbug (TOM BOSLEY). Also supplying singing and speaking voices were Theodore Bikel, DENNIS DAY, Robert MORSE, PAUL FREES, Darlene Conley, Sonny Melendrez, and Steffi Calli. While some thought the score was less impressive this time around, the animation was expert and the script by ROMEO MULLER was more satisfying. ARTHUR RANKIN, JR. and JULES BASS produced and directed.

STOKOWSKI, LEOPOLD [born Boleslawowicz Antonio Stanislaw] (1822–1977). Stage and film conductor and musician. A renowned, eccentric maestro of the concert world, the handsome, wild-haired conductor was one of the few of his profession widely known to the public because of his handful of film appearances. Stokowski was born in London, the son of a Polish cabinet maker, and was a child prodigy in music, playing the organ at St. James Church in London and going on to become one of the world's foremost conductors. He became an American citizen in 1915 and remained in Philadelphia where he made that city's symphony orchestra one of the finest anywhere. Stokowski made an appearance in the movie musical *BIG BROADCAST OF 1937* (1936) and was featured in *ONE HUNDRED MEN AND A GIRL* (1937). He persuaded WALT DISNEY to make *FANTASIA* (1940) and oversaw all the musical aspects of the film, as well as conducting it on screen. Stokowski also did a specialty in *Carnegie Hall* (1949). With his shock of long hair, fake eastern European accent, and flamboyant conducting techniques, he was to many the clichéd symphony maestro and was often parodied in live and animated films. However, the showy exterior hid one of the music world's most gifted talents. He was still making recordings when he died at the age of ninety-five. Biography: *The Mystery of Leopold Stokowski*, William Ander Smith (1990).

STOLL, GEORGE (1905–1985). Film musician and orchestrator. One of Hollywood's most respected and requested conductors, he supervised the music for many classic musicals. Stoll was born in Minneapolis and got his conducting experience on radio before going to MGM in the late 1930s. His many credits, which range from operetta to ELVIS PRESLEY vehicles, include *BROADWAY MELODY OF 1938* (1937), *BABES IN ARMS* (1939), *STRIKE UP THE BAND* (1940), *FOR ME AND MY GAL* (1942), *CABIN IN THE SKY* (1943), *MEET ME IN ST. LOUIS* (1945), *ANCHORS AWEIGH* (1945), *The Kissing Bandit* (1949), *THE STUDENT PRINCE* (1954), *Meet Me in Las Vegas*

(1956), *JUMBO* (1962), *VIVA LAS VEGAS* (1964), and *Made in Paris* (1966). Stoll composed background music for movies as well as songs for both musicals and nonmusicals. He also had a popular band that made many recordings and gave concerts.

STONE, FRED [born Va Alfred Andrew Stone] (1873–1959). Stage performer. A much-loved actor–singer–dancer who was half of a famous musical comedy team, the agile comic enjoyed a long career as a solo artist as well. Stone was born in Longmont, Colorado, and raised in Topeka, Kansas, where he first started doing acrobatic stunts with his brother Erwin. The siblings joined the circus as clowns and then Fred performed with a minstrel troupe with DAVID MONTGOMERY, with whom he later teamed up with to become a very popular act in vaudeville, British music halls, circuses, burlesque, and Wild West shows. The twosome were first seen on Broadway as comic pirates in *The Girl From Up There* (1901), which they repeated in London, but the show that made them Broadway stars was *THE WIZARD OF OZ* (1903) in which Stone played the Scarecrow to Montgomery's Tin Woodman. The team was a hit as two American tourists bumbling their way through Holland in *THE RED MILL* (1906) and as two Chinese sidekicks in *CHIN-CHIN* (1914). Montgomery and Stone's other musical credits together were *The Old Town* (1909) and *The Lady of the Slipper* (1912). Montgomery died in 1917 and Stone continued performing solo in such musicals as *Jack o' Lantern* (1917), *Tip Top* (1920), *Stepping Stones* (1923), *Criss Cross* (1926), *Ripples* (1930), and *Smiling Faces* (1932). He acted in a handful of silent and talking films, none of which utilized his musical comedy talents. In 1934 Stone turned to playing character parts in nonmusicals and then retired from Broadway in 1946. His daughters are actress–singer Dorothy Stone (1905–1974), actress–producer Paula Stone (1912–1997), and television actress Carol Stone (1915–). Autobiography: *Rolling Stone* (1945); biography: *Fred Stone: Circus Performer and Musical Comedy Star*, Armond Fields (2002).

STONE, PETER (1930–2003). Stage, film, and television writer. A very successful author of Broadway musical hits and film comedies, he was also a valued play "doctor" who made uncredited contributions to many stage works. Stone was born in Los Angeles, the son of a writer–producer, and educated at Bard College and Yale University. After graduation he wrote novels, plays, and television scripts, and his

Broadway bow came with his libretto for the musical *Kean* (1961). Two years later he wrote his first screenplay, *Charade*, based on his own novel, and went on to write *Father Goose* (1964), *Mirage* (1965), *The Taking of Pelham 123* (1974), and other movies. Stone frequently wrote for television, penning the teleplay for the TV musical ANDROCLES AND THE LION (1967). After writing the book for the short-lived stage musical *Skyscraper* (1965), he finally found acclaim on Broadway with his libretto for *1776* (1969) and went on to write the books for the musicals *TWO BY TWO* (1970), *SUGAR* (1972), *WOMAN OF THE YEAR* (1981), *THE WILL ROGERS FOLLIES* (1991), and *TITANIC* (1997), as well as the revised librettos for *MY ONE AND ONLY* (1983), *GRAND HOTEL* (1989), and *ANNIE GET YOUR GUN* (1999). Stone wrote the screenplay for the film version of *SWEET CHARITY* (1969) and adapted his *1776* libretto for the screen in 1972.

⚉ STOP THE WORLD—I WANT TO GET OFF

(Shubert Theatre 1962). A British import that was too offbeat for some tastes, the musical boasted some hit songs so the production ran 555 performances. In a circus tent, the allegorical tale of the clown-like Littlechap (ANTHONY NEWLEY) is enacted, showing his affairs with different women over the years (all played by Anna Quayle), and ending his life unfulfilled and wondering why he has been so foolish. Newley and LESLIE BRICUSSE wrote the libretto and score for the Everyman tale that was sometimes music hall jokes and other times broad anguish. Three hits came from the show, "What Kind of Fool Am I," "Gonna Build a Mountain," and "Once in a Lifetime," and audiences came to see Newley and to hear the hit songs that were given a lot of radio play at the time. DAVID MERRICK produced the London success and Newley directed.

▰ STORMY WEATHER

(Fox 1942). Offering the grandest collection of African American talent ever assembled in a major Hollywood film, the musical is an archival treasure trove. LENA HORNE, BILL "BOGANGLES" ROBINSON, THOMAS "FATS" WALLER, CAB CALLOWAY and his band, DOOLEY WILSON, the NICHOLAS BROTHERS, Flourney Miller, Ada Brown, Babe Wallace, Mae E. Johnson, Benny Carter, and Katherine Dunham and her dancers were all captured on film doing what they did best. Although it all seemed like a revue, the movie had a storyline by Frederick Jackson and others about the tap dancer Bill Williamson (Robinson) pursuing singer Selina Rogers

(Horne) from 1911 to 1936 and then winning her during World War II. Aside from the fact that it gave Robinson the only leading role of his film career, the plot was dispensable. But the songs and dances (choreographed by Clarence Robinson and NICK CASTLE) told a story of their own. Waller played the piano and warbled "Ain't Misbehavin'," Horne crooned the torchy "There's No Two Ways About Love," the Nicholas Brothers exploded with "Jumpin' Jive," Calloway joined Robinson for "Rhythm Cocktail," Johnson lamented "I Lost My Sugar in Salt Lake City," and Horne delivered the 1933 HAROLD ARLEN–TED KOEHLER title number for the first time in her screen career and it immediately became her signature song. Andrew Stone directed the WILLIAM LEBARON production that was not a blockbuster at the box office but a triumph all the same.

⬚ STORY OF RUDOLPH THE RED-NOSED REINDEER, THE

(NBC-TV 1964). Arguably the most popular musical ever produced for television, the stop-action animated fantasy has been broadcast every Christmas since 1964 and has rarely been bested in regards to storytelling, animation, and score.

Plot: When Rudolph is born in Christmasville, he has a red nose that flashes on and off at random. His parents try to hide the defect but cannot and Rudolph grows up being teased by the other young reindeer. Also not fitting into the scheme of things at Christmasville is Hermy, an elf who would rather be a dentist than make toys. Rudolph and Hermy run away from Christmasville and are nearly destroyed by the Abominable Snowman but are rescued by the prospector Yukon Cornelius. After visiting the Island of Misfit Toys, the two return to Christmasville to discover that Rudolph's parents have gone in search for their son and have been captured by the Snowman. Once again Cornelius saves the day. He discovers that the cause of the monster's anger is a toothache. He stuns the Snowman and Hermy pulls out his teeth, thereby curing the ache and making the monster harmless and happy to help the elves make toys. A blizzard threatens to cancel Christmas until Santa realizes that Rudolph's shiny nose can guide the sleigh through the storm. Adding the misfit toys to his sacks, Santa sets off on his rounds with Rudolph leading the way.

The sixty-minute musical was the first to use a process called Animagic in which stop-motion photography captured the three-dimensional figures and gave them smooth, life-like movements. (It was actually a more sophisticated

Cast for *The Story of Rudolph the Red-Nosed Reindeer*

Character	Performer (voice)
Sam the Snowman/Narrator	Burl Ives
Rudolph	Billie Mae Richards
Hermy the elf	Paul Soles
Yukon Cornelius	Larry Mann
Santa Claus/King Moonracer	Stan Francis
Comet/Donner	Paul Kligman
Clarice	Janet Orenstein
Head elf	Alfie Scopp

The Story of Rudolph the Red-Nosed Reindeer Musical Numbers

"Rudolph the Red-Nosed Reindeer"
"Jingle, Jingle, Jingle"
"There's Always Tomorrow"
"Silver and Gold"
"We Are Santa's Elves"
"Most Wonderful Day of the Year"
"Fame and Fortune"
"A Holly, Jolly Christmas"

The Story of Rudolph the Red Nosed Reindeer. Before computer animation there was stop-action animation, which was not so high tech yet very time consuming (and expensive). The simple, almost primitive look of stop-action can be endearing, as seen here with Santa Claus and the young Rudolph; their eyes tell you everything. (Photofest)

MULLER wrote the teleplay for the *General Electric Fantasy Hour* productions, adding the subplots that paralleled Rudolph's failure to fit in. Marks wrote seven new songs for the broadcast, with "A Holly, Jolly Christmas" already released and growing in popularity before the show was aired. It was a tuneful, contagiously catchy set of songs that gave the tale another level of whimsy and playfulness. ARTHUR RANKIN, JR. and JULES BASS produced and directed (with Larry Roemer) the celebrated musical and because it was so successful they brought their title character back for the TV musicals *Rudolph's Shiny New Year* (1976) and *RUDOLPH AND FROSTY'S CHRISTMAS IN JULY* (1979). Christmas specials have proliferated before and after *The Story of Rudolph the Red-Nosed Reindeer*, but it remains a masterwork in the field and represents a standard by which all others are judged.

version of the process used for the film *King Kong* thirty-one years before.) The painstaking preparation took a full year and cost NBC $500,000. The basic story of Rudolph goes back to 1939, a decade before Johnny Marks wrote the best-selling song that Gene Autry recorded with great success. There had also been a short cartoon version of Rudolph in 1944. ROMEO

▪ STORY OF VERNON AND IRENE CASTLE, THE (RKO 1939). More intriguing as a FRED ASTAIRE and GINGER ROGERS film than a biography of the famous dance team of pre–World War I, the plodding movie only comes alive when the two Hollywood starts set foot onto the dance floor. OSCAR HAMMERSTEIN and Dorothy Yost adapted IRENE CASTLE's memoir

My Husband and Richard Sherman wrote the dull screenplay. The famous couple is followed from their first meeting in 1910, their marriage and struggles for recognition, their introduction of the Castle Walk in Paris, their subsequent tour of America, and Vernon's death in a plane crash while preparing to go overseas to fight in the Great War. Because they were playing real people and Irene Castle was on the set as advisor, Rogers and Astaire seemed rather constricted in their dialogue scenes together. It was the team's least popular film, probably because it didn't have the glitzy, art deco look of their previous vehicles and somewhat because Astaire dies in the end, which audiences did not like. The supporting cast was exceptionally strong: Edna May Oliver, WALTER BRENNAN, LEW FIELDS, LEONID KINSKEY, Janet Beecher, MARGE CHAMPION, Clarence Derwent, and others. However, all of them made little impact and it was the dancing that mattered. HERMES PAN and Astaire choreographed the numbers, set to period songs such as "By the Beautiful Sea," "By the Light of the Silvery Moon," "Little Brown Jug," "Yama Yama Man," and "Waiting for the Robert E. Lee." BERT KALMAR, CON CONRAD, and HARRY RUBY wrote the one new song, the romantic ballad "Only When You're in My Arms," which could have been the cautionary evaluation of the movie. H. C. POTTER directed the George Haight production, which was the last Astaire–Rogers film for ten years.

STOTHART, HERBERT [Pope] (1885–1949). Stage and film composer, arranger, and musical director. Although little known today, he was a master craftsman who was involved in some famous Broadway and Hollywood musicals of the 1920s and 1930s. Stothart was born in Milwaukee, Wisconsin, and educated at the University of Wisconsin where he composed varsity shows. After graduation he taught drama at his alma mater but was drawn to music so he quit teaching and went to Chicago where he scored musicals between 1912 and 1915. Going to New York, Stothart made his Broadway debut with his score for OSCAR HAMMERSTEIN's first musical, *Always You* (1920). Much of the time he served as musical director and arranger for producer ARTHUR HAMMERSTEIN, but he did provide original music for other musicals, such as *Tickle Me* (1920), *Jimmie* (1920), *Daffy Dill* (1922), *WILDFLOWER* (1923), *Mary Jane McKane* (1923), *ROSE-MARIE* (1924), *Vogues of 1924*, *Marjorie* (1924), *Song of the Flame* (1925), *Golden Dawn* (1927), and *Good Boy* (1928).

Stothart went to Hollywood in 1928 and stayed on to orchestrate, arrange, and conduct dozens of musical films, such as *THE MERRY WIDOW* (1934), *NAUGHTY MARIETTA* (1935), *Rose Marie* (1936), *SAN FRANCISCO* (1936), *MAYTIME* (1937), *THE FIREFLY* (1937), *THE WIZARD OF OZ* (1939), and *NEW MOON* (1940). He also was musical director for nonmusicals such as *David Copperfield* (1935), *Mutiny on the Bounty* (1935), *The Good Earth* (1937), and *The Three Musketeers* (1948). Because he often collaborated with better-known composers, such as VINCENT YOUMANS and RUDOLF FRIML, Stothart never became a famous name for his own music, but in New York and Hollywood he was considered one of the most proficient musical talents in the business.

STRAUS, OSCAR [Nathan] (1870–1954). Stage composer. A major figure on the musical stages of Vienna and Berlin, the operetta composer was well represented on Broadway and in Hollywood. The Vienna-born Straus began his career conducting theatre orchestras in Germany and then turned to composing, scoring over forty operas and operettas. Many of these were seen in English-speaking countries, although sometimes the adaptations were far from faithful. Strauss's most familiar works on Broadway include *A Waltz Dream* (1908), *THE CHOCOLATE SOLDIER* (1909), *My Little Friend* (1913), *My Lady's Glove* (1917), *The Last Waltz* (1921), and *Three Waltzes* (1937). His music was used in creating a handful of movie musicals as well, although the story on screen rarely resembled the original European musical. Various American lyricists set his music to words for *Married in Hollywood* (1929), *A Lady's Morals* (1930), *THE SMILING LIEUTENANT* (1931), *ONE HOUR WITH YOU* (1932), *The Queen's Affair* (1934), *Make a Wish* (1937), and *The Chocolate Soldier* (1941), and his waltzing music was used in several nonmusical movies as well.

🎵 **STREET SCENE** (Adelphi Theatre 1947). Arguably KURT WEILL's most ambitious project, the musical drama bordered on opera and its future would lie in opera houses. As in Elmer Rice's 1929 drama of the same title, the musical looked at several residents of a Manhattan apartment building, particularly the young love developing between Sam Kaplan (Brian Sullivan) and Rose Maurrant (Anne Jeffreys), and the tragic fate of Rose's mother Anna (Polyna Stoska) whose infidelity leads her husband Willie (Peter Griffith) to murder her. Also featured in the strong cast were Sheila Bond, DANNY DANIELS, Don Saxon, Hope Emerson, and Norman Cordon. Rice wrote the libretto and LANGSTON HUGHES penned the lyrics for Weill's music, which utilized blues, jazz, jitterbug, and operatic turns. "Moon-Faced, Starry-Eyed," "I Got a Marble and a Star," "Lonely House," "Somehow I Never Could Believe," "Wouldn't You Like to Be on Broadway?," "What Good Would the Moon Be?," "Remember That I Care," and "We'll Go Away Together" were highlights in the sterling score. Reviewers praised the atmospheric piece and the splendid cast but audiences stayed away from such a demanding musical and it closed after 148 performances. DWIGHT DEERE WIMAN and the Playwrights' Company produced the musical, which later found life with opera companies, such as a laudable revival in 1959 by the New York City Light Opera.

STREISAND, BARBRA [Joan] (1942–). Stage, film, and television performer, director, and producer. The multitalented superstar who has remained a powerhouse in show business for over forty years, she began her career in musicals and has frequently returned to the genre in different media. The Brooklyn native began her career singing in nightclubs before getting her first professional legit job in the Off Broadway revue *Another Evening With Harry Stoones* (1961). She was first noticed on Broadway as the put-upon secretary Miss Marmelstein in *I CAN GET IT FOR YOU WHOLESALE* (1962) and then reached star status as FANNY BRICE in *FUNNY GIRL* (1964), a role she reprised on screen in 1968 affording her a remarkable Hollywood debut. One of the few female box office stars of her era, Streisand was cast in some big-budget movie musicals, playing matchmaker Dolly Levi in *HELLO, DOLLY!* (1969), the psychic Daisy Gamble in *ON A CLEAR DAY YOU CAN SEE FOREVER* (1969), and Brice again in *FUNNY LADY* (1975). She has also been popular in nonmusical films, eventually directing and producing some herself, but returned to the

Barbra Streisand. The unique singer–actress not only starred in her movie musicals, she had to carry them as well. Practically every scene and every song in *Funny Girl* (1968), *On a Clear Day You Can See Forever* (1970), *Yentl* (1983), and other musicals had Streisand holding the picture together. No one ever asked Bing Crosby or Jeanette MacDonald to be on screen all the time. Whenever Streisand is not seen, her movies flag a bit. That is not so much a condemnation of the films as a tribute to her star power. Pictured is Streisand in the screen version of *Funny Girl*. (Photofest)

musical genre with *A Star Is Born* (1976) and *Yentl* (1983), contributing to the scripts and the songs. Streisand has never returned to Broadway but has given many live performances over the years, with her concerts becoming legendary occasions. She also starred in a series of musical specials on television that rank among the most popular and renowned of their kind, just as her many recordings through the decades are prized by her legion of fans. Streisand was married to actor Elliott Gould (1938–) for a time and their son is actor Jason Gould (1966–); she is currently married to actor James Brolin (1940–). Biographies: *Barbra: The Way She Is*, Christopher Andersen (2006); *Streisand: The Intimate Biography*, James Spada (1995).

🐦 **Strike Up the Band** (Times Square Theatre 1930). The first of a handful of 1930s musicals that used political and social satire to deal with the grim reality of the Depression, the farcical show had a very serious subtext. George and Ira Gershwin teamed up with librettist George S. Kaufman in 1927 and wrote an incisive musical satire that was so dark that audiences bristled and the production closed out of town. With a new and more palatable libretto by Morrie Ryskind, the musical opened on Broadway in 1930 and was a success, running 191 performances. The plot, all in a dream, dealt with a war between the United States and Switzerland over tariffs on imported Swiss chocolate. Everything from White House pacifists to Swiss yodeling came under comic attack, and Ira Gershwin provided several comic lyrics, such as "A Typical Self-Made American," which parodied Gilbert and Sullivan. Also in the score were two popular love songs, "Soon" and "I've Got a Crush on You," and the satirically rousing title number. The cast featured comics Bobby Clark and Paul McCullough, belter Blanche Ring, Dudley Clements, Doris Carson, Jerry Goff, and the Red Nichols orchestra, which sounded terrific, having a young Benny Goodman, Gene Krupa, Glenn Miller, Jack Teagarden, and Jimmy Dorsey in the pit. While *Strike Up the Band* was not as polished as the later Gershwin–Kaufman–Ryslind musical *Of Thee I Sing* (1931), the Edgar Selwyn production, directed by Alexander Leftwich and choreographed by George Hale, was a bold and clever work that forecast one of the ways Broadway would react to the difficult 1930s.
▪ **Strike Up the Band** (MGM 1940) took only the title song from the Gershwin stage work, turned it into a straightforward

patriotic number, and created another Mickey Rooney–Judy Garland "let's put on a show" movie. High schooler Jimmy Connors (Rooney) has a jazz band with classmate Mary Holden (Garland) as his vocalist and he wants to take the whole gang to Chicago to enter an amateur band contest sponsored by orchestra conductor Paul Whiteman. The complications include lack of money for bus fare, Jimmy's mother (Ann Shoemaker) wanting him to give up music and become a doctor, and the arrival of rich and pretty Barbara Frances Morgan (June Preisser) who comes between Jimmy and Mary. The kids produce a hysterical musical melodrama to raise funds but they aren't needed because Barbara's family has hired Whiteman and his orchestra to come to town and play for her birthday party. Jimmy and the band audition for Whiteman and win the contest. There were some slow and maudlin stretches in the film but for the most part director–choreographer Busby Berkeley moved things along and came up with some engaging moments without using spectacle, such as Garland's wistful rendition of Roger Edens's "Nobody" in the local library and a number by Edens and producer Arthur Freed titled "Our Love Affair," which the young couple sang and then was performed by animated fruits as musicians conducted by Rooney. However, the finale, which used the title song, was spectacular with multiple bands and chorale groups with creative camera work, dramatic shadows, and clever editing.

Stritch, Elaine (1925–). Stage, film, and television performer. The unsentimental, raspy-voiced actress–singer who specializes in tough, sarcastic dames has given electric performances in plays and musicals over a period of sixty years. Stritch was born in Detroit and trained with Erwin Piscator at Manhattan's New School before she began working professionally in New York in 1945. She did not get noticed until she sang "Civilization" in the Broadway revue *Angel in the Wings* (1947) and then continued to attract attention in colorful supporting roles in *Pal Joey* (1952) and *On Your Toes* (1954). Stritch replaced Ethel Merman in *Call Me Madam* in 1953 and toured with it and then was the star of her own shows with *Goldilocks* (1958), in which she played the hapless actress Maggie Harris, and *Sail Away* (1961) for which Noel Coward wrote the role of shipboard recreation director Mimi Paragon just for her; she reprised the part on the London stage. After playing journalist Ruth Sherwood in a 1967 revival of *WONDERFUL TOWN*, Stritch gave one of her most renowned performances as the caustic New York alcoholic Joanne in *COMPANY* (1970), which she repeated in London. She played the scowling Parthy in the popular 1994 revival of *SHOW BOAT* and then was widely acclaimed for her autobiographical revue *Elaine Stritch: At Liberty* (2001), which was a hit Off Broadway, on Broadway, and in London. She made her first of many television appearances in 1948 and has been in films since 1946, but she was usually cast in minor roles in both media and rarely got to use her musical talents as she has on records and in nightclubs.

STROMAN, SUSAN (1954–). Stage and film director and choreographer. The much-praised choreographer-tuned-director has risen to the top of her profession in a relatively short time because of a string of splashy hits. Stroman was born in Wilmington, Delaware, and educated at the University of Delaware before pursuing a dance career until the mid-1980s, performing in such Broadway musicals as *CHICAGO* (1975), *WHOOPEE* (1979), and *PETER PAN* (1979). She began choreographing in regional theatre in 1987 and was first noticed in Manhattan for her clever staging of the musical numbers in the Off Broadway revue *And the World Goes 'Round* in 1991. Stroman provided vigorous and imaginative dances for *CRAZY FOR YOU* (1992), *SHOW BOAT* (1994), *Big* (1996), *Steel Pier* (1997), and *OKLAHOMA!* (2002). She began to direct as well as choreograph with the dance theatre piece *CONTACT* (2000) and has done both for most of her subsequent shows, including *THE MUSIC MAN* (2000), *Thou Shalt Not* (2001), *The Frogs* (2004), *THE PRODUCERS* (2001), which she also directed and choreographed for the screen, and *YOUNG FRANKENSTEIN* (2007). Her dances often employ props in ingenious ways and often she uses the dancers themselves as scenic devices, such as turning chorines into bass fiddles in the "Slap That Bass" number in *Crazy for You*. Stroman is also interested in the history of dance and frequently conjures up visions of past styles, such as the 1930s dances in *Steel Pier* and showing the development of African American dance in *Show Boat*. She was married to British director MIKE OCKRENT.

STROMBERG, HUNT (1894–1968). Film producer. A top MGM producer who worked with the studio's greatest female stars, he presented some widely popular musicals as well. Stromberg was born in Louisville, Kentucky, and worked as a sports reporter for a St. Louis newspaper before entering films as a public-ity man. By 1921 he was producing features, sometimes contributing to the scripts as well. Stromberg first teamed JEANETTE MACDONALD and NELSON EDDY together in *NAUGHTY MARIETTA* (1935) and also produced the team's musicals *ROSE MARIE* (1936), *MAYTIME* (1937), *SWEETHEARTS* (1938), and *I MARRIED AN ANGEL* (1942). His other musicals were *THE GREAT ZIEGFELD* (1936), *THE FIREFLY* (1937), and *Lady of Burlesque* (1943).

STROUSE, CHARLES. See ADAMS, Lee.

STUART, GLORIA [born Gloria Frances Stewart] (1910–). Film and television performer. A striking blonde beauty, she appeared in a handful of musicals even though she rarely sang or danced. Stuart was born in Santa Monica, California, and educated at the University of California at Berkeley before getting some stage experience and being signed by UNIVERSAL PICTURES. Usually cast as intelligent, glamorous ingénues in comedies and dramas, she also appeared in such musicals as *ROMAN SCANDALS* (1933), *It's Great to Be Alive* (1933), *Gift of Gab* (1934), *GOLD DIGGERS OF 1935*, *POOR LITTLE RICH GIRL* (1936), *REBECCA OF SUNNYBROOK FARM* (1938), *The Lady Objects* (1938), *The Three Musketeers* (1939), and *Here Comes Elmer* (1943). Stuart retired from the screen in the late 1940s and became a reputable artist. She started acting again on television in the 1970s and made quite a stir when she returned to the movies to play the aged Rose in the nonmusical *Titanic* (1997). Autobiography: *I Just Kept Hoping* (1999).

STUDENT PRINCE, THE (Jolson's 59th Street Theatre 1924). Arguably composer SIGMUND ROMBERG's finest operetta, the show boasts lyrics and a libretto by DOROTHY DONNELLY that are still engaging.

Plot: Before he takes up his duties as prince, Karl-Franz goes to Heidelberg University for a year, accompanied by his old tutor Dr. Engel who once attended the school himself and has fond memories of his youthful days there. The two reside at an inn called The Three Apples where the students gather to drink and sing and Karl-Franz falls in love with Kathie, the waitress at the tavern, even though she is a commoner. The two lovers find their romance is short-lived; word arrives that Karl-Franz's father the king has died and the prince returns home to be crowned king and marry Princess Margaret for political reasons. After he becomes king, Karl-Franz quietly returns to Heidelberg and he and Kathie bid each other farewell, vowing to never forget their love for each other.

Casts for *The Student Prince*

Character	1924 Broadway	1954 film
Prince Karl Franz	HOWARD MARSH	Edmund Purdom
Kathie	Ilse Marvenga	ANN BLYTH
Dr. Engel	Greek Evans	Edmund Gwenn
Lutz	George Hassell	John Williams
Princess	Roberta Beatty	Betta St. John
Capt. Tarnitz	John Coast	
Joseph Ruder	W. H. White	S. K. SAKALL

The Student Prince (stage) Musical Numbers

"By Our Bearings So Sedate"
"Golden Days"
"Garlands Bright"
"Drinking Song"
"To the Inn We're Marching"
"You're in Heidelberg"
"Welcome to Prince"
"Deep in My Heart, Dear"
"Serenade (Overhead the Moon Is Beaming"
"Come, Sir, Will You Join Our Noble Saxon Corps"
"Farmer Jacob (Lay-a-Snoring)"
"Student Life"
"Farewell, Dear"
"Waltz Ensemble"
"Just We Two"
"Gavotte"
"What Memories"
"Sing a Little Song"
"Come Boys (Let's All Be Gay, Boys)"

Titled *The Student Prince in Heidelberg* when it first opened but abridged to *The Student Prince* ever since, the operetta was based on the German play *Alt Heidelberg*, which had been adapted into a nonmusical years earlier. The musical was unusual in two respects: it had a bittersweet ending with the lovers separating instead of marrying and it featured a strong male chorus instead of a line of pretty chorines. The producing SHUBERTS worried about these unconventional aspects of the piece but audiences loved the tearful ending and the men's chorale was thrilling, particularly during the rousing "Drinking Song." The other hits to come from the indelible Romberg–Donnelly score were the nostalgic ballad "Golden Days" and the thrilling duets "Serenade (Overhead the Moon Is Beaming)" and "Deep in My Heart, Dear." The score was filled with variety, some of the numbers stirring, such as the opening "By Our Bearings So Sedate" and "To the Inn We're Marching," whereas others are light-hearted and frolicsome, as in "Student Life" and "Come Boys (Let's All Be Gay Boys)." J. C. HUFFMAN directed the original production, which was as romantic to look at as to hear, and the operetta ran 606 performances, the longest run of the decade. *The Student Prince* was also one of the most successful Broadway shows of the period on the road, with companies touring the country almost nonstop for twenty-five years. New York has seen revivals in 1931, 1943, 1980, 1981, 1985, 1987, and 1993. The operetta remains one of the most frequently produced by opera and light opera companies.

■ *The Student Prince* (MGM 1954) was certainly late in coming, not made until thirty years after the New York opening. A silent film version with Norma Shearer and Ramon Novarro was very popular in 1927 so it is surprising that Hollywood waited so long to make a movie of the popular piece. It was probably the popularity of tenor MARIO LANZA that prompted producer JOE PASTERNAK to make the film and Lanza was signed and recorded the score before he broke his contract and walked away from the project. His reasons have never been made clear, although the tenor had put on a great deal of weight and was suffering from alcoholism and depression, which must have been a factor. MGM used the Lanza recordings and cast handsome but wooden Edward Purdom as the prince and it was difficult to detect much passion for bar maid Kathie, played with zest by ANN BLYTH. The screenplay by SONYA LEVIEN and William Ludwig took a few liberties with the story and added humor to the script by building up the role of Kathie's father Joseph Ruder, played by the scene-stealing S. Z. SAKALL. The highlights of the stage score were retained and two new songs, "I'll Walk With God" and "Beloved" by NICHOLAS BRODSZKY (music) and PAUL FRANCIS WEBSTER (lyrics), were added. The production was visually beautiful, and RICHARD THORPE directed efficiently, but the movie lacks chemistry between the lovers and rarely is emotionally involving.

STYNE, JULE [born Jules Kerwin Stein] (1905–1994). Stage, film, and television composer and producer. One of Broadway's favorite songwriters, the prolific composer had a long Hollywood career before his first stage musical ever opened in New York. Styne was born in London but grew up in America where he was a child prodigy on the piano, but he threw over a concert career to form a jazz band and write popular music. He first went to Hollywood as a vocal arranger and was a singing coach for such stars as ALICE FAYE and SHIRLEY TEMPLE. By 1938 some of his songs were being used in films, although at first most were B pictures and he never became famous even if some of his songs were hits. Collaborating with FRANK LOESSER, HERB MAGIDSON, SAMMY CAHN, and other lyricists, Styne scored thirty movie musicals before his theatre career began in 1948, including *Melody and Moonlight* (1940), *Sis Hopkins* (1941), *Sleepy Time Gal* (1942), *Sweater Girl* (1942), *Youth on Parade* (1942), *Thumbs Up!* (1943), *KNICKERBOCKER HOLIDAY* (1944), *Step Lively* (1944), *Carolina Blues* (1944), *ANCHORS AWEIGH* (1945), *The Kid From Brooklyn* (1946), *Ladies' Man* (1947), *IT HAPPENED IN BROOKLYN* (1947), and *ROMANCE ON THE HIGH SEAS* (1948). With Cahn he scored his first Broadway musical, *HIGH BUTTON SHOES* (1948), and with LEO ROBIN he also had a hit with *GENTLEMEN PREFER BLONDES* (1949). Styne's most frequent Broadway collaborators were lyricist-librettists BETTY COMDEN and ADOLPH GREEN and together they wrote *TWO ON THE AISLE* (1951), *PETER PAN* (1954), *BELLS ARE RINGING* (1956), *Say, Darling* (1958), *DO RE MI* (1960), *SUBWAYS ARE FOR SLEEPING* (1961), *FADE OUT–FADE IN* (1964), and *HALLELUJAH, BABY!* (1967). With BOB MERRILL he scored *FUNNY GIRL* (1964) and *SUGAR* (1972) and with other partners wrote *Hazel Flagg* (1953), *Darling of the Day* (1968), *Look to the Lilies* (1970), and *The Red Shoes* (1993). Most agree that Styne's greatest Broadway score was *GYPSY* (1959) with lyrics by STEPHEN SONDHEIM. Many of Styne's stage works were filmed and after 1950 he concentrated on Broadway, but he occasionally returned to writing for the movies, as with *It's a Great Feeling* (1949), *The West Point Story* (1950), *Two Tickets to Broadway* (1951), *Double Dynamite* (1951), *MY SISTER EILEEN* (1955), and *What a Way to Go* (1964), as well as

songs for nonmusicals such as "Three Coins in the Fountain." Styne was active on television and, working with various lyricists, scored the original TV musicals *RUGGLES OF RED GAP* (1957), *MR. MAGOO'S CHRISTMAS* (1962), *THE DANGEROUS CHRISTMAS OF RED RIDING HOOD* (1965), *I'm Getting Married* (1968), and *The Night the Animals Talked* (1970). He was also a Broadway producer and presented the musicals *Make a Wish* (1951), the acclaimed 1952 revival of *PAL JOEY*, *MR. WONDERFUL* (1956), and *First Impressions* (1959). Styne's music is variable and accessible, often in the popular style of its time and in the Broadway tradition. Biography: *Jule: The Story of Composer Jule Styne*, Theodore Taylor (1979).

🕙 **SUBWAYS ARE FOR SLEEPING** (St. James Theatre 1961). One of the lesser efforts by JULE STYNE (music), BETTY COMDEN, and ADOLPH GREEN (book, lyrics), the unusual musical comedy still had its pleasurable moments. New Yorker Tom Bailey (SYDNEY CHAPLIN) has dropped out of society and rides on the subway all day. He falls in love with the magazine writer Angela McKay (CAROL LAWRENCE) who interviews him. Also riding the subway is beauty contest winner Martha Vail (PHYLLIS NEWMAN) who has been evicted and runs around in a towel, much to the bemusement of her sweetheart Charlie Smith (Orson Bean). It was an odd story and the characters didn't make much sense at times but the performers, under MICHAEL KIDD's direction and choreography, were spirited and the score was commendable, with the highlights being "Comes Once in a Lifetime," "Ride Through the Night," "Be a Santa," "Girls Like Me," and "I Just Can't Wait." The press disdained the show as a poor excuse for some sprightly performances and enjoyable musical numbers and prospects did not look promising so producer DAVID MERRICK pulled one of his most famous publicity stunts, running a newspaper ad filled with rave reviews by bogus theatre critics who happened to have the names of real critics. Theatre journalists fumed, there was a big fuss made about truth in advertising, and all the hoopla sold enough tickets to let the show run 205 performances.

🕙 **SUGAR** (Majestic Theatre 1972). One of those rare musicals that worked best when the libretto took over from the songs, the show was based on the hilarious film *Some Like It Hot* (1959) and, while the libretto by PETER STONE was no match for the movie, it was still funny.

During Prohibition, Chicago musicians Joe (TONY ROBERTS) and Jerry (ROBERT MORSE) witness the St. Valentine's Day massacre and are hunted by Spats Palazzo (Steve Condos) and his gang, so the two disguise themselves as females and get a job with an all-girl band run by Sweet Sue (Sheila Smith) that is going to Florida. Joe falls for the beautiful Sugar Kane (Elaine Joyce) and Jerry is pursued by the randy old millionaire Osgood Fielding, Jr. (CYRIL RITCHARD), with both couples finding some sort of happiness by the final curtain. JULE STYNE (music) and BOB MERRILL (lyrics) wrote the lackluster score that included "We Could Be Close," "November Song," "Beautiful Through and Through," "It's Always Love," and the title song. GOWER CHAMPION directed and choreographed the DAVID MERRICK production, and the performances were first rate but the musical never fell into place and the notices were mixed. All the same the show ran 500 performances on the strength of its stars and the audience's fond memory of the film.

SUGAR BABIES (Mark Hellinger Theatre 1979). A pleasing mixture of not-so-dirty burlesque and nostalgia, the revue became topflight entertainment thanks to its stars. Ralph G. Allen conceived and wrote the sketches for this idealized version of a burlesque show that contained better songs, sketches, and stars than one found in the days of Minsky's. Film stars MICKEY ROONEY (in his belated Broadway debut) and ANN MILLER led the cast of singers, dancers, and comics, directed and choreographed by Ernest Flatt, and memorable songs by JIMMY MCHUGH, DOROTHY FIELDS, RAY EVANS, JAY LIVINGSTON, and others offered a pleasant contrast with the comic sketches. There was even a dog act to fill out the evening's fun. Critical raves and strong word of mouth made the show a hit, running 1,208 performances and touring for four years.

SUMMER HOLIDAY (MGM 1947). An atmospheric piece of Americana in the vein of *MEET ME IN ST. LOUIS* (1944), the pleasing movie musical never caught on with the public even though it was exceptional in all departments. The screenplay by FRANCES GOODRICH and ALBERT HACKETT was closely based on Eugene O'Neill's Broadway hit *Ah, Wilderness!* (1933), the great playwright's only comedy and an idealized depiction of a life he never knew. At the turn of the twentieth century in a small Connecticut town, the Miller family is having its everyday headaches dealing with teenager Richard (MICKEY ROONEY) who is rebelling against traditional views, embracing radical literature such as poetry by Dowson and plays by Shaw, and falling in love with the sweet innocent Muriel McComber (GLORIA DeHAVEN). The young couple is separated by the girl's father and Richard goes to the local bar where he gets drunk and has a run-in with saloon singer Belle (MARILYN MAXWELL) before sobering up in time to be reunited with Muriel. Richards parents were played by Walter Huston and Selena Royle, and the spinster Aunt Lily (AGNES MOOREHEAD) and the tipsy Uncle Sid (FRANK MORGAN) who woos her made up the subplot. The performances were colorful yet genuine, and ROUBEN MAMOULIAN directed with precision and warmth. Although none of the songs became popular, the score by HARRY WARREN (music) and RALPH BLANE (lyrics) was filled with rich melodies and sincere sentiments. The amiable "Our Home Town" introduced the members of the Miller household, the young couple's "Afraid to Fall in Love" was a touching character song, they all took a ride and celebrated "The Stanley Steamer," and the father wryly looked back at youth and reflected "Spring Isn't Everything." With its lovely score, evocative sets and costumes, and engaging performances, *Summer Holiday* is an unpretentious little gem of a movie that is undeservedly neglected.

Casts for *Summer Holiday* and *Take Me Along*

	Summer Holiday	*Take Me Along*	
Character	*1948 film*	*1959 Broadway*	*1985 Broadway*
Richard Miller	MICKEY ROONEY	ROBERT MORSE	Gary Landon Wright
Nat Miller	Walter Huston	WALTER PIDGEON	Robert Nichols
Muriel	GLORIA DeHAVEN	Susan Luckey	Taryn Grimes
Uncle Sid	FRANK MORGAN	JACKIE GLEASON	Kurt Knudson
Lily	AGNES MOOREHEAD	Eileen Herle	BETH FOWLER
Mrs. Miller	Selena Royle	UNA MERKEL	Betty Johnson
Belle	MARILYN MAXWELL	Arlene Golonka	Nikki Sahagen

TAKE ME ALONG (Shubert Theatre 1959) was also based on O'Neill's play but had a whole new score by BOB MERRILL that was also commendable. "Staying Young," "I Get Embarrassed," "Little Green Snake," "Sid, Ol' Kid," and the bouncy title number were the notable songs. JOSEPH STEIN and Robert Russell wrote the libretto that shifted focus away from parents Nat (WALTER PIDGEON) and Essie Miller (UNA MERKEL) and their son Richard (ROBERT MORSE) and highlighted their boozing Uncle Sid played by television star JACKIE GLEASON. It threw the story off balance but it was Gleason who kept the musical on the boards for 448 performances. A 1985 revival, which originated at Connecticut's GOODSPEED OPERA HOUSE, opened on Broadway with no stars and a minimal advance so when it received mostly negative notices the production closed on opening night. Merrill wrote three new songs for the revival, "If Jesus Don't Love Ya," "In the Company of Men," and "Knights on White Horses."

SUMMER MAGIC (Disney 1963). An unabashedly sentimental musical from the DISNEY studios, it has much to offer if you can get past its heart-on-the-sleeve tone. Sally Benson's screenplay was based on the Kate Douglas Wiggin book *Mother Carey's Chickens*, which had been filmed several times, most memorably in 1938. This was the first musical version but it stayed close to the original story about the Boston widow Margaret Carey (Dorothy McGuire) who moves to Maine with her brood of children, befriends the local postman Osh Popham (Burl Ives), who sets them up in a neglected house, and has a series of domestic adventures involving sibling rivalry, petty jealousy, and young love. Haley Mills played the daughter Nancy, and the other supporting players included Eddie Hodges, Deborah Walley, Michael J. Pollard, UNA MERKEL, Jimmy Mathers, Wendy Turner, and Peter Brown. RICHARD M. and ROBERT B. SHERMAN wrote the pleasant score, with the best number being "The Ugly Bug Ball," which Ives sang as the film temporarily turned into a nature documentary showing insects frolicking. Other songs included "Femininity," "The Pink of Perfection," "Railroad Rag," and the title number.

SUMMER STOCK (MGM 1950). Although MICKEY ROONEY was replaced by GENE KELLY, this JUDY GARLAND vehicle differed little from the Rooney-Garland backstagers that the stu-dio had produced a decade earlier. The screenplay by GEORGE WELLS and Sy Gomberg even had the big show take place in the barn so there was something nostalgic about the film, even if Garland was no kid and was starting to show the ravages of her difficult life. Jane Falbury (Garland) is having trouble keeping her New England farm running so when some Manhattan actors are desperate for a place to rehearse and Jane's kid sister Abigail (GLORIA DeHAVEN) suggests the family barn, Jane is not pleased. She doesn't like show people and makes them work on the farm in exchange for room and board. The company's author–performer Joe D. Ross (Kelly) is Abigail's love interest but by the end of the picture his affections have shifted to Jane and she even takes over the leading role in the musical revue they put on for the producers. What was barely palatable with kids looked even more ridiculous with adults, but the spirited musical numbers relieved the tedium of the plot. HARRY WARREN (music) and MACK GORDON (lyrics) wrote most of the songs and, as choreographed by NICK CASTLE and Kelly, they all deserved a better vehicle. Garland sang the yearning ballads "Friendly Star" and the carefree "If You Feel Like Singing, Sing" while Kelly wooed her with "You, Wonderful You" (by JACK BROOKS, SAUL CHAPLIN, and Warren) and then performed a remarkable dance solo in which he tapped and ripped apart a newspaper. The musical highlight of the film was Garland's jazzy version of the 1930 standard "Get Happy" by HAROLD ARLEN and TED KOEHLER. The number was filmed months after the rest of the movie and a slimmer, more vital Garland is unmistakable. CHARLES WALTERS directed the frail script as best he could and got a lot of help from supporting cast members EDDIE BRACKEN, PHIL SILVERS, MARJORIE MAIN, Ray Collins, HANS CONREID, CAROL HANEY, CARLETON CARPENTER, and Nita Bieber.

SUN VALLEY SERENADE (Fox 1941). SONJA HENIE's best film, the vibrant Big Band musical also featured GLENN MILLER and a crack-erjack score by HARRY WARREN (music) and MACK GORDON (lyrics). Robert Ellis and Helen Logan's screenplay had an interesting twist that fit the war years time frame. Band leader Phil Carey (Miller) and his boys spon-sor a Norwegian child refugee but find them-selves saddled with grown-up Karen Benson (Henie). Pianist Ted Scott (JOHN PAYNE) is put in charge of her and they all head to a gig at a resort in Sun Valley, Idaho. The complications arising from Karen's falling in love with Ted while he tries to juggle the affections of other women in his life made up the plot, which seemed harmless enough when set on the snow-covered slopes. The cast also featured MILTON BERLE, LYNN BARI (dubbed by Pat Friday), JOAN DAVIS, and Martha Tilton, as well as Miller vocalists Ray Anthony, Bill May, Tex Beneke, Paula Kelly, Hal McIntyre, and the Modernaires. The biggest hit to come from the film was "Chattanooga Choo-Choo," played and vocalized by Miller and his group, and then sung by teenage DOROTHY DANDRIDGE and danced by the flying NICHOLAS BROTHERS. Also in the score were "It Happened in Sun Valley," "I Know Why (And So Do You)," and "The Kiss Polka." Miller's band played its signature number "In the Mood" (by Andy Razaf and Joe Garland), and for the finale there was a stunning ice-skating sequence choreographed by HERMES PAN that had Henie gliding across black ice. H. BRUCE HUMBERSTONE directed the Milton Sperling production that is still first-class fun.

📖 **SUNDAY IN THE PARK WITH GEORGE** (Booth Theatre 1984). A deeply personal musical play by STEPHEN SONDHEIM (music and lyrics) and JAMES LAPINE (book) that explored the creative process, the show looked and sounded like no other.

Plot: Artist George Seurat struggles against critical disapproval in 1880s Paris as he works on his large painting "A Sunday Afternoon on the Island of La Grande Jatte." His mistress Dot tires of George's supposed indifference to her so when she gets pregnant she weds a baker and emigrates to America just as George completes the painting. One hundred years later in Chicago, the modernist sculptor George tries to get funding for his expensive art projects and starts to lose faith in his talents until the ghost of Dot appears and urges him to move on with his work, just as his great-grandfather did.

Sunday in the Park with George. The plots for Broadway musicals have been based on a lot of things, from historical personages to sex farces, but this is probably the only one based on a painting. Luckily George Seurat's masterpiece had plenty of characters and lots of possibilities and the authors had an open canvas, so to speak, to work on. Pictured is the finale of Act One when the painting is being completed. The bearded figure center is the artist George, played by Mandy Patinkin, and he is gazing at his ex-mistress Dot (Bernadette Peters) in a tranquil pose before she bids him farewell for ever. (Photofest)

Cast for *Sunday in the Park With George*

Characters	1984 Broadway	2007 Broadway
George Seurat, George	MANDY PATINKIN	Daniel Evans
Dot, Marie, Dot	BERNADETTE PETERS	Jenna Russell
Old Lady, Blair Daniels	Barbara Byrne	Mary Beth Peil
Jules, Bob Greenberg	Charles Kimbrough	Michael Cumpsty
Yvonne, Naomi Eisen	Dana Ivey	Jessica Molaskey
Louis, Billy Webster	Cris Groendaal	Drew McVety
Soldier, Alex	ROBERT WESTENBERG	Santino Fontana
Frieda, Betty	Nancy Opel	Stacie Morgain Lewis
Franz, Dennis	Brent Spiner	David Turner, Alexander Germignnani
Louise	Danielle Ferland	Kelsey Fowler, Allison Horowitz

Inspired by the figures in Seraut's pointillist painting, the musical was both distant and engaging. Some characters were one-dimensional types, as flat as the painting, whereas others, such as the Georges and Dot, were complex and fascinating. Lapine directed the stunning production in which Tony Straiges's stylized scenery and Patricia Zipprodt and Ann Hould-Ward's costumes were very Seurat-like in the first act. The painting was seen in sections throughout the act, only coming together as a whole by the finale when George has finished it. The second act was slick in its look and style, with the fanciful kinetic sculpture with lasers bouncing throughout the theatre and serving as a startling contrast to the painting in the first act. Sondheim's songs were similarly different in each act, although they were all part of a whole. The delicate French impressionist sounds created by George's staccato pointillist painting techniques were far from the usual Broadway score and were difficult to digest on first hearing. There was a good deal of romanticism, also French in flavor, in the songs so the period was evoked even as the score sounded modern. In the second act the music was contemporary, although not rock or pop. Just as George's computer-generated art was funky and offbeat, so too were such numbers as the complaining "It's Hot Up Here" and the sly "Putting It Together." Other highlights in the remarkable score were the intoxicating duet "Color and Light," the revealing "Finishing the Hat," the flowing "Sunday," the encouraging "Move On," the wistful "Children and Art," and the sarcastic title number. *Sunday in the Park With George* received both raves and pans by the press and audiences were equally divided, although enough were curious to keep the show running in the small house for 540 performances. The musical won the PULITZER

Sunday in the Park With George Musical Numbers

"Sunday in the Park With George"
"No Life"
"Color and Light"
"Gossip"
"The Day Off"
"Everybody Loves Louis"
"Finishing the Hat"
"We Do Not Belong Together"
"Beautiful"
"Sunday"
"It's Hot Up Here"
"Chromolume No. 7"
"Putting It Together"
"Children and Art"
"Lesson No. 8"
"Move On"

PRIZE and over time has become more appreciated, produced successfully by ambitious theatres groups regionally and in Europe. An acclaimed London revival transfered to Broadway in 2008.

☐ The original New York cast of *Sunday in the Park With George* was videotaped in performance with a live audience and was broadcast on PBS-TV in 1986. Television director Terry Hughes filmed the show with taste and creativity and it is a stunning record of a brilliant production.

SUNDBERG, CLINTON (1906–1987). Film, television, and stage performer. A familiar Hollywood character actor who specialized in subservient butlers and sympathetic clerks, the meek, raspy-voiced actor appeared in several movie musicals. Sundberg was born in Appleton, Minnesota, and educated at Hamline

University in St. Paul for a career in education. After teaching a while, he turned to acting and got experience in stock before getting cast on the London stage. Sundberg made his Broadway debut in 1936 and was featured in the musical revue *Stars in Your Eyes* (1939). By 1946 he was in Hollywood and was kept busy for the next twenty-five years playing small but noticeable parts. His many musicals include *GOOD NEWS* (1947), *EASTER PARADE* (1948), *A DATE WITH JUDY* (1948), *The Kissing Bandit* (1948), *WORDS AND MUSIC* (1948), *THE BARKLEYS OF BROADWAY* (1949), *IN THE GOOD OLD SUMMERTIME* (1949), *ANNIE GET YOUR GUN* (1950, *THE TOAST OF NEW ORLEANS* (1950), *ON THE RIVIERA* (1951), *THE BELLE OF NEW YORK* (1952), *The Caddy* (1953), *Main Street to Broadway* (1953), and *The Wonderful World of the Brothers Grimm* (1962). Sundberg returned to Broadway in plays up until 1961 and acted in many television shows through the 1960s.

SUNNY (New Amsterdam Theatre 1925). The popular star MARILYN MILLER and composer JEROME KERN reunited for this musical that attempted to capture the allure of their earlier *SALLY* (1920) and for the most part they succeeded. The American bareback rider Sunny Peters (Miller) goes to England with the circus and falls in love with the American tourist Tom Warren (Paul Frawley). When Tom leaves for the States, Sunny stows aboard his ship in order to be with him but, since she has no papers, she cannot land in New York and will be shipped back to England. Tom's friend Jack Deming (JACK DONAHUE) takes pity on Sunny and marries her so she can legally go ashore. There they get a divorce and Sunny can be with Tom once again. The nonsensical libretto by OTTO HARBACH and OSCAR HAMMERSTEIN was so cockeyed that when the show was done in London, the ending was changed (she stays married to Jack) and barely

a line of dialogue had to be altered. Audiences didn't seem too worried about the logic of the show, especially with the interpolated circus acts, an impressive hunting scene in the British countryside, and Miller's sprightly singing and dancing. The songs by Kern, Harbach, and Hammerstein were also a compensation, with the merry score including "Who?," "Let's Say Goodnight Till It's Morning," "D'Ye Love Me?," "Two Little Bluebirds," and the vivacious title number. HASSARD SHORT directed the CHARLES DILLINGHAM production, which ran 517 performances.

Sunny (Warner/First National 1930) also starred Marilyn Miller so the awkward screenplay by Humphrey Pearson and Henry McCarthy could be easily overlooked when she was singing the five Kern songs that were retained for the screen. In this version, Sunny marries Jim Deming (Joe Donahue), which made a little more sense, and there were some ballet sequences choreographed by Theodore Kosloff that were quite impressive. WILLIAM A. SEITER directed with flair, and the result is the best of Miller's too-few screen vehicles. **Sunny** (RKO 1941) was less accomplished even if it utilized four of the Kern songs. Producer–director Herbert Wilcox made the film as a vehicle for his wife ANNA NEAGLE and it was not her finest hour. Sig Herzig wrote the screenplay in which Sunny is still a circus performer but now concentrates on winning over the aristocratic New Orleans family of the man she loves, Larry Warren (John Carroll). It was a routine and uninteresting tale and the movie only came to life when the supporting players took over, particularly RAY BOLGER with his frantic, eccentric dancing.

SUNNY SIDE UP (Fox 1929). An early musical talkie featuring one of America's favorite screen couples, JANET GAYNOR and CHARLES FARRELL, the film was an important

---

Casts for *Sunny*

Character	1925 Broadway	1930 film	1941 film
Sunny Peters	MARILYN MILLER	Marilyn Miller	ANNA NEAGLE
Jim Deering	JACK DONAHUE	Joe Donahue	
Tom/Larry Warren	Paul Frawley	Lawrence Gray	JOHN CARROLL
Marcia Manners	Elsa Peterson	Barbara Bedford	
Sue/Elizabeth Warren	Esther Howard	Judith Vosselli	Freida Inescort
Harold/Henry	CLIFTON WEBB	Mackenzie Ward	EDWARD EVERETT HORTON
Weenie	Mary Hay	Inez Courtney	
Siegfried Peters	Frank Doane	O. P. Heggie	
Bunny Billings			RAY BOLGER

step in the developing genre as it experimented with new ways to present song and dance outside the confines of a stage show. The team of DE SYLVA, BROWN, and HENDERSON wrote the score and the screenplay about the poor Yorkville girl Molly Carr (Gaynor) whose singing of the cheery title song so dazzled millionaire Jack Cromwell (Farrell) that he puts on a charity show at his Long Island estate featuring her. The story resembled a half a dozen Cinderella musicals seen on Broadway in the 1920s but director DAVID BUTLER and choreographer SEYMOUR FELIX placed the musical numbers on the street and in other nontheatre locales so it was all very cinematic. The songs were tuneful and memorable, especially the enchanting "I'm a Dreamer, Aren't We All?," the cozy "If I Had a Talking Picture of You," and the buoyant title number. There was also a clever production number for "Turn On the Heat," in which fur-clad chorines in the frozen North shed their coats to reveal bathing suits, palm trees came up out of the ice, fire rose from everywhere, and the girls escaped the heat by diving into a cool lagoon.

👓 **SUNSET BOULEVARD** (Minskoff Theatre 1994). One of the longest-running Broadway shows (997 performances) not to show a profit, the expensive and dazzling version of the classic 1950 movie was big in every way, from the performances to the scenery to the orchestrations. The fading silent screen star Norma Desmond (GLENN CLOSE), tended to in her ghostly mansion by her butler–ex-husband Max von Mayerling (GEORGE HEARN), coerces down-and-out scriptwriter Joe Gillis (Alan Campbell) to polish up her screenplay of *Salome* as her comeback vehicle and then makes him her kept lover. When Joe falls in love with the young scriptwriter Betty Schaefer (Alice Ripley) and finally finds the courage to leave Norma, the deranged star shoots him dead and makes a grand exit as the police take her away. Don Black and Christopher Hampton wrote the libretto and the lyrics for ANDREW LLOYD WEBBER's lush, movie soundtrack-like music. It was one of the very few Webber shows that was not sung-through but often the dialogue scenes were given busy underscoring, just as in the old films. "With One Look" and "As If We Never Said Goodbye" became hits and other songs included "New Ways to Dream," "Too Much in Love to Care," "The Greatest Star of All," and the title number. TREVOR NUNN directed the spectacular production, which featured gothic–romantic sets by John Napier and high-style costumes by Anthony Powell.

Webber's Really Useful Company produced the musical, which had already opened in London, and it received mixed notices and plenty of awards, running two and a half years without ever paying back its investment.

SUTHERLAND, A. EDWARD (1895–1974). Film director. A performer-turned-director, he specialized in comedies and musicals at PARAMOUNT. Sutherland was born in London to American parents in show business and was in vaudeville as a child, first breaking into movies as a stuntman. After appearing in many shorts, including some Keystone Kop comedies, he was assistant to Charles Chaplin on *A Woman of Paris* (1923) and then began directing features. Over the next twenty-five years Sutherland helmed eighteen musicals, including *Close Harmony* (1929), *The Dance of Life* (1929), *The Sap From Syracuse* (1930), *Palmy Days* (1931), *INTERNATIONAL HOUSE* (1933), *Too Much Harmony* (1933), *MISSISSIPPI* (1935), *Poppy* (1936), *Every Day's a Holiday* (1937), *THE BOYS FROM SYRACUSE* (1940), *ONE NIGHT IN THE TROPICS* (1942), *Dixie* (1943), and *Follow the Boys* (1944). He was married for a time to screen actress Louise Brooks (1906–1985).

SUTTON, GRADY [Harwell] (1908–1995). Film and television performer. A paunchy character actor who was expert at playing dull-witted, rural hicks, he popped up in many film musicals from the 1930s through the 1960s. Sutton was born in Chattanooga, Tennessee, and by the age of sixteen was acting in films and gained recognition for a series of comedy shorts in the 1930s called *Boy Friends*. In features he rarely was cast in a leading role but he was very noticeable in over 100 comedies, dramas, and musicals, such as *College Humor* (1933), *Pigskin Parade* (1936), *Waikiki Wedding* (1937), *ALEXANDER'S RAGTIME BAND* (1938), *Sing Your Way Home* (1945), *ANCHORS AWEIGH* (1945), *My Wild Irish Rose* (1947), *ROMANCE ON THE HIGH SEAS* (1948), *A STAR IS BORN* (1954), *WHITE CHRISTMAS* (1954), *JUMBO* (1962), *MY FAIR LADY* (1964), *Paradise Hawaiian Style* (1966), and *Rock 'n' Roll High School* (1979). He also acted on dozens of television shows up through the 1970s.

SWADOS, ELIZABETH (1951–). Stage composer, lyricist, director, and performer. One of the more unique creative songwriters of the 1970s and 1980s, the multihyphenate artist has pursued experimental and collage-like pieces using a variety of musical forms. Swados was born in Buffalo and was composing at the piano by the time she was five. She studied music at Bennington College for a time and then worked with such innovative directors as Ellen Stewart, Peter Brook, and Andrei Serban on classic plays for which she provided music. Her first music theatre work was *Nightclub Cantata* (1977) in which she wrote, staged, and performed in. Swados' other pieces from that era include *Runaways* (1978), *Dispatches* (1979), *Alice in Concert* (1980), and *Haggadah* (1981). Her most traditional musical was *Doonesbury* (1983) with libretto and lyrics by Gary Trudeau who also collaborated with her on the satirical musical *Rap Ronnie Master* (1988). Swados has written over fifty theatre pieces over the years, many performed Off Broadway, in churches, schools, and arts centers. Among her other works are *The New Americans* (1996), *Jewish Girlz* (2003), *Jabu* (2005), *Missionaries* (2006), and *Atonement* (2007). She also has scored television programs and films, children's pieces, and animated shorts. Swados often uses music and verse eclectically to express themes and concepts rather than traditional stories and characters. Autobiography: *The Four of Us: The Story of a Family* (1991).

SWARTHOUT, GLADYS (1904–1969). Stage and film performer. A renowned opera singer with a movie star's looks, she made a brief but memorable foray into Hollywood. Swarthout was born in Deepwater, Missouri, and began singing in church choirs as a preteen. She studied music at the Bush Conservatory in Chicago and made her professional debut with the Chicago Civic Opera. By 1929 she was at the Metropolitan Opera and over the years sang major mezzo-soprano roles. Swarthout was lured to Hollywood to compete with opera singer GRACE MOORE at COLUMBIA PICTURES and she was praised for both her singing and her acting in *Rose of the Rancho* (1935), *Give Us This Night* (1936), *Champagne Waltz* (1937), and *Romance in the Dark* (1938). However, the public did not embrace her so she returned to the opera and concert stage and, later on, radio and television. Autobiography: *Come Soon, Tomorrow* (1949).

🕭 **SWEENEY TODD, THE DEMON BARBER OF FLEET STREET** (Uris Theatre 1979). Perhaps the crowning achievement of songwriter STEPHEN SONDHEIM, the "musical thriller" was a challenging blend of Victorian melodrama, English operetta, Brechtian music drama, and a ghoulish sense of humor.

Plot: Barber Benjamin Barker is sent to prison on a trumped up charge by the cor-

Sweeney Todd. The ghoulish story of the mass murderer Sweeney Todd put off many Broadway theatregoers in 1979. Over the years audiences have become less squeamish about Sweeney (Len Cariou) and his cohort Mrs. Lovett (Angela Lansbury), pictured in the original production. (Photofest)

rupt Judge Turpin who lusts after Barker's wife Lucy, so when he returns to London he calls himself Sweeney Todd and sets up business over the meat pie shop of Mrs. Lovett. When the judge comes for a shave one day, Sweeney is interrupted before he can kill him, the barber loses what is left of his reason and starts murdering innocent customers, their bodies ground into meat pies by Mrs. Lovett. Pretending to help his daughter Johanna elope with the sailor Anthony Hope, Sweeney draws the judge back to his barber chair and takes his revenge. But soon he discovers that one of his victims is his wife who Mrs. Lovett implied was dead. Sweeney throws Mrs. Lovett into the bake oven and lets the waif Tobias slit the barber's throat.

Based on a nineteenth-century tale most recently dramatized by Christopher Bond in London, the libretto by HUGH WHEELER was sly and entertaining, never falling into camp and yet always remaining on a stylized Grand Guingol level. Much of the musical was sung, and the integration of song and story was more complete than in any other Sondheim musical. The songs were often pure Victorian romanticism, other times creepy in a KURT WEILL way. Only "Johanna" and "Not While I'm Around" could easily be removed from the context of the musical and stand on their own, for the numbers usually continued the plot and were very character driven. At a few points during

Casts for *Sweeney Todd*

Character	1979 Broadway	1989 Broadway	2005 Broadway	2008 film
Sweeney Todd	LEN CARIOU	BOB GUNTON	MICHAEL CERVERIS	Johnny Depp
Mrs. Lovett	ANGELA LANSBURY	BETH FOWLER	PATTI LUPONE	Helena Bonham Carter
Anthony Hope	VICTOR GARBER	Jim Walton	Benjamin Magnuso	Jamie Campbell Bower
Tobias	Ken Jennings	Eddie Korbich	Manoel Felciano	Ed Sanders
Johanna	Sarah Rice	Gretchen Kingsley	Lauren Molina	Jayne Wisener
Judge Turpin	Edmund Lyndeck	David Barron	Mark Jacoby	Alan Rickman
Beadle Bamford	Jack Eric Williams	Michael McCarthy	Alexander Gemignami	Timothy Spall
Beggar woman	Merle Louise	SuEllen Estey	Diana DiMarzio	Laura Michelle Kelly
Pirelli	Joaquin Romaquera	Bill Nabel	Donna Lynne Champlin	Sacha Baron Cohen

the show a lovely, caressing song with romantic lyrics was placed just at the point of danger or intrigue, making an upsetting contrast between the beautiful and the grisly. This happened with "Pretty Women," knowing that at any minute Sweeney might slit the judge's throat, and in the second act reprise of "Johanna" when Sweeney sings the flowing love song even as he calmly murders his victims and disposes of their bodies. Sondheim's wit was in full throttle with the risible "The Worst Pies in London" and the off-color "A Little Priest." "Parlor Songs," "Green Finch and Linnet Bird," and "By the Sea" were delightful Victorian pastiches, and the recurring theme "The Ballad of Sweeney Todd" was both enticing and chilling. *Sweeney Todd* was praised with reservations by the press, with critics applauding the score, the sterling performances by LEN CARIOU and ANGELA LANSBURY, and for producer–director HAROLD PRINCE's compelling production. All the same, many playgoers were put off by the unusual subject matter and the musical had to struggle to run 557 performances.

Over time, audiences have gotten used to *Sweeney Todd* and its dark humor and revivals are plentiful, particularly by opera companies. Broadway has seen two outstanding revivals. Scaled down, slightly abridged, and presented in a more intimate space, the 1989 revival at the Circle in the Square Uptown was directed by SUSAN H. SCHULMAN on the thrust stage with an immediacy that many found thrilling. BOB GUNTON and BETH FOWLER led the

Sweeney Todd Musical Numbers

"The Ballad of Sweeney Todd"
"No Place Like London"
"The Barber and His Wife"
"The Worst Pies in London"
"Poor Thing"
"My Friends"
"Green Finch and Linnet Bird"
"Ah, Miss"
"Johanna"
"Pirelli's Miracle Elixir"
"The Contest"
"Wait"
"Kiss Me"
"Ladies in Their Sensitivities"
"Quartet"
"Pretty Women"
"Epiphany"
"A Little Priest"
"God, That's Good"
"By the Sea"
"No While I'm Around"
"Parlor Songs"
"City on Fire"

cast of only fourteen performers and what had been close to grand opera was now a chamber piece. The musical was even more highly thought of by the press this time around and audiences seemed more open to the difficult piece so it ran 189 performances. Even smaller and more deadly was the 2005 revival in which director–designer John Doyle deconstructed the dark operetta, turning it into a macabre expressionistic piece. On a stark setting that suggested a lunatic asylum at times, the story of the demon barber was told by ten performers who also provided their own accompaniment by picking up a violin or tuba as needed. MICHAEL CERVERIS and PATTI LUPONE each gave a unique interpretations of the famous murderers, and other cast members also found new aspects of the characters, in particular Manoel Felciano who played Toby an as asylum victim with the entire Sweeney Todd legend haunting him from inside his head. The challenging production received rave reviews from the press and, more surprising, managed to find an audience for 349 performances, one of the few Sondheim revivals to turn a profit.

■ *Sweeney Todd: The Demon Barber of Fleet Street* (Warner-DreamWorks 2007) solved the debate over whether the show was opera or musical theatre; on screen it was a thriller. Cast with dynamic performers without operatic singing voices and given a stunning visual look by director Tim Burton, *Sweeney Todd* went back to its roots as a melodrama but a melodrama enhanced by music. The songs were not set pieces in a musical as much as they were extensions to the characters' psyches. Johnny Depp was a younger Todd but still weary and broken when we first see him. Revenge is not only his impetus to act, it is his drug and his addiction leads to mass murder. Helena Bonham Carter was a less flamboyant Mrs. Lovett, much as LuPone had been, and being younger makes her diabolical agenda more chilling. The supporting cast included some marvelous performances as well. Screenwriter John Logan and Burton rethought the musical in cinema terms and knew the power of the medium. For those hoping for a full-voiced, operatic *Sweeney Todd*, the film was a disappointment; for those looking for a musical masterpiece effectively reimagined, the film was a success.

SWEET ADELINE (Hammerstein's Theatre 1929). A poignant musical vehicle for HELEN MORGAN

put together by JEROME KERN (music) and OSCAR HAMMERSTEIN (book and lyrics) after her affecting performance in their *SHOW BOAT* (1927), the show had a superior score that included "Why Was I Born?," one of Morgan's signature torch songs for the rest of her tragic life. Addie Schmidt works in her family's beer garden in Hoboken, New Jersey, in 1898 and is in love with Tom Martin but loses him to her sister Nellie so Addie goes to New York and becomes a star thanks to the help of the rich Manhattanite James Day. She is not sure if she loves him or is just grateful, so when his snooty family disapproves of her, Addie leaves him and ends up with the playwright Sid Barnett. The nostalgic musical, produced by ARTHUR HAMMERSTEIN and directed by his brother Reginald Hammerstein, was filled with period touches in both the production and the score. "Here Am I," "Don't Ever Leave Me," "T'was Not So Long Ago," and "Some Girl Is on Your Mind" were the other estimable songs that Kern and Hammerstein wrote, most sung by Morgan whose performance was roundly hailed. Notices for the musical were also favorable but the stock market crash coming two months into the run hurt business and *Sweet Adeline* only managed to run 234 performances.

■ *Sweet Adeline* (Warner 1935) kept half of the stage songs, including the most famous numbers, and two new ones ("Lonely Feet" and "We Were So Young") by Kern and Hammerstein were added so musically the movie was as satisfying as the Broadway original. The screenplay by Erwin Gelsey juiced up the quietly involving story and made Addie's sister Nellie a spy during the Spanish-American War who is out to destroy her sister's romance and her Broadway show. IRENE DUNNE played Addie with skill but she lacked the desperate quality that Morgan exuded so what happened to the character was only of mild interest. MERVYN LEROY directed the Edward Chodorov production, and BOBBY CONNOLLY did the dances in the two stage shows which featured Addie.

Casts for *Sweet Adeline*

Character	1929 Broadway	1935 film
Addie	HELEN MORGAN	IRENE DUNNE
James Day	ROBERT CHISHOLM	LOUIS CALHERN
Tom Martin	Max Hoffman, Jr.	
Sid Barnett	John Seymour	Donald Woods
Nellie	Caryl Bergman	Nydia Westman
Rupert Rockingham		HUGH HERBERT

SWEET CHARITY (Palace Theatre 1966). A slick musical comedy vehicle for dancing star GWEN VERDON, the show boasted a funny libretto by NEIL SIMON and a dazzling production directed and choreographed by BOB FOSSE. The dance hall hostess Charity Hope Valentine is an optimist who believes in love but love doesn't seem to believe in her, eluding her with each bad relationship with men. It finally looks like Charity will find happiness with the neurotic but sweet Oscar, but on the day of their wedding he cannot go through with it and Charity is left to live "hopefully ever after." Simon's libretto, a freely adapted and Americanized version of Federico Fellini's 1957 film *Nights of Cabiria*, was a sarcastic fairy tale for modern times, and the songs by CY COLEMAN (music) and Dorothy Fields (lyric) were equally contemporary sounding and facile. "Big Spender," "If My Friends Could See Me Now," "Baby, Dream Your Dream," "I'm a Brass Band," "I Love to Cry at Weddings," "Where Am I Going?," and "There's Gotta Be Something Better Than This" were highlights in the tuneful bouncy score. The show was particularly strong in dance, and Fosse's satirical choreography as performed by Verdon made the show seem like gold. Notices were laudatory and the musical ran a happy 608 performances. Although *Sweet Charity* was a star vehicle, the musical remains very popular with amateur groups and in summer stock without name players. However, the two New York revivals depended on stars and they had them with television favorites DEBBIE ALLEN in 1986 and Christina Applegate in 2005. Fosse directed Allen and critics applauded her and her expert supporting cast, with the revival running 368 performances. The press was less in agreement about Applegate and her production, directed by WALTER BOBBIE and choreographed by Wayne Cilento, so it struggled to run 279 performances.

Sweet Charity (Universal 1969) marked Bob Fosse's directorial film debut and he filled the movie with jazzy crosscutting, stark camera angles, and big garish performances that impressed some critics and annoyed others. SHIRLEY MACLAINE played Charity and, as accomplished a dancer as she was, the film star could not carry a whole musical as Verdon had done, so the most dynamic choreography was saved for the ensemble and Charity's pals played by CHITA RIVERA and Paula Kelly. JOHN MCMARTIN reprised his stage performance as the weak-kneed Oscar, and SAMMY DAVIS, JR. was featured in the "Rhythm of Life" number. Much of the Coleman–Fields score made it to the screen and the team wrote two new numbers as well, "It's a Nice Face" and "My Personal Property." It is a bright, colorful movie, very much of its time, and an interesting record of Fosse's vibrant stage choreography.

SWEET ROSIE O'GRADY (Fox 1943). Another period musical featuring BETTY GRABLE, the movie was chock full of old standards and some pleasing new songs by HARRY WARREN (music) and MACK GORDON (lyrics). Ken Englund's screenplay centered on Broadway star Madeleine Marlowe (Grable) who returns to New York after a triumphant tour of Europe only to have her image tarnished by the newspaper reporter Sam MacKeever (ROBERT YOUNG). It seems that the glamorous Miss Marlowe is really simple Rosie O'Grady from Flugelman's Beer Garden in the Bowery. Rosie is furious and fights back by exposing MacKeever as a former and discontented suitor of hers. The two bicker for most of the movie before realizing that they love each other. The supporting cast was a rich one, including ADOLPHE MENJOU, REGINALD GARDINER, Virginias Grey, PHIL REGAN, SIG RUMANN, Alan Dinehart, and Hobart Cavanaugh. In addition to the title song, other oldies performed (mostly by Grable since Young was not a strong singer) included "Sidewalks of New York," "Two Little Girls in Blue," "Little Annie Rooney," and "Heaven Will Protect the Working Girl." The best of the new numbers was "My Heart Tells Me," which Grable

Casts for *Sweet Charity*				
Character	*1966 Broadway*	*1969 film*	*1986 Broadway*	*2005 Broadway*
Charity	GWEN VERDON	SHIRLEY MACLAINE	DEBBIE ALLEN	Christina Applegate
Oscar	JOHN MCMARTIN	John McMartin	MICHAEL RUPERT	Denis O'Hare
Helene	Thelma Oliver	Paula Kelly	Allison Williams	Kyra Da Costa
Nickie	HELEN GALLAGHER	CHITA RIVERA	BEBE NEUWIRTH	Janine LaManna
Vittorio Vidal	James Luisi	RICARDO MONTALBAN	Mark Jacoby	Paul Schoeffler
Herman	John Wheeler	STUBBY KAYE	Lee Wilkof	Ernie Sabella

sang in a bathtub. The other Warren–Gordon songs were "Get Your Police Gazette," "The Wishing Waltz," and "Going to the County Fair." IRVING CUMMINGS directed the WILLIAM PERLBERG production, which was choreographed by HERMES PAN who was the featured dancer in "The Wishing Waltz."

🕊️ **SWEETHEARTS** (New Amsterdam Theatre 1913). Although it had one of the most farfetched plots of any operetta, the VICTOR HERBERT musical had an enthralling score so all was forgiven for 136 performances. Librettists HARRY B. SMITH and Fred De Gresac claimed that the tale was based on a real fifteenth-century princess from Naples but nothing could be less plausible than the story of *Sweethearts*. The baby princess Sylvia from mythological Zilania is shipped off to Bruges during a war and is raised by a laundress named Mother Goose (Ethel De Fre Houston). Prince Franz (Thomas Conkey), the heir to the throne of Zilania who is traveling incognito, falls in love with the adult Sylvia (CHRISTIE MACDONALD) at first sight, but there is jealous Lieutenant Karl (Edwin Wilson), a trio of villains, and an old family friend disguised as a monk to keep the lovers apart until the finale when it is discovered that Sylvia is the long-lost princess and she and Franz can rule Zilania as king and queen. Smith provided the lyrics for Herbert's felicitous music and the title song became the most famous, although also memorable were "Pretty as a Picture," "Angelus," "Every Lover Must Meet His Fate," "The Cricket on the Hearth," and "Jeanette and Her Little Wooden Shoes." The romantic operetta was revived in New York in 1929 and 1947, the last with BOBBY CLARK in the built-up comic role of the political henchman Mikel Mikeloviz and running 288 performances.

■ *Sweethearts* (MGM 1938) was a rarity: an operetta set in contemporary times and one that downplayed sentiment and romance for interesting characters and sassy dialogue. Much of the credit was due to Dorothy Parker and Alan Campbell who wrote the screenplay, tossing out the stage libretto completely and coming up with a modern tale about a married couple, Gwen Marlowe (JEANETTE MACDONALD) and Ernest Lane (NELSON EDDY), who have been performing in a Broadway show called *Sweethearts* for six years. Bored with the theatre (and a little with each other too), the twosome are encouraged by the crafty agent Norman Trumpett (REGINALD GARDNER) to head to

Hollywood, much to the dismay of the show's producer Felix Lehman (FRANK MORGAN), author Leo Kronk (MISCHA AUER), and composer Oscar Engel (HERMAN BING). Once in Tinsel Town, the couple breaks up over a misunderstanding and is treated crassly by the movie community, so they are reconciled to each other and are back on Broadway for the big finale. ROBERT WRIGHT and GEORGE FORREST provided some new lyrics so the modern tone of the screenplay was continued when the characters broke into song. W. S. VAN DYKE directed the picture, which also featured Florence Rice, Douglas MacPhail, Allyn Joslyn, Gene Lockhart, Raymond Walburn, and RAY BOLGER who had fun with the "Wooden Shoes" number. The choreography was by ALBERTINA RASCH, and the production numbers were quite impressive, the movie being the first MGM musical to use the new three-color Technicolor process. However, the most interesting aspect of the film is to see MacDonald and Nelson in contemporary clothes and showing some spirit in delivering the slangy, funny dialogue.

SWENSON, INGA (1932–). Stage and television performer. A striking, statuesque lyric soprano in musicals, the blonde singer–actress gave some memorable performances on Broadway in the 1960s. Swenson was born in Omaha, Nebraska, and studied theatre at Northwestern University. She made her Broadway debut as one of the *NEW FACES OF 1956* and then gained further recognition for her performance in the play *The First Gentleman* (1959). After understudying JULIE ANDREWS in *CAMELOT* (1960), Swenson was cast in the leading role of the frustrated but eager spinster Lizzie Curry in *110 IN THE SHADE* (1963), followed by the clever actress Irene Adler in *Baker Street* (1965). She got to reprise her Lizzie in London in 1967. Swenson made some nonmusical films and many television appearances, such as the original TV musical *ANDROCLES AND THE LION* (1967) and several series, most memorably *Soap* and *Benson*. She retired from acting in 1990.

■ **SWING TIME** (RKO 1936). Even with its convoluted plot twists and turns, the movie still ranks as a strong candidate for the best of the FRED ASTAIRE and GINGER ROGERS musicals.

Plot: After the irresponsible gambler "Lucky" Garnett leaves his fiancée Margaret Watson at the altar while he's partying with his pal Pop Cardetti, Judge Watson tells Lucky he has to raise $25,000 in order to marry his

Casts for *Swing Time* and *Never Gonna Dance*

Character	*Swing Time* (1936)	*Never Gonna Dance* (2004)
John "Lucky" Garnett	FRED ASTAIRE	Noah Racey
Penny Carroll	GINGER ROGERS	Nancy Lemenager
Pop Cardetti	VICTOR MOORE	
Mabel Anderson/Pritt	HELEN BRODERICK	KAREN ZIEMBA
Mr. Pangborn		Peter Bartlett
Alfred J. Morganthal		Peter Gerety
Gordon	ERIC BLORE	
Margaret Watson/Chalfont	Betty Furness	Deborah Leamy
Ricardo Romero	Georges Metaxa	David Pittu
Judge Watson/Mr. Chalfont	Landers Stevens	Philip LeStrange

daughter. Lucky and Pop go to New York to try and raise the cash but he is sidetracked by the beautiful dance instructor Penny Carroll. He takes lessons just to be near her, but she's engaged to bandleader Ricardo Romero. Before you know it the quarreling Lucky and Penny have a successful dance act and are falling in love, although Ricardo and Margaret present a major obstacle until the final reel.

HOWARD LINDSAY and Allan Scott wrote the contrived screenplay that at least had some sparkling dialogue for the lovers and comic bits for the secondary couple made up of Victor Moore and Helen Broderick. It also left plenty of room for dance and all of it was superb: the couple's effervescent "Waltz in Swing Time," Astaire's rhythmic "Bojangles of Harlem," the seductive *pas de deux* "Never Gonna Dance," and the clever "Pick Yourself Up," in which Astaire pretends he cannot dance very well in order to keep getting lessons from Rogers. Astaire and HERMES PAN devised the choreography and it was quintessential Astaire and Rogers magic. GEORGE STEVENS directed the PANDRO S. BERMAN production, which was originally titled *I Won't Dance* and then *Never Gonna Dance* until the studio, worried that the public would not come and see a Fred Astaire picture where no one danced, changed it to *Swing Time* (although there is only one swing number in the film). Although the movie is remembered as one of the great dance musicals, it also boasts one of the best film scores of the 1930s. JEROME KERN (music) and DOROTHY FIELDS (lyrics) wrote the delectable songs that, in addition to the dance numbers already mentioned, included

Swing Time Musical Numbers
"It's Not in the Cards"
"Pick Yourself Up"
"The Way You Look Tonight"
"Waltz in Swing Time"
"A Fine Romance"
"Bojangles of Harlem"
"Never Gonna Dance"

two outstanding numbers that were presented to perfection. "A Fine Romance" was a wry musical conversation with the lovers quarreling in a snow-covered wood, with the song itself becoming a complete musical scene. And Astaire sang the Oscar-winning "The Way You Look Tonight" to Rogers as she lathered her head with shampoo. The offbeat way of setting the number made it all the more romantic.

🕭 ***Never Gonna Dance*** (Broadhurst Theatre 2004) was a stage version of *Swing Time* using the title that was once considered for the film. Jeffrey Hatcher's libretto stuck to the movie plot somewhat, although Pop Cardetti was dropped and some of the details changed. Most of the screen songs were used plus others by Kern, such as "Dearly Beloved," "Who?," "The Song Is You," "I'm Old-Fashioned," and "I'll Be Hard to Handle." The production, directed by Michael Greif, boasted some inventive choreography by JERRY MITCHELL but the charming leads lacked star charisma and critics found the musical more pleasant than exhilarating so it struggled to run eighty-four performances.

T

TABBERT, WILLIAM [Henry] (1921–1974). Stage and television performer. A youthful-looking, full-voiced singer, he enjoyed a limited but impressive Broadway career. Tabbert was born in Chicago, trained for an opera career, and then later apprenticed with the Chicago Civic Opera Company. His Broadway debut was a featured role in the short-lived Lerner and Loewe musical *What's Up* (1943) and then he appeared in *FOLLOW THE GIRLS* (1944), *Seven Lively Arts* (1944), and *Billion Dollar Baby* (1945) before originating the role of the doomed Lt. Joe Cable in *SOUTH PACIFIC* (1949) where he introduced "Younger Than Springtime." Tabbert's other important Broadway role was the French fisherman Marius in *FANNY* (1954). The rest of his career was in nightclubs and on television (where he was a regular on network shows under the name Billy Tabbert) and he occasionally returned to the musical stage in regional theatres.

TAKE A CHANCE (Apollo Theatre 1932). A musical comedy that went through so many rewrites and revisions on its pre-Broadway tour that it opened with three composers providing the score: HERB NACIO BROWN, RICHARD A. WHITING, and VINCENT YOUMANS. Harvard-educated Kenneth Raleigh is producing a musical revue about American history for Broadway and enlists the financial help of Toni Ray who brings in the crooked Duke Stanley and Louie Webb for financing. Kenneth falls for Toni but when he discovers that Duke and Louie are far from honest, he believes she set him up and it takes Toni's explaining and her starring in his show to set him straight. The musical had started as a revue called *Humpty Dumpty* that did so poorly during tryouts that producers LAURENCE SCHWAB and B. G. DE SYLVA brought in composer Youmans to spice up the score, rewrote the musical themselves, turning it from a revue to a book show, and ended up with a hit. ETHEL MERMAN, in a minor role, got to introduce the two best songs, "Eadie Was a Lady" and "Rise and Shine," and stopped the show both times. Also in the tuneful score were "(You're an Old) Smoothie," "I Got Religion," "Turn Out the Lights," and "Should I Be Sweet." After the musical had been running several months and business started to slack off, comics OLSEN and JOHNSON took over as producers, played Duke and Louie, and kept it on the boards a few more months, eventually running 243 performances in the darkest days of the Depression. EDGAR MACGREGOR directed, and BOBBY CONNOLLY did the choreography.

Take a Chance (Paramount 1933) kept the plot, most of the songs, and performer JUNE KNIGHT from the Broadway show but dropped Ethel Merman and gave LILLIAN ROTH the number "Rise and Shine" to sing. Lawrence Schwab adapted his own libretto into a routine screenplay and directed as well, and he was saved by the talented and playful cast. There were a few song interpolations, most memorably the little-known "It's Only a Paper Moon" by HAROLD ARLEN (music), E. Y. HARBURG, and BILLY ROSE (lyric) that became a hit after it was sung in the film by Knight, CHARLES "BUDDY" ROGERS, and CLIFF EDWARDS.

TAKE ME ALONG. See *SUMMER HOLIDAY*

TAKE ME OUT TO THE BALLGAME (MGM 1949). One of the few film musicals dealing with sports, it hedged its bets by making the main characters two turn-of-the-twentieth-century

Casts for *Take a Chance*		
Characters	*1932 Broadway*	*1933 film*
Kenneth Raleigh	JACK WHITING	CHARLES "BUDDY" ROGERS
Toni Ray	JUNE KNIGHT	June Knight
Duke Stanley	JACK HALEY	James Dunn
Wanda Brill	ETHEL MERMAN	LILLIAN ROTH
Louie Webb	SID SILVERS	CLIFF EDWARDS
Consuelo Raleigh	Mitzi Mayfair	Dorothy Lee

baseball players who worked in vaudeville during the off season. Scriptwriters Harry Turgend and GEORGE WELLS had their work cut out for them when swimming star ESTHER WILLIAMS was cast in the picture and they had to figure out how to sandwich in some aquatic opportunities in a baseball movie. (She ended up taking a balletic dip in a pool in one scene.) Shortstop Eddie O'Brien (GENE KELLY) and second baseman Dennis Ryan (FRANK SINATRA) are not thrilled when they hear their team, the Wolves, has been bought by one K. C. Higgins until Higgins turn out to be a woman (Williams) with brains and beauty. Dennis falls for his new boss but she has her eye on the brash Eddie while the oversexed Shirley Delwyn (BETTY GARRETT) is chasing after Dennis. The predictability of it all was relieved by several playful numbers staged by Kelly and STANLEY DONEN while BUSBY BERKELEY directed (for the last time) the tale breezily. ROGER EDENS, BETTY COMDEN, and ADOLPH GREEN penned most of the sprightly songs: Garrett trying to seduce Sinatra with "It's Fate, Baby, It's Fate," Sinatra dreaming of "The Right Girl for Me," Kelly, Sinatra, and team member JULES MUNSHIN singing the daffy trios "Yes, Indeedy" and "O'Brien to Ryan to Goldberg," and the ensemble's patriotic paean "Strictly U. S. A." Kelly's most impressive choreographic feat was a barrel dance set to "The Hat My Father Wore on St. Patrick's Day" (by William Jerome and JEAN SCHWARTZ), and he joined Sinatra for a soft-shoe version of the 1908 title song.

TALBOT, LYLE [born Lisle Henderson] (1902–1996). Film and television performer. A prolific actor who played heavies as easily as lightweight leading men, he made a dozen movie musicals playing both types. Talbot was born in Pittsburgh, the son of show boat entertainers, and started his career as a magician before turning to acting in stock. He ran his own theatre touring company in the late 1920s and was on screen by 1931. While he was cast as the likable hero in A pictures he was usually the gangster or Western outlaw in B movies. Between the two he was one of the busiest actors in Hollywood, making twenty-nine movies just in 1950 and 1951. When television started, he acted there in dozens of series and hundreds of episodes. Talbot's film musicals include *42ND STREET* (1933), *ONE NIGHT OF LOVE* (1934), *Broadway Hostess* (1935), *The Singing Kid* (1936), *SECOND FIDDLE* (1939), *UP IN ARMS* (1944), *Dixie Jamboree* (1944), *Sensations of 1945*, *Mississippi Rhythm* (1949), *Everybody's Dancin'* (1950),

WITH A SONG IN MY HEART (1952), and *THERE'S NO BUSINESS LIKE SHOW BUSINESS* (1954). He continued performing in films and on television until the late 1980s.

TAMARA [born Tamara Drasin] (1907–1943). Stage and film performer. The dark, exotic singer with a captivating throaty voice, she was popular in cabarets, on the radio, and in a handful of Broadway and Hollywood musicals. Tamara was born in Odessa, Russia, and was educated in the Ukraine and in New York City before she started singing professionally in nightclubs. She made her Broadway bow in the revue *Innocent Eyes* (1924) and was featured in *The New Yorkers* (1927), *Crazy Quilt* (1931), *Free for All* (1931), and *New Americana* (1932) before getting the plum role of the Russian princess Stephanie in *ROBERTA* (1933) and introducing "Smoke Gets in Your Eyes." Tamara was lauded for her phony wife Mimi in the short-lived *Right This Way* (1938), where she got to introduce another standard, "I'll Be Seeing You." Her final Broadway musical, *LEAVE IT TO ME!* (1938), was more successful and as the sassy Colette she sang "Get Out of Town." Tamara appeared in two Hollywood musicals, *Sweet Surrender* (1935) and *No, No, NANETTE* (1940), was popular on the radio during the Depression years, and was a favorite in swank supper clubs before her untimely death in the same plane crash in Portugal that crippled singer JANE FROMAN.

TAMBLYN, RUSS[ell] (1934–). Film and television performer. A highly athletic and agile dancer, the youthful-looking actor lit up several movie musicals. Tamblyn was born in Los Angeles and was a child performer on the stage, on the radio, and in films. He played many juvenile roles on screen but his dancing talent was not noticed until he played the youngest Pontipee brother Gideon in *SEVEN BRIDES FOR SEVEN BROTHERS* (1954). Tamblyn was also memorable as the sailor Danny Smith in *HIT THE DECK* (1955), the tiny hero of *TOM THUMB* (1958), and the gang leader Riff in *WEST SIDE STORY* (1961). His other screen musicals were *The Wonderful World of the Brothers Grimm* (1962) and *Follow the Boys* (1963). The quality of his films declined in the late 1960s but he was successful on television in dramatic series and TV movies.

TAMIRIS, HELEN [born Helen Becker] (1905–1966). Stage and film choreographer. One of Broadway's top choreographers in the 1940s and 1950s, she provided memorable moments in both hits and flops. Tamiris was born in New York City and studied dance with Michel Fokine before beginning her career as a dancer at the Metropolitan Opera. She made her Broadway debut in 1924 as a performer and then founded her own modern dance company in the 1930s. Tamiris choreographed the dance drama *Trojan Incident* for the Federal Theatre Project in 1938, made her Broadway choreography debut in 1944 with *Marianne*, and then found renown for her dances in *Up in Central Park* the next year. Among her hits were the 1946 revival of *Show Boat*, *Annie Get Your Gun* (1946), *Fanny* (1954), *Plain and Fancy* (1955), and the revues *Touch and Go* (1949) and *Inside U.S.A.* (1948). Tamiris's choreography was equally impressive in such short-lived musicals as *Park Avenue* (1946), *Flahooley* (1951), and *Carnival in Flanders* (1953). She recreated some of her dances for the 1948 film version of *Up in Central Park* and choreographed the film *Just for You* (1952). Tamiris used both modern dance and ballet in her musicals, and the variety in her work was considerable, from the lyrical "Currier and Ives" ballet for the ice skaters in *Up in Central Park* to the quirky, offbeat shenanigans in *Flahooley*, to the Amish folk dance in the barn raising scene in *Plain and Fancy*.

TAMIROFF, AKIM (1899–1972). Stage, film, and television performer. A heavyset character actor who often played heavies on screen, the thick-accented performer was often cast as silly foreigners in musicals. Tamiroff was born in Tiflis, Georgia, Russia, to Armenian parents and eventually became a member of the distinguished Moscow Art Theatre. When the troupe toured America in 1923, he remained in New York and enjoyed a productive career on Broadway acting in dramas. Tamiroff headed to Hollywood in 1931 and was soon cast in supporting roles. As the years passed the parts got better but rarely any bigger as he was cast as foreign villains, eccentric immigrants, corrupt authority figures, and sidekicks. His film musicals include *Here Is My Heart* (1934), *The Merry Widow* (1934), *Naughty Marietta* (1935), *Go Into Your Dance* (1935), *Big Broadcast of 1936* (1935), *High, Wide and Handsome* (1937), *Paris Honeymoon* (1939), *Can't Help Singing* (1944), and *Fiesta* (1947). Tamiroff made many television appearances in both series and specials, such as the original TV musical *Aladdin* (1958).

TANGUAY, EVA (1879–1947). Stage performer. One of vaudeville's most popular and highest-paid stars, the lively blonde comedienne wore outrageous feathered costumes and sang risqué songs to the delight of her fans. Tanguay was born in Marbleton, Canada, and was on the stage from childhood, playing the young Cedric Erroll in *Little Lord Fauntleroy* on the road for five years. She made her Broadway debut in the play *The Engineer* (1895), sang in the musical revue *Wine, Women and Song* (1998), and found fame three years later as Gabrielle in *The Three Musketeers* burlesque *My Lady* (1901), which was followed by other sassy, comic roles in *The Chaperons* (1902), *The Office Boy* (1903), and *The Sambo Girl* (1905). It was when she turned to vaudeville in 1906 that Tanguay became a major star, dubbed the "I Don't Care Girl" after one of her saucy ditties. Billed as "the girl who made vaudeville famous," she also appeared in three silent films. Only returning to Broadway as a featured star in *Ziegfeld Follies* (1909), Tanguay remained in variety until the Depression killed off the genre then she retired and went into seclusion. MITZI GAYNOR played her in the movie biomusical *The "I Don't Care" Girl* (1953).

⛟ *TAP DANCE KID, THE* (Broadhurst Theatre 1983). A musical play about African Americans and dance, it was an interesting twist on the too-familiar tale about making it in show business. The young Willie (Alphonso Ribeiro) dreams of being a great tap dancer like FRED ASTAIRE and "BOJANGLES" ROBINSON but his lawyer–father William (SAMUEL E. WRIGHT) refuses to let his son become an outdated black stereotype. With the help of his dancer–uncle Dipsey (HINTON BATTLE), Willie wins over his mother (Hattie Winston) and eventually his father and follows his dream. Also in the cast were Alan Weeks, Martine Allard, and Barbara Montgomery. Based on Louise Fitzhugh's novel *Nobody's Family Is Going to Change*, the libretto by Charles Blackwell was about much more than dancing and the characterizations throughout were real and engrossing. Henry Krieger (music) and Robert Lorick (lyrics) wrote the lively score that consisted of truthful characters' songs and vibrant dance numbers. "Fabulous Feet," "Like Him," "Dance If It Makes You Happy," "William's Song," "I Remember How It Was," and "Tap Tap" were among the notable numbers. Vivian Matalon directed and DANNY DANIELS choreographed the vivacious dances, including a tap number with sneakers. The musical met with critical approval and through word of mouth business slowly built until it became a hit, running 669 performances.

🎬 **TARZAN** (Disney 1999). The familiar tale became an engrossing animated musical that was not only exciting to watch but filled with reflections on prejudice and family. Tab Murphy, Noni White, and Bob Tzudiker took Edgar Rice Burroughs' oft-filmed story and fleshed out a screenplay in which two parallel words are presented, the human one and a community of gorillas living in Africa. The orphaned boy Tarzan is caught between both worlds, loved by his foster mother, the ape Kala, and seen as a threat by Kerchak, the leader of the gorilla family. The appearance of Jane and her father, Professor Archimedes Q. Porter, reveals to the adult Tarzan the world of humans, just as the devious hunter Clayton represents the evils of that world. Singing his own songs on the soundtrack was composer–performer Phil Collins. "Two Worlds," "Son of Man," "I Need to Know," and the Oscar-winning "You'll Be in My Heart" were contemporary sounding, yet their rhythmic momentum blended beautifully with the pulsating sounds of the jungle. Chris Buck and Kevin Lima directed with an eye on the beauty of nature and the expressive faces of both human and ape characters. The movie was very popular, as was the score, and the Disney magic was still alive as the century ended.

📖 **Tarzan** (Richard Rodgers Theatre 2006) was a dazzling stage version of the movie that did not try to depict the apes or the jungle realistically but created a stylized playground of sorts where just about all of the characters were swinging from ropes. DAVID HENRY HWANG adapted the screenplay into a workable libretto, building up the relationships of the characters over the adventure aspects of the story. Director–designer Bob Crowley came up with some startling images and memorable sequences, such as the shipwreck at the beginning of the show and making waterfalls and giant insects out of fabric and lights. Phil Collins wrote some additional character songs for the new version, including "Different," "Who Better Than Me?," "Everything That I Am," "For the First Time," and "Waiting for This Moment." Josh Strickland played the adult Tarzan with sincerity and humor, Shuler Hensley was a commanding Kerchak, Merle Dandridge was an affecting Kara, and Jenn Gambatese a forthright and plucky Jane. The press was unusually severe in its criticism, just as it had been with BEAUTY AND THE BEAST (1994), and it was clear the disdain many of them had for Disney on Broadway. Audience reactions were enthusiastic and the musical did brisk business, but not brisk enough for the expensive show so after 486 performances it closed in the red.

TAUROG, NORMAN (1899–1981). Film director. A favorite of the studios because his pictures always had a low budget and a high box office appeal, he helmed over seventy-five movies, half of them musicals. Taurog was born in Chicago and was on stage and in silents as a boy. He began directing in 1919 and over the next fifty years turned out every kind of genre from comedies such as *If I Had a Million* (1932) to melodramas such as *Boys Town* (1938). Taurog directed nine Elvis Presley musicals, including *GI Blues* (1960), *BLUE HAWAII* (1962), *Spinout* (1966), and *Love a Little Live a Little* (1968), and four DEAN MARTIN–JERRY LEWIS musicals, such as *The Stooge* (1952), *Living It Up* (1954), and *Pardners* (1956). Among his other screen musicals were *Lucky Boy* (1929), *THE PHANTOM PRESIDENT* (1932), *WE'RE NOT DRESSING* (1934), *COLLEGE RHYTHM* (1934), *BIG BROADCAST OF 1936* (1935), *Rhythm on the Range* (1936), *BROADWAY MELODY OF 1940*,

Casts for *Tarzan*

Character	1999 film (voices)	2006 Broadway
Adult Tarzan	Tony Goldwyn	Josh Strickland
Young Tarzan	Alex D. Linz	Daniel Manche
		Alex Rutherford
Jane Porter	Minnie Driver	Jenn Gambatese
Kala	GLENN CLOSE	Merle Dandridge
Kerchak	Lance Henrikson	Shuler Hensley
Terk	Rosie O'Donnell	Chester Gregory II
Prof. Porter	Nigel Hawthorne	Timothy Jerome
Clayton	Brian Blessed	Donnie R. Keshawarz

LITTLE NELLIE KELLY (1940), *Presenting Lily Mars* (1943), *GIRL CRAZY* (1943), *WORDS AND MUSIC* (1948), *THE TOAST OF NEW ORLEANS* (1950), *Rich, Young and Pretty* (1951), *The Stars Are Singing* (1953), *All Hands on Deck* (1961), *Girls! Girls! Girls!* (1962), *Tickle Me* (1965), *Double Trouble* (1967), and *Speedway* (1968).

TAYLOR, ELIZABETH [Rosemond] (1932–). Film, television, and stage performer. The beautiful cinema star who for decades represented Hollywood allure and glamour, she numbers a few musicals among her many movies made between 1942 and 1994. Taylor was born in London to American parents who were art dealers and she studied ballet as a young child. At the outbreak of World War II, her family relocated to Los Angeles and she was on the screen at the age of ten, her adult-like features and screen presence remarkable even in her early bit roles. The world watched Taylor grow up on screen as she was featured in MGM films, including the musical *A DATE WITH JUDY* (1948). Taylor's singing was weak and she was soon too important a star to waste in featured roles in musicals so she only was seen in a few screen musicals: *Rhapsody* (1954), *The Blue Bird* (1976), and *A LITTLE NIGHT MUSIC* (1978); none showed her at her best. Taylor started appearing on television in the 1970s and made a late Broadway debut as the scheming Regina in the drama *The Little Foxes* (1981), returning two years later with ex-husband Richard Burton (1925–1984) in the comedy *Private Lives* (1983). She has managed to remain a Hollywood icon decades after her prime years. Among her other husbands were actors Michael Wilding (1912–1979), singer Eddie Fisher (1928–), and producer MICHAEL TODD. Biographies: *Elizabeth*, J. Randy Taraborrelli (2006); *Elizabeth: The Life of Elizabeth Taylor*, Alexander Walker (2001).

TAYMOR, JULIE (1952–). Stage and film director, writer, and designer. An endlessly inventive stager of operas, Broadway musicals, films, and puppet performances, she became famous with her concept and direction for *THE LION KING* (1997) on Broadway, although she had been doing similarly dazzling things in regional theatre for years. Taymor was born in Boston, the daughter of a gynecologist and a political activist, was educated at Oberlin College, and studied puppetry with the Bread and Puppet Theatre and in Bali. She directed the classics in regional theatres while her puppet and mask creations were seen in such New

York productions as *The Haggadah* (1980) and *Black Elk Speaks* (1981). Taymor co-wrote, staged, and designed the theatrical fables *Juan Darién* (1996) and *The Green Bird* (2000), both of which began regionally and ended up on Broadway. After the success of *The Lion King*, Taymor was in great demand and staged *The Magic Flute* for the Metropolitan Opera. She has also directed some films, including the musical *ACROSS THE UNIVERSE* (2007). She uses both ancient performance techniques and modern innovative ideas to create theatrical works that are surprisingly accessible.

TEMPLE, SHIRLEY (1928–). Film and television performer. The most popular child star in the history of the movies, the blonde, curly moppet usually appeared in musicals so that her considerable singing and dancing talents could be displayed. Temple was born in Santa Monica, California, the daughter of a bank teller, and started taking dance lessons at the age of three. Before she was four Temple was featured in a series of film shorts called *Baby Burlesks* in which she and other tots imitated the stars of the day. After some bit parts in

Shirley Temple. When the adored moppet danced with adults, some of the cuteness disappeared and she met them as equals. This was particularly true in her four movies with the tap dancing phenomenon Bill "Bojangles" Robinson. Here the two are thrillingly matched in *The Littlest Rebel* (1935). (Photofest)

features, she caught attention singing "Baby Take a Bow" in *Stand Up and Cheer* (1934) and she was a star by the time she made *Little Miss Marker* (1934). Temple's other childhood musicals are *Baby Take a Bow* (1934), *Bright Eyes* (1934), *The Little Colonel* (1935), *CURLY TOP* (1935), *The Littlest Rebel* (1935), *CAPTAIN JANUARY* (1936), *POOR LITTLE RICH GIRL* (1936), *Dimples* (1936), *Stowaway* (1936), *REBECCA OF SUNNYBROOK FARM* (1938), *Little Miss Broadway* (1938), *Just Around the Corner* (1938), *The Little Princess* (1939), *The Blue Bird* (1940), and *Young People* (1940). While much of her appeal had to do with Depression-weary audiences seeing Temple as a symbol of innocence and optimism, there was no question she was one of the most talented kids ever put on the screen. Not only could Temple sing and dance (she was able to keep up with the veteran hoofer BILL ROBINSON in four films) but she had the acting know-how to make sentimentality warm and funny. Temple often played variations of the same character, the cheerful orphan who could make jaded adults behave with humanity, and when she outgrew that persona her popularity waned. Her only teenage musical was *Honeymoon* (1947) and her nonmusicals in the 1940s did not do well at the box office so she left Hollywood. Temple resurfaced on television in 1958 and again in 1960 but neither show was renewed so she retired from acting for good and went into politics in the 1960s where she had more success serving as a congresswoman and later an ambassador. Autobiography: *Child Star* (1988).

TEMPLETON, FAY (1865–1939). Stage performer. The beloved Broadway singing–acting star enjoyed a career of sixty-four years during which she was an ingénue in early developmental musicals, a mature comedienne in WEBER and FIELDS' burlesques, a leading lady in GEORGE M. COHAN's new form of book musical, and a featured character actress in a modern JEROME KERN musical. Templeton was born in Little Rock, Arkansas, the daughter of a singer and a theatre manager, and was on stage as a youngster. After working in vaudeville she made her Broadway debut at the age of eight as Puck in *A Midsummer Night's Dream* (1873). She appeared in the musicals *The Mascot* (1881) and *Billee Taylor* (1883) and then attracted attention in the "pants" role of Gabriel in a revival of *EVANGELINE* (1885). Templeton was also featured in *Hendrik Hudson* (1890), *Madame Favart* (1893), and *Excelsior, Jr.* (1895), as well as the London show *Monte Cristo, Jr.* (1886). Her career moved in a new

direction in 1898 when she joined with comics Weber and Fields and played saucy characters in a famed series of musical spoofs such as *Hurly Burly* (1898), *Fiddle-Dee-Dee* (1900), *Broadway to Tokio* (1900), *Hoity Toity* (1901), and *Twirly Whirly* (1902). Perhaps her finest characterization was the housekeeper–heiress Mary Jane Jenkins in Cohan's *FORTY-FIVE MINUTES FROM BROADWAY* (1906). Templeton retired from the stage in 1910 but returned for the Weber and Fields reunion *Hokey Pokey* (1912) and to play Little Buttercup in the operetta *H.M.S. PINAFORE* in 1911, 1924, 1926, and 1931. She made a final and memorable appearance as the aging dress salon owner Minnie in Kern's *ROBERTA* (1933). Irene Manning played Templeton in the Cohan movie bio-musical *YANKEE DOODLE DANDY* (1942).

TENDERLOIN (46th Street Theatre 1960). A satirical musical comedy about corruption and vice in nineteenth-century New York City, the show reunited the creative talents of the recent *FIORELLO!* (1959): JEROME WEIDMAN and director GEORGE ABBOTT (book), JERRY BOCK (music), SHELDON HARNICK (lyrics), and producers HAROLD PRINCE and Robert E. Griffith. Rev. Brock (Maurice Evans) leads a righteous campaign to clean up the vice in the Tenderloin district and enlists the help of journalist Tommy (RON HUSMANN) in his muckraking activities. But Tommy is out to frame the minister and he succeeds, even though he sees the error of his methods by the loving choir singer Laura (Wynne Miller). Also in the cast were Ralph Dunn, Eileen Rodgers, Lee Becker, Raymond Bramley, Irene Kane, and Rex Everhart. The story, based on the novel by Samuel Hopkins Adams, was problematic. Neither Brock nor Tommy was a very likable character so the audience never got involved with what happened to them. The performers, however, were more than interesting, as were the songs they sang. "Artificial Flowers," "Little Old New York," "Good Clean Fun," "The Picture of Happiness," "How the Money Changes Hands," and other numbers were as accomplished as the songs in *Fiorello!* (if not more so), but without a strong libretto the musical floundered. Aislesitters appreciated the tuneful score and the proficient cast, as well as JOE LAYTON's effervescent choreography, but the show managed only 216 performances, much of that due to the healthy advance.

TERRIS, NORMA [born Norma Allison] (1904–1989). Stage performer. An accomplished singer–actress who played several leading roles on Broadway before retiring early in life, she originated the part of Magnolia Hawks in *SHOW BOAT* (1927). A native of Columbus, Kansas, Terris was educated locally and in Chicago before going into the theatre to be a dramatic actress. She began working professionally as a singer in vaudeville and her first New York job was in the chorus of *Ziegfeld Midnight Frolic* (1920) when she was only sixteen years old. Her subsequent career was mostly in musicals, getting her first major part in *Queen 'o Hearts* (1922). Five years later she was in *Show Boat* where she introduced "Make Believe," "You Are Love," and other standards. Terris reprised her performance in the 1932 revival of *Show Boat*, but her other musicals, *The Well of Romance* (1930) and *Great Lady* (1938), failed to run. Realizing she would never get a role as satisfying as Magnolia, she retired to Connecticut in 1939 and lived there quietly for the next fifty years. The GOODSPEED OPERA HOUSE in nearby Chester named its second performance space the Terris Theatre in honor of the local actress. Terris appeared in only two films, *Married in Hollywood* (1929) and *Cameo Kirby* (1930), both of which are lost; since she made no recordings, there is no record of her exceptional singing voice.

TERRY, ETHELIND (1900–1984). Stage performer. A dark-haired beauty whose soprano voice made her ideal in operettas, she was very popular on Broadway in the 1920s but when she was only in her thirties her voice gave out and she disappeared into obscurity. Terry was born and educated in Philadelphia and then in 1920 went to New York where she took over the leading role in a revival of *FLORODORA*. After appearing in *Honeydew* (1920) and two editions of the *MUSIC BOX REVUE* (1922 and 1923), she was a hit in three book musicals: as the South American Carmen Mendoza in *Kid Boots* (1923), the hot-tempered Rita in *RIO RITA* (1927), and the Peruvian society lady Nina in *Nina Rosa* (1930). While Terry got to perform in these and a few other musicals on the road or in London, her career quickly faded away afterward. She tried for a comeback with the musical *Cocktail Bar* in 1937 but the show closed before reaching New York.

TERRY, RUTH [born Ruth Mae McMahon] (1920–). Film and television performer. An estimable song stylist, she was starred in a dozen Hollywood musicals but they were B pictures and she never became widely famous. Terry was born in Benton Harbor, Michigan, and sang in public as a child, win-

ning talent contests and performing in vaudeville. Her career started to take off when she sang on the radio and became a featured band singer for Ted Lewis and his orchestra. After a bit part in the movie musical *Love and Hisses* (1937), Terry was featured in *ALEXANDER'S RAGTIME BAND* (1938) and then was given bigger parts in smaller films, such as the musicals *Hold That Coed* (1938), *Blondie Goes Latin* (1941), *Heart of the Golden West* (1942), *Pistol Packin' Mama* (1943), *My Buddy* (1944), *Lake Placid Serenade* (1944), and *Jamboree* (1944). She retired from films in 1947 but returned to acting on television in the 1950s and 1960s.

TESORI, JEANINE (1961–). Stage composer. A gifted songwriter who has shown considerable versatility in her young career, she has quickly established herself as one of the most promising theatre composers. Tesori was born in Manhasset, New York, and studied music at Barnard College. She arranged dance music and orchestrations for several musicals on and Off Broadway before her country and gospel-flavored score for *VIOLET* (1997) was heard Off Broadway. Tesori proved just as capable writing 1920s pastiche music for *THOROUGHLY MODERN MILLIE* (2002) and then revealed a talent for blues and 1960s pop music for *CAROLINE, OR CHANGE* (2004). She has also written music for nonmusical theatre productions and is currently scoring the animated musical film, *Rapunzel* for DISNEY PICTURES and *Shrek* for Broadway.

TESTA, MARY (1955–). Stage, television, and film performer. A hefty, inspired comedienne–singer who often steals the show, usually in supporting or featured roles, she has also given some powerful serious performances in musicals. Testa was born in Philadelphia and educated at the University of Rhode Island before beginning her career as a singer with concert orchestras and in clubs. She made her New York legit debut Off Broadway in 1979 and gave some delightful comic performances in the little-seen musicals *In Trousers* (1979) and *Lucky Stiff* (1988) and replaced leading ladies on Broadway in *BARNUM* (1980) and *THE RINK* (1984). Testa's most memorable musical performances include the harridan wife Domina in *A FUNNY THING HAPPENED ON THE WAY TO THE FORUM* (1996), the drunken voice teacher Madame Dilly in *ON THE TOWN* (1998), the Chicago saloon singer Magdalena in the tragic *Marie Christine* (1999), the veteran trouper Maggie Jones in *42ND STREET* (2001), a replacement for the Matron in *CHICAGO*

(2005), and the muse of tragedy Melpomene in *XANADU* (2007). Her other musical credits include *Marilyn* (1983), *The Knife* (1987), *Hello Muddah, Hello Fadduh* (1992), *A NEW BRAIN* (1998), and *See What I Wanna See* (2005). Testa has appeared in several films and television program, although her musical abilities have not been utilized.

THACKER, RUSS (1946–). Stage and television performer. A boyish-looking singer–actor with an exuberant quality, he played leading juvenile roles in some musicals on and Off Broadway. Thacker was born in Washington, DC, and educated at Montgomery College. He made his New York acting debut in the 1967 revival of *Life With Father* and gained recognition as the rock-singing twin Sebastian in the Off Broadway musical hit *YOUR OWN THING* (1968). Thacker also shone as the oversexed youth Colin in *THE GRASS HARP* (1971). His other New York musicals include *Heathen* (1972), *Dear Oscar* (1972), *Home Sweet Homer* (1976), *Do Patent Leather Shoes Really Reflect Up?* (1982), and *Wings* (19893). Thacker has also acted on television and in a few films.

THANK YOUR LUCKY STARS (Warner 1943). Probably the best of the all-star revues the studios put out during World War II to entertain troops abroad and their families back home, it was a series of musical numbers strung together by the most negligible of plots. The screenplay by MELVIN FRANK, Norman Panama, and others followed songwriter Pat Dixon (JOAN LESLIE), crooner Tommy Randolph (DENNIS MORGAN), and fledgling song and dance man Joe Simpson (EDDIE CANTOR) as they try to break into the movies while producers Dr. Schlenna (S. K. SAKALL) and Farnsworth (EDWARD EVERETT HORTON) try to put together a big benefit show, with everybody and everything converging together for said show at the climax of the film. More intriguing than the story were the oddities to be found in the movie, such as Cantor also playing himself as an egotistical, talentless star who steps on everybody beneath him. ARTHUR SCHWARTZ (music) and FRANK LOESSER (lyrics) wrote the sparkling songs, and WARNER BROTHERS pulled in everyone on contract to sing them, even those not known for their musical talents. This led to some delightful surprises, such as Erroll Flynn spoofing his masculinity with "That's What You Jolly Well Get" and ANN SHERIDAN arguing "Love Isn't Born, It's Made," and also to some embarrassments, such as John Garfield trying to croon the HAROLD ARLEN–JOHNNY MERCER standard "Blues in the Night." Other memorable moments included DINAH SHORE singing the pastiche number "How Sweet You Are" to a group of Civil war soldiers, Willie Best and a chorus of Harlem residents encouraging "Ice Cold Katie" (HATTIE McDANIEL) to marry her G.I. sweetheart before he goes off to war, Leslie and Morgan's jaunty duet "I'm Ridin' for a Fall," Shore and company's cheery delivery of the title song, and, best of all, Bette Davis lamenting the lack of males during wartime with "They're Either Too Young or Too Old." Mark Hellinger and Jack L. Warner produced, DAVID BUTLER directed, and LEROY PRINZ choreographed.

THANKS A MILLION (Fox 1935). A sharp and knowing screenplay by Nunnally Johnson helped this musical satire become a hit, the first one for the newly merged 20TH CENTURY-FOX company. Vaudevillian Eric Land (DICK POWELL) and his fellow players are hired to entertain at a political rally for Judge Culliman (Raymond Walburn) who is running for governor. When the judge is too drunk to address the assembly, Dick does and, singing his way into the crowd's hearts, is picked up by Ned Allen (FRED ALLEN) and his political cronies as a serious candidate. Sally Mason (Ann Dvorak) loves Dick but walks out on him when he is elected unfairly. So Dick exposes his corrupt backers, resigns the governorship, and goes back to her. But the voters won't accept Dick's resignation so he returns to office with Sally's approval. It was sassy stuff and director ROY DEL RUTH pulled no punches in directing the mocking film, which also featured PATSY KELLY, Benny Baker, Alan Dinehart, Andrew Tombes, Paul Harvey, and PAUL WHITEMAN as himself. ARTHUR JOHNSTON (music) and GUS KAHN (lyrics) provided the songs, the best two being the cocky "I'm Sitting High on a Hilltop" and the heartfelt title number. The DARRYL F. ZANUCK film was remade as the musical *If I'm Lucky* (1946) with PERRY COMO as the candidate.

THAT NIGHT IN RIO. See *FOLIES BERGERE DE PARIS*

THAT THING YOU DO (Fox 1996). If it's possible to build an entire musical on one song, this film comes close to it. The movie told the tale of a pop-rock group, the Wonders, from Erie, Pennsylvania, who make one record (the catchy "That Thing You Do") and see it slowly climb the charts until they are (briefly) famous. But infighting within the group, including a romantic triangle, brings the boys down before they ever make a second record and their fifteen minutes of fame is over. Actor Tom Hanks wrote and directed the personable little film and played the record producer who discovers, nurtures, and promotes the Wonders. Also cast were Tom Everett Scott, Liv Tyler, Jonathan Schaech, Steve Zahn, Ethan Embry, Bill Cobbs, and Rita Wilson. Adam Schlesinger wrote the title number and, while there are plenty of other songs heard in the background, "That Thing You Do" was repeated so many times that it felt like a one-song movie.

THAT'S ENTERTAINMENT (MGM 1974). A documentary about the variety and genius of MGM musicals, the film did more to revitalize interest in the golden age of movie musicals than a hundred nights on the late late show. Jack Haley, Jr. compiled the anthology of musical numbers. Familiar classic moments from THE WIZARD OF OZ (1939), THE HARVEY GIRLS (1946), SINGIN' IN THE RAIN (1952), and others were nicely balanced with selections from oft-forgotten films such as THE GREAT ZIEGFELD (1936) and the ESTHER WILLIAMS aquatic vehicles. The on-screen narration by FRANK SINATRA, FRED ASTAIRE, ELIZABETH TAYLOR, GENE KELLY, and others struck some as gratuitous but the clips were everything. For some in the audience it was the first time they had seen much of the footage, and for most it was the first time on a movie screen. The popularity of the documentary prompted *That's Entertainment, Part Two* (MGM 1976), which suffered in comparison. Not only were the clips less thrilling but they were badly truncated and haphazardly presented. Aging Kelly and Astaire sang new lyrics to the ARTHUR SCHWARTZ–HOWARD DIETZ title tune, and the result was more embarrassing than nostalgic. Still, there were some pleasing moments and even an inept documentary about gold still shone on occasion. *That's Dancing* (1985) sought out footage not already covered in the previous films, and *That's Entertainment III* (1994) used "never before seen" footage to fill out its running time.

THAT'S LIFE (ABC 1968–1969). An ambitious first for network television, this weekly sixty-minute musical comedy series offered a continuing plot, characters, and six original songs with each episode. Executive producer Martin Marx oversaw the series in which Robert Dickson (ROBERT MORSE) meets and falls in love with Gloria Quigley (E. J. Peaker),

they marry and settle down in the community of Ridgeville, and eventually have a baby. The slice-of-life episodes were sometimes comic, sometimes sentimental, often clever. One of the last episodes viewed the young couple from the baby's point of view. Shelly Berman and KAY MEDFORD were regulars as Gloria's parents and there were guest stars who played other characters and sang as well. The scripts and the songs were by various writers and some existing songs were used as well. Critical reaction to the series was positive, particularly for the personable leads, but ratings were not high enough to justify a second season. Two decades later the same network offered an even more unlikely musical series, **Cop Rock** (ABC-TV 1990). The weekly sixty-minute show was not a comedy but a police and courtroom drama set in Los Angeles in which detectives, criminals, judges, and juries sang out in contemporary songs that ranged from rap and rock to gospel and pop. Even more daring, the characters often burst into dance a la WEST SIDE STORY (1957). Randy Newman wrote the series' theme song, "Under the Gun," and the numbers for the first episode. Others contributed to the four or five original songs heard each week. Recurring cast members included Ronny Cox, Zachary Thorne, Larry Joshua, James McDaniel, Kathleen Wilhoite, Steven Anderson, Sharon Brown, John Hancock, Peter Onorati, Ron McLarty, Anne Bobby, and Dean Scofield. Some critics found the concept original and thrilling, whereas others thought it too odd and quirky for mainstream tastes. Audiences didn't have much time to discover the series for themselves as it only lasted half a season. Steven Brochco, who had created the television series *Hill Street Blues* and *L. A. Law*, and William M. Finkelstein produced the unusual experiment, which was one of the most expensive series ever made, with each episode costing about $1.8 million.

THEATRE GUILD, THE. America's most durable, influential, and prestigious theatre organization, it played an instrumental part in the American theatre and was responsible for some classic Broadway musicals as well. The Guild was founded in 1919 as an outgrowth of the experimental Washington Square Players and was run by a board of actors, directors, and designers who believed in challenging theatre. Lawrence Langner and Theresa Helburn ran the Guild for much of its history and their offerings were highly eclectic. As well as introducing important American plays and playwrights, the organization was the first to present in New York works by George Bernard Shaw and other European dramatists. For over fifty years the Guild presented plays and musicals for its subscribers and the general public, although there were periods of turmoil and financial instability. The Guild's first musical effort was THE GARRICK GAIETIES (1925), a musical revue that was a fundraiser for the organization. It introduced RICHARD RODGERS and LORENZ HART to Broadway and was so successful subsequent editions were presented in 1926 and 1930. The most important musical contribution by the Guild in the 1930s was the Gershwins' PORGY AND BESS (1935), but it failed to make money and by the early 1940s the organization was on the brink of financial ruin. It was Helburn who suggested to Rodgers that the play *Green Grow the Lilacs*, which the Guild had produced in 1931, would make an exceptional musical. When Hart rejected the idea, the team of Rodgers and Hammerstein was born and OKLAHOMA! (1943) brought fame to the new collaborators and it saved the organization. The Guild produced the next two Rodgers and Hammerstein musicals, CAROUSEL (1945) and ALLEGRO (1947), but few of the Guild's other musicals were financially successful: *Parade* (1935), *Sing Out, Sweet Land* (1944), *Arms and the Girl* (1950), BELLS ARE RINGING (1956), THE UNSINKABLE MOLLY BROWN (1960), and *Darling of the Day* (1968). By the 1970s the Guild existed only on paper or as a co-producer for various New York productions. The last Broadway show to carry the Theatre Guild name was the stage version of STATE FAIR (1996).

THEODORE, LEE (1933–1987). Stage, film, and television choreographer and performer. A notable dancer-turned-choreographer, she was instrumental in preserving theatre dance for future generations. Theodore's birthplace and early life remain unconfirmed but she shows up for the first time on Broadway in the dancing chorus of GENTLEMEN PREFER BLONDES (1953), followed by appearances in the musicals THE KING AND I (1951), *John Murray Anderson's Almanac* (1953), *Seventh Heaven* (1955), DAMN YANKEES (1955), WEST SIDE STORY (1957), where she originated the role of the tomboy Anybodys, and *Tenderloin* (1960). Theodore also danced in the movie versions of *Gentlemen Prefer Blondes* (1953), *Damn Yankees* (1958), and *West Side Story* (1961), assisting with the choreography in the last. She turned to solo choreographing with *Baker Street* (1965), followed by FLORA, THE RED MENACE (1965), THE APPLE TREE (1966), *Darling of the Day* (1968),

Noel Coward's Sweet Potato (1968), *Park* (1970), and *Hard Job Being God* (1972), as well as the television version of KISS ME, KATE (1968) and the film version of SONG OF NORWAY (1970). In the 1970s Theodore concentrated on the American Dance Machine, a company she founded that recreated the dance numbers from Broadway musicals exactly as the original choreographers had set them. The company toured the country, made appearances on television, and performed on Broadway in 1978.

THERE'S NO BUSINESS LIKE SHOW BUSINESS (Fox 1954). The last musical that IRVING BERLIN worked on, it contained two new songs by the veteran songwriter amidst a dozen old established ones pulled out of the proverbial trunk. Phoebe and Henry Ephron wrote the screenplay, an epic soap opera that followed the ups and downs of a show business family over several years. Vaudevillians Terence (DAN DAILEY) and Molly Donahue (ETHEL MERMAN) put each of their three kids in the act, and the quintet is hitting the big time until as adults both the family and the act break up. Eldest son Tim (DONALD O'CONNOR) has a drinking problem, especially when he loses his heart to showgirl Vicky Hoffman (MARILYN MONROE); younger son Steve (Johnnie Ray) gives up performing to become a priest; and daughter Katy (MITZI GAYNOR) wants to make it on her own on Broadway. After a lot of heartache, the family is temporarily reunited and sings the title number in a big show. The musical numbers were a welcome escape from the plot. Some of the highlights included the family act in vaudeville singing "When the Midnight Choo-Choo Leaves for Alabam'," Merman and Dailey in the duets "Play a Simple Melody" and "A Pretty Girl Is Like a Melody," Monroe's sensual renditions of "Heat Wave" and "After You Get What You Want You Don't Want It," O'Connor's singing "A Man Chases a Girl (Until She Catches Him)" and then dancing with some statues come to life, and the ensemble having fun with "Alexander's Ragtime Band" by performing it as a French, Scottish, and Swiss number. The supporting cast included Richard Eastham, Hugh O'Brien, FRANK MCHUGH, Rhys Williams, Lee Patrick, and LYLE TALBOT. WALTER LANG directed the SOL C. SIEGEL production and the choreography was handled by ROBERT ALTON and JACK COLE.

THEY'RE PLAYING OUR SONG (Imperial Theatre 1979). Playwright NEIL SIMON returned to the musical theatre with this lightweight show, coming up with a hit if not a very accomplished libretto. Pop composer Vernon Gersch (Robert Klein) is put together with kookie lyricist Sonia Walsk (Lucie Arnaz) to write songs together and over time their professional and romantic relationship has a series of ups and downs. MARVIN HAMLISCH (music) and Carole Bayer Sager (lyrics) wrote the pop-sounding score that was catchy if not memorable. The songs included "If He Really Knew Me," "Workin' It Out," "Just for Tonight," "I Still Believe in Love," and the bouncy title number. Critics pointed out the paper-thin characters, clumsy jokes, and characterless songs but still recommended the musical as escapist entertainment. Playgoers did not quibble and kept the small musical on the boards for 1,082 performances. The economical, small-cast show was a favorite in summer stock and dinner theatre but seemed to disappear after a time.

THIRTEEN CLOCKS, THE (ABC-TV 1953). A musical fantasy based on a whimsical story by James Thurber, the sixty-minute *Motorola TV Hour* presentation boasted a sterling cast that was directed by Donald Richard and Ralph Nelson to walk the line between ardent passion and silliness. The Duke (Basil Rathbone) lives in a cold, dreary castle where the hands of the clocks are frozen still. He keeps his niece, the Princess Sara Linda (Roberta Peters), a prisoner there, frightening off any suitors with unfair contests and killing the ones who do not run away. The handsome Prince Zorn of Zorna (JOHN RAITT) disguises himself as a minstrel and, with the help of his oddball sidekick Golux (Cedric Hardwicke), outwits the Duke and wins the princess. ALICE PEARCE and RUSSELL NYPE were also in the cast. Fred Sadoff and John Crilly adapted the tale into a teleplay, and Thurber himself wrote the lyrics with Mark Bucci who composed the songs. The score, like the show itself, is lost and not even a kinescope of the broadcast is known to exist. What has survived are the rave notices by the press praising the entire enterprise.

THIS IS SPINAL TAP (Embassy 1984). A mock rockumentary that spoofed the tell-all films about rock groups on tour, the movie featured a set of original rock songs that were both silly and pleasing. Director Rob Reiner played a documentary director joining a has-been British rock band called Spinal Tap as they tour the States and find a less-than-enthusiastic reception. Interviews, cameo appearances, and footage of the rehearsals and concerts were devastatingly accurate and very funny, even a bit uncomfortable at times. Christopher Guest,

Harry Shearer, R. J. Parnell, and David Kaff were the members of the band and, with Reiner and Michael McKean, collaborated on the bogus heavy-metal songs such as "Big Bottom" and "Hell Hole." The comic documentary became a cult favorite and garnered such a following that the cast reassembled a decade later and made some music videos and went on tour for real. Guest and McKean came back with the mock documentary ***Waiting for Guffman*** (Castle Rock/SONY 1996) about a community theatre production. Guest co-wrote, directed, and played the leading role of the affected Corky St. Clair who is putting on an original musical for the town of Blaine, Missouri. McKean and others again came up with the songs that were again throwaway ditties but strangely appealing. The cast also included Eugene Levy, Fred Willard, Catherine O'Hara, Parker Posey, Bob Balaban, Don Lake, Michael Hitchcock, Larry Miller, and others who would become part of an unofficial repertory of actors appearing in later films by Guest. Their fiction documentary *A Mighty Wind* (2003) was a musical with a full score of bluegrass, folk, and country music songs, again written by McKean and some cast members.

THIS IS THE ARMY (Broadway Theatre 1942). A sequel of sorts to the famous World War I revue YIP YIP YAPHANK (1919), this patriotic fund-raiser for the Army Emergency Relief Fund boasted a new score by IRVING BERLIN but the musical highlight was his singing the old standard "Oh, How I Hate to Get Up in the Morning," which he had performed in the original revue. James McColl wrote the sketches about army life and the all-soldier cast included Earl Oxford, Stuart Churchill, Gary Merrill, Burl Ives, Ezra Stone, and Joe Cook, Jr. Berlin's new songs included "I Left My Heart at the Stage Door Canteen," "This Is the Army, Mr. Jones," "The Army's Made a Man Out of Me," "I'm Getting Tired So I Can Sleep," "This Time," "American Eagles," and "That's What the Well-Dressed Man in Harlem Will Wear." The show was indeed patriotic but there was also plenty of humor in both the skits and the musical numbers. The engagement of 113 performances in the large house quickly sold out and then the show toured for three years. ■ ***This Is the Army*** (Warner 1943) was also a fund-raiser but the movie discarded the revue format and offered a thin plot to supposedly tie together the parade of disjointed musical numbers. Claude Binyon and Casey Robinson wrote the screenplay, which started in 1918 and showed Jerry Jones

(GEORGE MURPHY) putting on a benefit show to raise money for the armed forces. A generation later, his son Johnny Jones (RONALD REAGAN) is producing a similar show and its preparation and presentation framed the Berlin songs. Also in the cast were JOAN LESLIE, GEORGE TOBIAS, ALAN HALE, CHARLES BUTTERWORTH, Kate Smith, GERTRUDE NIESEN, FRANCES LANGFORD, ROSEMARY DeCAMP, Earl Oxford, Dolores Costello, UNA MERKEL, Joe Louis, and James Burrell. The movie was very timely, of course, and reflected the spirit of the day, yet much of the movie is still entertaining and effective. Director MICHAEL CURTIZ moved the silly plot along quickly, and choreographers LeROY PRINZ and Robert Sidney found a nice balance between military maneuvers and dance. Most of the stage songs were kept and some Berlin favorites were added, such as "We're on Our Way to France' and "God Bless America." The finale, with 350 soldiers singing "This Is the Army, Mr. Jones," is still a power-packed ending.

THOMAS, DANNY [born Muzyad Yakhoob] (1914–1991). Television and film performer and producer. The hawk-nosed entertainer, who tried most forms of show business and found his greatest success in television, made a few notable appearances in movie musicals. Thomas was born in Deerfield, Michigan, the son of Catholic immigrants from Lebanon, and Americanized his name to Amos Jacobs in school. He started in burlesque before he worked in vaudeville and then nightclubs where he sang and proved an amiable emcee. Appearances in higher-class supper clubs and on the radio led to a Hollywood contract, and he was featured or starred in a handful of musicals, most memorably as songwriter GUS KAHN in the biography *I'll See You in My Dreams* (1952) and the Jewish singer Jerry Golding in the remake of *THE JAZZ SINGER* (1953). Thomas's other screen musicals were *The Unfinished Dance* (1947), *Big City* (1948), *CALL ME MISTER* (1951), and *Looking for Love* (1964). His *Make Room for Daddy* television series ran over a decade and he appeared on many other shows as well. Thomas was also a shrewd television producer who had a half dozen hit series running in the 1960s. His daughter is actress Marlo Thomas (1938–). Autobiography: *Make Room for Danny* (1990).

THOMPSON, KAY [born Katherine L. Fink] (1902–1998). Film and television performer, composer, lyricist, and musician. The stylish singer–pianist enlivened a few movie musi-

cals and entertained in nightclubs for decades but she was more influential behind the scenes where she did the vocal arrangements for many films and was instrumental in the success for several songwriters and performers. Thompson was born in St. Louis and showed extraordinary musical talents as a young girl. She was groomed for a concert pianist career and even was a soloist with the St. Louis Symphony Orchestra but she was sidetracked and started singing with various bands. She went to Hollywood in 1936 and worked closely with ROGER EDENS on several MGM musicals. Her own screen appearances were limited to a specialty in *Manhattan Merry-Go-Round* (1937), a bit part in *The Kid From Brooklyn* (1946), and the funny, flamboyant editor Maggie Prescott who urges everyone to "Think pink!" in *FUNNY FACE* (1957). Thomson contributed music and lyrics to different Hollywood projects, coached such stars as JUDY GARLAND and LENA HORNE, had a popular nightclub act with the Williams Brothers, made many television appearances, and wrote the *Eloise* books.

THOROUGHLY MODERN MILLIE (Universal 1967). A satiric look at the Roaring Twenties

Thoroughly Modern Millie. Hollywood never quite knew what to do with the unique comedienne Beatrice Lillie who was an oddball mixture of high class and low comedy on the stage. Here she is as the white slaver Mrs. Meers, preparing an apple with knockout drops. The half smile and look of satisfaction on her face is pure Lillie. (Photofest)

Casts for *Thoroughly Modern Millie*

Character	1967 film	2002 Broadway
Millie Dilmount	JULIE ANDREWS	SUTTON FOSTER
Mrs. Meers	BEATRICE LILLIE	Harriet Harris
Jimmy Smith	James Fox	Gavin Creel
Miss Dorothy	Mary Tyler Moore	Angela Christian
Muzzy	CAROL CHANNING	Sheryl Lee Ralph
Trevor Graydon	John Gavin	MARC KUDISCH

and silent films of that era, the musical was a lighthearted vehicle fashioned for JULIE ANDREWS who had first come to the attention of Broadway audiences in a similar show, the 1920s musical spoof *THE BOY FRIEND* (1954). Richard Morris's screenplay concerns the naive but spunky Millie Dilmount who arrives in New York City during the jazz age, bobs her hair, and looks for a job with a handsome, rich boss whom she can marry. Despite early setbacks, she mostly succeeds, only to fall in love with the penniless Jimmy who, to no one's surprise, turns out to be a millionaire. ROSS HUNTER produced the wry spoof, and director George Roy Hill filled it with slapstick, silent screen camera techniques, and high camp. Andrews was appealing as Millie but more interesting were BEATRICE LILLIE as the sinister landlady Mrs. Meers who runs a white slave ring, Mary Tyler Moore as the addlebrained debutante Miss Dorothy, and CAROL CHANNING as the wacky heiress Muzzy. Much of the score consisted of period favorites such as "Do It Again," "Jazz Baby," "Poor Butterfly," and "Baby Face," but JAMES VAN HEUSEN (music) and SAMMY CAHN (lyrics) provided four pastiche numbers, including the hit title song.

Thoroughly Modern Millie (Marquis Theatre 2002) was written by Richard Morris with Dick Scanlan who also wrote the lyrics for eight new songs with music by JEANINE TESORI. Numbers such as "Forget About the Boy," "Not for the Life of Me," "Gimme Gimme," and "What Do I Need With Love?" were as accurate to the period as they were pleasing in their own right. Both the script and the score were an improvement on the slapdash film and, as directed by Michael Mayer and choreographed by ROB ASHFORD, the stage version was highly entertaining. Newcomer SUTTON FOSTER triumphed as Millie, Gavin Creel and MARC KUDISCH were buoyant as Jimmy and Millie's boss Mr. Graydon, and Harriet Harris stole her scenes as Mrs. Meers. The musical was very popular, running 903 performances, followed by many summer stock and amateur productions.

THORPE, [Rollo Smolt] **RICHARD** (1896–1991). Film director. Although he directed over 150 films, including sixteen musicals, over a forty-five year period, he never turned out a classic but always delivered a polished, professional product. Thorpe was born in Hutchinson, Kansas, and began his career performing in vaudeville, musical comedy, and silents before he started directing shorts and low-budget pictures. By the mid-1930s he was helming first-class movies for MGM in a variety of genres. Thorpe's screen musicals include *TWO GIRLS AND A SAILOR* (1944), *Thrill of a Romance* (1945), *Fiesta* (1947), *A DATE WITH JUDY* (1948), *THREE LITTLE WORDS* (1950), *THE GREAT CARUSO* (1951), *THE STUDENT PRINCE* (1954), *Athena* (1954), *Ten Thousand Bedrooms* (1957), *JAILHOUSE ROCK* (1957), *Follow the Boys* (1963), and *Fun in Acapulco* (1963). His son is film and television producer–director Jerry Thorpe (1926–).

THREE CABALLEROS, THE (Disney/RKO 1945). A Donald Duck cartoon, an anthology program, a musical celebration of Latin America, and a travelogue all wrapped up with dizzying visuals and expert animation, the movie is a one-of-a-kind experience that still pleases audiences. The film is structured around a series of gifts that Donald (voice of Clarence Nash) receives in the mail for his birthday. Each package contains a story, pop-up book, or sequence that transports him to Mexico and Brazil where, with his pal the parrot Joe Carioca (José Olivera), they attend a bull fight, see some local folk tales animated for them, and ogle the lovely ladies south of the border. The songs, sung in Portuguese, Spanish, and English, ranged from the romantic "You Belong to My Heart" to the dreamy "Baia" to the raucous title number performed by Donald, Carioca, and the feathered Panchito (Joaquin Garay) in a surrealistic frenzy of animation. The finished print sat on the shelves for a year while WALT DISNEY waited for Technicolor film stock to become available during the wartime shortage. When the movie finally opened it was a box office hit and found a new audience four decades later when it was released on video.

THREE LITTLE GIRLS IN BLUE. See *MOON OVER MIAMI*

THREE LITTLE WORDS (MGM 1950). This biographical musical differed from most in that the central characters, lyricist BERT KALMAR and composer HARRY RUBY, were not household names and the George Ells's screenplay was more interested in the two men than in a series of lavish production numbers. Hoofer Kalmar (FRED ASTAIRE) turns to lyric writing after a knee injury ends his dancing days. Ruby (RED SKELTON) is more interested in baseball and girls than in songwriting and needs continual prodding by his partner to get down to composing. After the two men have a falling out, their wives Jessie Kalmar (VERA-ALLEN) and Eileen Ruby (Arlene Dahl) bring the songwriting team back together. Although some of the Kalmar–Ruby songs were instantly recognizable, there were many forgotten gems that were featured in the film and, as staged by choreographer HERMES PAN, they made for some delectable surprises. Astaire and Vera-Ellen (singing dubbed by Anita Ellis) sang the duet "Where Did You Get That Girl?" and danced to "Mr. and Mrs. Hoffer at Home," GLORIA DEHAVEN played her own mother, Mrs. Carter DeHaven, and sang "Who's Sorry Now," and Debbie Reynolds impersonated the "Boop-Boop-a-Doop" girl HELEN KANE and sang "I Wanna Be Loved By You" with the real Kane providing the vocals. Also in the cast were KEENAN WYNN, Gale Robbins, Harry Shannon, CARLETON CARPENTER, PHIL REGAN as himself, and the actual Harry Ruby in a cameo as a baseball player. RICHARD THORPE directed the JACK CUMMINGS production, which lost points on accuracy but was a treat all the same.

THREE MUSKETEERS, THE (Lyric Theatre 1928). Three years after DENNIS KING had played the swashbuckling hero in RUDOLF FRIML'S operetta *THE VAGABOND KING*, he returned in another Friml work as another swashbuckler, the musketeer d'Artagnan. WILLIAM ANTHONY McGUIRE'S libretto follows the Dumas classic up to a point, concentrating on the romance between d'Artagnan and Constance Bonacieux (VIVIENNE SEGAL) but leaving plenty of room for the title musketeers Athos (Douglass Dumbrille), Porthos (Detmar

Poppen), and Aramis (Joseph Macaulay) and their intrigues with the evil Cardinal Richelieu (REGINALD OWEN) who is trying to dishonor Queen Anne (Yvonne D'Arle). CLIFFORD GREY and P. G. WODEHOUSE wrote the lyrics for Friml's lilting music, and the score featured such memorable numbers as "March of the Musketeers," "Ma Belle,' "My Sword and I," "Your Eyes," and "Queen of My Heart." McGuire co-directed the FLORENZ ZIEGFELD production with Richard Boleslawsky and ALBERTINA RASCH did the choreography. The original production ran 318 performances, followed by road companies and many productions by light opera companies over the years. A revised version of *The Three Musketeers* played briefly on Broadway in 1984. Curiously, the operetta was never filmed by Hollywood and of the many movie and television versions of the Dumas tale made over the years, none took a musical approach.

THREEPENNY OPERA, THE (Empire Theatre 1933). A major work of music–theatre and one of the most influential of all foreign musicals, the piece was not welcomed the first time around

The Threepenny Opera. The Off Broadway cast of the the Brecht–Weill musical cast was filled with unknowns who went on to become very well known. Pictured is a young Beatrice Arthur as the jailer's daughter Lucy being seduced (once again) by Mack the Knife, played by Scott Merrill. (Photofest)

but eventually became a much-revived hit. In Victorian England, the dashing villain Macheath (ROBERT CHISHOLM), better known to the police and the underworld as Mack the Knife, hopes to marry Polly (Steffi Duna), the daughter of the crime syndicate boss Jonathan Peachum (Rex Weber), but Macheath is betrayed by Peachum and the whore Jenny Diver (Marjorie Dille). About to be hanged, Macheath is saved by a last-minute reprieve from the Queen, pointing out the irony of justice and goodness in the world. Based on John Gay's eighteenth-century ballad opera THE BEGGAR'S OPERA, the 1928 German musical *Die Dreigoschenoper* by KURT WEILL (music) and Bertolt Brecht (book and lyrics) was translated by Gifford Cochran and Jerrold Krimsky. The notable musical numbers included "The Legend of Mackie Messer," "The Pirate Jenny," "Love Duet," "Jealousy Duet," "Song of the Aimlessness of Life," "Farewell Song," and "Ballad of the Easy Life." Critics found it a puzzling, socialist diatribe and dismissed the show, although some complimented the strange but haunting Weill music. Because the production closed after twelve performances, most theatregoers were not even aware that the musical existed. Not until after Weill's premature death in 1950 did producers look at the composer's German works and in 1954 Carmen Capalbo and Stanley Chase presented MARC BLITZSTEIN's translation and adaptation of the musical at the Theatre de Lys Off Broadway with an outstanding cast that included some promising new talents: Scott Merrill (MacHeath), LOTTE LENYA (Jennie), Jo Sullivan (Polly), BEATRICE ARTHUR (Lucy), Frederic Downs (Peachum), JANE CONNELL (Mrs. Peachum), Richard Verney (Tiger Brown), and Tige Andrews (Streetsinger). Blitzstein's version was sharp, poetic, and gripping, his lyrics accessible but harsh. His adaptation of the main ballad into the song "Mack the Knife" was an immediate (if unlikely) hit and was on the pop charts. The Off Broadway production, directed by Capalbo, was acclaimed by the press as a strange and fascinating "new" work and the little show became the talk of the town. After its scheduled ninety-two performances, the cry for tickets was such that the show reopened and ran 2,611 performances, the longest-running Off Broadway musical up to that time.

In addition to the hundreds of productions over the years in colleges, regional theatres, and summer stock, there have been four major New York revivals. In 1966, the Stockholm Marionette Theatre of Fantasy visited Manhattan for two weeks and presented actors dressed as cut-out puppets performing the text in Blitzstein's English version. A 1976 Lincoln Center production used a new and purposely unpoetic translation by Ralph Manheim and John Willett, which most critics disdained but there was more approval for the very stylized production directed by avant gardist Richard Forman. The excellent cast included RAUL JULIA (MacHeath), Ellen Greene (Jenny), Caroline Kava (Polly), C. K. Alexander (Peachum), Elizabeth Wilson (Mrs. Peachum), and Blair Brown (Lucy). The JOSEPH PAPP-produced production was extended for a run of 307 performances, the longest-running Broadway revival of the show on record. Rock star Sting was the star of the 1989 revival, which was billed as *3 Penny Opera* but critics thought Sting's MacHeath a dull fellow and the singer's fans could keep him on the boards for only sixty-five performances. John Dexter directed and the cast also featured Alvin Epstein (Peachum), GEORGIA BROWN (Mrs. Peachum), Maureen McGovern (Polly), Kim Criswell (Lucy), and Ethyl Eichelberger (Ballad Singer). Unanimous pans greeted the 2006 ROUNDABOUT THEATRE COMPANY revival directed by Scott Elliott using a new version by Wallace Shawn. The main complaint concerned the vastly different acting styles used throughout the campy, overblown production, which featured a bisexual MacHeath by Alan Cumming, a vampy Jenny by Cyndi Lauper, a drag queen Lucy by Brian Charles Rooney, a shrill Mrs. Peachum by Ana Gasteyer, and a sly, understated Peachum by JIM DALE, who got the only good notices. There was no demand to extend the run beyond its scheduled seventy-seven performances.

🎬 *The Threepenny Opera* was filmed in Germany in 1931 by G. W. Pabst with Rudolf Forster as Mackie Messer and Lotte Lenya as Jenny, and again in 1962 with Curt Jurgens as MacHeath, Hildegarde Kneff as Jenny, and Gert Frobe as Peachum. Raul Julia reprised his MacHeath in an English-language film titled *Mack the Knife* (1990) written and directed by Menahem Golan. The score was greatly abridged but the cast was impressive: Julia Migenes (Jenny), Richard Harris (Peachum), Rachel Robertson (Polly), Julie Walters (Mrs. Peachum), Erin Donovan (Lucy), Bill Nighy (Tiger Brown), and Roger Daltry (Streetsinger).

🕊 ***THREE'S A CROWD*** (Selwyn Theatre 1930). Reuniting many of the talents from *The Little Show* (1929), the revue was similarly innovative and nearly as popular. HOWARD DIETZ, Arthur Skeekman, GROUCHO MARX, and others wrote the satirical sketches, and the songs were by ARTHUR SCHWARTZ (music) and Dietz (lyrics), the most memorable being "Something to Remember You By," "The Moment I Saw You," and "Right at the Start of It." The number "Body and Soul," by JOHNNY GREEN (music) and Edward Heyman (lyric), was already popular in England and was interpolated into the score, introducing the long, moaning musical line that would characterize much of the 1930s sound. CLIFTON WEBB, LIBBY HOLMAN, and FRED ALLEN led the cast that also included TAMARA GEVA, Earl Oxford, FRED MACMURRAY, and ALLAN JONES. Director–lighting designer HASSARD SHORT staged the piece without footlights, instead hanging the instruments from the balcony and creating the look of theatrical lighting to come. MAX GORDON produced, ALBERTINA RASCH devised the modern choreography, and the smart little revue ran 272 performances.

TIBBETT, LAURENCE [Mervil] (1895–1960). Stage and film performer. Arguably the greatest opera baritone of the 1920s, the handsome singer sang in six movie musicals. Tibbett was born in Bakersfield, California, the son of a sheriff, and took singing lessons in Los Angeles before singing professionally. He made his Metropolitan opera debut in 1923 and stayed for twenty-eight years. One of the first opera singers to try talkies, he played leading roles in the musicals *The Rogue Song* (1930), *NEW MOON* (1930), *The Prodigal* (1931), *Cuban Love Song* (1931), *Metropolitan* (1935), and *Under Your Spell* (1936). Tibbett proved to be an exceptional actor as well as a singer, getting an Oscar nomination for his first film. In the late 1930s he returned to the opera and concert stage. He made many popular recordings of opera, operetta, and musical theatre songs. In the 1950s Tibbett's powerful voice gave out and he turned to drink and a premature death.

TIERNEY, HARRY [Austin] and [Thomas] **JOSEPH MCCARTHY.** Stage composer and lyricist. An oft-forgotten songwriting team from the first two decades of the twentieth century, they scored some very popular Broadway musicals. Tierney (1890–1965) was born in Perth Amboy, New Jersey, into a musical family, and studied piano in New York for a concert career. As a juvenile he performed in concert halls in Europe and America but as an adult threw it over to become a song plugger at

Harrods department store in London where he was heard by theatrical producer C. B. Cochran who hired Tierney to write songs for the musical stage. His songs were interpolated into various West End musicals and he got to score *Keep Smiling* (1913) by himself before returning to America where he met lyricist McCarthy (1885–1943). He was born in Somerville, Massachusetts, and began his career as a music publisher and sometime singer. Before long his songs were sung in vaudeville by such stars as May Irwin and AL JOLSON. McCarthy's first score to be heard on Broadway was the short-lived *Oh, Look!* (1918) but when he teamed up with Tierney, the result was *IRENE* (1919), the biggest hit of its time. The two collaborated on five subsequent book musicals: *Up She Goes* (1922), *Glory* (1922), *Kid Boots* (1923), *RIO RITA* (1927), and *Cross My Heart* (1928), as well as some songs for the revues ZIEGFELD FOLLIES (1919) and *The Broadway Whirl* (1921). The two men rarely wrote together after 1927 and neither had much success on Broadway without the other. Tierney went to Hollywood where he oversaw the film versions of his hits and to write original scores for *Dixiana* (1930) and *Half Shot at Sunrise* (1930). He also composed several operettas that never made it to New York. McCathy wrote songs for several editions of the ZIEGFELD FOLLIES, for nonmusical films, and for Tin Pan Alley with others.

■ *TILL THE CLOUDS ROLL BY* (MGM 1946). A biographical musical that probably packed more stars into the film than any other of its genre, this movie about the life and career of JEROME KERN needed every one of those celebrities for it was as dull as it was inaccurate. The screenplay by Myles Connolly and Jean Holloway began in 1927 with the opening night of *Show Boat* and presented a fifteen-minute version of that landmark musical, featuring KATHRYN GRAYSON, TONY MARTIN, LENA HORNE, VIRGINIA O'BRIEN, Caleb Peterson, and others, that was beautifully done. Then the plot jumps back to the young and struggling Kern (Robert Walker) as he gets advice from his teacher and mentor James Hessler (Van Heflin), goes to England and meets his future bride Eva (Dorothy Patrick), and eventually becomes famous. Three different directors (GEORGE SIDNEY, VINCENTE MINNELLI, and Richard Whorf) contributed to the film and none of them could breathe any life into it anytime the music stopped. Luckily it didn't stop very often, and over two dozen Kern songs were paraded by with professional panache. JUDY GARLAND, as 1920s Broadway star MARILYN MILLER, sang "Who?" and "Look for the Silver Lining," a young ANGELA LANSBURY got to do her own vocals with the coy "How'd You Like to Spoon With Me?," DINAH SHORE recalled "The Last Time I Saw Paris," Grayson performed the dreamy "Long Ago and Far Away," Martin did justice to the entrancing "All the Things You Are," and JUNE ALLYSON showed a wry sense of humor with "Cleopatterer." ROBERT ALTON did the spirited choreography, with the dance highlight being Allyson and RAY MCDONALD'S vivacious version of the title song. Some numbers were oddly out of sync, such as a tuxedoed FRANK SINATRA crooning "Ol' Man River" like a lounge singer, but for the most part producer ARTHUR FREED knew how to use the talent available on the studio lot and he used them well.

TILLER, JOHN (1852?–1925). Stage choreographer. The influential British choreographer's dance routines were only seen for a short time on Broadway but his innovations were long lasting. Tiller was born in Manchester, England, and started as a businessman who staged church pageants as an avocation. His military-like maneuvers were so well received that Tiller opened a dance school and integrated various dance steps into his drill formations. His dancers, soon dubbed Tiller Girls, formed geometric patterns and dazzled audiences in several London musicals before he interpolated his girls and choreography into a handful of Broadway shows in the 1920s, mostly revues and most memorably four editions of the ZIEGFELD FOLLIES. After Tiller's death, his associate Mary Read continued his Tiller Girls and they appeared on Broadway in *She's My Baby* (1928) and *Yours Truly* (1928). By the 1930s, the expression "Tiller Girls" meant any chorus line of girls with military-like precision. While some dismissed Tiller's work as nothing more than glorified acrobatics, his influence was far reaching. Early director–choreographers such as JULIAN MITCHELL took Tiller's ideas and used them to create the modern chorus line. BUSBY BERKELEY was also inspired by Tiller and his geometric dance formations on Broadway, and in the WARNER BROTHERS film musicals of the 1930s he used extended versions of the original Tiller Girls. Variations of Tiller Girls can be seen in such later musicals as *CABARET* (1967) and *A CHORUS LINE* (1975). John Tiller's legacy can best be seen today in the patterns and precision of the high-kicking Rockettes at Radio City Music Hall.

TIMBUKTU! See *KISMET*

TIME, THE PLACE AND THE GIRL, THE (Wallack's Theatre 1907). A big hit in Chicago where it ran over 400 performances, the musical comedy was snubbed by New York but was a success on the road for several years. Drinking buddies Tom Cunningham (George Anderson) and Johnny Hicks (Arthur Deagon) have had one too many drunken brawls and end up in a sanitarium where Tom runs across an old love, Margaret Simpson (Violet McMillan), and Johnny finds a new sweetheart, Molly Kelly (Elene Foster). It looks like both men will lose their new-found romances when the two girls are released, but an outbreak of infection in the sanitarium forces the authorities to quarantine everyone inside, which gives the two boys time to woo and win their mates. Will M. Hough and Frank R. Adams wrote the silly but useful libretto and also provided the lyrics for Joe Howard's music, with the notable songs being "Waning Honeymoon," "Blow the Smoke Away," "It's Lonesome Tonight," and "Thursday's My Jonah Day." The dismissive critical reaction to the Midwestern musical in New York was typical of the time and forced the show to close after thirty-two performances. A 1942 Broadway revival of *The Time, the Place and the Girl* that kept the plot but replaced most of the score with new songs did not fare any better, closing after thirteen performances. Two movie musicals used the title *The Time, the Place and the Girl* (1929 and 1946) but neither had any connections, plot-wise or musically, with the stage show.

TIN PAN ALLEY (Fox 1940). The only musical to feature both of the 1940's favorite blondes, ALICE FAYE and BETTY GRABLE, the film tended to favor the established Faye over the up-and-coming Grable. In the Helen Logan and Robert Ellis screenplay, the stars played the performing sisters Katie (Faye) and Lili Blane (Grable) between the years 1915 and 1939 (although neither aged a day) who become involved with songwriters Skeets Harrigan (JOHN PAYNE) and Harry Calhoun (JACK OAKIE) as they struggle to make their music publishing company succeed on Tin Pan Alley. HARRY WARREN (music) and MACK GORDON (lyrics) wrote one new number for the film, the hit "You Say the Sweetest Things, Baby," and the rest of the score was comprised of old standards, some of which were not correct for the period. All four stars, joined by the NICHOLAS BROTHERS, Allen Jenkins, BILLY GILBERT,

Esther Ralston, and others, were in fine form as they delivered such favorites as "The Sheik of Araby," "K-K-K-Katy," "Honeysuckle Rose," and "Moonlight Bay." WALTER LANG directed and SEYMOUR FELIX choreographed the Kenneth Macgowan production. It wasn't much of a story but 20TH CENTURY-FOX retold it again in the musical *I'll Get By* (1950).

TIP-TOES (Liberty Theatre 1925). An art deco-styled musical comedy, the Gershwin brothers show did not offer many hit standards but was infectious fun all the same. Vaudevillians Tip-Toes Kaye (QUEENIE SMITH) and her two performing uncles Al (Andrew Tombes) and Harry (Harry Watson, Jr.) are stranded in Palm Beach, Florida, so they plot a scheme to try and pass Tip-Toes off as an aristocrat and snag her a rich husband among all the vacationing millionaires. Their target is the glue king Steve Burton (ALLEN KEARNS) but Tip-Toes falls in love with him for real so she is relieved to learn that he is just as penniless as her. The happy ending came about when Steve admitted he pretended to be poor to test her love. Also in the cast were JEANETTE MCDONALD, ROBERT HALLIDAY, and Gertrude McDonald. GUY BOLTON and Fred Thompson wrote the obvious but playful libretto, and GEORGE (music) and IRA GERSHWIN (lyrics) contributed the hit "That Certain Feeling," as well as such commendable songs as "Sweet and Low-Down," "These Charming People," "When Do We Dance?," "Looking for a Boy," and "Nice Baby." John Harwood directed the ALEX A. AARONS–VINTON FREEDLEY production, SAMMY LEE choreographed the jazzy dances, and the musical ran 194 performances.

TITANIC (Lunt-Fontanne Theatre 1997). An unlikely musical subject, a sea disaster with no happy ending, the ambitious show took itself very seriously and so did many playgoers. A handful of characters from the crew, first class, second class, and steerage were followed from the departure of the White Star Line ocean liner *Titanic* to its sinking in the mid-Atlantic, ending with an anthem of hope sung by the survivors. The cast included JOHN CUNNINGHAM, BRIAN D'ARCY JAMES, VICTORIA CLARK, David Garrison, MICHAEL CERVERIS, Judith Blazer, Jennifer Piech, Erin Hill, Theresa McCarthy, Larry Keith, Alma Cuervo, and Martin Moran. PETER STONE wrote the competent if not inspired libretto, and MAURY YESTON provided the songs, which ranged from lyrical pastiche numbers to rousing chorales. "In Every Age," "Barrett's Song," "Lady's Maid," "No Moon," "Still," "Autumn," and "We'll Meet Tomorrow" were among the notable numbers. Richard Jones directed with an obvious hand and the technical effects, which included the giant ship tilting more and more before it sank, were sometimes impressive. Technical troubles during previews led to many jokes in the theatre district and the reviewers could not help making their own snide comments about a show concerning a disaster, but slowly favorable word of mouth grew and a few months after the musical opened it started selling out. The run of 804 performances was not enough to pay back the $10 million investment but the tour was successful and there have been subsequent productions in summer and community theatres.

TOAST OF NEW ORLEANS, THE (MGM 1950). A MARIO LANZA vehicle that was filled with opera selections, the film gave the tenor one of his biggest nonopera hits, "Be My Love" by NICHOLAS BRODSZKY (music) and SAMMY CAHN (lyric). Scriptwriters Sy Gomberg and GEORGE WELLS cast Lanza as the poor Louisiana bayou fisherman Pepe Duvalle who is discovered by the music manager Jacques Riboudeaux (David Niven) who brings him to New Orleans and trains him. Riboudeaux's star client is the snooty opera singer Suzette Micheline (KATHRYN GRAYSON) who looks down on the uncouth Pepe but, to one one's surprise, eventually falls in love with him, much to Riboudeaux's distress. J. CARROL NAISH, James Mitchell, Richard Hageman, CLINTON SUNDBERG, Sig Arno, RITA MORENO, and Romo Vincent made up the supporting cast directed by NORMAN TAUROG. Lanza sang selections from *La Gioconda*, *La Traviata*, *Martha*, *Carmen*, and other operas, as well as such Brodszky–Cahn songs as "The Tina Lina" and "Boom Biddy Boom Boom," but the highlight of the film was when he exploded with the bombastic "Be My Love."

TOBIAS, GEORGE (1901–1980). Stage, film, and television performer. A dour-looking character actor who was versatile in his portrayals, he shone in supporting roles in Hollywood musicals. The native New Yorker studied acting at the Neighborhood Playhouse School and then began his professional career at the experimental Provincetown Playhouse Off Broadway and by 1924 was acting in dramas and comedies on Broadway, mostly for the THEATRE GUILD. He went to Hollywood in 1937 and was soon cast as everything from gangsters to buffoons. Tobias' musical credits include

BALALAIKA (1939), *Music in My Heart* (1940), *YANKEE DOODLE DANDY* (1942), *THIS IS THE ARMY* (1943), *THANK YOUR LUCKY STARS* (1943), *My Wild Irish Rose* (1947), *The GLENN MILLER STORY* (1954), *The Seven Little Foys* (1955), and *SILK STOCKINGS* (1957). He also acted in dozens of television dramas and comedies, most memorably *Bewitched* in the 1960s.

TODD, MICHAEL [born Avram Goldbogen] (1907–1958). Film and stage producer. The colorful showman who made sure each of his projects was launched with plenty of bally-hoo, he presented some memorable Broadway musicals. Todd was born in Minneapolis and made his name with his show at the 1933 Chicago World's Fair. Three years later he was producing plays on Broadway and made his musical bow with the jazzy *The Hot Mikado* (1939). His subsequent musicals were *Star and Garter* (1942), *SOMETHING FOR THE BOYS* (1943), *MEXICAN HAYRIDE* (1944), *UP IN CENTRAL PARK* (1945), *AS THE GIRLS GO* (1948), and *Mike Todd's Peep Show* (1950). Some of these were only a step above burlesque but he knew what audiences wanted, particularly G.I.s on leave in New York during the war years. Todd moved into movie producing in 1945, forming his own production company, and in the 1950s he offered wide-screen spectaculars to compete with television. In films such as *Around the World in 80 Days* (1956) he not only promoted his big-screen approach, but he also polished the concept of cameo appearances by stars. Todd was at the peak of his success when he died in a plane crash at the age of fifty-one. He was married to JOAN BLONDELL and then ELIZABETH TAYLOR. Biographies: *A Valuable Property: The Life Story of Mike Todd*, Michael Todd, Jr., Susan McCarthy Todd (1983); *The Nine Lives of Michael Todd*, Art Cohn (1959).

TOM THUMB (MGM 1958). A fairy tale musical that was live action yet used a lot of trick photography, the movie was uneven to say the least, but the entertainment level was high if you were young (very young) at heart. Ladislas Fodor adapted the Brothers Grimm tale for the screen, telling the story of the thumb-size boy Tom (RUSS TAMBLYN) alongside a subplot dealing with the romance between the commoner Woody (Alan Young) and the magical Forest Queen (June Thorburn). Bernard Miles and JESSIE MATTHEWS were Tom's simple country folk parents, and Peter Sellers and Terry-Thomas were the buffoonish villains Anthony and Ivan. PEGGY LEE, Kermit Goell, Janice Torre, and Fred Spielman wrote the pleasant if

unmemorable songs, although "The Yawning Song," sung by a puppet (Stan Freberg), was quite fun. Other numbers included "Tom Thumb's Tune," "After All These Years," and "Are You a Dream?" George Pal produced and directed, using his gift for special effects to place the tiny Tom into the decor. Tamblyn, in one of his few leading roles, was a delight-fully vivacious Tom and his dancing, choreo-graphed by Alex Romero, was a special effect all its own.

TOMMY (Hemdale 1975). KEN RUSSELL's spaced-out movie version of the trailblazing rock opera by Peter Townsend and The Who was filled with bizarre images, over-the-top performances, and pretentious symbolism. The story line of the opera is strange enough: the boy Tommy is struck deaf, dumb, and blind when he witnesses a murder and he survives the sexual abuse by his uncle to become the pinball-machine guru and the leader of a cult of pinball worshippers. Director–screenwriter Russell heaped on his own incongruities, such as a temple honoring MARILYN MONROE, Tommy's mother experiencing an orgasm

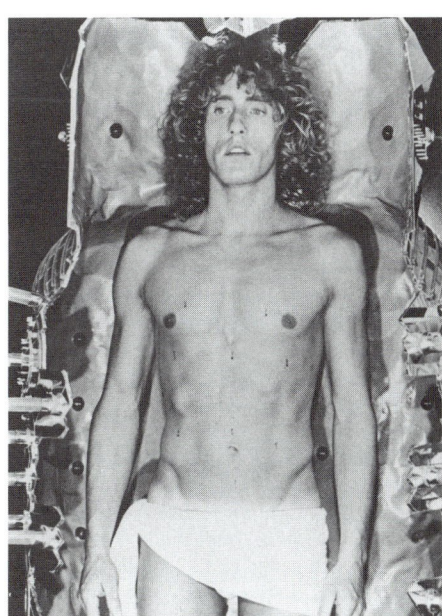

Tommy. If you like your symbolism delivered with a sledgehammer, director Ken Russell is your man. In the film version of *Tommy*, rock star Roger Daltry (pictured) played the title character and, in this scene, is portrayed as a Jesus-like martyr. (Alamy)

Casts for *Tommy*		
Character	*1975 film*	*1995 Broadway*
Adult Tommy	Roger Daltry	MICHAEL CERVERIS
Young Tommy	Barry Winch	Buddy Smith
Mrs. Walker	ANN-MARGARET	Marcia Mitzman
Frank Hobbs	Oliver Reed	
Uncle Ernie	Keith Moon	Paul Kandel
Local Lad	ELTON JOHN	Michael Arnold
Acid Queen	Tina Turner	

as colored liquids flood her apartment, and a crucified Tommy with a crown of flowers rather than thorns. Rock singer Roger Daltry captured the innocence of Tommy, ANN-MARGARET was stunning as the oddball mother, Tina Turner was the Acid Queen, ELTON JOHN the Pinball Wizard wearing giant platform shoes, and others, such as Eric Clapton, Oliver Reed, Keith Moon, and Jack Nicholson, did their best. Musically, the movie was more satisfying, and the most memorable passages from the rock opera were there in fine form, even if the visuals often got in the way. "I'm Free,' "Tommy Can You Hear Me?," "Captain Walker," "Sensation," "Eyesight to the Blind," "Pinball Wizard," and "See Me, Feel Me" were among the musical moments that survived Russell's overenthusiasm. The British film was a moderate success at its release but has gathered a cult following of sorts over the years.

🐸 **The Who's Tommy** (St. James Theatre 1993) turned the popular concert attraction into a truly theatrical performance, thanks to director DES MCANUFF who adapted the piece for Broadway and staged it with a sense of theatre rather than a rock concert. Tommy was played at different ages by Carly Jane Steinborn, Crista Macalush, Buddy Smith, and MICHAEL CERVERIS, and McAnuff sometimes created a reality on stage that was from the youth's point of view. Where Russell's approach had been bombastic, McAnuff's was high-tech, lucid, and exciting. The story was still considered weak by the press but the music, performances, and production were commended. The musical, which had originated at the La Jolla Playhouse in California, drew old and new fans of the rock opera and ran 900 performances.

TONE, [Stanilas Pascal] **FRANCHOT** (1905–1968). Film, stage, and television performer. A handsome, aristocratic-looking leading man who specialized in playing wealthy, cultivated heroes, he had no musical talents but was starred in eleven Hollywood musicals all

the same. Tone was born in Niagara Falls, New York, the son of a prosperous industrialist, and was educated at Cornell University where he first became interested in acting. He made his professional debut in Buffalo in 1927 and later that year was on Broadway, soon playing major roles in dramas and comedies. Tone was a member of the THEATRE GUILD and the Group Theatre and remained committed to challenging theatre even after his film career started in 1932, returning to the stage as late as 1967. On screen he was featured in nonsinging roles in such musicals as *DANCING LADY* (1933), *Reckless* (1935), *The King Steps Out* (1936), *True to Life* (1943), *That Night With You* (1945), *Because of Him* (1946), *Honeymoon* (1947), and *HERE COMES THE GROOM* (1951). Tone's popularity in movies waned in the 1950s so he turned to television and was successful in series and drama specials. One of his wives was actress JOAN CRAWFORD.

TONY AWARDS. Theatre awards for Broadway plays and musicals. The New York theatre's version of the Oscars, these awards have been presented annually by the American Theatre Wing since 1947. The awards are restricted to plays and musicals that have been presented in a contracted Broadway house so as Off and Off Off Broadway have grown over the decades, the Tonys no longer include a majority of theatre in New York City. No award for best musical was given during the first two years of the presentations and other categories have been added over the years, often separating musicals from plays when it comes to performances, direction, and even design. The ceremony in which the awards are given has grown from an intimate dinner in a hotel ballroom to a mammoth production in Radio City Music Hall, which is not even a Broadway theatre. The awards ceremony has been broadcast live on national television since 1967 so the Tonys have become Broadway's biggest advertising event of the year. Winning an award is sometimes less important than the impact the show

Tony Award–Winning Musicals

1949	*KISS ME KATE*		1978	*AIN'T MISBEHAVIN'*
1950	*SOUTH PACIFIC*		1979	*SWEENEY TODD …*
1951	*GUYS AND DOLLS*		1980	*EVITA*
1952	*THE KING AND I*		1981	*42ND STREET*
1953	*WONDERFUL TOWN*		1982	*NINE*
1954	*KISMET*		1983	*CATS*
1955	*THE PAJAMA GAME*		1984	*LA CAGE AUX FOLLES*
1956	*DAMN YANKEES*		1985	*BIG RIVER*
1957	*MY FAIR LADY*		1986	*THE MYSTERY*
1958	*THE MUSIC MAN*			*OF EDWIN DROOD*
1959	*REDHEAD*		1987	*LES MISÉRABLES*
1960	*FIORELLO!* and *THE SOUND OF MUSIC* (tie)		1988	*THE PHANTOM OF THE OPERA*
1961	*BYE BYE BIRDIE*		1989	*JEROME ROBBINS' BROADWAY*
1962	*HOW TO SUCCEED IN BUSINESS WITHOUT*		1990	*CITY OF ANGELS*
	REALLY TRYING		1991	*THE WILL ROGERS FOLLIES*
1963	*A FUNNY THING HAPPENED ON THE WAY*		1992	*CRAZY FOR YOU*
	TO THE FORUM		1993	*KISS OF THE SPIDER WOMAN*
1964	*HELLO, DOLLY!*		1994	*PASSION*
1965	*FIDDLER ON THE ROOF*		1995	*SUNSET BOULEVARD*
1966	*MAN OF LA MANCHA*		1996	*RENT*
1967	*CABARET*		1997	*TITANIC*
1968	*HALLELUJAH, BABY!*		1998	*THE LION KING*
1969	*1776*		1999	*FOSSE*
1970	*APPLAUSE*		2000	*CONTACT*
1971	*COMPANY*		2001	*THE PRODUCERS*
1972	*TWO GENTLEMEN OF VERONA*		2002	*THOROUGHLY MODERN MILLIE*
1973	*A LITTLE NIGHT MUSIC*		2003	*HAIRSPRAY*
1974	*RAISIN*		2004	*AVENUE Q*
1975	*THE WIZ*		2005	*SPAMALOT*
1976	*A CHORUS LINE*		2006	*JERSEY BOYS*
1977	*ANNIE*		2007	*SPRING AWAKENING*

can make on the broadcast. In 1994, for example, the musical *PASSION* won for best musical but it prompted little box office action. On the same broadcast, *BEAUTY AND THE BEAST* was featured and, although it only won one award (for costuming), the next day the box office take broke records. Like any awards organization, the competition often becomes a popularity contest or a political game. The voters for the Tony Awards are made up of professionals in different areas so there is some kind of cross section of opinions. However, the nominations are made by a relatively small committee and the choices of which shows and performers are selected for nominations have often been open to question. Also, among the voters are people who have their own special interests at stake. Voters who book or produce touring shows are more likely to vote for a musical that has wide appeal across the country rather than a more deserving production. As more and more money is at stake, the Tony Awards have echoed the Oscars in their bid for atten-

tion. Blatant advertising and direct appeals to voters, something long practiced with the Academy Awards, have started to become common within the theatre community. The day may come when the winners are determined by which producers have the most money to spend on self-promotion. See also the Awards appendix.

TOO MANY GIRLS (Imperial Theatre 1939). Utilizing a familiar but entertaining premise, this campus musical stood out because of its effervescent cast of mostly unknowns and some superior songs by RICHARD RODGERS (music) and LORENZ HART (lyrics). The wealthy Harvey Casey of Skohegan, Maine, has a wild daughter, Consuelo, so when he sends her to Stop Gap, New Mexico, to attend school at Pottawatomie College, he secretly hires four All-American football players to enroll as well and keep an eye on her. Clint Kelley arrives in New Mexico with his pals Jojo Jordan, Al Terwilliger, and Manuelito, and when they are put on the football team the college starts winning. Clint and Consuelo fall in love, just as the other three men are getting romantically involved with coeds, but on the night before the big game Consuelo finds out why Clint is really there and plans to return home. Since Clint and the boys have orders to stick to Consuelo, they will all miss the crucial football game if they follow her. Consuelo is finally convinced that Clint really loves her, everyone stays in New Mexico, and Pottawatomie is victorious on the field. George Marion, Jr. wrote the useful if unoriginal libretto, GEORGE ABBOTT produced and directed, and the choreography was by ROBERT ALTON. However, it was the Rodgers and Hart score that kept the show from becoming just another collegiate musical. The runaway hit was "I Didn't Know What Time It Was" but there was exceptional lyric work in the comic numbers as well and Rodgers' Latin-flavored music was fresh and contagious. "Give It Back to the Indians," "I Like to Recognize the Tune," "Love Never Went to College," "Spic and Spanish," and "She Could Shake the Maracas" were among the musical highlights. EDDIE BRACKEN and DESI ARNAZ were the most applauded newcomers, the former for his comic antics and the latter for his hot Spanish singing and drumming. *Too Many Girls* had a healthy run of 249 performances on Broadway and toured with success but has not been revived as frequently as the earlier campus musicals *LEAVE IT TO JANE* (1917) and *GOOD NEWS!* (1927) or the later *BEST FOOT FORWARD* (1941).

■ **Too Many Girls** (RKO 1940) featured Bracken, Arnaz, and HAL LEROY from the original company and VAN JOHNSON from the tour and, with half of the Broadway score carried over as well, it was a very faithful rendering of the stage hit. LUCILLE BALL (dubbed by Trudy Erwin) and Richard Carlson were Consuelo and Clint; Ball/Erwin got to sing the pleasing new Rodgers and Hart ballad "You're Nearer."

ANN MILLER and FRANCES LANGFORD were among the coeds and both got to show off their dancing and singing talents with the Broadway cast members. The screenplay by John Twist made no major changes to the story, and the movie, produced and directed by Abbott and choreographed by LEROY PRINZ, ended up being highly enjoyable and the most accurate transfer of a Rodgers and Hart musical to the screen.

■ **TOP HAT** (RKO 1935). Perhaps the quintessential FRED ASTAIRE and GINGER ROGERS musical if for no other reason than the fact that Astaire wears white tie, tails, and the titular hat for most of the film, the movie is a treasure for its many memorable scenes and indelible IRVING BERLIN score.

Plot: The American hoofer Jerry Travers is in London to do a show and falls in love with the American tourist Dale Tremont at first sight, following her and wooing her. Dale mistakenly finds out that his name is Horace Hardwicke, the husband of her dear friend Madge Hardwicke, so she leaves London and joins Marge at the Lido in Venice. Jerry and the real Horace, Jerry's fussy producer, follow and Dale, feeling guilty over starting to love her friend's husband, marries the Italian dress designer Beddini. The mistaken identity continues until Jerry and Horace are finally together in one place and Dale realizes her mistake. She can now let her true feelings of affection for Jerry surface and it turns out her wedding to Beddini is invalid because the ceremony was performed by Horace's valet Bates posing as a preacher.

The screenplay by Dwight Taylor and Allan Scott stretched mistaken identity to its limits, yet the players were so adept at this sort of thing that the story almost seemed to make logical sense. The romantic yet hesitant (on her

Casts for *Too Many Girls*		
Character	*1939 Broadway*	*1940 film*
Clint Kelley	Richard Kolmar	Richard Carlson
Consuelo Casey	Marcy Westcott	LUCILLE BALL
Jojo Jordan	EDDIE BRACKEN	Eddie Bracken
Al Terwilliger	HAL LEROY	Hal LeRoy
Manuelito	DESI ARNAZ	Desi Arnaz
Eileen Eilers	Mary Jane Walsh	FRANCES LANGFORD
Talullah Lou	Leila Ernst	Libby Bennett
Pepe	Diosa Costello	ANN MILLER
Harvey Casey	Clyde Fillmore	Harry Shannon

Cast for *Top Hat*

Character	Performer
Jerry Travers	FRED ASTAIRE
Dale Tremont	GINGER ROGERS
Horace Hardwicke	EDWARD EVERETT HORTON
Madge Hardwicke	HELEN BRODERICK
Alberto Beddini	ERIK RHODES
Bates	ERIC BLORE

***Top Hat* Musical Numbers**

"No Strings"
"Isn't This a Lovely Day?"
"Top Hat, White Tie and Tails"
"Cheek to Cheek"
"The Piccolino"

Top Hat. Looking at this elegant moment from the "Cheek to Cheek" number, you'd never suspect that Fred Astaire hated wearing tails and that during the filming Ginger Rogers' feathered dress kept shedding and feathers ended up in his mouth. What's on the screen looks like heavenly bliss. (Photofest)

part) relationship between Astaire and Rogers was one of their most amusing and romantic. EDWARD EVERETT HORTON was delightful as always but here his character is more entrenched in the plot, and HELEN BRODERICK shines as the deadpan wife who is disbelieving and a little pleased to hear that her fussbudget is such a ladies' man. MARK SANDRICH directed with a light touch, and HERMES PAN and Astaire did the choreography, which ranged from precision tapping to gliding fox-trot to BUSBY BERKELEY-like formations by the dancing couples on the Lido.

Because of the complicated plot, there are only five songs in the musical but they are by IRVING BERLIN at his best. Perhaps the most unforgettable one is "Cheek to Cheek" sung by Astaire and danced with Rogers, a classic moment of musical romance. He also sang and tapped the slaphappy "No Strings" and wooed Rogers with the intoxicating "Isn't This a Lovely Day (To Be Caught in the Rain)?" when they were caught in a London park during a rain shower. Astaire sang and danced the debonair "Top

Hat, White Tie and Tails" even as he "shot" down tuxedoed chorus boys with his cane, and just about everyone in the cast joined in singing and dancing the festive "The Piccolino." Not only was each number radiant but the songs actually had something to do with the plot. With its implausibly sleek art deco sets and highly stylized look, *Top Hat* is a fantasy of musical comedy and exists in its own wonderful reality.

TORMÉ, MEL[vin Howard] (1925–1999). Film performer and composer. A velvet-voiced singer and songwriter known for his distinctive scat singing and jazz interpretations of popular songs, the slight, light-haired artist appeared in eight movie musicals, although his acting abilities were suspect. Tormé was born in Chicago and was a child prodigy, singing professionally at the age of three and working as a drummer in CHICO MARX's band when he was a teenager. He formed his own group in the 1940s called the Mel-Tones, one of the first jazz vocal groups, and became very popular for his high baritone voice, getting him the nickname "The Velvet Fog." Tormé made his film debut in *HIGHER AND HIGHER* (1943), and went on to sing in the musicals *Pardon My Rhythm* (1944), *Ghost Catchers* (1944), *Let's Go Steady* (1945), *GOOD NEWS!* (1947), *WORDS AND MUSIC* (1948), *Duchess of Idaho* (1950), and *A Man Called Adam* (1960), as well as doing vocals for *So Dear to My Heart* (1949). In many of these he played himself or a nightclub singer–pianist much like himself. Tormé was very popular in supper clubs, concerts, television, and records. He wrote several songs, the most famous one by far being "The Christmas Song," better known as "Chestnuts Roasting on an Open Fire." Autobiography: *It Wasn't All Velvet* (1990).

TOWERS, CONSTANCE [Mary] (1934–). Stage, film, and television performer. A striking blonde singer–actress who was praised for her performances in revivals, she found herself in flops when she originated roles on Broadway. Towers was born in Whitefish, Montana, and sang on the radio as a child. When her family moved to New York, she studied music at Juilliard and acting at the American Academy of Dramatic Arts. Having played leading roles in musicals regionally, she made her Broadway debut as the lost Romanoff princess Anastasia in the short-lived musical *Anya* (1965). After giving a highly commended performance as Julie Jordan in *CAROUSEL* the next year, Towers became a favorite in Rodgers and Hammerstein revivals on Broadway. She played Maria in *THE SOUND OF MUSIC* in 1967, 1970, 1972, and 1980, and her Anna in *THE KING AND I* was seen on Broadway in 1968, 1972, and 1977. Towers also played Julie in a well-received 1966 revival of *SHOW BOAT*. Her other original role was Kitty Fremont in the unsuccessful musical *Ari* (1971). Towers made a few movies, mostly dramas and one musical, *Bring Your Smile Along* (1955). She has appeared in many television series, soap operas, and specials, and often tours with concerts and musicals. She is married to actor John Gavin (1931–).

TRAVOLTA, JOHN (1954–). Film, television, and stage performer. A popular heartthrob of the 1970s for his clowning on television and his disco dancing on screen, the handsome Italian Irish actor has matured into a versatile performer who returns to the musical on occasion. Travolta was born in Englewood, New Jersey, and dropped out of school at the age of sixteen to pursue a career in musicals in summer stock. He eventually got on Broadway as a replacement in *GREASE* in 1972 and was featured in *OVER HERE!* (1974) before finding stardom in 1975 as a cute but dense high schooler in the television sit-com *Welcome Back, Kotter*. Travolta secured his fame on screen as the disco-crazy Tony Manero in *SATURDAY NIGHT FEVER* (1977) and as greaser Danny Zuko in *Grease* (1979) and then suffered an up-and-down career with a series of flops, including the musical *Staying Alive* (1983). By the 1990s he established himself as a durable film actor in a variety of genres, including the musi-

cal *HAIRSPRAY* (2007) in which he played the hefty housewife Edna Turnblad. Biographies: *John Travolta, King of Cool*, Wensley Clarkson (2005); *Fever! The Biography of John Travolta*, Douglas Thompson (1997).

TREACHER, ARTHUR [Veary] (1894–1975). Film, stage, and television performer. The quintessential British butler in many Hollywood films, the tall, dry, and perfectly correct character actor was featured in several musicals. Treacher was born in Brighton, England, the son of a barrister, and trained for a legal career but, after serving in World War I, turned to acting and was soon on the London stage. He came to America in 1926 and acted in some Broadway shows, including the musicals *The Great Temptations* (1926) and *The Madcap* (1928) before making his Hollywood debut in 1929. Among his musical credits are *Fashions of 1934*, *Hollywood Party* (1934), *HERE COMES THE GROOM* (1934), *CURLY TOP* (1935), *GO INTO YOUR DANCE* (1935), *ANYTHING GOES* (1936), *Stowaway* (1936), *Mad About Music* (1938), *My Lucky Star* (1938), *The Little Princess* (1939), *IRENE* (1940), *STAR-SPANGLED RHYTHM* (1942), and *MARY POPPINS* (1964). Treacher returned to Broadway for such musicals as *Sweet and Low* (1930), *PANAMA HATTIE* (1940), *ZIEGFELD FOLLIES* (1943), and as a replacement for King Pellinore in *CAMELOT* in 1962. He was also a familiar face on television, particularly as Merv Griffin's sidekick, and then became a household name when he lent the Treacher moniker to a chain of fish and chips restaurants in the 1970s.

🎭 *TREE GROWS IN BROOKLYN, A* (Alvin Theatre 1951). A gentle, nostalgic period musical that only had a modest run (270 performances), the show is fondly remembered for its engaging score. In a turn-of-the-twentieth-century working-class neighborhood in Brooklyn, the hapless Johnny Nolan (JOHNNY JOHNSTON) has trouble keeping a job or staying sober but he is loved all the same by his adoring wife Katie (Marcia Van Dyke) and their adolescent daughter Francie (Nomi Mitty). Katie's flamboyant sister Cissy (SHIRLEY BOOTH) enters the picture with her own problems but ends up being some comfort to the family after Johnny dies. Betty Smith and director GEORGE ABBOTT adapted Smith's best-selling novel for the musical stage, and ARTHUR SCHWARTZ (music) and DOROTHY FIELDS (lyrics) wrote the resplendent score, which included the poignant "Make the Man Love Me," the lilting

"I'll Buy You a Star," the farcical character song "He Had Refinement," the catchy "Love Is the Reason," and the lively "Look Who's Dancin'." As accomplished as all the elements were, it was Booth's hilarious, pathetic Cissy that brought the show to life and allowed it to run as long as it did. *A Tree Grows in Brooklyn* has developed a cult following over the years, although it is rarely revived.

TRENTINI, EMMA (1885–1959). Stage performer. A small but overpowering opera singer, she had a short but memorable Broadway career. Trentini was born in Milan, Italy, and was singing in cabarets when impresario OSCAR HAMMERSTEIN I discovered her and brought her to America in 1906 to star in his Manhattan Opera Company's productions for four years. In 1910 she moved into operetta and originated the role of the New Orleans aristocrat Marietta D'Altena in VICTOR HERBERT'S *NAUGHTY MARIETTA*. Herbert was signed to write her next vehicle but the temperamental diva so infuriated the composer that he withdrew and RUDOLF FRIML scored *THE FIREFLY* (1912) in which Trentini played the Italian street singer Nina. Her other Broadway musical was *The Peasant Girl* (1915). Although Trentini's voice was considered one of the finest of her era, she was so egotistical and difficult that no producers or composers would work with her after 1915 so she performed briefly in vaudeville and in London music halls before returning to Italy where she lived in obscurity and relative poverty for the next forty years.

TRIP TO CHINATOWN, A (Madison Square Theatre 1891). A merry, madcap show that was one of the earliest and best musical comedies, the production ran 657 performances, a Broadway record for twenty-eight years. The libretto by CHARLES H. HOYT was a lively tale about a group of young adults in San Francisco who plan a night on the town so they tell their unsuspecting guardian Uncle Ben (George A. Beane) that they are going sightseeing in Chinatown. They write a letter to Mrs. Guyer (Anna Boyd) asking her to serve as chaperone and her positive reply is accidentally sent to Ben who thinks she is requesting an assignation at a fancy restaurant. Mrs. Guyer, Ben, and his young charges all show up at the restaurant and there is a lot of hiding and maneuvering to keep from being discovered. Ben gets drunk, loses his wallet, and chaos ensues. The next day when he tries to scold the young ones about their behavior, they turn around and gleefully

tease him about his own misadventure. The farcical piece was the forerunner of twentieth-century musical comedy (the similarities with *HELLO, DOLLY!* are significant) and boasted the finest score yet heard in an American musical. The runaway hits were "The Bowery" and "Reuben and Cynthia" by Percy Gaunt (music) and Hoyt (lyrics), and during the national tour Charles K. Harris' "After the Ball" was interpolated and used in other tours and revivals of the show; the waltzing favorite would become the most popular theatre song of the nineteenth century. Hoyt and JULIAN MITCHELL co-directed *A Trip to Chinatown*, one of the prolific Mitchell's early efforts, and the show was staged in the rapid, efficient manner that would characterize American musical comedy.

TRUEX, ERNEST (1889–1973). Stage, film, and television performer. A durable little comic with boyish looks and a raspy voice, he had a busy sixty-year career in all media. Born in Kansas City, Missouri, the son of a physician, and raised in nearby Rich Hill, Truex was on the stage at the age of five, and soon considered a prodigy for his singing and acting talents. While still a boy he played such diverse roles as Little Lord Fauntleroy and Hamlet on tour and in stock and then made his Broadway debut in 1908 still playing children even though he was twenty years old, as in the musicals *Girlies* (1910) and *Dr. De Luxe* (1911). Truex had no trouble moving into adult roles and was usually cast as naive dreamers or hen-pecked husbands, as with his touching performance as put-upon Eddie Kettle in the landmark PRINCESS MUSICAL *VERY GOOD EDDIE* (1915). He appeared in nearly fifty Broadway productions by 1965, including the musicals *Annie Dear* (1924), *The Third Little Show* (1931), *Frederika* (1937), *Helen Goes to Troy* (1944), and *FLAHOOLEY* (1951). Truex also enjoyed a long film career, from 1913 to 1965, appearing as an impish boy in silents opposite Mary Pickford to adult character parts in many comedies and musicals, including *Everybody Dance* (1936), *Start Cheering* (1938), *Freshman Year* (1938), *Swing That Cheer* (1938), *Swing, Sister, Swing* (1938), *LILLIAN RUSSELL* (1940), *Private Buckaroo* (1942), *STAR-SPANGLED RHYTHM* (1942), *Rhythm of the Islands* (1943), *THIS IS THE ARMY* (1943), and *Pan-Americana* (1945). He also found time for an extensive television career starting in the 1950s, appearing as a regular in four comedy series and performing in specials, such as the TV musical *OUR TOWN*

(1955). Truex was married to actress Sylvia Field (1901–1998).

TUCKER, SOPHIE [Born Sophia Kalish] (1884–1966). Stage, radio, and film performer. The legendary singer of blues, ragtime, jazz, and other forms of popular music was an American favorite for six decades. Tucker was born in Russia, came to America as an infant, and was raised in Hartford, Connecticut, where she started singing for customers in her father's eatery. She went into vaudeville in 1906 and soon rose to the top of her profession singing ribald songs and billing herself as "The Last of the Red Hot Mamas." By 1909 she was featured in ZIEGFELD FOLLIES and returned to Broadway for other revues such as *Shubert Gaieties* (1919), EARL CARROLL'S VANITIES (1924), and *Gay Paree* (1927), as well as a few shows in London. Tucker got to play character parts in two book musicals, *Hello Alexander* (1919) and LEAVE IT TO ME! (1938) in which she shone as the pushy diplomat's wife Mrs. Goodhue, and *High Kickers* (1941) where she played herself. When sound movies arrived, she was featured as a specialty in *Follow the Boys* (1944) and *Sensations of 1945* (1944) and played matronly roles in *Honky Tonk* (1929), *Thoroughbreds Don't Cry* (1937), and BROADWAY MELODY OF *1938* (1937) in which she belted out old favorite songs such as "Some of These Days," her signature tune. Tucker appeared in one British movie musical, *Gay Love* (1934), and made a final screen appearance in a guest bit in THE JOKER IS WILD (1957). She returned to vaudeville and nightclubs throughout her lifetime and made many recordings so her innovative and influential way of delivering a song is well preserved. Libi Staiger played Tucker in the short-lived Broadway musical *Sophie* (1963). Autobiography: *Some of These Days* (1945); biography: *Sophie Tucker: First Lady of Show Business*, Armond Fields (2003).

TUFTS, SONNY [born Bowen Charlton Tufts III] (1911–1970). Film and stage performer. A tall, blond, athletic leading man who enjoyed some popularity in the 1940s, the talented singer never found the vehicles to make him a durable star. Tufts was born in Boston into a prestigious banking family and was educated at Yale where he pursued musical activities and later trained as an opera singer. He appeared in a handful of Broadway shows before going to Hollywood and getting cast as the all-American boy in several films, including the musicals *Bring on the Girls* (1944), HERE COMES THE GROOM (1944),

Duffy's Tavern (1945), *Cross My Heart* (1946), and *Variety Girl* (1947). By the 1950s Tufts was playing supporting roles in Hollywood and soon his alcoholism and many scandals finished off his career, although he made a few television appearances before his death.

TUNE, TOMMY [born Thomas James Tune] (1939–). Stage and film performer, director, and choreographer. The tall, lanky dancer–singer who also directs and choreographs, he has found considerable success in all three fields. Tune was born in Wichita Falls, Texas, but raised in Houston where he began dance lessons at the age of five. After studying at the University of Texas at Austin and the University of Houston, he worked as a dancer in touring musicals and made his Broadway debut in 1965 in the chorus of *Baker Street*, followed by appearances in *A Joyful Noise* (1966) and *How Now Dow Jones* (1967). Tune danced on *The Dean Martin Show* on television and was featured in two film musicals, as artist Ambrose in HELLO, DOLLY! (1969) and

Tommy Tune. Whether one prefers Tune the choreographer–director or Tune the dancer, it all comes down to talent, which he has in abundance. Here he floats in air with Twiggy in *My One and Only* (1983), a Broadway show in which he seemed to do everything but pull up the curtain. (Photofest)

hoofer Tommy in *THE BOY FRIEND* (1971), before he began to choreograph and direct. His first New York credit as director was the Off Broadway musical *The Club (1976)*, although he had assisted with the choreography in *SEESAW* (1973), the MICHAEL BENNETT musical in which he was featured as the tap-dancing David. Tune's first Broadway hit was *THE BEST LITTLE WHOREHOUSE IN TEXAS* (1978), which he co-directed and choreographed. He staged and co-choreographed the revue *A DAY IN HOLLYWOOD/A NIGHT IN THE UKRAINE* (1980) before showing a dexterity with directing the nonmusicals *Cloud 9* (1981) and *Stepping Out* (1987). Tune's staging of *NINE* (1982), *GRAND HOTEL* (1989), and *THE WILL ROGERS FOLLIES* (1991) solidified his reputation as an ingenious creator of musical theatre but he stumbled badly with the sequel *The Best Little Whorehouse in Texas Goes Public* (1994). He was slated only to appear as flyer Billy Buck Chandler in *MY ONE AND ONLY* (1983) but during the difficult previews he ended up directing and co-choreographing. By the 1990s he concentrated on performing, as in his Broadway revues *Tommy Tune Tonite!* (1992) and *Tommy Tune: White Tie and Tails* (2002), which also toured successfully. Tune's style is flashy and clever, yet on occasion it can be haunting and poetic, as in some of the poignant flashback scenes in *Nine* and the surreal dance sequences in *Grand Hotel*. Autobiography: *Footsteps* (1997).

TUNICK, JONATHAN (1938–). Stage and film orchestrator. One of the most ingenious and consistently experimental arrangers of music, he has collaborated with STEPHEN SONDHEIM on some of his most adventurous scores. The native New Yorker made his Broadway debut orchestrating the revue *From A to Z* (1960) and over the past five decades has done inventive musical arrangements for such shows as *PROMISES, PROMISES* (1968), *THE GRASS HARP* (1971), *A CHORUS LINE* (1975), *NINE* (1982), *BABY* (1983), *TITANIC* (1997), *Marie Christine* (1999), *THE COLOR PURPLE* (2005), and *LoveMusik* (2007). Tunick first worked with Sondheim on *COMPANY* (1970) and went on to orchestrate most of his subsequent Broadway musicals up through *The Frogs* (2004), as well as the film soundtrack arrangements for *A LITTLE NIGHT MUSIC* (1978). His other film credits include *Reds* (1981), *THE FANTASTICKS* (1995), *The Birdcage* (1996), and several MEL BROOKS movies. He was the first orchestrator to win a TONY AWARD and has also won a

Grammy, an Oscar, and an Emmy. Tunick is a composer of note who has written the music for several films and television programs.

TURNER, LANA [born Julia Jean Mildred Frances Turner] (1921–1995). Film and television performer. The popular "Sweater Girl" and a favorite pinup of G.I.s in the 1940s, the blonde beauty was featured in eight movie musicals, although her singing was always dubbed. Turner was born in Wallace, Idaho, the daughter of a miner, and grew up in California where, legend insists, she was discovered by a talent scout as she sat at the counter of Schwab's Drugstore wearing a tight sweater and sipping a soda. She made her film debut in a bit part in *A Star Is Born* (1937) and soon was playing glamorous and voluptuous heroines, often of a sexy and wicked nature. Turner's musical credits are *Love Finds Andy Hardy* (1938), *Dancing Coed* (1939), *TWO GIRLS ON BROADWAY* (1940), *ZIEGFELD GIRL* (1941), *DUBARRY WAS A LADY* (1943), *Mr. Imperium* (1951), *THE MERRY WIDOW* (1952), and *Latin Lovers* (1953). It took a while for Turner to be considered a serious actress by the public and then her career suffered from a scandal involving her daughter killing her lover in 1958. However, she continued to appear in films through the 1970s and was featured in several television shows. Among her seven husbands was bandleader Artie Shaw (1910–2004). Autobiography: *Lana: The Lady, the Legend, the Truth* (1983); biography: *Lana: The Lives and Loves of Lana Turner*, Jane Ellen Wayne (1995).

TUTTLE, FRANK (1892–1963). Film director. A busy Hollywood director from the days of silent pictures, he helmed some dozen musicals during the first decade of the talkies, including six features with BING CROSBY. Tuttle was born in New York City and educated at Yale University where he directed campus stage productions. After working as a journalist, publicist, and screenwriter, he started directing for PARAMOUNT in 1922 and later helmed some early musicals for them, such as *Sweetie* (1929), *PARAMOUNT ON PARADE* (1930, *True to the Navy* (1930), *THE BIG BROADCAST* (1932), and *ROMAN SCANDALS* (1933). Among his subsequent musicals were *All the King's Horses* (1935), *Two for Tonight* (1935), *College Holiday* (1936), *Waikiki Wedding* (1937), *Doctor Rhythm* (1938), and *Paris Honeymoon* (1939). Tuttle was kept busy directing through the war years but during the McCarthy witch hunts for Communists in the 1950s, Tuttle admitted he had been a party member and named others, causing his career to unravel.

20TH CENTURY-FOX. The film studio was formed in 1935 with a merger between the established Fox Film Corporation, going back to the nickelodeon days and incorporated in 1915, and the newly formed Twentieth Century, a production company founded in 1933 by DARRYL F. ZANUCK and Joseph M. Schenck. Even before the merger, SHIRLEY TEMPLE rose as the predominant star at Fox and continued to remain box office gold for the rest of the decade. Other musical stars that shone at 20th Century-Fox were ALICE FAYE, SONJA HENIE, DON AMECHE, BETTY GRABLE, and MARILYN MONROE. Although the Fox musicals of the 1930s and 1940s were not as lavish or spectacular as at MGM and other studios, they had a glossy, polished look and high entertainment value as seen in *MUSIC IN THE AIR* (1934), *FOLIES BERGÉRE DE PARIS* (1935), *ON THE AVENUE* (1937), *ALEXANDER'S RAGTIME BAND* (1938), *DOWN ARGENTINE WAY* (1940), *SUN VALLEY SERENADE* (1941), *THE GANG'S ALL HERE* (1943), *MOTHER WORE TIGHTS* (1947), and others. The studio made Rodgers and Hammerstein's *STATE FAIR* (1945) and the screen versions of most of the team's stage works: *OKLAHOMA!* (1955) [with Magna Pictures], *CAROUSEL* (1956), *THE KING AND I* (1956), *SOUTH PACIFIC* (1958), the 1961 remake of *State Fair*, and *THE SOUND OF MUSIC* (1965), the most successful film in the studio's history. Fox also filmed Hammerstein's *CARMEN JONES* (1954). In the 1950s the studio countered the threat of television with wide-screen spectaculars, such as the musical *THERE'S NO BUSINESS LIKE SHOW BUSINESS* (1954). Expensive 1960s musicals such as *STAR!* (1968) and *HELLO, DOLLY!* (1969) put Fox in the red, and 1970s musicals such as *ALL THAT JAZZ* (1979) and *THE ROSE* (1979) were only moderately successful. Fox was rescued again in the 1990s by low-budget comedies, such as *Home Alone* (1990) and its sequels, and big-budget hits such as *Titanic* (1997). The only recent Fox musicals to make a profit were the surprise hit *MOULIN ROUGE* (2001) and the small-scale *WALK THE LINE* (2005).

📀 25TH ANNUAL PUTNAM COUNTY SPELLING BEE, THE (Circle in the Square 2005). An intimate, small-scale musical that seemed unlikely on Broadway, the clever and touching little show became a surprise hit all the same. The six finalists in the local spelling bee are an awkward bunch of young adolescents, some neglected by parents and others suffering from too much family. As they go through the elimination rounds, the characters break away from the bee and reveal aspects of themselves others do not see, from sexual frustration to yearning to be accepted. The talented cast included Dan Fogler, Celia Keenan-Bolger, Jose Ilana, Jesse Tyler Ferguson, Lisa Howard, and Sarah Saltzberg. Rachel Sheinkin wrote the humorous libretto, and WILLIAM FINN contributed the songs, which ranged from the incongruous to the heartfelt, including "Magic Foot," "Chip's Lament," "The I Love You Song," "Pandemonium," "I Speak Six Languages," "I'm Not That Smart," "My Friend, the Dictionary," and the title number. Part of the charm of the musical was seeing adults play the teens with dead-on accuracy and the use of some volunteers from the audience as fellow contestants. JAMES LAPINE directed the musical, which had originated in regional theatre and then played Off Broadway at the Second Stage before making the transfer to Broadway. After the propitious reviews came out, the box office slowly picked up and the show ran 1,136 performances.

TWIGGY [born Leslie Hornby] (1949–). Film, television, and stage performer. A pencil-thin blonde who found fame as a swinging London model in the 1960s, the tiny but personable Brit was very appealing in a handful of musicals. Twiggy was born in Neasden, England, and was nicknamed "sticks" and then "twigs" before she began modeling as "Twiggy." By the age of seventeen she was the most famous new model in the world, her shapeless figure and large innocent eyes gracing ads, magazine covers, and even a doll manufactured by Mattel. Twiggy made a notable film (and acting) debut singing and dancing as the gofer who played Polly in *THE BOY FRIEND* (1971), followed by her own television show and she appeared in many films and TV programs. Her Broadway debut was opposite TOMMY TUNE as the swimming champ Edythe Herbert in *MY ONE AND ONLY* (1983). Twiggy retuned to the New York stage as GERTRUDE LAWRENCE in the Off Broadway musical *If Love Were All* (1998), a role she had played previously in London under the title *Noël & Gertie*. She is married to British actor Leigh Lawson (1945–).

📀 TWO BY TWO (Imperial Theatre 1970). DANNY KAYE returned to a Broadway show after twenty-nine years in Hollywood with this Biblical musical and turned the piece into a one-man showcase, which pleased audiences if not its creators. When God commands Noah (Kaye) to build an ark because He is going to flood the earth, Noah's wife Esther (Joan Copeland) and his family think he has gone crazy. But the old patriarch gets them and all the animals into the boat just before the rains start. During the forty days adrift, Noah's faith is sometimes challenged, as when one of his sons falls in love with his sister-in-law and when Esther dies, but by the time the waters recede, God and Noah have reached a covenant and a rainbow appears to seal the deal. Also in the cast were Tricia O'Neil, Walter Willison, MADELINE KAHN, Harry Goz, MARILYN COOPER, and Michael Karm. PETER STONE penned the libretto, based on Clifford Odets' Jewish comedy *The Flowering Peach* (1954), and it wavered uncertainly between the reverent and the ridiculous, and RICHARD RODGERS (music) and MARTIN CHARNIN (lyrics) provided the score, which was equally uneven. The lovely ballad "I Do Not Know a Day I Did Not Love You" was the musical highlight of the show and among the other songs were "Something Doesn't Happen," "The Golden Ram," "When It Dries," and the title number. Expectations were high for a new Rodgers musical and the return of star Kaye to Broadway so the critics' disappointment was very vocal. Audiences were content to see Kaye clowning through the piece, ad-libbing and often turning the production into a nightclub act. When Kaye tore a ligament in his leg and was out of the show, the box office plummeted; he quickly returned and performed the piece in a wheelchair and then on crutches. Rodgers produced and JOE LAYTON directed and choreographed the musical that managed a profitable run of 351 performances. Revivals are rare, although a 1971 St. Louis Municipal Opera production with MILTON BERLE as Noah and NANCY ANDREWS as his wife Esther proved *Two By Two* could serve comedians other than Kaye.

🎭 **TWO GENTLEMEN OF VERONA** (St. James Theatre 1971). A clever if substandard musical version of the dark Shakespearean comedy, the show was such a hit in the NEW YORK SHAKESPEARE FESTIVAL's outdoor theatre in Central Park that producer JOSEPH PAPP brought it to Broadway where after a slow start it caught on and ran 627 performances. Shakespeare's play was reset in urban America with a Latino and African American flavor added to the plot, characters, and songs. Clifton Davis (Valentine) and RAUL JULIA (Proteus) were the two friends of the title, Jonelle Allen (Silvia) and Diana Davilla (Julia) their sweet-

hearts, and Norman Matlock as the Duke of Milan. John Guare wrote the adaptation that used little of Shakespeare's dialogue but was filled with modern slang, ethnic humor, and many topical references, including anti-war sentiments regarding the Viet Nam War. He also penned the lyrics for GALT MACDERMOT's reputable music, resulting in such songs as "I Love My Father," "I Am Not Interested in Love," "Bring All the Boys Back Home," "Love's Revenge," "Follow the Rainbow," and "Summer, Summer." The hip, tuneful musical was directed by Mel Shapiro and choreographed by Jean Erdman. A 2006 revival of the musical, also staged in Central Park, was a critical and popular success. KATHLEEN MARSHALL was the clever director and choreographer.

🎬 **TWO GIRLS AND A SAILOR** (MGM 1944). A thinly disguised revue, the film solved the problem of rationalizing all its songs and guest appearances by setting the action in an old warehouse that was turned into a servicemen's canteen. Sisters Patsy (JUNE ALLYSON) and Jean Deyo (GLORIA DEHAVEN) opened the canteen, ex-vaudevillian Billy Kipp (JIMMY DURANTE) managed it, and sailor John Dykeman III (VAN JOHNSON), who turned out to be a millionaire in disguise, financed the whole operation. John loves Jean but Patsy loves John and it wasn't so complicated that the plot by Richard Connell and Gladys Lehman got in the way of the musical numbers. Among the stars who stopped by were LENA HORNE singing "Paper Doll," GRACIE ALLEN knocking them silly with "Concerto for Index Finger," Ella Fitzgerald smoothly delivering "A-Tisket-a-Tasket," Amparo and JOSÉ ITURBI playing Falla's "Ritual Fire Dance," Durante doing his signature song "Inka Dinka Doo," VIRGINIA O'BRIEN singing "Take It Easy"(by Albert De Bru, Vic Mizzy, and Irving Taylor), and Allyson and the HARRY JAMES orchestra performing "Young Man With a Horn" (by GEORGE STOLL and Ralph Freed); the last two numbers were written for the film. RICHARD THORPE directed the JOE PASTERNAK production, which also featured Tom Drake, Henry Stephenson, HENRY O'NEILL, BEN BLUE, DONALD MEEK, Helen Forrest, XAVIER CUGAT, and Carlos Ramirez.

TWO GIRLS ON BROADWAY. *See BROADWAY MELODY, THE*

🎭 **TWO ON THE AISLE** (Mark Hellinger Theatre 1951). Considered the last of the great star revues on Broadway, this hilarious and tuneful show featured BERT LAHR and DOLORES

GRAY. BETTY COMDEN, ADOLPH GREEN, Nat Hiken, and William Friedberg wrote the jocular sketches and the lyrics for JULE STYNE's music. "Give a Little, Get a Little Love," "If You Hadn't, But You Did," "Hold Me Tight," and "There Never Was a Baby Like My Baby" were among the musical highlights. Lahr played a boozing baseball player, a bubble-headed space explorer, and a dimwitted trash collector, and Gray joined him in a buffoonish takeoff on opera. ABE BURROWS directed the raucous revue, which ran 281 performances.

U

UDELL, PETER (1934–). Stage lyricist and writer. Usually collaborating with composer GARY GELD, the Broadway writer penned a number of musicals in the 1970s and 1980s, two of them long-run hits. The Brooklyn-born Udell attended the University of Chicago briefly and then met Geld in 1960, the two of them writing pop songs and seeing a few of them climb the charts. Their interest in pop, country western, and rhythm and blues carried over to their first Broadway score, the rousing hit *PURLIE* (1970). A similar sound was also found in *SHENANDOAH* (1975), which ran even longer. Udell's subsequent musicals boasted fine scores but problematic books, such as *Angel* (1978), *Comin' Uptown* (1979), and *The Amen Corner* (1983). His lyrics are in the simple, straightforward, and sincere style of OSCAR HAMMERSTEIN and, although they lean toward the sentimental at times, are usually expert and effective.

UGGAMS, LESLIE (1943–). Television and stage performer. The vibrant African American singer who became famous as a youth on television, she has matured into a superb actress who occasionally returns to musicals. Uggams was born in New York, the daughter of a Cotton Club chorine, and attended the Professional Children's School and Juilliard, as well as training with ROBERT LEWIS. She made her television debut at the age of seven and was widely noticed in the early 1960s on Mitch Miller's variety programs. Uggams had her own television show when she was twenty-six years old and has remained a favorite on the tube in series and specials. She made an impressive Broadway debut as the ambitious Georgina who lives through different eras in the musical *HALLELUJAH, BABY!* (1967); her subsequent musicals, *Her First Roman* (1968), *Blues in the Night* (1982), and *Jerry's Girls* (1985), were short-lived, but she got to shine as replacement for Reno Sweeney in the popular revival of *ANYTHING GOES* (1989) and the nightclub star Muzzy in *THOROUGHLY MODERN MILLIE* (2003). Uggams turned to dramatic roles on and Off Broadway in the 1990s and was widely applauded, although she still returns to the concert stage and nightclubs.

UNITED ARTISTS. Because it never had such extensive production facilities and a glittering roster of stars, United Artists sometimes had trouble keeping up with the other studios, but that didn't stop it from producing beloved films, including musicals. The company was founded in 1919 by four screen artists, actors Charles Chaplin, Mary Pickford, and Douglas Fairbanks, and director D. W. Griffith, in order to have more control over their films. Producing and releasing features starring themselves and others, such as Buster Keaton, Rudolph Valentino, and Gloria Swanson, the new studio flourished in the 1920s. The arrival of sound took the company by surprise and it experienced a shaky history for a few years because it did not have the facilities or technology to make talkies right away. Most of the company's notable musicals were made by independents such as SAMUEL GOLDWYN and released through United Artists, such as the early *WHOOPEE!* (1930), *ROMAN SCANDALS* (1933), and *FOLIES BERGERE DE PARIS* (1935). Some of the studio's most memorable musicals of the 1930s were *HALLELUJAH, I'M A BUM* (1933), *KID MILLIONS* (1934), and *THE GOLDWYN FOLLIES* (1938). By the war years United Artists infrequently presented musicals until the 1960s when the studio found success with *WEST SIDE STORY* (1961), *A HARD DAY'S NIGHT* (1964), and *HELP!* (1965), followed by such 1970s moderate hits as *FIDDLER ON THE ROOF* (1971) and *HAIR* (1978). The company was bought by TransAmerica Corporation in 1967, and after some profitable dramas and comedies, such as *Rocky* (1976) and *Annie Hall* (1977), and some monumental flops, such as *Heaven's Gate* (1980), it merged with MGM and formed the new MGM/UA in 1981. When that company was bought out by a French bank, the name was changed to Metro-Goldwyn-Mayer, Inc., and the old United Artists identity was gone forever.

UNIVERSAL PICTURES. While the company was never as powerful a studio as some of its competitors, Universal usually managed to survive by arranging shrewd tie-ins with record companies, television, and tourism. Film exhibitor Carl Laemmle founded the studio in 1912 by merging several small moviemaking concerns. The company built its 230-acre studio lot Universal City in 1915, the most complete and up-to-date movie facility with the capability of filming both interior and exterior locations on the lot. Universal thrived through the silent picture era and in the early 1930s, mostly because of its horror films and popular melodramas. By the middle of the decade the studio struggled, although two impressive musicals came from Universal in the Depression, *KING OF JAZZ* (1930) and *SHOW BOAT* (1936). The studio was saved from bankruptcy later in the 1930s by the introduction of DEANNA DURBIN, whose musicals between 1936 and 1948 were the company's greatest asset. W. C. FIELDS, DONALD O'CONNOR, and Marlene Dietrich vehicles, as well as more horror pictures and some distinguished dramas, helped Universal pull though the decades, but only rarely did a musical hit arrive, such as *THE GLENN MILLER STORY* (1954). The 1960s and 1970s were a boom time for the studio with DORIS DAY–Rock Hudson comedies, disaster spectacles, and other nonmusicals leading the way. Again musicals were scarce with only a handful worth recalling, such as *THOROUGHLY MODERN MILLIE* (1967), *SWEET CHARITY* (1969), *JESUS CHRIST SUPERSTAR* (1973), and *COAL MINER'S DAUGHTER* (1980). More recently Universal had a hit with *RAY* (2004) and a miss with *THE PRODUCERS* (2005). The studio merged with Decca Records in 1962, and in the late 1960s the vast studio lot became one of television's busiest production factories. Today the company draws considerable income from tours of its California facility and its Florida theme park.

UNSINKABLE MOLLY BROWN, THE (Winter Garden Theatre 1960). A big musical comedy epic with a folktale quality to it, the show was highly anticipated because it was the first work by MEREDITH WILLSON after his popular *THE MUSIC MAN* (1957). The frontier gal Molly marries the miner Johnny Brown and when he strikes it rich she tries to break into Denver high society. The snobs will have nothing to do with her, so Molly travels across Europe and on the way back becomes a heroine manning one of the lifeboats of the *Titanic*, becoming famous and finally getting to move with the upper crust. Richard Morris penned the episodic libretto (loosely based on a real person) that was filled with more comedy than adventure, and Willson wrote a tuneful score that included the merry march "I Ain't Down Yet," the raucous "Belly Up to the Bar, Boys," the soaring ballad "I'll Never Say No," the revival-like "Are You Sure?," and the nostalgic "Colorado, My Home." The slaphappy musical was welcomed as a rousing good time by the press, and TAMMY GRIMES was lauded as a funny, likable Molly. Dore Schary directed, PETER GENNARO choreographed, and the THEATRE GUILD production ran 532 performances. All the same, the musical never became a perennial favorite like *The Music Man*.

The Unsinkable Molly Brown (MGM 1964) kept Harve Presnell but replaced Tammy Grimes with DEBBIE REYNOLDS who captured Molly's feisty quality with her lively performance. Helen Deutsch's screenplay changed some of the details of the plot and several of the secondary characters and only half the stage score was used (plus a new song, "He's My Friend," by Willson), yet the movie feels like the Broadway musical in its slaphappy approach to the folk tale-like story. CHARLES WALTERS directed and, although parts of the musical were filmed on location in Colorado, much of the picture looked like the big studio productions of a decade earlier. Gennaro got

Casts for *The Unsinkable Molly Brown*		
Character	*1960 Broadway*	*1964 film*
Molly	TAMMY GRIMES	DEBBIE REYNOLDS
Johnny Brown	HARVE PRESNELL	Harve Presnell
Shamus Tobin	Cameron Prud'homme	Ed Begley
Mrs. McGlone/McGraw	Edith Meiser	Audrey Christie
Princess DeLong	Mony Daimes	
Prince DeLong	Mitchell Gregg	
Monsignor Ryan	Jack Harrold	George Mitchell
Buttercup Grogan		Hermione Baddeley
Prince Louis de Laniere		Vassili Lambrinos
Grand Duchess	Patricia Kelly	Martita Hunt

to recreate his vigorous choreography for the screen and it is one of the highlights of the movie.

◼ UP IN ARMS (Avalon/RKO 1944). DANNY KAYE made his screen debut in this wartime musical and when moviegoers heard the hyperactive clown scat-sing, produce different accents, and race through tongue-twisting lyrics, it was love at first sight. Producer SAMUEL GOLDWYN brought Kaye from Broadway and had the movie built around his special talents. In the screenplay by Don Hartman, Allen Boretz, and Robert Pirosh, Kaye played Danny Weems, a hypochondriac who works as an elevator boy in a building full of doctors, so he's always near a physician. When Danny and his roommate Joe Nelson (Dana Andrews) are drafted, their girlfriends Virginia Merrill (DINAH SHORE) and Mary Morgan (Constance Dowling) sign up as nurses and follow the boys to the South Pacific where Danny bumbles everything but somehow manages to capture twenty Japanese soldiers so he becomes a hero. Sylvia Fine and MAX LIEBMAN wrote two specialty numbers for Kaye: "Theatre Lobby Number" (also known as "Manic Depressive Pictures Presents"), in which he acted out an entire film while waiting in line to get into a movie, and "Melody in 4-F" (which he had performed on stage in 1941), a rapid-fire scat song about the plight of a draftee. HAROLD ARLEN (music) and TED KOEHLER (lyrics) penned the rest of the score, with the best numbers being the swinging lament "Tess's Torch Song" and the gentle ballad "Now I Know," both sung by Shore. ELLIOTT NUGENT directed and DANNY DARE choreographed the film, which was a big hit and launched Kaye's screen career with a bang.

◐ UP IN CENTRAL PARK (Century Theatre 1945). Written decades after the golden age of American operetta, this nostalgic SIGMUND ROMBERG musical recalls the old genre effectively. *New York Times* reporter John Matthews sets out to expose the corruption of Boss Tweed and his cronies who are using the construction of Central Park in 1870 to their profit. Among the obstacles facing John is his romance with Rosie Moore, the daughter of one of Tweed's men, but John eventually gets the girl and Tweed gets caught up in a scandal. HERBERT FIELDS wrote the libretto, and DOROTHY FIELDS penned the graceful lyrics for Romberg's music. The felicitous songs include the cozy ballads "Close As Pages in a Book" and "April Snow," the exhilarating "Carousel in the Park," the gushing "When She Walks in the Room," the rowdy "The Big Back Yard," and the starry-eyed "It Doesn't Cost You Anything to Dream." The lilting score and nostalgic recreation of old New York were extolled by the reviewers even if the story was not much better than those for Romberg's operettas of two decades earlier. Howard Bay designed the evocative sets, and HELEN TAMIRIS choreographed the musical numbers, most memorably an ice skating scene right out of a Currier and Ives lithograph. The MICHAEL TODD production ran 504 performances, Romberg's last hit. Maureen Cannon reprised her Rosie Moore in a 1947 limited engagement at the City Center, which featured Earle MacVeigh as John and Malcolm Lee Beggs as Boss Tweed.

◼ Up in Central Park (Universal 1948) tossed out all but two of the stage songs and producer Karl Tunberg's screenplay removed much of the politics and concentrated on the lovers, played by the popular DEANNA DURBIN and DICK HAYMES. Romberg and Fields wrote one new song for the movie, "Oh Say, Do You See What I See?," and Durbin sang an opera selection from Verdi. WILLIAM A. SEITER directed clumsily, the movie not even looking as picturesque as the Broadway production, and the performances are uneven to say the least. Helen Tamiris was hired to redo her

Casts for *Up in Central Park*

Character	1945 Broadway	1948 film
Rosie Moore	Maureen Cannon	DEANNA DURBIN
John Matthews	Wilbur Evans	DICK HAYMES
William Marcy "Boss" Tweed	Noah Beery, Sr.	Vincent Price
Timothy Moore	Charles Irwin	Albert Sharpe
Bessie O'Cahane	Betty Bruce	
Joe Stewart	Fred Barry	
Rogan		Tom Powers
Mayor Oakley	Rowan Tudor	Hobart Cavanaugh

choreography but there is too little dance to save the tepid movie.

URINETOWN (Henry Miller Theatre 2001). A dark and satirical little musical that used Brechtian techniques as it spoofed everything from politics to musical theatre, the show went from an Off Off Broadway curiosity to a long-run hit on Broadway. Because of a severe water shortage, citizens in some future society are forced to use public pay-per-use conveniences owned by the corrupt Caldwell B. Caldwell (JOHN CULLUM). When his daughter Hope (Jennifer Laura Thompson) falls in love with the insurrectionist Bobby Strong (Hunter Foster), who is leading a revolt against Caldwell's monopoly, Caldwell arranges for Bobby's death. Hope takes up the cause and rebels against her father, bringing down the establishment. Also featured in the cast were Nancy Opel, Jeff McCarthy, Spencer Kayden, and John Doyle. Greg Kotis (book and lyrics) and Mark Hollmann (music and lyrics) set up a sarcastic tone from the top of the show and never let the audience forget that this was just an outrageous musical in questionable taste. "Follow Your Heart," "Don't Be the Bunny," "I See a River," "It's a Privilege to Pee," and "Run Freedom Run" were among the highlights in the score, which used pop, folk, country, and lite rock. The uniquely irreverent show, directed by John Rando and choreographed by John Carrafa, was a surprise hit, running 965 performances. *Urinetown* later received many productions by colleges and other ambitious theatre groups.

V

VAGABOND KING, THE (Casino Theatre 1925). Arguably composer RUDOLF FRIML'S finest score, the fervent operetta has a better story than most and the music is exhilarating. In fifteenth-century France, the romantic poet–outlaw Francois Villon woos the aristocratic Katherine de Vaucelles, repels the Duke of Burgundy's soldiers by raising an army of vagabonds, and takes over the throne of Louis XI to be king for one day. Just as Villon seems to have run out of luck, the ruffian outwits the gallows and weds his high-class sweetheart. It was all rip-roaring fun, based on the popular melodrama *If I Were King* (1901), and the lush music added to the romance and the derring-do. Brian Hooker wrote the lyrics for Friml's lilting melodies, resulting in such operetta favorites as "Only a Rose," "Song of the Vagabonds," "Some Day," "Hugette Waltz," "Love for Sale," and "Love Me Tonight." Operetta favorite DENNIS KING was a thrilling Villon, and the Russell Janney production was as beautiful to look at as to listen to. The show ran 511 performances and quickly joined the ranks of oft-produced American operettas across the country.

The Vagabond King (Paramount 1930) was a primitive, heavy film version of the operetta and not much fun. King got to reprise his Villon from the stage but he seems stiff and JEANETTE MACDONALD sounds fine as Katherine but doesn't have much of a character. The best thing in the film is LILLIAN ROTH's fiery Huguette, the commoner who is a pawn in all the intrigue and dies for her love. Herman Mankiewicz wrote the condensed screenplay, which only left room for half of the stage songs. *The Vagabond King* (Paramount 1956) had great production values and was directed efficiently by MICHAEL CURTIZ but again the movie lacks excitement. The opera singer Orestes Kirkop from Malta sings beautifully, as does KATHRYN GRAYSON as Catherine, but there is no chemistry between them. More interesting was Rita Moreno's Huguette and the atmospheric sets and costumes. Friml wrote some new songs for each of the two film versions but they could not compete with the familiar numbers from 1925.

VALLEE, [Hubert Prior] RUDY (1901–1986). Film, television, and stage performer. Although he had a small, nasal voice, often sung through his trademark megaphone, he was one of the most popular crooners in America from the 1920s into the 1950s. Vallee was born in Island Pond, Vermont, and studied at the University of Maine to be a pharmacist like his father, but started playing the saxophone in bands and turned toward a musical career. While at Yale he sang as well as played, and after graduation formed his own band, The Connecticut Yankees, which became very popular on radio and in clubs. The first singer to be dubbed a "crooner," Vallee became a sex symbol of sorts and was one of the first singers to cause swooning by his fans. His trademark song "The Vagabond Lover," which he co-wrote, provided the title for his first film in 1929 and he played romantic leads or did specialty spots in such musicals as *Glorifying the American Girl* (1929), *INTERNATIONAL HOUSE* (1933), *GEORGE WHITE'S SCANDALS* (1934), *Sweet Music* (1935), *GOLD DIGGERS IN PARIS* (1938), and *SECOND FIDDLE* (1939). By the 1940s he was playing stuffy millionaires and other character parts and sang less, although he made many more musicals, such as *Time Out for Rhythm* (1941), *Too Many Blondes* (1941), *HAPPY GO LUCKY* (1942), *People Are Funny* (1946), *Gentlemen Marry Brunettes* (1955), and *The Helen Morgan Story* (1957). Vallee appeared on Broadway in the revues *George White's Scandals* in 1931

Casts for *The Vagabond King*

Character	1925 Broadway	1930 film	1956 film
Francois Villon	DENNIS KING	Dennis King	Oreste Kirkop
Katherine de Vaucelles	Carolyn Thomson	JEANETTE MACDONALD	KATHRYN GRAYSON
Huguette du Hamel	Jane Carroll	LILLIAN ROTH	RITA MORENO
Louis XI	Max Figman	O. P. Heggie	Walter Hampden
Thibault	Bryan Lycan	Warner Oakland	Leslie Nielson

and 1935 and made a triumphal return as the grumpy executive J. B. Biggley in *How to Succeed in Business Without Really Trying* (1961), a role he reprised on screen in 1966. His last movie musicals were *The Night They Raided Minsky's* (1968), which he narrated, and *Live a Little Love a Little* (1968). Vallee was one of radio's earliest stars with his own show in the 1930s and later made many concert and television appearances, including the TV musical *Hansel and Gretel* (1958). Autobiographies: *Vagabond Dreams Come True* (1930); *My Time Is Your Time* (1962); *Let the Chips Fall* (1976); biography: *My Vagabond Lover: An Intimate Biography of Rudy Vallee*, Eleanor Vallee, Jill Amadio.

VAN, BOBBY [born Robert Stein King] (1930–1980). Film, television, and stage performer and choreographer. The high-flying song-and-dance man of the movies saw his career fade when film musicals waned but he found success on Broadway before his premature death. Van was born in the Bronx, the son of vaudevillians, and danced on the stage as a child, never taking lessons but refining his art in Catskills resorts until he made his Broadway debut in the revue *Alive and Kicking* (1950). Two years later he was in Hollywood and dancing in *Skirts Ahoy* (1952) and was then featured in *Because You're Mine* (1952), *Small Town Girl* (1953), *The Affairs of Dobie Gillis* (1953), and *Kiss Me, Kate* (1953). Van returned to Broadway to play the leading role of Phil Dolan in the short-lived revival of *On Your Toes* (1954) and then was back in California choreographing the JERRY LEWIS musicals *The Ladies Man* (1961) and *It's Only Money* (1962). He finally got wide recognition on Broadway as the hoofing lawyer Billy Early in the popular 1971 revival of *No, No, Nanette*, followed by major roles in the musical flops *Lost Horizon* (1973) on screen and *Doctor Jazz* (1975) on stage. Van choreographed musicals on occasion and frequently performed on radio, in nightclubs, and on television where he did everything from game shows to drama series before his untimely death from brain cancer. He was married to actress–singer Elaine Joyce (1945–).

VAN DYKE, DICK (1925–). Television, stage, and film performer. The tall and very physical comic actor has been a favorite on television in three series and has some memorable musical credits in other media. Born in West Plains, Missouri, and raised in Danville, Illinois, Van Dyke ran an advertising agency after he served

Dick Van Dyke. With such a busy and successful television career, Van Dyke's musical credits are limited, which is unfortunate because he is at heart a true song and dance man. Here he is as the genial, slightly goofy Albert Peterson in the Broadway production of *Bye Bye Birdie* (1960) with Chita Rivera. (Photofest)

in the Air Force during World War II and then started performing comedy on local television. By 1959 he was on Broadway in the revue *The Boys Against the Girls* and then the next year had the leading role of talent agent Albert Peterson in *Bye Bye Birdie*, reprising his performance in the 1963 movie, which was his screen debut. He shone as the Cockney chimney sweep Bert in *Mary Poppins* (1964) and that same year his first TV series made him one of the most popular performers on the tube. His film career was uneven, appearing in such musicals as *What a Way to Go!* (1964), *Chitty Chitty Bang Bang* (1968), and *Dick Tracy* (1990), and his Broadway return in *The Music Man* in 1980 was short-lived, so he concentrated on television where he has usually been very successful. His brother is comic Jerry Van Dyke (1931–).

VAN DYKE, W[oodbridge] **S**[trong], **II.** (1889–1943). Film director. Nicknamed "One Shot Woody" for his efficiency on the set and refusal to overshoot film footage, the prolific director did eight movie musicals in the 1930s, including five JEANETTE MACDONALD–NELSON EDDY pictures. Van Dyke was born in Seattle and as a youth traveled with his actress mother, working as a child in vaudeville and stock. He broke into movies as one of D. W. Griffith's assistants on *Intolerance* (1916) and helmed his first silent picture the next year. Van Dyke directed all genres of film, from Westerns such as *Wyoming* (1928) to urban comedies such as *The Thin Man* (1934), and in the last decade of his life turned out such musicals as *NAUGHTY MARIETTA* (1935), *ROSE MARIE* (1936), *ROSALIE* (1937), *SWEETHEARTS* (1938), *BITTER SWEET* (1940), and *I MARRIED AN ANGEL* (1942).

VAN HEUSEN, JAMES [born Edward Chester Babcock] (1913–1990). Film, stage, and television composer. In two careers with two different partners, he scored some thirty screen musicals and wrote hit songs for several nonmusicals as well. Born in Syracuse, New York, Van Heusen was playing piano professionally as a teenager and then studied music at Syracuse University before getting a job as a local radio announcer. In 1940 he was in Hollywood writing songs with lyricist JOHNNY BURKE and over the next dozen years scored such screen musicals as *LOVE THY NEIGHBOR* (1940), *Dixie* (1943), *GOING MY WAY* (1944), *And the Angels Sing* (1944), *Belle of the Yukon* (1944), *A CONNECTICUT YANKEE IN KING ARTHUR'S COURT* (1949), *Riding High* (1950), and *Mister Music* (1950), as well as four of the "ROAD" pictures with BING CROSBY and BOB HOPE. (Few wrote more songs for Crosby than Van Heusen.) When Burke retired from films in the 1950s, Van Heusen teamed up with lyricist SAMMY CAHN and enjoyed a second career writing ten musicals and many songs for FRANK SINATRA. His Cahn collaborations include *ANYTHING GOES* (1956), *Pardners* (1956), *Let's Make Love* (1960), *High Time* (1960), *THE ROAD TO HONG KONG* (1962), *ROBIN AND THE SEVEN HOODS* (1964), *THOROUGHLY MODERN MILLIE* (1967), and hit nonmusical movie songs such as "Call Me Irresponsible," "The Tender Trap," "All the Way," and "High Hopes." Van Heusen scored five Broadway musicals, none of which ran despite some commendable scores: *Swingin' the Dream* (1939), *Nellie Bly* (1946), *Carnival in Flanders* (1953), *Skyscraper* (1965), and *Walking Happy* (1966). He had better luck writing original material for nightclub and concert stars and on television where he scored the TV musicals *OUR TOWN* (1955), *JACK AND THE BEANSTALK* (1967), and *The Legend of Robin Hood* (1968). Van Heusen's song catalogue was celebrated in the Broadway revue *Swinging on*

a Star (1995) and his songs were heard in the stage musicals *FIVE GUYS NAMED MOE* (1992), *Dream* (1997), and *Thoroughly Modern Millie* (2002).

VANCE, VIVIAN [born Vivian Roberta Jones] (1909–1979). Television and stage performer. Forever remembered as the sidekick to LUCILLE BALL on television, the slightly frumpy character actress had a stage career that included some notable musicals. Vance was born in Cherryvale, Kansas, and was active in community theatre before studying acting with William Inge in Kansas and Eva Le Gallienne in New York. By 1932 she was on Broadway in *MUSIC IN THE AIR* and was in the original cast of *ANYTHING GOES* (1934) where she understudied ETHEL MERMAN. Vance got featured roles in the musicals *RED, HOT AND BLUE!* (1936), *HOORAY FOR WHAT!* (1937), *LET'S FACE IT!* (1941), and *THE CRADLE WILL ROCK* (1947), as well as in some comedies. Seen by actor–producer DESI ARNAZ in a California theatre production, Vance was cast as Ethel Mertz in the legendary TV sit-com *I Love Lucy* in 1953 and was associated with its star over the next twenty years. One of her few TV credits without Lucille Ball was the musical *High Pitch* (1955). Throughout her life she suffered from depression and had had a nervous breakdown in the 1950s; later in her life she promoted awareness of mental health issues. Biography: *The Other Side of Ethel Mertz: The Life Story of Vivian Vance*, Frank Casteluccio, Alvin Walker (2000).

■ VARSITY SHOW (Warner 1937). The biggest (if not the best) collegiate movie musical, the film featured plenty of spectacle, including a finale staged by BUSBY BERKELEY with hundreds of students spelling out the names of various colleges in an overhead shot. The screenplay by Sid Herzig and others concerned the Broadway producer Chuck Daly (DICK POWELL) who returns to his alma mater Winfield College to organize the annual musical show. The stuffy school administration, led by Dean Meredith (Halliwell Hobbes), objects to some of the things Chuck is putting in the show and gives him trouble, so Chuck quits and heads back to New York. The students, led by Willy Williams (Ted Healy), Betty Bradley (PRISCILLA LANE), and Babs Steward (ROSEMARY LANE), follow him and put their show on in a Broadway theatre. WALTER CATLETT, Buck and Bubbles, Johnnie Davis, STERLING HOLLOWAY, Mabel Todd, and Fred Waring and his Pennsylvanians were also featured in the large cast directed by William Keighley. RICHARD A. WHITING (music) and JOHNNY MERCER (lyrics) provided the songs, which included the romantic "You've Got Something There," the swaggering "Have You Any Castles, Baby?," the rousing "Love Is on the Air Tonight," and the pie-eyed musical claim "We're Working Our Way Through College." The silly musical was remade as *Fine and Dandy* (1950).

VELEZ, LUPE [born Maria Guadelupe Velez de Villa Lobos] (1908–1944). Film and stage performer. A fiery singer–dancer labeled the Mexican Spitfire, she was featured in several films during her short but active career. Velez was born in San Luis Potosi, Mexico, and was educated at a convent school in San Antonio, Texas, before beginning her career as a dancer in nightclubs in Mexico and Hollywood. In 1926 she made her screen debut appearing in comedy shorts by Hal Roach and then was Douglas Fairbanks' hot-blooded leading lady in *The Gaucho* (1926). When sound came in, Velez got to show off her singing and dancing talents in such early musicals as *Lady of the Pavements* (1929), *The Wolf Song* (1929), *Cuban Love Song* (1931), *Hollywood Party* (1934), and *Strictly Dynamite* (1934). After appearing in a few British movies and performing in the Broadway musicals *Hot-Cha!* (1932), *Strike Me Pink* (1933), and *You Never Know* (1938), she returned to Hollywood for the musicals *The Girl From Mexico* (1939), *Redhead From Manhattan* (1941), *Playmates* (1941), and *Six Lessons From Madam LaZonga* (1941). In the 1940s she costarred with LEON ERROLL in a series of comedies called the Mexican Spitfire films. On screen Velez played sexy, volatile Latins and her offscreen life was just as tempestuous, having many affairs that filled the gossip columns. After one of her relationships ended passionately, she had her hairdresser make her up to perfection, filled her room with flowers, and took an overdose of pills. Velez was married for a time to actor–athlete Johnny Weissmuller (1904–1984). Biography: *Lupe Velez and Her Lovers*, Floyd Conner (1993).

VERA-ELLEN [born Vera Ellen Westmeyr Rohe] (1921–1981). Film and stage performer. A petite, blonde dancer who had to be dubbed for her screen roles, she partnered with the greatest hoofers in Hollywood. Born in Cincinnati, Ohio, where she took dance lessons as a child with DORIS DAY, Vera-Ellen was one of the Radio City Music Hall Rockettes and danced in nightclubs before making her Broadway debut in the chorus of *VERY WARM FOR MAY* (1939). After appearing in *HIGHER AND HIGHER* (1940) and *PANAMA HATTIE* (1940), she was featured in *BY JUPITER* (1942) and *A CONNECTICUT YANKEE* (1943) and then was signed by Hollywood. She made her screen debut with the DANNY KAYE musical *Wonder Man* (1945) and appeared with him also in *The Kid From Brooklyn* (1946) and *WHITE CHRISTMAS* (1954). Vera-Ellen's most memorable screen roles include the lead dancer opposite GENE KELLY in the "Slaughter on Tenth Avenue" sequence of *WORDS AND MUSIC* (1948) and Kelly's idealized Ivy Smith in *ON THE TOWN* (1949), FRED ASTAIRE's partner Angela Bonfils in *THE BELLE OF NEW YORK* (1952), and the dancing Princess Maria worshipped by DONALD O'CONNOR in *CALL ME MADAM* (1953). Her other movie musicals were *THREE LITTLE GIRLS IN BLUE* (1946), *Carnival in Costa Rica* (1947), *THREE LITTLE WORDS* (1950), and the British films *Happy Go Lovely* (1951) and *Let's Be Happy* (1957). Vera-Ellen suffered from anorexia and arthritis and retired from public life in the late 1950s, living as a recluse until her death.

VERDON, GWEN [Evelyn] (1926–2000). Stage, film, and television performer. Arguably Broadway's finest dancing star in the second half of the twentieth century, the redheaded entertainer did not appear in many productions but in each one she gave an outstanding performance. Verdon was born in Culver City, California, the daughter of dancer Gertrude Standing who taught her beginning at a young age. Verdon also trained in New York with choreographer JACK COLE and acted as his assistant on several later projects. She made her Broadway bow in the revue *Alive and Kicking* (1950) and then returned to California where she danced in the screen musicals *ON THE RIVIERA* (1951), *Meet Me After the Show* (1951), *THE MERRY WIDOW* (1952), *The "I Don't Care" Girl* (1953), and *THE FARMER TAKES A WIFE* (1953). Verdon found recognition back on Broadway as the flighty cabaret dancer Claudine in *CAN-CAN* (1953), followed by her first starring role as the devil's assistant Lola in *DAMN YANKEES* (1955), her only stage role that she got to reprise on screen. Her other musical triumphs were the former prostitute Anna in *NEW GIRL IN TOWN* (1957), the Londoner Essie Whimple caught up in a murder investigation in *REDHEAD* (1959), the optimistic taxi dancer Charity in *SWEET CHARITY*

(1966), and the sensation-seeking murderess Roxie Hart in *CHICAGO* (1975). Late in her career she gave up dancing and played character roles in films and on television. Verdon's unique talent lay in the way she exuded sexuality and, at the same time, seemed vulnerable and funny. She was married for a time to BOB FOSSE who choreographed her in most of her Broadway musicals.

VEREEN, BEN [born Benjamin Augustus Middleton] (1946–). Stage, film, and television performer. An electric African American dancer–singer–actor, his seemingly boundless energy has made him a favorite in both musicals and dramatic pieces. Vereen was born in Miami, Florida, and grew up in New York City where he attended the High School of the Performing Arts. After making his Manhattan acting debut Off Broadway in 1965, he spent a few years doing musicals in stock and in tours and then was cast by BOB FOSSE as one of the dancers in the film musical *SWEET CHARITY* (1969). Vereen made his Broadway bow as a replacement in *HAIR* in 1969 and then won attention and applause for his tormented Judas Iscariot in the original New York production of *JESUS CHRIST SUPERSTAR* (1971). The next year he was further praised for his cat-like portrayal of the Leading Player in Fosse's *PIPPIN* (1972). Vereen then turned to films, where he was featured in the musicals *FUNNY LADY* (1975), *ALL THAT JAZZ* (1979), and *Mama, I Want to Sing!* (2007), and television, where he acted in miniseries, children's shows, sit-coms, dramas, his own variety show, and specials such as the TV versions of *Pippin* (1981) and *FOSSE* (2001). Back on Broadway he was featured as the burlesque comic Leroy in the short-lived *Grind* (1985) and was welcomed in replacement roles in *JELLY'S LAST JAM* (1993), *Fosse* (2001), and *WICKED* (2006). Vereen also played the Ghost of Christmas Present in the Madison Square Garden Theatre musical *A CHRISTMAS CAROL* (1995 and 1996) and frequently returns to the concert stage and nightclubs.

🔊 **VERY GOOD EDDIE** (Princess Theatre 1915). A landmark PRINCESS THEATRE MUSICAL that introduced the intimate, contemporary American musical comedy.

Plot: Diminutive and weak-willed Eddie Kettle has married the bossy harridan Georgina and they are off on their honeymoon, a boat ride up the Hudson River. Also on the steamer are the newlyweds Percy and Elsie Darling. After the boat makes a stop for touristing, Georgina and Percy are accidentally left behind and Eddie and Elsie are left with each other, spending time on the steamer and that night at an inn when a storm frightens Elsie and she goes to Eddie's room for protection. The experience makes a new man out of Eddie and, when Percy and Georgina catch up with their spouses, Eddie learns he can put Georgina in her place.

Producer F. Ray Comstock and Elisabeth Marbury conceived the idea of presenting small-scale, modern musicals in the small Princess Theatre. *Very Good Eddie* was their first success in the venture, running 341 performances, and the impact the show had was considerable. There were no long chorus lines, lavish sets, or period costumes. Instead audiences were treated to a witty, up-to-date musical comedy with a bright and sassy score. GUY BOLTON and Philip Batholomae penned the lively libretto, Schuyler Green, Herbert Reynolds, and others wrote the modern, conversational lyrics, and JEROME KERN composed the inventive, zesty music. Not only did some of the songs become popular, but the score as a whole was admired and seemed to be all of one spirited frame of mind. It wasn't an integrated score but several of the songs seemed to grow out of the situation and the blending of story and music was noticed by audiences and critics. The next generation of theatre songwriters (RICHARD RODGERS, LORENZ HART, GEORGE and IRA GERSHWIN, and COLE PORTER) also noticed and *Very Good Eddie* and the subsequent Princess Musicals would serve as their inspiration.

Casts for *Very Good Eddie*

Character	1915 Broadway	1975 Broadway
Eddie Kettle	ERNEST TRUEX	Charles Repole
Elsie Darling	Alice Dovey	Virginia Seidel
Georgina Kettle	Helen Raymond	Spring Fairbank
Percy Darling	John Willard	Nicholas Wyman
Dick Rivers	OSCAR SHAW	David Christmas
Mme. Matroppo	Ada Lewis	Travis Hudson

Very Good Eddie Musical Numbers

"We're on Our Way"
"The Same Old Game"
"Some Sort of Somebody"
"Isn't It Great to Be Married"
"Wedding Bells Are Calling Me"
"On the Shore at the Le Lei Wi"
"If I Find the Girl"
"Thirteen Collar"
"Old Boy Neutral"
"Babes in the Wood"
"Nodding Roses"

A production of *Very Good Eddie* at the GOODSPEED OPERA HOUSE in Connecticut was so well received that producer DAVID MERRICK brought it to Broadway in 1975 and the show ran 304 performances without benefit of star names in the cast. It was not a very authentic revival, adding several Kern songs from other shows and rewriting the script, particularly the ending in which the two honeymooning couples find out their marriage certificates are invalid and Eddie goes off with Elsie. However, the production, directed by Bill Gile and choreographed by DAN SIRETTA, was definitely in the spirit of the original, and presenting the musical in the small, intimate Booth Theatre gave audiences a taste of the Princess Musical experience.

🎵 **VERY WARM FOR MAY** (Alvin Theatre 1939). An outstanding score by JEROME KERN (music) and OSCAR HAMMERSTEIN (lyrics) was upstaged by this terribly uneventful musical comedy in which not much of anything happened. May Graham (GRACE McDONALD) doesn't want to go to summer school, as her father (DONALD BRIAN) insists; she'd rather further her stage career so she runs away to a summer theatre managed by Winnie Spofford (EVE ARDEN) where the temperamental director Ogden Quiller (HIRAM SHERMAN) does "progressive" theatre productions. May falls for Winnie's son Sonny (RICHARD QUINE) and when May's brother Johnny (JACK WHITING) comes looking for her, he falls for Sonny's sister Liz (Frances Mercer). May and Johnny's father comes to fetch them, but he gets entangled with his old flame Winnie and by the end all the couples are properly matched and the summer theatre is a big success. Critics were surprised that Hammerstein could write such a shallow and uninteresting libretto, but few of them knew that what Broadway saw was not

the satirical comedy making fun of pretentious art and the recent avant garde movement that Hammerstein saw jettisoned out of town by the producer MAX GORDON and director VINCENTE MINNELLI. All that was left were some fine performances and a glorious score that included "Heaven in My Arms," "In the Heart of the Dark," "In Other Words," "All in Fun," and the indelible "All the Things You Are," one of the musical theatre's greatest ballads. The song would not become popular until after the misguided show closed after fifty-nine performances. Sadly, *Very Warm for May* was Kern's last original Broadway musical. 🎵 Hollywood bought the screen rights and retitled the musical **Broadway Rhythm** (MGM 1944) but all it kept was "All the Things You Are" (sung by GINNY SIMMS) and the backstage setting. The screenplay by DOROTHY KINGSLEY and Henry Clark concerns Broadway producer Johnny Demming (GEORGE MURPHY) who is having trouble getting his latest project afloat and tries to land big-name talent for his show when there is plenty of talent in his own family, namely his father Sam (CHARLES WINNINGER) and his sister Patsy (GLORIA DE HAVEN). Johnny is blind to them and concentrates on getting the Hollywood star Helen Hoyt (Simms) and, when he gets her, Pa and Sis nearly go off and do their own show before Helen opens Johnny's eyes to their abilities. The thin plot allowed for specialty numbers and some of the performers were indeed special, such as LENA HORNE, NANCY WALKER, BEN BLUE, and TOMMY DORSEY and his orchestra. Three of the Hammerstein–Kern stage songs were heard briefly in a medley but the rest of the screen score ("Milkman, Keep Those Bottles Quiet," "Brazilian Boogie," "Who's Who in Your Love Life?," "What Do You Think I Am?," and "Solid Potato Salad") was by HUGH MARTIN, RALPH BLANE, GENE DE PAUL, DON RAYE, and others. The film was produced by JACK CUMMINGS, directed by ROY DEL RUTH, and choreographed by ROBERT ALTON and JACK DONOHUE.

VESTOFF, VIRGINIA (1939–1982). Stage, television, and film performer. A classy, redheaded actress who appeared in both plays and musicals, the singer–dancer rarely found herself originating a role in a hit but was kept busy replacing others in hit shows. The native New Yorker was the daughter of vaudevillians who died when she was young so Vestoff was raised in an orphanage. At the age of twelve she was a winner on *Ted Mack's Amateur Hour* and soon she was singing professionally in the children's chorus at the New York City Opera. After graduating from the New York High School of the Performing Arts, Vestoff worked as a dancer on tour and got to play major roles in productions of *THE BOY FRIEND*, *MY FAIR LADY*, *THE THREEPENNY OPERA*, and *CAMELOT*. She made her Broadway debut in the revue *From A to Z* (1960), was standby and took over leading roles in *IRMA LA DOUCE* (1960) and *Baker Street* (1965), and then got some recognition as the aristocratic Lady in the Off Broadway musical *MAN WITH A LOAD OF MISCHIEF* (1966). Vestoff's best role was Abigail Adams in the original cast of *1776* (1969) and she got to reprise her performance in the 1972 film version. Vestoff was also featured in the short-lived Broadway musicals *Via Galactica* (1972), *Nash at Nine* (1973), *A Doll's House* (1975), *Boccaccio* (1975), and *Spokesong* (1979). She acted in classic play revivals on the New York and regional theatre and was very active on television before her premature death from cancer.

■ *VICTOR/VICTORIA* (MGM 1982). JULIE ANDREWS got the best role she'd been handed in years in this musical, although she had to dress like a man to play it. BLAKE EDWARDS produced, directed, and wrote the screenplay about the starving British singer Victoria Grant who is having so much trouble getting work in Paris during the 1930s that she goes along with a crazy scheme by the gay nightclub performer Carroll "Toddy" Todd. She masquerades as Victor, a female impersonator who can hit the high notes when singing. Soon Victor/Victoria becomes the toast of Paris night life under Toddy's careful management. Complications set in when the American gangster King Marchand falls for Victoria while King's blonde mistress Norma Cassady has the hots for Victor. By the time the confusion is cleared, everyone's sexual preferences are revealed. Some critics thought the movie

a sophisticated romp, others a one-joke show, but all agreed the performances were first rate. HENRY MANCINI (music) and LESLIE BRICUSSE (lyrics) wrote the score, which included the facetious "Chicago, Illinois," the steamy "Le Jazz Hot," the soft-shoe "You and Me," and the flowing ballad "Crazy World."

🕭 *Victor/Victoria* (Marquis Theatre 1995) brought Julie Andrews back to Broadway for the first time since *CAMELOT* in 1960 and she was warmly welcomed, even if her vehicle was not. Blake Edwards adapted his screenplay into a libretto and there were added songs by Mancini, Bricusse and FRANK WILDHORN, such as "Paris By Night," "Louis Says," and "Living in the Shadows." Edwards co-produced and directed and the musical had excellent production values, as well as spirited choreography by ROB MARSHALL. Not the strongest of vehicles, the musical nevertheless had its charm and much of the second act played like a hit. The critics severely slammed all aspects of the show except Andrews but audiences were anxious to see her and kept the musical on the boards for 734 performances. When the TONY AWARDS committee granted no nominations to *Victor/Victoria* except for a nod to Andrews, she publicly refused the nomination. Because the musical was rarely a sellout during its long run, the production did not make money.

VIDOR, CHARLES (1900–1959). Film director. The Hungarian-born director helmed a half-dozen Hollywood musicals during the postwar years. Vidor was born in Budapest and, after serving in World War I and performing in opera for a time, he trained at the UFA studios in Berlin before emigrating to America in 1924. He served as an editor and scriptwriter before directing his first feature in 1932 and then went on to do a variety of movies that were popular, such as the sultry *Gilda* (1946). Vidor's musicals include *COVER GIRL* (1944), *A Song to Remember* (1945), *HANS CHRISTIAN*

Casts for *Victor/Victoria*

Character	1982 film	1995 Broadway
Victoria Grant	JULIE ANDREWS	Julie Andrews
Carroll Todd	ROBERT PRESTON	TONY ROBERTS
King Marchand	James Garner	Michael Nouri
Norma Cassady	Leslie Ann Warren	RACHEL YORK
Richard Di Nardo	Malcolm Jamieson	Michael Cripe
Henri Labisse	Peter Arne	Adam Heller
Squash Bernstein	Alex Karras	Gregory Jbara

ANDERSEN (1952), *LOVE ME OR LEAVE ME* (1955), and *Song Without End* (1960), which was completed by GEORGE CUKOR after Vidor's death.

VIOLET (Playwrights Horizons 1997). An intimate, oddly poignant Off Broadway musical, the chamber piece brought some recognition to promising composer JEANINE TESORI. The Southern girl Violet (Lauren Ward) is marked with a facial scar she's had since her father had an accident with his ax. In 1964 she sets out from Spruce Pine, North Carolina, by bus to attend a revivalist meeting held by a televangelist in Oklahoma with the hopes of getting cured. On the journey she befriends two servicemen, good ol' boy Monty (Michael Park) and the African American Flick (Michael McElroy). The faith healing at the revival does not remove the scar, but Violet does find the strength to overcome her prejudices and return the love of Flick. Based on Doris Betts' novel *The Ugliest Pilgrim*, the libretto and lyrics by Brian Crawley and the music by Tesori were praised by the press and plans were made to move the PLAYWRIGHTS HORIZONS production to a commercial venue after its one-month engagement, but a pan in the all-powerful *New York Times* scuttled the transfer. The work has since been slowly finding recognition in regional theatres and colleges, and such incisive songs as "Raise Me Up," "On My Way," "Let It Sing," and "Down the Mountain" have finally been heard by a wider audience.

VIVA LAS VEGAS (MGM 1964). The most popular of ELVIS PRESLEY's thirty-one films, the musical had more interesting characters than most of his vehicles and there was an engaging chemistry between the rock and roll star and ANN-MARGARET. Race car driver Lucky Jackson (Presley) comes to Las Vegas to enter the Grand Prix, but engine trouble puts him out of the race. He gets a job at a Vegas resort where he meets swimming instructor Rusty Martin (Ann-Margaret) and the two set off sparks. Cesare Danova, WILLIAM DEMAREST, Jack Carter, and Nickey Blaire where also in the cast directed with style by GEORGE SIDNEY and David Winters provided choreography that was much more interesting than the usual hip swiveling usually found in the King's movies. The songs, by various tunesmiths, included "My Rival," "The Lady Loves Me," "I Need Somebody to Lean On," and the rocking country-western title number.

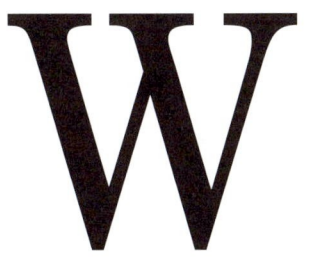

W

WABASH AVENUE. *See CONEY ISLAND*

WAITING FOR GUFFMAN. See *THIS IS SPINAL TAP*

WAKE UP AND LIVE (Fox 1937). Capitalizing on the current radio feud between columnist Walter Winchell and orchestra leader Ben Bernie, this musical had more fun with radio than most films about the airwaves. Harry Tugend and JACK YELLEN concocted the screenplay about crooner Eddie Kane (JACK HALEY) who freezes up every time he gets in front of a radio microphone. To overcome his fears, Eddie consults Alice Huntley (ALICE FAYE), an advice-giver with her own radio talk show called *Wake Up and Live*. When Eddie's singing is accidentally broadcast during Bernie's show, he becomes famous as the "Phantom Troubadour," and Winchell and Bernie fight over who discovered the new singer. It was mostly slaphappy nonsense with HARRY REVEL (music) and MACK GORDON (lyrics) supplying such songs as the silly "I Love You Much Too Much, Muchacha," the doting ballads "It's Swell of You" and "Never in a Million Years," the spirited title number, and the popular torch song "There's a Lull in My life," which was a bestseller for Faye. The cast also included Leah Ray, PATSY KELLY, NED SPARKS, GRACE BRADLEY, WALTER CATLETT, JOAN DAVIS, WILLIAM DEMAREST, EDDIE ANDERSON, the Condos Brothers, and the Brewster Twins. Ironically, Haley's singing voice was considered by producers DARRYL F. ZANUCK and Kenneth Macgowan too weak for the crooner who was supposed to conquer the airwaves, so his songs were dubbed by Buddy Clark. SIDNEY LANFIELD directed and Jack Haskell choreographed.

WALK THE LINE (Fox 2005). The musical biography of country music giant Johnny Cash (Joaquin Phoenix), the film was so well acted and the music so well presented that its appeal went far beyond Cash and country fans. The screenplay by Gill Dennis and James Mangold was based on Cash's autobiography and, although the singer's life had many cliché-ridden moments, the story was solid and the portrayal of the hero far from sentimentalized. The plot followed the life of Cash from his growing up in an Arkansas town during the Depression, his Air Force days in Germany where he starts singing, his unhappy marriage to Vivian (Ginnifer Goodwin) in Tennessee, the early recording years and his meeting June Carter (Reese Witherspoon), his dependency on drugs, fame on the road and then nationwide, and Carter's love helping him to stop the drugs and marry her. Several famous singers, from ELVIS PRESLEY (Tyler Hilton) to Jerry Lee Lewis (Waylon Payne) to Waylon Jennings (Shooter Jennings), were on hand to capture the flavor of the music business, and both Phoenix and Witherspoon were outstanding, both doing their own singing and performing on the guitar and Autoharp. James Mangold was the astute director.

WALKER, DON[ald John] J. (1907–1989). Stage orchestrator. A much-in-demand musical talent, he was a leading orchestrator on Broadway for over forty years. Walker was born in Lambertville, New Jersey, and educated at the University of Pennsylvania. He scored his first Broadway musical in 1934 and, before retiring in the mid-1980s, arranged the music for over 100 shows. Among his Broadway credits are *ZIEGFELD FOLLIES* (1936 and 1943), *LEAVE IT TO ME!* (1938), *BEST FOOT FORWARD* (1941), *ON THE TOWN* (1944), *CAROUSEL* (1945), *FINIAN'S RAINBOW* (1947), *GENTLEMEN PREFER BLONDES* (1949), *CALL ME MADAM* (1950), *WONDERFUL TOWN* (1953), *THE PAJAMA GAME* (1954), *DAMN YANKEES* (1955), *THE MOST HAPPY FELLA* (1956), *THE MUSIC MAN* (1957), *FIDDLER ON THE ROOF* (1964), *CABARET* (1966), and *SHENANDOAH* (1975), as well as the revivals of *PAL JOEY* (1952), *OF THEE I SING* (1952), and *ON YOUR TOES* (1954). Walker was so busy on Broadway that he rarely worked in other media, although he did orchestrate the TV musical *THE GIFT OF THE MAGI* (1958).

WALKER, [Harold] HAL (1896–1972). Film and television director. The former actor specialized in helming lightweight comedies and musicals, including two of the BOB HOPE–BING CROSBY *Road* pictures. Walker was born in Ottumwa, Iowa, and pursued an acting career until he went to Hollywood in the early 1930s and worked as an assistant at PARAMOUNT. His first directing assignment was *Out of This World* (1945), followed by such musicals as *Duffy's Tavern* (1945), *The Stork Club* (1945), ROAD TO UTOPIA (1945), *At War With the Army* (1950), *Sailor Beware* (1951), and ROAD TO BALI (1951). He left films in the early 1950s to direct television sit-coms, such as *I Married Joan*.

WALKER, NANCY [born Anna Myrtle Smoyer] (1922–1992). Stage, film, and television performer. The short, sour-faced, gravel-voiced comedienne enlivened and often stole any show she was in, usually in supporting parts. Walker was born in Philadelphia and performed on the radio until she made a hard-not-to-notice Broadway debut as the Blind Date in BEST FOOT FORWARD (1941), followed by a hilarious performance as the amorous taxi driver Hilda Esterhazy in ON THE TOWN (1944). Oddly, these were her only Broadway musical hits; instead she would shine in short-lived musicals, such as playing the would-be ballet dancer Lily Malloy in *Look, Ma, I'm Dancin'* (1948), the hapless policewoman Katey O'Shea in *Copper and Brass* (1957), and the persevering wife Kay Cram in *Do Re Mi* (1960). Walker's other New York musicals include *Barefoot Boy With Cheek* (1947), *Along Fifth Avenue* (1949), PAL JOEY (1952), *Phoenix '55* (1955), WONDERFUL TOWN (1958), and *The Girls Against the Boys* (1959). She got to reprise her Blind Date in the 1941 screen version of *Best Foot Forward* and was also in the film musicals GIRL CRAZY (1940), BROADWAY RHYTHM (1944), and *Lucky Me* (1954). Walker found her greatest success on television where he appeared in dozens of programs and commercials, was a regular in three series, had her own show in the 1970s, and was in the TV musicals WHOOPEE (1950) and *Three for the Girls* (1973). She directed some episodes

Nancy Walker. After stealing the show in supporting roles in *Best Foot Forward* (1941) and *On the Town* (1944), the comic actress starred in a half a dozen Broadway musicals but few of them ran. Here she is in one of her best performances, as the patient wife Kay Cram in *Do Re Mi* (1960) trying to reason with her husband Hubie (Phil Silvers) when he has another one of his get-rich-quick schemes. (Photofest)

of television sit-coms as well as the camp classic film musical *Can't Stop the Music* (1980).

WALLER, THOMAS [Wright] **"FATS"** (1904–1943). Stage and film composer, performer, and musician. The rotund African American pianist–singer had a distinctive way of delivering a song, many of which he wrote. Waller was born in Waverly, New York, the son of Reverend Edward Martin Waller who preached at the Abyssinian Baptist Church in Harlem. The young Waller learned to play the organ at the church and then in the 1920s made a living playing piano in Washington, DC movie houses before finding success in vaudeville and later major theatres in Chicago and New York. His freewheeling way of singing as he played and interjected ad libs along the way soon caught on and his recordings of his own songs and those by others became popular. Waller had started composing music in the 1920s and, working with such lyricists as Andy Razaf, wrote many jazz favorites, such as "Ain't Misbehavin'," "Honeysuckle Rose," "This Joint Is Jumpin'," "I've Got a Feeling I'm Falling," and "Keeping Out of Mischief Now." He scored two "Negro'" revues on Broadway, *Keep Shufflin'* (1928) and *Hot Chocolates* (1929), and appeared in three Hollywood movies performing his own songs: *Hooray for Love* (1935), *KING OF BURLESQUE* (1935), and *STORMY WEATHER* (1943). A heavy drinker and far overweight, Waller lived carelessly and few were surprised at his death at the age of thirty-nine as he rode the *Santa Fe Chief* train. Interest in Waller's works was revived with the long-running Broadway revue *AIN'T MISBEHAVIN'* (1978). Biographies: *Fats Waller: The Cheerful Little Earful*, Alyn Shipton (2005); *Ain't Misbehavin': The Story of Fats Waller*, W. T. and Ed Kirkeby (1988).

WALLIS, HAL B. [born Harold Brent Wallis] (1899–1986). Film producer. One of Hollywood's most prolific and influential producers, he headed **WARNER BROTHERS** throughout its golden age in the 1930s and later was a distinguished independent producer. Wallis was born in Chicago and quit school to work as an office boy, then a salesman, and ended up in Los Angeles where he managed a movie theatre. By 1928 he was managing the Warner studio and overseeing dozens of films each year. In 1944 he left Warners and founded his own company, Hal Wallis Productions, releasing his films through **PARAMOUNT** and then later **UNIVERSAL**. During his fifty-year career, Wallis produced over 400 films, including thirty-six musicals featuring stars ranging from **JAMES CAGNEY** to **JERRY LEWIS** to **ELVIS PRESLEY**. Among his notable musicals are *GOLD DIGGERS OF 1937* (1936), *The Singing Marine* (1937), *Going Places* (1938), *BLUES IN THE NIGHT* (1941), *YANKEE DOODLE DANDY* (1942), *THIS IS THE ARMY* (1943), *My Friend Irma* (1949), *Sailor Beware* (1951), *Scared Stiff* (1953), *ARTISTS AND MODELS* (1955), *KING CREOLE* (1958), *BLUE HAWAII* (1961), *Fun in Acapulco* (1963), and *Easy Come, Easy Go* (1967). Autobiography: *Starmaker*, with Charles Higham (1980); biography: *Hal Wallis: Producer to the Stars*, Bernard F. Dick (2004).

WALSH, RAOUL (1887–1980). Film director. Known for his rugged he-man touch in many male action pictures, he also directed a dozen movie musicals in the 1940s and 1950s. Walsh was born in New York City but ran away from home as a boy and had adventures at sea and in cattle ranches out west. He turned to acting in 1910 and worked for D. W. Griffith, first as an actor (he played John Wilkes Booth in the 1915 classic *The Birth of a Nation*) and then as an assistant director, before becoming a prolific director in his own right who helmed over 100 films. He is most known for outdoor adventures such as *The Thief of Bagdad* (1924) and blistering melodramas such as *The Roaring Twenties* (1939), yet he also helmed a number of sensitive dramas and stylish musicals, such as *GOING HOLLYWOOD* (1933), *EVERY NIGHT AT EIGHT* (1935), *ARTISTS AND MODELS* (1937), *St. Louis Blues* (1939), *The Man I Love* (1946), and *A Private Affair* (1959). Autobiography: *Each Man in His Time* (1974).

WALSH, THOMMIE (1950–2007). Stage choreographer and dancer. A very resourceful choreographer, he was once a protégé of **TOMMY TUNE** but later found renown on his own. Walsh was born in Auburn, New York, took dance lessons as a child, and then studied at the Boston Conservatory of Music before pursuing a career as a dancer. By the age of eighteen he was dancing on Broadway in *SEESAW* (1973), *Rachel Lily Rosenbloom … * (1973), and *A CHORUS LINE* (1975) in which he originated the role of Bobby. Walsh served as Tune's co-choreographer on *A DAY IN HOLLYWOOD— A NIGHT IN THE UKRAINE* (1980), *NINE* (1982), and *MY ONE AND ONLY* (1983), and on his own staged the musical numbers for *The 1940s Radio Hour* (1979), *Do Patent Leather Shoes Really Reflect Up?* (1982), *Lucky Stiff* (1988),

My Favorite Year (1992), and the national tour of *THE BEST LITTLE WHOREHOUSE IN TEXAS*. He was very active in regional theatre, staged shows for stars such as CHITA RIVERA, SANDY DUNCAN, and DONNA MCKECHNIE, and taught master classes at several universities across the country. Walsh was so busy in live theatre that he rarely ventured into television or film, although he was featured as Thaddeus in the movie version of *JESUS CHRIST SUPERSTAR* (1973).

WALSTON, RAY [born Herman Walston] (1914–2001). Stage, film, and television performer. A thin, redheaded comic actor, he played wisecracking sidekicks and other character parts for forty years. A native of New Orleans, Walston worked as a reporter and printer before turning to acting at a community theatre in Houston, Texas. He made his Broadway debut in the cast of Maurice Evans' *Hamlet* in 1945 and played colorful minor roles on stage before making his television bow in 1954 and his first film three years later. Walston's comic talents were well known enough by the 1950s that Rodgers and Hammerstein selected him to play the wheeler-dealer Luther Billis on tour and in the London company of *SOUTH PACIFIC* in 1951 and he reprised the role in the 1958 screen version. His most famous Broadway role was the devilish Mr. Applegate in *DAMN YANKEES* (1955), which he also recreated in the 1958 movie. Walston's other Broadway credits were in dramas, comedies, and classics, but he also shone in two musical roles: the quirky stage manager Mac in *ME AND JULIET* (1953) and the crafty Captain Jonas in *HOUSE OF FLOWERS* (1954). He appeared in a variety of films, including the musicals *Kiss Me, Stupid* (1964), *PAINT YOUR WAGON* (1969), and *Popeye* (1980), and he was very popular on television, particularly in the 1960s series *My Favorite Martian* and the 1990s series *Picket Fences*. He was still acting on television up to the year of his death.

WALT DISNEY PICTURES. Hollywood's most successful and comprehensive entertainment corporation with major activity in live-action and animated films, television, Broadway musicals, publishing, and theme parks, it started with a single and rather simple focus: movie cartoons. Founder WALT DISNEY and his brother Roy Disney began the company in 1923 and soon the character of Mickey Mouse became the figurehead of a series of cartoon shorts. The young studio produced its first

sound short, *Steamboat Willie*, in 1928 and the mouse's popularity soared. Over the years no one used the development of sound, color, multiplane camera shooting, split screen, and other innovations better than Disney, who assembled the most talented artists in the business and dominated the animation field for decades. The company's gamble with the expensive *SNOW WHITE AND THE SEVEN DWARFS* (1937), the first full-length animated featured, paid off a hundredfold, so Disney moved on to even more ambitious projects. While continuing to provide shorts featuring Mickey, Donald Duck, and other character favorites, the studio regularly turned out animated features, usually releasing them through RKO. Just as with the first effort, these movies utilized music effectively in the plot and created dozens of popular songs over the years. Other musicals based on classic tales include *PINOCCHIO* (1940), *SONG OF THE SOUTH* (1946), *CINDERELLA* (1950), *PETER PAN* (1953), *Sleeping Beauty* (1959), *The Sword in the Stone* (1963), and *THE JUNGLE BOOK* (1967). Lesser-known stories soon became classics after the Disney touch, as with *DUMBO* (1941), *Bambi* (1942), *LADY AND THE TRAMP* (1955), and *101 Dalmations* (1961). The studio experimented with anthology features, sometimes mixing live action and animation in a series of stories or musical specialties: *Saludos Amigos* (1943), *MAKE MINE MUSIC* (1946), *Fun and Fancy Free* (1947), *MELODY TIME* (1948), and others. Some entries were so unique that they defied simple description, as with *FANTASIA* (1940) and *THE THREE CABALLEROS* (1945). By the 1950s Disney had moved into television, built its first theme park, and produced live-action features including comedies, adventure tales, history stories, and nature documentaries. The studio's first foray into live-action musicals was the moderate hit *BABES IN TOYLAND* (1961), followed by the charming but unexceptional *SUMMER MAGIC* (1963). With *MARY POPPINS* (1964), the company came up with a movie musical that rivaled those of Hollywood's golden age. However, subsequent efforts, such as *The Happiest Millionaire* (1967) and *The One and Only, Genuine Original Family Band* (1968), failed to capture the magic (and the audiences) of *Mary Poppins*. Over the next three decades only occasionally would the studio produce a live-action musical of interest, such as *BEDKNOBS AND BROOMSTICKS* (1971). Walt Disney, who had involved himself in every aspect of the huge company, died in 1966 and the whole operation declined. Some memorable animated musicals were made during the 1970s and 1980s, such as

THE ARISTOCATS (1970), THE RESCUERS (1977), and OLIVER & COMPANY (1988), but mostly the studio turned out inferior comedies and some ambitious but unsatisfying efforts, such as *Return to Oz* (1985) and *The Black Caldron* (1985). The corporation's fortunes improved with new management in the mid-1980s and the establishment of Touchstone Pictures that made features not necessarily directed to the usual family audience. After a power struggle that left Michael Eisner in control and had Roy E. Disney (Walt's nephew) revitalizing the animation division, the company experienced a renaissance of sorts with a stronger presence in television, growth in the theme park sector, and a series of superb animated features that compared favorably to the classics of the past: THE LITTLE MERMAID (1989), BEAUTY AND THE BEAST (1991), ALADDIN (1992), THE LION KING (1994), POCAHONTAS (1995), THE HUNCHBACK OF NOTRE DAME (1996), HERCULES (1997), MULAN (1998), TARZAN (1999), and others. Disney developed stop-action musicals, such as THE NIGHTMARE BEFORE CHRISTMAS (1993) and *James and the Giant Peach* (1996), and with Pixar was the first to present a fully computerized feature, *Toy Story* (1995). Also in the 1990s, the company founded Disney Theatricals and produced musicals on Broadway: *Beauty and the Beast* (1994), *The Lion King* (1997), *AIDA* (2000), *Tarzan* (2006), *Mary Poppins* (2006), and *The Little Mermaid* (2008). With subsidiaries such as Miramax, the studio has presented various films, such as the musical *CHICAGO* (2002), and expanded its television programing in both network and cable divisions. Disney's outstanding musical hits on the small screen included CINDERELLA (1997), HIGH SCHOOL MUSICAL (2006), and HIGH SCHOOL MUSICAL 2 (2007). Also ever expanding are the theme parks, and the corporation knows how to sell them as well as many other kinds of merchandising. The conglomerate has grown too large and powerful for some people's taste, but like all business it is subject to financial setbacks and rough times, proving that the corporation is indeed mortal. Good times or bad, one aspect of the Disney operation is the high quality that it always pursues. There are no cheap, sloppy, or tawdry products, and that can be said for their movie, stage, and television musicals as well.

WALTERS, CHARLES (1911–1982). Film, stage, and television director, choreographer, and performer. A former Broadway dancer who choreographed a number of stage musicals, he later went to Hollywood and did the dances for many musical favorites before turning to directing. Walters was born in Brooklyn and by 1934 was performing on Broadway in such shows as NEW FACES (1934), JUBILEE (1935), BETWEEN THE DEVIL (1937), and *I MARRIED AN ANGEL* (1938). His first choreography assignment was *Sing Out the News* (1938), followed by LET'S FACE IT! (1941), *Banjo Eyes* (1941), and ST. LOUIS WOMAN (1946). Walters went to Hollywood in 1942 and choreographed such film musicals as *DuBARRY WAS A LADY* (1943), GIRL CRAZY (1943), BEST FOOT FORWARD (1943), BROADWAY RHYTHM (1943), MEET ME IN ST. LOUIS (1944), THE HARVEY GIRLS (1945), and SUMMER HOLIDAY (1948). His first directing credit was the popular EASTER PARADE (1948), followed by THE BARKLEYS OF BROADWAY (1949), SUMMER STOCK (1950), THE BELLE OF NEW YORK (1952), LILI (1953), *Dangerous When Wet* (1953), HIGH SOCIETY (1956), JUMBO (1962), THE UNSINKABLE MOLLY BROWN (1964), and others. Walters served as co-choreographer on many of the films he directed and sometimes returned to performing, usually as a featured dancer. He retired in the mid-1960s but came out of retirement a decade later to direct two LUCILLE BALL television specials.

WANG (Broadway Theatre 1891). A cock-eyed comic operetta that was a vehicle for popular comic DEWOLF HOPPER, it was a wacky cross between THE MIKADO and THE KING AND I. The conniving Regent of Siam, Wang (Hopper), is always looking for ways to take over the country, which doesn't bother the young Prince Mataya (Della Fox in a trouser role) because he is more concerned with his courtship of Gillette (Anna O'Keefe). Gillette's mother, La Veuve Frimousse (Marion Singer), is convinced that Mataya wants her daughter only for her money since, as the widow of a former French consul, Frimousse has managed to get her hands on the entire treasury of Siam. The resourceful Wang manipulates matters so that Gillette and Mataya are united and he himself weds the widow, relieving her of her money and saving the government at the same time. J. Cheever Goodwin wrote the funny libretto and lyrics, and Woolson Morse composed the tuneful music, the two hit songs being "Ask the Man in the Moon" and "A Pretty Girl." The silly show was very popular and, thanks to Hopper's expert clowning, ran 151 performances. So widespread was *Wang*'s appeal that forty years later when the King of Siam visited America, he asked to hear songs from the musical.

WARNER BROTHERS. This Hollywood studio virtually invented the movie musical and would dominate the market for the new genre during its early years. Founded by Jack L. Warner and his three brothers in 1923, the fledging company bought up some small studios like Vitagraph and First National Pictures, but by 1926 found themselves on the verge of bankruptcy. The brothers decided to sink their remaining assets into an experiment called Vitaphone, which provided sounds that coordinated with the images on the screen. After testing Vitaphone with a music soundtrack and sound effects for the swashbuckler *Don Juan* (1926), the studio opened up a world of sound with the partial talkies *THE JAZZ SINGER* (1927) and *THE SINGING FOOL* (1928). Other companies scrambled to incorporate sound, but Warner Brothers had the lead and maintained it with such early musicals as *ON WITH THE SHOW* (1929), the *GOLD DIGGERS* movies, *42ND STREET* (1933), *FOOTLIGHT PARADE* (1933), *WONDER BAR* (1934), and *DAMES* (1934). AL JOLSON, DICK POWELL, RUBY KEELER, JAMES CAGNEY, and JOAN BLONDELL were among the stars who made the Warner musicals sparkle, and with its popular series of gangster pictures, the studio flourished. Although the products of Warner Brothers never had the glossiness of some of the other major studios, there was a crisp, dramatic look to its films and even the musicals had a toughness and crude attractiveness about them. The 1940s and 1950s saw a decline in musicals at the studio, although there were the occasional hits such as *YANKEE DOODLE DANDY* (1942), *THANK YOUR LUCKY STARS* (1943), *RHAPSODY IN BLUE* (1944), *NIGHT AND DAY* (1946), *A STAR IS BORN* (1954), and *DAMN YANKEES* (1958). The 1960s saw some big-budget musicals that paid off, such as *THE MUSIC MAN* (1962), *GYPSY* (1962), *ROBIN AND THE SEVEN HOODS* (1964), and *MY FAIR LADY* (1964). The studio was bought up by Seven Arts Productions in 1967 and was known for a time as Warner Bros.-Seven Arts. Soon after it became Warner Communications, and then in 1989 a merger created Time Warner, an empire controlling music, television, and films. As with most studios, musicals at Warners were mostly abandoned in the 1970s, and the company remains one of the industry's most potent at the box office without them, although occasionally a musical is produced, such as *THE PHANTOM OF THE OPERA* (2004) and *SWEENEY TODD* (2007).

WARREN, HARRY [born Salvatore Anthony Guaragna] (1893–1981). Film and stage composer. The quintessential Hollywood composer, his long career included scores from the early musicals at WARNER BROTHERS through the 1960s. A native of Brooklyn, Warren began his career as a drummer in a carnival band and when he broke into movies at the Vitagraph studios it was as a prop man and an extra. While serving as an assistant director he wrote songs for Tin Pan Alley, some of which were hits in the 1920s, and in 1930 his work was heard on Broadway in the revue *Sweet and Low* and on screen in *Spring Is Here*. His subsequent stage efforts—*The Laugh Parade* (1931), *Chamberlain Brown's Scrap Book* (1932), and *Swingin' the Dream* (1939)—failed to run but his Hollywood career was established when he teamed up with lyricist AL DUBIN and scored *42ND STREET* (1933). With Dubin he wrote songs for twenty-two more WARNER BROTHERS musicals in the 1930s, most memorably *GOLD DIGGERS OF 1933*, *FOOTLIGHT PARADE* (1933), *ROMAN SCANDALS* (1933), *MOULIN ROUGE* (1934), *WONDER BAR* (1934), *DAMES* (1934), *GOLD DIGGERS OF 1935*, *GO INTO YOUR DANCE* (1935), *Colleen* (1936), *GOLD DIGGERS OF 1937* (1936), *The Singing Marine* (1937), *GOLD DIGGERS IN PARIS* (1938), and *Garden of the Moon* (1938). After Dubin's premature death, Warren wrote with various lyricists, turning out hit songs decade after decade. With JOHNNY MERCER he scored *Going Places* (1938), *Naughty But Nice* (1939), *THE HARVEY GIRLS* (1946), *THE BELLE OF NEW YORK* (1952); with RALPH BLANE he wrote *SUMMER HOLIDAY* (1948), *My Dream of Yours* (1949), and *Skirts Ahoy* (1952); he wrote music to Jack Brooks' lyrics in *The Caddy* (1953), *ARTISTS AND MODELS* (1955), *Cinderfella* (1960), and *Ladies Man* (1961); and with lyricist MACK GORDON he scored such films as *DOWN ARGENTINE WAY* (1940), *THAT NIGHT IN RIO* (1941), *SUN VALLEY SERENADE* (1941), *WEEKEND IN HAVANA* (1941), *ORCHESTRA WIVES* (1942), *ICELAND* (1942), *SPRINGTIME IN THE ROCKIES* (1942), *Sweet Rosie O'Grady* (1943), and *SUMMER STOCK* (1950). Warren also collaborated with IRA GERSHWIN, DOROTHY FIELDS, LEO ROBIN, SAMMY CAHN, ARTHUR FREED, GUS KAHN, and other outstanding lyricists, scoring such films as *Honolulu* (1939), *THE GANG'S ALL HERE* (1943), *Yolanda and the Thief* (1945), *ZIEGFELD FOLLIES* (1946), *THE BARKLEYS OF BROADWAY* (1949), *Texas Carnival* (1951), and *Rock-a-Bye Baby* (1958). He was less successful when he returned to Broadway to score *Shangri-La* (1956) but in 1980 his songs were heard in the hit stage version of *42nd Street*. No composer in Hollywood was more prolific and more adaptable to the changing styles in popular music. Warren's gift for melody, intoxicating harmony, and strong musical line helped him write such diverse song hits as "Shuffle Off to Buffalo," "Lullaby of Broadway," "Jeepers Creepers," "You'll Never Know," "On the Atchison, Topeka and the Sante Fe," and "That's Amore." Biography: *Harry Warren and the Hollywood Musical*, Tony Thomas (1975).

WASHINGTON, NED (1901–1976). Film and stage lyricist. A songwriter little known to the public, some of his movie songs are beloved by millions, none more so than "When You Wish Upon a Star." Washington was born in Scranton, Pennsylvania, and began his career in vaudeville as an agent and an emcee. He later started writing songs (music and lyrics) for variety acts and had some of his numbers interpolated into the Broadway revue *EARL CARROLL VANITIES* (1928). Working with composer collaborators he penned the lyrics for songs in *Murder at the Vanities* (1933) and *Blackbirds of 1933*. After one of Washington's lyrics was used in WARNER BROTHERS screen musical *THE SHOW OF SHOWS* (1929), he was given a contract and for the next thirty years turned out scores with various partners for thirteen musicals and songs for dozens of nonmusicals. He is best remembered for the songs he wrote for the DISNEY-animated musicals *PINOCCHIO* (1940) and *DUMBO* (1941), but there were commendable numbers also in *LITTLE JOHNNY JONES* (1930), *Bright Lights* (1931), *Tropic Holiday* (1938), *Hands Across the Border* (1943), *Mexicana* (1945), *Miss Sadie Thompson* (1953), and *Let's Do It Again* (1953), as well as interpolations into *NO, NO, NANETTE* (1930), *FOLIES BERGERE DE PARIS* (1935), and *A Night at the Opera* (1935). Among Washington's hits from nonmusicals are "Town Without Pity," "My Foolish Heart," and "High Noon (Do Not Forsake Me Oh My Darling)." He also wrote some television theme songs, most notably "Rawhide."

📖 *WATCH YOUR STEP* (New Amsterdam Theatre 1914). The musical that introduced ragtime to Broadway, the show was IRVING BERLIN's first complete score for a book show and it gave audiences a taste of a true dance musical. HARRY B. SMITH wrote the ridiculous libretto about the millionaire Ebeneezer Hardacre (Harry Kelly) who bequeaths a fortune on any of his male relatives who has never been in love, engaged, or married. What followed was a series of episodes about relatives trying to get the money but falling for the charms of women. VERNON and IRENE CASTLE were the main attraction, doing their cakewalk, fox trot, and other forms of ballroom dancing that they had made popular. Also in the cast were Frank Tinney, CHARLES KING, Elizabeth Brice, and Justine Johnstone. Berlin provided a very danceable score, including two songs that are still performed today, the catchy "The Syncopated Walk" and the clever double song "Play a Simple Melody." R. H. BURNSIDE directed the CHARLES DILLINGHAM production which ran 175 performances.

WATERS, ETHEL (1896–1977). Stage, television, and film performer. Few African Americans broke as many racial barriers as this gifted singer–actress whose warm stage persona, velvet flowing voice, expressive eyes, and infectiously radiant smile made her a favorite of both black and white audiences. Born in poverty in Chester, Pennsylvania, she worked as a servant until someone who heard her sing suggested she try vaudeville. She made her debut in 1917 and became one of the few black performers to succeed in both "colored" and mainstream variety. Soon Waters rose to become a recognized singer of jazz and blues in supper clubs and cabarets, some of which had never featured African Americans before. She first appeared on Broadway in the "all-Negro" revues *Africana* (1927), *LEW LESLIE'S BLACKBIRDS* (1930), and *Rhapsody in Black* (1931) and then in 1933 Waters became the first black performer to get star billing alongside whites in the popular revue *AS THOUSANDS CHEER*. Two years later she starred in the revue *At Home Abroad*, followed by her only book musical, *CABIN IN THE SKY* (1940), in which she played the steadfast wife Petunia Jackson. Waters' two most memorable nonmusical appearances were as the vengeful mother Hagar in *Mamba's Daughters* (1939) and the mother earth figure Berenice in *The Member of the Wedding* (1950). She reprised her Petunia Jackson in the 1943 film version of *Cabin in the Sky* and repeated her Berenice on screen in 1952; they remain a vibrant record of Water's remarkable talents. Her other Broadway musicals were *Laugh Time* (1943) and *Blue Holiday* (1945), returning to Broadway for *At Home With Ethel Waters* (1953) and *An Evening With Ethel Waters* (1959). She also made several recordings and was featured in a handful of other films, including the musicals *ON WITH THE SHOW* (1929), *Gift of Gab* (1934), *Cairo* (1942), and *STAGE DOOR CANTEEN* (1943).

"AMERICA'S FOREMOST EBONY COMEDIENNE"

ETHEL WATERS

"Society's Latest Fad"

Now Starred in
EARL DANCER'S

"AFRICANA"

GREATEST OF ALL COLORED REVUES
"ON TOUR"—ERLANGER BOOKING

Ethel Waters. In both revues, such as *Africana* (1927), and in book musicals, such as *Cabin in the Sky* (1940), Waters was a glowing presence on stage. How fortunate that she also made films for there is now a vivid record of this remarkable entertainer. Pictured is the advertisement that ran in the national directory for booking agents. (NYPL)

Waters was the first African American to have her own national radio show and in the 1950s she had her own television series, *Beulah*, and made guest appearances on all the top variety shows. Autobiographies: *His Eye Is on the Sparrow* (1951); *To Me It's Wonderful* (1972); biographies: *Ethel Waters, I Touched a Sparrow*, Twila Knaack (1978); *Ethel Waters: Stormy Weathers*, Stephen Bourne (2005).

WATSON, SUSAN [Elizabeth] (1938–). Stage and television performer. Perhaps the brightest Broadway musical ingénue of the 1960s, the round-faced singer–actress played lively teenagers and young ladies with spunk in new and revived works. Watson was born in Tulsa, Oklahoma, and studied at Juilliard and with Uta Hagen at the Herbert Berghof Studio. After getting experience in stock, she made her Off Broadway debut in 1959 as Luisa in the one-act version of *The Fantasticks*. Watson didn't

get to reprise her performance in the legendary 1960 production because by then she was playing the all-American teenager Kim McAfee in *BYE BYE BIRDIE* (1960) on Broadway. Her other memorable Broadway roles include a replacement for Lili in *CARNIVAL* (1962), the folk music lover Jenny Lee in *A Joyful Noise* (1966), the eager singer Angel in *CELEBRATION* (1969), and the strong-willed flapper Nanette in the popular revival of *NO, NO, NANETTE* (1971). Watson's other New York musicals were *Ben Franklin in Paris* (1964), *CAROUSEL* (1965), *OKLAHOMA!* (1965), *WHERE'S CHARLEY?* (1966), and *The Bone Room* (1975). She has acted in several television programs, from soap opera to variety shows, and got to play Luisa again the 1964 TV version of *The Fantasticks*.

WAYBURN, NED [born Edward Claudius Weyburn] (1874–1942). Stage director and choreographer. A colorful Broadway personality who was one of the earliest director–choreographers, he is possibly the inventor of tap dancing. Wayburn was born in Pittsburgh, Pennsylvania, the son of a prosperous businessman, and began in the family business, first in his hometown and then in Atlanta and Chicago. While working as an assistant hotel manager in Chicago, he ushered at the Grand Opera House and was entranced by show business. Wayburn wrote songs and sang and danced to them in vaudeville and eventually made it to Broadway where he appeared in a few musicals. His gift for staging the dances and sketches in minstrel shows, revues, and later book musicals was soon recognized and by the turn of the century Wayburn was a busy director and choreographer. Long before others, he developed a way of unifying the songs, dances, and book scenes with a rapid choreographic tempo and striking visuals. Although he was often negligent of the story and characters, his musicals moved like one extended musical number. Among his seventy Broadway shows were *Star and Garter* (1900), *The Governor's Son* (1901), *HUMPTY DUMPTY* (1904), *School Days* (1908), *The Midnight Sons* (1909), *The Rose of Algeria* (1909), *The Jolly Bachelors* (1910), *Tillie's Nightmare* (1910), *Peggy* (1911), *The Honeymoon Express* (1913), *The Century Girl* (1916), *Miss 1917* (1917), *Poor Little Ritz Girl* (1920), *The Night Boat* (1920), *Two Little Girls in Blue* (1921), *Smiles* (1930), and several editions of *THE PASSING SHOW* and the *ZIEGFELD FOLLIES*. Wayburn turned to producing his own musicals and gained and lost a fortune several times during his long career. He spent some years in London staging musicals and he often directed shows in Chicago, the most famous of them, *THE TIME, THE PLACE AND THE GIRL*, which transferred to Broadway in 1907. He opened his first of many dancing schools in 1905 and claimed to have invented tap dancing by nailing metal tips to his students' clogs for a rat-a-tat-tat sound. In 1925 he published a book, *The Art of Stage Dancing*, outlining his ideas. Few of Wayburn's musicals have stood the test of time and by the late 1920s he was overshadowed by younger and more up-to-date talents, but few artists were as influential in giving the Broadway musical the flash and fast-tempo flavor that dominated until "musical plays" were invented. Biography: *Ned Wayburn and the Dance Routine: From Vaudeville to the Ziegfeld Follies*, Barbara Stratyner (1996).

WAYNE, DAVID [born Wayne James McMeekan] (1914–1995). Stage, television, and film performer. An affable, light-footed character actor with a pixie-like persona, he became a stage favorite in supporting roles. Wayne was born in Traverse City, Michigan, the son of an insurance executive, and educated at Western Michigan College for an accounting career. After working as a statistician for a while, he turned to acting, getting experience regionally before making his Broadway bow in 1938. It was not until after he had served in World War II that he started getting significant roles such as the leprechaun Og discovering lust in *FINIAN'S RAINBOW* (1947). Wayne's other musical triumphs were Cap'n Andy in the 1966 revival *SHOW BOAT* and the bon vivant French Canadian grandpa Bonnard in *THE HAPPY TIME* (1968). He was also featured in the musicals *THE MERRY WIDOW* (1943), *Park Avenue* (1946), *Say, Darling* (1958), and *The Yearling* (1965). Wayne appeared in several films beginning with *My Blue Heaven* (1950), followed by the musicals *WITH A SONG IN MY HEART* (1952), *Wait 'Til the Sun Shines, Nellie* (1952), *The "I Don't Care" Girl* (1953), *Tonight We Sing* (1953), *Down Among the Sheltering Palms* (1953), and *Huckleberry Finn* (1974). In the 1950s he started concentrating on television, where he acted in several series and specials, such as the TV musicals *RUGGLES OF RED GAP* (1957), *JUNIOR MISS* (1957), and *Strawberry Blonde* (1959).

WEBB, CLIFTON [born Webb Parmallee] (1893–1966). Stage and film performer. The agile, dapper, sophisticated actor–singer–dancer whom many mistakenly thought was British because of his precise, affected manner, he had different performing careers during his unusual life. Webb was born in Indianapolis and, pushed by his legendary stage mother, was singing and dancing in public by the age of ten. As a teenager he gave up show business to study painting and music and then he pursued an opera career for a while, performing with the Boston Opera Company. After appearing in a few silent films, Webb became somewhat known in New York as a ballroom dancer and at the age of nineteen was on Broadway in supporting roles in plays and musicals. Of his many Broadway credits, he shone brightest in revues such as *THE LITTLE SHOW* (1929), *THREE'S A CROWD* (1930), *FLYING COLORS* (1932), and *AS THOUSANDS CHEER* (1933). His other musicals include *Dancing Around* (1914), *Town Topics* (1915), *SUNNY* (1925), *She's My Baby* (1928), *Treasure Girl* (1928), and *You Never Know* (1938). After his last musical, Webb retired from musicals and concentrated on comedies where he played witty, urban characters on Broadway as in *The Importance of Being Earnest* (1939), *Blithe Spirit* (1941), and *Present Laughter* (1946). He left the stage in the mid-1940s to concentrate on films, playing similarly waspish, pedantic characters.

WEBBER, ANDREW LLOYD (1948–). Stage and film composer and producer. The phenomenally successful British composer with plenty of stage hits on both sides of the Atlantic, he has seen much of his work transferred to the screen and the tube with variable success. The native Londoner was born into a family of classically trained and distinguished musicians. He studied classical music at Oxford but turned to rock and other popular forms when he first collaborated with lyricist TIM RICE on *JOSEPH AND THE AMAZING TECHNICOLOR DREAMCOAT* in 1968. The young songwriters rose to prominence with their rock opera *JESUS CHRIST SUPERSTAR*, which was a successful album and later a stage hit in London and then in New York in 1971, followed by the team's *EVITA* (1979). With various lyricists, Webber has scored a number of musicals of diverse subject matter, most of which played on Broadway and none more successful than *CATS* (1982) and *THE PHANTOM OF THE OPERA* (1988). His other New York credits include *Song and Dance* (1985), *STARLIGHT EXPRESS* (1987), *ASPECTS OF LOVE* (1990), *SUNSET BOULEVARD* (1994), *By Jeeves* (2001), and *The Woman in White* (2005). While *Jesus Christ Superstar* (1973), *Evita* (1996), and *The Phantom of the Opera* (2004) were filmed, some of his other works were made into videos, such as *Tell Me on a Sunday* (from *Song and Dance*) in 1979, *Joseph and the Amazing Technicolor Dreamcoat* (1991), *Aspects of Love* (1993), and *Cats* (1998). Webber is also an important theatre owner in London and has produced some of his own musicals and those by others, such as *Bombay Dreams* in London and in 2004 on Broadway. Although some of his most successful musicals have relied on spectacle and he is rarely a critics' favorite, Webber is very popular with theatregoers on two continents and has been instrumental in bringing modern musical idioms to the theatre. Biography: *Andrew Lloyd Webber: His Life and Works*, Michael Walsh (1989).

WEBER, JOE [Morris] (1867–1942). Stage performer and producer. The short, dumpy "Dutch" comic was extremely popular as part of the famous team of Weber and Fields in vaudeville and on Broadway. The native New Yorker grew up only a few blocks from where LEW FIELDS lived and the two formed a comedy act for vaudeville when they were still very young. In variety they developed and refined their form of ethnic humor using German Jewish stereotypes that pleased audiences of all backgrounds. By 1896 they were so successful that the team was able to purchase a Broadway theatre where they produced and performed in a series of musical comedy "burlesques" that parodied the shows and stars currently on Broadway. Among the most popular of these musical spoofs were *The Art of Maryland* (1896), *Hurly Burly* (1898), *Cyranose de Bricabrac* (1898), *Fiddle-Dee-Dee* (1900), *Hoity Toity* (1901), *Twirly Whirly* (1902), *Whoop-Dee-Doo* (1903), and *An English Daisy* (1904). The team split up in 1913 and Weber produced some book musicals that he did not appear in, such as *The Only Girl* (1914), *Eileen* (1917), *Her Regiment* (1917), and *Honeydew* (1920). Weber and Fields sometimes reteamed for a special event and they played themselves in the films *Two Flaming Youths* (1927), *Blossoms on Broadway* (1937), and *LILLIAN RUSSELL* (1940).

WEBSTER, PAUL FRANCIS (1907–1984). Film and stage lyricist. Writing with a variety of composers, he penned lyrics for award-winning songs from musicals and nonmusical movies. The native New Yorker was educated at New York University and Cornell before working as a seaman and a dance instructor. Webster started writing lyrics in the Depression and some of his songs were heard on Broadway in *Murder at the Vanities* (1933). He made his screen debut with the songs used in *Under the Pampas Moon* (1935) and then scored the musical *Rainbow on the River* (1936) with composer LOUIS ALTER. With collaborator HARRY REVEL, he provided scores for such movies as *It Ain't Hay* (1943), *Ghost Catchers* (1944), and *The Stork Club* (1945), and with composer SAMMY FAIN the songs for *CALAMITY JANE* (1953), *Lucky Me* (1954), *Hollywood or Bust* (1956), *April Love* (1957), *Mardi Gras* (1958), and *The Big Circus* (1959), as well as the television musical *A Diamond for Carla* (1959). With other collaborators Webster wrote songs for *Make a Wish* (1937), *THE MERRY WIDOW* (1952), *ROSE MARIE* (1954), *THE STUDENT PRINCE* (1954), *THE GREAT CARUSO* (1955), the British film *Let's Be Happy* (1957), and the TV musical *The Young Man From Boston* (1965). He returned to Broadway with the revues *Alive and Kicking* (1950) and

Catch a Star (1955), as well as the short-lived *Christine* (1960). Some of Webster's most popular songs were written for nonmusicals, such as "Love Is a Many-Spendored Thing" and "The Shadow of Your Smile." He contributed lyrics to the movies up through the 1970s.

WEEDE, ROBERT (1903–1972). Stage performer. A celebrated opera singer who turned to Broadway late in his career, he got to originate a major musical theatre role. Weede was born in Baltimore and studied for an opera career, eventually becoming one of the most popular baritones at the Metropolitan Opera between 1937 and 1950. He made a notable Broadway debut as the vineyard owner Tony in *THE MOST HAPPY FELLA* (1956) in which his operatic voice was ideal. Weede's other two musicals were not as successful, although he was praised for his American tourist Phil Arkin in *MILK AND HONEY* (1961) and the politician Edward Quinn in *Cry for Us All* (1970). He also played Marley's ghost in the TV musical *THE STINGIEST MAN IN TOWN* (1956). Weede continued to perform in concerts up to the year of his death.

WEEKEND IN HAVANA (Fox 1941). This ALICE FAYE and CARMEN MIRANDA vehicle may be hard to distinguish from the other 20TH CENTURY FOX south-of-the-border musicals featuring the two stars but that doesn't make it any less enjoyable. In Karl Tunberg and Darrel Ware's script, Faye is Nan Spencer, a Macy's Department store salesgirl, who takes a cruise to Cuba but threatens to sue the steamship company when her ship runs aground. Executive Jay Williams (JOHN PAYNE) takes Nan on an all-expenses-paid trip to Havana to get her to sign a release form but ends up head over heels in love with her. CESAR ROMERO was the Brooklyn-born Cuban Monte Blanca who was after the fortune he thinks Nan has, and Miranda was his jealous sweetheart Rosita Rivas. Corbina Wright, Jr., LEONID KINSKEY, GEORGE BARBIER, Sheldon Leonard, and BILLY GILBERT were added to the merriment, and HARRY REVEL (music) and MACK GORDON (lyrics) wrote such first-class songs as "Tropical Magic," "When I Love I Love," "Romance and Rhumba" (music by JAMES MONACO), the Latin-flavored title number, and "The Nango," a swinging tango that HERMES PAN staged with Miranda and the chorus girls tearing down the house. WALTER LANG directed the WILLIAM LeBARON production and it was as successful as all the other Latin Faye–Miranda musicals.

WEIDLER, VIRGINIA (1927–1968). Film performer. A perky child star from the late 1930s and 1940s, she specialized in outgoing brats and lovable preteens in a number of musicals and nonmusicals. Weidler was born in Eagle Rock, California, the daughter of an architect and a German-born opera singer, and was on the screen by the age of three. She first endeared herself to audiences as the rascally imp Europena in *Mrs. Wiggs of the Cabbage Patch* (1934) and was steadily employed for several years. Weidler's screen musicals include *THE BIG BROADCAST OF 1937* (1937), *BABES ON BROADWAY* (1942), *Born to Sing* (1942), and *BEST FOOT FORWARD* (1943). She appeared in many dramas and comedies and perhaps her finest musical moment on screen was singing "Lydia the Tattooed Lady" in the nonmusical *The Philadelphia Story* (1940). While making films she was educated at the Hollywood Professional School. When Weidler turned twenty, she was unable to find suitable roles and appeared regionally on stage and in concerts before retiring in 1945. She died of a heart attack at the age of forty.

WEIDMAN, JEROME (1913–1998) **AND JOHN** (1946–). Stage, film, and television writers. Father and son writers who did not work together, they have each contributed to a handful of memorable musical librettos. Jerome Weidman was a native New Yorker who was educated at New York University for a law career but turned to writing novels. He co-wrote the books for *FIORELLO* (1959) and *TENDERLOIN* (1960) with GEORGE ABBOTT as well as the musical *Pousse-Cafe* (1966). His novel *I CAN GET IT FOR YOU WHOLESALE* was filmed in 1951, which he turned into a musical in 1962. Jerome Weidman also wrote a few television scripts and screenplays, including the musical *The Eddie Cantor Story* (1953). His son John was born in New York and educated at Harvard where he wrote for the humor magazine *Lampoon*. He also studied law but at Yale then turned to writing. He made a notable Broadway debut with his libretto for STEPHEN SONDHEIM's musical *PACIFIC OVERTURES* (1976) and then worked with the songwriter again on *ASSASSINS* (1991). Weidman wrote the revised libretto for the 1987 revival of *ANYTHING GOES* as well as the musicals *Big* (1996), *CONTACT* (2000), and Sondheim's *Bounce* (2003), which closed before reaching Broadway. He has also written for television, including the children's show *Sesame Street*. John Weidman's scripts are often challenging pieces that eschew traditional storytelling and have bold concepts that match Sondheim's demanding scores.

WEILL, KURT (1900–1950). Stage and film composer. One of the musical theatre's most passionate and ambitious composers, he came to Broadway as a seasoned creator of opera and music–drama and made demands on theatregoers that were unique. Weill was born in Dessau, Germany, and studied music in Berlin, writing operas and instrumental pieces before he teamed up with playwright Bertolt Brecht (1898–1956) to create the bold musical *Die Dreigoschenoper* (1928) later known in America as *THE THREEPENNY OPERA*. Their similarly explosive works *Happy End* (1929) and *The Rise and Fall of Mahagony* (1930) drew attention and were not looked on favorably by the Nazi regime, particularly as both men were Jewish. Weill and his actress–wife LOTTE LENYA emigrated to Paris where he scored *Marie Galante* (1933) with French playwright Jacques Deval and composed the ballet *The Seven Deadly Sins*. Arriving in New York in 1935, Weill saw the Broadway musical stage as a place where music, drama, and explosive ideas could find a popular audience. His first American musical was the antiwar piece *JOHNNY JOHNSON* (1936) written with playwright Paul Green, followed by the satirical *KNICKERBOCKER HOLIDAY* (1938) with playwright MAXWELL ANDERSON. Neither show ran very long but *LADY IN THE DARK* (1941), with librettist MOSS HART and lyricist IRA GERSHWIN, was as popular as it was revolutionary. Poet Odgen Nash provided the lyrics for Weill's wry but successful satire *ONE TOUCH OF VENUS* (1943) but his sarcastic *The Firebrand of Florence* (1945) with Gershwin failed to run. Weill's last three musicals were perhaps his most ambitious: *STREET SCENE* (1947), *LOVE LIFE* (1948), and *LOST IN THE STARS* (1949). Each was a bold attempt to push the parameters of the Broadway musical further than previously seen but each would only be fully appreciated after Weill's premature death at the age of fifty. *The Threepenny Opera*, which had been produced unsuccessfully back in 1933 before Weill came to America, was given a new translation–adaptation by MARC BLITZSTEIN and opened Off Broadway in 1955, running for 2,611 performances and has frequently been revived ever since. Some of Weill's musicals were filmed in Germany and America and he contributed to the Hollywood musicals *You and Me* (1938) with lyricist SAM COSLOW and *Where Do We Go From Here?* (1945) with Gershwin. There is a distinct quality to all of Weill's music. It is hypnotic, exotic, and yet engaging. Much of his work was ahead of its time and has found continued life in theatres and opera houses around the world. Weill's theatre music was celebrated in the Off Broadway revue *Berlin to Broadway With Kurt Weill* (1963), and his life and work were explored in the Broadway musical *LoveMusik* (2007) where the composer was portrayed by MICHAEL CERVERIS. Biographies: *Kurt Weill*, David Farneth (2004); *The Days Grow Short: The Life and Music of Kurt Weill*, Ronald Sanders (1991).

WELCH, ELISABETH (1904–2003). Stage, film, and television performer. The deep-voiced ethnic singer, who spent most of her life in Great Britain, gave some glorious performances in a handful of Broadway revues. The native New Yorker, who was a mixture of Native and African American, sang in the church choir at the age of eight and worked as a social worker for children before going on the stage. Her Broadway debut was in the chorus of *Liza* (1922), and the next year she introduced the song and the dance "Charleston" in *Runnin' Wild* (1923). She was also featured in two "all-Negro" revues, *The Chocolate Dandies* (1924) and *BLACKBIRDS OF 1928*. Soon after the COLE PORTER musical *THE NEW YORKERS* (1931) opened, Welch was added to the cast to sing the risqué "Love for Sale." In 1933 she went to London where she remained for the rest of her long career, singing in nightclubs and appearing in West End revues and book musicals and acting in British films, such as the musicals *Soft Lights and Sweet Music* (1936), *Big Fella* (1937), and *Around the Town* (1938). Welch was on some television programs and continued making films for decades, singing "Stormy Weather" in the movie *The Tempest* (1979). When in her eighties she returned to the New York stage to sing in the London revue *Jerome Kern Goes to Hollywood* (1986) and performed a one-woman show Off Broadway the same year. Biography: *Elisabeth Welch: Soft Lights and Sweet Music*, Stephen Bourne (2005)

WELLS, GEORGE (1909–2000). Film writer and producer. Moving back and forth from comedies to musicals, he scripted some beloved MGM musicals. Wells was born in New York, the son of a vaudeville performer, and educated at New York University before starting his career as a radio writer. He went to Hollywood in the 1940s and wrote scripts alone or with others, specializing in light comedies and popular musicals such as *TILL THE CLOUDS ROLL BY* (1946), *TAKE ME OUT TO THE BALL*

GAME (1949), *THREE LITTLE WORDS* (1950), and *SUMMER STOCK* (1950). In the 1950s he also produced a number of feature films, including the musicals *Dangerous When Wet* (1953) and *Jupiter's Darling* (1955), and both writing and producing the musicals *Everything I Have Is Yours* (1952) and *I Love Melvin* (1953). His other writing credits include the musicals *THE TOAST OF NEW ORLEANS* (1950), *Texas Carnival* (1951), *LOVELY TO LOOK AT* (1952), and *Where the Boys Are* (1960).

■ **WE'RE NOT DRESSING** (Paramount 1934). BING CROSBY moved from crooner to light comic leading man with this silly but agreeable film in which he was charmingly offbeat as the carefree outsider, a persona he would perfect over the years. Horace Jackson, Frances Martin, and George Marion, Jr. adapted J. M. Barrie's Edwardian comedy *The Admirable Crichton* into a musical comedy about the spoiled heiress Doris Worthington (Carole Lombard) who is sailing the South Seas with some of her friends when they are shipwrecked on a desert island and it is the lowly sailor Stephen Jones (Crosby) who is the only one with the wherewithal to take charge. Doris resents him at first, but after a few songs and walks along the moonlit beach, she succumbs to his charms. Also on board were ETHEL MERMAN, LEON ERROL, and Ray Milland, with naturalists GRACIE ALLEN and GEORGE BURNS studying flora and fauna on the island and providing most of the jokes. It was a daffy adventure and one, under NORMAN TAUROG's direction, that worked effortlessly. HARRY REVEL (music) and MACK GORDON (lyrics) penned the songs and they were equally expert: the touching ballads "She Reminds Me of You" and "Once in a Blue Moon," the sly "May I?," the merry "Love Thy Neighbor," and the lullaby "Goodnight, Lovely Little Lady," which Crosby sang to his pet bear.

WEST, MAE [born Mary Jane West] (1893–1980). Stage and film performer and writer. The celebrated busty, blonde sex symbol who was more a parody than a seriously enticing siren, she found fame on Broadway and in Hollywood and then remained an American icon for decades afterwards. West was born in Brooklyn, the daughter of a heavyweight boxer, and was on the stage at the age of five, later touring in kid roles in melodramas such as *Little Nell of the Marchioness*, *Mrs. Wiggs of the Cabbage Patch*, and *East Lynne*. By 1911 she was on Broadway playing supporting roles in plays and musicals, such as *A La Broadway* (1911), *Vera Violetta* (1911), *A Winsome Widow* (1912), and *The Mimic World* (1921). West developed her satiric vamp persona singing ribald songs in vaudeville and was already becoming well known by the time she made headlines in 1926 for the play *Sex*, which she wrote, produced, directed, and starred in. Her infamy was established and she starred on Broadway in her own shows, most memorably *Diamond Lil* (1928), which she reprised in New York in 1949 and 1951. West made her screen debut in 1932, usually writing her own dialogue for her vehicles and always battling over the censors over what she could say and do on screen. Most of her movies were musicals and she got to introduce some standards such as "My Old Flame." Her screen musicals are *SHE DONE HIM WRONG* (1933), *I'm No Angel* (1933), *Belle of the Nineties* (1934), *Goin' to Town* (1935), *Klondike Annie* (1936), *Go West, Young Man* (1936), *Every Day's a Holiday* (1937), and *The Heat's On* (1943). After decades of being out of the public eye (but not forgotten), West returned to the limelight in the 1970s doing concerts in America and England and making the nonmusical movies *Myra Breckinridge* (1970) and *Sextet* (1978). Autobiographies: *Good Had Nothing to Do With It* (1959); *Life, Sex and ESP* (1975); biographies: *Mae West: It Ain't No Sin*, Simon Louvish (2006); *Becoming Mae West*, Emily Wortis (1997).

✧ **WEST SIDE STORY** (Winter Garden Theatre 1957). A familiar and perennial favorite, the powerful musical play by ARTHUR LAURENTS (book), LEONARD BERNSTEIN (music), and STEPHEN SONDHEIM (lyrics) was quite bold and daring in its day, breaking from convention and utilizing dance in new and exciting ways.

Plot: The street rivalry between the gang of Puerto Rican immigrants known as the Sharks and the native-New York gang called the Jets has intensified over the summer. The Jet leader Riff tries to get Tony, who co-founded the gang with him, to get more involved but Tony is restless and is outgrowing street fighting. Riff plans to challenge the Sharks at the dance where the two gangs and their girls will be together and it is there that Tony sees Maria, the newly arrived immigrant who is the sister of Bernardo, the leader of the Sharks. The two are immediately drawn to each other and that night they meet on the fire escape outside her bedroom window and profess their love for

West Side Story. Theatre dance had been used to illustrate many emotions over the years but never tension and pent-up frustration as it was seen in *West Side Story*. The number "Cool" (pictured above) allowed the street gang known as the Jets to explode into modern jazz dance as they tried to hide the anger and bitterness within them. Under Jerome Robins' direction and choreography, dance was used to explore feelings usually reserved for dialogue or song. The photo shows the replacement cast of the Broadway production with original cast member Lee Theodore (fourth from the right) as the tomboy Anybodys. (Photofest)

Casts for *West Side Story*

Character	1957 Broadway	1961 film	1980 Broadway
Maria	CAROL LAWRENCE	NATALIE WOOD	Josie de Guzman
Tony	LARRY KERT	Richard Beymer	Ken Marshall
Anita	CHITA RIVERA	RITA MORENO	DEBBIE ALLEN
Riff	Mickey Calin	RUSS TAMBLYN	James J. Mellon
Bernardo	Ken LeRoy	GEORGE CHAKIRIS	Hector Jaime Mercado
Doc	Art Smith	Ned Glass	Sammy Smith

each other. A rumble between the two gangs is planned and when Maria hears of it she makes Tony promise he will try and stop it. When Tony attempts to do so, Bernardo stabs and kills Riff and in anger Tony kills Bernardo. While the police are looking for Tony, Maria sends her friend Anita to take a message to Tony through the Jets, but the gang taunts Anita and in anger she tells them that Maria has been killed by her jealous fiancé Chino. When Tony gets word of this, he goes looking for Chino asking to be killed as well. Chino shoots Tony, he dies in Maria's arms, and then she takes the gun and vents her anger on both gangs, accusing them and their rivalry for all that has happened.

The musical updating of *Romeo and Juliet* was a risky undertaking, mixing harsh drama with music and modern dance, and telling such a tragic tale in the form of a Broadway musical. Instead of an overture, the piece opened with a danced prologue that showed how the gang rivalry developed and grew. The first act ended not with a musical number but with two dead bodies on stage and police sirens blaring. The dancing was sometime joyous but just as often was filled with tension and frustration. The score utilized opera techniques, such as the complex "Tonight Quintet" that contained the separate musical thoughts of various characters before the rumble. There are no musical numbers for the last portion of the show, relying instead on dialogue in order to avoid a neatly concluded finale. "Maria," "Tonight," and "Somewhere" were the most popular numbers from the score but several of the other songs became just as well known even if they could not work outside of the context of the musical. The score allows for some relief from the grim events taking place, but even the mocking "Gee, Officer Krupke" and "America" have a bitter subtext to them, with the wisecracking and mockery just a cover for truly deep frustration. JEROME ROBBINS's masterful direction and choreography were major factors in making the problematic show effective. There was so much dance in the piece that PETER GENNARO was brought on as co-choreographer. HAROLD PRINCE and Robert E. Griffith produced the musical, which did not receive unanimous raves but was much talked about and was able to find audiences for 732 performances. After touring the country, the same cast returned to Broadway in 1960 for another 249 performances. In 1964 the New York Light Opera Company and director Gerald Freedman recreated the staging and design of the original and the cast included Julia Migenes (Maria), Don McKay (Tony), Luba Lisa (Anita), James Moore (Riff), and Jay Norman (Bernardo). LEE THEODORE recreated Jerome Robbins's choreography and direction for the 1968 Lincoln Center revival that featured Kurt Peterson and Victoria Mallory as the tragic lovers. The most popular revival was the 1980 Broadway production in which Jerome Robbins recreated his original staging and choreography with television star DEBBIE ALLEN featured as Anita. The production ran 333 performances. *West Side Story* remains a frequently produced musical not only in the States, but around the world, with the show having an international appeal and a story that translates well for different cultures.

West Side Story (Mirisch/United Artists 1961) has been mockingly called "the *Ben-Hur* of movie musicals" and there is a bigness and majesty about the film that clamors for greatness. But it took such confidence to pull off a screen version that relied on dance and operatic-like singing to tell its story. Co-director ROBERT WISE worked with co-director and choreographer Robbins to create a movie that was gritty and real and yet was very stylized. Parts of the film were shot on location in Manhattan, other parts in the studio, yet there is a consistent sense of style throughout the movie that works. ERNEST LEHMAN's screenplay sticks close to the stage libretto and the entire stage score was used, although some numbers changed positions in the story and were sung by different characters. The very non-Hispanic NATALIE WOOD played Maria effectively (her singing was dubbed by MARNI NIXON), but Richard Beymer (singing dubbed by Jim Bryat) was a bland Tony and the love scenes never reached the heights that they had on Broadway. The supporting cast, however, was outstanding. Considering the acting, singing, and dancing demands of the gang members and their girls, it becomes clear that the movie works as well as it does because of them. *West Side Story* was a box office and critical hit and the stage work became better known because of it. Before the film was released, the musical was thought different and daring; after the movie, it joined the ranks of the Broadway classics.

West Side Story Musical Numbers

"Prologue"
"Jet Song"
"Something's Coming"
"Dance at the Gym"
"Maria"
"Tonight"
"America"
"Cool"
"One Hand, One Heart"
"Tonight Quintet"
"The Rumble"
"I Feel Pretty"
"Somewhere"
"Gee, Officer Krupke"
"A Boy Like That"
"I Have a Love"
"Taunting"

WESTENBERG, ROBERT (1953–). Stage performer. A tall, handsome leading man from regional theatre, he has given some impressive Broadway musical performances in a relatively short career. Westenberg was born in Miami Beach, educated at California State University at Fresno, and trained at the American Conservatory Theatre in San Francisco. He made his Off Broadway bow with the NEW YORK SHAKESPEARE FESTIVAL in 1981 playing classical roles and acting in new plays and then was on Broadway as Nikos in the revival of ZORBÁ (1983). Westenberg played supporting roles in SUNDAY IN THE PARK WITH GEORGE (1984) and eventually took over the part of George. Other memorable performances include the Wolf and Cinderella's Prince in INTO THE WOODS (1987), the jealous Dr. Craven in THE SECRET GARDEN (1991), and the alcohol-prone husband Harry in COMPANY (1995), as well as a replacement for the villainous Javert in LES MISÉRABLES in 1991. Westenberg's other New York musical credits are A CHRISTMAS CAROL (1994), VIOLET (1997), and 1776 (1997). He appeared in a few films and on television before retiring in 2001 to teach theatre at Drury University, although he has appeared in some regional productions since then. Westenberg is married to singer–actress Kim Crosby (1960–).

WESTLEY, HELEN [born Henrietta Meserole Maney] (1875–1942). Stage and film performer. A very busy character actress with a severe pinched face that made her ideal for spinsters and villainesses, she had an active theatre career followed by an equally impressive screen career. Westley was born in Brooklyn and studied at the American Academy of Dramatic Arts before making her Broadway bow in 1897. She then left New York and spent years in stock companies across the country, returning to Manhattan in 1915 to co-found the Washington Players, which later developed into the THEATRE GUILD where she was a principal player for twenty years. Westley acted in a variety of new and revived works but not musicals until her film career was launched in 1934. Her most remembered musical role on screen is the disapproving Parthy Hawks in the 1936 version of SHOW BOAT, but she was featured in other musicals as well, such as The Melody Lingers On (1935), ROBERTA (1935), Stowaway (1936), Dimples (1936), I'll Take Romance (1937), REBECCA OF SUNNYBROOK FARM (1938), ALEXANDER'S RAGTIME BAND (1938), LILLIAN RUSSELL (1940), SUNNY (1941), and My Favorite Spy (1942).

WHEELER, HUGH [Callingham] (1916–1987). Stage, television, and film writer. The British novelist, playwright, and screenwriter wrote a half-dozen Broadway musicals late in his career, most memorably those for songwriter STEPHEN SONDHEIM. Born in Hampstead, England, Wheeler spent much of his early career writing detective novels under the nom de plume Patrick Quentin and Q Patrick. He made his Broadway debut with the play Big Fish, Little Fish (1961) and scripted his first musical when he adapted the Ingmar Bergman screenplay Smiles of a Summer Night into A LITTLE NIGHT MUSIC (1973). Wheeler wrote the revised librettos for IRENE (1973) and CANDIDE (1973) on Broadway and THE STUDENT PRINCE (1980) for the New York City Opera. His most important adaptation was Sondheim's SWEENEY TODD, THE DEMON BARBER OF FLEET STREET (1979) based on a British play. He was also a noted play doctor who contributed to musical scripts, including HALF A SIXPENCE (1965), PACIFIC OVERTURES (1976), and MEET ME IN ST. LOUIS (1989). Wheeler wrote for American and British television and penned a few original screenplays, as well as the film script for A Little Night Music (1978).

WHEELER AND WOOLSEY. Stage and film performers. A comedy team who often played supporting roles on Broadway and in Hollywood, they livened up a handful of musicals as well. [Al]Bert [Jerome] Wheeler (1895–1968) was born in Patterson, New Jersey, and was on the vaudeville stage as a boy and later headlined with his wife Betty, making their Broadway debut in ZIEGFELD FOLLIES (1923). Robert Woolsey (1889–1938) was born in Oakland, California, and began his career as a jockey but was forced to give it up after a crippling accident. After various jobs he turned to the theatre and was in New York by 1919 and playing comic roles in the musicals Nothing But Love (1919), The Right Girl (1921), The Blue Kitten (1922), The Lady in Ermine (1922), POPPY (1923), and Mayflowers (1925). Producer FLORENZ ZIEGFELD teamed the two men together for comic relief in his production of the operetta RIO RITA (1927) and they were immediately an audience favorite. The team repeated their performances in the 1929 film version and went on to similar clowning in the screen musicals The Cuckoos (1930), Dixiana (1930), GIRL CRAZY (1932), Cockeyed Cavaliers (1934), Hips Hips Hooray (1934), and Nitwits (1935). The roly-poly Wheeler usually played the naive, squeaky-voiced dupe while the owl-glassed Woolsey was the fast-talking shyster. The twosome toured in vaudeville and appeared in several nonmusical films before Woolsey's premature death at the age of forty-nine. Wheeler performed alone in a handful of films, including the musical *Las Vegas Nights* (1941), and then returned to Broadway where he acted in a few plays and the musicals *New Priorities of 1943* (1942), *Laugh Time* (1943), *All for Love* (1949), and *Three Wishes for Jamie* (1952). He also appeared on tours, in nightclubs, and on television into the 1960s.

🎵 *WHERE'S CHARLEY?* (St. James Theatre 1948). FRANK LOESSER's first book musical for Broadway, this delightful show based on the 1892 British farce *Charley's Aunt* was also one of RAY BOLGER's greatest stage triumphs. GEORGE ABBOTT's tight libretto simplified the plotline somewhat, with the Oxford student Charley Wyckeham now being the one to dress up like his aunt from Brazil in order to provide a chaperone for himself as well as for his fellow student Jack Chesney as they court Amy Spettigue and Kitty Verdun. Complications for Charley increase when Amy's guardian Mr. Spettigue starts to woo the bewigged Charley and when the real aunt Donna Lucia shows up and turns out to be the long lost love of Jack's father. The runaway hit from Loesser's score was "Once in Love With Amy," which Bolger turned into a sing-along number with the audience. Also first rate were the sprightly duet "Make a Miracle," the rousing "The New Ashmolean Marching Society and Students' Conservatory Band," the lilting ballad "My Darling, My Darling," the waltzing "At the Red Rose Cotillion," and the comic number "Serenade With Asides." Reviews were mixed for the musical and for Loesser's first Broadway score but the critics were in agreement that Bolger was a dancing, comic delight. CY FEUER and ERNEST H. MARTIN produced, author Abbott directed, and GEORGE BALANCHINE did the sportive choreography. The produc-

tion ran 792 performances and then went on tour, returning to Broadway for six weeks in 1951 with Bolger before he went to Hollywood to recreate his performance on screen. Darryl Hickman played Charley in the 1966 New York City Light Opera production directed by Christopher Hewitt. The cast also included SUSAN WATSON (Amy), David Smith (Jack), Karen Shepard (Kitty), and opera star Eleanor Steber as Donna Lucia. In 1974, RAUL JULIA was complimented on his unique approach to the cross-dressing Charley and the Theodore Mann-directed production was generally well received. The limited engagement of seventy-six performances at the Circle in the Square was well attended.

🎬 *Where's Charley?* (Warner 1952) retained Bolger, Allyn Ann McLerie, and Horace Cooper from the stage version, as well as most of the score and much of the fun. Partially filmed on location in Oxford, the musical was very attractive, with even the studio-shot dream sequence filmed with style by director DAVID BUTLER. MICHAEL KIDD did the playful choreography and Bolger got to do more dancing than in the stage show. He also performed "Once in Love With Amy" as he had on Broadway, encouraging the movie audience to join in. The effect was not nearly as effective as with a live audience in a theatre but it gave the movie a silliness that was appropriate. Feuer and Martin produced the film as well so it was a commendable version of the original.

🎬 *WHITE CHRISTMAS* (Paramount 1954). IRVING BERLIN's last full movie score, the perennial favorite capitalized on the consistent popularity of the 1942 title song and offered some memorable new tunes as well.

Plot: Army buddies Bob Wallace and Phil Davis go into show business together after World War II and find themselves in a Florida nightclub where they meet the sister act of Betty and Judy Haynes. The four travel up to

Casts for *Where's Charley?*

Character	1948 Broadway	1952 film	1974 Broadway
Charley Wykeham	RAY BOLGER	Ray Bolger	RAUL JULIA
Amy Spettigue	Allyn Ann McLerie	Allyn Ann McLerie	Marcia McClain
Jack Chesney	Byron Palmer	Robert Shackleton	Jerry Lanning
Kitty Verdun	DORETTA MORROW	Mary Germaine	Carol Jo Lugenbeal
Mr. Spettigue	Horace Cooper	Horace Cooper	Tom Aldredge
Donna Lucia	Jane Lawrence	Margaretta Scott	Taina Elg
Sir Francis Chesney	Paul England	Howard Marion-Crawford	Peter Walker

Cast for *White Christmas*

Character	Performer
Bob Wallace	BING CROSBY
Phil Davis	DANNY KAYE
Betty Haynes	ROSEMARY CLOONEY
Judy Haynes	VERA-ELLEN
Maj. Gen. Waverly	Dean Jagger
Emma Allen	MARY WICKES
Susan Waverly	Anne Whitfield
John	John Brascia

White Christmas Musical Numbers

"(We'll Follow) The Old Man"
"Sisters"
"Snow"
"The Best Things Happen While You're
    Dancing"
"Let Me Sing"
"I'd Rather See a Minstrel Show"
"Mandy"
"Blue Skies"
"Heat Wave"
"Count Your Blessings Instead of Sheep"
"Abraham"
"Choreography"
"Love, You Didn't Do Right By Me"
"What Can You Do With a General?"
"Gee, I Wish I Was Back in the Army"
"White Christmas"

White Christmas. While the Haynes Sisters sneak out of a nightclub, the army buddies Bob Wallace (left), played by Bing Crosby, and Phil, portrayed by Danny Kaye, put on the record of "Sisters" and lip-sync to the girl's recording. It was an inspired bit of buffoonery that, once seen, can never be forgotten. (Photofest)

Vermont where the girls have a booking to sing at a ski lodge but when the foursome arrive there is no snow and the lodge is like a ghost town. When the ex-G.I.s find out that their old commander, Major General Waverly, is the proprietor and going bankrupt, Bob decides to rehearse and try out his Broadway-bound show at the inn to attract business and Bob even goes on television to encourage former servicemen who served under the general to come to New England for the bash. They do, a lover's quarrel between Bob and Betty is resolved, and it starts to snow as everyone sings the title song joyously.

Norman Krasna, Norman Panama, and MELVIN FRANK wrote the screenplay that went far on a thin premise and some unlikely plot turns but the characters were well defined and the stars shone; ROSEMARY CLOONEY, for example, giving her best screen performance. DONALD O'CONNOR was originally cast as Phil but after he injured his leg DANNY KAYE stepped in and

played what was primarily a dancing role and did very well with it. The supporting cast was solid, with Dean Jagger providing the substance and MARY WICKES the comedy. Robert Emmett Dolan produced the film, the first in colorful Vistavision, MICHAEL CURTIZ directed it at an efficient pace, and ROBERT ALTON did the choreography, which ranged from old-time soft shoes to satiric modern interpretive dance.

Berlin wrote nine new songs for the film and some joined the ranks of his beloved standards: the tender lullaby "Count Your Blessings Instead of Sheep," the torchy "Love, You Didn't Do Right By Me," and the frivolous but catchy "Sisters," which was sung with a wink by Clooney and VERA-ELLEN and then lip-synced by Crosby and Kaye in one of the movie's silliest but most beloved numbers. "The Best Things Happen While You're Dancing" was another commendable addition to the catalogue of Berlin dance songs, and "Gee, I Wish I Was Back in the Army" was a nostalgic soft shoe in the grand manner. The film was the top-grossing picture of the year and remains a holiday-time favorite.

WHITE, GEORGE [born George Weitz] (1890–1968). Stage producer, choreographer, director, and dancer. FLORENZ ZIEGFELD's most accomplished rival in producing lavish Broadway revues, White directed and choreographed most of his shows and also produced nightclub revues and Hollywood films. A native New Yorker, White ran away from home as a boy and danced in vaudeville and then on Broadway, appearing in two editions of the ZIEGFELD FOLLIES. In 1919 he produced his first revue, calling it the GEORGE WHITE SCANDALS and it was popular enough to warrant thirteen more editions between 1920 and 1939. In addition to directing his revues personally, White sometimes danced in them as well. He also produced other Broadway musicals, such as *Runnin' Wild* (1923), *Manhattan Mary* (1927), *Flying High* (1930), and *Melody* (1933). In Hollywood he produced two film versions of his *Scandals* in 1934 and 1935, as well as the screen version of *Flying High* (1931). White was a versatile talent, sometimes also writing sketches and lyrics for his shows, but his greatest contribution may be the introduction of so many outstanding artists through his revues, in particular songwriters B. G. DeSYLVA, LEW BROWN, RAY HENDERSON, and GEORGE GERSHWIN.

WHITE, LILLIAS (1951–). Stage, film, and television performer. An ample-figured, full-voiced African American singer–actress, she has lit up the stage many times, usually in supporting roles. The Brooklyn native was educated at City College of New York before working as a backup singer and later a soloist in concerts. White made her New York legit debut in 1975 and then went on to replace others in *BARNUM* (1981), *CATS* (1985), and *ONCE ON THIS ISLAND* (1991). Her first wide recognition came as singer Effie in the 1987 revival of *DREAMGIRLS* (1987) and her other memorable performances include the weary hooker Sonja in *THE LIFE* (Off Broadway in 1990, on Broadway in 1997), the corporate secretary Miss Jones in *HOW TO SUCCEED IN BUSINESS WITHOUT REALLY TRYING* (1995), and as a replacement as singer Dinah Washington in *Dinah Was* (1998) and Mama Morton in *CHICAGO* (2006). White's other Manhattan musicals include *Rock 'n' Roll: The First 5,000 Years* (1982), *Romance in Hard Times* (1989), *Back to Bacharach and David* (1993), and *Crowns* (2002). She has appeared in a handful of films and some television dramas but her musical talents have only been enjoyed on the concert and musical stages.

WHITE, ONNA (1922–2005). Stage and film choreographer. A highly respected choreographer on Broadway and in Hollywood, she had plenty of hits and misses over a period of two decades. White was born in Nova Scotia, Canada, and began her career as a ballet dancer, eventually performing with the San Francisco Ballet Company. She appeared in such Broadway musicals as *FINIAN'S RAINBOW* (1947), *GUYS AND DOLLS* (1950), and *SILK STOCKINGS* (1955) and served as an assistant to MICHAEL KIDD who directed the first two; White later recreated his choreography for both shows in Broadway revivals in 1955. White's first original choreography for Broadway was perhaps her best: the spirited dances for *THE MUSIC MAN* (1957). She also choreographed such hits as *TAKE ME ALONG* (1959), *IRMA LA DOUCE* (1960), *HALF A SIXPENCE* (1965), *MAME* (1966), *1776* (1969), and *I LOVE MY WIFE* (1977), yet her work shone also in such short-lived musicals as *I Had a Ball* (1964), *Illya Darling* (1967), *70, GIRLS, 70* (1971), *GIGI* (1973), *Goodtime Charley* (1975), *WORKING* (1978), and *Gantry* (1970), which she also directed. White was also a much-in-demand choreographer for movie musicals, recreating her dances for the screen versions of *The Music Man* (1962), *1776* (1972), and *Mame* (1974) and creating new ones for *BYE BYE BIRDIE* (1963), *OLIVER!* (1968), and *PETE'S DRAGON* (1977). She was an eclectic choreographer with no distinct style, yet her work was always inventive, vibrant, and highly polished.

WHITEMAN, PAUL (1891–1967). Stage and film conductor and musician. The first and most durable of the popular bandleaders, the rotund, mustached conductor appeared on Broadway and in films as well as in concert and dance halls where he was dubbed the King of Jazz. Whiteman was born in Denver, the son of a musician and a music teacher, and began his career as a viola player with the San Francisco Symphony. During World War I he conducted a navy band and then formed his own orchestra with an open mind to new musical forms. Whiteman and his band rose to fame in the 1920s introducing jazz and dance music to concert halls. He premiered GEORGE GERSHWIN's "Rhapsody in Blue" in 1924 and the piece became his signature song. Whiteman and his band performed in the Broadway musicals *GEORGE WHITE'S SCANDALS* (1922), *ZIEGFELD FOLLIES* (1923), and *Lucky* (1927). He played himself in a handful of films, often with his celebrated orchestra performing as part of the plot.

His movie musicals were *KING OF JAZZ* (1930), *THANKS A MILLION* (1935), *STRIKE UP THE BAND* (1940), *Lady, Let's Dance* (1944), *Atlantic City* (1944), *RHAPSODY IN BLUE* (1945), and *The Fabulous Dorseys* (1947). From the early 1940s into the 1960s, Whiteman was musical director for the American Broadcasting Company and in 1942 he co-founded Capitol Records. Over the years he discovered or promoted such musicians as Red Nichols, Bix Beiderbecke, and TOMMY DORSEY, as well as singers as diverse as BING CROSBY and Bobby Rydell. Biography: *Pops: Paul Whiteman, King of Jazz*, Thomas A. DeLong (1983).

WHITING, JACK (1901–1961). Stage and film performer. A smiling, blond leading man in Broadway comedies and musicals, he played juvenile roles far into his middle age. Whiting was born and educated in Philadelphia and worked as a stenographer before going on the vaudeville stage as a song-and-dance man. His Broadway bow was in the 1922 edition of ZIEGFELD FOLLIES, followed by many musicals in which he played the all-American boy who gets the all-American girl: *Orange Blossoms* (1922), *Cinders* (1923), *Stepping Stones* (1923), *When You Smile* (1926), *The Ramblers* (1926), *She's My Baby* (1928), HOLD EVERYTHING (1928), *HEADS UP!* (1929), *America's Sweetheart* (1931), *TAKE A CHANCE* (1932), *HOORAY FOR WHAT!* (1937), *VERY WARM FOR MAY* (1939), *Walk With Music* (1940), *OF THEE I SING* (1952), and others, as well as such popular London productions as *ANYTHING GOES* (1935), *Rise and Shine* (1936), and *ON YOUR TOES* (1937). While few of these characters were very substantial, Whiting got to introduce such song hits as "You're the Cream in My Coffee," "I've Got Five Dollars," "All Alone Monday," and "Down With Love." Some of his more interesting characterizations came near the end of his career, such as the jaunty mayor of New York in *Hazel Flagg* (1953) and the mythical Hector and the soft-shoe dancing stockbroker Charybdis in *THE GOLDEN APPLE* (1954). Whiting acted in a handful of films in the 1930s, including the musicals *Top Speed* (1930), *Men of the Sky* (1931), *Sailing Along* (1938), and *Give Me a Sailor* (1938), and in a few television programs in the 1950s. His last New York stage appearance was as agent Charlie Davenport in the 1958 revival of *ANNIE GET YOUR GUN*.

WHITING, RICHARD A. (1891–1938). Film and stage composer. A versatile Hollywood composer, he scored eighteen movie musicals and, in most cases, the songs were much better than the films and became popular. Whiting was born in Peoria, Illinois, and began his career on Broadway contributing songs to the musical revues *Toot Sweet* (1919), *GEORGE WHITE'S SCANDALS* (1919 and 1928), *THE PASSING SHOW OF 1921* (1920), and *TAKE A CHANCE* (1932). With his career stuck, he started writing background music for silent films and when sound came in he scored such early musicals as *INNOCENTS OF PARIS* (1929), *The Dance of Life* (1929), *Sweetie* (1929), *Safety in Numbers* (1930), and *MONTE CARLO* (1930). Working with such lyricists as LEO ROBIN, B. G. DESYLVA, GEORGE MARION, JR., and JOHNNY MERCER, Whiting remained in Hollywood where the popularity of song hits such as "Louise" and "Too Marvelous for Words" made him a studio favorite even if most of his movies were not hits. Before his premature death, he scored such musicals as *ONE HOUR WITH YOU* (1932), *Adorable* (1933), *Take a Chance* (1933), *Transatlantic Merry-Go-Round* (1934), *BIG BROADCAST OF 1936* (1935), *Coronado* (1935), *Ready, Willing and Able* (1937), *VARSITY SHOW* (1937), *HOLLYWOOD HOTEL* (1937), and *Cowboy From Brooklyn* (1938). Songs such as "Ain't We Got Fun?," "Hooray for Hollywood," "On the Good Ship Lollipop," " Beyond the Blue Horizon," and "Japanese Sandman" were not only popular but often typified the era in which they were written. Whiting's movie songs were celebrated as part of the Broadway musical *A DAY IN HOLLYWOOD–A NIGHT IN THE UKRAINE* (1980). His daughter is singer Margaret Whiting (1924–).

WHOOPEE! (New Amsterdam 1928). A zany musical comedy tailored to the considerable talents of comic EDDIE CANTOR, the show also boasted a topnotch score by WALTER DONALDSON (music) and GUS KAHN (lyrics). The hypochondriac Henry Williams flees the East coast and goes to California for health reasons only to get involved with Indians, the damsel Sally Morgan on the run from an amorous sheriff, and other Wild West antics, such as Henry disguising himself as a black-faced waiter on the reservation who sings "Mammy" songs. WILLIAM ANTHONY McGUIRE wrote the libretto, which was based on the 1923 play *The Nervous Wreck*, and it provided enough sticky situations for the hero and Cantor made the most of them. He got strong support from comedienne Ethel Shutta and torch singer RUTH ETTING, who introduced the song standard "Love Me or Leave Me," which was not at

Casts for *Whoopee!*			
Character	*1928 Broadway*	*1930 film*	*1979 Broadway*
Henry Williams	EDDIE CANTOR	Eddie Cantor	Charles Repole
Mary Custer	Ethel Shutta	Ethel Shutta	Carol Swarbrick
Wanenis	Paul Gregory	Paul Gregory	Franc Luz
Sally Morgan	Frances Upton	Eleanor Hunt	Beth Austin
Sheriff	Jack Rutherford	Jack Rutherford	J. Kevin Scannell
Black Eagle	Chief Capolican	Chief Capolican	Leonard Drum
Jerome Underwood	Spencer Charles	Spencer Charters	Peter Boyden
Chester Underwood	ALBERT HACKETT	Albert Hackett	Garrett M. Brown
Ma-ta-pe/Matafly	Sylvia Adam	Lou-Scha-Enya	Candy Darling
Leslie Daw	RUTH ETTING		

all in keeping with the frivolous nature of the show. Cantor got to sing the musical's other big hit, the sly and suggestive "Makin' Whoopee." Also heard were "(I'm Bringing a) Red Red Rose," "Until You Get Somebody Else," "Gypsy Joe," and "Stetson." McGuire directed the FLORENZ ZIEGFELD production, which was choreographed by SEYMOUR FELIX and TAMARA GEVA, and it ran 379 performances. A 1979 Broadway revival of *Whoopee!*, which originated at the GOODSPEED OPERA HOUSE in Connecticut, featured Cantor look-alike Charles Repole and was directed by Frank Coprsar and choreographed by DAN SIRETTA. The score was altered but the spirit of the original came through and the production ran 204 performances.

Whoopee! (Goldwyn/United Artists 1930) was sometimes stagy and frequently primitive, yet it is an important film in the developing movie musical for it has some wonderfully cinematic moments. Producer SAM GOLDWYN bought the rights and brought Cantor and several of the stage principals to Hollywood, although only three stage songs were retained from the Broadway score. William Conselman's screenplay is a simplified version of the libretto that is less wacky, and Thornton Freeland directed perfunctorily. It was choreographer BUSBY BERKELEY's choreography that made the picture unique. Berkeley promised Goldwyn that he would break away from the static way productions numbers in movie musicals were usually filmed. He made good on his claim, getting rid of multiple cameras so that each number had one specific point of view, filming the chorus girls in close up for the first time and putting the camera overhead and creating the first of his famous kaleidoscope shots of women making geometric patterns. *Whoopee!* also marked Cantor's first starring role on the screen and his daffy

performance made him a movie star. "Love Me or Leave Me" was dropped but "Makin' Whoopee" was retained as was "Stetson," which was filmed ingeniously by Berkeley with the chorines popping up in front of the camera sporting hats. The best of the new numbers was Donaldson and Kahn's "My Baby Just Cares for Me." Ziegfeld served as consultant on the film, which used a new two-color Technicolor process that was impressive.

WHO'S EARNEST? (1957 CBS-TV). Oscar Wilde's 1895 classic comedy of manners *The Importance of Being Earnest* was musicalized for this sixty-minute *U.S. Steel Hour* broadcast and, while the witty Irishman may have been shortchanged in the greatly abridged teleplay, there was a delightful Wildean score to help compensate. Both Jack Worthing (David Atkinson) and Algernon Moncrief (Edward Mulhare) claim their names to be Earnest in order to woo the ladies Gwendolyn (Louise Troy) and Cecily (Dorothy Collins). The pompous Lady Bracknell (Edith King) is not about to allow either relationship to get to the altar until the forgetful Miss Prism (Nydia Westman) reveals that Jack is really of noble birth and was named Earnest. Martyn Green, Rex O'Malley, and Gordon Peters rounded out the superior cast who handled the Wilde dialogue (what was left of it) with aplomb. Anne Croswell adapted the three-act comedy and provided the lyrics for Lee Pockriss's music. The songs, which were often delicious extensions of the play's risible and ridiculous sense of humor, included "Perfection," "A Wicked Man," "My Eternal Devotion," "Mr. Bunbury," and "Metaphorically Speaking." Critical reaction to the show was encouraging enough that Croswell and Pockriss expanded the piece into a full-length stage musical and it was produced Off Broadway in 1960 under the title

Earnest in Love. The new numbers included "A Handbag Is Not a Proper Mother," "The Muffin Song," "How Do You Find the Words?," and the title number. Reviews were favorable and the clever, intimate musical ran 111 performances.

WHO'S TOMMY, THE. *See TOMMY*

⧉ **WICKED** (Gershwin Theatre 2003). A big, colorful musical with performances as spectacular as the technical effects, the show was unique in that it was about the friendship of two dissimilar women rather than about romantic love. On the day that the Wicked Witch of the West melts, the citizens of Oz celebrate, but the good witch Glinda (KRISTIN CHENOWETH) recalls the full story of her friend Elphaba (IDINA MENZEL), an awkward loner who was born green and wanted to do good in the world. At school together, Glinda and Elphaba are mismatched roommates but gradually become friends and remain so even after Glinda's fiancée Fiyero (NORBERT LEO BUTZ) leaves her for Elphaba. When the two girls finally meet the Wizard (JOEL GREY), Elphaba realizes that the power-hungry sorcerer is truly evil and, defying him, she is labeled "wicked" by the establishment. Taking on the witch form thrust on her, Elphaba stages a fake death by melting and then runs off with Fieryo. Also featured in the large cast were Carole Shelley, Michelle Federer, and Christopher Fitzgerald. Winnie Holzman adapted Gregory Maguire's imaginative novel, and STEPHEN SCHWARTZ wrote the vibrant score, which included "Defying Gravity," "As Long As You're Mine," "Popular," "No One Mourns the Wicked," "For Good," "I'm Not That Girl," "The Wizard and I," "Wonderful," and "Dancing Through Life." JOE MANTELLO directed and WAYNE CILENTO choreographed the stunning production, which was dismissed by most of the press as a humdrum affair with some vivid performances. Audiences disagreed and the show soon became one of the most successful musicals of its era. The production also secured the promise of Chenoweth and made Menzel a bona fide Broadway star.

WICKES, MARY [born Mary Isabelle Wickenhauser] (1916–1995). Stage, film, and television performer. The tall, gawky character actress was one of the most familiar faces in films and on television, although she rarely had a major role; all the same she often stole the show playing wisecracking spinsters, aunts, housekeepers, and secretaries. Wickes was born in St. Louis and educated locally at Washington University before working in stock. She made her Broadway debut in 1934 and was cast as busybodies and sidekicks in comedies and musicals such as *Stars in Your Eyes* (1939), *Jackpot* (1944), *Hollywood Pinafore* (1945), and *Park Avenue* (1946). Wickes made her first film in 1935 and her wry comic touch played well on the screen. Among her musical credits were *Private Buckaroo* (1942), *HIGHER AND HIGHER* (1943), *Rhythm of the Islands* (1943), *On Moonlight Bay* (1951), *I'll See You in My Dreams* (1951), *By the Light of the Silvery Moon* (1953), *WHITE CHRISTMAS* (1954), *THE MUSIC MAN* (1962), *Sister Act* (1992), and *Sister Act 2: Back in the Habit* (1993). In 1979 she returned to Broadway to play Aunt Eller in a revival of *OKLAHOMA!* Wickes appeared in dozens of television programs and provided voices for animated movies, most memorably her last credit as one of the gargoyles in *THE HUNCHBACK OF NOTRE DAME* (1996).

WILCOX, HERBERT (1892–1977). Film director and producer. The Irish-born showman made a name for himself in Europe before coming to America and presenting some musicals for Hollywood. Wilcox was born in Cork County, Ireland, and after serving as a British flying ace in World War I entered the film business in England in 1922, quickly establishing himself as a producer and director who knew what the public wanted. He founded Elstree Studios in 1926 and used it to make ANNA NEAGLE (whom he later married) the biggest star in British cinema. Among the Wilcox–Neagle musicals in England were *BITTER SWEET* (1933), *The Courtneys of Curzon Street* (1947), and *King's Rhapsody* (1954). The duo came to America in 1939 to make a few musicals for RKO, most memorably *IRENE* (1940), *NO, NO, NANETTE* (1941), and *SUNNY* (1941). Wilcox never became a powerful Hollywood player but continued to make films in Europe through the 1950s. Autobiography: *Twenty-Five Thousand Sunsets* (1967).

⧉ **WILD PARTY, THE** (Virginia Theatre 2000). A dark musical play by MICHAEL JOHN LA CHIUSA (book, music, and lyrics) and George C. Wolfe (book), it was unrelenting in its nightmarish style and very demanding fare for Broadway. The 1920s vaudeville performers and lovers Queenie (Toni Collette) and Burrs (MANDY PATINKIN) throw a decadent, gin-soaked party for friends and their hangers-on. During the festivities, Queenie is attracted to the gangster Black (Yancey Arias), the kept man of her friend and rival Kate (TONYA PINKINS), which raises Burrs' jealousy and ends in bloodshed. Most memorable among the partygoers was the ageless EARTHA KITT as the show biz trouper Dolores still trying to make deals for her career. Also in the talented cast were MARC KUDISCH, Leah Hocking, Norm Lewis, Jane Summerhays, Sally Murphy, Brooke Sunny Moriber, Michael McElroy, Nathan Lee Graham, and Stuart Zagnit. The songs, excellent pastiches of the jazzy Roaring Twenties, included "People Like Us," "Uptown," "The Lights of Broadway," "How Many Women in the World?," "Wouldn't It Be Nice," "When It Ends," and "The Movin' Uptown Blues." Based on Joseph Moncure March's narrative poem, the challenging musical, directed by Wolfe and choreographed by JOEY MCKNEELY, and its gifted cast impressed reviewers without really pleasing them and so the notices were ambivalent. Confused playgoers patronized the difficult yet hypnotic show for sixty-eight performances. That same season saw another musical version of Moncure's poem, also titled *The Wild Party* (2000), that was produced Off Broadway by the Manhattan Theatre Club. Andrew Lippa wrote the libretto and the score and, since it stuck close to the source material, the characters and most of the story were identical to the La Chiusa musical. Only the songs were radically different, with Lippa using a more pop and rock sound in the score. Among the notable numbers were "Out of the Blue," "An Old-Fashioned Love Story," "Raise the Roof," "Look at Me Now," "Come With Me," and "Who Is This Man?" The Off Broadway cast, just as accomplished as the Broadway one, featured Julia Murney (Queenie), BRIAN D'ARCY JAMES (Burrs), Taye Diggs (Black), IDINA MENZEL (Kate), and Kena Tangi Dorsey (Dolores). Critical reaction was as mixed as it was for the Broadway effort but the limited engagement of fifty-four performances was well attended.

👁 *WILDCAT* (Alvin Theatre 1960). A raucous musical vehicle for television star LUCILLE BALL, the problematic show had a vivacious score but a story so thin that no star could save it. The gutsy Wildcat Jackson (Ball) arrives in the Wild West town of Centavo City in 1912 with her crippled sister Janie (Paula Stewart) and claims to have oil rights to the place. She hoodwinks Joe Dynamite (Keith Andes) into joining the scheme and soon everyone in town is drilling and digging for oil. Just as

she's about to be exposed as a fraud, Wildcat throws a stick of dynamite into a well and oil gushes forth. Ball's singing talents were limited but she threw all her energy into the part, getting more respect than praise from the press. Her supporting cast was very strong and included Swen Swenson, Edith King, Clifford David, Howard Fischer, and Charles Braswell. N. Richard Nash penned the tattered libretto and CY COLEMAN (music) and CAROLYN LEIGH (lyrics) provided the lively songs, with the two best being the hit "Hey, Look Me Over" and the hoe-down number "What Takes My Fancy," which MICHAEL KIDD choreographed masterfully. Despite lackluster notices, audiences wanted to see Lucy and came for 171 performances; when she left the show, it folded and hasn't been heard of since.

WILDER, [Samuel] **BILLY** (1906–2002). Film director and screenwriter. The celebrated creator of many Hollywood classics was equally adept at comedies as with taut melodramas and even worked on a handful of musical films. Wilder was born in Poland and worked as a newspaper reporter in Vienna and Berlin before breaking into movies by scripting German films in the early 1930s. The Jewish writer fled the Nazis in 1933 and worked on films in Paris before coming to America and by 1938 established himself as a scriptwriter with such successes as *Ninotchka* (1939) and *Ball of Fire* (1942). Wider's direction of *Double Indemnity* (1944) placed him in the top ranks of Hollywood directors, although he often continued writing or co-writing his films, as with *Sunset Boulevard* (1950), *Some Like It Hot* (1959), *The Apartment* (1960), and others. Throughout his career he had a passing acquaintance with musicals, scripting such Hollywood products as *MUSIC IN THE AIR* (1934), *RHYTHM ON THE RIVER* (1940), and *A Song Is Born* (1948), and directing *The Emperor Waltz* (1947), *A Foreign Affair* (1948), and *Kiss Me Stupid* (1964). Biography: *On Sunset Boulevard: The Life and Times of Billy Wilder*, Ed Sikov (1998).

👁 *WILDFLOWER* (Casino Theatre 1923). A long forgotten musical from the Roaring Twenties, the show was a showcase for the popular Broadway star EDITH DAY and the biggest hit of its season. The Lombardi farm girl Nina Benedetto (Day) has a fiery temper and it doesn't take much to set her off. All the same, she is loved by the local lad Guido (GUY ROBERTSON) and the two foresee a happy, if sometimes tempestuous, life together. Then Nina inherits a sizable amount of money and a villa on Lake Como but if she loses her temper, even once over the next six months, all the money goes to her cousin Bianca (Evelyn Cavanaugh). Bianca plots several different ways to provoke Nina to anger but, with the help of Guido, Nina perseveres and she gets the money and the man. OSCAR HAMMERSTEIN and OTTO HARBACH wrote the libretto and the lyrics for music by VINCENT YOUMANS and HERBERT STOTHART, and two hits came from the score, the vivacious "Bambalina" and the title song. Also heard were "April Blossoms," "I Love You, I Love You, I Love You," "If I Told You," "Goodbye, Little Rosebud," and "The World's Worst Woman." Critics balked at the feeble plot but audience favorite Edith Day lit up the stage and, backed by a fun score and plenty of dancing, the show ran 477 performances and then toured for two seasons. The ARTHUR HAMMERSTEIN production, directed by Oscar Eagle and choreographed by David Bennett, launched Youman's career but it marked the end of Day's Broadway days; after its run she moved to London where she remained for the rest of her long and successful career.

WILDHORN, FRANK (1960–). Stage composer and lyricist. Never a critics' favorite, the busy songwriter has conquered the world of pop music and Broadway, sometimes at the same time. Wildhorn was raised in Hollywood, Florida, and as a self-taught musician played in bands as a teenager. He attended Miami University for a while and then completed his studies at the University of Southern California where he wrote original musicals, which got him a contract writing pop songs. Over the years he has had some 250 of his songs recorded and/or published and has sold over 50 million records. However, Wildhorn's heart was in theatre and he struggled for years to bring his musical *JEKYLL & HYDE* (1990) to Broadway. The critics carped but the audiences embraced it, with some fans so dedicated that they were dubbed "Jekies." He followed this with the period musical *THE SCARLET PIMPERNEL* (1997), which went through three different revised versions on Broadway. *The Civil War* (1998) and *Dracula, the Musical* (2004) had short runs but he has seen other works produced regionally and workshopped in New York so Wildhorn's career is far from over. He also contributed to the stage version of *VICTOR/VICTORIA* (1995) when the film's composer HENRY MANCINI died.

WILL ROGERS FOLLIES, THE (Palace Theatre 1991). A musical biography that made little pretense of being an accurate account of the famous stage–screen–radio personality, its lack of content was covered by a lavish and clever production. PETER STONE's libretto about the life and times of comic commentator Will Rogers (Keith Carradine) was told as if it were an edition of the ZIEGFELD FOLLIES, complete with beautifully costumed girls parading down long staircases and extraneous acts showing off rope twirling and performing dogs. Also featured in the cast were Cady Huffman, Dee Hoty, and Paul Ukena, Jr. CY COLEMAN (music), BETTY COMDEN, and ADOLPH GREEN (lyrics) provided the songs, which were serviceable but not memorable. The score included "Never Met a Man I Didn't Like," "Will-a-Mania," "Presents for Mrs. Rogers," "Give a Man Enough Rope," "Favorite Son," and "My Big Mistake." Although it was practically plotless and what little story there was was deemed unexciting by the critics, the musical was satisfying entertainment for entertainment's sake only, thanks to the ingenious direction and choreography by TOMMY TUNE. Approving notices for the cast and the colorful production helped the show run 983 performances.

WILLIAMS, BERT [born Egbert Austin Williams] (1874?–1922). Stage and film performer. America's first (and arguably best) mainstream African American comedian, he performed in theatres that no black entertainer had played before and broke new ground by starring with white players on Broadway. Williams was born on the island of Antiqua in the West Indies and came to the States as a child. He was light-skinned, handsome, very intelligent, and had a deep, musical voice, but he learned to portray a shuffling, mumbling caricature on stage. Williams began in minstrel shows and then moved on to vaudeville; he and his partner George W. Walker (1880?–1911) became very popular and were featured in the Broadway musicals *IN DAHOMEY* (1903), *Abyssinia* (1906), *Bandanna Land* (1908), and *Mr. Lode of Koal* (1909), as well as Williams alone in *ZIEGFELD FOLLIES* (1910). After the premature death of Walker, Williams went solo and appeared in the star spot in seven more editions of the *Follies* between 1911 and 1919. His final Broadway appearance was in the revue *Broadway Brevities of 1920*. Williams produced, wrote, directed, and starred in two silent features in the 1910s, the first African American to become a filmmaker. His act stayed much the same throughout his career. He blacked his face to appear more negroid, dressed as a tramp with a tattered top hat, moaned about his troubles, and sang his signature song "Nobody," which he composed himself. Williams made many recordings, which were very popular in the 1920s, and he was still at the peak of his career when he died at the age of forty-seven.

WILLIAMS, ESTHER [born Ester Jane Williams] (1923–). Film and television performer. Dubbed the "Queen of the Surf" and "Hollywood's Mermaid," the attractive, shapely actress was the best (and only) swimming star of the movies and most of her vehicles were musicals. Williams was born in Los Angeles and by her teen years was already a champion swimmer. She studied at Los Angeles City College for a time while doing some modeling and then was hired for BILLY ROSE's Aquacade. A talent agent spotted her and she was cast in a few Andy Hardy films before taking to the water on screen for the first time in *Bathing Beauty* (1944). Williams was an immediate hit with the public so a series of films were written around her limited singing but outstanding swimming and diving talents. Among her musical credits are *Thrill of a Romance* (1945), *ZIEGFELD FOLLIES* (1946), *Fiesta* (1947), *This Time for Keeps* (1947), *On an Island With You* (1948), *TAKE ME OUT TO THE BALL GAME* (1949), *NEPTUNE'S DAUGHTER* (1949), *Duchess of Idaho* (1950), *Pagan Love Song* (1950), *Texas Carnival* (1951), *Skirts Ahoy* (1952), *Million Dollar Mermaid* (1952), *Dangerous When Wet* (1953), *Easy to Love* (1953), *Jupiter's Darling* (1955), and *The Big Show* (1960). When she turned to dramatic, nonswimming roles, Williams lost her popularity so she retired to promote swimming competitions and exhibitions. She has appeared occasionally on television and at special events. Among her husbands was FERNANDO LAMAS. Autobiography: *The Million Dollar Mermaid* (1999).

WILLIAMS, PAUL (1940–). Film and television composer, lyricist and performer. A pint-sized actor and singer with a full-size talent for writing pop songs, he has contributed both scores and individual songs for Hollywood movies. Williams was born in Omaha, Nebraska, and as a teenager was an apprentice jockey and tried other jobs until he turned to acting in summer stock productions. By the 1960s he was getting bit parts in films but became more famous in the 1970s for his songs on the charts. He scored and played the villain Swan in *PHANTOM OF THE PARADISE*

(1974), a rock satire of *Phantom of the Opera*, and did some of the vocals for the songs he wrote for the kids–gangster musical *BUGSY MALONE* (1976). Williams' other film scores include *A STAR IS BORN* (1976), *THE MUPPET MOVIE* (1979), *A Muppet Christmas Carol* (1992), and the original TV musical *The Night They Saved Christmas* (1984), as well as theme songs for a number of nonmusical movies and television shows, such as "The Love Boat." His other hit songs include "Just an Old-Fashioned Love Song," "We've Only Just Begun," "The Rainbow Connection," and "Evergreen." *Bugsy Malone* has been adapted for the stage, and his musical based on the TV series *Happy Days* has recently been produced in England, Australia, and regionally in the States. Williams has appeared on numerous television shows and continues to act in the movies. A former victim of drug abuse, he is a public advocate for awareness of drug and alcohol addiction.

WILLIAMS, [Richard] **TREAT** (1951–). Film, stage, and television performer. A rugged, good-looking leading man who has aged with grace, he occasionally dipped into musicals on Broadway and in Hollywood. Williams was born in Rowayton, Connecticut, the son of a business executive and a descendant of Robert Treat Payne, a signer of the Declaration of Independence. He was educated at Franklin and Marshall College and worked in regional theatre before making his Broadway debut as a replacement for Danny Zuko in *GREASE* (1973). Williams played the World War II G.I. Utah in *OVER HERE!* (1974) and then found fame in the movies playing in dramas, comedies, and in the screen version of *HAIR* (1979). He returned to Broadway as a replacement for the Pirate King in the popular revival of *THE PIRATES OF PENZANCE* (1981) and appeared Off Broadway as the Portuguese fisherman Manuel in the musical *Captains Courageous* (1999). Williams' most recent musical credit is the two-timing Buddy Plummer in the 2001 Broadway revival of *FOLLIES*. He has acted in many television drama specials and series but, as with his many movies, his musical talents are not utilized.

WILLS, CHILL [Theodore] (1903–1978). Film and television performer. A crusty character actor who added rustic flavor to many movies, he rarely sang on screen in musicals but often broke into song in westerns. Wills was born in Seagoville, Texas, and was on stage as a child performing in vaudeville and stock before forming a singing group called the Avalon

Boys in the 1930s. The group was featured in a few films, including the musical *ANYTHING GOES* (1936). By the late 1930s Wills was working solo and playing bit parts on the screen, eventually becoming a familiar favorite. His most famous role was never seen: as the voice of Francis the talking mule in a series of popular comedies in the 1950s. Among the musicals Wills was featured in were *Honky Tonk* (1941), *BEST FOOT FORWARD* (1943), *MEET ME IN ST. LOUIS* (1944), *THE HARVEY GIRLS* (1946), *Small Town Girl* (1953), and *Where the Boys Are* (1960). Wills appeared in many television shows, mostly westerns, and never gave up his singing; he released an album in 1975.

WILLSON, MEREDITH [born Robert Meredith Reinger] (1902–1984). Stage and television composer, lyricist, writer, and conductor. The veteran musical director had a late but impressive career writing Broadway musicals, most memorably *THE MUSIC MAN* (1957). Willson was born in Mason City, Iowa, the son of a piano teacher, and took piccolo and flute lessons and played in the civic band. After studying music at Juilliard, he played flute in JOHN PHILIP SOUSA's band and by 1924 was a member of the New York Philharmonic under Toscanini. Willson later became music director at ABC and conducted on several popular radio shows, writing songs for some of them, such as "You and I" and "May the Lord Bless and Keep You." His boyhood in Iowa served as the background for his first Broadway musical, the smash hit *The Music Man*, which he scripted with Franklin Lacy and wrote both music and lyrics, and it was turned into a very successful film in 1962. His two other musicals were not as popular but had admirable scores: *THE UNSINKABLE MOLLY BROWN* (1960), which was filmed in 1964, and *Here's Love* (1963), a musicalization of the film *The Miracle on 34th Street* (1947). Willson's remarkable talent for creating sentimental yet sly characters, highly rhythmic music, and mesmerizing lyrics made his work distinctive and, in the case of *The Music Man*, unforgettably unique. Autobiography: *But He Doesn't Know the Territory* (1959).

▦ WILLY WONKA AND THE CHOCOLATE FACTORY (Wolper/Paramount 1971). The odd but engaging musical version of Roald Dahl's story *Charlie and the Chocolate Factory* was supposed to be for kids but it had a dark subtext (as all of Dahl's books have) that made it more nightmarish than simple fantasy. David Seltzer's screenplay stuck fairly close to the

original, centering on the English lad Charlie Bucket (Peter Ostrum) who is one of the lucky winners of a candy manufacturer's contest and is invited, with four obnoxious kids from different parts of the globe, to tour the candy factory run by the eccentric Willy Wonka (Gene Wilder). The tour turns out to be a test of character, which the other children fail miserably and for which they are punished in ghastly ways. But Charlie and his Grandpa Joe (Jack Albertson) pass the test, inherit the factory, and go flying into the air in one of Wonka's many strange and wonderful contraptions. Dahl's book had verses in it that were chanted by the workers, called Oomp Loompas, but they were pretty much ignored and songs were written by ANTHONY NEWLEY and LESLIE BRICUSSE for the film, with "The Candy Man" being the big hit. More accomplished was the enchanting "Pure Imagination." Mel Stuart directed a cast that also included Roy Kinnear, Julie Dawn Cole, Leonard Stone, Denise Nickerson, Nora Denny, Paris Themmen, Ursula Reit, Michael Bollner, and Diana Sowle. Wilder gave a bizarre, intriguing performance as Wonka, and the set decor was often stunning. Sometimes maudlin, other times cruel, always fascinating, the movie took a while to gain the following it enjoys today on DVD. In 2005, Dahl's book was filmed again, this time using the original title *Charlie and the Chocolate Factory* and featuring Freddie Highmore as Charlie and Johnny Depp as Willy Wonka. Some of Dahl's verses were put to new music but the film was not a musical.

WILSON, DOOLEY [born Arthur Wilson] (1886?–1953). Stage and film performer. Forever remembered as the piano-playing Sam who crooned "As Time Goes By" in *Casablanca* (1943), the African American actor–singer played leading roles on Broadway before being reduced to a supporting player on screen. Wilson was born in Tyler, Texas, and started his career in vaudeville, singing and later playing the drums and leading a band. (He never learned the piano; his playing in *Casablanca* was by Eliot Carpenter.) After appearing in nightclubs in Chicago, New York, and Paris, Wilson made his Broadway debut as a detective in the comedy *Conjure Man Dies* (1938) and his talking film debut the next year. Wilson shone in the leading role of the troublesome Little Joe Jackson in the Broadway musical *CABIN IN THE SKY* opposite ETHEL WATERS, but the part was given to EDDIE ANDERSON for the 1943 film. Wilson's other major stage role was the escaped slave Pompey in *BLOOMER GIRL* (1944) in which he introduced "The Eagle and Me." On screen he played minor roles, although some were memorable. His musical movies include *Cairo* (1942), *STORMY WEATHER* (1943), *HIGHER AND HIGHER* (1943), and *Seven Days Ashore* (1944). Right before his death, Wilson was a regular on *Beulah*, the first television series starring African Americans.

WILSON, JOHN C[hapman]. (1899–1961). Stage producer and director. With a short but impressive list of Broadway credits, the producer-turned-director presented some musical favorites in the 1940s. Wilson was born in rural New Jersey and educated at Yale University where he prepared for a business career. After working as a stockbroker, Wilson became a Broadway producer when he befriended NOEL COWARD in 1925 and co-produced works by the British playwright as well as plays for the Lunts and the THEATRE GUILD. By the 1940s, Wilson was directing some of his own productions and proved to be adept at both sophisticated comedies and musicals. Among his works in the latter category were the 1941 revival of *A CONNECTICUT YANKEE*, *The Day Before Spring* (1945), *KISS ME, KATE* (1948), *GENTLEMEN PREFER BLONDES* (1949), *Make a Wish* (1951), and *Seventh Heaven* (1955).

WILSON, MARY LOUISE (1932–). Stage, television, and film performer. A pinch-faced, wiry character actress with a distinctive sharp voice and a talent for outspoken women, her musical credits are limited but include many memorable performances. Wilson was born in New Haven, Connecticut, and was educated at Northwestern University before making her Manhattan debut in a revival of *Our Town* (1959). After appearing in the musicals *Dime a Dozen* (1962) and *Hot Spot* (1963), she was noticed as the strident communist Ada in *FLORA, THE RED MENACE* (1965). Wilson's notable musical roles include a replacement for the tipsy Marge MacDougall in *PROMISES, PROMISES* (1970), the crafty Mrs. Peachum in *THE BEGGAR'S OPERA* (1972), the stripper Tessie Tura in the 1974 revival of *GYPSY*, the Berlin landlady Fraulein Schneider in the popular 1998 revival of *CABARET*, and the eccentric recluse Edith Bouvier Beale in *GREY GARDENS* (2006). In addition to many nonmusical plays, she has appeared in several television series and specials and in a handful of movies, including the musical *THE BEST LITTLE WHOREHOUSE IN TEXAS* (1982).

WILSON, PATRICK [Joseph] (1973–). Stage, film, and television performer. An affable, attractive, and traditional leading man in Broadway musicals, he has shone in both revivals and new works. Wilson was born in Norfolk, Virginia, the son of a TV anchorman, and educated at Carnegie-Mellon University where he studied theatre. He began his career in regional theatre and in tours of *MISS SAIGON* and *CAROUSEL*, playing Billy Bigelow in London as well, and then made his New York debut in the Off Broadway musical *Bright Lights, Big City* (1999). Wilson appeared on Broadway in *The Gershwin's Fascinating Rhythm* (1999) before landing the leading role of unemployed Jerry Ludowski in *THE FULL MONTY* (2000), followed by Curly in the 2002 Broadway revival of *OKLAHOMA!* He was chosen among many possibilities to play Raul in the film version of *THE PHANTOM OF THE OPERA* (2004). In addition to *Barefoot in the Park* (2006) on Broadway, he has acted in other nonmusicals on screen and television, most memorably *Angels in America* (2003). Wilson has also performed as soloist with leading symphony orchestras.

WIMAN, DWIGHT DEERE (1895–1951). Stage producer. The busy presenter of plays on Broadway, he also produced fourteen musicals, including five Rodgers and Hart shows. Wiman was born in Moline, Illinois, the son of a successful manufacturer, and was educated at Yale University where he studied theatre under MONTY WOOLLEY. He began his career as an actor and appeared in a few silent films in the early 1920s before turning to producing plays in partnership with William A. Brady, Jr. The team had a few hits and then Wiman went solo and presented the innovative musical revue *THE LITTLE SHOW* (1929), followed by new editions in 1930 and 1931. He presented the dance musical *ON YOUR TOES* (1936) by RICHARD RODGERS (music) and LORENZ HART (lyrics) and went on to produce the team's *BABES IN ARMS* (1937), *I Married an Angel* (1938), *HIGHER AND HIGHER* (1940), and *BY JUPITER* (1942). His other musical credits were *GAY DIVORCE* (1932), *Champagne, Sec* (1933), *Great Lady* (1938), *Stars in Your Eyes* (1939), *STREET SCENE* (1947), and *Dance Me a Song* (1950). Wiman also presented some forty nonmusicals during his career.

◻ **WIND IN THE WILLOWS, THE** (ABC-TV 1987). While sections of Kenneth Grahame's children's novel had been animated by WALT DISNEY and others, this two-hour animated musical includes all the major events and characters in the episodic book. The reckless and carefree Mr. Toad (voice of CHARLES NELSON REILLY) sets off on his adventures with his friends Badger (JOSÉ FERRER), Mole (EDDIE BRACKEN), and Ratty (Roddy McDowall), piloting a steamboat down the river, heading a gypsy caravan, and driving a Rolls Royce, all with erratic abandon. Toad ends up in jail but escapes with his friends and drives off the destructive animals that have taken over his mansion Toad Hall. ROMEO MULLER wrote the breezy teleplay, and JULES BASS penned the lyrics for MAURY LAWS' music, resulting in such fun songs as "We Don't Have Any Pate De Foie Gras," "A Party That Never Ceases," "Benefit of Doubt," "Messin' Around in Boats," "I Hate Company," and the title number. Bass co-produced and co-directed with ARTHUR RANKIN, JR. 🐝 A Broadway musical version of The Wind in the Willows ran for only four performances in 1985. Critics were unimpressed with the libretto and the score but commended the sprightly cast, which included NATHAN LANE (Toad), Vicki Lewis (Mole), DAVID CARROLL (Ratty), and Irving Barnes (Badger).

WING, [Martha Virginia] **TOBY** (1915–2001). Film performer. Playing only bit parts or being featured in a musical number was enough to make the baby-faced, platinum blonde famous and an icon of sorts of the 1930s dame. Wing was born in Amelia Court House, Virginia, the daughter of an army officer, and grew up in the American South and the Panama Canal Zone. When the family moved to Los Angeles she appeared in silent shorts and features, leading her to be chosen as one of the Goldwyn Girls. When sound came in, Wing was cast as sexy waitresses, admiring coeds, or peroxided chorines in talkies, including the musicals *Palmy Days* (1931), *The Kid From Spain* (1933), *42ND STREET* (1933), *College Humor* (1933), *Too Much Harmony* (1933), *Murder at the Vanities* (1934), *Kiss and Make-Up* (1934), *With Love and Kisses* (1936), and *Sing While You're Able* (1937). In each the camera would pick up Wing and she would be special, particularly when DICK POWELL sang "Young and Healthy" to her in *42nd Street*. After playing another bit part in *SWEETHEARTS* (1938), she went to Broadway where she was featured in Cole Porter's musical *You Never Know* (1938). When it failed to run, she retired from show business.

WINNINGER, CHARLES [born Karl Winninger] (1884–1969). Stage and film performer. A rotund, blustering comic actor, he usually played fathers, uncles, mayors, and other character types on Broadway and in Hollywood, including some important musicals. Born into a show business family in Athens, Wisconsin, Winninger quit school at the age of nine to tour the variety circuits with the Five Winninger Brothers. He also worked as a trapeze artist in the circus and in 1900 was employed on a show boat named (prophetically) *Cotton Blossom*. Winninger made his New York legit bow in the musical *The Yankee Girl* (1910) and appeared in book musicals, such as *The Wall Street Girl* (1912) and *Friendly Enemies* (1919), and revues, such as *The Cohan Revue* (1916 and 1917), *THE PASSING SHOW OF 1919*, and *ZIEGFELD FOLLIES* (1920). He created the role of the Bible salesman Jimmy Smith in *NO, NO, NANETTE* (1925), stopping the show with his rendition of "I Want to Be Happy." He was given an even better part in 1927 as Cap'n Andy Hawks in the original *SHOW BOAT*, a role he got to reprise on Broadway in 1932 and in the 1936 screen version. Winninger's other notable Broadway performances include the patriarch Dr. Owen Harding in *Through the Years* (1932), the Spanish plutocrat Don Emilio in *REVENGE WITH MUSIC* (1934), and the heroine's father, Dr. Walther Lessing, in the 1951 revival of *MUSIC IN THE AIR*. He made over thirty movies in Hollywood, including the musicals *Children of Dreams* (1931), *FLYING HIGH* (1931), *Three Smart Girls* (1937), *You Can't Have Everything* (1937), *Every Day's a Holiday* (1937), *BABES IN ARMS* (1939), *DESTRY RIDES AGAIN* (1939), *LITTLE NELLIE KELLY* (1941), *ZIEGFELD GIRL* (1941), *CONEY ISLAND* (1943), *BROADWAY RHYTHM* (1944), *STATE FAIR* (1945), *Living in a Big Way* (1947), and *Give My Regards to Broadway* (1948). He was married to actress–singer BLANCHE RING.

WISE, ROBERT [Earl] (1914–2005). Film director and producer. One of Hollywood's most respected directors, he only helmed five screen musicals in his career but two of them were landmarks. Wise was born in Winchester, Indiana, and attended Franklin College until his money ran out during the Depression. He began his film career as an assistant to a cutter and then did the sound effects for a handful of 1930s movies, including the musicals *THE GAY DIVORCEE* (1934) and *TOP HAT* (1935), before becoming a film editor for such important films as Orson Welles's *Citizen Kane* (1941) and *The Magnificent Ambersons* (1942). He started directing B movies in 1944 and immediately showed promise, although he would not graduate into the major league of filmmakers until his terse boxing film *The Set-Up* (1949). Wise directed dramas, comedies, and musicals, the most famous of the last category being WEST SIDE STORY (1961) and THE SOUND OF MUSIC, both of which he also produced. His other screen musicals were *Mystery in Mexico* (1948), *This Could Be the Night* (1957), and *STAR!* (1968).

🕭 **WISH YOU WERE HERE** (Imperial Theatre 1952). Songwriter HAROLD ROME's first book musical, the master of revue songs came up with a bright and engaging set of character songs. At the Jewish summer Camp Karefree where "friendships are formed to last a whole lifetime through," various romances between the staff and the campers develop, a few of them turning into marriage proposals. The cast, which included several promising performers, featured Patricia Marand, JACK CASSIDY, Sheila Bond, Paul Valentine, Sammy Smith, and Harry Clark. Director JOSHUA LOGAN and Arthur Kober wrote the libretto, based on Kober's popular comedy *Having Wonderful Time* (1936), and it was more disjointed than its source material but the bright performances and delectable Rome songs helped, particularly "Where Did the Night Go?," "Don José (of Far Rockaway)," "Social Director," and the flowing title number. The reviews were not encouraging but producers Logan and LELAND HAYWARD persevered and the show became an audience favorite, running 598 performances. It helped that there was a real swimming pool on stage for spectacle and that Eddie Fisher's recording of the title song was a bestseller.

📽 **WITH A SONG IN MY HEART** (Fox 1952). A biographical film whose plot, as they used to say, was torn right from the headlines, the musical was about the life of singer Jane Froman. The screenplay by producer Lamar Trotti was a two-handkerchief weeper so well acted by SUSAN HAYWARD and presented so smartly that it transcended its genre and still packs a wallop. Radio singer Froman (Hayward) from Cincinnati works her way to Broadway and is on the brink of stardom when World War II breaks out and she goes off to entertain the troops overseas. Her plane crashes in Portugal and Froman, left badly injured and partially paralyzed, undergoes years of treatment and operations before she makes her professional comeback. DAVID WAYNE was her husband Don Riss who shaped her career, Rory Calhoun was the pilot John Burn who rescued and then

fell in love with her, and Thelma Ritter was the nurse and friend Clancy who helped Froman survive her ordeal. Also in the cast were Robert Walker, UNA MERKEL, LYLE TALBOT, HELEN WESTCOTT, Robert Wagner, Leif Erickson, Richard Allan, and Max Showalter, directed by WALTER LANG with plenty of pathos. Froman herself did the vocals for Hayward and the twenty songs (all familiar hits ranging from "Blue Moon" to the title number) were beautifully presented. Most moving of all was the 1944 song "I'll Walk Alone" by JULE STYNE (music) and SAMMY CAHN (lyrics); Froman's recording of it became her biggest hit.

WITHERS, JANE (1926–). Film and television performer. The dark-haired, pudgy, bratty child star of the 1930s, she made an interesting contrast with her colleague SHIRLEY TEMPLE. Withers was born in Atlanta and was in vaudeville and on the radio as a young child. She made her screen debut at the age of six and was soon playing major kid roles, often being more mischievous and hyperactive than cute or charming. Wither's credits, which were usually B musicals, include *Bright Eyes* (1934), *This Is the Life* (1935), *Paddy O'Day* (1935), *Can This Be Dixie?* (1936), *The Holy Terror* (1937), and *Rascals* (1938). As a teenager she was cast in the musicals *Shooting High* (194), *Johnny Doughboy* (1942), and *My Best Gal* (1944), but as an adult she found little work and retired in 1947. Withers returned to public eye in a few films in the 1950s and 1960s and on television where she appeared in several shows but was mostly known for her commercials as Josephine the plumber. She has also done voices for Disney-animated films and television programs.

WIZ, THE. See *WIZARD OF OZ, THE*

WIZARD OF OZ, THE. One of the most timeless of all children's books in American literature, L. Frank Baum's 1900 story has inspired two movies and three popular Broadway musicals. All five versions are unique and reflect the spirit of the times in which they were created.

🕭 **The Wizard of Oz** (Majestic Theatre 1903). A musical spectacular that used the Baum book as an excuse for musical numbers and lavish pageantry, the show was popular in its day because it marked the legit debut of vaudeville clowns DAVID MONTGOMERY (Tin Man) and FRED STONE (Scarecrow). Although Baum himself wrote the libretto and the lyrics, the stage version differs somewhat from *The Wonderful Wizard of Oz*. A cyclone blows Dorothy and

The Wizard of Oz. In what other movie musical is every line of dialogue, every lyric, every face, and even every costume immediately recognized by young and old alike? The film is more than a classic, it is an American icon. For those who have been in a coma for the last seventy years, pictured are (left to right) Ray Bolger, Jack Haley, Judy Garland, and Bert Lahr. (Photofest)

her pet cow to the land of the Munchkins where she befriends the Scarecrow, Tin Man, and Lion and they travel to the Emerald City to meet the Wizard. Because of the casting of Montgomery and Stone, the role of the Lion was minor, as was the witch. Paul Tietjens and A. Baldwin Sloane wrote the music for such numbers as "Alas for a Man Without Brains" and "When You Love Love Love" but the more popular songs were by others and interpolated into the show, such as "Sammy" and "Hurrah for Baffin's Bay." Aside from the star comics, much of the success of the show was attributed to director–choreographer JULIAN MITCHELL who staged the extravaganza with flair. The musical ran 293 performances and inspired other large-scale family shows, most notably *BABES IN TOYLAND* (1903).

■ **The Wizard of Oz** (MGM 1939). Arguably the most beloved and continually popular Hollywood musical ever produced, the film has become such a part of American pop culture that it seems to have been created by magic. However, the troublesome movie went through a dozen scriptwriters, four directors, several cast changes (some after filming began), and one of the most complicated and difficult production histories on record.

Plot: Orphaned farm girl Dorothy Gale lives with her Uncle Henry and Aunt Em on a drab farm in Kansas and dreams of a world that is full of color and magic. When the local harridan Miss Gulch gets a sheriff's order to have Dorothy's troublesome dog Toto destroyed, Dorothy runs away with Toto, only to return home after visiting the traveling fortune teller Professor Marvel who tells her that her aunt needs her. A tornado lifts the farmhouse with Dorothy and Toto inside and it lands in Munchkinland, killing the Wicked Witch of the East. The pint-sized Munchkins are thrilled and celebrate the witch's death but the appearance of the deceased's sister, the Wicked Witch of the West, convinces Dorothy that she needs to return home to Kansas. The Good Witch Glinda instructs Dorothy to take the yellow brick road to the Emerald City where the mighty Wizard of Oz will grant her wish. On the way Dorothy befriends the Scarecrow, Tin Man, and Lion who accompany her to the Wizard in order to ask favors of their own. The Wizard will not see the four friends at first and when he does grant them an audience, he demands the broomstick of the Wicked Witch as payment for their wishes. After being captured and rescued from the witch's clutches, Dorothy accidentally melts the old crone by throwing water on her. With the broomstick in hand, Dorothy and her friends return to the Wizard only to find out that he is a fraud. Glinda reappears and tells Dorothy she only needs to wish herself home and the magic slippers she wears will make her wish come true. Dorothy awakes in Kansas, the whole experience in Oz being a dream she had after the tornado winds had knocked her unconscious, and she has a new appreciation of home.

Producers ARTHUR FREED and MERVYN LEROY both claimed credit for pitching the idea of a musical version of the Baum tale to MGM studio head Louis B. Mayer. Luckily the movie Mayer envisioned, with SHIRLEY TEMPLE as Dorothy and W. C. FIELDS as the Wizard, never materialized, and JUDY GARLAND shot to stardom for her innocent, sincere performance. RAY BOLGER, JACK HALEY, and BERT LAHR had the best screen roles of their careers as the Scarecrow, Tin Man, and Lion, and the rest of the cast was equally expert, including FRANK MORGAN who played a variety of roles, giving the cockeyed dream a kind of leitmotif. The production began filming with BUDDY EBSEN as the Tin Man but he got skin poisoning from the silver makeup and was hospitalized; Haley took over and a new makeup mixture was used. During filming MARGARET HAMILTON was burnt during one of the fiery explosions manufactured on the set. Trouble persisted even after filming as the length of the picture

Casts for *The Wizard of Oz* and *The Wiz*

Character	1903 Broadway	1939 film	*The Wiz* (Broadway)	*The Wiz* (film)
Dorothy	Anna Laughlin	JUDY GARLAND	Stephanie Mills	DIANA ROSS
Scarecrow	FRED STONE	RAY BOLGER	HINTON BATTLE	Michael Jackson
Tin Man	DAVID MONTGOMERY	JACK HALEY	TIGER HAYNES	Nipsey Russell
Lion	Arthur Hill	BERT LAHR	Ted Ross	Ted Ross
Wicked Witch of the West	Edith Hutchins	MARGARET HAMILTON		
Evelline Addaperle			Mabel King Clarice Taylor	Mabel King
Sir Dashemoff Daily	Bessie Wynn			
Tryxie Tryffle Glinda	Grace Kimball	BILLIE BURKE	Dee Dee Bridgewater	LENA HORNE
Wizard	Bobby Gaylor	FRANK MORGAN	ANDRE DE SHIELDS	Richard Pryor
Auntie Em		Clara Blandick	Tasha Thomas	THERESA MERRITT
Uncle Henry		Charley Grapewin		Stanley Greene

The Wizard of Oz and *The Wiz* Musical Numbers

1939 film *The Wizard of Oz*	1975 Broadway *The Wiz*
"Over the Rainbow"	"The Feeling We Once Had"
"Ding-Dong! The Witch Is Dead"	"Tornado Ballet"
"We're Off to See the Wizard"	"He's the Wizard"
"Follow the Yellow Brick Road"	"Soon As I Get Home"
"If I Only Had a Brian"	"I Was Born on the Day Before Yesterday"
"If I Only Had a Heart"	"Ease on Down the Road"
"If I Only Had the Nerve"	"Slide Some Oil to Me"
"The Merry Old Land of Oz"	"Mean Ol' Lion"
"If I Were King of the Forest"	"Be a Lion"
	"So You Wanted to Meet the Wizard"
	"To Be Able to Feel"
	"No Bad News"
	"Funky Monkeys"
	"Everybody Rejoice"
	"Who Do You Think You Are?"
	"Believe in Yourself"
	"Y'all Got It!"
	"Home"

worried the executives and musical numbers were cut, including the expensive, elaborate "The Jitterbug" dance and verses and dances by Dorothy's friends. Victor Fleming, KING VIDOR, GEORGE CUKOR, and RICHARD THORPE each directed different sections of the film, with BOBBY CONNOLLY doing the choreography, Cedric Gibbons and William Horning the imaginative sets, and Adrian the costumes.

Using twenty-nine sound stages and sixty-five different sets, the movie was one of the most expensive in the studio's record books.

HAROLD ARLEN (music) and E. Y. HARBURG (lyrics) penned one of filmdom's greatest scores, led by the Oscar-winning "Over the Rainbow," which was nearly left on the cutting room floor until wiser minds prevailed.

However, even that lovely song lost its introductory verse and much of the rest of the score was cut or abridged by the studio. Harburg foresaw a film with long extended musical scenes, a sort of fantasy operetta, and one can see how effectively it worked in the long Munchkinland sequence and the preparations in the Emerald City before Dorothy and her friends see the Wizard. Similar musical scenes were lost and the film ended up having no songs at all during its last twenty minutes. However, what is there is marvelous, from the jubilant "Ding-Dong! The Witch Is Dead" to the character numbers "If I Only Had a Brain/a Heart/the Nerve" to the farcical "If I Were King of the Forest." All of the numbers have become part of American folklore, just as every line in the screenplay is widely recognized even out of context. But even acknowledging the high quality of all the movie's elements doesn't quite explain why *The Wizard of Oz* is so special. Billed as a treat for "children of all ages," it goes beyond anyone's idea of a children's movie. It is very adult in many ways, from its expressionistic look (the change from back and white in Kansas to color for Oz was a bold idea) to its difficult themes of friendship and home. Arriving at the end of the Depression may have impacted the film, for it was immediately a hit with audiences and far beyond MGM's high hopes. However, the movie has been equally enjoyed by generations since. Perhaps *The Wizard of Oz* is the great American fantasy, a dream that still prevails within the hearts of moviegoers.

Stage versions of Hollywood's *The Wizard of Oz* have existed for amateur groups since the 1960s. These use the Arlen–Harburg songs but the script is very different from the film, leaving out major scenes and adding others. Not until the 1980s did regional theatres start producing the musical with a script that resembled the movie. New York saw a lavish stage version of the film script and score at Radio City Music Hall in 1989. There were no stars in the cast, yet the limited engagement of thirty-seven performances was very popular. In 1997 a huge production at the Madison Square Garden Theatre played for forty-seven performances. The cast included Jessica Grove (Dorothy), Roseanne Barr (Witch), Lara Teeter (Scarecrow), KEN PAGE (Lion), Michael Gruber (Tin Man), and Gerry Vichi (Wizard). The same production returned in 1998 with MICKEY ROONEY as the Wizard and EARTHA KITT as the Witch, and in 1999 with Rooney again and Joanne Worley as the Witch.

THE WIZ (Majestic Theatre 1975) was an updated version of Baum's tale with a funky, satirical flavor and peopled with African American characters and slangy street talk. William F. Brown wrote the lighthearted libretto in which Dorothy is blown away by a stylized cyclone to Munchkinland, the yellow brick road was represented by yellow-tuxedoed dancers, the Tin Man was made of modern garbage parts (hubcaps, beer cans, and so on), and the Wiz himself was a glittering revivalist with a rap-like patter. Charlie Smalls wrote the sparkling score, which had a Motown flavor, and the songs were often placed in the script differently from the movie so that there would be no direct comparisons. *The Wiz* was plagued with troubles on the road but when GEOFFREY HOLDER took over the direction and with GEORGE FAISON's vigorous choreography, the show pulled itself together and was joyously received by the press and the public, running 1,672 performances.

The Wiz (Universal 1978) was one of the most expensive, most misguided, and most reviled movies of the 1970s and it not only died at the box office but cast a shadow over the vibrant stage version, discouraging revivals for years. Producer Rob Cohen cast thirty-four-year-old DIANA ROSS, the only bankable female African American movie star, as Dorothy so Joel Schumacher's screenplay turned the heroine into a Harlem schoolteacher who is blown downtown which serves as a kind of Oz, although geographically Dorothy and her friends went in circles to end up at the World Trade Center as the Emerald City. Tony Walton's expressionistic sets were dazzling but made no sense, the actors were covered with so much makeup they may as well have been puppets, and the direction by Sidney Lumet was slow and vague. Louis Johnson's choreography had some lively moments, Mabel King was fun reprising her witch from the stage, and Richard Pryor was a fascinating Wiz, but much of the rest of the film was an embarrassment. Even the great LENA HORNE looked foolish singing her heart out in close-up, like a television special gone wrong. Making a movie out of *The Wiz* was not the easiest task, but no one expected such a fiasco. The most recent incarnation of Baum's story occurred in 2003 with the Broadway musical *WICKED*, which has its own entry. See also the animated *JOURNEY BACK TO OZ* (1972).

WODEHOUSE, P[elham] G[ranville] (1881–1975). Stage lyricist and writer. A prolific writer who only spent a small portion of his long career in the theatre, the British humorist greatly influenced the sound and shape of the Broadway musical. Born in Guildford, England, Wodehouse was educated at Dulwich College and worked in banking before turning to writing short stories in magazines for boys. He first made a name for himself as the author of comic short pieces and novels featuring such memorable characters as Bertie Wooster, Jeeves, Psmith, and Mr. Mulliner. Wodehouse came to America in 1915 and served as a drama critic for *Vanity Fair*, writing lyrics for *Miss Springtime* (1916) before meeting composer JEROME KERN and writer GUY BOLTON and contributing lyrics to their PRINCESS MUSICALS *Have a Heart* (1917), *Oh, Boy!* (1917), and *Oh, Lady! Lady!* (1918). His lyrics were sophisticated, yet colloquial, witty but highly accessible. The flowing words and deft rhymes were noticed by the critics and inspired a generation of young lyricists such as IRA GERSHWIN, COLE PORTER, and LORENZ HART, with the three men later publicly acknowledging Wodehouse as their idol and inspiration. Wodehouse collaborated with Kern on *LEAVE IT TO JANE* (1917), *Miss 1917* (1917), and *Sitting Pretty* (1924), and with other composers he wrote *The Riviera Girl* (1917), *Kitty Darlin'* (1917), *The Girl Behind the Gun* (1918), *The Canary* (1918), *Oh, My Dear* (1918), *The Rose of China* (1919), *The Nightingale* (1927), and *ROSALIE* (1928), as well as the books for *OH, KAY!* (1926) and *ANYTHING GOES* (1934). Wodehouse also contributed to a half-dozen London musicals in the early 1920s. By 1935 he had become disillusioned with the lack of control writers had in the musical theatre so he concentrated on nonmusical plays and novels, writing a total of ninety-six of the latter by the time he died. He also co-wrote the screenplay for the film musical *DAMSEL IN DISTRESS* (1937), which was based on one of his stories, as was the Broadway musical *By Jeeves* (2001). Autobiography: *Bring on the Girls! The Improbable Story of Our Life in Musical Comedy*, with Guy Bolton (1953); biography: *P. G. Wodehouse*, Francis Donaldson (2001).

WOLFE, GEORGE C. (1955–). Stage director, producer, and writer. One of the most successful of African American producing directors, he is also an accomplished playwright and a champion of new works, including some important musicals. Wolfe was born in Frankfort, Kentucky, the son of a government clerk and a teacher, and educated at Pomona College and New York University where he began to write and direct for the stage. In the 1970s he taught and directed in Los Angeles, making his professional directing debut in 1978. Wolfe relocated to New York in the 1980s, made his debut as a lyricist first, then as a playwright, and in 1990 as a director Off Broadway. Although the plays he wrote were often commended, in particular *The Colored Museum* (1986), Wolfe became more known for his staging of musicals, classic revivals, and new works. After working with the PUBLIC THEATRE for years, he was named its artistic director in 1993 where he staged a variety of theatre productions, some of which transferred to Broadway with success. His most notable nonmusical directing projects include *Angels in America* (1993) and *Topdog/Underdog* (2001). In many ways, Wolfe is at his boldest directing musicals, such as *JELLY'S LAST JAM* (1992), *BRING IN 'DA NOISE BRING IN 'DA FUNK* (1996), *THE WILD PARTY* (2000), and *CAROLINE, OR CHANGE* (2003), some of which he co-authored.

WOMAN OF THE YEAR (Palace Theatre 1981). Eleven years after her triumph in *APPLAUSE* (1970), LAUREN BACALL returned to the Broadway musical in this stage version of the popular 1942 Katherine Hepburn–Spencer Tracy film. PETER STONE wrote the libretto that changed the characters' occupations but kept the same battle of the sexes, updated to the 1980s. Brainy television talk-show hostess Tess Harding (Bacall) and satirical cartoonist Sam Craig (Harry Guardino) mock each other in public but when they finally meet face to face their disagreements lead to romance and then a tricky but hopeful marriage. Also featured in the cast were MARILYN COOPER, Roderick Cook, Grace Keagy, Eivind Harum, and Rex Everhart. The score by JOHN KANDER (music) and FRED EBB (lyrics) was far from their best, but there were still some pleasing numbers, such as "The Grass Is Always Greener," "One of the Boys," "So What Else Is New?," "When You're Right, You're Right," and "Sometimes a Day Goes By." ROBERT MOORE directed and Tony Charmoli choreographed the uneven musical and the reviews were not enthusiastic but the show ran 770 performances, thanks to the star power of Bacall whose limited singing–dancing talents did not stand in her way. After she left, *Woman of the Year* was kept afloat by star replacements Raquel Welch and DEBBIE REYNOLDS.

WONDER BAR (Warner 1934). A soft-boiled melodrama with songs, the AL JOLSON film told of the racy doings during one night at a Paris nightclub of the title. Earl Baldwin's screenplay focused on the club's proprietor, Al Wonder (Jolson), who has set his heart on cabaret singer Inez (DOLORES DEL RIO) but so has the club's crooner Tom (DICK POWELL). Inez cares for neither of them, with her affections going to her dancing partner Harry the Gigolo (Ricardo Cortez) who is, to say the least, not a one-woman man. Patrons Henry Simpson (GUY KIBBEE) and Corey Pratt (HUGH HERBERT) are trying to lose their wives (Louise Fazenda and Ruth Donnelly) in order to chase two of the Wonder Bar's hostesses, Mitzi (Fifi D'Orsay) and Claire (Merna Kennedy). The evening's complications climax when the socialite Liane Renaud (Kay Francis) sinks her hooks into Harry, he likes it, and Inez stabs him to death in a fit of jealousy. Based on one of Jolson's few Broadway flops, the musical was directed by LLOYD BACON in the tough WARNER BROTHERS style of the 1930s and BUSBY BERKELEY staged the dances in his usual fantasy vein. One sequence, "Goin' to Heaven on a Mule," in which heaven was depicted with hundreds of "Negroes" eating watermelon while they sang and danced, was considered in bad taste even in its day. Berkeley was in better form with "Don't Say Goodnight," which was staged with chorus girls dancing in front of revolving mirrors, with the handful of chorines turning into thousands in the many reflections. HARRY WARREN (music) and AL DUBIN (lyrics) wrote the score, which also included the enthralling ballad "Why Do I Dream Those Dreams?" and the snappy title tune.

Wonderful Town. The songwriters Bernstein, Comden, and Green celebrated New York City of the 1940s in *On the Town* (1944). A decade later they returned to New York of the 1930s with *Wonderful Town.* Pictured is Rosalind Russell as Ruth Sherwood, finding some Brazilian naval cadets obsessed with the "Conga!" (Photofest)

🎭 **WONDERFUL TOWN** (Winter Garden Theatre 1953). One of the best "New York" musicals, the sprightly show celebrated life in Greenwich Village in the 1930s. JOSEPH FIELDS and JEROME CHODOROV adapted their long-running comedy *My Sister Eileen* (1940) for the musical stage and it lost none of its laughs and gained a splendid score by LEONARD BERNSTEIN (music), BETTY COMDEN, and Adolph Green (lyrics). The acerbic Ruth Sherwood comes to New York City from Ohio with her pretty sister Eileen where they take lodgings in a Greenwich Village basement apartment. While Ruth pursues a writing career, Eileen hopes to become an actress. The city is not hospitable but eventually through new-made friends and cockeyed luck both end up with a sweetheart and a job. Among the highlights of the musical version were Ruth's riotous dance with some Brazilian sailors as they sang "Conga!" and a satirical nightclub act in a Greenwich Village

watering hole with everyone singing and dancing to the "Wrong Note Rag." Other delectable songs from the show include the homesick ballad "Ohio," the revelatory "It's Love," the comic lament "One Hundred Easy Ways (To Lose a Man)," and the soothing ballads "A Quiet Girl" and "Never Felt This Way Before (A Little Bit in Love)." ROSALIND RUSSELL got the best musical role of her career as Ruth, EDIE ADAMS became a Broadway star as Eileen, and their fellow players were also expert. GEORGE ABBOTT directed the Robert Fryer production, which was choreographed by DONALD SADDLER and (uncredited) JEROME ROBBINS. The notices were enthusiastic and the musical ran 559 performances. NANCY WALKER made a hilarious Ruth and Jo Sullivan was her sister Eileen in a 1958 New York City Light Opera production, which also featured Peter Cookson, Frank Maxwell, and George Givot. The same organization revived the musical in 1963 with KAYE BALLARD (Ruth) and Jacquelyn McKeever (Eileen) and in 1967 with ELAINE STRITCH (Ruth) and Linda Bennett (Eileen), and the New York City Opera did a production

Casts for *Wonderful Town*

Character	1953 Broadway	1958 television	2003 Broadway
Ruth Sherwood	ROSALIND RUSSELL	Rosalind Russell	DONNA MURPHY
Eileen Sherwood	EDITH ADAMS	Jacquelyn McKeever	Jennifer Westfeldt
Robert Baker	George Gaynes	SYDNEY CHAPLIN	GREGG EDELMAN
Frank Lippencott	Cris Alexander	Cris Alexander	Peter Benson
Appopolous	Henry Lascoe	Joseph Buloff	David Margulies
Chick Clark	Dort Clark	Dort Clark	Michael McGrath
Helen	Michele Burke	Michele Burke	Nancy Anderson
Wreck	Jordan Bentley	Jordan Bentley	Raymond McLeod

at Lincoln Center in 1994 with Kay McClelland (Ruth) and Crista Moore (Elieen) leading the cast. Because she was known mostly for her dramatic roles in musicals, DONNA MURPHY surprised and delighted reviewers and audiences with her farcical performance as Ruth in the 2003 Broadway revival based on an earlier *ENCORES!* concert. KATHLEEN MARSHALL directed and choreographed the production and it ran 497 performances. See also MY SISTER EILEEN.

▢ Rosalind Russell reprised her Ruth on a CBS-TV version in 1958 and much of the original cast joined her so it is noteworthy for archival purposes. It is unfortunate that the production was not better. None of the performers seemed as effective as they were on stage, and the 120-minute broadcast was directed (by HERBERT ROSS and Mel Ferber) and choreographed (by Ralph Beaumont) without much spirit.

WOOD, NATALIE [born Natasha Nikolaevna Zakharenko] (1938–1981). Film and television performer. A child actress who grew up to be an even more popular adult star, she appeared in some film musicals and sang in some nonmusicals, although she was usually dubbed. Wood was born in San Francisco, the daughter of a Russian architect and French ballet dancer, and took dance lessons as soon as she could walk. She made her film debut in a bit part in *Happy Land* (1943) and was immediately noticed and cast in several 1940s movies, most memorably in a major role in *Miracle on 34th Street* (1947). Wood was one of the few kid performers to make the transition into adult roles and appeared in a variety of comedies and dramas up until her premature death by drowning. Although she could not sing, she was cast in two plum musical roles in the 1960s: the Puerto Rican immigrant Maria in *WEST SIDE STORY* (1961) and the stripper GYPSY ROSE LEE in *GYPSY* (1962), with

her singing dubbed by MARNI NIXON in both. She also "sang" in the screen musical *Just for You* (1952) and the nonmusicals *The Great Race* (1965) and *Inside Daisy Clover* (1966). Wood also appeared in television dramas and miniseries. She was married to actor Robert Wagner (1930–). Biographies: *Natasha: The Biography of Natalie Wood*, Suzanne Finstad (2002); *Natalie Wood*, Gavin Lambert (2005); *Natalie: A Memoir By Her Sister*, Lana Wood (1986).

WOOD, PEGGY (1892–1978). Stage, television, and film performer. A striking soprano beauty who played the heroines in many Broadway musicals and operettas, she later became a popular character actress specializing in matronly roles. Born in Brooklyn, New York, the daughter of a newspaper writer, Wood was on Broadway by the age of eighteen, appearing in the chorus of *NAUGHTY MARIETTA* (1910). She played supporting roles and then replaced others in major parts until she found fame as the tragic Ottile in the popular operetta *MAYTIME* (1917). For the next fifty years she played everything from Shakespeare to musical comedy to melodramas on stage, including the musicals *Buddies* (1919), *Marjolaine* (1922), *The Clinging Vine* (1922), and *Champagne, Sec* (1933). Wood was very popular on the London stage where NOEL COWARD wrote for her the musical roles of Sarah Millick in *BITTER SWEET* (1929) and Rozanne Gray in *Operette* (1938) and the flustered wife Ruth in his comedy *Blithe Spirit* (1941). She appeared in a handful of nonmusical films between 1919 and 1965 but she became more famous on television where she appeared as the maternal lead in the series *I Remember Mama* for eight years in the 1950s. By the time the former beauty was cast in *THE SOUND OF MUSIC* (1964), her singing voice had deteriorated so much of her vocals had to be dubbed by Margery McKay, yet her performance was still penetrating. Autobiographies: *Actors and People* (1930); *How Young You Look* (1940); *Arts and Flowers* (1963).

WOOD, SAM[uel Grosvenor] (1883–1949). Film director. A pioneering filmmaker with dozens of features to his credit, he helmed five musicals, two for the MARX BROTHERS. Wood was born in Philadelphia and worked as an actor in silent two-reelers around 1908 before serving as an assistant to Cecil B. DeMille in 1915. He was directing features for PARAMOUNT by the 1920s and over the next thirty years worked in many different genres, helming such films as *Goodbye Mr. Chips* (1939), *Kings Row* (1942), and *For Whom the Bell Tolls* (1943). Wood's musical credits were *It's a Great Life* (1929), *So This Is College* (1929), *They Learned About Women* (1930), *A NIGHT AT THE OPERA* (1935), and *A DAY AT THE RACES* (1937).

■ **WOODSTOCK** (Warner 1970). The granddaddy of all rockumentaries, the film was about the granddaddy of all rock festivals and captured the "three days of peace and music" with split screen, dizzying montage, multipaneled images, and vibrant use of color. Michael Wadleigh was the inventive director who filmed interviews with patrons, performers, police, and even local farmers, put it together with exciting footage of the concert itself, and then sliced in fascinating scenes backstage and in the crowd. Not all the artists who performed in the 1969 festival got on film, but a "director's cut" version released in 1994 added forty more minutes of performances. Most memorable of the performers and/or groups were Jimi Hendrix, Joe Cocker, Sly and the Family Stone, Ten Years After, The Who, Arlo Guthrie, Joan Baez, Jefferson Airplane, Richie Havens, and Crosby, Stills and Nash. Most rockumentaries that came after *Woodstock* were influenced by its techniques and could not help copying it, although rarely did they measure up to the original.

WOOLLEY, MONTY [Edgar Montillion] (1888–1963). Stage and film director and performer. A colorful personality most remembered for playing the irascible Sheridan Whiteside in the stage and screen versions of *The Man Who Came to Dinner* (1939 and 1942), he was a respected director of Broadway musicals in the 1930s. Woolley was born in New York City and educated at Yale and Harvard Universities, returning to the former to teach dramatics until he went on the stage as the temperamental impresario Sergei Alexandrovitch in *ON YOUR TOES* (1936). The bearded performer made his film debut the next year and was a favorite character actor in Hollywood into the

1950s. Among the screen musicals he appeared in were *ARTISTS AND MODELS ABROAD* (1938), *Irish Eyes Are Smiling* (1944), *NIGHT AND DAY* (1946), and *KISMET* (1955). On Broadway, Woolley directed the COLE PORTER musicals *FIFTY MILLION FRENCHMEN* (1929), *THE NEW YORKERS* (1930), and *JUBILEE* (19335), as well as *The Second Little Show* (1930) and *Champagne, Sec* (1933).

■ **WORDS AND MUSIC** (MGM 1948). Supposedly about the lives and works of songwriters RICHARD RODGERS and LORENZ HART, the biographical musical was one of the most fictitious even by Hollywood's standards of fabrication. Rodgers' real life was simply dull and Hart's story, that of a tormented homosexual who died of alcoholism, was unfilmable at the time, so the screenplay by Ben Feiner, Jr. and Fred Finklehoffe told the tale of songwriter Hart who loved a nightclub singer but she didn't love him because he was short so he drank himself to death. Tom Drake was fitfully unexciting as Rodgers, MICKEY ROONEY was a petulant but energetic Hart, and Betty Garrett was Peggy McNeil, the fictional love of his life. Producer ARTHUR FREED had the good sense to fill the musical with seventeen Rodgers and Hart tunes and gathered a crackerjack cast to perform them. Among the highlights were Rooney and JUDY GARLAND (together on the big screen for the last time) recapturing the old magic with "I Wish I Were in Love Again," LENA HORNE's distinctive renditions of "The Lady Is a Tramp" and "Where or When," JUNE ALLYSON and the Blackburn Twins in a zesty version of "Thou Swell," Garland's exciting "Johnny One-Note," and the modern ballet "Slaughter on Tenth Avenue" choreographed and danced by GENE KELLY with VERA-ELLEN. Among the many other performers who strutted their stuff were CYD CHARISSE, MEL TORMÉ, PERRY COMO, ANN SOTHERN, JANET LEIGH, RICHARD QUINE, and Marshall Thompson. ROBERT ALTON choreographed the rest of the numbers, and NORMAN TAUROG directed the movie like a piece of backstage fiction, which it was.

❧ **WORKING** (46th Street Theatre 1978). This thought-provoking musical revue could not find an audience on Broadway but was later picked up by regional theatres. Songwriter STEPHEN SCHWARTZ compiled and directed the program based on portraits taken from Studs Terkel's nonfiction book of the same title. Various blue-collar and low-paying workers expressed themselves in song and in monologues, shedding light on the job and the people performing those jobs. The exceptional cast included PATTI LuPONE, Joe Mantegna, Lynne Thigpen, BOB GUNTON, Rex Everhart, Bobo Lewis, David Patrick Kelly, and Lenora Nemetz. The songs, by Schwartz, CRAIG CARNELIA, MICKI GRANT, MARY RODGERS, Susan Birkenhead, and James Taylor, were varied and quite perceptive, as with "Fathers and Sons," "Just a Housewife," "It's an Art," "The Mason," "Nobody Tells Me How," "Cleanin' Women," "Brother Trucker," "Lovin Al," and "Husbands and Wives." Critics were more admiring than enthusiastic about the potent little revue and it closed after twenty-four performances.

WRIGHT, ROBERT, AND GEORGE FORREST. Stage and film composers and lyricists. Over a period of fifty years, the gifted songwriters wrote original scores and adapted classical music into musicals, often with talent and taste. Robert [Craig] Wright (1914–2005) was born in Daytona Beach, Florida, and attended the University of Miami before working in various musical capacities. His career-long partner George Forrest [born George Forrest Chichester, Jr.] (1915–1999) was a native of Brooklyn who played piano on cruise liners and in clubs. The two men were still in their teens when they teamed up, both writing music and lyrics when they worked together. Their first Hollywood assignment was writing "The Donkey Serenade" for the screen version of *THE FIREFLY* (1937), with the song becoming an instant hit and the signature number for ALLAN JONES who introduced it on screen. Wright and Forrest songs were also heard in the movie musicals *SWEETHEARTS* (1938), *BALALAIKA* (1939), *Fiesta* (1942), and *I MARRIED AN ANGEL* (1942), while Wright alone worked on *Music in My Heart* (1940), *Dance Girl Dance* (1940), and *Blondie Goes Latin* (1941). The team's first Broadway score was *SONG OF NORWAY* (1944) in which they took melodies from Edvard Grieg and turned them into musical numbers for a biographical show about his life. They did similar adaptations for *Gypsy Lady* (1946), using VICTOR HERBERT music, *Magdalena* (1948), with Villa-Lobos music, and *Anya* (1965) with Rachmaninoff themes. Their greatest success was *KISMET* (1953) in which the music by Borodin became an entrancing Broadway musical score. Their original music was heard on Broadway in the short-lived *Kean* (1961) and the long-run *GRAND HOTEL* (1989).

Hollywood also filmed their *Kismet* (1955) and *Song of Norway* (1970).

WRIGHT, SAMUEL E. (1948–). Stage, film, and television performer. A deep-voiced African American actor–singer who has given many noteworthy performances in Broadway musicals without ever becoming a star, his voice will be forever remembered from animated television shows and films, particularly the voice of Sebastian the crab in *THE LITTLE MERMAID* (1989) and its many sequels. Wright was born in Camden, South Carolina, and was an acting teacher before making television commercials. He made his Broadway bow as one of the Apostles in the original company of *JESUS CHRIST SUPERSTAR* (1971) and took over leading roles in *TWO GENTLEMEN OF VERONA* (1972) and *PIPPIN* (1974). Wright's most accomplished musical performances were as the uptight, confused father William in *THE TAP DANCE KID* (1983) and as the majestic King Mufasa in the original cast of *THE LION KING* (1997). His other New York musicals include *OVER HERE!* (1974), *Potholes* (1979), and *Welcome to the Club* (1991). He has acted in many television shows and films, including the bio-musical *BIRD* (1988) in which he played Dizzy Gillespie.

WRUBEL, ALLIE (1905–1973). Film composer. A Tin Pan Alley songwriter with an impressive track record, he scored a dozen movie musicals and wrote some memorable songs. Wrubel was born in Middletown, Connecticut, and began his career as a musician. He eventually was a saxophone player for PAUL WHITEMAN's orchestra. His first movie score was with lyricist MORT DIXON for *Flirtation Walk* (1934), followed by *Happiness Ahead* (1934), *Bright Lights* (1935), *In Caliente* (1935), and *I Live for Love* (1935). With lyricist HERB MAGIDSON he wrote the songs for *Life of the Party* (1937), *Radio City Revels* (1938), and *Sing Your Way Home* (1945), and with MAXWELL ANDERSON he scored *Never Steal Anything Small* (1959). Perhaps Wrubel's finest work was with lyricist RAY GILBERT writing the songs for *SONG OF THE SOUTH* (1946), which introduced "Zip-a-Dee-Doo-Dah." He also contributed songs to the screen musicals *The Toast of New York* (1937), *MAKE MINE MUSIC* (19470, *The Fabulous Dorseys* (1947), and *MELODY TIME* (1948).

WYMAN, JANE [born Sarah Jane Fulks] (1914–2007). Film and television performer.

A versatile screen actress with many memorable comic and dramatic performances to her credit, she was featured in several musicals. Wyman was born in St. Joseph, Missouri, and attempted a screen career as a child actress in Hollywood but nothing came of it so the family moved back to the Midwest where she grew up and attended the University of Missouri. After working different jobs she broke into show business as a radio singer and was back in Hollywood by 1935 in the chorus of such musicals as KING OF BURLESQUE (1935), Cain and Mabel (1936), GOLD DIGGERS OF 1937 (1936), and Stage Struck (1936). Wyman graduated to supporting and then leading roles in the musicals The King and the Chorus Girl (1937), Ready, Willing and Able (1937), Mr. Dodd Takes the Air (1927), The Singing Marine (1937), My Favorite Spy (1942), Footlight Serenade (1942), HOLLYWOOD CANTEEN (1944), and NIGHT AND DAY (1945), yet she never achieved star status until her dramatic performance in The Lost Weekend (1945). From that point on she concentrated on dramas and comedies, making an occasional appearance in such musicals as It's a Great Feeling (1949), HERE COMES THE GROOM (1951), Starlift (1951), Just for You (1952), and Let's Do It Again (1953). By the 1970s Wyman left films and acted in television, most memorably Falcon Crest in the 1980s and into the 1990s. She was married to actor-turned-president RONALD REAGAN and then Fred Karger (1916–1979).

WYNN, ED [born Isaiah Edwin Leopold] (1886–1966). Stage, film, and television performer, producer, and director. A very distinctive American comic, he had a lisping voice, silly giggle, and fluttering mannerisms and, dressed in eccentric costumes, made outrageous puns and demonstrated ridiculous inventions. Wynn was born in Philadelphia, the son of an immigrant who had built up a successful hat company. The son wasn't interested in the family business and as a teenager went into vaudeville, touring the country as part of an act called the Rah Rah Boys. It was in variety that Wynn developed his character of the "perfect fool" and by the 1910s he was playing this character in Broadway revues such as ZIEGFELD FOLLIES (1914 and 1915), THE PASSING SHOW OF 1916, Doing Our Bit (1917), Over the Top (1917), and Shubert Gaieties (1919), as well as daffy characters in the book musicals The

Deacon and the Lady (1910), Sometime (1918), and Manhattan Mary (1927). He became so popular that shows were built around him and even his book musicals, such as SIMPLE SIMON (1930) and HOORAY FOR WHAT! (1937), made concessions to his unique talents. Wynn started producing and directing his musical revues and sometimes contributed to the sketches and songs, as with Ed Wynn Carnival (1920), The Perfect Fool (1921), The Grab Bag (1924), The Laugh Parade (1931), Boys and Girls Together (1940), and Laugh, Town, Laugh (1942). Wynn was very popular on the radio in the 1930s and on television in the 1950s, and his film career, while limited, stretched from 1927 to 1967. His screen musicals were Follow the Leader (1930), STAGE DOOR CANTEEN (1943), Cinderfella (1960), BABES AND TOYLAND (1961), and MARY POPPINS (1965) where he played the laughing Uncle Albert.

WYNN, [Francis Xavier Aloysius] **KEENAN** (1916–1986). Film, television, and stage performer. A versatile character actor who played everything from congenial con men to brash villains in nearly fifty movies, he lit up several musicals as irascible agents or lovable sidekicks. He was born in New York, the son of comic ED WYNN, and worked in radio and stock before making his Broadway debut in 1935. Wynn appeared in a handful of comedies and melodramas, as well as doing sketches in the musical revues One for the Money (1939) and Two for the Show (1940). By 1942 he was in Hollywood in a featured role in the musical FOR ME AND MY GAL (1942). Wynn was soon one of the most dependable and familiar character actors in movies. His most memorable musical roles were doing a comic specialty in ZIEGFELD FOLLIES (1946), the hassled businessman Joe Becket in NEPTUNE'S DAUGHTER (1949), the brash American Irving Klinger and his British brother Edgar in ROYAL WEDDING (1951), the gangster Lippy in KISS ME, KATE (1953), the bigoted Judge Rawkins in FINIAN'S RAINBOW (1968), and the aged Mr. Green in NASHVILLE (1975). Wynn's other musical credits include The Thrill of Brazil (1946), ANNIE GET YOUR GUN (1950), THREE LITTLE WORDS (1950), Texas Carnival (1951), THE BELLE OF NEW YORK (1952), The Glass Slipper (1955), and Bikini Beach (1964). He appeared in dozens of television programs and was still acting for the big and small screens up to the year of his death.

X

XANADU (Universal 1980). A camp classic of sorts, the movie had an odd fascination because its story was so bizarre and its look so cockeyed. Richard Christian Danus and Marc Reid Rubel concocted the hair-brained plot about the frustrated artist Sonny Malone who is inspired by the muse Clio, who comes down to earth as the mortal Kira, to open a roller disco in Southern California. He enlists the help of the millionaire Danny Maguire whom Clio had once inspired years ago to go into performing but he settled for business. Clio is not allowed to fall in love with any mortal so when Kira does she abandons Sonny and returns to Olympus. Danny intercedes and Zeus makes Clio mortal so that she and Sonny are together the day the roller disco opens with a splash. It was all fluffy nonsense and, less forgivable, it took itself seriously. Olivia Newton-John and Michael Beck made a lifeless, vapid couple and GENE KELLY (in his last screen musical) seemed tired and a bit embarrassed, which he had every right to be. However, the staging of the musical numbers by Jerry Trent and Kenny Ortega was inventive and, in their own weird way, beautiful. John Farrar, Jeff Lynne, and the group known as the Electric Light Orchestra wrote the disco score, which was tuneful and surprisingly catchy. Newton-John sang "Magic," "Dancin'," and "Suddenly," joined with Kelly for the soft-shoe duet "Whenever You're Away from Me," and performed "Suspended in Time" with Beck. The rest of the singing was covered by the Electric Light Orchestra, including "I'm Alive," "Don't Walk Away," "All Over the World," and the title song. The movie was a little-seen curiosity but the soundtrack recording was a major hit.

A very unlikely prospect for a remake or a stage version, the cockeyed fantasy was turned into a surprise hit on Broadway in 2007. Douglas Carter Beane did not stray far from the film in his libretto but it was completely different in tone and attitude. A spoof of the 1980s sensibility and the pretentious quest for art that resulted in movies like *Xanadu*, the stage work was a thorough delight. Kerry Butler was a spacy yet knowing Clio whose fake Australian accent when she becomes Kira was as appealing as it was irritating. TONY ROBERTS had no reason to be embarrassed as Danny, cutting through the featherbrained dreams of Sonny and yet enchanted by his own lost music. Adding to the fun were the muses, four women and two affected men who found the humans as silly as the script and relished the roller skating and dancing like children in a playpen. MARY TESTA and Jackie Hoffman stole the show as the two jealous muses who plot Clio's downfall by making her fall in love with Sonny. However, in the madcap revelations at the end, it turns out that Clio was impervious to their magic and it was true love after all. Farrar and Lynne wrote some new songs for the production, such as the ribald "Evil Woman" for the villainesses, and dug out the old Newton-John hit "Have You Never Been Mellow?" sung to soften the heart of Zeus (also played by Roberts). Cheyenne Jackson was the thickheaded artist Sonny and set the tone for the lightheaded musical. CHRISTOPHER ASHLEY was the clever director, and Dan Knechtges did the goofy choreography.

Casts for *Xanadu*		
Character	*1980 film*	*2007 Broadway*
Kira (Clio)	Olivia Newton-John	Kerry Butler
Sonny Malone	Michael Beck	Cheyenne Jackson
Danny Maguire	GENE KELLY	TONY ROBERTS
Muse/Melpomene	Sandahl Bergman	MARY TESTA
Muse/Calliope	Lynn Latham	Jackie Hoffman
Muse/Thalia	Melinda Phelps	Curtis Holbrook
Muse/Terpsicore	Juliette Marshall	André Ward
Muse/Erato	Marilyn Tokuda	Kenita Miller
Muse/Euterpe	Teri Beckerman	Anika Larsen

Y

YANKEE DOODLE DANDY (Warner 1942). The facts about the show business giant GEORGE M. COHAN may have been altered or bent, but the spirit of the man was certainly alive in this thrilling biographical musical in which JAMES CAGNEY gave his finest musical performance.

Plot: Little Georgie is born into a family of vaudeville performers and is on the stage at a young age, singing and dancing with his parents and sister Josie in variety and appearing in kid parts in plays. As a young man he is already writing songs and sketches for the family act but dreams of going to Broadway, which he does in 1904 with *LITTLE JOHNNY JONES*. After a string of hits over several years, George finds that the new fangled theatre is not for him so he retires to the country with his wife Mary. But the hyperactive performer cannot sit still so he returns to Broadway and has a triumph playing President Roosevelt in the musical *I'D RATHER BE RIGHT*. Having received the Congressional Medal of Honor from the real Roosevelt, George dances out of the White House and into history.

Robert Bruckner wrote the tight and efficient screenplay with some other scriptwriters, eliminating Cohan's unhappy first marriage and condensing his career so that the hits just kept on coming. MICHAEL CURTIZ directed with flair and plenty of humor, with none of the characters falling into historical blandness. The supporting cast was vibrant but the movie was really all Cagney's, making Cohan brash, funny, stubborn, and invigorating. His dancing was contagious and his showmanship in the stage sequences illustrated how one man could dazzle Broadway for years. The movie's most effective numbers were the two scenes from *Little Johnny Jones* in which Cagney got to sing the cocky "Yankee Doodle Boy" and the celebratory farewell song "Give My Regards to Broadway." Other notable Cohan songs featured were "Mary's a Grand Old Name," "You're a Grand Old Flag," "Over There," "Oh, You Wonderful Girl," "So Long Mary," "Forty-Five Minutes From Broadway," and "Harrigan." HAL B. WALLIS produced

Yankee Doodle Dandy. Cagney and Cohan were a perfect fit, as this popular musical biography can attest. Both were brash and thrilling performers. Seen behind Cagney in patriotic garb are (left to right) Jeanne Cagney, Joan Leslie, Rosemary DeCamp, and Walter Huston. (Photofest)

Casts for *Yankee Doodle Dandy*

Character	Performer
GEORGE M. COHAN	JAMES CAGNEY
Mary Cohan	JOAN LESLIE
Jerry Cohan	Walter Huston
Nellie Cohan	ROSEMARY DECAMP
Josie Cohan	Jeanne Cagney
SAM H. HARRIS	Richard Whorf
ABE ERLANGER	GEORGE BARBIER
Schwab	S. K. SAKALL
B. F. Albee	Minor Watson

the musical, and SEYMOUR FELIX, LEROY PRINZ, and John Boyle shared the choreography chores. *Yankee Doodle Dandy* was the first major Hollywood picture about an American songwriter and its success would launch many others, few coming even close to the original in quality. See also *GEORGE M!* (1968).

☐ **YEAR WITHOUT A SANTA CLAUS, THE** (ABC-TV 1974). Phyllis McGinley's children's book was given an animated musical treatment by scriptwriter William Keenan, composer MAURY LAWS, and lyricist JULES BASS. The sixty-minute show was packed with action, beginning with the announcement that Christmas is canceled because Santa (voice of MICKEY ROONEY) is tired, ill, and wondering if anyone cares about Christmas anymore. Mrs. Claus (SHIRLEY BOOTH) tries to remedy the situation by sending the elves Jingle (Bob McFadden) and Jangle (Bradley Bolke) to Southtown, USA, where it never snows and the people cannot get into the Christmas spirit unless the two elves can make a miracle and bring snow. Jingle and Jangle plead with Mother Nature (Rhoda Mann) to make Heat Miser (GEORGE S. IRVING) and Snow Miser (Dick Shawn) cooperate. When snow comes to Southtown, the people yearn again for Christmas so Santa, encouraged by their change of heart, sets off on his sleigh. While all the characters were vivid and enjoyable, Heat Miser and Snow Miser stole the show and their musical numbers were the standouts. The songs included "Anyone Can Be Santa," "Blue Christmas," "It's Gonna Snow," and the title number. Bass co-produced and co-directed with ARTHUR RANKIN, JR.

YELLEN, JACK [born Jacek Jelén] (1892–1991). Stage and film lyricist. The author of some 200 songs, he captured the feelings of America in the 1920s with the slaphappy "Ain't She Sweet?" and the yearning in the 1930s with "Happy Days Are Here Again." Yellen was born in Poland and emigrated to America when he was five years old. He was educated at the University of Michigan and then worked as a newspaper reporter in Buffalo before teaming up with composer MILTON AGER to write and publish songs. Yellen first found success when SOPHIE TUCKER sang his song "My Yiddishe Momme" in vaudeville and it became a hit. He worked for Tin Pan Alley, in Hollywood, and on Broadway throughout his long career, collaborating with a variety of composers. Yellen's stage works include *High Jinks* (1913), *What's*

in a Name? (1920), *ZIEGFELD FOLLIES* (1920 and 1943), *Rain or Shine* (1928), *John Murray Anderson's Almanac* (1929), *You Said It* (1931), *GEORGE WHITE'S SCANDALS* (1936 and 1939), *Boys and Girls Together* (1940), and *Sons o' Fun* (1943). For the movies he scored *Honky Tonk* (1929), *Chasing Rainbows* (1930), *KING OF JAZZ* (1930), *They Learned About Women* (1930), *George White's Scandals* (1934, 1935, and 1945), *Under Pressure* (1935), *Sing, Baby, Sing* (1936), *Happy Landing* (1938), and *Sensations of 1945* (1944).

▪ YELLOW SUBMARINE (United Artists 1968). One of the most imaginative animated films of the 1960s, this surreal fantasy featured cartoon images of the BEATLES, their voices, and song was a visual treat. The good-versus-evil tale was set in Pepperland where the Blue Meanies overcome the peaceful, music-loving kingdom and place it under a frozen spell. The Beatles leave their British homeland and travel in a yellow submarine through exotic, fantastical places before arriving in Pepperland, defeat the Meanies, and restore music to the land. Director George Dunning and the animators used plenty of psychedelic and pop-art design and there was nothing subtle about the drug-induced kind of imagination at work. However, the movie is also a simple, wholesome fable with a straightforward appreciation of a merry tale. Most of the songs were already hits from the group's albums, so it was probably the finest collection of Beatles songs ever heard in one film, including "Sgt. Pepper's Lonely Club Band," "When I'm Sixty-Four," "Nowhere Man," "Lucy in the Sky With Diamonds," "All You Need Is Love," "Eleanor Rigby," "All Together Now," and the title song.

▪ YENTL (United Artists/Barwood 1983). A powerhouse directing debut for BARBRA STREISAND, the period musical also had the singer–actress as producer, co-author, and star, and she shone in each job. Streisand and Jack Rosenthal adapted the Isaac Bashevis Singer story "Yentl, the Yeshiva Boy" (which had already been made into a Broadway play) into a musical fable about the young woman Yentl who lives in an eastern European village in 1904 and wishes to study the Torah rather than just marry and have children. When her father (Nehemiah Persoff) dies, she disguises herself as a boy and travels to a shiva where she studies, argues, and discusses the Torah with other bright males. Yentl finds herself attracted to the fellow student Avigdor (MANDY PATINKIN) but instead ends up marrying Avigdor's sweetheart Hadass (Amy Irving) before the truth is revealed. In the end, Yentl disposes of her disguise and sets off for America where a woman has more freedom. It was a far-fetched story told with warmth and care, and the songs by MICHEL LEGRAND (music) and ALAN and MARILYN BERGMAN (lyrics) were used mostly as interior soliloquies for the title character. "Papa, Can You Hear Me?," "No Wonder," "The Way He Makes Me Feel," "A Piece of Sky," and others were all expertly written and performed even though the score lacked variety and one longed to hear Patinkin and others sing as well. Yentl was one of the most visually beautiful movies of the decade, much of it filmed in the Czech Republic, and there was no question Streisand had learned a great deal about directing after appearing before the camera for fourteen years. Critics and some moviegoers were not so enthusiastic about the film, with much of the criticism aimed at Streisand's performance, which was considered too feminine for the boyish role. Perhaps it is a musical that only true Streisand fans can totally embrace.

YESTON, MAURY (1945–). Stage composer and lyricist. A recognized music theorist and teacher, he also managed to create some Broadway musicals in the popular vein. Yeston was born in Jersey City, New Jersey, and was educated at Yale and Cambridge University, writing orchestral pieces as a student. He returned to Yale as a faculty member teaching theory and running the celebrated BMI Workshops for promising theatre songwriters. Yeston made his Broadway songwriting debut with the successful *NINE* (1982) and then provided half of the songs for *GRAND HOTEL* (1989). His other Broadway hit was *TITANIC* (1997). Yeston also wrote the opera *Goya*, and his musical version of *The Phantom of the Opera* called *Phantom* has received many productions regionally. In addition to several concert pieces, he has written books on music theory. Yeston's theatre songs are sometimes very sophisticated but always accessible.

YIP YIP YAPHANK (Century Theatre 1918). More a fundraiser than a Broadway show, it had the score and the impact of a Broadway musical hit. IRVING BERLIN, as a member of the military getting ready to go to France to fight in World War I, put together the revue as a "military mess cooked up by the boys of Camp Upton." The show had a cast of 350 members of the armed forces and a Berlin score that included "I Can Always Find a Little Sunshine in the Y.M.C.A.," "Mandy," "We're on Our Way to France," and "Oh, How I Hate to Get Up in the Morning," the last sung by Berlin himself. The revue ran thirty-two performances and raised thousands of dollars for the war effort. Berlin did a similar project under the title *THIS IS THE ARMY* (1942) during World War II.

YORK, RACHEL (1971–). Stage, film, and television performer. An attractive blonde singer–actress, she has moved from playing sexy ingénues to more complex and mature roles in musicals. York was born in Orlando, Florida, and as a teenager won a scholarship to study at the American Center for Music Theatre in Los Angeles. By the age of seventeen she was on Broadway as a replacement for Fantine in *LES MISÉRABLES* and two years later originated the role of the oversexed Mallory Kingsley in *CITY OF ANGELS* (1989). York appeared Off Broadway with JULIE ANDREWS in the revue *Putting It Together* (1993) and then was applauded for her funny gangster's moll Norma Cassidy in *VICTOR/VICTORIA* (1995) also starring Andrews. Her other New York musical roles include the aristocrat Marguerite in the second Broadway version of *THE SCARLET PIMPERNEL* (1997), the Southern belle Ruth in *Dessa Rose* (2005), and the lonely wife Dorothy in *Summer of 42* (2006). York played leading roles in the tours of *RAGTIME* and *CAMELOT* and played Lilli Vanessi/Kate in the London revival of *KISS ME, KATE*, which was filmed for television in 2003. She has appeared in some films and many television programs.

◼ YOU WERE NEVER LOVELIER (Columbia 1942). Although this musical was set in Bueno Aires, Argentina, the characters, music, and plot seemed to have nothing to do with its location. Scriptwriters Ernest Pagano, Michael Fessier, and Delmar Daves based their tale on a story by Carlos Oliveri and Sixto Pondal Rios so they kept the Latin American setting and filled it with Americans. Manhattan nightclub hoofer Robert Davis (FRED ASTAIRE) goes to Argentina to gamble on the horses, loses all his money, and seeks a job at a ritzy hotel, only to have the owner Edouardo Acuna (ADOLPHE MENJOU) hire him because he thinks the young man is a good match for his daughter Maria (RITA HAYWORTH). Acuna even goes so far as to write love letters to his daughter signing Robert's name. JEROME KERN (music) and JOHNNY MERCER (lyrics) wrote a set of memorable songs to entertain audiences until the plot came to its inevitable conclusion, and Astaire and Hayworth had some sensational dance duets to fill in the dull stretches. "I'm Old Fashioned" was sung (Hayworth dubbed by Nan Wynn) and danced in a moonlit garden in one of the era's most romantic sequences. Also in the score were the snappy wedding number "Dearly Beloved" and the delectable title song. XAVIER CUGAT and his orchestra provided the only Hispanic touch, unless you count fifteen-year-old Fidel Castro, who was one of the extras in the film. WILLIAM A. SEITER directed and Astaire and Val Raset did the choreography.

YOU'LL NEVER GET RICH (Columbia 1941). RITA HAYWORTH became a musical film star to be reckoned with because of this movie in which she was teamed with FRED ASTAIRE for the first time and was able to match him step by step. COLUMBIA bet the bankroll on the production, spending more than they ever had before on a film. However, the highlights of the musical are not spectacle scenes but the duets by the two stars and the songs by COLE PORTER. In the screenplay by Ernest Pagano and Michael Fessier, Robert Curtis (Astaire) is smitten with the dancer Sheila Winthrop (Hayworth) when he directs her in a Broadway show. The romance is interrupted by the war and Robert is drafted and spends a good portion of the film tap dancing in the guard house. The two lovers are reunited for the big military show, the finale of which was the "Wedding Cake Walk" (choreographed by ROBERT ALTON) with a chorus of eighty dancing on a giant wedding cake that had an Army tank sitting on top. Other songs included the too-neglected ballad "Dream Dancing," the swinging torch song "Since I Kissed My Baby Goodbye," the rhythmic "So Near and Yet So Far," and the patriotic "Shootin' the Works for Uncle Sam." ROBERT BENCHLEY, John Hubbard, Osa Massen, Frieda Inescort, Ann Shoemaker, and the Delta Rhythm Boys were also featured, but the movie belonged to Hayworth who single-handedly kept the studio solvent for several years. SIDNEY LANFIELD directed the Samuel Bischoff production.

YOUMANS, VINCENT [Millie] (1898–1946). Stage and film songwriter. This brilliant and unique composer wrote only a limited number of shows during his short life but left some unforgettable scores. Born into a wealthy New York City family that manufactured hats, Youmans planned to become an engineer but,

while serving in the Navy during World War I, started composing music for service shows, including a concert by JOHN PHILIP SOUSA in which one of his songs was performed. After the armistice, Youmans worked as a song plugger and saw a few of his songs interpolated into Broadway shows, including a handful in *Two Little Girls in Blue* (1921). His first hit was *WILDFLOWER* (1923), followed by *Mary Jane McKane* (1923), *Lollipop* (1924), *NO, NO, NANETTE* (1925), *Oh, Please* (1926), *HIT THE DECK* (1927), *Rainbow* (1928), *Great Day!* (1929), and *Through the Years* (1932). Most of Youmans' Broadway hit shows were filmed—*Rainbow* was retitled by Hollywood as *Song of the West* (1930)—and he also wrote original scores for *What a Widow!* (1930), *TAKE A CHANCE* (1933), and *FLYING DOWN TO RIO* (1934), one of the most influential movie musicals of the period. His unusual but contagious rhythms, interesting melodic line, and ingenious use of repeated notes and phrases put Youmans' music in a class with GEORGE GERSHWIN, but his difficult personality, bad decisions, and battle with alcoholism cut short his life, leaving only speculation about what great things he might have accomplished. Biography: *Days to Be Happy, Years to Be Sad*, Gerald Bordman (1982).

YOUNG FRANKENSTEIN (Hilton Theatre 2007). A highly anticipated musical comedy taken from a popular film, the show reunited much of the creative staff from *THE PRODUCERS* (2001) but whether it will repeat the success of that Broadway blockbuster remains to be seen. MEL BROOKS and THOMAS MEEHAN adapted Brooks's 1974 screenplay about the American scientist Frederick Frankenstein (ROGER BART) who bids a temporary farewell to his uptight fiancée Elizabeth (Megan Mullally) and goes back to the Transylvania of his ancestors. The creepy castle of the late Victor Frankenstein is lorded over by the mysterious Frau Blucher (ANDREA MARTIN) who leaves Frederick clues about his ancestor's experiments with creation. With the assistance of the humpbacked Igor (Christopher Fitzgerald) and the romantic support of the local fraulein Inga (SUTTON FOSTER), Frederick repeats Victor Frankenstein's feat of bringing a monster of a man (Shuler Hensley) to life, only to have him rampage the countryside. Farcical shenanigans finally bring Frederick and Inga together and Elizabeth is more than happy with the sexually powerful monster as a mate. As in the film, IRVING BERLIN's "Puttin' on the Ritz" was used for the monster's public debut but the rest

Young Frankenstein. Everyone wondered if lightning would strike twice for Mel Brooks when he followed his *The Producers* (2001) with another musical based on one of his films. Lightning certainly struck on cue when it was time to bring the Monster to life. Shuler Hensley (pictured far left) played the Monster who learned the importance of white tie and tails. Here he is at the finale with Megan Mullally as his "bride of Frankenstein" Elizabeth, and Roger Bart as the doctor who gave the Monster life (and some dance lessons). (Getty)

of the score was new songs by Brooks, including "Together Again for the First Time," "He Vas My Boyfriend," "There Is Nothing Like a Brain," "Join the Family Business," "Roll in the Hay," "Deep Love," and "Transylvania Mania." SUSAN STROMAN was the clever director–choreographer and, with a superior cast and expert production values, the show was highly entertaining even if the reviews were disappointing.

YOUNG MAN WITH A HORN (Warner 1950). A dark melodrama with music, the film was based (not too accurately) on the career of jazz trumpet musician Bix Beiderbecke, played here by Kirk Douglas with HARRY JAMES providing the horn playing on the soundtrack. Carl Forman and Edmund North wrote the screenplay that centered on Rick Martin (Douglas), a neglected kid who grows up loving the sounds of jazz he heard African American musicians play. He studies the trumpet and gets a job in a band but is not happy being a subservient side man. Rick wants to make his own music, improvising as he goes along, but that's not what pays and he is continually frustrated. His high society wife Amy North (LAUREN BACALL) is not much help, belittling him and driving him to drink so that he can't hold a job. Only the band singer Jo Jordan (DORIS DAY) and Rick's old piano-playing pal Willie "Smoke" Willoughby (HOAGY CARMICHAEL) believe in him and try to help him get some recognition in the jazz world. MICHAEL CURTIZ directed with a somber look and tone, capturing the behind-the-scenes life of band musicians. The score consisted of standards from the band repertoire, and Day sang some fine renditions of "The Very Thought of You," "Too Marvelous for Words," "I May Be Wrong (But I Think You're Wonderful)," and other standards. In England, where "horn" is slang for an erection, the movie was titled *Young Man of Music.*

YOUNG, RIDA JOHNSON [born Ida Louise Johnson] (1869–1926). Stage lyricist, writer, and performer. A pioneering writer of musicals, she collaborated with America's three greatest operetta composers: VICTOR HERBERT, SIGMUND ROMBERG, and RUDOLF FRIML. Young was born in Baltimore and began her career as an actress in companies run by E. H. Sothern and Viola Allen in the late nineteenth century. After working in the music publishing business, she started to write plays and enjoyed some success before attempting her first operetta libretto and lyrics for Herbert's NAUGHTY MARIETTA (1910). Young's other giant hit was MAYTIME with composer Romberg. Her other New York musicals include *The Red Petticoat* (1912), *Lady Luxury* (1914), *Her Soldier Boy* (1916) with Romberg, *Sometime* (1918) with Friml, and *Little Simplicity* (1918). Young's last Broadway musical was *The Dream Girl* (1924) with her first collaborator Herbert. While much of her work may seem dated today, she was very important for establishing the American operetta format and some of her lyrics still sparkle.

YOUNG, ROBERT [George] (1907–1998). Television and film performer. A personable leading man of over 100 films and two very successful television series, the boyish-looking actor found himself in nine Hollywood musicals. Young was born in Chicago and raised in southern California where he began acting at the Pasadena Playhouse before getting bit parts in films. By 1931 he was cast in notable roles and soon became one of the industry's most durable and enduring performers, playing wholesome and romantic men for over twenty years. Young played similar types in his musicals, which included *The Kid From Spain* (1932), *Stowaway* (1936), *Honolulu* (1939), *LADY, BE GOOD* (1941), *Cairo* (1942), and *Sweet Rosie O'Grady* (1943). In the 1950s he turned to television and spent the rest of his long career playing an understanding father (*Father Knows Best*) and a kindly physician (*Marcus Welby, M.D.*).

YOUNG, VICTOR (1900–1956). Film and stage musician, orchestrator, and composer. A prolific music arranger and conductor, he worked on hundreds of movies before his untimely death. A Chicago native, he was a child prodigy on the violin and, after studying at the Warsaw Conservatory in Poland, made many concert appearances before giving up classical music for popular song. Young was signed by PARAMOUNT in 1930 to oversee the orchestra in both musical and nonmusical films. Among his musical credits are *ANYTHING GOES* (1936), *Klondike Annie* (1936), *BIG BROADCAST OF*

1937 (1936), *ARTISTS AND MODELS* (1937), *THE PALEFACE* (1948), *The Emperor Waltz* (1948), *My Favorite Spy* (1951), and *THE COUNTRY GIRL* (1954). Young also collaborated on several songs, most memorably "Golden Earrings" with JAY LIVINGSTON and RAY EVANS and "My Foolish Heart" with NED WASHINGTON.

YOUR ARMS TOO SHORT TO BOX WITH GOD (Lyceum Theatre 1976). A fervent but fun musical revue by VINNETTE CARROLL (book), Alex Bradford, and MICKI GRANT (music and lyrics), the show originated Off Broadway and was so well reviewed that it transferred to Broadway for a long run. Taking the form of a revival meeting, the *Gospel According to St. Matthew* was celebrated in revue format with plenty of gospel singing and stomping. The vibrant cast included Delores Hall, William Hardy, J., Clinton Derricks-Carroll, Salome Bey, and Bobby Hill, directed by Carroll, and the songs included "Didn't I Tell You," "On That Day," "Just a Little Bit of Jesus Goes a Long Way," "Beatitudes," and the zesty title number. Critics commended the gifted cast and strong word of mouth kept the musical on the boards for 578 performances in two separate engagements.

YOUR OWN THING (Orpheum Theatre 1968). A silly but endearing rock musical, the Off Broadway work spoofed Shakespeare's *Twelfth Night* as well as rock music itself. Librettist Donald Driver set the Elizabethan tale in contemporary Manhattan and put the characters in the music business. Siblings Viola (LELAND PALMER) and Sebastian (RUSTY THACKER) look alike and, because all the boys are wearing their hair long, Viola is able to disguise herself and get a job with the male rock group the Four Apocalypse. The expected confusions result, such as the record producer Olivia (Marian Mercer) falling for the male Viola and Orson (Tom Ligon), the manager for the rock group, wondering if he is homosexual since he too is attracted to the "boy." The slaphappy tale took time to stop intermittently and make sly comments on the generation gap, Shakespeare, the establishment, and love. Hal Hester and Danny Apolinar wrote the derivative but clever songs that sometimes used Shakespeare's lyrics, such as "Come Away, Death" and "She Never Told Her Love." Also in the score were "The Middle Years," "The Flowers," "I'm On My Way to the Top," "When You're Young and in Love," "Be Gentle," and the title number. Driver directed the small-cast show with spirit and it ran 933 performances.

Casts for *You're a Good Man, Charlie Brown*

Character	1967 Off Broadway	1973 television	1999 Broadway
Charlie Brown	Gary Burghoff	Wendell Burton	ANTHONY RAPP
Lucy	Reva Rose	Ruby Pearson	Ilans Levine
Linus	Bob Balaban	Barry Livingston	B. D. Wong
Snoopy	Bill Hinnant	Bill Hinnant	ROGER BART
Schroeder	Skip Hinnant	Mark Montgomery	Stanley Wayne Mathis
Patty	Karen Johnson	Noelle Matlovsky	
Sally			KRISTIN CHENOWETH

YOU'RE A GOOD MAN, CHARLIE BROWN (Theatre 80 St. Marks 1967). A modest little musical based on Charles Schulz's beloved comic strip *Peanuts*, the intimate piece was a long run hit Off Broadway and one of the most produced shows by amateur groups for many years.

During a typical day in the life of the boy Charlie Brown, he has encounters with his friends, such as the bossy Lucy, her philosophical brother Linus, and the Beethoven-loving Schroeder, as well as the unseen redheaded girl he loves and his very human dog Snoopy. Clark Gesner wrote the libretto, music, and lyrics, which were all delightfully unpretentious yet pointed. "Happiness," "Suppertime," "My Blanket and Me," "Book Report," and the marching title song were among the most memorable numbers. Joseph Hardy directed, PATRICIA BIRCH choreographed, and the chamber piece ran 1,597 performances. After touring successfully in larger houses, it tried Broadway in 1971 but critics felt the charm and intimacy of the original were lost even in the small John Golden Theatre and the show closed in a month. With a few new songs by Andrew Lippa, a reworked script, and a multi-racial cast, the little musical was given a bigger and brighter staging by Michael Mayer in 1999 and most reviewers again felt that something was lost. The only recurring compliments were for new faces ROGER BART (Snoopy) and KRISTIN CHENOWETH, who stole the show as Sally, a character not even in the original script. The revival managed to run an unprofitable 250 performances.

There have been two television versions of *You're a Good Man, Charlie Brown*. A 1973 production on *HALLMARK HALL OF FAME* was filmed in a studio and had the simple, unadorned look of the Off Broadway production. The cast, which included the original Snoopy of Bill Hinnant, was excellent, and Walter C. Miller directed the gentle piece with care and humor. A 1985 animated version on CBS-TV reduced the musical down to forty-nine minutes so both songs and script were cut severely. The voices by child actors and the original Schulz art work made the show seem just like another of the many other *Peanuts* specials on TV. All the same, it is superior television fare and the widely seen show was a potent introduction to the stage version for many young viewers.

Z

ZAKS, JERRY [born Byczek] (1946–). Stage director and performer. A popular and prodigious director with a wide repertoire and a bottomless barrel of creativity, he staged a number of memorable musical revivals. Zaks was born in Stuttgart, Germany, and emigrated to America with his father, finally settling in Patterson, New Jersey. Zaks studied law at Dartmouth College but left to pursue theatre studies at Smith College. After graduating he worked as an actor in plays and musicals, eventually appearing on Broadway in the revue *Tintypes* (1980) and other works. His directing career began Off Off Broadway in 1976 but he did not receive recognition until his witty and precise staging of Christopher Durang's satirical *Sister Mary Ignatius Explains It All for You* Off Broadway in 1981 and he was soon one of the most in-demand directors in New York. While Zaks made his reputation with comedies and farces, such as *Lend Me a Tenor* (1989) and *The Man Who Came to Dinner* (2000), his biggest successes have been musical revivals, such as *ANYTHING GOES* (1987), *A FUNNY THING HAPPENED ON THE WAY TO THE FORUM* (1996), and *GUYS AND DOLLS* (1992), and the record-breaking revue *SMOKEY JOE'S CAFE* (1995). His other musical credits include the new works *ASSASSINS* (1991) and *The Civil War* (1999) and the Broadway revivals of *LITTLE SHOP OF HORRORS* (2003) and *LA CAGE AUX FOLLES* (2004). Zaks has also triumphed staging more serious nonmusicals, such as *Six Degrees of Separation* (1990) and *The Caine Mutiny Court-Martial* (2006).

ZANUCK, DARRYL F[rancis]. (1902–1979). Film producer and writer. The legendary movie mogul who was instrumental in the development of talkies, he managed two famous studios and then continued presenting films as an independent producer. Zanuck was born in Wahoo, Nebraska, and began his career as a writer of adventures stories. After serving in World War I

and making a living as a boxer, he started writing scripts for silent movies and found success with his scenarios for canine star Rin Tin Tin. By 1928 he was managing WARNER BROTHERS and was responsible for the studio's experiment with sound and the subsequent success with *THE JAZZ SINGER* (1927), which he produced. Zanuck also presented the early musicals *My Man* (1928), *ON WITH THE SHOW* (1929), *Say It With Songs* (1929), *The Life of the Party* (1930), *42ND STREET* (1933), *GOLD DIGGERS OF 1933*, *FOOTLIGHT PARADE* (1933), and *Broadway Through a Keyhole* (1933), often contributing to the scripts as well. He left Warners in 1933 and helped form 20th Century Pictures, which merged with Fox with himself as studio head. Zanuck's musicals at 20TH CENTURY-Fox include *Folies Bergere de Paris* (1935), *Metropolitan* (1935), *THANKS A MILLION* (1935), *KING OF BURLESQUE* (1936), *CAPTAIN JANUARY* (1936), *Sing, Baby, Sing* (1936), *Pigskin Parade* (1936), *ON THE AVENUE* (1937), *IN OLD CHICAGO* (1938), *Little Miss Broadway* (1938), *ALEXANDER'S RAGTIME BAND* (1938), *SECOND FIDDLE* (1939), *The Little Princess* (1939), *LILLIAN RUSSELL* (1940), and *DOWN ARGENTINE WAY* (1940). He concentrated on nonmusicals for the rest of his career, which consisted of going independent in 1956 and producing into the 1960s. Zanuck was a temperamental workaholic who insisted on overseeing every aspect of his films, particularly the scripts. His son is film producer Richard Darryl Zanuck (1934–). Biographies: *Twentieth Century-Fox's Darryl F. Zanuck and the Culture of Hollywood*, George F. Custen (1997); *Don't Say Yes Until I Finish Talking*, Mel Gussow (1980).

ZIEGFELD, FLORENZ, JR. (1867–1932). Stage and film producer. Perhaps the most famous of all American theatrical showmen, he is most remembered for his lavish revues bearing his name but he also presented Broadway and Hollywood book musicals as well. Ziegfeld was born in Chicago, where his family ran a music conservatory, and was sent by his father to Europe to secure talent for the 1893 Colombian Exposition. It was the beginning of a life of searching out and promoting stage attractions, from the strongman Eugene Sandow to the provocative French coquette ANNA HELD. Ziegfeld's first Broadway production was in 1896 and he presented the first of his famous *Follies* in 1907, a series that he would repeat eighteen more times during his lifetime. He also presented book musicals, including *A Parlor Match* (1896), *The Little Duchess* (1901),

The Parisian Model (1906), *Miss Innocence* (1908), *A Winsome Widow* (1912), *The Century Girl* (1916), *SALLY* (1920), *Kid Boots* (1923), *Betsy* (1926), *RIO RITA* (1927), *ROSALIE* (1928), THE THREE MUSKETEERS (1928), *WHOOPEE* (1929), *BITTER SWEET* (1929), *SIMPLE SIMON* (1930), and *Hot-Cha!* (1932). Ziegfeld's least typical but most important Broadway production was the classic *SHOW BOAT* (1927); he also produced the 1932 revival of that musical. He produced and acted as consultant on some of the screen versions of his Broadway hits. Ziegfeld possessed a magnetic personality and exuded an extravagance in his life as he did in his spectacular revues. Although he lived and behaved like a king, his finances were always precarious and he died bankrupt. WILLIAM POWELL impersonated Ziegfeld in both *THE GREAT ZIEGFELD* (1936) and *ZIEGFELD FOLLIES* (1946), and WALTER PIDGEON played the

showman in *FUNNY GIRL* (1968). Ziegfeld was married to actresses ANNA HELD and BILLIE BURKE. Biographies: *Ziegfeld*, Charles Higham (1982); *The Ziegfeld Touch: The Life and Times of Florenz Ziegfeld, Jr.*, Richard and Paulette Ziegfeld (1993).

ZIEGFELD FOLLIES. Stage series. The most famous series of revues in the American theatre, the opulent shows were considered the hallmark of lavish but tasteful extravaganza. FLORENZ ZIEGFELD produced *Follies of 1907* at the rooftop Jardin de Paris and it was such a hit he moved it to Broadway for a total of seventy performances. The revue emphasized beautiful girls and dazzling scenery rather than songs and sketches; it was a pattern that was continued throughout the series, although many famous songs and performers would be featured in the shows later on. Before Ziegfeld died in 1932,

Ziegfeld Follies. Pretty girls with props were all Florenz Ziegfeld needed to make a production number. He understood that everything was in the presentation, not the content. This undated photo from one of his *Ziegfeld Follies* revues shows a number far from his most lavish yet the use of girls and props is unmistakably Ziegfeld. (Photofest)

he presented twenty-one editions of the revue. They were called *Follies of*... until 1911 when he changed the name to *Ziegfeld Follies*. As the shows got bigger, more girls were added and top stars were signed up. The most recurring performers were FANNY BRICE, ANN PENNINGTON, BERT WILLIAMS, W. C. FIELDS, EDDIE CANTOR, NORA BAYES, LEON ERROL, and WILL ROGERS. Joseph Urban, a noted architect, designed the scenery for several editions, and Ben Ali Haggin created many of the celebrated tableau vivants. Although Ziegfeld did not put much importance on songs, IRVING BERLIN, VICTOR HERBERT, HARRY TIERNEY, and other noted composers wrote *Follies* scores and several popular songs came from the shows, including Berlin's "A Pretty Girl Is a Like a Melody," the signature number for the series. In 1934, Ziegfeld's widow BILLIE BURKE sold the rights to the series' title and there were editions produced by others in the 1930s and 1940s but, as accomplished as some were, they did not compare favorably to the originals. It was Ziegfeld's careful eye, his demand for high-class production values, and his respectful but adoring presentation of beautiful women that made his shows unique.

Of the many revues billed as the *Follies* over the decades, a few stand out as exceptional. The 1915 edition was notable as the first of the extravagant productions designed by Urban and the beginning of a golden age for the *Follies*. In addition to stars W. C. Fields, GEORGE WHITE, Ann Pennington, Bert Williams, Ina Claire, Mae Murray, and Leon Errol, the show featured an underwater ballet and a number called "Elysian Fields," which featured live elephants. The 1918 edition starred MARILYN MILLER, Eddie Cantor, Will Rogers, and W. C. Fields and had a patriotic theme in the songs, production numbers, and tableaus. Irving Berlin wrote most of the songs for the 1919 *Ziegfeld Follies* and it was the best score of the entire series: "Mandy," "A Pretty Girl Is Like a Melody," "You'd Be Surprised," "You Cannot Make Your Shimmy Shake on Tea," "Tulip Time," and "My Baby's Arms." The 1921 edition is most remembered for Fanny Brice and her renditions of "Second Hand Rose" and "My Man," and joining her on stage were W. C. Fields, Van and Schenck, Raymond Hitchcock, and Mary Eaton. Brice was also in the 1934 edition, one of the best post-Ziegfeld entries in the series. The cast also included WILLIE and EUGENE HOWARD, JANE FROMAN, BUDDY and VILMA EBSEN, EVE ARDEN, ROBERT CUMMINGS, and Everett

Marshall, as well as such song hits as "I Like the Likes of You," "The Last Round-Up," "What Is There to Say," and "Wagon Wheels." *Ziegfeld Follies* of 1936 is considered the last of the exceptional shows. Fanny Brice made her last *Follies* appearance and she was joined by BOB HOPE, Josephine Baker, GERTRUDE NEISEN, JUDY CANOVA, and the NICHOLAS BROTHERS. VERNON DUKE (music) and IRA GERSHWIN (lyrics) wrote the songs, with the best one being the unforgettable "I Can't Get Started With You." The last Broadway revue to use the name *Ziegfeld Follies* was in 1957.

▪ ZIEGFELD FOLLIES (MGM 1946). The first time a major studio attempted a musical revue since the early days of the talkies, this colossal effort by MGM failed to win an audience and the coffin was sealed on cinema revues forever. However, the film is filled with musical gems since all the top talents at the studio were involved in the production. In a prologue, WILLIAM POWELL played producer FLORENZ ZIEGFELD up in heaven dreaming about the sort of *Follies* he could create using the talent at Hollywood's glossiest studio. What followed was a series of singing, dancing, and comedy acts put together by producer ARTHUR FREED and directed by VINCENTE MINNELLI and others. FANNY BRICE, KEENAN WYNN, RED SKELTON, WILLIAM FRAWLEY, VICTOR MOORE, and Edward Arnold were featured in the sketches, most of which were genuine in spirit to those in the *Follies* if not all that funny today. LENA HORNE's sultry rendition of "Love" (by RALPH BLANE and HUGH MARTIN) and JUDY GARLAND impersonating Greer Garson in the satirical "The Great Lady Gives an Interview" (by ROGER EDENS and KAY THOMPSON) were the best of the singing entries. But like a true *Follies*, the highlights were the dance pieces and opulent production numbers. The opening featured FRED ASTAIRE, LUCILLE BALL, and CYD CHARISSE in the dazzling "Bring on the Beautiful Girls" (by Earl Brent and Edens) complemented by VIRGINIA O'BRIEN's noticing the lack of males on stage and wryly suggesting "Bring on Those Wonderful Men." Freed and HARRY WARREN's "This Heart of Mine" was a partially sung ballet with Astaire as a jewel thief and LUCILLE BREMER as his victim, with whom he falls in love while stealing her diamond bracelet. Astaire and Bremer were also featured in a lush, oriental production number for the old standard "Limehouse Blues." The most remembered number from the movie was the GERSHWINS' droll duet "The

Babbitt and the Bromide" sung and danced by GENE KELLY and Astaire, the only time the two sang and danced together on film until a guest spot together in *That's Entertainment, Part Two* (1976). The first preview of the film ran over three hours so several numbers were deleted or edited, including a lengthy finale, and the studio tinkered further with the musical before releasing it to tepid reviews and lackluster box office. However, it remains an archival wonder and an oddball classic of sorts.

■ *ZIEGFELD GIRL* (MGM 1940). A backstage musical that followed the struggles of three girls who aim to star in the *Follies,* the film was really a tiresome soap opera with classy production numbers. Marguerite Roberts and SONYA LEVIEN were responsible for the story of elevator girl Sheila Hale (LANA TURNER) who dumps her boy friend Gil Young (JAMES STEWART) in order to be a kept woman and reach the top; but her plan fails and she is punished with Hollywood justice. Sandra Kolter (Hedy Lamarr), however, leaves her penniless violinist husband Franz (Philip Dorn) to go into show business but sees the error of her ways and gives up the stage to rejoin him in the final reel. Only eager vaudevillian Sue Gallagher (JUDY GARLAND) gets to become a Ziegfeld girl and is propped up on the top of a wedding cake setting (footage reused from *THE GREAT ZIEGFELD*) for the big finale. The musical numbers staged by BUSBY BERKELEY made the film watchable, especially Garland's frivolous rendition of "Minnie From Trinidad" (by ROGER EDENS), an exciting Spanish dance by Antonio and Rosario, and Tony Martin's warm delivery of "You Stepped Out of a Dream" by HERB NACIO BROWN and GUS KAHN. More interesting than the main characters were the expert supporting players such as Jackie Cooper, Ian Hunter, CHARLES WINNINGER, AL SHEAN (as himself), Paul Kelly, EDWARD EVERETT HORTON, DAN DAILEY, EVE ARDEN, and FELIX BRESSART. PANDRO S. BERMAN produced and ROBERT Z. LEONARD directed with a sluggishness atypical of his work.

ZIEMBA, KAREN (1957–). Stage and television performer. An animated singer–dancer who has not found widespread recognition outside of the theatre community, she has played major roles in Broadway musicals for twenty years. Ziemba was born in St. Joseph, Missouri, and was educated at the University of Akron before training at the Actors Institute and the American Place Theatre. She made her New York debut

in 1981 and then was a replacement in leading roles in *42ND STREET* (1983) and *A CHORUS LINE* (1982 and 1988). Ziemba was first noticed by the press in the Off Broadway revue *And the World Goes 'Round* (1991) and gave winning performances as the marathon dancer Rita Racine in *Steel Pier* (1997), the overimaginative Italian wife in *CONTACT* (1999), and the hoofer–songwriter Georgia Hendricks in *CURTAINS* (2007). Her other New York musicals include *I MARRIED AN ANGEL* (1986), *Teddy & Alice* (1987), *Sing for Your Supper* (1988), *THE MOST HAPPY FELLA* (1991), *110 IN THE SHADE* (1992), *I Do! I Do!* (1996), *NEVER GONNA DANCE* (2003), and replacement roles in *CRAZY FOR YOU* (1995) and *CHICAGO* (1998). Ziemba has sung in concerts and benefits and has appeared in some television drama series.

ZIEN, CHIP (1947–). Stage, television, and film performer. The short, wiry, hyperactive character actor has appeared in Broadway farces and musicals on and Off Broadway, usually in colorful supporting roles. Zien was born in Milwaukee and was educated at the University of Pennsylvania before making his New York debut Off Broadway in 1972. He is mostly known for his quirky characterizations in musicals by WILLIAM FINN: the gay husband Marvin in *In Trousers* (1979), the lovelorn psychiatrist Mendel in *March of the Falsettos* (1981), *Falsettoland* (1990), and *FALSETTOS* (1992), and the obnoxious children's TV star Mr. Bungee in *A NEW BRAIN* (1998). Zien originated the role of the Baker in *INTO THE WOODS* (1987) and was a replacement for the dying accountant Otto Klingeline in *GRAND HOTEL* (1990) and the conniving tavern owner Thenardier in *LES MISÉRABLES* (2007). His other New York musicals include *Ride the Winds* (1974), *Tuscaloosa's Calling Me ...* (1976), *Real Life Funnies* (1981), *Diamonds* (1984), *THE BOYS FROM SYRACUSE* (2002), and *CHITTY CHITTY BANG BANG* (2005). Zien has appeared in a few films and many television series.

🎭 *ZORBÁ* (Imperial Theatre 1968). A well-crafted but somewhat awkward musical play, it was based on Nikos Kazantzakis's novel *Zorbá the Greek,* which had been made into a very popular movie in 1964. The Englishman Nikos arrives in Crete to reopen a mine he has inherited and takes on the robust, life-affirming Zorbá as his right-hand man. Nikos has an affair with a local widow that ends tragically and Zorbá woos the aging courtesan Hortense but she dies.

Broadway casts for _Zorbá_

Character	1968 Broadway	1983 Broadway
Zorbá	Herschel Bernardi	Anthony Quinn
Nikos	John Cunningham	ROBERT WESTENBERG
Madame Hortense	MARIA KARNILOVA	Lila Kedrova
Leader	Lorraine Serabian	Debbie Shapiro
Widow	Carmen Alvarez	Taro Meyer

The mine is a disaster but Nikos learns to look at life differently because of his spirited companion. JOSEPH STEIN wrote the efficient libretto, and JOHN KANDER (music) and FRED EBB (lyrics) wrote the ethnic-sounding score that included "Life Is," "Only Love," "The Butterfly," "The First Time," "No Boom Boom," "I Am Free," and "Goodbye, Canavaro." HAROLD PRINCE produced and directed, using the format of a village circle led by the Leader to tell the story, and RON FIELD did the lively choreography. The production was professionally done in all areas, although many critics felt the flavor of the movie was not there and only the sterling performances by Hershel Bernardi and MARIA KARNILOVA as Zorbá and Hortense were very involving. All the same the musical ran 305 performances. Even more successful was the 1983 revival in which Anthony Quinn and Lila Kedrova, who had starred in the film _Zorbá the Greek_, took on the musical roles and, although neither was much of a singer, they triumphed once again in the parts. Michael Cacoyannis, who had directed the film, staged the revival, which was popular enough to run longer than the original: 354 performances.

ZORINA, VERA [born Eva Brigitta Hartwig] (1917–2003). Stage, film, and television performer. A world-renowned ballet dancer, she acted and sang in a few Broadway musicals. Zorina was born in Berlin to Norwegian parents, was a professional dancer by the age of seven, and later was a member of the Ballet Russe. She had danced on the stages of London and New York before playing the role of the ballerina Vera in the West End production of _ON YOUR TOES_. Zorina's Broadway bow was as the celestial heroine in _I MARRIED AN ANGEL_ (1938), which was followed by the seductive Marina in _LOUISIANA PURCHASE_ (1940); she got to reprise the last on screen. SAMUEL GOLDWYN brought Zorina to Hollywood and featured her in _THE GOLDWYN FOLLIES_ (1938). Her other screen musicals were _STAR-SPANGLED RHYTHM_ (1942) and _Follow the Boys_ (1944). She returned to Broadway to dance in the theatre–dance piece _Dream With Music_ (1944) and in 1954 reprised her Vera for New Yorkers in the Broadway revival of _On Your Toes_. She also appeared in a few television broadcasts in the early 1950s. Zorina retired from performing in the mid-1950s and concentrated on managing opera companies and record production. She was married to choreographer GEORGE BALANCHINE and then record producer Goddard Lieberson (1911–1977).

ZUCCO, GEORGE (1886–1960). Film and stage performer. A British character actor who played a variety of oddball types on the American stage and screen, he was often cast as heavies in his Hollywood musicals. Zucco was born in Manchester, England, and began his acting career in Canada in 1908. After appearing in vaudeville and stock he appeared on Broadway as Disraeli in the Helen Hayes play _Victoria Regina_ (1935). He first appeared in British films in 1931 but five years later was frequently seen in Hollywood features where he specialized in mad scientists and sinister henchmen. Zucco was seen in a slightly lighter vein in such musicals as _THE FIREFLY_ (1937), _ROSALIE_ (1937), _NEW MOON_ (1940), _THE PIRATE_ (1948), _THE BARKLEYS OF BROADWAY_ (1949), and _Let's Dance_ (1950).

Chronology of Musicals

All of the musicals that have their own entries or are discussed within an entry are listed below in the order in which they initially opened in New York or were released or first broadcast. Film and television remakes are included but not Broadway revivals.

1750
The Beggar's Opera 🕮

1866
The Black Crook 🕮

1868
Humpty Dumpty 🕮

1874
Evangeline 🕮

1875
Around the World in Eighty Days 🕮

1878
The Mulligan Guard's Picnic 🕮

1879
The Mulligan Guards' Ball 🕮
H. M. S. Pinafore 🕮
The Brook 🕮
The Pirates of Penzance 🕮

1883
Cordelia's Aspirations 🕮

1884
Adonis 🕮

1885
The Mikado 🕮

1891
Wang 🕮
Robin Hood 🕮
A Trip to Chinatown 🕮

1894
The Passing Show 🕮

1896
El Capitan 🕮

1897
The Belle of New York 🕮

1898
Clorindy 🕮
The Fortune Teller 🕮

1900
Florodora 🕮

1903
The Wizard of Oz 🕮
In Dahomey 🕮
Babes in Toyland 🕮

1904
Little Johnny Jones 🐱

1905
Mlle. Modiste 🐱

1906
Forty-five Minutes From Broadway 🐱
The Red Mill 🐱

1907
The Follies of 1907 🐱
The Time, the Place and the Girl 🐱
The Merry Widow 🐱

1909
The Chocolate Soldier 🐱

1910
Madame Sherry 🐱
Naughty Marietta 🐱

1911
The Pink Lady 🐱
Ziegfeld Follies 🐱

1912
The Firefly 🐱

1913
Sweethearts 🐱

1914
The Girl From Utah 🐱
Chin-Chin 🐱
Watch Your Step 🐱

1915
Ziegfeld Follies 🐱
The Blue Paradise 🐱
Very Good Eddie 🐱

1917
Oh, Boy! 🐱
Maytime 🐱
Leave It to Jane 🐱

1918
Oh, Lady! Lady! 🐱

Ziegfeld Follies 🐱
Sinbad 🐱
Yip Yip Yaphank 🐱

1919
Scandals of 1919 🐱
Ziegfeld Follies 🐱
Irene 🐱

1920
Mary 🐱
Sally 🐱

1921
Shuffle Along 🐱
Ziegfeld Follies 🐱
George White's Scandals 🐱
The Music Box Revue 🐱
Blossom Time 🐱
Bombo 🐱

1922
Little Nellie Kelly 🐱
Ziegfeld Follies 🐱
George White's Scandals 🐱

1923
Wildflower 🐱
Artists and Models 🐱
Earl Carroll Vanities 🐱

1924
Andre Charlot's Revue 🐱
Rose-Marie 🐱
Artists and Models 🐱
Earl Carroll's Vanities 🐱
Lady, Be Good! 🐱
The Student Prince 🐱

1925
Big Boy 🐱
The Garrick Gaieties 🐱
No, No, Nanette 🐱
Dearest Enemy 🐱
The Vagabond King 🐱
Sunny 🐱
The Cocoanuts 🐱
Tip-Toes 🐱

1926
George White's Scandals 🐱
Countess Maritza 🐱

Garrick Gaieties of 1926
Oh, Kay!
The Desert Song
Peggy-Ann

1927

Rio Rita
Hit the Deck!
Good News!
Artists and Models
Present Arms
The Jazz Singer
A Connecticut Yankee
Funny Face
Show Boat

1928

My Man
Rosalie
The Three Musketeers
Present Arms
Blackbirds of 1928
The New Moon
The Singing Fool
Hold Everything!
Animal Crackers
Whoopee!

1929

Follow Thru
The Broadway Melody
The Little Show
On With the Show
The Desert Song
Heads Up!
Paramount on Parade
Innocents of Paris
The Coconuts
Show Boat
The Hollywood Revue of 1929
Gold Diggers of Broadway
Sweet Adeline
Hallelujah
Sunny Side Up
Rio Rita
Bitter Sweet
The Love Parade
Applause
The Show of Shows
Little Johnny Jones
Fifty Million Frenchmen
Sally

1930

Strike Up the Band

No, No, Nanette
Garrick Gaieties of 1930
Leathernecking
Follow Thru
Sunny
Evergreen
Simple Simon
Hit the Deck!
The Vagabond King
Flying High
King of Jazz
Paramount on Parade
Monte Carlo
Animal Crackers
Heads Up!
Puttin' on the Ritz
Hold Everything!
Good News!
Fine and Dandy
Whoopee
Girl Crazy
Three's a Crowd
The New Yorkers
The New Moon

1931

The Smiling Lieutenant
Follow Through
Delicious
The Band Wagon
Earl Carroll Vanities
Flying High
Kiss Me Again
The Threepenny Opera
Leathernecking
Heads Up!
George White's Scandals
The Cat and the Fiddle
Of Thee I Sing
Sunny

1932

Face the Music
One Hour With You
Love Me Tonight
The Phantom President
Girl Crazy
The Big Broadcast
Flying Colors
Music in the Air
Take a Chance
Gay Divorce

1933

Hallelujah, I'm a Bum

42nd Street 🎬
She Done Him Wrong 🎬
The Threepenny Opera 🎭
International House 🎬
Gold Diggers of 1933 🎬
Take a Chance 🎬
Bitter Sweet 🎬
Footlight Parade 🎬
As Thousands Cheer 🎭
Roberta 🎭
Let 'Em Eat Cake 🎭
Dancing Lady 🎬
Roman Scandals 🎬
Flying Down to Rio 🎬
Going Hollywood 🎬
Duck Soup 🎬

1934

New Faces 🎭
Ziegfeld Follies 🎭
The Cat and the Fiddle 🎬
Wonder Bar 🎬
George White's Scandals 🎬
We're Not Dressing 🎬
Evergreen 🎬
One Night of Love 🎬
Life Begins at 8:40 🎭
Blossom Time 🎬
College Rhythm 🎬
Revenge With Music 🎭
Dames 🎬
The Merry Widow 🎬
The Great Waltz 🎭
The Gay Divorcee 🎬
Anything Goes 🎭
Kid Millions 🎬
Music in the Air 🎬
Babes in Toyland 🎬

1935

Sweet Adeline 🎬
Roberta 🎬
Folies Bergere de Paris 🎬
Gold Diggers of 1935 🎬
Go Into Your Dance 🎬
Naughty Marietta 🎬
Every Night at Eight 🎬
Mississippi 🎬
Top Hat 🎬
At Home Abroad 🎭
The Big Broadcast of 1936 🎬
Porgy and Bess 🎭
Thanks a Million 🎬
Jubilee 🎭
Jumbo 🎭
King of Burlesque 🎬

I Dream Too Much 🎬
Curly Top 🎬
A Night at the Opera 🎬

1936

Rose Marie 🎬
Anything Goes 🎬
Follow the Fleet 🎬
Poor Little Rich Girl 🎬
San Francisco 🎬
Swing Time 🎬
The Big Broadcast of 1937 🎬
Pennies From Heaven 🎬
Red, Hot and Blue! 🎭
New Faces 🎭
Born to Dance 🎬
Let's Sing Again 🎬
Ziegfeld Follies 🎭
On Your Toes 🎭
The Great Ziegfeld 🎬
Show Boat 🎬
Gold Diggers of 1937 🎬
One in a Million 🎬
The Show Is On 🎭
Johnny Johnson 🎭

1937

On the Avenue 🎬
Maytime 🎬
New Faces of 1937 🎬
Babes in Arms 🎭
Artists and Models 🎬
Wake Up and Live 🎬
Shall We Dance 🎬
Between the Devil 🎭
A Day at the Races 🎬
High, Wide and Handsome 🎬
Double or Nothing 🎬
Varsity Show 🎬
Broadway Melody of 1938 🎬
The Firefly 🎬
One Hundred Men and a Girl 🎬
I'd Rather Be Right 🎭
Damsel in Distress 🎬
Pins and Needles 🎭
Hooray for What! 🎭
Snow White and the Seven Dwarfs 🎬
Rosalie 🎬
Hollywood Hotel 🎬

1938

The Cradle Will Rock 🎭
The Goldwyn Follies 🎬
The Big Broadcast of 1938 🎬
Joy of Living 🎬
Artists and Models Abroad 🎬

I Married an Angel 🎬
Rebecca of Sunnybrook Farm 🎬
Alexander's Ragtime Band 🎬
Sing You Sinners 🎬
Gold Diggers of Paris 🎬
In Old Chicago 🎬
Carefree 🎬
Hellzapoppin' ✋
Knickerbocker Holiday ✋
Leave It to Me! ✋
The Great Waltz 🎬
The Boys From Syracuse ✋
Sweethearts 🎬

1939

The Story of Vernon and Irene Castle 🎬
Second Fiddle 🎬
The Wizard of Oz 🎬
On Your Toes 🎬
At the Circus 🎬
The Mikado 🎬
Rose of Washington Square 🎬
Gulliver's Travels 🎬
Very Warm for May ✋
Too Many Girls ✋
Babes in Arms 🎬
DuBarry Was a Lady ✋

1940

Irene 🎬
Higher and Higher ✋
Pinocchio 🎬
Bitter Sweet 🎬
Little Nellie Kelly 🎬
Love Thy Neighbor 🎬
Broadway Melody of 1940 🎬
The Boys From Syracuse 🎬
Rhythm on the River 🎬
Road to Singapore 🎬
New Moon 🎬
Lillian Russell 🎬
Louisiana Purchase ✋
Strike Up the Band 🎬
Cabin in the Sky ✋
Down Argentine Way 🎬
Panama Hattie ✋
One Night in the Tropics 🎬
Fantasia 🎬
Too Many Girls 🎬
Tin Pan Alley 🎬
No, No, Nanette 🎬
Pal Joey ✋
Lady in the Dark ✋

1941

That Night in Rio 🎬

Ziegfeld Girl 🎬
Sunny 🎬
Moon Over Miami 🎬
Dumbo 🎬
Buck Privates 🎬
The Chocolate Soldier 🎬
Sun Valley Serenade 🎬
Lady, Be Good! 🎬
Birth of the Blues 🎬
Road to Zanzibar 🎬
Louisiana Purchase 🎬
Weekend in Havana 🎬
You'll Never Get Rich 🎬
Best Foot Forward ✋
Blues in the Night 🎬
Let's Face It! ✋
Babes on Broadway 🎬
Hellzapoppin' 🎬

1942

Louisiana Purchase 🎬
The Fleet's In 🎬
I Married an Angel 🎬
My Gal Sal 🎬
Yankee Doodle Dandy 🎬
Rio Rita 🎬
Stormy Weather 🎬
By Jupiter ✋
Holiday Inn 🎬
This Is the Army ✋
Orchestra Wives 🎬
Springtime in the Rockies 🎬
You Were Never Lovelier 🎬
Road to Morocco 🎬
For Me and My Gal 🎬
Iceland 🎬
Panama Hattie 🎬
Star-Spangled Rhythm 🎬

1943

Something for the Boys ✋
Hello, Frisco, Hello 🎬
Happy Go Lucky 🎬
Oklahoma! ✋
Cabin in the Sky 🎬
Stagedoor Canteen 🎬
Higher and Higher 🎬
New Faces 🎬
Coney Island 🎬
This Is the Army 🎬
Thank Your Lucky Stars 🎬
Sweet Rosie O'Grady 🎬
One Touch of Venus ✋
Best Foot Forward 🎬
Let's Face It! 🎬
DuBarry Was a Lady 🎬

The Sky's the Limit 🎬
Girl Crazy 🎬
The Desert Song 🎬
The Gang's All Here 🎬
Carmen Jones 🖒

1944

Higher and Higher 🎬
Lady in the Dark 🎬
Mexican Hayride 🖒
Up in Arms 🎬
Going My Way 🎬
Here Come the Waves 🎬
Cover Girl 🎬
Follow the Girls 🖒
Two Girls and a Sailor 🎬
Knickerbocker Holiday 🎬
Broadway Rhythm 🎬
Song of Norway 🖒
Bloomer Girl 🖒
Can't Help Singing 🎬
Something for the Boys 🎬
The Boys From Boise 📺
Hollywood Canteen 🎬
Meet Me in St. Louis 🎬
On the Town 🖒

1945

Up in Central Park 🖒
Carousel 🖒
Rhapsody in Blue 🎬
Anchors Aweigh 🎬
The Three Caballeros 🎬
Earl Carroll Vanities 🎬
State Fair 🎬
The Dolly Sisters 🎬
George White's Scandals 🎬
The Bells of St. Mary's 🎬
Road to Utopia 🎬

1946

Ziegfeld Follies 🎬
The Harvey Girls 🎬
St. Louis Woman 🖒
Call Me Mister 🖒
Annie Get Your Gun 🖒
Make Mine Music 🎬
Centennial Summer 🎬
Night and Day 🎬
Around the World 🖒
Three Little Girls in Blue 🎬
The Jolson Story 🎬
Blue Skies 🎬
Song of the South 🎬
Till the Clouds Roll By 🎬

1947

Street Scene 🖒
Finian's Rainbow 🖒
The Shocking Miss Pilgrim 🎬
It Happened in Brooklyn 🎬
Brigadoon 🖒
New Orleans 🎬
Summer Holiday 🎬
Mother Wore Tights 🎬
High Button Shoes 🖒
Allegro 🖒
Road to Rio 🎬
Good News! 🎬

1948

Make Mine Manhattan 🖒
The Pirate 🎬
The Paleface 🎬
Inside U. S. A. 🖒
Up in Central Park 🎬
Melody Time 🎬
Easter Parade 🎬
Casbah 🎬
Love Life 🖒
Romance on the High Seas 🎬
Where's Charley? 🖒
As the Girls Go 🖒
A Date With Judy 🎬
One Touch of Venus 🎬
Lend an Ear 🖒
Words and Music 🎬
Kiss Me, Kate 🖒

1949

South Pacific 🖒
Take Me Out to the Ball Game 🎬
A Connecticut Yankee in King Arthur's Court 🎬
The Barkleys of Broadway 🎬
Neptune's Daughter 🎬
In the Good Old Summertime 🎬
Miss Liberty 🖒
Jolson Sings Again 🎬
Lost in the Stars 🖒
Regina 🖒
Gentlemen Prefer Blondes 🖒
On the Town 🎬

1950

Young Man With a Horn 🎬
Cinderella 🎬
The Toast of New Orleans 🎬
Annie Get Your Gun 🎬
Three Little Words 🎬 📺
Knickerbocker Holiday 📺

Peter Pan 📺
Summer Stock 🎬
Wabash Avenue 🎬
Call Me Madam 📺
Guys and Dolls 📺
Out of This World 📺

1951

On the Riviera 🎬
Royal Wedding 🎬
The King and I 📺
A Tree Grows in Brooklyn 📺
The Great Caruso 🎬
Call Me Mister 🎬
On the Riviera 🎬
Show Boat 🎬
Alice in Wonderland 🎬
Flahooley 📺
Here Comes the Groom 🎬
Two on the Aisle 📺
An American in Paris 🎬
Paint Your Wagon 📺

1952

With a Song in My Heart 🎬
The Belle of New York 🎬
The Merry Widow 🎬
Singin' in the Rain 🎬
New Faces of 1952 📺
The Jazz Singer 🎬
Lovely to Look At 🎬
Wish You Were Here 📺
Where's Charley? 🎬
Son of Paleface 🎬
Road to Bali 🎬
Hans Christian Andersen 🎬

1953

Wonderful Town 📺
Call Me Madam 🎬
The Desert Song 🎬
Thirteen Clocks 📺 🎬
The Beggar's Opera 🎬
Peter Pan 🎬
Lili 🎬
Can-Can 📺
The Farmer Takes a Wife 🎬
The 5,000 Fingers of Dr. T 🎬
Me and Juliet 📺
Gentlemen Prefer Blondes 🎬
The Band Wagon 🎬
Kiss Me, Kate 🎬
Kismet 📺
Calamity Jane 🎬
Give a Girl a Break 🎬

1954

New Faces 🎬
The Glenn Miller Story 🎬
The Threepenny Opera 📺
Rose Marie 🎬
The Country Girl 🎬
Lady in the Dark 🎬
Let's Face It! 📺
The Golden Apple 📺
By the Beautiful Sea 📺
Panama Hattie 📺
The Pajama Game 📺
Seven Brides for Seven Brothers 🎬
The Student Prince 🎬
White Christmas 🎬
Brigadoon 🎬
A Star Is Born 🎬
Satins and Spurs 📺
The Boy Friend 📺
Carmen Jones 🎬
Peter Pan 📺
Fanny 📺
Deep in My Heart 🎬
There's No Business Like Show Business 🎬
A Christmas Carol 📺
House of Flowers 📺

1955

Plain and Fancy 📺
Silk Stockings 📺
Peter Pan 📺
Hit the Deck! 🎬
Naughty Marietta 📺
Lady and the Tramp 🎬
Dearest Enemy 📺
Pipe Dream 📺
Damn Yankees 📺
Love Me or Leave Me 🎬
Artists and Models 🎬
Daddy Long Legs 🎬
The Desert Song 📺
The Great Waltz 📺
Pete Kelly's Blues 🎬
The Merry Widow 📺
It's Always Fair Weather 🎬
The Chocolate Soldier 📺
Our Town 📺
My Sister Eileen 🎬
One Touch of Venus 📺
Oklahoma! 🎬
Guys and Dolls 🎬
Kismet 🎬
I'll Cry Tomorrow 🎬

1956

The Court Jester 🎬

Carousel
The King and I
New Faces
Bloomer Girl
The Vagabond King
High Tor
My Fair Lady
High Button Shoes
The Adventures of Marco Polo
Mr. Wonderful
Anything Goes
Jack and the Beanstalk
Love Me Tender
The Best Things in Life Are Free
The Most Happy Fella
A Bell for Adano
The Bachelor
Invitation to the Dance
High Society
Li'l Abner
Bells Are Ringing
Candide
The Stingiest Man in Town

1957

Ruggles of Red Gap
Funny Face
Cinderella
New Girl in Town
Silk Stockings
Annie Get Your Gun
Pinocchio
The Pajama Game
The Joker Is Wild
Pal Joey
West Side Story
Les Girls
Who's Earnest?
Jamaica
The Music Man
Jailhouse Rock
The Pied Piper of Hamlin
Junior Miss

1958

Hans Brinker or the Silver Skates
Aladdin
The Seven Hills of Rome
South Pacific
Hansel and Gretel
Goldilocks
La Plume de Ma Tante
Gigi
Wonderful Town
Damn Yankees
King Creole

Kiss Me Kate
Tom Thumb
Little Women
Flower Drum Song
Gift of the Magi

1959

Redhead
Juno
The Five Pennies
Destry Rides Again
Saratoga
Once Upon a Mattress
Gypsy
Porgy and Bess
The Jazz Singer
Take Me Along
Meet Me in St. Louis
The Sound of Music
Li'l Abner
Little Mary Sunshine
Fiorello!

1960

Greenwillow
Can-Can
Bye Bye Birdie
The Fantasticks
Irma la Douce
Tenderloin
Peter Pan
So Help Me, Aphrodite
Bells Are Ringing
The Unsinkable Molly Brown
Earnest in Love
Camelot
Wildcat
Do Re Mi

1961

Carnival
West Side Story
Babes in Toyland
The Gay Life
Kwamina
Feathertop
Milk and Honey
How to Succeed in Business Without Really Trying
Flower Drum Song
Subways Are for Sleeping

1962

No Strings
The Music Man
The Road to Hong Kong

All American 📖
State Fair 🎬
New Faces 📖
The Threepenny Opera 🎬
Blue Hawaii 🎬
I Can Get It for You Wholesale 📖
Gypsy 🎬
Mr. President 📖
A Funny Thing Happened on the Way to the Forum 📖
Stop the World—I Want to Get Off 📖
Little Me 📖
Billy Rose's Jumbo 🎬
Mr. Magoo's Christmas Carol 📺
Gay Purr-ee 🎬

1963

Oliver! 📖
She Loves Me 📖
Bye Bye Birdie 🎬
Summer Magic 🎬
110 in the Shade 📖
Quillow and the Giant 📺

1964

Hello, Dolly! 📖
Funny Girl 📖
Anyone Can Whistle 📖
Viva Las Vegas 🎬
The Fantasticks 📺
The Unsinkable Molly Brown 🎬
Kiss Me, Kate 📺
Robin and the Seven Hoods 🎬
A Hard Day's Night 🎬
Once Upon a Mattress 📺
Fade Out—Fade In 📖
Mary Poppins 🎬
Fiddler on the Roof 📖
Golden Boy 📖
The Story of Rudolph the Red-Nosed Reindeer 📺
My Fair Lady 🎬

1965

Cinderella 📺
Do I Hear a Waltz? 📖
The Sound of Music 🎬
Half a Sixpence 📖
Flora, the Red Menace 📖
The Roar of the Greasepaint—The Smell of the Crowd 📖
Help! 🎬
On a Clear Day You Can See Forever 📖
The Court Jester 🎬
Pinocchio 📺
The Dangerous Christmas of Red Riding Hood 📺

1966

Man of La Mancha 📖
Sweet Charity 📖
How to Succeed in Business Without Really Trying 📖
Alice in Wonderland 📺
It's a Bird, It's a Plane, It's Superman 📖
Brigadoon 📺
Jack and the Beanstalk 📺
Mame 📖
A Funny Thing Happened on the Way to the Forum 🎬
When the Boys Meet the Girls 🎬
Man With a Load of Mischief 📖
Olympus 7-0000 📺
The Apple Tree 📖
The Canterville Ghost 📺
Cabaret 📖
I Do! I Do! 📖
Evening Primrose 📺
Alice Through the Looking Glass 📺
Dr. Seuss' How the Grinch Stole Christmas 📺

1967

Hallelujah, Baby! 📖
Jack and the Beanstalk 📺
You're a Good Man, Charlie Brown 📖
Carousel 📺
Thoroughly Modern Millie 🎬
Annie Get Your Gun 📺
Damn Yankees 📺
Half a Sixpence 🎬
Pinocchio 📺
Camelot 🎬
The Jungle Book 🎬
Kismet 📺
Aladdin 📺
Doctor Dolittle 🎬
Androcles and the Lion 📺

1968

Your Own Thing 📖
The Happy Time 📖
Jacques Brel Is Alive and Well and Living in Paris 📖
George M! 📖
New Faces 📖
Hair 📖
Kiss Me, Kate 📺
Finian's Rainbow 🎬
Funny Girl 🎬
Star! 🎬
Zorbá 📖
That's Life 📺
Yellow Submarine 🎬
Chitty Chitty Bang Bang 🎬

Promises, Promises 🖱️
Oliver! 📺
Babes in Toyland 📺
Dames at Sea 🖱️

1969

Sweet Charity 🎬
Celebration 🖱️
1776 🖱️
Coco 🖱️
Paint Your Wagon 🎬
Dear World 🖱️
Hello, Dolly! 🎬
Goodbye, Mr. Chips 🎬
Hans Brinker or the Silver Skates 📺
The Littlest Angel 📺

1970

Purlie 🖱️
Darling Lili 🎬
Applause 🖱️
Company 🖱️
On a Clear Day You Can See Forever 🎬
Woodstock 📺
George M! 📺
The Aristocats 🎬
The Rothschilds 🖱️
The Last Sweet Days of Isaac 🖱️
Song of Norway 🎬
Scrooge 🎬
Santa Claus Is Coming to Town 📺
Two By Two 🖱️
The Me Nobody Knows 🖱️

1971

Willy Wonka and the Chocolate Factory 🎬
Follies 🖱️
Dames at Sea 🖱️
Godspell 🖱️
Oh, Calcutta! 🖱️
Jesus Christ Superstar 🖱️
70, Girls, 70 🖱️
Fiddler on the Roof 🎬
Bedknobs and Broomsticks 🎬
The Boy Friend 🎬
Ain't Supposed to Die a Natural Death 🖱️
The Grass Harp 🖱️
Two Gentlemen of Verona 🖱️

1972

Cabaret 🎬
Grease 🖱️
Sugar 🖱️
The Great Waltz 🎬
Man of La Mancha 🎬

Don't Bother Me, I Can't Cope 🖱️
Of Thee I Sing 📺
Lady Sings the Blues 🎬
Pippin 🖱️
Oh, Calcutta! 🎬
1776 🎬

1973

A Little Night Music 🖱️
Dr. Jekyll and Mr. Hyde 📺
Seesaw 🖱️
Charlotte's Web 🎬
Applause 📺
Robin Hood 🎬
You're a Good Man, Charlie Brown 📺
Raisin 🖱️
Jesus Christ Superstar 🎬
Godspell 🎬
Gigi 🖱️

1974

Lost in the Stars 🎬
Lorelei 🖱️
Mame 🎬
Over Here! 🖱️
Journey Back to Oz 🎬
That's Entertainment 🎬
Phantom of the Paradise 🎬
The Magic Show 🖱️
The Year Without a Santa Claus 📺
Mack and Mabel 🖱️

1975

The Wiz 🖱️
Shenandoah 🖱️
Queen of the Stardust Ballroom 📺
Funny Lady 🎬
The Rocky Horror Show 🖱️
Chicago 🖱️
Tommy 🎬
Jacques Brel Is Alive and Well and Living in
Paris 🎬
Really Rosie 📺
A Chorus Line 🖱️
The Robber Bridegroom 🖱️
Nashville 🎬
The Rocky Horror Picture Show 🎬

1976

Pacific Overtures 🖱️
Bubbling Brown Sugar 🖱️
The Baker's Wife 🖱️
Bugsy Malone 🎬
The Slipper and the Rose 🎬
1600 Pennsylvania Avenue 🖱️

That's Entertainment, Part Two 🎬
Pinocchio ☐
Your Arms Too Short to Box With God 📺
Peter Pan ☐
A Star Is Born 🎬

1977

Once Upon a Brothers Grimm ☐
Minstrel Man ☐
I Love My Wife 📺
Starting Here, Starting Now 📺
The Rescuers 🎬
Annie 📺
New York, New York 🎬
The Act 📺
Pete's Dragon 🎬
Saturday Night Fever 🎬

1978

On the Twentieth Century 📺
Cindy ☐
Dancin' 📺
Ain't Misbehavin' 📺
I'm Getting My Act Together and Taking It on
the Road 📺
Ballroom 📺
A Little Night Music 🎬
Grease 🎬
Working 📺
She Loves Me ☐
Timbuktu! 📺
The Buddy Holly Story 🎬
The Wiz 🎬
Movie Movie 🎬
The Best Little Whorehouse in Texas 📺
The Stingiest Man in Town ☐

1979

They're Playing Our Song 📺
Sweeney Todd, the Demon Barber of Fleet Street 📺
Hair 🎬
The Muppet Movie 🎬
Evita 📺
The Wiz 🎬
Sugar Babies 📺
Rudolph and Frosty's Christmas ☐
The Rose 🎬

1980

All That Jazz 🎬
Coal Miner's Daughter 🎬
Fame 🎬
The Jazz Singer 🎬
Xanadu 🎬
Barnum 📺

A Day in Hollywood—A Night in the Ukraine 📺
42nd Street 📺

1981

Sophisticated Ladies 📺
Woman of the Year 📺
Dreamgirls 📺
Merrily We Roll Along 📺
Pennies From Heaven 🎬

1982

Forbidden Broadway 📺
Joseph and the Amazing Technicolor Dreamcoat 📺
Victor/Victoria 🎬
Seven Brides for Seven Brothers 📺
Annie 🎬
Grease 2 🎬
Nine 📺
Little Shop of Horrors 📺
Cats 📺

1983

Flashdance 🎬
My One and Only 📺
The Beggar's Opera ☐
La Cage aux Folles 📺
Baby 📺
Yentl 🎬
The Tap Dance Kid 📺

1984

Footloose 🎬
The Rink 📺
This Is Spinal Tap 🎬
The Human Comedy 📺
Sunday in the Park With George 📺
The Cotton Club 🎬

1985

Big River 📺
The Mystery of Edwin Drood 📺
Follow That Bird 🎬
Nunsense 📺
A Chorus Line 🎬
Copacabana ☐
You're a Good Man, Charlie Brown ☐
Alice in Wonderland ☐
The Life and Adventures of Santa Claus ☐

1986

Me and My Girl 📺
Rags 📺
Singin' in the Rain 📺
Little Shop of Horrors 🎬
Babes in Toyland ☐

1987

Les Misérables 🐝
Starlight Express 🐝
The Wind in the Willows 📺
La Bamba 🎬
Dirty Dancing 🎬
Into the Woods 🐝

1988

The Phantom of the Opera 🐝
Oliver & Company 🎬
Chess 🐝
Bird 🎬

1989

Jerome Robbins' Broadway 🐝
The Little Mermaid 🎬
Grand Hotel 🐝
Polly 📺
City of Angels 🐝
Meet Me in St. Louis 🐝
Closer Than Ever 🐝

1990

Aspects of Love 🐝
Forever Plaid 🐝
Buddy 🐝
Dick Tracy 🎬
Polly—Comin' Home! 📺
Cop Rock 📺
Mack the Knife 🎬
Once on This Island 🐝

1991

The Doors 🎬
Miss Saigon 🐝
The Secret Garden 🐝
Assassins 🐝
Joseph and the Amazing Technicolor Dreamcoat 📺
The Will Rogers Follies 🐝
The Commitments 🎬
For the Boys 🎬
Beauty and the Beast 🎬

1992

Jelly's Last Jam 🐝
Crazy for You 🐝
Five Guys Named Moe 🐝
Falsettos 🐝
Aladdin 🎬

1993

The Who's Tommy 🐝

Blood Brothers 🐝
Kiss of the Spider Woman 🐝
Cinderella 🐝
Gypsy 📺
The Nightmare Before Christmas 🎬

1994

Beauty and the Beast 🐝
Hello Again 🐝
Passion 🐝
The Lion King 🎬
Sunset Boulevard 🐝

1995

Pocahontas 🎬
Bye Bye Birdie 📺
A Christmas Carol 🐝
The Fantasticks 🎬
Smokey Joe's Cafe 🐝
Victor/Victoria 🐝

1996

State Fair 🐝
Bring in 'da Noise, Bring in 'da Funk 🐝
Rent 🐝
The Hunchback of Notre Dame 🎬
Floyd Collins 🐝
I Love You, You're Perfect, Now Change 🐝
The Preacher's Wife 🎬
That Thing You Do 🎬
Waiting for Guffman 🎬
Mrs. Santa Claus 📺

1997

Everyone Says I Love You 🎬
Violet 🐝
Evita 🎬
Titanic 🐝
The Life 🐝
Jekyll and Hyde 🐝
Hercules 🎬
The Scarlet Pimpernel 🐝
Cinderella 📺
The Lion King 🐝
Anastasia 🎬
Babes in Toyland 🎬

1998

Ragtime 🐝
High Society 🐝
Footloose 🐝
Mulan 🎬
Cats 📺
Hedwig and the Angry Inch 🐝

A New Brain 📺
Parade 📺
The Prince of Egypt 🎬

1999

Fosse 📺
James Joyce's The Dead 📺
Tarzan 🎬
The Cradle Will Rock 🎬
The King and I 🎬
Annie 📺
Joseph and the Amazing Technicolor Dreamcoat 📺
Saturday Night Fever 📺

2000

Contact 📺
Aida 📺
The Wild Party 📺
Fantasia 2000 🎬
Footloose 📺
The Full Monty 📺
Seussical 📺
Geppetto 📺

2001

The Producers 📺
Bat Boy 📺
Hedwig and the Angry Inch 🎬
Moulin Rouge! 🎬
South Pacific 📺
Urinetown 📺
Mamma Mia! 📺

2002

Thoroughly Modern Millie 📺
Hairspray 📺
Chicago 🎬
Movin' Out 📺

2003

Avenue Q 📺
The Boy From Oz 📺
Camp 🎬
The Music Man 📺
Wicked 📺

2004

Caroline or Change 📺
De-Lovely 🎬
Ray 🎬
The Phantom of the Opera 🎬
Little Women 📺
Never Gonna Dance 📺
A Christmas Carol 📺

2005

The Light in the Piazza 📺
Spamalot 📺
Chitty Chitty Bang Bang 📺
The 25th Annual Putnam County Spelling Bee 📺
Dirty Rotten Scoundrels 📺
Walk the Line 🎬
Once Upon a Mattress 📺
Jersey Boys 📺
The Color Purple 📺
Rent 🎬
The Producers 🎬

2006

The Drowsy Chaperone 📺
High School Musical 📺
Tarzan 📺
Grey Gardens 📺
Mary Poppins 📺
Spring Awakening 📺
Dreamgirls 🎬
Dr. Seuss' How the Grinch Stole Christmas 📺

2007

Curtains 📺
Legally Blonde 📺
Xanadu 📺
High School Musical 2 📺
Hairspray 🎬
Across the Universe 🎬
Young Frankenstein 📺
Sweeney Todd 🎬

2008

The Little Mermaid 📺
In the Heights 📺

Awards

Stage musicals that have won the PULITZER PRIZE and/or the NEW YORK DRAMA CRITICS CIRCLE AWARD are listed under those entries. What follows is a more detailed listing of ACADEMY AWARDS and TONY AWARDS than is found under their entries.

Academy Awards

Listed below are the major "Oscars" given to film musicals since sound came in. The year given is the date of the award ceremony, not the release date of the film. For a list of all movies nominated for an Academy Award for Best Picture, see the ACADEMY AWARDS entry.

1928

Special Oscar to Warner Brothers for *THE JAZZ SINGER*

1929

Picture: *THE BROADWAY MELODY*

1930

Interior decoration: *KING OF JAZZ*

1934

Interior decoration: *THE MERRY WIDOW*
Sound: *ONE NIGHT OF LOVE*
Song: "The Continental" from *THE GAY DIVORCE*
Score: *One Night of Love*

1935

Sound: *NAUGHTY MARIETTA*
Song: "Lullaby of Broadway" from *GOLD DIGGERS OF 1935*
Dance direction: DAVE GOULD for *BROADWAY MELODY OF 1936* and *FOLIES BERGERE DE PARIS*

1936

Picture: *THE GREAT ZIEGFELD*
Actress: LUISE RAINER in *The Great Ziegfeld*
Sound: *SAN FRANCISCO*
Song: "The Way You Look Tonight" from *SWING TIME*
Dance direction: SEYMOUR FELIX for *The Great Ziegfeld*

1937

Supporting actress: ALICE BRADY in *IN OLD CHICAGO*
Song: "Sweet Leilani" from *Waikiki Wedding*
Score: *ONE HUNDRED MEN AND A GIRL*
Dance direction: HERMES PAN for *DAMSEL IN DISTRESS*

1938

Cinematography: *THE GREAT WALTZ*
Song: "Thanks for the Memory" from *BIG BROADCAST OF 1938*
Score: *ALEXANDER'S RAGTIME BAND*

1939

Song: "Over the Rainbow" from *THE WIZARD OF OZ*
Score: *The Wizard of Oz*

1940

Sound: *STRIKE UP THE BAND*
Song: "When You Wish Upon a Star" from *PINOCCHIO*

Score: *TIN PAN ALLEY*
Original score: *Pinocchio*

1941

Song: "The Last Time I Saw Paris" from *LADY, BE GOOD*
Score (musical): *DUMBO*

1942

Actor: JAMES CAGNEY in *YANKEE DOODLE DANDY*
Interior decoration (color): *MY GAL SAL*
Sound: *Yankee Doodle Dandy*
Song: "White Christmas" from *HOLIDAY INN*
Score: *Yankee Doodle Dandy*

1943

Cinematography (color): *The Phantom of the Opera*
Interior decoration (color): *The Phantom of the Opera*
Song: "You'll Never Know" from *HELLO, FRISCO, HELLO*
Score (musical): *THIS IS THE ARMY*

1944

Picture: *GOING MY WAY*
Actor: BING CROSBY in *Going My Way*
Supporting actor: Barry Fitzgerald in *Going My Way*
Director: LEO MCCAREY for *Going My Way*
Original story: *Going My Way*
Screenplay: *Going My Way*
Song: "Swinging on a Star" from *Going My Way*
Score (musical): *COVER GIRL*

1945

Sound: *THE BELLS OF ST. MARY'S*
Song: "It Might as Well Be Spring" from *STATE FAIR*
Score (musical): *ANCHORS AWEIGH*

1946

Sound: *THE JOLSON STORY*
Song: "On the Atchison, Topeka and the Santa Fe" from *THE HARVEY GIRLS*
Scoring (musical): *The Jolson Story*

1947

Song: "Zip-a-Dee Doo-Dah" from *SONG OF THE SOUTH*
Score (musical): *MOTHER WORE TIGHTS*

1948

Art direction (color): *The Red Shoes*
Song: "Buttons and Bows" from *THE PALEFACE*
Score (drama): *The Red Shoes*
Score (musical): *EASTER PARADE*

1949

Song: "Baby, It's Cold Outside" from *NEPTUNE'S DAUGHTER*
Score (musical): *ON THE TOWN*

1950

Scoring (musical): *ANNIE GET YOUR GUN*

1951

Picture: *AN AMERICAN IN PARIS*
Story and screenplay: *An American in Paris*
Cinematography (color): *An American in Paris*
Art direction (color): *An American in Paris*
Sound: *THE GREAT CARUSO*
Song: "In the Cool, Cool, Cool of the Evening" from *HERE COMES THE GROOM*
Score (musical): *An American in Paris*
Costumes (color): *An American in Paris*

1952

Score (musical): *WITH A SONG IN MY HEART*

1953

Song: "Secret Love" from *CALAMITY JANE*
Score (musical): *CALL ME MADAM*

1954

Actress: Grace Kelly in *THE COUNTRY GIRL*
Screenplay: *The Country Girl*
Sound: *THE GLENN MILLER STORY*
Score (musical): *SEVEN BRIDES FOR SEVEN BROTHERS*

1955

Story: *LOVE ME OR LEAVE ME*
Screenplay: *Interrupted Melody*
Sound: *OKLAHOMA!*
Score (musical): *Oklahoma!*
Costumes (black and white): *I'LL CRY TOMORROW*

1956

Actor: YUL BRYNNER in *THE KING AND I*
Art direction (color): *The King and I*
Sound: *The King and I*
Score (musical): *The King and I*
Costumes (color): *The King and I*

1957

Song: "All the Way" from *The Joker Is Wild*
Costumes: *Les Girls*

1958

Picture: *Gigi*
Director: Vincente Minnelli for *Gigi*
Screenplay: *Gigi*
Cinematography (color): *Gigi*
Art direction: *Gigi*
Sound: *South Pacific*
Song: "Gigi" from *Gigi*
Score (musical): *Gigi*
Editing: *Gigi*
Costumes: *Gigi*

1959

Score (musical): *Porgy and Bess*

1960

Score (musical): *Song Without End*

1961

Picture: *West Side Story*
Supporting actor: George Chakiris in *West Side Story*
Supporting actress: Rita Moreno in *West Side Story*
Director: Robert Wise and Jerome Robbins for *West Side Story*
Cinematography (color): *West Side Story*
Art decoration (color): *West Side Story*
Sound: *West Side Story*
Score (musical): *West Side Story*
Editing: *West Side Story*
Costumes (color): *West Side Story*

1962

Score (adaptation): *The Music Man*
Costume (color): *The Wonderful World of the Brothers Grimm*

1964

Picture: *My Fair Lady*
Actor: Rex Harrison in *My Fair Lady*
Actress: Julie Andrews in *Mary Poppins*
Director: George Cukor for *My Fair Lady*
Cinematography (color): *My Fair Lady*
Art direction (color): *My Fair Lady*
Sound: *My Fair Lady*
Song: "Chim Chim Cher-ee" from *Mary Poppins*
Score (original): *Mary Poppins*
Score (adaptation): *My Fair Lady*

Editing: *Mary Poppins*
Costumes (color): *My Fair Lady*
Special visual effects: *Mary Poppins*

1965

Picture: *The Sound of Music*
Director: Robert Wise for *The Sound of Music*
Sound: *The Sound of Music*
Score (adaptation): *The Sound of Music*
Editing: *The Sound of Music*

1966

Score (adaptation): *A Funny Thing Happened on the Way to the Forum*

1967

Art decoration: *Camelot*
Song: "Talk to the Animals" from *Doctor Dolittle*
Score (original): *Thoroughly Modern Millie*
Score (adaptation): *Camelot*
Costumes: *Camelot*
Special visual effects: *Doctor Dolittle*

1968

Picture: *Oliver!*
Director: Carol Reed for *Oliver!*
Art direction: *Oliver!*
Sound: *Oliver!*
Score (musical): *Oliver!*

1969

Art direction: *Hello, Dolly!*
Sound: *Hello, Dolly!*
Score (adaptation): *Hello, Dolly!*

1970

Score: *Let It Be*
Documentary: *Woodstock*

1971

Cinematography: *Fiddler on the Roof*
Sound: *Fiddler on the Roof*
Score (adaptation): *Fiddler on the Roof*
Special visual effects: *Bednobs and Broomsticks*

1972

Actress: Liza Minnelli in *Cabaret*
Supporting actor: Joel Grey in *Cabaret*
Director: Bob Fosse for *Cabaret*
Cinematography: *Cabaret*
Art direction: *Cabaret*

Sound: *Cabaret*
Score (adaptation): *Cabaret*
Editing: *Cabaret*

1975

Song: "I'm Easy" from *NASHVILLE*

1976

Cinematography: *Bound for Glory*
Song: "Evergreen (Love Theme from *A Star Is Born*)"
Score (original): *Bound for Glory*

1977

Score (adaptation): *A LITTLE NIGHT MUSIC*

1978

Song: "Last Dance" from *Thank God It's Friday*
Score: *THE BUDDY HOLLY STORY*

1979

Art direction: *ALL THAT JAZZ*
Score: *All That Jazz*
Editing: *All That Jazz*
Costumes: *All That Jazz*

1980

Song: "Fame" from *FAME*
Score: *Fame*

1982

Score: *VICTOR/VICTORIA*

1983

Song: "Flashdance...What a Feeling" from *FLASHDANCE*
Score: *YENTL*

1987

Song: "(I've Had) The Time of My Life" from *DIRTY DANCING*

1988

Sound: *BIRD*

1989

Song: "Under the Sea" from *THE LITTLE MERMAID*
Score: *The Little Mermaid*

1990

Art direction: *DICK TRACY*
Song: "Sooner or Later" from *Dick Tracy*
Makeup: *Dick Tracy*

1991

Song: "Beauty and the Beast" from *BEAUTY AND THE BEAST*
Score: *Beauty and the Beast*

1992

Song: "A Whole New World" from *ALADDIN*
Score: *Aladdin*

1994

Song: "Can You Feel the Love Tonight" from *THE LION KING*
Score: *The Lion King*

1995

Song: "Colors of the Wing" from *POCAHONTAS*
Score (musical): *Pocahontas*

1997

Song: "You Must Love Me" from *EVITA*

1999

Song: "When You Believe" from *THE PRINCE OF EGYPT*

2000

Costumes: *Topsy Turvy*
Makeup: *Topsy Turvy*
Song: "You'll Be in My Heart" from *TARZAN*

2002

Art decoration: *MOULIN ROUGE!*
Costumes: *Moulin Rouge!*

2003

Picture: *CHICAGO*
Supporting actress: Catherine Zeta-Jones in *Chicago*
Art decoration: *Chicago*
Costumes: *Chicago*
Sound: *Chicago*
Editing: *Chicago*

2005

Actor: Jamie Foxx in *RAY*
Sound: *Ray*

2006
Actress: Reese Witherspoon in *WALK THE LINE*

2007
Supporting actress: Jennifer Hudson in *DREAM-GIRLS*
Sound: *Dreamgirls*

Tony Awards
The Anoinette Perry Awards, more familiarly known as the Tonys, have been presented since 1947 but an award for best musical was not given until 1949. Also, categories having to do with musicals have been added and eliminated over the years. For example, some years an award was given just to lyrics, other years to music and lyrics together, and some years both were eliminated. The years indicated below are the year of the awards ceremony, not the production dates. Each musical that won an award that year is given with its winning categories.

1947
FINIAN'S RAINBOW: actor (DAVID WAYNE), choreography (MICHAEL KIDD)
BRIGADOON: choreography (AGNES DE MILLE)

1948
Angel in the Wings: actor (Paul Hartman), actress (Grace Hartman)
HIGH BUTTON SHOES: choreography (JEROME ROBBINS)

1949
KISS ME, KATE: musical, producers, score (COLE PORTER), book (Bella and Samuel Spewack), costumes
LEND AN EAR: choreography (GOWER CHAMPION)
WHERE'S CHARLEY?: actor (RAY BOLGER)
LOVE LIFE: actress (NANETTE FABRAY)
AS THE GIRLS GO: conductor/musical director (Max Meth)

1950
SOUTH PACIFIC: musical, producers, composer (RICHARD RODGERS), book (OSCAR HAMMERSTEIN), actor (EZIO PINZA), actress (MARY MARTIN), featured actress (JUANITA HALL), featured actor (Myron McCormick), director (JOSHUA LOGAN)
REGINA: costumes, conductor/musical director (Maurice Abravanel)
Touch and Go: choreography (HELEN TAMIRIS)

1951
GUYS AND DOLLS: musical, producers, score (FRANK LOESSER), book (ABE BURROWS, Jo Swerling), actor (ROBERT ALDA), featured actress (Isabel Bigley), director (GEORGE S. KAUFMAN), choreography (MICHAEL KIDD)
CALL ME MADAM: score (IRVING BERLIN) actress (ETHEL MERMAN), featured actor (RUSSELL NYPE)
Bless You All: costumes
The Consul: conductor/musical director (LEHMAN ENGEL)

1952
THE KING AND I: musical, actress (GERTRUDE LAWRENCE), featured actor (YUL BRYNNER), scenic design, costumes
PAL JOEY: featured actress (HELEN GALLAGHER), choreography (ROBERT ALTON), conductor/musical director (Max Meth)
Top Banana: actor (PHIL SILVERS)

1953
WONDERFUL TOWN: musical, producer, composer (LEONARD BERNSTEIN), book (JOSEPH FIELDS, Jerome Chodorov), actress (ROSALIND RUSSELL), scenic design, choreography (DONALD SADDLER), conductor/musical director (LEHMAN ENGEL)
Hazel Flagg: actor (Thomas Mitchell), costumes
Two's Company: featured actor: HIRAM SHERMAN
WISH YOU WERE HERE: featured actress (Sheila Bond)

1954
KISMET: musical, producer, composer (Alexander Borodin), book (Charles Lederer, Luther Davis), actor (ALFRED DRAKE), musical conductor (Louis Adrian)
CAN-CAN: featured actress (GWEN VERDON), choreography (MICHAEL KIDD)
Carnival in Flanders: actress (DOLORES GRAY)
John Murray Anderson's Almanac: actor (Harry Belafonte)

1955
THE PAJAMA GAME: musical, producers, score (RICHARD ADLER, JERRY ROSS), book (GEORGE ABBOTT, Richard Bissell), featured actress (CAROL HANEY), choreography (BOB FOSSE)
PETER PAN: actress (MARY MARTIN), featured actor (CYRIL RITCHARD)
FANNY: actor (WALTER SLEZAK)
HOUSE OF FLOWERS: scenic design

1956

DAMN YANKEES: musical, producers, score (RICHARD ADLER, JERRY ROSS), book (GEORGE ABBOTT, Douglass Wallop), actor (RAY WALSTON), actress (GWEN VERDON), featured actor (Russ Brown), choreography (BOB FOSSE)

THE THREEPENNY OPERA: featured actress (LOTTE LENYA), special Tony for Off Broadway production

PIPE DREAM: costumes

1957

MY FAIR LADY: musical, producer, composer (FREDERICK LOEWE), book (ALAN JAY LERNER), actor (REX HARRISON), director (MOSS HART), conductor/musical director (Franz Allers), scenic design, costumes

BELLS ARE RINGING: actress (JUDY HOLLIDAY), featured actor (SYDNEY CHAPLIN)

LI'L ABNER: featured actress (EDITH ADAMS), choreography (MICHAEL KIDD)

1958

THE MUSIC MAN: musical, producer, score (MEREDITH WILLSON), book (Meredith Willson, Franklin Lacy), actor (ROBERT PRESTON), featured actor (DAVID BURNS), featured actress (BARBARA COOK), conductor/musical director (Herbert Greene)

WEST SIDE STORY: choreography (JEROME ROBBINS), scenic design

NEW GIRL IN TOWN: producers, book, composer (ALBERT HAGUE), featured actress (Thelma Ritter)

1959

REDHEAD: musical, actress (GWEN VERDON), actor (RICHARD KILEY), featured actor (Leonard Stone), choreography (BOB FOSSE), costumes

FLOWER DRUM SONG: conductor/musical director (SALVATORE DELL'ISOLA)

GOLDILOCKS: featured actor (RUSSELL NYPE), featured actress (Pat Stanley)

1960

THE SOUND OF MUSIC: musical (tie), producers, composer (RICHARD RODGERS), book (HOWARD LINDSAY, RUSSEL CROUSE), actress (MARY MARTIN), featured actress (Patricia Neway), conductor/musical director (Frederick Dvonch), scenic design

FIORELLO!: musical (tie), producers, composer (JERRY BOCK), book (JEROME WEIDMAN, GEORGE ABBOTT), featured actor (TOM BOSLEY), director (George Abbott)

TAKE ME ALONG: actor (JACKIE GLEASON)

DESTRY RIDES AGAIN: choreography (MICHAEL KIDD)

SARATOGA: costumes

1961

BYE BYE BIRDIE: musical, producer, book (MICHAEL STEWART), actor (DICK VAN DYKE), director, choreography (GOWER CHAMPION)

CAMELOT: actor (Richard Burton), conductor/musical director (Franz Allers), scenic design, costumes

IRMA LA DOUCE: actress (Elizabeth Seal)

THE UNSINKABLE MOLLY BROWN: actress (TAMMY GRIMES)

1962

HOW TO SUCCEED IN BUSINESS WITHOUT REALLY TRYING: musical, producers, book (ABE BURROWS), actor (ROBERT MORSE), featured actor (CHARLES NELSON REILLY), director (Abe Burrows), conductor/musical director (Elliot Lawrence)

CARNIVAL: actress (ANNA MARIA ALBERGHETTI), scenic design

SUBWAYS ARE FOR SLEEPING: featured actress (PHYLLIS NEWMAN)

NO STRINGS: composer (RICHARD RODGERS), actress (DIAHANN CARROLL)

KWAMINA: choreography (AGNES DE MILLE)

THE GAY LIFE: costumes

1963

A FUNNY THING HAPPENED ON THE WAY TO THE FORUM: musical, producer, book (BURT SHEVELOVE, LARRY GELBART), actor (ZERO MOSTEL), featured actor (DAVID BURNS), director (GEORGE ABBOTT)

OLIVER!: score (LIONEL BART), scenic design

STOP THE WORLD—I WANT TO GET OFF: featured actress (Anna Quayle)

Tovarich: actress (Vivien Leigh)

LITTLE ME: choreography (BOB FOSSE)

1964

HELLO, DOLLY!: musical, producer, book (MICHAEL STEWART), score (JERRY HERMAN), actress (CAROL CHANNING), director, choreography (GOWER CHAMPION), conductor/musical director (Shepard Coleman), scenic design, costumes

Foxy: actor (BERT LAHR)

SHE LOVES ME: featured actor (JACK CASSIDY)

The Girl Who Came to Supper: featured actress (Tessie O'Shea)

1965

FIDDLER ON THE ROOF: musical, producer, book (JOSEPH STEIN), score (JERRY BOCK, SHELDON HARNICK), actor (ZERO MOSTEL), featured actress (MARIA KARNILOVA), director, choreography (JEROME ROBBINS), costumes

FLORA, THE RED MENACE: actress (LIZA MINNELLI)

Oh, What a Lovely War!: featured actor (Victor Spinetti)

Baker Street: scenic design

1966

MAN OF LA MANCHA: musical, score (MITCH LEIGH, Joe Darion), actor (RICHARD KILEY), director (ALBERT MARRE), scenic design

MAME: actress (ANGELA LANSBURY), featured actress (BEATRICE ARTHUR), featured actor (Frankie Michaels)

SWEET CHARITY: choreography (BOB FOSSE)

1967

CABARET: musical, score (JOHN KANDER, FRED EBB), featured actor (JOEL GREY) featured actress (Peg Murray), director (HAROLD PRINCE), choreography (RON FIELD), scenic design, costumes

I Do! I Do!: actor (ROBERT PRESTON)

THE APPLE TREE: actress (BARBARA HARRIS)

1968

HALLELUJAH, BABY!: musical, producers, score (JULE STYNE, BETTY COMDEN, ADOLPH GREEN), actress (LESLIE UGGAMS), featured actress (Lillian Hayman)

THE HAPPY TIME: actor (ROBERT GOULET), director, choreography (GOWER CHAMPION)

DARLING OF THE DAY: actress (PATRICIA ROUTLEDGE)

1969

1776: musical, featured actor (RON HOLGATE), director (Peter Hunt)

PROMISES, PROMISES: actor (JERRY ORBACH), featured actress (Marian Mercer)

DEAR WORLD: actress (ANGELA LANSBURY)

How Now Dow Jones: featured actor (HIRAM SHERMAN)

GEORGE M!: choreography (JOE LAYTON)

ZORBA!: scenic design

Canterbury Tales: costumes

1970

APPLAUSE: musical, actress (LAUREN BACALL), director, choreography (RON FIELD)

PURLIE: actor (Cleavon Little), featured actress (MELBA MOORE)

COCO: featured actor (RENE AUBERJONOIS), costumes

1971

COMPANY: musical, producer, book (George Furth), score (STEPHEN SONDHEIM), director (HAROLD PRINCE), scenic design

THE ROTHSCHILDS: actor (HAL LINDEN), featured actor (Keene Curtis)

NO, NO, NANETTE: actress (HELEN GALLAGHER), featured actress (PATSY KELLY), choreography (DONALD SADDLER), costumes

1972

TWO GENTLEMEN OF VERONA: musical, book (John Guare, Mel Shapiro)

FOLLIES: score (STEPHEN SONDHEIM), actress (ALEXIS SMITH), director (HAROLD PRINCE, MICHAEL BENNETT), choreography (Michael Bennett), scenic design, costumes, lighting

A FUNNY THING HAPPENED ON THE WAY TO THE FORUM: actor (PHIL SILVERS), featured actor (LARRY BLYDEN)

Inner City: featured actress (LINDA HOPKINS)

1973

A LITTLE NIGHT MUSIC: musical, score (STEPHEN SONDHEIM), book (HUGH WHEELER), actress (Glynis Johns), featured actress (Patricia Elliott), costumes

PIPPIN: actor (BEN VEREEN), director, choreographer (BOB FOSSE), scenic design, lighting.

IRENE: featured actor (GEORGE S. IRVING)

1974

RAISIN: musical, actress (Virginia Capers)

SEESAW: featured actor (TOMMY TUNE), choreography (MICHAEL BENNETT)

OVER HERE!: featured actress (Janie Sell)

CANDIDE: book (HUGH WHEELER), director (HAROLD PRINCE), scenic design, costumes

Cyrano: actor (Christopher Plummer)

GIGI: score (ALAN JAY LERNER, FREDERICK LOEWE)

1975

THE WIZ: musical, score (Charlie Smalls), featured actor (Ted Ross), featured actress (Dee Dee Bridgewater), director (GEOFFREY HOLDER), choreography (George Faison), costumes

SHENANDOAH: book (James Lee Barrett, PHILIP ROSE, PETER UDELL), actor (JOHN CULLUM)

GYPSY: actress (ANGELA LANSBURY)

1976

A CHORUS LINE: musical, book (James Kirkwood, Nicholas Dante), score (MARVIN HAMLISCH, Edward Kleban), actress (DONNA MCKECHNIE), featured actor (Sammy Williams), featured actress (Carole Bishop), director (MICHAEL BENNETT), choreography (Michael Bennett, Bob Avian), lighting

MY FAIR LADY: actor (GEORGE ROSE)

PACIFIC OVERTURES: scenic design, costumes

1977

ANNIE: musical, book (THOMAS MEEHAN), score (CHARLES STROUSE, MARTIN CHARNIN), actress (DOROTHY LOUDON), choreography (PETER GENNARO), scenic design, costumes

I LOVE MY WIFE: featured actor (Lenny Baker), director (GENE SAKS)

THE ROBBER BRIDEGROOM: actor (BARRY BOSTWICK)

YOUR ARMS TOO SHORT TO BOX WITH GOD: featured actress (Delores Hall)

PORGY AND BESS: revival

1978

AIN'T MISBEHAVIN': musical, featured actress (Nell Carter), director (RICHARD MALTBY, JR.)

ON THE TWENTIETH CENTURY: book (BETTY COMDEN, ADOLPH GREEN), score (CY COLEMAN, Betty Comden, Adolph Green), actor (JOHN CULLUM), featured actor (KEVIN KLINE), scenic design

THE ACT: actress (LIZA MINNELLI)

DANCIN': choreography (BOB FOSSE), lighting

1979

SWEENEY TODD, THE DEMON BARBER OF FLEET STREET: musical, book (HUGH WHEELER), score (STEPHEN SONDHEIM), actor (LEN CARIOU), actress (ANGELA LANSBURY), director (HAROLD PRINCE), scenic design, costumes

THE BEST LITTLE WHOREHOUSE IN TEXAS: featured actor (Henderson Forsythe), featured actress (Carlin Glynn)

BALLROOM: choreography (MICHAEL BENNETT, Bob Avian)

1980

EVITA: musical, book (TIM RICE), score (ANDREW LLOYD WEBBER, Tim Rice), actress (PATTI LUPONE), featured actor (MANDY PATINKIN), director (HAROLD PRINCE), lighting

A DAY IN HOLLYWOOD/A NIGHT IN THE UKRAINE: featured actress (PRISCILLA LOPEZ), choreography (TOMMY TUNE, THOMMIE WALSH)

BARNUM: actor (JIM DALE), scenic design, costumes

1981

42ND STREET: musical, director, choreography (GOWER CHAMPION)

THE PIRATES OF PENZANCE: revival, actor (KEVIN KLINE)

WOMAN OF THE YEAR: book (PETER STONE), score (JOHN KANDER, FRED EBB), actress (LAUREN BACALL), featured actress (MARILYN COOPER)

SOPHISTICATED LADIES: featured actor (HINTON BATTLE), costumes

1982

NINE: musical, score (MAURY YESTON), featured actress (Liliane Montevecchi), director (TOMMY TUNE), costumes

DREAMGIRLS: book (Tom Eyen), actor (Ben Harney), actress (Jennifer Holliday), featured actor (Cleavant Derricks), choreography (MICHAEL BENNETT, Michael Peters), lighting

1983

CATS: musical, book (T. S. Eliot), score (ANDREW LLOYD WEBBER, T. S. Eliot), featured actress (BETTY BUCKLEY), director (TREVOR NUNN), costumes, lighting

MY ONE AND ONLY: actor (TOMMY TUNE), featured actor (Charles "Honi" Coles), choreography (Tommy Tune, THOMMIE WALSH)

ON YOUR TOES: revival, actress (Natalia Markarova)

1984

LA CAGE AUX FOLLES: musical, book (HARVEY FIERSTEIN), score (JERRY HERMAN), actor (GEORGE HEARN), director (ARTHUR LAURENTS), costumes

THE RINK: actress (CHITA RIVERA)

THE TAP DANCE KID: featured actor (HINTON BATTLE), choreography (DANNY DANIELS)

SUNDAY IN THE PARK WITH GEORGE: scenic design, lighting

ZORBÁ!: featured actress Lila Kedrova

1985

BIG RIVER: musical, book (William Hauptman), score (Roger Miller), featured actor (Ron Richardson), director (DES MCANUFF), scenic design, lighting

Grind: featured actress (Leilani Jones), costumes

1986

THE MYSTERY OF EDWIN DROOD: musical, book (Rupert Holmes), score (Rupert Holmes), actor (GEORGE ROSE), director (Wilfred Leach)

SWEET CHARITY: revival, featured actor (MICHAEL RUPERT), featured actress (BEBE NEUWIRTH), costumes

Big Deal: choreography (BOB FOSSE)

Song & Dance: actress (BERNADETTE PETERS)

1987

LES MISÉRABLES: musical, book, score (Claude-Michel Schonberg, Alain Boublil, Herbert Kretzmer), featured actor (Michael Maguire), featured actress (Frances Ruffelle), director (TREVOR NUNN, John Caird), scenic design, lighting

ME AND MY GIRL: actor (Robert Lindsay), actress (Maryann Plunkett), choreography (Gillian Gregory)

STARLIGHT EXPRESS: costumes

1988

THE PHANTOM OF THE OPERA: musical, actor (MICHAEL CRAWFORD), featured actress (JUDY KAYE), director (HAROLD PRINCE), scenic design, costumes, lighting

INTO THE WOODS: book (JAMES LAPINE), score (STEPHEN SONDHEIM), actress (JOHANNA GLEASON)

ANYTHING GOES: revival, featured actor (Bill McCutcheon), choreography (Michael Smuin)

1989

JEROME ROBBINS' BROADWAY: musical, actor (JASON ALEXANDER), featured actor (Scott Wise), featured actress (Debbie Shapiro), director (JEROME ROBBINS)

BLACK AND BLUE: actress (Ruth Brown), choreography (Cholly Atkins, Henry Le Tang, Frankie Manning, FAYARD NICHOLAS), costumes

1990

CITY OF ANGELS: musical, book (LARRY GELBART), score (CY COLEMAN, David Zippel), actor (JAMES NAUGHTON), featured (RANDY GRAFF), scenic design

GRAND HOTEL: featured actor (Michael Jeter), director, choreography (TOMMY TUNE), costumes, lighting

GYPSY: revival, actress (Tyne Daly)

1991

THE WILL ROGERS FOLLIES: musical, score (CY COLEMAN, BETTY COMDEN, ADOLPH GREEN), director, choreography (TOMMY TUNE), costumes, lighting

MISS SAIGON: actor (Jonathan Pryce), actress (LEA SALONGA), featured actor (HINTON BATTLE)

THE SECRET GARDEN: book (Marsha Norman), featured actress (Daisy Eagan), scenic design

FIDDLER ON THE ROOF: revival

1992

CRAZY FOR YOU: musical, choreography (SUSAN STROMAN), costumes

GUYS AND DOLLS: revival, actress (FAITH PRINCE), director (JERRY ZAKS), scenic design

JELLY'S LAST JAM: actor (GREGORY HINES), featured actress (TONYA PINKINS), lighting

FALSETTOS: book (WILLIAM FINN, JAMES LAPINE), score (William Finn)

THE MOST HAPPY FELLA: featured actor (Scott Waara)

1993

KISS OF THE SPIDER WOMAN: musical, book (TERRENCE MCNALLY), score (JOHN KANDER, FRED EBB), actor (BRENT CARVER), actress (CHITA RIVERA), featured actor (Anthony Crivello), costumes

THE WHO'S TOMMY: director (DES MCANUFF), choreography (Wayne Cilento), scenic design, lighting

My Favorite Year: featured actress (ANDREA MARTIN)

1994

PASSION: musical, book (JAMES LAPINE), score (STEPHEN SONDHEIM), actress (DONNA MURPHY)

CAROUSEL: revival, featured actress (AUDRA MCDONALD), director (NICHOLAS HYTNER), choreography (Kenneth MacMillan), scenic design

DAMN YANKEES: featured actor (Jarrod Emick)

SHE LOVES ME: actor (BOYD GAINES)

BEAUTY AND THE BEAST: costumes

1995

SUNSET BOULEVARD: musical, book (Don Black, Christopher Hampton), score (ANDREW LLOYD WEBBER, Don Black, Christopher Hampton), actress (GLENN CLOSE), featured actor (GEORGE HEARN), scenic design, lighting

SHOWBOAT: revival, featured actress (Gretha Boston), director (HAROLD PRINCE), choreography (SUSAN STROMAN), costumes

HOW TO SUCCEED IN BUSINESS WITHOUT REALLY TRYING: actor (MATTHEW BRODERICK)

1996

RENT: musical, book, score (JONATHAN LARSON), featured actor (Jermaine Heredia)

THE KING AND I: revival, actress (DONNA MURPHY), scenic design, costumes

A FUNNY THING HAPPENED ON THE WAY TO THE FORUM: actor (NATHAN LANE)

BRING IN 'DA NOISE BRING IN 'DA FUNK: featured actress (Ann Duquesnay), director (GEORGE C. WOLFE), choreography (SAVION GLOVER), lighting

1997

TITANIC: musical, book (PETER STONE), score (MAURY YESTON), orchestrations, scenic design

CHICAGO: revival, actor (JAMES NAUGHTON), actress (BEBE NEUWIRTH), director (WALTER BOBBIE), choreography (ANN REINKING), lighting

THE LIFE: featured actor (Chuck Cooper), featured actress (LILLIAS WHITE)

CANDIDE: costumes

1998

THE LION KING: musical, director (JULIE TAYMOR), choreography (Garth Fagan), scenic design, costumes, lighting

RAGTIME: book (TERRENCE MCNALLY), score (STEPHEN FLAHERTY, LYNN AHRENS), featured actress (AUDRA MCDONALD), orchestrations

CABARET: revival, actor (Alan Cumming), actress (Natasha Richardson), featured actor (Ron Rifkin)

1999

FOSSE: musical, orchestrations, lighting

ANNIE GET YOUR GUN: revival, actress (BERNADETTE PETERS)

YOU'RE A GOOD MAN, CHARLIE BROWN: featured actor (ROGER BART), featured actress (KRISTIN CHENOWETH)

Swan Lake: director, choreography (Matthew Bourne), costumes

PARADE: book (Alfred Uhry), score (JASON ROBERT BROWN)

LITTLE ME: actor (MARTIN SHORT)

2000

CONTACT: musical, featured actor (BOYD GAINES), featured actress (KAREN ZIEMBA), choreography (SUSAN STROMAN)

KISS ME, KATE: revival, actor (BRIAN STOKES MITCHELL), director (Michael Blakemore), orchestrations, costumes

AIDA: score (ELTON JOHN, TIM RICE), actress (Heather Headley), scenic design, lighting

JAMES JOYCE'S THE DEAD: book (Richard Nelson)

2001

THE PRODUCERS: musical, book (MEL BROOKS, THOMAS MEEHAN), score (Mel Brooks), actor (NATHAN LANE), featured actor (GARY BEACH), featured actress (Cady Huffman), director, choreographer (SUSAN STROMAN), orchestrations, scenic design, costumes, lighting

42ND STREET: revival, actress (CHRISTINE EBERSOLE)

2002

THOROUGHLY MODERN MILLIE: musical, actress (SUTTON FOSTER), featured actress (Harriet Harris), choreography (ROB ASHFORD), orchestrations, costumes

URINETOWN: book (Greg Kotis), score (Mark Hollmann, Greg Kotis), director (John Rando)

INTO THE WOODS: revival, lighting

OKLAHOMA!: featured actor (Shuler Hensley)

Sweet Smell of Success: actor (John Lithgow)

2003

HAIRSPRAY: musical, book (THOMAS MEEHAN, Mark O'Donnell), score (Scott Wittman, Marc Shaiman), actor (HARVEY FIERSTEIN), actress Marissa Jaret Winokur), featured actor (Dick Latessa), director (JACK O'BRIEN), costumes

NINE: revival, featured actress (Jane Krakowski)

La Boheme: scenic design, lighting

MOVIN' OUT: choreography (Twyla Tharp), orchestrations

2004

AVENUE Q: musical, book (Jeff Whitty), score (Robert Lopez, Jeff Marx)

WICKED: actress (IDINA MENZEL), scenic design, costumes

THE BOY FROM OZ: actor (Hugh Jackman)

ASSASSINS: revival, featured actor (MICHAEL CERVERIS), director (JOE MANTELLO), orchestrations, lighting

Caroline or Change: featured actress (Anika Noni Rose)
Wonderful Town: choreography (Kathleen Marshall)

2005

Spamalot: musical, featured actress (Sarah Ramirez), director (Mike Nichols)
The Light in the Piazza: score (Adam Guettel), actress (Victoria Clark), orchestrations, scenic design, costumes, lighting
25 Annual Putnam County Spelling Bee: book (Rachel Sheinkin), featured actor (Dan Fogler)
Dirty Rotten Scoundrels: actor (Norbert Leo Butz)
La Cage aux Folles: revival, choreography (Jerry Mitchell)

2006

Jersey Boys: musical, actor (John Lloyd Young), featured actor (Christian Hoff), lighting

The Drowsy Chaperone: book (Bob Martin, Dom McKellar), score (Lisa Lambert, Greg Morison), featured actress (Beth Leavel), scenic design, costumes
The Pajama Game: revival, choreography (Kathleen Marshall)
The Color Purple: actress (La Chanze)
Sweeney Todd: director (John Doyle), orchestrations

2007

Spring Awakening: musical, book (Steven Sater), score (Duncan Sheik, Steven Sater), featured actor (John Gallagher, Jr.), director (Michael Mayer), choreography (Bill T. Jones), orchestrations, lighting
Curtains: actor (David Hyde Pierce)
Grey Gardens: actress (Christine Ebersole), featured actress (Mary Louise Wilson), costumes
Mary Poppins: scenic design
Company: revival

GUIDE TO RECORDINGS

Compiled by Catherine Hischak

The scores from theatre, film, and television musicals have been issued in different formats over the years. The following list is meant as a guide to let the reader know what recordings were made, though some are not easy to locate today. Most of the recordings listed first came out long before CDs existed, although a good number have been reissued on CD. The rest can often be found in used record stores and via online services. However, one should keep in mind that old recordings are continually being reissued on CD and, hopefully, more of the recordings found here will be in that format by the time you read this.

The listing follows a simple format: After each title, the source of the recording (original Broadway cast, film soundtrack, revival, etc.) is followed by the year the recording was first released. Major singers on the recording are then identified and, finally, it is indicated if the recording is available on CD and if the production is available on DVD. Some musicals have received many recordings over the years in which case only major ones have been selected.

Across the Universe
Film soundtrack (2007) with Jim Sturgess, Evan Rachel Wood, Joe Anderson, Dana Fuchs, Bono, Joe Cocker. CD, DVD

Act, The
Original Broadway cast (1977) with Liza Minnelli, Gayle Crofoot, Roger Minami. CD

Adventures of Marco Polo, The
TV soundtrack (1956) with Alfred Drake, Doretta Morrow, Ray Drakeley. CD

Aida
Original Broadway cast (1999) with Heather Headley, Adam Pascal, Sherie Rene Scott. CD
Studio recording (1999) with Elton John, Heather Headley, Tina Turner. CD

Ain't Misbehavin'
Original Broadway cast (1978) with Nell Carter, Andre De Shields, Ken Page, Armelia McQueen, Charlaine Woodard. CD
Tour revival (1995) with the Pointer Sisters (highlights only). CD

Ain't Supposed to Die a Natural Death
Original Broadway cast (1971) with Arthur French, Minnie Gentry, Sati Jamal, Albert Hall, Marilyn B. Coleman. CD

Aladdin
TV soundtrack (1958) with Cyril Ritchard, Anna Maria Alberghetti, Sal Mineo.
Film soundtrack (1992) with (voices of) Robin Williams, Brad Kane, Lea Salonga. CD, DVD

Alexander's Ragtime Band

Film soundtrack (1938) with Alice Faye, Ethel Merman, Don Ameche. CD, DVD

Alice in Wonderland

Film soundtrack (1951) with (voices of) Kathryn Beaumont, Ed Wynn, Sterling Holloway. CD, DVD
TV soundtrack (1966) with (voices of) Sammy Davis, Jr., Hedda Hopper, Zsa Zsa Gabor, Bill Dana, Howard Morris.

Alice Through the Looking Glass

TV soundtrack (1966) with Jimmy Durante, Nanette Fabray, Ricardo Montalban. DVD

All American

Original Broadway cast (1962) with Ray Bolger, Eileen Herlie, Anita Gillette, Ron Husmann. CD

All That Jazz

Film soundtrack (1979) with Roy Scheider, Jessica Lange, Ann Reinking. CD, DVD

Allegro

Original Broadway cast (1947) with John Battles, Lisa Kirk, William Shing, Annamary Dickey. CD

American in Paris, An

Film soundtrack (1951) with Gene Kelly, Georges Guetary. CD, DVD

Anastasia

Film soundtrack (1997) with (voices of) Meg Ryan, Liz Callaway, John Cusak, Jonathan Dokuchitz. CD, DVD

Anchors Aweigh

Film soundtrack (1945) with Gene Kelly, Frank Sinatra, Kathryn Grayson. CD, DVD

Androcles and the Lion

TV soundtrack (1967) with Norman Wisdom, Noel Coward, Inga Swenson, John Cullum.

Animal Crackers

Film soundtrack (1930) with the Marx Brothers. CD, DVD

Annie

Original Broadway cast (1977) with Andrea McArdle, Reid Shelton, Dorothy Loudon. CD
Film soundtrack (1982) with Aileen Quinn, Albert Finney, Ann Reinking, Carol Burnett. CD, DVD
Studio recording (1998) with Ruthie Henshaw, Kim Criswell, Dorothy Loudon. CD
TV soundtrack (1999) with Alice Morton, Victor Garber, Kathy Bates, Audra McDonald. CD, DVD

Annie Get Your Gun

Original Broadway cast (1946) with Ethel Merman, Ray Middleton. CD
Film soundtrack (1950) with Betty Hutton, Howard Keel. CD, DVD
Original London cast (1947) with Dolores Gray, Bill Johnson. CD
TV soundtrack (1957) with Mary Martin, John Raitt.
Broadway revival (1966) with Ethel Merman, Bruce Yarnell. CD
Studio recording (1990) with Kim Criswell, Thomas Hampson. CD
Studio recording (1995) with Judy Kaye, Barry Bostwick. CD
Broadway revival (1999) with Bernadette Peters, Tom Wopat. CD

Anyone Can Whistle

Original Broadway cast (1964) with Angela Lansbury, Lee Remick, Harry Guardino. CD
Concert recording (1995) with Madeline Kahn, Bernadette Peters, Scott Bakula. CD

Anything Goes

Original Broadway cast (1934) with Ethel Merman, William Gaxton. CD
Film soundtrack (1936) with Bing Crosby, Ethel Merman.
Film soundtrack (1956) with Bing Crosby, Donald O' Connor, Mitzi Gaynor, Jeanmaire. CD, DVD
Off Broadway revival (1962) with Eileen Rodgers, Hal Linden, Mickey Deems. CD
Broadway revival (1987) with Patti LuPone, Howard McGillin, Bill McCutcheon. CD
Studio recording (1988) with Frederica von Stade, Cris Groenendaal, Kim Criswell. CD
London revival (1989) with Elaine Page, Howard McGillin. CD
London revival (2003) with Sally Ann Triplett, John Barrowman. CD

Applause

Film soundtrack (1929) with Helen Morgan.

Applause

Original Broadway cast (1970) with Lauren Bacall, Len Cariou, Penny Fuller. CD

Apple Tree, The

Original Broadway cast (1966) with Barbara Harris, Alan Alda, Larry Blyden. CD

Aristocats, The

Film soundtrack (1969) with (voices of) Phil Harris, Eva Gabor, Scatman Crothers, Maurice Chevalier. CD, DVD

Artists and Models

Film soundtrack (1937) with Martha Raye, Louis Armstrong.
Film Soundtrack (1955) with Dean Martin.

As the Girls Go

Original Broadway cast (1948) with Bobby Clark.

As Thousands Cheer

Off Broadway revival (1998) with Howard McGillin, Judy Kuhn, Paula Newsome, B. D. Wong. CD

Aspects of Love

Original London cast (1989) with Michael Ball, Ann Crumb, Kevin Colson. CD
Studio recording (2005) with Stephanie Lawrence, Dave Willetts, Jack Emblow. CD

Assassins

Original Off Broadway cast (1990) with Victor Garbor, Patrick Cassidy, Terrence Mann. CD
Broadway revival (2004) with Michael Cerveris, Neil Patrick Harrison, Marc Kudisch. CD

At Home Abroad

Original Broadway cast (1935) with Beatrice Lillie, Ethel Waters, Eleanor Powell. CD

At the Circus

Film soundtrack (1939) with Kenny Baker, Florence Rice, the Marx Brothers. DVD

Avenue Q

Original Broadway cast (2003) with John Tartaglia, Stephanie D'Abruzzo. CD

Babes in Arms

Original Broadway cast (1937) with Wynn Murray, Ray Heatherton (selections only).
Film soundtrack (1939) with Judy Garland, Mickey Rooney, Douglas McPhail, Betty Jaynes. DVD
Studio recording (1951) with Mary Martin, Mardi Bayne, Jack Cassidy.
Studio recording (1989) with Judy Blazer, Gregg Edelman, Judy Kaye, Jason Graae. CD
Concert recording (1999) with Erin Dilly, Melissa Rain Anderson, David Campbell. CD

Babes in Toyland

Studio recording (1903) with Mary Ellen Pracht, Jeanette Scovotti, Sara Endich.
Film soundtrack (1934) with Felix Knight, Charlotte Henry.
Film soundtrack (1961) with Annette Funicello, Tommy Sands, Ray Bolger, Ed Wynn. DVD

Babes on Broadway

Film soundtrack (1941) with Judy Garland, Mickey Rooney. DVD

Baby

Original Broadway cast (1983) with Liz Callaway, James Congdon, Beth Fowler, Martin Vidnovic. CD

Baker's Wife, The

Original tour cast (1976) with Patti LuPone, Paul Sorvino, Kurt Peterson. CD
Original London cast (1990) with Sharon Lee Hill, Alun Armstrong. CD

Balalaika

Studio recording (1936) with Valda Bagnall, Neill Williams.
Film soundtrack (1939) with Nelson Eddy, Ilona Massey. DVD

Ballroom

Original Broadway cast (1978) with Dorothy Loudon, Vincent Gardenia, Lynn Roberts, Bernie Knee. CD

Band Wagon, The

Studio recording (1931) with Fred Astaire, Adele Astaire.
Studio recording (1953) with Harold Lang, Edith Adams, George Britton.
Film soundtrack (1953) with Fred Astaire, Nanette Fabray, Jack Buchanan. CD, DVD

Barkleys of Broadway

Film soundtrack (1949) with Fred Astaire, Ginger Rogers. DVD

Barnum

Original Broadway cast (1980) with Jim Dale, Glenn Close. CD
London cast (1981) with Michael Crawford, Eileen Battye. DVD

Bat Boy

Original Off Broadway cast (2001) with Deven May, Josie Walker, David Shannon, Kerry Butler. CD

Beauty and the Beast

Film soundtrack (1991) with (voices of) Paige O'Hara, Angela Lansbury, Jerry Orbach. CD, DVD
Original Broadway cast (1994) with Susan Egan, Terrence Mann, Tom Bosley, Gary Beach. CD
Original Australian cast (1995) with Rachel Peck, Michael McCormick, Hugh Jackman. CD
Original London cast (1997) with Julie-Alanah Brighten, Alasdair Harvey. CD

Bednobs and Broomsticks

Film soundtrack (1971) with Angela Lansbury, David Tomlinson. CD, DVD

Beggar's Opera, The

Studio recording (1948) with Anne Sharp, Catherine Lawson. CD
Film soundtrack (1984) with Roger Daltry, Rosemary Ashe, Peter Bayliss. DVD
Studio recording (1992) with Roy Rashbrook, Sarah Walker, Roger Bryson, Anne Dawson, Ian Caddy. CD
Studio recording (2005) with George James, Flora Nielsen, Max Worthley. CD

Bell for Adano, A

TV soundtrack (1956) with Anna Maria Alberghetti, Edwin Steffe, Barry Sullivan.

Belle of New York, The

Film soundtrack (1952) with Fred Astaire, Anita Ellis (for Vera-Ellen). CD, DVD

Bells Are Ringing

Original Broadway cast (1956) with Judy Holliday, Sydney Chaplin. CD
Film soundtrack (1960) with Judy Holliday, Dean Martin. CD, DVD
Broadway revival (2001) with Faith Prince, Marc Kudisch. CD

Best Foot Forward

Film soundtrack (1943) with Gloria Grafton (for Lucille Ball), Tommy Dix. CD, DVD
Broadway revival (1963) with Paula Wayne, Glenn Walken, Liza Minnelli, Kay Cole. CD

Best Little Whorehouse in Texas, The

Original Broadway cast (1978) with Carlin Glynn, Delores Hall, Henderson Forsythe, Clint Allmon. CD
Film soundtrack (1982) with Dolly Parton, Burt Reynolds, Charles Durning. CD, DVD

Best Things in Life Are Free

Film soundtrack (1956) with Gordon MacRae, Dan Dailey.

Big Boy

Film soundtrack (1930) with Al Jolson.

Big Broadcast, The

Film soundtrack (1932) with Bing Crosby, George Burns, Gracie Allen.

Big Broadcast of 1936, The

Film soundtrack (1936) with Ethel Merman, Bing Crosby.

Big Broadcast of 1937, The

Film soundtrack (1937) with Shirley Ross.

Big Broadcast of 1938

Film soundtrack (1938) with Bob Hope, Martha Raye, Robert Cummings.

Big Broadcast of 1938, The

Film soundtrack (1938) with Bob Hope, Shirley Ross, W. C. Fields. DVD

Big River

Original Broadway cast (1985) with Daniel Jenkins, Ron Richardson. CD

Bird

Film soundtrack (1988) with Forest Whitaker, Diane Verona, Samuel Wright. CD, DVD

Birth of the Blues

Film soundtrack (1941) with Bing Crosby, Mary Martin, Jack Teagarden. DVD

Bitter Sweet

Studio recording (1962) with Vanessa Lee, Roberto Cardinali. CD
Studio recording (1969) with June Bronhill, Neville Jason. CD

Black and Blue

Original Broadway cast (1989) with Linda Hopkins, Ruth Brown. CD

Blackbirds of 1928

Original Broadway cast (1928) with Bill Robinson, Adelaide Hall.

Blood Brothers

Original London cast (1983) with Barbara Dixon, George Costigan. CD
London replacement cast (1988) with Kiki Dee, Con O'Neill, Robert Locke. CD
International recording (1995) Petula Clark, David and Sean Cassidy. CD
London revival (1995) with Stephanie Lawrence, Warwick Evans. CD

Bloomer Girl

Original Broadway cast (1944) with Celeste Holm, David Brooks, Joan McCracken, Dooley Wilson. CD

Blossom Time

Studio recording (1947) with Earl Wrightson, Donald Dame.
Studio recording (1961) with Jacqueline Delman, John Larsen.

Blue Hawaii

Film soundtrack (1961) with Elvis Presley. CD, DVD

Blue Skies

Film soundtrack (1946) with Bing Crosby, Fred Astaire. DVD

Born to Dance

Film soundtrack (1936) with Eleanor Powell, Virginia Bruce, James Stewart. CD, DVD

Boy Friend

Original London cast (1954) with Anne Rogers, Denise Hirst. CD
Original Broadway cast (1954) with Julie Andrews, John Hewer, Millicent Martin. CD
Broadway revival (1970) with Judy Carne, Sandy Duncan. CD
Film soundtrack (1971) with Twiggy, Christopher Gable.

Boy from Oz, The

Original Australian cast (1998) with Todd McKenney, Mathew Waters. CD
Original Broadway cast (2004) with Hugh Jackman, Stephanie Block, Isabel Keating, Beth Fowler. CD

Boys from Syracuse, The

Studio recording (1938) with Rudy Vallee, Frances Langford (selections only).
Film soundtrack (1940) with Allan Jones, Martha Raye, Joe Penner (selections only).
Studio recording (1953) with Portia Nelson, Jack Cassidy, Stanley Praeger, Bibi Osterwald, Holly Harris, Bob Shaver. CD
Off Broadway revival (1963) with Stuart Damon, Clifford David, Ellen Hanley, Karen Morrow, Danny Carroll, Cathryn Damon, Julienne Marie, Rudy Tronto, Matthew Tobin. CD
London revival (1963) with Bob Monkhouse, Denis Quilley, Ronnie Corbett, Maggie Fitzgibbon, John Adams, John Moore, Lynn Kennington, Pat Turner, Paula Hendrix. CD
Concert recording (1997) with Rebecca Luker, Sarah Uriarte Berry, Debbie Gravitte, Malcolm Gets, Davis Gaines, Mario Cantone, Patrick Quinn, Michael McGrath. CD

Brigadoon

Original Broadway cast (1947) with David Brooks, Marion Bell, Lee Sullivan. CD
Film soundtrack (1954) with Gene Kelly, Van Johnson, Carol Richards (for Cyd Charisse). CD, DVD
Studio recording (1991) with Brent Barrett, Rebecca Luker, Judy Kaye. CD

Bring in 'da Noise, Bring in 'da Funk

Original Broadway cast (1996) with Savion Glover, Ann Duquesnay. CD

Broadway Melody, The

Film soundtrack (1929) with Bessie Love, Charles King, Anita Page, James Burrows. DVD

Broadway Melody of 1938, The

Film soundtrack (1937) with Sophie Tucker, Judy Garland, George Murphy, Eleanor Powell. CD, DVD

Broadway Melody of 1940, The

Film soundtrack (1940) with Fred Astaire, George Murphy, Eleanor Powell. CD, DVD

Bubbling Brown Sugar

Original Broadway cast (1976) with Vivian Reed, Carolyn Byrd, Chip Garnett. CD

Buck Privates

Film soundtrack (1941) with the Andrews Sisters, Bud Abbott, Lou Costello. DVD

Buddy Holly Story, The

Film soundtrack (1978) with Gary Busey. CD, DVD

Bugsy Malone

Film Soundtrack (1976) with (voices of) Paul Williams, Julie McWirder. CD, DVD
Edinburgh production (1996) with National Youth Music Theatre Company. CD

By Jupiter

Off Broadway revival (1967) with Bob Dishy, Jackie Alloway, Irene Byatt, Rosemarie Heyer. CD

By the Beautiful Sea

Original Broadway cast (1954) with Shirley Booth, Wilbur Evans, Richard France. CD

Bye Bye Birdie

Original Broadway cast (1960) with Dick Van Dyke, Chita Rivera, Susan Watson. CD
Original London cast (1961) with Peter Marshall, Sylvia Tysick, Robert Nichols. CD
Film soundtrack (1963) with Dick Van Dyke, Janet Leigh, Ann-Margaret. CD, DVD
TV soundtrack (1995) with Jason Alexander, Vanessa Williams. CD, DVD

Cabaret

Original Broadway cast (1966) with Joel Grey, Bert Convy, Jill Haworth. CD
Original London cast (1968) with Judi Dench, Kevin Colson, Peter Sallis. CD
Film soundtrack (1972) with Liza Minnelli, Joel Grey, Michael York. CD, DVD
Broadway revival (1998) with Alan Cumming, Natasha Richardson, Ron Rifkin, Mary Wilson. CD
Studio recording (1999) with Marcus Cooper, Judi Dench, Caroline O'Connor. CD

Cabin in the Sky

Film soundtrack (1943) with Ethel Waters, Eddie Anderson, Lena Horne. CD, DVD
Off Broadway revival (1964) with Rosetta Le Noire, Ketty Lester, Sam Laws. CD

Calamity Jane

Film soundtrack (1953) with Doris Day, Howard Keel. CD, DVD

Call Me Madam

Original Broadway cast (1950) with Dinah Shore (for Ethel Merman), Russell Nype.
Original London cast (1952) with Billie Worth, Anton Walbrook. CD
Film soundtrack (1953) with Ethel Merman, Donald O'Connor, George Sanders. CD, DVD
Concert recording (1995) with Tyne Daly, Walter Charles, Lewis Cleale, Melissa Errico. CD

Call Me Mister

Original Broadway cast (1946) with Betty Garrett, Lawrence Winters, Jules Munshin. CD

Camelot

Original Broadway cast (1960) with Julie Andrews, Richard Burton, Robert Goulet. CD
Original London cast (1964) with Laurence Harvey, Elizabeth Larner, Barry Kent. CD
Film soundtrack (1967) with Vanessa Redgrave, Richard Harris, Gene Merlino (for Franco Nero). CD, DVD
London Revival (1982) with Richard Harris, Fiona Fullerton, Robert Meadmore. CD

Camp

Film soundtrack (2003) with Daniel Letterle, Robin de Jesus, Steven Cutts, Joanna Chilcoat. CD, DVD

Can-Can

Original Broadway cast (1953) with Lilo, Gwen Verdon, Peter Cookson, Hans Conried. CD
Film soundtrack (1960) with Shirley MacLaine, Frank Sinatra, Maurice Chevalier. DVD

Candide

Original Broadway cast (1956) with Barbara Cook, Robert Rounseville, Max Adrian. CD
Broadway revival (1973) with Maureen Brennan, Mark Baker, Lewis Stadlen, June Gable. CD
Studio recording (1989) with Jerry Hadley, Adolph Green, June Anderson, Crista Ludwig. CD
Broadway revival (1997) with Jim Dale, Jason Danieley, Harolyn Blackwell, Andrea Martin. CD
London revival (1999) with Simon Russell Beale, Daniel Evans, Alex Kelly, Beverly Klein. CD

Can't Help Singing

Film soundtrack (1944) with Deanna Durbin, Robert Paige. DVD

Canterville Ghost, The

TV soundtrack (1966) with Michael Redgrave, Natalie Schafer, Douglas Fairbanks, Jr., Mark Coleano, Peter Noone.

Captain January

Film soundtrack (1936) with Shirley Temple, Guy Kibbee, Slim Summerville. DVD

Carefree

Film soundtrack (1938) with Fred Astaire, Ginger Rogers. DVD

Carmen Jones

Original Broadway cast (1943) with Muriel Smith, Luther Saxon, Carlotta Franzell, Glenn Bryant, June Hawkins. CD
Film soundtrack (1954) with Marilyn Horne (for Dorothy Dandridge), LeVern Hutcherson (for Harry Belafonte), Marvin Hayes (for Joe Adams), Olga James, Pearl Bailey, Brock Peters, Bernice Peterson (for Diahann Carroll). DVD
Studio recording (1967) with Grace Bumbry, George Webb, Elisabeth Welch, Ena Babb, Thomas Baptiste, Ursula Connors. CD
London cast (1991) with Wilhelmenia Fernandez, Sharon Benson, Damon Evans, Michael Austin, Karen Parks, Gregg Baker. CD

Carnival

Original Broadway cast (1961) with Anna Maria Alberghetti, Jerry Orbach, Kaye Ballard, James Mitchell. CD

Caroline, or Change

Original Broadway cast (2004) with Tonya Pinkins, Veanne Cox, Anika Noni Rose. CD

Carousel

Original Broadway cast (1947) with John Raitt, Jan Clayton, Jean Darling, Christine Johnson, Eric Mattson, Murvyn Vye. CD
London cast (1950) with Stephen Douglass, Iva Withers, Marion Ross, Margo Moser, Eric Mattson, Morgan Davies.
Studio recording (1955) with Robert Merrill, Patrice Munsel, Florence Henderson, Gloria Lane, George S. Irving, Herbert Banke.
Film soundtrack (1956) with Gordon MacRae, Shirley Jones, Barbara Ruick, Claramae Turner, Robert Rounseville, Cameron Mitchell. CD, DVD
Studio recording (1960) with Harry Snow, Lois Hunt, Charmaine Harma, Clifford Young, Helena Seymour, Kay Lande, Charles Green.
Studio recording (1962) with Alfred Drake, Roberta Peters, Lee Venora, Claramae Turner, Norman Treigle, Jon Crain.
Broadway revival (1965) with John Raitt, Eileen Christy, Susan Watson, Reid Shelton, Katherine Hilgenberg, Jerry Orbach. CD
TV soundtrack (1967) with Robert Goulet, Mary Grover, Marilyn Mason, Patricia Neway, Jack De Lon, Pernell Roberts.
Studio recording (1987) with Samuel Ramey, Barbara Cook, Sarah Brightman, David Rendall, Maureen Forrester, John Parry. CD
London revival (1993) with Michael Hayden, Joanna Riding, Katrina Murphy, Meg Johnson, Clive Rowe, Phil Daniels. CD
Broadway revival (1994) with Michael Hayden, Sally Murphy, Audra McDonald, Shirley Verrett, Eddie Korbich, Fisher Stevens. CD

Cat and the Fiddle, The

Film soundtrack (1934) with Jeanette MacDonald, Vivienne Segal, Ramon Novarro, Earl Oxford. Studio recording (1958) Doreen Hume, Denis Quilley

Cats

Original London cast (1981) with Elaine Page, Brian Blessed, Paul Nicholas. CD
Original Broadway cast (1982) with Betty Buckley, Ken Page. CD
TV soundtrack (2000) with Elaine Paige, John Mills, Ken Page. DVD

Celebration

Original Broadway cast (1969) with Michael Glenn-Smith, Keith Charles, Susan Watson, Ted Thurston. CD

Centennial Summer

Film soundtrack (1946) with Louanne Hogan (for Jeanne Crain), Larry Stevens, Avon Long, Linda Darnell. CD

Charlotte's Web

Film soundtrack (1973) with (voices of) Debbie Reynolds, Agnes Moorehead, Paul Lynde. CD, DVD

Chess

Studio recording (1984) with Elaine Page, Murray Head, Tommy Korberg. CD
Original Broadway cast (1988) with Judy Kuhn, Philip Casnoff, David Carroll. CD

Chicago

Original Broadway cast (1975) with Chita Rivera, Gwen Verdon, Jerry Orbach. CD
Broadway revival (1996) with Ann Reinking, Bebe Neuwirth, James Naughton. CD
Film soundtrack (2002) with Renee Zellweger, Catherine Zeta-Jones, Richard Gere. CD, DVD

Chitty Chitty Bang Bang

Film soundtrack (1968) with Dick Van Dyke, Sally Ann Howes, Gert Forbe. CD, DVD
Original London cast (2002) with Michael Ball, Emma Williams, Brian Blessed. CD

Chocolate Soldier, The

Studio recording (1949) with Charles Fredericks, Ann Ayars, Jimmy Carroll.
Studio recording (1959) with Rise Stevens, Robert Merrill, Jo Sullivan.

Studio recording (1963) with Laurie Payne, Stephanie Voss, Barbara Elsy.
Studio recording (1999) with Boyd Mackus, Elizabeth Patterson, John Pickle, Suzanne Woods. CD

Chorus Line, A

Original Broadway cast (1975) with Donna McKechnie, Priscilla Lopez, Wayne Cilento. CD
Film soundtrack (1985) with Yamil Borges, Alyson Reed, Terrence Mann, Gregg Burge. CD, DVD
Broadway revival (2007) with Charlotte d'Amboise, Deidre Goodwin, Natalie Cortez, Jeffrey Schectet. CD

Christmas Carol, A

TV soundtrack (1954) with Basil Rathbone, Fredric March, Bob Sweeney, Queenie Leonard
Original Madison Square Theatre cast (1994) with Walter Charles, Robert Westenberg, Emily Skinner, Ken Jennings. CD
TV soundtrack (2004) with Kelsey Grammer, Jason Alexander, Jane Krakowski. CD, DVD

Cinderella

TV soundtrack (1957) with Julie Andrews, Jon Cypher, Ilka Chase, Kaye Ballard, Alice Ghostley, Edith Adams. CD, DVD
London stage cast (1958) with Yana, Tommy Steele, Robin Palmer, Bruce Trent, Kenneth Williams, Ted Durante, Enid Lowe.
TV soundtrack (1965) with Lesley Ann Warren, Stuart Damon, Celeste Holm, Jo Van Fleet, Pat Carroll, Barbara Ruick. CD, DVD
TV soundtrack (1997) with Brandy Norwood, Paolo Montalban, Bernadette Peters, Whitney Houston, Natalie Desselle, Veanne Cox. DVD

City of Angels

Original Broadway cast (1989) with Gregg Edelman, James Naughton, Randy Graff, Rene Auberjonois. CD
Original London cast (1993) with Roger Allam, Martin Smith, Susannah Fellows, Fiona Hendley. CD

Closer than Ever

Original Off Broadway cast (1989) with Brent Barrett, Sally Mayes, Lynne Wintersteller, Richard Munez. CD
Original London cast (1993) with Samantha Shaw, Michael Cantwell, Clare Burt. CD

Coal Miner's Daughter

Film soundtrack (1980) with Sissy Spacek, Beverly D'Angelo. CD, DVD

Coco

Original Broadway cast (1969) with Katherine Hepburn, Rene Auberjonois, George Rose. CD

Cocoanuts, The

Film soundtrack (1929) with the Marx Brothers, Mary Eaton, Oscar Shaw. DVD

Color Purple, The

Original Broadway cast (2005) with La Chanze, Felicia P. Fields, Renee Elise Goldsberry, Elisabeth Withers-Mendes, Brandon Victor Dixon. CD

Commitments, The

Film soundtrack (1991) with Andrew Strong, Niamh Kavanagh, Johnny Murphy, Dick Massey. CD, DVD

Company

Original Broadway cast (1970) with Dean Jones, Elaine Stritch, Charles Kimbrough, Barbara Barrie. CD
Broadway revival (1995) with Boyd Gaines, Debra Monk, Robert Westenberg. CD
London revival (1996) with Adrian Lester. CD
Broadway revival (2006) with Raul Esparza, Barbara Walsh, Robert Cunningham. CD, DVD

Coney Island

Film soundtrack (1943) with Betty Grable, Caesar Romero, Charles Winninger.

A Connecticut Yankee

Broadway revival (1943) with Vivienne Segal, Dick Foran, Julie Warren, Vera-Ellen, Robert Chisholm, Chester Stratton. CD
Studio recording (1952) with Earl Wrightson, Elaine Malbin (selections only).
TV soundtrack (1955) with Eddie Albert, Janet Blair, Boris Karloff. CD

Connecticut Yankee in King Arthur's Court, A

Film soundtrack (1949) with Bing Crosby, Rhonda Fleming. DVD

Contact

Original Broadway cast (2000) with various recording artists. CD

Copacabana

TV soundtrack (1985) Barry Manilow, Annette O'Toole, Joe Bologna. CD

Cotton Club, The

Film soundtrack (1984) with Gregory Hines, Lonette McKee. CD, DVD

Countess Maritza

Studio recording (1926) with Jeanette Scovotti, Patricia Clark, William Lewis.

Country Girl, The

Film soundtrack (1954) with Bing Crosby. DVD

Court Jester, The

Film soundtrack (1956) with Danny Kaye. CD, DVD

Cover Girl

Film soundtrack (1944) with Gene Kelly, Nan Wynn (for Rita Hayworth), Phil Silvers. CD, DVD

Cradle Will Rock, The

Original Off Broadway cast (1937) with Howard Da Silva, Will Geer, Blanche Collins. CD
Off Broadway revival (1964) with Jerry Orbach, Joseph Bova, Nancy Andrews, Gordon B. Clark, Rita Gardner.
London revival (1983) with Randell Mell, Patti LuPone, David Schramm, Michele-Denise Woods. CD
Film soundtrack (1999) with Emily Watson, Eddie Vetter, Susan Sarandon. CD, DVD

Crazy for You

Original Broadway cast (1992) with Harry Groener, Jodi Benson, Michele Pawk, Bruce Adler. CD
Original London cast (1993) with Ruthie Henshall, Kirby Ward, Nicola Hughes. CD

Curly Top

Film soundtrack (1935) with Shirley Temple. DVD

Curtains

Original Broadway cast (2007) with David Hyde Pierce, Debra Monk, Karen Ziemba. CD

Daddy Long Legs

Film soundtrack (1955) with Fred Astaire, Leslie Caron. DVD

Dames

Film soundtrack (1934) with Joan Blondell, Dick Powell. CD, DVD

Dames at Sea

Original Off Broadway cast (1968) with Bernadette Peters, David Christmas, Steve Elmore, Tamara Long. CD
London revival (1989) with Josephine Blake, Paul Robinson, Tina Doyle, Sandra Dickinson. CD

Damn Yankees

Original Broadway cast (1955) with Gwen Verdon, Ray Walston, Stephen Douglass. CD
Film soundtrack (1958) with Gwen Verdon, Ray Walston, Tab Hunter. CD, DVD
Broadway revival (1994) with Victor Garber, Bebe Neuwirth, Jarod Emick, Linda Stephens. CD

Damsel in Distress

Film soundtrack (1937) with Fred Astaire, George Burns, Gracie Allen. DVD

Dancing Lady

Film soundtrack (1933) with Fred Astaire, Joan Crawford, Art Jarrett. DVD

Dangerous Christmas of Red Riding Hood, The

TV soundtrack (1965) with Liza Minnelli, Cyril Ritchard, Vic Damone. DVD

Darling Lili

Film soundtrack (1969) with Julie Andrews, Gloria Paul. CD, DVD

Date with Judy, A

Film Soundtrack (1948) with Jane Powell, Scotty Beckett, Carmen Miranda. DVD

Day in Hollywood, A—A Night in the Ukraine

Original Broadway cast (1980) with David Garrison, Priscilla Lopez, Peggy Hewett. CD

De-Lovely

Film soundtrack (2004) with Kevin Kline, Elvis Costello, Sheryl Crow, Diana Krall, Natalie Cole, Robbie Williams. CD, DVD

Dear World

Original Broadway cast (1969) with Angela Lansbury, Jane Connell, Milo O'Shea. CD

Dearest Enemy

TV soundtrack (1955) with Cyril Ritchard, Anne Jeffreys, Robert Sterling, Cornelia Otis Skinner. CD
Studio recording (1981) with Michele Summers, Freddy Williams, Charles West, Patricia Whitmore, John Diedrich, Richard Day-Lewis. CD

Deep in My Heart

Film soundtrack (1954) with José Ferrer, Helen Traubel, Gene Kelly, Fred Kelly, Jane Powell, Vic Damone, Howard Keel, Ann Miller, Tony Martin, Rosemary Clooney, William Olvis. CD, DVD

Delicious

Film soundtrack (1931) with Janet Gaynor, Charles Farrell, Mischa Auer, Manya Roberti.

The Desert Song

London cast (1927) with Edith Day, Harry Welchman, Dennis Hoey, Sidney Pointer, Gene Gerrard. CD
Studio recording (1945) with Kitty Carlisle, Wilbur Evans, Felix Knight, Vicki Vola. CD
Studio recording (1952) with Nelson Eddy, Doretta Morrow, Wesley Dalton, Lee Cass, David Atkinson, Wilton Clary.
Film soundtrack (1953) with Kathryn Grayson, Gordon MacRae, Allyn McLerie.
Studio recording (1958) with Giorgio Tozzi, Kathy Barr, Peter Palmer, Eugene Morgan.
Studio recording (1961) with Mario Lanza, Judith Raskin, Raymond Murcell, Donald Arthur.
Studio recording (1962) with Dorothy Kirsten, Gordon MacRae, Gerald Shirkey, Lloyd Bunnell. CD

Destry Rides Again

Original Broadway cast (1959) with Andy Griffith, Dolores Gray, Rosetta LeNoire. CD London revival (1982) with Alfred Molina, Jill Gascoine. CD

Dick Tracy

Film soundtrack (1990) with Madonna, Mandy Patinkin. CD, DVD

Dirty Dancing

Film soundtrack (1987) with various recording artists. CD, DVD

Dirty Rotten Scoundrels

Original Broadway cast (2005) with John Lithgow, Norbert Leo Butz, Sherie Rene Scott. CD

Do I Hear a Waltz?

Original Broadway cast (1965) with Elizabeth Allen, Sergio Franchi, Carol Bruce. CD Pasadena Playhouse revival (2001) with Alyson Reed, Anthony Crivello. CD

Do Re Mi

Original Broadway cast (1960) with Phil Silvers, Nancy Walker, David Burns, Nancy Dussault. CD London cast (1961) with Max Bygraves, Maggie Fitzgibbon, Jan Warters, Steve Arlen. CD Concert recording (1999) with Nathan Lane, Randy Graff, Brian Stokes Mitchell, Heather Headley. CD

Doctor Doolittle

Film soundtrack (1967) with Rex Harrison, Samantha Eggar, Anthony Newley, William Dix. CD, DVD

Dr. Seuss' How the Grinch Stole Christmas

TV soundtrack (1966) with (voices of) Boris Karloff, Thuri Ravenscroft. CD, DVD

Dolly Sisters, The

Film soundtrack (1945) with Betty Grable, June Haver, John Payne. CD, DVD

Don't Bother Me, I Can't Cope

Original Broadway cast (1972) with Micki Grant, Alex Bradford, Hope Clarke. CD

Doors, The

Film soundtrack (1991) with Val Kilmer, Kathleen Quinlan. CD, DVD

Double or Nothing

Film soundtrack (1937) with Bing Crosby, Martha Raye.

Down Argentine Way

Film soundtrack (1940) with Don Ameche, Betty Grable, Carmen Miranda. DVD

Dreamgirls

Original Broadway cast (1982) with Jennifer Holliday, Sheryl Lee Ralph, Loretta Devine. CD Concert recording (2002) with Audra McDonald, Heather Headley, Lillias White. CD Film soundtrack (2006) with Beyonce Knowles, Eddie Murphy, Jennifer Hudson, Anika Noni Rose. CD, DVD

Drowsy Chaperone, The

Original Broadway cast (2006) with Sutton Foster, Bob Martin, Eddie Kobich, Danny Burstein, Georgia Engel, Beth Leavel. CD

Du Barry Was a Lady

Film soundtrack (1939) with Gene Kelly, Martha Mears (for Lucille Ball), Red Skelton. CD, DVD

Duck Soup

Film soundtrack (1933) with the Marx Brothers, Margaret Dumont. DVD

Dumbo

Film soundtrack (1941) with (the voice of) Betty Noyes, Sterling Holloway. CD, DVD

Earnest in Love

Original Off Broadway cast (1960) with John Irving, Leila Martin, Sara Seegar. CD

Easter Parade

Film soundtrack (1948) with Judy Garland, Fred Astaire, Ann Miller, Peter Lawford. CD, DVD

El Capitan

Studio recording (1998) with Gerald Dolter, Darryl Edwards, Lucille Beer. CD

Evening Primrose

Studio recording (1967) with Anthony Perkins. Studio recording (2001) with Neil Patrick Harris, Theresa McCarthy. CD

Evergreen

Film soundtrack (1934) with Jessie Matthews, Sonnie Hale.

Every Night at Eight

Film soundtrack (1935) with Frances Langford.

Everyone Says I Love You

Film soundtrack (1997) with Alan Alda, Edward Norton, Woody Allen, Goldie Hawn. CD, DVD

Evita

Studio recording (1976) with Julie Covington, Colm Wilkinson, Paul Jones. CD
Original London cast (1978) with Elaine Page, Joss Ackland, David Essex. CD
Original Broadway cast (1979) with Patti LuPone, Mandy Patinkin, Bob Gunton. CD
Film soundtrack (1996) with Madonna, Antonio Banderas, Jonathan Pryce. CD, DVD
London revival (2006) with Elena Roger, Matt Rawle, Philip Quast. CD

Face the Music

Concert recording (2007) with Judy Kaye, Lee Wilkof, Meredith Paterson. CD

Fade Out—Fade In

Original Broadway cast (1964) with Carol Burnett, Jack Cassidy, Dick Patterson. CD

Falsettoland

Original Off Broadway cast (1990) with Michael Rupert, Faith Prince, Stephen Bogardus. CD

Fame

Film soundtrack (1980) with Irene Cara, Paul McCrane. CD, DVD
London cast (1995) with Miquel Brown, Marcos D'Cruze. CD
American touring cast (1999) with Gavin Creel, Jennifer Gambatese, Kim Cea, Natasha Rennalls. CD

Fame on 42nd Street

Off Broadway cast (2003) with Nicole Leach, Cheryl Freeman, Nancy Hess. CD

Fanny

Original Broadway cast (1954) with Florence Henderson, Ezio Pinza, Walter Slezak, William Tabbert. CD

Fantasia

Film soundtrack (1940) with Philadelphia Symphony conducted by Leopold Stokowski. CD, DVD

Fantasia 2000

Film soundtrack (2000) with Chicago Symphony conducted by James Levine. CD, DVD

Fantasticks, The

Original Off Broadway cast (1960) with Jerry Orbach, Rita Gardner, Kenneth Nelson. CD
Film soundtrack (1995) with Jean Louisa Kelly, Joey McIntyre, Joel Grey, Bernard Hughes. DVD
Off Broadway revival (2006) with Burke Moses, Santino Fontana, Sara Jean Ford, Leo Burmester, Martin Vidnovic. CD

Farmer Takes a Wife

Film soundtrack (1953) with Betty Grable, Dale Robertson, Thelma Ritter.

Feathertop

TV soundtrack (1961) with Jane Powell, Hugh O'Brien, Hans Conried.

Fiddler on the Roof

Original Broadway cast (1964) with Zero Mostel, Maria Karnilova, Beatrice Arthur. CD
Original London cast (1967) with Topol, Miriam Karlin, Linda Gardner. CD
Studio recording (1968) with Robert Merrill, Molly Picon, Mary Thomas. CD
Film soundtrack (1971) with Topol, Norma Crane, Molly Picon, Leonard Frey. CD, DVD
Broadway revival (2004) with Alfred Molina, Randy Graff, John Cariani. CD

Fifty Million Frenchmen

Studio recording (1991) with Kim Criswell, Howard McGillin, Karen Ziemba, Jason Graae. CD

Fine and Dandy

Studio Recording (2004) with Jennifer Laura Thompson, Mario Cantone, Ann Kaufman, Gavin Creel, Carolee Carmello. CD

Finian's Rainbow

Original Broadway cast (1947) with Ella Logan, David Wayne, Donald Richards, Albert Sharpe. CD

Off Broadway revival (1960) with Jeannie Carson, Biff McGuire, Howard Morris, Sorell Booke. CD

Film soundtrack (1968) with Fred Astaire, Petula Clark, Tommy Steele, Don Francks. CD, DVD

Off Broadway revival (2004) with Melissa Errico, Max Von Essen, Malcolm Gets, Jonathan Freeman. CD

Fiorello!

Original Broadway cast (1959) with Tom Bosley, Howard Da Silva, Ellen Hanley, Eileen Rodgers, Patricia Wilson. CD

Firefly, The

Studio recording (1951) with Allan Jones, Elaine Malbin, Martha Wright.

Studio recording (1963) with Stephanie Voss, Laurie Payne.

Five Guys Named Moe

Original London cast (1991) with Dig Wayne, Kenny Andrews, Clarke Peters. CD

Original Broadway cast (1992) with Jerry Dixon, Kevin Ramsey, Doug Eskew. CD

Five Pennies, The

Film soundtrack (1959) with Danny Kaye, Louis Armstrong, Eileen Wilson (for Barbara Bel Geddes). CD, DVD

5,000 Fingers of Dr. T

Film soundtrack (1953) with Peter Lind Hayes, Mary Healy, Tommy Rettig, Hans Conreid. DVD

Flahooley

Original Broadway cast (1951) with Barbara Cook, Jerome Courtland, Yma Sumac. CD

Flashdance

Film soundtrack (1983) with various recording artists. CD, DVD

Fleet's In, The

Film soundtrack (1942) with Dorothy Lamour, Betty Hutton, Eddie Bracken.

Flora, the Red Menace

Original Off Broadway cast (1965) with Liza Minelli, Bob Dishy. CD

Off Broadway revival (1987) with Veanne Cox, Peter Frechette. CD

Florodora

Original London cast (1900–1915) with Ada Reeve, Kate Cutler. CD

Flower Drum Song

Original Broadway cast (1958) with Miyoshi Umeki, Larry Blyden, Pat Suzuki, Juanita Hall, Ed Kenny, Arabella Hong, Keye Luke. CD

London cast (1960) with Yama Saki, Tim Herbert, Kevin Scott, Yau San Tung, Ida Shepley, Joan Pethers, Ruth Silvestre, Leon Thau. CD

Film soundtrack (1961) with Miyoshi Umeki, Jack Soo, B. J. Baker (for Nancy Kwan), James Shigeta, Juanita Hall, Marilyn Horne (for Reiko Sato). CD, DVD

Broadway revival (2003) with Lea Salonga, José Llana, Sandra Allen, Randall Duk Kim, Jodi Long. CD

Floyd Collins

Original Off Broadway cast (1996) with Christopher Innvar, Theresa McCarthy, Don Chastain, Cass Morgan, Jason Danieley. CD

Flying Down to Rio

Film soundtrack (1933) with Fred Astaire, Ginger Rogers, Etta Moten, Raul Roulien. CD, DVD

Folies Bergere de Paris

Film soundtrack (1935) with Maurice Chevalier, Ann Southern, Merle Oberon.

Follies

Original Broadway cast (1971) with Alexis Smith, John McMartin, Gene Nelson, Dorothy Collins. CD

Concert cast (1985) with Barbara Cook, Mandy Patinkin, Lee Remick, George Hearn, Carol Burnett, Elaine Stritch, Phyllis Newman. CD, DVD

Original London cast (1987) with Diana Rigg, Julia McKenzie, Daniel Massey, Millicent Martin, David Healy. CD

Paper Mill Playhouse revival (1998) with Dee Hoty, Donna McKechnie, Tony Roberts, Laurence Guittard, Ann Miller, Eddie Bracken, Kaye Ballard. CD

Follow That Bird

Film soundtrack (1985) with Carroll Spinney, Jim Henson, Frank Oz. CD, DVD

Follow the Fleet

Film soundtrack (1936) with Fred Astaire, Ginger Rogers, Harriet Hilliard. DVD

Footlight Parade

Film soundtrack (1933) with James Cagney, Dick Powell, Ruby Keeler. CD, DVD

Footloose

Film soundtrack (1984) with various recording artists. CD, DVD
Original Broadway cast (1998) with Dee Hoty, Jeremy Kushnier, Jennifer Laura Thompson. CD

For Me and My Gal

Film soundtrack (1942) with Judy Garland, Gene Kelly, George Murphy. CD, DVD

For the Boys

Film soundtrack (1991) with Bette Midler, James Caan. CD, DVD

Forbidden Broadway

Original Off Broadway cast (1982) with Gerald Alessandrini, Chloe Webb, Fred Barton. CD
Original Off Broadway cast (1985) with Gerald Alessandrini, Michael McGrath. CD
Compilation album (1991) with Michael McGrath, Karen Murphy. CD
Off Off Broadway cast (1993) with Suzanne Blakeslee, CD

Forbidden Broadway: Special Victims Unit

Off Broadway cast (2005) with Jason Mills, Megan Lewis, Ron Bohmer, Jennifer Simard. CD

Forbidden Broadway Strikes Back!

Off Broadway cast (1996) with Tom Plotkin, Christine Pedi, Donna English. CD

Forbidden Broadway 2001: A Spoof Odyssey

Off Broadway cast (2000) with Danny Gurwin, Christine Pedi, Tony Nation. CD

Forever Plaid

Original Off Broadway cast (1990) with Stan Chandler, David Engel, Jason Graae, Guy Stroman. CD

Forty-Five Minutes From Broadway

TV soundtrack (1959) with Tammy Grimes, Polly Rowles, David Burns. CD

42nd Street

Film soundtrack (1933) with Ruby Keeler, Dick Powell, Ginger Rogers. DVD
Original Broadway cast (1980) with Jerry Orbach, Tammy Grimes, Wanda Richert, Lee Roy Reams. CD
Broadway revival (2001) with Michael Cumpsty, Christine Ebersole, Kate Levering. CD

Fosse

Original Broadway cast (199) with Jane Lanier, Scott Wise, Shannon Lewis, Alex Sanchez. CD

Full Monty, The

Original Broadway cast (2000) with Patrick Wilson, Jason Danieley, Andre DeShields, John Ellison Conlee, Annie Golden, Kathleen Freeman. CD

Funny Face

Reconstructed New York and London casts (1927–1928) with Fred Astaire, Adele Astaire. CD
Film soundtrack (1957) with Fred Astaire, Audrey Hepburn, Kay Thompson. CD, DVD

Funny Girl

Original Broadway cast (1964) with Barbra Streisand, Sydney Chaplin, Kay Medford. CD
Film soundtrack (1968) with Barbra Streisand, Omar Sharif, Kay Medford. CD, DVD

Funny Lady

Film soundtrack (1975) with Barbra Streisand, James Caan, Ben Vereen. CD, DVD

Funny Thing Happened on the Way to the Forum, A

Original Broadway cast (1962) with Zero Mostel, David Burns, Jack Gilford. CD
Original London cast (1963) with Frankie Howard, John Rye, Leon Greene. CD
Film soundtrack (1966) with Zero Mostel, Michael Crawford, Jack Gilford. CD, DVD
Broadway revival (1996) with Nathan Lane, Jim Stanek, Mark Linn-Baker. CD

Gang's All Here, The

Film soundtrack (1943) with Alice Faye, Phil Baker, Carmen Miranda. CD, DVD

Gay Divorcee, The

Film soundtrack (1934) with Fred Astaire, Ginger Rogers, Betty Grable. DVD

Gay Life, The

Original Broadway cast (1961) with Barbara Cook, Jules Munshin, Walter Chiari. CD

Gay Purr-ee

Film soundtrack (1962) with (voices of) Judy Garland, Robert Goulet, Red Buttons. CD, DVD

Gentlemen Prefer Blondes

Original Broadway cast (1949) with Carol Channing, Yvonne Adair, Jack McCauley. CD
Film soundtrack (1953) with Marilyn Monroe, Jane Russell. CD, DVD
Broadway revival (1995) with KT Sullivan, Karen Prunzik, George Dvorsky. CD

George M!

Original Broadway cast (1968) with Joel Grey, Bernadette Peters, Jerry Dodge, Jill O'Hara, Betty Ann Grove. CD

George White's Scandals of 1922

Studio recording (1976) with Joyce Andrews, Patrick Mason, Walter Richardson.

George White's Scandals of 1935

Film soundtrack (1935) with Alice Faye.

Geppetto

TV soundtrack (2000) with Drew Carey, Rene Auberjonois, Seth Adkins, Brent Spiner. CD, DVD

Gift of the Magi

TV soundtrack (1958) with Sally Ann Howes, Allen Case, Bibi Osterwald.

Gigi

Film soundtrack (1958) with Maurice Chevalier, Louis Jourdan, Betty Wand (for Leslie Caron), Hermione Gingold. CD, DVD
Original Broadway cast (1973) with Alfred Drake, Daniel Massey, Agnes Moorehead, Karin Wolfe, Maria Karnilova. CD

Girl Crazy

Film soundtrack (1943) with Judy Garland, Mickey Rooney, June Allyson. CD, DVD
Studio recording (1951) with Mary Martin. CD
Studio recording (1990) with Judy Blazer, David-James Carroll, Lorna Luft, David Garrison. CD

Give a Girl a Break

Film soundtrack (1953) with Marge Champion, Gower Champion, Debbie Reynolds.

Glenn Miller Story, The

Film soundtrack (1954) with June Allyson, Frances Langford, Louis Armstrong. DVD

Go Into Your Dance

Film soundtrack (1935) with Al Jolson, Ruby Keeler, Helen Morgan. DVD

Godspell

Original Off Broadway cast (1971) with Stephen Nathan, David Haskell. CD
Film soundtrack (1973) with Victor Garbor, Lynne Thigpen, David Haskell. CD, DVD
Original London cast (1972) with Jeremy Irons, Julie Covington. CD
Off Broadway revival (2000) with Barrett Foa, Will Erat, Capathia Jenkins. CD
National touring cast (2001) with Joe Carney, Michael Yuen, Sal Sabella. CD

Going Hollywood

Film soundtrack (1933) with Bing Crosby. CD

Going My Way

Film soundtrack (1944) with Bing Crosby. CD, DVD

Gold Diggers of Broadway

Film soundtrack (1929) with Winnie Lightner, Nick Lucas, Nancy Welford.

Gold Diggers of 1933

Film soundtrack (1933) with Joan Blondell, Ruby Keeler, Dick Powell, Ginger Rogers. DVD

Gold Diggers of 1935

Film soundtrack (1935) with Dick Powell. DVD

Gold Diggers of 1937

Film soundtrack (1936) with Joan Blondell, Dick Powell, Lee Dixon.

Golden Apple, The

Original Broadway cast (1954) with Priscilla Gillette, Bibi Osterwald, Stephen Douglass. CD

Golden Boy

Original Broadway cast (1964) with Sammy Davis, Louis Gossett, Paula Wayne, Billy Daniels. CD

Goldilocks

Original Broadway cast (1958) with Elaine Stritch, Don Ameche, Russell Nype. CD

Goldwyn Follies, The

Film soundtrack (1938) with Kenny Baker, the Ritz Brothers, Vera Zorina. DVD

Good News!

Film soundtrack (1947) with June Allyson, Peter Lawford, Mel Torme. CD, DVD
Studio recording (1996) with Ann Morrison, Michael Gruber, Kim Huber. CD

Goodbye, Mr. Chips

Film soundtrack (1969) with Petula Clark, Peter O'Toole. CD, DVD

Grand Hotel

Original Broadway cast (1989) with Brent Barrett, Liliane Montevecchi, Karen Akers, Michael Jeter. CD

Grand Tour, The

Original Broadway cast (1970) with Joel Grey, Ron Holgate, Florence Lacey. CD

Grass Harp, The

Original Broadway cast (1971) with Barbara Cook, Karen Morrow, Russ Thacker, Carol Brice. CD

Grease

Original Broadway cast (1972) with Barry Bostwick, Carole Demas, Adrienne Barbeau. CD
Film soundtrack (1978) with John Travolta, Olivia Newton-John, Stockard Channing. CD, DVD
Original London cast (1993) with Deborah Gibson, Craig McLachlan, Sally Ann Triplett. CD
Broadway revival (1994) with Sam Harris, Susan Wood, Rosie O'Donnell. CD
Studio recording (1994) with John Barrowman, Shona Lindsey. CD
Broadway revival (2007) with Max Crumm, Laura Osnes, Jenny Powers, Ryan Patrick Binder, Lindsay Mendez. CD

Grease 2

Film soundtrack (1982) with Michelle Pfeiffer, Maxwell Caulfield, Lorna Luft. CD, DVD

Great Caruso, The

Film soundtrack (1951) with Mario Lanza. CD, DVD

Great Waltz, The

Film soundtrack (1938) with Miliza Korjus, Fernand Gravet, Christian Rub, George Houston, Al Shean, Curt Bois, Leonid Kinsky. DVD
California revival (1965) with Giorgio Tozzi, Anita Gillette, Jean Finn. CD
London revival (1970) with Sari Barabas, David Watson, Diane Todd. CD
Film soundtrack (1972) with Mary Costa.

Great Ziegfeld, The

Film soundtrack (1936) with Luise Rainer, Ray Bolger, Fanny Brice. CD, DVD

Greenwillow

Original Broadway cast (1960) with Anthony Perkins, Ellen McCown, Pert Kelton, Cecil Kellaway. CD

Grey Gardens

Original Off Broadway cast (2006) with Christine Ebersole, Mary Louise Wilson, Sara Gettelfinger. CD

Broadway cast (2006) with Christine Ebersole, Mary Louise Wilson, Erin Davie. CD

Gulliver's Travels

Film soundtrack (1939) with Lanny Ross, Jessica Dragonette, Jack Mercer, Pinto Colvig. DVD

Guys and Dolls

Original Broadway cast (1950) with Robert Alda, Vivian Blaine, Sam Levene, Isabel Bigley, Stubby Kaye. CD
Original London cast (1953) with Jerry Wayne, Lizbeth Webb, Edmund Hockridge, Joyce Blair. CD
Film soundtrack (1955) with Vivian Blaine, Marlon Brando, Frank Sinatra, Jean Simmons. DVD
Broadway revival (1976) with Robert Guillaume, Ernestine Jackson, James Randolph, Norma Donaldson. CD
London revival (1982) with Ian Charleston, Julie Covington, Julia McKenzie, Bob Hoskins. CD
Studio recording (1986) with Gregg Edelman, Emily Loesser, Kim Criswell, Tim Flavin. CD
Broadway revival (1992) with Nathan Lane, Josie DeGuzman, Peter Gallagher, Faith Prince. CD
Touring cast (2001) with Maurice Hines, Brian Sutherland, Diane Sutherland, Alexandra Foucard. CD

Gypsy

Original Broadway cast (1959) with Ethel Merman, Sandra Church, Jack Klugman. CD
Film soundtrack (1962) with Natalie Wood, Lisa Kirk (for Rosalind Russell), Karl Malden. CD, DVD
Studio recording (1969) with Kay Medford. CD
London revival (1973) with Angela Lansbury, Barrie Ingham, Zan Charisse. CD
Broadway revival (1989) with Tyne Daly, Crista Moore, Jonathan Hadary. CD
TV soundtrack (1993) with Bette Midler, Cynthia Gibb, Peter Riegert. CD, DVD
Broadway revival (2003) with Bernadette Peters, Tammy Blanchard, John Dossett. CD

Hair

Original Off Broadway cast (1967) with Gerome Ragni, James Rado, Walker Daniels, Jill O'Hara, Suzannah Evans. CD
Film soundtrack (1979) with Treat Williams, John Savage, Don Dacus, Annie Golden, Nell

Carter, Beverly D'Angelo, Cheryl Barnes, Ronnie Dyson. CD, DVD
Concert recording (2005) with Gavin Creel, Christopher Sieber, Adam Pascal, Annie Golden, Lillias White, Liz Callaway, Raul Esparza. CD

Hairspray

Original Broadway cast (2002) with Harvey Fierstein, Marissa Jaret Winokur, Matthew Morrison, Dick Latessa, Kerry Butler. CD
Film soundtrack (2007) with John Travolta, Nikki Blonsky, Zac Efron, Michelle Pfeiffer, Christopher Walken. CD, DVD

Half a Sixpence

Original Broadway cast (1965) with Tommy Steele, Will Mackenzie, Polly James. CD
Film soundtrack (1967) with Tommy Steele, Marti Webb (for Julia Foster), Cyril Ritchard. DVD

Hallelujah

Film soundtrack (1929) with Daniel L. Haynes, Nina Mae McKinney. DVD

Hallelujah, Baby!

Original Broadway cast (1967) with Leslie Uggams, Robert Hooks, Allen Case, Lillian Hayman. CD

Hallelujah, I'm a Bum

Film soundtrack (1933) with Al Jolson, Frank Morgan, Madge Evans, Harry Langdon, Chester Conklin. DVD

Hans Brinker or the Silver Skates

TV soundtrack (1958) with Tab Hunter, Peggy King, Anna Maria Alberghetti.

Hans Christian Anderson

Film soundtrack (1952) with Danny Kaye. CD, DVD
London cast (1974) with Tommy Steele, Sally Ann Howes, Anthony Valentine. CD

Hansel and Gretel

TV soundtrack (1958) with Red Buttons, Barbara Cook, Rudy Vallee.

Happy Go Lucky

Film soundtrack (1943) with Mary Martin, Betty Hutton, Dick Powell.

Happy Time, The

Original Broadway cast (1968) with Robert Goulet, David Wayne, Mike Rupert, Julie Gregg. CD

Hard Day's Night, A

Film soundtrack (1964) with the Beatles. CD DVD

Harvey Girls, The

Film soundtrack (1946) with Judy Garland, Kenny Baker, Virginia O'Brien. CD, DVD

Heads Up!

Film soundtrack (1930) with Charles "Buddy" Rogers (selections only).

Hedwig and the Angry Inch

Original Off Broadway cast (1998) with John Cameron Mitchell. CD
Film soundtrack (2001) with John Cameron Mitchell. CD, DVD

Hello Again

Original Off Broadway cast (1994) with Donna Murphy, John Cameron Mitchell, Malcolm Gets, Dennis Parlato, Michele Pawk, Judy Blazer. CD

Hello, Dolly!

Original Broadway cast (1964) with Carol Channing, David Burns, Charles Nelson Reilly, Eileen Brennan. CD
Original London cast (1965) with Mary Martin, Loring Smith, Marilyn Lovell, Garrett Lewis. Broadway replacement cast (1967) Pearl Bailey, Cab Calloway. CD
Film soundtrack (1969) with Barbra Streisand, Walter Mattau, Michael Crawford. CD, DVD
Broadway revival (1995) with Carol Channing, Jay Garner, Florence Lacey. CD

Hello, Frisco, Hello

Film soundtrack (1943) with Alice Faye, John Payne, Jack Oakie. DVD

Help!

Film soundtrack (1965) with the Beatles. CD, DVD

Hellzapoppin'

Film soundtrack (1941) with Olsen & Johnson, Martha Raye, Hugh Herbert. DVD

Hercules

Film soundtrack (1997) with (voices of) Tate Donovan, Josh Keaton, Roger Bart, Danny De Vito. CD, DVD

Here Come the Waves

Film soundtrack (1944) with Bing Crosby, Betty Hutton. DVD

Here Comes the Groom

Film soundtrack (1951) with Bing Crosby, Jane Wyman. DVD

High Button Shoes

Original Broadway cast (1947) with Phil Silvers, Nanette Fabray, Jack McCauley, Mark Dawson. CD

High School Musical

TV soundtrack (2006) with Zac Efron, Vanessa Anne Hudgens, Ashley Tisdale. CD, DVD

High School Musical 2

TV soundtrack (2007) with Zac Efron, Vanessa Anne Hudgens, Ashley Tisdale. CD, DVD

High Society

Film soundtrack (1956) with Bing Crosby, Frank Sinatra, Grace Kelly, Louis Armstrong. CD, DVD
Studio recording (1994) with Carl Wayne, Dennis Lotis. CD
Broadway cast (1998) with Melissa Errico, Stephen Bogardus, Daniel McDonald, John McMartin. CD

High Tor

TV soundtrack (1956) with Bing Crosby, Julie Andrews, Everett Sloane.

High, Wide and Handsome

Film soundtrack (1937) with Irene Dunne, Dorothy Lamour, William Frawley (selections only).

Higher and Higher

Film soundtrack (1940) with Frank Sinatra, Michele Morgan, Marcy Maguire, Mel Tormé, Barbara Hale, Dooley Wilson. CD, DVD

Hit the Deck

Film soundtrack (1955) with Tony Martin, Ann Miller, Debbie Reynolds, Vic Damone. CD

Holiday Inn

Film soundtrack (1942) with Fred Astaire, Bing Crosby. CD, DVD

Hollywood Canteen

Film soundtrack (1944) with Jack Benny, Eddie Cantor, Kitty Carlisle. CD

Hollywood Hotel

Film soundtrack (1937) with Dick Powell, Harry James, Ted Healy. CD

Hollywood Revue of 1929

Film soundtrack (1929) with Joan Crawford, Marion Davies.

House of Flowers

Original Broadway cast (1954) with Pearl Bailey, Diahann Carroll, Juanita Hall, Ada Moore. CD

How the Grinch Stole Christmas

TV soundtrack (1966) with (voices of) Boris Karloff, Thuri Ravenscroft. CD, DVD

How to Succeed in Business Without Really Trying

Original Broadway cast (1961) with Robert Morse, Rudy Vallee, Bonnie Scott, Charles Nelson Reilly. CD
Film soundtrack (1967) with Robert Morse, Michele Lee, Rudy Vallee. CD, DVD
Broadway revival (1995) with Matthew Broderick, Ronn Carroll, Megan Mullally, Lillias White. CD

Human Comedy, The

Original Broadway cast (1984) with Rex Smith, Mary Elizabeth Mastrantonio, Bonnie Koloc, Stephen Geoffreys, Don Kehr. CD

Hunchback of Notre Dame, The

Film soundtrack (1996) with (voices of) Heidi Mollenhauer (for Demi Moore), Tom Hulce, Jason Alexander, Tony Jay. CD, DVD

I Can Get It for You Wholesale

Original Broadway cast (1962) with Elliott Gould, Sheree North, Lillian Roth, Marilyn Cooper, Barbra Streisand. CD

I Do! I Do!

Original Broadway cast (1966) with Mary Martin, Robert Preston. CD

Off Broadway revival (1996) with Karen Ziemba, David Garrison. CD

I Dream Too Much

Film soundtrack (1935) with Lily Pons.

I Love My Wife

Original Broadway cast (1977) with Lenny Baker, Joanna Gleason, Ilene Graff, James Naughton. CD

I'll Cry Tomorrow

Film soundtrack (1956) with Susan Hayward. DVD

I Love You, You're Perfect, Now Change

Original Off Broadway cast (1996) with Danny Burstein, Jennifer Simard, Melissa Weil. CD

I Married an Angel

Film soundtrack (1942) with Nelson Eddy, Jeanette MacDonald, Binnie Barnes.
Radio broadcast (1942) with Nelson Eddy, Jeanette MacDonald, Binnie Barnes, Edward Everett Horton.
Studio recording (1952) with Gordon MacRae, Lucille Norman, Audrey Christie, Wynn Murray, Eve Symington. CD

I'm Getting My Act Together and Taking It on the Road

Original Off Broadway cast (1978) with Gretchen Cryer. CD
London cast (1981) with Diane Langton, Ben Cross. CD

In Old Chicago

Film soundtrack (1938) with Alice Faye. DVD

In the Good Old Summertime

Film soundtrack (1949) with Judy Garland, Van Johnson. CD, DVD

Innocents of Paris

Film soundtrack (1929) with Maurice Chevalier.

Inside U.S.A.

Original Broadway cast (1948) with Jack Haley, Beatrice Lillie. CD

International House

Film soundtrack (1933) with Baby Rose Marie, Rudy Vallee, Cab Calloway. DVD

Into the Woods

Original Broadway cast (1987) with Kim Crosby, Joanna Gleason, Bernadette Peters, Chip Zien, Robert Westenberg. CD, DVD
Original London cast (1991) with Julia McKenzie, Ian Bartholomew. CD
Broadway revival (2002) with Laura Benanti, Stephen DeRosa, Vanessa Williams, Gregg Edelman, John McMartin, Kerry O'Malley. CD

Irene

Broadway revival (1973) with Debbie Reynolds, Patsy Kelly, George S. Irving. CD
London revival (1976) with Julie Anthony, Eric Flynn, Jon Pertwee, Jessie Evans. CD

Irma La Douce

Original London cast (1958) with Elizabeth Seal, Keith Michell, Clive Revill. CD
Original Broadway cast (1960) with Elizabeth Seal, Keith Michell, Clive Revill. CD

It Happened in Brooklyn

Film soundtrack (1947) with Frank Sinatra, Kathryn Grayson, Jimmy Durante. CD, DVD

It's a Bird...It's a Plane... It's Superman

Original Broadway cast (1966) with Bob Holliday, Jack Cassidy, Linda Lavin, Michael O'Sullivan. CD

It's Always Fair Weather

Film soundtrack (1955) with Gene Kelly, Dan Dailey, Dolores Gray. CD, DVD

Jack and the Beanstalk

TV soundtrack (1956) with Joel Grey, Celeste Holm, Cyril Ritchard, Peggy King.
TV soundtrack (1967) with Gene Kelly, Bobby Riha, Marni Nixon.

Jacques Brel Is Alive and Well and Living in Paris

Original Off Broadway cast (1966) with Shawn Elliott, Elly Stone, Mort Shuman, Alice Whitfield. CD

Film soundtrack (1975) with Elly Stone, Mort Shuman, Joe Masiell. DVD
London revival cast (1995) with Liz Greenaway, Michael Cahill, Alison Egan. CD

Jailhouse Rock

Film soundtrack (1957) with Elvis Presley. CD, DVD

Jamaica

Original Broadway cast (1957) with Lena Horne, Ricardo Montalban, Adelaide Hall. CD

Jazz Singer, The

Film soundtrack (1927) with Al Jolson. DVD
Film soundtrack (1953) with Danny Thomas.
Film soundtrack (1980) with Neil Diamond. DVD

Jekyll and Hyde

Studio recording (1990) with Colm Wilkinson, Linda Eder. CD
Studio recording (1994) with Carolee Carmello, Anthony Warlow. CD
Original Broadway cast (1997) with Linda Eder, Robert Cuccioli. CD

Jelly's Last Jam

Original Broadway cast (1992) with Gregory Hines, Tonya Pinkins, Savion Glover. CD

Jerome Robbins Broadway

Original Broadway cast (1989) with Jason Alexander, Debbie Shapiro, Faith Prince, Scott Wise, Charlotte D'Amboise. CD

Jersey Boys

Original Broadway cast (2005) with John Lloyd Young, Christian Hoff, Daniel Reichard, J. Robert Spencer. CD

Jesus Christ Superstar

Concept album (1970) with Ian Gillan, Murray Head, Yvonne Elliman. CD
Original Broadway cast (1971) with Jeff Fenholt, Ben Vereen, Bob Bingham, Yvonne Elliman. CD
Film soundtrack (1973) with Ted Neeley, Yvonne Ellima, Carl Anderson. CD, DVD
Studio recording (1992) with Paul Nicholas, Claire Moore, Keith Burns. CD

Studio recording (1996) with Clive Rowe, Dave Willett, Issy van Randwyck. CD
Studio recording (1996) with Steve Balsamo, Zubin Varla, Joana Ampil. CD
TV soundtrack (2000) with Glenn Carter, Jerome Pradon, Renee Castle. CD

Johnny Johnson

Studio recording (1956) with Burgess Meredith, Hiram Sherman, Scott Merrill, Lotte Lenya, Jane Connell. CD

Jolson Sings Again

Film soundtrack (1949) with Al Jolson (for Larry Parks). CD, DVD

Jolson Story, The

Film soundtrack (1946) with Al Jolson (for Larry Parks). CD, DVD

Joseph and the Amazing Technicolor Dreamcoat

Concept album (1968) with David Daltry, Tim Rice, Bryan Watson, Malcolm Parry.
Studio recording (1974) with Gary Bond, Peter Reeves. CD
Broadway cast (1982) with Bill Hutton, Laurie Beechman, Tom Carder. CD
London revival (1991) with Jason Donovan, Linzi Hately, David Easter. CD
Canadian revival (1992) with Donny Osmond, Janet Metz. CD
California revival (1993) with Michael Damian, Kelli Rabke, Clifford David. CD
Video soundtrack (1999) with Donny Osmond, Maria Friedman, Richard Attenborough. CD, DVD

Journey Back to Oz

Film soundtrack (1974) with (voices of) Liza Minnelli, Ethel Merman, Danny Thomas, Milton Berle, Rise Stevens. DVD

Joy of Living, The

Film soundtrack (1938) with Irene Dunne.

Jumbo

Studio recording (1953) with Lisa Kirk, Jack Cassidy, Jordan Bentley.
Film soundtrack (1962) with Doris Day, James Joyce (for Stephan Boyd), Jimmy Durante, Martha Raye. CD, DVD

Jungle Book, The

Film soundtrack (1967) with (voices of) Phil Harris, Sebastian Cabot, Louis Prima. CD, DVD

Junior Miss

TV soundtrack (1957) with Don Ameche, Joan Bennett, Carol Lynley, Diana Lynn, Jill St. John.

Juno

Original Broadway cast (1959) with Shirley Booth, Melvyn Douglas, Monte Amundsen, Jack MacGowran, Tommy Rall, Rico Froehlich. CD

Kid Millions

Film soundtrack (1963) with Eddie Cantor, Ethel Merman, George Murphy.

The King and I

Original Broadway cast (1951) with Gertrude Lawrence, Yul Brynner, Dorothy Sarnoff, Doretta Morrow, Larry Douglas. CD
Studio recording (1952) with Patrice Munsel, Robert Merrill, Dinah Shore, Tony Martin.
London production (1953) with Valerie Hobson, Herbert Lom, Muriel Smith, Jan Mazarus, Doreen Duke. CD
Film soundtrack (1956) with Marni Nixon (for Deborah Kerr), Yul Brynner, Terry Saunders, Rita Moreno, Reuben Fuentes (for Carlos Rivas). CD, DVD
Studio recording (1964) with Barbara Cook, Theodore Bikel, Anita Darian, Daniel Ferro, Jeanette Scovotti. CD
Lincoln Center revival (1964) with Rise Stevens, Darren McGavin, Lee Venora, Frank Poretta, Patricia Neway, James Harvey. CD
Broadway revival (1977) with Constance Towers, Yul Brynner, June Angela, Martin Vidnovic, Hye-Young Choi, Alan Amick, Gene Profanto. CD
Studio recording (1992) with Julie Andrews, Ben Kingsley, Marilyn Horne, Lea Salonga, Peabo Bryson. CD
Broadway revival (1996) with Donna Murphy, Lou Diamond Phillips, Joohee Choi, José Llana, Taewon Yi Kim. CD
Animated film soundtrack (1999) with (voices of) Christiane Noll, Martin Vidnovic, Barbra Streisand. CD, DVD
London revival (2000) with Elaine Paige, Jason Scott Lee, Taewon Yi Kim, Aura Deva, Sean Ghazi. CD

King Creole

Film soundtrack (1958) with Elvis Presley. CD
DVD

King of Burlesque

Film soundtrack (1935) with Alice Faye.

King of Jazz, The

Film soundtrack (1930) with Bing Crosby, the
Rhythm Boys.

Kismet

Original Broadway cast (1953) with Alfred Drake,
Joan Diener, Richard Kiley, Doretta Morrow. CD
Film soundtrack (1955) with Howard Keel, Ann
Blyth, Vic Damone, Dolores Gray. CD, DVD
Studio recording (1963) with Robert Merrill,
Regina Resnik, Adele Leigh. CD
Revival cast (1965) with Alfred Drake, Lee
Venora, Anne Jeffreys, Richard Banke. CD
Studio recording (1989) with Donald Maxwell,
David Rendall, Judy Kaye, Valerie Masterson.
CD
Studio recording (1991) with Samuel Ramsey,
Jerry Hadley, Julia Migenes, Ruth Ann Swenson.
CD

Kiss Me, Kate

Original Broadway cast (1948) with Alfred
Drake, Patricia Morison, Lisa Kirk, Harold
Lang. CD
Film soundtrack (1953) with Kathryn Grayson,
Howard Keel, Ann Miller, Tommy Rall. DVD
Studio recording (1989) with Thomas Hampson,
Josephine Barstow, Kim Criswell. CD
Studio recording (1990) with Josephine Barstow,
Thomas Hampson, Kim Criswell. CD
Studio recording (1996) with Thomas Allen, Diana
Montague, Diane Langton, Graham Bickley. CD
Broadway revival (2000) with Brian Stokes
Mitchell, Marin Mazzie, Amy Spanger, Michael
Berresse. CD

Kiss of the Spider Woman

Original Broadway cast (1993) with Brent
Carver, Anthony Crivello, Chita Rivera. CD
Broadway replacement cast (1995) with
Vanessa Williams, Brian Stokes Mitchell,
Howard McGillin. CD

Knickerbocker Holiday

Original Broadway cast (1938) with Walter
Huston, Ray Middleton, Jeanne Madden, Richard
Kollmar. CD

Film soundtrack (1944) with Charles Coburn,
Ernest Cossart, Nelson Eddy. CD

Kwamina

Original Broadway cast (1961) with Terry
Carter, Sally Ann Howes, Robert Guillaume,
Brock Peters. CD

La Bamba

Film soundtrack (1987) with Lou Diamond
Phillips, Esai Morales. CD, DVD

La Cage Aux Folles

Original Broadway cast (1983) with George
Hearn, Gene Barry. CD

Lady and the Tramp, The

Film soundtrack (1955) with (voices of) Peggy
Lee, Sonny Burke, George Givot. CD, DVD

Lady Be Good!

Film soundtrack (1941) with Ann Southern,
Eleanor Powell, Dan Dailey. CD
Original Broadway cast reconstruction (1977)
with Fred Astaire, Adele Astaire. CD
Studio recording (1992) with Ann Morrison,
John Pizzarelli, Jason Alexander. CD

Lady in the Dark

Original Broadway cast (1941) with Gertrude
Lawrence, Danny Kaye. CD
Film soundtrack (1944) with Ginger Rogers,
Ray Milland. CD
TV soundtrack (1954) with Ann Sothern,
MacDonald Carey. CD
Studio recording (1963) with Rise Stevens,
Adolph Green, John Reardon. CD
London revival (1997) with Maria Friedman,
Steven Edward Moore, James Dreyfuss. CD

Lady Sings the Blues

Film soundtrack (1972) with Diana Ross,
Michele Aller, Blinky Williams. CD, DVD

Last Sweet Days of Isaac, The

Original Off Broadway cast (1970) with Austin
Pendleton, Fredricka Weber.

Leave It to Jane

Off Broadway revival (1959) with Dorothy
Greener, Kathleen Murray, Jeanne Allen, Angelo
Mango. CD

Legally Blonde

Original Broadway cast (2007) with Laura Bell Bundy, Orfeh, Christian Borle. CD

Les Girls

Film soundtrack (1957) with Gene Kelly, Mitzi Gaynor, Taina Elg, Kay Kendall. DVD

Les Miserables

Original London cast (1985) with Colm Wilkinson, Patti LuPone, Michael Ball, Frances Ruffelle, Roger Allam. CD
Original Broadway cast (1985) with Colm Wilkinson, Terrence Mann, Randy Graff, Judy Kuhn, Michael Maguire. CD
Complete symphonic recording (1988) with Michael Ball, Tracy Shayne, Debbie Byrne. CD
Concert recording (1995) with Colm Wilkinson, Lea Salonga, Philip Quast. CD

Let 'Em Eat Cake

Studio recording (1987) with Larry Kert, Maureen McGovern, Paige O'Hara, David Garrison. CD

Let's Face It

Reconstruction of Broadway cast (1941) with Danny Kaye, Mary Jane Walsh, Hildegarde.
Film soundtrack (1943) with Bob Hope, Betty Hutton.
TV soundtrack (1954) with Gene Nelson, Vivian Blaine.

Let's Sing Again

Film soundtrack (1936) with George Houston, Bobby Breen, Ann Doran. DVD

Life, The

Concept album (1995) with Lou Rawls, Liza Minnelli, Bobby Short. CD
Original Broadway cast (1997) with Sam Harris, Lillias White, Chuck Cooper, Vernel Bagneris. CD

Life and Adventures of Santa Claus, The

TV soundtrack (1985) with (voices of) Earl Hammond, Earle Hyman, Larry Kenney.

Light in the Piazza, The

Original Broadway cast (2005) with Victoria Clark, Kelli O'Hara, Matthew Morrison. CD

Li'l Abner

Original Broadway cast (1956) with Peter Palmer, Stubby Kaye, Edith Adams, Charlotte Rae. CD
Film soundtrack (1959) with Peter Palmer, Stubby Kaye, Leslie Parrish. DVD

Lili

Film soundtrack (1953) with Leslie Caron, Mel Ferrer. CD, DVD

Lillian Russell

Film soundtrack (1940) with Alice Fay, Don Ameche. DVD

Lion King, The

Film soundtrack (1994) with (voices of) Matthew Broderick, Nathan Lane, Jim Cummings, Jeremy Irons, Jonathan Taylor Thomas. CD, DVD
Original Broadway cast (1997) with Samuel E. Wright, Jason Raize, John Vickery, Heather Headley, Max Casella. CD

Little Mary Sunshine

Original Off Broadway cast (1959) with Eileen Brennan, John McMartin, John Aniston. CD

Little Me

Original Broadway cast (1962) with Sid Caesar, Virginia Martin, Nancy Andrews, Joey Faye. CD
Original London cast (1964) with Bruce Forsyth, Swen Swenson. CD
Broadway revival (1998) with Martin Short, Faith Prince. CD

Little Mermaid, The

Film soundtrack (1989) with (voices of) Jodi Benson, Pat Carroll, Samuel Wright. CD, DVD
Original Broadway cast (2008) with Sierra Boggess, Sherie René Scott, Sean Palmer. CD

Little Nellie Kelly

Film soundtrack (1940) with Judy Garland.

Little Night Music, A

Original Broadway cast (1973) with Len Cariou, Glynis Johns, Hermione Gingold, Victoria Mallory, Patricia Elliott, Laurence Guittard. CD
Original London cast (1975) with Joss Ackland, Jean Simmons, Veronica Page, David Kernan. CD
Film soundtrack (1978) with Len Cariou, Elizabeth Taylor, Diana Rigg, Lesley-Anne

Down, Hermione Gingold, Laurence Guittard.
DVD
Studio recording (1990) with Eric Flynn, Jason
Howard, Sian Phillips.
London revival (1995) with Judi Dench,
Laurence Guittard, Lambert Wilson, Patricia
Hodge, Joanna Riding. CD

Little Shop of Horrors

Original Off Broadway cast (1982) with Ellen
Greene, Lee Wilkof, Hy Anzell. CD
Film soundtrack (1986) with Rick Moranis,
Ellen Greene, Levi Stubbs (for plant). CD DVD
Studio recording (1993) with Harry Formby,
Michaela Aughton, Charles de Trafford. CD
Broadway revival (2003) with Hunter Foster,
Kerry Butler. CD

Little Show, The

Studio recording (1953) with Carol Bruce,
Sheila Bond, Hiram Sherman.

Little Women

TV soundtrack (1958) with Jeanne Carson,
Florence Henderson, Rise Stevens.
Original Broadway cast (2004) with Sutton
Foster, Maureen McGovern, Janet Carroll.
CD

Littlest Angel, The

TV soundtrack (1969) with Johnnie Whitaker,
Fred Gwynne, Cab Calloway. DVD

Lorelei

Original Broadway cast (1974) with Carol
Channing, Peter Palmer, Tamara Long, Lee
Roy Reams. CD

Lost in the Stars

Original Broadway cast (1949) with Todd
Duncan, Inez Matthews, Frank Roane. CD
Studio recording (1993) with Arthur Woodley,
Gregory Hopkins, Cynthia Clarey. CD

Louisiana Purchase

Film soundtrack (1941) with Vera Zorina,
Victor Moore. DVD
TV soundtrack (1951) with Sandra Deel,
Victor Moore, Irene Bordoni.
Concert recording (1996) with Michael
McGrath, Judy Blazer, George S. Irving, Taina
Elg, Debbie Gravitte. CD

Love Me or Leave Me

Film soundtrack (1955) with Doris Day. CD,
DVD

Love Me Tender

Film soundtrack (1956) with Elvis Presley. CD,
DVD

Love Me Tonight

Film soundtrack (1932) with Jeanette
MacDonald, Maurice Chevalier, Joseph
Cawthorne, C. Aubrey Smith. DVD

Love Parade

Film soundtrack (1929) with Maurice Chevalier,
Jeannette MacDonald. DVD

Love Thy Neighbor

Film soundtrack (1945) with Jack Benny, Fred
Allen.

Lovely to Look At

Film Soundtrack (1952) with Kathryn Grayson,
Howard Keel, Red Skelton. CD, DVD

Mack and Mabel

Original Broadway cast (1974) with Robert
Preston, Bernadette Peters, Lisa Kirk. CD
Concert recording (1988) with George Hearn,
Denis Quilley, Tommy Tune. CD
Original London cast (1995) with Howard
McGillin, Caroline O'Connor. CD

Mack the Knife

Film soundtrack (1989) with Raul Julia, Rachel
Robertson, Richard Harris, Roger Daltry, Julia
Migenes, Julie Walters. CD

Mlle. Modeste

Studio recording (1952) with Dorothy Kirsten,
Robert Rounseville, Genevieve Warner.

Magic Show, The

Original Broadway cast (1974) with David
Ogden Stiers, Anita Morris, Cheryl Barnes,
Annie McGreevey. CD

Make Mine Manhattan

Studio recording (1978) with Helen Gallagher,
Arthur Siegel, Estelle Parsons. CD

Make Mine Music

Film soundtrack (1946) with (voices of) Nelson Eddy, Dinah Shore, Andrews Sisters. DVD

Mame

Original Broadway cast (1966) with Angela Lansbury, Beatrice Arthur, Jerry Lanning, Frankie Michaels, Jane Connell, Charles Braswell. CD
Film soundtrack (1974) with Lucille Ball, Beatrice Arthur, Robert Preston, Bruce Davison, Jane Connell. CD, DVD

Mamma Mia!

Original London cast (1999) with Lisa Stokke, Hilton McRae, Siobhan McCarthy, Jenny Galloway, Louise Plowright. CD

Man of La Mancha

Original Broadway cast (1965) with Richard Kiley, Joan Diener, Robert Rounseville, Irving Jacobson. CD
Original London cast (1968) with Keith Michell, Joan Diener, Alan Crofoot, Bernard Spear. CD
Film soundtrack (1972) with Simon Gilbert (for Peter O'Toole), Sophia Loren, James Coco, Ian Richardson. CD, DVD
Studio recording (1972) with Jim Nabors, Marilyn Horne, Jack Gilford. CD
Studio recording (1990) with Mandy Patinkin, Placido Domingo, Julia Migenes. CD
Broadway revival (2002) with Brian Stokes Mitchell, Mary Elizabeth Mastrantonio, Ernie Sabella, Mark Jacoby. CD

Man with a Load of Mischief

Original Off Broadway cast (1966) with Shelton Reid, Raymond Thorne, Tom Noel, Virginia Vestoff, Alice Cannon. CD

March of the Falsettos

Original Off Broadway cast (1981) with Michael Rupert, Chip Zen, Alison Fraser, Stephen Bogardus. CD

Mary Poppins

Film soundtrack (1964) with Julie Andrews, Dick Van Dyke, David Tomlinson, Glynis Johns. CD, DVD
Original London cast (2004) with Laura Mitchell, Gavin Lee, Linzi Hateley. CD

Maytime

Film soundtrack (1937) with Jeanette MacDonald, Nelson Eddy. DVD
Radio soundtrack (1944) with Jeanette MacDonald, Nelson Eddy.

Me and Juliet

Original Broadway cast (1953) with Isabel Bigley, Bill Hayes, Mark Dawson, Joan McCracken, Arthur Maxwell. CD

Me and My Girl

London revival (1985) with Robert Lindsey, Emma Thompson.
Original Broadway cast (1986) with Robert Lindsay, Maryann Plunkett, Jane Connell, George S. Irving. CD

Me Nobody Knows, The

Original Broadway cast (1970) with Irene Cara, Hattie Winston, José Fernandez, Melanie Henderson, Northern J. Calloway. CD

Meet Me in St. Louis

Film soundtrack (1944) with Judy Garland, Tom Drake, Margaret O'Brien. CD, DVD
Broadway cast (1989) with Donna Kane, George Hearn, Milo O'Shea, Courtney Peldon, Jason Workman, Betty Garrett. CD

Melody Time

Film soundtrack (1948) with the Andrew Sisters, Dennis Day. DVD

Merrily We Roll Along

Original Broadway cast (1981) with Jim Walton, Lonny Price, Ann Morrison, Jason Alexander. CD
London cast (1993) with Michael Cantwell, Jacqueline Dankworth, Maria Friedman, Evan Pappas. CD
Off Broadway cast (1994) Adam Heller, Amy Ryder, Malcolm Gets, Michele Pawk, Anne Bobby. CD

Merry Widow, The

Film soundtrack (1934) with Maurice Chevalier, Jeanette MacDonald. DVD
City Center revival (1944) with Kitty Carlisle, Wilbur Evans, Felix Knight.
Film soundtrack (1952) with Trudy Erwin (for Lana Turner), Richard Haydn, Fernando Lamas. CD
Studio recording (1952) with Dorothy Kirsten, Robert Rounseville, George S. Irving.

City Center revival (1964) with Patrice Munsel, Bob Wright, Mischa Auer.

City Opera revival (1978) with Beverly Sills, Alan Titus, Glenys Fowles.

Mexican Hayride

Original Broadway cast (1944) with Wilbur Evans, June Havoc, Corinna Mura. CD

Mikado, The

TV soundtrack (1959) with Groucho Marx, Robert Rounseville, Stanley Holloway. CD

Studio recording (1989) with Eric Roberts, Bonaventura Bottone, Deborah Rees. CD

Studio recording (1992) with Anthony Rolfe Johnson, Richard Van Allen, Anne Howells, Donald Adams, Richard Suart. CD

Milk and Honey

Original Broadway cast (1961) with Mimi Benzell, Robert Weede, Molly Picon. CD

Miss Liberty

Original Broadway cast (1949) with Eddie Albert, Allyn McLerie, Mary McCarty. CD

Miss Saigon

Original London cast (1989) with Jonathan Price, Lea Salonga, Simon Bowman. CD

Studio recording (1995) with Joanna Ampil, Kevin Gray, Peter Cousens. CD

Mississippi

Film soundtrack (1935) with Bing Crosby, Queenie Smith (selections only).

Mrs. Santa Claus

TV soundtrack (1996) with Angela Lansbury, Michael Jeter, Terrence Mann. CD, DVD

Mr. Magoo's Christmas Carol

TV soundtrack (1962) with (voices of) Jim Backus, Jack Cassidy. DVD

Mr. President

Original Broadway cast (1962) with Nanette Fabray, Anita Gillette, Robert Ryan. CD

Mr. Wonderful

Original Broadway cast (1956) with Sammy Davis, Jr., Pat Marshall, Chita Rivera. CD

Monte Carlo

Film soundtrack (1930) with Jeanette MacDonald, Jack Buchanan, John Roche.

Moon Over Miami

Film soundtrack (1941) with Betty Grable, Robert Cummings, Don Ameche. DVD

Most Happy Fella, The

Original Broadway cast (1956) with Robert Weede, Jo Sullivan, Susan Johnson, Art Lund. CD

Original London cast (1960) with Inia Te Wiata, Helena Scott, Libi Staiger, Jack DeLon. CD

Broadway revival (1992) with Spiro Malas, Sophie Hayden, Charles Pistone, Bill Nadel. CD

Studio recording (1999) with Louis Quilco, Emily Loesser, Nancy Shade, Jo Sullivan. CD

Mother Wore Tights

Film soundtrack (1947) with Betty Grable, Dan Dailey, Mona Freeman.

Moulin Rouge

Film soundtrack (2001) with various recording artists. CD, DVD

Movie Movie

Film soundtrack (1979) with Patricia Marshall, Gene Merlino, Jerry Whitman.

Movin' Out

Original Broadway cast (2002) with Michael Cavanaugh, John Selya, Elizabeth Parkinson, Keith Roberts. CD

Muppet Movie, The

Film soundtrack (1979) with (voices of) Jim Henson, Frank Oz, Dave Goelz. CD, DVD

Music in the Air

Studio recording (1932) with Robert Simmons, Jack Parker, Conrad Thibault, James Stanley, Marjorie Horton.

Film soundtrack (1934) with John Boles, Gloria Swanson, James O'Brien, Betty Hiestand (for June Lang), James O'Brien (for Douglass Montgomery).

Radio broadcast (1949) with Jane Powell, Gordon MacRae.

Music Man, The

Original Broadway cast (1957) with Robert Preston, Barbara Cook. CD
Original London cast (1961) with Van Johnson, Patricia Lambert. CD
Film soundtrack (1962) with Robert Preston, Shirley Jones. CD, DVD
Studio recording (1991) with Timothy Nolan, Kathleen Brett. CD
Broadway revival (2000) with Craig Bierko, Rebecca Luker. CD
Television soundtrack (2003) with Matthew Broderick, Kristin Chenoweth. CD, DVD

My Fair Lady

Original Broadway cast (1956) with Julie Andrews, Rex Harrison, Stanley Holloway, Robert Coote. CD
Original London cast (1959) with Julie Andrews, Rex Harrison, Stanley Holloway, Robert Coote. CD
Film soundtrack (1964) with Rex Harrison, Marni Nixon (for Audrey Hepburn), Stanley Holloway, Wilfred Hyde-White. CD, DVD
Broadway revival (1976) with Ian Richardson, Christine Andreas, George Rose, Robert Coote. CD
Studio recording (1987) with Kiri Te Kanawa, Jeremy Irons, Jerry Hadley, Warren Mitchell. CD
Studio recording (1994) with Alec McCowen, Tinuke Olafimihan, Michael Denison. CD
London cast (2001) with Martine McCutcheon, Jonathan Pryce, Mark Umber, Nicholas Le Prevost. CD

My Gal Sal

Film soundtrack (1942) with Victor Mature, Nan Wynn (for Rita Hayworth.)

My Man

Film soundtrack (1928) with Fanny Brice.

My One and Only

Original Broadway cast (1983) with Tommy Tune, Twiggy, Roscoe Lee Browne. CD

Mystery of Edwin Drood, The

Original Broadway cast (1985) with Betty Buckley, Howard McGillin, Cleo Laine, George Rose, Patti Cohenour. CD

Nashville

Film soundtrack (1975) with Ronee Blakely, Keith Carradine, Henry Gibson. CD, DVD

Naughty Marietta

Film soundtrack (1935) with Nelson Eddy, Jeannette MacDonald. DVD
Radio soundtrack (1944) with Jeanette MacDonald, Nelson Eddy.
Studio recording (1950) with Earl Wrightson, Elaine Malbin, Jimmy Carroll.
Studio recording (1954) with Gordon MacRae, Marguerite Piaza, Katherine Hilgenberg.
Studio recording (1965) with Mary Thomas, John McNally.

Neptune's Daughter

Film soundtrack (1949) with Esther Williams, Betty Garrett, Red Skelton. DVD

New Brain, A

Original Off Broadway cast (1998) with Malcolm Gets, Penny Fuller, Chip Zien, Norm Lewis. CD

New Faces

Film soundtrack (1954) with Eartha Kitt, Robert Clary, Paul Lynde. DVD

New Faces of 1952

Original Broadway cast (1952) with Eartha Kitt, Robert Clary, Alice Ghostly, Paul Lynde. CD

New Faces of 1956

Original Broadway cast (1956) with T. C. Jones, Tiger Haynes, John Reardon. CD

New Faces of 1968

Original Broadway cast (1968) with Madeline Kahn, Robert Kline. CD

New Girl in Town

Original Broadway cast (1957) with Gwen Verdon, George Wallace, Cameron Prud'homme. CD

New Moon, The

London cast (1929) with Evelyn Laye, Ben Williams, Howett Worster, Gene Gerrard, Dolores Farris. CD

Film soundtrack (1930) with Lawrence Tibbett, Grace Moore, Roland Young.

Film soundtrack (1940) with Jeanette MacDonald, Nelson Eddy. DVD

Studio recording (1950) with Lucille Norman, Gordon MacRae.

Studio recording: RCA (1952) with Earl Wrightson, Frances Greer, Donald Dame, Earl Oxford.

Studio recording (1962) with Peter Palmer, Arthur Rubin. CD

Studio recording (1963) with Gorgon MacCrae, Dorothy Kirsten. CD

Studio recording: Phillips (1967) with John Hanson, Patricia Michael.

Concert recording (2004) with Christiane Noll, Rodney Gilfry, Burke Moses, Lauren Ward, Peter Benson, Brandon Jovanovich. CD

New Orleans

Film soundtrack (1947) with Arturo de Cordova, Dorothy Patrick, Marjorie Lord. DVD

New York, New York

Film soundtrack (1977) with Liza Minnelli, Larry Kert, Robert De Niro. CD, DVD

Night and Day

Film soundtrack (1946) with Ginny Simms, Dorothy Malone, Mary Martin. CD, DVD

Night at the Opera, A

Film soundtrack (1935) with Allan Jones, Kitty Carlisle, the Marx Brothers. DVD

Nightmare Before Christmas, The

Film soundtrack (1993) with (voices of) Danny Elfman, Ken Page, Catherine O'Hara. CD, DVD

Nine

Original Broadway cast (1982) with Raul Julia, Anita Morris, Karen Akers. CD

London concert recording (1992) with Jonathan Pryce, Ann Crumb, Liliane Montevecchi. CD

Broadway revival (2003) with Antonio Banderas, Mary Stuart Masterson, Jane Krakowski. CD

No, No, Nanette

Film soundtrack (1930) with Anna Naegle, Victor Mature. DVD

Broadway revival (1971) with Susan Watson, Ruby Keeler, Helen Gallagher, Jack Gilford, Bobby Van. CD

No Strings

Original Broadway cast (1962) with Diahann Carroll, Richard Kiley. CD

London cast (1963) with Art Lund, Beverly Todd.

Nunsense

Original Off Broadway cast (1985) with Suzi Winson, Christine Anderson. CD

London cast (1987) with Honor Blackman, Anna Sharkey, Pip Hinton. CD

Nunsense II: The Second Coming

Original Off Broadway cast (1993) with Christine Anderson, Mary Gillis, Lyn Vaux. CD

Of Thee I Sing

Broadway revival (1952) with Jack Carson, Betty Oakes, Lenore Lonergan. CD

Television recording (1972) with Carroll O'Connor, Cloris Leachman, Michele Lee. CD

Studio recording (1987) with Larry Kert, Maureen McGovern, Jack Gilford. CD

Oh! Calcutta!

Original Broadway cast (1969) with Peter Schickele, Stanley Walden, CD

Oh, Kay!

Reconstruction of Original Broadway cast (1926) with Gertrude Lawrence.

Studio recording (1955) with Barbara Ruick, Jack Cassidy, Allen Case. CD

Off Broadway revival (1960) with Murray Matheson, Marti Stevens, Eddie Phillips.

Studio recording (1994) with Dawn Upshaw, Patrick Cassidy, Liz Larsen, Susan Lucci. CD

Oklahoma!

Original Broadway cast (1943) with Alfred Drake, Joan Roberts, Lee Dixon, Celeste Holm, Howard Da Silva, Betty Garde. CD

London cast (1947) with Howard Keel, Betty Jane Watson, Walter Donahue, Dorothea McFarland, Henry Clarke. CD

Studio recording (1952) with Nelson Eddy, Portia Nelson, Kaye Ballard, Wilton Clary, Virginia Haskins, David Morris, Lee Cass.

Studio recording (1953) with John Raitt, Patricia Northrup.

Film soundtrack (1955) with Gordon MacRae, Shirley Jones, Gloria Grahame, Gene Nelson, Charlotte Greenwood, Rod Steiger. CD, DVD

Studio recording (1964) with Florence Henderson, John Raitt, Phyllis Newman, Jack Elliott, Irene Carroll, Ara Berberian, Leonard Stokes. CD
Broadway revival (1979) with Laurence Guittard, Christine Andreas, Mary Wickes, Martin Vidnovic, Christine Ebersole, Bruce Adler, Harry Groener, Philip Rash. CD
London revival (1980) with John Diedrich, Rosamund Shelley, Madge Ryan, Alfred Molina, Jillian Mack. CD
London revival (1998) with Hugh Jackman, Josefina Gabrielle, Shuler Hensley, Maureen Lipman, Jimmy Johnston, Vicki Simon. CD, DVD

Oliver!

Original London cast (1960) with Ron Moody, Georgia Brown, Keith Hamshere. CD
Studio recording (1962) with Stanley Holloway, Alma Coga, Tony Tanner. CD
Original Broadway cast (1963) with Clive Revill, Georgia Brown, Bruce Prochnik. CD
Film soundtrack (1968) with Mark Lester, Ron Moody, Shani Wallis, Jack Wild. CD, DVD
Studio recording (1991) with Josephine Barstow, Stuart Kale, Julian Forsyth. CD
London revival (1994) with Jonathan Pryce, Sally Dexter, Adam Searles. CD

Oliver and Company

Film soundtrack (1988) with (voices of) Joseph Lawrence, Billy Joel, Cheech Marin, Bette Midler. CD, DVD

Olympus 7-0000

TV soundtrack (1966) with Donald O'Connor, Larry Blyden, Alan Alda.

On a Clear Day You Can See Forever

Original Broadway cast (1965) with Barbara Harris, John Cullum, William Daniels. CD
Film soundtrack (1969) with Barbra Streisand, Yves Montand. CD, DVD

On the Avenue

Film soundtrack (1937) with Alice Faye, Dick Powell, Madeline Carroll. DVD

On the Riviera

Film soundtrack (1951) with Danny Kaye, Gene Tierney, Corinne Calvert. DVD

On the Town

Film soundtrack (1949) with Frank Sinatra, Gene Kelly, Ann Miller, Betty Garrett. DVD
Studio recording (1960) with Nancy Walker, Betty Comden, Adolph Green. CD
Original London cast (1963) with Don McKay, Elliott Gould, Terry Kiser. CD
Studio recording (1992) with Tyne Daly, David Garrison, Frederica Von Stade. CD
Studio recording (1996) with Kin Criswell, Judy Kaye, Ethan Freeman. CD

On the Twentieth Century

Original Broadway cast (1978) with John Cullum, Madeline Kahn, Kevin Kline, Imogene Coca. CD

On Your Toes

Studio recording (1952) with Portia Nelson, Jack Cassidy, Laurel Shelby, Ray Hyson. CD
Broadway revival (1954) with Bobby Van, Kay Coulter, Elaine Stritch, Joshua Kelly, Jack Williams. CD
Broadway revival (1983) with Lara Teeter, Christine Andreas, Dina Merrill, George S. Irving. CD

Once on This Island

Original Broadway cast (1990) with Ellis E. Williams, La Chanze, Kecia Lewis-Evans. CD
Original London cast (1994) with Monique Mason. CD

Once Upon a Brothers Grimm

Television soundtrack (1977) with Dean Jones, Gordon Connell, Susan Silo.

Once Upon a Mattress

Original Broadway cast (1959) with Carol Burnett, Joe Bova, Jack Gilford. CD
Original London cast (1960) with Jane Connell, Patricia Lambert. CD
Broadway revival (1997) with Sarah Jessica Parker, Lawrence Clayton. CD
TV soundtrack (2005), Tracy Ullman, Carol Burnett, Denis O'Hare. DVD

One Hour with You

Film soundtrack (1932) with Jeanette MacDonald, Maurice Chevalier, Genevieve Tobin. CD, DVD

110 in the Shade

Original Broadway cast (1963) with Inga Swenson, Robert Horton, Stephen Douglass. CD
Studio recording (1997) with Karen Ziemba, Richard Muenz, Kristin Chenoweth. CD
Broadway revival (2007) with Audra McDonald, John Cullum, Steve Kazee. CD

One in a Million

Radio soundtrack (1936) with Arline Judge, the Ritz Brothers.

One Night in the Tropics

Film soundtrack (1940) with Bud Abbott, Lou Costello, Allan Jones. DVD

One Night of Love

Film soundtrack (1934) with Tullio Carminati, Grace Moore, Lyle Talbot.

One Touch of Venus

Original Broadway cast (1943) with Kenny Baker, Mary Martin. CD

Orchestra Wives

Film soundtrack (1942) with Tex Beneke, Pat Friday (for Lynn Bari), Ray Eberle. DVD

Our Town

TV soundtrack (1955) with Frank Sinatra.

Out of This World

Original Broadway cast (1950) with Charlotte Greenwood, Priscilla Gillette, William Redfield. CD
Concert revival (1995) with Andrea Martin, Gregg Edelman Marin Mazzie, Ken Page. CD

Over Here!

Original Broadway cast (1974) with Maxene Andrews, Patty Andrews, Janie Sell, April Shawhan, John Driver. CD

Pacific Overtures

Original Broadway cast (1976) with Mako, Alvin Ing, Ernest Haradia. CD
London cast (1989) with Richard Angas, Christopher Booth Jones. CD
Broadway revival (2004) with B. D. Wong, Paolo Montalban, Michael K. Lee. CD

Paint Your Wagon

Original Broadway cast (1951) with James Barton, Olga San Juan, Tony Bavaar. CD
Original London cast (1953) with Bobby Howes, Sally Ann Howes, Ken Cantril. CD
Film soundtrack (1969) with Lee Marvin, Clint Eastwood, Harve Presnell. CD, DVD

Pajama Game, The

Original Broadway cast (1954) with John Raitt, Janis Paige, Carol Haney, Eddie Foy, Jr. CD
Film soundtrack (1957) with Doris Day, John Raitt, Eddie Foy, Jr., Carol Haney. CD, DVD
Studio recording (1996) with Ron Raines, Kim Criswell, Judy Kaye. CD
Broadway revival (2006) with Harry Connick, Jr., Kelli O'Hara, Megan Lawrence, Michael McKean. CD

Pal Joey

Studio recording (1950) with Harold Lang, Vivienne Segal, Beverly Fite, Barbara Ashley, Kenneth Remo, Jo Hurt. CD
Broadway revival (1952) with Dick Beavers, Jane Froman, Elaine Stritch, Helen Gallagher, Patricia Northrop, Lewis Bolyard. CD
Film soundtrack (1957) with Frank Sinatra, Jo Ann Greer (for Rita Hayworth), Trudi Erwin (for Kim Novak). CD, DVD
London cast (1980) with Denis Lawson, Sian Phillips, Jane Gurnett, Darlene Johnson, Tracey Perry.
Concert recording (1995) with Patti LuPone, Peter Gallagher, Daisy Prince, Bebe Neuwirth, Vicki Lewis. CD

Paleface, The

Film soundtrack (1948) with Bob Hope, Jane Russell. DVD

Panama Hattie

Original Broadway cast (1940) with Ethel Merman, Joan Carroll. CD
TV soundtrack (1954) with Ethel Merman, Ray Middleton, Jack Leonard.

Parade

Original Broadway cast (1999) with Brent Carver, Carolee Carmello, Don Chastain, Rufus Bonds, Jr., Evan Pappas. CD

Paramount on Parade

Film soundtrack (1930) with Maurice Chevalier, Dennis King, Buddy Rogers.

Passion
Original Broadway cast (1994) with Donna Murphy, Marin Mazzie, Jere Shea. CD, DVD
Original London cast (1997) with Maria Friedman, Michael Ball, Helen Hobson. CD

Pennies from Heaven
Film soundtrack (1981) with various recording artists. DVD

Pete Kelly's Blues
Film soundtrack (1955) with Ella Fitzgerald, Peggy Lee. CD, DVD

Pete's Dragon
Film soundtrack (1977) with Helen Reddy, Jim Dale, Mickey Rooney. CD, DVD

Peter Pan (Bernstein)
Original Broadway cast (1950) with Jean Arthur, Boris Karloff, Marcia Henderson. CD

Peter Pan (Disney)
Film soundtrack (1953) with (voices of) Bobby Driscoll, Kathryn Beaumont, Hans Conried. CD, DVD

Peter Pan (Styne, etc.)
Original Broadway cast (1954) with Mary Martin, Cyril Ritchard, Kathy Nolan. CD
Studio recording (1997) with Kathy Rigby, Paul Schoeffler. CD

Phantom of the Opera
Original London cast (1986) with Michael Crawford, Sarah Brightman, Steve Barton. CD
Original Canadian cast (1990) with Colm Wilkinson, Rebecca Caine, Byron Nease. CD
Studio recording (2005) with Paul Jones, Stephanie Lawrence, Carl Wayne. CD
Film soundtrack (2004) with Gerard Butler, Emmy Rossum, Patrick Wilson. CD, DVD

Phantom of the Paradise
Film soundtrack (1974) with Paul Williams, Jessica Harper, Ray Kennedy. DVD

Phantom President, The
Film soundtrack (1932) with George M. Cohan, Jimmy Durante.

Pied Piper of Hamelin
TV soundtrack (1957) with Van Johnson.

Pinocchio
Film soundtrack (1940) with (voices of) Dickie Jones, Cliff Edwards, Walter Cantlett. CD, DVD
Studio recording (1957) with Paul Winchell, Jerry Mahoney, Johnny Haymer.
TV soundtrack (1957) with Mickey Rooney, Fran Allison, Jerry Colonna.
TV soundtrack (1965) with John Joy, David Life, Fred Grades.

Pins and Needles
Studio recording (1962) with Jack Carroll, Harold Rome, Rose Marie Jun, Barbra Streisand. CD

Pipe Dream
Original Broadway cast (1955) with William Johnson, Judy Tyler, Helen Traubel, Mike Kellin, G. D. Wallace. CD

Pippin
Original Broadway cast (1972) with John Rubenstein, Ben Vereen, Jill Clayburgh, Irene Ryan. CD
TV soundtrack (1981) with Ben Vereen, William Katt, Martha Raye. DVD

Pirate, The
Film soundtrack (1948) with Judy Garland, Gene Kelly. DVD

Pirates of Penzance, The
Broadway revival cast (1981) with Kevin Kline, Linda Ronstadt, Rex Smith, George Rose. CD, DVD
Studio recording (1993) Isidore Godfrey, Donald Adams, Owen Brannigan. CD

Plain and Fancy
Original Broadway cast (1955) with Gloria Marlowe, Barbara Cook, David Daniels, Shirl Conway. CD

Pocahontas
Film soundtrack (1995) with (voices of) Judy Kuhn, Linda Hunt, Mel Gibson, Jim Cummings. CD, DVD

Polly

TV soundtrack (1989) with Kamrock Hack (for Keshia Knight Pulliam), Vanessa Bell Calaway, T. K. Carter, Phylicia Rashad. CD, DVD

Poor Little Rich Girl

Film soundtrack (1936) with Shirley Temple, Alice Faye, Jack Haley. DVD

Porgy and Bess

Original Broadway cast (1940/1942) with Todd Duncan, Anne Brown, Avon Long. CD
Studio recording (1951) with Edward Matthews, J. Rosamond Johnson, Helen Dowdy. CD
Film soundtrack (1959) with Robert McFerrin (for Sidney Poitier), Adele Addison (for Dorothy Dandridge). DVD
Studio recording (1963) with Leontyne Price, William Warfield, McHenry Boatwright. CD
Studio recording (1976) with Ray Charles, Cleo Laine.
Houston Grand Opera cast (1976) with Betty Lane, Donnie Rae Albert, Larry Marshall. CD
Studio recording (1989) with Willard White, Cynthia Haymon, Gregg Baker. CD

Preacher's Wife, The

Film soundtrack (1996) with Whitney Houston. CD, DVD

Present Arms

Studio recording (2006) with James Anest, Danielle Vernengo, Brad Roseborough. CD

Prince of Egypt, The

Film soundtrack (1998) with (voices of) Val Kilmer, Ralph Fiennes. CD, DVD

Producers, The

Original Broadway cast (2001) with Nathan Lane, Matthew Broderick, Gary Beach, Cady Huffman. CD
Film soundtrack (2005) with Nathan Lane, Matthew Broderick, Gary Beach, Uma Thurman. CD, DVD

Promises, Promises

Original Broadway cast (1968) with Jerry Orbach, Jill O'Hara, Edward Winter, Marian Mercer. CD
Original London cast (1969) with Tony Roberts, Betty Buckley.

Purlie

Original Broadway cast (1970) with Cleavon Little, Melba Moore, Sherman Hemsley. CD

Puttin' on the Ritz

Film soundtrack (1930) with Harry Richman, Joan Bennett.

Queen of the Stardust Ballroom

TV soundtrack (1975) with Maureen Stapleton, Charles Durning, Michael Brandon. DVD

Rags

Original Broadway cast (1986) with Judy Kuhn, Julia Migenes, Terrence Mann, Larry Kert, Lonny Price. CD

Ragtime

Original Broadway cast (1998) with Brian Stokes Mitchell, Marin Mazzie, Audra McDonald, Mark Jacoby, Judy Kaye. CD

Raisin

Original Broadway cast (1973) with Joe Morton, Virginia Capers, Ernestine Jackson, Deborah Allen, Ralph Carter. CD

Ray

Film soundtrack (2004) with Jamie Fox, Kerry Washington, Regina King. CD, DVD

Really Rosie

TV soundtrack (1980) with Carole King. CD

Rebecca of Sunnybrook Farm

Film soundtrack (1938) with Shirley Temple. DVD

Red, Hot and Blue

Studio recording (1936) with Ethel Merman, Jimmy Durante, Bob Hope. CD

Red Mill, The

Studio recording (1946) with Earl Wrightson, Mary Martha Briney, Donald Dame.
Studio recording (1946) with Wilbur Evans, Eileen Farrell, Felix Knight.
Studio recording (1955) with Gordan MacRae, Lucille Norman.
Studio recording (1979) with Rosalind Rees, Leonard Van Camp, Michael Wilson.

Ohio Light Opera cast (2001) with Cassidy King, Anthony Maida, Megan Loomis, Lucas Meachum. CD

Redhead

Original Broadway cast (1959) with Gwen Verdon, Richard Kiley, Leonard Stone. CD

Rent

Original Broadway cast (1996) with Adam Pascal, Daphne Rubin-Vega, Anthony Rapp, Idina Menzel. CD
Film soundtrack (2005) with Adam Pascal, Rosario Dawson, Anthony Rapp, Idina Menzel. CD, DVD

Rescuers, The

Film soundtrack (1977) with (voices of) Eva Gabor, Bob Newhart, Michelle Stacy, Geraldine Page. DVD

Revenge with Music

Studio recording (1934) with Libby Holman (selections only).

Rhapsody in Blue

Film soundtrack (1945) with Al Jolson, Hazel Scott.

Rhythm on the River

Film soundtrack (1940) with Bing Crosby, Mary Martin. DVD

Rink, The

Original Broadway cast (1984) with Liza Minnelli, Chita Rivera, Jason Alexander. CD
Original London cast (1988) with Josephine Blake, Diane Langton. CD

Rio Rita

Original London cast (1930) with Edith Day, Geoffrey Gwyther.

Road to Bali

Film soundtrack (1953) with Bing Crosby, Bob Hope, Dorothy Lamour. DVD

Road to Hong Kong, The

Film soundtrack (1961) with Bing Crosby, Bob Hope, Joan Collins. DVD

Road to Morocco

Film soundtrack (1942) with Bing Crosby, Bob Hope, Dorothy Lamour. DVD

Road to Rio

Film soundtrack (1948) with Bing Crosby, Bob Hope, Dorothy Lamour, the Andrew Sisters. DVD

Road to Singapore

Film soundtrack (1940) with Bing Crosby, Bob Hope, Dorothy Lamour. DVD

Road to Utopia

Film soundtrack (1946) with Bing Crosby, Bob Hope, Dorothy Lamour. DVD

Road to Zanzibar

Film soundtrack (1941) with Bing Crosby, Bob Hope, Dorothy Lamour. DVD

Roar of the Greasepaint, The—The Smell of the Crowd

Original Broadway cast (1965) with Anthony Newley, Cyril Ritchard, Joyce Jillson. CD

Robber Bridegroom, The

Original Broadway cast (1976) with Barry Bostwick, Rhonda Coullet, Barbara Lang, Lawrence John Moss, Ernie Sabella. CD

Roberta

Film soundtrack (1935) with Fred Astaire, Ginger Rogers, Irene Dunne. DVD
Studio recording (1944) with Kitty Carlisle, Alfred Drake, Paula Lawrence. CD
Studio recording (1953) with Stephen Douglass, Joan Roberts, Jack Cassidy. CD

Robin and the Seven Hoods

Film soundtrack (1964) with Frank Sinatra, Bing Crosby, Dean Martin, Sammy Davis, Jr. CD, DVD

Rocky Horror Picture Show, The

Film soundtrack (1975) with Tim Curry, Barry Bostwick, Susan Sarandon. CD, DVD

Rocky Horror Show, The

Original London cast (1973) with Richard O'Brien, Little Nell, Jonathan Adams. CD

Original Roxy cast (1974) with B. Miller, Tim Curry, Bruce Scott. CD
Original Broadway cast (1975) with Tim Curry, Meat Loaf, Abigale Haness.
Studio recording (1995) with Brian May, Christopher Lee. CD
Broadway revival (2001) with Tom Hewitt, Alice Ripley, Jarod Emick. CD

Roman Scandals

Film soundtrack (1933) with Eddie Cantor, Ruth Etting.

Romance on the High Seas

Film soundtrack (1948) with Doris Day, Page Cavanaugh Trio. DVD

Rosalie

Film soundtrack (1937) with Nelson Eddy, Frank Morgan, Ilona Massey.

Rose, The

Film soundtrack (1979) with Bette Midler. CD, DVD

Rose-Marie

London cast (1925) with Edith Day, Derek Oldham, Billy Merson, Claire Hardwicke, John Dunsmure.
Film soundtrack (1936) with Jeanette Mac Donald, Nelson Eddy, Allan Jones, Gilda Gray. DVD
Studio recording (1951) with Dorothy Kirsten, Nelson Eddy (selections only).
Film soundtrack (1954) Ann Blyth, Howard Keel, Bert Lahr, Fernando Lamas, Marjorie Main. DVD
Studio recording (1958) with Julie Andrews, Giorgio Tozzi, Meier Tzelniker, Frances Day, Marion Keene, Frederick Harvey.

Rose of Washington Square

Film soundtrack (1939) with Alice Faye, Al Jolson. CD

Rothschilds, The

Original Broadway cast (1970) with Hal Linden, Paul Hecht, Jill Clayburgh. CD

Royal Wedding

Film soundtrack (1951) with Fred Astaire, Jane Powell. CD, DVD

Rudolph and Frosty's Christmas in July

TV soundtrack (1979) with (voices of) Red Buttons, Ethel Merman, Mickey Rooney. DVD

Rudolph the Red-Nosed Reindeer

TV soundtrack (1964) with (voices of) Burl Ives, Billie Mae Richards, Paul Soles. CD, DVD

Ruggles of Red Gap

TV soundtrack (1957) with Michael Redgrave, Peter Lawford, Imogene Coca.

St. Louis Woman

Original Broadway cast (1946) with Harold Nicholas, Pearl Bailey, June Hawkins, Ruby Hill. CD
Concert recording (1998) with Vanessa Williams, Helen Goldsby, Wayne Mathis, Victor Trent Cook. CD

Sally

Film soundtrack (1920) with Marilyn Miller, Alexander Gray.

San Francisco

Film soundtrack (1936) with Jeannette MacDonald. DVD

Santa Claus Is Coming to Town

TV soundtrack (1971) with Fred Astaire, Mickey Rooney, Keenan Wynn. CD DVD

Saratoga

Original Broadway cast (1959) with Howard Keel, Carol Lawrence, Carol Brice. CD

Satins and Spurs

Studio recording (1954) with Betty Hutton, Earl Wrightson. CD

Saturday Night Fever

Film soundtrack (1977) with Bee Gees, Yvonne Elliman. CD, DVD
Original London cast (1998) with Adam Garcia, Tara Wilkinson. CD

Scarlet Pimpernel, The

Original Broadway cast (1997) with Douglas Sills, Terrence Mann, Christina Andreas. CD

Concert recording (1999) with Rachel York, Rex Smith, Douglas Sills. CD

Scrooge
Film soundtrack (1970) with Albert Finney, Richard Beaumont, Alec Guinness. DVD

Second Fiddle
Film soundtrack (1939) with Sonja Henie, Tyrone Power. DVD

Secret Garden, The
Original Broadway cast (1991) with Mandy Patinkin, Rebecca Luker, Daisy Eagan, Robert Westenberg. CD
Original London cast (2001) with Linzi Hateley, Freddie Davies, Craig Purnell. CD

Seesaw
Original Broadway cast (1973) with Michele Lee, Ken Howard, Tommy Tune. CD

Seussical
Original Broadway cast (2000) with David Shiner, Kevin Chamberlain, Janine LaManna. CD

Seven Brides for Seven Brothers
Film soundtrack (1954) with Howard Keel, Jane Powell. CD, DVD

Seven Hills of Rome
Film soundtrack (1958) with Mario Lanza. DVD

1776
Original Broadway cast (1969) with William Daniels, Ronald Holgate, Betty Buckley. CD
Original London cast (1970) with Lewis Fiander, Ronald Radd, Cheryl Kennedy. CD
Film soundtrack (1972) with William Daniels, Howard Da Silva, John Cullum. DVD
Broadway revival (1997) with Brent Spiner, Pat Hingle, Paul Michael Valley, Gregg Edelman. CD

70, Girls, 70
Original Broadway cast (1971) with Mildred Natwick, Hans Conried, Lillian Roth. CD
Original London cast (1991) with Dora Bryan. CD

Shall We Dance
Film soundtrack (1937) with Fred Astaire, Ginger Rogers. CD, DVD

She Done Him Wrong
Film soundtrack (1933) with Mae West. DVD

She Loves Me
Original Broadway cast (1963) with Barbara Cook, Daniel Massey, Jack Cassidy. CD
Original London cast (1964) with Anne Rogers, Gary Raymond, Gary Miller. CD
Broadway revival (1993) with Boyd Gaines, Howard McGillin, Sally Mayes. CD
London revival (1994) with Ruthie Henshall, John Gordon Sinclair, Barry James. CD

Shenandoah
Original Broadway cast (1975) with John Cullum, Joel Higgins, Donna Theodore. CD

Shocking Miss Pilgrim, The
Film soundtrack (1947) with Betty Grable, Dick Haymes, Allyn Joslyn.

Show Boat
London cast (1928) with Edith Day, Howett Worster, Paul Robeson, Marie Burke, Norris Smith. CD
Film soundtrack (1936) with Irene Dunne, Allan Jones, Paul Robeson, Helen Morgan, Hattie McDaniel, Sammy White, Queenie Smith.
Broadway revival (1946) with Jan Clayton, Charles Fredericks, Carol Bruce, Kenneth Spencer, Colette Lyons, Helen Dowdy. CD
Film soundtrack (1951) with Kathryn Grayson, Howard Keel, William Warfield, Annette Warren (for Ava Gardner), Gower and Marge Champion. CD, DVD
Studio recording (1956) with Robert Merrill, Patrice Munsel, Rise Stevens, Janet Pavek, Kevin Scott, Katherine Graves.
Studio recording (1962) with John Raitt, Barbara Cook, William Warfield, Anita Darian, Fay DeWitt, Louise Parker, Jack Dabdoub. CD
Lincoln Center revival (1966) with Barbara Cook, Stephen Douglass, Constance Towers, William Warfield, Margaret Hamilton, David Wayne, Allyn McLerie, Rosetta LeNoire, Eddie Phillips. CD
Studio recording (1988) with Jerry Hadley, Frederica Von Stade, Teresa Stratas, Bruce

Hubbard, Paige O'Hara, Robert Nichols, David Garrison, Karla Burns. CD
Broadway revival (1994) with Rebecca Luker, Mark Jacoby, Lonette McKee, Michel Bell, Elaine Stritch, Gretha Boston. CD

Shuffle Along

Reconstruction (1921) with Flourney Miller, Aubrey Lyles, Noble Sissle.

Silk Stockings

Original Broadway cast (1955) with Don Ameche, Hildegarde Neff, Gretchen Wyler. CD
Film soundtrack (1957) with Fred Astaire, Carol Richards (for Cyd Charisse). CD, DVD

Sing You Sinners

Film soundtrack (1938) with Bing Crosby.

Singin' in the Rain

Film soundtrack (1952) with Gene Kelly, Donald O'Connor, Debbie Reynolds. CD DVD
Original London cast (1984) with Tommy Steele. CD
Studio recording (1996) with Michael Gruber. CD

Singing Fool, The

Film soundtrack (1928) with Al Jolson. DVD

1600 Pennsylvania Avenue

Concert recording (1976) with Thomas Hampson, June Anderson, Barbara Hendricks (called *White House Cantata*). CD

Sky's the Limit, The

Film soundtrack (1943) with Fred Astaire, Sally Sweetland (for Joan Leslie).

Slipper and the Rose, The

Film soundtrack (1976) with Richard Chamberlain, Christopher Gable, Gemma Craven. CD, DVD

Smiling Lieutenant, The

Film soundtrack (1931) with Maurice Chevalier, Claudette Colbert, Miriam Hopkins. DVD

Smokey Joe's Cafe

Original Broadway cast (1995) with Adrian Bailey, David Keyes, Ken Ard. CD

Snow White and the Seven Dwarfs

Film soundtrack (1937) with (voices of) Adriana Caselotti, Harry Stockwell, Billy Gilbert. CD, DVD

Something for the Boys

Original cast members (1944) with Ethel Merman, Paula Laurence, Bill Johnson. CD
San Francisco cast (1997) with Meg MacKay, Joseph Lustig, Lesley Hamilton. CD

Son of Paleface

Film soundtrack (1952) with Jane Russell, Bob Hope, Roy Rogers. DVD

Song of Norway

Original Broadway cast (1944) with Kitty Carlisle, Robert Shafer, Helena Bliss. CD
Off Broadway revival (1958) with Helena Scott, John Reardon, William Olvis. LP
Jones Beach cast (1959) with Brenda Lewis, John Reardon, Helana Scott. CD
Film soundtrack (1970) with Florence Henderson, Frank Porretta, Harry Secombe. DVD
Studio recording (1990) with Donald Maxwell, David Rendell, Valerie Masterson. CD

Song of the South

Film soundtrack (1946) with James Baskett, Hattie McDaniel. DVD

Sophisticated Ladies

Original Broadway cast (1981) with Hinton Battle, Gregory Hines, Judith Jamison. CD

Sound of Music, The

Original Broadway cast (1959) with Mary Martin, Theodore Bikel, Patricia Neway, Kurt Kasznar, Marian Marlowe, Lauri Peters, Brian Davies. CD
London cast (1961) with Jean Bayless, Olive Gilbert, Constance Skacklock, Roger Dann, Barbara Brown, Eunice Gayson, Harold Kasket.
Film soundtrack (1965) with Julie Andrews, Bill Lee (for Christopher Plummer), Marjorie McKay (for Peggy Wood), Charmian Carr, Dan Truhitte. CD, DVD
London revival (1981) with Petula Clark, Michael Jayston, June Bronhill, Honor Blackman.
Studio recording (1987) with Frederica von Stade, Hakan Hagegard, Eileen Ferrell, Neil

Jones, Lewis Dahle von Schlanbusch, Barbara Daniels.
Broadway revival (1998) with Rebecca Luker, Michael Silberry, Patti Cohenour, Sara Zelle, Dashiell Eaves, Jan Maxwell, Fred Applegate. CD

South Pacific

Original Broadway cast (1949) with Mary Martin, Ezio Pinza, Juanita Hall, William Tabbert, Barbara Luna. CD
Studio recording (1950) with Peggy Lee, Margaret Whiting, Gordon MacRae.
Film soundtrack (1958) with Mitzi Gaynor, Giorgio Tozzi (for Rossano Brazzi), Bill Lee (for John Kerr), Muriel Smith (for Juanita Hall), Ray Walston. CD, DVD
Lincoln Center revival (1967) with Florence Henderson, Giorgio Tozzi, Irene Byatt, Justin McDonough, Eleanor Cables, David Doyle. CD
Studio recording (1986) with Kiri Te Kanawa, José Carreras, Mandy Patinkin, Sarah Vaughn. CD
London revival (1988) with Gemma Craven, Emile Belcourt, Bertice Reading, Johnny Wade. CD
Studio recording (1997) with Justino Diaz, Paige O'Hara, Pat Suzuki, Sean McDermott. CD
Television soundtrack (2001) with Glenn Close, Rade Serbedzija, Harry Connick, Jr., Lori Tan Chinn, Robert Pastorelli. CD, DVD
London revival (2002) with Lauren Kennedy, Philip Quest, Sheila Francisco, Edward Baker Duly. CD
Concert recording (2006) with Reba McEntire, Brian Stokes Mitchell, Lillias White, Jason Danieley, Alec Baldwin. CD

Spamalot

Original Broadway cast (2005) with Tim Curry, Hank Azaria, David Hyde-Pierce. CD

Spring Awakening

Original Broadway cast (2006) with Lea Michele, Jonathan Groff, John Gallagher, Jr. CD

Springtime in the Rockies

Film soundtrack (1942) with Betty Grable, John Payne, Carmen Miranda. DVD

Stage Door Canteen

Film soundtrack (1943) with Ray Bolger, Ethel Merman, Gracie Fields. CD, DVD

Star!

Film Soundtrack (1968) with Julie Andrews, Bruce Forsyth, Garrett Lewis. CD, DVD

Star Is Born, A

Film soundtrack (1954) with Judy Garland. CD, DVD
Film soundtrack (1976) with Barbra Streisand, Kris Kristofferson. CD, DVD

Star-Spangled Rhythm

Film soundtrack (1942) with Dick Powell, Betty Hutton, Bing Crosby. CD, DVD

Starlight Express

Original London cast (1984) with Jeff Shankley, P. P. Arnold, Frances Ruffelle, Lon Satton. CD
Studio recording (1987) with Richie Havens, Josie Aiello, Marc Cohn. CD
Studio recording (1993) with Tara Wilkinson, Debbie Blankett, Greg Ellis. CD

Starting Here, Starting Now

Original Off Broadway cast (1977) with George Lee Andrews, Loni Ackerman, Margery Cohen. CD
Original London cast (1997) with Michael Cantwell, Clare Burt. CD

State Fair

Original film soundtrack (1945) with Dick Haymes, Luanne Hogan (for Jeanne Crain), Vivian Blaine, Charles Winninger, Fay Bainter, Dana Andrews. CD, DVD
Film remake (1962) with Pat Boone, Alice Faye, Ann-Margaret, Anita Gordon (for Pamela Tiffin), Bobby Darin, Tom Ewell, David. CD, DVD
Broadway version (1996) with John Davidson, Kathryn Crosby, Andrea McArdle, Ben Wright, Donna McKechnie, Scott Wise. CD

Stingiest Man in Town, The

TV soundtrack (1956) with Vic Damone, Johnny Desmond, Patrice Munsel.

Stop the World—I Want to Get Off

Original London cast (1961) with Anthony Newley, Anna Quayle. CD
Original Broadway cast (1962) with Anthony Newley, Anna Quayle. CD

Film soundtrack (1966) with Millicent Martin, Tony Tanner. CD

Broadway revival (1978) with Sammy Davis, Jr., Shelly Burch, Marion Mercer.

Studio recording (1996) Mike Holloway, Louise Gold. CD

Stormy Weather

Film soundtrack (1943) with Cab Calloway, Lena Horne, Fats Waller. CD, DVD

Story of Rudolph the Red-Nosed Reindeer, The

TV soundtrack (1954) with (voices of) Burl Ives, Billie Mae Richards, Paul Soles. CD, DVD

Story of Vernon and Irene Castle, The

Film soundtrack (1939) with Fred Astaire, Ginger Rogers. DVD

Street Scene

Original Broadway cast (1947) with Brian Sullivan, Anne Jeffreys, Hope Arden. CD

Original London cast (1989) with Philip Day, Catherine Zeta-Jones. CD

Studio recording (1990) with Josephine Barstow, Samuel Ramsey, Angelina Reaux. CD

Strike Up the Band

Film soundtrack (1940) with Judy Garland, Mickey Rooney. DVD

Studio recording (1991) with Rebecca Luker, Jason Graae, Juliet Lambert, Beth Fowler. CD

Student Prince, The

Studio recording (1950) with Lauritz Melchior, Jane Wilson. CD

Studio recording (1952) with Robert Rounseville, Dorothy Kirsten. CD

Film soundtrack (1954) with Mario Lanza (for Edmund Purdom), Ann Blyth. DVD

Studio recording (1960) with Mario Lanza, Elizabeth Doubleday.

Studio recording (1962) with Gordon MacRae, Dorothy Kirsten. CD

Studio recording (1962) with Roberta Peters, Jan Peerce, Giorgio Tozzi.

Studio recording (1989) with David Rendall, Norman Balley, Marilyn Hill Smith. CD

Subways Are for Sleeping

Original Broadway cast (1961) with Carol Lawrence, Sydney Chaplin, Orson Bean, Phyllis Newman. CD

Sugar

Original Broadway cast (1972) with Elaine Joyce, Robert Morse, Tony Roberts. CD

Sugar Babies

Original Broadway cast (1979) with Mickey Rooney, Ann Miller. CD

Summer Holiday

Film soundtrack (1948) with Walter Huston, Mickey Rooney, Gloria De Haven, Marilyn Maxwell. CD

Summer Magic

Film soundtrack (1962) with Hayley Mills, Eddie Hodges, Burl Ives. DVD

Summer Stock

Film soundtrack (1950) with Judy Garland, Gene Kelly, Phil Silvers. CD, DVD

Sun Valley Serenade

Film soundtrack (1941) with John Payne, Pat Friday. CD, DVD

Sunday in the Park with George

Original Broadway cast (1984) with Mandy Patinkin, Bernadette Peters, Barbara Byrne. CD, DVD

London revival (2006) with Daniel Evans, Jenna Russell. CD

Sunny

London cast (1926) with Jack Buchanan, Binnie Hale, Claude Hulbert, Elsie Randolph, Jack Hobbs.

Sunset Boulevard

Original London cast (1993) with Patti LuPone, Kevin Anderson, Daniel Benzali. CD

Original Broadway cast (1994) with Glenn Close, George Hearn, Judy Kuhn. CD

Original Canadian cast (1995) with Diahann Carroll, Rex Smith, Walter Charles. CD

Sweeney Todd, the Demon Barber of Fleet Street

Original Broadway cast (1979) with Len Cariou, Victor Garber, Angela Lansbury. CD

Touring production (1982) with George Hearn, Langela Lansbury. DVD

Concert recording (2000) with George Hearn, Patti LuPone, Davis Gaines. CD
Broadway revival (2005) with Michael Cerveris, Patti LuPone, Mark Jacoby. CD
Film soundtrack (2007) with Johnny Depp, Helena Bonham Carter, Alan Rickman. CD, DVD

Sweet Adeline

Film soundtrack (1935) with Irene Dunne, Phil Regan, Joseph Cawthorn.

Sweet Charity

Original Broadway cast (1966) with Gwen Verdon, John McMartin, Helen Gallagher. CD
Film soundtrack (1968) with Shirley MacLaine, Sammy Davis, Chita Rivera. CD, DVD
Broadway revival (1986) with Debbie Allen, Michael Rupert, Bebe Neuwirth. CD
Studio recording (1994) with Gregg Edelman, Jacqueline Dankworth, Clive Rowe. CD

Sweet Rosie O'Grady

Film soundtrack (1943) with Betty Grable, Phil Regan, Robert Young. DVD

Sweethearts

Radio soundtrack (1946) with Jeanette MacDonald, Nelson Eddy.
Studio recording (1947) with Earl Wrightson, Frances Greer, Jimmy Carroll.

Swing Time

Film soundtrack (1936) with Fred Astaire, Ginger Rogers, Victor Moore. DVD

Take a Chance

Film soundtrack (1933) with Lillian Roth, Dorothy Lee.

Take Me Along

Original Broadway cast (1959) with Jackie Gleason, Robert Morse, Walter Pidgeon. CD

Take Me Out to the Ball Game

Film soundtrack (1949) with Gene Kelly, Frank Sinatra, Betty Garrett. DVD

Tap Dance Kid, The

Original Broadway cast (1983) with Samuel Wright, Hinton Battle, Gail Nelson, Jimmy Tate. CD

Tarzan

Film soundtrack (1999) with Glenn Close, Tony Goldwyn, Minnie Driver. CD, DVD
Original Broadway cast (2006) with Josh Strickland, Jenn Gambatese, Shuler Hensley. CD

Tenderloin

Original Broadway cast (1960) with Maurice Evans, Eileen Rodgers, Ron Husmann. CD
Concert recording (2000) with Patrick Wilson, Debbie Gravitte, David Ogden Stiers. CD

Thank Your Lucky Stars

Film soundtrack (1943) with Eddie Cantor, Dennis Morgan, Bette Davis.

That Night in Rio

Film soundtrack (1941) with Don Ameche, Alice Faye, Carmen Miranda. DVD

That Thing You Do

Film soundtrack (1996) with various recording artists. CD, DVD

That's Entertainment

Film soundtrack (1974) with Fred Astaire, Judy Garland, Mickey Rooney, Judy Garland. CD, DVD

There's No Business Like Show Business

Film soundtrack (1954) with Ethel Merman, Donald O'Connor, Mitzi Gaynor, Dan Dailey, Marilyn Monroe. CD, DVD

They're Playing Our Song

Original Broadway cast (1979) with Lucie Arnaz, Robert Klein. CD
Original London cast (1981) with Tom Conti, Gemma Crave. CD
Original Australian cast (1996) with John Waters, Jacki Weaver. CD

This Is the Army

Original Broadway cast (1942) with Irving Berlin, Earl Oxford, Ezra Stone. CD
Film soundtrack (1943) with Irving Berlin, George Murphy, Robert Stanley. CD, DVD

This Is Spinal Tap

Film soundtrack (1984) with Christopher Guest, Dana Carvey. CD, DVD

Thoroughly Modern Millie

Film soundtrack (1967) with Julie Andrews, Carol Channing, James Fox. CD, DVD
Original Broadway cast (2002) with Sutton Foster, Harriet Harris, Marc Kudisch. CD

Three Caballeros, The

Film soundtrack (1944) with Nestor Amaral. DVD

Three Little Girls in Blue

Film soundtrack (1946) with Carol Stewart (for Vera-Ellen), Vivian Blaine.

Three Little Words

Film soundtrack (1950) with Fred Astaire, Arlene Dahl, Helen Kane (for Debbie Reynolds). CD, DVD

Threepenny Opera, The

Off Broadway revival (1954) with Scott Merrill, Beatrice Arthur, Lotte Lenya, Gerald Price. CD
Film soundtrack (1964) with Kurt Muhlhardt (for Sammy Davis), Curt Jurgens, Gert Forbe.
Broadway revival (1976) with C. K. Alexander, Raul Julia, Ellen Greene.

Till the Clouds Roll By

Film soundtrack (1946) with Judy Garland, Frank Sinatra, Kathryn Grayson, Tony Martin, June Allyson, Lena Horne, Virginia O'Brien, Dinah Shore, Caleb Peterson. CD, DVD

Tin Pan Alley

Film soundtrack (1940) with Alice Faye, Betty Grable, John Payne.

Tip-Toes

Concert recording (1998) with Emily Loesser, Andy Taylor, Lewis J. Stadlen, Lee Wilkof. CD

Titanic

Original Broadway cast (1997) with Michael Cerveris, Brian d'Arcy James, David Garrison. CD

Toast of New Orleans, The

Film soundtrack (1950) with Mario Lanza. DVD

Tom Thumb

Film soundtrack (1958) with Russ Tamblyn, Ian Wallace. DVD

Tommy

Studio recording (1969) with Roger Daltry. CD
Studio recording (1972) with Maggie Bell, Steve Winwood, Ringo Starr. CD
Film soundtrack (1975) with Ann-Margaret, Elton John, Eric Clapton, Elton John. CD, DVD
Original Broadway cast (1993) with Michael Cerveris, Marcia Mitzman, Jonathan Dokuchitz. CD

Too Many Girls

Studio recording (1977) with Anthony Perkins, Estelle Parsons, Nancy Andrews, Johnny Desmond, Nancy Grennan, Jerry Wyatt, Arthur Siegel. CD

Top Hat

Film soundtrack (1935) with Fred Astaire, Ginger Rogers. CD, DVD

Tree Grows in Brooklyn, A

Original Broadway cast (1951) with Shirley Booth, Johnny Johnston, Marcia Van Dyke, Nomi Mitty. CD

25th Annual Putnam County Spelling Bee, The

Original Broadway cast (2005) with Dan Fogler, Lisa Howard, Jose Llana. CD

Two by Two

Original Broadway cast (1970) with Danny Kaye, Joan Copeland, Harry Goz, Madeline Kahn, Michael Karm, Walter Willison, Tricia O'Neil, Marilyn Cooper. CD

Two Gentlemen of Verona

Original Off Broadway cast (1971) with Clifton Davis, Raul Julia, Joella Allen, Alix Elias. CD

Two Girls and a Sailor

Film soundtrack (1944) with June Allyson, Gloria DeHaven, Van Johnson.

Two on the Aisle

Original Broadway cast (1951) with Bert Lahr, Dolores Gray. CD

Unsinkable Molly Brown, The

Original Broadway cast (1960) with Tammy Grimes, Harve Presnell, Joseph Sirola. CD
Film soundtrack (1964) with Debbie Reynolds, Harve Presnell, Ed Begley. CD, DVD

Up in Arms

Film soundtrack (1944) with Danny Kaye, Dinah Shore.

Up in Central Park

Studio recording (1945) with Celeste Holm, Eileen Farrell, Wilbur Evans, Betty Bruce. CD

Urinetown

Original Broadway cast (2001) with Hunter Foster, Jennifer Laura Thompson, John Cullum, Spencer Kayden, Jeff McCarthy. CD

Vagabond King

Studio recording (1950) with Earl Wrightson, Frances Greer.
Studio recording (1951) with Alfred Drake, Mimi Benzell, Frances Bible.
Film soundtrack (1956) with Oreste, Jean Fenn. CD
Studio recording (1961) with Edwin Steffe, Melissa Gray, Dorothy Dorrow.

Varsity Show

Film soundtrack (1937) with Dick Powell.

Very Good Eddie

Broadway revival (1975) with Charles Repole, Spring Fairbank, David Christmas, Virginia Seidel, Cynthia Wells. CD

Very Warm for May

Original Broadway cast (1939) with Jack Whiting, Grace McDonald, Frances Mercer, Eve Arden, Hiram Sherman. CD

Victor/Victoria

Film soundtrack (1982) with Julia Andrews, Robert Preston, Lesley Ann Warren. CD, DVD
Original Broadway cast (1995) with Julie Andrews, Tony Roberts, Rachel York. CD

Violet

Original Off Broadway cast (1997) with Lauren Ward, Amanda Posner, Michael McElroy. CD

Viva Las Vegas

Film soundtrack (1964) with Elvis Presley. CD, DVD

Wabash Avenue

Film soundtrack (1950) with Betty Grable.

Waiting for Guffman

Film soundtrack (1996) with Christopher Guest, Catherine O'Hara. DVD

Wake Up and Live

Film soundtrack (1937) with Buddy Clark (for Jack Haley), Alice Faye.

Walk the Line

Film soundtrack (2005) with Joaquin Phoenix, Reese Witherspoon. CD, DVD

Watch Your Step

Off Broadway revival (2001) with Julian Brightman, Daniel Frank Kelly, Jennifer Miller. CD

Weekend in Havana

Film soundtrack (1941) with Alice Faye, John Payne, Cesar Romero. DVD

We're Not Dressing

Film soundtrack (1934) with Bing Crosby, Ethel Merman. DVD

West Side Story

Original Broadway cast (1957) with Carol Lawrence, Larry Kert, Chita Rivera. CD
Film soundtrack (1961) with Marni Nixon (for Natalie Woods), Jim Bryant (for Richard Beymer), Rita Moreno. CD, DVD
Studio recording (1985) with Jose Carreras, Tatiana Troyanos, Kurt Ollman. CD
Studio recording (1993) with Tinuke Olafmihan, Caroline O'Connor, Paul Manuel. CD
Studio recording (1993) with Michael Ball, Barbara Bonney, LaVerne Williams. CD
Studio recording (2001) with Mike Eldred, Betsi Morrison, Michelle Prentice. CD
Studio recording (2007) with Hayley Westenra, Vittorio Gtigolo, Melanie Marshall. CD

Where's Charlie?

Original London cast (1958) with Norman Wisdom, Pip Hinton, Pamela Gale, Jerry Desmond. CD

White Christmas

Film soundtrack (1954) with Bing Crosby, Danny Kaye, Rosemary Clooney. CD, DVD
Touring cast (2006) with Brian D'Arcy James, Jeffrey Denman, Anastasia Barzee, Karen Morrow. CD

Whoopie

Film soundtrack (1930) with Eddie Cantor, Claire Dodd, Betty Grable.

Who's Tommy, The

Original Broadway cast (1993) with Michael Cerveris, Marcia Mitzman, Jonathan Dokuchitz. CD

Wicked

Original Broadway cast (2003) with Idina Menzel, Kristin Chenoweth, Norbert Leo Butz. CD

Wild Party, The (LaChiusa)

Original Broadway cast (2000) with Toni Colette, Mandy Patinkin, Tonya Pinkins, Eartha Kitt. CD

Wild Party, The (Lippa)

Original Off Broadway cast (2000) with Julia Murney, Brian d'Arcy James, Idina Menzel. CD

Wildcat

Original Broadway cast (1960) with Lucille Ball, Keith Andes, Swen Swenson. CD

Wildflower

London cast (1926) with Kitty Reidy, Howett Worster, Evelyn Drewe.

Will Rogers Follies, The

Original Broadway cast (1991) with Keith Carradine, Dee Hoty, Cady Huffman. CD

Willy Wonka and the Chocolate Factory

Film soundtrack (1971) with Gene Wilder, Peter Ostrum, Frank Albertson. CD, DVD

Wish You Were Here

Original Broadway cast (1952) with Jack Cassidy, Sheila Bond, Sidney Armus, Patricia Marand, Harry Clark. CD

Original London cast (1953) with Christopher Hewett, Bruce Trent, Shani Wallis. CD

With a Song in My Heart

Film soundtrack (1952) with Jane Froman (for Susan Hayward.) CD, DVD

Wiz, The

Original Broadway cast (1975) with Stephanie Mills, Ted Ross, Mabel King, Andre DeShields, Tiger Naynes, Hinton Battle. CD
Film soundtrack (1978) with Diana Ross, Lena Horne, Nipsey Russell, Ted Ross, Mabel King, Richard Pryor, Michael Jackson. CD, DVD

Wizard of Oz, The

Film soundtrack (1939) with Judy Garland, Ray Bolger, Jack Haley, Burt Lahr. CD, DVD
Original London cast (1989) with Gillian Bevan, Joyce Grant, Bille Brown. CD
Concert recording (1996) with Natalie Cole, Jewel, Roger Daltrey. CD
Madison Square Garden cast (1998) with Mickey Rooney, Eartha Kitt, Jessica Grove. CD

Woman of the Year

Original Broadway cast (1981) with Lauren Bacall, Harry Guardino. CD

Wonder Bar

Film soundtrack (1934) with Al Jolson, Dick Powell, Deloris Del Rio. CD

Wonderful Town

Original Broadway cast (1953) with Rosalind Russell, Edith Adams, George Gaynes. CD
TV soundtrack (1958) with Rosalind Russell, Jacqueline McKeever, Sydney Chaplin. CD
London revival (1986) with Maureen Lipman, Emily Morgan, Ray Lonnen. CD
Studio recording (1996) with Rebecca Luker, Ron Raines, Karen Mason. CD
Studio recording (1998) with Kim Criswell, Audra McDonald, Thomas Hampson. CD
Broadway revival (2003) with Donna Murphy, Jennifer Westfeldt, Gregg Edelman. CD

Woodstock

Film soundtrack (1970) with Richie Havens, Joan Baez, Jimi Hendrix, Joe Cocker, Arlo Guthrie. CD, DVD

Words and Music

Film soundtrack (1948) with Mickey Rooney, Lena Horne, Judy Garland, Ann Sothern, Betty Garrett, June Allyson. DVD

Working

Original Broadway cast (1978) with Bob Gunton, Lynne Thigpen, Joe Mantegna, Lenora Nemetz, Rex Everhart. CD
Los Angeles cast (1999) with Orson Bean, Harry Groener, B. J. Ward. CD

Xanadu

Film soundtrack (1980) with Olivia Newton-John, Gene Kelly, Cliff Richard. CD, DVD
Broadway cast (2007) with Cheyenne Jackson, Kerry Butler, Tony Roberts, Mary Testa, Jackie Hoffman. CD

Yankee Doodle Dandy

Film soundtrack (1942) with James Cagney, Joan Leslie, Frances Langford. CD, DVD

Year Without Santa Claus, The

TV soundtrack (1976) with (voices of) Shirley Booth, Mickey Rooney, Dick Shawn. DVD

Yellow Submarine

Film soundtrack (1968) with (voices of) the Beatles. CD DVD

Yentl

Film soundtrack (1983) with Barbra Streisand, Amy Irving, Mandy Patinkin. CD

You Were Never Lovelier

Film soundtrack (1942) with Fred Astaire, Nan Wynn (for Rita Hayworth), Lina Romay. DVD

You'll Never Get Rich

Film soundtrack (1941) with Fred Astaire, Martha Tilton. DVD

Young Man With a Horn

Film soundtrack (1950) with Doris Day. CD, DVD

Your Arms Too Short to Box with God

Original Broadway cast (1976) with Vinnette Carroll, Clinton Derricks-Carroll, Delores Hall.

Your Own Thing

Original Off Broadway cast (1968) with Rusty Thacker, Leland Palmer, Marcia Rodd. CD

You're a Good Man, Charlie Brown

Studio recording (1966) with Orson Bean, Barbara Minkus, Bill Hinnant.
Original Off Broadway cast (1967) with Gary Burghoff, Bob Balaban, Reva Rose, Bill Hinnant. CD
Broadway cast (1999) with Kristin Chenoweth, Anthony Rapp, Roger Bart, Ilans Levine. CD

Ziegfeld Follies of 1919

Original cast (1919–1920) with Eddie Cantor, Bert Williams, Marilyn Miller. CD

Ziegfeld Follies of 1936

Concert recording (1999) with Christine Ebersole, Peter Scolari, Howard McGillin. CD

Ziegfeld Follies of 1946

Film soundtrack (1946) with Fred Astaire, Gene Kelly, William Powell. CD

Ziegfeld Girl

Film soundtrack (1941) with Judy Garland, Tony Martin, Charles Winninger. CD, DVD

Zorba

Original Broadway cast (1968) with Herschel Bernardi, John Cunningham, Maria Karnilova. CD
Broadway revival (1983) with Anthony Quinn, Robert Westenberg, Lila Kedrova. CD

BIBLIOGRAPHY

The books listed here are general works on stage, film, and television musicals. Autobiographies and biographies about individuals are noted at the end of each biographical entry.

Alpert, Hollis. *Broadway: 125 Years of Musical Theatre*. New York: Arcade Publishers, 1991.

Allvine, Glendon. *The Greatest Fox of Them All*. New York: Lyle Stuart, 1969.

Altman, Rick. *The American Film Musical*. Bloomington, Indiana University Press, 1987.

Atkinson, Brooks. *Broadway*. Rev. ed. New York: Macmillan Publishing Co., 1974.

Aylesworth, Thomas G. *Broadway to Hollywood*. New York: Gallery Books, W. H. Smith Publishers, 1985.

Balio, Tino. *United Artists*. Madison: University of Wisconsin Press, 1976.

Banham, Martin (ed.). *The Cambridge Guide to Theatre*. New York: Cambridge University Press, 1992.

Bawden, Liz-Anne. *The Oxford Companion to Film*. New York: Oxford University Press, 1976.

Baxter, Joan. *Television Musicals, 1944–1996*. Jefferson, NC: McFarland & Co., 1997.

Benjamin, Ruth, and Arthur Roseblatt. *Movie Song Catalog*. Jefferson, NC: McFarland, 1993.

The Best Plays. 86 editions. Editors: Garrison Sherwood and John Chapman (1894–1919); Burns Mantle (1919–1947); John Chapman (1947–1952); Louis Kronenberger (1952–1961); Henry Hewes (1961–1964); Otis Guernsey, Jr. (1964–2000); Jeffrey Eric Jenkins (2000–2005). New York: Dodd, Mead & Co., 1894–1988; New York: Applause Theatre Book Publishers, 1988–1993. New York: Limelight Editions, 1994–2005.

Bloom, Ken. *Broadway: An Encyclopedic Guide to the History, People and Places of Times Square*. New York: Facts on File Publications, 1991.

Bloom, Ken, and Frank Vlastnik. *Broadway Musicals: The 101 Greatest Shows of All Time*. New York: Black Dog & Leventhal Publishers, 2004.

Bordman, Gerald. *American Musical Theatre: A Chronicle*. 3rd ed. New York: Oxford University Press, 2001.

Bordman, Gerald. *American Operetta: From H.M.S. Pinafore to Sweeney Todd*. New York: Oxford University Press, 1981.

Bordman, Gerald, and Thomas S. Hischak. *The Oxford Companion to American Theatre*. 3rd ed. New York: Oxford University Press, 2004.

Contemporary Theatre, Film and Television: Who's Who. Volumes 1–60. Detroit: Gale Research, 1978–2004.

Crowther, Bosley. *The Lion's Share: The Story of an Entertainment Empire*. New York: E. P. Dutton & Co., 1957.

Denkirk, Darcia. *A Fine Romance: Hollywood and Broadway*. New York: Watson-Guptill Publications, 2005.

Druxman, Michael B. *The Musical From Broadway to Hollywood*. New York: Barnes, 1980.

Eames, John Douglas. *The MGM Story*. New York: Crown Publishers, 1975.

Eames, John Douglas. *The Paramount Story*. New York: Crown Publishers, 1985.

Everett, William A., and Paul R. Laird. *Historical Dictionary of the Broadway Musical*. Lanham, MD: Scarecrow Press, 2008.

Ewen, David. *American Popular Songs*. New York: Random House, 1966.

Feuer, Jane. *The Hollywood Musical*. Bloomington: Indiana University Press, 1982.

Fitzgerald, Michael G. *Universal Pictures: A Panoramic History*. Westport, CT: Arlington House, 1977.

Fordin, Hugh. *MGM's Greatest Musicals: The Arthur Freed Unit*. New York: Da Capo Press, 1996.

Furia, Philip. *The Poets of Tin Pan Alley: A History of America's Great Lyricists*. New York: Oxford University Press, 1990.

Ganzl, Kurt. *Ganzl's Encyclopedia of the Musical Theatre*. New York: Schirmer Books,1993.

Geduld, Harry M. *The Birth of the Talkies*. Bloomington: Indiana University Press, 1975.

Gottfried, Martin. *Broadway Musicals*. New York: Harry N. Abrams, 1980.

Gottfried, Martin. *More Broadway Musicals*. New York: Harry N. Abrams, 1991.

Grant, Mark N. *The Rise and Fall of the Broadway Musical*. Boston: Northeastern University Press, 2004.

Green, Stanley. *Broadway Musicals Show By Show*. 5th ed. Milwaukee: Hal Leonard Publishing Corp., 1999.

Green, Stanley. *Encyclopedia of Musical Film*. New York: Oxford University Press, 1981.

Green, Stanley. *Encyclopedia of the Musical Theatre*. New York: Dodd, Mead & Co., 1976.

Green, Stanley. *Hollywood Musicals Year by Year*. 2nd ed. Milwaukee: Hal Leonard Publishing Corp., 1999.

Green, Stanley. *The World of Musical Comedy*. New York: A.S. Barnes & Co., 1980.

Halliwell, Leslie. *Halliwell's Film Guide*. 7th ed. New York: Harper & Row, Publishers, 1989.

Henderson, Mary C. *Theater in America*. New York: Harry N. Abrams, 1986.

Herbert, Ian (ed.). *Who's Who in the Theatre*. 17 editions. London: Pitman Publishing, 1912/1981.

Hirschhorn, Clive. *The Hollywood Musical* (revised 2nd ed.) New York: Crown Publishers, 1983.

Hirschhorn, Clive. *The Universal Story*. New York: Crown Publishers, 1981.

Hirschhorn, Clive. *The Warner Bros. Story*. New York: Crown Publishers, 1979.

Hischak, Thomas S. *Film It with Music: An Encyclopedic Guide to the American Movie Musical*. Westport, CT: Greenwood Press, 2001.

Hischak, Thomas S. *Stage It with Music: An Encyclopedic Guide to the American Musical Theatre*. Westport, CT: Greenwood Press, 1993.

Hischak, Thomas S. *Through the Screen Door: What Happened to the Broadway Musical When It Went to Hollywood*. Lanham, MD: Scarecrow Press, 2004.

Hyland, William G. *The Song Is Ended: Songwriters and American Music, 1900–1950*. New York: Oxford University Press, 1995.

Jacobs, Lewis. *The Rise of the American Film*. New York: Harcourt, Brace & Co., 1939.

Jackson, Arthur. *The Best Musicals From Show Boat to A Chorus Line*. New York: Crown Publishers, 1977.

Jewell, Richard B., and Vernon Harbin. *The RKO Story*. New York: Arlington House, 1982.

Jones, John Bush. *Our Musicals, Ourselves*. Lebanon, NH: University Press of New England, 2003.

Kantor, Michael, and Laurence Maslon. *Broadway: The American Musical*. New York: Bullfinch Press, 2004.

Katz, Ephraim. *The Film Encyclopedia*. 3rd ed. New York: Harper-Perennial, 1998.

Konigsberg, Ira. *The Complete Film Dictionary*. 2nd ed. New York: Penguin, 1997.

Lamb, Andrew. *150 Years of Popular Musical Theatre*. New Haven, CT: Yale University Press, 2000.

Lasky, Betty. *RKO: The Biggest Little Major of Them All*. Englewood Cliffs, NJ: Prentice-Hall, 1984.

Laufe, Abe. *Anatomy of a Hit: Long-Run Plays on Broadway from 1900 to the Present Day*. New York: Hawthorn Books, Inc., 1966.

Laufe, Abe. *Broadway's Greatest Musicals*. New York: Funk and Wagnalls, 1977.

Leonard, William Torbert. *Theatre: Stage to Screen to Television*. Metuchen, NJ: Scarecrow Press, 1981.

Lerner, Alan Jay. *The Musical Theatre: A Celebration*. New York: McGraw-Hill Book Co., 1986.

Lewis, David H. *Broadway Musicals*. Jefferson, NC: McFarland & Co., Inc., 2002.

Maltin, Leonard. *Movie & Video Guide*. New York: Penguin Putnam, 2007.

Mast, Gerald. *Can't Help Singin': The American Musical on Stage and Screen*. Woodstock, NY: Overlook Press, 1987.

Mast, Gerald. *A Short History of the Movies*. Indianapolis: Pegasus, 1971.

Matthew-Walker, Robert. *Broadway to Hollywood: The Musical and the Cinema*. London: Sanctuary Publishing, 1996.

McNeil, Alex. *Total Television*. 4th ed. New York: Penguin Books, 1997.

Mordden, Ethan. *Beautiful Mornin': The Broadway Musical in the 1940s*. New York: Oxford University Press, 1999.

Mordden, Ethan. *Coming Up Roses: The Broadway Musical in the 1950s*. New York: Oxford University Press, 1998.

Mordden, Ethan. *The Happiest Corpse I've Ever Seen: The Last 25 Years of the Broadway Musical*. New York: Palgrave MacMillan, 2004.

Mordden, Ethan. *The Hollywood Musical*. New York: St. Martin's Press, 1982.

Mordden, Ethan. *One More Kiss: The Broadway Musical in the 1970s*. New York: Palgrave Macmillan, 2004.

Mordden, Ethan. *Open a New Window: The Broadway Musical in the 1960s*. New York: Palgrave Macmillan, 2002.

Norton, Richard C. *A Chronology of American Musical Theatre*. New York: Oxford University Press, 2002.

Portantier, Michael (ed.). *The Theatremania Guide to Musical Theatre Recordings*. New York: Backstage Books, 2004.

Raymond, Jack. *Show Music on Record, From the 1890s to the 1980s*. New York: Frederick Ungar Publishing Co., 1982.

Sennett, Ted. *Song and Dance: The Musicals of Broadway*. New York: Metro Books, 1998.

Sennett, Ted. *Warner Brothers Presents*. Secaucus, NJ: Castle Books, 1971.

Sheward, David. *It's a Hit: The Back Stage Book of Longest-Running Broadway Shows, 1884 to the Present*. New York: Watson-Guptill Publications-BPI Communications, Inc., 1994.

Shipman, David. *The Story of Cinema*. New York: St. Martin's Press, 1982.

Smith, Cecil, and Glenn Litton. *Musical Comedy in America*. 2nd ed. New York: Theatre Arts Books, 1981.

Suskin, Steven. *Opening Night on Broadway: A Critical Quotebook of the Golden Era of the Musical Theatre*. New York: Schirmer Books, 1990.

Suskin, Steven. *More Opening Nights on Broadway: A Critical Quotebook of the Musical Theatre, 1965–1981*. New York: Schirmer Books, 1997.

Swain, Joseph P. *The Broadway Musical: A Critical and Musical Survey*. New York: Oxford University Press, 1990.

Theatre World. 60 editions. Editors: Daniel C. Blum (1946–1964), John Willis (1964–2006); New York: Norman McDonald Associate, 1946–1949; New York: Greenberg, Publisher, 1949–1957; Philadelphia: Chilton, 1957–1964; New York: Crown Publishers: 1964–1991; New York: Applause Theatre Book Publishers, 1991–2006.

Thomas, Lawrence B. *The MGM Years*. New York: Arlington House, 1971.

Thomas, Tony, and Aubrey Solomon. *The Films of 20th Century Fox*. Secaucus, NJ: Citadel Press, 1979.

Traubner, Richard. *Operetta: A Theatrical History*. Garden City, NY: Doubleday & Co., 1983.

Wilmeth, Don. B., and Tice Miller (eds.). *Cambridge Guide to American Theatre*. New York: Cambridge University Press, 1993.

Wlaschin, Ken. *Opera on Screen*. Los Angeles: Beachwood Press, 1997.

INDEX

Page numbers in **bold** indicate main articles; page numbers in *italics* indicate photographs.